July 30, 2010

Dear Chaz,

We think your a wonderful grandson. Were very proud of you.

We love you lots,

Grampa + Bubbles

NEW CENTURY VERSION

THE YOUTH BIBLE

WORD BIBLES

Group

In grateful recognition of the significant contribution the World Bible Translation Center has made to the development of the New Century Version and to the promotion of God's Word in understandable language throughout the world, a portion of the purchase price of this Bible goes to support their mission.

The Youth Bible

The Holy Bible, New Century Version

The preliminary research and development on the New Century Version was done by the World Bible Translation Center, Inc., Fort Worth, Texas 76182.

Devotional and study materials were developed by Group Publishing, Inc., Loveland, CO 80539.

Library of Congress Cataloging-in-Publication Data

Bible, English. New Century. 1991.
The Youth Bible: New Century Version.
p. cm.
Summary: Illustrated Biblical text is accompanied by a related present-day "true-life" story, topical index, maps, timelines, and a study guide.
ISBN 0-8499-0821-3 (black hardback). – ISBN 0-8499-0925-2 (teal hardback) – ISBN 0-8499-3227-0 (black duraflex) – ISBN 0-8499-3339-0 (teal duraflex)
1. Teenagers–Religious life. I. Word Publishing. II. Title. 91-30800
BS195.N353 1991 CIP
220.5'208–dc20 AC

Published by Word Publishing. Printed in the United States of America. All rights reserved.
89 RRD 14131211

Acknowledgments

The following people contributed to *The Youth Bible:*

Group Publishing editorial team: Eugene C. Roehlkepartain (general editor), Thom Schultz, Joani Schultz, Paul Woods, Michael D. Warden, Chris Yount, Lee Sparks, Cindy Sauer, and DeAnne Trujillo.

Word, Inc. team: Dan Rich, Kip Jordon, Carol Bartley, Carey Moore, Dave Moberg, Rob Birkhead, Ed Curtis, Jill Sciacca, Jim Burns, and Matt Barnhill.

Writers: Timothy R. Anderson, Nancy Brumbaugh Bayne, J. Brent Bill, Ann B. Cannon, Michael C. Carson, Dave Carver, Rick Chromey, L. Katherine Cook, Vaughn CroweTipton, Bob Darden, Karen Dockrey, Thomas J. Everson, Jim Farris, Dean Feldmeyer, Karen J. Fisher, Marty Fuller, Mike Gillespie, Mark Gilroy, Vicki Grove, Sam D. Halverson, Cindy S. Hansen, Mike Hertenstein, Margaret R. Hinchey, Tom Klaus, Rick Lawrence, Cynthia Cornwell McCachern, Elaine McCalla, Robert J. McCarty, Kevin A. Miller, Amy L.W. Nappa, Mike D.F. Nappa, Jolene L. Roehlkepartain, Ron Scates, Bob Searl, Yvonne L.D. Steindal, Gary B. Swanson, Jeffrey E. Tucker, Ramona Cramer Tucker, Annie Wamberg, Steve Wamberg, Mark Winter, Twyla Gill Wright, and Carol Davis Younger.

Designers and artists: Richard Slaton, Brian Peterson, Pat Reinheimer, David Martin, and Glyn Powell.

We would also like to thank all the young people, families and youth leaders who allowed their stories to be used in this Bible. Names and details have been changed to maintain their privacy.

Preface

The Bible is God's message to humanity. He has spoken to all peoples and all generations. Of course, God first accomplished this by directly addressing his people, the Israelites in the Old Testament and the young church in the New Testament, in a language they could understand.

The original text of the Bible was written in Hebrew, Aramaic, and Greek—languages of the people. Since God intends to address all people of all ages through his Word, each generation and language group must translate the Bible into its own language.

These facts, that the Bible is God's message and that it is ultimately addressed to all people in every age, require that a translation be both accurate and clear. These are the two overarching principles that stand behind the *New Century Version.*

An Accurate Translation

The first concern of the *New Century Version* is that the translation be faithful to the manuscripts in the original languages. A team composed of the World Bible Translation Center and fifty additional, highly qualified and experienced Bible scholars and translators was assembled. This team included people with experience on the *New International Version*, the *New American Standard Bible*, and the *New King James Version.* The scholars came from a variety of theological colleges, universities, and seminaries in the United States, Canada, Australia, and Great Britain.

These translators recognize that the most accurate translations are those which pay close attention to the meanings of words in their broader context, rather than those which simply treat words as isolated entities. They understand that a contemporary English translation must sometimes depart from the word order of the original languages to reflect accurately the meaning of God's Word to a modern English-speaking audience.

Further, it is true that translation involves interpretive decisions. With this in mind, it is important to note that the breadth of scholarship which stands behind the *New Century Version* ensures an unbiased translation.

Last, it should be mentioned that the best available Hebrew and Greek texts were used, principally the third edition of the United Bible Societies' Greek text and the latest edition of the Biblia Hebraica, along with the Septuagint.

A Clear Translation

The second concern was to make the language clear enough for all people to read the Bible and understand it for themselves. In maintaining clear language, several guidelines were followed. Vocabulary choice has been based upon *The Living Word Vocabulary* by Dr. Edgar Dale and Dr. Joseph O'Rourke (Worldbook-Childcraft International, 1981), which is the standard used by the editors of *The World Book Encyclopedia* to determine appropriate vocabulary. For difficult words that have no simpler synonyms, footnotes and dictionary references are provided. Footnotes appear at the bottom of the page and are indicated in the text by a raised letter ([n]) for "note." The dictionary/topical concordance is located at the back of the Bible with references indicated in the text by a raised letter ([d]).

The *New Century Version* aids understanding by using contemporary references for measurements and geographical locations when it is feasible. For instance, terms such as "shekels," "cubits," "omer," and "hin" have been converted to modern equivalents. Where geographical references are identical, the modern name has been used, such as the "Mediterranean Sea" instead of "Great Sea" or "Western Sea." Also, to minimize confusion, the most familiar name for a place is used consistently, instead of using variant names for the same place. "Lake Galilee" is used throughout rather than its variant forms, "Sea of Kinnereth," "Lake Gennesaret," and "Sea of Tiberias."

Ancient customs are often unfamiliar to modern readers. Customs such as shaving a man's beard to shame him or ritually walking between the halves of a dead animal to seal an agreement are meaningless to many modern-day readers. So these are clarified either in the text or in a footnote.

Since *meanings* of words change with time, care has been taken to avoid potential misunderstandings. To do so, the *New Century Version* uses contemporary language in place of the archaic language often found in translations. Frequently in the Old Testament God tells his people to "devote" something to him, as when he tells the Israelites to devote Jericho and everything in it to him. While we might understand this to mean he is telling them to keep it safe and holy, the exact opposite is true. He is telling them to destroy it totally as an offering to him. The *New Century Version* communicates the idea clearly by translating "devoted," in these situations, as "destroyed as an offering to the Lord."

Where there was potential for confusion, *rhetorical questions* have been stated according to their implied answer. The psalmist's question, "Who, O God, is like you?" has been stated more directly as, "God, there is no one like you."

Figures of speech have been translated according to their meanings. For instance, the expression, "the Virgin Daughter of Zion," which is frequently used in the Old Testament, is simply and accurately translated "the people of Jerusalem" so that the meaning is not obscured by the figure of speech.

Idiomatic expressions of the biblical languages are translated to communicate the same meaning to today's reader that would have been understood by the original audience. For example, the Hebrew idiom "he rested with his fathers" is translated by its meaning—"he died."

Obscure terms have been clarified. Terms are often obscure in the Bible because they are part of the ancient culture which God directly addressed in his revelation. In the Old Testament, for instance, God frequently condemns the people for their "high places" and "Asherah poles." The *New Century Version* translates these according to their meanings, which would have been understood by the Hebrews. "High places" is translated "places where gods were worshiped" and "Asherah poles" is translated "Asherah idols."

Gender language has also been translated with a concern for clarity. To avoid the misconception that "man," "mankind," and "he" are exclusively masculine when they are being used in a generic sense, this translation has chosen to use less ambiguous language, such as "people," "humans," and "human beings," and has carefully worked throughout to choose gender language that would accurately convey the intent of the original writers. Specifically and exclusively masculine and feminine references in the text have been retained.

Following in the tradition of other English versions, the *New Century Version* indicates the divine name YHWH, the Tetragrammaton, by putting LORD, and sometimes GOD, in capital letters. This is to distinguish it from Adonai, another Hebrew word that is translated "Lord."

Every attempt has been made to maintain proper English style, while clarifying concepts and communication. The beauty of Hebrew parallelism in poetry has been retained, and the images of the ancient languages have been captured in equivalent English images wherever possible, but in all cases, clarity of communication with the modern reader has taken precedence over preservation of the ancient form.

Study Aids

Other features to enhance understanding of the text include full-color maps of Bible lands, subject headings throughout to identify speakers and topics, book introductions to give a synopsis of each book's theme, a dictionary/topical concordance of biblical words and concepts, and footnotes identifying Old Testament quotations in the New Testament.

Our Prayer

It is with great humility and prayerfulness that this Bible is presented. We acknowledge the infallibility of God's Word and yet our own human frailty. We pray that God has worked through us as his vessels so that we all might better learn his truth for ourselves and that it might richly grow in our lives. It is to his glory that this Bible is given.

THE PUBLISHER

NO DUSTING NECESSARY

According to a Search Institute study, 86 percent of Christian teenagers do not read the Bible when they are by themselves. Why?

"I sometimes don't understand it, so I stop."
–Mary in Nebraska

"I'm really confused."
–Andrew in Michigan

"I don't know how to read the Bible."
–Chris in Florida

If you are like most teenagers, you have had similar feelings. Sometimes the Bible seems hard to understand, hard to use, irrelevant, and even boring. So even though you know it's important, it often collects dust on a shelf.

The Youth Bible is designed specifically to help you find God's guidance in the everyday issues you face. It includes:

- The Bible text translated into clear, modern English. It's easier to read than a newspaper!
- Devotions that relate the Bible to everyday life.
- Introductions that help you understand each book of the Bible.
- "Sidelights" that give interesting–often humorous–insights into life in Bible times.

These features help you discover for yourself that the Bible is about everyday life. It's easy to use, interesting, and life-changing.

It's Easy to Use

You don't have to be a Bible scholar to use *The Youth Bible.* In fact, we have designed it so that people who have never studied the Bible can find help in God's Word. Here is all you have to do to use it.

- *Find what's on your mind* – When you are dealing with a topic or problem, just look it up in the "Topical Devotion Guide." This guide lists more than four hundred devotions on topics that interest teenagers.
- *Read the devotion* – The devotions tell true stories or give interesting information to help you think about the topic. Then read the related Bible passage and think about the questions, which will help you understand and apply the passage.
- *Find related passages* – Each devotion suggests other Bible passages that can speak to your need. Just look them up. And you don't have to already know where to find Malachi or 2 Timothy or 1 Chronicles in the Bible. Just use the page numbers listed beside each reference.
- *Learn about the Bible* – This Bible doesn't assume you know who people are or what events take place. It explains in simple language the ideas and events that are important for understanding Bible passages. And if you don't know where to find a story, use the quick guide "Where Do I Find . . . ?" to help you.

It's Interesting

On the surface, many parts of the Bible may seem boring. But when you start digging, you discover that even these kinds of books are fascinating. These features help bring the Bible to life:

- *Introductions* – Each book of the Bible has a short, easy-to-read introduction to help you understand the book and its purpose. Most introductions also include time lines and maps or diagrams to help you see when and where things happened.
- *Sidelights* – Throughout the Bible you'll find over three hundred boxes with interesting and fun information about life in Bible times and about the Bible itself. This information will

not only add interest to your Bible reading, but it will help you understand many passages. Besides, you will amaze your friends with your knowledge!

It's Life-Changing

One warning: Don't use this Bible unless you want your life to be changed. The devotions are written to challenge you to grow in your faith. They encourage you to examine your own life and to relate the scriptural principles to what you say, do, and think.

Of course, the Bible can do all these things even without the devotions, introductions, and sidelights that are added. It's God's Word, and it doesn't need our help. But sometimes *we* need help; we need guidance and direction to get us started. *The Youth Bible* gives that help. Once you start using it, it won't have much time to collect dust on the bookshelf.

The Editors, Group Publishing

FIVE BIBLE STUDY TIPS

1. Pray. Ask God to guide you as you read. Your prayer doesn't have to be fancy. You might just pray, "Help me, God, to discover you and your will as I read my Bible."

2. Read. Read a devotion and the Bible passage related to it. If the passage is not clear the first time you read it, read it again. Also check out the introduction at the beginning of the book that helps you understand the book's purpose.

3. Think. Think about the questions listed in the devotion. It may help to ask yourself: What's going on in the passage? How is the world similar or different than it was then? How does the passage fit into my faith?

4. Do. What is God saying to you through this passage? What changes or new directions does the passage call for? Decide what you can do to respond to the truth in the passage, and do it. Use the ideas in the devotional section labeled "Consider . . ." to get you started. It could change your life!

5. Ask. If a passage confuses or bothers you, talk to someone about it. Ask a parent, youth leader, pastor, Sunday school teacher, or trusted friend to help you understand.

USING THE YOUTH BIBLE IN GROUPS

Though designed especially for individual use, *The Youth Bible* has many features that also make it excellent for group use. Use it with your youth group or in a Bible study group with friends. Try these suggestions:

Decide – Find out what topics interest or concern group members. Then see the Topical Devotion Guide to find the devotions on those themes.

Compare – Have different people (or small groups) look at different devotions on the same topic. Compare the stories and the passages. Where do they overlap? What new insights do you gain from the differences?

Be open – Let people express their thoughts and feelings. Listen for different perspectives. When someone says something controversial, you might ask, "Would anyone like to respond to that?"

Commit – Decide specific ways group members can apply what they have learned from the Bible. Encourage each other to keep the commitments you make to yourselves and to God.

Topical Devotion Guide

This devotion guide helps you find devotions on topics that interest or concern you. Refer to it when you are dealing with a particular problem or issue, or use it as a topical reading plan. Simply decide what topic you want to study and then read one devotion each day on that topic until you have read all the devotions and passages.

Forgiveness

Freedom

Friends

Where Do I Find . . . ?

Have you ever known what you were looking for but didn't know where to find it in the Bible? A great event? A famous passage? A favorite story? Use this guide to help you find stories you remember but don't know where to find. The descriptions listed here are the common descriptions and are not always exactly the same as the descriptions in this Bible translation.

Contents

Old Testament

New Testament

Old Testament

GENESIS

Why Read This Book:

- Reflect on the beauty and wonder of God's creation (Genesis 1—2).
- Learn how God responds to rebellion against him (Genesis 3—11).
- Discover how God keeps his promises (Genesis 12—24).
- See how God works for good even during bad times (Genesis 37—50).

Behind the Scenes:

For a week, you work tediously in art class creating a clay sculpture. You carefully shape the soft clay. On Friday, you leave the almost-finished sculpture to harden. Monday you return. You find your clay twisted into a chaotic, unrecognizable blob. Rage and sadness swell up in you. You must begin the painstaking work all over again.

Genesis tells a similar story. It's the story of God's loving care in creating the world. But the story has a dark, twisted side. Genesis tells of human rebellion, murder, and other human evil as people rebel against God.

Genesis falls naturally into two parts. Chapters 1—11 talk about the beginnings of the world. Here you'll read the famous stories of Adam and Eve, Cain and Abel, Noah, and the tower of Babel. Each story shows how people often twist and destroy the gifts God has given them.

Then chapters 12—50 talk specifically about the beginnings of the Hebrew people, later known as Israelites. You'll read about Abraham, the father of the nation, and his sons. And the book concludes with the story of Joseph, whom God was able to use for great things even after his brothers had sold him into slavery.

Genesis is one of the most important books in the Bible. Not only does the rest of the Bible build on the foundation laid in this book, but the book shows how, from the beginning, God has used special people to play important roles in his world.

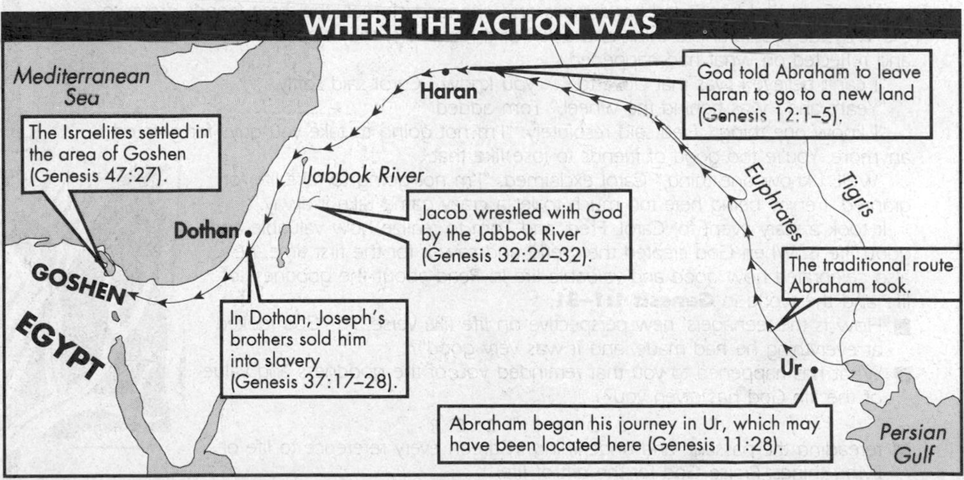
WHERE THE ACTION WAS
Mediterranean Sea
Haran
God told Abraham to leave Haran to go to a new land (Genesis 12:1-5).
The Israelites settled in the area of Goshen (Genesis 47:27).
Jabbok River
Euphrates
Tigris
Jacob wrestled with God by the Jabbok River (Genesis 32:22-32).
Dothan
GOSHEN
EGYPT
The traditional route Abraham took.
In Dothan, Joseph's brothers sold him into slavery (Genesis 37:17-28).
Ur
Abraham began his journey in Ur, which may have been located here (Genesis 11:28).
Persian Gulf

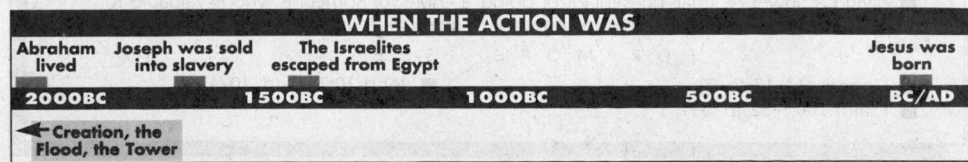

WHEN THE ACTION WAS

Abraham lived	Joseph was sold into slavery	The Israelites escaped from Egypt			Jesus was born
2000BC		1500BC	1000BC	500BC	BC/AD

← Creation, the Flood, the Tower

The Beginning of the World

1 In the beginning God created the sky and the
earth. 2The earth was empty and had no
form. Darkness covered the ocean, and God's
Spirit[d] was moving over the water.
3Then God said, "Let there be light," and there
was light. 4God saw that the light was good, so he
divided the light from the darkness. 5God named
the light "day" and the darkness "night." Evening
passed, and morning came. This was the first day.
6Then God said, "Let there be something to divide the water in two." 7So God made the air and
placed some of the water above the air and some
below it. 8God named the air "sky." Evening
passed, and morning came. This was the second
day.
9Then God said, "Let the water under the sky
be gathered together so the dry land will appear."
And it happened. 10God named the dry land
"earth" and the water that was gathered together
"seas." God saw that this was good.
11Then God said, "Let the earth produce
plants—some to make grain for seeds and others
to make fruits with seeds in them. Every seed will
produce more of its own kind of plant." And it
happened. 12The earth produced plants with grain
for seeds and trees that made fruits with seeds in
them. Each seed grew its own kind of plant. God

LIFE

The Good Things

Carol, Fred, and Tom had planned an evening packed with fun. The trunk of Tom's Honda was loaded with toilet paper and flashlights—the supplies they'd need to "t.p." Tanya's house in honor of her sixteenth birthday.

But first they went to the school parking lot for some fun with the car. Carol and Fred jumped on the hood, and Tom steered in wild, squealing circles. It was as fun as a roller coaster—until Carol lost her grip and flew off the hood. The tires screeched and swerved, barely missing Carol, who was lying on the ground. Her jeans were ripped, and one leg was bleeding.

"You okay?" Tom asked as he rushed out of the car.

"I think so," Carol responded, holding her leg. "Just shook up."

The three friends pulled themselves together, stunned by what had happened—and could have happened. Their original plans forgotten, they cautiously drove to Carol's house to explain to her parents the stupid thing they had done.

After Carol had bandaged her scrapes and changed clothes, the three friends drove to the Wayside Restaurant to think and talk. For three hours, they sipped on chocolate malts and reflected on what had happened.

"I can't believe I was that close to . . . you know," Carol said softly.

"Yeah, and I was behind the wheel," Tom added.

"I know one thing," Fred said resolutely. "I'm not going to take you guys for granted anymore. You're too good of friends to lose like that."

"Well, I know one thing," Carol exclaimed. "I'm not going to take life for granted. I enjoy being here too much to let a crazy game take it away."

It took a scary event for Carol, Fred, and Tom to realize how valuable and good life is. When God created the world and saw it for the first time, he also celebrated how good and valuable life is. Read about the goodness of life and the world in **Genesis 1:1–31**.

- How is the teenagers' new perspective on life like verse 31: "God looked at everything he had made, and it was very good"?
- What has happened to you that reminded you of the goodness and value of the life God has given you?

CONSIDER . . .

- rereading the passage and underlining in green every reference to life or living things. Praise God for the gift of life.
- giving a flower or small houseplant or doing a chore for someone who is valuable to you. Include a note that celebrates how he or she makes your life better.

FOR MORE, SEE . . .

- Genesis 2:4–17 (p. 3)
- Psalm 104:1–32 (p. 541)
- John 10:7–18 (p. 1074)

saw that all this was good. 13Evening passed, and
morning came. This was the third day.
14Then God said, "Let there be lights in the sky
to separate day from night. These lights will be
used for signs, seasons, days, and years. 15They
will be in the sky to give light to the earth." And
it happened.
16So God made the two large lights. He made
the brighter light to rule the day and made the
smaller light to rule the night. He also made the
stars. 17God put all these in the sky to shine on the
earth, 18to rule over the day and over the night,
and to separate the light from the darkness. God
saw that all these things were good. 19Evening
passed, and morning came. This was the fourth
day.
20Then God said, "Let the water be filled with
living things, and let birds fly in the air above the
earth."
21So God created the large sea animals and every living thing that moves in the sea. The sea is
filled with these living things, with each one producing more of its own kind. He also made every
bird that flies, and each bird produced more of its
own kind. God saw that this was good. 22God
blessed them and said, "Have many young ones
so that you may grow in number. Fill the water
of the seas, and let the birds grow in number on
the earth." 23Evening passed, and morning came.
This was the fifth day.
24Then God said, "Let the earth be filled with
animals, each producing more of its own kind. Let
there be tame animals and small crawling animals
and wild animals, and let each produce more of
its kind." And it happened.
25So God made the wild animals, the tame animals, and all the small crawling animals to produce more of their own kind. God saw that this
was good.
26Then God said, "Let us make human beings
in our image and likeness. And let them rule over
the fish in the sea and the birds in the sky, over
the tame animals, over all the earth, and over all
the small crawling animals on the earth."
27So God created human beings in his image. In
the image of God he created them. He created
them male and female. 28God blessed them and
said, "Have many children and grow in number.
Fill the earth and be its master. Rule over the fish
in the sea and over the birds in the sky and over
every living thing that moves on the earth."
29God said, "Look, I have given you all the
plants that have grain for seeds and all the trees
whose fruits have seeds in them. They will be
food for you. 30I have given all the green plants as
food for every wild animal, every bird of the air,
and every small crawling animal." And it happened. 31God looked at everything he had made,
and it was very good. Evening passed, and morning came. This was the sixth day.

The Seventh Day—Rest

2 So the sky, the earth, and all that filled them
were finished. 2By the seventh day God finished the work he had been doing, so he rested
from all his work. 3God blessed the seventh day
and made it a holy day, because on that day he
rested from all the work he had done in creating
the world.

The First People

4This is the story of the creation of the sky and
the earth. When the LORD God first made the
earth and the sky, 5there were still no plants on
the earth. Nothing was growing in the fields because the LORD God had not yet made it rain on
the land. And there was no person to care for the
ground, 6but a mist would rise up from the earth
and water all the ground.
7Then the LORD God took dust from the ground
and formed a man from it. He breathed the breath
of life into the man's nose, and the man became
a living person. 8Then the LORD God planted a
garden in the east, in a place called Eden, and put
the man he had formed into it. 9The LORD God
caused every beautiful tree and every tree that
was good for food to grow out of the ground. In
the middle of the garden, God put the tree that
gives life and also the tree that gives the knowledge of good and evil.
10A river flowed through Eden and watered the
garden. From there the river branched out to become four rivers. 11The first river, named Pishon,
flows around the whole land of Havilah, where
there is gold. 12The gold of that land is excellent.
Bdellium and onyx[n] are also found there. 13The
second river, named Gihon, flows around the
whole land of Cush. 14The third river, named Tigris, flows out of Assyria toward the east. The
fourth river is the Euphrates.
15The LORD God put the man in the garden of
Eden to care for it and work it. 16The LORD God
commanded him, "You may eat the fruit from any
tree in the garden, 17but you must not eat the fruit
from the tree which gives the knowledge of good
and evil. If you ever eat fruit from that tree, you
will die!"

The First Woman

18Then the LORD God said, "It is not good for
the man to be alone. I will make a helper who is
right for him."
19From the ground God formed every wild ani-

bdellium and onyx Bdellium is an expensive, sweet-smelling resin like myrrh, and onyx is a gem.

mal and every bird in the sky, and he brought
them to the man so the man could name them.

SIDELIGHT: Adam and Eve ate an apple in the garden, right? Probably not. The Bible never says what the fruit was. It's only described as "the fruit from the tree which gives the knowledge of good and evil" (Genesis 2:17). Doesn't sound much like the humble apple!

Whatever the man called each living thing, that
became its name. 20The man gave names to all the
tame animals, to the birds in the sky, and to all the
wild animals. But Adam[n] did not find a helper
that was right for him. 21So the LORD God caused
the man to sleep very deeply, and while he was
asleep, God removed one of the man's ribs. Then
God closed up the man's skin at the place where
he took the rib. 22The LORD God used the rib from
the man to make a woman, and then he brought
the woman to the man.

23And the man said,

"Now, this is someone whose bones came
from my bones,
whose body came from my body.
I will call her 'woman,'
because she was taken out of man."

24So a man will leave his father and mother and
be united with his wife, and the two will become
one body.

25The man and his wife were naked, but they
were not ashamed.

The Beginning of Sin

3 Now the snake was the most clever of all the
wild animals the LORD God had made. One
day the snake said to the woman, "Did God really

Adam This is the name of the first man. It also means "humans," including men and women.

CREATION

Will We Ever Learn?

Five hundred years ago, Christopher Columbus wrote about the lush forests on the Haitian island of La Gonave. He described "thousands of kinds of trees so tall that they seem to be scratching heaven."

Today, the mountains of that island are almost barren. When the rain comes, the rich topsoil is eroded away, causing regular, devastating floods.

One year, thirty-three people in the small island town of Anse-a-Galets died in a flood. Three years later, the people were ready for the flooding. No one died, but two churches, four homes, and a drinking-water system were destroyed.

Some say the floods are natural disasters. But they happen, in part, because the people don't care for the land. They cut down trees to make charcoal to cook with or to sell. It's the only way they know to survive.

But it hurts them. Without trees, the highlands aren't protected. When rainfall comes, the good soil washes away, and the lowlands flood. So the cutting of trees to survive actually makes survival more difficult.

The people of La Gonave are experiencing the problems that come when people don't take care of the environment. Read **Genesis 2:4–17**—particularly verse 15—to see how God expects us to care for his world.

- How well do you think the people of La Gonave are fulfilling the responsibility of caring for God's "garden"?
- In what ways have you taken responsibility for caring for the world or "garden" God has given you?

CONSIDER. . .

- noting everything you throw away in a day or week. Decide which items you could avoid throwing away by recycling, reusing, or not purchasing.
- contributing to or getting involved with the National Forestry Association's Global ReLeaf campaign (Box 2000, Washington, DC 20013) or another organization that plants trees to repair damage people have caused by cutting down trees.

FOR MORE, SEE. . .

- Leviticus 25:1–7 (p. 121)
- Psalm 8:1–9 (p. 485)
- Colossians 1:15–20 (p. 1239)

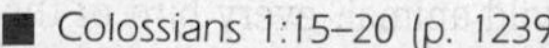

say that you must not eat fruit from any tree in the
garden?"
[2]The woman answered the snake, "We may eat
fruit from the trees in the garden. [3]But God told
us, 'You must not eat fruit from the tree that is in
the middle of the garden. You must not even
touch it, or you will die.' "
[4]But the snake said to the woman, "You will
not die. [5]God knows that if you eat the fruit from
that tree, you will learn about good and evil and
you will be like God!"
[6]The woman saw that the tree was beautiful,
that its fruit was good to eat, and that it would
make her wise. So she took some of its fruit and
ate it. She also gave some of the fruit to her husband, and he ate it.
[7]Then, it was as if their eyes were opened.
They realized they were naked, so they sewed fig
leaves together and made something to cover
themselves.
[8]Then they heard the LORD God walking in the
garden during the cool part of the day, and the
man and his wife hid from the LORD God among
the trees in the garden. [9]But the LORD God called
to the man and said, "Where are you?"
[10]The man answered, "I heard you walking in
the garden, and I was afraid because I was naked,
so I hid."
[11]God asked, "Who told you that you were naked? Did you eat fruit from the tree from which
I commanded you not to eat?"
[12]The man said, "You gave this woman to me
and she gave me fruit from the tree, so I ate it."
[13]Then the LORD God said to the woman,
"How could you have done such a thing?"
She answered, "The snake tricked me, so I ate
the fruit."
[14]The LORD God said to the snake,

"Because you did this,
 a curse will be put on you.
 You will be cursed as no other animal,
 tame or wild, will ever be.
You will crawl on your stomach,
 and you will eat dust all the days of your
 life.
[15]I will make you and the woman
 enemies to each other.
Your descendants[d] and her descendants
 will be enemies.
One of her descendants will crush your head,

MARRIAGE

One Body . . . Kind Of

"Connie, I'd like to talk about something."

"Sure, Jeff. Are you nervous about the wedding?"

"No, that's not it. I just wonder if you'd sign this with me. It's a pre-marriage agreement."

Connie scanned the document in disbelief. "This covers everything," she said. "Who'll get what if we divorce. How many children and how we'll raise them. How we'll pay the bills. Who's responsible for what around the house. . . . This reads like a business deal."

"Well, my lawyer . . ."

"Your lawyer! I thought we loved and trusted each other, Jeff."

"Of course I love you, Connie. I just want to be sure everything's clear. These agreements are good protection . . . you know, with the divorce rate and all."

"Will this piece of paper protect us more than sacred vows to love and cherish each other?"

Connie and Jeff discovered differences in their views of marriage—almost too late. Read **Genesis 2:18–24** to discover God's intention for marriage.

- How could this passage help Connie and Jeff sort out their conflicting expectations for marriage?
- How does this passage challenge or confirm your views of marriage?

C O N S I D E R . . .

- listing in order of priority all the things that would be important to you if you married. Then decide whether those priorities are compatible with the theme of this scripture passage.
- asking a parent or pastor to define a healthy Christian marriage.

F O R M O R E , S E E . . .

- Genesis 29:16–20 (p. 34)
- Matthew 19:3–6 (p. 941)
- Ephesians 5:21–33 (p. 1225)

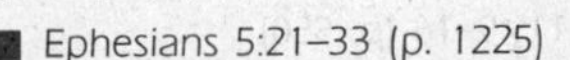

and you will bite his heel."

16Then God said to the woman,
"I will cause you to have much trouble
when you are pregnant,
and when you give birth to children,
you will have great pain.
You will greatly desire your husband,
but he will rule over you."

17Then God said to the man, "You listened to
what your wife said, and you ate fruit from the
tree from which I commanded you not to eat.
"So I will put a curse on the ground,
and you will have to work very hard for
your food.
In pain you will eat its food
all the days of your life.
18The ground will produce thorns and weeds
for you,
and you will eat the plants of the field.
19You will sweat and work hard
for your food.
Later you will return to the ground,
because you were taken from it.
You are dust,
and when you die, you will return to the
dust."

20The man named his wife Eve,[n] because she
is the mother of everyone who has ever lived.
21The LORD God made clothes from animal

Eve This name sounds like the Hebrew word meaning "alive."

SIN

An Expensive CD

Larry Rickers pulled the compact disc out from under his school jacket as he sauntered toward his car. His cool exterior disguised his excitement. A single from the CD had been at the top of the charts for five weeks straight, and he couldn't get it out of his head. He'd never wanted a recording this much, and now he had it. He couldn't wait to listen to it.

Suddenly, something came down hard on the back of his neck and made him crumple to his knees.

"Back inside, kid," an angry voice growled, as a security guard jerked Larry's arm behind his back. "I'll take that CD, thank you."

Larry felt humiliated as the guard escorted him through the mall, to the store manager's office. Then he sat awkwardly while the manager finished talking to the cops on the phone.

"An officer will be here in a few minutes," he said as he put down the receiver. "I won't press charges if you're a first-timer, but I need your home phone number. Your mom or dad will have to come get you."

Larry dictated the number as the manager dialed. "And, young man," the manager said as the phone rang, "I never want to see you in my store again."

Larry dreaded seeing his mom. She'd be so disappointed. Her eyes would be glassy-wet and red. She wouldn't look at him. That was the hardest part. He laid his head back and waited.

Larry experienced shame as Adam and Eve experienced shame when God caught them disobeying him. Read **Genesis 3:8–24** to learn what happened.

- How does the store manager's punishment for shoplifting compare to God's punishment of Adam and Eve? What resulted from Adam and Eve's sin? Was Larry's punishment—and Adam and Eve's—appropriate?
- In what ways do you, like Adam and Eve, try to hide from God when you disobey him?

CONSIDER . . .

- interrupting the "blame chain" ("somebody else made me do it") by accepting responsibility for things you do.
- talking to someone you trust about a sin you've been hiding inside, then confessing the sin to God. Discover how the confession affects you.

FOR MORE, SEE . . .

- Psalm 119:9–16 (p. 550)
- John 8:1–11 (p. 1070)
- 1 John 1:5–10 (p. 1316)

skins for the man and his wife and dressed them.
22Then the LORD God said, "The man has become
like one of us; he knows good and evil. We must
keep him from eating some of the fruit from the
tree of life, or he will live forever." 23So the LORD
God forced the man out of the garden of Eden to
work the ground from which he was taken. 24Af-
ter God forced the man out of the garden, he
placed angels and a sword of fire that flashed
around in every direction on its eastern border.
This kept people from getting to the tree of life.

The First Family

4 Adam had sexual relations with his wife Eve,
and she became pregnant and gave birth to
Cain.[n] Eve said, "With the LORD's help, I have
given birth to a man." 2After that, Eve gave birth
to Cain's brother Abel. Abel took care of flocks,
and Cain became a farmer.

3Later, Cain brought some food from the
ground as a gift to God. 4Abel brought the best
parts from some of the firstborn[d] of his flock. The
LORD accepted Abel and his gift, 5but he did not
accept Cain and his gift. So Cain became very angry and felt rejected.

6The LORD asked Cain, "Why are you angry?
Why do you look so unhappy? 7If you do things
well, I will accept you, but if you do not do them
well, sin is ready to attack you. Sin wants you, but
you must rule over it."

8Cain said to his brother Abel, "Let's go out
into the field." While they were out in the field,
Cain attacked his brother Abel and killed him.

9Later, the LORD said to Cain, "Where is your
brother Abel?"

Cain answered, "I don't know. Is it my job to
take care of my brother?"

10Then the LORD said, "What have you done?
Your brother's blood is crying out to me from the
ground. 11And now you will be cursed in your
work with the ground, the same ground where
your brother's blood fell and where your hands
killed him. 12You will work the ground, but it will
not grow good crops for you anymore, and you
will wander around on the earth."

13Then Cain said to the LORD, "This punishment is more than I can stand! 14Today you have
forced me to stop working the ground, and now
I must hide from you. I must wander around on
the earth, and anyone who meets me can kill
me."

15The LORD said to Cain, "No! If anyone kills
you, I will punish that person seven times more."
Then the LORD put a mark on Cain warning anyone who met him not to kill him.

Cain's Family

16So Cain went away from the LORD and lived
in the land of Nod,[n] east of Eden. 17He had sexual relations with his wife, and she became pregnant and gave birth to Enoch. At that time Cain
was building a city, which he named after his son
Enoch. 18Enoch had a son named Irad, Irad had
a son named Mehujael, Mehujael had a son
named Methushael, and Methushael had a son
named Lamech.

SIDELIGHT: If one wife is a good idea, two wives must be twice as good. That's what Lamech thought (Genesis 4:19). The idea really caught on by the time it reached Solomon, who ended up with seven hundred wives (1 Kings 11:3, p. 315).

19Lamech married two women, Adah and Zillah. 20Adah gave birth to Jabal, who became the
first person to live in tents and raise cattle. 21Ja-
bal's brother was Jubal, the first person to play the
harp and flute. 22Zillah gave birth to Tubal-Cain,
who made tools out of bronze and iron. The sister
of Tubal-Cain was Naamah.

23Lamech said to his wives:
"Adah and Zillah, hear my voice!
You wives of Lamech, listen to what I say.
I killed a man for wounding me,
a young man for hitting me.
24If Cain's killer is punished seven times,
then Lamech's killer will be punished
seventy-seven times."

Adam and Eve Have a New Son

25Adam had sexual relations with his wife Eve
again, and she gave birth to a son. She named him
Seth[n] and said, "God has given me another child.
He will take the place of Abel, who was killed by
Cain." 26Seth also had a son, and they named him
Enosh. At that time people began to pray to the
LORD.

Adam's Family History

5 This is the family history of Adam. When
God created human beings, he made them
in his own likeness. 2He created them male and
female, and on that day he blessed them and
named them human beings.

3When Adam was 130 years old, he became
the father of another son in his likeness and im-

Cain This name sounds like the Hebrew word for "I have given birth."
Nod This name sounds like the Hebrew word for "wander."
Seth This name sounds like the Hebrew word for "to give."

age, and Adam named him Seth. 4After Seth was
born, Adam lived 800 years and had other sons
and daughters. 5So Adam lived a total of 930
years, and then he died.

6When Seth was 105 years old, he had a son
named Enosh. 7After Enosh was born, Seth lived
807 years and had other sons and daughters. 8So
Seth lived a total of 912 years, and then he died.

9When Enosh was 90 years old, he had a son
named Kenan. 10After Kenan was born, Enosh
lived 815 years and had other sons and daughters.
11So Enosh lived a total of 905 years, and then he
died.

12When Kenan was 70 years old, he had a son
named Mahalalel. 13After Mahalalel was born, Kenan lived 840 years and had other sons and
daughters. 14So Kenan lived a total of 910 years,
and then he died.

15When Mahalalel was 65 years old, he had a
son named Jared. 16After Jared was born, Mahalalel lived 830 years and had other sons and daughters. 17So Mahalalel lived a total of 895 years, and
then he died.

18When Jared was 162 years old, he had a son
named Enoch. 19After Enoch was born, Jared
lived 800 years and had other sons and daughters.
20So Jared lived a total of 962 years, and then he
died.

21When Enoch was 65 years old, he had a son
named Methuselah. 22After Methuselah was
born, Enoch walked with God 300 years more
and had other sons and daughters. 23So Enoch
lived a total of 365 years. 24Enoch walked with
God; one day Enoch could not be found, because
God took him.

25When Methuselah was 187 years old, he had
a son named Lamech. 26After Lamech was born,
Methuselah lived 782 years and had other sons
and daughters. 27So Methuselah lived a total of
969 years, and then he died.

SIDELIGHT: If you think older adults tell too many stories about "when I was your age," imagine how Methuselah's kids must have felt. Genesis 5:27 says he lived to be 969 years old. If he were born when Christopher Columbus discovered the Americas in 1492, he would only be middle-aged today!

28When Lamech was 182, he had a son. 29La-
mech named his son Noah[n] and said, "He will
comfort us in our work, which comes from the
ground the LORD has cursed." 30After Noah was
born, Lamech lived 595 years and had other sons
and daughters. 31So Lamech lived a total of 777
years, and then he died.

32After Noah was 500 years old, he became the
father of Shem, Ham, and Japheth.

The Human Race Becomes Evil

6 The number of people on earth began to
grow, and daughters were born to them.
2When the sons of God saw that these girls were
beautiful, they married any of them they chose.
3The LORD said, "My Spirit[d] will not remain in
human beings forever, because they are flesh.
They will live only 120 years."

4The Nephilim[d] were on the earth in those days
and also later. That was when the sons of God had
sexual relations with the daughters of human beings. These women gave birth to children, who
became famous and were the mighty warriors of
long ago.

SIDELIGHT: Noah's boat described in Genesis 6:15 would have been huge for its time—about 450 feet long, the length of one and a half football fields. That's five times as long as the Mayflower in which the pilgrims sailed to North America in 1620. And it's more than half as long as a modern 860-foot ocean liner.

5The LORD saw that the human beings on the
earth were very wicked and that everything they
thought about was evil. 6He was sorry he had
made human beings on the earth, and his heart
was filled with pain. 7So the LORD said, "I will
destroy all human beings that I made on the
earth. And I will destroy every animal and everything that crawls on the earth and the birds of the
air, because I am sorry I have made them." 8But
Noah pleased the LORD.

Noah and the Great Flood

9This is the family history of Noah. Noah was
a good man, the most innocent man of his time,
and he walked with God. 10He had three sons:
Shem, Ham, and Japheth.

11People on earth did what God said was evil,
and violence was everywhere. 12When God saw
that everyone on the earth did only evil, 13he said
to Noah, "Because people have made the earth
full of violence, I will destroy all of them from the
earth. 14Build a boat of cypress wood for yourself.
Make rooms in it and cover it inside and outside
with tar. 15This is how big I want you to build the
boat: four hundred fifty feet long, seventy-five feet
wide, and forty-five feet high. 16Make an opening

Noah This name sounds like the Hebrew word for "rest."

around the top of the boat that is eighteen inches high from the edge of the roof down. Put a door in the side of the boat. Make an upper, middle, and lower deck in it. 17I will bring a flood of water on the earth to destroy all living things that live under the sky, including everything that has the breath of life. Everything on the earth will die. 18But I will make an agreement with you—you, your sons, your wife, and your sons' wives will all go into the boat. 19Also, you must bring into the boat two of every living thing, male and female. Keep them alive with you. 20Two of every kind of bird, animal, and crawling thing will come to you to be kept alive. 21Also gather some of every kind of food and store it on the boat as food for you and the animals."

22Noah did everything that God commanded him.

The Flood Begins

7 Then the LORD said to Noah, "I have seen that you are the best person among the people of this time, so you and your family can go into the boat. 2Take with you seven pairs, each male with its female, of every kind of clean[d] animal, and take one pair, each male with its female, of every kind of unclean animal. 3Take seven pairs of all the birds of the sky, each male with its female. This will allow all these animals to continue living on the earth after the flood. 4Seven days from now I will send rain on the earth. It will rain forty days and forty nights, and I will wipe off from the earth every living thing that I have made."

5Noah did everything the LORD commanded him.

6Noah was six hundred years old when the flood came. 7He and his wife and his sons and their wives went into the boat to escape the waters of the flood. 8The clean animals, the unclean animals, the birds, and everything that crawls on the ground 9came to Noah. They went into the boat in groups of two, male and female, just as God had commanded Noah. 10Seven days later the flood started.

11When Noah was six hundred years old, the flood started. On the seventeenth day of the second month of that year the underground springs

EVIL

Quiet Cancer

The symptoms don't seem that bad. You feel kind of tired and short of breath. Your blood doesn't clot as well as it should, and you bruise easily.

But these seemingly minor problems can be symptoms of acute leukemia, a potentially deadly cancer.

Though the outward signs don't seem that bad, inside, the body is under siege. Cancerous cells have invaded the bone marrow and bloodstream. The body no longer produces enough healthy white blood cells, taking away the body's ability to fight off infections. Suddenly, the body feels sick and needs immediate medical attention. Untreated, a person can die within six weeks. Treatment can involve intravenous chemotherapy with drugs that kill the cancerous cells, but also kill normal cells.

The hope is that healthy cells will grow again after treatment . . . and that cancerous ones won't.

Like leukemia, evil can spread without people really noticing it. Yet it's deadly and difficult to get rid of. See how God feels about evil in the world by reading **Genesis 6:5—7:24**.

- What parallels do you see between acute leukemia and the evil described in the passage? How is God's response to that evil like chemotherapy?
- What kinds of evil described in the passage still exist today? How is God working in the world today to stop the spread of evil?

CONSIDER . . .

- identifying a potential evil in your life and then talking to a parent or other trusted adult about how you can stop it before it grows into a bigger problem.
- clipping newspaper articles that show evil in the world. Each day this week, pray for people who are trapped by that evil.

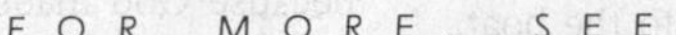

FOR MORE, SEE . . .

- Psalm 43:1–5 (p. 507)
- Romans 1:28–32 (p. 1141)
- 1 John 5:18–20 (p. 1321)

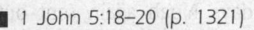

split open, and the clouds in the sky poured out
rain. 12The rain fell on the earth for forty days and
forty nights.
13On that same day Noah and his wife, his sons
Shem, Ham, and Japheth, and their wives went
into the boat. 14They had every kind of wild and
tame animal, every kind of animal that crawls on
the earth, and every kind of bird. 15Every creature
that had the breath of life came to Noah in the
boat in groups of two. 16One male and one female
of every living thing came, just as God had commanded Noah. Then the LORD closed the door
behind them.
17Water flooded the earth for forty days, and as
it rose it lifted the boat off the ground. 18The water continued to rise, and the boat floated on it
above the earth. 19The water rose so much that
even the highest mountains under the sky were
covered by it. 20It continued to rise until it was
more than twenty feet above the mountains.
21All living things that moved on the earth died.
This included all the birds, tame animals, wild animals, and creatures that swarm on the earth, as
well as all human beings. 22So everything on dry
land that had the breath of life in it died. 23God
destroyed from the earth every living thing that
was on the land — every man, animal, crawling
thing, and bird of the sky. All that was left was
Noah and what was with him in the boat. 24And
the waters continued to cover the earth for one
hundred fifty days.

The Flood Ends

8 But God remembered Noah and all the wild
and tame animals with him in the boat. He
made a wind blow over the earth, and the water
went down. 2The underground springs stopped
flowing, and the clouds in the sky stopped pouring down rain. 3-4The water that covered the earth
began to go down. After one hundred fifty days it
had gone down so much that the boat touched
land again. It came to rest on one of the mountains of Ararat[n] on the seventeenth day of the
seventh month. 5The water continued to go down
so that by the first day of the tenth month the tops
of the mountains could be seen.
6Forty days later Noah opened the window he
had made in the boat, and 7he sent out a raven.
It flew here and there until the water had dried
up from the earth. 8Then Noah sent out a dove to
find out if the water had dried up from the
ground. 9The dove could not find a place to land
because water still covered the earth, so it came
back to the boat. Noah reached out his hand and
took the bird and brought it back into the boat.
10After seven days Noah again sent out the
dove from the boat, 11and that evening it came
back to him with a fresh olive leaf in its mouth.
Then Noah knew that the ground was almost dry.
12Seven days later he sent the dove out again, but
this time it did not come back.
13When Noah was six hundred and one years
old, in the first day of the first month of that year,
the water was dried up from the land. Noah removed the covering of the boat and saw that the
land was dry. 14By the twenty-seventh day of the
second month the land was completely dry.
15Then God said to Noah, 16"You and your
wife, your sons, and their wives should go out of
the boat. 17Bring every animal out of the boat with
you — the birds, animals, and everything that
crawls on the earth. Let them have many young
ones so that they might grow in number."
18So Noah went out with his sons, his wife, and
his sons' wives. 19Every animal, everything that
crawls on the earth, and every bird went out of
the boat by families.
20Then Noah built an altar to the LORD. He
took some of all the clean[d] birds and animals, and
he burned them on the altar as offerings to God.
21The LORD was pleased with these sacrifices and
said to himself, "I will never again curse the
ground because of human beings. Their thoughts
are evil even when they are young, but I will
never again destroy every living thing on the earth
as I did this time.

22"As long as the earth continues,
planting and harvest,
cold and hot,
summer and winter,
day and night
will not stop."

The New Beginning

9 Then God blessed Noah and his sons and
said to them, "Have many children; grow in
number and fill the earth. 2Every animal on earth,
every bird in the sky, every animal that crawls on
the ground, and every fish in the sea will respect
and fear you. I have given them to you.
3"Everything that moves, everything that is
alive, is yours for food. Earlier I gave you the
green plants, but now I give you everything for
food. 4But you must not eat meat that still has
blood in it, because blood gives life. 5I will demand blood for life. I will demand the life of any
animal that kills a person, and I will demand the
life of anyone who takes another person's life.

6"Whoever kills a human being
will be killed by a human being,
because God made humans
in his own image.

7"As for you, Noah, I want you and your family

Ararat The ancient land of Urartu, an area in Eastern Turkey.

to have many children, to grow in number on the earth, and to become many."

8 Then God said to Noah and his sons, 9 "Now I am making my agreement with you and your people who will live after you, 10 and with every living thing that is with you — the birds, the tame and the wild animals, and with everything that came out of the boat with you — with every living thing on earth. 11 I make this agreement with you: I will never again destroy all living things by a flood. A flood will never again destroy the earth."

12 And God said, "This is the sign of the agreement between me and you and every living creature that is with you. 13 I am putting my rainbow in the clouds as the sign of the agreement between me and the earth. 14 When I bring clouds over the earth and a rainbow appears in them, 15 I will remember my agreement between me and you and every living thing. Floods will never again destroy all life on the earth. 16 When the rainbow appears in the clouds, I will see it and I will remember the agreement that continues forever between me and every living thing on the earth."

17 So God said to Noah, "The rainbow is a sign of the agreement that I made with all living things on earth."

Noah and His Sons

18 The sons of Noah who came out of the boat with him were Shem, Ham, and Japheth. (Ham was the father of Canaan.) 19 These three men were Noah's sons, and all the people on earth came from these three sons.

20 Noah became a farmer and planted a vineyard. 21 When he drank wine made from his grapes, he became drunk and lay naked in his tent. 22 Ham, the father of Canaan, looked at his naked father and told his brothers outside. 23 Then Shem and Japheth got a coat and, carrying it on both their shoulders, they walked backwards into the tent and covered their father. They turned their faces away so that they did not see their father's nakedness.

24 Noah was sleeping because of the wine. When he woke up and learned what his youngest son, Ham, had done to him, 25 he said,

"May there be a curse on Canaan!

FUTURE

A Hope-Filled Dream

The future looked bleak for Miguel Rodriquez. Friends in his Brooklyn, New York neighborhood used drugs, spent time in jail, and dropped out of school. For them, life seemed hopeless and the future painful.

But Miguel had a friend who believed in him — Phill Carlos Archbold, his youth minister. Phill Carlos encouraged and supported Miguel, helped him with homework, and invited him over for meals. Sometimes he would even pay Miguel's bus fare so he could get to school.

"He was a father-figure to me," Miguel says. "He was — and still is — always there for me."

Phill Carlos's support and encouragement gave Miguel hope for the future. Though his friends dropped out of high school, he graduated and went on to earn a mechanical engineering degree.

Because of Phill Carlos's ministry, Miguel looked forward to a bright future. God's promise to Noah also pointed to a bright future. Read about it in **Genesis 9:8–17**.

- How do you think God's promise to Noah gave him hope? How is that hope similar to the hope Phill Carlos gave to Miguel?
- What signs — like the rainbow for Noah — do you see that give you hope and courage for the future?

CONSIDER. . .

- drawing a rainbow on paper and posting it where you'll see it. Whenever something happens this week that encourages you about your future, write it on the paper.
- watching the evening news to look for signs of hope. Thank God for those people who are working for a positive future.

FOR MORE, SEE. . .

- Jeremiah 29:11 (p. 723)
- Matthew 6:25–34 (p. 918)
- 2 Corinthians 4:16–18 (p. 1196)

May he be the lowest slave to his
brothers."
[26]Noah also said,
"May the LORD, the God of Shem, be
praised!
May Canaan be Shem's slave.
[27]May God give more land to Japheth.
May Japheth live in Shem's tents,
and may Canaan be their slave."
[28]After the flood Noah lived 350 years. [29]He
lived a total of 950 years, and then he died.

Nations Grow and Spread

10 This is the family history of Shem, Ham, and Japheth, the sons of Noah. After the flood these three men had sons.

Japheth's Sons

[2]The sons of Japheth were Gomer, Magog,
Madai, Javan, Tubal, Meshech, and Tiras.
[3]The sons of Gomer were Ashkenaz, Riphath,
and Togarmah.
[4]The sons of Javan were Elishah, Tarshish, Kittim,[n] and Rodanim. [5]Those who lived in the
lands around the Mediterranean Sea came from
these sons of Japheth. All the families grew and
became different nations, each nation with its
own land and its own language.

Ham's Sons

[6]The sons of Ham were Cush, Mizraim,[n] Put,
and Canaan.
[7]The sons of Cush were Seba, Havilah, Sabtah,
Raamah, and Sabteca.
The sons of Raamah were Sheba and Dedan.
[8]Cush also had a descendant[d] named Nimrod,
who became a very powerful man on earth. [9]He
was a great hunter before the LORD, which is why
people say someone is "like Nimrod, a great
hunter before the LORD." [10]At first Nimrod's kingdom covered Babylon, Erech, Akkad, and Calneh
in the land of Babylonia. [11]From there he went to
Assyria, where he built the cities of Nineveh, Rehoboth Ir, and Calah. [12]He also built Resen, the
great city between Nineveh and Calah.
[13]Mizraim was the father of the Ludites, Ana-
mites, Lehabites, Naphtuhites, [14]Pathrusites, Casluhites, and the people of Crete. (The Philistines
came from the Casluhites.)
[15]Canaan was the father of Sidon, his first son,
and of Heth. [16]He was also the father of the Jebusites, Amorites, Girgashites, [17]Hivites, Arkites, Sinites, [18]Arvadites, Zemarites, and Hamathites.
The families of the Canaanites scattered. [19]Their
land reached from Sidon to Gerar as far as Gaza,
and then to Sodom, Gomorrah, Admah, and Zeboiim, as far as Lasha.
[20]All these people were the sons of Ham, and
all these families had their own languages, their
own lands, and their own nations.

Shem's Sons

[21]Shem, Japheth's older brother, also had sons.
One of his descendants[d] was the father of all the
sons of Eber.
[22]The sons of Shem were Elam, Asshur, Arphaxad, Lud, and Aram.
[23]The sons of Aram were Uz, Hul, Gether, and
Meshech.
[24]Arphaxad was the father of Shelah, who was
the father of Eber. [25]Eber was the father of two
sons—one named Peleg,[n] because the earth was
divided during his life, and the other was named
Joktan.
[26]Joktan was the father of Almodad, Sheleph,
Hazarmaveth, Jerah, [27]Hadoram, Uzal, Diklah,
[28]Obal, Abimael, Sheba, [29]Ophir, Havilah, and Jobab. All these people were the sons of Joktan.
[30]They lived in the area between Mesha and Se-
phar in the hill country in the East.
[31]These are the people from the family of
Shem, arranged by families, languages, countries,
and nations.
[32]This is the list of the families from the sons of
Noah, arranged according to their nations. From
these families came all the nations who spread
across the earth after the flood.

The Languages Confused

11 At this time the whole world spoke one
language, and everyone used the same
words. [2]As people moved from the east, they
found a plain in the land of Babylonia and settled
there.
[3]They said to each other, "Let's make bricks
and bake them to make them hard." So they used
bricks instead of stones, and tar instead of mortar.
[4]Then they said to each other, "Let's build a city
and a tower for ourselves, whose top will reach
high into the sky. We will become famous. Then
we will not be scattered over all the earth."
[5]The LORD came down to see the city and the
tower that the people had built. [6]The LORD said,
"Now, these people are united, all speaking the
same language. This is only the beginning of what
they will do. They will be able to do anything they
want. [7]Come, let us go down and confuse their
language so they will not be able to understand
each other."

Kittim His descendants were the people of Cyprus.
Mizraim This is another name for Egypt.
Peleg This name sounds like the Hebrew word for "divided."

8 So the LORD scattered them from there over all
the earth, and they stopped building the city. 9 The
place is called Babel[n] since that is where the
LORD confused the language of the whole world.
So the LORD caused them to spread out from there
over the whole world.

SIDELIGHT: The tower described in Genesis 11:1–9 was probably a ziggurat—a multi-storied temple built to worship Babylonian gods. The "temple towers," which looked like staircase pyramids, were built in most major Babylonian cities.

The Story of Shem's Family

10 This is the family history of Shem. Two years
after the flood, when Shem was 100 years old, his
son Arphaxad was born. 11 After that, Shem lived
500 years and had other sons and daughters.
12 When Arphaxad was 35 years old, his son
Shelah was born. 13 After that, Arphaxad lived 403
years and had other sons and daughters.
14 When Shelah was 30 years old, his son Eber
was born. 15 After that, Shelah lived 403 years and
had other sons and daughters.
16 When Eber was 34 years old, his son Peleg
was born. 17 After that, Eber lived 430 years and
had other sons and daughters.
18 When Peleg was 30 years old, his son Reu
was born. 19 After that, Peleg lived 209 years and
had other sons and daughters.
20 When Reu was 32 years old, his son Serug
was born. 21 After that, Reu lived 207 years and
had other sons and daughters.
22 When Serug was 30 years old, his son Nahor
was born. 23 After that, Serug lived 200 years and
had other sons and daughters.
24 When Nahor was 29 years old, his son Terah
was born. 25 After that, Nahor lived 119 years and
had other sons and daughters.
26 After Terah was 70 years old, his sons Abram,
Nahor, and Haran were born.

Babel This name sounds like the Hebrew word for "confused."

BRAGGING

Pride Hurts

Everyone was sure Susan Thompson would get the lead role of Maria in the spring musical, "West Side Story." Especially Susan. She regularly reminded everyone of her experience—being in every production since she was a freshman.

"I can make Maria come to life on the stage," she would proclaim. "Besides, this is my last high school show. Lots of people would be disappointed if I weren't cast as Maria."

Audition day came, and Susan was ready. She confidently sang and danced and acted. It felt great. "I was hot," she told her best friend, Dee, on the phone that evening. "This is a great part. It'll really stretch me."

The next morning Susan rushed to the drama room to see the cast list and confirm what she already knew.

But she stared at the list in disbelief. Her name wasn't next to Maria. It was way down the page—a little part with just a few lines in Act 2. Humiliated, Susan left in tears.

Pride was at the root of Susan's problem. And it was at the heart of the events in **Genesis 11:1–9**, where the people built a tower in disobedience to God.

- How did Susan's pride hurt her like pride hurt the tower builders?
- What "towers" of pride are you building in your own life?

C O N S I D E R . . .

- giving a compliment to another person when you're tempted to brag about yourself.
- listing everything about yourself that makes you proud. Then put checkmarks beside items you think are appropriate forms of pride, and x's beside those that aren't. Decide how you'll begin overcoming one of the x's this week.

F O R M O R E , S E E . . .

- Proverbs 16:18–19 (p. 581)
- Hosea 5:5–6 (p. 826)
- Philippians 2:1–11 (p. 1230)

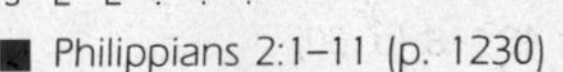

The Story of Terah's Family

27This is the family history of Terah. Terah was
the father of Abram, Nahor, and Haran. Haran
was the father of Lot. 28While his father, Terah,
was still alive, Haran died in Ur in Babylonia,
where he was born. 29Abram and Nahor both
married. Abram's wife was named Sarai, and Nahor's wife was named Milcah. She was the daughter of Haran, who was the father of both Milcah
and Iscah. 30Sarai was not able to have children.
31Terah took his son Abram, his grandson Lot
(Haran's son), and his daughter-in-law Sarai
(Abram's wife) and moved out of Ur of Babylonia.
They had planned to go to the land of Canaan, but
when they reached the city of Haran, they settled
there.
32Terah lived to be 205 years old, and then he
died in Haran.

God Calls Abram

12 The LORD said to Abram, "Leave your
country, your relatives, and your father's
family, and go to the land I will show you.
2I will make you a great nation,
and I will bless you.
I will make you famous,
and you will be a blessing to others.
3I will bless those who bless you,
and I will place a curse on those who harm
you.
And all the people on earth
will be blessed through you."

GOD'S WILL

Unknown Outcomes

Though it was the 1950s, the Auca Indians of Ecuador, South America were still a violent, Stone Age tribe.

But Jim Elliot felt God calling him to Ecuador to share the Gospel with the Aucas. Only one missionary had ever gone: Pedro Suarez, a Jesuit priest who, in 1667, was murdered at his remote jungle outpost.

Jim didn't let history deter him from what he knew God wanted. "My going to Ecuador is God's counsel," Jim wrote in his diary.

So Jim and four other missionaries left their families and boarded the ship for Ecuador. They built an encampment in Auca territory and began trying to befriend the Aucas. They would fly over their village in a small airplane, drop gifts and call out to them in the Auca language.

On January 6, 1956, they finally befriended one Auca, a young man they called "George." Now, they hoped, they could make more contact with the tribe.

That weekend, the Aucas attacked, killing all the missionaries, including Jim Elliot.

But that wasn't the end of the story. Jim's wife, Elisabeth, refused to let the murder of her husband keep her from following God's call to Ecuador. She and other missionaries returned to Auca territory.

Less than three years later, Elisabeth wrote: "Today I sit in a tiny leaf-thatched hut. . . . In another leaf house, just ten feet away, sit two of the seven men who killed my husband."

Jim Elliot followed God's will to seemingly tragic consequences. But God was at work even when his plan was difficult to see. And the missionary effort, started by Jim Elliot and continued by Elisabeth, prospered. Abram also left everything he knew to follow God to an unknown place. Read about his faith in **Genesis 12:1–9**.

- In what ways was Jim Elliot's call similar to Abram's call in the passage?
- Have you ever sensed that God wanted you to do something without your knowing what the result would be? How did you respond?

CONSIDER . . .

- taking a step of faith by doing something you believe God wants you to do, such as sharing your faith with a friend or working on a bad habit.
- making a bookmark for your Bible with two big eyes on it to remind you to look for God's will as you read.

FOR MORE, SEE . . .

- Genesis 45:1–8 (p. 50)
- Matthew 8:18–22 (p. 921)
- James 4:13–17 (p. 1298)

4So Abram left Haran as the LORD had told him,
and Lot went with him. At this time Abram was
75 years old. 5He took his wife Sarai, his nephew
Lot, and everything they owned, as well as all the
servants they had gotten in Haran. They set out
from Haran, planning to go to the land of Canaan,
and in time they arrived there.

> **SIDELIGHT:** When Abram left Egypt, he couldn't rent a moving truck to haul all his belongings when he moved from Haran to Canaan (Genesis 12:4–5). Instead, he probably lived in large animal-skin tents that were stretched over wooden poles. Some tents may have had several rooms.

6Abram traveled through that land as far as the
great tree of Moreh at Shechem. The Canaanites
were living in the land at that time. 7The LORD
appeared to Abram and said, "I will give this land
to your descendants."[d] So Abram built an altar
there to the LORD, who had appeared to him.
8Then he traveled from Shechem to the mountain
east of Bethel and set up his tent there. Bethel was
to the west, and Ai was to the east. There Abram
built another altar to the LORD and worshiped
him. 9After this, he traveled on toward southern
Canaan.

Abram Goes to Egypt

10At this time there was not much food in the
land, so Abram went down to Egypt to live because there was so little food. 11Just before they
arrived in Egypt, he said to his wife Sarai, "I know
you are a very beautiful woman. 12When the
Egyptians see you, they will say, 'This woman is
his wife.' Then they will kill me but let you live.
13Tell them you are my sister so that things will
go well with me and I may be allowed to live
because of you."

14When Abram came to Egypt, the Egyptians
saw that Sarai was very beautiful. 15The Egyptian
officers saw her and told the king of Egypt how
beautiful she was. They took her to the king's palace, and 16the king was kind to Abram because he
thought Abram was her brother. He gave Abram
sheep, cattle, male and female donkeys, male and
female servants, and camels.

17But the LORD sent terrible diseases on the
king and all the people in his house because of
Abram's wife Sarai. 18So the king sent for Abram
and said, "What have you done to me? Why
didn't you tell me Sarai was your wife? 19Why did
you say, 'She is my sister' so that I made her my
wife? Now, here is your wife. Take her and
leave!" 20Then the king commanded his men to
make Abram leave Egypt; so Abram and his wife
left with everything they owned.

Abram and Lot Separate

13 So Abram, his wife, and Lot left Egypt,
taking everything they owned, and traveled to southern Canaan. 2Abram was very rich in
cattle, silver, and gold.

3He left southern Canaan and went back to
Bethel where he had camped before, between
Bethel and Ai, 4and where he had built an altar.
So he worshiped the LORD there.

5During this time Lot was traveling with
Abram, and Lot also had flocks, herds, and tents.
6Abram and Lot had so many animals that the
land could not support both of them together, 7so
Abram's herdsmen and Lot's herdsmen began to
argue. The Canaanites and the Perizzites were living in the land at this time.

8Abram said to Lot, "There should be no arguing between you and me, or between your herdsmen and mine, because we are brothers. 9We
should separate. The whole land is there in front
of you. If you go to the left, I will go to the right.
If you go to the right, I will go to the left."

10Lot looked all around and saw the whole Jordan Valley and that there was much water there.
It was like the LORD's garden, like the land of
Egypt in the direction of Zoar. (This was before
the LORD destroyed Sodom and Gomorrah.) 11So
Lot chose to move east and live in the Jordan Valley. In this way Abram and Lot separated.
12Abram lived in the land of Canaan, but Lot lived
among the cities in the Jordan Valley, very near
to Sodom. 13Now the people of Sodom were very
evil and were always sinning against the LORD.

14After Lot left, the LORD said to Abram, "Look
all around you — to the north and south and east
and west. 15All this land that you see I will give
to you and your descendants[d] forever. 16I will
make your descendants as many as the dust of the
earth. If anyone could count the dust on the
earth, he could count your people. 17Get up! Walk
through all this land because I am now giving it
to you."

18So Abram moved his tents and went to live
near the great trees of Mamre at the city of Hebron. There he built an altar to the LORD.

Lot Is Captured

14 Now Amraphel was king of Babylonia,
Arioch was king of Ellasar, Kedorlaomer
was king of Elam, and Tidal was king of Goiim.
2All these kings went to war against several other
kings: Bera king of Sodom, Birsha king of Gomorrah, Shinab king of Admah, Shemeber king of Zeboiim, and the king of Bela. (Bela is also called
Zoar.)

3These kings who were attacked united their
armies in the Valley of Siddim (now the Dead
Sea[d]). 4They had served Kedorlaomer for twelve
years, but in the thirteenth year, they all turned
against him. 5Then in the fourteenth year, Kedorlaomer and the kings with him came and defeated
the Rephaites[d] in Ashteroth Karnaim, the Zuzites
in Ham, and the Emites in Shaveh Kiriathaim.
6They also defeated the Horites in the mountains
of Edom to El Paran (near the desert). 7Then they
turned back and went to En Mishpat (that is, Kadesh). They defeated all the Amalekites, as well as
the Amorites who lived in Hazazon Tamar.

8At that time the kings of Sodom, Gomorrah,
Admah, Zeboiim, and Bela went out to fight in the
Valley of Siddim. (Bela is called Zoar.) 9They
fought against Kedorlaomer king of Elam, Tidal
king of Goiim, Amraphel king of Babylonia, and
Arioch king of Ellasar — four kings fighting against
five. 10There were many tar pits in the Valley of
Siddim. When the kings of Sodom and Gomorrah
and their armies ran away, some of the soldiers
fell into the tar pits, but the others ran away to the
mountains.

11Now Kedorlaomer and his armies took everything the people of Sodom and Gomorrah owned,
including their food. 12They took Lot, Abram's
nephew who was living in Sodom, and everything
he owned. Then they left. 13One of the men who
was not captured went to Abram, the Hebrew,
and told him what had happened. At that time
Abram was camped near the great trees of Mamre
the Amorite. Mamre was a brother of Eshcol and
Aner, and they had all made an agreement to help
Abram.

Abram Rescues Lot

14When Abram learned that Lot had been captured, he called out his 318 trained men who had
been born in his camp. He led the men and
chased the enemy all the way to the town of Dan.
15That night he divided his men into groups, and
they made a surprise attack against the enemy.
They chased them all the way to Hobah, north of
Damascus. 16Then Abram brought back everything the enemy had stolen, the women and
the other people, and Lot, and everything Lot
owned.

17After defeating Kedorlaomer and the kings
who were with him, Abram went home. As he
was returning, the king of Sodom came out to
meet him in the Valley of Shaveh (now called
King's Valley).

18Melchizedek king of Salem brought out bread
and wine. He was a priest for God Most High
19and blessed Abram, saying,

"Abram, may you be blessed by God Most
High,
the God who made heaven and earth.
20And we praise God Most High,
who has helped you to defeat your
enemies."

Then Abram gave Melchizedek a tenth of everything he had brought back from the battle.

21The king of Sodom said to Abram, "You may
keep all these things for yourself. Just give me my
people who were captured."

22But Abram said to the king of Sodom, "I make
a promise to the LORD, the God Most High, who
made heaven and earth. 23I promise that I will not
keep anything that is yours. I will not keep even
a thread or a sandal strap so that you cannot say,
'I made Abram rich.' 24I will keep nothing but the
food my young men have eaten. But give Aner,
Eshcol, and Mamre their share of what we won,
because they went with me into battle."

God's Agreement with Abram

15 After these things happened, the LORD
spoke his word to Abram in a vision:
"Abram, don't be afraid. I will defend you, and I
will give you a great reward."

2But Abram said, "Lord GOD, what can you
give me? I have no son, so my slave Eliezer from
Damascus will get everything I own after I die."
3Abram said, "Look, you have given me no son,
so a slave born in my house will inherit everything
I have."

4Then the LORD spoke his word to Abram: "He
will not be the one to inherit what you have. You
will have a son of your own who will inherit what
you have."

5Then God led Abram outside and said, "Look
at the sky. There are so many stars you cannot
count them. Your descendants[d] also will be too
many to count."

6Abram believed the LORD. And the LORD accepted Abram's faith, and that faith made him
right with God.

7God said to Abram, "I am the LORD who led
you out of Ur of Babylonia so that I could give you
this land to own."

8But Abram said, "Lord GOD, how can I be sure
that I will own this land?"

9The LORD said to Abram, "Bring me a three-
year-old cow, a three-year-old goat, a three-year-
old male sheep, a dove, and a young pigeon."

10Abram brought them all to God. Then Abram
killed the animals and cut each of them into two
pieces, laying each half opposite the other half.
But he did not cut the birds in half. 11Later, large
birds flew down to eat the animals, but Abram
chased them away.

12As the sun was going down, Abram fell into
a deep sleep. While he was asleep, a very terrible
darkness came. 13Then the LORD said to Abram,
"You can be sure that your descendants will be

strangers and travel in a land they don't own. The
people there will make them slaves and be cruel
to them for four hundred years. 14But I will punish
the nation where they are slaves. Then your
descendants will leave that land, taking great
wealth with them. 15And you, Abram, will die in
peace and will be buried at an old age. 16After
your great-great-grandchildren are born, your people will come to this land again. It will take that
long, because I am not yet going to punish the
Amorites for their evil behavior."
17After the sun went down, it was very dark.
Suddenly a smoking firepot and a blazing torch
passed between the halves of the dead animals.[n]
18So on that day the LORD made an agreement
with Abram and said, "I will give to your descendants the land between the river of Egypt and the
great river Euphrates. 19This is the land of the Kenites, Kenizzites, Kadmonites, 20Hittites, Perizzites, Rephaites,[d] 21Amorites, Canaanites, Girgashites, and Jebusites."

Ishmael Is Born

16 Sarai, Abram's wife, had no children, but
she had a slave girl from Egypt named
Hagar. 2Sarai said to Abram, "Look, the LORD has
not allowed me to have children, so have sexual
relations with my slave girl. If she has a child,
maybe I can have my own family through her."
Abram did what Sarai said. 3It was after he had
lived ten years in Canaan that Sarai gave Hagar to
her husband Abram. (Hagar was her slave girl
from Egypt.)
4Abram had sexual relations with Hagar, and
she became pregnant. When Hagar learned she
was pregnant, she began to treat her mistress Sarai badly. 5Then Sarai said to Abram, "This is your
fault. I gave my slave girl to you, and when she
became pregnant, she began to treat me badly.
Let the LORD decide who is right—you or me."
6But Abram said to Sarai, "You are Hagar's mistress. Do anything you want to her." Then Sarai
was hard on Hagar, and Hagar ran away.

passed . . . animals This showed that God sealed the agreement between himself and Abram.

DISCOURAGEMENT

49,999 . . . and Counting

Thomas wanted to create something to store electricity. Time after time—in fact, fifty thousand times—he failed. But he kept trying and eventually succeeded. The first battery was invented.

Someone asked him, "Don't you get discouraged when you have to try fifty thousand experiments before you get any results?"

"Results?" Thomas replied. "Why, I've gotten a lot of results. I know fifty thousand things that won't work."

Thomas didn't get discouraged when he didn't get instant results. Perhaps that's why Thomas Edison is credited with almost thirteen hundred inventions, including record players, movies, microphones, light bulbs, and the transmitter that made telephones possible.

Just as Thomas Edison didn't expect instant results, Abram also waited for God's promises to come true. Read **Genesis 15:1–6** to see how he didn't give in to discouragement.

- What kept Thomas Edison from giving in to discouragement? What kept Abram from giving in? What's similar and different about the two situations?
- When have you been discouraged and tempted to give up on God as Abram was tempted? What happened?

C O N S I D E R . . .

- writing a letter of encouragement to yourself, then sealing the letter in an envelope to keep in your Bible. Open and read the letter sometime when you're discouraged.
- visiting a hospital's physical rehabilitation center. Ask a therapist what characteristics keep people from getting discouraged in recovery. Apply those characteristics in your own life.

F O R M O R E , S E E . . .

- Psalm 77:1–15 (p. 526)
- Isaiah 40:27–31 (p. 656)
- Hebrews 6:13–19 (p. 1282)

7The angel of the LORD found Hagar beside
a spring of water in the desert, by the road to
Shur. 8The angel said, "Hagar, Sarai's slave girl,
where have you come from? Where are you going?"
Hagar answered, "I am running away from my
mistress Sarai."
9The angel of the LORD said to her, "Go home
to your mistress and obey her." 10The angel also
said, "I will give you so many descendants[d] they
cannot be counted."
11The angel added,
"You are now pregnant,
and you will have a son.
You will name him Ishmael,[n]
because the LORD has heard your cries.
12Ishmael will be like a wild donkey.
He will be against everyone,
and everyone will be against him.
He will attack all his brothers."
13The slave girl gave a name to the LORD who
spoke to her: "You are 'God who sees me,'" because she said to herself, "Have I really seen God
who sees me?" 14So the well there, between Kadesh and Bered, was called Beer Lahai Roi.[n]
15Hagar gave birth to a son for Abram, and
Abram named him Ishmael. 16Abram was eighty-
six years old when Hagar gave birth to Ishmael.

Proof of the Agreement

17 When Abram was ninety-nine years old,
the LORD appeared to him and said, "I
am God Almighty. Obey me and do what is right.

Ishmael The Hebrew words for "Ishmael" and "has heard" sound similar.
Beer Lahai Roi This means "the well of the Living One who sees me."

PROMISES

Trusting the Pilot

The clouds hid the airport at Nairobi, Kenya. The twin-engine Cessna was running low on fuel.

"We're going to have to set down at the Athi River strip," the pilot said. "We can't fly into that storm."

The missionary passengers—the Partain family—listened nervously to the pilot's decision. Ruth, the mother, was unconscious, lying on a stretcher in the back after a near-fatal car accident. They had to get to Nairobi for better medical care.

The plane touched down and bounced to a stop on the grassy landing strip. When the storm had passed, the pilot stepped out and paced the runway. "I think we can make it now," he concluded. "But it's a bit muddy. I don't think we should try it with this load. We'll have to leave the luggage here. And we'll need Gene and David to wait too."

The two teenagers looked apprehensive, knowing that the landing strip was near a wild game park. "Don't worry," the pilot assured, "I'll be back to get you as quickly as I can. And it's safe here. The fence will keep wild animals out."

So Gene and David sat on the luggage and waited, watching for herds of wildebeests and zebras. They didn't worry much, though, because they knew the pilot would be back—as he had promised.

An hour later, a small dot in the sky showed the pilot's promise coming true. And the pilot's plan helped everyone arrive safely in Nairobi.

As the two teenagers trusted the pilot to come back, Abraham knew he could trust God's promise in **Genesis 17:1–10**.

- Why do you think Gene, David, and Abraham trusted the promises made to them?
- What kind of assurance do you get from God's promise to Abraham?

CONSIDER . . .

- changing something about yourself—such as a negative attitude or habit—as a sign that you believe and have responded to God's promise.
- drawing up a blank agreement between you and God, and posting it in your bedroom. When you find a promise from God in the Bible, write it on one side of the agreement. When you make a commitment to God, write it on the other side.

FOR MORE, SEE . . .

- Numbers 23:19 (p. 148)
- Matthew 28:16–20 (p. 962)
- Romans 4:18–25 (p. 1145)

2I will make an agreement between us, and I will
make you the ancestor of many people."
3Then Abram bowed facedown on the ground.
God said to him, 4"I am making my agreement
with you: I will make you the father of many nations. 5I am changing your name from Abram[n] to
Abraham[n] because I am making you a father of
many nations. 6I will give you many descendants.[d] New nations will be born from you, and
kings will come from you. 7And I will make an
agreement between me and you and all your
descendants from now on: I will be your God and
the God of all your descendants. 8You live in
the land of Canaan now as a stranger, but I will
give you and your descendants all this land
forever. And I will be the God of your descendants."

> **SIDELIGHT:** In the Bible, a change of name had great significance. That was certainly true when God changed Abram's name to Abraham (Genesis 17:5). Abram means "exalted father" in Hebrew, but Abraham means "father of a multitude"—a sign of God's promise.

9Then God said to Abraham, "You and your
descendants must keep this agreement from now
on. 10This is my agreement with you and all your
descendants, which you must obey: Every male
among you must be circumcised.[d] 11Cut away
your foreskin to show that you are prepared to
follow the agreement between me and you.
12From now on when a baby boy is eight days old,
you will circumcise him. This includes any boy
born among your people or any who is your slave,
who is not one of your descendants. 13Circumcise
every baby boy whether he is born in your family
or bought as a slave. Your bodies will be marked
to show that you are part of my agreement that
lasts forever. 14Any male who is not circumcised
will be cut off from his people, because he has
broken my agreement."

Isaac—the Promised Son

15God said to Abraham, "I will change the
name of Sarai,[n] your wife, to Sarah.[n] 16I will
bless her and give her a son, and you will be the
father. She will be the mother of many nations.
Kings of nations will come from her."
17Abraham bowed facedown on the ground
and laughed. He said to himself, "Can a man have
a child when he is a hundred years old? Can Sarah
give birth to a child when she is ninety?" 18Then
Abraham said to God, "Please let Ishmael be the
son you promised."
19God said, "No, Sarah your wife will have
a son, and you will name him Isaac.[n] I will
make my agreement with him to be an agreement that continues forever with all his descendants.[d]
20"As for Ishmael, I have heard you. I will bless
him and give him many descendants. And I will
cause their numbers to grow greatly. He will be
the father of twelve great leaders, and I will make
him into a great nation. 21But I will make my
agreement with Isaac, the son whom Sarah will
have at this same time next year." 22After God
finished talking with Abraham, God rose and left
him.
23Then Abraham gathered Ishmael, all the
males born in his camp, and the slaves he had
bought. So that day Abraham circumcised every
man and boy in his camp as God had told him to
do. 24Abraham was ninety-nine years old when he
was circumcised. 25And Ishmael, his son, was
thirteen years old when he was circumcised.
26Abraham and his son were circumcised on the
same day. 27Also on that day all the men in Abraham's camp were circumcised, including all those
born in his camp and all the slaves he had bought
from other nations.

The Three Visitors

18 Later, the LORD again appeared to Abraham near the great trees of Mamre.
Abraham was sitting at the entrance of his tent
during the hottest part of the day. 2He looked up
and saw three men standing near him. When
Abraham saw them, he ran from his tent to meet
them. He bowed facedown on the ground before
them 3and said, "Sir, if you think well of me,
please stay awhile with me, your servant. 4I will
bring some water so all of you can wash your feet.
You may rest under the tree, 5and I will get some
bread for you so you can regain your strength.
Then you may continue your journey."
The three men said, "That is fine. Do as you
said."
6Abraham hurried to the tent where Sarah was
and said to her, "Hurry, prepare twenty quarts of
fine flour, and make it into loaves of bread."

Abram This name means "honored father."
Abraham The end of the Hebrew word for "Abraham" sounds like the beginning of the Hebrew word for "many."
Sarai An Aramaic name meaning "princess."
Sarah A Hebrew name meaning "princess."
Isaac The Hebrew words for "he laughed" (vs. 17) and "Isaac" sound the same.

7Then Abraham ran to his herd and took one of
his best calves. He gave it to a servant, who hurried to kill it and to prepare it for food. 8Abraham
gave the three men the calf that had been cooked
and milk curds and milk. While they ate, he stood
under the tree near them.
9The men asked Abraham, "Where is your wife
Sarah?"
"There, in the tent," said Abraham.
10Then the LORD said, "I will certainly return to
you about this time a year from now. At that time
your wife Sarah will have a son."
Sarah was listening at the entrance of the tent
which was behind him. 11Abraham and Sarah
were very old. Since Sarah was past the age when
women normally have children, 12she laughed to
herself, "My husband and I are too old to have a
baby."
13Then the LORD said to Abraham, "Why did
Sarah laugh? Why did she say, 'I am too old to
have a baby'? 14Is anything too hard for the LORD?
No! I will return to you at the right time a year
from now, and Sarah will have a son."
15Sarah was afraid, so she lied and said, "I
didn't laugh."
But the LORD said, "No. You did laugh."
16Then the men got up to leave and started out
toward Sodom. Abraham walked along with them
a short time to send them on their way.

Abraham's Bargain with God

17The LORD said, "Should I tell Abraham what
I am going to do now? 18Abraham's children will
certainly become a great and powerful nation,
and all nations on earth will be blessed through
him. 19I have chosen him so he would command
his children and his descendants[d] to live the way
the LORD wants them to, to live right and be fair.
Then I, the LORD, will give Abraham what I promised him."

DOUBT

Who, Me?

Tony Matthews avoided his church's youth group. It was small, and none of his friends went. Plus, Tony was the youngest teenager in his church.

One Sunday, Tony's youth leader, Sharon, stopped him in the hall after worship. "Going with us on the retreat?" she asked.

Tony shook his head. "Uhhhh . . . It sounds all right, but I don't think so. Nobody my age will be there."

"That's a problem, isn't it?" Sharon mused. "Why don't you invite some of your friends?"

"I'm not very good at asking," Tony replied. "Besides, they wouldn't go anyway."

"Why not give it a try?" Sharon prodded. "I'd really like you to go."

Tony decided to try, but it was tough. He was shy, and he'd never talked to anyone about his church.

Most of the kids he asked said no, but Tony was persistent. Finally, he found two buddies to go with him, and they had a great time at the retreat.

The next youth group event was a miniature golf outing. Sharon figured about a dozen young people would come. But Tony and his friends liked golf, and he was part of the reason twenty-seven people showed up.

Being shy, Tony had doubted he had the gifts needed to persuade other kids to come to church, but God knew otherwise. Abraham and Sarah also doubted God could use them. Read their story in **Genesis 17:15–19**.

- How were Tony, Abraham, and Sarah similar and how were they different?
- Have you ever felt like laughing when someone suggested how God could use you? How did you deal with your doubts?

CONSIDER . . .

- asking a friend to tell you about gifts you have that you may not be aware of. Then commit yourself to using those gifts to serve God.
- doing something you're not sure you could ever do (such as writing a song, leading a Bible study, or sharing your faith) to see if God has given you gifts you doubted you had.

FOR MORE, SEE . . .

- Exodus 3:7–22 (p. 60)
- Psalm 77:1–15 (p. 526)
- John 20:24–29 (p. 1094)

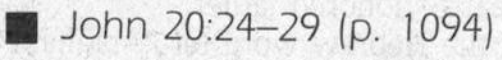

20 Then the LORD said, "I have heard many
complaints against the people of Sodom and Gomorrah. They are very evil. 21 I will go down and
see if they are as bad as I have heard. If not, I will
know."

22 So the men turned and went toward Sodom,
but Abraham stood there before the LORD. 23 Then
Abraham approached him and asked, "Do you
plan to destroy the good people along with
the evil ones? 24 What if there are fifty good people in that city? Will you still destroy it? Surely
you will save the city for the fifty good people living there. 25 Surely you will not destroy the
good people along with the evil ones; then
they would be treated the same. You are the
judge of all the earth. Won't you do what is
right?"

26 The LORD said, "If I find fifty good people in
the city of Sodom, I will save the whole city because of them."

27 Then Abraham said, "Though I am only dust
and ashes, I have been brave to speak to the Lord.
28 What if there are only forty-five good people in
the city? Will you destroy the whole city for the
lack of five good people?"

The LORD said, "If I find forty-five there, I will
not destroy the city."

29 Again Abraham said to him, "If you find only
forty good people there, will you destroy the
city?"

The LORD said, "If I find forty, I will not destroy
it."

30 Then Abraham said, "Lord, please don't be
angry with me, but let me ask you this. If you find
only thirty good people in the city, will you destroy it?"

He said, "If I find thirty good people there, I
will not destroy the city."

31 Then Abraham said, "I have been brave to
speak to the Lord. But what if there are twenty
good people in the city?"

He answered, "If I find twenty there, I will not
destroy the city."

32 Then Abraham said, "Lord, please don't be
angry with me, but let me bother you this one last
time. What if you find ten there?"

He said, "If I find ten there, I will not destroy
it."

33 When the LORD finished speaking to Abraham, he left, and Abraham returned home.

SERVICE

Gift for a Stranger

Unlike other leaders in India in the 1940s, V. P. Menon didn't have a fancy degree from a fancy university. He wasn't from a well-to-do or respected family. The oldest of thirteen children, he had to quit school at age thirteen to work in coal mines and factories.

As a young man, he went to Delhi to get a government job. On the way, everything he had—including his money and identification—was stolen at the railway station.

In desperation, he went to an elderly man standing nearby, explained his situation, and asked for a loan of fifteen rupees to buy food until he could get a job. The man gave him the money. Menon asked for his address so he could repay the loan, but the man said Menon didn't owe the debt to him, but owed any stranger in need. The help came from a stranger and should be repaid to a stranger.

Menon never forgot his debt, and his life was marked by constant generosity to those in need. The day before he died, a beggar came to the family home asking for money to buy new sandals. Menon asked his daughter to take fifteen rupees out of his wallet to give to the man.

It was his last conscious act.

V. P. Menon served strangers selflessly, just as Abraham provided food for strangers in **Genesis 18:1–16**. Read how that incident affected Abraham.

- What attitudes cause people to share as Menon, Abraham and Sarah did?
- How do you need to become more like Abraham and Sarah? When have you served God by serving people you didn't know?

C O N S I D E R . . .

- inviting someone who's new at your school home for a Coke.
- trying V. P. Menon's approach. Give five dollars to a stranger in need, and ask that he or she repay it to another stranger in need.

F O R   M O R E ,   S E E . . .

- 1 Kings 17:10–16 (p. 322)
- Hebrews 13:2 (p. 1290)
- James 2:1–13 (p. 1294)

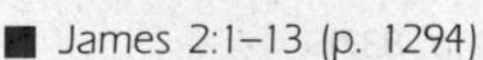

Lot Leaves Sodom

19 The two angels came to Sodom in the
evening as Lot was sitting near the city
gate. When he saw them, he got up and went to
them and bowed facedown on the ground. 2Lot
said, "Sirs, please come to my house and spend
the night. There you can wash your feet, and then
tomorrow you may continue your journey."
The angels answered, "No, we will spend the
night in the city's public square."
3But Lot begged them to come, so they agreed
and went to his house. Then Lot prepared a meal
for them. He baked bread without yeast, and they
ate it.
4Before bedtime, men both young and old and
from every part of Sodom surrounded Lot's
house. 5They called to Lot, "Where are the two
men who came to you tonight? Bring them out to
us so we can have sexual relations with them."
6Lot went outside to them, closing the door behind him. 7He said, "No, my brothers! Do not do
this evil thing. 8Look! I have two daughters who
have never slept with a man. I will give them to
you, and you may do anything you want with
them. But please don't do anything to these men.
They have come to my house, and I must protect
them."
9The men around the house answered, "Move
out of the way!" Then they said to each other,
"This man Lot came to our city as a stranger, and
now he wants to tell us what to do!" They said
to Lot, "We will do worse things to you than to
them." They started pushing him back and were
ready to break down the door.

GOD'S LOVE

A Second Chance

Most girls would love to have Amy Kennedy's looks. Her face. Her hair. Her figure. You would think she had it made.

But her good looks haven't kept her life from being a mess. At home, her alcoholic mom either neglected her or screamed at her. So she avoided home and hung out on street corners with other kids who didn't fit in.

At thirteen, Amy ran away from home for the fourth time and ended up in a juvenile detention center. While there, she decided to turn her life around and make something of herself—to give herself a second chance.

When she returned to school, things went great. She made new friends who didn't drink or party. Her life seemed to be coming together. But then a rumor started. "Amy sleeps around," people whispered at school. Nothing Amy said or did made any difference, and the rumor stuck. One by one, her new friends dumped her.

Except Mona. "I don't believe the rumor," she would tell Amy. "Besides, you deserve a second chance."

But Amy still felt rejected, so she went back to her old friends. She started dating Tim, who kept her comfortable with expensive gifts bought with drug money. "I love you," he would tell Amy. But she discovered that he only said it to get her to have sex with him. When she wouldn't, he dropped her, and so did all of her other old friends.

But Amy wasn't friendless. She still had Mona, and Mona's family took her in so she would have a place to live. Now, three years later, she feels like part of the family. She knows what it's like to have a second chance.

Like Amy, the people of Sodom and Gomorrah were given a second chance. Read how they responded to it in **Genesis 18:20—19:25**.

- How are Amy's friend Mona and Abraham similar? different?
- If you were Abraham, when would you have given up begging for the lives of the people?

CONSIDER . . .

- giving a friend a second chance when he or she blows it and does something that hurts you.
- keeping track of all the times people give you second chances. Thank them by baking cookies or running an errand—and learning from your mistake.

FOR MORE, SEE . . .

- Joel 2:12–13 (p. 837)
- Zephaniah 3:14–20 (p. 884)
- Acts 26:9–18 (p. 1135)

10But the two men staying with Lot opened the
door, pulled him back inside the house, and then
closed the door. 11They struck those outside the
door with blindness, so the men, both young and
old, could not find the door.
12The two men said to Lot, "Do you have any
other relatives in this city? Do you have any sons-
in-law, sons, daughters, or any other relatives? If
you do, tell them to leave now, 13because we are
about to destroy this city. The LORD has heard of
all the evil that is here, so he has sent us to destroy
it."
14So Lot went out and said to his future sons-in-
law who were pledged to marry his daughters,
"Hurry and leave this city! The LORD is about to
destroy it!" But they thought Lot was joking.
15At dawn the next morning, the angels begged
Lot to hurry. They said, "Go! Take your wife and
your two daughters with you so you will not be
destroyed when the city is punished."
16But Lot delayed. So the two men took the
hands of Lot, his wife, and his two daughters and
led them safely out of the city. So the LORD was
merciful to Lot and his family. 17After they
brought them out of the city, one of the men said,
"Run for your lives! Don't look back or stop anywhere in the valley. Run to the mountains, or you
will be destroyed."
18But Lot said to one of them, "Sir, please don't
force me to go so far! 19You have been merciful
and kind to me and have saved my life. But I can't
run to the mountains. The disaster will catch me,
and I will die. 20Look, that little town over there
is not too far away. Let me run there. It's really
just a little town, and I'll be safe there."
21The angel said to Lot, "Very well, I will allow
you to do this also. I will not destroy that town.
22But run there fast, because I cannot destroy
Sodom until you are safely in that town." (That
town is named Zoar,[n] because it is little.)

Sodom and Gomorrah Are Destroyed

23The sun had already come up when Lot entered Zoar. 24The LORD sent a rain of burning sulfur down from the sky on Sodom and Gomorrah
25and destroyed those cities. He also destroyed
the whole Jordan Valley, everyone living in the
cities, and even all the plants.
26At that point Lot's wife looked back. When
she did, she became a pillar of salt.
27Early the next morning, Abraham got up and
went to the place where he had stood before the
LORD. 28He looked down toward Sodom and Gomorrah and all the Jordan Valley and saw smoke
rising from the land, like smoke from a furnace.
29God destroyed the cities in the valley, but he
remembered what Abraham had asked. So God
saved Lot's life, but he destroyed the city where
Lot had lived.

SIDELIGHT: When God destroyed the cities of Sodom and Gomorrah (Genesis 19:23–29), he made sure they weren't built again. Archaeologists believe the two cities are now under water in a shallow part of the Dead Sea. The waters may have risen because of an earthquake around 2000 B.C.

Lot and His Daughters

30Lot was afraid to continue living in Zoar, so
he and his two daughters went to live in the
mountains in a cave. 31One day the older daughter said to the younger, "Our father is old. Everywhere on the earth women and men marry, but
there are no men around here for us to marry.
32Let's get our father drunk and have sexual relations with him. We can use him to have children
and continue our family."
33That night the two girls got their father
drunk, and the older daughter went and had sexual relations with him. But Lot did not know
when she lay down or when she got up.
34The next day the older daughter said to the
younger, "Last night I had sexual relations with
my father. Let's get him drunk again tonight so
you can go and have sexual relations with him,
too. In this way we can use our father to have
children to continue our family." 35So that night
they got their father drunk again, and the younger
daughter went and had sexual relations with him.
Again, Lot did not know when she lay down or
when she got up.
36So both of Lot's daughters became pregnant
by their father. 37The older daughter gave birth to
a son and named him Moab. He is the ancestor
of all the Moabite people who are still living today. 38The younger daughter also gave birth to a
son and named him Ben-Ammi. He is the father
of all the Ammonite people who are still living
today.

Abraham Tricks Abimelech

20 Abraham left Hebron and traveled to
southern Canaan where he stayed
awhile between Kadesh and Shur. When he
moved to Gerar, 2he told people that his wife
Sarah was his sister. Abimelech king of Gerar
heard this, so he sent some servants to take her.
3But one night God spoke to Abimelech in a

Zoar This name sounds like the Hebrew word for "little."

dream and said, "You will die. The woman you
took is married."

4But Abimelech had not gone near Sarah, so he
said, "Lord, would you destroy an innocent nation? 5Abraham himself told me, 'This woman is
my sister,' and she also said, 'He is my brother.'
I am innocent. I did not know I was doing anything wrong."

6Then God said to Abimelech in the dream,
"Yes, I know you did not realize what you were
doing. So I did not allow you to sin against me and
touch her. 7Give Abraham his wife back. He is a
prophet.[d] He will pray for you, and you will not
die. But if you do not give Sarah back, you and all
your family will surely die."

8So early the next morning, Abimelech called
all his officers and told them everything that had
happened in the dream. They were very afraid.
9Then Abimelech called Abraham to him and
said, "What have you done to us? What wrong
did I do against you? Why did you bring this trouble to my kingdom? You should not have done
these things to me. 10What were you thinking that
caused you to do this?"

11Then Abraham answered, "I thought no one
in this place respected God and that someone
would kill me to get Sarah. 12And it is true that
she is my sister. She is the daughter of my father,
but she is not the daughter of my mother. 13When
God told me to leave my father's house and wander in many different places, I told Sarah, 'You
must do a special favor for me. Everywhere we go
tell people I am your brother.' "

14Then Abimelech gave Abraham some sheep,
cattle, and male and female slaves. He also gave
Sarah, Abraham's wife, back to him 15and said,
"Look around you at my land. You may live anywhere you want."

16Abimelech said to Sarah, "I gave your brother
Abraham twenty-five pounds of silver to make up
for any wrong that people may think about you.
I want everyone to know that you are innocent."

17Then Abraham prayed to God, and God
healed Abimelech, his wife, and his servant girls
so they could have children. 18The LORD had kept
all the women in Abimelech's house from having
children as a punishment on Abimelech for taking
Abraham's wife Sarah.

A Baby for Sarah

21 The LORD cared for Sarah as he had said
and did for her what he had promised.
2Sarah became pregnant and gave birth to a son
for Abraham in his old age. Everything happened
at the time God had said it would. 3Abraham
named his son Isaac, the son Sarah gave birth to.
4He circumcised[d] Isaac when he was eight days
old as God had commanded.

5Abraham was one hundred years old when his
son Isaac was born. 6And Sarah said, "God has
made me laugh.[n] Everyone who hears about this
will laugh with me. 7No one thought that I would
be able to have Abraham's child, but even though
Abraham is old I have given him a son."

Hagar and Ishmael Leave

8Isaac grew, and when he became old enough
to eat food, Abraham gave a great feast. 9But
Sarah saw Ishmael making fun of Isaac. (Ishmael
was the son of Abraham by Hagar, Sarah's Egyptian slave.) 10So Sarah said to Abraham, "Throw
out this slave woman and her son. Her son should
not inherit anything; my son Isaac should receive
it all."

11This troubled Abraham very much because
Ishmael was also his son. 12But God said to Abraham, "Don't be troubled about the boy and the
slave woman. Do whatever Sarah tells you. The
descendants[d] I promised you will be from Isaac.
13I will also make the descendants of Ishmael into
a great nation because he is your son, too."

14Early the next morning Abraham took some
food and a leather bag full of water. He gave them
to Hagar and sent her away. Carrying these things
and her son, Hagar went and wandered in the
desert of Beersheba.

15Later, when all the water was gone from the
bag, Hagar put her son under a bush. 16Then she
went away a short distance and sat down. She
thought, "My son will die, and I cannot watch
this happen." She sat there and he began to cry.

17God heard the boy crying, and God's angel
called to Hagar from heaven. He said, "What is
wrong, Hagar? Don't be afraid! God has heard the
boy crying there. 18Help him up and take him by
the hand. I will make his descendants into a great
nation."

19Then God showed Hagar a well of water. So
she went to the well and filled her bag with water
and gave the boy a drink.

20God was with the boy as he grew up. Ishmael
lived in the desert and became an archer. 21He
lived in the Desert of Paran, and his mother found
a wife for him in Egypt.

Abraham's Bargain with Abimelech

22Then Abimelech came with Phicol, the commander of his army, and said to Abraham, "God
is with you in everything you do. 23So make a
promise to me here before God that you will be
fair with me and my children and my descendants.[d] Be kind to me and to this land where you

laugh The Hebrew words for "he laughed" and "Isaac" sound the same.

have lived as a stranger—as kind as I have been to you."

24And Abraham said, "I promise." 25Then Abraham complained to Abimelech about Abimelech's servants who had seized a well of water.

26But Abimelech said, "I don't know who did this. You never told me about this before today."

27Then Abraham gave Abimelech some sheep and cattle, and they made an agreement. 28Abraham also put seven female lambs in front of Abimelech.

29Abimelech asked Abraham, "Why did you put these seven female lambs by themselves?"

30Abraham answered, "Accept these lambs from me to prove that you believe I dug this well."

31So that place was called Beersheba[n] because they made a promise to each other there.

32After Abraham and Abimelech made the agreement at Beersheba, Abimelech and Phicol, the commander of his army, went back to the land of the Philistines.

33Abraham planted a tamarisk tree at Beersheba and prayed to the LORD, the God who lives forever. 34And Abraham lived as a stranger in the land of the Philistines for a long time.

God Tests Abraham

22 After these things God tested Abraham's faith. God said to him, "Abraham!"

And he answered, "Here I am."

2Then God said, "Take your only son, Isaac, the son you love, and go to the land of Moriah. Kill

Beersheba This name means "well of the promise" or "well of seven."

PRIORITIES

Worth a Sacrifice

Jesse Poling couldn't sleep. He tossed restlessly in bed, wondering what to do. He had been planning to take a summer job at a local machine shop. The pay and hours looked great, and the work didn't sound bad.

But then, last week at school, he had seen a poster about a camp for disabled kids that needed someone to teach swimming and canoeing. He loved water sports, and his youth minister had encouraged him to consider volunteering to help at the camp.

Jesse wasn't prepared for the reaction when he mentioned the camp possibility to his dad. "That's the craziest idea you've come up with in a long time, Jesse," his dad fumed. "Why would you want to work for free when you could get paid? It's not like you're independently wealthy. And then you'll come running to me to pay your college tuition."

His dad had a point, Jesse reasoned as he stared up at the dark bedroom ceiling. But no matter how hard he tried, he couldn't forget about the camp—or those kids.

When Jesse's alarm woke him the next morning, he knew what he had to do. "Dad," he explained at breakfast, "some things are worth sacrificing for. Helping at that camp is important to me." His dad didn't understand, but he agreed to let Jesse stick with his priorities. So Jesse called the camp director.

Like Jesse, Abraham had tough decisions, but he also stuck with what he believed was right. Check out **Genesis 22:1–18** to see what happened.

- What do Jesse's and Abraham's decisions say about their priorities?
- When have you, like Abraham, had to make a tough decision because of what you believed God wanted? What happened?

CONSIDER

- writing out the issues involved in a tough decision. Keep the list by your bed or on your desk for a few days. Whenever you think of an option, benefit, or disadvantage, write it on the paper. Pray about your decision through the week and then make the decision, sticking to what you know to be right.
- having a "What If" discussion over lunch with friends in the school cafeteria. Brainstorm together several situations that test your priorities. Then discuss what you would do if you were in a particular situation.

FOR MORE, SEE . . .

- Proverbs 3 (p. 570)
- Daniel 3:8–30 (p. 809)
- Matthew 6:19–24 (p. 918)

him there and offer him as a whole burnt offering on one of the mountains I will tell you about."

3Abraham got up early in the morning and saddled his donkey. He took Isaac and two servants with him. After he cut the wood for the sacrifice, they went to the place God had told them to go. 4On the third day Abraham looked up and saw the place in the distance. 5He said to his servants, "Stay here with the donkey. My son and I will go over there and worship, and then we will come back to you."

6Abraham took the wood for the sacrifice and gave it to his son to carry, but he himself took the knife and the fire. So he and his son went on together.

7Isaac said to his father Abraham, "Father!"

Abraham answered, "Yes, my son."

Isaac said, "We have the fire and the wood, but where is the lamb we will burn as a sacrifice?"

8Abraham answered, "God will give us the lamb for the sacrifice, my son."

So Abraham and his son went on together 9and came to the place God had told him about. Abraham built an altar there. He laid the wood on it and then tied up his son Isaac and laid him on the wood on the altar. 10Then Abraham took his knife and was about to kill his son.

11But the angel of the LORD called to him from heaven and said, "Abraham! Abraham!"

Abraham answered, "Yes."

12The angel said, "Don't kill your son or hurt him in any way. Now I can see that you trust God and that you have not kept your son, your only son, from me."

13Then Abraham looked up and saw a male sheep caught in a bush by its horns. So Abraham went and took the sheep and killed it. He offered it as a whole burnt offering to God, and his son was saved. 14So Abraham named that place The LORD Provides. Even today people say, "On the mountain of the LORD it will be provided."

15The angel of the LORD called to Abraham from heaven a second time 16and said, "The LORD says, 'Because you did not keep back your son, your only son, from me, I make you this promise by my own name: 17I will surely bless you and give you many descendants.[a] They will be as many as the stars in the sky and the sand on the seashore, and they will capture the cities of their enemies. 18Through your descendants all the nations on the earth will be blessed, because you obeyed me.' "

19Then Abraham returned to his servants. They all traveled back to Beersheba, and Abraham stayed there.

20After these things happened, someone told Abraham: "Your brother Nahor and his wife Milcah have children now. 21The first son is Uz, and the second is Buz. The third son is Kemuel (the father of Aram). 22Then there are Kesed, Hazo, Pildash, Jidlaph, and Bethuel." 23Bethuel became the father of Rebekah. Milcah was the mother of these eight sons, and Nahor, Abraham's brother, was the father. 24Also Nahor had four other sons by his slave woman[a] Reumah. Their names were Tebah, Gaham, Tahash, and Maacah.

> **SIDELIGHT:** If his name matches his sleeping habits, you probably wouldn't want to spend the night at Nahor's. His name means "snorer" (Genesis 22:23–24).

Sarah Dies

23 Sarah lived to be one hundred twenty-seven years old. 2She died in Kiriath Arba (that is, Hebron) in the land of Canaan. Abraham was very sad and cried because of her. 3After a while he got up from the side of his wife's body and went to talk to the Hittites. He said, 4"I am only a stranger and a foreigner here. Sell me some of your land so that I can bury my dead wife."

5The Hittites answered Abraham, 6"Sir, you are a great leader among us. You may have the best place we have to bury your dead. You may have any of our burying places that you want, and none of us will stop you from burying your dead wife."

7Abraham rose and bowed to the people of the land, the Hittites. 8He said to them, "If you truly want to help me bury my dead wife here, speak to Ephron, the son of Zohar for me. 9Ask him to sell me the cave of Machpelah at the edge of his field. I will pay him the full price. You can be the witnesses that I am buying it as a burial place."

10Ephron was sitting among the Hittites at the city gate. He answered Abraham, 11"No, sir. I will give you the land and the cave that is in it, with these people as witnesses. Bury your dead wife."

12Then Abraham bowed down before the Hittites. 13He said to Ephron before all the people, "Please let me pay you the full price for the field. Accept my money, and I will bury my dead there."

14Ephron answered Abraham, 15"Sir, the land is worth ten pounds of silver, but I won't argue with you over the price. Take the land, and bury your dead wife."

16Abraham agreed and paid Ephron in front of the Hittite witnesses. He weighed out the full price, ten pounds of silver, and they counted the weight as the traders normally did.

17-18So Ephron's field in Machpelah, east of Mamre, was sold. Abraham became the owner of the field, the cave in it, and all the trees that were in the field. The sale was made at the city gate, with the Hittites as witnesses. 19After this, Abraham buried his wife Sarah in the cave in the field of Machpelah, near Mamre. (Mamre was later called Hebron in the land of Canaan.) 20So Abraham bought the field and the cave in it from the Hittites to use as a burying place.

A Wife for Isaac

24 Abraham was now very old, and the LORD had blessed him in every way. 2Abraham said to his oldest servant, who was in charge of everything he owned, "Put your hand under my leg.[n] 3Make a promise to me before the LORD, the God of heaven and earth. Don't get a wife for my son from the Canaanite girls who live around here. 4Instead, go back to my country, to the land of my relatives, and get a wife for my son Isaac."

> **SIDELIGHT:** In Abraham's day, one way to show you'd keep your promise was to put your hand under the thigh of the person you were making the promise to (Genesis 24:2). Don't you like a simple promise better?

5The servant said to him, "What if this woman does not want to return with me to this land? Then, should I take your son with me back to your homeland?"

6Abraham said to him, "No! Don't take my son back there. 7The LORD, the God of heaven, brought me from the home of my father and the land of my relatives. And he promised me, 'I will give this land to your descendants.'[d] The LORD will send his angel before you to help you get a wife for my son there. 8If the girl won't come back with you, you will be free from this promise. But you must not take my son back there." 9So the servant put his hand under his master's leg and made a promise to Abraham about this.

10The servant took ten of Abraham's camels and left, carrying with him many different kinds of beautiful gifts. He went to Northwest Mesopotamia to Nahor's city. 11In the evening, when the women come out to get water, he made the camels kneel down at the well outside the city.

12The servant said, "LORD, God of my master Abraham, allow me to find a wife for his son today. Please show this kindness to my master Abraham. 13Here I am, standing by the spring, and the girls from the city are coming out to get water. 14I will say to one of them, 'Please put your jar down so I can drink.' Then let her say, 'Drink, and I will also give water to your camels.' If that happens, I will know she is the right one for your servant Isaac and that you have shown kindness to my master."

15Before the servant had finished praying, Rebekah, the daughter of Bethuel, came out of the city. (Bethuel was the son of Milcah and Nahor, Abraham's brother.) Rebekah was carrying her water jar on her shoulder. 16She was very pretty, a virgin;[d] she had never had sexual relations with a man. She went down to the spring and filled her jar, then came back up. 17The servant ran to her and said, "Please give me a little water from your jar."

18Rebekah said, "Drink, sir." She quickly lowered the jar from her shoulder and gave him a drink. 19After he finished drinking, Rebekah said, "I will also pour some water for your camels." 20So she quickly poured all the water from her jar into the drinking trough for the camels. Then she kept running to the well until she had given all the camels enough to drink.

21The servant quietly watched her. He wanted to be sure the LORD had made his trip successful. 22After the camels had finished drinking, he gave Rebekah a gold ring weighing one-fifth of an ounce and two gold arm bracelets weighing about four ounces each. 23He asked, "Who is your father? Is there a place in his house for me and my men to spend the night?"

24Rebekah answered, "My father is Bethuel, the son of Milcah and Nahor." 25Then she said, "And, yes, we have straw for your camels and a place for you to spend the night."

26The servant bowed and worshiped the LORD 27and said, "Blessed is the LORD, the God of my master Abraham. The LORD has been kind and truthful to him and has led me to my master's relatives."

28Then Rebekah ran and told her mother's family about all these things. 29She had a brother named Laban, who ran out to Abraham's servant, who was still at the spring. 30Laban had heard what she had said and had seen the ring and the bracelets on his sister's arms. So he ran out to the well, and there was the man standing by the camels at the spring. 31Laban said, "Sir, you are welcome to come in; you don't have to stand outside. I have prepared the house for you and also a place for your camels."

32So Abraham's servant went into the house. After Laban unloaded the camels and gave them straw and food, he gave water to Abraham's servant so he and the men with him could wash their feet. 33Then Laban gave the servant food,

Put . . . leg This showed that a person would keep the promise.

but the servant said, "I will not eat until I have told you why I came."

So Laban said, "Then tell us."

34He said, "I am Abraham's servant. 35The LORD has greatly blessed my master in everything, and he has become a rich man. The LORD has given him many flocks of sheep, herds of cattle, silver and gold, male and female servants, camels, and horses. 36Sarah, my master's wife, gave birth to a son when she was old, and my master has given everything he owns to that son. 37My master had me make a promise to him and said, 'Don't get a wife for my son from the Canaanite girls who live around here. 38Instead, you must go to my father's people and to my family. There you must get a wife for my son.' 39I said to my master, 'What if the woman will not come back with me?' 40But he said, 'I serve the LORD, who will send his angel with you and will help you. You will get a wife for my son from my family and my father's people. 41Then you will be free from the promise. But if they will not give you a wife for my son, you will be free from this promise.'

42"Today I came to this spring. I said, 'LORD, God of my master Abraham, please make my trip successful. 43I am standing by this spring. I will wait for a young woman to come out to get water, and I will say, "Please give me water from your jar to drink." 44Then let her say, "Drink this water, and I will also get water for your camels." By this I will know the LORD has chosen her for my master's son.'

45"Before I finished my silent prayer, Rebekah came out of the city with her water jar on her shoulder. She went down to the spring and got water. I said to her, 'Please give me a drink.' 46She quickly lowered the jar from her shoulder and said, 'Drink this. I will also get water for your camels.' So I drank, and she gave water to my camels too. 47When I asked her, 'Who is your father?' she answered, 'My father is Bethuel son of Milcah and Nahor.' Then I put the ring in her nose and the bracelets on her arms, 48and I bowed my head and thanked the LORD. I praised the LORD, the God of my master Abraham, because he led me on the right road to get the granddaughter of my master's brother for his son. 49Now, tell me, will you be kind and truthful to my master? And if not, tell me so. Then I will know what I should do."

50Laban and Bethuel answered, "This is clearly from the LORD, and we cannot change what must happen. 51Rebekah is yours. Take her and go. Let her marry your master's son as the LORD has commanded."

52When Abraham's servant heard these words, he bowed facedown on the ground before the LORD. 53Then he gave Rebekah gold and silver jewelry and clothes. He also gave expensive gifts to her brother and mother. 54The servant and the men with him ate and drank and spent the night there. When they got up the next morning, the servant said, "Now let me go back to my master."

55Rebekah's mother and her brother said, "Let Rebekah stay with us at least ten days. After that she may go."

56But the servant said to them, "Do not make me wait, because the LORD has made my trip successful. Now let me go back to my master."

57Rebekah's brother and mother said, "We will call Rebekah and ask her what she wants to do." 58They called her and asked her, "Do you want to go with this man now?"

She said, "Yes, I do."

59So they allowed Rebekah and her nurse to go with Abraham's servant and his men. 60They blessed Rebekah and said,

"Our sister, may you be the mother of
thousands of people,
and may your descendants[d] capture the
cities of their enemies."

61Then Rebekah and her servant girls got on the camels and followed the servant and his men. So the servant took Rebekah and left.

62At this time Isaac had left Beer Lahai Roi and was living in southern Canaan. 63One evening when he went out to the field to think, he looked up and saw camels coming. 64Rebekah also looked and saw Isaac. Then she jumped down from the camel 65and asked the servant, "Who is that man walking in the field to meet us?"

The servant answered, "That is my master." So Rebekah covered her face with her veil.

66The servant told Isaac everything that had happened. 67Then Isaac brought Rebekah into the tent of Sarah, his mother, and she became his wife. Isaac loved her very much, and so he was comforted after his mother's death.

Abraham's Family

25 Abraham married again, and his new wife was Keturah. 2She gave birth to Zimran, Jokshan, Medan, Midian, Ishbak, and Shuah. 3Jokshan was the father of Sheba and Dedan. Dedan's descendants[d] were the people of Assyria, Letush, and Leum. 4The sons of Midian were Ephah, Epher, Hanoch, Abida, and Eldaah. All these were descendants of Keturah. 5Abraham left everything he owned to Isaac. 6But before Abraham died, he did give gifts to the sons of his other wives, then sent them to the East to be away from Isaac.

7Abraham lived to be one hundred seventy-five years old. 8He breathed his last breath and died at an old age, after a long and satisfying life. 9His sons Isaac and Ishmael buried him in the cave of Machpelah in the field of Ephron east of Mamre.

(Ephron was the son of Zohar the Hittite.) [10]So
Abraham was buried with his wife Sarah in the
same field that he had bought from the Hittites.
[11]After Abraham died, God blessed his son Isaac.
Isaac was now living at Beer Lahai Roi.

[12]This is the family history of Ishmael, Abraham's son. (Hagar, Sarah's Egyptian servant, was
Ishmael's mother.) [13]These are the names of Ishmael's sons in the order they were born: Nebaioth, the first son, then Kedar, Adbeel, Mibsam,
[14]Mishma, Dumah, Massa, [15]Hadad, Tema, Jetur,
Naphish, and Kedemah. [16]These were Ishmael's
sons, and these are the names of the tribal leaders
listed according to their settlements and camps.
[17]Ishmael lived one hundred thirty-seven years
and then breathed his last breath and died. [18]His
descendants lived from Havilah to Shur, which is
east of Egypt stretching toward Assyria. They often attacked the descendants of his brothers.

Isaac's Family

[19]This is the family history of Isaac. Abraham
had a son named Isaac. [20]When Isaac was forty
years old, he married Rebekah, who came from
Northwest Mesopotamia. She was Bethuel's
daughter and the sister of Laban the Aramean.
[21]Isaac's wife could not have children, so Isaac
prayed to the LORD for her. The LORD heard
Isaac's prayer, and Rebekah became pregnant.

[22]While she was pregnant, the babies struggled
inside her. She asked, "Why is this happening to
me?" Then she went to get an answer from the
LORD.

[23]The LORD said to her,

"Two nations are in your body,
and two groups of people will be taken
from you.
One group will be stronger than the other,
and the older will serve the younger."

[24]When the time came, Rebekah gave birth to
twins. [25]The first baby was born red. Since his
skin was like a hairy robe, he was named Esau.*n*
[26]When the second baby was born, he was holding on to Esau's heel, so that baby was named

Esau This name may mean "hairy."

FAMILY

Sibling Rivalry

According to the American Chicle Youth Poll, most teenagers in North America have one brother and one sister. Only 8 percent of teenagers have no brothers or sisters. But 12 percent have three or more brothers and sisters.

So how do they get along with their brothers and sisters?

Only 62 percent of young people in the poll say they're happy with their relationships with their brothers and sisters. It's the area of home life they're least satisfied with.

About 40 percent say getting along better with their brothers and sisters would improve their home life more than anything else.

Only 15 percent of teenagers say they can talk about their problems with their brothers. And only 19 percent say they can talk about their problems with their sisters.

Some tension between brothers and sisters is normal. Relationships with siblings have been tough for a long time. **Genesis 25:19–34** describes fierce sibling rivalry between Esau and Jacob. Read how their rivalry made life difficult for them.

- If someone asked Jacob and Esau to respond to a survey about sibling relationships, what do you think the two of them would say?
- How is your relationship with your brother and/or sister like or unlike the relationship between Jacob and Esau? Which of the two brothers do you most closely identify with?

CONSIDER...

- sending your brother or sister a note—through the mail—giving a compliment for something he or she did recently.
- asking a trusted adult for some help with your family conflicts.

FOR MORE, SEE...

- Judges 9:1–6 (p. 225)
- Luke 10:38–42 (p. 1024)
- 1 John 3:11–18 (p. 1318)

Jacob.[n] Isaac was sixty years old when they were born.

27When the boys grew up, Esau became a skilled hunter. He loved to be out in the fields. But Jacob was a quiet man and stayed among the tents. 28Isaac loved Esau because he hunted the wild animals that Isaac enjoyed eating. But Rebekah loved Jacob.

29One day Jacob was boiling a pot of vegetable soup. Esau came in from hunting in the fields, weak from hunger. 30So Esau said to Jacob, "Let me eat some of that red soup, because I am weak with hunger." (That is why people call him Edom.[n])

31But Jacob said, "You must sell me your rights as the firstborn son."[n]

32Esau said, "I am almost dead from hunger. If I die, all of my father's wealth will not help me."

33But Jacob said, "First, promise me that you will give it to me." So Esau made a promise to Jacob and sold his part of their father's wealth to Jacob. 34Then Jacob gave Esau bread and vegetable soup, and he ate and drank, and then left. So Esau showed how little he cared about his rights as the firstborn son.

Isaac Lies to Abimelech

26 Now there was a time of hunger in the land, besides the time of hunger that happened during Abraham's life. So Isaac went to the town of Gerar to see Abimelech king of the Philistines. 2The LORD appeared to Isaac and said, "Don't go down to Egypt, but live in the land where I tell you to live. 3Stay in this land, and I will be with you and bless you. I will give you and your descendants[d] all these lands, and I will keep the oath I made to Abraham your father. 4I will give you many descendants, as hard to count as the stars in the sky, and I will give them all these lands. Through your descendants all the nations on the earth will be blessed. 5I will do this because your father Abraham obeyed me. He did what I said and obeyed my commands, my teachings, and my rules."

6So Isaac stayed in Gerar. 7His wife Rebekah was very beautiful, and the men of that place asked Isaac about her. Isaac said, "She is my sister," because he was afraid to tell them she was his wife. He thought they might kill him so they could have her.

8Isaac lived there a long time. One day as Abimelech king of the Philistines looked out his window, he saw Isaac holding his wife Rebekah tenderly. 9Abimelech called for Isaac and said, "This woman is your wife. Why did you say she was your sister?"

Isaac said to him, "I was afraid you would kill me so you could have her."

10Abimelech said, "What have you done to us? One of our men might have had sexual relations with your wife. Then we would have been guilty of a great sin."

11So Abimelech warned everyone, "Anyone who touches this man or his wife will be put to death."

Isaac Becomes Rich

12Isaac planted seed in that land, and that year he gathered a great harvest. The LORD blessed him very much, 13and he became rich. He gathered more wealth until he became a very rich man. 14He had so many slaves and flocks and herds that the Philistines envied him. 15So they stopped up all the wells the servants of Isaac's father Abraham had dug. (They had dug them when Abraham was alive.) The Philistines filled those wells with dirt. 16And Abimelech said to Isaac, "Leave our country because you have become much more powerful than we are."

17So Isaac left that place and camped in the Valley of Gerar and lived there. 18Long before this time Abraham had dug many wells, but after he died, the Philistines filled them with dirt. So Isaac dug those wells again and gave them the same names his father had given them. 19Isaac's servants dug a well in the valley, from which a spring of water flowed. 20But the herdsmen of Gerar argued with them and said, "This water is ours." So Isaac named that well Argue because they argued with him. 21Then his servants dug another well. When the people also argued about it, Isaac named that well Fight. 22He moved from there and dug another well. No one argued about this one, so he named it Room Enough. Isaac said, "Now the LORD has made room for us, and we will be successful in this land."

23From there Isaac went to Beersheba. 24The LORD appeared to him that night and said, "I am the God of your father Abraham. Don't be afraid, because I am with you. I will bless you and give you many descendants[d] because of my servant Abraham." 25So Isaac built an altar and worshiped the LORD there. He also made a camp there, and his servants dug a well.

26Abimelech came from Gerar to see Isaac. He brought with him Ahuzzath, who advised him, and Phicol, the commander of his army. 27Isaac asked them, "Why have you come to see me? You

Jacob This name sounds like the Hebrew word for "heel." "Grabbing someone's heel" is a Hebrew saying for tricking someone.
Edom This name sounds like the Hebrew word for "red."
rights . . . son Usually the firstborn son had a high rank in the family. The firstborn son usually became the new head of the family.

were my enemy and forced me to leave your
country."
28They answered, "Now we know that the
LORD is with you. Let us swear an oath to each
other. Let us make an agreement with you 29that
since we did not hurt you, you will not hurt us.
We were good to you and sent you away in peace.
Now the LORD has blessed you."
30So Isaac prepared food for them, and they all
ate and drank. 31Early the next morning the men
swore an oath to each other. Then Isaac sent
them away, and they left in peace.
32That day Isaac's servants came and told him
about the well they had dug, saying, "We found
water in that well." 33So Isaac named it Shibah[n]
and that city is called Beersheba even now.
34When Esau was forty years old, he married
two Hittite women—Judith daughter of Beeri
and Basemath daughter of Elon. 35These women
brought much sorrow to Isaac and Rebekah.

Shibah This name sounds like the Hebrew words for "seven" and "promise."

HONESTY

Truth and Consequences

Marcus Baker couldn't wait to show up at Julius's "spring fling" party with Maria. Every guy in school drooled over Maria. For months, he had wanted to ask her out. Then when he invited her to the party, she had actually said, "I'd love to go with you."

When he had told his parents about the date, they asked about the party. "Will Julius's parents be there?"

"Of course," he said, without thinking.

Then he found out Julius's parents would be out of town. "That's the whole idea, guy!" Julius had boasted. "This is going to be a real party!"

The Thursday before the party, Marcus's parents spent the whole breakfast asking for details about the party. Usually he liked it when they showed interest, but it felt like they were prying this time.

He tried not to lie. Instead, he carefully worded his answers to avoid the exact truth about Julius's parents being gone. "I'm not sure exactly about the plans," he explained awkwardly. "But I'm sure Julius and his parents have everything worked out."

His parents seemed satisfied, and Marcus spent the day trying to put the conversation—and his white lies—out of his mind. But he couldn't. When he went to bed that night, he couldn't sleep. He didn't want to blow their trust in him over one party—even if he was taking Maria.

Finally, at 2 A.M., he climbed out of bed and went to his parents' room to wake them. He had to tell them and risk the consequences. And he could not sleep until he did.

And he was right about what his parents would say. They didn't let him go to the party. Friday morning, when he called Maria to explain, she was relieved. "To be honest," she said, "I was worried when I heard what the party would be like. Maybe we can do something else instead."

Marcus had struggled with telling the whole truth. Similarly, Isaac feared for his life if he told the king the truth. Read what happened to him in **Genesis 26:1–11**.

- What were Marcus and Isaac afraid would happen if they told the truth? Was their concern legitimate?
- When have you, like Isaac, told a lie to avoid potential trouble? What happened?

CONSIDER . . .

- talking with your parent or a trusted adult friend about situations when you might be tempted not to tell the whole truth. Ask what he or she would do in that situation.
- starting an honesty piggy bank. Every time you tell the truth when it's tough, put in a penny. Every time you tell a lie, take out a penny. Try to improve your "bank balance."

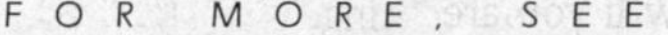
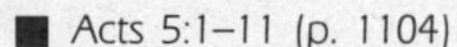

FOR MORE, SEE . . .

- Genesis 20:1–13 (p. 23)
- Proverbs 3:3–4 (p. 570)
- Acts 5:1–11 (p. 1104)

Jacob Tricks Isaac

27 When Isaac was old, his eyesight was
poor, so he could not see clearly. One
day he called his older son Esau to him and said,
"Son."
Esau answered, "Here I am."
2Isaac said, "I am old and don't know when I
might die. 3So take your bow and arrows and go
hunting in the field for an animal for me to eat.
4When you prepare the tasty food that I love,
bring it to me, and I will eat. Then I will bless you
before I die." 5So Esau went out in the field to
hunt.
Rebekah was listening as Isaac said this to his
son Esau. 6She said to her son Jacob, "Listen, I
heard your father saying to your brother Esau,
7'Kill an animal and prepare some tasty food for
me to eat. Then I will bless you in the presence
of the LORD before I die.' 8So obey me, my son,
and do what I tell you. 9Go out to our goats and
bring me two of the best young ones. I will prepare them just the way your father likes them.
10Then you will take the food to your father, and
he will bless you before he dies."
11But Jacob said to his mother Rebekah, "My
brother Esau is a hairy man, and I am smooth! 12If
my father touches me, he will know I am not
Esau. Then he will not bless me but will place a
curse on me because I tried to trick him."
13So Rebekah said to him, "If your father puts
a curse on you, I will accept the blame. Just do
what I said and go, get the goats for me."
14So Jacob went out and got two goats and
brought them to his mother, and she cooked
them in the special way Isaac enjoyed. 15She took
the best clothes of her older son Esau that were
in the house and put them on the younger son
Jacob. 16She also took the skins of the goats and
put them on Jacob's hands and neck. 17Then she
gave Jacob the tasty food and the bread she had
made.
18Jacob went in to his father and said, "Father."
And his father said, "Yes, my son. Who are
you?"
19Jacob said to him, "I am Esau, your first son.
I have done what you told me. Now sit up and eat
some meat of the animal I hunted for you. Then
bless me."
20But Isaac asked his son, "How did you find
and kill the animal so quickly?"
Jacob answered, "Because the LORD your God
helped me to find it."
21Then Isaac said to Jacob, "Come near so I can
touch you, my son. Then I will know if you are
really my son Esau."
22So Jacob came near to Isaac his father. Isaac
touched him and said, "Your voice sounds like
Jacob's voice, but your hands are hairy like the
hands of Esau." 23Isaac did not know it was Jacob,
because his hands were hairy like Esau's hands, so
Isaac blessed him. 24Isaac asked, "Are you really
my son Esau?"
Jacob answered, "Yes, I am."
25Then Isaac said, "Bring me the food, and I
will eat it and bless you." So Jacob gave him the
food, and he ate. Jacob gave him wine, and he
drank. 26Then Isaac said to him, "My son, come
near and kiss me." 27So Jacob went to his father
and kissed him. When Isaac smelled Esau's
clothes, he blessed him and said,

"The smell of my son
  is like the smell of the field
  that the LORD has blessed.
28May God give you plenty of rain
  and good soil
  so that you will have plenty of grain and
    new wine.
29May nations serve you
  and peoples bow down to you.
May you be master over your brothers,
  and may your mother's sons bow down to
    you.
May everyone who curses you be cursed,
  and may everyone who blesses you be
    blessed."

> **SIDELIGHT:** Jacob was the world's first make-up artist. With some help from his mom, Rebekah, and some fancy cosmetic work, he tricked his father, Isaac, into thinking he was his older brother, Esau (Genesis 27:14–29). By mistakenly blessing Jacob instead of Esau, Isaac fulfilled God's promise to Rebekah in Genesis 25:23 (p. 29).

30Isaac finished blessing Jacob. Then, just as Jacob left his father Isaac, Esau came in from hunting. 31He also prepared some tasty food and
brought it to his father. He said, "Father, rise and
eat the food that your son killed for you and then
bless me."
32Isaac asked, "Who are you?"
He answered, "I am your son—your firstborn[d]
son—Esau."
33Then Isaac trembled greatly and said, "Then
who was it that hunted the animals and brought
me food before you came? I ate it, and I blessed
him, and it is too late now to take back my blessing."
34When Esau heard the words of his father, he
let out a loud and bitter cry. He said to his father,
"Bless me—me, too, my father!"

35But Isaac said, "Your brother came and
tricked me. He has taken your blessing."
36Esau said, "Jacob[n] is the right name for him.
He has tricked me these two times. He took away
my share of everything you own, and now he has
taken away my blessing." Then Esau asked,
"Haven't you saved a blessing for me?"
37Isaac answered, "I gave Jacob the power to be
master over you, and all his brothers will be his
servants. And I kept him strong with grain and
new wine. There is nothing left to give you, my
son."
38But Esau continued, "Do you have only one
blessing, Father? Bless me, too, Father!" Then
Esau began to cry out loud.
39Isaac said to him,

"You will live far away from the best land,
far from the rain.
40You will live by using your sword,
and you will be a slave to your brother.
But when you struggle,
you will break free from him."

41After that Esau hated Jacob because of the
blessing from Isaac. He thought to himself, "My
father will soon die, and I will be sad for him.
Then I will kill Jacob."
42Rebekah heard about Esau's plan to kill Jacob.
So she sent for Jacob and said to him, "Listen,
your brother Esau is comforting himself by planning to kill you. 43So, my son, do what I say. My
brother Laban is living in Haran. Go to him at
once! 44Stay with him for a while, until your
brother is not so angry. 45In time, your brother
will not be angry, and he will forget what you did
to him. Then I will send a servant to bring you
back. I don't want to lose both of my sons on the
same day."
46Then Rebekah said to Isaac, "I am tired of
Hittite women. If Jacob marries one of these Hittite women here in this land, I want to die."

Jacob Searches for a Wife

28 Isaac called Jacob and blessed him and
commanded him, "You must not marry
a Canaanite woman. 2Go to the house of Bethuel,
your mother's father, in Northwest Mesopotamia.
Laban, your mother's brother, lives there. Marry
one of his daughters. 3May God Almighty bless
you and give you many children, and may you
become a group of many peoples. 4May he give
you and your descendants[d] the blessing of Abraham so that you may own the land where you are
now living as a stranger, the land God gave to
Abraham." 5So Isaac sent Jacob to Northwest
Mesopotamia, to Laban the brother of Rebekah.
Bethuel the Aramean was the father of Laban and
Rebekah, and Rebekah was the mother of Jacob
and Esau.
6Esau learned that Isaac had blessed Jacob and
sent him to Northwest Mesopotamia to find a
wife there. He also learned that Isaac had commanded Jacob not to marry a Canaanite woman
7and that Jacob had obeyed his father and mother
and had gone to Northwest Mesopotamia. 8So
Esau saw that his father Isaac did not want his
sons to marry Canaanite women. 9Now Esau already had wives, but he went to Ishmael son of
Abraham, and he married Mahalath, Ishmael's
daughter. Mahalath was the sister of Nebaioth.

Jacob's Dream at Bethel

10Jacob left Beersheba and set out for Haran.
11When he came to a place, he spent the night
there because the sun had set. He found a stone
and laid his head on it to go to sleep. 12Jacob
dreamed that there was a ladder resting on the
earth and reaching up into heaven, and he saw
angels of God going up and coming down the ladder. 13Then Jacob saw the LORD standing above
the ladder, and he said, "I am the LORD, the God
of Abraham your grandfather, and the God of
Isaac. I will give you and your descendants[d] the
land on which you are now sleeping. 14Your
descendants will be as many as the dust of the
earth. They will spread west and east, north and
south, and all the families of the earth will be
blessed through you and your descendants. 15I am
with you and will protect you everywhere you go
and will bring you back to this land. I will not
leave you until I have done what I have promised
you."
16Then Jacob woke from his sleep and said,
"Surely the LORD is in this place, but I did not
know it." 17He was afraid and said, "This place
frightens me! It is surely the house of God and the
gate of heaven."
18Jacob rose early in the morning and took the
stone he had slept on and set it up on its end.
Then he poured olive oil on the top of it. 19At first,
the name of that city was Luz, but Jacob named
it Bethel.[n]
20Then Jacob made a promise. He said, "I want
God to be with me and to protect me on this journey. I want him to give me food to eat and clothes
to wear 21so I will be able to return in peace to
my father's house. If the LORD does these things,
he will be my God. 22This stone which I have set
up on its end will be the house of God. And I will
give God one-tenth of all he gives me."

Jacob This name sounds like the Hebrew word for "heel." "Grabbing someone's heel" is a Hebrew saying for tricking someone.
Bethel This name means "house of God."

Jacob Arrives in Northwest Mesopotamia

29 Then Jacob continued his journey and came to the land of the people of the East. 2 He looked and saw a well in the field and three flocks of sheep lying nearby, because they drank water from this well. A large stone covered the mouth of the well. 3 When all the flocks would gather there, the shepherds would roll the stone away from the well and water the sheep. Then they would put the stone back in its place.

4 Jacob said to the shepherds there, "My brothers, where are you from?"

They answered, "We are from Haran."

5 Then Jacob asked, "Do you know Laban, grandson of Nahor?"

They answered, "We know him."

6 Then Jacob asked, "How is he?"

They answered, "He is well. Look, his daughter Rachel is coming now with his sheep."

7 Jacob said, "But look, it is still the middle of the day. It is not time for the sheep to be gathered for the night, so give them water and let them go back into the pasture."

8 But they said, "We cannot do that until all the flocks are gathered. Then we will roll away the stone from the mouth of the well and water the sheep."

9 While Jacob was talking with the shepherds, Rachel came with her father's sheep, because it was her job to care for the sheep. 10 When Jacob saw Laban's daughter Rachel and Laban's sheep, he went to the well and rolled the stone from its mouth and watered Laban's sheep. Now Laban was the brother of Rebekah, Jacob's mother. 11 Then Jacob kissed Rachel and cried. 12 He told her that he was from her father's family and that he was the son of Rebekah. So Rachel ran home and told her father.

13 When Laban heard the news about his sister's son Jacob, he ran to meet him. Laban hugged him and kissed him and brought him to his house, where Jacob told Laban everything that had happened.

14 Then Laban said, "You are my own flesh and blood."

Jacob Is Tricked

Jacob stayed there a month. 15 Then Laban said to Jacob, "You are my relative, but it is not right for you to work for me without pay. What would you like me to pay you?"

16 Now Laban had two daughters. The older was Leah, and the younger was Rachel. 17 Leah had weak eyes, but Rachel was very beautiful. 18 Jacob loved Rachel, so he said to Laban, "Let me marry your younger daughter Rachel. If you will, I will work seven years for you."

19 Laban said, "It would be better for her to marry you than someone else, so stay here with me." 20 So Jacob worked for Laban seven years so he could marry Rachel. But they seemed like just a few days to him because he loved Rachel very much.

21 After seven years Jacob said to Laban, "Give me Rachel so that I may marry her. The time I promised to work for you is over."

22 So Laban gave a feast for all the people there. 23 That evening he brought his daughter Leah to Jacob, and they had sexual relations. 24 (Laban gave his slave girl Zilpah to his daughter to be her servant.) 25 In the morning when Jacob saw that he had had sexual relations with Leah, he said to Laban, "What have you done to me? I worked hard for you so that I could marry Rachel! Why did you trick me?"

26 Laban said, "In our country we do not allow the younger daughter to marry before the older daughter. 27 But complete the full week of the marriage ceremony with Leah, and I will give you Rachel to marry also. But you must serve me another seven years."

28 So Jacob did this, and when he had completed the week with Leah, Laban gave him his daughter Rachel as a wife. 29 (Laban gave his slave girl Bilhah to his daughter Rachel to be her servant.) 30 So Jacob had sexual relations with Rachel also, and Jacob loved Rachel more than Leah. Jacob worked for Laban for another seven years.

> **SIDELIGHT:** If you think it's hard to get a date with the right guy or girl, imagine how Jacob felt. He worked seven years to marry beautiful Rachel, only to be tricked into marrying her "weak-eyed" sister Leah. Then Jacob was given Rachel too, but he had to work for seven more years (Genesis 29:16–30). Jacob might have been tricked because the bride is brought to the wedding festivities wearing a veil.

Jacob's Family Grows

31 When the LORD saw that Jacob loved Rachel more than Leah, he made it possible for Leah to have children, but not Rachel. 32 Leah became pregnant and gave birth to a son. She named him Reuben,[n] because she said, "The LORD has seen my troubles. Surely now my husband will love me."

Reuben This name sounds like the Hebrew word for "he has seen my troubles."

33 Leah became pregnant again and gave birth
to another son. She named him Simeon[n] and
said, "The LORD has heard that I am not loved, so
he has given me this son."
34 Leah became pregnant again and gave birth
to another son. She named him Levi[n] and said,
"Now, surely my husband will be close to me,
because I have given him three sons."
35 Then Leah gave birth to another son. She
named him Judah,[n] because she said, "Now I
will praise the LORD." Then Leah stopped having
children.

30 When Rachel saw that she was not having children for Jacob, she envied her sister Leah. She said to Jacob, "Give me children, or
I'll die!"
2 Jacob became angry with her and said, "Can
I do what only God can do? He is the one who
has kept you from having children."
3 Then Rachel said, "Here is my slave girl Bilhah. Have sexual relations with her so she can
give birth to a child for me. Then I can have my
own family through her."
4 So Rachel gave Bilhah, her slave girl, to Jacob
as a wife, and he had sexual relations with her.
5 She became pregnant and gave Jacob a son. 6 Rachel said, "God has judged me innocent. He has
listened to my prayer and has given me a son," so
she named him Dan.[n]
7 Bilhah became pregnant again and gave Jacob
a second son. 8 Rachel said, "I have struggled hard
with my sister, and I have won." So she named
that son Naphtali.[n]
9 Leah saw that she had stopped having children, so she gave her slave girl Zilpah to Jacob as
a wife. 10 When Zilpah had a son, 11 Leah said, "I
am lucky," so she named him Gad.[n] 12 Zilpah
gave birth to another son, 13 and Leah said, "I am
very happy! Now women will call me happy," so
she named him Asher.[n]
14 During the wheat harvest Reuben went into
the field and found some mandrake[n] plants and
brought them to his mother Leah. But Rachel said
to Leah, "Please give me some of your son's mandrakes."
15 Leah answered, "You have already taken
away my husband, and now you are trying to take
away my son's mandrakes."
But Rachel answered, "If you will give me your
son's mandrakes, you may sleep with Jacob tonight."
16 When Jacob came in from the field that night,
Leah went out to meet him. She said, "You will
have sexual relations with me tonight because I
have paid for you with my son's mandrakes." So
Jacob slept with her that night.
17 Then God answered Leah's prayer, and she
became pregnant again. She gave birth to a fifth
son 18 and said, "God has given me what I paid for,
because I gave my slave girl to my husband." So
Leah named her son Issachar.[n]
19 Leah became pregnant again and gave birth
to a sixth son. 20 She said, "God has given me a
fine gift. Now surely Jacob will honor me, because
I have given him six sons," so she named him
Zebulun.[n]
21 Later Leah gave birth to a daughter and
named her Dinah.
22 Then God remembered Rachel and answered
her prayer, making it possible for her to have children. 23 When she became pregnant and gave
birth to a son, she said, "God has taken away my
shame," 24 and she named him Joseph.[n] Rachel
said, "I wish the LORD would give me another
son."

Jacob Tricks Laban

25 After the birth of Joseph, Jacob said to Laban,
"Now let me go to my own home and country.
26 Give me my wives and my children and let me
go. I have earned them by working for you, and
you know that I have served you well."
27 Laban said to him, "If I have pleased you,
please stay. I know the LORD has blessed me because of you. 28 Tell me what I should pay you,
and I will give it to you."
29 Jacob answered, "You know that I have
worked hard for you, and your flocks have grown
while I cared for them. 30 When I came, you had
little, but now you have much. Every time I did
something for you, the LORD blessed you. But
when will I be able to do something for my own
family?"
31 Laban asked, "Then what should I give you?"
Jacob answered, "I don't want you to give me
anything. Just do this one thing, and I will come
back and take care of your flocks. 32 Today let me
go through all your flocks. I will take every speck-

Simeon This name sounds like the Hebrew word for "has heard."
Levi This name sounds like the Hebrew word for "be close to."
Judah This name sounds like the Hebrew word for "praise."
Dan This name means "he has judged."
Naphtali This name sounds like the Hebrew word for "my struggle."
Gad This name may mean "lucky."
Asher This name may mean "happy."
mandrake A plant which was believed to cause a woman to become pregnant.
Issachar This name sounds like the Hebrew word for "paid for."
Zebulun This name sounds like the Hebrew word for "honor."
Joseph This name sounds like the Hebrew word for "he adds."

led or spotted sheep, every black lamb, and every spotted or speckled goat. That will be my pay. 33In the future you can easily see if I am honest. When you come to look at my flocks, if I have any goat that isn't speckled or spotted or any lamb that isn't black, you will know I stole it."

34Laban answered, "Agreed! We will do what you ask." 35But that day Laban took away all the male goats that had streaks or spots, all the speckled and spotted female goats (all those that had white on them), and all the black sheep. He told his sons to watch over them. 36Then he took these animals to a place that was three days' journey away from Jacob. Jacob took care of all the flocks that were left.

37So Jacob cut green branches from poplar, almond, and plane trees and peeled off some of the bark so that the branches had white stripes on them. 38He put the branches in front of the flocks at the watering places. When the animals came to drink, they also mated there, 39so the flocks mated in front of the branches. Then the young that were born were streaked, speckled, or spotted. 40Jacob separated the young animals from the others, and he made them face the streaked and dark animals in Laban's flock. Jacob kept his animals separate from Laban's. 41When the stronger animals in the flock were mating, Jacob put the branches before their eyes so they would mate near the branches. 42But when the weaker animals mated, Jacob did not put the branches there. So the animals born from the weaker animals were Laban's, and those born from the stronger animals were Jacob's. 43In this way Jacob became very rich. He had large flocks, many male and female servants, camels, and donkeys.

Jacob Runs Away

31 One day Jacob heard Laban's sons talking. They said, "Jacob has taken everything our father owned, and in this way he has become rich." 2Then Jacob noticed that Laban was not as friendly as he had been before. 3The LORD said to Jacob, "Go back to the land where your ancestors lived, and I will be with you."

4So Jacob told Rachel and Leah to meet him in the field where he kept his flocks. 5He said to them, "I have seen that your father is not as friendly with me as he used to be, but the God of my father has been with me. 6You both know that I have worked as hard as I could for your father, 7but he cheated me and changed my pay ten times. But God has not allowed your father to harm me. 8When Laban said, 'You can have all the speckled animals as your pay,' all the animals gave birth to speckled young ones. But when he said, 'You can have all the streaked animals as your pay,' all the flocks gave birth to streaked babies. 9So God has taken the animals away from your father and has given them to me.

10"I had a dream during the season when the flocks were mating. I saw that the only male goats who were mating were streaked, speckled, or spotted. 11The angel of God spoke to me in that dream and said, 'Jacob!' I answered, 'Yes!' 12The angel said, 'Look! Only the streaked, speckled, or spotted male goats are mating. I have seen all the wrong things Laban has been doing to you. 13I am the God who appeared to you at Bethel, where you poured olive oil on the stone you set up on end and where you made a promise to me. Now I want you to leave here and go back to the land where you were born.' "

14Rachel and Leah answered Jacob, "Our father has nothing to give us when he dies. 15He has treated us like strangers. He sold us to you, and then he spent all of the money you paid for us. 16God took all this wealth from our father, and now it belongs to us and our children. So do whatever God has told you to do."

17So Jacob put his children and his wives on camels, 18and they began their journey back to Isaac, his father, in the land of Canaan. All the flocks of animals that Jacob owned walked ahead of them. He carried everything with him that he had gotten while he lived in Northwest Mesopotamia.

19While Laban was gone to cut the wool from his sheep, Rachel stole the idols that belonged to him. 20And Jacob tricked Laban the Aramean by not telling him he was leaving. 21Jacob and his family left quickly, crossed the Euphrates River, and traveled toward the mountains of Gilead.

22Three days later Laban learned that Jacob had run away, 23so he gathered his relatives and began to chase him. After seven days Laban found him in the mountains of Gilead. 24That night God came to Laban the Aramean in a dream and said, "Be careful! Do not say anything to Jacob, good or bad."

The Search for the Stolen Idols

25So Laban caught up with Jacob. Now Jacob had made his camp in the mountains, so Laban and his relatives set up their camp in the mountains of Gilead. 26Laban said to Jacob, "What have you done? You cheated me and took my daughters as if you had captured them in a war. 27Why did you run away secretly and trick me? Why didn't you tell me? Then I could have sent you away with joy and singing and with the music of tambourines[d] and harps. 28You did not even let me kiss my grandchildren and my daughters good-bye. You were very foolish to do this! 29I have the power to harm you, but last night the God of your father spoke to me and warned me not to say anything to you, good or bad. 30I know you want to go back to your home, but why did you steal my idols?"

31 Jacob answered Laban, "I left without telling you, because I was afraid you would take your daughters away from me. 32 If you find anyone here who has taken your idols, that person will be killed! Your relatives will be my witnesses. You may look for anything that belongs to you and take anything that is yours." (Now Jacob did not know that Rachel had stolen Laban's idols.)

33 So Laban looked in Jacob's tent, in Leah's tent, and in the tent where the two slave women stayed, but he did not find his idols. When he left Leah's tent, he went into Rachel's tent. 34 Rachel had hidden the idols inside her camel's saddle and was sitting on them. Although Laban looked through the whole tent, he did not find them. 35 Rachel said to her father, "Father, don't be angry with me. I am not able to stand up before you because I am having my monthly period." So Laban looked through the camp, but he did not find his idols.

36 Then Jacob became very angry and said, "What wrong have I done? What law have I broken to cause you to chase me? 37 You have looked through everything I own, but you have found nothing that belongs to you. If you have found anything, show it to everyone. Put it in front of your relatives and my relatives, and let them decide which one of us is right. 38 I have worked for you now for twenty years. During all that time none of the lambs and kids died during birth, and I have not eaten any of the male sheep from your flocks. 39 Any time an animal was killed by wild beasts, I did not bring it to you, but made up for the loss myself. You made me pay for any animal that was stolen during the day or night. 40 In the daytime the sun took away my strength, and at night I was cold and could not sleep. 41 I worked like a slave for you for twenty years—the first fourteen to get your two daughters and the last six to earn your flocks. During that time you changed my pay ten times. 42 But the God of my father, the God of Abraham and the God of Isaac, was with me. Otherwise, you would have sent me away with nothing. But he saw the trouble I had and the hard work I did, and last night he corrected you."

Jacob and Laban's Agreement

43 Laban said to Jacob, "These girls are my daughters. Their children belong to me, and these flocks are mine. Everything you see here belongs to me, but I can do nothing to keep my daughters and their children. 44 Let us make an agreement, and let us set up a pile of stones to remind us of it."

45 So Jacob took a large rock and set it up on its end. 46 He told his relatives to gather rocks, so they took the rocks and piled them up; then they ate beside the pile. 47 Laban named that place in his language A Pile to Remind Us, and Jacob gave the place the same name in Hebrew.

48 Laban said to Jacob, "This pile of rocks will remind us of the agreement between us." That is why the place was called A Pile to Remind Us. 49 It was also called Mizpah,[n] because Laban said, "Let the LORD watch over us while we are separated from each other. 50 Remember that God is our witness even if no one else is around us. He will know if you harm my daughters or marry other women. 51 Here is the pile of rocks that I have put between us and here is the rock I set up on end. 52 This pile of rocks and this rock set on end will remind us of our agreement. I will never go past this pile to hurt you, and you must never come to my side of them to hurt me. 53 Let the God of Abraham, who is the God of Nahor and the God of their fathers, punish either of us if we break this agreement."

So Jacob made a promise in the name of the God whom his father Isaac worshiped. 54 Then Jacob killed an animal and offered it as a sacrifice on the mountain, and he invited his relatives to share in the meal. After they finished eating, they spent the night on the mountain. 55 Early the next morning Laban kissed his grandchildren and his daughters and blessed them, and then he left to return home.

Jacob Meets Esau

32 When Jacob also went his way, the angels of God met him. 2 When he saw them, he said, "This is the camp of God!" So he named that place Mahanaim.[n]

3 Jacob's brother Esau was living in the area called Seir in the country of Edom. Jacob sent messengers to Esau, 4 telling them, "Give this message to my master Esau: 'This is what Jacob, your servant, says: I have lived with Laban and have remained there until now. 5 I have cattle, donkeys, flocks, and male and female servants. I send this message to you and ask you to accept us.' "

6 The messengers returned to Jacob and said, "We went to your brother Esau. He is coming to meet you and has four hundred men with him."

7 Then Jacob was very afraid and worried. He divided the people who were with him and all the flocks, herds, and camels into two camps. 8 Jacob thought, "Esau might come and destroy one

Mizpah This name sounds like the Hebrew word for "watch."
Mahanaim This name means "two camps."

camp, but the other camp can run away and be
saved."
9Then Jacob said, "God of my father Abraham!
God of my father Isaac! LORD, you told me to return to my country and my family. You said that
you would treat me well. 10I am not worthy of the
kindness and continual goodness you have shown
me. The first time I traveled across the Jordan
River, I had only my walking stick, but now I own
enough to have two camps. 11Please save me from
my brother Esau. I am afraid he will come and kill
all of us, even the mothers with the children.
12You said to me, 'I will treat you well and will
make your children as many as the sand of the
seashore. There will be too many to count.' "
13Jacob stayed there for the night and prepared
a gift for Esau from what he had with him: 14two
hundred female goats and twenty male goats, two
hundred female sheep and twenty male sheep,
15thirty female camels and their young, forty cows
and ten bulls, twenty female donkeys, and ten
male donkeys. 16Jacob gave each separate flock of
animals to one of his servants and said to them,
"Go ahead of me and keep some space between
each herd." 17Jacob gave them their orders. To
the servant with the first group of animals he said,
"My brother Esau will come to you and ask,
'Whose servant are you? Where are you going
and whose animals are these?' 18Then you will
answer, 'They belong to your servant Jacob. He
sent them as a gift to you, my master Esau, and
he also is coming behind us.' "
19Jacob ordered the second servant, the third
servant, and all the other servants to do the same
thing. He said, "Say the same thing to Esau when
you meet him. 20Say, 'Your servant Jacob is coming behind us.' " Jacob thought, "If I send these
gifts ahead of me, maybe Esau will forgive me.
Then when I see him, perhaps he will accept me."
21So Jacob sent the gifts to Esau, but he himself
stayed that night in the camp.

Jacob Wrestles with God

22During the night Jacob rose and crossed the

SPIRITUAL GROWTH

Wrestling With God

Donald Cho, sixteen, sat silently through the youth council meeting at church. Usually bubbling with ideas, he sat back in his chair with his arms folded. The summer trip being planned just didn't interest him.

He and some friends had visited a home for the mentally retarded early that day, and he couldn't get it out of his mind.

Then, without warning or prompting, he interrupted the planning. "I get so disgusted sometimes when we sit here and haggle about what amusement parks to visit on our trip and all that junk," Donald said. "I mean, there are people living in old people's homes and hospitals and places for mentally retarded people. And nobody cares about. . . ."

His voice trailed off when he noticed everyone staring at him. "I just wish we did something that really mattered," he concluded. "What's the point of being a Christian otherwise?"

Donald's visit to the home for mentally retarded people had challenged him to struggle with what it means to follow God. Jacob also struggled with God—literally. Read **Genesis 32:22–32** and see what happened when Jacob wrestled with God.

- How does Donald's struggle with what it means to follow God compare with Jacob's wrestling by the Jabbok River?
- When have you "wrestled with God" like Jacob and grown in your faith because of the struggle?

CONSIDER . . .

- writing a letter to God, honestly asking him the questions you have about him, your faith, and the world. Then decide one thing you'll start doing to discover some answers to those questions.
- asking an athlete to tell you how the struggle of practice and physical exertion helps him or her improve physically. Compare the response to how "wrestling with God" can help you grow in your faith.

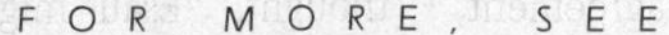

FOR MORE, SEE . . .

- Job 23:1–14 (p. 466)
- Jonah 2:1–7 (p. 857)
- John 20:24–29 (p. 1094)

Jabbok River at the crossing, taking with him his
two wives, his two slave girls, and his eleven
sons. 23He sent his family and everything he had
across the river. 24So Jacob was alone, and a man
came and wrestled with him until the sun came
up. 25When the man saw he could not defeat Jacob, he struck Jacob's hip and put it out of joint.
26Then he said to Jacob, "Let me go. The sun is
coming up."

But Jacob said, "I will let you go if you will bless
me."

27The man said to him, "What is your name?"

And he answered, "Jacob."

28Then the man said, "Your name will no
longer be Jacob. Your name will now be Israel,[n]
because you have wrestled with God and with
people, and you have won."

29Then Jacob asked him, "Please tell me your
name."

But the man said, "Why do you ask my name?"
Then he blessed Jacob there.

30So Jacob named that place Peniel,[n] saying, "I
have seen God face to face, but my life was
saved." 31Then the sun rose as he was leaving that
place, and Jacob was limping because of his leg.
32So even today the people of Israel do not eat the
muscle that is on the hip joint of animals, because
Jacob was touched there.

SIDELIGHT: The first wrestling match in the Bible was no mere three-period event. It lasted all night. Jacob's opponent had out-of-this-world strength, but Jacob still ended the match undefeated—though he sustained a sports-related injury and was given a prize-fighter's name, Israel, which means "he struggles with God" (Genesis 32:22–32).

Jacob Shows His Bravery

33 Jacob looked up and saw Esau coming,
and with him were four hundred men.
So Jacob divided his children among Leah, Rachel, and the two slave girls. 2Jacob put the slave
girls with their children first, then Leah and her
children behind them, and Rachel and Joseph last.
3Jacob himself went out in front of them and
bowed down flat on the ground seven times as he
was walking toward his brother.

4But Esau ran to meet Jacob and put his arms
around him and hugged him. Then Esau kissed
him, and they both cried. 5When Esau looked up
and saw the women and children, he asked,
"Who are these people with you?"

Jacob answered, "These are the children God
has given me. God has been good to me, your
servant."

6Then the two slave girls and their children
came up to Esau and bowed down flat on the
earth before him. 7Leah and her children also
came up to Esau and also bowed down flat on the
earth. Last of all, Joseph and Rachel came up to
Esau, and they, too, bowed down flat before him.

8Esau said, "I saw many herds as I was coming
here. Why did you bring them?"

Jacob answered, "They were to please you, my
master."

9But Esau said, "I already have enough, my
brother. Keep what you have."

10Jacob said, "No! Please! If I have pleased you,
then accept the gift I give you. I am very happy
to see your face again. It is like seeing the face of
God, because you have accepted me. 11So I beg
you to accept the gift I give you. God has been
very good to me, and I have more than I need."
And because Jacob begged, Esau accepted the gift.

12Then Esau said, "Let us be going. I will travel
with you."

13But Jacob said to him, "My master, you know
that the children are weak. And I must be careful
with my flocks and their young ones. If I force
them to go too far in one day, all the animals will
die. 14So, my master, you go on ahead of me, your
servant. I will follow you slowly and let the animals and the children set the speed at which we
travel. I will meet you, my master, in Edom."

15So Esau said, "Then let me leave some of my
people with you."

"No, thank you," said Jacob. "I only want to
please you, my master." 16So that day Esau started
back to Edom. 17But Jacob went to Succoth,
where he built a house for himself and shelters for
his animals. That is why the place was named
Succoth.[n]

18Jacob left Northwest Mesopotamia and arrived safely at the city of Shechem in the land of
Canaan. There he camped east of the city. 19He
bought a part of the field where he had camped
from the sons of Hamor father of Shechem for one
hundred pieces of silver. 20He built an altar there
and named it after God, the God of Israel.

Dinah Is Attacked

34 At this time Dinah, the daughter of Leah
and Jacob, went out to visit the women
of the land. 2When Shechem son of Hamor the
Hivite, the ruler of the land, saw her, he took her

Israel This name means "he wrestles with God."
Peniel This name means "the face of God."
Succoth This name means "shelters."

and forced her to have sexual relations with him. 3Shechem fell in love with Dinah, and he spoke kindly to her. 4He told his father, Hamor, "Please get this girl for me so I can marry her."

5Jacob learned how Shechem had disgraced his daughter, but since his sons were out in the field with the cattle, Jacob said nothing until they came home. 6While he waited, Hamor father of Shechem went to talk with Jacob.

7When Jacob's sons heard what had happened, they came in from the field. They were very angry that Shechem had done such a wicked thing to Israel. It was wrong for him to have sexual relations with Jacob's daughter; a thing like this should not be done.

8But Hamor talked to Dinah's brothers and said, "My son Shechem is deeply in love with Dinah. Please let him marry her. 9Marry our people. Give your women to our men as wives and take our women for your men as wives. 10You can live in the same land with us. You will be free to own land and to trade here."

11Shechem also talked to Jacob and to Dinah's brothers and said, "Please accept my offer. I will give anything you ask. 12Ask as much as you want for the payment for the bride, and I will give it to you. Just let me marry Dinah."

13Jacob's sons answered Shechem and his father with lies, because Shechem had disgraced their sister Dinah. 14The brothers said to them, "We cannot allow you to marry our sister, because you are not circumcised.[d] That would be a disgrace to us. 15But we will allow you to marry her if you do this one thing: Every man in your town must be circumcised like us. 16Then your men can marry our women, and our men can marry your women, and we will live in your land and become one people. 17If you refuse to be circumcised, we will take Dinah and leave."

18What they asked seemed fair to Hamor and Shechem. 19So Shechem quickly went to be circumcised because he loved Jacob's daughter.

Now Shechem was the most respected man in his family. 20So Hamor and Shechem went to the gate of their city and spoke to the men of their city, saying, 21"These people want to be friends with us. So let them live in our land and trade here. There is enough land for all of us. Let us marry their women, and we can let them marry our women. 22But we must agree to one thing: All our men must be circumcised as they are. Then they will agree to live in our land, and we will be one people. 23If we do this, their cattle and their animals will belong to us. Let us do what they say, and they will stay in our land." 24All the people who had come to the city gate heard this. They agreed with Hamor and Shechem, and every man was circumcised.

25Three days later the men who were circumcised were still in pain. Two of Jacob's sons, Simeon and Levi (Dinah's brothers), took their swords and made a surprise attack on the city, killing all the men there. 26They killed Hamor and his son Shechem and then took Dinah out of Shechem's house and left. 27Jacob's sons came upon the dead bodies and stole everything that was in the city, to pay them back for what Shechem had done to their sister. 28So the brothers took the flocks, herds, and donkeys, and everything in the city and in the fields. 29They took every valuable thing the people owned, even their wives and children and everything in the houses.

30Then Jacob said to Simeon and Levi, "You have caused me a lot of trouble. Now the Canaanites and the Perizzites who live in the land will hate me. Since there are only a few of us, if they join together to attack us, my people and I will be destroyed."

31But the brothers said, "We will not allow our sister to be treated like a prostitute."[d]

Jacob in Bethel

35 God said to Jacob, "Go to the city of Bethel and live there. Make an altar to the God who appeared to you there when you were running away from your brother Esau."

2So Jacob said to his family and to all who were with him, "Put away the foreign gods you have, and make yourselves clean,[d] and change your clothes. 3We will leave here and go to Bethel. There I will build an altar to God, who has helped me during my time of trouble. He has been with me everywhere I have gone." 4So they gave Jacob all the foreign gods they had, and the earrings they were wearing, and he hid them under the great tree near the town of Shechem. 5Then Jacob and his sons left there. But God caused the people in the nearby cities to be afraid, so they did not follow them. 6And Jacob and all the people who were with him went to Luz, which is now called Bethel, in the land of Canaan. 7There Jacob built an altar and named the place Bethel, after God, because God had appeared to him there when he was running from his brother.

8Deborah, Rebekah's nurse, died and was buried under the oak tree at Bethel, so they named that place Oak of Crying.

Jacob's New Name

9When Jacob came back from Northwest Mesopotamia, God appeared to him again and blessed him. 10God said to him, "Your name is Jacob, but you will not be called Jacob any longer. Your new name will be Israel." So he called him Israel. 11God said to him, "I am God Almighty. Have many children and grow in number as a nation. You will be the ancestor of many nations and kings. 12The same land I gave to Abraham and

Isaac I will give to you and your descendants."[d]
13Then God left him. 14Jacob set up a stone on
edge in that place where God had talked to him,
and he poured a drink offering and olive oil on it
to make it special for God. 15And Jacob named the
place Bethel.

Rachel Dies Giving Birth

16Jacob and his group left Bethel. Before they
came to Ephrath, Rachel began giving birth to her
baby, 17but she was having much trouble. When
Rachel's nurse saw this, she said, "Don't be
afraid, Rachel. You are giving birth to another
son." 18Rachel gave birth to the son, but she herself died. As she lay dying, she named the boy Son
of My Suffering, but Jacob called him Benjamin.[n]
19Rachel was buried on the road to Ephrath, a
district of Bethlehem, 20and Jacob set up a rock on
her grave to honor her. That rock is still there.
21Then Israel[n] continued his journey and camped
just south of Migdal Eder.
22While Israel was there, Reuben had sexual
relations with Israel's slave woman[d] Bilhah, and
Israel heard about it.

The Family of Israel

Jacob had twelve sons. 23He had six sons by his
wife Leah: Reuben, his first son, then Simeon,
Levi, Judah, Issachar, and Zebulun.
24He had two sons by his wife Rachel: Joseph
and Benjamin.
25He had two sons by Rachel's slave girl Bilhah:
Dan and Naphtali.
26And he had two sons by Leah's slave girl Zilpah: Gad and Asher.
These are Jacob's sons who were born in
Northwest Mesopotamia.
27Jacob went to his father Isaac at Mamre near
Hebron, where Abraham and Isaac had lived.
28Isaac lived one hundred eighty years. 29So Isaac
breathed his last breath and died when he was
very old, and his sons Esau and Jacob buried him.

Esau's Family

36 This is the family history of Esau (also
called Edom).
2Esau married women from the land of Canaan: Adah daughter of Elon the Hittite; and
Oholibamah daughter of Anah, the son of Zibeon
the Hivite; 3and Basemath, Ishmael's daughter,
the sister of Nebaioth.
4Adah gave birth to Eliphaz for Easu. Basemath
gave him Reuel, 5and Oholibamah gave him Jeush, Jalam, and Korah. These were Esau's sons
who were born in the land of Canaan.
6Esau took his wives, his sons, his daughters,
and all the people who lived with him, his herds
and other animals, and all the belongings he had
gotten in Canaan, and he went to a land away
from his brother Jacob. 7Esau's and Jacob's belongings were becoming too many for them to
live in the same land. The land where they had
lived could not support both of them, because
they had too many herds. 8So Esau lived in the
mountains of Edom. (Esau is also named Edom.)
9This is the family history of Esau. He is the
ancestor of the Edomites, who live in the mountains of Edom.
10Esau's sons were Eliphaz, son of Adah and
Esau, and Reuel, son of Basemath and Esau.
11Eliphaz had five sons: Teman, Omar, Zepho,
Gatam, and Kenaz. 12Eliphaz also had a slave
woman[d] named Timna, and Timna and Eliphaz
gave birth to Amalek. These were Esau's grandsons by his wife Adah.
13Reuel had four sons: Nahath, Zerah, Shammah, and Mizzah. These were Esau's grandsons
by his wife Basemath.
14Esau's third wife was Oholibamah the daughter of Anah. (Anah was the son of Zibeon.) Esau
and Oholibamah gave birth to Jeush, Jalam, and
Korah.
15These were the leaders that came from Esau:
Esau's first son was Eliphaz. From him came these
leaders: Teman, Omar, Zepho, Kenaz, 16Korah,
Gatam, and Amalek. These were the leaders that
came from Eliphaz in the land of Edom. They
were the grandsons of Adah.
17Esau's son Reuel was the father of these leaders: Nahath, Zerah, Shammah, and Mizzah.
These were the leaders that came from Reuel in
the land of Edom. They were the grandsons of
Esau's wife Basemath.
18Esau's wife Oholibamah gave birth to these
leaders: Jeush, Jalam, and Korah. These are the
leaders that came from Esau's wife Oholibamah
the daughter of Anah. 19These were the sons of
Esau (also called Edom), and these were their
leaders.
20These were the sons of Seir the Horite, who
were living in the land: Lotan, Shobal, Zibeon,
Anah, 21Dishon, Ezer, and Dishan. These sons of
Seir were the leaders of the Horites in Edom.
22The sons of Lotan were Hori and Homam.
(Timna was Lotan's sister.)
23The sons of Shobal were Alvan, Manahath,
Ebal, Shepho, and Onam.
24The sons of Zibeon were Aiah and Anah.
Anah is the man who found the hot springs in the
desert while he was caring for his father's donkeys.

Benjamin This name means "right-hand son" or "favorite son."
Israel Also called Jacob.

25The children of Anah were Dishon and Oholibamah daughter of Anah.
26The sons of Dishon were Hemdan, Eshban,
Ithran, and Keran.
27The sons of Ezer were Bilhan, Zaavan, and
Akan.
28The sons of Dishan were Uz and Aran.
29These were the names of the Horite leaders:
Lotan, Shobal, Zibeon, Anah, 30Dishon, Ezer, and
Dishan.
These men were the leaders of the Horite families who lived in the land of Edom.
31These are the kings who ruled in the land of
Edom before the Israelites ever had a king:
32Bela son of Beor was the king of Edom. He
came from the city of Dinhabah.
33When Bela died, Jobab son of Zerah became
king. Jobab was from Bozrah.
34When Jobab died, Husham became king. He
was from the land of the Temanites.
35When Husham died, Hadad son of Bedad,
who had defeated Midian in the country of Moab,
became king. Hadad was from the city of Avith.
36When Hadad died, Samlah became king. He
was from Masrekah.
37When Samlah died, Shaul became king. He
was from Rehoboth on the Euphrates River.
38When Shaul died, Baal-Hanan son of Acbor
became king.
39When Baal-Hanan son of Acbor died, Hadad
became king. He was from the city of Pau. His
wife's name was Mehetabel daughter of Matred,
who was the daughter of Me-Zahab.
40These Edomite leaders, listed by their families
and regions, came from Esau. Their names were
Timna, Alvah, Jetheth, 41Oholibamah, Elah, Pinon, 42Kenaz, Teman, Mibzar, 43Magdiel, and
Iram. They were the leaders of Edom. (Esau was
the father of the Edomites.) The area where each
of these families lived was named after that family.

Joseph the Dreamer

37 Jacob lived in the land of Canaan, where
his father had lived. 2This is the family
history of Jacob:
Joseph was a young man, seventeen years old.
He and his brothers, the sons of Bilhah and Zilpah, his father's wives, cared for the flocks. Joseph gave his father bad reports about his brothers. 3Since Joseph was born when his father
Israel[n] was old, Israel loved him more than his
other sons. He made Joseph a special robe with
long sleeves. 4When Joseph's brothers saw that
their father loved him more than he loved them,
they hated their brother and could not speak to
him politely.
5One time Joseph had a dream, and when he
told his brothers about it, they hated him even
more. 6Joseph said, "Listen to the dream I had.
7We were in the field tying bundles of wheat together. My bundle stood up, and your bundles of
wheat gathered around it and bowed down to it."

> **SIDELIGHT:** Joseph's "coat of many colors" was likely a long robe with sleeves. Laborers wore shorter garments that freed their arms and legs. The coat upset Joseph's brothers because it signified that Joseph was special and didn't have to do any manual labor (Genesis 37:3–4).

8His brothers said, "Do you really think you
will be king over us? Do you truly think you will
rule over us?" His brothers hated him even more
because of his dreams and what he had said.
9Then Joseph had another dream, and he told
his brothers about it also. He said, "Listen, I had
another dream. I saw the sun, moon, and eleven
stars bowing down to me."
10Joseph also told his father about this dream,
but his father scolded him, saying, "What kind of
dream is this? Do you really believe that your
mother, your brothers, and I will bow down to
you?" 11Joseph's brothers were jealous of him, but
his father thought about what all these things
could mean.
12One day Joseph's brothers went to Shechem
to graze their father's flocks. 13Israel said to Joseph, "Go to Shechem where your brothers are
grazing the flocks."
Joseph answered, "I will go."
14His father said, "Go and see if your brothers
and the flocks are all right. Then come back and
tell me." So Joseph's father sent him from the Valley of Hebron.
When Joseph came to Shechem, 15a man found
him wandering in the field and asked him, "What
are you looking for?"
16Joseph answered, "I am looking for my brothers. Can you tell me where they are grazing the
flocks?"
17The man said, "They have already gone. I
heard them say they were going to Dothan." So
Joseph went to look for his brothers and found
them in Dothan.

Joseph Sold into Slavery

18Joseph's brothers saw him coming from far
away. Before he reached them, they made a plan
to kill him. 19They said to each other, "Here

Israel Also called Jacob.

comes that dreamer. 20Let's kill him and throw
his body into one of the wells. We can tell our
father that a wild animal killed him. Then we will
see what will become of his dreams."
21But Reuben heard their plan and saved Joseph, saying, "Let's not kill him. 22Don't spill any
blood. Throw him into this well here in the
desert, but don't hurt him!" Reuben planned to
save Joseph later and send him back to his father.
23So when Joseph came to his brothers, they
pulled off his robe with long sleeves 24and threw
him into the well. It was empty, and there was no
water in it.
25While Joseph was in the well, the brothers sat
down to eat. When they looked up, they saw a
group of Ishmaelites traveling from Gilead to
Egypt. Their camels were carrying spices, balm,[d]
and myrrh.[d]
26Then Judah said to his brothers, "What will
we gain if we kill our brother and hide his death?
27Let's sell him to these Ishmaelites. Then we will
not be guilty of killing our own brother. After all,
he is our brother, our own flesh and blood." And
the other brothers agreed. 28So when the Midianite traders came by, the brothers took Joseph out
of the well and sold him to the Ishmaelites for
eight ounces of silver. And the Ishmaelites took
him to Egypt.

SIDELIGHT: Do you think your brother is mean? Joseph's brothers sold him as a slave into Egypt (Genesis 37:18–28). The payment of eight ounces of silver was the same amount the Israelites later gave when they dedicated a young man to God (see Leviticus 27:5, p. 124).

FAMILY

Family Feud

Another famous Wilson-sister fight was brewing. Usually Marianne was home from college for an hour or so before the anger boiled over. This time she didn't have her bag unpacked.

"How could you ruin my Creston High School jacket!" Marianne screamed the minute she opened her closet to hang up her clothes.

"I didn't fall off my bike on purpose," Sheila yelled from her room. "A car almost hit me. It's not my fault!"

"But you took my jacket," Marianne hissed, storming into her sister's room.

"Mom said I could wear anything in your closet," Sheila retorted hotly.

"But you should've known I'd never let you wear this. I can never replace it," Marianne shot back.

"It's just a stupid school jacket," Sheila sassed sarcastically. "I thought you were a big college girl now."

Marianne threw the torn jacket on Sheila's bed. "Mom lets you get away with everything," she said, seething with anger. "But not this time. You're going to pay, little sister." And she stormed out of the room.

Sheila sat down on the bed, and her anger turned to tears. Why do I have so much trouble with my sister?

Sheila and Marianne's constant clashes are a lot like the clashes between Joseph and his brothers. Read **Genesis 37:1–36** to see what their bad relationship led to.

- What problems do you see in Marianne and Sheila's relationship that also show up in the relationship between Joseph and his brothers?
- Are you more like Joseph (the one who gets picked on) or his brothers (the ones who become jealous)?

CONSIDER . . .

- writing an "I'm sorry" or "I forgive you" note to a family member and taping it to a mirror he or she uses.
- starting a "Something Nice" jar to collect notes about nice things other family members do for you. Look through the notes when you're angry at another family member.

FOR MORE, SEE . . .

- Genesis 27:1–41 (p. 32)
- Luke 10:38–41 (p. 1024)
- 1 John 2:9–11 (p. 1317)

29When Reuben came back to the well and Joseph was not there, he tore his clothes to show he
was upset. 30Then he went back to his brothers
and said, "The boy is not there! What shall I do?"
31The brothers killed a goat and dipped Joseph's
robe in its blood. 32Then they brought the long-
sleeved robe to their father and said, "We found
this robe. Look it over carefully and see if it is your
son's robe."

33Jacob looked it over and said, "It is my son's
robe! Some savage animal has eaten him. My son
Joseph has been torn to pieces!" 34Then Jacob tore
his clothes and put on rough cloth to show that
he was upset, and he continued to be sad about
his son for a long time. 35All of his sons and daughters tried to comfort him, but he could not be
comforted. He said, "I will be sad about my son
until the day I die." So Jacob cried for his son
Joseph.

36Meanwhile the Midianites who had bought
Joseph had taken him to Egypt. There they sold
him to Potiphar, an officer to the king of Egypt
and captain of the palace guard.

Judah and Tamar

38 About that time, Judah left his brothers
and went to stay with a man named Hirah in the town of Adullam. 2There Judah met a
Canaanite girl, the daughter of a man named
Shua, and married her. Judah had sexual relations
with her, 3and she became pregnant and gave
birth to a son, whom Judah named Er. 4Later she
gave birth to another son and named him Onan.
5Still later she had another son and named him
Shelah. She was at Kezib when this third son was
born.

6Judah chose a girl named Tamar to be the wife
of his first son Er. 7But Er, Judah's oldest son, did
what the LORD said was evil, so the LORD killed
him. 8Then Judah said to Er's brother Onan, "Go
and have sexual relations with your dead
brother's wife.[n] It is your duty to provide children for your brother in this way."

9But Onan knew that the children would not
belong to him, so when he was supposed to have
sexual relations with Tamar he did not complete
the sex act. This made it impossible for Tamar to
become pregnant and for Er to have descendants.[d] 10The LORD was displeased by this wicked
thing Onan had done, so the LORD killed Onan
also. 11Then Judah said to his daughter-in-law Tamar, "Go back to live in your father's house, and
don't marry until my young son Shelah grows
up." Judah was afraid that Shelah also would die
like his brothers. So Tamar returned to her father's home.

12After a long time Judah's wife, the daughter
of Shua, died. After Judah had gotten over his sorrow, he went to Timnah to his men who were
cutting the wool from his sheep. His friend Hirah
from Adullam went with him. 13Tamar learned
that Judah, her father-in-law, was going to Timnah to cut the wool from his sheep. 14So she took
off the clothes that showed she was a widow and
covered her face with a veil to hide who she was.
Then she sat down by the gate of Enaim on the
road to Timnah. She did this because Judah's
younger son Shelah had grown up, but Judah had
not made plans for her to marry him.

15When Judah saw her, he thought she was a
prostitute,[d] because she had covered her face
with a veil. 16So Judah went to her and said, "Let
me have sexual relations with you." He did not
know that she was Tamar, his daughter-in-law.

She asked, "What will you give me if I let you
have sexual relations with me?"

17Judah answered, "I will send you a young
goat from my flock."

She answered, "First give me something to
keep as a deposit until you send the goat."

18Judah asked, "What do you want me to give
you as a deposit?"

Tamar answered, "Give me your seal and its
cord,[n] and give me your walking stick." So Judah
gave these things to her. Then Judah and Tamar
had sexual relations, and Tamar became pregnant. 19When Tamar went home, she took off the
veil that covered her face and put on the clothes
that showed she was a widow.

20Judah sent his friend Hirah with the young
goat to find the woman and get back his seal and
the walking stick he had given her, but Hirah
could not find her. 21He asked some of the people
at the town of Enaim, "Where is the prostitute
who was here by the road?"

They answered, "There has never been a prostitute here."

22So he went back to Judah and said, "I could
not find the woman, and the people who lived
there said, 'There has never been a prostitute
here.' "

23Judah said, "Let her keep the things. I don't
want people to laugh at us. I sent her the goat as
I promised, but you could not find her."

24About three months later someone told Judah, "Tamar, your daughter-in-law, is guilty of
acting like a prostitute, and now she is pregnant."

Go . . . wife It was a custom in Israel that if a man died without children, one of his brothers would marry the widow. If a child was born, it would be considered the dead man's child.

seal . . . cord A seal was used like a rubber stamp, and people ran a string through it to tie around the neck. They wrote a contract, folded it, put wax or clay on the contract, and pressed the seal onto it as a signature.

Then Judah said, "Bring her out and let her be burned to death."

25When the people went to bring Tamar out, she sent a message to her father-in-law that said, "The man who owns these things has made me pregnant. Look at this seal and its cord and this walking stick, and tell me whose they are."

26Judah recognized them and said, "She is more in the right than I. She did this because I did not give her to my son Shelah as I promised." And Judah did not have sexual relations with her again.

27When the time came for Tamar to give birth, there were twins in her body. 28While she was giving birth, one baby put his hand out. The nurse tied a red string on his hand and said, "This baby came out first." 29But he pulled his hand back in, so the other baby was born first. The nurse said, "So you are able to break out first," and they named him Perez.[n] 30After this, the baby with the red string on his hand was born, and they named him Zerah.

Joseph Is Sold to Potiphar

39 Now Joseph had been taken down to Egypt. An Egyptian named Potiphar was an officer to the king of Egypt and the captain of the palace guard. He bought Joseph from the Ishmaelites who had brought him down there. 2The LORD was with Joseph, and he became a successful man. He lived in the house of his master, Potiphar the Egyptian.

3Potiphar saw that the LORD was with Joseph and that the LORD made Joseph successful in everything he did. 4So Potiphar was very happy with Joseph and allowed him to be his personal servant. He put Joseph in charge of the house, trusting him with everything he owned. 5When Joseph was put in charge of the house and everything Potiphar owned, the LORD blessed the people in Potiphar's house because of Joseph. And the LORD blessed everything that belonged to Potiphar, both in the house and in the field. 6So Potiphar left Joseph in charge of everything he owned and was not concerned about anything except the food he ate.

Joseph Is Put into Prison

Now Joseph was well built and handsome. 7After some time the wife of Joseph's master began to desire Joseph, and one day she said to him, "Have sexual relations with me."

8But Joseph refused and said to her, "My master trusts me with everything in his house. He has put me in charge of everything he owns. 9There is no one in his house greater than I. He has not kept anything from me except you, because you are his wife. How can I do such an evil thing? It is a sin against God."

10The woman talked to Joseph every day, but he refused to have sexual relations with her or even spend time with her.

11One day Joseph went into the house to do his work as usual and was the only man in the house at that time. 12His master's wife grabbed his coat and said to him, "Come and have sexual relations with me." But Joseph left his coat in her hand and ran out of the house.

13When she saw that Joseph had left his coat in her hands and had run outside, 14she called to the servants in her house and said, "Look! This Hebrew slave was brought here to shame us. He came in and tried to have sexual relations with me, but I screamed. 15My scream scared him and he ran away, but he left his coat with me." 16She kept his coat until her husband came home, 17and she told him the same story. She said, "This Hebrew slave you brought here came in to shame me! 18When he came near me, I screamed. He ran away, but he left his coat."

19When Joseph's master heard what his wife said Joseph had done, he became very angry. 20So Potiphar arrested Joseph and put him into the prison where the king's prisoners were put. And Joseph stayed there in the prison.

21But the LORD was with Joseph and showed him kindness and caused the prison warden to like Joseph. 22The prison warden chose Joseph to take care of all the prisoners, and he was responsible for whatever was done in the prison. 23The warden paid no attention to anything that was in Joseph's care because the LORD was with Joseph and made him successful in everything he did.

Joseph Interprets Two Dreams

40 After these things happened, two of the king's officers displeased the king—the man who served wine to the king and the king's baker. 2The king became angry with his officer who served him wine and his baker, 3so he put them in the prison of the captain of the guard, the same prison where Joseph was kept. 4The captain of the guard put the two prisoners in Joseph's care, and they stayed in prison for some time.

5One night both the king's officer who served him wine and the baker had a dream. Each had his own dream with its own meaning. 6When Joseph came to them the next morning, he saw they were worried. 7He asked the king's officers who were with him, "Why do you look so unhappy today?"

8The two men answered, "We both had dreams last night, but no one can explain their meaning to us."

Perez This name means "breaking out."

Joseph said to them, "God is the only One who can explain the meaning of dreams. Tell me your dreams."

9So the man who served wine to the king told Joseph his dream. He said, "I dreamed I saw a vine, and 10on the vine were three branches. I watched the branches bud and blossom, and then the grapes ripened. 11I was holding the king's cup, so I took the grapes and squeezed the juice into the cup. Then I gave it to the king."

12Then Joseph said, "I will explain the dream to you. The three branches stand for three days. 13Before the end of three days the king will free you, and he will allow you to return to your work. You will serve the king his wine just as you did before. 14But when you are free, remember me. Be kind to me, and tell the king about me so I can get out of this prison. 15I was taken by force from the land of the Hebrews, and I have done nothing here to deserve being put in prison."

16The baker saw that Joseph's explanation of the dream was good, so he said to him, "I also had a dream. I dreamed there were three bread baskets on my head. 17In the top basket were all kinds of baked food for the king, but the birds were eating this food out of the basket on my head."

18Joseph answered, "I will tell you what the dream means. The three baskets stand for three days. 19Before the end of three days, the king will cut off your head! He will hang your body on a pole, and the birds will eat your flesh."

20Three days later, on his birthday, the king gave a feast for all his officers. In front of his officers, he released from prison the chief officer who served his wine and the chief baker. 21The king gave his chief officer who served wine his old position, and once again he put the king's cup of wine into the king's hand. 22But the king hanged the baker on a pole. Everything happened just as Joseph had said it would, 23but the officer who served wine did not remember Joseph. He forgot all about him.

The King's Dreams

41 Two years later the king dreamed he was standing on the bank of the Nile River. 2He saw seven fat and beautiful cows come up out of the river, and they stood there, eating the grass. 3Then seven more cows came up out of the river, but they were thin and ugly. They stood beside the seven beautiful cows on the bank of the Nile. 4The seven thin and ugly cows ate the seven beautiful fat cows. Then the king woke up. 5The king slept again and dreamed a second time. In his dream he saw seven full and good heads of grain growing on one stalk. 6After that, seven more heads of grain sprang up, but they were thin and burned by the hot east wind. 7The thin heads of grain ate the seven full and good heads. Then the king woke up again, and he realized it was only a dream. 8The next morning the king was troubled about these dreams, so he sent for all the magicians and wise men of Egypt. The king told them his dreams, but no one could explain their meaning to him.

9Then the chief officer who served wine to the king said to him, "Now I remember something I promised to do, but I forgot about it. 10There was a time when you were angry with the baker and me, and you put us in prison in the house of the captain of the guard. 11In prison we each had a dream on the same night, and each dream had a different meaning. 12A young Hebrew man, a servant of the captain of the guard, was in the prison with us. When we told him our dreams, he explained their meanings to us. He told each man the meaning of his dream, and 13things happened exactly as he said they would: I was given back my old position, and the baker was hanged."

14So the king called for Joseph. The guards quickly brought him out of the prison, and he shaved, put on clean clothes, and went before the king.

15The king said to Joseph, "I have had a dream, but no one can explain its meaning to me. I have heard that you can explain a dream when someone tells it to you."

16Joseph answered the king, "I am not able to explain the meaning of dreams, but God will do this for the king."

17Then the king said to Joseph, "In my dream I was standing on the bank of the Nile River. 18I saw seven fat and beautiful cows that came up out of the river and ate the grass. 19Then I saw seven more cows come out of the river that were thin and lean and ugly—the worst looking cows I have seen in all the land of Egypt. 20And these thin and ugly cows ate the first seven fat cows, 21but after they had eaten the seven cows, no one could tell they had eaten them. They looked just as thin and ugly as they did in the beginning. Then I woke up.

22"I had another dream. I saw seven full and good heads of grain growing on one stalk. 23Then seven more heads of grain sprang up after them, but these heads were thin and ugly and were burned by the hot east wind. 24Then the thin heads ate the seven good heads. I told this dream to the magicians, but no one could explain its meaning to me."

Joseph Tells the Dreams' Meaning

25Then Joseph said to the king, "Both of these dreams mean the same thing. God is telling you what he is about to do. 26The seven good cows stand for seven years, and the seven good heads of grain stand for seven years. Both dreams mean the same thing. 27The seven thin and ugly cows stand for seven years, and the seven thin heads of grain burned by the hot east wind stand for seven years of hunger. 28This will happen as I told you. God is showing the king what he is about to do. 29You will have seven years of good crops and plenty to eat in all the land of Egypt. 30But after those seven years, there will come seven years of hunger, and all the food that grew in the land of Egypt will be forgotten. The time of hunger will eat up the land. 31People will forget what it was like to have plenty of food, because the hunger that follows will be so great. 32You had two dreams which mean the same thing. This shows that God has firmly decided that this will happen, and he will make it happen soon.

33"So let the king choose a man who is very wise and understanding and set him over the land of Egypt. 34And let the king also appoint officers over the land, who should take one-fifth of all the food that is grown during the seven good years. 35They should gather all the food that is produced during the good years that are coming, and under the king's authority they should store the grain in the cities and guard it. 36That food should be saved to use during the seven years of hunger that will come on the land of Egypt. Then the people in Egypt will not die during the seven years of hunger."

Joseph Is Made Ruler over Egypt

37This seemed like a very good idea to the king, and all his officers agreed. 38And the king asked them, "Can we find a better man than Joseph to take this job? God's spirit is truly in him!"

39So the king said to Joseph, "God has shown you all this. There is no one as wise and understanding as you are, so 40I will put you in charge of my palace. All the people will obey your orders, and only I will be greater than you."

41Then the king said to Joseph, "Look! I have put you in charge of all the land of Egypt." 42Then the king took off from his own finger his ring with the royal seal on it, and he put it on Joseph's finger. He gave Joseph fine linen clothes to wear, and he put a gold chain around Joseph's neck. 43The king had Joseph ride in the second royal chariot, and people walked ahead of his chariot calling, "Bow down!" By doing these things, the king put Joseph in charge of all of Egypt.

44The king said to him, "I am the king, and I say that no one in all the land of Egypt may lift a hand or a foot without your permission." 45The king gave Joseph the name Zaphenath-Paneah. He also gave Joseph a wife named Asenath, who was the daughter of Potiphera, priest of On. So Joseph traveled through all the land of Egypt.

46Joseph was thirty years old when he began serving the king of Egypt. And he left the king's court and traveled through all the land of Egypt.

SIDELIGHT: In Old Testament times, Middle Easterners depended on rainfall to grow crops. If rain didn't come, people often went to Egypt, because the Nile River flooded each year, making the ground moist and rich. So famine in Egypt could mean disaster. That's why Joseph's prediction of seven years of famine was taken so seriously (Genesis 41:25–43).

47During the seven good years, the crops in the land grew well. 48And Joseph gathered all the food which was produced in Egypt during those seven years of good crops and stored the food in the cities. In every city he stored grain that had been grown in the fields around that city. 49Joseph stored much grain, as much as the sand of the seashore—so much that he could not measure it.

50Joseph's wife was Asenath daughter of Potiphera, the priest of On. Before the years of hunger came, Joseph and Asenath had two sons. 51Joseph named the first son Manasseh[n] and said, "God has made me forget all the troubles I have had and all my father's family." 52Joseph named the second son Ephraim[n] and said, "God has given me children in the land of my troubles."

53The seven years of good crops came to an end in the land of Egypt. 54Then the seven years of hunger began, just as Joseph had said. In all the lands people had nothing to eat, but in Egypt there was food. 55The time of hunger became terrible in all of Egypt, and the people cried to the king for food. He said to all the Egyptians, "Go to Joseph and do whatever he tells you."

56The hunger was everywhere in that part of the world. And Joseph opened the storehouses and sold grain to the people of Egypt, because the time of hunger became terrible in Egypt. 57And all the people in that part of the world came to Joseph in Egypt to buy grain because the hunger was terrible everywhere in that part of the world.

The Dreams Come True

42 Jacob learned that there was grain in Egypt, so he said to his sons, "Why are you just sitting here looking at one another? 2I

Manasseh This name sounds like the Hebrew word for "made me forget."
Ephraim This name sounds like the Hebrew word for "given me children."

have heard that there is grain in Egypt. Go down
there and buy grain for us to eat, so that we will
live and not die."
3So ten of Joseph's brothers went down to buy
grain from Egypt. 4But Jacob did not send Benjamin, Joseph's brother, with them, because he was
afraid that something terrible might happen to
him. 5Along with many other people, the sons of
Israel[n] went to Egypt to buy grain, because the
people in the land of Canaan were also hungry.
6Now Joseph was governor over Egypt. He was
the one who sold the grain to people who came
to buy it. So Joseph's brothers came to him and
bowed facedown on the ground before him.
7When Joseph saw his brothers, he knew who
they were, but he acted as if he didn't know
them. He asked unkindly, "Where do you come
from?"

They answered, "We have come from the land
of Canaan to buy food."
8Joseph knew they were his brothers, but they
did not know who he was. 9And Joseph remembered his dreams about his brothers bowing to
him. He said to them, "You are spies! You came
to learn where the nation is weak!"
10But his brothers said to him, "No, my master.
We come as your servants just to buy food. 11We
are all sons of the same father. We are honest
men, not spies."
12Then Joseph said to them, "No! You have
come to learn where this nation is weak!"
13And they said, "We are ten of twelve brothers, sons of the same father, and we live in the
land of Canaan. Our youngest brother is there
with our father right now, and our other brother
is gone."
14But Joseph said to them, "I can see I was
right! You are spies! 15But I will give you a way
to prove you are telling the truth. As surely as the
king lives, you will not leave this place until your
youngest brother comes here. 16One of you must
go and get your brother. The rest of you will stay
here in prison. We will see if you are telling the
truth. If not, as surely as the king lives, you are
spies." 17Then Joseph put them all in prison for
three days.
18On the third day Joseph said to them, "I am
a God-fearing man. Do this and I will let you live:
19If you are honest men, let one of your brothers
stay here in prison while the rest of you go and
carry grain back to feed your hungry families.
20Then bring your youngest brother back here to
me. If you do this, I will know you are telling the
truth, and you will not die."

The brothers agreed to this. 21They said to each
other, "We are being punished for what we did to
our brother. We saw his trouble, and he begged
us to save him, but we refused to listen. That is
why we are in this trouble now."
22Then Reuben said to them, "I told you not to
harm the boy, but you refused to listen to me. So
now we are being punished for what we did to
him."
23When Joseph talked to his brothers, he used
an interpreter, so they did not know that Joseph
understood what they were saying. 24Then Joseph
left them and cried. After a short time he went
back and spoke to them. He took Simeon and tied
him up while the other brothers watched. 25Jo-
seph told his servants to fill his brothers' bags with
grain and to put the money the brothers had paid
for the grain back in their bags. The servants were
also to give them what they would need for their
trip back home. And the servants did this.
26So the brothers put the grain on their donkeys
and left. 27When they stopped for the night, one
of the brothers opened his sack to get food for his
donkey. Then he saw his money in the top of the
sack. 28He said to the other brothers, "The money
I paid for the grain has been put back. Here it is
in my sack!"

The brothers were very frightened. They said
to each other, "What has God done to us?"

The Brothers Return to Jacob

29The brothers went to their father Jacob in the
land of Canaan and told him everything that had
happened. 30They said, "The master of that land
spoke unkindly to us. He accused us of spying on
his country, 31but we told him that we were honest men, not spies. 32We told him that we were
ten of twelve brothers—sons of one father. We
said that one of our brothers was gone and that
our youngest brother was with our father in Canaan.
33"Then the master of the land said to us, 'Here
is a way I can know you are honest men: Leave
one of your brothers with me, and take grain to
feed your hungry families, and go. 34And bring
your youngest brother to me so I will know you
are not spies but honest men. Then I will give you
back your brother whom you leave with me, and
you can move about freely in our land.' "
35As the brothers emptied their sacks, each of
them found his money in his sack. When they and
their father saw it, they were afraid.
36Their father Jacob said to them, "You are robbing me of all my children. Joseph is gone, Simeon
is gone, and now you want to take Benjamin
away, too. Everything is against me."
37Then Reuben said to his father, "You may put
my two sons to death if I don't bring Benjamin
back to you. Trust him to my care, and I will bring
him back to you."

Israel Also called Jacob.

38But Jacob said, "I will not allow Benjamin to go with you. His brother is dead, and he is the only son left from my wife Rachel. I am afraid something terrible might happen to him during the trip to Egypt. Then I would be sad until the day I die."

The Brothers Go Back to Egypt

43 Still no food grew in the land of Canaan. 2When Jacob's family had eaten all the grain they had brought from Egypt, Jacob said to them, "Go to Egypt again and buy a little more grain for us to eat."

3But Judah said to Jacob, "The governor of that country strongly warned us, 'If you don't bring your brother back with you, you will not be allowed to see me.' 4If you will send Benjamin with us, we will go down and buy food for you. 5But if you refuse to send Benjamin, we will not go. The governor of that country warned us that we would not see him if we didn't bring Benjamin with us."

6Israel[n] said, "Why did you tell the man you had another brother? You have caused me a lot of trouble."

7The brothers answered, "He questioned us carefully about ourselves and our family. He asked us, 'Is your father still alive? Do you have another brother?' We just answered his questions. How could we know he would ask us to bring our other brother to him?"

8Then Judah said to his father Jacob, "Send Benjamin with me, and we will go at once so that we, you, and our children may live and not die. 9I will guarantee you that he will be safe, and I will be personally responsible for him. If I don't bring him back to you, you can blame me all my life. 10If we had not wasted all this time, we could have already made two trips."

11Then their father Jacob said to them, "If it has to be that way, then do this: Take some of the best foods in our land in your packs. Give them to the man as a gift: some balm,[d] some honey, spices, myrrh,[d] pistachio nuts, and almonds. 12Take twice as much money with you this time, and take back the money that was returned to you in your sacks last time. Maybe it was a mistake. 13And take Benjamin with you. Now leave and go to the man. 14I pray that God Almighty will cause the governor to be merciful to you and that he will allow Simeon and Benjamin to come back with you. If I am robbed of my children, then I am robbed of them!"

15So the brothers took the gifts. They also took twice as much money as they had taken the first time, and they took Benjamin. They hurried down to Egypt and stood before Joseph.

16When Joseph saw Benjamin with them, he said to the servant in charge of his house, "Bring those men into my house. Kill an animal and prepare a meal. Those men will eat with me today at noon." 17The servant did as Joseph told him and brought the men to Joseph's house.

18The brothers were afraid when they were brought to Joseph's house and thought, "We were brought here because of the money that was put in our sacks on the first trip. He wants to attack us, make us slaves, and take our donkeys." 19So the brothers went to the servant in charge of Joseph's house and spoke to him at the door of the house. 20They said, "Master, we came here once before to buy food. 21While we were going home, we stopped for the night and when we opened our sacks each of us found all his money in his sack. We brought that money with us to give it back to you. 22And we have brought more money to pay for the food we want to buy this time. We don't know who put that money in our sacks."

23But the servant answered, "It's all right. Don't be afraid. Your God, the God of your father, must have put the money in your sacks. I got the money you paid me for the grain last time." Then the servant brought Simeon out to them.

24The servant led the men into Joseph's house and gave them water, and they washed their feet. Then he gave their donkeys food to eat. 25The men prepared their gift to give to Joseph when he arrived at noon, because they had heard they were going to eat with him there.

26When Joseph came home, the brothers gave him the gift they had brought into the house and bowed down to the ground in front of him. 27Joseph asked them how they were doing. He said, "How is your aged father you told me about? Is he still alive?"

28The brothers answered, "Your servant, our father, is well. He is still alive." And they bowed low before Joseph to show him respect.

29When Joseph saw his brother Benjamin, who had the same mother as he, Joseph asked, "Is this your youngest brother you told me about?" Then he said to Benjamin, "God be good to you, my son!" 30Then Joseph hurried off because he had to hold back the tears when he saw his brother Benjamin. So Joseph went into his room and cried there. 31Then he washed his face and came out. He controlled himself and said, "Serve the meal."

32So they served Joseph at one table, his brothers at another table, and the Egyptians who ate with him at another table. This was because Egyptians did not like Hebrews and never ate with them. 33Joseph's brothers were seated in front of him in order of their ages, from oldest to youngest. They looked at each other because they

Israel Also called Jacob.

were so amazed. 34Food from Joseph's table was
taken to them, but Benjamin was given five times
more food than the others. Joseph's brothers ate
and drank freely with him.

Joseph Sets a Trap

44 Then Joseph gave a command to the servant in charge of his house. He said, "Fill
the men's sacks with as much grain as they can
carry, and put each man's money into his sack
with the grain. 2Put my silver cup in the sack of
the youngest brother, along with his money for
the grain." The servant did what Joseph told him.
3At dawn the brothers were sent away with
their donkeys. 4They were not far from the city
when Joseph said to the servant in charge of his
house, "Go after the men. When you catch up
with them, say, 'Why have you paid back evil for
good? 5The cup you have stolen is the one my
master uses for drinking and for explaining
dreams. You have done a very wicked thing!' "
6So the servant caught up with the brothers
and said to them what Joseph had told him to say.
7But the brothers said to the servant, "Why do
you say these things? We would not do anything
like that! 8We brought back to you from the land
of Canaan the money we found in our sacks. So
surely we would not steal silver or gold from your
master's house. 9If you find that silver cup in the
sack of one of us, then let him die, and we will
be your slaves."
10The servant said, "We will do as you say, but
only the man who has taken the cup will become
my slave. The rest of you may go free."
11Then every brother quickly lowered his sack
to the ground and opened it. 12The servant
searched the sacks, going from the oldest brother
to the youngest, and found the cup in Benjamin's
sack. 13The brothers tore their clothes to show
they were afraid. Then they put their sacks back
on the donkeys and returned to the city.
14When Judah and his brothers went back to
Joseph's house, Joseph was still there, so the
brothers bowed facedown on the ground before
him. 15Joseph said to them, "What have you
done? Didn't you know that a man like me can
learn things by signs and dreams?"
16Judah said, "Master, what can we say? And
how can we show we are not guilty? God has
uncovered our guilt, so all of us will be your
slaves, not just Benjamin."
17But Joseph said, "I will not make you all
slaves! Only the man who stole the cup will be
my slave. The rest of you may go back safely to
your father."
18Then Judah went to Joseph and said, "Master, please let me speak plainly to you, and please
don't be angry with me. I know that you are as
powerful as the king of Egypt himself. 19When we
were here before, you asked us, 'Do you have a
father or a brother?' 20And we answered you, 'We
have an old father. And we have a younger
brother, who was born when our father was old.
This youngest son's brother is dead, so he is the
only one of his mother's children left alive, and
our father loves him very much.' 21Then you said
to us, 'Bring that brother to me. I want to see
him.' 22And we said to you, 'That young boy cannot leave his father, because if he leaves him, his
father would die.' 23But you said to us, 'If you
don't bring your youngest brother, you will not be
allowed to see me again.' 24So we went back to
our father and told him what you had said.
25"Later, our father said, 'Go again and buy us
a little more food.' 26We said to our father, 'We
cannot go without our youngest brother. Without
our youngest brother, we will not be allowed to
see the governor.' 27Then my father said to us,
'You know that my wife Rachel gave me two
sons. 28When one son left me, I thought, "Surely
he has been torn apart by a wild animal," and I
haven't seen him since. 29Now you want to take
this son away from me also. But something terrible might happen to him, and I would be miserable until the day I die.' 30Now what will happen
if we go home to our father without our youngest
brother? He is so important in our father's life that
31when our father sees the young boy is not with
us, he will die. And it will be our fault. We will
cause the great sorrow that kills our father.
32"I gave my father a guarantee that the young
boy would be safe. I said to my father, 'If I don't
bring him back to you, you can blame me all my
life.' 33So now, please allow me to stay here and
be your slave, and let the young boy go back
home with his brothers. 34I cannot go back to my
father if the boy is not with me. I couldn't stand
to see my father that sad."

Joseph Reveals Who He Is

45 Joseph could not control himself in front
of his servants any longer, so he cried
out, "Have everyone leave me." When only the
brothers were left with Joseph, he told them who
he was. 2Joseph cried so loudly that the Egyptians
heard him, and the people in the king's palace
heard about it. 3He said to his brothers, "I am
Joseph. Is my father still alive?" But the brothers
could not answer him, because they were very
afraid of him.
4So Joseph said to them, "Come close to me."
When the brothers came close to him, he said to
them, "I am your brother Joseph, whom you sold
as a slave to go to Egypt. 5Now don't be worried
or angry with yourselves because you sold me
here. God sent me here ahead of you to save people's lives. 6No food has grown on the land for
two years now, and there will be five more years

without planting or harvest. 7So God sent me here ahead of you to make sure you have some descendants[d] left on earth and to keep you alive in an amazing way. 8So it was not you who sent me here, but God. God has made me the highest officer of the king of Egypt. I am in charge of his palace, and I am the master of all the land of Egypt.

9"So leave quickly and go to my father. Tell him, 'Your son Joseph says: God has made me master over all Egypt. Come down to me quickly. 10Live in the land of Goshen where you will be near me. Your children, your grandchildren, your flocks and herds, and all that you have will also be near me. 11I will care for you during the next five years of hunger so that you and your family and all that you have will not starve.'

12"Now you can see for yourselves, and so can my brother Benjamin, that the one speaking to you is really Joseph. 13So tell my father about how powerful I have become in Egypt. Tell him about everything you have seen. Now hurry and bring him back to me." 14Then Joseph hugged his brother Benjamin and cried, and Benjamin cried also. 15And Joseph kissed all his brothers and cried as he hugged them. After this, his brothers talked with him.

16When the king of Egypt and his officers learned that Joseph's brothers had come, they were very happy. 17So the king said to Joseph, "Tell your brothers to load their animals and go back to the land of Canaan 18and bring their father and their families back here to me. I will give them the best land in Egypt, and they will eat the best food we have here. 19Tell them to take some wagons from Egypt for their children and their wives and to bring their father back also. 20Tell them not to worry about bringing any of their things with them, because we will give them the best of what we have in Egypt."

21So the sons of Israel did this. Joseph gave them wagons as the king had ordered and food for their trip. 22He gave each brother a change of clothes, but he gave Benjamin five changes of clothes and about seven and one-half pounds of silver. 23Joseph also sent his father ten donkeys loaded with the best things from Egypt and ten female donkeys loaded with grain, bread, and other food for his father on his trip back. 24Then Joseph told his brothers to go. As they were leav-

REVENGE

A Violent Cycle

Spangler was a powerful gang leader in Cleveland, Ohio. He and his "homeboys" spent their days and nights partying with drugs and booze. The only times they interrupted their ongoing parties were to make drug deals or to "jam" a rival.

Spangler had everything. He was untouchable. Or so he thought. One day, an off-duty bus driver accidently bumped Spangler's Mercedes-Benz. Enraged that someone would dent his car, Spangler walked up and pumped four bullets into the man's face.

"Nobody does that to me," he howled.

But someone saw. And Spangler—who had killed dozens of Blood, Crip, Jamaican, and Colombian gang members as well as innocent bystanders—was arrested and charged with first-degree murder. For killing a man he didn't know. For minor damage to a car he didn't really care about.

Spangler's gang activity revolved around revenge and hurting countless people. In **Genesis 45:3–8**, Joseph also had a motive and opportunity for revenge. Read how he acted differently.

- What differences do you see between the attitudes of Joseph and Spangler? How did their attitudes affect their responses?
- What can you learn from Joseph about grabbing chances for revenge?

CONSIDER . . .

- looking through a school yearbook to find people who have done something to you out of revenge. Decide how you'll respond the next time they try to get you.
- evaluating the role revenge plays in a murder-mystery on television. Decide ways that characters could break the destructive cycle of revenge.

FOR MORE, SEE . . .

- Joshua 20:1–6 (p. 210)
- Luke 6:27–36 (p. 1013)
- Acts 7:51–60 (p. 1109)

ing, he said to them, "Don't quarrel on the way home."

25So the brothers left Egypt and went to their father Jacob in the land of Canaan. 26They told him, "Joseph is still alive and is the ruler over all the land of Egypt." Their father was shocked and did not believe them. 27But when the brothers told him everything Joseph had said, and when Jacob saw the wagons Joseph had sent to carry him back to Egypt, he felt better. 28Israel[n] said, "Now I believe you. My son Joseph is still alive, and I will go and see him before I die."

Jacob Goes to Egypt

46 So Israel[n] took all he had and started his trip. He went to Beersheba, where he offered sacrifices to the God of his father Isaac. 2During the night God spoke to Israel in a vision and said, "Jacob, Jacob."

And Jacob answered, "Here I am."

3Then God said, "I am God, the God of your father. Don't be afraid to go to Egypt, because I will make your descendants[d] a great nation there. 4I will go to Egypt with you, and I will bring you out of Egypt again. Joseph's own hands will close your eyes when you die."

5Then Jacob left Beersheba. The sons of Israel loaded their father, their children, and their wives in the wagons the king of Egypt had sent. 6They also took their farm animals and everything they had gotten in Canaan. So Jacob went to Egypt with all his descendants— 7his sons and grandsons, his daughters and granddaughters. He took all his family to Egypt with him.

Jacob's Family

8Now these are the names of the children of Israel who went into Egypt (Jacob and his descendants[d]).

Reuben was Jacob's first son. 9Reuben's sons were Hanoch, Pallu, Hezron, and Carmi.

10Simeon's sons were Jemuel, Jamin, Ohad, Jakin, Zohar, and Shaul (Simeon's son by a Canaanite woman).

11Levi's sons were Gershon, Kohath, and Merari.

12Judah's sons were Er, Onan, Shelah, Perez, and Zerah (but Er and Onan had died in the land of Canaan). Perez's sons were Hezron and Hamul.

13Issachar's sons were Tola, Puah, Jashub, and Shimron.

14Zebulun's sons were Sered, Elon, and Jahleel.

15These are the sons of Leah and Jacob born in Northwest Mesopotamia, in addition to his daughter Dinah. There were thirty-three persons in this part of Jacob's family.

16Gad's sons were Zephon, Haggi, Shuni, Ezbon, Eri, Arodi, and Areli.

17Asher's sons were Imnah, Ishvah, Ishvi, and Beriah, and their sister was Serah. Beriah's sons were Heber and Malkiel.

18These are Jacob's sons by Zilpah, the slave girl whom Laban gave to his daughter Leah. There were sixteen persons in this part of Jacob's family.

19The sons of Jacob's wife Rachel were Joseph and Benjamin. 20In Egypt, Joseph became the father of Manasseh and Ephraim by his wife Asenath, the daughter of Potiphera, priest of On.

21Benjamin's sons were Bela, Beker, Ashbel, Gera, Naaman, Ehi, Rosh, Muppim, Huppim, and Ard.

22These are the sons of Jacob by his wife Rachel. There were fourteen persons in this part of Jacob's family.

23Dan's son was Hushim.

24Naphtali's sons were Jahziel, Guni, Jezer, and Shillem.

25These are Jacob's sons by Bilhah, the slave girl whom Laban gave to his daughter Rachel. There were seven persons in this part of Jacob's family.

26So the total number of Jacob's direct descendants who went to Egypt was sixty-six, not counting the wives of Jacob's sons. 27Joseph had two sons born in Egypt, so the total number in the family of Jacob in Egypt was seventy.

Jacob Arrives in Egypt

28Jacob sent Judah ahead of him to see Joseph in Goshen. When Jacob and his people came into the land of Goshen, 29Joseph prepared his chariot and went to meet his father Israel in Goshen. As soon as Joseph saw his father, he hugged him, and cried there for a long time.

30Then Israel said to Joseph, "Now I am ready to die, because I have seen your face and I know you are still alive."

31Joseph said to his brothers and his father's family, "I will go and tell the king you are here. I will say, 'My brothers and my father's family have left the land of Canaan and have come here to me. 32They are shepherds and take care of farm animals, and they have brought their flocks and their herds and everything they own with them.' 33When the king calls you, he will ask, 'What work do you do?' 34This is what you should tell him: 'We, your servants, have taken care of farm animals all our lives. Our ancestors did the same thing.' Then the king will allow you to settle in the land of Goshen, away from the Egyptians because they don't like to be near shepherds."

Israel Also called Jacob.

Jacob Settles in Goshen

47 Joseph went in to the king and said, "My father and my brothers have arrived from Canaan with their flocks and herds and everything they own. They are now in the land of Goshen." 2Joseph chose five of his brothers to introduce to the king.

3The king said to the brothers, "What work do you do?"

And they said to him, "We, your servants, are shepherds, just as our ancestors were." 4They said to the king, "We have come to live in this land, because there is no grass in the land of Canaan for our animals to eat, and the hunger is terrible there. So please allow us to live in the land of Goshen."

5Then the king said to Joseph, "Your father and your brothers have come to you, 6and you may choose any place in Egypt for them to live. Give your father and your brothers the best land; let them live in the land of Goshen. And if any of them are skilled shepherds, put them in charge of my sheep and cattle."

7Then Joseph brought in his father Jacob and introduced him to the king, and Jacob blessed the king.

8Then the king said to Jacob, "How old are you?"

9Jacob said to him, "My life has been spent wandering from place to place. It has been short and filled with trouble — only one hundred thirty years. My ancestors lived much longer than I." 10Then Jacob blessed the king and left.

11Joseph obeyed the king and gave his father and brothers the best land in Egypt, near the city of Rameses. 12And Joseph gave his father, his brothers, and everyone who lived with them the food they needed.

Joseph Buys Land for the King

13The hunger became worse, and since there was no food anywhere in the land, Egypt and Canaan became very poor. 14Joseph collected all the money that was to be found in Egypt and Canaan. People paid for the grain they were buying, and he brought that money to the king's palace. 15After some time, when the people in Egypt and Canaan had no money left, they went to Joseph and said, "Please give us food. Our money is gone, and if we don't eat, we will die here in front of you."

16Joseph answered, "Since you have no money, give me your farm animals, and I will give you food in return." 17So people brought their farm animals to Joseph, and he gave them food in exchange for their horses, sheep, goats, cattle, and donkeys. And he kept them alive by trading food for their farm animals that year.

18The next year the people came to Joseph and said, "You know we have no money left, and all our animals belong to you. We have nothing left except our bodies and our land. 19Surely both we and our land will die here in front of you. Buy us and our land in exchange for food, and we will be slaves to the king, together with our land. Give us seed to plant so that we will live and not die, and the land will not become a desert."

20So Joseph bought all the land in Egypt for the king. Every Egyptian sold Joseph his field, because the hunger was very great. So the land became the king's, 21and Joseph made the people slaves from one end of Egypt to the other. 22The only land he did not buy was the land the priests owned. They did not need to sell their land because the king paid them for their work. So they had money to buy food.

23Joseph said to the people, "Now I have bought you and your land for the king, so I will give you seed and you can plant your fields. 24At harvest time you must give one-fifth to the king. You may keep four-fifths for yourselves to use as seed for the field and as food for yourselves, your families, and your children."

25The people said, "You have saved our lives. If you like, we will become slaves of the king."

26So Joseph made a law in Egypt, which continues today: One-fifth of everything from the land belongs to the king. The only land the king did not get was the priests' land.

"Don't Bury Me in Egypt"

27The Israelites continued to live in the land of Goshen in Egypt. There they got possessions and had many children and grew in number.

28Jacob[n] lived in Egypt seventeen years, so he lived to be one hundred forty-seven years old. 29When Israel knew he soon would die, he called his son Joseph to him and said to him, "If you love me, put your hand under my leg.[n] Promise me you will not bury me in Egypt. 30When I die, carry me out of Egypt, and bury me where my ancestors are buried."

Joseph answered, "I will do as you say."

31Then Jacob said, "Promise me." And Joseph promised him that he would do this. Then Israel worshiped as he leaned on the top of his walking stick.

Blessings for Manasseh and Ephraim

48 Some time later Joseph learned that his father was very sick, so he took his two sons Manasseh and Ephraim and went to his fa-

Jacob Also called Israel.
put . . . leg This showed that a person would keep a promise.

ther. 2When Joseph arrived, someone told Jacob,[n] "Your son Joseph has come to see you." Jacob was weak, so he used all his strength and sat up on his bed.

3Then Jacob said to Joseph, "God Almighty appeared to me at Luz in the land of Canaan and blessed me there. 4He said to me, 'I will give you many children. I will make you the father of many peoples, and I will give your descendants[d] this land forever.' 5Your two sons, who were born here in Egypt before I came, will be counted as my own sons. Ephraim and Manasseh will be my sons just as Reuben and Simeon are my sons. 6But if you have other children, they will be your own, and their land will be part of the land given to Ephraim and Manasseh. 7When I came from Northwest Mesopotamia, Rachel died in the land of Canaan, as we were traveling toward Ephrath. This made me very sad, and I buried her there beside the road to Ephrath." (Today Ephrath is Bethlehem.)

8Then Israel saw Joseph's sons and said, "Who are these boys?"

9Joseph said to his father, "They are my sons that God has given me here in Egypt."

Israel said, "Bring your sons to me so I may bless them."

10At this time Israel's eyesight was bad because he was old. So Joseph brought the boys close to him, and Israel kissed the boys and put his arms around them. 11He said to Joseph, "I thought I would never see you alive again, and now God has let me see you and also your children."

> **SIDELIGHT:** If you have older brothers and sisters and think they always get the best deal, take some comfort in Genesis 48:13–14. Though Israel blessed both Manasseh, the oldest, and Ephraim, the youngest, he crossed his hands and blessed Ephraim with his right hand. That made Ephraim's blessing more important.

12Then Joseph moved his sons off Israel's lap and bowed facedown to the ground. 13He put Ephraim on his right side and Manasseh on his left. (So Ephraim was near Israel's left hand, and Manasseh was near Israel's right hand.) Joseph brought the boys close to Israel. 14But Israel crossed his arms and put his right hand on the head of Ephraim, who was younger. He put his left hand on the head of Manasseh, the firstborn[d] son. 15And Israel blessed Joseph and said,

"My ancestors Abraham and Isaac served our
God,
and like a shepherd God has led me all my
life.
16He was the Angel who saved me from all my
troubles.
Now I pray that he will bless these boys.
May my name be known through these boys,
and may the names of my ancestors
Abraham and Isaac be known through
them.
May they have many descendants[d]
on the earth."

17When Joseph saw that his father put his right hand on Ephraim's head, he didn't like it. So he took hold of his father's hand, wanting to move it from Ephraim's head to Manasseh's head. 18Joseph said to his father, "You are doing it wrong, Father. Manasseh is the firstborn son. Put your right hand on his head."

19But his father refused and said, "I know, my son, I know. Manasseh will be great and have many descendants. But his younger brother will be greater, and his descendants will be enough to make a nation."

20So Israel blessed them that day and said,

"When a blessing is given in Israel, they will
say:
'May God make you like Ephraim and
Manasseh.'"

In this way he made Ephraim greater than Manasseh.

21Then Israel said to Joseph, "Look at me; I am about to die. But God will be with you and will take you back to the land of your fathers. 22I have given you something that I did not give your brothers—the land of Shechem that I took from the Amorite people with my sword and my bow."

Jacob Blesses His Sons

49 Then Jacob called his sons to him. He said, "Come here to me, and I will tell you what will happen to you in the future.

2"Come together and listen, sons of Jacob.
Listen to Israel, your father."

3"Reuben, my first son, you are my strength.
Your birth showed I could be a father.
You have the highest position among my
sons,
and you are the most powerful.
4But you are uncontrolled like water,
so you will no longer lead your brothers.
This is because you got into your father's bed
and shamed me by having sexual relations
with my slave girl.

5"Simeon and Levi are brothers
who used their swords to do violence.

Jacob Also called Israel.

[6]I will not join their secret talks,
and I will not meet with them to plan evil.
They killed men because they were angry,
and they crippled oxen just for fun.
[7]May their anger be cursed, because it is too violent.
May their violence be cursed, because it is too cruel.
I will divide them up among the tribes[d] of Jacob
and scatter them through all the tribes of Israel.

[8]"Judah, your brothers will praise you.
You will grab your enemies by the neck,
and your brothers will bow down to you.
[9]Judah is like a young lion.
You have returned from killing, my son.
Like a lion, he stretches out and lies down to rest,
and no one is brave enough to wake him.
[10]Kings will come from Judah's family;
someone from Judah will always be on the throne.
Judah will rule until Shiloh comes,
and the nations will obey him.
[11]He ties his donkey to a grapevine,
his young donkey to the best branch.
He can afford to use wine to wash his clothes
and the best wine to wash his robes.
[12]His eyes are dark like the color of wine,
and his teeth are as white as the color of milk.

[13]"Zebulun will live near the sea.
His shore will be a safe place for ships,
and his land will reach as far as Sidon.

[14]"Issachar is like a strong donkey
who lies down while carrying his load.
[15]When he sees his resting place is good
and how pleasant his land is,
he will put his back to the load
and become a slave.

[16]"Dan will rule his own people
like the other tribes in Israel.
[17]Dan will be like a snake by the side of the road,
a dangerous snake lying near the path.
That snake bites a horse's leg,
and the rider is thrown off backward.

[18]"LORD, I wait for your salvation.

[19]"Robbers will attack Gad,
but he will defeat them and drive them away.

[20]"Asher's land will grow much good food;
he will grow food fit for a king.

[21]"Naphtali is like a female deer that runs free,
that has beautiful fawns.

[22]"Joseph is like a grapevine that produces much fruit,
a healthy vine watered by a spring,
whose branches grow over the wall.
[23]Archers attack him violently
and shoot at him angrily,
[24]but he aims his bow well.
His arms are made strong.
He gets his power from the Mighty God of Jacob
and his strength from the Shepherd, the Rock[d] of Israel.
[25]Your father's God helps you.
God Almighty blesses you.
He blesses you with rain from above,
with water from springs below,
with many babies born to your wives,
and many young ones born to your animals.
[26]The blessings of your father are greater
than the blessings of the oldest mountains,
greater than the good things of the long-lasting hills.
May these blessings rest on the head of Joseph,
on the forehead of the one who was separated from his brothers.

[27]"Benjamin is like a hungry wolf.
In the morning he eats what he has caught,
and in the evening he divides what he has taken."

[28]These are the twelve tribes of Israel, and this
is what their father said to them. He gave each
son the blessing that was right for him. [29]Then
Israel gave them a command and said, "I am
about to die. Bury me with my ancestors in the
cave in the field of Ephron the Hittite. [30]That cave
is in the field of Machpelah east of Mamre in the
land of Canaan. Abraham bought the field and
cave from Ephron the Hittite for a burying place.
[31]Abraham and Sarah his wife are buried there.
Isaac and Rebekah his wife are buried there, and
I buried my wife Leah there. [32]The field and the
cave in it were bought from the Hittite people."
[33]After Jacob finished talking to his sons, he lay
down. He put his feet back on the bed, took his
last breath, and died.

Jacob's Burial

50 When Jacob died, Joseph hugged his father and cried over him and kissed him.
[2]He commanded the doctors who served him to
prepare his father's body, so the doctors prepared
Jacob's body to be buried. [3]It took the doctors
forty days to prepare his body (the usual time it
took). And the Egyptians had a time of sorrow for
Jacob that lasted seventy days.

4When this time of sorrow had ended, Joseph
spoke to the king's officers and said, "If you think
well of me, please tell this to the king: 5'When my
father was near death, I made a promise to him
that I would bury him in a cave in the land of
Canaan, in a burial place that he cut out for himself. So please let me go and bury my father, and
then I will return.' "

6The king answered, "Keep your promise. Go
and bury your father."

7So Joseph went to bury his father. All the
king's officers, the older leaders, and all the leading men of Egypt went with Joseph. 8Everyone
who lived with Joseph and his brothers went with
him, as well as everyone who lived with his father. They left only their children, their flocks,
and their herds in the land of Goshen. 9They went
with Joseph in chariots and on horses. It was a
very large group.

10When they came to the threshing[d] floor of
Atad, near the Jordan River, they cried loudly and
bitterly for his father. Joseph's time of sorrow continued for seven days. 11The people that lived in
Canaan saw the sadness at the threshing floor of
Atad and said, "Those Egyptians are showing
great sorrow!" So now that place is named Sorrow of the Egyptians.

12So Jacob's sons did as their father commanded. 13They carried his body to the land of
Canaan and buried it in the cave in the field of
Machpelah near Mamre. Abraham had bought
this cave and field from Ephron the Hittite to use
as a burial place. 14After Joseph buried his father,
he returned to Egypt, along with his brothers and
everyone who had gone with him to bury his father.

The Brothers Fear Joseph

15After Jacob died, Joseph's brothers said,
"What if Joseph is still angry with us? We did
many wrong things to him. What if he plans to
pay us back?" 16So they sent a message to Joseph
that said, "Your father gave this command before
he died. 17He said to us, 'You have done wrong
and have sinned and done evil to Joseph. Tell Joseph to forgive you, his brothers.' So now, Joseph,
we beg you to forgive our wrong. We are the servants of the God of your father." When Joseph
received the message, he cried.

18And his brothers went to him and bowed low
before him and said, "We are your slaves."

19Then Joseph said to them, "Don't be afraid.
Can I do what only God can do? 20You meant to
hurt me, but God turned your evil into good to
save the lives of many people, which is being
done. 21So don't be afraid. I will take care of you
and your children." So Joseph comforted his
brothers and spoke kind words to them.

22Joseph continued to live in Egypt with all
his father's family. He died when he was one
hundred ten years old. 23During Joseph's life
Ephraim had children and grandchildren, and
Joseph's son Manasseh had a son named Makir. Joseph accepted Makir's children as his
own.

The Death of Joseph

24Joseph said to his brothers, "I am about to
die, but God will take care of you. He will lead
you out of this land to the land he promised to
Abraham, Isaac, and Jacob." 25Then Joseph had
the sons of Israel make a promise. He said, "Promise me that you will carry my bones with you out
of Egypt."

26Joseph died when he was one hundred ten
years old. Doctors prepared his body for burial,
and then they put him in a coffin in Egypt.

EXODUS

Why Read This Book:

- Discover how God works in miraculous ways to set people free (Exodus 1—18).
- Learn guidelines for living as they are described in the Ten Commandments (Exodus 20).
- Compare ancient worship practices with worship today (Exodus 25—31, 35—40).

Behind the Scenes:

"Free at last, free at last; thank God Almighty, we are free at last."

This spiritual celebrated freedom from slavery in the United States. And it became an important song in the civil rights struggle in the 1950s and 1960s in the United States. But the spiritual also could have been sung by the Israelites as they escaped from Egypt with Moses as their leader.

The Israelites had settled in Egypt about four hundred years earlier when Joseph arranged for them to be Egypt's guests (see Genesis 47:1–12, p. 53). But, in time, Egypt's rulers died, and the new rulers turned the Israelites into slaves. The Israelites longed for freedom from the horrible slavery.

WHERE THE ACTION WAS

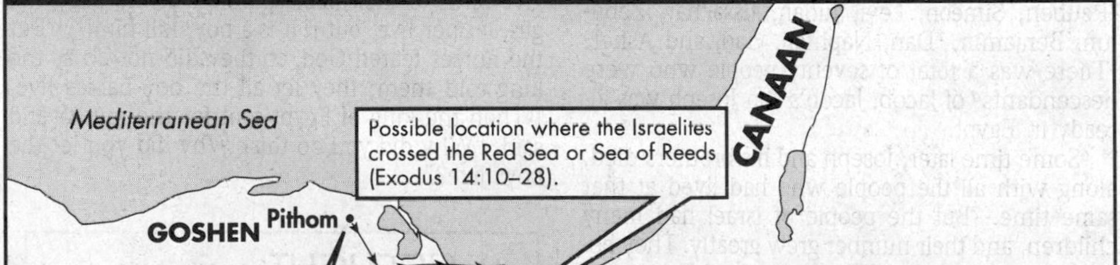

CANAAN
Mediterranean Sea
Possible location where the Israelites crossed the Red Sea or Sea of Reeds (Exodus 14:10–28).
GOSHEN
Pithom
EGYPT
Rameses
Possible alternate routes for the Exodus.
The Egyptian king made the Israelite slaves build the cities of Pithom and Rameses (Exodus 1:11).
The traditional route of the Exodus.
Moses fled to the land of Midian after killing an Egyptian (Exodus 2:13–15).
SINAI
Possible site of Mt. Sinai, where Moses received the Ten Commandments (Exodus 19:20–20:21).
MIDIAN
Note: Many of the places named in the book of Exodus are unknown. That's why scholars have different views of the route and where events took place.

WHEN THE ACTION WAS

The Israelites became slaves in Egypt
The Israelites received the Ten Commandments
Jesus was born
2000BC
1500BC
1000BC
500BC
BC/AD
The Israelites escaped from Egypt
The Israelites entered the promised land

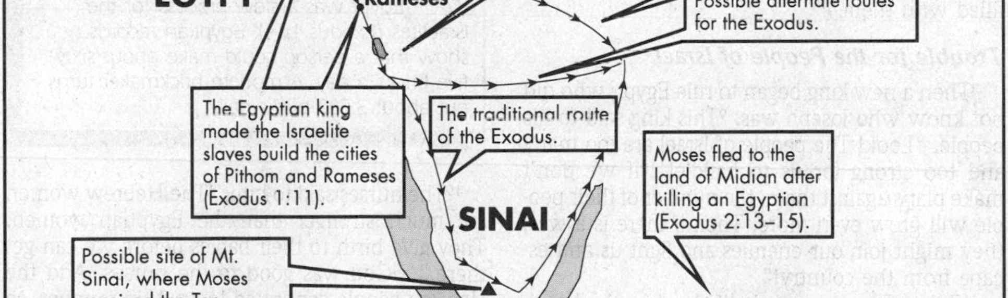

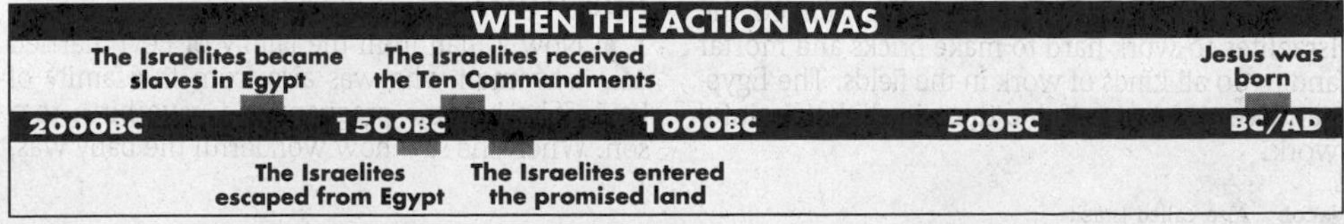

Behind the Scenes (cont.):

Exodus tells how God took the Hebrew people—descendants of Abraham—and shaped them into the free nation of Israel.

The book begins with the story of Moses being saved from slaughter. Rescued by the king's daughter, Moses grew up in the king's palace. When he became an adult, God called Moses to lead the Israelites to freedom.

Though filled with uncertainty, Moses answered God's call and negotiated with the Egyptian king. Again and again the king resisted, but God's miraculous power eventually convinced him to let Israel go. In joyous celebration, the Israelites left for the promised land, Canaan, only to be chased by the king's army. God's deliverance of Israel at the Red Sea is known as the Exodus.

Before reaching the promised land, however, the Israelites spent forty years in the wilderness. There they learned more about what God wanted them to do and be, as people and as a nation.

In Exodus 3:14, God reveals his name to Moses: I AM WHO I AM or Yahweh. It means "The One Who Is Always Present." And, indeed, God was always with Moses and the Israelites in the desert. And he is always with us today.

Jacob's Family Grows Strong

1 When Jacob[n] went to Egypt, he took his
sons, and each son took his own family with
him. These are the names of the sons of Israel:
2Reuben, Simeon, Levi, Judah, 3Issachar, Zebulun, Benjamin, 4Dan, Naphtali, Gad, and Asher.
5There was a total of seventy people who were
descendants[d] of Jacob. Jacob's son Joseph was already in Egypt.
6Some time later, Joseph and his brothers died,
along with all the people who had lived at that
same time. 7But the people of Israel had many
children, and their number grew greatly. They became very strong, and the country of Egypt was
filled with them.

Trouble for the People of Israel

8Then a new king began to rule Egypt, who did
not know who Joseph was. 9This king said to his
people, "Look! The people of Israel are too many
and too strong for us to handle! 10If we don't
make plans against them, the number of their people will grow even more. Then if there is a war,
they might join our enemies and fight us and escape from the country!"
11So the Egyptians made life hard for the Israelites. They put slave masters over them, who
forced the Israelites to build the cities Pithom and
Rameses as supply centers for the king. 12But the
harder the Egyptians forced the Israelites to work,
the more the Israelites grew in number and
spread out. So the Egyptians became very afraid
of them 13and demanded even more of them.
14They made their lives bitter. They forced the
Israelites to work hard to make bricks and mortar
and to do all kinds of work in the fields. The Egyptians were not merciful to them in all their painful
work.
15Two Hebrew nurses, named Shiphrah and
Puah, helped the Israelite women give birth to
their babies. The king of Egypt said to the nurses,
16"When you are helping the Hebrew women
give birth to their babies, watch! If the baby is a
girl, let her live, but if it is a boy, kill him!" 17But
the nurses feared God, so they did not do as the
king told them; they let all the boy babies live.
18Then the king of Egypt sent for the nurses and
said, "Why did you do this? Why did you let the
boys live?"

> **SIDELIGHT:** Making bricks in Egypt was a slow process for the Israelites (Exodus 1:14). Egyptian records show that a person could make about sixty-five bricks a day. A modern brickmaker turns out about 3,500 bricks daily.

19The nurses said to him, "The Hebrew women
are much stronger than the Egyptian women.
They give birth to their babies before we can get
there." 20God was good to the nurses. And the
Hebrew people continued to grow in number, so
they became even stronger. 21Because the nurses
feared God, he gave them families of their own.
22So the king commanded all his people, "Every time a boy is born to the Hebrews, you must
throw him into the Nile River, but let all the girl
babies live."

Baby Moses

2 Now a man from the family of Levi married
a woman who was also from the family of
Levi. 2She became pregnant and gave birth to a
son. When she saw how wonderful the baby was,

Jacob Also called Israel.

she hid him for three months. 3But after three
months she was not able to hide the baby any
longer, so she got a basket and covered it with tar
so that it would float. She put the baby in the
basket. Then she put the basket among the tall

> **SIDELIGHT:** If you think waterbeds are something new, read Exodus 2:3, where Moses is given the first waterbed in the Bible. The tall grass he was placed in was probably papyrus, which the Egyptians used for making paper.

stalks of grass at the edge of the Nile River. 4The
baby's sister stood a short distance away to see
what would happen to him.

5Then the daughter of the king of Egypt came
to the river to take a bath, and her servant girls
were walking beside the river. When she saw the
basket in the tall grass, she sent her slave girl to
get it. 6The king's daughter opened the basket and
saw the baby boy. He was crying, so she felt sorry
for him and said, "This is one of the Hebrew babies."
7Then the baby's sister asked the king's daughter, "Would you like me to go and find a Hebrew
woman to nurse the baby for you?"
8The king's daughter said, "Go!" So the girl
went and got the baby's own mother.
9The king's daughter said to the woman, "Take
this baby and nurse him for me, and I will pay
you." So the woman took her baby and nursed
him. 10When the child grew older, the woman
took him to the king's daughter, and she adopted

SUFFERING

Running for His Life

Sydney Maree felt like he didn't fit anywhere. A black in South Africa, he lived under harsh apartheid laws that restricted blacks in virtually all areas of life. He and his family could only live in black townships, and many things were off limits to them.

Sydney only felt at peace when he ran. Something about running gave him a sense of power in a world where he felt powerless because of unjust government policies. He'd run to school. He'd run more than a mile to the store. He'd run everywhere he went.

When he was sixteen, the high school track coach noticed Sydney's speed, and got him involved in track. Sydney trained tirelessly. "He was running for revenge," his trainer recalls, "running for liberation."

In 1976, his liberation began. He entered a major track meet in Port Elizabeth, South Africa, with the help of a white businessman. The only high schooler and the only black in the race, he won—and set a record for the fastest time ever by a high schooler.

Sydney's life changed that day. He became a national hero and then went to school in the United States. He set records running for Villanova University and joined the U.S. team in the 1984 Olympics.

The white businessman who helped Sydney begin racing in South Africa came to his college graduation. "Sydney started to tell me how he could never thank me enough," the supporter said. "I stopped him and said, 'No, it is I who must thank you.' Before I met him I'd only known blacks as people who did gardening for me. Now I know . . . that they too have goals and aspirations and can be like sons in my home."

Like Sydney, the Israelites faced extreme persecution as slaves in Egypt. Read about their situation in **Exodus 1:6—2:10**.

- How was Sydney's world like the world of the enslaved Israelites?
- How would you react if you faced the suffering the Israelites faced? How do you react to people suffering around you?

CONSIDER . . .

- writing a story that describes a time you experienced suffering. Thank God for getting you through that tough time.
- talking to someone who has been through tremendous suffering (such as a refugee or a war veteran). What helped him or her survive?

FOR MORE, SEE . . .

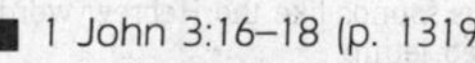

- Psalm 57:1–11 (p. 515)
- Philippians 4:14–19 (p. 1235)
- 1 John 3:16–18 (p. 1319)

the baby as her own son. The king's daughter
named him Moses,[n] because she had pulled him
out of the water.

Moses Tries to Help

11Moses grew and became a man. One day he
visited his people and saw that they were forced
to work very hard. He saw an Egyptian beating a
Hebrew man, one of Moses' own people. 12Moses
looked all around and saw that no one was watching, so he killed the Egyptian and hid his body in
the sand.
13The next day Moses returned and saw two
Hebrew men fighting each other. He said to the
one that was in the wrong, "Why are you hitting
one of your own people?"
14The man answered, "Who made you our
ruler and judge? Are you going to kill me as you
killed the Egyptian?"

Moses was afraid and thought, "Now everyone
knows what I did."
15When the king heard what Moses had done,
he tried to kill him. But Moses ran away from the
king and went to live in the land of Midian. There
he sat down near a well.

Moses in Midian

16There was a priest in Midian who had seven
daughters. His daughters went to that well to get
water to fill the water troughs for their father's
flock. 17Some shepherds came and chased the
girls away, but Moses defended the girls and watered their flock.
18When they went back to their father Reuel,[n]
he asked them, "Why have you come home early
today?"
19The girls answered, "The shepherds chased
us away, but an Egyptian defended us. He got water for us and watered our flock."
20He asked his daughters, "Where is this man?
Why did you leave him? Invite him to eat with
us."
21Moses agreed to stay with Jethro, and he gave
his daughter Zipporah to Moses to be his wife.
22Zipporah gave birth to a son. Moses named him
Gershom,[n] because Moses was a stranger in a
land that was not his own.
23After a long time, the king of Egypt died. The
people of Israel groaned, because they were
forced to work very hard. When they cried for
help, God heard them. 24God heard their cries,
and he remembered the agreement he had made
with Abraham, Isaac, and Jacob. 25He saw the
troubles of the people of Israel, and he was concerned about them.

The Burning Bush

3 One day Moses was taking care of Jethro's
flock. (Jethro was the priest of Midian and
also Moses' father-in-law.) When Moses led the
flock to the west side of the desert, he came to
Sinai, the mountain of God. 2There the angel of
the LORD appeared to him in flames of fire coming
out of a bush. Moses saw that the bush was on
fire, but it was not burning up. 3So he said, "I will
go closer to this strange thing. How can a bush
continue burning without burning up?"
4When the LORD saw Moses was coming to
look at the bush, God called to him from the bush,
"Moses, Moses!"

And Moses said, "Here I am."
5Then God said, "Do not come any closer. Take
off your sandals, because you are standing on holy
ground. 6I am the God of your ancestors—the
God of Abraham, the God of Isaac, and the God
of Jacob." Moses covered his face because he was
afraid to look at God.
7The LORD said, "I have seen the troubles my
people have suffered in Egypt, and I have heard
their cries when the Egyptian slave masters hurt
them. I am concerned about their pain, 8and I
have come down to save them from the Egyptians. I will bring them out of that land and lead
them to a good land with lots of room—a fertile
land. It is the land of the Canaanites, Hittites, Amorites, Perizzites, Hivites, and Jebusites. 9I have
heard the cries of the people of Israel, and I have
seen the way the Egyptians have made life hard
for them. 10So now I am sending you to the king
of Egypt. Go! Bring my people, the Israelites, out
of Egypt!"
11But Moses said to God, "I am not a great
man! How can I go to the king and lead the Israelites out of Egypt?"
12God said, "I will be with you. This will be the
proof that I am sending you: After you lead the
people out of Egypt, all of you will worship me on
this mountain."
13Moses said to God, "When I go to the Israelites, I will say to them, 'The God of your fathers
sent me to you.' What if the people say, 'What is
his name?' What should I tell them?"
14Then God said to Moses, "I AM WHO I AM.[n]
When you go to the people of Israel, tell them, 'I
AM sent me to you.' "
15God also said to Moses, "This is what you
should tell the people: 'The LORD is the God of

Moses The name Moses sounds like the Hebrew word for "to pull out."
Reuel He was also called Jethro.
Gershom This name sounds like the Hebrew word meaning "a stranger there."
I . . . I AM The Hebrew words are like the name "Yahweh." This Hebrew name for God, usually called "LORD," shows that God always lives and is always with his people.

your ancestors—the God of Abraham, the God of
Isaac, and the God of Jacob. He sent me to you.'
This will always be my name, by which people
from now on will know me.

> **SIDELIGHT:** In Exodus 3:14, God first says his name: I AM WHO I AM or Yahweh. This is the most common name for God in the Old Testament, appearing about 6,800 times in the original language, Hebrew. English Bibles often translate the name as LORD.

[16]"Go and gather the older leaders and tell
them this: 'The LORD, the God of your ancestors
Abraham, Isaac, and Jacob, has appeared to me.
He said, I care about you, and I have seen what
has happened to you in Egypt. [17]I promised I
would take you out of your troubles in Egypt. I
will lead you to the land of the Canaanites, Hittites, Amorites, Perizzites, Hivites, and Jebusites—a fertile land.'
[18]"The older leaders will listen to you. And
then you and the older leaders of Israel will go to
the king of Egypt and tell him, 'The LORD, the
God of the Hebrews, appeared to us. Let us travel
three days into the desert to offer sacrifices to the
LORD our God.'
[19]"But I know that the king of Egypt will not
let you go. Only a great power will force him to
let you go, [20]so I will use my great power against
Egypt. I will strike Egypt with all the miracles[d]
that will happen in that land. After I do that, he
will let you go. [21]I will cause the Egyptians to
think well of the Israelites. So when you leave,
they will give gifts to your people. [22]Each woman
should ask her Egyptian neighbor and any Egyptian woman living in her house for gifts—silver,
gold, and clothing. You should put those gifts on
your children when you leave Egypt. In this way
you will take with you the riches of the Egyp
tians."

LEADERSHIP

Somebody Do Something!

In 1981 in the United States, 11,005 people between the ages of sixteen and twenty-one died in car accidents. Under normal circumstances, that statistic wouldn't have meant much to Robert Anastas, a hockey coach at Wayland Public School in Wayland, Massachusetts.

But two of those 11,005 young people had been on his hockey team. They were killed in a car accident involving a drunk driver. Robert was stunned. It doesn't have to be this way, he thought.

Robert knew nothing would change if no one did anything to combat the problem. So he started Students Against Driving Drunk (SADD) and has dedicated his life to combating the drunk driving problem. The organization works to alert students to the dangers of drinking and driving.

Under Robert's leadership, SADD has grown to a national organization with four million members and chapters in all fifty U.S. states and Canada. And Robert has received dozens of awards for battling this serious problem.

Robert saw a problem and became a leader in the fight to overcome it. In the same way, Moses learned about the Israelites' persecution in Egypt and followed God's call to lead them to freedom. Read about it in **Exodus 3:1–20**.

- What similarities are there between Robert's call and Moses' call to leadership? What differences do you see?
- Have you, like Moses, felt called by God to take leadership in fighting a particular problem? How have you responded?

CONSIDER . . .

- watching the evening news and identifying leaders who are working to end suffering around the world. Pray for these leaders.
- listing problems in your school, church, community, or country that you're concerned about. Then decide one area where your leadership can make a difference.

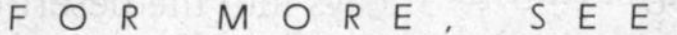

FOR MORE, SEE . . .

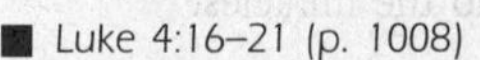

- Psalm 22:1–11 (p. 493)
- Micah 2:6–13 (p. 863)
- Luke 4:16–21 (p. 1008)

Proof for Moses

4 Then Moses answered, "What if the people of Israel do not believe me or listen to me? What if they say, 'The LORD did not appear to you'?"

[2]The LORD said to him, "What is that in your hand?"

Moses answered, "It is my walking stick."

[3]The LORD said, "Throw it on the ground."

So Moses threw it on the ground, and it became a snake. Moses ran from the snake, [4]but the LORD said to him, "Reach out and grab the snake by its tail." When Moses reached out and took hold of the snake, it again became a stick in his hand. [5]The LORD said, "This is so that the Israelites will believe that the LORD appeared to you. I am the God of their ancestors, the God of Abraham, the God of Isaac, and the God of Jacob."

[6]Then the LORD said to Moses, "Put your hand inside your coat." So Moses put his hand inside his coat. When he took it out, it was white with a skin disease.

[7]Then he said, "Now put your hand inside your coat again." So Moses put his hand inside his coat again. When he took it out, his hand was healthy again, like the rest of his skin.

[8]Then the LORD said, "If the people do not believe you or pay attention to the first miracle,[d] they may believe you when you show them this second miracle. [9]After these two miracles, if they still do not believe or listen to you, take some water from the Nile River and pour it on the dry ground. The water will become blood when it touches the ground."

[10]But Moses said to the LORD, "Please, Lord, I have never been a skilled speaker. Even now, after talking to you, I cannot speak well. I speak slowly and can't find the best words."

[11]Then the LORD said to him, "Who made a person's mouth? And who makes someone deaf or not able to speak? Or who gives a person sight or blindness? It is I, the LORD. [12]Now go! I will help you speak, and I will teach you what to say."

[13]But Moses said, "Please, Lord, send someone else."

[14]The LORD became angry with Moses and said, "Your brother Aaron, from the family of Levi, is a skilled speaker. He is already coming to meet you, and he will be happy when he sees you. [15]You will speak to Aaron and tell him what to say. I will help both of you to speak and will teach you what to do. [16]Aaron will speak to the people for you. You will tell him what God says, and he will speak for you. [17]Take your walking stick with you, and use it to do the miracles."

Moses Returns to Egypt

[18]Moses went back to Jethro, his father-in-law, and said to him, "Let me go back to my people in Egypt. I want to see if they are still alive."

Jethro said to Moses, "Go! I wish you well."

[19]While Moses was still in Midian, the LORD said to him, "Go back to Egypt, because the men who wanted to kill you are dead now."

[20]So Moses took his wife and his sons, put them on a donkey, and started back to Egypt. He took with him the walking stick of God.

[21]The LORD said to Moses, "When you get back to Egypt, do all the miracles[d] I have given you the power to do. Show them to the king of Egypt. But I will make the king very stubborn, and he will not let the people go. [22]Then say to the king, 'This is what the LORD says: Israel is my firstborn[d] son. [23]I told you to let my son go so he may worship me. But you refused to let Israel go, so I will kill your firstborn son.' "

[24]As Moses was on his way to Egypt, he stopped at a resting place for the night. The LORD met him there and tried to kill him. [25]But Zipporah took a flint knife and circumcised[d] her son. Taking the skin, she touched Moses' feet with it and said to him, "You are a bridegroom of blood to me." [26]She said, "You are a bridegroom of blood," because she had to circumcise her son. So the LORD let Moses alone.

[27]Meanwhile the LORD said to Aaron, "Go out into the desert to meet Moses." When Aaron went, he met Moses at Sinai, the mountain of God, and kissed him. [28]Moses told Aaron everything the LORD had said to him when he sent him to Egypt. He also told him about the miracles which the LORD had commanded him to do.

[29]Moses and Aaron gathered all the older leaders of the Israelites, [30]and Aaron told them everything that the LORD had told Moses. Then Moses did the miracles for all the people to see, [31]and the Israelites believed. When they heard that the LORD was concerned about them and had seen their troubles, they bowed down and worshiped him.

Moses and Aaron Before the King

5 After Moses and Aaron talked to the people, they went to the king of Egypt and said, "This is what the LORD, the God of Israel says: 'Let my people go so they may hold a feast for me in the desert.' "

[2]But the king of Egypt said, "Who is the LORD? Why should I obey him and let Israel go? I do not know the LORD, and I will not let Israel go."

[3]Then Aaron and Moses said, "The God of the Hebrews has met with us. Now let us travel three days into the desert to offer sacrifices to the LORD our God. If we don't do this, he may kill us with a disease or in war."

[4]But the king said to them, "Moses and Aaron, why are you taking the people away from their

work? Go back to your jobs! 5There are very many
Hebrews, and now you want them to quit working!"

6That same day the king gave a command to
the slave masters and foremen. 7He said, "Don't
give the people straw to make bricks as you used
to do. Let them gather their own straw. 8But they
must still make the same number of bricks as they
did before. Do not accept fewer. They have become lazy, and that is why they are asking me,
'Let us go to offer sacrifices to our God.' 9Make
these people work harder and keep them busy;
then they will not have time to listen to the lies
of Moses."

10So the slave masters and foremen went to the
Israelites and said, "This is what the king says: I
will no longer give you straw. 11Go and get your
own straw wherever you can find it. But you must
make as many bricks as you made before." 12So
the people went everywhere in Egypt looking for
dry stalks to use for straw. 13The slave masters
kept forcing the people to work harder. They said,
"You must make just as many bricks as you did
when you were given straw." 14The king's slave
masters had made the Israelite foremen responsible for the work the people did. The Egyptian
slave masters beat these men and asked them,
"Why aren't you making as many bricks as you
made in the past?"

15Then the Israelite foremen went to the king
and complained, "Why are you treating us, your
servants, this way? 16You give us no straw, but we
are commanded to make bricks. Our slave masters beat us, but it is your own people's fault."

17The king answered, "You are lazy! You don't
want to work! That is why you ask to leave here
and make sacrifices to the LORD. 18Now, go back
to work! We will not give you any straw, but you
must make just as many bricks as you did before."

19The Israelite foremen knew they were in
trouble, because the king had told them, "You
must make just as many bricks each day as you
did before." 20As they were leaving the meeting
with the king, they met Moses and Aaron, who
were waiting for them. 21So they said to Moses
and Aaron, "May the LORD punish you. You
caused the king and his officers to hate us. You
have given them an excuse to kill us."

Moses Complains to God

22Then Moses returned to the LORD and said,
"Lord, why have you brought this trouble on your
people? Is this why you sent me here? 23I went to
the king and said what you told me to say, but
ever since that time he has made the people suffer. And you have done nothing to save them."

6 Then the LORD said to Moses, "Now you will
see what I will do to the king of Egypt. I will
use my great power against him, and he will let
my people go. Because of my power, he will force
them out of his country."

2Then God said to Moses, "I am the LORD. 3I
appeared to Abraham, Isaac, and Jacob by the
name God Almighty, but they did not know me
by my name, the LORD. 4I also made my agreement with them to give them the land of Canaan.
They lived in that land, but it was not their own.
5Now I have heard the cries of the Israelites,
whom the Egyptians are treating as slaves, and I
remember my agreement. 6So tell the people of
Israel that I say to them, 'I am the LORD. I will
save you from the hard work the Egyptians force
you to do. I will make you free, so you will not
be slaves to the Egyptians. I will free you by my
great power, and I will punish the Egyptians terribly. 7I will make you my own people, and I will
be your God. You will know that I am the LORD
your God, the One who saves you from the hard
work the Egyptians force you to do. 8I will lead
you to the land that I promised to Abraham, Isaac,
and Jacob, and I will give you that land to own.
I am the LORD.'"

9So Moses told this to the Israelites, but they
would not listen to him. They were discouraged,
and their slavery was hard.

10Then the LORD said to Moses, 11"Go tell the
king of Egypt that he must let the Israelites leave
his land."

12But Moses answered, "The Israelites will not
listen to me, so surely the king will not listen to
me either. I am not a good speaker."

13But the LORD spoke to Moses and Aaron and
gave them orders about the Israelites and the king
of Egypt. He commanded them to lead the Israelites out of Egypt.

Families of Israel

14These are the leaders of the families of Israel:

Israel's first son, Reuben, had four sons: Hanoch, Pallu, Hezron, and Carmi. These are the
family groups of Reuben.

15Simeon's sons were Jemuel, Jamin, Ohad, Jakin, Zohar, and Shaul, the son of a Canaanite
woman. These are the family groups of Simeon.

16Levi lived one hundred thirty-seven years.
These are the names of his sons according to their
family history: Gershon, Kohath, and Merari.

17Gershon had two sons, Libni and Shimei,
with their families.

18Kohath lived one hundred thirty-three years.
The sons of Kohath were Amram, Izhar, Hebron,
and Uzziel.

19The sons of Merari were Mahli and Mushi.

These are the family groups of Levi, according
to their family history.

20Amram married his father's sister Jochebed,

who gave birth to Aaron and Moses. Amram lived
one hundred thirty-seven years.
21Izhar's sons were Korah, Nepheg, and Zicri.
22Uzziel's sons were Mishael, Elzaphan, and
Sithri.
23Aaron married Elisheba, the daughter of Amminadab and the sister of Nahshon. Elisheba gave
birth to Nadab, Abihu, Eleazar, and Ithamar.
24The sons of Korah were Assir, Elkanah, and
Abiasaph. These are the family groups of the Ko-
rahites.
25Eleazar son of Aaron married a daughter of
Putiel, and she gave birth to Phinehas.
These are the leaders of the family groups of
the Levites.
26This was the Aaron and Moses to whom the
LORD said, "Lead the people of Israel out of Egypt
by their divisions." 27Aaron and Moses are the
ones who talked to the king of Egypt and told him
to let the Israelites leave Egypt.

God Repeats His Call to Moses

28The LORD spoke to Moses in the land of Egypt
29and said, "I am the LORD. Tell the king of Egypt
everything I tell you."
30But Moses answered, "I am not a good
speaker. The king will not listen to me."

7 The LORD said to Moses, "I have made you
like God to the king of Egypt, and your
brother Aaron will be like a prophet[d] for you. 2Tell
Aaron your brother everything that I command
you, and let him tell the king of Egypt to let the
Israelites leave his country. 3But I will make the
king stubborn. I will do many miracles[d] in Egypt,
4but he will still refuse to listen. So then I will
punish Egypt terribly, and I will lead my divisions,
my people the Israelites, out of that land. 5I will
punish Egypt with my power, and I will bring the
Israelites out of that land. Then they will know I
am the LORD."
6Moses and Aaron did just as the LORD had
commanded them. 7Moses was eighty years old
and Aaron was eighty-three when they spoke to
the king.

Aaron's Walking Stick Becomes a Snake

8The LORD said to Moses and Aaron, 9"Moses,
when the king asks you to do a miracle,[d] tell
Aaron to throw his walking stick down in front of
the king, and it will become a snake."
10So Moses and Aaron went to the king as the
LORD had commanded. Aaron threw his walking
stick down in front of the king and his officers,
and it became a snake.
11So the king called in his wise men and his
magicians, and with their tricks the Egyptian magicians were able to do the same thing. 12They
threw their walking sticks on the ground, and
their sticks became snakes. But Aaron's stick
swallowed theirs. 13Still the king was stubborn
and refused to listen to Moses and Aaron, just as
the LORD had said.

The Water Becomes Blood

14Then the LORD said to Moses, "The king is
being stubborn and refuses to let the people go.
15In the morning the king will go out to the Nile
River. Go meet him by the edge of the river, and
take with you the walking stick that became a
snake. 16Tell him: The LORD, the God of the Hebrews, sent me to you. He said, 'Let my people go
worship me in the desert.' Until now you have
not listened. 17This is what the LORD says: 'This
is how you will know that I am the LORD. I will
strike the water of the Nile River with this stick
in my hand, and the water will change into blood.
18Then the fish in the Nile will die, and the river
will begin to stink. The Egyptians will not be able
to drink the water from the Nile.' "
19The LORD said to Moses, "Tell Aaron: 'Take
the walking stick in your hand and stretch your
hand over the rivers, canals, ponds, and pools in
Egypt.' The water will become blood everywhere
in Egypt, both in wooden buckets and in stone
jars."
20So Moses and Aaron did just as the LORD had
commanded. In front of the king and his officers,
Aaron raised his walking stick and struck the water in the Nile River. So all the water in the Nile
changed into blood. 21The fish in the Nile died,
and the river began to stink, so the Egyptians
could not drink water from it. Blood was everywhere in the land of Egypt.
22Using their tricks, the magicians of Egypt did
the same thing. So the king was stubborn and refused to listen to Moses and Aaron, just as the
LORD had said. 23The king turned and went into
his palace and ignored what Moses and Aaron had
done. 24The Egyptians could not drink the water
from the Nile, so all of them dug along the bank
of the river, looking for water to drink.

The Frogs

25Seven days passed after the LORD changed the
Nile River.

8 Then the LORD told Moses, "Go to the king
of Egypt and tell him, 'This is what the LORD
says: Let my people go to worship me. 2If you
refuse, I will punish Egypt with frogs. 3The Nile
River will be filled with frogs. They will come up
into your palace, into your bedroom, on your bed,
into the houses of your officers, and onto your
people. They will come into your ovens and into
your baking pans. 4The frogs will jump all over
you, your people, and your officers.' "
5Then the LORD said to Moses, "Tell Aaron to
hold his walking stick in his hand over the rivers,

canals, and ponds. Make frogs come up out of the
water onto the land of Egypt."
6So Aaron held his hand over all the waters of
Egypt, and the frogs came up out of the water and
covered the land of Egypt. 7The magicians used
their tricks to do the same thing, so even more
frogs came up onto the land of Egypt.

> **SIDELIGHT:** Lots of movies have been based on the Bible: The Ten Commandments, The Greatest Story Ever Told, David and Bathsheba. But what about the 1972 horror movie Frogs? Sounds an awful lot like Exodus 8:6–7, doesn't it?

8The king called for Moses and Aaron and said,
"Pray to the LORD to take the frogs away from me
and my people. I will let your people go to offer
sacrifices to the LORD."
9Moses said to the king, "Please set the time
when I should pray for you, your people, and your
officers. Then the frogs will leave you and your
houses and will remain only in the Nile."
10The king answered, "Tomorrow."
Moses said, "What you want will happen. By
this you will know that there is no one like the
LORD our God. 11The frogs will leave you, your
houses, your officers, and your people. They will
remain only in the Nile."
12After Moses and Aaron left the king, Moses
asked the LORD about the frogs he had sent to the
king. 13And the LORD did as Moses asked. The
frogs died in the houses, in the yards, and in the
fields. 14The Egyptians put them in piles, and
the whole country began to stink. 15But when
the king saw that they were free of the frogs,
he became stubborn again. He did not listen to
Moses and Aaron, just as the LORD had said.

The Gnats

16Then the LORD said to Moses, "Tell Aaron to
raise his walking stick and strike the dust on the
ground. Then everywhere in Egypt the dust will
change into gnats." 17They did this, and when
Aaron raised the walking stick that was in his
hand and struck the dust on the ground, everywhere in Egypt the dust changed into gnats. The
gnats got on the people and animals. 18Using their
tricks, the magicians tried to do the same thing,
but they could not make the dust change into
gnats. The gnats remained on the people and animals. 19So the magicians told the king that the
power of God had done this. But the king was
stubborn and refused to listen to them, just as the
LORD had said.

The Flies

20The LORD told Moses, "Get up early in the
morning, and meet the king of Egypt as he goes
out to the river. Tell him, 'This is what the LORD
says: Let my people go so they can worship me.
21If you don't let them go, I will send swarms of
flies into your houses. The flies will be on you,
your officers, and your people. The houses of
Egypt will be full of flies, and they will be all over
the ground, too. 22But I will not treat the Israelites
the same as the Egyptian people. There will not
be any flies in the land of Goshen, where my people live. By this you will know that I, the LORD,
am in this land. 23I will treat my people differently
from your people. This miracle[d] will happen tomorrow.' "
24So the LORD did as he had said, and great
swarms of flies came into the king's palace and his
officers' houses. All over Egypt flies were ruining
the land. 25The king called for Moses and Aaron
and told them, "Offer sacrifices to your God here
in this country."
26But Moses said, "It wouldn't be right to do
that, because the Egyptians hate the sacrifices we
offer to the LORD our God. If they see us offering
sacrifices they hate, they will throw stones at us
and kill us. 27Let us make a three-day journey into
the desert. We must offer sacrifices to the LORD
our God there, as the LORD told us to do."
28The king said, "I will let you go so that you
may offer sacrifices to the LORD your God in the
desert, but you must not go very far away. Now
go and pray for me."
29Moses said, "I will leave and pray to the
LORD, and he will take the flies away from you,
your officers, and your people tomorrow. But do
not try to trick us again. Do not stop the people
from going to offer sacrifices to the LORD."
30So Moses left the king and prayed to the
LORD, 31and the LORD did as he asked. He removed the flies from the king, his officers, and his
people so that not one fly was left. 32But the king
became stubborn again and did not let the people
go.

The Disease on the Farm Animals

9 Then the LORD told Moses, "Go to the king
of Egypt and tell him, 'This is what the LORD,
the God of the Hebrews, says: Let my people go
to worship me. 2If you refuse to let them go and
continue to hold them, 3the LORD will punish
you. He will send a terrible disease on your farm
animals that are in the fields. He will cause your
horses, donkeys, camels, cattle, goats, and sheep
to become sick. 4But the LORD will treat Israel's
animals differently from the animals of Egypt.
None of the animals that belong to the Israelites
will die. 5The LORD has set tomorrow as the time

he will do this in the land.' " 6The next day the LORD did as he promised. All the farm animals in Egypt died, but none of the animals belonging to Israelites died. 7The king sent people to see what had happened to the animals of Israel, and they found that not one of them had died. But the king was still stubborn and did not let the people go.

The Boils

8The LORD said to Moses and Aaron, "Fill your hands with ashes from a furnace. Moses, throw the ashes into the air in front of the king of Egypt. 9The ashes will spread like dust through all the land of Egypt. They will cause boils to break out and become sores on the skin of people and animals everywhere in the land."

10So Moses and Aaron took ashes from a furnace and went and stood before the king. Moses threw ashes into the air, which caused boils to break out and become sores on people and animals. 11The magicians could not stand before Moses, because all the Egyptians had boils, even the magicians. 12But the LORD made the king stubborn, so he refused to listen to Moses and Aaron, just as the LORD had said.

The Hail

13Then the LORD said to Moses, "Get up early in the morning and go to the king of Egypt. Tell him, 'This is what the LORD, the God of the Hebrews, says: Let my people go to worship me. 14If you don't, this time I will punish you, your officers, and your people, with all my power. Then you will know there is no one in the whole land like me. 15By now I could have used my power and caused a terrible disease that would have destroyed you and your people from the earth. 16But I have let you live for this reason: to show you my power so that my name will be talked about in all the earth. 17You are still against my people and do not want to let them go. 18So at this time tomorrow, I will send a terrible hailstorm, the worst in Egypt since it became a nation. 19Now send for your animals and whatever you have in the fields, and bring them into a safe place. The hail will fall on every person or animal that is still in the fields. If they have not been brought in, they will die.' " 20Some of the king's officers respected the word of the LORD and hurried to bring their slaves and animals inside. 21But others ignored the LORD's message and left their slaves and animals in the fields.

22The LORD told Moses, "Raise your hand toward the sky. Then the hail will start falling in all the land of Egypt. It will fall on people, animals, and on everything that grows in the fields of Egypt." 23When Moses raised his walking stick toward the sky, the LORD sent thunder and hail, and lightning flashed down to the earth. So he caused hail to fall upon the land of Egypt. 24There was hail, and lightning flashed as it hailed — the worst hailstorm in Egypt since it had become a nation. 25The hail destroyed all the people and animals that were in the fields in all the land of Egypt. It also destroyed everything that grew in the fields and broke all the trees in the fields. 26The only place it did not hail was in the land of Goshen, where the Israelites lived.

27The king sent for Moses and Aaron and told them, "This time I have sinned. The LORD is in the right, and I and my people are in the wrong. 28Pray to the LORD. We have had enough of God's thunder and hail. I will let you go; you do not have to stay here any longer."

29Moses told the king, "When I leave the city, I will raise my hands to the LORD in prayer, and the thunder and hail will stop. Then you will know that the earth belongs to the LORD. 30But I know that you and your officers do not yet fear the LORD God."

31The flax was in bloom, and the barley had ripened, so these crops were destroyed. 32But both wheat crops ripen later, so they were not destroyed.

33Moses left the king and went outside the city. He raised his hands to the LORD, and the thunder and hail stopped. The rain also stopped falling to the ground. 34When the king saw that the rain, hail, and thunder had stopped, he sinned again, and he and his officers became stubborn. 35So the king became stubborn and refused to let the Israelites go, just as the LORD had said through Moses.

The Locusts

10 The LORD said to Moses, "Go to the king of Egypt. I have made him and his officers stubborn so I could show them my powerful miracles.[d] 2I also did this so you could tell your children and your grandchildren how I was hard on the Egyptians. Tell them about the miracles I did among them so that all of you will know that I am the LORD."

3So Moses and Aaron went to the king and told him, "This is what the LORD, the God of the Hebrews, says: 'How long will you refuse to be sorry for what you have done? Let my people go to worship me. 4If you refuse to let my people go, tomorrow I will bring locusts[d] into your country. 5They will cover the land so that no one will be able to see the ground. They will eat anything that was left from the hailstorm and the leaves from every tree growing in the field. 6They will fill your palaces and all your officers' houses, as well as the houses of all the Egyptians. There will be more locusts than your fathers or ancestors have ever seen — more than there have been since people

began living in Egypt.' " Then Moses turned and
walked away from the king.
7The king's officers asked him, "How long will
this man make trouble for us? Let the Israelites go
to worship the LORD their God. Don't you know
that Egypt is ruined?"
8So Moses and Aaron were brought back to the
king. He said to them, "Go and worship the LORD
your God. But tell me, just who is going?"
9Moses answered, "We will go with our young
and old people, our sons and daughters, and our
flocks and herds, because we are going to have a
feast to honor the LORD."
10The king said to them, "The LORD will really
have to be with you if ever I let you and all of your
children leave Egypt. See, you are planning something evil! 11No! Only the men may go and worship the LORD, which is what you have been asking for." Then the king forced Moses and Aaron
out of his palace.
12The LORD told Moses, "Raise your hand over
the land of Egypt, and the locusts will come. They
will spread all over the land of Egypt and will eat
all the plants the hail did not destroy."
13So Moses raised his walking stick over the
land of Egypt, and the LORD caused a strong wind
to blow from the east. It blew across the land all
that day and night, and when morning came, the
east wind had brought the locusts. 14Swarms of
locusts covered all the land of Egypt and settled
everywhere. There were more locusts than ever
before or after, 15and they covered the whole land
so that it was black. They ate everything that was
left after the hail—every plant in the field and all
the fruit on the trees. Nothing green was left on
any tree or plant anywhere in Egypt.
16The king quickly called for Moses and Aaron.
He said, "I have sinned against the LORD your
God and against you. 17Now forgive my sin this
time. Pray to the LORD your God, and ask him to
stop this punishment that kills."
18Moses left the king and prayed to the LORD.
19So the LORD changed the wind. He made a very
strong wind blow from the west, and it blew the
locusts away into the Red Sea.[d] Not one locust
was left anywhere in Egypt. 20But the LORD
caused the king to be stubborn again, and he did
not let the Israelites go.

The Darkness

21Then the LORD told Moses, "Raise your hand
toward the sky, and darkness will cover the land
of Egypt. It will be so dark you will be able to feel
it." 22Moses raised his hand toward the sky, and
total darkness was everywhere in Egypt for three
days. 23No one could see anyone else, and no one
could go anywhere for three days. But the Israelites had light where they lived.
24Again the king of Egypt called for Moses. He
said, "All of you may go and worship the LORD.
You may take your women and children with
you, but you must leave your flocks and herds
here."
25Moses said, "You must let us have animals to
use as sacrifices and burnt offerings, because we
have to offer them to the LORD our God. 26So we
must take our animals with us; not a hoof will be
left behind. We have to use some of the animals
to worship the LORD our God. We won't know
exactly what we will need to worship the LORD
until we get there."
27But the LORD made the king stubborn again,
so he refused to let them go. 28Then he told Moses, "Get out of here, and don't come again! The
next time you see me, you will die."
29Then Moses told the king, "I'll do what you
say. I will not come to see you again."

The Death of the Firstborn

11 Now the LORD had told Moses, "I have
one more way to punish the king and the
people of Egypt. After this, the king will send all
of you away from Egypt. When he does, he will
force you to leave completely. 2Tell the men and
women of Israel to ask their neighbors for things
made of silver and gold." 3The LORD had caused
the Egyptians to respect the Israelites, and both
the king's officers and the Egyptian people considered Moses to be a great man.
4So Moses said to the king, "This is what the
LORD says: 'About midnight tonight I will go
through all Egypt. 5Every firstborn[d] son in the
land of Egypt will die—from the firstborn son of
the king, who sits on his throne, to the firstborn
of the slave girl grinding grain. Also the firstborn
farm animals will die. 6There will be loud outcries
everywhere in Egypt, worse than any time before
or after this. 7But not even a dog will bark at the
Israelites or their animals.' Then you will know
that the LORD treats Israel differently from Egypt.
8All your officers will come to me. They will bow
facedown to the ground before me and say,
'Leave and take all your people with you.' After
that, I will leave." Then Moses very angrily left
the king.
9The LORD had told Moses, "The king will not
listen to you and Aaron so that I may do many
miracles[d] in the land of Egypt." 10Moses and
Aaron did all these great miracles in front of the
king. But the LORD made him stubborn, and the
king would not let the Israelites leave his country.

The First Passover

12 The LORD spoke to Moses and Aaron in
the land of Egypt: 2"This month will be
the beginning of months, the first month of the
year for you. 3Tell the whole community of Israel

that on the tenth day of this month each man
must get one lamb for the people in his house. [4]If
there are not enough people in his house to eat a
whole lamb, he must share it with his closest
neighbor, considering the number of people.
There must be enough lamb for everyone to eat.
[5]The lamb must be a one-year-old male that has
nothing wrong with it. This animal can be either
a young sheep or a young goat. [6]Take care of the
animals until the fourteenth day of the month. On
that day all the people of the community of Israel
will kill them in the evening before dark. [7]The
people must take some of the blood and put it on
the sides and tops of the doorframes of the houses
where they eat the lambs. [8]On this night they
must roast the lamb over a fire. They must eat it
with bitter herbs and bread made without yeast.
[9]Do not eat the lamb raw or boiled in water. Roast
the whole lamb over a fire—with its head, legs,
and inner organs. [10]You must not leave any of it
until morning, but if any of it is left over until
morning, you must burn it with fire.

[11]"This is the way you must eat it: You must be
fully dressed as if you were going on a trip. You
must have your sandals on and your walking stick
in your hand. You must eat it in a hurry; this is
the LORD's Passover.[d]

[12]"That night I will go through the land of
Egypt and kill all the firstborn[d] animals and people
in the land of Egypt. I will also punish all the gods
of Egypt. I am the LORD. [13]But the blood will be
a sign on the houses where you are. When I see
the blood, I will pass over you. Nothing terrible
will hurt you when I punish the land of Egypt.

[14]"You are always to remember this day and
celebrate it with a feast to the LORD. Your descendants[d] are to honor the LORD with this feast from
now on. [15]For this feast you must eat bread made
without yeast for seven days. On the first day, you
are to remove all the yeast from your houses. No

GOD'S LOVE

Waiting for Miracles

When the children in George Müller's orphanage in Bristol, England, ate dinner that evening, they didn't know the food on their plates was the only food in the orphanage. No food or money was left for the next morning's breakfast. George prayed that something would arrive that evening, but nothing did. He went to bed, committing the need to God.

The next morning, George went out for his early morning walk and prayer. For some reason, he took a different route than usual, and a friend saw him. "I'm glad to see you," his friend said. "Please accept five pounds for the orphans."

"Thank you," George said graciously, never mentioning that the money would provide the kids' food for several days. "God bless you."

Because of his faith, George fed and housed hundreds of homeless kids in Bristol in the 1800s. But he never made public appeals for funds.

When the food ran out at the orphanage, George told no one but God. And, miraculously, God supplied it time and time again. When George was short on funds, only God knew. And the money arrived when George needed it.

George Müller would never have been able to help hundreds of orphans without God's love to provide for them. Similarly, the Israelites would never have escaped from Egypt without God's love to protect them. Read **Exodus 12:1–14** to see how God's love delivered them during the Passover.

- What similarities do you see between God's provisions for George Müller's orphanages and his protection of the Israelites during the Passover?
- Has God's love helped you through a situation you could never have survived on your own? How did the experience make you feel about God?

CONSIDER . . .

- thanking God for his love that has delivered you in the past from tough situations.
- writing on a card a tough situation you are experiencing. Put the card in a place where you will find it in a week or so to see how God helped you through that tough time.

FOR MORE, SEE . . .

- Psalm 34 (p. 501)
- Hosea 14:1–8 (p. 832)
- Romans 5:1–11 (p. 1145)

one should eat any yeast for the full seven days of
the feast, or that person will be cut off from Israel.
16You are to have holy meetings on the first and
last days of the feast. You must not do any work
on these days; the only work you may do is to
prepare your meals. 17You must celebrate the
Feast[d] of Unleavened Bread, because on this very
day I brought your divisions of people out of
Egypt. So all of your descendants must celebrate
this day. This is a law that will last from now on.
18In the first month of the year you are to eat
bread made without yeast, from the evening of
the fourteenth day until the evening of the
twenty-first day. 19For seven days there must not
be any yeast in your houses. Anybody who eats
yeast during this time, either an Israelite or non-
Israelite, must be cut off from the community of
Israel. 20During this feast you must not eat anything made with yeast. You must eat only bread
made without yeast wherever you live."

21Then Moses called all the older leaders of Israel together and told them, "Get the animals for
your families and kill the lamb for the Passover.
22Take a branch of the hyssop plant, dip it into the
bowl filled with blood, and then wipe the blood
on the sides and tops of the doorframes. No one
may leave that house until morning. 23When the
LORD goes through Egypt to kill the Egyptians, he
will see the blood on the sides and tops of the
doorframes, and he will pass over that house. He
will not let the one who brings death come into
your houses and kill you.

24"You must keep this command as a law for
you and your descendants from now on. 25Do this
when you go to the land the LORD has promised
to give you. 26When your children ask you, 'Why
are we doing these things?' 27you will say, 'This
is the Passover sacrifice to honor the LORD. When
we were in Egypt, the LORD passed over the
houses of Israel, and when he killed the Egyptians, he saved our homes.' " Then the people
bowed down and worshiped the LORD. 28They did
just as the LORD commanded Moses and Aaron.

29At midnight the LORD killed all the firstborn
sons in the land of Egypt—from the firstborn of
the king who sat on the throne to the firstborn of
the prisoner in jail. Also, all the firstborn farm animals died. 30The king, his officers, and all the
Egyptians got up during the night because someone had died in every house. So there was a loud
outcry everywhere in Egypt.

Israel Leaves Egypt

31During the night the king called for Moses
and Aaron and said, "Get up and leave my people.
You and your people may do as you have asked;
go and worship the LORD. 32Take all of your flocks
and herds as you have asked, and go. And also
bless me." 33The Egyptians also asked the Israelites to hurry and leave, saying, "If you don't leave,
we will all die!"

34So the people took their dough before the
yeast was added. They wrapped the bowls for
making dough in clothing and carried them on
their shoulders. 35The Israelites did what Moses
told them to do and asked their Egyptian neighbors for things made of silver and gold and for
clothing. 36The LORD caused the Egyptians to
think well of them, and the Egyptians gave the
people everything they asked for. So the Israelites
took rich gifts from them.

37The Israelites traveled from Rameses to Succoth. There were about six hundred thousand
men walking, not including the women and children. 38Many other people who were not Israelites went with them, as well as a large number of
sheep, goats, and cattle. 39The Israelites used the
dough they had brought out of Egypt to bake
loaves of bread without yeast. The dough had no
yeast in it, because they had been rushed out of
Egypt and had no time to get food ready for their
trip.

40The people of Israel had lived in Egypt for
four hundred thirty years; 41on the very day the
four hundred thirty years ended, the LORD's divisions of people left Egypt. 42That night the LORD
kept watch to bring them out of Egypt, and so on
this same night the Israelites are to keep watch to
honor the LORD from now on.

43The LORD told Moses and Aaron, "Here are
the rules for Passover:[d] No foreigner is to eat the
Passover. 44If someone buys a slave and circum-
cises[d] him, the slave may eat the Passover. 45But
neither a person who lives for a short time in your
country nor a hired worker may eat it.

46"The meal must be eaten inside a house; take
none of the meat outside the house. Don't break
any of the bones. 47The whole community of Israel must take part in this feast. 48A foreigner who
lives with you may share in the LORD's Passover
if all the males in his house become circumcised.
Then, since he will be like a citizen of Israel, he
may share in the meal. But a man who is not circumcised may not eat the Passover meal. 49The
same rules apply to an Israelite born in the country or to a foreigner living there."

50So all the Israelites did just as the LORD had
commanded Moses and Aaron. 51On that same
day the LORD led the Israelites out of Egypt by
their divisions.

The Law of the Firstborn

13 Then the LORD said to Moses, 2"Give every firstborn[d] male to me. Every firstborn
male among the Israelites belongs to me, whether
human or animal."

3Moses said to the people, "Remember this
day, the day you left Egypt. You were slaves in

that land, but the LORD with his great power brought you out of it. You must not eat bread made with yeast. 4Today, in the month of Abib,[d] you are leaving Egypt. 5The LORD will lead you to the land of the Canaanites, Hittites, Amorites, Hivites, and Jebusites. This is the land he promised your ancestors he would give you, a fertile land. There you must celebrate this feast during the first month of every year. 6For seven days you must eat bread made without yeast, and on the seventh day there will be a feast to honor the LORD. 7So for seven days you must not eat any bread made with yeast. There must be no bread made with yeast anywhere in your land. 8On that day you should tell your son: 'We are having this feast because of what the LORD did for me when I came out of Egypt.' 9This feast will help you remember, like a mark on your hand or a reminder on your forehead. This feast will remind you to speak the LORD's teachings, because the LORD used his great power to bring you out of Egypt. 10So celebrate this feast every year at the right time.

11"And when the LORD takes you into the land of the Canaanites, the land he promised to give you and your ancestors, 12you must give him every firstborn male. Also every firstborn male animal must be given to the LORD. 13Buy back every firstborn donkey by offering a lamb. But if you don't want to buy the donkey back, then break its neck. You must buy back from the LORD every firstborn of your sons.

14"From now on when your son asks you, 'What does this mean?' you will answer, 'With his great power, the LORD brought us out from Egypt, the land where we were slaves. 15The king of Egypt was stubborn and refused to let us leave. But the LORD killed every firstborn male in Egypt, both human and animal. That is why I sacrifice every firstborn male animal to the LORD, and that is why I buy back each of my firstborn sons from the LORD.' 16This feast is like a mark on your hand and a reminder on your forehead to help you remember that the LORD brought us out of Egypt with his great power."

The Way Out of Egypt

17When the king sent the people out of Egypt, God did not lead them on the road through the Philistine country, though that was the shortest way. God said, "If they have to fight, they might change their minds and go back to Egypt." 18So God led them through the desert toward the Red Sea.[d] The Israelites were dressed for fighting when they left the land of Egypt.

19Moses carried the bones of Joseph with him, because before Joseph died, he had made the Israelites promise to do this. He had said, "When God saves you, remember to carry my bones with you out of Egypt."

20The Israelites left Succoth and camped at Etham, on the edge of the desert. 21The LORD showed them the way; during the day he went ahead of them in a pillar of cloud, and during the night he was in a pillar of fire to give them light. In this way they could travel during the day or night. 22The pillar of cloud was always with them during the day, and the pillar of fire was always with them at night.

14 Then the LORD said to Moses, 2"Tell the Israelites to turn back to Pi Hahiroth and to camp between Migdol and the Red Sea. Camp across from Baal Zephon, on the shore of the sea. 3The king will think, 'The Israelites are lost, trapped by the desert.' 4I will make the king stubborn again so he will chase after them, but I will defeat the king and his army. This will bring honor to me, and the Egyptians will know that I am the LORD." The Israelites did just as they were told.

The King Chases the Israelites

5When the king of Egypt was told that the Israelites had left, he and his officers changed their minds about them. They said, "What have we done? We have let the Israelites leave. We have lost our slaves!" 6So the king prepared his war chariot and took his army with him. 7He took six hundred of his best chariots, together with all the other chariots of Egypt, each with an officer in it. 8The LORD made the king of Egypt stubborn, so he chased the Israelites, who were leaving victoriously. 9The Egyptians—with all the king's horses, chariot drivers, and army—chased the Israelites. They caught up with them while they were camped by the Red Sea,[d] near Pi Hahiroth and Baal Zephon.

10When the Israelites saw the king and his army coming after them, they were very frightened and cried to the LORD for help. 11They said to Moses, "What have you done to us? Why did you bring us out of Egypt to die in the desert? There were plenty of graves for us in Egypt. 12We told you in Egypt, 'Let us alone; we will stay and serve the Egyptians.' Now we will die in the desert."

13But Moses answered, "Don't be afraid! Stand still and you will see the LORD save you today. You will never see these Egyptians again after today. 14You only need to remain calm; the LORD will fight for you."

15Then the LORD said to Moses, "Why are you crying out to me? Command the Israelites to start moving. 16Raise your walking stick and hold it over the sea so that the sea will split and the people can cross it on dry land. 17I will make the Egyptians stubborn so they will chase the Israelites, but I will be honored when I defeat the king and all of his chariot drivers and chariots. 18When

I defeat the king, his chariot drivers, and chariots, the Egyptians will know that I am the
LORD."
19Now the angel of God that usually traveled in
front of Israel's army moved behind them. Also,
the pillar of cloud moved from in front of the people and stood behind them. 20So the cloud came
between the Egyptians and the Israelites. This
made it dark for the Egyptians but gave light to
the Israelites. So the cloud kept the two armies
apart all night.
21Then Moses held his hand over the sea. All
that night the LORD drove back the sea with a
strong east wind, making the sea become dry
ground. The water was split, 22and the Israelites
went through the sea on dry land, with a wall of
water on their right and on their left.
23Then all the king's horses, chariots, and chariot drivers followed them into the sea. 24When
morning came, the LORD looked down from the
pillar of cloud and fire at the Egyptian army and
made them panic. 25He kept the wheels of the
chariots from turning, making it hard to drive the
chariots. The Egyptians shouted, "Let's get away
from the Israelites! The LORD is fighting for them
and against Egypt."
26Then the LORD told Moses, "Hold your hand
over the sea so that the water will come back over
the Egyptians, their chariots, and chariot drivers."
27So Moses raised his hand over the sea, and at
dawn the sea returned to its place. The Egyptians
tried to run from it, but the LORD swept them
away into the sea. 28The water returned, covering
the chariots, chariot drivers, and all the king's
army that had followed the Israelites into the sea.
Not one of them survived.
29But the Israelites crossed the sea on dry land,
with a wall of water on their right and on their
left. 30So that day the LORD saved the Israelites
from the Egyptians, and the Israelites saw the
Egyptians lying dead on the seashore. 31When the
Israelites saw the great power the LORD had used

FREEDOM

A Place to Call Home

The hot August night made it too stuffy to sleep. Sharon McPherson-Mullins looked at her four children lying in the boxes in the back of her old car—the family's only home. She felt trapped in the world of homelessness with nowhere to go and no one to turn to. "Oh God, my God," she cried and prayed silently. "Where are you, God? Have you forsaken me?" And she fell into a restless sleep.

For the next week, she went from shelter to shelter, hoping to find a place to live. One shelter took only children, and her four kids wanted to be with their mom. When a shelter finally had room for all of them, it still wasn't a home.

Then a Christian friend gave Sharon hope. She arranged for the family to rent a house without having to pay a deposit first—and the first month was free. "God has told me to help you," the owner explained.

The new home gave Sharon a freedom from poverty that she had never known. "As a family, we've never been more secure," she says. "God solved my homeless problem by using his people."

Sharon experienced new freedom from poverty and hopelessness as God worked through his people. The Israelites gained freedom from slavery in Egypt through Moses' leadership and God's work. Read about how they gained their freedom in **Exodus 14:19–31**.

- What feelings do you think Sharon would have if she read the story of the Israelites' new freedom? What parts would be most meaningful to her?
- As God led the Israelites to freedom, when has he freed you from a tough situation? How did you celebrate?

CONSIDER . . .

- finding someone in your school or church who's trapped by poverty, prejudice, or some other form of captivity. Talk to the person to find a way you can help him or her gain freedom.
- contacting a chapter of Habitat for Humanity in your area and volunteering to help build or repair homes for low-income people to help them escape from poverty.

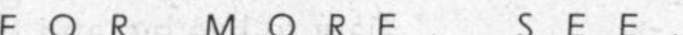

FOR MORE, SEE . . .

- Exodus 15:1–11 (p. 72)
- John 8:31–38 (p. 1072)
- Galatians 5:1–15 (p. 1212)

against the Egyptians, they feared the LORD, and they trusted him and his servant Moses.

The Song of Moses

15 Then Moses and the Israelites sang this song to the LORD:

"I will sing to the LORD,
because he is worthy of great honor.
He has thrown the horse and its rider
into the sea.
2The LORD gives me strength and makes me
sing;
he has saved me.
He is my God,
and I will praise him.
He is the God of my fathers,
and I will honor him.
3The LORD is a warrior;
the LORD is his name.
4The chariots and soldiers of the king of Egypt
he has thrown into the sea.
The king's best officers
are drowned in the Red Sea.[d]
5The deep waters covered them,
and they sank to the bottom like a rock.
6Your right hand, LORD,
is amazingly strong.
LORD, your right hand
broke the enemy to pieces.
7In your great victory
you destroyed those who were against you.
Your anger destroyed them,
like fire burning straw.
8Just a blast of your breath,
and the waters piled up.
The moving water stood like a wall;
the deep waters became solid in the middle
of the sea.

9"The enemy bragged,
'I'll chase them and catch them.
I'll take all their riches;
I'll take all I want.
I'll pull out my sword,
and my hand will destroy them.'
10But you blew on them with your breath
and covered them with the sea.
They sank like lead
in the raging water.

11"Are there any gods like you, LORD?
There are no gods like you.
You are wonderfully holy,
amazingly powerful,
a worker of miracles.[d]
12You reached out with your right hand,
and the earth swallowed our enemies.
13You keep your loving promise
and lead the people you have saved.
With your strength you will guide them
to your holy place.

14"The other nations will hear this and tremble
with fear;
terror will take hold of the Philistines.
15The leaders of the tribes[d] of Edom will be
very frightened;
the powerful men of Moab will shake with
fear;
the people of Canaan will lose all their
courage.
16Terror and horror will fall on them.
When they see your strength,
they will be as still as a rock.
They will be still until your people pass by,
LORD.
They will be still until the people you have
taken as your own pass by.
17You will lead your people and place them
on your very own mountain,
the place that you, LORD, made for yourself
to live,
the temple, Lord, that your hands have
made.
18The LORD will be king forever!"

19The horses, chariot drivers, and chariots of
the king of Egypt went into the sea, and the LORD
covered them with water from the sea. But the
Israelites walked through the sea on dry land.
20Then Aaron's sister Miriam, a prophetess,[d] took
a tambourine[d] in her hand. All the women followed her, playing tambourines and dancing.
21Miriam told them:
"Sing to the LORD,
because he is worthy of great honor;
he has thrown the horse and its rider
into the sea."

Bitter Water Becomes Good

22Moses led the Israelites away from the Red
Sea[d] into the Desert of Shur. They traveled for
three days in the desert but found no water.
23Then they came to Marah, where there was water, but they could not drink it because it was too
bitter. (That is why the place was named Marah.[n]) 24The people grumbled to Moses and
asked, "What will we drink?"
25So Moses cried out to the LORD, and the LORD
showed him a tree. When Moses threw the tree
into the water, the water became good to drink.
There the LORD gave the people a rule and a
law to live by, and there he tested their loyalty to
him. 26He said, "You must obey the LORD your
God and do what he says is right. If you obey all

Marah This name means "bitter."

his commands and keep his rules, I will not bring
on you any of the sicknesses I brought on the
Egyptians. I am the LORD who heals you."
27 Then the people traveled to Elim, where
there were twelve springs of water and seventy
palm trees. So the people camped there near the
water.

The People Demand Food

16 The whole Israelite community left Elim
and came to the Desert of Sin, which
was between Elim and Sinai; they arrived there
on the fifteenth day of the second month after
they had left Egypt. 2 Then the whole Israelite
community grumbled to Moses and Aaron in the
desert. 3 They said to them, "It would have been
better if the LORD had killed us in the land of
Egypt. There we had meat to eat and all the food
we wanted. But you have brought us into this
desert to starve us to death."

4 Then the LORD said to Moses, "I will cause
food to fall like rain from the sky for all of you.
Every day the people must go out and gather what
they need for that day. I want to see if the people
will do what I teach them. 5 On the sixth day of
each week, they are to gather twice as much as
they gather on other days. Then they are to prepare it."
6 So Moses and Aaron said to all the Israelites:
"This evening you will know that the LORD is
the one who brought you out of Egypt. 7 Tomorrow morning you will see the glory of
the LORD, because he has heard you grumble
against him. We are nothing, so you are not
grumbling against us, but against the LORD."
8 And Moses said, "Each evening the LORD
will give you meat to eat, and every morning he will give you all the bread you want,
because he has heard you grumble against
him. You are not grumbling against Aaron and

WORRYING

A Little Hope

Jimmy O'Neill, fifteen, has a lot to worry about. Born with cystic fibrosis, an inherited lung disease, he has been hospitalized five or six times a year since age six. Every day he takes twenty-five pills and spends twenty minutes in physical therapy.

Whenever he has a cold, he has to receive intravenous medication to fight off the infection. And if he feels a little sick, he immediately has to go to the hospital to see what's wrong. "My body is sort of like a car that everyone wants to keep in tip-top shape," he explains. As a result, he often misses fifty to sixty days of school each year.

Jimmy also has a future to worry about. "I have to realize that, no matter what, I'll never be totally independent," he says. "There's always going to have to be someone there for me."

Yet Jimmy doesn't worry. "There are some things in life you have choices about and there are things you don't," he explains. "God will take care of whatever is going to happen."

So instead of worrying, Jimmy has hope and faith in God. "You always have to have a little hope," he says, "because if you run out of that, there's nothing worth anything. You might as well give up right then and there."

Jimmy O'Neill has learned how faith helps overcome worries. In contrast, the Israelites in the desert worried about how to find food. Read **Exodus 16:2–15** to learn how God took care of their worries.

- How does Jimmy's faith in God contrast with the Israelites' worries about how to survive?
- What in the passage comforts you in an area of life that's had you worried lately?

CONSIDER . . .

- asking someone with a disability how God has helped him or her overcome worries that come with the disability.
- writing a list of your worries about the future. Then fold the sheet in half and write one of the Bible verses below on the back. Keep the sheet in your Bible as a reminder of God's promises.

FOR MORE, SEE

- Joshua 1:9 (p. 195)
- Luke 12:22–31 (p. 1028)
- James 4:13–15 (p. 1298)

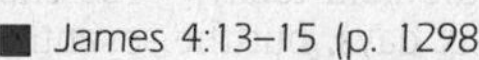

me, because we are nothing; you are grumbling against the LORD."

9Then Moses said to Aaron, "Speak to the whole community of the Israelites, and say to them, 'Meet together in the presence of the LORD, because he has heard your grumblings.' "

10While Aaron was speaking to the whole community of the Israelites, they looked toward the desert. There the glory of the LORD appeared in a cloud.

11The LORD said to Moses, 12"I have heard the grumblings of the people of Israel. So tell them, 'At twilight you will eat meat, and every morning you will eat all the bread you want. Then you will know I am the LORD your God.' "

13That evening quail came and covered the camp, and in the morning dew lay around the camp. 14When the dew was gone, thin flakes like frost were on the desert ground. 15When the Israelites saw it, they asked each other, "What is it?" because they did not know what it was.

So Moses told them, "This is the bread the LORD has given you to eat. 16The LORD has commanded, 'Each one of you must gather what he needs, about two quarts for every person in your family.' "

17So the people of Israel did this; some people gathered much, and some gathered little. 18Then they measured it. The person who gathered more did not have too much, nor did the person who gathered less have too little. Each person gathered just as much as he needed.

19Moses said to them, "Don't keep any of it to eat the next day." 20But some of the people did not listen to Moses and kept part of it to eat the next morning. It became full of worms and began to stink, so Moses was angry with those people.

21Every morning each person gathered as much food as he needed, but when the sun became hot, it melted away.

22On the sixth day the people gathered twice as much food—four quarts for every person. When all the leaders of the community came and told this to Moses, 23he said to them, "This is what the LORD commanded, because tomorrow is the Sabbath,[d] the LORD's holy day of rest. Bake what you want to bake, and boil what you want to boil today. Save the rest of the food until tomorrow morning."

24So the people saved it until the next morning, as Moses had commanded, and none of it began to stink or have worms in it. 25Moses told the people, "Eat the food you gathered yesterday. Today is a Sabbath, the LORD's day of rest; you will not find any out in the field today. 26You should gather the food for six days, but the seventh day is a Sabbath day. On that day there will not be any food on the ground."

27On the seventh day some of the people went out to gather food, but they couldn't find any. 28Then the LORD said to Moses, "How long will you people refuse to obey my commands and teachings? 29Look, the LORD has made the Sabbath a day of rest for you. So on the sixth day he will give you enough food for two days, but on the seventh day each of you must stay where you are. Do not go anywhere." 30So the people rested on the seventh day.

31The people of Israel called the food manna.[d] It was like small white seeds and tasted like wafers made with honey.

32Then Moses said, "The LORD said, 'Save two quarts of this food for your descendants.[d] Then they can see the food I gave you to eat in the desert when I brought you out of Egypt.' "

33Moses told Aaron, "Take a jar and fill it with two quarts of manna. Then place it before the LORD, and save it for your descendants." 34So Aaron did what the LORD had commanded Moses. He put the jar of manna in front of the Agreement to keep it safe. 35The Israelites ate manna for forty years, until they came to the land where they settled—the edge of the land of Canaan. 36The measure they used for the manna was two quarts, or one-tenth of an ephah.[n]

Water from a Rock

17 The whole Israelite community left the Desert of Sin and traveled from place to place, as the LORD commanded. They camped at Rephidim, but there was no water there for the people to drink. 2So they quarreled with Moses and said, "Give us water to drink."

Moses said to them, "Why do you quarrel with me? Why are you testing the LORD?"

3But the people were very thirsty for water, so they grumbled against Moses. They said, "Why did you bring us out of Egypt? Was it to kill us, our children, and our farm animals with thirst?"

4So Moses cried to the LORD, "What can I do with these people? They are almost ready to stone me to death."

5The LORD said to Moses, "Go ahead of the people, and take some of the older leaders of Israel with you. Carry with you the walking stick that you used to strike the Nile River. Now go! 6I will stand in front of you on a rock at Mount Sinai. Hit that rock with the stick, and water will come out of it so that the people can drink." Moses did these things as the older leaders of Israel watched. 7He named that place Massah,[n] because the Israelites tested the LORD when they asked, "Is the

ephah An ephah was a measure that equaled twenty quarts.
Massah This name is the Hebrew word for "testing."

LORD with us or not?" He also named it Meribah,[n] because they quarreled.

The Amalekites Fight Israel

8At Rephidim the Amalekites came and fought
the Israelites. 9So Moses said to Joshua, "Choose
some men and go and fight the Amalekites. Tomorrow I will stand on the top of the hill, holding
the walking stick of God in my hands."
10Joshua obeyed Moses and went to fight the
Amalekites, while Moses, Aaron, and Hur went to
the top of the hill. 11As long as Moses held his
hands up, the Israelites would win the fight, but
when Moses put his hands down, the Amalekites
would win. 12Later, when Moses' arms became
tired, the men put a large rock under him, and he
sat on it. Then Aaron and Hur held up Moses'
hands—Aaron on one side and Hur on the other.
They kept his hands steady until the sun went
down. 13So Joshua defeated the Amalekites in this
battle.
14Then the LORD said to Moses, "Write about
this battle in a book so people will remember. And
be sure to tell Joshua, because I will completely
destroy the Amalekites from the earth."

> **SIDELIGHT:** Ever do "the wave" at a sports event? You may not realize it, but Moses invented the cheer. Every time he lifted his arms, his "team" would start winning (Exodus 17:10–13).

15Then Moses built an altar and named it The
LORD is my Banner. 16Moses said, "I lifted my
hands toward the LORD's throne. The LORD will
fight against the Amalekites forever."

Meribah This name is the Hebrew word for "quarrel."

PATIENCE

When the Going Gets Tough

The van was jammed with volleyballs, Frisbees, two guitars, a box of scissors, markers, string and glue, a big cooler, a water jug, eleven sweaty teenagers, and eleven backpacks crammed with shirts, shoes, and towels.

After a day of teaching crafts, songs, and Bible stories to children near Mexicali, Mexico, the teenagers were sunburned, dusty, and tired—and ready to head home.

But as they approached the border leaving Mexico, their hopes of being home soon evaporated into the hot summer air. Cars and trucks were backed up in a two-hour traffic jam.

As the young people roasted in the van without air conditioning, the sweat rolled down their faces, the exhaust fumes poured in, and everyone got hungry. The leaders figured that complaining, whining, and bickering would erupt any minute from impatient teenagers.

But then someone shouted, "I've got an idea," and pulled bread, peanut butter, and jelly from under the backpacks. "Let's make sandwiches." The fun began. Someone else passed around the water jug. And rather than getting upset when the jelly spilled, everyone laughed and helped clean up the sticky mess.

Caught in a frustrating situation, the van-load of teenagers pulled together and kept their patience. Read how the Israelites had a different reaction to their predicament in **Exodus 17:1–7**.

- Do you think the teenagers could have been patient if their situation had been as serious as that of the Israelites?
- What ideas from the Israelites' story can help you be patient when things aren't going your way?

CONSIDER

- counting to ten next time you're tempted to blow up instead of being patient.
- trying a joke or a smile next time you're caught in a traffic jam or other uncontrollable predicament.

FOR MORE, SEE

- Proverbs 19:11 (p. 583)
- Colossians 1:9–14 (p. 1238)
- James 1:19 (p. 1294)

Jethro Visits Moses

18 Jethro, Moses' father-in-law, was the priest of Midian. He heard about everything that God had done for Moses and his people, the Israelites, and how the LORD had led the Israelites out of Egypt. 2Now Moses had sent his wife Zipporah to Jethro, his father-in-law, 3along with his two sons. The first son was named Gershom,[n] because when he was born, Moses said, "I am a stranger in a foreign country." 4The other son was named Eliezer,[n] because when he was born, Moses said, "The God of my father is my help. He saved me from the king of Egypt."

5So Jethro, Moses' father-in-law, took Moses' wife and his two sons and went to Moses. He was camped in the desert near the mountain of God.

> **SIDELIGHT:** The book of Exodus is quoted 250 times in the New Testament, making it the fourth-most-quoted book. Only Isaiah, Psalms, and Genesis are quoted more.

6Jethro had sent a message ahead to Moses that said, "I, Jethro, your father-in-law, am coming to you with your wife and her two sons."

7So Moses went out to meet his father-in-law and bowed down and kissed him. After the two men asked about each other's health, they went into Moses' tent. 8Moses told his father-in-law everything the LORD had done to the king and the Egyptians to help Israel. He told about all the problems they had faced along the way and how the LORD had saved them.

9Jethro was very happy to hear all the good things the LORD had done for Israel when he had saved them from the Egyptians. 10He said, "Praise the LORD. He has saved you from the Egyptians and their king, and he has saved the people from the power of the Egyptians. 11Now I know the LORD is greater than all gods, because he did this to those who looked down on Israel." 12Then Jethro, Moses' father-in-law, gave a whole burnt offering and other sacrifices to God. Aaron and all the older leaders of Israel came to Moses' father-in-law to eat the holy meal together before God.

13The next day Moses solved disagreements among the people, and the people stood around him from morning until night. 14When Moses' father-in-law saw all that Moses was doing for the people, he asked, "What is all this you are doing for the people? Why are you the only one to solve disagreements? All the people are standing around you from morning until night!"

15Then Moses said to his father-in-law, "It is because the people come to me for God's help in solving their disagreements. 16When people have a disagreement, they come to me, and I decide who is right. I tell them God's laws and teachings."

17Moses' father-in-law said to him, "You are not doing this right. 18You and the people who come to you will get too tired. This is too much work for you; you can't do it by yourself. 19Now listen to me, and I will give you some advice. I want God to be with you. You must speak to God for the people and tell him about their disagreements. 20Warn them about the laws and teachings, and teach them the right way to live and what they should do. 21But choose some capable men from among the people—men who respect God, who can be trusted, and who will not change their decisions for money. Make these men officers over the people, to rule over groups of thousands, hundreds, fifties, and tens. 22Let these officers solve the disagreements among the people all the time. They can bring the hard cases to you, but they can decide the simple cases themselves. That will make it easier for you, because they will share the work with you. 23If you do this as God commands you, then you will be able to do your job, and all the people will go home with their disagreements solved."

24So Moses listened to his father-in-law and did everything he said. 25He chose capable men from all the Israelites and made them leaders over the people; they were officers over groups of thousands, hundreds, fifties, and tens. 26These officers solved disagreements among the people all the time. They brought the hard cases to Moses, but they decided the simple cases themselves.

27So Moses sent his father-in-law on his way, and Jethro went back to his own home.

Israel Camps at Sinai

19 Exactly three months after the Israelites had left Egypt, they reached the Desert of Sinai. 2When they left Rephidim, they came to the Desert of Sinai and camped in the desert in front of the mountain. 3Then Moses went up on the mountain to God. The LORD called to him from the mountain and said, "Say this to the family of Jacob, and tell the people of Israel: 4'Every one of you has seen what I did to the people of Egypt. You saw how I carried you out of Egypt, as if on eagle's wings. And I brought you here to me. 5So now if you obey me and keep my agreement, you will be my own possession, chosen

Gershom This name sounds like the Hebrew word for "a stranger there."
Eliezer This name sounds like the Hebrew words "My God is my help."

from all nations. Even though the whole earth is
mine, [6]you will be my kingdom of priests and a
holy nation.' You must tell the Israelites these
words."
[7]So Moses went down and called the older
leaders of the people together. He told them all
the words the LORD had commanded him to say.
[8]All the people answered together, "We will do
everything he has said." Then Moses took their
answer back to the LORD.
[9]And the LORD said to Moses, "I will come to
you in a thick cloud and speak to you. The people
will hear me speaking with you and will always
trust you." Then Moses told the LORD what the
people had said.
[10]The LORD said to Moses, "Go to the people
and have them spend today and tomorrow preparing themselves. They must wash their clothes
[11]and be ready by the day after tomorrow. On that
day I, the LORD, will come down on Mount Sinai,
and all the people will see me. [12]But you must set
a limit around the mountain that the people are
not to cross. Tell them not to go up on the mountain and not to touch the foot of it. Anyone who
touches the mountain must be put to death [13]with
stones or shot with arrows. No one is allowed to
touch him. Whether it is a person or an animal,
he will not live. But the trumpet will make a long
blast, and only then may the people go up on the
mountain."

FOLLOWING GOD

A Trusted Leader

The entire drama class snickered when it was announced: Judson Zinder would be the student director for the spring production of "How to Succeed in Business."

Judson Zinder? He was a tall, lanky, freckle-faced sophomore with a squeaky voice. The only reason classmates liked him was because he was a natural clown. He was hardly someone they would look up to.

But no matter. Mr. Hall would be directing, and having Judson as the assistant wouldn't hurt.

Then one evening the cast arrived for rehearsal to find Judson sitting in Mr. Hall's chair. "Mr. Hall is sick," Judson announced. "He'll be okay, but he won't be back for a couple of weeks."

Groans echoed across the stage. "There goes our big hit," someone onstage quipped. "Kiss that Tony Award good-bye." And everyone laughed. The rehearsal was a disaster. People joked with their lines, missed their entrances, and talked to Judson with mock respect.

Suddenly, Judson threw his clipboard on the stage in frustration. "Okay," he said. "I know I'm just a sophomore, and I know you guys don't think I can do this. But we've got to do it together—for Mr. Hall."

Surprised by his honesty, the cast started paying attention, and they discovered Judson was a natural at blocking and staging. In his quiet way, he turned a mediocre school play into a big success.

The cast members began following Judson when they realized he could lead them. The Israelites made a bigger commitment and trusted God because they had seen his work before. Read about their agreement to follow God in **Exodus 19:1–8**.

- What similarities and differences do you see between Judson's speech to the cast and God's declaration to Moses? What parts of what they said provide the most motivation to follow them?
- How does God's leadership of the Israelites give you faith that you too can follow God?

CONSIDER . . .

- finding a calendar from the past month and writing ways God was with you through the month. Keep the calendar handy to remind you of God's guidance when you have trouble following him.
- memorizing Exodus 19:4 to boost your faith when you're discouraged.

FOR MORE, SEE . . .

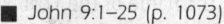

- Jeremiah 2:1–11 (p. 692)
- Ezekiel 16:59–63 (p. 774)
- John 9:1–25 (p. 1073)

14After Moses went down from the mountain to the people, he made them prepare themselves for service to God, and they washed their clothes. 15Then Moses said to the people, "Be ready in three days. Do not have sexual relations during this time."

16On the morning of the third day, there was thunder and lightning with a thick cloud on the mountain. There was a very loud blast from a trumpet, and all the people in the camp trembled. 17Then Moses led the people out of the camp to meet God, and they stood at the foot of the mountain. 18Mount Sinai was covered with smoke, because the LORD came down on it in fire. The smoke rose from the mountain like smoke from a furnace, and the whole mountain shook wildly. 19The sound from the trumpet became louder. Then Moses spoke, and the voice of God answered him.

20When the LORD came down on top of Mount Sinai, he called Moses to come up to the top of the mountain, and Moses went up. 21The LORD said to Moses, "Go down and warn the people that they must not force their way through to see me. If they do, many of them will die. 22Even the priests, who may come near me, must first prepare themselves. If they don't, I, the LORD, will punish them."

23Moses told the LORD, "The people cannot come up on Mount Sinai, because you yourself told us, 'Set a limit around the mountain, and set it apart as holy.' "

24The LORD said to him, "Go down and bring Aaron up with you, but don't allow the priests or the people to force their way through. They must not come up to the LORD, or I will punish them."

25So Moses went down to the people and told them these things.

The Ten Commandments

20 Then God spoke all these words:

2"I am the LORD your God, who brought you out of the land of Egypt where you were slaves.

3"You must not have any other gods except me.

4"You must not make for yourselves an idol that looks like anything in the sky above or on the earth below or in the water below the land. 5You must not worship or serve any idol, because I, the LORD your God, am a jealous God. If you hate me, I will punish your children, and even your grandchildren and great-grandchildren. 6But I show kindness to thousands who love me and obey my commands.

7"You must not use the name of the LORD your God thoughtlessly; the LORD will punish anyone who misuses his name.

8"Remember to keep the Sabbath[d] holy. 9Work and get everything done during six days each week, 10but the seventh day is a day of rest to honor the LORD your God. On that day no one may do any work: not you, your son or daughter, your male or female slaves, your animals, or the foreigners living in your cities. 11The reason is that in six days the LORD made everything — the sky, the earth, the sea, and everything in them. On the seventh day he rested. So the LORD blessed the Sabbath day and made it holy.

12"Honor your father and your mother so that you will live a long time in the land that the LORD your God is going to give you.

13"You must not murder anyone.

14"You must not be guilty of adultery.[d]

15"You must not steal.

16"You must not tell lies about your neighbor.

17"You must not want to take your neighbor's house. You must not want his wife or his male or female slaves, or his ox or his donkey, or anything that belongs to your neighbor."

SIDELIGHT: The Ten Commandments (Exodus 20:2–17) are twice as easy to find as most famous Bible passages. They're also listed in Deuteronomy 5:6–21 (p. 166), with only slight variations.

18When the people heard the thunder and the trumpet, and when they saw the lightning and the smoke rising from the mountain, they shook with fear and stood far away from the mountain. 19Then they said to Moses, "Speak to us yourself, and we will listen. But don't let God speak to us, or we will die."

20Then Moses said to the people, "Don't be afraid, because God has come to test you. He wants you to respect him so you will not sin."

21The people stood far away from the mountain while Moses went near the dark cloud where God was. 22Then the LORD told Moses to say these things to the Israelites: "You yourselves have seen that I talked with you from heaven. 23You must not use gold or silver to make idols for yourselves; do not worship these gods in addition to me.

24"Make an altar of dirt for me, and sacrifice on it your whole burnt offerings and fellowship offerings, your sheep and your cattle. Worship me in every place that I choose, and I will come and bless you. 25If you use stones to make an altar for me, don't use stones that you have shaped with tools. When you use any tools on them, you make them unsuitable for use in worship. 26And you must not go up to my altar on steps, or people will be able to see under your clothes."

Laws for Living

21 Then God said to Moses, "These are the
laws for living that you will give to the
Israelites:
2"If you buy a Hebrew slave, he will serve you
for six years. In the seventh year you are to set
him free, and he will have to pay nothing. 3If he
is not married when he becomes your slave, he
must leave without a wife. But if he is married
when he becomes your slave, he may take his
wife with him. 4If the slave's master gives him a
wife, and she gives birth to sons or daughters, the
woman and her children will belong to the master. When the slave is set free, only he may
leave.
5"But if the slave says, 'I love my master, my
wife and my children, and I don't want to go
free,' 6then the slave's master must take him to
God. The master is to take him to a door or door-
frame and punch a hole through the slave's ear
using a sharp tool. Then the slave will serve that
master all his life.
7"If a man sells his daughter as a slave, the rules
for setting her free are different from the rules for
setting the male slaves free. 8If the master wanted
to marry her but then decided he was not pleased

GOD'S WILL

Following the Guidelines

"I just don't understand," Teresa Vasquez cried, sitting on her bed looking at the mail scattered around her. Three weeks earlier—right after Christmas—she'd written to colleges to begin applying for the fall. But her excitement dwindled as she opened each form letter.

"Dear student: Due to high interest last fall, we are out of catalogs. We will send you one when the new catalogs are available in April."

"Dear student: Our final date for admissions in the fall is January 10. Therefore, we will not be able to consider any more applications for this fall. We invite you to apply next year."

Even the schools that sent catalogs didn't sound too promising. First, several schools required four years of English in high school. She had quit English after her junior year because she didn't like the senior teacher. Then they wanted to know her Scholastic Aptitude Test (SAT) scores. She hadn't taken the test yet, and it wasn't being offered for another month.

She walked into the kitchen and slumped into a chair. "I don't get it," she complained to her dad. "Why do colleges have to have all these rules?"

"What would it be like if they didn't have rules?" her dad asked.

"Well, getting into college wouldn't be so hard," Teresa responded.

"If you didn't meet college entrance requirements, would you be able to keep up with college courses?" Dad continued.

"I guess not. But. . . ."

"And what would have happened if you had started following the guidelines earlier?"

"Going to college would be a lot less hassle," Teresa finally admitted.

In the same way that following guidelines is necessary to get into college, following God's will is necessary to find meaning and purpose in life. Read the Ten Commandments in **Exodus 20:1–20** to learn what God requires of people.

- How does knowing a college's guidelines help students? How is that similar to knowing God's commandments?
- What do you think our world would be like if everyone followed the commandments in this passage?

CONSIDER. . .

- circling the commandment that's most difficult for you to follow. Then concentrate on following that commandment in the coming week.
- writing one key word from each commandment on a small card to keep in your purse or wallet as a reminder of God's will.

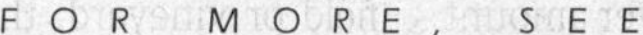

FOR MORE, SEE. . .

- Micah 6:6–8 (p. 866)
- Matthew 22:34–40 (p. 948)
- Romans 6:20–23 (p. 1148)

with her, he must let one of her close relatives
buy her back. He has no right to sell her to foreigners, because he has treated her unfairly. 9If
the man who bought her promises to let the
woman marry his son, he must treat her as a
daughter. 10If the man who bought her marries
another woman, he must not keep his first wife
from having food or clothing or sexual relations.
11If he does not give her these three things, she
may go free, and she owes him no money.

Laws About Injuries

12"Anyone who hits a person and kills him
must be put to death. 13But if a person kills someone accidentally, God allowed that to happen, so
the person must go to a place I will choose. 14But
if someone plans and murders another person on
purpose, put him to death, even if he has run to
my altar for safety.

15"Anyone who hits his father or his mother
must be put to death.

16"Anyone who kidnaps someone and either
sells him as a slave or still has him when he is
caught must be put to death.

17"Anyone who says cruel things to his father
or mother must be put to death.

> **SIDELIGHT:** Did you know that "Honor your father and mother" is a two-part commandment? If you do, "you will live a long time." According to Israelite law, if you didn't honor them, you could be put to death (Exodus 21:17). And you thought being grounded was tough!

18"If two men argue, and one hits the other
with a rock or with his fist, the one who is hurt
but not killed might have to stay in bed. 19Later
if he is able to get up and walk around outside
with his walking stick, the one who hit him is not
to be punished. But he must pay the injured man
for the loss of his time, and he must support the
injured man until he is completely healed.

20"If a man beats his male or female slave with
a stick, and the slave dies on the spot, the owner
must be punished. 21But if the slave gets well after
a day or two, the owner will not be punished
since the slave belongs to him.

22"Suppose two men are fighting and hit a pregnant woman, causing the baby to come out. If
there is no further injury, the man who caused
the accident must pay money — whatever amount
the woman's husband says and the court allows.
23But if there is further injury, then the punishment that must be paid is life for life, 24eye for eye,
tooth for tooth, hand for hand, foot for foot,
25burn for burn, wound for wound, and bruise for
bruise.

26"If a man hits his male or female slave in the
eye, and the eye is blinded, the man is to free the
slave to pay for the eye. 27If a master knocks out
a tooth of his male or female slave, the man is to
free the slave to pay for the tooth.

28"If a man's bull kills a man or woman, you
must kill that bull by throwing stones at it, and
you should not eat the bull. But the owner of the
bull is not guilty. 29However, suppose the bull has
hurt people in the past and the owner, though
warned, did not keep it in a pen. Then if it kills
a man or woman, the bull must be stoned to
death, and the owner must also be put to death.
30But if the family of the dead person accepts
money, the one who owned the bull may buy
back his life, but he must pay whatever is demanded. 31Use this same law if the bull kills a
person's son or daughter. 32If the bull kills a male
or female slave, the owner must pay the master
the price for a new slave, or twelve ounces of
silver, and the bull must also be stoned to death.

33"If a man takes the cover off a pit, or digs a
pit and does not cover it, and another man's ox
or donkey comes and falls into it, 34the owner of
the pit must pay the owner of the animal for the
loss. The dead animal will belong to the one who
pays.

35"If a man's bull kills another man's bull, they
must sell the bull that is alive. Both men will get
half of the money and half of the bull that was
killed. 36But if a person's bull has hurt other animals in the past and the owner did not keep it in
a pen, that owner must pay bull for bull, and the
dead animal is his.

Property Laws

22 "If a man steals a bull or a sheep and kills
or sells it, he must pay back five bulls for
the one bull he stole and four sheep for the one
sheep he stole.

2-4"The robber who is caught must pay back
what he stole. If he owns nothing, he must be
sold as a slave to pay for what he stole. If the
stolen animal is found alive with the robber, he
must give the owner two animals for every animal
he stole, whether it was a bull, donkey, or sheep.

"If a thief is killed while breaking into a house
at night, the one who killed him is not guilty of
murder. But if this happens during the day, he is
guilty of murder.

5"If a man lets his farm animal graze in his field
or vineyard, and it wanders into another man's
field or vineyard, the owner of the animal must
pay back the loss from the best of his crop.

6"Suppose a man starts a fire that spreads
through the thornbushes to his neighbor's field. If
the fire burns his neighbor's growing grain or

grain that has been stacked, or if it burns his
whole field, the person who started the fire must
pay for what was burned.
7“Suppose a man gives his neighbor money or
other things to keep for him and those things are
stolen from the neighbor’s house. If the thief is
caught, he must pay back twice as much as he
stole. 8But if the thief is never found, the owner
of the house must make a promise before God
that he has not stolen his neighbor’s things.
9“Suppose two men disagree about who owns
something—whether ox, donkey, sheep, clothing, or something else that is lost. If each says,
‘This is mine,’ each man must bring his case to
God. God’s judges will decide who is guilty, and
that person must pay the other man twice as
much as the object is worth.
10“Suppose a man asks his neighbor to keep his
donkey, ox, sheep, or some other animal for him,
and that animal dies, gets hurt, or is taken away,
without anyone seeing what happened. 11That
neighbor must promise before the LORD that he
did not harm or kill the other man’s animal, and
the owner of the animal must accept his promise
made before God. The neighbor does not have to
pay the owner for the animal. 12But if the animal
was stolen from the neighbor, he must pay the
owner for it. 13If wild animals killed it, the neighbor must bring the body as proof, and he will not
have to pay for the animal that was killed.
14“If a man borrows an animal from his neighbor, and it gets hurt or dies while the owner is not
there, the one who borrowed it must pay the
owner for the animal. 15But if the owner is with
the animal, the one who borrowed it does not
have to pay. If the animal was rented, the rental
price covers the loss.

Laws and Relationships

16“Suppose a man finds a woman who is not
pledged to be married and has never had sexual
relations with a man. If he tricks her into having
sexual relations with him, he must give her family
the payment to marry her, and she will become
his wife. 17But if her father refuses to allow his
daughter to marry him, the man must still give
the usual payment for a bride who has never had
sexual relations.
18“Put to death any woman who does evil
magic.
19“Put to death anyone who has sexual relations with an animal.
20“Destroy completely any person who makes
a sacrifice to any god except the LORD.
21“Do not cheat or hurt a foreigner, because
you were foreigners in the land of Egypt.
22“Do not cheat a widow or an orphan. 23If you
do, and they cry out to me for help, I certainly will
hear their cry. 24And I will be very angry and kill
you in war. Then your wives will become widows, and your children will become orphans.
25“If you lend money to one of my people who
is poor, do not treat him as a moneylender would.
Charge him nothing for using your money. 26If
your neighbor gives you his coat as a promise for
the money he owes you, you must give it back to
him by sunset, 27because it is the only cover to
keep his body warm. He has nothing else to sleep
in. If he cries out to me for help, I will listen,
because I am merciful.
28“You must not speak against God or curse a
leader of your people.
29“Do not hold back your offering from the first
of your harvest and the first wine that you make.
Also, you must give me your firstborn[d] sons.
30You must do the same with your bulls and your
sheep. Let the firstborn males stay with their
mothers for seven days, and on the eighth day you
must give them to me.
31“You are to be my holy people. You must not
eat the meat of any animal that has been killed by
wild animals. Instead, give it to the dogs.

Laws About Fairness

23 “You must not tell lies. If you are a witness in court, don’t help a wicked person
by telling lies.
2“You must not do wrong just because everyone else is doing it. If you are a witness in court,
you must not ruin a fair trial. You must not tell lies
just because everyone else is. 3If a poor person is
in court, you must not take his side just because
he is poor.
4“If you see your enemy’s ox or donkey wandering away, you must return it to him. 5If you see
that your enemy’s donkey has fallen because its
load is too heavy, do not leave it there. You must
help your enemy get the donkey back on its feet.
6“You must not be unfair to a poor person
when he is in court. 7You must not lie when you
accuse someone in court. Never allow an innocent or honest person to be put to death as punishment, because I will not treat guilty people as
if they were innocent.
8“You must not accept money from a person
who wants you to lie in court, because such
money will not let you see what is right. Such
money makes good people tell lies.
9“You must not mistreat a foreigner. You know
how it feels to be a foreigner, because you were
foreigners in Egypt.

Laws for the Sabbath

10“For six years you are to plant and harvest
crops on your land. 11Then during the seventh
year, do not plow or plant your land. If any food
grows there, allow the poor people to have it, and
let the wild animals eat what is left. You should

do the same with your vineyards and your orchards of olive trees.

12“You should work six days a week, but on the seventh day you must rest. This lets your ox and your donkey rest, and it also lets the slave born in your house and the foreigner be refreshed.

13“Be sure to do all that I have said to you. You must not even say the names of other gods; those names must not come out of your mouth.

Three Yearly Feasts

14“Three times each year you must hold a feast to honor me. 15You must celebrate the Feast[d] of Unleavened Bread in the way I commanded you. For seven days you must eat bread that is made without yeast at the set time during the month of Abib,[d] the month when you came out of Egypt. No one is to come to worship me without bringing an offering.

16“You must celebrate the Feast[d] of Weeks. Offer to God the first things you harvest from the crops you planted in your fields.

“You must celebrate the Feast[d] of Shelters in the fall, when you gather all the crops from your fields.

17“So three times during every year all your males must come to worship the LORD God.

18“You must not offer animal blood along with anything that has yeast in it.

“You must not save any of the fat from the sacrifice for the next day.

19“You must bring the best of the firstfruits[d] of your land to the Holy Tent[n] of the LORD your God.

“You must not cook a young goat in its mother's milk.

God Will Help Israel

20“I am sending an angel ahead of you, who will protect you as you travel. He will lead you to the place I have prepared. 21Pay attention to the angel and obey him. Do not turn against him; he will not forgive such turning against him because my power is in him. 22If you listen carefully to all he says and do everything that I tell you, I will be an enemy to your enemies. I will fight all who fight against you. 23My angel will go ahead of you and take you into the land of the Amorites, Hittites, Perizzites, Canaanites, Hivites, and Jebusites, and I will destroy them.

24“You must not bow down to their gods or worship them. You must not live the way those people live. You must destroy their idols, breaking into pieces the stone pillars they use in worship. 25If you worship the LORD your God, I will bless your bread and your water. I will take away sickness from you. 26None of your women will have her baby die before it is born, and all women will have children. I will allow you to live long lives.

27“I will make your enemies afraid of me. I will confuse any people you fight against, and I will make all your enemies run away from you. 28I will send terror ahead of you that will force the Hivites, Canaanites, and Hittites out of your way. 29But I will not force all those people out in only one year. If I did, the land would become a desert and the wild animals would become too many for you. 30Instead, I will force those people out slowly, until there are enough of you to take over the land.

31“I will give you the land from the Red Sea to the Mediterranean Sea, and from the desert to the Euphrates River. I will give you power over the people who now live in the land, and you will force them out ahead of you. 32You must not make an agreement with those people or with their gods. 33You must not let them live in your land, or they will make you sin against me. If you worship their gods, you will be caught in a trap.”

God and Israel Make Their Agreement

24 The LORD told Moses, “You, Aaron, Nadab, Abihu, and seventy of the older leaders of Israel must come up to me and worship me from a distance. 2Then Moses alone must come near me; the others must not come near. The rest of the people must not come up the mountain with Moses.”

3Moses told the people all the LORD's words and laws for living. Then all of the people answered out loud together, “We will do all the things the LORD has said.” 4So Moses wrote down all the words of the LORD. And he got up early the next morning and built an altar near the bottom of the mountain. He set up twelve stones, one stone for each of the twelve tribes[d] of Israel. 5Then Moses sent young Israelite men to offer whole burnt offerings and to sacrifice young bulls as fellowship offerings to the LORD. 6Moses put half of the blood of these animals in bowls, and he sprinkled the other half of the blood on the altar. 7Then he took the Book of the Agreement and read it so the people could hear him. And they said, “We will do everything that the LORD has said; we will obey.”

8Then Moses took the blood from the bowls and sprinkled it on the people, saying, “This is the blood that begins the Agreement, the Agreement which the LORD has made with you about all these words.”

9Moses, Aaron, Nadab, Abihu, and seventy of the older leaders of Israel went up the mountain 10and saw the God of Israel. Under his feet was a surface that looked as if it were paved with blue

Holy Tent Literally, “house of the LORD your God.” See Exodus 25:9.

sapphire stones, and it was as clear as the sky!
11These leaders of the Israelites saw God, but God
did not destroy them. Then they ate and drank
together.

God Promises Moses the Stone Tablets

12The LORD said to Moses, "Come up the
mountain to me. Wait there, and I will give you
two stone tablets. On these are the teachings and
the commands I have written to instruct the people."

13So Moses and his helper Joshua set out, and
Moses went up to Sinai, the mountain of God.
14Moses said to the older leaders, "Wait here for
us until we come back to you. Aaron and Hur are
with you, and anyone who has a disagreement
with others can take it to them."

Moses Meets with God

15When Moses went up on the mountain, the
cloud covered it. 16The glory of the LORD came
down on Mount Sinai, and the cloud covered it
for six days. On the seventh day the LORD called
to Moses from inside the cloud. 17To the Israelites
the glory of the LORD looked like a fire burning on
top of the mountain. 18Then Moses went into the
cloud and went higher up the mountain. He was
on the mountain for forty days and forty nights.

Gifts for the Lord

25 The LORD said to Moses, 2"Tell the Israelites to bring me gifts. Receive for me
the gifts each person wants to give. 3These are the
gifts that you should receive from them: gold, silver, bronze; 4blue, purple, and red thread; fine
linen, goat hair, 5sheepskins that are dyed red;
fine leather; acacia wood; 6olive oil to burn in the
lamps; spices for sweet-smelling incense,[d] and the
special olive oil poured on a person's head to
make him a priest; 7onyx stones, and other jewels
to be put on the holy vest[d] and the chest covering.

8"The people must build a holy place for me so
that I can live among them. 9Build this Holy Tent[d]
and everything in it by the plan I will show you.

The Ark of the Agreement

10"Use acacia wood and build an Ark[d] forty-five
inches long, twenty-seven inches wide, and
twenty-seven inches high. 11Cover the Ark inside
and out with pure gold, and put a gold strip all
around it. 12Make four gold rings for the Ark and
attach them to its four feet, two rings on each
side. 13Then make poles from acacia wood and
cover them with gold. 14Put the poles through the
rings on the sides of the Ark, and use these poles
to carry it. 15These poles must always stay in the
rings of the Ark. Do not take them out. 16Then put
in the Ark the Agreement which I will make with
you.

17"Then make a lid of pure gold for the Ark;
this is the mercy seat.[d] Make it forty-five inches
long and twenty-seven inches wide. 18Then hammer gold to make two creatures with wings, and
put one on each end of the lid. 19Attach one creature on one end of the lid and the other creature
on the other end. Make them to be one piece with
the lid at the ends. 20The creatures' wings should
be spread upward, covering the lid, and the creatures are to face each other across the lid. 21Put
this lid on top of the Ark, and put in the Ark the
Agreement which I will make with you. 22I will
meet with you there, above the lid between the
two winged creatures on the Ark of the Agreement. There I will give you all my commands for
the Israelites.

The Table

23"Make a table out of acacia wood, thirty-six
inches long, eighteen inches wide, and twenty-
seven inches high. 24Cover it with pure gold, and
put a gold strip around it. 25Make a frame three
inches high that stands up all around the edge,
and put a gold strip around it. 26Then make four
gold rings. Attach them to the four corners of the
table where the four legs are. 27Put the rings close
to the frame around the top of the table, because
they will hold the poles for carrying it. 28Make the
poles out of acacia wood, cover them with gold,
and carry the table with these poles. 29Make the
plates and bowls for the table, as well as the jars
and cups, out of pure gold. They will be used for
pouring out the drink offerings. 30On this table
put the bread that shows you are in my presence
so that it is always there in front of me.

The Lampstand

31"Hammer pure gold to make a lampstand. Its
base, stand, flower-like cups, buds, and petals
must all be joined together in one piece. 32The
lampstand must have six branches going out from
its sides—three on one side and three on the
other. 33Each branch must have three cups
shaped like almond flowers on it. Each cup must
have a bud and a petal. Each of the six branches
going out from the lampstand must be the same.
34And there must be four more cups made like
almond flowers on the lampstand itself. These
cups must also have buds and petals. 35Put a bud
under each pair of branches that goes out from
the lampstand. Each of the six branches going out
from the lampstand must be the same. 36The
branches, buds, and lampstand must be made of
one piece, hammered out of pure gold.

37"Then make seven small oil lamps and put
them on the lampstand so that they give light to
the area in front of it. 38The wick trimmers and
trays must be made of pure gold. 39Use seventy-
five pounds of pure gold to make the lampstand

and everything with it. 40Be very careful to make them by the plan I showed you on the mountain.

The Holy Tent

26 "Make for the Holy Tent[d] ten curtains of fine linen and blue, purple, and red thread. Have a skilled craftsman sew designs of creatures with wings on the pieces of cloth. 2Make each curtain the same size—forty-two feet long and six feet wide. 3Sew five curtains together for one set, and sew the other curtains together for the second set. 4Make loops of blue cloth on the edge of the end curtain of one set, and do the same for the end curtain of the other set. 5Make fifty loops on the end curtain of the first set and fifty loops on the end curtain of the second set. These loops must be opposite each other. 6And make fifty gold hooks to join the two sets of curtains so that the Holy Tent is one piece.

7"Then make another tent that will cover the Holy Tent, using eleven curtains made from goat hair. 8All these curtains must be the same size—forty-five feet long and six feet wide. 9Sew five of the curtains together into one set. Then sew the other six curtains together into the second set. Fold the sixth curtain double over the front of the Tent. 10Make fifty loops down the edge of the end curtain of one set, and do the same for the end curtain of the other set. 11Then make fifty bronze hooks and put them in the loops to join the tent together so that the covering is one piece. 12Let the extra half piece of cloth hang over the back of the Holy Tent. 13There will be eighteen inches hanging over the sides of the Holy Tent, to protect it. 14Make a covering for the Holy Tent from sheepskins colored red, and over that make a covering from fine leather.

15"Use acacia wood to make upright frames for the Holy Tent. 16Each frame must be fifteen feet long and twenty-seven inches wide, 17with two pegs side by side. Every frame must be made the same way. 18Make twenty frames for the south side of the Holy Tent. 19Each frame must have two silver bases to go under it, a peg fitting into each base. You must make forty silver bases for the frames. 20Make twenty more frames for the north side of the Holy Tent 21and forty silver bases for them—two bases for each frame. 22You must make six frames for the rear or west end of the Holy Tent 23and two frames for each corner at the rear. 24The two frames are to be doubled at the bottom and joined at the top with a metal ring. Both corner frames must be made this way. 25So there will be a total of eight frames at the rear of the Tent, and there will be sixteen silver bases—two bases under each frame.

26"Make crossbars of acacia wood to connect the upright frames of the Holy Tent. Make five crossbars to hold the frames together on one side 27and five to hold the frames together on the other side. Also make five crossbars to hold the frames together on the west end, at the rear. 28The middle crossbar is to be set halfway up the frames, and it is to run along the entire length of each side and rear. 29Make gold rings on the sides of the frames to hold the crossbars, and cover the frames and the crossbars with gold. 30Set up the Holy Tent by the plan shown to you on the mountain.

31"Make a curtain of fine linen and blue, purple, and red thread, and have a skilled craftsman sew designs of creatures with wings on it. 32Hang the curtain by gold hooks on four posts of acacia wood that are covered with gold, and set them in four silver bases. 33Hang the curtain from the hooks in the roof, and put the Ark[d] of the Agreement containing the two stone tablets behind it. This curtain will separate the Holy Place from the Most Holy Place. 34Put the lid on the Ark of the Agreement in the Most Holy Place.

35"Outside the curtain, put the table on the north side of the Holy Tent. Put the lampstand on the south side of the Holy Tent across from the table.

The Entrance of the Holy Tent

36"Then, for the entrance of the Tent,[d] make a curtain with fine linen and blue, purple, and red thread. Someone who can sew well is to sew designs on it. 37Make five posts of acacia wood covered with gold. Make gold hooks for them on which to hang the curtain, and make five bronze bases for them.

The Altar for Burnt Offerings

27 "Make an altar of acacia wood, four and one-half feet high. It should be square—seven and one-half feet long and seven and one-half feet wide. 2Make each of the four corners of the altar stick out like a horn, in such a way that the corners with their horns are all one piece. Then cover the whole altar with bronze.

3"Use bronze to make all the tools and dishes that will be used on the altar: the pots to remove the ashes, the shovels, the bowls for sprinkling blood, the meat forks, and the pans for carrying the burning wood.

4"Make a large bronze screen to hold the burning wood, and put a bronze ring at each of the four corners of it. 5Put the screen inside the altar, under its rim, halfway up from the bottom.

6"Make poles of acacia wood for the altar, and cover them with bronze. 7Put the poles through the rings on both sides of the altar to carry it. 8Make the altar out of boards and leave the inside hollow. Make it as you were shown on the mountain.

The Courtyard of the Holy Tent

9“Make a wall of curtains to form a courtyard
around the Holy Tent.[d] The south side should
have a wall of fine linen curtains one hundred fifty
feet long. 10Hang the curtain with silver hooks
and bands on twenty bronze posts with twenty
bronze bases. 11The north side must also be one
hundred fifty feet long. Hang its curtains on silver
hooks and bands on twenty bronze posts with
twenty bronze bases.

12“The west end of the courtyard must have a
wall of curtains seventy-five feet long, with ten
posts and ten bases on that wall. 13The east end
of the courtyard must also be seventy-five feet
long. 14On one side of the entry, there is to be a
wall of curtains twenty-two and one-half feet
long, held up by three posts on three bases. 15On
the other side of the entry, there is also to be a
wall of curtains twenty-two and one-half feet
long, held up by three posts on three bases.

16“The entry to the courtyard is to be a curtain
thirty feet wide, made of fine linen with blue, purple, and red thread. Someone who can sew well
is to sew designs on it. It is to be held up by four
posts on four bases. 17All the posts around the
courtyard must have silver bands and hooks and
bronze bases. 18The courtyard must be one hundred fifty feet long and seventy-five feet wide,
with a wall of curtains around it seven and one-
half feet high, made of fine linen. The bases in
which the posts are set must be bronze. 19All the
things used in the Holy Tent and all the tent pegs
for the Holy Tent and the wall around the courtyard must be made of bronze.

Oil for the Lamp

20“Command the people of Israel to bring you
pure olive oil, made from pressed olives, to keep
the lamps on the lampstand burning. 21Aaron and
his sons must keep the lamps burning before the
LORD from evening till morning. This will be in
the Meeting Tent,[d] outside the curtain which is in
front of the Ark.[d] The Israelites and their descendants[d] must obey this rule from now on.

Clothes for the Priests

28 “Tell your brother Aaron to come to you,
along with his sons Nadab, Abihu, Eleazar, and Ithamar. Separate them from the other
Israelites to serve me as priests. 2Make holy
clothes for your brother Aaron to give him honor
and beauty. 3Tell all the skilled craftsmen to
whom I have given wisdom to make special
clothes for Aaron—clothes to show that he belongs to me so that he may serve me as a priest.
4These are the clothes they must make: a chest
covering, a holy vest,[d] an outer robe, a woven
inner robe, a turban, and a cloth belt. The craftsmen must make these holy clothes for your
brother Aaron and his sons. Then they may serve
me as priests. 5The craftsmen must use gold and
blue, purple and red thread, and fine linen.

The Holy Vest

6“Use gold and blue, purple and red thread,
and fine linen to make the holy vest;[d] skilled
craftsmen are to make it. 7At each top corner of
this holy vest there will be a pair of shoulder
straps tied together over each shoulder.

8“The craftsmen will very carefully weave a
belt on the holy vest that is made with the same
materials—gold and blue, purple and red thread,
and fine linen.

9“Take two onyx stones and write the names of
the twelve sons of Israel on them, 10six on one
stone and six on the other. Write the names in
order, from the oldest son to the youngest.
11Carve the names of the sons of Israel on these
stones in the same way a person carves words and
designs on a seal.[d] Put gold around the stones to
hold them on the holy vest. 12Then put the two
stones on the two straps of the holy vest as reminders of the twelve sons of Israel. Aaron is to
wear their names on his shoulders in the presence
of the LORD as reminders of the sons of Israel.
13Make two gold pieces to hold the stones 14and
two chains of pure gold, twisted together like a
rope. Attach the chains to the two gold pieces that
hold the stones.

The Chest Covering

15“Make a chest covering to help in making decisions. The craftsmen should make it as they
made the holy vest,[d] using gold and blue, purple
and red thread, and fine linen. 16The chest covering must be square—nine inches long and nine
inches wide—and folded double to make a
pocket. 17Put four rows of beautiful gems on the
chest covering: The first row must have a ruby,
topaz, and yellow quartz; 18the second must have
turquoise, a sapphire, and an emerald; 19the third
must have a jacinth, an agate, and an amethyst;
20the fourth must have a chrysolite, an onyx, and
a jasper. Put gold around these jewels to attach
them to the chest covering. 21There must be
twelve jewels on the chest covering—one jewel
for each of the names of the sons of Israel. Carve
the name of one of the twelve tribes[d] on each of
the stones as you would carve a seal.[d]

22“Make chains of pure gold, twisted together
like rope, for the chest covering. 23Make two gold
rings and put them on the two upper corners of
the chest covering. 24Attach the two gold chains
to the two rings at the upper corners of the chest
covering. 25Attach the other ends of the two
chains to the two gold pieces on the shoulder
straps in the front of the holy vest.

26“Make two gold rings and put them at the two lower corners of the chest covering, on the inside edge next to the holy vest. 27Make two more gold rings and attach them to the bottom of the shoulder straps in the front of the holy vest. Put them close to the seam above the woven belt of the holy vest. 28Join the rings of the chest covering to the rings of the holy vest with blue ribbon, connecting it to the woven belt so the chest covering will not swing out from the holy vest.

29“When Aaron enters the Holy Place, he will wear the names of the sons of Israel over his heart, on the chest covering that helps in making decisions. This will be a continual reminder before the LORD. 30And put the Urim and Thummim[d] inside the chest covering so that they will be on Aaron's heart when he goes before the LORD. They will help in making decisions for the Israelites. So Aaron will always carry them with him when he is before the LORD.

31“Make the outer robe to be worn under the holy vest, using only blue cloth. 32Make a hole in the center for Aaron's head, with a woven collar around the hole so it will not tear. 33Make balls like pomegranates[d] of blue, purple, and red thread, and hang them around the bottom of the outer robe with gold bells between them. 34All around the bottom of the outer robe there should be a gold bell and a pomegranate ball, a gold bell and a pomegranate ball. 35Aaron must wear this robe when he serves as priest. The ringing of the bells will be heard when he enters and leaves the Holy Place before the LORD so that Aaron will not die.

SIDELIGHT: Worried about being noisy at church? Priests in the Old Testament had the opposite problem; they worried about being too quiet. So they wore special robes with bells on the bottom hem (Exodus 28:33–34). The bells may have been there so the priests wouldn't go into God's presence unannounced.

36“Make a strip of pure gold and carve these words on it as you would carve a seal:[d] ‘Holy to the LORD.’ 37Use blue ribbon to tie it to the turban; put it on the front of the turban. 38Aaron must wear this on his forehead. In this way, he will be blamed if anything is wrong with the gifts of the Israelites. Aaron must always wear this on his head so the LORD will accept the gifts of the people.

39“Make the woven inner robe of fine linen, and make the turban of fine linen also. Make the cloth belt with designs sewn on it. 40Also make woven inner robes, cloth belts, and headbands for Aaron's sons, to give them honor and beauty. 41Put these clothes on your brother Aaron and his sons, and pour olive oil on their heads to appoint them as priests. Make them belong to me so they may serve me as priests.

42“Make for them linen underclothes to cover them from the waist to the upper parts of the legs. 43Aaron and his sons must wear these underclothes when they enter the Meeting Tent[d] and anytime they come near the altar to serve as priests in the Holy Place. If they do not wear these clothes, they will be guilty of wrong, and they will die. This will be a law that will last from now on for Aaron and all his descendants.[d]

Appointing the Priests

29 “This is what you must do to appoint Aaron and his sons to serve me as priests. Take one young bull and two male sheep that have nothing wrong with them. 2Use fine wheat flour without yeast to make bread, cakes mixed with olive oil, and wafers brushed with olive oil. 3Put these in one basket, and bring them along with the bull and two male sheep. 4Bring Aaron and his sons to the entrance of the Meeting Tent[d] and wash them with water. 5Take the clothes and dress Aaron in the inner robe and the outer robe of the holy vest.[d] Then put on him the holy vest and the chest covering, and tie the holy vest on him with its skillfully woven belt. 6Put the turban on his head, and put the holy crown on the turban. 7Take the special olive oil and pour it on his head to make him a priest.

8“Then bring his sons and put the inner robes on them. 9Put the headbands on their heads, and tie cloth belts around their waists. Aaron and his descendants[d] will be priests in Israel, according to a rule that will continue from now on. This is how you will appoint Aaron and his sons as priests.

10“Bring the bull to the front of the Meeting Tent, and Aaron and his sons must put their hands on the bull's head. 11Then kill the bull before the LORD at the entrance to the Meeting Tent. 12Use your finger to put some of the bull's blood on the corners of the altar, and then pour the blood that is left at the bottom of the altar. 13Take all the fat that covers the inner organs, as well as the best part of the liver, both kidneys, and the fat around them, and burn them on the altar. 14Take the bull's meat, skin, and intestines, and burn them outside the camp. This is an offering to take away sin.

15“Take one of the male sheep, and have Aaron and his sons put their hands on its head. 16Kill it, and take its blood and sprinkle it on all four sides of the altar. 17Then cut it into pieces and wash its inner organs and its legs, putting them with its head and its other pieces. 18Burn the whole sheep on the altar; it is a burnt offering made by fire to the LORD. Its smell is pleasing to the LORD.

19“Take the other male sheep, and have Aaron and his sons put their hands on its head. 20Kill it and take some of its blood. Put the blood on the bottom of the right ears of Aaron and his sons and on the thumbs of their right hands and on the big toes of their right feet. Then sprinkle the rest of the blood against all four sides of the altar. 21Take some of the blood from the altar, and mix it with the special oil used in appointing priests. Sprinkle this on Aaron and his clothes and on his sons and their clothes. This will show that Aaron and his sons and their clothes are given to my service.

22“Then take the fat from the male sheep, the fat tail, and the fat that covers the inner organs. In addition, take the best part of the liver, both kidneys, and the fat around them, and the right thigh. (This is the male sheep to be used in appointing priests.)

23“Then take the basket of bread that you made without yeast, which you put before the LORD. From it take a loaf of bread, a cake made with olive oil, and a wafer. 24Put all of these in the hands of Aaron and his sons, and tell them to present them as an offering to the LORD. 25Then take them from their hands and burn them on the altar with the whole burnt offering. This is an offering made by fire to the LORD; its smell is pleasing to the LORD. 26Then take the breast of the male sheep used to appoint Aaron as priest, and present it before the LORD as an offering. This part of the animal will be your share. 27Set aside the breast and the thigh of the sheep that were used to appoint Aaron and his sons as priests. These parts belong to them. 28They are to be the regular share which the Israelites will always give to Aaron and his sons. It is the gift the Israelites must give to the LORD from their fellowship offerings.

29“The holy clothes made for Aaron will belong to his descendants so that they can wear these clothes when they are appointed as priests. 30Aaron's son, who will become high priest after Aaron, will come to the Meeting Tent to serve in the Holy Place. He is to wear these clothes for seven days.

31“Take the male sheep used to appoint priests and boil its meat in a place that is holy. 32Then at the entrance of the Meeting Tent, Aaron and his sons must eat the meat of the sheep and the bread that is in the basket. 33They should eat these offerings that were used to remove their sins and to make them holy when they were made priests. But no one else is to eat them, because they are holy things. 34If any of the meat from that sheep or any of the bread is left the next morning, it must be burned. It must not be eaten, because it is holy.

35“Do all these things that I commanded you to do to Aaron and his sons, and spend seven days appointing them. 36Each day you are to offer a bull to remove the sins of Aaron and his sons so they will be given for service to the LORD. Make the altar ready for service to the LORD, and pour oil on it to make it holy. 37Spend seven days making the altar ready for service to God and making it holy. Then the altar will become very holy, and anything that touches it must be holy.

The Daily Sacrifices

38“Every day from now on, offer on the altar two lambs that are one year old. 39Offer one lamb in the morning and the other in the evening before dark. 40In the morning, when you offer the first lamb, offer also two quarts of fine flour mixed with one quart of oil from pressed olives. Pour out a quart of wine as a drink offering. 41Offer the second lamb in the evening with the same grain offering and drink offering as you did in the morning. This is an offering made by fire to the LORD, and its smell is pleasing to him.

42“You must burn these things as an offering to the LORD every day, from now on, at the entrance of the Meeting Tent[d] before the LORD. When you make the offering, I, the LORD, will meet you there and speak to you. 43I will meet with the people of Israel there, and that place will be holy because of my glory.

44“So I will make the Meeting Tent and the altar holy; I will also make Aaron and his sons holy so they may serve me as priests. 45I will live with the people of Israel and be their God. 46And they will know that I am the LORD their God who led them out of Egypt so that I could live with them. I am the LORD their God.

The Altar for Burning Incense

30 “Make an altar out of acacia wood for burning incense.[d] 2Make it square—eighteen inches long and eighteen inches wide—and make it thirty-six inches high. The corners that stick out like horns must be one piece with the altar. 3Cover its top, its sides, and its corners with pure gold, and put a gold strip all around the altar. 4Make two gold rings beneath the gold strip on opposite sides of the altar, and slide poles through them to carry the altar. 5Make the poles from acacia wood and cover them with gold. 6Put the altar of incense in front of the curtain that is near the Ark[d] of the Agreement, in front of the lid that covers that Ark. There I will meet with you.

7“Aaron must burn sweet-smelling incense on the altar every morning when he comes to take care of the oil lamps. 8He must burn incense again in the evening when he lights the lamps, so incense will burn before the LORD every day from now on. 9Do not use this altar for offering any other incense, or burnt offering, or any kind of grain offering, or drink offering. 10Once a year Aaron must make the altar ready for service to God by putting blood on its corners — the blood of the animal offered to remove sins. He is to do this once a year from now on. This altar belongs completely to the LORD's service."

The Tax for the Meeting Tent

11The LORD said to Moses, 12"When you count the people of Israel, every person must buy back his life from the LORD so that no terrible things will happen to the people when you number them. 13Every person who is counted must pay one-fifth of an ounce of silver. (This is set by using one-half of the Holy Place measure, which weighs two-fifths of an ounce.) This amount is a gift to the LORD. 14Every person who is counted and is twenty years old or older must give this amount to the LORD. 15A rich person must not give more than one-fifth of an ounce, and a poor person must not give less. You are paying this to the LORD to buy back your lives. 16Gather from the people of Israel this money paid to buy back their lives, and spend it on things for the service in the Meeting Tent.[d] This payment will remind the LORD that the Israelites' lives have been bought back."

The Bronze Bowl

17The LORD said to Moses, 18"Make a bronze bowl, on a bronze stand, for washing. Put the bowl and stand between the Meeting Tent[d] and the altar, and put water in the bowl. 19Aaron and his sons must wash their hands and feet with the water from this bowl. 20Each time they enter the Meeting Tent they must wash with water so they will not die. Whenever they approach the altar to serve as priests and offer a sacrifice to the LORD by fire, 21they must wash their hands and their feet so they will not die. This is a rule which Aaron and his descendants[d] are to keep from now on."

Oil for Appointing

22Then the LORD said to Moses, 23"Take the finest spices: twelve pounds of liquid myrrh,[d] half that amount (that is, six pounds) of sweet-smelling cinnamon, six pounds of sweet-smelling cane, 24and twelve pounds of cassia.[d] Weigh all these by the Holy Place measure. Also take four quarts of olive oil, 25and mix all these things like a perfume to make a holy olive oil. This special oil must be put on people and things to make them ready for service to God. 26Put this oil on the Meeting Tent[d] and the Ark[d] of the Agreement, 27on the table and all its dishes, on the lampstand and all its tools, and on the incense[d] altar. 28Also, put the oil on the altar for burnt offerings and on all its tools, as well as on the bowl and the stand under the bowl. 29You will prepare all these things for service to God, and they will be very holy. Anything that touches these things must be holy.

30"Put the oil on Aaron and his sons to give them for service to me, that they may serve me as priests. 31Tell the Israelites, 'This is to be my holy olive oil from now on. It is to be put on people and things to make them ready for service to God. 32Do not pour it on the bodies of ordinary people, and do not make perfume the same way you make this oil. It is holy, and you must treat it as holy. 33If anyone makes perfume like it or puts it on someone who is not a priest, that person must be cut off from his people.' "

Incense

34Then the LORD said to Moses, "Take these sweet-smelling spices: resin, onycha, galbanum, and pure frankincense.[d] Be sure that you have equal amounts of each. 35Make incense[d] as a person who makes perfume would do. Add salt to it to keep it pure and holy. 36Beat some of the incense into a fine powder, and put it in front of the Ark[d] of the Agreement in the Meeting Tent,[d] where I will meet with you. You must use this incense powder only for its very special purpose. 37Do not make incense for yourselves the same way you make this incense. Treat it as holy to the LORD. 38Whoever makes incense like this to use as perfume must be cut off from his people."

SIDELIGHT: Kentucky Fried Chicken isn't the first company to have a secret recipe. In ancient Israel, priests had a secret recipe for the spices in the holy incense (Exodus 30:34–38). Three of the ingredients—resin, galbanum, and frankincense—were extracted from plants or trees. Onycha came from a shellfish in the Red Sea.

Bezalel and Oholiab Help

31 Then the LORD said to Moses, 2"See, I have chosen Bezalel son of Uri from the tribe[d] of Judah. (Uri was the son of Hur.) 3I have filled Bezalel with the Spirit[d] of God and have given him the skill, ability, and knowledge to do all kinds of work. 4He is able to design pieces to be made from gold, silver, and bronze, 5to cut jewels and put them in metal, to carve wood, and to do all kinds of work. 6I have also chosen Oholiab son of Ahisamach from the tribe of Dan to work with Bezalel. I have given skills to all the craftsmen, and they will be able to make all these things I have commanded you: 7the Meeting Tent,[d] the Ark[d] of the Agreement, the lid that covers the Ark, and everything in the Tent. 8This includes the table and everything on it, the pure gold lampstand and everything with it, the altar of incense,[d] 9the altar for burnt offerings and everything used with it, and the bowl and the stand under it. 10They will make the woven clothes and the holy clothes for Aaron and the clothes for his sons to wear when they serve as priests. 11They will also make the special olive oil used in appointing people and things to the service of the LORD, and the sweet-smelling incense for the Holy Place.

"These workers will make all these things just as I have commanded you."

The Day of Rest

12Then the LORD said to Moses, 13"Tell the Israelites, 'You must keep the rules about my Sabbaths,[d] because they will be a sign between you and me from now on. In this way you will know that I, the LORD, make you holy.

14" 'Make the Sabbath a holy day. If anyone treats the Sabbath like any other day, that person must be put to death; anyone who works on the Sabbath day must be cut off from his people. 15There are six days for working, but the seventh day is a day of rest, a day holy for the LORD. Anyone who works during the Sabbath day must be put to death. 16The Israelites must remember the Sabbath day as an agreement between them and me that will continue from now on. 17The Sabbath day will be a sign between me and the Israelites forever, because in six days I, the LORD, made the sky and the earth. On the seventh day I did not work; I rested.' "

18When the LORD finished speaking to Moses on Mount Sinai, he gave him the two stone tablets with the Agreement written on them, written by the finger of God.

The People Make a Gold Calf

32 The people saw that a long time had passed and Moses had not come down from the mountain. So they gathered around Aaron and said, "Moses led us out of Egypt, but we don't know what has happened to him. Make us gods who will lead us."

2Aaron said to the people, "Take off the gold earrings that your wives, sons, and daughters are wearing, and bring them to me." 3So all the people took their gold earrings and brought them to Aaron. 4He took the gold from the people and formed it with a tool and made a statue of a calf. Then the people said, "Israel, these are your gods who brought you out of the land of Egypt!"

5When Aaron saw all this, he built an altar before the calf and announced, "Tomorrow there will be a special feast to honor the LORD." 6The people got up early the next morning and offered whole burnt offerings and fellowship offerings. They sat down to eat and drink, and then they got up and sinned sexually.

7Then the LORD said to Moses, "Go down from this mountain, because your people, the people you brought out of the land of Egypt, have ruined themselves. 8They have quickly turned away from the things I commanded them to do. They have made for themselves a calf covered with gold, and they have worshiped it and offered sacrifices to it. They have said, 'Israel, these are your gods who brought you out of Egypt.' "

9The LORD said to Moses, "I have seen these people, and I know that they are very stubborn. 10So now do not stop me. I am so angry with them that I am going to destroy them. Then I will make you and your descendants[d] a great nation."

11But Moses begged the LORD his God and said, "LORD, don't let your anger destroy your people, whom you brought out of Egypt with your great power and strength. 12Don't let the people of Egypt say, 'The LORD brought the Israelites out of Egypt for an evil purpose. He planned to kill them in the mountains and destroy them from the earth.' So stop being angry, and don't destroy your people. 13Remember the men who served you—Abraham, Isaac, and Israel. You promised with an oath to them and said, 'I will make your descendants as many as the stars in the sky. I will give your descendants all this land that I have promised them, and it will be theirs forever.' " 14So the LORD changed his mind and did not destroy the people as he had said he might.

15Then Moses went down the mountain, and in his hands he had the two stone tablets with the Agreement on them. The commands were written on both sides of each stone, front and back. 16God himself had made the tablets, and God himself had written the commands on the tablets.

17When Joshua heard the sound of the people shouting, he said to Moses, "It sounds like war down in the camp."

18Moses answered:

"It is not a shout of victory;
  it is not a cry of defeat.
  It is the sound of singing that I hear."

19When Moses came close to the camp, he saw the gold calf and the dancing, and he became very angry. He threw down the stone tablets that he was carrying and broke them at the bottom of the mountain. 20Then he took the calf that the people had made and melted it in the fire. He ground it into powder. Then he threw the powder into the water and forced the Israelites to drink it.

21Moses said to Aaron, "What did these people do to you? Why did you cause them to do such a terrible sin?"

22Aaron answered, "Don't be angry, master. You know that these people are always ready to

do wrong. 23The people said to me, 'Moses led us
out of Egypt, but we don't know what has happened to him. Make us gods who will lead us.'
24So I told the people, 'Take off your gold jewelry.' When they gave me the gold, I threw it into
the fire and out came this calf!"
25Moses saw that the people were acting
wildly. Aaron had let them get out of control and
become fools in front of their enemies. 26So Moses
stood at the entrance to the camp and said, "Let
anyone who wants to follow the LORD come to
me." And all the people from the family of Levi
gathered around Moses.
27Then Moses said to them, "The LORD, the
God of Israel, says this: 'Every man must put on
his sword and go through the camp from one end
to the other. Each man must kill his brother, his
friend, and his neighbor.' " 28The people from the
family of Levi obeyed Moses, and that day about
three thousand of the Israelites died. 29Then Moses said, "Today you have been given for service
to the LORD. You were willing to kill your own
sons and brothers, and God has blessed you for
this."
30The next day Moses told the people, "You
have done a terrible sin. But now I will go up to
the LORD. Maybe I can do something so your sins
will be removed." 31So Moses went back to the
LORD and said, "How terribly these people have
sinned! They have made for themselves gods from
gold. 32Now, please forgive them of this sin. If you
will not, then erase my name from the book in
which you have written the names of your people."
33But the LORD told Moses, "I will erase from
my book the names of the people who sin against

SIN

I Told You So

Tyrone Gilker carefully laid the extra pillows on his bed, fluffing them to make them look bigger. Then he covered them with the sheets and bedspread. "That should do it," he whispered as he shut off the light.

He tiptoed to the window and opened it carefully. Climbing out, he stretched his legs to reach the porch roof below, shimmied to the edge and climbed down the trellis, carefully avoiding the climbing roses.

Mark and Sandy were waiting in the Toyota around the corner. "No problem," Tyrone said, hopping into the back seat. "They'll never know I'm gone. Six Flags, here we come."

The three friends didn't plan to stay at the theme park too long, but they didn't want to completely miss the park's all-night extravaganza for graduating seniors. Tyrone had tried to get permission to go, but his parents wouldn't give him a later curfew. So he decided to go without them knowing.

It would have worked, except the trellis wasn't as strong as he had thought. When he returned home four hours later, his foot found a loose board, and he screamed, "Aaaaaaaaah!" as he tumbled into the roses.

When the light came on in his parents' room, Tyrone knew he was in trouble. What would happen now? he wondered as he sat on the lawn and waited for his dad to appear.

Tyrone knew what he was doing was wrong, but he did it anyway. Similarly, the Israelites knew they shouldn't build an idol to worship. Read **Exodus 32:1–14** to see what happened when they did it anyway.

- What lesson might Tyrone have learned from the passage if he had read it before crawling out the window?
- When have you, like the Israelites, doubted God's leadership and disobeyed him? What did you learn about trusting God from that experience?

CONSIDER...

- praying that God will give you strength next time you're tempted to do something you know is wrong.
- listening to popular songs on the radio to find out what things people trust instead of God. How is their misplaced trust sinful?

FOR MORE, SEE...

- Deuteronomy 32:15–22 (p. 189)
- 1 Kings 18:22–39 (p. 324)
- Romans 6:1–7 (p. 1146)

me. 34So now, go. Lead the people where I have
told you, and my angel will lead you. When the
time comes to punish, I will punish them for their
sin."

35So the LORD caused terrible things to happen
to the people because of what they did with the
calf Aaron had made.

33 Then the LORD said to Moses, "You and
the people you brought out of Egypt
must leave this place. Go to the land that I promised with an oath to give to Abraham, Isaac, and
Jacob when I said, 'I will give that land to your
descendants.' 2I will send an angel to lead you,
and I will force these people out of the land: the
Canaanites, Amorites, Hittites, Perizzites, Hivites,
and Jebusites. 3Go up to a fertile land. But I will
not go with you, because I might destroy you on
the way, since you are such a stubborn people."

4When the people heard this bad news, they
became very sad, and none of them put on jewelry. 5This was because the LORD had said to Moses, "Tell the Israelites, 'You are a stubborn people. If I were to go with you even for a moment,
I would destroy you. So take off all your jewelry,
and I will decide what to do with you.' " 6So the
people of Israel took off their jewelry at Mount
Sinai.

The Meeting Tent

7Moses used to take a tent and set it up a long
way outside the camp; he called it the "Meeting
Tent."[d] Anyone who wanted to ask the LORD
about something would go to the Meeting Tent
outside the camp. 8Whenever Moses went out to
the Tent, all the people would rise and stand at
the entrances of their tents, watching him until he
entered the Meeting Tent. 9When Moses went
into the Tent, the pillar of cloud would always
come down and stay at the entrance of the Tent
while the LORD spoke with Moses. 10Whenever
the people saw the pillar of cloud at the entrance
of the Tent, they stood and worshiped, each person at the entrance of his own tent.

11The LORD spoke to Moses face to face as a
man speaks with his friend. Then Moses would
return to the camp, but Moses' young helper,
Joshua son of Nun, did not leave the Tent.

12Moses said to the LORD, "You have told me
to lead these people, but you did not say whom
you would send with me. You have said to me,
'I know you very well, and I am pleased with
you.' 13If I have truly pleased you, show me your
plans so that I may know you and continue to
please you. Remember that this nation is your
people."

14The LORD answered, "I myself will go with
you, and I will give you victory."

15Then Moses said to him, "If you yourself
don't go with us, then don't send us away from
this place. 16If you don't go with us, no one will
know that you are pleased with me and with your
people. These people and I will be no different
from any other people on earth."

17Then the LORD said to Moses, "I will do what
you ask, because I know you very well, and I am
pleased with you."

Moses Sees God's Glory

18Then Moses said, "Now, please show me
your glory."

19The LORD answered, "I will cause all my
goodness to pass in front of you, and I will announce my name, the LORD, so you can hear it.
I will show kindness to anyone to whom I want
to show kindness, and I will show mercy to anyone to whom I want to show mercy. 20But you
cannot see my face, because no one can see me
and live.

21"There is a place near me where you may
stand on a rock. 22When my glory passes that
place, I will put you in a large crack in the rock
and cover you with my hand until I have passed
by. 23Then I will take away my hand, and you will
see my back. But my face must not be seen."

Moses Gets New Stone Tablets

34 The LORD said to Moses, "Cut two more
stone tablets like the first two, and I will
write the same words on them that were on the
first two stones which you broke. 2Be ready tomorrow morning, and then come up on Mount
Sinai. Stand before me there on the top of the
mountain. 3No one may come with you or even
be seen any place on the mountain. Not even the
flocks or herds may eat grass near that mountain."

4So Moses cut two stone tablets like the first
ones. Then early the next morning he went up
Mount Sinai, just as the LORD had commanded
him, carrying the two stone tablets with him.
5Then the LORD came down in the cloud and
stood there with Moses, and the LORD called out
his name: the LORD.

6The LORD passed in front of Moses and said,
"I am the LORD. The LORD is a God who shows
mercy, who is kind, who doesn't become angry
quickly, who has great love and faithfulness 7and
is kind to thousands of people. The LORD forgives
people for evil, for sin, and for turning against
him, but he does not forget to punish guilty people. He will punish not only the guilty people,
but also their children, their grandchildren,
their great-grandchildren, and their great-great-
grandchildren."

8Then Moses quickly bowed to the ground and
worshiped. 9He said, "Lord, if you are pleased
with me, please go with us. I know that these are
stubborn people, but forgive our evil and our sin.
Take us as your own people."

[10]Then the LORD said, "I am making this agreement with you. I will do miracles[d] in front of all
your people—things that have never before been
done for any other nation on earth—and the people with you will see my work. I, the LORD, will
do wonderful things for you. [11]Obey the things I
command you today, and I will force out the Amorites, Canaanites, Hittites, Perizzites, Hivites,
and Jebusites ahead of you. [12]Be careful that you
don't make an agreement with the people who
live in the land where you are going, because it
will bring you trouble. [13]Destroy their altars,
break their stone pillars, and cut down their Asherah[d] idols. [14]Don't worship any other god, because I, the LORD, the Jealous One, am a jealous
God.

[15]"Be careful that you don't make an agreement with the people who live in that land. When
they worship their gods, they will invite you to
join them. Then you will eat their sacrifices. [16]If
you choose some of their daughters as wives for
your sons and those daughters worship gods, they
will lead your sons to do the same thing.

[17]"Do not make gods of melted metal.

[18]"Celebrate the Feast[d] of Unleavened Bread.
For seven days you must eat bread made without
yeast as I commanded you. Do this during the
month I have chosen, the month of Abib,[d] because in that month you came out of Egypt.

[19]"The firstborn[d] of every mother belongs to
me, including every firstborn male animal that is
born in your flocks and herds. [20]You may buy
back a donkey by paying for it with a lamb, but
if you don't want to buy back a donkey, you must
break its neck. You must buy back all your firstborn sons.

FORGIVENESS

Living With Consequences

Jay Jones had big plans for his life. When he graduated from high school, he would go to college to play basketball. He hoped to make it to the pros. If he didn't, he would go to law school and become a partner in his dad's firm.

Then Jay met Mindy at a school dance. They fell in love and became more and more involved. Even though they were Christians, they began having sex "because we love each other so much."

Several months passed. Then one day Mindy came to school sobbing. "I'm pregnant," she told Jay. "What am I going to do?"

As they talked—and cried—in the next few days, and faced up to their sin, they decided the best thing to do was to get married. They knew God would forgive them, but they also knew they would have to live with what they had done.

Jay quit the basketball team, dropped out of school, and started working at a fast-food restaurant to pay the doctor bills. He gave up his dream of playing pro basketball.

After the baby was born, Jay's life revolved around work and diapers. Sometimes he wanted to run away—to leave behind the stress and responsibility. But he didn't. Instead, he worked with Mindy to have the best possible family for their child.

By asking God's forgiveness, Jay and Mindy were able to keep going. But they had to live with what they had done. **Exodus 34:4–8** teaches that God forgives but doesn't take away the natural consequences of what we do.

- How did God's forgiveness affect the way Jay and Mindy were able to work together to create their family? How might their relationship have been different if they hadn't sought God's forgiveness?
- When have you asked for forgiveness but still had to live with the consequences of what you did? How did you feel?

CONSIDER . . .

- making a chart that shows the consequences of a particular sin, such as premarital sex. Put the sin at the top and then list below it everything that might happen as a result. How does forgiveness affect the consequences?
- asking God's forgiveness for something you have done, while also asking him to guide you as you deal responsibly with the consequences.

FOR MORE, SEE . . .

- 2 Chronicles 6:24–31 (p. 390)
- Psalm 51:1–13 (p. 511)
- Luke 17:1–4 (p. 1039)

“No one is to come before me without a gift.

21“You must work for six days, but on the seventh day you must rest—even during the planting season and the harvest season.

22“Celebrate the Feast[d] of Weeks when you gather the first grain of the wheat harvest. And celebrate the Feast[d] of Shelters in the fall.

23“Three times each year all your males must come before the Lord God, the God of Israel. 24I will force out nations ahead of you and expand the borders of your land. You will go before the LORD your God three times each year, and at that time no one will try to take your land from you.

25“Do not offer the blood of a sacrifice to me with anything containing yeast, and do not leave any of the sacrifice of the Feast[d] of Passover until the next morning.

26“Bring the best first crops that you harvest from your ground to the Tent[d] of the LORD your God.

“You must not cook a young goat in its mother’s milk.”

27Then the LORD said to Moses, “Write down these words, because with these words I have made an agreement with you and Israel.”

28Moses stayed there with the LORD forty days and forty nights, and during that time he did not eat food or drink water. And Moses wrote the words of the Agreement—the Ten Commandments—on the stone tablets.

The Face of Moses Shines

29Then Moses came down from Mount Sinai, carrying the two stone tablets of the Agreement in his hands. But he did not know that his face was shining because he had talked with the LORD. 30When Aaron and all the people of Israel saw that Moses’ face was shining, they were afraid to go near him. 31But Moses called to them, so Aaron and all the leaders of the people returned to Moses, and he talked with them. 32After that, all the people of Israel came near him, and he gave them all the commands that the LORD had given him on Mount Sinai.

33When Moses finished speaking to the people, he put a covering over his face. 34Anytime Moses went before the LORD to speak with him, Moses took off the covering until he came out. Then Moses would come out and tell the Israelites what the LORD had commanded. 35They would see that Moses’ face was shining. So he would cover his face again until the next time he went in to speak with the LORD.

Rules About the Sabbath

35 Moses gathered all the Israelite community together and said to them, “These are the things the LORD has commanded you to do. 2You are to work for six days, but the seventh day will be a holy day, a Sabbath[d] of rest to honor the LORD. Anyone who works on that day must be put to death. 3On the Sabbath day you must not light a fire in any of your houses.”

4Moses said to all the Israelites, “This is what the LORD has commanded: 5From what you have, take an offering for the LORD. Let everyone who is willing bring this offering to the LORD: gold, silver, bronze, 6blue, purple and red thread, and fine linen, goat hair 7and male sheepskins that are colored red. They may also bring fine leather, acacia wood, 8olive oil for the lamps, spices for the special olive oil used for appointing priests and for the sweet-smelling incense,[d] 9onyx stones, and other jewels to be put on the holy vest[d] and chest covering of the priests.

10“Let all the skilled workers come and make everything the LORD commanded: 11the Holy Tent,[d] its outer tent and its covering, the hooks, frames, crossbars, posts, and bases; 12the Ark[d] of the Agreement, its poles, lid, and the curtain in front of it; 13the table, and its poles, all the things that go with the table, and the bread that shows we are in God’s presence; 14the lampstand for the light and all the things that go with it, the lamps, and olive oil for the light; 15the altar of incense and its poles, the special oil and the sweet-smelling incense, the curtain for the entrance of the Meeting Tent; 16the altar of burnt offering and its bronze screen, its poles and all its tools, the bronze bowl and its base; 17the curtains around the courtyard, their posts and bases, and the curtain at the entry to the courtyard; 18the pegs of the Holy Tent and of the courtyard and their ropes; 19the special clothes that the priest will wear in the Holy Place. These are the holy clothes for Aaron the priest and his sons to wear when they serve as priests.”

20Then all the people of Israel went away from Moses. 21Everyone who wanted to give came and brought a gift to the LORD for making the Meeting Tent, all the things in the Tent, and the special clothes. 22All the men and women who wanted to give brought gold jewelry of all kinds—pins, earrings, rings, and bracelets. They all presented their gold to the LORD. 23Everyone who had blue, purple, and red thread, and fine linen, and anyone who had goat hair or male sheepskins colored red or fine leather brought them to the LORD. 24Everyone who could give silver or bronze brought that as a gift to the LORD, and everyone who had acacia wood to be used in the work brought it. 25Every skilled woman used her hands to make the blue, purple, and red thread, and fine linen, and they brought what they had made. 26All the women who were skilled and wanted to help made thread of the goat hair. 27The leaders brought onyx stones and other jewels to put on the holy vest and chest covering for the priest.

28They also brought spices and olive oil for the sweet-smelling incense, the special oil, and the oil to burn in the lamps. 29All the men and women of Israel who wanted to help brought gifts to the LORD for all the work the LORD had commanded Moses and the people to do.

30Then Moses said to the Israelites, "Look, the LORD has chosen Bezalel son of Uri the son of Hur, from the tribe[d] of Judah. 31The LORD has filled Bezalel with the Spirit[d] of God and has given him the skill, ability, and knowledge to do all kinds of work. 32He is able to design pieces to be made of gold, silver, and bronze, 33to cut stones and jewels and put them in metal, to carve wood, and to do all kinds of work. 34Also, the LORD has given Bezalel and Oholiab, the son of Ahisamach from the tribe of Dan, the ability to teach others. 35The LORD has given them the skill to do all kinds of work. They are able to cut designs in metal and stone. They can plan and sew designs in the fine linen with the blue, purple, and red thread. And they are also able to weave things.

36

1So Bezalel, Oholiab, and every skilled person will do the work the LORD has commanded, because he gave them the wisdom and understanding to do all the skilled work needed to build the Holy Tent."

2Then Moses called Bezalel, Oholiab, and all the other skilled people to whom the LORD had given skills, and they came because they wanted to help with the work. 3They received from Moses everything the people of Israel had brought as gifts to build the Holy Tent. The people continued to bring gifts each morning because they wanted to. 4So all the skilled workers left the work they were doing on the Holy Tent, 5and they said to Moses, "The people are bringing more than we need to do the work the LORD commanded."

6Then Moses sent this command throughout the camp: "No man or woman should make anything else as a gift for the Holy Tent." So the people were kept from giving more, 7because what they had was already more than enough to do all the work.

The Holy Tent

8Then the skilled workers made the Holy Tent.[d] They made the ten curtains of blue, purple, and red cloth, and they sewed designs of creatures with wings on the curtains. 9Each curtain was the same size—forty-two feet long and six feet wide. 10Five of the curtains were fastened together to make one set, and the other five were fastened together to make another set. 11Then they made loops of blue cloth along the edge of the end curtain on the first set of five, and they did the same thing with the other set of five. 12There were fifty loops on one curtain and fifty loops on the other curtain, with the loops opposite each other. 13They made fifty gold hooks to join the two curtains together so that the Holy Tent was joined together as one piece.

14Then the workers made another tent of eleven curtains made of goat hair, to put over the Holy Tent. 15All eleven curtains were the same size—forty-five feet long and six feet wide. 16The workers sewed five curtains together into one set and six together into another set. 17They made fifty loops along the edge of the outside curtain of one set and fifty loops along the edge of the outside curtain of the other set. 18Then they made fifty bronze rings to join the two sets of cloth together and make the tent one piece. 19They made two more coverings for the outer tent—one made of male sheepskins colored red and the other made of fine leather.

SIDELIGHT: Goat hair was good material for building the Holy Tent (Exodus 36:14–19). When it's dry, it's open and airy, making it cooler inside. But when it rains, the goat hairs expand and keep out the moisture.

20Then they made upright frames of acacia wood for the Holy Tent. 21Each frame was fifteen feet tall and twenty-seven inches wide, 22and there were two pegs side by side on each one. Every frame of the Holy Tent was made this same way. 23They made twenty frames for the south side of the Tent, 24and they made forty silver bases that went under the twenty frames. There were two bases for every frame—one for each peg of each frame. 25They also made twenty frames for the north side of the Holy Tent 26and forty silver bases—two to go under each frame. 27They made six frames for the rear or west end of the Holy Tent 28and two frames for the corners at the rear of the Holy Tent. 29These two frames were doubled at the bottom and joined at the top with a metal ring. They did this for each of these corners. 30So there were eight frames and sixteen silver bases—two bases under each frame.

31Then they made crossbars of acacia wood to connect the upright frames of the Holy Tent. Five crossbars held the frames together on one side of the Tent, 32and five held the frames together on the other side. Also, five crossbars held the frames together on the west end, at the rear of the Tent. 33They made the middle crossbar run along the entire length of each side and rear of the Tent. It was set halfway up the frames. 34They made gold rings on the sides of the frames to hold the crossbars, and they covered the frames and the crossbars with gold.

[35]Then they made the curtain of blue, purple, and red thread, and fine linen. A skilled craftsman sewed designs of creatures with wings on it. [36]They made four posts of acacia wood for it and covered them with gold. Then they made gold hooks for the posts, as well as four silver bases in which to set the posts. [37]For the entrance to the Tent, they made a curtain of blue, purple, and red thread, and fine linen. A person who sewed well sewed designs on it. [38]Then they made five posts and hooks for it. They covered the tops of the posts and their bands with gold, and they made five bronze bases for the posts.

The Ark of the Agreement

37 Bezalel made the Ark[d] of acacia wood; it was forty-five inches long, twenty-seven inches wide, and twenty-seven inches high. [2]He covered it, both inside and out, with pure gold, and he put a gold strip around it. [3]He made four gold rings for it and attached them to its four feet, with two rings on each side. [4]Then he made poles of acacia wood and covered them with gold. [5]He put the poles through the rings on each side of the Ark to carry it. [6]Then he made a lid of pure gold that was forty-five inches long and twenty-seven inches wide. [7]Then Bezalel hammered gold to make two creatures with wings and attached them to each end of the lid. [8]He made one creature on one end of the lid and the other creature on the other end. He attached them to the lid so that it would be one piece. [9]The creatures' wings were spread upward, covering the lid, and the creatures faced each other across the lid.

The Table

[10]Then he made the table of acacia wood; it was thirty-six inches long, eighteen inches wide, and twenty-seven inches high. [11]He covered it with pure gold and put a gold strip around it. [12]He made a frame three inches high that stood up all around the edge, and he put a gold strip around it. [13]Then he made four gold rings for the table and attached them to the four corners of the table where the four legs were. [14]The rings were put close to the frame around the top of the table, because they held the poles for carrying it. [15]The poles for carrying the table were made of acacia wood and were covered with gold. [16]He made of pure gold all the things that were used on the table: the plates, bowls, cups, and jars used for pouring the drink offerings.

The Lampstand

[17]Then he made the lampstand of pure gold, hammering out its base and stand. Its flower-like cups, buds, and petals were joined together in one piece with the base and stand. [18]Six branches went out from the sides of the lampstand — three on one side and three on the other. [19]Each branch had three cups shaped like almond flowers, and each cup had a bud and a petal. Each of the six branches going out from the lampstand was the same. [20]There were four more cups shaped like almond flowers on the lampstand itself, each with its buds and petals. [21]Three pairs of branches went out from the lampstand. A bud was under the place where each pair was attached to the lampstand. Each of the six branches going out from the lampstand was the same. [22]The buds, branches, and lampstand were all one piece of pure, hammered gold. [23]He made seven pure gold lamps for this lampstand, and he made pure gold wick trimmers and trays. [24]He used about seventy-five pounds of pure gold to make the lampstand and all the things that go with it.

The Altar for Burning Incense

[25]Then he made the altar of incense[d] out of acacia wood. It was square — eighteen inches long and eighteen inches wide — and it was thirty-six inches high. Each corner that stuck out like a horn was joined into one piece with the altar. [26]He covered the top and all the sides and the corners with pure gold, and he put gold trim around the altar. [27]He made two gold rings and put them below the trim on opposite sides of the altar; these rings held the poles for carrying it. [28]He made the poles of acacia wood and covered them with gold.

[29]Then he made the holy olive oil for appointing the priests and the pure, sweet-smelling incense. He made them like a person who mixes perfumes.

The Altar for Burnt Offerings

38 Then he built the altar for burnt offerings out of acacia wood. The altar was square — seven and one-half feet long and seven and one-half feet wide — and it was four and one-half feet high. [2]He made each corner stick out like a horn so that the horns and the altar were joined together in one piece. Then he covered the altar with bronze. [3]He made all the tools of bronze to use on the altar: the pots, shovels, bowls for sprinkling blood, meat forks, and pans for carrying the fire. [4]He made a large bronze screen to hold the burning wood for the altar and put it inside the altar, under its rim, halfway up from the bottom. [5]He made bronze rings to hold the poles for carrying the altar, and he put them at the four corners of the screen. [6]Then he made poles of acacia wood and covered them with bronze. [7]He put the poles through the rings on both sides of the altar, to carry it. He made the altar of boards and left the inside hollow.

The Bronze Bowl

8He made the bronze bowl for washing, and he built it on a bronze stand. He used the bronze from mirrors that belonged to the women who served at the entrance to the Meeting Tent.[d]

The Courtyard of the Holy Tent

9Then he made a wall of curtains to form a courtyard around the Holy Tent.[d] On the south side the curtains were one hundred fifty feet long and were made of fine linen. 10The curtains hung on silver hooks and bands, placed on twenty bronze posts with twenty bronze bases. 11On the north side the wall of curtains was also one hundred fifty feet long, and it hung on silver hooks and bands on twenty posts with twenty bronze bases.

12On the west side of the courtyard, the wall of curtains was seventy-five feet long. It was held up by silver hooks and bands on ten posts with ten bases. 13The east side was also seventy-five feet long. 14On one side of the entry there was a wall of curtains twenty-two and one-half feet long, held up by three posts and three bases. 15On the other side of the entry there was also a wall of curtains twenty-two and one-half feet long, held up by three posts and three bases. 16All the curtains around the courtyard were made of fine linen. 17The bases for the posts were made of bronze. The hooks and the bands on the posts were made of silver, and the tops of the posts were covered with silver also. All the posts in the courtyard had silver bands.

18The curtain for the entry of the courtyard was made of blue, purple, and red thread, and fine linen, sewn by a person who could sew well. The curtain was thirty feet long and seven and one-half feet high, the same height as the curtains around the courtyard. 19It was held up by four posts and four bronze bases. The hooks and bands on the posts were made of silver, and the tops on the posts were covered with silver. 20All the tent pegs for the Holy Tent and for the curtains around the courtyard were made of bronze.

21This is a list of the materials used to make the Holy Tent, where the Agreement is kept. Moses ordered the Levites to make this list, and Ithamar son of Aaron was in charge of keeping it. 22Bezalel son of Uri, the son of Hur of the tribe[d] of Judah, made everything the LORD commanded Moses. 23Oholiab son of Ahisamach of the tribe of Dan helped him. He could cut designs into metal and stone; he was a designer and also skilled at sewing the blue, purple, and red thread, and fine linen.

24The total amount of gold used to build the Holy Tent was presented to the LORD. It weighed over 2,000 pounds, as set by the Holy Place measure.

25The silver was given by the members of the community who were counted. It weighed 7,550 pounds, as set by the Holy Place measure. 26All the men twenty years old or older were counted. There were 603,550 men, and each man had to pay one-fifth of an ounce of silver, as set by the Holy Place measure. 27Of this silver, 7,500 pounds were used to make the one hundred bases for the Holy Tent and for the curtain — 75 pounds of silver in each base. 28They used 50 pounds of silver to make the hooks for the posts and to cover the tops of the posts and to make the bands on them.

29The bronze which was presented to the LORD weighed about 5,000 pounds. 30They used the bronze to make the bases at the entrance of the Meeting Tent, to make the altar and the bronze screen, and to make all the tools for the altar. 31This bronze was also used to make bases for the wall of curtains around the courtyard and bases for curtains at the entry to the courtyard, as well as to make the tent pegs for the Holy Tent and the curtains that surrounded the courtyard.

Clothes for the Priests

39 They used blue, purple, and red thread to make woven clothes for the priests to wear when they served in the Holy Place. They made the holy clothes for Aaron as the LORD had commanded Moses.

2They made the holy vest[d] of gold, and blue, purple, and red thread, and fine linen. 3They hammered the gold into sheets and then cut it into long, thin strips. They worked the gold into the blue, purple, and red thread, and fine linen. This was done by skilled craftsmen. 4They made the shoulder straps for the holy vest, which were attached to the top corners of the vest and tied together over each shoulder. 5The skillfully woven belt was made in the same way; it was joined to the holy vest as one piece. It was made of gold, and blue, purple, and red thread, and fine linen, the way the LORD commanded Moses.

6They put gold around the onyx stones and then wrote the names of the sons of Israel on these gems, as a person carves words and designs on a seal.[d] 7Then they attached the gems on the shoulder straps of the holy vest, as reminders of the twelve sons of Israel. This was done just as the LORD had commanded Moses.

8The skilled craftsmen made the chest covering like the holy vest; it was made of gold, and blue, purple, and red thread, and fine linen. 9The chest covering was square — nine inches long and nine inches wide — and it was folded double to make a pocket. 10Then they put four rows of beautiful jewels on it: In the first row there was a ruby, a topaz, and a yellow quartz; 11in the second there was a turquoise, a sapphire, and an emerald; 12in the third there was a jacinth, an agate, and an amethyst; 13in the fourth there was a chrysolite, an onyx, and a jasper. Gold was put around these jewels to attach them to the chest covering, 14and the names of the sons of Israel were carved on these twelve jewels as a person carves a seal. Each jewel had the name of one of the twelve tribes[d] of Israel.

15They made chains of pure gold, twisted together like a rope, for the chest covering. 16The workers made two gold pieces and two gold rings. They put the two gold rings on the two upper corners of the chest covering. 17Then they put two gold chains in the two rings at the ends of the chest covering, 18and they fastened the other two ends of the chains to the two gold pieces. They attached these gold pieces to the two shoulder straps in the front of the holy vest. 19They made two gold rings and put them at the lower corners of the chest covering on the inside edge next to the holy vest. 20They made two more gold rings on the bottom of the shoulder straps in front of the holy vest, near the seam, just above the woven belt of the holy vest. 21They used a blue ribbon and tied the rings of the chest covering to the rings of the holy vest, connecting it to the woven belt. In this way the chest covering would not swing out from the holy vest. They did all these things the way the LORD commanded.

22Then they made the outer robe to be worn under the holy vest. It was woven only of blue cloth. 23They made a hole in the center of the outer robe, with a woven collar sewn around it so it would not tear. 24Then they made balls like pomegranates[d] of blue, purple, and red thread, and fine linen and hung them around the bottom of the outer robe. 25They also made bells of pure gold and hung these around the bottom of the outer robe between the balls. 26So around the bottom of the outer robe there was a bell and a pomegranate ball, a bell and a pomegranate ball. The priest wore this outer robe when he served as priest, just as the LORD had commanded Moses.

27They wove inner robes of fine linen for Aaron and his sons, 28and they made turbans, headbands, and underclothes of fine linen. 29Then they made the cloth belt of fine linen, and blue, purple, and red thread, and designs were sewn onto it, just as the LORD had commanded Moses.

30They made a strip of pure gold, which is the holy crown, and carved these words in the gold, as one might carve on a seal: "Holy to the LORD." 31Then they tied this flat piece to the turban with a blue ribbon, as the LORD had commanded Moses.

32So all the work on the Meeting Tent[d] was finished. The Israelites did everything just as the LORD had commanded Moses. 33Then they brought the Holy Tent to Moses: the Tent and all its furniture, hooks, frames, crossbars, posts, and bases; 34the covering made of male sheepskins colored red, the covering made of fine leather, and the curtain that covered the entrance to the Most Holy Place; 35the Ark[d] of the Agreement, its poles and lid; 36the table, all its containers, and the bread that showed they were in God's presence; 37the pure gold lampstand with its lamps in a row, all its tools, and the olive oil for the light; 38the gold altar, the special olive oil used for appointing priests, the sweet-smelling incense,[d] and the curtain that covered the entrance to the Tent; 39the bronze altar and its screen, its poles and all its tools, the bowl and its stand; 40the curtains for the courtyard with their posts and bases, the curtain that covered the entry to the courtyard, the cords, pegs, and all the things in the Meeting Tent. 41They brought the clothes for the priests to wear when they served in the Holy Tent—the holy clothes for Aaron the priest and the clothes for his sons, which they wore when they served as priests.

42The Israelites had done all this work just as the LORD had commanded Moses. 43Moses looked closely at all the work and saw they had done it just as the LORD had commanded. So Moses blessed them.

Setting Up the Holy Tent

40 Then the LORD said to Moses: 2"On the first day of the first month, set up the Holy Tent,[d] which is the Meeting Tent. 3Put the Ark[d] of the Agreement in it and hang the curtain in front of the Ark. 4Bring in the table and arrange everything on the table that should be there. Then bring in the lampstand and set up its lamps. 5Put the gold altar for burning incense[d] in front of the Ark of the Agreement, and put the curtain at the entrance to the Holy Tent.

6"Put the altar of burnt offerings in front of the entrance of the Holy Tent, the Meeting Tent. 7Put the bowl between the Meeting Tent and the altar, and put water in it. 8Set up the courtyard around the Holy Tent, and put the curtain at the entry to the courtyard.

9"Use the special olive oil and pour it on the Holy Tent and everything in it, in order to give the Tent and all that is in it for service to the LORD. They will be holy. 10Pour the special oil on the altar for burnt offerings and on all its tools. Give the altar for service to God, and it will be very holy. 11Then pour the special olive oil on the bowl and the base under it so that they will be given for service to God.

12"Bring Aaron and his sons to the entrance of the Meeting Tent, and wash them with water. 13Then put the holy clothes on Aaron. Pour the

special oil on him, and give him for service to God
so that he may serve me as a priest. 14Bring
Aaron's sons and put the inner robes on them.
15Pour the special oil on them in the same way
that you appointed their father as priest so that
they may also serve me as priests. Pouring oil on
them will make them a family of priests, they and
their descendants[d] from now on." 16Moses did everything that the LORD commanded him.

17So the Holy Tent was set up on the first day
of the first month during the second year after
they left Egypt. 18When Moses set up the Holy
Tent, he put the bases in place, and he put the
frames on the bases. Next he put the crossbars
through the rings of the frames and set up the
posts. 19After that, Moses spread the cloth over
the Holy Tent and put the covering over it, just
as the LORD commanded.

20Moses put the stone tablets that had the
Agreement written on them into the Ark. He put
the poles through the rings of the Ark and put the
lid on it. 21Next he brought the Ark into the Tent
and hung the curtain to cover the Ark, just as the
LORD commanded him.

22Moses put the table in the Meeting Tent on
the north side of the Holy Tent in front of the
curtain. 23Then he put the bread on the table before the LORD, just as the LORD commanded him.
24Moses put the lampstand in the Meeting Tent
on the south side of the Holy Tent across from the
table. 25Then he put the lamps on the lampstand
before the LORD, just as the LORD commanded
him.

26Moses put the gold altar for burning incense
in the Meeting Tent in front of the curtain. 27Then
he burned sweet-smelling incense on it, just as the
LORD commanded him. 28Then he hung the curtain at the entrance to the Holy Tent.

29He put the altar for burnt offerings at the entrance to the Holy Tent, the Meeting Tent, and
offered a whole burnt offering and grain offerings
on it, just as the LORD commanded him. 30Moses
put the bowl between the Meeting Tent and the
altar for burnt offerings, and he put water in it for
washing. 31Moses, Aaron, and Aaron's sons used
this water to wash their hands and feet. 32They
washed themselves every time they entered the
Meeting Tent and every time they went near the
altar for burnt offerings, just as the LORD commanded Moses.

33Then Moses set up the courtyard around the
Holy Tent and the altar, and he put up the curtain
at the entry to the courtyard. So Moses finished
the work.

The Cloud over the Holy Tent

34Then the cloud covered the Meeting Tent,[d]
and the glory of the LORD filled the Holy Tent.
35Moses could not enter the Meeting Tent, because the cloud had settled on it, and the glory of
the LORD filled the Holy Tent.

36When the cloud rose from the Holy Tent, the
Israelites would begin to travel, 37but as long as
the cloud stayed on the Holy Tent, they did not
travel. They stayed in that place until the cloud
rose. 38So the cloud of the LORD was over the
Holy Tent during the day, and there was a fire in
the cloud at night. So all the Israelites could see
the cloud while they traveled.

LEVITICUS

Why Read This Book:

- Discover how worshiping God today is different than it used to be (Leviticus 1–7).
- Learn ancient laws people followed to obey God (Leviticus 18–20).
- Find out how people used to be punished for disobeying God's laws (Leviticus 24–26).

Behind the Scenes:

If you were a boy in ancient Israel and your great-great-great-grandfather were named Levi, you would be born with your career already planned. You would know where to live, what to wear, and exactly how to do your job. That's because the descendants of Levi—the Levites—were Israel's original priests. And Leviticus was the manual they followed in leading people in worship.

The priests were the religious leaders in the Old Testament. They served God by preparing sacrifices to God from the people. People offered sacrifices to thank God and to ask for forgiveness for sins.

Priests were also responsible for maintaining the Meeting Place or tabernacle. Many of the regulations in Leviticus deal with worship in the Meeting Tent—a portable sanctuary used as the Israelites wandered in the wilderness after being freed from slavery in Egypt. The worship regulations also applied to the Temple when it was built in Jerusalem about three hundred fifty years later.

This book is sometimes difficult for us to follow. It's filled with detailed (sometimes repulsive) instructions about animal sacrifices, building the Temple, and celebrating various religious festivals. It also contains explicit guidelines for all people about diet, sexuality, personal relationships, and other areas of life.

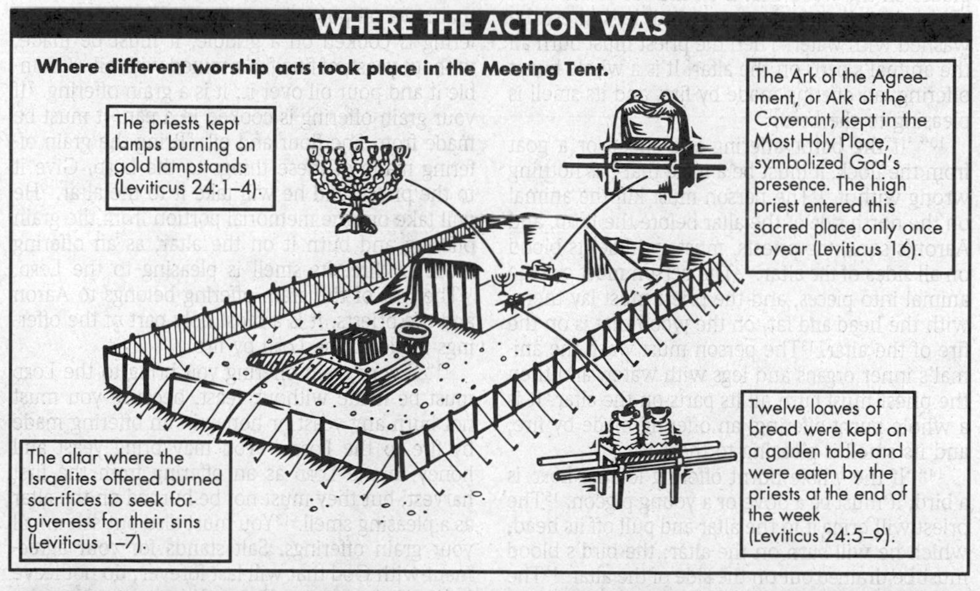

WHERE THE ACTION WAS
Where different worship acts took place in the Meeting Tent.
The priests kept lamps burning on gold lampstands (Leviticus 24:1–4).
The Ark of the Agreement, or Ark of the Covenant, kept in the Most Holy Place, symbolized God's presence. The high priest entered this sacred place only once a year (Leviticus 16).
Twelve loaves of bread were kept on a golden table and were eaten by the priests at the end of the week (Leviticus 24:5–9).
The altar where the Israelites offered burned sacrifices to seek forgiveness for their sins (Leviticus 1–7).

WHEN THE ACTION WAS

2000BC	1500BC	1000BC	500BC	BC/AD

- Abraham lived
- The Israelites became slaves in Egypt
- The Israelites escaped from Egypt
- The Israelites entered the promised land
- The Israelites wandered in the desert for forty years
- The Temple was built in Jerusalem for worship
- Jesus was born

Behind the Scenes (cont.): Many of the guidelines seem irrelevant to us today. But behind all the details are themes that help us understand what it means to follow God today. God wants a relationship with us, but we must first admit our sins and accept God's forgiveness. And God expects believers to live their lives in ways that are pleasing to him. As Leviticus 19:2 says: "I am the Lord your God. You must be holy because I am holy."

The Burnt Offering

1 The LORD called to Moses and spoke to him from the Meeting Tent,[d] saying, 2"Tell the people of Israel: 'When you bring an offering to the LORD, bring as your offering an animal from the herd or flock.

3" 'If the offering is a whole burnt offering from the herd, it must be a male that has nothing wrong with it. The person must take the animal to the entrance of the Meeting Tent so that the LORD will accept the offering. 4He must put his hand on the animal's head, and the LORD will accept it to remove the person's sin so he will belong to God. 5He must kill the young bull before the LORD, and Aaron's sons, the priests, must bring its blood and sprinkle it on all sides of the altar at the entrance to the Meeting Tent. 6After that he will skin the animal and cut it into pieces. 7The priests, when they have put wood and fire on the altar, 8are to lay the head, the fat, and other pieces on the wood that is on the fire of the altar. 9The animal's inner organs and legs must be washed with water. Then the priest must burn all the animal's parts on the altar. It is a whole burnt offering, an offering made by fire, and its smell is pleasing to the LORD.

10" 'If the burnt offering is a sheep or a goat from the flock, it must be a male that has nothing wrong with it. 11The person must kill the animal on the north side of the altar before the LORD, and Aaron's sons, the priests, must sprinkle its blood on all sides of the altar. 12The person must cut the animal into pieces, and the priest must lay them, with the head and fat, on the wood that is on the fire of the altar. 13The person must wash the animal's inner organs and legs with water, and then the priest must burn all its parts on the altar. It is a whole burnt offering, an offering made by fire, and its smell is pleasing to the LORD.

14" 'If the whole burnt offering for the LORD is a bird, it must be a dove or a young pigeon. 15The priest will bring it to the altar and pull off its head, which he will burn on the altar; the bird's blood must be drained out on the side of the altar. 16The priest must remove the bird's crop[n] and its contents and throw them on the east side of the altar, where the ashes are. 17Then he must tear the bird open by its wings without dividing it into two parts. He must burn the bird on the altar, on the wood which is on the fire. It is a whole burnt offering, an offering made by fire, and its smell is pleasing to the LORD.

The Grain Offering

2 " 'When anyone offers a grain offering to the LORD, it must be made from fine flour. The person must pour oil on it, put incense[d] on it, 2and then take it to Aaron's sons, the priests. The priest must take a handful of the fine flour and oil and all the incense, and burn it on the altar as a memorial portion. It is an offering made by fire, and its smell is pleasing to the LORD. 3The rest of the grain offering will belong to Aaron and the priests; it is a most holy part of the offerings made by fire to the LORD.

4" 'If you bring a grain offering that was baked in the oven, it must be made from fine flour. It may be loaves made without yeast and mixed with oil, or it may be wafers made without yeast that have oil poured over them. 5If your grain offering is cooked on a griddle, it must be made, without yeast, of fine flour mixed with oil. 6Crumble it and pour oil over it; it is a grain offering. 7If your grain offering is cooked in a pan, it must be made from fine flour and oil. 8Bring the grain offering made of these things to the LORD. Give it to the priest, and he will take it to the altar. 9He will take out the memorial portion from the grain offering and burn it on the altar, as an offering made by fire. Its smell is pleasing to the LORD. 10The rest of the grain offering belongs to Aaron and the priests. It is a most holy part of the offerings made to the LORD by fire.

11" 'Every grain offering you bring to the LORD must be made without yeast, because you must not burn any yeast or honey in an offering made by fire to the LORD. 12You may bring yeast and honey to the LORD as an offering from the first harvest, but they must not be burned on the altar as a pleasing smell. 13You must also put salt on all your grain offerings. Salt stands for your agreement with God that will last forever; do not leave it out of your grain offering. You must add salt to all your offerings.

14" 'If you bring a grain offering from the first harvest to the LORD, bring crushed heads of new

crop A small bag inside a bird's throat. When a bird eats, its food goes into this part first. There, the food is made soft before it goes into the stomach.

grain roasted in the fire. [15]Put oil and incense on
it; it is a grain offering. [16]The priest will burn the
memorial portion of the crushed grain and oil,
with the incense on it. It is an offering by fire to
the LORD.

The Fellowship Offering

3 " 'If a person's fellowship offering to the
LORD is from the herd, it may be a male or
female, but it must have nothing wrong with it.
[2]The person must put his hand on the animal's
head and kill it at the entrance to the Meeting
Tent.[d] Then Aaron's sons, the priests, must sprinkle the blood on all sides of the altar. [3]From the
fellowship offering he must make a sacrifice by
fire to the LORD. He must offer the fat of the animal's inner organs (both the fat that is in them
and that covers them), [4]both kidneys with the fat
that is on them near the lower back muscle, and
the best part of the liver, which he will remove
with the kidneys. [5]Then the priests will burn
these parts on the altar, on the whole burnt offering that is on the wood of the fire. It is an offering made by fire, and its smell is pleasing to the
LORD.

[6]" 'If a person's fellowship offering to the LORD
is a lamb or a goat, it may be a male or female,
but it must have nothing wrong with it. [7]If he
offers a lamb, he must bring it before the LORD
[8]and put his hand on its head. Then he must kill
the animal in front of the Meeting Tent, and the
priests must sprinkle its blood on all sides of the
altar. [9]From the fellowship offering the person
must make a sacrifice by fire to the LORD. He must
bring the fat, the whole fat tail cut off close to the
backbone, the fat of the inner organs (both the fat
that is in them and that covers them), [10]both kidneys with the fat that is on them, near the lower
back muscle, and the best part of the liver, which
he will remove with the kidneys. [11]Then the
priest will burn these parts on the altar as food;
it will be an offering made by fire to the LORD.

[12]" 'If a person's offering is a goat, he must offer
it before the LORD [13]and put his hand on the its
head. Then he must kill it in front of the Meeting
Tent, and the priests must sprinkle its blood on all
sides of the altar. [14]From this offering the person
must make a sacrifice by fire to the LORD. He must
offer all the fat of the goat's inner organs (both the
fat that is in them and that covers them), [15]both
kidneys with the fat that is on them near the
lower back muscle, and the best part of the liver,
which he will remove with the kidneys. [16]The
priest will burn these parts on the altar as food. It
is an offering made by fire, and its smell is pleasing
to the LORD. All the fat belongs to the LORD.

[17]" 'This law will continue for people from now
on, wherever you live: You must not eat any fat
or blood.' "

The Sin Offering

4 The LORD said to Moses, [2]"Tell the people of
Israel this: 'When a person sins by accident
and does some things the LORD has commanded
not to be done, that person must do these things:

[3]" 'If the appointed priest sins so that he brings
guilt on the people, then he must offer a young
bull to the LORD, one that has nothing wrong with
it, as a sin offering for the sin he has done. [4]He
will bring the bull to the entrance of the Meeting
Tent[d] in front of the LORD, put his hand on its
head, and kill it before the LORD. [5]Then the appointed priest must bring some of the bull's blood
into the Meeting Tent. [6]The priest is to dip his
finger into the blood and sprinkle it seven times
before the LORD in front of the curtain of the Most
Holy Place. [7]The priest must also put some of the
blood on the corners of the altar of incense[d] that
stands before the LORD in the Meeting Tent. The
rest of the blood he must pour out at the bottom
of the altar of burnt offering, which is at the entrance of the Meeting Tent. [8]He must remove all
the fat from the bull of the sin offering—the fat
on and around the inner organs, [9]both kidneys
with the fat that is on them near the lower back
muscle, and the best part of the liver which he
will remove with the kidneys. [10](He must do this
in the same way the fat is removed from the bull
of the fellowship offering.) Then the priest must
burn the animal parts on the altar of burnt offering. [11]But the priest must carry off the skin of the
bull and all its meat, along with the rest of the
bull—its head, legs, intestines, and other inner
organs. [12]He must take it outside the camp to the
special clean[d] place where the ashes are poured
out. He must burn it on a wood fire on the pile
of ashes.

> **SIDELIGHT:** Collecting the church offering these days is simple compared to the offerings described in Leviticus 4:4–12. Imagine removing livers, kidneys, intestines, and other inner organs from a sacrificed bull. Other animals sacrificed were sheep, goats, doves, and pigeons.

[13]" 'If the whole nation of Israel sins accidentally without knowing it and does something the
LORD has commanded not to be done, they are
guilty. [14]When they learn about the sin they have
done, they must offer a young bull as a sin offering
and bring it before the Meeting Tent. [15]The older
leaders of the group of people must put their
hands on the bull's head before the LORD, and it
must be killed before the LORD. [16]Then the appointed priest must bring some of the bull's blood

into the Meeting Tent. 17Dipping his finger in the
blood, he must sprinkle it seven times before the
LORD in front of the curtain. 18Then he must put
some of the blood on the corners of the altar that
is before the LORD in the Meeting Tent. The priest
must pour out the rest of the blood at the bottom
of the altar of burnt offering, which is at the entrance to the Meeting Tent. 19He must remove all
the fat from the animal and burn it on the altar;
20he will do the same thing with this bull that he
did with the first bull of the sin offering. In this
way the priest removes the sins of the people so
they will belong to the LORD and be forgiven.
21Then the priest must carry the bull outside the
camp and burn it, just as he did with the first bull.
This is the sin offering for the whole community.
22" 'If a ruler sins by accident and does something the LORD his God has commanded must not
be done, he is guilty. 23When he learns about his
sin, he must bring a male goat that has nothing
wrong with it as his offering. 24The ruler must put
his hand on the goat's head and kill it in the place
where they kill the whole burnt offering before
the LORD; it is a sin offering. 25The priest must
take some of the blood of the sin offering on his
finger and put it on the corners of the altar of
burnt offering. He must pour out the rest of the
blood at the bottom of the altar of burnt offering.
26He must burn all the goat's fat on the altar in the
same way he burns the fat of the fellowship offerings. In this way the priest removes the ruler's sin
so he belongs to the LORD, and the LORD will forgive him.
27" 'If any person in the community sins by accident and does something which the LORD has
commanded must not be done, he is guilty.
28When the person learns about his sin, he must
bring a female goat that has nothing wrong with
it as an offering for his sin. 29He must put his hand
on the animal's head and kill it at the place of the
whole burnt offering. 30Then the priest must take
some of the goat's blood on his finger and put it
on the corners of the altar of burnt offering. He
must pour out the rest of the goat's blood at the
bottom of the altar. 31Then the priest must remove all the goat's fat in the same way the fat is
removed from the fellowship offerings. He must
burn it on the altar as a smell pleasing to the
LORD. In this way the priest will remove that person's sin so he will belong to the LORD, and the
LORD will forgive him.
32" 'If this person brings a lamb as his offering
for sin, he must bring a female that has nothing
wrong with it. 33He must put his hand on the animal's head and kill it as a sin offering in the place
where the whole burnt offering is killed. 34The
priest must take some of the blood from the sin
offering on his finger and put it on the corners of
the altar of burnt offering. He must pour out the
rest of the lamb's blood at the bottom of the altar.
35Then the priest must remove all the lamb's fat
in the same way that the lamb's fat is removed
from the fellowship offerings. He must burn the
pieces on the altar on top of the offerings made by
fire for the LORD. In this way the priest will remove that person's sins so he will belong to the
LORD, and the LORD will forgive him.

Special Types of Accidental Sins

5 " 'If a person is ordered to tell in court what
he has seen or what he knows and he does
not tell the court, he is guilty of sin.
2" 'Or someone might touch something unclean,[d] such as the dead body of an unclean wild
animal or an unclean farm animal or an unclean
crawling animal. Even if he does not know that he
touched it, he will still be unclean and guilty of
sin.
3" 'Someone might touch human uncleanness—anything that makes someone unclean—
and not know it. But when he learns about it, he
will be guilty.
4" 'Or someone might make a promise before
the LORD without thinking. It might be a promise
to do something bad or something good; it might
be about anything. Even if he forgets about it,
when he remembers, he will be guilty.
5" 'When anyone is guilty of any of these
things, he must tell how he sinned. 6He must
bring an offering to the LORD as a penalty for sin;
it must be a female lamb or goat from the flock.
The priest will perform the acts to remove that
person's sin so he will belong to the LORD.
7" 'But if the person cannot afford a lamb, he
must bring two doves or two young pigeons to the
LORD as the penalty for his sin. One bird must be
for a sin offering, and the other must be for a
whole burnt offering. 8He must bring them to the
priest, who will first offer the one for the sin offering. He will pull the bird's head from its neck, but
he will not pull it completely off. 9He must sprinkle the blood from the sin offering on the side of
the altar, and then he must pour the rest of the
blood at the bottom of the altar; it is a sin offering.
10Then the priest must offer the second bird as a
whole burnt offering, as the law says. In this way
the priest will remove the person's sin so he will
belong to the LORD, and the LORD will forgive
him.
11" 'If the person cannot afford two doves or
two pigeons, he must bring about two quarts of
fine flour as an offering for sin. He must not put
oil or incense[d] on the flour, because it is a sin
offering. 12He must bring the flour to the priest.
The priest will take a handful of the flour as a
memorial offering and burn it on the altar on top
of the offerings made by fire to the LORD; it is a

sin offering. 13In this way the priest will remove the person's sins so he will belong to the LORD, and the LORD will forgive him. What is left of the sin offering belongs to the priest, like the grain offering.' "

The Penalty Offering

14The LORD said to Moses, 15"If a person accidentally sins and does something against the holy things of the LORD, he must bring from the flock a male sheep that has nothing wrong with it. This will be his penalty offering to the LORD. Its value in silver must be correct as set by the Holy Place measure. It is a penalty offering. 16That person must pay for the sin he did against the holy thing, adding one-fifth to its value. Then he must give it all to the priest. In this way the priest will remove the person's sin so he will belong to the LORD, by using the male sheep as the penalty offering. And the LORD will forgive the person.

17"If a person sins and does something the LORD has commanded not to be done, even if he does not know it, he is still guilty. He is responsible for his sin. 18He must bring the priest a male sheep from the flock, one that has nothing wrong with it and that is worth the correct amount. It will be a penalty offering. Though the person sinned without knowing it, with this offering the priest will remove the sin so the person will belong to the LORD, and the LORD will forgive him. 19The person is guilty of doing wrong, so he must give the penalty offering to the LORD."

6 The LORD said to Moses, 2"A person might sin against the LORD by doing one of these sins: He might lie about what happened to something he was taking care of for someone else, or he might lie about a promise he made. He might steal something or cheat someone. 3He might find something that had been lost and then lie about it. He might make a promise before the LORD about something and not mean it, or he might do some other sin. 4If he does any of these things, he is guilty of sin. He must bring back whatever he stole or whatever he took by cheating. He must bring back the thing he took care of for someone else. He must bring back what he found and lied about 5or what he made a false promise about. He must pay the full price plus an extra one-fifth of the value of what he took. He must give the money to the true owner on the day he brings his penalty offering. 6He must bring his penalty to the priest—a male sheep from the flock, one that does not have anything wrong with it and that is worth the correct amount. It will be a penalty offering to the LORD. 7Then the priest will perform the acts to remove that person's sin so he will belong to the LORD, and the LORD will forgive him for the sins that made him guilty."

The Whole Burnt Offering

8The LORD said to Moses, 9"Give this command to Aaron and the priests: 'These are the teachings about the whole burnt offering: The burnt offering must stay on the altar all night until morning, and the altar's fire must be kept burning. 10The priest must put on his linen robe and linen underclothes next to his body. Then he will remove the ashes from the burnt offering on the altar and put them beside the altar. 11Then he must take off those clothes and put on others and carry the ashes outside the camp to a special clean[d] place. 12But the fire must be kept burning on the altar; it must not be allowed to go out. The priest must put more firewood on the altar every morning, place the whole burnt offering on the fire, and burn the fat of the fellowship offerings. 13The fire must be kept burning on the altar all the time; it must not go out.

The Grain Offering

14" 'These are the teachings about the grain offering: The priests must bring it to the LORD in front of the altar. 15The priest must take a handful of fine flour, with the oil and all of the incense[d] on it, and burn the grain offering on the altar as a memorial offering to the LORD. Its smell is pleasing to him. 16Aaron and the priests may eat what is left, but it must be eaten without yeast in a holy place. They must eat it in the courtyard of the Meeting Tent.[d] 17It must not be cooked with yeast. I have given it as their share of the offerings made to me by fire; it is most holy, like the sin offering and the penalty offering. 18Any male descendant[d] of Aaron may eat it as his share of the offerings made to the LORD by fire, and this will continue from now on. Whatever touches these offerings shall become holy.' "

19The LORD said to Moses, 20"This is the offering Aaron and the priests must bring to the LORD on the day they appoint Aaron as high priest: They must bring two quarts of fine flour for a continual grain offering, half of it in the morning and half in the evening. 21The fine flour must be mixed with oil and cooked on a griddle. Bring it when it is well mixed. Present the grain offering that is broken into pieces, and it will be a smell that is pleasing to the LORD. 22One of the priests appointed to take Aaron's place as high priest must make the grain offering. It is a rule forever that the grain offering must be completely burned to the LORD. 23Every grain offering made by a priest must be completely burned; it must not be eaten."

The Sin Offering

24The LORD said to Moses, 25"Tell Aaron and the priests: 'These are the teachings about the sin offering: The sin offering must be killed in front of the LORD in the same place the whole burnt offering is killed; it is most holy. 26The priest who offers the sin offering must eat it in a holy place, in the courtyard of the Meeting Tent.[d] 27Whatever touches the meat of the sin offering must be holy, and if the blood is sprinkled on any clothes, you must wash them in a holy place. 28The clay pot the meat is cooked in must be broken, or if a bronze pot is used, it must be scrubbed and rinsed with water. 29Any male in a priest's family may eat the offering; it is most holy. 30But if the blood of the sin offering is taken into the Meeting Tent and used to remove sin in the Holy Place, that sin offering must be burned with fire. It must not be eaten.

The Penalty Offering

7 " 'These are the teachings about the penalty offering, which is most holy: 2The penalty offering must be killed where the whole burnt offering is killed. Then the priest must sprinkle its blood on all sides of the altar. 3He must offer all the fat from the penalty offering — the fat tail, the fat that covers the inner organs, 4both kidneys with the fat that is on them near the lower back muscle, and the best part of the liver, which is to be removed with the kidneys. 5The priest must burn all these things on the altar as an offering made by fire to the LORD. It is a penalty offering. 6Any male in a priest's family may eat it. It is most holy, so it must be eaten in a holy place.

7" 'The penalty offering is like the sin offering in that the teachings are the same for both. The priest who offers the sacrifice to remove sins will get the meat for food. 8The priest who offers the burnt offering may also have the skin from it. 9Every grain offering that is baked in an oven, cooked on a griddle, or baked in a dish belongs to the priest who offers it. 10Every grain offering, either dry or mixed with oil, belongs to the priests, and all priests will share alike.

The Fellowship Offering

11" 'These are the teachings about the fellowship offering a person may offer to the LORD: 12If he brings the fellowship offering to show his thanks, he should also bring loaves of bread made without yeast that are mixed with oil, wafers made without yeast that have oil poured over them, and loaves of fine flour that are mixed with oil. 13He must also offer loaves of bread made with yeast along with his fellowship offering, which he gives to show thanks. 14One of each kind of offering will be for the LORD; it will be given to the priest who sprinkles the blood of the fellowship offering. 15When the fellowship offering is given to thank the LORD, the meat from it must be eaten the same day it is offered; none of it must be left until morning.

16" 'If a person brings a fellowship offering just to give a gift to God or because of a special promise to him, the sacrifice should be eaten the same day he offers it. If there is any left, it may be eaten the next day. 17If any meat from this sacrifice is left on the third day, it must be burned up. 18Any meat of the fellowship offering eaten on the third day will not be accepted, nor will the sacrifice count for the person who offered it. It will become unclean,[d] and anyone who eats the meat will be guilty of sin.

19" 'People must not eat meat that touches anything unclean; they must burn this meat with fire. Anyone who is clean may eat other meat. 20But if anyone is unclean and eats the meat from the fellowship offering that belongs to the LORD, he must be cut off from his people.

21" 'If anyone touches something unclean — uncleanness that comes from people, from an animal, or from some hated thing — touching it will make him unclean. If he then eats meat from the fellowship offering that belongs to the LORD, he must be cut off from his people.' "

22The LORD said to Moses, 23"Tell the people of Israel: 'You must not eat any of the fat from cattle, sheep, or goats. 24If an animal is found dead or torn by wild animals, you may use its fat for other things, but you must not eat it. 25If someone eats fat from an animal offering made by fire to the LORD, he must be cut off from his people. 26No matter where you live, you must not eat blood from any bird or animal. 27Anyone who eats blood must be cut off from his people.' "

The Priests' Share

28The LORD said to Moses, 29"Tell the people of Israel: 'If someone brings a fellowship offering to the LORD, he must give part of it as his sacrifice to the LORD. 30He must carry that part of the gift in his own hands as an offering made by fire to the LORD. He must bring the fat and the breast of the animal to the priest, to be presented to the LORD as the priests' share. 31Then the priest must burn the fat on the altar, but the breast of the animal will belong to Aaron and the priests. 32You must also give the right thigh from the fellowship offering to the priest as a gift; 33it will belong to the priest who offers the blood and fat of the fellowship offering. 34I have taken the breast and the thigh from the fellowship offerings of the Israelites, and I have given these parts to Aaron and the priests as their share for all time from the Israelites.' "

35This is the portion that belongs to Aaron and his sons from the offerings made by fire to the LORD. They were given this share on the day they were presented to the LORD as priests. 36On the day the LORD appointed the priests, he commanded Israel to give this share to them, and it is to be given to the priests as their share from now on.

37These are the teachings about the whole burnt offering, the grain offering, the sin offering, the penalty offering, the offering for the appointment of priests, and the fellowship offering. 38The LORD gave these teachings to Moses on Mount Sinai on the day he commanded the Israelites to bring their offerings to the LORD in the Sinai Desert.

Aaron and His Sons Appointed

8 The LORD said to Moses, 2"Bring Aaron and his sons and their clothes, the special olive oil used in appointing people and things to the service of the LORD, the bull of the sin offering and the two male sheep, and the basket of bread made without yeast. 3Then gather the people together at the entrance to the Meeting Tent."[d] 4Moses did as the LORD commanded him, and the people met together at the entrance to the Meeting Tent.

5Then Moses spoke to the people and said, "This is what the LORD has commanded to be done." 6Bringing Aaron and his sons forward, Moses washed them with water. 7He put the inner robe on Aaron and tied the cloth belt around him. Then Moses put the outer robe on him and placed the holy vest[d] on him. He tied the skillfully woven belt around him so that the holy vest was tied to Aaron. 8Then Moses put the chest covering on him and put the Urim and the Thummim[d] in the chest covering. 9He also put the turban on Aaron's head. He put the strip of gold, the holy crown, on the front of the turban, as the LORD commanded him to do.

10Then Moses put the special oil on the Holy Tent[d] and everything in it, making them holy for the LORD. 11He sprinkled some oil on the altar seven times, sprinkling the altar and all its tools and the large bowl and its base. In this way he made them holy for the LORD. 12He poured some of the special oil on Aaron's head to make Aaron holy for the LORD. 13Then Moses brought Aaron's sons forward. He put the inner robes on them, tied cloth belts around them, and put headbands on them, as the LORD had commanded him.

14Then Moses brought the bull for the sin offering, and Aaron and his sons put their hands on its head. 15Moses killed the bull, took the blood, and with his finger put some of it on all the corners of the altar, to make it pure. Then he poured out the rest of the blood at the bottom of the altar. In this way he made it holy and ready for service to God. 16Moses took all the fat from the inner organs of the bull, the best part of the liver, and both kidneys with the fat that is on them, and he burned them on the altar. 17But he took the bull's skin, its meat, and its intestines and burned them in a fire outside the camp, as the LORD had commanded him.

18Next Moses brought the male sheep of the burnt offering, and Aaron and his sons put their hands on its head. 19Then Moses killed it and sprinkled the blood on all sides of the altar. 20He cut the male sheep into pieces and burned the head, the pieces, and the fat. 21He washed the inner organs and legs with water and burned the whole sheep on the altar as a burnt offering made by fire to the LORD; its smell was pleasing to the LORD. Moses did these things as the LORD had commanded him.

22Then Moses brought the other male sheep, the one used in appointing Aaron and his sons as priests, and Aaron and his sons put their hands on its head. 23Then Moses killed the sheep and put some of its blood on the bottom of Aaron's right ear, some on the thumb of Aaron's right hand, and some on the big toe of his right foot. 24Then Moses brought Aaron's sons close to the altar. He put some of the blood on the bottom of their right ears, some on the thumbs of their right hands, and some on the big toes of their right feet. Then he sprinkled blood on all sides of the altar. 25He took the fat, the fat tail, all the fat on the inner organs, the best part of the liver, both kidneys with their fat, and the right thigh. 26From the basket of bread made without yeast that is put before the LORD each day, Moses took a loaf of bread, a loaf made with oil, and a wafer. He put these pieces of bread on the fat and right thigh of the male sheep. 27All these things he put in the hands of Aaron and his sons and presented them as an offering before the LORD. 28Then Moses took them from their hands and burned them on the altar on top of the burnt offering. So this was the offering for appointing Aaron and his sons as priests. It was an offering made by fire to the LORD, and its smell was pleasing to him. 29Moses also took the breast and presented it as an offering before the LORD. It was Moses' share of the male sheep used in appointing the priests, as the LORD had commanded him.

30Moses took some of the special oil and some of the blood which was on the altar, and he sprinkled them on Aaron and Aaron's clothes and on Aaron's sons and their clothes. In this way Moses made Aaron, his clothes, his sons, and their clothes holy for the LORD.

31Then Moses said to Aaron and his sons, "I gave you a command, saying, 'Aaron and his sons will eat these things.' So take the meat and basket of bread from the offering for appointing priests. Boil the meat at the door of the Meeting Tent, and eat it there with the bread. 32If any of the meat or bread is left, burn it. 33The time of appointing will last seven days; you must not go outside the entrance of the Meeting Tent until that time is up. Stay there until the time of your appointing is finished. 34The LORD commanded the things that were done today to remove your sins so you will belong to him. 35You must stay at the entrance of the Meeting Tent day and night for seven days. If you don't obey the LORD's commands, you will die. The LORD has given me these commands."

36So Aaron and his sons did everything the LORD had commanded through Moses.

Aaron and His Sons Offer Sacrifices

9 On the eighth day after the time of appointing, Moses called for Aaron and his sons and for the older leaders of Israel. 2He said to Aaron, "Take a bull calf and a male sheep that have nothing wrong with them, and offer them to the LORD. The calf will be a sin offering, and the male sheep will be a whole burnt offering. 3Tell the people of Israel, 'Take a male goat for a sin offering and a calf and a lamb for a whole burnt offering; each must be one year old, and it must have nothing wrong with it. 4Also take a bull and a male sheep for fellowship offerings, along with a grain offering mixed with oil. Offer all these things to the LORD, because the LORD will appear to you today.' "

5So all the people came to the front of the Meeting Tent,[d] bringing the things Moses had commanded them to bring, and they stood before the LORD. 6Moses said, "You have done what the LORD commanded, so you will see the LORD's glory."

7Then Moses told Aaron, "Go to the altar and offer sin offerings and whole burnt offerings. Do this to remove your sins and the people's sins so you will belong to God. Offer the sacrifices for the people and perform the acts to remove their sins for them so they will belong to the LORD, as the LORD has commanded."

8So Aaron went to the altar and killed the bull calf as a sin offering for himself. 9Then his sons brought the blood to him, and he dipped his finger in the blood and put it on the corners of the altar. He poured out the rest of the blood at the bottom of the altar. 10Aaron took the fat, the kidneys, and the best part of the liver from the sin offering and burned them on the altar, in the way the LORD had commanded Moses. 11The meat and skin he burned outside the camp.

12Then Aaron killed the animal for the whole burnt offering. His sons brought the blood to him, and he sprinkled it on all sides of the altar. 13As they gave him the pieces and head of the burnt offering, Aaron burned them on the altar. 14He also washed the inner organs and the legs of the burnt offering and burned them on top of the burnt offering on the altar.

15Then Aaron brought the offering that was for the people. He took the goat of the people's sin offering and killed it and offered it for the sin offering, just as he had done the first sin offering.

16Then Aaron brought the whole burnt offering and offered it in the way that the LORD had commanded. 17He also brought the grain offering to the altar. He took a handful of the grain and burned it on the altar, in addition to the morning's burnt offering.

18Aaron also killed the bull and the male sheep as the fellowship offerings for the people. His sons brought him the blood, and he sprinkled it on all sides of the altar. 19Aaron's sons also brought to Aaron the fat of the bull and the male sheep — the fat tail, the fat covering the inner organs, the kidneys, and the best part of the liver. 20Aaron's sons put them on the breasts of the bull and the sheep. Then Aaron burned these fat parts on the altar. 21He presented the breasts and the right thigh before the LORD as the priests' share of the offering, as Moses had commanded.

22Then Aaron lifted his hands toward the people and blessed them. When he had finished offering the sin offering, the burnt offering, and the fellowship offering, he stepped down from the altar.

23Moses and Aaron went into the Meeting Tent. Then they came out and blessed the people, and the LORD's glory came to all the people. 24Fire came out from the LORD and burned up the burnt offering and fat on the altar. When the people saw this, they shouted with joy and bowed facedown on the ground.

God Destroys Nadab and Abihu

10 Aaron's sons Nadab and Abihu took their pans for burning incense,[d] put fire in them, and added incense; but they did not use the special fire Moses had commanded them to use in the presence of the LORD. 2So fire came down from the LORD and destroyed Nadab and Abihu, and they died in front of the LORD. 3Then Moses said to Aaron, "This is what the LORD was speaking about when he said,

'I must be respected as holy
by those who come near me;
before all the people
I must be given honor.' "

So Aaron did not say anything about the death of his sons.

4Aaron's uncle Uzziel had two sons named Mishael and Elzaphan. Moses said to them, "Come here and pick up your cousins' bodies. Carry them outside the camp away from the front of the Holy Place." 5So Mishael and Elzaphan obeyed Moses and carried the bodies of Nadab and Abihu, still clothed in the special priest's inner robes, outside the camp.

6Then Moses said to Aaron and his other sons,

Eleazar and Ithamar, "Don't show sadness by
tearing your clothes or leaving your hair uncombed. If you do, you will die, and the LORD will
be angry with all the people. All the people of
Israel, your relatives, may cry loudly about the
LORD burning Nadab and Abihu, 7but you must
not even leave the Meeting Tent.[d] If you go out
of the entrance, you will die, because the LORD
has appointed you to his service." So Aaron, Eleazar, and Ithamar obeyed Moses.
8Then the LORD said to Aaron, 9"You and your
sons must not drink wine or beer when you go
into the Meeting Tent. If you do, you will die.
This law will continue from now on. 10You must
keep what is holy separate from what is not holy;
you must keep what is clean[d] separate from what
is unclean. 11You must teach the people all the
laws that the LORD gave to them through Moses."
12Moses said to Aaron and his remaining sons,
Eleazar and Ithamar, "Eat the part of the grain
offering that is left from the sacrifices offered by
fire to the LORD, but do not add yeast to it. Eat it
near the altar because it is most holy. 13You must
eat it in a holy place, because this part of the offerings made by fire to the LORD belongs to you and
your sons. I have been commanded to tell you
this.
14"Also, you and your sons and daughters may
eat the breast and thigh of the fellowship offering
that was presented to the LORD. You must eat
them in a clean place; they are your share of the
fellowship offerings given by the Israelites. 15The
people must bring the fat from their animals that
was part of the offering made by fire, and they
must present it to the LORD along with the thigh
and the breast of the fellowship offering. They will
be the regular share of the offerings for you and
your children, as the LORD has commanded."
16Moses looked for the goat of the sin offering,
but it had already been burned up. So he became
very angry with Eleazar and Ithamar, Aaron's remaining sons. He said, 17"Why didn't you eat that
goat in a holy place? It is most holy, and the LORD
gave it to you to take away the guilt of the people,
to remove their sins so they will belong to the
LORD. 18You didn't bring the goat's blood inside
the Holy Place. You were supposed to eat the goat
in a holy place, as I commanded!"
19But Aaron said to Moses, "Today they
brought their sin offering and burnt offering before the LORD, but these terrible things have still
happened to me! Do you think the LORD would
be any happier if I ate the sin offering today?"
20When Moses heard this, he was satisfied.

Rules About What May Be Eaten

11 The LORD said to Moses and Aaron,
2"Tell the Israelites this: 'These are the
land animals you may eat: 3You may eat any animal that has split hoofs completely divided and
that chews the cud.[d]
4" 'Some animals only chew the cud or only
have split hoofs, and you must not eat them. The
camel chews the cud but does not have a split
hoof; it is unclean[d] for you. 5The rock badger
chews the cud but does not have a split hoof; it
is unclean for you. 6The rabbit chews the cud but
does not have a split hoof; it is unclean for you.
7Now the pig has a split hoof that is completely
divided, but it does not chew the cud; it is unclean for you. 8You must not eat the meat from
these animals or even touch their dead bodies;
they are unclean for you.
9" 'Of the animals that live in the sea or in a
river, if the animal has fins and scales, you may
eat it. 10But whatever lives in the sea or in a river
and does not have fins and scales—including the
things that fill the water and all other things that
live in it—you should hate. 11You must not eat
any meat from them or even touch their dead
bodies, because you should hate them. 12You
must hate any animal in the water that does not
have fins and scales.
13" 'Also, these are the birds you are to hate.
They are hateful and should not be eaten. You
must not eat eagles, vultures, black vultures,
14kites, any kind of falcon, 15any kind of raven,
16horned owls, screech owls, sea gulls, any kind
of hawk, 17little owls, cormorants, great owls,
18white owls, desert owls, ospreys, 19storks, any
kind of heron, hoopoes, or bats.
20" 'Don't eat insects that have wings and walk
on all four feet; they also are to be hated.
21" 'But you may eat certain insects that have
wings and walk on four feet. You may eat those
that have legs with joints above their feet so they
can jump. 22These are the insects you may eat: all
kinds of locusts, winged locusts, crickets, and
grasshoppers. 23But all other insects that have
wings and walk on four feet you are to hate.
24Those insects will make you unclean, and anyone who touches the dead body of one of these
insects will become unclean until evening. 25Any-
one who picks up one of these dead insects must
wash his clothes and be unclean until evening.
26" 'Some animals have split hoofs, but the
hoofs are not completely divided; others do not
chew the cud. They are unclean for you, and anyone who touches the dead body of one of these
animals will become unclean. 27Of all the animals
that walk on four feet, the animals that walk on
their paws are unclean for you. Anyone who
touches the dead body of one of these animals will
become unclean until evening. 28Anyone who
picks up their dead bodies must wash his clothes
and be unclean until evening; these animals are
unclean for you.
29" 'These crawling animals are unclean for

you: moles, rats, all kinds of great lizards, 30geckos, crocodiles, lizards, sand reptiles, and chameleons. 31These crawling animals are unclean for you; anyone who touches their dead bodies will be unclean until evening.

> **SIDELIGHT:** Ever have a craving for a leg o' lizard sandwich? If the Israelites did, they would have gone hungry. Their dietary laws forbade eating moles, rats, lizards, crocodiles, chameleons, and other slinky, slimy things (Leviticus 11:29–30). Many scholars believe this prohibition grew out of the fact that these animals transmitted diseases. Now there's a law we can live with!

32" 'If an unclean animal dies and falls on something, that item will also become unclean. This includes anything made from wood, cloth, leather, or rough cloth, regardless of its use. Whatever the animal falls on must be washed with water and be unclean until evening; then it will become clean again. 33If the dead, unclean animal falls into a clay bowl, anything in the bowl will become unclean, and you must break the bowl. 34If water from the unclean clay bowl gets on any food, that food will become unclean. 35If any dead, unclean animal falls on something, it becomes unclean. If it is a clay oven or a clay baking pan, it must be broken into pieces. These things will be unclean; they are unclean for you.

36" 'A spring or well that collects water will stay clean, but anyone who touches the dead body of any unclean animal will become unclean. 37If a dead, unclean animal falls on a seed to be planted, that seed is still clean. 38But if you put water on some seeds and a dead, unclean animal falls on them, they are unclean for you.

39" 'Also, if an animal which you use for food dies, anyone who touches its body will be unclean until evening. 40Anyone who eats meat from this animal's dead body must wash his clothes and be unclean until evening. Anyone who picks up the animal's dead body must wash his clothes and be unclean until evening.

41" 'Every animal that crawls on the ground is to be hated; it must not be eaten. 42You must not eat any of the animals that crawl on the ground, including those that crawl on their stomachs, that walk on all four feet, or on many feet. They are to be hated. 43Do not make yourself unclean by these animals; you must not become unclean by them. 44I am the LORD your God. Keep yourselves holy for me because I am holy. Don't make yourselves unclean with any of these crawling animals. 45I am the LORD who brought you out of Egypt to be your God; you must be holy because I am holy.

46" 'These are the teachings about all of the cattle, birds, and other animals on earth, as well as the animals in the sea and those that crawl on the ground. 47These teachings help people know the difference between unclean animals and clean animals; they help people know which animals may be eaten and which ones must not be eaten.' "

Rules for New Mothers

12 The LORD said to Moses, 2"Tell the people of Israel this: 'If a woman gives birth to a son, she will become unclean[d] for seven days, as she is unclean during her monthly period. 3On the eighth day the boy must be circumcised.[d] 4Then it will be thirty-three days before she becomes clean from her loss of blood. She must not touch anything that is holy or enter the Holy Tent until her time of cleansing is finished. 5But if she gives birth to a daughter, the mother will be unclean for two weeks, as she is unclean during her monthly period. It will be sixty-six days before she becomes clean from her loss of blood.

6" 'After she has a son or daughter and her days of cleansing are over, the new mother must bring certain sacrifices to the Meeting Tent.[d] She must give the priest at the entrance a year-old lamb for a burnt offering and a dove or young pigeon for a sin offering. 7He will offer them before the LORD to make her clean so she will belong to the LORD again; then she will be clean from her loss of blood. These are the teachings for a woman who gives birth to a boy or girl.

8" 'If she cannot afford a lamb, she is to bring two doves or two young pigeons, one for a burnt offering and one for a sin offering. In this way the priest will make her clean so she will belong to the LORD again, and she will be clean.' "

Rules About Skin Diseases

13 The LORD said to Moses and Aaron, 2"Someone might have on his skin a swelling or a rash or a bright spot. If the sore looks like a harmful skin disease, the person must be brought to Aaron the priest or to one of Aaron's sons, the priests. 3The priest must look at the sore on the person's skin. If the hair in the sore has become white, and the sore seems deeper than the person's skin, it is a harmful skin disease. When he has finished looking at the person, the priest must announce that the person is unclean.[d]

4"If there is a white spot on a person's skin, but the spot does not seem deeper than the skin, and if the hair from the spot has not turned white, the priest must separate that person from other people for seven days. 5On the seventh day the priest must look at the person again. If he sees that the

sore has not changed and it has not spread on the
skin, the priest must keep the person separated for
seven more days. 6On the seventh day the priest
must look at the person again. If the sore has
faded and has not spread on the skin, the priest
must announce that the person is clean. The sore
is only a rash. The person must wash his clothes,
and he will become clean again.

7"But if the rash spreads again after the priest
has announced him clean, the person must come
again to the priest. 8The priest must look at him,
and if the rash has spread on the skin, the priest
must announce that the person is unclean; it is a
harmful skin disease.

9"If a person has a harmful skin disease, he
must be brought to the priest, 10and the priest
must look at him. If there is a white swelling in
the skin, and the hair has become white, and the
skin looks raw in the swelling, 11it is a harmful
skin disease. It is one he has had for a long time.
The priest must announce that the person is unclean. He will not need to separate that person
from other people, because everyone already
knows that the person is unclean.

12"If the skin disease spreads all over a person's
body, covering his skin from his head to his feet,
as far as the priest can see, the priest must look
at the person's whole body. 13If the priest sees
that the disease covers the whole body and has
turned all of the person's skin white, he must announce that the person is clean.

14"But when the person has an open sore, he
is unclean. 15When the priest sees the open sore,
he must announce that the person is unclean. The
open sore is not clean; it is a harmful skin disease.
16If the open sore becomes white again, the person must come to the priest. 17The priest must
look at him, and if the sores have become white,
the priest must announce that the person with the
sores is clean. Then he will be clean.

18"Someone may have a boil on his skin that is
healed. 19If in the place where the boil was, there
is a white swelling or a bright red spot, this place
on the skin must be shown to the priest. 20And
the priest must look at it. If the spot seems deeper
than the skin and the hair on it has become white,
the priest must announce that the person is unclean. The spot is a harmful skin disease that has
broken out from inside the boil. 21But if the priest
looks at the spot and there are no white hairs in
it and the spot is not deeper than the skin and it
has faded, the priest must separate the person
from other people for seven days. 22If the spot
spreads on the skin, the priest must announce
that the person is unclean; it is a disease that will
spread. 23But if the bright spot does not spread
or change, it is only the scar from the old boil.
Then the priest must announce that the person is
clean.

24"When a person gets a burn on his skin, if the
open sore becomes white or red, 25the priest must
look at it. If the white spot seems deeper than the
skin and the hair at that spot has become white,
it is a harmful skin disease. The disease has broken out in the burn, and the priest must announce that the person is unclean. It is a harmful
skin disease. 26But if the priest looks at the spot
and there is no white hair in the bright spot, and
the spot is no deeper than the skin and has faded,
the priest must separate the person from other
people for seven days. 27On the seventh day the
priest must look at him again. If the spot has
spread on the skin, the priest must announce that
the person is unclean. It is a harmful skin disease.
28But if the bright spot has not spread on the skin
but has faded, it is the swelling from the burn.
The priest must announce that the person is
clean, because the spot is only a scar from the
burn.

29"When a man or a woman gets a sore on the
scalp or on the chin, 30a priest must look at the
sore. If it seems deeper than the skin and the hair
around it is thin and yellow, the priest must announce that the person is unclean. It is an itch, a
harmful skin disease of the head or chin. 31But if
the priest looks at it and it does not seem deeper
than the skin and there is no black hair in it, the
priest must separate the person from other people
for seven days. 32On the seventh day the priest
must look at the sore. If it has not spread, and
there are no yellow hairs growing in it, and the
sore does not seem deeper than the skin, 33the
person must shave himself, but he must not shave
the sore place. The priest must separate that person from other people for seven more days. 34On
the seventh day the priest must look at the sore.
If it has not spread on the skin and it does not
seem deeper than the skin, the priest must announce that the person is clean. So the person
must wash his clothes and become clean. 35But if
the sore spreads on the skin after the person has
become clean, 36the priest must look at him again.
If the sore has spread on the skin, the priest
doesn't need to look for the yellowish hair; the
person is unclean. 37But if the priest thinks the
sore has stopped spreading, and black hair is
growing in it, the sore has healed. The person
is clean, and the priest must announce that he is
clean.

38"When a man or a woman has white spots on
the skin, 39a priest must look at them. If the spots
on the skin are dull white, the disease is only a
harmless rash. That person is clean.

40"When anyone loses hair from his head and
is bald, he is clean. 41If he loses hair from the front
of his head and has a bald forehead, he is clean.
42But if there is a red-white sore on his bald head
or forehead, it is a skin disease breaking out in

those places. 43A priest must look at that person.
If the swelling of the sore on his bald head or
forehead is red-white, like a skin disease that
spreads, 44that person has a skin disease. He is
unclean. The priest must announce that the
person is unclean because of the sore on his
head.
45"If a person has a skin disease that spreads, he
must warn other people by shouting, 'Unclean,
unclean!' His clothes must be torn at the seams,
he must let his hair stay uncombed, and he must
cover his mouth. 46That person will be unclean
the whole time he has the disease; he is unclean.
He must live alone outside the camp.

Rules About Mildew

47"Clothing might have mildew[d] on it. It might
be clothing made of linen or wool 48(either woven
or knitted), or of leather, or something made from
leather. 49If the mildew in the clothing, leather, or
woven or knitted material is green or red, it is a
spreading mildew. It must be shown to the priest.
50The priest must look at the mildew, and he must
put that piece of clothing in a separate place for
seven days. 51On the seventh day he must look at
the mildew again. If the mildew has spread on the
cloth (either woven or knitted) or the leather, no
matter what the leather was used for, it is a mildew that destroys; it is unclean. 52The priest must
burn the clothing. It does not matter if it is woven
or knitted, wool or linen, or made of leather,
because the mildew is spreading. It must be
burned.
53"If the priest sees that the mildew has not
spread in the cloth (either knitted or woven) or
leather, 54he must order the people to wash that
piece of leather or cloth. Then he must separate
the clothing for seven more days. 55After the piece
with the mildew has been washed, the priest
must look at it again. If the mildew still looks the
same, the piece is unclean,[d] even if the mildew
has not spread. You must burn it in fire; it does
not matter if the mildew is on one side or the
other.
56"But when the priest looks at that piece of
leather or cloth, the mildew might have faded after the piece has been washed. Then the priest
must tear the mildew out of the piece of leather
or cloth (either woven or knitted). 57But if the
mildew comes back to that piece of leather or
cloth (either woven or knitted), the mildew is
spreading. And whatever has the mildew must be
burned with fire. 58When the cloth (either woven
or knitted) or the leather is washed and the mildew is gone, it must be washed again; then it will
be clean.
59"These are the teachings about mildew on
pieces of cloth (either woven or knitted) or
leather, to decide if they are clean or unclean."

Rules for Cleansing from Skin Diseases

14 The LORD said to Moses, 2"These are the
teachings for the time at which people
who had a harmful skin disease are made clean.[d]
"The person shall be brought to the priest, 3and
the priest must go outside the camp and look at
the one who had the skin disease. If the skin disease is healed, 4the priest will command that two
living, clean birds, a piece of cedar wood, a piece
of red string, and a hyssop plant be brought for
cleansing the person with the skin disease.
5"The priest must order one bird to be killed in
a clay bowl containing fresh water. 6Then he will
take the living bird, the piece of cedar wood, the
red string, and the hyssop; all these he will dip
into the blood of the bird that was killed over the
fresh water. 7The priest will sprinkle the blood
seven times on the person being cleansed from
the skin disease. He must announce that the person is clean and then go to an open field and let
the living bird go free.
8"The person to be cleansed must wash his
clothes, shave off all his hair, and bathe in water.
Then he will be clean and may go into the camp,
though he must stay outside his tent for the first
seven days. 9On the seventh day he must shave
off all his hair — the hair from his head, his beard,
his eyebrows, and the rest of his hair. He must
wash his clothes and bathe his body in water, and
he will be clean.
10"On the eighth day the person who had the
skin disease must take two male lambs that have
nothing wrong with them and a year-old female
lamb that has nothing wrong with it. He must also
take six quarts of fine flour mixed with oil for a
grain offering and two-thirds of a pint of olive oil.
11The priest who is to announce that the person
is clean must bring him and his sacrifices before
the LORD at the entrance of the Meeting Tent.[d]
12The priest will take one of the male lambs and
offer it with the olive oil as a penalty offering; he
will present them before the LORD as an offering.
13Then he will kill the male lamb in the holy
place, where the sin offering and the whole burnt
offering are killed. The penalty offering is like the
sin offering — it belongs to the priest and it is most
holy.
14"The priest will take some of the blood of the
penalty offering and put it on the bottom of the
right ear of the person to be made clean. He will
also put some of it on the thumb of the person's
right hand and on the big toe of the person's right
foot. 15Then the priest will take some of the oil
and pour it into his own left hand. 16He will dip
a finger of his right hand into the oil that is in his
left hand, and with his finger he will sprinkle
some of the oil seven times before the LORD.
17The priest will put some oil from his hand on the

bottom of the right ear of the person to be made
clean, some on the thumb of the person's right
hand, and some on the big toe of the person's
right foot. The oil will go on these places on top
of the blood for the penalty offering. 18He will put
the rest of the oil that is in his left hand on the
head of the person to be made clean. In this way
the priest will make that person clean so he can
belong to the LORD again.
19"Next the priest will offer the sin offering to
make that person clean so he can belong to the
LORD again. After this the priest will kill the animal for the whole burnt offering, 20and he will
offer the burnt offering and grain offering on the
altar. In this way he will make that person clean
so he can belong to the LORD again.
21"But if the person is poor and unable to afford
these offerings, he must take one male lamb for
a penalty offering. It will be presented to the LORD
to make him clean so he can belong to the LORD
again. The person must also take two quarts of
fine flour mixed with oil for a grain offering. He
must also take two-thirds of a pint of olive oil
22and two doves or two young pigeons, which he
can afford. One bird is for a sin offering and the
other for a whole burnt offering. 23On the eighth
day the person will bring them for his cleansing
to the priest at the entrance of the Meeting Tent,
before the LORD. 24The priest will take the lamb
for the penalty offering and the oil, and he will
present them as an offering before the LORD.
25Then he will kill the lamb of the penalty offering, take some of its blood, and put it on the bottom of the right ear of the person to be made
clean. The priest will put some of this blood on
the thumb of the person's right hand and some on
the big toe of the person's right foot. 26He will also
pour some of the oil into his own left hand.
27Then with a finger of his right hand, he will
sprinkle some of the oil from his left hand seven
times before the LORD. 28The priest will take some
of the oil from his hand and put it on the bottom
of the right ear of the person to be made clean. He
will also put some of it on the thumb of the person's right hand and some on the big toe of the
person's right foot. The oil will go on these places
on top of the blood from the penalty offering.
29The priest must put the rest of the oil that is in
his hand on the head of the person to be made
clean, to make him clean so he can belong to the
LORD again. 30Then the priest will offer one of the
doves or young pigeons, which the person can
afford. 31He must offer one of the birds for a sin
offering and the other for a whole burnt offering,
along with the grain offering. In this way the
priest will make the person clean so he can belong
to the LORD again; he will become clean.
32"These are the teachings for making a person clean after he has had a skin disease, if he
cannot afford the regular sacrifices for becoming
clean."

Rules for Cleaning Mildew

33The LORD also said to Moses and Aaron, 34"I
am giving the land of Canaan to your people.
When they enter that land, if I cause mildew[d] to
grow in someone's house in that land, 35the
owner of that house must come and tell the
priest. He should say, 'I have seen something like
mildew in my house.' 36Then the priest must order the people to empty the house before he goes
in to look at the mildew. This is so he will not
have to say that everything in the house is unclean.[d] After this, the priest will go in to look at
it. 37He will look at the mildew, and if the mildew
on the walls of the house is green or red and goes
into the wall's surface, 38he must go out and close
up the house for seven days. 39On the seventh day
the priest must come back and check the house.
If the mildew has spread on the walls of the
house, 40the priest must order the people to tear
out the stones with the mildew on them. They
should throw them away, at a certain unclean
place outside the city. 41Then the priest must have
all the inside of the house scraped. The people
must throw away the plaster they scraped off the
walls, at a certain unclean place outside the city.
42Then the owner must put new stones in the
walls, and he must cover the walls with new clay
plaster.
43"Suppose a person has taken away the old
stones and plaster and put in new stones and plaster. If mildew again appears in his house, 44the
priest must come back and check the house again.
If the mildew has spread in the house, it is a mildew that destroys things; the house is unclean.
45Then the owner must tear down the house, remove all its stones, plaster, and wood, and take
them to the unclean place outside the city. 46Any-
one who goes into that house while it is closed up
will be unclean until evening. 47Anyone who eats
in that house or lies down there must wash his
clothes.
48"Suppose after new stones and plaster have
been put in a house, the priest checks it again and
the mildew has not spread. Then the priest will

SIDELIGHT: The bathroom's dirty, and it's your job to clean it. You're out of cleanser. What do you do? Leviticus 14:33–45 gives a detailed process for cleaning mildew. Of course, your parents may not like you tearing out all the mildewy bricks—or tearing down the house.

announce that the house is clean, because the mildew is gone.

49“Then, to make the house clean, the priest must take two birds, a piece of cedar wood, a piece of red string, and a hyssop plant. 50He will kill one bird in a clay bowl containing fresh water. 51Then he will take the bird that is still alive, the cedar wood, the hyssop, and the red string, and he will dip them into the blood of the bird that was killed over the fresh water. The priest will sprinkle the blood on the house seven times. 52He will use the bird’s blood, the fresh water, the live bird, the cedar wood, the hyssop, and the red string to make the house clean. 53He will then go to an open field outside the city and let the living bird go free. This is how the priest makes the house clean and ready for service to the LORD.”

54These are the teachings about any kind of skin disease, 55mildew on pieces of cloth or in a house, 56swellings, rashes, or bright spots on the skin; 57they help people decide when things are unclean and when they are clean. These are the teachings about all these kinds of diseases.

Rules About a Person’s Body

15 The LORD also said to Moses and Aaron, 2“Say to the people of Israel: ‘When a fluid comes from a person’s body, the fluid is unclean.[d] 3It doesn’t matter if the fluid flows freely or if it is blocked from flowing; the fluid will make him unclean. This is the way the fluid makes him unclean:

4“ ‘If the person who discharges the body fluid lies on a bed, that bed becomes unclean, and everything he sits on becomes unclean. 5Anyone who touches his bed must wash his clothes and bathe in water, and the person will be unclean until evening. 6Whoever sits on something that the person who discharges the fluid sat on must wash his clothes and bathe in water; he will be unclean until evening. 7Anyone who touches the person who discharges the body fluid must wash his clothes and bathe in water; he will be unclean until evening.

8“ ‘If the person who discharges the body fluid spits on someone who is clean, that person must wash his clothes and bathe in water; he will be unclean until evening. 9Everything on which the person who is unclean sits when riding will become unclean. 10Anyone who touches something that was under him will be unclean until evening. And anyone who carries these things must wash his clothes and bathe in water; he will be unclean until evening.

11“ ‘If the person who discharges a body fluid has not washed his hands in water and touches another person, that person must wash his clothes and bathe in water; he will be unclean until evening.

12“ ‘If a person who discharges a body fluid touches a clay bowl, that bowl must be broken. If he touches a wooden bowl, that bowl must be washed in water.

13“ ‘When a person who discharges a body fluid is made clean, he must count seven days for himself for his cleansing. He must wash his clothes and bathe his body in fresh water, and he will be clean. 14On the eighth day he must take two doves or two young pigeons before the LORD at the entrance of the Meeting Tent.[d] He will give the two birds to the priest. 15The priest will offer the birds, one for a sin offering and the other for a burnt offering. And the priest will make that person clean so he can belong to the LORD again.

16“ ‘If semen[n] goes out from a man, he must bathe in water; he will be unclean until evening. 17If the fluid gets on any clothing or leather, it must be washed with water; it will be unclean until evening.

18“ ‘If a man has sexual relations with a woman and semen comes out, both people must bathe in water; they will be unclean until evening.

Rules About a Woman’s Body

19“ ‘When a woman has her monthly period, she is unclean[d] for seven days; anyone who touches her will be unclean until evening. 20Anything she lies on during this time will be unclean, and everything she sits on during this time will be unclean. 21Anyone who touches her bed must wash his clothes and bathe in water; that person will be unclean until evening. 22Anyone who touches something she has sat on must wash his clothes and bathe in water; that person will be unclean until evening. 23It does not matter if the person touched the woman’s bed or something she sat on; he will be unclean until evening.

24“ ‘If a man has sexual relations with a woman and her monthly period touches him, he will be unclean for seven days; every bed he lies on will be unclean.

25“ ‘If a woman has a loss of blood for many days and it is not during her regular monthly period, or if she continues to have a loss of blood after her regular period, she will be unclean, as she is during her monthly period. She will be unclean for as long as she continues to bleed. 26Any bed she lies on during all the time of her bleeding will be like her bed during her regular monthly period. Everything she sits on will be unclean, as during her regular monthly period.

27“ ‘Whoever touches those things will be unclean and must wash his clothes and bathe in water; he will be unclean until evening. 28When the

semen A man’s body fluid by which he can make a woman pregnant.

woman becomes clean from her bleeding, she
must wait seven days, and after this she will be
clean. 29Then on the eighth day she must take
two doves or two young pigeons and bring them
to the priest at the entrance of the Meeting Tent.[d]
30The priest must offer one bird for a sin offering
and the other for a whole burnt offering. In this
way the priest will make her clean so she can belong to the LORD again.
31" 'So you must warn the people of Israel to
stay separated from things that make them unclean. If you don't warn the people, they might
make my Holy Tent[d] unclean, and then they
would have to die!' "
32These are the teachings for the person who
discharges a body fluid and for the man who becomes unclean from semen[n] coming out of his
body. 33These are the teachings for the woman
who becomes unclean from her monthly period,
for a man or woman who has a discharge, and for
a man who becomes unclean by having sexual
relations with a woman who is unclean.

The Day of Cleansing

16 Now two of Aaron's sons had died while
offering incense[d] to the LORD, and after
that time the LORD spoke to Moses. 2The LORD
said to him, "Tell your brother Aaron that there
are times when he cannot go behind the curtain
into the Most Holy Place where the Ark[d] is. If he
goes in when I appear in a cloud over the lid on
the Ark, he will die.
3"This is how Aaron may enter the Most Holy
Place: Before he enters, he must offer a bull for
a sin offering and a male sheep for a whole burnt
offering. 4He must put on the holy linen inner
robe, with the linen underclothes next to his
body. His belt will be the cloth belt, and he will
wear the linen turban. These are holy clothes, so
he must bathe his body in water before he puts
them on.
5"Aaron must take from the people of Israel
two male goats for a sin offering and one male
sheep for a burnt offering. 6Then he will offer the
bull for the sin offering for himself to remove sins
from him and his family so they will belong to the
LORD.
7"Next Aaron will take the two goats and bring
them before the LORD at the entrance to the
Meeting Tent.[d] 8He will throw lots[d] for the two
goats — one will be for the LORD and the other for
the goat that removes sin. 9Then Aaron will take
the goat that was chosen for the LORD by throwing the lot, and he will offer it as a sin offering.
10The other goat, which was chosen by lot to remove the sin, must be brought alive before the
LORD. The priest will use it to perform the acts
that remove Israel's sin so they will belong to the
LORD. Then this goat will be sent out into the
desert as a goat that removes sin.
11"Then Aaron will offer the bull as a sin offering for himself, to remove the sins from him and
his family so they will belong to the LORD; he will
kill the bull for the sin offering for himself. 12Then
he must take a pan full of burning coals from the
altar before the LORD and two handfuls of sweet
incense that has been ground into powder. He
must bring it into the room behind the curtain.
13He must put the incense on the fire before the
LORD so that the cloud of incense will cover the
lid on the Ark. Then when Aaron comes in, he
will not die. 14Also, he must take some of the
blood from the bull and sprinkle it with his finger
on the front of the lid; with his finger he will
sprinkle the blood seven times in front of the lid.
15"Then Aaron must kill the goat of the sin offering for the people and bring its blood into the
room behind the curtain. He must do with the
goat's blood as he did with the bull's blood, sprinkling it on the lid and in front of the lid. 16Because
the people of Israel have been unclean,[d] Aaron
will perform the acts to make the Most Holy Place
ready for service to the LORD. Then it will be
clean from the sins and crimes of the Israelites. He
must also do this for the Meeting Tent, because
it stays in the middle of unclean people. 17When
Aaron makes the Most Holy Place ready for service to the LORD, no one is allowed in the Meeting Tent until he comes out. So Aaron will perform the acts to remove sins from himself, his
family, and all the people of Israel, so they will
belong to the LORD. 18Afterward he will go out to
the altar that is before the LORD and will make it
ready for service to the LORD. Aaron will take
some of the bull's blood and some of the goat's
blood and put it on the corners of the altar on all
sides. 19Then, with his finger, he will sprinkle
some of the blood on the altar seven times to
make the altar holy for the LORD and clean from
all the sins of the Israelites.
20"When Aaron has finished making the Most
Holy Place, the Meeting Tent, and the altar ready
for service to the LORD, he will offer the living
goat. 21He will put both his hands on the head of
the living goat, and he will confess over it all the
sins and crimes of Israel. In this way Aaron will
put the people's sins on the goat's head. Then he
will send the goat away into the desert, and a man
who has been appointed will lead the goat away.
22So the goat will carry on itself all the people's
sins to a lonely place in the desert. The man who
leads the goat will let it loose there.
23"Then Aaron will enter the Meeting Tent and
take off the linen clothes he had put on before he

semen A man's body fluid by which he can make a woman pregnant.

went into the Most Holy Place; he must leave
these clothes there. 24He will bathe his body in
water in a holy place and put on his regular
clothes. Then he will come out and offer the
whole burnt offering for himself and for the people, to remove sins from himself and the people
so they will belong to the LORD. 25Then he will
burn the fat of the sin offering on the altar.

26"The person who led the goat, the goat to
remove sins, into the desert must wash his clothes
and bathe his body in water. After that, he may
come back into the camp.

27"The bull and the goat for the sin offerings,
whose blood was brought into the Most Holy
Place to make it ready for service to the LORD,
must be taken outside the camp; the animals'
skins, bodies, and intestines will be burned in the
fire. 28Then the one who burns them must wash
his clothes and bathe his body in water. After that,
he may come back into the camp.

29"This law will always continue for you: On
the tenth day of the seventh month, you must not
eat and you must not do any work. The travelers
or foreigners living with you must not work either. 30It is on this day that the priests will make
you clean so you will belong to the LORD again.
All your sins will be removed. 31This is a very important day of rest for you, and you must not eat.
This law will continue forever.

32"The priest appointed to take his father's
place, on whom the oil was poured, will perform
the acts for making things ready for service to the
LORD. He must put on the holy linen clothes 33and
make the Most Holy Place, the Meeting Tent, and
the altar ready for service to the LORD. He must
also remove the sins of the priests and all the people of Israel so they will belong to the LORD.
34That law for removing the sins of the Israelites
so they will belong to the LORD will continue forever. You will do these things once a year."

So they did the things the LORD had commanded Moses.

Offering Sacrifices

17 The LORD said to Moses, 2"Speak to
Aaron, his sons, and all the people of Israel. Tell them: 'This is what the LORD has commanded. 3If an Israelite kills an ox, a lamb, or a
goat either inside the camp or outside it, 4when
he should have brought the animal to the entrance of the Meeting Tent[d] as a gift to the LORD
in front of the LORD's Holy Tent, he is guilty of
killing. He has killed, and he must be cut off from
the people. 5This rule is so people will bring their
sacrifices, which they have been sacrificing in the
open fields, to the LORD. They must bring those
animals to the LORD at the entrance of the Meeting Tent; they must bring them to the priest and
offer them as fellowship offerings. 6Then the
priest will sprinkle the blood from those animals
on the LORD's altar near the entrance of the Meeting Tent. And he will burn the fat from those animals on the altar, as a smell pleasing to the LORD.
7They must not offer any more sacrifices to their
goat idols, which they have chased like prostitutes.[d] These rules will continue for people from
now on.'

8"Tell the people this: 'If any citizen of Israel or
foreigner living with you offers a burnt offering or
sacrifice, 9that person must take his sacrifice to
the entrance of the Meeting Tent to offer it to the
LORD. If he does not do this, he must be cut off
from the people.

10" 'I will be against any citizen of Israel or foreigner living with you who eats blood. I will cut
off that person from the people. 11This is because
the life of the body is in the blood, and I have
given you rules for pouring that blood on the altar
to remove your sins so you will belong to the
LORD. It is the blood that removes the sins, because it is life. 12So I tell the people of Israel this:
"None of you may eat blood, and no foreigner
living among you may eat blood."

13" 'If any citizen of Israel or foreigner living
among you catches a wild animal or bird that can
be eaten, that person must pour the blood on the
ground and cover it with dirt. 14If blood is still in
the meat, the animal's life is still in it. So I give
this command to the people of Israel: "Don't eat
meat that still has blood in it, because the animal's
life is in its blood. Anyone who eats blood must
be cut off."

15" 'If a person, either a citizen or a foreigner,
eats an animal that died by itself or was killed by
another animal, he must wash his clothes and
bathe in water. He will be unclean until evening;
then he will be clean. 16If he does not wash his
clothes and bathe his body, he will be guilty of
sin.' "

Rules About Sexual Relations

18 The LORD said to Moses, 2"Tell the people of Israel: 'I am the LORD your God.
3In the past you lived in Egypt, but you must not
do what was done in that country. And you must
not do as they do in the land of Canaan, where
I am bringing you. Do not follow their customs.
4You must obey my rules and follow them. I am
the LORD your God. 5Obey my laws and rules; a
person who obeys them will live because of them.
I am the LORD.

6" 'You must never have sexual relations with
your close relatives. I am the LORD.

7" 'You must not shame your father by having
sexual relations with your mother. She is your
mother; do not have sexual relations with her.
8You must not have sexual relations with your
father's wife; that would shame your father.

9“ ‘You must not have sexual relations with
your sister, either the daughter of your father
or your mother. It doesn’t matter if she was born
in your house or somewhere else.

10“ ‘You must not have sexual relations with
your son’s daughter or your daughter’s daughter;
that would bring shame on you.

11“ ‘If your father and his wife have a daughter,
she is your sister. You must not have sexual relations with her.

12“ ‘You must not have sexual relations with
your father’s sister; she is your father’s close relative. 13You must not have sexual relations with
your mother’s sister; she is your mother’s close
relative. 14You must not have sexual relations
with the wife of your father’s brother, because
this would shame him. She is your aunt.

15“ ‘You must not have sexual relations with
your daughter-in-law; she is your son’s wife. Do
not have sexual relations with her.

16“ ‘You must not have sexual relations with
your brother’s wife. That would shame your
brother.

17“ ‘You must not have sexual relations with
both a woman and her daughter. And do not have
sexual relations with this woman’s granddaughter, either the daughter of her son or her daughter; they are her close relatives. It is evil to do this.

18“ ‘While your wife is still living, you must not
take her sister as another wife. Do not have sexual
relations with her.

19“ ‘You must not go near a woman to have
sexual relations with her during her monthly period, when she is unclean.[d]

20“ ‘You must not have sexual relations with
your neighbor’s wife and make yourself unclean
with her.

21“ ‘You must not give any of your children to
be sacrificed to Molech,[d] because this would
show that you do not respect your God. I am the
LORD.

22“ ‘You must not have sexual relations with a
man as you would a woman. That is a hateful sin.

23“ ‘You must not have sexual relations with an
animal and make yourself unclean with it. Also a
woman must not have sexual relations with an
animal; it is not natural.

24“ ‘Don’t make yourself unclean by any of
these wrong things. I am forcing nations out of
their countries because they did these sins, and I
am giving their land to you. 25The land has become unclean, and I punished it for its sins, so the
land is throwing out those people who live there.

26“ ‘You must obey my laws and rules, and you
must not do any of these hateful sins. These rules
are for the citizens of Israel and for the people
who live with you. 27The people who lived in the
land before you did all these hateful things and
made the land unclean. 28If you do these things,
you will also make the land unclean, and it will
throw you out as it threw out the nations before
you. 29Anyone who does these hateful sins must
be cut off from the people. 30Keep my command
not to do these hateful sins that were done by the
people who lived in the land before you. Don’t
make yourself unclean by doing them. I am the
LORD your God.’ ”

Other Laws

19 The LORD said to Moses, 2“Tell all the
people of Israel: ‘I am the LORD your
God. You must be holy because I am holy.

3“ ‘You must respect your mother and father,
and you must keep my Sabbaths.[d] I am the LORD
your God.

4“ ‘Do not worship idols or make statues or
gods for yourselves. I am the LORD your God.

5“ ‘When you sacrifice a fellowship offering to
the LORD, offer it in such a way that will be accepted. 6You may eat it the same day you offer it
or on the next day. But if any is left on the third
day, you must burn it up. 7If any of it is eaten on
the third day, it is unclean,[d] and it will not be
accepted. 8Anyone who eats it then will be guilty
of sin, because he did not respect the holy things
that belong to the LORD. He must be cut off from
the people.

9“ ‘When you harvest your crops on your land,
do not harvest all the way to the corners of your
fields. If grain falls onto the ground, don’t gather
it up. 10Don’t pick all the grapes in your vineyards,
and don’t pick up the grapes that fall to the
ground. You must leave those things for poor people and for people traveling through your country.
I am the LORD your God.

SIDELIGHT: They may not have had government welfare programs to help the poor in Old Testament times, but the Israelites were careful to take care of the poor. Farmers were told to leave grain in their field so that poor people and travelers would have something to eat (Leviticus 19:9–10). The story of Ruth (Ruth 2:2–9, p. 240) illustrates a time when someone used this law that provides for outsiders.

11“ ‘You must not steal. You must not cheat
people, and you must not lie to each other. 12You
must not make a false promise by my name, or
you will show that you don’t respect your God. I
am the LORD.

13“ ‘You must not cheat your neighbor or rob
him. You must not keep a hired worker’s salary

all night until morning. 14You must not curse a
deaf person or put something in front of a blind
person to make him fall. But you must respect
your God. I am the LORD.

15" 'Be fair in your judging. You must not show
special favor to poor people or great people, but
be fair when you judge your neighbor. 16You must
not spread false stories against other people, and
you must not do anything that would put your
neighbor's life in danger. I am the LORD.

17" 'You must not hate your fellow citizen in
your heart. If your neighbor does something
wrong, tell him about it, or you will be partly to
blame. 18Forget about the wrong things people do
to you, and do not try to get even. Love your
neighbor as you love yourself. I am the LORD.

19" 'Obey my laws. You must not mate two different kinds of cattle or sow your field with two
different kinds of seed. You must not wear clothing made from two different kinds of material
mixed together.

20" 'If a man has sexual relations with a slave
girl of another man, but this slave girl has not
been bought or given her freedom, there must be
punishment. But they are not to be put to death,
because the woman was not free. 21The man must
bring a male sheep as his penalty offering to the
LORD at the entrance to the Meeting Tent.[d] 22The
priest will offer the sheep as a penalty offering
before the LORD for the man's sin, to remove the
sins of the man so he will belong to the LORD.
Then he will be forgiven for his sin.

23" 'In the future, when you enter your country, you will plant many kinds of trees for food.
After planting a tree, wait three years before using
its fruit. 24In the fourth year the fruit from the tree
will be the LORD's, a holy offering of praise to him.
25Then in the fifth year, you may eat the fruit from

HONESTY

The Cover-Up

At first, Rick Johnson was reluctant. "I don't think it's a good idea to take this stuff from stores," he would tell his friends.

"It's no big deal," they would respond. "You're not taking much. Besides, they charge too much for this stuff."

Gradually, Rick joined the shoplifting sprees. Soon he was an expert.

Each time Rick brought something home, his parents would ask about it. "I bought it with my paper route money," he would lie. Or, "A friend gave it to me." Or, "I've had it for a long time."

He really didn't feel guilty about the lying or the shoplifting. "It was just a game—a challenge not to get caught," he recalls. "I thought I could ask God for forgiveness every time I took something, and God would wipe my slate clean again."

One day Rick let the truth slip. He gave his younger brother, Kevin, a stolen watch and bragged about how he had gotten it. Kevin told their parents, who made Rick return everything he had stolen—two hundred dollars worth.

At first Rick was angry with Kevin for telling, but soon he understood how telling the truth and getting caught were the best things that could have happened. Why? Because they made him realize he was wrong. And he never shoplifted again.

Rick finally understood that being honest is best for everyone, a point that's clear in **Leviticus 19:1–18**, particularly verses 11–16. Read God's commandments about getting along with other people.

- Which verses in the passage would have helped Rick avoid shoplifting and lying? How did his dishonesty go against verse 18?
- How could the honesty demanded in this passage help your relationships with people around you, and your relationship with God?

CONSIDER. . .

- underlining the "do not" and "you must not" commands in the passage that are most difficult for you to follow.
- going to a friend or family member and "coming clean" on something you've lied or misled others about.

FOR MORE, SEE. . .

- Proverbs 11:1–3 (p. 576)
- Matthew 5:33–37 (p. 915)
- Acts 5:1–11 (p. 1104)

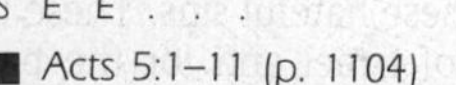

the tree. The tree will then produce more fruit for
you. I am the LORD your God.
26“ ‘You must not eat anything with the blood
in it.
“ ‘You must not try to tell the future by signs
or black magic.
27“ ‘You must not cut the hair on the sides of
your heads or cut the edges of your beard. 28You
must not cut your body to show sadness for someone who died or put tattoo marks on yourselves.
I am the LORD.
29“ ‘Do not dishonor your daughter by making
her become a prostitute.[d] If you do this, the country will be filled with all kinds of sin.
30“ ‘Obey the laws about Sabbaths, and respect
my Most Holy Place. I am the LORD.
31“ ‘Do not go to mediums[d] or fortune-tellers
for advice, or you will become unclean. I am the
LORD your God.
32“ ‘Show respect to old people; stand up in
their presence. Show respect also to your God. I
am the LORD.
33“ ‘Do not mistreat foreigners living in your
country, 34but treat them just as you treat your
own citizens. Love foreigners as you love yourselves, because you were foreigners one time in
Egypt. I am the LORD your God.
35“ ‘Do not cheat when you measure the length
or weight or amount of something. 36Your
weights and balances should weigh correctly,
with your weighing baskets the right size and
your jars holding the right amount of liquid. I am
the LORD your God. I brought you out of the land
of Egypt.
37“ ‘Remember all my laws and rules, and obey
them. I am the LORD.’ ”

Warnings About Various Sins

20 The LORD said to Moses, 2“You must
also tell the people of Israel these things:
‘If a person in your country gives one of his children to Molech,[d] that person must be killed. It
doesn’t matter if he is a citizen or a foreigner living in Israel; you must throw stones at him and
kill him. 3I will be against him and cut him off
from his people, because he gave his children to
Molech. He showed that he did not respect my
holy name, and he made my Holy Place unclean.[d]
4The people of the community might ignore that
person and not kill the one who gave his children
to Molech. 5But I will be against him and his family, and I will cut him off from his people. I will
do this to anyone who follows him in being unfaithful to me by worshiping Molech.
6“ ‘I will be against anyone who goes to mediums[d] and fortune-tellers for advice, because that
person is being unfaithful to me. So I will cut him
off from his people.
7“ ‘Be my holy people. Be holy because I am
the LORD your God. 8Remember and obey my
laws. I am the LORD, and I have made you holy.
9“ ‘Anyone who curses his father or mother
must be put to death. He has cursed his father or
mother, so he has brought his own death on himself.

Punishments for Sexual Sins

10“ ‘If a man has sexual relations with his
neighbor’s wife, both the man and the woman are
guilty of adultery[d] and must be put to death. 11If
a man has sexual relations with his father’s wife,
he has shamed his father, and both the man and
his father’s wife must be put to death. They have
brought it on themselves.
12“ ‘If a man has sexual relations with his
daughter-in-law, both of them must be put to
death. What they have done is not natural. They
have brought their own deaths on themselves.
13“ ‘If a man has sexual relations with another
man as a man does with a woman, these two men
have done a hateful sin. They must be put to
death. They have brought it on themselves.
14“ ‘If a man has sexual relations with both a
woman and her mother, this is evil. The people
must burn that man and the two women in fire
so that your people will not be evil.
15“ ‘If a man has sexual relations with an animal, he must be put to death. You must also kill
the animal. 16If a woman approaches an animal
and has sexual relations with it, you must kill the
woman and the animal. They must be put to
death. They have brought it on themselves.
17“ ‘It is shameful for a brother to marry his sister, the daughter of either his father or his
mother, and to have sexual relations with her. In
front of everyone they must both be cut off from
their people. The man has shamed his sister, and
he is guilty of sin.
18“ ‘If a man has sexual relations with a woman
during her monthly period, both the woman and
the man must be cut off from their people. They
sinned because they showed the source of her
blood.
19“ ‘Do not have sexual relations with your
mother’s sister or your father’s sister, because that
would shame a close relative. Both of you are
guilty of this sin.
20“ ‘If a man has sexual relations with his uncle’s wife, he has shamed his uncle. That man and
his uncle’s wife will die without children; they
are guilty of sin.
21“ ‘It is unclean for a man to marry his
brother’s wife. That man has shamed his brother,
and they will have no children.
22“ ‘Remember all my laws and rules, and obey
them. I am leading you to your own land, and if
you obey my laws and rules, that land will not
throw you out. 23I am forcing out ahead of you the

people who live there. Because they did all these sins, I have hated them. Do not live the way those people lived.

24" 'I have told you that you will get their land, which I will give to you as your very own; it is a fertile land. I am the LORD your God, and I have set you apart from other people and made you my own. 25So you must treat clean animals and birds differently from unclean animals and birds. Do not make yourselves unclean by any of these unclean birds or animals or things that crawl on the ground, which I have made unclean for you. 26So you must be holy to me because I, the LORD, am holy, and I have set you apart from other people to be my own.

27" 'A man or woman who is a medium[d] or a fortune-teller must be put to death. You must stone them to death; they have brought it on themselves.' "

How Priests Must Behave

21 The LORD said to Moses, "Tell these things to Aaron's sons, the priests: 'A priest must not make himself unclean[d] by touching a dead person. 2But if the dead person was one of his close relatives, he may touch him. The priest may make himself unclean if the dead person is his mother or father, son or daughter, brother or 3unmarried sister who is close to him because she has no husband. The priest may make himself unclean for her if she dies. 4But a priest must not make himself unclean if the dead person was only related to him by marriage.

5" 'Priests must not shave their heads, or shave off the edges of their beards, or cut their bodies. 6They must be holy to their God and show respect for God's name, because they present the offerings made by fire to the LORD, which is the food of their God. So they must be holy.

7" 'A priest must not marry an unclean prostitute[d] or a divorced woman, because he is holy to his God. 8Treat him as holy, because he offers up the food of your God. Think of him as holy; I am the LORD who makes you holy, and I am holy.

9" 'If a priest's daughter makes herself unclean by becoming a prostitute, she shames her father. She must be burned with fire.

10" 'The high priest, who was chosen from among his brothers, had the special olive oil poured on his head. He was also appointed to wear the priestly clothes. So he must not show his sadness by letting his hair go uncombed or tearing his clothes. 11He must not go into a house where there is a dead body. He must not make himself unclean, even if it is for his own father or mother. 12The high priest must not go out of the Holy Place, because if he does and becomes unclean, he will make God's Holy Place unclean. The special oil used in appointing priests was poured on his head to separate him from the rest of the people. I am the LORD.

13" 'The high priest must marry a woman who is a virgin.[d] 14He must not marry a widow, a divorced woman, or a prostitute. He must marry a virgin from his own people 15so the people will respect his children as his own. I am the LORD. I have set the high priest apart for his special job.' "

16The LORD said to Moses, 17"Tell Aaron: 'If any of your descendants[d] have something wrong with them, they must never come near to offer the special food of their God. 18Anyone who has something wrong with him must not come near: blind men, crippled men, men with damaged faces, deformed men, 19men with a crippled foot or hand, 20hunchbacks, dwarfs, men who have something wrong with their eyes, men who have an itching disease or a skin disease, or men who have damaged sex glands.

21" 'If one of Aaron's descendants[d] has something wrong with him, he cannot come near to make the offerings made by fire to the LORD. He has something wrong with him; he cannot offer the food of his God. 22He may eat the most holy food and also the holy food. 23But he may not go through the curtain into the Most Holy Place, and he may not go near the altar, because he has something wrong with him. He must not make my Holy Place unfit. I am the LORD who makes these places holy.' "

24So Moses told these things to Aaron, Aaron's sons, and all the people of Israel.

22 The LORD said to Moses, 2"Tell Aaron and his sons: 'The people of Israel will give offerings to me. These offerings are holy, and they are mine, so you must respect them to show that you respect my holy name. I am the LORD. 3Say to them: If any one of your descendants[d] from now on is unclean[d] and comes near the offerings that the Israelites made holy for me, that person must be cut off from appearing before me. I am the LORD.

4" 'If one of Aaron's descendants has a harmful skin disease, or if he discharges a body fluid, he cannot eat the holy offerings until he becomes clean. He could also become unclean from touching a dead body, from his own semen,[n] 5from touching any unclean crawling animal, or from touching an unclean person (no matter what made the person unclean). 6Anyone who touches those things will become unclean until evening. That person must not eat the holy offerings unless he washes with water. 7He will be clean only after the sun goes down. Then he may eat the holy offerings; the offerings are his food.

semen A man's body fluid by which he can make a woman pregnant.

8“ ‘If a priest finds an animal that died by itself
or that was killed by some other animal, he must
not eat it. If he does, he will become unclean. I
am the LORD.
9“ ‘If the priests keep all the rules I have given,
they will not become guilty; if they are careful,
they will not die. I am the LORD who has made
them holy. 10Only people in a priest’s family may
eat the holy offering. A visitor staying with the
priest or a hired worker must not eat it. 11But if
the priest buys a slave with his own money, that
slave may eat the holy offerings; slaves who were
born in his house may also eat his food. 12If a
priest’s daughter marries a person who is not a
priest, she must not eat any of the holy offerings.
13But if the priest’s daughter becomes widowed or
divorced, with no children to support her, and if
she goes back to her father’s house where she
lived as a child, she may eat some of her father’s
food. But only people from a priest’s family may
eat this food.
14“ ‘If someone eats some of the holy offering
by mistake, that person must pay back the priest
for that holy food, adding another one-fifth of the
price of that food.
15“ ‘When the Israelites give their holy offerings to the LORD, the priest must not treat these
holy things as though they were not holy. 16The
priests must not allow those who are not priests
to eat the holy offerings. If they do, they cause the
ones who eat the holy offerings to become guilty,
and they will have to pay for it. I am the LORD,
who makes them holy.’ ”
17The LORD said to Moses, 18“Tell Aaron and
his sons and all the people of Israel: ‘A citizen of
Israel or a foreigner living in Israel might want to
bring a whole burnt offering, either for some special promise he has made or for a special gift he
wants to give to the LORD. 19If he does, he must
bring a male animal that has nothing wrong with
it—a bull, a sheep, or a goat—so it might be accepted for him. 20He must not bring an animal
that has something wrong with it, or it will not be
accepted for him.
21“ ‘If someone brings a fellowship offering to
the LORD, either as payment for a special promise
the person has made or as a special gift the person
wants to give the LORD, it might be from the herd
or from the flock. But it must be healthy, with
nothing wrong with it, so that it will be accepted.
22You must not offer to the LORD any animal that
is blind, that has broken bones or is crippled, that
has running sores or any sort of skin disease. You
must not offer any animals like these on the altar
as an offering by fire to the LORD.
23“ ‘If an ox or lamb is smaller than normal or
is not perfectly formed, you may give it as a special gift to the LORD; it will be accepted. But it will
not be accepted as payment for a special promise
you have made.
24“ ‘If an animal has bruised, crushed, torn, or
cut sex glands, you must not offer it to the LORD.
You must not do this in your own land, 25and you
must not take such animals from foreigners as sacrifices to the LORD. Because the animals have
been hurt in some way and have something
wrong with them, they will not be accepted for
you.’ ”
26The LORD said to Moses, 27“When an ox, a
sheep, or a goat is born, it must stay seven days
with its mother. But from the eighth day on, this
animal will be accepted as a sacrifice by fire to the
LORD. 28But you must not kill the animal and its
mother on the same day, either an ox or a sheep.
29“If you want to offer some special offering of
thanks to the LORD, you must do it in a way that
pleases him. 30You must eat the whole animal that
same day and not leave any of the meat for the
next morning. I am the LORD.
31“Remember my commands and obey them; I
am the LORD. 32Show respect for my holy name.
You Israelites must remember that I am holy; I am
the LORD, who has made you holy. 33I brought
you out of Egypt to be your God. I am the LORD.”

Special Holidays

23 The LORD said to Moses, 2“Tell the people of Israel: ‘You will announce the
LORD’s appointed feasts as holy meetings. These
are my special feasts.

The Sabbath

3“ ‘There are six days for you to work, but the
seventh day will be a special day of rest. It is a day
for a holy meeting; you must not do any work. It
is a Sabbath[d] to the LORD in all your homes.

The Passover and Unleavened Bread

4“ ‘These are the LORD’s appointed feasts, the
holy meetings, which you will announce at the
times set for them. 5The LORD’s Passover[d] is on
the fourteenth day of the first month, beginning
at twilight. 6The Feast[d] of Unleavened Bread begins on the fifteenth day of the same month. You
will eat bread made without yeast for seven days.
7On the first day of this feast you will have a holy
meeting, and you must not do any work. 8For
seven days you will bring an offering made by fire
to the LORD. There will be a holy meeting on the
seventh day, and on that day you must not do any
regular work.’ ”

The First of the Harvest

9The LORD said to Moses, 10“Tell the people of
Israel: ‘You will enter the land I will give you and
gather its harvest. At that time you must bring the
first bundle of grain from your harvest to the

priest. 11The priest will present the bundle before the LORD, and it will be accepted for you; he will present the bundle on the day after the Sabbath.[d]

12" 'On the day when you present the bundle of grain, offer a male lamb, one year old, that has nothing wrong with it, as a burnt offering to the LORD. 13You must also offer a grain offering—four quarts of fine flour mixed with olive oil as an offering made by fire to the LORD; its smell will be pleasing to him. You must also offer a quart of wine as a drink offering. 14Until the day you bring your offering to your God, do not eat any new grain, roasted grain, or bread made from new grain. This law will always continue for people from now on, wherever you live.

The Feast of Weeks

15" 'Count seven full weeks from the morning after the Sabbath.[d] (This is the Sabbath that you bring the bundle of grain to present as an offering.) 16On the fiftieth day, the first day after the seventh week, you will bring a new grain offering to the LORD. 17On that day bring two loaves of bread from your homes to be presented as an offering. Use yeast and four quarts of flour to make those loaves of bread; they will be your gift to the LORD from the first wheat of your harvest.

18" 'Offer with the bread one young bull, two male sheep, and seven male lambs that are one year old and have nothing wrong with them. Offer them with their grain offerings and drink offerings, as a burnt offering to the LORD. They will be an offering made by fire, and the smell will be pleasing to the LORD. 19You must also offer one male goat for a sin offering and two male, one-year-old lambs as a fellowship offering.

20" 'The priest will present the two lambs as an offering before the LORD, along with the bread from the first wheat of the harvest. They are holy to the LORD, and they will belong to the priest. 21On that same day you will call a holy meeting; you must not do any work that day. This law will continue for you from now on, wherever you live.

22" 'When you harvest your crops on your land, do not harvest all the way to the corners of your field. If grain falls onto the ground, don't gather it up. Leave it for poor people and foreigners in your country. I am the LORD your God.' "

The Feast of Trumpets

23Again the LORD said to Moses, 24"Tell the people of Israel: 'On the first day of the seventh month you must have a special day of rest, a holy meeting, when you blow the trumpet for a special time of remembering. 25Do not do any work, and bring an offering made by fire to the LORD.' "

The Day of Cleansing

26The LORD said to Moses, 27"The Day of Cleansing will be on the tenth day of the seventh month. There will be a holy meeting, and you will give up eating and bring an offering made by fire to the LORD. 28Do not do any work on that day, because it is the Day of Cleansing. On that day the priests will go before the LORD and perform the acts to make you clean[d] so you will belong to the LORD.

29"Anyone who refuses to give up food on this day must be cut off from the people. 30If anyone works on this day, I will destroy that person from among the people. 31You must not do any work at all; this law will continue for people from now on wherever you live. 32It will be a special day of rest for you, and you must not eat. You will start this special day of rest on the evening after the ninth day of the month, and it will continue from that evening until the next evening."

The Feast of Shelters

33Again the LORD said to Moses, 34"Tell the people of Israel: 'On the fifteenth day of the seventh month is the Feast[d] of Shelters. This feast to the LORD will continue for seven days. 35There will be a holy meeting on the first day; do not do any work. 36You will bring an offering made by fire to the LORD each day for seven days. On the eighth day you will have another holy meeting, and you will bring an offering made by fire to the LORD. This will be a holy meeting; do not do any work.

37(" 'These are the LORD's special feasts, when there will be holy meetings and when you bring offerings made by fire to the LORD. You will bring whole burnt offerings, grain offerings, sacrifices, and drink offerings—each at the right time. 38These offerings are in addition to those for the LORD's Sabbath[d] days, in addition to offerings you give as payment for special promises, and in addition to special offerings you want to give to the LORD.)

39" 'So on the fifteenth day of the seventh month, after you have gathered in the crops of the land, celebrate the LORD's festival for seven days. You must rest on the first day and the eighth day. 40On the first day you will take good fruit from the fruit trees, as well as branches from palm trees, poplars, and other leafy trees. You will celebrate before the LORD your God for seven days. 41Celebrate this festival to the LORD for seven days each year. This law will continue from now on; you will celebrate it in the seventh month. 42Live in shelters for seven days. All the people born in Israel must live in shelters 43so that all your descendants[d] will know I made Israel live in shelters during the time I brought them out of Egypt. I am the LORD your God.' "

44So Moses told the people of Israel about all of the LORD's appointed feast days.

The Lampstand and the Holy Bread

24 The Lord said to Moses, 2“Command
the people of Israel to bring you pure oil
from crushed olives. That oil is for the lamps so
that these lamps may never go out. 3Aaron will
keep the lamps burning in the Meeting Tent[d]
from evening until morning before the Lord; this
is in front of the curtain of the Ark[d] of the Agreement. This law will continue from now on.
4Aaron must always keep the lamps burning on
the lampstands of pure gold before the Lord.

5“Take fine flour and bake twelve loaves of
bread with it, using four quarts of flour for each
loaf. 6Put them in two rows on the golden table
before the Lord, six loaves in each row. 7Put pure
incense[d] on each row as the memorial portion to
take the place of the bread. It is an offering made
by fire to the Lord. 8Every Sabbath[d] day Aaron
will put the bread in order before the Lord, as an
agreement with the people of Israel that will continue forever. 9That bread will belong to Aaron
and his sons. They will eat it in a holy place, because it is a most holy part of the offerings made
by fire to the Lord. That bread is their share forever.”

The Man Who Cursed God

10Now there was a son of an Israelite woman
and an Egyptian father who was walking among
the Israelites. A fight broke out in the camp between him and an Israelite. 11The son of the Israelite woman began cursing and speaking against
the Lord, so the people took him to Moses. (The
mother's name was Shelomith, the daughter of
Debri from the family of Dan.) 12The people held
him as a prisoner while they waited for the Lord's
command to be made clear to them.

13Then the Lord said to Moses, 14“Take the
one who spoke against me outside the camp.
Then all the people who heard him must put their
hands on his head, and all the people must throw
stones at him and kill him. 15Tell the people of
Israel this: ‘If anyone curses his God, he is guilty
of sin. 16Anyone who speaks against the Lord
must be put to death; all the people must kill him
by throwing stones at him. Foreigners must be
punished just like the people born in Israel; if they
speak against the Lord, they must be put to
death.

17“ ‘Whoever kills another person must be put
to death. 18Whoever kills an animal that belongs
to another person must give that person another
animal to take its place. 19And whoever causes an
injury to a neighbor must receive the same kind
of injury in return: 20Broken bone for broken
bone, eye for eye, tooth for tooth. Anyone who
injures another person must be injured in the
same way in return. 21Whoever kills another person's animal must give that person another animal to take its place. But whoever kills another
person must be put to death.

22“ ‘The law will be the same for the foreigner
as for those from your own country. I am the
Lord your God.’ ”

23Then Moses spoke to the people of Israel, and
they took the person who had cursed outside the
camp and killed him by throwing stones at him.
So the people of Israel did as the Lord had commanded Moses.

The Time of Rest for the Land

25 The Lord said to Moses at Mount Sinai,
2“Tell the people of Israel this: ‘When
you enter the land I will give you, let it have a
special time of rest, to honor the Lord. 3You may
plant seed in your field for six years, and you may
trim your vineyards for six years and bring in their
fruits. 4But during the seventh year, you must let
the land rest. This will be a special time to honor
the Lord. You must not plant seed in your field
or trim your vineyards. 5You must not cut the
crops that grow by themselves after harvest, or
gather the grapes from your vines that are not
trimmed. The land will have a year of rest.

6“ ‘You may eat whatever the land produces
during that year of rest. It will be food for your
men and women servants, for your hired workers,
and for the foreigners living in your country. 7It
will also be food for your cattle and the wild animals of your land. Whatever the land produces
may be eaten.

The Year of Jubilee

8“ ‘Count off seven groups of seven years, or
forty-nine years. During that time there will be
seven years of rest for the land. 9On the Day of
Cleansing,[d] you must blow the horn of a male
sheep; this will be on the tenth day of the seventh
month. You must blow the horn through the
whole country. 10Make the fiftieth year a special
year, and announce freedom for all the people living in your country. This time will be called Jubilee.[n] You will each go back to your own property, each to your own family and family group.
11The fiftieth year will be a special time for you to
celebrate. Don't plant seeds, or harvest the crops
that grow by themselves, or gather grapes from
the vines that are not trimmed. 12That year is Jubilee; it will be a holy time for you. You may eat
only the crops that come from the field. 13In the
year of Jubilee you each must go back to your own
property.

14“ ‘If you sell your land to your neighbor, or if

Jubilee This word comes from the Hebrew word for a horn of a male sheep.

you buy land from your neighbor, don't cheat each other. [15]If you want to buy your neighbor's land, count the number of years since the last Jubilee, and use that number to decide the right price. If your neighbor sells the land to you, count the number of years left for harvesting crops, and use that number to decide the right price. [16]If there are many years, the price will be high. But if there are only a few years, lower the price, because your neighbor is really selling only a few crops to you. [17]You must not cheat each other, but you must respect your God. I am the LORD your God.

[18]" 'Remember my laws and rules, and obey them so that you will live safely in the land. [19]The land will give good crops to you, and you will eat as much as you want and live safely in the land.

[20]" 'But you might ask, "If we don't plant seeds or gather crops, what will we eat the seventh year?" [21]I will send you such a great blessing during the sixth year that the land will produce enough crops for three years. [22]When you plant in the eighth year, you will still be eating from the old crop; you will eat the old crop until the harvest of the ninth year.

> **SIDELIGHT:** If you have ever been sorry you gave something away, you would like the idea of the Year of Jubilee (Leviticus 25:8–22). To protect the poor and to ensure justice, the law said that all property had to be returned to its original owners after forty-nine years. Of course, after forty-nine years, that sweater you loaned to your best friend might not fit well!

Property Laws

[23]" 'The land really belongs to me, so you can't sell it for all time. You are only foreigners and travelers living for a while on my land. [24]People might sell their land, but it must always be possible for the family to get its land back. [25]If a person in your country becomes very poor and sells some land, then close relatives must come and buy it back. [26]If there is not a close relative to buy the land back, but if the person makes enough money to be able to buy it back, [27]the years must be counted since the land was sold. That number must be used to decide how much the first owner should pay back the one who bought it. Then the land will belong to the first owner again. [28]But if there is not enough money to buy it back, the one who bought it will keep it until the year of Jubilee.[d] During that celebration, the land will go back to the first owner's family.

[29]" 'If someone sells a home in a walled city, for a full year after it is sold, the person has the right to buy it back. [30]But if the owner does not buy back the house before a full year is over, it will belong to the one who bought it and to his future sons. The house will not go back to the first owner at Jubilee. [31]But houses in small towns without walls are like open country; they can be bought back, and they must be returned to their first owner at Jubilee.

[32]" 'The Levites may always buy back their houses in the cities that belong to them. [33]If someone buys a house from a Levite, that house in the Levites' city will again belong to the Levites in the Jubilee. This is because houses in Levite cities belong to the people of Levi; the Israelites gave these cities to them. [34]Also the fields and pastures around the Levites' cities cannot be sold, because those fields belong to the Levites forever.

Rules for Slave Owners

[35]" 'If anyone from your country becomes too poor to support himself, help him to live among you as you would a stranger or foreigner. [36]Do not charge him any interest on money you loan to him, but respect your God; let the poor live among you. [37]Don't lend him money for interest, and don't try to make a profit from the food he buys. [38]I am the LORD your God, who brought you out of the land of Egypt to give the land of Canaan to you and to become your God.

[39]" 'If anyone from your country becomes very poor and sells himself as a slave to you, you must not make him work like a slave. [40]He will be like a hired worker and a visitor with you until the year of Jubilee.[d] [41]Then he may leave you, take his children, and go back to his family and the land of his ancestors. [42]This is because the Israelites are my servants, and I brought them out of slavery in Egypt. They must not become slaves again. [43]You must not rule this person cruelly, but you must respect your God.

[44]" 'Your men and women slaves must come from other nations around you; from them you may buy slaves. [45]Also you may buy as slaves children from the families of foreigners living in your land. These child slaves will belong to you, [46]and you may even pass them on to your children after you die; you can make them slaves forever. But you must not rule cruelly over your own people, the Israelites.

[47]" 'Suppose a foreigner or visitor among you becomes rich. If someone in your country becomes so poor that he has to sell himself as a slave to the foreigner living among you or to a member of the foreigner's family, [48]the poor person has the right to be bought back and become free. One of his relatives may buy him back: [49]His uncle, his uncle's son, or any one of his close relatives may

buy him back. Or, if he gets enough money, he
may pay the money to free himself.

50“ ‘He and the one who bought him must
count the time from when he sold himself up to
the next year of Jubilee. Use that number to decide the price, because the person really only
hired himself out for a certain number of years.
51If there are still many years before the year of
Jubilee, the person must pay back a large part of
the price. 52If there are only a few years left until
Jubilee, the person must pay a small part of the
first price. 53But he will live like a hired person
with the foreigner every year; don’t let the foreigner rule cruelly over him.

54“ ‘Even if no one buys him back, at the year
of Jubilee, he and his children will become free.
55This is because the people of Israel are servants
to me. They are my servants, whom I brought out
of Egypt. I am the LORD your God.

Rewards for Obeying God

26 “ ‘Don’t make idols for yourselves or set
up statues or memorials. Don’t put stone
statues in your land to bow down to, because I am
the LORD your God.

2“ ‘Remember my Sabbaths,[d] and respect my
Holy Place. I am the LORD.

3“ ‘If you remember my laws and commands
and obey them, 4I will give you rains at the right
season; the land will produce crops, and the trees
of the field will produce their fruit. 5Your threshing[d] will continue until the grape harvest, and
your grape harvest will continue until it is time to
plant. Then you will have plenty to eat and live
safely in your land. 6I will give peace to your country; you will lie down in peace, and no one will
make you afraid. I will keep harmful animals out
of your country, and armies will not pass through
it.

7“ ‘You will chase your enemies and defeat
them, killing them with your sword. 8Five of you
will chase a hundred men; a hundred of you will
chase ten thousand men. You will defeat your enemies and kill them with your sword.

9“ ‘Then I will show kindness to you and let
you have many children; I will keep my agreement with you. 10You will have enough crops to
last for more than a year. When you harvest the
new crops, you will have to throw out the old
ones to make room for them. 11Also I will place
my Holy Tent[d] among you, and I will not turn
away from you. 12I will walk with you and be your
God, and you will be my people. 13I am the LORD
your God, who brought you out of Egypt, where
you were slaves. I broke the heavy weights that
were on your shoulders and let you walk proudly
again.

Punishment for Not Obeying God

14“ ‘But if you do not obey me and keep all my
commands, 15and if you turn away from my rules
and hate my laws, refusing to obey all my commands, you have broken our agreement. 16As a
result, I will do this to you: I will cause terrible
things to happen to you. I will cause you to have
disease and fever that will destroy your eyes and
slowly kill you. You will not have success when
you plant your seed, and your enemy will eat your
crops. 17I will be against you, and your enemies
will defeat you. These people who hate you will
rule over you, and you will run away even when
no one is chasing you.

18“ ‘If after all this you still do not obey me, I
will punish you seven times more for your sins. 19I
will break your great pride, and I will make the
sky like iron and the earth like bronze.[n] 20You
will work hard, but it will not help. Your land will
not grow any crops, and your trees will not give
their fruit.

21“ ‘If you still turn against me and refuse to
obey me, I will beat you seven times harder. The
more you sin, the more you will be punished. 22I
will send wild animals to attack you, and they will
take your children away from you and destroy
your cattle. They will make you so few in number
the roads will be empty.

23“ ‘If you don’t learn your lesson after all these
things, and if you still turn against me, 24I will also
turn against you. I will punish you seven more
times for your sins. 25You broke my agreement,
and I will punish you. I will bring armies against
you, and if you go into your cities for safety, I will
cause diseases to spread among you so that your
enemy will defeat you. 26There will be very little
bread to eat; ten women will be able to cook all
your bread in one oven. They will measure each
piece of bread, and you will eat, but you will still
be hungry.

27“ ‘If you still refuse to listen to me and still
turn against me, 28I will show my great anger; I
will punish you seven more times for your sins.
29You will eat the bodies of your sons and daughters. 30I will destroy your places where gods are
worshiped and cut down your incense[d] altars. I
will pile your dead bodies on the lifeless forms of
your idols. I will hate you. 31I will destroy your
cities and make your holy places empty, and I will
not smell the pleasing smell of your offerings. 32I
will make the land empty so that your enemies
who come to live in it will be shocked at it. 33I will
scatter you among the nations, and I will pull out
my sword and destroy you. Your land will become
empty, your cities a waste. 34When you are taken
to your enemy’s country, your land will finally get

sky . . . bronze This means the sky will give no rain and the earth will produce no crops.

its rest. It will enjoy its time of rest all the time it lies empty. 35During the time the land is empty, it will have the rest you should have given it while you lived in it.

36" 'Those of you who are left alive will lose their courage in the land of their enemies. They will be frightened by the sound of a leaf being blown by the wind. They will run as if someone were chasing them with a sword, and they will fall even when no one is chasing them. 37They will fall over each other, as if someone were chasing them with a sword, even though no one is chasing them. You will not be strong enough to stand up against your enemies. 38You will die among other nations and disappear in your enemies' countries. 39So those who are left alive will rot away in their enemies' countries because of their sins. They will also rot away because of their ancestors' sins.

There Is Always Hope

40" 'But maybe the people will confess their sins and the sins of their ancestors; maybe they will admit they turned against me and sinned against me, 41which made me turn against them and send them into the land of their enemies. If these disobedient people are sorry for what they did and accept punishment for their sin, 42I will remember my agreement with Jacob, my agreement with Isaac, and my agreement with Abraham, and I will remember the land. 43The land will be left empty by its people, and it will enjoy its time of rest as it lies bare without them. Then those who are left alive will accept the punishment for their sins. They will learn that they were punished because they hated my laws and refused to obey my rules. 44But even though this is true, I will not turn away from them when they are in the land of their enemies. I will not hate them so much that I completely destroy them and break my agreement with them, because I am the LORD their God. 45For their good I will remember the agreement with their ancestors, whom I brought out of the land of Egypt so I could become their God; the other nations saw these things. I am the LORD.' "

46These are the laws, rules, and teachings the LORD made between himself and the Israelites through Moses at Mount Sinai.

Promises Are Important

27 The LORD said to Moses, 2"Speak to the people of Israel and tell them: 'If someone makes a special promise to give a person as a servant to the LORD by paying a price that is the same value as that person, 3the price for a man twenty to sixty years old is about one and one-fourth pounds of silver. (You must use the measure as set by the Holy Place.) 4The price for a woman twenty to sixty years old is about twelve ounces of silver. 5The price for a man five to twenty years old is about eight ounces of silver; for a woman it is about four ounces of silver. 6The price for a baby boy one month to five years old is about two ounces of silver; for a baby girl the price is about one and one-half ounces of silver. 7The price for a man sixty years old or older is about six ounces of silver; for a woman it is about four ounces of silver.

8" 'If anyone is too poor to pay the price, bring him to the priest, and the priest will set the price. The priest will decide how much money the person making the vow can afford to pay.

Gifts to the Lord

9" 'Some animals may be used as sacrifices to the LORD. If someone promises to bring one of these to the LORD, it will become holy. 10That person must not try to put another animal in its place or exchange it, a good animal for a bad one, or a bad animal for a good one. If this happens, both animals will become holy.

11" 'Unclean[d] animals cannot be offered as sacrifices to the LORD, and if someone brings one of them to the LORD, that animal must be brought to the priest. 12The priest will decide a price for the animal, according to whether it is good or bad; as the priest decides, that is the price for the animal. 13If the person wants to buy back the animal, an additional one-fifth must be added to the price.

Value of a House

14" 'If a person gives a house as holy to the LORD, the priest must decide its value, according to whether the house is good or bad; as the priest decides, that is the price for the house. 15But if the person who gives the house wants to buy it back, an additional one-fifth must be added to the price. Then the house will belong to that person again.

Value of Land

16" 'If a person gives some family property to the LORD, the value of the fields will depend on how much seed is needed to plant them. It will cost about one and one-fourth pounds of silver for each six bushels of barley seed needed. 17If the person gives a field at the year of Jubilee,[d] its value will stay at what the priest has decided. 18But if the person gives the field after the Jubilee, the priest must decide the exact price by counting the number of years to the next year of Jubilee. Then he will subtract that number from its value. 19If the person who gave the field wants to buy it back, one-fifth must be added to that price, and the field will belong to the first owner again.

20" 'If the person does not buy back the field, or if it is sold to someone else, the first person cannot ever buy it back. 21When the land is released at the year of Jubilee, it will become holy to the LORD, like land specially given to him. It will become the property of the priests.

22" 'If someone gives to the LORD a field he has bought, which is not a part of his family land, 23the priest must count the years to the next Jubilee. He must decide the price for the land, and the price must be paid on that day. Then that land will be holy to the LORD. 24At the year of Jubilee, the land will go back to its first owner, to the family who sold the land.

25" 'You must use the measure as set by the Holy Place in paying these prices; it weighs two-fifths of an ounce.

Value of Animals

26" 'If an animal is the first one born to its parent, it already belongs to the LORD, so people may not give it again. If it is a cow or a sheep, it is the LORD's. 27If the animal is unclean,[d] the person must buy it back for the price set by the priest, and the person must add one-fifth to that price. If it is not bought back, the priest must sell it for the price he had decided.

28" 'There is a special kind of gift that people set apart to give to the LORD; it may be a person, animal, or field from the family property. That gift cannot be bought back or sold. Every special kind of gift is most holy to the LORD.

29" 'If anyone is given for the purpose of being destroyed, he cannot be bought back; he must be put to death.

30" 'One-tenth of all crops belongs to the LORD, including the crops from fields and the fruit from trees. That one-tenth is holy to the LORD. 31If a person wants to get back that tenth, one-fifth must be added to its price.

32" 'The priest will take every tenth animal from a person's herd or flock, and it will be holy to the LORD. 33The owner should not pick out the good animals from the bad or exchange one animal for another. If that happens, both animals will become holy; they cannot be bought back.' "

34These are the commands the LORD gave to Moses at Mount Sinai for the people of Israel.

NUMBERS

Why Read This Book:

- Learn what can happen when you don't trust God's power (Numbers 13—14).
- See that God plans to be good to his people (Numbers 22—24).
- Read about the first equal rights for women (Numbers 27:1–11).

Behind the Scenes:

The offense has just made a sensational play that put the team in easy scoring position—first down and goal to go. The coach sends in the next play. But in the huddle, the excited quarterback decides to change the play. The play fails miserably, and the quarterback gets sacked back at the forty-yard line. The discouraged team faces a long struggle.

The book of Numbers tells a similar story about a much more difficult situation. The Hebrew people had just been set free from slavery in Egypt and were headed to God's promised land. But they disobeyed God, and, as a result, spent forty difficult years wandering in a hot, hostile desert.

Numbers tells how God punished his people who had lost faith in themselves and in him. It emphasizes the importance of wholehearted trust in and obedience

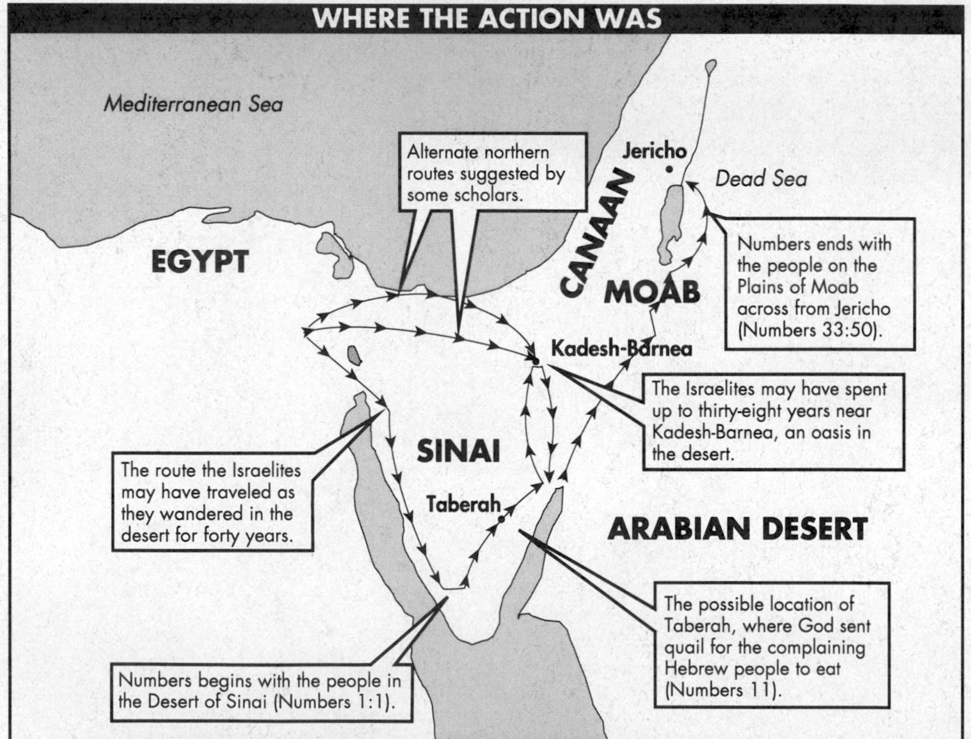

WHERE THE ACTION WAS
Mediterranean Sea
Alternate northern routes suggested by some scholars.
Jericho
Dead Sea
CANAAN
EGYPT
MOAB
Numbers ends with the people on the Plains of Moab across from Jericho (Numbers 33:50).
Kadesh-Barnea
The Israelites may have spent up to thirty-eight years near Kadesh-Barnea, an oasis in the desert.
SINAI
The route the Israelites may have traveled as they wandered in the desert for forty years.
Taberah
ARABIAN DESERT
The possible location of Taberah, where God sent quail for the complaining Hebrew people to eat (Numbers 11).
Numbers begins with the people in the Desert of Sinai (Numbers 1:1).

WHEN THE ACTION WAS

2000BC	1500BC	1000BC	500BC	BC/AD

- Abraham lived
- The Israelites became slaves in Egypt
- The Israelites escaped from Egypt
- The Israelites wandered in the desert for forty years
- The Israelites entered the promised land
- The Temple was built in Jerusalem for worship
- Jesus was born

Behind the Scenes (cont.): to God. And it shows how God patiently and persistently disciplines his stubborn children.

Numbers gets its name from the census taken near the beginning and end of the book. However, the book's original Hebrew name—"In the Desert" or "In the Wilderness"—more accurately describes it.

The People of Israel Are Counted

1 The LORD spoke to Moses in the Meeting Tent in the Desert of Sinai. This was on the first day of the second month in the second year after the Israelites left Egypt. He said to Moses: 2"You and Aaron must count all the people of Israel by families and family groups, listing the name of each man. 3You and Aaron must count every man twenty years old or older who will serve in the army of Israel, and list them by their divisions. 4One man from each tribe, the leader of his family, will help you. 5These are the names of the men who will help you:

from the tribe of Reuben—Elizur son of Shedeur;
6from the tribe of Simeon—Shelumiel son of Zurishaddai;
7from the tribe of Judah—Nahshon son of Amminadab;
8from the tribe of Issachar—Nethanel son of Zuar;
9from the tribe of Zebulun—Eliab son of Helon;
10from the tribe of Ephraim son of Joseph—Elishama son of Ammihud;
from the tribe of Manasseh son of Joseph—Gamaliel son of Pedahzur;
11from the tribe of Benjamin—Abidan son of Gideoni;
12from the tribe of Dan—Ahiezer son of Ammishaddai;
13from the tribe of Asher—Pagiel son of Ocran;
14from the tribe of Gad—Eliasaph son of Deuel;
15from the tribe of Naphtali—Ahira son of Enan."

16These were the men chosen from the people to be leaders of their tribes, the heads of Israel's family groups.

17Moses and Aaron took these men who had been picked 18and called all the people of Israel together on the first day of the second month. Then the people were listed by their families and family groups, and all the men who were twenty years old or older were listed by name. 19Moses did exactly what the LORD had commanded and listed the people while they were in the Desert of Sinai.

20The tribe of Reuben, the first son born to Israel, was counted; all the men twenty years old or older who were able to serve in the army were listed by name with their families and family groups. 21The tribe of Reuben totaled 46,500 men.

22The tribe of Simeon was counted; all the men twenty years old or older who were able to serve in the army were listed by name with their families and family groups. 23The tribe of Simeon totaled 59,300 men.

24The tribe of Gad was counted; all the men twenty years old or older who were able to serve in the army were listed by name with their families and family groups. 25The tribe of Gad totaled 45,650 men.

26The tribe of Judah was counted; all the men twenty years old or older who were able to serve in the army were listed by name with their families and family groups. 27The tribe of Judah totaled 74,600 men.

28The tribe of Issachar was counted; all the men twenty years old or older who were able to serve in the army were listed by name with their families and family groups. 29The tribe of Issachar totaled 54,400 men.

30The tribe of Zebulun was counted; all the men twenty years old or older who were able to serve in the army were listed by name with their families and family groups. 31The tribe of Zebulun totaled 57,400 men.

32The tribe of Ephraim, a son of Joseph, was counted; all the men twenty years old or older who were able to serve in the army were listed by name with their families and family groups. 33The tribe of Ephraim totaled 40,500 men.

34The tribe of Manasseh, also a son of Joseph, was counted; all the men twenty years old or older who were able to serve in the army were listed by name with their families and family groups. 35The tribe of Manasseh totaled 32,200 men.

36The tribe of Benjamin was counted; all the men twenty years old or older who were able to serve in the army were listed by name with their families and family groups. 37The tribe of Benjamin totaled 35,400 men.

38The tribe of Dan was counted; all the men twenty years old or older who were able to serve in the army were listed by name with their families and family groups. 39The tribe of Dan totaled 62,700 men.

40The tribe of Asher was counted; all the men

twenty years old or older who were able to serve in the army were listed by name with their families and family groups. 41The tribe of Asher totaled 41,500 men.

42The tribe of Naphtali was counted; all the men twenty years old or older who were able to serve in the army were listed by name with their families and family groups. 43The tribe of Naphtali totaled 53,400 men.

44Moses, Aaron, and the twelve leaders of Israel, one from each of the families, counted these men. 45Every man of Israel twenty years old or older who was able to serve in the army was counted and listed with his family. 46The total number of men was 603,550.

SIDELIGHT: Imagine the entire population of San Diego—more than two million—wandering through the Mojave Desert in Southern California. That would be about how many Israelites some scholars say escaped from Egypt and wandered in the desert, according to the figures in Numbers 1:45–46.

47The families from the tribe of Levi were not listed with the others, because 48the LORD had told Moses: 49"Do not count the tribe of Levi or include them with the other Israelites. 50Instead put the Levites in charge of the Holy Tent[d] of the Agreement and everything that is with it. They must carry the Holy Tent and everything in it, and they must take care of it and make their camp around it. 51Any time the Holy Tent is moved, the Levites must take it down, and any time it is set up, the Levites must do it. Anyone else who goes near the Holy Tent will be put to death. 52The Israelites will make their camps in separate divisions, each family near its flag. 53But the Levites must make their camp around the Holy Tent of the Agreement so that I will not be angry with the Israelites. The Levites will take care of the Holy Tent of the Agreement."

54So the Israelites did everything just as the LORD commanded Moses.

The Camp Arrangement

2 The LORD said to Moses and Aaron: 2"The Israelites should make their camps around the Meeting Tent,[d] but they should not camp too close to it. They should camp under their family flag and banners."

3The camp of Judah will be on the east side, where the sun rises, and they will camp by divisions there under their flag. The leader of the people of Judah is Nahshon son of Amminadab. 4There are 74,600 men in his division.

5Next to them the tribe[d] of Issachar will camp. The leader of the people of Issachar is Nethanel son of Zuar. 6There are 54,400 men in his division.

7Next is the tribe of Zebulun. The leader of the people of Zebulun is Eliab son of Helon. 8There are 57,400 men in his division.

9There are a total of 186,400 men in the camps of Judah and its neighbors, in all their divisions. They will be the first to march out of camp.

10The divisions of the camp of Reuben will be on the south side, where they will camp under their flag. The leader of the people of Reuben is Elizur son of Shedeur. 11There are 46,500 men in his division.

12Next to them the tribe of Simeon will camp. The leader of the people of Simeon is Shelumiel son of Zurishaddai. 13There are 59,300 men in his division.

14Next is the tribe of Gad. The leader of the people of Gad is Eliasaph son of Deuel. 15There are 45,650 men in his division.

16There are a total of 151,450 men in the camps of Reuben and its neighbors, in all their divisions. They will be the second group to march out of camp.

17When the Levites march out with the Meeting Tent, they will be in the middle of the other camps. The tribes will march out in the same order as they camp, each in its place under its flag.

18The divisions of the camp of Ephraim will be on the west side, where they will camp under their flag. The leader of the people of Ephraim is Elishama son of Ammihud. 19There are 40,500 men in his division.

20Next to them the tribe of Manasseh will camp. The leader of the people of Manasseh is Gamaliel son of Pedahzur. 21There are 32,200 men in his division.

22Next is the tribe of Benjamin. The leader of the people of Benjamin is Abidan son of Gideoni. 23There are 35,400 men in his division.

24There are a total of 108,100 men in the camps of Ephraim and its neighbors, in all their divisions. They will be the third group to march out of camp.

25The divisions of the camp of Dan will be on the north side, where they will camp under their flag. The leader of the people of Dan is Ahiezer son of Ammishaddai. 26There are 62,700 men in his division.

27Next to them the tribe of Asher will camp. The leader of the people of Asher is Pagiel son of Ocran. 28There are 41,500 men in his division.

29Next is the tribe of Naphtali. The leader of the people of Naphtali is Ahira son of Enan. 30There are 53,400 men in his division.

31There are 157,600 men in the camps of Dan and its neighbors. They will be the last to march out of camp, and they will travel under their own flag.

32These are the Israelites who were counted by families. The total number of Israelites in the camps, counted by divisions, is 603,550. 33Moses obeyed the LORD and did not count the Levites among the other people of Israel.

34So the Israelites obeyed everything the LORD commanded Moses. They camped under their flags and marched out by families and family groups.

Aaron's Family, the Priests

3 This is the family history of Aaron and Moses at the time the LORD talked to Moses on Mount Sinai.

2Aaron had four sons: Nadab, the oldest, Abihu, Eleazar, and Ithamar. 3These were the names of Aaron's sons, who were appointed to serve as priests. 4But Nadab and Abihu died in the presence of the LORD when they offered the wrong kind of fire before the LORD in the Desert of Sinai. They had no sons. So Eleazar and Ithamar served as priests during the lifetime of their father Aaron.

5The LORD said to Moses, 6"Bring the tribe[d] of Levi and present them to Aaron the priest to help him. 7They will help him and all the Israelites at the Meeting Tent,[d] doing the work in the Holy Tent. 8The Levites must take care of everything in the Meeting Tent and serve the people of Israel by doing the work in the Holy Tent. 9Give the Levites to Aaron and his sons; of all the Israelites, the Levites are given completely to him. 10Appoint Aaron and his sons to serve as priests, but anyone else who comes near the holy things must be put to death."

11The LORD also said to Moses, 12"I am choosing the Levites from all the Israelites to take the place of all the firstborn[d] children of Israel. The Levites will be mine, 13because the firstborn are mine. When you were in Egypt, I killed all the firstborn children of the Egyptians and took all the firstborn of Israel to be mine, both animals and children. They are mine. I am the LORD."

14The LORD again said to Moses in the Desert of Sinai, 15"Count the Levites by families and family groups. Count every male one month old or older." 16So Moses obeyed the LORD and counted them all.

17Levi had three sons, whose names were Gershon, Kohath, and Merari.

18The Gershonite family groups were Libni and Shimei.

19The Kohathite family groups were Amram, Izhar, Hebron, and Uzziel.

20The Merarite family groups were Mahli and Mushi.

These were the family groups of the Levites.

21The family groups of Libni and Shimei belonged to Gershon; they were the Gershonite family groups. 22The number that was counted was 7,500 males one month old or older. 23The Gershonite family groups camped on the west side, behind the Holy Tent. 24The leader of the families of Gershon was Eliasaph son of Lael. 25In the Meeting Tent the Gershonites were in charge of the Holy Tent, its covering, the curtain at the entrance to the Meeting Tent, 26the curtains in the courtyard, the curtain at the entry to the courtyard around the Holy Tent and the altar, the ropes, and all the work connected with these items.

27The family groups of Amram, Izhar, Hebron, and Uzziel belonged to Kohath; they were the Kohathite family groups. 28They had 8,600 males one month old or older, and they were responsible for taking care of the Holy Place. 29The Kohathite family groups camped south of the Holy Tent. 30The leader of the Kohathite families was Elizaphan son of Uzziel. 31They were responsible for the Ark,[d] the table, the lampstand, the altars, the tools of the Holy Place which they were to use, the curtain, and all the work connected with these items. 32The main leader of the Levites was Eleazar son of Aaron, the priest, who was in charge of all those responsible for the Holy Place.

33The family groups of Mahli and Mushi belonged to Merari; they were the Merarite family groups. 34The number that was counted was 6,200 males one month old or older. 35The leader of the Merari families was Zuriel son of Abihail, and they were to camp north of the Holy Tent. 36The Merarites were responsible for the frames of the Holy Tent, the braces, the posts, the bases, and all the work connected with these items. 37They were also responsible for the posts in the courtyard around the Holy Tent and their bases, tent pegs, and ropes.

38Moses, Aaron, and his sons camped east of the Holy Tent, toward the sunrise, in front of the Meeting Tent. They were responsible for the Holy Place for the Israelites. Anyone else who came near the Holy Place was to be put to death.

39Moses and Aaron counted the Levite men by their families, as the LORD commanded, and there were 22,000 males one month old or older.

Levites Take the Place of the Firstborn Sons

40The LORD said to Moses, "Count all the firstborn[d] sons in Israel one month old or older, and list their names. 41Take the Levites for me instead of the firstborn sons of Israel; take the animals of

the Levites instead of the firstborn animals from
the rest of Israel. I am the LORD."
42So Moses did what the LORD commanded
and counted all the firstborn sons of the Israelites.
43When he listed all the firstborn sons one month
old or older, there were 22,273 names.
44The LORD also said to Moses, 45"Take the Levites instead of all the firstborn sons of the Israelites, and take the animals of the Levites instead of
the animals of the other people. The Levites are
mine. I am the LORD. 46Since there are 273 more
firstborn sons than Levites, 47collect two ounces
of silver for each of the 273 sons. Use the measure
as set by the Holy Place, which is two-fifths of an
ounce. 48Give the silver to Aaron and his sons as
the payment for the 273 Israelites."
49So Moses collected the money for the people
the Levites could not replace. 50From the firstborn
of the Israelites, he collected thirty-five pounds of
silver, using the measure set by the Holy Place.
51Moses obeyed the command of the LORD and
gave the silver to Aaron and his sons.

The Jobs of the Kohath Family

4 The LORD said to Moses and Aaron, 2"Count
the Kohathites among the Levites by family
groups and families. 3Count the men from thirty
to fifty years old, all who come to serve in the
Meeting Tent.[d]
4"The Kohathites are responsible for the most
holy things in the Meeting Tent. 5When the Israelites are ready to move, Aaron and his sons must
go into the Holy Tent, take down the curtain, and
cover the Ark[d] of the Agreement with it. 6Over
this they must put a covering made from fine
leather, then spread the solid blue cloth over that,
and put the poles in place.
7"Then they must spread a blue cloth over the
table for the bread that shows a person is in God's
presence. They must put the plates, pans, bowls,
and the jars for drink offerings on the table; they
must leave the bread that is always there on the
table. 8Then they must put a red cloth over all of
these things, cover everything with fine leather,
and put the poles in place.
9"With a blue cloth they must cover the lampstand, its lamps, its wick trimmers, its trays, and
all the jars for the oil used in the lamps. 10Then
they must wrap everything in fine leather and put
all these things on a frame for carrying them.
11"They must spread a blue cloth over the gold
altar, cover it with fine leather, and put the poles
in place.
12"They must gather all the things used for
serving in the Holy Place and wrap them in a blue
cloth. Then they must cover that with fine leather
and put these things on a frame for carrying them.
13"They must clean the ashes off the bronze
altar and spread a purple cloth over it. 14They
must gather all the things used for serving at the
altar—the pans for carrying the fire, the meat
forks, the shovels, and the bowls—and put them
on the bronze altar. Then they must spread a covering of fine leather over it and put the poles in
place.
15"When the Israelites are ready to move, and
when Aaron and his sons have covered the holy
furniture and all the holy things, the Kohathites
may go in and carry them away. In this way they
won't touch the holy things and die. It is the Kohathites' job to carry the things that are in the
Meeting Tent.
16"Eleazar son of Aaron, the priest, will be responsible for the Holy Tent and for everything in
it, for all the holy things it has: the oil for the
lamp, the sweet-smelling incense,[d] the continual
grain offering, and the oil used to appoint priests
and things to the LORD's service."
17The LORD said to Moses and Aaron, 18"Don't
let the Kohathites be cut off from the Levites.
19Do this for the Kohathites so that they may go
near the Most Holy Place and not die: Aaron and
his sons must go in and show each Kohathite
what to do and what to carry. 20The Kohathites
must not enter and look at the holy things, even
for a second, or they will die."

The Jobs of the Gershon Family

21The LORD said to Moses, 22"Count the Gershonites by families and family groups. 23Count
the men from thirty to fifty years old, all who have
a job to do in the Meeting Tent.[d]
24"This is what the Gershonite family groups
must do and what they must carry. 25They must
carry the curtains of the Holy Tent,[d] the Meeting
Tent, its covering, and its outer covering made
from fine leather. They must also carry the curtains for the entrance to the Meeting Tent, 26the
curtains of the courtyard that goes around the
Holy Tent and the altar, the curtain for the entry
to the courtyard, the ropes, and all the things used
with the curtains. They must do everything connected with these things. 27Aaron and his sons are
in charge of what the Gershonites do or carry;
you tell them what they are responsible for carrying. 28This is the work of the Gershonite family
group at the Meeting Tent. Ithamar son of Aaron,
the priest, will direct their work.

The Jobs of the Merari Family

29"Count the Merarite families and family
groups. 30Count the men from thirty to fifty years
old, all who work at the Meeting Tent.[d] 31It is
their job to carry the following as they serve in the
Meeting Tent: the frames of the Holy Tent, the
crossbars, the posts, and bases, 32in addition to the
posts that go around the courtyard, their bases,
tent pegs, ropes, and everything that is used with

the poles around the courtyard. Tell each man exactly what to carry. 33This is the work the Merarite family group will do for the Meeting Tent. Ithamar son of Aaron, the priest, will direct their work."

The Levite Families

34Moses, Aaron, and the leaders of Israel counted the Kohathites by families and family groups, 35the men from thirty to fifty years old who were to work at the Meeting Tent.[d] 36There were 2,750 men in the family groups. 37This was the total of the Kohath family groups who worked at the Meeting Tent, whom Moses and Aaron counted as the LORD had commanded Moses.

38Also, the Gershonites were counted by families and family groups, 39the men from thirty to fifty years old who were given work at the Meeting Tent. 40The families and family groups had 2,630 men. 41This was the total of the Gershon family groups who worked at the Meeting Tent, whom Moses and Aaron counted as the LORD had commanded.

42Also, the men in the families and family groups of the Merari family were counted, 43the men from thirty to fifty years old who were to work at the Meeting Tent. 44The family groups had 3,200 men. 45This was the total of the Merari family groups, whom Moses and Aaron counted as the LORD had commanded Moses.

46So Moses, Aaron, and the leaders of Israel counted all the Levites by families and family groups. 47They counted the men from thirty to fifty who were given work at the Meeting Tent and who carried the Tent. 48The total number of these men was 8,580. 49Each man was counted as the LORD had commanded Moses; each man was given his work and told what to carry as the LORD had commanded Moses.

Rules About Cleanliness

5 The LORD said to Moses, 2"Command the Israelites to send away from camp anyone with a harmful skin disease. Send away anyone who gives off body fluid or who has become unclean by touching a dead body. 3Send both men and women outside the camp so that they won't spread the disease there, where I am living among you." 4So Israel obeyed the LORD's command and sent those people outside the camp. They did just as the LORD had told Moses.

Paying for Doing Wrong

5The LORD said to Moses, 6"Tell the Israelites: 'When a man or woman does something wrong to another person, that is really sinning against the LORD. That person is guilty 7and must admit the wrong that has been done. The person must fully pay for the wrong that has been done, adding one-fifth to it, and giving it to the person who was wronged. 8But if that person is dead and does not have any close relatives to receive the payment, the one who did wrong owes the LORD and must pay the priest. In addition, the priest must sacrifice a male sheep to remove the wrong so that the person will belong to the LORD. 9When an Israelite brings a holy gift, it should be given to the priest. 10No one has to give these holy gifts, but if someone does give them, they belong to the priest.' "

Suspicious Husbands

11Then the LORD said to Moses, 12"Tell the Israelites: 'A man's wife might be unfaithful to him 13and have sexual relations with another man. Her sin might be kept hidden from her husband so that he does not know about the wrong she did. Perhaps no one saw it, and she wasn't caught. 14But if her husband has feelings of jealousy and suspects she has sinned—whether she has or not— 15he should take her to the priest. The husband must also take an offering for her of two quarts of barley flour. He must not pour oil or incense[d] on it, because this is a grain offering for jealousy, an offering of remembrance. It is to find out if she is guilty.

16" 'The priest will bring in the woman and make her stand before the LORD. 17He will take some holy water in a clay jar, and he will put some dirt from the floor of the Holy Tent into the water. 18The priest will make the woman stand before the LORD, and he will loosen her hair. He will hand her the offering of remembrance, the grain offering for jealousy; he will hold the bitter water that brings a curse. 19The priest will make her take an oath and ask her, "Has another man had sexual relations with you? Have you been unfaithful to your husband? If you haven't, this bitter water that brings a curse won't hurt you. 20But if you have been unfaithful to your husband and have had sexual relations with a man besides him"— 21the priest will then put on her the curse that the oath will bring—"the LORD will make the people curse and reject you. He will make your stomach get big, and he will make your body unable to give birth to another baby. 22This water that brings a curse will go inside you and make your body unable to give birth to another baby."

" 'The woman must say, "I agree."

23" 'The priest should write these curses on a scroll, wash the words off into the bitter water, 24and make the woman drink the bitter water that brings a curse. If she is guilty, the water will make her sick. 25Then the priest will take the grain offering for jealousy from her. He will present it before the LORD and bring it to the altar. 26He will take a handful of the grain, which is a memorial offering, and burn it on the altar. After that he will make the woman drink the water 27to see if she is not pure and if she has sinned against her husband. When it goes into her, if her stomach gets big so that she is not able to have another baby, her people will reject her. 28But if the woman has not sinned, she is pure. She is not guilty, and she will be able to have babies.

29" 'So this is the teaching about jealousy. This is what to do when a woman does wrong and is unfaithful while she is married to her husband. 30It also should be done if the man gets jealous because he suspects his wife. The priest will have her stand before the LORD, and he will do all these things, just as the teaching commands. 31In this way the husband can be proven correct, and the woman will suffer if she has done wrong.' "

Rules for the Nazirites

6 The LORD said to Moses, 2"Tell the Israelites: 'If men or women want to promise to belong to the LORD in a special way, they will be called Nazirites. 3During this time, they must not drink wine or beer, or vinegar made from wine or beer. They must not even drink grape juice or eat grapes or raisins. 4While they are Nazirites, they must not eat anything that comes from the grapevine, even the seeds or the skin.

5" 'During the time they have promised to belong to the LORD, they must not cut their hair. They must be holy until this special time is over. They must let their hair grow long. 6During their special time of belonging to the LORD, Nazirites must not go near a dead body. 7Even if their own father, mother, brother, or sister dies, they must not touch them, or they will become unclean.[d] They must still keep their promise to belong to God in a special way. 8While they are Nazirites, they belong to the LORD in a special way.

> **SIDELIGHT:** What do you call a person who grows a beard, watches what he eats, and never cuts his hair? A Nazirite. Nazirites were men who took a special vow to dedicate their lives to God (Numbers 6:2–8). Samson, whose story is in Judges 13—16 (p. 229), was probably the most famous of these Nazirites.

9" 'If they are next to someone who dies suddenly, their hair, which was part of their promise, has been made unclean. So they must shave their head seven days later to be clean. 10Then on the eighth day, they must bring two doves or two young pigeons to the priest at the entrance to the Meeting Tent.[d] 11The priest will offer one as a sin offering and the other as a burnt offering. This removes sin so they will belong to the LORD. (They had sinned because they were near a dead body.) That same day they will again promise to let their hair grow 12and give themselves to the LORD for another special time. They must bring a male lamb a year old as a penalty offering. The days of the special time before don't count, because they became unclean during their first special time.

13" 'This is the teaching for the Nazirites. When the promised time is over, they must go the entrance of the Meeting Tent[d] 14and give their offerings to the LORD. They must offer a year-old male lamb that has nothing wrong with it, as a burnt offering, a year-old female lamb that has nothing wrong with it, as a sin offering, and a male sheep that has nothing wrong with it, for a fellowship offering. 15They must also bring the grain offerings and drink offerings that go with them. And they must bring a basket of bread made without yeast, loaves made with fine flour mixed with oil, and wafers made without yeast spread with oil.

16" 'The priest will give these offerings to the LORD and make the sin offering and the burnt offering. 17Then he will kill the male sheep as a fellowship offering to the LORD; along with it, he will present the basket of bread made without yeast, the grain offering, and the drink offering.

18" 'The Nazirites must go to the entrance of the Meeting Tent and shave off their hair that they grew for their promise. The hair will be put in the fire that is under the sacrifice of the fellowship offering.

19" 'After the Nazirites cut off their hair, the priest will give them a boiled shoulder from the male sheep. From the basket he will also give a loaf and a wafer, both made without yeast. 20Then the priest will present them to the LORD. They are holy and belong to the priest. Also, he is to present the breast and the thigh from the male sheep. After that, the Nazirites may drink wine.

21" 'This is the teaching for the Nazirites who make a promise. Everyone who makes the Nazirite promise must give all of these gifts to the LORD. If they promised to do more, they must keep their promise, according to the teaching of the Nazirites.' "

The Priests' Blessings

22The LORD said to Moses, 23"Tell Aaron and his sons, 'This is how you should bless the Israelites. Say to them:

24"May the LORD bless you and keep you.
25May the LORD show you his kindness
and have mercy on you.
26May the LORD watch over you
and give you peace." '

27"So Aaron and his sons will bless the Israelites with my name, and I will bless them."

The Holy Tent

7 When Moses finished setting up the Holy
Tent,[d] he gave it for service to the LORD by
pouring olive oil on the Tent and on everything
used in it. He also poured oil on the altar and all
its tools to prepare them for service to the LORD.
2Then the leaders of Israel made offerings. These
were the heads of the families, the leaders of each
tribe[d] who counted the people. 3They brought to
the LORD six covered carts and twelve oxen—
each leader giving an ox, and every two leaders
giving a cart. They brought these to the Holy
Tent.

4The LORD said to Moses, 5"Accept these gifts
from the leaders and use them in the work of the
Meeting Tent. Give them to the Levites as they
need them."

6So Moses accepted the carts and the oxen and
gave them to the Levites. 7He gave two carts and
four oxen to the Gershonites, which they needed
for their work. 8Then Moses gave four carts and
eight oxen to the Merarites, which they needed
for their work. Ithamar son of Aaron, the priest,
directed the work of all of them. 9Moses did not
give any oxen or carts to the Kohathites, because
their job was to carry the holy things on their
shoulders.

10When the oil was poured on the altar, the
leaders brought their offerings to it to give it to the
LORD's service; they presented them in front of
the altar. 11The LORD told Moses, "Each day one
leader must bring his gift to make the altar ready
for service to me."

12-83Each of the twelve leaders brought these
gifts. Each leader brought one silver plate that
weighed about three and one-fourth pounds, and
one silver bowl that weighed about one and
three-fourths pounds. These weights were set by
the Holy Place measure. The bowl and the plate
were filled with fine flour mixed with oil for a
grain offering. Each leader also brought a large
gold dish that weighed about four ounces and was
filled with incense.[d]

In addition, each of the leaders brought one
young bull, one male sheep, and one male lamb
a year old for a burnt offering; one male goat for
a sin offering; and two oxen, five male sheep, five
male goats, and five male lambs a year old for a
fellowship offering.

On the first day Nahshon son of Amminadab

PEACE

An Unlikely Gift

Adam, twenty-five, lives in a home with six handicapped people and four assistants. He can't speak, walk, or eat without help. His back is deformed, his movements are uncoordinated, and seizures grip his body daily.

But Adam's dependence on others has taught valuable lessons to those who know him. As people help Adam with things he can't do alone, they discover that Adam never hurries or worries. Without ever speaking, Adam communicates inner peace.

Some people would consider Adam worthless. But after being with Adam, people feel touched by an inner peace. As people help him, they are touched with a sense of tender affection that's much deeper than words, thoughts, or emotions. Though totally dependent on them, his gift is simply to be there with them. The peace Adam shares by his being with others far outweighs anything Adam can't do.

Adam shows that peace is a gift from God that's deeper than things we do. Consider the source of Adam's peace as you read **Numbers 6:22–27**.

- How is the peace talked about in this passage like the peace that Adam shows in his life?
- Are you experiencing these things in your life? If not, how can you begin to experience them?

CONSIDER. . .

- reading dictionary definitions of peace. Write the ones that apply to God's peace on a three-by-five card, and post it where you can see it every day.
- sitting silently for ten minutes in prayer, inviting God to give you inner peace. Think about how the experience affects the rest of your day.

FOR MORE, SEE. . .

- Psalm 119:165 (p. 554)
- John 14:27 (p. 1085)
- Romans 12:14–21 (p. 1158)

brought his gifts. He was the leader of the tribe of
Judah.
On the second day Nethanel son of Zuar
brought his gifts. He was the leader of the tribe of
Issachar.
On the third day Eliab son of Helon brought his
gifts. He was the leader of the tribe of Zebulun.
On the fourth day Elizur son of Shedeur
brought his gifts. He was the leader of the tribe of
Reuben.
On the fifth day Shelumiel son of Zurishaddai
brought his gifts. He was the leader of the tribe of
Simeon.
On the sixth day Eliasaph son of Deuel brought
his gifts. He was the leader of the tribe of Gad.
On the seventh day Elishama son of Ammihud
brought his gifts. He was the leader of the tribe of
Ephraim.
On the eighth day Gamaliel son of Pedahzur
brought his gifts. He was the leader of the tribe of
Manasseh.
On the ninth day Abidan son of Gideoni
brought his gifts. He was the leader of the tribe of
Benjamin.
On the tenth day Ahiezer son of Ammishaddai
brought his gifts. He was the leader of the tribe of
Dan.
On the eleventh day Pagiel son of Ocran
brought his gifts. He was the leader of the tribe of
Asher.
On the twelfth day Ahira son of Enan brought
his gifts. He was the leader of the tribe of Naphtali.
84So these were the gifts from the Israelite leaders when oil was poured on the altar and it was
given for service to the LORD: twelve silver plates,
twelve silver bowls, and twelve gold dishes.
85Each silver plate weighed about three and one-
fourth pounds, and each bowl weighed about one
and three-fourths pounds. All the silver plates and
silver bowls together weighed about sixty pounds
according to a weight set by the Holy Place measure. 86The twelve gold dishes filled with incense
weighed four ounces each, according to the
weight set by the Holy Place measure. Together
the gold dishes weighed about three pounds.
87The total number of animals for the burnt offering was twelve bulls, twelve male sheep, and
twelve male lambs a year old. There was also a
grain offering, and there were twelve male goats
for a sin offering. 88The total number of animals
for the fellowship offering was twenty-four bulls,
sixty male sheep, sixty male goats, and sixty male
lambs a year old. All these offerings were for giving the altar to the service of the LORD after the
oil had been poured on it.
89When Moses went into the Meeting Tent to
speak with the LORD, he heard the LORD speaking
to him. The voice was coming from between the
two gold creatures with wings that were above
the lid of the Ark[d] of the Agreement. In this way
the LORD spoke with him.

The Lampstand

8 The LORD said to Moses, 2"Speak to Aaron
and tell him, 'Put the seven lamps where
they can light the area in front of the lampstand.' "
3Aaron did this, putting the lamps so they
lighted the area in front of the lampstand; he
obeyed the command the LORD gave Moses. 4The
lampstand was made from hammered gold, from
its base to the flowers. It was made exactly the
way the LORD had showed Moses.

The Levites Are Given to God

5The LORD said to Moses, 6"Take the Levites
away from the other Israelites and make them
clean.[d] 7This is what you should do to make them
clean: Sprinkle the cleansing water on them, and
have them shave their bodies and wash their
clothes so they will be clean. 8They must take a
young bull and the grain offering of flour mixed
with oil that goes with it. Then take a second
young bull for a sin offering. 9Bring the Levites to
the front of the Meeting Tent,[d] and gather all the
Israelites around. 10When you bring the Levites
before the LORD, the Israelites should put their
hands on them.[n] 11Aaron will present the Levites
before the LORD as an offering presented from the
Israelites. Then the Levites will be ready to do the
work of the LORD.
12"The Levites will put their hands on the bulls'
heads—one bull will be a sin offering to the
LORD, and the other will be a burnt offering, to
remove the sins of the Levites so they will belong
to the LORD. 13Make the Levites stand in front of
Aaron and his sons and present the Levites as an
offering to the LORD. 14In this way you must set
apart the Levites from the other Israelites; the Levites will be mine.
15"Make the Levites pure, and present them as
an offering so that they may come to work at the
Meeting Tent. 16They will be given completely to
me from the Israelites; I have taken them for myself instead of the firstborn[d] of every Israelite
woman. 17All the firstborn in Israel—people or
animals—are mine. When I killed all the firstborn
in Egypt, I set the firstborn in Israel aside for myself. 18But I have taken the Levites instead of all
the firstborn in Israel. 19From all the Israelites I
have given the Levites to Aaron and his sons so
that they may serve the Israelites at the Meeting
Tent. They will help remove the Israelites' sins so

put . . . them This showed that the people had a part in giving the Levites their special work.

they will belong to the LORD and so that no disaster will strike the Israelites when they approach the Holy Place."

20So Moses, Aaron, and all the Israelites obeyed and did with the Levites what the LORD commanded Moses. 21The Levites made themselves clean and washed their clothes. Then Aaron presented them as an offering to the LORD. He also removed their sins so they would be pure. 22After that, the Levites came to the Meeting Tent to work, and Aaron and his sons told them what to do. They did with the Levites what the LORD commanded Moses.

23The LORD said to Moses, 24"This command is for the Levites. Everyone twenty-five years old or older must come to the Meeting Tent, because they all have jobs to do there. 25At the age of fifty, they must retire from their jobs and not work again. 26They may help their fellow Levites with their work at the Meeting Tent, but they must not do the work themselves. This is the way you are to give the Levites their jobs."

The Passover Is Celebrated

9 The LORD spoke to Moses in the Desert of Sinai in the first month of the second year after the Israelites left Egypt. He said, 2"Tell the Israelites to celebrate the Passover[d] at the appointed time. 3That appointed time is the fourteenth day of this month at twilight; they must obey all the rules about it."

4So Moses told the Israelites to celebrate the Passover, 5and they did; it was in the Desert of Sinai at twilight on the fourteenth day of the first month. The Israelites did everything just as the LORD commanded Moses.

6But some of the people could not celebrate the Passover on that day because they were unclean[d] from touching a dead body. So they went to Moses and Aaron that day and 7said to Moses, "We are unclean because of touching a dead body. But why should we be kept from offering gifts to the LORD at this appointed time? Why can't we join the other Israelites?"

8Moses said to them, "Wait, and I will find out what the LORD says about you."

9Then the LORD said to Moses, 10"Tell the Israelites this: 'If you or your descendants[d] become unclean because of a dead body, or if you are away on a trip during the Passover, you must still celebrate the LORD's Passover. 11But celebrate it at twilight on the fourteenth day of the second month. Eat the lamb with bitter herbs and bread made without yeast. 12Don't leave any of it until the next morning or break any of its bones. When you celebrate the Passover, follow all the rules. 13Anyone who is clean and is not away on a trip but does not eat the Passover must be cut off from the people. That person did not give an offering to the LORD at the appointed time and must be punished for the sin.

14" 'Foreigners among you may celebrate the LORD's Passover, but they must follow all the rules. You must have the same rules for foreigners as you have for yourselves.' "

The Cloud Above the Tent

15On the day the Holy Tent,[d] the Tent of the Agreement, was set up, a cloud covered it. From dusk until dawn the cloud above the Tent looked like fire. 16The cloud stayed above the Tent, and at night it looked like fire. 17When the cloud moved from its place over the Tent, the Israelites moved, and wherever the cloud stopped, the Israelites camped. 18So the Israelites moved at the LORD's command, and they camped at his command. While the cloud stayed over the Tent, they remained camped. 19Sometimes the cloud stayed over the Tent for a long time, but the Israelites obeyed the LORD and did not move. 20Sometimes the cloud was over it only a few days. At the LORD's command the people camped, and at his command they moved. 21Sometimes the cloud stayed only from dusk until dawn; when the cloud lifted the next morning, the people moved. When the cloud lifted, day or night, the people moved. 22The cloud might stay over the Tent for two days, a month, or a year. As long as it stayed, the people camped, but when it lifted, they moved. 23At the LORD's command the people camped, and at his command they moved. They obeyed the LORD's order that he commanded through Moses.

The Silver Trumpets

10 The LORD said to Moses, 2"Make two trumpets of hammered silver, and use them to call the people together and to march out of camp. 3When both trumpets are blown, the people should gather before you at the entrance to the Meeting Tent.[d] 4If you blow only one trumpet, the leaders, the heads of the family groups of Israel, should meet before you. 5When you loudly blow the trumpets, the tribes[d] camping on the east should move. 6When you loudly blow them again, the tribes camping on the south should move; the loud sound will tell them to move. 7When you want to gather the people, blow the trumpets, but don't blow them as loudly.

8"Aaron's sons, the priests, should blow the trumpets. This is a law for you and your descendants[d] from now on. 9When you are fighting an enemy who attacks you in your own land, blow the trumpets loudly. The LORD your God will take notice of you and will save you from your enemies. 10Also blow your trumpets at happy times and during your feasts and at New Moon[d] festivals. Blow them over your burnt offerings and fellowship offerings, because they will help you remember your God. I am the LORD your God."

The Israelites Move Camp

11The cloud lifted from the Tent[d] of the Agreement on the twentieth day of the second month of the second year. 12So the Israelites moved from the Desert of Sinai and continued until the cloud stopped in the Desert of Paran. 13This was their first time to move, and they did it as the LORD had commanded Moses.

14The divisions from the camp of Judah moved first under their flag. Nahshon son of Amminadab was the commander. 15Nethanel son of Zuar was over the division of the tribe[d] of Issachar. 16Eliab son of Helon was over the division of the tribe of Zebulun. 17Then the Holy Tent was taken down, and the Gershonites and Merarites, who carried it, moved next.

18Then came the divisions from the camp of Reuben under their flag, and Elizur son of Shedeur was the commander. 19Shelumiel son of Zurishaddai was over the division of the tribe of Simeon. 20Eliasaph son of Deuel was over the division of the tribe of Gad. 21Then came the Kohathites, who carried the holy things; the Holy Tent was to be set up before they arrived.

22Next came the divisions from the camp of Ephraim under their flag, and Elishama son of Ammihud was the commander. 23Gamaliel son of Pedahzur was over the division of the tribe of Manasseh, 24and Abidan son of Gideoni was over the division of the tribe of Benjamin.

25The last ones were the rear guard for all the tribes. These were the divisions from the camp of Dan under their flag, and Ahiezer son of Ammishaddai was the commander. 26Pagiel son of Ocran was over the division of the tribe of Asher; 27Ahira son of Enan was over the division of the tribe of Naphtali. 28This was the order the Israelite divisions marched in when they moved.

29Hobab was the son of Reuel the Midianite,[n] who was Moses' father-in-law. Moses said to Hobab, "We are moving to the land the LORD promised to give us. Come with us and we will be good to you, because the LORD has promised good things to Israel."

30But Hobab answered, "No, I will not go. I will go back to my own land where I was born."

31But Moses said, "Please don't leave us. You know where we can camp in the desert, and you can be our guide. 32Come with us. We will share with you all the good things the LORD gives us."

33So they left the mountain of the LORD and traveled for three days. The Ark[d] of the LORD's Agreement went in front of the people for those three days, as they looked for a place to camp. 34The LORD's cloud was over them during the day when they left their camp.

35When the Ark left the camp, Moses said,

"Rise up, LORD!
Scatter your enemies;
make those who hate you run from you."

36And when the Ark was set down, Moses said,

"Return, LORD,
to the thousands of people of Israel."

Fire from the Lord

11 Now the people complained to the LORD about their troubles, and when he heard them, he became angry. Then fire from the LORD burned among the people at the edge of the camp. 2The people cried out to Moses, and when he prayed to the LORD, the fire stopped burning. 3So that place was called Taberah,[n] because the LORD's fire had burned among them.

Seventy Older Leaders Help Moses

4Some troublemakers among them wanted better food, and soon all the Israelites began complaining. They said, "We want meat! 5We remember the fish we ate for free in Egypt. We also had cucumbers, melons, leeks, onions, and garlic. 6But now we have lost our appetite; we never see anything but this manna!"

7The manna was like small white seeds. 8The people would go to gather it, and then grind it in handmills, or crush it between stones. After they cooked it in a pot or made cakes with it, it tasted like bread baked with olive oil. 9When the dew fell on the camp each night, so did the manna.

10Moses heard every family crying as they stood in the entrances of their tents. Then the LORD became very angry, and Moses got upset. 11He asked the LORD, "Why have you brought me, your servant, this trouble? What have I done wrong that you made me responsible for all these people? 12I am not the father of all these people, and I didn't give birth to them. So why do you make me carry them to the land you promised to our ancestors? Must I carry them in my arms as a nurse carries a baby? 13Where can I get meat for all these people? They keep crying to me, 'We want meat!' 14I can't take care of all these people alone. It is too much for me. 15If you are going to continue doing this to me, then kill me now. If you care about me, put me to death, and then I won't have any more troubles."

16The LORD said to Moses, "Bring me seventy of Israel's older leaders, men that you know are leaders among the people. Bring them to the Meeting Tent,[d] and have them stand there with

Reuel the Midianite Also called Jethro.
Taberah This name means "burning."

you. 17I will come down and speak with you there. I will take some of the Spirit[d] that is in you, and I will give it to them. They will help you care for the people so that you will not have to care for them alone.

18"Tell the people this: 'Make yourselves holy for tomorrow, and you will eat meat. You cried to the LORD, "We want meat! We were better off in Egypt!" So now the LORD will give you meat to eat. 19You will eat it not for just one, two, five, ten, or even twenty days, 20but you will eat that meat for a whole month. You will eat it until it comes out your nose, and you will grow to hate it. This is because you have rejected the LORD, who is with you. You have cried to him, saying, "Why did we ever leave Egypt?" ' "

21Moses said, "LORD, here are six hundred thousand people standing around me, and you say, 'I will give them enough meat to eat for a month!' 22If we killed all the flocks and herds, that would not be enough. If we caught all the fish in the sea, that would not be enough."

23But the LORD said to Moses, "Do you think I'm weak? Now you will see if I can do what I say."

24So Moses went out to the people and told them what the LORD had said. He gathered seventy of the older leaders together and had them stand around the Tent. 25Then the LORD came down in the cloud and spoke to Moses. The LORD took some of the Spirit Moses had, and he gave it to the seventy leaders. With the Spirit in them, they prophesied,[d] but just that one time.

26Two men named Eldad and Medad were also listed as leaders, but they did not go to the Tent. They stayed in the camp, but the Spirit was also given to them, and they prophesied in the camp. 27A young man ran to Moses and said, "Eldad and Medad are prophesying in the camp."

28Joshua son of Nun said, "Moses, my master, stop them!" (Ever since he was a young boy, Joshua had been Moses' assistant.)

29But Moses answered, "Are you jealous for me? I wish all the LORD's people could prophesy. I wish the LORD would give his Spirit to all of them!" 30Then Moses and the leaders of Israel went back to the camp.

The Lord Sends Quail

31The LORD sent a strong wind from the sea, and it blew quail into the area all around the camp. The quail were about three feet deep on the ground, and there were quail a day's walk in any direction. 32The people went out and gathered quail all that day, that night, and the next day. Everyone gathered at least sixty bushels, and they spread them around the camp. 33But the LORD became very angry, and he gave the people a terrible sickness that came while the meat was still in their mouths. 34So the people named that place Kibroth Hattaavah,[n] because there they buried those who wanted other food.

35From Kibroth Hattaavah the people went to stay at Hazeroth.

> **SIDELIGHT:** If you get sick of Thanksgiving leftovers, imagine having one hundred eighty turkeys left! That's about how much quail the Israelites each gathered after complaining that God hadn't provided them with meat in the desert. No wonder they all got sick (Numbers 11:31–32).

Miriam and Aaron Speak Against Moses

12 Miriam and Aaron began to talk against Moses because of his Cushite wife (he had married a Cushite). 2They said, "Is Moses the only one the LORD speaks through? Doesn't he also speak through us?" And the LORD heard this.

3(Now Moses was very humble. He was the least proud person on earth.)

4So the LORD suddenly spoke to Moses, Aaron, and Miriam and said, "All three of you come to the Meeting Tent."[d] So they went. 5The LORD came down in a pillar of cloud and stood at the entrance to the Tent. He called to Aaron and Miriam, and they both came near. 6He said, "Listen to my words:

When a prophet[d] is among you,
I, the LORD, will show myself to him in visions;
I will speak to him in dreams.
7But this is not true with my servant Moses.
I trust him to lead all my people.
8I speak face to face with him—
clearly, not with hidden meanings.
He has even seen the form of the LORD.
You should be afraid
to speak against my servant Moses."

9The LORD was very angry with them, and he left.

10When the cloud lifted from the Tent and Aaron turned toward Miriam, she was as white as snow; she had a skin disease. 11Aaron said to Moses, "Please, my master, forgive us for our foolish sin. 12Don't let her be like a baby who is born dead. (Sometimes a baby is born with half of its flesh eaten away.)"

13So Moses cried out to the LORD, "God, please heal her!"

Kibroth Hattaavah This name in Hebrew means "graves of wanting."

14The LORD answered Moses, "If her father had spit in her face, she would have been shamed for seven days, so put her outside the camp for seven days. After that, she may come back." 15So Miriam was put outside of the camp for seven days, and the people did not move on until she came back.

16After that, the people left Hazeroth and camped in the Desert of Paran.

The Spies Explore Canaan

13 The LORD said to Moses, 2"Send men to explore the land of Canaan, which I will give to the Israelites. Send one leader from each tribe."[d]

3So Moses obeyed the LORD's command and sent the Israelite leaders out from the Desert of Paran. 4These are their names: from the tribe of Reuben, Shammua son of Zaccur; 5from the tribe of Simeon, Shaphat son of Hori; 6from the tribe of Judah, Caleb son of Jephunneh; 7from the tribe of Issachar, Igal son of Joseph; 8from the tribe of Ephraim, Hoshea son of Nun; 9from the tribe of Benjamin, Palti son of Raphu; 10from the tribe of Zebulun, Gaddiel son of Sodi; 11from the tribe of Manasseh (a tribe of Joseph), Gaddi son of Susi; 12from the tribe of Dan, Ammiel son of Gemalli; 13from the tribe of Asher, Sethur son of Michael; 14from the tribe of Naphtali, Nahbi son of Vophsi; 15from the tribe of Gad, Geuel son of Maki.

16These are the names of the men Moses sent to explore the land. (Moses gave Hoshea son of Nun the new name Joshua.)

17Moses sent them to explore Canaan and said, "Go through southern Canaan and then into the mountains. 18See what the land looks like. Are the people who live there strong or weak? Are there a few or many? 19What kind of land do they live in? Is it good or bad? What about the towns they live in—are they open like camps, or do they have walls? 20What about the soil? Is it fertile or poor? Are there trees there? Try to bring back some of the fruit from that land." (It was the season for the first grapes.)

21So they went up and explored the land, from the Desert of Zin all the way to Rehob by Lebo Hamath. 22They went through the southern area to Hebron, where Ahiman, Sheshai, and Talmai, the descendants[d] of Anak lived.[d] (The city of Hebron had been built seven years before Zoan in Egypt.) 23In the Valley of Eshcol, they cut off a branch of a grapevine that had one bunch of grapes on it and carried that branch on a pole between two of them. They also got some pomegranates[d] and figs. 24That place was called the Valley of Eshcol,[n] because the Israelites cut off the bunch of grapes there. 25After forty days of exploring the land, the men returned to the camp.

26They came back to Moses and Aaron and all the Israelites at Kadesh, in the Desert of Paran. The men reported to them and showed everybody the fruit from the land. 27They told Moses, "We went to the land where you sent us, and it is a fertile land! Here is some of its fruit. 28But the people who live there are strong. Their cities are walled and very large. We even saw some Anakites there. 29The Amalekites live in the southern area; the Hittites, Jebusites, and Amorites live in the mountains; and the Canaanites live near the sea and along the Jordan River."

30Then Caleb told the people near Moses to be quiet, and he said, "We should certainly go up and take the land for ourselves. We can certainly do it."

31But the men who had gone with him said, "We can't attack those people; they are stronger than we are." 32And those men gave the Israelites a bad report about the land they explored, saying, "The land that we explored is too large to conquer. All the people we saw are very tall. 33We saw the Nephilim[d] people there. (The Anakites come from the Nephilim people.) We felt like grasshoppers, and we looked like grasshoppers to them."

The People Complain Again

14 That night all the people in the camp began crying loudly. 2All the Israelites complained against Moses and Aaron, and all the people said to them, "We wish we had died in Egypt or in this desert. 3Why is the LORD bringing us to this land to be killed with swords? Our wives and children will be taken away. We would be better off going back to Egypt." 4They said to each other, "Let's choose a leader and go back to Egypt."

5Then Moses and Aaron bowed facedown in front of all the Israelites gathered there. 6Joshua son of Nun and Caleb son of Jephunneh, who had explored the land, tore their clothes. 7They said to all of the Israelites, "The land we explored is very good. 8If the LORD is pleased with us, he will lead us into that land and give us that fertile land. 9Don't turn against the LORD! Don't be afraid of the people in that land! We will chew them up. They have no protection, but the LORD is with us. So don't be afraid of them."

10Then all the people talked about killing them with stones. But the glory of the LORD appeared at the Meeting Tent[d] to all the Israelites. 11The LORD said to Moses, "How long will these people ignore me? How long will they not believe me in spite of the miracles[d] I have done among them? 12I will give them a terrible sickness and get rid of

Eshcol This name in Hebrew means "bunch."

them. But I will make you into a great nation that
will be stronger than they are."
13Then Moses said to the LORD, "The Egyptians
will hear about it! You brought these people from
there by your great power, 14and the Egyptians
will tell this to those who live in this land. They
have already heard about you, LORD. They know
that you are with your people and that you were
seen face to face. They know that your cloud stays
over your people and that you lead your people
with that cloud during the day and with fire at
night. 15If you put these people to death all at
once, the nations who have heard about your
power will say, 16'The LORD was not able to bring
them into the land he promised them. So he killed
them in the desert.'
17"So show your strength now, Lord. Do what
you said: 18'The LORD doesn't become angry
quickly, but he has great love. He forgives sin and
law breaking. But the LORD never forgets to punish guilty people. When parents sin, he will
also punish their children, their grandchildren,
their great-grandchildren, and their great-great-
grandchildren.' 19By your great love, forgive these
people's sin, just as you have forgiven them from
the time they left Egypt until now."
20The LORD answered, "I have forgiven them as
you asked. 21But, as surely as I live and as surely
as my glory fills the whole earth, I make this
promise: 22All these men saw my glory and the
miracles I did in Egypt and in the desert, but they
disobeyed me and tested me ten times. 23So not
one of them will see the land I promised to their
ancestors. No one who rejected me will see that
land. 24But my servant Caleb thinks differently
and follows me completely. So I will bring him
into the land he has already seen, and his children
will own that land. 25Since the Amalekites and
the Canaanites are living in the valleys, leave tomorrow and follow the desert road toward the
Red Sea."

The Lord Punishes the People

26The LORD said to Moses and Aaron, 27"How
long will these evil people complain about me? I
have heard the grumbling and complaining of
these Israelites. 28So tell them, 'This is what the
LORD says. I heard what you said, and as surely
as I live, I will do those very things to you: 29You
will die in this desert. Every one of you who is
twenty years old or older and who was counted
with the people—all of you who complained
against me—will die. 30Not one of you will enter
the land where I promised you would live; only
Caleb son of Jephunneh and Joshua son of Nun
will go in. 31You said that your children would be
taken away, but I will bring them into the land to
enjoy what you refused. 32As for you, you will die
in this desert. 33Your children will be shepherds
here for forty years. Because you were not loyal,
they will suffer until you lie dead in the desert.
34For forty years you will suffer for your sins—a
year for each of the forty days you explored the
land. You will know me as your enemy.' 35I, the
LORD, have spoken, and I will certainly do these
things to all these evil people who have come together against me. So they will all die here in this
desert."
36The men Moses had sent to explore the land
had returned and spread complaints among all the
people. They had given a bad report about the
land. 37The men who gave a very bad report died;
the LORD killed them with a terrible sickness.
38Only two of the men who explored the land did
not die—Joshua son of Nun and Caleb son of Jephunneh.
39When Moses told these things to all the Israelites, they were very sad. 40Early the next morning they started to go toward the top of the mountains, saying, "We have sinned. We will go where
the LORD told us."
41But Moses said, "Why are you disobeying the
LORD's command? You will not win! 42Don't go,
because the LORD is not with you and you will be
beaten by your enemies. 43You will run into the
Amalekites and Canaanites, who will kill you
with swords. You have turned away from the
LORD, so the LORD will not be with you."
44But they were proud. They went toward the
top of the mountains, but Moses and the Ark[d] of
the Agreement with the LORD did not leave the
camp. 45The Amalekites and the Canaanites who
lived in those mountains came down and attacked the Israelites and beat them back all the
way to Hormah.

Rules About Sacrifices

15 The LORD said to Moses, 2"Speak to the
Israelites and say to them, 'When you
enter the land that I am giving you as a home,
3give the LORD offerings made by fire. These may
be from your herds or flocks, as a smell pleasing
to the LORD. These may be burnt offerings or sacrifices for special promises, or as gifts to him, or
as festival offerings. 4The one who brings the offering shall also give the LORD a grain offering. It
should be two quarts of fine flour mixed with one
quart of olive oil. 5Each time you offer a lamb as
a burnt offering or sacrifice, also prepare a quart
of wine as a drink offering.
6" 'If you are giving a male sheep, also prepare
a grain offering of four quarts of fine flour mixed
with one and one-fourth quarts of olive oil. 7Also
prepare one and one-fourth quarts of wine as a
drink offering. Its smell will be pleasing to the
LORD.
8" 'If you prepare a young bull as a burnt offering or sacrifice, whether it is for a special promise

or a fellowship offering to the LORD, 9bring a grain offering with the bull. It should be six quarts of fine flour mixed with two quarts of olive oil. 10Also bring two quarts of wine as a drink offering. This offering is made by fire, and its smell will be pleasing to the LORD. 11Prepare each bull or male sheep, lamb or young goat this way. 12Do this for every one of the animals you bring.

13" 'All citizens must do these things in this way, and the smell of their offerings by fire will be pleasing to the LORD. 14From now on if foreigners who live among you want to make offerings by fire so the smell will be pleasing to the LORD, they must offer them the same way you do. 15The law is the same for you and for foreigners, and it will be from now on; you and the foreigners are alike before the LORD. 16The teachings and rules are the same for you and for the foreigners among you.' "

17The LORD said to Moses, 18"Tell the Israelites: 'You are going to another land, where I am taking you. 19When you eat the food there, offer part of it to the LORD. 20Offer a loaf of bread from the first of your grain, which will be your offering from the threshing[d] floor. 21From now on offer to the LORD the first part of your grain.

22" 'Now what if you forget to obey any of these commands the LORD gave Moses? 23These are the LORD's commands given to you through Moses, which began the day the LORD gave them to you and will continue from now on. 24If the people forget to obey one of these commands, all the people must offer a young bull as a burnt offering, a smell pleasing to the LORD. By law you must also give the grain offering and the drink offering with it, and you must bring a male goat as a sin offering.

25" 'The priest will remove that sin for all the Israelites so they will belong to the LORD. They are forgiven, because they didn't know they were sinning. For the wrong they did they brought offerings to the LORD, an offering by fire and a sin offering. 26So all of the people of Israel and the foreigners living among them will be forgiven. No one meant to do wrong.

27" 'If just one person sins without meaning to, a year-old female goat must be brought for a sin offering. 28The priest will remove the sin of the person who sinned accidentally. He will remove it before the LORD, and the person will be forgiven. 29The same teaching is for everyone who sins accidentally—for those born Israelites and for foreigners living among you.

30" 'But anyone who sins on purpose is against the LORD and must be cut off from the people, whether it is someone born among you or a foreigner. 31That person has turned against the LORD's word and has not obeyed his commands. Such a person must surely be cut off from the others. He is guilty.' "

A Man Worked on the Sabbath

32When the Israelites were still in the desert, they found a man gathering wood on the Sabbath[d] day. 33Those who found him gathering wood brought him to Moses and Aaron and all the people. 34They held the man under guard, because they did not know what to do with him. 35Then the LORD said to Moses, "The man must surely die. All the people must kill him by throwing stones at him outside the camp." 36So all the people took him outside the camp and stoned him to death, as the LORD commanded Moses.

The Tassels

37The LORD said to Moses, 38"Speak to the Israelites and tell them this: 'Tie several pieces of thread together and attach them to the corners of your clothes. Put a blue thread in each one of these tassels. Wear them from now on. 39You will have these tassels to look at to remind you of all the LORD's commands. Then you will obey them and not be disloyal by following what your bodies and eyes want. 40Then you will remember to obey all my commands, and you will be God's holy people. 41I am the LORD your God, who brought you out of Egypt to be your God. I am the LORD your God.' "

Korah, Dathan, Abiram, and On

16 Korah, Dathan, Abiram, and On turned against Moses. (Korah was the son of Izhar, the son of Kohath, the son of Levi; Dathan and Abiram were brothers, the sons of Eliab; and On was the son of Peleth; Dathan, Abiram, and On were from the tribe[d] of Reuben.) 2These men gathered two hundred fifty other Israelite men, well-known leaders chosen by the community, and challenged Moses. 3They came as a group to speak to Moses and Aaron and said, "You have gone too far. All the people are holy, every one of them, and the LORD is among them. So why do you put yourselves above all the people of the LORD?"

4When Moses heard this, he bowed facedown. 5Then he said to Korah and all his followers: "Tomorrow morning the LORD will show who belongs to him. He will bring the one who is holy near to him; he will bring to himself the person he chooses. 6So Korah, you and all your followers do this: Get some pans for burning incense.[d] 7Tomorrow put fire and incense in them and take them before the LORD. He will choose the man who is holy. You Levites have gone too far."

8Moses also said to Korah, "Listen, you Levites. 9The God of Israel has separated you from the rest of the Israelites. He brought you near to himself to do the work in the LORD's Holy Tent[d] and to stand before all the Israelites and serve them. Isn't that enough? 10He has brought you and all your fellow Levites near to himself, yet now you want to be priests. 11You and your followers have joined together against the LORD. Your complaint is not against Aaron."

12Then Moses called Dathan and Abiram, the sons of Eliab, but they said, "We will not come! 13You have brought us out of a fertile land to this desert to kill us, and now you want to order us around. 14You haven't brought us into a fertile land; you haven't given us any land with fields and vineyards. Will you put out the eyes of these men? No! We will not come!"

15Then Moses became very angry and said to the LORD, "Don't accept their gifts. I have not taken anything from them, not even a donkey, and I have not done wrong to any of them."

16Then Moses said to Korah, "You and all your followers must stand before the LORD tomorrow. And Aaron will stand there with you and them. 17Each of you must take your pan and put incense in it; present these two hundred fifty pans before the LORD. You and Aaron must also present your pans." 18So each man got his pan and put burning incense in it and stood with Moses and Aaron at the entrance to the Meeting Tent. 19Korah gathered all his followers who were against Moses and Aaron, and they stood at the entrance to the Meeting Tent. Then the glory of the LORD appeared to everyone.

20The LORD said to Moses and Aaron, 21"Move away from these men so I can destroy them quickly."

22But Moses and Aaron bowed facedown and cried out, "God, you are the God over the spirits of all people. Please don't be angry with this whole group. Only one man has really sinned."

23Then the LORD said to Moses, 24"Tell everyone to move away from the tents of Korah, Dathan, and Abiram."

25Moses stood and went to Dathan and Abiram; the older leaders of Israel followed him. 26Moses warned the people, "Move away from the tents of these evil men! Don't touch anything of theirs, or you will be destroyed because of their sins." 27So they moved away from the tents of Korah, Dathan, and Abiram. Dathan and Abiram were standing outside their tents with their wives, children, and little babies.

28Then Moses said, "Now you will know that the LORD has sent me to do all these things; it was not my idea. 29If these men die a normal death—the way men usually die—then the LORD did not really send me. 30But if the LORD does something new, you will know they have insulted the LORD. The ground will open and swallow them. They will be buried alive and will go to the place of the dead, and everything that belongs to them will go with them."

31When Moses finished saying these things, the ground under the men split open. 32The earth opened and swallowed them and all their families. All Korah's men and everything they owned went down. 33They were buried alive, going to the place of the dead, and everything they owned went with them. Then the earth covered them. They died and were gone from the community. 34The people of Israel around them heard their screams and ran away, saying, "The earth will swallow us, too!"

35Then a fire came down from the LORD and destroyed the two hundred fifty men who had presented the incense.

36The LORD said to Moses, 37"Tell Eleazar son of Aaron, the priest, to take all the incense pans out of the fire. Have him scatter the coals a long distance away. But the incense pans are still holy. 38Take the pans of these men who sinned and lost their lives, and hammer them into flat sheets that will be used to cover the altar. They are holy, because they were presented to the LORD, and they will be a sign to the Israelites."

39So Eleazar the priest gathered all the bronze pans that had been brought by the men who were burned up. He had the pans hammered into flat sheets to put on the altar, 40as the LORD had commanded him through Moses. These sheets were to remind the Israelites that only descendants[d] of Aaron should burn incense before the LORD. Anyone else would die like Korah and his followers.

Aaron Saves the People

41The next day all the Israelites complained against Moses and Aaron and said, "You have killed the LORD's people."

42When the people gathered to complain against Moses and Aaron, they turned toward the Meeting Tent,[d] and the cloud covered it. The glory of the LORD appeared. 43Then Moses and Aaron went in front of the Meeting Tent.

44The LORD said to Moses, 45"Move away from these people so I can destroy them quickly." So Moses and Aaron bowed facedown.

46Then Moses said to Aaron, "Get your pan, and put fire from the altar and incense[d] in it. Hurry to the people and remove their sin. The LORD is angry with them; the sickness has already started." 47So Aaron did as Moses said. He ran to the middle of the people, where the sickness had already started among them. So Aaron offered the incense to remove their sin. 48He stood between the dead and the living, and the sickness stopped there. 49But 14,700 people died from that sickness, in addition to those who died because of Korah. 50Then Aaron went back to Moses at the

entrance to the Meeting Tent. The terrible sickness had been stopped.

Aaron's Walking Stick Buds

17 The LORD said to Moses, 2"Speak to the
people of Israel and get twelve walking
sticks from them—one from the leader of each
tribe.[d] Write the name of each man on his stick,
and 3on the stick from Levi, write Aaron's name.
There must be one stick for the head of each tribe.
4Put them in the Meeting Tent[d] in front of the
Ark[d] of the Agreement, where I meet with you.
5I will choose one man whose walking stick will
begin to grow leaves; in this way I will stop the
Israelites from always complaining against
you."
6So Moses spoke to the Israelites. Each of the
twelve leaders gave him a walking stick—one
from each tribe—and Aaron's walking stick was
among them. 7Moses put them before the LORD
in the Tent of the Agreement.
8The next day, when Moses entered the Tent,
he saw that Aaron's stick (which stood for the
family of Levi) had grown leaves. It had even bud-
ded, blossomed, and produced almonds. 9So Moses brought out to the Israelites all the walking
sticks from the LORD's presence. They all looked,
and each man took back his stick.
10Then the LORD said to Moses, "Put Aaron's
walking stick back in front of the Ark of the Agreement. It will remind these people who are always
turning against me to stop their complaining
against me so they won't die." 11So Moses obeyed
what the LORD commanded him.
12The people of Israel said to Moses, "We are
going to die! We are destroyed. We are all destroyed! 13Anyone who even comes near the Holy
Tent of the LORD will die. Will we all die?"

The Work of the Priests and Levites

18 The LORD said to Aaron, "You, your
sons, and your family are now responsible for any wrongs done against the Holy Place;
you and your sons are responsible for any wrongs
done against the priests. 2Bring with you your fellow Levites from your tribe,[d] and they will help
you and your sons serve in the Tent[d] of the Agreement. 3They are under your control, to do all the
work that needs to be done in the Tent. But they
must not go near the things in the Holy Place or
near the altar. If they do, both you and they will
die. 4They will join you in taking care of the Meeting Tent. They must do the work at the Tent, and
no one else may come near you.
5"You must take care of the Holy Place and the
altar so that I won't become angry with the Israelites again. 6I myself chose your fellow Levites
from among the Israelites as a gift given for you
to the LORD, to work at the Meeting Tent. 7But
only you and your sons may serve as priests. Only
you may serve at the altar or go behind the curtain. I am giving you this gift of serving as a priest,
and anyone else who comes near the Holy Place
will be put to death."
8Then the LORD said to Aaron, "I myself make
you responsible for the offerings given to me. All
the holy offerings that the Israelites give to me, I
give to you and your sons as your share, your continual portion. 9Your share of the holy offerings is
that part which is not burned. When the people
bring me gifts as most holy offerings, whether
they are grain or sin or penalty offerings, they will
be set apart for you and your sons. 10You must eat
the offering in a most holy place. Any male may
eat it, but you must respect it as holy.
11"I also give you the offerings the Israelites
present to me. I give these to you and your sons
and daughters as your continual share. Anyone in
your family who is clean[d] may eat it.
12"And I give you all the best olive oil and all
the best new wine and grain. This is what the
Israelites give to me, the LORD, from the first
crops they harvest. 13When they bring to the
LORD all the first things they harvest, they will be
yours. Anyone in your family who is clean may
eat these things.
14"Everything in Israel that is given to the LORD
is yours. 15The first one born to any family,
whether people or animals, will be offered to the
LORD. And that will be yours. But you must make
a payment for every firstborn[d] child and every
firstborn animal that is unclean. 16When they are
one month old, you must make a payment for
them of two ounces of silver, as set by the Holy
Place measure.

> **SIDELIGHT:** Your parents may say you're priceless, but the ancient Hebrews knew exactly how much a baby was worth. Numbers 18:15–16 tells how parents had to offer their child to God and then buy it back for about two ounces of silver when the baby was a month old.

17"But you must not make a payment for the
firstborn ox or sheep or goat. Those animals are
holy. Sprinkle their blood on the altar and burn
their fat as an offering made by fire. The smell is
pleasing to the LORD. 18But the meat will be
yours, just as the breast that is presented and the
right thigh will be yours. 19Anything the Israelites
present as holy gifts I, the LORD, give to you, your
sons and daughters as your continual portion.

This is a lasting agreement of salt[n] before the
LORD for you and your children forever."
20The LORD also said to Aaron, "You will not
inherit any of the land, and you will not own any
land among the other people. I will be yours. Out
of all the Israelites, only you will inherit me.
21"When the people of Israel give me a tenth of
what they make, I will give that tenth to the Levites. This is their payment for the work they do
serving at the Meeting Tent. 22But the other Israelites must never go near the Meeting Tent, or
they will die for their sin. 23Only the Levites
should work in the Meeting Tent and be responsible for any sins against it. This is a rule from now
on. The Levites will not inherit any land among
the other Israelites, 24but when the Israelites give
a tenth of everything they make to me, I will give
that tenth to the Levites as a reward. That is why
I said about the Levites: 'They will not inherit any
land among the Israelites.' "
25The LORD said to Moses, 26"Speak to the Levites and tell them: 'You will receive a tenth of
everything the Israelites make, which I will give
to you. But you must give a tenth of that back to
the LORD. 27I will accept your offering just as
much as I accept the offerings from others, who
give new grain or new wine. 28In this way you
will present an offering to the LORD as the other
Israelites do. When you receive a tenth from the
Israelites, you will give a tenth of that to Aaron,
the priest, as the LORD's share. 29Choose the best
and holiest part from what you are given as the
portion you must give to the LORD.'
30"Say to the Levites: 'When you present the
best, it will be accepted as much as the grain and
wine from the other people. 31You and your families may eat all that is left anywhere, because it is
your pay for your work in the Meeting Tent.
32And if you always give the best part to the LORD,
you will never be guilty. If you do not sin against
the holy offerings of the Israelites, you will not
die.' "

The Offering for Cleansing

19 The LORD said to Moses and Aaron,
2"These are the teachings that the LORD
commanded. Tell the Israelites to get a young red
cow that does not have anything wrong with it
and that has never been worked. 3Give the cow
to Eleazar the priest; he will take it outside the
camp and kill it. 4Then Eleazar the priest must put
some of its blood on his finger and sprinkle it
seven times toward the front of the Meeting
Tent.[d] 5The whole cow must be burned while he
watches; the skin, the meat, the blood, and the
intestines must all be burned. 6Then the priest
must take a cedar stick, a hyssop branch, and a
red string and throw them onto the burning cow.
7After the priest has washed himself and his
clothes with water, he may come back into the
camp, but he will be unclean[d] until evening. 8The
man who burns the cow must wash himself and
his clothes in water; he will be unclean until evening.
9"Then someone who is clean will collect the
ashes from the cow and put them in a clean place
outside the camp. The Israelites will keep these
ashes to use in the cleansing water, in a special
ceremony to cleanse away sin. 10The man who
collected the cow's ashes must wash his clothes
and be unclean until evening. This is a lasting rule
for the Israelites and for the foreigners among
them.
11"Those who touch a dead person's body will
be unclean for seven days. 12They must wash
themselves with the cleansing water on the third
day and on the seventh day; then they will be
clean. But if they do not wash themselves on the
third day and the seventh day, they cannot be
clean. 13If those who touch a dead person's body
stay unclean and go to the LORD's Holy Tent, it
becomes unclean; they must be cut off from Israel. If the cleansing water is not sprinkled on
them, they are unclean and will stay unclean.
14"This is the teaching about someone who
dies in a tent: Anyone in the tent or anyone who
enters it will be unclean for seven days. 15And
every open jar or pot without a cover becomes
unclean. 16If anyone is outside and touches someone who was killed by a sword or who died a
natural death, or if anyone touches a human bone
or a grave, that person will be unclean for seven
days.
17"So you must use the ashes from the burnt
offering to make that person clean again. Pour
fresh water over the ashes into a jar. 18A clean
person must take a hyssop branch and dip it into
the water, and then he must sprinkle it over the
Tent and all its objects. He must also sprinkle the
people who were there, as well as anyone who
touched a bone, or the body of someone who was
killed, or a dead person, or a grave. 19The person
who is clean must sprinkle this water on the unclean people on the third day and on the seventh
day. On the seventh day they will become clean.
They must wash their clothes and take a bath, and
they will be clean that evening. 20If any who are
unclean do not become clean, they must be cut
off from the community. Since they were not
sprinkled with the cleansing water, they stay unclean, and they could make the LORD's Holy Tent

agreement of salt The meaning is not clear, but Leviticus 2:13 says, "Salt stands for your agreement with God that will last forever."

unclean. 21This is a lasting rule. Those who sprinkle the cleansing water must also wash their clothes, and anyone who touches the water will be unclean until evening. 22Anything an unclean person touches becomes unclean, and whoever touches it will be unclean until evening."

Moses Disobeys God

20 In the first month all the people of Israel arrived at the Desert of Zin, and they stayed at Kadesh. There Miriam died and was buried. 2There was no water for the people, so they came together against Moses and Aaron. 3They argued with Moses and said, "We should have died in front of the LORD as our brothers did. 4Why did you bring the LORD's people into this desert? Are we and our animals to die here? 5Why did you bring us from Egypt to this terrible place? It has no grain, figs, grapevines, or pomegranates,[d] and there's no water to drink!"

6So Moses and Aaron left the people and went to the entrance of the Meeting Tent.[d] There they bowed facedown, and the glory of the LORD appeared to them. 7The LORD said to Moses, 8"Take your walking stick, and you and your brother Aaron should gather the people. Speak to that rock in front of them so that its water will flow from it. When you bring the water out from that rock, give it to the people and their animals."

9So Moses took the stick from in front of the LORD, as he had said. 10Moses and Aaron gathered the people in front of the rock, and Moses said, "Now listen to me, you who turn against God! Do you want us to bring water out of this rock?" 11Then Moses lifted his hand and hit the rock twice with his stick. Water began pouring out, and the people and their animals drank it.

12But the LORD said to Moses and Aaron, "Because you did not believe me, and because you did not honor me as holy before the people, you will not lead them into the land I will give them."

13These are the waters of Meribah,[n] where the Israelites argued with the LORD and where he showed them he was holy.

Edom Will Not Let Israel Pass

14From Kadesh, Moses sent messengers to the king of Edom. He said, "Your brothers, the Israelites, say to you: You know about all the troubles we have had, 15how our ancestors went down into Egypt and we lived there for many years. The people of Egypt were cruel to us and our ancestors, 16but when we cried out to the LORD, he heard us and sent us an angel to bring us out of Egypt.

"Now we are here at Kadesh, a town on the edge of your land. 17Please let us pass through your country. We will not touch any fields of grain or vineyards, and will not drink water from the wells. We will travel only along the king's road, not turning right or left until we have passed through your country."

18But the king of Edom answered: "You may not pass through here. If you try, I will come and meet you with swords."

19The Israelites answered: "We will go along the main road, and if we or our animals drink any of your water, we will pay for it. We only want to walk through. That's all."

20But he answered: "You may not pass through here."

Then the Edomites went out to meet the Israelites with a large and powerful army. 21The Edomites refused to let them pass through their country, so the Israelites turned back.

Aaron Dies

22All the Israelites moved from Kadesh to Mount Hor, 23near the border of Edom. There the LORD said to Moses and Aaron, 24"Aaron will die. He will not enter the land that I'm giving to the Israelites, because you both acted against my command at the waters of Meribah. 25Take Aaron and his son Eleazar up on Mount Hor, 26and take off Aaron's special clothes and put them on his son Eleazar. Aaron will die there; he will join his ancestors."

27Moses obeyed the LORD's command. They climbed up Mount Hor, and all the people saw them go. 28Moses took off Aaron's clothes and put them on Aaron's son Eleazar. Then Aaron died there on top of the mountain. Moses and Eleazar came back down the mountain, 29and when all the people learned that Aaron was dead, everyone in Israel cried for him for thirty days.

War with the Canaanites

21 The Canaanite king of Arad lived in the southern area. When he heard that the Israelites were coming on the road to Atharim, he attacked them and captured some of them. 2Then the Israelites made this promise to the LORD: "If you will help us defeat these people, we will completely destroy their cities." 3The LORD listened to the Israelites, and he let them defeat the Canaanites. The Israelites completely destroyed the Canaanites and their cities, so the place was named Hormah.[n]

The Bronze Snake

4The Israelites left Mount Hor and went on the road toward the Red Sea, in order to go around

Meribah This name in Hebrew means "argument."
Hormah This name in Hebrew means "completely destroyed."

the country of Edom. But the people became impatient on the way 5and grumbled at God and
Moses. They said, "Why did you bring us out of
Egypt to die in this desert? There is no bread and
no water, and we hate this terrible food!"
6So the LORD sent them poisonous snakes; they
bit the people, and many of the Israelites died.
7The people came to Moses and said, "We sinned
when we grumbled at you and the LORD. Pray
that the LORD will take away these snakes." So
Moses prayed for the people.
8The LORD said to Moses, "Make a bronze
snake, and put it on a pole. When anyone who is
bitten looks at it, that person will live." 9So Moses
made a bronze snake and put it on a pole. Then
when a snake bit anyone, that person looked at
the bronze snake and lived.

The Journey to Moab

10The Israelites went and camped at Oboth.
11They went from Oboth to Iye Abarim, in the
desert east of Moab. 12From there they went and
camped in the Zered Valley. 13From there they
went and camped across the Arnon, in the desert
just inside the Amorite country. The Arnon is the
border between the Moabites and the Amorites.
14That is why the Book of the Wars of the LORD
says:

"... and Waheb in Suphah, and the ravines,
the Arnon, 15and the slopes of the ravines
that lead to the settlement of Ar.
These places are at the border of Moab."

16The Israelites went from there to Beer; a well
is there where the LORD said to Moses, "Gather
the people and I will give them water."

DISCOURAGEMENT

Specially Chosen

If there was anything Adrienne Rivera didn't want, it was attention. She felt self-conscious about her looks, and she was fairly sure no one really liked her.

Adrienne began having trouble with her right knee. Soon she could hardly walk on it, and nothing eased the pain. Finally, she went to a doctor.

She couldn't believe what the doctor found: a rare, cancerous tumor. And to save her life, he had to treat her with chemotherapy and then amputate her leg.

Amputate? Word spread fast through school. Adrienne—who avoided being in the spotlight—suddenly found herself the center of school gossip and the focus of curious stares. She hated it.

Adrienne was confused and angry. Was God punishing her? What had she done to deserve this?

Then one day during her chemo treatments, Adrienne was thinking about her three-in-a-million chance of getting this cancer. And a thought struck her. "Suppose God isn't punishing me? Suppose he chose me?"

Adrienne's new perspective gave her the courage to face surgery—and the world. During recovery, her shyness disappeared as she answered her classmates' questions and satisfied their curiosity.

With just one natural leg, she joined the school flag squad, swim team, and track team. Recently she started something she probably wouldn't have done with two legs: downhill competitive skiing. Now there's no stopping the girl who once had trouble standing on her own two feet.

Like Adrienne, the Israelites in the Bible faced a discouraging situation. Read how they dealt with discouragement in **Numbers 21:4–9**.

- How were Adrienne's questions like the questions the Israelites asked? How did God provide hope and healing for Adrienne and the Israelites in the midst of discouragement?
- When you're discouraged, how can this passage help your attitude?

CONSIDER . . .

- listing reasons you get discouraged. Then use a marker to write "But God . . ." boldly over each reason.
- asking a friend, parent, or trusted adult for help if your discouragement is overwhelming.

FOR MORE, SEE . . .

- Job 19:7–27(p. 463)
- Psalm 56:1–13 (p. 514)
- Romans 8:31–39 (p. 1152)

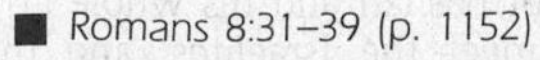

17Then the Israelites sang this song:
"Pour out water, well!
Sing about it.
18Princes dug this well.
Important men made it.
With their scepters[d] and poles, they dug it."
The people went from the desert to Mattanah.
19From Mattanah they went to Nahaliel and on to
Bamoth. 20From Bamoth they went to the valley
of Moab where the top of Mount Pisgah looks
over the desert.

Israel Kills Sihon and Og

21The Israelites sent messengers to Sihon, king
of the Amorites, saying, 22"Let us pass through
your country. We will not go through any fields
of grain or vineyards, or drink water from the
wells. We will travel only along the king's road
until we have passed through your country."
23But King Sihon would not let the Israelites
pass through his country. He gathered his whole
army together, and they marched out to meet Israel in the desert. At Jahaz they fought the Israelites. 24Israel killed the king and captured his land
from the Arnon River to the Jabbok River. They
took the land as far as the Ammonite border,
which was strongly defended. 25Israel captured all
the Amorite cities and lived in them, taking Heshbon and all the towns around it. 26Heshbon was
the city where Sihon, the Amorite king, lived. In
the past he had fought with the king of Moab and
had taken all the land as far as the Arnon.
27That is why the poets say:
"Come to Heshbon
and rebuild it;
rebuild Sihon's city.
28A fire began in Heshbon;
flames came from Sihon's city.
It destroyed Ar in Moab,
and it burned the Arnon highlands.
29How terrible for you, Moab!
The people of Chemosh[d] are ruined.
His sons ran away
and his daughters were captured
by Sihon, king of the Amorites.
30But we defeated those Amorites.
We ruined their towns from Heshbon to
Dibon,
and we destroyed them as far as Nophah,
near Medeba."
31So Israel lived in the land of the Amorites.
32After Moses sent spies to the town of Jazer,
they captured the towns around it, forcing out the
Amorites who lived there.
33Then the Israelites went up the road toward
Bashan. Og king of Bashan and his whole army
marched out to meet the Israelites, and they
fought at Edrei.
34The LORD said to Moses, "Don't be afraid of
him. I will hand him, his whole army, and his
land over to you. Do to him what you did to Sihon, the Amorite king who lived in Heshbon."
35So the Israelites killed Og and his sons and all
his army; no one was left alive. And they took his
land.

Balak Sends for Balaam

22 Then the people of Israel went to the
plains of Moab, and they camped near
the Jordan River across from Jericho.
2Balak son of Zippor saw everything the Israelites had done to the Amorites. 3And Moab was
scared of so many Israelites; truly, Moab was terrified by them.
4The Moabites said to the older leaders of Midian, "These people will take everything around us
like an ox eating grass."
Balak son of Zippor was the king of Moab at
this time. 5He sent messengers to Balaam son of
Beor at Pethor, near the Euphrates River in his
native land. Balak said, "A nation has come out of
Egypt that covers the land. They have camped
next to me, 6and they are too powerful for me. So
come and put a curse on them. Maybe then I can
defeat them and make them leave the area. I
know that if you bless someone, the blessings happen, and if you put a curse on someone, it happens."
7The older leaders of Moab and Midian went
with payment in their hands. When they found
Balaam, they told him what Balak had said.
8Balaam said to them, "Stay here for the night,
and I will tell you what the LORD tells me." So the
Moabite leaders stayed with him.
9God came to Balaam and asked, "Who are
these men with you?"
10Balaam said to God, "The king of Moab, Balak son of Zippor, sent them to me with this message: 11'A nation has come out of Egypt that covers the land. So come and put a curse on them,
and maybe I can fight them and force them out
of my land.' "
12But God said to Balaam, "Do not go with
them. Don't put a curse on those people, because
I have blessed them."
13The next morning Balaam awoke and said to
Balak's leaders, "Go back to your own country;
the LORD has refused to let me go with you."
14So the Moabite leaders went back to Balak
and said, "Balaam refused to come with us."
15So Balak sent other leaders—this time there
were more of them, and they were more important. 16They went to Balaam and said, "Balak son
of Zippor says this: Please don't let anything stop
you from coming to me. 17I will pay you very well,
and I will do what you say. Come and put a curse
on these people for me."
18But Balaam answered Balak's servants, "King

Balak could give me his palace full of silver and
gold, but I cannot disobey the LORD my God in
anything, great or small. 19You stay here tonight
as the other men did, and I will find out what
more the LORD tells me."

20That night God came to Balaam and said,
"These men have come to ask you to go with
them. Go, but only do what I tell you."

Balaam's Donkey Speaks

21Balaam got up the next morning and put a
saddle on his donkey. Then he went with the Moabite leaders. 22But God became angry because
Balaam went, so the angel of the LORD stood in
the road to stop Balaam. Balaam was riding his
donkey, and he had two servants with him.
23When the donkey saw the angel of the LORD
standing in the road with a sword in his hand, the
donkey left the road and went into the field. Balaam hit the donkey to force her back on the road.

24Later, the angel of the LORD stood on a narrow path between two vineyards, with walls on
both sides. 25Again the donkey saw the angel of
the LORD, and she walked close to one wall,
crushing Balaam's foot against it. So he hit her
again.

26The angel of the LORD went ahead again and
stood at a narrow place, too narrow to turn left or
right. 27When the donkey saw the angel of the
LORD, she lay down under Balaam. This made
him so angry that he hit her with his stick. 28Then
the LORD made the donkey talk, and she said to
Balaam, "What have I done to make you hit me
three times?"

29Balaam answered the donkey, "You have
made me look foolish! I wish I had a sword in my
hand! I would kill you right now!"

> **SIDELIGHT:** When pets talk, people listen. At least Balaam listened when his donkey talked (Numbers 22:21–30). And it's good that he listened, because the donkey's advice kept him out of some serious trouble. But Balaam later led the Israelites to sin (Numbers 31:16, p. 155), which is why Bible writers consider him evil (see, for example, 2 Peter 2:15–16, p. 1312, and Revelation 2:14, p. 1333).

30But the donkey said to Balaam, "I am your
very own donkey, which you have ridden for
years. Have I ever done this to you before?"

"No," Balaam said.

31Then the LORD let Balaam see the angel of the
LORD, who was standing in the road with his
sword drawn. Then Balaam bowed facedown on
the ground.

32The angel of the LORD asked Balaam, "Why
have you hit your donkey three times? I have
stood here to stop you, because what you are doing is wrong. 33The donkey saw me and turned
away from me three times. If she had not turned
away, I would have killed you by now, but I
would have let her live."

34Then Balaam said to the angel of the LORD, "I
have sinned; I did not know you were standing in
the road to stop me. If I am wrong, I will go
back."

35The angel of the LORD said to Balaam, "Go
with these men, but say only what I tell you." So
Balaam went with Balak's leaders.

36When Balak heard that Balaam was coming,
he went out to meet him at Ar in Moab, which
was beside the Arnon, at the edge of his country.
37Balak said to Balaam, "I had asked you before to
come quickly. Why didn't you come to me? I am
able to reward you well."

38But Balaam answered, "I have come to you
now, but I can't say just anything. I can only say
what God tells me to say."

39Then Balaam went with Balak to Kiriath Hu-
zoth. 40Balak offered cattle and sheep as a sacrifice
and gave some meat to Balaam and the leaders
with him.

41The next morning Balak took Balaam to Bamoth Baal; from there he could see the edge of
the Israelite camp.

Balaam's First Message

23 Balaam said to Balak, "Build me seven
altars here, and prepare seven bulls and
seven male sheep for me." 2Balak did what Balaam asked, and they offered a bull and a male
sheep on each of the altars.

3Then Balaam said to Balak, "Stay here beside
your burnt offering and I will go. If the LORD
comes to me, I will tell you whatever he shows
me." Then Balaam went to a higher place.

4God came to Balaam there, and Balaam said to
him, "I have prepared seven altars, and I have
offered a bull and a male sheep on each altar."

5The LORD told Balaam what he should say.
Then the LORD said, "Go back to Balak and give
him this message."

6So Balaam went back to Balak. Balak and all
the leaders of Moab were still standing beside his
burnt offering 7when Balaam gave them this message:

"Balak brought me here from Aram;
the king of Moab brought me from the
eastern mountains.
Balak said, 'Come, put a curse on the people
of Jacob for me.

Come, call down evil on the people of
Israel.'
8But God has not cursed them,
so I cannot curse them.
The LORD has not called down evil on them,
so I cannot call down evil on them.
9I see them from the top of the mountains;
I see them from the hills.
I see a people who live alone,
who think they are different from other
nations.
10No one can number the many people of
Jacob,
and no one can count a fourth of Israel.
Let me die like good men,
and let me end up like them!"
11Balak said to Balaam, "What have you done
to me? I brought you here to curse my enemies,
but you have only blessed them!"
12But Balaam answered, "I must say what the
LORD tells me to say."

Balaam's Second Message

13Then Balak said to him, "Come with me to
another place, where you can also see the people.
But you can only see part of them, not all of them.
Curse them for me from there." 14So Balak took
Balaam to the field of Zophim, on top of Mount
Pisgah. There Balak built seven altars and offered
a bull and a male sheep on each altar.
15So Balaam said to Balak, "Stay here by your
burnt offering, and I will meet with God over
there."
16So the LORD came to Balaam and told him
what to say. Then he said, "Go back to Balak and
say such and such."
17So Balaam went to Balak, where he and the
leaders of Moab were standing beside his burnt
offering. Balak asked him, "What did the LORD
say?"
18Then Balaam gave this message:
"Stand up, Balak, and listen.
Hear me, son of Zippor.
19God is not a human being, and he will not
lie.
He is not a human, and he does not change
his mind.
What he says he will do, he does.
What he promises, he makes come true.
20He told me to bless them,
so I cannot change the blessing.
21He has found no wrong in the people of
Jacob;
he saw no fault in Israel.
The LORD their God is with them,
and they praise their King.
22God brought them out of Egypt;
they are as strong as a wild ox.
23No tricks will work on the people of Jacob,
and no magic will work against Israel.
People now say about them,
'Look what God has done for Israel!'
24The people rise up like a lioness;
they get up like a lion.
Lions don't rest until they have eaten,
until they have drunk their enemies'
blood."
25Then Balak said to Balaam, "You haven't
cursed these people, so at least, don't bless
them!"
26Balaam answered Balak, "I told you before
that I can only do what the LORD tells me."

Balaam's Third Message

27Then Balak said to Balaam, "Come, I will take
you to another place. Maybe God will be pleased
to let you curse them from there." 28So Balak took
Balaam to the top of Peor, the mountain that
looks over the desert.
29Balaam told Balak, "Build me seven altars
here and prepare for me seven bulls and seven
male sheep." 30Balak did what Balaam asked, and
he offered a bull and a male sheep on each altar.

24 Balaam saw that the LORD wanted to
bless Israel, so he did not try to use any
magic but looked toward the desert. 2When Balaam saw the Israelites camped in their tribes,[d]
the Spirit[d] of God took control of him, 3and he
gave this message:
"This is the message of Balaam son of Beor,
the message of a man who sees clearly;
4this is the message of a man who hears the
words of God.
I see a vision from the Almighty,
and my eyes are open as I fall before him.
5Your tents are beautiful, people of Jacob!
So are your homes, Israel!
6Your tents spread out like valleys,
like gardens beside a river.
They are like spices planted by the LORD,
like cedar trees growing by the water.
7Israel's water buckets will always be full,
and their crops will have plenty of water.
Their king will be greater than Agag;
their kingdom will be very great.
8God brought them out of Egypt;
they are as strong as a wild ox.
They will defeat their enemies
and break their enemies' bones;
they will shoot them with arrows.
9Like a lion, they lie waiting to attack;
like a lioness, no one would be brave
enough to wake them.
Anyone who blesses you will be blessed,
and anyone who curses you will be
cursed."
10Then Balak was angry with Balaam, and he
pounded his fist. He said to Balaam, "I called you

here to curse my enemies, but you have continued to bless them three times. 11Now go home!
I said I would pay you well, but the LORD has
made you lose your reward."
12Balaam said to Balak, "When you sent messengers to me, I told them, 13'Balak could give me
his palace filled with silver and gold, but I still
cannot go against the LORD's commands. I could
not do anything, good or bad, on my own, but I
must say what the LORD says.' 14Now I am going
back to my own people, but I will tell you what
these people will do to your people in the future."

Balaam's Final Message

15Then Balaam gave this message:
"This is the message of Balaam son of Beor,
the message of a man who sees clearly;
16this is the message of a man who hears the
words of God.
I know well the Most High God.
I see a vision from the Almighty,
and my eyes are open as I fall before him.
17I see someone who will come some day,
someone who will come, but not soon.
A star will come from Jacob;
a ruler will rise from Israel.
He will crush the heads of the Moabites
and smash the skulls of the sons of Sheth.
18Edom will be conquered;
his enemy Edom will be conquered,
but Israel will grow wealthy.
19A ruler will come from the descendants[d] of
Jacob
and will destroy those left in the city."

20Then Balaam saw Amalek and gave this message:
"Amalek was the most important nation,
but Amalek will be destroyed at last."

21Then Balaam saw the Kenites and gave this
message:
"Your home is safe,
like a nest on a cliff.
22But you Kenites will be burned up;
Assyria will keep you captive."

23Then Balaam gave this message:
"No one can live when God does this.
24 Ships will sail from the shores of Cyprus
and defeat Assyria and Eber,
but they will also be destroyed."

25Then Balaam got up and returned home, and
Balak also went on his way.

Israel Worships Baal at Peor

25 While the people of Israel were still
camped at Acacia, the men began sinning sexually with Moabite women. 2The women
invited them to their sacrifices to their gods, and
the Israelites ate food there and worshiped these
gods. 3So the Israelites began to worship Baal[d] of
Peor, and the LORD was very angry with them.
4The LORD said to Moses, "Get all the leaders
of the people and kill them in open daylight in the
presence of the LORD. Then the LORD will not be
angry with the people of Israel."
5So Moses said to Israel's judges, "Each of you
must put to death your people who have become
worshipers of Baal of Peor."
6Moses and the Israelites were gathered at the
entrance to the Meeting Tent,[d] crying there. Then
an Israelite man brought a Midianite woman to
his brothers in plain sight of Moses and all the
people. 7Phinehas son of Eleazar, the son of
Aaron, the priest, saw this, so he left the meeting
and got his spear. 8He followed the Israelite into
his tent and drove his spear through both the Israelite man and the Midianite woman. Then the
terrible sickness among the Israelites stopped.
9This sickness had killed twenty-four thousand
people.
10The LORD said to Moses, 11"Phinehas son of
Eleazar, the son of Aaron, the priest, has saved the
Israelites from my anger. He hates sin as much as
I do. Since he tried to save my honor among
them, I will not kill them. 12So tell Phinehas that
I am making my peace agreement with him. 13He
and his descendants[d] will always be priests, because he had great concern for the honor of his
God. He removed the sins of the Israelites so they
would belong to God."
14The Israelite man who was killed with the
Midianite woman was named Zimri son of Salu.
He was the leader of a family in the tribe[d] of Simeon. 15And the name of the Midianite woman
who was put to death was Cozbi daughter of Zur,
who was the chief of a Midianite family.
16The LORD said to Moses, 17"The Midianites
are your enemies, and you should kill them.
18They have already made you their enemies, because they tricked you at Peor and because of
their sister Cozbi, the daughter of a Midianite
leader. She was the woman who was killed when
the sickness came because the people sinned at
Peor."

The People Are Counted

26 After the great sickness, the LORD said to
Moses and Eleazar son of Aaron, the
priest, 2"Count all the people of Israel by families.
Count all the men who are twenty years old or
older who will serve in the army of Israel." 3Mo-
ses and Eleazar the priest spoke to the people on
the plains of Moab near the Jordan River, across
from Jericho. They said, 4"Count the men twenty
years old or older, as the LORD commanded Moses."
Here are the Israelites who came out of Egypt:

[5]The tribe[a] of Reuben, the first son born to Israel, was counted. From Hanoch came the Ha-
nochite family group; from Pallu came the Pallu-
ite family group; [6]from Hezron came the
Hezronite family group; from Carmi came the
Carmite family group. [7]These were the family
groups of Reuben, and the total number of men
was 43,730.
[8]The son of Pallu was Eliab, [9]and Eliab's sons
were Nemuel, Dathan, and Abiram. Dathan and
Abiram were the leaders who turned against Moses and Aaron and followed Korah when he
turned against the LORD. [10]The earth opened up
and swallowed them and Korah; they died at the
same time the fire burned up the 250 men. This
was a warning, [11]but the children of Korah did not
die.
[12]These were the family groups in the tribe of
Simeon: From Nemuel came the Nemuelite family group; from Jamin came the Jaminite family
group; from Jakin came the Jakinite family group;
[13]from Zerah came the Zerahite family group;
from Shaul came the Shaulite family group.
[14]These were the family groups of Simeon, and
the total number of men was 22,200.
[15]These were the family groups in the tribe
of Gad: From Zephon came the Zephonite family group; from Haggi came the Haggite family group; from Shuni came the Shunite family
group; [16]from Ozni came the Oznite family
group; from Eri came the Erite family group;
[17]from Arodi came the Arodite family group; from
Areli came the Arelite family group. [18]These were
the family groups of Gad, and the total number of
men was 40,500.
[19]Two of Judah's sons, Er and Onan, died in
Canaan.
[20]These were the family groups in the tribe
of Judah: From Shelah came the Shelanite family group; from Perez came the Perezite family
group; from Zerah came the Zerahite family
group. [21]These were the family groups from Perez: From Hezron came the Hezronite family
group; from Hamul came the Hamulite family
group. [22]These were the family groups of Judah,
and the total number of men was 76,500.
[23]These were the family groups in the tribe of
Issachar: From Tola came the Tolaite family
group; from Puah came the Puite family group;
[24]from Jashub came the Jashubite family group;
from Shimron came the Shimronite family group.
[25]These were the family groups of Issachar, and
the total number of men was 64,300.
[26]These were the family groups in the tribe of
Zebulun: From Sered came the Seredite family
group; from Elon came the Elonite family group;
from Jahleel came the Jahleelite family group.
[27]These were the family groups of Zebulun, and
the total number of men was 60,500.

[28]These were the family groups of Joseph
through Manasseh and Ephraim.
[29]These were the family groups of Manasseh:
From Makir came the Makirite family group (Makir was the father of Gilead); from Gilead came
the Gileadite family group. [30]These were the family groups that came from Gilead: From Iezer
came the Iezerite family group; from Helek came
the Helekite family group; [31]from Asriel came the
Asrielite family group; from Shechem came the
Shechemite family group; [32]from Shemida came
the Shemidaite family group; from Hepher came
the Hepherite family group. [33](Zelophehad son of
Hepher had no sons; he had only daughters, and
their names were Mahlah, Noah, Hoglah, Milcah,
and Tirzah.) [34]These were the family groups of
Manasseh, and the total number of men was
52,700.
[35]These were the family groups in the tribe of
Ephraim: From Shuthelah came the Shuthelahite
family group; from Beker came the Bekerite family group; from Tahan came the Tahanite family
group. [36]This was the family group from Shuthelah: From Eran came the Eranite family group.
[37]These were the family groups of Ephraim, and
the total number of men was 32,500. These are
the family groups that came from Joseph.
[38]These were the family groups in the tribe
of Benjamin: From Bela came the Belaite family group; from Ashbel came the Ashbelite family
group; from Ahiram came the Ahiramite family
group; [39]from Shupham came the Shuphamite
family group; from Hupham came the Huphamite
family group. [40]These were the family groups
from Bela through Ard and Naaman: From Ard
came the Ardite family group; from Naaman
came the Naamite family group. [41]These were the
family groups of Benjamin, and the total number
of men was 45,600.
[42]This was the family group in the tribe of Dan:
From Shuham came the Shuhamite family group.
That was the family of Dan, [43]and the total number of men in the Shuhamite family group of Dan
was 64,400.
[44]These were the family groups in the tribe of
Asher: From Imnah came the Imnite family
group; from Ishvi came the Ishvite family group;
from Beriah came the Beriite family group.
[45]These were the family groups that came from
Beriah: From Heber came the Heberite family
group; from Malkiel came the Malkielite family
group. [46](Asher also had a daughter named Serah.) [47]These were the family groups of Asher,
and the total number of men was 53,400.
[48]These were the family groups in the tribe of
Naphtali: From Jahzeel came the Jahzeelite family
group; from Guni came the Gunite family group;
[49]from Jezer came the Jezerite family group; from
Shillem came the Shillemite family group. [50]These

were the family groups of Naphtali, and the total number of men was 45,400.

51So the total number of the men of Israel was 601,730.

52The LORD said to Moses, 53"Divide the land among these people by the number of names. 54A large tribe will get more land, and a small tribe will get less land; the amount of land each tribe gets will depend on the number of its people. 55Divide the land by drawing lots,[d] and the land each tribe gets will be named for that tribe. 56Divide the land between large and small groups by drawing lots."

57The tribe of Levi was also counted. These were the family groups of Levi: From Gershon came the Gershonite family group; from Kohath came the Kohathite family group; from Merari came the Merarite family group. 58These also were Levite family groups: the Libnite family group, the Hebronite family group, the Mahlite family group, the Mushite family group, and the Korahite family group. (Kohath was the ancestor of Amram, 59whose wife was named Jochebed. She was from the tribe of Levi and she was born in Egypt. She and Amram had two sons, Aaron and Moses, and their sister Miriam. 60Aaron was the father of Nadab, Abihu, Eleazar, and Ithamar. 61But Nadab and Abihu died because they made an offering before the LORD with the wrong kind of fire.)

62The total number of male Levites one month old or older was 23,000. But these men were not counted with the other Israelites, because they were not given any of the land among the other Israelites.

63Moses and Eleazar the priest counted all these people. They counted the Israelites on the plains of Moab across the Jordan River from Jericho. 64Moses and Aaron the priest had counted the Israelites in the Desert of Sinai, but no one Moses counted on the plains of Moab was in the first counting. 65The LORD had told the Israelites they would all die in the desert, and the only two left were Caleb son of Jephunneh and Joshua son of Nun.

Zelophehad's Daughters

27 Then the daughters of Zelophehad came near. Zelophehad was the son of Hepher, the son of Gilead, the son of Makir, the son of Manasseh. Zelophehad's daughters belonged to the family groups of Manasseh son of Joseph. The daughters' names were Mahlah, Noah, Hoglah, Milcah, and Tirzah. 2They went to the entrance of the Meeting Tent[d] and stood before Moses, Eleazar the priest, the leaders, and all the people. They said, 3"Our father died in the desert. He was not one of Korah's followers who came together against the LORD, but he died because of his own sin, and he had no sons. 4Our father's name will die out because he had no sons. Give us property among our father's relatives."

5So Moses brought their case to the LORD, 6and the LORD said to him, 7"The daughters of Zelophehad are right; they should certainly get what their father owned. Give them property among their father's relatives.

8"Tell the Israelites, 'If a man dies and has no son, then everything he owned should go to his daughter. 9If he has no daughter, then everything he owned should go to his brothers. 10If he has no brothers, then everything he owned should go to his father's brothers. 11And if his father had no brothers, then everything he owned should go to the nearest relative in his family group. This should be a rule among the people of Israel, as the LORD has given this command to Moses.' "

Joshua Is the New Leader

12Then the LORD said to Moses, "Climb this mountain in the Abarim Mountains, and look at the land I have given to the Israelites. 13After you have seen it, you will die and join your ancestors as your brother Aaron did, 14because you both acted against my command in the Desert of Zin. You did not honor me as holy before the people at the waters of Meribah." (This was at Meribah in Kadesh in the Desert of Zin.)

15Moses said to the LORD, 16"The LORD is the God of the spirits of all people. May he choose a leader for these people, 17who will go in and out before them. He must lead them out like sheep and bring them in; the LORD's people must not be like sheep without a shepherd."

18So the LORD said to Moses, "Take Joshua son of Nun, because my Spirit[d] is in him. Put your hand on him, 19and have him stand before Eleazar the priest and all the people. Then give him his orders as they watch. 20Let him share your honor so that all the Israelites will obey him. 21He must stand before Eleazar the priest, and Eleazar will get advice from the LORD by using the Urim.[d] At his command all the Israelites will go out, and at his command they will all come in."

22Moses did what the LORD told him. He took Joshua and had him stand before Eleazar the priest and all the people, 23and he put his hands on him and gave him orders, just as the LORD had told him.

Daily Offerings

28 The LORD said to Moses, 2"Give this command to the Israelites. Tell them: 'Bring me food offerings made by fire, for a smell that is pleasing to me, and be sure to bring them at the right time.' 3Say to them, 'These are the offerings you must bring to the LORD: two male lambs, a year old, as a burnt offering each day.

They must have nothing wrong with them. [4]Offer
one lamb in the morning and the other lamb at
twilight. [5]Also bring a grain offering of two quarts
of fine flour, mixed with one quart of oil from
pressed olives. [6]This is the daily burnt offering
which began at Mount Sinai; its smell is pleasing
to the LORD. [7]Offer one quart of wine with each
lamb as a drink offering; pour it out to the LORD
at the Holy Place. [8]Offer the second lamb at twilight. As in the morning, also give a grain offering
and a drink offering. This offering is made by fire,
and its smell is pleasing to the LORD.

Sabbath Offerings

[9]" 'On the Sabbath[d] day you must give two
male lambs, a year old, that have nothing wrong
with them. Also give a drink offering and a grain
offering; the grain offering must be four quarts of
fine flour mixed with olive oil. [10]This is the burnt
offering for every Sabbath, in addition to the daily
burnt offering and drink offering.

Monthly Offerings

[11]" 'On the first day of each month bring a
burnt offering to the LORD. This will be two young
bulls, one male sheep, and seven male lambs a
year old, and they must have nothing wrong with
them. [12]Give a grain offering with each bull of six
quarts of fine flour mixed with olive oil. Also give
a grain offering with the male sheep. It must be
four quarts of fine flour mixed with olive oil.
[13]And give a grain offering with each lamb of two
quarts of fine flour mixed with olive oil. This is a
burnt offering, and its smell is pleasing to the
LORD. [14]The drink offering with each bull will be
two quarts of wine, with the male sheep it will be
one and one-third quarts, and with each lamb it
will be one quart of wine. This is the burnt offering that must be offered each month of the year.
[15]Besides the daily burnt offerings and drink offerings, bring a sin offering of one goat to the
LORD.

LEADERSHIP

Walking in My Own Footsteps

Clarence Mitchell was a legend. For twenty-nine years, he had been the chief lobbyist in Washington, D.C., for the National Association for the Advancement of Colored People (NAACP).

Using his knowledge of the law and his persuasive powers, he pushed legislators to pass laws to protect the rights of black people. Every civil rights law passed by Congress during the turbulent 1960s had his fingerprints on it.

Then, in 1978, he retired, and Althea T. L. Simmons took his place. For years, she had dedicated her life to studying and practicing civil rights law. And she had worked for twenty-five years honing her skills and knowledge.

Soon after she took the new position, she went to the White House to meet with U.S. President Jimmy Carter. "Miss Simmons," he said, "you've got some very big shoes to fill."

She responded: "Mr. President, nobody can fill Clarence Mitchell's shoes. I'll have to walk in my own footsteps."

As a leader, Clarence Mitchell left a legacy. Moses—one of the Israelites' greatest leaders—left a legacy by leading them out of captivity in Egypt. When he died, Joshua became the new leader with a new agenda. Read about the challenge he faced in **Numbers 27:12–23**.

- How were Althea Simmons's years of experience and training similar to Joshua's forty years of preparation to become a leader?
- In what ways that are described in the passage are you being prepared to become a leader in your school, church, or community?

CONSIDER. . .

- asking your parent to list leadership skills, gifts, or qualities he or she would like to pass on to you. Then decide together ways for you to learn those skills.
- interviewing your pastor or another church leader about how he or she became a leader. Then write a short biography for the church newsletter.

FOR MORE, SEE. . .

- Judges 6:11–16 (p. 222)
- John 21:15–22 (p. 1095)
- 2 Timothy 2:1–7 (p. 1264)

The Passover

16“ ‘The LORD’s Passover[d] will be on the fourteenth day of the first month. 17The Feast[d] of Unleavened Bread begins on the fifteenth day of that month. For seven days, you may eat only bread made without yeast. 18Have a holy meeting on the first day of the festival, and don’t work that day. 19Bring to the LORD an offering made by fire, a burnt offering of two young bulls, one male sheep, and seven male lambs a year old. They must have nothing wrong with them. 20With each bull give a grain offering of six quarts of fine flour mixed with olive oil. With the male sheep it must be four quarts of fine flour mixed with oil. 21With each of the seven lambs, it must be two quarts of fine flour mixed with oil. 22Bring one goat as a sin offering, to remove your sins so you will belong to God. 23Bring these offerings in addition to the burnt offerings you give every morning. 24So bring food for the offering made by fire each day for seven days, for a smell that is pleasing to the LORD. Do it in addition to the daily burnt offering and its drink offering. 25On the seventh day have a holy meeting, and don’t work that day.

The Feast of Weeks

26“ ‘On the day of firstfruits[d] when you bring new grain to the LORD during the Feast[d] of Weeks, have a holy meeting. Don’t work that day. 27Bring this burnt offering to the LORD: two young bulls, one male sheep, and seven male lambs a year old. This smell is pleasing to the LORD. 28Also, with each bull give a grain offering of six quarts of fine flour mixed with oil. With the male sheep, it must be four quarts of flour, 29and with each of the seven lambs offer two quarts of flour. 30Offer one male goat to remove your sins so you will belong to God. 31Bring these offerings and their drink offerings in addition to the daily burnt offering and its grain offering. The animals must have nothing wrong with them.

The Feast of Trumpets

29 “ ‘Have a holy meeting on the first day of the seventh month, and don’t work on that day. That is the day you blow the trumpets. 2Bring these burnt offerings as a smell pleasing to the LORD: one young bull, one male sheep, and seven male lambs a year old. They must have nothing wrong with them. 3With the bull give a grain offering of six quarts of fine flour mixed with oil. With the male sheep offer four quarts, 4and with each of the seven lambs offer two quarts. 5Offer one male goat for a sin offering to remove your sins so you will belong to God. 6These offerings are in addition to the monthly and daily burnt offerings. Their grain offerings and drink offerings must be done as you have been told. These offerings are made by fire to the LORD, and their smell is pleasing to him.

The Day of Cleansing

7“ ‘Have a holy meeting on the tenth day of the seventh month. On that day do not eat and do not work. 8Bring these burnt offerings as a smell pleasing to the LORD: one young bull, one male sheep, and seven male lambs a year old. They must have nothing wrong with them. 9With the bull give a grain offering of six quarts of fine flour mixed with oil. With the male sheep it must be four quarts, 10and with each of the seven lambs it must be two quarts. 11Offer one male goat as a sin offering. This will be in addition to the sin offering which removes your sins, the daily burnt offering with its grain offering, and the drink offerings.

The Feast of Shelters

12“ ‘Have a holy meeting on the fifteenth day of the seventh month, and do not work on that day. Celebrate a festival to the LORD for seven days. 13Bring these burnt offerings, made by fire, as a smell pleasing to the LORD: thirteen young bulls, two male sheep, and fourteen male lambs a year old. They must have nothing wrong with them. 14With each of the thirteen bulls offer a grain offering of six quarts of fine flour mixed with oil. With each of the two male sheep it must be four quarts, 15and with each of the fourteen lambs it must be two quarts. 16Offer one male goat as a sin offering in addition to the daily burnt offering with its grain and drink offerings.

17“ ‘On the second day of this festival give an offering of twelve bulls, two male sheep, and fourteen male lambs a year old. They must have nothing wrong with them. 18Bring the grain and drink offerings for the bulls, sheep, and lambs, according to the number required. 19Offer one male goat as a sin offering, in addition to the daily burnt offering with its grain and drink offerings.

20“ ‘On the third day offer eleven bulls, two male sheep, and fourteen male lambs a year old. They must have nothing wrong with them. 21Bring the grain and drink offerings for the bulls, sheep, and lambs, according to the number required. 22Offer one male goat as a sin offering, in addition to the daily burnt offering with its grain and drink offerings.

23“ ‘On the fourth day offer ten bulls, two male sheep, and fourteen male lambs a year old. They must have nothing wrong with them. 24Bring the grain and drink offerings for the bulls, sheep, and lambs, according to the number required. 25Offer one male goat as a sin offering, in addition to the daily burnt offering with its grain and drink offerings.

26“ ‘On the fifth day offer nine bulls, two male sheep, and fourteen male lambs a year old. They

must have nothing wrong with them. 27Bring the
grain and drink offerings for the bulls, sheep, and
lambs, according to the number required. 28Offer
one male goat as a sin offering, in addition to the
daily burnt offering with its grain and drink offerings.
29" 'On the sixth day offer eight bulls, two male
sheep, and fourteen male lambs a year old. They
must have nothing wrong with them. 30Bring the
grain and drink offerings for the bulls, sheep, and
lambs, according to the number required. 31Offer
one male goat as a sin offering, in addition to the
daily burnt offering with its grain and drink offerings.
32" 'On the seventh day offer seven bulls, two
male sheep, and fourteen male lambs a year old.
They must have nothing wrong with them.
33Bring the grain and drink offerings for the bulls,
sheep, and lambs, according to the number required. 34Offer one male goat as a sin offering, in
addition to the daily burnt offering with its grain
and drink offerings.
35" 'On the eighth day have a closing meeting,
and do not work on that day. 36Bring an offering
made by fire, a burnt offering, as a smell pleasing
to the LORD. Offer one bull, one male sheep, and
seven male lambs a year old. They must have
nothing wrong with them. 37Bring the grain and
drink offerings for the bull, the male sheep, and
the lambs, according to the number required.
38Offer one male goat as a sin offering, in addition
to the daily burnt offering with its grain and drink
offerings.
39" 'At your festivals you should bring these to
the LORD: your burnt offerings, grain offerings,
drink offerings and fellowship offerings. These are
in addition to other promised offerings and special
gifts you want to give to the LORD.' "
40Moses told the Israelites everything the LORD
had commanded him.

Rules About Special Promises

30 Moses spoke with the leaders of the Israelite tribes.[d] He told them these commands from the LORD.
2"If a man makes a promise to the LORD or says
he will do something special, he must keep his
promise. He must do what he said. 3If a young
woman still living at home makes a promise to the
LORD or pledges to do something special, 4and if
her father hears about the promise or pledge and
says nothing, she must do what she promised. She
must keep her pledge. 5But if her father hears
about the promise or pledge and does not allow
it, then the promise or pledge does not have to be
kept. Her father would not allow it, so the LORD
will free her from her promise.
6"If a woman makes a pledge or a careless
promise and then gets married, 7and if her husband hears about it and says nothing, she must
keep her promise or the pledge she made. 8But if
her husband hears about it and does not allow it,
he cancels her pledge or the careless promise she
made. The LORD will free her from keeping it.
9"If a widow or divorced woman makes a
promise, she must do whatever she promised.
10"If a woman makes a promise or pledge while
she is married, 11and if her husband hears about
it but says nothing and does not stop her, she
must keep her promise or pledge. 12But if her husband hears about it and cancels it, she does not
have to do what she said. Her husband has canceled it, so the LORD will free her from it. 13A
woman's husband may make her keep or cancel
any promise or pledge she has made. 14If he says
nothing to her about it for several days, she must
keep her promises. If he hears about them and
says nothing, she must keep her promises. 15But
if he cancels them long after he heard about them,
he is responsible if she breaks her promise."
16These are commands that the LORD gave to
Moses for husbands and wives, and for fathers
with daughters living at home.

Israel Attacks the Midianites

31 The LORD spoke to Moses and said,
2"Pay back the Midianites for what they
did to the Israelites; after that you will die."
3So Moses said to the people, "Get some men
ready for war. The LORD will use them to pay
back the Midianites. 4Send to war a thousand
men from each of the tribes[d] of Israel." 5So twelve
thousand men got ready for war, a thousand men
from each tribe. 6Moses sent those men to war;
Phinehas son of Eleazar the priest was with them.
He took with him the holy things and the trumpets for giving the alarm. 7They fought the Midianites as the LORD had commanded Moses, and
they killed every Midianite man. 8Among those
they killed were Evi, Rekem, Zur, Hur, and Reba,
who were the five kings of Midian. They also
killed Balaam son of Beor with a sword.
9The Israelites captured the Midianite women
and children, and they took all their flocks, herds,
and goods. 10They burned all the Midianite towns
where they had settled and all their camps, 11but
they took all the people and animals and goods.
12Then they brought the captives, the animals,
and the goods back to Moses and Eleazar the
priest and all the Israelites. Their camp was on the
plains of Moab near the Jordan River, across from
Jericho.
13Moses, Eleazar the priest, and all the leaders
of the people went outside the camp to meet
them. 14Moses was angry with the army officers,
the commanders over a thousand men, and those
over a hundred men, who returned from war.
15He asked them, "Why did you let the women

live? 16They were the ones who followed Balaam's advice and turned the Israelites from the LORD at Peor. Then a terrible sickness struck the LORD's people. 17Kill all the Midianite boys, and kill all the Midianite women who have had sexual relations. 18But save for yourselves the girls who have not had sexual relations with a man.

19"All you men who killed anyone or touched a dead body must stay outside the camp for seven days. On the third and seventh days you and your captives must make yourselves clean.[d] 20You must clean all your clothes and anything made of leather, goat hair, or wood."

21Then Eleazar the priest said to the soldiers who had gone to war, "These are the teachings that the LORD gave to Moses: 22Put any gold, silver, bronze, iron, tin, or lead — 23anything that will not burn — into the fire, and then it will be clean. But also purify those things with the cleansing water. Then they will be clean. If something cannot stand the fire, wash it with the water. 24On the seventh day wash your clothes, and you will be clean. After that you may come into the camp."

Dividing the Goods

25The LORD said to Moses, 26"You, Eleazar the priest, and the leaders of the family groups should take a count of the goods, the men, and the animals that were taken. 27Then divide those possessions between the soldiers who went to war and the rest of the people. 28From the soldiers who went to war, take a tax for the LORD of one item out of every five hundred. This includes people, cattle, donkeys, or sheep. 29Take it from the soldiers' half, and give it to Eleazar the priest as the LORD's share. 30And from the people's half, take one item out of every fifty. This includes people, cattle, donkeys, sheep, or other animals. Give that to the Levites, who take care of the LORD's Holy Tent."[d] 31So Moses and Eleazar did as the LORD commanded Moses.

32There remained from what the soldiers had taken 675,000 sheep, 3372,000 cattle, 3461,000 donkeys, 35and 32,000 women who had not had sexual relations with a man. 36The soldiers who went to war got 337,000 sheep, 37and they gave 675 of them to the LORD. 38They got 36,000 cattle, and they gave 72 of them to the LORD. 39They got 30,500 donkeys, and they gave 61 of them to the LORD. 40They got 16,000 people, and they gave 32 of them to the LORD. 41Moses gave the LORD's share to Eleazar the priest, as the LORD had commanded him.

42Moses separated the people's half from the soldiers' half. 43The people got 337,500 sheep, 4436,000 cattle, 4530,500 donkeys, 46and 16,000 people. 47From the people's half Moses took one item out of every fifty for the LORD. This included the animals and the people. Then he gave them to the Levites, who took care of the LORD's Holy Tent. This was what the LORD had commanded Moses.

48Then the officers of the army, the commanders of a thousand men and commanders of a hundred men, came to Moses. 49They told Moses, "We, your servants, have counted our soldiers under our command, and not one of them is missing. 50So we have brought the LORD a gift of the gold things that each of us found: arm bands, bracelets, signet[d] rings, earrings, and necklaces. These are to remove our sins so we will belong to the LORD."

51So Moses and Eleazar the priest took the gold from them, which had been made into all kinds of objects. 52The commanders of a thousand men and the commanders of a hundred men gave the LORD the gold, and all of it together weighed about 420 pounds; 53each soldier had taken something for himself. 54Moses and Eleazar the priest took the gold from the commanders of a thousand men and the commanders of a hundred men. Then they put it in the Meeting Tent[d] as a memorial before the LORD for the people of Israel.

The Tribes East of the Jordan

32 The people of Reuben and Gad had large flocks and herds. When they saw that the lands of Jazer and Gilead were good for the animals, 2they came to Moses, Eleazar the priest, and the leaders of the people. 3-4They said, "We, your servants, have flocks and herds. The LORD has captured for the Israelites a land that is good for animals — the land around Ataroth, Dibon, Jazer, Nimrah, Heshbon, Elealeh, Sebam, Nebo, and Beon. 5If it pleases you, we would like this land to be given to us. Don't make us cross the Jordan River."

6Moses told the people of Gad and Reuben, "Shall your brothers go to war while you stay behind? 7You will discourage the Israelites from going over to the land the LORD has given them. 8Your ancestors did the same thing. I sent them from Kadesh Barnea to look at the land. 9They went as far as the Valley of Eshcol, and when they saw the land, they discouraged the Israelites from going into the land the LORD had given them. 10The LORD became very angry that day and made this promise: 11'None of the people who came from Egypt and who are twenty years old or older will see the land that I promised to Abraham, Isaac, and Jacob. These people have not followed me completely. 12Only Caleb son of Jephunneh the Kenizzite and Joshua son of Nun followed the LORD completely.'

13"The LORD was angry with Israel, so he made them wander in the desert for forty years. Finally all the people who had sinned against the LORD

died, [14]and now you are acting just like your ancestors! You sinful people are making the LORD
even more angry with Israel. [15]If you quit following him, it will add to their stay in the desert, and
you will destroy all these people."

[16]Then the Reubenites and Gadites came up to
Moses and said, "We will build pens for our animals and cities for our children here. [17]Then our
children will be in strong, walled cities, safe from
the people who live in this land. Then we will
prepare for war. We will help the other Israelites
get their land, [18]and we will not return home until
every Israelite has received his land. [19]We won't
take any of the land west of the Jordan River; our
part of the land is east of the Jordan."

[20]So Moses told them, "You must do these
things. You must go before the LORD into battle
[21]and cross the Jordan River armed, until the
LORD forces out the enemy. [22]After the LORD
helps us take the land, you may return home. You
will have done your duty to the LORD and Israel,
and you may have this land as your own.

[23]"But if you don't do these things, you will be
sinning against the LORD; know for sure that you
will be punished for your sin. [24]Build cities for
your children and pens for your animals, but then
you must do what you promised."

[25]The Gadites and Reubenites said to Moses,
"We are your servants, and we will do what you,
our master, command. [26]Our children, wives, and
all our cattle will stay in the cities of Gilead, [27]but
we, your servants, will prepare for battle. We will
go over and fight for the LORD, as you, our master,
have said."

[28]So Moses gave orders about them to Eleazar
the priest, to Joshua son of Nun, and to the leaders of the tribes[d] of Israel. [29]Moses said to them,
"If the Gadites and Reubenites prepare for battle
and cross the Jordan River with you, to go before
the LORD and help you take the land, give them
the land of Gilead for their own. [30]But if they do
not go over armed, they will not receive it; their
land will be in Canaan with you."

[31]The Gadites and Reubenites answered, "We
are your servants, and we will do as the LORD
said. [32]We will cross over into Canaan and go before the LORD ready for battle. But our land will
be east of the Jordan River."

[33]So Moses gave that land to the tribes of Gad,
Reuben, and East Manasseh. (Manasseh was Jo-
seph's son.) That land had been the kingdom of
Sihon, king of the Amorites, and the kingdom of
Og, king of Bashan, as well as all the cities and the
land around them.

[34]The Gadites rebuilt the cities of Dibon, Ataroth, Aroer, [35]Atroth Shophan, Jazer, Jogbehah,
[36]Beth Nimrah, and Beth Haran. These were
strong, walled cities. And they built sheep pens.

[37]The Reubenites rebuilt Heshbon, Elealeh, Kiriathaim, [38]Nebo, Baal Meon, and Sibmah. They
renamed Nebo and Baal Meon when they rebuilt
them.

[39]The descendants[d] of Makir son of Manasseh
went and captured Gilead and forced out the Amorites who were there. [40]So Moses gave Gilead to
the family of Makir son of Manasseh, and they
settled there. [41]Jair son of Manasseh went out and
captured the small towns there, and he called
them the Towns of Jair. [42]Nobah went and captured Kenath and the small towns around it; then
he named it Nobah after himself.

Israel's Journey from Egypt

33 These are the places the Israelites went
as Moses and Aaron led them out of
Egypt in divisions. [2]At the LORD's command Moses recorded the places they went, and these are
the places they went.

[3]On the fifteenth day of the first month, the day
after the Passover,[d] the Israelites left Rameses and
marched out boldly in front of all the Egyptians.
[4]The Egyptians were burying their firstborn[d] sons,
whom the LORD had killed; the LORD showed that
the gods of Egypt were false.

[5]The Israelites left Rameses and camped at Succoth.

[6]They left Succoth and camped at Etham, at the
edge of the desert.

[7]They left Etham and went back to Pi Hahiroth,
to the east of Baal Zephon, and camped near Migdol.

[8]They left Pi Hahiroth and walked through the
sea into the desert. After going three days through
the Desert of Etham, they camped at Marah.

[9]They left Marah and went to Elim; there were
twelve springs of water and seventy palm trees
where they camped.

[10]They left Elim and camped near the Red Sea.[d]

[11]They left the Red Sea and camped in the
Desert of Sin.

[12]They left the Desert of Sin and camped at
Dophkah.

[13]They left Dophkah and camped at Alush.

[14]They left Alush and camped at Rephidim,
where the people had no water to drink.

[15]They left Rephidim and camped in the Desert
of Sinai.

[16]They left the Desert of Sinai and camped at
Kibroth Hattaavah.

[17]They left Kibroth Hattaavah and camped at
Hazeroth.

[18]They left Hazeroth and camped at Rithmah.

[19]They left Rithmah and camped at Rimmon
Perez.

[20]They left Rimmon Perez and camped at Libnah.

[21]They left Libnah and camped at Rissah.

[22]They left Rissah and camped at Kehelathah.

23They left Kehelathah and camped at Mount
Shepher.
24They left Mount Shepher and camped at Haradah.
25They left Haradah and camped at Makheloth.
26They left Makheloth and camped at Tahath.
27They left Tahath and camped at Terah.
28They left Terah and camped at Mithcah.
29They left Mithcah and camped at Hashmonah.
30They left Hashmonah and camped at Moseroth.
31They left Moseroth and camped at Bene Jaakan.
32They left Bene Jaakan and camped at Hor
Haggidgad.
33They left Hor Haggidgad and camped at Jotbathah.
34They left Jotbathah and camped at Abronah.
35They left Abronah and camped at Ezion Geber.
36They left Ezion Geber and camped at Kadesh
in the Desert of Zin.
37They left Kadesh and camped at Mount Hor,
on the border of Edom. 38Aaron the priest obeyed
the LORD and went up Mount Hor. There he died
on the first day of the fifth month in the fortieth
year after the Israelites left Egypt. 39Aaron was
123 years old when he died on Mount Hor.
40The Canaanite king of Arad, who lived in the
southern area of Canaan, heard that the Israelites
were coming.
41The people left Mount Hor and camped at
Zalmonah.
42They left Zalmonah and camped at Punon.
43They left Punon and camped at Oboth.
44They left Oboth and camped at Iye Abarim,
on the border of Moab.
45They left Iye Abarim and camped at Dibon
Gad.
46They left Dibon Gad and camped at Almon
Diblathaim.
47They left Almon Diblathaim and camped in
the mountains of Abarim, near Nebo.
48They left the mountains of Abarim and
camped on the plains of Moab near the Jordan
River across from Jericho. 49They camped along
the Jordan on the plains of Moab, and their camp
went from Beth Jeshimoth to Abel Acacia.
50On the plains of Moab by the Jordan River
across from Jericho, the LORD spoke to Moses. He
said, 51"Speak to the Israelites and tell them,
'When you cross the Jordan River and go into Canaan, 52force out all the people who live there.
Destroy all of their carved statues and metal idols.
Wreck all of their places of worship. 53Take over
the land and settle there, because I have given
this land to you to own. 54Throw lots[d] to divide
up the land by family groups, giving larger portions to larger family groups and smaller portions
to smaller family groups. The land will be given
as the lots decide; each tribe[d] will get its own
land.
55" 'But if you don't force those people out of
the land, they will bring you trouble. They will be
like sharp hooks in your eyes and thorns in your
sides. They will bring trouble to the land where
you live. 56Then I will punish you as I had planned
to punish them.' "

The Borders of Canaan

34 The LORD said to Moses, 2"Give this
command to the people of Israel: 'You
will soon enter Canaan and it will be yours. These
shall be the borders: 3On the south you will get
part of the Desert of Zin near the border of Edom.
On the east side your southern border will start at
the south end of the Dead Sea,[d] 4cross south of
Scorpion Pass, and go through the Desert of Zin
and south of Kadesh Barnea. Then it will go to
Hazar Addar and over to Azmon. 5From Azmon
it will go to the brook of Egypt, and it will end at
the Mediterranean Sea.
6" 'Your western border will be the Mediterranean Sea.
7" 'Your northern border will begin at the
Mediterranean Sea and go to Mount Hor. 8From
Mount Hor it will go to Lebo Hamath, and on to
Zedad. 9Then the border will go to Ziphron, and
it will end at Hazar Enan. This will be your northern border.
10" 'Your eastern border will begin at Hazar
Enan and go to Shepham. 11From Shepham the
border will go east of Ain to Riblah and along the
hills east of Lake Galilee. 12Then the border will
go down along the Jordan River and end at the
Dead Sea.
" 'These are the borders around your country.' "
13So Moses gave this command to the Israelites: "This is the land you will receive. Throw
lots[d] to divide it among the nine and one-half
tribes,[d] because the LORD commanded that it
should be theirs. 14The tribes of Reuben, Gad, and
East Manasseh have already received their land.
15These two and one-half tribes received land east
of the Jordan River, across from Jericho."
16Then the LORD said to Moses, 17"These are
the men who will divide the land: Eleazar the
priest and Joshua son of Nun. 18Also take one
leader from each tribe to help divide the land.
19These are the names of the leaders: from the
tribe of Judah, Caleb son of Jephunneh; 20from
the tribe of Simeon, Shemuel son of Ammihud;
21from the tribe of Benjamin, Elidad son of Kislon;
22from the tribe of Dan, Bukki son of Jogli; 23from
the tribe of Manasseh son of Joseph, Hanniel son
of Ephod; 24from the tribe of Ephraim son of Jo-

seph, Kemuel son of Shiphtan; 25from the tribe of Zebulun, Elizaphan son of Parnach; 26from the tribe of Issachar, Paltiel son of Azzan; 27from the tribe of Asher, Ahihud son of Shelomi; 28from the tribe of Naphtali, Pedahel son of Ammihud."

29The LORD commanded these men to divide the land of Canaan among the Israelites.

The Levites' Towns

35 The LORD spoke to Moses on the plains of Moab across from Jericho by the Jordan River. He said, 2"Command the Israelites to give the Levites cities to live in from the land they receive. Also give the Levites the pastureland around these cities. 3Then the Levites will have cities where they may live and pastureland for their cattle, flocks, and other animals. 4The pastureland you give the Levites will extend fifteen hundred feet from the city wall. 5Also measure three thousand feet in each direction outside the city wall—three thousand feet east of the city, three thousand feet south of the city, three thousand feet west of the city, and three thousand feet north of the city, with the city in the center. This will be pastureland for the Levites' cities.

Cities of Safety

6"Six of the cities you give the Levites will be cities of safety.[d] A person who accidentally kills someone may run to one of those cities for safety. You must also give forty-two other cities to the Levites; 7give the Levites a total of forty-eight cities and their pastures. 8The larger tribes[d] of Israel must give more cities, and the smaller tribes must give fewer cities. Each tribe must give some of its cities to the Levites, but the number of cities they give will depend on the size of their land."

9Then the LORD said to Moses, 10"Tell the Israelites these things: 'When you cross the Jordan River and go into Canaan, 11you must choose cities to be cities of safety, so that a person who accidentally kills someone may run to them for safety. 12There the person will be safe from the dead person's relative who has the duty of punishing the killer. He will not die before he receives a fair trial in court. 13The six cities you give will be cities of safety. 14Give three cities east of the Jordan River and three cities in Canaan as cities of safety. 15These six cities will be places of safety for citizens of Israel, as well as for foreigners and other people living with you. Any of these people who accidentally kills someone may run to one of these cities.

16" 'Anyone who uses an iron weapon to kill someone is a murderer. He must be put to death. 17Anyone who takes a rock and kills a person with it is a murderer. He must be put to death. 18Anyone who picks up a piece of wood and kills someone with it is a murderer. He must be put to death. 19A relative of the dead person must put the murderer to death; when they meet, the relative must kill the murderer. 20A person might shove someone or throw something at someone and cause death. 21Or a person might hit someone with his hand and cause death. If it were done from hate, the person is a murderer and must be put to death. A relative of the dead person must kill the murderer when they meet.

22" 'But a person might suddenly shove someone, and not from hatred. Or a person might accidentally throw something and hit someone. 23Or a person might drop a rock on someone he couldn't see and kill that person. There was no plan to hurt anyone and no hatred for the one who was killed. 24If that happens, the community must judge between the relative of the dead person and the killer, according to these rules. 25They must protect the killer from the dead person's relative, sending the killer back to the original city of safety, to stay there until the high priest dies (the high priest had the holy oil poured on him).

26" 'Such a person must never go outside the limits of the city of safety. 27If a relative of the dead person finds the killer outside the city, the relative may kill that person and not be guilty of murder. 28The killer must stay in the city of safety until the high priest dies. After the high priest dies, the killer may go home.

SIDELIGHT: Today, if a person kills someone, a trial is held to determine guilt or innocence, and sentencing. In Old Testament times, such a person could be murdered. To protect people who accidentally killed, Numbers 35:6–28 tells of six cities of safety where someone could go to be safe from the victim's relatives. But if the killer left the city, the dead person's family could take revenge.

29" 'These laws are for you from now on, wherever you live.

30" 'If anyone kills a person, the murderer may be put to death only if there are witnesses. No one may be put to death with only one witness.

31" 'Don't take money to spare the life of a murderer who should be put to death. A murderer must be put to death.

32" 'If someone has run to a city of safety, don't take money to let the person go back home before the high priest dies.

33" 'Don't let murder spoil your land. The only way to remove the sin of killing an innocent person is for the murderer to be put to death. 34I am the LORD, and I live among the Israelites. I live in

that land with you, so do not spoil it with murder.' "

Land for Zelophehad's Daughters

36 The leaders of Gilead's family group
went to talk to Moses and the leaders of
the families of Israel. (Gilead was the son of Makir, the son of Manasseh, the son of Joseph.)
2They said, "The LORD commanded you, our master, to give the land to the Israelites by throwing
lots,[d] and the LORD commanded you to give the
land of Zelophehad, our brother, to his daughters.
3But if his daughters marry men from other tribes[d]
of Israel, then that land will leave our family, and
the people of the other tribes will get that land.
So we will lose some of our land. 4When the time
of Jubilee[d] comes for the Israelites, their land will
go to the tribes of the people they marry; their
land will be taken away from us, the land we received from our fathers."

5Then Moses gave the Israelites this command
from the LORD: "These men from the tribe of Joseph are right. 6This is the LORD's command to
Zelophehad's daughters: You may marry anyone
you wish, as long as the person is from your own
tribe. 7In this way the Israelites' land will not pass
from tribe to tribe, and each Israelite will keep the
land in the tribe that belonged to his ancestors. 8A
woman who inherits her father's land may marry,
but she must marry someone from her own tribe.
In this way every Israelite will keep the land that
belonged to his ancestors. 9The land must not
pass from tribe to tribe, and each Israelite tribe
will keep the land it received from its ancestors."

10Zelophehad's daughters obeyed the LORD's
command to Moses.

11So Zelophehad's daughters—Mahlah, Tirzah, Hoglah, Milcah, and Noah—married their
cousins, their father's relatives. 12Their husbands
were from the tribe of Manasseh son of Joseph, so
their land stayed in their father's family group and
tribe.

13These were the laws and commands that the
LORD gave to the Israelites through Moses on the
plains of Moab by the Jordan River, across from
Jericho.

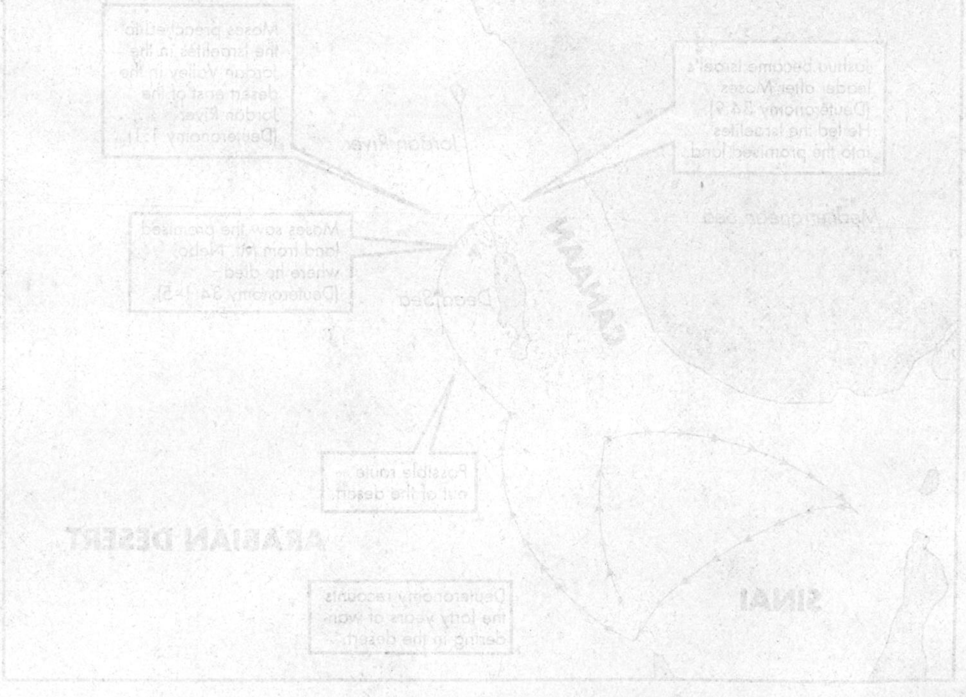

DEUTERONOMY

Why Read This Book:

- Be reminded of all the good things God has done for his people (Deuteronomy 1—4).
- Find out what God requires of people because of his special relationship with them (Deuteronomy 5—28).
- See what God has in store for his people, when they do right and when they do wrong (Deuteronomy 29—30).

Behind the Scenes:

You've spent weeks reading books, listening to lectures, and doing homework. You've learned lots of important information that will help you in the future. Then the week before the big test, your teacher reviews what you've learned and urges you to remember everything that has happened.

The book of Deuteronomy is a lot like that last week of review. The Israelites had escaped from slavery in Egypt. But because they would not do God's will, they had to wander in the desert for forty years until they died, and their children

WHERE THE ACTION WAS

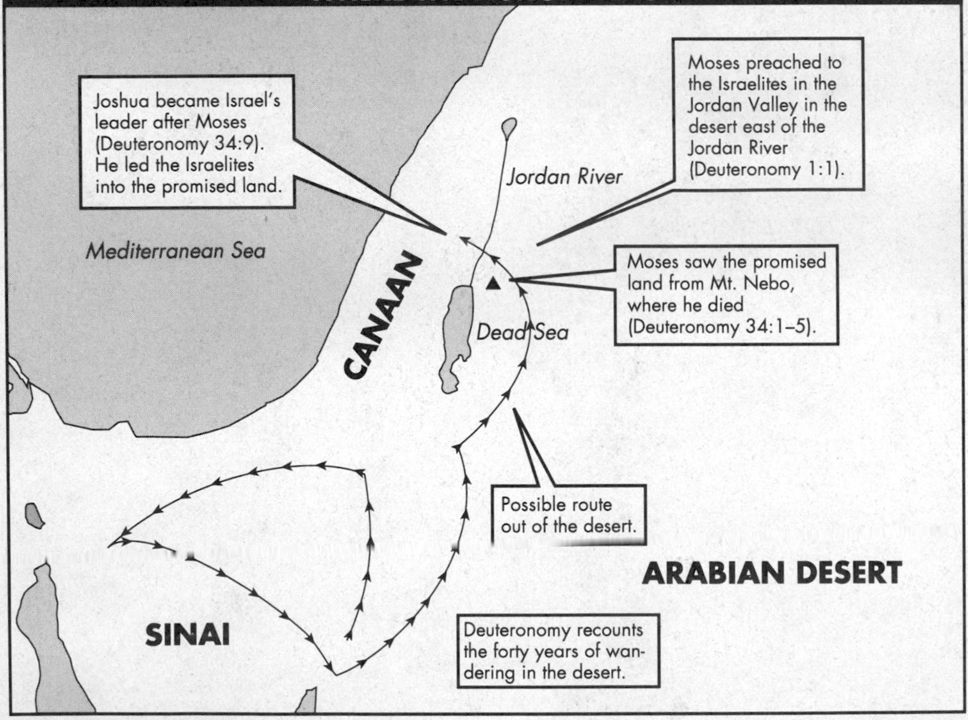

Joshua became Israel's leader after Moses (Deuteronomy 34:9). He led the Israelites into the promised land.
Moses preached to the Israelites in the Jordan Valley in the desert east of the Jordan River (Deuteronomy 1:1).
Jordan River
Mediterranean Sea
CANAAN
Moses saw the promised land from Mt. Nebo, where he died (Deuteronomy 34:1–5).
Dead Sea
Possible route out of the desert.
ARABIAN DESERT
SINAI
Deuteronomy recounts the forty years of wandering in the desert.

WHEN THE ACTION WAS

The Israelites escaped from Egypt
Moses died on Mt. Nebo
Jesus was born
2000BC
1500BC
1000BC
500BC
BC/AD
The Israelites wandered in the desert
Joshua led the Israelites into Canaan

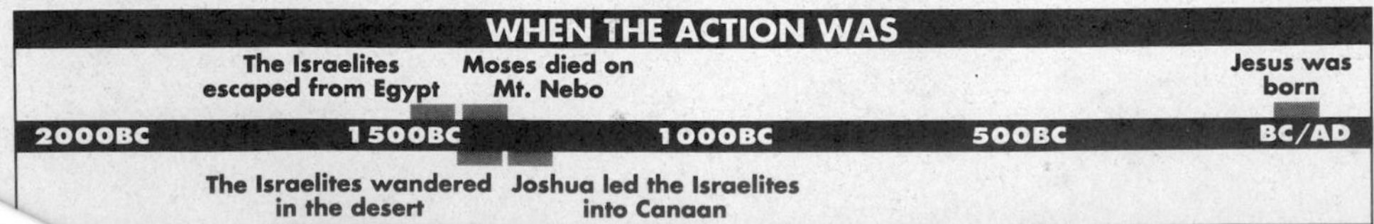

Behind the Scenes (cont.): took their places. In the desert, Moses, their leader, had received laws from God and had helped the new generation learn what it meant to be a nation that followed God.

Now the people were preparing for "finals week"—when they would enter the land of Canaan, the promised land. Just before his death, Moses gave the people three "review sessions" or sermons. He reminded them of what God had done for them, and he urged the people to keep God's commandments as they entered a new land with new temptations.

Deuteronomy means "second law" or "repetition of the law." It restates many of the laws the Israelites had received in the desert. But unlike other law books, it focuses more on why people should keep the laws, namely, out of gratitude for God's love.

Moses Talks to the Israelites

1 This is the message Moses gave to all the people of Israel in the desert east of the Jordan River. They were in the desert area near Suph, between Paran and the towns of Tophel, Laban, Hazeroth, and Dizahab.

2(The trip from Mount Sinai to Kadesh Barnea on the Mount Seir road takes eleven days.) 3Forty years after the Israelites had left Egypt, on the first day of the eleventh month, Moses told the people of Israel everything the LORD had commanded him to tell them. 4This was after the LORD had defeated Sihon and Og. Sihon was king of the Amorite people and lived in Heshbon. Og was king of Bashan and lived in Ashteroth and Edrei.

5Now the Israelites were east of the Jordan River in the land of Moab, and there Moses began to explain what God had commanded. He said:

6The LORD our God spoke to us at Mount Sinai and said, "You have stayed long enough at this mountain. 7Get ready, and go to the mountain country of the Amorites, and to all the places around there—the Jordan Valley, the mountains, the western hills, the southern area, the seacoast, the land of Canaan, and Lebanon. Go as far as the great river, the Euphrates. 8See, I have given you this land, so go in and take it for yourselves. The LORD promised it to your ancestors—Abraham, Isaac, and Jacob and their descendants."[d]

Moses Appoints Leaders

9At that time I said, "I am not able to take care of you by myself. 10The LORD your God has made you grow in number so that there are as many of you as there are stars in the sky. 11I pray that the LORD, the God of your ancestors, will give you a thousand times more people and do all the wonderful things he promised. 12But I cannot take care of your problems, your troubles, and your arguments by myself. 13So choose some men from each tribe[d]—wise men who have understanding and experience—and I will make them leaders over you."

14And you said, "That's a good thing to do."

15So I took the wise and experienced leaders of your tribes, and I made them your leaders. I appointed commanders over a thousand people, over a hundred people, over fifty people, and over ten people and made them officers over your tribes. 16Then I told your leaders, "Listen to the arguments between your people. Judge fairly between two Israelites or between an Israelite and a foreigner. 17When you judge, be fair to everyone; don't act as if one person is more important than another, and don't be afraid of anyone, because your decision comes from God. Bring the hard cases to me, and I will judge them." 18At that time I told you everything you must do.

Spies Enter the Land

19Then, as the LORD our God commanded us, we left Mount Sinai and went toward the mountain country of the Amorite people. We went through that large and terrible desert you saw, and then we came to Kadesh Barnea. 20I said to you, "You have now come to the mountain country of the Amorites, to the land the LORD our God will give us. 21Look, here it is! Go up and take it. The LORD, the God of your ancestors, told you to do this, so don't be afraid and don't worry."

22Then all of you came to me and said, "Let's send men before us to spy out the land. They can come back and tell us about the way we should go and the cities we will find."

23I thought that was a good idea, so I chose twelve of your men, one for each tribe.[d] 24They left and went up to the mountains, and when they came to the Valley of Eshcol they explored it. 25They took some of the fruit from that land and brought it down to us, saying, "It is a good land that the LORD our God is giving us."

Israel Refuses to Enter

26But you refused to go. You would not obey the command of the LORD your God, 27but grumbled in your tents, saying, "The LORD hates us. He brought us out of Egypt just to give us to the Amorites, who will destroy us. 28Where can we go now? The spies we sent have made us afraid, because they said, 'The people there are stronger

and taller than we are. The cities are big, with
walls up to the sky. And we saw the Anakites[d]
there!' "
29Then I said to you, "Don't be frightened;
don't be afraid of those people. 30The LORD your
God will go ahead of you and fight for you as he
did in Egypt; you saw him do it. 31And in the
desert you saw how the LORD your God carried
you, like one carries a child. And he has brought
you safely all the way to this place."
32But you still did not trust the LORD your God,
even though 33he had always gone before you to
find places for you to camp. In a fire at night and
in a cloud during the day, he showed you which
way to go.
34When the LORD heard what you said, he was
angry and made an oath, saying, 35"I promised a
good land to your ancestors, but none of you evil
people will see it. 36Only Caleb son of Jephunneh
will see it. I will give him and his descendants[d]
the land he walked on, because he followed the
LORD completely."
37Because of you, the LORD was also angry with
me and said, "You won't enter the land either,
38but your assistant, Joshua son of Nun, will enter
it. Encourage him, because he will lead Israel to
take the land for their own.
39"Your little children that you said would be
captured, who do not know right from wrong at
this time, will go into the land. I will give the land
to them, and they will take it for their own. 40But
you must turn around and follow the desert road
toward the Red Sea."
41Then you said to me, "We have sinned
against the LORD, but now we will go up and
fight, as the LORD our God commanded us." Then
all of you put on weapons, thinking it would be
easy to go into the mountains.
42But the LORD said to me, "Tell the people,
'You must not go up there and fight. I will not be
with you, and your enemies will defeat you.' "
43So I told you, but you would not listen. You
would not obey the LORD's command. You were
proud, so you went on up into the mountains,
44and the Amorites who lived in those mountains
came out and fought you. They chased you like
bees and defeated you from Edom to Hormah.
45So you came back and cried before the LORD,
but the LORD did not listen to you; he refused to
pay attention to you. 46So you stayed in Kadesh a
long time.

Israel Wanders in the Desert

2 Then we turned around, and we traveled on
the desert road toward the Red Sea, as the
LORD had told me to do. We traveled through the
mountains of Edom for many days.
2Then the LORD said to me, 3"You have traveled through these mountains long enough. Turn
north 4and give the people this command: 'You
will soon go through the land that belongs to your
relatives, the descendants[d] of Esau who live in
Edom. They will be afraid of you, but be very
careful. 5Do not go to war against them. I will not
give you any of their land—not even a foot of it,
because I have given the mountains of Edom to
Esau as his own. 6You must pay them in silver for
any food you eat or water you drink.' "
7The LORD your God has blessed everything
you have done; he has protected you while you
traveled through this great desert. The LORD your
God has been with you for the past forty years,
and you have had everything you needed.
8So we passed by our relatives, the descendants
of Esau who lived in Edom. We turned off the
Jordan Valley road that comes from the towns of
Elath and Ezion Geber and traveled along the
desert road to Moab.

The Land of Ar

9Then the LORD said to me, "Don't bother the
people of Moab. Don't go to war against them,
because I will not give you any of their land as
your own; I have given Ar to the descendants[d] of
Lot as their own." 10(The Emites, who lived in Ar
before, were strong people, and there were many
of them. They were very tall, like the Anakites.[d]
11The Emites were thought to be Rephaites,[d] like
the Anakites, but the Moabite people called them
Emites. 12The Horites also lived in Edom before,
but the descendants of Esau forced them out and
destroyed them, taking their place as Israel did in
the land the LORD gave them as their own.)
13And the LORD said to me, "Now get up and
cross the Zered Valley." So we crossed the valley.
14It had been thirty-eight years from the time we
left Kadesh Barnea until we crossed the Zered Valley. By then, all the fighting men from that time
had died, as the LORD had promised would happen. 15The LORD continued to work against them
to remove them from the camp until they were all
dead.
16When the last of those fighting men had died,
17the LORD said to me, 18"Today you will pass by
Ar, on the border of Moab. 19When you come
near the people of Ammon, don't bother them or
go to war against them, because I will not give
you any of their land as your own. I have given
it to the descendants of Lot for their own."
20(That land was also thought to be a land of
the Rephaites, because those people used to live
there, but the Ammonites called them Zamzummites. 21They were strong people, and there were
many of them; they were very tall, like the Anakites. The LORD destroyed the Zamzummites, and
the Ammonites forced them out of the land and
took their place. 22The LORD did the same thing
for the descendants of Esau, who lived in Edom,

when he destroyed the Horites. The Edomites forced them out of the land and took their place, and they live there to this day. 23The Cretan people came from Crete and destroyed the Avvites, who lived in towns all the way to Gaza; the Cretans destroyed them and took their place.)

Fighting the Amorites

24The LORD said, "Get up and cross the Arnon Ravine. See, I am giving you the power to defeat Sihon the Amorite, king of Heshbon, and I am giving you his land. So fight against him and begin taking his land. 25Today I will begin to make all the people in the world afraid of you. When they hear reports about you, they will shake with fear, and they will be terrified of you."

26I sent messengers from the desert of Kedemoth to Sihon king of Heshbon. They offered him peace, saying, 27"If you let us pass through your country, we will stay on the road and not turn right or left. 28We will pay you in silver for any food we eat or water we drink. We only want to walk through your country. 29The descendants[d] of Esau in Edom let us go through their land, and so did the Moabites in Ar. We want to cross the Jordan River into the land the LORD our God has given us." 30But Sihon king of Heshbon would not let us pass, because the LORD your God had made him stubborn. The LORD wanted you to defeat Sihon, and now this has happened.

31The LORD said to me, "See, I have begun to give Sihon and his country to you. Begin taking the land as your own."

32Then Sihon and all his army came out and fought us at Jahaz, 33but the LORD our God gave Sihon to us. We defeated him, his sons, and all his army. 34We captured all his cities at that time and completely destroyed them, as well as the men, women, and children. We left no one alive. 35But we kept the cattle and valuable things from the cities for ourselves. 36We defeated Aroer on the edge of the Arnon Ravine, and we defeated the town in the ravine, and even as far as Gilead. No town was too strong for us; the LORD our God gave us all of them. 37But you did not go near the land of the Ammonites, on the shores of the Jabbok River, or the towns in the mountains, as the LORD our God had commanded.

The Battle at Bashan

3 When we turned and went up the road toward Bashan, Og king of Bashan and all his army came out to fight us at Edrei. 2The LORD said to me, "Don't be afraid of Og, because I will hand him, his whole army, and his land over to you. Do to him what you did to Sihon king of the Amorites, who ruled in Heshbon."

3So the LORD our God gave us Og king of Bashan and all his army; we defeated them and left no one alive. 4Then we captured all of Og's cities, all sixty of them, and took the whole area of Argob, Og's kingdom in Bashan. 5All these were strong cities, with high walls and gates with bars. And there were also many small towns with no walls. 6We completely destroyed them, just like the cities of Sihon king of Heshbon. We killed all the men, women, and children, 7but we kept all the cattle and valuable things from the cities for ourselves.

8So at that time we took the land east of the Jordan River, from the Arnon Ravine to Mount Hermon, from these two Amorite kings. 9(Hermon is called Sirion by the Sidonian people, but The Amorites call it Senir.) 10We captured all the cities on the high plain and all of Gilead, and we took all of Bashan as far as Salecah and Edrei, towns in Og's kingdom of Bashan. 11(Only Og king of Bashan was left of the few Rephaites.[d] His bed was made of iron, and it was more than thirteen feet long and six feet wide! It is still in the Ammonite city of Rabbah.)

The Land Is Divided

12At that time we took this land to be our own. I gave the people of Reuben and Gad the land from Aroer by the Arnon Ravine, as well as half of the mountain country of Gilead and the cities in it. 13To the people of East Manasseh I gave the rest of Gilead and all of Bashan, the kingdom of Og. (The area of Argob in Bashan was called the land of the Rephaites.[d] 14Jair, a descendant[d] of Manasseh, took the whole area of Argob, all the way to the border of the Geshurites and Maacathites. So that land was named for Jair, and even today Bashan is called the Towns of Jair.) 15I gave Gilead to Makir. 16I gave the Reubenites and the Gadites the land that begins at Gilead and goes from the Arnon Ravine (the middle of the Arnon is the border) to the Jabbok River, which is the Ammonite border. 17The border on the west was the Jordan River in the Jordan Valley, and it goes from Lake Galilee to the Dead Sea[d] west of Mount Pisgah.

18At that time I gave you this command: "The LORD your God has given you this land as your own. Now your fighting men must take their weapons, and you must lead the other Israelites across the river. 19Your wives, your young children, and your cattle may stay here. I know you have many cattle, and they may stay here in the cities I have given you, 20until the LORD also gives your Israelite relatives a place to rest. They will receive the land the LORD your God has given them on the other side of the Jordan River. After that, you may each return to the land I have given you."

21Then I gave this command to Joshua: "You have seen for yourself all that the LORD your God

has done to these two kings. The LORD will do the
same thing to all the kingdoms where you are going. 22Don't be afraid of them, because the LORD
your God will fight for you."

Moses Cannot Enter the Land

23Then I begged the LORD: 24"Lord GOD, you
have begun to show me, your servant, how great
you are. You have great strength, and no other
god in heaven or on earth can do the powerful
things you do. There is no other god like you.
25Please let me cross the Jordan River so that I
may see the good land by the Jordan. I want to see
the beautiful mountains and Lebanon."
26But the LORD was angry with me because of
you, and he would not listen to me. The LORD
said to me, "That's enough. Don't talk to me anymore about it. 27Climb to the top of Mount Pisgah
and look west, north, south, and east. You can
look at the land, but you will not cross the Jordan
River. 28Appoint Joshua and help him be brave
and strong. He will lead the people across the
river and give them the land that they are to inherit, but you can only look at it." 29So we stayed
in the valley opposite Beth Peor.

Moses Tells Israel to Obey

4 Now, Israel, listen to the laws and commands I will teach you. Obey them so that
you will live and so that you will go over and take
the land the LORD, the God of your ancestors, is
giving to you. 2Don't add to these commands, and
don't leave anything out, but obey the commands
of the LORD your God that I give you.
3You have seen for yourselves what the LORD
did at Baal Peor, how the LORD your God destroyed everyone among you who followed Baal[d]
in Peor. 4But all of you who continued following
the LORD your God are still alive today.
5Look, I have taught you the laws and rules the
LORD my God commanded me. Now you can
obey the laws in the land you are entering, in the
land you will take. 6Obey these laws carefully, in
order to show the other nations that you have
wisdom and understanding. When they hear
about these laws, they will say, "This great nation
of Israel is wise and understanding." 7No other
nation is as great as we are. Their gods do not
come near them, but the LORD our God comes
near when we pray to him. 8And no other nation
has such good teachings and commands as those
I am giving to you today.
9But be careful! Watch out and don't forget the
things you have seen. Don't forget them as long
as you live, but teach them to your children and
grandchildren. 10Remember the day you stood before the LORD your God at Mount Sinai. He said
to me, "Bring the people together so I can tell
them what I have to say. Then they will respect
me as long as they live in the land, and they will
teach these things to their children." 11When you
came and stood at the bottom of the mountain, it
blazed with fire that reached to the sky, and black
clouds made it very dark. 12The LORD spoke to
you from the fire. You heard the sound of words,
but you did not see him; there was only a voice.
13The LORD told you about his Agreement, the
Ten Commandments. He told you to obey them,
and he wrote them on two stone tablets. 14Then
the LORD commanded me to teach you the laws
and rules that you must obey in the land you will
take when you cross the Jordan River.

Laws About Idols

15Since the LORD spoke to you from the fire at
Mount Sinai, but you did not see him, watch
yourselves carefully! 16Don't sin by making idols
of any kind, and don't make statues—of men or
women, 17of animals on earth or birds that fly in
the air, 18of anything that crawls on the ground,
or of fish in the water below. 19When you look up
at the sky, you see the sun, moon, and stars, and
everything in the sky. But don't bow down and
worship them, because the LORD your God has
made these things for all people everywhere.
20But the LORD brought you out of Egypt, which
tested you like a furnace for melting iron, and
he made you his very own people, as you are
now.
21The LORD was angry with me because of you,
and he swore that I would not cross the Jordan
River to go into the good land the LORD your God
is giving you as your own. 22I will die here in this
land and not cross the Jordan, but you will soon
go across and take that good land. 23Be careful.
Don't forget the Agreement of the LORD your God
that he made with you, and don't make any idols
for yourselves, as the LORD your God has commanded you not to do. 24The LORD your God is
a jealous God, like a fire that burns things up.
25Even after you have lived in the land a long
time and have had children and grandchildren,
don't do evil things. Don't make any kind of idol,
and don't do what the LORD your God says is evil,
because that will make him angry. 26If you do, I
ask heaven and earth to speak against you this day
that you will quickly be removed from this land
that you are crossing the Jordan River to take. You
will not live there long after that, but you will be
completely destroyed. 27The LORD will scatter you
among the other nations. Only a few of you will
be left alive, and those few will be in other nations
where the LORD will send you. 28There you will
worship gods made by people, gods made of wood
and stone, that cannot see, hear, eat, or smell.
29But even there you can look for the LORD your
God, and you will find him if you look for him
with your whole being. 30It will be hard when all

these things happen to you. But after that you will come back to the LORD your God and obey him, 31because the LORD your God is a merciful God. He will not leave you or destroy you. He will not forget the Agreement with your ancestors, which he swore to them.

The Lord Is Great

32Nothing like this has ever happened before! Look at the past, long before you were even born. Go all the way back to when God made humans on the earth, and look from one end of heaven to the other. Nothing like this has ever been heard of! 33No other people have ever heard God speak from a fire and have still lived. But you have. 34No other god has ever taken for himself one nation out of another. But the LORD your God did this for you in Egypt, right before your own eyes. He did it with tests, signs, miracles,[d] war, and great sights, by his great power and strength.

35He showed you things so you would know that the LORD is God, and there is no other God besides him. 36He spoke to you from heaven to teach you. He showed you his great fire on earth, and you heard him speak from the fire. 37Because the LORD loved your ancestors, he chose you, their descendants,[d] and he brought you out of Egypt himself by his great strength. 38He forced nations out of their land ahead of you, nations that were bigger and stronger than you were. The LORD did this so he could bring you into their land and give it to you as your own, and this land is yours today.

39Know and believe today that the LORD is God. He is God in heaven above and on the earth below. There is no other god! 40Obey his laws and commands that I am giving you today so that

GOD'S LOVE

Persistent Love

According to most people, Martha Henry should have hated Edward Henderson. After all, he had shot her son Calvin twice—once between the eyes and once in the neck.

Martha got the details of the shooting from Edward, who said he had intended to fire warning shots over the car, not into the car. He called the hospital almost every hour to see how Calvin was doing. Calvin died five days after the shooting, never having regained consciousness.

Martha believed Edward when he said the shooting was accidental. But the court didn't; he was sentenced to life in prison without parole.

Then Martha felt God nudging her to share God's love with Edward, now in prison for life. "I had a lot to think about while the Lord was pushing me to love Edward and not hold any bitterness against him," Martha says. "But, I'd learned from experience that when God tells you something, he means what he says."

On Martha's first visit, Edward suspected her motives and didn't want to see her again. "I'm praying for you," she told him as she left. But each succeeding visit helped him open up. Eventually, he committed his life to Christ and began calling Martha "Mother Henry."

When Edward began appealing for parole, Martha pleaded his case. Though he hasn't been released, Martha believes he eventually will be. "He's not staying in there forever," she says confidently. "The Lord has things for him to do!"

Martha reached out to Edward and believed he had a special role to play. God also reached out to the Israelites and chose them for a special role, revealing his incredible love in **Deuteronomy 4:32–40**.

- According to the passage, how were the Israelites like Edward?
- How did God make himself known to the Israelites? How are the reasons God worked in them similar to the reasons he has worked in you?

CONSIDER . . .

- writing a love letter to God, thanking him for the many things he's done for you.
- becoming a pen pal with a prison inmate. Offer God's love and encouragement in your letters.

FOR MORE, SEE . . .

- Psalm 91:14–16 (p. 535)
- Isaiah 43:1–4 (p. 659)
- Romans 5:6–8 (p. 1145)

things will go well for you and your children.
Then you will live a long time in the land that the
LORD your God is giving to you forever.

Cities of Safety

41Moses chose three cities east of the Jordan
River, 42where a person who accidentally killed
someone could go. If the person was not killed
because of hatred, the murderer's life could be
saved by running to one of these cities. 43These
were the cities: Bezer in the desert high plain was
for the Reubenites; Ramoth in Gilead was for the
Gadites; and Golan in Bashan was for the Manas-
sites.

The Laws Moses Gave

44These are the teachings Moses gave to the
people of Israel. 45They are the rules, commands,
and laws he gave them when they came out of
Egypt. 46They were in the valley near Beth Peor,
east of the Jordan River, in the land of Sihon. Sihon king of the Amorites ruled in Heshbon and
was defeated by Moses and the Israelites as they
came out of Egypt. 47The Israelites took his land
and the land of Og king of Bashan, the two Amorite kings east of the Jordan River. 48This land
went from Aroer, on the edge of the Arnon Ravine, to Mount Hermon. 49It included all the Jordan Valley east of the Jordan River, and it went
as far as the Dead Sea[d] below Mount Pisgah.

The Ten Commandments

5 Moses called all the people of Israel together
and said: Listen, Israel, to the commands
and laws I am giving you today. Learn them and
obey them carefully. 2The LORD our God made an
Agreement with us at Mount Sinai. 3He did not
make this Agreement with our ancestors, but he
made it with us, with all of us who are alive here
today. 4The LORD spoke to you face to face from
the fire on the mountain. 5(At that time I stood
between you and the LORD in order to tell you
what the LORD said; you were afraid of the fire,
so you would not go up on the mountain.) The
LORD said:

6"I am the LORD your God; I brought you out
of the land of Egypt where you were slaves.

7"You must not have any other gods except
me.

8"You must not make for yourselves any idols
or anything to worship that looks like something
in the sky above or on the earth below or in the
water below the land. 9You must not worship or
serve any idol, because I, the LORD your God, am
a jealous God. If people sin against me and hate
me, I will punish their children, even their grandchildren and great-grandchildren. 10But I will be
very kind for a thousand lifetimes to those who
love me and obey my commands.

11"You must not use the name of the LORD your
God thoughtlessly, because the LORD will punish
anyone who uses his name in this way.

12"Keep the Sabbath[d] as a holy day, as the LORD
your God has commanded you. 13You may work
and get everything done during six days each
week, 14but the seventh day is a day of rest to
honor the LORD your God. On that day no one
may do any work: not you, your son or daughter,
your male or female slaves, your ox, your donkey,
or any of your animals, or the foreigners living in
your cities. That way your servants may rest as
you do. 15Remember that you were slaves in
Egypt and that the LORD your God brought you
out of there by his great power and strength. So
the LORD your God has commanded you to rest
on the Sabbath day.

16"Honor your father and your mother as the
LORD your God has commanded you. Then you
will live a long time, and things will go well for
you in the land that the LORD your God is going
to give you.

17"You must not murder anyone.

18"You must not be guilty of adultery.[d]

19"You must not steal.

20"You must not tell lies about your neighbor.

21"You must not want to take your neighbor's
wife. You must not want to take your neighbor's
house or land, his male or female slaves, his ox or
his donkey, or anything that belongs to your
neighbor."

22The LORD spoke these commands to all of you
on the mountain in a loud voice out of the fire,
the cloud, and the deep darkness; he did not say
anything else. Then he wrote them on two stone
tablets, and he gave them to me.

23When you heard the voice from the darkness,
as the mountain was blazing with fire, all your
older leaders and leaders of your tribes[d] came to
me. 24And you said, "The LORD our God has
shown us his glory and majesty, and we have
heard his voice from the fire. Today we have seen
that a person can live even if God speaks to him.
25But now, we will die! This great fire will burn
us up, and we will die if we hear the LORD our
God speak anymore. 26No human being has ever
heard the living God speaking from a fire and still
lived, but we have. 27Moses, you go near and listen to everything the LORD our God says. Then
you tell us what the LORD our God tells you, and
we will listen and obey."

28The LORD heard what you said to me, and he
said to me, "I have heard what the people said to
you. Everything they said was good. 29I wish their
hearts would always respect me and that they
would always obey my commands so that things
would go well for them and their children forever!

30"Go and tell the people to return to their

tents, 31but you stay here with me so that I may
give you all the commands, rules, and laws that
you must teach the people to obey in the land I
am giving them as their own."
32So be careful to do what the LORD your God
has commanded you, and follow the commands
exactly. 33Live the way the LORD your God has
commanded you so that you may live and have
what is good and have a long life in the land you
will take.

The Command to Love God

6 These are the commands, rules, and laws
that the LORD your God told me to teach you
to obey in the land you are crossing the Jordan
River to take. 2You, your children, and your
grandchildren must respect the LORD your God as
long as you live. Obey all his rules and commands
I give you so that you will live a long time. 3Listen,
Israel, and carefully obey these laws. Then all will
go well for you, and you will become a great nation in a fertile land, just as the LORD, the God of
your ancestors, has promised you.
4Listen, people of Israel! The LORD our God is
the only LORD. 5Love the LORD your God with all
your heart, all your soul, and all your strength.
6Always remember these commands I give you
today. 7Teach them to your children, and talk
about them when you sit at home and walk along
the road, when you lie down and when you get
up. 8Write them down and tie them to your hands
as a sign. Tie them on your forehead to remind
you, 9and write them on your doors and gates.

SIDELIGHT: Deuteronomy 6:4–9 is as important to the Jews as the Lord's Prayer (Matthew 6:9–13, p. 918) is to Christians. The Deuteronomy passage is the basis for the Jewish Shema, which is recited morning and evening by many Jews. This classic declaration of faith is also recited just before death and in times of martyrdom.

10The LORD your God will bring you into the
land he promised to your ancestors, to Abraham,
Isaac, and Jacob, and he will give it to you. The
land has large, growing cities you did not build,
11houses full of good things you did not buy, wells
you did not dig, and vineyards and olive trees you
did not plant. You will eat as much as you want.
12But be careful! Do not forget the LORD, who

FOLLOWING GOD

Totally Committed

Joseph Clark, fifteen, was determined. So what if his 900-student high school had only thirty black students? He still believed the school should have a major, annual celebration to commemorate Martin Luther King, Jr.'s contribution to society.

School officials were reluctant. The school already had a black history program. But Joseph kept pushing and eventually succeeded in gaining approval for a special program for King's birthday. Then he planned the program and invited the speakers, who helped the students understand the leader's legacy.

But Joseph wasn't satisfied. He talked to his pastor about having a special worship service to honor Dr. King. With a little work, he convinced the minister too.

Joseph doesn't tire of his efforts. He's totally dedicated to promoting his black heritage. It's that kind of wholehearted commitment that God wants his people to have when following his will. Read **Deuteronomy 6:1–9** to learn about the importance of total commitment when following God.

- How does Joseph's commitment to his cause compare to the commitment called for in the passage? What is similar?
- How difficult is it for you to be completely dedicated to God as the passage challenges? How are you working on your commitment?

CONSIDER. . .

- rewriting in your own words what Deuteronomy 6:5 means to you.
- evaluating what area of your life is most difficult to give totally to God. Pray that God will give you the strength to commit that area to him.

FOR MORE, SEE. . .

- Deuteronomy 10:12–22 (p. 171)
- Luke 14:25–35 (p. 1034)

- Philippians 3:12–16 (p. 1232)

brought you out of the land of Egypt where you
were slaves.
13Respect the LORD your God. You must worship him and make your promises only in his
name. 14Do not worship other gods as the people
around you do, 15because the LORD your God is
a jealous God. He is present with you, and if you
worship other gods, he will become angry with
you and destroy you from the earth. 16Do not test
the LORD your God as you did at Massah. 17Be
sure to obey the commands of the LORD your God
and the rules and laws he has given you. 18Do
what the LORD says is good and right so that
things will go well for you. Then you may go in
and take the good land the LORD promised to your
ancestors. 19He will force all your enemies out as
you go in, as the LORD has said.
20In the future when your children ask you,
"What is the meaning of the laws, commands,
and rules the LORD our God gave us?" 21tell them,
"We were slaves to the king of Egypt, but the
LORD brought us out of Egypt by his great power.
22The LORD showed us great and terrible signs
and miracles,[d] which he did to Egypt, the king,
and his whole family. 23The LORD brought us out
of Egypt to lead us here and to give us the land
he promised our ancestors. 24The LORD ordered
us to obey all these commands and to respect the
LORD our God so that we will always do well and
stay alive, as we are today. 25The right thing for
us to do is this: Obey all these rules in the presence of the LORD our God, as he has commanded."

You Are God's People

7 The LORD your God will bring you into the
land that you are entering and that you will
have as your own. As you go in, he will force out
these nations: the Hittites, Girgashites, Amorites,
Canaanites, Perizzites, Hivites, and Jebusites—
seven nations that are stronger than you. 2The
LORD your God will hand these nations over to
you, and when you defeat them, you must destroy them completely. Do not make a peace
treaty with them or show them any mercy. 3Do
not marry any of them, or let your daughters
marry their sons, or let your sons marry their
daughters. 4If you do, those people will turn your
children away from me, to begin serving other
gods. Then the LORD will be very angry with you,
and he will quickly destroy you. 5This is what you
must do to those people: Tear down their altars,
smash their holy stone pillars, cut down their
Asherah[d] idols, and burn their idols in the fire.
6You are holy people who belong to the LORD
your God. He has chosen you from all the people
on earth to be his very own.
7The LORD did not care for you and choose you
because there were many of you—you are the
smallest nation of all. 8But the LORD chose you
because he loved you, and he kept his promise to
your ancestors. So he brought you out of Egypt by
his great power and freed you from the land of
slavery, from the power of the king of Egypt. 9So
know that the LORD your God is God, the faithful
God. He will keep his agreement of love for a
thousand lifetimes for people who love him and
obey his commands. 10But he will pay back those
people who hate him. He will destroy them, and
he will not be slow to pay back those who hate
him. 11So be careful to obey the commands, rules,
and laws I give you today.
12If you pay attention to these laws and obey
them carefully, the LORD your God will keep his
agreement and show his love to you, as he promised your ancestors. 13He will love and bless you.
He will make the number of your people grow; he
will bless you with children. He will bless your
fields with good crops and will give you grain,
new wine, and oil. He will bless your herds with
calves and your flocks with lambs in the land he
promised your ancestors he would give you.
14You will be blessed more than any other people.
Every husband and wife will have children, and
all your cattle will have calves. 15The LORD will
take away all disease from you; you will not have
the terrible diseases that were in Egypt, but he
will give them to all the people who hate you.
16You must destroy all the people the LORD your
God hands over to you. Do not feel sorry for
them, and do not worship their gods, or they will
trap you.
17You might say to yourselves, "Because these
nations are stronger than we are, we can't force
them out." 18But don't be afraid of them. Remember what the LORD your God did to all of Egypt
and its king. 19You saw for yourselves the troubles, signs, and miracles[d] he did, how the LORD's
great power and strength brought you out of
Egypt. The LORD your God will do the same thing
to all the nations you now fear. 20The LORD your
God will also send terror among them so that
even those who are alive and hiding from you will
die. 21Don't be afraid of them, because the LORD
your God is with you; he is a great God and people are afraid of him. 22When the LORD your God
forces those nations out of the land, he will do it
little by little ahead of you. You won't be able to
destroy them all at once; otherwise, the wild animals will grow too many in number. 23But the
LORD your God will hand those nations over to
you, confusing them until they are destroyed.
24The LORD will help you defeat their kings, and
the world will forget who they were. No one will
be able to stop you; you will destroy them all.
25Burn up their idols in the fire. Do not wish for
the silver and gold they have, and don't take it for
yourselves, or you will be trapped by it. The LORD

your God hates it. 26Do not bring one of those
hateful things into your house, or you will be
completely destroyed along with it. Hate and reject those things; they must be completely destroyed.

Remember the Lord

8 Carefully obey every command I give you today. Then you will live and grow in number,
and you will enter and take the land the LORD
promised your ancestors. 2Remember how the
LORD your God has led you in the desert for these
forty years, taking away your pride and testing
you, because he wanted to know what was in
your heart. He wanted to know if you would obey
his commands. 3He took away your pride when
he let you get hungry, and then he fed you with
manna,[d] which neither you nor your ancestors
had ever seen. This was to teach you that a person
does not live by eating only bread, but by everything the LORD says. 4During these forty years,
your clothes did not wear out, and your feet did
not swell. 5Know in your heart that the LORD your
God corrects you as a parent corrects a child.

6Obey the commands of the LORD your God,
living as he has commanded you and respecting
him. 7The LORD your God is bringing you into a
good land, a land with rivers and pools of water,
with springs that flow in the valleys and hills, 8a
land that has wheat and barley, vines, fig trees,
pomegranates,[d] olive oil, and honey. 9It is a land
where you will have plenty of food, where you
will have everything you need, where the rocks
are iron, and where you can dig copper out of the
hills.

10When you have all you want to eat, then
praise the LORD your God for giving you a good
land. 11Be careful not to forget the LORD your God
so that you fail to obey his commands, laws, and
rules that I am giving to you today. 12When you

THANKFULNESS

Remembering Love

Terrence Shaw, seventeen, bravely held back tears as he tossed a shovel of dirt into his mother's grave.

What would his family do now? He, his four younger brothers, and his dad had depended on their mom for everything. None of them knew how to cook, do laundry, or clean the house. And, making matters worse, his dad had been laid off from his job just a week before Mom's stroke.

After the burial, Terrence and his family went to the church where lunch was provided. Mrs. Hammer pulled Terrence aside. "I just spoke with your father, Terrence," she said. "Some of the women of the church want to help you and your brothers around the house. We'll be over tomorrow to do some cooking and cleaning."

Two women arrived the next morning and spent several hours in the home. And through the next month, different people came back. They patiently taught Terrence and the others how to cook meals, separate and wash the laundry, and clean the floors. Gradually, the family learned what it needed to cope without Mom.

Now a pastor, Terrence testifies: "I don't know what we would have done without our church family. Their love is what made me decide to become a minister. They helped make me what I am today."

Terrence has never forgotten how God provided for his family through the church. **Deuteronomy 8:10–18** reminds us never to forget that all good things come from God.

- How does Terrence's choice to be a pastor show the spirit of thankfulness spoken of in this passage?
- In what ways mentioned in the passage has God helped you? How have you expressed your thanks?

CONSIDER . . .

- writing a list of everything you can think of that God has given you in the past month. Then thank God for something different every day in the next week.
- taking a dessert or a meal to someone who's suffering as a way of saying thanks to God.

FOR MORE, SEE . . .

- Psalm 77:11–20 (p. 527)
- Psalm 92:1–5 (p. 536)
- 2 Corinthians 9:6–15 (p. 1201)

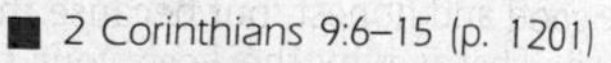

eat all you want and build nice houses and live in
them, 13when your herds and flocks grow large
and your silver and gold increase, when you have
more of everything, 14then your heart will become proud. You will forget the LORD your God,
who brought you out of the land of Egypt, where
you were slaves. 15He led you through the large
and terrible desert that was dry and had no water,
and that had poisonous snakes and stinging insects. He gave you water from a solid rock 16and
manna to eat in the desert. Manna was something
your ancestors had never seen. He did this to take
away your pride and to test you, so things would
go well for you in the end. 17You might say to
yourself, "I am rich because of my own power
and strength," 18but remember the LORD your
God! It is he who gives you the power to become
rich, keeping the agreement he promised to your
ancestors, as it is today.

19If you ever forget the LORD your God and follow other gods and worship them and bow down
to them, I warn you today that you will be destroyed. 20Just as the LORD destroyed the other
nations for you, you can be destroyed if you do
not obey the LORD your God.

SIDELIGHT: Most Christians pray or say grace before they eat a meal. But the ancient Israelites didn't just pray before they ate. They prayed afterward as well (Deuteronomy 8:10).

The Lord Will Be with Israel

9 Listen, Israel. You will soon cross the Jordan
River to go in and force out nations that are
bigger and stronger than you. They have large cities with walls up to the sky. 2The people there are
Anakites,[d] who are strong and tall. You know
about them, and you have heard it said: "No one
can stop the Anakites." 3But today remember that
the LORD your God goes in before you to destroy
them like a fire that burns things up. He will defeat them ahead of you, and you will force them
out and destroy them quickly, just as the LORD
has said.

4After the LORD your God has forced those nations out ahead of you, don't say to yourself, "The
LORD brought me here to take this land because
I am so good." No! It is because these nations are
evil that the LORD will force them out ahead of
you. 5You are going in to take the land, not because you are good and honest, but because these
nations are evil. That is why the LORD your God
will force them out ahead of you, to keep his
promise to your ancestors, to Abraham, Isaac, and
Jacob. 6The LORD your God is giving you this good
land to take as your own. But know this: It is not
because you are good; you are a stubborn people.

Remember the Lord's Anger

7Remember this and do not forget it: You made
the LORD your God angry in the desert. You
would not obey the LORD from the day you left
Egypt until you arrived here. 8At Mount Sinai you
made the LORD angry—angry enough to destroy
you. 9When I went up on the mountain to receive
the stone tablets, the tablets with the Agreement
the LORD had made with you, I stayed on the
mountain for forty days and forty nights; I did not
eat bread or drink water. 10The LORD gave me
two stone tablets, which God had written on with
his own finger. On them were all the commands
that the LORD gave to you on the mountain out
of the fire, on the day you were gathered there.

11When the forty days and forty nights were
over, the LORD gave me the two stone tablets, the
tablets with the Agreement on them. 12Then the
LORD told me, "Get up and go down quickly from
here, because the people you brought out from
Egypt are ruining themselves. They have quickly
turned away from what I commanded and have
made an idol for themselves."

13The LORD said to me, "I have watched these
people, and they are very stubborn! 14Get away so
that I may destroy them and make the whole
world forget who they are. Then I will make another nation from you that will be bigger and
stronger than they are."

15So I turned and came down the mountain
that was burning with fire, and the two stone tablets with the Agreement were in my hands.
16When I looked, I saw you had sinned against the
LORD your God and had made an idol in the shape
of a calf. You had quickly turned away from what
the LORD had told you to do. 17So I took the two
stone tablets and threw them down, breaking
them into pieces right in front of you.

18Then I again bowed facedown on the ground
before the LORD for forty days and forty nights; I
did not eat bread or drink water. You had sinned
by doing what the LORD said was evil, and you
made him angry. 19I was afraid of the LORD's anger and rage, because he was angry enough with
you to destroy you, but the LORD listened to me
again. 20And the LORD was angry enough with
Aaron to destroy him, but then I prayed for Aaron,
too. 21I took that sinful calf idol you had made and
burned it in the fire. I crushed it into a powder
like dust and threw the dust into a stream that
flowed down the mountain.

22You also made the LORD angry at Taberah,
Massah, and Kibroth Hattaavah.

23Then the LORD sent you away from Kadesh
Barnea and said, "Go up and take the land I have

given you." But you rejected the command of the LORD your God. You did not trust him or obey him. 24You have refused to obey the LORD as long as I have known you.

25The LORD had said he would destroy you, so I threw myself down in front of him for those forty days and forty nights. 26I prayed to the LORD and said, "Lord GOD, do not destroy your people, your own people, whom you freed and brought out of Egypt by your great power and strength. 27Remember your servants Abraham, Isaac, and Jacob. Don't look at how stubborn these people are, and don't look at their sin and evil. 28Otherwise, Egypt will say, 'It was because the LORD was not able to take his people into the land he promised them, and it was because he hated them that he took them into the desert to kill them.' 29But they are your people, LORD, your own people, whom you brought out of Egypt with your great power and strength."

New Stone Tablets

10 At that time the LORD said to me, "Cut two stone tablets like the first ones and come up to me on the mountain. Also make a wooden Ark.[d] 2I will write on the tablets the same words that were on the first tablets, which you broke, and you will put the new tablets in the Ark."

3So I made the Ark out of acacia wood, and I cut out two stone tablets like the first ones. Then I went up on the mountain with the two tablets in my hands. 4The LORD wrote the same things on these tablets he had written before—the Ten Commandments that he had told you on the mountain from the fire, on the day you were gathered there. And the LORD gave them to me. 5Then I turned and came down the mountain; I put the tablets in the Ark I had made, as the LORD had commanded, and they are still there.

6(The people of Israel went from the wells of the Jaakanites to Moserah. Aaron died there and was buried; his son Eleazar became priest in his place. 7From Moserah they went to Gudgodah, and from Gudgodah they went to Jotbathah, a place with streams of water. 8At that time the LORD chose the tribe[d] of Levi to carry the Ark of the Agreement with the LORD. They were to serve the LORD and to bless the people in his name, which they still do today. 9That is why the Levites did not receive any land of their own; instead, they received the LORD himself as their gift, as the LORD your God told them.)

10I stayed on the mountain forty days and forty nights just like the first time, and the LORD listened to me this time also. He did not want to destroy you. 11The LORD said to me, "Go and lead the people so that they will go in and take the land I promised their ancestors."

What the Lord Wants You To Do

12Now, Israel, this is what the LORD your God wants you to do: Respect the LORD your God, and do what he has told you to do. Love him. Serve the LORD your God with your whole being, 13and obey the LORD's commands and laws that I am giving you today for your own good.

14The LORD owns the world and everything in it—the heavens, even the highest heavens, are his. 15But the LORD cared for and loved your ancestors, and he chose you, their descendants,[d] over all the other nations, just as it is today. 16Give yourselves completely to serving him, and do not be stubborn any longer. 17The LORD your God is God of all gods and Lord of all lords. He is the great God, who is strong and wonderful. He does not take sides, and he will not be talked into doing evil. 18He helps orphans and widows, and he loves foreigners and gives them food and clothes. 19You also must love foreigners, because you were foreigners in Egypt. 20Respect the LORD your God and serve him. Be loyal to him and make your promises in his name. 21He is the one you should praise; he is your God, who has done great and wonderful things for you, which you have seen with your own eyes. 22There were only seventy of your ancestors when they went down to Egypt, and now the LORD your God has made you as many as the stars in the sky.

Great Things Israel Saw

11 Love the LORD your God and always obey his orders, rules, laws, and commands. 2Remember today it was not your children who saw and felt the correction of the LORD your God. They did not see his majesty, his power, his strength, 3or his signs and the things he did in Egypt to the king and his whole country. 4They did not see what he did to the Egyptian army, its horses and chariots, when he drowned them in the Red Sea[d] as they were chasing you. The LORD ruined them forever. 5They did not see what he did for you in the desert until you arrived here. 6They did not see what he did to Dathan and Abiram, the sons of Eliab the Reubenite, when the ground opened up and swallowed them, their families, their tents, and everyone who stood with them in Israel. 7It was you who saw all these great things the LORD has done.

8So obey all the commands I am giving you today so that you will be strong and can go in and take the land you are going to take as your own. 9Then you will live a long time in the land that the LORD promised to give to your ancestors and their descendants,[d] a fertile land. 10The land you are going to take is not like Egypt, where you were. There you had to plant your seed and water it, like a vegetable garden, by using your feet. 11But the land that you will soon cross the Jordan River to take is a land of hills and valleys, a land that drinks rain from heaven. 12It is a land the LORD your God cares for. His eyes are on it continually, and he watches it from the beginning of the year to the end.

13If you carefully obey the commands I am giving you today and love the LORD your God and serve him with your whole being, 14then he will send rain on your land at the right time, in the fall and spring, and you will be able to gather your grain, new wine, and oil. 15He will put grass in the fields for your cattle, and you will have plenty to eat.

16Be careful, or you will be fooled and will turn away to serve and worship other gods. 17If you do, the LORD will become angry with you and will shut the heavens so it will not rain. Then the land will not grow crops, and you will soon die in the good land the LORD is giving you. 18Remember my words with your whole being. Write them down and tie them to your hands as a sign; tie

SIDELIGHT: If you have trouble remembering scripture passages, you are not alone. The Israelites apparently did too. So God told his people to write down his words and tie them to their hands so they wouldn't forget them (Deuteronomy 11:18). This approach might get cumbersome if you memorized the whole Bible!

them on your foreheads to remind you. 19Teach them well to your children, talking about them when you sit at home and walk along the road, when you lie down and when you get up. 20Write them on your doors and gates 21so that both you and your children will live a long time in the land the LORD promised your ancestors, as long as the skies are above the earth.

22If you are careful to obey every command I am giving you to follow, and love the LORD your God, and do what he has told you to do, and are loyal to him, 23then the LORD will force all those nations out of the land ahead of you, and you will take the land from nations that are bigger and stronger than you. 24Everywhere you step will be yours. Your land will go from the desert to Lebanon and from the Euphrates River to the Mediterranean Sea. 25No one will be able to stop you. The LORD your God will do what he promised and will make the people afraid everywhere you go.

26See, today I am letting you choose a blessing or a curse. 27You will be blessed if you obey the commands of the LORD your God that I am giving you today. 28But you will be cursed if you disobey the commands of the LORD your God. So do not disobey the commands I am giving you today, and do not worship other gods you do not know. 29When the LORD your God brings you into the land you will take as your own, you are to announce the blessings from Mount Gerizim and the curses from Mount Ebal. 30(These mountains are on the other side of the Jordan River, to the west, toward the sunset. They are near the great trees of Moreh in the land of the Canaanites who live in the Jordan Valley opposite Gilgal.) 31You will soon cross the Jordan River to enter and take the land the LORD your God is giving you. When you take it over and live there, 32be careful to obey all the commands and laws I am giving you today.

The Place for Worship

12 These are the commands and laws you must carefully obey in the land the LORD, the God of your ancestors, is giving you. Obey them as long as you live in the land. 2When you inherit the lands of these nations, you must completely destroy all the places where they serve their gods, on high mountains and hills and under every green tree. 3Tear down their altars, smash their holy stone pillars, and burn their Asherah[d] idols in the fire. Cut down their idols and destroy their names from those places.

4Don't worship the LORD your God that way, 5but look for the place the LORD your God will choose — a place among your tribes[d] where he is to be worshiped. Go there, 6and bring to that place your burnt offerings and sacrifices; bring a tenth of what you gain and your special gifts; bring what you have promised and the special gifts you want to give the LORD, and bring the first animals born to your herds and flocks.

7There you will be together with the LORD your God. There you and your families will eat, and you will enjoy all the good things for which you have worked, because the LORD your God has blessed you.

8Do not worship the way we have been doing today, each person doing what he thinks is right. 9You have not yet come to a resting place, to the land the LORD your God will give you as your own. 10But soon you will cross the Jordan River to live in the land the LORD your God is giving you as your own, where he will give you rest from all your enemies and you will live in safety. 11Then the LORD your God will choose a place where he is to be worshiped. To that place you must bring everything I tell you: your burnt offerings and sacrifices, your offerings of a tenth of what you gain, your special gifts, and all your best things you promised to the LORD. 12There rejoice before the LORD your God. Everyone should rejoice: you, your sons and daughters, your male and female servants, and the Levites from your towns who have no land of their own. 13Be careful that you don't sacrifice your burnt offerings just anywhere you please. 14Offer them only in the place the LORD will choose. He will choose a place in one of your tribes, and there you must do everything I am commanding you.

15But you may kill your animals in any of your towns and eat as much of the meat as you want, as if it were a deer or a gazelle; this is the blessing the LORD your God is giving you. Anyone, clean[d] or unclean, may eat this meat, 16but do not eat the blood. Pour it out on the ground like water. 17Do not eat in your own towns what belongs to the LORD: one-tenth of your grain, new wine, or oil; the first animals born to your herds or flocks; whatever you have promised to give; the special gifts you want to give to the LORD, or any other gifts. 18Eat these things when you are together with the LORD your God, in the place the LORD your God chooses to be worshiped. Everyone must do this: you, your sons and daughters, your male and female servants, and the Levites from your towns. Rejoice in the LORD your God's presence about the things you have worked for. 19Be careful not to forget the Levites as long as you live in the land.

20When the LORD your God enlarges your country as he has promised, and you want some meat so you say, "I want some meat," you may eat as much meat as you want. 21If the LORD your God chooses a place where he is to be worshiped that is too far away from you, you may kill animals from your herds and flocks, which the LORD has given to you. I have commanded that you may do this. You may eat as much of them as you want in your own towns, 22as you would eat gazelle or deer meat. Both clean and unclean people may eat this meat, 23but be sure you don't eat the blood, because the life is in the blood. Don't eat the life with the meat. 24Don't eat the blood, but pour it out on the ground like water. 25If you don't eat it, things will go well for you and your children, because you will be doing what the LORD says is right.

26Take your holy things and the things you have promised to give, and go to the place the LORD will choose. 27Present your burnt offerings on the altar of the LORD your God, both the meat and the blood. The blood of your sacrifices should be poured beside the altar of the LORD your God, but you may eat the meat. 28Be careful to obey all the rules I am giving you so that things will always go well for you and your children, and you will be doing what the LORD your God says is good and right.

29You will enter the land and take it away from the nations that the LORD your God will destroy ahead of you. When you force them out and live in their land, 30they will be destroyed for you, but be careful not to be trapped by asking about their gods. Don't say, "How do these nations worship? I will do the same." 31Don't worship the LORD your God that way, because the LORD hates the evil ways they worship their gods. They even burn their sons and daughters as sacrifices to their gods!

32Be sure to do everything I have commanded you. Do not add anything to it, and do not take anything away from it.

False Prophets

13 Prophets[d] or those who tell the future with dreams might come to you and say they will show you a miracle[d] or a sign. 2The miracle or sign might even happen, and then they might say, "Let's serve other gods" (gods you have not known) "and let's worship them." 3But you must not listen to those prophets or dreamers. The LORD your God is testing you, to find out if you love him with your whole being. 4Serve only the LORD your God. Respect him, keep his commands, and obey him. Serve him and be loyal to him. 5The prophets or dreamers must be killed, because they said you should turn against the LORD your God, who brought you out of Egypt and saved you from the land where you were slaves. They tried to turn you from doing what the LORD your God commanded you to do. You must get rid of the evil among you.

6Someone might try to lead you to serve other gods—it might be your brother, your son or daughter, the wife you love, or a close friend. The person might say, "Let's go and worship other gods." (These are gods that neither you nor your ancestors have known, 7gods of the people who live around you, either nearby or far away, from one end of the land to the other.) 8Do not give in to such people. Do not listen or feel sorry for them, and do not let them go free or protect them. 9You must put them to death. You must be the first one to start to kill them, and then everyone else must join in. 10You must throw stones at them until they die, because they tried to turn you away from the LORD your God, who brought you out of the land of Egypt, where you were slaves. 11Then everyone in Israel will hear about this and be afraid, and no one among you will ever do such an evil thing again.

Cities to Destroy

12The LORD your God is giving you cities in which to live, and you might hear something about one of them. Someone might say 13that evil people have moved in among you. And they might lead the people of that city away from God, saying, "Let's go and worship other gods." (These are gods you have not known.) 14Then you must

ask about it, looking into the matter and checking
carefully whether it is true. If it is proved that a
hateful thing has happened among you, 15you
must kill with a sword everyone who lives in that
city. Destroy the city completely and kill everyone
in it, as well as the animals, with a sword.
16Gather up everything those people owned, and
put it in the middle of the city square. Then completely burn the city and everything they owned
as a burnt offering to the LORD your God. That
city should never be rebuilt; let it be ruined forever. 17Don't keep for yourselves any of the things
found in that city, so the LORD will not be angry
anymore. He will give you mercy and feel sorry
for you, and he will make your nation grow
larger, as he promised to your ancestors. 18You
will have obeyed the LORD your God by keeping
all his commands that I am giving to you today,
and you will be doing what the LORD says is right.

God's Special People

14 You are the children of the LORD your
God. When someone dies, do not cut
yourselves or shave your heads to show your sadness. 2You are holy people, who belong to the
LORD your God. He has chosen you from all the
people on earth to be his very own.

3Do not eat anything the LORD hates. 4These
are the animals you may eat: oxen, sheep, goats,
5deer, gazelle, roe deer, wild goats, ibex, antelope, and mountain sheep. 6You may eat any animal that has a split hoof and chews the cud,[d] 7but
you may not eat camels, rabbits, or rock badgers.
These animals chew the cud, but they do not
have split hoofs, so they are unclean[d] for you.
8Pigs are also unclean for you; they have split
hoofs, but they do not chew the cud. Do not eat
their meat or touch their dead bodies.

9There are many things that live in the water.
You may eat anything that has fins and scales,
10but do not eat anything that does not have fins
and scales. It is unclean for you.

11You may eat any clean bird. 12But do not eat
these birds: eagles, vultures, black vultures, 13red
kites, falcons, any kind of kite, 14any kind of raven, 15horned owls, screech owls, sea gulls, any
kind of hawk, 16little owls, great owls, white
owls, 17desert owls, ospreys, cormorants, 18storks,
any kind of heron, the hoopoes, or bats.

19All insects with wings are unclean for you; do
not eat them. 20Other things with wings are clean,
and you may eat them.

21Do not eat anything you find that is already
dead. You may give it to a foreigner living in your
town, and he may eat it, or you may sell it to a
foreigner. But you are holy people, who belong to
the LORD your God.

Do not cook a baby goat in its mother's milk.

Giving One-Tenth

22Be sure to save one-tenth of all your crops
each year. 23Take it to the place the LORD your
God will choose where he is to be worshiped.

> **SIDELIGHT:** If you've got a new recipe for goat meat boiled in goat's milk, don't try it. The cooking technique was forbidden in Deuteronomy 14:21—for a good reason. It was a practice associated with pagan worship.

There, where you will be together with the LORD,
eat the tenth of your grain, new wine, and oil, and
eat the animals born first to your herds and flocks.
Do this so that you will learn to respect the LORD
your God always. 24But if the place the LORD will
choose to be worshiped is too far away and he has
blessed you so much you cannot carry a tenth,
25exchange your one-tenth for silver. Then take
the silver with you to the place the LORD your
God shall choose. 26Use the silver to buy anything
you wish—cattle, sheep, wine, beer, or anything
you wish. Then you and your family will eat and
celebrate there before the LORD your God. 27Do
not forget the Levites in your town, because they
have no land of their own among you.

28At the end of every third year, everyone
should bring one-tenth of that year's crop and
store it in your towns. 29This is for the Levites so
they may eat and be full. (They have no land of
their own among you.) It is also for strangers,
orphans, and widows who live in your towns so
that all of them may eat and be full. Then the
LORD your God will bless you and all the work
you do.

The Special Seventh Year

15 At the end of every seven years, you
must tell those who owe you anything
that they do not have to pay you back. 2This is
how you must do it: Everyone who has loaned
money must cancel the loan and not make a
neighbor or relative pay it back. This is the LORD's
time for canceling what people owe. 3You may
make a foreigner pay what is owed to you,
but you must not collect what another Israelite
owes you. 4But there should be no poor people
among you, because the LORD your God will richly bless you in the land he is giving you as your
own. 5He will bless you if you obey the LORD your
God completely, but you must be careful to obey
all the commands I am giving you today. 6The
LORD your God will bless you as he promised, and
you will lend to other nations, but you will not

need to borrow from them. You will rule over many nations, but none will rule over you.

7If there are poor among you, in one of the towns of the land the LORD your God is giving you, do not be selfish or greedy toward them. 8But give freely to them, and freely lend them whatever they need. 9Beware of evil thoughts. Don't think, "The seventh year is near, the year to cancel what people owe." You might be mean to the needy and not give them anything. Then they will complain to the LORD about you, and he will find you guilty of sin. 10Give freely to the poor person, and do not wish that you didn't have to give. The LORD your God will bless your work and everything you touch. 11There will always be poor people in the land, so I command you to give freely to your neighbors and to the poor and needy in your land.

Letting Slaves Go Free

12If one of your own people sells himself to you as a slave, whether it is a Hebrew man or woman, that person will serve you for six years. But in the seventh year you must let the slave go free. 13When you let slaves go, don't send them away without anything. 14Give them some of your flock, your grain, and your wine, giving to them as the LORD has given to you. 15Remember that you were slaves in Egypt, and the LORD your God saved you. That is why I am commanding this to you today.

16But if your slave says to you, "I don't want to leave you," because he loves you and your family and has a good life with you, 17stick an awl[n] through his ear into the door; he will be your slave for life. Also do this to a female slave.

18Do not think of it as a hard thing when you let your slaves go free. After all, they served you six years and did twice the work of a hired person. The LORD your God will bless you in everything you do.

Rules About Firstborn Animals

19Save all the first male animals born to your herds and flocks. They are for the LORD your God. Do not work the first calf born to your oxen, and do not cut off the wool from the first lamb born to your sheep. 20Each year you and your family are to eat these animals in the presence of the LORD your God, in the place he will choose to be worshiped. 21If an animal is crippled or blind or has something else wrong, do not sacrifice it to the LORD your God. 22But you may eat that animal in your own town. Both clean[d] and unclean people may eat it, as they would eat a gazelle or a deer. 23But don't eat its blood; pour it out on the ground like water.

The Passover

16 Celebrate the Passover[d] of the LORD your God during the month of Abib,[d] because it was during Abib that he brought you out of Egypt at night. 2As the sacrifice for the Passover to the LORD your God, offer an animal from your flock or herd at the place the LORD will choose to be worshiped. 3Do not eat it with bread made with yeast. But for seven days eat bread made without yeast, the bread of suffering, because you left Egypt in a hurry. So all your life you will remember the time you left Egypt. 4There must be no yeast anywhere in your land for seven days. Offer the sacrifice on the evening of the first day, and eat all the meat before morning; do not leave it overnight.

5Do not offer the Passover sacrifice in just any town the LORD your God gives you, 6but offer it in the place he will choose to be worshiped. Offer it in the evening as the sun goes down, which is when you left Egypt. 7Roast the meat and eat it at the place the LORD your God will choose. The next morning go back to your tents. 8Eat bread made without yeast for six days. On the seventh day have a special meeting for the LORD your God, and do not work that day.

The Feast of Weeks

9Count seven weeks from the time you begin to harvest the grain, 10and then celebrate the Feast[d] of Weeks for the LORD your God. Bring an offering as a special gift to him, giving to him just as he has blessed you. 11Rejoice before the LORD your God at the place he will choose to be worshiped. Everybody should rejoice: you, your sons and daughters, your male and female servants, the Levites in your town, the strangers, orphans, and widows living among you. 12Remember that you were slaves in Egypt, and carefully obey all these laws.

The Feast of Shelters

13Celebrate the Feast[d] of Shelters for seven days, after you have gathered your harvest from the threshing[d] floor and winepress.[d] 14Everybody should rejoice at your Feast: you, your sons and daughters, your male and female servants, the Levites, strangers, orphans, and widows who live in your towns. 15Celebrate the Feast to the LORD your God for seven days at the place he will choose, because the LORD your God will bless all your harvest and all the work you do, and you will be completely happy.

16All your men must come before the LORD three times a year to the place he will choose. They must come at these times: the Feast[d] of Un-

awl A tool like a big needle with a handle at one end.

leavened Bread, the Feast[d] of Weeks, and the Feast of Shelters. No man should come before the LORD without a gift. 17Each of you must bring a gift that will show how much the LORD your God has blessed you.

Judges for the People

18Appoint judges and officers for your tribes[d] in every town the LORD your God is giving you; they must judge the people fairly. 19Do not judge unfairly or take sides. Do not let people pay you to make wrong decisions, because that kind of payment makes wise people seem blind, and it changes the words of good people. 20Always do what is right so that you will live and always have the land the LORD your God is giving you.

God Hates Idols

21Do not set up a wooden Asherah[d] idol next to the altar you build for the LORD your God, 22and do not set up holy stone pillars. The LORD your God hates them.

17 If an ox or sheep has something wrong with it, do not offer it as a sacrifice to the LORD your God. He would hate that.

2A man or woman in one of the towns the LORD gave you might be found doing something evil and breaking the Agreement. 3That person may have served other gods and bowed down to them or to the sun or moon or stars of the sky, which I have commanded should not be done. 4If someone has told you about it, you must look into the matter carefully. If it is true that such a hateful thing has happened in Israel, 5take the man or woman who has done the evil thing to the city gates and throw stones at that person until he dies. 6There must be two or three witnesses that it is true before the person is put to death; if there is only one witness, the person should not be put to death. 7The witnesses must be the first to throw stones at the person, and then everyone else will follow. You must get rid of the evil among you.

Courts of Law

8Some cases that come before you, such as murder, quarreling, or attack, may be too difficult to judge. Take these cases to the place the LORD your God will choose. 9Go to the priests who are Levites and to the judge who is on duty at that time. Ask them about the case, and they will decide. 10You must follow the decision they give you at the place the LORD your God will choose. Be careful to do everything they tell you. 11Follow the teachings they give you, and do whatever they decide, exactly as they tell you. 12The person who does not show respect for the judge or priest who is there serving the LORD your God must be put to death. You must get rid of that evil from Israel. 13Then everyone will hear about this and will be afraid, and they will not show disrespect anymore.

Choosing a King

14When you enter the land the LORD your God is giving you, taking it as your own and living in it, you will say, "Let's appoint a king over us like the nations all around us." 15Be sure to appoint over you the king the LORD your God chooses. He must be one of your own people. Do not appoint as your king a foreigner who is not a fellow Israelite. 16The king must not have too many horses for himself, and he must not send people to Egypt to get more horses, because the LORD has told you, "Don't return that way again." 17The king must not have many wives, or his heart will be led away from God. He must not have too much silver and gold.

18When he becomes king, he should write a copy of the teachings on a scroll for himself, a copy taken from the priests and Levites. 19He should keep it with him all the time and read from it every day of his life. Then he will learn to respect the LORD his God, and he will obey all the teachings and commands. 20He should not think he is better than his fellow Israelites, and he must not stop obeying the law in any way so that he and his descendants[d] may rule the kingdom for a long time.

Shares for Priests and Levites

18 The priests are from the tribe[d] of Levi, and that tribe will not receive a share of the land with the Israelites. They will eat the offerings made to the LORD by fire, which is their share. 2They will not inherit any of the land like their brothers, but they will inherit the LORD himself, as he has promised them.

3When you offer a bull or sheep as a sacrifice, you must share with the priests, giving them the shoulder, the cheeks, and the inner organs. 4Give them the first of your grain, new wine, and oil, as well as the first wool you cut from your sheep. 5The LORD your God has chosen the priests and their descendants[d] out of all your tribes to stand and serve the LORD always.

6If a Levite moves from one of your towns anywhere in Israel where he lives and comes to the place the LORD will choose, because he wants to serve the LORD there, 7he may serve the LORD his God. He will be like his fellow Levites who serve there before the LORD. 8They all will have an equal share of the food. That is separate from what he has received from the sale of family possessions.

Do Not Follow Other Nations

9When you enter the land the LORD your God

is giving you, don't learn to do the hateful things
the other nations do. 10Don't let anyone among
you offer a son or daughter as a sacrifice in the
fire. Don't let anyone use magic or witchcraft,[d] or
try to explain the meaning of signs. 11Don't let
anyone try to control others with magic, and
don't let them be mediums[d] or try to talk with the
spirits of dead people. 12The LORD hates anyone
who does these things. Because the other nations
do these things, the LORD your God will force
them out of the land ahead of you. 13But you must
be innocent in the presence of the LORD your
God.

The Lord's Special Prophet

14The nations you will force out listen to people
who use magic and witchcraft,[d] but the LORD
your God will not let you do those things. 15The
LORD your God will give you a prophet[d] like me,
who is one of your own people. Listen to him.
16This is what you asked the LORD your God to do
when you were gathered at Mount Sinai. You
said, "Don't make us listen to the voice of the
LORD our God again, and don't make us look at
this terrible fire anymore, or we will die."
17So the LORD said to me, "What they have said
is good. 18So I will give them a prophet like you,
who is one of their own people. I will tell him
what to say, and he will tell them everything I
command. 19This prophet will speak for me; anyone who does not listen when he speaks will answer to me. 20But if a prophet says something I
did not tell him to say as though he were speaking

LEADERSHIP

Standing for Right

George Fox had a message from God, and he was not going to let anyone stop him from preaching it. In England in the 1600s, he urged people to listen to Christ, to be honest in business, and to be compassionate to the poor. Central to his message was the idea of religious liberty and that God worked through individual people, not just through the established church.

Though many people believed him and were converted, others opposed him. On many occasions, he was thrown down church steps or beaten. Once he was thrown into jail for six months. But he would not bend his beliefs and so got sentenced to six more months as a result. "Truth can live in the jails," he wrote. "Be valiant for Truth upon the earth and tread upon deceit."

Despite the government's efforts to stop him from challenging the official church, Fox's message got through to people because of his conviction and honesty. Within eight years of beginning his ministry, fifty thousand people had heard his message and had become followers. Young followers, known as "the valiant sixty," joined Fox in preaching at fairs, in markets, in fields, in jails, and in courts.

When he died in 1691, about one hundred thousand people had joined Fox's movement, which became known as the Society of Friends. Today the Friends (or Quakers) span the world, spreading a message of peace, holiness, service, and religious liberty.

George Fox's ministry had a long-term impact because his message was a true message from God. In his farewell speech, Moses urged the Israelites to listen carefully to prophets' messages to learn if they are true or not. Read **Deuteronomy 18:15–20** to see the guidelines he established.

- In what ways did George Fox's message fit with the message of the prophets as described in this passage?
- How can this passage help you evaluate messages you hear from people who have leadership roles?

CONSIDER. . .

- choosing key words from this passage to make a checklist for evaluating leaders. Use it whenever you wonder whether to believe what someone tells you.
- praying for Christian leaders around the world who sometimes have to risk their lives to speak God's truth.

FOR MORE, SEE. . .

- Jeremiah 37:1–21 (p. 734)
- Luke 4:23–30 (p. 1009)
- Hebrews 11:32–40 (p. 1288)

for me, or if a prophet speaks in the name of other gods, that prophet must be killed."

21You might be thinking, "How can we know if a message is not from the LORD?" 22If what a prophet says in the name of the LORD does not happen, it is not the LORD's message. That prophet was speaking his own ideas. Don't be afraid of him.

Cities of Safety

19 When the LORD your God gives you land that belongs to the other nations, nations that he will destroy, you will force them out and live in their cities and houses. 2Then choose three cities in the middle of the land the LORD your God is giving you as your own. 3Build roads to these cities, and divide the land the LORD is giving you into three parts so that someone who kills another person may run to these cities.

4This is the rule for someone who kills another person and runs to one of these cities in order to save his life. But the person must have killed a neighbor without meaning to, not out of hatred. 5For example, suppose someone goes into the forest with a neighbor to cut wood and swings an ax to cut down a tree. If the ax head flies off the handle, hitting and killing the neighbor, the one who killed him may run to one of these cities to save his life. 6Otherwise, the dead person's relative who has the duty of punishing a murderer might be angry and chase him. If the city is far away, the relative might catch and kill the person, even though he should not be killed because there was no intent to kill his neighbor. 7This is why I command you to choose these three cities.

8-9Carefully obey all these laws I'm giving you today. Love the LORD your God, and always do what he wants you to do. Then the LORD your God will enlarge your land as he promised your ancestors, giving you the whole land he promised to them. After that, choose three more cities of safety 10so that innocent people will not be killed in your land, the land that the LORD your God is giving you as your own. By doing this you will not be guilty of allowing the death of innocent people.

11But if a person hates his neighbor and, after hiding and waiting, attacks and kills him and then runs to one of these cities for safety, 12the older leaders of his own city should send for the murderer. They should bring the person back from the city of safety and hand him over to the relative who has the duty of punishing the murderer. 13Show no mercy. You must remove from Israel the guilt of murdering innocent people so that things will go well for you.

14Do not move the stone that marks the border of your neighbor's land, which people long ago set in place. It marks what you inherit in the land the LORD your God is giving you as your own.

Rules About Witnesses

15One witness is not enough to accuse a person of a crime or sin. A case must be proved by two or three witnesses.

16If a witness lies and accuses a person of a crime, 17the two people who are arguing must stand in the presence of the LORD before the priests and judges who are on duty. 18The judges must check the matter carefully. The witness who is a liar, lying about a fellow Israelite, 19must be punished. He must be punished in the same way the other person would have been punished. You must get rid of the evil among you. 20The rest of the people will hear about this and be afraid, and no one among you will ever do such an evil thing again. 21Show no mercy. A life must be paid for a life, an eye for an eye, a tooth for a tooth, a hand for a hand, a foot for a foot.

Laws for War

20 When you go to war against your enemies and you see horses and chariots and an army that is bigger than yours, don't be afraid of them. The LORD your God, who brought you out of Egypt, will be with you. 2The priest must come and speak to the army before you go into battle. 3He will say, "Listen, Israel! Today you are going into battle against your enemies. Don't lose your courage or be afraid. Don't panic or be frightened, 4because the LORD your God goes with you, to fight for you against your enemies and to save you."

5The officers should say to the army, "Has anyone built a new house but not given it to God? He may go home, because he might die in battle and someone else would get to give his house to God. 6Has anyone planted a vineyard and not begun to enjoy it? He may go home, because he might die in battle and someone else would enjoy his vineyard. 7Is any man engaged to a woman and not yet married to her? He may go home, because he might die in battle and someone else would marry her." 8Then the officers should also say, "Is anyone here afraid? Has anyone lost his courage? He may go home so that he will not cause others to lose their courage, too." 9When the officers finish

SIDELIGHT: If the military had had chaplains in Old Testament times, they would not have performed many weddings for soldiers. That's because engaged men didn't have to serve in the military (Deuteronomy 20:7). And newly married men were exempt from military duty for a year (Deuteronomy 24:5, p. 181)!

speaking to the army, they should appoint commanders to lead it.

10When you march up to attack a city, first make them an offer of peace. 11If they accept your offer and open their gates to you, all the people of that city will become your slaves and work for you. 12But if they do not make peace with you and fight you in battle, you should surround that city. 13The LORD your God will give it to you. Then kill all the men with your swords, 14and you may take everything else in the city for yourselves. Take the women, children, and animals, and you may use these things the LORD your God gives you from your enemies. 15Do this to all the cities that are far away, that do not belong to the nations nearby.

16But leave nothing alive in the cities of the land the LORD your God is giving you. 17Completely destroy these people: the Hittites, Amorites, Canaanites, Perizzites, Hivites, and Jebusites, as the LORD your God has commanded. 18Otherwise, they will teach you what they do for their gods, and if you do these hateful things, you will sin against the LORD your God.

19If you surround and attack a city for a long time, trying to capture it, do not destroy its trees with an ax. You can eat the fruit from the trees, but do not cut them down. These trees are not the enemy, so don't make war against them. 20But you may cut down trees that you know are not fruit trees and use them to build devices to attack the city walls, until the city is captured.

A Person Found Murdered

21 Suppose someone is found murdered, lying in a field in the land the LORD your God is giving you as your own, and no one knows who killed the person. 2Your older leaders and judges should go to where the body was found, and they should measure how far it is to the nearby cities. 3The older leaders of the city nearest the body must take a young cow that has never worked or worn a yoke,[d] 4and they must lead her down to a valley that has never been plowed or planted, with a stream flowing through it. There they must break the young cow's neck. 5The priests, the sons of Levi, should come forward, because they have been chosen by the LORD your God to serve him and to give blessings in the LORD's name. They are the ones who decide cases of quarreling and attacks. 6Then all the older leaders of the city nearest the murdered person should wash their hands over the young cow whose neck was broken in the valley. 7They should declare: "We did not kill this person, and we did not see it happen. 8LORD, remove this sin from your people Israel, whom you have saved. Don't blame your people, the Israelites, for the murder of this innocent person." And so the murder will be paid for. 9Then you will have removed from yourselves the guilt of murdering an innocent person, because you will be doing what the LORD says is right.

Captive Women as Wives

10When you go to war against your enemies, the LORD will help you defeat them so that you will take them captive. 11If you see a beautiful woman among the captives and are attracted to her, you may take her as your wife. 12Bring her into your home, where she must shave her head and cut her nails 13and change the clothes she was wearing when you captured her. After she has lived in your house and cried for her parents for a month, you may marry her. You will be her husband, and she will be your wife. 14But if you are not pleased with her, you must let her go anywhere she wants. You must not sell her for money or make her a slave, because you have taken away her honor.

The Oldest Son

15A man might have two wives, one he loves and one he doesn't. Both wives might have sons by him. If the older son belongs to the wife he does not love, 16when that man wills his property to his sons he must not give the son of the wife he loves what belongs to the older son, the son of the wife he does not love. 17He must agree to give the older son two shares of everything he owns, even though the older son is from the wife he does not love. That son was the first to prove his father could have children, so he has the rights that belong to the older son.

Sons Who Refuse to Obey

18If someone has a son who is stubborn, who turns against his father and mother and doesn't obey them or listen when they correct him, 19his parents must take him to the older leaders at the city gate. 20They will say to the leaders, "Our son is stubborn and turns against us. He will not obey us. He eats too much, and he is always drunk." 21Then all the men in his town must throw stones at him until he dies. Get rid of the evil among you, because then all the people of Israel will hear about this and be afraid.

Other Laws

22If someone is guilty of a sin worthy of death, he must be put to death and his body displayed on a tree. 23But don't leave his body hanging on the tree overnight; be sure to bury him that same day, because anyone whose body is displayed on a tree is cursed by God. You must not ruin the land the LORD your God is giving you as your own.

22 If you see your fellow Israelite's ox or sheep wandering away, don't ignore it. Take it back to its owner. 2If the owner does not live close to you, or if you do not know who the owner is, take the animal home with you. Keep it until the owner comes looking for it; then give it back. 3Do the same thing if you find a donkey or coat or anything someone lost. Don't just ignore it.

4If you see your fellow Israelite's donkey or ox fallen on the road, don't ignore it. Help the owner get it up.

5A woman must not wear men's clothes, and a man must not wear women's clothes. The LORD your God hates anyone who does that.

6If you find a bird's nest by the road, either in a tree or on the ground, and the mother bird is sitting on the young birds or eggs, do not take the mother bird with the young birds. 7You may take the young birds, but you must let the mother bird go free. Then things will go well for you, and you will live a long time.

8When you build a new house, build a low wall around the edge of the roof[n] so you will not be guilty if someone falls off the roof.

9Don't plant two different kinds of seeds in your vineyard. Otherwise, both crops will be ruined.

10Don't plow with an ox and a donkey tied together.

11Don't wear clothes made of wool and linen woven together.

12Tie several pieces of thread together; then put these tassels on the four corners of your coat.

Marriage Laws

13If a man marries a girl and has sexual relations with her but then decides he does not like her, 14he might talk badly about her and give her a bad name. He might say, "I married this woman, but when I had sexual relations with her, I did not find that she was a virgin."[d] 15Then the girl's parents must bring proof that she was a virgin to the older leaders at the city gate. 16The girl's father will say to the leaders, "I gave my daughter to this man to be his wife, but now he does not want her. 17This man has told lies about my daughter. He has said, 'I did not find your daughter to be a virgin,' but here is the proof that my daughter was a virgin." Then her parents are to show the sheet to the city leaders, 18and the leaders must take the man and punish him. 19They must make him pay about two and one-half pounds of silver to the girl's father, because the man has given an Israelite virgin a bad name. The girl will continue to be the man's wife, and he may not divorce her as long as he lives.

20But if the things the husband said about his wife are true, and there is no proof that she was a virgin, 21the girl must be brought to the door of her father's house. Then the men of the town must put her to death by throwing stones at her. She has done a disgraceful thing in Israel by having sexual relations before she was married. You must get rid of the evil among you.

22If a man is found having sexual relations with another man's wife, both the woman and the man who had sexual relations with her must die. Get rid of this evil from Israel.

23If a man meets a virgin in a city and has sexual relations with her, but she is engaged to another man, 24you must take both of them to the city gate and put them to death by throwing stones at them. Kill the girl, because she was in a city and did not scream for help. And kill the man for having sexual relations with another man's wife. You must get rid of the evil among you.

25But if a man meets an engaged girl out in the country and forces her to have sexual relations with him, only the man who had sexual relations with her must be put to death. 26Don't do anything to the girl, because she has not done a sin worthy of death. This is like the person who attacks and murders a neighbor; 27the man found the engaged girl in the country and she screamed, but no one was there to save her.

28If a man meets a virgin who is not engaged to be married and forces her to have sexual relations with him and people find out about it, 29the man must pay the girl's father about one and one-fourth pounds of silver. He must also marry the girl, because he has dishonored her, and he may never divorce her for as long as he lives.

30A man must not marry his father's wife; he must not dishonor his father in this way.

The Lord's People

23 No man who has had part of his sex organ cut off may come into the meeting to worship the LORD.

2No one born to parents who were forbidden by law to marry may come into the meeting to worship the LORD. The descendants for ten generations may not come in either.

3No Ammonite or Moabite may come into the meeting to worship the LORD, and none of their descendants for ten generations may come in. 4This is because the Ammonites and Moabites did not give you bread and water when you came out of Egypt. And they hired Balaam son of Beor, from

roof In Bible times houses were built with flat roofs. The roof was used for drying things such as flax and fruit. And it was used as an extra room, as a place for worship, and as a place to sleep in the summer.

Pethor in Northwest Mesopotamia, to put a curse
on you. 5But the LORD your God would not listen
to Balaam. He turned the curse into a blessing for
you, because the LORD your God loves you.
6Don't wish for their peace or success as long as
you live.
7Don't hate Edomites; they are your close relatives. Don't hate Egyptians, because you were foreigners in their country. 8The great-grandchildren
of these two peoples may come into the meeting
to worship the LORD.

Keeping the Camp Clean

9When you are camped in time of war, keep
away from unclean[d] things. 10If a man becomes
unclean during the night, he must go outside the
camp and not come back. 11But when evening
comes, he must wash himself, and at sunset he
may come back into the camp.
12Choose a place outside the camp where people may go to relieve themselves. 13Carry a tent
peg with you, and when you relieve yourself, dig
a hole and cover up your dung. 14The LORD your
God moves around through your camp to protect
you and to defeat your enemies for you, so the
camp must be holy. He must not see anything
unclean among you so that he will not leave you.

Other Laws

15If an escaped slave comes to you, do not hand
over the slave to his master. 16Let the slave live
with you anywhere he likes, in any town he
chooses. Do not mistreat him.
17No Israelite man or woman must ever become a temple prostitute.[d] 18Do not bring a male
or female prostitute's pay to the Temple[d] of the
LORD your God to pay what you have promised
to the LORD, because the LORD your God hates
prostitution.
19If you loan your fellow Israelites money or
food or anything else, don't make them pay back
more than you loaned them. 20You may charge
foreigners, but not fellow Israelites. Then the
LORD your God will bless everything you do in the
land you are entering to take as your own.
21If you make a promise to give something to
the LORD your God, do not be slow to pay it, because the LORD your God demands it from you.
Do not be guilty of sin. 22But if you do not make
the promise, you will not be guilty. 23You must do
whatever you say you will do, because you chose
to make the promise to the LORD your God.
24If you go into your neighbor's vineyard, you
may eat as many grapes as you wish, but do not
put any grapes into your basket. 25If you go into
your neighbor's grainfield, you may pick grain
with your hands, but you must not cut down your
neighbor's grain with your sickle.

24 A man might marry a woman but later
decide she doesn't please him because
he has found something bad about her. He writes
out divorce papers for her, gives them to her, and
sends her away from his house. 2After she leaves
his house, she goes and marries another man, 3but
her second husband does not like her either. So
he writes out divorce papers for her, gives them
to her, and sends her away from his house. Or the
second husband might die. 4In either case, her
first husband who divorced her must not marry
her again, because she has become unclean.[d] The
LORD would hate this. Don't bring this sin into the
land the LORD your God is giving you as your
own.
5A man who has just married must not be sent
to war or be given any other duty. He should be
free to stay home for a year to make his new wife
happy.
6If someone owes you something, do not take
his two stones for grinding grain—not even the
upper one—in place of what he owes, because
this is how the person makes a living.
7If someone kidnaps a fellow Israelite, either to
make him a slave or sell him, the kidnapper must
be killed. You must get rid of the evil among you.
8Be careful when someone has a skin disease.
Do exactly what the priests, the Levites, teach
you, being careful to do what I have commanded
them. 9Remember what the LORD your God did
to Miriam on your way out of Egypt.
10When you make a loan to your neighbors,
don't go into their homes to get something in
place of it. 11Stay outside and let them go in and
get what they promised you. 12If a poor person
gives you a coat to show he will pay the loan back,
don't keep it overnight. 13Give the coat back at
sunset, because your neighbor needs that coat to
sleep in, and he will be grateful to you. And the
LORD your God will see that you have done a
good thing.
14Don't cheat hired servants who are poor and
needy, whether they are fellow Israelites or foreigners living in one of your towns. 15Pay them
each day before sunset, because they are poor and
need the money. Otherwise,they may complain
to the LORD about you, and you will be guilty of
sin.
16Parents must not be put to death if their children do wrong, and children must not be put to
death if their parents do wrong. Each person must
die for his own sin.
17Do not be unfair to a foreigner or an orphan.
Don't take a widow's coat to make sure she pays
you back. 18Remember that you were slaves in
Egypt, and the LORD your God saved you from
there. That is why I am commanding you to do
this.
19When you are gathering your harvest in the

field and leave behind a bundle of grain, don't go back and get it. Leave it there for foreigners, orphans, and widows so that the LORD your God can bless everything you do. 20When you beat your olive trees to knock the olives off, don't beat the trees a second time. Leave what is left for foreigners, orphans, and widows. 21When you harvest the grapes in your vineyard, don't pick the vines a second time. Leave what is left for foreigners, orphans, and widows. 22Remember that you were slaves in Egypt; that is why I am commanding you to do this.

25 If two people have an argument and go to court, the judges will decide the case. They will declare one person right and the other guilty. 2If the guilty person has to be punished with a beating, the judge will make that person lie down and be beaten in front of him. The number of lashes should match the crime. 3But don't hit a person more than forty times, because more than that would disgrace him before others.

4When an ox is working in the grain, do not cover its mouth to keep it from eating.

5If two brothers are living together, and one of them dies without having a son, his widow must not marry someone outside her husband's family. Her husband's brother must marry her, which is his duty to her as a brother-in-law. 6The first son she has counts as the son of the dead brother so that his name will not be forgotten in Israel.

7But if a man does not want to marry his brother's widow, she should go to the older leaders at the town gate. She should say, "My brother-in-law will not carry on his brother's name in Israel. He refuses to do his duty for me."

SIDELIGHT: If you have a married brother, be glad if you like his wife. In Old Testament times, a man was supposed to marry his brother's wife if the brother died, to carry on his brother's name. If the man didn't want to marry her, she would publicly spit in his face, take off one of his sandals, and curse him (Deuteronomy 25:5–9).

8Then the older leaders of the town must call for the man and talk to him. But if he is stubborn and says, "I don't want to marry her," 9the woman must go up to him in front of the leaders. She must take off one of his sandals and spit in his face and say, "This is for the man who won't continue his brother's family!" 10Then that man's family shall be known in Israel as the Family of the Unsandaled.

11If two men are fighting and one man's wife comes to save her husband from his attacker, grabbing the attacker by his sex organs, 12you must cut off her hand. Show her no mercy.

13Don't carry two sets of weights with you, one heavy and one light. 14Don't have two different sets of measures in your house, one large and one small. 15You must have true and honest weights and measures so that you will live a long time in the land the LORD your God is giving you. 16The LORD your God hates anyone who is dishonest and uses dishonest measures.

17Remember what the Amalekites did to you when you came out of Egypt. 18When you were tired and worn out, they met you on the road and attacked all those lagging behind. They were not afraid of God. 19When the LORD your God gives you rest from all the enemies around you in the land he is giving you as your own, you shall destroy any memory of the Amalekites on the earth. Do not forget!

The First Harvest

26 When you go into the land the LORD your God is giving you as your own, to take it over and live in it, 2you must take some of the first harvest of crops that grow from the land the LORD your God is giving you. Put the food in a basket and go to the place where the LORD your God will choose to be worshiped. 3Say to the priest on duty at that time, "Today I declare before the LORD your God that I have come into the land the LORD promised our ancestors that he would give us." 4The priest will take your basket and set it down in front of the altar of the LORD your God. 5Then you shall announce before the LORD your God: "My father was a wandering Aramean. He went down to Egypt with only a few people, but they became a great, powerful, and large nation there. 6But the Egyptians were cruel to us, making us suffer and work very hard. 7So we prayed to the LORD, the God of our ancestors, and he heard us. When he saw our trouble, hard work, and suffering, 8the LORD brought us out of Egypt with his great power and strength, using great terrors, signs, and miracles.[d] 9Then he brought us to this place and gave us this fertile land. 10Now I bring part of the first harvest from this land that you, LORD, have given me." Place the basket before the LORD your God and bow down before him. 11Then you and the Levites and foreigners among you should rejoice, because the LORD your God has given good things to you and your family.

12Bring a tenth of all your harvest the third year (the year to give a tenth of your harvest). Give it to the Levites, foreigners, orphans, and widows so that they may eat in your towns and be full. 13Then say to the LORD your God, "I have taken

out of my house the part of my harvest that belongs to God, and I have given it to the Levites,
foreigners, orphans, and widows. I have done everything you commanded me; I have not broken
your commands, and I have not forgotten any of
them. 14I have not eaten any of the holy part
while I was in sorrow. I have not removed any of
it while I was unclean,[d] and I have not offered it
for dead people. I have obeyed you, the LORD my
God, and have done everything you commanded
me. 15So look down from heaven, your holy
home. Bless your people Israel and bless the land
you have given us, which you promised to our
ancestors—a fertile land."

Obey the Lord's Commands

16Today the LORD your God commands you to
obey all these rules and laws; be careful to obey
them with your whole being. 17Today you have
said that the LORD is your God, and you have
promised to do what he wants you to do—to
keep his rules, commands, and laws. You have
said you will obey him. 18And today the LORD has
said that you are his very own people, as he has
promised you. But you must obey his commands.
19He will make you greater than all the other nations he made. He will give you praise, fame, and
honor, and you will be a holy people to the LORD
your God, as he has said.

The Law Written on Stones

27 Then Moses, along with the older leaders of Israel, commanded the people,
saying, "Keep all the commands I have given you
today. 2Soon you will cross the Jordan River to go
into the land the LORD your God is giving you. On
that day set up some large stones and cover them
with plaster. 3When you cross over, write all the
words of these teachings on them. Then you may
enter the land the LORD your God is giving you,
a fertile land, just as the LORD, the God of your
ancestors, promised. 4After you have crossed the
Jordan River, set up these stones on Mount Ebal,
as I command you today, and cover them with
plaster. 5Build an altar of stones there to the LORD
your God, but don't use any iron tool to cut the
stones; 6build the altar of the LORD your God with
stones from the field. Offer burnt offerings on it to
the LORD your God, 7and offer fellowship offerings there, and eat them and rejoice before the
LORD your God. 8Then write clearly all the words
of these teachings on the stones."

GIVING

Sharing With Joy

Jennie Meehl didn't realize what she was getting into when she agreed to go on a two-and-a-half-week mission trip to an orphanage in Mexico with her youth group.

"It was culture shock," she admits. For the first time ever, she realized how much she had been given in her life.

After returning home, Jennie couldn't get the kids in the orphanage out of her mind. So she went back—by herself. She traveled more than two thousand miles from Minnesota to spend her entire next summer helping the children in the orphanage. She bathed them, played games with them, fed them, and helped take care of them.

"It helped me realize the important things in life," she explains. "Sharing my love helped me grow."

Jennie had learned the importance of giving to God and others because of what God has given to us. "Help others," she challenges, "because the rewards are greater than you can imagine." Similarly, **Deuteronomy 26:5–11** challenged the Israelites to give to God because of all he had given them.

- How does Jennie's story model the giving discussed in the passage?
- What can you bring to God from your "first harvest" in thanks for the many things God gives you?

CONSIDER . . .

- participating in a service project at your church as a way of giving back to God part of the love and time he has given you.
- taking ten percent of the money in your purse or wallet and giving it to God.

FOR MORE, SEE . . .

- Genesis 28:22 (p. 33)
- Malachi 3:8–10 (p. 901)
- Luke 11:42 (p. 1026)

Curses of the Law

9Then Moses and the Levites who were priests
spoke to all Israel and said, "Be quiet, Israel. Listen! Today you have become the people of the
LORD your God. 10Obey the LORD your God, and
keep his commands and laws that I give you today."
11That day Moses also gave the people this
command:
12When you cross the Jordan River, these
tribes[d] must stand on Mount Gerizim to bless the
people: Simeon, Levi, Judah, Issachar, Joseph and
Benjamin. 13And these tribes must stand on
Mount Ebal to announce the curses: Reuben,
Gad, Asher, Zebulun, Dan, and Naphtali.
14The Levites will say to all the people of Israel
in a loud voice:
15"Anyone will be cursed who makes an idol or
statue and secretly sets it up, because the LORD
hates the idols people make."
Then all the people will say, "Amen!"
16"Anyone will be cursed who dishonors his father or mother."
Then all the people will say, "Amen!"
17"Anyone will be cursed who moves the stone
that marks a neighbor's border."
Then all the people will say, "Amen!"
18"Anyone will be cursed who sends a blind
person down the wrong road."
Then all the people will say, "Amen!"
19"Anyone will be cursed who is unfair to foreigners, orphans, or widows."
Then all the people will say, "Amen!"
20"A man will be cursed who has sexual relations with his father's wife, because it is a dishonor to his father."
Then all the people will say, "Amen!"
21"Anyone will be cursed who has sexual relations with an animal."
Then all the people will say, "Amen!"
22"A man will be cursed who has sexual relations with his sister, whether she is his father's
daughter or his mother's daughter."
Then all the people will say, "Amen!"
23"A man will be cursed who has sexual relations with his mother-in-law."
Then all the people will say, "Amen!"
24"Anyone will be cursed who kills a neighbor
secretly."
Then all the people will say, "Amen!"
25"Anyone will be cursed who takes money to
murder an innocent person."
Then all the people will say, "Amen!"
26"Anyone will be cursed who does not agree
with the words of these teachings and does not
obey them."
Then all the people will say, "Amen!"

Blessings for Obeying

28 You must completely obey the LORD
your God, and you must carefully follow
all his commands I am giving you today. Then the
LORD your God will make you greater than any
other nation on earth. 2Obey the LORD your God
so that all these blessings will come and stay with
you:
3You will be blessed in the city and blessed in
the country.
4Your children will be blessed, as well as your
crops; your herds will be blessed with calves and
your flocks with lambs.
5Your basket and your kitchen will be blessed.
6You will be blessed when you come in and
when you go out.
7The LORD will help you defeat the enemies
that come to fight you. They will attack you from
one direction, but they will run from you in seven
directions.
8The LORD your God will bless you with full
barns, and he will bless everything you do. He
will bless the land he is giving you.
9The LORD will make you his holy people, as he
promised. But you must obey his commands and
do what he wants you to do. 10Then everyone on
earth will see that you are the LORD's people, and
they will be afraid of you. 11The LORD will make
you rich: You will have many children, your animals will have many young, and your land will
give good crops. It is the land that the LORD promised your ancestors he would give to you.
12The LORD will open up his heavenly storehouse so that the skies send rain on your land at
the right time, and he will bless everything you
do. You will lend to other nations, but you will
not need to borrow from them. 13The LORD will
make you like the head and not like the tail; you
will be on top and not on bottom. But you must
obey the commands of the LORD your God that I
am giving you today, being careful to keep them.
14Do not disobey anything I command you today.
Do exactly as I command, and do not follow other
gods or serve them.

Curses for Disobeying

15But if you do not obey the LORD your God
and carefully follow all his commands and laws I
am giving you today, all these curses will come
upon you and stay:
16You will be cursed in the city and cursed in
the country.
17Your basket and your kitchen will be cursed.
18Your children will be cursed, as well as your
crops; the calves of your herds and the lambs of
your flocks will be cursed.
19You will be cursed when you go in and when
you go out.

20The LORD will send you curses, confusion,
and punishment in everything you do. You will be
destroyed and suddenly ruined because you did
wrong when you left him. 21The LORD will give
you terrible diseases and destroy you from the
land you are going to take. 22The LORD will punish
you with disease, fever, swelling, heat, lack of
rain, plant diseases, and mildew[d] until you die.
23The sky above will be like bronze,[n] and the
ground below will be like iron. 24The LORD will
turn the rain into dust and sand, which will fall
from the skies until you are destroyed.

25The LORD will help your enemies defeat you.
You will attack them from one direction, but you
will run from them in seven directions. And you
will become a thing of horror among all the kingdoms on earth. 26Your dead bodies will be food for
all the birds and wild animals, and there will be
no one to scare them away. 27The LORD will punish you with boils like those the Egyptians had.
You will have bad growths, sores, and itches that
can't be cured. 28The LORD will give you mad-
ness, blindness, and a confused mind. 29You will
have to feel around in the daylight like a blind
person. You will fail in everything you do. People
will hurt you and steal from you every day, and
no one will save you.

30You will be engaged to a woman, but another
man will force her to have sexual relations with
him. You will build a house, but you will not live
in it. You will plant a vineyard, but you will not
get its grapes. 31Your ox will be killed before your
eyes, but you will not eat any of it. Your donkey
will be taken away from you, and it will not be
brought back. Your sheep will be given to your
enemies, and no one will save you. 32Your sons
and daughters will be given to another nation,
and you will grow tired looking for them every
day, but there will be nothing you can do. 33Peo-
ple you don't know will eat the crops your land
and hard work have produced. You will be mistreated and abused all your life. 34The things you
see will cause you to go mad. 35The LORD will give
you sore boils on your knees and legs that cannot
be cured, and they will go from the soles of your
feet to the tops of your heads.

36The LORD will send you and your king away
to a nation neither you nor your ancestors know,
where you will serve other gods made of wood
and stone. 37You will become a hated thing to the
nations where the LORD sends you; they will
laugh at you and make fun of you.

38You will plant much seed in your field, but
your harvest will be small, because locusts[d] will
eat the crop. 39You will plant vineyards and work
hard in them, but you will not pick the grapes or
drink the wine, because the worms will eat them.
40You will have olive trees in all your land, but
you will not get any olive oil, because the olives
will drop off the trees. 41You will have sons and
daughters, but you will not be able to keep them,
because they will be taken captive. 42Locusts will
destroy all your trees and crops.

43The foreigners who live among you will get
stronger and stronger, and you will get weaker
and weaker. 44Foreigners will lend money to you,
but you will not be able to lend to them. They will
be like the head, and you will be like the tail.
45All these curses will come upon you. They
will chase you and catch you and destroy you,
because you did not obey the LORD your God and
keep the commands and laws he gave you. 46The
curses will be signs and miracles[d] to you and your
descendants[d] forever. 47You had plenty of everything, but you did not serve the LORD your God
with joy and a pure heart, 48so you will serve the
enemies the LORD sends against you. You will be
hungry, thirsty, naked, and poor, and the LORD
will put a load on you until he has destroyed
you.

The Curse of an Enemy Nation

49The LORD will bring a nation against you from
far away, from the end of the world, and it will
swoop down like an eagle. You won't understand
their language, 50and they will look mean. They
will not respect old people or feel sorry for the
young. 51They will eat the calves from your herds
and the harvest of your field, and you will be destroyed. They will not leave you any grain, new
wine or oil, or any calves from your herds or
lambs from your flocks. You will be ruined. 52That
nation will surround and attack all your cities.
You trust in your high, strong walls, but they will
fall down. That nation will surround all your cities
everywhere in the land the LORD your God is giving you.

53Your enemy will surround you. Those people
will make you starve so that you will eat your
own babies, the bodies of the sons and daughters
the LORD your God gave you. 54Even the most
gentle and kind man among you will become
cruel to his brother, his wife whom he loves, and
his children who are still alive. 55He will not even
give them any of the flesh of his children he is
eating, because it will be all he has left. Your enemy will surround you and make you starve in all
your cities. 56The most gentle and kind woman
among you, so gentle and kind she would hardly
even walk on the ground, will be cruel to her
husband whom she loves and to her son and
daughter. 57She will give birth to a baby, but she
will plan to eat the baby and what comes after the
birth itself. She will eat them secretly while the

sky . . . bronze This means the sky will give no rain and the earth will produce no crops.

enemy surrounds the city. Those people will make you starve in all your cities.

58Be careful to obey everything in these teachings that are written in this book. You must respect the glorious and wonderful name of the LORD your God, 59or the LORD will give terrible diseases to you and your descendants.[d] You will have long and serious diseases, and long and miserable sicknesses. 60He will give you all the diseases of Egypt that you dread, and the diseases will stay with you. 61The LORD will also give you every disease and sickness not written in this Book of the Teachings, until you are destroyed. 62You people may have outnumbered the stars, but only a few of you will be left, because you did not obey the LORD your God. 63Just as the LORD was once happy with you and gave you good things and made you grow in number, so then the LORD will be happy to ruin and destroy you, and you will be removed from the land you are entering to take as your own.

64Then the LORD will scatter you among the nations—from one end of the earth to the other. There you will serve other gods of wood and stone, gods that neither you nor your ancestors have known. 65You will have no rest among those nations and no place that is yours. The LORD will make your mind worried, your sight weak, and your soul sad. 66You will live with danger and be afraid night and day. You will not be sure that you will live. 67In the morning you will say, "I wish it were evening," and in the evening you will say, "I wish it were morning." Terror will be in your heart, and the things you have seen will scare you. 68The LORD will send you back to Egypt in ships, even though I, Moses, said you would never go back to Egypt. And there you will try to sell yourselves as slaves to your enemies, but no one will buy you.

The Agreement in Moab

29 The LORD commanded Moses to make an agreement with the Israelites in Moab in addition to the agreement he had made with them at Mount Sinai. These are the words of that agreement.

2Moses called all the Israelites together and said to them:

You have seen everything the LORD did before your own eyes to the king of Egypt and to the king's leaders and to the whole country. 3With your own eyes you saw the great troubles, signs, and miracles.[d] 4But to this day the LORD has not given you a mind that understands; you don't really understand what you see with your eyes or hear with your ears. 5I led you through the desert for forty years, and during that time neither your clothes nor sandals wore out. 6You ate no bread and drank no wine or beer. This was so you would understand that I am the LORD your God.

7When you came to this place, Sihon king of Heshbon and Og king of Bashan came out to fight us, but we defeated them. 8We captured their land and gave it to the tribes[d] of Reuben, Gad, and East Manasseh to be their own.

9You must carefully obey everything in this agreement so that you will succeed in everything you do. 10Today you are all standing here before the LORD your God—your leaders and important men, your older leaders, officers, and all the other men of Israel, 11your wives and children and the foreigners who live among you, who chop your wood and carry your water. 12You are all here to enter into an agreement and a promise with the LORD your God, an agreement the LORD your God is making with you today. 13This will make you today his own people. He will be your God, as he told you and as he promised your ancestors Abraham, Isaac, and Jacob. 14But I am not just making this agreement and its promises with you 15who are standing here before the LORD your God today, but also with those who are not here today.

16You know how we lived in Egypt and how we passed through the countries when we came here. 17You saw their hateful idols made of wood, stone, silver, and gold. 18Make sure no man, woman, family group, or tribe among you leaves the LORD our God to go and serve the gods of those nations. They would be to you like a plant that grows bitter, poisonous fruit.

19These are the kind of people who hear these curses but bless themselves, thinking, "We will be safe even though we continue doing what we want to do." Those people may destroy all of your land, both wet and dry. 20The LORD will not forgive them. His anger will be like a burning fire against those people, and all the curses written in this book will come on them. The LORD will destroy any memory of them on the earth. 21He will separate them from all the tribes of Israel for punishment. All the curses of the Agreement that are written in this Book of the Teachings will happen to them.

22Your children who will come after you, as well as foreigners from faraway lands, will see the disasters that come to this land and the diseases the LORD will send on it. They will say, 23"The land is nothing but burning cinders and salt. Nothing is planted, nothing grows, and nothing blooms. It is like Sodom and Gomorrah, and Admah and Zeboiim, which the LORD destroyed because he was very angry." 24All the other nations will ask, "Why has the LORD done this to the land? Why is he so angry?"

25And the answer will be, "It is because the people broke the Agreement of the LORD, the God of their ancestors, which he made with them when he brought them out of Egypt. 26They went

and served other gods and bowed down to gods
they did not even know. The LORD did not allow
that, 27so he became very angry at the land and
brought all the curses on it that are written in this
book. 28Since the LORD became angry and furious
with them, he took them out of their land and put
them in another land where they are today."
29There are some things the LORD our God has
kept secret, but there are some things he has let
us know. These things belong to us and our children forever so that we will do everything in
these teachings.

The Israelites Will Return

30 When all these blessings and curses I
have described happen to you, and the
LORD your God has sent you away to other nations, think about these things. 2Then you and
your children will return to the LORD your God,
and you will obey him with your whole being in
everything I am commanding you today. 3Then
the LORD your God will give you back your freedom. He will feel sorry for you, and he will bring
you back again from the nations where he scattered you. 4He may send you to the ends of the
earth, but he will gather you and bring you back
from there, 5back to the land that belonged to
your ancestors. It will be yours. He will give you
success, and there will be more of you than there
were of your ancestors. 6The LORD your God will
prepare you and your descendants[d] to love him
with your whole being so that you will live. 7The
LORD your God will put all these curses on your
enemies, who hate you and are cruel to you. 8And
you will again obey the LORD, keeping all his commands that I give you today. 9The LORD your God
will make you successful in everything you do.
You will have many children, your cattle will
have many calves, and your fields will produce
good crops, because the LORD will again be happy
with you, just as he was with your ancestors.
10But you must obey the LORD your God by keeping all his commands and rules that are written in
this Book of the Teachings. You must return to
the LORD your God with your whole being.

Choose Life or Death

11This command I give you today is not too

DECISION MAKING

Living With Deadlines

Wayne Holsten had never kissed a girl—until he met Karen Mills at youth camp. It was love at first sight. Karen and Wayne were good for each other, and they encouraged each other in their faith.

But there was Andrea to think about—Wayne's girlfriend back home. She was cynical about the church, and she made fun of Wayne's efforts to grow in his faith. Wayne decided he needed to end this unhealthy relationship.

When Wayne got back home at the end of July, he had mixed emotions. It was hard breaking away from the past. So he decided he would go back to his old girlfriend if he didn't get a letter from Karen by August 15.

Each day, he checked his mail. No letters. On August 15, he nervously flipped through the mail. Nothing.

So he called Andrea.

On August 16, Karen's letter came, but Wayne had already made his choice.

In the same way Wayne had to decide what to do, the Israelites had a choice to make in **Deuteronomy 30:11–20**. Theirs was a much more important choice: whether or not to follow God.

- With this passage in mind, how would you advise Wayne if he came to you for advice about his dilemma?
- What principles from this passage can help you make wise choices?

CONSIDER . . .

- circling the things in the passage that God asks people to do. Underline the "not to do" items.
- writing out an important decision you face. List all the pros and cons of your choices. Then circle any reasons that fit the scripture passage. Cross out any that contradict it. Your decision may be easier now.

FOR MORE, SEE . . .

- Genesis 39:6–23 (p. 45)
- Joshua 24:14–15 (p. 214)
- Matthew 25:1–13 (p. 953)

hard for you; it is not beyond what you can do.
12It is not up in heaven. You do not have to ask,
"Who will go up to heaven and get it for us so we
can obey it and keep it?" 13It is not on the other
side of the sea. You do not have to ask, "Who will
go across the sea and get it? Who will tell it to us
so we can keep it?" 14No, the word is very near
you. It is in your mouth and in your heart so you
may obey it.

15Look, today I offer you life and success, death
and destruction. 16I command you today to love
the LORD your God, to do what he wants you to
do, and to keep his commands, his rules, and his
laws. Then you will live and grow in number, and
the LORD your God will bless you in the land you
are entering to take as your own.

17But if you turn away from the LORD and do
not obey him, if you are led to bow and serve
other gods, 18I tell you today that you will surely
be destroyed. And you will not live long in the
land you are crossing the Jordan River to enter
and take as your own.

19Today I ask heaven and earth to be witnesses.
I am offering you life or death, blessings or curses.
Now, choose life! Then you and your children
may live. 20To choose life is to love the LORD your
God, obey him, and stay close to him. He is your
life, and he will let you live many years in the
land, the land he promised to give your ancestors
Abraham, Isaac, and Jacob.

Joshua Takes Moses' Place

31 Then Moses went and spoke these
words to all the Israelites: 2"I am now
one hundred twenty years old, and I cannot lead
you anymore. The LORD told me I would not cross
the Jordan River; 3the LORD your God will lead
you across himself. He will destroy those nations
for you, and you will take over their land. Joshua
will also lead you across, as the LORD has said.
4The LORD will do to those nations what he did
to Sihon and Og, the kings of the Amorites, when
he destroyed them and their land. 5The LORD will
give those nations to you; do to them everything
I told you. 6Be strong and brave. Don't be afraid
of them and don't be frightened, because the
LORD your God will go with you. He will not
leave you or forget you."

7Then Moses called Joshua and said to him in
front of the people, "Be strong and brave, because
you will lead these people into the land the LORD
promised to give their ancestors, and help them
take it as their own. 8The LORD himself will go
before you. He will be with you; he will not leave
you or forget you. Don't be afraid and don't
worry."

Moses Writes the Teachings

9So Moses wrote down these teachings and
gave them to the priests and all the older leaders
of Israel. (The priests are the sons of Levi, who
carry the Ark[d] of the Agreement with the LORD.)
10-11Then Moses commanded them: "Read these
teachings for all Israel to hear at the end of every
seven years, which is the year to cancel what people owe. Do it during the Feast[d] of Shelters, when
all the Israelites will come to appear before the
LORD your God and stand at the place he will
choose. 12Gather all the people: the men, women,
children, and foreigners living in your towns so
that they can listen and learn to respect the LORD
your God and carefully obey everything in this
law. 13Since their children do not know this law,
they must hear it. They must learn to respect the
LORD your God for as long as they live in the land
you are crossing the Jordan River to take for your
own."

The Lord Calls Moses and Joshua

14The LORD said to Moses, "Soon you will die.
Get Joshua and come to the Meeting Tent[d] so that
I may command him." So Moses and Joshua went
to the Meeting Tent.

15The LORD appeared at the Meeting Tent in a
cloud; the cloud stood over the entrance of the
Tent. 16And the LORD said to Moses, "You will
soon die. Then these people will not be loyal to
me but will worship the foreign gods of the land
they are entering. They will leave me, breaking
the Agreement I made with them. 17Then I will
become very angry at them, and I will leave them.
I will turn away from them, and they will be destroyed. Many terrible things will happen to
them. Then they will say, 'It is because God is not
with us that these terrible things are happening.'
18I will surely turn away from them then, because
they have done wrong and have turned to other
gods.

19"Now write down this song and teach it to
the Israelites. Then have them sing it, because it
will be my witness against them. 20When I bring
them into the land I promised to their ancestors,
a fertile land, they will eat as much as they want
and get fat. Then they will turn to other gods and
serve them. They will reject me and break my
Agreement. 21Then when many troubles and terrible things happen to them, this song will testify
against them, because the song will not be forgotten by their descendants.[d] I know what they plan
to do, even before I take them into the land I
promised them." 22So Moses wrote down the
song that day, and he taught it to the Israelites.

23Then the LORD gave this command to Joshua
son of Nun: "Be strong and brave, because you
will lead the people of Israel to the land I promised them, and I will be with you."

24After Moses finished writing all the words of
the teachings in a book, 25he gave a command to

the Levites, who carried the Ark[d] of the Agreement with the LORD. 26He said, "Take this Book of the Teachings and put it beside the Ark of the Agreement with the LORD your God. It must stay

SIDELIGHT: Have you ever done a research paper and found that an important book is out of print? Bible scholars often have that problem. The Bible mentions several books that no longer exist. Deuteronomy 31:26 mentions the "Book of the Teachings." Others include: the "Book of the Wars of the Lord" (Numbers 21:14–15, p. 145), and the "Book of Jashar" (Joshua 10:13, p. 202).

there as a witness against you. 27I know how stubborn and disobedient you are. You have disobeyed the LORD while I am alive and with you, and you will disobey even more after I die! 28Gather all the older leaders of your tribes[d] and all your officers to me so that I may say these things for them to hear, and so that I may ask heaven and earth to testify against them. 29I know that after I die you will become completely evil. You will turn away from the commands I have given you. Terrible things will happen to you in the future when you do what the LORD says is evil, and you will make him angry with the idols you have made."

Moses' Song

30And Moses spoke this whole song for all the people of Israel to hear:

32 Hear, heavens, and I will speak.
Listen, earth, to what I say.
2My teaching will drop like rain;
my words will fall like dew.
They will be like showers on the grass;
they will pour down like rain on young plants.
3I will announce the name of the LORD.
Praise God because he is great!
4He is like a rock; what he does is perfect,
and he is always fair.
He is a faithful God who does no wrong,
who is right and fair.

5They have done evil against him.
To their shame they are no longer his children;
they are an evil and lying people.
6This is not the way to repay the LORD,
you foolish and unwise people.
He is your Father and Maker,
who made you and formed you.

7Remember the old days.
Think of the years already passed.
Ask your father and he will tell you;
ask your older leaders and they will inform you.
8God Most High gave the nations their lands,
dividing up the human race.
He set up borders for the people
and even numbered the Israelites.
9The LORD took his people as his share,
the people of Jacob as his very own.

10He found them in a desert,
a windy, empty land.
He surrounded them and brought them up,
guarding them as those he loved very much.
11He was like an eagle building its nest
that flutters over its young.
It spreads its wings to catch them
and carries them on its feathers.
12The LORD alone led them,
and there was no foreign god helping him.

13The LORD brought them to the heights of the land
and fed them the fruit of the fields.
He gave them honey from the rocks,
bringing oil from the solid rock.
14There were milk curds from the cows and milk from the flock;
there were fat sheep and goats.
There were sheep and goats from Bashan
and the best of the wheat.
You drank the juice of grapes.

15Israel grew fat and kicked;
they were fat and full and firm.
They left the God who made them
and rejected the Rock[d] who saved them.
16They made God jealous with foreign gods
and angry with hateful idols.
17They made sacrifices to demons,[d] not God,
to gods they had never known,
new gods from nearby,
gods your ancestors did not fear.
18You left God who is the Rock, your Father,
and you forgot the God who gave you birth.

19The LORD saw this and rejected them;
his sons and daughters had made him angry.
20He said, "I will turn away from them
and see what will happen to them.
They are evil people,
unfaithful children.
21They used things that are not gods to make me jealous
and worthless idols to make me angry.

So I will use those who are not a nation to
make them jealous;
I will use a nation that does not understand
to make them angry.
22My anger has started a fire
that burns down to the place of the dead.
It will burn up the ground and its crops,
and it will set fire to the base of the
mountains.

23"I will pile troubles upon them
and shoot my arrows at them.
24They will be starved and sick,
destroyed by terrible diseases.
I will send them vicious animals
and gliding, poisonous snakes.
25In the streets the sword will kill;
in their homes there will be terror.
Young men and women will die,
and so will babies and gray-haired men.
26I will scatter them as I said,
and no one will remember them.
27But I didn't want their enemy to brag;
their enemy might misunderstand
and say, 'We have won!
The LORD has done none of this.' "

28Israel has no sense;
they do not understand.
29I wish they were wise and understood this;
I wish they could see what will happen to
them.
30One person cannot chase a thousand people,
and two people cannot fight ten thousand
unless their Rock has sold them,
unless the LORD has given them up.
31The rock of these people is not like our
Rock;
our enemies agree to that.
32Their vine comes from Sodom,
and their fields are like Gomorrah.
Their grapes are full of poison;
their bunches of grapes are bitter.
33Their wine is like snake poison,
like the deadly poison of cobras.

34"I have been saving this,
and I have it locked in my storehouses.
35I will punish those who do wrong; I will
repay them.
Soon their foot will slip,
because their day of trouble is near,
and their punishment will come quickly."

36The LORD will defend his people
and have mercy on his servants.
He will see that their strength is gone,
that nobody is left, slaves or free.
37Then he will say, "Where are their gods?
Where is the rock they trusted?
38Who ate the fat from their sacrifices,
and who drank the wine of their drink
offerings?
Let those gods come to help you!
Let them protect you!

39"Now you will see that I am the one God!
There is no god but me.
I send life and death;
I can hurt, and I can heal.
No one can escape from me.
40I raise my hand toward heaven and make this
promise:
As surely as I live forever,
41I will sharpen my flashing sword,
and I will take it in my hand to judge.
I will punish my enemies
and pay back those who hate me.
42My arrows will be covered with their blood;
my sword will eat their flesh.
The blood will flow from those who are
killed and the captives.
The heads of the enemy leaders will be cut
off."
43Be happy, nations, with his people,
because he will repay you for the blood of
his servants.
He will punish his enemies,
and he will remove the sin of his land and
people.

44Moses came with Joshua son of Nun, and
they spoke all the words of this song for the people to hear. 45When Moses finished speaking
these words to all Israel, 46he said to them: "Pay
careful attention to all the words I have said
to you today, and command your children to
obey carefully everything in these teachings.
47These should not be unimportant words for
you, but rather they mean life for you! By these
words you will live a long time in the land you
are crossing the Jordan River to take as your
own."

Moses Goes Up to Mount Nebo

48The LORD spoke to Moses again that same
day and said, 49"Go up the Abarim Mountains, to
Mount Nebo in the country of Moab, across from
Jericho. Look at the land of Canaan that I am giving to the Israelites as their own. 50On that mountain that you climb, you will die and join your
ancestors, just as your brother Aaron died on
Mount Hor and joined his ancestors. 51You both
sinned against me at the waters of Meribah Kadesh in the Desert of Zin, and you did not honor
me as holy there among the Israelites. 52So now
you will only look at the land from far away. You
will not enter the land I am giving the people of
Israel."

Moses Blesses the People

33 Moses, the man of God, gave this blessing to the Israelites before he died. 2He said:

"The LORD came from Mount Sinai
and rose like the sun from Edom;
he showed his greatness from Mount Paran.
He came with thousands of angels
from the southern mountains.
3The LORD surely loves his people
and takes care of all those who belong to him.
They bow down at his feet,
and they are taught by him.
4Moses gave us the teachings
that belong to the people of Jacob.
5The LORD became king of Israel
when the leaders of the people gathered,
when the tribes[d] of Israel came together.

6"Let the people of Reuben live and not die,
but let the people be few."

7Moses said this about the people of Judah:
"LORD, listen to Judah's prayer;
bring them back to their people.
They defend themselves with their hands.
Help them fight their enemies!"

8Moses said this about the people of Levi:
"LORD, your Thummim and Urim[d] belong
to Levi, whom you love.
LORD, you tested him at Massah
and argued with him at the waters of Meribah.
9He said about his father and mother,
'I don't care about them.'
He did not treat his brothers as favorites
or give special favors to his children,
but he protected your word
and guarded your agreement.
10He teaches your laws to the people of Jacob
and your teachings to the people of Israel.

GOD'S POWER

Stronger Than Hatred

Andrew Casindola was livid. He had come to pick up his son Rob from church camp. While waiting for the last session to end, he had overheard his son telling other campers how he hated his dad because of abuse. But Christ had changed Rob's life that week. "And I know Christ can change my dad, too," he had concluded.

Andrew stormed to camp director Enoch Olson's office and verbally abused the director for what he had overheard.

Enoch calmed Andrew down and responded, "If your son is worse because of this camp experience, call me. I'll personally apologize. But, if your son is better, write to thank me."

Andrew picked up his son, still steaming with anger. The two drove silently in the car listening to the radio. About a hundred miles from camp, Rob's dad pulled into a rest area. As they looked at the view, Rob awkwardly put his arms around his dad and said, "Dad, I've hated you ever since I can remember. Will you forgive me?"

Two hours later, Enoch Olson found Rob's dad sitting at a picnic table back at the camp. "Christ made my son better," he told Enoch. "Can he do it in my life too?"

That day, Rob's dad began the long process of healing and recovery. It was not easy for either Rob or his dad to let go of the feelings of anger and hatred. But, in the process, they discovered God's power in the world and in their own lives. Read a description of God's power in **Deuteronomy 32:36–33:4**.

- How might Rob's father have responded to this passage in the first part of the story? How might he have responded at the end?
- What characteristic of God in the passage helps you understand God's power the most? What comfort do you gain from knowing that power?

CONSIDER . . .

- confessing a way you've tried to escape from God (such as making decisions for selfish reasons), then letting God's power work in that area of your life.
- sharing your faith in God's power with someone who has no hope.

FOR MORE, SEE . . .

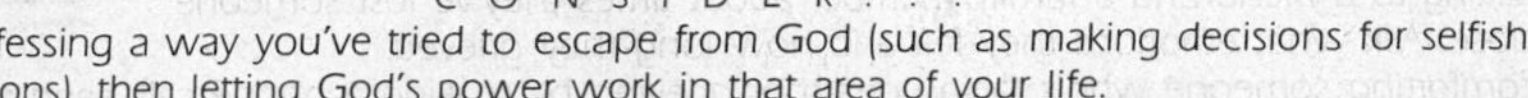

- Job 9:4–10 (p. 457)
- Isaiah 46:8–12 (p. 664)
- Ephesians 1:19–22 (p. 1218)

He burns incense[d] before you
and makes whole burnt offerings on your altar.
11LORD, make them strong;
be pleased with the work they do.
Defeat those who attack them,
and don't let their enemies rise up again."

12Moses said this about the people of Benjamin:
"The LORD's loved ones will lie down in safety,
because he protects them all day long.
The ones he loves rest with him."

13Moses said this about the people of Joseph:
"May the LORD bless their land with wonderful dew from heaven,
with water from the springs below,
14with the best fruits that the sun brings,
and with the best fruits that the moon brings.
15Let the old mountains give the finest crops,
and let the everlasting hills give the best fruits.
16Let the full earth give the best fruits,
and let the LORD who lived in the burning bush be pleased.
May these blessings rest on the head of Joseph,
on the forehead of the one who was blessed among his brothers.
17Joseph has the majesty of a firstborn[d] bull;
he is as strong as a wild ox.
He will stab other nations,
even those nations far away.
These are the ten thousands of Ephraim,
and these are the thousands of Manasseh."

18Moses said this about the people of Zebulun:
"Be happy when you go out, Zebulun,
and be happy in your tents, Issachar.
19They will call the people to the mountain,
and there they will offer the right sacrifices.
They will do well from all that is in the sea,
and they will do well from the treasures hidden in the sand on the shore."

20Moses said this about the people of Gad:

DEATH

He's Gone

Cory Weskamp will never graduate from high school. He'll never have a date. He won't ever play in another band concert. He lost the battle to cancer before he turned sixteen. Cory didn't broadcast his illness. While some friends knew he was sick, they hadn't expected him to die.

The word rolled quickly down the halls of Goodrich Junior High. "Cory is dead." Students were stunned. Shocked. Afraid.

"I don't know what to think," said Ron, one of Cory's friends.

"It makes me look at life differently," Fred explained, worrying about his other friends getting sick. "Death could happen to anyone. It doesn't matter how old you are."

"It left an empty feeling knowing that I'd never be able to talk or laugh with him again," one student admitted. "I got scared."

Another shared, "I felt kind of sick. I didn't think someone of his age and strength would die."

When someone dies, people need time to grieve. When their great leader Moses died, the Israelites grieved for a long time. Read about how they dealt with Moses' death in **Deuteronomy 34:1–12**.

- How do the students' statements about Cory's death compare to what the Israelites must have felt when Moses died?
- When have you experienced the loss of someone you respected? How was that experience like the Israelites' experience when Moses died?

CONSIDER . . .

- talking to a friend and a family member about times they've lost someone close. Ask what emotions they felt and how long they grieved.
- comforting someone who's facing death or grieving by making a phone call, sending a card, visiting, or giving a hug.

FOR MORE, SEE . . .

- 2 Samuel 1:17–27 (p. 245)
- John 11:28–44 (p. 1077)
- Revelation 21:1–4 (p. 1347)

"Praise God who gives Gad more land!
Gad lives there like a lion,
who tears off arms and heads.
21They chose the best land for themselves.
They received a large share, like that given
to an officer.
When the leaders of the people gathered,
the people of Gad did what the LORD said
was right,
and they judged Israel fairly."

22Moses said this about the people of Dan:
"Dan is like a lion's cub,
who jumps out of Bashan."

23Moses said this about the people of Naphtali:
"Naphtali enjoys special kindnesses,
and they are full of the LORD's blessings.
Take as your own the west and south."

24Moses said this about the people of Asher:
"Asher is the most blessed of the sons;
let him be his brothers' favorite.
Let him bathe his feet in olive oil.
25Your gates will have locks of iron and bronze,
and you will be strong as long as you live.

26"There is no one like the God of Israel,
who rides through the skies to help you,
who rides on the clouds in his majesty.
27The everlasting God is your place of safety,
and his arms will hold you up forever.
He will force your enemy out ahead of you,
saying, 'Destroy the enemy!'
28The people of Israel will lie down in safety.
Jacob's spring is theirs alone.
Theirs is a land full of grain and new wine,
where the skies drop their dew.
29Israel, you are blessed!
No one else is like you,
because you are a people saved by the
LORD.
He is your shield and helper,
your glorious sword.
Your enemies will be afraid of you,
and you will walk all over their holy
places."

Moses Dies

34 Then Moses climbed Mount Nebo from
the plains of Moab to the top of Mount
Pisgah, across from Jericho. From there the LORD
showed him all the land from Gilead to Dan, 2all
of Naphtali and the lands of Ephraim and Manasseh, all the land of Judah as far as the Mediterranean Sea, 3as well as the southern desert and
the whole Valley of Jericho up to Zoar. (Jericho is
called the city of palm trees.) 4Then the LORD said
to Moses, "This is the land I promised to Abraham, Isaac, and Jacob when I said to them, 'I will
give this land to your descendants.'[d] I have let you
look at it, Moses, but you will not cross over
there."

5Then Moses, the servant of the LORD, died
there in Moab, as the LORD had said. 6He buried
Moses in Moab in the valley opposite Beth Peor,
but even today no one knows where his grave is.
7Moses was one hundred twenty years old when
he died. His eyes were not weak, and he was still
strong. 8The Israelites cried for Moses for thirty
days, staying in the plains of Moab until the time
of sadness was over.

9Joshua son of Nun was then filled with wisdom, because Moses had put his hands on him.
So the Israelites listened to Joshua, and they did
what the LORD had commanded Moses.

10There has never been another prophet[d] in Is
rael like Moses. The LORD knew Moses face to
face 11and sent him to do signs and miracles[d] in
Egypt—to the king, to all his officers, and to the
whole land of Egypt. 12Moses had great power,
and he did great and wonderful things for all the
Israelites to see.

JOSHUA

Why Read This Book:

- See how God leads people to victory when they are faithful (Joshua 1—12).
- Learn how God takes care of people's needs (Joshua 13—21).
- Be challenged to stay faithful to God (Joshua 22—24).

Behind the Scenes:

The book of Joshua could be a great script for an action-packed movie. It's filled with spies, surprise attacks, guerrilla warfare, courageous leaders, unusual battles, and victory celebrations.

The central hero is Joshua, a creative military mind with great organizational skills. But above all, he is absolutely loyal to and dependent on God.

The plot tells how the Israelites conquered land God promised to their ancestor Abram (Genesis 12:7, p. 15). Their parents had escaped from Egypt but had not followed God. So the whole generation that left Egypt had died in the desert, leaving the children—under Joshua's leadership—to cross the Jordan River and conquer the land of Canaan.

Canaan consisted of many independent cities, each with its own king and army,

WHERE THE ACTION WAS

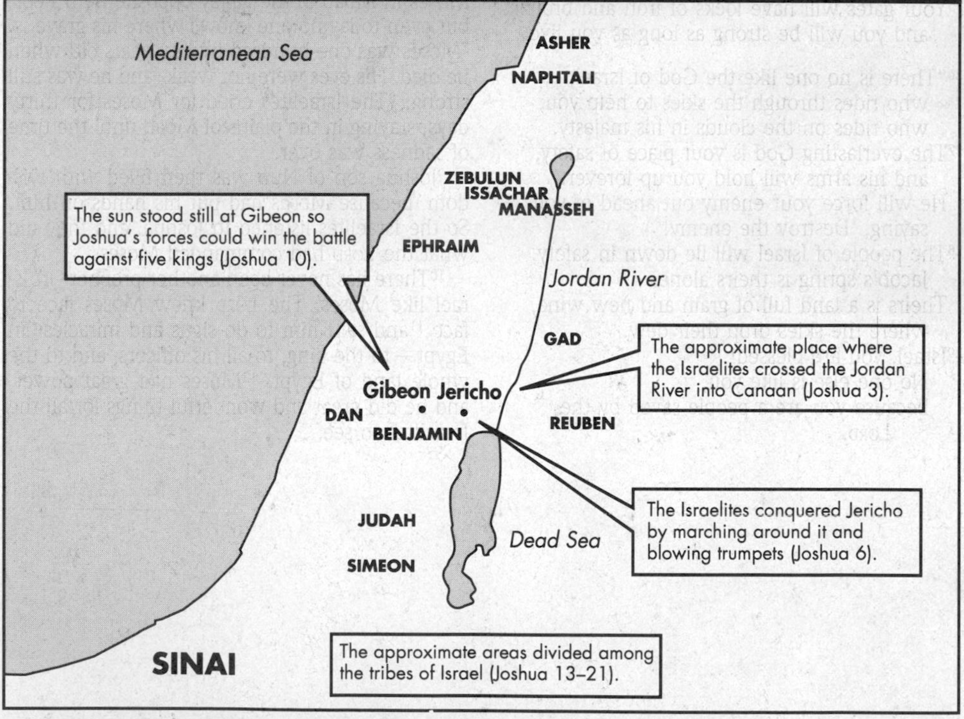

Mediterranean Sea
ASHER
NAPHTALI
ZEBULUN
ISSACHAR
MANASSEH
EPHRAIM
Jordan River
GAD
Gibeon Jericho
DAN
BENJAMIN
REUBEN
JUDAH
SIMEON
Dead Sea
SINAI
The sun stood still at Gibeon so Joshua's forces could win the battle against five kings (Joshua 10).
The approximate place where the Israelites crossed the Jordan River into Canaan (Joshua 3).
The Israelites conquered Jericho by marching around it and blowing trumpets (Joshua 6).
The approximate areas divided among the tribes of Israel (Joshua 13–21).

WHEN THE ACTION WAS

The Israelites escaped from Egypt
Saul was Israel's king
Jesus was born
2000BC
1500BC
1000BC
500BC
BC/AD
Joshua led the Israelites into Canaan

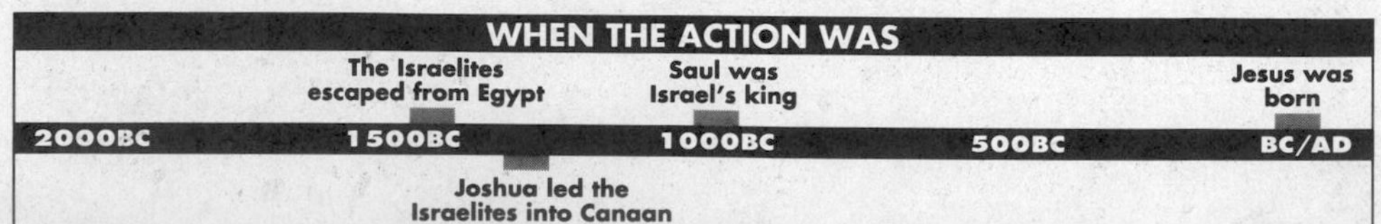

Behind the Scenes (cont.): and many had strong, high walls. So the Israelites had to defeat the cities one by one, beginning with the famous battle of Jericho (Joshua 6, p. 198).

Two major themes flow through Joshua. First, the book shows how God works through people to fulfill his purposes on earth. And it emphasizes the importance of loyally following God, depending on God's power in all things.

God's Command to Joshua

1 After Moses, the servant of the LORD, died,
the LORD spoke to Joshua son of Nun, Moses' assistant. 2The LORD said, "My servant Moses
is dead. Now you and all these people go across
the Jordan River into the land I am giving to the
Israelites. 3I promised Moses I would give you this
land, so I will give you every place you go in the
land. 4All the land from the desert in the south to
Lebanon in the north will be yours. All the land
from the great river, the Euphrates, in the east, to
the Mediterranean Sea in the west will be yours,
too, including the land of the Hittites. 5No one
will be able to defeat you all your life. Just as I was
with Moses, so I will be with you. I will not leave
you or forget you.

> **SIDELIGHT:** The Hebrew name Joshua means "The Lord saves." It's a more famous name than you might think. When you translate it to English, it's Jesus.

6"Joshua, be strong and brave! You must lead
these people so they can take the land that I promised their fathers I would give them. 7Be strong
and brave. Be sure to obey all the teachings my
servant Moses gave you. If you follow them exactly, you will be successful in everything you do.
8Always remember what is written in the Book of
the Teachings. Study it day and night to be sure
to obey everything that is written there. If you do
this, you will be wise and successful in everything. 9Remember that I commanded you to be
strong and brave. Don't be afraid, because the
LORD your God will be with you everywhere you
go."

Joshua's Orders to the People

10Then Joshua gave orders to the officers of the
people: 11"Go through the camp and tell the people, 'Get your supplies ready. Three days from
now you will cross the Jordan River and take the
land the LORD your God is giving you.'"
12Then Joshua said to the people of Reuben,
Gad, and East Manasseh, 13"Remember what Moses, the servant of the LORD, told you. He said the
LORD your God would give you rest and would
give you this land. 14Now the LORD has given you
this land east of the Jordan River. Your wives, children, and animals may stay here, but your fighting
men must dress for war and cross the Jordan River
ahead of your brothers to help them. 15The LORD
has given you a place to rest and will do the same
for your brothers. But you must help them until
they take the land the LORD their God is giving
them. Then you may return to your own land east
of the Jordan River, the land that Moses, the servant of the LORD, gave you."
16Then the people answered Joshua, "Anything
you command us to do, we will do. Any place you
send us, we will go. 17Just as we fully obeyed Moses, we will obey you. We ask only that the LORD
your God be with you just as he was with Moses.
18Whoever refuses to obey your commands or
turns against you will be put to death. Just be
strong and brave!"

Spies Sent to Jericho

2 Joshua son of Nun secretly sent out two spies
from Acacia and said to them, "Go and look
at the land, particularly at the city of Jericho."
So the men went to Jericho and stayed at the
house of a prostitute[d] named Rahab.
2Someone told the king of Jericho, "Some men
from Israel have come here tonight to spy out the
land."
3So the king of Jericho sent this message to Rahab: "Bring out the men who came to you and
entered your house. They have come to spy out
our whole land."
4But the woman had hidden the two men. She
said, "They did come here, but I didn't know
where they came from. 5In the evening, when it
was time to close the city gate, they left. I don't
know where they went, but if you go quickly,
maybe you can catch them." 6(The woman had
taken the men up to the roof[n] and had hidden
them there under stalks of flax[d] that she had
spread out.) 7So the king's men went out looking
for the spies on the road that leads to the crossings
of the Jordan River. The city gate was closed just
after the king's men left the city.
8Before the spies went to sleep for the night,
Rahab went up to the roof. 9She said to them, "I
know the LORD has given this land to your people.
You frighten us very much. Everyone living in this
land is terribly afraid of you 10because we have

roof In Bible times houses were built with flat roofs. The roof was used for drying things such as flax and fruit. It was also used as an extra room, as a place for worship, and as a place to sleep in the summer.

heard how the LORD dried up the Red Sea[d] when
you came out of Egypt. We have heard how you
destroyed Sihon and Og, two Amorite kings who
lived east of the Jordan. 11When we heard this,
we were very frightened. Now our men are afraid
to fight you because the LORD your God rules the
heavens above and the earth below! 12So now,
promise me before the LORD that you will show
kindness to my family just as I showed kindness
to you. Give me some proof that you will do this.
13Allow my father, mother, brothers, sisters, and
all of their families to live. Save us from death."
14The men agreed and said, "It will be our lives
for your lives if you don't tell anyone what we are
doing. When the LORD gives us the land, we will
be kind and true to you."
15The house Rahab lived in was built on the
city wall, so she used a rope to let the men down
through a window. 16She said to them, "Go into
the hills so the king's men will not find you. Hide
there for three days. After the king's men return,
you may go on your way."

SIDELIGHT: Rahab, the prostitute, could help the Israelite spies escape from the king because her house was built into the city wall (Joshua 2:15). It's another one of those stories about a beautiful girl from the wrong side of the wall!

17The men said to her, "You must do as we say.
If not, we cannot be responsible for keeping this
oath you have made us swear. 18When we return

BIBLE STUDY

Where's Your Focus?

Gary Richards was appalled when he saw the tapes in his friend Tim Fellman's car. "How can you listen to this trash?" he asked as he read the sexually explicit and raunchy song titles.

"Give it a rest," Tim shot back. "These groups know music. Who cares about the words? Stop being a crusader."

The conversation came back to haunt Tim that Wednesday night in Bible study. The group read the Bible and tried to apply its principles to their lives. They focused on how being a Christian shapes your priorities and interests in life and how it affects everything you do.

Tim was challenged by the discussion and wanted to talk about it with Gary. On the way home from the Bible study, they talked about friendships and being honest. Then Gary asked, "What does all this say about your music, Tim? Can you listen to raunchy songs and read your Bible at the same time?"

Tim was steamed. "Sure I can!" he shouted, hoping Gary would back off. Which he did. They rode in silence until Tim dropped off Gary at home.

Two weeks later Gary found a note stuffed through the slot in his school locker. "You were right," it simply said. "The songs I liked and God's Word don't mix. I've changed to more positive music. Thanks."

Tim had discovered how focusing on God's Word can change your values and priorities. God gave Joshua the same advice, and it guided him to be successful as God's leader. Read the advice in **Joshua 1:6–9**.

- How did studying the Bible help Tim learn more about what it means to follow God? How did it change the way he lived?
- How has reading the Bible given you courage or success in the past? How can it guide you in a particular area of your life right now?

CONSIDER . . .

- reading three or four devotions on a topic with which you're struggling right now. (See the devotion guide on page 11 for suggestions.) Discover how Bible study changes how you think and what you do.
- writing Joshua 1:9 on a three-by-five card and carrying it in your pocket for a week or two. Glance at it occasionally to remind you God is with you.

FOR MORE, SEE . . .

- Deuteronomy 11:16–21 (p. 172)
- Psalm 119:105–120 (p. 553)
- Romans 15:4–6 (p. 1161)

to this land, you must tie this red rope in the window through which you let us down. Bring your
father, mother, brothers, and all your family into
your house. 19If anyone leaves your house and is
killed, it is his own fault. We cannot be responsible for him. If anyone in your house is hurt, we
will be responsible. 20But if you tell anyone about
this, we will be free from the oath you made us
swear."
21Rahab answered, "I agree to this." So she sent
them away, and they left. Then she tied the red
rope in the window.
22The men left and went into the hills where
they stayed for three days. The king's men looked
for them all along the road, but after three days,
they returned to the city without finding them.
23Then the two men started back. They left the
hills and crossed the river and came to Joshua son
of Nun and told him everything that had happened to them. 24They said, "The LORD surely has
given us all of the land. All the people in that land
are terribly afraid of us."

Crossing the Jordan

3 Early the next morning Joshua and all the
Israelites left Acacia. They traveled to the
Jordan River and camped there before crossing it.
2After three days the officers went through the
camp 3and gave orders to the people: "When you
see the priests and Levites carrying the Ark[d] of the
Agreement with the LORD your God, leave where
you are and follow it. 4That way you will know
which way to go since you have never been here
before. But do not follow too closely. Stay about
a thousand yards behind the Ark."
5Then Joshua told the people, "Make yourselves holy, because tomorrow the LORD will do
amazing things among you."
6Joshua said to the priests, "Take the Ark of the
Agreement and go ahead of the people." So the
priests lifted the Ark and carried it ahead of the
people.
7Then the LORD said to Joshua, "Today I will
begin to make you great in the opinion of all the
Israelites so the people will know I am with you
just as I was with Moses. 8Tell the priests who
carry the Ark of the Agreement to go to the edge
of the Jordan River and stand in the water."
9Then Joshua said to the Israelites, "Come here
and listen to the words of the LORD your God.
10Here is proof that the living God is with you and
that he will force out the Canaanites, Hittites, Hivites, Perizzites, Girgashites, Amorites, and Jebusites. 11The Ark of the Agreement with the Lord
of the whole world will go ahead of you into the
Jordan River. 12Now choose twelve men from
among you, one from each of the twelve tribes[d]
of Israel. 13The priests will carry the Ark of the
LORD, the Master of the whole world, into the
Jordan ahead of you. When they step into the water, it will stop. The river will stop flowing and
will stand up in a heap."
14So the people left the place where they had
camped, and they followed the priests who carried the Ark of the Agreement across the Jordan
River. 15During harvest the Jordan overflows its
banks. When the priests carrying the Ark came to
the edge of the river and stepped into the water,
16the water upstream stopped flowing. It stood up
in a heap a great distance away at Adam, a town
near Zarethan. The water flowing down to the
Sea of Arabah (the Dead Sea[d]) was completely cut
off. So the people crossed the river near Jericho.
17The priests carried the Ark of the Agreement
with the LORD to the middle of the river and stood
there on dry ground. They waited there while all
the people of Israel walked across the Jordan
River on dry land.

Rocks to Remind the People

4 After all the people had finished crossing the
Jordan, the LORD said to Joshua, 2"Choose
twelve men from among the people, one from
each tribe.[d] 3Tell them to get twelve rocks from
the middle of the river, from where the priests
stood. Carry the rocks and put them down where
you stay tonight."
4So Joshua chose one man from each tribe.
Then he called the twelve men together 5and said
to them, "Go out into the river where the Ark[d] of
the LORD your God is. Each of you bring back one
rock, one for each tribe of Israel, and carry it on
your shoulder. 6They will be a sign among you. In
the future your children will ask you, 'What do
these rocks mean?' 7Tell them the water stopped
flowing in the Jordan when the Ark of the Agreement with the LORD crossed the river. These
rocks will always remind the Israelites of this."
8So the Israelites obeyed Joshua and carried
twelve rocks from the middle of the Jordan River,
one rock for each of the twelve tribes of Israel,
just as the LORD had commanded Joshua. They
carried the rocks with them and put them down
where they made their camp. 9Joshua also put
twelve rocks in the middle of the Jordan River
where the priests had stood while carrying the
Ark of the Agreement. These rocks are still there
today.
10The priests carrying the Ark continued standing in the middle of the river until everything was
done that the LORD had commanded Joshua to tell
the people, just as Moses had told Joshua. The
people hurried across the river. 11After they finished crossing the river, the priests carried the Ark
of the LORD to the other side as the people
watched. 12The men from the tribes of Reuben,
Gad, and East Manasseh obeyed what Moses had
told them. They were dressed for war, and they

crossed the river ahead of the other people.
13About forty thousand soldiers prepared for war
passed before the LORD as they marched across
the river, going toward the plains of Jericho.
14That day the LORD made Joshua great in the
opinion of all the Israelites. They respected Joshua
all his life, just as they had respected Moses.
15Then the LORD said to Joshua, 16"Command
the priests to bring the Ark of the Agreement out
of the river."
17So Joshua commanded the priests, "Come up
out of the Jordan."
18Then the priests carried the Ark of the Agreement with the LORD out of the river. As soon as
their feet touched dry land, the water began flowing again. The river again overflowed its banks,
just as it had before they crossed.
19The people crossed the Jordan on the tenth
day of the first month and camped at Gilgal, east
of Jericho. 20They carried with them the twelve
rocks taken from the Jordan, and Joshua set them
up at Gilgal. 21Then he spoke to the Israelites: "In
the future your children will ask you, 'What do
these rocks mean?' 22Tell them, 'Israel crossed the
Jordan River on dry land. 23The LORD your God
caused the water to stop flowing until you finished crossing it, just as the LORD did to the Red
Sea.[d] He stopped the water until we crossed it.
24The LORD did this so all people would know he
has great power and so you would always respect
the LORD your God.' "

5 All the kings of the Amorites west of the Jordan and the Canaanite kings living by the
Mediterranean Sea heard that the LORD dried up
the Jordan River until the Israelites had crossed it.
After that they were scared and too afraid to face
the Israelites.

The Israelites Are Circumcised

2At that time the LORD said to Joshua, "Make
knives from flint stones and circumcise[d] the Israelites." 3So Joshua made knives from flint stones
and circumcised the Israelites at Gibeath Haara-
loth.
4This is why Joshua circumcised the men: After
the Israelites left Egypt, all the men old enough to
serve in the army died in the desert on the way
out of Egypt. 5The men who had come out of
Egypt had been circumcised, but none of those
who were born in the desert on the trip from
Egypt had been circumcised. 6The Israelites had
moved about in the desert for forty years. During
that time all the fighting men who had left Egypt
had died because they had not obeyed the LORD.
So the LORD swore they would not see the land
he had promised their ancestors to give them, a
fertile land. 7Their sons took their places. But
none of the sons born on the trip from Egypt had
been circumcised, so Joshua circumcised them.
8After all the Israelites had been circumcised, they
stayed in camp until they were healed.
9Then the LORD said to Joshua, "As slaves in
Egypt you were ashamed, but today I have removed that shame." So Joshua named that place
Gilgal, which it is still named today.
10The people of Israel were camped at Gilgal on
the plains of Jericho. It was there, on the evening
of the fourteenth day of the month, they celebrated the Passover[d] Feast. 11The day after the
Passover, the people ate food grown on that land:
bread made without yeast and roasted grain.
12The day they ate this food, the manna[d] stopped
coming. The Israelites no longer got the manna
from heaven. They ate the food grown in the land
of Canaan that year.
13Joshua was near Jericho when he looked up
and saw a man standing in front of him with a
sword in his hand. Joshua went to him and asked,
"Are you a friend or an enemy?"
14The man answered, "I am neither. I have
come as the commander of the LORD's army."
Then Joshua bowed facedown on the ground
and asked, "Does my master have a command for
me, his servant?"
15The commander of the LORD's army answered, "Take off your sandals, because the place
where you are standing is holy." So Joshua did.

The Fall of Jericho

6 The people of Jericho were afraid because
the Israelites were near. They closed the city
gates and guarded them. No one went into the
city, and no one came out.
2Then the LORD said to Joshua, "Look, I have
given you Jericho, its king, and all its fighting
men. 3March around the city with your army
once a day for six days. 4Have seven priests carry
trumpets made from horns of male sheep and
have them march in front of the Ark.[d] On the
seventh day march around the city seven times
and have the priests blow the trumpets as they
march. 5They will make one long blast on the
trumpets. When you hear that sound, have all
the people give a loud shout. Then the walls
of the city will fall so the people can go straight
into the city."
6So Joshua son of Nun called the priests together and said to them, "Carry the Ark of the
Agreement. Tell seven priests to carry trumpets
and march in front of it." 7Then Joshua ordered
the people, "Now go! March around the city. The
soldiers with weapons should march in front of
the Ark of the Agreement with the LORD."
8When Joshua finished speaking to the people,
the seven priests began marching before the
LORD. They carried the seven trumpets and blew
them as they marched. The priests carrying the

Ark of the Agreement with the LORD followed
them. 9Soldiers with weapons marched in front of
the priests, and armed men walked behind the
Ark. The priests were blowing their trumpets.
10But Joshua had told the people not to give a war
cry. He said, "Don't shout. Don't say a word until
the day I tell you. Then shout." 11So Joshua had
the Ark of the LORD carried around the city one
time. Then they went back to camp for the
night.

12Early the next morning Joshua got up, and
the priests carried the Ark of the LORD again.
13The seven priests carried the seven trumpets
and marched in front of the Ark of the LORD,
blowing their trumpets. Soldiers with weapons
marched in front of them, and other soldiers
walked behind the Ark of the LORD. All this time
the priests were blowing their trumpets. 14So on
the second day they marched around the city one
time and then went back to camp. They did this
every day for six days.

15On the seventh day they got up at dawn and
marched around the city, just as they had on the
days before. But on that day they marched around
the city seven times. 16The seventh time around
the priests blew their trumpets. Then Joshua gave
the command: "Now, shout! The LORD has given
you this city! 17The city and everything in it are
to be destroyed as an offering to the LORD. Only
Rahab the prostitute[d] and everyone in her house
should remain alive. They must not be killed, because Rahab hid the two spies we sent out.
18Don't take any of the things that are to be destroyed as an offering to the LORD. If you take
them and bring them into our camp, you yourselves will be destroyed, and you will bring trouble to all of Israel. 19All the silver and gold and
things made from bronze and iron belong to the
LORD and must be saved for him."

> **SIDELIGHT:** Jericho (Joshua 6:1–19) has been called "the oldest walled town in the world." Many archaeologists believe it was settled as early as 10,000 B.C., and walls were built by 8,000 B.C. After it was destroyed, it wasn't rebuilt for about 400 years. Today the ancient city of Jericho is a seventy-foot-high mound near the modern city of Jericho in Israel.

20When the priests blew the trumpets, the people shouted. At the sound of the trumpets and the
people's shout, the walls fell, and everyone ran
straight into the city. So the Israelites defeated
that city. 21They completely destroyed with the
sword every living thing in the city—men and
women, young and old, cattle, sheep, and donkeys.

22Joshua said to the two men who had spied
out the land, "Go into the prostitute's house.
Bring her out and bring out those who are with
her, because of the promise you made to her."
23So the two men went into the house and
brought out Rahab, her father, mother, brothers,
and all those with her. They put all of her family
in a safe place outside the camp of Israel.

24Then Israel burned the whole city and everything in it, but they did not burn the things made
from silver, gold, bronze, and iron. These were
saved for the LORD. 25Joshua saved Rahab the
prostitute, her family, and all who were with her,
because Rahab had helped the men he had sent
to spy out Jericho. Rahab still lives among the Israelites today.

26Then Joshua made this oath:

"Anyone who tries to rebuild this city of
Jericho
will be cursed by the LORD.
The one who lays the foundation of this city
will lose his oldest son,
and the one who sets up the gates
will lose his youngest son."

27So the LORD was with Joshua, and Joshua became famous through all the land.

The Sin of Achan

7 But the Israelites did not obey the LORD.
There was a man from the tribe[d] of Judah
named Achan. (He was the son of Carmi and
grandson of Zabdi, who was the son of Zerah.)
Because Achan kept some of the things that were
to be given to the LORD, the LORD became very
angry at the Israelites.

2Joshua sent some men from Jericho to Ai,
which was near Beth Aven, east of Bethel. He told
them, "Go to Ai and spy out the area." So the men
went to spy on Ai.

3Later they came back to Joshua and said,
"There are only a few people in Ai, so we will not
need all our people to defeat them. Send only two
or three thousand men to fight. There is no need
to send all of our people." 4So about three thousand men went up to Ai, but the people of Ai beat
them badly. 5The people of Ai killed about thirty-
six Israelites and then chased the rest from the
city gate all the way down to the canyon, killing
them as they went down the hill. When the Israelites saw this, they lost their courage.

6Then Joshua tore his clothes in sorrow. He
bowed facedown on the ground before the Ark[d]
of the LORD and stayed there until evening. The
leaders of Israel did the same thing. They also
threw dirt on their heads to show their sorrow.
7Then Joshua said, "Lord GOD, you brought our

people across the Jordan River. Why did you bring
us this far and then let the Amorites destroy us?
We would have been happy to stay on the other
side of the Jordan. 8Lord, there is nothing I can say
now. Israel has been beaten by the enemy. 9The
Canaanites and all the other people in this country will hear about this and will surround and kill
us all! Then what will you do for your own great
name?"

10The LORD said to Joshua, "Stand up! Why are
you down on your face? 11The Israelites have
sinned; they have broken the agreement I commanded them to obey. They took some of the
things I commanded them to destroy. They have
stolen and lied and have taken those things for
themselves. 12That is why the Israelites cannot
face their enemies. They turn away from the fight
and run, because I have commanded that they be
destroyed. I will not help you anymore unless you
destroy everything as I commanded you.

13"Now go! Make the people holy. Tell them,
'Set yourselves apart to the LORD for tomorrow.
The LORD, the God of Israel, says some of you are
keeping things he commanded you to destroy.
You will never defeat your enemies until you
throw away those things.

14" 'Tomorrow morning you must be present
with your tribes. The LORD will choose one tribe
to stand alone before him. Then the LORD will
choose one family group from that tribe to stand
before him. Then the LORD will choose one family
from that family group to stand before him, person by person. 15The one who is keeping what
should have been destroyed will himself be destroyed by fire. Everything he owns will be destroyed with him. He has broken the agreement
with the LORD and has done a disgraceful thing
among the people of Israel!' "

16Early the next morning Joshua led all of Israel
to present themselves in their tribes, and the
LORD chose the tribe of Judah. 17So the family
groups of Judah presented themselves, and the
LORD then chose the family group of Zerah. When
all the families of Zerah presented themselves, the
family of Zabdi was chosen. 18And Joshua told all
the men in that family to present themselves. The
LORD chose Achan son of Carmi. (Carmi was the
son of Zabdi, who was the son of Zerah.)

19Then Joshua said to Achan, "My son, tell the
truth. Confess to the LORD, the God of Israel. Tell
me what you did, and don't try to hide anything
from me."

20Achan answered, "It is true! I have sinned
against the LORD, the God of Israel. This is what
I did: 21Among the things I saw was a beautiful
coat from Babylonia and about five pounds of silver and more than one and one-fourth pounds of
gold. I wanted these things very much for myself,
so I took them. You will find them buried in the
ground under my tent, with the silver underneath."

22So Joshua sent men who ran to the tent and
found the things hidden there, with the silver.
23The men brought them out of the tent, took
them to Joshua and all the Israelites, and spread
them out on the ground before the LORD. 24Then
Joshua and all the people led Achan son of Zerah
to the Valley of Trouble. They also took the silver,
the coat, the gold, Achan's sons, daughters, cattle,
donkeys, sheep, tent, and everything he owned.
25Joshua said, "I don't know why you caused so
much trouble for us, but now the LORD will bring
trouble to you." Then all the people threw stones
at Achan and his family until they died. Then the
people burned them. 26They piled rocks over
Achan's body, and they are still there today. That
is why it is called the Valley of Trouble. After this
the LORD was no longer angry.

Ai Is Destroyed

8 Then the LORD said to Joshua, "Don't be
afraid or give up. Lead all your fighting men
to Ai. I will help you defeat the king of Ai, his
people, his city, and his land. 2You will do to Ai
and its king what you did to Jericho and its king.
Only this time you may take all the wealth and
keep it for yourselves. Now tell some of your soldiers to set up an ambush behind the city."

3So Joshua led his whole army toward Ai. Then
he chose thirty thousand of his best fighting men
and sent them out at night. 4Joshua gave them
these orders: "Listen carefully. You must set up
an ambush behind the city. Don't go far from it,
but continue to watch and be ready. 5I and the
men who are with me will march toward the city,
and the men in the city will come out to fight us,
just as they did before. Then we will turn and run
away from them. 6They will chase us away from
the city, thinking we are running away from them
as we did before. When we run away, 7come out
from your ambush and take the city. The LORD
your God will give you the power to win. 8After
you take the city, burn it. See to it! You have your
orders."

9Then Joshua sent them to wait in ambush between Bethel and Ai, to the west of Ai. But Joshua
stayed the night with his people.

10Early the next morning Joshua gathered his
men together. He and the older leaders of Israel
led them up to Ai. 11All of the soldiers who were
with Joshua marched up to Ai and stopped in
front of the city and made camp north of it. There
was a valley between them and the city. 12Then
Joshua chose about five thousand men and set
them in ambush in the area west of the city between Bethel and Ai. 13So the people took their
positions; the main camp was north of the city,

and the other men were hiding to the west. That night Joshua went down into the valley.

[14]Now when the king of Ai saw the army of Israel, he and his people got up early the next morning and hurried out to fight them. They went out to a place east of the city, but the king did not know soldiers were waiting in ambush behind the city. [15]Joshua and all the men of Israel let the army of Ai push them back. Then they ran toward the desert. [16]The men in Ai were called to chase Joshua and his men, so they left the city and went after them. [17]All the men of Ai and Bethel chased the army of Israel. The city was left open; not a man stayed to protect it.

[18]Then the LORD said to Joshua, "Hold your spear toward Ai, because I will give you that city." So Joshua held his spear toward the city of Ai. [19]When the Israelites who were in ambush saw this, they quickly came out of their hiding place and hurried toward the city. They entered the city, took control of it, and quickly set it on fire.

[20]When the men of Ai looked back, they saw smoke rising from their city. At the same time the Israelites stopped running and turned against the men of Ai, who could not escape in any direction. [21]When Joshua and all his men saw that the army had taken control of the city and saw the smoke rising from it, they stopped running and turned to fight the men of Ai. [22]The men who were in ambush also came out of the city to help with the fight. So the men of Ai were caught between the armies of Israel. None of the enemy escaped. The Israelites fought until not one of the men of Ai was left alive, except [23]the king of Ai, and they brought him to Joshua.

A Review of the Fighting

[24]During the fighting the army of Israel chased the men of Ai into the fields and desert and killed all of them. Then they went back to Ai and killed everyone there. [25]All the people of Ai died that day, twelve thousand men and women. [26]Joshua had held his spear toward Ai, as a sign to destroy the city, and did not draw it back until all the people of Ai were destroyed. [27]The people of Israel kept for themselves the animals and the other things the people of Ai had owned, as the LORD had commanded Joshua to do.

[28]Then Joshua burned the city of Ai and made it a pile of ruins. And it is still like that today. [29]Joshua hanged the king of Ai on a tree and left him there until evening. At sunset Joshua told his men to take the king's body down from the tree and to throw it down at the city gate. Then they covered it with a pile of rocks, which is still there today.

[30]Joshua built an altar for the LORD, the God of Israel, on Mount Ebal, as [31]Moses, the LORD's servant, had commanded. Joshua built the altar as it was explained in the Book of the Teachings of Moses. It was made from uncut stones; no tool was ever used on them. On that altar the Israelites offered burnt offerings to the LORD and fellowship offerings. [32]There Joshua wrote the teachings of Moses on stones for all the people of Israel to see. [33]The older leaders, officers, judges, and all the Israelites were there; Israelites and non-Israelites were all standing around the Ark[d] of the Agreement with the LORD in front of the priests, the Levites who had carried the Ark. Half of the people stood in front of Mount Ebal, and half stood in front of Mount Gerizim. This was the way the LORD's servant Moses had earlier commanded the people to be blessed.

[34]Then Joshua read all the words of the teachings, the blessings and the curses, exactly as they were written in the Book of the Teachings. [35]All the Israelites were gathered together—men, women, and children—along with the non-Israelites who lived among them. Joshua read every command that Moses had given.

The Gibeonite Trickery

9 All the kings west of the Jordan River heard about these things: the kings of the Hittites, Amorites, Canaanites, Perizzites, Hivites, and Jebusites. They lived in the mountains and on the western hills and along the whole Mediterranean Sea coast. [2]So all these kings gathered to fight Joshua and the Israelites.

[3]When the people of Gibeon heard how Joshua had defeated Jericho and Ai, [4]they decided to trick the Israelites. They gathered old sacks and old leather wine bags that were cracked and mended, and they put them on the backs of their donkeys. [5]They put old sandals on their feet and wore old clothes, and they took some dry, moldy bread. [6]Then they went to Joshua in the camp near Gilgal.

The men said to Joshua and the Israelites, "We have traveled from a faraway country. Make a peace agreement with us."

[7]The Israelites said to these Hivites, "Maybe you live near us. How can we make a peace agreement with you?"

[8]The Hivites said to Joshua, "We are your servants."

But Joshua asked, "Who are you? Where do you come from?"

[9]The men answered, "We are your servants who have come from a far country, because we heard of the fame of the LORD your God. We heard about what he has done and everything he did in Egypt. [10]We heard that he defeated the two kings of the Amorites from the east side of the Jordan River—Sihon king of Heshbon and Og king of Bashan who ruled in Ashtaroth. [11]So our older leaders and our people said to us, 'Take food

for your journey and go and meet the Israelites.
Tell them, "We are your servants. Make a peace
agreement with us." '
12"Look at our bread. On the day we left home
to come to you it was warm and fresh, but now
it is dry and moldy. 13Look at our leather wine
bags. They were new and filled with wine, but
now they are cracked and old. Our clothes and
sandals are worn out from the long journey."
14The men of Israel tasted the bread, but they
did not ask the LORD what to do. 15So Joshua
agreed to make peace with the Gibeonites and to
let them live. And the leaders of the Israelites
swore an oath to keep the agreement.

16Three days after they had made the agreement, the Israelites learned that the Gibeonites
lived nearby. 17So the Israelites went to where
they lived and on the third day came to their cities: Gibeon, Kephirah, Beeroth, and Kiriath Jearim. 18But the Israelites did not attack those cities,
because they had made a promise to them before
the LORD, the God of Israel.

All the Israelites grumbled against the leaders.
19But the leaders answered, "We have given our
promise before the LORD, the God of Israel, so we
cannot attack them now. 20This is what we must
do. We must let them live. Otherwise, God's anger will be against us for breaking the oath we
swore to them. 21So let them live, but they will
cut wood and carry water for our people." So the
leaders kept their promise to them.

22Joshua called for the Gibeonites and asked,
"Why did you lie to us? Your land was near our
camp, but you told us you were from a far country. 23Now, you will be placed under a curse to be
our slaves. You will have to cut wood and carry
water for the house of my God."

24The Gibeonites answered Joshua, "We lied to
you because we were afraid you would kill us. We
heard that the LORD your God commanded his
servant Moses to give you all of this land and to
kill all the people who lived in it. That is why we
did this. 25Now you can decide what to do with
us, whatever you think is right."

26So Joshua saved their lives by not allowing
the Israelites to kill them, 27but he made the Gibeonites slaves. They cut wood and carried water
for the Israelites, and they did it for the altar of the
LORD—wherever he chose it to be. They are still
doing this today.

The Sun Stands Still

10 At this time Adoni-Zedek king of Jerusalem heard that Joshua had defeated Ai
and completely destroyed it, as he had also done
to Jericho and its king. The king also learned that
the Gibeonites had made a peace agreement with
Israel and that they lived nearby. 2Adoni-Zedek
and his people were very afraid because of this.
Gibeon was not a little town like Ai; it was a large
city, as big as a city that had a king, and all its men
were good fighters. 3So Adoni-Zedek king of Jerusalem sent a message to Hoham king of Hebron,
Piram king of Jarmuth, Japhia king of Lachish, and
Debir king of Eglon. He begged them, 4"Come
with me and help me attack Gibeon, which has
made a peace agreement with Joshua and the Israelites."

5Then these five Amorite kings—the kings of
Jerusalem, Hebron, Jarmuth, Lachish, and Eglon—gathered their armies, went to Gibeon, surrounded it, and attacked it.

6The Gibeonites sent this message to Joshua in
his camp at Gilgal: "Don't let us, your servants,
be destroyed. Come quickly and help us! Save us!
All the Amorite kings from the mountains have
joined their armies and are fighting against us."
7So Joshua marched out of Gilgal with his
whole army, including his best fighting men. 8The
LORD said to Joshua, "Don't be afraid of those armies, because I will hand them over to you. None
of them will be able to stand against you."

9Joshua and his army marched all night from
Gilgal for a surprise attack. 10The LORD confused
those armies when Israel attacked, so Israel defeated them in a great victory at Gibeon. They
chased them along the road going up to Beth Horon and killed men all the way to Azekah and
Makkedah. 11As they chased the enemy down the
Beth Horon Pass to Azekah, the LORD threw large
hailstones on them from the sky and killed them.
More people were killed by the hailstones than by
the Israelites' swords.

12On the day that the LORD gave up the Amorites to the Israelites, Joshua stood before all the
people of Israel and said to the LORD:

"Sun, stand still over Gibeon.
Moon, stand still over the Valley of
Aijalon."
13So the sun stood still,
and the moon stopped
until the people defeated their enemies.

These words are written in the Book of Jashar.

The sun stopped in the middle of the sky and
waited to go down for a full day. 14That has never
happened at any time before that day or since.
That was the day the LORD listened to a human
being. Truly the LORD was fighting for Israel!

15After this, Joshua and his army went back to
the camp at Gilgal.

16During the fight the five kings ran away and
hid in a cave near Makkedah, 17but someone
found them hiding in the cave at Makkedah and
told Joshua. 18So he said, "Cover the opening of
the cave with large rocks. Put some men there to
guard it, 19but don't stay there yourselves. Continue chasing the enemy and attacking them from
behind. Don't let them get to their cities, because

the LORD your God will hand them over to
you."
20So Joshua and the Israelites killed the enemy,
but a few were able to get back to their strong,
walled cities. 21After the fighting, Joshua's men
came back safely to him at Makkedah. No one
was brave enough to say a word against the Israelites.
22Joshua said, "Move the rocks that are covering the opening of the cave and bring those five
kings out to me." 23So Joshua's men brought the
five kings out of the cave—the kings of Jerusalem, Hebron, Jarmuth, Lachish, and Eglon.
24When they brought the five kings out to Joshua,
he called for all his men. He said to the commanders of his army, "Come here! Put your feet on the
necks of these kings." So they came close and put
their feet on their necks.
25Joshua said to his men, "Be strong and brave!
Don't be afraid, because I will show you what the
LORD will do to the enemies you will fight in the
future." 26Then Joshua killed the five kings and
hung their bodies on five trees, where he left
them until evening.
27At sunset Joshua told his men to take the bodies down from the trees. Then they threw them
into the same cave where they had been hiding
and covered the opening of the cave with large
rocks, which are still there today.
28That day Joshua defeated Makkedah. He
killed the king and completely destroyed all the
people in that city as an offering to the LORD; no
one was left alive. He did the same thing to the
king of Makkedah that he had done to the king
of Jericho.

Defeating Southern Cities

29Joshua and all the Israelites traveled from
Makkedah to Libnah and attacked it. 30The LORD
handed over the city and its king. They killed every person in the city; no one was left alive. And
they did the same thing to that king that they had
done to the king of Jericho.
31Then Joshua and all the Israelites left Libnah
and went to Lachish, which they surrounded and
attacked. 32The LORD handed over Lachish on the
second day. The Israelites killed everyone in that
city just as they had done to Libnah. 33During this
same time Horam king of Gezer came to help Lachish, but Joshua also defeated him and his army;
no one was left alive.

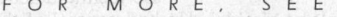

GOD'S POWER

In Just Fifteen Seconds

At 5:04 P.M. on October 17, 1989, the San Francisco area shook like Jell-O under the force of a major earthquake. The quake lasted just fifteen seconds, but it left massive devastation.

- 67 people were killed.
- 3,757 people were injured.
- 1,018 houses were destroyed.
- 366 businesses were destroyed.
- 1.4 million customers lost electricity.
- $6 billion in property damage was caused.
- 64,159 people sought shelter from the Red Cross.

If the earth stores up that much power for destruction, imagine God's power to do good in the world he created. Read **Joshua 10:5–14** to see how God used that power to give victory to Joshua and the Israelites.

- What similarities do you see between God's power in the passage and the effects of the earthquake? What is different about the two displays of power?
- Have you experienced God's power when you've been surrounded by enemies? How can you begin to trust God's power in a new way?

CONSIDER . . .

- throwing a quick celebration party when God's power gives you victory over problems you face. (Hint: The sun doesn't have to stop in the sky for God to be at work!)
- praying that God's power will be with you next time you feel you're being attacked by enemies.

FOR MORE, SEE . . .

- Exodus 14:19–31 (p. 71)
- 1 Kings 18:20–39 (p. 324)
- 1 Corinthians 1:18–31 (p. 1168)

34Then Joshua and all the Israelites went from Lachish to Eglon. They surrounded Eglon, attacked it, and 35captured it the same day. They killed all its people and completely destroyed everything in it as an offering to the LORD, just as they had done to Lachish.

36Then Joshua and the Israelites went from Eglon to Hebron and attacked it, 37capturing it and all the little towns near it. The Israelites killed everyone in Hebron; no one was left alive there. Just as they had done to Eglon, they completely destroyed the city and all its people as an offering to the LORD.

38Then Joshua and the Israelites went back to Debir and attacked it. 39They captured that city, its king, and all the little towns near it, completely destroying everyone in Debir as an offering to the LORD; no one was left alive there. Israel did to Debir and its king just as they had done to Libnah and its king, just as they had done to Hebron. 40So Joshua defeated all the kings of the cities of these areas: the mountains, southern Canaan, the western hills, and the slopes. The LORD, the God of Israel, had told Joshua to completely destroy all the people as an offering to the LORD, so he left no one alive in those places. 41Joshua captured all the cities from Kadesh Barnea to Gaza, and from Goshen to Gibeon. 42He captured all these cities and their kings on one trip, because the LORD, the God of Israel, was fighting for Israel.

43Then Joshua and all the Israelites returned to their camp at Gilgal.

Defeating Northern Kings

11 When Jabin king of Hazor heard about all that had happened, he sent messages to Jobab king of Madon, to the king of Shimron, and to the king of Acshaph. 2He sent messages to the kings in the northern mountains and also to the kings in the Jordan Valley south of Lake Galilee and in the western hills. He sent a message to the king of Naphoth Dor in the west 3and to the kings of the Canaanites in the east and in the west. He sent messages to the Amorites, Hittites, Perizzites, and Jebusites in the mountains. Jabin also sent one to the Hivites, who lived below Mount Hermon in the area of Mizpah. 4So the armies of all these kings came together with their horses and chariots. There were as many soldiers as grains of sand on the seashore.

5All of these kings met together at the waters of Merom, joined their armies together into one camp, and made plans to fight against the Israelites.

6Then the LORD said to Joshua, "Don't be afraid of them, because at this time tomorrow I will give them to you. You will cripple their horses and burn all their chariots."

7So Joshua and his whole army surprised the enemy by attacking them at the waters of Merom. 8The LORD handed them over to Israel. They chased them to Greater Sidon, Misrephoth Maim, and the Valley of Mizpah in the east. Israel fought until none of the enemy was left alive. 9Joshua did what the LORD said to do; he crippled their horses and burned their chariots.

10Then Joshua went back and captured the city of Hazor and killed its king. (Hazor had been the leader of all the kingdoms that fought against Israel.) 11Israel killed everyone in Hazor, completely destroying them; no one was left alive. Then they burned Hazor itself.

SIDELIGHT: Joshua's victory over Hazor was remarkable, considering that the city was huge for its day (Joshua 11:10). It had forty thousand residents, and its walls were about fifty feet high—about four to five stories. But despite the city's power, it was never rebuilt after Israel destroyed it.

12Joshua captured all of these cities, killed all of their kings, and completely destroyed everything in these cities. He did this just as Moses, the servant of the LORD, had commanded. 13But the Israelites did not burn any cities that were built on their mounds, except Hazor; only that city was burned by Joshua. 14The people of Israel kept for themselves everything they found in the cities, including all the animals. But they killed all the people there; they left no one alive. 15Long ago the LORD had commanded his servant Moses to do this, and then Moses had commanded Joshua to do it. Joshua did everything the LORD had commanded Moses.

SIDELIGHT: It's probably a good idea to clean your room from time to time. When war destroyed an ancient city, the people never cleaned away the rubble. They simply built on top of it. Before long, the cities looked like they were built on hills (Joshua 11:13). As many as five thousand of these hills (which archaeologists call "tells") exist today.

16So Joshua defeated all the people in the land. He had control of the mountains and the area of southern Canaan, all the areas of Goshen, the western hills, and the Jordan Valley. He controlled the mountains of Israel and all the hills

near them. 17Joshua controlled all the land from
Mount Halak near Edom to Baal Gad in the Valley
of Lebanon, below Mount Hermon. Joshua also
captured all the kings in the land and killed them.
18He fought against them for many years. 19The
people of only one city in all the land had made
a peace agreement with Israel — the Hivites living
in Gibeon. All the other cities were defeated in
war. 20The LORD made those people stubborn so
they would fight against Israel and he could completely destroy them without mercy. This is what
the LORD had commanded Moses to do.

21Now Joshua fought the Anakites[d] who lived
in the mountains of Hebron, Debir, Anab, Judah,
and Israel, and he completely destroyed them and
their towns. 22There were no Anakites left living
in the land of the Israelites and only a few were
left in Gaza, Gath, and Ashdod. 23Joshua took
control of all the land of Israel as the LORD had
told Moses to do long ago. He gave the land to
Israel, because he had promised it to them. Then
Joshua divided the land among the tribes[d] of Israel, and there was peace in the land.

Kings Defeated by Israel

12 The Israelites took control of the land
east of the Jordan River from the Arnon
Ravine to Mount Hermon and all the land along
the eastern side of the Jordan Valley. These lands
belonged to the kings whom the Israelites defeated.

2Sihon king of the Amorites lived in the city of
Heshbon and ruled the land from Aroer at the
Arnon Ravine to the Jabbok River. His land started
in the middle of the ravine, which was their border with the Ammonites. Sihon ruled over half
the land of Gilead 3and over the eastern side of
the Jordan Valley from Lake Galilee to the Dead
Sea.[d] And he ruled from Beth Jeshimoth south to
the slopes of Pisgah.

4Og king of Bashan was one of the last of the
Rephaites.[d] He ruled the land in Ashtaroth and
Edrei. 5He ruled over Mount Hermon, Salecah,
and all the area of Bashan up to where the people
of Geshur and Maacah lived. Og also ruled half
the land of Gilead up to the border of Sihon king
of Heshbon.

6The LORD's servant Moses and the Israelites
defeated all these kings, and Moses gave that land
to the tribes[d] of Reuben and Gad and to East Manasseh as their own.

7Joshua and the Israelites also defeated kings in
the land west of the Jordan River. He gave the
people the land and divided it among the twelve
tribes to be their own. It was between Baal Gad
in the Valley of Lebanon and Mount Halak near
Edom. 8This included the mountains, the western
hills, the Jordan Valley, the slopes, the desert, and
southern Canaan. This was the land where the
Hittites, Amorites, Canaanites, Perizzites, Hivites, and Jebusites had lived. The Israelites defeated the king of each of the following cities:
9Jericho, Ai (near Bethel), 10Jerusalem, Hebron,
11Jarmuth, Lachish, 12Eglon, Gezer, 13Debir, Geder, 14Hormah, Arad, 15Libnah, Adullam, 16Makke-
dah, Bethel, 17Tappuah, Hepher, 18Aphek, Lasha-
ron, 19Madon, Hazor, 20Shimron Meron, Acshaph,
21Taanach, Megiddo, 22Kedesh, Jokneam in Carmel, 23Dor (in Naphoth Dor), Goyim in Gilgal,
and 24Tirzah.

The total number of kings was thirty-one.

Land Still to Be Taken

13 When Joshua was very old, the LORD
said to him, "Joshua, you have grown
old, but there is still much land for you to take.
2This is what is left: the regions of Geshur and of
the Philistines; 3the area from the Shihor River at
the border of Egypt to Ekron in the north, which
belongs to the Canaanites; the five Philistine leaders at Gaza, Ashdod, Ashkelon, Gath, and Ekron;
the Avvites, 4who live south of the Canaanite
land; 5the Gebalites, and the area of Lebanon east
of Baal Gad below Mount Hermon to Lebo Hamath.

6"The Sidonians are living in the hill country
from Lebanon to Misrephoth Maim, but I will
force all of them out ahead of the Israelites. Be
sure to remember this land when you divide the
land among the Israelites, as I told you.
7"Now divide the land among the nine tribes[d]
and West Manasseh."

Dividing the Land

8East Manasseh and the tribes of Reuben and
Gad had received their land. The LORD's servant
Moses had given them the land east of the Jordan
River. 9Their land started at Aroer at the Arnon
Ravine and continued to the town in the middle
of the ravine, and it included the whole plain from
Medeba to Dibon. 10All the towns ruled by Sihon
king of the Amorites, who ruled in the city of
Heshbon, were in that land. The land continued
to the area where the Ammonites lived. 11Gilead
was also there, as well as the area where the people of Geshur and Maacah lived, and all of Mount
Hermon and Bashan as far as Salecah. 12All the
kingdom of Og king of Bashan was in the land. Og
was one of the last of the Rephaites, and in the
past he ruled in Ashtaroth and Edrei. Moses had
defeated them and had taken their land. 13Be-
cause the Israelites did not force out the people of
Geshur and Maacah, they still live among the Israelites today.

14The tribe of Levi was the only one that did
not get any land. Instead, they were given all the
burned sacrifices made to the LORD, the God of
Israel, as he had promised them.

15Moses had given each family group from the tribe of Reuben some land: 16Theirs was the land from Aroer near the Arnon Ravine to the town of Medeba, including the whole plain and the town in the middle of the ravine; 17Heshbon and all the towns on the plain: Dibon, Bamoth Baal, and Beth Baal Meon, 18Jahaz, Kedemoth, Mephaath, 19Kiriathaim, Sibmah, Zereth Shahar on the hill in the valley, 20Beth Peor, the hills of Pisgah, and Beth Jeshimoth. 21So that land included all the towns on the plain and all the area that Sihon king of the Amorites had ruled from the town of Heshbon. Moses had defeated him along with the leaders of the Midianites, including Evi, Rekem, Zur, Hur, and Reba. All these leaders fought together with Sihon and lived in that country. 22The Israelites killed many people during the fighting, including Balaam of Beor, who tried to use magic to tell the future. 23The land given to Reuben stopped at the shore of the Jordan River. So the land given to the family groups of Reuben included all these towns and their villages that were listed.

24This is the land Moses gave to the tribe of Gad, to all its family groups: 25the land of Jazar and all the towns of Gilead; half the land of the Ammonites that went as far as Aroer near Rabbah; 26the area from Heshbon to Ramath Mizpah and Betonim; the area from Mahanaim to the land of Debir; 27in the valley, Beth Haram, Beth Nimrah, Succoth, and Zaphon, the other land Sihon king of Heshbon had ruled east of the Jordan River and continuing to the end of Lake Galilee. 28All this land went to the family groups of Gad, including all these towns and their villages.

29This is the land Moses had given to East Manasseh. Half of all the family groups in the tribe of Manasseh were given this land: 30The land started at Mahanaim and included all of Bashan and the land ruled by Og king of Bashan; all the towns of Jair in Bashan, sixty cities in all; 31half of Gilead, Ashtaroth, and Edrei, the cities where Og king of Bashan had ruled. All this went to the family of Makir son of Manasseh, and half of all his sons were given this land.

32Moses had given this land to these tribes on the plains of Moab across the Jordan River east of Jericho. 33But Moses had given no land to the tribe of Levi because the LORD, the God of Israel, promised that he himself would be the gift for the Levites.

14 Eleazar the priest, Joshua son of Nun, and the leaders of all the tribes of Israel decided what land to give to the people in the land of Canaan. 2The LORD had commanded Moses long ago how he wanted the people to choose their land. The people of the nine-and-a-half tribes threw lots[d] to decide which land they would receive. 3Moses had already given the two-and-a-half tribes their land east of the Jordan River. But the tribe of Levi was not given any land like the others. 4The sons of Joseph had divided into two tribes — Manasseh and Ephraim. The tribe of Levi was not given any land. It was given only some towns in which to live and pastures for its animals. 5The LORD had told Moses how to give the land to the tribes of Israel, and the Israelites divided the land.

Caleb's Land

6One day some men from the tribe[d] of Judah went to Joshua at Gilgal. Among them was Caleb son of Jephunneh the Kenizzite. He said to Joshua, "You remember what the LORD said at Kadesh Barnea when he was speaking to the prophet Moses about you and me. 7Moses, the LORD's servant, sent me to look at the land where we were going. I was forty years old then. When I came back, I told Moses what I thought about the land. 8The other men who went with me frightened the people, but I fully believed the LORD would allow us to take the land. 9So that day Moses promised me, 'The land where you went will become your land, and your children will own it forever. I will give you that land because you fully believed in the LORD, my God.'

10"Now then, the LORD has kept his promise. He has kept me alive for forty-five years from the time he said this to Moses during the time we all wandered in the desert. Now here I am, eighty-five years old. 11I am still as strong today as I was the day Moses sent me out, and I am just as ready to fight now as I was then. 12So give me the mountain country the LORD promised me that day long ago. Back then you heard that the Anakite[d] people lived there and the cities were large and well protected. But now with the LORD helping me, I will force them out, just as the LORD said."

13Joshua blessed Caleb son of Jephunneh and gave him the city of Hebron as his own. 14Hebron still belongs to the family of Caleb son of Jephunneh the Kenizzite because he had faith and obeyed the LORD, the God of Israel. 15(In the past it was called Kiriath Arba, named for Arba, the greatest man among the Anakites.)

After this there was peace in the land.

Land for Judah

15 The land that was given to the tribe[d] of Judah was divided among all the family groups. It went all the way to the Desert of Zin in the far south, at the border of Edom.

2The southern border of Judah's land started at the south end of the Dead Sea[d] 3and went south of Scorpion Pass to Zin. From there it passed to the south of Kadesh Barnea and continued past Hezron to Addar. From Addar it turned and went to Karka. 4It continued to Azmon, the brook of Egypt, and then to the Mediterranean Sea. This was the southern border.

5The eastern border was the shore of the Dead Sea, as far as the mouth of the Jordan River.

The northern border started at the bay of the sea at the mouth of the Jordan River. 6Then it went to Beth Hoglah and continued north of Beth Arabah to the stone of Bohan son of Reuben. 7Then the northern border went through the Valley of Achor to Debir where it turned toward the north and went to Gilgal. Gilgal is across from the road that goes through Adummim Pass, on the south side of the ravine. The border continued to the waters of En Shemesh and stopped at En Rogel. 8Then it went through the Valley of Ben Hinnom, next to the southern side of the Jebusite city (which is called Jerusalem). There the border went to the top of the hill on the west side of Hinnom Valley, at the northern end of the Valley of Giants. 9From there it went to the spring of the waters of Nephtoah and then it went to the cities near Mount Ephron. There it turned and went toward Baalah, which is called Kiriath Jearim. 10At Baalah the border turned west and went toward Mount Seir. It continued along the north side of Mount Jearim (also called Kesalon) and came to Beth Shemesh. From there it went past Timnah 11to the hill north of Ekron. Then it turned toward Shikkeron and went past Mount Baalah and continued on to Jabneel, ending at the sea.

12The Mediterranean Sea was the western border. Inside these borders lived the family groups of Judah.

13The LORD had commanded Joshua to give Caleb son of Jephunneh part of the land in Judah, so he gave Caleb the town of Kiriath Arba, also called Hebron. (Arba was the father of Anak.[d]) 14Caleb forced out the three Anakite families living in Hebron: Sheshai, Ahiman, and Talmai, the descendants[d] of Anak. 15Then he left there and went to fight against the people living in Debir. (In the past Debir had been called Kiriath Sepher.) 16Caleb said, "I will give Acsah, my daughter, as a wife to the man who attacks and captures the city of Kiriath Sepher." 17Othniel son of Kenaz, Caleb's brother, captured the city, so Caleb gave his daughter Acsah to Othniel to be his wife. 18When Acsah came to Othniel, she told him to ask her father for a field.

So Acsah went to her father. When she got down from her donkey, Caleb asked her, "What do you want?"

19Acsah answered, "Do me a special favor. Since you have given me land in southern Canaan, also give me springs of water." So Caleb gave her the upper and lower springs.

20The tribe of Judah got the land God had promised them. Each family group got part of the land.

21The tribe of Judah got all these towns in the southern part of Canaan near the border of Edom: Kabzeel, Eder, Jagur, 22Kinah, Dimonah, Adadah, 23Kedesh, Hazor, Ithnan, 24Ziph, Telem, Bealoth, 25Hazor Hadattah, Kerioth Hezron (also called Hazor), 26Amam, Shema, Moladah, 27Hazar Gaddah, Heshmon, Beth Pelet, 28Hazar Shual, Beersheba, Biziothiah, 29Baalah, Iim, Ezem, 30Eltolad, Kesil, Hormah, 31Ziklag, Madmannah, Sansannah, 32Lebaoth, Shilhim, Ain, and Rimmon. There were twenty-nine towns and their villages.

33The tribe of Judah got these towns in the western hills: Eshtaol, Zorah, Ashnah, 34Zanoah, En Gannim, Tappuah, Enam, 35Jarmuth, Adullam, Socoh, Azekah, 36Shaaraim, Adithaim, and Gederah (also called Gederothaim). There were fourteen towns and their villages.

37Judah was also given these towns in the western hills: Zenan, Hadashah, Migdal Gad, 38Dilean, Mizpah, Joktheel, 39Lachish, Bozkath, Eglon, 40Cabbon, Lahmas, Kitlish, 41Gederoth, Beth Dagon, Naamah, and Makkedah. There were sixteen towns and their villages.

42Judah was also given these towns in the western hills: Libnah, Ether, Ashan, 43Iphtah, Ashnah, Nezib, 44Keilah, Aczib, and Mareshah. There were nine towns and their villages.

45The tribe of Judah was also given these towns: Ekron and all the small towns and villages near it; 46the area west of Ekron and all the villages and small towns near Ashdod; 47Ashdod and the small towns and villages around it; the villages and small towns around Gaza as far as the brook of Egypt and along the coast of the Mediterranean Sea.

48The tribe of Judah was also given these towns in the mountains: Shamir, Jattir, Socoh, 49Dannah, Kiriath Sannah (also called Debir), 50Anab, Eshtemoh, Anim, 51Goshen, Holon, and Giloh. There were eleven towns and their villages.

52They were also given these towns in the mountains: Arab, Dumah, Eshan, 53Janim, Beth Tappuah, Aphekah, 54Humtah, Kiriath Arba (also called Hebron), and Zior. There were nine towns and their villages.

55Judah was also given these towns in the mountains: Maon, Carmel, Ziph, Juttah, 56Jezreel, Jokdeam, Zanoah, 57Kain, Gibeah, and Timnah. There were ten towns and their villages.

58They were also given these towns in the mountains: Halhul, Beth Zur, Gedor, 59Maarath, Beth Anoth, and Eltekon. There were six towns and their villages.

60The people of Judah were also given the two towns of Rabbah and Kiriath Baal (also called Kiriath Jearim) and their villages.

61Judah was given these towns in the desert:

Beth Arabah, Middin, Secacah, 62Nibshan, the
City of Salt, and En Gedi. There were six towns
and all their villages.

63The army of Judah was not able to force out
the Jebusites living in Jerusalem, so the Jebusites
still live among the people of Judah to this day.

Land for Ephraim and Manasseh

16 This is the land the tribe[d] of Joseph received. It started at the Jordan River near
Jericho and continued to the waters of Jericho,
just east of the city. The border went up from
Jericho to the mountains of Bethel. 2Then it continued from Bethel (also called Luz) to the Arkite
border at Ataroth. 3From there it went west to the
border of the Japhletites and continued to the area
of the Lower Beth Horon. Then it went to Gezer
and ended at the sea.

4So Manasseh and Ephraim, sons of Joseph, received their land.

5This is the land that was given to the family
groups of Ephraim: Their border started at Ataroth Addar in the east, went to Upper Beth Horon, 6and then to the sea. From Micmethath it
turned eastward toward Taanath Shiloh and continued eastward to Janoah. 7Then it went down
from Janoah to Ataroth and to Naarah. It continued until it touched Jericho and stopped at the
Jordan River. 8The border went from Tappuah
west to Kanah Ravine and ended at the sea. This
is all the land that was given to each family group
in the tribe of the Ephraimites. 9Many of the
towns were actually within Manasseh's borders,
but the people of Ephraim got those towns and
their villages. 10The Ephraimites could not force
the Canaanites to leave Gezer, so the Canaanites
still live among the Ephraimites today, but they
became slaves of the Ephraimites.

17 Then land was given to the tribe of Manasseh, Joseph's first son. Manasseh's
first son was Makir, the father of Gilead. Makir
was a great soldier, so the lands of Gilead and
Bashan were given to his family. 2Land was also
given to the other family groups of Manasseh—
Abiezer, Helek, Asriel, Shechem, Hepher, and
Shemida. These were all the other sons of Manasseh son of Joseph.

3Zelophehad was the son of Hepher, who was
the son of Gilead, who was the son of Makir, who
was the son of Manasseh. Zelophehad had no
sons, but he had five daughters, named Mahlah,
Noah, Hoglah, Milcah, and Tirzah. 4They went to
Eleazar the priest and to Joshua son of Nun and
all the leaders. They said, "The LORD told Moses
to give us land like the men received." So Eleazar
obeyed the LORD and gave the daughters some
land, just like the brothers of their father. 5So the
tribe of Manasseh had ten sections of land west of
the Jordan River and two more sections, Gilead
and Bashan, on the east side of the Jordan River.
6The daughters of Manasseh received land just as
the sons did. Gilead was given to the rest of the
families of Manasseh.

7The lands of Manasseh were in the area between Asher and Micmethath, near Shechem.
The border went south to the En Tappuah area,
8which belonged to Manasseh, except for the
town of Tappuah. It was along the border of Manasseh's land and belonged to the sons of
Ephraim. 9The border of Manasseh continued
south to Kanah Ravine. The cities in this area of
Manasseh belonged to Ephraim. Manasseh's border was on the north side of the ravine and went
to the sea. 10The land to the south belonged to
Ephraim, and the land to the north belonged to
Manasseh. The Mediterranean Sea was the western border. The border touched Asher's land on
the north and Issachar's land on the east.

11In the areas of Issachar and Asher, the people
of Manasseh owned these towns: Beth Shan and
its small towns; Ibleam and its small towns; the
people who lived in Dor and its small towns; the
people in Naphoth Dor and its small towns;
the people who lived in Taanach and its small
towns; the people in Megiddo and its small
towns. 12Manasseh was not able to defeat those
cities, so the Canaanites continued to live
there. 13When the Israelites grew strong, they
forced the Canaanites to work for them, although they did not force them to leave the
land.

SIDELIGHT: When we think of nations, we think of united territory. But when the Israelites conquered Canaan, they really only conquered parts of it at first. So they divided the land among the twelve tribes before they really controlled it (Joshua 17:11–13). Later, individual tribes would conquer cities to unite their areas.

14The people from the tribes of Joseph said to
Joshua, "You gave us only one area of land, but
we are many people. Why did you give us only
one part of all the land the LORD gave his people?"

15And Joshua answered them, "If you have too
many people, go up to the forest and make a place
for yourselves to live there in the land of the Perizzites and the Rephaites.[d] The mountain country
of Ephraim is too small for you."

16The people of Joseph said, "It is true. The
mountain country of Ephraim is not enough for
us, but the land where the Canaanites live is dangerous. They are skilled fighters. They have powerful weapons in Beth Shan and all the small

towns in that area, and they are also in the Valley
of Jezreel."
17Then Joshua said to the people of Joseph—to
Ephraim and Manasseh, "There are many of you,
and you have great power. You should be given
more than one share of land. 18You also will have
the mountain country. It is a forest, but you can
cut down the trees and make it a good place to
live. You will own all of it because you will force
the Canaanites to leave the land even though they
have powerful weapons and are strong."

The Rest of the Land Divided

18 All of the Israelites gathered together at
Shiloh where they set up the Meeting
Tent.[d] The land was now under their control.
2But there were still seven tribes[d] of Israel that
had not yet received their land.
3So Joshua said to the Israelites: "Why do you
wait so long to take your land? The LORD, the God
of your ancestors, has given this land to you.
4Choose three men from each tribe, and I will
send them out to study the land. They will describe in writing the land their tribe wants as its
share, and then they will come back to me. 5They
will divide the land into seven parts. The people
of Judah will keep their land in the south, and the
people of Joseph will keep their land in the north.
6You should describe the seven parts of land in
writing and bring what you have written to me.
Then I will throw lots[d] in the presence of the
LORD our God. 7But the Levites do not get any
part of these lands, because they are priests, and
their work is to serve the LORD. Gad, Reuben, and
East Manasseh have received the land promised
to them, which is east of the Jordan River. Moses,
the servant of the LORD, gave it to them."
8So the men who were chosen to map the land
started out. Joshua told them, "Go and study the
land and describe it in writing. Then come back
to me, and I will throw lots in the presence of the
LORD here in Shiloh." 9So the men left and went
into the land. They described in a scroll each
town in the seven parts of the land. Then they
came back to Joshua, who was still at the camp
at Shiloh. 10There Joshua threw lots in the presence of the LORD to choose the lands that should
be given to each tribe.

Land for Benjamin

11The first part of the land was given to the
tribe[d] of Benjamin. Each family group received
some land between the land of Judah and the land
of Joseph. This is the land chosen for Benjamin:
12The northern border started at the Jordan River
and went along the northern edge of Jericho, and
then it went west into the mountains. That
boundary continued until it was just east of Beth
Aven. 13From there it went south to Luz (also
called Bethel) and then down to Ataroth Addar,
which is on the hill south of Lower Beth Horon.
14At the hill to the south of Beth Horon, the
border turned and went south near the western
side of the hill. It went to Kiriath Baal (also called
Kiriath Jearim), a town where people of Judah
lived. This was the western border.
15The southern border started near Kiriath Jearim and went west to the waters of Nephtoah.
16Then it went down to the bottom of the hill,
which was near the Valley of Ben Hinnom, on the
north side of the Valley of Rephaim. The border
continued down the Hinnom Valley just south of
the Jebusite city to En Rogel. 17There it turned
north and went to En Shemesh. It continued to
Geliloth near the Adummim Pass. Then it went
down to the great Stone of Bohan son of Reuben.
18The border continued to the northern part of
Beth Arabah and went down into the Jordan Val
ley. 19From there it went to the northern part of
Beth Hoglah and ended at the north shore of the
Dead Sea,[d] where the Jordan River flows into the
sea. This was the southern border.
20The Jordan River was the border on the eastern side. So this was the land given to the family
groups of Benjamin with the borders on all sides.
21The family groups of Benjamin received these
cities: Jericho, Beth Hoglah, Emek Keziz, 22Beth
Arabah, Zemaraim, Bethel, 23Avvim, Parah, Ophrah, 24Kephar Ammoni, Ophni, and Geba. There
were twelve towns and all their villages.
25The tribe of Benjamin also received Gibeon,
Ramah, Beeroth, 26Mizpah, Kephirah, Mozah,
27Rekem, Irpeel, Taralah, 28Zelah, Haeleph, the
Jebusite city (Jerusalem), Gibeah, and Kiriath.
There were fourteen towns and their villages. All
these areas are the lands the family groups of Benjamin were given.

Land for Simeon

19 The second part of the land was given to
the tribe[d] of Simeon. Each family group
received some of the land inside the area of Judah.
2They received Beersheba (also called Sheba),
Moladah, 3Hazar Shual, Balah, Ezem, 4Eltolad,
Bethul, Hormah, 5Ziklag, Beth Marcaboth, Hazar
Susah, 6Beth Lebaoth, and Sharuhen. There were
thirteen towns and their villages.
7They received the towns of Ain, Rimmon,
Ether, and Ashan, four towns and their villages.
8They also received all the very small areas with
people living in them as far as Baalath Beer (this
is the same as Ramah in southern Canaan). So
these were the lands given to the family groups in
the tribe of Simeon. 9The land of the Simeonites
was taken from part of the land of Judah. Since
Judah had much more land than they needed, the
Simeonites received part of their land.

Land for Zebulun

10The third part of the land was given to the tribe[d] of Zebulun. Each family group of Zebulun received some of the land. The border of Zebulun went as far as Sarid. 11Then it went west to Maralah and came near Dabbesheth and then near Jokneam. 12Then it turned to the east. It went from Sarid to the area of Kisloth Tabor and on to Daberath and to Japhia. 13It continued eastward to Gath Hepher and Eth Kazin, ending at Rimmon. There the border turned and went toward Neah. 14At Neah it turned again and went to the north to Hannathon and continued to the Valley of Iphtah El. 15Inside this border were the cities of Kattath, Nahalal, Shimron, Idalah, and Bethlehem. There were twelve towns and their villages.

16So these are the towns and the villages that were given to the family groups of Zebulun.

Land for Issachar

17The fourth part of the land was given to the tribe[d] of Issachar. Each family group of Issachar received some of the land. 18Their land included Jezreel, Kesulloth, Shunem, 19Hapharaim, Shion, Anaharath, 20Rabbith, Kishion, Ebez, 21Remeth, En Gannim, En Haddah, and Beth Pazzez.

22The border of their land touched the area called Tabor, Shahazumah, and Beth Shemesh and stopped at the Jordan River. There were sixteen towns and their villages.

23These cities and towns were part of the land that was given to the family groups of Issachar.

Land for Asher

24The fifth part of the land was given to the tribe[d] of Asher. Each family group of Asher received some of the land. 25Their land included Helkath, Hali, Beten, Acshaph, 26Allammelech, Amad, and Mishal.

The western border touched Mount Carmel and Shihor Libnath. 27Then it turned east and went to Beth Dagon, touching Zebulun and the Valley of Iphtah El. Then it went north of Beth Emek and Neiel and passed north to Cabul. 28From there it went to Abdon, Rehob, Hammon, and Kanah and continued to Greater Sidon. 29Then the border went back south toward Ramah and continued to the strong, walled city of Tyre. There it turned and went toward Hosah, ending at the sea. This was in the area of Aczib, 30Ummah, Aphek, and Rehob. There were twenty-two towns and their villages.

31These cities and their villages were part of the land that was given to the family groups of Asher.

Land for Naphtali

32The sixth part of the land was given to the tribe[d] of Naphtali. Each family group of Naphtali received some of the land. 33The border of their land started at the large tree in Zaanannim, which is near Heleph. Then it went through Adami Nekeb and Jabneel, as far as Lakkum, and ended at the Jordan River. 34Then it went to the west through Aznoth Tabor and stopped at Hukkok. It went to the area of Zebulun on the south, Asher on the west, and Judah, at the Jordan River, on the east. 35The strong, walled cities inside these borders were called Ziddim, Zer, Hammath, Rakkath, Kinnereth, 36Adamah, Ramah, Hazor, 37Kedesh, Edrei, En Hazor, 38Iron, Migdal El, Horem, Beth Anath, and Beth Shemesh. There were nineteen towns and all their villages.

39The towns and the villages around them were in the land that was given to the family groups of Naphtali.

Land for Dan

40The seventh part of the land was given to the tribe[d] of Dan. Each family group of Dan received some of the land. 41Their land included Zorah, Eshtaol, Ir Shemesh, 42Shaalabbin, Aijalon, Ithlah, 43Elon, Timnah, Ekron, 44Eltekeh, Gibbethon, Baalath, 45Jehud, Bene Berak, Gath Rimmon, 46Me Jarkon, Rakkon, and the area near Joppa.

47(But the Danites had trouble taking their land. They went and fought against Leshem, defeated it, and killed the people who lived there. So the Danites moved into the town of Leshem and changed its name to Dan, because he was the father of their tribe.) 48All of these towns and villages were given to the family groups of Dan.

Land for Joshua

49After the leaders finished dividing the land and giving it to the different tribes,[d] the Israelites gave Joshua son of Nun his land also. 50They gave Joshua the town he asked for, Timnath Serah in the mountains of Ephraim, just as the LORD commanded. He built up the town and lived there.

51So these lands were given to the different tribes of Israel. Eleazar the priest, Joshua son of Nun, and the leaders of each tribe divided up the land by lots at Shiloh. They met in the presence of the LORD at the entrance to the Meeting Tent.[d] Now they were finished dividing the land.

Cities of Safety

20 Then the LORD said to Joshua: 2"Tell the Israelites to choose the special cities of safety,[d] as I had Moses command you to do. 3If a person kills someone accidentally and without meaning to kill him, that person may go to a city of safety to hide. There the killer will be safe from the relative who has the duty of punishing a murderer.

4"When the killer runs to one of those cities, he must stop at the entrance gate, stand there, and

tell the leaders of the people what happened.
Then that person will be allowed to enter the city
and will be given a place to live among them. 5But
if the one who is chasing him follows him to that
city, the leaders of the city must not hand over the
killer. It was an accident. He did not hate him
beforehand or kill him on purpose. 6The killer
must stay in the city until a court comes to a decision and until the high priest dies. Then he may
go back home to the town from which he ran
away."

7So the Israelites chose these cities to be cities
of safety: Kedesh in Galilee in the mountains of
Naphtali; Shechem in the mountains of Ephraim;
Kiriath Arba (also called Hebron) in the mountains of Judah; 8Bezer on the east side of the Jordan River near Jericho in the desert in the land of
Reuben; Ramoth in Gilead in the land of Gad; and
Golan in Bashan in the land of Manasseh. 9Any
Israelite or anyone living among them who killed
someone accidentally was to be allowed to run to
one of these cities of safety. There he would not
be killed, before he was judged, by the relative
who had the duty of punishing a murderer.

Towns for the Levites

21 The heads of the Levite families went to
talk to Eleazar the priest, to Joshua son
of Nun, and to the heads of the families of all the
tribes[d] of Israel. 2At Shiloh in the land of Canaan,
the heads of the Levite families said to them, "The
LORD commanded Moses that you give us towns
where we may live and pastures for our animals."
3So the Israelites obeyed this command of the
LORD and gave the Levite people these towns and
pastures for their own land: 4The Kohath family
groups were part of the tribe of Levi. Some of the
Levites in the Kohath family groups were from the
family of Aaron the priest. To these Levites were
given thirteen towns in the areas of Judah, Simeon, and Benjamin. 5The other family groups of
Kohath were given ten towns in the areas of
Ephraim, Dan, and West Manasseh.

6The people from the Gershon family groups
were given thirteen towns in the land of Issachar,
Asher, Naphtali, and the East Manasseh in Bashan.

7The family groups of Merari were given
twelve towns in the areas of Reuben, Gad, and
Zebulun.

8So the Israelites gave the Levites these towns
and the pastures around them, just as the LORD
had commanded Moses.

9These are the names of the towns that came
from the lands of Judah and Simeon. 10The first
choice of towns was given to the Kohath family
groups of the Levites. 11They gave them Kiriath
Arba, also called Hebron, and all its pastures in
the mountains of Judah. (Arba was the father of
Anak.[d]) 12But the fields and the villages around
Kiriath Arba had been given to Caleb son of Jephunneh.

13So they gave the city of Hebron to the descen-
dants[d] of Aaron (Hebron was a city of safety[d]).
They also gave them the towns of Libnah, 14Jattir,
Eshtemoa, 15Holon, Debir, 16Ain, Juttah, and Beth
Shemesh, and all the pastures around them. Nine
towns were given from these two tribes.

17They also gave the people of Aaron these cities that belonged to the tribe of Benjamin: Gibeon, Geba, 18Anathoth, and Almon. They gave
them these four towns and the pastures around
them.

19So these thirteen towns with their pastures
were given to the priests, who were from the family of Aaron.

20The other Kohathite family groups of the Levites were given these towns from the tribe of
Ephraim: 21Shechem in the mountains of Ephraim
(which was a city of safety), Gezer, 22Kibzaim,
and Beth Horon. There were four towns and their
pastures.

23The tribe of Dan gave them Eltekeh, Gibbethon, 24Aijalon, and Gath Rimmon. There were
four towns and their pastures.

25West Manasseh gave them Taanach and Gath
Rimmon and the pastures around these two
towns.

26So these ten towns and the pastures around
them were given to the rest of the Kohathite family groups.

27The Gershonite family groups of the Levite
tribe were given these towns: East Manasseh
gave them Golan in Bashan, which was a city of
safety, and Be Eshtarah, and the pastures around
these two towns.

28The tribe of Issachar gave them Kishion, Daberath, 29Jarmuth, and En Gannim, and the pastures around these four towns.

30The tribe of Asher gave them Mishal, Abdon,
31Helkath, and Rehob, and the pastures around
these four towns.

32The tribe of Naphtali gave them Kedesh in
Galilee (a city of safety), Hammoth Dor, and Kar-
tan, and the pastures around these three towns.
33So the Gershonite family groups received thirteen towns and the pastures around them.

34The Merarite family groups (the rest of the
Levites) were given these towns: The tribe of Zebulun gave them Jokneam, Kartah, 35Dimnah, and
Nahalal, and the pastures around these four
towns.

36The tribe of Reuben gave them Bezer, Jahaz,
37Kedemoth, and Mephaath, along with the pastures around these four towns.

38The tribe of Gad gave them Ramoth in Gilead
(a city of safety), Mahanaim, 39Heshbon, and Jazer, and the pastures around these four towns.

40So the total number of towns given to the Merarite family groups was twelve.

41A total of forty-eight towns with their pastures in the land of Israel were given to the Levites. 42Each town had pastures around it.

43So the LORD gave the people all the land he had promised their ancestors. The people took the land and lived there. 44The LORD gave them peace on all sides, as he had promised their ancestors. None of their enemies defeated them; the LORD handed all their enemies over to them. 45He kept every promise he had made to the Israelites; each one came true.

Three Tribes Go Home

22 Then Joshua called a meeting of all the people from the tribes[d] of Reuben, Gad, and East Manasseh. 2He said to them, "You have done everything Moses, the LORD's servant, told you to do. You have also obeyed all my commands. 3For a long time you have supported the other Israelites. You have been careful to obey the commands the LORD your God gave you. 4The LORD your God promised to give the Israelites peace, and he has kept his promise. Now you may go back to your homes, to the land that Moses, the LORD's servant, gave you, on the east side of the Jordan River. 5But be careful to obey the teachings and laws Moses, the LORD's servant, gave you: to love the LORD your God and obey his commands, to continue to follow him and serve him the very best you can."

6Then Joshua said good-bye to them, and they left and went away to their homes. 7Moses had given the land of Bashan to East Manasseh. Joshua gave land on the west side of the Jordan River to West Manasseh. And he sent them to their homes and he blessed them. 8He said, "Go back to your homes and your riches. You have many animals, silver, gold, bronze, and iron, and many beautiful clothes. Also, you have taken many things from your enemies that you should divide among yourselves."

9So the people from the tribes of Reuben, Gad, and East Manasseh left the other Israelites at Shiloh in Canaan and went back to Gilead. It was their own land, given to them by Moses as the LORD had commanded.

10The people of Reuben, Gad, and East Manasseh went to Geliloth, near the Jordan River in the land of Canaan. There they built a beautiful altar. 11The other Israelites still at Shiloh heard about the altar these three tribes built at the border of Canaan at Geliloth, near the Jordan River on Israel's side. 12All the Israelites became very angry at these three tribes, so they met together and decided to fight them.

13The Israelites sent Phinehas son of Eleazar the priest to Gilead to talk to the people of Reuben, Gad, and East Manasseh. 14They also sent one leader from each of the ten tribes at Shiloh. Each of them was a leader of his family group of Israelites.

15These leaders went to Gilead to talk to the people of Reuben, Gad, and East Manasseh. They said: 16"All the Israelites ask you: 'Why did you turn against the God of Israel by building an altar for yourselves? You know that this is against God's law. 17Remember what happened at Peor? We still suffer today because of that sin, for which God made many Israelites very sick. 18And now are you turning against the LORD and refusing to follow him?

" 'If you don't stop what you're doing today, the LORD will be angry with everyone in Israel tomorrow. 19If your land is unclean,[d] come over into our land where the LORD's Tent is. Share it with us. But don't turn against the LORD and us by building another altar for the LORD our God. 20Remember how Achan son of Zerah refused to obey the command about what must be completely destroyed. That one man broke God's law, but all the Israelites were punished. Achan died because of his sin, but others also died.' "

21The people from Reuben, Gad, and East Manasseh answered, 22"The LORD is God of gods! The LORD is God of gods! God knows, and we want you to know also. If we have done something wrong, you may kill us. 23If we broke God's law, we ask the LORD himself to punish us. We did not build this altar to offer burnt offerings or grain and fellowship offerings.

24"We did not build it for that reason. We feared that some day your people would not accept us as part of your nation. Then they might say, 'You cannot worship the LORD, the God of Israel. 25The LORD made the Jordan River a border between us and you people of Reuben and Gad. You cannot worship the LORD.' So we feared that your children might make our children stop worshiping the LORD.

26"That is why we decided to build this altar. But it is not for burnt offerings and sacrifices. 27This altar is proof to you and us and to all our children who will come after us that we worship the LORD with our whole burnt offerings, grain, and fellowship offerings. This was so your children would not say to our children, 'You are not the LORD's.'

28"In the future if your children say that, our children can say, 'See the altar made by our ancestors. It is exactly like the LORD's altar, but we do not use it for sacrifices. It shows that we are part of Israel.'

29"Truly, we don't want to be against the LORD or to stop following him by building an altar for burnt offerings, grain offerings, or sacrifices. We know the only true altar to the LORD our God is in front of the Holy Tent.[d]"

30When Phinehas the priest and the ten leaders heard the people of Reuben, Gad, and East Manasseh, they were pleased. 31So Phinehas, son of Eleazar the priest, said, "Now we know the LORD is with us and that you didn't turn against him. Now the Israelites will not be punished by the LORD."

32Then Phinehas and the leaders left the people of Reuben and Gad in Gilead and went back to Canaan where they told the Israelites what had happened. 33They were pleased and thanked God. So they decided not to fight the people of Reuben and Gad and destroy those lands.

34And the people of Reuben and Gad named the altar Proof That We Believe the LORD Is God.

SIDELIGHT: It's okay to worship God anywhere, right? Well, that wasn't always the case. In Joshua's time, Israel only presented its sacrifices at the tabernacle. When three tribes built an altar by the Jordan River, other tribes thought they might sacrifice to a pagan god. They almost went to war, but talked out their differences instead (Joshua 22:9–34).

The Last Words of Joshua

23 The LORD gave Israel peace from their enemies around them. Many years passed, and Joshua grew very old. 2He called a meeting of all the older leaders, heads of families, judges, and officers of Israel. He said, "I am now very old. 3You have seen what the LORD has done to our enemies to help us. The LORD your God fought for you. 4Remember that your people have been given their land between the Jordan River and the Mediterranean Sea in the west, the land I promised to give you. 5The LORD your God will force out the people living there. The LORD will push them out ahead of you. And you will own the land, as he has promised you.

6"Be strong. You must be careful to obey everything commanded in the Book of the Teachings of Moses. Do exactly as it says. 7Don't become friends with the people living among us who are not Israelites. Don't say the names of their gods or make anyone swear by them. Don't serve or worship them. 8You must continue to follow the LORD your God, as you have done in the past.

9"The LORD has forced many great and powerful nations to leave ahead of you. No nation has been able to defeat you. 10With his help, one Israelite could defeat a thousand, because the LORD your God fights for you, as he promised to do. 11So you must be careful to love the LORD your God.

12"If you turn away from the way of the LORD and become friends with these people who are not part of Israel and marry them, 13the LORD your God will not help you defeat your enemies. They will be like traps for you, like whips on your back and thorns in your eyes, and none of you will be left in this good land the LORD your God has given you.

14"It's almost time for me to die. You know and fully believe that the LORD has done great things for you. You know that he has not failed to keep any of his promises. 15Every good promise that the LORD your God made has come true, and in the same way, his other promises will come true. He promised that evil will come to you and that he will destroy you from this good land that he gave you. 16This will happen if you don't keep your agreement with the LORD your God. If you go and serve other gods and worship them, the LORD will become very angry with you. Then none of you will be left in this good land he has given you."

24 Joshua gathered all the tribes[d] of Israel together at Shechem. He called the older leaders, heads of families, judges, and officers of Israel to stand before God.

2Then Joshua said to all the people, "Here's what the LORD, the God of Israel, says to you: 'A long time ago your ancestors lived on the other side of the Euphrates River. Terah, the father of Abraham and Nahor, worshiped other gods. 3But I, the LORD, took your ancestor Abraham from the other side of the river and led him through the land of Canaan. And I gave him many children, including his son Isaac. 4I gave Isaac two sons named Jacob and Esau. I gave the land around the mountains of Edom to Esau, but Jacob and his sons went down to Egypt. 5Then I sent Moses and Aaron to Egypt, where I brought many disasters on the Egyptians. Afterwards I brought you out. 6When I brought your ancestors out of Egypt, they came to the Red Sea,[d] and the Egyptians chased them with chariots and men on horses. 7So the people called out to the LORD. And I brought darkness between you and the Egyptians and made the sea to cover them. You yourselves saw what I did to the army of Egypt. After that, you lived in the desert for a long time.

8" 'Then I brought you to the land of the Amorites, east of the Jordan River. They fought against you, but I handed them over to you. I destroyed them before you, and you took control of that land. 9But the king of Moab, Balak son of Zippor, prepared to fight against the Israelites. The king sent for Balaam son of Beor to curse you, 10but I refused to listen to Balaam. So he asked for good things to happen to you! I saved you and brought you out of his power.

11" 'Then you crossed the Jordan River and came to Jericho, where the people of Jericho fought against you. Also, the Amorites, Perizzites, Canaanites, Hittites, Girgashites, Hivites, and Jebusites fought against you. But I handed them over to you. 12I sent terror ahead of you to force out two Amorite kings. You took the land without using swords and bows. 13I gave you that land where you did not have to work. I gave you cities that you did not have to build. And now you live in that land and in those cities, and you eat from vineyards and olive trees that you did not plant.' "

14Then Joshua said to the people, "Now respect the LORD and serve him fully and sincerely. Throw away the gods that your ancestors worshiped on the other side of the Euphrates River and in Egypt. Serve the LORD. 15But if you don't want to serve the LORD, you must choose for yourselves today whom you will serve. You may serve the gods that your ancestors worshiped when they lived on the other side of the Euphrates River, or you may serve the gods of the Amorites who lived in this land. As for me and my family, we will serve the LORD."

16Then the people answered, "We will never stop following the LORD to serve other gods! 17It was the LORD our God who brought our ancestors out of Egypt. We were slaves in that land, but the LORD did great things for us there. He brought us out and protected us while we traveled through other lands. 18Then he forced out all the people living in these lands, even the Amorites. So we will serve the LORD, because he is our God."

19Then Joshua said, "You are not able to serve the LORD, because he is a holy God and a jealous God. If you turn against him and sin, he will not forgive you. 20If you leave the LORD and serve other gods, he will send you great trouble. The LORD may have been good to you, but if you turn against him, he will destroy you."

21But the people said to Joshua, "No! We will serve the LORD."

22Then Joshua said, "You are your own witnesses that you have chosen to serve the LORD."

The people said, "Yes, we are."

23Then Joshua said, "Now throw away the gods that you have. Love the LORD, the God of Israel, with all your heart."

24Then the people said to Joshua, "We will serve the LORD our God, and we will obey him."

25On that day at Shechem Joshua made an agreement for the people. He made rules and laws for them to follow. 26Joshua wrote these things in the Book of the Teachings of God. Then he took a large stone and set it up under the oak tree near the LORD's Holy Tent.[a]

27Joshua said to all the people, "See this stone! It will remind you of what we did today. It was here the LORD spoke to us today. It will remind you of what happened so you will not turn against your God."

Joshua Dies

28Then Joshua sent the people back to their land.

29After that, Joshua son of Nun died at the age of one hundred ten. 30They buried him in his own land at Timnath Serah, in the mountains of Ephraim, north of Mount Gaash.

31The Israelites served the LORD during the lifetime of Joshua and during the lifetimes of the older leaders who lived after Joshua who had seen what the LORD had done for Israel.

SIDELIGHT: When Joseph's bones were buried (Joshua 24:32), the people didn't dig a grave as we do today. Rather, the bones were probably placed in a family cave or a tomb cut from rock, large enough for several family members.

Joseph Comes Home

32When the Israelites left Egypt, they carried the bones of Joseph with them. They buried them at Shechem, in the land Jacob had bought for a hundred pieces of silver from the sons of Hamor (Hamor was the father of Shechem). This land now belonged to Joseph's children.

33And Eleazar son of Aaron died and was buried at Gibeah in the mountains of Ephraim, which had been given to Eleazar's son Phinehas.

JUDGES

Why Read This Book:

- See how God does not want his people to follow the crowd (Judges 1—2).
- Discover how sin can capture people, but God can set them free if they ask for forgiveness (Judges 3—16).
- Understand how people can become corrupt when they don't follow God (Judges 17—21).

Behind the Scenes:

Working in a fast-food restaurant can be a disaster if the work isn't organized. Fries aren't ready when the burgers are done. The soft-serve ice cream runs empty. Customers receive the wrong orders. During the dinner-hour rush, lettuce can fly, mayonnaise can spill, and tempers can flare as each person tries frantically to catch up.

The chaos of an unorganized fast-food restaurant is similar to the chaos in Israel during the book of Judges. The last verse of the book summarizes what it was like: "In those days Israel did not have a king. Everyone did what seemed right" (Judges 21:25, p. 237).

Under the leadership of Joshua (see the book of Joshua, p. 195), the Israelites

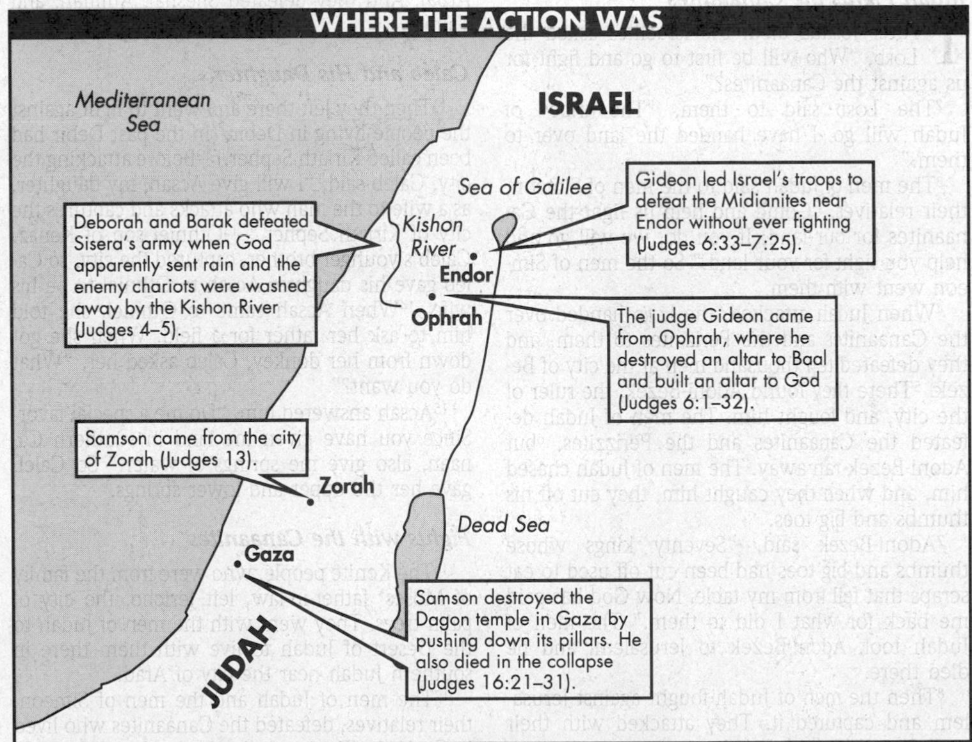
WHERE THE ACTION WAS
Mediterranean Sea
ISRAEL
Sea of Galilee
Gideon led Israel's troops to defeat the Midianites near Endor without ever fighting (Judges 6:33–7:25).
Deborah and Barak defeated Sisera's army when God apparently sent rain and the enemy chariots were washed away by the Kishon River (Judges 4–5).
Kishon River
Endor
Ophrah
The judge Gideon came from Ophrah, where he destroyed an altar to Baal and built an altar to God (Judges 6:1–32).
Samson came from the city of Zorah (Judges 13).
Zorah
Dead Sea
Gaza
Samson destroyed the Dagon temple in Gaza by pushing down its pillars. He also died in the collapse (Judges 16:21–31).
JUDAH

WHEN THE ACTION WAS

2000BC	1500BC	1000BC	500BC	BC/AD
	The Israelites escaped from Egypt; Joshua led the Israelites into Canaan	Saul was Israel's king; The judges led the Israelites in times of trouble		Jesus was born

Behind the Scenes (cont.):

had conquered major Canaanite cities and divided the land among the twelve Israelite tribes. But many Canaanites and other people still remained. They didn't believe in God, but worshiped idols and pagan gods.

These other people threatened the Israelites in two ways. First, they wanted the land back that the Israelites had taken away. So the Israelites constantly had to defend themselves. Second, the Israelites married Canaanites, which God had said not to do; then they accepted the Canaanites' religious practices, forgetting the true God.

Like workers in fast-food restaurants, the Israelites needed leaders to organize them and keep them on track. So in times of crisis, God chose different judges to bring the twelve tribes together to fight their enemies. These judges—such as Deborah, Samson, and Gideon—became national heroes for the Israelites.

Judges illustrates a common theme in the Old Testament. When a judge or leader was faithful to God, the people remained loyal to God and prospered. But when the judge died, the people sinned and were conquered. Then in their suffering, they confessed their sin, and God called a new judge to deliver them. This cycle continued for several generations.

Judges reminds us of the importance of always following God—and the dangers of ignoring God. At the same time, it shows that God is always willing to forgive us when we come back to him.

Judah Fights the Canaanites

1 After Joshua died, the Israelites asked the
LORD, "Who will be first to go and fight for
us against the Canaanites?"
2The LORD said to them, "The tribe[d] of
Judah will go. I have handed the land over to
them."
3The men of Judah said to the men of Simeon,
their relatives, "Come and help us fight the Canaanites for our land. If you do, we will go and
help you fight for your land." So the men of Simeon went with them.
4When Judah attacked, the LORD handed over
the Canaanites and the Perizzites to them, and
they defeated ten thousand men at the city of Bezek. 5There they found Adoni-Bezek, the ruler of
the city, and fought him. The men of Judah defeated the Canaanites and the Perizzites, 6but
Adoni-Bezek ran away. The men of Judah chased
him, and when they caught him, they cut off his
thumbs and big toes.
7Adoni-Bezek said, "Seventy kings whose
thumbs and big toes had been cut off used to eat
scraps that fell from my table. Now God has paid
me back for what I did to them." The men of
Judah took Adoni-Bezek to Jerusalem, and he
died there.
8Then the men of Judah fought against Jerusalem and captured it. They attacked with their
swords and burned the city.
9Later, they went down to fight the Canaanites
who lived in the mountains, in the dry country to
the south, and in the western hills. 10The men of
Judah went to fight against the Canaanites in the
city of Hebron (which used to be called Kiriath
Arba). And they defeated Sheshai, Ahiman, and
Talmai.

Caleb and His Daughter

11Then they left there and went to fight against
the people living in Debir. (In the past Debir had
been called Kiriath Sepher.) 12Before attacking the
city, Caleb said, "I will give Acsah, my daughter,
as a wife to the man who attacks and captures the
city of Kiriath Sepher." 13Othniel son of Kenaz,
Caleb's younger brother, captured the city, so Caleb gave his daughter Acsah to Othniel to be his
wife. 14When Acsah came to Othniel, she told
him to ask her father for a field. When she got
down from her donkey, Caleb asked her, "What
do you want?"
15Acsah answered him, "Do me a special favor.
Since you have given me land in southern Canaan, also give me springs of water." So Caleb
gave her the upper and lower springs.

Fights with the Canaanites

16The Kenite people, who were from the family
of Moses' father-in-law, left Jericho, the city of
palm trees. They went with the men of Judah to
the Desert of Judah to live with them there in
southern Judah near the city of Arad.
17The men of Judah and the men of Simeon,
their relatives, defeated the Canaanites who lived
in Zephath. They completely destroyed the city,
so they called it Hormah.[n] 18The men of Judah
captured Gaza, Ashkelon, Ekron, and the lands
around them.
19The LORD was with the men of Judah. They
took the land in the mountains, but they could

Hormah Hormah sounds like the Hebrew word meaning "to destroy completely."

not force out the people living on the plain, because they had iron chariots. 20As Moses had
promised, Hebron was given to Caleb, and Caleb
forced out the three sons of Anak.[d] 21But the people of Benjamin could not make the Jebusite people leave Jerusalem. Since that time the Jebusites
have lived with the Benjaminites in Jerusalem.
22The men of Joseph went to fight against the
city of Bethel, and the LORD was with them.
23They sent some spies to Bethel (which used to
be called Luz). 24The spies saw a man coming out
of the city and said to him, "Show us a way into
the city, and we will be kind to you." 25So the
man showed them the way into the city. The men
of Joseph attacked with swords the people in
Bethel, but they let the man and his family go
free. 26He went to the land where the Hittites
lived and built a city. He named it Luz, which it
is called even today.
27There were Canaanites living in the cities of
Beth Shan, Taanach, Dor, Ibleam, Megiddo, and
the small towns around them. The people of Manasseh did not force those people out of their
towns, because the Canaanites were determined
to stay there. 28Later, the Israelites grew strong
and forced the Canaanites to work as slaves, but
they did not make all the Canaanites leave their
land. 29The people of Ephraim did not force out
all of the Canaanites living in Gezer. So the Canaanites continued to live in Gezer with the people of Ephraim. 30The people of Zebulun did not
force out the Canaanites living in the cities of Kit-
ron and Nahalol. They stayed and lived with the
people of Zebulun, but Zebulun made them work
as slaves.
31The people of Asher did not force the Canaanites from the cities of Acco, Sidon, Ahlab, Aczib,
Helbah, Aphek, and Rehob. 32Since the people of
Asher did not force them out, the Canaanites continued to live with them. 33The people of Naphtali
did not force out the people of the cities of Beth
Shemesh and Beth Anath. So they continued to
live with the Canaanites in those cities, and the
Canaanites worked as slaves. 34The Amorites
forced the Danites back into the mountains and
would not let them come down to live in the
plain. 35The Amorites were determined to stay in
Mount Heres, Aijalon, and Shaalbim. But when
the Israelites grew stronger, they made the Amorites work as slaves. 36The land of the Amorites
was from Scorpion Pass to Sela and beyond.

The Angel of the Lord at Bokim

2 The angel of the LORD went up from Gilgal
to Bokim and said, "I brought you up from
Egypt and led you to the land I promised to give
your ancestors. I said, 'I will never break my
agreement with you. 2But you must not make an
agreement with the people who live in this land.
You must destroy their altars.' But you did not
obey me. How could you do this? 3Now I tell you,
'I will not force out the people in this land. They
will be your enemies, and their gods will be a trap
for you.' "
4After the angel gave Israel this message from
the LORD, they cried loudly. 5So they named the
place Bokim.[n] There they offered sacrifices to the
LORD.

Joshua Dies

6Then Joshua sent the people back to their
land. 7The people served the LORD during the lifetime of Joshua and during the lifetimes of the
older leaders who lived after Joshua and who had
seen what great things the LORD had done for Israel. 8Joshua son of Nun, the servant of the LORD,
died at the age of one hundred ten. 9They buried
him in his own land at Timnath Serah in the
mountains of Ephraim, north of Mount Gaash.

The People Disobey

10After those people had died, their children
grew up and did not know the LORD or what he
had done for Israel. 11So they did what the LORD
said was wrong, and they worshiped the Baal[d]
idols. 12They quit following the LORD, the God of
their ancestors who had brought them out of
Egypt. They began to worship the gods of the
people who lived around them, and that made
the LORD angry. 13The Israelites quit following the
LORD and worshiped Baal and Ashtoreth.[d] 14The
LORD was angry with the people of Israel, so he
handed them over to robbers who took their possessions. He let their enemies who lived around
them defeat them; they could not protect themselves. 15When the Israelites went out to fight,
they always lost, because the LORD was not with
them. The LORD had sworn to them this would
happen. So the Israelites suffered very much.

> **SIDELIGHT:** The Israelites sinned when they worshiped Baal (Judges 2:11), not only because Baal was a false god, but also because of the religion's worship practices. Archaeologists have found that the Canaanites practiced infant sacrifice and prostitution in their temples. Baal worship included sexual elements intended to make the gods bring rain and fertility.

Bokim This name means "crying."

God Chooses Judges

16Then the LORD chose leaders called judges,[n]
who saved the Israelites from the robbers. 17But
the Israelites did not listen to their judges. They
were not faithful to God but worshiped other gods
instead. Their ancestors had obeyed the LORD's
commands, but they quickly turned away and did
not obey. 18When their enemies hurt them, the
Israelites cried for help. So the LORD felt sorry for
them and sent judges to save them from their enemies. The LORD was with those judges all their
lives. 19But when the judges died, the Israelites
again sinned and worshiped other gods. They became worse than their ancestors. The Israelites
were very stubborn and refused to change their
evil ways.

> **SIDELIGHT:** Judges in the Old Testament wouldn't fit in well in today's court system. Instead of making judgments in court, the ancient judges were leaders in battle and heroes for the people (Judges 2:16). Imagine what that would do to our law schools!

20So the LORD became angry with the Israelites.
He said, "These people have broken the agreement I made with their ancestors. They have not
listened to me. 21I will no longer defeat the nations who were left when Joshua died. 22I will use
them to test Israel, to see if Israel will keep the
LORD's commands as their ancestors did." 23In the
past the LORD had permitted those nations to stay
in the land. He did not quickly force them out or
help Joshua's army defeat them.

3 These are the nations the LORD did not force
to leave. He wanted to test the Israelites who
had not fought in the wars of Canaan. 2(The only
reason the LORD left those nations in the land was
to teach the descendants[d] of the Israelites who
had not fought in those wars how to fight.) 3These
are the nations: the five rulers of the Philistines,
all the Canaanites, the people of Sidon, and the
Hivites who lived in the Lebanon mountains from
Mount Baal Hermon to Lebo Hamath. 4Those nations were in the land to test the Israelites — to
see if they would obey the commands the LORD
had given to their ancestors by Moses.

5The people of Israel lived with the Canaanites,
Hittites, Amorites, Perizzites, Hivites, and Jebusites. 6The Israelites began to marry the daughters
of those people, and they allowed their daughters
to marry the sons of those people. Israel also
served their gods.

Othniel, the First Judge

7The Israelites did what the LORD said was
wrong. They forgot about the LORD their God and
served the idols of Baal[d] and Asherah.[d] 8So the
LORD was angry with Israel and allowed Cushan-
Rishathaim king of Northwest Mesopotamia to
rule over the Israelites for eight years. 9When Israel cried to the LORD, the LORD sent someone to
save them. Othniel son of Kenaz, Caleb's younger
brother, saved the Israelites. 10The Spirit[d] of
the LORD entered Othniel, and he became Israel's judge. When he went to war, the LORD
handed over to him Cushan-Rishathaim king
of Northwest Mesopotamia. 11So the land was
at peace for forty years. Then Othniel son of
Kenaz died.

Ehud, the Judge

12Again the people of Israel did what the LORD
said was wrong. So the LORD gave Eglon king of
Moab power to defeat Israel because of the evil
Israel did. 13Eglon got the Ammonites and the
Amalekites to join him. Then he attacked Israel
and took Jericho, the city of palm trees. 14So the
people of Israel were ruled by Eglon king of Moab
for eighteen years.

15When the people cried to the LORD, he sent
someone to save them. He was Ehud, son of Gera
from the people of Benjamin, who was left-
handed. Israel sent Ehud to give Eglon king of
Moab the payment he demanded. 16Ehud made
himself a sword with two edges, about eighteen
inches long, and he tied it to his right hip under
his clothes. 17Ehud gave Eglon king of Moab the
payment he demanded. Now Eglon was a very fat
man. 18After he had given Eglon the payment,
Ehud sent away the people who had carried it.
19When he passed the statues near Gilgal, he
turned around and said to Eglon, "I have a secret
message for you, King Eglon."

The king said, "Be quiet!" Then he sent all of
his servants out of the room. 20Ehud went to King
Eglon, as he was sitting alone in the room above
his summer palace.

Ehud said, "I have a message from God for
you." As the king stood up from his chair, 21Ehud
reached with his left hand and took out the sword
that was tied to his right hip. Then he stabbed the
sword deep into the king's belly! 22Even the handle sank in, and the blade came out his back. The
king's fat covered the whole sword, so Ehud left
the sword in Eglon. 23Then he went out of the
room and closed and locked the doors behind
him.

24When the servants returned just after Ehud

judges They were not judges in courts of law, but leaders of the people in times of emergency.

left, they found the doors to the room locked. So
they thought the king was relieving himself.
25They waited for a long time. Finally they became worried because he still had not opened the
doors. So they got the key and unlocked them and
saw their king lying dead on the floor!
26While the servants were waiting, Ehud had
escaped. He passed by the statues and went to
Seirah. 27When he reached the mountains of
Ephraim he blew the trumpet. The people of Israel heard it and went down from the hills with
Ehud leading them.
28He said to them, "Follow me! The LORD has
helped you to defeat your enemies, the Moabites." So Israel followed Ehud and captured the
crossings of the Jordan River. They did not allow
the Moabites to cross the Jordan River. 29Israel
killed about ten thousand strong and able men
from Moab; not one escaped. 30So that day Moab
was forced to be under the rule of Israel, and
there was peace in the land for eighty years.

Shamgar, the Judge

31After Ehud, Shamgar son of Anath saved Israel. Shamgar killed six hundred Philistines with
a sharp stick used to guide oxen.

Deborah, the Woman Judge

4 After Ehud died, the Israelites again did
what the LORD said was wrong. 2So he let
Jabin, a king of Canaan who ruled in the city of
Hazor, defeat Israel. Sisera, who lived in Harosheth Haggoyim, was the commander of Jabin's
army. 3Because he had nine hundred iron chariots
and was very cruel to the people of Israel for
twenty years, they cried to the LORD for help.
4A prophetess[d] named Deborah, the wife of
Lappidoth, was judge of Israel at that time. 5Debo-
rah would sit under the Palm Tree of Deborah,
which was between the cities of Ramah and
Bethel, in the mountains of Ephraim. And the
people of Israel would come to her to settle their
arguments.
6Deborah sent a message to Barak son of Abinoam. Barak lived in the city of Kedesh, which is
in the area of Naphtali. Deborah said to Barak,
"The LORD, the God of Israel, commands you:
'Go and gather ten thousand men of Naphtali and
Zebulun and lead them to Mount Tabor. 7I will
make Sisera, the commander of Jabin's army, and
his chariots, and his army meet you at the Kishon
River. I will hand Sisera over to you.' "
8Then Barak said to Deborah, "I will go if you

LEADERSHIP

Pass the Paintbrush

Leonardo da Vinci was one of the greatest artists who has ever lived. In the late 1400s and early 1500s, this Italian genius was revered for his painting, sculpting, architecture, engineering, and inventing.

One day a student walked into da Vinci's studio to find the master working on a huge canvas. He had chosen the subject, planned the perspective, sketched the outline, and begun painting. Then, suddenly, he stopped and asked the student to finish the painting.

The student protested, saying he could never do justice to the great painter's work. He felt he was unworthy to complete such an important job.

Da Vinci cut him off. "Will not what I have done inspire you to do your best?" he asked.

In the same way that da Vinci hoped to encourage his student, Deborah wanted to motivate Barak and the Israelites in battle. Read how she challenged Barak in **Judges 4:4–16**.

- How was da Vinci's challenge to the student similar to Deborah's challenge to Barak?
- How can you use God's power to help you inspire others the way Deborah inspired Barak to overcome a challenge?

CONSIDER . . .

- asking someone you admire for support to deal with a challenge you're facing.
- sending a thank-you note to someone—a parent, a friend, someone at church—who has inspired you in your faith in recent months.

FOR MORE, SEE . . .

- Judges 5:1–31 (p. 220)
- 1 Corinthians 1:10–17 (p. 1168)
- Hebrews 12:1–3 (p. 1289)

will go with me, but if you won't go with me, I
won't go."
9"Of course I will go with you," Deborah answered, "but you will not get credit for the victory. The LORD will let a woman defeat Sisera."
So Deborah went with Barak to Kedesh. 10At Kedesh, Barak called the people of Zebulun and
Naphtali together. From them, he gathered ten
thousand men to follow him, and Deborah went
with him also.
11Now Heber the Kenite had left the other Kenites, the descendants[d] of Hobab, Moses' brother-
in-law. Heber had put up his tent by the great tree
in Zaanannim, near Kedesh.
12When Sisera was told that Barak son of Abinoam had gone to Mount Tabor, 13Sisera gathered
his nine hundred iron chariots and all the men
with him, from Harosheth Haggoyim to the Kishon River.
14Then Deborah said to Barak, "Get up! Today
is the day the LORD will hand over Sisera. The
LORD has already cleared the way for you." So
Barak led ten thousand men down Mount Tabor.
15As Barak approached, the LORD confused Sisera
and his army and chariots. The LORD defeated
them with the sword, but Sisera left his chariot
and ran away on foot. 16Barak and his men chased
Sisera's chariots and army to Harosheth Haggoyim. With their swords they killed all of Sisera's
men; not one of them was left alive.
17But Sisera himself ran away to the tent where
Jael lived. She was the wife of Heber, one of the
Kenite family groups. Heber's family was at peace
with Jabin king of Hazor. 18Jael went out to meet
Sisera and said to him, "Come into my tent, master! Come in. Don't be afraid." So Sisera went
into Jael's tent, and she covered him with a rug.
19Sisera said to Jael, "I am thirsty. Please give
me some water to drink." So she opened a leather
bag of milk and gave him a drink. Then she covered him up.

SIDELIGHT: When Jael gave Sisera milk to drink, it probably wasn't ice cold (Judges 4:19). Because of the hot climate, people often curdled milk to preserve it. The nutritious result (known as kefir) is similar to yogurt. Unfortunately, you couldn't get it with strawberries and bananas mixed in.

20He said to her, "Go stand at the entrance to
the tent. If anyone comes and asks you, 'Is anyone
here?' say, 'No.' "
21But Jael, the wife of Heber, took a tent peg
and a hammer and quietly went to Sisera. Since
he was very tired, he was in a deep sleep. She
hammered the tent peg through the side of Sisera's head and into the ground. And so Sisera
died.
22At that very moment Barak came by Jael's
tent, chasing Sisera. Jael went out to meet him
and said, "Come. I will show you the man you are
looking for." So Barak entered her tent, and there
Sisera lay dead, with the tent peg in his head.
23On that day God defeated Jabin king of Canaan in the sight of Israel.
24Israel became stronger and stronger against
Jabin king of Canaan until finally they destroyed
him.

The Song of Deborah

5 On that day Deborah and Barak son of Abinoam sang this song:

2"The leaders led Israel.
The people volunteered to go to battle.
Praise the LORD!
3Listen, kings.
Pay attention, rulers!
I myself will sing to the LORD.
I will make music to the LORD, the God of
Israel.

4"LORD, when you came from Edom,
when you marched from the land of Edom,
the earth shook,
the skies rained,
and the clouds dropped water.
5The mountains shook before the LORD, the
God of Mount Sinai,
before the LORD, the God of Israel!

6"In the days of Shamgar son of Anath,
in the days of Jael, the main roads were
empty.
Travelers went on the back roads.
7There were no warriors in Israel
until I, Deborah, arose,
until I arose to be a mother to Israel.
8At that time they chose to follow new gods.
Because of this, enemies fought us at our
city gates.
No one could find a shield or a spear
among the forty thousand people of Israel.
9My heart is with the commanders of Israel.
They volunteered freely from among the
people.
Praise the LORD!

10"You who ride on white donkeys
and sit on saddle blankets,
and you who walk along the road, listen!
11Listen to the sound of the singers
at the watering holes.
There they tell about the victories of the
LORD,

the victories of the LORD's warriors in
Israel.
Then the LORD's people went down to the
city gates.

12"Wake up, wake up, Deborah!
Wake up, wake up, sing a song!
Get up, Barak!
Go capture your enemies, son of Abinoam!

13"Then those who were left came down to
the important leaders.
The LORD's people came down to me with
strong men.
14They came from Ephraim in the mountains of
Amalek.
Benjamin was among the people who
followed you.
From the family group of Makir, the
commanders came down.
And from Zebulun came those who lead.
15The princes of Issachar were with Deborah.
The people of Issachar were loyal to Barak
and followed him into the valley.
The Reubenites thought hard
about what they would do.
16Why did you stay by the sheepfold?
Was it to hear the music played for your
sheep?
The Reubenites thought hard
about what they would do.
17The people of Gilead stayed east of the
Jordan River.
People of Dan, why did you stay by the
ships?
The people of Asher stayed at the seashore,
at their safe harbors.
18But the people of Zebulun risked their lives,
as did the people of Naphtali on the
battlefield.

19"The kings came, and they fought.
At that time the kings of Canaan fought
at Taanach, by the waters of Megiddo.
But they took away no silver or possessions
of Israel.
20The stars fought from heaven;
from their paths, they fought Sisera.
21The Kishon River swept Sisera's men away,
that old river, the Kishon River.
March on, my soul, with strength!
22Then the horses' hoofs beat the ground.
Galloping, galloping go Sisera's mighty
horses.
23'May the town of Meroz be cursed,' said the
angel of the LORD.
'Bitterly curse its people,
because they did not come to help the LORD.
They did not fight the strong enemy.'
24"May Jael, the wife of Heber the Kenite,
be blessed above all women who live in
tents.
25Sisera asked for water,
but Jael gave him milk.
In a bowl fit for a ruler,
she brought him cream.
26Jael reached out and took the tent peg.
Her right hand reached for the workman's
hammer.
She hit Sisera! She smashed his head!
She crushed and pierced the side of his
head!
27At Jael's feet he sank.
He fell, and he lay there.
At her feet he sank. He fell.
Where Sisera sank, there he fell, dead!

28"Sisera's mother looked out through the
window.
She looked through the curtains and cried
out,
'Why is Sisera's chariot so late in coming?
Why are sounds of his chariots' horses
delayed?'
29The wisest of her servant ladies answer her,
and Sisera's mother says to herself,
30'Surely they are robbing the people they
defeated!
Surely they are dividing those things among
themselves!
Each soldier is given a girl or two.
Maybe Sisera is taking pieces of dyed cloth.
Maybe they are even taking
pieces of dyed, embroidered cloth for the
necks of the victors!'

31"Let all your enemies die this way, LORD!
But let all the people who love you
be as strong as the rising sun!"

Then there was peace in the land for forty
years.

The Midianites Attack Israel

6 Again the Israelites did what the LORD said
was wrong. So for seven years the LORD
handed them over to Midian. 2Because the Midianites were very powerful and were cruel to Israel, the Israelites made hiding places in the
mountains, in caves, and in safe places. 3When-
ever the Israelites planted crops, the Midianites,
Amalekites, and other peoples from the east
would come and attack them. 4They camped in
the land and destroyed the crops that the Israelites had planted as far away as Gaza. They left
nothing for Israel to eat, and no sheep, cattle, or
donkeys. 5The Midianites came with their tents
and their animals like swarms of locusts[d] to ruin
the land. There were so many people and camels
they could not be counted. 6Israel became very

poor because of the Midianites, so they cried out to the LORD.

7When the Israelites cried out to the LORD against the Midianites, 8the LORD sent a prophet[d] to them. He said, "This is what the LORD, the God of Israel, says: I brought you out of Egypt, the land of slavery. 9I saved you from the Egyptians and from all those who were against you. I forced the Canaanites out of their land and gave it to you. 10Then I said to you, 'I am the LORD your God. Live in the land of the Amorites, but do not worship their gods.' But you did not obey me."

The Angel of the Lord Visits Gideon

11The angel of the LORD came and sat down under the oak tree at Ophrah that belonged to Joash, one of the Abiezrite people. Gideon, Joash's son, was separating some wheat from the chaff[d] in a winepress[d] to keep the wheat from the Midianites. 12The angel of the LORD appeared to Gideon and said, "The LORD is with you, mighty warrior!"

13Then Gideon said, "Sir, if the LORD is with us, why are we having so much trouble? Where are the miracles[d] our ancestors told us he did when the LORD brought them out of Egypt? But now he has left us and has handed us over to the Midianites."

14The LORD turned to Gideon and said, "Go with your strength and save Israel from the Midianites. I am the one who is sending you."

15But Gideon answered, "Lord, how can I save Israel? My family group is the weakest in Manasseh, and I am the least important member of my family."

16The LORD answered him, "I will be with you. It will seem as if the Midianites you are fighting are only one man."

17Then Gideon said to the LORD, "If you are pleased with me, give me proof that it is really you talking with me. 18Please wait here until I come back to you. Let me bring my offering and set it in front of you."

And the LORD said, "I will wait until you return."

19So Gideon went in and cooked a young goat, and with twenty quarts of flour, made bread without yeast. Then he put the meat into a basket and the broth into a pot. He brought them out and gave them to the angel under the oak tree.

20The angel of God said to Gideon, "Put the meat and the bread without yeast on that rock over there. Then pour the broth on them." And Gideon did as he was told. 21The angel of the LORD touched the meat and the bread with the end of the stick that was in his hand. Then fire jumped up from the rock and completely burned up the meat and the bread! And the angel of the LORD disappeared! 22Then Gideon understood he had been talking to the angel of the LORD. So Gideon cried out, "Lord GOD! I have seen the angel of the LORD face to face!"

23But the LORD said to Gideon, "Calm down! Don't be afraid! You will not die!"

24So Gideon built an altar there to worship the LORD and named it The LORD Is Peace. It still stands at Ophrah, where the Abiezrites live.

Gideon Tears Down the Altar of Baal

25That same night the LORD said to Gideon, "Take the bull that belongs to your father and a second bull seven years old. Pull down your father's altar to Baal,[d] and cut down the Asherah[d] idol beside it. 26Then build an altar to the LORD your God with its stones in the right order on this high ground. Kill and burn a second bull on this altar, using the wood from the Asherah idol."

27So Gideon got ten of his servants and did what the LORD had told him to do. But Gideon was afraid that his family and the men of the city might see him, so he did it at night, not in the daytime.

28When the men of the city got up the next morning, they saw that the altar for Baal had been destroyed and that the Asherah idol beside it had been cut down! They also saw the altar Gideon had built and the second bull that had been sacrificed on it. 29The men of the city asked each other, "Who did this?"

After they asked many questions, someone told them, "Gideon son of Joash did this."

30So they said to Joash, "Bring your son out. He has pulled down the altar of Baal and cut down the Asherah idol beside it. He must die!"

31But Joash said to the angry crowd around him, "Are you going to take Baal's side? Are you going to defend him? Anyone who takes Baal's side will be killed by morning! If Baal is a god, let him fight for himself. It's his altar that has been pulled down." 32So on that day Gideon got the name Jerub-Baal, which means "let Baal fight against him," because Gideon pulled down Baal's altar.

Gideon Defeats Midian

33All the Midianites, the Amalekites, and other peoples from the east joined together and came across the Jordan River and camped in the Valley of Jezreel. 34But the Spirit[d] of the LORD entered Gideon, and he blew a trumpet to call the Abiezrites to follow him. 35He sent messengers to all of Manasseh, calling them to follow him. He also sent messengers to the people of Asher, Zebulun, and Naphtali. So they also went up to meet Gideon and his men.

36Then Gideon said to God, "You said you would help me save Israel. 37I will put some wool on the threshing[d] floor. If there is dew only on the

wool but all of the ground is dry, then I will know
that you will use me to save Israel, as you said."
38And that is just what happened. When Gideon
got up early the next morning and squeezed the
wool, he got a full bowl of water from it.
39Then Gideon said to God, "Don't be angry
with me if I ask just one more thing. Please let me
make one more test. Let only the wool be dry
while the ground around it gets wet with dew."
40That night God did that very thing. Just the
wool was dry, but the ground around it was wet
with dew.

7 Early in the morning Jerub-Baal (also called
Gideon) and all his men set up their camp at
the spring of Harod. The Midianites were camped
north of them in the valley at the bottom of the
hill called Moreh. 2Then the LORD said to Gideon,
"You have too many men to defeat the Midianites. I don't want the Israelites to brag that they
saved themselves. 3So now, announce to the people, 'Anyone who is afraid may leave Mount Gilead and go back home.'" So twenty-two thousand men returned home, but ten thousand
remained.
4Then the LORD said to Gideon, "There are still
too many men. Take the men down to the water,
and I will test them for you there. If I say, 'This
man will go with you,' he will go. But if I say,
'That one will not go with you,' he will not go."
5So Gideon led the men down to the water.
There the LORD said to him, "Separate them into
those who drink water by lapping it up like a dog

DOUBT

Conquering Doubt

The ropes course was almost over. A one hundred-foot steel cable—a zip line—swung between two trees. Carol Berry was strapped into the harness fifty feet above the ground, in position to zoom down the line to a soft landing at the other end.

But she wasn't ready—at least not mentally.

Crossing the high beam had been scary enough. "Let me be last," she had pleaded. "I don't want to slow the group down." But everyone knew the real reason she wanted to wait was to build up her own confidence.

Now Carol faced the terrifying free fall down the zip line. Even I'll-go-first Kevin had hesitated. He had stood on the platform five minutes before he gave a horrifying scream and shot down the line. And, one by one, the rest of the group had followed and cheered.

Except Carol. She stood alone on the platform, crying. The group was silent, except for gentle encouragement. "You can do this, Carol. We know you can."

Fifteen minutes passed.

Suddenly, she stepped off the platform and whooshed down the line, so fast it took her breath away.

"I did it!" she shouted with joy when she landed on the ground. "I really did it!"

Carol's friends cheered her accomplishment. "I couldn't have done it without you guys," she finally said. "Thanks for reassuring me."

Just as Carol needed reassurance to help her conquer doubt, Gideon needed assurance that God would be with him as he led the Israelites into battle. Read how he got God's reassurance in **Judges 6:33–40**.

- How was the group's confidence in Carol like God's patience with Gideon?
- When have you wanted to "test" God before trusting him? What did you do? What happened?

CONSIDER . . .

- writing on a sheet of paper a doubt you have about God or the world, then thinking about it through the week. Be alert for new insights as you read the Bible, talk with friends or a parent, or watch television. Whenever you have new insights, jot them down. Then evaluate what you have learned about doubt.
- asking a friend or a parent to tell about a time he or she doubted God. Find out how that person dealt with the doubt and what you can learn from the experience.

FOR MORE, SEE . . .

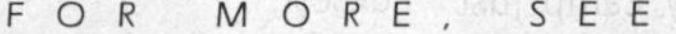
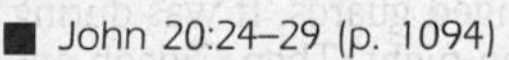

- Genesis 18:1–15 (p. 19)
- John 20:24–29 (p. 1094)
- Matthew 14:22–33 (p. 934)

and those who bend down to drink." 6There were
three hundred men who used their hands to bring
water to their mouths, lapping it as a dog does. All
the rest got down on their knees to drink.
7Then the LORD said to Gideon, "Using the
three hundred men who lapped the water, I will
save you and hand Midian over to you. Let all the
others go home." 8So Gideon sent the rest of Israel to their homes. But he kept three hundred
men and took the jars and the trumpets of those
who left.
Now the camp of Midian was in the valley below Gideon. 9That night the LORD said to Gideon,
"Get up. Go down and attack the camp of the
Midianites, because I will give them to you. 10But
if you are afraid to go down, take your servant
Purah with you. 11When you come to the camp
of Midian, you will hear what they are saying.
Then you will not be afraid to attack the camp."

Gideon Is Encouraged

So Gideon and his servant Purah went down to
the edge of the enemy camp. 12The Midianites,
the Amalekites, and all the peoples from the east
were camped in that valley. There were so many
of them they seemed like locusts.[d] Their camels
could not be counted because they were as many
as the grains of sand on the seashore!
13When Gideon came to the enemy camp, he
heard a man telling his friend about a dream. He
was saying, "I dreamed that a loaf of barley bread
rolled into the camp of Midian. It hit the tent so
hard that the tent turned over and fell flat!"
14The man's friend said, "Your dream is about
the sword of Gideon son of Joash, a man of Israel.
God will hand Midian and the whole army over
to him!"
15When Gideon heard about the dream and
what it meant, he worshiped God. Then Gideon
went back to the camp of Israel and called out to
them, "Get up! The LORD has handed the army of
Midian over to you!" 16Gideon divided the three
hundred men into three groups. He gave each
man a trumpet and an empty jar with a burning
torch inside.
17Gideon told the men, "Watch me and do
what I do. When I get to the edge of the camp,
do what I do. 18Surround the enemy camp. When
I and everyone with me blow our trumpets, you
blow your trumpets, too. Then shout, 'For the
LORD and for Gideon!' "

Midian Is Defeated

19So Gideon and the one hundred men with
him came to the edge of the enemy camp just
after they had changed guards. It was during the
middle watch of the night. Then Gideon and his
men blew their trumpets and smashed their jars.
20All three groups of Gideon's men blew their
trumpets and smashed their jars. They held the
torches in their left hands and the trumpets in
their right hands. Then they shouted, "A sword
for the LORD and for Gideon!" 21Each of Gideon's
men stayed in his place around the camp, but the
Midianites began shouting and running to escape.
22When Gideon's three hundred men blew
their trumpets, the LORD made all the Midianites
fight each other with their swords! The enemy
army ran away to the city of Beth Shittah toward
Zererah. They ran as far as the border of Abel Meholah, near the city of Tabbath. 23Then men of
Israel from Naphtali, Asher, and all of Manasseh
were called out to chase the Midianites. 24Gideon
sent messengers through all the mountains of
Ephraim, saying, "Come down and attack the
Midianites. Take control of the Jordan River as far
as Beth Barah before the Midianites can get to it."
So they called out all the men of Ephraim, who
took control of the Jordan River as far as Beth
Barah. 25The men of Ephraim captured two
princes of Midian named Oreb and Zeeb. They
killed Oreb at the rock of Oreb and Zeeb at the
winepress[d] of Zeeb, and they continued chasing
the Midianites. They brought the heads of Oreb
and Zeeb to Gideon, who was east of the Jordan
River.

8 The men of Ephraim asked Gideon, "Why
did you treat us this way? Why didn't you
call us when you went to fight against Midian?"
They argued angrily with Gideon.
2But he answered them, "I have not done as
well as you! The small part you did was better
than all that my people of Abiezer did. 3God let
you capture Oreb and Zeeb, the princes of Midian. How can I compare what I did with what you
did?" When the men of Ephraim heard Gideon's
answer, they were not as angry anymore.

Gideon Captures Two Kings

4When Gideon and his three hundred men
came to the Jordan River, they were tired, but
they chased the enemy across to the other side.
5Gideon said to the men of Succoth, "Please give
my soldiers some bread because they are very
tired. I am chasing Zebah and Zalmunna, the
kings of Midian."
6But the leaders of Succoth said, "Why should
we give your soldiers bread? You haven't caught
Zebah and Zalmunna yet."
7Then Gideon said, "The LORD will surrender
Zebah and Zalmunna to me. After that, I will
whip your skin with thorns and briers from the
desert."
8Gideon left Succoth and went to the city of
Peniel and asked them for food. But the people of
Peniel gave him the same answer as the people of
Succoth. 9So Gideon said to the men of Peniel,

"After I win the victory, I will return and pull down this tower."

10Zebah and Zalmunna and their army were in the city of Karkor. About fifteen thousand men were left of the armies of the peoples of the east. Already one hundred twenty thousand soldiers had been killed. 11Gideon went up the road of those who live in tents east of Nobah and Jogbehah, and he attacked the enemy army when they did not expect it. 12Zebah and Zalmunna, the kings of Midian, ran away, but Gideon chased and captured them and frightened away their army.

13Then Gideon son of Joash returned from the battle by the Pass of Heres. 14Gideon captured a young man from Succoth and asked him some questions. So the young man wrote down for Gideon the names of seventy-seven officers and older leaders of Succoth.

Gideon Punishes Succoth

15When Gideon came to Succoth, he said to the people of that city, "Here are Zebah and Zalmunna. You made fun of me by saying, 'Why should we give bread to your tired men? You have not caught Zebah and Zalmunna yet.' " 16So Gideon took the older leaders of the city and punished them with thorns and briers from the desert. 17He also pulled down the tower of Peniel and killed the people in that city.

18Gideon asked Zebah and Zalmunna, "What were the men like that you killed on Mount Tabor?"

They answered, "They were like you. Each one of them looked like a prince."

19Gideon said, "Those were my brothers, my mother's sons. As surely as the LORD lives, I would not kill you if you had spared them." 20Then Gideon said to Jether, his oldest son, "Kill them." But Jether was only a boy and was afraid, so he did not take out his sword.

21Then Zebah and Zalmunna said to Gideon, "Come on. Kill us yourself. As the saying goes, 'It takes a man to do a man's job.' " So Gideon got up and killed Zebah and Zalmunna and took the decorations off their camels' necks.

Gideon Makes an Idol

22The people of Israel said to Gideon, "You saved us from the Midianites. Now, we want you and your son and your grandson to rule over us."

23But Gideon told them, "The LORD will be your ruler. I will not rule over you, nor will my son rule over you." 24He said, "I want you to do this one thing for me. I want each of you to give me a gold earring from the things you took in the fighting." (The Ishmaelites[n] wore gold earrings.)

25They said, "We will gladly give you what you want." So they spread out a coat, and everyone threw down an earring from what he had taken. 26The gold earrings weighed about forty-three pounds. This did not count the decorations, necklaces, and purple robes worn by the kings of Midian, nor the chains from the camels' necks. 27Gideon used the gold to make a holy vest, which he put in his hometown of Ophrah. But all the Israelites were unfaithful to God and worshiped it, so it became a trap for Gideon and his family.

SIDELIGHT: People today wear earrings for decoration, but that has not always been the only reason. Three thousand years ago, people also wore earrings because they thought they had magical power—which may be one reason the Israelites took away the Ishmaelites' earrings in battle (Judges 8:23–27).

The Death of Gideon

28So Midian was under the rule of Israel; they did not cause trouble anymore. And the land had peace for forty years, as long as Gideon was alive.

29Gideon[n] son of Joash went to his home to live. 30He had seventy sons of his own, because he had many wives. 31He had a slave woman[d] who lived in Shechem, and he had a son by her, whom he named Abimelech. 32So Gideon son of Joash died at a good old age. He was buried in the tomb of Joash, his father, in Ophrah, where the Abiezrites live.

33As soon as Gideon died, the people of Israel were again unfaithful to God and followed the Baals.[d] They made Baal-Berith their god. 34The Israelites did not remember the LORD their God, who had saved them from all their enemies living all around them. 35And they were not kind to the family of Jerub-Baal, also called Gideon, for all the good he had done for Israel.

Abimelech Becomes King

9 Abimelech son of Gideon[n] went to his uncles in the city of Shechem. He said to his uncles and all of his mother's family group, 2"Ask the leaders of Shechem, 'Is it better for the seventy sons of Gideon to rule over you or for one man to rule?' Remember, I am your relative."

3Abimelech's uncles spoke to all the leaders of Shechem about this. And they decided to follow Abimelech, because they said, "He is our relative." 4So the leaders of Shechem gave Abimelech

Ishmaelites Another name for the Midianites. See Genesis 37:25-28.
Gideon Also called Jerub-Baal.

about one and three-quarter pounds of silver from the temple of the god Baal-Berith. Abimelech used the silver to hire some worthless, reckless men, who followed him wherever he went. 5He went to Ophrah, the hometown of his father, and murdered his seventy brothers, the sons of Gideon. He killed them all on one stone. But Gideon's youngest son, Jotham, hid from Abimelech and escaped. 6Then all of the leaders of Shechem and Beth Millo gathered beside the great tree standing in Shechem. There they made Abimelech their king.

Jotham's Story

7When Jotham heard this, he went and stood on the top of Mount Gerizim. He shouted to the people: "Listen to me, you leaders of Shechem, so that God will listen to you! 8One day the trees decided to appoint a king to rule over them. They said to the olive tree, 'You be king over us!'

9"But the olive tree said, 'Men and gods are honored by my oil. Should I stop making it and go and sway over the other trees?'

10"Then the trees said to the fig tree, 'Come and be king over us!'

11"But the fig tree answered, 'Should I stop making my sweet and good fruit and go and sway over the other trees?'

12"Then the trees said to the vine, 'Come and be king over us!'

13"But the vine answered, 'My new wine makes men and gods happy. Should I stop making it and go and sway over the trees?'

14"Then all the trees said to the thornbush, 'Come and be king over us.'

15"But the thornbush said to the trees, 'If you really want to appoint me king over you, come and find shelter in my shade! But if not, let fire come out of the thornbush and burn up the cedars of Lebanon!'

16"Now, were you completely honest and sincere when you made Abimelech king? Have you been fair to Gideon[n] and his family? Have you treated Gideon as you should? 17Remember, my father fought for you and risked his life to save you from the power of the Midianites. 18But now you have turned against my father's family and have killed his seventy sons on one stone. You have made Abimelech, the son of my father's slave girl, king over the leaders of Shechem just because he is your relative! 19So then, if you have been honest and sincere to Gideon and his family today, be happy with Abimelech as your king. And may he be happy with you! 20But if not, may fire come out of Abimelech and completely burn you leaders of Shechem and Beth Millo! Also may fire come out of the leaders of Shechem and Beth Millo and burn up Abimelech!"

21Then Jotham ran away and escaped to the city of Beer. He lived there because he was afraid of his brother Abimelech.

Abimelech Fights Against Shechem

22Abimelech ruled Israel for three years. 23Then God sent an evil spirit to make trouble between Abimelech and the leaders of Shechem so that the leaders of Shechem turned against him. 24Abimelech had killed Gideon's[n] seventy sons, his own brothers, and the leaders of Shechem had helped him. So God sent the evil spirit to punish them. 25The leaders of Shechem were against Abimelech then. They put men on the hilltops in ambush who robbed everyone going by. And Abimelech was told.

26A man named Gaal son of Ebed and his brothers moved into Shechem, and the leaders of Shechem trusted him. 27They went out to the vineyards to pick grapes, and they squeezed the grapes. Then they had a feast in the temple of their god, where they ate and drank and cursed Abimelech. 28Gaal son of Ebed said, "We are the men of Shechem. Who is Abimelech that we should serve him? Isn't he one of Gideon's sons, and isn't Zebul his officer? We should serve the men of Hamor, Shechem's father. Why should we serve Abimelech? 29If you made me commander of these people, I would get rid of Abimelech. I would say to him, 'Get your army ready and come out to battle.' "

30Now when Zebul, the ruler of Shechem, heard what Gaal son of Ebed said, he was very angry. 31He sent secret messengers to Abimelech, saying, "Gaal son of Ebed and Gaal's brothers have come to Shechem, and they are turning the city against you! 32You and your men should get up during the night and hide in the fields outside the city. 33As soon as the sun comes up in the morning, attack the city. When Gaal and his men come out to fight you, do what you can to them."

34So Abimelech and all his soldiers got up during the night and hid near Shechem in four groups. 35Gaal son of Ebed went out and was standing at the entrance to the city gate. As he was standing there, Abimelech and his soldiers came out of their hiding places.

36When Gaal saw the soldiers, he said to Zebul, "Look! There are people coming down from the mountains!"

But Zebul said, "You are seeing the shadows of the mountains. The shadows just look like people."

37But again Gaal said, "Look, there are people coming down from the center of the land, and

Gideon Also called Jerub-Baal.

there is a group coming from the fortune-tellers' tree!"

38Zebul said to Gaal, "Where is your bragging now? You said, 'Who is Abimelech that we should serve him?' You made fun of these men. Now go out and fight them."

39So Gaal led the men of Shechem out to fight Abimelech. 40Abimelech and his men chased them, and many of Gaal's men were killed before they could get back to the city gate. 41While Abimelech stayed at Arumah, Zebul forced Gaal and his brothers to leave Shechem.

42The next day the people of Shechem went out to the fields. When Abimelech was told about it, 43he separated his men into three groups and hid them in the fields. When he saw the people coming out of the city, he jumped up and attacked them. 44Abimelech and his group ran to the entrance gate to the city. The other two groups ran out to the people in the fields and struck them down. 45Abimelech and his men fought the city of Shechem all day until they captured it and killed its people. Then he tore it down and threw salt[n] over the ruins.

The Tower of Shechem Burns

46When the leaders who were in the Tower of Shechem heard what had happened to Shechem, they gathered in the safest room of the temple of El Berith. 47Abimelech heard that all the leaders of the Tower of Shechem had gathered there. 48So he and all his men went up Mount Zalmon, near Shechem. Abimelech took an ax and cut some branches and put them on his shoulders. He said to all those with him, "Hurry! Do what I have done!" 49So all those men cut branches and followed Abimelech and piled them against the safest room of the temple. Then they set them on fire and burned the people inside. So all the people who were at the Tower of Shechem also died—about a thousand men and women.

Abimelech's Death

50Then Abimelech went to the city of Thebez. He surrounded the city, attacked it, and captured it. 51But inside the city was a strong tower, so all the men, women, and leaders of that city ran to the tower. When they got inside, they locked the door behind them. Then they climbed up to the roof of the tower. 52Abimelech came to the tower to attack it. He approached the door of the tower to set it on fire, 53but as he came near, a woman dropped a grinding stone on his head, crushing his skull.

54He quickly called to the officer who carried his armor and said, "Take out your sword and kill me. I don't want people to say, 'A woman killed Abimelech.'" So the officer stabbed Abimelech, and he died. 55When the people of Israel saw Abimelech was dead, they all returned home.

56In that way God punished Abimelech for all the evil he had done to his father by killing his seventy brothers. 57God also punished the men of Shechem for the evil they had done. So the curse spoken by Jotham, the youngest son of Gideon,[n] came true.

Tola, the Judge

10 After Abimelech died, another judge came to save Israel. He was Tola son of Puah, the son of Dodo. Tola was from the people of Issachar and lived in the city of Shamir in the mountains of Ephraim. 2Tola was a judge for Israel for twenty-three years. Then he died and was buried in Shamir.

Jair, the Judge

3After Tola died, Jair from the region of Gilead became judge. He was a judge for Israel for twenty-two years. 4Jair had thirty sons, who rode thirty donkeys. These thirty sons controlled thirty towns in Gilead, which are called the Towns of Jair to this day. 5Jair died and was buried in the city of Kamon.

The Ammonites Trouble Israel

6Again the Israelites did what the LORD said was wrong. They worshiped Baal[d] and Ashtoreth,[d] the gods of Aram, Sidon, Moab, and Ammon, and the gods of the Philistines. The Israelites left the LORD and stopped serving him. 7So the LORD was angry with them and handed them over to the Philistines and the Ammonites. 8In the same year those people destroyed the Israelites who lived east of the Jordan River in the region of Gilead, where the Amorites lived. So the Israelites suffered for eighteen years. 9The Ammonites then crossed the Jordan River to fight the people of Judah, Benjamin, and Ephraim, causing much trouble to the people of Israel. 10So the Israelites cried out to the LORD, "We have sinned against you. We left our God and worshiped the Baal idols."

11The LORD answered the Israelites, "When the Egyptians, Amorites, Ammonites, Philistines, 12Sidonians, Amalekites, and Maonites were cruel to you, you cried out to me, and I saved you. 13But now you have left me again and have worshiped other gods. So I refuse to save you again. 14You have chosen those gods. So go call to them for help. Let them save you when you are in trouble."

15But the people of Israel said to the LORD, "We

salt The salt would keep crops from growing there.
Gideon Also called Jerub-Baal.

have sinned. Do to us whatever you want, but please save us today!" 16Then the Israelites threw away the foreign gods among them, and they worshiped the LORD again. So he felt sorry for them when he saw their suffering.

17The Ammonites gathered for war and camped in Gilead. The Israelites gathered and camped at Mizpah. 18The leaders of the people of Gilead said, "Who will lead us to attack the Ammonites? He will become the head of all those who live in Gilead."

Jephthah Is Chosen as Leader

11 Jephthah was a strong soldier from Gilead. His father was named Gilead, and his mother was a prostitute.[d] 2Gilead's wife had several sons. When they grew up, they forced Jephthah to leave his home, saying to him, "You will not get any of our father's property, because you are the son of another woman." 3So Jephthah ran away from his brothers and lived in the land of Tob. There some worthless men began to follow him.

4After a time the Ammonites fought against Israel. 5When the Ammonites made war against Israel, the older leaders of Gilead went to Jephthah to bring him back from Tob. 6They said to him, "Come and lead our army so we can fight the Ammonites."

7But Jephthah said to them, "Didn't you hate me? You forced me to leave my father's house. Why are you coming to me now that you are in trouble?"

8The older leaders of Gilead said to Jephthah, "It is because of those troubles that we come to you now. Please come with us and fight against the Ammonites. You will be the ruler over everyone who lives in Gilead."

9Then Jephthah answered, "If you take me back to Gilead to fight the Ammonites and the LORD helps me win, I will be your ruler."

10The older leaders of Gilead said to him, "The LORD is listening to everything we are saying. We promise to do all that you tell us to do." 11So Jephthah went with the older leaders of Gilead, and the people made him their leader and commander of their army. Jephthah repeated all of his words in front of the LORD at Mizpah.

Jephthah Sends Messengers to the Ammonite King

12Jephthah sent messengers to the king of the Ammonites, asking, "What have you got against Israel? Why have you come to attack our land?"

13The king of the Ammonites answered the messengers of Jephthah, "We are fighting Israel because you took our land when you came up from Egypt. You took our land from the Arnon River to the Jabbok River to the Jordan River. Now give our land back to us peacefully."

14Jephthah sent the messengers to the Ammonite king again. 15They said:

"This is what Jephthah says: Israel did not take the land of the people of Moab or Ammon. 16When the Israelites came out of Egypt, they went into the desert to the Red Sea and then to Kadesh. 17Israel sent messengers to the king of Edom, saying, 'Let the people of Israel go across your land.' But the king of Edom refused. We sent the same message to the king of Moab, but he also refused. So the Israelites stayed at Kadesh.

18"Then the Israelites went into the desert around the borders of the lands of Edom and Moab. Israel went east of the land of Moab and camped on the other side of the Arnon River, the border of Moab. They did not cross it to go into the land of Moab.

19"Then Israel sent messengers to Sihon king of the Amorites, king of the city of Heshbon, asking, 'Let the people of Israel pass through your land to go to our land.' 20But Sihon did not trust the Israelites to cross his land. So he gathered all of his people and camped at Jahaz and fought with Israel.

21"But the LORD, the God of Israel, handed Sihon and his army over to Israel. All the land of the Amorites became the property of Israel. 22So Israel took all the land of the Amorites from the Arnon River to the Jabbok River, from the desert to the Jordan River.

23"It was the LORD, the God of Israel, who forced out the Amorites ahead of the people of Israel. So do you think you can make them leave? 24Take the land that your god Chemosh[d] has given you. We will live in the land the LORD our God has given us!

25"Are you any better than Balak son of Zippor, king of Moab? Did he ever quarrel or fight with the people of Israel? 26For three hundred years the Israelites have lived in Heshbon and Aroer and the towns around them and in all the cities along the Arnon River. Why have you not taken these cities back in all that time? 27I have not sinned against you, but you are sinning against me by making war on me. May the LORD, the Judge, decide whether the Israelites or the Ammonites are right."

28But the king of the Ammonites ignored this message from Jephthah.

Jephthah's Promise

29Then the Spirit[d] of the LORD entered Jephthah. Jephthah passed through Gilead and Manasseh and the city of Mizpah in Gilead to the land of the Ammonites. 30Jephthah made a promise to the LORD, saying, "If you will hand over the Ammonites to me, 31I will give you as a burnt offering the first thing that comes out of my house to meet me when I return from the victory. It will be the LORD's."

32Then Jephthah went over to fight the Ammonites, and the LORD handed them over to him. 33In a great defeat Jephthah struck them down from the city of Aroer to the area of Minnith, and twenty cities as far as the city of Abel Keramim. So the Ammonites were defeated by the Israelites.

34When Jephthah returned to his home in Mizpah, his daughter was the first one to come out to meet him, playing a tambourine[d] and dancing. She was his only child; he had no other sons or daughters. 35When Jephthah saw his daughter, he tore his clothes to show his sorrow. He said, "My daughter! You have made me so sad because I made a promise to the LORD, and I cannot break it!"

36Then his daughter said, "Father, you made a promise to the LORD. So do to me just what you promised, because the LORD helped you defeat your enemies, the Ammonites." 37She also said, "But let me do one thing. Let me be alone for two months to go to the mountains. Since I will never marry, let me and my friends go and cry together."

38Jephthah said, "Go." So he sent her away for two months. She and her friends stayed in the mountains and cried for her because she would never marry. 39After two months she returned to her father, and Jephthah did to her what he had promised. Jephthah's daughter never had a husband.

From this came a custom in Israel that 40every year the young women of Israel would go out for four days to remember the daughter of Jephthah from Gilead.

> **SIDELIGHT:** Have you ever made a promise you later regretted? Judge Jephthah did. He promised to sacrifice the first thing that came out of his house after battle. Jephthah may have expected to see an animal, since houses in that day often included space for cattle. But when his only daughter appeared, he tore his clothes in sorrow (Judges 11:30–40).

Jephthah and Ephraim

12 The men of Ephraim called all their soldiers together and crossed the river to the town of Zaphon. They said to Jephthah, "Why didn't you call us to help you fight the Ammonites? We will burn your house down with you in it."

2Jephthah answered them, "My people and I fought a great battle against the Ammonites. I called you, but you didn't come to help me. 3When I saw that you would not help me, I risked my own life and went against the Ammonites. The LORD handed them over to me. So why have you come to fight against me today?"

4Then Jephthah called the men of Gilead together and fought the men of Ephraim. The men of Gilead struck them down because the Ephraimites had said, "You men of Gilead are nothing but deserters from Ephraim—living between Ephraim and Manasseh." 5The men of Gilead captured the crossings of the Jordan River that led to the country of Ephraim. A person from Ephraim trying to escape would say, "Let me cross the river." Then the men of Gilead would ask him, "Are you from Ephraim?" If he replied no, 6they would say to him, "Say the word 'Shibboleth.'" The men of Ephraim could not say that word correctly. So if the person from Ephraim said, "Sibboleth," the men of Gilead would kill him at the crossing. So forty-two thousand people from Ephraim were killed at that time.

7Jephthah was a judge for Israel for six years. Then Jephthah, the man from Gilead, died and was buried in a town in Gilead.

Ibzan, the Judge

8After Jephthah died, Ibzan from Bethlehem was a judge for Israel. 9He had thirty sons and thirty daughters. He let his daughters marry men who were not in his family group, and he brought thirty women who were not in his tribe[d] to be wives for his sons. Ibzan judged Israel for seven years. 10Then he died and was buried in Bethlehem.

Elon, the Judge

11After Ibzan died, Elon from the tribe[d] of Zebulun was a judge for Israel. He judged Israel for ten years. 12Then Elon, the man of Zebulun, died and was buried in the city of Aijalon in the land of Zebulun.

Abdon, the Judge

13After Elon died, Abdon son of Hillel from the city of Pirathon was a judge for Israel. 14He had forty sons and thirty grandsons, who rode on seventy donkeys. He judged Israel for eight years. 15Then Abdon son of Hillel died and was buried in Pirathon in the land of Ephraim, in the mountains where the Amalekites lived.

The Birth of Samson

13 Again the people of Israel did what the LORD said was wrong. So he handed them over to the Philistines for forty years.

2There was a man named Manoah from the tribe[d] of Dan, who lived in the city of Zorah. He had a wife, but she could not have children. 3The angel of the LORD appeared to Manoah's wife and said, "You have not been able to have children, but you will become pregnant and give birth to a son. 4Be careful not to drink wine or beer or eat anything that is unclean,[d] 5because you will become pregnant and have a son. You must never cut his hair, because he will be a Nazirite,[d] given to God from birth. He will begin to save Israel from the power of the Philistines."

6Then Manoah's wife went to him and told him what had happened. She said, "A man from God came to me. He looked like an angel from God; his appearance was frightening. I didn't ask him where he was from, and he didn't tell me his name. 7But he said to me, 'You will become pregnant and will have a son. Don't drink wine or beer or eat anything that is unclean, because the boy will be a Nazirite to God from his birth until the day of his death.' "

8Then Manoah prayed to the LORD: "Lord, I beg you to let the man of God come to us again. Let him teach us what we should do for the boy who will be born to us."

9God heard Manoah's prayer, and the angel of God came to Manoah's wife again while she was sitting in the field. But her husband Manoah was not with her. 10So she ran to tell him, "He is here! The man who appeared to me the other day is here!"

11Manoah got up and followed his wife. When he came to the man, he said, "Are you the man who spoke to my wife?"

The man said, "I am."

12So Manoah asked, "When what you say happens, what kind of life should the boy live? What should he do?"

13The angel of the LORD said, "Your wife must be careful to do everything I told her to do. 14She must not eat anything that grows on a grapevine, or drink any wine or beer, or eat anything that is unclean. She must do everything I have commanded her."

15Manoah said to the angel of the LORD, "We would like you to stay awhile so we can cook a young goat for you."

16The angel of the LORD answered, "Even if I stay awhile, I would not eat your food. But if you want to prepare something, offer a burnt offering to the LORD." (Manoah did not understand that the man was really the angel of the LORD.)

17Then Manoah asked the angel of the LORD, "What is your name? Then we will honor you when what you have said really happens."

18The angel of the LORD said, "Why do you ask my name? It is too amazing for you to understand." 19So Manoah sacrificed a young goat on a rock and offered some grain as a gift to the LORD. Then an amazing thing happened as Manoah and his wife watched. 20The flames went up to the sky from the altar. As the fire burned, the angel of the LORD went up to heaven in the flame. When Manoah and his wife saw that, they bowed facedown on the ground. 21The angel of the LORD did not appear to them again. Then Manoah understood that the man was really the angel of the LORD. 22Manoah said, "We have seen God, so we will surely die."

23But his wife said to him, "If the LORD wanted to kill us, he would not have accepted our burnt offering or grain offering. He would not have shown us all these things or told us all this."

24So the woman gave birth to a boy and named him Samson. He grew, and the LORD blessed him. 25The Spirit[d] of the LORD began to work in Samson while he was in the city of Mahaneh Dan, between the cities of Zorah and Eshtaol.

Samson's First Marriage

14 Samson went down to the city of Timnah where he saw a Philistine woman. 2When he returned home, he said to his father and mother, "I saw a Philistine woman in Timnah. I want you to get her for me so I can marry her."

3His father and mother answered, "Surely there is a woman from Israel you can marry. Do you have to marry a woman from the Philistines, who are not circumcised?"[d]

But Samson said, "Get that woman for me! She is the one I want!" 4(Samson's parents did not know that the LORD wanted this to happen because he was looking for a way to challenge the Philistines, who were ruling over Israel at this time.) 5Samson went down with his father and mother to Timnah, as far as the vineyard near there. Suddenly, a young lion came roaring toward Samson! 6The Spirit[d] of the LORD entered Samson with great power, and he tore the lion apart with his bare hands. For him it was as easy as tearing apart a young goat. But Samson did not tell his father or mother what he had done. 7Then he went down to the city and talked to the Philistine woman, and he liked her.

8Several days later Samson went back to marry her. On his way he went over to look at the body of the dead lion and found a swarm of bees and honey in it. 9Samson got some of the honey with his hands and walked along eating it. When he came to his parents, he gave some to them. They ate it, too, but Samson did not tell them he had taken the honey from the body of the dead lion.

10Samson's father went down to see the Philistine woman. And Samson gave a feast, as was the custom for the bridegroom. 11When the people saw him, they sent thirty friends to be with him.

Samson's Riddle

12Samson said to them, "Let me tell you a riddle. Try to find the answer during the seven days of the feast. If you can, I will give you thirty linen shirts and thirty changes of clothes. 13But if you can't, you must give me thirty linen shirts and thirty changes of clothes."

So they said, "Tell us your riddle so we can hear it."

14Samson said,

"Out of the eater comes something to eat.
  Out of the strong comes something sweet."

After three days, they had not found the answer.

15On the fourth[n] day they said to Samson's wife, "Did you invite us here to make us poor? Trick your husband into telling us the answer to the riddle. If you don't, we will burn you and everyone in your father's house."

16So Samson's wife went to him, crying, and said, "You hate me! You don't really love me! You told my people a riddle, but you won't tell me the answer."

Samson said, "I haven't even told my father or mother. Why should I tell you?"

17Samson's wife cried for the rest of the seven days of the feast. So he finally gave her the answer on the seventh day, because she kept bothering him. Then she told her people the answer to the riddle.

18Before sunset on the seventh day of the feast, the Philistine men had the answer. They came to Samson and said,

"What is sweeter than honey?
  What is stronger than a lion?"

Then Samson said to them,

"If you had not plowed with my young cow,
  you would not have solved my riddle!"

19Then the Spirit[d] of the LORD entered Samson and gave him great power. Samson went down to the city of Ashkelon and killed thirty of its men and took all that they had and gave the clothes to the men who had answered his riddle. Then he went to his father's house very angry. 20And Samson's wife was given to his best man.

Samson Troubles the Philistines

15 At the time of the wheat harvest, Samson went to visit his wife, taking a young goat with him. He said, "I'm going to my wife's room," but her father would not let him go in.

2He said to Samson, "I thought you really hated your wife, so I gave her to your best man. Her younger sister is more beautiful. Take her instead."

3But Samson said to them, "This time no one will blame me for hurting you Philistines!" 4So Samson went out and caught three hundred foxes. He took two foxes at a time, tied their tails together, and then tied a torch to the tails of each pair of foxes. 5After he lit the torches, he let the foxes loose in the grainfields of the Philistines so that he burned up their standing grain, the piles of grain, their vineyards, and their olive trees.

6The Philistines asked, "Who did this?"

Someone told them, "Samson, the son-in-law of the man from Timnah, did because his father-in-law gave his wife to his best man."

So the Philistines burned Samson's wife and her father to death. 7Then Samson said to the Philistines, "Since you did this, I won't stop until I pay you back!" 8Samson attacked the Philistines and killed many of them. Then he went down and stayed in a cave in the rock of Etam.

> **SIDELIGHT:** Samson was not only strong, but he could also have been a good wrestler. In the original language, Judges 15:8 describes how he beat the Philistines "hip and thigh." This phrase may have been an old wrestling term, such as "half-nelson" and "flying scissors" used by wrestlers today.

9The Philistines went up and camped in the land of Judah, near a place named Lehi. 10The men of Judah asked them, "Why have you come here to fight us?"

They answered, "We have come to make Samson our prisoner, to pay him back for what he did to our people."

11Then three thousand men of Judah went to the cave in the rock of Etam and said to Samson, "What have you done to us? Don't you know that the Philistines rule over us?"

Samson answered, "I only paid them back for what they did to me."

12Then they said to him, "We have come to tie you up and to hand you over to the Philistines."

Samson said to them, "Promise me you will not hurt me yourselves."

13The men from Judah said, "We agree. We will just tie you up and give you to the Philistines. We will not kill you." So they tied Samson with two new ropes and led him up from the cave in the rock. 14When Samson came to the place named Lehi, the Philistines came to meet him, shouting for joy. Then the Spirit[d] of the LORD entered Samson and gave him great power. The ropes on him weakened like burned strings and fell off his hands! 15Samson found the jawbone of

fourth The Hebrew word is "seventh." Some old translations say "fourth," which fits the order of events better.

a dead donkey, took it, and killed a thousand men with it!

16Then Samson said,

"With a donkey's jawbone
I made donkeys out of them.
With a donkey's jawbone
I killed a thousand men!"

17When he finished speaking, he threw away the jawbone. So that place was named Ramath Lehi.[n]

18Samson was very thirsty, so he cried out to the LORD, "You gave me, your servant, this great victory. Do I have to die of thirst now? Do I have to be captured by people who are not circumcised?"[d] 19Then God opened up a hole in the ground at Lehi, and water came out. When Samson drank, he felt better; he felt strong again. So he named that spring Caller's Spring, which is still in Lehi.

20Samson judged Israel for twenty years in the days of the Philistines.

Samson Goes to the City of Gaza

16 One day Samson went to Gaza and saw a prostitute[d] there. He went in to spend the night with her. 2When the people of Gaza heard, "Samson has come here!" they surrounded the place and waited for him near the city gate all night. They whispered to each other, "When dawn comes, we will kill Samson!"

3But Samson only stayed with the prostitute until midnight. Then he got up and took hold of the doors and the two posts of the city gate and tore them loose, along with the bar. He put them on his shoulders and carried them to the top of the hill that faces the city of Hebron.

Samson and Delilah

4After this, Samson fell in love with a woman named Delilah, who lived in the Valley of Sorek. 5The Philistine rulers went to Delilah and said, "Find out what makes Samson so strong. Trick him into telling you how we can overpower him and capture him and tie him up. If you do this, each one of us will give you twenty-eight pounds of silver."

6So Delilah said to Samson, "Tell me why you are so strong. How can someone tie you up and capture you?"

7Samson answered, "Someone would have to tie me up with seven new bowstrings that have not been dried. Then I would be as weak as any other man."

8The Philistine rulers brought Delilah seven new bowstrings that had not been dried, and she tied Samson with them. 9Some men were hiding in another room. Delilah said to him, "Samson, the Philistines are here!" But Samson broke the bowstrings like pieces of burned string. So the Philistines did not find out the secret of Samson's strength.

10Then Delilah said to Samson, "You made a fool of me. You lied to me. Now tell me how someone can tie you up."

11Samson said, "They would have to tie me with new ropes that have not been used before. Then I would become as weak as any other man."

12So Delilah took new ropes and tied Samson. Some men were hiding in another room. She called out to him, "Samson, the Philistines are here!" But he broke the ropes as easily as if they were threads.

13Then Delilah said to Samson, "Again you have made a fool of me. You lied to me. Tell me how someone can tie you up."

He said, "Using the loom,[n] weave the seven braids of my hair into the cloth, and tighten it with a pin. Then I will be as weak as any other man."

While Samson slept, Delilah wove the seven braids of his hair into the cloth. 14Then she fastened it with a pin.

Again she said to him, "Samson, the Philistines are here!" Samson woke up and pulled out the pin and the loom with the cloth.

15Then Delilah said to him, "How can you say, 'I love you,' when you don't even trust me? This is the third time you have made a fool of me. You haven't told me the secret of your great strength." 16She kept bothering Samson about his secret day after day until he felt he was going to die!

17So he told her everything. He said, "I have never had my hair cut, because I have been set apart to God as a Nazirite[d] since I was born. If someone shaved my head, I would lose my strength and be as weak as any other man."

18When Delilah saw that he had told her everything sincerely, she sent a message to the Philistine rulers. She said, "Come back one more time, because he has told me everything." So the Philistine rulers came back to Delilah and brought the silver with them. 19Delilah got Samson to sleep, lying in her lap. Then she called in a man to shave off the seven braids of Samson's hair. In this way she began to make him weak, and his strength left him.

20Then she said, "Samson, the Philistines are here!"

He woke up and thought, "I'll leave as I did before and shake myself free." But he did not know that the LORD had left him.

21Then the Philistines captured Samson and

Ramath Lehi This name means Jawbone Hill.
loom A machine for making cloth from thread.

tore out his eyes. They took him down to Gaza,
where they put bronze chains on him and made
him grind grain in the prison. 22But his hair began
to grow again.

SIDELIGHT: When Samson was forced to grind grain as a prisoner, the punishment was severe (Judges 16:21). The millstone he would have turned was probably made of limestone and was at least two feet across with a hole in the middle. Only large animals and extremely strong people could operate the grinding mills.

Samson Dies

23The Philistine rulers gathered to celebrate
and to offer a great sacrifice to their god Dagon.[d]
They said, "Our god has handed Samson our enemy over to us." 24When the people saw him,
they praised their god, saying,

"This man destroyed our country.
He killed many of us!
But our god handed over
our enemy to us."

25While the people were enjoying the celebration, they said, "Bring Samson out to perform for
us." So they brought Samson from the prison, and
he performed for them. They made him stand between the pillars. 26Samson said to the servant
holding his hand, "Let me feel the pillars that hold
up the temple so I can lean against them." 27Now
the temple was full of men and women. All the
Philistine rulers were there, and about three thousand men and women were on the roof[n] watching Samson perform. 28Then Samson prayed to
the LORD, "Lord GOD, remember me. God, please
give me strength one more time so I can pay these
Philistines back for putting out my two eyes!"
29Then Samson turned to the two center pillars
that supported the whole temple. He braced himself between the two pillars, with his right hand
on one and his left hand on the other. 30Samson
said, "Let me die with these Philistines!" Then he
pushed as hard as he could, causing the temple to
fall on the rulers and all the people in it. So Samson killed more of the Philistines when he died
than when he was alive.

31Samson's brothers and his whole family went
down to get his body. They brought him back and
buried him in the tomb of Manoah, his father,
between the cities of Zorah and Eshtaol. Samson
was a judge for the people of Israel for twenty
years.

Micah's Idols

17 There was a man named Micah who
lived in the mountains of Ephraim. 2He
said to his mother, "I heard you speak a curse
about the twenty-eight pounds of silver that were
taken from you. I have the silver with me; I took
it."

His mother said, "The LORD bless you, my
son!"

3Micah gave the twenty-eight pounds of silver
to his mother. Then she said, "I will give this silver to the LORD. I will have my son make an idol
and a statue. So I will give the silver back to you."

4When he gave the silver back to his mother,
she took about five pounds and gave it to a silversmith. With it he made an idol and a statue,
which stood in Micah's house. 5Micah had a special holy place, and he made a holy vest[d] and
some household idols. Then Micah chose one of
his sons to be his priest. 6At that time Israel did
not have a king, so everyone did what seemed
right.

7There was a young man who was a Levite[n]
from the city of Bethlehem in Judah who was
from the people of Judah. 8He left Bethlehem to
look for another place to live, and on his way he
came to Micah's house in the mountains of
Ephraim. 9Micah asked him, "Where are you
from?"

He answered, "I'm a Levite from Bethlehem in
Judah. I'm looking for a place to live."

10Micah said to him, "Live with me and be my
father and my priest. I will give you four ounces
of silver each year and clothes and food." So the
Levite went in. 11He agreed to live with Micah
and became like one of Micah's own sons. 12Mi-
cah made him a priest, and he lived in Micah's
house. 13Then Micah said, "Now I know the
LORD will be good to me, because I have a Levite
as my priest."

Dan's Family Captures Laish

18 At that time Israel did not have a king.
And at that time the tribe[d] of Dan was
still looking for a land where they could live, a
land of their own. The Danites had not yet been
given their own land among the tribes of Israel.
2So, from their family groups, they chose five soldiers from the cities of Zorah and Eshtaol to spy
out and explore the land. They were told, "Go,
explore the land."

They came to the mountains of Ephraim, to Mi-

roof In Bible times houses were built with flat roofs. The roof was used for drying things such as flax and fruit. And it was used as an extra room, as a place for worship, and as a place to sleep in the summer.
Levite The Levites were the only ones God had appointed as priests.

cah's house, where they spent the night. [3]When they came near Micah's house, they recognized the voice of the young Levite.[n] So they stopped there and asked him, "Who brought you here? What are you doing here? Why are you here?"

[4]He told them what Micah had done for him, saying "He hired me. I am his priest."

[5]They said to him, "Please ask God if our journey will be successful."

[6]The priest said to them, "Go in peace. The LORD is pleased with your journey."

[7]So the five men left. When they came to the city of Laish, they saw that the people there lived in safety, like the people of Sidon. They thought they were safe and had plenty of everything. They lived a long way from the Sidonians and had no dealings with anyone else.

[8]When the five men returned to Zorah and Eshtaol, their relatives asked them, "What did you find?"

[9]They answered, "We have seen the land, and it is very good. We should attack them. Aren't you going to do something? Don't wait! Let's go and take that land! [10]When you go, you will see there is plenty of land — plenty of everything! The people are not expecting an attack. Surely God has handed that land over to us!"

[11]So six hundred Danites left Zorah and Eshtaol ready for war. [12]On their way they set up camp near the city of Kiriath Jearim in Judah. That is why the place west of Kiriath Jearim is named Mahaneh Dan[n] to this day. [13]From there they traveled on to the mountains of Ephraim. Then they came to Micah's house.

[14]The five men who had explored the land around Laish said to their relatives, "Do you know in one of these houses there are a holy vest,[d] household gods, an idol, and a statue? You know what to do." [15]So they stopped at the Levite's house, which was also Micah's house, and greeted the Levite. [16]The six hundred Danites stood at the entrance gate, wearing their weapons of war. [17]The five spies went into the house and took the idol, the holy vest, the household idols, and the statue. The priest and the six hundred men armed for war stood by the entrance gate.

[18]When the spies went into Micah's house and took the image, the holy vest, the household idols, and the statue, the priest asked them, "What are you doing?"

[19]They answered, "Be quiet! Don't say a word. Come with us and be our father and priest. Is it better for you to be a priest for one man's house or for a tribe and family group in Israel?" [20]This made the priest happy. So he took the holy vest, the household idols, and the idol and went with the Danites. [21]They left Micah's house, putting their little children, their animals, and everything they owned in front of them.

[22]When they had gone a little way from Micah's house, the men who lived near Micah were called out and caught up with them. [23]The men with Micah shouted at the Danites, who turned around and said to Micah, "What's the matter with you? Why have you been called out to fight?"

[24]Micah answered, "You took my gods that I made and my priest. What do I have left? How can you ask me, 'What's the matter?' "

[25]The Danites answered, "You should not argue with us. Some of our angry men might attack you, killing you and your family." [26]Then the Danites went on their way. Micah knew they were too strong for him, so he turned and went back home.

[27]Then the Danites took what Micah had made and his priest and went on to Laish. They attacked those peaceful people and killed them with their swords and then burned the city. [28]There was no one to save the people of Laish. They lived too far from Sidon, and they had no dealings with anyone else. Laish was in a valley near Beth Rehob.

The people of Dan rebuilt the city and lived there. [29]They changed the name of Laish to Dan, naming it for their ancestor Dan, one of the sons of Israel.

[30]The people of Dan set up the idols in the city of Dan. Jonathan son of Gershom, Moses' son, and his sons served as priests for the tribe of Dan until the land was captured. [31]The people of Dan set up the idols Micah had made as long as the Holy Tent[d] of God was in Shiloh.

A Levite and His Servant

19 At that time Israel did not have a king. There was a Levite who lived in the faraway mountains of Ephraim. He had taken a slave woman[d] from the city of Bethlehem in the land of Judah to live with him, [2]but she was unfaithful to him. She left him and went back to her father's house in Bethlehem in Judah and stayed there for four months. [3]Then her husband went to ask her to come back to him, taking with him his servant and two donkeys. When the Levite came to her father's house, she invited him to come in, and her father was happy to see him. [4]The father-in-law, the young woman's father, asked him to stay. So he stayed for three days and ate, drank, and slept there.

[5]On the fourth day they got up early in the morning. The Levite was getting ready to leave, but the woman's father said to his son-in-law,

Levite The Levites were the only ones God had appointed as priests.
Mahaneh Dan This name means "the camp of Dan."

"Refresh yourself by eating something. Then go."
6So the two men sat down to eat and drink together. After that, the father said to him, "Please
stay tonight. Relax and enjoy yourself." 7When
the man got up to go, his father-in-law asked him
to stay. So he stayed again that night. 8On the fifth
day the man got up early in the morning to leave.
The woman's father said, "Refresh yourself. Wait
until this afternoon." So the two men ate together.

9When the Levite, his slave woman, and his
servant got up to leave, the father-in-law, the
young woman's father, said, "It's almost night.
The day is almost gone. Spend the night here and
enjoy yourself. Tomorrow morning you can get
up early and go home." 10But the Levite did not
want to stay another night. So he took his two
saddled donkeys and his slave woman and traveled toward the city of Jebus (also called Jerusalem).

11As the day was almost over, they came near
Jebus. So the servant said to his master, "Let's
stop at this city of the Jebusites, and spend the
night here."

12But his master said, "No. We won't go inside
a foreign city. Those people are not Israelites. We
will go on to the city of Gibeah." 13He said,
"Come on. Let's try to make it to Gibeah or Ramah so we can spend the night in one of those
cities." 14So they went on. The sun went down as
they came near Gibeah, which belongs to the
tribe[d] of Benjamin. 15They stopped there to spend
the night. They came to the public square of the
city and sat down, but no one invited them home
to spend the night.

16Finally, in the evening an old man came in
from his work in the fields. His home was in the
mountains of Ephraim, but now he was living in
Gibeah. (The people of Gibeah were from the
tribe of Benjamin.) 17He saw the traveler in the
public square and asked, "Where are you going?
Where did you come from?"

18The Levite answered, "We are traveling from
Bethlehem in Judah to my home in the mountains
of Ephraim. I have been to Bethlehem in Judah,
but now I am going to the Holy Tent[d] of the LORD.
No one has invited me to stay in his house. 19We
already have straw and food for our donkeys and
bread and wine for me, the young woman, and
my servant. We don't need anything."

20The old man said, "You are welcome to stay
at my house. Let me give you anything you need,
but don't spend the night in the public square."
21So the old man took the Levite into his house,
and he fed their donkeys. They washed their feet
and had something to eat and drink.

22While they were enjoying themselves, some
wicked men of the city surrounded the house and
beat on the door. They shouted to the old man
who owned the house, "Bring out the man who
came to your house. We want to have sexual relations with him."

23The owner of the house went outside and
said to them, "No, my friends. Don't be so evil.
This man is a guest in my house. Don't do this
terrible thing! 24Look, here are my daughter, who
has never had sexual relations before, and the
man's slave woman. I will bring them out to you
now. Do anything you want with them, but don't
do such a terrible thing to this man."

25But the men would not listen to him. So the
Levite took his slave woman and sent her outside
to them. They forced her to have sexual relations
with them, and they abused her all night long.
Then, at dawn, they let her go. 26She came back
to the house where her master was staying and
fell down at the door and lay there until day
light.

27In the morning when the Levite got up, he
opened the door of the house and went outside to
go on his way. But his slave woman was lying at
the doorway of the house, with her hands on the
doorsill. 28The Levite said to her, "Get up; let's
go." But she did not answer. So he put her on his
donkey and went home.

29When the Levite got home, he took a knife
and cut his slave woman into twelve parts, limb
by limb. Then he sent a part to each area of Israel.
30Everyone who saw this said, "Nothing like this
has ever happened before, not since the people of
Israel came out of Egypt. Think about it. Tell us
what to do."

The War Between Israel and Benjamin

20 So all the Israelites from Dan to Beersheba,[n] including the land of Gilead,
joined together before the LORD in the city of Mizpah. 2The leaders of all the tribes[d] of Israel took
their places in the meeting of the people of God.
There were 400,000 soldiers with swords. 3(The
people of Benjamin heard that the Israelites had
gone up to Mizpah.) Then the Israelites said to the
Levite, "Tell us how this evil thing happened."

4So the husband of the murdered woman answered, "My slave woman[d] and I came to Gibeah
in Benjamin to spend the night. 5During the night
the men of Gibeah came after me. They surrounded the house and wanted to kill me. They
forced my slave woman to have sexual relations
and she died. 6I took her and cut her into parts
and sent one part to each area of Israel because
the people of Benjamin did this wicked and terri-

Dan . . . Beersheba Dan was the city farthest north in Israel. Beersheba was the city farthest south. So this means all the people of Israel.

ble thing in Israel. 7Now, all you Israelites, speak
up. What is your decision?"
8Then all the people stood up at the same time,
saying, "None of us will go home. Not one of us
will go back to his house! 9Now this is what we
will do to Gibeah. We will throw lots.[d] 10That
way we will choose ten men from every hundred
men from all the tribes of Israel, and we will
choose a hundred men from every thousand, and
a thousand men from every ten thousand. These
will find supplies for the army. Then the army will
go to the city of Gibeah of Benjamin to repay them
for the terrible thing they have done in Israel."
11So all the men of Israel were united and gathered against the city.
12The tribes of Israel sent men throughout the
tribe of Benjamin demanding, "What is this evil
thing some of your men have done? 13Hand over
the wicked men in Gibeah so that we can put
them to death. We must remove this evil from
Israel."
But the Benjaminites would not listen to their
fellow Israelites. 14The Benjaminites left their
own cities and met at Gibeah to fight the Israelites. 15In only one day the Benjaminites got
26,000 soldiers together who were trained with
swords. They also had 700 chosen men from Gibeah. 16Seven hundred of these trained soldiers
were left-handed, each of whom could sling a
stone at a hair and not miss!

SIDELIGHT: Looking for a good left-handed pitcher for your baseball team? Check out Judges 20:16, which tells about the Benjaminite army that included seven hundred lefties who were such good aims they could hit a hair with a stone from a sling. They would probably be all-stars today.

17The Israelites, except for the Benjaminites,
gathered 400,000 soldiers with swords.
18The Israelites went up to the city of Bethel
and asked God, "Which tribe shall be first to attack the Benjaminites?"
The LORD answered, "Judah shall go first."
19The next morning the Israelites got up and
made a camp near Gibeah. 20The men of Israel
went out to fight the Benjaminites and took their
battle position at Gibeah. 21Then the Benjaminites
came out of Gibeah and killed 22,000 Israelites
during the battle that day. 22-23The Israelites went
before the LORD and cried until evening. They
asked the LORD, "Shall we go to fight our relatives, the Benjaminites, again?"
The LORD answered, "Go up and fight them."
The men of Israel encouraged each other. So they
took the same battle positions they had taken the
first day.
24The Israelites came to fight the Benjaminites
the second day. 25The Benjaminites came out of
Gibeah to attack the Israelites. This time, the Benjaminites killed 18,000 Israelites, all of whom carried swords.
26Then the Israelites went up to Bethel. There
they sat down and cried to the LORD and went
without food all day until evening. They also
brought burnt offerings and fellowship offerings to
the LORD. 27The Israelites asked the LORD a question. (In those days the Ark[d] of the Agreement
with God was there at Bethel. 28A priest named
Phinehas son of Eleazar, the son of Aaron, served
before the Ark of the Agreement.) They asked,
"Shall we go to fight our relatives, the Benjaminites, again, or shall we stop fighting?"
The LORD answered, "Go, because tomorrow I
will hand them over to you."
29Then the Israelites set up ambushes all
around Gibeah. 30They went to fight against the
Benjaminites at Gibeah on the third day, getting
into position for battle as they had done before.
31When the Benjaminites came out to fight them,
the Israelites backed up and led the Benjaminites
away from the city. The Benjaminites began to kill
some of the Israelites as they had done before.
About thirty Israelites were killed—some in the
fields and some on the roads leading to Bethel and
to Gibeah.
32The Benjaminites said, "We are winning as
before!"
But the Israelites said, "Let's run. Let's trick
them into going farther away from their city and
onto the roads."
33All the Israelites moved from their places and
got into battle positions at a place named Baal Tamar. Then the Israelites ran out from their hiding
places west of Gibeah. 34Ten thousand of the best
trained soldiers from all of Israel attacked Gibeah.
The battle was very hard. The Benjaminites did
not know disaster was about to come to them.
35The LORD used the Israelites to defeat the Benjaminites. On that day the Israelites killed 25,100
Benjaminites, all armed with swords. 36Then the
Benjaminites saw that they were defeated.
The Israelites had moved back because they
were depending on the surprise attack they had
set up near Gibeah. 37The men in hiding rushed
into Gibeah, spread out, and killed everyone in
the city with their swords. 38Now the Israelites
had set up a signal with the men in hiding. The
men in the surprise attack were to send up a
cloud of smoke from the city. 39Then the army of
Israel turned around in the battle.
The Benjaminites had killed about thirty Israelites. They were saying, "We are winning, as in the

first battle!" 40But then a cloud of smoke began to rise from the city. The Benjaminites turned around and saw that the whole city was going up in smoke. 41Then the Israelites turned and began to fight. The Benjaminites were terrified because they knew that disaster was coming to them. 42So the Benjaminites ran away from the Israelites toward the desert, but they could not escape the battle. And the Israelites who came out of the cities killed them. 43They surrounded the Benjaminites and chased them and caught them in the area east of Gibeah. 44So 18,000 brave Benjaminite fighters were killed. 45The Benjaminites ran toward the desert to the rock of Rimmon, but the Israelites killed 5,000 Benjaminites along the roads. They chased them as far as Gidom and killed 2,000 more Benjaminites there.

46On that day 25,000 Benjaminites were killed, all of whom had fought bravely with swords. 47But 600 Benjaminites ran to the rock of Rimmon in the desert, where they stayed for four months. 48Then the Israelites went back to the land of Benjamin and killed the people in every city and also the animals and everything they could find. And they burned every city they found.

Wives for the Men of Benjamin

21 At Mizpah the men of Israel had sworn, "Not one of us will let his daughter marry a man from the tribe[d] of Benjamin."

2The people went to the city of Bethel and sat before God until evening, crying loudly. 3They said, "LORD, God of Israel, why has this terrible thing happened to us so that one tribe of Israel is missing today?"

4Early the next day the people built an altar and put burnt offerings and fellowship offerings to God on it.

5Then the Israelites asked, "Did any tribe of Israel not come here to meet with us in the presence of the LORD?" They asked this question because they had sworn that anyone who did not meet with them at Mizpah would be killed.

6The Israelites felt sorry for their relatives, the Benjaminites. They said, "Today one tribe has been cut off from Israel. 7We swore before the LORD that we would not allow our daughters to marry a Benjaminite. How can we make sure that the remaining men of Benjamin will have wives?" 8Then they asked, "Which one of the tribes of Israel did not come here to Mizpah?" They found that no one from the city of Jabesh Gilead had come. 9The people of Israel counted everyone, but there was no one from Jabesh Gilead.

10So the whole group of Israelites sent twelve thousand soldiers to Jabesh Gilead to kill the people with their swords, even the women and children.

11"This is what you must do: Kill every man in Jabesh Gilead and every married woman." 12The soldiers found four hundred young unmarried women in Jabesh Gilead, so they brought them to the camp at Shiloh in Canaan.

13Then the whole group of Israelites sent a message to the men of Benjamin, who were at the rock of Rimmon, offering to make peace with them. 14So the men of Benjamin came back at that time. The Israelites gave them the women from Jabesh Gilead who had not been killed, but there were not enough women.

15The people of Israel felt sorry for the Benjaminites because the LORD had separated the tribes of Israel. 16The older leaders of the Israelites said, "The women of Benjamin have been killed. Where can we get wives for the men of Benjamin who are still alive? 17These men must have children to continue their families so a tribe in Israel will not die out. 18But we cannot allow our daughters to marry them, because we swore, 'Anyone who gives a wife to a man of Benjamin is cursed.' 19We have an idea! There is a yearly festival of the LORD at Shiloh, which is north of the city of Bethel, east of the road that goes from Bethel to Shechem, and south of the city of Lebonah."

20So the older leaders told the men of Benjamin, "Go and hide in the vineyards. 21Watch for the young women from Shiloh to come out to join the dancing. Then run out from the vineyards and take one of the young Shiloh women and return to the land of Benjamin. 22If their fathers or brothers come to us and complain, we will say: 'Be kind to the men of Benjamin. We did not get wives for Benjamin during the war, and you did not give the women to the men from Benjamin. So you are not guilty.' "

23So that is what the Benjaminites did. While the young women were dancing, each man caught one of them, took her away, and married her. Then they went back to the land God had given them and rebuilt their cities and lived there.

24Then the Israelites went home to their own tribes and family groups, to their own land that God had given them.

25In those days Israel did not have a king. Everyone did what seemed right.

RUTH

Why Read This Book:

- See how relationships grow strong (Ruth 1—2).
- Discover the importance of keeping agreements (Ruth 3—4).

Behind the Scenes:

The story of Ruth would never have made the evening news. There are no wars, no twisted plots, no villains. In fact, much more "important" things were happening at the time. The story took place during the period of the judges (see Judges, p. 215), and Israel faced moral decline, foreign attacks and national chaos.

But in the midst of other seemingly important events, the Bible tells the simple, beautiful story of Ruth. It's a story of loyalty and faithfulness, a story of how ordinary people kept following God even when the nation of Israel was abandoning God.

The story opens in Moab, a non-Jewish area, where Naomi had gone to live. Her son had married a Moabite woman, Ruth. After only ten years, Ruth's husband died. Even though Naomi could have left Ruth, she took her in, and the two became close friends.

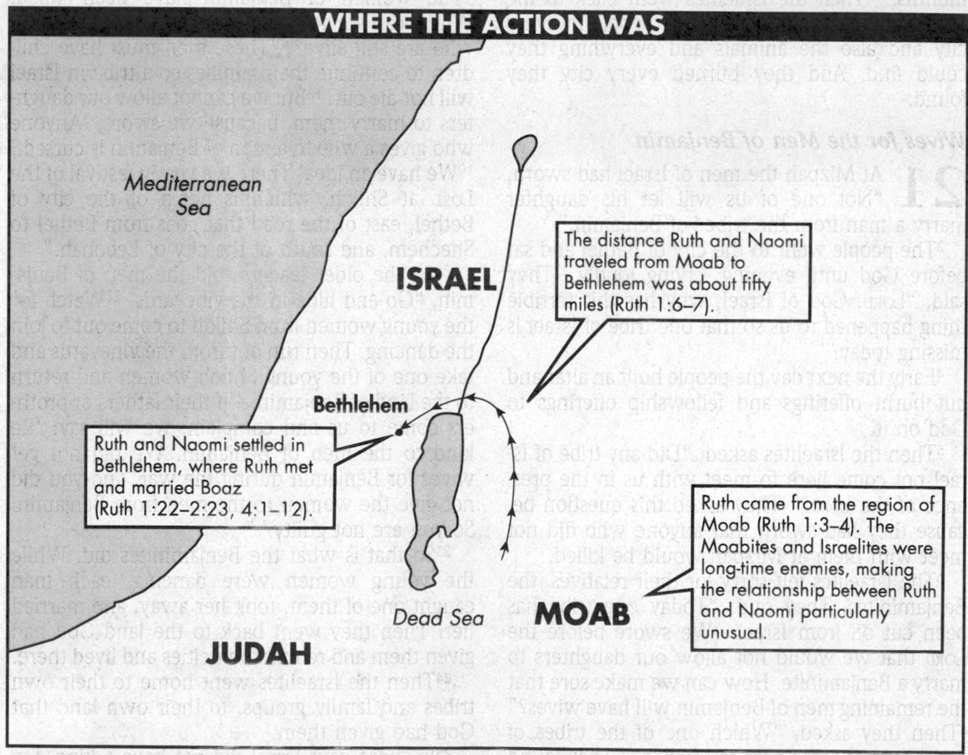
WHERE THE ACTION WAS
Mediterranean Sea
ISRAEL
The distance Ruth and Naomi traveled from Moab to Bethlehem was about fifty miles (Ruth 1:6–7).
Bethlehem
Ruth and Naomi settled in Bethlehem, where Ruth met and married Boaz (Ruth 1:22–2:23, 4:1–12).
Ruth came from the region of Moab (Ruth 1:3–4). The Moabites and Israelites were long-time enemies, making the relationship between Ruth and Naomi particularly unusual.
Dead Sea
MOAB
JUDAH

WHEN THE ACTION WAS

2000BC	1500BC	1000BC	500BC	BC/AD

- The Israelites escaped from Egypt
- Joshua led the Israelites into Canaan
- Saul was Israel's king
- Ruth lived during the time of the judges
- Jesus was born

Behind the Scenes (cont.): Then Ruth and Naomi moved to Israel, Naomi's homeland, where Ruth was a foreigner. There Ruth met Boaz, who married her so Ruth's family name could continue. Years later, one of Ruth's descendants, David, became the greatest king of Israel. Even more important, Ruth thus was included in the family of Jesus Christ (see Matthew 1:5, p. 906).

The story of Ruth emphasizes the importance of faithfulness and loyalty—of one person to another and to God. Each main character—Ruth, Naomi, Boaz—shows a loyalty beyond what's required.

The story also reminds us that we don't have to be famous or do great things to be important to God. What is most important to God is that people are faithful in whatever they do, whether or not they are famous.

1

1-2 Long ago when the judges[n] ruled Israel,
there was a shortage of food in the land. So
a man named Elimelech left the town of Bethlehem in Judah to live in the country of Moab with
his wife and his two sons. His wife was named
Naomi, and his two sons were named Mahlon
and Kilion. They were Ephrathahites from Bethlehem in Judah. When they came to Moab, they
settled there.
3 Then Naomi's husband, Elimelech, died, and
she was left with her two sons. 4 These sons married women from Moab. One was named Orpah,
and the other was named Ruth. Naomi and her
sons had lived in Moab about ten years 5 when
Mahlon and Kilion also died. So Naomi was left
alone without her husband or her two sons.
6 While Naomi was in Moab, she heard that the
Lord had come to help his people and had given
them food again. So she and her daughters-in-law
got ready to leave Moab and return home. 7 Naomi and her daughters-in-law left the place where
they had lived and started back to the land of Judah. 8 But Naomi said to her two daughters-in-law,
"Go back home, each of you to your own

judges They were not judges in courts of law, but leaders of the people in times of emergency.

FRIENDS

A Little Encouragement

Dean Agnew would lie awake nights waiting to hear the sound of a car driving up. When he did, he would run to the front door to unlock it. Then he would cry with fear as his stepfather stumbled in, reeking of alcohol.

Doors slammed. Dishes broke in the kitchen. And yelling—the horrible yelling at his mother—made Dean wish his alcoholic stepfather would die.

Dean might have gone crazy if it hadn't been for friends like Tom Kruger. Tom was a year older than Dean. The two laughed a lot together, and Tom, a mechanical wizard, taught Dean how to fix cars.

Whenever Tom gave Dean a ride somewhere, he would end the trip by saying, "Stay cool, guy." Dean knew he meant, "Hang in there."

Those were tough times for Dean, but he survived because of his friends—people like Tom.

Ruth and Naomi also faced tough times. Both lost their husbands, and Naomi also lost her only sons. But because of their friendship with each other, they made it through. Read about their relationship in **Ruth 1:1–19**.

- How were Dean's and Ruth's situations made better by the friendships of Tom and Naomi?
- How can Ruth's example help you be a more committed friend?

CONSIDER

- befriending a newcomer at school or someone with a different background from you.
- being a committed friend to someone who is facing tough times by letting him or her talk openly about the problems.

FOR MORE, SEE

- Leviticus 19:9–10 (p. 115)
- 1 Samuel 20:11–17 (p. 263)
- 1 John 3:11–18 (p. 1318)

mother's house. May the LORD be as kind to you
as you have been to me and my sons who are now
dead. 9May the LORD give you another happy
home and a new husband."

When Naomi kissed the women good-bye, they
began to cry out loud. 10They said to her, "No, we
want to go with you to your people."

11But Naomi said, "My daughters, return to
your own homes. Why do you want to go with
me? I cannot give birth to more sons to give you
new husbands; 12go back, my daughters, to your
own homes. I am too old to have another husband. Even if I told myself, 'I still have hope' and
had another husband tonight, and even if I had
more sons, 13should you wait until they were
grown into men? Should you live for so many
years without husbands? Don't do that, my
daughters. My life is much too sad for you to
share, because the LORD has been against me!"

14The women cried together out loud again.
Then Orpah kissed her mother-in-law Naomi
good-bye, but Ruth held on to her tightly.

15Naomi said to Ruth, "Look, your sister-in-law
is going back to her own people and her own
gods. Go back with her."

Ruth Stays with Naomi

16But Ruth said, "Don't beg me to leave you or
to stop following you. Where you go, I will go.
Where you live, I will live. Your people will be my
people, and your God will be my God. 17And
where you die, I will die, and there I will be buried. I ask the LORD to punish me terribly if I do
not keep this promise: Not even death will separate us."

18When Naomi saw that Ruth had firmly made
up her mind to go with her, she stopped arguing
with her. 19So Naomi and Ruth went on until they
came to the town of Bethlehem. When they entered Bethlehem, all the people became very excited. The women of the town said, "Is this really
Naomi?"

20Naomi answered the people, "Don't call me
Naomi.[n] Call me Mara,[n] because the Almighty
has made my life very sad. 21When I left, I had all
I wanted, but now, the LORD has brought me
home with nothing. Why should you call me Naomi when the LORD has spoken against me and
the Almighty has given me so much trouble?"

22So Naomi and her daughter-in-law Ruth, the
Moabite, returned from Moab and arrived at
Bethlehem at the beginning of the barley harvest.

Ruth Meets Boaz

2 Now Naomi had a rich relative named Boaz,
from Elimelech's family.

2One day Ruth, the Moabite, said to Naomi, "I
am going to the fields. Maybe someone will be
kind enough to let me gather the grain he leaves
behind."

Naomi said, "Go, my daughter."

3So Ruth went to the fields and gathered the
grain that the workers cutting the grain had left
behind. It just so happened that the field belonged
to Boaz, from Elimelech's family.

> **SIDELIGHT:** When Ruth went to Boaz's field to harvest barley (Ruth 2:1–3), she wasn't stealing. Deuteronomy 24:19–21 (p. 181) commanded farmers to leave some of the grain in the field so the poor could harvest it.

4Soon Boaz came from Bethlehem and greeted
his workers, "The LORD be with you!"

And the workers answered, "May the LORD
bless you!"

5Then Boaz asked his servant in charge of the
workers, "Whose girl is that?"

6The servant answered, "She is the young Moabite woman who came back with Naomi from
the country of Moab. 7She said, 'Please let me
follow the workers cutting grain and gather what
they leave behind.' She came and has remained
here, from morning until just now. She has
stopped only a few moments to rest in the shelter."

8Then Boaz said to Ruth, "Listen, my daughter.
Don't go to gather grain for yourself in another
field. Don't even leave this field at all, but continue following closely behind my women workers. 9Watch to see into which fields they go to cut
grain and follow them. I have warned the young
men not to bother you. When you are thirsty, you
may go and drink from the water jugs that the
young men have filled."

10Then Ruth bowed low with her face to the
ground and said to him, "I am not an Israelite.
Why have you been so kind to notice me?"

11Boaz answered her, "I know about all the
help you have given your mother-in-law after your
husband died. You left your father and mother
and your own country to come to a nation where
you did not know anyone. 12May the LORD reward you for all you have done. May your wages
be paid in full by the LORD, the God of Israel,
under whose wings you have come for shelter."

13Then Ruth said, "I hope I can continue to
please you, sir. You have said kind and encourag-

Naomi This name means "happy" or "pleasant."
Mara This name means "bitter" or "sad."

ing words to me, your servant, though I am not
one of your servants."
14At mealtime Boaz told Ruth, "Come here. Eat
some of our bread and dip it in our sauce."
So Ruth sat down beside the workers. Boaz
handed her some roasted grain, and she ate until
she was full; she even had some food left over.
15When Ruth rose and went back to work, Boaz
commanded his workers, "Let her gather even
around the piles of cut grain. Don't tell her to go
away. 16In fact, drop some full heads of grain for
her from what you have in your hands, and let her
gather them. Don't tell her to stop."
17So Ruth gathered grain in the field until evening. Then she separated the grain from the
chaff,[d] and there was about one-half bushel of barley. 18Ruth carried the grain into town, and her
mother-in-law saw how much she had gathered.
Ruth also took out the food that was left over from
lunch and gave it to Naomi.
19Naomi asked her, "Where did you gather all
this grain today? Where did you work? Blessed be
whoever noticed you!"
Ruth told her mother-in-law whose field she
had worked in. She said, "The man I worked with
today is named Boaz."
20Naomi told her daughter-in-law, "The LORD
bless him! He continues to be kind to us—both
the living and the dead!" Then Naomi told Ruth,
"Boaz is one of our close relatives,[n] one who
should take care of us."
21Then Ruth, the Moabite, said, "Boaz also told
me, 'Keep close to my workers until they have
finished my whole harvest.' "
22But Naomi said to her daughter-in-law Ruth,
"It is better for you to continue working with his
women workers. If you work in another field,
someone might hurt you." 23So Ruth continued
working closely with the workers of Boaz, gathering grain until the barley harvest and the wheat
harvest were finished. And she continued to live
with Naomi, her mother-in-law.

Naomi's Plan

3 Then Naomi, Ruth's mother-in-law, said to
her, "My daughter, I must find a suitable
home for you, one that will be good for you.
2Now Boaz, whose young women you worked
with, is our close relative.[n] Tonight he will be
working at the threshing[d] floor. 3Wash yourself,
put on perfume, change your clothes, and go
down to the threshing floor. But don't let him
know you're there until he has finished his dinner. 4Watch him so you will know where he lies
down to sleep. When he lies down, go and lift the
cover off his feet[n] and lie down. He will tell you
what you should do."
5Then Ruth answered, "I will do everything
you say."
6So Ruth went down to the threshing floor and
did all her mother-in-law told her to do. 7After his
evening meal, Boaz felt good and went to sleep
lying beside the pile of grain. Ruth went to him
quietly and lifted the cover from his feet and lay
down.
8About midnight Boaz was startled and rolled
over. There was a woman lying near his feet!
9Boaz asked, "Who are you?"
She said, "I am Ruth, your servant girl. Spread
your cover over me, because you are a relative
who is supposed to take care of me."[n]
10Then Boaz said, "The LORD bless you, my
daughter. This act of kindness is greater than the
kindness you showed to Naomi in the beginning.
You didn't look for a young man to marry, either
rich or poor. 11Now, my daughter, don't be afraid.
I will do everything you ask, because all the people in our town know you are a good woman. 12It
is true that I am a relative who is to take care of
you, but you have a closer relative than I. 13Stay
here tonight, and in the morning we will see if he
will take care of you. If he decides to take care of
you, that is fine. But if he refuses, I will take care
of you myself, as surely as the LORD lives. So stay
here until morning."
14So Ruth stayed near his feet until morning but
got up while it was still too dark to recognize anyone. Boaz thought, "People in town must not
know that the woman came here to the threshing[d] floor." 15So Boaz said to Ruth, "Bring me
your shawl and hold it open."
So Ruth held her shawl open, and Boaz poured
six portions of barley into it. Boaz then put it on
her head and went back to the city.
16When Ruth went back to her mother-in-law,
Naomi asked, "How did you do, my daughter?"
Ruth told Naomi everything that Boaz did for
her. 17She said, "Boaz gave me these six portions
of barley, saying, 'You must not go home without
a gift for your mother-in-law.' "
18Naomi answered, "Ruth, my daughter, wait
here until you see what happens. Boaz will not
rest until he has finished doing what he should do
today."

Boaz Marries Ruth

4 Boaz went to the city gate and sat there until
the close relative he had mentioned passed

close relatives In Bible times the closest relative could marry a widow without children so she could have children. He would care for this family, but they and their property would not belong to him. They would belong to the dead husband.
lift . . . feet This showed Ruth was asking him to be her husband.
Spread . . . me By this, Ruth was asking Boaz to marry her.

by. Boaz called to him, "Come here, friend, and
sit down." So the man came over and sat down.
2Boaz gathered ten of the older leaders of the city
and told them, "Sit down here!" So they sat
down.
3Then Boaz said to the close relative, "Naomi,
who has come back from the country of Moab,
wants to sell the piece of land that belonged to
our relative Elimelech. 4So I decided to tell you
about it: If you want to buy back the land, then
buy it in front of the people who are sitting here
and in front of the older leaders of my people. But
if you don't want to buy it, tell me, because you
are the only one who can buy it, and I am next
after you."

The close relative answered, "I will buy back
the land."
5Then Boaz explained, "When you buy the
land from Naomi, you must also marry Ruth, the
Moabite, the dead man's wife. That way, the land
will stay in the dead man's name."
6The close relative answered, "I can't buy back
the land. If I did, I might harm what I can pass on
to my own sons. I cannot buy the land back, so
buy it yourself."

SIDELIGHT: "Proof of purchase" coupons like those on cereal boxes are nothing new. In the Old Testament, people gave away one sandal as a proof of purchase (Ruth 4:7). Today's coupon is a definite improvement—especially when the other person's feet are smaller than yours!

7Long ago in Israel when people traded or
bought back something, one person took off his
sandal and gave it to the other person. This was
the proof of ownership in Israel.

MARRIAGE

Ask Her, John!

John Anderson and Kim Mayo were special youth leaders. John's energy and Kim's spiritual insight made them a dynamic team. Everyone could see how they complemented each other. They were natural together.

John and Kim joined a two-year Bible study program and found themselves together again. In the study, they talked often about the Bible and their growing faith.

The youth group kids began taunting John and Kim. "Hey John! " they would tease. "When are you going to open your eyes and ask Kim out?"

He would blush. She would smile.

Finally, John asked her for a date. And another. And another. For two years, the youth group enjoyed watching the two leaders fall in love.

"When are you going to pop the question?" kids would tease John.

"We really love each other," John would reply, "but getting married is a big commitment. . . . We don't want to rush it."

Six months later, the couple walked into the youth room beaming. Kim proudly displayed a beautiful ring on her left hand. The whole youth group cheered, knowing this marriage would last a lifetime. When Boaz married Ruth, he also committed himself to her, even though his commitment was different from John's. Read about how Boaz made a marriage commitment in **Ruth 4:7–17**.

- How did Boaz show that his commitment to Ruth was strong? How is what he did similar to and different from a wedding ceremony today?
- What can you learn from Boaz and Ruth about what's most important in choosing a spouse?

CONSIDER . . .

- writing a list of characteristics you hope to find in a spouse if you marry. Then evaluate the list in light of your faith and your commitments.
- asking a husband and wife you respect to explain how commitment holds their relationship together.

FOR MORE, SEE . . .

- Genesis 29:15–30 (p. 34)
- Matthew 19:6 (p. 941)
- Ephesians 5:21–33 (p. 1225)

8So the close relative said to Boaz, "Buy the
land yourself," and he took off his sandal.
9Then Boaz said to the older leaders and to all
the people, "You are witnesses today. I am buying from Naomi everything that belonged to
Elimelech and Kilion and Mahlon. 10I am also
taking Ruth, the Moabite who was the wife of
Mahlon, as my wife. I am doing this so her dead
husband's property will stay in his name and
his name will not be separated from his family and his hometown. You are witnesses today."
11So all the people and older leaders who were
at the city gate said, "We are witnesses. May the
LORD make this woman, who is coming into your
home, like Rachel and Leah, who had many children and built up the people of Israel. May you
become powerful in the district of Ephrathah and
famous in Bethlehem. 12As Tamar gave birth to
Judah's son Perez,[n] may the LORD give you many
children through Ruth. May your family be great
like his."

13So Boaz took Ruth home as his wife and had
sexual relations with her. The LORD let her become pregnant, and she gave birth to a son. 14The
women told Naomi, "Praise the LORD who gave
you this grandson. May he become famous in Israel. 15He will give you new life and will take care
of you in your old age because of your daughter-
in-law who loves you. She is better for you than
seven sons, because she has given birth to your
grandson."
16Naomi took the boy, held him in her arms,
and cared for him. 17The neighbors gave the boy
his name, saying, "This boy was born for Naomi."
They named him Obed. Obed was the father of
Jesse, and Jesse was the father of David.
18This is the family history of Perez, the father
of Hezron. 19Hezron was the father of Ram, who
was the father of Amminadab. 20Amminadab was
the father of Nahshon, who was the father of Salmon. 21Salmon was the father of Boaz, who was
the father of Obed. 22Obed was the father of Jesse,
and Jesse was the father of David.

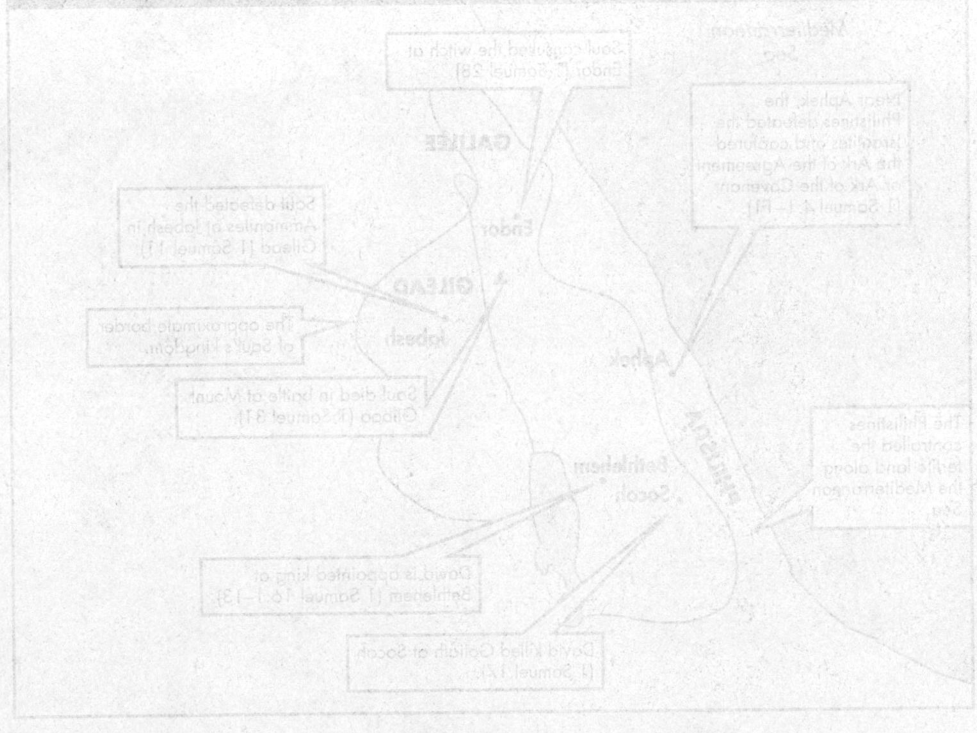

Perez One of Boaz's ancestors.

1 SAMUEL

Why Read This Book:

- See how God uses great leaders (1 Samuel 1—7).
- Discover what can happen when leaders don't obey God (1 Samuel 8—15).
- Find out how God can unite a nation under a holy leader (1 Samuel 16—31).

Behind the Scenes:

After the American Revolution in the 1770s, the thirteen states were almost like independent countries. Each had its own laws, and they constantly bickered. Only after the country had a new constitution and a strong president, George Washington, did the states unite.

The Israelites in Samuel's time lived in a similar situation. They didn't have any central government or regular army. For about a hundred years, the tribes had come together only during crises.

But the Israelites lived in constant fear of the Philistines. This warlike nation with superior iron weapons controlled the fertile plains along the Mediterranean Sea and wanted to add to its territory. So the Philistines wanted to conquer the Israelites and take their land.

To survive, the independent tribes had to unite and stop the invaders. They

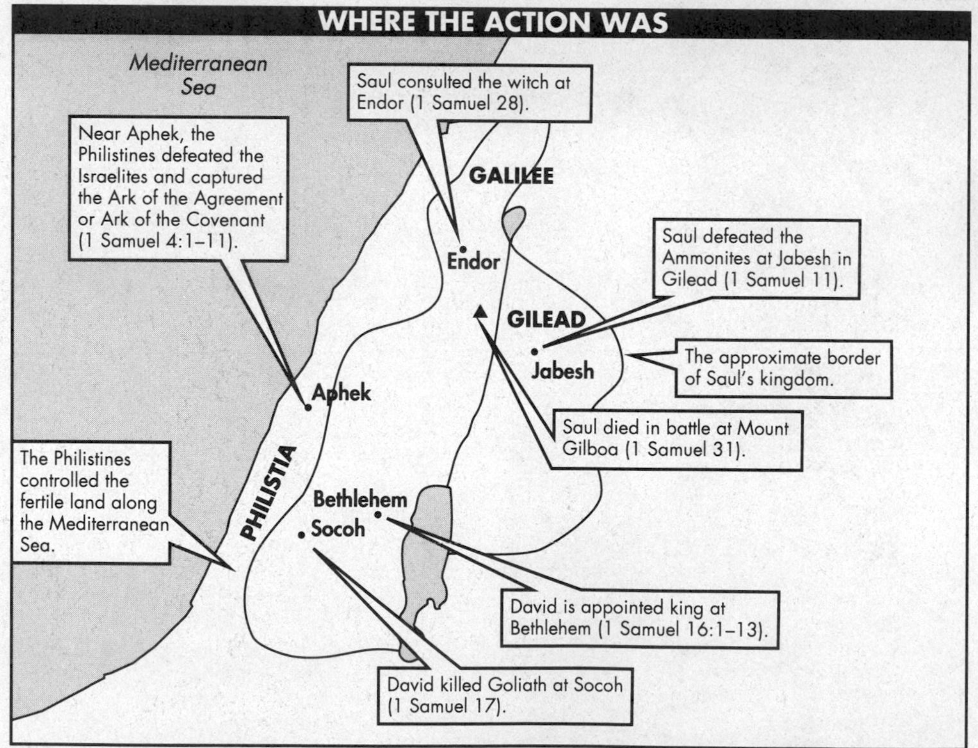
WHERE THE ACTION WAS
Mediterranean Sea
Saul consulted the witch at Endor (1 Samuel 28).
Near Aphek, the Philistines defeated the Israelites and captured the Ark of the Agreement or Ark of the Covenant (1 Samuel 4:1–11).
GALILEE
Endor
Saul defeated the Ammonites at Jabesh in Gilead (1 Samuel 11).
GILEAD
Jabesh
The approximate border of Saul's kingdom.
Aphek
Saul died in battle at Mount Gilboa (1 Samuel 31).
The Philistines controlled the fertile land along the Mediterranean Sea.
PHILISTIA
Bethlehem
Socoh
David is appointed king at Bethlehem (1 Samuel 16:1–13).
David killed Goliath at Socoh (1 Samuel 17).

WHEN THE ACTION WAS

2000BC — 1500BC — 1000BC — 500BC — BC/AD

- The Israelites escaped from Egypt
- Joshua led the Israelites into Canaan
- Samuel served as Israel's last judge
- Saul was Israel's king
- David was Israel's king
- Jesus was born

Behind the Scenes (cont.): needed a leader to unite them to stand up to the threat. That leader would be Samuel.

As it turned out, Samuel changed Israel's history. He stopped the Philistines from advancing, and, even more important, he appointed Israel's first two kings: King Saul and King David.

First Samuel contains some of the most thrilling stories in the Bible, including Saul's spectacular victories over the Philistines, David's battle with Goliath, David's friendship with Jonathan, and Saul's final days. Through all the stories, 1 Samuel shows the importance of having leaders who follow God.

Samuel's Birth

1 There was a man named Elkanah son of Jeroham from Ramathaim in the mountains of Ephraim. Elkanah was from the family of Zuph. (Jeroham was Elihu's son. Elihu was Tohu's son, and Tohu was the son of Zuph from the family group of Ephraim.) 2Elkanah had two wives named Hannah and Peninnah. Peninnah had children, but Hannah had none.

> **SIDELIGHT:** First and Second Samuel were originally one book. The prophet Samuel—after whom the books were named—doesn't even appear in 2 Samuel.

3Every year Elkanah left his town of Ramah and went up to Shiloh to worship the LORD All-Powerful and to offer sacrifices to him. Shiloh was where Hophni and Phinehas, the sons of Eli, served as priests of the LORD. 4When Elkanah offered sacrifices, he always gave a share of the meat to his wife Peninnah and to her sons and daughters. 5But Elkanah always gave a special share of the meat to Hannah, because he loved Hannah and because the LORD had kept her from having children. 6Peninnah would tease Hannah and upset her, because the LORD had made her unable to have children. 7This happened every year when they went up to the house of the LORD at Shiloh. Peninnah would upset Hannah until Hannah would cry and not eat anything. 8Her husband Elkanah would say to her, "Hannah, why are you crying and why won't you eat? Why are you sad? Don't I mean more to you than ten sons?"

9Once, after they had eaten their meal in Shiloh, Hannah got up. Now Eli the priest was sitting on a chair near the entrance to the LORD's house. 10Hannah was so sad that she cried and prayed to the LORD. 11She made a promise, saying, "LORD All-Powerful, see how sad I am. Remember me and don't forget me. If you will give me a son, I will give him back to you all his life, and no one will ever cut his hair with a razor."[n]

12While Hannah kept praying, Eli watched her mouth. 13She was praying in her heart so her lips moved, but her voice was not heard. Eli thought she was drunk 14and said to her, "Stop getting drunk! Throw away your wine!"

15Hannah answered, "No, sir, I have not drunk any wine or beer. I am a deeply troubled woman, and I was telling the LORD about all my problems. 16Don't think I am an evil woman. I have been praying because I have many troubles and am very sad."

17Eli answered, "Go! I wish you well. May the God of Israel give you what you asked of him."

18Hannah said, "May I always please you." When she left and ate something, she was not sad anymore.

19Early the next morning Elkanah's family got up and worshiped the LORD. Then they went back home to Ramah. Elkanah had sexual relations with his wife Hannah, and the LORD remembered her. 20So Hannah became pregnant, and in time she gave birth to a son. She named him Samuel,[n] saying, "His name is Samuel because I asked the LORD for him."

Hannah Gives Samuel to God

21Every year Elkanah went with his whole family to Shiloh to offer sacrifices and to keep the promise he had made to God. 22But one time Hannah did not go with him. She told him, "When the boy is old enough to eat solid food, I will take him to Shiloh. Then I will give him to the LORD, and he will always live there."

23Elkanah, Hannah's husband, said to her, "Do what you think is best. You may stay home until the boy is old enough to eat. May the LORD do what you have said." So Hannah stayed at home to nurse her son until he was old enough to eat.

24When Samuel was old enough to eat, Hannah

cut . . . razor People who made special promises not to cut their hair or to drink wine or beer were called Nazirites. These people gave a specific time in their lives, or sometimes their entire lives, to the Lord. See Numbers 6:1-5.
Samuel This name sounds like the Hebrew word for "God heard."

took him to the house of the LORD at Shiloh, along
with a three-year-old bull, one-half bushel of flour,
and a leather bag filled with wine. 25After they
had killed the bull for the sacrifice, Hannah
brought Samuel to Eli. 26She said to Eli, "As surely
as you live, sir, I am the same woman who stood
near you praying to the LORD. 27I prayed for this
child, and the LORD answered my prayer and gave
him to me. 28Now I give him back to the LORD.
He will belong to the LORD all his life." And he
worshiped the LORD there.

Hannah Gives Thanks

2 Hannah prayed:

"The LORD has filled my heart with joy;
I feel very strong in the LORD.
I can laugh at my enemies;
I am glad because you have helped me!

2"There is no one holy like the LORD.
There is no God but you;
there is no Rock[d] like our God.

3"Don't continue bragging,
don't speak proud words.
The LORD is a God who knows everything,
and he judges what people do.

4"The bows of warriors break,
but weak people become strong.
5Those who once had plenty of food now
must work for food,
but people who were hungry are hungry no
more.
The woman who could not have children
now has seven,
but the woman who had many children
now is sad.

6"The LORD sends death,
and he brings to life.
He sends people to the grave,
and he raises them to life again.
7The LORD makes some people poor,
and others he makes rich.
He makes some people humble,
and others he makes great.
8The LORD raises the poor up from the dust,
and he lifts the needy from the ashes.

BRAGGING

She Spoke Too Soon

Arlis Jordan was gorgeous. Stylish hair. Perfect complexion. Long eyelashes. Five-foot-five, one hundred eight pounds. Flawless figure. Everyone knew she was the best-looking girl at Westmont High.

Everyone, including Arlis. Whenever she had a chance, she would point out her own beauty and slam the "plain" girls. "Don't you care how you look?" she would chide if someone's hair wasn't carefully curled or if make-up didn't hide every blemish. "You really should take care of yourself . . . like I do."

When it was time for the Westmont Beauty Pageant, everyone knew Arlis would enter. And Arlis knew she would win. "Come on," she would sneer if someone questioned her. "Who in this city can give me any competition?"

As it turned out, Kris Jackson could. Kris entered the pageant because she wanted scholarship money for college. And though she wasn't as strikingly beautiful as Arlis, her vibrant personality and smile gave her the edge.

When Kris was crowned Miss Westmont, Arlis didn't even congratulate her. She burst into tears and stormed off the stage. "The judges are just stupid!" she cried, alone in the dressing room. "This whole thing is stupid!"

Arlis discovered how dangerous and humiliating bragging can be. Read **1 Samuel 2:1–10** to see what God thinks of braggers.

- How does the passage describe what happened to Arlis? What does it say about Kris?
- What caution about bragging do you see in the passage?

CONSIDER . . .

- stopping yourself next time you're tempted to brag about a good grade, honor or public recognition. Instead, use your gifts to help others.
- thanking God for the gifts you have, instead of bragging about them.

FOR MORE, SEE . . .

- Proverbs 16:18–20 (p. 581)
- Jeremiah 9:23–24 (p. 703)
- Luke 1:46–55 (p. 1001)

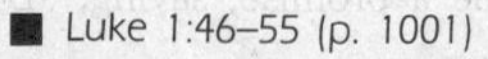

He lets the poor sit with princes
and receive a throne of honor.

"The foundations of the earth belong to the
LORD,
and the LORD set the world upon them.
9He protects those who are loyal to him,
but evil people will be silenced in darkness.
Power is not the key to success.
10The LORD destroys his enemies;
he will thunder in heaven against them.
The LORD will judge all the earth.
He will give power to his king
and make his appointed king strong."

Eli's Evil Sons

11Then Elkanah went home to Ramah, but the
boy continued to serve the LORD under Eli the
priest.
12Now Eli's sons were evil men; they did not
care about the LORD. 13This is what the priests
would normally do to the people: Every time
someone brought a sacrifice, the meat would be
cooked in a pot. The priest's servant would then
come carrying a fork that had three prongs. 14He
would plunge the fork into the pot or the kettle.
Whatever the fork brought out of the pot belonged to the priest. But this is how they treated
all the Israelites who came to Shiloh to offer sacrifices. 15Even before the fat was burned, the
priest's servant would come to the person offering
sacrifices and say, "Give the priest some meat to
roast. He won't accept boiled meat from you, only
raw meat."
16If the one who offered the sacrifice said, "Let
the fat be burned up first as usual, and then take
anything you want," the priest's servant would
answer, "No, give me the meat now. If you don't,
I'll take it by force."
17The LORD saw that the sin of the servants was
very great because they did not show respect for
the offerings made to the LORD.

Samuel Grows Up

18But Samuel obeyed the LORD. As a boy he
wore a linen holy vest.[d] 19Every year Samuel's
mother made a little coat for him and took it to
him when she went with her husband to Shiloh
for the sacrifice. 20When Eli blessed Elkanah and
his wife, he would say, "May the LORD repay you
with children through Hannah to take the place
of the boy Hannah prayed for and gave back to the
LORD." Then Elkanah and Hannah would go
home. 21The LORD was kind to Hannah, so she
became the mother of three sons and two daughters. And the boy Samuel grew up serving the
LORD.
22Now Eli was very old. He heard about everything his sons were doing to all the Israelites and
how his sons had sexual relations with the
women who served at the entrance to the Meeting Tent.[d] 23Eli said to his sons, "Why do you do
these evil things that the people tell me about?
24No, my sons. The LORD's people are spreading
a bad report about you. 25If you sin against someone, God can help you. But if you sin against the
LORD himself, no one can help you!" But Eli's
sons would not listen to him, because the LORD
had decided to put them to death.
26The boy Samuel grew physically. He pleased
the LORD and the people.
27A man of God came to Eli and said, "This is
what the LORD says: 'I clearly showed myself to
the family of your ancestor Aaron when they were
slaves to the king of Egypt. 28I chose them from
all the tribes[d] of Israel to be my priests. I wanted
them to go up to my altar, to burn incense,[d] and
to wear the holy vest. I also let the family of your
ancestor have part of all the offerings sacrificed by
the Israelites. 29So why don't you respect the sacrifices and gifts? You honor your sons more than
me. You grow fat on the best parts of the meat the
Israelites bring to me.'
30"So the LORD, the God of Israel, says: 'I promised that your family and your ancestor's family
would serve me always.' But now the LORD says:
'This must stop! I will honor those who honor
me, but I will dishonor those who ignore me.
31The time is coming when I will destroy the
descendants[d] of both you and your ancestors. No
man will grow old in your family. 32You will see
trouble in my house. No matter what good things
happen to Israel, there will never be an old man
in your family. 33I will not totally cut off your family from my altar. But your eyes will cry and your
heart be sad, because all your descendants will
die.
34" 'I will give you a sign. Both your sons,
Hophni and Phinehas, will die on the same day.
35I will choose a loyal priest for myself who will
listen to me and do what I want. I will make his
family continue, and he will always serve before
my appointed king. 36Then everyone left in your
family will come and bow down before him. They
will beg for a little money or a little food and say,
"Please give me a job as priest so I can have food
to eat." ' "

God Calls Samuel

3 The boy Samuel served the LORD under Eli.
In those days the LORD did not speak directly
to people very often; there were very few visions.
2Eli's eyes were so weak he was almost blind.
One night he was lying in bed. 3Samuel was also
in bed in the LORD's house, where the Ark[d] of the
Agreement was. God's lamp was still burning.

4Then the LORD called Samuel, and Samuel an-
swered, "I am here!" 5He ran to Eli and said, "I
am here. You called me."
But Eli said, "I didn't call you. Go back to bed."
So Samuel went back to bed.
6The LORD called again, "Samuel!"
Samuel again went to Eli and said, "I am here.
You called me."
Again Eli said, "I didn't call you. Go back to
bed."
7Samuel did not yet know the LORD, and the
LORD had not spoken directly to him yet.
8The LORD called Samuel for the third time.
Samuel got up and went to Eli and said, "I am
here. You called me."
Then Eli realized the LORD was calling the boy.
9So he told Samuel, "Go to bed. If he calls you
again, say, 'Speak, LORD. I am your servant and I
am listening.' " So Samuel went and lay down in
bed.
10The LORD came and stood there and called as
he had before, "Samuel, Samuel!"
Samuel said, "Speak, LORD. I am your servant
and I am listening."
11The LORD said to Samuel, "Watch, I am going
to do something in Israel that will shock those
who hear about it. 12At that time I will do to Eli
and his family everything I promised, from beginning to end. 13I told Eli I would punish his family
always, because he knew his sons were evil. They
acted without honor, but he did not stop them.
14So I swore to Eli's family, 'Your guilt will never
be removed by sacrifice or offering.' "
15Samuel lay down until morning. Then he

FOLLOWING GOD

Did Someone Call?

From the time she learned to play the flute, Ramona Sanchez wanted to be a marching band director. She spent hours practicing flute and learning marching patterns for her high school band.

When Ramona wasn't practicing her music, she was working on the school newspaper or yearbook. She hadn't planned on doing them, but the yearbook adviser had asked her to be yearbook editor. Then the newspaper editor asked her to write features.

"I know you love music," her yearbook adviser told her, "but maybe you're overlooking your writing gifts."

Ramona dismissed the thought and kept concentrating on music. She regularly entered music competitions, hoping to get into a good music school. She did well in regional competitions, but never in state. However, when the yearbook was entered in state competition, it won first place.

"What's going on?" Ramona wondered, as she filled out applications for music schools. Her adviser's thoughts came to mind: "Maybe you're overlooking your writing gifts."

Ramona went to music school, but didn't do well. She didn't enjoy all the theory and hours of practice. To lift her spirits, she went to work at the college newspaper. Now that was fun!

After the first semester, she knew what she had to do. She dropped her music major and majored in English and communications. "It took me a while to figure out what to do," she recalls. "I'm glad I finally paid attention to the gifts God gave me."

It took several years for Ramona to understand how God wanted her to use her gifts. Similarly, Samuel didn't recognize God's call right away in **1 Samuel 3:1–20**. But by listening to the advice of Eli the priest, Samuel heard and followed God's call.

■ What signs did Ramona see that were similar to the calls Samuel heard?
■ When have you, like Samuel, had trouble knowing what God wanted you to do?

CONSIDER . . .

■ silently listening for God's direction when you pray.
■ asking someone you respect to help you figure out ways God might want you to follow him.

FOR MORE, SEE . . .

■ Isaiah 6:1–8 (p. 622)
■ Mark 1:16–20 (p. 964)
■ Acts 9:1–19 (p. 1112)

opened the doors of the house of the LORD. He was afraid to tell Eli about the vision, 16but Eli called to him, "Samuel, my son!"

Samuel answered, "I am here."

17Eli asked, "What did the LORD say to you? Don't hide it from me. May God punish you terribly if you hide from me anything he said to you." 18So Samuel told Eli everything and did not hide anything from him. Then Eli said, "He is the LORD. Let him do what he thinks is best."

19The LORD was with Samuel as he grew up; he did not let any of Samuel's messages fail to come true. 20Then all Israel, from Dan to Beersheba,[n] knew Samuel was a true prophet[d] of the LORD. 21And the LORD continued to show himself at Shiloh, and he showed himself to Samuel through his word.

4 So, news about Samuel spread through all of Israel.

The Philistines Capture the Ark of the Agreement

At that time the Israelites went out to fight the Philistines. The Israelites camped at Ebenezer and the Philistines at Aphek. 2The Philistines went to meet the Israelites in battle. And as the battle spread, they defeated the Israelites, killing about four thousand soldiers on the battlefield. 3When some Israelite soldiers went back to their camp, the older leaders of Israel asked, "Why did the LORD let the Philistines defeat us? Let's bring the Ark[d] of the Agreement with the LORD here from Shiloh and take it with us into battle. Then God will save us from our enemies."

4So the people sent men to Shiloh. They brought back the Ark of the Agreement with the LORD All-Powerful, who sits between the gold creatures with wings. Eli's two sons, Hophni and Phinehas, were there with the Ark.

5When the Ark of the Agreement with the LORD came into the camp, all the Israelites gave a great shout of joy that made the ground shake. 6When the Philistines heard Israel's shout, they asked, "What's all this shouting in the Hebrew camp?"

Then the Philistines found out that the Ark of the LORD had come into the Hebrew camp. 7They were afraid and said, "A god has come into the Hebrew camp! We're in trouble! This has never happened before! 8How terrible it will be for us! Who can save us from these powerful gods? They are the ones who struck the Egyptians with all kinds of disasters in the desert. 9Be brave, Philistines! Fight like men! In the past they were our slaves. So fight like men, or we will become their slaves."

10So the Philistines fought hard and defeated the Israelites, and every Israelite soldier ran away to his own home. It was a great defeat for Israel, because thirty thousand Israelite soldiers were killed. 11The Ark of God was taken by the Philistines, and Eli's two sons, Hophni and Phinehas, died.

12That same day a man from the tribe[d] of Benjamin ran from the battle. He tore his clothes and put dust on his head to show his great sadness. 13When he arrived in Shiloh, Eli was by the side of the road. He was sitting there in a chair, watching, because he was worried about the Ark of God. When the Benjaminite entered Shiloh, he told the bad news. Then all the people in town cried loudly. 14Eli heard the crying and asked, "What's all this noise?"

The Benjaminite ran to Eli and told him what had happened. 15Eli was now ninety-eight years old, and he was blind. 16The Benjaminite told him, "I have come from the battle. I ran all the way here today."

Eli asked, "What happened, my son?"

17The Benjaminite answered, "Israel ran away from the Philistines, and the Israelite army has lost many soldiers. Your two sons are both dead, and the Philistines have taken the Ark of God."

18When he mentioned the Ark of God, Eli fell backward off his chair. He fell beside the gate, broke his neck, and died, because he was old and fat. He had led Israel for forty years.

> **SIDELIGHT:** Ever get yelled at for leaning back in your chair? It's dangerous. You could fall over backwards. Eli did . . . and died (1 Samuel 4:18).

The Glory Is Gone

19Eli's daughter-in-law, the wife of Phinehas, was pregnant and was about to give birth. When she heard the news that the Ark[d] of God had been taken and that Eli, her father-in-law, and Phinehas, her husband, were both dead, she began to give birth to her child. The child was born, but the mother had much trouble in giving birth. 20As she was dying, the women who helped her said, "Don't worry! You've given birth to a son!" But she did not answer or pay attention. 21She named the baby Ichabod,[n] saying, "Israel's glory is gone." She said this because the Ark of God had been taken and her father-in-law and husband

Dan to Beersheba Dan was the city farthest north in Israel, and Beersheba was the city farthest south. So this means all the people of Israel.

Ichabod This name means "no glory."

were dead. 22She said, "Israel's glory is gone, because the Ark of God has been taken away."

Trouble for the Philistines

5 After the Philistines had captured the Ark[d] of God, they took it from Ebenezer to Ashdod. 2They carried it into Dagon's[d] temple and put it next to Dagon. 3When the people of Ashdod rose early the next morning, they found that Dagon had fallen on his face on the ground before the Ark of the LORD. So they put Dagon back in his place. 4The next morning when they rose, they again found Dagon fallen on the ground before the Ark of the LORD. His head and hands had broken off and were lying in the doorway. Only his body was still in one piece. 5So, even today, Dagon's priests and others who enter his temple at Ashdod refuse to step on the doorsill.

6The LORD was hard on the people of Ashdod and their neighbors. He caused them to suffer and gave them growths on their skin. 7When the people of Ashdod saw what was happening, they said, "The Ark of the God of Israel can't stay with us. God is punishing us and Dagon our god." 8The people of Ashdod called all five Philistine kings together and asked them, "What should we do with the Ark of the God of Israel?"

The rulers answered, "Move the Ark of the God of Israel to Gath." So the Philistines moved it to Gath.

9But after they moved it to Gath, there was a great panic. The LORD was hard on that city also, and he gave both old and young people in Gath growths on their skin. 10Then the Philistines sent the Ark of God to Ekron.

But when it came into Ekron, the people of Ekron yelled, "Why are you bringing the Ark of the God of Israel to our city? Do you want to kill us and our people?" 11So they called all the kings of the Philistines together and said, "Send the Ark of the God of Israel back to its place before it kills us and our people!" All the people in the city were struck with terror because God was so hard on them there. 12The people who did not die were troubled with growths on their skin. So the people of Ekron cried loudly to heaven.

The Ark of God Is Sent Home

6 The Philistines kept the Ark[d] of God in their land seven months. 2Then they called for their priests and magicians and said, "What should we do with the Ark of the LORD? Tell us how to send it back home!"

3The priests and magicians answered, "If you send back the Ark of the God of Israel, don't send it back empty. You must give a penalty offering. If you are then healed, you will know that it was because of the Ark that you had such trouble."

4The Philistines asked, "What kind of penalty offering should we send to Israel's God?"

They answered, "Make five gold models of the growths on your skin and five gold models of rats. The number of models must match the number of Philistine kings, because the same sickness has come on you and your kings. 5Make models of the growths and the rats that are ruining the country, and give honor to Israel's God. Then maybe he will stop being so hard on you, your gods, and your land. 6Don't be stubborn like the king of Egypt and the Egyptians. After God punished them terribly, they let the Israelites leave Egypt.

7"You must build a new cart and get two cows that have just had calves. These must be cows that have never had yokes[d] on their necks. Hitch the cows to the cart, and take the calves home, away from their mothers. 8Put the Ark of the LORD on the cart and the gold models for the penalty offering in a box beside the Ark. Then send the cart straight on its way. 9Watch the cart. If it goes toward Beth Shemesh in Israel's own land, the LORD has given us this great sickness. But if it doesn't, we will know that Israel's God has not punished us. Our sickness just happened by chance."

10The Philistines did what the priests and magicians said. They took two cows that had just had calves and hitched them to the cart, but they kept their calves at home. 11They put the Ark of the LORD and the box with the gold rats and models of growths on the cart. 12Then the cows went straight toward Beth Shemesh. They stayed on the road, mooing all the way, and did not turn right or left. The Philistine kings followed the cows as far as the border of Beth Shemesh.

13Now the people of Beth Shemesh were harvesting their wheat in the valley. When they looked up and saw the Ark of the LORD, they were very happy. 14The cart came to the field belonging to Joshua of Beth Shemesh and stopped near a large rock. The people of Beth Shemesh chopped up the wood of the cart. Then they sacrificed the cows as burnt offerings to the LORD. 15The Levites took down the Ark of the LORD and the box that had the gold models, and they put both on the large rock. That day the people of Beth Shemesh offered whole burnt offerings and made sacrifices to the LORD. 16After the five Philistine kings saw this, they went back to Ekron the same day.

17The Philistines had sent these gold models of the growths as penalty offerings to the LORD. They sent one model for each Philistine town: Ashdod, Gaza, Ashkelon, Gath, and Ekron. 18And the Philistines also sent gold models of rats. The number of rats matched the number of towns belonging to the Philistine kings, including both strong, walled cities and country villages. The large rock on which they put the Ark of the LORD is still there in the field of Joshua of Beth Shemesh.

19But some of the men of Beth Shemesh looked into the Ark of the LORD. So God killed seventy of them. The people of Beth Shemesh cried because the LORD had struck them down. 20They said, "Who can stand before the LORD, this holy God? Whom will he strike next?"

21Then they sent messengers to the people of Kiriath Jearim, saying, "The Philistines have brought back the Ark of the LORD. Come down and take it to your city."

7 The men of Kiriath Jearim came and took the Ark of the LORD to Abinadab's house on a hill. There they made Abinadab's son Eleazar holy for the LORD so he could guard the Ark of the LORD.

The Lord Saves the Israelites

2The Ark[d] stayed at Kiriath Jearim a long time—twenty years in all. And the people of Israel began to follow the LORD again. 3Samuel spoke to the whole group of Israel, saying, "If you're turning back to the LORD with all your hearts, you must remove your foreign gods and your idols of Ashtoreth.[d] You must give yourselves fully to the LORD and serve only him. Then he will save you from the Philistines."

4So the Israelites put away their idols of Baal[d] and Ashtoreth, and they served only the LORD.

5Samuel said, "All Israel must meet at Mizpah, and I will pray to the LORD for you." 6So the Israelites met together at Mizpah. They drew water from the ground and poured it out before the LORD and did not eat that day. They confessed, "We have sinned against the LORD." And Samuel served as judge of Israel at Mizpah.

7The Philistines heard the Israelites were meeting at Mizpah, so the Philistine kings came up to attack them. When the Israelites heard they were coming, they were afraid. 8They said to Samuel, "Don't stop praying to the LORD our God for us! Ask him to save us from the Philistines!" 9Then Samuel took a baby lamb and offered it to the LORD as a whole burnt offering. He called to the LORD for Israel's sake, and the LORD answered him.

10While Samuel was burning the offering, the Philistines came near to attack Israel. But the LORD thundered against them with loud thunder. They were so frightened they became confused. So the Israelites defeated the Philistines in battle. 11The men of Israel ran out of Mizpah and chased the Philistines almost to Beth Car, killing the Philistines along the way.

Peace Comes to Israel

12After this happened Samuel took a stone and set it up between Mizpah and Shen. He named the stone Ebenezer,[n] saying, "The LORD has helped us to this point." 13So the Philistines were defeated and did not enter the Israelites' land again.

The LORD was against the Philistines all Samuel's life. 14Earlier the Philistines had taken towns from the Israelites, but the Israelites won them back, from Ekron to Gath. They also took back from the Philistines the lands near these towns. There was peace also between Israel and the Amorites.

15Samuel continued as judge of Israel all his life. 16Every year he went from Bethel to Gilgal to Mizpah and judged the Israelites in all these towns. 17But Samuel always went back to Ramah, where his home was. There he judged Israel and built an altar to the LORD.

Israel Asks for a King

8 When Samuel was old, he made his sons judges for Israel. 2His first son was named Joel, and his second son was named Abijah. Joel and Abijah were judges in Beersheba. 3But Samuel's sons did not live as he did. They tried to get money dishonestly, and they accepted money secretly to make wrong judgments.

4So all the older leaders came together and met Samuel at Ramah. 5They said to him, "You're old, and your sons don't live as you do. Give us a king to rule over us like all the other nations."

6When the older leaders said that, Samuel was not pleased. He prayed to the LORD, 7and the LORD told Samuel, "Listen to whatever the people say to you. They have not rejected you. They have rejected me from being their king. 8They are doing as they have always done. When I took them out of Egypt, they left me and served other gods. They are doing the same to you. 9Now listen to the people, but warn them what the king who rules over them will do."

10So Samuel told those who had asked him for a king what the LORD had said. 11Samuel said, "If you have a king ruling over you, this is what he will do: He will take your sons and make them serve with his chariots and his horses, and they will run in front of the king's chariot. 12The king will make some of your sons commanders over thousands or over fifties. He will make some of your other sons plow his ground and reap his harvest. He will take others to make weapons of war and equipment for his chariots. 13He will take your daughters to make perfume and cook and bake for him. 14He will take your best fields, vine-

Ebenezer This name means "stone of help."

yards, and olive groves and give them to his servants. 15He will take one-tenth of your grain and grapes and give it to his officers and servants. 16He will take your male and female servants, your best cattle, and your donkeys and use them all for his own work. 17He will take one-tenth of your flocks, and you yourselves will become his slaves. 18When that time comes, you will cry out because of the king you chose. But the LORD will not answer you then."

19But the people would not listen to Samuel. They said, "No! We want a king to rule over us. 20Then we will be the same as all the other nations. Our king will judge for us and go with us and fight our battles."

21After Samuel heard all that the people said, he repeated their words to the LORD. 22The LORD answered, "You must listen to them. Give them a king."

Then Samuel told the people of Israel, "Go back to your towns."

Saul Looks for His Father's Donkeys

9 Kish, son of Abiel from the tribe[d] of Benjamin, was an important man. (Abiel was the son of Zeror, who was the son of Becorath, who was the son of Aphiah of Benjamin.) 2Kish had a son named Saul, who was a fine young man. There was no Israelite better than he. Saul stood a head taller than any other man in Israel.

3Now the donkeys of Saul's father, Kish, were lost. So Kish said to Saul, his son, "Take one of the servants, and go and look for the donkeys." 4Saul went through the mountains of Ephraim and the land of Shalisha, but he and the servant could not find the donkeys. They went into the land of Shaalim, but the donkeys were not there. They went through the land of Benjamin, but they still did not find them. 5When they arrived in the area of Zuph, Saul said to his servant, "Let's go back or my father will stop thinking about the donkeys and will start worrying about us."

6But the servant answered, "A man of God is in this town. People respect him because everything he says comes true. Let's go into the town now. Maybe he can tell us something about the journey we have taken."

7Saul said to his servant, "If we go into the town, what can we give him? The food in our bags is gone. We have no gift to give him. Do we have anything?"

8Again the servant answered Saul. "Look, I have one-tenth of an ounce of silver. Give it to the man of God. Then he will tell us about our journey." 9(In the past, if someone in Israel wanted to ask something from God, he would say, "Let's go to the seer."[d] We call the person a prophet[d] today, but in the past he was called a seer.)

10Saul said to his servant, "That's a good idea. Come, let's go." So they went toward the town where the man of God was.

11As Saul and the servant were going up the hill to the town, they met some young women coming out to get water. Saul and the servant asked them, "Is the seer here?"

12The young women answered, "Yes, he's here. He's ahead of you. Hurry now. He has just come to our town today, because the people will offer a sacrifice at the place of worship. 13As soon as you enter the town, you will find him before he goes up to the place of worship to eat. The people will not begin eating until the seer comes, because he must bless the sacrifice. After that, the guests will eat. Go now, and you should find him."

Saul Meets Samuel

14Saul and the servant went up to the town. Just as they entered it, they saw Samuel coming toward them on his way up to the place of worship.

15The day before Saul came, the LORD had told Samuel: 16"About this time tomorrow I will send you a man from the land of Benjamin. Appoint him to lead my people Israel. He will save my people from the Philistines. I have seen the suffering of my people, and I have listened to their cry."

17When Samuel first saw Saul, the LORD said to Samuel, "This is the man I told you about. He will organize my people."

18Saul approached Samuel at the gate and said, "Please tell me where the seer's[d] house is."

19Samuel answered, "I am the seer. Go with me to the place of worship. Today you and your servant are to eat with me. Tomorrow morning I will answer all your questions and send you home. 20Don't worry about the donkeys you lost three days ago, because they have been found. Soon all the wealth of Israel will belong to you and your family."

21Saul answered, "But I am from the tribe[d] of Benjamin, the smallest tribe in Israel. And my family group is the smallest in the tribe of Benjamin. Why are you saying such things?"

22Then Samuel took Saul and his servant into a large room and gave them a choice place at the table. About thirty guests were there. 23Samuel said to the cook, "Bring the meat I gave you, the portion I told you to set aside."

24So the cook took the thigh and put it on the table in front of Saul. Samuel said, "This is the meat saved for you. Eat it, because it was set aside for you for this special time. As I said, 'I had invited the people.' " So Saul ate with Samuel that day.

25After they finished eating, they came down from the place of worship and went to the town.

Then Samuel talked with Saul on the roof[n] of his house. 26At dawn they got up, and Samuel called to Saul on the roof. He said, "Get up, and I will send you on your way." So Saul got up and went out of the house with Samuel. 27As Saul, his servant, and Samuel were getting near the edge of the city, Samuel said to Saul, "Tell the servant to go on ahead of us, but you stay, because I have a message from God for you."

Samuel Appoints Saul

10 Samuel took a jar of olive oil and poured it on Saul's head. He kissed Saul and said, "The LORD has appointed you to lead his people. 2After you leave me today, you will meet two men near Rachel's tomb on the border of Benjamin at Zelzah. They will say to you, 'The donkeys you were looking for have been found. But now your father has stopped thinking about his donkeys and is worrying about you. He is asking, "What will I do about my son?" '

3"Then you will go on until you reach the big tree at Tabor. Three men on their way to worship God at Bethel will meet you there. One man will be carrying three goats. Another will be carrying three loaves of bread. And the third will have a leather bag full of wine. 4They will greet you and offer you two loaves of bread, which you must accept. 5Then you will go to Gibeah of God, where a Philistine camp is. When you approach this town, a group of prophets[d] will come down from the place of worship. They will be playing harps, tambourines,[d] flutes, and lyres,[d] and they will be prophesying. 6Then the Spirit[d] of the LORD will rush upon you with power. You will prophesy with these prophets, and you will be changed into a different man. 7After these signs happen, do whatever you find to do, because God will help you.

8"Go ahead of me to Gilgal. I will come down to you to offer whole burnt offerings and fellowship offerings. But you must wait seven days. Then I will come and tell you what to do."

Saul Made King

9When Saul turned to leave Samuel, God changed Saul's heart. All these signs came true that day. 10When Saul and his servant arrived at Gibeah, Saul met a group of prophets.[d] The Spirit[d] of God rushed upon him, and he prophesied with the prophets. 11When people who had known Saul before saw him prophesying with the prophets, they asked each other, "What has happened to Kish's son? Is even Saul one of the prophets?"

12A man who lived there said, "Who is the father of these prophets?" So this became a famous saying: "Is even Saul one of the prophets?" 13When Saul finished prophesying, he entered the place of worship.

14Saul's uncle asked him and his servant, "Where have you been?"

Saul said, "We were looking for the donkeys. When we couldn't find them, we went to talk to Samuel."

15Saul's uncle asked, "Please tell me. What did Samuel say to you?"

16Saul answered, "He told us the donkeys had already been found." But Saul did not tell his uncle what Samuel had said about his becoming king.

17Samuel called all the people of Israel to meet with the LORD at Mizpah. 18He said, "This is what the LORD, the God of Israel, says: 'I led Israel out of Egypt. I saved you from Egypt's control and from other kingdoms that were troubling you.' 19But now you have rejected your God. He saves you from all your troubles and problems, but you said, 'No! We want a king to rule over us.' Now come, stand before the LORD in your tribes[d] and family groups."

20When Samuel gathered all the tribes of Israel, the tribe of Benjamin was picked. 21Samuel had them pass by in family groups, and Matri's family was picked. Then he had each man of Matri's family pass by, and Saul son of Kish was picked. But when they looked for Saul, they could not find him. 22They asked the LORD, "Has Saul come here yet?"

The LORD said, "Yes. He's hiding behind the baggage."

23So they ran and brought him out. When Saul stood among the people, he was a head taller than anyone else. 24Then Samuel said to the people, "See the man the LORD has chosen. There is no one like him among all the people."

Then the people shouted, "Long live the king!"

SIDELIGHT: Even if you're shy, you could still be president. Saul, Israel's first king, was so shy that when the people tried to crown him, he hid in the baggage (1 Samuel 10:20–24).

25Samuel explained the rights and duties of the king and then wrote them in a book and put it before the LORD. Then he told the people to go to their homes.

26Saul also went to his home in Gibeah. God touched the hearts of certain brave men who

roof In Bible times houses were built with flat roofs. The roof was used for drying things such as flax and fruit. And it was used as an extra room, as a place for worship, and as a place to sleep in the summer.

went along with him. 27But some troublemakers
said, "How can this man save us?" They disapproved of Saul and refused to bring gifts to him.
But Saul kept quiet.

Nahash Troubles Jabesh Gilead

11 About a month later Nahash the Ammonite and his army surrounded the city
of Jabesh in Gilead. All the people of Jabesh said
to Nahash, "Make a treaty with us, and we will
serve you."

2But he answered, "I will make a treaty with
you only if I'm allowed to poke out the right eye
of each of you. Then all Israel will be ashamed!"

3The older leaders of Jabesh said to Nahash,
"Give us seven days to send messengers through
all Israel. If no one comes to help us, we will give
ourselves up to you."

4When the messengers came to Gibeah where
Saul lived and told the people the news, they
cried loudly. 5Saul was coming home from plowing the fields with his oxen when he heard the
people crying. He asked, "What's wrong with the
people that they are crying?" Then they told Saul
what the messengers from Jabesh had said.
6When Saul heard their words, God's Spirit[d]
rushed upon him with power, and he became
very angry. 7So he took a pair of oxen and cut
them into pieces. Then he gave the pieces of the
oxen to messengers and ordered them to carry
them through all the land of Israel.

The messengers said, "This is what will happen
to the oxen of anyone who does not follow Saul
and Samuel." So the people became very afraid of
the LORD. They all came together as if they were
one person. 8Saul gathered the people together at
Bezek. There were three hundred thousand men
from Israel and thirty thousand men from Judah.

9They said to the messengers who had come,
"Tell the people at Jabesh Gilead this: 'Before the
day warms up tomorrow, you will be saved.' " So
the messengers went and reported this to the people at Jabesh, and they were very happy. 10The
people said to Nahash the Ammonite, "Tomorrow
we will come out to meet you. Then you can do
anything you want to us."

11The next morning Saul divided his soldiers
into three groups. At dawn they entered the Ammonite camp and defeated them before the heat
of the day. The Ammonites who escaped were
scattered; no two of them were still together.

12Then the people said to Samuel, "Who didn't
want Saul as king? Bring them here and we will
kill them!"

13But Saul said, "No! No one will be put to
death today. Today the LORD has saved Israel!"

14Then Samuel said to the people, "Come, let's
go to Gilgal. There we will again promise to obey
the king." 15So all the people went to Gilgal, and
there, before the LORD, the people made Saul
king. They offered fellowship offerings to the
LORD, and Saul and all the Israelites had a great
celebration.

> **SIDELIGHT:** Modern military recruiters might not have much luck enlisting volunteers if they used Saul's methods in 1 Samuel 11:7. He cut two oxen into pieces and gave the pieces to messengers to carry around the country to mobilize people for war. (The act symbolized uniting all the people.) The approach worked for Saul; his army walloped the Ammonites (1 Samuel 11:11).

Samuel's Farewell Speech

12 Samuel said to all Israel, "I have done
everything you wanted me to do and
have put a king over you. 2Now you have a king
to lead you. I am old and gray, and my sons are
here with you. I have been your leader since I was
young. 3Here I am. If I have done anything wrong,
you must testify against me before the LORD and
his appointed king. Did I steal anyone's ox or donkey? Did I hurt or cheat anyone? Did I ever secretly accept money to pretend not to see something wrong? If I did any of these things, I will
make it right."

4The Israelites answered, "You have not
cheated us, or hurt us, or taken anything unfairly
from anyone."

5Samuel said to them, "The LORD is a witness
to what you have said. His appointed king is also
a witness today that you did not find anything
wrong in me."

"He is our witness," they said.

6Then Samuel said to the people, "It is the
LORD who chose Moses and Aaron and brought
your ancestors out of Egypt. 7Now, stand there,
and I will remind you of all the good things the
LORD did for you and your ancestors.

8"After Jacob entered Egypt, his descendants[d]
cried to the LORD for help. So the LORD sent Moses and Aaron, who took your ancestors out of
Egypt and brought them to live in this place.

9"But they forgot the LORD their God. So he
handed them over as slaves to Sisera, the commander of the army of Hazor, and as slaves to the
Philistines and the king of Moab. They all fought
against your ancestors. 10Then your ancestors
cried to the LORD and said, 'We have sinned. We
have left the LORD and served the Baals[d] and the
Ashtoreths.[d] But now save us from our enemies,
and we will serve you.' 11So the LORD sent Gid-

eon,[n] Barak, Jephthah, and Samuel. He saved you from your enemies around you, and you lived in safety. 12But when you saw Nahash king of the Ammonites coming against you, you said, 'No! We want a king to rule over us!'—even though the LORD your God was your king. 13Now here is the king you chose, the one you asked for. The LORD has put him over you. 14You must honor the LORD and serve him. You must obey his word and not turn against his commands. Both you and the king ruling over you must follow the LORD your God. If you do, it will be well with you. 15But if you don't obey the LORD, and if you turn against his commands, he will be against you. He will do to you what he did to your ancestors.

16"Now stand still and see the great thing the LORD will do before your eyes. 17It is now the time of the wheat harvest.[n] I will pray for the LORD to send thunder and rain. Then you will know what an evil thing you did against the LORD when you asked for a king."

18Then Samuel prayed to the LORD, and that same day the LORD sent thunder and rain. So the people were very afraid of the LORD and Samuel. 19They said to Samuel, "Pray to the LORD your God for us, your servants! Don't let us die! We've added to all our sins the evil of asking for a king."

20Samuel answered, "Don't be afraid. It's true that you did wrong, but don't turn away from the LORD. Serve the LORD with all your heart. 21Idols are of no use, so don't worship them. They can't help you or save you. They are useless! 22For his own sake, the LORD won't leave his people. Instead, he was pleased to make you his own people. 23I will surely not stop praying for you, because that would be sinning against the LORD. I will teach you what is good and right. 24You must honor the LORD and truly serve him with all your heart. Remember the wonderful things he did for you! 25But if you are stubborn and do evil, he will sweep you and your king away."

13 Saul was thirty years old when he became king, and he was king over Israel forty-two years.[n] 2Saul chose three thousand men from Israel. Two thousand men stayed with him at Micmash in the mountains of Bethel, and one thousand men stayed with Jonathan at Gibeah in Benjamin. Saul sent the other men in the army back home.

3Jonathan attacked the Philistine camp in Geba, and the other Philistines heard about it. Saul said, "Let the Hebrews hear what happened." So he told the men to blow trumpets through all the land of Israel. 4All the Israelites heard the news. The men said, "Saul has defeated the Philistine camp. Now the Philistines will really hate us!" Then the Israelites were called to join Saul at Gilgal.

5The Philistines gathered to fight Israel with three thousand[n] chariots and six thousand men to ride in them. Their soldiers were as many as the grains of sand on the seashore. The Philistines went and camped at Micmash, which is east of Beth Aven. 6When the Israelites saw that they were in trouble, they went to hide in caves and bushes, among the rocks, and in pits and wells. 7Some Hebrews even went across the Jordan River to the land of Gad and Gilead.

But Saul stayed at Gilgal, and all the men in his army were shaking with fear. 8Saul waited seven days, because Samuel had said he would meet him then. But Samuel did not come to Gilgal, and the soldiers began to leave.

9So Saul said, "Bring me the whole burnt offering and the fellowship offerings." Then Saul offered the whole burnt offering. 10Just as he finished, Samuel arrived, and Saul went to greet him.

11Samuel asked, "What have you done?"

Saul answered, "I saw the soldiers leaving me, and you were not here when you said you would be. The Philistines were gathering at Micmash. 12Then I thought, 'The Philistines will come against me at Gilgal, and I haven't asked for the LORD's approval.' So I forced myself to offer the whole burnt offering."

13Samuel said, "You acted foolishly! You haven't obeyed the command of the LORD your God. If you had obeyed him, the LORD would have made your kingdom continue in Israel always, 14but now your kingdom will not continue. The LORD has looked for the kind of man he wants. He has appointed him to rule his people, because you haven't obeyed his command."

15Then Samuel left Gilgal and went to Gibeah in Benjamin. Saul counted the men who were still with him, and there were about six hundred.

Hard Times for Israel

16Saul and his son Jonathan and the soldiers with him stayed in Gibeah in the land of Benjamin. The Philistines made their camp at Micmash. 17Three groups went out from the Philistine camp to make raids. One group went on the Ophrah road in the land of Shual. 18The second group went on the Beth Horon road. The third group went on the border road that overlooks the Valley of Zeboim toward the desert.

Gideon Also called Jerub-Baal.
time . . . harvest This was a dry time in the summer when no rains fell.
Saul . . . years This is how the verse is worded in some early Greek copies. The Hebrew is not clear here.
three thousand Some Greek copies say three thousand. The Hebrew copies say thirty thousand.

19The whole land of Israel had no blacksmith because the Philistines had said, "The Hebrews might make swords and spears." 20So all the Israelites had to go down to the Philistines to have their plows, hoes, axes, and sickles sharpened. 21The Philistine blacksmiths charged about one-fourth of an ounce of silver for sharpening plows and hoes. And they charged one-eighth of an ounce of silver for sharpening picks, axes, and the sticks used to guide oxen.

22So when the battle came, the soldiers with Saul and Jonathan had no swords or spears. Only Saul and his son Jonathan had them.

SIDELIGHT: The Philistines were so threatening to the Israelites partly because they held a monopoly on iron weapons. Only Israelite royalty had spears or swords (1 Samuel 13:19–22), and they were probably smuggled in from other countries.

Israel Defeats the Philistines

23A group from the Philistine army had gone out to the pass at Micmash.

14 One day Jonathan, Saul's son, said to the officer who carried his armor, "Come, let's go over to the Philistine camp on the other side." But Jonathan did not tell his father.

2Saul was sitting under a pomegranate[d] tree at the threshing[d] floor near Gibeah. He had about six hundred men with him. 3One man was Ahijah who was wearing the holy vest.[d] (Ahijah was a son of Ichabod's brother Ahitub. Ichabod was the son of Phinehas, the son of Eli, the LORD's priest in Shiloh.) No one knew Jonathan had left.

4There was a steep slope on each side of the pass that Jonathan planned to go through to reach the Philistine camp. The cliff on one side was named Bozez, and the cliff on the other side was named Seneh. 5One cliff faced north toward Micmash. The other faced south toward Geba.

6Jonathan said to his officer who carried his armor, "Come. Let's go to the camp of those men who are not circumcised.[d] Maybe the LORD will help us. The LORD can give us victory if we have many people, or just a few."

7The officer who carried Jonathan's armor said to him, "Do whatever you think is best. Go ahead. I'm with you."

8Jonathan said, "Then come. We will cross over to the Philistines and let them see us. 9If they say to us, 'Stay there until we come to you,' we will stay where we are. We won't go up to them. 10But if they say, 'Come up to us,' we will climb up, and the LORD will let us defeat them. This will be the sign for us."

11When both Jonathan and his officer let the Philistines see them, the Philistines said, "Look! The Hebrews are crawling out of the holes they were hiding in!" 12The Philistines in the camp shouted to Jonathan and his officer, "Come up to us. We'll teach you a lesson!"

Jonathan said to his officer, "Climb up behind me, because the LORD has given the Philistines to Israel!" 13So Jonathan climbed up, using his hands and feet, and his officer climbed just behind him. Jonathan struck down the Philistines as he went, and his officer killed them as he followed behind him. 14In that first fight Jonathan and his officer killed about twenty Philistines over a half acre of ground.

15All the Philistine soldiers panicked—those in the camp and those in the raiding party. The ground itself shook! God had caused the panic.

16Saul's guards were at Gibeah in the land of Benjamin when they saw the Philistine soldiers running in every direction. 17Saul said to his army, "Check to see who has left our camp." When they checked, they learned that Jonathan and his officer were gone.

18So Saul said to Ahijah the priest, "Bring the Ark[d] of God." (At that time it was with the Israelites.) 19While Saul was talking to the priest, the confusion in the Philistine camp was growing. Then Saul said to Ahijah, "Put your hand down!"

20Then Saul gathered his army and entered the battle. They found the Philistines confused, striking each other with their swords! 21Earlier, there were Hebrews who had served the Philistines and had stayed in their camp, but now they joined the Israelites with Saul and Jonathan. 22When all the Israelites hidden in the mountains of Ephraim heard that the Philistine soldiers were running away, they also joined the battle and chased the Philistines. 23So the LORD saved the Israelites that day, and the battle moved on past Beth Aven.

Saul Makes Another Mistake

24The men of Israel were miserable that day because Saul had made an oath for all of them. He had said, "No one should eat food before evening and before I finish defeating my enemies. If he does, he will be cursed!" So no Israelite soldier ate food.

25Now the army went into the woods, where there was some honey on the ground. 26They came upon some honey, but no one took any because they were afraid of the oath. 27Jonathan had not heard the oath Saul had put on the army, so he dipped the end of his stick into the honey and lifted some out and ate it. Then he felt better. 28Then one of the soldiers told Jonathan, "Your father made an oath for all the soldiers. He said any man who eats today will be cursed! That's why they are so weak."

29Jonathan said, "My father has made trouble for the land! See how much better I feel after just tasting a little of this honey! 30It would have been much better for the men to eat the food they took from their enemies today. We could have killed many more Philistines!"

31That day the Israelites defeated the Philistines from Micmash to Aijalon. After that, they were very tired. 32They had taken sheep, cattle, and calves from the Philistines. Now they were so hungry they killed the animals on the ground and ate them, without draining the blood from them! 33Someone said to Saul, "Look! The men are sinning against the LORD. They're eating meat without draining the blood from it!"

Saul said, "You have sinned! Roll a large stone over here now!" 34Then he said, "Go to the men and tell them that each person must bring his ox and sheep to me and kill it here and eat it. Don't sin against the LORD by eating meat without draining the blood from it."

That night everyone brought his animals and killed them there. 35Then Saul built an altar to the LORD. It was the first altar he had built to the LORD.

36Saul said, "Let's go after the Philistines tonight and rob them. We won't let any of them live!"

The men answered, "Do whatever you think is best."

But the priest said, "Let's ask God."

37So Saul asked God, "Should I chase the Philistines? Will you let us defeat them?" But God did not answer Saul at that time. 38Then Saul said to all the leaders of his army, "Come here. Let's find out what sin has been done today. 39As surely as the LORD lives who has saved Israel, even if my son Jonathan did the sin, he must die." But no one in the army spoke.

40Then Saul said to all the Israelites, "You stand on this side. I and my son Jonathan will stand on the other side."

The men answered, "Do whatever you think is best."

41Then Saul prayed to the LORD, the God of Israel, "Give me the right answer."

And Saul and Jonathan were picked; the other men went free. 42Saul said, "Now let us discover if it is I or Jonathan my son who is guilty." And Jonathan was picked.

43Saul said to Jonathan, "Tell me what you have done."

So Jonathan told Saul, "I only tasted a little honey from the end of my stick. And must I die now?"

44Saul said, "Jonathan, if you don't die, may God punish me terribly."

45But the soldiers said to Saul, "Must Jonathan die? Never! He is responsible for saving Israel today! As surely as the LORD lives, not even a hair of his head will fall to the ground! Today Jonathan fought against the Philistines with God's help!" So the army saved Jonathan, and he did not die.

46Then Saul stopped chasing the Philistines, and they went back to their own land.

Saul Fights Israel's Enemies

47When Saul became king over Israel, he fought against Israel's enemies all around. He fought Moab, the Ammonites, Edom, the king of Zobah, and the Philistines. Everywhere Saul went he defeated Israel's enemies. 48He fought bravely and defeated the Amalekites. He saved the Israelites from their enemies who had robbed them.

49Saul's sons were Jonathan, Ishvi, and Malki-Shua. His older daughter was named Merab, and his younger daughter was named Michal. 50Saul's wife was Ahinoam daughter of Ahimaaz. The commander of his army was Abner son of Ner, Saul's uncle. 51Saul's father Kish and Abner's father Ner were sons of Abiel.

52All Saul's life he fought hard against the Philistines. When he saw strong or brave men, he took them into his army.

Saul Rejected as King

15 Samuel said to Saul, "The LORD sent me to appoint you king over Israel. Now listen to his message. 2This is what the LORD All-Powerful says: 'When the Israelites came out of Egypt, the Amalekites tried to stop them from going to Canaan. So I will punish them. 3Now go, attack the Amalekites and destroy everything they own as an offering to the LORD. Don't let anything live. Put to death men and women, children and small babies, cattle and sheep, camels and donkeys.' "

4So Saul called the army together at Telaim. There were two hundred thousand foot soldiers and ten thousand men from Judah. 5Then Saul went to the city of Amalek and set up an ambush in the ravine. 6He said to the Kenites, "Go away. Leave the Amalekites so that I won't destroy you with them, because you showed kindness to the Israelites when they came out of Egypt." So the Kenites moved away from the Amalekites.

7Then Saul defeated the Amalekites. He fought them all the way from Havilah to Shur, at the border of Egypt. 8He took King Agag of the Amalekites alive, but he killed all of Agag's army with the sword. 9Saul and the army let Agag live, along with the best sheep, fat cattle, and lambs. They let every good animal live, because they did not want to destroy them. But when they found an animal that was weak or useless, they killed it.

10Then the LORD spoke his word to Samuel: 11"I am sorry I made Saul king, because he has stopped following me and has not obeyed my

commands." Samuel was upset, and he cried out
to the LORD all night long.
12Early the next morning Samuel got up and
went to meet Saul. But the people told Samuel,
"Saul has gone to Carmel, where he has put up
a monument in his own honor. Now he has gone
down to Gilgal."
13When Samuel came to Saul, Saul said, "May
the LORD bless you! I have obeyed the LORD's
commands."
14But Samuel said, "Then why do I hear cattle
mooing and sheep bleating?"
15Saul answered, "The soldiers took them from
the Amalekites. They saved the best sheep and
cattle to offer as sacrifices to the LORD your God,
but we destroyed all the other animals."
16Samuel said to Saul, "Stop! Let me tell you
what the LORD said to me last night."
Saul answered, "Tell me."
17Samuel said, "Once you didn't think much of
yourself, but now you have become the leader of
the tribes[d] of Israel. The LORD appointed you to
be king over Israel. 18And he sent you on a mission. He said, 'Go and destroy those evil people,
the Amalekites. Make war on them until all of
them are dead.' 19Why didn't you obey the LORD?
Why did you take the best things? Why did you
do what the LORD said was wrong?"
20Saul said, "But I did obey the LORD. I did
what the LORD told me to do. I destroyed all the
Amalekites, and I brought back Agag their king.
21The soldiers took the best sheep and cattle to
sacrifice to the LORD your God at Gilgal."
22But Samuel answered,

"What pleases the LORD more:
burnt offerings and sacrifices
or obedience to his voice?
It is better to obey than to sacrifice.
It is better to listen to God than to offer the
fat of sheep.
23Disobedience is as bad as the sin of sorcery.[d]
Pride is as bad as the sin of worshiping
idols.
You have rejected the LORD's command.
Now he rejects you as king."

24Then Saul said to Samuel, "I have sinned. I
didn't obey the LORD's commands and your
words. I was afraid of the people, and I did what
they said. 25Now, I beg you, forgive my sin. Come
back with me so I may worship the LORD."
26But Samuel said to Saul, "I won't go back
with you. You rejected the LORD's command, and
now he rejects you as king of Israel."
27As Samuel turned to leave, Saul caught his
robe, and it tore. 28Samuel said to him, "The LORD
has torn the kingdom of Israel from you today and
has given it to one of your neighbors who is better
than you. 29The LORD is the Eternal One of Israel.
He does not lie or change his mind. He is not a
human being, so he does not change his mind."
30Saul answered, "I have sinned. But please
honor me in front of the older leaders of my people and in front of the Israelites. Come back with
me so that I can worship the LORD your God."
31So Samuel went back with Saul, and Saul worshiped the LORD.
32Then Samuel said, "Bring me King Agag of
the Amalekites."
Agag came to Samuel in chains, but Agag
thought, "Surely the threat of death has passed."
33Samuel said to him, "Your sword made other
mothers lose their children. Now your mother
will have no children." And Samuel cut Agag to
pieces before the LORD at Gilgal.
34Then Samuel left and went to Ramah, but
Saul went up to his home in Gibeah. 35And Samuel never saw Saul again the rest of his life, but
he was sad for Saul. And the LORD was very sorry
he had made Saul king of Israel.

Samuel Goes to Bethlehem

16 The LORD said to Samuel, "How long
will you continue to feel sorry for Saul?
I have rejected him as king of Israel. Fill your container with olive oil and go. I am sending you to
Jesse who lives in Bethlehem, because I have chosen one of his sons to be king."
2But Samuel said, "If I go, Saul will hear the
news and will try to kill me."
The LORD said, "Take a young calf with you.
Say, 'I have come to offer a sacrifice to the LORD.'
3Invite Jesse to the sacrifice. Then I will tell you
what to do. You must appoint the one I show
you."
4Samuel did what the LORD told him to do.
When he arrived at Bethlehem, the older leaders
of Bethlehem shook with fear. They met him and
asked, "Are you coming in peace?"
5Samuel answered, "Yes, I come in peace. I
have come to make a sacrifice to the LORD. Set
yourselves apart to the LORD and come to the sacrifice with me." Then he set Jesse and his sons
apart to the LORD, and he invited them to come
to the sacrifice.
6When they arrived, Samuel saw Eliab, and he
thought, "Surely the LORD has appointed this person standing here before him."
7But the LORD said to Samuel, "Don't look at
how handsome Eliab is or how tall he is, because
I have not chosen him. God does not see the same
way people see. People look at the outside of a
person, but the LORD looks at the heart."
8Then Jesse called Abinadab and told him to
pass by Samuel. But Samuel said, "The LORD has
not chosen this man either." 9Then Jesse had
Shammah pass by. But Samuel said, "No, the
LORD has not chosen this one." 10Jesse had seven
of his sons pass by Samuel. But Samuel said to

him, "The LORD has not chosen any of these."
11Then he asked Jesse, "Are these all the sons
you have?"
Jesse answered, "I still have the youngest son.
He is out taking care of the sheep."
Samuel said, "Send for him. We will not sit
down to eat until he arrives."
12So Jesse sent and had his youngest son
brought in. He was a fine boy, tanned, and handsome.
The LORD said to Samuel, "Go, appoint him,
because he is the one."
13So Samuel took the container of olive oil and
poured it on Jesse's youngest son to appoint him
in front of his brothers. From that day on, the
LORD's Spirit[d] worked in David. Samuel then
went back to Ramah.

David Serves Saul

14But the LORD's Spirit[d] had left Saul, and an
evil spirit from the LORD troubled him.
15Saul's servants said to him, "See, an evil spirit
from God is troubling you. 16Give us the command to look for someone who can play the harp.
When the evil spirit from God troubles you, he
will play, and you will feel better."
17So Saul said to his servants, "Find someone
who can play well and bring him to me."
18One of the servants said, "I have seen a son
of Jesse of Bethlehem play the harp. He is brave
and courageous. He is a good speaker and handsome, and the LORD is with him."
19Then Saul sent messengers to Jesse, saying,
"Send me your son David, who is with the
sheep." 20So Jesse loaded a donkey with bread, a
leather bag full of wine, and a young goat, and he
sent them with his son David to Saul.
21When David came to Saul, he began to serve
him. Saul liked David and made him the officer
who carried his armor. 22Saul sent a message to
Jesse, saying, "Let David stay and serve me because I like him."
23When the evil spirit from God troubled Saul,
David would take his harp and play. Then the evil

SELF-ESTEEM

Bigger Isn't Always Better

"Too short."

That was the assessment of basketball coaches at Wilmer-Hutchins High School near Dallas. At five-foot-seven, Spud Webb didn't look like he was varsity basketball material.

But Spud thought they were wrong, and he played hard every day. He became the team's best passer, dribbler, and outside shooter.

Coaches at Midland Junior College told Spud the same thing: He was too short for the team. But Spud believed in himself and proved them wrong.

Coaches at North Carolina State also thought Spud was too short to play major-college ball. But Spud believed in himself, and he not only started for NC State, but he became an All-Atlantic Coast Conference player.

When Spud graduated, the sports commentators said he was too short to play in the National Basketball Association. But the Atlanta Hawks drafted him in 1985, and he proved the commentators wrong.

In a league where some players towered two feet above him, Spud's slashing, driving style made him one of the most feared guards in professional basketball.

Spud Webb became a superstar—despite people's predictions. Likewise, David became king of Israel, even though he wasn't the tallest, smartest, or strongest choice. Read why God chose him in **1 Samuel 16:1–13**.

- What might have happened if Spud Webb and David had believed what others said?
- What qualities did David have that you see in yourself?

C O N S I D E R . . .

- identifying some good things about yourself that someone looking at you from the outside might not notice. Decide how you'll use those qualities to serve God.
- finding out some good things that are hidden in someone who is unpopular at school or church, then encouraging him or her in those things.

F O R M O R E , S E E . . .

- Psalm 147:10–11 (p. 564)
- Galatians 2:6 (p. 1207)
- Ephesians 1:3–6 (p. 1217)

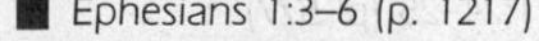

spirit would leave him, and Saul would feel better.

David and Goliath

17 The Philistines gathered their armies for
war. They met at Socoh in Judah and
camped at Ephes Dammim between Socoh and
Azekah. 2Saul and the Israelites gathered in the
Valley of Elah and camped there and took their
positions to fight the Philistines. 3The Philistines
controlled one hill while the Israelites controlled
another. The valley was between them.
4The Philistines had a champion fighter from
Gath named Goliath. He was about nine feet, four
inches tall. He came out of the Philistine camp
5with a bronze helmet on his head and a coat of
bronze armor that weighed about one hundred
twenty-five pounds. 6He wore bronze protectors
on his legs, and he had a bronze spear on his back.
7The wooden part of his larger spear was like a
weaver's rod, and its blade weighed about fifteen
pounds. The officer who carried his shield walked
in front of him.
8Goliath stood and shouted to the Israelite soldiers, "Why have you taken positions for battle?
I am a Philistine, and you are Saul's servants!
Choose a man and send him to fight me. 9If he
can fight and kill me, we will be your servants.
But if I can kill him, you will be our servants."
10Then he said, "Today I stand and dare the army
of Israel! Send one of your men to fight me!"
11When Saul and the Israelites heard the Philistine's words, they were very scared.
12Now David was the son of Jesse, an Ephrath-
ite from Bethlehem in Judah. Jesse had eight sons.
In Saul's time Jesse was an old man. 13His three
oldest sons followed Saul to the war. The first son
was Eliab, the second was Abinadab, and the
third was Shammah. 14David was the youngest.
Jesse's three oldest sons followed Saul, 15but David went back and forth from Saul to Bethlehem,
where he took care of his father's sheep.
16For forty days the Philistine came out every
morning and evening and stood before the Israelite army.
17Jesse said to his son David, "Take this half
bushel of cooked grain and ten loaves of bread to
your brothers in the camp. 18Also take ten pieces

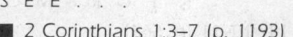

SERVICE

When People Can't Say Thanks

Rick Marty's friends couldn't believe he was taking a summer job at the nursing home after graduation. When he described his job, they gagged.

"I'll be working with eight Alzheimer's patients," he explained. "Waking them up. Changing their adult diapers. Taking them to breakfast. Feeding them."

And that's what he did for three months. Every day, he would wake people and get them ready for the day. And even though he was always there, they never recognized him. In fact, some would slap him and yell at him without any reason. And they never thanked him or even recognized all the work he did for them.

"How do you do it?" his amazed friends asked one Saturday night when the gang went out for pizza. "It sounds terrible."

"You have to realize what these people are going through," Rick said. "They're frustrated with themselves, not you. You just have to help them be as comfortable as they can be."

Rick had learned what it means to serve someone even when it's tough. David had similar experiences with service in a tough situation. Read about it in **1 Samuel 16:14–23**.

- How does Rick's servant attitude compare with David's dedicated service to King Saul? Read 1 Samuel 18:10–11 (p. 262) to see what happened later. How does this information change your view of David's dedication?
- When have you comforted someone who, like King Saul, could never express gratitude? How did you feel?

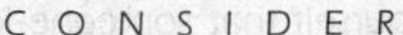

CONSIDER . . .

- volunteering at a nursing home or day care center for people who need special help.
- writing a letter of encouragement to someone who is doing a thankless, but necessary, service.

FOR MORE, SEE . . .

- Proverbs 11:24–25 (p. 577)
- Matthew 10:5–8 (p. 922)
- 2 Corinthians 1:3–7 (p. 1193)

of cheese to the commander and to your brothers.
See how your brothers are and bring back some
proof to show me that they are all right. 19Your
brothers are with Saul and the army in the Valley
of Elah, fighting against the Philistines."

20Early in the morning David left the sheep
with another shepherd. He took the food and left
as Jesse had told him. When David arrived at the
camp, the army was going out to their battle positions, shouting their war cry. 21The Israelites and
Philistines were lining up their men to face each
other in battle.

22David left the food with the man who kept
the supplies and ran to the battle line to talk to his
brothers. 23While he was talking with them, Goliath, the Philistine champion from Gath, came out.
He shouted things against Israel as usual, and David heard him. 24When the Israelites saw Goliath,
they were very much afraid and ran away.

25They said, "Look at this man! He keeps coming out to challenge Israel. The king will give
much money to whoever kills him. He will also
let whoever kills him marry his daughter. And his
father's family will not have to pay taxes in Israel."

26David asked the men who stood near him,
"What will be done to reward the man who kills
this Philistine and takes away the shame from Israel? Who does this uncircumcised[d] Philistine
think he is? Does he think he can speak against
the armies of the living God?"

27The Israelites told David what would be done
for the man who would kill Goliath.

28When David's oldest brother Eliab heard David talking with the soldiers, he was angry with
David. He asked David, "Why did you come
here? Who's taking care of those few sheep of
yours in the desert? I know you are proud and
wicked at heart. You came down here just to
watch the battle."

29David asked, "Now what have I done wrong?
Can't I even talk?" 30When he turned to other
people and asked the same questions, they gave
him the same answer as before. 31Yet what David
said was told to Saul, and he sent for David.

32David said to Saul, "Don't let anyone be discouraged. I, your servant, will go and fight this
Philistine!"

33Saul answered, "You can't go out against this
Philistine and fight him. You're only a boy. Goliath has been a warrior since he was a young
man."

34But David said to Saul, "I, your servant, have
been keeping my father's sheep. When a lion or
bear came and took a sheep from the flock, 35I
would chase it. I would attack it and save the
sheep from its mouth. When it attacked me, I
caught it by its fur and hit it and killed it. 36I, your
servant, have killed both a lion and a bear! This
uncircumcised Philistine will be like them, because he has spoken against the armies of the living God. 37The LORD who saved me from a lion
and a bear will save me from this Philistine."

Saul said to David, "Go, and may the LORD be
with you." 38Saul put his own clothes on David.
He put a bronze helmet on his head and dressed
him in armor. 39David put on Saul's sword and
tried to walk around, but he was not used to all
the armor Saul had put on him.

He said to Saul, "I can't go in this, because I'm
not used to it." Then David took it all off. 40He
took his stick in his hand and chose five smooth
stones from a stream. He put them in his shepherd's bag and grabbed his sling. Then he went to
meet the Philistine.

41At the same time, the Philistine was coming
closer to David. The man who held his shield
walked in front of him. 42When Goliath looked at
David and saw that he was only a boy, tanned and
handsome, he looked down on David with disgust. 43He said, "Do you think I am a dog, that
you come at me with a stick?" He used his gods'
names to curse David. 44He said to David, "Come
here. I'll feed your body to the birds of the air and
the wild animals!"

45But David said to him, "You come to me using a sword and two spears. But I come to you in
the name of the LORD All-Powerful, the God of
the armies of Israel! You have spoken against him.
46Today the LORD will hand you over to me, and
I'll kill you and cut off your head. Today I'll feed
the bodies of the Philistine soldiers to the birds of
the air and the wild animals. Then all the world
will know there is a God in Israel! 47Everyone
gathered here will know the LORD does not need
swords or spears to save people. The battle belongs to him, and he will hand you over to us."

48As Goliath came near to attack him, David
ran quickly to meet him. 49He took a stone from
his bag, put it into his sling, and slung it. The
stone hit the Philistine and went deep into his
forehead, and Goliath fell facedown on the
ground.

50So David defeated the Philistine with only a
sling and a stone. He hit him and killed him. He
did not even have a sword in his hand. 51Then
David ran and stood beside him. He took Goliath's sword out of its holder and killed him by
cutting off his head.

When the Philistines saw that their champion
was dead, they turned and ran. 52The men of Israel and Judah shouted and chased the Philistines
all the way to the entrance of the city of Gath and
to the gates of Ekron.

The Philistines' bodies lay on the Shaaraim
road as far as Gath and Ekron. 53The Israelites returned after chasing the Philistines and robbed
their camp. 54David took Goliath's head to Jerusa-

lem and put Goliath's weapons in his own tent.
55When Saul saw David go out to meet Goliath,
Saul asked Abner, commander of the army, "Abner, who is that young man's father?"

SIDELIGHT: Slam-dunking would have been easy for Goliath. At nine-foot-four, his head would have been just a few inches below the basketball rim. But he was still no match for David, who was good at "long shots" (1 Samuel 17:41–54).

Abner answered, "As surely as you live, my
king, I don't know."
56The king said, "Find out whose son he is."
57When David came back from killing Goliath,
Abner brought him to Saul. David was still holding Goliath's head.
58Saul asked him, "Young man, who is your father?"
David answered, "I am the son of your servant
Jesse of Bethlehem."

Saul Fears David

18 When David finished talking with Saul,
Jonathan felt very close to David. He
loved David as much as he loved himself. 2Saul
kept David with him from that day on and did not
let him go home to his father's house. 3Jonathan
made an agreement with David, because he loved
David as much as himself. 4He took off his coat
and gave it to David, along with his armor, including his sword, bow, and belt.
5Saul sent David to fight in different battles,
and David was very successful. Then Saul put David over the soldiers, which pleased Saul's officers
and all the other people.
6After David had killed the Philistine, he and
the men returned home. Women came out from
all the towns of Israel to meet King Saul. They
sang songs of joy, danced, and played tambourines[d] and stringed instruments. 7As they played,
they sang,

"Saul has killed thousands of his enemies,
but David has killed tens of thousands."

8The women's song upset Saul, and he became
very angry. He thought, "The women say David
has killed tens of thousands, but they say I have
killed only thousands. The only thing left for him
to have is the kingdom!" 9So Saul watched David
closely from then on, because he was jealous.
10The next day an evil spirit from God rushed
upon Saul, and he prophesied[d] in his house. David was playing the harp as he usually did, but
Saul had a spear in his hand. 11He threw the
spear, thinking, "I'll pin David to the wall." But
David escaped from him twice.
12The LORD was with David but had left Saul.
So Saul was afraid of David. 13He sent David away
and made him commander of a thousand soldiers.
So David led them in battle. 14He had great success in everything he did because the LORD was
with him. 15When Saul saw that David was very
successful, he feared David even more. 16But all
the people of Israel and Judah loved David because he led them well in battle.

Saul's Daughter Marries David

17Saul said to David, "Here is my older daughter Merab. I will let you marry her. All I ask is that
you remain brave and fight the LORD's battles."
Saul thought, "I won't have to kill David. The
Philistines will do that."
18But David answered Saul, saying, "Who am
I? My family is not important enough for me to
become the king's son-in-law." 19So, when the
time came for Saul's daughter Merab to marry David, Saul gave her instead to Adriel of Meholah.
20Now Saul's other daughter, Michal, loved
David. When they told Saul, he was pleased. 21He
thought, "I will let her marry David. Then she
will be a trap for him, and the Philistines will defeat him." So Saul said to David a second time,
"You may become my son-in-law."
22And Saul ordered his servants to talk with David in private and say, "Look, the king likes you.
His servants love you. You should be his son-in-
law."
23Saul's servants said these words to David, but
David answered, "Do you think it is easy to become the king's son-in-law? I am poor and unimportant."
24When Saul's servants told him what David
had said, 25Saul said, "Tell David, 'The king
doesn't want money for the bride. All he wants is
a hundred Philistine foreskins to get even with his
enemies.' " Saul planned to let the Philistines kill
David.
26When Saul's servants told this to David, he
was pleased to become the king's son-in-law. 27So
he and his men went out and killed two hundred
Philistines. David brought all their foreskins to
Saul so he could be the king's son-in-law. Then
Saul gave him his daughter Michal for his wife.
28Saul saw that the LORD was with David and that
his daughter Michal loved David. 29So he grew
even more afraid of David, and he was David's
enemy all his life.
30The Philistine commanders continued to go
out to fight the Israelites, but every time, David
was more skillful than Saul's officers. So he became famous.

Saul Tries to Kill David

19 Saul told his son Jonathan and all his servants to kill David, but Jonathan liked David very much. 2So he warned David, "My father Saul is looking for a chance to kill you. Watch out in the morning. Hide in a secret place. 3I will go out and stand with my father in the field where you are hiding, and I'll talk to him about you. Then I'll let you know what I find out."

4When Jonathan talked to Saul his father, he said good things about David. Jonathan said, "The king should do no wrong to your servant David since he has done nothing wrong to you. What he has done has helped you greatly. 5David risked his life when he killed Goliath the Philistine, and the LORD won a great victory for all Israel. You saw it and were happy. Why would you do wrong against David? He's innocent. There's no reason to kill him!"

6Saul listened to Jonathan and then made this promise: "As surely as the LORD lives, David won't be put to death."

7So Jonathan called to David and told him everything that had been said. He brought David to Saul, and David was with Saul as before.

8When war broke out again, David went out to fight the Philistines. He defeated them, and they ran away from him.

9But once again an evil spirit from the LORD rushed upon Saul as he was sitting in his house with his spear in his hand. David was playing the harp. 10Saul tried to pin David to the wall with his spear, but David jumped out of the way. So Saul's spear went into the wall, and David ran away that night.

11Saul sent messengers to David's house to watch it and to kill him in the morning. But Michal, David's wife, warned him, saying, "Tonight you must run for your life. If you don't, you will be dead in the morning." 12So she let David down out of a window, and he ran away and escaped. 13Then Michal took an idol, laid it on the bed, covered it with clothes, and put goats' hair at its head.

14Saul sent messengers to take David prisoner, but Michal said, "He is sick."

15Saul sent them back to see David, saying, "Bring him to me on his bed so I can kill him." 16When the messengers entered David's house, they found just an idol on the bed with goats' hair on its head.

17Saul said to Michal, "Why did you trick me this way? You let my enemy go so he could run away!"

Michal answered Saul, "David told me if I did not help him escape, he would kill me."

18After David had escaped from Saul, he went to Samuel at Ramah and told him everything Saul had done to him. Then David and Samuel went to Naioth and stayed there. 19Saul heard that David was in Naioth at Ramah. 20So he sent messengers to capture him. But they met a group of prophets[d] prophesying, with Samuel standing there leading them. So the Spirit[d] of God entered Saul's men, and they also prophesied.

21When Saul heard the news, he sent more messengers, but they also prophesied. Then he sent messengers a third time, but they also prophesied. 22Finally, Saul himself went to Ramah, to the well at Secu. He asked, "Where are Samuel and David?"

The people answered, "In Naioth at Ramah."

23When Saul went to Naioth at Ramah, the Spirit of God also rushed upon him. And he walked on, prophesying until he came to Naioth at Ramah. 24He took off his robes and prophesied in front of Samuel. He lay that way all day and all night. That is why people ask, "Is even Saul one of the prophets?"

Jonathan Helps David

20 Then David ran away from Naioth in Ramah. He went to Jonathan and asked, "What have I done? What is my crime? How did I sin against your father? Why is he trying to kill me?"

2Jonathan answered, "No! You won't die! See, my father doesn't do anything great or small without first telling me. Why would he keep this from me? It's not true!"

3But David took an oath, saying, "Your father knows very well that you like me. He says to himself, 'Jonathan must not know about it, or he will tell David.' As surely as the LORD lives and as you live, I am only a step away from death!"

4Jonathan said to David, "I'll do anything you want me to do."

5So David said, "Look, tomorrow is the New Moon[d] festival. I am supposed to eat with the king, but let me hide in the field until the third evening. 6If your father notices I am gone, tell him, 'David begged me to let him go to his hometown of Bethlehem. Every year at this time his family group offers a sacrifice.' 7If your father says, 'Fine,' I am safe. But if he becomes angry, you will know that he wants to hurt me. 8Jonathan, be loyal to me, your servant. You have made an agreement with me before the LORD. If I am guilty, you may kill me yourself! Why hand me over to your father?"

9Jonathan answered, "No, never! If I learn that my father plans to hurt you, I will warn you!"

10David asked, "Who will let me know if your father answers you unkindly?"

11Then Jonathan said, "Come, let's go out into the field." So the two of them went out into the field.

12Jonathan said to David, "I promise this before the LORD, the God of Israel: At this same time the day after tomorrow, I will find out how my father feels. If he feels good toward you, I will send word to you and let you know. 13But if my father plans to hurt you, I will let you know and send you away safely. May the LORD punish me terribly if I don't do this. And may the LORD be with you as he has been with my father. 14But show me the kindness of the LORD as long as I live so that I may not die. 15You must never stop showing your kindness to my family, even when the LORD has destroyed all your enemies from the earth."

16So Jonathan made an agreement with David. He said, "May the LORD hold David's enemies responsible." 17And Jonathan asked David to repeat his promise of love for him, because he loved David as much as he loved himself.

18Jonathan said to David, "Tomorrow is the New Moon festival. Your seat will be empty, so my father will miss you. 19On the third day go to the place where you hid when this trouble began. Wait by the rock Ezel. 20On the third day I will shoot three arrows to the side of the rock as if I am shooting at a target. 21Then I will send a boy to find the arrows. If I say to him, 'The arrows are near you; bring them here,' you may come out of hiding. You are safe. As the LORD lives, there is no danger. 22But if I say to the boy, 'Look, the arrows are beyond you,' you must go, because the LORD is sending you away. 23Remember what we talked about. The LORD is a witness between you and me forever."

24So David hid in the field. When the New Moon festival came, the king sat down to eat. 25He sat where he always sat, near the wall. Jonathan sat across from him, and Abner sat next to Saul, but David's place was empty. 26That day Saul said nothing. He thought, "Maybe something has happened to David so that he is unclean."[d] 27But the next day was the second day of the month, and David's place was still empty. So Saul said to Jonathan, "Why hasn't the son of Jesse come to the feast yesterday or today?"

28Jonathan answered, "David begged me to let him go to Bethlehem. 29He said, 'Let me go, because our family has a sacrifice in the town, and my brother has ordered me to be there. Now if I am your friend, please let me go to see my brothers.' That is why he has not come to the king's table."

30Then Saul became very angry with Jonathan. He said, "You son of a wicked, worthless woman! I know you are on the side of David son of Jesse! You bring shame on yourself and on your mother who gave birth to you. 31As long as Jesse's son lives, you will never be king or have a kingdom. Now send for David and bring him to me. He must die!"

32Jonathan asked his father, "Why should David be killed? What wrong has he done?" 33Then Saul threw his spear at Jonathan, trying to kill him. So Jonathan knew that his father really wanted to kill David. 34Jonathan was very angry and left the table. That second day of the month he refused to eat. He was ashamed of his father and upset over David.

35The next morning Jonathan went out to the field to meet David as they had agreed. He had a young boy with him. 36Jonathan said to the boy, "Run and find the arrows I shoot." When he ran, Jonathan shot an arrow beyond him. 37The boy ran to the place where Jonathan's arrow fell, but Jonathan called, "The arrow is beyond you!" 38Then he shouted, "Hurry! Go quickly! Don't stop!" The boy picked up the arrow and brought it back to his master. 39(The boy knew nothing about what this meant; only Jonathan and David knew.) 40Then Jonathan gave his weapons to the boy and told him, "Go back to town."

41When the boy left, David came out from the south side of the rock. He bowed facedown on the ground before Jonathan three times. Then David and Jonathan kissed each other and cried together, but David cried the most.

42Jonathan said to David, "Go in peace. We have promised by the LORD that we will be friends. We said, 'The LORD will be a witness between you and me, and between our descendants[d] always.' " Then David left, and Jonathan went back to town.

David Goes to See Ahimelech

21 David went to Nob to see Ahimelech the priest. Ahimelech shook with fear when he saw David, and he asked, "Why are you alone? Why is no one with you?"

2David answered him, "The king gave me a special order. He told me, 'No one must know what I am sending you to do or what I told you to do.' I told my men where to meet me. 3Now, what food do you have with you? Give me five loaves of bread or anything you find."

4The priest said to David, "I don't have any plain bread here, but I do have some holy bread.[n] You may eat it if your men have kept themselves from women."

5David answered, "No women have been near us for days. My men always keep themselves holy, even when we do ordinary work. And this is especially true when the work is holy."

6So the priest gave David the holy bread from the presence of God because there was no other.

holy bread This was the bread that showed the people were in the presence of God. Normally only the priests ate this bread.

Each day the holy bread was replaced with hot
bread.
7One of Saul's servants happened to be there
that day. He had been held there before the LORD.
He was Doeg the Edomite, the chief of Saul's
shepherds.
8David asked Ahimelech, "Do you have a spear
or sword here? The king's business was very important, so I left without my sword or any other
weapon."
9The priest answered, "The sword of Goliath
the Philistine, the one you killed in the Valley of
Elah, is here. It is wrapped in a cloth behind the
holy vest.[d] If you want it, you may take it. There's
no other sword here but that one."
David said, "There is no other sword like it.
Give it to me."

David Goes to Gath

10That day David ran away from Saul and went
to Achish king of Gath. 11But the servants of
Achish said to him, "This is David, the king of the
Israelites. He's the man they dance and sing
about, saying:

'Saul has killed thousands of his enemies,
but David has killed tens of thousands.' "

12David paid attention to these words and was
very much afraid of Achish king of Gath. 13So he
pretended to be crazy in front of Achish and his
servants. While he was with them, he acted like
a madman and clawed on the doors of the gate
and let spit run down his beard.
14Achish said to his servants, "Look at the man!
He's crazy! Why do you bring him to me? 15I have
enough madmen. I don't need you to bring him
here to act like this in front of me! Don't let him
in my house!"

> **SIDELIGHT:** Most people know David was a musician. Did you know he was an actor, too? When he was afraid of being captured by the Philistine King Achish, he drooled in his beard and acted crazy. He must have been good, because the king let him go (1 Samuel 21:12–15).

David at Adullam and Mizpah

22 David left Gath and escaped to the cave
of Adullam. When his brothers and other
relatives heard that he was there, they went to see
him. 2Everyone who was in trouble, or who owed
money, or who was unsatisfied gathered around
David, and he became their leader. About four
hundred men were with him.
3From there David went to Mizpah in Moab
and spoke to the king of Moab. He said, "Please
let my father and mother come and stay with you
until I learn what God is going to do for me." 4So
he left them with the king of Moab, and they
stayed with him as long as David was hiding in
the stronghold.[d]
5But the prophet[d] Gad said to David, "Don't
stay in the stronghold. Go to the land of Judah."
So David left and went to the forest of Hereth.

Saul Destroys Ahimelech's Family

6Saul heard that David and his men had been
seen. Saul was sitting under the tamarisk tree on
the hill at Gibeah, and all his officers were standing around him. He had a spear in his hand. 7Saul
said to them, "Listen, men of Benjamin! Do you
think the son of Jesse will give all of you fields and
vineyards? Will David make you commanders
over thousands of men or hundreds of men? 8You
have all made plans against me! No one tells me
when my son makes an agreement with the son
of Jesse! No one cares about me! No one tells me
when my son has encouraged my servant to am
bush me this very day!"
9Doeg the Edomite, who was standing there
with Saul's officers, said, "I saw the son of Jesse.
He came to see Ahimelech son of Ahitub at Nob.
10Ahimelech prayed to the LORD for David and
gave him food and gave him the sword of Goliath
the Philistine."
11Then the king sent for the priest Ahimelech
son of Ahitub and for all of Ahimelech's relatives
who were priests at Nob. And they all came to the
king. 12Saul said to Ahimelech, "Listen now, son
of Ahitub."
Ahimelech answered, "Yes, master."
13Saul said, "Why are you and Jesse's son
against me? You gave him bread and a sword! You
prayed to God for him. David has turned against
me and is waiting to attack me even now!"
14Ahimelech answered, "You have no other
servant who is as loyal as David, your own son-in-
law and captain of your bodyguards. Everyone in
your house respects him. 15That was not the first
time I prayed to God for David. Don't blame me
or any of my relatives. I, your servant, know nothing about what is going on."
16But the king said, "Ahimelech, you and all
your relatives must die!" 17Then he told the
guards at his side, "Go and kill the priests of the
LORD, because they are on David's side. They
knew he was running away, but they didn't tell
me."
But the king's officers refused to kill the priests
of the LORD.
18Then the king ordered Doeg, "Go and kill the
priests." So Doeg the Edomite went and killed the
priests. That day he killed eighty-five men who
wore the linen holy vest.[d] 19He also killed the peo-

ple of Nob, the city of the priests. With the sword he killed men, women, children, babies, cattle, donkeys, and sheep.

20But Abiathar, a son of Ahimelech, who was the son of Ahitub, escaped. He ran away and joined David. 21He told David that Saul had killed the LORD's priests. 22Then David told him, "Doeg the Edomite was there at Nob that day. I knew he would surely tell Saul. So I am responsible for the death of all your father's family. 23Stay with me. Don't be afraid. The man who wants to kill you also wants to kill me. You will be safe with me."

David Saves the People of Keilah

23 Someone told David, "Look, the Philistines are fighting against Keilah and stealing grain from the threshing[d] floors."

2David asked the LORD, "Should I go and fight these Philistines?"

The LORD answered him, "Go. Attack them, and save Keilah."

3But David's men said to him, "We're afraid here in Judah. We will be more afraid if we go to Keilah where the Philistine army is."

4David again asked the LORD, and the LORD answered, "Go down to Keilah. I will help you defeat the Philistines." 5So David and his men went to Keilah and fought the Philistines and took their cattle. David killed many Philistines and saved the people of Keilah. 6(Now Abiathar son of Ahimelech had brought the holy vest[d] with him when he came to David at Keilah.)

Saul Chases David

7Someone told Saul that David was now at Keilah. Saul said, "God has handed David over to me! He has trapped himself, because he has entered a town with gates and bars." 8Saul called all his army together for battle, and they prepared to go down to Keilah to attack David and his men.

9David learned Saul was making evil plans against him. So he said to Abiathar the priest, "Bring the holy vest."[d] 10David prayed, "LORD, God of Israel, I have heard that Saul plans to come to Keilah to destroy the town because of me. 11Will the leaders of Keilah hand me over to Saul? Will Saul come down to Keilah, as I heard? LORD, God of Israel, tell me, your servant!"

The LORD answered, "Saul will come down."

12Again David asked, "Will the leaders of Keilah hand me and my men over to Saul?"

The LORD answered, "They will."

13So David and his six hundred men left Keilah and kept moving from place to place. When Saul found out that David had escaped from Keilah, he did not go there.

14David stayed in the desert hideouts and in the hills of the Desert of Ziph. Every day Saul looked for David, but the LORD did not surrender David to him.

15While David was at Horesh in the Desert of Ziph, he learned that Saul was coming to kill him. 16But Saul's son Jonathan went to David at Horesh and strengthened his faith in God. 17Jonathan told him, "Don't be afraid, because my father won't touch you. You will be king of Israel, and I will be second to you. Even my father Saul knows this." 18The two of them made an agreement before the LORD. Then Jonathan went home, but David stayed at Horesh.

19The people from Ziph went to Saul at Gibeah and told him, "David is hiding in our land. He's at the hideouts of Horesh, on the hill of Hakilah, south of Jeshimon. 20Now, our king, come down anytime you want. It's our duty to hand David over to you."

21Saul answered, "The LORD bless you for helping me. 22Go and learn more about him. Find out where he is staying and who has seen him there. I have heard that he is clever. 23Find all the hiding places he uses, and come back and tell me everything. Then I'll go with you. If David is in the area, I will track him down among all the families in Judah."

24So they went back to Ziph ahead of Saul. Now David and his men were in the Desert of Maon[n] in the desert area south of Jeshimon. 25Saul and his men went to look for David, but David heard about it and went down to a rock and stayed in the Desert of Maon. When Saul heard that, he followed David into the Desert of Maon.

26Saul was going along one side of the mountain, and David and his men were on the other side. They were hurrying to get away from Saul, because Saul and his men were closing in on them. 27But a messenger came to Saul, saying, "Come quickly! The Philistines are attacking our land!" 28So Saul stopped chasing David and went to challenge the Philistines. That is why people call this place Rock of Parting. 29David also left the Desert of Maon and stayed in the hideouts of En Gedi.

David Shames Saul

24 After Saul returned from chasing the Philistines, he was told, "David is in the Desert of En Gedi." 2So he took three thousand chosen men from all Israel and began looking for David and his men near the Rocks of the Wild Goats.

3Saul came to the sheep pens beside the road. A cave was there, and he went in to relieve him-

Maon Some early Greek copies say "Maon." The Hebrew copies say "Paran."

self. Now David and his men were hiding far back in the cave. 4The men said to David, "Today is the day the LORD spoke of when he said, 'I will give your enemy over to you. Do anything you want with him.' "

Then David crept up to Saul and quietly cut off a corner of Saul's robe. 5Later David felt guilty because he had cut off a corner of Saul's robe. 6He said to his men, "May the LORD keep me from doing such a thing to my master! Saul is the LORD's appointed king. I should not do anything against him, because he is the LORD's appointed king!" 7David used these words to stop his men; he did not let them attack Saul. Then Saul left the cave and went his way.

8When David came out of the cave, he shouted to Saul, "My master and king!" Saul looked back, and David bowed facedown on the ground. 9He said to Saul, "Why do you listen when people say, 'David wants to harm you'? 10You have seen something with your own eyes today. The LORD put you in my power in the cave. They said I should kill you, but I was merciful. I said, 'I won't harm my master, because he is the LORD's appointed king.' 11My father, look at this piece of your robe in my hand! I cut off the corner of your robe, but I didn't kill you. Now understand and know I am not planning any evil against you. I did nothing wrong to you, but you are hunting me to kill me. 12May the LORD judge between us, and may he punish you for the wrong you have done to me! But I am not against you. 13There is an old saying: 'Evil things come from evil people.' But I am not against you. 14Whom is the king of Israel coming out against? Whom are you chasing? It's as if you are chasing a dead dog or a flea. 15May the LORD be our judge and decide between you and me. May he support me and show that I am right. May he save me from you!"

16When David finished saying these words, Saul asked, "Is that your voice, David my son?" And he cried loudly. 17He said, "You are a better man than I am. You have been good to me, but I have done wrong to you. 18You told me what good things you did. The LORD handed me over to you, but you did not kill me. 19If a person finds his enemy, he doesn't just send him on his way, does he? May the LORD reward you because you were good to me today. 20I know you will surely be king, and you will rule the kingdom of Israel. 21Now swear to me by the LORD that you will not kill my descendants[d] and that you won't wipe out my name from my father's family."

22So David made the promise to Saul. Then Saul went back home, and David and his men went up to their hideout.

Nabal Insults David

25 Now Samuel died, and all the Israelites met and had a time of sadness for him. Then they buried him at his home in Ramah.

David moved to the Desert of Maon.[n] 2A man in Maon who had land at Carmel was very rich. He had three thousand sheep and a thousand goats. He was cutting the wool off his sheep at Carmel. 3His name was Nabal, and he was a descendant[d] of Caleb. His wife was named Abigail. She was wise and beautiful, but Nabal was cruel and mean.

4While David was in the desert, he heard that Nabal was cutting the wool from his sheep. 5So he sent ten young men and told them, "Go to Nabal at Carmel, and greet him for me. 6Say to Nabal, 'May you and your family and all who belong to you have good health! 7I have heard that you are cutting the wool from your sheep. When your shepherds were with us, we did not harm them. All the time your shepherds were at Carmel, we stole nothing from them. 8Ask your servants, and they will tell you. We come at a happy time, so be kind to my young men. Please give anything you can find for them and for your son David.' "

9When David's men arrived, they gave the message to Nabal, but Nabal insulted them. 10He answered them, "Who is David? Who is this son of Jesse? Many slaves are running away from their masters today! 11I have bread and water, and I have meat that I killed for my servants who cut the wool. But I won't give it to men I don't know."

12David's men went back and told him all Nabal had said. 13Then David said to them, "Put on your swords!" So they put on their swords, and David put on his also. About four hundred men went with David, but two hundred men stayed with the supplies.

14One of Nabal's servants said to Abigail, Nabal's wife, "David sent messengers from the desert to greet our master, but Nabal insulted them. 15These men were very good to us. They did not harm us. They stole nothing from us during all the time we were out in the field with them. 16Night and day they protected us. They were like a wall around us while we were with them caring for the sheep. 17Now think about it, and decide what you can do. Terrible trouble is coming to our master and all his family. Nabal is such a wicked man that no one can even talk to him."

18Abigail hurried. She took two hundred loaves of bread, two leather bags full of wine, five cooked sheep, a bushel of cooked grain, a hundred cakes of raisins, and two hundred cakes of

Maon Some early Greek copies say "Maon." The Hebrew copies say "Paran."

pressed figs and put all these on donkeys. 19Then
she told her servants, "Go on. I'll follow you." But
she did not tell her husband.
20Abigail rode her donkey and came down toward the mountain hideout. There she met David
and his men coming down toward her.
21David had just said, "It's been useless! I
watched over Nabal's property in the desert. I
made sure none of his sheep was missing. I did
good to him, but he has paid me back with evil.
22May God punish my enemies even more. I will
not leave one of Nabal's men alive until morning."
23When Abigail saw David, she quickly got off
her donkey and bowed facedown on the ground
before him. 24She fell at David's feet and said,
"My master, let the blame be on me! Please let
me talk to you. Listen to what I say. 25My master,
don't pay attention to this worthless man Nabal.
He is like his name. His name means 'fool,' and
he is truly a fool. But I, your servant, didn't see
the men you sent. 26The LORD has kept you from
killing and punishing anyone. As surely as the
LORD lives and as surely as you live, may your
enemies become like Nabal! 27I have brought a
gift to you for the men who follow you. 28Please
forgive my wrong. The LORD will certainly let
your family have many kings, because you fight
his battles. As long as you live, may you do nothing bad. 29Someone might chase you to kill you,
but the LORD your God will keep you alive. He
will throw away your enemies' lives as he would
throw a stone from a sling. 30The LORD will keep
all his promises of good things for you. He will
make you leader over Israel. 31Then you won't
feel guilty or troubled because you killed innocent
people and punished them. Please remember me
when the LORD brings you success."
32David answered Abigail, "Praise the LORD,
the God of Israel, who sent you to meet me.
33May you be blessed for your wisdom. You have
kept me from killing or punishing people today.
34As surely as the LORD, the God of Israel, lives,
he has kept me from hurting you. If you hadn't
come quickly to meet me, not one of Nabal's men
would have lived until morning."
35Then David accepted Abigail's gifts. He told
her, "Go home in peace. I have heard your words,
and I will do what you have asked."

Nabal's Death

36When Abigail went back to Nabal, he was in
the house, eating like a king. He was very drunk
and in a good mood. So she told him nothing until
the next morning. 37In the morning when he was
not drunk, his wife told him everything. His heart
stopped, and he became like stone. 38About ten
days later the LORD struck Nabal and he died.
39When David heard that Nabal was dead, he
said, "Praise the LORD! Nabal insulted me, but the
LORD has supported me! He has kept me from
doing wrong. The LORD has punished Nabal for
his wrong."
Then David sent a message to Abigail, asking
her to be his wife. 40His servants went to Carmel
and said to Abigail, "David sent us to take you so
you can become his wife."
41Abigail bowed facedown on the ground and
said, "I am your servant. I'm ready to serve you
and to wash the feet of my master's servants."
42Abigail quickly got on a donkey and went with
David's messengers, with her five maids following
her. And she became David's wife.
43David also had married Ahinoam of Jezreel.
So they were both David's wives. 44Saul's daughter Michal was also David's wife, but Saul had
given her to Paltiel son of Laish, who was from
Gallim.

David Shames Saul Again

26 The people of Ziph went to Saul at Gibeah and said to him, "David is hiding on
the hill of Hakilah opposite Jeshimon."
2So Saul went down to the Desert of Ziph with
three thousand chosen men of Israel to look for
David there. 3Saul made his camp beside the road
on the hill of Hakilah opposite Jeshimon, but David stayed in the desert. When he heard Saul had
followed him, 4he sent out spies and learned for
certain that Saul had come to Hakilah.
5Then David went to the place where Saul had
camped. He saw where Saul and Abner son of
Ner, the commander of Saul's army, were sleeping. Saul was sleeping in the middle of the camp
with all the army around him.
6David asked Ahimelech the Hittite and
Abishai son of Zeruiah, Joab's brother, "Who will
go down into Saul's camp with me?"
Abishai answered, "I'll go with you."
7So that night David and Abishai went into
Saul's camp. Saul was asleep in the middle of the
camp with his spear stuck in the ground near his
head. Abner and the army were sleeping around
Saul. 8Abishai said to David, "Today God has
handed your enemy over to you. Let me pin Saul
to the ground with my spear. I'll only have to do
it once. I won't need to hit him twice."
9But David said to Abishai, "Don't kill Saul! No
one can harm the LORD's appointed king and still
be innocent! 10As surely as the LORD lives, the
LORD himself will punish Saul. Maybe Saul will
die naturally, or maybe he will go into battle and
be killed. 11But may the LORD keep me from
harming his appointed king! Take the spear and
water jug that are near Saul's head. Then let's
go."
12So David took the spear and water jug that
were near Saul's head, and they left. No one saw

them or knew about it or woke up, because the LORD had put them sound asleep.

13David crossed over to the other side of the hill and stood on top of the mountain far from Saul's camp. They were a long way away from each other. 14David shouted to the army and to Abner son of Ner, "Won't you answer me, Abner?"

Abner answered, "Who is calling for the king? Who are you?"

15David said, "You're the greatest man in Israel. Isn't that true? Why didn't you guard your master the king? Someone came into your camp to kill your master the king! 16You have not done well. As surely as the LORD lives, you and your men should die. You haven't guarded your master, the LORD's appointed king. Look! Where are the king's spear and water jug that were near his head?"

17Saul knew David's voice. He said, "Is that your voice, David my son?"

David answered, "Yes, it is, my master and king." 18David also said, "Why are you chasing me, my master? What wrong have I done? What evil am I guilty of? 19My master and king, listen to me. If the LORD made you angry with me, let him accept an offering. But if people did it, may the LORD curse them! They have made me leave the land the LORD gave me. They have told me, 'Go and serve other gods.' 20Now don't let me die far away from the LORD's presence. The king of Israel has come out looking for a flea! You're just hunting a bird in the mountains!"

21Then Saul said, "I have sinned. Come back, David my son. Today you respected my life, so I will not try to hurt you. I have been very stupid and foolish."

22David answered, "Here is your spear. Let one of your young men come here and get it. 23The LORD rewards us for the things we do right and for our loyalty to him. The LORD handed you over to me today, but I wouldn't harm the LORD's appointed king. 24As I respected your life today, may the LORD also respect my life and save me from all trouble."

25Then Saul said to David, "You are blessed, my son David. You will do great things and succeed."

So David went on his way, and Saul went back home.

David Lives with the Philistines

27 But David thought to himself, "Saul will catch me someday. The best thing I can do is escape to the land of the Philistines. Then he will give up looking for me in Israel, and I can get away from him."

2So David and his six hundred men left Israel and went to Achish son of Maoch, king of Gath. 3David, his men, and their families made their home in Gath with Achish. David had his two wives with him—Ahinoam of Jezreel and Abigail of Carmel, the widow of Nabal. 4When Saul heard that David had run away to Gath, he stopped looking for him.

5Then David said to Achish, "If you are pleased with me, give me a place in one of the country towns where I can live. I don't need to live in the royal city with you."

6That day Achish gave David the town of Ziklag, and Ziklag has belonged to the kings of Judah ever since. 7David lived in the Philistine land a year and four months.

8David and his men raided the people of Geshur, Girzi, and Amalek. (These people had lived for a long time in the land that reached to Shur and Egypt.) 9When David fought them, he killed all the men and women and took their sheep, cattle, donkeys, camels, and clothes. Then he returned to Achish.

10Achish would ask David, "Where did you go raiding today?" And David would tell him that he had gone to the southern part of Judah, or Jerahmeel, or to the land of the Kenites. 11David never brought a man or woman alive to Gath. He thought, "If we bring people alive, they may tell Achish, 'This is what David really did.' " David did this all the time he lived in the Philistine land. 12So Achish trusted David and said to himself, "David's own people, the Israelites, now hate him very much. He will serve me forever."

Saul and the Witch of Endor

28 Later, the Philistines gathered their armies to fight against Israel. Achish said to David, "You understand that you and your men must join my army."

2David answered, "You will see for yourself what I, your servant, can do!"

Achish said, "Fine, I'll make you my permanent bodyguard."

3Now Samuel was dead, and all the Israelites had shown their sadness for him. They had buried Samuel in his hometown of Ramah.

And Saul had forced out the mediums[d] and fortune-tellers from the land.

4The Philistines came together and made camp at Shunem. Saul gathered all the Israelites and made camp at Gilboa. 5When he saw the Philistine army, he was afraid, and his heart pounded with fear. 6He prayed to the LORD, but the LORD did not answer him through dreams, Urim,[d] or prophets.[d] 7Then Saul said to his servants, "Find me a woman who is a medium[d] so I may go and ask her what will happen."

His servants answered, "There is a medium in Endor."

8Then Saul put on other clothes to disguise himself, and at night he and two of his men went to see the woman. Saul said to her, "Talk to a spirit for me. Bring up the person I name."

9But the woman said to him, "Surely you know what Saul has done. He has forced the mediums and fortune-tellers from the land. You are trying to trap me and get me killed."

10Saul made a promise to the woman in the name of the LORD. He said, "As surely as the LORD lives, you won't be punished for this."

11The woman asked, "Whom do you want me to bring up?"

He answered, "Bring up Samuel."

12When the woman saw Samuel, she screamed. She said, "Why have you tricked me? You are Saul!"

13The king said to the woman, "Don't be afraid! What do you see?"

The woman said, "I see a spirit coming up out of the ground."

14Saul asked, "What does he look like?"

The woman answered, "An old man wearing a coat is coming up."

Then Saul knew it was Samuel, and he bowed facedown on the ground.

15Samuel asked Saul, "Why have you disturbed me by bringing me up?"

Saul said, "I am greatly troubled. The Philistines are fighting against me, and God has left me. He won't answer me anymore, either by prophets or in dreams. That's why I called for you. Tell me what to do."

16Samuel said, "The LORD has left you and has become your enemy. So why do you call on me? 17He has done what he said he would do—the things he said through me. He has torn the kingdom out of your hands and given it to one of your neighbors, David. 18You did not obey the LORD; you did not show the Amalekites how angry he was with them. That's why he has done this to you today. 19The LORD will hand over both Israel and you to the Philistines. Tomorrow you and your sons will be with me. The LORD will hand over the army of Israel to the Philistines."

20Saul quickly fell flat on the ground and was afraid of what Samuel had said. He was also very weak because he had eaten nothing all that day and night.

21Then the woman came to Saul and saw that he was really frightened. She said, "Look, I, your servant, have obeyed you. I have risked my life and done what you told me to do. 22Now please listen to me. Let me give you some food so you may eat and have enough strength to go on your way."

23But Saul refused, saying, "I won't eat."

His servants joined the woman in asking him to eat, and he listened to them. So he got up from the ground and sat on the bed.

24At the house the woman had a fat calf, which she quickly killed. She took some flour and mixed dough with her hands. Then she baked some bread without yeast. 25She put the food before them, and they ate. That same night they got up and left.

David Goes Back to Ziklag

29 The Philistines gathered all their soldiers at Aphek. Israel camped by the spring at Jezreel. 2The Philistine kings were marching with their groups of a hundred and a thousand men. David and his men were marching behind Achish. 3The Philistine commanders asked, "What are these Hebrews doing here?"

Achish told them, "This is David. He served Saul king of Israel, but he has been with me for over a year now. I have found nothing wrong in David since the time he left Saul."

4But the Philistine commanders were angry with Achish and said, "Send David back to the city you gave him. He cannot go with us into battle. If he does, we'll have an enemy in our own camp. He could please his king by killing our own men. 5David is the one the Israelites dance and sing about, saying:

'Saul has killed thousands of his enemies,
but David has killed tens of thousands.' "

6So Achish called David and said to him, "As surely as the LORD lives, you are loyal. I would be pleased to have you serve in my army. Since the day you came to me, I have found no wrong in you. But the other kings don't trust you. 7Go back in peace. Don't do anything to displease the Philistine kings."

8David asked, "What wrong have I done? What evil have you found in me from the day I came to you until now? Why can't I go fight your enemies, my lord and king?"

9Achish answered, "I know you are as good as an angel from God. But the Philistine commanders have said, 'David must not go with us into battle.' 10Early in the morning you and your master's servants should leave. Get up as soon as it is light and go."

11So David and his men got up early in the morning and went back to the country of the Philistines. And the Philistines went up to Jezreel.

David's War with the Amalekites

30 On the third day, when David and his men arrived at Ziklag, he found that the Amalekites had raided southern Judah and Ziklag, attacking Ziklag and burning it. 2They captured the women and everyone, young and old, but they had not killed anyone. They had only taken them away.

3When David and his men came to Ziklag, they found the town had been burned and their wives,

sons, and daughters had been taken as prisoners.
4Then David and his army cried loudly until they
were too weak to cry anymore. 5David's two

> **SIDELIGHT:** If you think it's not manly to cry, read 1 Samuel 30:3–4. When they found their town burned and their families carted off into captivity, David and his army cried so much that they were too weak to cry anymore.

wives had also been taken—Ahinoam of Jezreel
and Abigail the widow of Nabal from Carmel.
6The men in the army were threatening to kill
David with stones, which greatly upset David.
Each man was sad and angry because his sons and
daughters had been captured, but David found
strength in the LORD his God. 7David said to Abiathar the priest, "Bring me the holy vest."[d]
8Then David asked the LORD, "Should I chase
the people who took our families? Will I catch
them?"

The LORD answered, "Chase them. You will
catch them, and you will succeed in saving your
families."

9David and the six hundred men with him
came to the Besor Ravine, where some of the men
stayed. 10David and four hundred men kept up
the chase. The other two hundred men stayed behind because they were too tired to cross the ravine.

11They found an Egyptian in a field and brought
him to David. They gave the Egyptian some water
to drink and some food to eat. 12And they gave
him a piece of a fig cake and two clusters of raisins. Then he felt better, because he had not eaten
any food or drunk any water for three days and
nights.

13David asked him, "Who is your master?
Where do you come from?"

He answered, "I'm an Egyptian, the slave of an
Amalekite. Three days ago my master left me, because I was sick. 14We had raided the southern
area of the Kerethites, the land of Judah, and the
southern area of Caleb. We burned Ziklag, as
well.

15David asked him, "Can you lead me to the
people who took our families?"

He answered, "Yes, if you promise me before
God that you won't kill me or give me back to my
master. Then I will take you to them."

16So the Egyptian led David to the Amalekites.
They were lying around on the ground, eating
and drinking and celebrating with the things they
had taken from the land of the Philistines and
from Judah. 17David fought them from sunset until the evening of the next day. None of them escaped, except four hundred young men who rode
off on their camels. 18David got his two wives
back and everything the Amalekites had taken.
19Nothing was missing. David brought back everyone, young and old, sons and daughters. He
recovered the valuable things and everything the
Amalekites had taken. 20David took all the sheep
and cattle, and his men made these animals go in
front, saying, "They are David's prize."

21Then David came to the two hundred men
who had been too tired to follow him, who had
stayed at the Besor Ravine. They came out to
meet David and the people with him. When he
came near, David greeted the men at the ravine.

22But the evil men and troublemakers among
those who followed David said, "Since these two
hundred men didn't go with us, we shouldn't give
them any of the things we recovered. Just let each
man take his wife and children and go."

23David answered, "No, my brothers. Don't do
that after what the LORD has given us. He has
protected us and given us the enemy who attacked us. 24Who will listen to what you say? The
share will be the same for the one who stayed
with the supplies as for the one who went into
battle. All will share alike." 25David made this an
order and rule for Israel, which continues even
today.

26When David arrived in Ziklag, he sent some
of the things he had taken from the Amalekites to
his friends, the leaders of Judah. He said, "Here
is a present for you from the things we took from
the LORD's enemies."

27David also sent some things to the leaders in
Bethel, Ramoth in the southern part of Judah, Jattir, 28Aroer, Siphmoth, Eshtemoa, 29Racal, the cities of the Jerahmeelites and the Kenites, 30Hor-
mah, Bor Ashan, Athach, 31Hebron, and to the
people in all the other places where he and his
men had been.

The Death of Saul

31 The Philistines fought against Israel, and
the Israelites ran away from them. Many
Israelites were killed on Mount Gilboa. 2The Philistines fought hard against Saul and his sons, killing his sons Jonathan, Abinadab, and Malki-Shua.
3The fighting was heavy around Saul. The archers
shot him, and he was badly wounded. 4He said to
the officer who carried his armor, "Pull out your
sword and kill me. Then those uncircumcised[d]
men won't make fun of me and kill me." But
Saul's officer refused, because he was afraid. So
Saul took his own sword and threw himself on it.
5When the officer saw that Saul was dead, he
threw himself on his own sword, and he died
with Saul. 6So Saul, his three sons, and the officer
who carried his armor died together that day.

[7]When the Israelites who lived across the Jezreel Valley and those who lived across the Jordan
River saw how the Israelite army had run away,
and that Saul and his sons were dead, they left
their cities and ran away. Then the Philistines
came and lived there.

[8]The next day when the Philistines came to
take all the valuable things from the dead soldiers,
they found Saul and his three sons dead on Mount
Gilboa. [9]They cut off Saul's head and took off his
armor. Then they sent messengers through all the
land of the Philistines to tell the news in the temple of their idols and to their people. [10]They put
Saul's armor in the temple of the Ashtoreths[d] and
hung his body on the wall of Beth Shan.

[11]When the people living in Jabesh Gilead
heard what the Philistines had done to Saul, [12]the
brave men of Jabesh marched all night and came
to Beth Shan. They removed the bodies of Saul
and his sons from the wall of Beth Shan and
brought them to Jabesh. There they burned the
bodies. [13]They took their bones and buried them
under the tamarisk tree in Jabesh. Then the people of Jabesh gave up eating for seven days.

2 SAMUEL

Why Read This Book:

- Learn how leaders can encourage people to follow God (2 Samuel 1—6).
- Discover how God can use people for good in spite of their faults (2 Samuel 7—12).
- See how family problems can hurt leaders (2 Samuel 13–20).

Behind the Scenes:

War was inevitable. King Saul was dead. David—a popular hero among southern tribes—had the charisma and leadership skills needed in a king. But while David was being crowned king in Judah (the southern half of the nation), Saul's son Ish-Bosheth took control of the northern part of the kingdom, Israel.

It took seven and a half years of civil war, but David finally united the kingdom when Ish-Bosheth was murdered. Then with decisive and effective leadership, David began building the country to the height of its military and political power. The kingdom he established would last four hundred years.

David's power came from following God. But he wasn't perfect. In 2 Samuel, David commits adultery with Bathsheba and then has her husband killed so that

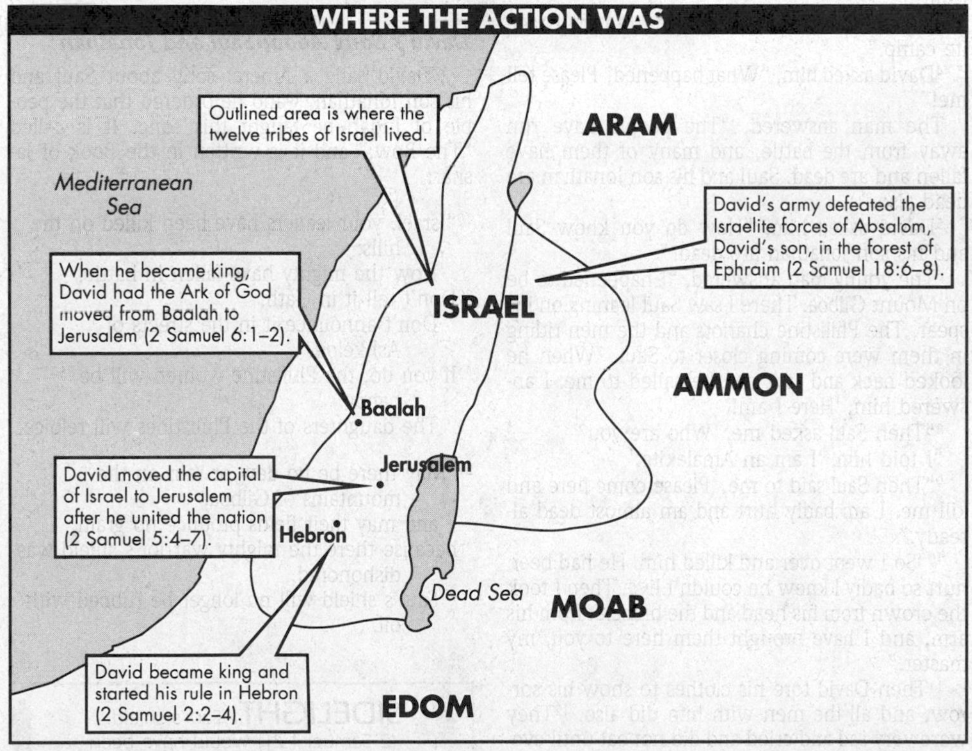
WHERE THE ACTION WAS
Outlined area is where the twelve tribes of Israel lived.
ARAM
Mediterranean Sea
David's army defeated the Israelite forces of Absalom, David's son, in the forest of Ephraim (2 Samuel 18:6–8).
When he became king, David had the Ark of God moved from Baalah to Jerusalem (2 Samuel 6:1–2).
ISRAEL
AMMON
Baalah
Jerusalem
David moved the capital of Israel to Jerusalem after he united the nation (2 Samuel 5:4–7).
Hebron
Dead Sea
MOAB
David became king and started his rule in Hebron (2 Samuel 2:2–4).
EDOM

WHEN THE ACTION WAS

2000BC	1500BC	1000BC	500BC	BC/AD

- The Israelites escaped from Egypt
- Joshua led the Israelites into Canaan
- Samuel served as Israel's last judge
- Saul was Israel's king
- David was Israel's king
- Jesus was born

Behind the Scenes (cont.): he can cover his sin and can marry her. We see David struggling with family problems that led to bloodshed and the death of his son Absalom.

Yet in the midst of his problems and sinfulness, David always tried to follow God. When God's prophet confronted him, he admitted his sin and sought forgiveness. When his family was torn apart, he asked for God's help. Because he relied on God, David became known as Israel's greatest king.

David's dramatic story reminds all people of the importance of following God and relying on God. Even when we fail, God is with us, ready to pick us up and give us another chance.

David Learns About Saul's Death

1 Now Saul was dead. After David had defeated the Amalekites, he returned to Ziklag and stayed there two days. 2On the third day a young man from Saul's camp came to Ziklag. To show his sadness, his clothes were torn and he had dirt on his head. He came and bowed facedown on the ground before David.

3David asked him, "Where did you come from?"

The man answered, "I escaped from the Israelite camp."

4David asked him, "What happened? Please tell me!"

The man answered, "The people have run away from the battle, and many of them have fallen and are dead. Saul and his son Jonathan are dead also."

5David asked him, "How do you know Saul and his son Jonathan are dead?"

6The young man answered, "I happened to be on Mount Gilboa. There I saw Saul leaning on his spear. The Philistine chariots and the men riding in them were coming closer to Saul. 7When he looked back and saw me, he called to me. I answered him, 'Here I am!'

8"Then Saul asked me, 'Who are you?'

"I told him, 'I am an Amalekite.'

9"Then Saul said to me, 'Please come here and kill me. I am badly hurt and am almost dead already.'

10"So I went over and killed him. He had been hurt so badly I knew he couldn't live. Then I took the crown from his head and the bracelet from his arm, and I have brought them here to you, my master."

11Then David tore his clothes to show his sorrow, and all the men with him did also. 12They were very sad and cried and did not eat until evening. They cried for Saul and his son Jonathan and for all the people of the LORD and for all the Israelites who had died in the battle.

David Orders the Amalekite Killed

13David asked the young man who brought the report, "Where are you from?"

The young man answered, "I am the son of a foreigner, an Amalekite."

14David asked him, "Why were you not afraid to kill the LORD's appointed king?"

15Then David called one of his men and told him, "Go! Kill the Amalekite!" So the Israelite killed him. 16David had said to the Amalekite, "You are responsible for your own death. You confessed by saying, 'I have killed the LORD's appointed king.' "

David's Song About Saul and Jonathan

17David sang a funeral song about Saul and his son Jonathan, 18and he ordered that the people of Judah be taught this song. It is called "The Bow," and it is written in the Book of Jashar:

19"Israel, your leaders have been killed on the
hills.
How the mighty have fallen in battle!
20Don't tell it in Gath.
Don't announce it in the streets of
Ashkelon.
If you do, the Philistine women will be
happy.
The daughters of the Philistines will rejoice.

21"May there be no dew or rain on the
mountains of Gilboa,
and may their fields produce no grain,
because there the mighty warrior's shield was
dishonored.
Saul's shield will no longer be rubbed with
oil.

SIDELIGHT: Saul's shield (2 Samuel 1:21) would have been made of leather. If the shield was "no longer rubbed with oil," it would dry up, crack, and fall apart.

22Jonathan's bow did not fail
to kill many soldiers.

Saul's sword did not fail
to wound many strong men.

23"We loved Saul and Jonathan
and enjoyed them while they lived.
They are together even in death.
They were faster than eagles.
They were stronger than lions.

24"You daughters of Israel, cry for Saul.
Saul clothed you with red dresses
and put gold decorations on them.

25"How the mighty have fallen in battle!
Jonathan is dead on Gilboa's hills.
26I cry for you, my brother Jonathan.
I enjoyed your friendship so much.
Your love to me was wonderful,
better than the love of women.

27"How the mighty have fallen!
The weapons of war are gone."

David Is Made King of Judah

2 Later, David prayed to the LORD, saying,
"Should I go up to any of the cities of Judah?"
The LORD said to David, "Go."
David asked, "Where should I go?"
The LORD answered, "To Hebron."
2So David went up to Hebron with his two
wives: Ahinoam from Jezreel and Abigail, the
widow of Nabal from Carmel. 3David also
brought his men and their families, and they all
made their homes in the cities of Hebron. 4Then
the men of Judah came to Hebron and appointed
David king over Judah.
They told David that the men of Jabesh Gilead
had buried Saul. 5So David sent messengers to the
men of Jabesh Gilead and said to them, "The
LORD bless you. You have shown loyalty to your
master Saul by burying him. 6May the LORD now
be loyal and true to you. I will also treat you well
because you have done this. 7Now be strong and

DEATH

A Tribute

Dennis Olson was the popular band teacher at Fridley Junior High. Not only did he patiently help students learn music, but he cared about each band member. He would send kids birthday cards and was sure to ask, "How're you doing?" if he heard one of them had been sick.

So the band sat silently as the principal explained. "I'm sorry to have to tell you that Mr. Olson was in a car accident yesterday. He's in serious—actually, critical—condition. We'll be getting a new teacher next week."

In the weeks that followed, band members sent cards and regularly visited Mr. Olson in the hospital as his condition got worse and worse.

Then Mr. Olson died, and the principal came back to the band class. "You all know about Mr. Olson," he began. "I talked to Mrs. Olson today, and she said her husband wanted this band to play at his funeral. Would you?"

The band members were willing, even though it meant extra practices. They wanted to do something to show their respect for their former teacher.

On the day of the funeral, band members played with tears in their eyes. Then they each filed past the casket and laid a white carnation on top. It was hard, but they were glad they had done it for Mr. Olson.

In **2 Samuel 1:17–27**, David also felt great loss when Saul and his son Jonathan—David's friend—died in battle. Read how David expressed his grief for these people he respected and loved.

- How is David's song like the band's tribute at Mr. Olson's funeral?
- When have you felt the grief that David expresses in the passage?

CONSIDER . . .

- reading the obituaries in your newspaper, and praying each day for one family that has experienced a death.
- making a scrapbook about deceased family members—so their memories will live on.

FOR MORE, SEE . . .

- Deuteronomy 34:1–12 (p. 193)
- Isaiah 61:1–3 (p. 680)
- Matthew 5:4 (p. 912)

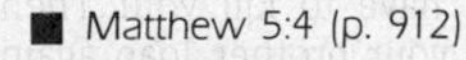

brave. Saul your master is dead, and the people of Judah have appointed me their king."

War Between Judah and Israel

[8]Abner son of Ner was the commander of Saul's army. Abner took Saul's son Ish-Bosheth to Mahanaim [9]and made him king of Gilead, Ashuri, Jezreel, Ephraim, Benjamin, and all Israel. [10]Saul's son Ish-Bosheth was forty years old when he became king over Israel, and he ruled two years. But the people of Judah followed David. [11]David was king in Hebron for seven years and six months.

[12]Abner son of Ner and the servants of Ish-Bosheth son of Saul left Mahanaim and went to Gibeon. [13]Joab son of Zeruiah and David's men also went there and met Abner and Ish-Bosheth's men at the pool of Gibeon. Abner's group sat on one side of the pool; Joab's group sat on the other.

[14]Abner said to Joab, "Let the young men have a contest here."

Joab said, "Yes, let them have a contest."

[15]Then the men got up and were counted—twelve from the people of Benjamin for Ish-Bosheth son of Saul, and twelve from David's men. [16]Each man grabbed the one opposite him by the head and stabbed him in the side with a knife. So the men fell down together. For that reason, that place in Gibeon is called the Field of Knives. [17]That day there was a terrible battle, and David's men defeated Abner and the Israelites.

SIDELIGHT: The pool of Gibeon—where Saul's and David's armies fought—was a huge well (2 Samuel 2:8–17). Archaeologists have discovered what was probably the pool. It is thirty-seven feet in diameter, and has a seventy-nine-step winding stairway down to the water level, which is thirty-three feet below the ground.

Abner Kills Asahel

[18]Zeruiah's three sons, Joab, Abishai, and Asahel, were there. Now Asahel was a fast runner, as fast as a deer in the field. [19]Asahel chased Abner, going straight toward him. [20]Abner looked back and asked, "Is that you, Asahel?"

Asahel said, "Yes, it is."

[21]Then Abner said to Asahel, "Turn to your right or left and catch one of the young men and take his armor." But Asahel refused to stop chasing him.

[22]Abner again said to Asahel, "Stop chasing me! If you don't stop, I'll have to kill you! Then I won't be able to face your brother Joab again!"

[23]But Asahel refused to stop chasing Abner. So using the back end of his spear, Abner stabbed Asahel in the stomach, and the spear came out of his back. Asahel died right there, and everyone stopped when they came to the place where Asahel's body lay.

[24]But Joab and Abishai continued chasing Abner. As the sun was going down, they arrived at the hill of Ammah, near Giah on the way to the desert near Gibeon. [25]The men of Benjamin came to Abner, and all stood together at the top of the hill.

[26]Abner shouted to Joab, "Must the sword kill forever? Surely you must know this will only end in sadness! Tell the people to stop chasing their own brothers!"

[27]Then Joab said, "As surely as God lives, if you had not said anything, the people would have chased their brothers until morning." [28]Then Joab blew a trumpet, and his people stopped chasing the Israelites. They did not fight them anymore.

[29]Abner and his men marched all night through the Jordan Valley. They crossed the Jordan River, and after marching all day, arrived at Mahanaim.

[30]After he had stopped chasing Abner, Joab came back and gathered the people together. Asahel and nineteen of David's men were missing. [31]But David's men had killed three hundred sixty Benjaminites who had followed Abner. [32]David's men took Asahel and buried him in the tomb of his father at Bethlehem. Then Joab and his men marched all night. The sun came up as they reached Hebron.

3 There was a long war between the people who supported Saul's family and those who supported David's family. The supporters of David's family became stronger and stronger, but the supporters of Saul's family became weaker and weaker.

David's Sons

[2]Sons were born to David at Hebron. The first was Amnon, whose mother was Ahinoam from Jezreel. [3]The second son was Kileab, whose mother was Abigail, the widow of Nabal from Carmel. The third son was Absalom, whose mother was Maacah daughter of Talmai, the king of Geshur. [4]The fourth son was Adonijah, whose mother was Haggith. The fifth son was Shephatiah, whose mother was Abital. [5]The sixth son was Ithream, whose mother was Eglah, David's wife. These sons were born to David at Hebron.

Abner Joins David

[6]During the war between the supporters of Saul's family and the supporters of David's family, Abner made himself a main leader among the supporters of Saul.

[7]Saul once had a slave woman[d] named Rizpah, who was the daughter of Aiah. Ish-Bosheth said

to Abner, "Why did you have sexual relations
with my father's slave woman?"
8Abner was very angry because of what Ish-
Bosheth said, and he replied, "I have been loyal
to Saul and his family and friends! I didn't hand
you over to David. I am not a traitor working for
Judah! But now you are saying I did something
wrong with this woman! 9May God help me if I
don't join David! I will make sure that what the
LORD promised does happen! 10I will take the
kingdom from the family of Saul and make David
king of Israel and Judah, from Dan to Beersheba!"[n]
11Ish-Bosheth couldn't say anything to Abner,
because he was afraid of him.
12Then Abner sent messengers to ask David,
"Who is going to rule the land? Make an agreement with me, and I will help you unite all Israel."
13David answered, "Good! I will make an
agreement with you, but I ask you one thing. I
will not meet with you unless you bring Saul's
daughter Michal to me." 14Then David sent messengers to Saul's son Ish-Bosheth, saying, "Give
me my wife Michal. She was promised to me, and
I killed a hundred Philistines to get her."
15So Ish-Bosheth sent men to take Michal from
her husband Paltiel son of Laish. 16Michal's husband went with her, crying as he followed her to
Bahurim. But Abner said to Paltiel, "Go back
home." So he went home.

SIDELIGHT: If you feel like your parent interferes with your dating life, imagine how David felt. He married Saul's daughter, Michal (1 Samuel 18:20–29, p. 262). But when Saul got angry with David, he took back his daughter and gave her to someone else to marry (1 Samuel 25:44, p. 268). Later she returned to David as part of a political bargain (2 Samuel 3:12–16).

17Abner sent this message to the older leaders
of Israel: "You have been wanting to make David
your king. 18Now do it! The LORD said of David,
'Through my servant David, I will save my people
Israel from the Philistines and all their enemies.' "
19Abner also said these things to the people of
Benjamin. He then went to Hebron to tell David
what the Benjaminites and Israel wanted to do.
20Abner came with twenty men to David at Hebron. There David prepared a feast for them. 21Ab-
ner said to David, "My master and king, I will go
and bring all the Israelites to you. Then they will
make an agreement with you so you will rule over
all Israel as you wanted." So David let Abner go,
and he left in peace.

Abner's Death

22Just then Joab and David's men came from a
battle, bringing many valuable things they had
taken from the enemy. David had let Abner leave
in peace, so he was not with David at Hebron.
23When Joab and all his army arrived at Hebron,
the army said to Joab, "Abner son of Ner came to
King David, and David let him leave in peace."
24Joab came to the king and said, "What have
you done? Abner came to you. Why did you let
him go? Now he's gone. 25You know Abner son
of Ner! He came to trick you! He came to learn
about everything you are doing!"
26After Joab left David, he sent messengers after
Abner, and they brought him back from the well
of Sirah. But David did not know this. 27When
Abner arrived at Hebron, Joab took him aside into
the gateway. He acted as though he wanted to
talk with Abner in private, but Joab stabbed him
in the stomach, and Abner died. Abner had killed
Joab's brother Asahel, so Joab killed Abner to pay
him back.
28Later when David heard the news, he said,
"My kingdom and I are innocent forever of the
death of Abner son of Ner. The LORD knows this.
29Joab and his family are responsible for this. May
his family always have someone with sores or
with a skin disease. May they always have someone who must lean on a crutch. May some of his
family be killed in war. May they always have
someone without food to eat."
30(Joab and his brother Abishai killed Abner,
because he had killed their brother Asahel in the
battle at Gibeon.)
31Then David said to Joab and to all the people
with Joab, "Tear your clothes and put on rough
cloth to show how sad you are. Cry for Abner."
King David himself followed the body of Abner.
32They buried Abner in Hebron, and David and all
the people cried at Abner's grave.
33King David sang this funeral song for Abner.

"Did Abner die like a fool?
34 His hands were not tied.
His feet were not in chains.
He fell at the hands of evil men."

Then all the people cried again for Abner.
35They came to encourage David to eat while it
was still day. But he made a promise, saying,
"May God punish me terribly if I eat bread or anything else before the sun sets!"
36All the people saw what happened, and they

Dan to Beersheba Dan was the city farthest north in Israel, and Beersheba was the city farthest south. So this means all the people of Israel.

agreed with what the king was doing, just as they agreed with everything he did. 37That day all the people of Judah and Israel understood that David did not order the killing of Abner son of Ner.

38David said to his officers, "You know that a great man died today in Israel. 39Even though I am the appointed king, I feel empty. These sons of Zeruiah are too much for me. May the LORD give them the punishment they should have."

Ish-Bosheth's Death

4 When Ish-Bosheth son of Saul heard that Abner had died at Hebron, he was shocked and all Israel became frightened. 2Two men who were captains in Saul's army came to Ish-Bosheth. One was named Baanah, and the other was named Recab. They were the sons of Rimmon of Beeroth, who was a Benjaminite. (The town Beeroth belonged to the tribe[d] of Benjamin. 3The people of Beeroth ran away to Gittaim, and they still live there as foreigners today.)

4(Saul's son Jonathan had a son named Mephibosheth, who was crippled in both feet. He was five years old when the news came from Jezreel that Saul and Jonathan were dead. Mephibosheth's nurse had picked him up and run away. But as she hurried to leave, she dropped him, and now he was lame.)

5Recab and Baanah, sons of Rimmon from Beeroth, went to Ish-Bosheth's house in the afternoon while he was taking a nap. 6-7They went into the middle of the house as if to get some wheat. Ish-Bosheth was lying on his bed in his bedroom. Then Recab and Baanah stabbed him in the stomach, killed him, cut off his head, and took it with them. They escaped and traveled all night through the Jordan Valley. 8When they arrived at Hebron, they gave his head to David and said to the king, "Here is the head of Ish-Bosheth son of Saul, your enemy. He tried to kill you! Today the LORD has paid back Saul and his family for what they did to you!"

9David answered Recab and his brother Baanah, the sons of Rimmon of Beeroth, "As surely as the LORD lives, he has saved me from all trouble! 10Once a man thought he was bringing me good news. When he told me, 'Saul is dead!' I seized him and killed him at Ziklag. That was the reward I gave him for his news! 11So even more I must put you evil men to death because you have killed an innocent man on his own bed in his own house!"

12So David commanded his men to kill Recab and Baanah. They cut off the hands and feet of Recab and Baanah and hung them over the pool of Hebron. Then they took Ish-Bosheth's head and buried it in Abner's tomb at Hebron.

David Is Made King of Israel

5 Then all the tribes[d] of Israel came to David at Hebron and said to him, "Look, we are your own family. 2Even when Saul was king, you were the one who led Israel in battle. The LORD said to you, 'You will be a shepherd for my people Israel. You will be their leader.' "

3So all the older leaders of Israel came to King David at Hebron, and he made an agreement with them in Hebron in the presence of the LORD. Then they poured oil on David to make him king over Israel.

4David was thirty years old when he became king, and he ruled forty years. 5He was king over Judah in Hebron for seven years and six months, and he was king over all Israel and Judah in Jerusalem for thirty-three years.

6When the king and his men went to Jerusalem to attack the Jebusites who lived there, the Jebusites said to David, "You can't get inside our city. Even the blind and the crippled can stop you." They thought David could not enter their city. 7But David did take the city of Jerusalem with its strong walls, and it became the City of David.

8That day David said to his men, "To defeat the Jebusites you must go through the water tunnel. Then you can reach those 'crippled' and 'blind' enemies. This is why people say, 'The blind and the crippled may not enter the palace.' "

9So David lived in the strong, walled city and called it the City of David. David built more buildings around it, beginning where the land was filled in. He also built more buildings inside the

> **SIDELIGHT:** Jerusalem wasn't very big by modern standards when King David captured it (2 Samuel 5:6–9). It covered only eleven acres—smaller than the thirteen-acre Superdome stadium in New Orleans, Louisiana.

city. 10He became stronger and stronger, because the LORD God All-Powerful was with him.

11Hiram king of the city of Tyre sent messengers to David, along with cedar logs, carpenters, and stonecutters. They built a palace for David. 12Then David knew that the LORD really had made him king of Israel and that the LORD had made his kingdom great because the LORD loved his people Israel.

13After he came from Hebron, David took for himself more slave women[d] and wives in Jerusalem. More sons and daughters were born to David. 14These are the names of the sons born to

David in Jerusalem: Shammua, Shobab, Nathan,
Solomon, 15Ibhar, Elishua, Nepheg, Japhia,
16Elishama, Eliada, and Eliphelet.

David Defeats the Philistines

17When the Philistines heard that David had
been made king over Israel, all the Philistines
went to look for him. But when David heard the
news, he went down to the stronghold.[d] 18The
Philistines came and camped in the Valley of
Rephaim. 19David asked the LORD, "Should I attack the Philistines? Will you hand them over to
me?"

The LORD said to David, "Go! I will certainly
hand them over to you."

20So David went to Baal Perazim and defeated
the Philistines there. David said, "Like a flood of
water, the LORD has broken through my enemies
in front of me." So David named the place Baal
Perazim.[n] 21The Philistines left their idols behind
at Baal Perazim, so David and his men carried
them away.

22Once again the Philistines came and camped
at the Valley of Rephaim. 23When David prayed to
the LORD, he answered, "Don't attack the Philistines from the front. Instead, go around and attack
them in front of the balsam trees. 24When you
hear the sound of marching in the tops of the balsam trees, act quickly. I, the LORD, will have gone
ahead of you to defeat the Philistine army." 25So
David did what the LORD commanded. He defeated the Philistines and chased them all the way
from Gibeon to Gezer.

The Ark Is Brought to Jerusalem

6 David again gathered all the chosen men of
Israel—thirty thousand of them. 2Then he
and all his people went to Baalah in Judah[n] to
bring back the Ark[d] of God. The Ark is called by
the Name, the name of the LORD All-Powerful,

Baal Perazim This name means "the Lord breaks through."
Baalah in Judah Another name for Kiriath Jearim.

LEADERSHIP

Earned Respect

The other track team members didn't know what to think when Anne Cleveland walked into the locker room the first day of practice. She was a sophomore, and everyone else on the team was a junior or senior. "How's everybody doing?" she said cheerfully.

But as the other team members ran their warm-up laps, they couldn't ignore Anne's rhythmic stride and seemingly effortless pace. And by the end of the afternoon, they all knew this girl would fit in. She worked hard, did well and encouraged others.

Within weeks, Anne had become a star, setting the state record in the 400-meter dash. But when the school newspaper reporter asked her about it, she replied: "I'm glad the team did well. The whole team encouraged me in that race. We work hard together."

Anne never would take glory for her performance. And, gradually, the older girls began asking her for pointers. By the end of the season, the whole team had become one of the best in the state.

When it came to picking a captain for the next year, no one questioned whom to pick. Sure she was only a junior, and a senior usually led the team, but Anne was the team's natural leader.

Like Anne, David had proven his leadership skills for years. So when it came time to find a new king, he was a natural choice, even though he was young. Read how the country chose him in **2 Samuel 5:1–5**.

- How did both Anne and David earn respect so that they were chosen as leaders? How did their humility help them both as leaders?
- How can you, like David, work to earn respect so you can be a leader?

CONSIDER...

- talking to a leader you respect about how he or she became a leader. Then put into practice one tip you learned.
- working to be a team player at church, school and work, then watching to see what leadership role you might play.

FOR MORE, SEE...

- Jeremiah 1:4–10 (p. 691)
- Matthew 20:20–28 (p. 944)
- 1 Corinthians 3:5–9 (p. 1170)

whose throne is between the gold creatures with
wings. 3They put the Ark of God on a new cart
and brought it out of Abinadab's house on the hill.
Uzzah and Ahio, sons of Abinadab, led the new
cart 4which had the Ark of God on it. Ahio was
walking in front of it. 5David and all the Israelites
were celebrating in the presence of the LORD.
They were playing wooden instruments: lyres,[d]
harps, tambourines,[d] rattles, and cymbals.
6When David's men came to the threshing[d]
floor of Nacon, the oxen stumbled. So Uzzah
reached out to steady the Ark of God. 7The LORD
was angry with Uzzah and killed him because of
what he did. So Uzzah died there beside the Ark
of God. 8David was angry because the LORD had
killed Uzzah. Now that place is called the Punishment of Uzzah.
9David was afraid of the LORD that day, and he
said, "How can the Ark of the LORD come to me
now?" 10So David would not move the Ark of the
LORD to be with him in Jerusalem. Instead, he
took it to the house of Obed-Edom, a man from
Gath. 11The Ark of the LORD stayed in Obed-
Edom's house for three months, and the LORD
blessed Obed-Edom and all his family.
12The people told David, "The LORD has
blessed the family of Obed-Edom and all that belongs to him, because the Ark of God is there." So
David went and brought it up from Obed-Edom's
house to Jerusalem with joy. 13When the men carrying the Ark of the LORD had walked six steps,
David sacrificed a bull and a fat calf. 14Then David
danced with all his might before the LORD. He
had on a holy linen vest.[d] 15David and all the Israelites shouted with joy and blew the trumpets as
they brought the Ark of the LORD to the city.
16As the Ark of the LORD came into the city,
Saul's daughter Michal looked out the window.
When she saw David jumping and dancing in the
presence of the LORD, she hated him.
17David put up a tent for the Ark of the LORD,
and then the Israelites put it in its place inside the
tent. David offered whole burnt offerings and fellowship offerings before the LORD. 18When David
finished offering the whole burnt offerings and
the fellowship offerings, he blessed the people in
the name of the LORD All-Powerful. 19David gave
a loaf of bread, a cake of dates, and a cake of raisins to every Israelite, both men and women.
Then all the people went home.
20David went back to bless the people in his
home, but Saul's daughter Michal came out to
meet him. She said, "With what honor the king
of Israel acted today! You took off your clothes in
front of the servant girls of your officers like one
who takes off his clothes without shame!"
21Then David said to Michal, "I did it in the
presence of the LORD. The LORD chose me, not
your father or anyone from Saul's family. The
LORD appointed me to be over Israel. So I will
celebrate in the presence of the LORD. 22Maybe I
will lose even more honor, and maybe I will be
brought down in my own opinion, but the girls
you talk about will honor me!"
23And Saul's daughter Michal had no children
to the day she died.

David Wants to Build a Temple

7 King David was living in his palace, and the
LORD had given him peace from all his enemies around him. 2Then David said to Nathan the
prophet,[d] "Look, I am living in a palace made of
cedar wood, but the Ark[d] of God is in a tent!"
3Nathan said to the king, "Go and do what you
really want to do, because the LORD is with you."
4But that night the LORD spoke his word to Nathan, 5"Go and tell my servant David, 'This is
what the LORD says: Will you build a house for
me to live in? 6From the time I brought the Israelites out of Egypt until now I have not lived in a
house. I have been moving around all this time
with a tent as my home. 7As I have moved with
the Israelites, I have never said to the tribes,[d]
whom I commanded to take care of my people
Israel, "Why haven't you built me a house of cedar?" '
8"You must tell my servant David, 'This is what
the LORD All-Powerful says: I took you from the
pasture and from tending the sheep and made you
leader of my people Israel. 9I have been with you
everywhere you have gone and have defeated
your enemies for you. I will make you as famous
as any of the great people on the earth. 10Also I
will choose a place for my people Israel, and I will
plant them so they can live in their own homes.
They will not be bothered anymore. Wicked people will no longer bother them as they have in the
past 11when I chose judges for my people Israel.
But I will give you peace from all your enemies.
I also tell you that I will make your descendants[d]
kings of Israel after you.
12" 'When you die and join your ancestors, I
will make one of your sons the next king, and I
will set up his kingdom. 13He will build a house
for me, and I will let his kingdom rule always. 14I
will be his father, and he will be my son. When
he sins, I will use other people to punish him.
They will be my whips. 15I took away my love
from Saul, whom I removed before you, but I will
never stop loving your son. 16But your family and
your kingdom will continue always before me.
Your throne will last forever.' "
17Nathan told David everything God had said
in this vision.

David Prays to God

18Then King David went in and sat in front of
the LORD. David said, "Lord GOD, who am I?

What is my family? Why did you bring me to this
point? 19But even this is not enough for you, Lord
God. You have also made promises about my future family. This is not normal, Lord God.
20"What more can I say to you, Lord God,
since you know me, your servant, so well! 21You
have done this great thing because you said you
would and because you wanted to, and you have
let me know about it. 22This is why you are great,
Lord God! There is no one like you. There is no
God except you. We have heard all this ourselves!
23There is no nation like your people Israel. They
are the only people on earth that God chose to be
his own. You made your name well known. You
did great and wonderful miracles[d] for them. You
went ahead of them and forced other nations and
their gods out of the land. You freed your people
from slavery in Egypt. 24You made the people of
Israel your very own people forever, and, Lord,
you are their God.
25"Now, Lord God, keep the promise forever
that you made about my family and me, your servant. Do what you have said. 26Then you will be
honored always, and people will say, 'The Lord
All-Powerful is God over Israel!' And the family of
your servant David will continue before you.
27"Lord All-Powerful, the God of Israel, you
have said to me, 'I will make your family great.'
So I, your servant, am brave enough to pray to
you. 28Lord God, you are God, and your words
are true. And you have promised these good
things to me, your servant. 29Please, bless my family. Let it continue before you always. Lord God,
you have said so. With your blessing let my family
always be blessed."

David Wins Many Wars

8 Later, David defeated the Philistines, conquered them, and took the city of Metheg
Ammah.
2He also defeated the people of Moab. He made
them lie on the ground, and then he used a rope
to measure them. Those who were measured
within two rope lengths were killed, but those
who were within the next rope length were allowed to live. So the people of Moab became servants of David and gave him the payment he demanded.
3David also defeated Hadadezer son of Rehob,
king of Zobah, as he went to take control again at
the Euphrates River. 4David captured one thousand chariots, seven thousand men who rode in
chariots, and twenty thousand foot soldiers. He
crippled all but a hundred of the chariot horses.

THANKFULNESS

Unnoticed Gifts

If you have trouble thinking of things to thank God for, start with this list of things he has given you:

- A defense against tiny bacteria and larger critters such as scorpions, fleas, and bugs.
- Something to keep some things in while keeping other things out.
- A radiator to cool you.
- Padding that takes the shape of objects it touches.
- Half a million transmitters that send messages through your body.
- A unique pattern that identifies you.

All these things are in just one part of your body: your skin. Imagine how much else you have to be thankful for in your life and world!

David recognized the gifts God had given him and his family. Read his prayer of thanksgiving in **2 Samuel 7:18–29**.

- Why does David say God gives good things? What is David's response?
- What has God given you that reminds you of how important you are? How have you thanked God for that?

CONSIDER

- making a list of people and things for which you are most thankful. Thank God for each of these people or things this week, and call or write each person a thank-you message.
- tracing your family tree back as far as you can. Then talk with your parent about the strengths and weaknesses of each generation. Pray that God will guide and bless you and future generations.

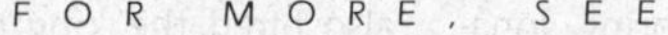

FOR MORE, SEE...

- Psalm 98:1–9 (p. 538)
- Isaiah 63:7–9 (p. 683)
- Colossians 1:9–13 (p. 1238)

5Arameans from Damascus came to help Hadadezer king of Zobah, but David killed twenty-two thousand of them. 6Then David put groups of soldiers in Damascus in Aram. The Arameans became David's servants and gave him the payment he demanded. The LORD gave David victory everywhere he went.

7David took the shields of gold that had belonged to Hadadezer's officers and brought them to Jerusalem. 8David also took many things made of bronze from Tebah and Berothai, which had been cities under Hadadezer's control.

9Toi king of Hamath heard that David had defeated all the army of Hadadezer. 10So Toi sent his son Joram to greet and congratulate King David for defeating Hadadezer. (Hadadezer had been at war with Toi.) Joram brought items made of silver, gold, and bronze. 11King David gave them to the LORD, along with the silver and gold he had taken from the other nations he had defeated. 12These nations were Edom, Moab, Ammon, Philistia, and Amalek. David also gave the LORD what he had taken from Hadadezer son of Rehob, king of Zobah.

13David was famous after he returned from defeating eighteen thousand Arameans in the Valley of Salt. 14He put groups of soldiers all over Edom, and all the Edomites became his servants. The LORD gave David victory everywhere he went.

15David was king over all Israel, and he did what was fair and right for all his people. 16Joab son of Zeruiah was commander over the army. Jehoshaphat son of Ahilud was the recorder. 17Zadok son of Ahitub and Abiathar son of Ahimelech were priests. Seraiah was the royal secretary. 18Benaiah son of Jehoiada was over the Kerethites and Pelethites.[n] And David's sons were priests.

David Helps Saul's Family

9 David asked, "Is anyone still left in Saul's family? I want to show kindness to that person for Jonathan's sake!"

2Now there was a servant named Ziba from Saul's family. So David's servants called Ziba to him. King David said to him, "Are you Ziba?"

He answered, "Yes, I am your servant."

3The king asked, "Is anyone left in Saul's family? I want to show God's kindness to that person."

Ziba answered the king, "Jonathan has a son still living who is crippled in both feet."

4The king asked Ziba, "Where is this son?"

Ziba answered, "He is at the house of Makir son of Ammiel in Lo Debar."

5Then King David had servants bring Jonathan's son from the house of Makir son of Ammiel in Lo Debar. 6Mephibosheth, Jonathan's son, came before David and bowed facedown on the floor.

David said, "Mephibosheth!"

Mephibosheth said, "I am your servant."

7David said to him, "Don't be afraid. I will be kind to you for your father Jonathan's sake. I will give you back all the land of your grandfather Saul, and you will always eat at my table."

8Mephibosheth bowed to David again and said, "You are being very kind to me, your servant! And I am no better than a dead dog!"

9Then King David called Saul's servant Ziba. David said to him, "I have given your master's grandson everything that belonged to Saul and his family. 10You, your sons, and your servants will farm the land and harvest the crops. Then your family will have food to eat. But Mephibosheth, your master's grandson, will always eat at my table."

(Now Ziba had fifteen sons and twenty servants.) 11Ziba said to King David, "I, your servant, will do everything my master, the king, commands me."

So Mephibosheth ate at David's table as if he were one of the king's sons. 12Mephibosheth had a young son named Mica. Everyone in Ziba's family became Mephibosheth's servants. 13Mephibosheth lived in Jerusalem, because he always ate at the king's table. And he was crippled in both feet.

War with the Ammonites and Arameans

10 When Nahash king of the Ammonites died, his son Hanun became king after him. 2David said, "Nahash was loyal to me, so I will be loyal to his son Hanun." So David sent his messengers to comfort Hanun about his father's death.

David's officers went to the land of the Ammonites. 3But the Ammonite leaders said to Hanun, their master, "Do you think David wants to honor your father by sending men to comfort you? No! David sent them to study the city and spy it out and capture it!" 4So Hanun arrested David's officers. To shame them he shaved off half their beards and cut off their clothes at the hips. Then he sent them away.

5When the people told David, he sent messengers to meet his officers because they were very ashamed. King David said, "Stay in Jericho until your beards have grown back. Then come home."

6The Ammonites knew that they had insulted David. So they hired twenty thousand Aramean foot soldiers from Beth Rehob and Zobah. They also hired the king of Maacah with a thousand men and twelve thousand men from Tob.

Kerethites and Pelethites These were probably special units of the army that were responsible for the king's safety, a kind of palace guard.

[7]When David heard about this, he sent Joab with the whole army. [8]The Ammonites came out and prepared for battle at the city gate. The Arameans from Zobah and Rehob and the men from Tob and Maacah were out in the field by themselves.

[9]Joab saw that there were enemies both in front of him and behind him. So he chose some of the best soldiers of Israel and sent them out to fight the Arameans. [10]Joab put the rest of the army under the command of Abishai, his brother. Then he sent them out to fight the Ammonites. [11]Joab said to Abishai, "If the Arameans are too strong for me, you must help me. Or, if the Ammonites are too strong for you, I will help you. [12]Be strong. We must fight bravely for our people and the cities of our God. The LORD will do what he thinks is right."

[13]Then Joab and the army with him went to attack the Arameans, and the Arameans ran away. [14]When the Ammonites saw that the Arameans were running away, they also ran away from Abishai and went back to their city. So Joab returned from the battle with the Ammonites and came to Jerusalem.

[15]When the Arameans saw that Israel had defeated them, they came together into one big army. [16]Hadadezer sent messengers to bring the Arameans from east of the Euphrates River, and they went to Helam. Their leader was Shobach, the commander of Hadadezer's army.

[17]When David heard about this, he gathered all the Israelites together. They crossed over the Jordan River and went to Helam. There the Arameans prepared for battle and attacked him. [18]But the Arameans ran away from the Israelites. David killed seven hundred Aramean chariot drivers and forty thousand Aramean horsemen. He also killed Shobach, the commander of the Aramean army.

SIDELIGHT: If you wanted to shame a man in ancient Israel, you could shave off his beard. But if you did it, you had better be prepared for him to strike back in revenge. In 2 Samuel 10:1–19, a shaving party resulted in a war that took about 40,700 lives.

[19]When the kings who served Hadadezer saw that the Israelites had defeated them, they made peace with the Israelites and served them. And the Arameans were afraid to help the Ammonites again.

David Sins with Bathsheba

11 In the spring, when the kings normally went out to war, David sent out Joab, his servants, and all the Israelites. They destroyed the Ammonites and attacked the city of Rabbah. But David stayed in Jerusalem. [2]One evening David got up from his bed and walked around on the roof[n] of his palace. While he was on the roof, he saw a woman bathing. She was very beautiful. [3]So David sent his servants to find out who she was. A servant answered, "That woman is Bathsheba daughter of Eliam. She is the wife of Uriah the Hittite." [4]So David sent messengers to bring Bathsheba to him. When she came to him, he had sexual relations with her. (Now Bathsheba had purified herself from her monthly period.) Then she went back to her house. [5]But Bathsheba became pregnant and sent word to David, saying, "I am pregnant."

[6]So David sent a message to Joab: "Send Uriah the Hittite to me." And Joab sent Uriah to David. [7]When Uriah came to him, David asked him how Joab was, how the soldiers were, and how the war was going. [8]Then David said to Uriah, "Go home and rest."

So Uriah left the palace, and the king sent a gift to him. [9]But Uriah did not go home. Instead, he slept outside the door of the palace as all the king's officers did.

[10]The officers told David, "Uriah did not go home."

Then David said to Uriah, "You came from a long trip. Why didn't you go home?"

[11]Uriah said to him, "The Ark[d] and the soldiers of Israel and Judah are staying in tents. My master Joab and his officers are camping out in the fields. It isn't right for me to go home to eat and drink and have sexual relations with my wife!"

[12]David said to Uriah, "Stay here today. Tomorrow I'll send you back to the battle." So Uriah stayed in Jerusalem that day and the next. [13]Then David called Uriah to come to see him, so Uriah ate and drank with David. David made Uriah drunk, but he still did not go home. That evening Uriah again slept with the king's officers.

[14]The next morning David wrote a letter to Joab and sent it by Uriah. [15]In the letter David wrote, "Put Uriah on the front lines where the fighting is worst and leave him there alone. Let him be killed in battle."

[16]Joab watched the city and saw where its strongest defenders were and put Uriah there. [17]When the men of the city came out to fight against Joab, some of David's men were killed. And Uriah the Hittite was one of them.

[18]Then Joab sent David a complete account of

roof In Bible times houses were built with flat roofs. The roof was used for drying things such as flax and fruit. And it was used as an extra room, as a place for worship, and as a place to sleep in the summer.

the war. 19Joab told the messenger, "Tell King David what happened in the war. 20After you finish, the king may be angry and ask, 'Why did you go so near the city to fight? Didn't you know they would shoot arrows from the city wall? 21Do you remember who killed Abimelech son of Jerub-Besheth?[n] It was a woman on the city wall. She threw a large stone for grinding grain on Abimelech and killed him there in Thebez. Why did you go so near the wall?' If King David asks that, tell him, 'Your servant Uriah the Hittite also died.' "

22The messenger left and went to David and told him everything Joab had told him to say. 23The messenger told David, "The men of Ammon were winning. They came out and attacked us in the field, but we fought them back to the city gate. 24The archers on the city wall shot at your servants, and some of your men were killed. Your servant Uriah the Hittite also died."

25David said to the messenger, "Say this to Joab: 'Don't be upset about this. The sword kills everyone the same. Make a stronger attack against the city and capture it.' Encourage Joab with these words."

26When Bathsheba heard that her husband was dead, she cried for him. 27After she finished her time of sadness, David sent servants to bring her to his house. She became David's wife and gave birth to his son, but the LORD did not like what David had done.

David's Son Dies

12 The LORD sent Nathan to David. When he came to David, he said, "There were two men in a city. One was rich, but the other was poor. 2The rich man had many sheep and cattle. 3But the poor man had nothing except one little female lamb he had bought. The poor man fed the lamb, and it grew up with him and his

Jerub-Besheth Another name for Gideon.

SEXUALITY

Risking Everything

Something about LaDonna King turned Allan Gentry's head. Maybe her figure. Maybe her playful smile. Maybe her piercing eyes. Whatever it was, Allan couldn't get her out of his mind.

After two weeks of nervous planning, he finally found the courage to ask her out. He did everything he could to impress her. He waxed his vintage Mustang and took her to the fanciest restaurant in town. He turned on his charm, making sure she knew how important he was.

After that first date, they kissed at the door. But over the next few weeks, Allan wanted more. Each time, he would try to go a little farther. Each time she would resist.

As their dizzying romance continued, Allan became more aggressive. LaDonna bravely continued to resist, but Allan applied even more pressure. "If you really loved me," he said, "you wouldn't make me stop."

"But I do love you, Allan," she replied.

"Well, I can't be sure unless you show me."

Frightened at the prospect of losing Allan, LaDonna finally gave in. Three months later, she discovered she was pregnant.

Out of her fear of losing Allan, she lost so much more.

Like LaDonna, David risked everything to have Bathsheba. And it nearly cost him everything. Read **2 Samuel 11:1–15** to see what happened.

- How did Allan and David abuse their power? What choices did LaDonna and Bathsheba have?
- What would you have done if you had been in David's situation? What about Bathsheba's?

CONSIDER . . .

- writing on a small card three things you could say to someone who pressures you to have sex. Keep the card in your wallet or purse.
- praying regularly that God will give you strength to resist sexual temptation.

FOR MORE, SEE . . .

- 2 Samuel 12:1–14 (p. 284)
- Matthew 5:27–30 (p. 914)
- 1 Thessalonians 4:3–8 (p. 1247)

children. It shared his food and drank from his
cup and slept in his arms. The lamb was like a
daughter to him.
4“Then a traveler stopped to visit the rich man.
The rich man wanted to feed the traveler, but he
didn’t want to take one of his own sheep or cattle.
Instead, he took the lamb from the poor man and
cooked it for his visitor.”
5David became very angry at the rich man. He
said to Nathan, “As surely as the LORD lives, the
man who did this should die! 6He must pay for the
lamb four times for doing such a thing. He had no
mercy!”
7Then Nathan said to David, “You are the man!
This is what the LORD, the God of Israel, says: ‘I
appointed you king of Israel and saved you from
Saul. 8I gave you his kingdom and his wives. And
I made you king of Israel and Judah. And if that
had not been enough, I would have given you
even more. 9So why did you ignore the LORD’s
command? Why did you do what he says is
wrong? You killed Uriah the Hittite with the
sword of the Ammonites and took his wife to be
your wife! 10Now there will always be people in
your family who will die by a sword, because you
did not respect me; you took the wife of Uriah the
Hittite for yourself!’
11“This is what the LORD says: ‘I am bringing
trouble to you from your own family. While you
watch, I will take your wives from you and give
them to someone who is very close to you. He
will have sexual relations with your wives, and
everyone will know it. 12You had sexual relations
with Bathsheba in secret, but I will do this so all
the people of Israel can see it.’ ”
13Then David said to Nathan, “I have sinned
against the LORD.”
Nathan answered, “The LORD has taken away
your sin. You will not die. 14But what you did
caused the LORD’s enemies to lose all respect for

SIN

Hidden Sins

- It wasn’t a big crash. Just a little nudge in the parking lot. From what Joni Snyder could tell, just the taillight was broken. She would get it fixed before her parents returned from their weekend getaway, and they would never know she had taken the Volvo without permission.

  She didn’t notice that the license plate was also bent.
- When Terrence Ball’s parents asked him if he smoked pot, he was furious. “Of course not!” he shouted. “Don’t you trust me?”

  But his parents could smell the smoke in his jean jacket.
- It would be harmless. No one would know that Terri Walker’s English term paper was just like Amy Woods’s paper from four years ago. Amy had gotten an A on it, so Terri figured she could too—with a lot less work.

  But she wasn’t prepared when the teacher asked for an oral report too.
- The lawn in front of the school looked like a moonscape. The tires had torn the sod so badly that the whole lawn would have to be replaced. The principal demanded that anyone who knew what had happened report it. Almost everyone knew it was Don Hunter and Gary Richards, the football stars.

  But no one said anything.

Just as people try to hide their sins today, David tried to hide his sin when he committed adultery with Bathsheba. But, as **2 Samuel 12:1–25** reveals, God saw the sin.

- What might the prophet Nathan say to the teenagers who tried to hide their sins?
- Just as David suffered the consequences of his sin, how have you suffered the consequences of something you’ve done wrong?

CONSIDER...

- confessing to a parent or friend something you’ve done wrong but have kept hidden. Also confess it to God and accept his forgiveness.
- being honest and open next time you’re confronted about something you did. See how the approach affects what happens.

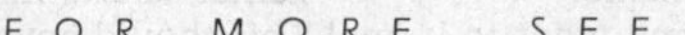

FOR MORE, SEE...

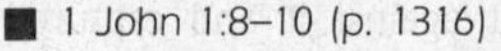

- Psalm 51:1–13 (p. 511)
- Isaiah 29:15–16 (p. 645)
- 1 John 1:8–10 (p. 1316)

him. For this reason the son who was born to you will die."

15Then Nathan went home. And the LORD caused the son of David and Bathsheba, Uriah's widow, to be very sick. 16David prayed to God for the baby. David refused to eat or drink. He went into his house and stayed there, lying on the ground all night. 17The older leaders of David's family came to him and tried to pull him up from the ground, but he refused to get up or to eat food with them.

18On the seventh day the baby died. David's servants were afraid to tell him that the baby was dead. They said, "Look, we tried to talk to David while the baby was alive, but he refused to listen to us. If we tell him the baby is dead, he may do something awful."

19When David saw his servants whispering, he knew that the baby was dead. So he asked them, "Is the baby dead?"

They answered, "Yes, he is dead."

20Then David got up from the floor, washed himself, put lotions on, and changed his clothes. Then he went into the LORD's house to worship. After that, he went home and asked for something to eat. His servants gave him some food, and he ate.

21David's servants said to him, "Why are you doing this? When the baby was still alive, you refused to eat and you cried. Now that the baby is dead, you get up and eat food."

22David said, "While the baby was still alive, I refused to eat, and I cried. I thought, 'Who knows? Maybe the LORD will feel sorry for me and let the baby live.' 23But now that the baby is dead, why should I go without food? I can't bring him back to life. Some day I will go to him, but he cannot come back to me."

24Then David comforted Bathsheba his wife. He slept with her and had sexual relations with her. She became pregnant again and had another son, whom David named Solomon. The LORD loved Solomon. 25The LORD sent word through Nathan the prophet[d] to name the baby Jedidiah,[n] because the LORD loved the child.

David Captures Rabbah

26Joab fought against Rabbah, a royal city of the Ammonites, and he was about to capture it. 27Joab sent messengers to David and said, "I have fought against Rabbah and have captured its water supply. 28Now bring the other soldiers together and attack this city. Capture it before I capture it myself and it is called by my name!"

29So David gathered all the army and went to Rabbah and fought against it and captured it. 30David took the crown off their king's head and had it placed on his own head. That gold crown weighed about seventy-five pounds, and it had valuable gems in it. And David took many valuable things from the city. 31He also brought out the people of the city and forced them to work with saws, iron picks, and axes. He also made them build with bricks. David did this to all the Ammonite cities. Then David and all his army returned to Jerusalem.

Amnon and Tamar

13 David had a son named Absalom and a son named Amnon. Absalom had a beautiful sister named Tamar, and Amnon loved her. 2Tamar was a virgin.[d] Amnon made himself sick just thinking about her, because he could not find any chance to be alone with her.

3Amnon had a friend named Jonadab son of Shimeah, David's brother. Jonadab was a very clever man. 4He asked Amnon, "Son of the king, why do you look so sad day after day? Tell me what's wrong!"

Amnon told him, "I love Tamar, the sister of my half-brother Absalom."

5Jonadab said to Amnon, "Go to bed and act as if you are sick. Then your father will come to see you. Tell him, 'Please let my sister Tamar come in and give me food to eat. Let her make the food in front of me so I can watch and eat it from her hand.' "

6So Amnon went to bed and acted sick. When King David came in to see him, Amnon said to him, "Please let my sister Tamar come in. Let her make two of her special cakes for me while I watch. Then I will eat them from her hands."

7David sent for Tamar in the palace, saying, "Go to your brother Amnon's house and make some food for him." 8So Tamar went to her brother Amnon's house, and he was in bed. Tamar took some dough and pressed it together with her hands. She made some special cakes while Amnon watched. Then she baked them. 9Next she took the pan and served him, but he refused to eat.

He said to his servants, "All of you, leave me alone!" So they all left him alone. 10Amnon said to Tamar, "Bring the food into the bedroom so I may eat from your hand."

Tamar took the cakes she had made and brought them to her brother Amnon in the bedroom. 11She went to him so he could eat from her hands, but Amnon grabbed her. He said, "Sister, come and have sexual relations with me."

12Tamar said to him, "No, brother! Don't force me! This should never be done in Israel! Don't do this shameful thing! 13I could never get rid of my shame! And you will be like the shameful fools in

Jedidiah This name means "loved by the LORD."

Israel! Please talk with the king, and he will let you marry me."

14But Amnon refused to listen to her. He was stronger than she was, so he forced her to have sexual relations with him. 15After that, Amnon hated Tamar. He hated her more than he had loved her before. Amnon said to her, "Get up and leave!"

16Tamar said to him, "No! Sending me away would be worse than what you've already done!"

But he refused to listen to her. 17He called his young servant back in and said, "Get this woman out of here and away from me! Lock the door after her." 18So his servant led her out of the room and bolted the door after her.

Tamar was wearing a special robe with long sleeves, because the king's virgin daughters wore this kind of robe. 19To show how upset she was, Tamar put ashes on her head and tore her special robe and put her hand on her head. Then she went away, crying loudly.

20Absalom, Tamar's brother, said to her, "Has Amnon, your brother, forced you to have sexual relations with him? For now, sister, be quiet. He is your half-brother. Don't let this upset you so much!" So Tamar lived in her brother Absalom's house and was sad and lonely.

21When King David heard the news, he was very angry. 22Absalom did not say a word, good or bad, to Amnon. But he hated Amnon for disgracing his sister Tamar.

Absalom's Revenge

23Two years later Absalom had some men come to Baal Hazor, near Ephraim, to cut the wool from his sheep. Absalom invited all the king's sons to come also. 24Absalom went to the king and said, "I have men coming to cut the wool. Please come with your officers and join me."

25King David said to Absalom, "No, my son. We won't all go, because it would be too much trouble for you." Although Absalom begged David, he would not go, but he did give his blessing.

26Absalom said, "If you don't want to come, then please let my brother Amnon come with us."

King David asked, "Why should he go with you?"

27Absalom kept begging David until he let Amnon and all the king's sons go with Absalom.

28Then Absalom instructed his servants, "Watch Amnon. When he is drunk, I will tell you, 'Kill Amnon.' Right then, kill him! Don't be afraid, because I have commanded you! Be strong and brave!" 29So Absalom's young men killed Amnon as Absalom commanded, but all of David's other sons got on their mules and escaped.

30While the king's sons were on their way, the news came to David, "Absalom has killed all of the king's sons! Not one of them is left alive!" 31King David tore his clothes and lay on the ground to show his sadness. All his servants standing nearby tore their clothes also.

32Jonadab son of Shimeah, David's brother, said to David, "Don't think all the young men, your sons, are killed. No, only Amnon is dead! Absalom has planned this ever since Amnon forced his sister Tamar to have sexual relations with him. 33My master and king, don't think that all of the king's sons are dead. Only Amnon is dead!"

34In the meantime Absalom had run away.

A guard standing on the city wall saw many people coming from the other side of the hill. 35So Jonadab said to King David, "Look, I was right! The king's sons are coming!"

36As soon as Jonadab had said this, the king's sons arrived, crying loudly. David and all his servants began crying also. 37David cried for his son every day.

But Absalom ran away to Talmai[n] son of Ammihud, the king of Geshur. 38After Absalom ran away to Geshur, he stayed there for three years. 39When King David got over Amnon's death, he missed Absalom greatly.

Joab Sends a Wise Woman to David

14 Joab son of Zeruiah knew that King David missed Absalom very much. 2So Joab sent messengers to Tekoa to bring a wise woman from there. He said to her, "Pretend to be very sad. Put on funeral clothes and don't put lotion on yourself. Act like a woman who has been crying many days for someone who died. 3Then go to the king and say these words." Then Joab told her what to say.

4So the woman from Tekoa spoke to the king. She bowed facedown on the ground to show respect and said, "My king, help me!"

5King David asked her, "What is the matter?"

The woman said, "I am a widow; my husband is dead. 6I had two sons. They were out in the field fighting, and no one was there to stop them. So one son killed the other son. 7Now all the family group is against me. They said to me, 'Bring the son who killed his brother so we may kill him for killing his brother. That way we will also get rid of the one who would receive what belonged to his father.' My son is like the last spark of a fire. He is all I have left. If they kill him, my husband's name and property will be gone from the earth."

8Then the king said to the woman, "Go home. I will take care of this for you."

9The woman of Tekoa said to him, "Let the

Talmai He was Absalom's grandfather.

blame be on me and my father's family. My master and king, you and your throne are innocent."

10King David said, "Bring me anyone who says anything bad to you. Then he won't bother you again."

11The woman said, "Please promise in the name of the LORD your God. Then my relative who has the duty of punishing a murderer won't add to the destruction by killing my son."

David said, "As surely as the LORD lives, no one will hurt your son. Not one hair from his head will fall to the ground."

12The woman said, "Let me say something to you, my master and king."

The king said, "Speak."

13Then the woman said, "Why have you decided this way against the people of God? When you judge this way, you show that you are guilty for not bringing back your son who was forced to leave home. 14We will all die some day. We're like water spilled on the ground; no one can gather it back. But God doesn't take away life. Instead, he plans ways that those who have been sent away will not have to stay away from him! 15My master and king, I came to say this to you because the people have made me afraid! I thought, 'Let me talk to the king. Maybe he will do what I ask. 16Maybe he will listen. Perhaps he will save me from those who want to keep both me and my son from getting what God gave us.'

17"Now I say, 'May the words of my master the king give me rest. Like an angel of God, you know what is good and what is bad. May the LORD your God be with you!' "

18Then King David said, "Do not hide the truth. Answer me one question."

The woman said, "My master the king, please ask your question."

19The king said, "Did Joab tell you to say all these things?"

The woman answered, "As you live, my master the king, no one could avoid that question. You are right. Your servant Joab did tell me to say these things. 20Joab did it so you would see things differently. My master, you are wise like an angel of God who knows everything that happens on earth."

Absalom Returns to Jerusalem

21The king said to Joab, "Look, I will do what I promised. Bring back the young man Absalom."

22Joab bowed facedown on the ground and blessed the king. Then he said, "Today I know you are pleased with me, because you have done what I asked."

23Then Joab got up and went to Geshur and brought Absalom back to Jerusalem. 24But King David said, "Absalom must go to his own house. He may not come to see me." So Absalom went to his own house and did not go to see the king.

25Absalom was greatly praised for his handsome appearance. No man in Israel was as handsome as he. No blemish was on him from his head to his foot. 26At the end of every year, Absalom would cut his hair, because it became too heavy. When he weighed it, it would weigh about five pounds by the royal measure.

27Absalom had three sons and one daughter. His daughter's name was also Tamar, and she was a beautiful woman.

28Absalom lived in Jerusalem for two full years without seeing King David. 29Then Absalom sent for Joab so he could send him to the king, but Joab would not come. Absalom sent a message a second time, but Joab still refused to come. 30Then Absalom said to his servants, "Look, Joab's field is next to mine, and he has barley growing there. Go burn it." So Absalom's servants set fire to Joab's field.

31Then Joab went to Absalom's house and said to him, "Why did your servants burn my field?"

32Absalom said to Joab, "I sent a message to you, asking you to come here. I wanted to send you to the king to ask him why he brought me home from Geshur. It would have been better for me to stay there! Now let me see the king. If I have sinned, he can put me to death!"

33So Joab went to the king and told him Absalom's words. Then the king called for Absalom. Absalom came and bowed facedown on the ground before the king, and the king kissed him.

Absalom Plans to Take David's Kingdom

15 After this, Absalom got a chariot and horses for himself and fifty men to run before him. 2Absalom would get up early and stand near the city gate.[n] Anyone who had a problem for the king to settle would come here. When someone came, Absalom would call out and say, "What city are you from?"

The person would answer, "I'm from one of the tribes[d] of Israel."

3Then Absalom would say, "Look, your claims are right, but the king has no one to listen to you." 4Absalom would also say, "I wish someone would make me judge in this land! Then people with problems could come to me, and I could help them get justice."

5People would come near Absalom to bow to him. When they did, Absalom would reach out his hand and take hold of them and kiss them. 6Absalom did that to all the Israelites who came to King David for decisions. In this way, Absalom stole the hearts of all Israel.

city gate People came here to conduct business. Public meetings and court cases were also held here.

7After four years Absalom said to King David,
"Please let me go to Hebron. I want to carry out
my promise that I made to the LORD 8while I was
living in Geshur in Aram. I said, 'If the LORD takes
me back to Jerusalem, I will worship him in Hebron.' "

SIDELIGHT: Got a complaint about city government? If you lived in ancient Israel, you wouldn't take your problem to city hall. You would go to the city's gates, where people made business and legal deals. That's where Absalom took his complaints about his dad, King David, and plotted an overthrow (2 Samuel 15:2–4).

9The king said, "Go in peace."
So Absalom went to Hebron. 10But he sent secret messengers through all the tribes of Israel.
They told the people, "When you hear the trumpets, say this: 'Absalom is the king at Hebron!' "
11Absalom had invited two hundred men to go
with him. So they went from Jerusalem with him,
but they didn't know what he was planning.
12While Absalom was offering sacrifices, he sent
for Ahithophel, one of the people who advised
David, to come from his hometown of Giloh. So
Absalom's plans were working very well. More
and more people began to support him.
13A messenger came to David, saying, "The Israelites are giving their loyalty to Absalom."
14Then David said to all his officers who were
with him in Jerusalem, "We must leave quickly!
If we don't, we won't be able to get away from
Absalom. We must hurry before he catches us and
destroys us and kills the people of Jerusalem."
15The king's officers said to him, "We will do
anything you say."
16The king set out with everyone in his house,
but he left ten slave women[d] to take care of the
palace. 17The king left with all his people following him, and they stopped at a house far away.
18All the king's servants passed by him — the Kerethites and Pelethites,[n] all those from Gath, and
the six hundred men who had followed him.
19The king said to Ittai, a man from Gath, "Why
are you also going with us? Turn back and stay
with King Absalom because you are a foreigner.
This is not your homeland. 20You joined me only
a short time ago. Should I make you wander with
us when I don't even know where I'm going?
Turn back and take your brothers with you. May
kindness and loyalty be shown to you."
21But Ittai said to the king, "As surely as the
LORD lives and as you live, I will stay with you,
whether it means life or death."
22David said to Ittai, "Go, march on." So Ittai
from Gath and all his people with their children
marched on. 23All the people cried loudly as everyone passed by. King David crossed the Kidron
Valley, and then all the people went on to the
desert. 24Zadok and all the Levites with him carried the Ark[d] of the Agreement with God. They
set it down, and Abiathar offered sacrifices until
all the people had left the city.
25The king said to Zadok, "Take the Ark of God
back into the city. If the LORD is pleased with me,
he will bring me back and will let me see both it
and Jerusalem again. 26But if the LORD says he is
not pleased with me, I am ready. He can do what
he wants with me."
27The king also said to Zadok the priest, "Aren't
you a seer?[d] Go back to the city in peace and take
your son Ahimaaz and Abiathar's son Jonathan
with you. 28I will wait near the crossings into the
desert until I hear from you." 29So Zadok and Abiathar took the Ark of God back to Jerusalem and
stayed there.
30David went up the Mount of Olives,[d] crying
as he went. He covered his head and went barefoot. All the people with David covered their
heads also and cried as they went. 31Someone told
David, "Ahithophel is one of the people with Absalom who made secret plans against you."
So David prayed, "LORD, please make Ahithophel's advice foolish."
32When David reached the top of the mountain
where people used to worship God, Hushai the
Arkite came to meet him. Hushai's coat was torn,
and there was dirt on his head to show how sad
he was. 33David said to Hushai, "If you go with
me, you will be just one more person for me to
take care of. 34But if you return to the city, you
can make Ahithophel's advice useless. Tell Absalom, 'I am your servant, my king. In the past I
served your father, but now I will serve you.'
35The priests Zadok and Abiathar will be with
you. Tell them everything you hear in the royal
palace. 36Zadok's son Ahimaaz and Abiathar's son
Jonathan are with them. Send them to tell me
everything you hear." 37So David's friend Hushai
entered Jerusalem just as Absalom arrived.

Ziba Meets David

16 When David had passed a short way
over the top of the Mount of Olives,[d]
Ziba, Mephibosheth's servant, met him. Ziba had
a row of donkeys loaded with two hundred loaves
of bread, one hundred cakes of raisins, one hundred cakes of figs, and leather bags full of wine.

Kerethites and Pelethites These were probably special units of the army that were responsible for the king's safety, a kind of palace guard.

2The king asked Ziba, "What are these things
for?"
Ziba answered, "The donkeys are for your family to ride. The bread and cakes of figs are for the
servants to eat. And the wine is for anyone to
drink who might become weak in the desert."
3The king asked, "Where is Mephibosheth?"
Ziba answered him, "Mephibosheth is staying
in Jerusalem because he thinks, 'Today the Israelites will give my father's kingdom back to me!' "
4Then the king said to Ziba, "All right. Everything that belonged to Mephibosheth, I now give
to you!"
Ziba said, "I bow to you. I hope I will always
be able to please you."

Shimei Curses David

5As King David came to Bahurim, a man came
out and cursed him. He was from Saul's family
group, and his name was Shimei son of Gera. 6He
threw stones at David and his officers, but the
people and soldiers gathered all around David.
7Shimei cursed David, saying, "Get out, get out,
you murderer, you troublemaker. 8The LORD is
punishing you for the people in Saul's family you
killed! You took Saul's place as king, but now the
LORD has given the kingdom to your son Absalom! Now you are ruined because you are a murderer!"
9Abishai son of Zeruiah said to the king, "Why
should this dead dog curse you, the king? Let me
go over and cut off his head!"
10But the king answered, "This does not concern you, sons of Zeruiah! If he is cursing me because the LORD told him to, who can question
him?"
11David also said to Abishai and all his officers,
"My own son is trying to kill me! This man is a
Benjaminite and has more right to kill me! Leave
him alone, and let him curse me because the
LORD told him to do this. 12Maybe the LORD will
see my misery and repay me with something good
for Shimei's curses today!"
13So David and his men went on down the
road, but Shimei followed on the nearby hillside.
He kept cursing David and throwing stones and
dirt at him. 14When the king and all his people
arrived at the Jordan, they were very tired, so they
rested there.
15Meanwhile, Absalom, Ahithophel, and all the
Israelites arrived at Jerusalem. 16David's friend
Hushai the Arkite came to Absalom and said to
him, "Long live the king! Long live the king!"
17Absalom asked, "Why are you not loyal to
your friend David? Why didn't you leave Jerusalem with your friend?"
18Hushai said, "I belong to the one chosen by
the LORD and by these people and everyone in
Israel. I will stay with you. 19In the past I served
your father. So whom should I serve now? David's son! I will serve you as I served him."

Ahithophel's Advice

20Absalom said to Ahithophel, "Tell us what we
should do."
21Ahithophel said, "Your father left behind
some of his slave women[d] to take care of the palace. Have sexual relations with them. Then all
Israel will hear that your father is your enemy,
and all your people will be encouraged to give you
more support." 22So they put up a tent for Absalom on the roof[n] of the palace where everyone
in Israel could see it. And Absalom had sexual
relations with his father's slave women.
23At that time people thought Ahithophel's advice was as reliable as God's own word. Both David and Absalom thought it was that reliable.

17 Ahithophel said to Absalom, "Let me
choose twelve thousand men and chase
David tonight. 2I'll catch him while he is tired and
weak, and I'll frighten him so all his people will
run away. But I'll kill only King David. 3Then I'll
bring everyone back to you. If the man you are
looking for is dead, everyone else will return
safely." 4This plan seemed good to Absalom and
to all the leaders of Israel.
5But Absalom said, "Now call Hushai the Arkite, so I can hear what he says." 6When Hushai
came to Absalom, Absalom said to him, "This is
the plan Ahithophel gave. Should we follow it? If
not, tell us."
7Hushai said to Absalom, "Ahithophel's advice
is not good this time." 8Hushai added, "You know
your father and his men are strong. They are as
angry as a bear that is robbed of its cubs. Your
father is a skilled fighter. He won't stay all night
with the army. 9He is probably already hiding in
a cave or some other place. If the first attack fails,
people will hear the news and think, 'Absalom's
followers are losing!' 10Then even the men who
are as brave as lions will be frightened, because all
the Israelites know your father is a fighter. They
know his men are brave!
11"This is what I suggest: Gather all the Israelites from Dan to Beersheba.[n] There will be as
many people as grains of sand by the sea. Then
you yourself must go into the battle. 12We will go
to David wherever he is hiding. We will fall on

roof In Bible times houses were built with flat roofs. The roof was used for drying things such as flax and fruit. And it was used as an extra room, as a place for worship, and as a place to sleep in the summer.

Dan to Beersheba Dan was the city farthest north in Israel, and Beersheba was the city farthest south. So this means all the people of Israel.

him as dew falls on the ground. We will kill him
and all of his men so that no one will be left alive.
13If David escapes into a city, all the Israelites will
bring ropes to that city and pull it into the valley.
Not a stone will be left!"
14Absalom and all the Israelites said, "The advice of Hushai the Arkite is better than that of
Ahithophel." (The LORD had planned to destroy
the good advice of Ahithophel so the LORD could
bring disaster on Absalom.)
15Hushai told Zadok and Abiathar, the priests,
what Ahithophel had suggested to Absalom and
the older leaders of Israel. He also reported to
them what he himself had suggested. Hushai said,
16"Quickly! Send a message to David. Tell him
not to stay tonight at the crossings into the desert
but to cross over the Jordan River at once. If he
crosses the river, he and all his people won't be
destroyed."
17Jonathan and Ahimaaz were waiting at En
Rogel. They did not want to be seen going into the
city, so a servant girl would go out to them and
give them messages. Then Jonathan and Ahimaaz
would go and tell King David.
18But a boy saw Jonathan and Ahimaaz and
told Absalom. So Jonathan and Ahimaaz left
quickly and went to a man's house in Bahurim.
He had a well in his courtyard, and they climbed
down into it. 19The man's wife spread a sheet
over the opening of the well and covered it with
grain. No one could tell that anyone was hiding
there.
20Absalom's servants came to the woman at the
house and asked, "Where are Ahimaaz and Jonathan?"

She said to them, "They have already crossed
the brook."

Absalom's servants then went to look for Jonathan and Ahimaaz, but they could not find them.
So they went back to Jerusalem.
21After Absalom's servants left, Jonathan and
Ahimaaz climbed out of the well and went to tell
King David. They said, "Hurry, cross over the
river! Ahithophel has said these things against
you!" 22So David and all his people crossed the
Jordan River. By dawn, everyone had crossed the
Jordan.
23When Ahithophel saw that the Israelites did
not accept his advice, he saddled his donkey and
went to his hometown. He left orders for his family and property, and then he hanged himself. He
died and was buried in his father's tomb.

War Between David and Absalom

24David arrived at Mahanaim. And Absalom
and all his Israelites crossed over the Jordan River.
25Absalom had made Amasa captain of the army
instead of Joab. Amasa was the son of a man
named Jether the Ishmaelite. Amasa's mother
was Abigail daughter of Nahash and sister of Zeruiah, Joab's mother. 26Absalom and the Israelites
camped in the land of Gilead.
27Shobi, Makir, and Barzillai were at Mahanaim when David arrived. Shobi son of Nahash
was from the Ammonite town of Rabbah. Makir
son of Ammiel was from Lo Debar, and Barzillai
was from Rogelim in Gilead. 28They brought beds,
bowls, clay pots, wheat, barley, flour, roasted
grain, beans, small peas, 29honey, milk curds,
sheep, and cheese made from cows' milk for David and his people. They said, "The people are
hungry and tired and thirsty in the desert."

18 David counted his men and placed over
them commanders of thousands and
commanders of hundreds. 2He sent the troops out
in three groups. Joab commanded one-third of the
men. Joab's brother Abishai son of Zeruiah commanded another third. And Ittai from Gath commanded the last third. King David said to them,
"I will also go with you."
3But the men said, "You must not go with us!
If we run away in the battle, Absalom's men
won't care. Even if half of us are killed, Absalom's
men won't care. But you're worth ten thousand
of us! You can help us most by staying in the city."
4The king said to his people, "I will do what
you think is best." So the king stood at the side
of the gate as the army went out in groups of a
hundred and a thousand.
5The king commanded Joab, Abishai, and Ittai,
"Be gentle with young Absalom for my sake." Everyone heard the king's orders to the commanders about Absalom.
6David's army went out into the field against
Absalom's Israelites, and they fought in the forest
of Ephraim. 7There David's army defeated the Israelites. Many died that day—twenty thousand
men. 8The battle spread through all the country,
but that day more men died in the forest than in
the fighting.

SIDELIGHT: If you haven't gotten your hair cut lately, be careful. Absalom's long hair got caught in a tree when his mule rode under it, leaving Absalom hanging (2 Samuel 18:9). It's no wonder, either. He only cut it once a year when it became too heavy—weighing five pounds (2 Samuel 14:26)!

Absalom Dies

9Then Absalom happened to meet David's
troops. As Absalom was riding his mule, it went
under the thick branches of a large oak tree. Absa-

lom's head got caught in the tree, and his mule
ran out from under him. So Absalom was left
hanging above the ground.
10When one of the men saw it happen, he told
Joab, "I saw Absalom hanging in an oak tree!"
11Joab said to him, "You saw him? Why didn't
you kill him and let him fall to the ground? I
would have given you a belt and four ounces of
silver!"
12The man answered, "I wouldn't touch the
king's son even if you gave me twenty-five pounds
of silver. We heard the king command you,
Abishai, and Ittai, 'Be careful not to hurt young
Absalom.' 13If I had killed him, the king would
have found out, and you would not have protected me!"
14Joab said, "I won't waste time here with
you!" Absalom was still alive in the oak tree, so
Joab took three spears and stabbed him in the
heart. 15Ten young men who carried Joab's armor
also gathered around Absalom and struck him and
killed him.
16Then Joab blew the trumpet, so the troops
stopped chasing the Israelites. 17Then Joab's men
took Absalom's body and threw it into a large pit
in the forest and filled the pit with many stones.
All the Israelites ran away to their homes.
18When Absalom was alive, he had set up a
pillar for himself in the King's Valley. He said, "I
have no son to keep my name alive." So he
named the pillar after himself, and it is called Absalom's Monument even today.
19Ahimaaz son of Zadok said to Joab, "Let me
run and take the news to King David. I'll tell him
the LORD has saved him from his enemies."
20Joab answered Ahimaaz, "No, you are not the
one to take the news today. You may do it another time, but do not take it today, because the
king's son is dead."
21Then Joab said to a man from Cush, "Go, tell
the king what you have seen." The Cushite
bowed to Joab and ran to tell David.
22But Ahimaaz son of Zadok begged Joab again,
"No matter what happens, please let me go along
with the Cushite!"
Joab said, "Son, why do you want to carry the
news? You won't get any reward."
23Ahimaaz answered, "No matter what happens, I will run."
So Joab said to Ahimaaz, "Run!" Then Ahimaaz
ran by way of the Jordan Valley and passed the
Cushite.
24David was sitting between the inner and
outer gates of the city. The watchman went up to
the roof of the gate by the walls, and as he looked
up, he saw a man running alone. 25He shouted
the news to the king.
The king said, "If he is alone, he is bringing
good news!"
The man came nearer and nearer to the city.
26Then the watchman saw another man running,
and he called to the gatekeeper, "Look! Another
man is running alone!"
The king said, "He is also bringing good news!"
27The watchman said, "I think the first man
runs like Ahimaaz son of Zadok."
The king said, "Ahimaaz is a good man. He
must be bringing good news!"
28Then Ahimaaz called a greeting to the king.
He bowed facedown on the ground before the
king and said, "Praise the LORD your God! The
LORD has defeated those who were against you,
my king."
29The king asked, "Is young Absalom all right?"
Ahimaaz answered, "When Joab sent me, I saw
some great excitement, but I don't know what it
was."
30The king said, "Step over here and wait." So
Ahimaaz stepped aside and stood there.
31Then the Cushite arrived. He said, "Master
and king, hear the good news! Today the LORD
has punished those who were against you!"
32The king asked the Cushite, "Is young Absalom all right?"
The Cushite answered, "May your enemies
and all who come to hurt you be like that young
man!"
33Then the king was very upset, and he went
to the room over the city gate and cried. As he
went, he cried out, "My son Absalom, my son
Absalom! I wish I had died and not you. Absalom,
my son, my son!"

Joab Scolds David

19 People told Joab, "Look, the king is sad
and crying because of Absalom." 2Da-
vid's army had won the battle that day. But it
became a very sad day for all the people, because
they heard that the king was very sad for his son.
3The people came into the city quietly that day.
They were like an army that had been defeated in
battle and had run away. 4The king covered his
face and cried loudly, "My son Absalom! Absalom, my son, my son!"
5Joab went into the king's house and said, "Today you have shamed all your men. They saved
your life and the lives of your sons, daughters,
wives, and slave women.[d] 6You have shamed
them because you love those who hate you, and
you hate those who love you. Today you have
made it clear that your commanders and men
mean nothing to you. What if Absalom had lived
and all of us were dead? I can see you would be
pleased. 7Now go out and encourage your servants. I swear by the LORD that if you don't go
out, no man will be left with you by tonight! That
will be worse than all the troubles you have had
from your youth until today."

[8]So the king went to the city gate.[n] When the
news spread that the king was at the gate, everyone came to see him.

David Goes Back to Jerusalem

All the Israelites who had followed Absalom
had run away to their homes. [9]People in all the
tribes[d] of Israel began to argue, saying, "The king
saved us from the Philistines and our other enemies, but he left the country because of Absalom.
[10]We appointed Absalom to rule us, but now he
has died in battle. We should make David the
king again."

[11]King David sent a message to Zadok and Abiathar, the priests, that said, "Speak to the older
leaders of Judah. Say, 'Even in my house I have
heard what all the Israelites are saying. So why
are you the last tribe to bring the king back to his
palace? [12]You are my brothers, my own family.
Why are you the last tribe to bring back the king?'
[13]And say to Amasa, 'You are part of my own family. May God punish me terribly if I don't make
you commander of the army in Joab's place!' "

city gate People came here to conduct business. Public meetings and court cases were also held here.

REBELLION

Donna's Diary

October 15—I got drunk last night. Again. I had to do something to ease the tensions at home. Mom and Dad keep hassling me about what I'm going to do with my life. Why won't they leave me alone? Why won't they let me grow up? I'm sixteen—old enough to make my own decisions.

I can't take it! The rules. The curfews. The restrictions. They're driving me crazy. Just tonight, Jerry called. When I told Mom and Dad, they blew up. "Why do you hang out with that scum?" Mom cried.

October 23—Mom and Dad caught me coming home drunk last night. I've never seen them so angry. So this morning they packed me into the car and brought me to this funny farm.

January 29—I just got out of the alcohol-abuse treatment program this week. I thought things would be better when I got home, but I was wrong. Mom and Dad watch me constantly. They're so paranoid I'll do something wrong again.

Well, I don't have to deal with this anymore. Jerry said I could move in with him. I think I will. Tomorrow it's good-bye to this place and hello to a new, free life.

April 18. It wasn't supposed to be this way. I mean, Jerry seemed like such a great guy. But I hadn't seen him angry—really angry. Like he was last night. Now the side of my face is swollen, and I can't open my left eye.

What can I do? He said he'd kill me if I told anyone. And, after last night, I believe him. Should I tell Mom and Dad? We used to be so close. But, since I left home, I don't know. Would they help me? Do they still love me?

Does anyone really love me? What went wrong?

Donna's diary describes rebellion from a teenager's perspective. Read about rebellion from a parent's perspective in **2 Samuel 18:24–33**, where King David expresses deep pain at his son Absalom's rebellion when he learns about Absalom's death.

- If Absalom had written a diary, what do you think he might have said to his father, King David?
- When have you wanted to rebel against your parent or parents? What did you do? What happened?

CONSIDER . . .

- praying for families that are torn apart by rebellion. Ask God to help the families communicate and come back together.
- negotiating with your parents to decide together what to do if you feel overly restricted or stifled.

FOR MORE, SEE . . .

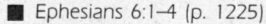

- Hosea 11:1–11 (p. 831)
- Luke 15:11–32 (p. 1035)
- Ephesians 6:1–4 (p. 1225)

14David touched the hearts of all the people of Judah at once. They sent a message to the king that said, "Return with all your men." 15Then the king returned as far as the Jordan River. The men of Judah came to Gilgal to meet him and to bring him across the Jordan.

16Shimei son of Gera, a Benjaminite who lived in Bahurim, hurried down with the men of Judah to meet King David. 17With Shimei came a thousand Benjaminites. Ziba, the servant from Saul's family, also came, bringing his fifteen sons and twenty servants with him. They all hurried to the Jordan River to meet the king. 18The people went across the Jordan to help bring the king's family back to Judah and to do whatever the king wanted. As the king was crossing the river, Shimei son of Gera came to him and bowed face-down on the ground in front of the king. 19He said to the king, "My master, don't hold me guilty. Don't remember the wrong I did when you left Jerusalem! Don't hold it against me. 20I know I have sinned. That is why I am the first person from Joseph's family to come down and meet you today, my master and king!"

21But Abishai son of Zeruiah said, "Shimei should die because he cursed you, the LORD's appointed king!"

22David said, "This does not concern you, sons of Zeruiah! Today you're against me! No one will be put to death in Israel today. Today I know I am king over Israel!" 23Then the king promised Shimei, "You won't die."

24Mephibosheth, Saul's grandson, also went down to meet King David. Mephibosheth had not cared for his feet, cut his beard, or washed his clothes from the time the king had left Jerusalem until he returned safely. 25When Mephibosheth came from Jerusalem to meet the king, the king asked him, "Mephibosheth, why didn't you go with me?"

26He answered, "My master, my servant Ziba tricked me! I said to Ziba, 'I am crippled, so saddle a donkey. Then I will ride it so I can go with the king.' 27But he lied about me to you. You, my master and king, are like an angel from God. Do what you think is good. 28You could have killed all my grandfather's family. Instead, you put me with those people who eat at your own table. So I don't have a right to ask anything more from the king!"

29The king said to him, "Don't say anything more. I have decided that you and Ziba will divide the land."

30Mephibosheth said to the king, "Let Ziba take all the land now that my master the king has arrived safely home."

31Barzillai of Gilead came down from Rogelim to cross the Jordan River with the king. 32Barzillai was a very old man, eighty years old. He had taken care of the king when David was staying at Mahanaim, because Barzillai was a very rich man. 33David said to Barzillai, "Cross the river with me. Come with me to Jerusalem, and I will take care of you."

34But Barzillai answered the king, "Do you know how old I am? Do you think I can go with you to Jerusalem? 35I am eighty years old! I am too old to taste what I eat or drink. I am too old to hear the voices of men and women singers. Why should you be bothered with me? 36I am not worthy of a reward from you, but I will cross the Jordan River with you. 37Then let me go back so I may die in my own city near the grave of my father and mother. But here is Kimham, your servant. Let him go with you, my master and king. Do with him whatever you want."

38The king answered, "Kimham will go with me. I will do for him anything you wish, and I will do anything for you that you wish." 39The king kissed Barzillai and blessed him. Then Barzillai returned home, and the king and all the people crossed the Jordan.

40When the king crossed over to Gilgal, Kimham went with him. All the troops of Judah and half the troops of Israel led David across the river.

41Soon all the Israelites came to the king and said to him, "Why did our relatives, the people of Judah, steal you away? Why did they bring you and your family across the Jordan River with your men?"

42All the people of Judah answered the Israelites, "We did this because the king is our close relative. Why are you angry about it? We have not eaten food at the king's expense or taken anything for ourselves!"

43The Israelites answered the people of Judah, "We have ten tribes in the kingdom, so we have more right to David than you do! But you ignored us! We were the first ones to talk about bringing our king back!"

But the people of Judah spoke even more unkindly than the people of Israel.

Sheba Leads Israel Away from David

20 It happened that a troublemaker named Sheba son of Bicri from the tribe[d] of Benjamin was there. He blew the trumpet and said:

"We have no share in David!
We have no part in the son of Jesse!
People of Israel, let's go home!"

2So all the Israelites left David and followed Sheba son of Bicri. But the people of Judah stayed with their king all the way from the Jordan River to Jerusalem.

3David came back to his palace in Jerusalem. He had left ten of his slave women[d] there to take care of the palace. Now he put them in a locked house. He gave them food, but he did not have sexual relations with them. So they lived like widows until they died.

4The king said to Amasa, "Tell the men of Judah to meet with me in three days, and you must also be here." 5So Amasa went to call the men of Judah together, but he took more time than the king had said.

6David said to Abishai, "Sheba son of Bicri is more dangerous to us than Absalom was. Take my men and chase him before he finds walled cities and escapes from us." 7So Joab's men, the Kerethites and the Pelethites,[n] and all the soldiers went with Abishai. They went out from Jerusalem to chase Sheba son of Bicri.

8When Joab and the army came to the great rock at Gibeon, Amasa came out to meet them. Joab was wearing his uniform, and at his waist he wore a belt that held his sword in its case. As Joab stepped forward, his sword fell out of its case. 9Joab asked Amasa, "Brother, is everything all right with you?" Then with his right hand he took Amasa by the beard to kiss him. 10Amasa was not watching the sword in Joab's hand. So Joab pushed the sword into Amasa's stomach, causing Amasa's insides to spill onto the ground. Joab did not have to stab Amasa again; he was already dead. Then Joab and his brother Abishai continued to chase Sheba son of Bicri.

11One of Joab's young men stood by Amasa's body and said, "Everyone who is for Joab and David should follow Joab!" 12Amasa lay in the middle of the road, covered with his own blood. When the young man saw that everyone was stopping to look at the body, he dragged it from the road, laid it in a field, and put a cloth over it. 13After Amasa's body was taken off the road, all the men followed Joab to chase Sheba son of Bicri.

14Sheba went through all the tribes of Israel to Abel Beth Maacah. All the Berites also came together and followed him. 15So Joab and his men came to Abel Beth Maacah and surrounded it. They piled dirt up against the city wall, and they began hacking at the walls to bring them down.

16But a wise woman shouted out from the city, "Listen! Listen! Tell Joab to come here. I want to talk to him!"

17So Joab came near her. She asked him, "Are you Joab?"

He answered, "Yes, I am."

Then she said, "Listen to what I say."

Joab said, "I'm listening."

18Then the woman said, "In the past people would say, 'Ask for advice at Abel,' and the problem would be solved. 19I am one of the peaceful, loyal people of Israel. You are trying to destroy an important city of Israel. Why must you destroy what belongs to the LORD?"

20Joab answered, "I would prefer not to destroy or ruin anything! 21That is not what I want. But there is a man here from the mountains of Ephraim, who is named Sheba son of Bicri. He has turned against King David. If you bring him to me, I will leave the city alone."

The woman said to Joab, "His head will be thrown over the wall to you."

22Then the woman spoke very wisely to all the people of the city. They cut off the head of Sheba son of Bicri and threw it over the wall to Joab. So he blew the trumpet, and the army left the city. Every man returned home, and Joab went back to the king in Jerusalem.

23Joab was commander of all the army of Israel. Benaiah son of Jehoiada led the Kerethites and Pelethites. 24Adoniram was in charge of the men who were forced to do hard work. Jehoshaphat son of Ahilud was the recorder. 25Sheba was the royal secretary. Zadok and Abiathar were the priests, 26and Ira the Jairite was David's priest.

The Gibeonites Punish Saul's Family

21 During the time David was king, there was a shortage of food that lasted for three years. So David prayed to the LORD.

The LORD answered, "Saul and his family of murderers are the reason for this shortage, because he killed the Gibeonites." 2(Now the Gibeonites were not Israelites; they were a group of Amorites who were left alive. The Israelites had promised not to hurt the Gibeonites, but Saul had tried to kill them, because he was eager to help the people of Israel and Judah.)

King David called the Gibeonites together and spoke to them. 3He asked, "What can I do for you? How can I make up for the harm done so you can bless the LORD's people?"

4The Gibeonites said to David, "We cannot demand silver or gold from Saul or his family. And we don't have the right to kill anyone in Israel."

Then David asked, "What do you want me to do for you?"

5The Gibeonites said, "Saul made plans against us and tried to destroy all our people who are left in the land of Israel. 6So bring seven of his sons to us. Then we will kill them and hang them on stakes in the presence of the LORD at Gibeah, the hometown of Saul, the LORD's chosen king."

The king said, "I will give them to you." 7But the king protected Mephibosheth, the son of Jonathan, the son of Saul, because of the promise he had made to Jonathan in the LORD's name. 8The

Kerethites and Pelethites These were probably special units of the army that were responsible for the king's safety, a kind of palace guard.

king did take Armoni and Mephibosheth,[n] sons
of Rizpah and Saul. (Rizpah was the daughter of
Aiah.) And the king took the five sons of Saul's
daughter Merab. (Adriel son of Barzillai the Me-
holathite was the father of Merab's five sons.)
9David gave these seven sons to the Gibeonites.
Then the Gibeonites killed them and hung them
on stakes on a hill in the presence of the LORD. All
seven sons died together. They were put to death
during the first days of the harvest season at the
beginning of barley harvest.

10Aiah's daughter Rizpah took the rough cloth
that was worn to show sadness and put it on a
rock for herself. She stayed there from the beginning of the harvest until the rain fell on her sons'
bodies. During the day she did not let the birds of
the sky touch her sons' bodies, and during the
night she did not let the wild animals touch them.

11People told David what Aiah's daughter Rizpah, Saul's slave woman,[d] was doing. 12Then David took the bones of Saul and Jonathan from the
men of Jabesh Gilead. (The Philistines had hung
the bodies of Saul and Jonathan in the public
square of Beth Shan after they had killed Saul at
Gilboa. Later the men of Jabesh Gilead had secretly taken them from there.) 13David brought
the bones of Saul and his son Jonathan from Gilead. Then the people gathered the bodies of Saul's
seven sons who were hanged on stakes. 14The
people buried the bones of Saul and his son Jonathan at Zela in Benjamin in the tomb of Saul's
father Kish. The people did everything the king
commanded.

Then God answered the prayers for the land.

Wars with the Philistines

15Again there was war between the Philistines
and Israel. David and his men went out to fight
the Philistines, but David became tired. 16Ishbi-
Benob, one of the sons of Rapha,[d] had a bronze
spearhead weighing about seven and one-half
pounds and a new sword. He planned to kill David, 17but Abishai son of Zeruiah killed the Philistine and saved David's life.

Then David's men made a promise to him, saying, "Never again will you go out with us to battle. If you were killed, Israel would lose its greatest leader."

18Later, at Gob, there was another battle with
the Philistines. Sibbecai the Hushathite killed
Saph, another one of the sons of Rapha.

19Later, there was another battle at Gob with
the Philistines. Elhanan son of Jaare-Oregim from
Bethlehem killed Goliath[n] from Gath. His spear
was as large as a weaver's rod.

20At Gath another battle took place. A huge
man was there; he had six fingers on each hand
and six toes on each foot—twenty-four fingers
and toes in all. This man also was one of the sons
of Rapha. 21When he challenged Israel, Jonathan
son of Shimeah, David's brother, killed him.

22These four sons of Rapha from Gath were
killed by David and his men.

SIDELIGHT: One person in the Bible was not only big, but he had six toes on each foot and six fingers on each hand (2 Samuel 21:20). The extras probably came in handy in math class when counting numbers above twenty.

David's Song of Praise

22 David sang this song to the LORD when
the LORD saved him from Saul and all his
other enemies. 2He said:

"The LORD is my rock, my protection, my
Savior.
3My God is my rock.
I can run to him for safety.
He is my shield and my saving strength,
my defender and my place of safety.
The LORD saves me from those who want
to harm me.
4I will call to the LORD, who is worthy of
praise,
and I will be saved from my enemies.

5"The waves of death came around me;
the deadly rivers overwhelmed me.
6The ropes of death wrapped around me.
The traps of death were before me.
7In my trouble I called to the LORD;
I cried out to my God.
From his temple he heard my voice;
my call for help reached his ears.
8"The earth trembled and shook.
The foundations of heaven began to shake.
They trembled because the LORD was
angry.
9Smoke came out of his nose,
and burning fire came out of his mouth.
Burning coals went before him.
10He tore open the sky and came down
with dark clouds under his feet.
11He rode a creature with wings and flew.
He raced on the wings of the wind.
12He made darkness his shelter,
surrounded by fog and clouds.

Mephibosheth This is not Jonathan's son but another man with the same name.
Goliath In 1 Chronicles 20:5 he is called Lahmi brother of Goliath.

13Out of the brightness of his presence
came flashes of lightning.
14The LORD thundered from heaven;
the Most High raised his voice.
15He shot his arrows and scattered his enemies.
His bolts of lightning confused them with fear.
16The LORD spoke strongly.
The wind blew from his nose.
Then the valleys of the sea appeared,
and the foundations of the earth were seen.

17"The LORD reached down from above and took me;
he pulled me from the deep water.
18He saved me from my powerful enemies,
from those who hated me, because they were too strong for me.
19They attacked me at my time of trouble,
but the LORD supported me.
20He took me to a safe place.
Because he delights in me, he saved me.

21"The LORD spared me because I did what was right.
Because I have not done evil, he has rewarded me.
22I have followed the ways of the LORD;
I have not done evil by turning from my God.
23I remember all his laws
and have not broken his rules.
24I am innocent before him;
I have kept myself from doing evil.
25The LORD rewarded me because I did what was right,
because I did what the LORD said was right.

26"LORD, you are loyal to those who are loyal,
and you are good to those who are good.
27You are pure to those who are pure,
but you are against those who are evil.
28You save the humble,
but you bring down those who are proud.
29LORD, you give light to my lamp.
The LORD brightens the darkness around me.
30With your help I can attack an army.
With God's help I can jump over a wall.

31"The ways of God are without fault;
the LORD's words are pure.
He is a shield to those who trust him.
32Who is God? Only the LORD.
Who is the Rock?[d] Only our God.
33God is my protection.
He makes my way free from fault.
34He makes me like a deer that does not stumble;
he helps me stand on the steep mountains.
35He trains my hands for battle
so my arms can bend a bronze bow.
36You protect me with your saving shield.
You have stooped to make me great.
37You give me a better way to live,
so I live as you want me to.
38I chased my enemies and destroyed them.
I did not quit till they were destroyed.
39I destroyed and crushed them
so they couldn't rise up again.
They fell beneath my feet.
40You gave me strength in battle.
You made my enemies bow before me.
41You made my enemies turn back,
and I destroyed those who hated me.
42They called for help,
but no one came to save them.
They called to the LORD,
but he did not answer them.
43I beat my enemies into pieces,
like dust on the ground.
I poured them out and walked on them
like mud in the streets.

44"You saved me when my people attacked me.
You kept me as the leader of nations.
People I never knew serve me.
45Foreigners obey me.
As soon as they hear me, they obey me.
46They all become afraid
and tremble in their hiding places.

47"The LORD lives!
May my Rock be praised!
Praise God, the Rock, who saves me!
48God gives me victory over my enemies
and brings people under my rule.
49He frees me from my enemies.

"You set me over those who hate me.
You saved me from cruel men.
50So I will praise you, LORD, among the nations.
I will sing praises to your name.
51The LORD gives great victories to his king.
He is loyal to his appointed king,
to David and his descendants[d] forever."

David's Last Words

23 These are the last words of David.

This is the message of David son of Jesse.
The man made great by the Most High God speaks.
He is the appointed king of the God of Jacob;
he is the sweet singer of Israel:

2"The LORD's Spirit[d] spoke through me,
and his word was on my tongue.
3The God of Israel spoke;
the Rock[d] of Israel said to me:

'Whoever rules fairly over people,
who rules with respect for God,
4is like the morning light at dawn,
like a morning without clouds.
He is like sunshine after a rain
that makes the grass sprout from the ground.'

5"This is how God has cared for my family.
God made a lasting agreement with me,
right and sure in every way.
He will accomplish my salvation
and satisfy all my desires.

6"But all evil people will be thrown away like thorns
that cannot be held in a hand.
7No one can touch them
except with a tool of iron or wood.
They will be thrown in the fire and burned
where they lie."

David's Army

8These are the names of David's warriors:
Josheb-Basshebeth, the Tahkemonite, was head
of the Three.[n] He killed eight hundred men at
one time.
9Next was Eleazar son of Dodai the Ahohite.
Eleazar was one of the three soldiers who were
with David when they challenged the Philistines.
The Philistines were gathered for battle, and the
Israelites drew back. 10But Eleazar stayed where
he was and fought the Philistines until he was so
tired his hand stuck to his sword. The LORD gave
a great victory for the Israelites that day. The
troops came back after Eleazar had won the battle, but only to take weapons and armor from the
enemy.
11Next there was Shammah son of Agee the
Hararite. The Philistines came together to fight
in a vegetable field. Israel's troops ran away from
the Philistines, 12but Shammah stood in the
middle of the field and fought for it and killed
the Philistines. And the LORD gave a great victory.
13Once, three of the Thirty, David's chief soldiers, came down to him at the cave of Adullam
during harvest. The Philistine army had camped
in the Valley of Rephaim. 14At that time David

Three These were David's most powerful soldiers. See 1 Chronicles 11:11.

GOVERNMENT

Respected Leaders

Judge Bill Logue is a rare judge. He's respected by prosecuting attorneys and defense lawyers, by police officers and convicted felons alike. He knows the law, and his decisions are rarely overturned by a higher court.

Even with his back-breaking load of court cases, Judge Logue finds time each week to help underprivileged kids who have criminal records. He tutors them and helps them start constructive lives so he won't have to sentence them again.

Recently Judge Logue was stricken with throat cancer. Cards, letters, flowers and presents swamped the hospital. People from around the state wrote of their sympathy and prayers.

But nothing touched the judge as much as the fistful of letters he received from prisoners—prisoners he had sent to jail. "You helped me get my life back on track," they told him. "I'll never forget you. Thanks."

Judge Logue shows how God's followers can make a difference for good in government. When King David was dying, he celebrated how God had worked in his life for good. Read about it in **2 Samuel 23:1–7**.

- How do verses 3 and 4 describe Judge Logue and other Christians like him who serve in government?
- Do leaders today have the same opportunities to serve God as they did in David's time? How can you support and encourage them to do good?

CONSIDER . . .

- praying that God will guide your country's leaders as they make important decisions.
- writing a letter to government officials to express your opinion on an important issue they are confronting.

FOR MORE, SEE. . .

- Psalm 2:1–11 (p. 483)
- Proverbs 16:10–15 (p. 581)
- 1 Timothy 2:1–3 (p. 1256)

was in the stronghold,[d] and some of the Philistines were in Bethlehem.
15David had a strong desire for some water. He
said, "Oh, I wish someone would get me water
from the well near the city gate of Bethlehem!"
16So the three warriors broke through the Philistine army and took water from the well near the
city gate of Bethlehem. Then they brought it to
David, but he refused to drink it. He poured it out
before the LORD, 17saying, "May the LORD keep
me from drinking this water! It would be like
drinking the blood of the men who risked their
lives!" So David refused to drink it. These were
the brave things that the three warriors did.
18Abishai, brother of Joab son of Zeruiah, was
captain of the Three. Abishai fought three hundred soldiers with his spear and killed them. He
became as famous as the Three 19and was more
honored than the Three. He became their commander even though he was not one of them.
20Benaiah son of Jehoiada was a brave fighter
from Kabzeel who did mighty things. He killed
two of the best warriors from Moab. He also went
down into a pit and killed a lion on a snowy day.
21Benaiah killed a large Egyptian who had a spear
in his hand. Benaiah had a club, but he grabbed
the spear from the Egyptian's hand and killed him
with his own spear. 22These were the things Benaiah son of Jehoiada did. He was as famous as the
Three. 23He received more honor than the Thirty,
but he did not become a member of the Three.
David made him leader of his bodyguards.

The Thirty Chief Soldiers

24The following men were among the Thirty:

Asahel brother of Joab;
Elhanan son of Dodo from Bethlehem;
25Shammah the Harodite;
Elika the Harodite;
26Helez the Paltite;
Ira son of Ikkesh from Tekoa;
27Abiezer the Anathothite;
Mebunnai the Hushathite;
28Zalmon the Ahohite;
Maharai the Netophathite;
29Heled son of Baanah the Netophathite;
Ithai son of Ribai from Gibeah in Benjamin;
30Benaiah the Pirathonite;
Hiddai from the ravines of Gaash;
31Abi-Albon the Arbathite;
Azmaveth the Barhumite;
32Eliahba the Shaalbonite;
the sons of Jashen;
Jonathan 33son of Shammah the Hararite;
Ahiam son of Sharar the Hararite;
34Eliphelet son of Ahasbai the Maacathite;
Eliam son of Ahithophel the Gilonite;
35Hezro the Carmelite;
Paarai the Arbite;
36Igal son of Nathan of Zobah;
the son of Hagri;
37Zelek the Ammonite;
Naharai the Beerothite, who carried the armor of Joab son of Zeruiah;
38Ira the Ithrite;
Gareb the Ithrite,
39and Uriah the Hittite.

There were thirty-seven in all.

David Counts His Army

24 The LORD was angry with Israel again,
and he caused David to turn against the
Israelites. He said, "Go, count the people of Israel
and Judah."
2So King David said to Joab, the commander of
the army, "Go through all the tribes[d] of Israel,
from Dan to Beersheba,[n] and count the people.
Then I will know how many there are."
3But Joab said to the king, "May the LORD your
God give you a hundred times more people, and
may my master the king live to see this happen.
Why do you want to do this?"
4But the king commanded Joab and the commanders of the army, so they left the king to
count the Israelites.
5After crossing the Jordan River, they camped
near Aroer on the south side of the city in the
ravine. They went through Gad and on to Jazer.
6Then they went to Gilead and the land of Tahtim
Hodshi and to Dan Jaan and around to Sidon.
7They went to the strong, walled city of Tyre and
to all the cities of the Hivites and Canaanites. Finally, they went to southern Judah, to Beersheba.
8After nine months and twenty days, they had
gone through all the land. Then they came back
to Jerusalem.
9Joab gave the list of the people to the king.
There were eight hundred thousand men in Israel
who could use the sword and five hundred thousand men in Judah.
10David felt ashamed after he had counted the
people. He said to the LORD, "I have sinned
greatly by what I have done. LORD, I beg you to
forgive me, your servant, because I have been
very foolish."
11When David got up in the morning, the LORD

Dan to Beersheba Dan was the city farthest north in Israel, and Beersheba was the city farthest south. So this means all the people of Israel.

spoke his word to Gad, who was a prophet[d] and
David's seer.[d] 12The LORD told Gad, "Go and tell
David, 'This is what the LORD says: I offer you
three choices. Choose one of them and I will do
it to you.' "

13So Gad went to David and said to him,
"Should three years of hunger come to you and
your land? Or should your enemies chase you for
three months? Or should there be three days of
disease in your land? Think about it. Then decide
which of these things I should tell the LORD who
sent me."

14David said to Gad, "I am in great trouble. Let
the LORD punish us, because the LORD is very
merciful. Don't let my punishment come from human beings!"

15So the LORD sent a terrible disease on Israel.
It began in the morning and continued until the
chosen time to stop. From Dan to Beersheba seventy thousand people died. 16When the angel
raised his arm toward Jerusalem to destroy it,
the LORD felt very sorry about the terrible things
that had happened. He said to the angel who
was destroying the people, "That is enough!
Put down your arm!" The angel of the LORD was
then by the threshing[d] floor of Araunah the Jebusite.

17When David saw the angel that killed the
people, he said to the LORD, "I am the one who
sinned and did wrong. These people only followed me like sheep. They did nothing wrong.
Please punish me and my family."

18That day Gad came to David and said, "Go
and build an altar to the LORD on the threshing
floor of Araunah the Jebusite." 19So David did
what Gad told him to do, just as the LORD commanded.

20Araunah looked and saw the king and his servants coming to him. So he went out and bowed
facedown on the ground before the king. 21He
said, "Why has my master the king come to me?"

David answered, "To buy the threshing floor
from you so I can build an altar to the LORD. Then
the terrible disease will stop."

22Araunah said to David, "My master and king,
you may take anything you want for a sacrifice.
Here are some oxen for the whole burnt offering
and the threshing boards and the yokes[d] for the
wood. 23My king, I give everything to you." Araunah also said to the king, "May the LORD your
God be pleased with you."

24But the king answered Araunah, "No, I will
pay you for the land. I won't offer to the LORD my
God burnt offerings that cost me nothing."

So David bought the threshing floor and the
oxen for one and one-fourth pounds of silver.
25He built an altar to the LORD there and offered
whole burnt offerings and fellowship offerings.
Then the LORD answered his prayer for the country, and the disease in Israel stopped.

1 KINGS

Why Read This Book:

- See how God blesses those who follow him (1 Kings 1—11).
- Recognize how faithfulness can help all parts of life (1 Kings 12—16).
- Discover what can happen to a country that turns away from God (1 Kings 17—22).

Behind the Scenes:

Imagine how history books would be different if they evaluated presidents and other world leaders based on whether they followed God. Their political, economic and military feats would only be important when they showed obedience to God. Which presidents, kings and leaders would be judged good? Which ones would be judged bad?

That's the kind of history we find in 1 and 2 Kings, which were one continuous book in the original text. The story begins with King David turning over the country to his son Solomon. Solomon inherited a strong and united nation, exploding with energy. Through political and economic maneuvering, Solomon made the country—and himself—rich and powerful.

Solomon seemed headed for greatness. But in the end, the writer says,

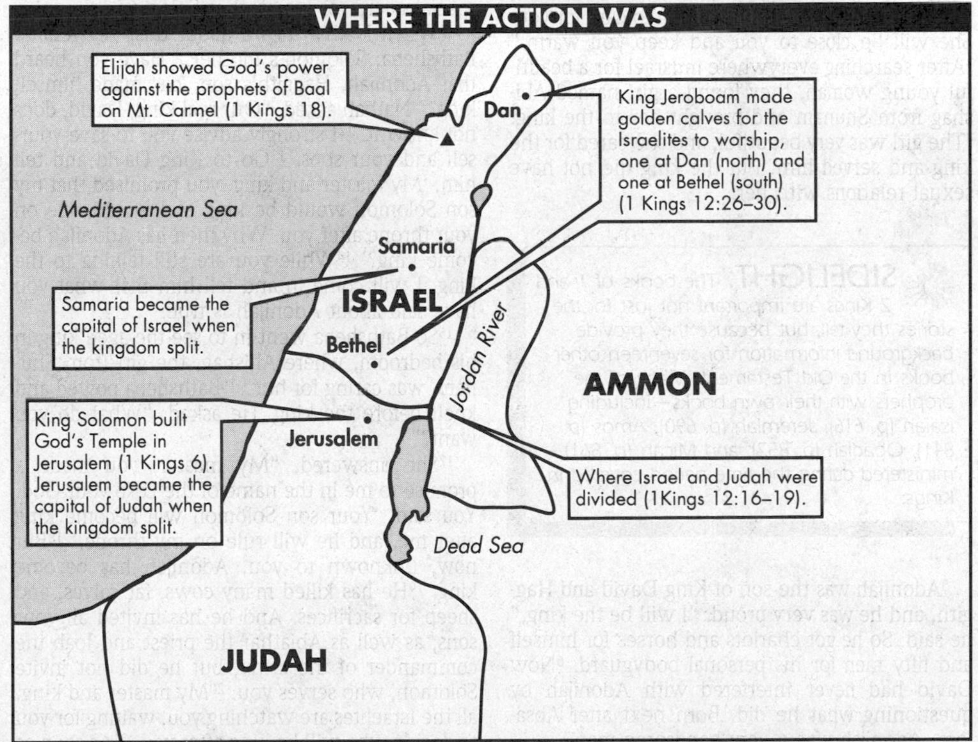

WHERE THE ACTION WAS
Elijah showed God's power against the prophets of Baal on Mt. Carmel (1 Kings 18).
Dan
King Jeroboam made golden calves for the Israelites to worship, one at Dan (north) and one at Bethel (south) (1 Kings 12:26–30).
Mediterranean Sea
Samaria
Samaria became the capital of Israel when the kingdom split.
ISRAEL
Bethel
Jordan River
AMMON
King Solomon built God's Temple in Jerusalem (1 Kings 6). Jerusalem became the capital of Judah when the kingdom split.
Jerusalem
Where Israel and Judah were divided (1Kings 12:16–19).
Dead Sea
JUDAH

WHEN THE ACTION WAS

2000BC	1500BC	1000BC	500BC	BC/AD
	Joshua led the Israelites into Canaan	The kingdom was split between Israel and Judah	Jerusalem fell to the Babylonians	Jesus was born
	The Israelites escaped from Egypt	Solomon was Israel's king	The Northern Kingdom (Israel) fell to Assyria	

Behind the Scenes (cont.):

"Solomon did what the Lord said was wrong and did not follow the Lord completely as his father David had done" (1 Kings 11:6, p. 315).

What happened? He began seeing the wealth and power as his own, not as gifts from God. Though he spent seven years building a beautiful temple for God (1 Kings 6), he spent thirteen years building his own palace. Soon his power and prestige became more important than following God. He began worshiping false gods.

The kingdom started to crumble. First it split between Israel (in the north) and Judah (in the south). Then one king after another didn't follow God, and the people suffered as a result. When kings did follow God, the people prospered. But by the end of 2 Kings, both kingdoms have been overthrown and the people taken away as slaves.

In telling about the rise and fall of good and bad kings, 1 Kings has a consistent theme: The longterm welfare of Israel and its people depended on obedience to God. And these stories remind us that—no matter what other forces are at play—God still works to accomplish his will in the world.

Adonijah Tries to Become King

1 At this time King David was very old, and
although his servants covered him with blankets, he could not keep warm. 2They said to him,
"We will look for a young woman to care for you.
She will lie close to you and keep you warm."
3After searching everywhere in Israel for a beautiful young woman, they found a girl named Abishag from Shunam and brought her to the king.
4The girl was very beautiful, and she cared for the
king and served him. But the king did not have
sexual relations with her.

SIDELIGHT: The books of 1 and 2 Kings are important not just for the stories they tell, but because they provide background information for seventeen other books in the Old Testament. Many of the prophets with their own books—including Isaiah (p. 616), Jeremiah (p. 690), Amos (p. 841), Obadiah (p. 852), and Micah (p. 861)—ministered during the time period covered in Kings.

5Adonijah was the son of King David and Haggith, and he was very proud. "I will be the king,"
he said. So he got chariots and horses for himself
and fifty men for his personal bodyguard. 6Now
David had never interfered with Adonijah by
questioning what he did. Born next after Absalom, Adonijah was a very handsome man.
7Adonijah spoke with Joab son of Zeruiah and
Abiathar the priest, and they agreed to help him.
8But Zadok the priest, Benaiah son of Jehoiada,
Nathan the prophet,[d] Shimei, Rei, and King David's special guard did not join Adonijah.
9Then Adonijah killed some sheep, cows, and
fat calves for sacrifices at the Stone of Zoheleth
near the spring of Rogel. He invited all his brothers, the other sons of King David, to come, as well
as all the men of Judah. 10But Adonijah did not
invite Nathan the prophet, Benaiah, his father's
special guard, or his brother Solomon.
11When Nathan heard about this, he went to
Bathsheba, Solomon's mother. "Have you heard
that Adonijah, Haggith's son, has made himself
king?" Nathan asked. "Our real king, David, does
not know it. 12I strongly advise you to save yourself and your sons. 13Go to King David and tell
him, 'My master and king, you promised that my
son Solomon would be king and would rule on
your throne after you. Why then has Adonijah become king?' 14While you are still talking to the
king, I will come in and tell him that what you
have said about Adonijah is true."
15So Bathsheba went in to see the aged king in
his bedroom, where Abishag, the girl from Shunam, was caring for him. 16Bathsheba bowed and
knelt before the king. He asked, "What do you
want?"
17She answered, "My master, you made a
promise to me in the name of the LORD your God.
You said, 'Your son Solomon will become king
after me, and he will rule on my throne.' 18But
now, unknown to you, Adonijah has become
king. 19He has killed many cows, fat calves, and
sheep for sacrifices. And he has invited all your
sons, as well as Abiathar the priest and Joab the
commander of the army, but he did not invite
Solomon, who serves you. 20My master and king,
all the Israelites are watching you, waiting for you
to decide who will be king after you. 21As soon as
you die, Solomon and I will be treated as criminals."
22While Bathsheba was still talking with the
king, Nathan the prophet arrived. 23The servants
told the king, "Nathan the prophet is here." So
Nathan went to the king and bowed facedown on
the ground before him.

24Nathan said, "My master and king, have you
said that Adonijah will be the king after you and
that he will rule on your throne? 25Today he has
sacrificed many cows, fat calves, and sheep, and
he has invited all your other sons, the commanders of the army, and Abiathar the priest. Right
now they are eating and drinking with him. They
are saying, 'Long live King Adonijah!' 26But he did
not invite me, your own servant, or Zadok the
priest, or Benaiah son of Jehoiada, or your son
Solomon. 27Did you do this? Since we are your
servants, why didn't you tell us who should be
king after you?"

David Makes Solomon King

28Then the king said, "Tell Bathsheba to come
in!" So she came in and stood before the king.
29Then the king made this promise, "The LORD
has saved me from all trouble. As surely as he
lives, 30I will do today what I have promised you
in the name of the LORD, the God of Israel. I
promised that your son Solomon would be king
after me and rule on my throne in my place."
31Then Bathsheba bowed facedown on the
ground and knelt before the king and said, "Long
live my master King David!"
32Then King David said, "Tell Zadok the priest,
Nathan the prophet,[d] and Benaiah son of Jehoiada
to come in." When they came before the king,
33he said to them, "Take my servants with you
and put my son Solomon on my own mule. Take
him down to the spring called Gihon. 34There Zadok the priest and Nathan the prophet should
pour olive oil on him and make him king over
Israel. Blow the trumpet and shout, 'Long live
King Solomon!' 35Then come back up here with
him. He will sit on my throne and rule in my
place, because he is the one I have chosen to be
the ruler over Israel and Judah."
36Benaiah son of Jehoiada answered the king,
"Amen! This is what the LORD, the God of my
master, has declared! 37The LORD has always
helped you, our king. May he also help Solomon
and make King Solomon's throne an even greater
throne than yours."
38So Zadok the priest, Nathan the prophet, and
Benaiah son of Jehoiada left with the Kerethites
and Pelethites.[n] They put Solomon on King David's mule and took him to the spring called Gihon. 39Zadok the priest took the container of olive
oil from the Holy Tent[d] and poured the oil on
Solomon's head to show he was the king. Then
they blew the trumpet, and all the people
shouted, "Long live King Solomon!" 40All the people followed Solomon into the city. Playing flutes
and shouting for joy, they made so much noise
the ground shook.
41At this time Adonijah and all the guests with
him were finishing their meal. When he heard the
sound from the trumpet, Joab asked, "What does
all that noise from the city mean?"
42While Joab was speaking, Jonathan son of
Abiathar the priest arrived. Adonijah said, "Come
in! You are an important man, so you must be
bringing good news."
43But Jonathan answered, "No! Our master
King David has made Solomon the new king.
44King David sent Zadok the priest, Nathan the
prophet, Benaiah son of Jehoiada, and all the
king's bodyguards with him, and they have put
Solomon on the king's own mule. 45Then Zadok
the priest and Nathan the prophet poured olive oil
on Solomon at Gihon to make him king. After that
they went into the city, shouting with joy. Now
the whole city is excited, and that is the noise you
hear. 46Solomon has now become the king. 47All
the king's officers have come to tell King David
that he has done a good thing. They are saying,
'May your God make Solomon even more famous
than you and an even greater king than you.' "
Jonathan continued, "And King David bowed
down on his bed to worship God, 48saying, 'Bless
the LORD, the God of Israel. Today he has made
one of my sons the king and allowed me to see
it.' "
49Then all of Adonijah's guests were afraid, and
they left quickly and scattered. 50Adonijah was
also afraid of Solomon, so he went and took hold
of the corners of the altar.[n] 51Then someone told
Solomon, "Adonijah is afraid of you, so he is at the
altar, holding on to its corners. He says, 'Tell King
Solomon to promise me today that he will not kill
me.' "
52So Solomon answered, "Adonijah must show
that he is a man of honor. If he does that, I promise he will not lose even a single hair from his
head. But if he does anything wrong, he will die."
53Then King Solomon sent some men to get Adonijah. When he was brought from the altar, he
came before King Solomon and bowed down. Solomon told him, "Go home."

The Death of David

2 Since it was almost time for David to die, he
gave his son Solomon his last commands.
2David said, "My time to die is near. Be a good
and strong leader. 3Obey the LORD your God. Follow him by obeying his demands, his commands,

Kerethites and Pelethites These were probably special units of the army that were responsible for the king's safety, a kind of palace guard.

corners of the altar If a person were innocent of a crime, he could run into the Holy Place where the altar was. If he held on to the corners of the altar, which looked like horns, he would be safe.

his laws, and his rules that are written in the
teachings of Moses. If you do these things, you
will be successful in all you do and wherever you
go. 4And if you obey the LORD, he will keep the
promise he made to me. He said: 'If your descendants[d] live as I tell them and have complete faith
in me, a man from your family will always be king
over the people of Israel.'
5"Also, you remember what Joab son of Zeruiah did to me. He killed the two commanders of
Israel's armies: Abner son of Ner and Amasa son
of Jether. He did this as if he and they were at
war, although it was a time of peace. He put their
blood on the belt around his waist and on his sandals on his feet. 6Punish him in the way you think
is wisest, but do not let him die peacefully of old
age.
7"Be kind to the children of Barzillai of Gilead,
and allow them to eat at your table. They welcomed me when I ran away from your brother
Absalom.
8"And remember, Shimei son of Gera, the Benjaminite, is here with you. He cursed me the day
I went to Mahanaim. But when he came down to
meet me at the Jordan River, I promised him before the LORD, 'Shimei, I will not kill you.' 9But

LEADERSHIP

The Measure of a Leader

During his lifetime, General Douglas MacArthur personified the best of America to millions of people. His determination and courage during the tumultuous years of World War II established him as a leading figure in world history. And his fairness as a military ruler of a conquered Japan made him a role model for all those who stood for justice and generosity.

But among all the general's great leadership achievements during those years, there was one achievement that towered above them all.

Douglas MacArthur had a son.

MacArthur spent the last years of his life in New England with his wife, Jean, and his son, Arthur. During that time, this great historical figure wrote a prayer that revealed what he believed was the true measure of leadership:

"Build me a son, O Lord, who will be strong enough to know when he is weak, and brave enough to face himself when he is afraid; one who will be proud and unbending in honest defeat, and humble and gentle in victory.

"Build me a son whose wishes will not take the place of deeds; a son who will know Thee . . . and that to know himself is the foundation stone of knowledge.

"Build me a son whose heart will be clear, whose goal will be high, a son who will master himself before he seeks to master other men; one who will reach into the future, yet never forget the past.

"And after all these things are his, add, I pray, enough of a sense of humor, so that he may always be serious, yet never take himself too seriously. Give him humility so that he may always remember the simplicity of true greatness, the open mind of true wisdom and the meekness of true strength.

"Then I, his father, will dare to whisper, 'I have not lived in vain.' "

For all his contributions to world events, General MacArthur believed the true measure of his leadership was in the raising of his son. King David was also a great leader who had dreams for his son's future. Read about David's wishes for Solomon in **1 Kings 2:1–12**.

- What leadership traits did MacArthur and King David both show in their final days?
- According to this passage, what responsibilities do we have to our leaders?

CONSIDER. . .

- memorizing 1 Timothy 4:12.
- asking your father or youth pastor how you can become a better Christian leader at church and at school.

FOR MORE, SEE. . .

- Psalm 132:11–18 (p. 558)
- John 16:4–15 (p. 1086)
- 2 Timothy 4:1–5 (p. 1266)

you should not leave him unpunished. You are a
wise man, and you will know what to do to him,
but you must be sure he is killed."
10Then David died and was buried with his ancestors in Jerusalem. 11He had ruled over Israel
forty years—seven years in Hebron and thirty-
three years in Jerusalem.

Solomon Takes Control as King

12Solomon became king after David, his father,
and he was in firm control of his kingdom.
13At this time Adonijah son of Haggith went to
Bathsheba, Solomon's mother. "Do you come in
peace?" Bathsheba asked.
"Yes. This is a peaceful visit," Adonijah answered. 14"I have something to say to you."
"You may speak," she said.
15"You remember that at one time the kingdom
was mine," Adonijah said. "All the people of Israel
recognized me as their king, but things have
changed. Now my brother is the king, because
the LORD chose him. 16Now I have one thing to
ask you; please do not refuse me."
Bathsheba answered, "What do you want?"
17"I know King Solomon will do anything you
ask him," Adonijah continued. "Please ask him to
give me Abishag the Shunammite to be my wife."
18"Very well," she answered. "I will speak to
the king for you."
19So Bathsheba went to King Solomon to speak
to him for Adonijah. When Solomon saw her, he
stood up to meet her, then bowed down, and sat
on the throne. He told some servants to bring another throne for his mother. Then she sat down
at his right side.
20Bathsheba said, "I have one small thing to ask
you. Please do not refuse me."
"Ask, mother," the king answered. "I will not
refuse you."
21So she said, "Allow Abishag the Shunammite
to marry your brother Adonijah."
22King Solomon answered his mother, "Why
do you ask me to give him Abishag? Why don't
you also ask for him to become the king since he
is my older brother? Abiathar the priest and Joab
son of Zeruiah would support him!"
23Then King Solomon swore by the name of the
LORD, saying, "May God punish me terribly if this
doesn't cost Adonijah his life! 24By the LORD who
has given me the throne that belonged to my father David and who has kept his promise and
given the kingdom to me and my people, Adonijah will die today!" 25Then King Solomon gave
orders to Benaiah son of Jehoiada, and he went
and killed Adonijah.
26King Solomon said to Abiathar the priest, "I
should kill you too, but I will allow you to go back
to your fields in Anathoth. I will not kill you at
this time, because you helped carry the Ark[d] of
the Lord GOD while marching with my father David. And I know you shared in all the hard times
with him." 27Then Solomon removed Abiathar
from being the LORD's priest. This happened as
the LORD had said it would, when he was speaking in Shiloh about the priest Eli and his descendants.[d]
28When Joab heard about what had happened,
he was afraid. He had supported Adonijah but not
Absalom. So Joab ran to the Tent[d] of the LORD and
took hold of the corners of the altar.[n] 29Someone
told King Solomon that Joab had run to the Tent
of the LORD and was beside the altar. Then Solomon ordered Benaiah to go and kill him.
30Benaiah went into the Tent of the LORD and
said to Joab, "The king says, 'Come out!' "
But Joab answered, "No, I will die here."
So Benaiah went back to the king and told him
what Joab had said. 31Then the king ordered Benaiah, "Do as he says! Kill him there and bury
him. Then my family and I will be free of the guilt
of Joab, who has killed innocent people. 32With-
out my father knowing it, he killed two men who
were much better than he was—Abner son of
Ner, the commander of Israel's army, and Amasa
son of Jether, the commander of Judah's army. So
the LORD will pay him back for those deaths.
33Joab and his family will be forever guilty for
their deaths, but there will be peace from the
LORD for David, his descendants, his family, and
his throne forever."
34So Benaiah son of Jehoiada killed Joab, and he
was buried near his home in the desert. 35The
king then made Benaiah son of Jehoiada commander of the army in Joab's place. He also made
Zadok the new high priest in Abiathar's place.
36Next the king sent for Shimei. Solomon said
to him, "Build a house for yourself in Jerusalem
and live there. Don't leave the city. 37The very
day you leave and cross the Kidron Valley, someone will kill you, and it will be your own fault."
38So Shimei answered the king, "I agree with
what you say. I will do what you say, my master
and king." So Shimei lived in Jerusalem for a long
time.
39But three years later two of Shimei's slaves
ran away to Achish king of Gath, who was the son
of Maacah. Shimei heard that his slaves were in
Gath, 40so he put his saddle on his donkey and
went to Achish at Gath to find them. Then he
brought them back from Gath.
41Someone told Solomon that Shimei had gone
from Jerusalem to Gath and had returned. 42So

corners of the altar If a person were innocent of a crime, he could run into the Holy Place where the altar was. If he held on to the corners of the altar, which looked like horns, he would be safe.

Solomon sent for Shimei and said, "I made you promise in the name of the LORD not to leave Jerusalem. I warned you if you went out anywhere you would die, and you agreed to what I said. 43Why did you break your promise to the LORD and disobey my command?" 44The king also said, "You know the many wrong things you did to my father David, so now the LORD will punish you for those wrongs. 45But the LORD will bless me and make the rule of David safe before the LORD forever."

46Then the king ordered Benaiah to kill Shimei, and he did. Now Solomon was in full control of his kingdom.

Solomon Asks for Wisdom

3 Solomon made an agreement with the king of Egypt by marrying his daughter and bringing her to Jerusalem. At this time Solomon was still building his palace and the Temple[d] of the LORD, as well as a wall around Jerusalem. 2The Temple for the worship of the LORD had not yet been finished, so people were still sacrificing at altars in many places of worship. 3Solomon showed he loved the LORD by following the commands his father David had given him, except many other places of worship were still used to offer sacrifices and to burn incense.[d]

4King Solomon went to Gibeon to offer a sacrifice, because it was the most important place of worship. He offered a thousand burnt offerings on that altar. 5While he was at Gibeon, the LORD appeared to him in a dream during the night. God said, "Ask for whatever you want me to give you."

6Solomon answered, "You were very kind to your servant, my father David. He obeyed you, and he was honest and lived right. You showed great kindness to him when you allowed his son to be king after him. 7LORD my God, now you have made me, your servant, king in my father's place. But I am like a little child; I don't know how to do what must be done. 8I, your servant, am here among your chosen people, and there are too many of them to count. 9I ask that you give me an obedient heart so I can rule the people in the right way and will know the difference between right and wrong. Otherwise, it is impossible to rule this great people of yours."

10The Lord was pleased that Solomon had asked this. 11So God said to him, "You did not ask for a long life, or riches for yourself, or the death of your enemies. Since you asked for wisdom to make the right decisions, 12I will do what you asked. I will give you wisdom and understanding that is greater than anyone has had in the past or will have in the future. 13I will also give you what you did not ask for: riches and honor. During your life no other king will be as great as you. 14If you follow me and obey my laws and commands, as your father David did, I will also give you a long life."

15After Solomon woke up from the dream, he went to Jerusalem. He stood before the Ark[d] of the Agreement with the Lord, where he made burnt offerings and fellowship offerings. After that, he gave a feast for all his leaders and officers.

Solomon Makes a Wise Decision

16One day two women who were prostitutes[d] came to Solomon. As they stood before him, 17one of the women said, "My master, this woman and I live in the same house. I gave birth to a baby while she was there with me. 18Three days later this woman also gave birth to a baby. No one else was in the house with us; it was just the two of us. 19One night this woman rolled over on her baby, and he died. 20So she took my son from my bed during the night while I was asleep, and she carried him to her bed. Then she put the dead baby in my bed. 21The next morning when I got up to feed my baby, I saw that he was dead! When I looked at him more closely, I realized he was not my son."

22"No!" the other woman cried. "The living baby is my son, and the dead baby is yours!"

But the first woman said, "No! The dead baby is yours, and the living one is mine!" So the two women argued before the king.

23Then King Solomon said, "One of you says, 'My son is alive and your son is dead.' Then the other one says, 'No! Your son is dead and my son is alive.' "

24The king sent his servants to get a sword. When they brought it to him, 25he said, "Cut the living baby into two pieces, and give each woman half."

> **SIDELIGHT:** Many people have half-brothers or half-sisters these days because of stepfamilies. But Solomon suggested another approach: settling a dispute by cutting the baby in half and giving each mother a half (1 Kings 3:16–28). Scholars have found twenty-two similar stories of wisdom in other cultures of ancient times.

26The real mother of the living child was full of love for her son. So she said to the king, "Please, my master, don't kill him! Give the baby to her!"

But the other woman said, "Neither of us will have him. Cut him into two pieces!"

27Then King Solomon said, "Don't kill him. Give the baby to the first woman, because she is the real mother."

28When the people of Israel heard about King Solomon's decision, they respected him very much. They saw he had wisdom from God to make the right decisions.

Solomon's Officers

4 King Solomon ruled over all Israel. 2These are the names of his leading officers:

Azariah son of Zadok was the priest;

3Elihoreph and Ahijah, sons of Shisha, recorded what happened in the courts;

Jehoshaphat son of Ahilud recorded the history of the people;

4Benaiah son of Jehoiada was commander of the army;

Zadok and Abiathar were priests;

5Azariah son of Nathan was in charge of the district governors;

Zabud son of Nathan was a priest and adviser to the king;

6Ahishar was responsible for everything in the palace;

Adoniram son of Abda was in charge of the labor force.

7Solomon placed twelve governors over the districts of Israel, who gathered food from their districts for the king and his family. Each governor was responsible for bringing food to the king one month of each year. 8These are the names of the twelve governors:

Ben-Hur was governor of the mountain country of Ephraim.

9Ben-Deker was governor of Makaz, Shaalbim, Beth Shemesh, and Elon Bethhanan.

10Ben-Hesed was governor of Arubboth, Socoh, and all the land of Hepher.

11Ben-Abinadab was governor of Naphoth Dor. (He was married to Taphath, Solomon's daughter.)

12Baana son of Ahilud was governor of Taanach, Megiddo, and all of Beth Shan next to Zarethan. This was below Jezreel from Beth Shan to Abel Meholah across from Jokmeam.

13Ben-Geber was governor of Ramoth in Gilead. (He was governor of all the towns of Jair in Gilead. Jair was the son of Manasseh. Ben-Geber was also over the district of Argob in Bashan, which had sixty large, walled cities with bronze bars on their gates.)

14Ahinadab son of Iddo was governor of Mahanaim.

15Ahimaaz was governor of Naphtali. (He was married to Basemath, Solomon's daughter.)

16Baana son of Hushai was governor of Asher and Aloth.

17Jehoshaphat son of Paruah was governor of Issachar.

18Shimei son of Ela was governor of Benjamin.

19Geber son of Uri was governor of Gilead. Gilead had been the country of Sihon king of the Amorites and Og king of Bashan. But Geber was the only governor over this district.

Solomon's Kingdom

20There were as many people in Judah and Israel as grains of sand on the seashore. The people ate, drank, and were happy. 21Solomon ruled over all the kingdoms from the Euphrates River to the land of the Philistines, as far as the border of Egypt. These countries brought Solomon the payments he demanded, and they were under his control all his life.

22Solomon needed much food each day to feed himself and all the people who ate at his table: one hundred ninety-five bushels of fine flour, three hundred ninety bushels of grain, 23ten cows that were fed on good grain, twenty cows that were raised in the fields, one hundred sheep, three kinds of deer, and fattened birds.

SIDELIGHT: Each day it took thirty cattle (plus lots of other food) to feed all the people at Solomon's table (1 Kings 4:23). That would be about 120,000 Big Macs a day.

24Solomon controlled all the countries west of the Euphrates River—the land from Tiphsah to Gaza. And he had peace on all sides of his kingdom. 25During Solomon's life Judah and Israel, from Dan to Beersheba,[n] also lived in peace; all of his people were able to sit under their own fig trees and grapevines.

26Solomon had four thousand stalls for his chariot horses and twelve thousand horses. 27Each month one of the district governors gave King Solomon all the food he needed—enough for every person who ate at the king's table. The governors made sure he had everything he needed. 28They also brought enough barley and straw for Solomon's chariot and work horses; each person brought this grain to the right place.

Solomon's Wisdom

29God gave Solomon great wisdom so he could understand many things. His wisdom was as hard to measure as the grains of sand on the seashore. 30His wisdom was greater than any wisdom of the

Dan to Beersheba Dan was the city farthest north in Israel, and Beersheba was the city farthest south. So this means all the people of Israel.

East, or any wisdom in Egypt. [31]He was wiser than anyone on earth. He was even wiser than Ethan the Ezrahite, as well as Heman, Calcol, and Darda — the three sons of Mahol. King Solomon became famous in all the surrounding countries. [32]During his life he spoke three thousand wise sayings and also wrote one thousand five songs. [33]He taught about many kinds of plants — everything from the great cedar trees of Lebanon to the weeds that grow out of the walls. He also taught about animals, birds, crawling things, and fish. [34]People from all nations came to listen to King Solomon's wisdom. The kings of all nations sent them to him, because they had heard of Solomon's wisdom.

Preparing to Build the Temple

5 Hiram, the king of Tyre, had always been David's friend. When Hiram heard that Solomon had been made king in David's place, he sent his messengers to Solomon. [2]Solomon sent this message back to King Hiram: [3]"You remember my father David had to fight many wars with the countries around him, so he was never able to build a temple for worshiping the LORD his God. David was waiting until the LORD allowed him to defeat all his enemies. [4]But now the LORD my God has given me peace on all sides of my country. I have no enemies now, and no danger threatens my people.

[5]"The LORD promised my father David, 'I will make your son king after you, and he will build a temple for worshiping me.' Now, I plan to build that temple for worshiping the LORD my God. [6]So send your men to cut down cedar trees for me from Lebanon. My servants will work with yours, and I will pay them whatever wages you decide. We don't have anyone who can cut down trees as well as the people of Sidon."

[7]When Hiram heard what Solomon asked, he was very happy. He said, "Praise the LORD today! He has given David a wise son to rule over this great nation!" [8]Then Hiram sent back this message to Solomon: "I received the message you sent, and I will give you all the cedar and pine trees you want. [9]My servants will bring them down from Lebanon to the sea. There I will tie them together and float them along the shore to the place you choose. Then I will separate the logs there, and you can take them away. In return it is my wish that you give food to all those who live with me." [10]So Hiram gave Solomon as much cedar and pine as he wanted. [11]And Solomon gave Hiram about one hundred twenty-five thousand bushels of wheat each year to feed the people who lived with him. Solomon also gave him about one hundred fifteen thousand gallons of pure olive oil every year.

[12]The LORD gave Solomon wisdom as he had promised. And there was peace between Hiram and Solomon; these two kings made a treaty between themselves.

> **SIDELIGHT:** The cedars Solomon imported from Lebanon were in high demand as building materials (1 Kings 5:6–10). The wood is red and resists insects and decay, making it ideal for buildings, musical instruments, chests and household furnishings. Though these trees have almost become extinct, the Lebanese flag still features the pyramid-shaped tree.

[13]King Solomon forced thirty thousand men of Israel to help in this work. [14]He sent a group of ten thousand men each month to Lebanon. Each group worked in Lebanon one month, then went home for two months. A man named Adoniram was in charge. [15]Solomon forced eighty thousand men to work in the hill country, cutting stone, and he had seventy thousand men to carry the stones. [16]There were also thirty-three hundred men who directed the workers. [17]King Solomon commanded them to cut large blocks of fine stone to be used for the foundation of the Temple.[d] [18]Solomon's and Hiram's builders and the men from Byblos carved the stones and prepared the stones and the logs for building the Temple.

Solomon Builds the Temple

6 Solomon began to build the Temple[d] four hundred eighty years after the people of Israel had left Egypt. This was during the fourth year of King Solomon's rule over Israel. It was the second month, the month of Ziv.

[2]The Temple was ninety feet long, thirty feet wide, and forty-five feet high. [3]The porch in front of the main room of the Temple was fifteen feet deep and thirty feet wide. This room ran along the front of the Temple itself. Its width was equal to that of the Temple. [4]The Temple also had windows that opened and closed. [5]Solomon also built some side rooms against the walls of the main room and the inner room of the Temple. He built rooms all around. [6]The rooms on the bottom floor were seven and one-half feet wide. Those on the middle floor were nine feet wide, and the rooms above them were ten and one-half feet wide. The Temple wall that formed the side of each room was thinner than the wall in the room below. These rooms were pushed against the Temple wall, but they did not have their main beams built into this wall.

[7]The stones were prepared at the same place where they were cut from the ground. Since these

stones were the only ones used to build the Temple, there was no noise of hammers, axes, or any other iron tools at the Temple.

> **SIDELIGHT:** Solomon's Temple was one of the largest structures in Israel at the time, but it wasn't very big by today's standards. It only had about twenty-seven hundred square feet of floor space—no larger than many good-sized homes today (1 Kings 6:2–38).

8The entrance to the lower rooms beside the Temple was on the south side. From there, stairs went up to the second-floor rooms. And from there, stairs went on to the third-floor rooms. 9Solomon put a roof made from beams and cedar boards on the Temple. So he finished building the Temple 10as well as the bottom floor that was beside the Temple. This bottom floor was seven and one half feet high and was attached to the Temple by cedar beams.

11The LORD said to Solomon: 12"If you obey all my laws and commands, I will do for you what I promised your father David. 13I will live among the Israelites in this Temple, and I will never leave my people Israel."

14So Solomon finished building the Temple. 15The inside walls were covered from floor to ceiling with cedar boards. The floor was made from pine boards. 16A room thirty feet long was built in the back part of the Temple. This room, called the Most Holy Place, was separated from the rest of the Temple by cedar boards which reached from floor to ceiling. 17The main room, the one in front of the Most Holy Place, was sixty feet long. 18Everything inside the Temple was covered with cedar, which was carved with pictures of flowers and plants. A person could not see the stones of the wall, only the cedar.

19Solomon prepared the inner room at the back of the Temple to keep the Ark[d] of the Agreement with the LORD. 20This inner room was thirty feet long, thirty feet wide, and thirty feet high. He covered this room with pure gold, and he also covered the altar of cedar. 21He covered the inside of the Temple with pure gold, placing gold chains across the front of the inner room, which was also covered with gold. 22So all the inside of the Temple, as well as the altar of the Most Holy Place, was covered with gold.

23Solomon made two creatures from olive wood and placed them in the Most Holy Place. Each creature was fifteen feet tall 24and had two wings. Each wing was seven and one-half feet long, so it was fifteen feet from the end of one wing to the end of the other. 25The creatures were the same size and shape; 26each was fifteen feet tall. 27These creatures were put beside each other in the Most Holy Place with their wings spread out. One creature's wing touched one wall, and the other creature's wing touched the other wall with their wings touching each other in the middle of the room. 28These two creatures were covered with gold.

29All the walls around the Temple were carved with pictures of creatures with wings, as well as palm trees and flowers. This was true for both the main room and the inner room. 30The floors of both rooms were covered with gold.

> **SIDELIGHT:** Building Solomon's Temple would ruin any church's budget (1 Kings 6:21). According to one estimate, just the gold overlay in the Temple might be worth almost thirty-six billion dollars on today's gold market.

31Doors made from olive wood were placed at the entrance to the Most Holy Place. These doors had five-sided frames. 32Creatures with wings, as well as palm trees and flowers, were also carved on the two olive wood doors that were covered with gold. The creatures and the palm trees on the doors were covered with gold as well. 33At the entrance to the main room there was a square door frame made of olive wood. 34Two doors were made from pine. Each door had two parts so the doors folded. 35The doors were covered with pictures of creatures with wings, as well as palm trees and flowers. All of the carvings were covered with gold, which was evenly spread over them.

36The inner courtyard was enclosed by walls, which were made of three rows of cut stones and one row of cedar boards.

37Work began on the Temple in Ziv, the second month, during the fourth year Solomon was king over Israel. 38The Temple was finished during the eleventh year he was king, in the eighth month, the month of Bul. It was built exactly as it was planned. Solomon had spent seven years building it.

Solomon's Palace

7 King Solomon also built a palace for himself; it took him thirteen years to finish it. 2Built of cedars from the Forest of Lebanon, it was one hundred fifty feet long, seventy-five feet wide, and forty-five feet high. It had four rows of cedar columns which supported the cedar beams. 3There were forty-five beams on the roof, with fifteen

beams in each row, and the ceiling was covered
with cedar above the beams. 4Windows were
placed in three rows facing each other. 5All the
doors were square, and the three doors at each
end faced each other.

6Solomon also built the porch that had pillars.
This porch was seventy-five feet long and forty-
five feet wide. Along the front of the porch was
a roof supported by pillars.

7Solomon also built a throne room where he
judged people, called the Hall of Justice. This
room was covered with cedar from the floor to
the ceiling. 8The palace where Solomon lived was
built like the Hall of Justice, and it was behind this
hall. Solomon also built the same kind of palace
for his wife, who was the daughter of the king of
Egypt.

9All these buildings were made with blocks of
fine stone. First they were carefully cut. Then
they were trimmed with a saw in the front and
back. These fine stones went from the foundations of the buildings to the top of the walls. Even
the courtyard was made with blocks of stone.
10The foundations were made with large blocks of
fine stone, some as long as fifteen feet. Others
were twelve feet long. 11On top of these foundation stones were other blocks of fine stone and
cedar beams. 12The palace courtyard, the courtyard inside the Temple,[d] and the porch of the
Temple were surrounded by walls. All of these
walls had three rows of stone blocks and one row
of cedar beams.

The Temple Is Completed Inside

13King Solomon sent to Tyre and had Huram
brought to him. 14Huram's mother was a widow
from the tribe[d] of Naphtali. His father was from
Tyre and had been skilled in making things from
bronze. Huram was also very skilled and experienced in bronze work. So he came to King Solomon and did all the bronze work.

15He made two bronze pillars, each one
twenty-seven feet tall and eighteen feet around.
16He also made two bronze capitals[d] that were
seven and one-half feet tall, and he put them on
top of the pillars. 17Then he made a net of seven
chains for each capital, which covered the capitals
on top of the two pillars. 18He made two rows of
bronze pomegranates[d] to go on the nets. These
covered the capitals at the top of the pillars. 19The
capitals on top of the pillars in the porch were
shaped like lilies, and they were six feet tall. 20The
capitals were on top of both pillars, above the
bowl-shaped section and next to the nets. At that
place there were two hundred pomegranates in
rows all around the capitals. 21Huram put these
two bronze pillars at the porch of the Temple.[d] He
named the south pillar He Establishes and the
north pillar In Him Is Strength. 22The capitals on
top of the pillars were shaped like lilies. So the
work on the pillars was finished.

23Then Huram made from bronze a large round
bowl, which was called the Sea. It was forty-five
feet around, fifteen feet across, and seven and
one-half feet deep. 24Around the outer edge of the
bowl was a rim. Under this rim were two rows of
bronze plants which surrounded the bowl. There
were ten plants every eighteen inches, and these
plants were made in one piece with the bowl.
25The bowl rested on the backs of twelve bronze
bulls that faced outward from the center of the
bowl. Three bulls faced north, three faced west,
three faced south, and three faced east. 26The
sides of the bowl were four inches thick, and it
held about eleven thousand gallons. The rim of
the bowl was like the rim of a cup or like a lily
blossom.

27Then Huram made ten bronze stands, each
one six feet long, six feet wide, and four and one-
half feet high. 28The stands were made from
square sides, which were put on frames. 29On the
sides were bronze lions, bulls, and creatures with
wings. On the frames above and below the lions
and bulls were designs of flowers hammered into
the bronze. 30Each stand had four bronze wheels
with bronze axles. At the corners there were
bronze supports for a large bowl, and the supports
had designs of flowers. 31There was a frame on
top of the bowls, eighteen inches high above the
bowls. The opening of the bowl was round,
twenty-seven inches deep. Designs were carved
into the bronze on the frame, which was square,
not round. 32The four wheels, placed under the
frame, were twenty-seven inches high. The axles
between the wheels were made as one piece
with the stand. 33The wheels were like a chariot's wheels. Everything on the wheels—the
axles, rims, spokes, and hubs—were made of
bronze.

34The four supports were on the four corners of
each stand. They were made as one piece with
the stand. 35A strip of bronze around the top of
each stand was nine inches deep. It was also
made as one piece with the stand. 36The sides of
the stand and the frames were covered with carvings of creatures with wings, as well as lions, palm
trees, and flowers. 37This is the way Huram made
the ten stands. The bronze for each stand was
melted and poured into a mold, so all the stands
were the same size and shape.

38Huram also made ten bronze bowls, one
bowl for each of the ten stands. Each bowl was six
feet across and could hold about two hundred
thirty gallons. 39Huram put five stands on the
south side of the Temple and five on the north
side. He put the large bowl in the southeast corner of the Temple. 40Huram also made bowls,
shovels, and small bowls.

So Huram finished all his work for King Solomon on the Temple of the LORD:

41 two pillars;
two large bowls for the capitals on top of the pillars;
two nets to cover the two large bowls for the capitals on top of the pillars;
42 four hundred pomegranates for the two nets (there were two rows of pomegranates for each net covering the bowls for the capitals on top of the pillars);
43 ten stands with a bowl on each stand;
44 the large bowl with twelve bulls under it;
45 the pots, shovels, small bowls, and all the utensils for the Temple of the LORD.

Huram made everything King Solomon wanted from polished bronze. 46 The king had these things poured into clay molds that were made in the plain of the Jordan River between Succoth and Zarethan. 47 Solomon never weighed the bronze used to make these things, because there was too much to weigh. So the total weight of all the bronze was never known.

48 Solomon also made all the items for the Temple of the LORD:

the golden altar;
the golden table which held the bread that shows God's people are in his presence;
49 the lampstands of pure gold (five on the right side and five on the left side in front of the Most Holy Place);
the flowers, lamps, and tongs of gold;
50 the pure gold bowls, wick trimmers, small bowls, pans, and dishes used to carry coals;
the gold hinges for the doors of the Most Holy Place and the main room of the Temple.

51 Finally the work King Solomon did for the Temple of the LORD was finished. Solomon brought in everything his father David had set apart for the Temple—silver, gold, and other articles. He put everything in the treasuries of the Temple of the LORD.

The Ark Is Brought into the Temple

8 King Solomon called for the older leaders of Israel, the heads of the tribes,[d] and the leaders of the families to come to him in Jerusalem. He wanted them to bring the Ark[d] of the Agreement with the LORD from the older part of the city. 2 So all the Israelites came together with King Solomon during the festival in the month of Ethanim, the seventh month.

3 When all the older leaders of Israel arrived, the priests lifted up the Ark. 4 They carried the Ark of the LORD, the Meeting Tent,[d] and the holy utensils; the priests and the Levites brought them up. 5 King Solomon and all the Israelites gathered before the Ark and sacrificed so many sheep and cattle no one could count them all. 6 Then the priests put the Ark of the Agreement with the LORD in its place inside the Most Holy Place in the Temple,[d] under the wings of the golden creatures. 7 The wings of these creatures were spread out over the place for the Ark, covering it and its carrying poles. 8 The carrying poles were so long that anyone standing in the Holy Place in front of the Most Holy Place could see the ends of the poles, but no one could see them from outside the Holy Place. The poles are still there today. 9 The only things inside the Ark were two stone tablets[n] that Moses had put in the Ark at Mount Sinai. That was where the LORD made his agreement with the Israelites after they came out of Egypt.

10 When the priests left the Holy Place, a cloud filled the Temple of the LORD. 11 The priests could not continue their work, because the Temple was filled with the glory of the LORD.

Solomon Speaks to the People

12 Then Solomon said, "The LORD said he would live in a dark cloud. 13 LORD, I have truly built a wonderful Temple[d] for you—a place for you to live forever."

14 While all the Israelites were standing there, King Solomon turned to them and blessed them. 15 Then he said, "Praise the LORD, the God of Israel. He has done what he promised to my father David. The LORD said, 16 'Since the time I brought my people Israel out of Egypt, I have not chosen a city in any tribe[d] of Israel where a temple will be built for me. But I have chosen David to lead my people Israel.'

17 "My father David wanted to build a temple for the LORD, the God of Israel. 18 But the LORD said to my father David, 'It was good that you wanted to build a temple for me. 19 But you are not the one to build it. Your son, who comes from your own body, is the one who will build my temple.'

20 "Now the LORD has kept his promise. I am the king now in place of David my father. Now I rule Israel as the LORD promised, and I have built the Temple for the LORD, the God of Israel. 21 I have made a place there for the Ark, in which is the Agreement the LORD made with our ancestors when he brought them out of Egypt."

stone tablets They were the two tablets on which God wrote the Ten Commandments.

Solomon's Prayer

22Then Solomon stood facing the LORD's altar,
and all the Israelites were standing behind him.
He spread out his hands toward the sky 23and
said:

"LORD, God of Israel, there is no god like you
in heaven above or on earth below. You keep
your agreement of love with your servants who
truly follow you. 24You have kept the promise you
made to your servant David, my father. You spoke
it with your own mouth and finished it with your
hands today. 25Now LORD, God of Israel, keep the
promise you made to your servant David, my father. You said, 'If your sons are careful to obey me
as you have obeyed me, there will always be
someone from your family ruling Israel.' 26Now,
God of Israel, please continue to keep that promise you made to your servant David, my father.

27"But, God, can you really live here on the
earth? The sky and the highest place in heaven
cannot contain you. Surely this house which I
have built cannot contain you. 28But please listen
to my prayer and my request, because I am your
servant. LORD my God, hear this prayer your servant prays to you today. 29Night and day please
watch over this Temple[d] where you have said, 'I
will be worshiped there.' Hear the prayer I pray
facing this Temple. 30Hear my prayers and the
prayers of your people Israel when we pray facing

PRAYER

Praying About Real Life

When seventeen-year-old Shelley Lundberg and her mom talked about Shelley's ex-boyfriend one evening, the conversation quickly escalated into a fight.

"LeRoy seems like such a nice young man, Shelley," Mom complained. "I really think you handled the whole thing wrong."

"I didn't ask your opinion, Mom. Thanks anyway." Shelley's words dripped with sarcasm. She felt as if she were about to explode.

"Now, just wait a minute, Miss. . . ."

"No, you wait a minute, Mother," Shelley's voice was strained with anger. "I'm tired of your constant meddling. I can't even put my shoes on without getting your approval first. I have a life, Mother. Why don't you let me live it by myself?"

Then Shelley stormed away. She didn't know or care what her mother thought—she just wanted to leave.

Shelley ended up at a nearby park for the next few hours. There, she discovered how much prayer can help. At first, she was angry with God. "Why does this stuff happen to me?" she asked God. "I shouldn't be having so much trouble with this! I'm a Christian." Shelley felt she should be able to deal with her family problems.

Soon, Shelley asked God to help her calm down. She sang a few worship songs, and she started feeling better. Once she had calmed down, Shelley asked God to help her understand her mom's side of the argument.

Shelley got home late, but in the morning, she and her mother apologized. That evening, they talked about how they could have dealt with their feelings better. And Shelley decided to talk to LeRoy. "It'll give me the chance to let him know I still care," she told her mom, smiling.

Shelley's relationship with her mom isn't perfect, but she knows she can turn to God in prayer for real-life issues like this one.

King Solomon also turned to God and prayed about real-life issues. Read his prayer after God's Temple was built in **1 Kings 8:22–30**.

- What elements do Shelley's prayer and King Solomon's prayer have in common? What's different?
- How does King Solomon's prayer compare with the kind of prayers you usually pray?

CONSIDER . . .

- listing all the concerns of your life on paper and then talking to God about each one.
- offering to pray with others who are going through rough times.

FOR MORE, SEE . . .

- 2 Samuel 22:1–51 (p. 296)
- Luke 1:46–55 (p. 1001)
- John 17:20–26 (p. 1089)

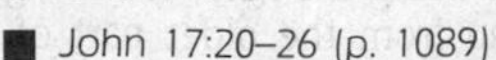

this place. Hear from your home in heaven, and
when you hear, forgive us.
31“If someone wrongs another person, he will
be brought to the altar in this Temple. If he swears
an oath that he is not guilty, 32then hear in
heaven. Judge the case, punish the guilty, but declare that the innocent person is not guilty.
33“When your people, the Israelites, sin against
you, their enemies will defeat them. But if they
come back to you and praise you and pray to you
in this Temple, 34then hear them in heaven. Forgive the sins of your people Israel, and bring them
back to the land you gave to their ancestors.
35“When they sin against you, you will stop the
rain from falling on their land. Then they will
pray, facing this place and praising you; they will
stop sinning when you make them suffer. 36When
this happens, please hear their prayer in heaven,
and forgive the sins of your servants, the Israelites. Teach them to do what is right. Then please
send rain to this land you have given particularly
to them.
37“At times the land will become so dry that no
food will grow, or a great sickness will spread
among the people. Sometimes all the crops will be
destroyed by locusts[d] or grasshoppers. Your people will be attacked in their cities by their enemy
or will become sick. 38When any of these things
happen, the people will become truly sorry. If
your people spread their hands in prayer toward
this Temple, 39then hear their prayers from your
home in heaven. Forgive and treat each person as
he should be treated because you know what is
in a person’s heart. Only you know what is in
everyone’s heart. 40Then your people will respect
you as long as they live in this land you gave to
our ancestors.
41-42“People who are not Israelites, foreigners
from other lands, will hear about your greatness
and power. They will come from far away to pray
at this Temple. 43Then hear from your home in
heaven, and do whatever they ask you. Then people everywhere will know you and respect you,
just as your people in Israel do. Then everyone
will know I built this Temple as a place to worship
you.
44“When your people go out to fight their enemies along some road on which you send them,
your people will pray to you, facing the city which
you have chosen and the Temple I have built for
you. 45Then hear in heaven their prayers, and do
what is right.
46“Everyone sins, so your people will also sin
against you. You will become angry with them
and hand them over to their enemies. Their enemies will capture them and take them away to
their countries far or near. 47Your people will be
sorry for their sins when they are held as prisoners
in another country. They will be sorry and pray to
you in the land where they are held as prisoners,
saying, ‘We have sinned. We have done wrong
and acted wickedly.’ 48They will truly turn back
to you in the land of their enemies. They will pray
to you, facing this land you gave their ancestors,
this city you have chosen, and the Temple I have
built for you. 49Then hear their prayers from your
home in heaven, and do what is right. 50Forgive
your people of all their sins and for turning against
you. Make those who have captured them show
them mercy. 51Remember, they are your special
people. You brought them out of Egypt, as if you
were pulling them out of a blazing furnace.
52“Give your attention to my prayers and the
prayers of your people Israel. Listen to them anytime they ask you for help. 53You chose them from
all the nations on earth to be your very own people. This is what you promised through Moses
your servant when you brought our ancestors out
of Egypt, Lord God.”
54Solomon prayed this prayer to the LORD,
kneeling in front of the altar with his arms raised
toward heaven. When he finished praying, he got
up. 55Then, in a loud voice, he stood and blessed
all the people of Israel, saying: 56“Praise the LORD!
He promised he would give rest to his people Israel, and he has given us rest. The LORD has kept
all the good promises he gave through his servant
Moses. 57May the LORD our God be with us as he
was with our ancestors. May he never leave us,
58and may he turn us to himself so we will follow
him. Let us obey all the laws and commands he
gave our ancestors. 59May the LORD our God remember this prayer day and night and do what is
right for his servant and his people Israel day by
day. 60Then all the people of the world will know
the LORD is the only true God. 61You must fully
obey the LORD our God and follow all his laws and
commands. Continue to obey in the future as you
do now.”

Sacrifices Are Offered

62Then King Solomon and all Israel with him
offered sacrifices to the LORD. 63Solomon killed
twenty-two thousand cattle and one hundred
twenty thousand sheep as fellowship offerings. So
the king and all the people gave the Temple[d] to
the LORD.
64On that day King Solomon made holy the
middle part of the courtyard which is in front of
the Temple of the LORD. There he offered whole
burnt offerings, grain offerings, and the fat of the
fellowship offerings. He offered them in the courtyard, because the bronze altar before the LORD
was too small to hold all the burnt offerings, the
grain offerings, and the fat of the fellowship offerings.
65Solomon and all the Israelites celebrated the
other festival that came at that time. People came

from as far away as Lebo Hamath and the brook of Egypt. A great many people celebrated before the LORD for seven days, then seven more days, for a total of fourteen days. 66On the following day Solomon sent the people home. They blessed the king as they went, happy because of all the good things the LORD had done for his servant David and his people Israel.

The Lord Appears to Solomon Again

9 Solomon finished building the Temple[d] of the LORD and his royal palace and everything he wanted to build. 2Then the LORD appeared to him again just as he had done before, in Gibeon. 3The LORD said to him: "I have heard your prayer and what you have asked me to do. You built this Temple, and I have made it a holy place. I will be worshiped there forever and will watch over it and protect it always.

4"But you must serve me as your father David did; he was fair and sincere. You must obey all I have commanded and keep my laws and rules. 5If you do, I will make your kingdom strong. This is the promise I made to your father David—that someone from his family would always rule Israel.

6"But you and your children must follow me and obey the laws and commands I have given you. You must not serve or worship other gods. 7If you do, I will force Israel to leave the land I have given them, and I will leave this Temple that I have made holy. All the nations will make fun of Israel and speak evil about them. 8If the Temple is destroyed, everyone who passes by will be shocked. They will make fun of you and ask, 'Why did the LORD do this terrible thing to this land and this Temple?' 9People will answer, 'This happened because they left the LORD their God. This was the God who brought their ancestors out of Egypt, but they decided to follow other gods. They worshiped and served those gods, so the LORD brought all this disaster on them.' "

Solomon's Other Achievements

10By the end of twenty years, King Solomon had built two buildings—the Temple[d] of the LORD and the royal palace. 11At that time King Solomon gave twenty towns in Galilee to Hiram king of Tyre, because Hiram had helped with the buildings. Hiram had given Solomon all the cedar, pine, and gold he wanted. 12So Hiram traveled from Tyre to see the towns Solomon had given him, but when he saw them, he was not pleased. 13He asked, "What good are these towns you have given me, my brother?" So he named them the Land of Cabul,[n] and they are still called that today. 14Hiram had sent Solomon about nine thousand pounds of gold.

15This is the account of the forced labor Solomon used to build the Temple and the palace. He had them fill in the land and build the wall around Jerusalem. He also had them rebuild the cities of Hazor, Megiddo, and Gezer. 16(In the past the king of Egypt had attacked and captured Gezer. After burning it, he killed the Canaanites who lived there. Then he gave it as a wedding present to his daughter, who married Solomon. 17So Solomon rebuilt it.) He also built the cities of Lower Beth Horon 18and Baalath, as well as Tadmor, which is in the desert. 19King Solomon also built cities for storing grain and supplies and cities for his chariots and horses. He built whatever he wanted in Jerusalem, Lebanon, and everywhere he ruled.

20There were other people in the land who were not Israelites—Amorites, Hittites, Perizzites, Hivites, and Jebusites. 21They were descendants[d] of people that the Israelites had not destroyed. Solomon forced them to work for him as slaves, as is still true today. 22But Solomon did not make slaves of the Israelites. They were his soldiers, government leaders, officers, captains, chariot commanders, and drivers.

23These were his most important officers over the work. There were five hundred fifty supervisors over the people who did the work on Solomon's projects.

24The daughter of the king of Egypt moved from the old part of Jerusalem to the palace that Solomon had built for her. Then Solomon filled in the surrounding land.

25Three times each year Solomon offered whole burnt offerings and fellowship offerings on the altar he had built for the LORD. He also burned incense[d] before the LORD. So he finished the work on the Temple.

26King Solomon also built ships at Ezion Geber, a town near Elath on the shore of the Red Sea, in the land of Edom. 27Hiram had skilled sailors, so he sent them to serve in these ships with Solomon's men. 28The ships sailed to Ophir and brought back about thirty-two thousand pounds of gold to King Solomon.

The Queen of Sheba Visits Solomon

10 When the queen of Sheba heard about Solomon, she came to test him with hard questions. 2She traveled to Jerusalem with a large group of servants and camels carrying spices, jewels, and much gold. When she came to Solomon, she talked with him about all she had in mind, 3and Solomon answered all her questions. Nothing was too hard for him to explain to her. 4The queen of Sheba learned that Solomon was very wise. She saw the palace he had built, 5the food

Cabul This name sounds like the Hebrew word for "worthless."

on his table, his many officers, the palace servants, and their good clothes. She saw the servants who served him at feasts and the whole burnt offerings he made in the Temple[d] of the LORD. All these things amazed her.

6So she said to King Solomon, "What I heard in my own country about your achievements and wisdom is true. 7I could not believe it then, but now I have come and seen it with my own eyes. I was not told even half of it! Your wisdom and wealth are much greater than I had heard. 8Your men and officers are very lucky, because in always serving you, they are able to hear your wisdom. 9Praise the LORD your God, who was pleased to make you king of Israel. The LORD has constant love for Israel, so he made you king to keep justice and to rule fairly."

10Then she gave the king about nine thousand pounds of gold and many spices and jewels. No one since that time has brought more spices than the queen of Sheba gave to King Solomon.

11(Hiram's ships brought gold from Ophir, as well as much juniper wood and jewels. 12Solomon used the juniper wood to build supports for the Temple of the LORD and the palace, and to make harps and lyres[d] for the musicians. Such fine juniper wood has not been brought in or been seen since that time.)

13King Solomon gave the queen of Sheba everything she wanted and asked for, in addition to what he had already given her of his wealth. Then she and her servants returned to her own country.

Solomon's Wealth

14Every year King Solomon received about fifty thousand pounds of gold. 15Besides that, he also received gold from the traders and merchants, as well as from the kings of Arabia and governors of the land.

16King Solomon made two hundred large shields of hammered gold, each of which contained about seven and one-half pounds of gold. 17He also made three hundred smaller shields of hammered gold, each of which contained about four pounds of gold. The king put them in the Palace of the Forest of Lebanon.

18The king built a large throne of ivory and covered it with fine gold. 19The throne had six steps on it, and its back was round at the top. There were armrests on both sides of the chair, and each armrest had a lion beside it. 20Twelve lions stood on the six steps, one lion at each end of each step. Nothing like this had ever been made for any other kingdom. 21All of Solomon's drinking cups, as well as the dishes in the Palace of the Forest of Lebanon, were made of pure gold. Nothing was made from silver, because silver was not valuable in Solomon's time.

22King Solomon also had many trading ships at sea, along with Hiram's ships. Every three years the ships returned, bringing back gold, silver, ivory, apes, and baboons.

23So Solomon had more riches and wisdom than all the other kings on earth. 24People everywhere wanted to see King Solomon and listen to the wisdom God had given him. 25Every year those who came brought gifts of silver and gold, clothes, weapons, spices, horses, and mules.

26Solomon had fourteen hundred chariots and twelve thousand horses. He kept some in special cities for the chariots, and others he kept with him in Jerusalem. 27In Jerusalem Solomon made silver as common as stones and cedar trees as common as the fig trees on the western hills. 28He imported horses from Egypt and Kue. His traders bought them in Kue. 29A chariot from Egypt cost about fifteen pounds of silver, and a horse cost nearly four pounds of silver. Solomon's traders also sold horses and chariots to all the kings of the Hittites and the Arameans.

Solomon's Many Wives

11 King Solomon loved many women who were not from Israel. He loved the daughter of the king of Egypt, as well as women of the Moabites, Ammonites, Edomites, Sidonians, and Hittites. 2The LORD had told the Israelites, "You must not marry people of other nations. If you do, they will cause you to follow their gods." But Solomon fell in love with these women. 3He had seven hundred wives who were from royal families and three hundred slave women[d] who gave birth to his children. His wives caused him to turn away from God. 4As Solomon grew old, his wives caused him to follow other gods. He did not follow the LORD completely as his father David had done. 5Solomon worshiped Ashtoreth,[d] the goddess of the people of Sidon, and Molech,[d] the hated god of the Ammonites. 6So Solomon did what the LORD said was wrong and did not follow the LORD completely as his father David had done.

7On a hill east of Jerusalem, Solomon built two places for worship. One was a place to worship Chemosh,[d] the hated god of the Moabites, and the other was a place to worship Molech, the hated god of the Ammonites. 8Solomon did the same thing for all his foreign wives so they could burn incense[d] and offer sacrifices to their gods.

9The LORD had appeared to Solomon twice, but the king turned away from following the LORD, the God of Israel. The LORD was angry with Solomon, 10because he had commanded Solomon not to follow other gods. But Solomon did not obey the LORD's command. 11So the LORD said to Solomon, "Because you have chosen to break your agreement with me and have not obeyed my com-

mands, I will tear your kingdom away from you
and give it to one of your officers. 12But I will not
take it away while you are alive because of my
love for your father David. I will tear it away from
your son when he becomes king. 13I will not tear
away all the kingdom from him, but I will leave
him one tribe[d] to rule. I will do this because of
David, my servant, and because of Jerusalem, the
city I have chosen."

Solomon's Enemies

14The LORD caused Hadad the Edomite, a
member of the family of the king of Edom, to become Solomon's enemy. 15Earlier, David had defeated Edom. When Joab, the commander of David's army, went into Edom to bury the dead, he
killed all the males. 16Joab and all the Israelites
stayed in Edom for six months and killed every
male in Edom. 17At that time Hadad was only a
young boy, so he ran away to Egypt with some of
his father's officers. 18They left Midian and went
to Paran, where they were joined by other men.
Then they all went to Egypt to see the king, who
gave Hadad a house, some food, and some land.
19The king liked Hadad so much he gave Hadad
a wife—the sister of Tahpenes, the king's wife.
20They had a son named Genubath. Queen Tahpenes brought him up in the royal palace with the
king's own children.
21While he was in Egypt, Hadad heard that David had died and that Joab, the commander of the
army, was dead also. So Hadad said to the king,
"Let me go; I will return to my own country."
22"Why do you want to go back to your own
country?" the king asked. "What haven't I given
you here?"
"Nothing," Hadad answered, "but please, let
me go."
23God also caused another man to be Solomon's enemy—Rezon son of Eliada. Rezon had
run away from his master, Hadadezer king of Zobah. 24After David defeated the army of Zobah,
Rezon gathered some men and became the leader
of a small army. They went to Damascus and settled there, and Rezon became king of Damascus.
25Rezon ruled Aram, and he hated Israel. So he
was an enemy of Israel all the time Solomon was
alive. Both Rezon and Hadad made trouble for
Israel.
26Jeroboam son of Nebat was one of Solomon's
officers. He was an Ephraimite from the town of
Zeredah, and he was the son of a widow named
Zeruah. Jeroboam turned against the king.
27This is the story of how Jeroboam turned
against the king. Solomon was filling in the land
and repairing the wall of Jerusalem, the city of
David, his father. 28Jeroboam was a capable man,
and Solomon saw that this young man was a good
worker. So Solomon put him over all the workers
from the tribes[d] of Ephraim and Manasseh.
29One day as Jeroboam was leaving Jerusalem,
Ahijah, the prophet[d] from Shiloh, who was wearing a new coat, met him on the road. The two
men were alone out in the country. 30Ahijah took
his new coat and tore it into twelve pieces. 31Then
he said to Jeroboam, "Take ten pieces of this coat
for yourself. The LORD, the God of Israel, says: 'I
will tear the kingdom away from Solomon and
give you ten tribes. 32But I will allow him to control one tribe. I will do this for the sake of my
servant David and for Jerusalem, the city I have
chosen from all the tribes of Israel. 33I will do this
because Solomon has stopped following me and
has worshiped the Sidonian god Ashtoreth,[d] the
Moabite god Chemosh,[d] and the Ammonite god
Molech. Solomon has not obeyed me by doing
what I said is right and obeying my laws and commands, as his father David did.
34" 'But I will not take all the kingdom away
from Solomon. I will let him rule all his life because of my servant David, whom I chose, who
obeyed all my commands and laws. 35But I will
take the kingdom away from his son, and I will
allow you to rule over the ten tribes. 36I will allow
Solomon's son to continue to rule over one tribe
so that there will always be a descendant of David, my servant, in Jerusalem, the city where I
chose to be worshiped. 37But I will make you rule
over everything you want. You will rule over all
of Israel, 38and I will always be with you if you do
what I say is right. You must obey all my commands. If you obey my laws and commands as
David did, I will be with you. I will make your
family a lasting family of kings, as I did for David,
and give Israel to you. 39I will punish David's children because of this, but I will not punish them
forever.' "

Solomon's Death

40Solomon tried to kill Jeroboam, but he ran
away to Egypt, to Shishak king of Egypt, where he
stayed until Solomon died.
41Everything else King Solomon did, and the
wisdom he showed, is written in the book of the
history of Solomon. 42Solomon ruled in Jerusalem
over all Israel for forty years. 43Then he died and
was buried in Jerusalem, the city of David, his
father. And his son Rehoboam became king in his
place.

Israel Turns Against Rehoboam

12 Rehoboam went to Shechem, where all
the Israelites had gone to make him
king. 2Jeroboam son of Nebat was still in Egypt,
where he had gone to escape from Solomon.
When Jeroboam heard about Rehoboam being
made king, he was living in Egypt. 3After the peo-

ple sent for him, he and the people went to Rehoboam and said to him, 4“Your father forced us to work very hard. Now, make it easier for us, and don’t make us work as hard as he did. Then we will serve you.”

5Rehoboam answered, “Go away for three days, and then come back to me.” So the people left.

6King Rehoboam asked the older leaders who had advised Solomon during his lifetime, “How do you think I should answer these people?”

7They said, “You should be like a servant to them today. If you serve them and give them a kind answer, they will serve you always.”

8But Rehoboam rejected this advice. Instead, he asked the young men who had grown up with him and who served as his advisers. 9Rehoboam asked them, “What is your advice? How should we answer these people who said, ‘Don’t make us work as hard as your father did’?”

10The young men who had grown up with him answered, “Those people said to you, ‘Your father forced us to work very hard. Now make our work easier.’ You should tell them, ‘My little finger is bigger than my father’s legs. 11He forced you to work hard, but I will make you work even harder. My father beat you with whips, but I will beat you with whips that have sharp points.’ ”

12Rehoboam had told the people, “Come back to me in three days.” So after three days Jeroboam and all the people returned to Rehoboam. 13King Rehoboam spoke cruel words to them, because he had rejected the advice the older leaders had given him. 14He followed the advice of the young men and said to the people, “My father forced you to work hard, but I will make you work even harder. My father beat you with whips, but I will beat you with whips that have sharp points.” 15So the king did not listen to the people. The LORD caused this to happen to keep the promise he had made to Jeroboam son of Nebat through Ahijah, a prophet[d] from Shiloh.

16When all the Israelites saw that the new king refused to listen to them, they said to the king,

“We have no share in David!
  We have no part in the son of Jesse!
People of Israel, let’s go to our own homes!
  Let David’s son rule his own people!”

So the Israelites went home. 17But Rehoboam still ruled over the Israelites who lived in the towns of Judah.

18Adoniram was in charge of the forced labor. When Rehoboam sent him to the people of Israel, they threw stones at him until he died. But King Rehoboam ran to his chariot and escaped to Jerusalem. 19Since then, Israel has been against the family of David.

20When all the Israelites heard that Jeroboam had returned, they called him to a meeting and made him king over all Israel. Only the tribe[d] of Judah continued to follow the family of David.

21When Rehoboam arrived in Jerusalem, he gathered one hundred eighty thousand of the best soldiers from the tribes of Judah and Benjamin. As son of Solomon, Rehoboam wanted to fight the people of Israel to take back his kingdom.

SIDELIGHT: When the kingdom was divided (1 Kings 12:16–19), Israel (the northern kingdom) was stronger economically, had more people, controlled major roads, and possessed the best land. Judah was smaller and had fewer resources. Yet Judah survived about one hundred fifty years longer than Israel. It didn’t face as many attacks from hostile nations, and more of the kings followed God’s leadership.

22But God spoke his word to Shemaiah, a man of God, saying, 23“Speak to Solomon’s son Rehoboam, the king of Judah, and to all the people of Judah and Benjamin and the rest of the people. Say to them, 24‘The LORD says you must not go to war against your brothers, the Israelites. Every one of you should go home, because I made all these things happen.’ ” So they obeyed the LORD’s command and went home as the LORD had commanded.

25Then Jeroboam made Shechem in the mountains of Ephraim a very strong city, and he lived there. He also went to the city of Peniel and made it stronger.

Jeroboam Builds Golden Calves

26Jeroboam said to himself, “The kingdom will probably go back to David’s family. 27If the people continue going to the Temple[d] of the LORD in Jerusalem to offer sacrifices, they will want to be ruled again by Rehoboam. Then they will kill me and follow Rehoboam king of Judah.”

28King Jeroboam asked for advice. Then he made two golden calves. “It is too long a journey for you to go to Jerusalem to worship,” he said to the people. “Israel, here are your gods who brought you out of Egypt.” 29Jeroboam put one golden calf in the city of Bethel and the other in the city of Dan. 30This became a very great sin, because the people traveled as far as Dan to worship the calf there.

31Jeroboam built temples on the places of worship. He also chose priests from all the people, not just from the tribe[d] of Levi. 32And he started a new festival on the fifteenth day of the eighth month, just like the festival in Judah. During that time the king offered sacrifices on the altar, along with sacrifices to the calves in Bethel he had made. He also chose priests in Bethel to serve at the places of worship he had made. 33So Jeroboam chose his own time for a festival for the Israelites—the fifteenth day of the eighth month. During that time he offered sacrifices on the altar he had built in Bethel. He set up a festival for the Israelites and offered sacrifices on the altar.

The Man of God Speaks Against Bethel

13 The LORD commanded a man of God from Judah to go to Bethel. When he arrived, Jeroboam was standing by the altar to offer a sacrifice. 2The LORD had commanded the man of God to speak against the altar. The man said, "Altar, altar, the LORD says to you: 'David's family will have a son named Josiah. The priests for the places of worship now make their sacrifices on you, but Josiah will sacrifice those priests on you. Human bones will be burned on you.' " 3That same day the man of God gave proof that these things would happen. "This is the LORD's sign that this will happen," he said. "This altar will break apart, and the ashes on it will fall to the ground."

4When King Jeroboam heard what the man of God said about the altar in Bethel, the king raised his hand from the altar and pointed at the man. "Take him!" he said. But when the king said this, his arm was paralyzed, and he could not move it. 5The altar also broke into pieces, and its ashes fell to the ground. This was the sign the LORD had told the man of God to give.

6Then the king said to the man of God, "Please pray to the LORD your God for me, and ask him to heal my arm."

So the man of God prayed to the LORD, and the king's arm was healed, becoming as it was before.

7Then the king said to the man of God, "Please come home and eat with me, and I will give you a gift."

8But the man of God answered the king, "Even if you gave me half of your kingdom, I would not go with you. I will not eat or drink anything in this place. 9The LORD commanded me not to eat or drink anything nor to return on the same road by which I came." 10So he took a different road and did not return on the same road by which he had come to Bethel.

11Now an old prophet[d] was living in Bethel. His sons came and told him what the man of God had done there that day. They also told their father what he had said to King Jeroboam. 12The father asked, "Which road did he use when he left?" So his sons showed him the road the man of God from Judah had taken. 13Then the prophet told his sons to put a saddle on his donkey. So they saddled the donkey, and he left.

14He went after the man of God and found him sitting under an oak tree. The prophet asked, "Are you the man of God who came from Judah?"

The man answered, "Yes, I am."

15The prophet said, "Please come home and eat with me."

16"I can't go home with you," the man of God answered. "I can't eat or drink with you in this place. 17The LORD said to me, 'Don't eat or drink anything there or return on the same road by which you came.' "

18Then the old prophet said, "But I also am a prophet like you." Then he told a lie. He said, "An angel from the LORD came to me and told me to bring you to my home. He said you should eat and drink with me." 19So the man of God went to the old prophet's house, and he ate and drank with him there.

20While they were sitting at the table, the LORD spoke his word to the old prophet. 21The old prophet cried out to the man of God from Judah, "The LORD said you did not obey him! He said you did not do what the LORD your God commanded you. 22The LORD commanded you not to eat or drink anything in this place, but you came back and ate and drank. So your body will not be buried in your family grave."

23After the man of God finished eating and drinking, the prophet put a saddle on his donkey for him, and the man left. 24As he was traveling home, a lion attacked and killed him. His body lay on the road, with the donkey and the lion standing nearby. 25Some men who were traveling on that road saw the body and the lion standing nearby. So they went to the city where the old prophet lived and told what they had seen.

26The old prophet who had brought back the man of God heard what had happened. "It is the man of God who did not obey the LORD's command," he said. "So the LORD sent a lion to kill him, just as he said he would."

27Then the prophet said to his sons, "Put a saddle on my donkey," which they did. 28The old prophet went out and found the body lying on the road, with the donkey and the lion still standing nearby. The lion had not eaten the body or hurt the donkey. 29The prophet put the body on his donkey and carried it back to the city to have a time of sadness for him and to bury him. 30The prophet buried the body in his own family grave, and they were sad for the man of God and said, "Oh, my brother."

31After the prophet buried the body, he said to his sons, "When I die, bury me in this same grave. Put my bones next to his. 32Through him the LORD spoke against the altar at Bethel and against the places of worship in the towns of Samaria. What the LORD spoke through him will certainly come true."

33After this incident King Jeroboam did not stop

doing evil. He continued to choose priests for the places of worship from among all the people. Anyone who wanted to be a priest for the places of worship was allowed to be one. [34]In this way the family of Jeroboam sinned, and this sin caused its ruin and destruction from the earth.

Jeroboam's Son Dies

14 At that time Jeroboam's son Abijah became very sick. [2]So Jeroboam said to his wife, "Go to Shiloh to see the prophet[d] Ahijah. He is the one who said I would become king of Israel. But dress yourself so people won't know you are my wife. [3]Take the prophet ten loaves of bread, some cakes, and a jar of honey. Then ask him what will happen to our son, and he will tell you." [4]So the king's wife did as he said and went to Ahijah's home in Shiloh.

Now Ahijah was very old and blind. [5]The LORD said to him, "Jeroboam's son is sick, and Jeroboam's wife is coming to ask you about him. When she arrives, she will pretend to be someone else." Then the LORD told Ahijah what to say.

[6]When Ahijah heard her walking to the door, he said, "Come in, wife of Jeroboam. Why are you pretending to be someone else? I have bad news for you. [7]Go back and tell Jeroboam that this is what the LORD, the God of Israel, says: 'Jeroboam, I chose you from among all the people and made you the leader of my people Israel. [8]I tore the kingdom away from David's family, and I gave it to you. But you are not like my servant David, who always obeyed my commands and followed me with all his heart. He did only what I said was right. [9]But you have done more evil than anyone who ruled before you. You have quit following me and have made other gods and idols of metal. This has made me very angry, [10]so I will soon bring disaster to your family. I will kill all the men in your family, both slaves and free men. I will destroy your family as completely as fire burns up manure. [11]Anyone from your family who dies in the city will be eaten by dogs, and those who die in the fields will be eaten by the birds. The LORD has spoken.' "

[12]Then Ahijah said to Jeroboam's wife, "Go home now. As soon as you enter your city, your son will die, [13]and all Israel will be sad for him and bury him. He is the only one of Jeroboam's family who will be buried, because he is the only one in the king's family who pleased the LORD, the God of Israel.

[14]"The LORD will put a new king over Israel, who will destroy Jeroboam's family, and this will happen soon. [15]Then the LORD will punish Israel, which will be like grass moving in the water. The LORD will pull up Israel from this good land, the land he gave their ancestors. He will scatter Israel beyond the Euphrates River, because he is angry with the people. They made the LORD angry when they set up idols to worship Asherah.[d] [16]Jeroboam sinned, and then he made the people of Israel sin. So the LORD will let the people of Israel be defeated."

[17]Then Jeroboam's wife left and returned to Tirzah. As soon as she entered her home, the boy died. [18]After they buried him, all Israel had a time of sadness for him, just as the LORD had said through his servant, the prophet Ahijah.

[19]Everything else Jeroboam did is written in the book of the history of the kings of Israel. He fought wars and continued to rule the people, [20]serving as king for twenty-two years. Then he died, and his son Nadab became king in his place.

The Death of Rehoboam

[21]Solomon's son Rehoboam was forty-one years old when he became king of Judah. His mother was Naamah from Ammon. Rehoboam ruled in Jerusalem for seventeen years. (The LORD had chosen that city from all the land of Israel as the place where he would be worshiped.)

[22]The people of Judah did what the LORD said was wrong. Their sins made the LORD very angry, even more angry than he had been at their ancestors. [23]The people built stone pillars and places to worship gods and Asherah[d] idols on every high hill and under every green tree. [24]There were even male prostitutes[d] in the land. They acted like the people who had lived in the land before the Israelites. They had done many evil things, and God had taken the land away from them.

[25]During the fifth year Rehoboam was king, Shishak king of Egypt attacked Jerusalem. [26]He took the treasures from the Temple[d] of the LORD and the king's palace. He took everything, even the gold shields Solomon had made. [27]So King Rehoboam made bronze shields to put in their place and gave them to the commanders of the guards for the palace gates. [28]Whenever the king went to the Temple of the LORD, the guards carried the shields. Later, they would put them back in the guardroom.

[29]Everything else King Rehoboam did is written in the book of the history of the kings of Judah. [30]There was war between Rehoboam and Jeroboam the whole time. [31]Rehoboam, son of Naamah from Ammon, died and was buried with his ancestors in Jerusalem, and his son Abijah became king in his place.

Abijah King of Judah

15 Abijah became king of Judah during the eighteenth year Jeroboam son of Nebat was king of Israel. [2]Abijah ruled in Jerusalem for three years. His mother was Maacah daughter of Abishalom. [3]He did all the same sins his father before him had done. Abijah was not faithful to

the LORD his God as David, his great-grandfather,
had been. 4Because the LORD loved David, the
LORD gave him a kingdom in Jerusalem and allowed him to have a son to be king after him. The
LORD also kept Jerusalem safe. 5David always did
what the LORD said was right and obeyed his commands all his life, except the one time when David sinned against Uriah the Hittite.

6There was war between Abijah and Jeroboam
during Abijah's lifetime. 7Everything else Abijah
did is written in the book of the history of the
kings of Judah. During the time Abijah ruled,
there was war between Abijah and Jeroboam.
8Abijah died and was buried in Jerusalem, and his
son Asa became king in his place.

Asa King of Judah

9During the twentieth year Jeroboam was king
of Israel, Asa became king of Judah. 10His grandmother's name was Maacah, the daughter of
Abishalom. Asa ruled in Jerusalem for forty-one
years.

11Asa did what the LORD said was right, as his
ancestor David had done. 12He forced the male
prostitutes[d] at the worship places to leave the
country. He also took away the idols that his ancestors had made. 13His grandmother Maacah had
made a terrible Asherah[d] idol, so Asa removed her
from being queen mother. He cut down that idol
and burned it in the Kidron Valley. 14The places
of worship to gods were not removed. Even so,
Asa was faithful to the LORD all his life. 15Asa
brought into the Temple[d] of the LORD the gifts he
and his father had given: gold, silver, and utensils.

16There was war between Asa and Baasha king
of Israel all the time they were kings. 17Baasha
attacked Judah, and he made the town of Ramah
strong so he could keep people from leaving or
entering Judah, Asa's country.

18Asa took the rest of the silver and gold from
the treasuries of the Temple of the LORD and his
own palace and gave it to his officers. Then he
sent them to Ben-Hadad son of Tabrimmon, who
was the son of Hezion. Ben-Hadad was the king
of Aram and ruled in the city of Damascus. Asa
said, 19"Let there be a treaty between you and me
as there was between my father and your father.
I am sending you a gift of silver and gold. Break
your treaty with Baasha king of Israel so he will
leave my land."

20Ben-Hadad agreed with King Asa, so he sent
the commanders of his armies to attack the towns
of Israel. They defeated the towns of Ijon, Dan,
and Abel Beth Maacah, as well as all Galilee and
the area of Naphtali. 21When Baasha heard about
these attacks, he stopped building up Ramah and
returned to Tirzah. 22Then King Asa gave an order
to all the people of Judah; everyone had to help.
They carried away all the stones and wood Baasha
had been using in Ramah, and they used them to
build up Geba and Mizpah in the land of Benjamin.

23Everything else Asa did—his victories and
the cities he built—is written in the book of the
history of the kings of Judah. When he became
old, he got a disease in his feet. 24After Asa died,
he was buried with his ancestors in Jerusalem, the
city of David, his ancestor. Then Jehoshaphat,
Asa's son, became king in his place.

Nadab King of Israel

25Nadab son of Jeroboam became king of Israel
during the second year Asa was king of Judah.
Nadab was king of Israel for two years, 26and he
did what the LORD said was wrong. Jeroboam had
led the people of Israel to sin, and Nadab sinned
in the same way as his father Jeroboam.

27Baasha son of Ahijah, from the tribe[d] of Issachar, made plans to kill Nadab. Nadab and all
Israel were attacking the Philistine town of
Gibbethon, so Baasha killed Nadab there. 28This
happened during Asa's third year as king of Judah,
and Baasha became the next king of Israel.

Baasha King of Israel

29As soon as Baasha became king, he killed all
of Jeroboam's family, leaving no one in Jeroboam's family alive. He destroyed them all as the
LORD had said would happen through his servant
Ahijah from Shiloh. 30King Jeroboam had sinned
very much and had led the people of Israel to sin,
so he made the LORD, the God of Israel, very angry.

31Everything else Nadab did is written in the
book of the history of the kings of Israel. 32There
was war between Asa king of Judah and Baasha
king of Israel all the time they ruled.

33Baasha son of Ahijah became king of Israel
during Asa's third year as king of Judah. Baasha
ruled in Tirzah for twenty-four years, 34and he did
what the LORD said was wrong. Jeroboam had led
the people of Israel to sin, and Baasha sinned in
the same way as Jeroboam.

16 Jehu son of Hanani spoke the word of
the LORD against King Baasha. 2The
LORD said, "You were nothing, but I took you and
made you a leader over my people Israel. But you
have followed the ways of Jeroboam and have led
my people Israel to sin. Their sins have made me
angry, 3so, Baasha, I will soon destroy you and
your family. I will do to you what I did to the
family of Jeroboam son of Nebat. 4Anyone from
your family who dies in the city will be eaten by
dogs, and anyone from your family who dies in
the fields will be eaten by birds."

5Everything else Baasha did and all his victories
are written down in the book of the history of the
kings of Israel. 6So Baasha died and was buried

in Tirzah, and his son Elah became king in his place.

7The LORD spoke his word against Baasha and his family through the prophet[d] Jehu son of Hanani. Baasha had done many things the LORD said were wrong, which made the LORD very angry. He did the same evil deeds that Jeroboam's family had done before him. The LORD also spoke against Baasha because he killed all of Jeroboam's family.

Elah King of Israel

8Elah son of Baasha became king of Israel during Asa's twenty-sixth year as king of Judah, and Elah ruled in Tirzah for two years.

9Zimri, one of Elah's officers, commanded half of Elah's chariots. Zimri made plans against Elah while the king was in Tirzah, getting drunk at Arza's home. (Arza was in charge of the palace at Tirzah.) 10Zimri went into Arza's house and killed Elah during Asa's twenty-seventh year as king of Judah. Then Zimri became king of Israel in Elah's place.

Zimri King of Israel

11As soon as Zimri became king, he killed all of Baasha's family, not allowing any of Baasha's family or friends to live. 12So Zimri destroyed all of Baasha's family just as the LORD had said it would happen through the prophet[d] Jehu. 13Baasha and his son Elah sinned and led the people of Israel to sin, and they made the LORD, the God of Israel, angry because of their worthless idols.

14Everything else Elah did is written in the book of the history of the kings of Israel.

15So during Asa's twenty-seventh year as king of Judah, Zimri became king of Israel and ruled in Tirzah seven days.

The army of Israel was camped near Gibbethon, a Philistine town. 16The men in the camp heard that Zimri had made secret plans against King Elah and had killed him. So that day in the camp they made Omri, the commander of the army, king over Israel. 17So Omri and all the Israelite army left Gibbethon and attacked Tirzah. 18When Zimri saw that the city had been captured, he went into the palace and set it on fire, burning the palace and himself with it. 19So Zimri died because he had sinned by doing what the LORD said was wrong. Jeroboam had led the people of Israel to sin, and Zimri sinned in the same way as Jeroboam.

20Everything else Zimri did and the story of how he turned against King Elah are written down in the book of the history of the kings of Israel.

Omri King of Israel

21The people of Israel were divided into two groups. Half of the people wanted Tibni son of Ginath to be king, while the other half wanted Omri. 22Omri's followers were stronger than the followers of Tibni son of Ginath, so Tibni died, and Omri became king.

23Omri became king of Israel during the thirty-first year Asa was king of Judah. Omri ruled Israel for twelve years, six of those years in the city of Tirzah. 24He bought the hill of Samaria from Shemer for about one hundred fifty pounds of silver. Omri built a city on that hill and called it Samaria after the name of its earlier owner, Shemer.

25But Omri did what the LORD said was wrong; he did more evil than all the kings who came before him. 26Jeroboam son of Nebat had led the people of Israel to sin, and Omri sinned in the same way as Jeroboam. The Israelites made the LORD, the God of Israel, very angry because they worshiped worthless idols.

27Everything else Omri did and all his successes are written in the book of the history of the kings of Israel. 28So Omri died and was buried in Samaria, and his son Ahab became king in his place.

> **SIDELIGHT:** King Omri doesn't get much press in the Bible (1 Kings 16:23–28), but he probably was one of the most powerful leaders of the northern kingdom. According to other sources, he established a strong rule and conquered the Moabites, long-term enemies. But, the Bible says, "he did more evil than all the kings who came before him."

Ahab King of Israel

29Ahab son of Omri became king of Israel during Asa's thirty-eighth year as king of Judah, and Ahab ruled Israel in the city of Samaria for twenty-two years. 30More than any king before him, Ahab son of Omri did many things the LORD said were wrong. 31He sinned in the same ways as Jeroboam son of Nebat, but he did even worse things. He married Jezebel daughter of Ethbaal, the king of Sidon. Then Ahab began to serve Baal[d] and worship him. 32He built a temple in Samaria for worshiping Baal and put an altar there for Baal. 33Ahab also made an idol for worshiping Asherah.[d] He did more things to make the LORD, the God of Israel, angry than all the other kings before him.

34During the time of Ahab, Hiel from Bethel rebuilt the city of Jericho. It cost Hiel the life of Abiram, his oldest son, to begin work on the city, and it cost the life of Segub, his youngest son, to build the city gates. This happened just as the

LORD, speaking through Joshua son of Nun, said
it would happen.[n]

Elijah Stops the Rain

17 Now Elijah the Tishbite was a prophet[d]
from the settlers in Gilead. "I serve the
LORD, the God of Israel," Elijah said to Ahab. "As
surely as the LORD lives, no rain or dew will fall
during the next few years unless I command it."
2Then the LORD spoke his word to Elijah:
3"Leave this place and go east and hide near Kerith Ravine east of the Jordan River. 4You may
drink from the stream, and I have commanded
ravens to bring you food there." 5So Elijah did
what the LORD said; he went to Kerith Ravine,
east of the Jordan, and lived there. 6The birds
brought Elijah bread and meat every morning
and evening, and he drank water from the
stream.
7After a while the stream dried up because
there was no rain. 8Then the LORD spoke his word
to Elijah, 9"Go to Zarephath in Sidon and live
there. I have commanded a widow there to take
care of you."
10So Elijah went to Zarephath. When he
reached the town gate, he saw a widow gathering
wood for a fire. Elijah asked her, "Would you
bring me a little water in a cup so I may have a
drink." 11As she was going to get his water, Elijah
said, "Please bring me a piece of bread, too."
12The woman answered, "As surely as the
LORD your God lives, I have no bread. I have only
a handful of flour in a jar and only a little olive oil
in a jug. I came here to gather some wood so I

the LORD . . . happen When Joshua destroyed Jericho, he said whoever rebuilt the city would lose his oldest and youngest sons. See Joshua 6:26.

HUNGER AND POVERTY

Letting God Use You

Jon Ralston went to help at the Rescue Mission mostly because someone asked him to go. He had never done anything like this in all of his fifteen years. But a friend asked him to help out this Sunday, and Jon couldn't think of any reason not to. So he went.

When they got there, Jon and his friends did simple tasks—preparing food, setting places, washing dishes, cleaning tables. "We just helped where we were needed," he says.

The Rescue Mission was run-down and dirty, Jon recalls. The people they served were dirty from the streets, and they didn't seem to appreciate what Jon and his friends were doing for them. Some of Jon's friends really didn't like it and didn't go back when they were asked to help out again.

But Jon went back. And he would go again.

"I'm needed there," he says. "And it's fun to give to people when you know they can't pay you back."

Jon was impressed with the staff at the Rescue Mission, too. They had a good attitude toward the people they served. "Even though the staff acts tough," Jon recalls, "they really care for the people who come there."

There's been hunger and poverty in the world almost since the beginning of time. God wants Christians—every Christian—to offer help and God's love to the poor and hungry. God even used the great prophet Elijah to help a widow and her son in **1 Kings 17:8–16**.

- What's the difference between the widow in this passage and the people Jon helped? What motives did Jon have for helping the poor? What motives did Elijah have for helping the widow?
- How does God keep the "jars of flour and jugs of oil" full for poor and hungry people today? What role can you play in providing food for hungry people?

CONSIDER . . .

- skipping dinner tonight and spending that time praying for poor and hungry people.
- following Jon's example by volunteering to work in a soup kitchen or a homeless shelter.

FOR MORE, SEE . . .

- Exodus 16:1–15 (p. 73)
- Mark 6:34–44 (p. 974)
- John 6:30–35 (p. 1067)

could go home and cook our last meal. My son
and I will eat it and then die from hunger."
13"Don't worry," Elijah said to her. "Go home
and cook your food as you have said. But first
make a small loaf of bread from the flour you
have, and bring it to me. Then cook something for
yourself and your son. 14The LORD, the God of
Israel, says, 'That jar of flour will never be empty,
and the jug will always have oil in it, until the day
the LORD sends rain to the land.' "
15So the woman went home and did what Elijah told her to do. And the woman and her son
and Elijah had enough food every day. 16The jar
of flour and the jug of oil were never empty, just
as the LORD, through Elijah, had promised.

Elijah Brings a Boy Back to Life

17Some time later the son of the woman who
owned the house became sick. He grew worse
and worse and finally stopped breathing. 18The
woman said to Elijah, "Man of God, what have
you done to me? Did you come here to remind
me of my sin and to kill my son?"
19Elijah said to her, "Give me your son." Elijah
took the boy from her, carried him upstairs, and
laid him on the bed in the room where he was
staying. 20Then he prayed to the LORD: "LORD my
God, this widow is letting me stay in her house.
Why have you done this terrible thing to her and
caused her son to die?" 21Then Elijah lay on top
of the boy three times. He prayed to the LORD,
"LORD my God, let this boy live again!"
22The LORD answered Elijah's prayer; the boy
began breathing again and was alive. 23Elijah carried the boy downstairs and gave him to his
mother and said, "See! Your son is alive!"
24"Now I know you really are a man from
God," the woman said to Elijah. "I know that the
LORD truly speaks through you!"

Elijah Kills the Prophets of Baal

18 During the third year without rain, the
LORD spoke his word to Elijah: "Go and
meet King Ahab, and I will soon send rain." 2So
Elijah went to meet Ahab.
By this time there was no food in Samaria.
3King Ahab sent for Obadiah, who was in charge
of the king's palace. (Obadiah was a true follower
of the LORD. 4When Jezebel was killing all the
LORD's prophets,[d] Obadiah hid a hundred of them
in two caves, fifty in one cave and fifty in another.
He also brought them food and water.) 5Ahab said

SIN

What's the Connection?

"Oh, my back! Help, it hurts!"

When Jen Freeman hurt her back trying to push a car out of the snow, the doctor confined her to bed for a week. At the end of the week, Jen felt much better, so she went on a retreat she had signed up for two months earlier. Everything went fine until the third day, when Jen slipped on some ice. Then her back was worse than ever.

People helped Jen stand up and get around, and they brought things to her. Even more important, they prayed for her and comforted her. She began to talk about how difficult it was for her to rely on other people.

"I'm really independent," she said. "Relying on other people is hard for me, but here on the retreat, I have no choice. I can't even walk!"

God used Jen's injury to help her see how she was trying to isolate herself too much. Jen had to learn to rely on others.

In Old Testament times, most people believed illnesses were caused by sin. But that is not necessarily true. Read **1 Kings 17:17–24** to see how God used a boy's illness to show that Elijah was a man of God.

- What connection is there between illness and sin for Jen and for the woman in the passage?
- In what ways does God use illness, both in Bible times and today?

CONSIDER . . .

- praying that God will use your next illness as a time of spiritual healing or renewal.
- asking to visit a hospital with your pastor or a hospital chaplain so you can join in caring for the sick.

FOR MORE, SEE . . .

- Deuteronomy 28:15–24 (p. 184)
- John 9:1–7 (p. 1073)
- Acts 3:1–19 (p. 1100)

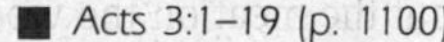

to Obadiah, "Let's check every spring and valley in the land. Maybe we can find enough grass to keep our horses and mules alive and not have to kill our animals." 6So each one chose a part of the country to search; Ahab went in one direction and Obadiah in another.

7While Obadiah was on his way, Elijah met him. Obadiah recognized Elijah, so he bowed down to the ground and said, "Elijah? Is it really you, master?"

8"Yes," Elijah answered. "Go tell your master that I am here."

9Then Obadiah said, "What wrong have I done for you to hand me over to Ahab like this? He will put me to death. 10As surely as the LORD your God lives, the king has sent people to every country to search for you. If the ruler said you were not there, Ahab forced the ruler to swear you could not be found in his country. 11Now you want me to go to my master and tell him, 'Elijah is here'? 12The Spirit[d] of the LORD may carry you to some other place after I leave. If I go tell King Ahab you are here, and he comes and doesn't find you, he will kill me! I have followed the LORD since I was a boy. 13Haven't you been told what I did? When Jezebel was killing the LORD's prophets, I hid a hundred of them, fifty in one cave and fifty in another. I brought them food and water. 14Now you want me to go and tell my master you are here? He will kill me!"

15Elijah answered, "As surely as the LORD All-Powerful lives, whom I serve, I will be seen by Ahab today."

16So Obadiah went to Ahab and told him where Elijah was. Then Ahab went to meet Elijah.

17When he saw Elijah, he asked, "Is it you—the biggest troublemaker in Israel?"

18Elijah answered, "I have not made trouble in Israel. You and your father's family have made all this trouble by not obeying the LORD's commands. You have gone after the Baals.[d] 19Now tell all Israel to meet me at Mount Carmel. Also bring the four hundred fifty prophets of Baal and the four hundred prophets of Asherah,[d] who eat at Jezebel's table."

20So Ahab called all the Israelites and those prophets to Mount Carmel. 21Elijah approached the people and said, "How long will you not decide between two choices? If the LORD is the true God, follow him, but if Baal is the true God, follow him!" But the people said nothing.

22Elijah said, "I am the only prophet of the LORD here, but there are four hundred fifty prophets of Baal. 23Bring two bulls. Let the prophets of Baal choose one bull and kill it and cut it into pieces. Then let them put the meat on the wood, but they are not to set fire to it. I will prepare the other bull, putting the meat on the wood but not setting fire to it. 24You prophets of Baal, pray to your god, and I will pray to the LORD. The god who answers by setting fire to his wood is the true God."

All the people agreed that this was a good idea.

SIDELIGHT: The four hundred fifty prophets of Baal had a home-court advantage in the contest against Elijah and God (1 Kings 18:20–46). Baal was considered the god of Mt. Carmel, and he was also the rain-giving god. When Elijah was the one who prayed and brought fire and ended the drought, the false prophets might have died of embarrassment if Elijah hadn't executed them first.

25Then Elijah said to the prophets of Baal, "There are many of you, so you go first. Choose a bull and prepare it. Pray to your god, but don't start the fire."

26So they took the bull that was given to them and prepared it. They prayed to Baal from morning until noon, shouting "Baal, answer us!" But there was no sound, and no one answered. They danced around the altar they had built.

27At noon Elijah began to make fun of them. "Pray louder!" he said. "If Baal really is a god, maybe he is thinking, or busy, or traveling! Maybe he is sleeping so you will have to wake him!" 28The prophets prayed louder, cutting themselves with swords and spears until their blood flowed, which was the way they worshiped. 29The afternoon passed, and the prophets continued to act like this until it was time for the evening sacrifice. But no voice was heard; Baal did not answer, and no one paid attention.

30Then Elijah said to all the people, "Now come to me." So they gathered around him, and Elijah rebuilt the altar of the LORD, which had been torn down. 31He took twelve stones, one stone for each of the twelve tribes,[d] the number of Jacob's sons. (The LORD changed Jacob's name to Israel.) 32Elijah used these stones to rebuild the altar in honor of the LORD. Then he dug a ditch around the altar that was big enough to hold about thirteen quarts of seed. 33Elijah put the wood on the altar, cut the bull into pieces, and laid the pieces on the wood. 34Then he said, "Fill four jars with water, and pour it on the meat and on the wood." Then Elijah said, "Do it again," and they did it again. Then he said, "Do it a third time," and they did it the third time. 35So the water ran off the altar and filled the ditch.

36At the time for the evening sacrifice, the prophet Elijah went near the altar. "LORD, you are the God of Abraham, Isaac, and Israel," he prayed. "Prove that you are the God of Israel and that I am your servant. Show these people that you commanded me to do all these things. 37LORD, answer my prayer so these people will know that you, LORD, are God and that you will change their minds."

38Then fire from the LORD came down and burned the sacrifice, the wood, the stones, and the ground around the altar. It also dried up the water in the ditch. 39When all the people saw this, they fell down to the ground, crying, "The LORD is God! The LORD is God!"

40Then Elijah said, "Capture the prophets of Baal! Don't let any of them run away!" The people captured all the prophets. Then Elijah led them down to the Kishon Valley, where he killed them.

The Rain Comes Again

41Then Elijah said to Ahab, "Now, go, eat, and drink, because a heavy rain is coming." 42So King Ahab went to eat and drink. At the same time Elijah climbed to the top of Mount Carmel, where he bent down to the ground with his head between his knees.

43Then Elijah said to his servant, "Go and look toward the sea."

The servant went and looked. "I see nothing," he said.

Elijah told him to go and look again. This happened seven times. 44The seventh time, the servant said, "I see a small cloud, the size of a human fist, coming from the sea."

Elijah told the servant, "Go to Ahab and tell him to get his chariot ready and go home now. Otherwise, the rain will stop him."

45After a short time the sky was covered with dark clouds. The wind began to blow, and soon a heavy rain began to fall. Ahab got in his chariot and started back to Jezreel. 46The LORD gave his power to Elijah, who tightened his clothes around him and ran ahead of King Ahab all the way to Jezreel.

> **SIDELIGHT:** For a short time, Elijah may have been the fastest runner in the world. Fearing the rain would start while he was on the mountain, Elijah received God's power and ran from Mt. Carmel to Jezreel—about ten miles—faster than the king's chariots (1 Kings 18:46). Some people will do anything to keep from getting their hair wet!

Elijah Runs Away

19 King Ahab told Jezebel everything Elijah had done and how Elijah had killed all the prophets[a] with a sword. 2So Jezebel sent a messenger to Elijah, saying, "May the gods punish me terribly if by this time tomorrow I don't kill you just as you killed those prophets."

3When Elijah heard this, he was afraid and ran for his life, taking his servant with him. When they came to Beersheba in Judah, Elijah left his servant there. 4Then Elijah walked for a whole day into the desert. He sat down under a bush and asked to die. "I have had enough, LORD," he prayed. "Let me die. I am no better than my ancestors." 5Then he lay down under the tree and slept.

Suddenly an angel came to him and touched him. "Get up and eat," the angel said. 6Elijah saw near his head a loaf baked over coals and a jar of water, so he ate and drank. Then he went back to sleep.

7Later the LORD's angel came to him a second time. The angel touched him and said, "Get up and eat. If you don't, the journey will be too hard for you." 8So Elijah got up and ate and drank. The food made him strong enough to walk for forty days and nights to Mount Sinai, the mountain of God. 9There Elijah went into a cave and stayed all night.

Then the LORD spoke his word to him: "Elijah! Why are you here?"

10He answered, "LORD God All-Powerful, I have always served you as well as I could. But the people of Israel have broken their agreement with you, destroyed your altars, and killed your prophets with swords. I am the only prophet left, and now they are trying to kill me, too."

11The LORD said to Elijah, "Go, stand in front of me on the mountain, and I will pass by you." Then a very strong wind blew until it caused the mountains to fall apart and large rocks to break in front of the LORD. But the LORD was not in the wind. After the wind, there was an earthquake, but the LORD was not in the earthquake. 12After the earthquake, there was a fire, but the LORD was not in the fire. After the fire, there was a quiet, gentle sound. 13When Elijah heard it, he covered his face with his coat and went out and stood at the entrance to the cave.

Then a voice said to him, "Elijah! Why are you here?"

14He answered, "LORD God All-Powerful, I have always served you as well as I could. But the people of Israel have broken their agreement with you, destroyed your altars, and killed your prophets with swords. I am the only prophet left, and now they are trying to kill me, too."

15The LORD said to him, "Go back on the road

that leads to the desert around Damascus. Enter
that city, and pour olive oil on Hazael to make
him king over Aram. 16Then pour oil on Jehu son
of Nimshi to make him king over Israel. Next,
pour oil on Elisha son of Shaphat from Abel Meholah to make him a prophet in your place. 17Jehu
will kill anyone who escapes from Hazael's
sword, and Elisha will kill anyone who escapes
from Jehu's sword. 18I have seven thousand people left in Israel who have never bowed down
before Baal[d] and whose mouths have never kissed
his idol."

Elisha Becomes a Prophet

19So Elijah left that place and found Elisha son
of Shaphat plowing a field with a team of oxen.
He owned twelve teams of oxen and was plowing with the twelfth team. Elijah came up to
Elisha, took off his coat, and put it on Elisha.
20Then Elisha left his oxen and ran to follow
Elijah. "Let me kiss my father and my mother
good-bye," Elisha said. "Then I will go with
you."

Elijah answered, "Go back. It does not matter
to me."

21So Elisha went back and took his pair of oxen
and killed them. He used their wooden yoke[d] for
a fire. Then he cooked the meat and gave it to the
people. After they ate it, Elisha left and followed
Elijah and became his helper.

LONELINESS

You Against the World

Cindy Barrington used to hang out with the popular crowd. That is, until one day on the school bus, when one of the guys got hold of a note that wasn't his. It belonged to Cindy's little sister Liz.

This guy decided to have some fun at Liz's expense. "Hey, listen to this everybody," Brad yelled. " 'Hey, Shannon, did you see that new guy at school yesterday? What a dream! We accidently bumped into each other in the hall, and he smiled at me. I almost died! I've got to find out his name. Signed, Liz.' "

"Hey, Liz," he added, "that was no 'accidental' bumping scene, now was it?" Everyone laughed. Liz shrunk in her seat.

As much as she wanted to go along with the popular crowd, Cindy couldn't let Brad hurt her sister like this.

"You know, I really pity you, Brad," Cindy said angrily. "I never knew you felt so bad about yourself that you'd stoop this low just for a laugh." Brad stopped laughing. "So why don't you just give me the note, Brad, and sit down. The real joke is on you."

The next day, the popular kids snubbed Cindy. They talked about her, loudly enough so she could hear, and they ignored her when she tried to talk. Cindy felt alone and lonely—all for standing up for what she believed was right.

Fortunately, her loneliness didn't last long. Soon, a few people told Cindy they were glad she stuck up for her sister. Before long, Cindy made new friends—kids she could be herself with. Cindy and Liz also grew closer together, and now they're better friends than ever.

After Elijah stood up for what he believed in and defeated the prophets of Baal, he thought he was alone against the world, too. But God showed Elijah there were other people on his side. Check out Elijah's conversation with God in **1 Kings 19:11–18**.

- How did God show Elijah that he was with him, even when the situation seemed overwhelming? How did God show Cindy he was with her too?
- How would you have reacted if you were in Elijah's place? Do you stand up for what is right, even when your beliefs go against the crowd? Why or why not?

CONSIDER . . .

- taking a walk alone in a park and looking for the quiet ways God reveals himself.
- reading this passage and the passages listed below the next time you feel lonely. Then write a letter to God that expresses your feelings.

FOR MORE, SEE . . .

- Psalm 13:1–6 (p. 488)
- Matthew 5:3–12 (p. 912)
- Romans 11:1–5 (p. 1155)

Ben-Hadad and Ahab Go to War

20 Ben-Hadad king of Aram gathered together all his army. There were thirty-two kings with their horses and chariots who went with him and surrounded Samaria and attacked it. 2The king sent messengers into the city to Ahab king of Israel.

This was his message: "Ben-Hadad says, 3'Your silver and gold belong to me, as well as the best of your wives and children.' "

4Ahab king of Israel answered, "My master and king, I agree to what you say. I and everything I have belong to you."

5Then the messengers came to Ahab again. They said, "Ben-Hadad says, 'I told you before that you must give me your silver and gold, your wives and your children. 6About this time tomorrow I will send my men, who will search everywhere in your palace and in the homes of your officers. Whatever they want they will take and carry off.' "

7Then Ahab called a meeting of all the older leaders of his country. He said, "Ben-Hadad is looking for trouble. First he said I had to give him my wives, my children, my silver, and my gold, and I have not refused him."

8The older leaders and all the people said, "Don't listen to him or agree to this."

9So Ahab said to Ben-Hadad's messengers, "Tell my master the king: 'I will do what you said at first, but I cannot allow this second command.' " And King Ben-Hadad's men carried the message back to him.

10Then Ben-Hadad sent another message to Ahab: "May the gods punish me terribly if I don't completely destroy Samaria. There won't be enough left for each of my men to get a handful of dust!"

11Ahab answered, "Tell Ben-Hadad, 'The man who puts on his armor should not brag. It's the man who lives to take it off who has the right to brag.' "

12Ben-Hadad was drinking in his tent with the other rulers when the message came from Ahab. Ben-Hadad commanded his men to prepare to attack the city, and they moved into place for battle.

13At the same time a prophet[d] came to Ahab king of Israel. The prophet said, "Ahab, the LORD says to you, 'Do you see that big army? I will hand it over to you today so you will know I am the LORD.' "

14Ahab asked, "Who will you use to defeat them?"

The prophet answered, "The LORD says, 'The young officers of the district governors will defeat them.' "

Then the king asked, "Who will command the main army?"

The prophet answered, "You will."

15So Ahab gathered the young officers of the district governors, two hundred thirty-two of them. Then he called together the army of Israel, about seven thousand people in all.

16They marched out at noon, while Ben-Hadad and the thirty-two rulers helping him were getting drunk in their tents. 17The young officers of the district governors attacked first. Ben-Hadad sent out scouts who told him that soldiers were coming from Samaria. 18Ben-Hadad said, "They may be coming to fight, or they may be coming to ask for peace. In either case capture them alive."

19The young officers of the district governors led the attack, followed by the army of Israel. 20Each officer of Israel killed the man who came against him. The men from Aram ran away as Israel chased them, but Ben-Hadad king of Aram escaped on a horse with some of his horsemen. 21Ahab king of Israel led the army and destroyed the Arameans' horses and chariots. King Ahab thoroughly defeated the Aramean army.

22Then the prophet went to Ahab king of Israel and said, "The king of Aram will attack you again next spring. So go home now and strengthen your army and see what you need to do."

23Meanwhile the officers of Ben-Hadad king of Aram said to him, "The gods of Israel are mountain gods. Since we fought in a mountain area, Israel won. Let's fight them on the flat land, and then we will win. 24This is what you should do. Don't allow the thirty-two rulers to command the armies, but put other commanders in their places. 25Gather an army like the one that was destroyed and as many horses and chariots as before. We will fight the Israelites on flat land, and then we will win." Ben-Hadad agreed with their advice and did what they said.

26The next spring Ben-Hadad gathered the army of Aram and went up to Aphek to fight against Israel.

27The Israelites also had prepared for war. They marched out to meet the Arameans and camped opposite them. The Israelites looked like two small flocks of goats, but the Arameans covered the area.

28A man of God came to the king of Israel with this message: "The LORD says, 'The people of Aram say that I, the LORD, am a god of the mountains, not a god of the valleys. So I will allow you to defeat this huge army, and then you will know I am the LORD.' "

29The armies were camped across from each other for seven days. On the seventh day the battle began. The Israelites killed one hundred thousand Aramean soldiers in one day. 30The rest of them ran away to the city of Aphek, where a city wall fell on twenty-seven thousand of them. Ben-Hadad also ran away to the city and hid in a room.

31His officers said to him, "We have heard that the kings of Israel are trustworthy. Let's dress in rough cloth to show our sadness, and wear ropes on our heads. Then we will go to the king of Israel, and perhaps he will let you live."

32So they dressed in rough cloth and wore ropes on their heads and went to the king of Israel. They said, "Your servant Ben-Hadad says, 'Please let me live.' "

Ahab answered, "Is he still alive? He is my brother."

33Ben-Hadad's men had wanted a sign from Ahab. So when Ahab called Ben-Hadad his brother, they quickly said, "Yes! Ben-Hadad is your brother."

Ahab said, "Bring him to me." When Ben-Hadad came, Ahab asked him to join him in the chariot.

34Ben-Hadad said to him, "Ahab, I will give you back the cities my father took from your father. And you may put shops in Damascus, as my father did in Samaria."

Ahab said, "If you agree to this, I will allow you to go free." So the two kings made a peace agreement. Then Ahab let Ben-Hadad go free.

A Prophet Speaks Against Ahab

35One prophet from one of the groups of prophets[d] told another, "Hit me!" He said this because the LORD had commanded it, but the other man refused. 36The prophet said, "You did not obey the LORD's command, so a lion will kill you as soon as you leave me." When the man left, a lion found him and killed him.

37The prophet went to another man and said, "Hit me, please!" So the man hit him and hurt him. 38The prophet wrapped his face in a cloth so no one could tell who he was. Then he went and waited by the road for the king. 39As Ahab king of Israel passed by, the prophet called out to him. "I went to fight in the battle," the prophet said. "One of our men brought an enemy soldier to me. Our man said, 'Guard this man. If he runs away, you will have to give your life in his place. Or, you will have to pay a fine of seventy-five pounds of silver.' 40But I was busy doing other things, so the man ran away."

The king of Israel answered, "You have already said what the punishment is. You must do what the man said."

41Then the prophet quickly took the cloth from his face. When the king of Israel saw him, he knew he was one of the prophets. 42The prophet said to the king, "This is what the LORD says: 'You freed the man I said should die, so your life will be taken instead of his. The lives of your people will also be taken instead of the lives of his people.' "

43Then King Ahab went back to his palace in Samaria, angry and upset.

> **SIDELIGHT:** Outside the Bible, the earliest mention of any Israelite king refers to King Ahab (1 Kings 20:1–43). An Assyrian monument commemorating a battle says Ahab contributed ten thousand soldiers and two thousand chariots to an alliance of countries that fought the Assyrians.

Ahab Takes Naboth's Vineyard

21 After these things had happened, this is what followed. A man named Naboth owned a vineyard in Jezreel, near the palace of Ahab king of Israel. 2One day Ahab said to Naboth, "Give me your vineyard. It is near my palace, and I want to make it into a vegetable garden. I will give you a better vineyard in its place, or, if you prefer, I will pay you what it is worth."

3Naboth answered, "May the LORD keep me from ever giving my land to you. It belongs to my family."

4Ahab went home angry and upset, because he did not like what Naboth from Jezreel had said. (Naboth had said, "I will not give you my family's land.") Ahab lay down on his bed, turned his face to the wall, and refused to eat.

5His wife, Jezebel, came in and asked him, "Why are you so upset that you refuse to eat?"

6Ahab answered, "I talked to Naboth, the man from Jezreel. I said, 'Sell me your vineyard, or, if you prefer, I will give you another vineyard for it.' But Naboth refused."

7Jezebel answered, "Is this how you rule as king over Israel? Get up, eat something, and cheer up. I will get Naboth's vineyard for you."

8So Jezebel wrote some letters, signed Ahab's name to them, and used his own seal[d] to seal them. Then she sent them to the older leaders and important men who lived in Naboth's town. 9The letter she wrote said: "Declare a day during which the people are to give up eating. Call the people together, and give Naboth a place of honor among them. 10Seat two troublemakers across from him, and have them say they heard Naboth speak against God and the king. Then take Naboth out of the city and kill him with stones."

11The older leaders and important men of Jezreel obeyed Jezebel's command, just as she wrote in the letters. 12They declared a special day on which the people were to give up eating. And they put Naboth in a place of honor before the people. 13Two troublemakers sat across from Naboth and said in front of everybody that they had heard him speak against God and the king. So the people carried Naboth out of the city and killed him with stones. 14Then the leaders sent a message to Jezebel, saying, "Naboth has been killed."

15When Jezebel heard that Naboth had been killed, she told Ahab, "Naboth of Jezreel is dead. Now you may go and take for yourself the vineyard he would not sell to you." 16When Ahab heard that Naboth of Jezreel was dead, he got up and went to the vineyard to take it for his own. 17At this time the LORD spoke his word to the prophet Elijah the Tishbite. The LORD said, 18"Go to Ahab king of Israel in Samaria. He is at Naboth's vineyard, where he has gone to take it as his own. 19Tell Ahab that I, the LORD, say to him, 'You have murdered Naboth and taken his land. So I tell you this: In the same place the dogs licked up Naboth's blood, they will also lick up your blood!' "

20When Ahab saw Elijah, he said, "So you have found me, my enemy!"

Elijah answered, "Yes, I have found you. You have always chosen to do what the LORD says is wrong. 21So the LORD says to you, 'I will soon destroy you. I will kill you and every male in your family, both slave and free. 22Your family will be like the family of King Jeroboam son of Nebat and like the family of King Baasha son of Ahijah. I will destroy you, because you have made me angry and have led the people of Israel to sin.'

23"And the LORD also says, 'Dogs will eat the body of Jezebel in the city of Jezreel.'

24"Anyone in your family who dies in the city will be eaten by dogs, and anyone who dies in the fields will be eaten by birds."

25There was no one like Ahab who had chosen so often to do what the LORD said was wrong, because his wife Jezebel influenced him to do evil. 26Ahab sinned terribly by worshiping idols, just as the Amorite people did. And the LORD had taken away their land and given it to the people of Israel.

27After Elijah finished speaking, Ahab tore his clothes. He put on rough cloth, refused to eat, and even slept in the rough cloth to show how sad and upset he was.

28The LORD spoke his word to Elijah the Tishbite: 29"I see that Ahab is now sorry for what he has done. So I will not cause the trouble to come to him during his life, but I will wait until his son is king. Then I will bring this trouble to Ahab's family."

The Death of Ahab

22 For three years there was peace between Israel and Aram. 2During the third year Jehoshaphat king of Judah went to visit Ahab king of Israel.

3At that time Ahab asked his officers, "Do you remember that the king of Aram took Ramoth in Gilead from us? Why have we done nothing to get it back?" 4So Ahab asked King Jehoshaphat, "Will you go with me to fight at Ramoth in Gilead?"

"I will go with you," Jehoshaphat answered. "My soldiers are yours, and my horses are yours." 5Jehoshaphat also said to Ahab, "But first we should ask if this is the LORD's will."

6Ahab called about four hundred prophets[d] together and asked them, "Should I go to war against Ramoth in Gilead or not?"

They answered, "Go, because the Lord will hand them over to you."

7But Jehoshaphat asked, "Isn't there a prophet of the LORD here? Let's ask him what we should do."

8Then King Ahab said to Jehoshaphat, "There is one other prophet. We could ask the LORD through him, but I hate him. He never prophesies anything good about me, but something bad. He is Micaiah son of Imlah."

Jehoshaphat said, "King Ahab, you shouldn't say that!"

9So Ahab king of Israel told one of his officers to bring Micaiah to him at once.

10Ahab king of Israel and Jehoshaphat king of Judah had on their royal robes and were sitting on their thrones at the threshing[d] floor, near the entrance to the gate of Samaria. All the prophets were standing before them, speaking their messages. 11Zedekiah son of Kenaanah had made some iron horns. He said to Ahab, "This is what the LORD says, 'You will use these horns to fight the Arameans until they are destroyed.' "

12All the other prophets said the same thing. "Attack Ramoth in Gilead and win, because the LORD will hand the Arameans over to you."

13The messenger who had gone to get Micaiah said to him, "All the other prophets are saying King Ahab will succeed. You should agree with them and give the king a good answer."

14But Micaiah answered, "As surely as the LORD lives, I can tell him only what the LORD tells me."

15When Micaiah came to Ahab, the king asked him, "Micaiah, should we attack Ramoth in Gilead or not?"

Micaiah answered, "Attack and win! The LORD will hand them over to you."

16But Ahab said to Micaiah, "How many times do I have to tell you to speak only the truth to me in the name of the LORD?"

17So Micaiah answered, "I saw the army of Israel scattered over the hills like sheep without a shepherd. The LORD said, 'They have no leaders. They should go home and not fight.' "

18Then Ahab king of Israel said to Jehoshaphat, "I told you! He never prophesies anything good about me, but only bad."

19But Micaiah said, "Hear the message from the

LORD: I saw the LORD sitting on his throne with his heavenly army standing near him on his right and on his left. 20The LORD said, 'Who will trick Ahab into attacking Ramoth in Gilead where he will be killed?'

"Some said one thing; some said another. 21Then one spirit came and stood before the LORD and said, 'I will trick him.'

22"The LORD asked, 'How will you do it?'

"The spirit answered, 'I will go to Ahab's prophets and make them tell lies.'

"So the LORD said, 'You will succeed in tricking him. Go and do it.'"

23Micaiah said, "Ahab, the LORD has made your prophets lie to you, and the LORD has decided that disaster should come to you."

24Then Zedekiah son of Kenaanah went up to Micaiah and slapped him in the face. Zedekiah said, "Has the LORD's spirit left me to speak through you?"

25Micaiah answered, "You will find out on the day you go to hide in an inside room."

26Then Ahab king of Israel ordered, "Take Micaiah and send him to Amon, the governor of the city, and to Joash, the king's son. 27Tell them I said to put this man in prison and give him only bread and water until I return safely from the battle."

28Micaiah said, "Ahab, if you come back safely from battle, the LORD has not spoken through me. Remember my words, all you people!"

29So Ahab king of Israel and Jehoshaphat king of Judah went to Ramoth in Gilead. 30King Ahab said to Jehoshaphat, "I will go into battle, but I will wear other clothes so no one will recognize me. But you wear your royal clothes." So Ahab wore other clothes and went into battle.

31The king of Aram had ordered his thirty-two chariot commanders, "Don't fight with anyone—important or unimportant—except the king of Israel." 32When these commanders saw Jehoshaphat, they thought he was certainly the king of Israel, so they turned to attack him. But Jehoshaphat began shouting. 33When they saw he was not King Ahab, they stopped chasing him.

34By chance, a soldier shot an arrow, but he hit Ahab king of Israel between the pieces of his armor. King Ahab said to his chariot driver, "Turn around and get me out of the battle, because I am hurt!" 35The battle continued all day. King Ahab was held up in his chariot and faced the Arameans. His blood flowed down to the bottom of the chariot. That evening he died. 36Near sunset a cry went out through the army of Israel: "Each man go back to his own city and land."

37In that way King Ahab died. His body was carried to Samaria and buried there. 38The men cleaned Ahab's chariot at a pool in Samaria where prostitutes[d] bathed, and the dogs licked his blood from the chariot. These things happened as the LORD had said they would.

39Everything else Ahab did is written in the book of the history of the kings of Israel. It tells about the palace Ahab built and decorated with ivory and the cities he built. 40So Ahab died, and his son Ahaziah became king in his place.

Jehoshaphat King of Judah

41Jehoshaphat son of Asa became king of Judah during Ahab's fourth year as king of Israel. 42Jehoshaphat was thirty-five years old when he became king, and he ruled in Jerusalem for twenty-five years. His mother's name was Azubah daughter of Shilhi. 43Jehoshaphat was good, like his father Asa, and he did what the LORD said was right. But Jehoshaphat did not destroy the places where gods were worshiped, so the people continued offering sacrifices and burning incense[d] there. 44Jehoshaphat was at peace with the king of Israel. 45Jehoshaphat fought many wars, and these wars and his successes are written in the book of the history of the kings of Judah. 46There were male prostitutes[d] still in the places of worship from the days of his father, Asa. So Jehoshaphat forced them to leave.

47During this time the land of Edom had no king; it was ruled by a governor.

48King Jehoshaphat built trading ships to sail to Ophir for gold. But the ships were wrecked at Ezion Geber, so they never set sail. 49Ahaziah son of Ahab went to help Jehoshaphat, offering to give Jehoshaphat some men to sail with his men, but Jehoshaphat refused.

50Jehoshaphat died and was buried with his ancestors in Jerusalem, the city of David, his ancestor. Then his son Jehoram became king in his place.

Ahaziah King of Israel

51Ahaziah son of Ahab became king of Israel in Samaria during Jehoshaphat's seventeenth year as king over Judah. Ahaziah ruled Israel for two years, 52and he did what the LORD said was wrong. He did the same evil his father Ahab, his mother Jezebel, and Jeroboam son of Nebat had done. All these rulers led the people of Israel into more sin. 53Ahaziah worshiped and served the god Baal,[d] and this made the LORD, the God of Israel, very angry. In these ways Ahaziah did what his father had done.

2 KINGS

Why Read This Book:

- See how God uses leaders to encourage people to follow him (2 Kings 1—8).
- Learn how unfaithfulness to God can destroy a nation (2 Kings 9—17).
- Be encouraged that God keeps his promises even when people don't keep theirs (2 Kings 18—23).

Behind the Scenes:

The land was in shambles. The kingdom that David and Solomon built had split into Israel (in the north) and Judah (in the south), and both countries faced attack from the outside and unrest from within. Making matters worse, the people kept turning to the false god Baal for help, ignoring and forgetting the true God.

But even in this difficult situation, God hadn't forgotten his people. He sent the prophet Elisha to challenge them to turn back to God. Unlike his combative predecessor Elijah (1 Kings 16—19, p. 320), Elisha was more of a healer and comforter. He performed numerous miracles to ease people's pain (2 Kings 4), and he also performed miracles on behalf of the nation (2 Kings 5). He showed that

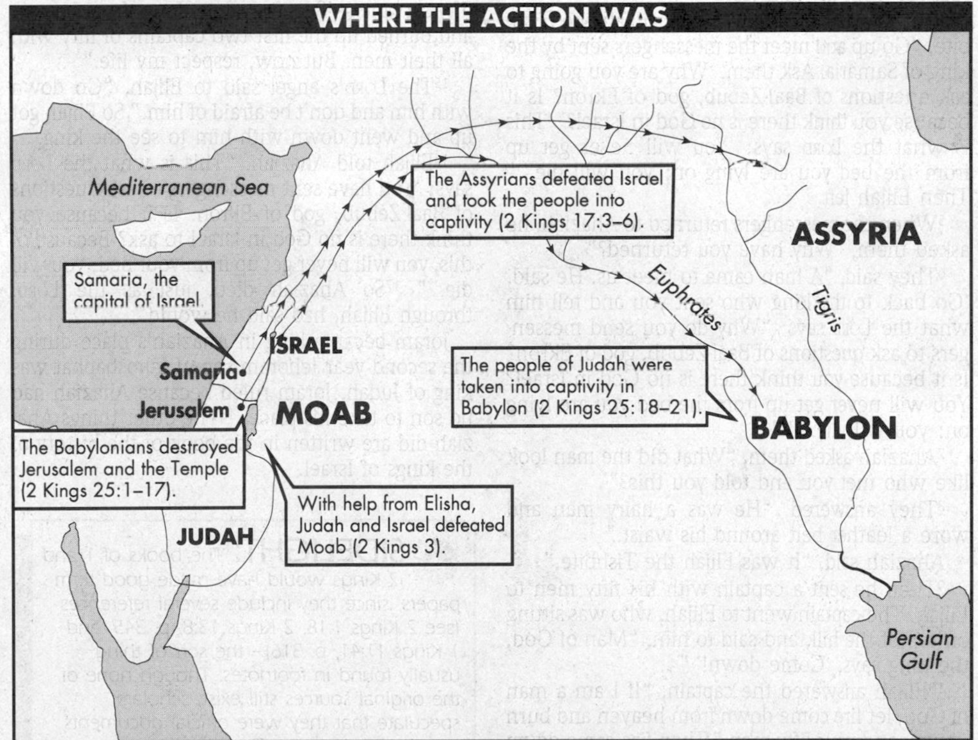
WHERE THE ACTION WAS
Mediterranean Sea
The Assyrians defeated Israel and took the people into captivity (2 Kings 17:3–6).
ASSYRIA
Samaria, the capital of Israel
Euphrates
Tigris
ISRAEL
Samaria
The people of Judah were taken into captivity in Babylon (2 Kings 25:18–21).
Jerusalem
MOAB
BABYLON
The Babylonians destroyed Jerusalem and the Temple (2 Kings 25:1–17).
With help from Elisha, Judah and Israel defeated Moab (2 Kings 3).
JUDAH
Persian Gulf

WHEN THE ACTION WAS

2000BC	1500BC	1000BC	500BC	BC/AD

- Joshua led the Israelites into Canaan
- Saul was Israel's king
- The kingdom was split between Israel and Judah
- Elisha was a prophet in Israel
- Israel fell to the Assyrians.
- Jerusalem fell to the Babylonians
- Jesus was born

Behind the Scenes (cont.): God hadn't given up on his people and would accept the Israelites if they would come back to him.

The northern kingdom did experience a brief revival under King Jeroboam II. But the overall decline continued, until Samaria—the northern capital—was destroyed and the people were taken into exile.

The southern kingdom also experienced some good years—under King Josiah, who repaired the Temple and led a religious revival in Judah. But in the end, Judah fell, the Temple was destroyed, and the Babylonians took the people into exile.

Despite the Israelites' unfaithfulness, God remained faithful. During this time he sent great prophets to call the people back to God. Even after Israel and Judah fell, God kept his promise to keep King David's descendants alive. And from those descendants eventually came Jesus.

Elijah and King Ahaziah

1 After Ahab died, Moab broke away from Israel's rule. 2Ahaziah fell down through the
wooden bars in his upstairs room in Samaria and
was badly hurt. He sent messengers and told
them, "Go, ask Baal-Zebub, god of Ekron, if I will
recover from my injuries."
3But the LORD's angel said to Elijah the Tishbite, "Go up and meet the messengers sent by the
king of Samaria. Ask them, 'Why are you going to
ask questions of Baal-Zebub, god of Ekron? Is it
because you think there is no God in Israel?' 4This
is what the LORD says: 'You will never get up
from the bed you are lying on; you will die.' "
Then Elijah left.
5When the messengers returned to Ahaziah, he
asked them, "Why have you returned?"
6They said, "A man came to meet us. He said,
'Go back to the king who sent you and tell him
what the LORD says: "Why do you send messengers to ask questions of Baal-Zebub, god of Ekron?
Is it because you think there is no God in Israel?
You will never get up from the bed you are lying
on; you will die." ' "
7Ahaziah asked them, "What did the man look
like who met you and told you this?"
8They answered, "He was a hairy man and
wore a leather belt around his waist."
Ahaziah said, "It was Elijah the Tishbite."
9Then he sent a captain with his fifty men to
Elijah. The captain went to Elijah, who was sitting
on top of the hill, and said to him, "Man of God,
the king says, 'Come down!' "
10Elijah answered the captain, "If I am a man
of God, let fire come down from heaven and burn
up you and your fifty men." Then fire came down
from heaven and burned up the captain and his
fifty men.
11Ahaziah sent another captain and fifty men to
Elijah. The captain said to him, "Man of God, this
is what the king says: 'Come down quickly!' "
12Elijah answered, "If I am a man of God, let
fire come down from heaven and burn up you and
your fifty men!" Then fire came down from
heaven and burned up the captain and his fifty
men.
13Ahaziah then sent a third captain with his
fifty men. The third captain came and fell down
on his knees before Elijah and begged, "Man of
God, please respect my life and the lives of your
fifty servants. 14See, fire came down from heaven
and burned up the first two captains of fifty with
all their men. But now, respect my life."
15The LORD's angel said to Elijah, "Go down
with him and don't be afraid of him." So Elijah got
up and went down with him to see the king.
16Elijah told Ahaziah, "This is what the LORD
says: 'You have sent messengers to ask questions
of Baal-Zebub, god of Ekron. Is it because you
think there is no God in Israel to ask? Because of
this, you will never get up from your bed; you will
die.' " 17So Ahaziah died, just as the LORD,
through Elijah, had said he would.
Joram became king in Ahaziah's place during
the second year Jehoram son of Jehoshaphat was
king of Judah. Joram ruled because Ahaziah had
no son to take his place. 18The other things Ahaziah did are written in the book of the history of
the kings of Israel.

SIDELIGHT: The books of 1 and 2 Kings would have made good term papers, since they include several references (see 2 Kings 1:18, 2 Kings 13:8, p. 345, and 1 Kings 11:41, p. 316)—the sort of thing usually found in footnotes. Though none of the original sources still exist, scholars speculate that they were official documents kept in the palace or Temple.

Elijah Is Taken to Heaven

2 It was almost time for the LORD to take Elijah
by a whirlwind up into heaven. While Elijah
and Elisha were leaving Gilgal, 2Elijah said to Eli-

sha, "Please stay here. The LORD has told me to go to Bethel."

SIDELIGHT: The prophets Elijah and Elisha had similar names but different styles. Elijah—whose name means "the Lord is my God"—preached judgment and repentance, and lived alone. Elisha—whose name means "the Lord is salvation"—stressed hope and grace, and lived among the people, especially the poor. Yet God used these two different people to accomplish his work.

But Elisha said, "As the LORD lives, and as you live, I won't leave you." So they went down to
Bethel. 3The groups of prophets at Bethel came
out to Elisha and said to him, "Do you know the LORD will take your master away from you today?"

Elisha said, "Yes, I know, but don't talk about it."

4Elijah said to him, "Stay here, Elisha, because the LORD has sent me to Jericho."

But Elisha said, "As the LORD lives, and as you live, I won't leave you."

So they went to Jericho. 5The groups of proph-
ets at Jericho came to Elisha and said, "Do you know that the LORD will take your master away from you today?"

Elisha answered, "Yes, I know, but don't talk about it."

6Elijah said to Elisha, "Stay here. The LORD has sent me to the Jordan River."

Elisha answered, "As the LORD lives, and as you live, I won't leave you."

So the two of them went on. 7Fifty men of the
groups of prophets came and stood far from
where Elijah and Elisha were by the Jordan. 8Eli-
jah took off his coat, rolled it up, and hit the water. The water divided to the right and to the left, and Elijah and Elisha crossed over on dry ground.

FRIENDS

Saying Good-Bye

Laura Eggers remembers vividly when she first found out that her best friend, Micky, would be moving away. "I was staying the night at her house when she told me," Laura said. "And we cried."

"It was really hard, because we didn't know exactly when she'd be moving," she continued. Micky's father was being transferred, and his company couldn't say exactly when.

Laura explained, "We even got kind of distant at one point, drawing back to avoid the pain of separation. We recognized it before it got too far along, and we said, 'Wait a minute, what are we doing?' "

Laura and Micky spent as much time together as they could over the next few months. When Micky finally left, Laura felt sad, lonely, anxious, angry, even depressed. But the two friends were glad they had spent those last few months together.

And Laura is glad Micky and she are still friends, even though they are far away from each other.

In **2 Kings 2:1–12**, two other friends had to say good-bye. See how Elisha handled saying good-bye when it came time for Elijah to go to heaven.

- What are the similarities between Laura and Micky's good-bye and Elijah and Elisha's good-bye?
- Elijah promised Elisha a double share of his spirit when they said good-bye. What kinds of things has a friend left you when you've had to say good-bye?

CONSIDER . . .

- what you would say to or do with a friend who was leaving—and say and do those things now, before you ever have to say good-bye.
- watching the movie Brian's Song with friends and then discussing how to say good-bye to a friend.

FOR MORE, SEE

- Ruth 1:14–18 (p. 240)
- 1 Samuel 20:41–42 (p. 264)
- John 17:13–26 (p. 1089)

9After they had crossed over, Elijah said to Elisha, "What can I do for you before I am taken from you?"

Elisha said, "Leave me a double share of your spirit."[n]

10Elijah said, "You have asked a hard thing. But if you see me when I am taken from you, it will be yours. If you don't, it won't happen."

SIDELIGHT: The prophet Elijah was whisked into heaven by a whirlwind, a chariot, and horses of fire—the first hot rod mentioned in the Bible (2 Kings 2:11). He is only one of two people mentioned in the Old Testament who never died. The other is Enoch (Genesis 5:24, p. 8).

11As they were walking and talking, a chariot and horses of fire appeared and separated Elijah from Elisha. Then Elijah went up to heaven in a whirlwind. 12Elisha saw it and shouted, "My father! My father! The chariots of Israel and their horsemen!" And Elisha did not see him anymore. Then Elisha grabbed his own clothes and tore them to show how sad he was.

13He picked up Elijah's coat that had fallen from him. Then he returned and stood on the bank of the Jordan. 14Elisha hit the water with Elijah's coat and said, "Where is the LORD, the God of Elijah?" When he hit the water, it divided to the right and to the left, and Elisha crossed over.

15The groups of prophets at Jericho were watching and said, "Elisha now has the spirit Elijah had." And they came to meet him, bowing down to the ground before him. 16They said to him, "There are fifty strong men with us. Please let them go and look for your master. Maybe the Spirit[d] of the LORD has taken Elijah up and set him down on some mountain or in some valley."

But Elisha answered, "No, don't send them."

17When the groups of prophets had begged Elisha until he couldn't refuse them anymore, he said, "Send them." So they sent fifty men who looked for three days, but they could not find him. 18Then they came back to Elisha at Jericho where he was staying. He said to them, "I told you not to go, didn't I?"

Elisha Makes the Water Pure

19The people of the city said to Elisha, "Look, master, this city is a nice place to live as you can see. But the water is so bad the land cannot grow crops."

20Elisha said, "Bring me a new bowl and put salt in it." So they brought it to him.

21Then he went out to the spring and threw the salt in it. He said, "This is what the LORD says: 'I have healed this water. From now on it won't cause death, and it won't keep the land from growing crops.' " 22So the water has been healed to this day just as Elisha had said.

Boys Make Fun of Elisha

23From there Elisha went up to Bethel. On the way some boys came out of the city and made fun of him. They said to him, "Go up too, you baldhead! Go up too, you baldhead!" 24Elisha turned around, looked at them, and put a curse on them in the name of the LORD. Then two mother bears came out of the woods and tore forty-two of the boys to pieces. 25Elisha went to Mount Carmel and from there he returned to Samaria.

SIDELIGHT: If you like making fun of bald people, be careful. Some young men made fun of the prophet Elisha's baldness, and they got mauled by bears (2 Kings 2:23–25). Why was their teasing so bad? Elisha had shaved his head to show his role as a prophet of God, and they were jeering him to "go up" to heaven like Elijah. So they were really making fun of his faith.

War Between Israel and Moab

3 Joram son of Ahab became king over Israel at Samaria in Jehoshaphat's eighteenth year as king of Judah. And Joram ruled twelve years. 2He did what the LORD said was wrong, but he was not like his father and mother; he removed the stone pillars his father had made for Baal.[d] 3But he continued to sin like Jeroboam son of Nebat who had led Israel to sin. Joram did not stop doing these same sins.

4Mesha king of Moab raised sheep. He paid the king of Israel one hundred thousand lambs and the wool of one hundred thousand sheep. 5But when Ahab died, the king of Moab turned against the king of Israel. 6So King Joram went out from Samaria and gathered Israel's army. 7He also sent messengers to Jehoshaphat king of Judah. "The king of Moab has turned against me," he said. "Will you go with me to fight Moab?"

Jehoshaphat replied, "I will go with you. My soldiers and my horses are yours."

8Jehoshaphat asked, "Which way should we attack?"

Leave . . . spirit By law, the first son in a family would inherit a double share of his father's possessions. Elisha is asking to inherit a share of his master's power as his follower. He is not asking for twice as much power as Elijah had.

Joram answered, "Through the Desert of Edom."

9So the king of Israel went with the king of Judah and the king of Edom. After they had marched seven days, there was no more water for the army or for their animals that were with them. 10The king of Israel said, "This is terrible! The LORD has called us three kings together to hand us over to the Moabites!"

11But Jehoshaphat asked, "Is there a prophet[d] of the LORD here? We can ask the LORD through him."

An officer of the king of Israel answered, "Elisha son of Shaphat is here. He was Elijah's servant."

12Jehoshaphat said, "He speaks the LORD's truth." So the king of Israel and Jehoshaphat and the king of Edom went down to see Elisha.

13Elisha said to the king of Israel, "I have nothing to do with you. Go to the prophets of your father and to the prophets of your mother!"

The king of Israel said to Elisha, "No, the LORD has called us three kings together to hand us over to the Moabites."

14Elisha said, "As surely as the LORD All-Powerful lives, whom I serve, I tell you the truth. I wouldn't even look at you or notice you if Jehoshaphat king of Judah were not here. I respect him. 15Now bring me someone who plays the harp."

While the harp was being played, the LORD gave Elisha power. 16Then Elisha said, "The LORD says to dig holes in the valley. 17The LORD says you won't see wind or rain, but the valley will be filled with water. Then you, your cattle, and your other animals can drink. 18This is easy for the LORD to do; he will also hand Moab over to you. 19You will destroy every strong, walled city and every important town. You will cut down every good tree and stop up all springs. You will ruin every good field with rocks."

20The next morning, about the time the sacrifice was offered, water came from the direction of Edom and filled the valley.

21All the Moabites heard that the kings had come up to fight against them. So they gathered everyone old enough to put on armor and waited at the border. 22But when the Moabites got up early in the morning, the sun was shining on the water. They saw the water across from them, and it looked as red as blood. 23Then they said, "This is blood! The kings must have fought and killed each other! Come, Moabites, let's take the valuables from the dead bodies!"

24When the Moabites came to the camp of Israel, the Israelites came out and fought them until they ran away. Then the Israelites went on into the land, killing the Moabites. 25They tore down the cities and threw rocks all over every good field. They stopped up all the springs and cut down all the good trees. Kir Hareseth was the only city with its stones still in place, but the men with slingshots surrounded it and conquered it, too.

26When the king of Moab saw that the battle was too much for him, he took seven hundred men with swords to try to break through to the king of Edom. But they could not break through. 27Then the king of Moab took his oldest son, who would have been king after him, and offered him as a burnt offering on the wall. So there was great anger against the Israelites, who left and went back to their own land.

SIDELIGHT: If you judge prophets' power by the number of miracles they perform, Elisha was almost twice as powerful as his predecessor Elijah. The Bible tells of thirteen miracles Elisha performed (see 2 Kings 4—6 for examples), but only seven that Elijah performed. Miracles were important at that time to show that God was more powerful than the false god Baal.

A Widow Asks Elisha for Help

4 The wife of a man from the groups of prophets[d] said to Elisha, "Your servant, my husband, is dead. You know he honored the LORD. But now the man he owes money to is coming to take my two boys as his slaves!"

2Elisha answered, "How can I help you? Tell me, what do you have in your house?"

The woman said, "I don't have anything there except a pot of oil."

3Then Elisha said, "Go and get empty jars from all your neighbors. Don't ask for just a few. 4Then go into your house and shut the door behind you and your sons. Pour oil into all the jars, and set the full ones aside."

5So she left Elisha and shut the door behind her and her sons. As they brought the jars to her, she poured out the oil. 6When the jars were all full, she said to her son, "Bring me another jar."

But he said, "There are no more jars." Then the oil stopped flowing.

7She went and told Elisha. And the prophet said to her, "Go, sell the oil and pay what you owe. You and your sons can live on what is left."

The Shunammite Woman

8One day Elisha went to Shunem, where an important woman lived. She begged Elisha to stay and eat. So every time Elisha passed by, he stopped there to eat. 9The woman said to her hus-

band, "I know that this is a holy man of God who
passes by our house all the time. 10Let's make a
small room on the roof[n] and put a bed in the
room for him. We can put a table, a chair, and a
lampstand there. Then when he comes by, he can
stay there."

11One day Elisha came to the woman's house.
After he went to his room and rested, 12he said
to his servant Gehazi, "Call the Shunammite
woman."

When the servant had called her, she stood in
front of him. 13Elisha had told his servant, "Now
say to her, 'You have gone to all this trouble for
us. What can I do for you? Do you want me to
speak to the king or the commander of the army
for you?' "

She answered, "I live among my own people."

14Elisha said to Gehazi, "But what can we do
for her?"

He answered, "She has no son, and her husband is old."

15Then Elisha said to Gehazi, "Call her." When
he called her, she stood in the doorway. 16Then
Elisha said, "About this time next year, you will
hold a son in your arms."

The woman said, "No, master, man of God,
don't lie to me, your servant!"

17But the woman became pregnant and gave
birth to a son at that time the next year, just as
Elisha had told her.

18The boy grew up and one day went out to his
father, who was with the grain harvesters. 19The
boy said to his father, "My head! My head!"

The father said to his servant, "Take him to his
mother!" 20The servant took him to his mother,
and he lay on his mother's lap until noon. Then
he died. 21So she took him up and laid him on
Elisha's bed. Then she shut the door and left.

22She called to her husband, "Send me one of
the servants and one of the donkeys. Then I can
go quickly to the man of God and return."

23The husband said, "Why do you want to go
to him today? It isn't the New Moon[d] or the Sabbath[d] day."

She said, "It will be all right."

24Then she saddled the donkey and said to her
servant, "Lead on. Don't slow down for me unless
I tell you." 25So she went to Elisha, the man of
God, at Mount Carmel.

When he saw her coming from far away, he
said to his servant Gehazi, "Look, there's the Shunammite woman! 26Run to meet her and ask, 'Are
you all right? Is your husband all right? Is the boy
all right?' "

She answered, "Everything is all right."

27Then she came to Elisha at the hill and
grabbed his feet. Gehazi came near to pull her
away, but Elisha said to him, "Leave her alone.
She's very upset, and the LORD has not told me
about it. He has hidden it from me."

28She said, "Master, did I ask you for a son?
Didn't I tell you not to lie to me?"

29Then Elisha said to Gehazi, "Get ready. Take
my walking stick in your hand and go quickly. If
you meet anyone, don't say hello. If anyone greets
you, don't respond. Lay my walking stick on the
boy's face."

30The boy's mother said, "As surely as the LORD
lives and as you live, I won't leave you!" So Elisha
got up and followed her.

31Gehazi went on ahead and laid the walking
stick on the boy's face, but the boy did not talk
or move. Then Gehazi went back to meet Elisha.
"The boy has not awakened," he said.

32When Elisha came into the house, the boy
was lying dead on his bed. 33Elisha entered the
room and shut the door, so only he and the boy
were in the room. Then he prayed to the LORD.
34He went to the bed and lay on the boy, putting
his mouth on the boy's mouth, his eyes on the
boy's eyes, and his hands on the boy's hands. He
stretched himself out on top of the boy. Soon the
boy's skin became warm. 35Elisha turned away
and walked around the room. Then he went back
and put himself on the boy again. The boy
sneezed seven times and opened his eyes.

36Elisha called Gehazi and said, "Call the Shunammite!" So he did. When she came, Elisha
said, "Pick up your son." 37She came in and fell
at Elisha's feet, bowing facedown to the floor.
Then she picked up her son and went out.

Elisha and the Stew

38When Elisha returned to Gilgal, there was a
shortage of food in the land. While the groups of
prophets[d] were sitting in front of him, he said to
his servant, "Put the large pot on the fire, and boil
some stew for these men."

39One of them went out into the field to gather
plants. Finding a wild vine, he picked fruit from
the vine and filled his robe with it. Then he came
and cut up the fruit into the pot. But they didn't
know what kind of fruit it was. 40They poured out
the stew for the others to eat. When they began
to eat it, they shouted, "Man of God, there's
death in the pot!" And they could not eat it.

41Elisha told them to bring some flour. He
threw it into the pot and said, "Pour it out for the
people to eat." Then there was nothing harmful
in the pot.

roof In Bible times houses were built with flat roofs. The roof was used for drying things such as flax and fruit. And it was used as an extra room, as a place for worship, and as a place to sleep in the summer.

Elisha Feeds the People

42A man from Baal Shalishah came to Elisha, bringing him twenty loaves of barley bread from the first harvest. He also brought fresh grain in his sack. Elisha said, "Give it to the people to eat."

43Elisha's servant asked, "How can I feed a hundred people with so little?"

"Give the bread to the people to eat," Elisha said. "This is what the LORD says: 'They will eat and will have food left over.' " 44After he gave it to them, the people ate and had food left over, as the LORD had said.

Naaman Is Healed

5 Naaman was commander of the army of the king of Aram. He was honored by his master, and he had much respect because the LORD used him to give victory to Aram. He was a mighty and brave man, but he had a skin disease.

2The Arameans had gone out to raid the Israelites and had taken a little girl as a captive. This little girl served Naaman's wife. 3She said to her mistress, "I wish my master would meet the prophet[d] who lives in Samaria. He would cure him of his disease."

4Naaman went to the king and told him what the girl from Israel had said. 5The king of Aram said, "Go ahead, and I will send a letter to the king of Israel." So Naaman left and took with him about seven hundred fifty pounds of silver, as well as one hundred fifty pounds of gold and ten changes of clothes. 6He brought the letter to the king of Israel, which read, "I am sending my servant Naaman to you so you can heal him of his skin disease."

7When the king of Israel read the letter, he tore his clothes to show how upset he was. He said, "I'm not God! I can't kill and make alive again! Why does this man send someone with a skin disease for me to heal? You can see that the king of Aram is trying to start trouble with me."

8When Elisha, the man of God, heard that the king of Israel had torn his clothes, he sent the king this message: "Why have you torn your clothes? Let Naaman come to me. Then he will know there is a prophet in Israel." 9So Naaman went with his horses and chariots to Elisha's house and stood outside the door.

10Elisha sent Naaman a messenger who said, "Go and wash in the Jordan River seven times.

S I C K N E S S

Take Your Medicine

Although the lightweight brace could be worn under her clothes, Allison Atkinson felt self-conscious about wearing it. She dreaded people's comments the first day she went to school with the "contraption." She thought everyone would notice it and make fun of her.

But if Allison didn't wear the brace, she would probably need to have surgery. Allison has a curvature of the spine known as scoliosis, a condition that can be stopped if she wears the back brace twenty-three hours a day during her growing years. Without the brace, the curvature can progress so that she will not be able to stand up straight.

Allison wore the brace. And as it turned out, no one noticed. "No one even knew I had it," she recalls.

That made the choice to wear the brace much easier. But it still seems like a nuisance. Every day over the past two years, Allison has had to choose: Will she wear her back brace or not?

Sometimes, people avoid medical treatment just because it's strange or embarrassing. But people won't get better if they don't follow the doctor's—or God's—orders. That was Naaman's predicament in **2 Kings 5:1–14**.

- What does God have to do with Allison's and Naaman's medical treatments?
- What kinds of things can keep God from working in our lives?

C O N S I D E R . . .

- talking with someone at school who has to wear some kind of medical device and finding out how he or she feels about wearing it.
- encouraging patients in a hospital to participate in God's healing processes by following doctor's orders.

F O R M O R E , S E E . . .

- Psalm 41 (p. 506)
- John 9:1–11 (p. 1073)
- Acts 3:1–10 (p. 1100)

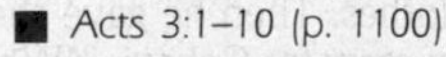

Then your skin will be healed, and you will be clean."

11Naaman became angry and left. He said, "I thought Elisha would surely come out and stand before me and call on the name of the LORD his God. I thought he would wave his hand over the place and heal the disease. 12The Abana and the Pharpar, the rivers of Damascus, are better than all the waters of Israel. Why can't I wash in them and become clean?" So Naaman went away very angry.

13Naaman's servants came near and said to him, "My father, if the prophet had told you to do some great thing, wouldn't you have done it? Doesn't it make more sense just to do it? After all, he only told you, 'Wash, and you will be clean.' " 14So Naaman went down and dipped in the Jordan seven times, just as Elisha had said. Then his skin became new again, like the skin of a child. And he was clean.

15Naaman and all his group returned to Elisha. He stood before Elisha and said, "Look, I now know there is no God in all the earth except in Israel. Now please accept a gift from me."

16But Elisha said, "As surely as the LORD lives whom I serve, I won't accept anything." Naaman urged him to take the gift, but he refused.

17Then Naaman said, "If you won't take the gift, then please give me some soil—as much as two of my mules can carry. From now on I'll not offer any burnt offering or sacrifice to any other gods but the LORD. 18But let the LORD pardon me for this: When my master goes into the temple of Rimmon[n] to worship, he leans on my arm. Then I must bow in that temple. May the LORD pardon me when I do that."

19Elisha said to him, "Go in peace."

Naaman left Elisha and went a short way. 20Gehazi, the servant of Elisha the man of God, thought, "My master has not accepted what Naaman the Aramean brought. As surely as the LORD lives, I'll run after him and get something from him." 21So Gehazi went after Naaman.

When Naaman saw someone running after him, he got off the chariot to meet Gehazi. He asked, "Is everything all right?"

22Gehazi said, "Everything is all right. My master has sent me. He said, 'Two young men from the groups of prophets in the mountains of Ephraim just came to me. Please give them seventy-five pounds of silver and two changes of clothes.' "

23Naaman said, "Please take one hundred fifty pounds," and he urged Gehazi to take it. He tied one hundred fifty pounds of silver in two bags with two changes of clothes. Then he gave them to two of his servants to carry for Gehazi. 24When they came to the hill, Gehazi took these things from Naaman's servants and put them in the house. Then he let Naaman's servants go, and they left.

25When he came in and stood before his master, Elisha said to him, "Where have you been, Gehazi?"

"I didn't go anywhere," he answered.

26But Elisha said to him, "My spirit was with you. I knew when the man turned from his chariot to meet you. This isn't a time to take money, clothes, olives, grapes, sheep, oxen, male servants, or female servants. 27So Naaman's skin disease will come on you and your children forever." When Gehazi left Elisha, the he had the disease and was as white as snow.

An Axhead Floats

6 The groups of prophets[d] said to Elisha, "The place where we meet with you is too small for us. 2Let's go to the Jordan River. There everyone can get a log, and let's build a place there to live."

Elisha said, "Go."

3One of them said, "Please go with us."

Elisha answered, "I will go," 4so he went with them. When they arrived at the Jordan, they cut down some trees. 5As one man was cutting down a tree, the head of his ax fell into the water. He yelled, "Oh, my master! I borrowed that ax!"

6Elisha asked, "Where did it fall?" The man showed him the place. Then Elisha cut down a stick and threw it into the water, and it made the iron head float. 7Elisha said, "Pick up the axhead." Then the man reached out and took it.

> **SIDELIGHT:** You've heard of a root beer float. How about an axhead float? You need an axhead, a river, and a prophet. The recipe is in 2 Kings 6:1–7.

Elisha and the Blinded Arameans

8The king of Aram was at war with Israel. He had a council meeting with his officers and said, "I will set up my camp in this place."

9Elisha, the man of God, sent a message to the king of Israel, saying, "Be careful! Don't pass that place, because the Arameans are going down there!"

10The king of Israel checked the place about which Elisha had warned him. Elisha warned him several times, so the king protected himself there.

11The king of Aram was angry about this. He called his officers together and demanded, "Tell

temple of Rimmon The place where the Aramean people worshiped the god Rimmon.

me who of us is working for the king of Israel."

12One of the officers said, "None, my master and king. It's Elisha, the prophet[d] from Israel. He can tell you what you speak in your bedroom."

13The king said, "Go and find him so I can send men and catch him."

The servants came back and reported, "He is in Dothan."

14Then the king sent horses, chariots, and many troops to Dothan. They arrived at night and surrounded the city.

15Elisha's servant got up early, and when he went out, he saw an army with horses and chariots all around the city. The servant said to Elisha, "Oh, my master, what can we do?"

16Elisha said, "Don't be afraid. The army that fights for us is larger than the one against us."

17Then Elisha prayed, "LORD, open my servant's eyes, and let him see."

The LORD opened the eyes of the young man, and he saw that the mountain was full of horses and chariots of fire all around Elisha.

18As the enemy came down toward Elisha, he prayed to the LORD, "Make these people blind." So he made the Aramean army blind, as Elisha had asked.

19Elisha said to them, "This is not the right road or the right city. Follow me and I'll take you to the man you are looking for." Then Elisha led them to Samaria.

20After they entered Samaria, Elisha said, "LORD, open these men's eyes so they can see." So the LORD opened their eyes, and the Aramean army saw that they were inside the city of Samaria!

21When the king of Israel saw the Aramean army, he said to Elisha, "My father, should I kill them? Should I kill them?"

22Elisha answered, "Don't kill them. You wouldn't kill people whom you captured with your sword and bow. Give them food and water, and let them eat and drink and then go home to their master." 23So he prepared a great feast for the Aramean army. After they ate and drank, the king sent them away, and they went home to their master. The soldiers of Aram did not come anymore into the land of Israel.

A Shortage of Food

24Later, Ben-Hadad king of Aram gathered his whole army and surrounded and attacked Samaria. 25There was a shortage of food in Samaria. It was so bad that a donkey's head sold for about two pounds of silver, and half of a pint of dove's dung sold for about two ounces of silver.

26As the king of Israel was passing by on the wall, a woman yelled out to him, "Help me, my master and king!"

27The king said, "If the LORD doesn't help you, how can I? Can I get help from the threshing[d] floor or from the winepress?"[d] 28Then the king said to her, "What is your trouble?"

She answered, "This woman said to me, 'Give up your son so we can eat him today. Then we will eat my son tomorrow.' 29So we boiled my son and ate him. Then the next day I said to her, 'Give up your son so we can eat him.' But she had hidden him."

30When the king heard the woman's words, he tore his clothes in grief. As he walked along the wall, the people looked and saw he had on rough cloth under his clothes to show his sadness. 31He said, "May God punish me terribly if the head of Elisha son of Shaphat isn't cut off from his body today!"

32The king sent a messenger to Elisha, who was sitting in his house with the older leaders. But before the messenger arrived, Elisha said to them, "See, this murderer is sending men to cut off my head. When the messenger arrives, shut the door and hold it; don't let him in. The sound of his master's feet is behind him."

33Elisha was still talking with the leaders when the messenger arrived. The king said, "This trouble has come from the LORD. Why should I wait for the LORD any longer?"

7 Elisha said, "Listen to the LORD's word. This is what the LORD says: 'About this time tomorrow seven quarts of fine flour will be sold for two-fifths of an ounce of silver, and thirteen quarts of barley will be sold for two-fifths of an ounce of silver. This will happen at the gate of Samaria.' "

2Then the officer who was close to the king answered Elisha, "Even if the LORD opened windows in the sky, that couldn't happen."

Elisha said, "You will see it with your eyes, but you will not eat any of it."

3There were four men with a skin disease at the entrance to the city gate. They said to each other, "Why do we sit here until we die? 4There is no food in the city. So if we go into the city, we will die there. If we stay here, we will die. So let's go to the Aramean camp. If they let us live, we will live. If they kill us, we die."

5So they got up at twilight and went to the Aramean camp, but when they arrived, no one was there. 6The Lord had caused the Aramean army to hear the sound of chariots, horses, and a large army. They had said to each other, "The king of Israel has hired the Hittite and Egyptian kings to attack us!" 7So they got up and ran away in the twilight, leaving their tents, horses, and donkeys. They left the camp standing and ran for their lives.

8When the men with the skin disease came to the edge of the camp, they went into one of the tents and ate and drank. They carried silver, gold, and clothes out of the camp and hid them. Then

they came back and entered another tent. They
carried things from this tent and hid them, also.
9Then they said to each other, "We're doing
wrong. Today we have good news, but we are
silent. If we wait until the sun comes up, we'll be
discovered. Let's go right now and tell the people
in the king's palace."

10So they went and called to the gatekeepers of
the city. They said, "We went to the Aramean
camp, but no one is there; we didn't hear anyone.
The horses and donkeys were still tied up, and the
tents were still standing." 11Then the gatekeepers
shouted out and told the people in the palace.

12The king got up in the night and said to his
officers, "I'll tell you what the Arameans are doing to us. They know we are starving. They have
gone out of the camp to hide in the field. They're
saying, 'When the Israelites come out of the city,
we'll capture them alive. Then we'll enter the
city.'"

13One of his officers answered, "Let some men
take five of the horses that are still left in the city.
These men are like all the Israelites who are left;
they are also about to die. Let's send them to see
what has happened."

14So the men took two chariots with horses.
The king sent them after the Aramean army, saying, "Go and see what has happened." 15The men
followed the Aramean army as far as the Jordan
River. The road was full of clothes and equipment
that the Arameans had thrown away as they had
hurriedly left. So the messengers returned and
told the king. 16Then the people went out and
took valuables from the Aramean camp. So seven
quarts of fine flour were sold for two-fifths of an
ounce of silver, and thirteen quarts of barley were
sold for two-fifths of an ounce of silver, just as the
LORD had said.

17The king chose the officer who was close to
him to guard the gate, but the people trampled
the officer to death. This happened just as Elisha
had told the king when the king came to his
house. 18He had said, "Thirteen quarts of barley
and seven quarts of fine flour will each sell for
two-fifths of an ounce of silver about this time
tomorrow at the gate of Samaria."

19But the officer had answered, "Even if the
LORD opened windows in the sky, that couldn't
happen." And Elisha had told him, "You will see
it with your eyes, but you won't eat any of it." 20It
happened to the officer just that way. The people
trampled him in the gateway, and he died.

The Shunammite Regains Her Land

8 Elisha spoke to the woman whose son he
had brought back to life. He said, "Get up
and go with your family. Stay any place you can,
because the LORD has called for a time without
food that will last seven years." 2So the woman
got up and did as the man of God had said. She
left with her family, and they stayed in the land
of the Philistines for seven years. 3After seven
years she returned from the land of the Philistines
and went to beg the king for her house and land.
4The king was talking with Gehazi, the servant of
the man of God. The king had said, "Please tell
me all the great things Elisha has done." 5Gehazi
was telling the king how Elisha had brought a
dead boy back to life. Just then the woman whose
son Elisha had brought back to life came and
begged the king for her house and land.

Gehazi said, "My master and king, this is the
woman, and this is the son Elisha brought back to
life."

6The king asked the woman, and she told him
about it. Then the king chose an officer to help
her. "Give the woman everything that is hers,"
the king said. "Give her all the money made from
her land from the day she left until now."

Ben-Hadad Is Killed

7Then Elisha went to Damascus, where Ben-
Hadad king of Aram was sick. Someone told him,
"The man of God has arrived."

8The king said to Hazael, "Take a gift in your
hand and go meet him. Ask the LORD through
him if I will recover from my sickness."

9So Hazael went to meet Elisha, taking with
him a gift of forty camels loaded with every good
thing in Damascus. He came and stood before Elisha and said, "Your son Ben-Hadad king of Aram
sent me to you. He asks if he will recover from his
sickness."

10Elisha said to Hazael, "Go and tell Ben-
Hadad, 'You will surely recover,' but the LORD
has told me he will really die." 11Hazael stared at
Elisha until he felt ashamed. Then Elisha cried.
12Hazael asked, "Why are you crying, master?"

Elisha answered, "Because I know what evil
you will do to the Israelites. You will burn their
strong, walled cities with fire and kill their young
men with swords. You will throw their babies to
the ground and split open their pregnant
women."

13Hazael said, "Am I a dog? How could I do
such things?"

Elisha answered, "The LORD has shown me
that you will be king over Aram."

14Then Hazael left Elisha and came to his master. Ben-Hadad said to him, "What did Elisha say
to you?"

Hazael answered, "He told me that you will
surely recover." 15But the next day Hazael took a
blanket and dipped it in water. Then he put it
over Ben-Hadad's face, and he died. So Hazael
became king in Ben-Hadad's place.

Jehoram King of Judah

16While Jehoshaphat was king in Judah, Jehoram son of Jehoshaphat became king of Judah. This was during the fifth year Joram son of Ahab was king of Israel. 17Jehoram was thirty-two years old when he began to rule, and he ruled eight years in Jerusalem. 18He followed the ways of the kings of Israel, just as the family of Ahab had done, because he married Ahab's daughter. Jehoram did what the LORD said was wrong. 19But the LORD would not destroy Judah because of his servant David. The LORD had promised that one of David's descendants would always rule.

20In Jehoram's time Edom broke away from Judah's rule and chose their own king. 21So Jehoram and all his chariots went to Zair. The Edomites surrounded him and his chariot commanders. Jehoram got up and attacked the Edomites at night, but his army ran away to their tents. 22From then until now the country of Edom has fought against the rule of Judah. At the same time Libnah also broke away from Judah's rule.

23The other acts of Jehoram and all the things he did are written in the book of the history of the kings of Judah. 24Jehoram died and was buried with his ancestors in Jerusalem, and Jehoram's son Ahaziah ruled in his place.

25Ahaziah son of Jehoram became king of Judah during the twelfth year Joram son of Ahab was king of Israel. 26Ahaziah was twenty-two years old when he became king, and he ruled one year in Jerusalem. His mother's name was Athaliah, a granddaughter of Omri king of Israel. 27Ahaziah followed the ways of Ahab's family. He did what the LORD said was wrong, as Ahab's family had done, because he was a son-in-law to Ahab.

28Ahaziah went with Joram son of Ahab to Ramoth in Gilead, where they fought against Hazael king of Aram. The Arameans wounded Joram. 29So King Joram returned to Jezreel to heal from the wound he had received from the Arameans at Ramoth when he fought Hazael king of Aram. Ahaziah son of Jehoram king of Judah went down to visit Joram son of Ahab at Jezreel, because he had been wounded.

Jehu Is Chosen King

9 At the same time, Elisha the prophet[d] called a man from the groups of prophets. Elisha said, "Get ready, and take this small bottle of olive oil in your hand. Go to Ramoth in Gilead. 2When you arrive, find Jehu son of Jehoshaphat, the son of Nimshi. Go in and make Jehu get up from among his brothers, and take him to an inner room. 3Then take the bottle and pour the oil on Jehu's head and say, 'This is what the LORD says: I have appointed you king over Israel.' Then open the door and run away. Don't wait!"

4So the young man, the prophet, went to Ramoth in Gilead. 5When he arrived, he saw the officers of the army sitting together. He said, "Commander, I have a message for you."

Jehu asked, "For which one of us?"

The young man said, "For you, commander."

6Jehu got up and went into the house. Then the young prophet poured the olive oil on Jehu's head and said to him, "This is what the LORD, the God of Israel says: 'I have appointed you king over the LORD's people Israel. 7You must destroy the family of Ahab your master. I will punish Jezebel for the deaths of my servants the prophets and for all the LORD's servants who were murdered. 8All of Ahab's family must die. I will not let any male child in Ahab's family live in Israel, whether slave or free. 9I will make Ahab's family like the family of Jeroboam son of Nebat and like the family of Baasha son of Ahijah. 10The dogs will eat Jezebel at Jezreel, and no one will bury her.' "

Then the young prophet opened the door and ran away.

11When Jehu went back to his master's officers, one of them said to Jehu, "Is everything all right? Why did this crazy man come to you?"

Jehu answered, "You know the man and how he talks."

12They answered, "That's not true. Tell us."

Jehu said, "He said to me, 'This is what the LORD says: I have appointed you to be king over Israel.' "

13Then the officers hurried, and each man took off his own coat and put it on the stairs for Jehu. They blew the trumpet and shouted, "Jehu is king!"

Joram and Ahaziah Are Killed

14So Jehu son of Jehoshaphat, the son of Nimshi, made plans against Joram. Now Joram and all Israel had been defending Ramoth in Gilead from Hazael king of Aram. 15But King Joram had to return to Jezreel to heal from the injuries the Arameans had given him when he fought against Hazael king of Aram.

Jehu said, "If you agree with this, don't let anyone leave the city. They might tell the news in Jezreel." 16Then he got into his chariot and set out for Jezreel, where Joram was resting. Ahaziah king of Judah had gone down to see him.

17The lookout was standing on the watchtower in Jezreel when he saw Jehu's troops coming. He said, "I see some soldiers!"

Joram said, "Take a horseman and send him to meet them. Tell him to ask, 'Is all in order?' "

18The horseman rode out to meet Jehu, and he said, "This is what the king says: 'Is all in order?' "

Jehu said, "Why bother yourself with order? Come along behind me."

The lookout reported, "The messenger reached them, but he is not coming back."

19Then Joram sent out a second horseman. This rider came to Jehu's group and said, "This is what the king says: 'Is all in order?' "

Jehu answered, "Why bother yourself with order? Come along behind me."

20The lookout reported, "The second man reached them, but he is not coming back. The man in the chariot is driving like Jehu son of Nimshi. He drives as if he were crazy!"

SIDELIGHT: The first record of bad driving in the Bible is in 2 Kings 9:20. King Jehu was such a bad driver that people could recognize his chariot driving from a distance. They said he drove "as if he were crazy." But since he was king, he never got a ticket.

21Joram said, "Get my chariot ready." Then the servant got Joram's chariot ready. Joram king of Israel and Ahaziah king of Judah went out, each in his own chariot, to meet Jehu at the property of Naboth the Jezreelite.

22When Joram saw Jehu, he said, "Is all in order, Jehu?"

Jehu answered, "There will never be any order as long as your mother Jezebel worships idols and uses witchcraft."[d]

23Joram turned the horses to run away and yelled to Ahaziah, "It's a trick, Ahaziah!"

24Then Jehu drew his bow and shot Joram between his shoulders. The arrow went through Joram's heart, and he fell down in his chariot.

25Jehu ordered Bidkar, his chariot officer, "Pick up Joram's body, and throw it into the field of Naboth the Jezreelite. Remember when you and I rode together with Joram's father Ahab. The LORD made this prophecy[d] against him:
26'Yesterday I saw the blood of Naboth and his sons, says the LORD, so I will punish Ahab in his field, says the LORD.' Take Joram's body and throw it into the field, as the LORD has said."

27When Ahaziah king of Judah saw this, he ran away toward Beth Haggan. Jehu chased him, saying, "Shoot Ahaziah, too!" Ahaziah was wounded in his chariot on the way up to Gur near Ibleam. He got as far as Megiddo but died there.
28Ahaziah's servants carried his body in a chariot to Jerusalem and buried him with his ancestors in his tomb in Jerusalem.
29(Ahaziah had become king over Judah in the eleventh year Joram son of Ahab was king.)

Death of Jezebel

30When Jehu came to Jezreel, Jezebel heard about it. She put on her eye makeup and fixed her hair. Then she looked out the window.
31When Jehu entered the city gate, Jezebel said, "Have you come in peace, you Zimri,[n] you who killed your master?"

32Jehu looked up at the window and said, "Who is on my side? Who?" Two or three servants looked out the window at Jehu.
33He said to them, "Throw her down." So they threw Jezebel down, and the horses ran over her. Some of her blood splashed on the wall and on the horses.

SIDELIGHT: When wicked Queen Jezebel put on make-up (2 Kings 9:30–33), it was probably quite elaborate. Women in those days used black eye liner, blue eye shadow, red lipstick and nail polish, powders, and perfume. None of it did much good, though, when she was thrown out the window and trampled by horses.

34Jehu went into the house and ate and drank. Then he said, "Now see about this cursed woman. Bury her, because she is a king's daughter."

35The men went to bury Jezebel, but they could not find her. They found only her skull, feet, and the palms of her hands.
36When they came back and told Jehu, he said, "The LORD said this through his servant Elijah the Tishbite: 'The dogs will eat Jezebel at Jezreel.
37Her body will be like manure on the field in the land at Jezreel. No one will be able to say that this is Jezebel.' "

Families of Ahab and Ahaziah Killed

10 Ahab had seventy sons in Samaria. Jehu wrote letters and sent them to Samaria to the officers and older leaders of Jezreel and to the guardians of the sons of Ahab. Jehu said,
2"You have your master's sons with you, and you have chariots, horses, a city with strong walls, and weapons. When you get this letter,
3choose the best and most worthy person among your master's sons, and make him king. Then fight for your master's family."

4But the officers and leaders of Jezreel were frightened. They said, "Two kings could not stand up to Jehu, so how can we?"

5The palace manager, the city governor, the leaders, and the guardians sent a message to Jehu. "We are your servants," they said. "We will do

Zimri He was the man who killed Elah and the family of Baasha. Read 1 Kings 16:8-12.

everything you tell us to do. We won't make any man king, so do whatever you think is best."

6Then Jehu wrote a second letter, saying, "If you are on my side and will obey me, cut off the heads of your master's sons and come to me at Jezreel tomorrow about this time."

Now the seventy sons of the king's family were with the leading men of the city who were their guardians. 7When the leaders received the letter, they took the king's sons and killed all seventy of them. They put their heads in baskets and sent them to Jehu at Jezreel. 8The messenger came to Jehu and told him, "They have brought the heads of the king's sons."

Then Jehu said, "Lay the heads in two piles at the city gate until morning."

9In the morning, Jehu went out and stood before the people and said to them, "You are innocent. Look, I made plans against my master and killed him. But who killed all these? 10You should know that everything the LORD said about Ahab's family will come true. The LORD has spoken through his servant Elijah, and the LORD has done what he said." 11So Jehu killed everyone of Ahab's family in Jezreel who was still alive. He also killed all Ahab's leading men, close friends, and priests. No one who had helped Ahab was left alive.

12Then Jehu left and went to Samaria by way of the road to Beth Eked of the Shepherds. 13There Jehu met some relatives of Ahaziah king of Judah. Jehu asked, "Who are you?"

They answered, "We are relatives of Ahaziah. We have come down to get revenge for the families of the king and the king's mother."

14Then Jehu said, "Take them alive!" So they captured Ahaziah's relatives alive and killed them at the well near Beth Eked—forty-two of them. Jehu did not leave anyone alive.

15After Jehu left there, he met Jehonadab son of Recab, who was also on his way to meet Jehu. Jehu greeted him and said, "Are you as good a friend to me as I am to you?"

Jehonadab answered, "Yes, I am."

Jehu said, "If you are, then give me your hand." So Jehonadab gave him his hand, and Jehu pulled him into the chariot. 16"Come with me," Jehu said. "You can see how strong my feelings are for the LORD." So Jehu had Jehonadab ride in his chariot.

17When Jehu came to Samaria, he killed all of Ahab's family in Samaria. He destroyed all those who were left, just as the LORD had told Elijah it would happen.

Baal Worshipers Killed

18Then Jehu gathered all the people together and said to them, "Ahab served Baal[d] a little, but Jehu will serve Baal much. 19Now call for me all Baal's prophets and priests and all the people who worship Baal. Don't let anyone miss this meeting, because I have a great sacrifice for Baal. Anyone who is not there will not live." But Jehu was tricking them so he could destroy the worshipers of Baal. 20He said, "Prepare a holy meeting for Baal." So they announced the meeting. 21Then Jehu sent word through all Israel, and all the worshipers of Baal came; not one stayed home. They came into the temple of Baal, and the temple was filled from one side to the other.

22Jehu said to the man who kept the robes, "Bring out robes for all the worshipers of Baal." After he brought out robes for them, 23Jehu and Jehonadab son of Recab went into the temple of Baal. Jehu said to the worshipers of Baal, "Look around, and make sure there are no servants of the LORD with you. Be sure there are only worshipers of Baal." 24Then the worshipers of Baal went in to offer sacrifices and burnt offerings.

Jehu had eighty men waiting outside. He had told them, "Don't let anyone escape. If you do, you must pay with your own life."

25As soon as Jehu finished offering the burnt offering, he ordered the guards and the captains, "Go in and kill the worshipers of Baal. Don't let anyone come out." So the guards and captains killed the worshipers of Baal with the sword and threw their bodies out. Then they went to the inner rooms of the temple 26and brought out the pillars of the temple of Baal and burned them. 27They tore down the stone pillar of Baal, as well as the temple of Baal. And they made it into a sewage pit, as it is today.

28So Jehu destroyed Baal worship in Israel, 29but he did not stop doing the sins Jeroboam son of Nebat had done. Jeroboam had led Israel to sin by worshiping the golden calves in Bethel and Dan.

30The LORD said to Jehu, "You have done well in obeying what I said was right. You have done to the family of Ahab as I wanted. Because of this, your descendants[d] as far as your great-great-grandchildren will be kings of Israel." 31But Jehu was not careful to follow the teachings of the LORD, the God of Israel, with all his heart. He did not stop doing the same sins Jeroboam had done, by which he had led Israel to sin.

32At that time the LORD began to make Israel smaller. Hazael defeated the Israelites in all the land of Israel, 33taking all the land of the Jordan known as the land of Gilead. (It was the region of Gad, Reuben, and Manasseh.) He took land from Aroer by the Arnon Ravine through Gilead to Bashan.

34The other things Jehu did—everything he did and all his victories—are recorded in the book of the history of the kings of Israel. 35Jehu died and was buried in Samaria, and his son Jehoahaz became king in his place. 36Jehu was king over Israel in Samaria for twenty-eight years.

Athaliah and Joash

11 When Ahaziah's mother, Athaliah, saw that her son was dead, she killed all the royal family. 2But Jehosheba, King Jehoram's daughter and Ahaziah's sister, took Joash, Ahaziah's son. She stole him from among the other sons of the king who were about to be murdered. She put Joash and his nurse in a bedroom to hide him from Athaliah, so he was not killed. 3He hid with her in the Temple[d] of the LORD for six years. During that time Athaliah ruled the land.

> **SIDELIGHT:** It may seem like a modern idea to have a woman as president, but one woman, Athaliah, ruled Judah for seven years (2 Kings 11:1–3). She didn't get her position by popular vote!

4In the seventh year Jehoiada sent for the commanders of groups of a hundred men, as well as the Carites.[n] He brought them together in the Temple of the LORD and made an agreement with them. There, in the Temple of the LORD, he made them promise loyalty, and then he showed them the king's son. 5He commanded them, "This is what you must do. A third of you who go on duty on the Sabbath[d] will guard the king's palace. 6A third of you will be at the Sur Gate, and another third will be at the gate behind the guard. This way you will guard the Temple. 7The two groups who go off duty on the Sabbath must protect the Temple of the LORD for the king. 8All of you must stand around the king, each man with his weapons in his hand. If anyone comes near, kill him. Stay close to the king when he goes out and when he comes in."

9The commanders over a hundred men obeyed everything Jehoiada the priest had commanded. Each one took his men who came on duty on the Sabbath and those who went off duty on the Sabbath, and they came to Jehoiada the priest. 10He gave the commanders the spears and shields that had belonged to King David and that were kept in the Temple of the LORD.

Joash Becomes King

11Then each guard took his place with his weapons in his hand. There were guards from the south side of the Temple[d] to the north side. They stood by the altar and the Temple and around the king. 12Jehoiada brought out the king's son and put the crown on him and gave him a copy of the agreement. They appointed him king and poured olive oil on him. Then they clapped their hands and said, "Long live the king!"

13When Athaliah heard the noise of the guards and the people, she went to them at the Temple of the LORD. 14She looked, and there was the king, standing by the pillar, as the custom was. The officers and trumpeters were standing beside him, and all the people of the land were very happy and were blowing trumpets. Then Athaliah tore her clothes and screamed, "Traitors! Traitors!"

15Jehoiada the priest gave orders to the commanders of a hundred men, who led the army. He said, "Surround her with soldiers and kill with a sword anyone who follows her." He commanded this because he had said, "Don't put Athaliah to death in the Temple of the LORD." 16So they caught her when she came to the horses' entrance near the palace. There she was put to death.

17Then Jehoiada made an agreement between the LORD and the king and the people that they would be the LORD's special people. He also made an agreement between the king and the people. 18All the people of the land went to the temple of Baal[d] and tore it down, smashing the altars and idols. They also killed Mattan, the priest of Baal, in front of the altars.

Then Jehoiada the priest placed guards at the Temple of the LORD. 19He took with him the commanders of a hundred men and the Carites, the royal bodyguards, as well as the guards and all the people of the land. Together they took the king out of the Temple of the LORD and went into the palace through the gate of the guards. Then the king sat on the royal throne. 20So all the people of

> **SIDELIGHT:** If anyone asked Joash if he had "grown up in the church" he could have easily said yes. In fact, he was hidden in the Temple for six years to keep from getting killed. At age seven, he became the youngest king in the Bible (2 Kings 11:1–3, 21).

the land were very happy, and Jerusalem had peace, because Athaliah had been put to death with the sword at the palace.

21Joash was seven years old when he became king.

Carites This was probably a special unit of the army that was responsible for the king's safety, a kind of palace guard similar to the Kerethites and the Pelethites.

12 Joash became king of Judah in Jehu's seventh year as king of Israel, and he ruled for forty years in Jerusalem. His mother's name was Zibiah, and she was from Beersheba. 2Joash did what the LORD said was right as long as Jehoiada the priest taught him. 3But the places where gods were worshiped were not removed; the people still made sacrifices and burned incense[d] there.

Joash Repairs the Temple

4Joash said to the priests, "Take all the money brought as offerings to the Temple[d] of the LORD. This includes the money each person owes in taxes and the money each person promises or brings freely to the LORD. 5Each priest will take the money from the people he serves. Then the priests must repair any damage they find in the Temple."

6But by the twenty-third year Joash was king, the priests still had not repaired the Temple. 7So King Joash called for Jehoiada the priest and the other priests and said to them, "Why aren't you repairing the damage of the Temple? Don't take any more money from the people you serve, but hand over the money for the repair of the Temple." 8The priests agreed not to take any more money from the people and not to repair the Temple themselves.

9Jehoiada the priest took a box and made a hole in the top of it. Then he put it by the altar, on the right side as the people came into the Temple of the LORD. The priests guarding the doorway put all the money brought to the Temple of the LORD into the box.

10Each time the priests saw that the box was full of money, the king's royal secretary and the high priest came. They counted the money that had been brought to the Temple of the LORD, and they put it into bags. 11Next they weighed the money and gave it to the people in charge of the work on the Temple. With it they paid the carpenters and the builders who worked on the Temple of the LORD, 12as well as the bricklayers and stonecutters. They also used the money to buy timber and cut stone to repair the damage of the Temple of the LORD. It paid for everything.

13The money brought into the Temple of the LORD was not used to make silver cups, wick trimmers, bowls, trumpets, or gold or silver vessels. 14They paid the money to the workers, who used it to repair the Temple of the LORD. 15They did not demand to know how the money was spent, because the workers were honest. 16The money from the penalty offerings and sin offerings was not brought into the Temple of the LORD, because it belonged to the priests.

Joash Saves Jerusalem

17About this time Hazael king of Aram attacked Gath and captured it. Then he went to attack Jerusalem. 18Joash king of Judah took all the holy things given by his ancestors, the kings of Judah—Jehoshaphat, Jehoram, and Ahaziah. He also took his own holy things as well as the gold that was found in the treasuries of the Temple[d] of the LORD and the gold from the palace. Joash sent all this treasure to Hazael king of Aram, who turned away from Jerusalem.

19Everything else Joash did is written in the book of the history of the kings of Judah. 20His officers made plans against him and killed him at Beth Millo on the road down to Silla. 21The officers who killed him were Jozabad son of Shimeath and Jehozabad son of Shomer. Joash was buried with his ancestors in Jerusalem, and Amaziah, his son, became king in his place.

Jehoahaz King of Israel

13 Jehoahaz son of Jehu became king over Israel in Samaria during the twenty-third year Joash son of Ahaziah was king of Judah. Jehoahaz ruled seventeen years, 2and he did what the LORD said was wrong. Jehoahaz did the same sins Jeroboam son of Nebat had done. Jeroboam had led Israel to sin, and Jehoahaz did not stop doing these same sins. 3So the LORD was angry with Israel and handed them over to Hazael king of Aram and his son Ben-Hadad for a long time.

4Then Jehoahaz begged the LORD, and the LORD listened to him. The LORD had seen the troubles of Israel; he saw how terribly the king of Aram was treating them. 5He gave Israel a man to save them, and they escaped from the Arameans. The Israelites then lived in their own homes as they had before, 6but they still did not stop doing the same sins that the family of Jeroboam had done. He had led Israel to sin, and they continued doing those sins. The Asherah[d] idol also was left standing in Samaria.

7Nothing was left of Jehoahaz's army except fifty horsemen, ten chariots, and ten thousand foot soldiers. The king of Aram had destroyed them and made them like chaff.[d]

8Everything else Jehoahaz did and all his victories are written in the book of the history of the kings of Israel. 9Jehoahaz died and was buried in Samaria, and his son Jehoash became king in his place.

Jehoash King of Israel

10Jehoash son of Jehoahaz became king of Israel in Samaria during Joash's thirty-seventh year as king of Judah. Jehoash ruled sixteen years, 11and he did what the LORD said was wrong. He did not stop doing the same sins Jeroboam son of Nebat had done. Jeroboam had led Israel to sin, and Jehoash continued to do the same thing. 12Everything else he did and all his victories, including his war against Amaziah king of Judah, are written in the book of the history of the kings of Israel. 13Jehoash died, and Jeroboam took his place on the throne. Jehoash was buried in Samaria with the kings of Israel.

The Death of Elisha

14At this time Elisha became sick. Before he died, Jehoash king of Israel went to Elisha and cried for him. Jehoash said, "My father, my father! The chariots of Israel and their horsemen!"

15Elisha said to Jehoash, "Take a bow and arrows." So he took a bow and arrows. 16Then Elisha said to him, "Put your hand on the bow." So Jehoash put his hand on the bow. Then Elisha put his hands on the king's hands. 17Elisha said, "Open the east window." So Jehoash opened the window. Then Elisha said, "Shoot," and Jehoash shot. Elisha said, "The LORD's arrow of victory over Aram! You will defeat the Arameans at Aphek until you destroy them."

18Elisha said, "Take the arrows." So Jehoash took them. Then Elisha said to him, "Strike the ground." So Jehoash struck the ground three times and stopped. 19The man of God was angry with him. "You should have struck five or six times!" Elisha said. "Then you would have struck Aram until you had completely destroyed it. But now you will defeat it only three times."

20Then Elisha died and was buried.

At that time groups of Moabites would rob the land in the springtime. 21Once as some Israelites were burying a man, suddenly they saw a group of Moabites coming. The Israelites threw the dead man into Elisha's grave. When the man touched Elisha's bones, the man came back to life and stood on his feet.

War with Aram

22During all the days Jehoahaz was king, Hazael king of Aram troubled Israel. 23But the LORD was kind to the Israelites; he had mercy on them and helped them because of his agreement with Abraham, Isaac, and Jacob. To this day he has never wanted to destroy them or reject them.

24When Hazael king of Aram died, his son Ben-Hadad became king in his place. 25During a war Hazael had taken some cities from Jehoahaz, Jehoash's father. Now Jehoash took back those cities from Hazael's son Ben-Hadad. He defeated Ben-Hadad three times and took back the cities of Israel.

Amaziah King of Judah

14 Amaziah son of Joash became king of Judah during the second year Jehoash son of Jehoahaz was king of Israel. 2Amaziah was twenty-five years old when he became king, and he ruled twenty-nine years in Jerusalem. His mother was named Jehoaddin, and she was from Jerusalem. 3Amaziah did what the LORD said was right. He did everything his father Joash had done, but he did not do as his ancestor David had done. 4The places where gods were worshiped were not removed, so the people still sacrificed and burned incense[d] there.

5As soon as Amaziah took control of the kingdom, he executed the officers who had murdered his father the king. 6But he did not put to death the children of the murderers because of the rule written in the Book of the Teachings of Moses. The LORD had commanded: "Parents must not be put to death when their children do wrong, and children must not be put to death when their parents do wrong. Each must die for his own sins."[n]

7In battle Amaziah killed ten thousand Edomites in the Valley of Salt. He also took the city of Sela. He called it Joktheel, as it is still called today.

8Amaziah sent messengers to Jehoash son of Jehoahaz, the son of Jehu, king of Israel. They said, "Come, let's meet face to face."

9Then Jehoash king of Israel answered Amaziah king of Judah, "A thornbush in Lebanon sent a message to a cedar tree in Lebanon. It said, 'Let your daughter marry my son.' But then a wild animal from Lebanon came by, walking on and crushing the thornbush. 10You have defeated Edom, but you have become proud. Stay at home and brag. Don't ask for trouble, or you and Judah will be defeated."

11But Amaziah would not listen, so Jehoash king of Israel went to attack. He and Amaziah king of Judah faced each other in battle at Beth Shemesh in Judah. 12Israel defeated Judah, and every man of Judah ran away to his home. 13At Beth Shemesh Jehoash king of Israel captured Amaziah king of Judah. (Amaziah was the son of Joash, who was the son of Ahaziah.) Jehoash went up to Jerusalem and broke down the wall of Jerusalem from the Gate of Ephraim to the Corner Gate, which was about six hundred feet. 14He took all the gold and silver and all the utensils in the Temple[d] of the LORD, and he took the treasuries of the palace and some hostages. Then he returned to Samaria.

15The other acts of Jehoash and his victories, including his war against Amaziah king of Judah, are written in the book of the history of the kings of Israel. 16Jehoash died and was buried in Sa-

"Parents . . . sins." See Deuteronomy 24:16.

maria with the kings of Israel, and his son Jeroboam became king in his place.

17Amaziah son of Joash, the king of Judah, lived fifteen years after the death of Jehoash son of Jehoahaz, the king of Israel. 18The other things Amaziah did are written in the book of the history of the kings of Judah. 19The people in Jerusalem made plans against him. So he ran away to the town of Lachish, but they sent men after him to Lachish and killed him. 20They brought his body back on horses, and he was buried with his ancestors in Jerusalem, in the city of David.

21Then all the people of Judah made Uzziah[n] king in place of his father Amaziah. Uzziah was sixteen years old. 22He rebuilt the town of Elath and made it part of Judah again after Amaziah died.

Jeroboam King of Israel

23Jeroboam son of Jehoash became king of Israel in Samaria during the fifteenth year Amaziah was king of Judah. (Amaziah was the son of Joash.) Jeroboam ruled forty-one years, 24and he did what the LORD said was wrong. Jeroboam son of Nebat had led Israel to sin, and Jeroboam son of Jehoash did not stop doing the same sins. 25Jeroboam won back Israel's border from Lebo Hamath to the Dead Sea.[d] This happened as the LORD, the God of Israel, had said through his servant Jonah son of Amittai, the prophet[d] from Gath Hepher. 26The LORD had seen how the Israelites, both slave and free, were suffering terribly. No one was left who could help Israel. 27The LORD had not said he would completely destroy Israel from the world, so he saved the Israelites through Jeroboam son of Jehoash.

28Everything else Jeroboam did is written down—all his victories and how he won back from Judah the towns of Damascus and Hamath for Israel. All this is written in the book of the history of the kings of Israel. 29Jeroboam died and was buried with his ancestors, the kings of Israel. Jeroboam's son Zechariah became king in his place.

Uzziah King of Judah

15 Uzziah[n] son of Amaziah became king of Judah during Jeroboam's twenty-seventh year as king of Israel. 2Uzziah was sixteen years old when he became king, and he ruled fifty-two years in Jerusalem. His mother was named Jecoliah, and she was from Jerusalem. 3He did what the LORD said was right, just as his father Amaziah had done. 4But the places where gods were worshiped were not removed, so the people still made sacrifices and burned incense[d] there.

5The LORD struck Uzziah with a skin disease, which he had until the day he died. So he had to live in a separate house. Jotham, the king's son, was in charge of the palace, and he governed the people of the land.

6All the other things Uzziah did are written in the book of the history of the kings of Judah. 7Uzziah died and was buried near his ancestors in Jerusalem, and his son Jotham became king in his place.

Zechariah King of Israel

8Zechariah son of Jeroboam was king over Israel in Samaria. He ruled for six months during Uzziah's[n] thirty-eighth year as king of Judah. 9Zechariah did what the LORD said was wrong, just as his ancestors had done. Jeroboam son of Nebat had led the people of Israel to sin, and Zechariah did not stop doing the same sins.

10Shallum son of Jabesh made plans against Zechariah and killed him in front of the people. Then Shallum became king in his place. 11The other acts of Zechariah are written in the book of the history of the kings of Israel. 12The LORD had told Jehu: "Your sons down to your great-great-grandchildren will be kings of Israel," and the LORD's word came true.

Shallum King of Israel

13Shallum son of Jabesh became king during Uzziah's thirty-ninth year as king of Judah. Shallum ruled for a month in Samaria. 14Then Menahem son of Gadi came up from Tirzah to Samaria and attacked Shallum son of Jabesh in Samaria. He killed him and became king in Shallum's place.

15The other acts of Shallum and his secret plans are written in the book of the history of the kings of Israel.

Menahem King of Israel

16Menahem started out from Tirzah and attacked Tiphsah, destroying the city and the area nearby. This was because the people had refused to open the city gate for him. He defeated them and ripped open all their pregnant women.

17Menahem son of Gadi became king over Israel during Uzziah's thirty-ninth year as king of Judah. Menahem ruled ten years in Samaria, 18and he did what the LORD said was wrong. Jeroboam son of Nebat had led Israel to sin, and all the time Menahem was king, he did not stop doing the same sins.

19Pul king of Assyria came to attack the land. Menahem gave him about seventy-four thousand pounds of silver so Pul would support him and make his hold on the kingdom stronger. 20Menahem taxed Israel to pay about one and one-fourth

Uzziah Also called Azariah.

pounds of silver to each soldier of the king of Assyria. So the king left and did not stay in the land. 21 Everything else Menahem did is written in the book of the history of the kings of Israel. 22 Then Menahem died, and his son Pekahiah became king in his place.

Pekahiah King of Israel

23 Pekahiah son of Menahem became king over Israel in Samaria during Uzziah's[n] fiftieth year as king of Judah. Pekahiah ruled two years, 24 and he did what the LORD said was wrong. Jeroboam son of Nebat had led Israel to sin, and Pekahiah did not stop doing the same sins.

25 Pekah son of Remaliah was one of Pekahiah's captains, and he made plans against Pekahiah. He took fifty men of Gilead with him and killed Pekahiah, as well as Argob and Arieh, in the palace at Samaria. Then Pekah became king in Pekahiah's place.

26 Everything else Pekahiah did is written in the book of the history of the kings of Israel.

Pekah King of Israel

27 Pekah son of Remaliah became king over Israel in Samaria during Uzziah's[n] fifty-second year as king of Judah. Pekah ruled twenty years, 28 and he did what the LORD said was wrong. Jeroboam son of Nebat had led Israel to sin, and Pekah did not stop doing the same sins.

29 Tiglath-Pileser[n] was king of Assyria. He attacked while Pekah was king of Israel, capturing the cities of Ijon, Abel Beth Maacah, Janoah, Kedesh, and Hazor. He also captured Gilead and Galilee and all the land of Naphtali and carried the people away to Assyria. 30 Then Hoshea son of Elah made plans against Pekah son of Remaliah and attacked and killed him. Then Hoseah became king in Pekah's place during the twentieth year Jotham son of Uzziah was king.

31 Everything else Pekah did is written in the book of the history of the kings of Israel.

Jotham King of Judah

32 Jotham son of Uzziah became king of Judah during the second year Pekah son of Remaliah was king of Israel. 33 Jotham was twenty-five years old when he became king, and he ruled sixteen years in Jerusalem. His mother's name was Jerusha daughter of Zadok. 34 Jotham did what the LORD said was right, just as his father Uzziah had done. 35 But the places where gods were worshiped were not removed, and the people still made sacrifices and burned incense[d] there. Jotham rebuilt the Upper Gate of the Temple[d] of the LORD.

36 The other things Jotham did while he was king are written in the book of the history of the kings of Judah. 37 At that time the LORD began to send Rezin king of Aram and Pekah son of Remaliah against Judah. 38 Jotham died and was buried with his ancestors in Jerusalem, the city of David, his ancestor. Then Jotham's son Ahaz became king in his place.

Ahaz King of Judah

16 Ahaz was the son of Jotham king of Judah. Ahaz became king of Judah in the seventeenth year Pekah son of Remaliah was king of Israel. 2 Ahaz was twenty years old when he became king, and he ruled sixteen years in Jerusalem. Unlike his ancestor David, he did not do what the LORD his God said was right. 3 Ahaz did the same things the kings of Israel had done. He even made his son pass through fire. He did the same hateful sins as the nations had done whom the LORD had forced out of the land ahead of the Israelites. 4 Ahaz offered sacrifices and burned incense[d] at the places where gods were worshiped, on the hills, and under every green tree.

5 Rezin king of Aram and Pekah son of Remaliah, the king of Israel, came up to attack Jerusalem. They surrounded Ahaz but could not defeat him. 6 At that time Rezin king of Aram took back the city of Elath for Aram, and he forced out all the people of Judah. Then Edomites moved into Elath, and they still live there today.

7 Ahaz sent messengers to Tiglath-Pileser king of Assyria, saying, "I am your servant and your friend. Come and save me from the king of Aram and the king of Israel, who are attacking me." 8 Ahaz took the silver and gold that was in the Temple[d] of the LORD and in the treasuries of the palace, and he sent these as a gift to the king of Assyria. 9 So the king of Assyria listened to Ahaz. He attacked Damascus and captured it and sent all its people away to Kir. And he killed Rezin.

10 Then King Ahaz went to Damascus to meet Tiglath-Pileser king of Assyria. Ahaz saw an altar at Damascus, and he sent plans and a pattern of this altar to Uriah the priest. 11 So Uriah the priest built an altar, just like the plans King Ahaz had sent him from Damascus. Uriah finished the altar before King Ahaz came back from Damascus. 12 When the king arrived from Damascus, he saw the altar and went near and offered sacrifices on it. 13 He burned his burnt offerings and grain offerings and poured out his drink offering. He also sprinkled the blood of his fellowship offerings on the altar.

14 Ahaz moved the bronze altar that was before the LORD at the front of the Temple. It was be-

Uzziah Also called Azariah.
Tiglath-Pileser Also called Pul.

tween Ahaz's altar and the Temple of the LORD, but he put it on the north side of his altar. 15King Ahaz commanded Uriah the priest, "On the large altar burn the morning burnt offering, the evening grain offering, the king's burnt offering and grain offering, and the whole burnt offering, the grain offering, and the drink offering for all the people of the land. Sprinkle on the altar all the blood of the burnt offering and of the sacrifice. But I will use the bronze altar to ask questions of God." 16So Uriah the priest did everything as King Ahaz commanded him.

17Then King Ahaz took off the side panels from the bases and removed the washing bowls from the top of the bases. He also took the large bowl, which was called the Sea, off the bronze bulls that held it up, and he put it on a stone base. 18Ahaz took away the platform for the royal throne, which had been built at the Temple of the LORD. He also took away the outside entrance for the king. He did these things because of the king of Assyria.

19The other things Ahaz did as king are written in the book of the history of the kings of Judah. 20Ahaz died and was buried with his ancestors in Jerusalem, and Ahaz's son Hezekiah became king in his place.

Hoshea, Last King of Israel

17 Hoshea son of Elah became king over Israel during Ahaz's twelfth year as king of Judah. Hoshea ruled in Samaria nine years. 2He did what the LORD said was wrong, but he was not as bad as the kings of Israel who had ruled before him.

3Shalmaneser king of Assyria came to attack Hoshea. Hoshea had been Shalmaneser's servant and had made the payments to Shalmaneser that he had demanded. 4But the king of Assyria found out that Hoshea had made plans against him by sending messengers to So, the king of Egypt. Hoshea had also stopped giving Shalmaneser the payments, which he had paid every year in the past. For that, the king put Hoshea in prison. 5Then the king of Assyria came and attacked all the land of Israel. He surrounded Samaria and attacked it for three years. 6He defeated Samaria in the ninth year Hoshea was king, and he took the Israelites away to Assyria. He settled them in Halah, in Gozan on the Habor River, and in the cities of the Medes.

Israelites Punished for Sin

7All these things happened because the Israelites had sinned against the LORD their God. He had brought them out of Egypt and had rescued them from the power of the king of Egypt, but the Israelites had honored other gods. 8They lived like the nations the LORD had forced out of the land ahead of them. They lived as their evil kings had shown them, 9secretly sinning against the LORD their God. They built places to worship gods in all their cities, from the watchtower to the strong, walled city. 10They put up stone pillars to gods and Asherah[d] idols on every high hill and under every green tree. 11The Israelites burned incense[d] everywhere gods were worshiped, just as the nations who lived there before them had done, whom the LORD had forced out of the land. The Israelites did wicked things that made the LORD angry. 12They served idols when the LORD had said, "You must not do this." 13The LORD used every prophet[d] and seer[d] to warn Israel and Judah. He said, "Stop your evil ways and obey my commands and laws. Follow all the teachings that I commanded your ancestors, the teachings that I gave you through my servants the prophets."

14But the people would not listen. They were stubborn, just as their ancestors had been who did not believe in the LORD their God. 15They rejected the LORD's laws and the agreement he had made with their ancestors. And they refused to listen to his warnings. They worshiped useless idols and became useless themselves. They did what the nations around them did, which the LORD had warned them not to do.

16The people rejected all the commands of the LORD their God. They molded statues of two calves, and they made an Asherah idol. They worshiped all the stars of the sky and served Baal.[d] 17They made their sons and daughters pass through fire and tried to find out the future by magic and witchcraft.[d] They always chose to do what the LORD said was wrong, which made him angry. 18Because he was very angry with the people of Israel, he removed them from his presence. Only the tribe[d] of Judah was left.

Judah Is Also Guilty

19But even Judah did not obey the commands of the LORD their God. They did what the Israelites had done, 20so the LORD rejected all the people of Israel. He punished them and let others destroy them; he threw them out of his presence. 21When the LORD separated them from the family of David, the Israelites made Jeroboam son of Nebat their king. Jeroboam led the Israelites away from the LORD and led them to sin greatly. 22So they continued to do all the sins Jeroboam did. They did not stop doing these sins 23until the LORD removed the Israelites from his presence, just as he had said through all his servants the prophets.[d] So the Israelites were taken out of their land to Assyria, and they have been there to this day.

The Beginning of the Samaritan People

24The king of Assyria brought people from Babylon, Cuthah, Avva, Hamath, and Sepharvaim and put them in the cities of Samaria to replace the Israelites. These people took over Samaria and lived in the cities. 25At first they did not worship the LORD, so he sent lions among them which killed some of them. 26The king of Assyria was told, "You sent foreigners into the cities of Samaria who do not know the law of the god of the land. This is why he has sent lions among them. The lions are killing them because they don't know what the god wants."

27Then the king of Assyria commanded, "Send back one of the priests you took away. Let him live there and teach the people what the god wants." 28So one of the priests who had been carried away from Samaria returned to live in Bethel. And he taught the people how to honor the LORD.

29But each nation made gods of its own and put them in the cities where they lived and in the temples where gods were worshiped. These temples had been built by the Samaritans. 30The people from Babylon made Succoth Benoth their god. The people from Cuthah worshiped Nergal. The people of Hamath worshiped Ashima. 31The Avvites worshiped Nibhaz and Tartak. The Sepharvites burned their children in the fire, sacrificing them to Adrammelech and Anammelech, the gods of Sepharvaim. 32They also honored the LORD, but they chose priests for the places where gods were worshiped. The priests were chosen from among themselves, and they made sacrifices for the people. 33The people honored the LORD but also served their own gods, just as the nations did from which they had been brought. 34Even today they do as they did in the past. They do not worship the LORD nor obey his rules and commands. They do not obey the teachings or the commands of the LORD, which he gave to the children of Jacob, whom he had named Israel. 35The LORD had made an agreement with them and had commanded them, "Do not honor other gods. Do not bow down to them or worship them or offer sacrifices to them. 36Worship the LORD who brought you up out of the land of Egypt with great power and strength. Bow down to him and offer sacrifices to him. 37Always obey the rules, orders, teachings, and commands he wrote for you. Do not honor other gods. 38Do not forget the agreement I made with you, and do not honor other gods. 39Instead worship the LORD your God, who will save you from all your enemies."

40But the Israelites did not listen. They kept on doing the same things they had done before. 41So these nations honored the LORD but also worshiped their idols, and their children and grandchildren still do as their ancestors did.

Hezekiah King of Judah

18 Hezekiah son of Ahaz king of Judah became king during the third year Hoshea son of Elah was king of Israel. 2Hezekiah was twenty-five years old when he became king, and he ruled twenty-nine years in Jerusalem. His mother's name was Abijah daughter of Zechariah. 3Hezekiah did what the LORD said was right, just as his ancestor David had done. 4He removed the places where gods were worshiped. He smashed the stone pillars and cut down the Asherah[d] idols. Also the Israelites had been burning incense[d] to Nehushtan, the bronze snake Moses had made. But Hezekiah broke it into pieces.

5Hezekiah trusted in the LORD, the God of Israel. There was no one like him among all the kings of Judah, either before him or after him. 6Hezekiah was loyal to the LORD and did not stop following him; he obeyed the commands the LORD had given Moses. 7And the LORD was with Hezekiah, so he had success in everything he did. He turned against the king of Assyria and stopped serving him. 8Hezekiah defeated the Philistines all the way to Gaza and its borders, including the watchtowers and the strong, walled cities.

The Assyrians Capture Samaria

9Shalmaneser king of Assyria surrounded Samaria and attacked it in the fourth year Hezekiah was king. This was the seventh year Hoshea son of Elah was king of Israel. 10After three years the Assyrians captured Samaria. This was in the sixth year Hezekiah was king, which was Hoshea's ninth year as king of Israel. 11The king of Assyria took the Israelites away to Assyria and settled them in Halah, in Gozan on the Habor River, and in the cities of the Medes. 12This happened because they did not obey the LORD their God. They broke his agreement and did not obey all that Moses, the LORD's servant, had commanded. They would not listen to the commands or do them.

Assyria Attacks Judah

13During Hezekiah's fourteenth year as king, Sennacherib king of Assyria attacked all the strong, walled cities of Judah and captured them. 14Then Hezekiah king of Judah sent a message to the king of Assyria at Lachish. He said, "I have done wrong. Leave me alone, and I will pay anything you ask." So the king of Assyria made Hezekiah pay about twenty-two thousand pounds of silver and two thousand pounds of gold. 15Hezekiah gave him all the silver that was in the Temple[d] of the LORD and in the palace treasuries. 16Hezekiah stripped all the gold that covered the doors and doorposts of the Temple of the LORD. Hezekiah had put gold on these doors himself, but he gave it all to the king of Assyria.

17The king of Assyria sent out his supreme commander, his chief officer, and his field commander. They went with a large army from Lachish to King Hezekiah in Jerusalem. When they
came near the waterway from the upper pool on
the road where people do their laundry, they
stopped. 18They called for the king, so the king
sent Eliakim, Shebna, and Joah out to meet them.
Eliakim son of Hilkiah was the palace manager,
Shebna was the royal secretary, and Joah son of
Asaph was the recorder.

19The field commander said to them, "Tell Hezekiah this:

" 'The great king, the king of Assyria, says:
What can you trust in now? 20You say you have
battle plans and power for war, but your words
mean nothing. Whom are you trusting for help so
that you turn against me? 21Look, you are depending on Egypt to help you, but Egypt is like a splint-
ered walking stick. If you lean on it for help, it will
stab your hand and hurt you. The king of Egypt
will hurt all those who depend on him. 22You
might say, "We are depending on the LORD our
God," but Hezekiah destroyed the LORD's altars
and the places of worship. Hezekiah told Judah
and Jerusalem, "You must worship only at this
one altar in Jerusalem."

23" 'Now make an agreement with my master,
the king of Assyria: I will give you two thousand
horses if you can find enough men to ride them.
24You cannot defeat one of my master's least important officers, so why do you depend on Egypt
to give you chariots and horsemen? 25I have not
come to attack and destroy this place without an
order from the LORD. The LORD himself told me
to come to this country and destroy it.' "

26Then Eliakim son of Hilkiah, Shebna, and
Joah said to the field commander, "Please speak
to us in the Aramaic language. We understand it.
Don't speak to us in Hebrew, because the people
on the city wall can hear you."

27"No," the commander said, "my master did
not send me to tell these things only to you and
your king. He sent me to speak also to those people sitting on the wall who will have to eat their
own dung and drink their own urine like you."

28Then the commander stood and shouted
loudly in the Hebrew language, "Listen to what
the great king, the king of Assyria, says! 29The
king says you should not let Hezekiah fool you,
because he can't save you from my power.
30Don't let Hezekiah talk you into trusting the
LORD by saying, 'The LORD will surely save us.
This city won't be handed over to the king of Assyria.'

31"Don't listen to Hezekiah. The king of Assyria
says, 'Make peace with me, and come out of the
city to me. Then everyone will be free to eat the
fruit from his own grapevine and fig tree and to
drink water from his own well. 32After that I will
come and take you to a land like your own—a
land with grain and new wine, bread and vineyards, olives, and honey. Choose to live and not
to die!'

"Don't listen to Hezekiah. He is fooling you
when he says, 'The LORD will save us.' 33Has a
god of any other nation saved his people from the
power of the king of Assyria? 34Where are the
gods of Hamath and Arpad? Where are the gods
of Sepharvaim, Hena, and Ivvah? They did not
save Samaria from my power. 35Not one of all the
gods of these countries has saved his people from
me. Neither can the LORD save Jerusalem from
my power."

36The people were silent. They didn't answer
the commander at all, because King Hezekiah had
ordered, "Don't answer him."

37Then Eliakim, Shebna, and Joah tore their
clothes to show how upset they were. (Eliakim
son of Hilkiah was the palace manager, Shebna
was the royal secretary, and Joah son of Asaph
was the recorder.) The three men went to Hezekiah and told him what the field commander had
said.

SIDELIGHT: The Assyrians' attack on Jerusalem led by Sennacherib isn't recorded only in the Bible (2 Kings 18:13–37). Archaeologists have found "Sennacherib's Prism," which gives the invaders' view of the situation. Another source tells how a plague of mice attacked Sennacherib's army to make the Assyrians retreat.

Jerusalem Will Be Saved

19 When King Hezekiah heard the message, he tore his clothes and put on
rough cloth to show how sad he was. Then he
went into the Temple[d] of the LORD. 2Hezekiah
sent Eliakim, the palace manager, and Shebna,
the royal secretary, and the older priests to Isaiah.
They were all wearing rough cloth when they
came to Isaiah the prophet,[d] the son of Amoz.
3They told Isaiah, "This is what Hezekiah says:
Today is a day of sorrow and punishment and disgrace, as when a child should be born, but the
mother is not strong enough to give birth to it.
4The king of Assyria sent his field commander to
make fun of the living God. Maybe the LORD your
God will hear what the commander said and will
punish him for it. So pray for the few of us who
are left alive."

5When Hezekiah's officers came to Isaiah, 6he
said to them, "Tell your master this: The LORD

says, 'Don't be afraid of what you have heard.
Don't be frightened by the words the servants of
the king of Assyria have spoken against me. 7Lis-
ten! I am going to put a spirit in the king of Assyria. He will hear a report that will make him
return to his own country, and I will cause him
to die by the sword there.' "

8The field commander heard that the king of
Assyria had left Lachish. When he went back, he
found the king fighting against the city of Libnah.

9The king received a report that Tirhakah, the
Cushite king of Egypt, was coming to attack him.
When the king of Assyria heard this, he sent messengers to Hezekiah, saying, 10"Tell Hezekiah
king of Judah: Don't be fooled by the god you
trust. Don't believe him when he says Jerusalem
will not be handed over to the king of Assyria.
11You have heard what the kings of Assyria have
done. They have completely defeated every country, so do not think you will be saved. 12Did the
gods of those people save them? My ancestors destroyed them, defeating the cities of Gozan, Haran, and Rezeph, and the people of Eden living in
Tel Assar. 13Where are the kings of Hamath and
Arpad? Where are the kings of Sepharvaim, Hena,
and Ivvah?"

Hezekiah Prays to the Lord

14When Hezekiah received the letter from the
messengers and read it, he went up to the Temple[d] of the LORD. He spread the letter out before
the LORD 15and prayed to the LORD: "LORD, God
of Israel, whose throne is between the gold creatures with wings, only you are God of all the kingdoms of the earth. You made the heavens and the
earth. 16Hear, LORD, and listen. Open your eyes,
LORD, and see. Listen to the words Sennacherib
has said to insult the living God. 17It is true, LORD,
that the kings of Assyria have destroyed these
countries and their lands. 18They have thrown the
gods of these nations into the fire, but they were
only wood and rock statues that people made. So
the kings have destroyed them. 19Now, LORD our
God, save us from the king's power so that all the
kingdoms of the earth will know that you, LORD,
are the only God."

God Answers Hezekiah

20Then Isaiah son of Amoz sent a message to
Hezekiah that said, "This is what the LORD, the
God of Israel, says: I have heard your prayer to me
about Sennacherib king of Assyria. 21This is what
the LORD has said against Sennacherib:

'The people of Jerusalem
hate you and make fun of you.
The people of Jerusalem
laugh at you as you run away.
22You have insulted me and spoken against me;
you have raised your voice against me.
You have a proud look on your face,
which is against me, the Holy One of Israel.
23You have sent your messengers to insult the Lord.
You have said, "With my many chariots
I have gone to the tops of the mountains,
to the highest mountains of Lebanon.
I have cut down its tallest cedars
and its best pine trees.
I have gone to its farthest places
and to its best forests.
24I have dug wells in foreign countries
and drunk water there.
By the soles of my feet,
I have dried up all the rivers of Egypt."

25" 'King of Assyria, surely you have heard.
Long ago I, the LORD, planned these things.
Long ago I designed them,
and now I have made them happen.
I allowed you to turn those strong, walled cities
into piles of rocks.
26The people in those cities were weak;
they were frightened and put to shame.
They were like grass in the field,
like tender, young grass,
like grass on the housetop
that is burned by the wind before it can grow.

27" 'I know when you rest,
when you come and go,
and how you rage against me.
28Because you rage against me,
and because I have heard your proud words,
I will put my hook in your nose
and my bit in your mouth.
Then I will force you to leave my country
the same way you came.'

29"Then the LORD said, 'Hezekiah, I will give
you this sign:
This year you will eat the grain that grows wild,
and the second year you will eat what grows wild from that.
But in the third year, plant grain and harvest it.
Plant vineyards and eat their fruit.
30Some of the people in the family of Judah will escape.
Like plants that take root,
they will grow strong and have many children.
31A few people will come out of Jerusalem alive;
a few from Mount Zion[d] will live.

The strong love of the LORD All-Powerful
will make this happen.'

32"So this is what the LORD says about the king
of Assyria:
'He will not enter this city
or even shoot an arrow here.
He will not fight against it with shields
or build a ramp to attack the city walls.
33He will return to his country the same way
he came,
and he will not enter this city,'
says the LORD.
34'I will defend and save this city
for my sake and for the sake of David, my
servant.' "

35That night the angel of the LORD went out
and killed one hundred eighty-five thousand men
in the Assyrian camp. When the people got up
early the next morning, they saw all the dead bodies. 36So Sennacherib king of Assyria left and went
back to Nineveh and stayed there.
37One day as Sennacherib was worshiping in
the temple of his god Nisroch, his sons Adrammelech and Sharezer killed him with a sword. Then
they escaped to the land of Ararat. So Sennacherib's son Esarhaddon became king of Assyria.

Hezekiah's Illness

20 At that time Hezekiah became so sick he
almost died. The prophet[d] Isaiah son of
Amoz went to see him and told him, "This is
what the LORD says: Make arrangements because
you are not going to live, but die."
2Hezekiah turned toward the wall and prayed
to the LORD, 3"LORD, please remember that I have
always obeyed you. I have given myself completely to you and have done what you said was
right." Then Hezekiah cried loudly.
4Before Isaiah had left the middle courtyard,
the LORD spoke his word to Isaiah: 5"Go back and
tell Hezekiah, the leader of my people: 'This is
what the LORD, the God of your ancestor David,
says: I have heard your prayer and seen your
tears, so I will heal you. Three days from now you
will go up to the Temple[d] of the LORD. 6I will add
fifteen years to your life. I will save you and this
city from the king of Assyria; I will protect the city
for my sake and for the sake of my servant David.' "
7Then Isaiah said, "Make a paste from figs." So
they made it and put it on Hezekiah's boil, and he
got well.
8Hezekiah had asked Isaiah, "What will be the
sign that the LORD will heal me and that I will go
up to the Temple[d] of the LORD on the third day?"
9Isaiah said, "The LORD will do what he says.
This is the sign from the LORD to show you: Do
you want the shadow to go forward ten steps or
back ten steps?"
10Hezekiah answered, "It's easy for the shadow
to go forward ten steps. Instead, let it go back ten
steps."
11Then Isaiah the prophet called to the LORD,
and the LORD brought the shadow ten steps back
up the stairway of Ahaz that it had gone down.

Messengers from Babylon

12At that time Merodach-Baladan son of Baladan was king of Babylon. He sent letters and a gift
to Hezekiah, because he had heard that Hezekiah
was sick. 13Hezekiah listened to the messengers,
so he showed them what was in his storehouses:
the silver, gold, spices, expensive perfumes, his
swords and shields, and all his wealth. He showed
them everything in his palace and his kingdom.
14Then Isaiah the prophet[d] went to King Hezekiah and asked him, "What did these men say?
Where did they come from?"
Hezekiah said, "They came from a faraway
country—from Babylon."
15So Isaiah asked him, "What did they see in
your palace?"
Hezekiah said, "They saw everything in my palace. I showed them all my wealth."
16Then Isaiah said to Hezekiah, "Listen to the
words of the LORD: 17'In the future everything in
your palace and everything your ancestors have
stored up until this day will be taken away to Babylon. Nothing will be left,' says the LORD. 18'Some
of your own children, those who will be born to
you, will be taken away. And they will become
servants in the palace of the king of Babylon.' "
19Hezekiah told Isaiah, "These words from the
LORD are good." He said this because he thought,
"There will be peace and security in my lifetime."
20Everything else Hezekiah did—all his victories, his work on the pool, his work on the tunnel
to bring water into the city—is written in the
book of the history of the kings of Judah. 21Then
Hezekiah died, and his son Manasseh became
king in his place.

SIDELIGHT: *The tunnel King Hezekiah dug to provide water for Jerusalem during the Assyrian siege (2 Kings 20:20) was cut through 1,748 feet of solid limestone—almost 200 feet longer than the longest span of Brooklyn Bridge in New York City. An inscription on "Hezekiah's Tunnel" says workers started digging at each end and met in the middle. People still walk through the tunnel today.*

Manasseh King of Judah

21 Manasseh was twelve years old when he became king, and he was king fifty-five years in Jerusalem. His mother's name was Hephzibah. 2He did what the LORD said was wrong. He did the hateful things the other nations had done—the nations that the LORD had forced out of the land ahead of the Israelites. 3Manasseh's father, Hezekiah, had destroyed the places where gods were worshiped, but Manasseh rebuilt them. He built altars for Baal,[d] and he made an Asherah[d] idol as Ahab king of Israel had done. Manasseh also worshiped all the stars of the sky and served them. 4The LORD had said about the Temple,[d] "I will be worshiped in Jerusalem," but Manasseh built altars in the Temple of the LORD. 5He built altars to worship the stars in the two courtyards of the Temple of the LORD. 6He made his own son pass through fire. He practiced magic and told the future by explaining signs and dreams, and he got advice from mediums[d] and fortune-tellers. He did many things the LORD said were wrong, which made the LORD angry.

> **SIDELIGHT:** The longest reign in the Bible was that of Manasseh. He reigned fifty-five years (2 Kings 21:1). That would be about like Franklin D. Roosevelt being U.S. president still. Despite his long rule, Manasseh was considered one of the most evil kings of Judah (2 Chronicles 33:9, p. 411). The king with the shortest reign was Zimri (1 Kings 16:15, p. 321), who lasted only seven days!

7Manasseh carved an Asherah idol and put it in the Temple. The LORD had said to David and his son Solomon about the Temple, "I will be worshiped forever in this Temple and in Jerusalem, which I have chosen from all the tribes[d] of Israel. 8I will never again make the Israelites wander out of the land I gave their ancestors. But they must obey everything I have commanded them and all the teachings my servant Moses gave them." 9But the people did not listen. Manasseh led them to do more evil than the nations the LORD had destroyed ahead of the Israelites.

10The LORD said through his servants the prophets,[d] 11"Manasseh king of Judah has done these hateful things. He has done more evil than the Amorites before him. He also has led Judah to sin with his idols. 12So this is what the LORD, the God of Israel, says: 'I will bring so much trouble on Jerusalem and Judah that anyone who hears about it will be shocked. 13I will stretch the measuring line of Samaria over Jerusalem, and the plumb line[d] used against Ahab's family will be used on Jerusalem. I will wipe out Jerusalem as a person wipes a dish and turns it upside down. 14I will throw away the rest of my people who are left. I will give them to their enemies, and they will be robbed by all their enemies, 15because my people did what I said was wrong. They have made me angry from the day their ancestors left Egypt until now.' "

16Manasseh also killed many innocent people, filling Jerusalem from one end to the other with their blood. This was besides the sin he led Judah to do; he led Judah to do what the LORD said was wrong.

17The other things Manasseh did as king, even the sin he did, are written in the book of the history of the kings of Judah. 18Manasseh died and was buried in the garden of his own palace, the garden of Uzza. Then Manasseh's son Amon became king in his place.

Amon King of Judah

19Amon was twenty-two years old when he became king, and he was king for two years in Jerusalem. His mother's name was Meshullemeth daughter of Haruz, who was from Jotbah. 20Amon did what the LORD said was wrong, as his father Manasseh had done. 21He lived in the same way his father had lived: he worshiped the idols his father had worshiped, and he bowed down before them. 22Amon rejected the LORD, the God of his ancestors, and did not follow the ways of the LORD.

23Amon's officers made plans against him and killed him in his palace. 24Then the people of the land killed all those who had made plans to kill King Amon, and they made his son Josiah king in his place.

25Everything else Amon did is written in the book of the history of the kings of Judah. 26He was buried in his grave in the garden of Uzza, and his son Josiah became king in his place.

Josiah King of Judah

22 Josiah was eight years old when he became king, and he ruled thirty-one years in Jerusalem. His mother's name was Jedidah daughter of Adaiah, who was from Bozkath. 2Josiah did what the LORD said was right. He lived as his ancestor David had lived, and he did not stop doing what was right.

3In Josiah's eighteenth year as king, he sent Shaphan to the Temple[d] of the LORD. Shaphan son of Azaliah, the son of Meshullam, was the royal secretary. Josiah said, 4"Go up to Hilkiah the high priest, and have him empty out the money the gatekeepers have gathered from the people. This is the money they have brought into the Temple of the LORD. 5Have him give the money to the supervisors of the work on the Temple of the LORD. They must pay the workers who repair the Temple of the LORD— 6the carpenters, builders, and bricklayers. Also use the money to buy timber and cut stone to repair the Temple. 7They do not need to report how they use the money given to them, because they are working honestly."

The Book of the Teachings Is Found

8Hilkiah the high priest said to Shaphan the royal secretary, "I've found the Book of the Teachings in the Temple[d] of the LORD." He gave it to Shaphan, who read it.

9Then Shaphan the royal secretary went to the king and reported to Josiah, "Your officers have paid out the money that was in the Temple of the LORD. They have given it to the workers and supervisors at the Temple." 10Then Shaphan the royal secretary told the king, "Hilkiah the priest has given me a book." And Shaphan read from the book to the king.

11When the king heard the words of the Book of the Teachings, he tore his clothes to show how upset he was. 12He gave orders to Hilkiah the priest, Ahikam son of Shaphan, Acbor son of Micaiah, Shaphan the royal secretary, and Asaiah the king's servant. These were the orders: 13"Go and ask the LORD about the words in the book that was found. Ask for me, for all the people, and for all Judah. The LORD's anger is burning against us, because our ancestors did not obey the words of this book; they did not do all the things written for us to do."

14So Hilkiah the priest, Ahikam, Acbor, Shaphan, and Asaiah went to talk to Huldah the prophetess.[d] She was the wife of Shallum son of Tikvah, the son of Harhas, who took care of the king's clothes. Huldah lived in Jerusalem, in the new area of the city.

15She said to them, "This is what the LORD, the God of Israel, says: Tell the man who sent you to me, 16'This is what the LORD says: I will bring trouble to this place and to the people living here, as it is written in the book which the king of Judah has read. 17The people of Judah have left me and have burned incense[d] to other gods. They have made me angry by all that they have done. My anger burns against this place like a fire, and it will not be put out.' 18Tell the king of Judah, who sent you to ask the LORD, 'This is what the LORD, the God of Israel, says about the words you heard: 19When you heard my words against this place and its people, you became sorry for what you had done and humbled yourself before me. I said they would be cursed and would be destroyed. You tore your clothes to show how upset you were, and you cried in my presence. This is why I have heard you, says the LORD. 20So I will let you die, and you will be buried in peace. You won't see all the trouble I will bring to this place.'"

So they took her message back to the king.

The People Hear the Agreement

23 Then the king gathered all the older leaders of Judah and Jerusalem together. 2He went up to the Temple[d] of the LORD, and all the people from Judah and Jerusalem went with him. The priests, prophets,[d] and all the people—from the least important to the most important—went with him. He read to them all the words of the Book of the Agreement that was found in the Temple of the LORD. 3The king stood by the pillar and made an agreement in the presence of the LORD to follow the LORD and obey his commands, rules, and laws with his whole being, and to obey the words of the agreement written in this book. Then all the people promised to obey the agreement.

Josiah Destroys the Places for Idol Worship

4The king commanded Hilkiah the high priest and the priests of the next rank and the gatekeepers to bring out of the Temple[d] of the LORD everything made for Baal,[d] Asherah,[d] and all the stars of the sky. Then Josiah burned them outside Jerusalem in the open country of the Kidron Valley and carried their ashes to Bethel. 5The kings of Judah had chosen priests for these gods. These priests burned incense[d] in the places where gods were worshiped in the cities of Judah and the towns around Jerusalem. They burned incense to Baal, the sun, the moon, the planets, and all the stars of the sky. But Josiah took those priests away. 6He removed the Asherah idol from the Temple of the LORD and took it outside Jerusalem to the Kidron Valley, where he burned it and beat it into dust. Then he threw the dust on the graves of the common people. 7He also tore down the houses of the male prostitutes[d] who were in the Temple of the LORD, where the women did weaving for Asherah.

8King Josiah brought all the false priests from the cities of Judah. He ruined the places where gods were worshiped, where the priests had burned incense, from Geba to Beersheba. He destroyed the places of worship at the entrance to the Gate of Joshua, the ruler of the city, on the left side of the city gate. 9The priests at the places where gods were worshiped were not allowed to serve at the LORD's altar in Jerusalem. But they could eat bread made without yeast with their brothers.

10Josiah ruined Topheth, in the Valley of Ben Hinnom, so no one could sacrifice his son or daughter to Molech.[d] 11Judah's kings had placed

horses at the front door of the Temple of the LORD
in the courtyard near the room of Nathan-Melech,
an officer. These horses were for the worship of
the sun. So Josiah removed them and burned the
chariots that were for sun worship also.
12The kings of Judah had built altars on the
roof[n] of the upstairs room of Ahaz. Josiah broke
down these altars and the altars Manasseh had
made in the two courtyards of the Temple of the
LORD. Josiah smashed them to pieces and threw
their dust into the Kidron Valley. 13King Josiah
ruined the places where gods were worshiped
east of Jerusalem, south of the Mount of Olives.[n]
Solomon king of Israel had built these places. One
was for Ashtoreth,[d] the hated goddess of the Sidonians. One was for Chemosh,[d] the hated god of
Moab. And one was for Molech, the hated god
of the Ammonites. 14Josiah smashed to pieces
the stone pillars they worshiped, and he cut down
the Asherah idols. Then he covered the places
with human bones.
15Josiah also broke down the altar at Bethel—
the place of worship made by Jeroboam son of
Nebat, who had led Israel to sin. Josiah burned
that place, broke the stones of the altar into
pieces, then beat them into dust. He also burned
the Asherah idol. 16When he turned around, he
saw the graves on the mountain. He had the
bones taken from the graves, and he burned them
on the altar to ruin it. This happened as the LORD
had said it would through the man of God.
17Josiah asked, "What is that monument I see?"
The people of the city answered, "It's the grave
of the man of God who came from Judah. This
prophet announced the things you have done
against the altar of Bethel."
18Josiah said, "Leave the grave alone. No one
may move this man's bones." So they left his
bones and the bones of the prophet who had
come from Samaria.
19The kings of Israel had built temples for worshiping gods in the cities of Samaria, which had
caused the LORD to be angry. Josiah removed all
those temples and did the same things as he had
done at Bethel. 20He killed all the priests of those
places of worship; he killed them on the altars
and burned human bones on the altars. Then he
went back to Jerusalem.

Josiah Celebrates the Passover

21The king commanded all the people, "Celebrate the Passover[d] to the LORD your God as it is
written in this Book of the Agreement." 22The
Passover had not been celebrated like this since
the judges led Israel. Nor had one like it happened
while there were kings of Israel and kings of Judah. 23This Passover was celebrated to the LORD
in Jerusalem in the eighteenth year of King Josiah's rule.
24Josiah destroyed the mediums,[d] fortune-
tellers, house gods, and idols. He also destroyed
all the hated gods seen in the land of Judah and
Jerusalem. This was to obey the words of the
teachings written in the book Hilkiah the priest
had found in the Temple[d] of the LORD.
25There was no king like Josiah before or after
him. He obeyed the LORD with all his heart, soul,
and strength, following all the Teachings of Moses.
26Even so, the LORD did not stop his strong and
terrible anger. His anger burned against Judah because of all Manasseh had done to make him angry. 27The LORD said, "I will send Judah out of my
sight, as I have sent Israel away. I will reject Jerusalem, which I chose. And I will take away the
Temple about which I said, 'I will be worshiped
there.' "
28Everything else Josiah did is written in the
book of the history of the kings of Judah.
29While Josiah was king, Neco king of Egypt
went to help the king of Assyria at the Euphrates
River. King Josiah marched out to fight against
Neco, but at Megiddo, Neco faced him and killed
him. 30Josiah's servants carried his body in a chariot from Megiddo to Jerusalem and buried him in
his own grave. Then the people of Judah chose
Josiah's son Jehoahaz and poured olive oil on him
to make him king in his father's place.

Jehoahaz King of Judah

31Jehoahaz was twenty-three years old when
he became king, and he was king in Jerusalem for
three months. His mother's name was Hamutal,
who was the daughter of Jeremiah from Libnah.
32Jehoahaz did what the LORD said was wrong,
just as his ancestors had done.
33King Neco took Jehoahaz prisoner at Riblah
in the land of Hamath so that Jehoahaz could
not rule in Jerusalem. Neco made the people of
Judah pay about seventy-five hundred pounds
of silver and about seventy-five pounds of gold.
34King Neco made Josiah's son Eliakim the king
in place of Josiah his father. Then Neco changed
Eliakim's name to Jehoiakim. But Neco took Jehoahaz to Egypt, where he died. 35Jehoiakim gave
King Neco the silver and gold he demanded. Jehoiakim taxed the land and took silver and gold
from the people of the land to give to King Neco.
Each person had to pay his share.

roof In Bible times houses were built with flat roofs. The roof was used for drying things such as flax and fruit. And it was used as an extra room, as a place for worship, and as a place to sleep in the summer.

Mount of Olives Literally, "The Mountain of Ruin."

Jehoiakim King of Judah

36Jehoiakim was twenty-five years old when he became king, and he was king in Jerusalem for eleven years. His mother's name was Zebidah daughter of Pedaiah, who was from Rumah. 37Jehoiakim did what the LORD said was wrong, just as his ancestors had done.

24 While Jehoiakim was king, Nebuchadnezzar king of Babylon attacked the land of Judah. So Jehoiakim became Nebuchadnezzar's servant for three years. Then he turned against Nebuchadnezzar and broke away from his rule. 2The LORD sent raiding parties from Babylon, Aram, Moab, and Ammon against Jehoiakim to destroy Judah. This happened as the LORD had said it would through his servants the prophets.[d]

3The LORD commanded this to happen to the people of Judah, to remove them from his presence, because of all the sins of Manasseh. 4He had killed many innocent people and had filled Jerusalem with their blood. And the LORD would not forgive these sins.

5The other things that happened while Jehoiakim was king and all he did are written in the book of the history of the kings of Judah. 6Jehoiakim died, and his son Jehoiachin became king in his place.

7The king of Egypt did not leave his land again, because the king of Babylon had captured all that belonged to the king of Egypt, from the brook of Egypt to the Euphrates River.

Jehoiachin King of Judah

8Jehoiachin was eighteen years old when he became king, and he was king three months in Jerusalem. His mother's name was Nehushta daughter of Elnathan from Jerusalem. 9Jehoiachin did what the LORD said was wrong, just as his father had done.

10At that time the officers of Nebuchadnezzar king of Babylon came up to Jerusalem. When they reached the city, they attacked it. 11Nebuchadnezzar himself came to the city while his officers were attacking it. 12Jehoiachin king of Judah surrendered to the king of Babylon, along with Jehoiachin's mother, servants, older leaders, and officers. So Nebuchadnezzar made Jehoiachin a prisoner in the eighth year he was king of Babylon. 13Nebuchadnezzar took all the treasures from the Temple[d] of the LORD and from the palace. He cut up all the gold objects Solomon king of Israel had made for the Temple of the LORD. This happened as the LORD had said it would. 14Nebuchadnezzar took away all the people of Jerusalem, including all the leaders, all the wealthy people, and all the craftsmen and metal workers. There were ten thousand prisoners in all. Only the poorest people in the land were left. 15Nebuchadnezzar carried away Jehoiachin to Babylon, as well as the king's mother and his wives, the officers, and the leading men of the land. They were taken captive from Jerusalem to Babylon. 16The king of Babylon also took all seven thousand soldiers, who were strong and able to fight in war, and about a thousand craftsmen and metal workers. Nebuchadnezzar took them as prisoners to Babylon. 17Then he made Mattaniah, Jehoiachin's uncle, king in Jehoiachin's place. He also changed Mattaniah's name to Zedekiah.

Zedekiah King of Judah

18Zedekiah was twenty-one years old when he became king, and he was king in Jerusalem for eleven years. His mother's name was Hamutal daughter of Jeremiah[n] from Libnah. 19Zedekiah did what the LORD said was wrong, just as Jehoiakim had done. 20All this happened in Jerusalem and Judah because the LORD was angry with them. Finally, he threw them out of his presence.

The Fall of Jerusalem

Zedekiah turned against the king of Babylon.

25 Nebuchadnezzar king of Babylon marched against Jerusalem with his whole army during Zedekiah's ninth year as king, on the tenth day of the tenth month. He made a camp around the city and piled dirt against the city walls to attack it. 2The city was under attack until Zedekiah's eleventh year as king. 3By the ninth day of the fourth month, the hunger was terrible in the city. There was no food for the people to eat. 4Then the city was broken into, and the whole army ran away at night through the gate between the two walls by the king's garden. While the Babylonians were still surrounding the city, Zedekiah and his men ran away toward the Jordan Valley. 5But the Babylonian army chased King Zedekiah and caught up with him in the plains of Jericho. All of his army was scattered from him, 6so they captured Zedekiah and took him to the king of Babylon at Riblah. There he passed sentence on Zedekiah. 7They killed Zedekiah's sons as he watched. Then they put out his eyes and put bronze chains on him and took him to Babylon.

8Nebuzaradan was the commander of the king's special guards. This officer of the king of Babylon came to Jerusalem on the seventh day of the fifth month, in Nebuchadnezzar's nineteenth year as king of Babylon. 9Nebuzaradan set fire to the Temple[d] of the LORD and the palace and all the houses of Jerusalem. Every important building was burned.

Jeremiah This is not the prophet Jeremiah, but a different man with the same name.

10The whole Babylonian army, led by the commander of the king's special guards, broke down
the walls around Jerusalem. 11Nebuzaradan, the
commander of the guards, captured the people
left in Jerusalem, those who had surrendered to
the king of Babylon, and the rest of the people.
12But the commander left behind some of the
poorest people of the land to take care of the vineyards and fields.
13The Babylonians broke up the bronze pillars,
the bronze stands, and the large bronze bowl,
which was called the Sea, in the Temple of the
LORD. Then they carried the bronze to Babylon.
14They also took the pots, shovels, wick trimmers,
dishes, and all the bronze objects used to serve in
the Temple. 15The commander of the king's special guards took away the pans for carrying hot
coals, the bowls, and everything made of pure
gold or silver. 16There were two pillars and the
large bronze bowl and the movable stands which
Solomon had made for the Temple of the LORD.
There was so much bronze that it could not be
weighed. 17Each pillar was about twenty-seven
feet high. The bronze capital[d] on top of the pillar
was about four and one-half feet high. It was decorated with a net design and bronze pomegranates[d] all around it. The other pillar also had a net
design and was like the first pillar.

Judah Is Taken Prisoner

18The commander of the guards took some prisoners—Seraiah the chief priest, Zephaniah the
priest next in rank, and the three doorkeepers.
19Of the people who were still in the city, he took
the officer in charge of the fighting men, as well
as five people who advised the king. He took the
royal secretary who selected people for the army
and sixty other men who were in the city. 20Neb-
uzaradan, the commander, took all these people
and brought them to the king of Babylon at Riblah. 21There at Riblah, in the land of Hamath, the
king had them killed. So the people of Judah were
led away from their country as captives.

Gedaliah Becomes Governor

22Nebuchadnezzar king of Babylon left some
people in the land of Judah. He appointed Gedaliah son of Ahikam, the son of Shaphan, as governor.
23The army captains and their men heard that
the king of Babylon had made Gedaliah governor,
so they came to Gedaliah at Mizpah. They were
Ishmael son of Nethaniah, Johanan son of Kareah,
Seraiah son of Tanhumeth the Netophathite, Jaazaniah son of the Maacathite, and their men.
24Then Gedaliah promised these army captains
and their men, "Don't be afraid of the Babylonian
officers. Live in the land and serve the king of
Babylon, and everything will go well for you."
25In the seventh month Ishmael son of Nethaniah, son of Elishama from the king's family, came
with ten men and killed Gedaliah. They also
killed the men of Judah and Babylon who were
with Gedaliah at Mizpah. 26Then all the people,
from the least important to the most important,
along with the army leaders, ran away to Egypt,
because they were afraid of the Babylonians.

Jehoiachin Is Set Free

27Jehoiachin king of Judah was held in Babylon
for thirty-seven years. In the thirty-seventh year
Evil-Merodach became king of Babylon, and he
let Jehoiachin out of prison on the twenty-seventh
day of the twelfth month. 28Evil-Merodach spoke
kindly to Jehoiachin and gave him a seat of honor
above the seats of the other kings who were with
him in Babylon. 29So Jehoiachin put away his
prison clothes. For the rest of his life, he ate at the
king's table. 30Every day, for as long as Jehoiachin
lived, the king gave him an allowance.

1 CHRONICLES

Why Read This Book:

- See God's faithfulness traced through history (1 Chronicles 1—9).
- Find out how David's relationship with God affected every area of his life (1 Chronicles 10—29).

Behind the Scenes:

In 1976, Alex Haley's book (and, later, TV mini-series), Roots, swept North America. People were entranced with the story Haley reconstructed of his ancestors' capture in Africa, of their being sold as slaves, and of their living on plantations with sometimes-brutal owners. Suddenly thousands of people began looking for their own "roots"—their own sense of where they had come from.

The books of 1 and 2 Chronicles (which were originally one book) are like the book Roots. They were written hundreds of years after the events to tell the Israelites where they had come from. The Israelites had been exiles—prisoners of war—in Babylon, where they had been taken because they did not follow God. They had returned to Jerusalem and were rebuilding their city, their history, and their lives.

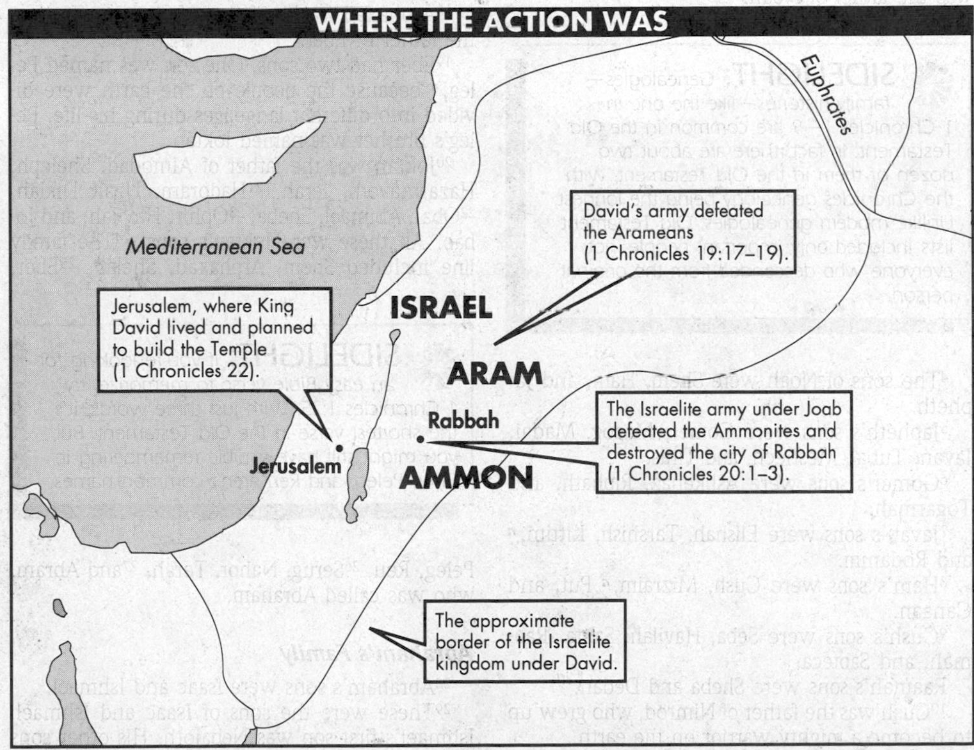
WHERE THE ACTION WAS
Euphrates
David's army defeated the Arameans (1 Chronicles 19:17–19).
Mediterranean Sea
Jerusalem, where King David lived and planned to build the Temple (1 Chronicles 22).
ISRAEL
ARAM
Rabbah
The Israelite army under Joab defeated the Ammonites and destroyed the city of Rabbah (1 Chronicles 20:1–3).
Jerusalem
AMMON
The approximate border of the Israelite kingdom under David.

WHEN THE ACTION WAS

1000BC	750BC	500BC	250BC	BC/AD
Solomon was Israel's king	People returned to Jerusalem from exile	1 and 2 Chronicles were written		Jesus was born
David was Israel's king	The Northern Kingdom (Israel) fell to Assyria	The Southern Kingdom (Judah) fell to Babylon		

Behind the Scenes (cont.):

First Chronicles was written to inspire these Israelites to return not only to Jerusalem but also to God. To do this, the author traced Israel's family roots and then told the story of the nation's greatest ruler, King David. Throughout the book one message is clear: The nation's success is directly linked to the people's relationship with God.

The two books of Chronicles weren't written to give a precise history of the Israelites. For example, the stories of David and Solomon are idealized here, leaving out some of the negative stories found in 1 and 2 Samuel (p. 245 and p. 274), and in 1 and 2 Kings (p. 302 and p. 332), which cover the same time period.

Instead, 1 and 2 Chronicles were written to point out how God had guided people in the past and to remind readers—including us—of the importance of following God.

From Adam to Abraham

1 Adam was the father of Seth. Seth was the
father of Enosh. Enosh was the father of Kenan. 2Kenan was the father of Mahalalel. Mahalalel was the father of Jared. Jared was the father of
Enoch. 3Enoch was the father of Methuselah. Methuselah was the father of Lamech, and Lamech
was the father of Noah.

> **SIDELIGHT:** Genealogies—family histories—like the one in 1 Chronicles 1—9 are common in the Old Testament. In fact, there are about two dozen of them in the Old Testament, with the Chronicles genealogy being the longest. Unlike modern genealogies, Old Testament lists included only important people, not everyone who descended from the original person.

4The sons of Noah were Shem, Ham, and Japheth.
5Japheth's sons were Gomer, Magog, Madai,
Javan, Tubal, Meshech, and Tiras.
6Gomer's sons were Ashkenaz, Riphath, and
Togarmah.
7Javan's sons were Elishah, Tarshish, Kittim,[n]
and Rodanim.
8Ham's sons were Cush, Mizraim,[n] Put, and
Canaan.
9Cush's sons were Seba, Havilah, Sabta, Raamah, and Sabteca.
Raamah's sons were Sheba and Dedan.
10Cush was the father of Nimrod, who grew up
to become a mighty warrior on the earth.
11Mizraim was the father of the Ludites, Ana-
mites, Lehabites, and Naphtuhites,
12Pathrusites, Casluhites, and Caphtorites.
(The Philistines came from the Casluhites.)
13Canaan's first child was Sidon. He was also
the father of the Hittites, 14Jebusites, Amorites,
Girgashites, 15Hivites, Arkites, Sinites, 16Arvad-
ites, Zemarites, and Hamathites.
17Shem's sons were Elam, Asshur, Arphaxad,
Lud, and Aram.
Aram's sons were Uz, Hul, Gether, and Meshech.
18Arphaxad was the father of Shelah, who was
the father of Eber.
19Eber had two sons. One son was named Peleg,[n] because the people on the earth were divided into different languages during his life. Peleg's brother was named Joktan.
20Joktan was the father of Almodad, Sheleph,
Hazarmaveth, Jerah, 21Hadoram, Uzal, Diklah,
22Obal, Abimael, Sheba, 23Ophir, Havilah, and Jobab. All these were Joktan's sons. 24The family
line included Shem, Arphaxad, Shelah, 25Eber,

> **SIDELIGHT:** If you're looking for an easy Bible verse to memorize, try 1 Chronicles 1:25. With just three words, it's the shortest verse in the Old Testament. But you might still have trouble remembering it; Eber, Peleg, and Reu aren't common names.

Peleg, Reu, 26Serug, Nahor, Terah, 27and Abram,
who was called Abraham.

Abraham's Family

28Abraham's sons were Isaac and Ishmael.
29These were the sons of Isaac and Ishmael.
Ishmael's first son was Nebaioth. His other sons
were Kedar, Adbeel, Mibsam, 30Mishma, Dumah, Massa, Hadad, Tema, 31Jetur, Naphish, and
Kedemah. These were Ishmael's sons. 32Ketu-
rah, Abraham's slave woman,[d] gave birth to

Kittim His descendants were the people of Cyprus.
Mizraim This is another name for Egypt.
Peleg This name sounds like the Hebrew word for "divided."

Zimran, Jokshan, Medan, Midian, Ishbak, and
Shuah.
Jokshan's sons were Sheba and Dedan.
33Midian's sons were Ephah, Epher, Hanoch,
Abida, and Eldaah. All these were descendants[d] of
Keturah.
34Abraham was the father of Isaac, and Isaac's
sons were Esau and Israel.
35Esau's sons were Eliphaz, Reuel, Jeush, Jalam, and Korah.
36Eliphaz's sons were Teman, Omar, Zepho,
Gatam, Kenaz, Timna, and Amalek.
37Reuel's sons were Nahath, Zerah, Shammah,
and Mizzah.

The Edomites from Seir

38Seir's sons were Lotan, Shobal, Zibeon, Anah,
Dishon, Ezer, and Dishan.
39Lotan's sons were Hori and Homam, and his
sister was Timna.
40Shobal's sons were Alvan, Manahath, Ebal,
Shepho, and Onam.
Zibeon's sons were Aiah and Anah.
41Anah's son was Dishon.
Dishon's sons were Hemdan, Eshban, Ithran,
and Keran.
42Ezer's sons were Bilhan, Zaavan, and Akan.
Dishan's sons were Uz and Aran.

The Kings of Edom

43These kings ruled in Edom before there were
kings in Israel. Bela son of Beor was king of Edom,
and his city was named Dinhabah.
44When Bela died, Jobab son of Zerah became
king. He was from Bozrah.
45When Jobab died, Husham became king. He
was from the land of the Temanites.
46When Husham died, Hadad son of Bedad became king, and his city was named Avith. Hadad
defeated Midian in the country of Moab.
47When Hadad died, Samlah became king. He
was from Masrekah.
48When Samlah died, Shaul became king. He
was from Rehoboth by the river.
49When Shaul died, Baal-Hanan son of Acbor
became king.
50When Baal-Hanan died, Hadad became king,
and his city was named Pau. Hadad's wife was
named Mehetabel, and she was the daughter of
Matred, who was the daughter of Me-Zahab.
51Then Hadad died.
The leaders of the family groups of Edom
were Timna, Alvah, Jetheth, 52Oholibamah,
Elah, Pinon, 53Kenaz, Teman, Mibzar,
54Magdiel, and Iram. These were the leaders of
Edom.

Israel's Family

2 The sons of Israel[n] were Reuben, Simeon,
Levi, Judah, Issachar, Zebulun, 2Dan, Joseph, Benjamin, Naphtali, Gad, and Asher.

Judah's Family

3Judah's sons were Er, Onan, and Shelah. A Canaanite woman, the daughter of Shua, was their
mother. Judah's first son, Er, did what the LORD
said was wicked, so the LORD put him to death.
4Judah's daughter-in-law Tamar gave birth to Perez and Zerah. Judah was the father, so Judah had
five sons.
5Perez's sons were Hezron and Hamul.
6Zerah had five sons: Zimri, Ethan, Heman,
Calcol, and Darda.
7Carmi's son was Achan, who caused trouble
for Israel because he took things that had been
given to the LORD to be destroyed.
8Ethan's son was Azariah.
9Hezron's sons were Jerahmeel, Ram, and Caleb.
10Ram was Amminadab's father, and Amminadab was Nashon's father. Nahshon was the leader of the people of Judah. 11Nahshon was the
father of Salmon, who was the father of Boaz.
12Boaz was the father of Obed, and Obed was
the father of Jesse.
13Jesse's first son was Eliab. His second son was
Abinadab, his third was Shimea, 14his fourth
was Nethanel, his fifth was Raddai, 15his sixth
was Ozem, and his seventh son was David.
16Their sisters were Zeruiah and Abigail. Zeruiah's three sons were Abishai, Joab, and Asahel.
17Abigail was the mother of Amasa, and his father was Jether, an Ishmaelite.

Caleb's Family

18Caleb son of Hezron had children by his wife
Azubah and by Jerioth. Caleb and Azubah's sons
were Jesher, Shobab, and Ardon. 19When Azubah
died, Caleb married Ephrath. They had a son
named Hur, 20who was the father of Uri, who was
the father of Bezalel.
21Later, when Hezron was sixty years old, he
married the daughter of Makir, Gilead's father.
Hezron had sexual relations with Makir's daughter, and she had a son named Segub. 22Segub was
the father of Jair. Jair controlled twenty-three cities in the country of Gilead. 23(But Geshur and
Aram captured the Towns of Jair, as well as Kenath and the small towns around it—sixty towns
in all.) All these were descendants[d] of Makir, the
father of Gilead.
24After Hezron died in Caleb Ephrathah, his

Israel Another name for Jacob.

wife Abijah had his son, named Ashhur. Ashhur became the father of Tekoa.

Jerahmeel's Family

25 Hezron's first son was Jerahmeel. Jerahmeel's sons were Ram, Bunah, Oren, Ozem, and Ahijah. Ram was Jerahmeel's first son. 26 Jerahmeel had another wife, named Atarah. She was the mother of Onam.

27 Jerahmeel's first son, Ram, had sons. They were Maaz, Jamin, and Eker.

28 Onam's sons were Shammai and Jada.

Shammai's sons were Nadab and Abishur.

29 Abishur's wife was named Abihail, and their sons were Ahban and Molid.

30 Nadab's sons were Seled and Appaim. Seled died without having children.

31 Appaim's son was Ishi, who became the father of Sheshan.

Sheshan was the father of Ahlai.

32 Jada was Shammai's brother, and Jada's sons were Jether and Jonathan. Jether died without having children.

33 Jonathan's sons were Peleth and Zaza.

These were Jerahmeel's descendants.[d]

34 Sheshan did not have any sons, only daughters. He had a servant from Egypt named Jarha. 35 Sheshan let his daughter marry his servant Jarha, and she had a son named Attai.

36 Attai was the father of Nathan. Nathan was the father of Zabad. 37 Zabad was the father of Ephlal. Ephlal was the father of Obed. 38 Obed was the father of Jehu. Jehu was the father of Azariah. 39 Azariah was the father of Helez. Helez was the father of Eleasah. 40 Eleasah was the father of Sismai. Sismai was the father of Shallum. 41 Shallum was the father of Jekamiah, and Jekamiah was the father of Elishama.

Caleb's Family

42 Caleb was Jerahmeel's brother. Caleb's first son was Mesha. Mesha was the father of Ziph, and his son Mareshah was the father of Hebron.

43 Hebron's sons were Korah, Tappuah, Rekem, and Shema. 44 Shema was the father of Raham, who was the father of Jorkeam. Rekem was the father of Shammai. 45 Shammai was the father of Maon, and Maon was the father of Beth Zur.

46 Caleb's slave woman[d] was named Ephah, and she was the mother of Haran, Moza, and Gazez. Haran was the father of Gazez.

47 Jahdai's sons were Regem, Jotham, Geshan, Pelet, Ephah, and Shaaph.

48 Caleb had another slave woman named Maacah. She was the mother of Sheber, Tirhanah, 49 Shaaph, and Sheva. Shaaph was the father of Madmannah. Sheva was the father of Macbenah and Gibea. Caleb's daughter was Acsah.

50-51 These were Caleb's descendants:[d] Caleb's son Hur was the first son of his mother Ephrathah. Hur's sons were Shobal, Salma, and Hareph. Shobal was the father of Kiriath Jearim. Salma was the father of Bethlehem. And Hareph was the father of Beth Gader.

52 Shobal was the father of Kiriath Jearim. Shobal's descendants were Haroeh, half the Manahathites, 53 and the family groups of Kiriath Jearim: the Ithrites, Puthites, Shumathites, and Mishraites. The Zorathites and the Eshtaolites came from the Mishraite people.

54 Salma's descendants were Bethlehem, the Netophathites, Atroth Beth Joab, half the Manahathites, and the Zorites. 55 His descendants included the families who lived at Jabez, who wrote and copied important papers. They were called the Tirathites, Shimeathites, and Sucathites and were from the Kenite family group who came from Hammath. He was the father of the people living in Recab.

David's Family

3 These are David's sons who were born in Hebron. The first was Amnon, whose mother was Ahinoam from Jezreel. The second son was Daniel, whose mother was Abigail from Carmel. 2 The third son was Absalom, whose mother was Maacah daughter of Talmai, the king of Geshur. The fourth son was Adonijah, whose mother was Haggith. 3 The fifth son was Shephatiah, whose mother was Abital. The sixth son was Ithream, whose mother was Eglah. 4 These six sons of David were born to him in Hebron, where David ruled for seven and one-half years.

David ruled in Jerusalem thirty-three years. 5 These were his children who were born in Jerusalem: Shammua, Shobab, Nathan, and Solomon — the four children of David and Bathsheba, Ammiel's daughter. 6-8 David's other nine children were Ibhar, Elishua, Eliphelet, Nogah, Nepheg, Japhia, Elishama, Eliada, and Eliphelet. 9 These were all of David's sons, except for those born to his slave women.[d] David also had a daughter named Tamar.

The Kings of Judah

10 Solomon's son was Rehoboam. Rehoboam's son was Abijah. Abijah's son was Asa. Asa's son was Jehoshaphat. 11 Jehoshaphat's son was Jehoram. Jehoram's son was Ahaziah. Ahaziah's son was Joash. 12 Joash's son was Amaziah. Amaziah's son was Azariah. Azariah's son was Jotham. 13 Jotham's son was Ahaz. Ahaz's son was Hezekiah. Hezekiah's son was Manasseh. 14 Manasseh's son was Amon, and Amon's son was Josiah.

15 These were Josiah's sons: His first son was Johanan, his second was Jehoiakim, his third was Zedekiah, and his fourth was Shallum.

16 Jehoiakim was followed by Jehoiachin, and he was followed by Zedekiah.

David's Descendants After the Babylonian Captivity

17 Jehoiachin was taken as a prisoner. His sons were Shealtiel, 18 Malkiram, Pedaiah, Shenazzar, Jekamiah, Hoshama, and Nedabiah.

19 Pedaiah's sons were Zerubbabel and Shimei.

Zerubbabel's sons were Meshullam and Hananiah, and their sister was Shelomith. 20 Zerubbabel also had five other sons: Hashubah, Ohel, Berekiah, Hasadiah, and Jushab-Hesed.

21 Hananiah's descendants[d] were Pelatiah and Jeshaiah, and the sons of Rephaiah, Arnan, Obadiah, and Shecaniah.

22 Shecaniah's son was Shemaiah. Shemaiah's sons were Hattush, Igal, Bariah, Neariah, and Shaphat. There were six in all.

23 Neariah had three sons: Elioenai, Hizkiah, and Azrikam.

24 Elioenai had seven sons: Hodaviah, Eliashib, Pelaiah, Akkub, Johanan, Delaiah, and Anani.

Other Family Groups of Judah

4 Judah's descendants[d] were Perez, Hezron, Carmi, Hur, and Shobal.

2 Reaiah was Shobal's son. Reaiah was the father of Jahath, and Jahath was the father of Ahumai and Lahad. They were the family groups of the Zorathite people.

3-4 Hur was the oldest son of Caleb and his wife Ephrathah. Hur was the leader of Bethlehem. His three sons were Etam, Penuel, and Ezer. Etam's sons were Jezreel, Ishma, and Idbash. They had a sister named Hazzelelponi. Penuel was the father of Gedor, and Ezer was the father of Hushah.

5 Tekoa's father was Ashhur. Ashhur had two wives named Helah and Naarah.

6 The sons of Ashhur and Naarah were Ahuzzam, Hepher, Temeni, and Haahashtari. These were the descendants of Naarah.

7 Helah's sons were Zereth, Zohar, Ethnan, 8 and Koz. Koz was the father of Anub, Hazzobebah, and the Aharhel family group. Aharhel was the son of Harum.

9 There was a man named Jabez, who was respected more than his brothers. His mother named him Jabez[n] because she said, "I was in much pain when I gave birth to him." 10 Jabez prayed to the God of Israel, "Please do good things for me and give me more land. Stay with me, and don't let anyone hurt me. Then I won't have any pain." And God did what Jabez had asked.

11 Kelub, Shuhah's brother, was the father of Mehir. Mehir was the father of Eshton. 12 Eshton was the father of Beth Rapha, Paseah, and Tehinnah. Tehinnah was the father of the people from the town of Nahash. These people were from Recah.

13 The sons of Kenaz were Othniel and Seraiah.

Othniel's sons were Hathath and Meonothai. 14 Meonothai was the father of Ophrah.

Seraiah was the father of Joab. Joab was the ancestor of the people from Craftsmen's Valley, named that because the people living there were craftsmen.

> **SIDELIGHT:** Have you ever wondered where Sears gets its tools? Maybe from Joab's descendants. They all lived in Craftsmen's Valley (1 Chronicles 4:14).

15 Caleb was Jephunneh's son. Caleb's sons were Iru, Elah, and Naam. Elah's son was Kenaz.

16 Jehallelel's sons were Ziph, Ziphah, Tiria, and Asarel.

17-18 Ezrah's sons were Jether, Mered, Epher, and Jalon. Mered married Bithiah, the daughter of the king of Egypt. The children of Mered and Bithiah were Miriam, Shammai, and Ishbah. Ishbah was the father of Eshtemoa. Mered also had a wife from Judah, who gave birth to Jered, Heber, and Jekuthiel. Jered became the father of Gedor. Heber became the father of Soco. And Jekuthiel became the father of Zanoah.

19 Hodiah's wife was Naham's sister. The sons of Hodiah's wife were Eshtemoa and the father of Keilah. Keilah was from the Garmite people, and Eshtemoa was from the Maacathite people.

20 Shimon's sons were Amnon, Rinnah, Ben-Hanan, and Tilon.

Ishi's sons were Zoheth and Ben-Zoheth.

21-22 Shelah was Judah's son. Shelah's sons were Er, Laadah, Jokim, the men from Cozeba, Joash, and Saraph. Er was the father of Lecah. Laadah was the father of Mareshah and the family groups of linen workers at Beth Ashbea. Joash and Saraph ruled in Moab and Jashubi Lehem. The writings about this family are very old. 23 These sons of Shelah were potters. They lived in Netaim and Gederah and worked for the king.

Simeon's Children

24 Simeon's sons were Nemuel, Jamin, Jarib, Zerah, and Shaul. 25 Shaul's son was Shallum. Shallum's son was Mibsam. Mibsam's son was Mishma.

26 Mishma's son was Hammuel. Hammuel's son was Zaccur. Zaccur's son was Shimei. 27 Shimei

Jabez This name in Hebrew sounds like the word for "pain."

had sixteen sons and six daughters, but his brothers did not have many children, so there were not as many people in their family group as there were in Judah.

[28]Shimei's children lived in Beersheba, Moladah, Hazar Shual, [29]Bilhah, Ezem, Tolad, [30]Bethuel, Hormah, Ziklag, [31]Beth Marcaboth, Hazar Susim, Beth Biri, and Shaaraim. They lived in these cities until David became king. [32]The five villages near these cities were Etam, Ain, Rimmon, Token, and Ashan. [33]There were also other villages as far away as Baalath. This is where they lived. And they wrote the history of their family.

[34-38]The men in this list were leaders of their family groups: Meshobab, Jamlech, Joshah son of Amaziah, Joel, Jehu son of Joshibiah (Joshibiah was the son of Seraiah, who was the son of Asiel), Elioenai, Jaakobah, Jeshohaiah, Asaiah, Adiel, Jesimiel, Benaiah, and Ziza. (Ziza was the son of Shiphi, who was the son of Allon. Allon was the son of Jedaiah, who was the son of Shimri. And Shimri was the son of Shemaiah.)

These families grew very large. [39]They went outside the city of Gedor to the east side of the valley to look for pasture for their flocks. [40]They found good pastures with plenty of grass, and the land was open country and peaceful and quiet. Ham's descendants[d] had lived there in the past.

[41]These men who were listed came to Gedor while Hezekiah was king of Judah. They fought against the Hamites, destroying their tents, and also against the Meunites who lived there, and completely destroyed them. So there are no Meunites there even today. Then these men began to live there, because there was pasture for their flocks. [42]Ishi's sons, Pelatiah, Neariah, Rephaiah, and Uzziel, led five hundred of the Simeonites and attacked the people living in the mountains of Edom. [43]They killed the few Amalekites who were still alive. From that time until now these Simeonites have lived in Edom.

Reuben's Children

5 Reuben was Israel's first son. Reuben should have received the special privileges of the oldest son, but he had sexual relations with his father's slave woman.[d] So those special privileges were given to Joseph's sons. (Joseph was a son of Israel.) In the family history Reuben's name is not listed as the first son. [2]Judah became stronger than his brothers, and a leader came from his family. But Joseph's family received the privileges that belonged to the oldest son. [3]Reuben was Israel's first son. Reuben's sons were Hanoch, Pallu, Hezron, and Carmi.

[4]These were the children of Joel: Shemaiah was Joel's son. Gog was Shemaiah's son. Shimei was Gog's son. [5]Micah was Shimei's son. Reaiah was Micah's son. Baal was Reaiah's son.[6]Beerah was Baal's son. Beerah was a leader of the tribe[d] of Reuben. Tiglath-Pileser king of Assyria captured him and took him away.

[7]Joel's brothers and all his family groups are listed just as they are written in their family histories: Jeiel was the first, then Zechariah, [8]and Bela. (Bela was the son of Azaz. Azaz was the son of Shema, and Shema was the son of Joel.) They lived in the area of Aroer all the way to Nebo and Baal Meon. [9]Bela's people lived to the east—as far as the edge of the desert, which is beside the Euphrates River—because they had too many cattle for the land of Gilead.

[10]When Saul was king, Bela's people fought a war against the Hagrite people and defeated them. Then Bela's people lived in the tents that had belonged to the Hagrites in all the area east of Gilead.

Gad's Children

[11]The people from the tribe[d] of Gad lived near the Reubenites. The Gadites lived in the area of Bashan all the way to Salecah. [12]Joel was the main leader, Shapham was second, and then Janai and Shaphat were leaders in Bashan.

[13]The seven relatives in their families were Michael, Meshullam, Sheba, Jorai, Jacan, Zia, and Eber. [14]They were the descendants[d] of Abihail. Abihail was Huri's son. Huri was Jaroah's son. Jaroah was Gilead's son. Gilead was Michael's son. Michael was Jeshishai's son. Jeshishai was Jahdo's son, and Jahdo was the son of Buz. [15]Ahi was Abdiel's son, and Abdiel was Guni's son. Ahi was the leader of their family.

[16]The Gadites lived in Gilead, Bashan and the small towns around it, and on all the pasturelands in the Plain of Sharon all the way to the borders.

[17]All these names were written in the family history of Gad during the time Jotham was king of Judah and Jeroboam was king of Israel.

Soldiers Skilled in War

[18]There were forty-four thousand seven hundred sixty soldiers from the tribes[d] of Reuben and Gad and East Manasseh who carried shields and swords and bows. They were skilled in war. [19]They started a war against the Hagrites and the people of Jetur, Naphish, and Nodab. [20]The men from the tribes of Manasseh, Reuben, and Gad prayed to God during the war, asking him to help them. So he helped them because they trusted him. He handed over to them the Hagrites and all those who were with them. [21]They took the animals that belonged to the Hagrites: fifty thousand camels, two hundred fifty thousand sheep, and two thousand donkeys. They also captured one hundred thousand people. [22]Many Hagrites were killed because God helped the people of Reuben,

Gad, and Manasseh. Then they lived there until Babylon captured them and took them away.

East Manasseh

23There were many people in East Manasseh, and they lived in the area of Bashan all the way to Baal Hermon, Senir, and Mount Hermon.

24These were the family leaders: Epher, Ishi, Eliel, Azriel, Jeremiah, Hodaviah, and Jahdiel. They were all strong, brave, and famous men, and leaders in their families. 25But they sinned against the God that their ancestors had worshiped. They began worshiping the gods of the people in that land, and those were the people God was destroying. 26So the God of Israel made Pul king of Assyria want to go to war. (Pul was also called Tiglath-Pileser.) He captured the people of Reuben, Gad, and East Manasseh, and he took them away to Halah, Habor, Hara, and near the Gozan River. They have lived there from that time until this day.

Levi's Children

6 Levi's sons were Gershon, Kohath, and Merari.

2Kohath's sons were Amram, Izhar, Hebron, and Uzziel.

3Amram's children were Aaron, Moses, and Miriam.

Aaron's sons were Nadab, Abihu, Eleazar, and Ithamar. 4Eleazar was the father of Phinehas. Phinehas was the father of Abishua. 5Abishua was the father of Bukki. Bukki was the father of Uzzi. 6Uzzi was the father of Zerahiah. Zerahiah was the father of Meraioth. 7Meraioth was the father of Amariah. Amariah was the father of Ahitub. 8Ahitub was the father of Zadok. Zadok was the father of Ahimaaz. 9Ahimaaz was the father of Azariah. Azariah was the father of Johanan. 10Johanan was the father of Azariah. (Azariah was a priest in the Temple[d] Solomon built in Jerusalem.) 11Azariah was the father of Amariah. Amariah was the father of Ahitub. 12Ahitub was the father of Zadok. Zadok was the father of Shallum. 13Shallum was the father of Hilkiah. Hilkiah was the father of Azariah. 14Azariah was the father of Seraiah, and Seraiah was the father of Jehozadak.

15Jehozadak was forced to leave his home when the LORD sent Judah and Jerusalem into captivity under the control of Nebuchadnezzar.

16Levi's sons were Gershon, Kohath, and Merari.

17The names of Gershon's sons were Libni and Shimei.

18Kohath's sons were Amram, Izhar, Hebron, and Uzziel.

19Merari's sons were Mahli and Mushi.

This is a list of the family groups of Levi, listed by the name of the father of each group.

20Gershon's son was Libni. Libni's son was Jehath. Jehath's son was Zimmah. 21Zimmah's son was Joah. Joah's son was Iddo. Iddo's son was Zerah. And Zerah's son was Jeatherai.

22Kohath's son was Amminadab. Amminadab's son was Korah. Korah's son was Assir. 23Assir's son was Elkanah. Elkanah's son was Ebiasaph. Ebiasaph's son was Assir. 24Assir's son was Tahath. Tahath's son was Uriel. Uriel's son was Uzziah, and Uzziah's son was Shaul.

25Elkanah's sons were Amasai and Ahimoth. 26Ahimoth's son was Elkanah. Elkanah's son was Zophai. Zophai's son was Nahath. 27Nahath's son was Eliab. Eliab's son was Jeroham. Jeroham's son was Elkanah, and Elkanah's son was Samuel.

28Samuel's sons were Joel, the first son, and Abijah, the second son.

29Merari's son was Mahli. Mahli's son was Libni. Libni's son was Shimei. Shimei's son was Uzzah. 30Uzzah's son was Shimea. Shimea's son was Haggiah, and Haggiah's son was Asaiah.

The Temple Musicians

31David chose some people to be in charge of the music in the house of the LORD. They began their work after the Ark[d] of the Agreement was put there. 32They served by making music at the Holy Tent[d] (also called the Meeting Tent), and they served until Solomon built the Temple[d] of the LORD in Jerusalem. They followed the rules for their work.

> **SIDELIGHT:** According to 1 Chronicles 6:31–32, King David may have started the first professional Jerusalem Philharmonic Orchestra and Chorus to lead music in the Temple. Today the musicians would probably go on strike: First Chronicles 9:33 says they were on duty "day and night."

33These are the musicians and their sons:

From Kohath's family there was Heman the singer. Heman was Joel's son. Joel was Samuel's son. 34Samuel was Elkanah's son. Elkanah was Jeroham's son. Jeroham was Eliel's son. Eliel was Toah's son. 35Toah was Zuph's son. Zuph was Elkanah's son. Elkanah was Mahath's son. Mahath was Amasai's son. 36Amasai was Elkanah's son. Elkanah was Joel's son. Joel was Azariah's son. Azariah was Zephaniah's son. 37Zephaniah was Tahath's son. Tahath was Assir's son. Assir was Ebiasaph's son. Ebiasaph was Korah's son. 38Korah was Izhar's son. Izhar was Kohath's son. Kohath was Levi's son. Levi was Israel's son.

39There was Heman's helper Asaph, whose group stood by Heman's right side. Asaph was

Berekiah's son. Berekiah was Shimea's son. 40Shimea was Michael's son. Michael was Baaseiah's son. Baaseiah was Malkijah's son. 41Malkijah was Ethni's son. Ethni was Zerah's son. Zerah was Adaiah's son. 42Adaiah was Ethan's son. Ethan was Zimmah's son. Zimmah was Shimei's son. 43Shimei was Jahath's son. Jahath was Gershon's son, and Gershon was Levi's son.

44Merari's family were the helpers of Heman and Asaph, and they stood by Heman's left side. In this group was Ethan son of Kishi. Kishi was Abdi's son. Abdi was Malluch's son. 45Malluch was Hashabiah's son. Hashabiah was Amaziah's son. Amaziah was Hilkiah's son. 46Hilkiah was Amzi's son. Amzi was Bani's son. Bani was Shemer's son. 47Shemer was Mahli's son. Mahli was Mushi's son. Mushi was Merari's son, and Merari was Levi's son.

48The other Levites served by doing their own special work in the Holy Tent, the house of God. 49Aaron and his descendants[d] offered the sacrifices on the altar of burnt offering and burned the incense on the altar of incense. They offered the sacrifices that removed the Israelites' sins so they could belong to God. They did all the work in the Most Holy Place and followed all the laws that Moses, God's servant, had commanded.

50These were Aaron's sons: Eleazar was Aaron's son. Phinehas was Eleazar's son. Abishua was Phinehas' son. 51Bukki was Abishua's son. Uzzi was Bukki's son. Zerahiah was Uzzi's son. 52Meraioth was Zerahiah's son. Amariah was Meraioth's son. Ahitub was Amariah's son. 53Zadok was Ahitub's son, and Ahimaaz was Zadok's son.

Land for the Levites

54These are the places where Aaron's descendants[d] lived. His descendants from the Kohath family group received the first share of the land. 55They were given the city of Hebron in Judah and the pastures around it, 56but the fields farther from the city and the villages near Hebron were given to Caleb son of Jephunneh. 57So the descendants of Aaron were given Hebron, one of the cities of safety.[n] They also received the towns and pastures of Libnah, Jattir, Eshtemoa, 58Hilen, Debir, 59Ashan, Juttah, and Beth Shemesh. 60They also received these towns and pastures from the tribe of Benjamin: Gibeon, Geba, Alemeth, and Anathoth.

The Kohath family groups received a total of thirteen towns.

61The rest of the Kohath family group was given ten towns from the family groups of West Manasseh. The towns were chosen by throwing lots.[d]

62The Gershon family group received thirteen towns from the tribes of Issachar, Asher, Naphtali, and the part of Manasseh living in Bashan.

63The Merari family group received twelve towns from the tribes of Reuben, Gad, and Zebulun. Those towns were chosen by throwing lots.

64So the Israelites gave these towns and their pastures to the Levites. 65The towns from the tribes of Judah, Simeon, and Benjamin, which were named, were chosen by throwing lots.

66Some of the Kohath family groups received towns and pastures from the tribe of Ephraim. 67They received Shechem, one of the cities of safety, with its pastures in the mountains of Ephraim. They also received the towns and pastures of Gezer, 68Jokmeam, Beth Horon, 69Aijalon, and Gath Rimmon.

70The rest of the people in the Kohath family group received the towns of Aner and Bileam and their pastures from West Manasseh.

71From East Manasseh, the Gershon family received the towns and pastures of Golan in Bashan and Ashtaroth.

72-73From the tribe of Issachar, the Gershon family received the towns and pastures of Kedesh, Daberath, Ramoth, and Anem.

74-75From the tribe of Asher, the Gershon family received the towns and pastures of Mashal, Abdon, Hukok, and Rehob.

76From the tribe of Naphtali, the Gershon family received the towns and pastures of Kedesh in Galilee, Hammon, and Kiriathaim.

77The rest of the Levites, the people from the Merari family, received from the tribe of Zebulun the towns and pastures of Jokneam, Kartah, Rimmono, and Tabor.

78-79From the tribe of Reuben, the Merari family received the towns and pastures of Bezer in the desert, Jahzah, Kedemoth, and Mephaath. (The tribe of Reuben lived east of the Jordan River, across from Jericho.)

80-81From the tribe of Gad, the Merari family received the towns and pastures of Ramoth in Gilead, Mahanaim, Heshbon, and Jazer.

Issachar's Children

7 Issachar had four sons: Tola, Puah, Jashub, and Shimron.

2Tola's sons were Uzzi, Rephaiah, Jeriel, Jahmai, Ibsam, and Samuel, and they were leaders of their families. In the family history of Tola's descendants,[d] twenty-two thousand six hundred men were listed as fighting men during the time David was king.

3Uzzi's son was Izrahiah.

Izrahiah's sons were Michael, Obadiah, Joel,

cities of safety A person who had accidentally killed someone could go to one of the six cities of safety to receive protection and a fair trial.

and Isshiah. All five of them were leaders. 4Their
family history shows they had thirty-six thousand
men ready to serve in the army, because they had
many wives and children.

5The records of the family groups of Issachar
show there were eighty-seven thousand fighting
men.

Benjamin's Children

6Benjamin had three sons: Bela, Beker, and Jediael.

7Bela had five sons: Ezbon, Uzzi, Uzziel, Jerimoth, and Iri, and they were leaders of their families. Their family history shows they had twenty-
two thousand thirty-four fighting men.

8Beker's sons were Zemirah, Joash, Eliezer, Elioenai, Omri, Jeremoth, Abijah, Anathoth, and Alemeth. They all were Beker's sons. 9Their family
history listed the family leaders and twenty thousand two hundred fighting men.

10Jediael's son was Bilhan.

Bilhan's sons were Jeush, Benjamin, Ehud, Kenaanah, Zethan, Tarshish, and Ahishahar. 11All
these sons of Jediael were leaders of their families.
They had seventeen thousand two hundred fighting men ready to serve in the army.

12The Shuppites and Huppites were descendants[d] of Ir, and the Hushites were descendants
of Aher.

Naphtali's Children

13Naphtali's sons were Jahziel, Guni, Jezer, and
Shillem. They were Bilhah's grandsons.

Manasseh's Children

14These are Manasseh's descendants.[d] Manasseh had an Aramean slave woman,[d] who was the
mother of Asriel and Makir. Makir was Gilead's
father. 15Makir took a wife from the Huppites and
Shuppites. His sister was named Maacah. His second son was named Zelophehad, and he had only
daughters. 16Makir's wife Maacah had a son
whom she named Peresh. Peresh's brother was
named Sheresh. Sheresh's sons were Ulam and
Rakem.

17Ulam's son was Bedan.

These were the sons of Gilead, who was the
son of Makir. Makir was Manasseh's son. 18Ma-
kir's sister Hammoleketh gave birth to Ishhod,
Abiezer, and Mahlah.

19The sons of Shemida were Ahian, Shechem,
Likhi, and Aniam.

Ephraim's Children

20These are the names of Ephraim's descendants.[d] Ephraim's son was Shuthelah. Shuthelah's
son was Bered. Bered's son was Tahath. Tahath's
son was Eleadah. Eleadah's son was Tahath. 21Ta-
hath's son was Zabad. Zabad's son was Shuthelah.

Ezer and Elead went to Gath to steal cows and
sheep and were killed by some men who grew up
in that city. 22Their father Ephraim cried for them
many days, and his family came to comfort him.
23Then he had sexual relations with his wife
again. She became pregnant and gave birth to a
son whom Ephraim named Beriah[n] because of
the trouble that had happened to his family.
24Ephraim's daughter was Sheerah. She built
Lower Beth Horon, Upper Beth Horon, and Uz-
zen Sheerah.

25Rephah was Ephraim's son. Resheph was Re-
phah's son. Telah was Resheph's son. Tahan was
Telah's son. 26Ladan was Tahan's son. Ammihud
was Ladan's son. Elishama was Ammihud's son.
27Nun was Elishama's son, and Joshua was the
son of Nun.

28Ephraim's descendants lived in these lands
and towns: Bethel and the villages near it, Naaran
on the east, Gezer and the villages near it on
the west, and Shechem and the villages near it.
These villages went all the way to Ayyah and its
villages. 29Along the borders of Manasseh's land
were the towns of Beth Shan, Taanach, Megiddo, and Dor, and the villages near them. The
descendants of Joseph son of Israel lived in these
towns.

Asher's Children

30Asher's sons were Imnah, Ishvah, Ishvi, and
Beriah. Their sister was Serah.

31Beriah's sons were Heber and Malkiel. Malkiel was Birzaith's father.

32Heber was the father of Japhlet, Shomer, Hotham, and their sister Shua.

33Japhlet's sons were Pasach, Bimhal, and Ash-
vath. They were Japhlet's children.

34Japhlet's brother was Shomer. Shomer's sons
were Rohgah, Hubbah, and Aram.

35Shomer's brother was Hotham. Hotham's
sons were Zophah, Imna, Shelesh, and Amal.

36Zophah's sons were Suah, Harnepher, Shual,
Beri, Imrah, 37Bezer, Hod, Shamma, Shilshah, Ithran, and Beera.

38Jether's sons were Jephunneh, Pispah, and
Ara.

39Ulla's sons were Arah, Hanniel, and Rizia.

40All these men were descendants of Asher and
leaders of their families. They were powerful warriors and outstanding leaders. Their family history
lists that they had twenty-six thousand soldiers
ready to serve in the army.

The Family History of King Saul

8 Benjamin was the father of Bela, his first son.
Ashbel was his second son, Aharah was his

Beriah This name sounds like the Hebrew word for "trouble."

third, 2Nohah was his fourth, and Rapha was his fifth son.

3Bela's sons were Addar, Gera, Abihud, 4Abishua, Naaman, Ahoah, 5Gera, Shephuphan, and Huram.

6These were the descendants[d] of Ehud and leaders of their families in Geba. They were forced to move to Manahath. 7Ehud's descendants were Naaman, Ahijah, and Gera. Gera forced them to leave. He was the father of Uzza and Ahihud.

8-11Shaharaim and his wife Hushim had sons named Abitub and Elpaal. In Moab, Shaharaim divorced his wives Hushim and Baara. Shaharaim and his wife Hodesh had these sons: Jobab, Zibia, Mesha, Malcam, Jeuz, Sakia, and Mirmah. They were leaders of their families.

12-13Elpaal's sons were Eber, Misham, Shemed, Beriah, and Shema. Shemed built the towns of Ono and Lod and the villages around them. Beriah and Shema were leaders of the families living in Aijalon, and they forced out the people who lived in Gath.

14Beriah's sons were Ahio, Shashak, Jeremoth, 15Zebadiah, Arad, Eder, 16Michael, Ishpah, and Joha.

17Elpaal's sons were Zebadiah, Meshullam, Hizki, Heber, 18Ishmerai, Izliah, and Jobab.

19Shimei's sons were Jakim, Zicri, Zabdi, 20Elienai, Zillethai, Eliel, 21Adaiah, Beraiah, and Shimrath.

22Shashak's sons were Ishpan, Eber, Eliel, 23Abdon, Zicri, Hanan, 24Hananiah, Elam, Anthothijah, 25Iphdeiah, and Penuel.

26Jeroham's sons were Shamsherai, Shehariah, Athaliah, 27Jaareshiah, Elijah, and Zicri.

28The family histories show that all these men were leaders of their families and lived in Jerusalem.

29Jeiel lived in the town of Gibeon, where he was the leader. His wife was named Maacah. 30Jeiel's first son was Abdon. His other sons were Zur, Kish, Baal, Ner, Nadab, 31Gedor, Ahio, Zeker, 32and Mikloth. Mikloth was the father of Shimeah. These sons also lived near their relatives in Jerusalem.

33Ner was the father of Kish. Kish was the father of Saul, and Saul was the father of Jonathan, Malki-Shua, Abinadab, and Esh-Baal.

34Jonathan's son was Merib-Baal, who was the father of Micah.

35Micah's sons were Pithon, Melech, Tarea, and Ahaz. 36Ahaz was the father of Jehoaddah. Jehoaddah was the father of Alemeth, Azmaveth, and Zimri. Zimri was the father of Moza. 37Moza was the father of Binea. Raphah was Binea's son. Eleasah was Raphah's son, and Azel was Eleasah's son.

38Azel had six sons: Azrikam, Bokeru, Ishmael, Sheariah, Obadiah, and Hanan. All these were Azel's sons.

39Azel's brother was Eshek. Eshek's first son was Ulam, his second was Jeush, and Eliphelet was his third. 40Ulam's sons were mighty warriors and good archers. They had many sons and grandsons—one hundred fifty of them in all.

All these men were Benjamin's descendants.

9 The names of all the people of Israel were listed in their family histories, and those family histories were put in the book of the kings of Israel.

The People in Jerusalem

The people of Judah were captured and forced to go to Babylon, because they were not faithful to God. 2The first people to come back and live in their own lands and towns were some Israelites, priests, Levites, and Temple[d] servants.

3People from the tribes[d] of Judah, Benjamin, Ephraim, and Manasseh lived in Jerusalem. This is a list of those people.

4There was Uthai son of Ammihud. (Ammihud was Omri's son. Omri was Imri's son. Imri was Bani's son. Bani was a descendant[d] of Perez, and Perez was Judah's son.)

5Of the Shilonite people there were Asaiah and his sons. Asaiah was the oldest son in his family.

6Of the Zerahite people there were Jeuel and other relatives of Zerah. There were six hundred ninety of them in all.

7From the tribe of Benjamin there was Sallu son of Meshullam. (Meshullam was Hodaviah's son, and Hodaviah was Hassenuah's son.) 8There was also Ibneiah son of Jeroham and Elah son of Uzzi. (Uzzi was Micri's son.) And there was Meshullam son of Shephatiah. (Shephatiah was Reuel's son, and Reuel was Ibnijah's son.) 9The family history of Benjamin lists nine hundred fifty-six people living in Jerusalem, and all these were leaders of their families.

10Of the priests there were Jedaiah, Jehoiarib, Jakin, and 11Azariah son of Hilkiah. (Hilkiah was Meshullam's son. Meshullam was Zadok's son. Zadok was Meraioth's son. Meraioth was Ahitub's son. Ahitub was the officer responsible for the Temple of God.) 12Also there was Adaiah son of Jeroham. (Jeroham was Pashhur's son, and Pashhur was Malkijah's son.) And there was Maasai son of Adiel. (Adiel was Jahzerah's son. Jahzerah was Meshullam's son. Meshullam was Meshillemith's son, and Meshillemith was Immer's son.) 13There were one thousand seven hundred sixty priests. They were leaders of their families, and they were responsible for serving in the Temple of God.

14Of the Levites there was Semaiah son of Hasshub. (Hasshub was Azrikam's son, and Azrikam was Hashabiah's son. Hashabiah was from the family of Merari.) 15There were also Bakbakkar, Heresh, Galal, and Mattaniah son of Mica. (Mica was Zicri's son, and Zicri was Asaph's son.) 16There was also Obadiah son of Shemaiah. (Shemaiah was Galal's son, and Galal was Jeduthun's son.) And there was Berekiah son of Asa. (Asa was the son of Elkanah, who lived in the villages of the Netophathites.)

17Of the gatekeepers there were Shallum, Akkub, Talmon, Ahiman, and their relatives. Shallum was their leader. 18These gatekeepers from the tribe of Levi still stand next to the King's Gate on the east side of the city. 19Shallum was Kore's son. Kore was Ebiasaph's son, and Ebiasaph was Korah's son. Shallum and his relatives from the family of Korah were gatekeepers and were responsible for guarding the gates of the Temple. Their ancestors had also been responsible for guarding the entrance to the Temple of the LORD. 20In the past Phinehas, Eleazar's son, was in charge of the gatekeepers, and the LORD was with Phinehas. 21Zechariah son of Meshelemiah was the gatekeeper at the entrance to the Temple.

22In all, two hundred twelve men were chosen to guard the gates, and their names were written in their family histories in their villages. David and Samuel the seer[d] chose these men because they were dependable. 23The gatekeepers and their descendants had to guard the gates of the Temple of the LORD. (The Temple took the place of the Holy Tent.[d]) 24There were gatekeepers on all four sides of the Temple: east, west, north, and south. 25The gatekeepers' relatives who lived in the villages had to come and help them at times. Each time they came they helped the gatekeepers for seven days. 26Because they were dependable, four gatekeepers were made the leaders of all the gatekeepers. They were Levites, and they were responsible for the rooms and treasures in the Temple of God. 27They stayed up all night guarding the Temple of God, and they opened it every morning.

28Some of the gatekeepers were responsible for the utensils used in the Temple services. They counted these utensils when people took them out and when they brought them back. 29Other gatekeepers were chosen to take care of the furniture and utensils in the Holy Place. They also took care of the flour, wine, oil, incense,[d] and spices, 30but some of the priests took care of mixing the spices. 31There was a Levite named Mattithiah who was dependable and had the job of baking the bread used for the offerings. He was the first son of Shallum, who was from the family of Korah. 32Some of the gatekeepers from the Kohath family had the job of preparing the special bread that was put on the table every Sabbath[d] day.

33Some of the Levites were musicians in the Temple. The leaders of these families stayed in the rooms of the Temple. Since they were on duty day and night, they did not do other work in the Temple.

SIDELIGHT: If being a gatekeeper sounds like a cushy job, read 1 Chronicles 9:28–32 before applying. The Temple gatekeepers were probably priests who washed dishes, kept inventory, baked bread, and mixed spices.

34These are the leaders of the Levite families. Their names were listed in their family histories, and they lived in Jerusalem.

The Family History of King Saul

35Jeiel lived in the town of Gibeon, where he was the leader. His wife was named Maacah. 36Jeiel's first son was Abdon. His other sons were Zur, Kish, Baal, Ner, Nadab, 37Gedor, Ahio, Zechariah, and Mikloth. 38Mikloth was Shimeam's father. Jeiel's family lived near their relatives in Jerusalem.

39Ner was Kish's father. Kish was Saul's father. Saul was the father of Jonathan, Malki-Shua, Abinadab, and Esh-Baal.

40Jonathan's son was Merib-Baal, who was the father of Micah.

41Micah's sons were Pithon, Melech, Tahrea, and Ahaz. 42Ahaz was Jadah's father. Jadah was the father of Alemeth, Azmaveth, and Zimri. Zimri was Moza's father. 43Moza was Binea's father. Rephaiah was Binea's son. Eleasah was Rephaiah's son, and Azel was Eleasah's son.

44Azel had six sons: Azrikam, Bokeru, Ishmael, Sheariah, Obadiah, and Hanan. They were Azel's sons.

The Death of King Saul

10 The Philistines fought against Israel, and the Israelites ran away from them. Many Israelites were killed on Mount Gilboa. 2The Philistines fought hard against Saul and his sons, killing his sons Jonathan, Abinadab, and Malki-Shua. 3The fighting was heavy around Saul, and the archers shot him with their arrows and wounded him.

4Then Saul said to the officer who carried his armor, "Pull out your sword and stab me. If you don't, these Philistines who are not circumcised will come and hurt me." But Saul's officer refused, because he was afraid. So Saul took his own sword and threw himself on it. 5When the officer saw that Saul was dead, he threw himself on his own sword and died. 6So Saul and three of his sons died; all his family died together.

7When the Israelites living in the valley saw that their army had run away and that Saul and his sons were dead, they left their towns and ran away. Then the Philistines came and settled in them.

8The next day when the Philistines came to strip the dead soldiers, they found Saul and his sons dead on Mount Gilboa. 9The Philistines stripped Saul's body and took his head and his armor. Then they sent messengers through all their country to tell the news to their idols and to their people. 10The Philistines put Saul's armor in the temple of their idols and hung his head in the temple of Dagon.[d]

11All the people in Jabesh Gilead heard what the Philistines had done to Saul. 12So the brave men of Jabesh went and got the bodies of Saul and his sons and brought them to Jabesh. They buried their bones under the large tree in Jabesh. Then the people of Jabesh gave up eating for seven days.

13Saul died because he was not faithful to the LORD and did not obey the LORD. He even went to a medium[d] and asked her for advice 14instead of asking the LORD. This is why the LORD put Saul to death and gave the kingdom to Jesse's son David.

David Becomes King

11 Then the people of Israel came to David at the town of Hebron and said, "Look, we are your own family. 2Even when Saul was king, you were the one who led Israel in battle. The LORD your God said to you, 'You will be the shepherd for my people Israel. You will be their leader.' "

3So all the older leaders of Israel came to King David at Hebron. He made an agreement with them in Hebron in the presence of the LORD. Then they poured oil on David to make him king over Israel. The LORD had promised through Samuel that this would happen.

David Captures Jerusalem

4David and all the Israelites went to the city of Jerusalem. At that time Jerusalem was called Jebus, and the people living there were named Jebusites. 5They said to David, "You can't get inside our city." But David did take the city of Jerusalem with its strong walls, and it became the City of David.

6David had said, "The person who leads the attack against the Jebusites will become the commander over all my army." Joab son of Zeruiah led the attack, so he became the commander of the army.

7Then David made his home in the strong, walled city, which is why it was named the City of David. 8David rebuilt the city, beginning where the land was filled in and going to the wall that was around the city. Joab repaired the other parts of the city. 9David became stronger and stronger, and the LORD All-Powerful was with him.

David's Mighty Warriors

10This is a list of the leaders over David's warriors who helped make David's kingdom strong. All the people of Israel also supported David's kingdom. These heroes and all the people of Israel made David king, just as the LORD had promised.

11This is a list of David's warriors:

Jashobeam was from the Hacmonite people. He was the head of the Three,[n] David's most powerful soldiers. He used his spear to fight three hundred men at one time, and he killed them all.

12Next was Eleazar, one of the Three. Eleazar was Dodai's son from the Ahohite people. 13Eleazar was with David at Pas-Dammim when the Philistines came there to fight. There was a field of barley at that place. The Israelites ran away from the Philistines, 14but they stopped in the middle of that field and fought for it and killed the Philistines. The LORD gave them a great victory.

15Once, three of the Thirty, David's chief soldiers, came down to him at the rock by the cave near Adullam. At the same time the Philistine army had camped in the Valley of Rephaim.

16At that time David was in a stronghold,[d] and some of the Philistines were in Bethlehem. 17David had a strong desire for some water. He said, "Oh, I wish someone would get me water from the well near the city gate of Bethlehem!" 18So the Three broke through the Philistine army and took water from the well near the city gate in Bethlehem. Then they brought it to David, but he refused to drink it. He poured it out before the LORD, 19saying, "May God keep me from drinking this water! It would be like drinking the blood of the men who risked their lives to bring it to me!" So David refused to drink it.

These were the brave things that the three warriors did.

20Abishai brother of Joab was the captain of the Three. Abishai fought three hundred soldiers with his spear and killed them. He became as famous as the Three 21and was more honored than the Three. He became their commander even though he was not one of them.

22Benaiah son of Jehoiada was a brave fighter from Kabzeel who did mighty things. He killed two of the best warriors from Moab. He also went down into a pit and killed a lion on a snowy day. 23Benaiah killed an Egyptian who was about seven and one-half feet tall and had a spear as

Three Or maybe "Thirty." These were David's most powerful soldiers. See 2 Samuel 23:8.

large as a weaver's rod. Benaiah had a club, but
he grabbed the spear from the Egyptian's hand
and killed him with his own spear. 24These were
the things Benaiah son of Jehoiada did. He was as
famous as the Three. 25He received more honor
than the Thirty, but he did not become a member
of the Three. David made him leader of his bodyguards.

The Thirty Chief Soldiers

26These were also mighty warriors:
Asahel brother of Joab;
Elhanan son of Dodo from Bethlehem;
27Shammoth the Harorite;
Helez the Pelonite;
28Ira son of Ikkesh from Tekoa;
Abiezer the Anathothite;
29Sibbecai the Hushathite;
Ilai the Ahohite;
30Maharai the Netophathite;
Heled son of Baanah the Netophathite;
31Ithai son of Ribai from Gibeah in Benja-
min;
Benaiah the Pirathonite;
32Hurai from the ravines of Gaash;
Abiel the Arbathite;
33Azmaveth the Baharumite;
Eliahba the Shaalbonite;
34the sons of Hashem the Gizonite;
Jonathan son of Shagee the Hararite;
35Ahiam son of Sacar the Hararite;
Eliphal son of Ur;
36Hepher the Mekerathite;
Ahijah the Pelonite;
37Hezro the Carmelite;
Naarai son of Ezbai;
38Joel brother of Nathan;
Mibhar son of Hagri;
39Zelek the Ammonite;
Naharai the Berothite, the officer who
carried the armor for Joab son of
Zeruiah;
40Ira the Ithrite;
Gareb the Ithrite;
41Uriah the Hittite;
Zabad son of Ahlai;
42Adina son of Shiza the Reubenite, who
was the leader of the Reubenites,
and his thirty soldiers;
43Hanan son of Maacah;
Joshaphat the Mithnite;
44Uzzia the Ashterathite;
Shama and Jeiel sons of Hotham the
Aroerite;
45Jediael son of Shimri;
Joha, Jediael's brother, the Tizite;
46Eliel the Mahavite;
Jeribai and Joshaviah, Elnaam's sons;
Ithmah the Moabite;
47Eliel, Obed, and Jaasiel the Mezobaites.

Warriors Join David

12 These were the men who came to David
at Ziklag when David was hiding from
Saul son of Kish. They were among the warriors
who helped David in battle. 2They came with
bows for weapons and could use either their right
or left hands to shoot arrows or to sling rocks.
They were Saul's relatives from the tribe[d] of Benjamin. 3Ahiezer was their leader, and there was
Joash. (Ahiezer and Joash were sons of Shemaah,
who was from the town of Gibeah.) There were
also Jeziel and Pelet, the sons of Azmaveth. There
were Beracah and Jehu from the town of Anathoth. 4And there was Ishmaiah from the town of
Gibeon; he was one of the Thirty. In fact, he was
the leader of the Thirty. There were Jeremiah, Jahaziel, Johanan, and Jozabad from Gederah.
5There were Eluzai, Jerimoth, Bealiah, and Shemariah. There was Shephatiah from Haruph. 6There
were Elkanah, Isshiah, Azarel, Joezer, and Jashobeam from the family group of Korah. 7And there
were Joelah and Zebadiah, the sons of Jeroham,
from the town of Gedor.

8Part of the people of Gad joined David at his
stronghold[d] in the desert. They were brave warriors trained for war and skilled with shields and
spears. They were as fierce as lions and as fast as
gazelles[d] over the hills.

9Ezer was the leader of Gad's army, and Obadiah was second in command. Eliab was third,
10Mishmannah was fourth, Jeremiah was fifth,
11Attai was sixth, Eliel was seventh, 12Johanan
was eighth, Elzabad was ninth, 13Jeremiah was
tenth, and Macbannai was eleventh in command.

14They were the commanders of the army from
Gad. The least of these leaders was in charge of
a hundred soldiers, and the greatest was in charge
of a thousand. 15They crossed the Jordan River
and chased away the people living in the valleys,
to the east and to the west. This happened in the
first month of the year when the Jordan floods the
valley.

16Other people from the tribes[d] of Benjamin
and Judah also came to David at his stronghold.
17David went out to meet them and said to them,
"If you have come peacefully to help me, I welcome you. Join me. But if you have come to turn
me over to my enemies, even though I have done
nothing wrong, the God of our fathers will see
this and punish you."

18Then the Spirit[d] entered Amasai, the leader of
the Thirty, and he said:

"We belong to you, David.
We are with you, son of Jesse.
Success, success to you.
Success to those who help you,
because your God helps you."

So David welcomed these men and made them
leaders of his army.
19Some of the men from Manasseh also joined
David when he went with the Philistines to fight
Saul. But David and his men did not really help
the Philistines. After talking about it, the Philistine leaders decided to send David away. They
said, "If David goes back to his master Saul, we
will be killed." 20These are the men from Manasseh who joined David when he went to Ziklag:
Adnah, Jozabad, Jediael, Michael, Jozabad, Elihu,
and Zillethai. Each of them was a leader of a thousand men from Manasseh. 21All these men of Manasseh were brave soldiers, and they helped David fight against groups of men who went around
the country robbing people. These soldiers became commanders in David's army. 22Every day
more men joined David, and his army became
large, like the army of God.

Others Join David at Hebron

23These are the numbers of the soldiers ready
for battle who joined David at Hebron. They came
to help turn the kingdom of Saul over to David,
just as the LORD had said.
24There were sixty-eight hundred men with
their weapons from Judah. They carried shields
and spears.
25There were seventy-one hundred men from
Simeon. They were warriors ready for war.
26There were forty-six hundred men from Levi.
27Jehoiada, a leader from Aaron's family, was in
that group. There were thirty-seven hundred with
him. 28Zadok was also in that group. He was a
strong young warrior, and with him came twenty-
two leaders from his family.
29There were three thousand men from Benjamin, who were Saul's relatives. Most of them had
remained loyal to Saul's family until then.
30There were twenty thousand eight hundred
men from Ephraim. They were brave warriors
and were famous men in their own family groups.
31There were eighteen thousand men from
West Manasseh. Each one was especially chosen
to make David king.
32There were two hundred leaders from Issachar. They knew what Israel should do, and they
knew the right time to do it. Their relatives were
with them and under their command.
33There were fifty thousand men from Zebulun. They were trained soldiers and knew how to
use every kind of weapon of war. They followed
David completely.
34There were one thousand officers from Naphtali. They had thirty-seven thousand soldiers with
them who carried shields and spears.
35There were twenty-eight thousand six hundred men from Dan, who were ready for war.
36There were forty thousand trained soldiers
from Asher, who were ready for war.
37There were one hundred twenty thousand
soldiers from the east side of the Jordan River
from the people of Reuben, Gad, and East Manasseh. They had every kind of weapon.
38All these fighting men were ready to go to
war. They came to Hebron fully agreed to make
David king of all Israel. All the other Israelites also
agreed to make David king. 39They spent three
days there with David, eating and drinking, because their relatives had prepared food for them.
40Also, their neighbors came from as far away as
Issachar, Zebulun, and Naphtali, bringing food on
donkeys, camels, mules, and oxen. They brought
much flour, fig cakes, raisins, wine, oil, cows, and
sheep, because the people of Israel were very
happy.

Bringing Back the Ark

13 David talked with all the officers of his
army, the commanders of a hundred
men and the commanders of a thousand men.
2Then David called the people of Israel together
and said, "If you think it is a good idea, and if it
is what the LORD our God wants, let's send a message. Let's tell our fellow Israelites in all the areas
of Israel and the priests and Levites living with
them in their towns and pastures to come and join
us. 3Let's bring the Ark[d] of our God back to us.
We did not use it to ask God for help while Saul
was king." 4All the people agreed with David, because they all thought it was the right thing to do.
5So David gathered all the Israelites, from the
Shihor River in Egypt to Lebo Hamath, to bring
the Ark of God back from the town of Kiriath Jearim. 6David and all the Israelites with him went
to Baalah of Judah, which is Kiriath Jearim, to get
the Ark of God the LORD. God's throne is between the golden, winged creatures on the Ark,
and the Ark is called by his name.
7The people carried the Ark of God from Abinadab's house on a new cart, and Uzzah and Ahio
guided it. 8David and all the Israelites were celebrating in the presence of God. With all their
strength they were singing and playing lyres,[d]
harps, tambourines,[d] cymbals, and trumpets.
9When David's men came to the threshing[d]
floor of Kidon, the oxen stumbled, and Uzzah
reached out his hand to steady the Ark. 10The
LORD was angry with Uzzah and killed him, because he had touched the Ark. So Uzzah died
there in the presence of God.
11David was angry because the LORD had punished Uzzah in his anger. Now that place is called
The Punishment of Uzzah.
12David was afraid of God that day and asked,
"How can I bring the Ark of God home to me?"
13So David did not take the Ark with him to Jeru-

salem. Instead, he took it to the house of Obed-Edom who was from Gath. 14The Ark of God stayed with Obed-Edom's family in his house for three months, and the LORD blessed Obed-Edom's family and everything he owned.

David's Kingdom Grows

14 Hiram king of the city of Tyre sent messengers to David. He also sent cedar logs, bricklayers, and carpenters to build a palace for David. 2Then David knew that the LORD really had made him king of Israel and that he had made his kingdom great. The LORD did this because he loved his people Israel.

3David married more women in Jerusalem and had more sons and daughters. 4These are the names of David's children born in Jerusalem: Shammua, Shobab, Nathan, Solomon, 5Ibhar, Elishua, Elpelet, 6Nogah, Nepheg, Japhia, 7Elishama, Beeliada, and Eliphelet.

David Defeats the Philistines

8When the Philistines heard that David had been made king of all Israel, they went to look for him. But David heard about it and went out to fight them. 9The Philistines had attacked and robbed the people in the Valley of Rephaim. 10David asked God, "Should I go and attack the Philistines? Will you hand them over to me?"

The LORD answered him, "Go, I will hand them over to you."

11So David and his men went up to the town of Baal Perazim and defeated the Philistines. David said, "Like a flood of water, God has broken through my enemies by using me." So that place was named Baal Perazim.[n] 12The Philistines had left their idols there, so David ordered his men to burn them.

13Soon the Philistines attacked the people in the valley again. 14David prayed to God again, and God answered him, saying, "Don't attack the Philistines from the front. Instead, go around them and attack them in front of the balsam trees. 15When you hear the sound of marching in the tops of the balsam trees, then attack. I, God, will have gone out before you to defeat the Philistine army." 16David did as God commanded, and he and his men defeated the Philistine army all the way from Gibeon to Gezer.

17So David became famous in all the countries, and the LORD made all nations afraid of him.

The Ark Is Brought to Jerusalem

15 David built houses for himself in Jerusalem. Then he prepared a place for the Ark[d] of God, and he set up a tent for it. 2David said, "Only the Levites may carry the Ark of God. The LORD chose them to carry the Ark of the LORD and to serve him forever."

3David called all the people of Israel to come to Jerusalem. He wanted to bring the Ark of the LORD to the place he had made for it. 4David called together the descendants[d] of Aaron and the Levites. 5There were one hundred twenty people from Kohath's family group, with Uriel as their leader. 6There were two hundred twenty people from Merari's family group, with Asaiah as their leader. 7There were one hundred thirty people from Gershon's family group, with Joel as their leader. 8There were two hundred people from Elizaphan's family group, with Shemaiah as their leader. 9There were eighty people from Hebron's family group, with Eliel as their leader. 10And there were one hundred twelve people from Uzziel's family group, with Amminadab as their leader.

11Then David asked the priests Zadok and Abiathar and these Levites to come to him: Uriel, Asaiah, Joel, Shemaiah, Eliel, and Amminadab. 12David said to them, "You are the leaders of the families of Levi. You and the other Levites must give yourselves for service to the LORD. Bring up the Ark of the LORD, the God of Israel, to the place I have made for it. 13The last time we did not ask the LORD how to carry it. You Levites didn't carry it, so the LORD our God punished us."

14Then the priests and Levites prepared themselves for service to the LORD so they could carry the Ark of the LORD, the God of Israel. 15The Levites used special poles to carry the Ark of God on their shoulders, as Moses had commanded, just as the LORD had said they should.

16David told the leaders of the Levites to appoint their brothers as singers to play their lyres,[d] harps, and cymbals and to sing happy songs.

17So the Levites appointed Heman and his relatives Asaph and Ethan. Heman was Joel's son. Asaph was Berekiah's son. And Ethan, from the Merari family group, was Kushaiah's son. 18There was also a second group of Levites: Zechariah, Jaaziel, Shemiramoth, Jehiel, Unni, Eliab, Benaiah, Maaseiah, Mattithiah, Eliphelehu, Mikneiah, Obed-Edom, and Jeiel. They were the Levite guards.

19The singers Heman, Asaph, and Ethan played bronze cymbals. 20Zechariah, Jaaziel, Shemiramoth, Jehiel, Unni, Eliab, Maaseiah, and Benaiah played the lyres. 21Mattithiah, Eliphelehu, Mikneiah, Obed-Edom, Jeiel, and Azaziah played the harps. 22The Levite leader Kenaniah was in charge of the singing, because he was very good at it.

23Berekiah and Elkanah were two of the guards for the Ark of the Agreement. 24The priests Shebaniah, Joshaphat, Nethanel, Amasai, Zechariah, Be-

Baal Perazim This name means "the Lord breaks through."

naiah, and Eliezer had the job of blowing trumpets in front of the Ark of God. Obed-Edom and
Jehiah were also guards for the Ark.
25David, the leaders of Israel, and the commanders of a thousand soldiers went to get the
Ark of the Agreement with the LORD. They all
went to bring the Ark from Obed-Edom's house
with great joy. 26Because God helped the Levites
who carried the Ark of the Agreement with the
LORD, they sacrificed seven bulls and seven male
sheep. 27All the Levites who carried the Ark, and
Kenaniah, the man in charge of the singing, and
all the singers wore robes of fine linen. David also
wore a robe of fine linen and a holy vest[d] of fine
linen. 28So all the people of Israel brought up the
Ark of the Agreement with the LORD. They
shouted, blew horns and trumpets, and played
cymbals, lyres, and harps.
29As the Ark of the Agreement with the LORD
entered Jerusalem, Saul's daughter Michal
watched from a window. When she saw King David dancing and celebrating, she hated him.

16 They brought the Ark of God and put it
inside the tent that David had set up for
it. Then they offered burnt offerings and fellowship offerings to God. 2When David had finished
giving the burnt offerings and fellowship offerings, he blessed the people in the name of the
LORD. 3He gave a loaf of bread, some dates, and
raisins to every Israelite man and woman.
4Then David appointed some of the Levites to
serve before the Ark of the LORD. They had the
job of leading the worship and giving thanks and
praising the LORD, the God of Israel. 5Asaph, who
played the cymbals, was the leader. Zechariah
was second to him. The other Levites were Jaaziel, Shemiramoth, Jehiel, Mattithiah, Eliab, Benaiah, Obed-Edom, and Jeiel. They played the
lyres and harps. 6Benaiah and Jahaziel were
priests who blew the trumpets regularly before
the Ark of the Agreement with God. 7That day
David first gave Asaph and his relatives the job of
singing praises to the LORD.

David's Song of Thanks

8Give thanks to the LORD and pray to him.
Tell the nations what he has done.
9Sing to him; sing praises to him.
Tell about all his miracles.[d]
10Be glad that you are his;
let those who seek the LORD be happy.
11Depend on the LORD and his strength;
always go to him for help.
12Remember the miracles he has done,
his wonders, and his decisions.
13You are the descendants[d] of his servant,
Israel;
you are the children of Jacob, his chosen
people.
14He is the LORD our God.
His laws are for all the world.
15He will keep his agreement forever;
he will keep his promises always.
16He will keep the agreement he made with
Abraham
and the promise he made to Isaac.
17He made it a law for the people of Jacob;
he made it an agreement with Israel to last
forever.
18He said, "I will give the land of Canaan to
you,
to belong to you."

19Then God's people were few in number,
and they were strangers in the land.
20They went from one nation to another,
from one kingdom to another.
21But he did not let anyone hurt them;
he warned kings not to harm them.
22He said, "Don't touch my chosen people,
and don't harm my prophets."[d]

23Sing to the LORD, all the earth.
Every day tell how he saves us.
24Tell the nations about his glory;
tell all peoples the miracles he does.
25The LORD is great; he should be praised.
He should be respected more than all the
gods.
26All the gods of the nations are only idols,
but the LORD made the skies.
27He has glory and majesty;
he has power and joy in his Temple.[d]

28Praise the LORD, all nations on earth.
Praise the LORD's glory and power;
29 praise the glory of the LORD's name.
Bring an offering and come to him.
Worship the LORD because he is holy.
30Tremble before him, everyone on earth.
The earth is set, and it cannot be moved.
31Let the skies rejoice and the earth be glad.
Let people everywhere say, "The LORD is
king!"
32Let the sea and everything in it shout;
let the fields and everything in them
rejoice.
33Then the trees of the forest will sing
for joy before the LORD.
They will sing because he is coming to
judge the world.

34Thank the LORD because he is good.
His love continues forever.
35Say to him, "Save us, God our Savior,
and bring us back and save us from other
nations.
Then we will thank you
and will gladly praise you."
36Praise the LORD, the God of Israel.

He always was and always will be.

All the people said "Amen" and praised the LORD.
37Then David left Asaph and the other Levites
there in front of the Ark[d] of the Agreement with
the LORD. They were to serve there every day.
38David also left Obed-Edom and sixty-eight other
Levites to serve with them. Hosah and Obed-
Edom son of Jeduthun were guards.
39David left Zadok the priest and the other
priests who served with him in front of the Tent
of the LORD at the place of worship in Gibeon.
40Every morning and evening they offered burnt
offerings on the altar of burnt offerings, following
the rules written in the Teachings of the LORD,
which he had given Israel. 41With them were Heman and Jeduthun and other Levites. They were
chosen by name to sing praises to the LORD because his love continues forever. 42Heman and Jeduthun also had the job of playing the trumpets
and cymbals and other musical instruments when
songs were sung to God. Jeduthun's sons guarded
the gates.
43Then all the people left. Each person went
home, and David also went home to bless the
people in his home.

God's Promise to David

17 When David moved into his palace, he
said to Nathan the prophet, "Look, I am
living in a palace made of cedar, but the Ark[d] of
the Agreement with the LORD sits in a tent."
2Nathan said to David, "Do what you want to
do, because God is with you."
3But that night God spoke his word to Nathan,
saying, 4"Go and tell David my servant, 'This is
what the LORD says: You are not the person to
build a house for me to live in. 5From the time I
brought Israel out of Egypt until now I have not
lived in a house. I have moved from one tent site
to another and from one place to another. 6As I
have moved with the Israelites to different places,
I have never said to the leaders, whom I commanded to take care of my people, "Why haven't
you built me a house of cedar?" '
7"Now, tell my servant David: 'This is what the
LORD All-Powerful says: I took you from the pasture and from tending the sheep and made you
king of my people Israel. 8I have been with you
everywhere you have gone. I have defeated your
enemies for you. I will make you as famous as any
of the great people on the earth. 9I will choose a
place for my people Israel, and I will plant them
so they can live in their own homes. They will not
be bothered anymore. Wicked people will no
longer hurt them as they have in the past 10when
I chose judges for my people Israel. I will defeat
all your enemies.
" 'I tell you that the LORD will make your
descendants[d] kings of Israel after you. 11When
you die and join your ancestors, I will make one
of your sons the new king, and I will set up his
kingdom. 12He will build a house for me, and I
will let his kingdom rule always. 13I will be his
father, and he will be my son. I took away my love
from Saul, who ruled before you, but I will never
stop loving your son. 14I will put him in charge of
my house and kingdom forever. His family will
rule forever.' "
15Nathan told David everything God had said
in this vision.

David Prays to God

16Then King David went in and sat in front of
the LORD. David said, "LORD God, who am I?
What is my family? Why did you bring me to this
point? 17But that was not enough for you, God.
You have also made promises about my future
family. LORD God, you have treated me like a very
important person.
18"What more can I say to you for honoring me,
your servant? You know me so well. 19LORD, you
have done this wonderful thing for my sake and
because you wanted to. You have made known all
these great things.
20"There is no one like you, LORD. There is no
God except you. We have heard all this ourselves!
21There is no nation like your people Israel. They
are the only people on earth that God chose to be
his own. You made your name well known by the
great and wonderful things you did for them. You
went ahead of them and forced other nations out
of the land. You freed your people from slavery in
Egypt. 22You made the people of Israel your very
own people forever, and, LORD, you are their
God.
23"LORD, keep the promise forever that you
made about my family and me, your servant. Do
what you have said. 24Then you will be honored
always, and people will say, 'The LORD All-
Powerful, the God over Israel, is Israel's God!'
And the family of your servant David will continue before you.
25"My God, you have told me that you would
make my family great. So I, your servant, am
brave enough to pray to you. 26LORD, you are
God, and you have promised these good things to
me, your servant. 27You have chosen to bless my
family. Let it continue before you always. LORD,
you have blessed my family, so it will always be
blessed."

David Defeats Nations

18 Later, David defeated the Philistines,
conquered them, and took the city of
Gath and the small towns around it.
2He also defeated the people of Moab. So the

people of Moab became servants of David and
gave him the payment he demanded.
3David also defeated Hadadezer king of Zobah
all the way to the town of Hamath as he tried to
spread his kingdom to the Euphrates River. 4Da-
vid captured one thousand of his chariots, seven
thousand men who rode in chariots, and twenty
thousand foot soldiers. He crippled all but a hundred of the chariot horses.
5Arameans from Damascus came to help Hadadezer king of Zobah, but David killed twenty-
two thousand of them. 6Then David put groups of
soldiers in Damascus in Aram. The Arameans became David's servants and gave him the payments he demanded. So the LORD gave David victory everywhere he went.
7David took the shields of gold that had belonged to Hadadezer's officers and brought them
to Jerusalem. 8David also took many things made
of bronze from Tebah and Cun, which had been
cities under Hadadezer's control. Later, Solomon
used this bronze to make things for the Temple:[d]
the large bronze bowl, which was called the Sea,
the pillars, and other bronze utensils.
9Toi king of Hamath heard that David had defeated all the army of Hadadezer king of Zobah.
10So Toi sent his son Hadoram to greet and congratulate King David for defeating Hadadezer.
(Hadadezer had been at war with Toi.) Hadoram
brought items made of gold, silver, and bronze.
11King David gave them to the LORD, along with
the silver and gold he had taken from these nations: Edom, Moab, the Ammonites, the Philistines, and Amalek.
12Abishai son of Zeruiah killed eighteen thousand Edomites in the Valley of Salt. 13David put
groups of soldiers in Edom, and all the Edomites
became his servants. The LORD gave David victory everywhere he went.

David's Important Officers

14David was king over all of Israel, and he did
what was fair and right for all his people. 15Joab
son of Zeruiah was commander over the army.
Jehoshaphat son of Ahilud was the recorder. 16Za-
dok son of Ahitub and Abiathar son of Ahimelech
were priests. Shavsha was the royal secretary.
17Benaiah son of Jehoiada was over the Kerethites
and Pelethites.[n] And David's sons were important officers who served at his side.

War with the Ammonites and Arameans

19 When Nahash king of the Ammonites
died, his son became king after him. 2Da-
vid said, "Nahash was loyal to me, so I will be
loyal to his son Hanun." So David sent messengers to comfort Hanun about his father's death.
David's officers went to the land of the Ammonites to comfort Hanun. 3But the Ammonite
leaders said to Hanun, "Do you think David
wants to honor your father by sending men to
comfort you? No! David sent them to study the
land and capture it and spy it out." 4So Hanun
arrested David's officers. To shame them he
shaved their beards and cut off their clothes at the
hips. Then he sent them away.
5When the people told David what had happened to his officers, he sent messengers to meet
them, because they were very ashamed. King David said, "Stay in Jericho until your beards have
grown back. Then come home."
6The Ammonites knew that they had insulted
David. So Hanun and the Ammonites sent about
seventy-four thousand pounds of silver to hire
chariots and chariot drivers from Northwest Mesopotamia, Aram Maacah, and Zobah. 7The Ammonites hired thirty-two thousand chariots and
the king of Maacah and his army. So they came
and set up camp near the town of Medeba. The
Ammonites themselves came out of their towns
and got ready for battle.
8When David heard about this, he sent Joab
with the whole army. 9The Ammonites came out
and prepared for battle at the city gate. The kings
who had come to help were out in the field by
themselves.
10Joab saw that there were enemies both in
front of him and behind him. So he chose some
of the best soldiers of Israel and sent them out to
fight the Arameans. 11Joab put the rest of the army
under the command of Abishai, his brother. Then
they went out to fight the Ammonites. 12Joab said
to Abishai, "If the Arameans are too strong for me,
you must help me. Or, if the Ammonites are too
strong for you, I will help you. 13Be strong. We
must fight bravely for our people and the cities of
our God. The LORD will do what he thinks is
right."
14Then Joab and the army with him went to
attack the Arameans, and the Arameans ran
away. 15When the Ammonites saw that the Arameans were running away, they also ran away
from Joab's brother Abishai and went back to
their city. So Joab went back to Jerusalem.
16When the Arameans saw that Israel had defeated them, they sent messengers to bring other
Arameans from east of the Euphrates River. Their
leader was Shophach, the commander of Hadadezer's army.
17When David heard about this, he gathered all
the Israelites, and they crossed over the Jordan
River. He prepared them for battle, facing the Ara-

Kerethites and Pelethites These were probably special units of the army that were responsible for the king's safety, a kind of palace guard.

means. The Arameans fought with him, 18but they ran away from the Israelites. David killed seven thousand Aramean chariot drivers and forty thousand Aramean foot soldiers. He also killed Shophach, the commander of the Aramean army.

19When those who served Hadadezer saw that the Israelites had defeated them, they made peace with David and served him. So the Arameans refused to help the Ammonites again.

> **SIDELIGHT:** Ecclesiastes 3:1 (p. 600) says, "There is a time for everything." Apparently the right time for war in the Old Testament was springtime (1 Chronicles 20:1). Kings would go to war right after the spring harvest when there wasn't much to do on the farm and when the soldiers could live off the land.

Joab Destroys the Ammonites

20 In the spring, the time of year when kings normally went out to battle, Joab led out the army of Israel. But David stayed in Jerusalem. The army of Israel destroyed the land of Ammon and went to the city of Rabbah and attacked it. 2David took the crown off the head of their king,[n] and had it placed on his own head. That gold crown weighed about seventy-five pounds, and it had valuable gems in it. And David took many valuable things from the city. 3He also brought out the people of the city and forced them to work with saws, iron picks, and axes. David did this to all the Ammonite cities. Then David and all his army returned to Jerusalem.

Philistine Giants Are Killed

4Later, at Gezer, war broke out with the Philistines. Sibbecai the Hushathite killed Sippai, who was one of the descendants[d] of the Rephaites.[d] So those Philistines were defeated.

5Later, there was another battle with the Philistines. Elhanan son of Jair killed Lahmi, the brother of Goliath, who was from the town of Gath. His spear was as large as a weaver's rod.

6At Gath another battle took place. A huge man was there; he had six fingers on each hand and six toes on each foot—twenty-four fingers and toes in all. This man also was one of the sons of Rapha.[d] 7When he spoke against Israel, Jonathan son of Shimea, David's brother, killed him.

8These descendants of Rapha from Gath were killed by David and his men.

David Counts the Israelites

21 Satan was against Israel, and he caused David to count the people of Israel. 2So David said to Joab and the commanders of the troops, "Go and count all the Israelites from Beersheba to Dan.[n] Then tell me so I will know how many there are."

3But Joab said, "May the LORD give the nation a hundred times more people. My master the king, all the Israelites are your servants. Why do you want to do this, my master? You will make Israel guilty of sin."

4But the king commanded Joab, so Joab left and went through all Israel. Then he returned to Jerusalem. 5Joab gave the list of the people to David. There were one million one hundred thousand men in all of Israel who could use the sword, and there were four hundred seventy thousand men in Judah who could use the sword. 6But Joab did not count the tribes[d] of Levi and Benjamin, because he didn't like King David's order. 7David had done something God had said was wrong, so God punished Israel.

8Then David said to God, "I have sinned greatly by what I have done! Now, I beg you to forgive me, your servant, because I have been very foolish."

9The LORD said to Gad, who was David's seer,[d] 10"Go and tell David, 'This is what the LORD says: I offer you three choices. Choose one of them and I will do it.'"

11So Gad went to David and said to him, "This is what the LORD says: 'Choose for yourself 12three years of hunger. Or choose three months of running from your enemies as they chase you with their swords. Or choose three days of punishment from the LORD, in which a terrible disease will spread through the country. The angel of the LORD will go through Israel destroying the people.' Now, David, decide which of these things I should tell the LORD who sent me."

13David said to Gad, "I am in great trouble. Let the LORD punish me, because the LORD is very merciful. Don't let my punishment come from human beings."

14So the LORD sent a terrible disease on Israel, and seventy thousand people died. 15God sent an angel to destroy Jerusalem, but when the angel started to destroy it, the LORD saw it and felt very sorry about the terrible things that had happened. So he said to the angel who was destroying, "That is enough! Put down your arm!" The angel of the LORD was then standing at the threshing[d] floor of Araunah the Jebusite.

16David looked up and saw the angel of the

their king Or, "Milcom," the god of the Ammonite people.
Beersheba to Dan Beersheba was the city farthest south in Israel. Dan was the city farthest north. So this means all the people of Israel.

LORD in the sky, holding his sword drawn and
pointed at Jerusalem. Then David and the older
leaders bowed facedown on the ground. They
were wearing rough cloth to show their grief.
17David said to God, "I am the one who sinned
and did wrong. I gave the order for the people
to be counted. These people only followed
me like sheep. They did nothing wrong. LORD
my God, please punish me and my family, but
stop the terrible disease that is killing your people."

18Then the angel of the LORD told Gad to tell
David that he should build an altar to the LORD
on the threshing floor of Araunah the Jebusite.
19So David did what Gad told him to do, in the
name of the LORD.

20Araunah was separating the wheat from the
straw. When he turned around, he saw the angel.
Araunah's four sons who were with him hid.
21David came to Araunah, and when Araunah
saw him, he left the threshing floor and bowed
facedown on the ground before David.

22David said to him, "Sell me your threshing
floor so I can build an altar to the LORD here. Then
the terrible disease will stop. Sell it to me for the
full price."

23Araunah said to David, "Take this threshing
floor. My master the king, do anything you want.
Look, I will also give you oxen for the whole
burnt offerings, the threshing boards for the
wood, and wheat for the grain offering. I give everything to you."

24But King David answered Araunah, "No, I
will pay the full price for the land. I won't take
anything that is yours and give it to the LORD. I
won't offer a burnt offering that costs me nothing."

25So David paid Araunah about fifteen pounds
of gold for the place. 26David built an altar to the
LORD there and offered whole burnt offerings and
fellowship offerings. David prayed to the LORD,
and he answered him by sending down fire from
heaven on the altar of burnt offering. 27Then the
LORD commanded the angel to put his sword back
into its holder.

28When David saw that the LORD had answered him on the threshing floor of Araunah, he
offered sacrifices there. 29The Holy Tent[d] that Moses made while the Israelites were in the desert
and the altar of burnt offerings were in Gibeon at
the place of worship. 30But David could not go to
the Holy Tent to speak with God, because he was
afraid of the angel of the LORD and his sword.

22 David said, "The Temple[d] of the LORD
God and the altar for Israel's burnt offerings will be built here."

David Makes Plans for the Temple

2So David ordered all foreigners living in Israel
to gather together. From that group David chose
stonecutters to cut stones to be used in building
the Temple[d] of God. 3David supplied a large
amount of iron to be used for making nails and
hinges for the gate doors. He also supplied more
bronze than could be weighed, 4and he supplied
more cedar logs than could be counted. Much of
the cedar had been brought to David by the people from Sidon and Tyre.

5David said, "We should build a great Temple
for the LORD, which will be famous everywhere
for its greatness and beauty. But my son Solomon
is young. He hasn't yet learned what he needs to
know, so I will prepare for the building of it." So
David got many of the materials ready before he
died.

6Then David called for his son Solomon and
told him to build the Temple for the LORD, the
God of Israel. 7David said to him, "My son, I
wanted to build a temple for worshiping the LORD
my God. 8But the LORD spoke his word to me,
'David, you have killed many people. You have
fought many wars. You cannot build a temple for
worship to me, because you have killed many
people. 9But, you will have a son, a man of peace
and rest. I will give him rest from all his enemies
around him. His name will be Solomon,[n] and I
will give Israel peace and quiet while he is king.
10Solomon will build a temple for worship to me.
He will be my son, and I will be his father. I will
make his kingdom strong; someone from his family will rule Israel forever.' "

11David said, "Now, my son, may the LORD be
with you. May you build a temple for the LORD
your God, as he said you would. 12He will make
you the king of Israel. May the LORD give you
wisdom and understanding so you will be able to
obey the teachings of the LORD your God. 13Be
careful to obey the rules and laws the LORD gave
Moses for Israel. If you obey them, you will have
success. Be strong and brave. Don't be afraid or
discouraged.

14"Solomon, I have worked hard getting many
of the materials for building the Temple of the
LORD. I have supplied about seven and one-half
million pounds of gold, about seventy-five million
pounds of silver, so much bronze and iron it cannot be weighed, and wood and stone. You may
add to them. 15You have many workmen — stonecutters, bricklayers, carpenters, and people skilled
in every kind of work. 16They are skilled in working with gold, silver, bronze, and iron. You have
more craftsmen than can be counted. Now begin
the work, and may the LORD be with you."

Solomon This name sounds like the Hebrew word for "peace."

17Then David ordered all the leaders of Israel to help his son Solomon. 18David said to them, "The LORD your God is with you. He has given you rest from our enemies. He has handed over to me the people living around us. The LORD and his people are in control of this land. 19Now give yourselves completely to obeying the LORD your God. Build the holy place of the LORD God; build the Temple for worship to the LORD. Then bring the Ark[d] of the Agreement with the LORD and the holy items that belong to God into the Temple."

The Levites

23 After David had lived long and was old, he made his son Solomon the new king of Israel. 2David gathered all the leaders of Israel, along with the priests and Levites. 3He counted the Levites who were thirty years old and older. In all, there were thirty-eight thousand Levites. 4David said, "Of these, twenty-four thousand Levites will direct the work of the Temple[d] of the LORD, six thousand Levites will be officers and judges, 5four thousand Levites will be gatekeepers, and four thousand Levites will praise the LORD with musical instruments I made for giving praise."

6David separated the Levites into three groups that were led by Levi's three sons: Gershon, Kohath, and Merari.

The People of Gershon

7From the people of Gershon, there were Ladan and Shimei.

8Ladan had three sons. His first son was Jehiel, and his other sons were Zetham and Joel.

9Shimei's sons were Shelomoth, Haziel, and Haran. These three sons were leaders of Ladan's families. 10Shimei had four sons: Jahath, Ziza, Jeush, and Beriah. 11Jahath was the first son, and Ziza was the second son. But Jeush and Beriah did not have many children, so they were counted as if they were one family.

The People of Kohath

12Kohath had four sons: Amram, Izhar, Hebron, and Uzziel.

13Amram's sons were Aaron and Moses. Aaron and his descendants[d] were chosen to be special forever. They were chosen to prepare the holy things for the LORD's service, to offer sacrifices before the LORD, and to serve him as priests. They were to give blessings in his name forever.

14Moses was the man of God, and his sons were counted as part of the tribe[d] of Levi. 15Moses' sons were Gershom and Eliezer. 16Gershom's first son was Shubael. 17Eliezer's first son was Rehabiah. Eliezer had no other sons, but Rehabiah had many sons.

18Izhar's first son was Shelomith.

19Hebron's first son was Jeriah, his second was Amariah, his third was Jahaziel, and his fourth was Jekameam.

20Uzziel's first son was Micah and his second was Isshiah.

The People of Merari

21Merari's sons were Mahli and Mushi. Mahli's sons were Eleazar and Kish. 22Eleazar died without sons; he had only daughters. Eleazar's daughters married their cousins, the sons of Kish. 23Mushi's three sons were Mahli, Eder, and Jerimoth.

The Levites' Work

24These were Levi's descendants[d] listed by their families. They were the leaders of families. Each person who was twenty years old or older was listed. They served in the LORD's Temple.[d]

25David had said, "The LORD, the God of Israel, has given rest to his people. He has come to live in Jerusalem forever. 26So the Levites don't need to carry the Holy Tent[d] or any of the things used in its services anymore." 27David's last instructions were to count the Levites who were twenty years old and older.

28The Levites had the job of helping Aaron's descendants in the service of the Temple of the LORD. They cared for the Temple courtyard and side rooms, and they made all the holy things pure. Their job was to serve in the Temple of God. 29They were responsible for putting the holy bread on the table, for the flour in the grain offerings, for the bread made without yeast, for the baking and mixing, and for the measuring. 30The Levites also stood every morning and gave thanks and praise to the LORD. They also did this every evening. 31The Levites offered all the burnt offerings to the LORD on the special days of rest, at the New Moon[d] festivals, and at all appointed feasts. They served before the LORD every day. They were to follow the rules for how many Levites should serve each time. 32So the Levites took care of the Meeting Tent and the Holy Place. And they helped their relatives, Aaron's descendants, with the services at the Temple of the LORD.

The Groups of the Priests

24 These were the groups of Aaron's sons: Aaron's sons were Nadab, Abihu, Eleazar, and Ithamar. 2But Nadab and Abihu died before their father did, and they had no sons. So Eleazar and Ithamar served as the priests. 3David, with the help of Zadok, a descendant[d] of Eleazar, and Ahimelech, a descendant of Ithamar, separated their family groups into two different groups. Each group had certain duties. 4There were more leaders from Eleazar's family than from Ithamar's—sixteen leaders from Eleazar's family and eight leaders from Ithamar's family.

5Men were chosen from Eleazar's and Ithamar's
families by throwing lots.[d] Some men from each
family were chosen to be in charge of the Holy
Place, and some were chosen to serve as priests.
6Shemaiah son of Nethanel, from the tribe[d] of
Levi, was the secretary. He recorded the names of
those descendants in front of King David, the officers, Zadok the priest, Ahimelech son of Abiathar,
and the leaders of the families of the priests and
Levites. The work was divided by lots among the
families of Eleazar and Ithamar. The following
men with their groups were chosen.
7The first one chosen was Jehoiarib. The second was Jedaiah. 8The third was Harim. The
fourth was Seorim. 9The fifth was Malkijah. The
sixth was Mijamin. 10The seventh was Hakkoz.
The eighth was Abijah. 11The ninth was Jeshua.
The tenth was Shecaniah. 12The eleventh was
Eliashib. The twelfth was Jakim. 13The thirteenth
was Huppah. The fourteenth was Jeshebeab.
14The fifteenth was Bilgah. The sixteenth was
Immer. 15The seventeenth was Hezir. The
eighteenth was Happizzez. 16The nineteenth
was Pethahiah. The twentieth was Jehezkel. 17The
twenty-first was Jakin. The twenty-second was
Gamul. 18The twenty-third was Delaiah. The
twenty-fourth was Maaziah.
19These were the groups chosen to serve in the
Temple of the LORD. They obeyed the rules given
them by Aaron, just as the LORD, the God of Israel, had commanded him.

The Other Levites

20These are the names of the rest of Levi's
descendants:[d]
Shubael was a descendant of Amram, and Jehdeiah was a descendant of Shubael.
21Isshiah was the first son of Rehabiah.
22From the Izhar family group, there was Shelomoth, and Jahath was a descendant of Shelomoth.
23Hebron's first son was Jeriah, Amariah was
his second, Jahaziel was his third, and Jekameam
was his fourth.
24Uzziel's son was Micah. Micah's son was
Shamir. 25Micah's brother was Isshiah, and Isshiah's son was Zechariah.
26Merari's descendants were Mahli and Mushi.
Merari's son was Jaaziah. 27Jaaziah son of Merari
had sons named Shoham, Zaccur, and Ibri.
28Mahli's son was Eleazar, but Eleazar did not
have any sons.
29Kish's son was Jerahmeel.
30Mushi's sons were Mahli, Eder, and Jerimoth.
These are the Levites, listed by their families.
31They were chosen for special jobs by throwing
lots[d] in front of King David, Zadok, Ahimelech,
the leaders of the families of the priests, and the
Levites. They did this just as their relatives, the
priests, Aaron's descendants, had done. The families of the oldest brother and the youngest brother
were treated the same.

SIDELIGHT: It might seem strange if your pastor started singing during a sermon. But 1 Chronicles 25:1 describes people who were chosen to preach—and play harps, lyres, and cymbals. The cymbals must have helped if the sermon got boring.

The Music Groups

25 David and the commanders of the army
chose some of the sons of Asaph, Heman, and Jeduthun to preach and play harps,
lyres,[d] and cymbals. Here is a list of the men who
served in this way:
2Asaph's sons who served were Zaccur, Joseph,
Nethaniah, and Asarelah. King David chose
Asaph to preach, and Asaph directed his sons.
3Jeduthun's sons who served were Gedaliah,
Zeri, Jeshaiah, Shimei, Hashabiah, and Mattithiah. There were six of them, and Jeduthun directed them. He preached and used a harp to give
thanks and praise to the LORD.
4Heman's sons who served were Bukkiah, Mattaniah, Uzziel, Shubael, Jerimoth, Hananiah, Hanani, Eliathah, Giddalti, Romamti-Ezer, Joshbekashah, Mallothi, Hothir, and Mahazioth. 5All these
were sons of Heman, David's seer.[d] God promised to make Heman strong, so Heman had many
sons. God gave him fourteen sons and three
daughters. 6Heman directed all his sons in making
music for the Temple[d] of the LORD with cymbals,
lyres, and harps; that was their way of serving in
the Temple of God. King David was in charge of
Asaph, Jeduthun, and Heman. 7These men and
their relatives were trained and skilled in making
music for the LORD. There were two hundred
eighty-eight of them. 8Everyone threw lots[d] to
choose the time his family was to serve at the
Temple. The young and the old, the teacher and
the student, had to throw lots.
9First, the lot fell to Joseph, from the family of
Asaph.
Second, twelve men were chosen from Gedaliah, his sons and relatives.
10Third, twelve men were chosen from Zaccur,
his sons and relatives.
11Fourth, twelve men were chosen from Izri,
his sons and relatives.
12Fifth, twelve men were chosen from Nethaniah, his sons and relatives.
13Sixth, twelve men were chosen from Bukkiah, his sons and relatives.

14Seventh, twelve men were chosen from Jesarelah, his sons and relatives.

15Eighth, twelve men were chosen from Jeshaiah, his sons and relatives.

16Ninth, twelve men were chosen from Mattaniah, his sons and relatives.

17Tenth, twelve men were chosen from Shimei, his sons and relatives.

18Eleventh, twelve men were chosen from Azarel, his sons and relatives.

19Twelfth, twelve men were chosen from Hashabiah, his sons and relatives.

20Thirteenth, twelve men were chosen from Shubael, his sons and relatives.

21Fourteenth, twelve men were chosen from Mattithiah, his sons and relatives.

22Fifteenth, twelve men were chosen from Jerimoth, his sons and relatives.

23Sixteenth, twelve men were chosen from Hananiah, his sons and relatives.

24Seventeenth, twelve men were chosen from Joshbekashah, his sons and relatives.

25Eighteenth, twelve men were chosen from Hanani, his sons and relatives.

26Nineteenth, twelve men were chosen from Mallothi, his sons and relatives.

27Twentieth, twelve men were chosen from Eliathah, his sons and relatives.

28Twenty-first, twelve men were chosen from Hothir, his sons and relatives.

29Twenty-second, twelve men were chosen from Giddalti, his sons and relatives.

30Twenty-third, twelve men were chosen from Mahazioth, his sons and relatives.

31Twenty-fourth, twelve men were chosen from Romamti-Ezer, his sons and relatives.

The Gatekeepers

26 These are the groups of the gatekeepers. From the family of Korah, there was Meshelemiah son of Kore, who was from Asaph's family. 2Meshelemiah had sons. Zechariah was his first son, Jediael was second, Zebadiah was third, Jathniel was fourth, 3Elam was fifth, Jehohanan was sixth, and Eliehoenai was seventh.

4Obed-Edom had sons. Shemaiah was his first son, Jehozabad was second, Joah was third, Sacar was fourth, Nethanel was fifth, 5Ammiel was sixth, Issachar was seventh, and Peullethai was eighth. God blessed Obed-Edom with children.

6Obed-Edom's son Shemaiah also had sons. They were leaders in their father's family because they were capable men. 7Shemaiah's sons were Othni, Rephael, Obed, Elzabad, Elihu, and Semakiah. Elihu, and Semakiah were skilled workers. 8All these were Obed-Edom's descendants.[d] They and their sons and relatives were capable men and strong workers. Obed-Edom had sixty-two descendants in all.

9Meshelemiah had sons and relatives who were skilled workers. In all, there were eighteen.

10From the Merari family, Hosah had sons. Shimri was chosen to be in charge. Although he was not the oldest son, his father chose him to be in charge. 11Hilkiah was his second son, Tabaliah was third, and Zechariah was fourth. In all, Hosah had thirteen sons and relatives.

12These were the leaders of the groups of gatekeepers, and they served in the Temple[d] of the LORD. Their relatives also worked in the Temple. 13By throwing lots,[d] each family chose a gate to guard. Young and old threw lots.

14Meshelemiah was chosen by lot to guard the East Gate. Then lots were thrown for Meshelemiah's son Zechariah. He was a wise counselor and was chosen for the North Gate. 15Obed-Edom was chosen for the South Gate, and Obed-Edom's sons were chosen to guard the storehouse. 16Shuppim and Hosah were chosen for the West Gate and the Shalleketh Gate on the upper road.

Guards stood side by side with guards. 17Six Levites stood guard every day at the East Gate; four Levites stood guard every day at the North Gate; four Levites stood guard every day at the South Gate; and two Levites at a time guarded the storehouse. 18There were two guards at the western court and four guards on the road to the court.

19These were the groups of the gatekeepers from the families of Korah and Merari.

Other Leaders

20Other Levites were responsible for guarding the treasuries of the Temple[d] of God and for the places where the holy items were kept.

21Ladan was Gershon's son and the ancestor of several family groups. Jehiel was a leader of one of the family groups. 22His sons were Zetham and Joel his brother, and they were responsible for the treasuries of the Temple of the LORD.

23Other leaders were chosen from the family groups of Amram, Izhar, Hebron, and Uzziel. 24Shubael, the descendant[d] of Gershom, who was Moses' son, was the leader responsible for the treasuries. 25These were Shubael's relatives from Eliezer: Eliezer's son Rehabiah, Rehabiah's son Jeshaiah, Jeshaiah's son Joram, Joram's son Zicri, and Zicri's son Shelomith. 26Shelomith and his relatives were responsible for everything that had been collected for the Temple by King David, by the heads of families, by the commanders of a thousand men and of a hundred men, and by other army commanders. 27They also gave some of the things they had taken in wars to be used in repairing the Temple of the LORD. 28Shelomith and his relatives took care of all the holy items. Some had been given by Samuel the seer,[d] Saul

son of Kish, Abner son of Ner, and Joab son of
Zeruiah.
29Kenaniah was from the Izhar family. He and
his sons worked outside the Temple as officers
and judges in different places in Israel.
30Hashabiah was from the Hebron family. He
and his relatives were responsible for the LORD's
work and the king's business in Israel west of the
Jordan River. There were seventeen hundred
skilled men in Hashabiah's group. 31The history of
the Hebron family shows that Jeriah was their
leader. In David's fortieth year as king, the
records were searched, and some capable men of
the Hebron family were found living at Jazer in
Gilead. 32Jeriah had twenty-seven hundred relatives who were skilled men and leaders of families. King David gave them the responsibility of
directing the tribes[d] of Reuben, Gad, and East Manasseh in God's work and the king's business.

Army Divisions

27 This is the list of the Israelites who
served the king in the army. Each division was on duty one month each year. There
were leaders of families, commanders of a hundred men, commanders of a thousand men, and
other officers. Each division had twenty-four
thousand men.
2Jashobeam son of Zabdiel was in charge of the
first division for the first month. There were
twenty-four thousand men in his division. 3Jasho-
beam, one of the descendants[d] of Perez, was
leader of all the army officers for the first month.
4Dodai, from the Ahohites, was in charge of the
division for the second month. Mikloth was a
leader in the division. There were twenty-four
thousand men in Dodai's division.
5The third commander, for the third month,
was Benaiah son of Jehoiada the priest. There
were twenty-four thousand men in his division.
6He was the Benaiah who was one of the Thirty[n]
soldiers. Benaiah was a brave warrior who led
those men. Benaiah's son Ammizabad was in
charge of Benaiah's division.
7The fourth commander, for the fourth month,
was Asahel, the brother of Joab. Later, Asahel's
son Zebadiah took his place as commander. There
were twenty-four thousand men in his division.
8The fifth commander, for the fifth month, was
Shamhuth, from Izrah's family. There were
twenty-four thousand men in his division.
9The sixth commander, for the sixth month,
was Ira son of Ikkesh from the town of Tekoa.
There were twenty-four thousand men in his division.
10The seventh commander, for the seventh
month, was Helez. He was from the Pelonites and
a descendant of Ephraim. There were twenty-four
thousand men in his division.
11The eighth commander, for the eighth
month, was Sibbecai. He was from Hushah and
was from Zerah's family. There were twenty-four
thousand men in his division.
12The ninth commander, for the ninth month,
was Abiezer. He was from Anathoth in Benjamin.
There were twenty-four thousand men in his division.
13The tenth commander, for the tenth month,
was Maharai. He was from Netophah and was
from Zerah's family. There were twenty-four
thousand men in his division.
14The eleventh commander, for the eleventh
month, was Benaiah. He was from Pirathon in
Ephraim. There were twenty-four thousand men
in his division.
15The twelfth commander, for the twelfth
month, was Heldai. He was from Netophah and
was from Othniel's family. There were twenty-
four thousand men in his division.

Leaders of the Tribes

16These were the leaders of the tribes[d] of Israel.
Eliezer son of Zicri was over the tribe of Reuben.
Shephatiah son of Maacah was over the tribe of
Simeon. 17Hashabiah son of Kemuel was over the
tribe of Levi. Zadok was over the people of Aaron.
18Elihu, one of David's brothers, was over the tribe
of Judah. Omri son of Michael was over the
tribe of Issachar. 19Ishmaiah son of Obadiah was
over the tribe of Zebulun. Jerimoth son of Azriel
was over the tribe of Naphtali. 20Hoshea son of
Azaziah was over the tribe of Ephraim. Joel son
of Pedaiah was over West Manasseh. 21Iddo
son of Zechariah was over East Manasseh. Jaasiel son of Abner was over the tribe of Benjamin.
22Azarel son of Jeroham was over the tribe of Dan.
These were the leaders of the tribes of Israel.
23The LORD had promised to make the Israelites
as many as the stars in the sky. So David only
counted the men who were twenty years old and
older. 24Joab son of Zeruiah began to count the
people, but he did not finish. God became angry
with Israel for counting the people, so the number
of the people was not put in the history book
about King David's rule.

The King's Directors

25Azmaveth son of Adiel was in charge of the
royal storehouses.
Jonathan son of Uzziah was in charge of the
storehouses in the country, towns, villages, and
towers.
26Ezri son of Kelub was in charge of the field
workers who farmed the land.

Thirty These were David's most powerful soldiers. See 2 Samuel 23:28.

27Shimei, from the town of Ramah, was in
charge of the vineyards.

Zabdi, from Shapham, was in charge of storing
the wine that came from the vineyards.

28Baal-Hanan, from Geder, was in charge of the
olive trees and sycamore trees in the western
hills.

Joash was in charge of storing the olive oil.

29Shitrai, from Sharon, was in charge of the
herds that fed in the Plain of Sharon.

Shaphat son of Adlai was in charge of the herds
in the valleys.

30Obil, an Ishmaelite, was in charge of the camels.

Jehdeiah, from Meronoth, was in charge of the
donkeys.

31Jaziz, from the Hagrites, was in charge of the
flocks.

All these men were the officers who took care
of King David's property.

32Jonathan was David's uncle, and he advised
David. Jonathan was a wise man and a teacher of
the law. Jehiel son of Hacmoni took care of the
king's sons. 33Ahithophel advised the king. Hushai, from the Arkite people, was the king's
friend. 34Jehoiada and Abiathar later took Ahithophel's place in advising the king. Jehoiada was Benaiah's son. Joab was the commander of the
king's army.

David's Plans for the Temple

28 David commanded all the leaders of Israel to come to Jerusalem. There were
the leaders of the tribes,[d] commanders of the divisions serving the king, commanders of a thousand
men and of a hundred men, leaders who took
care of the property and animals that belonged to
the king and his sons, men over the palace, the
powerful men, and all the brave warriors.

2King David stood up and said, "Listen to me,
my relatives and my people. I wanted to build a
place to keep the Ark[d] of the Agreement with the
LORD. I wanted it to be God's footstool. So I made
plans to build a temple. 3But God said to me, 'You
must not build a temple for worshiping me, because you are a soldier and have killed many people.'

4"But the LORD, the God of Israel, chose me
from my whole family to be king of Israel forever.
He chose the tribe of Judah to lead, and from the
people of Judah, he chose my father's family.
From that family God was pleased to make me
king of Israel. 5The LORD has given me many sons,
and from those sons he has chosen Solomon to be
the new king of Israel. Israel is the LORD's kingdom. 6The LORD said to me, 'Your son Solomon
will build my Temple[d] and its courtyards. I have
chosen Solomon to be my son, and I will be his
father. 7He is obeying my laws and commands
now. If he continues to obey them, I will make his
kingdom strong forever.' "

8David said, "Now, in front of all Israel, the
assembly of the LORD, and in the hearing of God,
I tell you these things: Be careful to obey all the
commands of the LORD your God. Then you will
keep this good land and pass it on to your descendants[d] forever.

9"And you, my son Solomon, accept the God of
your father. Serve him completely and willingly,
because the LORD knows what is in everyone's
mind. He understands everything you think. If
you go to him for help, you will get an answer.
But if you turn away from him, he will leave you
forever. 10Solomon, you must understand this.
The LORD has chosen you to build the Temple as
his holy place. Be strong and finish the job."

11Then David gave his son Solomon the plans
for building the Temple and the courtyard around
the Temple. They included its buildings, its storerooms, its upper rooms, its inside rooms, and the
place where the people's sins were removed.
12David gave him plans for everything he had in
mind: the courtyards around the LORD's Temple
and all the rooms around it, the Temple treasuries, and the treasuries of the holy items used in
the Temple. 13David gave Solomon directions for
the groups of the priests and Levites. David told
him about all the work of serving in the Temple
of the LORD and about the items to be used in the
Temple service 14that were made of gold or silver.
David told Solomon how much gold or silver
should be used to make each thing. 15David told
him how much gold to use for each gold lampstand and its lamps and how much silver to use
for each silver lampstand and its lamps. The different lampstands were to be used where needed.
16David told how much gold should be used for
each table that held the holy bread and how much
silver should be used for the silver tables. 17He
told how much pure gold should be used to make
the forks, bowls, and pitchers and how much gold
should be used to make each gold dish. He told
how much silver should be used to make each
silver dish 18and how much pure gold should be
used for the altar of incense.[d] He also gave Solomon the plans for the chariot of the golden creatures that spread their wings over the Ark[d] of the
Agreement with the LORD.

19David said, "All these plans were written
with the LORD guiding me. He helped me understand everything in the plans."

20David also said to his son Solomon, "Be
strong and brave, and do the work. Don't be
afraid or discouraged, because the LORD God, my
God, is with you. He will not fail you or leave you
until all the work for the Temple of the LORD is
finished. 21The groups of the priests and Levites
are ready for all the work on the Temple of God.

Every skilled worker is ready to help you with all
the work. The leaders and all the people will obey
every command you give."

Gifts for Building the Temple

29 King David said to all the Israelites who
were gathered, "God chose my son Solomon, who is young and hasn't yet learned what
he needs to know, but the work is important. This
palace is not for people; it is for the LORD God. 2I
have done my best to prepare for building the
Temple[d] of God. I have given gold for the things
made of gold and silver for the things made of
silver. I have given bronze for the things made of
bronze and iron for the things made of iron. I have
given wood for the things made of wood and onyx
for the settings. I have given turquoise gems of
many different colors, valuable stones, and white
marble. I have given much of all these things. 3I
have already given this for the Temple, but now
I am also giving my own treasures of gold and
silver, because I really want the Temple of my
God to be built. 4I have given about two hundred
twenty thousand pounds of pure gold from Ophir
and about five hundred twenty thousand pounds
of pure silver. They will be used to cover the walls
of the buildings 5and for all the gold and silver
work. Skilled men may use the gold and silver to
make things for the Temple. Now, who is ready
to give himself to the service of the LORD today?"

6The family leaders and the leaders of the tribes
of Israel, the commanders of a thousand men and
of a hundred men, and the leaders responsible for
the king's work gave their valuable things. 7They
donated about three hundred eighty thousand
pounds of gold, about seven hundred fifty thousand pounds of silver, about one million three
hundred fifty thousand pounds of bronze, and
about seven million five hundred thousand
pounds of iron to the Temple of God. 8People who
had valuable gems gave them to the treasury of
the Temple of the LORD, and Jehiel, from the Gershon family, took care of the valuable gems. 9The
leaders gave willingly and completely to the
LORD. The people rejoiced to see their leaders give
so gladly, and King David was also very happy.

David's Prayer

10David praised the LORD in front of all the peo-
ple who were gathered. He said:
"We praise you, LORD,
God of our father Israel.
We praise you forever and ever.
11LORD, you are great and powerful.

THANKFULNESS

A Letter to Dad

Jody Pearson was twenty when she moved to another state to work for the summer. While she was away she wrote this letter.

Dear Dad,

Lately I've thought of you often and wanted to thank you for many things!

I guess I've started seeing the simple things you and Mom taught us. The basics—like manners and respect—but also contentment with what we have, finding joy in each other, listening, forgiving, and understanding! You taught us that those things not only make life flow more smoothly, but they also show Jesus to the world. Now I understand!

Dad, I miss being able to share things with you. You always listen and understand. Thank you for all your time, love, and care. You've planted many seeds. I know I'll be reaping from this garden for a lifetime!

Love, Jody

Jody showed her appreciation for her father through a letter. In **1 Chronicles 29:10–13**, King David thanked his heavenly father for all he had done for Israel.

- How are Jody's letter and David's prayer alike?
- How can you, like David, express your praise to God?

CONSIDER . . .

- writing a poem expressing your thanks to God for something.
- sending a card to thank someone for something he or she has done for you.

FOR MORE, SEE . . .

- Psalm 100 (p. 539)
- Ephesians 1:15–16 (p. 1218)
- Revelation 7:9–12 (p. 1337)

You have glory, victory, and honor.
Everything in heaven and on earth belongs to you.
The kingdom belongs to you, LORD;
you are the ruler over everything.
12Riches and honor come from you.
You rule everything.
You have the power and strength
to make anyone great and strong.
13Now, our God, we thank you
and praise your glorious name.

14"These things did not really come from me and my people.
Everything comes from you;
we have given you back what you gave us.
15We are like foreigners and strangers,
as our ancestors were.
Our time on earth is like a shadow.
There is no hope.
16LORD our God, we have gathered all this
to build your Temple for worship to you.
But everything has come from you;
everything belongs to you.
17I know, my God, that you test people's hearts.
You are happy when people do what is right.
I was happy to give all these things,
and I gave with an honest heart.
Your people gathered here are happy to give to you,
and I rejoice to see their giving.
18LORD, you are the God of our ancestors,
the God of Abraham, Isaac, and Jacob.
Make your people want to serve you always,
and make them want to obey you.
19Give my son Solomon a desire to serve you.
Help him always obey your commands, laws, and rules.
Help him build the Temple
for which I have prepared."

20Then David said to all the people who were
gathered, "Praise the LORD your God." So they all
praised the LORD, the God of their ancestors, and
they bowed to the ground to give honor to the
LORD and the king.

Solomon Becomes King

21The next day the people sacrificed to the
LORD. They offered burnt offerings to him of a
thousand bulls, a thousand male sheep, and a
thousand male lambs. They also brought drink offerings. Many sacrifices were made for all the people of Israel.
22That day the people ate and drank
with much joy, and the LORD was with them.

And they made David's son Solomon king for
the second time. They poured olive oil on Solomon to appoint him king in the presence of the
LORD. And they poured oil on Zadok to appoint
him as priest.
23Then Solomon sat on the LORD's
throne as king and took his father David's place.
Solomon was very successful, and all the people
of Israel obeyed him.
24All the leaders and soldiers
and King David's sons accepted Solomon as king
and promised to obey him.
25The LORD made Solomon great before all the Israelites and gave Solomon much honor. No king of Israel before Solomon had such honor.

David's Death

26David son of Jesse was king over all Israel.
27He had ruled over Israel forty years — seven
years in Hebron and thirty-three years in Jerusalem.
28David died when he was old. He had lived
a good, long life and had received many riches
and honors. His son Solomon became king after
him.

29Everything David did as king, from beginning
to end, is recorded in the records of Samuel the
seer,[d] the records of Nathan the prophet, and the
records of Gad the seer.
30Those writings tell what
David did as king of Israel. They tell about his
power and what happened to him and to Israel
and to all the kingdoms around them.

2 CHRONICLES

Why Read This Book:

- See how following God can unite people and help them prosper (2 Chronicles 1—9).
- Learn what can happen when people turn away from God (2 Chronicles 10—36).

Behind the Scenes:

If God offered to grant you a wish, what would you request? Popularity? Lots of money? Good looks? Fame? A new sports car?

Second Chronicles begins with such a situation. Solomon had inherited Israel from his father, David, and God promised to give him whatever he asked for. Instead of asking for wealth or military power, Solomon requested wisdom to govern Israel the way God wanted it governed. His wish was granted. Second Chronicles describes a glorious, prosperous and peaceful reign for Solomon. Central to Solomon's grandeur was the spectacular Temple he built for God in Jerusalem. (See the introduction to 1 Kings for the rest of the story.)

Unfortunately, the nation struggled after Solomon's death. First a civil war divided Israel into two kingdoms. The North—keeping the name Israel—rejected rule by David's descendants and chose its own king. The South—adopting the name Judah—kept David's descendants in power but had trouble maintaining a relationship with God.

Picking up where 1 Chronicles left off, 2 Chronicles traces the history of the Israelites after King David, beginning with the united kingdom under Solomon and then focusing on Judah after the kingdom divided. The story is similar to the accounts in 1 and 2 Kings (p. 301 and p. 331).

Second Chronicles continues the message of 1 Chronicles, since they were originally one book (see 1 Chronicles introduction, p. 359). The writer is retelling the history of Israel and Judah as a reminder and warning that the nation's success is directly linked to its relationship with God.

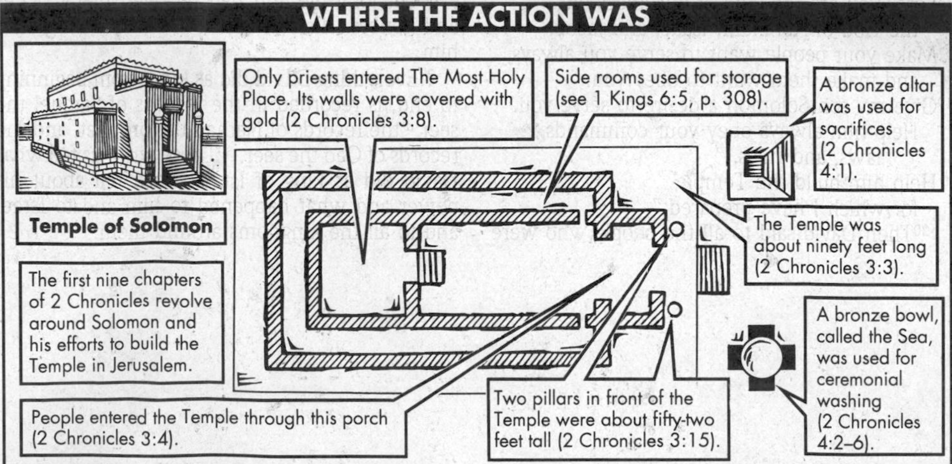

WHERE THE ACTION WAS
Temple of Solomon
The first nine chapters of 2 Chronicles revolve around Solomon and his efforts to build the Temple in Jerusalem.
Only priests entered The Most Holy Place. Its walls were covered with gold (2 Chronicles 3:8).
Side rooms used for storage (see 1 Kings 6:5, p. 308).
A bronze altar was used for sacrifices (2 Chronicles 4:1).
The Temple was about ninety feet long (2 Chronicles 3:3).
A bronze bowl, called the Sea, was used for ceremonial washing (2 Chronicles 4:2–6).
Two pillars in front of the Temple were about fifty-two feet tall (2 Chronicles 3:15).
People entered the Temple through this porch (2 Chronicles 3:4).

WHEN THE ACTION WAS

1000BC	750BC	500BC	250BC	BC/AD
Solomon was Israel's king; David was Israel's king	The Northern Kingdom (Israel) fell to Assyria	People returned to Jerusalem from exile; 1 and 2 Chronicles were written; The Southern Kingdom (Judah) fell to Babylon		Jesus was born

Solomon Asks for Wisdom

1 Solomon, David's son, became a powerful
king, because the LORD his God was with
him and made him very great.
2Solomon spoke to all the people of Israel — the
commanders of a hundred men and of a thousand
men, the judges, every leader in all Israel, and the
leaders of the families. 3Then Solomon and all the
people with him went to the place of worship at
the town of Gibeon. God's Meeting Tent,[d] which
Moses the LORD's servant had made in the desert,
was there. 4David had brought the Ark[d] of God
from Kiriath Jearim to Jerusalem, where he had
made a place for it and had set up a tent for it.
5The bronze altar that Bezalel son of Uri, who was
the son of Hur, had made was in Gibeon in front
of the Holy Tent. So Solomon and the people worshiped there. 6Solomon went up to the bronze
altar in the presence of the LORD at the Meeting
Tent and offered a thousand burnt offerings on it.
7That night God appeared to Solomon and said
to him, "Ask for whatever you want me to give
you."
8Solomon answered, "You have been very kind
to my father David, and you have made me king
in his place. 9Now, LORD God, may your promise
to my father David come true. You have made me
king of a people who are as many as the dust of
the earth. 10Now give me wisdom and knowledge
so I can lead these people in the right way, because no one can rule them without your help."
11God said to Solomon, "You have not asked
for wealth or riches or honor, or for the death of
your enemies, or for a long life. But since you
have asked for wisdom and knowledge to lead my
people, over whom I have made you king, 12I will
give you wisdom and knowledge. I will also give
you more wealth, riches, and honor than any king
who has lived before you or any who will live
after you."
13Then Solomon left the place of worship, the
Meeting Tent, at Gibeon and went back to Jerusalem. There King Solomon ruled over Israel.

Solomon's Wealth

14Solomon had fourteen hundred chariots and
twelve thousand horses. He kept some in special
cities for the chariots, and others he kept with
him in Jerusalem. 15In Jerusalem Solomon made
silver and gold as plentiful as stones and cedar
trees as plentiful as the fig trees on the western
hills. 16He imported horses from Egypt and Kue;
his traders bought them in Kue. 17They imported
chariots from Egypt for about fifteen pounds of
silver apiece, and horses cost nearly four pounds
of silver apiece. Then they sold the horses and
chariots to all the kings of the Hittites and the
Arameans.

Solomon Prepares for the Temple

2 Solomon decided to build a temple[d] as a
place to worship the LORD and also a palace
for himself. 2He chose seventy thousand men to
carry loads, eighty thousand men to cut stone in
the hill country, and thirty-six hundred men to
direct the workers.
3Solomon sent this message to Hiram king of
the city of Tyre: "Help me as you helped my father David by sending him cedar logs so he could
build himself a palace to live in. 4I will build a
temple for worshiping the LORD my God, and I
will give this temple to him. There we will burn
sweet-smelling spices in his presence. We will
continually set out the holy bread in God's presence. And we will burn sacrifices every morning
and evening, on Sabbath[d] days and New Moons,[d]
and on the other feast days commanded by the
LORD our God. This is a rule for Israel to obey
forever.
5"The temple I build will be great, because our
God is greater than all gods. 6But no one can
really build a house for our God. Not even the
highest of heavens can hold him. How then can
I build a temple for him except as a place to burn
sacrifices to him?
7"Now send me a man skilled in working with
gold, silver, bronze, and iron, and with purple,
red, and blue thread. He must also know how to
make engravings. He will work with my skilled
craftsmen in Judah and Jerusalem, whom my father David chose.
8"Also send me cedar, pine, and juniper logs
from Lebanon. I know your servants are experienced at cutting down the trees in Lebanon, and
my servants will help them. 9Send me a lot of
wood, because the temple I am going to build will
be large and wonderful. 10I will give your servants
who cut the wood one hundred twenty-five thousand bushels of wheat, one hundred twenty-five
thousand bushels of barley, one hundred fifteen
thousand gallons of wine, and one hundred fifteen thousand gallons of oil."
11Then Hiram king of Tyre answered Solomon
with this letter: "Solomon, because the LORD
loves his people, he chose you to be their king."
12Hiram also said: "Praise the LORD, the God of
Israel, who made heaven and earth! He has given
King David a wise son, one with wisdom and understanding, who will build a temple for the LORD
and a palace for himself.
13"I will send you a skilled and wise man
named Huram-Abi. 14His mother was from the
people of Dan, and his father was from Tyre.
Huram-Abi is skilled in working with gold, silver,
bronze, iron, stone, and wood, and with purple,
blue, and red thread, and expensive linen. He is
skilled in making engravings and can make any

design you show him. He will help your craftsmen and the craftsmen of your father David.
15“Now send my servants the wheat, barley,
oil, and wine you promised. 16We will cut as
much wood from Lebanon as you need and will
bring it on rafts by sea to Joppa. Then you may
carry it to Jerusalem.”
17Solomon counted all the foreigners living in
Israel. (This was after the time his father David
had counted the people.) There were one hundred fifty-three thousand six hundred foreigners
in the country. 18Solomon chose seventy thousand of them to carry loads, eighty thousand of
them to cut stone in the mountains, and thirty-six
hundred of them to direct the workers and to
keep the people working.

SIDELIGHT: Mount Moriah, where Solomon built the Temple (2 Chronicles 3:1), is a highly sacred spot for modern-day Christians, Jews and Muslims. It is traditionally where Abraham offered his son Isaac as a sacrifice (Genesis 22:2, p. 25) and where Gad came to David (2 Samuel 24:18, p. 300). The Dome of the Rock, a Muslim shrine, has occupied this traditional spot since the seventh century A.D.

Solomon Builds the Temple

3 Then Solomon began to build the Temple[d] of
the LORD in Jerusalem on Mount Moriah.
This was where the LORD had appeared to David,
Solomon's father. Solomon built the Temple on
the place David had prepared on the threshing[d]
floor of Araunah the Jebusite. 2Solomon began
building in the second month of the fourth year
he ruled Israel.
3Solomon used these measurements for building the Temple of God. It was ninety feet long and
thirty feet wide, using the old measurement. 4The
porch in front of the main room of the Temple
was thirty feet long and thirty feet high.

He covered the inside of the porch with pure
gold. 5He put panels of pine on the walls of the
main room and covered them with pure gold.
Then he put designs of palm trees and chains in
the gold. 6He decorated the Temple with gems
and gold from Parvaim.[n] 7He put gold on the
Temple's ceiling beams, doorposts, walls, and
doors, and he carved creatures with wings on the
walls.
8Then he made the Most Holy Place. It was
thirty feet long and thirty feet wide, as wide as the
Temple. He covered its walls with about forty-six
thousand pounds of pure gold. 9The gold nails
weighed over a pound. He also covered the upper
rooms with gold.
10He made two creatures with wings for the
Most Holy Place and covered them with gold.
11The wings of the gold creatures were thirty feet
across. One wing of one creature was seven and
one-half feet long and touched the Temple wall.
The creature's other wing was also seven and
one-half feet long, and it touched a wing of the
second creature. 12One wing of the second creature touched the other side of the room and was
also seven and one-half feet long. The second
creature's other wing touched the first creature's
wing, and it was also seven and one-half feet long.
13Together, the creatures' wings were thirty feet
across. The creatures stood on their feet, facing
the main room.
14He made the curtain of blue, purple, and red
thread, and expensive linen, and he put designs
of creatures with wings in it.
15He made two pillars to stand in front of the
Temple. They were about fifty-two feet tall, and
the capital[d] of each pillar was over seven feet tall.
16He made a net of chains and put them on the
tops of the pillars. He made a hundred pomegranates[d] and put them on the chains. 17Then he put
the pillars up in front of the Temple. One pillar
stood on the south side, the other on the north.
He named the south pillar He Establishes and the
north pillar In Him Is Strength.

Things for the Temple

4 He made a bronze altar thirty feet long,
thirty feet wide, and fifteen feet tall. 2Then
he made from bronze a large round bowl, which
was called the Sea. It was forty-five feet around,
fifteen feet across, and seven and one-half feet
deep. 3There were carvings of bulls under the rim
of the bowl—ten bulls every eighteen inches.
They were in two rows and were made in one
piece with the bowl.
4The bowl rested on the backs of twelve bronze
bulls that faced outward from the center of the
bowl. Three bulls faced north, three faced west,
three faced south, and three faced east. 5The sides
of the bowl were four inches thick, and it held
about seventeen thousand five hundred gallons.
The rim of the bowl was like the rim of a cup or
like a lily blossom.
6He made ten smaller bowls and put five on the
south side and five on the north. They were for
washing the animals for the burnt offerings, but
the large bowl was for the priests to wash in.
7He made ten lampstands of gold, following the
plans. He put them in the Temple,[d] five on the
south side and five on the north.

Parvaim There was much gold there. It may have been in the country of Ophir.

8He made ten tables and put them in the Temple, five on the south side and five on the north.
And he used gold to make a hundred other bowls.
9He also made the priests' courtyard and the
large courtyard. He made the doors that opened
to the courtyard and covered them with bronze.
10Then he put the large bowl in the southeast corner of the Temple.
11Huram also made bowls, shovels, and small
bowls. So he finished his work for King Solomon
on the Temple of God:

12two pillars;
two large bowls for the capitals on top of the
pillars;
two nets to cover the two large bowls for the
capitals on top of the pillars;
13four hundred pomegranates[d] for the two
nets (there were two rows of pomegranates for each net covering the bowls for
the capitals on top of the pillars);
14the stands with a bowl on each stand;
15the large bowl with twelve bulls under it;
16the pots, shovels, forks, and all the things to
go with them.

All the things that Huram-Abi made for King
Solomon for the Temple of the LORD were made
of polished bronze. 17The king had these things
poured into clay molds that were made in the
plain of the Jordan River between Succoth and
Zarethan. 18Solomon had so many things made
that the total weight of all the bronze was never
known.
19Solomon also made all the things for God's
Temple: the golden altar; tables which held the
bread that shows God's people are in his presence; 20the lampstands and their lamps of pure
gold, to burn in front of the Most Holy Place as
planned; 21the flowers, lamps, and tongs of pure
gold; 22the pure gold wick trimmers, small bowls,
pans, and dishes used to carry coals, the gold
doors for the Temple, and the inside doors of the
Most Holy Place and of the main room.

5 Finally all the work Solomon did for the
Temple of the LORD was finished. He
brought in everything his father David had set
apart for the Temple—all the silver and gold and
other articles. And he put everything in the treasuries of God's Temple.

The Ark Is Brought into the Temple

2Solomon called for the older leaders of Israel,
the heads of the tribes,[d] and the leaders of the
families to come to him in Jerusalem. He wanted
them to bring the Ark[d] of the Agreement with the
LORD from the older part of the city. 3So all the
Israelites came together with the king during the
festival in the seventh month.
4When all the older leaders of Israel arrived,
the Levites lifted up the Ark. 5They carried the
Ark of the Agreement, the Meeting Tent,[d] and the
holy utensils in it; the priests and the Levites
brought them up. 6King Solomon and all the Israelites gathered before the Ark of the Agreement
and sacrificed so many sheep and bulls no one
could count them.
7Then the priests put the Ark of the Agreement
with the LORD in its place inside the Most Holy
Place in the Temple,[d] under the wings of the
golden creatures. 8The wings of these creatures
were spread out over the place for the Ark, covering it and its carrying poles. 9The carrying poles
were so long that anyone standing in the Holy
Place in front of the Most Holy Place could see the
ends of the poles. But no one could see them from
outside the Holy Place. The poles are still there
today. 10The only things inside the Ark were two
stone tablets[n] that Moses had put in the Ark at
Mount Sinai. That was where the LORD made his
agreement with the Israelites after they came out
of Egypt.
11Then all the priests left the Holy Place. (All
the priests from each group had made themselves
ready to serve the LORD.) 12All the Levite musicians—Asaph, Heman, Jeduthun, and all their
sons and relatives—stood on the east side of the
altar. They were dressed in white linen and
played cymbals, harps, and lyres.[d] With them
were one hundred twenty priests who blew trumpets. 13Those who blew the trumpets and those
who sang together sounded like one person as
they praised and thanked the LORD. They sang as
others played their trumpets, cymbals, and other
instruments. They praised the LORD with this
song:
"He is good;
his love continues forever."
Then the Temple of the LORD was filled with
a cloud. 14The priests could not continue their

SIDELIGHT: Imagine having worship services on the church lawn outside your sanctuary. That's what the ancient Israelites did. The Temple was considered God's house, which was symbolized by putting the Ark of the Agreement in it (2 Chronicles 5:2, 7). It wasn't really a place to gather for worship or study. They had assemblies outside the Temple.

stone tablets They were the two stone tablets on which God wrote the Ten Commandments.

work because of the cloud, because the LORD's
glory filled the Temple of God.

Solomon Speaks to the People

6 Then Solomon said, "The LORD said he
would live in the dark cloud. 2LORD, I have
built a wonderful Temple for you—a place for
you to live forever."
3While all the Israelites were standing there,
King Solomon turned to them and blessed them.
4Then he said, "Praise the LORD, the God of Israel.
He has done what he promised to my father David. The LORD said, 5'Since the time I brought my
people out of Egypt, I have not chosen a city in
any tribe[d] of Israel where a temple[d] will be built
for me. I did not choose a man to lead my people
Israel. 6But now I have chosen Jerusalem as the
place I am to be worshiped, and I have chosen
David to lead my people Israel.'
7"My father David wanted to build a temple for
the LORD, the God of Israel. 8But the LORD said to
my father David, 'It was good that you wanted to
build a temple for me. 9But you are not the one
to build it. Your son, who comes from your own
body, is the one who will build my temple.'
10"Now the LORD has kept his promise. I am
the king now in place of David my father. Now
I rule Israel as the LORD promised, and I have built
the Temple for the LORD, the God of Israel.
11There I have put the Ark,[d] in which is the Agreement the LORD made with the Israelites."

Solomon's Prayer

12Then Solomon stood facing the LORD's altar,
and all the Israelites were standing behind him.
He spread out his hands. 13He had made a bronze
platform seven and one-half feet long, seven and
one-half feet wide, and seven and one-half feet
high, and he had placed it in the middle of the
outer courtyard. Solomon stood on the platform.
Then he kneeled in front of all the people of Israel
gathered there, and he spread out his hands toward the sky. 14He said, "LORD, God of Israel,
there is no god like you in heaven or on earth.
You keep your agreement of love with your servants who truly follow you. 15You have kept the
promise you made to your servant David, my father. You spoke it with your own mouth and finished it with your hands today.
16"Now, LORD, God of Israel, keep the promise
you made to your servant David, my father. You
said, 'If your sons are careful to obey my teachings
as you have obeyed, there will always be someone
from your family ruling Israel.' 17Now, LORD, God
of Israel, please continue to keep that promise you
made to your servant.
18"But, God, can you really live here on the
earth with people? The sky and the highest place
in heaven cannot contain you. Surely this house
which I have built cannot contain you. 19But
please listen to my prayer and my request, because I am your servant. LORD my God, hear this
prayer your servant prays to you. 20Day and night
please watch over this Temple where you have
said you would be worshiped. Hear the prayer I
pray facing this Temple. 21Hear my prayers and
the prayers of your people Israel when we pray
facing this place. Hear from your home in heaven,
and when you hear, forgive us.
22"If someone wrongs another person, he will
be brought to the altar in this Temple. If he swears
an oath that he is not guilty, 23then hear in
heaven. Judge the case, punish the guilty, but declare that the innocent person is not guilty.
24"When your people, the Israelites, sin against
you, their enemies will defeat them. But if they
come back to you and praise you and pray to you
in this Temple, 25then listen from heaven. Forgive
the sin of your people Israel, and bring them back
to the land you gave to them and their ancestors.
26"When they sin against you, you will stop the
rain from falling on their land. Then they will
pray, facing this place and praising you; they will
stop sinning when you make them suffer. 27When
this happens, hear their prayer in heaven, and forgive the sins of your servants, the Israelites. Teach
them to do what is right. Then please send rain
to this land you have given particularly to them.
28"At times the land will get so dry that no food
will grow, or a great sickness will spread among
the people. Sometimes the crops will be destroyed
by locusts[d] or grasshoppers. Your people will be
attacked in their cities by their enemies, or will
become sick. 29When any of these things happens,
the people will become truly sorry. If your people
spread their hands in prayer toward this Temple,
30then hear their prayers from your home in
heaven. Forgive and treat each person as he
should be treated because you know what is in a
person's heart. Only you know what is in people's
hearts. 31Then the people will respect and obey
you as long as they live in this land you gave our
ancestors.
32"People who are not Israelites, foreigners
from other lands, will hear about your greatness
and power. They will come from far away to pray
at this Temple. 33Then hear from your home in
heaven, and do whatever they ask you. Then people everywhere will know you and respect you,
just as your people Israel do. Then everyone will
know that I built this Temple as a place to worship you.
34"When your people go out to fight their enemies along some road on which you send them,
your people will pray to you, facing this city
which you have chosen and the Temple I have
built for you. 35Then hear in heaven their prayers,
and do what is right.

36"Everyone sins, so your people will also sin
against you. You will become angry with them
and will hand them over to their enemies. Their
enemies will capture them and take them away to
a country far or near. 37Your people will be sorry
for their sins when they are held as prisoners in
another country. They will be sorry and pray to
you in the land where they are held as prisoners,
saying, 'We have sinned. We have done wrong
and acted wickedly.' 38They will truly turn back
to you in the land where they are captives. They
will pray, facing this land you gave their ancestors, this city you have chosen, and the Temple I
have built for you. 39Then hear their prayers from
your home in heaven and do what is right. Forgive your people who have sinned against you.
40"Now, my God, look at us. Listen to the
prayers we pray in this place.
41Now, rise, LORD God, and come to your
resting place.
Come with the Ark[d] of the Agreement that
shows your strength.
Let your priests receive your salvation, LORD
God,
and may your holy people be happy
because of your goodness.
42LORD God, do not reject your appointed one.
Remember your love for your servant
David."

The Temple Is Given to the Lord

7 When Solomon finished praying, fire came
down from the sky and burned up the burnt
offering and the sacrifices. The LORD's glory filled
the Temple.[d] 2The priests could not enter the
Temple of the LORD, because the LORD's glory
filled it. 3When all the people of Israel saw the fire
come down from heaven and the LORD's glory on
the Temple, they bowed down on the pavement
with their faces to the ground. They worshiped
and thanked the LORD, saying,
"He is good;
his love continues forever."
4Then King Solomon and all the people offered
sacrifices to the LORD. 5King Solomon offered a
sacrifice of twenty-two thousand cattle and one
hundred twenty thousand sheep. So the king and
all the people gave the Temple to God. 6The
priests stood ready to do their work. The Levites
also stood with the instruments of the LORD's music that King David had made for praising the
LORD. The priests and Levites were saying, "His
love continues forever." The priests, who stood
across from the Levites, blew their trumpets, and
all the Israelites were standing.
7Solomon made holy the middle part of the
courtyard, which is in front of the Temple of the
LORD. There he offered whole burnt offerings and
the fat of the fellowship offerings. He offered
them in the courtyard, because the bronze altar
he had made could not hold the burnt offerings,
grain offerings, and fat.
8Solomon and all the Israelites celebrated the
festival for seven days. There were many people,
and they came from as far away as Lebo Hamath
and the brook of Egypt. 9For seven days they celebrated giving the altar for the worship of God.
Then they celebrated the festival for seven days.
On the eighth day they had a meeting. 10On the
twenty-third day of the seventh month Solomon
sent the people home, full of joy. They were
happy because the LORD had been so good to David, Solomon, and his people Israel.

The Lord Appears to Solomon

11Solomon finished the Temple[d] of the LORD
and his royal palace. He had success in doing everything he planned in the Temple of the LORD
and his own palace. 12Then the LORD appeared to
Solomon at night and said to him, "I have heard
your prayer and have chosen this place for myself
to be a Temple for sacrifices.
13"I may stop the sky from sending rain. I may
command the locusts[d] to destroy the land. I may
send sicknesses to my people. 14Then if my people, who are called by my name, are sorry for
what they have done, if they pray and obey me
and stop their evil ways, I will hear them from
heaven. I will forgive their sin, and I will heal
their land. 15Now I will see them, and I will listen
to the prayers prayed in this place. 16I have chosen
this Temple and made it holy. So I will be worshiped there forever. Yes, I will always watch over
it and love it.
17"But you must serve me as your father David
did. You must obey all I have commanded and
keep my laws and rules. 18If you do, I will make
your kingdom strong. This is the agreement I
made with your father David, saying, 'Someone
from your family will always rule in Israel.'
19"But you must follow me and obey the laws
and commands I have given you. You must not
serve or worship other gods. 20If you do, I will
take the Israelites out of my land, the land I have
given them, and I will leave this Temple that I
have made holy. All the nations will make fun of
it and speak evil about it. 21This Temple is honored now, but then, everyone who passes by will
be shocked. They will ask, 'Why did the LORD do
this terrible thing to this land and this Temple?'
22People will answer, 'This happened because
they left the LORD, the God of their ancestors, the
God who brought them out of Egypt. They decided to follow other gods and worshiped and
served them, so he brought all this disaster on
them.' "

Solomon's Other Achievements

8 By the end of twenty years, Solomon had
built the Temple[d] of the LORD and the royal
palace. 2Solomon rebuilt the towns that Hiram
had given him, and Solomon sent Israelites to live
in them. 3Then he went to Hamath Zobah and
captured it. 4Solomon also built the town of Tadmor in the desert, and he built all the towns in
Hamath as towns for storing grain and supplies.
5He rebuilt the towns of Upper Beth Horon and
Lower Beth Horon, protecting them with strong
walls, gates, and bars in the gates. 6He also rebuilt
the town of Baalath. And he built all the other
towns for storage and all the cities for his chariots
and horses. He built all he wanted in Jerusalem,
Lebanon, and everywhere he ruled.
7There were other people in the land who were
not Israelites — the Hittites, Amorites, Perizzites,
Hivites, and Jebusites. 8They were descendants[d]
of the people that the Israelites had not destroyed.
Solomon forced them to be slave workers, as is
still true today. 9But Solomon did not make slaves
of the Israelites. They were his soldiers, chief captains, commanders of his chariots, and his chariot
drivers. 10These were his most important officers.
There were two hundred fifty of them to direct
the people.
11Solomon brought the daughter of the king of
Egypt from the older part of Jerusalem to the palace he had built for her. Solomon said, "My wife
must not live in King David's palace, because the
places where the Ark[d] of the Agreement has been
are holy."
12Then Solomon offered burnt offerings to the
LORD on the altar he had built for the LORD in
front of the Temple porch. 13He offered sacrifices
every day as Moses had commanded. They were
offered on the Sabbath[d] days, New Moons,[d] and
the three yearly feasts — the Feast[d] of Unleavened
Bread, the Feast of Weeks, and the Feast of Shelters. 14Solomon followed his father David's instructions and chose the groups of priests for their
service and the Levites to lead the praise and to
help the priests do their daily work. And he chose
the gatekeepers by their groups to serve at each
gate, as David, the man of God, had commanded.
15They obeyed all of Solomon's commands to the
priests and Levites, as well as his commands
about the treasuries.
16All Solomon's work was done as he had said
from the day the foundation of the Temple of the
LORD was begun, until it was finished. So the
Temple was finished.
17Then Solomon went to the towns of Ezion
Geber and Elath near the Red Sea[d] in the land of
Edom. 18Hiram sent ships to Solomon that were
commanded by his own men, who were skilled
sailors. Hiram's men went with Solomon's men to
Ophir and brought back about thirty-four thousand pounds of gold to King Solomon.

The Queen of Sheba Visits

9 When the queen of Sheba heard about Solomon's fame, she came to Jerusalem to test
him with hard questions. She had a large group of
servants with her and camels carrying spices, jewels, and much gold. When she came to Solomon,
she talked with him about all she had in mind,
2and Solomon answered all her questions. Nothing was too hard for him to explain to her. 3The
queen of Sheba saw that Solomon was very wise.
She saw the palace he had built, 4the food on his
table, his many officers, the palace servants and
their good clothes, the servants who served Solomon his wine and their good clothes. She saw the
whole burnt offerings he made in the Temple[d] of
the LORD. All these things amazed her.
5So she said to King Solomon, "What I heard in
my own country about your achievements and
wisdom is true. 6I did not believe it then, but now
I have come and seen it with my own eyes. I was
not told even half of your great wisdom! You are
much greater than I had heard. 7Your men and
officers are very lucky, because in always serving
you, they are able to hear your wisdom. 8Praise
the LORD your God who was pleased to make you
king. He has put you on his throne to rule for the
LORD your God, because your God loves the people of Israel and supports them forever. He has
made you king over them to keep justice and to
rule fairly."
9Then she gave the king about nine thousand
pounds of gold and many spices and jewels. No
one had ever given such spices as the queen of
Sheba gave to King Solomon.
10Hiram's men and Solomon's men brought
gold from Ophir, juniper wood, and jewels. 11King
Solomon used the juniper wood to build steps for
the Temple of the LORD and the palace and to
make lyres[d] and harps for the musicians. No one
in Judah had ever seen such beautiful things as
these.
12King Solomon gave the queen of Sheba everything she wanted and asked for, even more than
she had brought to him. Then she and her servants returned to her own country.

Solomon's Wealth

13Every year King Solomon received about fifty
thousand pounds of gold. 14Besides that, he also
received gold from traders and merchants. All the
kings of Arabia and the governors of the land also
brought gold and silver.
15King Solomon made two hundred large
shields of hammered gold, each of which contained about seven and one-half pounds of hammered gold. 16He also made three hundred

smaller shields of hammered gold, each of which
contained about four pounds of gold. The king put
them in the Palace of the Forest of Lebanon.
17The king built a large throne of ivory and covered it with pure gold. 18The throne had six steps
on it and a gold footstool. There were armrests on
both sides of the chair, and each armrest had a
lion beside it. 19Twelve lions stood on the six
steps, one lion at each end of each step. Nothing
like this had ever been made for any other kingdom. 20All of Solomon's drinking cups, as well as
the dishes in the Palace of the Forest of Lebanon,
were made of pure gold. In Solomon's time people did not think silver was valuable.
21King Solomon had many ships that he sent
out to trade, with Hiram's men as the crews. Every three years the ships returned, bringing back
gold, silver, ivory, apes, and baboons.
22King Solomon had more riches and wisdom
than all the other kings on earth. 23All the kings
of the earth wanted to see Solomon and listen to
the wisdom God had given him. 24Year after year
everyone who came brought gifts of silver and
gold, clothes, weapons, spices, horses, and mules.
25Solomon had four thousand stalls for horses
and chariots, and he had twelve thousand horses.
He kept some in special cities for the chariots, and
others he kept with him in Jerusalem. 26Solomon
ruled over all the kingdoms from the Euphrates
River to the land of the Philistines, as far as the
border of Egypt. 27In Jerusalem the king made silver as common as stones and cedar trees as plentiful as the fig trees on the western hills. 28Solomon
imported horses from Egypt and all other countries.

Solomon's Death

29Everything else Solomon did, from the beginning to the end, is written in the records of Nathan the prophet,[d] and in the prophecy of Ahijah
the Shilonite, and in the visions of Iddo the seer,[d]
who wrote about Jeroboam, Nebat's son. 30Solo-
mon ruled in Jerusalem over all Israel for forty
years. 31Then Solomon died and was buried in Jerusalem, the city of David, his father. And Solomon's son Rehoboam became king in his place.

Israel Turns Against Rehoboam

10 Rehoboam went to Shechem, where all
the Israelites had gone to make him
king. 2Jeroboam son of Nebat was in Egypt, where
he had gone to escape from King Solomon. When
Jeroboam heard about Rehoboam being made
king, he returned from Egypt. 3After the people
sent for him, he and the people went to Rehoboam and said to him, 4"Your father forced us to
work very hard. Now, make it easier for us, and
don't make us work as he did. Then we will serve
you."
5Rehoboam answered, "Come back to me in
three days." So the people left.

> **SIDELIGHT:** Second Chronicles 10—36 is a lot like a Reader's Digest condensed version of 1 and 2 Kings (p. 301 and p. 331). In 2 Chronicles, the material on the divided kingdom takes up twenty-seven chapters, but Kings devotes thirty-six chapters to the same period.

6King Rehoboam asked the older leaders who
had advised Solomon during his lifetime, "How
do you think I should answer these people?"
7They answered, "Be kind to these people. If
you please them and give them a kind answer,
they will serve you always."
8But Rehoboam rejected this advice. Instead,
he asked the young men who had grown up with
him and who served as his advisers. 9Rehoboam
asked them, "What is your advice? How should
we answer these people who said, 'Don't make us
work as hard as your father did'?"
10The young men who had grown up with him
answered, "The people said to you, 'Your father
forced us to work very hard. Now make our work
easier.' You should tell them, 'My little finger is
bigger than my father's legs. 11He forced you to
work hard, but I will make you work even harder.
My father beat you with whips, but I will beat you
with whips that have sharp points.' "
12Rehoboam had told the people, "Come back
to me in three days." So after three days Jeroboam
and all the people returned to Rehoboam. 13King
Rehoboam spoke cruel words to them, because he
had rejected the advice of the older leaders. 14He
followed the advice of the young men and said,
"My father forced you to work hard, but I will
make you work even harder. My father beat you
with whips, but I will beat you with whips that
have sharp points." 15So the king did not listen to
the people. God caused this to happen so that the
LORD could keep the promise he had made to Jeroboam son of Nebat through Ahijah, a prophet[d]
from Shiloh.
16When all the Israelites saw that the king refused to listen to them, they said to the king,
"We have no share in David!
We have no part in the son of Jesse!
People of Israel, let's go to our own homes!
Let David's son rule his own people."
So all the Israelites went home. 17But Rehoboam
still ruled over the Israelites who lived in the
towns of Judah.
18Adoniram was in charge of the forced labor.
When Rehoboam sent him to the people, they

threw stones at him until he died. But King Rehoboam ran to his chariot and escaped to Jerusalem. [19]Since then, Israel has been against the family of David.

11 When Rehoboam arrived in Jerusalem, he gathered one hundred eighty thousand of the best soldiers from Judah and Benjamin. He wanted to fight Israel to take back his kingdom. [2]But the LORD spoke his word to Shemaiah, a man of God, saying, [3]"Speak to Solomon's son Rehoboam, the king of Judah, and to all the Israelites living in Judah and Benjamin. Say to them, [4]'The LORD says you must not go to war against your brothers. Every one of you should go home, because I made all these things happen.' " So they obeyed the LORD's command and turned back and did not attack Jeroboam.

Rehoboam Makes Judah Strong

[5]Rehoboam lived in Jerusalem and built strong cities in Judah to defend it. [6]He built up the cities of Bethlehem, Etam, Tekoa, [7]Beth Zur, Soco, Adullam, [8]Gath, Mareshah, Ziph, [9]Adoraim, Lachish, Azekah, [10]Zorah, Aijalon, and Hebron. These were strong, walled cities in Judah and Benjamin. [11]When Rehoboam made those cities strong, he put commanders and supplies of food, oil, and wine in them. [12]Also, Rehoboam put shields and spears in all the cities and made them very strong. Rehoboam kept the people of Judah and Benjamin under his control.

[13]The priests and the Levites from all over Israel joined Rehoboam. [14]The Levites even left their pasturelands and property and came to Judah and Jerusalem, because Jeroboam and his sons refused to let them serve as priests to the LORD. [15]Jeroboam chose his own priests for the places of worship and for the goat and calf idols he had made. [16]There were people from all the tribes[d] of Israel who wanted to obey the LORD, the God of Israel. So they went to Jerusalem with the Levites to sacrifice to the LORD, the God of their fathers. [17]These people made the kingdom of Judah strong, and they supported Solomon's son Rehoboam for three years. During this time they lived the way David and Solomon had lived.

Rehoboam's Family

[18]Rehoboam married Mahalath, the daughter of Jerimoth and Abihail. Jerimoth was David's son, and Abihail was the daughter of Eliab, Jesse's son. [19]Mahalath gave Rehoboam these sons: Jeush, Shemariah, and Zaham. [20]Then Rehoboam married Absalom's daughter Maacah, and she gave Rehoboam these children: Abijah, Attai, Ziza, and Shelomith. [21]Rehoboam loved Maacah more than his other wives and slave women.[d] Rehoboam had eighteen wives and sixty slave women and was the father of twenty-eight sons and sixty daughters.

[22]Rehoboam chose Abijah son of Maacah to be the leader of his own brothers, because he planned to make Abijah king. [23]Rehoboam acted wisely. He spread his sons through all the areas of Judah and Benjamin, sending them to every strong, walled city. He gave plenty of supplies to his sons, and he also found wives for them.

Shishak Attacks Jerusalem

12 After Rehoboam's kingdom was set up and he became strong, he and the people of Judah stopped obeying the teachings of the LORD. [2]During the fifth year Rehoboam was king, Shishak king of Egypt attacked Jerusalem, because Rehoboam and the people were unfaithful to the LORD. [3]Shishak had twelve hundred chariots and sixty thousand horsemen. He brought troops of Libyans, Sukkites, and Cushites from Egypt with him, so many they couldn't be counted. [4]Shishak captured the strong, walled cities of Judah and came as far as Jerusalem.

[5]Then Shemaiah the prophet[d] came to Rehoboam and the leaders of Judah who had gathered in Jerusalem because they were afraid of Shishak. Shemaiah said to them, "This is what the LORD says: 'You have left me, so now I will leave you to face Shishak alone.' "

[6]Then the leaders of Judah and King Rehoboam were sorry for what they had done. They said, "The LORD does what is right."

[7]When the LORD saw they were sorry for what they had done, the LORD spoke his word to Shemaiah, saying, "The king and the leaders are sorry. So I will not destroy them but will save them soon. I will not use Shishak to punish Jerusalem in my anger. [8]But the people of Jerusalem will become Shishak's servants so they may learn that serving me is different than serving the kings of other nations."

[9]Shishak king of Egypt attacked Jerusalem and took the treasures from the Temple[d] of the LORD and the king's palace. He took everything, even the gold shields Solomon had made. [10]So King Rehoboam made bronze shields to take their place and gave them to the commanders of the guards for the palace gates. [11]Whenever the king went to the Temple of the LORD, the guards went with him, carrying the shields. Later, they would put them back in the guardroom.

[12]When Rehoboam was sorry for what he had done, the LORD held his anger back and did not fully destroy Rehoboam. There was some good in Judah.

[13]King Rehoboam made himself a strong king in Jerusalem. He was forty-one years old when he became king, and he was king in Jerusalem for seventeen years. Jerusalem is the city that the

LORD chose from all the tribes[d] of Israel in which
he was to be worshiped. Rehoboam's mother was
Naamah from the country of Ammon. 14Reho-
boam did evil because he did not want to obey the
LORD.

15The things Rehoboam did as king, from the
beginning to the end, are written in the records
of Shemaiah the prophet and Iddo the seer,[d] in
the family histories. There were wars between Rehoboam and Jeroboam all the time they ruled.
16Rehoboam died and was buried in Jerusalem,
and his son Abijah became king in his place.

Abijah King of Judah

13 Abijah became the king of Judah during
the eighteenth year Jeroboam was king
of Israel. 2Abijah ruled in Jerusalem for three
years. His mother was Maacah daughter of Uriel
from the town of Gibeah.

And there was war between Abijah and Jeroboam. 3Abijah led an army of four hundred thousand capable soldiers into battle, and Jeroboam
prepared to fight him with eight hundred thousand capable soldiers.

4Abijah stood on Mount Zemaraim in the
mountains of Ephraim and said, "Jeroboam and
all Israel, listen to me! 5You should know that the
LORD, the God of Israel, gave David and his sons
the right to rule Israel forever by an agreement of
salt. 6But Jeroboam son of Nebat, one of the officers of Solomon, David's son, turned against his
master. 7Then worthless, evil men joined Jeroboam against Rehoboam, Solomon's son. He was
young and didn't know what to do, so he could
not stop them.

8"Now you people are making plans against the
LORD's kingdom, which belongs to David's sons.
There are many of you, and you have the gold
calves Jeroboam made for you as gods. 9You have
thrown out the Levites and the LORD's priests,
Aaron's sons. You have chosen your own priests
as people in other countries do. Anyone who
comes with a young bull and seven male sheep
can become a priest of idols that are not gods.

10"But as for us, the LORD is our God; we have
not left him. The priests who serve the LORD are
Aaron's sons, and the Levites help them. 11They
offer burnt offerings and sweet-smelling incense[d]
to the LORD every morning and evening. They put
the bread on the special table in the Temple.[d] And
they light the lamps on the gold lampstand every
evening. We obey the command of the LORD our
God, but you have left him. 12God himself is with
us as our ruler. His priests blow the trumpet to
call us to war against you. Men of Israel, don't
fight against the LORD, the God of your ancestors,
because you won't succeed."

13But Jeroboam had sent some troops to sneak
behind Judah's army. So while Jeroboam was in
front of Judah's army, Jeroboam's soldiers were
behind them. 14When the soldiers of Judah turned
around, they saw Jeroboam's army attacking both
in front and back. So they cried out to the LORD,
and the priests blew the trumpets. 15Then the
men of Judah gave a battle cry. When they
shouted, God caused Jeroboam and the army of
Israel to run away from Abijah and the army
of Judah. 16When the army of Israel ran away
from the men of Judah, God handed them over
to Judah. 17Abijah's army struck Israel so that
five hundred thousand of Israel's best men
were killed. 18So at that time the people of Israel were defeated. And the people of Judah
won, because they depended on the LORD, the
God of their ancestors.

19Abijah's army chased Jeroboam's army and
captured from him the towns of Bethel, Jeshanah,
and Ephron, and the small villages near them.
20Jeroboam never became strong again while Abijah was alive. The LORD struck Jeroboam, and he
died.

21But Abijah became strong. He married fourteen women and was the father of twenty-two
sons and sixteen daughters. 22Everything else Abijah did—what he said and what he did—is recorded in the writings of the prophet Iddo.

14 Abijah died and was buried in Jerusalem.
His son Asa became king in his place,
and there was peace in the country for ten years
during Asa's time.

Asa King of Judah

2Asa did what the LORD his God said was good
and right. 3He removed the foreign altars and the
places where gods were worshiped. He smashed
the stone pillars that honored other gods, and he
tore down the Asherah[d] idols. 4Asa commanded
the people of Judah to follow the LORD, the God
of their ancestors, and to obey his teachings and
commandments. 5He also removed the places
where gods were worshiped and the incense altars from every town in Judah. So the kingdom
had peace while Asa was king. 6Asa built strong,
walled cities in Judah during the time of peace.
He had no war in these years, because the LORD
gave him peace.

7Asa said to the people of Judah, "Let's build up
these towns and put walls around them. Let's
make towers, gates, and bars in the gates. This
country is ours, because we have obeyed the
LORD our God. We have followed him, and he has
given us peace all around." So they built and had
success.

8Asa had an army of three hundred thousand
men from Judah and two hundred eighty thousand men from Benjamin. The men from Judah
carried large shields and spears. The men from

Benjamin carried small shields and bows and arrows. All of them were brave fighting men.
9Then Zerah from Cush came out to fight them
with an enormous army and three hundred chariots. They came as far as the town of Mareshah.

> **SIDELIGHT:** Today, Zerah from Cush (2 Chronicles 14:9) would be "Zerah from Ethiopia," a country southeast of Egypt in Africa.

10So Asa went out to fight Zerah and prepared for
battle in the Valley of Zephathah at Mareshah.
11Asa called out to the LORD his God, saying,
"LORD, only you can help weak people against the
strong. Help us, LORD our God, because we depend on you. We fight against this enormous
army in your name. LORD, you are our God. Don't
let anyone win against you."
12So the LORD defeated the Cushites when
Asa's army from Judah attacked them, and the
Cushites ran away. 13Asa's army chased them as
far as the town of Gerar. So many Cushites were
killed that the army could not fight again; they
were crushed by the LORD and his army. Asa and
his army carried many valuable things away from
the enemy. 14They destroyed all the towns near
Gerar, because the people living in these towns
were afraid of the LORD. Since these towns had
many valuable things, Asa's army took them
away. 15Asa's army also attacked the camps
where the shepherds lived and took many sheep
and camels. Then they returned to Jerusalem.

Asa's Changes

15 The Spirit[d] of God entered Azariah son
of Oded. 2Azariah went to meet Asa and
said, "Listen to me, Asa and all you people of Judah and Benjamin. The LORD is with you when
you are with him. If you obey him, you will find
him, but if you leave him, he will leave you. 3For
a long time Israel was without the true God and
without a priest to teach them and without the
teachings. 4But when they were in trouble, they
turned to the LORD, the God of Israel. They
looked for him and found him. 5In those days no
one could travel safely. There was much trouble
in all the nations. 6One nation would destroy another nation, and one city would destroy another
city, because God troubled them with all kinds of
distress. 7But you should be strong. Don't give up,
because you will get a reward for your good
work."
8Asa felt brave when he heard these words and
the message from Azariah son of Oded the
prophet.[d] So he removed the hateful idols from all
of Judah and Benjamin and from the towns he had
captured in the hills of Ephraim. He repaired the
LORD's altar that was in front of the porch of the
Temple[d] of the LORD.
9Then Asa gathered all the people from Judah
and Benjamin and from the tribes[d] of Ephraim,
Manasseh, and Simeon who were living in Judah.
Many people came to Asa even from Israel, because they saw that the LORD, Asa's God, was
with him.
10Asa and these people gathered in Jerusalem in
the third month of the fifteenth year of Asa's rule.
11At that time they sacrificed to the LORD seven
hundred bulls and seven thousand sheep and
goats from the valuable things Asa's army had
taken from their enemies. 12Then they made an
agreement to obey the LORD, the God of their ancestors, with their whole being. 13Anyone who
refused to obey the LORD, the God of Israel, was
to be killed. It did not matter if that person was
important or unimportant, a man or woman.
14Then Asa and the people made a promise before
the LORD, shouting with a loud voice and blowing
trumpets and sheep's horns. 15All the people of
Judah were happy about the promise, because
they had promised with all their heart. They
looked for God and found him. So the LORD gave
them peace in all the country.
16King Asa also removed Maacah, his grandmother, from being queen mother, because she
had made a terrible Asherah[d] idol. Asa cut down
that idol, smashed it into pieces, and burned it in
the Kidron Valley. 17But the places of worship to
gods were not removed from Judah. Even so, Asa
was faithful all his life.
18Asa brought into the Temple of God the gifts
he and his father had given: silver, gold, and utensils.
19There was no more war until the thirty-fifth
year of Asa's rule.

Asa's Last Years

16 In the thirty-sixth year of Asa's rule, Baasha king of Israel attacked Judah. He
made the town of Ramah strong so he could keep
people from leaving or entering Judah, Asa's
country.
2Asa took silver and gold from the treasuries of
the Temple[d] of the LORD and out of his own palace. Then he sent it with messengers to Ben-
Hadad king of Aram, who lived in Damascus. Asa
said, 3"Let there be a treaty between you and me
as there was between my father and your father.
I am sending you silver and gold. Break your
treaty with Baasha king of Israel so he will leave
my land."
4Ben-Hadad agreed with King Asa and sent the
commanders of his armies to attack the towns of
Israel. They defeated the towns of Ijon, Dan, and

Abel Beth Maacah, and all the towns in Naphtali
where treasures were stored. 5When Baasha
heard about this, he stopped building up Ramah
and left his work. 6Then King Asa brought all the
people of Judah to Ramah, and they carried away
the rocks and wood that Baasha had used. And
they used them to build up Geba and Mizpah.
7At that time Hanani the seer[d] came to Asa king
of Judah and said to him, "You depended on the
king of Aram to help you and not on the LORD
your God. So the king of Aram's army escaped
from you. 8The Cushites and Libyans had a large
and powerful army and many chariots and horsemen. But you depended on the LORD to help you,
so he handed them over to you. 9The LORD
searches all the earth for people who have given
themselves completely to him. He wants to make
them strong. Asa, you did a foolish thing, so from
now on you will have wars."
10Asa was angry with Hanani the seer because
of what he had said; he was so angry that he put
Hanani in prison. And Asa was cruel to some of
the people at the same time.
11Everything Asa did as king, from the beginning to the end, is written in the book of the kings
of Judah and Israel. 12In the thirty-ninth year of his
rule, Asa got a disease in his feet. Though his disease was very bad, he did not ask for help from
the LORD, but only from the doctors. 13Then Asa
died in the forty-first year of his rule. 14The people
buried Asa in the tomb he had made for himself
in Jerusalem. They laid him on a bed filled with
spices and different kinds of mixed perfumes, and
they made a large fire to honor him.

> **SIDELIGHT:** Did King Asa have one of the world's first cases of athlete's foot (2 Chronicles 16:12)? Probably not. He may have had dropsy, which makes the feet swell like a tumor. Or the phrase may be a polite way to say he had a venereal disease.

Jehoshaphat King of Judah

17 Jehoshaphat, Asa's son, became king of
Judah in his place. Jehoshaphat made Judah strong so they could fight against Israel. 2He
put troops in all the strong, walled cities of Judah,
in the land of Judah, and in the towns of Ephraim
that his father Asa had captured.
3The LORD was with Jehoshaphat, because he
lived as his ancestor David had lived when he first
became king. Jehoshaphat did not ask for help
from the Baal[d] idols, 4but from the God of his father. He obeyed God's commands and did not live
as the people of Israel lived. 5The LORD made Jehoshaphat a strong king over Judah. All the people of Judah brought gifts to Jehoshaphat, so he
had much wealth and honor. 6He wanted very
much to obey the LORD. He also removed the
places for worshiping gods and the Asherah[d] idols
from Judah.
7During the third year of his rule, Jehoshaphat
sent his officers to teach in the towns of Judah.
These officers were Ben-Hail, Obadiah, Zechariah, Nethanel, and Micaiah. 8Jehoshaphat sent
with them these Levites: Shemaiah, Nethaniah,
Zebadiah, Asahel, Shemiramoth, Jehonathan, Adonijah, Tobijah, and Tob-Adonijah. He also sent
the priests Elishama and Jehoram. 9These leaders,
Levites, and priests taught the people in Judah.
They took the Book of the Teachings of the LORD
and went through all the towns of Judah and
taught the people.
10The nations near Judah were afraid of the
LORD, so they did not start a war against Jehoshaphat. 11Some of the Philistines brought gifts and
silver to Jehoshaphat as he demanded. Some
Arabs brought him flocks: seventy-seven hundred
sheep and seventy-seven hundred goats.
12Jehoshaphat grew more and more powerful.
He built strong, walled cities and towns for storing supplies in Judah. 13He kept many supplies in
the towns of Judah, and he kept trained soldiers
in Jerusalem. 14These soldiers were listed by families. From the families of Judah, these were the
commanders of groups of a thousand men: Adnah
was the commander of three hundred thousand
soldiers; 15Jehohanan was the commander of two
hundred eighty thousand soldiers; 16Amasiah was
the commander of two hundred thousand soldiers. Amasiah son of Zicri had volunteered to
serve the LORD.
17These were the commanders from the families of Benjamin: Eliada, a brave soldier, had two
hundred thousand soldiers who used bows and
shields. 18And Jehozabad had one hundred eighty
thousand men armed for war.
19All these soldiers served King Jehoshaphat.
The king also put other men in the strong, walled
cities through all of Judah.

Micaiah Warns King Ahab

18 Jehoshaphat had much wealth and
honor, and he made an agreement with
King Ahab through marriage.[n] 2A few years later
Jehoshaphat went to visit Ahab in Samaria. Ahab
sacrificed many sheep and cattle as a great feast
to honor Jehoshaphat and the people with him.
He encouraged Jehoshaphat to attack Ramoth in

agreement . . . through marriage Jehoshaphat's son Jehoram married Athaliah, Ahab's daughter. See 2 Chronicles 21:6.

Gilead. 3Ahab king of Israel asked Jehoshaphat
king of Judah, "Will you go with me to attack
Ramoth in Gilead?"
Jehoshaphat answered, "I will go with you, and
my soldiers are yours. We will join you in the
battle." 4Jehoshaphat also said to Ahab, "But first
we should ask if this is the LORD's will."
5So King Ahab called four hundred prophets[d]
together and asked them, "Should we go to war
against Ramoth in Gilead or not?"
They answered, "Go, because God will hand
them over to you."
6But Jehoshaphat asked, "Isn't there a prophet
of the LORD here? Let's ask him what we should
do."
7Then King Ahab said to Jehoshaphat, "There
is one other prophet. We could ask the LORD
through him, but I hate him. He never prophesies
anything good about me, but always something
bad. He is Micaiah son of Imlah."
Jehoshaphat said, "King Ahab, you shouldn't
say that!"
8So Ahab king of Israel told one of his officers
to bring Micaiah to him at once.
9Ahab king of Israel and Jehoshaphat king of
Judah had on their royal robes and were sitting on
their thrones at the threshing[d] floor, near the entrance to the gate of Samaria. All the prophets
were standing before them speaking their messages. 10Zedekiah son of Kenaanah had made
some iron horns. He said to Ahab, "This is what
the LORD says: 'You will use these horns to fight
the Arameans until they are destroyed.' "
11All the other prophets said the same thing,
"Attack Ramoth in Gilead and win, because the
LORD will hand the Arameans over to you."
12The messenger who had gone to get Micaiah
said to him, "All the other prophets are saying
King Ahab will win. You should agree with them
and give the king a good answer."
13But Micaiah answered, "As surely as the
LORD lives, I can tell him only what my God
says."
14When Micaiah came to Ahab, the king asked
him, "Micaiah, should we attack Ramoth in Gilead or not?"
Micaiah answered, "Attack and win! They will
be handed over to you."
15But Ahab said to Micaiah, "How many times
do I have to tell you to speak only the truth to me
in the name of the LORD?"
16So Micaiah answered, "I saw the army of Israel scattered over the hills like sheep without a
shepherd. The LORD said, 'They have no leaders.
They should go home and not fight.' "
17Then Ahab king of Israel said to Jehoshaphat,
"I told you! He never prophesies anything good
about me, but only bad."
18But Micaiah said, "Hear the message from the
LORD: I saw the LORD sitting on his throne with
his heavenly army standing on his right and on his
left. 19The LORD said, 'Who will trick King Ahab
of Israel into attacking Ramoth in Gilead where
he will be killed?'
"Some said one thing; some said another.
20Then one spirit came and stood before the LORD
and said, 'I will trick him.'
"The LORD asked, 'How will you do it?'
21"The spirit answered, 'I will go to Ahab's
prophets and make them tell lies.'
"So the LORD said, 'You will succeed in tricking
him. Go and do it.' "
22Micaiah said, "Ahab, the LORD has made your
prophets lie to you, and the LORD has decided that
disaster should come to you."
23Then Zedekiah son of Kenaanah went up to
Micaiah and slapped him in the face. Zedekiah
said, "Has the LORD's Spirit[d] left me to speak
through you?"
24Micaiah answered, "You will find out on the
day you go to hide in an inside room."
25Then Ahab king of Israel ordered, "Take Micaiah and send him to Amon, the governor of the
city, and to Joash, the king's son. 26Tell them I
said to put this man in prison and give him only
bread and water until I return safely from the battle."
27Micaiah said, "Ahab, if you come back safely
from the battle, the LORD has not spoken through
me. Remember my words, all you people!"

Ahab Is Killed

28So Ahab king of Israel and Jehoshaphat king
of Judah went to Ramoth in Gilead. 29King Ahab
said to Jehoshaphat, "I will go into battle, but I
will wear other clothes so no one will recognize
me. But you wear your royal clothes." So Ahab
wore other clothes, and they went into battle.
30The king of Aram ordered his chariot commanders, "Don't fight with anyone—important
or unimportant—except the king of Israel."
31When these commanders saw Jehoshaphat,
they thought he was the king of Israel, so they
turned to attack him. But Jehoshaphat began
shouting, and the LORD helped him. God made
the chariot commanders turn away from Jehoshaphat. 32When they saw he was not King Ahab,
they stopped chasing him.
33By chance, a soldier shot an arrow which hit
Ahab king of Israel between the pieces of his armor. King Ahab said to his chariot driver, "Turn
around and get me out of the battle, because I am
hurt!" 34The battle continued all day. King Ahab
held himself up in his chariot and faced the Arameans until evening. Then he died at sunset.

19 Jehoshaphat king of Judah came back
safely to his palace in Jerusalem. 2Jehu
son of Hanani, a seer,[d] went out to meet him and

said to the king, "Why did you help evil people? Why do you love those who hate the LORD? That is the reason the LORD is angry with you. 3But there is some good in you. You took the Asherah[d] idols out of this country, and you have tried to obey God."

Jehoshaphat Chooses Judges

4Jehoshaphat lived in Jerusalem. He went out again to be with the people, from Beersheba to the mountains of Ephraim, and he turned them back to the LORD, the God of their ancestors. 5Jehoshaphat appointed judges in all the land, in each of the strong, walled cities of Judah. 6Jehoshaphat said to them, "Watch what you do, because you are not judging for people but for the LORD. He will be with you when you make a decision. 7Now let each of you fear the LORD. Watch what you do, because the LORD our God wants people to be fair. He wants all people to be treated the same, and he doesn't want decisions influenced by money."

8And in Jerusalem Jehoshaphat appointed some of the Levites, priests, and leaders of Israelite families to be judges. They were to decide cases about the law of the LORD and settle problems between the people who lived in Jerusalem. 9Jehoshaphat commanded them, "You must always serve the LORD completely, and you must fear him. 10Your people living in the cities will bring you cases about killing, about the teachings, commands, rules, or some other law. In all these cases you must warn the people not to sin against the LORD. If you don't, he will be angry with you and your people. But if you warn them, you won't be guilty.

11"Amariah, the leading priest, will be over you in all cases about the LORD. Zebadiah son of Ishmael, a leader in the tribe[d] of Judah, will be over you in all cases about the king. Also, the Levites will serve as officers for you. Have courage. May the LORD be with those who do what is right."

Jehoshaphat Faces War

20 Later the Moabites, Ammonites, and some Meunites came to start a war with Jehoshaphat. 2Messengers came and told Jehoshaphat, "A large army is coming against you from Edom, from the other side of the Dead Sea.[d] They are already in Hazazon Tamar!" (Hazazon Tamar is also called En Gedi.) 3Jehoshaphat was afraid, so he decided to ask the LORD what to do. He announced that no one in Judah should eat during this special time of prayer to God. 4The people of Judah came together to ask the LORD for help; they came from every town in Judah.

5The people of Judah and Jerusalem met in front of the new courtyard in the Temple[d] of the LORD. Then Jehoshaphat stood up, 6and he said, "LORD, God of our ancestors, you are the God in heaven. You rule over all the kingdoms of the nations. You have power and strength, so no one can stand against you. 7Our God, you forced out the people who lived in this land as your people Israel moved in. And you gave this land forever to the descendants[d] of your friend Abraham. 8They lived in this land and built a Temple for you. They said, 9'If trouble comes upon us, or war, punishment, sickness, or hunger, we will stand before you and before this Temple where you have chosen to be worshiped. We will cry out to you when we are in trouble. Then you will hear and save us.'

10"But now here are men from Ammon, Moab, and Edom. You wouldn't let the Israelites enter their lands when the Israelites came from Egypt. So the Israelites turned away and did not destroy them. 11But see how they repay us for not destroying them! They have come to force us out of your land, which you gave us as our own. 12Our God, punish those people. We have no power against this large army that is attacking us. We don't know what to do, so we look to you for help."

13All the men of Judah stood before the LORD with their babies, wives, and children. 14Then the Spirit[d] of the LORD entered Jahaziel. (Jahaziel was Zechariah's son. Zechariah was Benaiah's son. Benaiah was Jeiel's son, and Jeiel was Mattaniah's son.) Jahaziel, a Levite and a descendant of Asaph, stood up in the meeting. 15He said, "Listen to me, King Jehoshaphat and all you people living in Judah and Jerusalem. The LORD says this to you: 'Don't be afraid or discouraged because of this large army. The battle is not your battle, it is God's. 16Tomorrow go down there and fight those people. They will come up through the Pass of Ziz. You will find them at the end of the ravine that leads to the Desert of Jeruel. 17You won't need to fight in this battle. Just stand strong in your places, and you will see the LORD save you. Judah and Jerusalem, don't be afraid or discouraged, because the LORD is with you. So go out against those people tomorrow.' "

18Jehoshaphat bowed facedown on the ground. All the people of Judah and Jerusalem bowed down before the LORD and worshiped him. 19Then some Levites from the Kohathite and Korahite people stood up and praised the LORD, the God of Israel, with very loud voices.

20Jehoshaphat's army went out into the Desert of Tekoa early in the morning. As they were starting out, Jehoshaphat stood and said, "Listen to me, people of Judah and Jerusalem. Have faith in the LORD your God, and you will stand strong. Have faith in his prophets,[d] and you will succeed." 21Jehoshaphat listened to the people's advice. Then he chose men to be singers to the LORD, to praise him because he is holy and wonderful. As they marched in front of the army, they said,

"Thank the LORD,
because his love continues forever."

22As they began to sing and praise God, the LORD set ambushes for the people of Ammon, Moab, and Edom who had come to attack Judah. And they were defeated. 23The Ammonites and Moabites attacked the Edomites, destroying them completely. After they had killed the Edomites, they killed each other.

24When the men from Judah came to a place where they could see the desert, they looked at the enemy's large army. But they only saw dead bodies lying on the ground; no one had escaped. 25When Jehoshaphat and his army came to take their valuables, they found many supplies, much clothing, and other valuable things. There was more than they could carry away; there was so much it took three days to gather it all. 26On the fourth day Jehoshaphat and his army met in the Valley of Beracah and praised the LORD. That is why that place has been called the Valley of Beracah[n] to this day.

27Then Jehoshaphat led all the men from Judah and Jerusalem back to Jerusalem. The LORD had made them happy because their enemies were defeated. 28They entered Jerusalem with harps, lyres,[d] and trumpets and went to the Temple of the LORD.

29When all the kingdoms of the lands around them heard how the LORD had fought Israel's enemies, they feared God. 30So Jehoshaphat's kingdom was not at war. His God gave him peace from all the countries around him.

Jehoshaphat's Rule Ends

31Jehoshaphat ruled over the country of Judah. He was thirty-five years old when he became king, and he ruled in Jerusalem for twenty-five years. His mother's name was Azubah daughter of Shilhi. 32Jehoshaphat was good like his father Asa, and he did what the LORD said was right. 33But the places where gods were worshiped were not removed, and the people did not really want to follow the God of their ancestors.

34The other things Jehoshaphat did as king, from the beginning to the end, are written in the records of Jehu son of Hanani, which are in the book of the kings of Israel.

35Later, Jehoshaphat king of Judah made a treaty with Ahaziah king of Israel, which was a wrong thing to do. 36Jehoshaphat agreed with Ahaziah to build trading ships, which they built in the town of Ezion Geber. 37Then Eliezer son of Dodavahu from the town of Mareshah spoke against Jehoshaphat. He said, "Jehoshaphat, because you joined with Ahaziah, the LORD will destroy what you have made." The ships were wrecked so they could not sail out to trade.

21 Jehoshaphat died and was buried with his ancestors in Jerusalem, the city of David. Then his son Jehoram became king in his place. 2Jehoram's brothers were Azariah, Jehiel, Zechariah, Azariahu, Michael, and Shephatiah. They were the sons of Jehoshaphat king of Judah. 3Jehoshaphat gave his sons many gifts of silver, gold, and valuable things, and he gave them strong, walled cities in Judah. But Jehoshaphat gave the kingdom to Jehoram, because he was the first son.

Jehoram King of Judah

4When Jehoram took control of his father's kingdom, he killed all his brothers with a sword and also killed some of the leaders of Judah. 5He was thirty-two years old when he began to rule, and he ruled eight years in Jerusalem. 6He followed in the ways of the kings of Israel, just as the family of Ahab had done, because he married Ahab's daughter. Jehoram did what the LORD said was wrong. 7But the LORD would not destroy David's family because of the agreement he had made with David. He had promised that one of David's descendants[d] would always rule.

8In Jehoram's time, Edom broke away from Judah's rule and chose their own king. 9So Jehoram went to Edom with all his commanders and chariots. The Edomites surrounded him and his chariot commanders, but Jehoram got up and attacked the Edomites at night. 10From then until now the country of Edom has fought against the rule of Judah. At the same time the people of Libnah also broke away from Jehoram because Jehoram left the LORD, the God of his ancestors.

11Jehoram also built places to worship gods on the hills in Judah. He led the people of Jerusalem to sin, and he led the people of Judah away from the LORD. 12Then Jehoram received this letter from Elijah the prophet:

> This is what the LORD, the God of your ancestor David, says, "Jehoram, you have not lived as your father Jehoshaphat lived and as Asa king of Judah lived. 13But you have lived as the kings of Israel lived, leading the people of Judah and Jerusalem to sin against God, as Ahab and his family did. You have killed your brothers, and they were better than you. 14So now the LORD is about to punish your people, your children, wives, and everything you own. 15You will have a terrible disease in your intestines that will

Beracah This name means "blessing" or "praise."

become worse every day. Finally it will
cause your intestines to come out."

> **SIDELIGHT:** The "terrible disease in your intestines" that was prophesied for King Jehoram by Elijah (2 Chronicles 21:15) was probably dysentery, a common ailment in the Middle East and other parts of the world. The king's case may have been chronic, resulting in intestinal blockage and death.

16The LORD caused the Philistines and the
Arabs who lived near the Cushites to be angry
with Jehoram. 17So the Philistines and Arabs attacked Judah and carried away all the wealth of
Jehoram's palace, as well as his sons and wives.
Only Jehoram's youngest son, Ahaziah, was left.
18After these things happened, the LORD gave
Jehoram a disease in his intestines that could not
be cured. 19After he was sick for two years, Jehoram's intestines came out because of the disease,
and he died in terrible pain. The people did not
make a fire to honor Jehoram as they had done for
his ancestors.
20Jehoram was thirty-two years old when he
became king, and he ruled eight years in Jerusalem. No one was sad when he died. He was buried in Jerusalem, but not in the graves for the
kings.

Ahaziah King of Judah

22 The people of Jerusalem chose Ahaziah,
Jehoram's youngest son, to be king in his
place. The robbers who had come with the Arabs
to attack Jehoram's camp had killed all of Jehoram's older sons. So Ahaziah began to rule Judah.
2Ahaziah was twenty-two years old when he became king, and he ruled one year in Jerusalem.
His mother's name was Athaliah, a granddaughter
of Omri. 3Ahaziah followed the ways of Ahab's
family, because his mother encouraged him to do
wrong. 4Ahaziah did what the LORD said was
wrong, as Ahab's family had done. They gave advice to Ahaziah after his father died, and their bad
advice led to his death. 5Following their advice,
Ahaziah went with Joram son of Ahab to Ramoth
in Gilead, where they fought against Hazael king
of Aram. The Arameans wounded Joram. 6So Joram returned to Jezreel to heal from the wounds
he received at Ramoth when he fought Hazael
king of Aram.
Ahaziah son of Jehoram and king of Judah went
down to visit Joram son of Ahab at Jezreel because he had been wounded.
7God caused Ahaziah's death when he went to
visit Joram. Ahaziah arrived and went out with
Joram to meet Jehu son of Nimshi, whom the
LORD had appointed to destroy Ahab's family.
8While Jehu was punishing Ahab's family, he
found the leaders of Judah and the sons of Ahaziah's relatives who served Ahaziah, and Jehu
killed them all. 9Then Jehu looked for Ahaziah.
Jehu's men caught him hiding in Samaria, so they
brought him to Jehu. Then they killed and buried
him. They said, "Ahaziah is a descendant[d] of Jehoshaphat, and Jehoshaphat obeyed the LORD
with all his heart." No one in Ahaziah's family
had the power to take control of the kingdom of
Judah.

Athaliah and Joash

10When Ahaziah's mother, Athaliah, saw that
her son was dead, she killed all the royal family
in Judah. 11But Jehosheba, King Jehoram's daugh
ter, took Joash, Ahaziah's son. She stole him from
among the other sons of the king who were going
to be murdered and put him and his nurse in a
bedroom. So Jehosheba, who was King Jehoram's
daughter and Ahaziah's sister and the wife of Jehoiada the priest, hid Joash so Athaliah could not
kill him. 12He hid with them in the Temple[d] of
God for six years. During that time Athaliah ruled
the land.

23 In the seventh year Jehoiada decided to
do something. He made an agreement
with the commanders of the groups of a hundred
men: Azariah son of Jeroham, Ishmael son of Jehohanan, Azariah son of Obed, Maaseiah son of
Adaiah, and Elishaphat son of Zicri. 2They went
around in Judah and gathered the Levites from all
the towns, and they gathered the leaders of the
families of Judah. Then they went to Jerusalem.
3All the people together made an agreement with
the king in the Temple of God.
Jehoiada said to them, "The king's son will
rule, as the LORD promised about David's descendants.[d] 4Now this is what you must do: You
priests and Levites go on duty on the Sabbath.[d] A
third of you will guard the doors. 5A third of you
will be at the king's palace, and a third of you will
be at the Foundation Gate. All the other people
will stay in the courtyards of the Temple of the
LORD. 6Don't let anyone come into the Temple of
the LORD except the priests and Levites who
serve. They may come because they have been
made ready to serve the LORD, but all the others
must do the job the LORD has given them. 7The
Levites must stay near the king, each man with
his weapon in his hand. If anyone tries to enter
the Temple, kill him. Stay close to the king when
he goes in and when he goes out."

Joash Becomes King

8The Levites and all the people of Judah obeyed

everything Jehoiada the priest had commanded.
He did not excuse anyone from the groups of the
priests. So each commander took his men who
came on duty on the Sabbath with those who
went off duty on the Sabbath. 9Jehoiada gave the
commanders of a hundred men the spears and the
large and small shields that had belonged to King
David and that were kept in the Temple of God.
10Then Jehoiada told the men where to stand,
each man with his weapon in his hand. There
were guards from the south side of the Temple to
the north side. They stood by the altar and the
Temple and around the king.

11Jehoiada and his sons brought out the king's
son and put the crown on him and gave him a
copy of the agreement. Then they appointed him
king and poured olive oil on him and shouted,
"Long live the king!"

12When Athaliah heard the noise of the people
running and praising the king, she went to them
at the Temple of the LORD. 13She looked, and
there was the king standing by his pillar at the
entrance. The officers and the trumpeters were
standing beside him, and all the people of the land
were happy and blowing trumpets. The singers
were playing musical instruments and leading
praises. Then Athaliah tore her clothes and
screamed, "Traitors! Traitors!"

14Jehoiada the priest sent out the commanders
of a hundred men, who led the army. He said,
"Surround her with soldiers and take her out of
the Temple area. Kill with a sword anyone who
follows her." He had said, "Don't put Athaliah to
death in the Temple of the LORD." 15So they
caught her when she came to the entrance of the
Horse Gate near the palace. There they put her to
death.

16Then Jehoiada made an agreement with the
people and the king that they would be the
LORD's special people. 17All the people went to
the temple of Baal[d] and tore it down, smashing
the altars and idols. They killed Mattan, the priest
of Baal, in front of the altars.

18Then Jehoiada chose the priests, who were
Levites, to be responsible for the Temple of the
LORD. David had given them duties in the Temple
of the LORD. They were to offer the burnt offerings to the LORD as the Teachings of Moses commanded, and they were to offer them with much
joy and singing as David had commanded. 19Jehoi-
ada put guards at the gates of the Temple of the
LORD so that anyone who was unclean[d] in any
way could not enter.

20Jehoiada took with him the commanders of a
hundred men, the important men, the rulers of
the people, and all the people of the land to take
the king out of the Temple of the LORD. They
went through the Upper Gate into the palace, and
then they seated the king on the throne. 21So all
the people of the land were very happy, and Jerusalem had peace, because Athaliah had been put
to death with the sword.

Joash Repairs the Temple

24 Joash was seven years old when he became king, and he ruled forty years in
Jerusalem. His mother's name was Zibiah, and
she was from Beersheba. 2Joash did what the
LORD said was right as long as Jehoiada the priest
was alive. 3Jehoiada chose two wives for Joash,
and Joash had sons and daughters.

4Later, Joash decided to repair the Temple[d] of
the LORD. 5He called the priests and the Levites
together and said to them, "Go to the towns of
Judah and gather the money all the Israelites have
to pay every year. Use it to repair the Temple of
your God. Do this now." But the Levites did not
hurry.

6So King Joash called for Jehoiada the leading
priest and said to him, "Why haven't you made
the Levites bring in from Judah and Jerusalem the
tax money that Moses, the LORD's servant, and
the people of Israel used for the Holy Tent?"[d]

7In the past the sons of wicked Athaliah had
broken into the Temple of God and used its holy
things for worshiping the Baal[d] idols.

8King Joash commanded that a box for contributions be made. They put it outside, at the gate
of the Temple of the LORD. 9Then the Levites
made an announcement in Judah and Jerusalem,
telling people to bring to the LORD the tax money
Moses, the servant of God, had made the Israelites give while they were in the desert. 10All the
officers and people were happy to bring their
money, and they put it in the box until the box
was full. 11When the Levites would take the box
to the king's officers, they would see that it was
full of money. Then the king's royal secretary and
the leading priest's officer would come and take
out the money and return the box to its place.
They did this often and gathered much money.
12King Joash and Jehoiada gave the money to the
people who worked on the Temple of the LORD.
And they hired stoneworkers and carpenters to
repair the Temple of the LORD. They also hired
people to work with iron and bronze to repair the
Temple.

13The people worked hard, and the work to repair the Temple went well. They rebuilt the Temple of God to be as it was before, but even stronger. 14When the workers finished, they brought
the money that was left to King Joash and Jehoiada. They used that money to make utensils for
the Temple of the LORD, utensils for the service
in the Temple and for the burnt offerings, and
bowls and other utensils from gold and silver.
Burnt offerings were given every day in the Temple of the LORD while Jehoiada was alive.

15Jehoiada grew old and lived many years.
Then he died when he was one hundred thirty
years old. 16Jehoiada was buried in Jerusalem with
the kings, because he had done much good in Judah for God and his Temple.

Joash Does Evil

17After Jehoiada died, the officers of Judah
came and bowed down to King Joash, and he listened to them. 18The king and these leaders
stopped worshiping in the Temple[d] of the LORD,
the God of their ancestors. Instead, they began
to worship the Asherah[d] idols and other idols.
Because they did wrong, God was angry
with the people of Judah and Jerusalem. 19Even
though the LORD sent prophets[d] to the people
to turn them back to him and even though
the prophets warned them, they refused to listen.
20Then the Spirit[d] of God entered Zechariah
son of Jehoiada the priest. Zechariah stood before
the people and said, "This is what God says: 'Why
do you disobey the LORD's commands? You will
not be successful. Because you have left the LORD,
he has also left you.' "
21But the king and his officers made plans
against Zechariah. At the king's command they
threw stones at him in the courtyard of the Temple of the LORD until he died. 22King Joash did not
remember Jehoiada's kindness to him, so Joash
killed Zechariah, Jehoiada's son. Before Zechariah
died, he said, "May the LORD see what you are
doing and punish you."
23At the end of the year, the Aramean army
came against Joash. They attacked Judah and Jerusalem, killed all the leaders of the people, and sent
all the valuable things to their king in Damascus.
24The Aramean army came with only a small
group of men, but the LORD handed over to them
a very large army from Judah, because the people
of Judah had left the LORD, the God of their ancestors. So Joash was punished. 25When the Arameans left, Joash was badly wounded. His own officers made plans against him because he had killed
Zechariah son of Jehoiada the priest. So they
killed Joash in his own bed. He died and was bur-

REBELLION

This Is My Life

"Eleven p.m. No exceptions."

"Eleven? But I'm sixteen! Everyone's gonna laugh at me! Nobody has to be home that early!"

Mitch Rayburn couldn't believe his parents were so unfair. Maybe he had ignored their rules lately, but he was old enough to run his own life.

"I'm leaving!" he yelled and stormed out of the house. After spending the night with a friend, he came home, hoping his parents would be good and worried.

But his dad didn't yell or ask questions. He simply took away Mitch's car keys.

Not to be beaten, Mitch took his life savings of four hundred dollars and bought an old car. It was in bad shape, but he defiantly drove it home. Now what could his parents do?

That night Mitch decided to go cruising in his "new" car. He put the key in the ignition. Nothing happened. And Mitch didn't have any money for repairs. The car sat on the street until the police towed it away.

Mitch never saw his car or his four hundred dollars again. And he didn't drive the family car for two months.

By rebelling against his parents, Mitch lost money and privileges. Read **2 Chronicles 24:17–25** to learn how King Joash's rebellion against God affected his life.

- What were common factors in Mitch's and Joash's rebellion?
- Joash's rebellion against God resulted in a murder. If you've ever rebelled against God, what has been a result of that rebellion?

CONSIDER . . .

- evaluating your own life for signs of rebellion against God and then working on ways to get rid of the rebellion.
- visiting a jail or juvenile detention center and telling inmates that God can forgive them.

FOR MORE, SEE

- Proverbs 1:8–9 (p. 568)
- Romans 3:9–20 (p. 1142)
- 1 Peter 2:13–25 (p. 1304)

ied in Jerusalem but not in the graves of the kings.

26The officers who made plans against Joash were Jozabad and Jehozabad. Jozabad was the son of Shimeath, a woman from Ammon. And Jehozabad was the son of Shimrith, a woman from Moab. 27The story of Joash's sons, the great prophecies[d] against him, and how he repaired the Temple of God are written in the book of the kings. Joash's son Amaziah became king in his place.

Amaziah King of Judah

25 Amaziah was twenty-five years old when he became king, and he ruled for twenty-nine years in Jerusalem. His mother's name was Jehoaddin, and she was from Jerusalem. 2Amaziah did what the LORD said was right, but he did not really want to obey him. 3As soon as Amaziah took strong control of the kingdom, he executed the officers who had murdered his father the king. 4But Amaziah did not put to death their children. He obeyed what was written in the Book of Moses, where the LORD commanded, "Parents must not be put to death when their children do wrong, and children must not be put to death when their parents do wrong. Each must die for his own sins."[n]

5Amaziah gathered the people of Judah together. He grouped all the people of Judah and Benjamin by families, and he put commanders over groups of a thousand and over groups of a hundred. He counted the men who were twenty years old and older. In all there were three hundred thousand soldiers ready to fight and skilled with spears and shields. 6Amaziah also hired one hundred thousand soldiers from Israel for about seventy-five hundred pounds of silver. 7But a man of God came to Amaziah and said, "My king, don't let the army of Israel go with you. The LORD is not with Israel or the people from the tribe[d] of Ephraim. 8You can make yourself strong for war, but God will defeat you. He has the power to help you or to defeat you."

9Amaziah said to the man of God, "But what about the seventy-five hundred pounds of silver I paid to the Israelite army?"

The man of God answered, "The LORD can give you much more than that."

10So Amaziah sent the Israelite army back home to Ephraim. They were very angry with the people of Judah and went home angry.

11Then Amaziah became very brave and led his army to the Valley of Salt in the country of Edom. There Amaziah's army killed ten thousand Edomites. 12The army of Judah also captured ten thousand and took them to the top of a cliff and threw them off so that they split open.

13At the same time the Israelite troops that Amaziah had not let fight in the war were robbing towns in Judah. From Samaria to Beth Horon they killed three thousand people and took many valuable things.

14When Amaziah came home after defeating the Edomites, he brought back the idols they worshiped and started to worship them himself. He bowed down to them and offered sacrifices to them. 15The LORD was very angry with Amaziah, so he sent a prophet[d] to him who said, "Why have you asked their gods for help? They could not even save their own people from you!"

16As the prophet spoke, Amaziah said to him, "We never gave you the job of advising the king. Stop, or you will be killed."

The prophet stopped speaking except to say, "I know that God has decided to destroy you because you have done this. You did not listen to my advice."

17Amaziah king of Judah talked with those who advised him. Then he sent a message to Jehoash son of Jehoahaz, who was the son of Jehu king of Israel. Amaziah said to Jehoash, "Come, let's meet face to face."

18Then Jehoash king of Israel answered Amaziah king of Judah, "A thornbush in Lebanon sent a message to a cedar tree in Lebanon. It said, 'Let your daughter marry my son.' But then a wild animal from Lebanon came by, walking on and crushing the thornbush. 19You say to yourself that you have defeated Edom, but you have become proud, and you brag. But you stay at home! Don't ask for trouble, or you and Judah will be defeated."

20But Amaziah would not listen. God caused this to happen so that Jehoash would defeat Judah, because Judah asked for help from the gods of Edom. 21So Jehoash king of Israel went to attack. He and Amaziah king of Judah faced each other in battle at Beth Shemesh in Judah. 22Israel defeated Judah, and every man of Judah ran away to his home. 23At Beth Shemesh Jehoash king of Israel captured Amaziah king of Judah. (Amaziah was the son of Joash, who was the son of Ahaziah.) Then Jehoash brought him to Jerusalem. Jehoash broke down the wall of Jerusalem, from the Gate of Ephraim to the Corner Gate, about six hundred feet. 24He took all the gold and silver and all the utensils from the Temple[d] of God that Obed-Edom had taken care of. He also took the treasures from the palace and some hostages. Then he returned to Samaria.

25Amaziah son of Joash, the king of Judah, lived fifteen years after the death of Jehoash son of Jehoahaz, the king of Israel. 26The other things Amaziah did as king, from the beginning to the end,

"Parents . . . sins." See Deuteronomy 24:16.

are written in the book of the kings of Judah and Israel. 27When Amaziah stopped obeying the LORD, the people in Jerusalem made plans against him. So he ran away to the town of Lachish, but they sent men after him to Lachish and killed him. 28They brought his body back on horses, and he was buried with his ancestors in Jerusalem, the city of David.

Uzziah King of Judah

26 Then all the people of Judah made Uzziah[n] king in place of his father Amaziah. Uzziah was sixteen years old. 2He rebuilt the town of Elath and made it part of Judah again after Amaziah died.

3Uzziah was sixteen years old when he became king, and he ruled fifty-two years in Jerusalem. His mother's name was Jecoliah, and she was from Jerusalem.

> **SIDELIGHT:** Wouldn't it be nice if everyone obeyed your slightest command? Uzziah must have felt that way when he became king at age sixteen (2 Chronicles 26:3). Do you suppose his first decree was to outlaw homework?

4He did what the LORD said was right, just as his father Amaziah had done. 5Uzziah obeyed God while Zechariah was alive, because he taught Uzziah how to respect and obey God. And as long as Uzziah obeyed the LORD, God gave him success.

6Uzziah fought a war against the Philistines. He tore down the walls around their towns of Gath, Jabneh, and Ashdod and built new towns near Ashdod and in other places among the Philistines. 7God helped Uzziah fight the Philistines, the Arabs living in Gur Baal, and the Meunites. 8Also, the Ammonites made the payments Uzziah demanded. He was very powerful, so his name became famous all the way to the border of Egypt.

9Uzziah built towers in Jerusalem at the Corner Gate, the Valley Gate, and where the wall turned, and he made them strong. 10He also built towers in the desert and dug many wells, because he had many cattle on the western hills and in the plains. He had people who worked his fields and vineyards in the hills and in the fertile lands, because he loved the land.

11Uzziah had an army of trained soldiers. They were counted and put in groups by Jeiel the royal secretary and Maaseiah the officer. Hananiah, one of the king's commanders, was their leader. 12There were twenty-six hundred leaders over the soldiers. 13They were in charge of an army of three hundred seven thousand five hundred men who fought with great power to help the king against the enemy. 14Uzziah gave his army shields, spears, helmets, armor, bows, and stones for their slings. 15In Jerusalem Uzziah made devices that were invented by clever men. These devices on the towers and corners of the city walls were used to shoot arrows and large rocks. So Uzziah became famous in faraway places, because he had much help until he became powerful.

> **SIDELIGHT:** Modern military experts debate whether their weapons are offensive or defensive. But ancient city walls (2 Chronicles 26:15) served both purposes. Massive in size, the walls offered a strong defense against battering and invasion. They also gave people on the walls an offensive position from which to drop rocks, shoot arrows, or pour hot oil on attackers.

16But when Uzziah became powerful, his pride led to his ruin. He was unfaithful to the LORD his God; he went into the Temple[d] of the LORD to burn incense[d] on the altar for incense. 17Azariah and eighty other brave priests who served the LORD followed Uzziah into the Temple. 18They told him he was wrong and said to him, "You don't have the right to burn incense to the LORD. Only the priests, Aaron's descendants,[d] should burn the incense, because they have been made holy. Leave this holy place. You have been unfaithful, and the LORD God will not honor you for this."

19Uzziah was standing beside the altar for incense in the Temple of the LORD, and in his hand was a pan for burning incense. He was very angry with the priests. As he was standing in front of the priests, a skin disease broke out on his forehead. 20Azariah, the leading priest, and all the other priests looked at him and saw the skin disease on his forehead. So they hurried him out of the Temple. Uzziah also rushed out, because the LORD was punishing him. 21So King Uzziah had the skin disease until the day he died. He had to live in a separate house and could not enter the Temple of the LORD. His son Jotham was in charge of the palace, and he governed the people of the land.

22The other things Uzziah did as king, from beginning to end, were written down by the prophet Isaiah son of Amoz. 23Uzziah died and was buried near his ancestors in a graveyard that

Uzziah Also called Azariah.

belonged to the kings. This was because people said, "He had a skin disease." And his son Jotham became king in his place.

Jotham King of Judah

27 Jotham was twenty-five years old when he became king, and he ruled sixteen years in Jerusalem. His mother's name was Jerusha daughter of Zadok. 2Jotham did what the LORD said was right, just as his father Uzziah had done. But Jotham did not enter the Temple[d] of the LORD to burn incense[d] as his father had. But the people continued doing wrong. 3Jotham rebuilt the Upper Gate of the Temple of the LORD, and he added greatly to the wall at Ophel. 4He also built towns in the hill country of Judah, as well as walled cities and towers in the forests.

5Jotham also fought the king of the Ammonites and defeated them. So each year for three years they gave Jotham about seventy-five hundred pounds of silver, about sixty-two thousand bushels of wheat, and about sixty-two thousand bushels of barley. 6Jotham became powerful, because he always obeyed the LORD his God.

7The other things Jotham did while he was king and all his wars are written in the book of the kings of Israel and Judah. 8Jotham was twenty-five years old when he became king, and he ruled sixteen years in Jerusalem. 9Jotham died and was buried in Jerusalem, the city of David. Then Jotham's son Ahaz became king in his place.

Ahaz King of Judah

28 Ahaz was twenty years old when he became king, and he ruled sixteen years in Jerusalem. Unlike his ancestor David, he did not do what the LORD said was right. 2Ahaz did the same things the kings of Israel had done. He made metal idols to worship Baal.[d] 3He burned incense[d] in the Valley of Ben Hinnom and made his children pass through the fire. He did the same hateful sins as the nations had done whom the LORD had forced out of the land ahead of the Israelites. 4Ahaz offered sacrifices and burned incense at the places where gods were worshiped, and on the hills, and under every green tree.

5So the LORD his God handed over Ahaz to the king of Aram. The Arameans defeated Ahaz and took many people of Judah as prisoners to Damascus.

He also handed over Ahaz to Pekah king of Israel, and Pekah's army killed many soldiers of Ahaz. 6The army of Pekah son of Remaliah killed one hundred twenty thousand brave soldiers from Judah in one day. Pekah defeated them because they had left the LORD, the God of their ancestors. 7Zicri, a warrior from Ephraim, killed King Ahaz's son Maaseiah. He also killed Azrikam, the officer in charge of the palace, and Elkanah, who was second in command to the king. 8The Israelite army captured two hundred thousand of their own relatives. They took women, sons and daughters, and many valuable things from Judah and carried them back to Samaria. 9But a prophet[d] of the LORD named Oded was there. He met the Israelite army when it returned to Samaria and said to them, "The LORD, the God of your ancestors, handed Judah over to you, because he was angry with those people. But God has seen the cruel way you killed them. 10Now you plan to make the people of Judah and Jerusalem your slaves, but you also have sinned against the LORD your God. 11Now listen to me. Send back your brothers and sisters whom you captured, because the LORD is very angry with you."

12Then some of the leaders in Ephraim—Azariah son of Jehohanan, Berekiah son of Meshillemoth, Jehizkiah son of Shallum, and Amasa son of Hadlai—met the Israelite soldiers coming home from war. 13They warned the soldiers, "Don't bring the prisoners from Judah here. If you do, we will be guilty of sin against the LORD, and that will make our sin and guilt even worse. Our guilt is already so great that he is angry with Israel."

14So the soldiers left the prisoners and valuable things in front of the officers and people there. 15The leaders who were named took the prisoners and gave those who were naked the clothes that the Israelite army had taken. They gave the prisoners clothes, sandals, food, drink, and medicine. They put the weak prisoners on donkeys and took them back to their families in Jericho, the city of palm trees. Then they returned home to Samaria.

16-17At that time the Edomites came again and attacked Judah and carried away prisoners. So King Ahaz sent to the king of Assyria for help. 18The Philistines also robbed the towns in the western hills and in southern Judah. They captured the towns of Beth Shemesh, Aijalon, Gederoth, Soco, Timnah, and Gimzo, and the villages around them. Then the Philistines lived in those towns. 19The LORD brought trouble on Judah because Ahaz their king led the people of Judah to sin, and he was unfaithful to the LORD. 20Tiglath-Pileser king of Assyria came to Ahaz, but he gave Ahaz trouble instead of help. 21Ahaz took some valuable things from the Temple[d] of the LORD, from the palace, and from the princes, and he gave them to the king of Assyria, but it did not help.

22During Ahaz's troubles he was even more unfaithful to the LORD. 23He offered sacrifices to the gods of the people of Damascus, who had defeated him. He thought, "The gods of the kings of Aram helped them. If I offer sacrifices to them, they will help me also." But this brought ruin to Ahaz and all Israel.

24Ahaz gathered the things from the Temple of

God and broke them into pieces. Then he closed
the doors of the Temple of the LORD. He made
altars and put them on every street corner in Jerusalem. 25In every town in Judah, Ahaz made
places for burning sacrifices to worship other
gods. So he made the LORD, the God of his ancestors, very angry.

26The other things Ahaz did as king, from beginning to end, are written in the book of the
kings of Judah and Israel. 27Ahaz died and was
buried in the city of Jerusalem, but not in the
graves of the kings of Israel. Ahaz's son Hezekiah
became king in his place.

Hezekiah Purifies the Temple

29 Hezekiah was twenty-five years old
when he became king, and he ruled
twenty-nine years in Jerusalem. His mother's
name was Abijah daughter of Zechariah. 2Heze-
kiah did what the LORD said was right, just as his
ancestor David had done.

3Hezekiah opened the doors of the Temple[d] of
the LORD and repaired them in the first month of
the first year he was king. 4Hezekiah brought in
the priests and Levites and gathered them in the
courtyard on the east side of the Temple. 5Heze-
kiah said, "Listen to me, Levites. Make yourselves
ready for the LORD's service, and make holy the
Temple of the LORD, the God of your ancestors.
Remove from the Temple everything that makes
it impure. 6Our ancestors were unfaithful to God
and did what the LORD said was wrong. They left
the LORD and stopped worshiping at the Temple
where he lives. They rejected him. 7They shut the
doors of the porch of the Temple, and they let the
fire go out in the lamps. They stopped burning
incense[d] and offering burnt offerings in the holy
place to the God of Israel. 8So the LORD became
very angry with the people of Judah and Jerusalem, and he punished them. Other people are
frightened and shocked by what he did to them.
So they insult the people of Judah. You know
these things are true. 9That is why our ancestors
were killed in battle and our sons, daughters, and
wives were taken captive. 10Now I, Hezekiah,
have decided to make an agreement with the
LORD, the God of Israel, so he will not be angry
with us anymore. 11My sons, don't waste any
more time. The LORD chose you to stand before
him, to serve him, to be his servants, and to burn
incense to him."

12These are the Levites who started to work.
From the Kohathite family there were Mahath
son of Amasai and Joel son of Azariah. From the
Merarite family there were Kish son of Abdi and
Azariah son of Jehallelel. From the Gershonite
family there were Joah son of Zimmah and Eden
son of Joah. 13From Elizaphan's family there were
Shimri and Jeiel. From Asaph's family there
were Zechariah and Mattaniah. 14From Heman's
family there were Jehiel and Shimei. From Jeduthun's family there were Shemaiah and Uzziel.

15These Levites gathered their brothers together and made themselves holy for service in
the Temple. Then they went into the Temple of
the LORD to purify it. They obeyed the king's command that had come from the LORD. 16When the
priests went into the Temple of the LORD to purify
it, they took out all the unclean[d] things they
found in the Temple of the LORD and put them in
the Temple courtyard. Then the Levites took
these things out to the Kidron Valley. 17Beginning
on the first day of the first month, they made the
Temple holy for the LORD's service. On the eighth
day of the month, they came to the porch of the
Temple, and for eight more days they made the
Temple of the LORD holy. So they finished on the
sixteenth day of the first month.

18Then they went to King Hezekiah and said,
"We have purified the entire Temple of the LORD,
the altar for burnt offerings and its utensils, and
the table for the holy bread and all its utensils.
19When Ahaz was king, he was unfaithful to God
and removed some things from the Temple. But
we have put them back and made them holy for
the LORD. They are now in front of the LORD's
altar."

20Early the next morning King Hezekiah gathered the leaders of the city and went up to the
Temple of the LORD. 21They brought seven bulls,
seven male sheep, seven lambs, and seven male
goats. These animals were an offering to remove
the sin of the people and the kingdom of Judah
and to make the Temple ready for service to God.
King Hezekiah commanded the priests, the
descendants[d] of Aaron, to offer these animals on
the LORD's altar. 22So the priests killed the bulls
and sprinkled their blood on the altar. They killed
the sheep and sprinkled their blood on the altar.
Then they killed the lambs and sprinkled their
blood on the altar. 23Then the priests brought the
male goats for the sin offering before the king and
the people there. After the king and the people
put their hands on the goats, 24the priests killed
them. With the goats' blood they made an offering on the altar to remove the sins of the Israelites
so they would belong to God. The king had said
that the burnt offering and sin offering should be
made for all Israel.

25King Hezekiah put the Levites in the Temple
of the LORD with cymbals, harps, and lyres,[d] as
David, Gad, and Nathan had commanded. (Gad
was the king's seer,[d] and Nathan was a prophet.[d])
This command came from the LORD through his
prophets. 26So the Levites stood ready with David's instruments of music, and the priests stood
ready with their trumpets.

27Then Hezekiah gave the order to sacrifice the

burnt offering on the altar. When the burnt offering began, the singing to the LORD also began. The
trumpets were blown, and the musical instruments of David king of Israel were played. 28All
the people worshiped, the singers sang, and the
trumpeters blew their trumpets until the burnt offering was finished.
29When the sacrifices were completed, King
Hezekiah and everyone with him bowed down
and worshiped. 30King Hezekiah and his officers
ordered the Levites to praise the LORD, using the
words David and Asaph the seer had used. So
they praised God with joy and bowed down and
worshiped.
31Then Hezekiah said, "Now that you people of
Judah have given yourselves to the LORD, come
near to the Temple of the LORD. Bring sacrifices
and offerings, to show thanks to him." So the people brought sacrifices and thank offerings, and
anyone who was willing also brought burnt offerings. 32For burnt offerings they brought a total of
seventy bulls, one hundred male sheep, and two
hundred lambs; all these animals were sacrificed
as burnt offerings to the LORD. 33The holy offerings totaled six hundred bulls and three thousand
sheep and goats. 34There were not enough priests
to skin all the animals for the burnt offerings. So
their relatives the Levites helped them until the
work was finished and other priests could be
made holy. The Levites had been more careful to
make themselves holy for the LORD's service than
the priests. 35There were many burnt offerings
along with the fat of fellowship offerings and
drink offerings. So the service in the Temple of
the LORD began again. 36And Hezekiah and the
people were very happy that God had made it
happen so quickly for his people.

The Passover Celebration

30 King Hezekiah sent messages to all the
people of Israel and Judah, and he wrote
letters to the people of Ephraim and Manasseh.
Hezekiah invited all these people to come to the
Temple[d] of the LORD in Jerusalem to celebrate the
Passover[d] for the LORD, the God of Israel. 2King
Hezekiah, his officers, and all the people in Jerusalem agreed to celebrate the Passover in the second month. 3They could not celebrate it at the
normal time, because not enough priests had
made themselves ready to serve the LORD, and
the people had not yet gathered in Jerusalem.
4This plan satisfied King Hezekiah and all the people. 5So they made an announcement everywhere
in Israel, from Beersheba to Dan,[n] telling the
people to come to Jerusalem to celebrate the Passover for the LORD, the God of Israel. For a long
time most of the people had not celebrated the
Passover as the law commanded. 6At the king's
command, the messengers took letters from him
and his officers all through Israel and Judah. This
is what the letters said:

People of Israel, return to the LORD, the
God of Abraham, Isaac, and Israel. Then
God will return to you who are still alive,
who have escaped from the kings of Assyria.
7Don't be like your ancestors or your relatives. They turned against the LORD, the God
of their ancestors, so he caused other people
to be disgusted with them. You know this is
true. 8Don't be stubborn as your ancestors
were, but obey the LORD willingly. Come to
the Temple, which he has made holy forever. Serve the LORD your God so he will not
be angry with you. 9Come back to the LORD.
Then the people who captured your relatives
and children will be kind to them and will let
them return to this land. The LORD your God
is kind and merciful. He will not turn away
from you if you return to him.

10The messengers went to every town in
Ephraim and Manasseh, and all the way to Zebulun, but the people laughed at them and made fun
of them. 11But some men from Asher, Manasseh,
and Zebulun were sorry for what they had done
and went to Jerusalem. 12And God united all the
people of Judah in obeying King Hezekiah and his
officers, because their command had come from
the LORD.
13In the second month a large crowd came together in Jerusalem to celebrate the Feast[d] of Unleavened Bread. 14The people removed the altars
and incense[d] altars to gods in Jerusalem and
threw them into the Kidron Valley.
15They killed the Passover lamb on the fourteenth day of the second month. The priests and
the Levites were ashamed, so they made themselves holy and brought burnt offerings into the
Temple of the LORD. 16They took their regular
places in the Temple as the Teachings of Moses,
the man of God, commanded. The Levites gave
the blood of the sacrifices to the priests, who
sprinkled it on the altar. 17Since many people in
the crowd had not made themselves holy, the Levites killed the Passover lambs for everyone who
was not clean.[d] The Levites made each lamb holy
for the LORD. 18-19Although many people from
Ephraim, Manasseh, Issachar, and Zebulun had
not purified themselves for the feast, they ate the
Passover even though it was against the law. So
Hezekiah prayed for them, saying, "LORD, you are
good. You are the LORD, the God of our ancestors.

Beersheba to Dan Dan was the city farthest north in Israel, and Beersheba was the city farthest south. So this means all the people of Israel.

Please forgive all those who try to obey you even if they did not make themselves clean as the rules of the Temple command." 20The LORD listened to Hezekiah's prayer, and he healed the people. 21The Israelites in Jerusalem celebrated the Feast of Unleavened Bread for seven days with great joy to the LORD. The Levites and priests praised the LORD every day with loud music. 22Hezekiah encouraged all the Levites who showed they understood well how to do their service for the LORD. The people ate the feast for seven days, offered fellowship offerings, and praised the LORD, the God of their ancestors.

23Then all the people agreed to stay seven more days, so they celebrated with joy for seven more days. 24Hezekiah king of Judah gave one thousand bulls and seven thousand sheep to the people. The officers gave one thousand bulls and ten thousand sheep to the people. Many priests made themselves holy. 25All the people of Judah, the priests, the Levites, those who came from Israel, the foreigners from Israel, and the foreigners living in Judah were very happy. 26There was much joy in Jerusalem, because there had not been a celebration like this since the time of Solomon son of David and king of Israel. 27The priests and Levites stood up and blessed the people, and God heard them because their prayer reached heaven, his holy home.

The Collection for the Priests

31 When the Passover[d] celebration was finished, all the Israelites in Jerusalem went out to the towns of Judah. There they smashed the stone pillars used to worship gods. They cut down the Asherah[d] idols and destroyed the altars and places for worshiping gods in all of Judah, Benjamin, Ephraim, and Manasseh. After they had destroyed all of them, the Israelites returned to their own towns and homes.

2King Hezekiah appointed groups of priests and Levites for their special duties. They were to offer burnt offerings and fellowship offerings, to worship, and to give thanks and praise at the gates of the LORD's house. 3Hezekiah gave some of his own animals for the burnt offerings, which were given every morning and evening, on Sabbath[d] days, during New Moons,[d] and at other feasts commanded in the LORD's Teachings.

4Hezekiah commanded the people living in Jerusalem to give the priests and Levites the portion that belonged to them. Then the priests and Levites could give all their time to the LORD's Teachings. 5As soon as the king's command went out to the Israelites, they gave freely of the first portion of their grain, new wine, oil, honey, and everything they grew in their fields. They brought a large amount, one-tenth of everything. 6The people of Israel and Judah who lived in Judah also brought one-tenth of their cattle and sheep and one-tenth of the holy things that were given to the LORD their God, and they put all of them in piles. 7The people began the piles in the third month and finished in the seventh month. 8When Hezekiah and his officers came and saw the piles, they praised the LORD and his people, the people of Israel. 9Hezekiah asked the priests and Levites about the piles. 10Azariah, the leading priest from Zadok's family, answered Hezekiah, "Since the people began to bring their offerings to the Temple[d] of the LORD, we have had plenty to eat and plenty left over, because the LORD has blessed his people. So we have all this left over."

11Then Hezekiah commanded the priests to prepare the storerooms in the Temple of the LORD. So this was done. 12Then the priests brought in the offerings and the things given to the LORD and one-tenth of everything the people had given. Conaniah the Levite was in charge of these things, and his brother Shimei was second to him. 13Conaniah and his brother Shimei were over these supervisors: Jehiel, Azaziah, Nahath, Asahel, Jerimoth, Jozabad, Eliel, Ismakiah, Mahath, and Benaiah. King Hezekiah and Azariah the officer in charge of the Temple of God had chosen them.

14Kore son of Imnah the Levite was in charge of the special gifts the people wanted to give to God. He was responsible for giving out the contributions made to the LORD and the holy gifts. Kore was the guard at the East Gate. 15Eden, Miniamin, Jeshua, Shemaiah, Amariah, and Shecaniah helped Kore in the towns where the priests lived. They gave from what was collected to the other groups of priests, both young and old.

16From what was collected, these men also gave to the males three years old and older who had their names in the Levite family histories. They were to enter the Temple of the LORD for their daily service, each group having its own responsibilities. 17The priests were given their part of the collection, by families, as listed in the family histories. The Levites twenty years old and older were given their part of the collection, based on their responsibilities and their groups. 18The Levites' babies, wives, sons, and daughters also got part of the collection. This was done for all the Levites who were listed in the family histories, because they always kept themselves ready to serve the LORD.

19Some of Aaron's descendants,[d] the priests, lived on the farmlands near the towns or in the towns. Men were chosen by name to give part of the collection to these priests. All the males and those named in the family histories of the Levites received part of the collection.

20This is what King Hezekiah did in Judah. He did what was good and right and obedient before

the LORD his God. 21Hezekiah tried to obey God
in his service of the Temple of God, and he tried
to obey God's teachings and commands. He gave
himself fully to his work for God. So he had success.

Assyria Attacks Judah

32 After Hezekiah did all these things to
serve the LORD, Sennacherib king of Assyria came and attacked Judah. He and his army
surrounded and attacked the strong, walled cities,
hoping to take them for himself. 2Hezekiah knew
that Sennacherib had come to Jerusalem to attack
it. 3So Hezekiah and his officers and army commanders decided to cut off the water from the
springs outside the city. So the officers and commanders helped Hezekiah. 4Many people came
and cut off all the springs and the stream that
flowed through the land. They said, "The king of
Assyria will not find much water when he comes
here." 5Then Hezekiah made Jerusalem stronger.
He rebuilt all the broken parts of the wall and put
towers on it. He also built another wall outside
the first one and strengthened the area that was
filled in on the east side of the old part of Jerusalem. He also made many weapons and shields.
6Hezekiah put army commanders over the people and met with them at the open place near the
city gate. Hezekiah encouraged them, saying,
7"Be strong and brave. Don't be afraid or worried
because of the king of Assyria or his large army.
There is a greater power with us than with him.
8He only has men, but we have the LORD our God
to help us and to fight our battles." The people
were encouraged by the words of Hezekiah king
of Judah.

> **SIDELIGHT:** The Assyrian attack on Lachish (2 Chronicles 32:9) was horrible for its citizens. Archaeologists have found the bones of fifteen hundred bodies in a pit there, a sign of the terrible siege.

9After this King Sennacherib of Assyria and all
his army surrounded and attacked Lachish. Then
he sent his officers to Jerusalem with this message
for King Hezekiah of Judah and all the people of
Judah in Jerusalem:

10Sennacherib king of Assyria says this:
"You have nothing to trust in to help you. It
is no use for you to stay in Jerusalem under
attack. 11Hezekiah says to you, 'The LORD
our God will save us from the king of Assyria,' but he is fooling you. If you stay in
Jerusalem, you will die from hunger and
thirst. 12Hezekiah himself removed your
LORD's places of worship and altars. He told
you people of Judah and Jerusalem that you
must worship and burn incense[d] on only one
altar.

13"You know what my ancestors and I
have done to all the people in other nations.
The gods of those nations could not save
their people from my power. 14My ancestors
destroyed those nations; none of their gods
could save them from me. So your god cannot save you from my power. 15Do not let
Hezekiah fool you or trick you, and do not
believe him. No god of any nation or kingdom has been able to save his people from
me or my ancestors. Your god is even less
able to save you from me."

16Sennacherib's officers said worse things
against the LORD God and his servant Hezekiah.
17King Sennacherib also wrote letters insulting the
LORD, the God of Israel. They spoke against him,
saying, "The gods of the other nations could not
save their people from me. In the same way Hezekiah's god won't be able to save his people from
me." 18Then the king's officers shouted in Hebrew, calling out to the people of Jerusalem who
were on the city wall. The officers wanted to
scare the people away so they could capture Jerusalem. 19They spoke about the God of Jerusalem
as though he were like the gods the people of the
world worshiped, which are made by human
hands.
20King Hezekiah and the prophet[d] Isaiah son of
Amoz prayed to heaven about this. 21Then the
LORD sent an angel who killed all the soldiers,
leaders, and officers in the camp of the king of
Assyria. So the king went back to his own country
in disgrace. When he went into the temple of his
god, some of his own sons killed him with a
sword.
22So the LORD saved Hezekiah and the people
in Jerusalem from Sennacherib king of Assyria and
from all other people. He took care of them on
every side. 23Many people brought gifts for the
LORD to Jerusalem, and they also brought valuable
gifts to King Hezekiah of Judah. From then on all
the nations respected Hezekiah.

Hezekiah Dies

24At that time Hezekiah became so sick he almost died. When he prayed to the LORD, the
LORD spoke to him and gave him a sign.[n] 25But
Hezekiah did not thank God for his kindness, because he was so proud. So the LORD was angry
with him and the people of Judah and Jerusalem.

sign See Isaiah 38:1-8. It tells the story about the sign and how the Lord gave Hezekiah fifteen more years to live.

26But later Hezekiah and the people of Jerusalem
were sorry and stopped being proud, so the LORD
did not punish them while Hezekiah was alive.
27Hezekiah had many riches and much honor.
He made treasuries for his silver, gold, gems,
spices, shields, and other valuable things. 28He
built storage buildings for grain, new wine, and oil
and stalls for all the cattle and pens for the sheep.
29He also built many towns. He had many flocks
and herds, because God had given Hezekiah
much wealth.
30It was Hezekiah who cut off the upper pool
of the Gihon spring and made those waters flow
straight down to the west side of the older part of
Jerusalem. And Hezekiah was successful in everything he did. 31But one time the leaders of Babylon sent messengers to Hezekiah, asking him
about a strange sign[n] that had happened in the
land. When they came, God left Hezekiah alone
to test him so he could know everything that was
in Hezekiah's heart.[n]
32Hezekiah's love for God and the other things
he did as king are written in the vision of the
prophet[d] Isaiah son of Amoz. This is in the book
of the kings of Judah and Israel. 33Hezekiah died
and was buried on a hill, where the graves of David's ancestors are. All the people of Judah and
Jerusalem honored Hezekiah when he died, and
his son Manasseh became king in his place.

Manasseh King of Judah

33 Manasseh was twelve years old when he
became king, and he was king for fifty-
five years in Jerusalem. 2He did what the LORD
said was wrong. He did the hateful things the na
tions had done—the nations that the LORD had
forced out of the land ahead of the Israelites. 3Ma-
nasseh's father, Hezekiah, had torn down the
places where gods were worshiped, but Manasseh rebuilt them. He also built altars for the Baal[d]
gods, and he made Asherah[d] idols and worshiped
all the stars of the sky and served them. 4The
LORD had said about the Temple,[d] "I will be worshiped in Jerusalem forever," but Manasseh built
altars in the Temple of the LORD. 5He built altars
to worship the stars in the two courtyards of the
Temple of the LORD. 6He made his children pass
through fire in the Valley of Ben Hinnom. He
practiced magic and witchcraft[d] and told the future by explaining signs and dreams. He got advice from mediums[d] and fortune-tellers. He did
many things the LORD said were wrong, which
made the LORD angry.
7Manasseh carved an idol and put it in the
Temple of God. God had said to David and his son
Solomon about the Temple, "I will be worshiped
forever in this Temple and in Jerusalem, which I
have chosen from all the tribes[d] of Israel. 8I will
never again make the Israelites leave the land I
gave to their ancestors. But they must obey everything I have commanded them in all the teachings, rules, and commands I gave them through
Moses." 9But Manasseh led the people of Judah
and Jerusalem to do wrong. They did more evil
than the nations the LORD had destroyed ahead of
the Israelites.
10The LORD spoke to Manasseh and his people,
but they did not listen. 11So the LORD brought the
king of Assyria's army commanders to attack Judah. They captured Manasseh, put hooks in him,
placed bronze chains on his hands, and took him
to Babylon. 12As Manasseh suffered, he begged
the LORD his God for help and humbled himself
before the God of his ancestors. 13When Manasseh prayed, the LORD heard him and had pity on
him. So the LORD let him return to Jerusalem and
to his kingdom. Then Manasseh knew that the
LORD is the true God.
14After that happened, Manasseh rebuilt the
outer wall of Jerusalem and made it higher. It was
in the valley on the west side of the Gihon spring
and went to the entrance of the Fish Gate and
around the hill of Ophel. Then he put commanders in all the strong, walled cities in Judah.
15Manasseh removed the idols of other nations,
including the idol in the Temple of the LORD. He
removed all the altars he had built on the Temple
hill and in Jerusalem and threw them out of the
city. 16Then he set up the LORD's altar and sacrificed on it fellowship offerings and offerings to
show thanks to God. Manasseh commanded all
the people of Judah to serve the LORD, the God of
Israel. 17The people continued to offer sacrifices at
the places of worship, but their sacrifices were
only to the LORD their God. 18The other things
Manasseh did as king, his prayer to his God, and
what the seers[d] said to him in the name of the
LORD, the God of Israel—all are recorded in the
book of the history of the kings of Israel. 19Manas-
seh's prayer and God's pity for him, his sins, his
unfaithfulness, the places he built for worshiping
gods and the Asherah[d] idols before he humbled
himself—all are written in the book of the seers.
20Manasseh died and was buried in his palace.
Then Manasseh's son Amon became king in his
place.

Amon King of Judah

21Amon was twenty-two years old when he became king, and he was king for two years in Jerusalem. 22He did what the LORD said was wrong,
as his father Manasseh had done. Amon wor-

sign See Isaiah 38:1-8. It tells the story about the sign and how the Lord gave Hezekiah fifteen more years to live.
God . . . heart See 2 Kings 20:12-19.

shiped and offered sacrifices to all the carved idols Manasseh had made. [23]Amon did not humble himself before the LORD as his father Manasseh had done. Instead, Amon sinned even more.

[24]King Amon's officers made plans against him and killed him in his palace. [25]Then the people of the land killed all those who had made plans to kill King Amon, and they made his son Josiah king in his place.

Josiah King of Judah

34 Josiah was eight years old when he became king, and he ruled thirty-one years in Jerusalem. [2]He did what the LORD said was right. He lived as his ancestor David had lived, and he did not stop doing what was right.

[3]In his eighth year as king while he was still young, Josiah began to obey the God of his ancestor David. In his twelfth year as king, Josiah began to remove from Judah and Jerusalem the gods, the places for worshiping gods, the Asherah[d] idols, and the wooden and metal idols. [4]The people tore down the altars for the Baal[d] gods as Josiah directed. Then Josiah cut down the incense[d] altars that were above them. He broke up the Asherah idols and the wooden and metal idols and beat them into powder. Then he sprinkled the powder on the graves of the people who had offered sacrifices to these gods. [5]He burned the bones of their priests on their own altars. So Josiah removed idol worship from Judah and Jerusalem, [6]and from the towns in the areas of Manasseh, Ephraim, and Simeon all the way to Naphtali, and in the ruins near these towns. [7]Josiah broke down the altars and Asherah idols and beat the idols into powder. He cut down all the incense altars in all of Israel. Then he went back to Jerusalem.

> **SIDELIGHT:** The "places" or "high places" where people worshiped false gods weren't necessarily hills or mountains (2 Chronicles 34:3–7). They were sacred platforms on which idols stood. The only way to get people to stop worshiping at them was to destroy them completely as King Josiah did.

[8]In Josiah's eighteenth year as king, he made Judah and the Temple[d] pure again. He sent Shaphan son of Azaliah, Maaseiah the city leader, and Joah son of Joahaz the recorder to repair the Temple of the LORD, the God of Josiah. [9]These men went to Hilkiah the high priest and gave him the money the Levite gatekeepers had gathered from the people of Manasseh, Ephraim, and all the Israelites who were left alive, and also from all the people of Judah, Benjamin, and Jerusalem. This is the money they had brought into the Temple of God. [10]Then the Levites gave it to the supervisors of the work on the Temple of the LORD, and they paid the workers who rebuilt and repaired the Temple. [11]They gave money to carpenters and builders to buy cut stone and wood. The wood was used to rebuild the buildings and to make beams for them, because the kings of Judah had let the buildings fall into ruin. [12]The men did their work well. Their supervisors were Jahath and Obadiah, who were Levites from the family of Merari, and Zechariah and Meshullam, who were from the family of Kohath. These Levites were all skilled musicians. [13]They were also in charge of the workers who carried loads and all the other workers. Some Levites worked as secretaries, officers, and gatekeepers.

> **SIDELIGHT:** If you don't think secretaries are important, read 2 Chronicles 34:13, which tells that the Levites served as honored secretaries in the Temple. Do you think they had to take a typing test?

The Book of the Teachings Is Found

[14]The Levites brought out the money that was in the Temple[d] of the LORD. As they were doing this, Hilkiah the priest found the Book of the LORD's Teachings that had been given through Moses. [15]Hilkiah said to Shaphan the royal secretary, "I've found the Book of the Teachings in the Temple of the LORD!" Then he gave it to Shaphan.

[16]Shaphan took the book to the king and reported to Josiah, "Your officers are doing everything you told them to do. [17]They have paid out the money that was in the Temple of the LORD and have given it to the supervisors and the workers." [18]Then Shaphan the royal secretary told the king, "Hilkiah the priest has given me a book." And Shaphan read from the book to the king.

[19]When the king heard the words of the Teachings, he tore his clothes to show how upset he was. [20]He gave orders to Hilkiah, Ahikam son of Shaphan, Acbor son of Micaiah, Shaphan the royal secretary, and Asaiah, the king's servant. These were the orders: [21]"Go and ask the LORD about the words in the book that was found. Ask for me and for the people who are left alive in Israel and Judah. The LORD is very angry with us, because our ancestors did not obey the LORD's word; they did not do everything this book says to do."

[22]So Hilkiah and those the king sent with him went to talk to Huldah the prophetess.[d] She was

the wife of Shallum son of Tikvah, the son of Harhas, who took care of the king's clothes. Huldah lived in Jerusalem, in the new area of the city.

23She said to them, "This is what the LORD, the God of Israel, says: Tell the man who sent you to me, 24'This is what the LORD says: I will bring trouble to this place and to the people living here. I will bring all the curses that are written in the book that was read to the king of Judah. 25The people of Judah have left me and have burned incense[d] to other gods. They have made me angry by all the evil things they have made. So I will punish them in my anger, which will not be put out.' 26Tell the king of Judah, who sent you to ask the LORD, 'This is what the LORD, the God of Israel, says about the words you heard: 27When you heard my words against this place and its people, you became sorry for what you had done and you humbled yourself before me. You tore your clothes to show how upset you were, and you cried in my presence. This is why I have heard you, says the LORD. 28So I will let you die and be buried in peace. You won't see all the trouble I will bring to this place and the people living here.' "

So they took her message back to the king.

29Then the king gathered all the older leaders of Judah and Jerusalem together. 30He went up to the Temple of the LORD, and all the people from Judah and from Jerusalem went with him. The priests, the Levites, and all the people — from the most important to the least important — went with him. He read to them all the words in the Book of the Agreement that was found in the Temple of the LORD. 31The king stood by his pillar and made an agreement in the presence of the LORD to follow the LORD and obey his commands, rules, and laws with his whole being and to obey the words of the agreement written in this book. 32Then Josiah made all the people in Jerusalem and Benjamin promise to accept the agreement. So the people of Jerusalem obeyed the agreement of God, the God of their ancestors.

33And Josiah threw out the hateful idols from all the land that belonged to the Israelites. He led everyone in Israel to serve the LORD their God. While Josiah lived, the people obeyed the LORD, the God of their ancestors.

Josiah Celebrates the Passover

35 King Josiah celebrated the Passover[d] to the LORD in Jerusalem. The Passover lamb was killed on the fourteenth day of the first month. 2Josiah chose the priests to do their duties, and he encouraged them as they served in the Temple[d] of the LORD. 3The Levites taught the Israelites and were made holy for service to the LORD. Josiah said to them, "Put the Holy Ark[d] in the Temple that David's son Solomon, the king of Israel, built. Do not carry it from place to place on your shoulders anymore. Now serve the LORD your God and his people Israel. 4Prepare yourselves by your family groups for service, and do the jobs that King David and his son Solomon gave you to do.

5"Stand in the holy place with a group of the Levites for each family group of the people. 6Kill the Passover lambs, and make yourselves holy to the LORD. Prepare the lambs for your relatives, the people of Israel, as the LORD through Moses commanded us to do."

7Josiah gave the Israelites thirty thousand sheep and goats to kill for the Passover sacrifices, and he gave them three thousand cattle. They were all his own animals.

8Josiah's officers also gave willingly to the people, the priests, and the Levites. Hilkiah, Zechariah, and Jehiel, the officers in charge of the Temple, gave the priests twenty-six hundred lambs and goats and three hundred cattle for Passover sacrifices. 9Conaniah, his brothers Shemaiah and Nethanel, and Hashabiah, Jeiel, and Jozabad gave the Levites five thousand sheep and goats and five hundred cattle for Passover sacrifices. These men were leaders of the Levites.

10When everything was ready for the Passover service, the priests and Levites went to their places, as the king had commanded. 11The Passover lambs were killed. Then the Levites skinned the animals and gave the blood to the priests, who sprinkled it on the altar. 12Then they gave the animals for the burnt offerings to the different family groups so the burnt offerings could be offered to the LORD as was written in the book of Moses. They also did this with the cattle. 13The Levites roasted the Passover sacrifices over the fire as they were commanded, and they boiled the holy offerings in pots, kettles, and pans. Then they quickly gave the meat to the people. 14After this was finished, the Levites prepared meat for themselves and for the priests, the descendants[d] of Aaron. The priests worked until night, offering the burnt offerings and burning the fat of the sacrifices.

15The Levite singers from Asaph's family stood in the places chosen for them by King David, Asaph, Heman, and Jeduthun, the king's seer.[d] The gatekeepers at each gate did not have to leave their places, because their fellow Levites had prepared everything for them for the Passover.

16So everything was done that day for the worship of the LORD, as King Josiah commanded. The Passover was celebrated, and the burnt offerings were offered on the LORD's altar. 17The Israelites who were there celebrated the Passover and the Feast[d] of Unleavened Bread for seven days. 18The Passover had not been celebrated like this in Israel since the prophet[d] Samuel was alive. None of the kings of Israel had ever celebrated a Passover like it was celebrated by King Josiah, the priests, the Levites, the people of Judah and Israel who were there, and the people of Jerusalem. 19This Passover was celebrated in the eighteenth year Josiah was king.

The Death of Josiah

20After Josiah did all this for the Temple,[d] Neco king of Egypt led an army to attack Carchemish, a town on the Euphrates River. And Josiah marched out to fight against Neco. 21But Neco sent messengers to Josiah, saying, "King Josiah, there should not be war between us. I did not come to fight you, but my enemies. God told me to hurry, and he is on my side. So don't fight God, or he will destroy you."

22But Josiah did not go away. He wore different clothes so no one would know who he was. Refusing to listen to what Neco said at God's command, Josiah went to fight on the plain of Megiddo. 23In the battle King Josiah was shot by archers. He told his servants, "Take me away because I am badly wounded." 24So they took him out of his chariot and put him in another chariot and carried him to Jerusalem. There he died and was buried in the graves where his ancestors were buried. All the people of Judah and Jerusalem were very sad because he was dead.

SIDELIGHT: If you want to buy a house on the plain of Megiddo (2 Chronicles 35:22), expect to pay high "war insurance." This plain may be one of the bloodiest battlegrounds in the world. Archaeologists have uncovered twenty cities—one on top of the other—that have been destroyed at this site.

25Jeremiah wrote some sad songs about Josiah. Even to this day all the men and women singers remember and honor Josiah with these songs. It became a custom in Israel to sing these songs that are written in the collection of sad songs.

26-27The other things Josiah did as king, from beginning to end, are written in the book of the kings of Israel and Judah. It tells how he loved what was written in the LORD's teachings.

Jehoahaz King of Judah

36 The people of Judah chose Josiah's son Jehoahaz and made him king in Jerusalem in his father's place.

2Jehoahaz was twenty-three years old when he became king, and he was king in Jerusalem for three months. 3Then King Neco of Egypt removed Jehoahaz from being king in Jerusalem. Neco made the people of Judah pay about seventy-five hundred pounds of silver and about seventy-five pounds of gold. 4The king of Egypt made Jehoahaz's brother Eliakim the king of Judah and Jerusalem and changed his name to Jehoiakim. But Neco took his brother Jehoahaz to Egypt.

Jehoiakim King of Judah

5Jehoiakim was twenty-five years old when he became king, and he was king in Jerusalem for eleven years. He did what the LORD his God said was wrong. 6King Nebuchadnezzar of Babylon attacked Judah, captured Jehoiakim, put bronze chains on him, and took him to Babylon. 7Nebuchadnezzar removed some of the things from the Temple[d] of the LORD, took them to Babylon, and put them in his own palace.

8The other things Jehoiakim did as king, the hateful things he did, and everything he was guilty of doing, are written in the book of the kings of Israel and Judah. And Jehoiakim's son Jehoiachin became king in his place.

Jehoiachin King of Judah

9Jehoiachin was eighteen years old when he became king of Judah, and he was king in Jerusalem for three months and ten days. He did what the LORD said was wrong. 10In the spring King Nebuchadnezzar sent for Jehoiachin and brought him and some valuable treasures from the Temple[d] of the LORD to Babylon. Then Nebuchadnezzar made Jehoiachin's uncle Zedekiah the king of Judah and Jerusalem.

Zedekiah King of Judah

11Zedekiah was twenty-one years old when he became king of Judah, and he was king in Jerusalem for eleven years. 12Zedekiah did what the LORD his God said was wrong. The prophet[d] Jeremiah spoke messages from the LORD, but Zedekiah did not obey. 13Zedekiah turned against King Nebuchadnezzar, who had forced him to swear in God's name to be loyal to him. But Zedekiah became stubborn and refused to obey the LORD, the God of Israel. 14Also, all the leaders of the priests and the people of Judah became more wicked, following the evil example of the other nations. The LORD had made the Temple[d] in Jerusalem holy, but the leaders made it unholy.

The Fall of Jerusalem

15The LORD, the God of their ancestors, sent prophets[d] again and again to warn his people, because he had pity on them and on his Temple. 16But they made fun of God's prophets and hated God's messages. They refused to listen to the prophets until, finally, the LORD became so angry with his people that he could not be stopped. 17So God brought the king of Babylon to attack them.

The king killed the young men even when they
were in the Temple. He had no mercy on the
young men or women, the old men or those who
were sick. God handed all of them over to Nebuchadnezzar. 18Nebuchadnezzar carried away to
Babylon all the things from the Temple of God,
both large and small, and all the treasures from
the Temple of the LORD and from the king and his
officers. 19Nebuchadnezzar and his army set fire
to God's Temple and broke down Jerusalem's
wall and burned all the palaces. They took or destroyed every valuable thing in Jerusalem.
20Nebuchadnezzar took captive to Babylon the
people who were left alive, and he forced them to
be slaves for him and his descendants.[d] They remained there as slaves until the Persian kingdom
defeated Babylon. 21And so what the LORD had
told Israel through the prophet Jeremiah happened: The country was an empty wasteland for
seventy years to make up for the years of Sabbath
rest[n] that the people had not kept.
22In the first year Cyrus was king of Persia, the
LORD had Cyrus send an announcement to his
whole kingdom. This happened so the LORD's
message spoken by Jeremiah would come true.
He wrote:

23This is what Cyrus king of Persia says:
The LORD, the God of heaven, has given
me all the kingdoms of the earth, and he has
appointed me to build a Temple for him at
Jerusalem in Judah. Now may the LORD your
God be with all of you who are his people.
You are free to go to Jerusalem.

Sabbath rest The Law said that every seventh year the land was not to be farmed. See Leviticus 25:1-7.

ANGER

One Mad Mom

Cari Lightner was only thirteen years old when a drunk driver swerved off the road and killed her.

When the police arrested the driver, they discovered he had been arrested many times before for drunk driving. Still, they told Cari's mother, Candy, that this man would probably go free. There were no laws that could keep him in jail.

How could someone kill her daughter and go free? In her anger, Candy declared to friends, "I'm going to start an organization." She created Mothers Against Drunk Drivers (MADD), a group that would work to pass tough laws that would punish drunk drivers. And the work paid off. Within five years, every state in the United States had made its drunk-driving laws more strict.

MADD has made people aware of the problem of drinking and driving, and its efforts have saved lives.

Candy Lightner and the thousands of MADD members put their anger to work and brought about change. In **2 Chronicles 36:14–21**, you can see changes that occurred when God became angry with his people.

- What part did anger play in Candy's—and God's—actions?
- Based on this passage, what kinds of things make God angry?

CONSIDER . . .

- writing your congressional representative about an issue you think needs to be changed.
- thinking of one issue that makes you angry and then doing three specific things to change the situation.

FOR MORE, SEE . . .

- Exodus 32:19–35 (p. 89)
- Psalm 103:8 (p. 540)
- Luke 19:45–48 (p. 1045)

EZRA

Why Read This Book:

- See how God uses world events to help his people (Ezra 1).
- Learn how to trust God in the face of opposition (Ezra 4—6).
- Examine the cost of compromising beliefs (Ezra 7—10).

Behind the Scenes:

If you have moved from one community to another, you know what it's like to visit the old community. Nothing seems the same. Trees look larger, buildings older and people different. Everything seems a little familiar, but it's also very different. It's no longer home.

The people of Judah had been gone from Israel for seventy years, captives of the Babylonian Empire. The Persians had then conquered Babylon and let the captives go home. The Jews could return to Jerusalem and worship their God. What a cause for celebration!

But things were different now. The people were different. Now they were called Jews, not Israelites. Many of them spoke primarily Aramaic, not the old Hebrew. They used to be rural people; now they were urban people.

Their world was different too. Instead of being an independent nation, the returning Jews were more like a religious community. The people who had stayed behind resented the exiles for wanting their land back. And Jerusalem, which the Babylonians had destroyed, lay in ruins. So, despite the excitement, home wasn't like they left it. There was work to do.

The books of Ezra and Nehemiah (p. 427), which were originally one book, tell the story of these returning exiles. In general, the books focus on the rebuilding of the Temple (Ezra 1—7), the preserving of the faith (Ezra 8—10), and the rebuilding of Jerusalem's walls (Nehemiah).

Through it all, we often see people wanting to give up. We see leaders

WHERE THE ACTION WAS

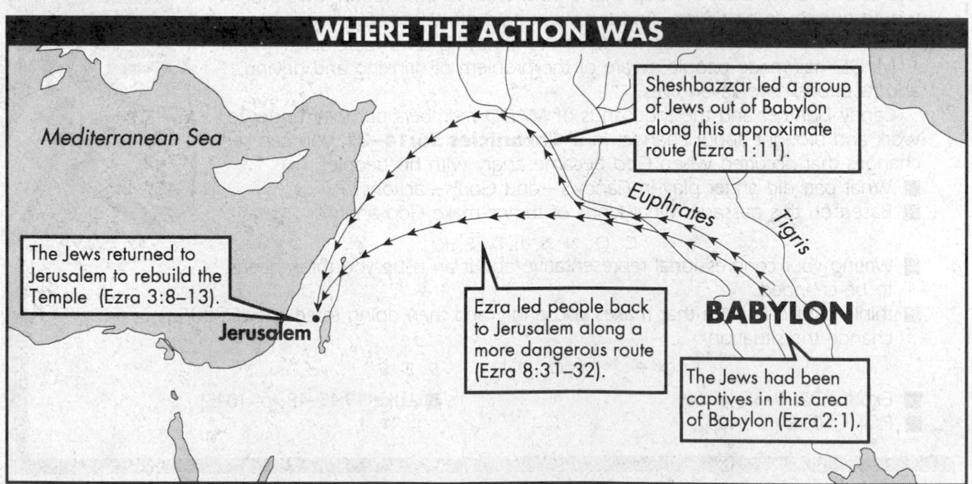
Mediterranean Sea
Sheshbazzar led a group of Jews out of Babylon along this approximate route (Ezra 1:11).
Euphrates
Tigris
The Jews returned to Jerusalem to rebuild the Temple (Ezra 3:8–13).
Jerusalem
Ezra led people back to Jerusalem along a more dangerous route (Ezra 8:31–32).
BABYLON
The Jews had been captives in this area of Babylon (Ezra 2:1).

WHEN THE ACTION WAS

1000BC — David was Israel's king
750BC — The Northern Kingdom (Israel) fell to Assyria; People of Judah taken into exile in Babylon
500BC — Jews began returning to Jerusalem from exile; Ezra returned to Jerusalem from exile; Nehemiah returned to Jerusalem from exile
250BC
BC/AD — Jesus was born

Behind the Scenes (cont.): challenging them and renewing their energy. And we see the people's faithfulness even when the obstacles seem impossible. Their story can be a comfort and a challenge to help us stick with our faith in tough times.

Cyrus Helps the Captives Return

1 In the first year Cyrus was king of Persia, the LORD caused Cyrus to send an announcement to his whole kingdom and to put it in writing. This happened so the LORD's message spoken by Jeremiah would come true. He wrote:

2This is what Cyrus king of Persia says:

The LORD, the God of heaven, has given all the kingdoms of the earth to me, and he has appointed me to build a Temple[d] for him at Jerusalem in Judah. 3May God be with all of you who are his people. You are free to go to Jerusalem in Judah and build the Temple of the LORD, the God of Israel, who is in Jerusalem. 4Those who stay behind, wherever they live, should support those who want to go. Give them silver and gold, supplies and cattle, and special gifts for the Temple of God in Jerusalem.

> **SIDELIGHT:** King Cyrus's decree granting religious freedom to the Jews apparently wasn't a special privilege for them alone (Ezra 1:4). Archaeologists have unearthed The Cyrus Cylinder, which reveals that Cyrus's policy extended to all people who had been taken captive by Babylon.

5Then the family leaders of Judah and Benjamin and the priests and Levites got ready to go to Jerusalem—everyone God had caused to want to go to Jerusalem to build the Temple of the LORD. 6All their neighbors helped them, giving them things made of silver and gold, along with supplies, cattle, valuable gifts, and special gifts for the Temple. 7Also, King Cyrus brought out the bowls and pans that belonged in the Temple of the LORD, which Nebuchadnezzar had taken from Jerusalem and put in the temple of his own god. 8Cyrus king of Persia had Mithredath the treasurer bring them and count them out for Sheshbazzar, the prince of Judah.

9He listed thirty gold dishes, one thousand silver dishes, twenty-nine pans, 10thirty gold bowls, four hundred ten matching silver bowls, and one thousand other pieces.

11There was a total of fifty-four hundred pieces of gold and silver. Sheshbazzar brought all these things along when the captives went from Babylon to Jerusalem.

The Captives Who Returned

2 These are the people of the area who returned from captivity, whom Nebuchadnezzar king of Babylon had taken away to Babylon.

> **SIDELIGHT:** When Cyrus sent the Jews back to Jerusalem, he had them take thirty gold dishes, one thousand silver dishes, twenty-nine silver pans, thirty gold bowls, and four hundred ten silver bowls (Ezra 1:9)—valuables that had been taken from the Temple in Jerusalem by King Nebuchadnezzar when he destroyed it (2 Kings 25:8–17, p. 357). Hope he sent a dishwasher, too!

They returned to Jerusalem and Judah, each going back to his own town. 2These people returned with Zerubbabel, Jeshua, Nehemiah, Seraiah, Reelaiah, Mordecai, Bilshan, Mispar, Bigvai, Rehum, and Baanah.

These are the people from Israel: 3the descendants[d] of Parosh—2,172; 4the descendants of Shephatiah—372; 5the descendants of Arah—775; 6the descendants of Pahath-Moab (through the family of Jeshua and Joab)—2,812; 7the descendants of Elam—1,254; 8the descendants of Zattu—945; 9the descendants of Zaccai—760; 10the descendants of Bani—642; 11the descendants of Bebai—623; 12the descendants of Azgad—1,222; 13the descendants of Adonikam—666; 14the descendants of Bigvai—2,056; 15the descendants of Adin—454; 16the descendants of Ater (through the family of Hezekiah)—98; 17the descendants of Bezai—323; 18the descendants of Jorah—112; 19the descendants of Hashum—223; 20the descendants of Gibbar—95.

21These are the people from the towns: of Bethlehem—123; 22of Netophah—56; 23of Anathoth—128; 24of Azmaveth—42; 25of Kiriath Jearim, Kephirah, and Beeroth—743; 26of Ramah and Geba—621; 27of Micmash—122; 28of Bethel and Ai—223; 29of Nebo—52; 30of Magbish—156; 31of the other town of Elam—1,254; 32of Harim—320; 33of Lod, Hadid and Ono—725; 34of Jericho—345; 35of Senaah—3,630.

36These are the priests: the descendants of Jedaiah (through the family of Jeshua)—973; 37the descendants of Immer—1,052; 38the descendants of Pashhur—1,247; 39the descendants of Harim—1,017.

40These are the Levites: the descendants of Jeshua and Kadmiel (through the family of Hodaviah)—74.

41These are the singers: the descendants of Asaph—128.

42These are the gatekeepers of the Temple:[d] the descendants of Shallum, Ater, Talmon, Akkub, Hatita, and Shobai—139.

43These are the Temple servants: the descendants of Ziha, Hasupha, Tabbaoth, 44Keros, Siaha, Padon, 45Lebanah, Hagabah, Akkub, 46Hagab, Shalmai, Hanan, 47Giddel, Gahar, Reaiah, 48Rezin, Nekoda, Gazzam, 49Uzza, Paseah, Besai, 50Asnah, Meunim, Nephussim, 51Bakbuk, Hakupha, Harhur, 52Bazluth, Mehida, Harsha, 53Barkos, Sisera, Temah, 54Neziah, and Hatipha.

55These are the descendants of the servants of Solomon: the descendants of Sotai, Hassophereth, Peruda, 56Jaala, Darkon, Giddel, 57Shephatiah, Hattil, Pokereth-Hazzebaim, and Ami.

58The Temple servants and the descendants of the servants of Solomon numbered 392.

59Some people came to Jerusalem from the towns of Tel Melah, Tel Harsha, Kerub, Addon, and Immer, but they could not prove that their ancestors came from Israel. 60They were the descendants of Delaiah, Tobiah, and Nekoda—652.

61Also these priests: the descendants of Hobaiah, Hakkoz, and Barzillai, who had married a daughter of Barzillai from Gilead and was called by her family name.

62These people searched for their family records but could not find them. So they could not be priests, because they were thought to be unclean. 63The governor ordered them not to eat any of the food offered to God until a priest had settled this matter by using the Urim and Thummim.[d]

SIDELIGHT: Not all the Jews returned from exile when the Persians let them leave (Ezra 2:1–2). According to Babylonian records, some Jews had become prominent bankers, business people, and government officials in Babylon.

64The total number of those who returned was 42,360. 65This is not counting their 7,337 male and female servants and the 200 male and female singers they had with them. 66They had 736 horses, 245 mules, 67435 camels, and 6,720 donkeys.

68When they arrived at the Temple of the LORD in Jerusalem, some of the leaders of families gave offerings to rebuild the Temple of God on the same site as before. 69They gave as much as they could to the treasury to rebuild the Temple—about 1,100 pounds of gold, about 6,000 pounds of silver, and 100 pieces of clothing for the priests.

70All the Israelites settled in their hometowns. The priests, Levites, singers, gatekeepers, and Temple servants, along with some of the other people, settled in their own towns as well.

Rebuilding the Altar

3 In the seventh month, after the Israelites were settled in their hometowns, they met together in Jerusalem. 2Then Jeshua son of Jozadak and his fellow priests joined Zerubbabel son of Shealtiel and began to build the altar of the God of Israel where they could offer burnt offerings, just as it is written in the Teachings of Moses, the man of God. 3Even though they were afraid of the people living around them, they built the altar where it had been before. And they offered burnt offerings on it to the LORD morning and evening. 4Then, to obey what was written, they celebrated the Feast[d] of Shelters. They offered the right number of sacrifices for each day of the festival. 5After the Feast of Shelters, they had regular sacrifices every day, as well as sacrifices for the New Moon[d] and all the festivals commanded by the LORD. Also there were special offerings brought as gifts to the LORD. 6On the first day of the seventh month they began to bring burnt offerings to the LORD, but the foundation of the LORD's Temple[d] had not yet been laid.

Rebuilding the Temple

7Then they gave money to the bricklayers and carpenters. They also gave food, wine, and oil to the cities of Sidon and Tyre so they would float cedar logs from Lebanon to the seacoast town of Joppa. Cyrus king of Persia had given permission for this.

8In the second month of the second year after their arrival at the Temple[d] of God in Jerusalem, Zerubbabel son of Shealtiel, Jeshua son of Jozadak, their fellow priests and Levites, and all who had returned from captivity to Jerusalem began to work. They chose Levites twenty years old and older to be in charge of the building of the Temple of the LORD. 9These men were in charge of the work of building the Temple of God: Jeshua and his sons and brothers; Kadmiel and his sons who were the descendants of Hodaviah; and the sons of Henadad and their sons and brothers. They were all Levites.

10The builders finished laying the foundation of the Temple of the LORD. Then the priests, dressed in their robes, stood with their trumpets, and the Levites, the sons of Asaph, stood with their cymbals. They all took their places and praised the LORD just as David king of Israel had said to do.

11With praise and thanksgiving, they sang to the LORD:

"He is good;
his love for Israel continues forever."

And then all the people shouted loudly, "Praise the LORD! The foundation of his Temple has been laid." 12But many of the older priests, Levites, and family leaders who had seen the first Temple cried when they saw the foundation of this Temple. Most of the other people were shouting with joy. 13The people made so much noise it could be heard far away, and no one could tell the difference between the joyful shouting and the sad crying.

Enemies of the Rebuilding

4 When the enemies of the people of Judah and Benjamin heard that the returned captives were building a Temple[d] for the LORD, the God of Israel, 2they came to Zerubbabel and the leaders of the families. The enemies said, "Let us help you build, because we are like you and want to worship your God. We have been offering sacrifices to him since the time of Esarhaddon king of Assyria, who brought us here."

3But Zerubbabel, Jeshua, and the leaders of Israel answered, "You will not help us build a Temple to our God. We will build it ourselves for the LORD, the God of Israel, as King Cyrus, the king of Persia, commanded us to do."

4Then the people around them tried to discourage the people of Judah by making them afraid to build. 5Their enemies hired others to delay the building plans during the time Cyrus was king of Persia. And it continued to the time Darius was king of Persia.

More Problems for the Builders

6When Xerxes first became king, those enemies wrote a letter against the people of Judah and Jerusalem.

7When Artaxerxes became king of Persia, Bishlam, Mithredath, Tabeel, and those with them wrote a letter to Artaxerxes. It was written in the Aramaic language and translated.

8Rehum the governor and Shimshai the governor's secretary wrote a letter against Jerusalem to Artaxerxes the king. It said:

9This letter is from Rehum the governor, Shimshai the secretary, and their fellow workers — the judges and important officers over the men who came from Tripolis, Persia, Erech, and Babylon, the Elamite people of Susa, 10and those whom the great and honorable Ashurbanipal forced out of their countries and settled in the city of Samaria and in other places of the Trans-Euphrates.

11(This is a copy of the letter they sent to Artaxerxes.)

To King Artaxerxes.
From your servants who live in Trans-Euphrates.

12King Artaxerxes, you should know that the Jewish people who came to us from you have gone to Jerusalem to rebuild that evil city that refuses to obey. They are fixing the walls and repairing the foundations of the buildings.

13Now, King Artaxerxes, you should know that if Jerusalem is built and its walls are fixed, Jerusalem will not pay taxes of any kind. Then the amount of money your government collects will be less. 14Since we must be loyal to the government, we don't want to see the king dishonored. So we are writing to let the king know. 15We suggest you search the records of the kings who ruled before you. You will find out that the city of Jerusalem refuses to obey and makes trouble for kings and areas controlled by Persia. Since long ago it has been a place where disobedience has started. That is why it was destroyed. 16We want you to know, King Artaxerxes, that if this city is rebuilt and its walls fixed, you will be left with nothing in Trans-Euphrates.

17King Artaxerxes sent this answer:

To Rehum the governor and Shimshai the secretary, to all their fellow workers living in Samaria, and to those in other places in Trans-Euphrates.

Greetings.

18The letter you sent to us has been translated and read to me. 19I ordered the records to be searched, and it was done. We found that Jerusalem has a history of disobedience to kings and has been a place of problems and trouble. 20Jerusalem has had powerful kings who have ruled over the whole area of Trans-Euphrates, and taxes of all kinds have

SIDELIGHT: The Old Testament was originally written in Hebrew, right? Well, not all of it. Ezra 4:8—6:18 and 7:12–26 were written in Aramaic, which was the language Jesus would speak centuries later. Three other Old Testament passages were also written in Aramaic (Genesis 31:47, p. 37; Jeremiah 10:11, p. 703; and Daniel 2:4—7:28, p. 807).

been paid to them. 21Now, give an order for
those men to stop work. The city of Jerusalem will not be rebuilt until I say so. 22Make
sure you do this, because if they continue, it
will hurt the government.

23A copy of the letter that King Artaxerxes sent
was read to Rehum and Shimshai the secretary
and the others. Then they quickly went to the
Jewish people in Jerusalem and forced them to
stop building.

24So the work on the Temple[d] of God in Jerusalem stopped until the second year Darius was king
of Persia.

Tattenai's Letter to Darius

5 The prophets Haggai and Zechariah, a
descendant of Iddo, prophesied to the Jewish
people in Judah and Jerusalem in the name of the
God of Israel, who was over them. 2Then Zerubbabel son of Shealtiel and Jeshua son of Jozadak
started working again to rebuild the Temple[d] of
God in Jerusalem. And the prophets of God were
there, helping them.

3At that time Tattenai, the governor of Trans-
Euphrates, and Shethar-Bozenai, and their fellow
workers went to the Jewish people and asked,
"Who gave you permission to rebuild this Temple
and fix these walls?" 4They also asked, "What are
the names of the men working on this building?"
5But their God was watching over the older leaders of the Jewish people. The builders were not
stopped until a report could go to King Darius and
his written answer could be received.

6This is a copy of the letter that was sent to
King Darius by Tattenai, the governor of Trans-
Euphrates, Shethar-Bozenai, and the other important officers of Trans-Euphrates. 7This is what was
said in the report they sent to him:

To King Darius.

Greetings. May you have peace.

8King Darius, you should know that we
went to the district of Judah where the Temple of the great God is. The people are building that Temple with large stones, and they
are putting timbers in the walls. They are
working very hard and are building very fast.

9We asked their older leaders, "Who gave
you permission to rebuild this Temple and
these walls?" 10We also asked for their
names, and we wrote down the names of
their leaders so you would know who they
are.

11This is the answer they gave to us: "We
are the servants of the God of heaven and
earth. We are rebuilding the Temple that a
great king of Israel built and finished many
years ago. 12But our ancestors made the God
of heaven angry, so he handed them over to
Nebuchadnezzar king of Babylon, who destroyed this Temple and took the people to
Babylon as captives.

13"Later, in the first year Cyrus was king
of Babylon, he gave a special order for this
Temple to be rebuilt. 14Cyrus brought out
from the temple in Babylon the gold and silver bowls and pans that came from the Temple of God. Nebuchadnezzar had taken them
from the Temple in Jerusalem and had put
them in the temple in Babylon.

"Then King Cyrus gave them to Sheshbazzar, his appointed governor. 15Cyrus said to
him, 'Take these gold and silver bowls and
pans, and put them back in the Temple in
Jerusalem and rebuild the Temple of God
where it was.' 16So Sheshbazzar came and
laid the foundations of the Temple of God in
Jerusalem. From that day until now the
work has been going on, but it is not yet
finished."

17Now, if the king wishes, let a search be
made in the royal records of Babylon. See if
King Cyrus gave an order to rebuild this
Temple in Jerusalem. Then let the king write
us and tell us what he has decided.

The Order of Darius

6 So King Darius gave an order to search the
records kept in the treasury in Babylon. 2A
scroll was found in Ecbatana, the capital city of
Media. This is what was written on it:

Note:

3King Cyrus gave an order about the Temple[d] of God in Jerusalem in the first year he
was king. This was the order:

"Let the Temple be rebuilt as a place to
present sacrifices. Let its foundations be laid;
it should be ninety feet high and ninety feet
wide. 4It must have three layers of large
stones and then one layer of timbers. The
costs should be paid from the king's treasury.
5The gold and silver utensils from the Temple of God should be put back in their places.
Nebuchadnezzar took them from the Temple in Jerusalem and brought them to Babylon, but they are to be put back in the Temple of God in Jerusalem."

6Now then, Tattenai, governor of Trans-
Euphrates, Shethar-Bozenai, and all the officers of that area, stay away from there. 7Do
not bother the work on that Temple of God.
Let the governor of the Jewish people and
the older Jewish leaders rebuild this Temple
where it was before.

8Also, I order you to do this for those older
leaders of the Jewish people who are build-

ing this Temple: The cost of the building is
to be fully paid from the royal treasury, from
taxes collected from Trans-Euphrates. Do
this so the work will not stop. 9Give those
people anything they need—young bulls,
male sheep, or lambs for burnt offerings to
the God of heaven, or wheat, salt, wine, or
olive oil. Give the priests in Jerusalem anything they ask for every day without fail.
10Then they may offer sacrifices pleasing to
the God of heaven, and they may pray for
the life of the king and his sons.
11Also, I give this order: If anyone changes
this order, a wood beam is to be pulled from
his house and driven through his body. Because of his crime, make his house a pile of

SIDELIGHT: King Darius didn't like his orders to be questioned. If you changed what he said, a wooden beam was to be taken from your house and driven through your body (Ezra 6:11). According to other sources, Darius impaled three thousand Babylonians when he captured their city.

ruins. 12God has chosen Jerusalem as the
place he is to be worshiped. May he punish
any king or person who tries to change this
order and destroy this Temple.

I, Darius, have given this order. Let it be obeyed quickly and carefully.

Completion of the Temple

13So, Tattenai, the governor of Trans-
Euphrates, Shethar-Bozenai, and their fellow
workers carried out King Darius' order quickly
and carefully. 14The older Jewish leaders continued to build and were successful because of the
preaching of Haggai the prophet[d] and Zechariah,
a descendant of Iddo. They finished building the
Temple[d] as the God of Israel had commanded and
as kings Cyrus, Darius, and Artaxerxes of Persia
had ordered. 15The Temple was finished on the
third day of the month of Adar in the sixth year
Darius was king.
16Then the people of Israel celebrated and gave
the Temple to God to honor him. Everybody was
happy: the priests, the Levites, and the rest of the
Jewish people who had returned from captivity.
17They gave the Temple to God by offering a hundred bulls, two hundred male sheep, and four
hundred lambs as sacrifices. And as an offering to
forgive the sins of all Israel, they offered twelve
male goats, one goat for each tribe[d] in Israel.
18Then they put the priests and the Levites into
their separate groups. Each group had a certain
time to serve God in the Temple at Jerusalem as
it is written in the Book of Moses.

The Passover Is Celebrated

19The Jewish people who returned from captivity celebrated the Passover[d] on the fourteenth day
of the first month. 20The priests and Levites had
made themselves clean.[d] Then the Levites killed
the Passover lambs for all the people who had returned from captivity, for their relatives the
priests, and for themselves. 21So all the people of
Israel who returned from captivity ate the Passover lamb. So did the people who had given up
the unclean ways of their non-Jewish neighbors in
order to worship the LORD, the God of Israel.
22For seven days they celebrated the Feast[d] of Unleavened Bread in a very joyful way. The LORD
had made them happy by changing the mind of
the king of Assyria so that he helped them in the
work on the Temple of the God of Israel.

Ezra Comes to Jerusalem

7 After these things[n] during the rule of Artaxerxes king of Persia, Ezra came up from Babylon. Ezra was the son of Seraiah, the son of Azariah, the son of Hilkiah, 2the son of Shallum, the
son of Zadok, the son of Ahitub, 3the son of Amariah, the son of Azariah, the son of Meraioth, 4the
son of Zerahiah, the son of Uzzi, the son of Bukki,
5the son of Abishua, the son of Phinehas, the son
of Eleazar, the son of Aaron the high priest. 6This
Ezra came to Jerusalem from Babylon. He was a
teacher and knew well the Teachings of Moses
that had been given by the LORD, the God of Israel. Ezra received everything he asked for from
the king, because the LORD his God was helping
him. 7In the seventh year of King Artaxerxes more
Israelites came to Jerusalem. Among them were
priests, Levites, singers, gatekeepers, and Temple[d]
servants.
8Ezra arrived in Jerusalem in the fifth month of
Artaxerxes' seventh year as king. 9Ezra had left
Babylon on the first day of the first month, and he
arrived in Jerusalem on the first day of the fifth

SIDELIGHT: Ezra's journey from Babylon to Jerusalem was about nine hundred miles—about the distance from Chicago to Dallas. But because there were no freeways in the Near East, the trip took about four months (Ezra 7:9).

After these things There is a time period of about sixty years between chapters six and seven.

month, because God was helping him. 10Ezra had worked hard to know and obey the Teachings of the LORD and to teach his rules and commands to the Israelites.

SIDELIGHT: Ezra is known as the "Father of Judaism" for his role in preserving the faith (Ezra 7:10). Tradition credits him with dictating from memory ninety-four books (including twenty-four in the Old Testament) that might otherwise have been lost or burned during the Exile.

Artaxerxes' Letter to Ezra

11King Artaxerxes had given a letter to Ezra, a priest and teacher who taught about the commands and laws the LORD gave Israel. This is a copy of the letter:

12From Artaxerxes, king of kings, to Ezra the priest, a teacher of the Law of the God of heaven.

Greetings.

13Now I give this order: Any Israelite in my kingdom who wishes may go with you to Jerusalem, including priests and Levites. 14Ezra, you are sent by the king and the seven people who advise him to ask how Judah and Jerusalem are obeying the Law of your God, which you are carrying with you. 15Also take with you the silver and gold that the king and those who advise him have given freely to the God of Israel, whose Temple[d] is in Jerusalem. 16Also take the silver and gold you receive from the area of Babylon. Take the offerings the Israelites and their priests have given as gifts for the Temple of your God in Jerusalem. 17With this money buy bulls, male sheep, and lambs, and the grain offerings and drink offerings that go with those sacrifices. Then sacrifice them on the altar in the Temple of your God in Jerusalem.

18You and your fellow Jews may spend the silver and gold left over as you want and as God wishes. 19Take to the God of Jerusalem all the utensils for worship in the Temple of your God, 20which we have given you. Use the royal treasury to pay for anything else you need for the Temple of your God.

21Now I, King Artaxerxes, give this order to all the men in charge of the treasury of Trans-Euphrates: Give Ezra, a priest and a teacher of the Law of the God of heaven, whatever he asks for. 22Give him up to seventy-five hundred pounds of silver, six hundred bushels of wheat, six hundred gallons of wine, and six hundred gallons of olive oil. And give him as much salt as he wants. 23Carefully give him whatever the God of heaven wants for the Temple of the God of heaven. We do not want God to be angry with the king and his sons. 24Remember, you must not make these people pay taxes of any kind: priests, Levites, singers, gatekeepers, Temple servants, and other workers in this Temple of God.

25And you, Ezra, use the wisdom you have from your God to choose judges and lawmakers to rule the Jewish people of Trans-Euphrates. They know the laws of your God, and you may teach anyone who does not know them. 26Whoever does not obey the law of your God or of the king must be punished. He will be killed, or sent away, or have his property taken away, or be put in jail.

27Praise the LORD, the God of our ancestors. He caused the king to want to honor the Temple of the LORD in Jerusalem. 28The LORD has shown me, Ezra, his love in the presence of the king, those who advise the king, and the royal officers. Because the LORD my God was helping me, I had courage, and I gathered the leaders of Israel to return with me.

Leaders Who Returned with Ezra

8 These are the leaders of the family groups and those who were listed with them who came back with me from Babylon during the rule of King Artaxerxes.

2From the descendants[d] of Phinehas: Gershom.

From the descendants of Ithamar: Daniel.

From the descendants of David: Hattush 3of the descendants of Shecaniah.

From the descendants of Parosh: Zechariah, with one hundred fifty men.

4From the descendants of Pahath-Moab: Eliehoenai son of Zerahiah, with two hundred men.

5From the descendants of Zattu: Shecaniah son of Jahaziel, with three hundred men.

6From the descendants of Adin: Ebed son of Jonathan, with fifty men.

7From the descendants of Elam: Jeshaiah son of Athaliah, with seventy men.

8From the descendants of Shephatiah: Zebadiah son of Michael, with eighty men.

9From the descendants of Joab: Obadiah son of Jehiel, with two hundred eighteen men.

10From the descendants of Bani: Shelomith son of Josiphiah, with one hundred sixty men.

11From the descendants of Bebai: Zechariah son of Bebai, with twenty-eight men.

12From the descendants of Azgad: Johanan son of Hakkatan, with one hundred ten men. 13From the descendants of Adonikam, these were the last ones: Eliphelet, Jeuel, and Shemaiah, with sixty men. 14From the descendants of Bigvai: Uthai and Zaccur, with seventy men.

The Return to Jerusalem

15I called all those people together at the canal that flows toward Ahava, where we camped for three days. I checked all the people and the priests, but I did not find any Levites. 16So I called these leaders: Eliezer, Ariel, Shemaiah, Elnathan, Jarib, Elnathan, Nathan, Zechariah, and Meshullam. And I called Joiarib and Elnathan, who were teachers. 17I sent these men to Iddo, the leader at Casiphia, and told them what to say to Iddo and his relatives, who are the Temple[d] servants in Casiphia. I sent them to bring servants to us for the Temple[d] of our God. 18Our God was helping us, so Iddo's relatives gave us Sherebiah, a wise man from the descendants of Mahli son of Levi, who was the son of Israel. And they brought Sherebiah's sons and brothers, for a total of eighteen men. 19And they brought to us Hashabiah and Jeshaiah from the descendants of Merari, and his brothers and nephews. In all there were twenty men. 20They also brought two hundred twenty of the Temple servants, a group David and the officers had set up to help the Levites. All of those men were listed by name.

21There by the Ahava Canal, I announced we would all give up eating and humble ourselves before our God. We would ask God for a safe trip for ourselves, our children, and all our possessions. 22I was ashamed to ask the king for soldiers and horsemen to protect us from enemies on the road. We had said to the king, "Our God helps everyone who obeys him, but he is very angry with all who reject him." 23So we gave up eating and prayed to our God about our trip, and he answered our prayers.

24Then I chose twelve of the priests who were leaders, Sherebiah, Hashabiah, and ten of their relatives. 25I weighed the offering of silver and gold and the utensils given for the Temple of our God, and I gave them to the twelve priests I had chosen. The king, the people who advised him, his officers, and all the Israelites there with us had given these things for the Temple. 26I weighed out and gave them about fifty thousand pounds of silver, about seventy-five hundred pounds of silver objects, and about seventy-five hundred pounds of gold. 27I gave them twenty gold bowls that weighed about nineteen pounds and two fine pieces of polished bronze that were as valuable as gold.

28Then I said to the priests, "You and these utensils belong to the LORD for his service. The silver and gold are gifts to the LORD, the God of your ancestors. 29Guard these things carefully. In Jerusalem, weigh them in front of the leading priests, Levites, and the leaders of the family groups of Israel in the rooms of the Temple of the LORD." 30So the priests and Levites accepted the silver, the gold, and the utensils that had been weighed to take them to the Temple of our God in Jerusalem.

31On the twelfth day of the first month we left the Ahava Canal and started toward Jerusalem. Our God helped us and protected us from enemies and robbers along the way. 32Finally we arrived in Jerusalem where we rested three days.

33On the fourth day we weighed out the silver, the gold, and the utensils in the Temple of our God. We handed them to the priest Meremoth son of Uriah. Eleazar son of Phinehas was with him, as were the Levites Jozabad son of Jeshua and Noadiah son of Binnui. 34We checked everything by number and by weight, and the total weight was written down.

35Then the captives who returned made burnt offerings to the God of Israel. They sacrificed twelve bulls for all Israel, ninety-six male sheep, and seventy-seven lambs. For a sin offering there were twelve male goats. All this was a burnt offering to the LORD. 36They took King Artaxerxes' orders to the royal officers and to the governors of Trans-Euphrates. Then these men gave help to the people and the Temple of God.

Ezra's Prayer

9 After these things had been done, the leaders came to me and said, "Ezra, the Israelites, including the priests and Levites, have not kept themselves separate from the people around us. Those neighbors do evil things, as the Canaanites, Hittites, Perizzites, Jebusites, Ammonites, Moabites, Egyptians, and Amorites did. 2The Israelite men and their sons have married these women. They have mixed the people who belong to God with the people around them. The leaders and officers of Israel have led the rest of the Israelites to do this unfaithful thing."

3When I heard this, I angrily tore my robe and coat, pulled hair from my head and beard, and sat down in shock. 4Everyone who trembled in fear at the word of the God of Israel gathered around me because of the unfaithfulness of the captives who had returned. I sat there in shock until the evening sacrifice.

5At the evening sacrifice I got up from where I had shown my shame. My robe and coat were torn, and I fell on my knees with my hands spread out to the LORD my God. 6I prayed,

"My God, I am too ashamed and embarrassed to lift up my face to you, my God, because our sins are so many. They are higher than our heads. Our guilt even reaches up to the sky. 7From the days of our ancestors until now, our guilt has been great. Because of our sins, we, our kings, and our priests have been punished by the sword and captivity. Foreign kings have taken away our things and shamed us, even as it is today.

SIDELIGHT: When Ezra got upset, he tore his clothes and pulled hair out of his head and beard—the only person to do that in the Bible (Ezra 9:3). Nehemiah had a less painful approach—for him, at least. He pulled out the hair of people at whom he was angry (Nehemiah 13:25, p. 440).

8"But now, for a short time, the LORD our God has been kind to us. He has let some of us come back from captivity and has let us live in safety in his holy place. And so our God gives us hope and a little relief from our slavery. 9Even though we are slaves, our God has not left us. He caused the kings of Persia to be kind to us and has given us new life. We can rebuild the Temple[d] and repair its ruins. And he has given us a wall to protect us in Judah and Jerusalem.

10"But now, our God, what can we say after you have done all this? We have disobeyed your commands 11that you gave through your servants the prophets.[d] You said, 'The land you are entering to own is ruined; the people living there have spoiled it by the evil they do. Their evil filled the land with uncleanness[d] from one end to the other. 12So do not let your daughters marry their sons, and do not let their daughters marry your sons. Do not wish for their peace or success. Then you will be strong and eat the good things of the land. Then you can leave this land to your descendants[d] forever.'

13"What has happened to us is our own fault. We have done evil things, and our guilt is great. But you, our God, have punished us less than we deserve; you have left a few of us alive. 14We should not again break your commands by allowing marriages with these wicked people. If we did, you would get angry enough to destroy us, and none of us would be left alive. 15LORD, God of Israel, by your goodness a few of us are left

FORGIVENESS

An Unexpected Visitor

"The Pope has been shot!" These words echoed throughout the world on May 13, 1981. Pope John Paul II had been shot in the stomach by Mehmet Ali Agca.

It took hours of surgery and weeks of painful rehabilitation for the Pope to regain his health. Yet he survived and returned to his duties. The terrorist was captured and imprisoned. It seemed the end of a near-fatal story.

But it wasn't.

Less than three years after the shooting, the Pope visited Agca in Rome's Rebibbia prison. Sitting in Agca's cell, John Paul held Agca's hand and spoke softly with him for twenty minutes.

What did the Pope say to the man who had tried to kill him? "I spoke to him as a brother whom I have pardoned, and who has my complete trust. . . . I was able to meet my assailant and repeat to him the pardon I gave him immediately."

Pope John Paul II showed love to Mehmet Ali Agca by forgiving him. **Ezra 9:1–9** tells how God showed love to his people by forgiving them.

- Did Agca or the Israelites deserve the love and forgiveness they received? Why or why not?
- When has God forgiven you when you felt you didn't deserve it?

CONSIDER. . .

- making a list of people who have offended you and then forgiving them in the same way God has forgiven you.
- doing one loving thing for someone who has been hard for you to love.

FOR MORE, SEE. . .

- Isaiah 1:18–20 (p. 618)
- Matthew 6:9–15 (p. 918)
- Romans 5:6–11 (p. 1145)

alive today. We admit that we are guilty and
none of us should be allowed to stand before
you."

The People Confess Sin

10 As Ezra was praying and confessing and
crying and throwing himself down in
front of the Temple,[d] a large group of Israelite
men, women, and children gathered around him
who were also crying loudly. 2Then Shecaniah
son of Jehiel the Elamite said to Ezra, "We have
been unfaithful to our God by marrying women
from the peoples around us. But even so, there is
still hope for Israel. 3Now let us make an agreement before our God. We will send away all these
women and their children as you and those who
respect the commands of our God advise. Let it be
done to obey God's Teachings. 4Get up, Ezra. You
are in charge, and we will support you. Have
courage and do it."

5So Ezra got up and made the priests, Levites,
and all the people of Israel promise to do what
was suggested; and they promised. 6Then Ezra
left the Temple and went to the room of Jehohanan son of Eliashib. While Ezra was there, he did
not eat or drink, because he was still sad about
the unfaithfulness of the captives who had returned.

7They sent an order in Judah and Jerusalem for
all the captives who had returned to meet together in Jerusalem. 8Whoever did not come to
Jerusalem within three days would lose his property and would no longer be a member of the
community of the returned captives. That was the
decision of the officers and older leaders.

9So within three days all the people of Judah
and Benjamin gathered in Jerusalem. It was the
twentieth day of the ninth month. All the people
were sitting in the open place in front of the Temple and were upset because of the meeting and
because it was raining. 10Ezra the priest stood up
and said to them, "You have been unfaithful and
have married non-Jewish women. You have made
Israel more guilty. 11Now, confess it to the LORD,
the God of your ancestors. Do his will and separate yourselves from the people living around you
and from your non-Jewish wives."

12Then the whole group answered Ezra with a
loud voice, "Ezra, you're right! We must do what
you say. 13But there are many people here, and
it's the rainy season. We can't stand outside, and
this problem can't be solved in a day or two, because we have sinned badly. 14Let our officers
make a decision for the whole group. Then let
everyone in our towns who has married a non-
Jewish woman meet with the older leaders and
judges of each town at a planned time, until the
hot anger of our God turns away from us." 15Only
Jonathan son of Asahel, Jahzeiah son of Tikvah,
Meshullam, and Shabbethai the Levite were
against the plan.

16So the returned captives did what was suggested. Ezra the priest chose men who were leaders of the family groups and named one from each
family division. On the first day of the tenth
month they sat down to study each case. 17By
the first day of the first month, they had finished
with all the men who had married non-Jewish
women.

Those Guilty of Marrying Non-Jewish Women

18These are the descendants[d] of the priests who
had married foreign women:

From the descendants of Jeshua son of Jozadak
and Jeshua's brothers: Maaseiah, Eliezer, Jarib,
and Gedaliah. 19(They all promised to divorce
their wives, and each one brought a male sheep
from the flock as a penalty offering.)

20From the descendants of Immer: Hanani and
Zebadiah.

21From the descendants of Harim: Maaseiah,
Elijah, Shemaiah, Jehiel, and Uzziah.

22From the descendants of Pashhur: Elioenai,
Maaseiah, Ishmael, Nethanel, Jozabad, and Elasah.

23Among the Levites: Jozabad, Shimei, Kelaiah
(also called Kelita), Pethahiah, Judah, and Eliezer.

24Among the singers: Eliashib.

Among the gatekeepers: Shallum, Telem, and
Uri.

25And among the other Israelites, these married
non-Jewish women:

From the descendants of Parosh: Ramiah, Iz-
ziah, Malkijah, Mijamin, Eleazar, Malkijah, and
Benaiah.

26From the descendants of Elam: Mattaniah,
Zechariah, Jehiel, Abdi, Jeremoth, and Elijah.

27From the descendants of Zattu: Elioenai, Eliashib, Mattaniah, Jeremoth, Zabad, and Aziza.

28From the descendants of Bebai: Jehohanan,
Hananiah, Zabbai, and Athlai.

29From the descendants of Bani: Meshullam,
Malluch, Adaiah, Jashub, Sheal, and Jeremoth.

30From the descendants of Pahath-Moab:
Adna, Kelal, Benaiah, Maaseiah, Mattaniah, Bezalel, Binnui, and Manasseh.

31From the descendants of Harim: Eliezer, Ishi-
jah, Malkijah, Shemaiah, Shimeon, 32Benjamin,
Malluch, and Shemariah.

33From the descendants of Hashum: Mattenai,
Mattattah, Zabad, Eliphelet, Jeremai, Manasseh,
and Shimei.

34From the descendants of Bani: Maadai, Am-
ram, Uel, 35Benaiah, Bedeiah, Keluhi, 36Vaniah,
Meremoth, Eliashib, 37Mattaniah, Mattenai, and
Jaasu.

38From the descendants of Binnui: Shimei,

39Shelemiah, Nathan, Adaiah, 40Macnadebai, Sha-
shai, Sharai, 41Azarel, Shelemiah, Shemariah,
42Shallum, Amariah, and Joseph.
43From the descendants of Nebo: Jeiel, Mattithiah, Zabad, Zebina, Jaddai, Joel, and Benaiah.
44All these men had married non-Jewish
women, and some of them had children by these
wives.

NEHEMIAH

Why Read This Book:

- Understand the importance of acting on what you believe (Nehemiah 1—5).
- Recognize how serving God sometimes means standing against those who don't serve him (Nehemiah 6—7).
- See the life-changing effects of believing God's word (Nehemiah 8—13).

Behind the Scenes:

Imagine a member of the president's cabinet leaving that prestigious office to trek on foot across a desert to rebuild a city destroyed one hundred forty years earlier.

That's about what Nehemiah did. He held a high office in the kingdom of Persia, which ruled virtually all of the Near East. He had power, prestige, and money.

Unlike many leaders in biblical times, whose high positions led them away from God, Nehemiah was not happy in his high office. He had heard about his own people, the Jews, struggling to rebuild the walls around Jerusalem. Ezra (see p. 416) had rebuilt the Temple and started religious reforms. But the city wall lay in ruin, leaving the city vulnerable to attackers.

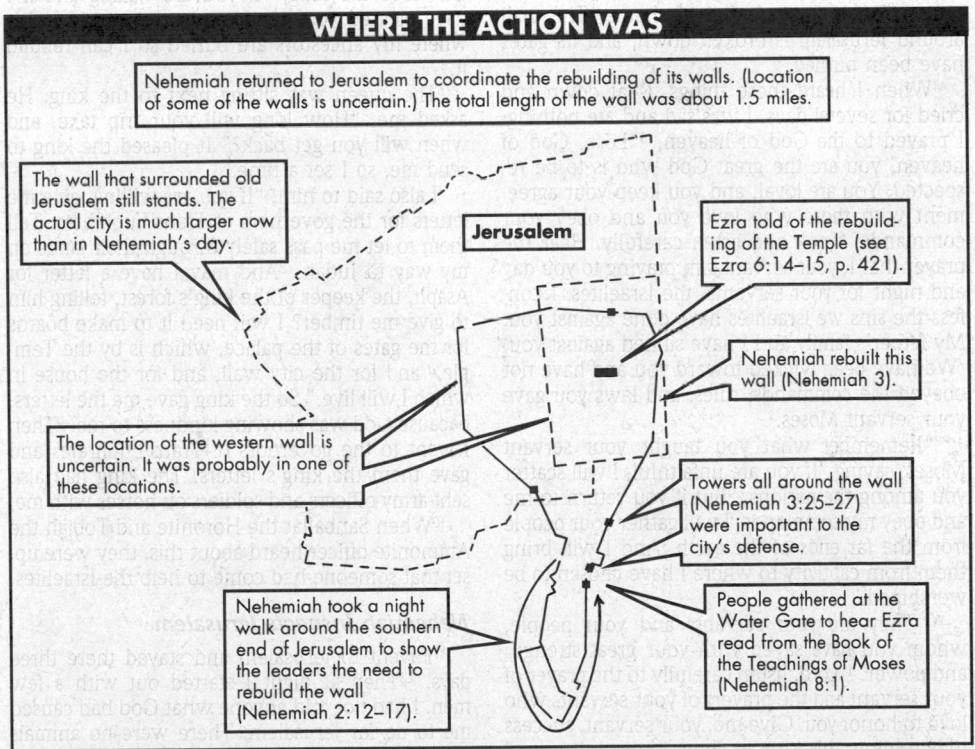

WHERE THE ACTION WAS

Nehemiah returned to Jerusalem to coordinate the rebuilding of its walls. (Location of some of the walls is uncertain.) The total length of the wall was about 1.5 miles.

The wall that surrounded old Jerusalem still stands. The actual city is much larger now than in Nehemiah's day.

Jerusalem

Ezra told of the rebuilding of the Temple (see Ezra 6:14–15, p. 421).

Nehemiah rebuilt this wall (Nehemiah 3).

The location of the western wall is uncertain. It was probably in one of these locations.

Towers all around the wall (Nehemiah 3:25–27) were important to the city's defense.

People gathered at the Water Gate to hear Ezra read from the Book of the Teachings of Moses (Nehemiah 8:1).

Nehemiah took a night walk around the southern end of Jerusalem to show the leaders the need to rebuild the wall (Nehemiah 2:12–17).

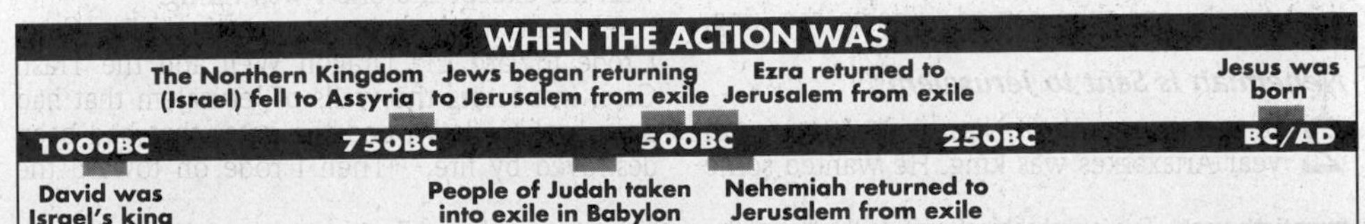

Behind the Scenes (cont.):

So Nehemiah asked for a change of assignment and was appointed governor of Jerusalem. He returned to the city to rally the people to rebuild the walls. Once the walls were up, he returned to his duties. But when religious corruption started, he returned to Jerusalem for a second term as governor.

The book of Nehemiah tells the story of this great leader. Parts of it (such as Nehemiah 1—7) read like a private journal, showing the joys and frustrations of trying to lead the people. Reading the book gives us a glimpse of a great leader. Nehemiah's organizational skills, prayer life, dependence on God, and commitment to justice shine as an example for everyone.

Nehemiah's Prayer

1 These are the words of Nehemiah son of Hacaliah.

In the month of Kislev in the twentieth year,[n] I, Nehemiah, was in the capital city of Susa. 2One of my brothers named Hanani came with some other men from Judah. I asked them about Jerusalem and the Jewish people who lived through the captivity.

3They answered me, "Those who are left from the captivity are back in Judah, but they are in much trouble and are full of shame. The wall around Jerusalem is broken down, and its gates have been burned."

4When I heard these things, I sat down and cried for several days. I was sad and ate nothing. I prayed to the God of heaven, 5"LORD, God of heaven, you are the great God who is to be respected. You are loyal, and you keep your agreement with those who love you and obey your commands. 6Look and listen carefully. Hear the prayer that I, your servant, am praying to you day and night for your servants, the Israelites. I confess the sins we Israelites have done against you. My father's family and I have sinned against you. 7We have been wicked toward you and have not obeyed the commands, rules, and laws you gave your servant Moses.

8"Remember what you taught your servant Moses, saying, 'If you are unfaithful, I will scatter you among the nations. 9But if you return to me and obey my commands, I will gather your people from the far ends of the earth. And I will bring them from captivity to where I have chosen to be worshiped.'

10"They are your servants and your people, whom you have saved with your great strength and power. 11Lord, listen carefully to the prayer of your servant and the prayers of your servants who love to honor you. Give me, your servant, success today; allow this king to show kindness to me."

I was the one who served wine to the king.

Nehemiah Is Sent to Jerusalem

2 It was the month of Nisan in the twentieth year Artaxerxes was king. He wanted some wine, so I took some and gave it to the king. I had not been sad in his presence before. 2So the king said, "Why does your face look sad even though you are not sick? Your heart must be sad."

Then I was very afraid. 3I said to the king, "May the king live forever! My face is sad because the city where my ancestors are buried lies in ruins, and its gates have been destroyed by fire."

4Then the king said to me, "What do you want?"

First I prayed to the God of heaven. 5Then I answered the king, "If you are willing and if I have pleased you, send me to the city in Judah where my ancestors are buried so I can rebuild it."

6The queen was sitting next to the king. He asked me, "How long will your trip take, and when will you get back?" It pleased the king to send me, so I set a time.

7I also said to him, "If you are willing, give me letters for the governors of Trans-Euphrates. Tell them to let me pass safely through their lands on my way to Judah. 8And may I have a letter for Asaph, the keeper of the king's forest, telling him to give me timber? I will need it to make boards for the gates of the palace, which is by the Temple,[d] and for the city wall, and for the house in which I will live." So the king gave me the letters, because God was showing kindness to me. 9Then I went to the governors of Trans-Euphrates and gave them the king's letters. The king had also sent army officers and soldiers on horses with me.

10When Sanballat the Horonite and Tobiah the Ammonite officer heard about this, they were upset that someone had come to help the Israelites.

Nehemiah Inspects Jerusalem

11I went to Jerusalem and stayed there three days. 12Then at night I started out with a few men. I had not told anyone what God had caused me to do for Jerusalem. There were no animals with me except the one I was riding.

13I went out at night through the Valley Gate. I rode toward the Dragon Well and the Trash Gate, inspecting the walls of Jerusalem that had been broken down and the gates that had been destroyed by fire. 14Then I rode on toward the

twentieth year This is probably referring to the twentieth year King Artaxerxes I ruled Persia.

Fountain Gate and the King's Pool, but there was not enough room for the animal I was riding to pass through. 15So I went up the valley at night, inspecting the wall. Finally, I turned and went back in through the Valley Gate. 16The guards did not know where I had gone or what I was doing. I had not yet said anything to the Jewish people, the priests, the important men, the officers, or any of the others who would do the work.

17Then I said to them, "You can see the trouble we have here. Jerusalem is a pile of ruins, and its gates have been burned. Come, let's rebuild the wall of Jerusalem so we won't be full of shame any longer." 18I also told them how God had been kind to me and what the king had said to me.

Then they answered, "Let's start rebuilding." So they began to work hard.

19But when Sanballat the Horonite, Tobiah the Ammonite officer, and Geshem the Arab heard about it, they made fun of us and laughed at us. They said, "What are you doing? Are you turning against the king?"

20But I answered them, "The God of heaven will give us success. We, his servants, will start rebuilding, but you have no share, claim, or memorial in Jerusalem."

Builders of the Wall

3 Eliashib the high priest and his fellow priests went to work and rebuilt the Sheep Gate. They gave it to the Lord's service and set its doors in place. They worked as far as the Tower of the Hundred and gave it to the Lord's service. Then they went on to the Tower of Hananel. 2Next to them, the men of Jericho built part of the wall, and Zaccur son of Imri built next to them.

3The sons of Hassenaah rebuilt the Fish Gate, laying its boards and setting its doors, bolts, and bars in place. 4Meremoth son of Uriah, the son of Hakkoz, made repairs next to them. Meshullam son of Berekiah, the son of Meshezabel, made repairs next to Meremoth. And Zadok son of Baana made repairs next to Meshullam. 5The men from Tekoa made repairs next to them, but the leading men of Tekoa would not work under their supervisors.

6Joiada son of Paseah and Meshullam son of Besodeiah repaired the Old Gate. They laid its boards and set its doors, bolts, and bars in place. 7Next to them, Melatiah from Gibeon, other men from Gibeon and Mizpah, and Jadon from Meronoth made repairs. These places were ruled by the governor of Trans-Euphrates. 8Next to them, Uzziel son of Harhaiah, a goldsmith, made repairs. And next to him, Hananiah, a perfume maker, made repairs. These men rebuilt Jerusalem as far as the Broad Wall. 9The next part of the wall was repaired by Rephaiah son of Hur, the ruler of half of the district of Jerusalem. 10Next to him, Jedaiah son of Harumaph made repairs opposite his own house. And next to him, Hattush son of Hashabneiah made repairs. 11Malkijah son of Harim and Hasshub son of Pahath-Moab repaired another part of the wall and the Tower of the Ovens. 12Next to them Shallum son of Hallohesh, the ruler of half of the district of Jerusalem, and his daughters made repairs.

SIDELIGHT: Did you know that women held construction jobs in Old Testament times? Check out Nehemiah 3:12.

13Hanun and the people of Zanoah repaired the Valley Gate, rebuilding it and setting its doors, bolts, and bars in place. They also repaired the five hundred yards of the wall to the Trash Gate.

14Malkijah son of Recab, the ruler of the district of Beth Hakkerem, repaired the Trash Gate. He rebuilt that gate and set its doors, bolts, and bars in place.

15Shallun son of Col-Hozeh, the ruler of the district of Mizpah, repaired the Fountain Gate. He rebuilt it, put a roof over it, and set its doors, bolts, and bars in place. He also repaired the wall of the Pool of Siloam next to the King's Garden all the way to the steps that went down from the older part of the city. 16Next to Shallun was Nehemiah[n] son of Azbuk, the ruler of half of the district of Beth Zur. He made repairs opposite the tombs of David and as far as the man-made pool and the House of the Heroes.

17Next to him, the Levites made repairs, working under Rehum son of Bani. Next to him, Hashabiah, the ruler of half of the district of Keilah, for his district. 18Next to him, Binnui son of Henadad and his Levites made repairs. Binnui was the ruler of the other half of the district of Keilah. 19Next to them, Ezer son of Jeshua, the ruler of Mizpah, repaired another part of the wall. He worked across from the way up to the armory, as far as the bend. 20Next to him, Baruch son of Zabbai worked hard on the wall that went from the bend to the entrance to the house of Eliashib, the high priest. 21Next to him, Meremoth son of Uriah, the son of Hakkoz, repaired the wall that went from the entrance to Eliashib's house to the far end of it.

22Next to him worked the priests from the surrounding area. 23Next to them, Benjamin and Hasshub made repairs in front of their own house. Next to them, Azariah son of Maaseiah, the son

Nehemiah This is a different Nehemiah than the one who wrote this book.

of Ananiah, made repairs beside his own house. 24Next to him, Binnui son of Henadad repaired the wall that went from Azariah's house to the bend and on to the corner. 25Palal son of Uzai worked across from the bend and by the tower on the upper palace, which is near the courtyard of the king's guard. Next to Palal, Pedaiah son of Parosh made repairs. 26The Temple[d] servants who lived on the hill of Ophel made repairs as far as a point opposite the Water Gate. They worked toward the east and the tower that extends from the palace. 27Next to them, the people of Tekoa repaired the wall from the great tower that extends from the palace to the wall of Ophel.

28The priests made repairs above the Horse Gate, each working in front of his own house. 29Next to them, Zadok son of Immer made repairs across from his own house. Next to him, Shemaiah son of Shecaniah, the guard of the East Gate, made repairs. 30Next to him, Hananiah son of Shelemiah, and Hanun, the sixth son of Zalaph, made repairs on another part of the wall. Next to them, Meshullam son of Berekiah made repairs across from where he lived. 31Next to him, Malkijah, one of the goldsmiths, made repairs. He worked as far as the house of the Temple servants and the traders, which is across from the Inspection Gate, and as far as the room above the corner of the wall. 32The goldsmiths and the traders made repairs between the room above the corner of the wall and the Sheep Gate.

Those Against the Rebuilding

4 When Sanballat heard we were rebuilding the wall, he was very angry, even furious. He made fun of the Jewish people. 2He said to his friends and those with power in Samaria, "What are these weak Jews doing? Will they rebuild the wall? Will they offer sacrifices? Can they finish it in one day? Can they bring stones back to life from piles of trash and ashes?"

> **SIDELIGHT:** Rebuilding the walls may have seemed impossible to people who opposed the work (Nehemiah 4:2–3), partly because many of the stones had cracked when the city was burned by the Babylonians. The Jews did rebuild some existing walls with the old materials, but they had to build brand new walls in some places.

3Tobiah the Ammonite, who was next to Sanballat, said, "If a fox climbed up on the stone wall they are building, it would break it down."

4I prayed, "Hear us, our God. We are hated. Turn the insults of Sanballat and Tobiah back on their own heads. Let them be captured and stolen like valuables. 5Do not hide their guilt or take away their sins so that you can't see them, because they have insulted the builders."

6So we rebuilt the wall to half its height, because the people were willing to work.

7But Sanballat, Tobiah, the Arabs, the Ammonites, and the people from Ashdod were very angry when they heard that the repairs to Jerusalem's walls were continuing and that the holes in the wall were being closed. 8So they all made plans to come to Jerusalem and fight and stir up trouble. 9But we prayed to our God and appointed guards to watch for them day and night.

10The people of Judah said, "The workers are getting tired. There is so much trash we cannot rebuild the wall."

11And our enemies said, "The Jews won't know or see anything until we come among them and kill them and stop the work."

12Then the Jewish people who lived near our enemies came and told us ten times, "Everywhere you turn, the enemy will attack us." 13So I put people behind the lowest places along the wall—the open places—and I put families together with their swords, spears, and bows. 14Then I looked around and stood up and said to the important men, the leaders, and the rest of the people: "Don't be afraid of them. Remember the Lord, who is great and powerful. Fight for your brothers, your sons and daughters, your wives, and your homes."

15Then our enemies heard that we knew about their plans and that God had ruined their plans. So we all went back to the wall, each to his own work.

16From that day on, half my people worked on the wall. The other half was ready with spears, shields, bows, and armor. The officers stood in back of the people of Judah 17who were building the wall. Those who carried materials did their work with one hand and carried a weapon with the other. 18Each builder wore his sword at his side as he worked. The man who blew the trumpet to warn the people stayed next to me.

19Then I said to the important men, the leaders, and the rest of the people, "This is a very big job. We are spreading out along the wall so that we are far apart. 20Wherever you hear the sound of the trumpet, assemble there. Our God will fight for us."

21So we continued to work with half the men holding spears from sunrise till the stars came out. 22At that time I also said to the people, "Let every man and his helper stay inside Jerusalem at night. They can be our guards at night and workmen during the day." 23Neither I, my brothers, my workers, nor the guards with me ever took off our

clothes. Each person carried his weapon even
when he went for water.

Nehemiah Helps Poor People

5 The men and their wives complained loudly
against their fellow Jews. 2Some of them
were saying, "We have many sons and daughters
in our families. To eat and stay alive, we need
grain."
3Others were saying, "We are borrowing
money against our fields, vineyards, and homes to
get grain because there is not much food."
4And still others were saying, "We are borrowing money to pay the king's tax on our fields and
vineyards. 5We are just like our fellow Jews, and
our sons are like their sons. But we have to
sell our sons and daughters as slaves. Some of our
daughters have already been sold. But there is
nothing we can do, because our fields and vineyards already belong to other people."
6When I heard their complaints about these
things, I was very angry. 7After I thought about it,
I accused the important people and the leaders,
"You are charging your own brothers too much
interest." So I called a large meeting to deal with
them. 8I said to them, "As much as possible, we
have bought freedom for our fellow Jews who had
been sold to foreigners. Now you are selling your
fellow Jews to us!" The leaders were quiet and
had nothing to say.
9Then I said, "What you are doing is not right.
Don't you fear God? Don't let our foreign enemies shame us. 10I, my brothers, and my men are
also lending money and grain to the people. But
stop charging them so much for this. 11Give back
their fields, vineyards, olive trees, and houses
right now. Also give back the extra amount you
charged—the hundredth part of the money,
grain, new wine, and oil."
12They said, "We will give it back and not demand anything more from them. We will do as
you say."
Then I called for the priests, and I made the
important men and leaders take an oath to do
what they had said. 13Also I shook out the folds
of my robe and said, "In this way may God shake
out everyone who does not keep his promise.
May God shake him out of his house and out of

HUNGER AND POVERTY

A Blanket of Love

Eleven-year-old Trevor Ferrell learned there were people living on the streets of Philadelphia—not far from his suburban home. Curious, he talked his parents into taking him downtown. There Trevor got out of the car and gave a homeless person a blanket.

When Trevor returned home, he searched for extra blankets and clothing, and he convinced his parents to take him downtown again and again to deliver such items. He talked to people at his church, and they donated food, clothing, and even a van to take things to the homeless.

Soon Trevor was in the newspapers, on television, even meeting the President of the United States! Trevor wanted to tell others what they could do to help those in need.

Now there is a home in Philadelphia called "Trevor's Place." People can live and be fed there. Trevor Ferrell began by giving a little of himself and was able to challenge others to do the same.

"One person can make a difference," Trevor says. "Just do what you can and follow your heart."

Nehemiah was also a person who made a difference for the poor. See how he helped them in **Nehemiah 5:1–11**.

- How did Nehemiah use his political power as governor of Judah to help the poor? How were Trevor's actions like Nehemiah's?
- How can you, like Trevor and Nehemiah, help people who are hungry?

CONSIDER

- helping low-income people in your community by giving nonperishable food to a food bank that distributes supplies to people in need.
- encouraging your government to take care of the needs of the poor by joining a Christian organization such as Bread for the World (801 Rhode Island Ave., NE, Washington, DC 20018).

FOR MORE, SEE

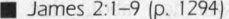

- Deuteronomy 15:7–8 (p. 175)
- Matthew 25:31–46 (p. 954)
- James 2:1–9 (p. 1294)

the things that are his. Let that person be shaken out and emptied!"

Then the whole group said, "Amen," and they praised the LORD. So the people did what they had promised.

14I was appointed governor in the land of Judah in the twentieth year of King Artaxerxes' rule. I was governor of Judah for twelve years, until his thirty-second year. During that time neither my brothers nor I ate the food that was allowed for a governor. 15But the governors before me had placed a heavy load on the people. They took about one pound of silver from each person, along with food and wine. The governors' helpers before me also controlled the people, but I did not do that, because I feared God. 16I worked on the wall, as did all my men who were gathered there. We did not buy any fields.

17Also, I fed one hundred fifty Jewish people and officers at my table, as well as those who came from the nations around us. 18This is what was prepared every day: one ox, six good sheep, and birds. And every ten days there were all kinds of wine. But I never demanded the food that was due a governor, because the people were already working very hard.

19Remember to be kind to me, my God, for all the good I have done for these people.

More Problems for Nehemiah

6 Then Sanballat, Tobiah, Geshem the Arab, and our other enemies heard that I had rebuilt the wall and that there was not one gap in it. But I had not yet set the doors in the gates. 2So Sanballat and Geshem sent me this message: "Come, Nehemiah, let's meet together in Kephirim on the plain of Ono."

But they were planning to harm me. 3So I sent messengers to them with this answer: "I am doing a great work, and I can't come down. I don't want the work to stop while I leave to meet you." 4Sanballat and Geshem sent the same message to me four times, and each time I sent back the same answer.

5The fifth time Sanballat sent his helper to me with the message, and in his hand was an unsealed letter. 6This is what was written:

> A report is going around to all the nations, and Geshem says it is true, that you and the Jewish people are planning to turn against the king and that you are rebuilding the wall. They say you are going to be their king 7and that you have appointed prophets[d] to announce in Jerusalem: "There is a king of Judah!" The king will hear about this. So come, let's discuss this together.

8So I sent him back this answer: "Nothing you are saying is really happening. You are just making it up in your own mind."

9Our enemies were trying to scare us, thinking, "They will get too weak to work. Then the wall will not be finished."

But I prayed, "God, make me strong."

10One day I went to the house of Shemaiah son of Delaiah, the son of Mehetabel. Shemaiah had to stay at home. He said, "Nehemiah, let's meet in the Temple[d] of God. Let's go inside the Temple and close the doors, because men are coming at night to kill you."

11But I said, "Should a man like me run away? Should I run for my life into the Temple? I will not go." 12I knew that God had not sent him but that Tobiah and Sanballat had paid him to prophesy against me. 13They paid him to frighten me so I would do this and sin. Then they could give me a bad name to shame me.

14I prayed, "My God, remember Tobiah and Sanballat and what they have done. Also remember the prophetess Noadiah and the other prophets who have been trying to frighten me."

> **SIDELIGHT:** Building the wall around Jerusalem took only fifty-two days (Nehemiah 6:15). But some archaeologists believe the wall would have been stronger if Nehemiah had slowed down some. Portions of the wall that have been uncovered show signs of the hasty construction. But Nehemiah might not have been able to slow down (see Nehemiah 4:15–18, p. 430)!

The Wall Is Finished

15The wall of Jerusalem was completed on the twenty-fifth day of the month of Elul. It took fifty-two days to rebuild. 16When all our enemies heard about it and all the nations around us saw it, they were shamed. They then understood that the work had been done with the help of our God.

17Also in those days the important men of Judah sent many letters to Tobiah, and he answered them. 18Many Jewish people had promised to be faithful to Tobiah, because he was the son-in-law of Shecaniah son of Arah. And Tobiah's son Jehohanan had married the daughter of Meshullam son of Berekiah. 19These important men kept telling me about the good things Tobiah was doing, and then they would tell Tobiah what I said about him. So Tobiah sent letters to frighten me.

7 After the wall had been rebuilt and I had set the doors in place, the gatekeepers, singers, and Levites were chosen. 2I put my brother Ha-

nani, along with Hananiah, the commander of the
palace, in charge of Jerusalem. Hananiah was
honest and feared God more than most people. 3I
said to them, "The gates of Jerusalem should not
be opened until the sun is hot. While the gatekeepers are still on duty, have them shut and bolt
the doors. Appoint people who live in Jerusalem
as guards, and put some at guard posts and some
near their own houses."

SIDELIGHT: Though Nehemiah says the city of Jerusalem was large (Nehemiah 7:4), two and a half Jerusalems would fit inside the U.S. Pentagon building in Washington, D.C. The ancient city probably took up only thirty or forty acres—one-sixteenth of a square mile.

The Captives Who Returned

4The city was large and roomy, but there were
few people in it, and the houses had not yet been
rebuilt. 5Then my God caused me to gather the
important men, the leaders, and the common
people so I could register them by families. I
found the family history of those who had returned first. This is what I found written there:

6These are the people of the area who returned
from captivity, whom Nebuchadnezzar king of
Babylon had taken away. They returned to Jerusalem and Judah, each going back to his own town.
7These people returned with Zerubbabel, Jeshua,
Nehemiah, Azariah, Raamiah, Nahamani, Mordecai, Bilshan, Mispereth, Bigvai, Nehum, and Baanah.

These are the people from Israel: 8the descendants[d] of Parosh—2,172; 9the descendants of
Shephatiah—372; 10the descendants of Arah—
652; 11the descendants of Pahath-Moab (through
the family of Jeshua and Joab)—2,818; 12the
descendants of Elam—1,254; 13the descendants
of Zattu—845; 14the descendants of Zaccai—
760; 15the descendants of Binnui—648; 16the
descendants of Bebai—628; 17the descendants of
Azgad—2,322; 18the descendants of Adonikam—667; 19the descendants of Bigvai—2,067;
20the descendants of Adin—655; 21the descendants of Ater (through Hezekiah)—98; 22the
descendants of Hashum—328; 23the descendants
of Bezai—324; 24the descendants of Hariph—
112; 25the descendants of Gibeon—95.

26These are the people from the towns of Bethlehem and Netophah—188; 27of Anathoth—
128; 28of Beth Azmaveth—42; 29of Kiriath Jearim, Kephirah, and Beeroth—743; 30of Ramah
and Geba—621; 31of Micmash—122; 32of
Bethel and Ai—123; 33of the other Nebo—52;
34of the other Elam—1,254; 35of Harim—320;
36of Jericho—345; 37of Lod, Hadid, and Ono—
721; 38of Senaah—3,930.

39These are the priests: the descendants of Jedaiah (through the family of Jeshua)—973; 40the
descendants of Immer—1,052; 41the descendants of Pashhur—1,247; 42the descendants
of Harim—1,017.

43These are the Levites: the descendants of
Jeshua (through Kadmiel through the family
of Hodaviah)—74.

44These are the singers: the descendants of
Asaph—148.

45These are the gatekeepers: the descendants
of Shallum, Ater, Talmon, Akkub, Hatita, and
Shobai—138.

46These are the Temple[d] servants: the descen-
dants of Ziha, Hasupha, Tabbaoth, 47Keros, Sia,
Padon, 48Lebana, Hagaba, Shalmai, 49Hanan, Gid-
del, Gahar, 50Reaiah, Rezin, Nekoda, 51Gazzam,
Uzza, Paseah, 52Besai, Meunim, Nephussim,
53Bakbuk, Hakupha, Harhur, 54Bazluth, Mehida,
Harsha, 55Barkos, Sisera, Temah, 56Neziah, and
Hatipha.

57These are the descendants of the servants of
Solomon: the descendants of Sotai, Sophereth,
Perida, 58Jaala, Darkon, Giddel, 59Shephatiah,
Hattil, Pokereth-Hazzebaim, and Amon.

60The Temple servants and the descendants of
the servants of Solomon totaled 392 people.

61Some people came to Jerusalem from the
towns of Tel Melah, Tel Harsha, Kerub, Addon,
and Immer, but they could not prove that their
ancestors came from Israel. Here are their names
and their number: 62the descendants of Delaiah,
Tobiah, and Nekoda—642.

63And these priests could not prove that their
ancestors came from Israel: the descendants of
Hobaiah, Hakkoz, and Barzillai. (He had married
a daughter of Barzillai from Gilead and was called
by her family name.)

64These people searched for their family
records, but they could not find them. So they
could not be priests, because they were thought
to be unclean.[d] 65The governor ordered them not
to eat any of the holy food until a priest settled
this matter by using the Urim and Thummim.[d]

66The total number of those who returned was
42,360. 67This is not counting their 7,337 male
and female servants and the 245 male and female
singers with them. 68They had 736 horses, 245
mules, 69435 camels, and 6,720 donkeys.

70Some of the family leaders gave to the work.
The governor gave to the treasury about 19
pounds of gold, 50 bowls, and 530 pieces of clothing for the priests. 71Some of the family leaders
gave about 375 pounds of gold and about 2,660
pounds of silver to the treasury for the work.
72The total of what the other people gave was

about 375 pounds of gold, about 2,250 pounds of silver, and 67 pieces of clothing for the priests. [73]So these people all settled in their own towns: the priests, the Levites, the gatekeepers, the singers, the Temple servants, and all the other people of Israel.

Ezra Reads the Teachings

By the seventh month the Israelites were settled in their own towns.

8 All the people of Israel gathered together in the square by the Water Gate. They asked Ezra the teacher to bring out the Book of the Teachings of Moses, which the LORD had given to Israel.

[2]So on the first day of the seventh month, Ezra the priest brought out the Teachings for the crowd. Men, women, and all who could listen and understand had gathered. [3]At the square by the Water Gate Ezra read the Teachings out loud from early morning until noon to the men, women, and everyone who could listen and understand. All the people listened carefully to the Book of the Teachings.

[4]Ezra the teacher stood on a high wooden platform that had been built just for this time. On his right were Mattithiah, Shema, Anaiah, Uriah, Hilkiah, and Maaseiah. And on his left were Pedaiah, Mishael, Malkijah, Hashum, Hashbaddanah, Zechariah, and Meshullam.

[5]Ezra opened the book in full view of everyone, because he was above them. As he opened it, all the people stood up. [6]Ezra praised the LORD, the great God, and all the people held up their hands and said, "Amen! Amen!" Then they bowed down and worshiped the LORD with their faces to the ground.

[7]These Levites explained the Teachings to the people as they stood there: Jeshua, Bani, Sherebiah, Jamin, Akkub, Shabbethai, Hodiah, Maaseiah, Kelita, Azariah, Jozabad, Hanan, and Pelaiah. [8]They read from the Book of the Teachings of God and explained what it meant so the people understood what was being read.

[9]Then Nehemiah the governor, Ezra the priest and teacher, and the Levites who were teaching said to all the people, "This is a holy day to the LORD your God. Don't be sad or cry." All the people had been crying as they listened to the words of the Teachings.

[10]Nehemiah said, "Go and enjoy good food and sweet drinks. Send some to people who have none, because today is a holy day to the Lord. Don't be sad, because the joy of the LORD will make you strong."

[11]The Levites helped calm the people, saying, "Be quiet, because this is a holy day. Don't be sad."

[12]Then all the people went away to eat and drink, to send some of their food to others, and to celebrate with great joy. They finally understood what they had been taught.

[13]On the second day of the month, the leaders of all the families, the priests, and the Levites met with Ezra the teacher. They gathered to study the words of the Teachings. [14]This is what they found written in the Teachings: The LORD commanded through Moses that the people of Israel were to live in shelters during the feast of the seventh month. [15]The people were supposed to preach this message and spread it through all their towns and in Jerusalem: "Go out into the mountains, and bring back branches from olive and wild olive trees, myrtle trees, palms, and shade trees. Make shelters with them, as it is written."

[16]So the people went out and got tree branches. They built shelters on their roofs,[n] in their courtyards, in the courtyards of the Temple,[d] in the square by the Water Gate, and in the square next to the Gate of Ephraim. [17]The whole group that had come back from captivity built shelters and lived in them. The Israelites had not done this since the time of Joshua son of Nun. And they were very happy.

[18]Ezra read to them every day from the Book of the Teachings, from the first day to the last. The people of Israel celebrated the feast for seven days, and then on the eighth day the people gathered as the law said.

Israel Confesses Sins

9 On the twenty-fourth day of that same month, the people of Israel gathered. They did not eat, and they wore rough cloth and put dust on their heads to show their sadness. [2]Those people whose ancestors were from Israel had separated themselves from all foreigners. They stood and confessed their sins and their ancestors' sins. [3]For a fourth of the day they stood where they were and read from the Book of the Teachings of the LORD their God. For another fourth of the day they confessed their sins and worshiped the LORD their God. [4]These Levites were standing on the stairs: Jeshua, Bani, Kadmiel, Shebaniah, Bunni, Sherebiah, Bani, and Kanani. They called out to the LORD their God with loud voices. [5]Then these Levites spoke: Jeshua, Kadmiel, Bani, Hashabneiah, Sherebiah, Hodiah, Shebaniah, and Pethahiah. They said, "Stand up and praise the LORD your God, who lives forever and ever."

roofs In Bible times houses were built with flat roofs. The roof was used for drying things such as flax and fruit. And it was used as an extra room, as a place for worship, and as a place to sleep in the summer.

The People's Prayer

"Blessed be your wonderful name.
It is more wonderful than all blessing and praise.
6You are the only LORD.
You made the heavens, even the highest heavens,
with all the stars.
You made the earth and everything on it,
the seas and everything in them;
you give life to everything.
The heavenly army worships you.

7"You are the LORD,
the God who chose Abram
and brought him out of Ur in Babylonia
and named him Abraham.
8You found him faithful to you,
so you made an agreement with him
to give his descendants[d] the land of the Canaanites,
Hittites, Amorites,
Perizzites, Jebusites, and Girgashites.
You have kept your promise,
because you do what is right.

9"You saw our ancestors suffering in Egypt
and heard them cry out at the Red Sea.[d]
10You did signs and miracles[d] against the king of Egypt,
and against all his officers and all his people,
because you knew how proud they were.
You became as famous as you are today.
11You divided the sea in front of our ancestors;
they walked through on dry ground.
But you threw the people chasing them into the deep water,
like a stone thrown into mighty waters.
12You led our ancestors with a pillar of cloud by day
and with a pillar of fire at night.
It lit the way
they were supposed to go.
13You came down to Mount Sinai
and spoke from heaven to our ancestors.
You gave them fair rules and true teachings,
good orders and commands.
14You told them about your holy Sabbath[d]
and gave them commands, orders, and teachings
through your servant Moses.
15When they were hungry, you gave them bread from heaven.
When they were thirsty, you brought them water from the rock.
You told them to enter and take over
the land you had promised to give them.

16"But our ancestors were proud and stubborn
and did not obey your commands.
17They refused to listen;
they forgot the miracles[d] you did for them.
So they became stubborn and turned against you,
choosing a leader to take them back to slavery.
But you are a forgiving God.
You are kind and full of mercy.
You do not become angry quickly, and you have great love.
So you did not leave them.
18Our ancestors even made an idol of a calf for themselves.
They said, 'This is your god, Israel,
who brought you up out of Egypt.'
They spoke against you.

19"You have great mercy,
so you did not leave them in the desert.
The pillar of cloud guided them by day,
and the pillar of fire led them at night,
lighting the way they were to go.
20You gave your good Spirit[d] to teach them.
You gave them manna[d] to eat
and water when they were thirsty.
21You took care of them for forty years in the desert;
they needed nothing.
Their clothes did not wear out,
and their feet did not swell.

22"You gave them kingdoms and nations;
you gave them more land.
They took over the country of Sihon king of Heshbon
and the country of Og king of Bashan.
23You made their children as many as the stars in the sky,
and you brought them into the land
that you told their fathers to enter and take over.
24So their children went into the land and took over.
The Canaanites lived there, but you defeated them for our ancestors.
You handed over to them the Canaanites,
their kings, and the people of the land.
Our ancestors could do what they wanted with them.
25They captured strong, walled cities and fertile land.
They took over houses full of good things,
wells that were already dug,
vineyards, olive trees, and many fruit trees.
They ate until they were full and grew fat;
they enjoyed your great goodness.

26"But they were disobedient and turned against you

and ignored your teachings.
Your prophets[d] warned them to come back to you,
but they killed those prophets
and spoke against you.
27So you handed them over to their enemies,
and their enemies treated them badly.
But in this time of trouble our ancestors cried out to you,
and you heard from heaven.
You had great mercy
and gave them saviors who saved them from the power of their enemies.
28But as soon as they had rest,
they again did what was evil.
So you left them to their enemies
who ruled over them.
When they cried out to you again,
you heard from heaven.
Because of your mercy, you saved them again and again.
29You warned them to return to your teachings,
but they were proud and did not obey your commands.
If someone obeys your laws, he will live,
but they sinned against your laws.
They were stubborn, unwilling, and disobedient.
30You were patient with them for many years
and warned them by your Spirit through the prophets,
but they did not pay attention.
So you handed them over to other countries.
31But because your mercy is great, you did not kill them all or leave them.
You are a kind and merciful God.
32"And so, our God, you are the great and mighty and wonderful God.
You keep your agreement of love.
Do not let all our trouble seem unimportant to you.
This trouble has come to us, to our kings and our leaders,
to our priests and prophets,
to our ancestors and all your people
from the days of the kings of Assyria
until today.
33You have been fair in everything that has happened to us;
you have been loyal, but we have been wicked.
34Our kings, leaders, priests, and ancestors did not obey your teachings;
they did not pay attention to the commands and warnings you gave them.
35Even when our ancestors were living in their kingdom,
enjoying all the good things you had given them,
enjoying the land that was fertile and full of room,
they did not stop their evil ways.
36"Look, we are slaves today
in the land you gave our ancestors.
They were to enjoy its fruit and its good things,
but look, we are slaves here.
37The land's great harvest belongs to the kings you have put over us
because of our sins.
Those kings rule over us and our cattle as they please,
so we are in much trouble.

The People's Agreement

38"Because of all this, we are making an agreement in writing, and our leaders, Levites, and priests are putting their seals[d] on it."

10 These are the men who sealed the agreement:
Nehemiah the governor, son of Hacaliah.
2Zedekiah, Seraiah, Azariah, Jeremiah, 3Pash-
hur, Amariah, Malkijah, 4Hattush, Shebaniah,
Malluch, 5Harim, Meremoth, Obadiah, 6Daniel,
Ginnethon, Baruch, 7Meshullam, Abijah, Mijamin, 8Maaziah, Bilgai, and Shemaiah. These
are the priests.
9These are the Levites who sealed it: Jeshua
son of Azaniah, Binnui of the sons of Henadad,
Kadmiel, 10and their fellow Levites: Shebaniah,
Hodiah, Kelita, Pelaiah, Hanan, 11Mica, Rehob,
Hashabiah, 12Zaccur, Sherebiah, Shebaniah, 13Ho-
diah, Bani, and Beninu.
14These are the leaders of the people who
sealed the agreement: Parosh, Pahath-Moab,
Elam, Zattu, Bani, 15Bunni, Azgad, Bebai, 16Ado-
nijah, Bigvai, Adin, 17Ater, Hezekiah, Azzur,
18Hodiah, Hashum, Bezai, 19Hariph, Anathoth,
Nebai, 20Magpiash, Meshullam, Hezir, 21Me-
shezabel, Zadok, Jaddua, 22Pelatiah, Hanan, Anaiah, 23Hoshea, Hananiah, Hasshub, 24Hallohesh,
Pilha, Shobek, 25Rehum, Hashabnah, Maaseiah,
26Ahiah, Hanan, Anan, 27Malluch, Harim, and Baanah.
28The rest of the people took an oath. They
were the priests, Levites, gatekeepers, singers,
Temple[d] servants, all those who separated themselves from foreigners to keep the Teachings of
God, and also their wives and their sons and
daughters who could understand. 29They joined
their fellow Israelites and their leading men in taking an oath, which was tied to a curse in case they

broke the oath. They promised to follow the Teachings of God, which they had been given through Moses the servant of God, and to obey all the commands, rules, and laws of the LORD our God.

30 They said:

> We promise not to let our daughters marry foreigners nor to let our sons marry their daughters. 31 Foreigners may bring goods or grain to sell on the Sabbath,[d] but we will not buy on the Sabbath or any holy day. Every seventh year we will not plant, and that year we will forget all that people owe us.
>
> 32 We will be responsible for the commands to pay for the service of the Temple of our God. We will give an eighth of an ounce of silver each year. 33 It is for the bread that is set out on the table; the regular grain offerings and burnt offerings; the offerings on the Sabbaths, New Moon[d] festivals, and special feasts; the holy offerings; the offerings to remove the sins of the Israelites so they will belong to God; and for the work of the Temple of our God.
>
> 34 We, the priests, the Levites, and the people, have thrown lots[d] to decide at what time of year each family must bring wood to the Temple. The wood is for burning on the altar of the LORD our God, and we will do this as it is written in the Teachings.
>
> 35 We also will bring the first fruits from our crops and the first fruits of every tree to the Temple each year.
>
> 36 We will bring to the Temple our firstborn[d] sons and cattle and the firstborn of our herds and flocks, as it is written in the Teachings. We will bring them to the priests who are serving in the Temple.
>
> 37 We will bring to the priests at the storerooms of the Temple the first of our ground meal, our offerings, the fruit from all our trees, and our new wine and oil. And we will bring a tenth of our crops to the Levites, who will collect these things in all the towns where we work. 38 A priest of Aaron's family must be with the Levites when they receive the tenth of the people's crops. The Levites must bring a tenth of all they receive to the Temple of our God to put in the storerooms of the treasury. 39 The people of Israel and the Levites are to bring to the storerooms the gifts of grain, new wine, and oil. That is where the utensils for the Temple are kept and where the priests who are serving, the gatekeepers, and singers stay.
>
> We will not ignore the Temple of our God.

New People Move into Jerusalem

11 The leaders of Israel lived in Jerusalem. But the rest of the people threw lots[d] to choose one person out of every ten to come and live in Jerusalem, the holy city. The other nine could stay in their own cities. 2 The people blessed those who volunteered to live in Jerusalem.

3 These are the area leaders who lived in Jerusalem. (Some people lived on their own land in the cities of Judah. These included Israelites, priests, Levites, Temple servants, and descendants[d] of Solomon's servants. 4 Others from the families of Judah and Benjamin lived in Jerusalem.)

These are the descendants of Judah who moved into Jerusalem. There was Athaiah son of Uzziah. (Uzziah was the son of Zechariah, the son of Amariah. Amariah was the son of Shephatiah, the son of Mahalalel. Mahalalel was a descendant of Perez.) 5 There was also Masseiah son of Baruch. (Baruch was the son of Col-Hozeh, the son of Hazaiah. Hazaiah was the son of Adaiah, the son of Joiarib. Joiarib was the son of Zechariah, a descendant of Shelah.) 6 All the descendants of Perez who lived in Jerusalem totaled 468 men. They were soldiers.

7 These are descendants of Benjamin who moved into Jerusalem. There was Sallu son of Meshullam. (Meshullam was the son of Joed, the son of Pedaiah. Pedaiah was the son of Kolaiah, the son of Maaseiah. Maaseiah was the son of Ithiel, the son of Jeshaiah.) 8 Following him were Gabbai and Sallai, for a total of 928 men. 9 Joel son of Zicri was appointed over them, and Judah son of Hassenuah was second in charge of the new area of the city.

10 These are the priests who moved into Jerusalem. There was Jedaiah son of Joiarib, Jakin, 11 and Seraiah son of Hilkiah, the supervisor in the Temple. (Hilkiah was the son of Meshullam, the son of Zadok. Zadok was the son of Meraioth, the son of Ahitub.) 12 And there were others with them who did the work for the Temple. All together there were 822 men. Also there was Adaiah son of Jeroham. (Jeroham was the son of Pelaliah, the son of Amzi. Amzi was the son of Zechariah, the son of Pashhur. Pashhur was the son of Malkijah.) 13 And there were family heads with him. All together there were 242 men. Also there was Amashsai son of Azarel. (Azarel was the son of Ahzai, the son of Meshillemoth. Meshillemoth was the son of Immer.) 14 And there were brave men with Amashsai. All together there were 128 men. Zabdiel son of Haggedolim was appointed over them.

15 These are the Levites who moved into Jerusalem. There was Shemaiah son of Hasshub. (Hasshub was the son of Azrikam, the son of Hashabiah. Hashabiah was the son of Bunni.) 16 And

there were Shabbethai and Jozabad, two of the leaders of the Levites who were in charge of the work outside the Temple. 17There was Mattaniah son of Mica. (Mica was the son of Zabdi, the son of Asaph.) Mattaniah was the director who led the people in thanksgiving and prayer. There was Bakbukiah, who was second in charge over his fellow Levites. And there was Abda son of Shammua. (Shammua was the son of Galal, the son of Jeduthun.) 18All together 284 Levites lived in the holy city of Jerusalem.

19The gatekeepers who moved into Jerusalem were Akkub, Talmon, and others with them. There was a total of 172 men who guarded the city gates.

20The other Israelites, priests, and Levites lived on their own land in all the cities of Judah.

21The Temple servants lived on the hill of Ophel, and Ziha and Gishpa were in charge of them.

22Uzzi son of Bani was appointed over the Levites in Jerusalem. (Bani was the son of Hashabiah, the son of Mattaniah. Mattaniah was the son of Mica.) Uzzi was one of Asaph's descendants, who were the singers responsible for the service of the Temple. 23The singers were under the king's orders, which regulated them day by day.

24Pethahiah son of Meshezabel was the king's spokesman. (Meshezabel was a descendant of Zerah, the son of Judah.)

25Some of the people of Judah lived in villages with their surrounding fields. They lived in Kiriath Arba and its surroundings, in Dibon and its surroundings, in Jekabzeel and its surroundings, 26in Jeshua, Moladah, Beth Pelet, 27Hazar Shual, Beersheba and its surroundings, 28in Ziklag and Meconah and its surroundings, 29in En Rimmon, Zorah, Jarmuth, 30Zanoah, Adullam and their villages, in Lachish and the fields around it, and in Azekah and its surroundings. So they settled from Beersheba all the way to the Valley of Hinnom.

31The descendants of the Benjaminites from Geba lived in Micmash, Aija, Bethel and its surroundings, 32in Anathoth, Nob, Ananiah, 33Hazor, Ramah, Gittaim, 34Hadid, Zeboim, Neballat, 35Lod, Ono, and in the Valley of the Craftsmen.

36Some groups of the Levites from Judah settled in the land of Benjamin.

Priests and Levites

12 These are the priests and Levites who returned with Zerubbabel son of Shealtiel and with Jeshua. There were Seraiah, Jeremiah, Ezra, 2Amariah, Malluch, Hattush, 3Shecaniah, Rehum, Meremoth, 4Iddo, Ginnethon, Abijah, 5Mijamin, Moadiah, Bilgah, 6Shemaiah, Joiarib, Jedaiah, 7Sallu, Amok, Hilkiah, and Jedaiah. They were the leaders of the priests and their relatives in the days of Jeshua.

8The Levites were Jeshua, Binnui, Kadmiel, Sherebiah, Judah, and Mattaniah. Mattaniah and his relatives were in charge of the songs of thanksgiving. 9Bakbukiah and Unni, their relatives, stood across from them in the services.

10Jeshua was the father of Joiakim. Joiakim was the father of Eliashib. Eliashib was the father of Joiada. 11Joiada was the father of Jonathan, and Jonathan was the father of Jaddua.

12In the days of Joiakim, these priests were the leaders of the families of priests: Meraiah, from Seraiah's family; Hananiah, from Jeremiah's family; 13Meshullam, from Ezra's family; Jehohanan, from Amariah's family; 14Jonathan, from Malluch's family; Joseph, from Shecaniah's family; 15Adna, from Harim's family; Helkai, from Meremoth's family; 16Zechariah, from Iddo's family; Meshullam, from Ginnethon's family; 17Zicri, from Abijah's family; Piltai, from Miniamin's and Moadiah's families; 18Shammua, from Bilgah's family; Jehonathan, from Shemaiah's family; 19Mattenai, from Joiarib's family; Uzzi, from Jedaiah's family; 20Kallai, from Sallu's family; Eber, from Amok's family; 21Hashabiah, from Hilkiah's family; and Nethanel, from Jedaiah's family.

22The leaders of the families of the Levites and the priests were written down in the days of Eliashib, Joiada, Johanan, and Jaddua, while Darius the Persian was king. 23The family leaders among the Levites were written down in the history book, but only up to the time of Johanan son of Eliashib. 24The leaders of the Levites were Hashabiah, Sherebiah, Jeshua son of Kadmiel, and their relatives. Their relatives stood across from them and gave praise and thanksgiving to God. One group answered the other group, as David, the man of God, had commanded.

25These were the gatekeepers who guarded the storerooms next to the gates: Mattaniah, Bakbukiah, Obadiah, Meshullam, Talmon, and Akkub. 26They served in the days of Joiakim son of Jeshua, the son of Jozadak. They also served in the days of Nehemiah the governor and Ezra the priest and teacher.

The Wall of Jerusalem

27When the wall of Jerusalem was offered as a gift to God, they asked the Levites to come from wherever they lived to Jerusalem to celebrate with joy the gift of the wall. They were to celebrate with songs of thanksgiving and with the music of cymbals, harps, and lyres.[a] 28They also brought together singers from all around Jerusalem, from the Netophathite villages, 29from Beth Gilgal, and from the areas of Geba and Azmaveth. The singers had built villages for themselves around Jerusalem. 30The priests and Levites made themselves pure, and they also made the people, the gates, and the wall of Jerusalem pure.

31I had the leaders of Judah go up on top of the wall, and I appointed two large choruses to give thanks. One chorus went to the right on top of the wall, toward the Trash Gate. 32Behind them went Hoshaiah and half the leaders of Judah. 33Azariah, Ezra, Meshullam, 34Judah, Benjamin, Shemaiah, and Jeremiah also went. 35Some priests with trumpets also went, along with Zechariah son of Jonathan. (Jonathan was the son of Shemaiah, the son of Mattaniah. Mattaniah was the son of Micaiah, the son of Zaccur. Zaccur was the son of Asaph.) 36Zechariah's relatives also went. They were Shemaiah, Azarel, Milalai, Gilalai, Maai, Nethanel, Judah, and Hanani. These men played the musical instruments of David, the man of God, and Ezra the teacher walked in front of them. 37They went from the Fountain Gate straight up the steps to the highest part of the wall by the older part of the city. They went on above the house of David to the Water Gate on the east.

38The second chorus went to the left, while I followed them on top of the wall with half the people. We went from the Tower of the Ovens to the Broad Wall, 39over the Gate of Ephraim to the Old Gate and the Fish Gate, to the Tower of Hananel and the Tower of the Hundred. We went as far as the Sheep Gate and stopped at the Gate of the Guard.

40The two choruses took their places at the Temple.[d] Half of the leaders and I did also. 41These priests were there with their trumpets: Eliakim, Maaseiah, Miniamin, Micaiah, Elioenai, Zechariah, and Hananiah. 42These people were also there: Maaseiah, Shemaiah, Eleazar, Uzzi, Jehohanan, Malkijah, Elam, and Ezer. The choruses sang, led by Jezrahiah. 43The people offered many sacrifices that day and were happy because God had given them great joy. The women and children were happy. The sound of happiness in Jerusalem could be heard far away.

SIDELIGHT: *When the Jews dedicated the completed wall around Jerusalem (Nehemiah 12:27–43), they didn't cut a ribbon or break a bottle of champagne. They probably offered an animal sacrifice and sprinkled blood or holy water on the wall.*

44At that time the leaders appointed men to be in charge of the storerooms. These rooms were for the gifts, the first fruits, and the ten percent that the people brought. The Teachings said they should bring a share for the priests and Levites from the fields around the towns. The people of Judah were happy to do this for the priests and Levites who served. 45They performed the service of their God in making things pure. The singers and gatekeepers also did their jobs, as David had commanded his son Solomon. 46Earlier, in the time of David and Asaph, there was a leader of the singers and of the songs of praise and thanksgiving to God. 47So it was in the days of Zerubbabel and Nehemiah. All the people of Israel gave something to the singers and gatekeepers, and they also set aside part for the Levites. Then the Levites set aside part for the descendants[d] of Aaron.

Foreign People Are Sent Away

13 On that day they read the Book of Moses to the people, and they found that it said no Ammonite or Moabite should ever be allowed in the meeting to worship. 2The Ammonites and Moabites had not welcomed the Israelites with food and water. Instead, they had hired Balaam to put a curse on Israel. (But our God turned the curse into a blessing.) 3When the people heard this teaching, they separated all foreigners from Israel.

Nehemiah Returns to Jerusalem

4Before that happened, Eliashib the priest, who was in charge of the Temple[d] storerooms, was friendly with Tobiah. 5Eliashib let Tobiah use one of the large storerooms. Earlier it had been used for grain offerings, incense,[d] the utensils, and the tenth offerings of grain, new wine, and olive oil that belonged to the Levites, singers, and gatekeepers. It had also been used for gifts for the priests.

6I was not in Jerusalem when this happened. I had gone back to Artaxerxes king of Babylon in the thirty-second year he was king. Finally I asked the king to let me leave. 7When I returned to Jerusalem, I found out the evil Eliashib had done by letting Tobiah have a room in the Temple courtyard. 8I was very upset at this, so I threw all of Tobiah's goods out of the room. 9I ordered the rooms to be purified, and I brought back the utensils for God's Temple, the grain offerings, and the incense.[d]

10Then I found out the people were not giving the Levites their shares. So the Levites and singers who served had gone back to their own farms. 11I argued with the officers, saying, "Why haven't you taken care of the Temple?" Then I gathered the Levites and singers and put them back at their places.

12All the people of Judah then brought to the storerooms a tenth of their crops, new wine, and olive oil. 13I put these men in charge of the storerooms: Shelemiah the priest, Zadok the teacher, and Pedaiah a Levite. I made Hanan son of Zaccur, the son of Mattaniah, their helper. Everyone knew they were honest men. They gave out the portions that went to their relatives.

[14]Remember me, my God, for this. Do not ignore my love for the Temple and its service.

[15]In those days I saw people in Judah working in the winepresses[d] on the Sabbath[d] day. They were bringing in grain and loading it on donkeys. And they were bringing loads of wine, grapes, and figs into Jerusalem on the Sabbath day. So I warned them about selling food on that day. [16]People from the city of Tyre who were living in Jerusalem brought in fish and other things and sold them there on the Sabbath day to the people of Judah. [17]I argued with the important men of Judah and said to them, "What is this evil thing you are doing? You are ruining the Sabbath day. [18]This is just what your ancestors did. So our God did terrible things to us and this city. Now you are making him even more angry at Israel by ruining the Sabbath day."

[19]So I ordered that the doors be shut at sunset before the Sabbath and not be opened until the Sabbath was over. I put my servants at the gates so no load could come in on the Sabbath. [20]Once or twice traders and sellers of all kinds of goods spent the night outside Jerusalem. [21]So I warned them, "Why are you spending the night by the wall? If you do it again, I will force you away." After that, they did not come back on the Sabbath. [22]Then I ordered the Levites to purify themselves and to guard the city gates to make sure the Sabbath remained holy.

Remember me, my God, for this. Have mercy on me because of your great love.

[23]In those days I saw men of Judah who had married women from Ashdod, Ammon, and Moab. [24]Half their children were speaking the language of Ashdod or some other place, and they couldn't speak the language of Judah. [25]I argued with those people, put curses on them, hit some of them, and pulled out their hair. I forced them to make a promise to God, saying, "Do not let your daughters marry the sons of foreigners, and do not take the daughters of foreigners as wives for your sons or yourselves. [26]Foreign women made King Solomon of Israel sin. There was never a king like him in any of the nations. God loved Solomon and made him king over all Israel, but foreign women made him sin. [27]And now you are not obedient when you do this evil thing. You are unfaithful to our God when you marry foreign wives."

[28]Joiada was the son of Eliashib the high priest. One of Joiada's sons married a daughter of Sanballat the Horonite, so I sent him away from me.

[29]Remember them, my God, because they made the priesthood unclean[d] and the agreement of the priests and Levites unclean.

[30]So I purified them of everything that was foreign. I appointed duties for the priests and Levites, giving each man his own job. [31]I also made sure wood was brought for the altar at regular times and that the first fruits were brought.

Remember me, my God; be kind to me.

ESTHER

Why Read This Book:

- Recognize God's work in life's circumstances (Esther 1—2).
- Discover how an obedient person can have a major impact in the world (Esther 4—10).

Behind the Scenes:

How do you respond in a crisis? Does your fear make you freeze up so you can't do anything to help? Or do you reveal heroic strength and skill—far more than you would normally have?

Esther faced a tough situation. She might be able to save thousands of Jewish lives by stopping the decree of King Xerxes to exterminate all the Jews in the Persian Empire. But if she tried, she could lose her own life. Would she "freeze up," or would she take heroic action? This book tells how Esther responded.

The story begins when King Xerxes dumped Queen Vashti because she wouldn't obey him. Four years later, the king picked a new queen, Esther, not knowing that she was a Jew.

Then the plot thickens. Esther's cousin, Mordecai, refused to bow down to Haman, a court official. Haman became furious and convinced the king to order the killing of all the Jews. Through a messenger, Mordecai told Esther about the death decree and convinced her to use her influence to stop the order. Esther agreed, saying: "I will go to the king, even though it is against the law, and if I die, I die" (Esther 4:16). So she went to the king to plead for the Jews, including herself. She succeeded. Then Haman was executed and Mordecai honored.

Esther is one of the most unusual books in the Bible. In some ways, it's a "secular" book; nowhere does it mention God, worship, prayer, or other religious

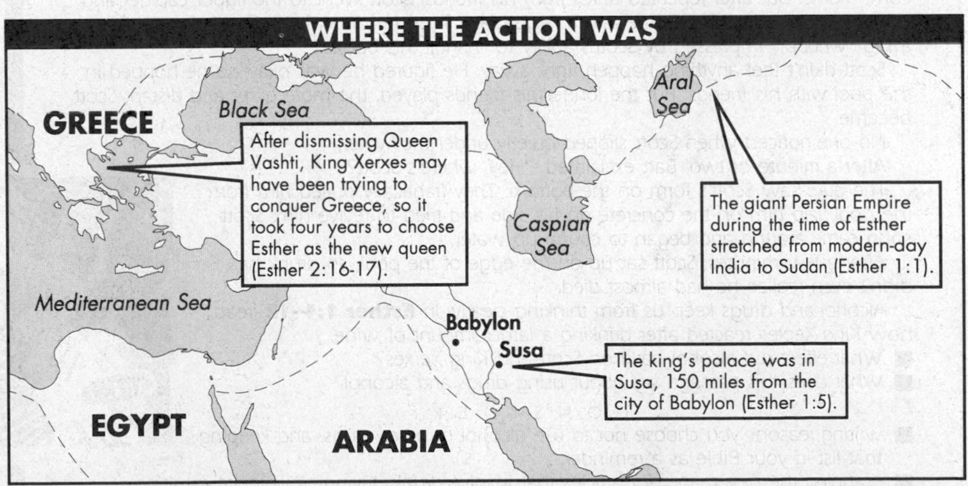

WHEN THE ACTION WAS

1000BC	David was Israel's king
750BC	The Northern Kingdom (Israel) fell to Assyria
	The Southern Kingdom (Judah) fell to Babylon
500BC	Jews began returning to Jerusalem from exile when Persia conquered Babylon
	King Xerxes ruled Persia and the story of Esther took place during this time
250BC	
BC/AD	Jesus was born

Behind the Scenes (cont.): practices. Yet God's protection is clear throughout. The number of "coincidences" in the book illustrate that God's hand is at work in events, even when we don't realize it.

Queen Vashti Disobeys the King

1 This is what happened during the time of
King Xerxes, the king who ruled the one
hundred twenty-seven states from India to Cush.
2In those days King Xerxes ruled from his capital
city of Susa. 3In the third year of his rule, he gave
a banquet for all his important men and royal officers. The army leaders from the countries of Persia and Media and the important men from all
Xerxes' empire were there.
4The banquet lasted one hundred eighty days.
All during that time King Xerxes was showing off
the great wealth of his kingdom and his own great
riches and glory. 5When the one hundred eighty

DRUGS AND ALCOHOL

Under the Influence

"I wonder what it's like to drown," Scott Walters mused aloud. He quietly exhaled, then slipped under the water in his backyard pool.

Scott was in junior high when he began sampling drinks from his father's liquor cabinet. No one in the family seemed to notice or care, so he continued to drink occasionally—in small amounts.

One afternoon several of Scott's friends came over to swim. Scott began to brag about his free access to the family liquor cabinet.

"My family lets me drink whenever I want to," Scott claimed. "In fact, my dad and I drink together all the time."

"You're lying," scowled Bart, one of Scott's friends. "Your dad doesn't let you drink."

"What do you know?" countered Scott. "You've probably never had anything stronger than milk."

"Okay, then," Bart said, "prove it. Prove to us that you drink."

Scott didn't really want to drink right then, because he never knew when his dad would come home. But after repeated dares from his friends, Scott went to the liquor cabinet and poured a little from each bottle into a large glass. Then he drank it all. Scott's friends let out a big "whoop," impressed by Scott's ability to "handle his booze."

Scott didn't feel anything happen right away. He figured he was okay, so he hopped in the pool with his friends. But the longer his friends played, the more quiet and distant Scott became.

No one noticed when Scott slipped quietly under the water.

After a minute or two, Bart exclaimed, "Hey, where's Scott?"

The guys saw Scott's form on the bottom. They frantically pulled him from the pool, laid him on the concrete on his side and tried to revive him. Scott soon came around and began to cough up water.

After a few minutes, Scott sat up on the edge of the pool, so drunk he didn't even realize he had almost died.

Alcohol and drugs keep us from thinking clearly. In **Esther 1:4–12**, read how King Xerxes reacted after drinking a large amount of wine.

- What effect did alcohol have on Scott and King Xerxes?
- What does this passage say about using drugs and alcohol?

CONSIDER . . .

- writing reasons you choose not to use alcohol or other drugs, and keeping that list in your Bible as a reminder.
- scanning the newspaper for articles that involve drunk driving or violence resulting from drug or alcohol use; then consider asking God to help the people in each of those situations.

FOR MORE, SEE . . .

- Proverbs 23:29–35 (p. 588)
- Galatians 5:19–23 (p. 1213)
- Ephesians 5:15–18 (p. 1224)

days were over, the king gave another banquet. It was held in the courtyard of the palace garden for seven days, and it was for everybody in the palace

SIDELIGHT: Some people in ancient times really knew how to throw parties. King Xerxes, for example, had one that lasted one hundred eighty days (Esther 1:4). But the party didn't have a happy ending. Some scholars believe the partygoers also planned a disastrous war campaign against Greece.

at Susa, from the greatest to the least. [6]The courtyard had fine white curtains and purple drapes that were tied to silver rings on marble pillars by white and purple cords. And there were gold and silver couches on a floor set with tiles of white marble, shells, and gems. [7]Wine was served in gold cups of various kinds. And there was plenty of the king's wine, because he was very generous. [8]The king commanded that the guests be permitted to drink as much as they wished. He told the wine servers to serve each person what he wanted.

SIDELIGHT: If you like taking a nap after eating, you would have loved the Persian palace in Esther's day. When people feasted at a royal party, they reclined on gold and silver couches—the beds of that day (Esther 1:4–8). Ordinary people had wooden beds with nets of cords for mattresses, and poor people slept on the ground and covered themselves with their clothes.

[9]Queen Vashti also gave a banquet for the women in the royal palace of King Xerxes.

[10]On the seventh day of the banquet, King Xerxes was very happy, because he had been drinking much wine. He gave a command to the seven eunuchs[d] who served him—Mehuman, Biztha, Harbona, Bigtha, Abagtha, Zethar, and Carcas. [11]He commanded them to bring him Queen Vashti, wearing her royal crown. She was to come to show her beauty to the people and important men, because she was very beautiful. [12]The eunuchs told Queen Vashti about the king's command, but she refused to come. Then the king became very angry; his anger was like a burning fire.

[13]It was a custom for the king to ask advice from experts about law and order. So King Xerxes spoke with the wise men who would know the right thing to do. [14]The wise men the king usually talked to were Carshena, Shethar, Admatha, Tarshish, Meres, Marsena, and Memucan, seven of the important men of Persia and Media. These seven had special privileges to see the king and had the highest rank in the kingdom. [15]The king asked them, "What does the law say must be done to Queen Vashti? She has not obeyed the command of King Xerxes, which the eunuchs took to her."

[16]Then Memucan said to the king and the other important men, "Queen Vashti has not done wrong to the king alone. She has also done wrong to all the important men and all the people in all the empire of King Xerxes. [17]All the wives of the important men of Persia and Media will hear about the queen's actions. Then they will no longer honor their husbands. They will say, 'King Xerxes commanded Queen Vashti to be brought to him, but she refused to come.' [18]Today the wives of the important men of Persia and Media have heard about the queen's actions. So they will speak in the same way to their husbands, and there will be no end to disrespect and anger.

[19]"So, our king, if it pleases you, give a royal order, and let it be written in the laws of Persia and Media, which cannot be changed. The law should say Vashti is never again to enter the presence of King Xerxes. Also let the king give her place as queen to someone who is better than she is. [20]And let the king's order be announced everywhere in his enormous kingdom. Then all the women will respect their husbands, from the greatest to the least."

[21]The king and his important men were happy with this advice, so King Xerxes did as Memucan suggested. [22]He sent letters to all the states of the kingdom in the writing of each state and in the language of each group of people. These letters announced that each man was to be the ruler of his own family.

Esther Is Made Queen

2 Later, when King Xerxes was not so angry, he remembered Vashti and what she had done and his order about her. [2]Then the king's personal servants suggested, "Let a search be made for beautiful young girls for the king. [3]Let the king choose supervisors in every state of his kingdom to bring every beautiful young girl to the palace at Susa. They should be taken to the women's quarters and put under the care of Hegai, the king's eunuch[d] in charge of the women. And let beauty treatments be given to them. [4]Then let the girl who most pleases the king become queen in place of Vashti." The king liked this idea, so he did as they said.

[5]Now there was a Jewish man in the palace of

Susa whose name was Mordecai son of Jair. Jair was the son of Shimei, the son of Kish. Mordecai was from the tribe[d] of Benjamin, 6which had been taken captive from Jerusalem by Nebuchadnezzar king of Babylon. They were part of the group taken into captivity with Jehoiachin king of Judah. 7Mordecai had a cousin named Hadassah, who had no father or mother, so Mordecai took care of her. Hadassah was also called Esther, and she had a very pretty figure and face. Mordecai had adopted her as his own daughter when her father and mother died.

8When the king's command and order had been heard, many girls had been brought to the palace in Susa and put under the care of Hegai. Esther was also taken to the king's palace and put under the care of Hegai, who was in charge of the women. 9Esther pleased Hegai, and he liked her. So Hegai quickly began giving Esther her beauty treatments and special food. He gave her seven servant girls chosen from the king's palace. Then he moved her and her seven servant girls to the best part of the women's quarters.

10Esther did not tell anyone about her family or who her people were, because Mordecai had told her not to. 11Every day Mordecai walked back and forth near the courtyard where the king's women lived to find out how Esther was and what was happening to her.

12Before a girl could take her turn with King Xerxes, she had to complete twelve months of beauty treatments that were ordered for the women. For six months she was treated with oil and myrrh[d] and for six months with perfumes and cosmetics. 13Then she was ready to go to the king. Anything she asked for was given to her to take with her from the women's quarters to the king's palace. 14In the evening she would go to the king's palace, and in the morning she would return to another part of the women's quarters. There she would be placed under the care of Shaashgaz, the king's eunuch in charge of the slave women.[d] The girl would not go back to the king again unless he was pleased with her and asked for her by name.

SIDELIGHT: If you think your sister takes too long in the bathroom, just be glad she isn't Esther. It took Esther a year of beauty treatments to get ready for the king (Esther 2:12–13).

15The time came for Esther daughter of Abihail, Mordecai's uncle, who had been adopted by Mordecai, to go to the king. She asked for only what Hegai suggested she should take. (Hegai was the king's eunuch who was in charge of the women.) Everyone who saw Esther liked her. 16So Esther was taken to King Xerxes in the royal palace in the tenth month, the month of Tebeth, during Xerxes' seventh year as king.

17And the king was pleased with Esther more than with any of the other girls. He liked her more than any of the other girls, so he put a royal crown on her head and made her queen in place of Vashti. 18Then the king gave a great banquet for Esther and invited all his important men and royal officers. He announced a holiday for all the empire and had the government give away gifts.

Mordecai Discovers an Evil Plan

19Now Mordecai was sitting at the king's gate when the girls were gathered the second time. 20Esther still had not told anyone about her family or who her people were, just as Mordecai had commanded her. She obeyed Mordecai just as she had done when she was under his care.

21Now Bigthana and Teresh were two of the king's officers who guarded the doorway. While Mordecai was sitting at the king's gate, they became angry and began to make plans to kill King Xerxes. 22But Mordecai found out about their plans and told Queen Esther. Then Esther told the king how Mordecai had discovered the evil plan. 23When the report was investigated, it was found to be true, and the two officers who had planned to kill the king were hanged. All this was written down in the daily court record in the king's presence.

Haman Plans to Destroy the Jewish People

3 After these things happened, King Xerxes honored Haman son of Hammedatha the Agagite. He gave him a new rank that was higher than all the important men. 2All the royal officers at the king's gate would bow down and kneel before Haman, as the king had ordered. But Mordecai would not bow down or show him honor.

3Then the royal officers at the king's gate asked Mordecai, "Why don't you obey the king's command?" 4And they said this to him every day. When he did not listen to them, they told Haman about it. They wanted to see if Haman would accept Mordecai's behavior because Mordecai had told them he was Jewish.

5When Haman saw that Mordecai would not bow down to him or honor him, he became very angry. 6He thought of himself as too important to try to kill only Mordecai. He had been told who the people of Mordecai were, so he looked for a way to destroy all of Mordecai's people, the Jews, in all of Xerxes' kingdom.

7It was in the first month of the twelfth year of King Xerxes' rule — the month of Nisan. Pur (that is, the lot[d]) was thrown before Haman to choose a day and a month. So the twelfth month, the month of Adar, was chosen.

8Then Haman said to King Xerxes, "There is a certain group of people scattered among the other people in all the states of your kingdom. Their customs are different from those of all the other people, and they do not obey the king's laws. It is not right for you to allow them to continue living in your kingdom. 9If it pleases the king, let an order be given to destroy those people. Then I will pay seven hundred fifty thousand pounds of silver to those who do the king's business, and they will put it into the royal treasury."

10So the king took his signet[d] ring off and gave it to Haman son of Hammedatha, the Agagite, the enemy of the Jewish people. 11Then the king said to Haman, "The money and the people are yours. Do with them as you please."

12On the thirteenth day of the first month, the royal secretaries were called, and they wrote out all of Haman's orders. They wrote to the king's governors and to the captains of the soldiers in each state and to the important men of each group of people. The orders were written in the writing of each state and in the language of each people. They were written in the name of King Xerxes and sealed with his signet ring. 13Letters were sent by messengers to all the king's empire ordering them to destroy, kill, and completely wipe out all the Jewish people. That meant young and old, women and little children, too. It was to happen on a single day — the thirteenth day of the twelfth month, which was Adar. And they could take everything the Jewish people owned. 14A copy of the order was given out as a law in every state so all the people would be ready for that day.

15The messengers set out, hurried by the king's command, as soon as the order was given in the palace at Susa. The king and Haman sat down to drink, but the city of Susa was in confusion.

Mordecai Asks Esther to Help

4 When Mordecai heard about all that had been done, he tore his clothes, put on rough cloth and ashes, and went out into the city crying loudly and painfully. 2But Mordecai went only as far as the king's gate, because no one was allowed to enter that gate dressed in rough cloth. 3As the king's order reached every area, there was great sadness and loud crying among the Jewish people. They gave up eating and cried out loud, and many of them lay down on rough cloth and ashes to show how sad they were.

4When Esther's servant girls and eunuchs[d] came to her and told her about Mordecai, she was very upset and afraid. She sent clothes for Mordecai to put on instead of the rough cloth, but he would not wear them. 5Then Esther called for Hathach, one of the king's eunuchs chosen by the king to serve her. Esther ordered him to find out what was bothering Mordecai and why.

6So Hathach went to Mordecai, who was in the city square in front of the king's gate. 7Mordecai told Hathach everything that had happened to him, and he told Hathach about the amount of money Haman had promised to pay into the king's treasury for the killing of the Jewish people. 8Mordecai also gave him a copy of the order to kill the Jewish people, which had been given in Susa. He wanted Hathach to show it to Esther and to tell her about it. And Mordecai told him to order Esther to go into the king's presence to beg for mercy and to plead with him for her people.

9Hathach went back and reported to Esther everything Mordecai had said. 10Then Esther told Hathach to tell Mordecai, 11"All the royal officers and people of the royal states know that no man or woman may go to the king in the inner courtyard without being called. There is only one law about this: Anyone who enters must be put to death unless the king holds out his gold scepter.[d] Then that person may live. And I have not been called to go to the king for thirty days."

12Esther's message was given to Mordecai. 13Then Mordecai sent back word to Esther: "Just because you live in the king's palace, don't think that out of all the Jewish people you alone will escape. 14If you keep quiet at this time, someone else will help and save the Jewish people, but you and your father's family will all die. And who knows, you may have been chosen queen for just such a time as this."

15Then Esther sent this answer to Mordecai: 16"Go and get all the Jewish people in Susa together. For my sake, give up eating; do not eat or drink for three days, night and day. I and my servant girls will also give up eating. Then I will go to the king, even though it is against the law, and if I die, I die."

17So Mordecai went away and did everything Esther had told him to do.

Esther Speaks to the King

5 On the third day Esther put on her royal robes and stood in the inner courtyard of the king's palace, facing the king's hall. The king was sitting on his royal throne in the hall, facing the doorway. 2When the king saw Queen Esther standing in the courtyard, he was pleased. He held out to her the gold scepter[d] that was in his hand, so Esther went forward and touched the end of it.

3The king asked, "What is it, Queen Esther? What do you want to ask me? I will give you as much as half of my kingdom."

4Esther answered, "My king, if it pleases you, come today with Haman to a banquet that I have prepared for him."

[5]Then the king said, "Bring Haman quickly so we may do what Esther asks."

SIDELIGHT: If you're afraid to go talk to someone in authority over you, imagine how Esther must have felt about going to the king (Esther 5:1–2). Frequent political assassinations at that time made security around a king extremely tight, and anyone—including the queen—who approached the king without being invited could be in danger of being killed.

So the king and Haman went to the banquet Esther had prepared for them. [6]As they were drinking wine, the king said to Esther, "Now, what are you asking for? I will give it to you. What is it you want? I will give you as much as half of my kingdom."

[7]Esther answered, "This is what I want and what I ask for. [8]My king, if you are pleased with me and if it pleases you, give me what I ask for and do what I want. Come with Haman tomorrow to the banquet I will prepare for you. Then I will answer your question about what I want."

Haman's Plans Against Mordecai

[9]Haman left the king's palace that day happy and content. But when he saw Mordecai at the king's gate and saw that Mordecai did not stand up or tremble with fear before him, Haman became very angry with Mordecai. [10]But he controlled his anger and went home.

Then Haman called together his friends and his wife, Zeresh. [11]He told them how wealthy he was and how many sons he had. He also told them all the ways the king had honored him and how the king had placed him higher than his important men and his royal officers. [12]He also said, "I'm the only person Queen Esther invited to come with the king to the banquet she gave. And tomorrow

HEROES

Risky Business

"They were chasing a little boy, about ten years old. They caught up with him, and one of them took his gun and bashed the child's head in. They killed him."

Those are the words of Giorgio Perlasca, who witnessed this murder in Hungary in 1944. It was World War II, and the Nazis were killing the Jews, regardless of their age. Perlasca couldn't sit back and watch this happen.

Although he was Italian, Perlasca was able to get a passport to Hungary that identified him as a Spaniard. Because of Spain's close ties with Germany, he could masquerade as a top Spanish diplomat and help save the Jews.

For three months, Perlasca distributed letters to all the Jews he could find. The letters stated that the Jews had been granted the protection of the Spanish government. When he saw Jews being herded onto trains, headed for death, he confronted the Nazis and ordered them to return the people to him. He housed more than five thousand Jews in eleven apartment buildings where he hung Spain's flag to protect the occupants.

Historians estimate Perlasca helped save more than ten thousand people before his cover was blown when Spain cut off diplomatic relations with Hungary at the end of 1944.

Giorgio Perlasca heroically risked his own life to save the lives of others. Queen Esther also put her life on the line for the Jews. Read her story in **Esther 4:9–16**.

- What risks did both Perlasca and Esther take to save the Jews?
- We may not all have the chance to save thousands of people from dying, but we can still make a difference. How can you be a hero for God?

CONSIDER. . .

- making a hero sandwich and sharing it with someone who is a hero to you.
- who your heroes are and how well they measure up to the standards of Esther. Then decide if you need to change heroes.

FOR MORE, SEE. . .

- Exodus 14:5–31 (p. 70)
- Joshua 2:1–22 (p. 195)
- Hebrews 11:29–40 (p. 1288)

also the queen has asked me to be her guest with the king. 13But all this does not really make me happy when I see that Jew Mordecai sitting at the king's gate."

14Then Haman's wife, Zeresh, and all his friends said, "Have a seventy-five foot platform built, and in the morning ask the king to have Mordecai hanged on it. Then go to the banquet with the king and be happy." Haman liked this suggestion, so he ordered the platform to be built.

Mordecai Is Honored

6 That same night the king could not sleep. So he gave an order for the daily court record to be brought in and read to him. 2It was found recorded that Mordecai had warned the king about Bigthana and Teresh, two of the king's officers who guarded the doorway and who had planned to kill the king.

3The king asked, "What honor and reward have been given to Mordecai for this?"

The king's personal servants answered, "Nothing has been done for Mordecai."

4The king said, "Who is in the courtyard?" Now Haman had just entered the outer court of the king's palace. He had come to ask the king about hanging Mordecai on the platform he had prepared.

5The king's personal servants said, "Haman is standing in the courtyard."

The king said, "Bring him in."

6So Haman came in. And the king asked him, "What should be done for a man whom the king wants very much to honor?"

And Haman thought to himself, "Whom would the king want to honor more than me?" 7So he answered the king, "This is what you could do for the man you want very much to honor. 8Have the servants bring a royal robe that the king himself has worn. And also bring a horse with a royal crown on its head, a horse that the king himself has ridden. 9Let the robe and the horse be given to one of the king's most important men. Let the servants put the robe on the man the king wants to honor, and let them lead him on the horse through the city streets. As they are leading him, let them announce: 'This is what is done for the man whom the king wants to honor!' "

10The king commanded Haman, "Go quickly. Take the robe and the horse just as you have said, and do all this for Mordecai the Jew who sits at the king's gate. Do not leave out anything you have suggested."

11So Haman took the robe and the horse, and he put the robe on Mordecai. Then he led him on horseback through the city streets, announcing before Mordecai: "This is what is done for the man whom the king wants to honor!"

12Then Mordecai returned to the king's gate, but Haman hurried home with his head covered, because he was embarrassed and ashamed. 13He told his wife, Zeresh, and all his friends everything that had happened to him.

Haman's wife and the men who gave him advice said, "You are starting to lose power to Mordecai. Since he is a Jew, you cannot win against him. You will surely be ruined." 14While they were still talking, the king's eunuchs[d] came to Haman's house and made him hurry to the banquet Esther had prepared.

Haman Is Hanged

7 So the king and Haman went in to eat with Queen Esther. 2As they were drinking wine on the second day, the king asked Esther again, "What are you asking for? I will give it to you. What is it you want? I will give you as much as half of my kingdom."

3Then Queen Esther answered, "My king, if you are pleased with me, and if it pleases you, let me live. This is what I ask. And let my people live, too. This is what I want. 4My people and I have been sold to be destroyed, to be killed and completely wiped out. If we had been sold as male and female slaves, I would have kept quiet, because that would not be enough of a problem to bother the king."

5Then King Xerxes asked Queen Esther, "Who is he, and where is he? Who has done such a thing?"

6Esther said, "Our enemy and foe is this wicked Haman!"

Then Haman was filled with terror before the king and queen. 7The king was very angry, so he got up, left his wine, and went out into the palace garden. But Haman stayed inside to beg Queen Esther to save his life. He could see that the king had already decided to kill him.

> **SIDELIGHT:** Going to the palace garden to cool off was probably a good idea for the angry king (Esther 7:7). The palace at Susa was the king's winter palace because it was warmer than the government headquarters in Persepolis.

8When the king returned from the palace garden to the banquet hall, he saw Haman falling on the couch where Esther was lying. The king said, "Will he even attack the queen while I am in the house?"

As soon as the king said that, servants came in and covered Haman's face. 9Harbona, one of the eunuchs[d] there serving the king, said, "Look, a seventy-five foot platform stands near Haman's house. This is the one Haman had prepared for Mordecai, who gave the warning that saved the king."

The king said, "Hang Haman on it!" 10So they hanged Haman on the platform he had prepared for Mordecai. Then the king was not so angry anymore.

SIDELIGHT: The execution planned by Haman for Mordecai, but carried out by the king on Haman (Esther 7:8–10), probably wouldn't have been a hanging in the modern sense. It probably involved impaling him on a sharp stake and then hanging the body in the city for display. Romans adapted this method to develop execution on crosses.

The King Helps the Jewish People

8 That same day King Xerxes gave Queen Esther everything Haman, the enemy of the Jewish people, had left when he died. And Mordecai came in to see the king, because Esther had told the king how he was related to her. 2Then the king took off his signet[d] ring that he had taken back from Haman, and he gave it to Mordecai. Esther put Mordecai in charge of everything Haman left when he died.

3Once again Esther spoke to the king. She fell at the king's feet and cried and begged him to stop the evil plan that Haman the Agagite had planned against the Jews. 4The king held out the gold scepter[d] to Esther. So Esther got up and stood in front of him.

5She said, "My king, if you are pleased with me, and if it pleases you to do this, if you think it is the right thing to do, and if you are happy with me, let an order be written to cancel the letters Haman wrote. Haman the Agagite sent messages to destroy all the Jewish people in all of your kingdom. 6I could not stand to see that terrible thing happen to my people. I could not stand to see my family killed."

7King Xerxes answered Queen Esther and Mordecai the Jew, "Because Haman was against the Jewish people, I have given his things to Esther, and my soldiers have hanged him. 8Now, in the king's name, write another order to the Jewish people as it seems best to you. Then seal the order with the king's signet[d] ring, because no letter written in the king's name and sealed with his signet ring can be canceled."

9At that time the king's secretaries were called. This was the twenty-third day of the third month, which is Sivan. The secretaries wrote out all of Mordecai's orders to the Jews, to the governors, to the captains of the soldiers in each state, and to the important men of the one hundred twenty-seven states that reached from India to Cush. They wrote in the writing of each state and in the language of each people. They also wrote to the Jewish people in their own writing and language.

SIDELIGHT: The longest verse in the Bible is Esther 8:9. It's eighty-eight words long.

10Mordecai wrote orders in the name of King Xerxes and sealed the letters with the king's signet ring. Then he sent the king's orders by messengers on fast horses, horses that were raised just for the king.

11These were the king's orders: The Jewish people in every city have the right to gather together to protect themselves. They may destroy, kill, and completely wipe out the army of any state or people who attack them. And they are to do the same to the women and children of that army. They may also take by force the property of their enemies. 12The one day set for the Jewish people to do this in all the empire of King Xerxes was the thirteenth day of the twelfth month, the month of Adar. 13A copy of the king's order was to be sent out as a law in every state. It was to be made known to the people of every nation living in the kingdom so the Jewish people would be ready on that set day to strike back at their enemies.

14The messengers hurried out, riding on the royal horses, because the king commanded those messengers to hurry. And the order was also given in the palace at Susa.

SIDELIGHT: They may not have had overnight mail, but the Persians had an excellent postal system to deliver Mordecai's letter (Esther 8:10). The Persian Empire was organized into twenty satrapies (or provinces), which were connected by efficient mail service begun by King Cyrus around 535 B.C.

15Mordecai left the king's presence wearing royal clothes of blue and white and a large gold crown. He also had a purple robe made of the best linen. And the people of Susa shouted for joy. 16It was a time of happiness, joy, gladness, and honor for the Jewish people. 17As the king's order went to every state and city, there was joy and gladness

among the Jewish people. In every state and city
to which the king's order went, they were having
feasts and celebrating. And many people through
all the empire became Jews, because they were
afraid of the Jewish people.

Victory for the Jewish People

9 The order the king had commanded was to
be done on the thirteenth day of the twelfth
month, the month of Adar. That was the day the
enemies of the Jewish people had hoped to defeat
them, but that was changed. So the Jewish people
themselves defeated those who hated them. 2The
Jews met in their cities in all the empire of King
Xerxes in order to attack those who wanted to
harm them. No one was strong enough to fight
against them, because all the other people living
in the empire were afraid of them. 3All the important men of the states, the governors, captains of
the soldiers, and the king's officers helped the
Jewish people, because they were afraid of Mordecai. 4Mordecai was very important in the king's
palace. He was famous in all the empire, because
he was becoming a leader of more and more people.

5And, with their swords, the Jewish people defeated all their enemies, killing and destroying
them. And they did what they wanted with those
people who hated them. 6In the palace at Susa,
they killed and destroyed five hundred men.
7They also killed: Parshandatha, Dalphon, Aspa-
tha, 8Poratha, Adalia, Aridatha, 9Parmashta,
Arisai, Aridai, and Vaizatha, 10the ten sons of Haman, son of Hammedatha, the enemy of the Jewish people. But the Jewish people did not take
their belongings.

11On that day the number killed in the palace
at Susa was reported to the king. 12The king said
to Queen Esther, "The Jewish people have killed
and destroyed five hundred people in the palace
at Susa, and they have also killed Haman's ten
sons. What have they done in the rest of the
king's empire! Now what else are you asking? I
will do it! What else do you want? It will be
done!"

13Esther answered, "If it pleases the king, give
the Jewish people who are in Susa permission to
do again tomorrow what the king ordered for today. And let the bodies of Haman's ten sons be
hanged on the platform."

14So the king ordered that it be done. A law
was given in Susa, and the bodies of the ten sons
of Haman were hanged. 15The Jewish people in
Susa came together on the fourteenth day of the
month of Adar. They killed three hundred people
in Susa, but they did not take their belongings.

16At that same time, all the Jewish people in the
king's empire also met to protect themselves and
get rid of their enemies. They killed seventy-five
thousand of those who hated them, but they did
not take their belongings. 17This happened on the
thirteenth day of the month of Adar. On the fourteenth day they rested and made it a day of joyful
feasting.

The Feast of Purim

18But the Jewish people in Susa met on the thirteenth and fourteenth days of the month of Adar.
Then they rested on the fifteenth day and made
it a day of joyful feasting.

19This is why the Jewish people who live in the
country and small villages celebrate on the fourteenth day of the month of Adar. It is a day of
joyful feasting and a day for exchanging gifts.

20Mordecai wrote down everything that had
happened. Then he sent letters to all the Jewish
people in all the empire of King Xerxes, far and
near. 21He told them to celebrate every year on
the fourteenth and fifteenth days of the month of
Adar, 22because that was when the Jewish people
got rid of their enemies. They were also to celebrate it as the month their sadness was turned to
joy and their crying for the dead was turned into
celebration. He told them to celebrate those days
as days of joyful feasting and as a time for giving
food to each other and presents to the poor.

23So the Jewish people agreed to do what Mordecai had written to them, and they agreed to
hold the celebration every year. 24Haman son of
Hammedatha, the Agagite, was the enemy of all
the Jewish people. He had made an evil plan
against the Jewish people to destroy them, and he
had thrown the Pur (that is, the lot[d]) to choose a
day to ruin and destroy them. 25But when the
king learned of the evil plan, he sent out written
orders that the evil plans Haman had made
against the Jewish people would be used against
him. And those orders said that Haman and his
sons should be hanged on the platform. 26So these
days were called Purim, which comes from the
word "Pur" (the lot). Because of everything written in this letter and what they had seen and what
happened to them, 27the Jewish people set up this
custom. They and their descendants[d] and all
those who join them are always to celebrate these
two days every year. They should do it in the right
way and at the time Mordecai had ordered them
in the letter. 28These two days should be remembered and celebrated from now on in every family, in every state, and in every city. These days
of Purim should always be celebrated by the Jewish people, and their descendants should always
remember to celebrate them, too.

29So Queen Esther daughter of Abihail, along
with Mordecai the Jew, wrote this second letter
about Purim. Using the power they had, they
wrote to prove the first letter was true. 30And
Mordecai sent letters to all the Jewish people in

the one hundred twenty-seven states of the kingdom of Xerxes, writing them a message of peace
and truth. 31He wrote to set up these days of Purim at the chosen times. Mordecai the Jew and

> **SIDELIGHT:** Looking for a reason to celebrate? Try the Feast of Purim, a joyous occasion Jews celebrate each year in February or March with parties, gift-giving and aid to the poor. The book of Esther describes the traditional beginning of this two-day festival (Esther 9:18–32).

Queen Esther had sent out the order for the Jewish people, just as they had set up things for themselves and their descendants: On these two days
the people should give up eating and cry loudly.
32Esther's letter set up the rules for Purim, and
they were written down in the records.

The Greatness of Mordecai

10 King Xerxes demanded taxes everywhere, even from the cities on the seacoast. 2And all the great things Xerxes did by his
power and strength are written in the record
books of the kings of Media and Persia. Also written in those record books are all the things done
by Mordecai, whom the king made great. 3Mor-
decai the Jew was second in importance to King
Xerxes, and he was the most important man
among the Jewish people. His fellow Jews respected him very much, because he worked for
the good of his people and spoke up for the safety
of all the Jewish people.

JOB

Why Read This Book:

- Learn patience from someone who is suffering unfairly (Job 1:21—2:10; 16; 19).
- Realize it's okay to question God (Job 10, 13, 23).
- See how God is always there, even when he doesn't seem to be (Job 38—42).

Behind the Scenes:

Why do good people suffer? Why do bad people seem to get away with everything? How can God love us if he lets bad things happen to us? If you have ever asked those questions, you are not alone. For centuries, people have asked them and struggled with them.

The book of Job addresses those questions as it tells about Job, an upright and wealthy man. Like others of his day, he believed that all of his blessings were the result of his goodness. He accepted traditional answers to life's questions.

Then his life fell apart. He lost everything—his family, his health, and his belongings. Life wasn't supposed to work out this way. In his pain, he angrily cried out to God, "Why do innocent people suffer?"

Four friends made matters worse by telling Job the same old thing: God

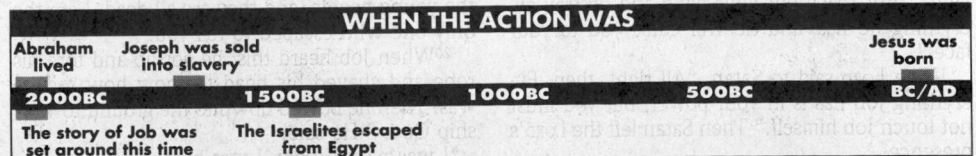

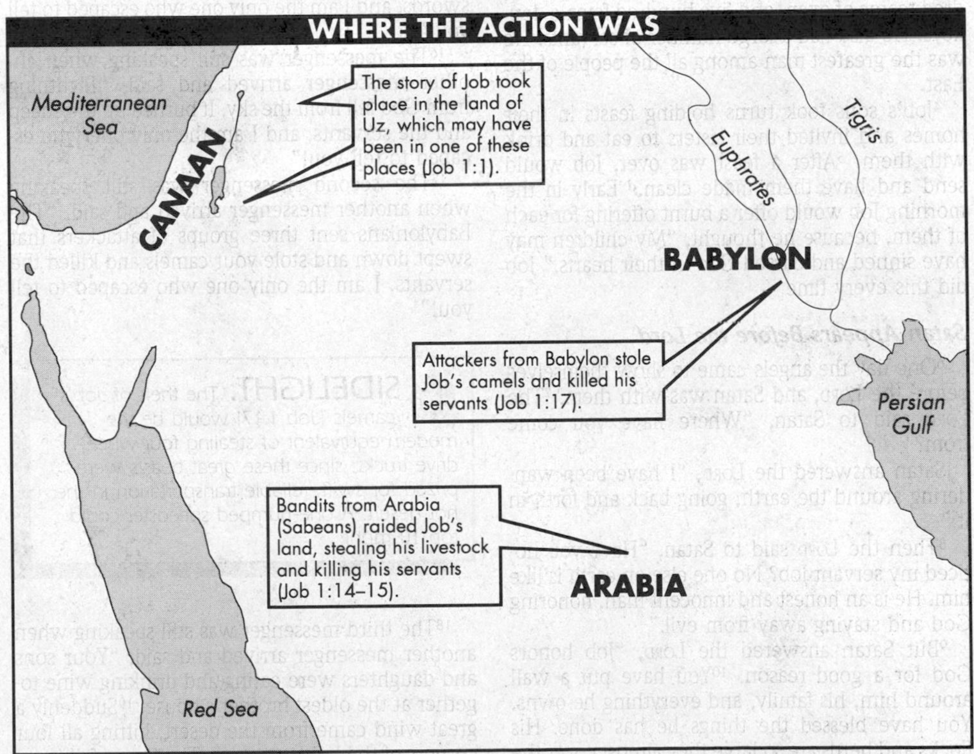
WHERE THE ACTION WAS
Mediterranean Sea
CANAAN
The story of Job took place in the land of Uz, which may have been in one of these places (Job 1:1).
Tigris
Euphrates
BABYLON
Attackers from Babylon stole Job's camels and killed his servants (Job 1:17).
Persian Gulf
Bandits from Arabia (Sabeans) raided Job's land, stealing his livestock and killing his servants (Job 1:14–15).
ARABIA
Red Sea

WHEN THE ACTION WAS

2000BC	1500BC	1000BC	500BC	BC/AD
Abraham lived; The story of Job was set around this time	Joseph was sold into slavery; The Israelites escaped from Egypt			Jesus was born

Behind the Scenes (cont.):

rewards the righteous and punishes sinners (Job 3—37). Job sincerely believed he was innocent, but he couldn't explain the suffering. He felt betrayed by God. Yet he patiently kept his faith in God and waited for God's answers to his questions.

Job and his friends never settled their debate. Suddenly God appeared on the scene through a storm, in chapters 38—41. He didn't answer Job, though he did speak to him. God reminded Job that his greatness and wisdom are beyond human understanding. Job then realized that it wasn't his place to try to understand God. Instead, he was to follow God faithfully no matter what happened.

People continue to struggle with why good people suffer. The book of Job tells us it's okay to ask God tough questions. It also challenges us to remain faithful in spite of suffering. In the end, we can trust in God's goodness, justice, and wisdom—even when we can't see it ourselves.

Job, the Good Man

1 A man named Job lived in the land of Uz. He
was an honest and innocent man; he honored God and stayed away from evil. 2Job had
seven sons and three daughters. 3He owned seven
thousand sheep, three thousand camels, five hundred teams of oxen, and five hundred female donkeys. He also had a large number of servants. He
was the greatest man among all the people of the
East.
4Job's sons took turns holding feasts in their
homes and invited their sisters to eat and drink
with them. 5After a feast was over, Job would
send and have them made clean.[d] Early in the
morning Job would offer a burnt offering for each
of them, because he thought, "My children may
have sinned and cursed God in their hearts." Job
did this every time.

Satan Appears Before the Lord

6One day the angels came to show themselves
before the LORD, and Satan was with them. 7The
LORD said to Satan, "Where have you come
from?"
Satan answered the LORD, "I have been wandering around the earth, going back and forth in
it."
8Then the LORD said to Satan, "Have you noticed my servant Job? No one else on earth is like
him. He is an honest and innocent man, honoring
God and staying away from evil."
9But Satan answered the LORD, "Job honors
God for a good reason. 10You have put a wall
around him, his family, and everything he owns.
You have blessed the things he has done. His
flocks and herds are so large they almost cover the
land. 11But reach out your hand and destroy everything he has, and he will curse you to your
face."
12The LORD said to Satan, "All right, then. Everything Job has is in your power, but you must
not touch Job himself." Then Satan left the LORD's
presence.
13One day Job's sons and daughters were eating
and drinking wine together at the oldest brother's
house. 14A messenger came to Job and said, "The
oxen were plowing and the donkeys were eating
grass nearby, 15when the Sabeans attacked and
carried them away. They killed the servants with
swords, and I am the only one who escaped to tell
you!"
16The messenger was still speaking when another messenger arrived and said, "Lightning
from God fell from the sky. It burned up the sheep
and the servants, and I am the only one who escaped to tell you!"
17The second messenger was still speaking
when another messenger arrived and said, "The
Babylonians sent three groups of attackers that
swept down and stole your camels and killed the
servants. I am the only one who escaped to tell
you!"

SIDELIGHT: The theft of Job's camels (Job 1:17) would be the modern equivalent of stealing four-wheel-drive trucks, since these great beasts were prized for swift, reliable transportation in the hot desert. A one-humped speedster could top 10 mph!

18The third messenger was still speaking when
another messenger arrived and said, "Your sons
and daughters were eating and drinking wine together at the oldest brother's house. 19Suddenly a
great wind came from the desert, hitting all four
corners of the house at once. The house fell in on
the young people, and they are all dead. I am the
only one who escaped to tell you!"
20When Job heard this, he got up and tore his
robe and shaved his head to show how sad he
was. Then he bowed down to the ground to worship God. 21He said:

"I was naked when I was born,

and I will be naked when I die.
The LORD gave these things to me,
and he has taken them away.
Praise the name of the LORD."
22In all this Job did not sin or blame God.

Satan Appears Before the Lord Again

2 On another day the angels came to show
themselves before the LORD, and Satan was
with them again. 2The LORD said to Satan,
"Where have you come from?"
Satan answered the LORD, "I have been wandering around the earth, going back and forth in
it."
3Then the LORD said to Satan, "Have you noticed my servant Job? No one else on earth is like
him. He is an honest and innocent man, honoring
God and staying away from evil. You caused me
to ruin him for no good reason, but he continues
to be without blame."
4"One skin for another!" Satan answered. "A
man will give all he has to save his own life. 5But
reach out your hand and destroy his flesh and
bones, and he will curse you to your face."
6The LORD said to Satan, "All right, then. Job
is in your power, but you may not take his life."
7So Satan left the LORD's presence. He put painful sores on Job's body, from the top of his head
to the soles of his feet. 8Job took a piece of broken
pottery to scrape himself, and he sat in ashes in
misery.
9Job's wife said to him, "Why are you trying to
stay innocent? Curse God and die!"
10Job answered, "You are talking like a foolish
woman. Should we take only good things from
God and not trouble?" In spite of all this Job did
not sin in what he said.

Job's Three Friends Come to Help

11Now Job had three friends: Eliphaz the Temanite, Bildad the Shuhite, and Zophar the Naamathite. When these friends heard about Job's
troubles, they agreed to meet and visit him. They
wanted to show their concern and to comfort
him. 12They saw Job from far away, but he looked
so different they almost didn't recognize him.
They began to cry loudly and tore their robes and
put dirt on their heads to show how sad they
were. 13Then they sat on the ground with Job
seven days and seven nights. No one said a word
to him because they saw how much he was suffering.

Job Curses His Birth

3 After seven days Job cried out and cursed the
day he had been born, 2saying:

3"Let the day I was born be destroyed,
and the night it was said, 'A boy is born!'
4Let that day turn to darkness.
Don't let God care about it.
Don't let light shine on it.
5Let darkness and gloom have that day.
Let a cloud hide it.
Let thick darkness cover its light.
6Let thick darkness capture that night.
Don't count it among the days of the year
or put it in any of the months.
7Let that night be empty,
with no shout of joy to be heard.
8Let those who curse days curse that day.
Let them prepare to wake up the sea
monster Leviathan.[d]
9Let that day's morning stars never appear;
let it wait for daylight that never comes.
Don't let it see the first light of dawn,
10because it allowed me to be born
and did not hide trouble from my eyes.

11"Why didn't I die as soon as I was born?
Why didn't I die when I came out of the
womb?
12Why did my mother's knees receive me,
and my mother's breasts feed me?
13If they had not been there,
I would be lying dead in peace;
I would be asleep and at rest
14with kings and wise men of the earth
who built places for themselves that are
now ruined.
15I would be asleep with rulers
who filled their houses with gold and silver.
16Why was I not buried like a child born dead,
like a baby who never saw the light of day?
17In the grave the wicked stop making trouble,
and the weary workers are at rest.
18In the grave there is rest for the captives
who no longer hear the shout of the slave
driver.
19People great and small are in the grave,
and the slave is freed from his master.

20"Why is light given to those in misery?
Why is life given to those who are so
unhappy?
21They want to die, but death does not come.
They search for death more than for hidden
treasure.
22They are very happy
when they get to the grave.
23They cannot see where they are going.
God has hidden the road ahead.
24I make sad sounds as I eat;
my groans pour out like water.
25Everything I feared and dreaded
has happened to me.
26I have no peace or quietness.
I have no rest, only trouble."

Eliphaz Speaks

4 Then Eliphaz the Temanite answered:
2"If someone tried to speak with you,
would you be upset?
I cannot keep from speaking.
3Think about the many people you have
taught
and the weak hands you have made strong.
4Your words have comforted those who fell,
and you have strengthened those who
could not stand.
5But now trouble comes to you, and you are
discouraged;
trouble hits you, and you are terrified.
6You should have confidence because you
respect God;
you should have hope because you are
innocent.

7"Remember that the innocent will not die;
honest people will never be destroyed.
8I have noticed that people who plow evil
and plant trouble, harvest it.
9God's breath destroys them,
and a blast of his anger kills them.
10Lions may roar and growl,
but when the teeth of a strong lion are
broken,
11that lion dies of hunger.
The cubs of the mother lion are scattered.

12"A word was brought to me in secret,
and my ears heard a whisper of it.
13It was during a nightmare
when people are in deep sleep.
14I was trembling with fear;
all my bones were shaking.
15A spirit glided past my face,
and the hair on my body stood on end.
16The spirit stopped,
but I could not see what it was.
A shape stood before my eyes,
and I heard a quiet voice.
17It said, 'Can a human be more right than
God?
Can a person be pure before his maker?
18God does not trust his angels;
he blames them for mistakes.
19So he puts even more blame on people who
live in clay houses,[n]
whose foundations are made of dust,
who can be crushed like a moth.
20Between dawn and sunset many people are
broken to pieces;
without being noticed, they die and are
gone forever.
21The ropes of their tents are pulled up,
and they die without wisdom.'

5 "Call if you want to, Job, but no one will
answer you.
You can't turn to any of the holy ones.
2Anger kills the fool,
and jealousy slays the stupid.
3I have seen a fool succeed,
but I cursed his home immediately.
4His children are far from safety
and are crushed in court with no defense.
5The hungry eat his harvest,
even taking what grew among the thorns,
and thirsty people want his wealth.
6Hard times do not come up from the ground,
and trouble does not grow from the earth.
7People produce trouble
as surely as sparks fly upward.

8"But if I were you, I would call on God
and bring my problem before him.
9God does wonders that cannot be
understood;
he does so many miracles[d] they cannot be
counted.
10He gives rain to the earth
and sends water on the fields.
11He makes the humble person important
and lifts the sad to places of safety.
12He ruins the plans of those who trick others
so they have no success.
13He catches the wise in their own clever traps
and sweeps away the plans of those who
try to trick others.
14Darkness covers them up in the daytime;
even at noon they feel around in the dark.
15God saves the needy from their lies
and from the harm done by powerful
people.
16So the poor have hope,
while those who are unfair are silenced.

17"The one whom God corrects is happy,
so do not hate being corrected by the
Almighty.
18God hurts, but he also bandages up;
he injures, but his hands also heal.
19He will save you from six troubles;
even seven troubles will not harm you.
20God will buy you back from death in times of
hunger,
and in battle he will save you from the
sword.
21You will be protected from the tongue that
strikes like a whip,
and you will not be afraid when destruction
comes.
22You will laugh at destruction and hunger,

clay houses This is probably talking about people's bodies.

and you will not fear the wild animals,
23because you will have an agreement with the
stones in the field,
and the wild animals will be at peace with
you.
24You will know that your tent is safe,
because you will check the things you own
and find nothing missing.
25You will know that you will have many
children,
and your descendants[d] will be like the grass
on the earth.
26You will come to the grave with all your
strength,
like bundles of grain gathered at the right
time.

27"We have checked this, and it is true,
so hear it and decide what it means to
you."

Job Answers Eliphaz

6 Then Job answered:

2"I wish my suffering could be weighed
and my misery put on scales.
3My sadness would be heavier than the sand
of the seas.
No wonder my words seem careless.
4The arrows of the Almighty are in me;
my spirit drinks in their poison;
God's terrors are gathered against me.

> **SIDELIGHT:** You may have never called God "King of the Hill," but the characters in Job did. "God Almighty" is the translation of a Hebrew name that literally means "Lord of the Mountain" (for example, Job 6:4).

5A wild donkey does not bray when it has
grass to eat,
and an ox is quiet when it has feed.
6Tasteless food is not eaten without salt,
and there is no flavor in the white of an
egg.
7I refuse to touch it;
such food makes me sick.

8"How I wish that I might have what I ask for
and that God would give me what I hope
for.
9How I wish God would crush me
and reach out his hand to destroy me.
10Then I would have this comfort
and be glad even in this unending pain,
because I would know I did not reject the
words of the Holy One.

11"I do not have the strength to wait.
There is nothing to hope for,
so why should I be patient?
12I do not have the strength of stone;
my flesh is not bronze.
13I have no power to help myself,
because success has been taken away from
me.

14"They say, 'A man's friends should be kind to
him when he is in trouble,
even if he stops fearing the Almighty.'
15But my brothers cannot be counted on.
They are like streams that do not always
flow,
streams that sometimes run over.
16They are made dark by melting ice
and rise with melting snow.
17But they stop flowing in the dry season;
they disappear when it is hot.
18Travelers turn away from their paths
and go into the desert and die.
19The groups of travelers from Tema look for
water,
and the traders of Sheba look hopefully.
20They are upset because they had been sure;
when they arrive, they are disappointed.
21You also have been no help.
You see something terrible, and you are
afraid.
22I have never said, 'Give me a gift.
Use your wealth to pay my debt.
23Save me from the enemy's power.
Buy me back from the clutches of cruel
people.'

24"Teach me, and I will be quiet.
Show me where I have been wrong.
25Honest words are painful,
but your arguments prove nothing.
26Do you mean to correct what I say?
Will you treat the words of a troubled man
as if they were only wind?
27You would even gamble for orphans
and would trade away your friend.

28"But now please look at me.
I would not lie to your face.
29Change your mind; do not be unfair;
think again, because my innocence is being
questioned.
30What I am saying is not wicked;
I can tell the difference between right and
wrong.

7 "People have a hard task on earth,
and their days are like those of a laborer.
2They are like a slave wishing for the evening
shadows,
like a laborer waiting to be paid.

[3]But I am given months that are empty,
and nights of misery have been given to me.
[4]When I lie down, I think, 'How long until I get up?'
The night is long, and I toss until dawn.
[5]My body is covered with worms and scabs,
and my skin is broken and full of sores.

[6]"My days go by faster than a weaver's tool,
and they come to an end without hope.
[7]Remember, God, that my life is only a breath.
My eyes will never see happy times again.
[8]Those who see me now will see me no more;
you will look for me, but I will be gone.
[9]As a cloud disappears and is gone,
people go to the grave and never return.
[10]They will never come back to their houses again,
and their places will not know them anymore.

[11]"So I will not stay quiet;
I will speak out in the suffering of my spirit.
I will complain because I am so unhappy.
[12]I am not the sea or the sea monster.
So why have you set a guard over me?
[13]Sometimes I think my bed will comfort me
or that my couch will stop my complaint.
[14]Then you frighten me with dreams
and terrify me with visions.
[15]My throat prefers to be choked;
my bones welcome death.
[16]I hate my life; I don't want to live forever.
Leave me alone, because my days have no meaning.

[17]"Why do you make people so important
and give them so much attention?
[18]You examine them every morning
and test them every moment.
[19]Will you never look away from me
or leave me alone even long enough to swallow?

DEPRESSION

Stirring Up Life

Mandy Lewis sat beside the swirling river that ran through town. Her fright and hurt had changed into a deadly heaviness. It stifled her. It dulled all hope.

Only last week everything had seemed okay. Then Josh McKinley dumped her—just put his arm around her best friend and took off. It nearly killed Mandy. How could he . . . when he said he loved her? And how could Sheila?

Mandy tried to talk to her mom, but the whole house was a constant battlefield, everyone yelling at each other. Her stepdad was out of work and there wasn't enough money to go around.

The water invited her into its depths. It offered an easy way out. Then she would never have to hurt again.

"Can I sit here with you?"

Mandy looked up at a tall girl. She had seen her a few times at school, always by herself, but self-assured, at ease.

"If you want."

"I'm nobody to you, but . . . I know what happened, and I care." The girl sat down. "I've been there. And even though it doesn't seem possible now, things will get better. Just hang in there, okay?"

Mandy looked into the girl's brown eyes. Their sincerity stirred life inside Mandy.

Like Mandy, Job felt overwhelmed by a sense of loss and depression. Read his story in **Job 7:1–8**.

- How does Mandy's depression compare with Job's?
- When you feel like Job did in verses 3 and 7, what do you need most?

CONSIDER . . .

- talking to a trusted friend about a problem that's getting you down.
- organizing a peer counseling program at your church or school. Talk to your youth pastor or school counselor for ideas.

FOR MORE, SEE . . .

- Psalm 139:1–24 (p. 561)
- 2 Corinthians 1:3–7 (p. 1193)
- Philippians 2:1–4 (p. 1230)

20If I have sinned, what have I done to you,
you watcher of humans?
Why have you made me your target?
Have I become a heavy load for you?
21Why don't you pardon my wrongs
and forgive my sins?
I will soon lie down in the dust of death.
Then you will search for me, but I will be no more."

Bildad Speaks to Job

8 Then Bildad the Shuhite answered:

2"How long will you say such things?
Your words are no more than wind.
3God does not twist justice;
the Almighty does not make wrong what is right.
4Your children sinned against God,
and he punished them for their sins.
5But you should ask God for help
and pray to the Almighty for mercy.
6If you are good and honest,
he will stand up for you
and bring you back where you belong.
7Where you began will seem unimportant,
because your future will be so successful.

8"Ask old people;
find out what their ancestors learned,
9because we were only born yesterday and know nothing.
Our days on earth are only a shadow.
10Those people will teach you and tell you
and speak about what they know.
11Papyrus[d] plants cannot grow where there is no swamp,
and reeds cannot grow tall without water.
12While they are still growing and not yet cut,
they will dry up quicker than grass.
13That is what will happen to those who forget God;
the hope of the wicked will be gone.
14What they hope in is easily broken;
what they trust is like a spider's web.
15They lean on the spider's web, but it breaks.
They grab it, but it does not hold up.
16They are like well-watered plants in the sunshine
that spread their roots all through the garden.
17They wrap their roots around a pile of rocks
and look for a place among the stones.
18But if a plant is torn from its place,
then that place rejects it and says, 'I never saw you.'
19Now joy has gone away;
other plants grow up from the same dirt.

20"Surely God does not reject the innocent
or give strength to those who do evil.
21God will yet fill your mouth with laughter
and your lips with shouts of joy.
22Your enemies will be covered with shame,
and the tents of the wicked will be gone."

Job Answers Bildad

9 Then Job answered:

2"Yes, I know that this is true,
but how can anyone be right in the presence of God?
3Someone might want to argue with God,
but no one could answer God,
not one time out of a thousand.
4God's wisdom is deep, and his power is great;
no one can fight him without getting hurt.
5God moves mountains without anyone knowing it
and turns them over when he is angry.
6He shakes the earth out of its place
and makes its foundations tremble.
7He commands the sun not to shine
and shuts off the light of the stars.
8He alone stretches out the skies
and walks on the waves of the sea.
9It is God who made the Bear, Orion, and the Pleiades[n]
and the groups of stars in the southern sky.
10He does wonders that cannot be understood;
he does so many miracles[d] they cannot be counted.
11When he passes me, I cannot see him;
when he goes by me, I do not recognize him.
12If he snatches something away, no one can stop him
or say to him, 'What are you doing?'
13God will not hold back his anger.
Even the helpers of the monster Rahab[d] lie at his feet in fear.
14So how can I argue with God,
or even find words to argue with him?
15Even if I were right, I could not answer him;
I could only beg God, my Judge, for mercy.
16If I called to him and he answered,
I still don't believe he would listen to me.
17He would crush me with a storm
and multiply my wounds for no reason.
18He would not let me catch my breath
but would overwhelm me with misery.
19When it comes to strength, God is stronger than I;
when it comes to justice, no one can accuse him.

Bear . . . Pleiades Names of well-known groups of stars.

[20]Even if I were right, my own mouth would say I was wrong;
if I were innocent, my mouth would say I was guilty.

[21]"I am innocent,
but I don't care about myself.
I hate my own life.
[22]It is all the same. That is why I say,
'God destroys both the innocent and the guilty.'
[23]If the whip brings sudden death,
God will laugh at the suffering of the innocent.
[24]When the land falls into the hands of evil people,
he covers the judges' faces so they can't see it.
If it is not God who does this, then who is it?

[25]"My days go by faster than a runner;
they fly away without my seeing any joy.
[26]They glide past like paper boats.
They attack like eagles swooping down to feed.
[27]Even though I say, 'I will forget my complaint;
I will change the look on my face and smile,'
[28]I still dread all my suffering.
I know you will hold me guilty.
[29]I have already been found guilty,
so why should I struggle for no reason?
[30]I might wash myself with soap
and scrub my hands with strong soap,
[31]but you would push me into a dirty pit,
and even my clothes would hate me.

[32]"God is not a man like me, so I cannot answer him.
We cannot meet each other in court.
[33]I wish there were someone to make peace between us,
someone to decide our case.
[34]Maybe he could remove God's punishment
so his terror would no longer frighten me.
[35]Then I could speak without being afraid,
but I am not able to do that.

10 "I hate my life,
so I will complain without holding back;
I will speak because I am so unhappy.
[2]I will say to God: Do not hold me guilty,
but tell me what you have against me.
[3]Does it make you happy to trouble me?
Don't you care about me, the work of your hands?
Are you happy with the plans of evil people?
[4]Do you have human eyes
that see as we see?
[5]Are your days like the days of humans,
and your years like our years?
[6]You look for the evil I have done
and search for my sin.
[7]You know I am not guilty,
but no one can save me from your power.

[8]"Your hands shaped and made me.
Do you now turn around and destroy me?
[9]Remember that you molded me like a piece of clay.
Will you now turn me back into dust?
[10]You formed me inside my mother
like cheese formed from milk.
[11]You dressed me with skin and flesh;
you sewed me together with bones and muscles.
[12]You gave me life and showed me kindness,
and in your care you watched over my life.

[13]"But in your heart you hid other plans.
I know this was in your mind.
[14]If I sinned, you would watch me
and would not let my sin go unpunished.
[15]How terrible it will be for me if I am guilty!
Even if I am right, I cannot lift my head.
I am full of shame
and experience only pain.
[16]If I hold up my head, you hunt me like a lion
and again show your terrible power against me.
[17]You bring new witnesses against me
and increase your anger against me.
Your armies come against me.

[18]"So why did you allow me to be born?
I wish I had died before anyone saw me.
[19]I wish I had never lived,
but had been carried straight from birth to the grave.
[20]The few days of my life are almost over.
Leave me alone so I can have a moment of joy.
[21]Soon I will leave; I will not return
from the land of darkness and gloom,
[22]the land of darkest night,
from the land of gloom and confusion,
where even the light is darkness."

Zophar Speaks to Job

11 Then Zophar the Naamathite answered:
[2]"Should these words go unanswered?
Is this talker in the right?
[3]Your lies do not make people quiet;
people should correct you when you make fun of God.
[4]You say, 'My teachings are right,
and I am clean[d] in God's sight.'

5I wish God would speak
and open his lips against you
6and tell you the secrets of wisdom,
because wisdom has two sides.
Know this: God has even forgotten some of
your sin.

7"Can you understand the secrets of God?
Can you search the limits of the Almighty?
8His limits are higher than the heavens;
you cannot reach them!
They are deeper than the grave;
you cannot understand them!
9His limits are longer than the earth
and wider than the sea.

10"If God comes along and puts you in prison
or calls you into court, no one can stop
him.
11God knows who is evil,
and when he sees evil, he takes note of it.
12A fool cannot become wise
any more than a wild donkey can be born
tame.

13"You must give your whole heart to him
and hold out your hands to him for help.
14Put away the sin that is in your hand;
let no evil remain in your tent.
15Then you can lift up your face without
shame,
and you can stand strong without fear.
16You will forget your trouble
and remember it only as water gone by.
17Your life will be as bright as the noonday
sun,
and darkness will seem like morning.
18You will feel safe because there is hope;
you will look around and rest in safety.
19You will lie down, and no one will scare you.
Many people will want favors from you.
20But the wicked will not be able to see,
so they will not escape.
Their only hope will be to die."

Job Answers Zophar

12 Then Job answered:
2"You really think you are the only
wise people
and that when you die, wisdom will die
with you!
3But my mind is as good as yours;
you are not better than I am.
Everyone knows all these things.
4My friends all laugh at me
when I call on God and expect him to
answer me;
they laugh at me even though I am right
and innocent!
5Those who are comfortable don't care that
others have trouble;
they think it right that those people should
have troubles.
6The tents of robbers are not bothered,
and those who make God angry are safe.
They have their god in their pocket.

7"But ask the animals, and they will teach
you,
or ask the birds of the air, and they will tell
you.
8Speak to the earth, and it will teach you,
or let the fish of the sea tell you.
9Every one of these knows
that the hand of the LORD has done this.
10The life of every creature
and the breath of all people are in God's
hand.
11The ear tests words
as the tongue tastes food.
12Older people are wise,
and long life brings understanding.

13"But only God has wisdom and power,
good advice and understanding.
14What he tears down cannot be rebuilt;
anyone he puts in prison cannot be let out.
15If God holds back the waters, there is no
rain;
if he lets the waters go, they flood the land.
16He is strong and victorious;
both the one who fools others and the one
who is fooled belong to him.
17God leads the wise away as captives
and turns judges into fools.
18He takes off chains that kings put on
and puts a garment on their bodies.
19He leads priests away naked
and destroys the powerful.
20He makes trusted people be silent
and takes away the wisdom of older
leaders.
21He brings disgrace on important people
and takes away the weapons of the strong.
22He uncovers the deep things of darkness
and brings dark shadows into the light.
23He makes nations great and then destroys
them;
he makes nations large and then scatters
them.
24He takes understanding away from the
leaders of the earth
and makes them wander through a pathless
desert.
25They feel around in darkness with no light;
he makes them stumble like drunks.

13 "Now my eyes have seen all this;
my ears have heard and understood it.

2What you know, I also know.
You are not better than I am.
3But I want to speak to the Almighty
and to argue my case with God.
4But you smear me with lies.
You are worthless doctors, all of you!
5I wish you would just stop talking;
then you would really be wise!
6Listen to my argument,
and hear the pleading of my lips.
7You should not speak evil in the name of God;
you cannot speak God's truth by telling lies.
8You should not unfairly choose his side against mine;
you should not argue the case for God.
9You will not do well if he examines you;
you cannot fool God as you might fool humans.
10God would surely scold you
if you unfairly took one person's side.
11His bright glory would scare you,
and you would be very much afraid of him.
12Your wise sayings are worth no more than ashes,
and your arguments are as weak as clay.

13"Be quiet and let me speak.
Let things happen to me as they will.
14Why should I put myself in danger
and take my life in my own hands?
15Even if God kills me, I have hope in him;
I will still defend my ways to his face.
16This is my salvation.
The wicked cannot come before him.
17Listen carefully to my words;
let your ears hear what I say.
18See, I have prepared my case,
and I know I will be proved right.
19No one can accuse me of doing wrong.
If someone can, I will be quiet and die.

20"God, please just give me these two things,
and then I will not hide from you:
21Take your punishment away from me,
and stop frightening me with your terrors.
22Then call me, and I will answer,
or let me speak, and you answer.
23How many evil things and sins have I done?
Show me my wrong and my sin.
24Don't hide your face from me;
don't think of me as your enemy.
25Don't punish a leaf that is blown by the wind;
don't chase after straw.
26You write down cruel things against me
and make me suffer for my boyhood sins.
27You put my feet in chains
and keep close watch wherever I go.
You even mark the soles of my feet.
28"Everyone wears out like something rotten,
like clothing eaten by moths.

14 "All of us born to women
live only a few days and have lots of trouble.
2We grow up like flowers and then dry up and die.
We are like a passing shadow that does not last.
3Lord, do you need to watch me like this?
Must you bring me before you to be judged?
4No one can bring something clean from something dirty.
5Our time is limited.
You have given us only so many months to live
and have set limits we cannot go beyond.
6So look away from us and leave us alone
until we put in our time like a laborer.

7"If a tree is cut down,
there is hope that it will grow again
and will send out new branches.
8Even if its roots grow old in the ground,
and its stump dies in the dirt,
9at the smell of water it will bud
and put out new shoots like a plant.
10But we die, and our bodies are laid in the ground;
we take our last breath and are gone.
11Water disappears from a lake,
and a river loses its water and dries up.
12In the same way, we lie down and do not rise again;
we will not get up or be awakened
until the heavens disappear.

13"I wish you would hide me in the grave;
hide me until your anger is gone.
I wish you would set a time
and then remember me!
14If a person dies, will he live again?
All my days are a struggle;
I will wait until my change comes.
15You will call, and I will answer you;
you will desire the creature your hands have made.
16Then you will count my steps,
but you will not keep track of my sin.
17My wrongs will be closed up in a bag,
and you will cover up my sin.

18"A mountain washes away and crumbles;
and a rock can be moved from its place.
19Water washes over stones and wears them down,
and rushing waters wash away the dirt.
In the same way, you destroy my hope.
20You defeat a person forever, and he is gone;

you change his appearance and send him
away.
21His sons are honored, but he does not know
it;
his sons are disgraced, but he does not
see it.
22He only feels the pain of his body
and feels sorry for himself."

Eliphaz Answers Job

15 Then Eliphaz the Temanite answered:
2"A wise person would not answer
with empty words
or fill his stomach with the hot east wind.
3He would not argue with useless words
or make speeches that have no value.
4But you even destroy respect for God
and limit the worship of him.
5Your sin teaches your mouth what to say;
you use words to trick others.
6It is your own mouth, not mine, that shows
you are wicked;
your own lips testify against you.

7"You are not the first man ever born;
you are not older than the hills.
8You did not listen in on God's secret council.
But you limit wisdom to yourself.
9You don't know any more than we know.
You don't understand any more than we
understand.
10Old people with gray hair are on our side;
they are even older than your father.

SIDELIGHT: While adults may try to hide their age today, growing old was a mark of dignity and respect in the Old Testament. That's why Eliphaz supported his argument by saying people with gray hair were on his side (Job 15:10).

11Is the comfort God gives you not enough for
you,
even when words are spoken gently to
you?
12Has your heart carried you away from God?
Why do your eyes flash with anger?
13Why do you speak out your anger against
God?
Why do these words pour out of your
mouth?

14"How can anyone be pure?
How can someone born to a woman be
good?
15God places no trust in his holy ones,
and even the heavens are not pure in his
eyes.
16How much less pure is one who is terrible
and rotten
and drinks up evil as if it were water!

17"Listen to me, and I will tell you about it;
I will tell you what I have seen.
18These are things wise men have told;
their fathers told them, and they have
hidden nothing.
19(The land was given to their fathers only,
and no foreigner lived among them.)
20The wicked suffer pain all their lives;
the cruel suffer during all the years saved
up for them.
21Terrible sounds fill their ears,
and when things seem to be going well,
robbers attack them.
22Evil people give up trying to escape from the
darkness;
it has been decided that they will die by
the sword.
23They wander around and will become food
for vultures.
They know darkness will soon come.
24Worry and suffering terrify them;
they overwhelm them, like a king ready to
attack,
25because they shake their fists at God
and try to get their own way against the
Almighty.
26They stubbornly charge at God
with thick, strong shields.

27"Although the faces of the wicked are thick
with fat,
and their bellies are fat with flesh,
28they will live in towns that are ruined,
in houses where no one lives,
which are crumbling into ruins.
29The wicked will no longer get rich,
and the riches they have will not last;
the things they own will no longer spread
over the land.
30They will not escape the darkness.
A flame will dry up their branches;
God's breath will carry the wicked away.
31The wicked should not fool themselves by
trusting what is useless.
If they do, they will get nothing in return.
32Their branches will dry up before they finish
growing
and will never turn green.
33They will be like a vine whose grapes are
pulled off before they are ripe,
like an olive tree that loses its blossoms.
34People without God can produce nothing.
Fire will destroy the tents of those who
take money to do evil,

35who plan trouble and give birth to evil,
whose hearts plan ways to trick others."

Job Answers Eliphaz

16 Then Job answered:
2"I have heard many things like these.
You are all painful comforters!
3Will your long-winded speeches never end?
What makes you keep on arguing?
4I also could speak as you do
if you were in my place.
I could make great speeches against you
and shake my head at you.
5But, instead, I would encourage you,
and my words would bring you relief.

6"Even if I speak, my pain is not less,
and if I don't speak, it still does not go away.
7God, you have surely taken away my strength
and destroyed my whole family.
8You have made me thin and weak,
and this shows I have done wrong.
9God attacks me and tears me with anger;
he grinds his teeth at me;
my enemy stares at me with his angry eyes.
10People open their mouths to make fun of me
and hit my cheeks to insult me.
They join together against me.
11God has turned me over to evil people
and has handed me over to the wicked.
12Everything was fine with me,
but God broke me into pieces;
he held me by the neck and crushed me.
He has made me his target;
13 his archers surround me.
He stabs my kidneys without mercy;
he spills my blood on the ground.
14Again and again God attacks me;
he runs at me like a soldier.

15"I have sewed rough cloth over my skin to show my sadness
and have buried my face in the dust.
16My face is red from crying;
I have dark circles around my eyes.
17Yet my hands have never done anything cruel,
and my prayer is pure.

18"Earth, please do not cover up my blood.
Don't let my cry ever stop being heard!
19Even now I have one who speaks for me in heaven;
the one who is on my side is high above.
20The one who speaks for me is my friend.
My eyes pour out tears to God.
21He begs God on behalf of a human
as a person begs for his friend.

22"Only a few years will pass
before I go on the journey of no return.

17 My spirit is broken;
the days of my life are almost gone.
The grave is waiting for me.
2Those who laugh at me surround me;
I watch them insult me.

3"God, make me a promise.
No one will make a pledge for me.
4You have closed their minds to understanding.
Do not let them win over me.
5A person might speak against his friends for money,
but if he does, the eyes of his children go blind.

6"God has made my name a curse word;
people spit in my face.
7My sight has grown weak because of my sadness,
and my body is as thin as a shadow.
8Honest people are upset about this;
innocent people are upset with those who do wrong.
9But those who do right will continue to do right,
and those whose hands are not dirty with sin will grow stronger.

10"But, all of you, come and try again!
I do not find a wise person among you.
11My days are gone, and my plans have been destroyed,
along with the desires of my heart.
12These men think night is day;
when it is dark, they say, 'Light is near.'
13If the only home I hope for is the grave,
if I spread out my bed in darkness,
14if I say to the grave, 'You are my father,'
and to the worm, 'You are my mother' or 'You are my sister,'
15where, then, is my hope?
Who can see any hope for me?
16Will hope go down to the gates of death?
Will we go down together into the dust?"

Bildad Answers Job

18 Then Bildad the Shuhite answered:
2"When will you stop these speeches?
Be sensible, and then we can talk.
3You think of us as cattle,
as if we are stupid.
4You tear yourself to pieces in your anger.
Should the earth be vacant just for you?
Should the rocks move from their places?

5"The lamp of the wicked will be put out,

and the flame in their lamps will stop
burning.
6The light in their tents will grow dark,
and the lamps by their sides will go out.
7Their strong steps will grow weak;
they will fall into their own evil traps.
8Their feet will be caught in a net
when they walk into its web.
9A trap will catch them by the heel
and hold them tight.
10A trap for them is hidden on the ground,
right in their path.
11Terrible things startle them from every side
and chase them at every step.
12Hunger takes away their strength,
and disaster is at their side.
13Disease eats away parts of their skin;
death gnaws at their arms and legs.
14They are torn from the safety of their tents
and dragged off to Death, the King of
Terrors.
15Their tents are set on fire,
and sulfur is scattered over their homes.
16Their roots dry up below ground,
and their branches die above ground.
17People on earth will not remember them;
their names will be forgotten in the land.
18They will be driven from light into darkness
and chased out of the world.
19They have no children or descendants[d]
among their people,
and no one will be left alive where they
once lived.
20People of the west will be shocked at what
has happened to them,
and people of the east will be very
frightened.
21Surely this is what will happen to the
wicked;
such is the place of one who does not
know God."

Job Answers Bildad

19 Then Job answered:
2"How long will you hurt me
and crush me with your words?
3You have insulted me ten times now
and attacked me without shame.
4Even if I have sinned,
it is my worry alone.
5If you want to make yourselves look better
than I,
you can blame me for my suffering.
6Then know that God has wronged me
and pulled his net around me.
7"I shout, 'I have been wronged!'
But I get no answer.
I scream for help
but I get no justice.
8God has blocked my way so I cannot pass;
he has covered my paths with darkness.
9He has taken away my honor
and removed the crown from my head.
10He beats me down on every side until I am
gone;
he destroys my hope like a fallen tree.
11His anger burns against me,
and he treats me like an enemy.
12His armies gather;
they prepare to attack me.
They camp around my tent.

13"God has made my brothers my enemies,
and my friends have become strangers.
14My relatives have gone away,
and my friends have forgotten me.
15My guests and my female servants treat me
like a stranger;
they look at me as if I were a foreigner.
16I call for my servant, but he does not answer,
even when I beg him with my own mouth.
17My wife can't stand my breath,
and my own family dislikes me.
18Even the little boys hate me
and talk about me when I leave.
19All my close friends hate me;
even those I love have turned against me.
20I am nothing but skin and bones;
I have escaped by the skin of my teeth.
21Pity me, my friends, pity me,
because the hand of God has hit me.
22Why do you chase me as God does?
Haven't you hurt me enough?

23"How I wish my words were written down,
written on a scroll.
24I wish they were carved with an iron pen
into lead,
or carved into stone forever.
25I know that my Defender lives,
and in the end he will stand upon the
earth.
26Even after my skin has been destroyed,
in my flesh I will see God.
27I will see him myself;
I will see him with my very own eyes.
How my heart wants that to happen!

28"If you say, 'We will continue to trouble
Job,
because the problem lies with him,'
29you should be afraid of the sword yourselves.
God's anger will bring punishment by the
sword.
Then you will know there is judgment."

Zophar Answers

20 Then Zophar the Naamathite answered:
2"My troubled thoughts cause me to answer,
because I am very upset.
3You correct me and I am insulted,
but I understand how to answer you.

4"You know how it has been for a long time,
ever since people were first put on the earth.
5The happiness of evil people is brief,
and the joy of the wicked lasts only a moment.
6Their pride may be as high as the heavens,
and their heads may touch the clouds,
7but they will be gone forever, like their own dung.
People who knew them will say, 'Where are they?'
8They will fly away like a dream
and not be found again;
they will be chased away like a vision in the night.
9Those who saw them will not see them again;
the places where they lived will see them no more.
10Their children will have to pay back the poor,
and they will have to give up their wealth.
11They had the strength of their youth in their bones,
but it will lie with them in the dust of death.

12"Evil may taste sweet in their mouths,
and they may hide it under their tongues.
13They cannot stand to let go of it;
they keep it in their mouths.
14But their food will turn sour in their stomachs,
like the poison of a snake inside them.
15They have swallowed riches, but they will spit them out;
God will make them vomit their riches up.
16They will suck the poison of snakes,
and the snake's fangs will kill them.

> **SIDELIGHT:** Snakes were dangerous desert residents in Bible times (Job 20:14–16). Numerous varieties of snakes lived in the desert, and about half a dozen of the species were poisonous. In one instance, snakes invaded an Israelite camp (Numbers 21:6–8, p. 145), and many of the Israelites died from the bites.

17They will not admire the sparkling streams
or the rivers flowing with honey and cream.
18They must give back what they worked for
without eating it;
they will not enjoy the money they made
from their trading,
19because they troubled the poor and left them
with nothing.
They have taken houses they did not build.

20"Evil people never lack an appetite,
and nothing escapes their selfishness.
21But nothing will be left for them to eat;
their riches will not continue.
22When they still have plenty, trouble will
catch up to them,
and great misery will come down on them.
23When the wicked fill their stomachs,
God will send his burning anger against them,
and blows of punishment will fall on them like rain.
24The wicked may run away from an iron weapon,
but a bronze arrow will stab them.
25They will pull the arrows out of their backs
and pull the points out of their livers.
Terrors will come over them;
26 total darkness waits for their treasure.
A fire not fanned by people will destroy them
and burn up what is left of their tents.
27The heavens will show their guilt,
and the earth will rise up against them.
28A flood will carry their houses away,
swept away on the day of God's anger.
29This is what God plans for evil people;
this is what he has decided they will receive."

Job Answers Zophar

21 Then Job answered:
2"Listen carefully to my words,
and let this be the way you comfort me.
3Be patient while I speak.
After I have finished, you may continue to make fun of me.

4"My complaint is not just against people;
I have reason to be impatient.
5Look at me and be shocked;
put your hand over your mouth in shock.
6When I think about this, I am terribly afraid
and my body shakes.
7Why do evil people live a long time?
They grow old and become more powerful.
8They see their children around them;
they watch them grow up.
9Their homes are safe and without fear;

God does not punish them.
10Their bulls never fail to mate;
their cows have healthy calves.
11They send out their children like a flock;
their little ones dance about.
12They sing to the music of tambourines[d] and harps,
and the sound of the flute makes them happy.
13Evil people enjoy successful lives
and then go peacefully to the grave.
14They say to God, 'Leave us alone!
We don't want to know your ways.
15Who is the Almighty that we should serve him?
What would we gain by praying to him?'
16The success of the wicked is not their own doing.
Their way of thinking is different from mine.
17Yet how often are the lamps of evil people turned off?
How often does trouble come to them?
How often do they suffer God's angry punishment?
18How often are they like straw in the wind
or like chaff[d] that is blown away by a storm?
19It is said, 'God saves up a person's punishment for his children.'
But God should punish the wicked themselves so they will know it.
20Their eyes should see their own destruction,
and they should suffer the anger of the Almighty.
21They do not care about the families they leave behind
when their lives have come to an end.

22"No one can teach knowledge to God;
he is the one who judges even the most important people.
23One person dies while he still has all his strength,
feeling completely safe and comfortable.
24His body was well fed,
and his bones were strong and healthy.
25But another person dies with an unhappy heart,
never enjoying any happiness.
26They are buried next to each other,
and worms cover them both.

27"I know very well your thoughts
and your plans to wrong me.
28You ask about me, 'Where is this great man's house?
Where are the tents where the wicked live?'
29Have you never asked those who travel?
Have you never listened to their stories?
30On the day of God's anger and punishment,
it is the wicked who are spared.
31Who will accuse them to their faces?
Who will pay them back for the evil they have done?
32They are carried to their graves,
and someone keeps watch over their tombs.
33The dirt in the valley seems sweet to them.
Everybody follows after them,
and many people go before them.

34"So how can you comfort me with this nonsense?
Your answers are only lies!"

Eliphaz Answers

22 Then Eliphaz the Temanite answered:
2"Can anyone be of real use to God?
Can even a wise person do him good?
3Does it help the Almighty for you to be good?
Does he gain anything if you are innocent?
4Does God punish you for respecting him?
Does he bring you into court for this?
5No! It is because your evil is without limits
and your sins have no end.
6You took your brothers' things for a debt they didn't owe;
you took clothes from people and left them naked.
7You did not give water to tired people,
and you kept food from the hungry.
8You were a powerful man who owned land;
you were honored and lived in the land.
9But you sent widows away empty-handed,
and you mistreated orphans.
10That is why traps are all around you
and sudden danger frightens you.
11That is why it is so dark you cannot see
and a flood of water covers you.

12"God is in the highest part of heaven.
See how high the highest stars are!
13But you ask, 'What does God know?
Can he judge us through the dark clouds?
14Thick clouds cover him so he cannot see us
as he walks around high up in the sky.'
15Are you going to stay on the old path
where evil people walk?
16They were carried away before their time was up,
and their foundations were washed away by a flood.
17They said to God, 'Leave us alone!
The Almighty can do nothing to us.'
18But it was God who filled their houses with good things.

Their way of thinking is different from
mine.

19"Good people can watch and be glad;
the innocent can laugh at them and say,
20'Surely our enemies are destroyed,
and fire burns up their wealth.'

21"Obey God and be at peace with him;
this is the way to happiness.
22Accept teaching from his mouth,
and keep his words in your heart.
23If you return to the Almighty, you will be
blessed again.
So remove evil from your house.
24Throw your gold nuggets into the dust
and your fine gold among the rocks in the
ravines.
25Then the Almighty will be your gold
and the best silver for you.
26You will find pleasure in the Almighty,
and you will look up to him.
27You will pray to him, and he will hear you,
and you will keep your promises to him.
28Anything you decide will be done,
and light will shine on your ways.
29When people are made humble and you say,
'Have courage,'
then the humble will be saved.
30Even a guilty person will escape
and be saved because your hands are
clean."[d]

Job Answers

23 Then Job answered:
2"My complaint is still bitter today.
I groan because God's heavy hand is on
me.
3I wish I knew where to find God
so I could go to where he lives.
4I would present my case before him
and fill my mouth with arguments.
5I would learn how he would answer me
and would think about what he would say.
6Would he not argue strongly against me?
No, he would really listen to me.
7Then an honest person could present his case
to God,
and I would be saved forever by my judge.

8"If I go to the east, God is not there;
if I go to the west, I do not see him.
9When he is at work in the north, I catch no
sight of him;
when he turns to the south, I cannot see
him.
10But God knows the way that I take,
and when he has tested me, I will come
out like gold.
11My feet have closely followed his steps;
I have stayed in his way;
I did not turn aside.
12I have never left the commands he has
spoken;
I have treasured his words more than my
own.

13"But he is the only God.
Who can come against him?
He does anything he wants.
14He will do to me what he said he would do,
and he has many plans like this.
15That is why I am frightened of him;
when I think of this, I am afraid of him.
16God has made me afraid;
the Almighty terrifies me.
17But I am not hidden by the darkness,
by the thick darkness that covers my face.

24 "I wish the Almighty would set a time
for judging.
Those who know God do not see such a
day.
2Wicked people take other people's land;
they steal flocks and take them to new
pastures.
3They chase away the orphan's donkey
and take the widow's ox when she has no
money.
4They push needy people off the path;
all the poor of the land hide from them.
5The poor become like wild donkeys in the
desert
who go about their job of finding food.
The desert gives them food for their
children.
6They gather hay and straw in the fields
and pick up leftover grapes from the
vineyard of the wicked.
7They spend the night naked, because they
have no clothes,
nothing to cover themselves in the cold.
8They are soaked from mountain rains
and stay near the large rocks because they
have no shelter.
9The fatherless child is grabbed from its
mother's breast;
they take a poor mother's baby to pay for
what she owes.
10So the poor go around naked without any
clothes;
they carry bundles of grain but still go
hungry;
11they crush olives to get oil
and grapes to get wine, but they still go
thirsty.
12Dying people groan in the city,
and the injured cry out for help,
but God accuses no one of doing wrong.

[13]"Those who fight against the light
do not know God's ways
or stay in his paths.
[14]When the day is over, the murderers get up
to kill the poor and needy.
At night they go about like thieves.
[15]Those who are guilty of adultery[d] watch for
the night,
thinking, 'No one will see us,'
and they keep their faces covered.
[16]In the dark, evil people break into houses.
In the daytime they shut themselves up in
their own houses,
because they want nothing to do with the
light.
[17]Darkness is like morning to all these evil
people
who make friends with the terrors of
darkness.

[18]"They are like foam floating on the water.
Their part of the land is cursed;
no one uses the road that goes by their
vineyards.
[19]As heat and dryness quickly melt the snow,
so the grave quickly takes away the sinners.
[20]Their mothers forget them,
and worms will eat their bodies.
They will not be remembered,
so wickedness is broken in pieces like a
stick.
[21]These evil people abuse women who cannot
have children
and show no kindness to widows.
[22]But God drags away the strong by his power.
Even though they seem strong, they do not
know how long they will live.
[23]God may let these evil people feel safe,
but he is watching their ways.
[24]For a little while they are important, and
then they die;
they are laid low and buried like everyone
else;
they are cut off like the heads of grain.
[25]If this is not true, who can prove I am
wrong?
Who can show that my words are worth
nothing?"

Bildad Answers

25 Then Bildad the Shuhite answered:
[2]"God rules and he must be honored;
he set up order in his high heaven.
[3]No one can count God's armies.
His light shines on all people.
[4]So no one can be good in the presence of
God,
and no one born to a woman can be pure.
[5]Even the moon is not bright
and the stars are not pure in his eyes.
[6]People are much less! They are like insects.
They are only worms!"

Job Answers Bildad

26 Then Job answered:
[2]"You are no help to the helpless!
You have not aided the weak!
[3]Your advice lacks wisdom!
You have shown little understanding!
[4]Who has helped you say these words?
And where did you get these ideas?

[5]"The spirits of the dead tremble,
those who are beneath and in the waters.
[6]Death is naked before God;
destruction is uncovered before him.
[7]God stretches the northern sky out over
empty space
and hangs the earth on nothing.
[8]He wraps up the waters in his thick clouds,
but the clouds do not break under their
weight.
[9]He covers the face of the moon,
spreading his clouds over it.
[10]He draws the horizon like a circle on the
water
at the place where light and darkness meet.
[11]Heaven's foundations shake
when he thunders at them.
[12]With his power he quiets the sea;
by his wisdom he destroys Rahab,[d] the sea
monster.
[13]He breathes, and the sky clears.
His hand stabs the fleeing snake.
[14]And these are only a small part of God's
works.
We only hear a small whisper of him.
Who could understand God's thundering
power?"

27 And Job continued speaking:
[2]"As surely as God lives, who has
taken away my rights,
the Almighty, who has made me unhappy,
[3]as long as I am alive
and God's breath of life is in my nose,
[4]my lips will not speak evil,
and my tongue will not tell a lie.
[5]I will never agree you are right;
until I die, I will never stop saying I am
innocent.
[6]I will insist that I am right; I will not back
down.
My conscience will never bother me.

[7]"Let my enemies be like evil people,
my foes like those who are wrong.

8What hope do the wicked have when they
die,
when God takes their life away?
9God will not listen to their cries
when trouble comes to them.
10They will not find joy in the Almighty,
even though they call out to God all the
time.

11"I will teach you about the power of God
and will not hide the ways of the Almighty.
12You have all seen this yourselves.
So why are we having all this talk that
means nothing?

13"Here is what God has planned for evil
people,
and what the Almighty will give to cruel
people:
14They may have many children, but the sword
will kill them.
Their children who are left will never have
enough to eat.
15Then they will die of disease and be buried,
and the widows will not even cry for them.
16The wicked may heap up silver like piles of
dirt
and have so many clothes they are like
piles of clay.
17But good people will wear what evil people
have gathered,
and the innocent will divide up their
silver.
18The houses the wicked build are like a
spider's web,
like a hut that a guard builds.
19The wicked are rich when they go to bed,
but they are rich for the last time;
when they open their eyes, everything is
gone.
20Fears come over them like a flood,
and a storm snatches them away in the
night.
21The east wind will carry them away, and
then they are gone,
because it sweeps them out of their place.
22The wind will hit them without mercy
as they try to run away from its power.
23It will be as if the wind is clapping its hands;
it will whistle at them as they run from
their place.

28 "There are mines where people dig
silver
and places where gold is made pure.
2Iron is taken from the ground,
and copper is melted out of rocks.
3Miners bring lights
and search deep into the mines
for ore in thick darkness.
4Miners dig a tunnel far from where people
live,
where no one has ever walked;
they work far from people, swinging and
swaying from ropes.
5Food grows on top of the earth,
but below ground things are changed as if
by fire.
6Sapphires are found in rocks,
and gold dust is also found there.
7No hawk knows that path;
the falcon has not seen it.
8Proud animals have not walked there,
and no lions cross over it.
9Miners hit the rocks of flint
and dig away at the bottom of the
mountains.
10They cut tunnels through the rock
and see all the treasures there.
11They search for places where rivers begin
and bring things hidden out into the light.

12"But where can wisdom be found,
and where does understanding live?
13People do not understand the value of
wisdom;
it cannot be found among those who are
alive.
14The deep ocean says, 'It's not in me;'
the sea says, 'It's not in me.'
15Wisdom cannot be bought with gold,
and its cost cannot be weighed in silver.
16Wisdom cannot be bought with fine gold
or with valuable onyx or sapphire gems.
17Gold and crystal are not as valuable as
wisdom,
and you cannot buy it with jewels of gold.
18Coral and jasper are not worth talking about,
and the price of wisdom is much greater
than rubies.
19The topaz from Cush cannot compare to
wisdom;
it cannot be bought with the purest gold.

20"So where does wisdom come from,
and where does understanding live?
21It is hidden from the eyes of every living
thing,
even from the birds of the air.
22The places of destruction and death say,
'We have heard reports about it.'
23Only God understands the way to wisdom,
and he alone knows where it lives,
24because he looks to the farthest parts of the
earth
and sees everything under the sky.
25When God gave power to the wind
and measured the water,
26when he made rules for the rain
and set a path for a thunderstorm to follow,

[27]then he looked at wisdom and decided its
worth;
he set wisdom up and tested it.
[28]Then he said to humans,
'The fear of the Lord is wisdom;
to stay away from evil is understanding.' "

Job Continues

29 Job continued to speak:
[2]"How I wish for the months that
have passed
and the days when God watched over me.
[3]God's lamp shined on my head,
and I walked through darkness by his light.
[4]I wish for the days when I was strong,
when God's close friendship blessed my
house.
[5]The Almighty was still with me,
and my children were all around me.
[6]It was as if my path were covered with
cream
and the rocks poured out olive oil for me.
[7]I would go to the city gate
and sit in the public square.
[8]When the young men saw me, they would
step aside,
and the old men would stand up in respect.
[9]The leading men stopped speaking
and covered their mouths with their hands.
[10]The voices of the important men were quiet,
as if their tongues stuck to the roof of their
mouths.
[11]Anyone who heard me spoke well of me,
and those who saw me praised me,
[12]because I saved the poor who called out
and the orphan who had no one to help.
[13]The dying person blessed me,
and I made the widow's heart sing.
[14]I put on right living as if it were clothing;
I wore fairness like a robe and a turban.
[15]I was eyes for the blind
and feet for the lame.
[16]I was like a father to needy people,
and I took the side of strangers who were
in trouble.

DECISION MAKING

To Fly or Not

Sixteen-year-old Neil stared at the model plane on his desk. He had loved planes all his life. Every penny he earned went for flying lessons, but now he wasn't sure if he ever wanted to fly.

The day before, Neil had watched helplessly as a friend's plane crashed before his eyes. He had rushed to the plane to try to help, but the crash was fatal. Neil could still feel his friend's head in his lap; he remembered his dying breath. What now? Should he go on with his own flying plans? He didn't want to die too.

For two days Neil sat in his bedroom. He analyzed the risks, struggled through his fears and dreams, and recalled the conflicting advice given to him. "Follow your dream!" "Dreams are worthless when you're dead!" He didn't know what to do.

Then he took out an old Sunday school notebook he had made. On its cover was a picture of Jesus; inside he had listed qualities of the Savior—"He was sinless"; "He championed the poor"; "He was unselfish"; "He was close to God." Neil studied them closely and then closed his eyes in thanksgiving and made his choice. "Mom," he said, "I hope you and Dad understand, but with God's help, I must go on flying."

Neil Armstrong's decision that day would eventually take him to the moon, to become the first human on its surface.

Neil learned that wisdom in making decisions is sometimes tough to find, as the writer said in **Job 28:20–28.**

- How did Neil and the writer of Job find wisdom?
- If wisdom is as difficult to find as verse 21 states, how do you find it?

CONSIDER . . .

- asking God to give you wisdom concerning an important relationship in your life.
- listing the pros and cons of decisions you must make soon. Pray that God will guide you.

FOR MORE, SEE . . .

- Deuteronomy 30:11–20 (p. 187)
- Joshua 24:14–15 (p. 214)
- Matthew 26:36–45 (p. 957)

[17]I broke the fangs of evil people
and snatched the captives from their teeth.

[18]"I thought, 'I will live for as many days as
there are grains of sand,
and I will die in my own house.
[19]My roots will reach down to the water.
The dew will lie on the branches all night.
[20]New honors will come to me continually,
and I will always have great strength.'

[21]"People listened to me carefully
and waited quietly for my advice.
[22]After I finished speaking, they spoke no more.
My words fell very gently on their ears.
[23]They waited for me as they would for rain
and drank in my words like spring rain.
[24]I smiled at them when they doubted,
and my approval was important to them.
[25]I chose the way for them and was their
leader.
I lived like a king among his army,
like a person who comforts sad people.

30 "But now men who are younger
than I
make fun of me.
I would not have even let their fathers
sit with my sheep dogs.
[2]What use did I have for their strength
since they had lost their strength to work?
[3]They were thin from hunger
and wandered the dry and ruined land at
night.
[4]They gathered desert plants among the brush
and ate the root of the broom tree.
[5]They were forced to live away from people;
people shouted at them as if they were
thieves.
[6]They lived in dried up streambeds,
in caves, and among the rocks.
[7]They howled like animals among the bushes
and huddled together in the brush.
[8]They are worthless people without names
and were forced to leave the land.

[9]"Now they make fun of me with songs;
my name is a joke among them.
[10]They hate me and stay far away from me,
but they do not mind spitting in my face.
[11]God has taken away my strength and made
me suffer,
so they attack me with all their anger.
[12]On my right side they rise up like a mob.
They lay traps for my feet
and prepare to attack me.
[13]They break up my road
and work to destroy me,
and no one helps me.
[14]They come at me as if through a hole in the
wall,
and they roll in among the ruins.
[15]Great fears overwhelm me.
They blow my honor away as if by a great
wind,
and my safety disappears like a cloud.

[16]"Now my life is almost over;
my days are full of suffering.
[17]At night my bones ache;
gnawing pains never stop.
[18]In his great power God grabs hold of my
clothing
and chokes me with the collar of my coat.
[19]He throws me into the mud,
and I become like dirt and ashes.

[20]"I cry out to you, God, but you do not
answer;
I stand up, but you just look at me.
[21]You have turned on me without mercy;
with your powerful hand you attacked me.
[22]You snatched me up and threw me into the
wind
and tossed me about in the storm.
[23]I know you will bring me down to death,
to the place where all living people must
go.

[24]"Surely no one would hurt a ruined man
when he cries for help in his time of
trouble.
[25]I cried for those who were in trouble;
I have been very sad for poor people.
[26]But when I hoped for good, only evil came to
me;
when I looked for light, darkness came.
[27]I never stop being upset;
days of suffering are ahead of me.
[28]I have turned black, but not by the sun.
I stand up in public and cry for help.
[29]I have become a brother to wild dogs
and a friend to ostriches.
[30]My skin has become black and peels off,
as my body burns with fever.
[31]My harp is tuned to sing a sad song,
and my flute is tuned to moaning.

31 "But I made an agreement with my
eyes
not to look with desire at a girl.
[2]What has God above promised for people?
What has the Almighty planned from on
high?
[3]It is ruin for evil people
and disaster for those who do wrong.
[4]God sees my ways
and counts every step I take.

[5]"If I have been dishonest
or lied to others,
[6]then let God weigh me on honest scales.

Then he will know I have done nothing
wrong.
7If I have turned away from doing what is
right,
or my heart has been led by my eyes to do
wrong,
or my hands have been made unclean,[d]
8then let other people eat what I have
planted,
and let my crops be plowed up.

9"If I have desired another woman
or have waited at my neighbor's door for
his wife,
10then let my wife grind another man's grain,
and let other men have sexual relations
with her.
11That would be shameful,
a sin to be punished.
12It is like a fire that burns and destroys;
all I have done would be plowed up.

13"If I have been unfair to my male and female
slaves
when they had a complaint against me,
14how could I tell God what I did?
What will I answer when he asks me to
explain what I've done?
15God made me in my mother's womb, and he
also made them;
the same God formed both of us in our
mothers' wombs.

16"I have never refused the appeals of the poor
or let widows give up hope while looking
for help.
17I have not kept my food to myself
but have given it to the orphans.
18Since I was young, I have been like a father
to the orphans.
From my birth I guided the widows.
19I have not let anyone die for lack of clothes
or let a needy person go without a coat.
20That person's heart blessed me,
because I warmed him with the wool of
my sheep.
21I have never hurt an orphan
even when I knew I could win in court.
22If I have, then let my arm fall off my
shoulder
and be broken at the joint.
23I fear destruction from God,
and I fear his majesty, so I could not do
such things.

24"I have not put my trust in gold
or said to pure gold, 'You are my security.'
25I have not celebrated my great wealth
or the riches my hands had gained.
26I have not thought about worshiping the sun
in its brightness
nor admired the moon moving in glory
27so that my heart was pulled away from God.
My hand has never offered the sun and
moon a kiss of worship.
28If I had, these also would have been sins to
be punished,
because I would have been unfaithful to
God.

29"I have not been happy when my enemy fell
or laughed when he had trouble.
30I have not let my mouth sin
by cursing my enemy's life.
31The men of my house have always said,
'Everyone has eaten all he wants of Job's
food.'
32No stranger ever had to spend the night in
the street,
because I always let travelers stay in my
home.
33I have not hidden my sin as others do,
secretly keeping my guilt to myself.
34I was not so afraid of the crowd
that I kept quiet and stayed inside
because I feared being hated by other
families.

35("How I wish a court would hear my case!
Here I sign my name to show I have told
the truth.
Now let the Almighty answer me;
let the one who accuses me write it down.
36I would wear the writing on my shoulder;
I would put it on like a crown.
37I would explain to God every step I took,
and I would come near to him like a
prince.)

38"If my land cries out against me
and its plowed rows are not wet with tears,
39if I have taken the land's harvest without
paying
or have broken the spirit of those who
worked the land,
40then let thorns come up instead of wheat,
and let weeds come up instead of barley."

The words of Job are finished.

Elihu Speaks

32 These three men stopped trying to answer Job, because he was so sure he was
right. 2But Elihu son of Barakel the Buzite, from
the family of Ram, became very angry with Job,
because Job claimed he was right instead of God.
3Elihu was also angry with Job's three friends who
had no answer to show that Job was wrong, yet
continued to blame him. 4Elihu had waited before
speaking to Job, because the three friends were
older than he was. 5But when Elihu saw that the

three men had nothing more to say, he became
very angry.
6So Elihu son of Barakel the Buzite said this:

"I am young,
and you are old.
That is why I was afraid
to tell you what I know.
7I thought, 'Older people should speak,
and those who have lived many years
should teach wisdom.'
8But it is the spirit in a person,
the breath of the Almighty, that gives
understanding.
9It is not just older people who are wise;
they are not the only ones who understand
what is right.
10So I say, listen to me.
I too will tell you what I know.
11I waited while you three spoke,
and listened to your explanations.
While you looked for words to use,
12 I paid close attention to you.
But not one of you has proved Job wrong;
none of you has answered his arguments.
13Don't say, 'We have found wisdom;
only God will show Job to be wrong, not
people.'
14Job has not spoken his words against me,
so I will not use your arguments to answer
Job.

15"These three friends are defeated and have
no more to say;
words have failed them.
16Now they are standing there with no answers
for Job.
Now that they are quiet, must I wait to
speak?
17No, I too will speak
and tell what I know.
18I am full of words,
and the spirit in me causes me to speak.
19I am like wine that has been bottled up;
I am ready to burst like a new leather wine
bag.
20I must speak so I will feel relief;
I must open my mouth and answer.
21I will be fair to everyone
and not flatter anyone.
22I don't know how to flatter,
and if I did, my Maker would quickly take
me away.

33 "Now, Job, listen to my words.
Pay attention to everything I say.
2I open my mouth
and am ready to speak.
3My words come from an honest heart,
and I am sincere in saying what I know.
4The Spirit[d] of God created me,
and the breath of the Almighty gave me
life.
5Answer me if you can;
get yourself ready and stand before me.
6I am just like you before God;
I too am made out of clay.
7Don't be afraid of me;
I will not be hard on you.

8"But I heard what you have said;
I heard every word.
9You said, 'I am pure and without sin;
I am innocent and free from guilt.
10But God has found fault with me;
he considers me his enemy.
11He locks my feet in chains
and closely watches everywhere I go.'

12"But I tell you, you are not right in saying
this,
because God is greater than we are.
13Why do you accuse God
of not answering anyone?
14God does speak—sometimes one way and
sometimes another—
even though people may not understand it.
15He speaks in a dream or a vision of the night
when people are in a deep sleep,
lying on their beds.
16He speaks in their ears
and frightens them with warnings
17to turn them away from doing wrong
and to keep them from being proud.
18God does this to save a person from death,
to keep him from dying.
19A person may be corrected while in bed in
great pain;
he may have continual pain in his very
bones.
20He may be in such pain that he even hates
food,
even the very best meal.
21His body becomes so thin there is almost
nothing left of it,
and his bones that were hidden now stick
out.
22He is near death,
and his life is almost over.

23"But there may be an angel to speak for
him,
one out of a thousand, who will tell him
what to do.
24The angel will beg for mercy and say:
'Save him from death.
I have found a way to pay for his life.'
25Then his body is made new like a child's.
It will return to the way it was when he
was young.

[26]That person will pray to God, and God will
listen to him.
He will see God's face and will shout with
happiness.
And God will set things right for him again.
[27]Then he will say to others,
'I sinned and twisted what was right,
but I did not receive the punishment I
should have received.
[28]God bought my life back from death,
and I will continue to enjoy life.'

[29]"God does all these things to a person
two or even three times
[30]so he won't die as punishment for his sins
and so he may still enjoy life.

[31]"Job, pay attention and listen to me;
be quiet, and I will speak.
[32]If you have anything to say, answer me;
speak up, because I want to prove you
right.
[33]But if you have nothing to say, then listen to
me;
be quiet, and I will teach you wisdom."

34

Then Elihu said:

[2]"Hear my words, you wise men;
listen to me, you who know a lot.
[3]The ear tests words
as the tongue tastes food.
[4]Let's decide for ourselves what is right,
and let's learn together what is good.

[5]"Job says, 'I am not guilty,
and God has refused me a fair trial.
[6]Instead of getting a fair trial,
I am called a liar.
I have been seriously hurt,
even though I have not sinned.'
[7]There is no other man like Job;
he takes insults as if he were drinking
water.
[8]He keeps company with those who do evil
and spends time with wicked men,
[9]because he says, 'It is no use
to try to please God.'

[10]"So listen to me, you who can understand.
God can never do wrong!
It is impossible for the Almighty to do evil.
[11]God pays a person back for what he has done
and gives him what his actions deserve.
[12]Truly God will never do wrong;
the Almighty will never twist what is right.
[13]No one chose God to rule over the earth
or put him in charge of the whole world.
[14]If God should decide
to take away life and breath,
[15]then everyone would die together
and turn back into dust.

[16]"If you can understand, hear this;
listen to what I have to say.
[17]Can anyone govern who hates what is right?
How can you blame God who is both fair
and powerful?
[18]God is the one who says to kings, 'You are
worthless,'
or to important people, 'You are evil.'
[19]He is not nicer to princes than other people,
nor kinder to rich people than poor people,
because he made them all with his own
hands.
[20]They can die in a moment, in the middle of
the night.
They are struck down, and then they pass
away;
powerful people die without help.

[21]"God watches where people go;
he sees every step they take.
[22]There is no dark place or deep shadow
where those who do evil can hide from
him.
[23]He does not set a time
for people to come before him for judging.
[24]Without asking questions, God breaks
powerful people into pieces
and puts others in their place.
[25]Because God knows what people do,
he defeats them in the night, and they are
crushed.
[26]He punishes them for the evil they do
so that everyone else can watch,
[27]because they stopped following God
and did not care about any of his ways.
[28]The cry of the poor comes to God;
he hears the cry of the needy.
[29]But if God keeps quiet, who can blame him?
If he hides his face, who can see him?
God still rules over both nations and persons
alike.
[30] He keeps the wicked from ruling
and from trapping others.

[31]"But suppose someone says to God,
'I am guilty, but I will not sin anymore.
[32]Teach me what I cannot see.
If I have done wrong, I will not do it
again.'
[33]So, Job, should God reward you as you want
when you refuse to change?
You must decide, not I,
so tell me what you know.

[34]"Those who understand speak,
and the wise who hear me say,
[35]'Job speaks without knowing what is true;
his words show he does not understand.'
[36]I wish Job would be tested completely,
because he answered like an evil man!

37 Job now adds to his sin by turning against God.
He claps his hands in protest,
speaking more and more against God."

35

Then Elihu said:
2 "Do you think this is fair?
You say, 'God will show that I am right,'
3 but you also ask, 'What's the use?
I don't gain anything by not sinning.'

4 "I will answer you
and your friends who are with you.
5 Look up at the sky
and see the clouds so high above you.
6 If you sin, it does nothing to God;
even if your sins are many, they do nothing to him.
7 If you are good, you give nothing to God;
he receives nothing from your hand.
8 Your evil ways only hurt a man like yourself,
and the good you do only helps other human beings.

9 "People cry out when they are in trouble;
they beg for relief from powerful people.
10 But no one asks, 'Where is God, my Maker,
who gives us songs in the night,
11 who makes us smarter than the animals of the earth
and wiser than the birds of the air?'
12 God does not answer evil people when they cry out,
because the wicked are proud.
13 God does not listen to their useless begging;
the Almighty pays no attention to them.
14 He will listen to you even less
when you say that you do not see him,
that your case is before him,
that you must wait for him,
15 that his anger never punishes,
and that he doesn't notice evil.
16 So Job is only speaking nonsense,
saying many words without knowing what is true."

Elihu's Speech Continues

36

Elihu continued:
2 "Listen to me a little longer, and I will show you
that there is more to be said for God.
3 What I know comes from far away.
I will show that my Maker is right.
4 You can be sure that my words are not false;
one who really knows is with you.

5 "God is powerful, but he does not hate people;
he is powerful and sure of what he wants to do.
6 He will not keep evil people alive,
but he gives the poor their rights.
7 He always watches over those who do right;
he sets them on thrones with kings
and they are honored forever.
8 If people are bound in chains,
or if trouble, like ropes, ties them up,
9 God tells them what they have done,
that they have sinned in their pride.
10 God makes them listen to his warning
and commands them to change from doing evil.
11 If they obey and serve him,
the rest of their lives will be successful,
and the rest of their years will be happy.
12 But if they do not listen,
they will die by the sword,
and they will die without knowing why.

13 "Those who have wicked hearts hold on to anger.
Even when God punishes them, they do not cry for help.
14 They die while they are still young,
and their lives end in disgrace.
15 But God saves those who suffer through their suffering;
he gets them to listen through their pain.

16 "God is gently calling you from the jaws of trouble
to an open place of freedom
where he has set your table full of the best food.
17 But now you are being punished like the wicked;
you are getting justice.
18 Be careful! Don't be led away from God by riches;
don't let much money turn you away.
19 Neither your wealth nor all your great strength
will keep you out of trouble.
20 Don't wish for the night
when people are taken from their homes.
21 Be careful not to turn to evil,
which you seem to want more than suffering.

22 "God is great and powerful;
no other teacher is like him.
23 No one has planned his ways for him;
no one can say to God, 'You have done wrong.'
24 Remember to praise his work,
about which people have sung.
25 Everybody has seen it;
people look at it from far off.
26 God is so great, greater than we can understand!

No one knows how old he is.
27"He evaporates the drops of water from the earth
and turns them into rain.
28The rain then pours down from the clouds,
and showers fall on people.
29No one understands how God spreads out the clouds
or how he sends thunder from where he lives.
30Watch how God scatters his lightning around him,
lighting up the deepest parts of the sea.
31This is the way God governs the nations;
this is how he gives us enough food.
32God fills his hands with lightning
and commands it to strike its target.
33His thunder announces the coming storm,
and even the cattle know it is near.

37 "At the sound of his thunder, my heart pounds
as if it will jump out of my chest.
2Listen! Listen to the thunder of God's voice
and to the rumbling that comes from his mouth.
3He turns his lightning loose under the whole sky
and sends it to the farthest parts of the earth.
4After that you can hear the roar
when he thunders with a great sound.
He does not hold back the flashing
when his voice is heard.
5God's voice thunders in wonderful ways;
he does great things we cannot understand.
6He says to the snow, 'Fall on the earth,'
and to the shower, 'Be a heavy rain.'
7With it, he stops everyone from working
so everyone knows it is the work of God.
8The animals take cover from the rain
and stay in their dens.
9The storm comes from where it was stored;
the cold comes with the strong winds.
10The breath of God makes ice,
and the wide waters become frozen.
11He fills the clouds with water
and scatters his lightning through them.
12At his command they swirl around
over the whole earth,
doing whatever he commands.
13He uses the clouds to punish people
or to water his earth and show his love.
14"Job, listen to this:
Stop and notice God's miracles.[d]
15Do you know how God controls the clouds
and makes his lightning flash?
16Do you know how the clouds hang in the sky?
Do you know the miracles of God, who knows everything?
17You suffer in your clothes
when the land is silenced by the hot, south wind.
18You cannot stretch out the sky like God
and make it look as hard as polished bronze.
19Tell us what we should say to him;
we cannot get our arguments ready because we do not have enough understanding.
20Should God be told that I want to speak?
Would a person ask to be swallowed up?
21No one can look at the sun
when it is bright in the sky
after the wind has blown all the clouds away.
22God comes out of the north in golden light,
in overwhelming greatness.
23The Almighty is too high for us to reach.
He has great strength;
he is always right and never punishes unfairly.
24That is why people honor him;
he does not respect those who say they are wise."

The Lord Questions Job

38 Then the LORD answered Job from the storm. He said:
2"Who is this that makes my purpose unclear
by saying things that are not true?
3Be strong like a man!
I will ask you questions,
and you must answer me.
4Where were you when I made the earth's foundation?
Tell me, if you understand.
5Who marked off how big it should be?
Surely you know!
Who stretched a ruler across it?
6What were the earth's foundations set on,
or who put its cornerstone[d] in place

> **SIDELIGHT:** Ancient cultures envisioned the earth resting on everything from pillars to sea turtles (Job 38:4–6). Everyone probably sleeps a little better since Isaac Newton discovered gravity.

7while the morning stars sang together
and all the angels shouted with joy?
8"Who shut the doors to keep the sea in

when it broke through and was born,
9when I made the clouds like a coat for the
sea
and wrapped it in dark clouds,
10when I put limits on the sea
and put its doors and bars in place,
11when I said to the sea, 'You may come this
far, but no farther;
this is where your proud waves must stop'?

12"Have you ever ordered the morning to
begin,
or shown the dawn where its place was
13in order to take hold of the earth by its edges
and shake evil people out of it?
14At dawn the earth changes like clay being
pressed by a seal;[d]
the hills and valleys stand out like folds in
a coat.
15Light is not given to evil people;
their arm is raised to do harm, but it is
broken.

16"Have you ever gone to where the sea begins
or walked in the valleys under the sea?
17Have the gates of death been opened to you?
Have you seen the gates of the deep
darkness?
18Do you understand how wide the earth is?
Tell me, if you know all these things.

19"What is the path to light's home,
and where does darkness live?
20Can you take them to their places?
Do you know the way to their homes?
21Surely you know, if you were already born
when all this happened!
Have you lived that many years?

22"Have you ever gone into the storehouse of
the snow
or seen the storehouses for hail,
23which I save for times of trouble,
for days of war and battle?
24Where is the place from which light comes?
Where is the place from which the east
winds blow over the earth?
25Who cuts a waterway for the heavy rains
and sets a path for the thunderstorm?
26Who waters the land where no one lives,
the desert that has no one in it?
27Who sends rain to satisfy the empty land
so the grass begins to grow?
28Does the rain have a father?
Who is father to the drops of dew?
29Who is the mother of the ice?
Who gives birth to the frost from the sky
30when the water becomes hard as stone,
and even the surface of the ocean is
frozen?

31"Can you tie up the stars of the Pleiades
or loosen the ropes of the stars in Orion?
32Can you bring out the stars on time
or lead out the stars of the Bear with its
cubs?
33Do you know the laws of the sky
and understand their rule over the earth?

34"Can you shout an order to the clouds
and cover yourself with a flood of water?
35Can you send lightning bolts on their way?
Do they come to you and say, 'Here we
are'?
36Who put wisdom inside the mind
or understanding in the heart?
37Who has the wisdom to count the clouds?
Who can pour water from the jars of the
sky
38when the dust becomes hard
and the clumps of dirt stick together?

39"Do you hunt food for the female lion
to satisfy the hunger of the young lions
40while they lie in their dens
or hide in the bushes waiting to attack?
41Who gives food to the birds
when their young cry out to God
and wander about without food?

39 "Do you know when the mountain
goats give birth?
Do you watch when the deer gives birth to
her fawn?
2Do you count the months until they give
birth
and know the right time for them to give
birth?
3They lie down, their young are born,
and then the pain of giving birth is over.
4Their young ones grow big and strong in the
wild country.
Then they leave their homes and do not
return.

5"Who let the wild donkey go free?
Who untied its ropes?
6I am the one who gave the donkey the desert
as its home;
I gave it the desert lands as a place to live.
7The wild donkey laughs at the confusion in
the city,
and it does not hear the drivers shout.
8It roams the hills looking for pasture,
looking for anything green to eat.

9"Will the wild ox agree to serve you
and stay by your feeding box at night?
10Can you hold it to the plowed row with a
harness
so it will plow the valleys for you?

11Will you depend on the wild ox for its great strength
and leave your heavy work for it to do?
12Can you trust the ox to bring in your grain
and gather it to your threshing[d] floor?

13"The wings of the ostrich flap happily,
but they are not like the feathers of the stork.
14The ostrich lays its eggs on the ground
and lets them warm in the sand.
15It does not stop to think that a foot might step on them and crush them;
it does not care that some animal might walk on them.
16The ostrich is cruel to its young, as if they were not even its own.
It does not care that its work is for nothing,
17because God did not give the ostrich wisdom;
God did not give it a share of good sense.
18But when the ostrich gets up to run, it is so fast
that it laughs at the horse and its rider.

19"Job, are you the one who gives the horse its strength
or puts a flowing mane on its neck?
20Do you make the horse jump like a locust?[d]
It scares people with its proud snorting.
21It paws wildly, enjoying its strength,
and charges into battle.
22It laughs at fear and is afraid of nothing;
it does not run away from the sword.
23The bag of arrows rattles against the horse's side,
along with the flashing spears and swords.
24With great excitement, the horse races over the ground;
and it cannot stand still when it hears the trumpet.
25When the trumpet blows, the horse snorts, 'Aha!'
It smells the battle from far away;
it hears the shouts of commanders and the battle cry.

26"Is it through your wisdom that the hawk flies
and spreads its wings toward the south?
27Are you the one that commands the eagle to fly
and build its nest so high?
28It lives on a high cliff and stays there at night;
the rocky peak is its protected place.
29From there it looks for its food;
its eyes can see it from far away.
30Its young eat blood,
and where there is something dead, the eagle is there."

40

The LORD said to Job:
2"Will the person who argues with the Almighty correct him?
Let the person who accuses God answer him."

3Then Job answered the LORD:
4"I am not worthy; I cannot answer you anything,
so I will put my hand over my mouth.
5I spoke one time, but I will not answer again;
I even spoke two times, but I will say nothing more."

6Then the LORD spoke to Job from the storm:
7"Be strong, like a man!
I will ask you questions,
and you must answer me.
8Would you say that I am unfair?
Would you blame me to make yourself look right?
9Are you as strong as God?
Can your voice thunder like his?
10If so, then decorate yourself with glory and beauty;
dress in honor and greatness as if they were clothing.
11Let your great anger punish;
look at the proud and bring them down.
12Look at the proud and make them humble.
Crush the wicked wherever they are.
13Bury them all in the dirt together;
cover their faces in the grave.
14If you can do that, then I myself will praise you,
because you are strong enough to save yourself.

15"Look at the behemoth,[n]
which I made just as I made you.
It eats grass like an ox.
16Look at the strength it has in its body;
the muscles of its stomach are powerful.
17Its tail is like a cedar tree;
the muscles of its thighs are woven together.
18Its bones are like tubes of bronze;
its legs are like bars of iron.
19It is one of the first of God's works,
but its Maker can destroy it.
20The hills, where the wild animals play,
provide food for it.
21It lies under the lotus plants,
hidden by the tall grass in the swamp.

behemoth A large land animal. It could refer to the hippopotamus, the elephant, or a monster.

22The lotus plants hide it in their shadow;
the poplar trees by the streams surround it.
23If the river floods, it will not be afraid;
it is safe even if the Jordan River rushes to its mouth.
24Can anyone blind its eyes and capture it?
Can anyone put hooks in its nose?

41 "Can you catch the leviathan[n] on a fishhook
or tie its tongue down with a rope?
2Can you put a cord through its nose
or a hook in its jaw?
3Will it keep begging you for mercy
and speak to you with gentle words?
4Will it make an agreement with you
and let you take it as your slave for life?
5Can you make a pet of the leviathan as you would a bird
or put it on a leash for your girls?
6Will traders try to bargain with you for it?
Will they divide it up among the merchants?
7Can you stick darts all over its skin
or fill its head with fishing spears?
8If you put one hand on it,
you will never forget the battle,
and you will never do it again!
9There is no hope of defeating it;
just seeing it overwhelms people.
10No one is brave enough to make it angry,
so who would be able to stand up against me?
11No one has ever given me anything that I must pay back,
because everything under the sky belongs to me.

12"I will speak about Leviathan's arms and legs,
its great strength and well-formed body.
13No one can tear off its outer hide
or poke through its double armor.
14No one can force open its great jaws;
they are filled with frightening teeth.
15It has rows of shields on its back
that are tightly sealed together.
16Each shield is so close to the next one
that no air can go between them.
17They are joined strongly to one another;
they hold on to each other and cannot be separated.
18When it snorts, flashes of light are thrown out,
and its eyes look like the light at dawn.
19Flames blaze from its mouth;
sparks of fire shoot out.
20Smoke pours out of its nose,
as if coming from a large pot over a hot fire.
21Its breath sets coals on fire,
and flames come out of its mouth.
22There is great strength in its neck.
People are afraid and run away.
23The folds of its skin are tightly joined;
they are set and cannot be moved.
24Its chest is as hard as a rock,
even as hard as a grinding stone.
25The powerful fear its terrible looks
and draw back in fear as it moves.
26The sword that hits it does not hurt it,
nor the arrows, darts, and spears.
27It treats iron as if it were straw
and bronze metal as if it were rotten wood.
28It does not run away from arrows;
stones from slings are like chaff[d] to it.
29Clubs feel like pieces of straw to it,
and it laughs when they shake a spear at it.
30The underside of its body is like broken pieces of pottery.
It leaves a trail in the mud like a threshing[d] board.
31It makes the deep sea bubble like a boiling pot;
it stirs up the sea like a pot of oil.
32When it swims, it leaves a shining path in the water
that makes the sea look as if it had white hair.
33Nothing else on earth is equal to it;
it is a creature without fear.
34It looks down on all those who are too proud;
it is king over all proud creatures."

Job Answers the Lord

42 Then Job answered the LORD:
2"I know that you can do all things
and that no plan of yours can be ruined.
3You asked, 'Who is this that made my purpose unclear by saying things that are not true?'
Surely I spoke of things I did not understand;
I talked of things too wonderful for me to know.
4You said, 'Listen now, and I will speak.
I will ask you questions,
and you must answer me.'
5My ears had heard of you before,
but now my eyes have seen you.
6So now I hate myself;
I will change my heart and life.
I will sit in the dust and ashes."

leviathan Possibly a crocodile or a sea monster.

End of the Story

7After the LORD had said these things to Job, he
said to Eliphaz the Temanite, "I am angry with
you and your two friends, because you have not
said what is right about me, as my servant Job did.
8Now take seven bulls and seven male sheep, and
go to my servant Job, and offer a burnt offering for
yourselves. My servant Job will pray for you, and
I will listen to his prayer. Then I will not punish
you for being foolish. You have not said what is
right about me, as my servant Job did." 9So Eliphaz the Temanite, Bildad the Shuhite, and Zophar the Naamathite did as the LORD said, and the
LORD listened to Job's prayer.
10After Job had prayed for his friends, the LORD
gave him success again. The LORD gave Job twice
as much as he had owned before. 11Job's brothers
and sisters came to his house, along with everyone who had known him before, and they all ate
with him there. They comforted him and made
him feel better about the trouble the LORD had
brought on him, and each one gave Job a piece of
silver and a gold ring.

SIDELIGHT: If unusual names were a source of pride, Job's daughters must have been downright arrogant. Their Hebrew names in Job 42:14 translate "dove," "cinnamon," and "container of eyeshadow."

12The LORD blessed the last part of Job's life
even more than the first part. Job had fourteen
thousand sheep, six thousand camels, a thousand
teams of oxen, and a thousand female donkeys.
13Job also had seven sons and three daughters.
14He named the first daughter Jemimah, the sec-

FOLLOWING GOD

His Presence

"There came into my soul . . . a sense of the glory of the divine being; a new sense, quite different from anything I had ever experienced before."

Jonathan Edwards (1703–1758)

Edwards followed God by devoting his life to proclaiming and defending the gospel as one of the leaders of the Great Awakening in New England.

"Down in my deep well, shrouded with blackness, feeling helpless and devoid of hope, I cried out for help. Now, at last, I was ready to go to any length to achieve sobriety. And God heard my cry and answered." "Michael"

"Michael" felt God's presence in his time of need and began the long road to recovery from alcoholism through Alcoholics Anonymous. He follows God day-by-day as a pastor who helps others recover from alcoholism.

"At this moment I feel something 'let go' inside and lo, God is here! It is a heart-melting 'here-ness,' a lovely whispering of father to child."

Frank Laubauch (1884–1970)

Laubauch became a missionary and developed a world-wide method of teaching people to read.

The experience of God's presence led these three to act on their faith. Job was also changed as he experienced God's presence. Read **Job 42:1–6**.

- How does Job's reaction to meeting God compare to these three people's sense of God's presence with them? How is it different?
- How would your faith change if you suddenly sensed God's presence, as in verses 4 and 5?

CONSIDER . . .

- praying for God to give you a clear picture of what he wants you to do for him.
- writing down what you value most, why you value it, and how your feelings about it would change if you considered it a loan from God.

FOR MORE, SEE . . .

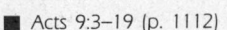

- 1 Kings 19:11–13 (p. 325)
- Psalm 63:1–8 (p. 518)
- Acts 9:3–19 (p. 1112)

ond daughter Keziah, and the third daughter Keren-Happuch. [15]There were no other women in all the land as beautiful as Job's daughters. And their father Job gave them land to own along with their brothers.

[16]After this, Job lived one hundred forty years. He lived to see his children, grandchildren, great-grandchildren, and great-great-grandchildren. [17]Then Job died; he was old and had lived many years.

PSALMS

Why Read This Book:

- Be inspired to express your feelings through songs about tough and joyful situations (such as Psalms 4, 27, 55, 147).
- Improve your prayer life by following the many models of prayer in the Psalms (such as Psalms 6, 32, 51, 102, 130, 143).
- Learn to praise and worship God through songs of praise (such as Psalms 8, 47, 81, 84, 108, 150).

Behind the Scenes:

If you flip through a church hymnbook, you see lots of different songs. Some are upbeat; others are meditative. Some are for special occasions; others can be used almost any time. Some are favorites; others you barely know. Different hymns were written by different authors at different times.

The book of Psalms is a lot like a church hymnbook. In fact, it was the hymnbook for Jews and Christians for many centuries. Each psalm is really a song for worship. And, like modern hymnbooks, Psalms contains a wide variety of songs that express many different emotions—joy, sadness, celebration, loneliness and many others. Different psalms were written by different people over several centuries, so the book is rich with diversity.

MUSIC IN THIS SONGBOOK

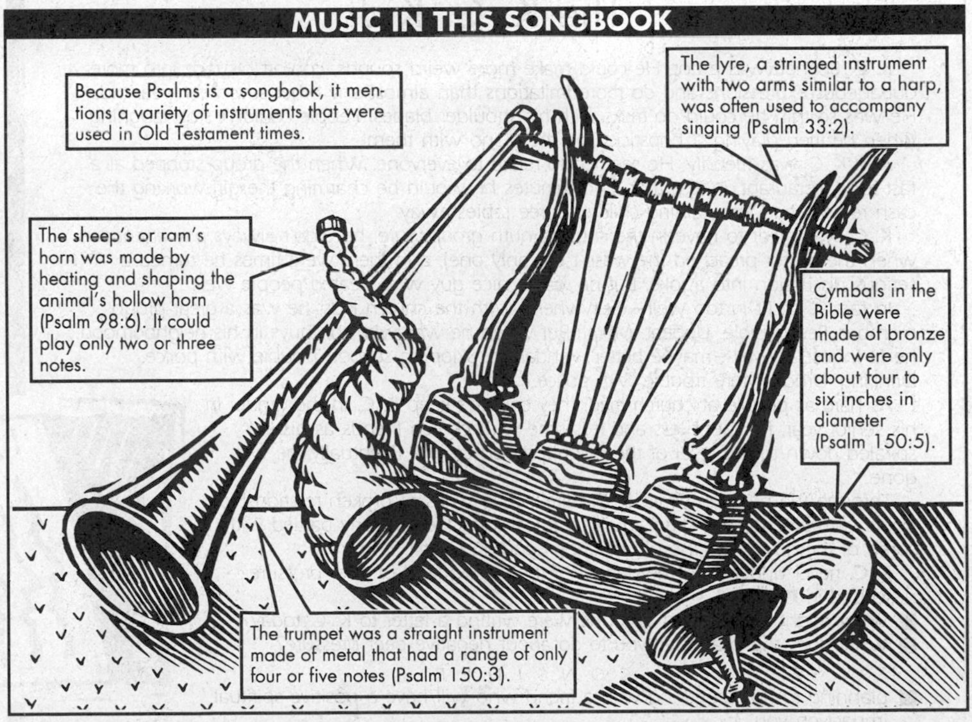

WHEN THE ACTION WAS

2000BC	
1500BC	The Israelites escaped from Egypt
1000BC	King David ruled Israel and almost half the psalms refer to him
	Judah fell to the Babylonians
500BC	Jews began returning to Jerusalem from exile
	Final collection of psalms was probably completed
BC/AD	Jesus was born

Behind the Scenes (cont.): The New Testament quotes from Psalms more than it quotes from any other book in the Old Testament, with the exception of Isaiah. Psalms is also the longest book of the Bible and contains some of the most popular reading in the Bible. Through these poetic words we can better understand our own hearts' longings to be close to God.

Book 1

Two Ways to Live

1 Happy are those who don't listen to the
wicked,
who don't go where sinners go,
who don't do what evil people do.
2They love the LORD's teachings,
and they think about those teachings day
and night.
3They are strong, like a tree planted by a
river.
The tree produces fruit in season,
and its leaves don't die.
Everything they do will succeed.
4But wicked people are not like that.
They are like chaff[d] that the wind blows
away.
5So the wicked will not escape God's
punishment.

PEER PRESSURE

The K. C. Kid

K. C. Bennett was a riot. He could make more weird sounds, contort his face into more outrageous expressions and do more imitations than almost any other seventeen-year-old. He was so thin he could do tricks with his shoulder blades. People couldn't stop laughing when he tried playing "Chopsticks" on the piano with them!

And K. C. was friendly. He seemed to relate to everyone. When the group stopped at a fast-food restaurant, in less than two minutes he would be charming the girl working the cash register and entertaining children three tables away.

K. C. was great to have in the church youth group. Sure, he didn't always pay attention when the pastor preached (he wasn't the only one), and there were times he turned a serious discussion into a joke. But he was a nice guy who treated people well.

In fact, K. C. fit in too well—everywhere. With the church kids, he was a great group member. Responsible. Upbeat. Moral. But when he was with the guys in his neighborhood, he fit in just as well—maybe better. Vandalism. Skipping school. Trouble with police. Drinking. Drugs. More trouble with police.

As hard as people at church tried, they couldn't keep K. C. in the group. In his senior year, he spent less and less time with church friends as his life spiraled down to the level of the neighborhood crowd. Eventually, he was gone.

Through the next ten years, K. C.'s life was a series of broken relationships, bouts with alcohol and drug abuse, and lost jobs. He regularly partied with some of the guys from the old neighborhood. K. C. still fit in.

K. C. never understood the danger of the wrong kind of peer pressure described in **Psalm 1**.

- What might the psalmist say if he were writing a letter to K. C. today?
- What does this psalm tell you to do about negative peer pressure?

CONSIDER. . .

- planning to do something with a friend who will have a positive spiritual impact on you.
- writing your own psalm (a song or a poem) that expresses your desire to do God's will rather than follow the crowd.

FOR MORE, SEE. . .

- Genesis 26:1–11 (p. 30)
- 2 Corinthians 6:14–18 (p. 1199)
- Hebrews 10:24–25 (p. 1286)

Sinners will not worship with God's
people.
6This is because the LORD takes care of his
people,
but the wicked will be destroyed.

SIDELIGHT: The book of Psalms is actually made up of five separate books (see heading above chapter 1). Psalms 1—41 are Book One. Psalms 42—72 are Book Two. Psalms 73—89 are Book Three. Psalms 90—106 are Book Four. And Psalms 107—150 are Book Five. Each "book" may have been collected at a different time.

The Lord's Chosen King

2 Why are the nations so angry?
Why are the people making useless
plans?
2The kings of the earth prepare to fight,
and their leaders make plans together
against the LORD
and his appointed one.
3They say, "Let's break the chains that hold us
back
and throw off the ropes that tie us down."

4But the one who sits in heaven laughs;
the Lord makes fun of them.
5Then the LORD warns them
and frightens them with his anger.
6He says, "I have appointed my own king
to rule in Jerusalem on my holy mountain,
Zion."

7Now I will tell you what the LORD has
declared:
He said to me, "You are my son.
Today I have become your father.
8If you ask me, I will give you the
nations;
all the people on earth will be yours.
9You will rule over them with an iron
rod.
You will break them into pieces like
pottery."

10So, kings, be wise;
rulers, learn this lesson.
11Obey the LORD with great fear.
Be happy, but tremble.
12Show that you are loyal to his son,
or you will be destroyed by his
anger,
because he can quickly become angry.
But happy are those who trust him for
protection.

A Morning Prayer

David sang this when he ran away
from his son Absalom.

3 LORD, I have many enemies!
Many people have turned against me.
2Many are saying about me,
"God won't rescue him." *Selah*[d]

3But, LORD, you are my shield,
my wonderful God who gives me courage.
4I will pray to the LORD,
and he will answer me from his holy
mountain. *Selah*

5I can lie down and go to sleep,
and I will wake up again,
because the LORD gives me strength.
6Thousands of troops may surround me,
but I am not afraid.

7LORD, rise up!
My God, come save me!
You have struck my enemies on the cheek;
you have broken the teeth of the wicked.
8The LORD can save his people.
LORD, bless your people. *Selah*

An Evening Prayer

For the director of music. With stringed instruments.
A psalm of David.

4 Answer me when I pray to you,
my God who does what is right.
Make things easier for me when I am in
trouble.
Have mercy on me and hear my prayer.

2People, how long will you turn my honor
into shame?
How long will you love what is false and
look for new lies? *Selah*[d]
3You know that the LORD has chosen for
himself those who are loyal to him.
The LORD listens when I pray to him.
4When you are angry, do not sin.
Think about these things quietly
as you go to bed. *Selah*

SIDELIGHT: The way citizens in Bible times showed their loyalty to royalty (Psalm 2:12) was by kissing the feet of the king or prince.

5Do what is right as a sacrifice to the LORD
and trust the LORD.

6Many people ask,
"Who will give us anything good?"

LORD, be kind to us.
7But you have made me very happy,
happier than they are,
even with all their grain and new wine.
8I go to bed and sleep in peace,
because, LORD, only you keep me safe.

A Morning Prayer for Protection

For the director of music. For flutes. A psalm of David.

5 LORD, listen to my words.
Understand my sadness.
2Listen to my cry for help, my King and my God,
because I pray to you.
3LORD, every morning you hear my voice.
Every morning, I tell you what I need,
and I wait for your answer.
4You are not a God who is pleased with the wicked;
you do not live with those who do evil.
5Those people who make fun of you cannot stand before you.
You hate all those who do evil.
6You destroy liars;
the LORD hates those who kill and trick others.

7Because of your great love,
I can come into your Temple.[d]
Because I fear and respect you,
I can worship in your holy Temple.

ANGER

He Lost His Grip

The school paper's sports headline said it all: "Tom Harley Loses Tennis Tournament With a Smash."

Tom read the biting article and then let out a sigh. He had felt so dumb for letting his anger get to him at the tournament that day. But the deed was done. Nothing could repair his tennis racket. He had hurled the stringed beast at the fence in a spark of rage. And his brand new racket abruptly met the fence post.

"C'mon, Tom," his partner, Jim, had whispered intensely. "Relax. Your temper's gonna throw this match for us."

"I'm fine," Tom had snapped. "Where's your extra racket?"

They probably would have lost anyway, but Tom was still mad about having to play with a racket he was unfamiliar with. They only won three games in the next two sets.

The coach didn't say a word that day, but Tom could tell he was furious. The next week at practice, he made Tom and Jim do extra "hate drills."

"Any doubles team with enough extra energy to waste on destroying tennis rackets," Coach said, "can surely handle a little extra running." So the twosome painfully ran the width of six tennis courts, frontward and backward, again and again.

And then there was the teasing from Tom's teammates.

"Hey, Tantrum Tom, fought off any attacking fence posts lately?"

"So, Tom, how many tennis rackets have you bought this month?"

Even with all this abuse, Tom hadn't learned his lesson. It took several more temper tantrums and broken rackets for him to learn the simple truth that anger wasn't going to make him play better tennis, or improve his life in any way!

Anger can sometimes be constructive. But, the psalmist reminds us how destructive anger can become. He warns us in **Psalm 4**, "When you are angry, do not sin." Hold on to the racket!

- Do you think throwing a tennis racket in a fit of anger is a sin? Why or why not?
- How can you avoid doing wrong things when you're angry?

CONSIDER . . .

- seeking forgiveness from someone you've sinned against because of your anger.
- picturing the place or situation in which you get the angriest, and asking God to help you stay calm the next time you're there.

FOR MORE, SEE . . .

- Exodus 32 (p. 89)
- Mark 11:15–19 (p. 995)
- Ephesians 4:26–27 (p. 1224)

8LORD, since I have many enemies,
show me the right thing to do.
Show me clearly how you want me to live.

9My enemies' mouths do not tell the truth;
in their hearts they want to destroy others.
Their throats are like open graves;
they use their tongues for telling lies.
10God, declare them guilty!
Let them fall into their own traps.
Send them away because their sins are many;
they have turned against you.

11But let everyone who trusts you be happy;
let them sing glad songs forever.
Protect those who love you
and who are happy because of you.
12LORD, you bless those who do what is right;
you protect them like a soldier's shield.

A Prayer for Mercy in Troubled Times

For the director of music. With stringed instruments. Upon the sheminith.[d] A psalm of David.

6 LORD, don't correct me when you are angry;
don't punish me when you are very angry.
2LORD, have mercy on me because I am weak.
Heal me, LORD, because my bones ache.
3I am very upset.
LORD, how long will it be?
4LORD, return and save me;
save me because of your kindness.
5Dead people don't remember you;
those in the grave don't praise you.

6I am tired of crying to you.
Every night my bed is wet with tears;
my bed is soaked from my crying.
7My eyes are weak from so much crying;
they are weak from crying about my enemies.

8Get away from me, all you who do evil,
because the LORD has heard my crying.
9The LORD has heard my cry for help;
the LORD will answer my prayer.
10All my enemies will be ashamed and troubled.
They will turn and suddenly leave in shame.

A Prayer for Fairness

A shiggaion[d] of David which he sang to the LORD about Cush, from the tribe of Benjamin.

7 LORD my God, I trust in you for protection.
Save me and rescue me
from those who are chasing me.
2Otherwise, like a lion they will tear me apart.
They will rip me to pieces, and no one can save me.

3LORD my God, what have I done?
Have my hands done something wrong?
4Have I done wrong to my friend
or stolen without reason from my enemy?
5If I have, let my enemy chase me and capture me.
Let him trample me into the dust
and bury me in the ground. *Selah*[d]

6LORD, rise up in your anger;
stand up against my enemies' anger.
Get up and demand fairness.
7Gather the nations around you
and rule them from above.
8LORD, judge the people.
LORD, defend me because I am right,
because I have done no wrong, God Most High.
9God, you do what is right.
You know our thoughts and feelings.
Stop those wicked actions done by evil people,
and help those who do what is right.

10God protects me like a shield;
he saves those whose hearts are right.
11God judges by what is right,
and God is always ready to punish the wicked.
12If they do not change their lives,
God will sharpen his sword;
he will string his bow and take aim.
13He has prepared his deadly weapons;
he has made his flaming arrows.

14There are people who think up evil
and plan trouble and tell lies.
15They dig a hole to trap others,
but they will fall into it themselves.
16They will get themselves into trouble;
the violence they cause will hurt only themselves.

17I praise the LORD because he does what is right.
I sing praises to the LORD Most High.

The Lord's Greatness

For the director of music. On the gittith.[d] A psalm of David.

8 LORD our Lord,
your name is the most wonderful name in all the earth!
It brings you praise in heaven above.
2You have taught children and babies
to sing praises to you
because of your enemies.
And so you silence your enemies

and destroy those who try to get even.

3I look at your heavens,
which you made with your fingers.
I see the moon and stars,
which you created.
4But why are people important to you?
Why do you take care of human beings?
5You made them a little lower than the angels
and crowned them with glory and honor.
6You put them in charge of everything you made.
You put all things under their control:
7all the sheep, the cattle,
and the wild animals,
8the birds in the sky,
the fish in the sea,
and everything that lives under water.
9LORD our Lord,
your name is the most wonderful name in all the earth!

Thanksgiving for Victory

For the director of music. To the tune of "The Death of the Son." A psalm of David.

9 I will praise you, LORD, with all my heart.
I will tell all the miracles[a] you have done.
2I will be happy because of you;
God Most High, I will sing praises to your name.

3My enemies turn back;

SELF-ESTEEM

A Speck?

When you look up in the sky at night, it's easy to see that the Earth is little more than a tiny speck in a giant universe. And within our solar system are nine planets, each of them unique and wonderful.

Mercury, the closest planet to the sun, is still 36 million miles from the sun. Venus, the next closest planet, is just a little smaller than the Earth and is covered by a layer of clouds that hide its surface.

Next beyond Earth is Mars, which is like a red desert of rock, sand, and soil. Jupiter, the largest planet, comes next. Its diameter is eleven times that of Earth. Saturn is next and is the last planet we can see with an unaided eye. The next planet, Uranus, is 1.8 billion miles from the sun. Beyond it are Neptune and Pluto, which have eccentric rotation patterns, so they sometimes switch places, making Pluto closer to the sun than Neptune.

It's kind of overwhelming, isn't it? It makes us seem so insignificant.

But wait!

Mercury's temperature can reach 780 degrees. Clouds on Venus drip pure sulphuric acid. The atmosphere on Mars is like car exhaust. A mixture of sulphur and phosphorus make Jupiter like a giant match head, ready to ignite.

On Saturn, raindrops are liquified methane gas. Uranus is covered in radioactive smog. One hemisphere of Neptune will not see sunlight until the year 2030. And Pluto is frozen solid.

Makes you think God cares specially for us on Earth, doesn't it?

When the psalmist looked to the heavens in **Psalm 8**, he, too, was overwhelmed and felt insignificant. But he recognized how special the Earth and its people are to God.

- How do these scientific facts about the solar system relate to the message of Psalm 8?
- Do you ever struggle with the thought that God values you and finds you important? What's the message of Psalm 8 for you?

CONSIDER . . .

- listing the different ways you strive to feel important and comparing them to the reasons you believe that God truly values you. The Bible passages listed under "For More, See" can get you started.
- doing something special for yourself—such as going to a fun athletic event or buying yourself flowers—as a way of recognizing how special you are to God!

FOR MORE, SEE . . .

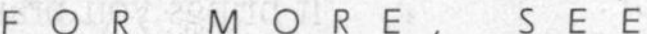

- Genesis 1:26–31 (p. 3)
- John 3:16–17 (p. 1062)
- Romans 5:6–8 (p. 1145)

they are overwhelmed and die because of
you.
4You have heard my complaint;
you sat on your throne and judged by what
was right.
5You spoke strongly against the foreign nations
and destroyed the wicked;
you wiped out their names forever and
ever.
6The enemy is gone forever.
You destroyed their cities;
no one even remembers them.

7But the LORD rules forever.
He sits on his throne to judge,
8and he will judge the world in fairness;
he will decide what is fair for the nations.
9The LORD defends those who suffer;
he defends them in times of trouble.
10Those who know the LORD trust him,
because he will not leave those who come
to him.

11Sing praises to the LORD who is king on
Mount Zion.[d]
Tell the nations what he has done.
12He remembers who the murderers are;
he will not forget the cries of those who
suffer.
13LORD, have mercy on me.
See how my enemies hurt me.
Do not let me go through the gates of
death.
14Then, at the gates of Jerusalem, I will praise
you;
I will rejoice because you saved me.
15The nations have fallen into the pit they dug.
Their feet are caught in the nets they laid.
16The LORD has made himself known by his
fair decisions;
the wicked get trapped by what they do.
Higgaion.[d] *Selah*[d]
17Wicked people will go to the grave,
and so will all those who forget God.
18But those who have troubles will not be
forgotten.
The hopes of the poor will never die.

19LORD, rise up and judge the nations.
Don't let people think they are strong.
20Teach them to fear you, LORD.
The nations must learn that they are only
human. *Selah*

A Complaint About Evil People

10 LORD, why are you so far away?
Why do you hide when there is
trouble?
2Proudly the wicked chase down those who
suffer.
Let them be caught in their own traps.
3They brag about the things they want.
They bless the greedy but hate the LORD.
4The wicked people are too proud.
They do not look for God;
there is no room for God in their thoughts.
5They always succeed.
They are far from keeping your laws;
they make fun of their enemies.
6They say to themselves, "Nothing bad will
ever happen to me;
I will never be ruined."
7Their mouths are full of curses, lies, and
threats;
they use their tongues for sin and evil.
8They hide near the villages.
They look for innocent people to kill;
they watch in secret for the helpless.
9They wait in hiding like a lion.
They wait to catch poor people;
they catch the poor in nets.
10The poor are thrown down and crushed;
they are defeated because the others are
stronger.
11The wicked think, "God has forgotten us.
He doesn't see what is happening."

12LORD, rise up and punish the wicked.
Don't forget those who need help.
13Why do wicked people hate God?
They say to themselves, "God won't punish
us."
14LORD, surely you see these cruel and evil
things;
look at them and do something.
People in trouble look to you for help.
You are the one who helps the orphans.
15Break the power of wicked people.
Punish them for the evil they have done.

16The LORD is King forever and ever.
Destroy from your land those nations that
do not worship you.
17LORD, you have heard what the poor people
want.
Do what they ask, and listen to them.
18Protect the orphans and put an end to
suffering
so they will no longer be afraid of evil
people.

Trust in the Lord

For the director of music. Of David.

11 I trust in the LORD for protection.
So why do you say to me,
"Fly like a bird to your mountain.
2Like hunters, the wicked string their
bows;
they set their arrows on the bowstrings.

They shoot from dark places
at those who are honest.
3When all that is good falls apart,
what can good people do?"

4The LORD is in his holy temple;
the LORD sits on his throne in heaven.
He sees what people do;
he keeps his eye on them.
5The LORD tests those who do right,
but he hates the wicked and those who
love to hurt others.
6He will send hot coals and burning sulfur on
the wicked.
A whirlwind is what they will get.

SIDELIGHT: You would want an air-conditioned tent if the whirlwind of Psalm 11:6 blew in. Called a sirocco, this hot desert wind could blow for days, killing most vegetation.

7The LORD does what is right, and he loves
justice,
so honest people will see his face.

A Prayer Against Liars

For the director of music. Upon the sheminith.[d] A psalm of David.

12 Save me, LORD, because the good
people are all gone;
no true believers are left on earth.
2Everyone lies to his neighbors;
they say one thing and mean another.
3The LORD will stop those flattering
lips
and cut off those bragging tongues.
4They say, "Our tongues will help us win.
We can say what we wish; no one is our
master."
5But the LORD says,
"I will now rise up,
because the poor are being hurt.
Because of the moans of the helpless,
I will give them the help they want."
6The LORD's words are pure,
like silver purified by fire,
like silver purified seven times over.

7LORD, you will keep us safe;
you will always protect us from such
people.
8But the wicked are all around us;
everyone loves what is wrong.

A Prayer for God to Be Near

For the director of music. A psalm of David.

13 How long will you forget me, LORD?
Forever?
How long will you hide from me?
2How long must I worry
and feel sad in my heart all day?
How long will my enemy win over me?

3LORD, look at me.
Answer me, my God;
tell me, or I will die.
4Otherwise my enemy will say, "I have won!"
Those against me will rejoice that I've been
defeated.

5I trust in your love.
My heart is happy because you saved me.
6I sing to the LORD
because he has taken care of me.

The Unbelieving Fool

For the director of music. Of David.

14 Fools say to themselves,
"There is no God."
Fools are evil and do terrible things;
there is no one who does anything good.

2The LORD looked down from heaven on all
people
to see if anyone understood,
if anyone was looking to God for help.
3But all have turned away.
Together, everyone has become evil.
There is no one who does anything good,
not even one.
4Don't the wicked understand?
They destroy my people as if they were
eating bread.
They do not ask the LORD for help.
5But the wicked are filled with terror,
because God is with those who do what is
right.
6The wicked upset the plans of the poor,
but the LORD will protect them.

7I pray that victory will come to Israel from
Mount Zion![d]
May the LORD bring them back.
Then the people of Jacob will rejoice,
and the people of Israel will be glad.

What the Lord Demands

A psalm of David.

15 LORD, who may enter your Holy
Tent?[d]
Who may live on your holy mountain?

[2]Only those who are innocent
and who do what is right.
Such people speak the truth from their hearts
3 and do not tell lies about others.
They do no wrong to their neighbors
and do not gossip.
[4]They do not respect hateful people
but honor those who honor the LORD.
They keep their promises to their neighbors,
even when it hurts.
[5]They do not charge interest on money they lend
and do not take money to hurt innocent people.

Whoever does all these things will never be destroyed.

The Lord Takes Care of His People

A miktam[d] of David.

16 Protect me, God,
because I trust in you.
[2]I said to the LORD, "You are my Lord.
Every good thing I have comes from you."
[3]As for the godly people in the world,
they are the wonderful ones I enjoy.
[4]But those who turn to idols
will have much pain.
I will not offer blood to those idols
or even speak their names.

[5]No, the LORD is all I need.
He takes care of me.
[6]My share in life has been pleasant;
my part has been beautiful.

[7]I praise the LORD because he advises me.
Even at night, I feel his leading.
[8]I keep the LORD before me always.
Because he is close by my side,
I will not be hurt.
[9]So I rejoice and am glad.
Even my body has hope,
[10]because you will not leave me in the grave.
You will not let your holy one rot.
[11]You will teach me how to live a holy life.
Being with you will fill me with joy;

DOUBT

She Loves Me?

Mark Donigan nearly died emotionally while dating Sharon. She was his first real girlfriend. He really didn't understand how this "falling in love" stuff worked.

Mark just knew that sometimes when he saw Sharon, she was absolutely in love with him—that big smile, sparkling eyes, tight handhold. Other times, it was like she could barely stand him—no eye contact, nothing to say, arms folded, nothing but frowns.

About the time Mark's friends would convince him to break up, she would write a wonderful note, bake him some cookies, or do some other nice thing that convinced him she really did love him.

Doubt took its toll on Mark. One day up and the next down. One day she loved him; the next day she seemed distant. Finally, after about six months of roller-coaster emotions, Mark ended his relationship with Sharon.

The breakup hurt, but deep down Mark was relieved. He finally realized that real love doesn't turn on and off unpredictably.

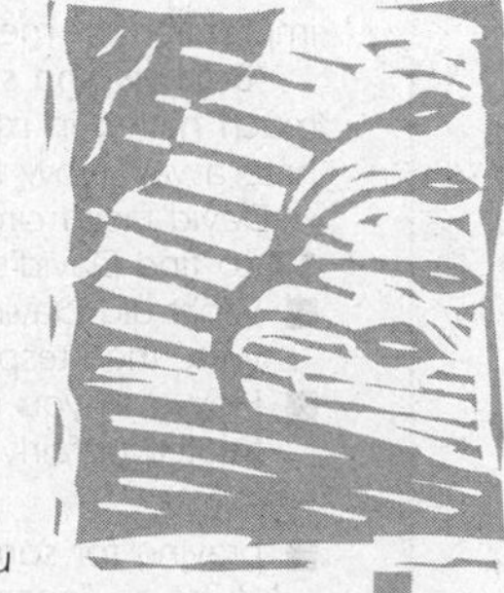

Mark doubted Sharon's love because her actions seemed inconsistent. In the same way, David's circumstances became so difficult that he began to wonder whether God loved him. But there was no break in this relationship. Read **Psalm 13** to discover the different conclusion David reached.

- Why, based on this psalm, could David be so confident in God's love? How is this different from Mark's doubts about Sharon's love?
- When was the last time you doubted God's love for you? How did you work through your doubt?

CONSIDER . . .

- starting a special prayer time for the relationship in your life that gives you the most doubts.
- writing a letter to "Mr. Doubt," letting him know how you plan to handle him with God's help.

FOR MORE, SEE . . .

- Jeremiah 1:4–10 (p. 691)
- John 20:24–29 (p. 1094)
- Romans 4:18–25 (p. 1145)

at your right hand I will find pleasure
forever.

A Prayer for Protection

A prayer of David.

17 LORD, hear me begging for fairness;
listen to my cry for help.
Pay attention to my prayer,
because I speak the truth.
2You will judge that I am right;
your eyes can see what is true.
3You have examined my heart;
you have tested me all night.
You questioned me without finding anything
wrong;
I have not sinned with my mouth.
4I have obeyed your commands,
so I have not done what evil people do.
5I have done what you told me;
I have not failed.

6I call to you, God,
and you answer me.
Listen to me now,
and hear what I say.
7Your love is wonderful.
By your power you save those who trust
you
from their enemies.
8Protect me as you would protect your own
eye.
Hide me under the shadow of your wings.
9Keep me from the wicked who attack me,
from my enemies who surround me.
10They are selfish
and brag about themselves.
11They have chased me until they have
surrounded me.
They plan to throw me to the ground.
12They are like lions ready to kill;
like lions, they sit in hiding.
13LORD, rise up, face the enemy, and throw
them down.
Save me from the wicked with your
sword.
14LORD, save me by your power
from those whose reward is in this life.
They have plenty of food.
They have many sons
and leave much money to their children.

15Because I have lived right, I will see your
face.

REVENGE

Hate Stealer

I can't remember his name. I'm really not sure how old he was. I can hardly remember his face. His broken English was tough to understand. But, I've never forgotten his story.

Before being baptized, this Vietnamese refugee stood before our church to tell how Jesus Christ had changed his life. He spoke of the horrors of war—of escape through jungles and rivers and over the border into Thailand, of hunger and near starvation in overcrowded camps, and of the joy of coming to America.

But above all his captivating stories, one part of his testimony left a lasting impression on me.

"Brothers and sisters," he said. "I came to America alone, and I came with much hatred in my heart. But when Jesus came into my heart, he stole my hate away. Now I can say that I love even my enemies."

David faced circumstances similar to this Vietnamese refugee. Read **Psalm 17** to find David's response to his enemies.

- What did David have in common with this Vietnamese refugee? How were their responses to their enemies different?
- How can you leave matters in God's hands—as David did—when you are treated unfairly?

CONSIDER . . .

- praying for someone who has treated you unfairly and whom you consider to be an "enemy."
- listing ways the world would be different if people and nations would turn away from revenge. Then pray for world peace—starting in your own home and school.

FOR MORE, SEE . . .

- 1 Samuel 24 (p. 266)
- Matthew 5:38–48 (p. 915)
- Romans 12:14–21 (p. 1158)

When I wake up, I will see your likeness
and be satisfied.

A Song of Victory

For the director of music. By the LORD's servant, David. David sang this song to the LORD when the LORD had saved him from Saul and all his other enemies.

18 I love you, LORD. You are my strength.

2The LORD is my rock, my protection, my Savior.
My God is my rock.
I can run to him for safety.
He is my shield and my saving strength, my defender.
3I will call to the LORD, who is worthy of praise,
and I will be saved from my enemies.

4The ropes of death came around me;
the deadly rivers overwhelmed me.
5The ropes of death wrapped around me.
The traps of death were before me.
6In my trouble I called to the LORD.
I cried out to my God for help.
From his temple he heard my voice;
my call for help reached his ears.

7The earth trembled and shook.
The foundations of the mountains began to shake.
They trembled because the LORD was angry.
8Smoke came out of his nose,
and burning fire came out of his mouth.
Burning coals went before him.
9He tore open the sky and came down
with dark clouds under his feet.
10He rode a creature with wings and flew.
He raced on the wings of the wind.
11He made darkness his covering, his shelter around him,
surrounded by fog and clouds.
12Out of the brightness of his presence came clouds
with hail and lightning.
13The LORD thundered from heaven;
the Most High raised his voice,
and there was hail and lightning.
14He shot his arrows and scattered his enemies.
His many bolts of lightning confused them with fear.
15LORD, you spoke strongly.
The wind blew from your nose.
Then the valleys of the sea appeared,
and the foundations of the earth were seen.

16The LORD reached down from above and took me;
he pulled me from the deep water.
17He saved me from my powerful enemies,
from those who hated me, because they were too strong for me.
18They attacked me at my time of trouble,
but the LORD supported me.
19He took me to a safe place.
Because he delights in me, he saved me.

20The LORD spared me because I did what was right.
Because I have not done evil, he has rewarded me.
21I have followed the ways of the LORD;
I have not done evil by turning away from my God.
22I remember all his laws
and have not broken his rules.
23I am innocent before him;
I have kept myself from doing evil.
24The LORD rewarded me because I did what was right,
because I did what the LORD said was right.

25LORD, you are loyal to those who are loyal,
and you are good to those who are good.
26You are pure to those who are pure,
but you are against those who are bad.
27You save the humble,
but you bring down those who are proud.
28LORD, you give light to my lamp.
My God brightens the darkness around me.
29With your help I can attack an army.
With God's help I can jump over a wall.

30The ways of God are without fault.
The LORD's words are pure.
He is a shield to those who trust him.
31Who is God? Only the LORD.
Who is the Rock?[d] Only our God.
32God is my protection.
He makes my way free from fault.
33He makes me like a deer that does not stumble;
he helps me stand on the steep mountains.
34He trains my hands for battle
so my arms can bend a bronze bow.
35You protect me with your saving shield.
You support me with your right hand.
You have stooped to make me great.
36You give me a better way to live,
so I live as you want me to.
37I chased my enemies and caught them.
I did not quit until they were destroyed.
38I crushed them so they couldn't rise up again.
They fell beneath my feet.
39You gave me strength in battle.

You made my enemies bow before me.
40You made my enemies turn back,
and I destroyed those who hated me.
41They called for help,
but no one came to save them.
They called to the LORD,
but he did not answer them.
42I beat my enemies into pieces, like dust in the wind.
I poured them out like mud in the streets.

43You saved me when the people attacked me.
You made me the leader of nations.
People I never knew serve me.
44As soon as they hear me, they obey me.
Foreigners obey me.
45They all become afraid
and tremble in their hiding places.

46The LORD lives!
May my Rock be praised.
Praise the God who saves me!
47God gives me victory over my enemies
and brings people under my rule.
48He saves me from my enemies.
You set me over those who hate me.
You saved me from cruel men.
49So I will praise you, LORD, among the nations.
I will sing praises to your name.
50The LORD gives great victories to his king.
He is loyal to his appointed king,
to David and his descendants[d] forever.

God's Works and Word

For the director of music. A psalm of David.

19 The heavens tell the glory of God,
and the skies announce what his hands have made.
2Day after day they tell the story;
night after night they tell it again.
3They have no speech or words;
they have no voice to be heard.
4But their message goes out through all the world;
their words go everywhere on earth.
The sky is like a home for the sun.
5 The sun comes out like a bridegroom from his bedroom.
It rejoices like an athlete eager to run a race.
6The sun rises at one end of the sky
and follows its path to the other end.
Nothing hides from its heat.

7The teachings of the LORD are perfect;
they give new strength.
The rules of the LORD can be trusted;
they make plain people wise.
8The orders of the LORD are right;
they make people happy.
The commands of the LORD are pure;
they light up the way.
9Respect for the LORD is good;
it will last forever.
The judgments of the LORD are true;
they are completely right.
10They are worth more than gold,
even the purest gold.
They are sweeter than honey,
even the finest honey.
11By them your servant is warned.
Keeping them brings great reward.

12People cannot see their own mistakes.
Forgive me for my secret sins.
13Keep me from the sins of pride;
don't let them rule me.
Then I can be pure
and innocent of the greatest of sins.

14I hope my words and thoughts please you.
LORD, you are my Rock,[d] the one who saves me.

A Prayer for the King

For the director of music. A psalm of David.

20 May the LORD answer you in times of trouble.
May the God of Jacob protect you.
2May he send you help from his Temple[d]
and support you from Mount Zion.[d]
3May he remember all your offerings
and accept all your sacrifices. *Selah*[d]
4May he give you what you want
and make all your plans succeed,
5and we will shout for joy when you succeed,
and we will raise a flag in the name of our God.
May the LORD give you all that you ask for.

6Now I know the LORD helps his appointed king.
He answers him from his holy heaven
and saves him with his strong right hand.
7Some trust in chariots, others in horses,
but we trust the LORD our God.
8They are overwhelmed and defeated,
but we march forward and win.
9LORD, save the king!
Answer us when we call for help.

Thanksgiving for the King

For the director of music. A psalm of David.

21 LORD, the king rejoices because of your strength;
he is so happy when you save him!
2You gave the king what he wanted

and did not refuse what he asked for. *Selah*[d]
3You put good things before him
and placed a gold crown on his head.
4He asked you for life,
and you gave it to him,
so his years go on and on.
5He has great glory because you gave him
victories;
you gave him honor and praise.
6You always gave him blessings;
you made him glad because you were with
him.
7The king truly trusts the LORD.
Because God Most High always loves him,
he will not be overwhelmed.
8Your hand is against all your enemies;
those who hate you will feel your power.
9When you appear,
you will burn them as in a furnace.
In your anger you will swallow them up,
and fire will burn them up.
10You will destroy their families from the earth;
their children will not live.
11They made evil plans against you,
but their traps won't work.
12You will make them turn their backs
when you aim your arrows at them.
13Be supreme, LORD, in your power.
We sing and praise your greatness.

The Prayer of a Suffering Man

For the director of music. To the tune of "The Doe of Dawn." A psalm of David.

22 My God, my God, why have you
rejected me?
You seem far from saving me,
far from the words of my groaning.

BIBLE STUDY

You'll Make It

Life began for Trisha Jones when she was seventeen years old. At summer camp she was introduced to Jesus Christ for the first time.

"I felt a mixture of relief and joy," says Trisha. "Relief, because I'd come to camp with my life in turmoil—I had destructive habits and relationships that just weren't right. And joy, because I really believed all things could be new for me as a Christian."

But with her joy over becoming a Christian, Trisha secretly wondered if it would last.

"I had so many problems," she recalls. "And even with Jesus in my life, I knew they weren't all just going to go away. I wasn't sure I was strong enough to make it through."

Returning home, Trisha wasn't in the camp's beautiful surroundings anymore. And the temptations she had given in to so many times before were back in full force.

"I couldn't believe so many things could go wrong in one week," Trisha says. "I had a major emotional letdown just from being away from the new friends I'd met at camp. My old friends pressured me to do the things I used to, and when I said no, they rejected me. And before the week was over, I'd failed to keep my commitment to Christ several times."

However, Trisha also started studying the Bible—sometimes joyfully and sometimes out of duty. And spending time with God through his Word helped Trisha learn about following Christ and encouraged her to do what was right. As she grew closer to Christ, it became easier to resist the temptations.

Trisha discovered how the Bible could help her change to be more like Christ. Read **Psalm 19** to discover how God's Word made a big difference in David's life!

- What does David say about God's Word—referred to as "the Lord's teachings," his "rules," his "commands"—in Psalm 19 that would have helped Trisha in those early days?
- How can you apply the truth in Psalm 19 to your life this week?

CONSIDER. . .

- highlighting or underlining a verse in this psalm that has special meaning for you.
- finding a friend who will meet with you once a week to study the Bible.

FOR MORE, SEE. . .

- Psalm 119:1–48 (p. 550)
- John 14:23–24 (p. 1085)
- 2 Timothy 3:14–17 (p. 1266)

[2]My God, I call to you during the day,
but you do not answer.
I call at night;
I am not silent.

[3]You sit as the Holy One.
The praises of Israel are your throne.
[4]Our ancestors trusted you;
they trusted, and you saved them.
[5]They called to you for help
and were rescued.
They trusted you
and were not disappointed.

[6]But I am like a worm instead of a man.
People make fun of me and hate me.
[7]Those who look at me laugh.
They stick out their tongues and shake
their heads.
[8]They say, "Turn to the LORD for help.
Maybe he will save you.
If he likes you,
maybe he will rescue you."

[9]You had my mother give birth to me.
You made me trust you
while I was just a baby.
[10]I have leaned on you since the day I was
born;
you have been my God since my mother
gave me birth.
[11]So don't be far away from me.
Now trouble is near,
and there is no one to help.
[12]People have surrounded me like angry bulls.
Like the strong bulls of Bashan, they are on
every side.

SIDELIGHT: Travelers through the region of Bashan, northeast of Galilee, might have needed professional bodyguards. In addition to "strong bulls" (Psalm 22:12), Bashan was notorious for fierce lions and giant people.

[13]Like hungry, roaring lions
they open their mouths at me.
[14]My strength is gone,
like water poured out onto the ground,
and my bones are out of joint.
My heart is like wax;
it has melted inside me.
[15]My strength has dried up like a clay pot,
and my tongue sticks to the top of my
mouth.
You laid me in the dust of death.
[16]Evil people have surrounded me;
like dogs they have trapped me.
They have bitten my arms and legs.
[17]I can count all my bones;
people look and stare at me.
[18]They divided my clothes among them,
and they threw lots[d] for my clothing.

[19]But, LORD, don't be far away.
You are my strength; hurry to help
me.
[20]Save me from the sword;
save my life from the dogs.
[21]Rescue me from the lion's mouth;
save me from the horns of the bulls.

[22]Then I will tell my fellow Israelites about
you;
I will praise you in the public meeting.
[23]Praise the LORD, all you who respect him.
All you descendants[d] of Jacob, honor
him;
fear him, all you Israelites.
[24]He does not ignore those in trouble.
He doesn't hide from them
but listens when they call out to him.
[25]LORD, I praise you in the great meeting of
your people;
these worshipers will see me do what I
promised.
[26]Poor people will eat until they are full;
those who look to the LORD will praise
him.
May your hearts live forever!
[27]People everywhere will remember
and will turn to the LORD.
All the families of the nations
will worship him
[28]because the LORD is King,
and he rules the nations.

[29]All the powerful people on earth will eat and
worship.
Everyone will bow down to him,
all who will one day die.
[30]The people in the future will serve him;
they will always be told about the Lord.
[31]They will tell that he does what is right.
People who are not yet born
will hear what God has done.

SIDELIGHT: Psalm 23 has always been one of the favorite, most-quoted passages in the Old Testament. The early Christian church sang this song when people were baptized.

The Lord the Shepherd

A psalm of David.

23 The LORD is my shepherd;
I have everything I need.
2He lets me rest in green pastures.
He leads me to calm water.
3He gives me new strength.
He leads me on paths that are right
for the good of his name.
4Even if I walk through a very dark valley,
I will not be afraid,
because you are with me.
Your rod and your walking stick[n] comfort
me.

5You prepare a meal for me
in front of my enemies.
You pour oil on my head;[n]
you fill my cup to overflowing.
6Surely your goodness and love will be with
me
all my life,
and I will live in the house of the LORD
forever.

A Welcome for God into the Temple

A psalm of David.

24 The earth belongs to the LORD, and
everything in it—
the world and all its people.
2He built it on the waters
and set it on the rivers.

walking stick The stick a shepherd uses to guide and protect his sheep.
pour oil . . . head This can mean that God gave him great wealth and blessed him.

HAPPINESS

Heart Strokes

Joe Castillo taught science at an inner-city high school in Kansas City. Some of the students were rough. He often had to break up fights. A student pulled a gun on him once, and knives were as common as notebooks.

But it didn't matter. Joe loved his students and did all he could to make science come alive for them. He would sell gum between classes to raise money for lab equipment the school district couldn't afford. He organized a clothes drive so his students could have winter coats. Most of his students loved him because they understood how much he cared. That's just the way he was.

When Joe had a stroke, it devastated his students. With incredible sadness, they watched him fight death every day. He lost many of his motor skills. He couldn't walk without a cane, and his speech began to slur. Many cried the day the principal told them the doctors wouldn't let Joe teach anymore. He had persevered ten months longer than the doctors thought he possibly could.

When students visited Joe in the hospital, they would go to his room sad. But when they would leave, they would be happy.

"I went to encourage him, and I left encouraged," one of Joe's seniors said. "Joe had me laughing so hard I almost forgot I was in the hospital. I don't know how anyone can be so happy in a place like that."

Despite awful pain, Joe held onto the truth that David declared in **Psalm 23**.

- What phrase in Psalm 23 best describes the reason for Joe's happiness despite such terrible circumstances?
- How can you make the truths of Psalm 23 the foundation for your happiness?

CONSIDER . . .

- taking a personal inventory of the sources of your happiness, by writing as many responses as you can to this phrase: "Happiness, for me, is . . ."
- taking a walk and talking to God about a "dark valley" you're going through right now.

FOR MORE, SEE . . .

- Psalm 100 (p. 539)
- Matthew 5:1–12 (p. 912)
- Philippians 4:4–7 (p. 1234)

3Who may go up on the mountain of the
LORD?
Who may stand in his holy Temple?[d]
4Only those with clean hands and pure hearts,
who have not worshiped idols,
who have not made promises in the name
of a false god.
5They will receive a blessing from the LORD;
the God who saves them will declare them
right.
6They try to follow God;
they look to the God of Jacob for help.
Selah[d]

7Gates, open all the way.
Open wide, aged doors
so the glorious King will come in.
8Who is this glorious King?
The LORD, strong and mighty.
The LORD, the powerful warrior.
9Gates, open all the way.
Open wide, aged doors
so the glorious King will come in.
10Who is this glorious King?
The LORD All-Powerful—
he is the glorious King. *Selah*

A Prayer for God to Guide

Of David.

25 LORD, I give myself to you;
2 my God, I trust you.
Do not let me be disgraced;
do not let my enemies laugh at me.
3No one who trusts you will be disgraced,
but those who sin without excuse will be
disgraced.

4LORD, tell me your ways.
Show me how to live.
5Guide me in your truth,
and teach me, my God, my Savior.
I trust you all day long.
6LORD, remember your mercy and love
that you have shown since long ago.
7Do not remember the sins
and wrong things I did when I was young.
But remember to love me always
because you are good, LORD.

8The LORD is good and right;
he points sinners to the right way.
9He shows those who are humble how to do
right,
and he teaches them his ways.
10All the LORD's ways are loving and true
for those who follow the demands of his
agreement.
11For the sake of your name, LORD,
forgive my many sins.
12Are there those who respect the LORD?
He will point them to the best way.
13They will enjoy a good life,
and their children will inherit the land.
14The LORD tells his secrets to those who
respect him;
he tells them about his agreement.
15My eyes are always looking to the LORD for
help.
He will keep me from any traps.
16Turn to me and have mercy on me,
because I am lonely and hurting.
17My troubles have grown larger;
free me from my problems.
18Look at my suffering and troubles,
and take away all my sins.
19Look at how many enemies I have!
See how much they hate me!
20Protect me and save me.
I trust you, so do not let me be disgraced.
21My hope is in you,
so may goodness and honesty guard
me.
22God, save Israel from all their troubles!

The Prayer of an Innocent Believer

Of David.

26 LORD, defend me because I have lived
an innocent life.
I have trusted the LORD and never doubted.
2LORD, try me and test me;
look closely into my heart and mind.
3I see your love,
and I live by your truth.
4I do not spend time with liars,
nor do I make friends with those who hide
their sin.
5I hate the company of evil people,
and I won't sit with the wicked.
6I wash my hands to show I am innocent,
and I come to your altar, LORD.
7I raise my voice in praise
and tell of all the miracles[d] you have
done.
8LORD, I love the Temple[d] where you
live,
where your glory is.
9Do not kill me with those sinners
or take my life with those murderers.
10Evil is in their hands,
and they do wrong for money.
11But I have lived an innocent life,
so save me and have mercy on me.
12I stand in a safe place.
LORD, I praise you in the great meeting.

A Song of Trust in God

Of David.

27 The LORD is my light and the one
who saves me.
I fear no one.
The LORD protects my life;
I am afraid of no one.
2Evil people may try to destroy my body.
My enemies and those who hate me attack
me,
but they are overwhelmed and defeated.
3If an army surrounds me,
I will not be afraid.
If war breaks out,
I will trust the LORD.

4I ask only one thing from the LORD.
This is what I want:
Let me live in the LORD's house
all my life.
Let me see the LORD's beauty
and look with my own eyes at his Temple.[d]
5During danger he will keep me safe in his
shelter.
He will hide me in his Holy Tent,[d]
or he will keep me safe on a high
mountain.
6My head is higher than my enemies around
me.
I will offer joyful sacrifices in his Holy Tent.
I will sing and praise the LORD.

7LORD, hear me when I call;
have mercy and answer me.
8My heart said of you, "Go, worship him."

FEAR

An Antidote for Fear

Dr. Martin Luther King, Jr., a minister, was one of the foremost spokespeople for the civil rights movement that began in the United States in the 1950s. He risked his life and career around the country participating in nonviolent protests and preaching equality for all people. He was arrested many times and received numerous threats on his life before he was assassinated in 1968.

One Monday evening after a particularly tension-packed week, King spoke at a mass meeting. "I attempted to convey an overt impression of strength and courage," he said, "although I was inwardly depressed and fear-stricken."

After his talk, Mother Pollard—an elderly woman who had been instrumental in early civil rights victories—came to the front of the church and called, "Come here, son." King embraced her warmly as usual, but she wasn't going to let him move on just yet.

"Something is wrong with you. You didn't talk strong tonight."

"Oh, no, Mother Pollard, nothing is wrong," King assured her. "I'm feeling as fine as ever."

"Now you can't fool me," she said. "I knows something is wrong. Is it that we ain't doing things to please you? Or is it that the white folks is bothering you? I done told you we is with you all the way. But even if we ain't with you, God's gonna take care of you."

"Since that dreary night, I have known very few quiet days," King later said. "But as the years have unfolded, the eloquently simple words of Mother Pollard have come back again and again to give light and peace and guidance to my troubled soul."

As you read **Psalm 27**, you'll find David expressing the same eloquently simple truth. He too found that the best antidote to fear is knowing "God's gonna take care of you."

- What verses from Psalm 27 might have inspired Mother Pollard's assurance to Martin Luther King, Jr.?
- What verse brings you the most assurance to face a fearful situation?

CONSIDER . . .

- memorizing the verse from Psalm 27 that you most want to remember the next time you are afraid.
- asking friends from school and church how they handle fear.

FOR MORE, SEE . . .

- 1 Kings 19:1–18 (p. 325)
- Luke 8:22–25 (p. 1017)
- 1 John 4:17–18 (p. 1319)

So I come to worship you, LORD.
9Do not turn away from me.
Do not turn your servant away in anger;
you have helped me.
Do not push me away or leave me alone,
God, my Savior.
10If my father and mother leave me,
the LORD will take me in.
11LORD, teach me your ways,
and guide me to do what is right
because I have enemies.
12Do not hand me over to my enemies,
because they tell lies about me
and say they will hurt me.

13I truly believe
I will live to see the LORD's goodness.
14Wait for the LORD's help.
Be strong and brave,
and wait for the LORD's help.

A Prayer in Troubled Times

Of David.

28 LORD, my Rock,[d] I call out to you for help.
Do not be deaf to me.
If you are silent,
I will be like those in the grave.
2Hear the sound of my prayer,
when I cry out to you for help.
I raise my hands
toward your Most Holy Place.
3Don't drag me away with the wicked,
with those who do evil.
They say "Peace" to their neighbors,
but evil is in their hearts.
4Pay them back for what they have done,
for their evil deeds.
Pay them back for what they have done;
give them their reward.
5They don't understand what the LORD has done
or what he has made.
So he will knock them down
and not lift them up.

6Praise the LORD,
because he heard my prayer for help.
7The LORD is my strength and shield.
I trust him, and he helps me.
I am very happy,
and I praise him with my song.
8The LORD is powerful;
he gives victory to his chosen one.
9Save your people
and bless those who are your own.
Be their shepherd and carry them forever.

God in the Thunderstorm

A psalm of David.

29 Praise the LORD, you angels;
praise the LORD's glory and power.
2Praise the LORD for the glory of his name;
worship the LORD because he is holy.

3The LORD's voice is heard over the sea.
The glorious God thunders;
the LORD thunders over the ocean.
4The LORD's voice is powerful;
the LORD's voice is majestic.
5The LORD's voice breaks the trees;
the LORD breaks the cedars of Lebanon.

SIDELIGHT: God's power was indeed great to break the cedars of Lebanon (Psalm 29:5). These trees grew seventy to eighty feet tall, with trunks sometimes more than twelve feet in diameter. Imagine how many strings of lights you would need to decorate one of those for Christmas!

6He makes the land of Lebanon dance like a calf
and Mount Hermon jump like a baby bull.
7The LORD's voice makes the lightning flash.
8The LORD's voice shakes the desert;
the LORD shakes the Desert of Kadesh.
9The LORD's voice shakes the oaks
and strips the leaves off the trees.
In his Temple[d] everyone says, "Glory to God!"

10The LORD controls the flood.
The LORD will be King forever.
11The LORD gives strength to his people;
the LORD blesses his people with peace.

Thanksgiving for Escaping Death

A psalm of David. A song for giving the Temple[d] to the LORD.

30 I will praise you, LORD,
because you rescued me.
You did not let my enemies laugh at me.
2LORD, my God, I prayed to you,
and you healed me.
3You lifted me out of the grave;
you spared me from going down to the place of the dead.

4Sing praises to the LORD, you who belong to him;
praise his holy name.
5His anger lasts only a moment,

but his kindness lasts for a lifetime.
Crying may last for a night,
but joy comes in the morning.

6When I felt safe, I said,
"I will never fear."
7LORD, in your kindness you made my mountain safe.
But when you turned away, I was frightened.

8I called to you, LORD,
and asked you to have mercy on me.
9I said, "What good will it do if I die
or if I go down to the grave?
Dust cannot praise you;
it cannot speak about your truth.
10LORD, hear me and have mercy on me.
LORD, help me."
11You changed my sorrow into dancing.
You took away my clothes of sadness,
and clothed me in happiness.
12I will sing to you and not be silent.
LORD, my God, I will praise you forever.

A Prayer of Faith in Troubled Times

For the director of music. A psalm of David.

31 LORD, I trust in you;
let me never be disgraced.
Save me because you do what is right.
2Listen to me
and save me quickly.
Be my rock of protection,
a strong city to save me.
3You are my rock and my protection.
For the good of your name, lead me and guide me.

DEPRESSION

The Wall Came Tumbling Down

On August 13, 1961, at 2:30 A.M., with floodlights to illuminate their work and soldiers to ensure no interruptions, engineering crews began sinking posts in the pavement of Berlin. Then they attached massive sheets of barbed wire.

Many thought it was a farce, but from that middle-of-the-night beginning, the Berlin Wall was built. It divided families, friends and nations. About ten thousand East Germans attempted to cross the wall in the next twenty-nine years, by tunneling, driving, flying, even blasting. At least 191 died trying.

The best-known "defector," Peter Fechter, was shot down by border guards in front of photographers and TV crews in 1962. Countless others were imprisoned for attempting to cross the wall.

Nothing portrayed the division of an entire country more dramatically than the Berlin Wall. And nothing else so well symbolized the broken people of this war-torn territory.

On November 17, 1989, Egon Krenz, the premier of East Germany, ordered the wall torn down. In no time, sledge hammers wielded by East and West Berliners broke through, opening the way for millions to cross back and forth in one joyous parade. No papers were checked. Even the border guards fought to keep from smiling.

"The wall is gone!" the people chanted. "The wall is gone." From both sides of the city they climbed atop undamaged portions of the ten-foot structure, laughing, crying, embracing, singing, and dancing.

When David was delivered from his enemies, he expressed the same joyous feeling in his prayer, "You changed my sorrow into dancing." Read **Psalm 30** to find out how your sorrow and depression can be turned to joy.

- How was the destruction of the Berlin Wall like David's deliverance from his enemies?
- What "walls" of sorrow and depression need to be broken down by God in your life? What sorrow in your life would you like God to turn into dancing?

CONSIDER . . .

- expressing thanks to people you turn to when you're depressed.
- planning a personal "party" complete with your favorite dessert to celebrate a victory God has gained in your life.

FOR MORE, SEE . . .

- Isaiah 61:3 (p. 681)
- Jonah 2 (p. 857)
- Luke 15:11–32 (p. 1035)

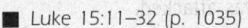

4Set me free from the trap they set for me,
because you are my protection.
5I give you my life.
Save me, LORD, God of truth.

6I hate those who worship false gods.
I trust only in the LORD.
7I will be glad and rejoice in your love,
because you saw my suffering;
you knew my troubles.
8You have not handed me over to my enemies
but have set me in a safe place.

9LORD, have mercy, because I am in misery.
My eyes are weak from so much crying,
and my whole being is tired from grief.
10My life is ending in sadness,
and my years are spent in crying.
My troubles are using up my strength,
and my bones are getting weaker.
11Because of all my troubles, my enemies hate
me,
and even my neighbors look down on me.
When my friends see me,
they are afraid and run.
12I am like a piece of a broken pot.
I am forgotten as if I were dead.
13I have heard many insults.
Terror is all around me.
They make plans against me
and want to kill me.

14LORD, I trust you.
I have said, "You are my God."
15My life is in your hands.
Save me from my enemies
and from those who are chasing me.
16Show your kindness to me, your servant.
Save me because of your love.
17LORD, I called to you,
so do not let me be disgraced.
Let the wicked be disgraced
and lie silent in the grave.
18With pride and hatred
they speak against those who do right.
So silence their lying lips.

19How great is your goodness
that you have stored up for those who fear
you,
that you have given to those who trust you.
You do this for all to see.
20You protect them by your presence
from what people plan against them.
You shelter them from evil words.
21Praise the LORD.
His love to me was wonderful
when my city was attacked.
22In my distress, I said,
"God cannot see me!"
But you heard my prayer
when I cried out to you for help.
23Love the LORD, all you who belong to him.
The LORD protects those who truly believe,
but he punishes the proud as much as they
have sinned.
24All you who put your hope in the LORD
be strong and brave.

It Is Better to Confess Sin

A maskil[d] of David.

32 Happy is the person
whose sins are forgiven,
whose wrongs are pardoned.
2Happy is the person
whom the LORD does not consider guilty
and in whom there is nothing false.

3When I kept things to myself,
I felt weak deep inside me.
I moaned all day long.
4Day and night you punished me.
My strength was gone as in the summer
heat. *Selah*[d]
5Then I confessed my sins to you
and didn't hide my guilt.
I said, "I will confess my sins to the LORD,"
and you forgave my guilt. *Selah*

6For this reason, all who obey you
should pray to you while they still can.
When troubles rise like a flood,
they will not reach them.
7You are my hiding place.
You protect me from my troubles
and fill me with songs of salvation. *Selah*

8The LORD says, "I will make you wise and
show you where to go.
I will guide you and watch over you.
9So don't be like a horse or donkey,
that doesn't understand.
They must be led with bits and reins,
or they will not come near you."

10Wicked people have many troubles,
but the LORD's love surrounds those who
trust him.
11Good people, rejoice and be happy in the
LORD.
Sing all you whose hearts are right.

Praise God Who Creates and Saves

33 Sing to the LORD, you who do what is
right;
honest people should praise him.
2Praise the LORD on the harp;
make music for him on a ten-stringed lyre.[d]
3Sing a new song to him;
play well and joyfully.

4God's word is true,
and everything he does is right.
5He loves what is right and fair;
the LORD's love fills the earth.

6The sky was made at the LORD's command.
By the breath from his mouth, he made all the stars.
7He gathered the water of the sea into a heap.
He made the great ocean stay in its place.
8All the earth should worship the LORD;
the whole world should fear him.
9He spoke, and it happened.
He commanded, and it appeared.
10The LORD upsets the plans of nations;
he ruins all their plans.
11But the LORD's plans will stand forever;
his ideas will last from now on.
12Happy is the nation whose God is the LORD,
the people he chose for his very own.
13The LORD looks down from heaven
and sees every person.
14From his throne he watches
all who live on earth.
15He made their hearts
and understands everything they do.
16No king is saved by his great army.
No warrior escapes by his great strength.
17Horses can't bring victory;
they can't save by their strength.
18But the LORD looks after those who fear him,
those who put their hope in his love.
19He saves them from death
and spares their lives in times of hunger.
20So our hope is in the LORD.
He is our help, our shield to protect us.
21We rejoice in him,
because we trust his holy name.
22LORD, show your love to us
as we put our hope in you.

SIDELIGHT: Have you ever made an acrostic in which you use each letter of a word to start a new word or phrase? Some psalms (such as Psalms 34, 37, 111 and 146) use this structure. In Hebrew, each unit of those psalms begins with a successive letter of the alphabet.

Praise God Who Judges and Saves

David's song from the time he acted crazy so Abimelech would send him away, and David did leave.

34 I will praise the LORD at all times;
his praise is always on my lips.
2My whole being praises the LORD.
The poor will hear and be glad.
3Glorify the LORD with me,
and let us praise his name together.

4I asked the LORD for help, and he answered me.
He saved me from all that I feared.
5Those who go to him for help are happy,
and they are never disgraced.
6This poor man called, and the LORD heard him
and saved him from all his troubles.
7The angel of the LORD camps around those who fear God,
and he saves them.

8Examine and see how good the LORD is.
Happy is the person who trusts him.
9You who belong to the LORD, fear him!
Those who fear him will have everything they need.
10Even lions may get weak and hungry,
but those who look to the LORD will have every good thing.
11Children, come and listen to me.
I will teach you to worship the LORD.
12You must do these things
to enjoy life and have many happy days.
13You must not say evil things,
and you must not tell lies.
14Stop doing evil and do good.
Look for peace and work for it.

15The LORD sees the good people
and listens to their prayers.
16But the LORD is against those who do evil;
he makes the world forget them.
17The LORD hears good people when they cry out to him,
and he saves them from all their troubles.
18The LORD is close to the brokenhearted,
and he saves those whose spirits have been crushed.
19People who do what is right may have many problems,
but the LORD will solve them all.
20He will protect their very bones;
not one of them will be broken.
21Evil will kill the wicked;
those who hate good people will be judged guilty.
22But the LORD saves his servants' lives;
no one who trusts him will be judged guilty.

A Prayer for Help

Of David.

35 LORD, battle with those who battle with me.
Fight against those who fight against me.

2Pick up the shield and armor.
Rise up and help me.
3Lift up your spears, both large and small,
against those who chase me.
Tell me, "I will save you."

4Make those who want to kill me
be ashamed and disgraced.
Make those who plan to harm me
turn back and run away.
5Make them like chaff[a] blown by the wind
as the angel of the LORD forces them away.
6Let their road be dark and slippery
as the angel of the LORD chases them.
7For no reason they spread out their net to trap me;
for no reason they dug a pit for me.
8So let ruin strike them suddenly.
Let them be caught in their own nets;
let them fall into the pit and die.
9Then I will rejoice in the LORD;
I will be happy when he saves me.
10Even my bones will say,
"LORD, who is like you?
You save the weak from the strong,
the weak and poor from robbers."

11Men without mercy stand up to testify.
They ask me things I do not know.
12They repay me with evil for the good I have done,
and they make me very sad.
13Yet when they were sick, I put on clothes of sadness
and showed my sorrow by going without food.
But my prayers were not answered.
14 I acted as if they were my friends or brothers.
I bowed in sadness as if I were crying for my mother.
15But when I was in trouble, they gathered and laughed;
they gathered to attack before I knew it.
They insulted me without stopping.
16They made fun of me and were cruel to me
and ground their teeth at me in anger.

17Lord, how long will you watch this happen?
Save my life from their attacks;
save me from these people who are like lions.
18I will praise you in the great meeting.
I will praise you among crowds of people.
19Do not let my enemies laugh at me;
they hate me for no reason.
Do not let them make fun of me;
they have no cause to hate me.
20Their words are not friendly
but are lies about peace-loving people.
21They speak against me
and say, "Aha! We saw what you did!"
22LORD, you have been watching. Do not keep quiet.
Lord, do not leave me alone.
23Wake up! Come and defend me!
My God and Lord, fight for me!
24LORD my God, defend me with your justice.
Don't let them laugh at me.
25Don't let them think, "Aha! We got what we wanted!"
Don't let them say, "We destroyed him."
26Let them be ashamed and embarrassed,
because they were happy when I hurt.
Cover them with shame and disgrace,
because they thought they were better than I was.
27May my friends sing and shout for joy.
May they always say, "Praise the greatness of the LORD,
who loves to see his servants do well."
28I will tell of your goodness
and will praise you every day.

Wicked People and a Good God

For the director of music. Of David,
the servant of the LORD.

36 Sin speaks to the wicked in their hearts.
They have no fear of God.
2They think too much of themselves
so they don't see their sin and hate it.
3Their words are wicked lies;
they are no longer wise or good.
4At night they make evil plans;
what they do leads to nothing good.
They don't refuse things that are evil.

5LORD, your love reaches to the heavens,
your loyalty to the skies.
6Your goodness is as high as the mountains.
Your justice is as deep as the great ocean.
LORD, you protect both people and animals.
7God, your love is so precious!
You protect people in the shadow of your wings.
8They eat the rich food in your house,
and you let them drink from your river of pleasure.
9You are the giver of life.
Your light lets us enjoy life.

10Continue to love those who know you
and to do good to those who are good.
11Don't let proud people attack me
and the wicked force me away.
12Those who do evil have been defeated.
They are overwhelmed;
they cannot do evil any longer.

God Will Reward Fairly

Of David.

37 Don't be upset because of evil people.
Don't be jealous of those who do wrong,
2because like the grass, they will soon dry up.
Like green plants, they will soon die away.

3Trust the LORD and do good.
Live in the land and feed on truth.
4Enjoy serving the LORD,
and he will give you what you want.
5Depend on the LORD;
trust him, and he will take care of you.
6Then your goodness will shine like the sun,
and your fairness like the noonday sun.

7Wait and trust the LORD.
Don't be upset when others get rich
or when someone else's plans succeed.
8Don't get angry.
Don't be upset; it only leads to trouble.
9Evil people will be sent away,
but those who trust the LORD will inherit the land.
10In a little while the wicked will be no more.
You may look for them, but they will be gone.
11People who are not proud will inherit the land
and will enjoy complete peace.

12The wicked make evil plans against good people.
They grind their teeth at them in anger.
13But the Lord laughs at the wicked,
because he sees that their day is coming.
14The wicked draw their swords
and bend their bows
to kill the poor and helpless,
to kill those who are honest.
15But their swords will stab their own hearts,
and their bows will break.

16It is better to have little and be right
than to have much and be wrong.
17The power of the wicked will be broken,

JEALOUSY

The Donald

During the 1980s, Donald Trump was one of the most-admired and most-envied men alive. His fortune grew from $100 million in 1982 to at least $1.7 billion in 1989. He claimed that his worth was closer to $5 billion. He bought an airline and named it after himself. He built hotels and casinos and named many of them after himself. He bought one of the finest yachts in the world and then decided to build one twice as nice. He had a beautiful wife, Ivana. His best-selling book, Trump: The Art of the Deal, drew in would-be entrepreneurs looking for words of financial wisdom.

People thought Trump was arrogant and greedy, but many still envied him. Who wouldn't want to be in his shoes?

In late 1989 and throughout 1990 Trump's fortune plummeted. He wasn't exactly in the poor house, still claiming to be worth around $500 million. But with all his debts, the threat of bankruptcy loomed. He left Ivana and filed for divorce. Many claimed he was estranged from his children, especially Donald, Jr.

Suddenly, few were saying they wanted to be like "The Donald." He became the butt of jokes. He symbolized the ruin of wasteful greed. Those who had envied him most now gloated most happily at his downfall.

If people had read and heeded **Psalm 37**, they would not have been jealous of Trump. Check out the psalmist's advice to people concerning the rich or the wicked.

- What verse in Psalm 37 best applies to the Donald Trump story?
- What should you do when you feel jealous of someone who gets ahead?

CONSIDER . . .

- listing at least twenty reasons why being jealous of anyone, especially people who do wrong, is senseless.
- talking to your parent or youth minister about why you feel jealous and how you can overcome those feelings.

FOR MORE, SEE . . .

- Proverbs 24:1–2 (p. 588)
- Matthew 6:19–24 (p. 918)
- James 1:9–11 (p. 1294)

but the LORD supports those who do right.
18The LORD watches over the lives of the innocent,
and their reward will last forever.
19They will not be ashamed when trouble comes.
They will be full in times of hunger.
20But the wicked will die.
The LORD's enemies will be like the flowers of the fields;
they will disappear like smoke.
21The wicked borrow and don't pay back,
but those who do right give freely to others.
22Those whom the LORD blesses will inherit the land,
but those he curses will be sent away.

23When a person's steps follow the LORD,
God is pleased with his ways.
24If he stumbles, he will not fall,
because the LORD holds his hand.

25I was young, and now I am old,
but I have never seen good people left helpless
or their children begging for food.
26Good people always lend freely to others,
and their children are a blessing.

27Stop doing evil and do good,
so you will live forever.
28The LORD loves justice
and will not leave those who worship him.
He will always protect them,
but the children of the wicked will die.
29Good people will inherit the land
and will live in it forever.

30A good person speaks with wisdom,
and he says what is fair.
31The teachings of his God are in his heart,
so he does not fail to keep them.
32The wicked watch for good people
so that they may kill them.
33But the LORD will not take away his protection
or let good people be judged guilty.

34Wait for the LORD's help
and follow him.
He will honor you and give you the land,
and you will see the wicked sent away.

35I saw a wicked and cruel man
who looked strong like a healthy tree in good soil.
36But he died and was gone;
I looked for him, but he couldn't be found.

37Think of the innocent person,
and watch the honest one.
The man who has peace
will have children to live after him.
38But sinners will be destroyed;
in the end the wicked will die.

39The LORD saves good people;
he is their strength in times of trouble.
40The LORD helps them and saves them;
he saves them from the wicked,
because they trust in him for protection.

A Prayer in Time of Sickness

A psalm of David to remember.

38 LORD, don't correct me when you are angry.
Don't punish me when you are furious.
2Your arrows have wounded me,
and your hand has come down on me.
3My body is sick from your punishment.
Even my bones are not healthy because of my sin.
4My guilt has overwhelmed me;
like a load it weighs me down.

5My sores stink and become infected
because I was foolish.
6I am bent over and bowed down;
I am sad all day long.
7I am burning with fever,
and my whole body is sore.
8I am weak and faint.
I moan from the pain I feel.

9Lord, you know everything I want;
my cries are not hidden from you.
10My heart pounds, and my strength is gone.
I am losing my sight.
11Because of my wounds, my friends and neighbors avoid me,
and my relatives stay far away.
12Some people set traps to kill me.
Those who want to hurt me plan trouble;
all day long they think up lies.

13I am like a deaf man; I cannot hear.
Like a mute, I cannot speak.
14I am like a person who does not hear,
who has no answer to give.
15I trust you, LORD.
You will answer, my Lord and God.
16I said, "Don't let them laugh at me
or brag when I am defeated."
17I am about to die,
and I cannot forget my pain.
18I confess my guilt;
I am troubled by my sin.
19My enemies are strong and healthy,
and many hate me for no reason.
20They repay me with evil for the good I did.
They lie about me because I try to do good.

21 LORD, don't leave me;
my God, don't go away.
22 Quickly come and help me,
my Lord and Savior.

Life Is Short

For the director of music. For Jeduthun.
A psalm of David.

39 I said, "I will be careful how I act
and will not sin by what I say.
I will be careful what I say
around wicked people."
2 So I kept very quiet.
I didn't even say anything good,
but I became even more upset.
3 I became very angry inside,
and as I thought about it, my anger burned.
So I spoke:
4 "LORD, tell me when the end will come
and how long I will live.
Let me know how long I have.
5 You have given me only a short life;
my lifetime is like nothing to you.
Everyone's life is only a breath. *Selah*[d]
6 People are like shadows moving about.
All their work is for nothing;
they collect things but don't know who will
get them.

7 "So, Lord, what hope do I have?
You are my hope.
8 Save me from all my sins.
Don't let wicked fools make fun of me.
9 I am quiet; I do not open my mouth,
because you are the one who has done
this.
10 Quit punishing me;
your beating is about to kill me.
11 You correct and punish people for their sins;
like a moth, you destroy what they love.
Everyone's life is only a breath. *Selah*

12 "LORD, hear my prayer,
and listen to my cry.
Do not ignore my tears.
I am like a visitor with you.
Like my ancestors, I'm only here a short
time.
13 Leave me alone so I can be happy
before I leave and am no more."

Praise and Prayer for Help

For the director of music. A psalm of David.

40 I waited patiently for the LORD.
He turned to me and heard my cry.
2 He lifted me out of the pit of destruction,
out of the sticky mud.
He stood me on a rock
and made my feet steady.
3 He put a new song in my mouth,
a song of praise to our God.
Many people will see this and worship
him.
Then they will trust the LORD.
4 Happy is the person
who trusts the LORD,
who doesn't turn to those who are proud
or to those who worship false gods.
5 LORD my God, you have done many
miracles.[d]
Your plans for us are many.
If I tried to tell them all,
there would be too many to count.
6 You do not want sacrifices and offerings.
But you have made a hole in my ear
to show that my body and life are yours.
You do not ask for burnt offerings
and sacrifices to take away sins.
7 Then I said, "Look, I have come.
It is written about me in the book.
8 My God, I want to do what you want.
Your teachings are in my heart."
9 I will tell about your goodness in the great
meeting of your people.
LORD, you know my lips are not silent.
10 I do not hide your goodness in my heart;
I speak about your loyalty and salvation.
I do not hide your love and truth
from the people in the great meeting.
11 LORD, do not hold back your mercy from me;
let your love and truth always protect me.
12 Troubles have surrounded me;
there are too many to count.
My sins have caught me
so that I cannot see a way to escape.
I have more sins than hairs on my head,
and I have lost my courage.
13 Please, LORD, save me.
Hurry, LORD, to help me.
14 People are trying to kill me.
Shame them and disgrace them.
People want to hurt me.
Let them run away in disgrace.
15 People are making fun of me.
Let them be shamed into silence.
16 But let those who follow you
be happy and glad.
They love you for saving them.
May they always say, "Praise the LORD!"
17 Lord, because I am poor and helpless,
please remember me.
You are my helper and savior.
My God, do not wait.

PSALM 41

A Prayer in Time of Sickness

For the director of music. A psalm of David.

41 Happy is the person who thinks about the poor.
When trouble comes, the LORD will save him.
2The LORD will protect him and spare his life
and will bless him in the land.
He will not let his enemies take him.
3The LORD will give him strength when he is sick,
and he will make him well again.

4I said, "LORD, have mercy on me.
Heal me, because I have sinned against you."
5My enemies are saying evil things about me.
They say, "When will he die and be forgotten?"
6Some people come to see me,
but they lie.
They just come to get bad news.
Then they go and gossip.
7All my enemies whisper about me
and think the worst about me.
8They say, "He has a terrible disease.
He will never get out of bed again."
9My best and truest friend, who ate at my table,
has even turned against me.

10LORD, have mercy on me.
Give me strength so I can pay them back.
11Because my enemies do not defeat me,
I know you are pleased with me.
12Because I am innocent, you support me
and will let me be with you forever.

13Praise the LORD, the God of Israel.
He has always been,
and he will always be.
Amen and amen.

GOD'S POWER

Against All Odds

It was June 18, 1940, one of Britain's grimmest historical moments. Nazi Germany had already wiped out the French army—one of the largest in the world—in forty days. Joseph Stalin of Russia had signed a nonaggression pact with Hitler. The United States was still officially neutral in what became World War II. Hitler's air force, the Luftwaffe, was mercilessly pounding London and the English countryside.

Germany had more than eleven hundred fighter planes and fifteen hundred light bombers facing fewer than seven hundred British Spitfires and Hurricanes. Before the Battle of Britain was over, forty-five thousand in London alone were killed or injured.

Sir Winston Churchill—a great leader for Britain during those dark years—was never known as a particularly religious man. But during the darkest hours of the battle, something in him seemed to understand that only God could save his country from the Nazi pounding: "If the Almighty God in his mercy should lighten or shorten our labors and the torment of all mankind, all his servants will be thankful. Let God defend the right; heed the call of duty and honor, and see that our policy and conduct are upon the highest level, and that honor should be our guide."

Against all odds, the British prevailed.

King David also called on God to save him from his enemies. Nowhere is David's cry for help expressed more strongly than in **Psalm 40**.

- How do you think Churchill would have responded to verses 1 through 3 if he had read them while Germany was bombing London?
- If you were writing a modern version of Psalm 40, what tough situations from your own life and the world would you include?

CONSIDER . . .

- praying for God's deliverance in what you believe is the world's most pressing crisis.
- scanning news reports of current world crises and looking for references to dependence on God for help.

FOR MORE, SEE . . .

- Exodus 14:5–31 (p. 70)
- Daniel 6 (p. 813)
- 2 Peter 1:3–4 (p. 1311)

Book 2

Wishing to Be Near God

For the director of music. A maskil[d]
of the sons of Korah.

42 As a deer thirsts for streams of water,
so I thirst for you, God.
2I thirst for the living God.
When can I go to meet with him?
3Day and night, my tears have been my food.
People are always saying,
"Where is your God?"
4When I remember these things,
I speak with a broken heart.
I used to walk with the crowd
and lead them to God's Temple[d]
with songs of praise.

5Why am I so sad?
Why am I so upset?
I should put my hope in God
and keep praising him,
my Savior and 6my God.

I am very sad.
So I remember you where the Jordan River
begins,
near the peaks of Hermon and Mount Mizar.
7Troubles have come again and again,
sounding like waterfalls.
Your waves are crashing all around me.
8The LORD shows his true love every day.
At night I have a song,
and I pray to my living God.
9I say to God, my Rock,[d]
"Why have you forgotten me?
Why am I sad
and troubled by my enemies?"
10My enemies' insults make me feel
as if my bones were broken.
They are always saying,
"Where is your God?"

11Why am I so sad?
Why am I so upset?
I should put my hope in God
and keep praising him,
my Savior and my God.

A Prayer for Protection

43 God, defend me.
Argue my case against those who
don't follow you.
Save me from liars and those who do evil.
2God, you are my strength.
Why have you rejected me?
Why am I sad
and troubled by my enemies?
3Send me your light and truth
to guide me.
Let them lead me to your holy mountain,
to where you live.
4Then I will go to the altar of God,
to God who is my joy and happiness.
I will praise you with a harp,
God, my God.

5Why am I so sad?
Why am I so upset?
I should put my hope in God
and keep praising him,
my Savior and my God.

A Prayer for Help

For the director of music. A maskil[d]
of the sons of Korah.

44 God, we have heard about you.
Our ancestors told us
what you did in their days,
in days long ago.
2With your power you forced the nations out
of the land
and placed our ancestors here.
You destroyed those other nations,
but you made our ancestors grow strong.
3It wasn't their swords that took the land.
It wasn't their power that gave them
victory.
But it was your great power and strength.
You were with them because you loved
them.

4My God, you are my King.
Your commands led Jacob's people to
victory.
5With your help we pushed back our enemies.
In your name we trampled those who came
against us.
6I don't trust my bow to help me,
and my sword can't save me.
7You saved us from our foes,
and you made our enemies ashamed.
8We will praise God every day;
we will praise your name forever. *Selah*[d]

9But you have rejected us and shamed us.
You don't march with our armies anymore.
10You let our enemies push us back,
and those who hate us have taken our
wealth.
11You gave us away like sheep to be eaten
and have scattered us among the nations.
12You sold your people for nothing
and made no profit on the sale.

13You made us a joke to our neighbors;
those around us laugh and make fun of us.
14You made us a joke to the other nations;
people shake their heads.
15I am always in disgrace,

and I am covered with shame.
16My enemy is getting even
with insults and curses.

17All these things have happened to us,
but we have not forgotten you
or failed to keep our agreement with you.
18Our hearts haven't turned away from you,
and we haven't stopped following you.
19But you crushed us in this place where wild
dogs live,
and you covered us with deep darkness.

20If we had forgotten our God
or lifted our hands in prayer to foreign
gods,
21God would have known,
because he knows what is in our hearts.
22But for you we are in danger of death all the
time.
People think we are worth no more than
sheep to be killed.

23Wake up, Lord! Why are you sleeping?
Get up! Don't reject us forever.
24Why do you hide from us?
Have you forgotten our pain and troubles?

25We have been pushed down into the dirt;
we are flat on the ground.
26Get up and help us.
Because of your love, save us.

A Song for the King's Wedding

For the director of music. To the tune of "Lilies."
A maskil.[d] A love song of the sons of Korah.

45 Beautiful words fill my mind.
I am speaking of royal things.
My tongue is like the pen of a skilled
writer.

2You are more handsome than anyone,
and you are an excellent speaker,
so God has blessed you forever.
3Put on your sword, powerful warrior.
Show your glory and majesty.
4In your majesty win the victory
for what is true and right.
Your power will do amazing things.
5Your sharp arrows will enter
the hearts of the king's enemies.
Nations will be defeated before you.
6God, your throne will last forever and ever.
You will rule your kingdom with fairness.
7You love right and hate evil,
so God has chosen you from among your
friends;
he has set you apart with much joy.
8Your clothes smell like myrrh,[d] aloes,[d] and
cassia.[d]
From palaces of ivory
music comes to make you happy.
9Kings' daughters are among your honored
women.
Your bride stands at your right side
wearing gold from Ophir.

SIDELIGHT: King Solomon could have made a giant wedding ring for the bride in Psalm 45:9. He received thirty-two thousand pounds of gold from the Arabian regions of Ophir! (See 1 Kings 9:28, p. 314.)

10Listen to me, daughter; look and pay
attention.
Forget your people and your father's family.
11The king loves your beauty.
Because he is your master, you should obey
him.
12People from the city of Tyre have brought a
gift.
Wealthy people will want to meet you.

13The princess is very beautiful.
Her gown is woven with gold.
14In her beautiful clothes she is brought to the
king.
Her bridesmaids follow behind her,
and they are also brought to him.
15They come with happiness and joy;
they enter the king's palace.

16You will have sons to replace your fathers.
You will make them rulers through all the
land.
17I will make your name famous from now on,
so people will praise you forever and ever.

God Protects His People

For the director of music. By alamoth.[d] A psalm of
the sons of Korah.

46 God is our protection and our
strength.
He always helps in times of trouble.
2So we will not be afraid even if the earth
shakes,
or the mountains fall into the sea,
3even if the oceans roar and foam,
or the mountains shake at the raging sea.
Selah[d]

4There is a river that brings joy to the city of
God,
the holy place where God Most High lives.
5God is in that city, and so it will not be
shaken.
God will help her at dawn.

6Nations tremble and kingdoms shake.
God shouts and the earth crumbles.

7The LORD All-Powerful is with us;
the God of Jacob is our defender. *Selah*

8Come and see what the LORD has done,
the amazing things he has done on the earth.
9He stops wars everywhere on the earth.
He breaks all bows and spears
and burns up the chariots with fire.
10God says, "Be quiet and know that I am God.
I will be supreme over all the nations;
I will be supreme in the earth."

11The LORD All-Powerful is with us;
the God of Jacob is our defender. *Selah*

God, the King of the World

For the director of music. A psalm of the sons of Korah.

47 Clap your hands, all you people.
Shout to God with joy.
2The LORD Most High is wonderful.
He is the great King over all the earth!
3He defeated nations for us
and put them under our control.
4He chose the land we would inherit.
We are the children of Jacob, whom he loved. *Selah*[d]

5God has risen with a shout of joy;
the LORD has risen as the trumpets sounded.
6Sing praises to God. Sing praises.
Sing praises to our King. Sing praises.
7God is King of all the earth,
so sing a song of praise to him.
8God is King over the nations.
God sits on his holy throne.
9The leaders of the nations meet
with the people of the God of Abraham,
because the leaders of the earth belong to God.
He is supreme.

Jerusalem, the City of God

A psalm of the sons of Korah.

48 The LORD is great; he should be praised
in the city of our God, on his holy mountain.
2It is high and beautiful
and brings joy to the whole world.
Mount Zion[d] is like the high mountains of the north;
it is the city of the Great King.
3God is within its palaces;
he is known as its defender.
4Kings joined together
and came to attack the city.
5But when they saw it, they were amazed.
They ran away in fear.
6Fear took hold of them;
they hurt like a woman having a baby.
7You destroyed the large trading ships
with an east wind.
8First we heard
and now we have seen
that God will always keep his city safe.
It is the city of the LORD All-Powerful,
the city of our God. *Selah*[d]

9God, we come into your Temple[d]
to think about your love.
10God, your name is known everywhere;
all over the earth people praise you.
Your right hand is full of goodness.
11Mount Zion is happy
and all the towns of Judah rejoice,
because your decisions are fair.

12Walk around Jerusalem
and count its towers.
13Notice how strong they are.
Look at the palaces.
Then you can tell your children about them.
14This God is our God forever and ever.
He will guide us from now on.

Trusting Money Is Foolish

For the director of music. A psalm of the sons of Korah.

49 Listen to this, all you nations;
listen, all you who live on earth.
2Listen, both great and small,
rich and poor together.
3What I say is wise,
and my heart speaks with understanding.
4I will pay attention to a wise saying;
I will explain my riddle on the harp.

5Why should I be afraid of bad days?
Why should I fear when evil men surround me?
6They trust in their money
and brag about their riches.
7No one can buy back the life of another.
No one can pay God for his own life,
8because the price of a life is high.
No payment is ever enough.
9Do people live forever?
Don't they all face death?

10See, even wise people die.
Fools and stupid people also die

and leave their wealth to others.
11Their graves will always be their homes.
They will live there from now on,
even though they named places after
themselves.
12Even rich people do not live forever;
like the animals, people die.

13This is what will happen to those who trust
in themselves
and to their followers who believe them.
Selah[d]

14Like sheep, they must die,
and death will be their shepherd.
Honest people will rule over them in the
morning,
and their bodies will rot in a grave far from
home.
15But God will save my life
and will take me from the grave. *Selah*

16Don't be afraid of rich people
because their houses are more beautiful.
17They don't take anything to the grave;
their wealth won't go down with
them.

WORSHIP

Clapping, Shouting, Singing

"Okay, then, it's a date," Mike Frazier said over the phone. "I'll meet you guys at the church at 6:00."

Five guys from Mike's youth group had wanted to go to a Christian rock concert in the Chicago area. All five were enthusiastic Christians and diehard rock 'n' roll fanatics. As their youth minister, Mike encouraged their interest and offered to take them.

The night was going to be super. Great friends. A Christian band that played great music. Nothing could spoil the plans for the evening. Except . . .

One of the guys, Tony Murelli, showed up with his dad, Bart, who didn't attend church. That made Mike nervous.

"What are you up to tonight?" Mike asked Bart.

"I decided to come to the concert," he responded.

Gulp. Tony's dad looked like he would be more comfortable watching a Lawrence Welk rerun. Mike wondered how Bart's attitude toward his son being a part of a church group would be affected by a high-decibel concert.

Mike didn't enjoy the concert nearly as much as he thought he would. He was too busy trying to watch everyone's reactions.

The guys? They loved it. They never sat down. They praised God all evening—stomping their feet, clapping their hands, and singing.

Tony's dad? Hard to tell. That is, until after the concert when, with his ears still ringing, Mike heard these amazing words:

"Frankly, Mike, I've wondered what Tony has been getting into, with all the time he spends at your church. I wanted to see one of your activities for myself."

Uh, oh.

"And I want you to know I've never been as impressed with a group of young people as I was tonight. That band, the kids, the way they expressed themselves—you can tell they really believe in something good."

What Bart observed was a group of Christians following the advice of the psalmist in **Psalm 47**. Read about how you too should lift praise to God.

- If Tony's dad were to read Psalm 47, what insight might he gain about his son's attitude toward God?
- What can you start doing in your time alone with God to follow the psalmist's call to "clap your hands," "shout to God with joy," and "sing praises"?

CONSIDER . . .

- asking other Christians whom you respect how they build worship into their lives.
- finding Christian tapes you can use in your devotion times to help you joyfully worship God.

FOR MORE, SEE . . .

- 1 Chronicles 16:7–36 (p. 374)
- Isaiah 6:1–4 (p. 622)
- Revelation 7:9–17 (p. 1337)

18Even though they were praised when they
were alive—
and people may praise you when you
succeed—
19they will go to where their ancestors are.
They will never see light again.
20Rich people with no understanding
are just like animals that die.

God Wants True Worship

A psalm of Asaph.

50 The God of gods, the LORD, speaks.
He calls the earth from the rising to
the setting sun.
2God shines from Jerusalem,
whose beauty is perfect.
3Our God comes, and he will not be silent.
A fire burns in front of him,
and a powerful storm surrounds him.
4He calls to the sky above and to the earth
that he might judge his people.
5He says, "Gather around, you who worship
me,
who have made an agreement with me,
using a sacrifice."
6God is the judge,
and even the skies say he is right. *Selah*[d]

7God says, "My people, listen to me;
Israel, I will testify against you.
I am God, your God.
8I do not scold you for your sacrifices.
You always bring me your burnt offerings.
9But I do not need bulls from your stalls
or goats from your pens,
10because every animal of the forest is already
mine.
The cattle on a thousand hills are mine.
11I know every bird on the mountains,
and every living thing in the fields is mine.
12If I were hungry, I would not tell you,
because the earth and everything in it are
mine.
13I don't eat the meat of bulls
or drink the blood of goats.
14Give an offering to show thanks to God.
Give God Most High what you have
promised.
15Call to me in times of trouble.
I will save you, and you will honor me."

16But God says to the wicked,
"Why do you talk about my laws?
Why do you mention my agreement?
17You hate my teachings
and turn your back on what I say.
18When you see a thief, you join him.
You take part in adultery.[d]
19You don't stop your mouth from speaking
evil,
and your tongue makes up lies.
20You speak against your brother
and lie about your mother's son.
21I have kept quiet while you did these things,
so you thought I was just like you.
But I will scold you
and accuse you to your face.

22"Think about this, you who forget God.
Otherwise, I will tear you apart,
and no one will save you.
23Those people honor me
who bring me offerings to show thanks.
And I, God, will save those who do that."

A Prayer for Forgiveness

For the director of music. A psalm of David when the prophet[d] Nathan came to David after David's sin with Bathsheba.

51 God, be merciful to me
because you are loving.
Because you are always ready to be merciful,
wipe out all my wrongs.
2Wash away all my guilt
and make me clean again.
3I know about my wrongs,
and I can't forget my sin.
4You are the only one I have sinned against;
I have done what you say is wrong.
You are right when you speak
and fair when you judge.
5I was brought into this world in sin.
In sin my mother gave birth to me.
6You want me to be completely truthful,
so teach me wisdom.
7Take away my sin, and I will be clean.
Wash me, and I will be whiter than snow.
8Make me hear sounds of joy and gladness;
let the bones you crushed be happy again.
9Turn your face from my sins
and wipe out all my guilt.

10Create in me a pure heart, God,
and make my spirit right again.
11Do not send me away from you
or take your Holy Spirit[d] away from me.
12Give me back the joy of your salvation.
Keep me strong by giving me a willing
spirit.
13Then I will teach your ways to those who do
wrong,
and sinners will turn back to you.

14God, save me from the guilt of murder,
God of my salvation,
and I will sing about your goodness.

15Lord, let me speak
so I may praise you.
16You are not pleased by sacrifices, or I would
give them.
You don't want burnt offerings.
17The sacrifice God wants is a broken spirit.
God, you will not reject a heart that is
broken and sorry for sin.

18Do whatever good you wish for Jerusalem.
Rebuild the walls of Jerusalem.
19Then you will be pleased with right sacrifices
and whole burnt offerings,
and bulls will be offered on your altar.

God Will Punish the Proud

For the director of music. A maskil[d] of David. When Doeg the Edomite came to Saul and said to him, "David is in Ahimelech's house."

52 Mighty warrior, why do you brag
about the evil you do?
God's love will continue forever.
2You think up evil plans.
Your tongue is like a sharp razor,
making up lies.
3You love wrong more than right
and lies more than truth. *Selah*[d]

SEXUALITY

Whiter Than Snow

Kimberly Johnson didn't understand what was happening to her.

She stood in church while the minister led the congregation in a benediction. But Kimberly felt weird. Her heart was racing, her eyes were welling up with tears. All she could think of was kneeling right there on the floor and asking God to help her.

One of the youth workers, Jan, noticed that Kimberly looked upset and approached her after the service.

"What's the matter, Kim?" Jan asked. But Kimberly started to cry and couldn't answer. Jan took her by the arm and led her to a corner, where they sat down together.

After a few minutes, Kimberly could finally talk.

"God could never love me," Kimberly said. "I've done too much to hurt him. I'm not worth it."

"Why do you think God doesn't love you?" Jan asked.

With more tears, Kimberly told Jan how she had been physically and sexually abused by an uncle when she was nine. At age thirteen she was sexually active with numerous guys and often dated guys four and five years older than she was.

"It's almost as if the last five years have been a bad dream and tonight somebody woke me up," she said.

"God does love you, Kimberly," Jan said confidently. "I'd like to pray with you for God to show you the special love he has for you."

As Kimberly and Jan prayed, something happened to Kimberly that radically changed her life. She understood the simple message about God's forgiveness, and believed it. Without reservation, she embraced God's healing and cleansing power.

"I came to church feeling like a tramp," she told Jan after they prayed. "But now I feel like God has made me clean again."

Kimberly grasped what David also understood when he prayed: "Take away my sin, and I will be clean. Wash me, and I will be whiter than snow." Read the rest of David's prayer for forgiveness in **Psalm 51**.

- According to this psalm, what else does Kimberly need for God to do in her life? (See especially verses 10, 12.)
- What verse from Psalm 51 best expresses your desire for God to forgive you for your sin—sexual or otherwise?

CONSIDER . . .

- praying that God will give you the strength to stay away from sexual sin.
- writing a verse from Psalm 51 on paper and keeping it with you as a reminder that God has forgiven you and can keep you from sin in the days ahead.

FOR MORE, SEE . . .

- 2 Samuel 11—12:14 (p. 283)
- John 8:1–11 (p. 1070)
- 1 Corinthians 6:12–20 (p. 1174)

[4]You love words that bite
and tongues that lie.

[5]But God will ruin you forever.
He will grab you and throw you out of your tent;
he will tear you away from the land of the living. *Selah*

[6]Those who do right will see this and fear God.
They will laugh at you and say,
[7]"Look what happened to the man
who did not depend on God
but depended on his money.
He grew strong by his evil plans."

[8]But I am like an olive tree
growing in God's Temple.[d]
I trust God's love
forever and ever.
[9]God, I will thank you forever for what you have done.
With those who worship you, I will trust you because you are good.

The Unbelieving Fool

For the director of music. By mahalath.[d] A maskil[d] of David.

53 Fools say to themselves,
"There is no God."
Fools are evil and do terrible things;
none of them does anything good.

[2]God looked down from heaven on all people
to see if anyone was wise,
if anyone was looking to God for help.
[3]But all have turned away.
Together, everyone has become evil;
none of them does anything good.
Not a single person.

[4]Don't the wicked understand?
They destroy my people as if they were eating bread.
They do not ask God for help.
[5]The wicked are filled with terror
where there had been nothing to fear.
God will scatter the bones of your enemies.
You will defeat them,
because God has rejected them.

[6]I pray that victory will come to Israel from Mount Zion![d]
May God bring them back.
Then the people of Jacob will rejoice,
and the people of Israel will be glad.

A Prayer for Help

For the director of music. With stringed instruments. A maskil[d] of David when the Ziphites went to Saul and said, "We think David is hiding among our people."

54 God, save me because of who you are.
By your strength show that I am innocent.

> **SIDELIGHT:** Feeling down? Then praise God! That's the attitude of even the saddest psalms, which are called "laments." These laments (such as Psalms 54–61) show individuals and the nation of Israel praying in times of crisis. Of all the types of psalms, the lament is most common.

[2]Hear my prayer, God;
listen to what I say.
[3]Strangers turn against me,
and cruel men want to kill me.
They do not care about God. *Selah*[d]

[4]See, God will help me;
the Lord will support me.
[5]Let my enemies be punished with their own evil.
Destroy them because you are loyal to me.

[6]I will offer a sacrifice as a special gift to you.
I will thank you, LORD, because you are good.
[7]You have saved me from all my troubles,
and I have seen my enemies defeated.

A Prayer About a False Friend

For the director of music. With stringed instruments. A maskil[d] of David.

55 God, listen to my prayer
and do not ignore my cry for help.
[2]Pay attention to me and answer me.
I am troubled and upset
[3]by what the enemy says
and how the wicked look at me.
They bring troubles down on me,
and in anger they attack me.

[4]I am frightened inside;
the terror of death has attacked me.
[5]I am scared and shaking,
and terror grips me.
[6]I said, "I wish I had wings like a dove.
Then I would fly away and rest.
[7]I would wander far away
and stay in the desert. *Selah*[d]
[8]I would hurry to my place of escape,
far away from the wind and storm."

[9]Lord, destroy and confuse their words,
because I see violence and fighting in the city.
[10]Day and night they are all around its walls,
and evil and trouble are everywhere inside.
[11]Destruction is everywhere in the city;
trouble and lying never leave its streets.

[12]It was not an enemy insulting me.
I could stand that.
It was not someone who hated me.
I could hide from him.
[13]But it is you, a person like me,
my companion and good friend.
[14]We had a good friendship
and walked together to God's Temple.[d]

[15]Let death take away my enemies.
Let them die while they are still young
because evil lives with them.
[16]But I will call to God for help,
and the LORD will save me.
[17]Morning, noon, and night I am troubled and upset,
but he will listen to me.
[18]Many are against me,
but he keeps me safe in battle.
[19]God who lives forever
will hear me and punish them. *Selah*
But they will not change;
they do not fear God.

[20]The one who was my friend attacks his friends
and breaks his promises.
[21]His words are slippery like butter,
but war is in his heart.
His words are smoother than oil,
but they cut like knives.

[22]Give your worries to the LORD,
and he will take care of you.
He will never let good people down.
[23]But, God, you will bring down
the wicked to the grave.
Murderers and liars will live
only half a lifetime.
But I will trust in you.

Trusting God for Help

For the director of music. To the tune of "The Dove in the Distant Oak." A miktam[d] of David when the Philistines captured him in Gath.

56 God, be merciful to me because
people are chasing me;
the battle has pressed me all day long.

FRIENDS

Betrayed

Gail Miller and Breck Peterson had been going out for well over a year. Deep down, Breck hoped that someday, probably after college, they would get married. But, just days before the beginning of their senior year in high school, Gail broke up with him.

Breck struggled to cope with the loss. His mind whirled as he tried to think of what to say and how to get Gail to change her mind.

Breck's best friend, Rick Leo, knew Breck was having a hard time, but Rick asked Gail out himself. Gail and Rick dated off and on for several months. They never really hit it off, and things ended quietly.

Breck's friendship with Rick, on the other hand, was ripped apart like a ship in a raging storm. Breck had never felt so betrayed. He found it hard to talk to Rick because every conversation reminded him of Gail—and Rick's betrayal.

Like Breck, many people know how it hurts to be betrayed by a friend. Read **Psalm 55** to discover David's anguish over a friend who betrayed him.

- Why was betrayal by a friend so hard for Breck and David to take?
- How can David's advice in verse 22 help you when you feel betrayed by a friend?

CONSIDER . . .

- asking God for forgiveness if you've betrayed a friend, or asking God to help you forgive a friend who's betrayed you.
- trying to reconcile a relationship that has been ruined by betrayal, by having a heart-to-heart talk.

FOR MORE, SEE . . .

- I Samuel 20 (p. 263)
- Proverbs 17:9 (p. 582)
- John 15:12–17 (p. 1085)

2My enemies have chased me all day;
there are many proud people fighting me.
3When I am afraid,
I will trust you.
4I praise God for his word.
I trust God, so I am not afraid.
What can human beings do to me?
5All day long they twist my words;
all their evil plans are against me.
6They wait. They hide.
They watch my steps,
hoping to kill me.
7God, do not let them escape;
punish the foreign nations in your anger.
8You have recorded my troubles.
You have kept a list of my tears.
Aren't they in your records?
9On the day I call for help, my enemies will
be defeated.
I know that God is on my side.
10I praise God for his word to me;
I praise the LORD for his word.
11I trust in God. I will not be afraid.
What can people do to me?

12God, I must keep my promises to you.
I will give you my offerings to thank you,
13because you have saved me from death.
You have kept me from being defeated.
So I will walk with God
in light among the living.

A Prayer in Troubled Times

For the director of music. To the tune of "Do Not Destroy." A miktam[d] of David when he escaped from Saul in the cave.

57 Be merciful to me, God; be merciful
to me
because I come to you for protection.
Let me hide under the shadow of your wings
until the trouble has passed.

2I cry out to God Most High,
to the God who does everything for me.
3He sends help from heaven and saves me.
He punishes those who chase me. *Selah*[d]
God sends me his love and truth.

4Enemies, like lions, are all around me;
I must lie down among them.
Their teeth are like spears and arrows,
their tongues as sharp as swords.

5God is supreme over the skies;
his majesty covers the earth.

6They set a trap for me.
I am very worried.
They dug a pit in my path,
but they fell into it themselves. *Selah*

7My heart is steady, God; my heart is steady.
I will sing and praise you.
8Wake up, my soul.
Wake up, harp and lyre![d]
I will wake up the dawn.
9Lord, I will praise you among the nations;
I will sing songs of praise about you to all
the nations.
10Your great love reaches to the skies,
your truth to the clouds.
11God, you are supreme above the skies.
Let your glory be over all the earth.

Unfair Judges

For the director of music. To the tune of "Do Not Destroy." A miktam[d] of David.

58 Do you rulers really say what is right?
Do you judge people fairly?
2No, in your heart you plan evil;
you think up violent crimes in the land.
3From birth, evil people turn away from God;
they wander off and tell lies as soon as they
are born.
4They are like poisonous snakes,
like deaf cobras that stop up their ears
5so they cannot hear the music of the snake
charmer
no matter how well he plays.

6God, break the teeth in their mouths!
Tear out the fangs of those lions, LORD!
7Let them disappear like water that flows
away.
Let them be cut short like a broken arrow.
8Let them be like snails that melt as they
move.
Let them be like a child born dead who
never saw the sun.
9His anger will blow them away alive
faster than burning thorns can heat a pot.
10Good people will be glad when they see him
get even.
They will wash their feet in the blood of
the wicked.
11Then people will say,
"There really are rewards for doing what is
right.
There really is a God who judges the
world."

A Prayer for Protection

For the director of music. To the tune of "Do Not Destroy." A miktam[d] of David when Saul sent men to watch David's house to kill him.

59 God, save me from my enemies.
Protect me from those who come
against me.

[2]Save me from those who do evil
and from murderers.

[3]Look, men are waiting to ambush
me.
Cruel men attack me,
but I have not sinned or done wrong,
LORD.
[4]I have done nothing wrong, but they are
ready to attack me.
Wake up to help me, and look.
[5]You are the LORD God All-Powerful, the God
of Israel.
Arise and punish those people.
Do not give those traitors any mercy. *Selah*[d]

[6]They come back at night.
Like dogs they growl and roam around the
city.
[7]Notice what comes from their mouths.
Insults come from their lips,
because they say, "Who's listening?"
[8]But, LORD, you laugh at them;
you make fun of all of them.

[9]God, my strength, I am looking to you,
because God is my defender.
[10]My God loves me, and he goes in front of
me.
He will help me defeat my enemies.
[11]Lord, our protector, do not kill them, or my
people will forget.
With your power scatter them and defeat
them.
[12]They sin by what they say;
they sin with their words.
They curse and tell lies,
so let their pride trap them.
[13]Destroy them in your anger;
destroy them completely!
Then they will know
that God rules over Israel
and to the ends of the earth. *Selah*

[14]They come back at night.
Like dogs they growl
and roam around the city.
[15]They wander about looking for food,
and they howl if they do not find
enough.
[16]But I will sing about your strength.
In the morning I will sing about your
love.
You are my defender,
my place of safety in times of trouble.
[17]God, my strength, I will sing praises to
you.
God, my defender, you are the God who
loves me.

A Prayer After a Defeat

For the director of music. To the tune of "Lily of the Agreement." A miktam[d] of David. For teaching. When David fought the Arameans of Northwest Mesopotamia and Zobah, and when Joab returned and defeated twelve thousand Edomites at the Valley of Salt.

60 God, you have rejected us and
scattered us.
You have been angry, but please come back
to us.
[2]You made the earth shake and crack.
Heal its breaks because it is shaking.
[3]You have given your people trouble.
You made us unable to walk straight, like
people drunk with wine.
[4]You have raised a banner to gather those
who fear you.
Now they can stand up against the enemy.
Selah[d]

[5]Answer us and save us by your power
so the people you love will be rescued.

[6]God has said from his Temple,[d]
"When I win, I will divide Shechem
and measure off the Valley of Succoth.
[7]Gilead and Manasseh are mine.
Ephraim is like my helmet.
Judah holds my royal scepter.[d]
[8]Moab is like my washbowl.
I throw my sandals at Edom.
I shout at Philistia."

[9]Who will bring me to the strong, walled city?
Who will lead me to Edom?
[10]God, surely you have rejected us;
you do not go out with our armies.
[11]Help us fight the enemy.
Human help is useless,
[12]but we can win with God's help.
He will defeat our enemies.

A Prayer for Protection

For the director of music. With stringed instruments. Of David.

61 God, hear my cry;
listen to my prayer.
[2]I call to you from the ends of the earth
when I am afraid.
Carry me away to a high mountain.
[3]You have been my protection,
like a strong tower against my enemies.
[4]Let me live in your Holy Tent[d] forever.
Let me find safety in the shelter of your
wings. *Selah*[d]
[5]God, you have heard my promises.
You have given me what belongs to those
who fear you.
[6]Give the king a long life;

let him live many years.
7Let him rule in the presence of God forever.
Protect him with your love and truth.
8Then I will praise your name forever,
and every day I will keep my promises.

Trust Only in God

For the director of music. For Jeduthun.
A psalm of David.

62 I find rest in God;
only he can save me.
2He is my rock and my salvation.
He is my defender;
I will not be defeated.

3How long will you attack someone?
Will all of you kill that person?
Who is like a leaning wall, like a fence
ready to fall?
4They are planning to make that person fall.
They enjoy telling lies.
With their mouths they bless,
but in their hearts they curse. *Selah*[d]

5I find rest in God;
only he gives me hope.
6He is my rock and my salvation.
He is my defender;
I will not be defeated.
7My honor and salvation come from God.
He is my mighty rock and my protection.

8People, trust God all the time.
Tell him all your problems,
because God is our protection. *Selah*

9The least of people are only a breath,
and even the greatest are just a lie.
On the scales, they weigh nothing;
together they are only a breath.
10Do not trust in force.
Stealing is of no use.
Even if you gain more riches,
don't put your trust in them.

11God has said this,
and I have heard it over and over:
God is strong.

WORRYING

Geronimo-o-o-o!

Seven friends made plans to drive to the small municipal airport in southern Indiana. But only Larry Cramer and Pete Sanchez ended up going. As they drove to the terminal, Larry joked about the "chickens" who didn't show up. The two of them were calm, cool, and confident about their first experience with sky diving.

For two and a half hours that morning they learned about taking that first jump from an airplane. As Pete and Larry listened to the instructor, it got tougher and tougher to stay calm, cool, and confident. They heard about every potential jump catastrophe imaginable. By the time they finished their tumbling drills and headed for the little Cessna 150, Pete was worried. Real worried.

"The flight master warned us not to look down," he says. "I did anyway. Farm houses look tiny at three thousand feet. Yes, I was worried. I had planned to shout 'Geronimo-o-o-o' when I jumped, but I could barely talk. The worst moment was leaning forward from the plane to position my foot on the wing brace.

"But when the flight master yelled to jump, I jumped. And seconds later, all my worry was replaced by an unbelievable calm as my chute opened and I slowly floated three thousand feet to the ground."

David had a fail-proof "parachute" to rescue him from the worries he faced. He describes his "parachute" in **Psalm 62**.

- How is David's trust in God like a sky diver's trust in a parachute?
- How would your life change if you replaced the first word of verse 8 with your name and really believed what the psalmist has to say?

CONSIDER . . .

- memorizing a verse from Psalm 62 that will help you cope with worry.
- listing the things in your life that act as "parachutes" to relieve your worries and praying for God to become your ultimate parachute in life.

FOR MORE, SEE . . .

- Proverbs 3:5–6 (p. 570)
- Matthew 6:25–34 (p. 918)
- Philippians 4:6–8 (p. 1234)

12The Lord is loving.
You reward people for what they have done.

Wishing to Be Near God

A psalm of David when he was in the desert of Judah.

63 God, you are my God.
I search for you.
I thirst for you
like someone in a dry, empty land
where there is no water.
2I have seen you in the Temple[d]
and have seen your strength and glory.
3Because your love is better than life,
I will praise you.
4I will praise you as long as I live.
I will lift up my hands in prayer to your name.
5I will be content as if I had eaten the best foods.
My lips will sing, and my mouth will praise you.

6I remember you while I'm lying in bed;
I think about you through the night.
7You are my help.
Because of your protection, I sing.
8I stay close to you;
you support me with your right hand.

9Some people are trying to kill me,
but they will go down to the grave.
10They will be killed with swords
and eaten by wild dogs.
11But the king will rejoice in his God.
All who make promises in his name will praise him,
but the mouths of liars will be shut.

A Prayer Against Enemies

For the director of music. A psalm of David.

64 God, listen to my complaint.
I am afraid of my enemies;
protect my life from them.
2Hide me from those who plan wicked things,
from that gang who does evil.
3They sharpen their tongues like swords
and shoot bitter words like arrows.
4From their hiding places they shoot at innocent people;
they shoot suddenly and are not afraid.
5They encourage each other to do wrong.
They talk about setting traps,
thinking no one will see them.
6They plan wicked things and say,
"We have a perfect plan."
The mind of human beings is hard to understand.

7But God will shoot them with arrows;
they will suddenly be struck down.
8Their own words will be used against them.
All who see them will shake their heads.
9Then everyone will fear God.
They will tell what God has done,
and they will learn from what he has done.
10Good people will be happy in the LORD
and will find protection in him.
Let everyone who is honest praise the LORD.

A Hymn of Thanksgiving

For the director of music. A psalm of David. A song.

65 God, you will be praised in Jerusalem.
We will keep our promises to you.
2You hear our prayers.
All people will come to you.
3Our guilt overwhelms us,
but you forgive our sins.
4Happy are the people you choose
and invite to stay in your court.
We are filled with good things in your house,
your holy Temple.[d]

5You answer us in amazing ways,
God our Savior.
People everywhere on the earth
and beyond the sea trust you.
6You made the mountains by your strength;
you are dressed in power.
7You stopped the roaring seas,
the roaring waves,
and the uproar of the nations.
8Even those people at the ends of the earth
fear your miracles.[d]
You are praised from where the sun rises to where it sets.

9You take care of the land and water it;
you make it very fertile.
The rivers of God are full of water.
Grain grows because you make it grow.
10You send rain to the plowed fields;
you fill the rows with water.
You soften the ground with rain,
and then you bless it with crops.
11You give the year a good harvest,
and you load the wagons with many crops.
12The desert is covered with grass
and the hills with happiness.

[13]The pastures are full of flocks,
and the valleys are covered with grain.
Everything shouts and sings for joy.

Praise God for What He Has Done

For the director of music. A song. A psalm.

66 Everything on earth, shout with joy to God!
[2]Sing about his glory!
Make his praise glorious!
[3]Say to God, "Your works are amazing!
Because your power is great,
your enemies fall before you.
[4]All the earth worships you
and sings praises to you.
They sing praises to your name." *Selah*[d]

[5]Come and see what God has done,
the amazing things he has done for people.
[6]He turned the sea into dry land.
The people crossed the river on foot.
So let us rejoice because of what he did.
[7]He rules forever with his power.
He keeps his eye on the nations,
so people should not turn against him. *Selah*

[8]You people, praise our God;
loudly sing his praise.
[9]He protects our lives
and does not let us be defeated.
[10]God, you have tested us;
you have purified us like silver.
[11]You let us be trapped
and put a heavy load on us.
[12]You let our enemies walk on our heads.
We went through fire and flood,
but you brought us to a place with good things.
[13]I will come to your Temple[d] with burnt offerings.
I will give you what I promised,
[14] things I promised when I was in trouble.
[15]I will bring you offerings of fat animals,
and I will offer sheep, bulls, and goats. *Selah*

[16]All of you who fear God, come and listen,
and I will tell you what he has done for me.
[17]I cried out to him with my mouth
and praised him with my tongue.
[18]If I had known of any sin in my heart,
the Lord would not have listened to me.
[19]But God has listened;
he has heard my prayer.
[20]Praise God,
who did not ignore my prayer
or hold back his love from me.

Everyone Should Praise God

For the director of music. With stringed instruments.
A psalm. A song.

67 God, have mercy on us and bless us
and show us your kindness *Selah*[d]
[2]so the world will learn your ways,
and all nations will learn that you can save.

[3]God, the people should praise you;
all people should praise you.
[4]The nations should be glad and sing
because you judge people fairly.
You guide all the nations on earth. *Selah*
[5]God, the people should praise you;
all people should praise you.

[6]The land has given its crops.
God, our God, blesses us.
[7]God blesses us
so people all over the earth will fear him.

Praise God Who Saved the Nation

For the director of music. A psalm of David. A song.

68 Let God rise up and scatter his enemies;
let those who hate him run away from him.
[2]Blow them away as smoke
is driven away by the wind.
As wax melts before a fire,
let the wicked be destroyed before God.
[3]But those who do right should be glad
and should rejoice before God;
they should be happy and glad.

[4]Sing to God; sing praises to his name.
Prepare the way for him
who rides through the desert,
whose name is the LORD.
Rejoice before him.
[5]God is in his holy Temple.[d]
He is a father to orphans,
and he defends the widows.

SIDELIGHT: Israelite con artists should have known better than to bother orphans and widows, two groups of people who had a special place in God's heart (Psalm 68:5). Look up the nasty penalty for cheating the defenseless in Exodus 22:22–24, p. 81.

[6]God gives the lonely a home.
He leads prisoners out with joy,
but those who turn against God will live in a dry land.

7God, you led your people out
when you marched through the desert. *Selah*[d]

8The ground shook
and the sky poured down rain
before God, the God of Mount Sinai,
before God, the God of Israel.
9God, you sent much rain;
you refreshed your tired land.
10Your people settled there.
God, in your goodness
you took care of the poor.

11The Lord gave the command,
and a great army told the news:
12"Kings and their armies run away.
In camp they divide the wealth taken in war.
13Those who stayed by the campfires
will share the riches taken in battle."
14The Almighty scattered kings
like snow on Mount Zalmon.

15The mountains of Bashan are high;
the mountains of Bashan have many peaks.
16Why do you mountains with many peaks
look with envy
on the mountain that God chose for his home?
The LORD will live there forever.
17God comes with millions of chariots;
the Lord comes from Mount Sinai to his holy place.
18When you went up to the heights,
you led a parade of captives.
You received gifts from the people,
even from those who turned against you.
And the LORD God will live there.

19Praise the Lord, God our Savior,
who helps us every day. *Selah*
20Our God is a God who saves us;
the LORD God saves us from death.

21God will crush his enemies' heads,
the hairy skulls of those who continue to sin.
22The Lord said, "I will bring the enemy back from Bashan;
I will bring them back from the depths of the sea.
23Then you can stick your feet in their blood,
and your dogs can lick their share."

24God, people have seen your victory march;
God my King marched into the holy place.

LONELINESS

On the Road Again

"Sometimes I think we're Gypsies," Rebekah confesses, describing the way her family has moved seven times in four years. "When your father's in the air force, you get used to it."

She laughs, but it sounds forced, and she looks away. There's a sadness in her voice, and she seems a little scared.

"You know, it's not that easy leaving friends and making new ones. When you're new, it helps a lot if people come up and introduce themselves," she says softly. "Or ask you to go to a club or church group meeting with them, or just to get a Coke. Loneliness must be one of the worst feelings in the world."

Everyone feels lonely sometimes. But, like Rebekah, we all have a home with God no matter how alone we may feel. Read **Psalm 68:1–10** to find God's assurance that he gives the lonely a place to belong.

- How do you think Rebekah would define the word "home" in this psalm?
- When you're feeling lonely, what sort of "home" do you think faith in God's love can help you build?

CONSIDER . . .

- organizing a "Welcome Wagon" of kids to greet newcomers to your school or church.
- widening your circle of friends by making a list of talents God has given you, including personality traits, such as a sense of humor or the ability to listen, and using the list to guide you to new clubs and activities.

FOR MORE, SEE . . .

- Job 19:13–27 (p. 463)
- Matthew 28:18–20 (p. 962)
- 2 Timothy 4:16–18 (p. 1268)

25The singers are in front and the instruments
are behind.
In the middle are the girls with the
tambourines.[d]
26Praise God in the meeting place;
praise the LORD in the gathering of Israel.
27There is the smallest tribe,[d] Benjamin, leading
them.
And there are the leaders of Judah with
their group.
There also are the leaders of Zebulun and
of Naphtali.

28God, order up your power;
show the mighty power you have used for
us before.
29Kings will bring their wealth to you,
to your Temple in Jerusalem.
30Punish Egypt, the beast in the tall grass along
the river.
Punish the leaders of nations, those bulls
among the cows.
Defeated, they will bring you their silver.
Scatter those nations that love war.
31Messengers will come from Egypt;
the people of Cush will pray to God.

32Kingdoms of the earth, sing to God;
sing praises to the Lord. *Selah*
33Sing to the one who rides through the skies,
which are from long ago.
He speaks with a thundering voice.
34Announce that God is powerful.
He rules over Israel,
and his power is in the skies.
35God, you are wonderful in your Temple.
The God of Israel gives his people strength
and power.

Praise God!

A Cry for Help

For the director of music. To the tune of "Lilies."
A psalm of David.

69 God, save me,
because the water has risen to my
neck.
2I'm sinking down into the mud,
and there is nothing to stand on.
I am in deep water,
and the flood covers me.
3I am tired from calling for help;
my throat is sore.
My eyes are tired from waiting
for God to help me.
4There are more people who hate me for no
reason than hairs on my head;
powerful enemies want to destroy me for
no reason.
They make me pay back
what I did not steal.
5God, you know what I have done wrong;
I cannot hide my guilt from you.
6Lord GOD All-Powerful,
do not let those who hope in you be
ashamed because of me.
God of Israel,
do not let your worshipers be disgraced
because of me.
7For you, I carry this shame,
and my face is covered with disgrace.
8I am like a stranger to my closest relatives
and a foreigner to my mother's children.
9My strong love for your Temple[d] completely
controls me.
When people insult you, it hurts me.
10When I cry and go without food,
they make fun of me.
11When I wear clothes of sadness,
they joke about me.
12They make fun of me in public places,
and the drunkards make up songs about
me.

13But I pray to you, LORD, for favor.
God, because of your great love, answer me.
You are truly able to save.
14Pull me from the mud,
and do not let me sink.
Save me from those who hate me
and from the deep water.
15Do not let the flood drown me
or the deep water swallow me
or the grave close its mouth over me.
16LORD, answer me because your love is so
good.
Because of your great kindness, turn to me.
17Do not hide from me, your servant.
I am in trouble. Hurry to help me!
18Come near and save me;
rescue me from my enemies.

19You see my shame and disgrace.
You know all my enemies and what they
have said.
20Insults have broken my heart
and left me weak.
I looked for sympathy, but there was none;
I found no one to comfort me.
21They put poison in my food
and gave me vinegar to drink.

22Let their own feasts cause their ruin;
let their feasts trap them and pay them
back.
23Let their eyes be closed so they cannot see
and their backs be forever weak from
troubles.
24Pour your anger out on them;
let your anger catch up with them.

25May their place be empty;
leave no one to live in their tents.
26They chase after those you have hurt,
and they talk about the pain of those you
have wounded.
27Charge them with crime after crime,
and do not let them have anything good.
28Wipe their names from the book of life,
and do not list them with those who do
what is right.

29I am sad and hurting.
God, save me and protect me.

30I will praise God in a song
and will honor him by giving thanks.
31That will please the LORD more than offering
him cattle,
more than sacrificing a bull with horns and
hoofs.
32Poor people will see this and be glad.
Be encouraged, you who worship
God.
33The LORD listens to those in need
and does not look down on captives.

34Heaven and earth should praise him,
the seas and everything in them.
35God will save Jerusalem
and rebuild the cities of Judah.
Then people will live there and own the
land.
36 The descendants[d] of his servants will inherit
that land,
and those who love him will live there.

FRIENDS

Everyone Welcome (Almost)

Everybody was surprised when Max Chezik showed up in Sunday school class. Shocked might be a better word.

"Somebody guard the collection plate," Jeanie Hackle whispered, and the rest of the class stifled giggles. Max had been suspended three times for breaking into lockers at school.

After announcements, the kids gathered in the sanctuary for group singing. Max lagged behind in the classroom. When the group returned ten minutes later, the class collection plate was empty. Every penny of the $6.47 was gone. Max Chezik had even stolen from God!

No one said anything, but the kids were obviously angry. What a total jerk, Jeanie thought. I hope he never shows his face around here again.

Then after class, something happened that made everyone stop dead in their tracks. Randy Jenks put his arm across Max's skinny shoulders as he was walking out.

He said, "Max, we enjoyed having you this morning, and we want you to come back next week."

What? Are you crazy, Randy? the kids' looks seemed to say.

"Thanks," said Max. "I'll try."

Everyone thought Randy had lost his brain. But the next week, Max came! And everyone watched as he gave a crumpled ten dollar bill.

Randy smiled. No one knew if that was Max's own money, or God's with interest. And no one really seemed to care anymore. He had shown what was most important—accepting Max as he was without judging him.

Like Randy, King David knew the dangers of judging people harshly. Read **Psalm 69:6–15** to see how David coped when others judged him.

- Which verses in this psalm describe Max?
- Based on this passage, what will you do the next time you're judged unfairly? How about the next time you're tempted to judge someone else?

C O N S I D E R . . .

- making friends with others who are often shunned by the "in" crowd.
- making a list of all the people you've made negative judgments about and then asking God to forgive you.

F O R M O R E , S E E . . .

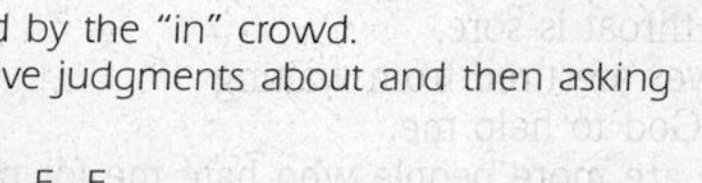

- Leviticus 19:15–18 (p. 116)
- Matthew 7:1–5 (p. 918)
- Romans 2:1–16 (p. 1141)

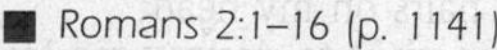

A Cry for God to Help Quickly

For the director of music. A psalm of David. To help people remember.

70 God, come quickly and save me.
LORD, hurry to help me.
2Let those who are trying to kill me
be ashamed and disgraced.
Let those who want to hurt me
run away in disgrace.
3Let those who make fun of me
stop because of their shame.
4But let all those who worship you
rejoice and be glad.
Let those who love your salvation
always say, "Praise the greatness of God."
5I am poor and helpless;
God, hurry to me.
You help me and save me.
LORD, do not wait.

An Old Person's Prayer

71 In you, LORD, is my protection.
Never let me be ashamed.
2Because you do what is right, save and
rescue me;
listen to me and save me.
3Be my place of safety
where I can always come.
Give the command to save me,
because you are my rock and my strong,
walled city.
4My God, save me from the power of the
wicked
and from the hold of evil and cruel people.
5LORD, you are my hope.
LORD, I have trusted you since I was
young.
6I have depended on you since I was born;
you helped me even on the day of my
birth.
I will always praise you.

7I am an example to many people,
because you are my strong protection.
8I am always praising you;
all day long I honor you.
9Do not reject me when I am old;
do not leave me when my strength is gone.
10My enemies make plans against me,
and they meet together to kill me.
11They say, "God has left him.
Go after him and take him,
because no one will save him."

12God, don't be far off.
My God, hurry to help me.
13Let those who accuse me
be ashamed and destroyed.
Let those who are trying to hurt me
be covered with shame and disgrace.
14But I will always have hope
and will praise you more and more.
15I will tell how you do what is right.
I will tell about your salvation all day long,
even though it is more than I can tell.
16I will come and tell about your powerful
works, Lord GOD.
I will remind people that only you do what
is right.

17God, you have taught me since I was young.
To this day I tell about the miracles[d] you
do.
18Even though I am old and gray,
do not leave me, God.
I will tell the children about your power;
I will tell those who live after me about
your might.

19God, your justice reaches to the skies.
You have done great things;
God, there is no one like you.
20You have given me many troubles and bad
times,
but you will give me life again.
When I am almost dead,
you will keep me alive.
21You will make me greater than ever,
and you will comfort me again.

22I will praise you with the harp.
I trust you, my God.
I will sing to you with the lyre,[d]
Holy One of Israel.
23I will shout for joy when I sing praises to
you.
You have saved me.
24I will tell about your justice all day long.
And those who want to hurt me
will be ashamed and disgraced.

A Prayer for the King

Of Solomon.

72 God, give the king your good
judgment
and the king's son your goodness.
2Help him judge your people fairly
and decide what is right for the poor.
3Let there be peace on the mountains
and goodness on the hills for the people.
4Help him be fair to the poor
and save the needy
and punish those who hurt them.

5May they respect you as long as the sun
shines
and as long as the moon glows.
6Let him be like rain on the grass,
like showers that water the earth.

[7]Let goodness be plentiful while he lives.
Let peace continue as long as there is a moon.

[8]Let his kingdom go from sea to sea,
and from the Euphrates River to the ends of the earth.
[9]Let the people of the desert bow down to him,
and make his enemies lick the dust.
[10]Let the kings of Tarshish and the faraway lands
bring him gifts.
Let the kings of Sheba and Seba
bring their presents to him.
[11]Let all kings bow down to him
and all nations serve him.

[12]He will help the poor when they cry out
and will save the needy when no one else will help.
[13]He will be kind to the weak and poor,
and he will save their lives.
[14]He will save them from cruel people who try to hurt them,
because their lives are precious to him.

[15]Long live the king!
Let him receive gold from Sheba.
Let people always pray for him
and bless him all day long.
[16]Let the fields grow plenty of grain
and the hills be covered with crops.
Let the land be as fertile as Lebanon,
and let the cities grow like the grass in a field.
[17]Let the king be famous forever;
let him be remembered as long as the sun shines.
Let the nations be blessed because of him,
and may they all bless him.

[18]Praise the LORD God, the God of Israel,
who alone does such miracles.[d]
[19]Praise his glorious name forever.
Let his glory fill the whole world.
Amen and amen.

[20]This ends the prayers of David son of Jesse.

HUNGER AND POVERTY

One Friend at a Time

When a few of her friends signed up to help at the Springfield community Salvation Army one Saturday, Jill Christy went along grudgingly.

"I figured you couldn't really change things for poor people in our town," she remembers. "It was just too big a problem."

About midday, Jill was straightening the sweater racks when Carolyn Harper came in with her three small children.

"I was really shocked," Jill recalls. "Carolyn seemed to be about my age."

Jill asked Carolyn if she needed any help.

"I need skirts and blouses," Carolyn whispered, sounding embarrassed. "The employment lady says she's found a good job for me that'll get us off welfare. If . . . you know . . . I can . . . well . . . look okay for an office."

Jill's heart ached for Carolyn. She quickly realized Carolyn needed a friend—someone to understand—as much as she needed clothes. Along with skirts, blouses, and shoes, Jill gave a listening ear, a smile and a little of her heart that afternoon.

Jill has never been the same since that encounter. Like the writer of **Psalm 72**, *Jill realized the importance of dealing compassionately with people in need.*

- *In what ways is Jill doing what the psalmist suggests?*
- *The psalmist uses the term "fair." How can you become more fair in your attitudes and actions toward needy people in your community?*

CONSIDER . . .

- *setting aside the same amount of money you've spent on "fun" this week and giving that amount to a hunger project.*
- *volunteering at a local clothes distribution center or food pantry.*

FOR MORE, SEE . . .

- Deuteronomy 14:28–29 (p. 174)
- Proverbs 14:31 (p. 580)
- 2 Corinthians 9:6–11 (p. 1201)

Book 3

Should the Wicked Be Rich?

A psalm of Asaph.

73 God is truly good to Israel,
to those who have pure hearts.
2But I had almost stopped believing;
I had almost lost my faith
3because I was jealous of proud people.
I saw wicked people doing well.

4They are not suffering;
they are healthy and strong.
5They don't have troubles like the rest of us;
they don't have problems like other people.
6They wear pride like a necklace
and put on violence as their clothing.
7They are looking for profits
and do not control their selfish desires.
8They make fun of others and speak evil;
proudly they speak of hurting others.
9They brag to the sky.
They say that they own the earth.
10So their people turn to them
and give them whatever they want.
11They say, "How can God know?
What does God Most High know?"
12These people are wicked,
always at ease, and getting richer.
13So why have I kept my heart pure?
Why have I kept my hands from doing wrong?
14I have suffered all day long;
I have been punished every morning.

15God, if I had decided to talk like this,
I would have let your people down.
16I tried to understand all this,
but it was too hard for me to see
17until I went to the Temple[d] of God.
Then I understood what will happen to them.
18You have put them in danger;
you cause them to be destroyed.
19They are destroyed in a moment;
they are swept away by terrors.
20It will be like waking from a dream.
Lord, when you rise up, they will disappear.

21When my heart was sad
and I was angry,
22I was senseless and stupid.
I acted like an animal toward you.
23But I am always with you;
you have held my hand.
24You guide me with your advice,
and later you will receive me in honor.
25I have no one in heaven but you;
I want nothing on earth besides you.
26My body and my mind may become weak,
but God is my strength.
He is mine forever.

27Those who are far from God will die;
you destroy those who are unfaithful.
28But I am close to God, and that is good.
The Lord GOD is my protection.
I will tell all that you have done.

A Nation in Trouble Prays

A maskil[d] of Asaph.

74 God, why have you rejected us for so long?
Why are you angry with us, the sheep of your pasture?
2Remember the people you bought long ago.
You saved us, and we are your very own.
After all, you live on Mount Zion.[d]
3Make your way through these old ruins;
the enemy wrecked everything in the Temple.[d]

4Those who were against you shouted in your meeting place
and raised their flags there.
5They came with axes raised
as if to cut down a forest of trees.
6They smashed the carved panels
with their axes and hatchets.
7They burned your Temple to the ground;
they have made the place where you live unclean.[d]
8They thought, "We will completely crush them!"
They burned every place where God was worshiped in the land.
9We do not see any signs.
There are no more prophets,
and no one knows how long this will last.
10God, how much longer will the enemy make fun of you?
Will they insult you forever?
11Why do you hold back your power?
Bring your power out in the open and destroy them!

12God, you have been our king for a long time.
You bring salvation to the earth.
13You split open the sea by your power
and broke the heads of the sea monster.
14You smashed the heads of the monster Leviathan[d]
and gave him to the desert creatures as food.

15You opened up the springs and streams
and made the flowing rivers run dry.
16Both the day and the night are yours;
you made the sun and the moon.
17You set all the limits on the earth;
you created summer and winter.

18LORD, remember how the enemy insulted
you.
Remember how those foolish people made
fun of you.
19Do not give us, your doves, to those wild
animals.
Never forget your poor people.
20Remember the agreement you made with us,
because violence fills every dark corner of
this land.
21Do not let your suffering people be disgraced.
Let the poor and helpless praise you.

22God, arise and defend yourself.
Remember the insults that come from those
foolish people all day long.
23Don't forget what your enemies said;
don't forget their roar as they rise against
you always.

God the Judge

For the director of music. To the tune of "Do Not Destroy." A psalm of Asaph. A song.

75 God, we thank you;
we thank you because you are near.
We tell about the miracles[d] you do.

2You say, "I set the time for trial,
and I will judge fairly.
3The earth with all its people may shake,
but I am the one who holds it steady. *Selah*[d]
4I say to those who are proud, 'Don't brag,'
and to the wicked, 'Don't show your
power.
5Don't try to use your power against heaven.
Don't be stubborn.' "

6No one from the east or the west
or the desert can judge you.
7God is the judge;
he judges one person as guilty and another
as innocent.
8The LORD holds a cup of anger in his hand;
it is full of wine mixed with spices.
He pours it out even to the last drop,
and the wicked drink it all.

9I will tell about this forever;
I will sing praise to the God of Jacob.
10He will take all power away from the
wicked,
but the power of good people will grow.

The God Who Always Wins

For the director of music. With stringed instruments. A psalm of Asaph. A song.

76 People in Judah know God;
his fame is great in Israel.
2His Tent[d] is in Jerusalem;
his home is on Mount Zion.[d]
3There God broke the flaming arrows,
the shields, the swords, and the weapons of
war. *Selah*[d]

4God, how wonderful you are!
You are more splendid than the hills full of
animals.
5The brave soldiers were stripped
as they lay asleep in death.
Not one warrior
had the strength to stop it.
6God of Jacob, when you spoke strongly,
horses and riders fell dead.
7You are feared;
no one can stand against you when you are
angry.
8From heaven you gave the decision,
and the earth was afraid and silent.
9God, you stood up to judge
and to save the needy people of the earth.
Selah
10People praise you for your anger against evil.
Those who live through your anger are
stopped from doing more evil.

11Make and keep your promises to the LORD
your God.
From all around, gifts should come to the
God we worship.
12God breaks the spirits of great leaders;
the kings on earth fear him.

Remembering God's Help

For the director of music. For Jeduthun. A psalm of Asaph.

77 I cry out to God;
I call to God, and he will hear me.
2I look for the Lord on the day of trouble.
All night long I reach out my hands,
but I cannot be comforted.
3When I remember God, I become upset;
when I think, I become afraid. *Selah*[d]

4You keep my eyes from closing.
I am too upset to say anything.
5I keep thinking about the old days,
the years of long ago.
6At night I remember my songs.
I think and I ask myself:
7"Will the Lord reject us forever?
Will he never be kind to us again?
8Is his love gone forever?

Has he stopped speaking for all time?
9Has God forgotten mercy?
Is he too angry to pity us?" *Selah*
10Then I say "This is what makes me sad:
For years the power of God Most High was with us."

11I remember what the LORD did;
I remember the miracles[d] you did long ago.
12I think about all the things you did
and consider your deeds.

13God, your ways are holy.
No god is as great as our God.
14You are the God who does miracles;
you have shown people your power.
15By your power you have saved your people,
the descendants[d] of Jacob and Joseph. *Selah*

16God, the waters saw you;
they saw you and became afraid;
the deep waters shook with fear.
17The clouds poured down their rain.
The sky thundered.
Your lightning flashed back and forth like arrows.
18Your thunder sounded in the whirlwind.
Lightning lit up the world.
The earth trembled and shook.
19You made a way through the sea
and paths through the deep waters,
but your footprints were not seen.
20You led your people like a flock
by using Moses and Aaron.

God Saved Israel from Egypt

A maskil[d] of Asaph.

78 My people, listen to my teaching;
listen to what I say.
2I will speak using stories;
I will tell secret things from long ago.
3We have heard them and known them
by what our ancestors have told us.
4We will not keep them from our children;
we will tell those who come later
about the praises of the LORD.
We will tell about his power
and the miracles[d] he has done.

5The LORD made an agreement with Jacob
and gave the teachings to Israel,
which he commanded our ancestors
to teach to their children.
6Then their children would know them,
even their children not yet born.
And they would tell their children.
7So they would all trust God
and would not forget what he had done
but would obey his commands.
8They would not be like their ancestors
who were stubborn and disobedient.
Their hearts were not loyal to God,
and they were not true to him.

9The men of Ephraim had bows for weapons,
but they ran away on the day of battle.
10They didn't keep their agreement with God
and refused to live by his teachings.
11They forgot what he had done
and the miracles he had shown them.
12He did miracles while their ancestors watched,
in the fields of Zoan in Egypt.
13He divided the Red Sea[d] and led them through.
He made the water stand up like a wall.
14He led them with a cloud by day
and by the light of a fire by night.
15He split the rocks in the desert
and gave them more than enough water, as if from the deep ocean.
16He brought streams out of the rock
and caused water to flow down like rivers.

17But the people continued to sin against him;
in the desert they turned against God Most High.
18They decided to test God
by asking for the food they wanted.
19Then they spoke against God,
saying, "Can God prepare food in the desert?
20When he hit the rock, water poured out
and rivers flowed down.
But can he give us bread also?
Will he provide his people with meat?"
21When the LORD heard them, he was very angry.
His anger was like fire to the people of Jacob;
his anger grew against the people of Israel.
22They had not believed God
and had not trusted him to save them.
23But he gave a command to the clouds above
and opened the doors of heaven.
24He rained manna[d] down on them to eat;
he gave them grain from heaven.
25So they ate the bread of angels.
He sent them all the food they could eat.
26He sent the east wind from heaven
and led the south wind by his power.
27He rained meat on them like dust.
The birds were as many as the sand of the sea.
28He made the birds fall inside the camp,
all around the tents.
29So the people ate and became very full.
God had given them what they wanted.
30While they were still eating,

and while the food was still in their
mouths,
31God became angry with them.
He killed some of the healthiest of them;
he struck down the best young men of
Israel.

32But they kept on sinning;
they did not believe even with the miracles.
33So he ended their days without meaning
and their years in terror.
34Anytime he killed them, they would look to
him for help;
they would come back to God and follow
him.
35They would remember that God was their
Rock,[d]
that God Most High had saved them.
36But their words were false,
and their tongues lied to him.
37Their hearts were not really loyal to God;
they did not keep his agreement.
38Still God was merciful.
He forgave their sins
and did not destroy them.
Many times he held back his anger
and did not stir up all his anger.
39He remembered that they were only human,
like a wind that blows and does not come
back.

40They turned against God so often in the
desert
and grieved him there.
41Again and again they tested God
and brought pain to the Holy One of Israel.
42They did not remember his power
or the time he saved them from the enemy.
43They forgot the signs he did in Egypt
and his wonders in the fields of Zoan.
44He turned their rivers to blood
so no one could drink the water.
45He sent flies that bit the people.
He sent frogs that destroyed them.
46He gave their crops to grasshoppers
and what they worked for to locusts.[d]
47He destroyed their vines with hail
and their sycamore trees with sleet.
48He killed their animals with hail
and their cattle with lightning.
49He showed them his hot anger.
He sent his strong anger against them,
his destroying angels.
50He found a way to show his anger.
He did not keep them from dying
but let them die by a terrible disease.
51God killed all the firstborn[d] sons in Egypt,
the oldest son of each family of Ham.[n]
52But God led his people out like sheep
and he guided them like a flock through
the desert.
53He led them to safety so they had nothing to
fear,
but their enemies drowned in the sea.
54So God brought them to his holy land,
to the mountain country he took with his
own power.
55He forced out the other nations,
and he had his people inherit the land.
He let the tribes[d] of Israel settle there in
tents.

56But they tested God
and turned against God Most High;
they did not keep his rules.
57They turned away and were disloyal just like
their ancestors.
They were like a crooked bow that does
not shoot straight.
58They made God angry by building places to
worship gods;
they made him jealous with their idols.
59When God heard them, he became very
angry
and rejected the people of Israel completely.
60He left his dwelling at Shiloh,
the Tent where he lived among the people.
61He let the Ark,[d] his power, be captured;
he let the Ark, his glory, be taken by
enemies.
62He let his people be killed;
he was very angry with his children.
63The young men died by fire,
and the young women had no one to
marry.
64Their priests fell by the sword,
but their widows were not allowed to cry.

65Then the Lord got up as if he had been
asleep;
he awoke like a man who had been drunk
with wine.
66He struck down his enemies
and disgraced them forever.
67But God rejected the family of Joseph;
he did not choose the tribe of Ephraim.
68Instead, he chose the tribe of Judah
and Mount Zion,[d] which he loves.
69And he built his Temple[d] high like the
mountains.
Like the earth, he built it to last forever.
70He chose David to be his servant
and took him from the sheep pens.
71He brought him from tending the sheep
so he could lead the flock, the people of
Jacob,

Ham The people in Egypt were descendants of Ham, one of Noah's sons. See Genesis 10:6.

his own people, the people of Israel.
72And David led them with an innocent heart
and guided them with skillful hands.

The Nation Cries for Jerusalem

A psalm of Asaph.

79 God, nations have come against your
chosen people.
They have ruined your holy Temple.[d]
They have turned Jerusalem into ruins.
2They have given the bodies of your servants
as food to the wild birds.
They have given the bodies of those who
worship you to the wild animals.
3They have spilled blood like water all around
Jerusalem.
No one was left to bury the dead.
4We are a joke to the other nations;
they laugh and make fun of us.

5LORD, how long will this last?
Will you be angry forever?
How long will your jealousy burn like a
fire?
6Be angry with the nations that do not know
you
and with the kingdoms that do not honor
you.
7They have gobbled up the people of Jacob
and destroyed their land.
8Don't punish us for our past sins.
Show your mercy to us soon,
because we are helpless!
9God our Savior, help us
so people will praise you.
Save us and forgive our sins
so people will honor you.
10Why should the nations say,
"Where is their God?"
Tell the other nations in our presence
that you punish those who kill your
servants.
11Hear the moans of the prisoners.
Use your great power
to save those sentenced to die.

12Repay those around us seven times over
for their insults to you, Lord.
13We are your people, the sheep of your flock.
We will thank you always;
forever and ever we will praise you.

A Prayer to Bring Israel Back

For the director of music. To the tune of "Lilies of the Agreement." A psalm of Asaph.

80 Shepherd of Israel, listen to us.
You lead the people of Joseph like a
flock.
You sit on your throne between the gold
creatures with wings.
Show your greatness 2to the people of
Ephraim, Benjamin, and Manasseh.
Use your strength,
and come to save us.

3God, take us back.
Show us your kindness so we can be
saved.

4LORD God All-Powerful,
how long will you be angry
at the prayers of your people?
5You have fed your people with tears;
you have made them drink many tears.
6You made those around us fight over us,
and our enemies make fun of us.

7God All-Powerful, take us back.
Show us your kindness so we can be
saved.

8You brought us out of Egypt as if we were a
vine.
You forced out other nations and planted us
in the land.
9You cleared the ground for us.
Like a vine, we took root and filled the
land.
10We covered the mountains with our shade.
We had limbs like the mighty cedar tree.
11Our branches reached the Mediterranean
Sea,
and our shoots went to the Euphrates
River.

12So why did you pull down our walls?
Now everyone who passes by steals from
us.
13Like wild pigs they walk over us;
like wild animals they feed on us.

14God All-Powerful, come back.
Look down from heaven and see.
Take care of us, your vine.
15 You planted this shoot with your own
hands
and strengthened this child.
16Now it is cut down and burned with fire;
you destroyed us by your angry looks.
17With your hand,
strengthen the one you have chosen for
yourself.
18Then we will not turn away from you.
Give us life again, and we will call to you
for help.

19LORD God All-Powerful, take us back.
Show us your kindness so we can be
saved.

A Song for a Holiday

For the director of music. By the gittith.[d]
A psalm of Asaph.

81 Sing for joy to God, our strength;
shout out loud to the God of Jacob.
2Begin the music. Play the tambourines.[d]
Play pleasant music on the harps and
lyres.[d]
3Blow the trumpet at the time of the New
Moon,[d]
when the moon is full, when our feast
begins.

> **SIDELIGHT:** The sheep's horn was used like a trumpet (Psalm 81:3). It is the only ancient instrument mentioned in the Bible that's still used in Jewish synagogues. It's made by heating and shaping the animal's hollow horn.

4This is the law for Israel;
it is the command of the God of Jacob.
5He gave this rule to the people of Joseph
when they went out of the land of Egypt.

I heard a language I did not know, saying:

6"I took the load off their shoulders;
I let them put down their baskets.
7When you were in trouble, you called, and I
saved you.
I answered you with thunder.
I tested you at the waters of Meribah. *Selah*[d]
8My people, listen. I am warning you.
Israel, please listen to me!
9You must not have foreign gods;
you must not worship any false god.
10I, the LORD, am your God,
who brought you out of Egypt.
Open your mouth and I will feed
you.

11"But my people did not listen to me;
Israel did not want me.
12So I let them go their stubborn way
and follow their own advice.
13I wish my people would listen to me;
I wish Israel would live my way.
14Then I would quickly defeat their enemies
and turn my hand against their foes.
15Those who hate the LORD would bow before
him.
Their punishment would continue
forever.
16But I would give you the finest wheat
and fill you with honey from the
rocks."

CELEBRATING

Shout Out Loud!

Imagine . . .

- Christmas without Christmas carols
- a wedding without the "Wedding March"
- a football game without a band
- Graduation without "Pomp and Circumstance"

Now for a really hard one. Imagine turning a year older without a group of friends and relatives singing "Happy Birthday"!

Pretty dismal, huh?

People have used music to celebrate life's joys for generations, dating all the way back to ancient writings such as the Psalms. **Psalm 81:1–10** calls people to shout and "sing for joy to God, our strength" for God's goodness and gifts.

- Why do you think the psalmist included a variety of methods for celebrating?
- What way of celebrating God do you enjoy most?

CONSIDER . . .

- putting a simple prayer to music and singing it to God.
- learning a new song or joining a music group to find new ways to worship God.

FOR MORE, SEE . . .

- 1 Chronicles 13:6–8 (p. 372)
- Psalm 149 (p. 565)
- Ephesians 5:15–20 (p. 1224)

A Cry for Justice

A psalm of Asaph.

82 God is in charge of the great meeting;
he judges among the "gods."
2He says, "How long will you defend evil
people?
How long will you show greater kindness
to the wicked? *Selah*[d]
3Defend the weak and the orphans;
defend the rights of the poor and suffering.
4Save the weak and helpless;
free them from the power of the wicked.

5"You know nothing. You don't understand.
You walk in the dark,
while the world is falling apart.
6I said, 'You are "gods."
You are all sons of God Most High.'
7But you will die like any other person;
you will fall like all the leaders."

8God, come and judge the earth,
because you own all the nations.

A Prayer Against the Enemies

A song. A psalm of Asaph.

83 God, do not keep quiet;
God, do not be silent or still.
2Your enemies are making noises;
those who hate you are getting ready to
attack.
3They are making secret plans against your
people;
they plot against those you love.
4They say, "Come, let's destroy them as a
nation.
Then no one will ever remember the name
'Israel.' "
5They are united in their plan.
These have made an agreement against
you:
6the families of Edom and the Ishmaelites,
Moab and the Hagrites,
7the people of Byblos, Ammon, Amalek,
Philistia, and Tyre.
8Even Assyria has joined them
to help Ammon and Moab, the
descendants[d] of Lot. *Selah*[d]

9God, do to them what you did to Midian,
what you did to Sisera and Jabin at the
Kishon River.
10They died at Endor,
and their bodies rotted on the ground.
11Do to their important leaders what you did to
Oreb and Zeeb.
Do to their princes what you did to Zebah
and Zalmunna.
12They said, "Let's take for ourselves
the pasturelands that belong to God."
13My God, make them like tumbleweed,
like chaff[d] blown away by the wind.
14Be like a fire that burns a forest
or like flames that blaze through the hills.
15Chase them with your storm,
and frighten them with your wind.
16Cover them with shame.
Then people will look for you, LORD.
17Make them afraid and ashamed forever.
Disgrace them and destroy them.
18Then they will know that you are the LORD,
that only you are God Most High over all
the earth.

SIDELIGHT: Psalms 84 and 122—among others—were "songs for the road" or pilgrim songs. Three times a year, faithful Jews packed up the family camel and traveled to Jerusalem to celebrate, singing along the way (see Deuteronomy 16:16, p. 175).

Wishing to Be in the Temple

For the director of music. On the gittith.[d] A psalm of the sons of Korah.

84 LORD All-Powerful,
how lovely is your Temple![d]
2I want more than anything
to be in the courtyards of the LORD's
Temple.
My whole being wants
to be with the living God.
3The sparrows have found a home,
and the swallows have nests.
They raise their young near your altars,
LORD All-Powerful, my King and my God.
4Happy are the people who live at your
Temple;
they are always praising you. *Selah*[d]

5Happy are those whose strength comes from
you,
who want to travel to Jerusalem.
6As they pass through the Valley of Baca,
they make it like a spring.
The autumn rains fill it with pools of water.
7The people get stronger as they go,
and everyone meets with God in Jerusalem.

8LORD God All-Powerful, hear my prayer;
God of Jacob, listen to me. *Selah*
9God, look at our shield;
be kind to your appointed king.

10One day in the courtyards of your Temple is
better

than a thousand days anywhere else.
I would rather be a doorkeeper in the
Temple of my God
than live in the homes of the wicked.
11The LORD God is like a sun and shield;
the LORD gives us kindness and honor.
He does not hold back anything good
from those whose lives are innocent.
12LORD All-Powerful,
happy are the people who trust you!

A Prayer for the Nation

For the director of music. A psalm
of the sons of Korah.

85 LORD, you have been kind to your
land;
you brought back the people of Jacob.
2You forgave the guilt of the people
and covered all their sins. *Selah*[d]
3You stopped all your anger;
you turned back from your strong anger.

4God our Savior, bring us back again.
Stop being angry with us.
5Will you be angry with us forever?
Will you stay angry from now on?
6Won't you give us life again?
Your people would rejoice in you.
7LORD, show us your love,
and save us.

8I will listen to God the LORD.
He has ordered peace for those who
worship him.
Don't let them go back to foolishness.
9God will soon save those who respect him,
and his glory will be seen in our land.
10Love and truth belong to God's people;
goodness and peace will be theirs.
11On earth people will be loyal to God,
and God's goodness will shine down from
heaven.
12The LORD will give his goodness,
and the land will give its crops.
13Goodness will go before God
and prepare the way for him.

A Cry for Help

A prayer of David.

86 LORD, listen to me and answer me.
I am poor and helpless.
2Protect me, because I worship you.
My God, save me, your servant who trusts
in you.
3Lord, have mercy on me,
because I have called to you all day.

WORSHIP

Happy Are Those

Su Ling admits that for years she took her church for granted. "It was a place to meet my friends on Sunday morning. We'd share the back pew and sometimes write notes to each other on the offering envelopes especially when the sermon got boring."

But then Su's grandmother died, and the sadness that settled into Su seemed endless. Grandma had been her best friend—the only person Su felt loved her without reservation. Now, Su felt a hole inside where that wonderful, happy love had been.

"I went to the church alone one night when I couldn't stop crying," Su recalls, "and when I prayed in the empty sanctuary, I felt suddenly calm. I realized God was there, waiting for me. I could tell because I felt surrounded again by the same kind of special love I'd always felt with Grandma. Now, I feel God close to me every time I pray or worship wherever I am."

Su Ling learned the special joy of living in God's presence. The writer of **Psalm 84** knew that same joy. Read about how he yearned to live in God's presence "in the courtyards of the Lord's Temple."

- To which verses of this psalm might Su Ling relate?
- What do you experience in your church that helps you worship?

CONSIDER . . .

- shocking the pastor by sitting in the front of the sanctuary one Sunday.
- finding a special time to go into your church to pray quietly, alone with God.

FOR MORE, SEE . . .

- 1 Chronicles 16:25–29 (p. 374)
- Psalm 132:7–9 (p. 558)
- John 4:19–26 (p. 1063)

[4]Give happiness to me, your servant,
because I give my life to you, Lord.
[5]Lord, you are kind and forgiving
and have great love for those who call to you.
[6]LORD, hear my prayer,
and listen when I ask for mercy.
[7]I call to you in times of trouble,
because you will answer me.

[8]Lord, there is no god like you
and no works like yours.
[9]Lord, all the nations you have made
will come and worship you.
They will honor you.
[10]You are great and you do miracles.[d]
Only you are God.

[11]LORD, teach me what you want me to do,
and I will live by your truth.
Teach me to respect you completely.
[12]Lord, my God, I will praise you with all my heart,
and I will honor your name forever.
[13]You have great love for me.
You have saved me from death.

[14]God, proud men are attacking me;
a gang of cruel men is trying to kill me.
They do not respect you.
[15]But Lord, you are a God who shows mercy and is kind.
You don't become angry quickly.
You have great love and faithfulness.
[16]Turn to me and have mercy.
Give me, your servant, strength.
Save me, the son of your female servant.
[17]Show me a sign of your goodness.
When my enemies look, they will be ashamed.
You, LORD, have helped me and comforted me.

God Loves Jerusalem

A song. A psalm of the sons of Korah.

87 The LORD built Jerusalem on the holy mountain.
[2] He loves its gates
more than any other place in Israel.
[3]City of God,
wonderful things are said about you. *Selah*[d]
[4]God says, "I will put Egypt and Babylonia
on the list of nations that know me.
People from Philistia, Tyre, and Cush
will be born there."

[5]They will say about Jerusalem,
"This one and that one were born there.
God Most High will strengthen her."
[6]The LORD will keep a list of the nations.
He will note, "This person was born there." *Selah*

[7]They will dance and sing,
"All good things come from Jerusalem."

A Sad Complaint

A song. A psalm of the sons of Korah. For the director of music. By the mahalath leannoth.[d] A maskil[d] of Heman the Ezrahite.

88 LORD, you are the God who saves me.
I cry out to you day and night.
[2]Receive my prayer,
and listen to my cry.

[3]My life is full of troubles,
and I am nearly dead.
[4]They think I am on the way to my grave.
I am like a man with no strength.
[5]I have been left as dead,
like a body lying in a grave
whom you don't remember anymore,
cut off from your care.
[6]You have brought me close to death;
I am almost in the dark place of the dead.
[7]You have been very angry with me;
all your waves crush me. *Selah*[d]
[8]You have taken my friends away from me
and have made them hate me.
I am trapped and cannot escape.
[9] My eyes are weak from crying.
LORD, I have prayed to you every day;
I have lifted my hands in prayer to you.

[10]Do you show your miracles[d] for the dead?
Do their spirits rise up and praise you? *Selah*
[11]Will your love be told in the grave?
Will your loyalty be told in the place of death?
[12]Will your miracles be known in the dark grave?
Will your goodness be known in the land of forgetfulness?

[13]But, LORD, I have called out to you for help;
every morning I pray to you.
[14]LORD, why do you reject me?
Why do you hide from me?
[15]I have been weak and dying since I was young.
I suffer from your terrors, and I am helpless.
[16]You have been angry with me,
and your terrors have destroyed me.
[17]They surround me daily like a flood;
they are all around me.
[18]You have taken away my loved ones and friends.
Darkness is my only friend.

A Song About God's Loyalty

A maskil[d] of Ethan the Ezrahite.

89 I will always sing about the LORD's love;
I will tell of his loyalty from now on.
2I will say, "Your love continues forever;
your loyalty goes on and on like the sky."
3You said, "I made an agreement with the man of my choice;
I made a promise to my servant David.
4I told him, 'I will make your family continue forever.
Your kingdom will go on and on.' " *Selah*[d]

5LORD, the heavens praise you for your miracles[d]
and for your loyalty in the meeting of your holy ones.
6Who in heaven is equal to the LORD?
None of the angels is like the LORD.
7When the holy ones meet, it is God they fear.
He is more frightening than all who surround him.
8Lord GOD All-Powerful, who is like you?
LORD, you are powerful and completely trustworthy.
9You rule the mighty sea
and calm the stormy waves.
10You crushed the sea monster Rahab;[d]
by your power you scattered your enemies.

11The skies and the earth belong to you.
You made the world and everything in it.
12You created the north and the south.
Mount Tabor and Mount Hermon sing for joy at your name.
13Your arm has great power.
Your hand is strong; your right hand is lifted up.
14Your kingdom is built on what is right and fair.
Love and truth are in all you do.

15Happy are the people who know how to praise you.
LORD, let them live in the light of your presence.
16In your name they rejoice
and continually praise your goodness.
17You are their glorious strength,
and in your kindness you honor our king.
18Our king, our shield, belongs to the LORD,
to the Holy One of Israel.

19Once, in a vision, you spoke
to those who worship you.
You said, "I have given strength to a warrior;
I have raised up a young man from my people.
20I have found my servant David;
I appointed him by pouring holy oil on him.
21I will steady him with my hand
and strengthen him with my arm.
22No enemy will make him give forced payments,
and wicked people will not defeat him.
23I will crush his enemies in front of him;
I will defeat those who hate him.
24My loyalty and love will be with him.
Through me he will be strong.
25I will give him power over the sea
and control over the rivers.
26He will say to me, 'You are my father,
my God, the Rock,[d] my Savior.'
27I will make him my firstborn[d] son,
the greatest king on earth.
28My love will watch over him forever,
and my agreement with him will never end.
29I will make his family continue,
and his kingdom will last as long as the skies.

30"If his descendants[d] reject my teachings
and do not follow my laws,
31if they ignore my demands
and disobey my commands,
32then I will punish their sins with a rod
and their wrongs with a whip.
33But I will not hold back my love from David,
nor will I stop being loyal.
34I will not break my agreement
nor change what I have said.
35I have promised by my holiness,
I will not lie to David.
36His family will go on forever.
His kingdom will last before me like the sun.
37It will continue forever, like the moon,
like a dependable witness in the sky." *Selah*

38But now you have refused and rejected your appointed king.
You have been angry with him.
39You have abandoned the agreement with your servant
and thrown his crown to the ground.
40You have torn down all his city walls;
you have turned his strong cities into ruins.
41Everyone who passes by steals from him.
His neighbors insult him.
42You have given strength to his enemies
and have made them all happy.
43You have made his sword useless;
you did not help him stand in battle.
44You have kept him from winning
and have thrown his throne to the ground.
45You have cut his life short

and covered him with shame. *Selah*

46LORD, how long will this go on?
Will you ignore us forever?
How long will your anger burn like a fire?
47Remember how short my life is.
Why did you create us? For nothing?
48What person alive will not die?
Who can escape the grave? *Selah*

49Lord, where is your love from times past,
which in your loyalty you promised to David?
50Lord, remember how they insulted your servant;
remember how I have suffered the insults of the nations.
51LORD, remember how your enemies insulted you
and how they insulted your appointed king wherever he went.

52Praise the LORD forever!
Amen and amen.

Book 4

God Is Eternal, and We Are Not

A prayer of Moses, the man of God.

90 Lord, you have been our home
since the beginning.
2Before the mountains were born
and before you created the earth and the world,
you are God.
You have always been, and you will always be.
3You turn people back into dust.
You say, "Go back into dust, human beings."
4To you, a thousand years
is like the passing of a day,
or like a few hours in the night.
5While people sleep, you take their lives.
They are like grass that grows up in the morning.
6In the morning they are fresh and new,
but by evening they dry up and die.

7We are destroyed by your anger;
we are terrified by your hot anger.
8You have put the evil we have done right in front of you;
you clearly see our secret sins.
9All our days pass while you are angry.
Our years end with a moan.
10Our lifetime is seventy years
or, if we are strong, eighty years.
But the years are full of hard work and pain.
They pass quickly, and then we are gone.
11Who knows the full power of your anger?
Your anger is as great as our fear of you should be.
12Teach us how short our lives really are
so that we may be wise.

13LORD, how long before you return
and show kindness to your servants?
14Fill us with your love every morning.
Then we will sing and rejoice all our lives.
15We have seen years of trouble.
Now give us as much joy as you gave us sorrow.
16Show your servants the wonderful things you do;
show your greatness to their children.
17Lord our God, treat us well.
Give us success in what we do;
yes, give us success in what we do.

Safe in the Lord

91 Those who go to God Most High for safety
will be protected by the Almighty.
2I will say to the LORD, "You are my place of safety and protection.
You are my God and I trust you."

3God will save you from hidden traps
and from deadly diseases.
4He will cover you with his feathers,
and under his wings you can hide.
His truth will be your shield and protection.
5You will not fear any danger by night
or an arrow during the day.
6You will not be afraid of diseases that come in the dark
or sickness that strikes at noon.
7At your side one thousand people may die,
or even ten thousand right beside you,
but you will not be hurt.
8You will only watch
and see the wicked punished.

9The LORD is your protection;
you have made God Most High your place of safety.
10Nothing bad will happen to you;
no disaster will come to your home.
11He has put his angels in charge of you
to watch over you wherever you go.
12They will catch you in their hands
so that you will not hit your foot on a rock.
13You will walk on lions and cobras;
you will step on strong lions and snakes.

14The LORD says, "Whoever loves me, I will save.
I will protect those who know me.

15They will call to me, and I will answer them.
I will be with them in trouble;
I will rescue them and honor them.
16I will give them a long, full life,
and they will see how I can save."

Thanksgiving for God's Goodness

A psalm. A song for the Sabbath[d] day.

92 It is good to praise you, LORD,
to sing praises to God Most High.
2It is good to tell of your love in the morning
and of your loyalty at night.
3It is good to praise you with the ten-stringed lyre[d]
and with the soft-sounding harp.

4LORD, you have made me happy by what you have done;
I will sing for joy about what your hands have done.
5LORD, you have done such great things!
How deep are your thoughts!
6Stupid people don't know these things,
and fools don't understand.
7Wicked people grow like the grass.
Evil people seem to do well,
but they will be destroyed forever.
8But, LORD, you will be honored forever.

9LORD, surely your enemies,
surely your enemies will be destroyed,
and all who do evil will be scattered.
10But you have made me as strong as an ox.
You have poured fine oils on me.
11When I looked, I saw my enemies;
I heard the cries of those who are against me.

12But good people will grow like palm trees;
they will be tall like the cedars of Lebanon.
13Like trees planted in the Temple of the LORD,
they will grow strong in the courtyards of our God.
14When they are old, they will still produce fruit;
they will be healthy and fresh.
15They will say that the LORD is good.
He is my Rock,[d] and there is no wrong in him.

The Majesty of the Lord

93 The LORD is king. He is clothed in majesty.
The LORD is clothed in majesty
and armed with strength.
The world is set,
and it cannot be moved.
2LORD, your kingdom was set up long ago;
you are everlasting.
3LORD, the seas raise,
the seas raise their voice.
The seas raise up their pounding waves.
4The sound of the water is loud;
the ocean waves are powerful,
but the LORD above is much greater.
5LORD, your laws will stand forever.
Your Temple[d] will be holy forevermore.

God Will Pay Back His Enemies

94 The LORD is a God who punishes.
God, show your greatness and punish!
2Rise up, Judge of the earth,
and give the proud what they deserve.
3How long will the wicked be happy?
How long, LORD?
4They are full of proud words;
those who do evil brag about what they have done.
5LORD, they crush your people
and make your children suffer.
6They kill widows and foreigners
and murder orphans.
7They say, "The LORD doesn't see;
the God of Jacob doesn't notice."
8You stupid ones among the people, pay attention.
You fools, when will you understand?
9Can't the creator of ears hear?
Can't the maker of eyes see?
10Won't the one who corrects nations punish you?
Doesn't the teacher of people know everything?
11The LORD knows what people think.
He knows their thoughts are just a puff of wind.

12LORD, those you correct are happy;
you teach them from your law.
13You give them rest from times of trouble
until a pit is dug for the wicked.
14The LORD won't leave his people
nor give up his children.
15Judgment will again be fair,
and all who are honest will follow it.

16Who will help me fight against the wicked?
Who will stand with me against those who do evil?
17If the LORD had not helped me,
I would have died in a minute.
18I said, "I am about to fall,"
but, LORD, your love kept me safe.
19I was very worried,
but you comforted me and made me happy.

20Crooked leaders cannot be your friends.
They use the law to cause suffering.

21 They join forces against people who do right
and sentence to death the innocent.
22 But the LORD is my defender;
my God is the rock of my protection.
23 God will pay them back for their sins
and will destroy them for their evil.
The LORD our God will destroy them.

A Call to Praise and Obedience

95 Come, let's sing for joy to the LORD.
Let's shout praises to the Rock[d] who
saves us.
2 Let's come to him with thanksgiving.
Let's sing songs to him,
3 because the LORD is the great God,
the great King over all gods.
4 The deepest places on earth are his,
and the highest mountains belong to him.
5 The sea is his because he made it,
and he created the land with his own
hands.

6 Come, let's worship him and bow down.
Let's kneel before the LORD who made us,
7 because he is our God
and we are the people he takes care of
and the sheep that he tends.

Today listen to what he says:
8 "Do not be stubborn, as your ancestors
were at Meribah,
as they were that day at Massah in the
desert.
9 There your ancestors tested me
and tried me even though they saw what I
did.
10 I was angry with those people for forty years.
I said, 'They are not loyal to me
and have not understood my ways.'
11 I was angry and made a promise,
'They will never enter my rest.' "

Praise for the Lord's Glory

96 Sing to the LORD a new song;
sing to the LORD, all the earth.
2 Sing to the LORD and praise his name;
every day tell how he saves us.
3 Tell the nations of his glory;
tell all peoples the miracles[d] he does,

4 because the LORD is great; he should be
praised at all times.
He should be honored more than all the
gods,
5 because all the gods of the nations are only
idols,
but the LORD made the heavens.
6 The LORD has glory and majesty;
he has power and beauty in his Temple.[d]

7 Praise the LORD, all nations on earth;
praise the LORD's glory and power.
8 Praise the glory of the LORD's name.
Bring an offering and come into his Temple
courtyards.
9 Worship the LORD because he is holy.
Tremble before him, everyone on earth.
10 Tell the nations, "The LORD is king."
The earth is set, and it cannot be moved.
He will judge the people fairly.
11 Let the skies rejoice and the earth be glad;
let the sea and everything in it shout.
12 Let the fields and everything in them
rejoice.
Then all the trees of the forest will sing for
joy
13 before the LORD, because he is coming.
He is coming to judge the world;
he will judge the world with fairness
and the peoples with truth.

A Hymn About the Lord's Power

97 The LORD is king. Let the earth
rejoice;
faraway lands should be glad.
2 Thick, dark clouds surround him.
His kingdom is built on what is right and
fair.
3 A fire goes before him
and burns up his enemies all around.
4 His lightning lights up the world;
when the people see it, they tremble.
5 The mountains melt like wax before the
LORD,
before the Lord of all the earth.
6 The heavens tell about his goodness,
and all the people see his glory.

7 Those who worship idols should be ashamed;
they brag about their gods.
All the gods should worship the LORD.
8 When Jerusalem hears this, she is glad,
and the towns of Judah rejoice.
They are happy because of your judgments,
LORD.
9 You are the LORD Most High over all the
earth;
you are supreme over all gods.

10 People who love the LORD hate evil.
The LORD watches over those who follow
him
and frees them from the power of the
wicked.
11 Light shines on those who do right;
joy belongs to those who are honest.
12 Rejoice in the LORD, you who do right.
Praise his holy name.

The Lord of Power and Justice

A psalm.

98 Sing to the LORD a new song,
because he has done miracles.[d]
By his right hand and holy arm
he has won the victory.
2The LORD has made known his power to
save;
he has shown the other nations his victory
for his people.
3He has remembered his love
and his loyalty to the people of Israel.
All the ends of the earth have seen
God's power to save.

4Shout with joy to the LORD, all the earth;
burst into songs and make music.
5Make music to the LORD with harps,
with harps and the sound of singing.
6Blow the trumpets and the sheep's horns;
shout for joy to the LORD the King.

7Let the sea and everything in it shout;
let the world and everyone in it sing.
8Let the rivers clap their hands;
let the mountains sing together for joy.
9Let them sing before the LORD,
because he is coming to judge the world.
He will judge the world fairly;
he will judge the peoples with fairness.

The Lord, the Fair and Holy King

99 The LORD is king.
Let the peoples shake with fear.
He sits between the gold creatures with
wings.
Let the earth shake.
2The LORD in Jerusalem is great;
he is supreme over all the peoples.
3Let them praise your name;
it is great, holy and to be feared.

4The King is powerful and loves justice.
LORD, you made things fair;
you have done what is fair and right
for the people of Jacob.
5Praise the LORD our God,
and worship at the Temple,[d] his footstool.
He is holy.

6Moses and Aaron were among his priests,
and Samuel was among his worshipers.
They called to the LORD,
and he answered them.
7He spoke to them from the pillar of cloud.

EVIL

Taking a Stand

When Ron Daly dozed off during math class, Rose giggled like everybody else. But Ron didn't stir when Ms. Shaster called on him ten minutes later. And he still didn't stir when she shook his shoulder, hard. The class laughter turned to panic and an ambulance was called. He was revived in the hospital several hours later, just barely.

Rose went to the hospital that evening to see how Ron was. He looked exhausted—pale, weak, and depressed—and Rose was amazed at how close Ron had come to death.

"Until I'd seen the effects of a drug overdose up close like that, I just thought of cocaine as a bad habit—gross, sure, but no big deal," Rose says. She got involved the next week in the school's anti-drug campaign.

"Ron's a good friend," Rose adds, "and now I know his habit is evil—a killer! Because I care about Ron, I have to hate his addiction."

"People who love the Lord hate evil," says the writer of **Psalm 97**. Read the passage for more of the psalmist's reflections on evil.

- Rose decided to take a stand against evil. What does the psalmist say about people who go out of their way to do what's right, like Rose?
- In what areas of your life do you need to take a stand against evil?

CONSIDER . . .

- writing a definition of "evil" based on Psalm 97 and carrying that definition in your pocket or purse this week to increase your awareness of the evil around you.
- talking with an adult friend about an addiction you cannot break.

FOR MORE, SEE . . .

- Proverbs 22:1–5, 8 (p. 586)
- Isaiah 5 (p. 621)
- Colossians 3:1–14 (p. 1241)

They kept the rules and laws he gave them.
8LORD our God, you answered them.
You showed them that you are a forgiving God,
but you punished them for their wrongs.
9Praise the LORD our God,
and worship at his holy mountain,
because the LORD our God is holy.

A Call to Praise the Lord

A psalm of thanks.

100 Shout to the LORD, all the earth.
2 Serve the LORD with joy;
come before him with singing.
3Know that the LORD is God.
He made us, and we belong to him;
we are his people, the sheep he tends.

4Come into his city with songs of thanksgiving
and into his courtyards with songs of praise.
Thank him and praise his name.
5The LORD is good. His love is forever,
and his loyalty goes on and on.

A Promise to Rule Well

A psalm of David.

101 I will sing of your love and fairness;
LORD, I will sing praises to you.
2I will be careful to live an innocent life.
When will you come to me?

I will live an innocent life in my house.
3 I will not look at anything wicked.
I hate those who turn against you;
they will not be found near me.
4Let those who want to do wrong stay away from me;
I will have nothing to do with evil.
5If anyone secretly says things against his neighbor,
I will stop him.
I will not allow people
to be proud and look down on others.

6I will look for trustworthy people
so I can live with them in the land.
Only those who live innocent lives
will be my servants.
7No one who is dishonest will live in my house;
no liars will stay around me.
8Every morning I will destroy the wicked in the land.
I will rid the LORD's city of people who do evil.

A Cry for Help

A prayer of a person who is suffering when he is discouraged and tells the LORD his complaints.

102 LORD, listen to my prayer;
let my cry for help come to you.
2Do not hide from me
in my time of trouble.
Pay attention to me.
When I cry for help, answer me quickly.

3My life is passing away like smoke,
and my bones are burned up with fire.
4My heart is like grass
that has been cut and dried.
I forget to eat.
5Because of my grief,
my skin hangs on my bones.
6I am like a desert owl,
like an owl living among the ruins.
7I lie awake.
I am like a lonely bird on a housetop.
8All day long enemies insult me;
those who make fun of me use my name as a curse.
9I eat ashes for food,
and my tears fall into my drinks.
10Because of your great anger,
you have picked me up and thrown me away.
11My days are like a passing shadow;
I am like dried grass.

12But, LORD, you rule forever,
and your fame goes on and on.
13You will come and have mercy on Jerusalem,
because the time has now come to be kind to her;
the right time has come.
14Your servants love even her stones;
they even care about her dust.
15Nations will fear the name of the LORD,
and all the kings on earth will honor you.

SIDELIGHT: If you repeat yourself too much, just tell people you're making up Hebrew poetry. One characteristic of this poetry—called parallelism—was that two consecutive lines would each say essentially the same thing in a different way. (For example, see Psalm 101:7.)

16The LORD will rebuild Jerusalem;
there his glory will be seen.
17He will answer the prayers of the needy;
he will not reject their prayers.

[18]Write these things for the future
so that people who are not yet born will
praise the LORD.
[19]The LORD looked down from his holy place
above;
from heaven he looked down at the earth.
[20]He heard the moans of the prisoners,
and he freed those sentenced to die.
[21]The name of the LORD will be heard in
Jerusalem;
his praise will be heard there.
[22]People will come together,
and kingdoms will serve the LORD.

[23]God has made me tired of living;
he has cut short my life.
[24]So I said, "My God, do not take me in the
middle of my life.
Your years go on and on.
[25]In the beginning you made the earth,
and your hands made the skies.
[26]They will be destroyed, but you will remain.
They will all wear out like clothes.
And, like clothes, you will change them
and throw them away.
[27]But you never change,
and your life will never end.
[28]Our children will live in your presence,
and their children will remain with you."

Praise to the Lord of Love

Of David.

103 My whole being, praise the LORD;
all my being, praise his holy name.
[2]My whole being, praise the LORD
and do not forget all his kindnesses.
[3]He forgives all my sins
and heals all my diseases.
[4]He saves my life from the grave
and loads me with love and mercy.
[5]He satisfies me with good things
and makes me young again, like the eagle.

[6]The LORD does what is right and fair
for all who are wronged by others.
[7]He showed his ways to Moses
and his deeds to the people of Israel.
[8]The LORD shows mercy and is kind.
He does not become angry quickly, and he
has great love.
[9]He will not always accuse us,
and he will not be angry forever.
[10]He has not punished us as our sins should be
punished;

GOD'S LOVE

Easy to Take for Granted

It's invisible—easy to take for granted.

Your hand will go right through it.

It combines with practically everything, and if it didn't, life couldn't exist. It's a part of hundreds of thousands of things we use daily, and it makes up two-thirds of your body . . . nine-tenths of the oceans . . . one-fifth of the air you breathe.

Try living without it. You can't. Nothing can.

It's invisible. You take it for granted and never think about it because it's everywhere.

You guessed it—it's oxygen.

In many ways, God's love is like oxygen. They're both invisible, and they're both everywhere.

But God's love is even more essential than oxygen for life. The writer of **Psalm 103** knew the importance of God's love for living.

- What phrases in this psalm reflect God's active, aggressive love for us?
- How is God's love alive in the attitudes and actions of people you know?

CONSIDER . . .

- thinking about what God has done in your life and writing two-word sentences combining the noun "He . . ." and an active, descriptive verb, such as "He strengthens" or "He listens."
- choosing three ways you can become more active in showing God's love to others, starting this week.

FOR MORE, SEE . . .

- Genesis 1:26–31 (p. 3)
- Proverbs 3:11–12 (p. 570)
- John 3:16–21 (p. 1062)

he has not repaid us for the evil we have
done.
11As high as the sky is above the earth,
so great is his love for those who respect
him.
12He has taken our sins away from us
as far as the east is from west.
13The LORD has mercy on those who respect
him,
as a father has mercy on his children.
14He knows how we were made;
he remembers that we are dust.

15Human life is like grass;
we grow like a flower in the field.
16After the wind blows, the flower is gone,
and there is no sign of where it was.
17But the LORD's love for those who respect
him
continues forever and ever,
and his goodness continues to their
grandchildren
18and to those who keep his agreement
and who remember to obey his orders.

19The LORD has set his throne in heaven,
and his kingdom rules over everything.
20You who are his angels, praise the LORD.
You are the mighty warriors who do what
he says
and who obey his voice.
21You, his armies, praise the LORD;
you are his servants who do what he
wants.
22Everything the LORD has made
should praise him in all the places he rules.
My whole being, praise the LORD.

Praise to God Who Made the World

104 My whole being, praise the LORD.
LORD my God, you are very great.
You are clothed with glory and majesty;
2 you wear light like a robe.
You stretch out the skies like a tent.
3 You build your room above the clouds.
You make the clouds your chariot,
and you ride on the wings of the wind.
4You make the winds your messengers,
and flames of fire are your servants.

5You built the earth on its foundations
so it can never be moved.
6You covered the earth with oceans;
the water was above the mountains.
7But at your command, the water rushed
away.
When you thundered your orders, it
hurried away.
8The mountains rose; the valleys sank.
The water went to the places you made for
it.
9You set borders for the seas that they cannot
cross,
so water will never cover the earth again.
10You make springs pour into the ravines;
they flow between the mountains.
11They water all the wild animals;
the wild donkeys come there to drink.
12Wild birds make nests by the water;
they sing among the tree branches.
13You water the mountains from above.
The earth is full of the things you made.
14You make the grass for cattle
and vegetables for the people.
You make food grow from the earth.
15You give us wine that makes happy hearts
and olive oil that makes our faces shine.
You give us bread that gives us strength.
16The LORD's trees have plenty of water;
they are the cedars of Lebanon, which he
planted.
17The birds make their nests there;
the stork's home is in the fir trees.
18The high mountains belong to the wild goats.
The rocks are hiding places for the badgers.

19You made the moon to mark the seasons,
and the sun always knows when to set.
20You make it dark, and it becomes night.
Then all the wild animals creep around.
21The lions roar as they attack.
They look to God for food.
22When the sun rises, they leave
and go back to their dens to lie down.
23Then people go to work
and work until evening.

24LORD, you have made many things;
with your wisdom you made them all.
The earth is full of your riches.
25Look at the sea, so big and wide,
with creatures large and small that cannot
be counted.
26Ships travel over the ocean,
and there is the sea monster Leviathan,[d]
which you made to play there.

27All these things depend on you
to give them their food at the right time.
28When you give it to them,
they gather it up.
When you open your hand,
they are filled with good food.
29When you turn away from them,
they become frightened.
When you take away their breath,
they die and turn to dust.
30When you breathe on them,
they are created,

and you make the land new again.

31May the glory of the LORD be forever.
May the LORD enjoy what he has made.
32He just looks at the earth, and it shakes.
He touches the mountains, and they smoke.

33I will sing to the LORD all my life;
I will sing praises to my God as long as I
live.
34May my thoughts please him;
I am happy in the LORD.
35Let sinners be destroyed from the earth,
and let the wicked live no longer.

My whole being, praise the LORD.
Praise the LORD.

God's Love for Israel

105 Give thanks to the LORD and pray
to him.
Tell the nations what he has done.
2Sing to him; sing praises to him.
Tell about all his miracles.[d]
3Be glad that you are his;
let those who seek the LORD be happy.
4Depend on the LORD and his strength;
always go to him for help.
5Remember the miracles he has done;
remember his wonders and his decisions.
6You are descendants[d] of his servant Abraham,
the children of Jacob, his chosen people.
7He is the LORD our God.
His laws are for all the world.

8He will keep his agreement forever;
he will keep his promises always.
9He will keep the agreement he made with
Abraham
and the promise he made to Isaac.
10He made it a law for the people of Jacob;
he made it an agreement with Israel to last
forever.
11The LORD said, "I will give you the land of
Canaan,
and it will belong to you."

12Then God's people were few in number.
They were strangers in the land.
13They went from one nation to another,
from one kingdom to another.
14But the LORD did not let anyone hurt them;
he warned kings not to harm them.
15He said, "Don't touch my chosen people,
and don't harm my prophets."[d]

16God ordered a time of hunger in the land,
and he destroyed all the food.
17Then he sent a man ahead of them—
Joseph, who was sold as a slave.
18They put chains around his feet
and an iron ring around his neck.
19Then the time he had spoken of came,
and the LORD's words proved that Joseph
was right.
20The king of Egypt sent for Joseph and freed
him;
the ruler of the people set him free.
21He made him the master of his house;
Joseph was in charge of his riches.
22He could order the princes as he wished.
He taught the older men to be wise.
23Then his father Israel came to Egypt;
Jacob[n] lived in Egypt.[n]
24The LORD made his people grow in number,
and he made them stronger than their
enemies.
25He caused the Egyptians to hate his people
and to make plans against his servants.
26Then he sent his servant Moses,
and Aaron, whom he had chosen.
27They did many signs among the Egyptians
and worked wonders in Egypt.
28The LORD sent darkness and made the land
dark,
but the Egyptians turned against what he
said.
29So he changed their water into blood
and made their fish die.
30Then their country was filled with frogs,
even in the bedrooms of their rulers.
31The LORD spoke and flies came,
and gnats were everywhere in the country.
32He made hail fall like rain
and sent lightning through their land.
33He struck down their grapevines and fig
trees,
and he destroyed every tree in the country.
34He spoke and grasshoppers came;
the locusts[d] were too many to count.
35They ate all the plants in the land
and everything the earth produced.
36The LORD also killed all the firstborn[d] sons in
the land,
the oldest son of each family.

37Then he brought his people out,
and they carried with them silver and gold.
Not one of his people stumbled.
38The Egyptians were glad when they left,
because the Egyptians were afraid of them.
39The LORD covered them with a cloud
and lit up the night with fire.
40When they asked, he brought them quail

Jacob Also called Israel.
Egypt Literally, "the land of Ham." Also in verse 27. The people in Egypt were descendants of Ham, one of Noah's sons. See Genesis 10:6.

and filled them with bread from heaven.
41God split the rock, and water flowed out;
it ran like a river through the desert.
42He remembered his holy promise
to his servant Abraham.

43So God brought his people out with joy,
his chosen ones with singing.
44He gave them lands of other nations,
so they received what others had worked for.
45This was so they would keep his orders
and obey his teachings.

Praise the LORD!

Israel's Failure to Trust God

106 Praise the LORD!
Thank the LORD because he is good.
His love continues forever.
2No one can tell all the mighty things the LORD has done;
no one can speak all his praise.
3Happy are those who do right,
who do what is fair at all times.

4LORD, remember me when you are kind to your people;
help me when you save them.
5Let me see the good things you do for your chosen people.
Let me be happy along with your happy nation;
let me join your own people in praising you.

6We have sinned just as our ancestors did.
We have done wrong; we have done evil.
7Our ancestors in Egypt
did not learn from your miracles.[d]
They did not remember all your kindnesses,
so they turned against you at the Red Sea.[d]
8But the LORD saved them for his own sake,
to show his great power.
9He commanded the Red Sea, and it dried up.
He led them through the deep sea as if it were a desert.
10He saved them from those who hated them.
He saved them from their enemies,
11and the water covered their foes.
Not one of them escaped.
12Then the people believed what the LORD said,
and they sang praises to him.

13But they quickly forgot what he had done;
they did not wait for his advice.
14They became greedy for food in the desert,
and they tested God there.
15So he gave them what they wanted,
but he also sent a terrible disease among them.

16The people in the camp were jealous of Moses
and of Aaron, the holy priest of the LORD.
17Then the ground opened up and swallowed Dathan
and closed over Abiram's group.
18A fire burned among their followers,
and flames burned up the wicked.

19The people made a gold calf at Mount Sinai
and worshiped a metal statue.
20They exchanged their glorious God
for a statue of a bull that eats grass.
21They forgot the God who saved them,
who had done great things in Egypt,
22who had done miracles in Egypt[n]
and amazing things by the Red Sea.
23So God said he would destroy them.
But Moses, his chosen one, stood before him
and stopped God's anger from destroying them.

24Then they refused to go into the beautiful land of Canaan;
they did not believe what God promised.
25They grumbled in their tents
and did not obey the LORD.
26So he swore to them
that they would die in the desert.
27He said their children would be killed by other nations
and that they would be scattered among other countries.

28They joined in worshiping Baal[d] at Peor
and ate meat that had been sacrificed to lifeless statues.
29They made the LORD angry by what they did,
so many people became sick with a terrible disease.
30But Phinehas prayed to the LORD,
and the disease stopped.
31Phinehas did what was right,
and it will be remembered from now on.

32The people also made the LORD angry at Meribah,
and Moses was in trouble because of them.
33The people turned against the Spirit[d] of God,
so Moses spoke without stopping to think.

34The people did not destroy the other nations
as the LORD had told them to do.
35Instead, they mixed with the other nations

Egypt Literally, "the land of Ham." The people in Egypt were descendants of Ham, one of Noah's sons. See Genesis 10:6.

and learned their customs.
36They worshiped other nations' idols
and were trapped by them.
37They even killed their sons and daughters
as sacrifices to demons.[d]
38They killed innocent people,
their own sons and daughters,
as sacrifices to the idols of Canaan.
So the land was made unholy by their blood.
39The people became unholy by their sins;
they were unfaithful to God in what they did.

40So the LORD became angry with his people
and hated his own children.
41He handed them over to other nations
and let their enemies rule over them.
42Their enemies were cruel to them
and kept them under their power.
43The LORD saved his people many times,
but they continued to turn against him.
So they became even more wicked.

44But God saw their misery
when he heard their cry.
45He remembered his agreement with them,
and he felt sorry for them because of his great love.
46He caused them to be pitied
by those who held them captive.

47LORD our God, save us
and bring us back from other nations.
Then we will thank you
and will gladly praise you.

48Praise the LORD, the God of Israel.
He always was and always will be.
Let all the people say, "Amen!"

Praise the LORD!

Book 5

God Saves from Many Dangers

107 Thank the LORD because he is good.
His love continues forever.
2That is what those whom the LORD has saved should say.
He has saved them from the enemy
3and has gathered them from other lands,
from east and west, north and south.

4Some people had wandered in the desert lands.
They found no city in which to live.
5They were hungry and thirsty,
and they were discouraged.
6In their misery they cried out to the LORD,
and he saved them from their troubles.
7He led them on a straight road
to a city where they could live.
8Let them give thanks to the LORD for his love
and for the miracles[d] he does for people.
9He satisfies the thirsty
and fills up the hungry.

10Some sat in gloom and darkness;
they were prisoners suffering in chains.
11They had turned against the words of God
and had refused the advice of God Most High.
12So he broke their pride by hard work.
They stumbled, and no one helped.
13In their misery they cried out to the LORD,
and he saved them from their troubles.
14He brought them out of their gloom and darkness
and broke their chains.
15Let them give thanks to the LORD for his love
and for the miracles he does for people.
16He breaks down bronze gates
and cuts apart iron bars.

17Some fools turned against God
and suffered for the evil they did.
18They refused to eat anything,
so they almost died.
19In their misery they cried out to the LORD,
and he saved them from their troubles.
20God gave the command and healed them,
so they were saved from dying.
21Let them give thanks to the LORD for his love
and for the miracles he does for people.
22Let them offer sacrifices to thank him.
With joy they should tell what he has done.

23Others went out to sea in ships
and did business on the great oceans.
24They saw what the LORD could do,
the miracles he did in the deep oceans.
25He spoke, and a storm came up,
which blew up high waves.
26The ships were tossed as high as the sky and fell low to the depths.
The storm was so bad that they lost their courage.
27They stumbled and fell like people who were drunk.
They did not know what to do.
28In their misery they cried out to the LORD,
and he saved them from their troubles.
29He stilled the storm
and calmed the waves.
30They were happy that it was quiet,
and God guided them to the port they wanted.
31Let them give thanks to the LORD for his love
and for the miracles he does for people.

[32]Let them praise his greatness in the meeting
of the people;
let them praise him in the meeting of the
older leaders.

[33]He changed rivers into a desert
and springs of water into dry ground.
[34]He made fertile land salty,
because the people there did evil.
[35]He changed the desert into pools of water
and dry ground into springs of water.
[36]He had the hungry settle there
so they could build a city in which to live.
[37]They planted seeds in the fields and
vineyards,
and they had a good harvest.
[38]God blessed them, and they grew in number.
Their cattle did not become fewer.

[39]Because of disaster, troubles, and sadness,
their families grew smaller and weaker.
[40]He showed he was displeased with their
leaders
and made them wander in a pathless
desert.
[41]But he lifted the poor out of their suffering
and made their families grow like flocks of
sheep.
[42]Good people see this and are happy,
but the wicked say nothing.

[43]Whoever is wise will remember these things
and will think about the love of the LORD.

A Prayer for Victory

A song. A psalm of David.

108 God, my heart is steady.
I will sing and praise you with all
my being.
[2]Wake up, harp and lyre![d]
I will wake up the dawn.
[3]LORD, I will praise you among the nations;
I will sing songs of praise about you to all
the nations.
[4]Your great love reaches to the skies,
your truth to the heavens.
[5]God, you are supreme above the skies.
Let your glory be over all the earth.

[6]Answer us and save us by your power
so the people you love will be rescued.
[7]God has said from his Temple,[d]
"When I win, I will divide Shechem
and measure off the Valley of Succoth.
[8]Gilead and Manasseh are mine.
Ephraim is like my helmet.
Judah holds my royal scepter.[d]
[9]Moab is like my washbowl.
I throw my sandals at Edom.
I shout at Philistia."
[10]Who will bring me to the strong, walled
city?
Who will lead me to Edom?
[11]God, surely you have rejected us;
you do not go out with our armies.
[12]Help us fight the enemy.
Human help is useless,
[13]but we can win with God's help.
He will defeat our enemies.

SIDELIGHT: Not all the psalms are positive and upbeat. Psalm 109, for example, sounds downright nasty. Verses 6–20 are written in the form of ancient Near Eastern curses, which were said to try to speed justice upon enemies and guilty people. A curse was intended to go into effect only if the person was guilty (see Numbers 5:18–28, p. 131, and Deuteronomy 27:15–26, p. 184).

A Prayer Against an Enemy

For the director of music. A psalm of David.

109 God, I praise you.
Do not be silent.
[2]Wicked people and liars have spoken against
me;
they have told lies about me.
[3]They have said hateful things about me
and attack me for no reason.
[4]They attacked me, even though I loved them
and prayed for them.
[5]I was good to them, but they repay me with
evil.
I loved them, but they hate me in return.

[6]They say about me, "Have an evil person
work against him,
and let an accuser stand against him.
[7]When he is judged, let him be found guilty,
and let even his prayers show his guilt.
[8]Let his life be cut short,
and let another man replace him as leader.
[9]Let his children become orphans
and his wife a widow.
[10]Make his children wander around, begging
for food.
Let them be forced out of the ruins in
which they live.
[11]Let the people to whom he owes money take
everything he owns,
and let strangers steal everything he has
worked for.
[12]Let no one show him love
or have mercy on his orphaned children.
[13]Let all his descendants[d] die

and be forgotten by those who live after
him.
14LORD, remember how wicked his ancestors
were,
and don't let the sins of his mother be
wiped out.
15LORD, always remember their sins.
Then make people forget about them
completely.

16"He did not remember to be loving.
He hurt the poor, the needy, and those
who were sad
until they were nearly dead.
17He loved to put curses on others,
so let those same curses fall on him.
He did not like to bless others,
so do not let good things happen to him.
18He cursed others as often as he wore
clothes.
Cursing others filled his body and his
life,
like drinking water and using olive oil.
19So let curses cover him like clothes
and wrap around him like a belt."
20May the LORD do these things to those who
accuse me,
to those who speak evil against me.

21But you, Lord GOD,
be kind to me so others will know you are
good.
Because your love is good, save me.
22I am poor and helpless
and very sad.
23I am dying like an evening shadow;
I am shaken off like a locust.[d]
24My knees are weak from hunger,
and I have grown thin.
25My enemies insult me;
they look at me and shake their heads.

26LORD my God, help me;
because you are loving, save me.
27Then they will know that your power has
done this;
they will know that you have done it,
LORD.
28They may curse me, but you bless me.
They may attack me, but they will be
disgraced.
Then I, your servant, will be glad.
29Let those who accuse me be disgraced
and covered with shame like a coat.
30I will thank the LORD very much;
I will praise him in front of many people.
31He defends the helpless
and saves them from those who accuse
them.

The Lord Appoints a King

A psalm of David.

110 The LORD said to my Lord,
"Sit by me at my right side
until I put your enemies under your
control."
2The LORD will enlarge your kingdom beyond
Jerusalem,
and you will rule over your enemies.
3Your people will join you on your day of
battle.
You have been dressed in holiness from
birth;
you have the freshness of a child.

4The LORD has made a promise
and will not change his mind.
He said, "You are a priest forever,
a priest like Melchizedek."

5The Lord is beside you to help you.
When he becomes angry, he will crush
kings.
6He will judge those nations, filling them with
dead bodies;
he will defeat rulers all over the world.
7The king will drink from the brook on the
way.
Then he will be strengthened.

Praise the Lord's Goodness

111 Praise the LORD!
I will thank the LORD with all my
heart
in the meeting of his good people.
2The LORD does great things;
those who enjoy them seek them.
3What he does is glorious and splendid,
and his goodness continues forever.
4His miracles[d] are unforgettable.
The LORD is kind and merciful.
5He gives food to those who fear him.
He remembers his agreement forever.
6He has shown his people his power
when he gave them the lands of other
nations.

7Everything he does is good and fair;
all his orders can be trusted.
8They will continue forever.
They were made true and right.
9He sets his people free.
He made his agreement everlasting.
He is holy and wonderful.

10Wisdom begins with respect for the LORD;
those who obey his orders have good
understanding.
He should be praised forever.

Honest People Are Blessed

112 Praise the LORD!

Happy are those who respect the
LORD,
who want what he commands.
2Their descendants[d] will be powerful in the
land;
the children of honest people will be
blessed.
3Their houses will be full of wealth and riches,
and their goodness will continue forever.
4A light shines in the dark for honest people,
for those who are merciful and kind and
good.
5It is good to be merciful and generous.
Those who are fair in their business
6will never be defeated.
Good people will always be remembered.
7They won't be afraid of bad news;
their hearts are steady because they trust
the LORD.
8They are confident and will not be afraid;
they will look down on their enemies.
9They give freely to the poor.
The things they do are right and will
continue forever.
They will be given great honor.
10The wicked will see this and become angry;
they will grind their teeth in anger and
then disappear.
The wishes of the wicked will come to
nothing.

SIDELIGHT: When Jesus and his disciples sang on the night Judas betrayed Jesus (Matthew 26:30, p. 957), they probably sang Psalms 113—114 or Psalms 115—118. These songs were customarily sung during the Passover, which was being celebrated at the time.

Praise for the Lord's Kindness

113 Praise the LORD!

Praise him, you servants of the
LORD;
praise the name of the LORD.
2The LORD's name should be praised
now and forever.
3The LORD's name should be praised
from where the sun rises to where it sets.
4The LORD is supreme over all the nations;
his glory reaches to the skies.

HONESTY

Slow But Sure

Almost everyone cheated in Mrs. Yount's algebra class. It was just so incredibly easy. The three class "brains" were generous with whispered answers on tests and would lend homework papers for copying. Mrs. Yount didn't seem to catch on, or else she ignored it, not knowing how to put a stop to it.

Chuck Cameron didn't believe in cheating, though. He plugged along, doing his own work, pulling B's or B-'s. That's why everybody was surprised when he got the best math college entrance test scores of anybody at Marshall High—even better than the "brains"—and was accepted into a top-rate college.

"How did you do it, Chuck?" asked one of the brains from algebra.

"I just knew the stuff," Chuck said with a smile. "I learned it, slowly but surely."

Honesty carries its own rewards today, just as it did in ancient times. **Psalm 112** talks about many of those rewards.

- How would the phrase "fair in their business" in verse 5 apply to Chuck?
- What are ways honesty can keep you "steady" (verse 7) as you go about your business at school, work, and home?

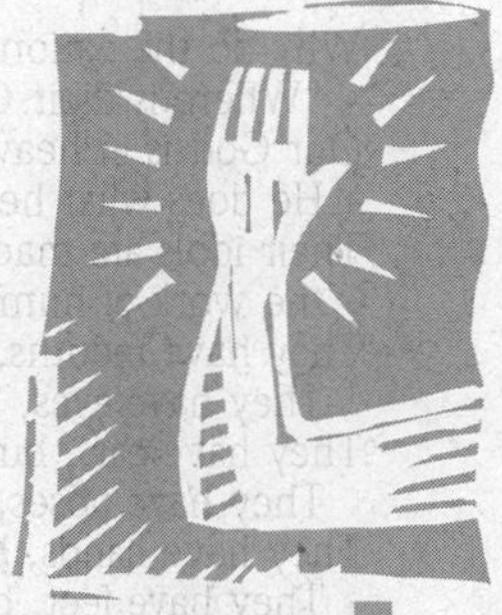

CONSIDER . . .

- rewriting this psalm using your own words and applying it to your own circumstances.
- committing to God never to cheat in school.

FOR MORE, SEE . . .

- 1 Samuel 12:1–5 (p. 254)
- Isaiah 33:15–17 (p. 649)
- Colossians 3:9–10 (p. 1241)

5No one is like the LORD our God,
who rules from heaven,
6who bends down to look
at the skies and the earth.
7The LORD lifts the poor from the dirt
and takes the helpless from the ashes.
8He seats them with princes,
the princes of his people.
9He gives children to the woman who has none
and makes her a happy mother.

Praise the LORD!

God Brought Israel from Egypt

114 When the Israelites went out of Egypt,
the people of Jacob left that foreign country.
2Then Judah became God's holy place;
Israel became the land he ruled.

3The Red Sea[d] looked and ran away;
the Jordan River turned back.
4The mountains danced like sheep
and the hills like little lambs.
5Sea, why did you run away?
Jordan, why did you turn back?
6Mountains, why did you dance like sheep?
Hills, why did you dance like little lambs?

7Earth, shake with fear before the Lord,
before the God of Jacob.
8He turned a rock into a pool of water,
a hard rock into a spring of water.

The One True God

115 It does not belong to us, LORD.
The glory belongs to you
because of your love and loyalty.

2Why do the nations ask,
"Where is their God?"
3Our God is in heaven.
He does what he pleases.
4Their idols are made of silver and gold,
the work of human hands.
5They have mouths, but they cannot speak.
They have eyes, but they cannot see.
6They have ears, but they cannot hear.
They have noses, but they cannot smell.
7They have hands, but they cannot feel.
They have feet, but they cannot walk.
No sounds come from their throats.
8People who make idols will be like them,
and so will those who trust them.

9Family of Israel, trust the LORD;
he is your helper and your protection.
10Family of Aaron, trust the LORD;
he is your helper and your protection.
11You who respect the LORD should trust him;
he is your helper and your protection.

12The LORD remembers us and will bless us.
He will bless the family of Israel;
he will bless the family of Aaron.
13The LORD will bless those who respect him,
from the smallest to the greatest.

14May the LORD give you success,
and may he give you and your children success.
15May you be blessed by the LORD,
who made heaven and earth.
16Heaven belongs to the LORD,
but he gave the earth to people.
17Dead people do not praise the LORD;
those in the grave are silent.
18But we will praise the LORD
now and forever.

Praise the LORD!

Thanksgiving for Escaping Death

116 I love the LORD,
because he listens to my prayers for help.
2He paid attention to me,
so I will call to him for help as long as I live.

3The ropes of death bound me,
and the fear of the grave took hold of me.
I was troubled and sad.
4Then I called out the name of the LORD.
I said, "Please, LORD, save me!"

5The LORD is kind and does what is right;
our God is merciful.
6The LORD watches over the foolish;
when I was helpless, he saved me.
7I said to myself, "Relax,
because the LORD takes care of you."
8LORD, you saved me from death.
You stopped my eyes from crying;
you kept me from being defeated.
9So I will walk with the LORD
in the land of the living.
10I believed, so I said,
"I am completely ruined."
11In my distress I said,
"All people are liars."

12What can I give the LORD
for all the good things he has given to me?
13I will lift up the cup of salvation,
and I will pray to the LORD.
14I will give the LORD what I promised
in front of all his people.

15The death of one that belongs to the LORD
is precious in his sight.

16LORD, I am your servant;
I am your servant and the son of your female servant.
You have freed me from my chains.
17I will give you an offering to show thanks to you,
and I will pray to the LORD.
18I will give the LORD what I promised
in front of all his people,
19in the Temple[d] courtyards
in Jerusalem.

Praise the LORD!

SIDELIGHT: The shortest chapter in the Bible—Psalm 117—is long on praise. The psalmist encourages the whole world to make music to God, which would make the Guinness Book of World Records for the Largest Community Sing-a-Long.

A Hymn of Praise

117 All you nations, praise the LORD.
All you people, praise him
2because the LORD loves us very much,
and his truth is everlasting.

Praise the LORD!

Thanksgiving for Victory

118 Thank the LORD because he is good.
His love continues forever.
2Let the people of Israel say,
"His love continues forever."
3Let the family of Aaron say,
"His love continues forever."
4Let those who respect the LORD say,
"His love continues forever."

5I was in trouble, so I called to the LORD.
The LORD answered me and set me free.
6I will not be afraid, because the LORD is with me.

THANKFULNESS

Thanks, But No Thanks

Kyle Pierce is a polite guy. He's always careful to say "no, thank you" when he turns down the supper his mother makes, choosing instead a few fast-food tacos.

Kyle isn't interested in fitness, but when someone invites him to jog or shoot some baskets he always remembers his manners. "No, thanks," he says.

Recently, his girlfriend, Cora, got the same polite response when she urged him to attend a seminar to help him kick his smoking habit.

"Not interested," he said, then smiled. "But thanks."

"Don't you dare use that word with me!" she fumed.

"What word?" Kyle asked, innocently.

"The word 'thanks'! God's given you good health, and you choose to blow it away with lousy nutrition, no exercise, and nicotine. You're obviously not thankful at all!"

Cora's outburst made Kyle stop, think, and begin to make changes. For instance, he and Cora have taken up playing tennis together. And when someone offers him a cigarette now, he declines—politely, of course.

The writer of **Psalm 116** was also in a potentially life-threatening situation, and God saved him. Read the psalmist's heart-felt words to discover the kind of thankful heart God wants.

- How would you use this psalm to advise Kyle about his attitude and actions?
- In what areas of your own life are you making choices that say "thanks, but no thanks," to God?

CONSIDER . . .

- listing all the things you're thankful for.
- keeping track of all your "no thank you's" for a week and seeing what they say about your lifestyle choices.

FOR MORE, SEE

- 1 Chronicles 29:10–20 (p. 384)
- Colossians 3:12–17 (p. 1232)
- 1 Thessalonians 5:16–18 (p. 1249)

People can't do anything to me.
7The LORD is with me to help me,
so I will see my enemies defeated.
8It is better to trust the LORD
than to trust people.
9It is better to trust the LORD
than to trust princes.

10All the nations surrounded me,
but I defeated them in the name of the LORD.
11They surrounded me on every side,
but with the LORD's power I defeated them.
12They surrounded me like a swarm of bees,
but they died as quickly as thorns burn.
By the LORD's power, I defeated them.
13They chased me until I was almost defeated,
but the LORD helped me.
14The LORD gives me strength and a song.
He has saved me.
15Shouts of joy and victory
come from the tents of those who do right:
"The LORD has done powerful things."
16The power of the LORD has won the victory;
with his power the LORD has done mighty things.

17I will not die, but live,
and I will tell what the LORD has done.
18The LORD has taught me a hard lesson,
but he did not let me die.

19Open for me the Temple[d] gates.
Then I will come in and thank the LORD.
20This is the LORD's gate;
only those who are good may enter through it.
21LORD, I thank you for answering me.
You have saved me.

22The stone that the builders rejected
became the cornerstone.[d]
23The LORD did this,
and it is wonderful to us.
24This is the day that the LORD has made.
Let us rejoice and be glad today!

25Please, LORD, save us;
please, LORD, give us success.
26God bless the one who comes in the name of the LORD.
We bless all of you from the Temple of the LORD.
27The LORD is God,
and he has shown kindness to us.
With branches in your hands, join the feast.
Come to the corners of the altar.

28You are my God, and I will thank you;
you are my God, and I will praise your greatness.

29Thank the LORD because he is good.
His love continues forever.

SIDELIGHT: "Ah, your eyes, your lips, your regulations!" You've probably never written a love song to a book of laws, but the writer of Psalm 119 did. The longest chapter in the Bible serenades God's commandments—probably as written in Genesis through Deuteronomy.

The Word of God

119 Happy are those who live pure lives,
who follow the LORD's teachings.
2Happy are those who keep his rules,
who try to obey him with their whole heart.
3They don't do what is wrong;
they follow his ways.
4LORD, you gave your orders
to be obeyed completely.
5I wish I were more loyal
in obeying your demands.
6Then I would not be ashamed
when I study your commands.
7When I learned that your laws are fair,
I praised you with an honest heart.
8I will obey your demands,
so please don't ever leave me.

9How can a young person live a pure life?
By obeying your word.
10With all my heart I try to obey you.
Don't let me break your commands.
11I have taken your words to heart
so I would not sin against you.
12LORD, you should be praised.
Teach me your demands.
13My lips will tell about
all the laws you have spoken.
14I enjoy living by your rules
as people enjoy great riches.
15I think about your orders
and study your ways.
16I enjoy obeying your demands,
and I will not forget your word.

17Do good to me, your servant, so I can live,
so I can obey your word.
18Open my eyes to see
the miracles[d] in your teachings.
19I am a stranger on earth.
Do not hide your commands from me.
20I wear myself out with desire
for your laws all the time.
21You scold proud people;

those who ignore your commands are
cursed.
22Don't let me be insulted and hated
because I keep your rules.
23Even if princes speak against me,
I, your servant, will think about your
demands.
24Your rules give me pleasure;
they give me good advice.

25I am about to die.
Give me life, as you have promised.
26I told you about my life, and you answered
me.
Teach me your demands.
27Help me understand your orders.
Then I will think about your miracles.
28I am sad and tired.
Make me strong again as you have
promised.
29Don't let me be dishonest;
have mercy on me by helping me obey
your teachings.
30I have chosen the way of truth;
I have obeyed your laws.
31I hold on to your rules.
LORD, do not let me be disgraced.
32I will quickly obey your commands,
because you have made me happy.

33LORD, teach me your demands,
and I will keep them until the end.
34Help me understand, so I can keep your
teachings,
obeying them with all my heart.
35Lead me in the path of your commands,
because that makes me happy.
36Make me want to keep your rules
instead of wishing for riches.
37Keep me from looking at worthless things.
Let me live by your word.
38Keep your promise to me, your servant,
so you will be respected.
39Take away the shame I fear,
because your laws are good.
40How I want to follow your orders.
Give me life because of your goodness.

41LORD, show me your love,
and save me as you have promised.
42I have an answer for people who insult me,
because I trust what you say.
43Never keep me from speaking your truth,
because I depend on your fair laws.
44I will obey your teachings
forever and ever.
45So I will live in freedom,
because I want to follow your orders.
46I will discuss your rules with kings

FOLLOWING GOD

To Live in Freedom

Reward posters offered large sums of money for her capture, dead or alive. Though she was barely five feet tall and subject to fainting spells because of a head injury inflicted by an owner when she was younger, many regarded her as extremely dangerous. Some even called her "the devil."

But others, many others, called her "Moses." She had, after all, led more than two hundred men, women, and children out of slavery to freedom in Canada via the Underground Railroad.

Her real name was Harriet Tubman, and in the years just before America's Civil War in the 1800s, she risked her life repeatedly to return to the South and guide escaped slaves to freedom in the North.

In **Psalm 119:33–48**, the psalmist yearns for guidance to "live in freedom," as so many slaves did long ago. As the slaves depended on Harriet Tubman, the psalmist depended on God to show him the way.

- Which verses of the passage would Harriet Tubman have identified with?
- According to this passage, how can God set you free?

CONSIDER . . .

- writing what total freedom means to you and what you think God would say it means.
- becoming a "Moses" to someone else by helping him or her overcome an enslaving problem, such as drug abuse or a negative attitude.

FOR MORE, SEE . . .

- Joshua 1:8–9 (p. 195)
- John 8:34–47 (p. 1072)
- Romans 6:15–23 (p. 1147)

and will not be ashamed.
[47]I enjoy obeying your commands,
which I love.
[48]I praise your commands, which I love,
and I think about your demands.

[49]Remember your promise to me, your servant;
it gives me hope.
[50]When I suffer, this comforts me:
Your promise gives me life.
[51]Proud people always make fun of me,
but I do not reject your teachings.
[52]I remember your laws from long ago,
and they comfort me, LORD.
[53]I become angry with wicked people
who do not keep your teachings.
[54]I sing about your demands
wherever I live.
[55]LORD, I remember you at night,
and I will obey your teachings.
[56]This is what I do:
I follow your orders.

[57]LORD, you are my share in life;
I have promised to obey your words.
[58]I prayed to you with all my heart.
Have mercy on me as you have promised.
[59]I thought about my life,
and I decided to follow your rules.
[60]I hurried and did not wait
to obey your commands.
[61]Wicked people have tied me up,
but I have not forgotten your teachings.
[62]In the middle of the night, I get up to thank
you
because your laws are right.
[63]I am a friend to everyone who fears you,
to anyone who obeys your orders.
[64]LORD, your love fills the earth.
Teach me your demands.

[65]You have done good things for your servant,
as you have promised, LORD.
[66]Teach me wisdom and knowledge
because I trust your commands.
[67]Before I suffered, I did wrong,
but now I obey your word.
[68]You are good, and you do what is good.
Teach me your demands.
[69]Proud people have made up lies about me,
but I will follow your orders with all my
heart.
[70]Those people have no feelings,
but I love your teachings.
[71]It was good for me to suffer
so I would learn your demands.
[72]Your teachings are worth more to me
than thousands of pieces of gold and silver.

[73]You made me and formed me with your
hands.
Give me understanding so I can learn your
commands.
[74]Let those who respect you rejoice when they
see me,
because I put my hope in your word.
[75]LORD, I know that your laws are right
and that it was right for you to punish me.
[76]Comfort me with your love,
as you promised me, your servant.
[77]Have mercy on me so that I may live.
I love your teachings.
[78]Make proud people ashamed because they
lied about me.
But I will think about your orders.
[79]Let those who respect you return to me,
those who know your rules.
[80]Let me obey your demands perfectly
so I will not be ashamed.

[81]I am weak from waiting for you to save me,
but I hope in your word.
[82]My eyes are tired from looking for your
promise.
When will you comfort me?
[83]Even though I am like a wine bag going up
in smoke,
I do not forget your demands.
[84]How long will I live?
When will you judge those who are hurting
me?
[85]Proud people have dug pits to trap me.
They have nothing to do with your
teachings.
[86]All of your commands can be trusted.
Liars are hurting me. Help me!
[87]They have almost put me in the grave,
but I have not rejected your orders.
[88]Give me life by your love
so I can obey your rules.

[89]LORD, your word is everlasting;
it continues forever in heaven.
[90]Your loyalty will go on and on;
you made the earth, and it still stands.
[91]All things continue to this day because of
your laws,
because all things serve you.
[92]If I had not loved your teachings,
I would have died from my sufferings.
[93]I will never forget your orders,
because you have given me life by them.
[94]I am yours. Save me.
I want to obey your orders.
[95]Wicked people are waiting to destroy me,
but I will think about your rules.
[96]Everything I see has its limits,
but your commands have none.

[97]How I love your teachings!
I think about them all day long.

98Your commands make me wiser than my
enemies,
because they are mine forever.
99I am wiser than all my teachers,
because I think about your rules.
100I have more understanding than the older
leaders,
because I follow your orders.
101I have avoided every evil way
so I could obey your word.
102I haven't walked away from your laws,
because you yourself are my teacher.
103Your promises are sweet to me,
sweeter than honey in my mouth!
104Your orders give me understanding,
so I hate lying ways.

105Your word is like a lamp for my feet
and a light for my path.
106I will do what I have promised
and obey your fair laws.
107I have suffered for a long time.
LORD, give me life by your word.
108LORD, accept my willing praise
and teach me your laws.
109My life is always in danger,
but I haven't forgotten your teachings.
110Wicked people have set a trap for me,
but I haven't strayed from your orders.
111I will follow your rules forever,
because they make me happy.
112I will try to do what you demand
forever, until the end.

113I hate disloyal people,
but I love your teachings.
114You are my hiding place and my shield;
I hope in your word.
115Get away from me, you who do evil,
so I can keep my God's commands.
116Support me as you promised so I can live.
Don't let me be embarrassed because of my
hopes.
117Help me, and I will be saved.
I will always respect your demands.
118You reject those who ignore your demands,
because their lies mislead them.
119You throw away the wicked of the world
like trash.
So I will love your rules.
120I shake in fear of you;
I respect your laws.

121I have done what is fair and right.
Don't leave me to those who wrong me.
122Promise that you will help me, your servant.
Don't let proud people wrong me.
123My eyes are tired from looking for your
salvation
and for your good promise.
124Show your love to me, your servant,
and teach me your demands.
125I am your servant. Give me wisdom
so I can understand your rules.
126LORD, it is time for you to do something,
because people have disobeyed your
teachings.
127I love your commands
more than the purest gold.
128I respect all your orders,
so I hate lying ways.

129Your rules are wonderful.
That is why I keep them.
130Learning your words gives wisdom
and understanding for the foolish.
131I am nearly out of breath.
I really want to learn your commands.
132Look at me and have mercy on me
as you do for those who love you.
133Guide my steps as you promised;
don't let any sin control me.
134Save me from harmful people
so I can obey your orders.
135Show your kindness to me, your servant.
Teach me your demands.
136Tears stream from my eyes,
because people do not obey your teachings.

137LORD, you do what is right,
and your laws are fair.
138The rules you commanded are right
and completely trustworthy.
139I am so upset I am worn out,
because my enemies have forgotten your
words.
140Your promises are proven,
so I, your servant, love them.
141I am unimportant and hated,
but I have not forgotten your orders.
142Your goodness continues forever,
and your teachings are true.
143I have had troubles and misery,
but I love your commands.
144Your rules are always good.
Help me understand so I can live.

145LORD, I call to you with all my heart.
Answer me, and I will keep your demands.
146I call to you.
Save me so I can obey your rules.
147I wake up early in the morning and cry out.
I hope in your word.
148I stay awake all night
so I can think about your promises.
149Listen to me because of your love;
LORD, give me life by your laws.
150Those who love evil are near,
but they are far from your teachings.

151But, LORD, you are also near,
and all your commands are true.
152Long ago I learned from your rules
that you made them to continue forever.

153See my suffering and rescue me,
because I have not forgotten your
teachings.
154Argue my case and save me.
Let me live by your promises.
155Wicked people are far from being saved,
because they do not want your demands.
156LORD, you are very kind;
give me life by your laws.
157Many enemies are after me,
but I have not rejected your rules.
158I see those traitors, and I hate them,
because they do not obey what you
say.
159See how I love your orders.
LORD, give me life by your love.
160Your words are true from the start,
and all your laws will be fair forever.

161Leaders attack me for no reason,
but I fear your law in my heart.
162I am as happy over your promises
as if I had found a great treasure.
163I hate and despise lies,
but I love your teachings.
164Seven times a day I praise you
for your fair laws.
165Those who love your teachings will find true
peace,
and nothing will defeat them.
166I am waiting for you to save me, LORD.
I will obey your commands.
167I obey your rules,
and I love them very much.
168I obey your orders and rules,
because you know everything I do.

169Hear my cry to you, LORD.
Let your word help me understand.
170Listen to my prayer;
save me as you promised.
171Let me speak your praise,
because you have taught me your demands.
172Let me sing about your promises,
because all your commands are fair.
173Give me your helping hand,
because I have chosen your commands.
174I want you to save me, LORD.
I love your teachings.
175Let me live so I can praise you,
and let your laws help me.
176I have wandered like a lost sheep.
Look for your servant, because I have not
forgotten your commands.

A Prayer of Someone Far from Home

A psalm for going up to worship.

120 When I was in trouble, I called to
the LORD,
and he answered me.
2LORD, save me from liars
and from those who plan evil.

3You who plan evil, what will God do to you?
How will he punish you?
4He will punish you with the sharp arrows of
a warrior
and with burning coals of wood.

5How terrible it is for me to live in the land of
Meshech,
to live among the people of Kedar.
6I have lived too long
with people who hate peace.
7When I talk peace,
they want war.

The Lord Guards His People

A song for going up to worship.

121 I look up to the hills,
but where does my help come
from?
2My help comes from the LORD,
who made heaven and earth.

3He will not let you be defeated.
He who guards you never sleeps.
4He who guards Israel
never rests or sleeps.
5The LORD guards you.
The LORD is the shade that protects you
from the sun.
6The sun cannot hurt you during the day,
and the moon cannot hurt you at night.
7The LORD will protect you from all dangers;
he will guard your life.
8The LORD will guard you as you come and
go,
both now and forever.

Happy People in Jerusalem

A song for going up to worship. Of David.

122 I was happy when they said to
me,
"Let's go to the Temple[d] of the LORD."
2Jerusalem, we are standing
at your gates.

3Jerusalem is built as a city
with the buildings close together.
4The tribes[d] go up there,
the tribes who belong to the LORD.

It is the rule in Israel
to praise the LORD at Jerusalem.
5There the descendants[d] of David
set their thrones to judge the people.

6Pray for peace in Jerusalem:
"May those who love her be safe.
7May there be peace within her walls
and safety within her strong towers."
8To help my relatives and friends,
I say, "Let Jerusalem have peace."
9For the sake of the Temple of the LORD our God,
I wish good for her.

A Prayer for Mercy

A song for going up to worship.

123 LORD, I look upward to you,
you who live in heaven.
2Slaves depend on their masters,
and a female servant depends on her mistress.
In the same way, we depend on the LORD our God;
we wait for him to show us mercy.

3Have mercy on us, LORD. Have mercy on us,
because we have been insulted.
4We have suffered many insults from lazy people
and much cruelty from the proud.

The Lord Saves His People

A song for going up to worship. Of David.

124 What if the LORD had not been on our side?
(Let Israel repeat this.)
2What if the LORD had not been on our side
when we were attacked?
3When they were angry with us,
they would have swallowed us alive.
4They would have been like a flood drowning us;
they would have poured over us like a river.
5 They would have swept us away like a mighty stream.

6Praise the LORD,
who did not let them chew us up.
7We escaped like a bird
from the hunter's trap.
The trap broke,
and we escaped.
8Our help comes from the LORD,
who made heaven and earth.

God Protects Those Who Trust Him

A song for going up to worship.

125 Those who trust the LORD are like Mount Zion,[d]
which sits unmoved forever.
2As the mountains surround Jerusalem,
the LORD surrounds his people
now and forever.

3The wicked will not rule
over those who do right.
If they did, the people who do right
might use their power to do evil.

4LORD, be good to those who are good,
whose hearts are honest.
5But, LORD, when you remove those who do evil,
also remove those who stop following you.

Let there be peace in Israel.

Lord, Bring Your People Back

A song for going up to worship.

126 When the LORD brought the prisoners back to Jerusalem,
it seemed as if we were dreaming.
2Then we were filled with laughter,
and we sang happy songs.
Then the other nations said,
"The LORD has done great things for them."
3The LORD has done great things for us,
and we are very glad.

4LORD, return our prisoners again,
as you bring streams to the desert.
5Those who cry as they plant crops
will sing at harvest time.
6Those who cry
as they carry out the seeds
will return singing
and carrying bundles of grain.

All Good Things Come from God

A song for going up to worship. Of Solomon.

127 If the LORD doesn't build the house,
the builders are working for nothing.
If the LORD doesn't guard the city,
the guards are watching for nothing.
2It is no use for you to get up early
and stay up late,
working for a living.
The LORD gives sleep to those he loves.
3Children are a gift from the LORD;
babies are a reward.
4Children who are born to a young man
are like arrows in the hand of a warrior.

5Happy is the man
who has his bag full of arrows.
They will not be defeated
when they fight their enemies at the city gate.

The Happy Home

A song for going up to worship.

128 Happy are those who respect the LORD
and obey him.
2You will enjoy what you work for,
and you will be blessed with good things.
3Your wife will give you many children,
like a vine that produces much fruit.
Your children will bring you much good,
like olive branches that produce many olives.
4This is how the man who respects the LORD
will be blessed.
5May the LORD bless you from Mount Zion;[d]
may you enjoy the good things of Jerusalem
all your life.
6May you see your grandchildren.

Let there be peace in Israel.

A Prayer Against the Enemies

A song for going up to worship.

129 They have treated me badly all my life.
(Let Israel repeat this.)
2They have treated me badly all my life,
but they have not defeated me.
3Like farmers plowing, they plowed over my back,
making long wounds.
4But the LORD does what is right;
he has set me free from those wicked people.
5Let those who hate Jerusalem
be turned back in shame.
6Let them be like the grass on the roof
that dries up before it has grown.

FAMILY

A Father's Love

"Where to first: burgers or the mall?" Jo Carasco called to Rosa Martinez over the music on the radio.

"Let's go to Fast Jack's for burgers!" Rosa called back. "It'll be crawling with cute guys."

They both laughed as Jo looked down to turn the radio up a notch. That's the last thing she remembers clearly—before the spin and the sickening jolt as the car turned on its side and then slammed to a stop against a concrete divider.

"I saw the stop sign, but it was too late to stop," Jo remembers. "When Rosa and I crawled out my window and I knew we were both okay, my next thought was, Dad will kill us! The hardest thing I ever had to do was call him from the police station to tell him I had just totaled his car."

But her father didn't even ask for details about the car. Over and over, while Jo clutched the phone and sobbed, he only asked for assurance that she and Rosa were okay.

"How can he love me like that?" she still asks today, four years later. "I'll tell you one thing. That love convinced me to drive differently. I try to live up to it."

Jo's father cared for his family. God cares about families too. Read **Psalm 127** to discover God's unselfish, protective love for families.

- According to verse 1, what's the danger of trying to build a family without God's guidance?
- How can you help make God a more prominent part of your family?

CONSIDER . . .

- stopping activities in your life that make your parents worry.
- writing and signing an agreement with your parents that makes God the central focus of your family.

FOR MORE, SEE . . .

- Joshua 24:14–15 (p. 214)
- 2 Corinthians 6:14–18 (p. 1199)
- Ephesians 5:21—6:4 (p. 1225)

7There is not enough of it to fill a hand
or to make into a bundle to fill one's arms.
8Let those who pass by them not say,
"May the LORD bless you.
We bless you by the power of the
LORD."

A Prayer for Mercy

A song for going up to worship.

130 LORD, I am in great trouble,
so I call out to you.
2Lord, hear my voice;
listen to my prayer for help.
3LORD, if you punished people for all their
sins,
no one would be left, Lord.
4But you forgive us,
so you are respected.

5I wait for the LORD to help me,
and I trust his word.
6I wait for the Lord to help me
more than night watchmen wait for the
dawn,
more than night watchmen wait for the
dawn.

7People of Israel, put your hope in the
LORD
because he is loving
and able to save.
8He will save Israel
from all their sins.

SIN

What Harm?

Sarah Furstie guessed it was stealing, in a way at least. But what choice did she have? Mr. Tanhover, the band director, had talked her into taking a solo to contests, but her flute was old and unreliable. It sounded more like a tin pipe than a flute when she played it.

Ann Filburgh, on the other hand, had a new, top-of-the-line flute that made each note sound like liquid silver. Ann didn't like other people playing her instrument, but what would be the harm if Sarah just switched the flutes in their cases the day before the contest?

For days Sarah agonized over her decision but finally decided, right or wrong, she just had to do it. She was nearly sick with nerves as she sneaked into the deserted band room the day before the contest, but the actual switch was easy. Nobody was anywhere around to see her.

Sarah played her solo for the judges the next day. Ann's flute sounded lovely, but Sarah made lots of dumb mistakes. Her fingers felt like rubber. She couldn't concentrate.

Afterward, she found Ann warming up for the band's contest number, using, of course, Sarah's old tin-pipe flute. As Sarah sat down in her own second-chair place beside Ann's first-chair spot, Ann stopped playing and turned to face her.

"Are you ready to trade back?" Ann asked quietly. Sarah heard, or thought she heard, hurt and anger in Ann's voice.

"Ann, I'm so sorry," Sarah whispered, her face burning. "I'm so ashamed. I just feel sick, and have all day."

Ann looked in Sarah's eyes for a long minute and then smiled. "Let's just forget it happened," she said. "It's okay. Really."

But Sarah knew it wasn't okay. Not quite. Ann had forgiven her, but it would be harder for Sarah to forgive herself. She had let herself down.

People like Sarah have always faced temptation, and sometimes they've given in. **Psalm 130** shows the need for forgiveness of these sins.

- What might the psalmist advise Sarah to do next in her situation?
- What temptations do you face that you need to ask God to help you sort out?

CONSIDER . . .

- writing on a slip of paper the major temptations you face today and then asking God each week to help you overcome them.
- apologizing to someone for something you did that hurt him or her.

FOR MORE, SEE . . .

- Isaiah 44:22–23 (p. 663)
- Jeremiah 31:31–34 (p. 727)
- 1 Corinthians 15:1–5 (p. 1187)

Childlike Trust in the Lord

A song for going up to worship. Of David.

131 LORD, my heart is not proud;
I don't look down on others.
I don't do great things,
and I can't do miracles.[d]
2But I am calm and quiet,
like a baby with its mother.
I am at peace, like a baby with its mother.

3People of Israel, put your hope in the LORD
now and forever.

In Praise of the Temple

A song for going up to worship.

132 LORD, remember David
and all his suffering.
2He made an oath to the LORD,
a promise to the Mighty God of Jacob.
3He said, "I will not go home to my house,
or lie down on my bed,
4or close my eyes,
or let myself sleep
5until I find a place for the LORD.
I want to provide a home for the Mighty
God of Jacob."

6We heard about the Ark[d] in Bethlehem.
We found it at Kiriath Jearim.
7Let's go to the LORD's house.
Let's worship at his footstool.
8Rise, LORD, and come to your resting place;
come with the Ark that shows your
strength.
9May your priests do what is right.
May your people sing for joy.

10For the sake of your servant David,
do not reject your appointed king.
11The LORD made a promise to David,
a sure promise that he will not take back.
He promised, "I will make one of your
descendants[d]
rule as king after you.
12If your sons keep my agreement
and the rules that I teach them,
then their sons after them will rule
on your throne forever and ever."

13The LORD has chosen Jerusalem;
he wants it for his home.
14He says, "This is my resting place forever.
Here is where I want to stay.
15I will bless her with plenty;
I will fill her poor with food.
16I will cover her priests with salvation,
and those who worship me will really sing
for joy.
17"I will make a king come from the family of
David.
I will provide my appointed one
descendants[d] to rule after him.
18I will cover his enemies with shame,
but his crown will shine."

The Love of God's People

A song for going up to worship. Of David.

133 It is good and pleasant
when God's people live together in
peace!
2It is like perfumed oil poured on the priest's
head
and running down his beard.
It ran down Aaron's beard
and on to the collar of his robes.
3It is like the dew of Mount Hermon
falling on the hills of Jerusalem.
There the LORD gives his blessing
of life forever.

> **SIDELIGHT:** The night servants in the Temple (Psalm 134:1) were the security guards of their day. They kept the keys to the Temple gates and made sure the furnishings didn't "walk off." (See 1 Chronicles 9:22, p. 369.)

Temple Guards, Praise the Lord

A song for going up to worship.

134 Praise the LORD, all you servants
of the LORD,
you who serve at night in the Temple[d] of
the LORD.
2Raise your hands in the Temple
and praise the LORD.

3May the LORD bless you from Mount Zion,[d]
he who made heaven and earth.

The Lord Saves, Idols Do Not

135 Praise the LORD!

Praise the name of the LORD;
praise him, you servants of the LORD,
2you who stand in the LORD's Temple[d]
and in the Temple courtyards.
3Praise the LORD, because he is good;
sing praises to him, because it is pleasant.
4The LORD has chosen the people of Jacob for
himself;
he has chosen the people of Israel for his
very own.
5I know that the LORD is great.

Our Lord is greater than all the gods.
[6]The LORD does what he pleases,
in heaven and on earth,
in the seas and the deep oceans.
[7]He brings the clouds from the ends of the earth.
He sends the lightning with the rain.
He brings out the wind from his storehouses.
[8]He destroyed the firstborn[d] sons in Egypt
the firstborn of both people and animals.
[9]He did many signs and miracles[d] in Egypt
against the king and his servants.
[10]He defeated many nations
and killed powerful kings:
[11]Sihon king of the Amorites,
Og king of Bashan,
and all the kings of Canaan.
[12]Then he gave their land as a gift,
a gift to his people, the Israelites.

[13]LORD, your name is everlasting;
LORD, you will be remembered forever.
[14]The LORD defends his people
and has mercy on his servants.

[15]The idols of other nations are made of silver and gold,
the work of human hands.
[16]They have mouths, but they cannot speak.
They have eyes, but they cannot see.
[17]They have ears, but they cannot hear.
They have no breath in their mouths.
[18]People who make idols will be like them,
and so will those who trust them.

[19]Family of Israel, praise the LORD.
Family of Aaron, praise the LORD.
[20]Family of Levi, praise the LORD.
You who respect the LORD should praise him.
[21]You people of Jerusalem, praise the LORD on Mount Zion.[d]
Praise the LORD!

God's Love Continues Forever

136 Give thanks to the LORD because he is good.
His love continues forever.
[2]Give thanks to the God of gods.
His love continues forever.
[3]Give thanks to the Lord of lords.
His love continues forever.

[4]Only he can do great miracles.[d]
His love continues forever.
[5]With his wisdom he made the skies.
His love continues forever.
[6]He spread out the earth on the seas.
His love continues forever.
[7]He made the sun and the moon.
His love continues forever.
[8]He made the sun to rule the day.
His love continues forever.
[9]He made the moon and stars to rule the night.
His love continues forever.

[10]He killed the firstborn[d] sons of the Egyptians.
His love continues forever.
[11]He brought the people of Israel out of Egypt.
His love continues forever.
[12]He did it with his great power and strength.
His love continues forever.
[13]He parted the water of the Red Sea.[d]
His love continues forever.
[14]He brought the Israelites through the middle of it.
His love continues forever.
[15]But the king of Egypt and his army drowned in the Red Sea.
His love continues forever.
[16]He led his people through the desert.
His love continues forever.
[17]He defeated great kings.
His love continues forever.
[18]He killed powerful kings.
His love continues forever.
[19]He defeated Sihon king of the Amorites.
His love continues forever.
[20]He defeated Og king of Bashan.
His love continues forever.
[21]He gave their land as a gift.
His love continues forever.
[22]It was a gift to his servants, the Israelites.
His love continues forever.
[23]He remembered us when we were in trouble.
His love continues forever.
[24]He freed us from our enemies.
His love continues forever.
[25]He gives food to every living creature.
His love continues forever.

[26]Give thanks to the God of heaven.
His love continues forever.

Israelites in Captivity

137 By the rivers in Babylon we sat and cried
when we remembered Jerusalem.
[2]On the poplar trees nearby
we hung our harps.
[3]Those who captured us asked us to sing;
our enemies wanted happy songs.
They said, "Sing us a song about Jerusalem!"

[4]But we cannot sing songs about the LORD
while we are in this foreign country!

5Jerusalem, if I forget you,
let my right hand lose its skill.
6Let my tongue stick to the roof of my mouth
if I do not remember you,
if I do not think about Jerusalem
as my greatest joy.

7LORD, remember what the Edomites did
on the day Jerusalem fell.
They said, "Tear it down!
Tear it down to its foundations!"
8People of Babylon, you will be destroyed.
The people who pay you back for what you did to us will be happy.
9They will grab your babies
and throw them against the rocks.

A Hymn of Thanksgiving

A psalm of David.

138 LORD, I will thank you with all my heart;
I will sing to you before the gods.
2I will bow down facing your holy Temple,[d]
and I will thank you for your love and loyalty.
You have made your name and your word
greater than anything.
3On the day I called to you, you answered me.
You made me strong and brave.

4LORD, let all the kings of the earth praise you
when they hear the words you speak.
5They will sing about what the LORD has done,
because the LORD's glory is great.

6Though the LORD is supreme,
he takes care of those who are humble,
but he stays away from the proud.
7LORD, even when I have trouble all around me,
you will keep me alive.
When my enemies are angry,
you will reach down and save me by your power.
8LORD, you do everything for me.
LORD, your love continues forever.
Do not leave us, whom you made.

LONELINESS

Left, But Not Forgotten

Somvilay's family came to America as refugees, and Somvilay will never forget the way his mother sat silently in the ship on the way to the new country, endlessly weaving small Laotian luck charms from delicate thread. Her eyes were downcast.

"I was the first in my family to learn English," Somvilay says proudly. "I learn in school. Now, after six years, all in my family know American speech, American ways. Well . . . somewhat."

Somvilay smiles with a shrug that reveals that Americans can still seem strange, with unfamiliar customs, styles and ways of thinking.

"Sometimes it is lonely," Somvilay confesses. "I miss my village in Laos, the people, my friends. America is different, not like home. I feel alone here."

Psalm 137:1–6 expresses the loneliness Somvilay and his family must sometimes feel as strangers in a strange land. Read the passage to see how the psalmist dealt with his loneliness as he expressed the Israelites' feelings as captives in a foreign land.

- In what ways are you like Somvilay and the psalmist? In what ways are you different?
- How can you overcome lonely feelings when it seems you're isolated—as if in a foreign country?

C O N S I D E R . . .

- listing the names of everyone who cares about you and then writing each one a thank-you note for his or her love and loyalty.
- calling a trusted friend to talk about your loneliness and discussing ways to deal with it.

F O R M O R E , S E E . . .

- Leviticus 19:33–34 (p. 117)
- Philippians 2:25–30 (p. 1231)
- Hebrews 13:1–2 (p. 1290)

God Knows Everything

For the director of music. A psalm of David.

139 LORD, you have examined me
and know all about me.
[2]You know when I sit down and when I get up.
You know my thoughts before I think them.
[3]You know where I go and where I lie down.
You know thoroughly everything I do.
[4]LORD, even before I say a word,
you already know it.
[5]You are all around me—in front and in back—
and have put your hand on me.
[6]Your knowledge is amazing to me;
it is more than I can understand.

[7]Where can I go to get away from your Spirit?[d]
Where can I run from you?
[8]If I go up to the heavens, you are there.
If I lie down in the grave, you are there.
[9]If I rise with the sun in the east
and settle in the west beyond the sea,
[10]even there you would guide me.
With your right hand you would hold me.

[11]I could say, "The darkness will hide me.
Let the light around me turn into night."
[12]But even the darkness is not dark to you.
The night is as light as the day;
darkness and light are the same to you.

[13]You made my whole being;
you formed me in my mother's body.
[14]I praise you because you made me in an amazing and wonderful way.
What you have done is wonderful.
I know this very well.
[15]You saw my bones being formed
as I took shape in my mother's body.
When I was put together there,
[16] you saw my body as it was formed.
All the days planned for me
were written in your book
before I was one day old.

[17]God, your thoughts are precious to me.
They are so many!
[18]If I could count them,
they would be more than all the grains of sand.
When I wake up,
I am still with you.

[19]God, I wish you would kill the wicked!
Get away from me, you murderers!
[20]They say evil things about you.
Your enemies use your name thoughtlessly.
[21]LORD, I hate those who hate you;
I hate those who rise up against you.
[22]I feel only hate for them;
they are my enemies.
[23]God, examine me and know my heart;
test me and know my nervous thoughts.
[24]See if there is any bad thing in me.
Lead me on the road to everlasting life.

A Prayer for Protection

For the director of music. A psalm of David.

140 LORD, rescue me from evil people;
protect me from cruel people
[2]who make evil plans,
who always start fights.
[3]They make their tongues sharp as a snake's;
their words are like snake poison. *Selah*[d]

[4]LORD, guard me from the power of wicked people;
protect me from cruel people
who plan to trip me up.
[5]The proud hid a trap for me.
They spread out a net beside the road;
they set traps for me. *Selah*

[6]I said to the LORD, "You are my God."
LORD, listen to my prayer for help.
[7]LORD God, my mighty savior,
you protect me in battle.
[8]LORD, do not give the wicked what they want.
Don't let their plans succeed,
or they will become proud. *Selah*

[9]Those around me have planned trouble.
Now let it come to them.
[10]Let burning coals fall on them.
Throw them into the fire
or into pits from which they cannot escape.
[11]Don't let liars settle in the land.
Let evil quickly hunt down cruel people.

[12]I know the LORD will get justice for the poor
and will defend the needy in court.
[13]Good people will praise his name;
honest people will live in his presence.

A Prayer Not to Sin

A psalm of David.

141 LORD, I call to you. Come quickly.
Listen to me when I call to you.
[2]Let my prayer be like incense[d] placed before you,
and my praise like the evening sacrifice.

[3]LORD, help me control my tongue;
help me be careful about what I say.
[4]Take away my desire to do evil

or to join others in doing wrong.
Don't let me eat tasty food
with those who do evil.

5If a good person punished me, that would be kind.
If he corrected me, that would be like perfumed oil on my head.
I shouldn't refuse it.
But I pray against those who do evil.
6 Let their leaders be thrown down the cliffs.
Then people will know that I have spoken correctly:
7"The ground is plowed and broken up.
In the same way, our bones have been scattered at the grave."

8GOD, I look to you for help.
I trust in you, LORD. Don't let me die.
9Protect me from the traps they set for me
and from the net that evil people have spread.
10Let the wicked fall into their own nets,
but let me pass by safely.

A Prayer for Safety

A maskil[d] of David when he was in the cave. A prayer.

142 I cry out to the LORD;
I pray to the LORD for mercy.
2I pour out my problems to him;
I tell him my troubles.
3When I am afraid,
you, LORD, know the way out.
In the path where I walk,
a trap is hidden for me.
4Look around me and see.
No one cares about me.
I have no place of safety;
no one cares if I live.

5LORD, I cry out to you.
I say, "You are my protection.
You are all I want in this life."
6Listen to my cry,
because I am helpless.
Save me from those who are chasing me,
because they are too strong for me.
7Free me from my prison,
and then I will praise your name.
Then good people will surround me,
because you have taken care of me.

A Prayer Not to Be Killed

A psalm of David.

143 LORD, hear my prayer;
listen to my cry for mercy.
Answer me
because you are loyal and good.
2Don't judge me, your servant,
because no one alive is right before you.
3My enemies are chasing me;
they crushed me to the ground.
They made me live in darkness
like those long dead.
4I am afraid;
my courage is gone.

5I remember what happened long ago;
I consider everything you have done.
I think about all you have made.
6I lift my hands to you in prayer.
As a dry land needs rain, I thirst for you.
Selah[d]

7LORD, answer me quickly,
because I am getting weak.
Don't turn away from me,
or I will be like those who are dead.
8Tell me in the morning about your love,
because I trust you.
Show me what I should do,
because my prayers go up to you.
9LORD, save me from my enemies;
I hide in you.
10Teach me to do what you want,
because you are my God.
Let your good Spirit[d]
lead me on level ground.

11LORD, let me live
so people will praise you.
In your goodness
save me from my troubles.
12In your love defeat my enemies.
Destroy all those who trouble me,
because I am your servant.

A Prayer for Victory

Of David.

144 Praise the LORD, my Rock,[d]
who trains me for war,
who trains me for battle.
2He protects me like a strong, walled city, and he loves me.
He is my defender and my Savior,
my shield and my protection.
He helps me keep my people under control.

3LORD, why are people important to you?
Why do you even think about human beings?
4People are like a breath;
their lives are like passing shadows.

5LORD, tear open the sky and come down.
Touch the mountains so they will smoke.
6Send the lightning and scatter my enemies.
Shoot your arrows and force them away.

[7]Reach down from above.
Save me and rescue me out of this sea of enemies,
from these foreigners.
[8]They are liars;
they are dishonest.

[9]God, I will sing a new song to you;
I will play to you on the ten-stringed harp.
[10]You give victory to kings.
You save your servant David from cruel swords.
[11]Save me, rescue me from these foreigners.
They are liars; they are dishonest.

[12]Let our sons in their youth
grow like plants.
Let our daughters be
like the decorated stones in the Temple.[d]
[13]Let our barns be filled
with crops of all kinds.
Let our sheep in the fields have
thousands and tens of thousands of lambs.
[14] Let our cattle be strong.
Let no one break in.
Let there be no war,
no screams in our streets.

[15]Happy are those who are like this;
happy are the people whose God is the LORD.

SIDELIGHT: If you're looking for something new to pray before each meal, try Psalm 145. This psalm is still recited in the morning, at noon and in the evening in Jewish synagogues. A fourth-century rabbi believed that reciting the psalm three times a day would assure one a place in the world to come.

Praise to God the King

A psalm of praise. Of David.

145

I praise your greatness, my God the King;
I will praise you forever and ever.
[2]I will praise you every day;
I will praise you forever and ever.
[3]The LORD is great and worthy of our praise;
no one can understand how great he is.

[4]Parents will tell their children what you have done.
They will retell your mighty acts,
[5]wonderful majesty, and glory.
And I will think about your miracles.[d]
[6]They will tell about the amazing things you do,
and I will tell how great you are.
[7]They will remember your great goodness
and will sing about your fairness.

[8]The LORD is kind and shows mercy.
He does not become angry quickly but is full of love.
[9]The LORD is good to everyone;
he is merciful to all he has made.
[10]LORD, everything you have made will praise you;
those who belong to you will bless you.
[11]They will tell about the glory of your kingdom
and will speak about your power.
[12]Then everyone will know the mighty things you do
and the glory and majesty of your kingdom.
[13]Your kingdom will go on and on,
and you will rule forever.

The LORD will keep all his promises;
he is loyal to all he has made.
[14]The LORD helps those who have been defeated
and takes care of those who are in trouble.
[15]All living things look to you for food,
and you give it to them at the right time.
[16]You open your hand,
and you satisfy all living things.

[17]Everything the LORD does is right.
He is loyal to all he has made.
[18]The LORD is close to everyone who prays to him,
to all who truly pray to him.
[19]He gives those who respect him what they want.
He listens when they cry, and he saves them.
[20]The LORD protects everyone who loves him,
but he will destroy the wicked.

[21]I will praise the LORD.
Let everyone praise his holy name forever.

Praise God Who Helps the Weak

146

Praise the LORD!
My whole being, praise the LORD.
[2]I will praise the LORD all my life;
I will sing praises to my God as long as I live.

[3]Do not put your trust in princes
or other people, who cannot save you.
[4]When people die, they are buried.
Then all of their plans come to an end.
[5]Happy are those who are helped by the God of Jacob.

Their hope is in the LORD their God.
6He made heaven and earth,
the sea and everything in it.
He remains loyal forever.
7He does what is fair for those who have been wronged.
He gives food to the hungry.
The LORD sets the prisoners free.
8 The LORD gives sight to the blind.
The LORD lifts up people who are in trouble.
The LORD loves those who do right.
9The LORD protects the foreigners.
He defends the orphans and widows,
but he blocks the way of the wicked.

10The LORD will be King forever.
Jerusalem, your God is everlasting.

Praise the LORD!

Praise God Who Helps His People

147 Praise the LORD!

It is good to sing praises to our God;
it is good and pleasant to praise him.
2The LORD rebuilds Jerusalem;
he brings back the captured Israelites.
3He heals the brokenhearted
and bandages their wounds.

4He counts the stars
and names each one.
5Our Lord is great and very powerful.
There is no limit to what he knows.
6The LORD defends the humble,
but he throws the wicked to the ground.

7Sing praises to the LORD;
praise our God with harps.
8He fills the sky with clouds
and sends rain to the earth
and makes grass grow on the hills.
9He gives food to cattle
and to the little birds that call.

10He does not enjoy the strength of a horse
or the strength of a man.
11The LORD is pleased with those who respect him,
with those who trust his love.

12Jerusalem, praise the LORD;

HUNGER AND POVERTY

The Numbers Tell the Story

Suppose you were sitting in a classroom of thirty people and that your classroom represented the world. How would your classroom "world" look? Check it out:

- Only two of you would live to age seventy-four.
- Seventeen of you would make less than six hundred dollars a year.
- Two of you would be so malnourished that your growth would be stunted.
- Ten of you would suffer some form of nutritional deficiency.
- Only fifteen of you would have access to clean drinking water.
- One of you would control 80 percent of the farmland.
- Only six of you would live in safe, sturdy homes.

Startling, isn't it? According to Worldwatch Institute, about 1.2 billion people live today without sufficient food, clothing, and shelter to meet their basic needs. Though North Americans tend to think of hunger as a Third World problem, statistics show that nearly 20 percent of Americans live below the poverty level, with that percentage even higher among children.

God wants to use the church to protect and help the less fortunate. Read **Psalm 146** to find out more about God's promises to people in need.

- The psalmist says the Lord "loves those who do right." What does this phrase mean with respect to helping the poor?
- How can you join with God in helping the "orphans and widows" in your community?

CONSIDER . . .

- keeping a jar by the washing machine and putting all your family's loose change into it. Give this to your church to help the disadvantaged.
- volunteering your time and energy to help repair the homes of the less fortunate.

FOR MORE, SEE . . .

- Psalm 140:12–13 (p. 561)
- Matthew 25:31–46 (p. 954)
- 2 Corinthians 9:7–9 (p. 1201)

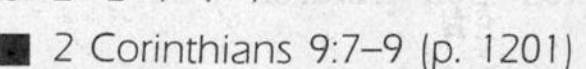

Jerusalem, praise your God.
13He makes your city gates strong
and blesses your children inside.
14He brings peace to your country
and fills you with the finest grain.

15He gives a command to the earth,
and it quickly obeys him.
16He spreads the snow like wool
and scatters the frost like ashes.
17He throws down hail like rocks.
No one can stand the cold he sends.
18Then he gives a command, and it melts.
He sends the breezes, and the waters flow.

19He gave his word to Jacob,
his laws and demands to Israel.
20He didn't do this for any other nation.
They don't know his laws.

Praise the LORD!

The World Should Praise the Lord

148 Praise the LORD!

Praise the LORD from the skies.
Praise him high above the earth.
2Praise him, all you angels.
Praise him, all you armies of heaven.
3Praise him, sun and moon.
Praise him, all you shining stars.
4Praise him, highest heavens
and you waters above the sky.
5Let them praise the LORD,
because they were created by his command.
6He put them in place forever and ever;
he made a law that will never change.

7Praise the LORD from the earth,
you large sea animals and all the oceans,
8lightning and hail, snow and mist,
and stormy winds that obey him,
9mountains and all hills,
fruit trees and all cedars,
10wild animals and all cattle,
crawling animals and birds,
11kings of the earth and all nations,
princes and all rulers of the earth,
12young men and women,
old people and children.

13Praise the LORD,
because he alone is great.
He is more wonderful than heaven and earth.
14God has given his people a king.
He should be praised by all who belong to him;
he should be praised by the Israelites, the people closest to his heart.

Praise the LORD!

Praise the God of Israel

149 Praise the LORD!

Sing a new song to the LORD;
sing his praise in the meeting of his people.

2Let the Israelites be happy because of God, their Maker.
Let the people of Jerusalem rejoice because of their King.
3They should praise him with dancing.
They should sing praises to him with tambourines[d] and harps.
4The LORD is pleased with his people;
he saves the humble.
5Let those who worship him rejoice in his glory.
Let them sing for joy even in bed!

6Let them shout his praise
with their two-edged swords in their hands.
7They will punish the nations
and defeat the people.
8They will put those kings in chains
and those important men in iron bands.
9They will punish them as God has written.
God is honored by all who worship him.

Praise the LORD!

Praise the Lord with Music

150 Praise the LORD!

Praise God in his Temple;[d]
praise him in his mighty heaven.
2Praise him for his strength;
praise him for his greatness.
3Praise him with trumpet blasts;
praise him with harps and lyres.[d]
4Praise him with tambourines[d] and dancing;
praise him with stringed instruments and flutes.
5Praise him with loud cymbals;
praise him with crashing cymbals.
6Let everything that breathes praise the LORD.

Praise the LORD!

WORSHIP

Time Out!

Tara Donagie often takes time out to worship, especially when something good happens in her life, as when she makes a new friend, finds a notebook that's been lost, or even gets over the flu.

Sometimes, she uses her guitar to praise God with a song.

"Especially if some friends are around and we're all celebrating," Tara says. "We may sing a couple of songs, laugh because we feel so good, and maybe say a prayer together."

Late last spring, things got really hectic. Tara began forgetting to take time out to worship God. "I lost my ability to be thankful in the shuffle of final exams and looking for a summer job," she says.

But that didn't last long.

"I couldn't handle it," Tara confesses. "Without taking time out to worship God, I took everything in my life for granted. I didn't feel thankful. This sounds weird, but the good stuff just didn't feel as good without the celebration."

Tara understood the unique blessings that come from worshiping God. **Psalm 150** expresses much of what Tara feels as she worships.

- How is Tara's attitude like the psalmist's in this passage?
- Why do you think it is good to practice worshiping and thanking God? What happens to our attitude if we don't?

CONSIDER . . .

- writing a list of items beginning with the phrase "Praise the Lord for . . ."
- keeping a diary of "blessings" so you won't get busy and forget to praise God and celebrate the things he gives you.

FOR MORE, SEE . . .

- 1 Chronicles 23:1–5 (p. 379)
- Psalm 147 (p. 564)
- Luke 2:8–14 (p. 1003)

PROVERBS

Why Read This Book:

- Discover life's basic goal (Proverbs 2:1–15).
- Find clear guidance on right and wrong (Proverbs 3, 10—23).
- Learn how to be wise instead of foolish (Proverbs 4, 6, 8, 9, 24).

Behind the Scenes:

If you like "quotable quotes" or bumper sticker slogans, you'll love Proverbs. Unlike other books of the Bible, Proverbs is mostly a collection of one- and two-line sayings on various everyday subjects—family life, work, money, getting along with others, honesty and many more. These sayings represent the heart of important truths about life and relationships. This is the wisdom of God for every day.

The book is filled with sharp phrases, dramatic contrasts, and vivid scenes from everyday life. A chapter may deal with dozens of different subjects (for example, see chapter 14). Because of their short, catchy style, these proverbs are easy to memorize. Other parts of Proverbs are longer, unified poems about wisdom, which is personified as a woman (see Proverbs 1:20–33).

Proverbs is divided into eight main sections. It begins with an introduction on wisdom (Proverbs 1—9), then has six collections of sayings by various "wise men" (Proverbs 10—31:9). It concludes with an acrostic poem on a perfect wife (Proverbs 31:10–31). Many scholars note that the perfect wife fulfills the virtues described in the rest of the book.

Collected hundreds of years ago to teach young people principles for life, Proverbs can still help guide us to make smart choices. And though many parts of Proverbs don't explicitly mention God, the sayings were gathered to help us follow God in everything we do.

WHEN THE ACTION WAS

1000BC	750BC	500BC	250BC	BC/AD
Solomon ruled Israel and many proverbs are attributed to him	Jerusalem fell to the Babylonians	Jews began returning to Jerusalem from exile	Proverbs was probably put into its final form	Jesus was born

The Importance of Proverbs

1 These are the wise words of Solomon son of David, king of Israel.

2They teach wisdom and self-control;
they will help you understand wise words.

> **SIDELIGHT:** Proverbs—short, catchy sayings—aren't found just in the book of Proverbs. They were a common type of writing in ancient times, and Jesus used them regularly in his teaching. See some examples in Matthew 6:21 (p. 918) and Matthew 7:13 (p. 919).

3They will teach you how to be wise and
self-controlled
and will teach you to do what is honest
and fair and right.
4They make the uneducated smarter
and give knowledge and sense to the
young.
5Wise people can also listen and learn;
even smart people can find good advice in
these words.
6Then anyone can understand wise words and
stories,
the words of the wise and their riddles.

7Knowledge begins with respect for the LORD,
but fools hate wisdom and self-control.

Warnings Against Evil

8My child, listen to your father's teaching
and do not forget your mother's advice.
9Their teaching will be like flowers in your
hair
or a necklace around your neck.

10My child, if sinners try to lead you into sin,
do not follow them.
11They will say, "Come with us.
Let's ambush and kill someone;
let's attack some innocent people just for
fun.
12Let's swallow them alive, as death does;
let's swallow them whole, as the grave
does.
13We will take all kinds of valuable things
and fill our houses with stolen goods.
14Come join us,
and we will share with you stolen goods."
15My child, do not go along with them;
do not do what they do.
16They are eager to do evil
and are quick to kill.
17It is useless to spread out a net
right where the birds can see it.
18But sinners will fall into their own traps;
they will only catch themselves!
19All greedy people end up this way;
greed kills selfish people.

Wisdom Speaks

20Wisdom is like a woman shouting in the
street;
she raises her voice in the city squares.
21She cries out in the noisy street
and shouts at the city gates:
22"You fools, how long will you be foolish?
How long will you make fun of wisdom
and hate knowledge?
23If only you had listened when I corrected
you,
I would have told you what's in my heart;
I would have told you what I am thinking.
24I called, but you refused to listen;
I held out my hand, but you paid no
attention.
25You did not follow my advice
and did not listen when I corrected you.
26So I will laugh when you are in trouble.
I will make fun when disaster strikes you,
27when disaster comes over you like a storm,
when trouble strikes you like a whirlwind,
when pain and trouble overwhelm you.

28"Then you will call to me,
but I will not answer.
You will look for me,
but you will not find me.
29It is because you rejected knowledge
and did not choose to respect the LORD.
30You did not accept my advice,
and you rejected my correction.
31So you will get what you deserve;
you will get what you planned for others.
32Fools will die because they refuse to listen;
they will be destroyed because they do not
care.
33But those who listen to me will live in safety
and be at peace, without fear of injury."

Rewards of Wisdom

2 My child, listen to what I say
and remember what I command you.
2Listen carefully to wisdom;
set your mind on understanding.
3Cry out for wisdom,
and beg for understanding.
4Search for it like silver,
and hunt for it like hidden treasure.
5Then you will understand respect for the
LORD,
and you will find that you know God.
6Only the LORD gives wisdom;
he gives knowledge and understanding.

7He stores up wisdom for those who are
honest.
Like a shield he protects the innocent.
8He makes sure that justice is done,
and he protects those who are loyal to him.
9Then you will understand what is honest and
fair
and what is the good and right thing to do.
10Wisdom will come into your mind,
and knowledge will be pleasing to you.
11Good sense will protect you;
understanding will guard you.
12It will keep you from the wicked,
from those whose words are bad,
13who don't do what is right
but what is evil.
14They enjoy doing wrong
and are happy to do what is crooked and
evil.
15What they do is wrong,
and their ways are dishonest.
16It will save you from the unfaithful wife
who tries to lead you into adultery[d] with
pleasing words.
17She leaves the husband she married when
she was young.
She ignores the promise she made before
God.
18Her house is on the way to death;
those who took that path are now all dead.
19No one who goes to her comes back
or walks the path of life again.
20But wisdom will help you be good
and do what is right.
21Those who are honest will live in the land,
and those who are innocent will remain in
it.
22But the wicked will be removed from the
land,
and the unfaithful will be thrown out of it.

SCHOOL

Stunned Into Action

Over the past three years, Kelly Hunt had come to respect and trust Mr. Hudson. Sometimes she would pop into his office to share good news or ask advice about her classes or boyfriend. Other times she would share an orange with him as they walked across campus. Always, he cared—and listened.

But today she sat in his office, watching a worried Mr. Hudson collect his thoughts.

Finally, he spoke. "Kelly, I'm concerned about you. Let me tell you what I see." Mr. Hudson leaned forward in his chair. "Your grades are falling. You've dropped your old friends and taken up with another group—one that's on the fringe of trouble. And I've heard you talking about dropping out of school."

Kelly swallowed.

"In your eyes I see rebellion and fear. Something has control of you. How about talking to your folks about it?"

Kelly walked out of the office, stunned. If wise, objective, Mr. Hudson thought she had a problem, then she must have one. She had been fooling herself about her drinking—she could admit that now. Kelly decided she didn't want to destroy her whole future by messing up at school.

A few days later Kelly sat down with her parents and told them she needed help. That was her first step on her way to recovery.

Kelly was rewarded for staying in school and following Mr. Hudson's wisdom. **Proverbs 2:1–10** describes the rewards wisdom and education bring.

- According to this passage, what things had to happen before Kelly received wisdom's reward?
- What rewards, described in these verses, would you like to have?

CONSIDER . . .

- copying different verses from the scripture passage onto your class notebooks.
- talking to a teacher you consider wise and asking for tips on how to get more out of your education.

FOR MORE, SEE

- 1 Kings 3:4–15 (p. 306)
- Colossians 2:1–4 (p. 1240)
- James 1:5–8 (p. 1294)

Advice to Children

3 My child, do not forget my teaching,
but keep my commands in mind.
2Then you will live a long time,
and your life will be successful.

3Don't ever forget kindness and truth.
Wear them like a necklace.
Write them on your heart as if on a tablet.
4Then you will be respected
and will please both God and people.

5Trust the LORD with all your heart,
and don't depend on your own
understanding.
6Remember the LORD in all you do,
and he will give you success.

7Don't depend on your own wisdom.
Respect the LORD and refuse to do wrong.
8Then your body will be healthy,
and your bones will be strong.

9Honor the LORD with your wealth
and the firstfruits[d] from all your crops.
10Then your barns will be full,
and your wine barrels will overflow with
new wine.

11My child, do not reject the LORD's discipline,
and don't get angry when he corrects you.
12The LORD corrects those he loves,
just as parents correct the child they delight
in.

13Happy is the person who finds wisdom,
the one who gets understanding.
14Wisdom is worth more than silver;
it brings more profit than gold.
15Wisdom is more precious than rubies;
nothing you could want is equal to it.
16With her right hand wisdom offers you a long
life,
and with her left hand she gives you riches
and honor.
17Wisdom will make your life pleasant
and will bring you peace.
18As a tree produces fruit, wisdom gives life to
those who use it,
and everyone who uses it will be happy.

19The LORD made the earth, using his wisdom.
He set the sky in place, using his
understanding.
20With his knowledge, he made springs flow
into rivers
and the clouds drop rain on the earth.

21My child, hold on to wisdom and good sense.
Don't let them out of your sight.
22They will give you life
and beauty like a necklace around your
neck.
23Then you will go your way in safety,
and you will not get hurt.
24When you lie down, you won't be afraid;
when you lie down, you will sleep in
peace.
25You won't be afraid of sudden trouble;
you won't fear the ruin that comes to the
wicked,
26because the LORD will keep you safe.
He will keep you from being trapped.

27Whenever you are able,
do good to people who need help.
28If you have what your neighbor asks for,
don't say, "Come back later.
I will give it to you tomorrow."
29Don't make plans to hurt your neighbor
who lives nearby and trusts you.
30Don't accuse a person for no good reason;
don't accuse someone who has not harmed
you.
31Don't be jealous of those who use violence,
and don't choose to be like them.
32The LORD hates those who do wrong,
but he is a friend to those who are honest.
33The LORD will curse the evil person's house,
but he will bless the home of those who do
right.
34The LORD laughs at those who laugh at him,
but he gives grace to those who are not
proud.
35Wise people will receive honor,
but fools will be disgraced.

Wisdom Is Important

4 My children, listen to your father's
teaching;
pay attention so you will understand.
2What I am telling you is good,
so do not forget what I teach you.
3When I was a young boy in my father's
house
and like an only child to my mother,
4my father taught me and said,
"Hold on to my words with all your heart.
Keep my commands and you will live.
5Get wisdom and understanding.
Don't forget or ignore my words.
6Hold on to wisdom, and it will take care of
you.
Love it, and it will keep you safe.
7Wisdom is the most important thing; so get
wisdom.
If it costs everything you have, get
understanding.
8Treasure wisdom, and it will make you great;
hold on to it, and it will bring you honor.

[9]It will be like flowers in your hair
and like a beautiful crown on your head."

[10]My child, listen and accept what I say.
Then you will have a long life.
[11]I am guiding you in the way of wisdom,
and I am leading you on the right path.
[12]Nothing will hold you back;
you will not be overwhelmed.
[13]Always remember what you have been taught,
and don't let go of it.
Keep all that you have learned;
it is the most important thing in life.
[14]Don't follow the ways of the wicked;
don't do what evil people do.
[15]Avoid their ways, and don't follow them.
Stay away from them and keep on going,
[16]because they cannot sleep until they do evil.
They cannot rest until they harm someone.
[17]They feast on wickedness and cruelty
as if they were eating bread and drinking wine.
[18]The way of the good person is like the light of dawn,
growing brighter and brighter until full daylight.
[19]But the wicked walk around in the dark;
they can't even see what makes them stumble.

[20]My child, pay attention to my words;
listen closely to what I say.
[21]Don't ever forget my words;
keep them always in mind.
[22]They are the key to life for those who find them;
they bring health to the whole body.
[23]Be careful what you think,
because your thoughts run your life.
[24]Don't use your mouth to tell lies;
don't ever say things that are not true.
[25]Keep your eyes focused on what is right,
and look straight ahead to what is good.
[26]Be careful what you do,
and always do what is right.
[27]Don't turn off the road of goodness;
keep away from evil paths.

Warning About Adultery

5 My son, pay attention to my wisdom;
listen to my words of understanding.
[2]Be careful to use good sense,
and watch what you say.
[3]The words of another man's wife may seem sweet as honey;
they may be as smooth as olive oil.
[4]But in the end she will bring you sorrow,
causing you pain like a two-edged sword.
[5]She is on the way to death;
her steps are headed straight to the grave.
[6]She gives little thought to life.
She doesn't even know that her ways are wrong.

[7]Now, my sons, listen to me,
and don't ignore what I say.
[8]Stay away from such a woman.
Don't even go near the door of her house,
[9]or you will give your riches to others,
and the best years of your life will be given to someone cruel.
[10]Strangers will enjoy your wealth,
and what you worked so hard for will go to someone else.
[11]You will groan at the end of your life
when your health is gone.
[12]Then you will say, "I hated being told what to do!
I would not listen to correction!
[13]I would not listen to my teachers
or pay attention to my instructors.
[14]I came close to being completely ruined
in front of a whole group of people."

[15]Be faithful to your own wife,
just as you drink water from your own well.
[16]Don't pour your water in the streets;
don't give your love to just any woman.
[17]These things are yours alone
and shouldn't be shared with strangers.
[18]Be happy with the wife you married when you were young.
She gives you joy, as your fountain gives you water.
[19]She is as lovely and graceful as a deer.
Let her love always make you happy;
let her love always hold you captive.
[20]My son, don't be held captive by a woman who takes part in adultery.[d]
Don't hug another man's wife.

[21]The LORD sees everything you do,
and he watches where you go.
[22]An evil man will be caught in his wicked ways;
the ropes of his sins will tie him up.
[23]He will die because he does not control himself,
and he will be held captive by his foolishness.

Dangers of Being Foolish

6 My child, be careful about giving a guarantee for somebody else's loan,
about promising to pay what someone else owes.
[2]You might get trapped by what you say;

you might be caught by your own words.
3My child, if you have done this and are
under your neighbor's control,
here is how to get free.
Don't be proud. Go to your neighbor
and beg to be free from your promise.
4Don't go to sleep
or even rest your eyes,
5but free yourself like a deer running from a
hunter,
like a bird flying away from a trapper.

6Go watch the ants, you lazy person.
Watch what they do and be wise.
7Ants have no commander,
no leader or ruler,
8but they store up food in the summer
and gather their supplies at harvest.
9How long will you lie there, you lazy person?
When will you get up from sleeping?
10You sleep a little; you take a nap.
You fold your hands and lie down to rest.
11So you will be as poor as if you had been
robbed;
you will have as little as if you had been
held up.

SIDELIGHT: Sleeping until noon would be a no-no for the writer of Proverbs 6:6–11. The book of Proverbs constantly blasts laziness and warns that lazy people will end up poor. Yet it doesn't say all poor people are lazy. Read the other side of the story in Proverbs 13:23 (p. 579) and Proverbs 22:1–2, 22–23 (p. 586).

12Some people are wicked and no good.
They go around telling lies,
13winking with their eyes, tapping with their
feet,
and making signs with their fingers.
14They make evil plans in their hearts
and are always starting arguments.
15So trouble will strike them in an instant;
suddenly they will be so hurt no one can
help them.

16There are six things the LORD hates.
There are seven things he cannot stand:
17 a proud look,
a lying tongue,
hands that kill innocent people,
18 a mind that thinks up evil plans,
feet that are quick to do evil,
19 a witness who lies,
and someone who starts arguments
among families.

Warning About Adultery

20My son, keep your father's commands,
and don't forget your mother's teaching.
21Keep their words in mind forever
as though you had them tied around your
neck.
22They will guide you when you walk.
They will guard you when you sleep.
They will speak to you when you are
awake.
23These commands are like a lamp;
this teaching is like a light.
And the correction that comes from them
will help you have life.
24They will keep you from sinful women
and from the pleasing words of another
man's unfaithful wife.
25Don't desire her because she is beautiful.
Don't let her capture you by the way she
looks at you.
26A prostitute[d] will treat you like a loaf of
bread,
and a woman who takes part in adultery[d]
may cost you your life.
27You cannot carry hot coals against your
chest
without burning your clothes,
28and you cannot walk on hot coals
without burning your feet.
29The same is true if you have sexual relations
with another man's wife.
Anyone who does so will be punished.

30People don't hate a thief
when he steals because he is hungry.
31But if he is caught, he must pay back seven
times what he stole,
and it may cost him everything he owns.
32A man who takes part in adultery has no
sense;
he will destroy himself.
33He will be beaten up and disgraced,
and his shame will never go away.
34Jealousy makes a husband very angry,
and he will have no pity when he gets
revenge.
35He will accept no payment for the wrong;
he will take no amount of money.

The Woman of Adultery

7 My son, remember what I say,
and treasure my commands.
2Obey my commands, and you will live.
Guard my teachings as you would your
own eyes.
3Remind yourself of them;
write them on your heart as if on a tablet.
4Treat wisdom as a sister,
and make understanding your closest friend.

5 Wisdom and understanding will keep you
away from adultery,[d]
away from the unfaithful wife and her
pleasing words.
6 Once while I was at the window of my
house
I looked out through the shutters
7 and saw some foolish, young men.
I noticed one of them had no wisdom.
8 He was walking down the street near the
corner
on the road leading to her house.
9 It was the twilight of the evening;
the darkness of the night was just
beginning.
10 Then the woman approached him,
dressed like a prostitute[d]
and planning to trick him.
11 She was loud and stubborn
and never stayed at home.
12 She was always out in the streets or in the
city squares,
waiting around on the corners of the
streets.
13 She grabbed him and kissed him.
Without shame she said to him,
14 "I made my fellowship offering and took
some of the meat home.
Today I have kept my special promises.
15 So I have come out to meet you;
I have been looking for you and have found
you.
16 I have covered my bed
with colored sheets from Egypt.
17 I have made my bed smell sweet
with myrrh,[d] aloes,[d] and cinnamon.
18 Come, let's make love until morning.
Let's enjoy each other's love.
19 My husband is not home;
he has gone on a long trip.
20 He took a lot of money with him
and won't be home for weeks."
21 By her clever words she made him give in;
by her pleasing words she led him into
doing wrong.
22 All at once he followed her,
like an ox led to the butcher,
like a deer caught in a trap
23 and shot through the liver with an arrow.
Like a bird caught in a trap,
he didn't know what he did would kill
him.

24 Now, my sons, listen to me;
pay attention to what I say.
25 Don't let yourself be tricked by such a
woman;
don't go where she leads you.
26 She has ruined many good men,
and many have died because of her.
27 Her house is on the road to death,
the road that leads down to the grave.

Listen to Wisdom

8 Wisdom calls to you like someone
shouting;
understanding raises her voice.
2 On the hilltops along the road
and at the crossroads, she stands calling.
3 Beside the city gates,
at the entrances into the city, she calls out:
4 "Listen, everyone, I'm calling out to you;
I am shouting to all people.
5 You who are uneducated, be smarter.
You who are foolish, get understanding.
6 Listen, because I have important things to
say,
and what I tell you is right.
7 What I say is true,
I refuse to speak evil.
8 Everything I say is honest;
nothing I say is crooked or false.
9 People with good sense know what I say is
true;
and those with knowledge know my words
are right.
10 Choose my teachings instead of silver,
and knowledge rather than the finest gold.
11 Wisdom is more precious than rubies.
Nothing you could want is equal to it.

12 "I am wisdom, and I am smart.
I also have knowledge and good sense.
13 If you respect the LORD, you will also hate
evil.
I hate pride and bragging,
evil ways and lies.
14 I have good sense and advice,
and I have understanding and power.
15 I help kings to govern
and rulers to make fair laws.
16 Princes use me to lead,
and so do all important people who judge
fairly.
17 I love those who love me,
and those who seek me find me.
18 Riches and honor are mine to give.
So are wealth and lasting success.
19 What I give is better than the finest gold,
better than the purest silver.
20 I do what is right
and follow the path of justice.
21 I give wealth to those who love me,
filling their houses with treasures.

22 "I, wisdom, was with the LORD when he
began his work,
long before he made anything else.
23 I was created in the very beginning,

even before the world began.
24I was born before there were oceans,
or springs overflowing with water,
25before the hills were there,
before the mountains were put in place.
26God had not made the earth or fields,
not even the first dust of the earth.
27I was there when God put the skies in place,
when he stretched the horizon over the oceans,
28when he made the clouds above
and put the deep underground springs in place.
29I was there when he ordered the sea
not to go beyond the borders he had set.
I was there when he laid the earth's foundation.
30 I was like a child by his side.
I was delighted every day,
enjoying his presence all the time,
31enjoying the whole world,
and delighted with all its people.

32"Now, my children, listen to me,
because those who follow my ways are happy.
33Listen to my teaching, and you will be wise;
do not ignore it.
34Happy are those who listen to me,
watching at my door every day,
waiting at my open doorway.
35Those who find me find life,
and the LORD will be pleased with them.
36Those who do not find me hurt themselves.
Those who hate me love death."

Being Wise or Foolish

9 Wisdom has built her house;
she has made its seven columns.
2She has prepared her food and wine;
she has set her table.
3She has sent out her servant girls,
and she calls out from the highest place in the city.
4She says to those who are uneducated,
"Come in here, you foolish people!
5Come and eat my food
and drink the wine I have prepared.
6Stop your foolish ways, and you will live;
take the road of understanding.

7"If you correct someone who makes fun of wisdom, you will be insulted.
If you correct an evil person, you will get hurt.

CREATION

Moment of Wonder

Waves on the Sea of Cortez rolled under Marty Stypes's kayak. One crested behind her and broke, spewing foam over her back. Panic gripped her. She leaned into the wind, paddling hard. Her muscles ached. Why had she taken this wilderness course?

The answer echoed within her, "to test myself, to get back in touch with God."

But where was he?

When she rounded the rocky point, stillness surrounded her. Sunlight broke through the clouds, sparkling into the turquoise depths of the protected cove. Marty rested her paddle and looked beneath her. Sea fans waved their purple lace. Yellow fish darted. She leaned back and gazed at the horizon. Pelicans skimmed inches above the water.

Suddenly the sea split beside her. A dolphin arched high, then dove, circling her. She sucked in her breath, overcome with wonder.

"Lord, oh Lord, you're everywhere!"

The voice of Wisdom, in Proverbs, speaks about the joy in observing God's creation. Read about it in **Proverbs 8:22–31**.

- What might Wisdom's voice say to Marty from this passage?
- Where do you most strongly sense God's presence? Why?

C O N S I D E R . . .

- searching for the tiny forms of God's creation as you walk across a yard or a vacant lot, and thanking God for them.
- finding a special place in nature where you can go regularly to be with God.

F O R M O R E , S E E . . .

- Psalm 104:1–35 (p. 541)
- Luke 8:22–26 (p. 1017)
- Revelation 4:11 (p. 1335)

8Do not correct those who make fun of
wisdom, or they will hate you.
But correct the wise, and they will love
you.
9Teach the wise, and they will become even
wiser;
teach good people, and they will learn even
more.

10"Wisdom begins with respect for the LORD,
and understanding begins with knowing the
Holy One.
11If you live wisely, you will live a long time;
wisdom will add years to your life.
12The wise person is rewarded by wisdom,
but whoever makes fun of wisdom will
suffer for it."

13Foolishness is like a loud woman;
she does not have wisdom or knowledge.
14She sits at the door of her house
at the highest place in the city.
15She calls out to those who are passing by,
who are going along, minding their own
business.
16She says to those who are uneducated,
"Come in here, you foolish people!
17Stolen water is sweeter,
and food eaten in secret tastes better."
18But these people don't know that everyone
who goes there dies,
that her guests end up deep in the grave.

SIDELIGHT: Two sections of Proverbs (Proverbs 10:1—22:16 and 25:1—29:27, p. 589) are attributed to Solomon, the king who was said to have spoken three thousand wise sayings (1 Kings 4:32–34, p. 308).

The Wise Words of Solomon

10 These are the wise words of Solomon:

A wise son makes his father happy,
but a foolish son makes his mother sad.

2Riches gotten by doing wrong have no value,
but right living will save you from death.

SCHOOL

Crossroads

Chad Monroe's cane tapped from side to side, sweeping across the sidewalk. He approached a street intersection, but veered left. As his cane tip struck metal, he stopped.

"Mr. Wright? Where am I?" he called.

Chad's mobility instructor from the school for the blind stood at a safe distance, observing Chad's cane technique.

"What have you hit?" he asked. "Listen to the sound of it. Feel it."

Chad swung his cane again, turning his head as he listened to the metallic ring. "It's a car." He felt its fender.

"Good. Get back on the walk, and cross the street." The instructor tensed. Would Chad follow what he had been taught? Or would he step in the path of a car?

Trucks raced in front of Chad. "I'm scared!"

"Listen for the parallel traffic to start. You can do it," the instructor said.

Finally, Chad stepped into the crosswalk. The instructor let out a relieved breath; Chad had picked the right time.

Proverbs 9:8–12 describes the rewards for a wise student who learns from a good teacher, as Chad did.

- According to this passage, where does true wisdom begin?
- How have you been rewarded by wisdom at school, as mentioned in verse 12?

CONSIDER . . .

- telling a teacher whom you admire how he or she has helped you in life.
- offering to tutor classmates who are having trouble in school so you can pass on to others what your teachers have taught you.

FOR MORE, SEE . . .

- Psalm 16:5–11 (p. 489)
- Daniel 1:3–18 (p. 807)
- John 7:14–18 (p. 1069)

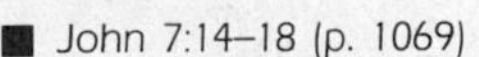

[3]The LORD does not let good people go
hungry,
but he keeps evil people from getting what
they want.

[4]A lazy person will end up poor,
but a hard worker will become rich.

[5]Those who gather crops on time are wise,
but those who sleep through the harvest
are a disgrace.

[6]Good people will have rich blessings,
but the wicked will be overwhelmed by
violence.

[7]Good people will be remembered as a
blessing,
but evil people will soon be forgotten.

[8]The wise do what they are told,
but a talkative fool will be ruined.

[9]The honest person will live in safety,
but the dishonest will be caught.

[10]A wink may get you into trouble,
and foolish talk will lead to your ruin.

[11]The words of a good person give life, like a
fountain of water,
but the words of the wicked contain
nothing but violence.

[12]Hatred stirs up trouble,
but love forgives all wrongs.

[13]Smart people speak wisely,
but people without wisdom should be
punished.

[14]The wise don't tell everything they know,
but the foolish talk too much and are
ruined.

[15]Having lots of money protects the rich,
but having no money destroys the poor.

[16]Good people are rewarded with life,
but evil people are paid with punishment.

[17]Whoever accepts correction is on the way to
life,
but whoever ignores correction will lead
others away from life.

[18]Whoever hides hate is a liar.
Whoever tells lies is a fool.

[19]If you talk a lot, you are sure to sin;
if you are wise, you will keep quiet.

[20]The words of a good person are like pure
silver,
but an evil person's thoughts are worth
very little.

[21]Good people's words will help many others,
but fools will die because they don't have
wisdom.

[22]The LORD's blessing brings wealth,
and no sorrow comes with it.

[23]A foolish person enjoys doing wrong,
but a person with understanding enjoys
doing what is wise.

[24]Evil people will get what they fear most,
but good people will get what they want
most.

[25]A storm will blow the evil person away,
but a good person will always be safe.

[26]A lazy person affects the one he works for
like vinegar on the teeth or smoke in the
eyes.

[27]Whoever respects the LORD will have a long
life,
but the life of an evil person will be cut
short.

[28]A good person can look forward to happiness,
but an evil person can expect nothing.

[29]The LORD will protect good people
but will ruin those who do evil.

[30]Good people will always be safe,
but evil people will not remain in the land.

[31]A good person says wise things,
but a liar's tongue will be stopped.

[32]Good people know the right thing to say,
but evil people only tell lies.

11 The LORD hates dishonest scales,
but he is pleased with honest weights.

SIDELIGHT: Since they didn't have digital scales in Bible times, people had to use stones and metal objects to figure out how heavy something was before buying or selling it. They probably used hand-held scales and put the merchandise on one side and the weight on the other. Proverbs 11:1 warns against using inaccurate scales to cheat someone.

[2]Pride leads only to shame;
it is wise to be humble.

[3]Good people will be guided by honesty;
dishonesty will destroy those who are not
trustworthy.

[4]Riches will not help when it's time to die,
but right living will save you from death.

5 The goodness of the innocent makes life easier,
but the wicked will be destroyed by their wickedness.

6 Doing right brings freedom to honest people,
but those who are not trustworthy will be caught by their own desires.

7 When the wicked die, hope dies with them;
their hope in riches will come to nothing.

8 The good person is saved from trouble;
it comes to the wicked instead.

9 With words an evil person can destroy a neighbor,
but a good person will escape by being smart.

10 When good people succeed, the city is happy.
When evil people die, there are shouts of joy.

11 Good people bless and build up their city,
but the wicked can destroy it with their words.

12 People without good sense find fault with their neighbors,
but those with understanding keep quiet.

13 Gossips can't keep secrets,
but a trustworthy person can.

14 Without leadership a nation falls,
but lots of good advice will save it.

15 Whoever guarantees to pay somebody else's loan will suffer.
It is safer to avoid such promises.

16 A kind woman gets respect,
but cruel men get only wealth.

17 Kind people do themselves a favor,
but cruel people bring trouble on themselves.

18 An evil person really earns nothing,
but a good person will surely be rewarded.

19 Those who are truly good will live,
but those who chase after evil will die.

20 The LORD hates those with evil hearts
but is pleased with those who are innocent.

21 Evil people will certainly be punished,
but those who do right will be set free.

22 A beautiful woman without good sense
is like a gold ring in a pig's snout.

23 Those who do right only wish for good,
but the wicked can expect to be defeated by God's anger.

24 Some people give much but get back even more.
Others don't give what they should and end up poor.

25 Whoever gives to others will get richer;
those who help others will themselves be helped.

26 People curse those who keep all the grain,
but they bless the one who is willing to sell it.

27 Whoever looks for good will find kindness,
but whoever looks for evil will find trouble.

28 Those who trust in riches will be ruined,
but a good person will be healthy like a green leaf.

29 Whoever brings trouble to his family
will be left with nothing but the wind.
A fool will be a servant to the wise.

30 A good person gives life to others;
the wise person teaches others how to live.

31 Good people will be rewarded on earth,
and the wicked and the sinners will be punished.

12 Anyone who loves learning accepts correction,
but a person who hates being corrected is stupid.

2 The LORD is pleased with a good person,
but he will punish anyone who plans evil.

3 Doing evil brings no safety at all,
but a good person has safety and security.

4 A good wife is like a crown for her husband,
but a disgraceful wife is like a disease in his bones.

5 The plans that good people make are fair,
but the advice of the wicked will trick you.

6 The wicked talk about killing people,
but the words of good people will save them.

7 Wicked people die and they are no more,
but a good person's family continues.

8 The wisdom of the wise wins praise,
but there is no respect for the stupid.

9 A person who is not important but has a servant is better off
than someone who acts important but has no food.

10 Good people take care of their animals,
but even the kindest acts of the wicked are cruel.

[11]Those who work their land will have plenty
of food,
but the one who chases empty dreams is
not wise.

[12]The wicked want what other evil people have
stolen,
but good people want to give what they
have to others.

[13]Evil people are trapped by their evil talk,
but good people stay out of trouble.

[14]People will be rewarded for what they say,
and they will also be rewarded for what
they do.

[15]Fools think they are doing right,
but the wise listen to advice.

[16]Fools quickly show that they are upset,
but the wise ignore insults.

[17]An honest witness tells the truth,
but a dishonest witness tells lies.

[18]Careless words stab like a sword,
but wise words bring healing.

[19]Truth will continue forever,
but lies are only for a moment.

[20]Those who plan evil are full of lies,
but those who plan peace are happy.

[21]No harm comes to a good person,
but an evil person's life is full of trouble.

[22]The LORD hates those who tell lies
but is pleased with those who keep their
promises.

[23]Wise people keep what they know to
themselves,
but fools can't keep from showing how
foolish they are.

[24]Hard workers will become leaders,
but those who are lazy will be slaves.

[25]Worry is a heavy load,
but a kind word cheers you up.

[26]Good people take advice from their friends,
but an evil person is easily led to do wrong.

[27]The lazy catch no food to cook,
but a hard worker will have great wealth.

[28]Doing what is right is the way to life,
but there is another way that leads to
death.

13

Wise children take their parents'
advice,
but whoever makes fun of wisdom won't
listen to correction.

[2]People will be rewarded for what they say,
but those who can't be trusted want only
violence.

[3]Those who are careful about what they say
protect their lives,
but whoever speaks without thinking will
be ruined.

[4]The lazy will not get what they want,
but those who work hard will.

[5]Good people hate what is false,
but the wicked do shameful and disgraceful
things.

[6]Doing what is right protects the honest
person,
but doing evil ruins the sinner.

[7]Some people pretend to be rich but really
have nothing.
Others pretend to be poor but really are
wealthy.

[8]The rich may have to pay a ransom for their
lives,
but the poor will face no such danger.

[9]Good people can look forward to a bright
future,
but the future of the wicked is like a flame
going out.

[10]Pride only leads to arguments,
but those who take advice are wise.

[11]Money that comes easily disappears quickly,
but money that is gathered little by little
will grow.

[12]It is sad not to get what you hoped for.
But wishes that come true are like eating
fruit from the tree of life.

[13]Those who reject what they are taught will
pay for it,
but those who obey what they are told will
be rewarded.

[14]The teaching of a wise person gives life.
It is like a fountain that can save people
from death.

[15]People with good understanding will be well
liked,
but the lives of those who are not
trustworthy are hard.

[16]Every wise person acts with good sense,
but fools show how foolish they are.

[17]A wicked messenger brings nothing but
trouble,
but a trustworthy one makes everything
right.

[18]A person who refuses correction will end up
poor and disgraced,
but the one who accepts correction will be
honored.

[19]It is so good when wishes come true,
but fools hate to stop doing evil.

[20]Spend time with the wise and you will
become wise,
but the friends of fools will suffer.

[21]Trouble always comes to sinners,
but good people enjoy success.

[22]Good people leave their wealth to their
grandchildren,
but a sinner's wealth is stored up for good
people.

[23]A poor person's field might produce plenty of
food,
but others often steal it away.

[24]If you do not punish your children, you don't
love them,
but if you love your children, you will
correct them.

[25]Good people have enough to eat,
but the wicked will go hungry.

14 A wise woman strengthens her family,
but a foolish woman destroys hers by
what she does.

[2]People who live good lives respect the LORD,
but those who live evil lives don't.

[3]Fools will be punished for their proud words,
but the words of the wise will protect
them.

[4]When there are no oxen, no food is in the
barn.
But with a strong ox, much grain can be
grown.

SIDELIGHT: In ancient times, oxen were more valuable to the Israelites than a stereo is to a teenager (Proverbs 14:4). These great beasts were used to plow, tread corn, and pull carts. They even had a day off on the Sabbath (Exodus 23:12, p. 82).

[5]A truthful witness does not lie,
but a false witness tells nothing but lies.

[6]Those who make fun of wisdom look for it
and do not find it,
but knowledge comes easily to those with
understanding.

[7]Stay away from fools,
because they can't teach you anything.

[8]A wise person will understand what to do,
but a foolish person is dishonest.

[9]Fools don't care if they sin,
but honest people work at being right.

[10]No one else can know your sadness,
and strangers cannot share your joy.

[11]The wicked person's house will be destroyed,
but a good person's tent will still be
standing.

[12]Some people think they are doing right,
but in the end it leads to death.

[13]Someone who is laughing may be sad inside,
and joy may end in sadness.

[14]Evil people will be paid back for their evil
ways,
and good people will be rewarded for their
good ones.

[15]Fools will believe anything,
but the wise think about what they do.

[16]Wise people are careful and stay out of
trouble,
but fools are careless and quick to act.

[17]Someone with a quick temper does foolish
things,
but someone with understanding remains
calm.

[18]Fools are rewarded with nothing but more
foolishness,
but the wise are rewarded with knowledge.

[19]Evil people will bow down to those who are
good;
the wicked will bow down at the door of
those who do right.

[20]The poor are rejected, even by their
neighbors,
but the rich have many friends.

[21]It is a sin to hate your neighbor,
but being kind to the needy brings
happiness.

[22]Those who make evil plans will be ruined,
but those who plan to do good will be
loved and trusted.

[23]Those who work hard make a profit,
but those who only talk will be poor.

[24]Wise people are rewarded with wealth,
but fools only get more foolishness.

25A truthful witness saves lives,
but a false witness is a traitor.

26Those who respect the LORD will have security,
and their children will be protected.

27Respect for the LORD gives life.
It is like a fountain that can save people from death.

28A king is honored when he has many people to rule,
but a prince is ruined if he has none.

29Patient people have great understanding,
but people with quick tempers show their foolishness.

30Peace of mind means a healthy body,
but jealousy will rot your bones.

31Whoever mistreats the poor insults their Maker,
but whoever is kind to the needy honors God.

32The wicked are ruined by their own evil,
but those who do right are protected even in death.

33Wisdom lives in those with understanding,
and even fools recognize it.

34Doing what is right makes a nation great,
but sin will bring disgrace to any people.

35A king is pleased with a wise servant,
but he will become angry with one who causes him shame.

15 A gentle answer will calm a person's anger,
but an unkind answer will cause more anger.

2Wise people use knowledge when they speak,
but fools pour out foolishness.

3The LORD's eyes see everything;
he watches both evil and good people.

4As a tree gives fruit, healing words give life,
but dishonest words crush the spirit.

5Fools reject their parents' correction,
but anyone who accepts correction is wise.

6Much wealth is in the houses of good people,
but evil people get nothing but trouble.

7Wise people use their words to spread knowledge,
but there is no knowledge in the thoughts of fools.

8The LORD hates the sacrifice that the wicked offer,
but he likes the prayers of honest people.

9The LORD hates what evil people do,
but he loves those who do what is right.

10The person who quits doing what is right will be punished,
and the one who hates to be corrected will die.

11The LORD knows what is happening in the world of the dead,
so he surely knows the thoughts of the living.

12Those who make fun of wisdom don't like to be corrected;
they will not ask the wise for advice.

13Happiness makes a person smile,
but sadness can break a person's spirit.

14People with understanding want more knowledge,
but fools just want more foolishness.

15Every day is hard for those who suffer,
but a happy heart is like a continual feast.

16It is better to be poor and respect the LORD
than to be wealthy and have much trouble.

17It is better to eat vegetables with those who love you
than to eat meat with those who hate you.

18People with quick tempers cause trouble,
but those who control their tempers stop a quarrel.

19A lazy person's life is like a patch of thorns,
but an honest person's life is like a smooth highway.

20A wise son makes his father happy,
but a foolish son disrespects his mother.

21A person without wisdom enjoys being foolish,
but someone with understanding does what is right.

22Plans fail without good advice,
but they succeed with the advice of many others.

23People enjoy giving good advice.
Saying the right word at the right time is so pleasing.

24Wise people's lives get better and better.
They avoid whatever would cause their death.

25The LORD will tear down the proud person's house,
but he will protect the widow's property.

26The LORD hates evil thoughts
but is pleased with kind words.

27Greedy people bring trouble to their families,
but the person who can't be paid to do
wrong will live.

28Good people think before they answer,
but the wicked simply pour out evil.

29The LORD does not listen to the wicked,
but he hears the prayers of those who do
right.

30Good news makes you feel better.
Your happiness will show in your eyes.

31If you listen to correction to improve your
life,
you will live among the wise.

32Those who refuse correction hate themselves,
but those who accept correction gain
understanding.

33Respect for the LORD will teach you wisdom.
If you want to be honored, you must be
humble.

16 People may make plans in their minds,
but only the LORD can make them
come true.

2You may believe you are doing right,
but the LORD will judge your reasons.

3Depend on the LORD in whatever you do,
and your plans will succeed.

4The LORD makes everything go as he pleases.
He has even prepared a day of disaster for
evil people.

5The LORD hates those who are proud.
They will surely be punished.

6Love and truth bring forgiveness of sin.
By respecting the LORD you will avoid evil.

7When people live so that they please the
LORD,
even their enemies will make peace with
them.

8It is better to be poor and right
than to be wealthy and dishonest.

9People may make plans in their minds,
but the LORD decides what they will do.

10The words of a king are like a message from
God,
so his decisions should be fair.

11The LORD wants honest balances and scales;
all the weights are his work.

12Kings hate those who do wrong,
because governments only continue if they
are fair.

13Kings like honest people;
they value someone who speaks the truth.

14An angry king can put someone to death,
so a wise person will try to make him
happy.

15A smiling king can give people life;
his kindness is like a spring shower.

16It is better to get wisdom than gold,
and to choose understanding rather than
silver!

17Good people stay away from evil.
By watching what they do, they protect
their lives.

18Pride will destroy a person;
a proud attitude leads to ruin.

19It is better to be humble and be with those
who suffer
than to share stolen property with the
proud.

20Whoever listens to what is taught will
succeed,
and whoever trusts the LORD will be happy.

21The wise are known for their understanding.
Their pleasant words make them better
teachers.

22Understanding is like a fountain which gives
life to those who use it,
but foolishness brings punishment to fools.

23Wise people's minds tell them what to say,
and that helps them be better teachers.

24Pleasant words are like a honeycomb,
making people happy and healthy.

25Some people think they are doing right,
but in the end it leads to death.

26The workers' hunger helps them,
because their desire to eat makes them
work.

27Useless people make evil plans,
and their words are like a burning fire.

28A useless person causes trouble,
and a gossip ruins friendships.

29Cruel people trick their neighbors
and lead them to do wrong.

30Someone who winks is planning evil,
and the one who grins is planning
something wrong.

31Gray hair is like a crown of honor;

it is earned by living a good life.

32 Patience is better than strength.
Controlling your temper is better than capturing a city.

33 People throw lots[d] to make a decision,
but the answer comes from the LORD.

17 It is better to eat a dry crust of bread in peace
than to have a feast where there is quarreling.

2 A wise servant will rule over the master's disgraceful child
and will even inherit a share of what the master leaves his children.

3 A hot furnace tests silver and gold,
but the LORD tests hearts.

4 Evil people listen to evil words.
Liars pay attention to cruel words.

5 Whoever mistreats the poor insults their Maker;
whoever enjoys someone's trouble will be punished.

6 Old people are proud of their grandchildren,
and children are proud of their parents.

7 Fools should not be proud,
and rulers should not be liars.

8 Some people think they can pay others to do anything they ask.
They think it will work every time.

9 Whoever forgives someone's sin makes a friend,
but gossiping about the sin breaks up friendships.

10 A wise person will learn more from a warning
than a fool will learn from a hundred lashings.

11 Disobedient people look only for trouble,
so a cruel messenger will be sent against them.

12 It is better to meet a bear robbed of her cubs
than to meet a fool doing foolish things.

13 Whoever gives evil in return for good
will always have trouble at home.

14 Starting a quarrel is like a leak in a dam,
so stop it before a fight breaks out.

15 The LORD hates both of these things:
freeing the guilty and punishing the innocent.

16 It won't do a fool any good to try to buy wisdom,
because he doesn't have the ability to be wise.

17 A friend loves you all the time,
and a brother helps in time of trouble.

18 It is not wise to promise
to pay what your neighbor owes.

19 Whoever loves to argue loves to sin.
Whoever brags a lot is asking for trouble.

20 A person with an evil heart will find no success,
and the person whose words are evil will get into trouble.

21 It is sad to have a foolish child;
there is no joy in being the parent of a fool.

22 A happy heart is like good medicine,
but a broken spirit drains your strength.

23 When the wicked accept money to do wrong
there can be no justice.

24 The person with understanding is always looking for wisdom,
but the mind of a fool wanders everywhere.

25 A foolish son makes his father sad
and causes his mother great sorrow.

26 It is not good to punish the innocent
or to beat leaders for being honest.

27 The smart person says very little,
and one with understanding stays calm.

28 Even fools seem to be wise if they keep quiet;
if they don't speak, they appear to understand.

18 Unfriendly people are selfish
and hate all good sense.

2 Fools do not want to understand anything.
They only want to tell others what they think.

3 Do something evil, and people won't like you.
Do something shameful, and they will make fun of you.

4 Spoken words can be like deep water,
but wisdom is like a flowing stream.

5 It is not good to honor the wicked
or to be unfair to the innocent.

6 The words of fools start quarrels.
They make people want to beat them.

7 The words of fools will ruin them;

their own words will trap them.

8The words of a gossip are like tasty bits of
food.
People like to gobble them up.

9A person who doesn't work hard
is just like someone who destroys things.

10The LORD is like a strong tower;
those who do right can run to him for
safety.

11Rich people trust their wealth to protect
them.
They think it is like the high walls of a city.

12Proud people will be ruined,
but the humble will be honored.

13Anyone who answers without listening
is foolish and confused.

14The will to live can get you through sickness,
but no one can live with a broken spirit.

15The mind of a person with understanding
gets knowledge;
the wise person listens to learn more.

16Taking a gift to an important man
will help get you in to see him.

17The person who tells one side of a story
seems right,
until someone else comes and asks
questions.

18Throwing lots[d] can settle arguments
and keep the two sides from fighting.

19A brother who has been insulted is harder to
win back than a walled city,
and arguments separate people like the
barred gates of a palace.

20People will be rewarded for what they say;
they will be rewarded by how they speak.

21What you say can mean life or death.
Those who speak with care will be
rewarded.

22When a man finds a wife, he finds something
good.
It shows that the LORD is pleased with him.

23The poor beg for mercy,
but the rich give rude answers.

24Some friends may ruin you,
but a real friend will be more loyal than a
brother.

19 It is better to be poor and honest
than to be foolish and tell lies.

2Enthusiasm without knowledge is not good.
If you act too quickly, you might make a
mistake.

3People's own foolishness ruins their lives,
but in their minds they blame the LORD.

4Wealthy people are always finding more
friends,
but the poor lose all theirs.

5A witness who lies will not go free;
liars will never escape.

6Many people want to please a leader,
and everyone is friends with those who
give gifts.

7Poor people's relatives avoid them;
even their friends stay far away.
They run after them, begging,
but they are gone.

8Those who get wisdom do themselves a
favor,
and those who love learning will succeed.

9A witness who lies will not go free,
liars will die.

10A fool should not live in luxury.
A slave should not rule over princes.

11Smart people are patient;
they will be honored if they ignore insults.

12An angry king is like a roaring lion,
but his kindness is like the dew on the
grass.

13A foolish son will ruin his father,
and a quarreling wife is like dripping water.

SIDELIGHT: When we think of dripping water, we most often think of a leaking faucet. But the dripping water of Proverbs 19:13 was much more annoying. It probably referred to a leaking roof. In Bible times, homes were made of mud and had flat roofs. With good care, roofs stayed pretty watertight, but leaky roofs were a common problem—and the source of many jokes.

14Houses and wealth are inherited from
parents,
but a wise wife is a gift from the LORD.

15Lazy people sleep a lot,
and idle people will go hungry.

16Those who obey the commands protect
themselves,
but those who are careless will die.

[17]Being kind to the poor is like lending to the LORD;
he will reward you for what you have done.

[18]Correct your children while there is still hope;
do not let them destroy themselves.

[19]People with quick tempers will have to pay for it.
If you help them out once, you will have to do it again.

[20]Listen to advice and accept correction,
and in the end you will be wise.

[21]People can make all kinds of plans,
but only the LORD's plan will happen.

[22]People want others to be loyal,
so it is better to be poor than to be a liar.

[23]Those who respect the LORD will live
and be satisfied, unbothered by trouble.

[24]Though the lazy person puts his hand in the dish,
he won't lift the food to his mouth.

[25]Whip those who make fun of wisdom, and perhaps foolish people will gain some wisdom.
Correct those with understanding, and they will gain knowledge.

[26]A son who robs his father and sends away his mother
brings shame and disgrace on himself.

[27]Don't stop listening to correction, my child,
or you will forget what you have already learned.

[28]An evil witness makes fun of fairness,
and wicked people love what is evil.

[29]People who make fun of wisdom will be punished,
and the backs of foolish people will be beaten.

20

Wine and beer make people loud and uncontrolled;
it is not wise to get drunk on them.

[2]An angry king is like a roaring lion.
Making him angry may cost you your life.

[3]Foolish people are always fighting,
but avoiding quarrels will bring you honor.

[4]Lazy farmers don't plow when they should;
they expect a harvest, but there is none.

[5]People's thoughts can be like a deep well,
but someone with understanding can find the wisdom there.

[6]Many people claim to be loyal,
but it is hard to find a trustworthy person.

[7]The good people who live honest lives
will be a blessing to their children.

[8]When a king sits on his throne to judge,
he knows evil when he sees it.

[9]No one can say, "I am innocent;
I have never done anything wrong."

[10]The LORD hates both these things:
dishonest weights and dishonest measures.

[11]Even children are known by their behavior;
their actions show if they are innocent and good.

[12]The LORD has made both these things:
ears to hear and eyes to see.

[13]If you love to sleep, you will be poor.
If you stay awake, you will have plenty of food.

[14]Buyers say, "This is bad. It's no good."
Then they go away and brag about what they bought.

[15]There is gold and plenty of rubies,
but only a few people speak with knowledge.

[16]Take the coat of someone who promises to pay a stranger's debts,
and keep it until he pays what the stranger owes.

[17]Stolen food may taste sweet at first,
but later it will feel like a mouth full of gravel.

[18]Get advice if you want your plans to work.
If you go to war, get the advice of others.

[19]Gossips can't keep secrets,
so avoid people who talk too much.

[20]Those who curse their father or mother
will be like a light going out in darkness.

[21]Wealth inherited quickly in the beginning
will do you no good in the end.

[22]Don't say, "I'll pay you back for the wrong you did."
Wait for the LORD, and he will make things right.

[23]The LORD hates dishonest weights,
and dishonest scales do not please him.

[24]The LORD decides what a person will do;

no one understands what his life is all about.

25It's dangerous to promise something to God too quickly.
After you've thought about it, it may be too late.

26A wise king sorts out the evil people,
and he punishes them as they deserve.

27The LORD looks deep inside people
and searches through their thoughts.

28Loyalty and truth keep a king in power;
he continues to rule if he is loyal.

29Young men glory in their strength,
and old men are honored for their gray hair.

30Hard punishment will get rid of evil,
and whippings can change an evil heart.

21

The LORD can control a king's mind as he controls a river;
he can direct it as he pleases.

2You may believe you are doing right,
but the LORD judges your reasons.

3Doing what is right and fair
is more important to the LORD than sacrifices.

4Proud looks, proud thoughts,
and evil actions are sin.

5The plans of hard-working people earn a profit,
but those who act too quickly become poor.

6Wealth that comes from telling lies
vanishes like a mist and leads to death.

7The violence of the wicked will destroy them,
because they refuse to do what is right.

8Guilty people live dishonest lives,
but honest people do right.

9It is better to live in a corner on the roof[n]
than inside the house with a quarreling wife.

10Evil people only want to harm others.
Their neighbors get no mercy from them.

11If you punish those who make fun of wisdom, a foolish person may gain some wisdom.
But if you teach the wise, they will get knowledge.

12God, who is always right, watches the house of the wicked
and brings ruin on every evil person.

13Whoever ignores the poor when they cry for help
will also cry for help and not be answered.

14A secret gift will calm an angry person;
a present given in secrecy will quiet great anger.

15When justice is done, good people are happy,
but evil people are ruined.

16Whoever does not use good sense
will end up among the dead.

17Whoever loves pleasure will become poor;
whoever loves wine and perfume will never be rich.

18Wicked people will suffer instead of good people,
and those who cannot be trusted will suffer instead of those who do right.

19It is better to live alone in the desert
than with a quarreling and complaining wife.

20Wise people's houses are full of the best foods and olive oil,
but fools waste everything they have.

21Whoever tries to live right and be loyal
finds life, success, and honor.

22A wise person can defeat a city full of warriors
and tear down the defenses they trust in.

23Those who are careful about what they say
keep themselves out of trouble.

24People who act with stubborn pride
are called "proud," "bragger," and "mocker."

25Lazy people's desire for sleep will kill them,
because they refuse to work.
26All day long they wish for more,
but good people give without holding back.

27The LORD hates sacrifices brought by evil people,
particularly when they offer them for the wrong reasons.

28A lying witness will be forgotten,
but a truthful witness will speak on.

29Wicked people are stubborn,

roof In Bible times houses were built with flat roofs. The roof was used for drying things such as flax and fruit. And it was used as an extra room, as a place for worship, and as a place to sleep in the summer.

but good people think carefully about what
they do.

30There is no wisdom, understanding, or advice
that can succeed against the LORD.

31You can get the horses ready for battle,
but it is the LORD who gives the victory.

22 Being respected is more important
than having great riches.
To be well thought of is better than silver
or gold.

2The rich and the poor are alike
in that the LORD made them all.

3The wise see danger ahead and avoid it,
but fools keep going and get into trouble.

4Respecting the LORD and not being proud
will bring you wealth, honor, and life.

5Evil people's lives are like paths covered with
thorns and traps.
People who guard themselves don't have
such problems.

6Train children how to live right,
and when they are old, they will not
change.

7The rich rule over the poor,
and borrowers are servants to lenders.

8Those who plan evil will receive trouble.
Their cruel anger will come to an end.

9Generous people will be blessed,

FAMILY

Trust

"Whirr, whirr, whirr, whirr!"

No, not a speeding ticket! Tanya Parker thought. At the worst possible time, too.

Tanya pulled over and waited for the police officer to come to the window. Tanya almost felt like crying. She had been planning to drive to an out-of-town concert this weekend, but getting a speeding ticket would jeopardize her concert plans—if her parents knew. As the police officer handed her the pink slip, she decided it would be better to tell Mom and Dad about the ticket after the concert. Then she returned home and kept quiet.

That night Tanya tossed and turned. Her parents had always trusted her to tell the truth. Finally, around midnight, she got up and went to her older brother to ask his advice. He was still up listening to music.

Tanya told him what had happened and then asked what he thought.

"You'd better tell them," he said. "They'll find out, and then you'll really be in trouble!"

The next morning at breakfast, Tanya spilled the whole story to her parents. She told them about the ticket, and how bad she felt about it, and how she had struggled about telling them.

Disappointment clouded their eyes.

"I don't like the thought of your speeding in our car," Dad said firmly.

"I know, Dad. I'm sorry," Tanya said. "I'll never do it again."

Mom and Dad left the room for a few minutes to talk. Then they returned.

"You have to pay the fine," Mom said and then paused. "And if you agree never to speed again, we won't take away your driving privileges."

"And you can still drive to the concert," Dad added with a grin.

Thrilled, Tanya determined never to betray her parents' trust. And she kept that promise.

Read how **Proverbs 22:1–9** reflects Tanya's family values of honesty and generosity.

- Which verse in this passage best summarizes Tanya's story?
- What would you pay to gain your family's respect and trust? As much as is stated in verse 1?

C O N S I D E R . . .

- talking with a parent about building trust in your relationship.
- writing on a card four things you can do to build your family's trust in you. Post it where only you can see it.

F O R M O R E , S E E . . .

- Genesis 4:1–12 (p. 7)
- Genesis 45:1–11 (p. 50)
- 2 Timothy 3:14–15 (p. 1266)

because they share their food with the
poor.

10Get rid of the one who makes fun of
wisdom.
Then fighting, quarrels, and insults will
stop.

11Whoever loves pure thoughts and kind words
will have even the king as a friend.

12The LORD guards knowledge,
but he destroys false words.

13The lazy person says, "There's a lion outside!
I might get killed out in the street!"

14The words of an unfaithful wife are like a
deep trap.
Those who make the LORD angry will get
caught by them.

15Every child is full of foolishness,
but punishment can get rid of it.

16Whoever gets rich by mistreating the poor,
and gives presents to the wealthy, will
become poor.

Other Wise Sayings

17Listen carefully to what wise people say;
pay attention to what I am teaching you.
18It will be good to keep these things in mind
so that you are ready to repeat them.
19I am teaching them to you now
so that you will put your trust in the LORD.
20I have written thirty sayings for you,
which give knowledge and good advice.
21I am teaching you true and reliable words
so that you can give true answers to
anyone who asks.

22Do not abuse poor people because they are
poor,
and do not take away the rights of the
needy in court.
23The LORD will defend them in court
and will take the life of those who take
away their rights.

24Don't make friends with quick-tempered
people
or spend time with those who have bad
tempers.
25If you do, you will be like them.
Then you will be in real danger.

26Don't promise to pay what someone else
owes,
and don't guarantee anyone's loan.
27If you cannot pay the loan,
your own bed may be taken right out from
under you.

28Don't move an old stone that marks a border,
because those stones were set up by your
ancestors.

29Do you see people skilled in their work?
They will work for kings, not for ordinary
people.

23 If you sit down to eat with a ruler,
notice the food that is in front of you.
2Control yourself
if you have a big appetite.
3Don't be greedy for his fine foods,
because that food might be a trick.

4Don't wear yourself out trying to get rich;
be wise enough to control yourself.
5Wealth can vanish in the wink of an eye.
It can seem to grow wings
and fly away like an eagle.

6Don't eat the food of selfish people;
don't be greedy for their fine foods.
7Selfish people are always worrying
about how much the food costs.
They tell you, "Eat and drink,"
but they don't really mean it.
8You will throw up the little you have eaten,
and you will have wasted your kind words.

9Don't speak to fools;
they will only ignore your wise words.

10Don't move an old stone that marks a border,
and don't take fields that belong to
orphans.
11God, their defender, is strong;
he will take their side against you.

12Remember what you are taught,
and listen carefully to words of knowledge.

13Don't fail to punish children.
If you spank them, they won't die.
14If you spank them,
you will save them from death.

15My child, if you are wise,
then I will be happy.
16I will be so pleased
if you speak what is right.

17Don't envy sinners,
but always respect the LORD.
18Then you will have hope for the future,
and your wishes will come true.

19Listen, my child, and be wise.
Keep your mind on what is right.
20Don't drink too much wine
or eat too much food.
21Those who drink and eat too much become
poor.

They sleep too much and end up wearing
rags.

22Listen to your father, who gave you life,
and do not forget your mother when she is
old.
23Learn the truth and never reject it.
Get wisdom, self-control, and
understanding.
24The father of a good child is very happy;
parents who have wise children are glad
because of them.
25Make your father and mother happy;
give your mother a reason to be glad.

26My son, pay attention to me,
and watch closely what I do.
27A prostitute[d] is as dangerous as a deep pit,
and an unfaithful wife is like a narrow well.
28They ambush you like robbers
and cause many men to be unfaithful to
their wives.

29Who has trouble? Who has pain?
Who fights? Who complains?
Who has unnecessary bruises?
Who has bloodshot eyes?
30It is people who drink too much wine,
who try out all different kinds of strong
drinks.
31Don't stare at the wine when it is red,
when it sparkles in the cup,
when it goes down smoothly.
32Later it bites like a snake
with poison in its fangs.
33Your eyes will see strange sights,
and your mind will be confused.
34You will feel dizzy as if you're in a storm on
the ocean,
as if you're on top of a ship's sails.
35You will think, "They hit me, but I'm not
hurt.
They beat me up, but I don't remember it.
I wish I could wake up.
Then I would get another drink."

24 Don't envy evil people
or try to be friends with them.
2Their minds are always planning violence,
and they always talk about making trouble.

3It takes wisdom to have a good family,
and it takes understanding to make it
strong.
4It takes knowledge to fill a home
with rare and beautiful treasures.

5Wise people have great power,
and those with knowledge have great
strength.
6So you need advice when you go to war.
If you have lots of good advice, you will
win.

7Foolish people cannot understand wisdom.
They have nothing to say in a discussion.

8Whoever makes evil plans
will be known as a troublemaker.
9Making foolish plans is sinful,
and making fun of wisdom is hateful.

10If you give up when trouble comes,
it shows that you are weak.

11Save those who are being led to their death;
rescue those who are about to be killed.
12If you say, "We don't know anything about
this,"
God, who knows what's in your mind, will
notice.
He is watching you, and he will know.
He will reward each person for what he
has done.

13My child, eat honey because it is good.
Honey from the honeycomb tastes sweet.
14In the same way, wisdom is pleasing to you.
If you find it, you have hope for the future,
and your wishes will come true.

15Don't be wicked and attack a good family's
house;
don't rob the place where they live.
16Even though good people may be bothered
by trouble seven times, they are never
defeated,
but the wicked are overwhelmed by
trouble.

17Don't be happy when your enemy is
defeated;
don't be glad when he is overwhelmed.
18The LORD will notice and be displeased.
He may not be angry with them anymore.

19Don't envy evil people,
and don't be jealous of the wicked.
20An evil person has nothing to hope for;
the wicked will die like a flame that is put
out.

21My child, respect the LORD and the king.
Don't join those people who refuse to obey
them.
22The LORD and the king will quickly destroy
such people.
Those two can cause great disaster!

More Words of Wisdom

23These are also sayings of the wise:

It is not good to take sides when you are the
judge.
24Don't tell the wicked that they are innocent;

people will curse you, and nations will hate
you.
25But things will go well if you punish the
guilty,
and you will receive rich blessings.

26An honest answer is as pleasing
as a kiss on the lips.

27First, finish your outside work
and prepare your fields.
After that, you can build your house.

28Don't testify against your neighbor for no
good reason.
Don't say things that are false.
29Don't say, "I'll get even;
I'll do to him what he did to me."

30I passed by a lazy person's field
and by the vineyard of someone with no
sense.
31Thorns had grown up everywhere.
The ground was covered with weeds,
and the stone walls had fallen down.
32I thought about what I had seen;
I learned this lesson from what I saw.
33You sleep a little; you take a nap.
You fold your hands and lie down to rest.
34Soon you will be as poor as if you had been
robbed;
you will have as little as if you had been
held up.

More Wise Sayings of Solomon

25 These are more wise sayings of Solomon, copied by the men of Hezekiah king of Judah.

2God is honored for what he keeps secret.
Kings are honored for what they can
discover.

3No one can measure the height of the skies
or the depth of the earth.
So also no one can understand the mind of
a king.

SIDELIGHT: Need a good brain teaser to fool your friends? Proverbs is filled with ancient riddles (see Proverbs 25:2–3, for example). Unfortunately, the punch lines have lost some of their luster over the years and in the translation, so they are not as intriguing as they used to be.

4Remove the scum from the silver,
so the silver can be used by the silversmith.
5Remove wicked people from the king's
presence;
then his government will be honest and last
a long time.

6Don't brag to the king
and act as if you are great.
7It is better for him to give you a higher
position
than to bring you down in front of the
prince.

Because of something you have seen,
8 do not quickly take someone to court.
What will you do later
when your neighbor proves you wrong?

9If you have an argument with your neighbor,
don't tell other people what was said.
10Whoever hears it might shame you,
and you might not ever be respected again.

11The right word spoken at the right time
is as beautiful as gold apples in a silver
bowl.

12A wise warning to someone who will listen
is as valuable as gold earrings or fine gold
jewelry.

13Trustworthy messengers refresh those who
send them,
like the coolness of snow in the
summertime.

14People who brag about gifts they never give
are like clouds and wind that give no rain.

15With patience you can convince a ruler,
and a gentle word can get through to the
hard-headed.

16If you find honey, don't eat too much,
or it will make you throw up.
17Don't go to your neighbor's house too often;
too much of you will make him hate you.

18When you lie about your neighbors,
it hurts them as much as a club, a sword,
or a sharp arrow.
19Trusting unfaithful people when you are in
trouble
is like eating with a broken tooth or
walking with a crippled foot.

20Singing songs to someone who is sad
is like taking away his coat on a cold day
or pouring vinegar on soda.

21If your enemy is hungry, feed him.
If he is thirsty, give him a drink.
22Doing this will be like pouring burning coals
on his head,
and the LORD will reward you.

[23]As the north wind brings rain,
telling gossip brings angry looks.

[24]It is better to live in a corner on the roof[n]
than inside the house with a quarreling wife.

[25]Good news from a faraway place
is like a cool drink when you are tired.

[26]A good person who gives in to evil
is like a muddy spring or a dirty well.

[27]It is not good to eat too much honey,
nor does it bring you honor to brag about yourself.

[28]Those who do not control themselves
are like a city whose walls are broken down.

26

It shouldn't snow in summer or rain at harvest.
Neither should a foolish person ever be honored.

[2]Curses will not harm someone who is innocent;
they are like sparrows or swallows that fly around and never land.

[3]Whips are for horses, and harnesses are for donkeys,
so paddles are good for fools.

[4]Don't give fools a foolish answer,
or you will be just like them.

[5]But answer fools as they should be answered,
or they will think they are really wise.

[6]Sending a message by a foolish person
is like cutting off your feet or drinking poison.

[7]A wise saying spoken by a fool
is as useless as the legs of a crippled person.

[8]Giving honor to a foolish person
is like tying a stone in a slingshot.

[9]A wise saying spoken by a fool
is like a thorn stuck in the hand of a drunk.

roof In Bible times houses were built with flat roofs. The roof was used for drying things such as flax and fruit. And it was used as an extra room, as a place for worship, and as a place to sleep in the summer.

BRAGGING

All Puffed Up

Porcupine puffer fish dart in and out of coral reefs as they feed. Their pale brown color blends magically with the buff coral. But let a predator, such as a barracuda, threaten them, and they immediately become defensive. They pump water into themselves, almost doubling their size. They inflate into spine-covered balls. The attacker usually retreats, unwilling to swallow such large, thorny creatures.

However, when they puff up, human predators can spot them. These floating curiosities are worth a lot of money. Once netted and brought to the surface, puffer fish inflate themselves with air. In that condition they die. Then they are dried and eventually hung on walls or heaped on shelves of coastal curio shops.

People who brag and boast are like spiny puffers. Take in what **Proverbs 25:6–7** says about puffed-up people.

- What are the puffer fish and the "braggart" in this passage trying to hide?
- In what situations are you tempted to exaggerate your knowledge, abilities, or material possessions? What might happen to you if you didn't pretend to be "great" as this passage directs?

CONSIDER . . .

- writing on a ribbon three things you're tempted to brag about. Then tie the ribbon to your keychain or purse as a reminder not to brag.
- writing a note to at least three people you admire for not being "people-pleasers," telling how you admire that quality in them.

FOR MORE, SEE . . .

- Daniel 4:28–37 (p. 811)
- Mark 9:33–35 (p. 980)
- Luke 18:9–14 (p. 1041)

[10]Hiring a foolish person or anyone just passing
by
is like an archer shooting at just anything.

[11]A fool who repeats his foolishness
is like a dog that goes back to what it has
thrown up.

[12]There is more hope for a foolish person
than for those who think they are wise.

[13]The lazy person says, "There's a lion in the
road!
There's a lion in the streets!"

[14]Like a door turning back and forth on its
hinges,
the lazy person turns over and over in bed.

[15]Lazy people may put their hands in the dish,
but they are too tired to lift the food to
their mouths.

[16]The lazy person thinks he is wiser
than seven people who give sensible
answers.

[17]Interfering in someone else's quarrel as you
pass by
is like grabbing a dog by the ears.

[18]Like a madman shooting
deadly, burning arrows
[19]is the one who tricks a neighbor
and then says, "I was just joking."

[20]Without wood, a fire will go out,
and without gossip, quarreling will stop.

[21]Just as charcoal and wood keep a fire going,
a quarrelsome person keeps an argument
going.

[22]The words of a gossip are like tasty bits of
food;
people like to gobble them up.

[23]Kind words from a wicked mind
are like a shiny coating on a clay pot.

[24]Those who hate you may try to fool you with
their words,
but in their minds they are planning evil.
[25]People's words may be kind, but don't
believe them,
because their minds are full of evil
thoughts.
[26]Lies can hide hate,
but the evil will be plain to everyone.

[27]Whoever digs a pit for others will fall into it.
Whoever tries to roll a boulder down on
others will be crushed by it.

[28]Liars hate the people they hurt,
and false praise can ruin others.

27 Don't brag about tomorrow;
you don't know what may happen
then.

[2]Don't praise yourself. Let someone else do it.
Let the praise come from a stranger and not
from your own mouth.

[3]Stone is heavy, and sand is weighty,
but a complaining fool is worse than either.

[4]Anger is cruel and destroys like a flood,
but no one can put up with jealousy!

[5]It is better to correct someone openly
than to have love and not show it.

[6]The slap of a friend can be trusted to help
you,
but the kisses of an enemy are nothing but
lies.

[7]When you are full, not even honey tastes
good,
but when you are hungry, even something
bitter tastes sweet.

[8]A person who leaves his home
is like a bird that leaves its nest.

[9]The sweet smell of perfume and oils is
pleasant,
and so is good advice from a friend.

SIDELIGHT: If you don't like taking baths, slap on some extra after-shave or perfume. Water was usually scarce in Israel in Old Testament times, and that's what people did. No wonder putting on oil and perfume made people happy (Proverbs 27:9). It probably made everyone nearby even happier!

[10]Don't forget your friend or your parent's
friend.
Don't always go to your family for help
when trouble comes.
A neighbor close by is better than a family
far away.

[11]Be wise, my child, and make me happy.
Then I can respond to any insult.

[12]The wise see danger ahead and avoid it,
but fools keep going and get into trouble.

[13]Take the coat of someone who promises to
pay a stranger's loan,
and keep it until he pays what the stranger
owes.

14If you loudly greet your neighbor early in the
morning,
he will think of it as a curse.

15A quarreling wife is as bothersome
as a continual dripping on a rainy day.
16Stopping her is like stopping the wind
or trying to grab oil in your hand.

17As iron sharpens iron,
so people can improve each other.

18Whoever tends a fig tree gets to eat its fruit,
and whoever takes care of his master will
receive honor.

19As water reflects your face,
so your mind shows what kind of person
you are.

20People will never stop dying and being
destroyed,
and they will never stop wanting more than
they have.

21A hot furnace tests silver and gold,
and people are tested by the praise they
receive.

22Even if you ground up a foolish person like
grain in a bowl,
you couldn't remove the foolishness.

23Be sure you know how your sheep are doing,
and pay attention to the condition of your
cattle.
24Riches will not go on forever,
nor do governments go on forever.
25Bring in the hay, and let the new grass
appear.
Gather the grass from the hills.
26Make clothes from the lambs' wool,
and sell some goats to buy a field.
27There will be plenty of goat's milk
to feed you and your family
and to make your servant girls healthy.

28

Evil people run even though no one is
chasing them,
but good people are as brave as a lion.

2When a country is lawless, it has one ruler
after another;
but when it is led by a man with
understanding and knowledge, it
continues strong.

3Rulers who mistreat the poor
are like a hard rain that destroys the crops.

4Those who disobey what they have been
taught praise the wicked,
but those who obey what they have been
taught are against them.

5Evil people do not understand justice,
but those who follow the LORD understand
it completely.

6It is better to be poor and innocent
than to be rich and wicked.

7Children who obey what they have been
taught are smart,
but friends of troublemakers disgrace their
parents.

8Some people get rich by overcharging others,
but their wealth will be given to those who
are kind to the poor.

9If you refuse to obey what you have been
taught,
your prayers will not be heard.

10Those who lead good people to do wrong
will be ruined by their own evil,
but the innocent will be rewarded with
good things.

11Rich people may think they are wise,
but the poor with understanding will prove
them wrong.

12When good people triumph, there is great
happiness,
but when the wicked get control,
everybody hides.

13If you hide your sins, you will not succeed.
If you confess and reject them, you will
receive mercy.

14Those who are always respectful will be
happy,
but those who are stubborn will get into
trouble.

15A wicked ruler is as dangerous to poor people
as a roaring lion or a charging bear.

16A ruler without wisdom will be cruel,
but the one who refuses to take dishonest
money will rule a long time.

17Don't help those who are guilty of murder;
let them run until they die.

18Innocent people will be kept safe,
but those who are dishonest will suddenly
be ruined.

19Those who work their land will have plenty
of food,
but the ones who chase empty dreams
instead will end up poor.

20A truthful person will have many blessings,
but those eager to get rich will be
punished.

21It is not good for a judge to take sides,

but some will sin for only a piece of bread.

22Selfish people are in a hurry to get rich
and do not realize they soon will be poor.

23Those who correct others will later be liked
more than those who give false praise.

24Whoever robs his father or mother
and says, "It's not wrong,"
is just like someone who destroys things.

25A greedy person causes trouble,
but the one who trusts the LORD will
succeed.

26Those who trust in themselves are foolish,
but those who live wisely will be kept safe.

27Whoever gives to the poor will have
everything he needs,
but the one who ignores the poor will
receive many curses.

28When the wicked get control, everybody
hides,
but when they die, good people do well.

29 Whoever is stubborn after being
corrected many times
will suddenly be hurt beyond cure.

2When good people do well, everyone is
happy,
but when evil people rule, everyone groans.

3Those who love wisdom make their parents
happy,
but friends of prostitutes[d] waste their
money.

4If a king is fair, he makes his country strong,
but if he takes gifts dishonestly, he tears his
country down.

5Those who give false praise to their neighbors
are setting a trap for them.

6Evil people are trapped by their own sin,
but good people can sing and be happy.

7Good people care about justice for the poor,
but the wicked are not concerned.

8People who make fun of wisdom cause
trouble in a city,
but wise people calm anger down.

9When a wise person takes a foolish person to
court,
the fool only shouts or laughs, and there is
no peace.

10Murderers hate an honest person
and try to kill those who do right.

11Foolish people lose their tempers,
but wise people control theirs.

12If a ruler pays attention to lies,
all his officers will become wicked.

13The poor person and the cruel person are
alike
in that the LORD gave eyes to both of them.

14If a king judges poor people fairly,
his government will continue forever.

15Correction and punishment make children
wise,
but those left alone will disgrace their
mother.

16When there are many wicked people, there is
much sin,
but those who do right will see them
destroyed.

17Correct your children, and you will be proud;
they will give you satisfaction.

18Where there is no word from God, people
are uncontrolled,
but those who obey what they have been
taught are happy.

19Words alone cannot correct a servant,
because even if he understands, he won't
respond.

20Do you see people who speak too quickly?
There is more hope for a foolish person
than for them.

21If you spoil your servants when they are
young,
they will bring you grief later on.

22An angry person causes trouble;
a person with a quick temper sins a lot.

23Pride will ruin people,
but those who are humble will be honored.

24Partners of thieves are their own worst
enemies.
If they have to testify in court, they are
afraid to say anything.

25Being afraid of people can get you into
trouble,
but if you trust the LORD, you will be safe.

26Many people want to speak to a ruler,
but justice comes only from the LORD.

27Good people hate those who are dishonest,
and the wicked hate those who are honest.

Wise Words from Agur

30 These are the words of Agur son of Jakeh.

This is his message to Ithiel and Ucal:

2“I am the most stupid person there is,
and I have no understanding.
3I have not learned to be wise,
and I don’t know much about God, the Holy One.
4Who has gone up to heaven and come back down?
Who can hold the wind in his hand?
Who can gather up the waters in his coat?
Who has set in place the ends of the earth?
What is his name or his son’s name?
Tell me, if you know!

5“Every word of God is true.
He guards those who come to him for safety.
6Do not add to his words,
or he will correct you and prove you are a liar.

7“I ask two things from you, LORD.
Don’t refuse me before I die.
8Keep me from lying and being dishonest.
And don’t make me either rich or poor;
just give me enough food for each day.
9If I have too much, I might reject you
and say, ‘I don’t know the LORD.’
If I am poor, I might steal
and disgrace the name of my God.

10“Do not say bad things about servants to their masters,
or they will curse you, and you will suffer for it.

11“Some people curse their fathers
and do not bless their mothers.
12Some people think they are pure,
but they are not really free from evil.
13Some people have such a proud look!
They look down on others.
14Some people have teeth like swords;
their jaws seem full of knives.
They want to remove the poor from the earth
and the needy from the land.

15“Greed has two daughters
named ‘Give’ and ‘Give.’
There are three things that are never satisfied,
really four that never say, ‘I’ve had enough!’:
16the cemetery, the childless mother,
the land that never gets enough rain,
and fire that never says, ‘I’ve had enough!’

17“If you make fun of your father
and refuse to obey your mother,
the birds of the valley will peck out your eyes,
and the vultures will eat them.

18“There are three things that are too hard for me,
really four I don’t understand:
19the way an eagle flies in the sky,
the way a snake slides over a rock,
the way a ship sails on the sea,
and the way a man and a woman fall in love.

20“This is the way of a woman who takes part in adultery:[d]
She acts as if she had eaten and washed her face;
she says, ‘I haven’t done anything wrong.’

21“There are three things that make the earth tremble,
really four it cannot stand:
22a servant who becomes a king,
a foolish person who has plenty to eat,
23a hated woman who gets married,
and a maid who replaces her mistress.

24“There are four things on earth that are small,
but they are very wise:
25Ants are not very strong,
but they store up food in the summer.
26Rock badgers are not very powerful,
but they can live among the rocks.
27Locusts[d] have no king,
but they all go forward in formation.
28Lizards can be caught in the hand,
but they are found even in kings’ palaces.

29“There are three things that strut proudly,
really four that walk as if they were important:
30a lion, the proudest animal,
which is strong and runs from nothing,
31a rooster, a male goat,
and a king when his army is around him.

32“If you have been foolish and proud,
or if you have planned evil, shut your mouth.
33Just as stirring milk makes butter,
and twisting noses makes them bleed,
so stirring up anger causes trouble.”

Wise Words of King Lemuel

31 These are the words of King Lemuel, the message his mother taught him:

2“My son, I gave birth to you.
You are the son I prayed for.
3Don’t waste your strength on women
or your time on those who ruin kings.

4“Kings should not drink wine, Lemuel,
and rulers should not desire beer.
5If they drink, they might forget the law

and keep the needy from getting their
rights.
6Give beer to people who are dying
and wine to those who are sad.
7Let them drink and forget their need
and remember their misery no more.

8"Speak up for those who cannot speak for
themselves;
defend the rights of all those who have
nothing.
9Speak up and judge fairly,
and defend the rights of the poor and
needy."

The Good Wife

10It is hard to find a good wife,
because she is worth more than rubies.
11Her husband trusts her completely.
With her, he has everything he needs.
12She does him good and not harm
for as long as she lives.
13She looks for wool and flax
and likes to work with her hands.
14She is like a trader's ship,
bringing food from far away.
15She gets up while it is still dark
and prepares food for her family
and feeds her servant girls.
16She inspects a field and buys it.
With money she earned, she plants a
vineyard.
17She does her work with energy,
and her arms are strong.
18She knows that what she makes is good.
Her lamp burns late into the night.

SIDELIGHT: The "good wife" of Proverbs 31:10–31 would have been a "supermom" centuries before that term was common. Not only did she do everything around the house; she also farmed (verse 16), worked in manufacturing (verse 24), and did volunteer work (verse 20). Makes you wonder what her husband did!

MARRIAGE

Like Great-Grandmother

Tracy Bilmer stood in her great-grandmother's wedding dress, watching her mother fit the new sleeves into place. "I'm scared."

"Of what, sweetie?"

"Marriage." Tracy stared into the mirror. "I'm scared of being an adult. Of being responsible for building a new life with Chris."

"I know." Her mother pushed back her hair. "But follow your great-grandmother's example. She built a grand life for herself and her husband."

Her mother smiled, remembering. "She helped clear the Colorado homestead, bore babies, worked beside my granddad in the fields, set her children's broken bones, canned a thousand jars of food each summer, sewed clothes, and prayed beside her children's beds each night. And through it all she was a loving lady. She and Granddad truly loved each other, and they made a great team. As Granddad lay dying, after sixty-six years of marriage, he said she was still his angel."

"Funny, she seems modern—a working woman, besides being a wife and mother," Tracy said.

"Loving determination, that's what she had. That and her faith in God."

The good wife in Proverbs also possessed some of the great-grandmother's qualities. Read **Proverbs 31:10–31**.

- In what ways is the great-grandmother like the wife described in this passage?
- Which qualities, listed in these verses, do you most want in your life?

CONSIDER . . .

- looking for qualities of a godly wife or husband at your church, then asking God to help you build those qualities in yourself so you will be a godly spouse if you marry.
- asking couples you admire for their secret of a successful marriage.

FOR MORE, SEE . . .

- Ruth 3—4 (p. 241)
- Ephesians 5:21–33 (p. 1225)
- 1 Peter 3:1–7 (p. 1306)

19She makes thread with her hands
and weaves her own cloth.
20She welcomes the poor
and helps the needy.
21She does not worry about her family when it snows,
because they all have fine clothes to keep them warm.
22She makes coverings for herself;
her clothes are made of linen and other expensive material.
23Her husband is known at the city meetings,
where he makes decisions as one of the leaders of the land.
24She makes linen clothes and sells them
and provides belts to the merchants.
25She is strong and is respected by the people.
She looks forward to the future with joy.
26She speaks wise words
and teaches others to be kind.
27She watches over her family
and never wastes her time.
28Her children speak well of her.
Her husband also praises her,
29saying, "There are many fine women,
but you are better than all of them."
30Charm can fool you, and beauty can trick you,
but a woman who respects the LORD should be praised.
31Give her the reward she has earned;
she should be praised in public for what she has done.

ECCLESIASTES

Why Read This Book:

- See the results of living a variety of lifestyles (Ecclesiastes 1—2).
- Find companionship when bad things happen (Ecclesiastes 4—5).
- Explore the problem of injustice and the mystery of God (Ecclesiastes 9—10).
- Accept and enjoy life as God has given it (Ecclesiastes 3, 6, 11—12).

Behind the Scenes:

What brings happiness? What gives life meaning? People look in all kinds of places for answers to these questions.

Some people spend their lives making money to buy happiness. Then they die feeling empty and lonely.

Other people work hard on the job, hoping to find a way to leave a lasting impression on the world. Then they die, and people forget them.

Some people study and learn all they can in a quest for knowledge and understanding. Yet the world still holds mysteries they can't understand.

Other people spend all their time on the "party scene," trying to have fun and feel good. But afterward, life seems hollow and purposeless.

The writer of Ecclesiastes—often called the Preacher or the Teacher—walked down all these paths looking for happiness. Yet he never found it. Life was too complex and contradictory to understand through simple formulas. Good people suffered. Bad people prospered. It didn't make sense.

The book of Ecclesiastes contains the Teacher's thoughts about life and its meaning. Sometimes he seems skeptical and cynical, because nothing in life seems meaningful (Ecclesiastes 1:2 and 12:8). Sometimes he says God is so distant we can't know him (Ecclesiastes 5:2).

Yet Ecclesiastes also gives insight and comfort on several levels.

- First, the book affirms the importance of exploring and reflecting on what it means to follow God. Not only does Ecclesiastes remind us it's okay to ask tough questions, but the author's arguments can help us think through those questions.
- Second, the author's philosophical thoughts show the emptiness of life without God. True wisdom and meaning can't be found with human effort; they are gifts from God.
- Third, the author believes life is worth living, even with its problems. He urges people to grab onto and enjoy the good things God gives us.
- Finally, the author affirms that God is in control—even when we can't see his work. "Honor God and obey his commands," he urges, "because this is all people must do" (Ecclesiastes 12:13).

WHEN THE ACTION WAS

1000BC	King Solomon ruled Israel and many people believe he wrote Ecclesiastes
750BC	
	Jerusalem fell to the Babylonians
500BC	Jews began returning to Jerusalem from exile
	Ecclesiastes may have been written
250BC	
BC/AD	Jesus was born

1 These are the words of the Teacher, a son of
David, king in Jerusalem.
2The Teacher says,
"Useless! Useless!
Completely useless!
Everything is useless."

3What do people really gain
from all the hard work they do here on
earth?

Things Never Change

4People live, and people die,
but the earth continues forever.
5The sun rises, the sun sets,
and then it hurries back to where it rises
again.
6The wind blows to the south;
it blows to the north.
It blows from one direction and then another.
Then it turns around and repeats the same
pattern, going nowhere.

SIDELIGHT: The title of Ecclesiastes is, itself, a mystery. It's translated from the Hebrew word "Qoheleth," but no one is sure what it means. Some scholars think it might be a proper name; others say it means "The Preacher," "The Teacher," or "Speaker." But still others think it could mean "The Arguer," which captures the book's content well!

7All the rivers flow to the sea,
but the sea never becomes full.
8Everything is boring,

DISCOURAGEMENT

Failure Turned Around

Charles sat on the steps in misery. He watched his classmates pass by him as if he were invisible. The yearbook committee rejection note in his hands branded him "First Class Loser"—a label he had worn many times. He had hoped this time would be different. He had hoped that his one ability, cartooning, would help promote him from his self-imposed "loser" status. But the note unceremoniously crushed his hopes.

"The yearbook committee has decided not to use your submission this year. Thank you for submitting your material."

Why should he be surprised? Failure slugged him regularly. He recounted his blunders:

- An F in Latin
- An F in Algebra
- Failed every class in the 8th grade
- A klutz in sports
- Last place in the school golf tournament and its consolation match
- Too scared to ask any girl out on a date

With a resigned sigh, Charles turned toward home. He believed nothing was ever going to change for him.

He continued to create imaginary worlds on paper, unable to stop drawing. Repeatedly, through the years, his cartoons were rejected. Then one day he created a character like himself—a habitual failure.

And Charlie Brown was born.

In Ecclesiastes, the writer is discouraged because he feels like nothing ever changes, just as Charles Schulz once did. But Schulz later created the famous Peanuts comic strip. Read **Ecclesiastes 1:2–11**.

- Which of these verses best describe Charles's feelings?
- Which verses best describe you when you're discouraged?

CONSIDER . . .

- identifying your strongest interest and writing yourself a promise to develop it to the fullest.
- asking a friend this week to encourage you by telling you what positive qualities he or she sees in you.

FOR MORE, SEE

- Isaiah 43:18–21 (p. 660)
- Matthew 6:25–27 (p. 918)
- Romans 15:1–7 (p. 1161)

so boring that you don't even want to talk
about it.
Words come again and again to our ears,
but we never hear enough,
nor can we ever really see all we want to
see.
9All things continue the way they have been
since the beginning.
What has happened will happen again;
there is nothing new here on earth.
10Someone might say,
"Look, this is new,"
but really it has always been here.
It was here before we were.
11People don't remember what happened long
ago,
and in the future people will not remember
what happens now.
Even later, other people will not remember
what was done before them.

Does Wisdom Bring Happiness?

12I, the Teacher, was king over Israel in Jerusalem. 13I decided to use my wisdom to learn about
everything that happens on earth. I learned that
God has given us terrible things to face. 14I looked
at everything done on earth and saw that it is all
useless, like chasing the wind.

15If something is crooked,
you can't make it straight.
If something is missing,
you can't say it is there.

16I said to myself, "I have become very wise
and am now wiser than anyone who ruled Jerusalem before me. I know what wisdom and knowledge really are." 17So I decided to find out about
wisdom and knowledge and also about foolish
thinking, but this turned out to be like chasing the
wind.

18With much wisdom comes much
disappointment;
the person who gains more knowledge also
gains more sorrow.

Does "Having Fun" Bring Happiness?

2 I said to myself, "I will try having fun. I will
enjoy myself." But I found that this is also
useless. 2It is foolish to laugh all the time, and
having fun doesn't accomplish anything. 3I decided to cheer myself up with wine while my
mind was still thinking wisely. I wanted to find a
way to enjoy myself and see what was good for
people to do during their few days of life.

Does Hard Work Bring Happiness?

4Then I did great things: I built houses and
planted vineyards for myself. 5I made gardens and
parks, and I planted all kinds of fruit trees in them.
6I made pools of water for myself and used them
to water my growing trees. 7I bought male and
female slaves, and slaves were also born in my
house. I had large herds and flocks, more than
anyone in Jerusalem had ever had before. 8I also
gathered silver and gold for myself, treasures from
kings and other areas. I had male and female singers and all the women a man could ever want. 9I
became very famous, even greater than anyone
who had lived in Jerusalem before me. My wisdom helped me in all this.

10Anything I saw and wanted, I got for myself;
I did not miss any pleasure I desired.
I was pleased with everything I did,
and this pleasure was the reward for all my
hard work.
11But then I looked at what I had done,
and I thought about all the hard work.
Suddenly I realized it was useless, like
chasing the wind.
There is nothing to gain from anything we
do here on earth.

SIDELIGHT: The Teacher mentions hard work more than thirty times in Ecclesiastes (for example, Ecclesiastes 2:4–11). Yet he considers it useless activity apart from God. Maybe he should have joined Workaholics Anonymous.

Maybe Wisdom Is the Answer

12Then I began to think again about being
wise,
and also about being foolish and doing
crazy things.
But after all, what more can anyone do?
He can't do more than what the other king
has already done.
13I saw that being wise is certainly better than
being foolish,
just as light is better than darkness.
14Wise people see where they are going,
but fools walk around in the dark.
Yet I saw that
both wise and foolish people end the same
way.
15I thought to myself,
"What happens to a fool will happen to me,
too,
so what is the reward for being wise?"
I said to myself,
"Being wise is also useless."
16The wise person and the fool
will both die,

and no one will remember either one for
long.
In the future, both will be forgotten.

Is There Real Happiness in Life?

17So I hated life. It made me sad to think that
everything here on earth is useless, like chasing
the wind. 18I hated all the things I had worked for
here on earth, because I must leave them to someone who will live after me. 19Someone else will
control everything for which I worked so hard
here on earth, and I don't know if he will be wise
or foolish. This is also useless. 20So I became sad
about all the hard work I had done here on earth.
21People can work hard using all their wisdom,
knowledge, and skill, but they will die, and other
people will get the things for which they worked.
They did not do the work, but they will get everything. This is also unfair and useless. 22What do
people get for all their work and struggling here
on earth? 23All of their lives their work is full of
pain and sorrow, and even at night their minds
don't rest. This is also useless.
24The best that people can do is eat, drink, and
enjoy their work. I saw that even this comes from
God, 25because no one can eat or enjoy life without him. 26If people please God, God will give
them wisdom, knowledge, and joy. But sinners
will get only the work of gathering and storing
wealth that they will have to give to the ones who
please God. So all their work is useless, like chasing the wind.

There Is a Time for Everything

3 There is a time for everything,
and everything on earth has its special
season.
2There is a time to be born
and a time to die.
There is a time to plant
and a time to pull up plants.
3There is a time to kill
and a time to heal.
There is a time to destroy
and a time to build.
4There is a time to cry
and a time to laugh.
There is a time to be sad
and a time to dance.
5There is a time to throw away stones

HAPPINESS

In the Here and Now

At dawn Jay Norris lay in his lakeside tent and replayed the state track meet in his head. He was running the 3200-meter race, pushing toward the finish line. His only chance for an athletic scholarship was riding on the finish. He had to place in the top three.

He came in seventh.

"Jay, pancakes on!" Uncle Carl called from the campfire. Uncle Carl had always been there for him, ever since Dad had left. He crawled out and joined Uncle Carl.

"I want to tell you something, boy," Uncle Carl said, serving Jay's plate. "You lost that race . . . that's life." He looked straight at Jay. "The point is—God has given you legs to enjoy running with."

"So?"

"I'm talking about enjoying the moment—the feel of your feet in your shoes, the pounding of your shoes on the track, and the tingle in your arms and legs!" He grinned at Jay. "Now, that's living."

Uncle Carl's words didn't mean much to Jay then. But over the years they've shaped the way he looks at life. Now he strives to enjoy what God's given to him.

The writer of Ecclesiastes tried to find happiness in the middle of loss also. Read **Ecclesiastes 2:18–26**.

- How does Uncle Carl's advice compare with the advice in Ecclesiastes?
- How can you apply the advice in the passage to your life this week?

CONSIDER . . .

- focusing only on your body sensations while washing the car, or eating or exercising.
- going for a walk in the woods and then recording in a journal all the fun moments you experienced.

FOR MORE, SEE . . .

- Psalm 16:7–11 (p. 489)
- Luke 12:22–31 (p. 1028)
- 2 Corinthians 4:7–9 (p. 1195)

and a time to gather them.
There is a time to hug
and a time not to hug.
6There is a time to look for something
and a time to stop looking for it.
There is a time to keep things
and a time to throw things away.
7There is a time to tear apart
and a time to sew together.
There is a time to be silent
and a time to speak.
8There is a time to love
and a time to hate.
There is a time for war
and a time for peace.

God Controls His World

9Do people really gain anything from their
work? 10I saw the hard work God has given people to do. 11God has given them a desire to know
the future. He does everything just right and on
time, but people can never completely understand what he is doing. 12So I realize that the best
thing for them is to be happy and enjoy themselves as long as they live. 13God wants all people
to eat and drink and be happy in their work,
which are gifts from God. 14I know that everything God does will continue forever. People cannot add anything to what God has done, and they
cannot take anything away from it. God does it
this way to make people respect him.

15What happens now has happened in the past,
and what will happen in the future has
happened before.
God makes the same things happen again
and again.

Unfairness on Earth

16I also saw this here on earth:
Where there should have been justice, there
was evil;
where there should have been right, there
was wrong.
17I said to myself,
God has planned a time for every thing and
every action,
so he will judge both good people and bad.

18I decided that God leaves it the way it is to
test people and to show them they are just like

SADNESS

Death Watch

Derek Grimm's grandfather lay quietly in his bed at home, shriveled to the bone by Parkinson's disease.

Derek held his calloused hand and whispered. "I love you, Gramps."

"I love you too," the old man whispered back, barely able to talk.

Tears sprang to Derek's eyes. "What will I do without you?"

"Remember our good times." The old man closed his eyes. "Enjoy your life . . . and follow the Lord."

"I don't want to let you go," Derek began to cry.

"It's all right," Gramps said. "It's my time to go. God knows what he's doing."

Derek fought back tears as he watched his grandfather struggle to breathe.

"Will you play 'Take My Hand, Precious Lord'? It soothes me," Gramps asked.

Derek sat at the piano in the next room and played the song Gramps had heard so many times before. Derek's heart broke with each note. But there was also a distant joy for the times he and Gramps had shared and the fact that the pain would finally end.

Even the sadness of death can be seen as a natural part of life, according to **Ecclesiastes 3:1–13**.

- Where in these verses are there words like Gramps spoke?
- How do these verses help you cope with sadness?

CONSIDER . . .

- writing an example for each of the "times" listed in the passage.
- looking through family photos and remembering times like those listed in Ecclesiastes.

FOR MORE, SEE . . .

- Psalm 88 (p. 533)
- Romans 5:3–5 (p. 1145)
- Philippians 3:4–7 (p. 1232)

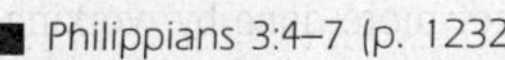

animals. 19The same thing happens to animals and to people; they both have the same breath, so they both die. People are no better off than the animals, because everything is useless. 20Both end up the same way; both came from dust and both will go back to dust. 21Who can be sure that the human spirit goes up to God and that the spirit of an animal goes down into the ground? 22So I saw that the best thing people can do is to enjoy their work, because that is all they have. No one can help another person see what will happen in the future.

Is It Better to Be Dead?

4 Again I saw all the people who were mistreated here on earth.

I saw their tears
and that they had no one to comfort them.
Cruel people had all the power,
and there was no one to comfort those they hurt.
2I decided that the dead
are better off than the living.
3But those who have never been born
are better off still;
they have not seen the evil
that is done here on earth.

Why Work So Hard?

4I realized the reason people work hard and try to succeed: They are jealous of each other. This, too, is useless, like chasing the wind.

5Some say it is foolish to fold your hands and do nothing,
because you will starve to death.
6Maybe so, but I say it is better to be content with what little you have.
Otherwise, you will always be struggling for more,
and that is like chasing the wind.

7Again I saw something here on earth that was useless:
8I saw a man who had no family,
no son or brother.
He always worked hard
but was never satisfied with what he had.
He never asked himself, "For whom am I working so hard?
Why don't I let myself enjoy life?"
This also is very sad and useless.

Friends and Family Give Strength

9Two people are better than one,
because they get more done by working together.
10If one falls down,
the other can help him up.
But it is bad for the person who is alone and falls,
because no one is there to help.
11If two lie down together, they will be warm,
but a person alone will not be warm.
12An enemy might defeat one person,
but two people together can defend themselves;
a rope that is woven of three strings is hard to break.

Fame and Power Are Useless

13A poor but wise boy is better than a foolish but old king who doesn't listen to advice. 14A boy became king. He had been born poor in the kingdom and had even gone to prison before becoming king. 15I watched all the people who live on earth follow him and make him their king. 16Many followed him at first, but later, they did not like him, either. So fame and power are useless, like chasing the wind.

Be Careful About Making Promises

5 Be careful when you go to worship at the Temple.[d] It is better to listen than to offer foolish sacrifices without even knowing you are doing wrong.

2Think before you speak,
and be careful about what you say to God.
God is in heaven,
and you are on the earth,
so say only a few words to God.
3The saying is true: Bad dreams come from too much worrying,
and too many words come from foolish people.

4If you make a promise to God, don't be slow to keep it. God is not happy with fools, so give God what you promised. 5It is better not to promise anything than to promise something and not do it. 6Don't let your words cause you to sin, and don't say to the priest at the Temple, "I didn't mean what I promised." If you do, God will become angry with your words and will destroy everything you have worked for. 7Many useless promises are like so many dreams; they mean nothing. You should respect God.

SIDELIGHT: Making a promise in biblical times (Ecclesiastes 5:4–7) was more like signing an important legal contract (such as a marriage license) today. Once you made a promise, you couldn't really get out of it.

Officers Cheat Each Other

[8]In some places you will see poor people mistreated. Don't be surprised when they are not treated fairly or given their rights. One officer is cheated by a higher officer who in turn is cheated by even higher officers. [9]The wealth of the country is divided up among them all. Even the king makes sure he gets his share of the profits.

Wealth Cannot Buy Happiness

[10]Whoever loves money
will never have enough money;
Whoever loves wealth
will not be satisfied with it.
This is also useless.
[11]The more wealth people have,
the more friends they have to help spend it.
So what do people really gain?
They gain nothing except to look at their riches.
[12]Those who work hard sleep in peace;
it is not important if they eat little or much.
But rich people worry about their wealth
and cannot sleep.

[13]I have seen real misery here on earth:
Money saved is a curse to its owners.
[14] They lose it all in a bad deal
and have nothing to give to their children.
[15]People come into this world with nothing,
and when they die they leave with nothing.
In spite of all their hard work,
they leave just as they came.
[16]This, too, is real misery:
They leave just as they came.
So what do they gain from chasing the wind?
[17]All they get are days full of sadness and sorrow,
and they end up sick, defeated, and angry.

Enjoy Your Life's Work

[18]I have seen what is best for people here on
earth. They should eat and drink and enjoy their
work, because the life God has given them on
earth is short. [19]God gives some people the ability
to enjoy the wealth and property he gives them,
as well as the ability to accept their state in life
and enjoy their work. [20]They do not worry about
how short life is, because God keeps them busy
with what they love to do.

6 I have seen something else wrong here on
earth that causes serious problems for people. [2]God gives great wealth, riches, and honor to
some people; they have everything they want.
But God does not let them enjoy such things; a
stranger enjoys them instead. This is useless and
very wrong. [3]A man might have a hundred children and live a long time, but what good is it if
he can't enjoy the good God gives him or have a
proper burial? I say a baby born dead is better off
than he is. [4]A baby born dead is useless. It returns
to darkness without even a name. [5]That baby
never saw the sun and never knew anything, but
it finds more rest than that man. [6]Even if he lives
two thousand years, he doesn't enjoy the good
God gives him. Everyone is going to the same
place.

[7]People work just to feed themselves,
but they never seem to get enough to eat.
[8]In this way a wise person
is no better off than a fool.
Then, too, it does a poor person little good
to know how to get along in life.
[9]It is better to see what you have
than to want more.
Wanting more is useless—
like chasing the wind.

Who Can Understand God's Plan?

[10]Whatever happens was planned long ago.
Everyone knows what people are like.
No one can argue with God,
who is stronger than anyone.
[11]The more you say,
the more useless it is.
What good does it do?

[12]People have only a few useless days of life on
the earth; their short life passes like a shadow.
Who knows what is best for them while they live?
Who can tell them what the future will bring?

Some Benefits of Serious Thinking

7 It is better to have respect than good perfume.
The day of death is better than the day of birth.
[2]It is better to go to a funeral
than to a party.
We all must die,
and everyone living should think about this.
[3]Sorrow is better than laughter,
and sadness has a good influence on you.
[4]A wise person thinks about death,
but a fool thinks only about having a good time.
[5]It is better to be criticized by a wise person
than to be praised by a fool.
[6]The laughter of fools
is like the crackling of thorns in a cooking fire.
Both are useless.

[7]Even wise people are fools
if they let money change their thinking.

[8]It is better to finish something
than to start it.

It is better to be patient
than to be proud.
9Don't become angry quickly,
because getting angry is foolish.

10Don't ask, "Why was life better in the 'good old days'?"
It is not wise to ask such questions.

11Wisdom is better when it comes with money.
They both help those who are alive.
12Wisdom is like money:
they both help.
But wisdom is better,
because it can save whoever has it.

13Look at what God has done:
No one can straighten what he has bent.
14When life is good, enjoy it.
But when life is hard, remember:
God gives good times and hard times,
and no one knows what tomorrow will bring.

It Is Impossible to Be Truly Good

15In my useless life I have seen both of these:
I have seen good people die in spite of their goodness
and evil people live a long time in spite of their evil.
16Don't be too right,
and don't be too wise.
Why destroy yourself?
17Don't be too wicked,
and don't be foolish.
Why die before your time?
18It is good to grab the one and not let go of the other;
those who honor God will hold them both.

19Wisdom makes a person stronger
than ten leaders in a city.

20Surely there is not a good person on earth
who always does good and never sins.

21Don't listen to everything people say,
or you might hear your servant insulting you.
22You know that many times
you have insulted others.

23I used wisdom to test all these things.
I wanted to be wise,
but it was too hard for me.
24I cannot understand why things are as they are.
It is too hard for anyone to understand.
25I studied and tried very hard to find wisdom,
to find some meaning for everything.
I learned that it is foolish to be evil,
and it is crazy to act like a fool.

26I found that some women are worse than death
and are as dangerous as traps.
Their love is like a net,
and their arms hold men like chains.
A man who pleases God will be saved from them,
but a sinner will be caught by them.

27The Teacher says, "This is what I learned:
I added all these things together
to find some meaning for everything.
28While I was searching,
I did not find one man among the thousands I found.
Nor did I find a woman among all these.
29One thing I have learned:
God made people good,
but they have found all kinds of ways to be bad."

Obey the King

8 No one is like the wise person
who can understand what things mean.
Wisdom brings happiness;
it makes sad faces happy.

2Obey the king's command, because you made
a promise to God. 3Don't be too quick to leave the
king. Don't support something that is wrong, because the king does whatever he pleases. 4What
the king says is law; no one tells him what to do.

5Whoever obeys the king's command will be safe.
A wise person does the right thing at the right time.
6There is a right time and a right way for everything,
yet people often have many troubles.
7They do not know what the future holds,
and no one can tell them what will happen.
8No one can control the wind
or stop his own death.
No soldier is released in times of war,
and evil does not set free those who do evil.

Justice, Rewards, and Punishment

9I saw all of this as I considered all that is done
here on earth. Sometimes men harm those they
control. 10I saw the funerals of evil people who
used to go in and out of the holy place. They were
honored in the same towns where they had done
evil. This is useless, too.

11When evil people are not punished right
away, it makes others want to do evil, too.
12Though a sinner might do a hundred evil things
and might live a long time, I know it will be better

for those who honor God. 13I also know it will not
go well for evil people, because they do not honor
God. Like a shadow, they will not last. 14Some-
times something useless happens on earth. Bad
things happen to good people, and good things
happen to bad people. I say that this is also useless. 15So I decided it was more important to enjoy
life. The best that people can do here on earth is
to eat, drink, and enjoy life, because these joys
will help them do the hard work God gives them
here on earth.

We Cannot Understand All God Does

16I tried to understand all that happens on
earth. I saw how busy people are, working day
and night and hardly ever sleeping. 17I also saw all
that God has done. Nobody can understand what
God does here on earth. No matter how hard people try to understand it, they cannot. Even if wise
people say they understand, they cannot; no one
can really understand it.

Is Death Fair?

9 I thought about all this and tried to understand it. I saw that God controls good people
and wise people and what they do, but no one
knows if they will experience love or hate.

2Good and bad people end up the same—
those who are right and those who are wrong,
those who are good and those who are evil,
those who are clean and those who are unclean,
those who sacrifice and those who do not.
The same things happen to a good person
as happen to a sinner,
to a person who makes promises to God
and to one who does not.

3This is something wrong that happens here on
earth: What happens to one happens to all. So
people's minds are full of evil and foolish thoughts
while they live. After that, they join the dead.
4But anyone still alive has hope; even a live dog
is better off than a dead lion!

5The living know they will die,
but the dead know nothing.
Dead people have no more reward,
and people forget them.
6After people are dead,
they can no longer love or hate or envy.
They will never again share
in what happens here on earth.

Enjoy Life While You Can

7So go eat your food and enjoy it;
drink your wine and be happy,
because that is what God wants you to do.
8Put on nice clothes
and make yourself look good.

9Enjoy life with the wife you love. Enjoy all the
useless days of this useless life God has given you
here on earth, because it is all you have. So enjoy
the work you do here on earth. 10Whatever work
you do, do your best, because you are going to the
grave, where there is no working, no planning, no
knowledge, and no wisdom.

> **SIDELIGHT:** Like most ancient Jews, the Teacher believed that death brought only "the grave" (Ecclesiastes 9:10). The Hebrew word "Sheol" referred to a silent, gloomy, mysterious world where the early Jews believed that departed spirits went. The idea of heaven is more appealing, don't you think?

Time and Chance

11I also saw something else here on earth:
The fastest runner does not always win the race,
the strongest soldier does not always win the battle,
the wisest does not always have food,
the smartest does not always become wealthy,
and the talented one does not always receive praise.
Time and chance happen to everyone.
12No one knows what will happen next.
Like a fish caught in a net,
or a bird caught in a trap,
people are trapped by evil
when it suddenly falls on them.

Wisdom Does Not Always Win

13I also saw something wise here on earth that
impressed me. 14There was a small town with
only a few people in it. A great king fought against
it and put his armies all around it. 15Now there
was a poor but wise man in the town who used
his wisdom to save his town. But later on, everyone forgot about him. 16I still think wisdom is better than strength. But those people forgot about
the poor man's wisdom and stopped listening to
what he said.

17The quiet words of a wise person are better
than the shouts of a foolish ruler.
18Wisdom is better than weapons of war,
but one sinner can destroy much good.

10 Dead flies can make even perfume
stink.

In the same way, a little foolishness can
spoil wisdom.
2The heart of the wise leads to right,
but the heart of a fool leads to wrong.
3Even in the way fools walk along the road,
they show they are not wise;
they show everyone how stupid they are.
4Don't leave your job
just because your boss is angry with you.
Remaining calm solves great problems.

5There is something else wrong that happens
here on earth.
It is the kind of mistake rulers make:
6Fools are given important positions
while gifted people are given lower ones;
7I have seen servants ride horses
while princes walk like servants on foot.
8Anyone who digs a pit might fall into it;
anyone who knocks down a wall might be
bitten by a snake;
9anyone who moves boulders might be hurt
by them;
and anyone who cuts logs might be harmed
by them.
10A dull ax means
harder work.
Being wise will make it easier.
11If a snake bites the tamer before it is tamed,
what good is the tamer?

12The words of the wise bring them praise,
but the words of a fool will destroy them.
13A fool begins by saying foolish things
and ends by saying crazy and wicked
things.
14A fool talks too much.
No one knows the future,
and no one can tell what will happen after
death.

15Work wears fools out;
they don't even know how to get home.

The Value of Work

16How terrible it is for a country whose king is
a child
and whose leaders eat all morning.
17How lucky a country is whose king comes
from a good family,
whose leaders eat only at mealtime
and for strength, not to get drunk.

18If someone is lazy, the roof will begin to fall.
If he doesn't fix it, the house will leak.

19A party makes you feel good,
wine makes you feel happy,
and money buys anything.

20Don't make fun of the king,
and don't make fun of rich people, even in
your bedroom.
A little bird might carry your words;
a bird might fly and tell what you said.

Boldly Face the Future

11 Invest what you have,
because after a while you will get a
return.
2Invest what you have in several different
businesses,
because you don't know what disasters
might happen.

3If clouds are full of rain,
they will shower on the earth.
A tree can fall to the north or south,
but it will stay where it falls.
4Those who wait for perfect weather
will never plant seeds;
those who look at every cloud
will never harvest crops.

5You don't know where the wind will blow,
and you don't know how a baby grows
inside the mother.
In the same way, you don't know what God
is doing,
or how he created everything.
6Plant early in the morning,
and work until evening,
because you don't know if this or that will
succeed.
They might both do well.

Serve God While You Are Young

7Sunshine is sweet;
it is good to see the light of day.
8People ought to enjoy every day of their lives,
no matter how long they live.
But they should also remember this:
You will be dead a long time.
Everything that happens then is useless.
9Young people, enjoy yourselves while you are
young;
be happy while you are young.
Do whatever your heart desires,
whatever you want to do.
But remember that God will judge you
for everything you do.
10Don't worry,
and forget the troubles of your body,
because youth and childhood are useless.

The Problems of Old Age

12 Remember your Creator
while you are young,
before the days of trouble come
and the years when you say,
"I find no pleasure in them."

2When you get old,
the light from the sun, moon, and stars will grow dark;
the rain clouds will never seem to go away.
3At that time your arms will shake
and your legs will become weak.
Your teeth will fall out so you cannot chew,
and your eyes will not see clearly.
4Your ears will be deaf to the noise in the streets,
and you will barely hear the millstone grinding grain.
You'll wake up when a bird starts singing,
but you will barely hear singing.
5You will fear high places
and will be afraid to go for a walk.
Your hair will become white like the flowers on an almond tree.
You will limp along like a grasshopper when you walk.
Your appetite will be gone.
Then you will go to your everlasting home,
and people will go to your funeral.

6Soon your life will snap like a silver chain
or break like a golden bowl.
You will be like a broken pitcher at a spring,
or a broken wheel at a well.
7You will turn back into the dust of the earth again,
but your spirit will return to God who gave it.

8Everything is useless!
The Teacher says that everything is useless.

Conclusion: Honor God

9The Teacher was very wise and taught the
people what he knew. He very carefully thought
about, studied, and set in order many wise teachings. 10The Teacher looked for just the right
words to write what is dependable and true.

SIDELIGHT: When the homework piles up, quote the last part of Ecclesiastes 12:12. Maybe someone will take pity on you. The words "my son" were a common way for teachers to address pupils in Old Testament times.

11Words from wise people are like sharp sticks used to guide animals. They are like nails that have been driven in firmly. Altogether they are wise teachings that come from one Shepherd.
12So be careful, my son, about other teachings. People are always writing books, and too much study will make you tired.

13Now, everything has been heard,
so I give my final advice:
Honor God and obey his commands,
because this is all people must do.
14God will judge everything,
even what is done in secret,
the good and the evil.

SONG OF SOLOMON

Why Read This Book:

- Identify with lovers' longing for each other (Song of Solomon 1—2).
- Celebrate true love and affection for a lover (Song of Solomon 3—5).
- Watch true love develop into commitment (Song of Solomon 6—8).

Behind the Scenes:

Romance. We read about it, dream about it, and fantasize about it. We each hope that someone wonderful will choose us, marry us, share passionate, lasting love with us. But we don't expect to find much about this kind of romance in the Bible.

That's what's so surprising about the Song of Solomon, also known as Song of Songs. Using graphic imagery and language, this unusual book in the Bible celebrates God's gifts of love and sexuality. It appears to tell about a king and a shepherd both pursuing a beautiful peasant woman. Through poetry, the book shows admiration, yearning for love, physical attractiveness and dedicated commitment.

Scholars have debated the Song of Solomon for centuries—beginning before Jesus was born. They suggest several possible ways to interpret this unusual book:

- Symbolic—The book has a hidden or symbolic religious meaning about the relationship between God and Israel or between Christ and the church. Beneath the pictures of physical love lies the spiritual truth that God loves us completely.
- Literal—The book is what it appears to be: Love songs about a beautiful courtship between a man and a woman. Thus these poems affirm a place for beautiful expressions of human love within our faith.
- Dramatic—The book is a drama about sexual love. The songs were written to be sung or performed by two to four actors and a chorus. The drama may have been performed as entertainment during weddings.

Whatever your view on the book's purpose, Song of Solomon should be treasured, because it gives beautiful images of committed love—both physical and spiritual—and celebrates human love as a gift from God.

WHEN THE ACTION WAS

Jerusalem fell to the Babylonians

Jews began returning to Jerusalem from exile

Jesus was born

1000BC | **750BC** | **500BC** | **250BC** | **BC/AD**

King Solomon ruled and may have written Song of Solomon

1

Solomon's Greatest Song.

The Woman Speaks to the Man She Loves

[2]Kiss me with the kisses of your mouth,
because your love is better than wine.

> **SIDELIGHT:** Song of Solomon is also known as the "Song of Songs." Repeating the word meant it was great. So this book could be called "Greatest Song" or "Most Beautiful Song." Wonder if it made the top ten?

[3]The smell of your perfume is pleasant,
and your name is pleasant like expensive perfume.
That's why the young women love you.
[4]Take me with you; let's run together.
The king takes me into his rooms.

Friends Speak to the Man

We will rejoice and be happy with you;
we praise your love more than wine.
With good reason, the young women love you.

The Woman Speaks

[5]I'm dark but lovely,
women of Jerusalem,
dark like the tents of Kedar,
like the curtains of Solomon.
[6]Don't look at how dark I am,
at how dark the sun has made me.
My brothers were angry with me
and made me tend the vineyards,
so I haven't tended my own vineyard!
[7]Tell me, you whom I love,
where do you feed your sheep?
Where do you let them rest at noon?
Why should I look for you near your friend's sheep,
like a woman who wears a veil?[n]

The Man Speaks to the Woman

[8]You are the most beautiful of women.
Surely you know to follow the sheep
and feed your young goats
near the shepherds' tents.
[9]My darling, you are like a mare
among the king's stallions.
[10]Your cheeks are beautiful with ornaments,
and your neck with jewels.
[11]We will make for you gold earrings
with silver hooks.

The Woman Speaks

[12]The smell of my perfume spreads out
to the king on his couch.
[13]My lover is like a bag of myrrh[d]
that lies all night between my breasts.
[14]My lover is like a bunch of flowers
from the vineyards at En Gedi.

> **SIDELIGHT:** Ancient lovers didn't have designer perfumes, but they were still into being attractive to others. Women wore sachets of fragrance around their necks (Song of Solomon 1:12–14), while men splashed perfume on their beards and robes.

The Man Speaks

[15]My darling, you are beautiful!
Oh, you are beautiful,
and your eyes are like doves.

The Woman Answers the Man

[16]You are so handsome, my lover,
and so pleasant!
Our bed is the grass.
[17]Cedar trees form our roof;
our ceiling is made of juniper wood.

The Woman Speaks Again

2

I am a rose in the Plain of Sharon,
a lily in the valleys.

The Man Speaks Again

[2]Among the young women, my darling
is like a lily among thorns!

The Woman Answers

[3]Among the young men, my lover
is like an apple tree in the woods!
I enjoy sitting in his shadow;
his fruit is sweet to my taste.
[4]He brought me to the banquet room,
and his banner over me is love.
[5]Strengthen me with raisins,
and refresh me with apples,
because I am weak with love.
[6]My lover's left hand is under my head,
and his right arm holds me tight.

veil This was the way a prostitute usually dressed.

The Woman Speaks to the Friends

7Women of Jerusalem, promise me
by the gazelles[d] and the deer
not to awaken
or excite my feelings of love
until it is ready.

The Woman Speaks Again

8I hear my lover's voice.
Here he comes jumping across the mountains,
skipping over the hills.
9My lover is like a gazelle[d] or a young deer.
Look, he stands behind our wall
peeking through the windows,
looking through the blinds.
10My lover spoke and said to me,
"Get up, my darling;
let's go away, my beautiful one.
11Look, the winter is past;
the rains are over and gone.
12Blossoms appear through all the land.
The time has come to sing;
the cooing of doves is heard in our land.
13There are young figs on the fig trees,
and the blossoms on the vines smell sweet.
Get up, my darling;
let's go away, my beautiful one."

The Man Speaks

14My beloved is like a dove hiding in the cracks of the rock,
in the secret places of the cliff.
Show me your face,
and let me hear your voice.
Your voice is sweet,
and your face is lovely.
15Catch the foxes for us—
the little foxes that ruin the vineyards
while they are in blossom.

The Woman Speaks

16My lover is mine, and I am his.
He feeds among the lilies
17until the day dawns
and the shadows disappear.
Turn, my lover.
Be like a gazelle[d] or a young deer
on the mountain valleys.

The Woman Dreams

3 At night on my bed,
I looked for the one I love;
I looked for him, but I could not find him.
2I got up and went around the city,
in the streets and squares,
looking for the one I love.

LOVE

Am I Really in Love?

Test yourself to discover whether you're really in love.

"I love you if . . ." I value your uniqueness. I freely give my joy, interests, knowledge, understanding, humor and sadness to you. I give you freedom to be true to yourself. I am happy to be with you most of the time. I really like, trust and respect you. I want our relationship to be permanent. I focus on your personality, not just sexual feelings. I care about your pleasure and well-being as much as my own. I feel like I "belong" to you. Our relationship has deepened during the past six months.

When we're really in love, we can honestly answer "yes" to these questions. The lovers in Song of Solomon are enthralled with each other. Read **Song of Solomon 2:10–17**.

- Which of the conditions above do you think apply to the couple in this passage?
- Based on this passage and the checklist, what would your checklist be for knowing if you are in love?

CONSIDER. . .

- talking to a couple you know who have a strong relationship, and asking them what makes their marriage so strong.
- making a list of action-oriented goals based on the passage that you can use when you're in a special relationship that you want to grow.

FOR MORE, SEE. . .

- Hosea 3 (p. 825)
- John 15:9–17 (p. 1085)
- 1 John 4:7–21 (p. 1319)

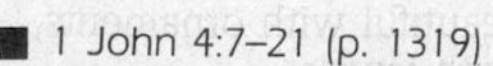

I looked for him, but I could not find him.
3The watchmen found me as they patrolled
the city,
so I asked, "Have you seen the one I
love?"
4As soon as I had left them,
I found the one I love.
I held him and would not let him go
until I brought him to my mother's house,
to the room where I was born.

The Woman Speaks to the Friends

5Women of Jerusalem, promise me
by the gazelles[d] and the deer
not to awaken
or excite my feelings of love
until it is ready.
6Who is this coming out of the desert
like a cloud of smoke?
Who is this that smells like myrrh,[d] incense,[d]
and other spices?
7Look, it's Solomon's couch[n]
with sixty soldiers around it,
the finest soldiers of Israel.
8These soldiers all carry swords
and have been trained in war.
Every man wears a sword at his side
and is ready for the dangers of the night.
9King Solomon had a couch made for himself
of wood from Lebanon.
10He made its posts of silver
and its braces of gold.
The seat was covered with purple cloth
that the women of Jerusalem wove with
love.
11Women of Jerusalem, go out and see King
Solomon.
He is wearing the crown his mother put on
his head
on his wedding day,
when his heart was happy!

The Man Speaks to the Woman

4 How beautiful you are, my darling!
Oh, you are beautiful!
Your eyes behind your veil are like doves.
Your hair is like a flock of goats streaming
down Mount Gilead.
2Your teeth are white like newly sheared
sheep
just coming from their bath.
Each one has a twin,
and none of them is missing.
3Your lips are like red silk thread,
and your mouth is lovely.
Your cheeks behind your veil
are like slices of a pomegranate.[d]
4Your neck is like David's tower,
built with rows of stones.
A thousand shields hang on its walls;
each shield belongs to a strong soldier.
5Your breasts are like two fawns,
like twins of a gazelle,[d]
feeding among the lilies.
6Until the day dawns
and the shadows disappear,
I will go to that mountain of myrrh[d]
and to that hill of incense.[d]
7My darling, everything about you is beautiful,
and there is nothing at all wrong with you.

SIDELIGHT: The poem in Song of Solomon 4:1–7 contains comparisons that may seem gross to us today, but they were quite appealing in ancient times. . . . Honest!

8Come with me from Lebanon, my bride.
Come with me from Lebanon,
from the top of Mount Amana,
from the tops of Mount Senir and Mount
Hermon.
Come from the lions' dens
and from the leopards' hills.
9My sister, my bride,
you have thrilled my heart;
you have thrilled my heart
with a glance of your eyes,
with one sparkle from your necklace.
10Your love is so sweet, my sister, my bride.
Your love is better than wine,
and your perfume smells better than any
spice.
11My bride, your lips drip honey;
honey and milk are under your tongue.
Your clothes smell like the cedars of
Lebanon.
12My sister, my bride, you are like a garden
locked up,
like a walled-in spring, a closed-up fountain.
13Your limbs are like an orchard
of pomegranates with all the best fruit,
filled with flowers and nard,[d]
14nard and saffron,[d] calamus,[d] and cinnamon,
with trees of incense, myrrh, and aloes[d]—
all the best spices.
15You are like a garden fountain—
a well of fresh water
flowing down from the mountains of
Lebanon.

couch Something like a bed carried by slaves on which the king lay or sat while traveling.

The Woman Speaks

16Awake, north wind.
Come, south wind.
Blow on my garden,
and let its sweet smells flow out.
Let my lover enter the garden
and eat its best fruits.

The Man Speaks

5 I have entered my garden, my sister, my bride.
I have gathered my myrrh[d] with my spice.
I have eaten my honeycomb and my honey.
I have drunk my wine and my milk.

The Friends Speak

Eat, friends, and drink;
yes, drink deeply, lovers.

The Woman Dreams

2I sleep, but my heart is awake.
I hear my lover knocking.
"Open to me, my sister, my darling,
my dove, my perfect one.
My head is wet with dew,
and my hair with the dampness of the night."
3I have taken off my garment
and don't want to put it on again.
I have washed my feet
and don't want to get them dirty again.
4My lover put his hand through the opening,
and I felt excited inside.
5I got up to open the door for my lover.
Myrrh[d] was dripping from my hands
and flowing from my fingers,
onto the handles of the lock.
6I opened the door for my lover,
but my lover had left and was gone.
When he spoke, he took my breath away.
I looked for him, but I could not find him;
I called for him, but he did not answer.
7The watchmen found me
as they patrolled the city.
They hit me and hurt me;
the guards on the wall took away my veil.
8Promise me, women of Jerusalem,

SEXUALITY

How Far?

Sherry Loomis leaned into Greg's muscular arms. His masculine scent, heightened by cologne, aroused a hunger in her. They kissed, again and again. Tonight her parents were gone, leaving them alone in the house.

"You're everything I want," Greg breathed. His hands moved over her eagerly. "Please," he urged.

Sherry pulled away. "I'm not sure . . ."

"I love you." He smiled, his eyes dark with passion.

The door bell rang. After straightening her clothes, Sherry opened the door and found her best friend standing there. Friends from church waited in the car.

"We're going out for pizza. Want to go with us?" Beth asked. Sherry took a deep breath; she was disappointed, yet relieved. "Yeah." She turned toward Greg. "Let's go with them, okay?"

The passion that Sherry and Greg feel is described in **Song of Solomon 5:2–6**. Although passion is a normal part of a love relationship, God has reserved it for marriage, because only a marriage agreement has the power to sustain the kind of intimacy that comes from passion.

- How is Sherry's experience like that of the woman in the passage?
- Sherry stopped short of going "all the way" with Greg. What are good reasons for you not to have sex until you're married?

CONSIDER . . .

- writing on a secret card exactly how far you'll go physically with a casual date, your boyfriend or girlfriend, and the person you're engaged to. Keep the card in your Bible as a promise to yourself and to God.
- controlling the temptation to "go too far" by dating in groups, avoiding alcohol, and staying away from secluded areas.

FOR MORE, SEE . . .

- Genesis 2:24–25 (p. 4)
- 1 Thessalonians 4:3–8 (p. 1247)
- 1 John 1:9 (p. 1316)

if you find my lover,
tell him I am weak with love.

The Friends Answer the Woman

9How is your lover better than other lovers,
most beautiful of women?
How is your lover better than other lovers?
Why do you want us to promise this?

The Woman Answers the Friends

10My lover is healthy and tan,
the best of ten thousand men.
11His head is like the finest gold;
his hair is wavy and black like a raven.
12His eyes are like doves
by springs of water.
They seem to be bathed in cream
and are set like jewels.
13His cheeks are like beds of spices;
they smell like mounds of perfume.
His lips are like lilies
flowing with myrrh.[d]
14His hands are like gold hinges,
filled with jewels.
His body is like shiny ivory
covered with sapphires.
15His legs are like large marble posts,
standing on bases of fine gold.
He is like a cedar of Lebanon,
like the finest of the trees.
16His mouth is sweet to kiss,
and I desire him very much.
Yes, daughters of Jerusalem,
this is my lover
and my friend.

The Friends Speak to the Woman

6 Where has your lover gone,
most beautiful of women?
Which way did your lover turn?
We will look for him with you.

The Woman Answers the Friends

2My lover has gone down to his garden,
to the beds of spices,
to feed in the gardens
and to gather lilies.
3I belong to my lover,
and my lover belongs to me.
He feeds among the lilies.

The Man Speaks to the Woman

4My darling, you are as beautiful as the city of Tirzah,
as lovely as the city of Jerusalem,
like an army flying flags.
5Turn your eyes from me,
because they excite me too much.
Your hair is like a flock of goats
streaming down Mount Gilead.
6Your teeth are white like sheep
just coming from their bath;
each one has a twin,
and none of them is missing.
7Your cheeks behind your veil
are like slices of a pomegranate.[d]

SIDELIGHT: You might not say your sweetheart has "fruity" cheeks, but that was a compliment in ancient times (Song of Solomon 6:7). The pomegranate is a small, red fruit that's especially refreshing in a hot climate like Israel's (Song of Solomon 8:2, p. 614). The round fruit is filled with pulp and seeds, somewhat like the inside of an orange in texture.

8There may be sixty queens and eighty slave women[d]
and so many girls you cannot count them,
9but there is only one like my dove, my perfect one.
She is her mother's only daughter,
the brightest of the one who gave her birth.
The young women saw her and called her happy;
the queens and the slave women also praised her.

The Young Women Praise the Woman

10Who is that young woman
that shines out like the dawn?
She is as pretty as the moon,
as bright as the sun,
as wonderful as an army flying flags.

The Man Speaks

11I went down into the orchard of nut trees
to see the blossoms of the valley,
to look for buds on the vines,
to see if the pomegranate[d] trees had bloomed.
12Before I realized it, my desire for you made me feel
like a prince in a chariot.

The Friends Call to the Woman

13Come back, come back, woman of Shulam.
Come back, come back,
so we may look at you!

The Woman Answers the Friends

Why do you want to look at the woman of Shulam
as you would at the dance of two armies?

The Man Speaks to the Woman

7 Your feet are beautiful in sandals,
you daughter of a prince.
Your round thighs are like jewels
shaped by an artist.
2Your navel is like a round drinking cup
always filled with wine.
Your stomach is like a pile of wheat
surrounded with lilies.
3Your breasts are like two fawns,
like twins of a gazelle.[d]
4Your neck is like an ivory tower.
Your eyes are like the pools in Heshbon
near the gate of Bath Rabbim.
Your nose is like the mountain of Lebanon
that looks down on Damascus.
5Your head is like Mount Carmel,
and your hair is like purple cloth;
the king is captured in its folds.
6You are beautiful and pleasant;
my love, you are full of delights.
7You are tall like a palm tree,
and your breasts are like its bunches of
fruit.
8I said, "I will climb up the palm tree
and take hold of its fruit."
Let your breasts be like bunches of grapes,
the smell of your breath like apples,
9 and your mouth like the best wine.

The Woman Speaks to the Man

Let this wine go down sweetly for my lover;
may it flow gently past the lips and teeth.
10I belong to my lover,
and he desires only me.
11Come, my lover,
let's go out into the country
and spend the night in the fields.
12Let's go early to the vineyards
and see if the buds are on the vines.
Let's see if the blossoms have already opened
and if the pomegranates[d] have bloomed.
There I will give you my love.
13The mandrake flowers give their sweet smell,
and all the best fruits are at our gates.
I have saved them for you, my lover,
the old delights and the new.

SIDELIGHT: The mandrake flower (Song of Solomon 7:13) not only gave a sweet smell but was also thought to arouse sexual desire. The yellow-red fruit was also thought to increase fertility (see Genesis 30:14–16, p. 35). No wonder it was called the "love apple"!

8 I wish you were like my brother
who fed at my mother's breasts.
If I found you outside,
I would kiss you,
and no one would look down on me.
2I would lead you and bring you
to my mother's house;
she is the one who taught me.
I would give you a drink of spiced wine
from my pomegranates.

The Woman Speaks to the Friends

3My lover's left hand is under my head,
and his right arm holds me tight.
4Women of Jerusalem,
promise not to awaken
or excite my feelings of love
until it is ready.

The Friends Speak

5Who is this coming out of the desert,
leaning on her lover?

The Man Speaks to the Woman

I woke you under the apple tree
where you were born;
there your mother gave birth to you.
6Put me like a seal on your heart,
like a seal on your arm.
Love is as strong as death;
jealousy is as strong as the grave.
Love bursts into flames
and burns like a hot fire.
7Even much water cannot put out the flame of
love;
floods cannot drown love.
If a man offered everything in his house for
love,
people would totally reject it.

The Woman's Brothers Speak

8We have a little sister,
and her breasts are not yet grown.
What should we do for our sister
on the day she becomes engaged?
9If she is a wall,
we will put silver towers on her.
If she is a door,
we will protect her with cedar boards.

The Woman Speaks

10I am a wall,
and my breasts are like towers.
So I was to him,
as one who brings happiness.
11Solomon had a vineyard at Baal Hamon.

He rented the vineyards for others to
tend,
and everyone who rented had to pay
twenty-five pounds of silver for the fruit.
12But my own vineyard is mine to give.

SIDELIGHT: If girls think their brothers are overprotective today, imagine how they would have felt in biblical times (Song of Solomon 8:8–9). Brothers were responsible for a sister until marriage, so they kept other men from taking advantage of her innocence. They would probably ride in the back seat on her dates today!

Solomon, the twenty-five pounds of silver
are for you,
and five pounds are for those who tend the
fruit.

The Man Speaks to the Woman

13You who live in the gardens,
my friends are listening for your voice;
let me hear it.

The Woman Speaks to the Man

14Hurry, my lover,
be like a gazelle[d]
or a young deer
on the mountains where spices grow.

ISAIAH

Why Read This Book:

- See how God works through world events to bring people to himself (Isaiah 1—35).
- Discover what can happen when people trust in things other than God (Isaiah 36—39).
- Be assured that God is working in the world, even when life seems hopeless (Isaiah 40—66).

Behind the Scenes:

Isaiah could have had a simple life in Judah. He was probably well-educated and may have been a priest. He knew "movers and shakers" in Jerusalem, including the king.

But Isaiah saw trouble brewing, and the Lord called him to be a prophet. Though his country had been peaceful and prosperous under King Uzziah's leadership (see 2 Chronicles 26:1–23, p. 405), Isaiah could tell the good situation was changing. God would have him speak out!

First, he watched as the Assyrians conquered neighboring Israel and threatened

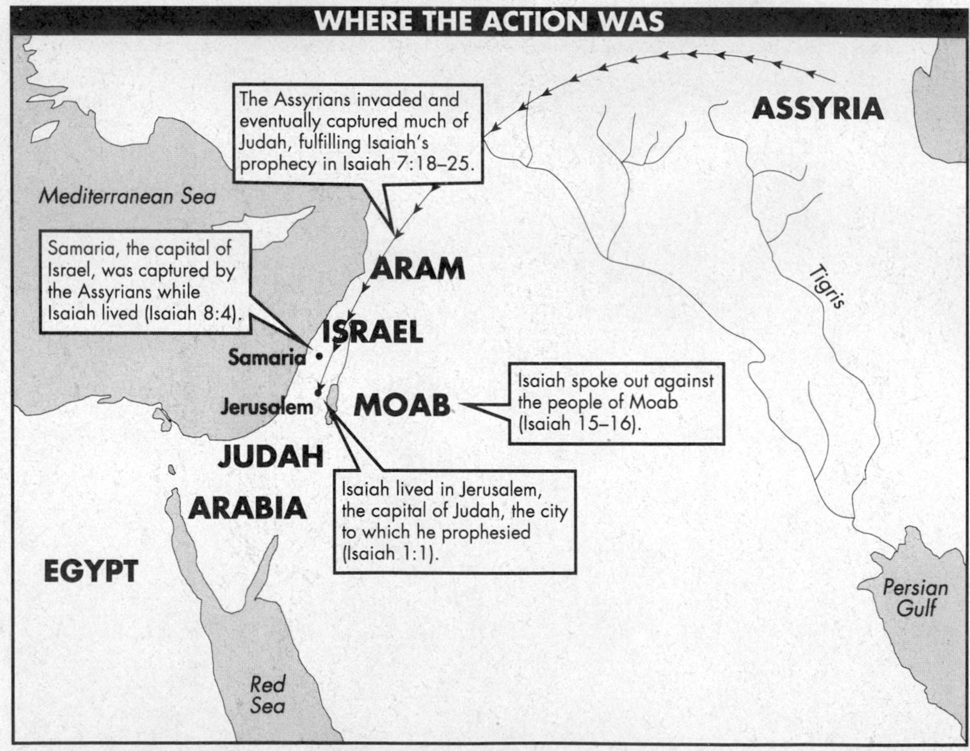
WHERE THE ACTION WAS
The Assyrians invaded and eventually captured much of Judah, fulfilling Isaiah's prophecy in Isaiah 7:18–25.
ASSYRIA
Mediterranean Sea
Samaria, the capital of Israel, was captured by the Assyrians while Isaiah lived (Isaiah 8:4).
ARAM
Tigris
ISRAEL
Samaria
Isaiah spoke out against the people of Moab (Isaiah 15–16).
Jerusalem
MOAB
JUDAH
ARABIA
Isaiah lived in Jerusalem, the capital of Judah, the city to which he prophesied (Isaiah 1:1).
EGYPT
Persian Gulf
Red Sea

WHEN THE ACTION WAS

1000BC	750BC	500BC	250BC	BC/AD
Saul was Israel's king; The kingdom was split between Israel and Judah	Isaiah began his prophetic ministry; The Northern Kingdom (Israel) fell to Assyria	The Southern Kingdom (Judah) fell to Babylon		Jesus was born

Behind the Scenes (cont.): Judah. The king of Judah was tempted to form military alliances to protect the nation; Isaiah believed Judah should rely on God instead.

Second, while people paid lip service to God, they didn't really follow him. Instead, they took advantage of the poor.

The book of Isaiah has two distinct parts:

Chapters 1—39 deal with events in the eighth century before Christ, when Judah was independent but constantly threatened by the Assyrians. During this time, the prophet blasted out against the rich and powerful who neglected and oppressed the poor. And he challenged the nation not to rely on military power to defend itself, but to rely on God.

Chapters 40—66 zoom forward to about two hundred years later, when the Persian Empire controlled Judah. After being in exile, the Jews were trying to rebuild their lives. Through this section, the prophet constantly comforts the people, assuring them that the past, present, and future are all in God's hands. God's presence and love gave them hope.

Isaiah's message of hope points to a time when God would deliver his people through God's suffering servant (Isaiah 52—57). Since New Testament times, Christians have believed these promises were fulfilled in the coming of Jesus Christ, who suffered and died for the sins of the world. (For example, see Isaiah 53.)

---

1 This is the vision Isaiah son of Amoz saw
about what would happen to Judah and Jerusalem. Isaiah saw these things while Uzziah, Jotham, Ahaz, and Hezekiah were kings of Judah.

SIDELIGHT: The book of Isaiah is quoted more in the New Testament than any other book—and more than all the other prophetic books combined. The New Testament refers to Isaiah one hundred fifty times and actually quotes it fifty times.

God's Case Against His Children

2Heaven and earth, listen,
because the LORD is speaking:
"I raised my children and helped them grow up,
but they have turned against me.
3An ox knows its master,
and a donkey knows where its owner feeds it,
but the people of Israel do not know me;
my people do not understand."

4How terrible! Israel is a nation of sin,
a people loaded down with guilt,
a group of children doing evil,
children who are full of evil.
They have left the LORD;
they hate God, the Holy One of Israel,
and have turned away from him as if he were a stranger.
5Why should you continue to be punished?
Why do you continue to turn against him?
Your whole head is hurt,
and your whole heart is sick.
6There is no healthy spot
from the bottom of your foot to the top of your head;
you are covered with wounds, hurts, and open sores
that are not cleaned and covered,
and no medicine takes away the pain.

7Your land is ruined;
your cities have been burned with fire.
While you watch,
your enemies are stealing everything from your land;
it is ruined like a country destroyed by enemies.
8Jerusalem is left alone
like an empty shelter in a vineyard,
like a hut left in a field of melons,
like a city surrounded by enemies.
9The LORD All-Powerful
allowed a few of our people to live.
Otherwise we would have been completely destroyed
like the cities of Sodom and Gomorrah.

10Jerusalem, your rulers are like those of Sodom,
and your people are like those of Gomorrah.
Hear the word of the LORD;
listen to the teaching of our God!
11The LORD says,
"I do not want all these sacrifices.
I have had enough of your burnt sacrifices
of male sheep and fat from fine animals.

I am not pleased
by the blood of bulls, lambs, and goats.
12You come to meet with me,
but who asked you to do
all this running in and out of my Temple's[d] rooms?
13Don't continue bringing me worthless sacrifices!
I hate the incense[d] you burn.
I can't stand your New Moons,[d] Sabbaths,[d]
and other feast days;
I can't stand the evil you do in your holy meetings.
14I hate your New Moon feasts
and your other yearly feasts.
They have become a heavy weight on me,
and I am tired of carrying it.
15When you raise your arms to me in prayer,
I will refuse to look at you.
Even if you say many prayers,
I will not listen to you,
because your hands are full of blood.
16Wash yourselves and make yourselves clean.[d]
Stop doing the evil things I see you do.
Stop doing wrong.
Learn to do good.
Seek justice.
Punish those who hurt others.
Help the orphans.
Stand up for the rights of widows."

18The LORD says,
"Come, let us talk about these things.
Though your sins are like scarlet,
they can be as white as snow.
Though your sins are deep red,
they can be white like wool.
19If you become willing and obey me,
you will eat good crops from the land.
20But if you refuse to obey and if you turn against me,
you will be destroyed by your enemies' swords."
The LORD himself said these things.

Jerusalem Is Not Loyal to God

21The city of Jerusalem once followed the LORD,
but she is no longer loyal to him.
She used to be filled with fairness;
people there lived the way God wanted.
But now, murderers live there.
22Jerusalem, you have become like the scum left when silver is purified;
you are like wine mixed with water.
23Your rulers are rebels
and friends of thieves.
They all accept money for doing wrong,
and they are paid to cheat people.
They don't seek justice for the orphans
or listen to the widows' needs.
24So the Lord GOD All-Powerful,
the Mighty One of Israel, says:
"You, my enemies, will not cause me any more trouble.
I will pay you back for what you did.
25I will turn against you
and clean away all your wrongs as if with soap;
I will take all the worthless things out of you.
26I will bring back judges as you had long ago;
your counselors will be like those you had in the beginning.
Then you will be called the City That Is Right with God,
the Loyal City."

27By doing what is fair,
Jerusalem will be free again.
By doing what is right,
her people who come back to the LORD will have freedom.
28But sinners and those who turn against him will be destroyed;
those who have left the LORD will die.

29"You will be ashamed,
because you have worshiped gods under the oak trees.
You will be disgraced,
because you have worshiped idols in your gardens.
30You will be like an oak whose leaves are dying
or like a garden without water.
31Powerful people will be like small, dry pieces of wood,
and their works will be like sparks.
They will burn together,
and no one will be able to put out that fire."

The Message About Jerusalem

2 Isaiah son of Amoz saw this message about Judah and Jerusalem:
2In the last days
the mountain on which the LORD's Temple[d] stands
will become the most important of all mountains.
It will be raised above the hills,
and people from all nations will come streaming to it.
3Many nations will come and say,
"Come, let us go up to the mountain of the LORD,
to the Temple of the God of Jacob.

Then God will teach us his ways,
and we will obey his teachings."
His teachings will go out from Jerusalem;
the message of the LORD will go out from Jerusalem.
4He will settle arguments among the nations
and will make decisions for many nations.
Then they will make their swords into plows
and their spears into hooks for trimming trees.
Nations will no longer fight other nations,
nor will they train for war anymore.

5Come, family of Jacob,
and let us follow the way of the LORD.

A Terrible Day Is Coming

6LORD, you have left your people,
the family of Jacob,
because they have become filled with wrong ideas from people in the East.
They try to tell the future like the Philistines,
and they have completely accepted those foreign ideas.
7Their land has been filled with silver and gold;
there are a great many treasures there.
Their land has been filled with horses;
there are many chariots there.
8Their land is full of idols.
The people worship these idols they made with their own hands
and shaped with their own fingers.
9People will not be proud any longer
but will bow low with shame.
God, do not forgive them.

10Go into the caves of the cliffs;
dig holes and hide in the ground
from the anger of the LORD
and from his great power!
11Proud people will be made humble,
and they will bow low with shame.
At that time only the LORD will still be praised.

PEACE

Sibling Rivalry

Almost anything can make Jason and Rick Lewis argue:

"You're supposed to help me take out the garbage."

"Dad told you to do it!"

"No, Dad told us to do it!"

"I did it yesterday!"

"You never do it."

"Just drop it, okay? I'll do it later!"

Sometimes the Lewis home sounds like a war zone in the Middle East.

Despite their fighting, Jason and Rick love each other and stand up for each other. Anytime someone begins to argue with one of the brothers, the other will immediately lend support.

Jason and Rick argue about little things, but they are bonded together when it comes to big things such as love, loyalty and support. One reason for their closeness is their shared family name, which lets them know they're part of something that will last no matter how they feel. They're family.

Jason and Rick still argue even though they deeply love each other. But according to **Isaiah 2:1–5**, one day God will settle all our arguments, strife and struggles forever.

- According to this passage, what's the only way true peace—at home or in the world—can be achieved?
- How does this passage's picture of God challenge you to make peace in your family? church? school? world?

CONSIDER . . .

- reestablishing ties with someone you used to be friends with.
- writing a prayer to God for peace in your home, school, city, nation, and world. Listen for one way God might use you to bring about that peace.

FOR MORE, SEE . . .

- Isaiah 60:15–20 (p. 680)
- John 14:27–29 (p. 1085)
- 1 Thessalonians 5:12–18 (p. 1249)

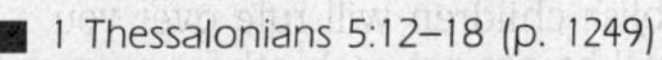

12The LORD All-Powerful has a certain day
planned
when he will punish the proud and those
who brag,
and they will no longer be important.
13He will bring down the tall cedar trees from
Lebanon
and the great oak trees of Bashan,
14all the tall mountains
and the high hills,
15every tall tower
and every high, strong wall,
16all the trading ships
and the beautiful ships.
17At that time proud people will be made
humble,
and they will bow low with shame.
At that time only the LORD will be praised,
18 but all the idols will be gone.

19People will run to caves in the rocky cliffs
and will dig holes and hide in the ground
from the anger of the LORD
and his great power,
when he stands to shake the earth.
20At that time people will throw away
their gold and silver idols,
which they made for themselves to worship;
they will throw them away to the bats and
moles.
21Then the people will hide in caves
and cracks in the rocks
from the anger of the LORD
and his great power,
when he stands to shake the earth.

22You should stop trusting in people to save
you,
because people are only human;
they aren't able to help you.

God Will Punish Judah and Jerusalem

3 Understand this:
The Lord GOD All-Powerful
will take away everything Judah and
Jerusalem need—
all the food and water,
2the heroes and great soldiers,
the judges and prophets,[d]
people who do magic and older leaders,
3the military leaders and government leaders,
the counselors, the skilled craftsmen, and
those who try to tell the future.
4The LORD says, "I will cause young boys to
be your leaders,
and foolish children will rule over you.
5People will be against each other; everyone
will be against his neighbor.
Young people will not respect older people,
and common people will not respect
important people."
6At that time a man will grab one of his
brothers
from his own family and say,
"You have a coat, so you will be our leader.
These ruins will be under your control."
7But that brother will stand up and say,
"I cannot help you,
because I do not have food or clothes in my
house.
You will not make me your leader."
8This will happen because Jerusalem has
stumbled,
and Judah has fallen.
The things they say and do are against the
LORD;
they turn against him.
9The look on their faces shows they are guilty;
like the people of Sodom, they are proud of
their sin.
They don't care who sees it.
How terrible it will be for them,
because they have brought much trouble on
themselves.

10Tell those who do what is right that things
will go well for them,
because they will receive a reward for what
they do.
11But how terrible it will be for the wicked!
They will be punished for all the wrong
they have done.
12Children treat my people cruelly,
and women rule over them.
My people, your guides lead you in the
wrong way
and turn you away from what is right.

13The LORD takes his place in court
and stands to judge the people.
14The LORD presents his case
against the older leaders and other leaders
of his people:
"You have burned the vineyard.
Your houses are full of what you took from
the poor.
15What gives you the right to crush my people
and grind the faces of the poor into the
dirt?"
The Lord GOD All-Powerful says this.

A Warning to Women of Jerusalem

16The LORD says,
"The women of Jerusalem are proud.
They walk around with their heads held
high,

and they flirt with their eyes.
They take quick, short steps,
making noise with their ankle bracelets."
17So the Lord will put sores on the heads of
those women in Jerusalem,
and he will make them lose their hair.

18At that time the Lord will take away everything that makes them proud: their beautiful ankle bracelets, their headbands, their necklaces
shaped like the moon, 19their earrings, bracelets,
and veils, 20their scarves, ankle chains, the cloth
belts worn around their waists, their bottles of
perfume, and charms, 21their signet[d] rings, nose
rings, 22their fine robes, capes, shawls, and
purses, 23their mirrors, linen dresses, turbans, and
long shawls.

24Instead of wearing sweet-smelling perfume,
they will stink.
Instead of fine cloth belts, they will wear
the ropes of captives.
Instead of having their hair fixed in fancy
ways, they will be bald.
Instead of fine clothes, they will wear
clothes of sadness.
Instead of being beautiful, they will wear
the brand of a captive.
25At that time your men will be killed with
swords,
and your heroes will die in war.
26There will be crying and sadness near the
city gates.
Jerusalem will be like a woman who has
lost everything and sits on the ground.

4 At that time seven women
will grab one man
and say, "We will eat our own bread
and make our own clothes,
but please marry us!
Please, take away our shame."

The Branch of the Lord

2At that time the LORD's branch will be very
beautiful and great. The people still living in Israel
will be proud of what the land grows. 3Those who
are still living in Jerusalem will be called holy;
their names are recorded among the living in Jerusalem. 4The Lord will wash away the filth from
the women of Jerusalem. He will wash the blood-
stains out of Jerusalem and clean the city with the
spirit of fairness and the spirit of fire. 5Then the
LORD will cover Mount Zion and the people who
meet there with a cloud of smoke during the day
and with a bright, flaming fire at night. There will
be a covering over every person. 6This covering
will protect the people from the heat of the sun
and will provide a safe place to hide from the
storm and rain.

Israel, the Lord's Vineyard

5 Now I will sing for my friend a song about
his vineyard.
My friend had a vineyard
on a hill with very rich soil.
2He dug and cleared the field of stones
and planted the best grapevines there.
He built a tower in the middle of it
and cut out a winepress[d] as well.
He hoped good grapes would grow there,
but only bad ones grew.

3My friend says, "You people living in
Jerusalem,
and you people of Judah,
judge between me and my vineyard.
4What more could I have done for my
vineyard
than I have already done?
Although I expected good grapes to grow,
why were there only bad ones?
5Now I will tell you
what I will do to my vineyard:
I will remove the hedge,
and it will be burned.
I will break down the stone wall,
and it will be walked on.
6I will ruin my field.
It will not be trimmed or hoed,
and weeds and thorns will grow there.
I will command the clouds
not to rain on it."

7The vineyard belonging to the LORD
All-Powerful
is the nation of Israel;
the garden that he loves
is the people of Judah.
He looked for justice, but there was only
killing.
He hoped for right living, but there were
only cries of pain.

8How terrible it will be for you who add more
houses to your houses
and more fields to your fields
until there is no room left for other people.
Then you are left alone in the land.

9The LORD All-Powerful said this to me:
"The fine houses will be destroyed;
the large and beautiful houses will be left
empty.
10At that time a ten-acre vineyard will make
only six gallons of wine,
and ten bushels of seed will grow only half
a bushel of grain."

11How terrible it will be for people who rise
early in the morning
to look for strong drink,

who stay awake late at night,
becoming drunk with wine.
12At their parties they have lyres,[d] harps,
tambourines,[d] flutes, and wine.
They don't see what the LORD has done
or notice the work of his hands.
13So my people will be captured and taken away,
because they don't really know me.
All the great people will die of hunger,
and the common people will die of thirst.
14So the place of the dead wants more and more people,
and it opens wide its mouth.
Jerusalem's important people and common people will go down into it,
with their happy and noisy ones.
15So the common people and the great people will be brought down;
those who are proud will be humbled.
16The LORD All-Powerful will receive glory by judging fairly;
the holy God will show himself holy by doing what is right.
17Then the sheep will go anywhere they want,
and lambs will feed on the land that rich people once owned.

18How terrible it will be for those people!
They pull their guilt and sins behind them
as people pull wagons with ropes.
19They say, "Let God hurry;
let him do his work soon
so we may see it.
Let the plan of the Holy One of Israel happen soon
so that we will know what it is."

20How terrible it will be for people who call good things bad
and bad things good,
who think darkness is light
and light is darkness,
who think sour is sweet
and sweet is sour.

21How terrible it will be for people who think they are wise
and believe they are clever.

22How terrible it will be for people who are famous for drinking wine
and are champions at mixing drinks.
23They take money to set the guilty free
and don't allow good people to be judged fairly.
24They will be destroyed
just as fire burns straw or dry grass.
They will be destroyed
like a plant whose roots rot
and whose flower dies and blows away like dust.
They have refused to obey the teachings of the LORD All-Powerful
and have hated the message from the Holy God of Israel.
25So the LORD has become very angry with his people,
and he has raised his hand to punish them.
Even the mountains are frightened.
Dead bodies lie in the streets like garbage.
But the LORD is still angry;
his hand is still raised to strike down the people.
26He raises a banner for the nations far away.
He whistles to call those people from the ends of the earth.
Look! The enemy comes quickly!
27Not one of them becomes tired or falls down.
Not one of them gets sleepy and falls asleep.
Their weapons are close at hand,
and their sandal straps are not broken.
28Their arrows are sharp,
and all of their bows are ready to shoot.
The horses' hoofs are hard as rocks,
and their chariot wheels move like a whirlwind.
29Their shout is like the roar of a lion;
it is loud like a young lion.
They growl as they grab their captives.
There is no one to stop them from taking their captives away.
30On that day they will roar
like the waves of the sea.
And when people look at the land,
they will see only darkness and pain;
all light will become dark in this thick cloud.

Isaiah Becomes a Prophet

6 In the year that King Uzziah died, I saw the
Lord sitting on a very high throne. His long
robe filled the Temple.[d] 2Heavenly creatures of
fire stood above him. Each creature had six
wings: It used two wings to cover its face, two
wings to cover its feet, and two wings for flying.
3Each creature was calling to the others:
"Holy, holy, holy is the LORD All-Powerful.
His glory fills the whole earth."
4Their calling caused the frame around the door
to shake, as the Temple filled with smoke.
5I said, "Oh, no! I will be destroyed. I am not
pure, and I live among people who are not pure,
but I have seen the King, the LORD All-Powerful."
6One of the heavenly creatures used a pair of
tongs to take a hot coal from the altar. Then he
flew to me with the hot coal in his hand. 7The

creature touched my mouth with the hot coal and said, "Look, your guilt is taken away, because this hot coal has touched your lips. Your sin is taken away."

[8]Then I heard the Lord's voice, saying, "Whom can I send? Who will go for us?"
So I said, "Here I am. Send me!"
[9]Then the Lord said, "Go and tell this to the people:
'You will listen and listen, but you will not
understand.
You will look and look, but you will not
learn.'
[10]Make the minds of these people dumb.
Shut their ears. Cover their eyes.
Otherwise, they might really understand
what they see with their eyes
and hear with their ears.
They might really understand in their minds
and come back to me and be healed."

SIDELIGHT: Isaiah is a hot book! It includes thirty-two references to fire, including Isaiah 6:6–7. Throughout the Bible, fire is a common symbol of God's presence, action, and judgment. See, for example, Genesis 15:17 (p. 17), Exodus 13:21–32 (p. 70), Acts 2:3 (p. 1098), Hebrews 12:29 (p. 1290), and Revelation 2:18 (p. 1334).

WORSHIP

Understanding God's Heart

When John Wesley was rescued from a blazing house as a child, he was convinced God had saved him for a purpose. As he grew up in eighteenth-century England, he applied all his energy toward accomplishing God's will for his life. While studying at Oxford University, John led a group of men known as the Holy Club. They met for Bible study and prayer, and cared for the sick, poor and imprisoned. Not long after completing his work at the university, John and his brother, Charles, sailed to America to spread Christ's message to native Americans.

John had good intentions but still felt like a failure. He knew God had given him a purpose in life, but he couldn't seem to carry it out. He needed to know and experience God's heart before he could offer it to anyone else. John and Charles returned to England discouraged and disillusioned. "I went to America to convert the Indians," John said. "But, oh, who shall convert me?"

Then something wonderful happened. On May 24, 1738, John attended a Christian meeting in London, and his life was changed. In his journal, John described what happened.

"I felt my heart strangely warmed," he wrote. "I felt I did trust in Christ, Christ alone for salvation; and an assurance was given to me that he had taken away my sins, even mine, and saved me from the law of sin and death."

John Wesley became one of the most influential men in the history of Christianity. During the fifty-two years following that experience in 1738, he preached over forty thousand sermons and traveled over two hundred thousand miles, sharing the message of Christ with hundreds of thousands.

John needed to understand and worship God before trying to serve him. The prophet Isaiah had a similar experience that launched his ministry. Read about Isaiah's encounter with God in **Isaiah 6:1–8**.

- Why did both John Wesley and Isaiah need to understand God's heart and worship him before they could adequately serve God?
- According to this passage, what do you know about God's character?

CONSIDER . . .

- asking God to reveal himself to you the way he did to Isaiah or to John Wesley.
- writing a poem or song of worship to God, praising him for the qualities about him that you know are true.

FOR MORE, SEE . . .

- 2 Chronicles 29:18–36 (p. 407)
- Psalm 50 (p. 511)
- Revelation 19:1–9 (p. 1345)

[11]Then I asked, "Lord, how long should I do this?"

He answered,

"Until the cities are destroyed
and the people are gone,
until there are no people left in the houses,
until the land is destroyed and left empty.
[12]The LORD will send the people far away,
and the land will be left empty.
[13]One-tenth of the people will be left in the land,
but it will be destroyed again.
These people will be like an oak tree
whose stump is left when the tree is chopped down.
The people who remain will be like a stump that will sprout again."

Trouble with Aram

7 Now Ahaz was the son of Jotham, who was the son of Uzziah. When Ahaz was king of Judah, Rezin king of Aram and Pekah son of Remaliah, the king of Israel, went up to Jerusalem to fight against it. But they were not able to defeat the city.

[2]Ahaz king of Judah received a message saying, "The armies of Aram and Israel[n] have joined together."

When Ahaz heard this, he and the people were frightened. They shook with fear like trees of the forest blown by the wind.

[3]Then the LORD told Isaiah, "You and your son Shear-Jashub[n] should go and meet Ahaz at the place where the water flows into the upper pool, on the road where people do their laundry. [4]Tell Ahaz, 'Be careful. Be calm and don't worry. Don't let those two men, Rezin and Pekah son of Remaliah, scare you. Don't be afraid of their anger or Aram's anger, because they are like two barely burning sticks that are ready to go out. [5]They have made plans against you, saying, [6]"Let's fight against Judah and tear it apart. We will divide the land for ourselves and make the son of Tabeel the new king of Judah." [7]But I, the Lord GOD, say,

" 'Their plan will not succeed;
it will not happen,
[8]because Aram is led by the city of Damascus,
and Damascus is led by its weak king, Rezin.
Within sixty-five years Israel will no longer be a nation.
[9]Israel is led by the city of Samaria,
and Samaria is led by its weak king, the son of Remaliah.
If your faith is not strong,
you will not have strength enough to last.' "

Immanuel—God Is with Us

[10]Then the LORD spoke to Ahaz again, saying, [11]"Ask for a sign from the LORD your God to prove to yourself that these things are true. It may be a sign from as deep as the place of the dead or as high as the heavens."

[12]But Ahaz said, "I will not ask for a sign or test the LORD."

[13]Then Isaiah said, "Ahaz, descendant[d] of David, listen carefully! Isn't it bad enough that you wear out the patience of people? Do you also have to wear out the patience of my God? [14]The Lord himself will give you a sign: The virgin[n] will be pregnant. She will have a son, and she will name him Immanuel.[n] [15]He will be eating milk curds and honey when he learns to reject what is evil and to choose what is good. [16]You are afraid of the kings of Israel and Aram now. But before the child learns to choose good and reject evil, the lands of Israel and Aram will be empty. [17]The LORD will bring troubled times to you, your people, and to the people of your father's family. They will be worse than anything that has happened since Israel separated from Judah. The LORD will bring the king of Assyria to fight against you.

[18]"At that time the LORD will whistle for the Egyptians, and they will come like flies from Egypt's faraway streams. He will call for the Assyrians, and they will come like bees. [19]These enemies will camp in the deep ravines and in the cliffs, by the thornbushes and watering holes. [20]The Lord will hire Assyria and use it like a razor to punish Judah. It will be as if the Lord is shaving the hair from Judah's head and legs and removing Judah's beard.

[21]"At that time a person will be able to keep only one young cow and two sheep alive. [22]There will be only enough milk for that person to eat milk curds. All who remain in the land will go back to eating just milk curds and honey. [23]In this land there are now vineyards that have a thousand grapevines, which are worth about twenty-five pounds of silver. But these fields will become full of weeds and thorns. [24]The land will become wild and useful only as a hunting ground. [25]People once worked and grew food on these hills, but at that time people will not go there, because the land will be filled with weeds and thorns. Only sheep and cattle will go to those places."

Israel Literally, "Ephraim." Isaiah often uses "Ephraim" to mean all of Israel.
Shear-Jashub This name means "a part of the people will come back."
virgin The Hebrew word means "a young woman." Often this meant a girl who was not married and had not yet had sexual relations with anyone.
Immanuel This name means "God is with us."

Assyria Will Come Soon

8 The LORD told me, "Take a large scroll and
write on it with an ordinary pen: 'Maher-
Shalal-Hash-Baz.' [2]I will gather some men to be
reliable witnesses: Uriah the priest and Zechariah
son of Jeberekiah."
[3]Then I went to the prophetess,[d] and she became pregnant and had a son. The LORD told me,
"Name the boy Maher-Shalal-Hash-Baz,[n] [4]be-
cause the king of Assyria will take away all the
wealth and possessions of Damascus and Samaria
before the boy learns to say 'my father' or 'my
mother.'"

[5]Again the LORD spoke to me, saying,
[6]"These people refuse to accept
the slow-moving waters of the pool of Shiloah
and are terrified of Rezin
and Pekah son of Remaliah.
[7]So I, the Lord, will bring
the king of Assyria and all his power against them,
like a powerful flood of water from the Euphrates River.
The Assyrians will be like water rising over the banks of the river,
flowing over the land.
[8]That water will flow into Judah and pass through it,
rising to Judah's throat.
Immanuel, this army will spread its wings like a bird
until it covers your whole country."

[9]Be broken, all you nations,
and be smashed to pieces.
Listen, all you faraway countries.
Prepare for battle and be smashed to pieces!
Prepare for battle and be smashed to pieces!

Maher-Shalal-Hash-Baz This name means "there will soon be looting and stealing."

DOUBT

Having Confidence

Jon Krause had a problem talking with girls.

While it seemed all of Jon's friends in high school had steady girlfriends, he couldn't even approach a girl without breaking out in a cold sweat. It was bad enough being a freshman in a new school, without also having to suffer the embarrassment of a glistening forehead and sweaty palms.

One night, Jon sought comfort and advice from his older brother, Mike. "I guess I'll never have a girlfriend," Jon confessed. "I just don't know what to say to girls. I'm not like the other guys. All of them have girlfriends."

"That's ridiculous," Mike said flatly. "Those guys don't have anything you haven't got. You've just got to believe in yourself. Take a risk. It's much easier to talk to girls after that first conversation."

Jon went to his room to think and pray about what Mike said. That night, he asked God to help him see himself the way God does. He prayed for God to help him develop confidence.

Two months later Jon began going steady with Diane.

Jon needed help from God to ease his doubts and build his confidence. In **Isaiah 7:10–16**, King Ahaz also needed God's help to ease his doubts.

- What do King Ahaz and Jon have in common?
- Why do you sometimes hesitate to ask God for something, even if you feel you really need it?

CONSIDER...

- listing ways God could help you ease your doubt about him or any situation in your life and then asking him to give you that help.
- asking your parent or youth pastor about ways you can overcome specific doubts in your life.

FOR MORE, SEE...

- Judges 6:11–24 (p. 222)
- Matthew 14:22–33 (p. 934)
- James 1:6–8 (p. 1294)

[10]Make your plans for the fight,
but they will be defeated.
Give orders to your armies,
but they will be useless,
because God is with us.

Warnings to Isaiah

[11]The LORD spoke to me with his great power and warned me not to follow the lead of the rest of the people. He said,
[12]"People are saying that others make plans
against them,
but you should not believe them.
Don't be afraid of what they fear;
do not dread those things.
[13]But remember that the LORD All-Powerful is
holy.
He is the one you should fear;
he is the one you should dread.
[14]Then he will be a place of safety for you.
But for the two families of Israel,
he will be like a stone that causes people to
stumble,
like a rock that makes them fall.
He will be like a trap for the people of
Jerusalem,
and he will catch them in his trap.
[15]Many people will fall over this rock.
They will fall and be broken;
they will be trapped and caught."

[16]Make an agreement.
Seal up the teaching while my followers are
watching.
[17]I will wait for the LORD to help us,
the LORD who is ashamed of the family of
Israel.
I will wait for him.

[18]I am here, and with me are the children the
LORD has given me. We are signs and proofs for
the people of Israel from the LORD All-Powerful,
who lives on Mount Zion.[d]
[19]Some people say, "Ask the mediums[d] and
fortune-tellers, who whisper and mutter, what to
do." But I tell you that people should ask their
God for help. Why should people who are still
alive ask something from the dead? [20]You should
follow the teachings and the agreement with the
LORD. The mediums and fortune-tellers do not
speak the word of the LORD, so their words are
worth nothing.
[21]People will wander through the land troubled
and hungry. When they become hungry, they will
become angry and will look up and curse their
king and their God. [22]They will look around them
at their land and see only trouble, darkness, and
awful gloom. And they will be forced into the
darkness.

A New Day Is Coming

9 But suddenly there will be no more gloom
for the land that suffered. In the past God
made the lands of Zebulun and Naphtali hang
their heads in shame, but in the future those lands
will be made great. They will stretch from the
road along the Mediterranean Sea to the land beyond the Jordan River and north to Galilee, the
land of people who are not Israelites.

[2]Before those people lived in darkness,
but now they have seen a great light.
They lived in a dark land,
but a light has shined on them.
[3]God, you have caused the nation to grow
and made the people happy.
And they have shown their happiness to you,
like the joy during harvest time,
like the joy of people
taking what they have won in war.
[4]Like the time you defeated Midian,
you have taken away their heavy load
and the heavy pole from their backs
and the rod the enemy used to punish
them.
[5]Every boot that marched in battle
and every uniform stained with blood
has been thrown into the fire.
[6]A child has been born to us;
God has given a son to us.
He will be responsible for leading the
people.
His name will be Wonderful Counselor,
Powerful God,
Father Who Lives Forever, Prince of Peace.
[7]Power and peace will be in his kingdom
and will continue to grow forever.
He will rule as king on David's throne
and over David's kingdom.
He will make it strong
by ruling with justice and goodness
from now on and forever.
The LORD All-Powerful will do this
because of his strong love for his people.

God Will Punish Israel

[8]The Lord sent a message against the people
of Jacob;
it says that God will judge Israel.
[9]Then everyone in Israel, even the leaders in
Samaria,
will know that God has sent it.
Those people are proud and brag by saying,
[10]"These bricks have fallen,
but we will build again with cut stones.
These small trees have been chopped down,
but we will put great cedars there."
[11]But the LORD has brought the enemies of
Rezin against them;

he has stirred up their enemies against
them.
12The Arameans came from the east
and the Philistines from the west,
and they ate up Israel with their armies.

But the LORD was still angry;
his hand was still raised to punish the
people.

13But the people did not return to the one who
had struck them;
they did not follow the LORD All-Powerful.
14So the LORD cut off Israel's head and tail,
taking away both the branch and stalk in
one day.
15The older leaders and important men were
the head,
and the prophets[d] who speak lies were the
tail.
16Those who led the people led them in the
wrong direction,
and those who followed them were
destroyed.
17So the Lord is not happy with the young
people,
nor will he show mercy to the orphans and
widows.
All the people are separated from God and
are very evil;
they all speak lies.

But the LORD is still angry;
his hand is still raised to strike down the
people.

18Evil is like a small fire.
First, it burns weeds and thorns.
Next, it burns the larger bushes in the forest,
and they all go up in a column of smoke.
19The LORD All-Powerful is angry,
so the land will be burned.
The people are like fuel for the fire;
no one will try to save his brother or sister.
20People will grab something on the right,
but they will still be hungry.
They will eat something on the left,
but they will not be filled.
Then they will each turn and eat their own
children.
21The people of Manasseh will fight against the
people of Ephraim,

JUSTICE

She Died in a Box

Rebecca Smith grew up enjoying the pine trees and fresh smells of spring in Virginia. One of thirteen children, Rebecca excelled in school and graduated as valedictorian of her class at the prestigious Hampton Institute.

Forty-three years later, Rebecca died from overexposure to the cold on a New York City street in January. She was living in a rug-covered cardboard box on the corner of Tenth Avenue and West Seventeenth Street. Few people on the city streets knew anything about her besides her name. She was considered by many to be a "crazy" or a throw-away.

What happened to Rebecca in those forty-three years? Years earlier, she had been hospitalized for schizophrenia and underwent involuntary shock therapy. For twenty years, she was in and out of hospitals and was often put on strong medication. Because of her state of mind, she failed to go to necessary interviews, and she lost her public assistance and benefits. In the end, through no fault of her own, she lived and died on the streets.

In our world, thousands of people experience the kind of injustice Rebecca experienced. But the Bible tells of a time when a child will rule with "goodness and fair judgment." Read about this promised time in **Isaiah 9:1–7**.

- Isaiah says people then lived in darkness. How does that apply now to people like Rebecca? What is the "light" Isaiah talks about?
- What's one area of your life that needs God's light?

CONSIDER

- praying for God to intervene in a bad situation you're concerned about.
- scanning the newspaper for examples of injustice and then writing down ideas for what can be done to solve the problems.

FOR MORE, SEE

- Psalm 82 (p. 531)
- John 5:30 (p. 1066)
- 1 Corinthians 6:9–11 (p. 1173)

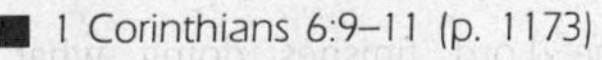

and Ephraim will fight against Manasseh.
Then both of them will turn against Judah.

But the LORD is still angry;
his hand is still raised to strike down the people.

10 How terrible it will be for those who make unfair laws,
and those who write laws that make life hard for people.
2They are not fair to the poor,
and they rob my people of their rights.
They allow people to steal from widows
and to take from orphans what really belongs to them.
3How will you explain the things you have done?
What will you do when your destruction comes from far away?
Where will you run for help?
Where will you hide your riches then?
4You will have to bow down among the captives
or fall down among the dead bodies.

But the LORD is still angry;
his hand is still raised to strike down the people.

God Will Punish Assyria

5God says, "How terrible it will be for the king of Assyria.
I use him like a rod to show my anger;
in anger I use Assyria like a club.
6I send it to fight against a nation that is separated from God.
I am angry with those people,
so I command Assyria to fight against them,
to take their wealth from them,
to trample them down like dirt in the streets.
7But Assyria's king doesn't understand that I am using him;
he doesn't know he is a tool for me.
He only wants to destroy other people
and to defeat many nations.
8The king of Assyria says to himself,
'All of my commanders are like kings.
9The city Calno is like the city Carchemish.
The city Hamath is like the city Arpad.
The city Samaria is like the city Damascus.
10I defeated those kingdoms that worship idols,
and those idols were more than the idols of Jerusalem and Samaria.
11As I defeated Samaria and her idols,
I will also defeat Jerusalem and her idols.' "

12When the Lord finishes doing what he
planned to Mount Zion[d] and Jerusalem, he will
punish Assyria. The king of Assyria is very proud,
and his pride has made him do these evil things,
so God will punish him. 13The king of Assyria says
this:
"By my own power I have done these things;
by my wisdom I have defeated many nations.
I have taken their wealth,
and, like a mighty one, I have taken their people.
14I have taken the riches of all these people,
like a person reaching into a bird's nest.
I have taken these nations,
like a person taking eggs.
Not one raised a hand
or opened its mouth to stop me."

15An ax is not better than the person who swings it.
A saw is not better than the one who uses it.
A stick cannot control the person who picks it up.
A club cannot pick up the person!
16So the Lord GOD All-Powerful
will send a terrible disease upon Assyria's soldiers.
The strength of Assyria will be burned up
like a fire burning until everything is gone.

SIDELIGHT: When the Assyrian army rolled into town, the locals could count on disaster (Isaiah 10:12–16). The Assyrians were known for flattening cities with battering rams, shooting defenders from mobile archery towers, and skinning survivors alive.

17God, the Light of Israel, will be like a fire;
the Holy One will be like a flame.
He will be like a fire
that suddenly burns the weeds and thorns.
18The fire burns away the great trees and rich farmlands,
destroying everything.
It will be like a sick person who wastes away.
19The trees left standing will be so few
that even a child could count them.

20At that time some people will be left alive in Israel
from the family of Jacob.
They will not continue to depend
on the person who defeated them.
They will learn truly to depend on the LORD,
the Holy One of Israel.
21Those who are left alive in Jacob's family

will again follow the powerful God.
22Israel, your people are many,
like the grains of sand by the sea.
But only a few of them will be left alive to return to the LORD.
God has announced that he will destroy the land
completely and fairly.
23The Lord GOD All-Powerful will certainly destroy this land,
as he has announced.

24This is what the Lord GOD All-Powerful says:
"My people living in Jerusalem,
don't be afraid of the Assyrians,
who beat you with a rod
and raise a stick against you, as Egypt did.
25After a short time my anger against you will stop,
and then I will turn my anger to destroying them."

26Then the LORD All-Powerful will beat the Assyrians with a whip
as he defeated Midian at the rock of Oreb.
He will raise his stick over the waters
as he did in Egypt.
27Then the troubles that Assyria puts on you
will be removed,
and the load they make you carry
will be taken away.

Assyria Invades Israel

28The army of Assyria will enter near Aiath.
Its soldiers will walk through Migron.
They will store their food in Micmash.
29The army will go over the pass.
The soldiers will sleep at Geba.
The people of Ramah will be afraid,
and the people at Gibeah of Saul will run away.
30Cry out, Bath Gallim!
Laishah, listen!
Poor Anathoth!
31The people of Madmenah are running away;
the people of Gebim are hiding.
32This day the army will stop at Nob.
They will shake their fist at Mount Zion,[d]
at the hill of Jerusalem.

33Watch! The Lord GOD All-Powerful
with his great power will chop them down
like a great tree.
Those who are great will be cut down;
those who are important will fall to the ground.
34He will cut them down
as a forest is cut down with an ax.
And the great trees of Lebanon
will fall by the power of the Mighty One.

The King of Peace Is Coming

11 A new branch will grow
from a stump of a tree;
so a new king will come
from the family of Jesse.[n]
2The Spirit[d] of the LORD will rest upon that king.
The Spirit will give him wisdom and understanding, guidance and power.
The Spirit will teach him to know and respect the LORD.
3This king will be glad to obey the LORD.
He will not judge by the way things look
or decide by what he hears.
4But he will judge the poor honestly;
he will be fair in his decisions for the poor people of the land.
At his command evil people will be punished,
and by his words the wicked will be put to death.
5Goodness and fairness will give him strength,
like a belt around his waist.
6Then wolves will live in peace with lambs,
and leopards will lie down to rest with goats.
Calves, lions, and young bulls will eat together,
and a little child will lead them.
7Cows and bears will eat together in peace.
Their young will lie down to rest together.
Lions will eat hay as oxen do.
8A baby will be able to play near a cobra's hole,
and a child will be able to put his hand
into the nest of a poisonous snake.

SIDELIGHT: Until God fully sets up the peaceful, new kingdom, you'll want to steer clear of the cobra (Isaiah 11:8). Some varieties of this snake—which can grow up to six feet long—spit venom into their victims' eyes.

9They will not hurt or destroy each other
on all my holy mountain,
because the earth will be full of the knowledge of the LORD,
as the sea is full of water.

10At that time the new king from the family of
Jesse will stand as a banner for all peoples. The

Jesse King David's father.

nations will come together around him, and the
place where he lives will be filled with glory. 11At
that time the Lord will again reach out and take
his people who are left alive in Assyria, North
Egypt, South Egypt, Cush, Elam, Babylonia, Hamath, and all the islands of the sea.

12God will raise a banner as a sign for all
nations,
and he will gather the people of Israel who
were forced from their country.
He will gather the scattered people of Judah
from all parts of the earth.
13At that time Israel will not be jealous
anymore,
and Judah will have no more enemies.
Israel will not be jealous of Judah,
and Judah will not hate Israel.
14But Israel and Judah will attack the Philistines
on the west.
Together they will take the riches from the
people of the east.
They will conquer Edom and Moab,
and the people of Ammon will be under
their control.
15The LORD will dry up
the Red Sea[a] of Egypt.
He will wave his arm over the Euphrates
River
and dry it up with a scorching wind.
He will divide it into seven small rivers

FUTURE

Assurance of Hope

Desmond Tutu is a small man with a big laugh. He bounces into rooms like a joyful elf who simultaneously puts others at ease and captures their attention. His eyes sparkle behind his gold-rimmed glasses. And his hands gesture wildly as he speaks about the issues that motivate his life in South Africa—God, Christianity, humanity and apartheid (the government system that denies basic rights to anyone who is not white).

Tutu has been leading his people in the war against apartheid for many years. Progress is slow. Yet he is convinced that he—and his people— will win. His confidence isn't based on political scheming or the possibility of civil war. His confidence is based on God. Tutu has a vision for a future free of racism and injustice in South Africa. He has shared his vision with kings, presidents and other leaders, all with the hope of creating a better future for his people.

"What we are looking for is not driving white people into the sea. What we are looking for is a new society where we are saying . . . 'Hey, let's go hand-in-hand together, black and white, into this glorious future that God opened up for us in this wonderful land so that we together—black and white—can walk tall and know that we count not because of the color of our skin, but we count because we are each creatures of infinite value made in the image of God.'

"What chance does the South African government stand?" asks Tutu. "There is just no hope for them. And they really ought to listen to us when we say, 'We are asking you to join the winning side.' When we say we are on the winning side, it isn't that God is on our side because we are good; it is because he is that kind of God."

Desmond Tutu is confident of the future because he believes in God's faithfulness and power to deliver those who cry to him. The writer of **Isaiah 11:1–10** also looks hopefully to the future, for God has promised a time in the future when peace will reign on the earth.

- How is Desmond Tutu's view of the future like Isaiah's in this passage? How is it different?
- How does this passage apply to your future?

CONSIDER . . .

- writing all the dreams you have for your future and then committing them each to God.
- choosing one goal you have for your future and committing yourself to achieve that goal this year.

FOR MORE, SEE . . .

- Psalm 42 (p. 507)
- Luke 19:11–27 (p. 1091)

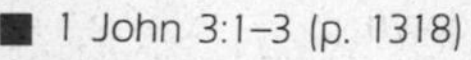

- 1 John 3:1–3 (p. 1318)

so that people can walk across them
with their sandals on.
16So God's people who are left alive
will have a way to leave Assyria,
just like the time the Israelites
came out of Egypt.

A Song of Praise to God

12 At that time you will say:
"I praise you, LORD!
You were angry with me,
but you are not angry with me now!
You have comforted me.
2God is the one who saves me;
I will trust him and not be afraid.
The LORD, the LORD gives me strength and
makes me sing.
He has saved me."
3You will receive your salvation with joy
as you would draw water from a well.
4At that time you will say,
"Praise the LORD and worship him.
Tell everyone what he has done
and how great he is.
5Sing praise to the LORD, because he has
done great things.
Let all the world know what he has
done.
6Shout and sing for joy, you people of
Jerusalem,
because the Holy One of Israel does great
things before your eyes."

God's Message to Babylon

13 God showed Isaiah son of Amoz this message about Babylon:
2Raise a flag on the bare mountain.
Call out to the men.
Raise your hand to signal them
to enter through the gates for important
people.
3I myself have commanded those people
whom I have separated as mine.
I have called those warriors to carry out my
anger.
They rejoice and are glad to do my will.

4Listen to the loud noise in the mountains,
the sound of many people.
Listen to the noise among the kingdoms,
the sound of nations gathering together.
The LORD All-Powerful is calling
his army together for battle.
5This army is coming from a faraway land,
from the edge of the horizon.
In anger the LORD is using this army like a
weapon

ETERNAL LIFE

Safe Under the Falls

From a distance, Niagara Falls is a spectacular sight. But up close, it can be terrifying. Millions of gallons of water rush over the cliff, falling one hundred sixty feet with tremendous force. Anyone caught in the falls would die instantly from the crushing impact on the jagged rocks below.

But with the help of guides, visitors can put on rubber suits and carefully make their way behind the falls. With water roaring and spraying just a few feet away, they can stand in a particular spot known as the Cave of the Winds and be perfectly safe.

Sometimes life can seem like the crushing pressure of Niagara Falls. But, as **Isaiah 12** promises, we can trust God to save and protect us with his gift of eternal life.

- What similarities are there between the Cave of the Winds and God's promise of eternal life?
- How does reading this passage give you assurance of God's gift when you are surrounded by troubles?

CONSIDER . . .

- blowing up a balloon and writing on it reasons you have to celebrate God's gift of eternal life. Keep the balloon in your room as a reminder.
- following Isaiah 12:4 by telling a non-Christian friend about the joy you have found in God's love, comfort, and salvation.

FOR MORE, SEE . . .

- Micah 7:7–9 (p. 868)
- John 3:1–16 (p. 1061)
- 2 Peter 1:3–11 (p. 1311)

to destroy the whole country.

6Cry, because the LORD's day of judging is near;
the Almighty is sending destruction.
7People will be weak with fear,
and their courage will melt away.
8Everyone will be afraid.
Pain and hurt will grab them;
they will hurt like a woman giving birth to a baby.
They will look at each other in fear,
with their faces red like fire.

God's Judgment Against Babylon

9Look, the LORD's day of judging is coming—
a terrible day, a day of God's anger.
He will destroy the land
and the sinners who live in it.
10The stars will not show their light;
the skies will be dark.
The sun will grow dark as it rises,
and the moon will not give its light.
11The LORD says, "I will punish the world for its evil
and wicked people for their sins.
I will cause proud people to lose their pride,
and I will destroy the pride of those who are cruel to others.
12People will be harder to find than pure gold;
there will be fewer people than there is fine gold in Ophir.
13I will make the sky shake,
and the earth will be moved from its place
by the anger of the LORD All-Powerful
at the time of his burning anger.
14"Then the people from Babylon will run away like hunted deer
or like sheep who have no shepherd.
Everyone will turn back to his own people;
each will run back to his own land.
15Everyone who is captured will be killed;
everyone who is caught will be killed with a sword.
16Their little children will be beaten to death in front of them.
Their houses will be robbed
and their wives raped.

17"Look, I will cause the armies of Media to attack Babylon.
They do not care about silver
or delight in gold.
18Their soldiers will shoot the young men with arrows;
they will show no mercy on children,
nor will they feel sorry for little ones.
19Babylon is the most beautiful of all kingdoms,
and the Babylonians are very proud of it.
But God will destroy it
like Sodom and Gomorrah.
20No one will ever live there
or settle there again.
No Arab will put a tent there;
no shepherd will bring sheep there.
21Only desert animals will live there,
and their houses will be full of wild dogs.
Owls will live there,
and wild goats will leap about in the houses.
22Wolves will howl within the strong walls,
and wild dogs will bark in the beautiful buildings.
The end of Babylon is near;
its time is almost over."

Israel Will Return Home

14 The LORD will show mercy to the people
of Jacob, and he will again choose the
people of Israel. He will settle them in their own
land. Then non-Israelite people will join the Israelites and will become a part of the family of Jacob.
2Nations will take the Israelites back to their land.
Then those men and women from the other nations will become slaves to Israel in the LORD's
land. In the past the Israelites were their slaves,
but now the Israelites will defeat those nations
and rule over them.

The King of Babylon Will Fall

3The LORD will take away the Israelites' hard
work and will comfort them. They will no longer
have to work hard as slaves. 4On that day Israel
will sing this song about the king of Babylon:
The cruel king who ruled us is finished;
his angry rule is finished!
5The LORD has broken the scepter[d] of evil rulers
and taken away their power.
6The king of Babylon struck people in anger
again and again.
He ruled nations in anger
and continued to hurt them.
7But now, the whole world rests and is quiet.
Now the people begin to sing.
8Even the pine trees are happy,
and the cedar trees of Lebanon rejoice.
They say, "The king has fallen,
so no one will ever cut us down again."
9The place of the dead is excited
to meet you when you come.
It wakes the spirits of the dead,
the leaders of the world.
It makes kings of all nations
stand up from their thrones to greet you.
10All these leaders will make fun of you
and will say,

"Now you are weak, as we are.
Now you are just like us."
11Your pride has been sent down to the place of the dead.
The music from your harps goes with it.
Flies are spread out like your bed beneath you,
and worms cover your body like a blanket.

12King of Babylon, morning star, you have fallen from heaven,
even though you were as bright as the rising sun!
In the past all the nations on earth bowed down before you,
but now you have been cut down.
13You told yourself,
"I will go up to heaven.
I will put my throne
above God's stars.
I will sit on the mountain of the gods,
on the slopes of the sacred mountain.
14I will go up above the tops of the clouds.
I will be like God Most High."
15But you were brought down to the grave,
to the deep places where the dead are.

16Those who see you stare at you.
They think about what has happened to you
and say, "Is this the same man who caused great fear on earth,
who shook the kingdoms,
17who turned the world into a desert,
who destroyed its cities,
who captured people in war
and would not let them go home?"

18Every king of the earth has been buried with honor,
each in his own grave.
19But you are thrown out of your grave,
like an unwanted branch.
You are covered by bodies
that died in battle,
by bodies to be buried in a rocky pit.
You are like a dead body other soldiers walk on.
20 You will not be buried with those bodies,
because you ruined your own country
and killed your own people.
The children of evil people
will never be mentioned again.

21Prepare to kill his children,
because their father is guilty.
They will never again take control of the earth;
they will never again fill the world with their cities.

22The LORD All-Powerful says this:
"I will fight against those people;
I will destroy Babylon and its people,
its children and their descendants,"[d] says the LORD.
23"I will make Babylon fit only for owls
and for swamps.
I will sweep Babylon as with a broom of destruction,"
says the LORD All-Powerful.

God Will Punish Assyria

24The LORD All-Powerful has made this promise:
"These things will happen exactly as I planned them;
they will happen exactly as I set them up.
25I will destroy the king of Assyria in my country;
I will trample him on my mountains.
He placed a heavy load on my people,
but that weight will be removed.

26"This is what I plan to do for all the earth.
And this is the hand that I have raised over all nations."
27When the LORD All-Powerful makes a plan,
no one can stop it.
When the LORD raises his hand to punish people,
no one can stop it.

God's Message to Philistia

28This message was given in the year that King
Ahaz died:
29Country of Philistia, don't be happy
that the king who struck you is now dead.
He is like a snake that will give birth to another dangerous snake.
The new king will be like a quick, dangerous snake to bite you.
30Even the poorest of my people will be able to eat safely,
and people in need will be able to lie down in safety.
But I will kill your family with hunger,
and all your people who are left will die.

31People near the city gates, cry out!
Philistines, be frightened,
because a cloud of dust comes from the north.
It is an army, full of men ready to fight.
32What shall we tell the messengers from Philistia?
Say that the LORD has made Jerusalem strong
and that his poor people will go there for safety.

God's Message to Moab

15 This is a message about Moab:
In one night armies took the wealth
from Ar in Moab,
and it was destroyed.
In one night armies took the wealth from Kir
in Moab,
and it was destroyed.

> **SIDELIGHT:** Even though the Moabites (Isaiah 15:1) were distant cousins of the Israelites, the two groups had been enemies ever since Moses tried to enter Canaan about seven hundred years before Isaiah (Judges 11:17, p. 228).

2The people of Dibon go to the places of
worship to cry.
The people of Moab cry for the cities of
Nebo and Medeba.
Every head and beard has been shaved to
show how sad Moab is.
3In the streets they wear rough cloth to show
their sadness.
On the roofs[n] and in the public squares,
they are crying loudly.
4People in the cities Heshbon and Elealeh cry
out loud.
You can hear their voices far away in the
city Jahaz.
Even the soldiers are frightened;
they are shaking with fear.

5My heart cries with sorrow for Moab.
Its people run away to Zoar for safety;
they run to Eglath Shelishiyah.
People are going up the mountain road to
Luhith,
crying as they go.
People are going on the road to Horonaim,
crying over their destruction.
6But the water of Nimrim has dried up.
The grass has dried up,
and all the plants are dead;
nothing green is left.
7So the people gather up what they have
saved
and carry it across the Ravine of the
Poplars.
8Crying is heard everywhere in Moab.
Their crying is heard as far away as the city
Eglaim;
it is heard as far away as Beer Elim.
9The water of the city Dibon is full of blood,
and I, the LORD, will bring even more
troubles to Dibon.
A few people living in Moab have escaped
the enemy,
but I will send lions to kill them.

16 Send the king of the land
the payment he demands.
Send a lamb from Sela through the desert
to the mountain of Jerusalem.
2The women of Moab
try to cross the river Arnon
like little birds
that have fallen from their nest.

3They say: "Help us.
Tell us what to do.
Protect us from our enemies
as shade protects us from the noon sun.
Hide us, because we are running for safety!
Don't give us to our enemies.
4Let those of us who were forced out of Moab
live in your land.
Hide us from our enemies."

The robbing of Moab will stop.
The enemy will be defeated;
those who hurt others will disappear from
the land.
5Then a new loyal king will come;
this faithful king will be from the family of
David.
He will judge fairly
and do what is right.

6We have heard that the people of Moab are
proud
and very conceited.
They are very proud and angry,
but their bragging means nothing.
7So the people of Moab will cry;
they will all be sad.
They will moan and groan
for the raisin cakes they had in Kir
Hareseth.
8But the fields of Heshbon and the vines of
Sibmah cannot grow grapes;
foreign rulers have destroyed the
grapevines.
The grapevines once spread as far as the city
of Jazer and into the desert;
they had spread as far as the sea.
9I cry with the people of Jazer
for the grapevines of Sibmah.
I will cry with the people of Heshbon and
Elealeh.
There will be no shouts of joy,

roofs In Bible times houses were built with flat roofs. The roof was used for drying things such as flax and fruit. And it was used as an extra room, as a place for worship, and as a place to sleep in the summer.

because there will be no harvest or ripe
fruit.
10There will be no joy and happiness in the
orchards
and no songs or shouts of joy in the
vineyards.
No one makes wine in the winepresses,[d]
because I have put an end to shouts of joy.
11My heart cries for Moab like a harp playing a
funeral song;
I am very sad for Kir Hareseth.
12The people of Moab will go to their places of
worship
and will try to pray.
But when they go to their temple to pray,
they will not be able.

13Earlier the LORD said these things about
Moab. 14Now the LORD says, "In three years all
those people and what they take pride in will be
hated. (This is three years as a hired helper would
count time.) There will be a few people left, but
they will be weak."

God's Message to Aram

17 This is a message about Damascus:
"The city of Damascus will be
destroyed;
only ruins will remain.
2People will leave the cities of Aroer.
Flocks will wander freely in those empty
towns,
and there will be no one to bother them.
3The strong, walled cities of Israel will be
destroyed.
The government in Damascus will end.
Those left alive of Aram will be
like the glory of Israel," says the LORD
All-Powerful.

4"At that time Israel's wealth will all be gone.
Israel will be like someone who has lost
much weight from sickness.
5That time will be like the grain harvest in the
Valley of Rephaim.
The workers cut the wheat.
Then they cut the heads of grain from the
plants
and collect the grain.
6That time will also be like the olive harvest,
when a few olives are left.
Two or three olives are left in the top
branches.
Four or five olives are left on full
branches," says the LORD, the God of
Israel.

7At that time people will look to God, their
Maker;
their eyes will see the Holy One of Israel.
8They will not trust the altars they have made,
nor will they trust what their hands have
made,
not even the Asherah[d] idols
and altars.

9In that day all their strong cities will be empty.
They will be like the cities the Hivites and the
Amorites left when the Israelites came to take the
land. Everything will be ruined.

10You have forgotten the God who saves you;
you have not remembered that God is your
place of safety.
You plant the finest grapevines
and grapevines from faraway places.
11You plant your grapevines one day and try to
make them grow,
and the next day you make them blossom.
But at harvest time everything will be dead;
a sickness will kill all the plants.

12Listen to the many people!
Their crying is like the noise from the sea.
Listen to the nations!
Their crying is like the crashing of great
waves.
13The people roar like the waves,
but when God speaks harshly to them, they
will run away.
They will be like chaff[d] on the hills being
blown by the wind,
or like tumbleweeds blown away by a
storm.
14At night the people will be very frightened.
Before morning, no one will be left.
So our enemies will come to our land,
but they will become nothing.

God's Message to Cush

18 How terrible it will be for the land
beyond the rivers of Cush.
It is filled with the sound of wings.
2That land sends messengers across the sea;
they go on the water in boats made of
reeds.

Go, quick messengers,
to a people who are tall and
smooth-skinned,
who are feared everywhere.
They are a powerful nation that defeats other
nations.
Their land is divided by rivers.

3All you people of the world, look!
Everyone who lives in the world, look!
You will see a banner raised on a mountain.
You will hear a trumpet sound.
4The LORD said to me,
"I will quietly watch from where I live,

like heat in the sunshine,
like the dew in the heat of harvest time."
5The time will come, after the flowers have bloomed and before the harvest,
when new grapes will be budding and growing.
The enemy will cut the plants with knives;
he will cut down the vines and take them away.
6They will be left for the birds of the mountains
and for the wild animals.
Birds will feed on them all summer,
and wild animals will eat them that winter."

7At that time a gift will be brought to the LORD All-Powerful
from the people who are tall and smooth-skinned,
who are feared everywhere.
They are a powerful nation that defeats other nations.
Their land is divided by rivers.
These gifts will be brought to the place of the LORD All-Powerful,
to Mount Zion.[d]

God's Message to Egypt

19 This is a message about Egypt:
Look, the LORD is coming on a fast cloud
to enter Egypt.
The idols of Egypt will tremble before him,
and Egypt's courage will melt away.

2The LORD says, "I will cause the Egyptians to fight against themselves.
People will fight with their relatives;
neighbors will fight neighbors;
cities will fight cities;
kingdoms will fight kingdoms.
3The Egyptians will be afraid,
and I will ruin their plans.
They will ask advice from their idols and spirits of the dead,
from their mediums[d] and fortune-tellers."
4The Lord GOD All-Powerful says,
"I will hand Egypt over to a hard master,
and a powerful king will rule over them."

5The sea will become dry,
and the water will disappear from the Nile River.
6The canals will stink;
the streams of Egypt will decrease and dry up.
All the water plants will rot;
7 all the plants along the banks of the Nile will die.
Even the planted fields by the Nile
will dry up, blow away, and disappear.
8The fishermen, all those who catch fish from the Nile,
will groan and cry;
those who fish in the Nile will be sad.
9All the people who make cloth from flax will be sad,
and those who weave linen will lose hope.
10Those who weave cloth will be broken.
All those who work for money will be sad.

11The officers of the city of Zoan are fools;
the wise men who advise the king of Egypt give wrong advice.
How can you say to him, 'I am wise'?
How can you say, 'I am from the old family of the kings'?
12Egypt, where are your wise men?
Let them show you
what the LORD All-Powerful has planned for Egypt.
13The officers of Zoan have been fooled;
the leaders of Memphis have believed false things.
So the leaders of Egypt
lead that nation the wrong way.
14The LORD has made the leaders confused.
They have led Egypt to wander in the wrong ways,
like drunk people stumbling in their own vomit.
15There is nothing Egypt can do;
no one there can help.

16In that day the Egyptians will be like women.
They will be afraid of the LORD All-Powerful, because he will raise his hand to strike them down.
17The land of Judah will bring fear to Egypt.
Anyone there who hears the name Judah will
be afraid, because the LORD All-Powerful has
planned terrible things for them. 18At that time
five cities in Egypt will speak Hebrew, the language of Canaan, and they will promise to be loyal
to the LORD All-Powerful. One of these cities will
be named the City of Destruction. 19At that time
there will be an altar for the LORD in the middle
of Egypt and a monument to the LORD at the border of Egypt. 20This will be a sign and a witness
to the LORD All-Powerful in the land of Egypt.
When the people cry to the LORD for help, he will
send someone to save and defend them. He will
rescue them from those who hurt them.
21So the LORD will show himself to the Egyptians, and then they will know he is the LORD.
They will worship God and offer many sacrifices.
They will make promises to the LORD and will
keep them. 22The LORD will punish the Egyptians,
but then he will heal them. They will come back

to the LORD, and he will listen to their prayers and
heal them.
23 At that time there will be a highway from
Egypt to Assyria, and the Assyrians will go to
Egypt, and the Egyptians will go to Assyria. The
Egyptians and Assyrians will worship God together. 24 At that time Israel, Assyria, and Egypt
will join together, which will be a blessing for the
earth. 25 The LORD All-Powerful will bless them,
saying, "Egypt, you are my people. Assyria, I
made you. Israel, I own you. You are all blessed!"

SIDELIGHT: Sargon, an Assyrian king during Isaiah's time (Isaiah 20:1), was not only a powerful military leader, but must have also been quite a scholar. He built the oldest library archaeologists have discovered, where twenty-five hundred books were found. Of course, that's a small number compared to modern libraries, which can have several million books.

Assyria Will Defeat Egypt and Cush

20 Sargon king of Assyria sent a military
commander to Ashdod to attack that
city. So the commander attacked and captured it.
2 Then the LORD spoke through Isaiah son of
Amoz, saying, "Take the rough cloth off your
body, and take your sandals off your feet." So Isaiah obeyed and walked around naked and barefoot.
3 Then the LORD said, "Isaiah my servant has
walked around naked and barefoot for three years
as a sign against Egypt and Cush. 4 The king of
Assyria will carry away prisoners from Egypt and
Cush. Old people and young people will be led
away naked and barefoot, with their buttocks
bare. So the Egyptians will be shamed. 5 People
who looked to Cush for help will be afraid, and
those who were amazed by Egypt's glory will be
shamed. 6 People who live near the sea will say,
'Look at those countries. We trusted them to help
us. We ran to them so they would save us from
the king of Assyria. So how will we be able to
escape?' "

God's Message to Babylon

21 This is a message about the Desert by the
Sea:[n]

Disaster is coming from the desert
like wind blowing in the south.
It is coming from a terrible country.
2 I have seen a terrible vision.
I see traitors turning against you
and people taking your wealth.

Elam, attack the people!
Media, surround the city and attack it!
I will bring an end to the pain the city
causes.

3 I saw those terrible things, and now I am in
pain;
my pains are like the pains of giving birth.
What I hear makes me very afraid;
what I see causes me to shake with fear.
4 I am worried,
and I am shaking with fear.
My pleasant evening
has become a night of fear.
5 They set the table;
they spread the rugs;
they eat and drink.
Leaders, stand up.
Prepare the shields for battle!

6 The Lord said to me,
"Go, place a lookout for the city
and have him report what he sees.
7 If he sees chariots and teams of horses,
donkeys, or camels,
he should pay very close attention."
8 Then the lookout called out,
"My master, each day I stand in the
watchtower watching;
every night I have been on guard.
9 Look, I see a man coming in a chariot
with a team of horses."
The man gives back the answer,
"Babylon has fallen. It has fallen!
All the statues of her gods
lie broken on the ground."

10 My people are crushed like grain on the
threshing[d] floor.
My people, I tell you what I have heard
from the LORD All-Powerful,
from the God of Israel.

God's Message to Edom

11 This is a message about Dumah:[n]
Someone calls to me from Edom,
"Watchman, how much of the night is left?
Watchman, how much longer will it be
night?"
12 The watchman answers,
"Morning is coming, but then night will
come again.
If you have something to ask,
then come back and ask."

Desert by the Sea Probably Babylon.
Dumah Another name for Edom.

God's Message to Arabia

13This is a message about Arabia:
A group of traders from Dedan
spent the night near some trees in
Arabia.
14 They gave water to thirsty travelers;
the people of Tema gave food
to those who were escaping.
15They were running from swords,
from swords ready to kill,
from bows ready to shoot,
from a hard battle.

16This is what the Lord said to me: "In one year
all the glory of the country of Kedar will be gone.
(This is a year as a hired helper counts time.) 17At
that time only a few of the archers, the soldiers of
Kedar, will be left alive." The LORD, the God of
Israel, has spoken.

God's Message to Jerusalem

22 This is a message about the Valley of Vision:[n]
What is wrong with you people?
Why are you on your roofs?[n]
2This city was a very busy city,
full of noise and wild parties.
Now your people have been killed,
but not with swords,
nor did they die in battle.
3All your leaders ran away together,
but they have been captured without using
a bow.
All you who were captured
tried to run away before the enemy came.
4So I say, "Don't look at me.
Let me cry loudly.
Don't hurry to comfort me
about the destruction of Jerusalem."
5The Lord GOD All-Powerful has chosen a
special day
of riots and confusion.
People will trample each other in the Valley
of Vision.
The city walls will be knocked down,
and the people will cry out to the
mountain.
6The soldiers from Elam will gather their
arrows
and their chariots and men on horses.
Kir will prepare their shields.
7Your nicest valleys will be filled with chariots.
Horsemen will be ordered to guard the
gates of the city.
8 The walls protecting Judah will fall.
At that time the people of Jerusalem
depended on
the weapons kept at the Palace of the
Forest.
9You saw that the walls of Jerusalem
had many cracks that needed repairing.
You stored up water in the lower pool.
10You counted the houses of Jerusalem,
and you tore down houses to repair the
walls with their stones.
11You made a pool between the two walls
to save water from the old pool,
but you did not trust the God who made
these things;
you did not respect the One who planned
them long ago.

12The Lord GOD All-Powerful told the people
to cry and be sad,
to shave their heads and wear rough cloth.
13But look, the people are happy
and are having wild parties.
They kill the cattle and the sheep;
they eat the food and drink the wine.
They say, "Let us eat and drink,
because tomorrow we will die."

14The LORD All-Powerful said to me: "You people will die before this guilt is forgiven." The Lord
GOD All-Powerful said this.

God's Message to Shebna

15This is what the Lord GOD All-Powerful says:
"Go to this servant Shebna,
the manager of the palace.
16Say to him, 'What are you doing here?
Who said you could cut out a tomb for
yourself here?
Why are you preparing your tomb in a high
place?
Why are you carving out a tomb from the
rock?
17Look, mighty one! The LORD will throw you
away.
He will take firm hold of you
18and roll you tightly into a ball
and throw you into another country.
There you will die,
and there your fine chariots will remain.
You are a disgrace to your master's house.
19I will force you out of your important job,
and you will be thrown down from your
important place.'

20"At that time I will call for my servant Eliakim
son of Hilkiah. 21I will take your robe and put it
on him and give him your belt. I will hand over

Valley of Vision This probably means a valley near Jerusalem.
roofs In Bible times houses were built with flat roofs. The roof was used for drying things such as flax and fruit. And it was used as an extra room, as a place for worship, and as a place to sleep in the summer.

to him the important job you have, and he will be
like a father to the people of Jerusalem and the
family of Judah. 22I will put the key to the house
of David around his neck. If he opens a door, no
one will be able to close it; if he closes a door, no
one will be able to open it. 23He will be like an
honored chair in his father's house. I will make
him strong like a peg that is hammered into a
strong board. 24All the honored and important
things of his family will depend on him; all the
adults and little children will depend on him.
They will be like bowls and jars hanging on him.
25"At that time," says the LORD All-Powerful,
"the peg hammered into the strong board will
weaken. It will break and fall, and everything
hanging on it will be destroyed." The LORD says
this.

God's Message to Lebanon

23 This is a message about Tyre:
You trading ships, cry!
The houses and harbor of Tyre are
destroyed.
This news came to the ships
from the land of Cyprus.
2Be silent, you who live on the island of Tyre;
you merchants of Sidon, be silent.
Sailors have made you rich.
3They traveled the sea to bring grain from
Egypt;
the sailors of Tyre brought grain from the
Nile Valley
and sold it to other nations.
4Sidon, be ashamed.
Strong city of the sea, be ashamed, because
the sea says:
"I have not felt the pain of giving birth;
I have not reared young men or women."
5Egypt will hear the news about Tyre,
and it will make Egypt hurt with sorrow.

6You ships should return to Tarshish.
You people living near the sea should be
sad.
7Look at your once happy city!
Look at your old, old city!
People from that city have traveled
far away to live.
8Who planned Tyre's destruction?
Tyre made others rich.
Its merchants were treated like princes,
and its traders were greatly respected.
9It was the LORD All-Powerful who planned
this.
He decided to make these proud people
unimportant;
he decided to disgrace those who were
greatly respected.
10Go through your land, people of Tarshish,
like the Nile goes through Egypt.
There is no harbor for you now!
11The LORD has stretched his hand over the sea
and made its kingdoms tremble.
He commands that Canaan's
strong, walled cities be destroyed.
12He said, "Sidon, you will not rejoice any
longer,
because you are destroyed.
Even if you cross the sea to Cyprus,
you will not find a place to rest."
13Look at the land of the Babylonians;
it is not a country now.
Assyria has made it a place for wild animals.
Assyria built towers to attack it;
the soldiers took all the treasures from its
cities,
and they turned it into ruins.
14So be sad, you trading ships,
because your strong city is destroyed.
15At that time people will forget about Tyre for
seventy years, which is the length of a king's life.
After seventy years, Tyre will be like the prostitute[a] in this song:

16"Oh woman, you are forgotten.
Take your harp and walk through the city.
Play your harp well. Sing your song often.
Then people will remember you."

17After seventy years the LORD will deal with
Tyre, and it will again have trade. It will be like
a prostitute for all the nations of the earth. 18The
profits will be saved for the LORD. Tyre will not
keep the money she earns but will give them to
the people who serve the LORD, so they will have
plenty of food and nice clothes.

The Lord Will Punish the World

24 Look! The LORD will destroy the earth
and leave it empty;
he will ruin the surface of the land and
scatter its people.
2At that time the same thing will happen to
everyone:
to common people and priests,
to slaves and masters,
to women slaves and their women masters,
to buyers and sellers,
to those who borrow and those who lend,
to bankers and those who owe the bank.
3The earth will be completely empty.
The wealth will all be taken,
because the LORD has commanded it.
4The earth will dry up and die;
the world will grow weak and die;
the great leaders in this land will become
weak.
5The people of the earth have ruined it,
because they do not follow God's teachings

or obey God's laws
or keep their agreement with God that was to last forever.
6So a curse will destroy the earth.
The people of the world are guilty,
so they will be burned up;
only a few will be left.
7The new wine will be bad, and the grapevines will die.
People who were happy will be sad.
8The happy music of the tambourines[d] will end.
The happy sounds of wild parties will stop.
The joyful music from the harps will end.
9People will no longer sing while they drink their wine.
The beer will taste bitter to those who drink it.
10The ruined city will be empty,
and people will hide behind closed doors.
11People in the streets will ask for wine,
but joy will have turned to sadness;
all the happiness will have left.
12The city will be left in ruins,
and its gates will be smashed to pieces.
13This is what will happen all over the earth
and to all the nations.
The earth will be like an olive tree after the harvest
or like the few grapes left on a vine after harvest.
14The people shout for joy.
From the west they praise the greatness of the LORD.
15People in the east, praise the LORD.
People in the islands of the sea,
praise the name of the LORD, the God of Israel.
16We hear songs from every part of the earth
praising God, the Righteous One.

But I said, "I am dying! I am dying!
How terrible it will be for me!
Traitors turn against people;
with their dishonesty, they turn against people."
17There are terrors, holes, and traps
for the people of the earth.
18Anyone who tries to escape from the sound of terror
will fall into a hole.
Anyone who climbs out of the hole
will be caught in a trap.
The clouds in the sky will pour out rain,
and the foundations of the earth will shake.
19The earth will be broken up;
the earth will split open;
the earth will shake violently.
20The earth will stumble around like someone who is drunk;
it will shake like a hut in a storm.
Its sin is like a heavy weight on its back;
it will fall and never rise again.

21At that time the LORD will punish
the powers in the sky above
and the rulers on earth below.
22They will be gathered together
like prisoners thrown into a dungeon;
they will be shut up in prison.
After much time they will be punished.
23The moon will be embarrassed,
and the sun will be ashamed,
because the LORD All-Powerful will rule as king
on Mount Zion[d] in Jerusalem.
Jerusalem's leaders will see his greatness.

A Song of Praise to God

25 LORD, you are my God.
I honor you and praise you,
because you have done amazing things.
You have always done what you said you would do;
you have done what you planned long ago.
2You have made the city a pile of rocks
and have destroyed her walls.
The city our enemies built with strong walls is gone;
it will never be built again.
3People from powerful nations will honor you;
cruel people from strong cities will fear you.
4You protect the poor;
you protect the helpless when they are in danger.
You are like a shelter from storms,
like shade that protects them from the heat.
The cruel people attack
like a rainstorm beating against the wall,
5 like the heat in the desert.
But you, God, stop their violent attack.
As a cloud cools a hot day,
you silence the songs of those who have no mercy.

God's Banquet for His Servants

6The LORD All-Powerful will prepare a feast
on this mountain for all people.
It will be a feast with all the best food and wine,
the finest meat and wine.
7On this mountain God will destroy
the veil that covers all nations,
the veil that stretches over all peoples;
8 he will destroy death forever.

The Lord God will wipe away every tear
from every face.
He will take away the shame of his people
from the earth.
The Lord has spoken.

9At that time people will say,
"Our God is doing this!
We have waited for him, and he has come to
save us.
This is the Lord. We waited for him,
so we will rejoice and be happy when he
saves us."

10The Lord will protect Jerusalem,
but he will crush our enemy Moab
like straw that is trampled down in the
manure.

11They will spread their arms in it
like a person who is swimming.
But God will bring down their pride,
and all the clever things they have made
will mean nothing.

SIDELIGHT: Lawn care services may be new, but fertilizer has been around for a long time. The ancient Israelite farmers would mix together straw and manure to make fertilizer (Isaiah 25:10). If they were around today, those farmers could sell their produce at all-organic stores.

12Moab's high walls protect them,
but God will destroy these walls.
He will throw them down to the ground,
even to the dust.

DEATH

Bittersweet

Jacob Blevins was a rebel. He didn't like church or the kids who went there. But something inside him kept drawing him to the youth group. Perhaps it was the way the kids treated each other: They truly cared. Or perhaps it was just the fun events.

For whatever reason, Jacob came to the harvest hayride. He arrived early and walked quietly around the church. He talked to a few people, but mostly kept to himself.

Just before the hayride trailer took off, Jacob saw Kellie, a girl he knew—and liked—from school. Jacob knew she was a Christian, and wondered whether she would talk to him. Despite his fears, he plopped down beside her on the front of one side of the trailer, and they took off.

Jacob and Kellie had a great time. They talked and laughed, and even wrestled playfully in the hay.

Then it happened. Kellie just suddenly wasn't there. There was no scream, no sound at all. It was like a weird dream, but Jacob couldn't wake himself up. He sat stunned as the trailer came to an abrupt halt.

Kellie was dead. While she and Jacob were wrestling, her foot had gotten caught in the trailer wheel. The turning of the wheel pulled her off the trailer, and under the tire.

Jacob struggled to get over the pain of that night. But through the months that followed, he developed a relationship with God that remains strong. Jacob knows he'll never see Kellie again in this lifetime. But now that he knows Christ, he's assured that he'll see her again . . . in heaven.

Isaiah 25:6–9 describes how God will destroy death and bring all his people together at the end of time. Read the passage to see what Jacob and Kellie's reunion will be like.

- Verse 7 describes death as a "veil." How is death like a "veil" separating Jacob and Kellie?
- According to this passage, why should we not fear death?

CONSIDER . . .

- writing all the positive things about someone you love who has died and then looking at your list every time you feel sad about that person's death.
- spending time with someone you know who has lost someone he or she loved.

FOR MORE, SEE . . .

- Psalm 23 (p. 495)
- 1 Corinthians 15:50–57 (p. 1189)
- 1 Thessalonians 4:13–18 (p. 1248)

A Song of Praise to God

26 At that time people will sing this song in Judah:

We have a strong city.
God protects us with its strong walls and defenses.
2Open the gates,
and the good people will enter,
those who follow God.
3You, LORD, give true peace
to those who depend on you,
because they trust you.
4So, trust the LORD always,
because he is our Rock[d] forever.
5He will destroy the proud city,
and he will punish the people living there.
He will bring that high city down to the ground
and throw it down into the dust.
6Then those who were hurt by the city will walk on its ruins;
those who were made poor by the city will trample it under their feet.

7The path of life is level for those who are right with God;
LORD, you make the way of life smooth for those people.
8But, LORD, we are waiting
for your way of justice.
Our souls want to remember
you and your name.
9My soul wants to be with you at night,
and my spirit wants to be with you at the dawn of every day.
When your way of justice comes to the land,
people of the world will learn the right way of living.
10Evil people will not learn to do good
even if you show them kindness.
They will continue doing evil, even if they live in a good world;
they never see the LORD's greatness.
11LORD, you are ready to punish those people,
but they do not see that.
Show them your strong love for your people.
Then those who are evil will be ashamed.
Burn them in the fire
you have prepared for your enemies.
12LORD, all our success is because of what you have done,
so give us peace.
13LORD, our God, other masters besides you have ruled us,
but we honor only you.
14Those masters are now dead;
their ghosts will not rise from death.
You punished and destroyed them
and erased any memory of them.
15LORD, you multiplied the number of your people;
you multiplied them and brought honor to yourself.
You made the borders of the land wide.
16LORD, people remember you when they are in trouble;
they say quiet prayers to you when you punish them.
17LORD, when we are with you,
we are like a woman giving birth to a baby;
she cries and has pain from the birth.
18In the same way, we had pain.
We gave birth, but only to wind.
We don't bring salvation to the land
or make new people for the world.
19Your people have died, but they will live again;
their bodies will rise from death.
You who lie in the ground,
wake up and be happy!
The dew covering you is like the dew of a new day;
the ground will give birth to the dead.

Judgment: Reward or Punishment

20My people, go into your rooms
and shut your doors behind you.
Hide in your rooms for a short time
until God's anger is finished.
21The LORD will leave his place
to punish the people of the world for their sins.
The earth will show the blood of the people who have been killed;
it will not cover the dead any longer.

27 At that time the LORD will punish Leviathan,[d] the gliding snake.
He will punish Leviathan, the coiled snake,
with his great and hard and powerful sword.
He will kill the monster in the sea.

2At that time
people will sing about the pleasant vineyard.
3"I, the LORD, will care for that vineyard;
I will water it at the right time.
No one will hurt it,
because I will guard it day and night.
4I am not angry.
If anyone builds a wall of thornbushes in war,
I will march to it and burn it.
5But if anyone comes to me for safety
and wants to make peace with me,
he should come and make peace with me."

[6]In the days to come, the people of Jacob will
be like a plant with good roots;
Israel will grow like a plant beginning to
bloom.
Then the world will be filled with their
children.

The Lord Will Send Israel Away

[7]The LORD has not hurt his people as he hurt
their enemies;
his people have not been killed like those
who tried to kill them.
[8]He will settle his argument with Israel by
sending it far away.
Like a hot desert wind, he will drive it
away.
[9]This is how Israel's guilt will be forgiven;
this is how its sins will be taken away:
Israel will crush the rocks of the altar to dust,
and no statues or altars will be left standing
for the Asherah[d] idols.
[10]At that time the strong, walled city will be
empty
like a desert.
Calves will eat grass there.
They will lie down there
and eat leaves from the branches.
[11]The limbs will become dry and break off,
so women will use them for firewood.
The people refuse to understand,
so God will not comfort them;
their Maker will not be kind to them.

[12]At that time the LORD will begin gathering his
people one by one from the Euphrates River to the
brook of Egypt. He will separate them from others
as grain is separated from chaff.[d] [13]Many of my
people are now lost in Assyria. Some have run
away to Egypt. But at that time a great trumpet
will be blown, and all those people will come and
worship the LORD on that holy mountain in Jerusalem.

Warnings to Israel

28 How terrible it will be for Samaria, the
pride of Israel's drunken people!
That beautiful crown of flowers is just a
dying plant
set on a hill above a rich valley where
drunkards live.
[2]Look, the Lord has someone who is strong
and powerful.
Like a storm of hail and strong wind,
like a sudden flood of water pouring over the
country,
he will throw Samaria down to the ground.
[3]That city, the pride of Israel's drunken
people,
will be trampled underfoot.
[4]That beautiful crown of flowers is just a
dying plant
set on a hill above a rich valley.
That city will be like the first fig of summer.
Anyone who sees it
quickly picks it and eats it.

[5]At that time the LORD All-Powerful
will be like a beautiful crown,
like a wonderful crown of flowers
for his people who are left alive.
[6]Then he will give wisdom to the judges who
must decide cases
and strength to those who battle at the city
gate.
[7]But now those leaders are drunk with wine;
they stumble from drinking too much beer.
The priests and prophets[d] are drunk with
beer
and are filled with wine.
They stumble from too much beer.
The prophets are drunk when they see
their visions;
the judges stumble when they make their
decisions.
[8]Every table is covered with vomit,
so there is not a clean place anywhere.

[9]The LORD is trying to teach the people a
lesson;
he is trying to make them understand his
teachings.
But the people are like babies too old for
breast milk,
like those who no longer nurse at their
mother's breast.
[10]So they make fun of the LORD's prophet and
say:
"A command here, a command there.
A rule here, a rule there.
A little lesson here, a little lesson there."
[11]So the LORD will use strange words and
foreign languages
to speak to these people.
[12]God said to them,
"Here is a place of rest;
let the tired people come and rest.
This is the place of peace."
But the people would not listen.
[13]So the words of the LORD will be,
"A command here, a command there.
A rule here, a rule there.
A little lesson here, a little lesson there."
They will fall back and be defeated;
they will be trapped and captured.

[14]So listen to the LORD's message, you who
brag,
you leaders in Jerusalem.

[15]You say, "We have made an agreement with death;
we have a contract with death.
When terrible punishment passes by,
it won't hurt us.
Our lies will keep us safe,
and our tricks will hide us."

[16]Because of these things, this is what the Lord
GOD says:
"I will put a stone in the ground in Jerusalem,
a tested stone.
Everything will be built on this important and precious rock.
Anyone who trusts in it will never be disappointed.
[17]I will use justice as a measuring line
and goodness as the standard.
The lies you hide behind will be destroyed as if by hail.
They will be washed away as if in a flood.
[18]Your agreement with death will be erased;
your contract with death will not help you.
When terrible punishment comes,
you will be crushed by it.
[19]Whenever punishment comes, it will take you away.
It will come morning after morning;
it will defeat you by day and by night.
Those who understand this punishment will be terrified."
[20]You will be like the person who tried to sleep
on a bed that was too short
and with a blanket that was too narrow
to wrap around himself.
[21]The LORD will fight as he did at Mount Perazim.
He will be angry as he was in the Valley of Gibeon.
He will do his work, his strange work.
He will finish his job, his strange job.
[22]Now, you must not make fun of these things,
or the ropes around you will become tighter.
The Lord GOD All-Powerful has told me
how the whole earth will be destroyed.

The Lord Punishes Fairly

[23]Listen closely to what I tell you;
listen carefully to what I say.
[24]A farmer does not plow his field all the time;
he does not go on working the soil.
[25]He makes the ground flat and smooth.
Then he plants the dill and scatters the cumin.
He plants the wheat in rows,
the barley in its special place,
and other wheat as a border around the field.
[26]His God teaches him
and shows him the right way.
[27]A farmer doesn't use heavy boards to crush dill;
he doesn't use a wagon wheel to crush cumin.
He uses a small stick to break open the dill,
and with a stick he opens the cumin.
[28]The grain is ground to make bread.
People do not ruin it by crushing it forever.
The farmer separates the wheat from the chaff[d] with his cart,
but he does not let his horses grind it.
[29]This lesson also comes from the LORD All-Powerful,
who gives wonderful advice, who is very wise.

Warnings to Jerusalem

29 How terrible it will be for you, Jerusalem,
the city where David camped.
Your festivals have continued
year after year.
[2]I will attack Jerusalem,
and that city will be filled with sadness and crying.
It will be like an altar to me.
[3]I will put armies all around you, Jerusalem;
I will surround you with towers
and with devices to attack you.
[4]You will be pulled down and will speak from the ground;
I will hear your voice rising from the ground.
It will sound like the voice of a ghost;
your words will come like a whisper from the dirt.

[5]Your many enemies will become like fine dust;
the many cruel people will be like chaff[d] that is blown away.
Everything will happen very quickly.
[6] The LORD All-Powerful will come
with thunder, earthquakes, and great noises,
with storms, strong winds, and a fire that destroys.
[7]Then all the nations that fight against Jerusalem
will be like a dream;
all the nations that attack her
will be like a vision in the night.
[8]They will be like a hungry man who dreams he is eating,
but when he awakens, he is still hungry.

They will be like a thirsty man who dreams
he is drinking,
but when he awakens, he is still weak and
thirsty.
It will be the same way with all the nations
who fight against Mount Zion.[d]
9Be surprised and amazed.
Blind yourselves so that you cannot see.
Become drunk, but not from wine.
Trip and fall, but not from beer.
10The LORD has made you go into a deep sleep.
He has closed your eyes. (The prophets are
your eyes.)
He has covered your heads. (The seers[d] are
your heads.)

11This vision is like the words of a book that is
closed and sealed. You may give the book to
someone who can read and tell that person to
read it. But he will say, "I can't read the book,
because it is sealed." 12Or you may give the book
to someone who cannot read and tell him to read
it. But he will say, "I don't know how to read."

13The Lord says:
"These people say they love me;
they show honor to me with words,
but their hearts are far from me.
The honor they show me
is nothing but human rules.
14So I will continue to amaze these people
by doing more and more miracles.[d]
Their wise men will lose their wisdom;
their wise men will not be able to
understand."

Warnings About Other Nations

15How terrible it will be for those who try
to hide things from the LORD
and who do their work in darkness.
They think no one will see them or know
what they do.
16You are confused.
You think the clay is equal to the potter.
You think that an object can tell the one who
made it,
"You didn't make me."
This is like a pot telling its maker,
"You don't know anything."

A Better Time Is Coming

17In a very short time, Lebanon will become
rich farmland,
and the rich farmland will seem like a
forest.
18At that time the deaf will hear the words in a
book.
Instead of having darkness and gloom, the
blind will see.
19The LORD will make the poor people happy;
they will rejoice in the Holy One of Israel.
20Then the people without mercy will come to
an end;
those who do not respect God will
disappear.
Those who enjoy doing evil will be gone:
21those who lie about others in court,
those who trap people in court,
those who lie and take justice from
innocent people in court.

22This is what the LORD who set Abraham free
says to the family of Jacob:
"Now the people of Jacob will not be
ashamed
or disgraced any longer.
23When they see all their children,
the children I made with my hands,
they will say my name is holy.
They will agree that the Holy One of Jacob
is holy,
and they will respect the God of Israel.
24People who do wrong will now understand.
Those who complain will accept being
taught."

Warnings to the Stubborn Nation

30 The LORD said,
"How terrible it will be for these
stubborn children.
They make plans, but they don't ask me to
help them.
They make agreements with other nations,
without asking my Spirit.[d]
They are adding more and more sins to
themselves.
2They go down to Egypt for help
without asking me about it first.
They hope they will be saved by the king of
Egypt;
they want Egypt to protect them.
3But hiding in Egypt will bring you only
shame;
Egypt's protection will only disappoint you.
4Your officers have gone to Zoan,
and your messengers have gone to Hanes,
5but they will be put to shame,
because Egypt is useless to them.
It will give no help and will be of no use;
it will cause them only shame and
embarrassment."

God's Message to Judah

6This is a message about the animals in southern Judah:
Southern Judah is a dangerous place
full of lions and lionesses,
poisonous snakes and darting snakes.

The messengers travel through there with
their wealth on the backs of donkeys
and their treasure on the backs of camels.
They carry them to a nation that cannot help
them,
7 to Egypt whose help is useless.
So I call that country Rahab[d] the Do-Nothing.

8Now write this on a sign for the people,
write this on a scroll,
so that for the days to come
this will be a witness forever.
9These people are like children who lie and
refuse to obey;
they refuse to listen to the LORD's
teachings.
10They tell the seers,[d]
"Don't see any more visions!"
They say to the prophets,[d]
"Don't tell us the truth!
Say things that will make us feel good;
see only good things for us.
11Stop blocking our path.
Get out of our way.
Stop telling us
about God, the Holy One of Israel."

12So this is what the Holy One of Israel says:
"You people have refused to accept this
message
and have depended on cruelty and lies to
help you.
13You are guilty of these things.
So you will be like a high wall with cracks
in it
that falls suddenly and breaks into small
pieces.
14You will be like a clay jar that breaks,
smashed into many pieces.
Those pieces will be too small
to take coals from the fire
or to get water from a well."

15This is what the Lord GOD, the Holy One of
Israel, says:
"If you come back to me and trust me, you
will be saved.
If you will be calm and trust me, you will
be strong."
But you don't want to do that.
16You say, "No, we need horses to run away
on."
So you will run away on horses.
You say, "We will ride away on fast horses."
So those who chase you will be fast.
17One enemy will make threats,
and a thousand of your men will run
away.
Five enemies will make threats,
and all of you will run from them.
You will be left alone like a flagpole on a
hilltop,
like a banner on a hill.
18The LORD wants to show his mercy to you.
He wants to rise and comfort you.
The LORD is a fair God,
and everyone who waits for his help will be
happy.

The Lord Will Help His People

19You people who live on Mount Zion[d] in Jerusalem will not cry anymore. The LORD will hear
your crying, and he will comfort you. When he
hears you, he will help you. 20The Lord has given
you sorrow and hurt like the bread and water you
ate every day. He is your teacher; he will not continue to hide from you, but you will see your
teacher with your own eyes. 21If you go the
wrong way—to the right or to the left—you will
hear a voice behind you saying, "This is the right
way. You should go this way." 22You have statues
covered with silver and gold, but you will ruin
them for further use. You will throw them away
like filthy rags and say, "Go away!"

23At that time the LORD will send rain for the
seeds you plant in the ground, and the ground
will grow food for you. The harvest will be rich
and great, and you will have plenty of food in the
fields for your animals. 24Your oxen and donkeys
that work the soil will have all the food they need.
You will have to use shovels and pitchforks to
spread all their food. 25Every mountain and hill
will have streams filled with water. These things
will happen after many people are killed and the
towers are pulled down. 26At that time the light
from the moon will be bright like the sun, and the
light from the sun will be seven times brighter
than now, like the light of seven days. These
things will happen when the LORD bandages his
broken people and heals the hurts he gave them.

27Look! The LORD comes from far away.
His anger is like a fire with thick clouds of
smoke.
His mouth is filled with anger,
and his tongue is like a burning fire.
28His breath is like a rushing river,
which rises to the throat.
He will judge the nations as if he is sifting
them through the strainer of
destruction.
He will place in their mouths a bit that will
lead them the wrong way.
29You will sing happy songs
as on the nights you begin a festival.
You will be happy like people listening to
flutes
as they come to the mountain of the LORD,
to the Rock[d] of Israel.

[30]The LORD will cause all people to hear his great voice
and to see his powerful arm come down with anger,
like a great fire that burns everything,
like a great storm with much rain and hail.

SIDELIGHT: About the only similarity between the flute mentioned in Isaiah 30:29 and the flutes people play today is that you blow into both. Many ancient flutes (or pipes) were made from two separate pipes, each with one hole in it to control pitch. These high-pitched instruments were used mostly for weddings and funerals.

[31]Assyria will be afraid when it hears the voice of the LORD,
because he will strike Assyria with a rod.
[32]When the LORD punishes Assyria with a rod,
he will beat them to the music of tambourines[d] and harps;
he will fight against them with his mighty weapons.
[33]Topheth[n] has been made ready for a long time;
it is ready for the king.
It was made deep and wide
with much wood and fire.
And the LORD's breath will come
like a stream of burning sulfur and set it on fire.

Warnings About Relying on Egypt

31 How terrible it will be for those people who go down to Egypt for help.
They think horses will save them.
They think their many chariots
and strong horsemen will save them.
But they don't trust God, the Holy One of Israel,
or ask the LORD for help.
[2]But he is wise and can bring them disaster.
He does not change his warnings.
He will rise up and fight against the evil people
and against those who try to help evil people.
[3]The Egyptians are only people and are not God.
Their horses are only animals and are not spirit.
The LORD will stretch out his arm,
and the one who helps will stumble,
and the people who wanted help will fall.
All of them will be destroyed together.

[4]The LORD says this to me:
"When a lion or a lion's cub kills an animal to eat,
it stands over the dead animal and roars.
A band of shepherds
may be assembled against it,
but the lion will not be afraid of their yelling
or upset by their noise.
So the LORD All-Powerful will come down
to fight on Mount Zion[d] and on its hill.
[5]The LORD All-Powerful will defend Jerusalem
like birds flying over their nests.
He will defend and save it;
he will 'pass over' and save Jerusalem."

[6]You children of Israel, come back to the God
you fought against. [7]The time is coming when
each of you will stop worshiping idols of gold and
silver, which you sinned by making.

[8]"Assyria will be defeated by a sword, but not the sword of a person;
Assyria will be destroyed, but not by a person's sword.
Assyria will run away from the sword of God,
but its young men will be caught and made slaves.
[9]They will panic, and their protection will be destroyed.
Their commanders will be terrified when they see God's battle flag,"
says the LORD,
whose fire is in Jerusalem
and whose furnace is in Jerusalem.

A Good Kingdom Is Coming

32 A king will rule in a way that brings justice,
and leaders will make fair decisions.
[2]Then each ruler will be like a shelter from the wind,
like a safe place in a storm,
like streams of water in a dry land,
like a cool shadow from a large rock in a hot land.

[3]People will look to the king for help,
and they will truly listen to what he says.
[4]People who are now worried will be able to understand.
Those who cannot speak clearly now will then be able to speak clearly and quickly.
[5]Fools will not be called great,
and people will not respect the wicked.
[6]A fool says foolish things,

Topheth Gehenna; the Valley of Hinnom. Here people burned the bodies of criminals and animals, along with garbage.

and in his mind he plans evil.
A fool does things that are wicked,
and he says wrong things about the LORD.
A fool does not feed the hungry
or let thirsty people drink water.
7The wicked person uses evil like a tool.
He plans ways to take everything from the poor.
He destroys the poor with lies,
even when the poor person is in the right.
8But a good leader plans to do good,
and those good things make him a good leader.

Hard Times Are Coming

9You women who are calm now,
stand up and listen to me.
You women who feel safe now,
hear what I say.
10You women feel safe now,
but after one year you will be afraid.
There will be no grape harvest
and no summer fruit to gather.
11Women, you are calm now, but you should shake with fear.
Women, you feel safe now, but you should tremble.
Take off your nice clothes
and put rough cloth around your waist to show your sadness.
12Beat your breasts in grief, because the fields that were pleasant are now empty.
Cry, because the vines that once had fruit now have no more grapes.
13Cry for the land of my people,
in which only thorns and weeds now grow.
Cry for the city that once was happy
and for all the houses that once were filled with joy.
14The palace will be empty;
people will leave the noisy city.
Strong cities and towers will be empty.
Wild donkeys will love to live there, and sheep will go there to eat.

Things Will Get Better

15This will continue until God pours his Spirit[d] from above upon us.
Then the desert will be like a fertile field
and the fertile field like a forest.
16Justice will be found even in the desert,
and fairness will be found in the fertile fields.
17That fairness will bring peace,
and it will bring calm and safety forever.
18My people will live in peaceful places
and in safe homes
and in calm places of rest.
19Hail will destroy the forest,
and the city will be completely destroyed.
20But you will be happy as you plant seeds near every stream
and as you let your cattle and donkeys wander freely.

Warnings to Assyria and Promises to God's People

33 How terrible it will be for you who destroy others
but have not been destroyed yet.
How terrible it will be for you, traitor,
whom no one has turned against yet.
When you stop destroying,
others will destroy you.
When you stop turning against others,
they will turn against you.

2LORD, be kind to us.
We have waited for your help.
Give us strength every morning.
Save us when we are in trouble.
3Your powerful voice makes people run away in fear;
your greatness causes the nations to run away.
4Like locusts,[d] your enemies will take away the things you stole in war.
Like locusts rushing about, they will take your wealth.
5The LORD is very great, and he lives in a high place.
He fills Jerusalem with fairness and justice.
6He will be your safety.
He is full of salvation, wisdom, and knowledge.
Respect for the LORD is the greatest treasure.

7See, brave men are crying out in the streets;
those who tried to bring peace are crying loudly.
8There is no one on the roads,
no one walking in the paths.
People have broken the agreements they made.
They refuse to believe the proof from witnesses.
No one respects other people.
9The land is sick and dying;
Lebanon is ashamed and dying.
The Plain of Sharon is dry like the desert,
and the trees of Bashan and Carmel are dying.

10The LORD says, "Now, I will stand up
and show my greatness.
Now, I will become important to the people.
11You people do useless things

that are like hay and straw.
A destructive wind will burn you like fire.
12People will be burned until their bones
become like lime;
they will burn quickly like dry
thornbushes."

13You people in faraway lands, hear what I
have done.
You people who are near me, learn about
my power.
14The sinners in Jerusalem are afraid;
those who are separated from God shake
with fear.
They say, "Can any of us live through this
fire that destroys?
Who can live near this fire that burns on
and on?"
15A person who does what is right
and speaks what is right,
who refuses to take money unfairly,
who refuses to take money to hurt others,
who does not listen to plans of murder,
who refuses to think about evil—
16this is the kind of person who will be safe.
He will be protected as he would be in a
high, walled city.
He will always have bread,
and he will not run out of water.
17Your eyes will see the king in his beauty.
You will see the land that stretches far
away.
18You will think about the terror of the past:
"Where is that officer?
Where is the one who collected the taxes?
Where is the officer in charge of our
defense towers?"
19No longer will you see those proud people
from other countries,
whose strange language you couldn't
understand.

God Will Protect Jerusalem

20Look at Jerusalem, the city of our festivals.
Look at Jerusalem, that beautiful place of
rest.
It is like a tent that will never be moved;
the pegs that hold her in place will never
be pulled up,
and her ropes will never be broken.
21There the LORD will be our Mighty One.
That land is a place with streams and wide
rivers,
but there will be no enemy boats on those
rivers;
no powerful ship will sail on them.
22This is because the LORD is our judge.
The LORD makes our laws.
The LORD is our king.
He will save us.
23You sailors from other lands, hear:
The ropes on your boats hang loose.
The mast is not held firm.
The sails are not spread open.
Then your great wealth will be divided.
There will be so much wealth that even
the crippled people will carry off a
share.
24No one living in Jerusalem will say, "I am
sick."
The people who live there will have their
sins forgiven.

God Will Punish His Enemies

34 All you nations, come near and listen.
Pay attention, you peoples!
The earth and all the people in it should
listen,
the world and everything in it.
2The LORD is angry with all the nations;
he is angry with their armies.
He will destroy them and kill them all.
3Their bodies will be thrown outside.
The stink will rise from the bodies,
and the blood will flow down the
mountains.
4The sun, moon, and stars will dissolve,
and the sky will be rolled up like a scroll.
The stars will fall
like dead leaves from a vine
or dried-up figs from a fig tree.
5The LORD's sword in the sky is covered with
blood.
It will cut through Edom
and destroy those people as an offering to
the LORD.
6The LORD's sword will be covered with
blood;
it will be covered with fat,
with the blood from lambs and goats,
with the fat from the kidneys of sheep.
This is because the LORD decided there will
be a sacrifice in Bozrah
and much killing in Edom.
7The oxen will be killed,
and the cattle and the strong bulls.
The land will be filled with their blood,
and the dirt will be covered with their fat.
8The LORD has chosen a time for punishment.
He has chosen a year when people must
pay for the wrongs they did to
Jerusalem.
9Edom's rivers will be like hot tar.
Its dirt will be like burning sulfur.
Its land will be like burning tar.
10The fires will burn night and day;
the smoke will rise from Edom forever.

Year after year that land will be empty;
no one will ever travel through that land again.
11Birds and small animals will own that land,
and owls and ravens will live there.
God will make it an empty wasteland;
it will have nothing left in it.
12The important people will have no one left to rule them;
the leaders will all be gone.
13Thorns will take over the strong towers,
and wild bushes will grow in the walled cities.
It will be a home for wild dogs
and a place for owls to live.
14Desert animals will live with the hyenas,
and wild goats will call to their friends.
Night animals will live there
and find a place of rest.
15Owls will nest there and lay eggs.
When they hatch open, the owls will gather their young under their wings.
Hawks will gather
with their own kind.

16Look at the LORD's scroll and read what is
written there:
None of these will be missing;
none will be without its mate.
God has given the command,
so his Spirit[d] will gather them together.
17God has divided the land among them,
and he has given them each their portion.
So they will own that land forever
and will live there year after year.

God Will Comfort His People

35 The desert and dry land will become happy;
the desert will be glad and will produce flowers.
Like a flower, 2it will have many blooms.
It will show its happiness, as if it were shouting with joy.

DEPRESSION

Positive

"Are you sure you did the test right?" asked Jan Dempsy as she gently coaxed the instruction sheet out of Sheila Burk's trembling hand. "Each one of these home kits is different, and you have to follow the directions just so." Jan began to read the instructions.

Sheila stood shaking as the tears ran silently down her blushed cheeks. She could barely muster a reply.

"I've taken this test three times, and it's the same every time." Sheila's voice began to crack. "I'm pregnant. I'm going to have a baby. But I don't want a baby . . . not now. I'm only sixteen years old. Jan, I'm so afraid, and so sad. Why did this have to happen to me?"

Sheila walked across the room and collapsed into the old brown chair that had comforted her so many times when she was a little girl. But there was no comfort in that chair now.

With no words left, Jan quietly sat down next to Sheila, put her arms around her and began to pray.

Sheila's sin may cause her to face many bouts with depression, but God can help her. Read **Isaiah 35** to discover the comfort God can bring for Sheila and others who turn to him.

- If you could talk to Sheila, which verses of Isaiah 35 would you use to encourage her?
- Think about how you feel when you're depressed. What does Isaiah 35 say to you about your depression?

CONSIDER . . .

- suggesting that your Sunday school teacher put a box marked "Teenage Problems" in your Sunday school room, and encouraging class members to submit, anonymously, any situations they are having problems with. Spend time each week discussing the problems and finding biblical solutions.
- talking to a trusted friend about the cause of your depression.

FOR MORE, SEE . . .

- Job 19:7–27 (p. 463)
- Psalm 88 (p. 533)
- 2 Corinthians 1:3–5 (p. 1193)

It will be beautiful like the forest of Lebanon,
as beautiful as the hill of Carmel and the
Plain of Sharon.
Everyone will see the glory of the LORD
and the splendor of our God.

3Make the weak hands strong
and the weak knees steady.
4Say to people who are frightened,
"Be strong. Don't be afraid.
Look, your God will come,
and he will punish your enemies.
He will make them pay for the wrongs they
did,
but he will save you."

5Then the blind people will see again,
and the deaf will hear.
6Crippled people will jump like deer,
and those who can't talk now will shout
with joy.
Water will flow in the desert,
and streams will flow in the dry land.
7The burning desert will have pools of water,
and the dry ground will have springs.
Where wild dogs once lived,
grass and water plants will grow.
8A road will be there;
this highway will be called "The Road to
Being Holy."
Evil people will not be allowed to walk on
that road;
only good people will walk on it.
No fools will go on it.
9No lions will be there,
nor will dangerous animals be on that road.
They will not be found there.
That road will be for the people God saves;
10 the people the LORD has freed will return
there.
They will enter Jerusalem with joy,
and their happiness will last forever.
Their gladness and joy will fill them
completely,
and sorrow and sadness will go far away.

The Assyrians Invade Judah

36 During Hezekiah's fourteenth year as
king, Sennacherib king of Assyria attacked all the strong, walled cities of Judah and
captured them. 2The king of Assyria sent out his
field commander with a large army from Lachish
to King Hezekiah in Jerusalem. When the commander came near the waterway from the upper
pool on the road where people do their laundry,
he stopped. 3Eliakim, Shebna, and Joah went out
to meet him. Eliakim son of Hilkiah was the palace manager, Shebna was the royal secretary, and
Joah son of Asaph was the recorder.
4The field commander said to them, "Tell Hezekiah this:
" 'The great king, the king of Assyria, says:
What can you trust in now? 5You say you have
battle plans and power for war, but your words
mean nothing. Whom are you trusting for help so
that you turn against me? 6Look, you are depending on Egypt to help you, but Egypt is like a splint-
ered walking stick. If you lean on it for help, it will
stab your hand and hurt you. The king of Egypt
will hurt all those who depend on him. 7You
might say, "We are depending on the LORD our
God," but Hezekiah destroyed the LORD's altars
and the places of worship. Hezekiah told Judah
and Jerusalem, "You must worship only at this
one altar."
8" 'Now make an agreement with my master,
the king of Assyria: I will give you two thousand
horses if you can find enough men to ride them.
9You cannot defeat one of my master's least important officers, so why do you depend on Egypt
to give you chariots and horsemen? 10I have
not come to attack and destroy this country without an order from the LORD. The LORD himself
told me to come to this country and destroy
it.' "
11Then Eliakim, Shebna, and Joah said to the
field commander, "Please speak to us in the Aramaic language. We understand it. Don't speak to
us in Hebrew, because the people on the city wall
can hear you."
12But the commander said, "My master did not
send me to tell these things only to you and your
king. He sent me to speak also to those people
sitting on the wall who will have to eat their own
dung and drink their own urine like you."
13Then the commander stood and shouted
loudly in the Hebrew language, "Listen to what
the great king, the king of Assyria says, 14The king
says you should not let Hezekiah fool you, because he can't save you. 15Don't let Hezekiah talk
you into trusting the LORD by saying, 'The LORD
will surely save us. This city won't be handed
over to the king of Assyria.'
16"Don't listen to Hezekiah. The king of Assyria
says, 'Make peace with me, and come out of the
city to me. Then everyone will be free to eat the
fruit from his own grapevine and fig tree and to
drink water from his own well. 17After that I will
come and take you to a land like your own—a
land with grain and new wine, bread and vineyards.'
18"Don't let Hezekiah fool you, saying, 'The
LORD will save us.' Has a god of any other nation
saved his people from the power of the king of
Assyria? 19Where are the gods of Hamath and Arpad? Where are the gods of Sepharvaim? They did
not save Samaria from my power. 20Not one of all
the gods of these countries has saved his people

from me. Neither can the LORD save Jerusalem
from my power."
21The people were silent. They didn't answer
the commander at all, because King Hezekiah had
ordered, "Don't answer him."
22Then Eliakim, Shebna, and Joah tore their
clothes to show how upset they were. (Eliakim
son of Hilkiah was the palace manager, Shebna
was the royal secretary, and Joah son of Asaph
was the recorder.) The three men went to Hezekiah and told him what the field commander had
said.

Hezekiah Asks God to Help

37 When King Hezekiah heard the message, he tore his clothes and put on
rough cloth to show how sad he was. Then he
went into the Temple[d] of the LORD. 2Hezekiah
sent Eliakim, the palace manager, and Shebna,
the royal secretary, and the older priests to Isaiah.
They were all wearing rough cloth when they
came to Isaiah the prophet,[d] the son of Amoz.
3They told Isaiah, "This is what Hezekiah says:
Today is a day of sorrow and punishment and disgrace, as when a child should be born, but the
mother is not strong enough to give birth to it.
4The king of Assyria sent his field commander to
make fun of the living God. Maybe the LORD your
God will hear what the commander said and will
punish him for it. So pray for the few of us who
are left alive."
5When Hezekiah's officers came to Isaiah, 6he
said to them, "Tell your master this: The LORD
says, 'Don't be afraid of what you have heard.
Don't be frightened by the words the servants of
the king of Assyria have spoken against me. 7Lis-
ten! I am going to put a spirit in the king of Assyria. He will hear a report that will make him
return to his own country, and I will cause him
to die by the sword there.' "
8The field commander heard that the king of
Assyria had left Lachish. When he went back, he
found the king fighting against the city of Libnah.
9The king received a report that Tirhakah, the
Cushite king of Egypt, was coming to attack him.
When the king of Assyria heard this, he sent messengers to Hezekiah, saying, 10"Tell Hezekiah
king of Judah: Don't be fooled by the god you
trust. Don't believe him when he says Jerusalem
will not be handed over to the king of Assyria.
11You have heard what the kings of Assyria have
done. They have completely defeated every country, so do not think you will be saved. 12Did the
gods of those people save them? My ancestors destroyed them, defeating the cities of Gozan, Haran, and Rezeph, and the people of Eden living in
Tel Assar. 13Where are the kings of Hamath and
Arpad? Where are the kings of Sepharvaim, Hena,
and Ivvah?"

Hezekiah Prays to the Lord

14When Hezekiah received the letter from the
messengers and read it, he went up to the Temple[d] of the LORD. He spread the letter out before
the LORD 15and prayed to the LORD: 16"LORD All-
Powerful, you are the God of Israel, whose throne
is between the gold creatures with wings, only
you are God of all the kingdoms of the earth. You
made the heavens and the earth. 17Hear, LORD,
and listen. Open your eyes, LORD, and see. Listen
to all the words Sennacherib has said to insult the
living God.
18"It is true, LORD, that the kings of Assyria
have destroyed all these countries and their lands.
19They have thrown the gods of these nations into
the fire, but they were only wood and rock statues
that people made. So the kings have destroyed
them. 20Now, LORD our God, save us from the
king's power so that all the kingdoms of the earth
will know that you, LORD, are the only God."

The Lord Answers Hezekiah

21Then Isaiah son of Amoz sent a message to
Hezekiah that said, "This is what the LORD, the
God of Israel, says: 'You prayed to me about Sen-
nacherib king of Assyria. 22So this is what the
LORD has said against Sennacherib:

The people of Jerusalem
  hate you and make fun of you;
the people of Jerusalem
  laugh at you as you run away.
23You have insulted me and spoken against me;
  you have raised your voice against me.
You have a proud look on your face,
  which is against me, the Holy One of
    Israel!
24You have sent your messengers to insult the
    Lord.
  You have said, "With my many chariots
I have gone to the tops of the mountains,
  to the highest mountains of Lebanon.
I have cut down its tallest cedars
  and its best pine trees.
I have gone to its greatest heights
  and its best forests.
25I have dug wells in foreign countries
  and drunk water there.
By the soles of my feet,
  I have dried up all the rivers of Egypt."
26" 'King of Assyria, surely you have heard.
  Long ago I, the LORD, planned these things.
Long ago I designed them,
  and now I have made them happen.
I allowed you to turn those strong, walled
    cities
  into piles of rocks.
27The people in those cities were weak;
  they were frightened and put to shame.

They were like grass in the field,
like tender, young grass,
like grass on the housetop
that is burned by the wind before it can grow.

28" 'I know when you rest,
when you come and go,
and how you rage against me.
29Because you rage against me,
and because I have heard your proud words,
I will put my hook in your nose
and my bit in your mouth.
Then I will force you to leave my country
the same way you came.'

30"Then the LORD said, 'Hezekiah, I will give
you this sign:
This year you will eat the grain that grows wild,
and the second year you will eat what grows wild from that.
But in the third year, plant grain and harvest it.
Plant vineyards and eat their fruit.
31Some of the people in the family of Judah
will escape.
Like plants that take root,
they will grow strong and have many children.
32A few people will come out of Jerusalem alive;
a few from Mount Zion[d] will live.
The strong love of the LORD All-Powerful
will make this happen.'

33"So this is what the LORD says about the king
of Assyria:
'He will not enter this city
or even shoot an arrow here.
He will not fight against it with shields
or build a ramp to attack the city walls.
34He will return to his country the same way he came,
and he will not enter this city,'
says the LORD.
35'I will defend and save this city
for my sake and for David, my servant.' "

36Then the angel of the LORD went out and
killed one hundred eighty-five thousand men in
the Assyrian camp. When the people got up early
the next morning, they saw all the dead bodies.
37So Sennacherib king of Assyria left and went
back to Nineveh and stayed there.
38One day as Sennacherib was worshiping in
the temple of his god Nisroch, his sons Adrammelech and Sharezer killed him with a sword.
Then they escaped to the land of Ararat. So Sennacherib's son Esarhaddon became king of
Assyria.

Hezekiah's Illness

38 At that time Hezekiah became very sick;
he was almost dead. The prophet[d] Isaiah
son of Amoz went to see him and told him, "This
is what the LORD says: Make arrangements, because you are not going to live, but die."
2Hezekiah turned toward the wall and prayed
to the LORD, 3"LORD, please remember that I have
always obeyed you. I have given myself completely to you and have done what you said was
right." Then Hezekiah cried loudly.
4Then the LORD spoke his word to Isaiah: 5"Go
to Hezekiah and tell him: 'This is what the LORD,
the God of your ancestor David, says: I have
heard your prayer and seen your tears. So I will
add fifteen years to your life. 6I will save you and
this city from the king of Assyria; I will defend this
city.
7" 'The LORD will do what he says. This is the
sign from the LORD to show you: 8The sun has
made a shadow go down the stairway of Ahaz,
but I will make it go back ten steps.' " So the
shadow made by the sun went back up the ten
steps it had gone down.
9After Hezekiah king of Judah got well, he
wrote this song:
10I said, "I am in the middle of my life.
Do I have to go through the gates of death?
Will I have the rest of my life taken away from me?"
11I said, "I will not see the LORD
in the land of the living again.
I will not again see the people
who live on the earth.
12Like a shepherd's tent,
my home has been pulled down and taken from me.
I am finished
like the cloth a weaver rolls up and cuts from the loom.[n]
In one day you brought me to this end.
13All night I cried loudly.
Like a lion, he crushed all my bones.
In one day you brought me to this end.
14I cried like a bird
and moaned like a dove.
My eyes became tired as I looked to the heavens.
Lord, I have troubles. Please help me."

15What can I say?

loom A machine for making cloth from thread.

The Lord told me what would happen and
then made it happen.
I have had these troubles in my soul,
so now I will be humble all my life.
16Lord, because of you, people live.
Because of you, my spirit also lives;
you made me well and let me live.
17It was for my own good
that I had such troubles.
Because you love me very much,
you did not let me die
but threw my sins
far away.
18People in the place of the dead cannot praise
you;
those who have died cannot sing praises to
you;
those who die don't trust you
to help them.
19The people who are alive are the ones who
praise you.
They praise you as I praise you today.
A father should tell his children
that you provide help.

20The LORD saved me,
so we will play songs on stringed
instruments
in the Temple of the LORD
all the days of our lives.

21Then Isaiah said, "Make a paste from figs and
put it on Hezekiah's boil. Then he will get well."
22Hezekiah then asked Isaiah, "What will be the
sign? What will show that I will go up to the Temple[d] of the LORD?"

Messengers from Babylon

39 At that time Merodach-Baladan son of
Baladan was king of Babylon. He sent
letters and a gift to Hezekiah, because he had
heard that Hezekiah had been sick and was
now well. 2Hezekiah was pleased and showed
the messengers what was in his storehouses:
the silver, gold, spices, expensive perfumes,
his swords and shields, and all his wealth. He
showed them everything in his palace and in
his kingdom.
3Then Isaiah the prophet[d] went to King Hezekiah and asked him, "What did these men say?
Where did they come from?"

Hezekiah said, "They came from a faraway country—from Babylon."
4So Isaiah asked him, "What did they see in
your palace?"

Hezekiah said, "They saw everything in my palace. I showed them all my wealth."
5Then Isaiah said to Hezekiah: "Listen to the
words of the LORD All-Powerful: 6'In the future
everything in your palace and everything your ancestors have stored up until this day will be taken
away to Babylon. Nothing will be left,' says the
LORD. 7Some of your own children, those who
will be born to you, will be taken away, and they
will become servants in the palace of the king of
Babylon."
8Hezekiah told Isaiah, "These words from the
LORD are good." He said this because he thought,
"There will be peace and security in my lifetime."

SIDELIGHT: Isaiah's vocal challenges to the different kings of Judah didn't make him popular (see Isaiah 39:1–8, for example). According to tradition, the evil king Manasseh had Isaiah killed by tying him between two planks of wood and sawing him in half.

Israel's Punishment Will End

40 Your God says,
"Comfort, comfort my people.
2Speak kindly to the people of Jerusalem
and tell them
that their time of service is finished,
that they have paid for their sins,
that the LORD has punished Jerusalem
twice for every sin they did."

3This is the voice of one who calls
out:
"Prepare in the desert
the way for the LORD.
Make a straight road in the dry lands
for our God.
4Every valley should be raised up,
and every mountain and hill should be
made flat.
The rough ground should be made level,
and the rugged ground should be made
smooth.
5Then the glory of the LORD will be shown,
and all people together will see it.
The LORD himself said these things."

6A voice says, "Cry out!"
Then I said, "What shall I cry out?"

"Say all people are like the grass,
and all their glory is like the flowers of the
field.
7The grass dies and the flowers fall
when the breath of the LORD blows on
them.
Surely the people are like grass.

8The grass dies and the flowers fall,
but the word of our God will live forever."
9Jerusalem, you have good news to tell.
Go up on a high mountain.
Jerusalem, you have good news to tell.
Shout out loud the good news.
Shout it out and don't be afraid.
Say to the towns of Judah,
"Here is your God."
10Look, the Lord GOD is coming with power
to rule all the people.
Look, he will bring reward for his people;
he will have their payment with him.
11He takes care of his people like a shepherd.
He gathers them like lambs in his arms
and carries them close to him.
He gently leads the mothers of the lambs.

God Is Supreme

12Who has measured the oceans in the palm of his hand?
Who has used his hand to measure the sky?
Who has used a bowl to measure all the dust of the earth
and scales to weigh the mountains and hills?
13Who has known the mind of the LORD
or been able to give him advice?
14Whom did he ask for help?
Who taught him the right way?
Who taught him knowledge
and showed him the way to understanding?

15The nations are like one small drop in a bucket;
they are no more than the dust on his measuring scales.
To him the islands are no more than fine dust on his scales.
16All the trees in Lebanon are not enough for the altar fires,
and all the animals in Lebanon are not enough for burnt offerings.
17Compared to the LORD all the nations are worth nothing;
to him they are less than nothing.

CELEBRATING

Ha!

Need a reason to laugh? Consider these:

- It takes seventy-two muscles to frown, but only fourteen to smile.
- Laughing relieves stress. After you laugh, your blood pressure briefly falls below normal, breathing slows, and tension subsides.
- A Stanford University doctor says laughing one hundred times each day is about the same amount of exercise as ten minutes of rowing a boat.
- Laughing may release natural painkillers in your body that have been found to combat arthritis and other painful conditions.
- "Happy patients usually work harder to recover," says the humor coordinator at Sunnyview Hospital and Rehabilitation Center in Schenectady, New York. So the hospital has a "humor room" where patients can check out funny books, tapes, music, and other mirth-makers.
- You could get in the Guinness Book of World Records by smiling longer than the current world record of ten hours and five minutes.

Isaiah 40:1–11 gives an even better reason to celebrate, smile, and laugh with joy. Read a promise that will bring a smile to your face!

- What parts of this passage give you a good reason to laugh—or shout—with joyful celebration?
- How does it make you feel to know the promise of God's comfort and love that this passage celebrates?

CONSIDER . . .

- keeping a "celebration first-aid kit" where you place reminders of God's goodness to you. When you are feeling down, look through the kit to remind yourself that you have something to celebrate every day.
- throwing a party for friends just to have fun together.

FOR MORE, SEE . . .

- Ezra 6:13–22 (p. 421)
- Luke 15 (p. 1034)
- Romans 15:8–13 (p. 1161)

18Can you compare God to anything?
Can you compare him to an image of anything?
19An idol is formed by a craftsman,
and a goldsmith covers it with gold
and makes silver chains for it.
20A poor person cannot buy those expensive statues,
so he finds a tree that will not rot.
Then he finds a skilled craftsman
to make it into an idol that will not fall over.

21Surely you know. Surely you have heard.
Surely from the beginning someone told you.
Surely you understand how the earth was created.
22God sits on his throne above the circle of the earth,
and compared to him, people are like grasshoppers.
He stretches out the skies like a piece of cloth
and spreads them out like a tent to sit under.
23He makes rulers unimportant
and the judges of this world worth nothing.
24They are like plants that are placed in the ground,
like seeds that are planted.
As soon as they begin to grow strong,
he blows on them and they die,
and the wind blows them away like chaff.[d]

25God, the Holy One, says, "Can you compare me to anyone?
Is anyone equal to me?"
26Look up to the skies.
Who created all these stars?
He leads out the army of heaven one by one
and calls all the stars by name.
Because he is strong and powerful,
not one of them is missing.

27People of Jacob, why do you complain?
People of Israel, why do you say,
"The LORD does not see what happens to me;
he does not care if I am treated fairly"?
28Surely you know.
Surely you have heard.
The LORD is the God who lives forever,
who created all the world.
He does not become tired or need to rest.
No one can understand how great his wisdom is.
29He gives strength to those who are tired
and more power to those who are weak.
30Even children become tired and need to rest,
and young people trip and fall.
31But the people who trust the LORD will become strong again.
They will rise up as an eagle in the sky;
they will run and not need rest;
they will walk and not become tired.

The Lord Will Help Israel

41 The LORD says, "Faraway countries, listen to me.
Let the nations become strong.
Come to me and speak;
we will meet together to decide who is right.
2"Who caused the one to come from the east?
Who gives him victories everywhere he goes?
The one who brought him gives nations over to him
and defeats kings.
He uses his sword, and kings become like dust.
He uses his bow, and they are blown away like chaff.[d]
3He chases them and is never hurt,
going places he has never been before.
4Who caused this to happen?
Who has controlled history since the beginning?
I, the LORD, am the one. I was here at the beginning,
and I will be here when all things are finished."

5All you faraway places, look and be afraid;
all you places far away on the earth, shake with fear.
Come close and listen to me.
6 The workers help each other
and say to each other, "Be strong!"
7The craftsman encourages the goldsmith,
and the workman who smooths the metal with a hammer encourages the one who shapes the metal.
He says, "This metal work is good."
He nails the statue to a base so it can't fall over.

Only the Lord Can Save Us

8The LORD says, "People of Israel, you are my servants.
People of Jacob, I chose you.
You are from the family of my friend Abraham.
9I took you from places far away on the earth
and called you from a faraway country.
I said, 'You are my servants.'
I have chosen you and have not turned against you.

10So don't worry, because I am with you.
Don't be afraid, because I am your God.
I will make you strong and will help you;
I will support you with my right hand that saves you.

11"All those people who are angry with you
will be ashamed and disgraced.
Those who are against you
will disappear and be lost.
12You will look for your enemies,
but you will not find them.
Those who fought against you
will vanish completely.
13I am the LORD your God,
who holds your right hand,
and I tell you, 'Don't be afraid.
I will help you.'
14You few people of Israel who are left,
do not be afraid even though you are weak as a worm.
I myself will help you," says the LORD.
"The one who saves you is the Holy One of Israel.
15Look, I have made you like a new threshing[d] board
with many sharp teeth.
So you will walk on mountains and crush them;
you will make the hills like chaff.[d]
16You will throw them into the air, and the wind will carry them away;
a windstorm will scatter them.
Then you will be happy in the LORD;
you will be proud of the Holy One of Israel.

17"The poor and needy people look for water,
but they can't find any.
Their tongues are dry with thirst.
But I, the LORD, will answer their prayers;
I, the God of Israel, will not leave them to die.
18I will make rivers flow on the dry hills
and springs flow through the valleys.
I will change the desert into a lake of water
and the dry land into fountains of water.
19I will make trees grow in the desert—
cedars, acacia, myrtle, and olive trees.
I will put pine, fir, and cypress trees
growing together in the desert.
20People will see these things and understand;
they will think carefully about these things and learn
that the LORD's power did this,
that the Holy One of Israel made these things."

The Lord Challenges False Gods

21The LORD says, "Present your case."
The King of Jacob says, "Tell me your arguments.
22Bring in your idols to tell us
what is going to happen.
Have them tell us what happened in the beginning.
Then we will think about these things,
and we will know how they will turn out.
Or tell us what will happen in the future.
23 Tell us what is coming next
so we will believe that you are gods.
Do something, whether it is good or bad,
and make us afraid.
24You gods are less than nothing;
you can't do anything.
Those who worship you should be hated.

25"I have brought someone to come out of the north.[n]
I have called by name a man from the east,
and he knows me.
He walks on kings as if they were mud,
just as a potter walks on the clay.
26Who told us about this before it happened?
Who told us ahead of time so we could say, 'He was right'?
None of you told us anything;
none of you told us before it happened;
no one heard you tell about it.
27I, the LORD, was the first one to tell
Jerusalem that the people were coming home.
I sent a messenger to Jerusalem with the good news.
28I look at the idols, but there is not one that can answer.
None of them can give advice;
none of them can answer my questions.
29Look, all these idols are false.
They cannot do anything;
they are worth nothing.

The Lord's Special Servant

42 "Here is my servant, the one I support.
He is the one I chose, and I am pleased with him.
I have put my Spirit[d] upon him,
and he will bring justice to all nations.
2He will not cry out or yell
or speak loudly in the streets.
3He will not break a crushed blade of grass
or put out even a weak flame.
He will truly bring justice;
4 he will not lose hope or give up

someone . . . north This probably means Cyrus, a king of Persia.

until he brings justice to the world.
And people far away will trust his teachings."

5God, the LORD, said these things.
He created the skies and stretched them out.
He spread out the earth and everything on it.
He gives life to all people on earth,
to everyone who walks on the earth.
6The LORD says, "I, the LORD, called you to do right,
and I will hold your hand
and protect you.
You will be the sign of my agreement with the people,
a light to shine for all people.
7You will help the blind to see.
You will free those who are in prison,
and you will lead those who live in darkness out of their prison.

8"I am the LORD. That is my name.
I will not give my glory to another;
I will not let idols take the praise that should be mine.
9The things I said would happen have happened,
and now I tell you about new things.
Before those things happen,
I tell you about them."

A Song of Praise to the Lord

10Sing a new song to the LORD;
sing his praise everywhere on the earth.
Praise him, you people who sail on the seas and you animals who live in them.

SERVICE

Called to Compassion

Claudia was blind, autistic, and in pain. Put in an institution when she was young, Claudia was angry and withdrawn. She would scream, eat her clothes, and refuse to cooperate with others.

Now Claudia is fifteen. She is still blind, and she is still autistic. She cannot really communicate with people. But now she is peaceful, loving, and trusting. What has changed?

When she was nine or ten, Claudia became part of a l'Arche community in Honduras. The love, compassion, and care she experienced in this Christian community helped her discover inner peace.

Founded by Canadian-born Jean Vanier, more than seventy l'Arche (which means "the Ark" in French) communities around the world are home to handicapped people who are forgotten or rejected by their society. For about thirty years, Vanier has given his life to these "little people," as he calls them.

For Vanier, his work is his ministry in Christ's name. "When we love others," Vanier says, "we can walk with them and share their pain. . . . I believe that Jesus is calling us to be men and women of compassion, to walk with people in their pain. . . . And then we discover how the pain and the cross are intimately linked with the joy of the resurrection."

Through his work with mentally handicapped people around the world, Jean Vanier lives a life that reflects the spirit of **Isaiah 42:1–9**, which promises a special servant who would lead the people—a promise that was fulfilled in Jesus Christ.

- What parallels are there between the ministry of Jean Vanier and the description in the passage?
- How can you follow in the footsteps of the special servant described in the passage?

CONSIDER . . .

- giving a few hours of your free time to work with mentally or physically handicapped people in your community. Afterwards, talk with a parent, friend, or trusted adult about the experience.
- reaching out to someone in need even when it may be inconvenient for you.

FOR MORE, SEE . . .

- Deuteronomy 11:13–15 (p. 172)
- 1 Samuel 3:1–10 (p. 247)
- 1 Corinthians 9:19–23 (p. 1178)

Praise him, you people living in faraway
places.
11The deserts and their cities should praise him.
The settlements of Kedar should praise him.
The people living in Sela should sing for joy;
they should shout from the mountaintops.
12They should give glory to the LORD.
People in faraway lands should praise him.
13The LORD will march out like a strong
soldier;
he will be excited like a man ready to fight
a war.
He will shout out the battle cry
and defeat his enemies.

14The LORD says, "For a long time I have said
nothing;
I have been quiet and held myself back.
But now I will cry out
and strain like a woman giving birth to a
child.
15I will destroy the hills and mountains
and dry up all their plants.
I will make the rivers become dry land
and dry up the pools of water.
16Then I will lead the blind along a way they
never knew;
I will guide them along paths they have not
known.
I will make the darkness become light for
them,
and the rough ground smooth.
These are the things I will do;
I will not leave my people.
17But those who trust in idols,
who say to their statues,
'You are our gods'
will be rejected in disgrace.

Israel Refused to Listen to the Lord

18"You who are deaf, hear me.
You who are blind, look and see.
19No one is more blind than my servant Israel
or more deaf than the messenger I send.
No one is more blind than the person I own
or more blind than the servant of the LORD.
20Israel, you have seen much, but you have not
obeyed.
You hear, but you refuse to listen."
21The LORD made his teachings wonderful,
because he is good.
22These people have been defeated and robbed.
They are trapped in pits
or locked up in prison.
Like robbers, enemies have taken them away,
and there is no one to save them.
Enemies carried them off,
and no one said, "Bring them back."

23Will any of you listen to this?
Will you listen carefully in the future?
24Who let the people of Jacob be carried off?
Who let robbers take Israel away?
The LORD allowed this to happen,
because we sinned against him.
We did not live the way he wanted us to live
and did not obey his teaching.
25So he became very angry with us
and brought terrible wars against us.
It was as if the people of Israel had fire all
around them,
but they didn't know what was happening.
It was as if they were burning,
but they didn't pay any attention.

God Is Always with His People

43 Now this is what the LORD says.
He created you, people of Jacob;
he formed you, people of Israel.
He says, "Don't be afraid, because I have
saved you.
I have called you by name, and you are
mine.
2When you pass through the waters, I will be
with you.
When you cross rivers, you will not drown.
When you walk through fire, you will not be
burned,
nor will the flames hurt you.
3This is because I, the LORD, am your God,
the Holy One of Israel, your Savior.
I gave Egypt to pay for you,
and I gave Cush and Seba to make you
mine.
4Because you are precious to me,
because I give you honor and love you,
I will give other people in your place;
I will give other nations to save your life.
5Don't be afraid, because I am with you.
I will bring your children from the east
and gather you from the west.
6I will tell the north: Give my people to me.
I will tell the south: Don't keep my people
in prison.
Bring my sons from far away
and my daughters from faraway places.
7Bring to me all the people who are mine,
whom I made for my glory,
whom I formed and made."

Judah Is God's Witness

8Bring out the people who have eyes but don't
see
and those who have ears but don't hear.
9All the nations gather together,
and all the people come together.
Which of their gods said this would happen?
Which of their gods can tell what happened
in the beginning?

Let them bring their witnesses to prove they
were right.
Then others will say, "It is true."
10The LORD says, "You are my witnesses
and the servant I chose.
I chose you so you would know and believe
me,
so you would understand that I am the true
God.
There was no God before me,
and there will be no God after me.
11I myself am the LORD;
I am the only Savior.
12I myself have spoken to you, saved you, and
told you these things.
It was not some foreign god among you.
You are my witnesses, and I am God,"
says the LORD.
13 "I have always been God.
No one can save people from my power;
when I do something, no one can change
it."

14This is what the LORD, who saves you,
the Holy One of Israel, says:
"I will send armies to Babylon for you,
and I will knock down all its locked gates.
The Babylonians will shout their cries of
sorrow.
15I am the LORD, your Holy One,
the Creator of Israel, your King."

God Will Save His People Again

16This is what the LORD says.
He is the one who made a road through
the sea
and a path through rough waters.
17He is the one who defeated the chariots and
horses
and the mighty armies.
They fell together and will never rise again.
They were destroyed as a flame is put out.
18The LORD says, "Forget what happened
before,
and do not think about the past.

SIN

Taking the Weight Off

Miriam Arkin didn't want to be in Sunday school. Lately, she felt distant from God. As she entered the classroom, her teacher handed her paper and a pencil.

"Write down whatever's bothering you," Sarah Evans said, "mistakes you've made or worries you have."

Miriam watched other kids working on their lists. She thought about the party she had gone to two weeks earlier. To fit in, she had let the other kids talk her into drinking several beers. Then she made out with this popular guy she didn't even really like. The whole experience made her feel cheap, like she wasn't worthy of anyone's respect. She started writing: "acting wild," "going further than I wanted to."

"When we give our problems to God, he makes the weight lighter," Sarah said, after everyone finished. She passed a metal wastebasket around the circle, and Miriam dropped her list in quickly. Sarah struck a match and set fire to the lists. As Miriam watched her list of sins burning, she felt God's love within her "burn away" the hurt of the sins she had committed. She took a deep breath and felt relieved for the first time in days. She realized that by admitting her mistakes to God she felt closer to him. Maybe she could start over now.

Sin keeps people from being what God wants them to be. **Isaiah 43:16–25** reminds us that God is willing to forgive sin so we can be close to him.

- How would Miriam have reacted to reading this passage?
- Which verses in this passage help you understand God's forgiveness of your sin?

CONSIDER . . .

- making a list of sins you've committed recently. Ask God to forgive you for each sin. Then burn the list in a metal trash can outside.
- giving God a thank-you present because he forgives you. Choose a gift God would appreciate, such as something for the needy, a gift to your church, or a time commitment from you.

FOR MORE, SEE . . .

- Psalm 32:1–7 (p. 500)
- Micah 7:18–20 (p. 868)
- Romans 3:23–26 (p. 1143)

19Look at the new thing I am going to do.
It is already happening. Don't you see it?
I will make a road in the desert
and rivers in the dry land.
20Even the wild animals will be thankful to me—
the wild dogs and owls.
They will honor me when I put water in the desert
and rivers in the dry land
to give water to my people, the ones I chose.
21 The people I made
will sing songs to praise me.

22"People of Jacob, you have not called to me;
people of Israel, you have become tired of me.
23You have not brought me your sacrifices of sheep
nor honored me with your sacrifices.
I did not weigh you down with sacrifices to offer
or make you tired with incense[d] to burn.
24So you did not buy incense for me;
you did not freely bring me fat from your sacrifices.
Instead you have weighed me down with your many sins;
you have made me tired of your many wrongs.

25"I, I am the One who forgives all your sins,
for my sake;
I will not remember your sins.
26But you should remind me.
Let's meet and decide what is right.
Tell what you have done and show you are right.
27Your first father sinned,
and your leaders have turned against me.
28So I will make your holy rulers unholy.
I will bring destruction on the people of Jacob,
and I will let Israel be insulted."

The Lord Is the Only God

44 The LORD says, "People of Jacob, you are my servants. Listen to me!
People of Israel, I chose you."
2This is what the LORD says, who made you,
who formed you in your mother's body,
who will help you:

SELF-ESTEEM

Are You Okay?

Take a simple quiz to measure your self-esteem. After each situation, decide whether your self-esteem rises, falls, or stays the same.

1. Your parent wakes you with a hug, calling you a dream of a teenager.
2. Your parent wakes you, complaining about the state of your room. Terms like "slob" and "pigpen" fly.
3. You miss the school bus.
4. The person you want to date drives by and offers you a ride.
5. You get an A on your term paper.
6. You get a C— on your math test.
7. You want to be in the upcoming school play, but your name is not on the cast list when it is posted.

How did your self-esteem do? Did you balance the good and bad with a healthy dose of self-respect? Or, did you end up in the dumps?

Life brings ups and downs that affect self-esteem, but God offers a better way to see ourselves. Read **Isaiah 44:1–8** to learn how God wants us to feel about who we are.

- What does the passage say to someone whose self-esteem is based on life's ups and downs?
- How does belonging to God affect how you feel about yourself?

CONSIDER . . .

- making a list of what you like about yourself. For each item suggest one way you could use this characteristic to serve God.
- asking your youth pastor for advice on how to boost your self-esteem.

FOR MORE, SEE . . .

- Deuteronomy 7:6–9 (p. 168)
- Psalm 139:1–16 (p. 561)
- 1 Peter 2:9–10 (p. 1303)

"People of Jacob, my servants, don't be
afraid.
Israel, I chose you.
3I will pour out water for the thirsty land
and make streams flow on dry land.
I will pour out my Spirit[d] into your children
and my blessing on your descendants.
4Your children will grow like a tree in the
grass,
like poplar trees growing beside streams of
water.
5One person will say, 'I belong to the LORD,'
and another will use the name Jacob.
Another will sign his name 'I am the LORD's,'
and another will use the name Israel."

6The LORD, the king of Israel,
is the LORD All-Powerful, who saves Israel.
This is what he says: "I am the beginning
and the end.
I am the only God.
7Who is a god like me?
That god should come and prove it.
Let him tell and explain all that has happened
since I set up my ancient people.
He should also tell what will happen in the
future.
8Don't be afraid! Don't worry!
I have always told you what will happen.
You are my witnesses.
There is no other God but me.
I know of no other Rock;[d] I am the only
One."

Idols Are Useless

9Some people make idols, but they are worth
nothing.
People treasure them, but they are useless.
Those people are witnesses for the statues,
but those people cannot see.
They know nothing, so they will be
ashamed.
10Who made these gods?
Who made these useless idols?
11The workmen who made them will be
ashamed,
because they are only human.
If they all would come together,
they would all be ashamed and afraid.

12One workman uses tools to heat iron,
and he works over hot coals.
With his hammer he beats the metal and
makes a statue,
using his powerful arms.
But when he becomes hungry, he loses his
power.
If he does not drink water, he becomes
tired.
13Another workman uses a line and a compass
to draw on the wood.
Then he uses his chisels to cut a statue
and his calipers to measure the statue.
In this way, the workman makes the wood
look exactly like a person,
and this statue of a person sits in the
house.
14He cuts down cedars
or cypress or oak trees.
Those trees grew by their own power in the
forest.
Or he plants a pine tree, and the rain
makes it grow.
15Then he burns the tree.
He uses some of the wood for a fire to
keep himself warm.
He also starts a fire to bake his bread.
But he uses part of the wood to make a god,
and then he worships it!
He makes the idol and bows down to it!
16The man burns half of the wood in the fire.
He uses the fire to cook his meat,
and he eats the meat until he is full.
He also burns the wood to keep himself
warm. He says,
"Good! Now I am warm. I can see because
of the fire's light."
17But he makes a statue from the wood that is
left and calls it his god.
He bows down to it and worships it.
He prays to it and says,
"You are my god. Save me!"
18Those people don't know what they are
doing. They don't understand!
It is as if their eyes are covered so they
can't see.
Their minds don't understand.
19They have not thought about these things;
they don't understand.
They have never thought to themselves,
"I burned half of the wood in the fire
and used the hot coals to bake my bread.
I cooked and ate my meat.
And I used the wood that was left to make
this hateful thing.
I am worshiping a block of wood!"
20He doesn't know what he is doing;
his confused mind leads him the wrong
way.
He cannot save himself
or say, "This statue I am holding is a false
god."

The Lord Is the True God

21"People of Jacob, remember these things!
People of Israel, remember you are my
servants.
I made you, and you are my servants.

So Israel, I will not forget you.
22I have swept away your sins like a big cloud;
I have removed your sins like a cloud that disappears into the air.
Come back to me because I saved you."

23Skies, sing for joy because the LORD did great things!
Earth, shout for joy, even in your deepest parts!
Sing, you mountains, with thanks to God.
Sing, too, you trees in the forest!
The LORD saved the people of Jacob!
He showed his glory when he saved Israel.
24This is what the LORD says, who saved you,
who formed you in your mother's body:
"I, the LORD, made everything,
stretching out the skies by myself
and spreading out the earth all alone.
25I show that the lying prophets'[d] signs are false;
I make fools of those who do magic.
I confuse even wise men;
they think they know much, but I make them look foolish.
26I make the messages of my servants come true;
I make the advice of my messengers come true.
I say to Jerusalem,
'People will live in you again!'
I say to the towns of Judah,
'You will be built again!'
I say to Jerusalem's ruins,
'I will repair you.'
27I tell the deep waters, 'Become dry!
I will make your streams become dry!'
28I say of Cyrus,[n] 'He is my shepherd
and will do all that I want him to do.
He will say to Jerusalem, "You will be built again!"
He will tell the Temple,[d] "Your foundations will be rebuilt." ' "

God Chooses Cyrus to Free Israel

45 This is what the LORD says to Cyrus,
his appointed king:
"I hold your right hand
and will help you defeat nations
and take away other kings' power.
I will open doors for you
so city gates will not stop you.
2I will go before you
and make the mountains flat.
I will break down the bronze gates of the cities
and cut through their iron bars.
3I will give you the wealth that is stored away
and the hidden riches
so you will know I am the LORD,
the God of Israel, who calls you by name.
4I do these things for my servants, the people of Jacob,
and for my chosen people, the Israelites.
Cyrus, I call you by name,
and I give you a title of honor even though you don't know me.
5I am the LORD. There is no other God;
I am the only God.
I will make you strong,
even though you don't know me,
6so that everyone will know
there is no other God.
From the east to the west they will know
I alone am the LORD.
7I made the light and the darkness.
I bring peace, and I cause troubles.
I, the LORD, do all these things.

8"Sky above, make victory fall like rain;
clouds, pour down victory.
Let the earth receive it,
and let salvation grow,
and let victory grow with it.
I, the LORD, have created it.

9"How terrible it will be for those who argue with the God who made them.
They are like a piece of broken pottery among many pieces.
The clay does not ask the potter,
'What are you doing?'
The thing that is made doesn't say to its maker,
'You have no hands.'
10How terrible it will be for the child who says to his father,
'Why are you giving me life?'
How terrible it will be for the child who says to his mother,
'Why are you giving birth to me?' "

11This is what the LORD,
the Holy One of Israel, and its Maker, says:
"You ask me about what will happen.
You question me about my children.
You give me orders about what I have made.
12I made the earth
and all the people living on it.
With my own hands I stretched out the skies,
and I commanded all the armies in the sky.
13I will bring Cyrus to do good things,
and I will make his work easy.
He will rebuild my city

Cyrus A king of Persia who ruled from about 550-530 B.C.

and set my people free
without any payment or reward.
The LORD All-Powerful says this."

14The LORD says,
"The goods made in Egypt and Cush
and the tall people of Seba
will come to you
and will become yours.
The Sabeans will walk behind you,
coming along in chains.
They will bow down before you
and pray to you, saying,
'God is with you,
and there is no other God.' "

15God and Savior of Israel,
you are a God that people cannot see.
16All the people who make idols will be put to great shame;
they will go off together in disgrace.
17But Israel will be saved by the LORD,
and that salvation will continue forever.
Never again will Israel be put to shame.

18The LORD created the heavens.
He is the God who formed the earth and made it.
He did not want it to be empty,
but he wanted life on the earth.
This is what the LORD says:
"I am the LORD. There is no other God.
19I did not speak in secret
or hide my words in some dark place.
I did not tell the family of Jacob
to look for me in empty places.
I am the LORD, and I speak the truth;
I say what is right.

20"You people who have escaped from other nations,
gather together and come before me;
come near together.
People who carry idols of wood don't know what they are doing.
They pray to a god who cannot save them.
21Tell these people to come to me.
Let them talk about these things together.
Who told you long ago that this would happen?
Who told about it long ago?
I, the LORD, said these things.
There is no other God besides me.
I am the only good God. I am the Savior.
There is no other God.

22"All people everywhere,
follow me and be saved.
I am God. There is no other God.
23I will make a promise by my own power,
and my promise is true;
what I say will not be changed.
I promise that everyone will bow before me
and will promise to follow me.
24People will say about me, 'Goodness and power
come only from the LORD.' "
Everyone who has been angry with him
will come to him and be ashamed.
25But with the LORD's help, the people of Israel
will be found to be good,
and they will praise him.

SIDELIGHT: The god Bel wasn't nice (Isaiah 46:1). According to mythology, Bel killed a dragon-goddess named Tiamat, cut her up, and formed the universe from her remains.

False Gods Are Useless

46 Bel[d] and Nebo[d] bow down.
Their idols are carried by animals.
The statues are only heavy loads that must be carried;
they only make people tired.
2These gods will all bow down.
They cannot save themselves
but will all be carried away like prisoners.

3"Family of Jacob, listen to me!
All you people from Israel who are still alive, listen!
I have carried you since you were born;
I have taken care of you from your birth.
4Even when you are old, I will be the same.
Even when your hair has turned gray, I will take care of you.
I made you and will take care of you.
I will carry you and save you.

5"Can you compare me to anyone?
No one is equal to me or like me.
6Some people are rich with gold
and weigh their silver on the scales.
They hire a goldsmith, and he makes it into a god.
Then they bow down and worship it.
7They put it on their shoulders and carry it.
They set it in its place, and there it stands;
it cannot move from its place.
People may yell at it, but it cannot answer.
It cannot save them from their troubles.

8"Remember this, and do not forget it!
Think about these things, you who turn against God.
9Remember what happened long ago.

Remember that I am God, and there is no other God.
I am God, and there is no one like me.
10From the beginning I told you what would happen in the end.
A long time ago I told you things that have not yet happened.
When I plan something, it happens.
What I want to do, I will do.
11I am calling a man from the east to carry out my plan;
he will come like a hawk from a country far away.
I will make what I have said come true;
I will do what I have planned.
12Listen to me, you stubborn people,
who are far from what is right.
13I will soon do the things that are right.
I will bring salvation soon.
I will save Jerusalem
and bring glory to Israel."

God Will Destroy Babylon

47 The LORD says, "City of Babylon,
go down and sit in the dirt.
People of Babylon, sit on the ground.
You are no longer the ruler.
You will no longer be called
tender or beautiful.
2 You must use large stones to grind grain into flour.
Remove your veil and your nice skirts.
Uncover your legs and cross the rivers.
3People will see your nakedness;
they will see your shame.
I will punish you;
I will punish every one of you."

4Our Savior is named the LORD All-Powerful;
he is the Holy One of Israel.

5"Babylon, sit in darkness and say nothing.
You will no longer be called the queen of kingdoms.
6I was angry with my people,
so I rejected those who belonged to me.
I gave them to you,
but you showed them no mercy.
You even made the old people
work very hard.
7You said, 'I will live forever
as the queen.'
But you did not think about these things
or consider what would happen.

8"Now, listen, you lover of pleasure.
You think you are safe.
You tell yourself,
'I am the only important person.
I will never be a widow
or lose my children.'
9Two things will happen to you suddenly, in a single day.
You will lose your children and your husband.
These things will truly happen to you,
in spite of all your magic,
in spite of your powerful tricks.
10You do evil things, but you feel safe
and say, 'No one sees what I do.'
Your wisdom and knowledge
have fooled you.
You say to yourself,
'I am God, and no one is equal to me.'
11But troubles will come to you,
and you will not know how to stop them.
Disaster will fall on you,
and you will not be able to keep it away.
You will be destroyed quickly;
you will not even see it coming.

12"Keep on using your tricks
and doing all your magic
that you have used since you were young.
Maybe they will help you;
maybe you will be able to scare someone.
13You are tired of the advice you have received.
So let those who study the sky—
those who tell the future by looking at the stars and the new moons—
let them save you from what is about to happen to you.
14But they are like straw;
fire will quickly burn them up.
They cannot save themselves
from the power of the fire.
They are not like coals that give warmth
nor like a fire that you may sit beside.
15You have worked with these people,
and they have been with you since you were young,
but they will not be able to help you.
Everyone will go his own way,
and there will be no one left to save you."

God Controls the Future

48 The LORD says, "Family of Jacob, listen to me.
You are called Israel,
and you come from the family of Judah.
You swear by the LORD's name
and praise the God of Israel,
but you are not honest or sincere.
2You call yourselves people of the holy city,
and you depend on the God of Israel,
who is named the LORD All-Powerful.
3Long ago I told you what would happen.
I said these things and made them known;

suddenly I acted, and these things
happened.
4I knew you were stubborn;
your neck was like an iron muscle,
and your head was like bronze.
5So a long time ago I told you about these
things;
I told you about them before they
happened
so you couldn't say, 'My idols did this,
and my wooden and metal statues made
these things happen.'

6"You heard and saw everything that
happened,
so you should tell this news to others.
Now I will tell you about new things,
hidden things that you don't know yet.
7These things are happening now, not long
ago;
you have not heard about them before
today.
So you cannot say, 'We already knew about
that.'
8But you have not heard me; you have not
understood.
Even long ago you did not listen to me.
I knew you would surely turn against me;
you have fought against me since you were
born.
9But for my own sake I will be patient.
People will praise me for not becoming
angry
and destroying you.
10I have made you pure, but not by fire, as
silver is made pure.
I have purified you by giving you troubles.
11I do this for myself, for my own sake.
I will not let people speak evil against me,
and I will not let some god take my glory.

Israel Will Be Free

12"People of Jacob, listen to me.
People of Israel, I have called you to be my
people.
I am God;
I am the beginning and the end.
13I made the earth with my own hands.
With my right hand I spread out the skies.
When I call them,
they come together before me."

14All of you, come together and listen.
None of the gods said these things would
happen.
The LORD has chosen someone
to attack the Babylonians;
he will carry out his wishes against
Babylon.
15"I have spoken; I have called him.[n]
I have brought him, and I will make him
successful.
16Come to me and listen to this.
From the beginning I have spoken openly.
From the time it began, I was there."

Now, the Lord GOD
has sent me with his Spirit.[d]

17This is what the LORD, who saves you,
the Holy One of Israel, says:
"I am the LORD your God,
who teaches you to do what is good,
who leads you in the way you should go.
18If you had obeyed me,
you would have had peace like a
full-flowing river.
Good things would have flowed to you like
the waves of the sea.
19You would have had many children,
as many as the grains of sand.
They would never have died out
nor been destroyed."

20My people, leave Babylon!
Run from the Babylonians!
Tell this news with shouts of joy to the
people;
spread it everywhere on earth.
Say, "The LORD has saved his servants, the
people of Jacob."
21They did not become thirsty when he led
them through the deserts.
He made water flow from a rock for them.
He split the rock,
and water flowed out.

22"There is no peace for evil people," says the
LORD.

God Calls His Special Servant

49 All of you people in faraway places,
listen to me.
Listen, all you nations far away.
Before I was born, the LORD called me to
serve him.
The LORD named me while I was still in
my mother's body.
2He made my tongue like a sharp sword.
He hid me in the shadow of his hand.
He made me like a sharp arrow.
He hid me in the holder for his arrows.
3He told me, "Israel, you are my servant.
I will show my glory through you."
4But I said, "I have worked hard for nothing;

him This probably refers to Cyrus king of Persia.

I have used all my power, but I did nothing
useful.
But the LORD will decide what my work is
worth;
God will decide my reward."
5The LORD made me in the body of my
mother
to be his servant,
to lead the people of Jacob back to him
so that Israel might be gathered to him.
The LORD will honor me,
and I will get my strength from my God.
6Now he told me,
"You are an important servant to me
to bring back the tribes[d] of Jacob,
to bring back the people of Israel who are
left alive.
But, more importantly, I will make you a
light for all nations
to show people all over the world the way
to be saved."

7The LORD who saves you
is the Holy One of Israel.
He speaks to the one who is hated by the
people,
to the servant of rulers.
This is what he says: "Kings will see you and
stand to honor you;
great leaders will bow down before you,
because the LORD can be trusted.
He is the Holy One of Israel, who has
chosen you."

The Day of Salvation

8This is what the LORD says:
"At the right time I will hear your prayers.
On the day of salvation I will help you.
I will protect you,
and you will be the sign of my agreement
with the people.
You will bring back the people to the land
and give the land that is now ruined back
to its owners.
9You will tell the prisoners, 'Come out of your
prison.'
You will tell those in darkness, 'Come into
the light.'
The people will eat beside the roads,
and they will find food even on bare hills.
10They will not be hungry or thirsty.

GOD'S WILL

What Will You Do?

"Instead of spending spring break on the ski slopes this year, we're going on a mission trip to Mexico!" The new youth minister looked at a sea of blank faces.

"But we always go skiing," they responded.

Nevertheless, at spring break a caravan headed for Mexico, packed with supplies and the California teenagers who were willing to try something new. They arrived just in time to overwhelm a tiny, Spanish-speaking congregation that was meeting for worship.

"We didn't think you'd really come," said the Mexican pastor. When the crew translated their desire to help build or fix whatever was needed, the pastor cried.

"You are an answer to prayer," he told them. "We've been praying that we could build a church, and here you are." What started out as something to fill spring break became part of God's mission in the world.

God has a purpose for his people, even when they are not sure what it is. Listen for the purpose God has for you in **Isaiah 49:1–13**.

- What might Isaiah have said to the California group as it planned its spring break?
- How does this passage encourage you as you make decisions about what to do with your life?

CONSIDER . . .

- rewriting Isaiah 49:1–13 in your own words, emphasizing how each verse might apply to God's will for you.
- asking your parent or youth pastor to pray for you to discover God's will for your future.

FOR MORE, SEE . . .

- 1 Chronicles 29:17–18 (p. 385)
- Romans 12:1–2 (p. 1157)
- 1 Thessalonians 4:3–10 (p. 1247)

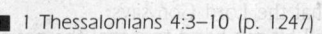

Neither the hot sun nor the desert wind
will hurt them.
The God who comforts them will lead them
and guide them by springs of water.
11I will make my mountains into roads,
and the roads will be raised up.
12Look, people are coming to me from far
away,
from the north and from the west,
from Aswan in southern Egypt."

13Heavens and earth, be happy.
Mountains, shout with joy,
because the LORD comforts his people
and will have pity on those who suffer.

Jerusalem and Her Children

14But Jerusalem said, "The LORD has left me;
the Lord has forgotten me."
15The LORD answers, "Can a woman forget the
baby she nurses?
Can she feel no kindness for the child to
which she gave birth?
Even if she could forget her children,
I will not forget you.
16See, I have written your name on my hand.
Jerusalem, I always think about your walls.
17Your children will soon return to you,
and the people who defeated you and
destroyed you will leave.
18Look up and look around you.
All your children are gathering to return to
you."
The LORD says, "As surely as I live,
your children will be like jewels
that a bride wears proudly.

19"You were destroyed and defeated,
and your land was made useless.
But now you will have more people than the
land can hold,
and those people who destroyed you will
be far away.
20Children were born to you while you were
sad,
but they will say to you,
'This place is too small for us.
Give us a bigger place to live.'
21Then you will say to yourself,
'Who gave me all these children?
I was sad and lonely,
defeated and separated from my people.
So who reared these children?
I was left all alone.
Where did all these children come from?' "

22This is what the Lord GOD says:
"See, I will lift my hand to signal the nations;
I will raise my banner for all the people to
see.
Then they will bring your sons back to you in
their arms,
and they will carry your daughters on their
shoulders.
23Kings will teach your children,
and daughters of kings will take care of
them.
They will bow down before you
and kiss the dirt at your feet.
Then you will know I am the LORD.
Anyone who trusts in me will not be
disappointed."

24Can the wealth a soldier wins in war be
taken away from him?
Can a prisoner be freed from a powerful
soldier?
25This is what the LORD says:
"The prisoners will be taken from the strong
soldiers.
What the soldiers have taken will be saved.
I will fight your enemies,
and I will save your children.
26I will force those who trouble you to eat
their own flesh.
Their own blood will be the wine that
makes them drunk.
Then everyone will know
I, the LORD, am the One who saves you;
I am the Powerful One of Jacob who saves
you."

Israel Was Punished for Its Sin

50 This is what the LORD says:
"People of Israel, you say I divorced
your mother.
Then where is the paper that proves it?
Or do you think I sold you
to pay a debt?
Because of the evil things you did, I sold you.
Because of the times she turned against me,
your mother was sent away.
2I came home and found no one there;
I called, but no one answered.
Do you think I am not able to save you?
Do I not have the power to save you?
Look, I need only to shout and the sea
becomes dry.
I change rivers into a desert,
and their fish rot because there is no water;
they die of thirst.
3I can make the skies dark;
I can make them black like clothes of
sadness."

God's Servant Obeys

4The Lord GOD gave me the ability to teach
so that I know what to say to make the
weak strong.

Every morning he wakes me.
He teaches me to listen like a student.
5 The Lord GOD helps me learn,
and I have not turned against him
nor stopped following him.
6 I offered my back to those who beat me.
I offered my cheeks to those who pulled
my beard.
I won't hide my face from them
when they make fun of me and spit
at me.
7 The Lord GOD helps me,
so I will not be ashamed.
I will be determined,
and I know I will not be disgraced.
8 He shows that I am innocent, and he is close
to me.
So who can accuse me?
If there is someone, let us go to court
together.
If someone wants to prove I have done
wrong,
he should come and tell me.
9 Look! It is the Lord GOD who helps me.
So who can prove me guilty?
Look! All those who try will become useless
like old clothes;
moths will eat them.

10 Who among you fears the LORD
and obeys his servant?
That person may walk in the dark
and have no light.
Then let him trust in the LORD
and depend on his God.
11 But instead, some of you want to light your
own fires
and make your own light.
So, go, walk in the light of your fires,
and trust your own light to guide you.
But this is what you will receive from me:
You will lie down in a place of pain.

Jerusalem Will Be Saved

51 The LORD says, "Listen to me,
those of you who try to live right and
follow the LORD.
Look at the rock from which you were cut;
look at the stone quarry from which you
were dug.

REVENGE

Different Strength

Tex, Pueblo, and Goat were leaders of Chicago street gangs. They grew up surrounded by poverty, poor schools and violence. Striking out with violence was their way to be recognized.

A black leader took interest in these boys. He listened to their stories and persuaded them to try nonviolence as a way to be seen and heard.

So in 1966, carloads of Chicago gang members drove to Mississippi to participate in their first nonviolent demonstration, a Freedom March. The marchers were treated unfairly; they were attacked with tear gas. But the experience changed the lives of these young men and women. They realized that nonviolence was a better way to respond.

Back in Chicago the gangs marched again. During this march a brick was hurled at the demonstrators. Goat jumped up and protected a woman from the brick by catching it with his bare hands. Instead of hurling it back, he continued marching peacefully.

Revenge harms the person who seeks it. **Isaiah 50:4–9** explains how God has a better way to handle tough situations.

- How was the gang members' new attitude similar to Isaiah's in this passage?
- How can this scripture help you when you're tempted to get even with those who have done you wrong?

CONSIDER . . .

- listing ways people try to get revenge for something and then making a second list of positive things you could do when confronted with an unfair situation.
- inviting someone who has wronged you to an activity that you or your group is planning. Include this person as you would a good friend.

FOR MORE, SEE . . .

- Leviticus 19:17–18 (p. 116)
- Matthew 5:38–48 (p. 915)

- Romans 12:17–21 (p. 1158)

2Look at Abraham, your ancestor,
and Sarah, who gave birth to your ancestors.
Abraham had no children when I called him,
but I blessed him and gave him many descendants.[d]
3So the LORD will comfort Jerusalem;
he will show mercy to those who live in her ruins.
He will change her deserts into a garden like Eden;
he will make her empty lands like the garden of the LORD.
People there will be very happy;
they will give thanks and sing songs.

4"My people, listen to me;
my nation, pay attention to me.
I will give the people my teachings,
and my decisions will be like a light to all people.
5I will soon show that I do what is right.
I will soon save you.
I will use my power and judge all nations.
All the faraway places are waiting for me;
they wait for my power to help them.
6Look up to the heavens.
Look around you at the earth below.
The skies will disappear like clouds of smoke.
The earth will become useless like old clothes,
and its people will die like flies.
But my salvation will continue forever,
and my goodness will never end.

7"You people who know what is right should listen to me;
you people who follow my teachings should hear what I say.
Don't be afraid of the evil things people say,
and don't be upset by their insults.
8Moths will eat those people as if they were clothes,
and worms will eat them as if they were wool.
But my goodness will continue forever,
and my salvation will continue from now on."

9Wake up, wake up, and use your strength,
powerful LORD.
Wake up as you did in the old times,
as you did a long time ago.
With your own power, you cut Rahab[d] into pieces
and killed that sea monster.
10You dried up the sea
and the waters of the deep ocean.
You made the deepest parts of the sea into a road
for your people to cross over and be saved.
11The people the LORD has freed will return
and enter Jerusalem with joy.
Their happiness will last forever.
They will have joy and gladness,
and all sadness and sorrow will be gone far away.

SIDELIGHT: When Isaiah 51:9 talks about cutting Rahab into little pieces, it's not referring to a person named Rahab. Rather, it refers to a sea monster of chaos that, according to an old legend, God killed in battle when he created the world. That's why the name was a put-down when it was used to refer to Egypt in Isaiah 30:7 (p. 646).

12The LORD says, "I am the one who comforts you.
So why should you be afraid of people, who die?
Why should you fear people who die like the grass?
13Have you forgotten the LORD who made you,
who stretched out the skies
and made the earth?
Why are you always afraid
of those angry people who trouble you
and who want to destroy?
But where are those angry people now?
14 People in prison will soon be set free;
they will not die in prison,
and they will have enough food.
15I am the LORD your God,
who stirs the sea and makes the waves roar.
My name is the LORD All-Powerful.
16I will give you the words I want you to say.
I will cover you with my hands and protect you.
I made the heavens and the earth,
and I say to Jerusalem, 'You are my people.' "

God Punished Israel

17Awake! Awake!
Get up, Jerusalem.
The LORD was very angry with you;
your punishment was like wine in a cup.
The LORD made you drink that wine;
you drank the whole cup until you stumbled.
18Jerusalem had many people,
but there was not one to lead her.

Of all the people who grew up there,
no one was there to guide her.
19 Troubles came to you two by two,
but no one will feel sorry for you.
There was ruin and disaster, great hunger and fighting.
No one can comfort you.
20 Your people have become weak.
They fall down and lie on every street corner,
like animals caught in a net.
They have felt the full anger of the LORD
and have heard God's angry shout.

21 So listen to me, poor Jerusalem,
you who are drunk but not from wine.
22 Your God will defend his people.
This is what the LORD your God says:
"The punishment I gave you is like a cup of wine.
You drank it and could not walk straight.
But I am taking that cup of my anger away from you,
and you will never be punished by my anger again.
23 I will now give that cup of punishment to those who gave you pain,
who told you,
'Bow down so we can walk over you.'
They made your back like dirt for them to walk on;
you were like a street for them to travel on."

Jerusalem Will Be Saved

52 Wake up, wake up, Jerusalem!
Become strong!
Be beautiful again,
holy city of Jerusalem.
The people who do not worship God and who are not pure

FREEDOM

Tearing Down the Walls

Angela Baxter looked like she had stepped out of the pages of Glamour magazine. She never went anywhere unless her outfit and makeup were perfect. As she walked up the stairs at Jackson Street Chapel, however, she looked out of place. "Excuse me," she mumbled to a group of street people around the doorway, "I'm here to volunteer." She heard snickers as she walked inside.

Gradually, over a period of months, as she worked several hours weekly at the chapel, Angela became a fixture there. She worked in the clothes closet. She planned after-school children's programs and visited with senior adults. She made a difference.

At the end of her visits, Angela would spend a few minutes alone in the sanctuary. Hanging at the front was a banner that pictured a crumbling wall and the words, "Tearing Down Walls." Here at the chapel, rich and poor, young and old, black and white became friends. The love of Jesus Christ and the freedom he offers tore down the barriers that usually come between people. She would glance at her clothes—usually a comfortable sweatshirt, jeans, and well-worn shoes. She would remember the walls that were there when she had first come to Jackson Street in her expensive outfits.

Maybe I've found freedom too, she thought, freedom to see what's most important.

God wants to set people free from anything that keeps them from serving him. Read about the freedom God offers in **Isaiah 52:1–10**.

- How is Angela's story like Jerusalem's story in this passage?
- What things hold you back and keep you from the freedom Isaiah talks about in this passage?

CONSIDER...

- writing down things in your life that might keep you from following Christ and then asking God to free you from those obstacles.
- sharing your time, talent, or money with an organization that helps the needy. Plan an activity for which you could volunteer, or organize an offering or fund-raiser.

FOR MORE, SEE...

- Psalm 118:5–17 (p. 549)
- John 8:31–36 (p. 1072)
- Romans 6:15–23 (p. 1147)

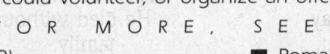

will not enter you again.
[2]Jerusalem, you once were a prisoner.
Now shake off the dust and stand up.
Jerusalem, you once were a prisoner.
Now free yourself from the chains around your neck.
[3]This is what the LORD says:
"You were not sold for a price,
so you will be saved without cost."
[4]This is what the Lord GOD says:
"First my people went down to Egypt to live.
Later Assyria made them slaves.

[5]"Now see what has happened," says the LORD.
"Another nation has taken away my people for nothing.
This nation who rules them makes fun of me," says the LORD.
"All day long they speak against me.
[6]This has happened so my people will know who I am,
and so, on that future day, they will know
that I am the one speaking to them.
It will really be me."

[7]How beautiful is the person
who comes over the mountains to bring good news,
who announces peace
and brings good news,
who announces salvation
and says to Jerusalem,
"Your God is King."
[8]Listen! Your guards are shouting.
They are all shouting for joy!
They all will see with their own eyes
when the LORD returns to Jerusalem.
[9]Jerusalem, your buildings are destroyed now,
but shout and rejoice together,
because the LORD has comforted his people.
He has saved Jerusalem.
[10]The LORD will show his holy power
to all the nations.
Then everyone on earth
will see the salvation of our God.

[11]You people, leave, leave; get out of Babylon!
Touch nothing that is unclean.[d]
You men who carry the LORD's things used in worship,
leave there and make yourselves pure.
[12]You will not be forced to leave Babylon quickly;
you will not be forced to run away,
because the LORD will go before you,
and the God of Israel will guard you from behind.

The Lord's Suffering Servant

[13]The LORD says, "See, my servant will act wisely.
People will greatly honor and respect him.
[14]Many people were shocked when they saw him.
His appearance was so changed he did not look like a man;
his form was changed so much they could barely tell he was human.
[15]But now he will surprise many nations.
Kings will be amazed and shut their mouths.
They will see things they had not been told about him,
and they will understand things they had not heard."

53

Who would have believed what we heard?
Who saw the LORD's power in this?
[2]He grew up like a small plant before the LORD,
like a root growing in a dry land.
He had no special beauty or form to make us notice him;
there was nothing in his appearance to make us desire him.
[3]He was hated and rejected by people.
He had much pain and suffering.
People would not even look at him.
He was hated, and we didn't even notice him.

[4]But he took our suffering on him
and felt our pain for us.
We saw his suffering
and thought God was punishing him.
[5]But he was wounded for the wrong we did;
he was crushed for the evil we did.
The punishment, which made us well, was given to him,
and we are healed because of his wounds.
[6]We all have wandered away like sheep;
each of us has gone his own way.
But the LORD has put on him the punishment
for all the evil we have done.

[7]He was beaten down and punished,
but he didn't say a word.
He was like a lamb being led to be killed.
He was quiet, as a sheep is quiet while its wool is being cut;
he never opened his mouth.
[8]Men took him away roughly and unfairly.
He died without children to continue his family.
He was put to death;
he was punished for the sins of my people.

[9]He was buried with wicked men,
and he died with the rich.
He had done nothing wrong,
and he had never lied.

[10]But it was the LORD who decided
to crush him and make him suffer.
The LORD made his life a penalty offering,
but he will still see his descendants[d] and live
a long life.
He will complete the things the LORD
wants him to do.
[11]"After his soul suffers many things,
he will see life and be satisfied.
My good servant will make many people
right with God;
he will carry away their sins.
[12]For this reason I will make him a great man
among people,
and he will share in all things with those
who are strong.
He willingly gave his life
and was treated like a criminal.
But he carried away the sins of many people
and asked forgiveness for those who
sinned."

People Will Return to Jerusalem

54 The LORD says, "Sing, Jerusalem.
You are like a woman who never gave
birth to children.
Start singing and shout for joy.
You never felt the pain of giving birth,
but you will have more children
than the woman who has a husband.
[2]Make your tent bigger;
stretch it out and make it wider.
Do not hold back.
Make the ropes longer
and its stakes stronger,
[3]because you will spread out to the right and
to the left.
Your children will take over other nations,
and they will again live in cities that once
were destroyed.

[4]"Don't be afraid, because you will not be
ashamed.
Don't be embarrassed, because you will not
be disgraced.
You will forget the shame you felt earlier;
you will not remember the shame you felt
when you lost your husband.

JESUS CHRIST

What Love Looks Like

Robert Nichols was an MK, a missionary kid; his parents served in South Asia. Sitting around a table with American friends one night, he and some friends started talking about missions and how to know whether a person was "cut out" to be a missionary. Robert thought about his parents. He knew the commitment and love it took to be effective for Christ.

"It takes love to do missions," Robert stated. "And do you know what love looks like?

"Once I watched my dad hold a man's diseased feet in his hands," Robert continued. "The feet were swollen and full of pus, but he wasn't afraid to touch him, because he cared for that person. His only concern was loving that man like Jesus does. That's the kind of love I want to have."

Because of Jesus' deep love for us, he experienced extreme pain and suffering. **Isaiah 52:13—53:12** is a prophetic picture of this servant of God, the Son of God.

- How was the love of Robert's father for the sick man like the love of God's servant in this passage?
- What kind of suffering could you face as God's servant today?

CONSIDER . . .

- writing a description of how Jesus might live today. What would he wear? How would he spend his time? With whom would he associate? Where would he go?
- "adopting" a person who serves God through missions work, ministry, or some kind of service by writing a note of appreciation, praying for the work he or she does, or offering your assistance.

FOR MORE, SEE . . .

- Isaiah 11:1–10 (p. 629)
- John 1:1–18 (p. 1058)
- Philippians 2:1–11 (p. 1230)

[5]The God who made you is like your
husband.
His name is the LORD All-Powerful.
The Holy One of Israel is the one who saves
you.
He is called the God of all the earth.
[6]You were like a woman whose husband left
her,
and you were very sad.
You were like a wife who married young
and then her husband left her.
But the LORD called you to be his,"
says your God.
[7]God says, "I left you for a short time,
but with great kindness I will bring you
back again.
[8]I became very angry
and hid from you for a time,
but I will show you mercy with kindness
forever,"
says the LORD who saves you.
[9]The LORD says, "This day is like the time of
Noah to me.
I promised then that I would never flood
the world again.
In the same way, I promise I will not be
angry with you
or punish you again.
[10]The mountains may disappear,
and the hills may come to an end,
but my love will never disappear;
my promise of peace will not come to an
end,"
says the LORD who shows mercy to you.

[11]"You poor city. Storms have hurt you,
and you have not been comforted.
But I will rebuild you with turquoise stones,
and I will build your foundations with
sapphires.
[12]I will use rubies to build your walls
and shining jewels for the gates
and precious jewels for all your outer walls.
[13]All your children will be taught by the LORD,
and they will have much peace.
[14]I will build you using fairness.
You will be safe from those who would hurt
you,
so you will have nothing to fear.
Nothing will come to make you afraid.
[15]I will not send anyone to attack you,
and you will defeat those who do attack
you.

[16]"See, I made the blacksmith.
He fans the fire to make it hotter,
and he makes the kind of tool he wants.
In the same way I have made the destroyer
to destroy.
[17]So no weapon that is used against you will
defeat you.
You will show that those who speak against
you are wrong.
These are the good things my servants
receive.
Their victory comes from me," says the
LORD.

God Gives What Is Good

55 The LORD says, "All you who are
thirsty,
come and drink.
Those of you who do not have money,
come, buy and eat!
Come buy wine and milk
without money and without cost.
[2]Why spend your money on something that is
not real food?
Why work for something that doesn't really
satisfy you?
Listen closely to me, and you will eat what is
good;
your soul will enjoy the rich food that
satisfies.
[3]Come to me and listen;
listen to me so you may live.
I will make an agreement with you that will
last forever.
I will give you the blessings I promised to
David.
[4]I made David a witness of my power for all
nations,
a ruler and commander of many nations.
[5]You will call for nations that you don't yet
know.
And these nations that do not know you
will run to you
because of the LORD your God,
because of the Holy One of Israel who
honors you."

[6]So you should look for the LORD before it is
too late;
you should call to him while he is near.
[7]The wicked should stop doing wrong,
and they should stop their evil thoughts.
They should return to the LORD so he may
have mercy on them.
They should come to our God, because he
will freely forgive them.

[8]The LORD says, "My thoughts are not like
your thoughts.
Your ways are not like my ways.
[9]Just as the heavens are higher than the earth,
so are my ways higher than your ways
and my thoughts higher than your
thoughts.
[10]Rain and snow fall from the sky

and don't return without watering the
ground.
They cause the plants to sprout and grow,
making seeds for the farmer
and bread for the people.
11The same thing is true of the words I speak.
They will not return to me empty.
They make the things happen that I want to
happen,
and they succeed in doing what I send
them to do.

12"So you will go out with joy
and be led out in peace.
The mountains and hills will burst into song
before you,
and all the trees in the fields will clap their
hands.
13Large cypress trees will grow where
thornbushes were.
Myrtle trees will grow where weeds were.
These things will be a reminder of the LORD's
promise,
and this reminder will never be destroyed."

SIDELIGHT: Replacing thornbushes with myrtle would require more than a little plant food (Isaiah 55:13). Thornbushes and weeds (or briars) are scraggly desert plants that survive with little nourishment. The myrtle is an evergreen shrub that grows along rivers and streams, and it symbolizes peace, joy, generosity, and justice—which fits the prophet's vision for the future.

All Nations Will Obey the Lord

56 This is what the LORD says:
"Give justice to all people,
and do what is right,
because my salvation will come to you soon.
Soon everyone will know that I do what is
right.
2The person who obeys the law about the
Sabbath[d]
will be blessed,
and the person who does no evil
will be blessed."

3Foreigners who have joined the LORD should
not say,
"The LORD will not accept me with his
people."
The eunuch[d] should not say,
"Because I cannot have children, the LORD
will not accept me."
4This is what the LORD says:
"The eunuchs should obey the law about the
Sabbath
and do what I want
and keep my agreement.
5If they do, I will make their names
remembered
within my Temple[d] and its walls.
It will be better for them than children.
I will give them a name that will last forever,
that will never be forgotten.
6Foreigners will join the LORD
to worship him and love him,
to serve him,
to obey the law about the Sabbath,
and to keep my agreement.
7I will bring these people to my holy
mountain
and give them joy in my house of prayer.
The offerings and sacrifices
they place on my altar will please me,
because my Temple will be called
a house for prayer for people from all
nations."
8The Lord GOD says—
he who gathers the Israelites that were
forced to leave their country:
"I will bring together other people
to join those who are already gathered."

Israel's Leaders Are Evil

9All you animals of the field,
all you animals of the forest, come to eat.
10The leaders who are to guard the people are
blind;
they don't know what they are doing.
All of them are like quiet dogs
that don't know how to bark.
They lie down and dream
and love to sleep.
11They are like hungry dogs
that are never satisfied.
They are like shepherds
who don't know what they are doing.
They all have gone their own way;
all they want to do is satisfy themselves.
12They say, "Come, let's drink some wine;
let's drink all the beer we want.
And tomorrow we will do this again,
or, maybe we will have an even better
time."

Israel Does Not Follow God

57 Those who are right with God may
die,
but no one pays attention.
Good people are taken away,
but no one understands.
Those who do right are being taken away
from evil

2 and are given peace.
Those who live as God wants
find rest in death.

3"Come here, you magicians!
Come here, you sons of prostitutes[d] and those who take part in adultery![d]
4Of whom are you making fun?
Whom are you insulting?
At whom do you stick out your tongue?
You turn against God,
and you are liars.
5You have sexual relations under every green tree
to worship your gods.
You kill children in the ravines
and sacrifice them in the rocky places.
6You take the smooth rocks from the ravines
as your portion.
You pour drink offerings on them to worship them,
and you give grain offerings to them.
Do you think this makes me want to show you mercy?
7You make your bed on every hill and mountain,
and there you offer sacrifices.
8You have hidden your idols
behind your doors and doorposts.
You have left me, and you have uncovered yourself.
You have pulled back the covers and climbed into bed.
You have made an agreement with those whose beds you love,
and you have looked at their nakedness.
9You use your oils and perfumes
to look nice for Molech.[d]
You have sent your messengers to faraway lands;
you even tried to send them to the place of the dead.
10You were tired from doing these things,
but you never gave up.
You found new strength,
so you did not quit.
11"Whom were you so afraid of
that you lied to me?
You have not remembered me
or even thought about me.
I have been quiet for a long time.
Is that why you are not afraid of me?
12I will tell about your 'goodness' and what you do,
and those things will do you no good.
13When you cry out for help,
let the gods you have gathered help you.
The wind will blow them all away;
just a puff of wind will take them away.
But the person who depends on me will receive the land
and own my holy mountain."

The Lord Will Save His People

14Someone will say, "Build a road! Build a road! Prepare the way!
Make the way clear for my people."
15And this is the reason: God lives forever and is holy.
He is high and lifted up.
He says, "I live in a high and holy place,
but I also live with people who are sad and humble.
I give new life to those who are humble
and to those whose hearts are broken.
16I will not accuse forever,
nor will I always be angry,
because then human life would grow weak.
Human beings, whom I created, would die.
17I was angry because they were dishonest in order to make money.
I punished them and turned away from them in anger,
but they continued to do evil.
18I have seen what they have done, but I will heal them.
I will guide them and comfort them and those who felt sad for them.
They will all praise me.
19I will give peace, real peace, to those far and near,
and I will heal them," says the LORD.
20But evil people are like the angry sea,
which cannot rest,
whose waves toss up waste and mud.
21"There is no peace for evil people," says my God.

How to Honor God

58 The LORD says, "Shout out loud. Don't hold back.
Shout out loud like a trumpet.
Tell my people what they have done against their God;
tell the family of Jacob about their sins.
2They still come every day looking for me
and want to learn my ways.
They act just like a nation that does what is right,
that obeys the commands of its God.
They ask me to judge them fairly.
They want God to be near them.
3They say, 'To honor you we had special days when we gave up eating,
but you didn't see.
We humbled ourselves to honor you,
but you didn't notice.' "

But the LORD says, "You do what pleases
yourselves on these special days,
and you are unfair to your workers.
4On these special days when you do not eat,
you argue and fight
and hit each other with your fists.
You cannot do these things as you do
now
and believe your prayers are heard in
heaven.
5This kind of special day is not what I want.
This is not the way I want people to be
sorry for what they have done.
I don't want people just to bow their heads
like a plant
and wear rough cloth and lie in ashes to
show their sadness.
This is what you do on your special days
when you do not eat,
but do you think this is what the LORD
wants?

6"I will tell you the kind of special day I
want:
Free the people you have put in prison
unfairly
and undo their chains.
Free those to whom you are unfair
and stop their hard labor.
7Share your food with the hungry
and bring poor, homeless people into your
own homes.
When you see someone who has no clothes,
give him yours,
and don't refuse to help your own relatives.
8Then your light will shine like the dawn,
and your wounds will quickly heal.
Your God will walk before you,
and the glory of the LORD will protect you
from behind.
9Then you will call out, and the LORD will
answer.
You will cry out, and he will say, 'Here I
am.'

"If you stop making trouble for others,
if you stop using cruel words and pointing
your finger at others,

HYPOCRISY

Are You for Real?

The bus was packed with everything, except servant attitudes. Compact disc players and hairspray were more important than the Bible Club materials crumpled under the seats. Efforts to work on club lessons were half-hearted.

"We'll help later," some in the group groaned, "it's just too hot right now."

Attitudes didn't improve much that missions week. While teenagers talked about Jesus' love, they rarely showed love to any of the children. "Jesus is your friend," Sam Cooper told the boys and girls during his turn to tell the story. But after the story, he left their circle and joined his own friends under a tree.

On the last Bible Club day, the teenagers brought cameras. "Matt, get our picture," yelled Kristy Land, surrounded by her friends. Seven-year-old Bobby grinned and jumped into the pose.

"Not you," Kristy smiled, pushing him out of camera range. Embarrassed, Bobby walked away. He guessed God's love was just a story they told.

The Bible says that many people pretend to serve God when they are only pleasing themselves. Read **Isaiah 58:3–9a** to discover what God wants from his people.

■ If the teenagers had used this passage as a guide, how might their week have been different?

■ If the passage were addressed to you, how would you change the way you show love to God?

CONSIDER . . .

■ confessing to God a time when you treated someone unkindly. Ask God to help you find a way to make amends for your actions.

■ choosing a person you often overlook and having an Appreciation Day for him or her. Volunteer your time, write a note, or make something special.

FOR MORE, SEE . . .

■ Micah 6:6–8 (p. 866)
■ Matthew 23:23–26 (p. 949)
■ James 1:22–27 (p. 1294)

10if you feed those who are hungry
and take care of the needs of those who are troubled,
then your light will shine in the darkness,
and you will be bright like sunshine at noon.
11The LORD will always lead you.
He will satisfy your needs in dry lands
and give strength to your bones.
You will be like a garden that has much water,
like a spring that never runs dry.
12Your people will rebuild the old cities that are now in ruins;
you will rebuild their foundations.
You will be known for repairing the broken places
and for rebuilding the roads and houses.

13"You must obey God's law about the Sabbath[d]
and not do what pleases yourselves on that holy day.
You should call the Sabbath a joyful day
and honor it as the LORD's holy day.
You should honor it by not doing whatever you please
nor saying whatever you please on that day.
14Then you will find joy in the LORD,
and I will carry you to the high places above the earth.
I will let you eat the crops of the land your ancestor Jacob had."
The LORD has said these things.

The Evil That People Do

59 Surely the LORD's power is enough to save you.
He can hear you when you ask him for help.
2It is your evil that has separated
you from your God.
Your sins cause him to turn away from you,
so he does not hear you.
3With your hands you have killed others,
and with your fingers you have done wrong.
With your lips you have lied,
and with your tongue you say evil things.
4People take each other to court unfairly,
and no one tells the truth in arguing his case.
They accuse each other falsely and tell lies.
They cause trouble and create more evil.
5They hatch evil like eggs from poisonous snakes.
If you eat one of those eggs, you will die,
and if you break one open, a poisonous snake comes out.
People tell lies as they would spin a spider's web.
6 The webs they make cannot be used for clothes;
you can't cover yourself with those webs.
The things they do are evil,
and they use their hands to hurt others.
7They eagerly run to do evil,
and they are always ready to kill innocent people.
They think evil thoughts.
Everywhere they go they cause ruin and destruction.
8They don't know how to live in peace,
and there is no fairness in their lives.
They are dishonest.
Anyone who lives as they live will never have peace.

Israel's Sin Brings Trouble

9Fairness has gone far away;
goodness is nowhere to be found.
We wait for the light, but there is only darkness now.
We hope for a bright light, but all we have is darkness.
10We are like the blind feeling our way along a wall.
We feel our way as if we had no eyes.
In the brightness of day we trip as if it were night.
We are like dead men among the strong.
11All of us growl like the bears.
We call out sadly like the doves.
We look for justice, but there isn't any.
We want to be saved, but salvation is far away.
12We have done many wrong things against our God;
our sins show we are wrong.
We know we have turned against God;
we know the evil things we have done:
13sinning and rejecting the LORD,
turning away from our God,
planning to hurt others and to disobey God,
planning and speaking lies.
14So we have driven away justice,
and we have kept away from what is right.
Truth is not spoken in the streets;
what is honest is not allowed to enter the city.
15Truth cannot be found anywhere,
and people who refuse to do evil are attacked.

The LORD looked and could not find any justice,
and he was displeased.

16He could not find anyone to help the people,
and he was surprised that there was no one
to help.
So he used his own power to save the
people;
his own goodness gave him strength.
17He covered himself with goodness like armor.
He put the helmet of salvation on his head.
He put on the clothes of punishment
and wrapped himself in the coat of his
strong love.
18The LORD will pay back his enemies for what
they have done.
He will show his anger to those who were
against him;
he will punish the people in faraway places
as they deserve.
19Then people from the west will fear the
LORD,
and people from the east will fear his glory.
The LORD will come quickly like a
fast-flowing river,
driven by the breath of the LORD.

20"Then a Savior will come to Jerusalem
and to the people of Jacob who have
turned from sin,"
says the LORD.

21The LORD says, "This is my agreement with
these people: My Spirit[d] and my words that I give
you will never leave you or your children or your
grandchildren, now and forever."

Jerusalem Will Be Great

60 "Jerusalem, get up and shine, because
your light has come,
and the glory of the LORD shines on you.
2Darkness now covers the earth;
deep darkness covers her people.
But the LORD shines on you,
and people see his glory around you.
3Nations will come to your light;
kings will come to the brightness of your
sunrise.

4"Look around you.
People are gathering and coming to you.
Your sons are coming from far away,
and your daughters are coming with them.

SHARING FAITH

How Can I Tell You?

Dona Smith usually ate lunch on a park bench by the White House. She loved her summer job as a subway attendant: the work, the subway, and the city. Each noon she wrote about her experiences in a notebook.

"Lord," she wrote one day, "how can I tell Matt about you?" She thought of the employee she had befriended. With no family, Matt was used to street life and had never been to church. Dona talked with him everyday. While she knew a lot about him, she had never said much about herself. She had never said, "I'm a Christian."

"He needs to know," she wrote. "Help me know what to say and the time to say it."

That afternoon Matt stopped by her desk. He asked, "Why do you smile so much? You just always seem so happy." Dona's faith had shown before she said anything. Her opportunity was obvious.

"You've told me about your life," she began. "Let me tell you about mine." When the conversation was over, Matt agreed to visit Dona's church and spend a Sunday with her family.

When people reflect God's light, they draw others to God. See in **Isaiah 60:1–6** how God shines on his followers to make them witnesses.

- How does this passage apply to Dona's situation?
- How can you reflect the kind of light Isaiah describes?

CONSIDER. . .

- using a permanent marker to write on a light bulb words that describe how you might show God's love to others. Place the light in your bedroom.
- keeping a prayer journal for one month. Write about situations where you could be God's light.

FOR MORE, SEE. . .

- Isaiah 9:2–7 (p. 626)
- Mark 16:15–20 (p. 997)
- Colossians 4:5–6 (p. 1243)

5When you see them, you will shine with
happiness;
you will be excited and full of joy,
because the wealth of the nations across the
seas will be given to you;
the riches of the nations will come to you.
6Herds of camels will cover your land,
young camels from Midian and Ephah.
People will come from Sheba
bringing gold and incense,[d]
and they will sing praises to the LORD.

SIDELIGHT: The promise to Jerusalem that people from Sheba would come to Jerusalem to worship was quite an impressive promise (Isaiah 60:6). Sheba was at least fourteen hundred miles away—across the desert of present-day Saudi Arabia. Years earlier, the queen of Sheba had visited King Solomon and seen all his wealth (1 Kings 10:1–13, p. 314).

7All the sheep from Kedar will be given to
you;
the sheep from Nebaioth will be brought to
you.
They will be pleasing sacrifices on my altar,
and I will make my beautiful Temple[d] more
beautiful.
8"The people are returning to you like clouds,
like doves flying to their nests.
9People in faraway lands are waiting for me.
The great trading ships will come first,
bringing your children from faraway lands,
and with them silver and gold.
This will honor the LORD your God,
the Holy One of Israel,
who does wonderful things for you.

10"Jerusalem, foreigners will rebuild your walls,
and their kings will serve you.
When I was angry, I hurt you,
but now I want to be kind to you and
comfort you.
11Your gates will always be open;
they will not be closed day or night
so the nations can bring their wealth to you,
and their kings will be led to you.
12The nation or kingdom that doesn't serve you
will be destroyed;
it will be completely ruined.

13"The great trees of Lebanon will be given to
you:
its pine, fir, and cypress trees together.
You will use them to make my Temple
beautiful,
and I will give much honor to this place
where I rest my feet.
14The people who have hurt you will bow
down to you;
those who hated you will bow down at
your feet.
They will call you The City of the LORD,
Jerusalem, city of the Holy One of Israel.

15"You have been hated and left empty
with no one passing through.
But I will make you great from now on;
you will be a place of happiness forever and
ever.
16You will be given what you need from the
nations,
like a child drinking milk from its mother.
Then you will know that it is I, the LORD,
who saves you.
You will know that the Powerful One of
Jacob protects you.
17I will bring you gold in place of bronze,
silver in place of iron,
bronze in place of wood,
iron in place of rocks.
I will change your punishment into peace,
and you will be ruled by what is right.
18There will be no more violence in your
country;
it will not be ruined or destroyed.
You will name your walls Salvation
and your gates Praise.
19The sun will no longer be your light during
the day
nor will the brightness from the moon be
your light,
because the LORD will be your light forever,
and your God will be your glory.
20Your sun will never set again,
and your moon will never be dark,
because the LORD will be your light forever,
and your time of sadness will end.
21All of your people will do what is right.
They will receive the earth forever.
They are the plant I have planted,
the work of my own hands
to show my greatness.
22The smallest family will grow to a thousand.
The least important of you will become a
powerful nation.
I am the LORD,
and when it is time, I will make these
things happen quickly."

The Lord's Message of Freedom

61 The Lord GOD has put his Spirit[d] in
me,
because the LORD has appointed me to tell
the good news to the poor.

He has sent me to comfort those whose
hearts are broken,
to tell the captives they are free,
and to tell the prisoners they are released.
2He has sent me to announce the time when
the LORD will show his kindness
and the time when our God will punish
evil people.
He has sent me to comfort all those who are
sad
3 and to help the sorrowing people of
Jerusalem.
I will give them a crown to replace their
ashes,
and the oil of gladness to replace their
sorrow,
and clothes of praise to replace their spirit
of sadness.
Then they will be called Trees of Goodness,
trees planted by the LORD to show his
greatness.

4They will rebuild the old ruins
and restore the places destroyed long ago.
They will repair the ruined cities
that were destroyed for so long.

5My people, foreigners will come to tend your
sheep.
People from other countries will tend your
fields and vineyards.
6You will be called priests of the LORD;
you will be named the servants of our
God.
You will have riches from all the nations on
earth,
and you will take pride in them.
7Instead of being ashamed, my people will
receive twice as much wealth.

SADNESS

Chasing the Blues Away

Are you ever sad or depressed? You're not alone:

- Twenty percent of all American teenagers report feeling emotionally empty, while another 20 percent feel confused most of the time.
- Sixty-one percent of teenagers feel extremely sad or depressed at least ten times during their teenage years.
- More than 60 percent of kids "worry a lot" about getting a bad report card, being in a plane crash, being in a car accident, or experiencing the death of a parent.
- More than 30 percent of high school students have experienced moderate or severe levels of symptoms of depression.

How do people get rid of the blues once they have them? Here are the top seven coping techniques most teenagers use:

1. listening to music
2. thinking of a solution by yourself
3. daydreaming
4. watching television
5. swearing
6. going shopping
7. going to a video arcade

There are lots of ways—both good and bad—to ease the weight of depression, but their benefits are almost always short-lived. God offers a way to get rid of the blues. Hear of the hope offered to depressed people in **Isaiah 61:1–11**.

- What's the difference between the way people try to escape their trouble and the way God suggests in this passage?
- How can these words of Isaiah help you when you feel depressed?

CONSIDER . . .

- listing all the things that make you sad and then thanking God that he can turn sadness into joy.
- making a new list of coping techniques based on the Bible passage and then doing one of them this week.

FOR MORE, SEE . . .

- Psalm 42 (p. 507)
- Romans 8:18–28 (p. 1151)
- 2 Corinthians 4:7–18 (p. 1210)

Instead of being disgraced, they will be
happy because of what they receive.
They will receive a double share of the land,
so their happiness will continue forever.
8"I, the LORD, love justice.
I hate stealing and everything that is
wrong.
I will be fair and give my people what they
should have,
and I will make an agreement with them
that will continue forever.
9Everyone in all nations will know the
children of my people,
and their children will be known among
the nations.
Anyone who sees them will know
that they are people the LORD has blessed."

10The LORD makes me very happy;
all that I am rejoices in my God.
He has covered me with clothes of salvation
and wrapped me with a coat of goodness,
like a bridegroom dressed for his wedding,
like a bride dressed in jewels.
11The earth causes plants to grow,
and a garden causes the seeds planted in it
to grow.
In the same way the Lord GOD will make
goodness and praise
come from all the nations.

New Jerusalem

62 Because I love Jerusalem, I will
continue to speak for her;
for Jerusalem's sake I will not stop speaking
until her goodness shines like a bright light,
until her salvation burns bright like a flame.
2Jerusalem, the nations will see your goodness,
and all kings will see your glory.
Then you will have a new name,
which the LORD himself will give you.
3You will be like a beautiful crown in the
LORD's hand,
like a king's crown in your God's hand.
4You will never again be called the People
that God Left,

PATIENCE

He's Still at Work

Barbara Davis heard crying, but didn't see anyone. Finally, she spotted Maggie Howard leaning against the back wall of the chapel, feet under the last pew.

"I'm tired of my life," Maggie cried. "I'm tired of nothing working out. I'll never find anyone to be with. I'll never be the person everyone at church expects me to be." For the moment, she only saw the things she wasn't.

Barbara saw her friend differently. She remembered what Maggie was like a year before, when she first came to the youth group. She was only interested in getting rowdy and causing trouble. Barbara could see that this life, given to God, was growing. Maggie read the Bible now, and really tried to absorb what was said at youth meetings. Barbara sat next to Maggie and held her close. They cried together a few minutes and then Barbara spoke. "Be patient," she said, "and keep praying. Good things are happening."

Growing spiritually takes time. Find encouragement to keep working at it in **Isaiah 62:1–12**.

- How is Barbara's advice to Maggie similar to Isaiah's words to God's people?
- According to these verses, why do you need both prayer and patience in your Christian life?

CONSIDER...

- writing a description of the person you hope to be five years from now. Include qualities you want to have. Keep this in your Bible and pray that God will help you grow.
- designing a step-by-step "Patience Program" to use during times when you're impatient. Include scriptures on patience (such as 1 Thessalonians 5:12–14, p. 1249 and James 5:7–8, p. 1299), the benefits of waiting, and a list of things to pray about and do in the meantime.

FOR MORE, SEE...

- Psalm 37:3–9 (p. 503)
- Luke 18:1–8 (p. 1041)
- Romans 5:3–5 (p. 1145)

nor your land the Land that God
Destroyed.
You will be called the People God Loves,
and your land will be called the Bride of
God,
because the LORD loves you.
And your land will belong to him as a bride
belongs to her husband.
5As a young man marries a woman,
so your children will marry your land.
As a man rejoices over his new wife,
so your God will rejoice over you.

6Jerusalem, I have put guards on the walls to
watch.
They must not be silent day or night.
You people who remind the LORD of your
needs in prayer
should never be quiet.
7You should not stop praying to him until he
builds up Jerusalem
and makes it a city all people will praise.

8The LORD has made a promise,
and by his power he will keep his promise.
He said, "I will never again give your grain
as food to your enemies.
I will not let your enemies drink the new
wine
that you have worked to make.
9The person who gathers food will eat it,
and he will praise the LORD.
The person who gathers the grapes will drink
the wine
in the courts of my Temple."[d]
10Go through, go through the gates!
Make the way ready for the people.
Build up, build up the road!
Move all the stones off the road.
Raise the banner as a sign for the people.
11The LORD is speaking
to all the faraway lands:
"Tell the people of Jerusalem,
'Look, your Savior is coming.
He is bringing your reward to you;
he is bringing his payment with him.' "
12His people will be called the Holy People,
the Saved People of the LORD,
and Jerusalem will be called the City God
Wants,
the City God Has Not Rejected.

The Lord Judges His People

63 Who is this coming from Edom,
from the city of Bozrah, dressed in
red?
Who is this dressed in fine clothes
and marching forward with his great
power?
He says, "I, the LORD, speak what is right.
I have the power to save you."

2Someone asks, "Why are your clothes bright
red
as if you had walked on the grapes to make
wine?"

3The LORD answers, "I have walked in the
winepress[d] alone,
and no one among the nations helped me.
I was angry and walked on the nations
and crushed them because of my anger.
Blood splashed on my clothes,
and I stained all my clothing.
4I chose a time to punish people,
and the time has come for me to save.
5I looked around, but I saw no one to help
me.
I was surprised that no one supported me.
So I used my own power to save my people;
my own anger supported me.
6While I was angry, I walked on the nations.
In my anger I punished them
and poured their blood on the ground."

The Lord's Kindness to His People

7I will tell about the LORD's kindness
and praise him for everything he has done.
I will praise the LORD for the many good
things he has given us
and for his goodness to the people of Israel.
He has shown great mercy to us
and has been very kind to us.
8He said, "These are my people;
my children will not lie to me."
So he saved them.
9When they suffered, he suffered also.
He sent his own angel to save them.
Because of his love and kindness, he saved
them.
Since long ago he has picked them up and
carried them.
10But they turned against him
and made his Holy Spirit[d] very sad.
So he became their enemy,
and he fought against them.

11But then his people remembered what
happened long ago,
in the days of Moses and the Israelites with
him.
Where is the LORD who brought the people
through the sea,
with the leaders of his people?
Where is the one
who put his Holy Spirit among them,
12who led Moses by the right hand
with his wonderful power,
who divided the water before them

to make his name famous forever,
13who led the people through the deep waters?
Like a horse walking through a desert,
the people did not stumble.
14Like cattle that go down to the valley,
the Spirit of the LORD gave the people a place to rest.
LORD, that is the way you led your people,
and by this you won for yourself wonderful fame.

A Prayer for Help

15LORD, look down from the heavens and see;
look at us from your wonderful and holy home in heaven.
Where is your strong love and power?
Why are you keeping your love and mercy from us?
16You are our father.
Abraham doesn't know we are his children,
and Israel doesn't recognize us.
LORD, you are our father.
You are called "the one who has always saved us."
17LORD, why are you making us wander from your ways?
Why do you make us stubborn so that we don't honor you?
For our sake come back to us,
your servants, who belong to you.
18Your people had your Temple[d] for a while,
but now our enemies have walked on your holy place and crushed it.
19We have become like people you never ruled over,
like those who have never worn your name.

64 Tear open the skies and come down to earth
so that the mountains will tremble before you.
2Like a fire that burns twigs,
like a fire that makes water boil,
let your enemies know who you are.
Then all nations will shake with fear when they see you.
3You have done amazing things we did not expect.

SUFFERING

In Sickness and in Health

The dresses, tuxes, and flowers were beautiful. On this fine day, Marshall Younger and Stephanie Eubank promised their love to each other for life. Guests released helium balloons when the couple left the church. It was a gorgeous wedding.

But just hours after the decorations were gone, the groom came down with the flu. In the middle of the night Stephanie went to find medication for Marshall. She stayed up all night caring for him.

When Marshall felt better, they watched a video of their wedding. They heard the words "in sickness and in health" and started laughing.

"I didn't realize how soon I'd be tested on that promise," said Stephanie, "Maybe what happened to us is a better picture of a good marriage than any wedding picture—feeling what the other one feels, taking care of each other no matter what."

Just as Stephanie shared in Marshall's sickness, God is so close to his people that he hurts when they hurt. Read about how he cares in **Isaiah 63:7–9**.

- Why do you think God chooses to hurt when his people hurt?
- According to the passage, what are ways you can know God cares for you when you're hurting?

CONSIDER . . .

- designing a "first-aid" plan to help hurting people. List things you could give to care for people in pain, such as visits, prayers, cards and food.
- filling a one-month calendar with names of people, groups and countries that experience suffering. For example, the homeless, Ethiopia or a cerebral palsy victim you know. Write a different name, group or country on each day of the month, and use this as a prayer calendar.

FOR MORE, SEE . . .

- Psalm 103:1–14 (p. 540)
- John 11:28–44 (p. 1077)
- Hebrews 13:1–3 (p. 1290)

You came down, and the mountains
trembled before you.
4From long ago no one has ever heard of a
God like you.
No one has ever seen a God besides you,
who helps the people who trust you.
5You help those who enjoy doing good,
who remember how you want them to live.
But you were angry because we sinned.
For a long time we disobeyed,
so how can we be saved?
6All of us are dirty with sin.
All the right things we have done are like
filthy pieces of cloth.
All of us are like dead leaves,
and our sins, like the wind, have carried us
away.
7No one worships you
or even asks you to help us.
That is because you have turned away
from us
and have let our sins destroy us.
8But LORD, you are our father.
We are like clay, and you are the potter;
your hands made us all.
9LORD, don't continue to be angry with us;
don't remember our sins forever.
Please, look at us,
because we are your people.
10Your holy cities are empty like the desert.
Jerusalem is like a desert;
it is destroyed.
11Our ancestors worshiped you
in our holy and wonderful Temple,
but now it has been burned with fire,
and all our precious things have been
destroyed.
12When you see these things, will you hold
yourself back from helping us, LORD?
Will you be silent and punish us beyond
what we can stand?

All People Will Learn About God

65 The LORD says, "I made myself known
to people who were not looking for
me.
I was found by those who were not asking
me for help.
I said, 'Here I am. Here I am,'
to a nation that was not praying to me.
2All day long I stood ready to accept
people who turned against me,

FOLLOWING GOD

Where Am I?

Stay calm. Don't worry—yet, Tessa Gore said to herself as she walked. After half an hour on the Ridgecrest Mountain she knew she was lost. Why did I come alone? She remembered how she'd wanted time to think, away from the noise of her group's cabin.

Don't panic, she thought, biting her lip. She had never felt lost before. She kept watching for landmarks and listening for sounds that seemed familiar. After wandering for almost an hour, she sat on a log and began to cry.

"Lord, help me out of here," she prayed.

In the distance she heard faint laughter and conversation. She wasn't completely alone! She followed the sounds until she found other campers—and the way home.

"Next time I go for a walk," she told her friends later, "I'll take a guide or a map—or both!"

The scripture describes how lost we feel when we're not following God. Hear what life is like without God in **Isaiah 63:16—64:8**.

■ How is being physically lost similar to wandering away from God, like the Israelites in the passage?
■ When have you wandered from God as the Israelites did?

CONSIDER. . .

■ creating a timeline of your life that highlights times you followed God and times you felt lost. Then ask God to help you follow him more.
■ packing a survival kit to use as you follow God. Include a list of people you could call when you run into trouble, a Bible, a Christian songbook, a journal, and a pen.

FOR MORE, SEE. . .

■ Psalm 25 (p. 496)
■ Jeremiah 18:1–10 (p. 711)
■ John 14:1–14 (p. 1083)

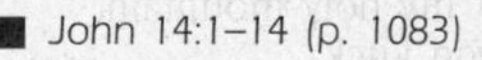

but the way they continue to live is not
good;
they do anything they want to do.
3Right in front of me
they continue to do things that make me
angry.
They offer sacrifices to their gods in their
gardens,
and they burn incense[d] on altars of brick.
4They sit among the graves
and spend their nights waiting to get
messages from the dead.
They eat the meat of pigs,
and their pots are full of soup made from
meat that is wrong to eat.
5But they tell others, 'Stay away, and don't
come near me.
I am too holy for you.'
These people are like smoke in my nose.
Like a fire that burns all the time, they
continue to make me angry.

6"Look, it is written here before me.
I will not be quiet; instead, I will repay you
in full.
I will punish you for what you have done.
7I will punish you for your sins and your
ancestors' sins,"
says the LORD.
"They burned incense to gods on the
mountains
and shamed me on those hills.
So I will punish them as they should be
punished
for what they did."

8This is what the LORD says:
"When there is juice left in the grapes,
people do not destroy them,
because they know there is good left in
them.
So I will do the same thing to my servants—
I will not completely destroy them.
9I will leave some of the children of Jacob,
and some of the people of Judah will
receive my mountain.
I will choose the people who will live there;
my servants will live there.
10Then the Plain of Sharon will be a field for
flocks,
and the Valley of Achor will be a place for
herds to rest.
They will be for the people who want to
follow me.

11"But as for you who left the LORD,
who forgot about my holy mountain,
who worship the god Luck,
who hold religious feasts for the god Fate,
12I decide your fate, and I will punish you with
my sword.
You will all be killed,
because I called you, but you refused to
answer.
I spoke to you, but you wouldn't listen.
You did the things I said were evil
and chose to do things that displease me."

13So this is what the Lord GOD says:
"My servants will eat,
but you evil people will be hungry.
My servants will drink,
but you evil people will be thirsty.
My servants will be happy,
but you evil people will be shamed.
14My servants will shout for joy
because of the goodness of their hearts,
but you evil people will cry,
because you will be sad.
You will cry loudly, because your spirits
will be broken.
15Your names will be like curses to my
servants,
and the Lord GOD will put you to death.
But he will call his servants by another
name.
16People in the land who ask for blessings
will ask for them from the faithful God.
And people in the land who make a promise
will promise in the name of the faithful
God,
because the troubles of the past will be
forgotten.
I will make those troubles go away.

A New Time Is Coming

17"Look, I will make new heavens and a new
earth,
and people will not remember the past
or think about those things.
18My people will be happy forever
because of the things I will make.
I will make a Jerusalem that is full of joy,
and I will make her people a delight.
19Then I will rejoice over Jerusalem
and be delighted with my people.
There will never again be heard in that city
the sounds of crying and sadness.
20There will never be a baby from that city
who lives only a few days.
And there will never be an older person
who doesn't have a long life.
A person who lives a hundred years will be
called young,
and a person who dies before he is a
hundred will be thought of as a sinner.

21In that city those who build houses will live
there.
Those who plant vineyards will get to eat
their grapes.
22No more will one person build a house and
someone else live there.
One person will not plant a garden and
someone else eat its fruit.
My people will live a long time,
as trees live long.
My chosen people will live there
and enjoy the things they make.
23They will never again work for nothing.
They will never again give birth to children
who die young.
All my people will be blessed by the LORD;
they and their children will be blessed.
24I will provide for their needs before they ask,
and I will help them while they are still
asking for help.
25Wolves and lambs will eat together in peace.
Lions will eat hay like oxen,
and a snake on the ground will not hurt
anyone.
They will not hurt or destroy each other
on all my holy mountain,"
says the LORD.

The Lord Will Judge All Nations

66 This is what the LORD says:
"Heaven is my throne,
and the earth is my footstool.
So do you think you can build a house for me?
Do I need a place to rest?
2My hand made all things.
All things are here because I made them,"
says the LORD.

"These are the people I am pleased with:
those who are not proud or stubborn
and who fear my word.
3But those people who kill bulls as a sacrifice
to me
are like those who kill people.
Those who kill sheep as a sacrifice
are like those who break the necks of dogs.
Those who give me grain offerings
are like those who offer me the blood of
pigs.[n]
Those who burn incense[d]
are like those who worship idols.
These people choose their own ways, not
mine,
and they love the terrible things they do.
4So I will choose their punishments,
and I will punish them with what they fear
most.
This is because I called to them, but they did
not listen.
I spoke to them, but they did not hear me.
They did things I said were evil;
they chose to do things I did not like."

5You people who obey the words of the LORD,
listen to what he says:
"Your brothers hated you
and turned against you because you
followed me.
Your brothers said, 'Let the LORD be honored
so we may see you rejoice,'
but they will be punished.
6Listen to the loud noise coming from the
city;
hear the noise from the Temple.[d]
It is the LORD punishing his enemies,
giving them the punishment they should
have.

7"A woman does not give birth before she
feels the pain;
she does not give birth to a son before the
pain starts.
8No one has ever heard of that happening;
no one has ever seen that happen.
In the same way no one ever saw a country
begin in one day;
no one has ever heard of a new nation
beginning in one moment.
But Jerusalem will give birth to her children
just as soon as she feels the birth pains.
9In the same way I will not cause pain
without allowing something new to be
born," says the LORD.
"If I cause you the pain,
I will not stop you from giving birth to
your new nation," says your God.
10"Jerusalem, rejoice.
All you people who love Jerusalem, be
happy.
Those of you who felt sad for Jerusalem
should now feel happy with her.
11You will take comfort from her and be
satisfied,
as a child is nursed by its mother.
You will receive her good things
and enjoy her wealth."
12This is what the LORD says:

"I will give her peace that will flow to her
like a river.
The wealth of the nations will come to her
like a river overflowing its banks.
Like babies you will be nursed and held in
my arms
and bounced on my knees.

dogs . . . pigs God did not want his people to offer dogs and pigs as sacrifices because they were unclean animals.

13I will comfort you
as a mother comforts her child.
You will be comforted in Jerusalem."

14When you see these things, you will be
happy,
and you will grow like the grass.
The LORD's servants will see his power,
but his enemies will see his anger.
15Look, the LORD is coming with fire
and his armies with clouds of dust.
He will punish those people with his anger;
he will punish them with flames of fire.
16The LORD will judge the people with fire,
and he will destroy many people with his
sword;
he will kill many people.

17"These people make themselves holy and
pure to go to worship their gods in their gardens.
Following each other into their special gardens,
they eat the meat of pigs and rats and other hateful things. But they will all be destroyed together," says the LORD.
18"I know they have evil thoughts and do evil
things, so I am coming to punish them. I will
gather all nations and all people, and they will
come together and see my glory.

SIDELIGHT: Isaiah is the "Bible-in-miniature." It has sixty-six chapters—as compared to sixty-six biblical books. Both Isaiah and the Bible end with "new heavens and the new earth" (Isaiah 66:22 and Revelation 21:1, p. 1347).

19"I will put a mark on some of the people, and
I will send some of these saved people to the nations: to Tarshish, Libya, Lud (the land of archers), Tubal, Greece, and all the faraway lands.
These people have never heard about what I have
done nor seen my glory. So the saved people will
tell the nations about my glory. 20And they will
bring all your fellow Israelites from all nations to
my holy mountain in Jerusalem. Your fellow Israelites will come on horses, donkeys, and camels
and in chariots and wagons. They will be like the

GOD'S LOVE

You'll Always Be My Baby

She was usually on the phone. "Come by and pick up diapers," she would say. Or, "I'll meet you at the emergency room in ten minutes." Stacks of baby clothes and cribs lined the walls of her office.

Susan Brown directed the Infant Resource Center in Louisville, Kentucky. Located near a cluster of hospitals, the center ministered to "rock-bottom poor" mothers, often in their teens. Many times the women had nothing to put their babies in when they came home from the hospital, and often they used dresser drawers for cribs. Sometimes poor prenatal care meant the babies needed emergency treatment after birth.

Susan loved the teenagers and their babies as a good mother would. She gave them basic supplies and information. She spent hours in doctors' offices and hospitals, holding the hands of scared mothers. As she cared for these women, she told them about God's love.

A new mother needs more than baby clothes and supplies. She needs the strength that comes from Christ. Susan Brown made a difference by offering young mothers that kind of strength.

God loves his people as a mother loves her children. **Isaiah 66:10–14** describes God's love and care for us.

- How did Susan demonstrate the love this passage describes?
- In what ways does God comfort and care for you?

CONSIDER . . .

- writing a thank-you note to someone who has shown you the kind of love this passage describes.
- writing a description of the "perfect" parent and then thanking God for being a perfect parent to you.

FOR MORE, SEE . . .

- Deuteronomy 32:9–12 (p. 189)
- Hosea 11:1–4 (p. 831)
- 1 John 4:7–10 (p. 1319)

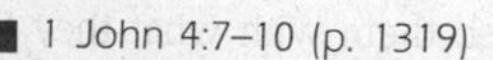

grain offerings that the people bring in clean containers to the Temple," says the LORD. 21"And I
will choose even some of these people to be
priests and Levites," says the LORD.
22"I will make new heavens and the new earth,
which will last forever," says the LORD. "In the
same way, your names and your children will always be with me. 23All people will come to worship me every Sabbath[d] and every New Moon,"[d]
says the LORD. 24"They will go out and see the
dead bodies of the people who sinned against me.
The worms that eat them will never die, and the
fires that burn them will never stop, and everyone
will hate to see those bodies."

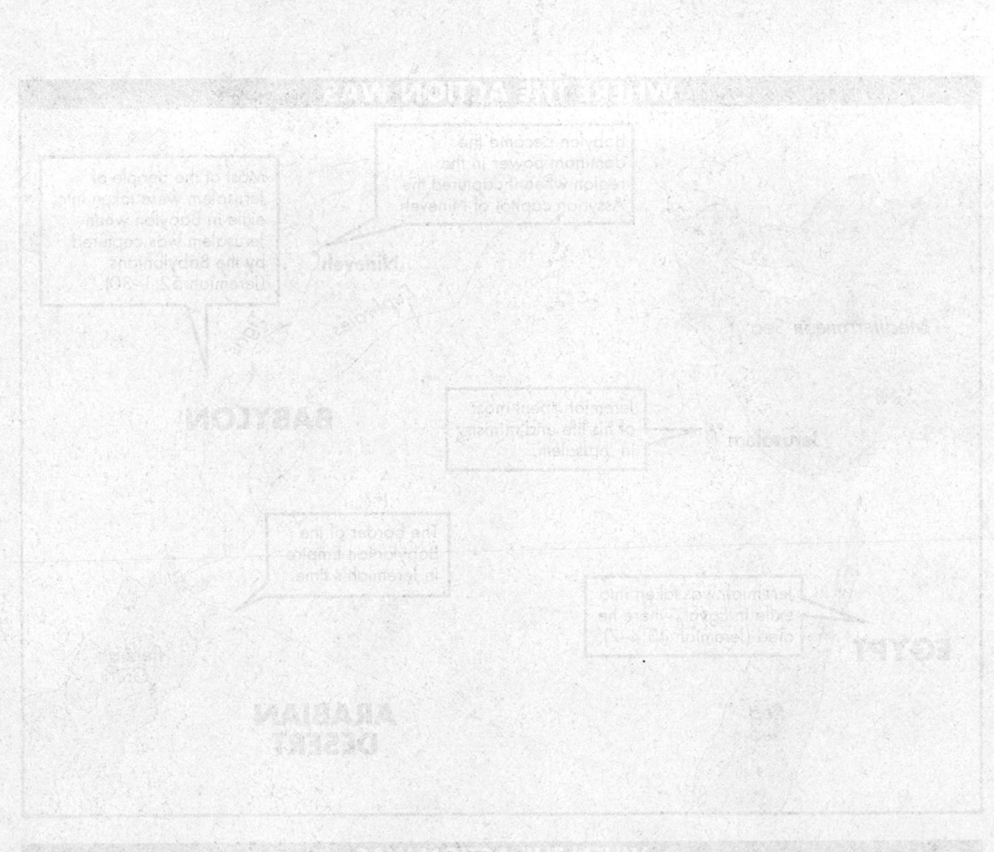

JEREMIAH

Why Read This Book:

- Learn responsibilities that come with belonging to God (Jeremiah 1—25).
- See God's continuing love for people even when they have sinned (Jeremiah 26—36).
- Find hope even in times of suffering (Jeremiah 37—45).

Behind the Scenes:

The nation of Judah was like a child caught in the crossfire between warring inner-city gangs. Like gangs fighting over turf, three world powers were fighting for control of the area we call the Near East. The Assyrians had been in control for quite a while, but the Egyptians and Babylonians would each take power within Jeremiah's lifetime. And Judah was caught in the middle.

But Judah was not like an innocent victim. Judah had stopped following God and was forming partnerships with pagan nations to try to protect itself. The people needed a word from God, and Jeremiah became the one whom God would use to proclaim that word—a word that Judah did not want to hear.

Jeremiah warned the people of Judah that they needed to obey God and rely

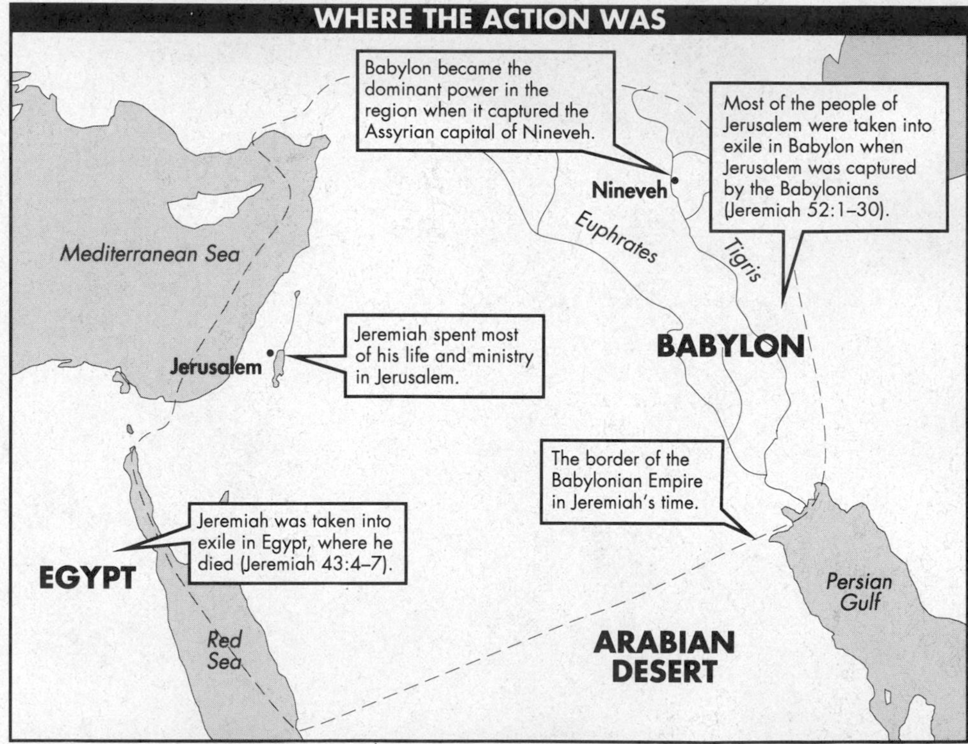

WHERE THE ACTION WAS
Babylon became the dominant power in the region when it captured the Assyrian capital of Nineveh.
Most of the people of Jerusalem were taken into exile in Babylon when Jerusalem was captured by the Babylonians (Jeremiah 52:1–30).
Nineveh
Euphrates
Tigris
Mediterranean Sea
Jeremiah spent most of his life and ministry in Jerusalem.
Jerusalem
BABYLON
The border of the Babylonian Empire in Jeremiah's time.
Jeremiah was taken into exile in Egypt, where he died (Jeremiah 43:4–7).
EGYPT
Persian Gulf
Red Sea
ARABIAN DESERT

WHEN THE ACTION WAS

The Northern Kingdom (Israel) fell to Assyria · Jeremiah began his ministry · The Jews began returning from exile · Jesus was born

1000BC · 750BC · 500BC · 250BC · BC/AD

The kingdom was split between Israel and Judah · King Josiah began reforms in Judah · Jerusalem was destroyed by the Babylonians

Behind the Scenes (cont.): on him. He condemned the false prophets and emphasized the need to repent and seek a personal relationship with God.

Jeremiah's tough message wasn't easy to accept—for Jeremiah or for the people of Judah. At first, Jeremiah was reluctant even to take the job (Jeremiah 1:6). He was abused, ridiculed, exiled to Egypt, and, in the end, possibly killed for what he said. The pain he faced and the pain he saw his people experiencing saddened him.

His book—which was dictated to his secretary Baruch (Jeremiah 36:4)—is sometimes difficult to follow. The poems (or oracles) aren't arranged in logical order. Events jump back and forth in history. To get a better feel for the historical events surrounding the book, read either 2 Kings 23—24 (p. 355) or 2 Chronicles 34—36 (p. 412).

Through poems, stories, and object lessons, the book of Jeremiah shows the personal struggles, depression, and anger Jeremiah experienced during his career. But through it all, Jeremiah continued doing the tough job he had been given. And even when he felt like giving up, he remembered that God would stand by him and comfort him.

Jeremiah was faithful to God's call—even when it was unpopular. And he was honest with God and faithful to God, even in the midst of his doubts, frustrations, and anger. His life can be a valuable model for us today.

---

1 These are the words of Jeremiah son of Hilkiah. He belonged to the family of priests
who lived in the town of Anathoth in the land of
Benjamin. 2The LORD spoke his word to Jeremiah
during the thirteenth year that Josiah son of Amon
was king of Judah. 3The LORD also spoke to Jeremiah while Jehoiakim son of Josiah was king of
Judah and during the eleven years that Zedekiah
son of Josiah was king of Judah. In the fifth month
of his last year, the people of Jerusalem were
taken away as captives.

The Lord Calls Jeremiah

4The LORD spoke his word to me, saying:
5"Before I made you in your mother's womb,
I chose you.
Before you were born, I set you apart for a
special work.
I appointed you as a prophet[d] to the
nations."

6Then I said, "But Lord GOD, I don't know how
to speak. I am only a boy."

SIDELIGHT: Jeremiah was probably about twenty years old when he began his ministry (Jeremiah 1:6). Josiah was only eight when he became king—and sixteen when he began to follow God. Youth power!

7But the LORD said to me, "Don't say, 'I am
only a boy.' You must go everywhere I send you,
and you must say everything I tell you to say.
8Don't be afraid of anyone, because I am with you
to protect you," says the LORD.
9Then the LORD reached out his hand and
touched my mouth. He said to me, "See, I am
putting my words in your mouth. 10Today I have
put you in charge of nations and kingdoms. You
will pull up and tear down, destroy and overthrow, build up and plant."

Jeremiah Sees Two Visions

11The LORD spoke his word to me, saying: "Jeremiah, what do you see?"
I answered, "I see a stick of almond wood."
12The LORD said to me, "You have seen correctly, because I am watching to make sure my
words come true."
13The LORD spoke his word to me again: "What
do you see?"
I answered, "I see a pot of boiling water, tip-
ping over from the north."
14The LORD said to me, "Disaster will come
from the north and strike all the people who live
in this country. 15In a short time I will call all of
the people in the northern kingdoms," said the
LORD.
"Those kings will come and set up their
thrones
near the entrance of the gates of Jerusalem.
They will attack all the city walls around
Jerusalem
and all the cities in Judah.
16And I will announce my judgments against
my people
because of their evil in turning away from
me.
They offered sacrifices to other gods

and worshiped idols they had made with
their own hands.

17"Jeremiah, get ready. Stand up and tell them everything I command you to say. Don't be afraid of the people, or I will give you good reason to be afraid of them. 18Today I am going to make you a strong city, an iron pillar, a bronze wall. You will be able to stand against everyone in the land: Judah's kings, officers, priests, and the people of the land. 19They will fight against you, but they will not defeat you, because I am with you to protect you!" says the LORD.

Israel Turns from God

2 The LORD spoke his word to me, saying:
2"Go and speak to the people of Jerusalem,
saying: This is what the LORD says:
'I remember how faithful you were to me
when you were a young nation.
You loved me like a young bride.
You followed me through the desert,
a land that had never been planted.
3The people of Israel were holy to the LORD,
like the first fruits from his harvest.
Those who tried to hurt Israel were judged guilty.
Disasters struck them,' " says the LORD.

4Hear the word of the LORD, family of Jacob,
all you family groups of Israel.
5This is what the LORD says:
"I was fair to your ancestors,
so why did they turn away from me?
Your ancestors worshiped useless idols
and became useless themselves.
6Your ancestors didn't say,
'Where is the LORD who brought us out of Egypt?
He led us through the desert,
through a dry and rocky land,
through a dark and dangerous land.
He led us where no one travels or lives.'
7I brought you into a fertile land

SELF-ESTEEM

The New Kid in the Group

As the newest member of the theater group, Adam Sanchez felt a little intimidated. There were good actors in the group. Plus, Adam was afraid that friendships—and cliques—had already formed and that he would be an outsider.

On top of that, people in theater learn to be very honest with their feelings, even blunt. Adam feared someone would criticize him and tell him he was a lousy actor. What if he didn't measure up?

But Adam's fears evaporated as he got involved. The group figured out pretty quickly that Adam was a good actor. People accepted him at first because of his talent, and later they accepted him as a good friend too.

Adam was a little shy about sharing his friendship with God with his newfound friends. Before long, however, he found himself in deep conversations about faith with people who hadn't really given God much thought. He invited them to church, and some went.

Although he started as an intimidated newcomer, with God's help Adam discovered his own value to the group and to God. As a result, he grew as a respected leader and a faithful witness.

Jeremiah was a young man when God first called him. Read how God responded to Jeremiah's fears and lack of self-esteem, in **Jeremiah 1:4–10**.

- Why were both Adam and Jeremiah at first fearful of what they had to do?
- When you sense that God wants you to do something, how do your feelings and thoughts compare to young Jeremiah's?

CONSIDER . . .

- writing verses 6–8 on a piece of paper and carrying it with you for times you need a confidence boost.
- giving three friends a self-esteem boost this week by telling them each a reason you like or respect them.

FOR MORE, SEE . . .

- Isaiah 6:1–8 (p. 622)
- Galatians 1:1–20 (p. 1206)
- 1 Timothy 4:12–16 (p. 1259)

so you could eat its fruit and produce.
But you came and made my land unclean;[d]
you made it a hateful place.
8The priests didn't ask,
'Where is the LORD?'
The people who know the teachings didn't
know me.
The leaders turned against me.
The prophets[d] prophesied in the name of
Baal[d]
and worshiped useless idols.

9"So now I will again tell what I have against
you," says the LORD.
"And I will tell what I have against your
grandchildren.
10Go across the sea to the island of Cyprus and
see.
Send someone to the land of Kedar to look
closely.
See if there has ever been anything like
this.
11Has a nation ever exchanged its gods?
(Of course, its gods are not really gods at
all.)
But my people have exchanged their glorious
God
for idols worth nothing.
12Skies, be shocked at the things that have
happened
and shake with great fear!" says the LORD.
13"My people have done two evils:
They have turned away from me,
the spring of living water.
And they have dug their own wells,
which are broken wells that cannot hold
water.
14Have the people of Israel become slaves?
Have they become like someone who was
born a slave?
Why were they taken captive?
15Enemies have roared like lions at Israel;
they have growled at Israel.
They have destroyed the land of Israel.
The cities of Israel lie in ruins,
and all the people have left.
16The men from the cities of Memphis and
Tahpanhes
have disgraced you by shaving the top of
your head.
17Haven't you brought this on yourselves
by turning away from the LORD your God
when he was leading you in the right
way?
18It did not help to go to Egypt
and drink from the Shihor River.
It did not help to go to Assyria
and drink from the Euphrates River.
19Your evil will bring punishment to you,
and the wrong you have done will teach
you a lesson.
Think about it and understand
that it is a terrible evil to turn away from the
LORD your God.
It is wrong not to fear me,"
says the Lord GOD All-Powerful.

20"Long ago you refused to obey me as an ox
breaks its yoke.[d]
You broke the ropes I used to hold you
and said, 'I will not serve you!'
In fact, on every high hill
and under every green tree
you lay down as a prostitute.[d]
21But I planted you as a special vine,
as a very good seed.
How then did you turn
into a wild vine that grows bad fruit?
22Although you wash yourself with cleanser
and use much soap,
I can still see the stain of your guilt," says
the Lord GOD.
23"How can you say to me, 'I am not guilty.
I have not worshiped the Baal[d] idols'?
Look at the things you did in the valley.
Think about what you have done.
You are like a she-camel in mating season
that runs from place to place.
24You are like a wild donkey that lives in the
desert
and sniffs the wind at mating time.
At that time who can hold her back?
Any male who chases her will easily catch
her;
at mating time, it is easy to find her.
25Don't run until your feet are bare
or until your throat is dry.
But you say, 'It's no use!
I love those other gods,
and I must chase them!'

26"A thief is ashamed when someone catches
him stealing.
In the same way, the family of Israel is
ashamed—
they, their kings, their officers,
their priests, and their prophets.
27They say to things of wood, 'You are my
father,'
and to idols of stone, 'You gave birth to
me.'
Those people won't look at me;
they have turned their backs to me.
But when they get into trouble, they say,
'Come and save us!'
28Where are the idols you made for yourselves?
Let them come and save you
when you are in trouble!
People of Judah, you have as many idols

as you have towns!

29"Why do you complain to me?
All of you have turned against me," says the LORD.
30"I punished your people, but it did not help.
They didn't come back when they were punished.
With your swords you killed your prophets like a hungry lion.

31"People of Judah, pay attention to the word of the LORD:
Have I been like a desert to the people of Israel
or like a dark and dangerous land?
Why do my people say, 'We are free to wander.
We won't come to you anymore'?
32A young woman does not forget her jewelry,
and a bride does not forget the decorations for her dress.
But my people have forgotten me
for more days than can be counted.
33You really know how to chase after love.
Even the worst women can learn evil ways from you.
34Even on your clothes you have the blood
of poor and innocent people,
but they weren't thieves you caught breaking in.
You do all these things,
35 but you say, 'I am innocent.
God is not angry with me.'
But I will judge you guilty of lying,
because you say, 'I have not sinned.'
36It is so easy for you to change your mind.
Even Egypt will let you down,
as Assyria let you down.
37You will eventually leave that place
with your hands on your head, like captives.
You trusted those countries,
but you will not be helped by them,
because the LORD has rejected them.

Judah Is Unfaithful

3 "If a man divorces his wife
and she leaves him and marries another man,
should her first husband come back to her again?
If he went back to her, wouldn't the land become completely unclean?[d]
But you have acted like a prostitute[d] with many lovers,
and now you want to come back to me?"
says the LORD.
2"Look up to the bare hilltops, Judah.
Is there any place where you have not been a prostitute?
You have sat by the road waiting for lovers,
like an Arab in the desert.
You made the land unclean,
because you did evil and were like a prostitute.
3So the rain has not come,
and there have not been any spring rains.
But your face still looks like the face of a prostitute.
You refuse even to be ashamed of what you did.

> **SIDELIGHT:** If you're planning a barbecue in the Middle East, most of the year you don't have to worry about getting rained out. Almost all the rain falls during spring (May) and fall (October). Since crops depended on this rain, good rains were considered a sign of God's blessing, and a lack of rain was considered a curse (Jeremiah 3:3).

4Now you are calling to me,
'My father, you have been my friend since I was young.
5Will you always be angry at me?
Will your anger last forever?'
Judah, you said this,
but you did as much evil as you could!"

Judah and Israel Are like Sisters

6When King Josiah was ruling Judah, the LORD
said to me, "Did you see what unfaithful Israel
did? She was like a prostitute[d] with her idols on
every hill and under every green tree. 7I said to
myself, 'Israel will come back to me after she does
this evil,' but she didn't come back. And Israel's
wicked sister Judah saw what she did. 8Judah saw
that I divorced unfaithful Israel because of her
adultery,[d] but that didn't make Israel's wicked sister Judah afraid. She also went out and acted like
a prostitute! 9And she didn't care that she was
acting like a prostitute. So she made her country
unclean[d] and was guilty of adultery, because she
worshiped idols made of stone and wood. 10Is-
rael's wicked sister didn't even come back to me
with her whole heart, but only pretended," says
the LORD.

11The LORD said to me, "Unfaithful Israel had
a better excuse than wicked Judah. 12Go and
speak this message toward the north:
'Come back, unfaithful people of Israel,' says the LORD.
'I will stop being angry at you,

because I am full of mercy,' says the LORD.
'I will not be angry with you forever.
13All you have to do is admit your sin—
that you turned against the LORD your God
and worshiped gods under every green tree
and didn't obey me,' " says the LORD.

14"Come back to me, you unfaithful children,"
says the LORD, "because I am your master. I will
take one person from every city and two from every family group, and I will bring you to Jerusalem. 15Then I will give you new rulers who will
be faithful to me, who will lead you with knowledge and understanding. 16In those days there
will be many of you in the land," says the LORD.
"At that time people will no longer say, 'I remember the Ark[d] of the Agreement.' They won't think
about it anymore or remember it or miss it or
make another one. 17At that time people will call
Jerusalem The Throne of the LORD, and all nations will come together in Jerusalem to show respect to the LORD. They will not follow their stubborn, evil hearts anymore. 18In those days the
family of Judah will join the family of Israel. They
will come together from a land in the north to the
land I gave their ancestors.

19"I, the LORD, said,
'How happy I would be to treat you as my
own children
and give you a pleasant land,
a land more beautiful than that of any other
nation.'
I thought you would call me 'My Father'
and not turn away from me.
20But like a woman who is unfaithful to her
husband,
family of Israel, you have been unfaithful to
me," says the LORD.

21You can hear crying on the bare hilltops.
It is the people of Israel crying and praying
for mercy.
They have become very evil
and have forgotten the LORD their God.
22"Come back to me, you unfaithful children,
and I will forgive you for being unfaithful."

"Yes, we will come to you,
because you are the LORD our God.
23It was foolish to worship idols on the hills
and on the mountains.
Surely the salvation of Israel
comes from the LORD our God.
24Since our youth, shameful gods have eaten
up in sacrifice
everything our ancestors worked for—
their flocks and herds,
their sons and daughters.
25Let us lie down in our shame,
and let our disgrace cover us like a blanket.
We have sinned against the LORD our God,
both we and our ancestors.
From our youth until now,
we have not obeyed the LORD our God."

4 "If you will return, Israel,
then return to me," says the LORD.
"If you will throw away your idols that I
hate,
then don't wander away from me.
2If you say when you make a promise,
'As surely as the LORD lives,'
and you can say it in a truthful, honest,
and right way,
then the nations will be blessed by him,
and they will praise him for what he has
done."

3This is what the LORD says to the people of
Judah and to Jerusalem:
"Plow your unplowed fields,
and don't plant seeds among thorns.
4Give yourselves to the service of the LORD,
and decide to obey him,
people of Judah and people of Jerusalem.
If you don't, my anger will spread among you
like a fire,
and no one will be able to put it out,
because of the evil you have done.

Trouble from the North

5"Announce this message in Judah and say it
in Jerusalem:
'Blow the trumpet throughout the country!'
Shout out loud and say,
'Come together!
Let's all escape to the strong, walled cities!'
6Raise the signal flag toward Jerusalem!
Run for your lives, and don't wait,
because I am bringing disaster from the
north.
There will be terrible destruction."
7A lion has come out of his den;
a destroyer of nations has begun to march.
He has left his home
to destroy your land.
Your towns will be destroyed
with no one left to live in them.
8So put on rough cloth,
show how sad you are, and cry loudly.
The terrible anger of the LORD
has not turned away from us.

9"When this happens," says the LORD,
"the king and officers will lose their
courage.
The priests will be terribly afraid,
and the prophets[d] will be shocked!"

10Then I said, "Lord GOD, you have tricked the
people of Judah and Jerusalem. You said, 'You will

have peace,' but now the sword is pointing at our throats!"

11At that time this message will be given to Judah and Jerusalem: "A hot wind blows from the bare hilltops of the desert toward the LORD's people. It is not a gentle wind to separate grain from chaff.[d] 12I feel a stronger wind than that. Now even I will announce judgments against the people of Judah."

13Look! The enemy rises up like a cloud,
and his chariots come like a tornado.
His horses are faster than eagles.
How terrible it will be for us! We are ruined!
14People of Jerusalem, clean the evil from your hearts so that you can be saved.
Don't continue making evil plans.
15A voice from Dan makes an announcement
and brings bad news from the mountains of Ephraim.
16"Report this to the nations.
Spread this news in Jerusalem:
'Invaders are coming from a faraway country,
shouting words of war against the cities of Judah.
17The enemy has surrounded Jerusalem as men guard a field,
because Judah turned against me,'" says the LORD.
18"The way you have lived and acted
has brought this trouble to you.
This is your punishment.
How terrible it is!
The pain stabs your heart!"

Jeremiah's Cry

19Oh, how I hurt! How I hurt!
I am bent over in pain.
Oh, the torture in my heart!
My heart is pounding inside me.
I cannot keep quiet,
because I have heard the sound of the trumpet.
I have heard the shouts of war.
20Disaster follows disaster;
the whole country has been destroyed.
My tents are destroyed in only a moment.
My curtains are torn down quickly.
21How long must I look at the war flag?
How long must I listen to the war trumpet?

22The LORD says, "My people are foolish.
They do not know me.
They are stupid children;
they don't understand.
They are skillful at doing evil,
but they don't know how to do good."

Disaster Is Coming

23I looked at the earth,
and it was empty and had no shape.
I looked at the sky,
and its light was gone.
24I looked at the mountains,
and they were shaking.
All the hills were trembling.
25I looked, and there were no people.
Every bird in the sky had flown away.
26I looked, and the good, rich land had become a desert.
All its towns had been destroyed
by the LORD and his great anger.

27This is what the LORD says:
"All the land will be ruined,
but I will not completely destroy it.
28So the people in the land will cry loudly,
and the sky will grow dark,
because I have spoken and will not change my mind.
I have made a decision, and I will not change it."
29At the sound of the horsemen and the archers,
all the people in the towns run away.
They hide in the thick bushes
and climb up into the rocks.
All of the cities of Judah are empty;
no one lives in them.
30Judah, you destroyed nation, what are you doing?
Why do you put on your finest dress
and decorate yourself with gold jewelry?
Why do you put color around your eyes?
You make yourself beautiful, but it is all useless.
Your lovers hate you;
they want to kill you.

31I hear a cry like a woman having a baby,
distress like a woman having her first child.
It is the sound of Jerusalem gasping for breath.
She lifts her hands in prayer and says,
"Oh! I am about to faint
before my murderers!"

No One Is Right

5 The LORD says, "Walk up and down the streets of Jerusalem.
Look around and discover these things.
Search the public squares of the city.
If you can find one person who does honest things,
who searches for the truth,
I will forgive this city.

[2]Although the people say, 'As surely as the
LORD lives!'
they don't really mean it."
[3]LORD, don't you look for truth in people?
You struck the people of Judah,
but they didn't feel any pain.
You crushed them,
but they refused to learn what is right.
They became more stubborn than a rock;
they refused to turn back to God.
[4]But I thought,
"These are only the poor, foolish people.
They have not learned the way of the LORD
and what their God wants them to do.
[5]So I will go to the leaders of Judah
and talk to them.
Surely they understand the way of the LORD
and know what God wants them to do."
But even the leaders had all joined together
to break away from the LORD;
they had broken their ties with him.
[6]So a lion from the forest will attack them.
A wolf from the desert will kill them.
A leopard is waiting for them near their
towns.
It will tear to pieces anyone who comes out
of the city,
because the people of Judah have sinned
greatly.
They have wandered away from the LORD
many times.
[7]The LORD said, "Tell me why I should forgive
you.
Your children have left me
and have made promises to idols that are
not gods at all.
I gave your children everything they needed,
but they still were like an unfaithful wife to
me.
They spent much time in houses of
prostitutes.[d]
[8]They are like well-fed horses filled with
sexual desire;
each one wants another man's wife.
[9]Shouldn't I punish the people of Judah for
doing these things?" says the LORD.
"Shouldn't I give a nation such as this the
punishment it deserves?

[10]"Go along and cut down Judah's vineyards,
but do not completely destroy them.
Cut off all her people as if they were
branches,
because they do not belong to the LORD.
[11]The families of Israel and Judah
have been completely unfaithful to me,"
says the LORD.
[12]Those people have lied about the LORD
and said, "He will not do anything to us!
Nothing bad will happen to us!
We will never see war or hunger!
[13]The prophets[d] are like an empty wind;
the word of God is not in them.
Let the bad things they say happen to
them."

[14]So this is what the LORD God All-Powerful
says:
"The people said I would not punish them.
So, the words I give you will be like fire,
and these people will be like wood that it
burns up.
[15]Listen, family of Israel," says the LORD,
"I will soon bring a nation from far away to
attack you.
It is an old nation that has lasted a long time.
The people there speak a language you do
not know;
you cannot understand what they say.
[16]Their arrows bring death.
All their people are strong warriors.
[17]They will eat your crops and your food.
They will eat your sons and daughters.
They will eat your flocks and herds.
They will eat your grapes and figs.
They will destroy with their swords
the strong, walled cities you trust.

[18]"Yet even then," says the LORD, "I will not
destroy you completely. [19]When the people of Judah ask, 'Why has the LORD our God done all
these terrible things to us?' then give them this
answer: 'You have left the LORD and served foreign idols in your own land. So now you will
serve foreigners in a land that does not belong to
you.'

[20]"Announce this message to the family of
Jacob,
and tell it to the nation of Judah:
[21]Hear this message, you foolish people who
have no sense.
They have eyes, but they don't really see.
They have ears, but they don't really listen.
[22]Surely you are afraid of me," says the LORD.
"You should shake with fear in my
presence.
I am the one who made the beaches to be a
border for the sea,
a border the water can never go past.
The waves may pound the beach, but they
can't win over it.
They may roar, but they cannot go beyond
it.
[23]But the people of Judah are stubborn and
have turned against me.
They have turned aside and gone away
from me.

24They do not say to themselves,
'We should fear the LORD our God,
who gives us autumn and spring rains in their seasons,
who makes sure we have the harvest at the right time.'
25But your evil has kept away both rain and harvest.
Your sins have kept you from enjoying good things.
26There are wicked men among my people.
Like those who make nets for catching birds,
they set their traps to catch people.
27Like cages full of birds,
their houses are full of lies.
They have become rich and powerful.
28 They have grown big and fat.
There is no end to the evil things they do.
They won't plead the case of the orphan
or help the poor be judged fairly.
29Shouldn't I punish the people of Judah for doing these things?" says the LORD.
"Shouldn't I give a nation such as this the punishment it deserves?

30"A terrible and shocking thing
has happened in the land of Judah:
31The prophets speak lies,
and the priests take power into their own hands,
and my people love it this way.
But what will you do when the end comes?

Jerusalem Is Surrounded

6 "Run for your lives, people of Benjamin!
Run away from Jerusalem!
Blow the war trumpet in the town of Tekoa!
Raise the warning flag over the town of Beth Hakkerem!
Disaster is coming from the north;
terrible destruction is coming to you.
2Jerusalem, I will destroy you,
you who are fragile and gentle.
3Shepherds with their flocks will come against Jerusalem.
They will set up their tents all around her,
each shepherd taking care of his own section."
4They say, "Get ready to fight against Jerusalem!
Get up! We will attack at noon!
But it is already getting late;
the evening shadows are growing long.
5So get up! We will attack at night.
We will destroy the strong towers of Jerusalem!"

6This is what the LORD All-Powerful says:
"Cut down the trees around Jerusalem,
and build an attack ramp to the top of its walls.
This city must be punished.
Inside it is nothing but slavery.
7Jerusalem pours out her evil
as a well pours out its water.
The sounds of violence and destruction are heard within her.
I can see the sickness and hurts of Jerusalem.
8Listen to this warning, Jerusalem,
or I will turn my back on you
and make your land an empty desert
where no one can live."

9This is what the LORD All-Powerful says:
"Gather the few people of Israel who are left alive,
as you would gather the last grapes on a grapevine.
Check each vine again,
like someone who gathers grapes."

10To whom can I speak? Whom can I warn?
Who will listen to me?
The people of Israel have closed ears,
so they cannot hear my warnings.
They don't like the word of the LORD;
they don't want to listen to it!
11But I am full of the anger of the LORD,
and I am tired of holding it in.

"Pour out my anger on the children who play in the street
and on the young men gathered together.
A husband and his wife will both be caught in his anger,
as will the very old.
12Their houses will be turned over to others,
along with their fields and wives,
because I will raise my hand
and punish the people of Judah," says the LORD.
13"Everyone, from the least important to the greatest,
is greedy for money.
Even the prophets[d] and priests
all tell lies.
14They tried to heal my people's serious injuries
as if they were small wounds.
They said, 'It's all right, it's all right.'
But really, it is not all right.
15They should be ashamed of the terrible way they act,
but they are not ashamed at all.
They don't even know how to blush about their sins.
So they will fall, along with everyone else.
They will be thrown to the ground when I punish them," says the LORD.

[16]This is what the LORD says:
"Stand where the roads cross and look.
Ask where the old way is,
where the good way is, and walk on it.
If you do, you will find rest for yourselves.
But they have said, 'We will not walk on
the good way.'
[17]I set watchmen over you
and told you, 'Listen for the sound of the
war trumpet!'
But they said, 'We will not listen.'
[18]So listen, all you nations,
and pay attention, you witnesses.
Watch what I will do to the people of
Judah.
[19]Hear this, people of the earth:
I am going to bring disaster to the people of
Judah
because of the evil they plan.
They have not listened to my messages
and have rejected my teachings.
[20]Why do you bring me offerings of incense[d]
from the land of Sheba?
Why do you bring me sweet-smelling cane
from a faraway land?
Your burnt offerings will not be accepted;
your sacrifices do not please me."

[21]So this is what the LORD says:
"I will put problems in front of Judah.
Fathers and sons will stumble over them
together.
Neighbors and friends will die."

[22]This is what the LORD says:
"Look, an army is coming
from the land of the north;
a great nation is coming
from the far sides of the earth.
[23]The soldiers carry bows and spears.
They are cruel and show no mercy.
They sound like the roaring ocean
when they ride their horses.
That army is coming lined up for battle,
ready to attack you, Jerusalem."

[24]We have heard the news about that army
and are helpless from fear.
We are gripped by our pain,
like a woman having a baby.
[25]Don't go out into the fields
or walk down the roads,
because the enemy has swords.
There is terror on every side.
[26]My people, put on rough cloth
and roll in the ashes to show how sad you
are.
Cry loudly for those who are dead,
as if your only son were dead,
because the destroyer
will soon come against us.
[27]"Jeremiah, I have made you like a worker
who tests metal,
and my people are like the ore.
You must observe their ways
and test them.
[28]All my people have turned against me and
are stubborn.
They go around telling lies about others.
They are like bronze and iron
that became covered with rust.
They all act dishonestly.
[29]The fire is fanned to make it hotter,
but the lead does not melt.
The pure metal does not come out;
the evil is not removed from my people.
[30]My people will be called rejected silver,
because the LORD has rejected them."

Jeremiah's Temple Message

7 This is the word that the LORD spoke to Jeremiah: [2]"Stand at the gate of the Temple[d] and
preach this message there:
" 'Hear the word of the LORD, all you people of
the nation of Judah! All you who come through
these gates to worship the LORD, listen to this
message! [3]This is what the LORD All-Powerful, the
God of Israel, says: Change your lives and do
what is right! Then I will let you live in this place.
[4]Don't trust the lies of people who say, "This is
the Temple of the LORD. This is the Temple of the
LORD. This is the Temple of the LORD!" [5]You must
change your lives and do what is right. Be fair to
each other. [6]You must not be hard on strangers,
orphans, and widows. Don't kill innocent people
in this place! Don't follow other gods, or they will
ruin your lives. [7]If you do these things, I will let
you live in this land that I gave to your ancestors
to keep forever.
[8]" 'But look, you are trusting lies, which is useless. [9]Will you steal and murder and be guilty of
adultery?[d] Will you falsely accuse other people?
Will you burn incense[d] to the god Baal[d] and follow other gods you have not known? [10]If you do
that, do you think you can come before me and
stand in this place where I have chosen to be worshiped? Do you think you can say, "We are safe!"
when you do all these hateful things? [11]This place
where I have chosen to be worshiped is nothing
more to you than a hideout for robbers. I have
been watching you, says the LORD.
[12]" 'You people of Judah, go now to the town
of Shiloh, where I first made a place to be worshiped. See what I did to it because of the evil
things the people of Israel had done. [13]You people
of Judah have done all these evil things too, says
the LORD. I spoke to you again and again, but you
did not listen to me. I called you, but you did not

answer. 14So I will destroy the place where I have
chosen to be worshiped in Jerusalem. You trust in
that place, which I gave to you and your ancestors, but I will destroy it just as I destroyed Shiloh.
15I will push you away from me just as I pushed
away your relatives, the people of Israel!'

16"As for you, Jeremiah, don't pray for these
people. Don't cry out for them or ask anything for
them or beg me to help them, because I will not
listen to you. 17Don't you see what they are doing
in the towns of Judah and in the streets of Jerusalem? 18The children gather wood, and the fathers
use the wood to make a fire. The women make
the dough for cakes of bread, and they offer them
to the Queen Goddess.[d] They pour out drink offerings to other gods to make me angry. 19But I
am not the one the people of Judah are really hurting, says the LORD. They are only hurting themselves and bringing shame upon themselves.

20" 'So this is what the Lord GOD says: I will
pour out my anger on this place, on people and
animals, on the trees in the field and the crops in
the ground. My anger will be like a hot fire that
no one can put out.

Obedience Is More than Sacrifice

21" 'This is what the LORD All-Powerful, the
God of Israel, says: Offer burnt offerings along
with your other sacrifices, and eat the meat yourselves! 22When I brought your ancestors out of
Egypt, I did not speak to them and give them commands only about burnt offerings and sacrifices.
23I also gave them this command: Obey me, and
I will be your God and you will be my people. Do
all that I command so that good things will happen to you. 24But your ancestors did not listen or
pay attention to me. They were stubborn and did
whatever their evil hearts wanted. They went
backward, not forward. 25Since the day your ancestors left Egypt, I have sent my servants, the
prophets, again and again to you. 26But your ancestors did not listen or pay attention to me. They
were very stubborn and did more evil than their
ancestors.'

27"Jeremiah, you will tell all these things to the
people of Judah, but they will not listen to you.
You will call to them, but they will not answer
you. 28So say to them, 'This is the nation that has
not obeyed the LORD its God. These people do

FOLLOWING GOD

No Exceptions

As one of ten prefects in her private school, Amy Harmon represents the student body to the administration. She considers her office an honor and privilege, and she tries to keep the trust of both teachers and students.

Other prefects are not as conscientious as Amy. Because of their special status, they know they can bend—even break—the school rules, and get away with it. Past prefects have been caught drinking and cheating—serious violations at Amy's school.

"Some lied their way out, and others have gotten off easy because they were prefects," she says. They see their prefect title not as an honor, but as a license to break school rules.

Like the prefects who abuse their privilege, the people in Jerusalem in Jeremiah's time thought their special status allowed them to do whatever they wanted. In **Jeremiah 7:1–15**, the prophet warns the people not to use title or status as an excuse for not following God.

- How are the other prefects' actions like the actions of the people described in the passage? How is Amy's commitment like the commitment God wants?
- In the passage, God tells the people how they must change their lives to follow him. If God were to speak to you through Jeremiah today, what might he ask you to change?

CONSIDER. . .

- listing some of the common excuses people use for not following God's commands. Then commit yourself to not using those excuses yourself.
- taking an honest inventory of what needs to change in your life. Then seek out people, groups, or programs to support your efforts to change.

FOR MORE, SEE. . .

- 1 Kings 9:1–9 (p. 314)
- Luke 3:7–9 (p. 1006)
- John 8:31–47 (p. 1072)

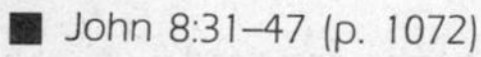

nothing when I correct them. They do not tell the truth; it has disappeared from their lips.

The Valley of Killing

29" 'Cut off your hair and throw it away. Go up
to the bare hilltop and cry out, because the LORD
has rejected these people. He has turned his back
on them, and in his anger will punish them. 30The
people of Judah have done what I said was evil,
says the LORD. They have set up their hateful idols
in the place where I have chosen to be worshiped
and have made it unclean.[d] 31The people of Judah
have built places of worship at Topheth in the
Valley of Ben Hinnom. There they burned their
own sons and daughters as sacrifices, something
I never commanded. It never even entered my
mind. 32So, I warn you. The days are coming, says
the LORD, when people will not call this place Topheth or the Valley of Ben Hinnom anymore.
They will call it the Valley of Killing. They will
bury the dead in Topheth until there is no room
to bury anyone else. 33Then the bodies of the dead
will become food for the birds of the sky and for
the wild animals. There will be no one left alive
to chase them away. 34I will end the happy sounds
of the bride and bridegroom. There will be no
happy sounds in the cities of Judah or in the
streets of Jerusalem, because the land will become
an empty desert!

8 " 'The LORD says: At that time they will remove from their tombs the bones of Judah's
kings and officers, priests and prophets,[d] and the
people of Jerusalem. 2The bones will be spread on
the ground under the sun, moon, and stars that
the people loved and served and went after and
searched for and worshiped. No one will gather
up the bones and bury them. So they will be like
dung thrown on the ground. 3I will force the people of Judah to leave their homes and their land.
Those of this evil family who are not dead will
wish they were, says the LORD All-Powerful.'

Sin and Punishment

4"Say to the people of Judah: 'This is what the LORD says:

When people fall down, don't they get up
again?
And when someone goes the wrong way,
doesn't he turn back?
5Why, then, have the people of Jerusalem
gone the wrong way
and not turned back?
They believe their own lies
and refuse to turn around and come back.
6I have listened to them very carefully,
but they do not say what is right.
They do not feel sorry about their wicked
ways,
saying, "What have I done?"
Each person goes his own way,
like a horse charging into a battle.
7Even the birds in the sky
know the right times to do things.
The storks, doves, swifts, and thrushes
know when it is time to migrate.
But my people don't know
what the LORD wants them to do.

8" 'You keep saying, "We are wise,
because we have the teachings of the
LORD."
But actually, those who explain the Scriptures
have written lies with their pens.
9These wise men refused to listen to the word
of the LORD,
so they are not really wise at all.
They will be ashamed.
They will be shocked and trapped.
10So I will give their wives to other men
and their fields to new owners.
Everyone, from the least important to the
greatest,
is greedy for money.
Even the prophets[d] and priests
all tell lies.
11They tried to heal my people's serious injuries
as if they were small wounds.
They said, "It's all right, it's all right."
But really, it is not all right.
12They should be ashamed of the terrible way
they act,
but they are not ashamed at all.
They don't even know how to blush about
their sins.
So they will fall, along with everyone else.
They will be thrown to the ground when I
punish them, says the LORD.

13" 'I will take away their crops, says the LORD.
There will be no grapes on the vine
and no figs on the fig tree.
Even the leaves will dry up and die.
I will take away what I gave them.' "

14"Why are we just sitting here?
Let's get together!
We have sinned against the LORD,
so he has given us poisoned water to drink.
Come, let's run to the strong, walled cities.
The LORD our God has decided that we
must die,
so let's die there.
15We hoped to have peace,
but nothing good has come.
We hoped for a time when he would heal
us,
but only terror has come.
16From the land of Dan,
the snorting of the enemy's horses is heard.

The ground shakes from the neighing of their large horses.
They have come and destroyed
the land and everything in it,
the city and all who live there."

17"Look! I am sending poisonous snakes to attack you.
These snakes cannot be charmed,
and they will bite you," says the LORD.

Jeremiah's Sadness

18God, you are my comfort when I am very sad
and when I am afraid.
19Listen to the sound of my people.
They cry from a faraway land:
"Isn't the LORD still in Jerusalem?
Isn't Jerusalem's king still there?"

But God says, "Why did the people make me angry by worshiping idols,
useless foreign idols?"

20And the people say, "Harvest time is over;
summer has ended,
and we have not been saved."

21Because my people are crushed, I am crushed.
I cry loudly and am afraid for them.
22Isn't there balm[d] in the land of Gilead?
Isn't there a doctor there?
So why aren't the hurts of my people healed?

SIDELIGHT: The "balm of Gilead" (Jeremiah 8:22) was a gummy substance taken from bushes in an area east of the Jordan River. As early as Genesis 37:25 (p. 43), when Joseph was sold to traders from Gilead, it was famous for its fragrant healing powers. But was it "no-sting, no-stain"?

9 I wish my head were like a spring of water
and my eyes like a fountain of tears!
Then I could cry day and night
for my people who have been killed.
2I wish I had a place in the desert—
a house where travelers spend the night—
so I could leave my people.
I could go away from them,
because they are all unfaithful to God;
they are all turning against him.

Judah's Failures

3"They use their tongues like a bow,
shooting lies from their mouths like arrows.
Lies, not truth,
have grown strong in the land.
They go from one evil thing to another.
They do not know who I am," says the LORD.
4"Watch out for your friends,
and don't trust your own relatives,
because every relative is a cheater,
and every friend tells lies about you.
5Everyone lies to his friend,
and no one speaks the truth.
The people of Judah have taught their tongues to lie.
They have become tired from sinning.
6Jeremiah, you live in the middle of lies.
With their lies the people refuse to know me," says the LORD.

7So this is what the LORD All-Powerful says:
"I will test the people of Judah as a person tests metal in a fire.
I have no other choice,
because my people have sinned.
8Their tongues are like sharp arrows.
Their mouths speak lies.
Everyone speaks nicely to his neighbor,
but he is secretly planning to attack him.
9Shouldn't I punish the people for doing this?"
says the LORD.
"Shouldn't I give a nation like this the punishment it deserves?"
10I, Jeremiah, will cry loudly for the mountains
and sing a funeral song for the empty fields.
They are empty, and no one passes through.
The mooing of cattle cannot be heard.
The birds have flown away,
and the animals are gone.

11"I, the LORD, will make the city of Jerusalem a heap of ruins,
a home for wild dogs.
I will destroy the cities of Judah
so no one can live there."

12What person is wise enough to understand
these things? Is there someone who has been
taught by the LORD who can explain them? Why
was the land ruined? Why has it been made like
an empty desert where no one goes?

13The LORD answered, "It is because Judah quit
following my teachings that I gave them. They
have not obeyed me or done what I told them to
do. 14Instead, they were stubborn and followed
the Baals,[d] as their ancestors taught them to do.
15So this is what the LORD All-Powerful, the God
of Israel, says: "I will soon make the people of
Judah eat bitter food and drink poisoned water.
16I will scatter them through other nations that
they and their ancestors never knew about. I will

chase the people of Judah with the sword until they are all killed."

[17]This is what the LORD All-Powerful says:
"Now, think about these things!
Call for the women who cry at funerals to come.
Send for those women who are good at that job.
[18]Let them come quickly
and cry loudly for us.
Then our eyes will fill with tears,
and streams of water will flow from our eyelids.
[19]The sound of loud crying is heard from Jerusalem:
'We are truly ruined!
We are truly ashamed!
We must leave our land,
because our houses are in ruins.' "

[20]Now, women of Judah, listen to the word of the LORD;
open your ears to hear the words of his mouth.
Teach your daughters how to cry loudly.
Teach one another a funeral song.
[21]Death has climbed in through our windows
and has entered our strong cities.
Death has taken away our children who play in the streets
and the young men who meet in the city squares.

[22]Say, "This is what the LORD says:
'The dead bodies of people will lie
in the open field like dung.
They will lie like grain a farmer has cut,
but there will be no one to gather them.' "

[23]This is what the LORD says:
"The wise must not brag about their wisdom.
The strong must not brag about their strength.
The rich must not brag about their money.
[24]But if someone wants to brag, let him brag
that he understands and knows me.
Let him brag that I am the LORD,
and that I am kind and fair,
and that I do things that are right on earth.
This kind of bragging pleases me," says the LORD.

[25]The LORD says, "The time is coming when I
will punish all those who are circumcised[d] only in
the flesh: [26]the people of Egypt, Judah, Edom,
Ammon, Moab, and the desert people who cut
their hair short. The men in all those countries are
not circumcised. And the whole family of Israel
does not give itself to serving me."

The Lord and the Idols

10 Family of Israel, listen to what the LORD says to you. [2]This is what he says:
"Don't live like the people from other nations,
and don't be afraid of special signs in the sky,
even though the other nations are afraid of them.
[3]The customs of other people are worth nothing.
Their idols are just wood cut from the forest,
shaped by a worker with his chisel.
[4]They decorate their idols with silver and gold.
With hammers and nails they fasten them down
so they won't fall over.
[5]Their idols are like scarecrows in melon fields;
they cannot talk.
Since they cannot walk,
they must be carried.
Do not be afraid of those idols,
because they can't hurt you,
and they can't help you either."

[6]LORD, there is no one like you.
You are great,
and your name is great and powerful.
[7]Everyone should respect you, King of the nations;
you deserve respect.
Of all the wise people among the nations
and in all the kingdoms,
none of them is as wise as you.
[8]Those wise people are stupid and foolish.
Their teachings come from worthless wooden idols.
[9]Hammered silver is brought from Tarshish
and gold from Uphaz,
so the idols are made by craftsmen and goldsmiths.
They put blue and purple clothes on the idols.
All these things are made by skilled workers.
[10]But the LORD is the only true God.
He is the only living God, the King forever.
The earth shakes when he is angry,
and the nations cannot stand up to his anger.

[11]"Tell them this message: 'These gods did not
make heaven and earth; they will be destroyed
and disappear from heaven and earth.' "

[12]God made the earth by his power.
He used his wisdom to build the world

and his understanding to stretch out the skies.
13When he thunders, the waters in the skies roar.
He makes clouds rise in the sky all over the earth.
He sends lightning with the rain
and brings out the wind from his storehouses.

14People are so stupid and know so little.
Goldsmiths are made ashamed by their idols,
because those statues are only false gods.
They have no breath in them.
15They are worth nothing; people make fun of them.
When they are judged, they will be destroyed.
16But God, who is Jacob's Portion,[d] is not like the idols.
He made everything,
and he chose Israel to be his special people.
The LORD All-Powerful is his name.

Destruction Is Coming

17Get everything you own and prepare to leave,
you people who are trapped by your enemies.
18This is what the LORD says:
"At this time I will throw out the people
who live in this land.
I will bring trouble to them
so that they may be captured."
19How terrible it will be for me because of my injury.
My wound cannot be healed.
Yet I told myself,
"This is my sickness; I must suffer through it."
20My tent is ruined,
and all its ropes are broken.
My children have gone away and left me.
No one is left to put up my tent again
or to set up a shelter for me.
21The shepherds are stupid
and don't ask the LORD for advice.
So they do not have success,
and all their flocks are scattered and lost.
22Listen! The news is coming.
A loud noise comes from the north
to make the towns of Judah an empty desert
and a home for wild dogs!

Jeremiah's Prayer

23LORD, I know that a person's life doesn't really belong to him.
No one can control his own life.
24LORD, correct me, but be fair.
Don't punish me in your anger,
or you will destroy me.
25Pour out your anger on other nations
that do not know you
and do not pray to you.
Those nations have destroyed Jacob's family.
They have eaten him up completely
and destroyed his homeland.

The Agreement Is Broken

11 These are the words that the LORD spoke
to Jeremiah: 2"Listen to the words of this
agreement and tell them to the people of Judah
and those living in Jerusalem. 3Tell them this is
what the LORD, the God of Israel, says: 'Cursed
is the person who does not obey the words of this
agreement 4that I made with your ancestors when
I brought them out of Egypt. Egypt was like a furnace for melting iron!' I told them, 'Obey me and
do everything I command you. Then you will be
my people, and I will be your God. 5Then I will
keep the promise I made to your ancestors to give
them a fertile land.' And you are living in that
country today."
I answered, "Amen, LORD."
6The LORD said to me, "Announce[d] this message in the towns of Judah and in the streets of
Jerusalem: 'Listen to the words of this agreement
and obey them. 7I warned your ancestors to obey
me when I brought them out of Egypt. I have
warned them again and again to this very day:
"Obey me!" 8But your ancestors did not listen to
me. They were stubborn and did what their own
evil hearts wanted. So I made all the curses of this
agreement come upon them. I commanded them
to obey the agreement, but they did not.'"
9Then the LORD said to me, "I know the people
of Judah and those living in Jerusalem have made
secret plans. 10They have gone back to the same
sins their ancestors did. Their ancestors refused to
listen to my message and followed and worshiped
other gods instead. The families of Israel and Judah have broken the agreement I made with their
ancestors. 11So this is what the LORD says: 'I will
soon bring a disaster on the people of Judah which
they will not be able to escape. They will cry to
me for help, but I will not listen to them. 12The
people living in the towns of Judah and the city
of Jerusalem will pray to their idols to whom they
burn incense.[d] But those idols will not be able to
help when disaster comes. 13Look, people of Judah, you have as many idols as there are towns in
Judah. You have built as many altars to burn incense to that shameful god Baal[d] as there are
streets in Jerusalem.'
14"As for you, Jeremiah, don't pray for these
people or cry out for them or ask anything for
them. I will not listen when they call to me in the
time of their trouble.

15"What is my beloved Judah doing in my
Temple[d]
when she makes many evil plans?
Do you think animal sacrifices will stop
your punishment?
When you do your evil, then you are happy."
16The LORD called you "a leafy olive tree,
with beautiful fruit and shape."
But with the roar of a strong storm
he will set that tree on fire,
and its branches will be burned up.

17The LORD All-Powerful, who planted you, has
announced that disaster will come to you. This is
because the families of Israel and Judah have done
evil and have made him angry by burning incense
to Baal.

Evil Plans Against Jeremiah

18The LORD showed me that men were making
plans against me. Because he showed me what
they were doing, I knew they were against me.
19Before this, I was like a gentle lamb waiting to
be butchered. I did not know they had made
plans against me, saying:
"Let us destroy the tree and its fruit.
Let's kill him so people will forget him."
20But, LORD All-Powerful, you are a fair judge.
You know how to test peoples' hearts and
minds.
I have told you what I have against them.
So let me see you give them the
punishment they deserve.

21So the LORD speaks about the men from Anathoth who plan to kill Jeremiah and say, "Don't
prophesy[d] in the name of the LORD, or we will kill
you!" 22So this is what the LORD All-Powerful
says: "I will soon punish the men from Anathoth.
Their young men will die in war. Their sons and
daughters will die from hunger. 23No one from
the city of Anathoth will be left alive, because I
will cause a disaster to happen to them that year."

Jeremiah's First Complaint

12 LORD, when I bring my case to you,
you are always right.
But I want to ask you about the justice you
give.
Why are evil people successful?
Why do dishonest people have such easy
lives?
2You have put the evil people here
like plants with strong roots.
They grow and produce fruit.
With their mouths they speak well of you,
but their hearts are really far away from
you.
3But you know my heart, LORD.
You see me and test my thoughts about
you.
Drag the evil people away like sheep to be
butchered.
Set them aside for the day of killing.
4How much longer will the land stay dried up
and the grass in every field be dead?
The animals and birds in the land have died,
because the people are evil.
Yes, they are even saying,
"God does not see what happens to us."

SIDELIGHT: How would you like to have a complaint named after you? Jeremiah's protesting to God (Jeremiah 12:1–4) made its way into the dictionary as a "jeremiad"—"a lamentation or tale of woe."

The Lord's Answer to Jeremiah

5"If you get tired while racing against people,
how can you race against horses?
If you stumble in a country that is safe,
what will you do in the thick thornbushes
along the Jordan River?
6Even your own brothers and members of
your own family
are making plans against you.
They are crying out against you.
Don't trust them,
even when they say nice things to you!

7"I have left Israel;
I have left my people.
I have given the people I love
over to their enemies.
8My people have become to me
like a lion in the forest.
They roar at me,
so I hate them.
9My people have become to me
like a speckled bird attacked on all sides by
hawks.
Go, gather the wild animals.
Bring them to get something to eat.
10Many shepherds have ruined my vineyards
and trampled the plants in my field.
They have turned my beautiful field
into an empty desert.
11They have turned my field into a desert
that is wilted and dead.
The whole country is an empty desert,
because no one who lives there cares.
12Many soldiers have marched over those
barren hills.
The LORD is using the armies to punish that
land

from one end to the other.
No one is safe.
13The people have planted wheat,
but they have harvested only thorns.
They have worked hard until they were very
tired,
but they have nothing for all their work.
They are ashamed of their poor harvest,
because the LORD's terrible anger has
caused this."

14This is what the LORD said to me: "Here is
what I will do to all my wicked neighbors who
take the land I gave my people Israel. I will pull
them up and throw them out of their land. And
I will pull up the people of Judah from among
them. 15But after I pull them up, I will feel sorry
for them again. I will bring each person back to
his own property and to his own land. 16I want
them to learn their lessons well. In the past they
taught my people to swear by Baal's[d] name. But
if they will now learn to swear by my name, saying 'As surely as the LORD lives . . .' I will allow
them to rebuild among my people. 17But if a nation will not listen to my message, I will pull it up
completely and destroy it," says the LORD.

Jeremiah's Linen Belt

13 This is what the LORD said to me: "Go
and buy a linen belt and put it around
your waist. Don't let the belt get wet."

2So I bought a linen belt, just as the LORD told
me, and put it around my waist. 3Then the LORD
spoke his word to me a second time: 4"Take the
belt you bought and are wearing, and go to Perath. Hide the belt there in a crack in the rocks."
5So I went to Perath and hid the belt there, just
as the LORD told me.

6Many days later the LORD said to me, "Now
go to Perath and get the belt I told you to hide
there." 7So I went to Perath and dug up the belt
and took it from where I had hidden it. But now
it was ruined; it was good for nothing.

8Then the LORD spoke his word to me. 9This is
what the LORD said: "In the same way I will ruin
the pride of the people of Judah and the great
pride of Jerusalem. 10These evil people refuse to
listen to my warnings. They stubbornly do only
what they want to do, and they follow other gods
to serve and worship them. So they will become
like this linen belt—good for nothing. 11As a belt
is wrapped tightly around a person's waist, I
wrapped the families of Israel and Judah around
me," says the LORD. "I did that so they would be
my people and bring fame, praise, and honor to
me. But my people would not listen.

Warnings About Leather Wine Bags

12"Say to them: 'This is what the LORD, the
God of Israel, says: All leather bags for holding
wine should be filled with wine.' People will say
to you: 'Of course, we know all wine bags should
be filled with wine.' 13Then you will say to them,

> **SIDELIGHT:** If Jeremiah were around today, he might get the "Teacher of the Year" award for his creative techniques. Check out his innovative teaching methods in Jeremiah 13:1–11; 19:1–15 (p. 712) and 32:1–15 (p. 728).

'This is what the LORD says: I will make everyone
in this land like a drunken person—the kings
who sit on David's throne, the priests and the
prophets,[d] and all the people who live in Jerusalem. 14I will make them smash against one another, fathers and sons alike, says the LORD. I will
not feel sorry or have pity on them or show mercy
that would stop me from destroying them.' "

Threat of Slavery

15Listen and pay attention.
Don't be too proud,
because the LORD has spoken to you.
16Give glory to the LORD your God
before he brings darkness
and before you slip and fall
on the dark hills.
You hope for light,
but he will turn it into thick darkness;
he will change it into deep gloom.
17If you don't listen to him,
I will cry secretly
because of your pride.
I will cry painfully,
and my eyes will overflow with tears,
because the LORD's people will be captured.

18Tell this to the king and the queen mother:
"Come down from your thrones,
because your beautiful crowns
have fallen from your heads."
19The cities of southern Judah are locked up,
and no one can open them.
All Judah will be taken as captives to a
foreign land;
they will be carried away completely.

20Jerusalem, look up and see
the people coming from the north.
Where is the flock God gave you to care for,
the flock you bragged about?
21What will you say when they appoint as your
heads
those you had thought were your friends?
Won't you have much pain and trouble,

like a woman giving birth to a baby?
22You might ask yourself,
"Why has this happened to me?"
It happened because of your many sins.
Because of your sins, your skirt was torn off
and your body has been treated badly.
23Can a person from Cush change the color of his skin?
Can a leopard change his spots?
In the same way, Jerusalem, you cannot change and do good,
because you are accustomed to doing evil.

24"I will scatter you like chaff[d] that is blown away by the desert wind.
25This is what will happen to you;
this is your part in my plans," says the LORD.
"Because you forgot me
and trusted in false gods,
26I will pull your skirts up over your face
so everyone will see your shame.
27I have seen the terrible things you have done:
your acts of adultery[d] and your snorting,
your prostitution,[d]
your hateful acts
on the hills and in the fields.
How terrible it will be for you, Jerusalem.
How long will you continue being unclean?"[d]

A Time Without Rain

14 These are the words that the LORD spoke to Jeremiah about the time when there was no rain:
2"The nation of Judah cries as if someone has died,
and her cities are very sad.
They are distressed over the land.
A cry goes up to God from Jerusalem.
3The important men send their servants to get water.
They go to the wells,
but they find no water.
So they return with empty jars.
They are ashamed and embarrassed
and cover their heads in shame.
4The ground is dry and cracked open,
because no rain falls on the land.
The farmers are upset and sad,
so they cover their heads in shame.
5Even the mother deer in the field
leaves her newborn fawn to die,
because there is no grass.
6Wild donkeys stand on the bare hills
and sniff the wind like wild dogs.
But their eyes go blind,
because there is no food."

7We know that we suffer because of our sins.
LORD, do something to help us for the good of your name.
We have left you many times;
we have sinned against you.
8God, the Hope of Israel,
you have saved Israel in times of trouble.
Why are you like a stranger in the land,
or like a traveler who only stays one night?
9Why are you like someone who has been attacked by surprise,
like a warrior who is not able to save anyone?
But you are among us, LORD,
and we are called by your name
so don't leave us without help!

10This is what the LORD says about the people
of Judah:
"They really love to wander from me;
they don't stop themselves from leaving me.
So now the LORD will not accept them.
He will now remember the evil they do
and will punish them for their sins."

11Then the LORD said, "Don't pray for good
things to happen to the people of Judah. 12Even if
they give up eating, I will not listen to their
prayers. Even if they offer burnt offerings and
grain offerings to me, I will not accept them. Instead, I will destroy the people of Judah with war,
hunger, and terrible diseases."

13But I said, "Oh, Lord GOD, the prophets[d]
keep telling the people, 'You will not suffer from
an enemy's sword or from hunger. I, the LORD,
will give you peace in this land.' "

14Then the LORD said to me, "Those prophets
are prophesying lies in my name. I did not send
them or appoint them or speak to them. They
have been prophesying false visions, idolatries,
worthless magic, and their own wishful thinking.
15So this is what I say about the prophets who are
prophesying in my name. I did not send them.
They say, 'No enemy will attack this country with
swords. There will never be hunger in this land.'
So those prophets will die from hunger and from
an enemy's sword. 16And the people to whom the
prophets speak will be thrown into the streets of
Jerusalem. There they will die from hunger and
from an enemy's sword. And no one will be there
to bury them, or their wives, or their sons, or their
daughters. I will punish them.

17"Jeremiah, speak this message to the people
of Judah:
'Let my eyes be filled with tears
night and day, without stopping.
My people have received a terrible blow;
they have been hurt badly.
18If I go into the country,

I see people killed by swords.
If I go into the city,
I see much sickness, because the people have no food.
Both the priests and the prophets
have been taken to a foreign land.' "

19LORD, have you completely rejected the nation of Judah?
Do you hate Jerusalem?
Why have you hurt us so badly
that we cannot be made well again?
We hoped for peace,
but nothing good has come.
We looked for a time of healing,
but only terror came.
20LORD, we admit that we are wicked
and that our ancestors did evil things.
We have sinned against you.
21For your sake, do not hate us.
Do not take away the honor from your glorious throne.
Remember your agreement with us,
and do not break it.
22Do foreign idols have the power to bring rain?
Does the sky itself have the power to send down showers?
No, it is you, LORD our God.
You are our only hope,
because you are the one who made all these things.

15 Then the LORD said to me: "I would not
feel sorry for the people of Judah even if
Moses and Samuel prayed for them. Send them
away from me! Tell them to go! 2When they ask
you, 'Where will we go?' tell them: 'This is what
the LORD says:
Those who are meant to die
will die.
Those who are meant to die in war
will die in war.
Those who are meant to die from hunger
will die from hunger.
Those who are meant to be taken captive
will be taken captive.'

3"I will send four kinds of destroyers against
them," says the LORD. "I will send war to kill,
dogs to drag the bodies away, and the birds of the
air and wild animals to eat and destroy the bodies.
4I will make the people of Judah hated by everyone on earth because of what Manasseh did in
Jerusalem. (Manasseh son of Hezekiah was king
of the nation of Judah.)

5"Who will feel sorry for you, Jerusalem?
Who will be sad and cry for you?
Who will go out of his way to ask how you are?
6Jerusalem, you have left me," says the LORD.
"You keep going farther and farther away,
so I have taken hold of you and destroyed you.
I was tired of holding back my anger.
7I have separated the people of Judah with my pitchfork
and scattered them at the city gates of the land.
My people haven't changed their ways.
So I have destroyed them
and taken away their children.
8There are more widows than grains of sand in the sea.
I brought a destroyer at noontime
against the mothers of the young men of Judah.
I suddenly brought pain and fear
on the people of Judah.
9When the enemy attacked, a woman with seven sons felt faint because they would all die.
She became weak and unable to breathe.
Her bright day became dark from sadness.
She felt shame and disgrace.
And everyone else left alive in Judah
I will hand over to the enemies, too!" says the LORD.

Jeremiah's Second Complaint

10Mother, I am sorry that you gave birth to me
since I must accuse and criticize the whole land.
I have not loaned or borrowed anything,
but everyone curses me.
11The LORD said,
"I have saved you for a good reason.
I have made your enemies beg you
in times of disaster and trouble.
12No one can smash a piece of iron or bronze
that comes from the north.
13Your wealth and treasures
I will give to others free of charge,
because the people of Judah have sinned
throughout the country.
14I will make you slaves to your enemies
in a land you have never known.
My anger is like a hot fire,
and it will burn against you."

15LORD, you understand.
Remember me and take care of me.
Punish for me those who are hurting me.
Don't destroy me while you remain patient with them.
Think about the shame I suffer for you.
16Your words came to me, and I listened carefully to them.

Your words made me very happy,
because I am called by your name,
LORD God All-Powerful.
[17]I never sat with the crowd
as they laughed and had fun.
I sat by myself, because you were there,
and you filled me with anger at the evil
around me.
[18]I don't understand why my pain has no end.
I don't understand why my injury is not
cured or healed.
Will you be like a brook that goes dry?
Will you be like a spring that stops flowing?

SIDELIGHT: Reading Jeremiah is like cracking open a diary full of private anguish and loud weeping (for example, see Jeremiah 15:10–18 and 20:7–18, p. 713). No wonder Jeremiah became known as the "weeping prophet."

[19]So this is what the LORD says:
"If you change your heart and return to me, I
will take you back.
Then you may serve me.
And if you speak things that have worth,
not useless words,
then you may speak for me.
Let the people of Judah turn to you,
but you must not change and be like them.
[20]I will make you as strong as a wall to this
people,
as strong as a wall of bronze.
They will fight against you,
but they will not defeat you,
because I am with you.
I will rescue you and save you," says the
LORD.
[21]"I will save you from these wicked people
and rescue you from these cruel people."

The Day of Disaster

16 Then the LORD spoke his word to me:
[2]"You must not get married or have sons
or daughters in this place."
[3]The LORD says this about the sons and daughters born in this land and their mothers and fathers: [4]"They will die of terrible diseases, and no
one will cry for them or bury them. Their bodies
will lie on the ground like dung. They will die in
war, or they will starve to death. Their bodies will
be food for the birds of the sky and for the wild
animals."
[5]So this is what the LORD says: "Jeremiah, do
not go into a house where there is a funeral meal.
Do not go there to cry for the dead or to show
your sorrow for them, because I have taken back
my blessing, my love, and my pity from these people," says the LORD. [6]"Important people and common people will die in the land of Judah. No one
will bury them or cry for them or cut himself
or shave his head to show sorrow for them. [7]No
one will bring food to comfort those who are
crying for the dead. No one will offer a drink to
comfort someone whose mother or father has
died.
[8]"Do not go into a house where the people are
having a feast to sit down to eat and drink, [9]be-
cause this is what the LORD All-Powerful, the God
of Israel, says: I will soon stop the sounds of joy
and gladness and the happy sounds of brides and
bridegrooms in this place. This will happen during
your lifetime.
[10]"When you tell the people of Judah these
things, they will ask you, 'Why has the LORD said
these terrible things to us? What have we done
wrong? What sin have we done against the LORD
our God?'
[11]"Then say to them: 'This is because your ancestors quit following me,' says the LORD. 'And
they followed other gods and served and worshiped them. Your ancestors left me and quit
obeying my teaching. [12]But you have done even
more evil than your ancestors. You are very stubborn and do only what you want to do; you have
not obeyed me. [13]So I will throw you out of this
country and send you into a land that you and
your ancestors never knew. There you can serve
other gods day and night, because I will not help
you or show you any favors.'
[14]"People say, 'As surely as the LORD lives, who
brought the people of Israel out of Egypt . . .'
But the time is coming," says the LORD, "when
people will not say this anymore. [15]They will say
instead, 'As surely as the LORD lives, who brought
the Israelites from the northern land and from all
the countries where he had sent them . . .'
And I will bring them back to the land I gave
to their ancestors.
[16]"I will soon send for many fishermen to come
to this land," says the LORD. "And they will catch
the people of Judah. After that, I will send for
many hunters to come to this land. And they will
hunt the people of Judah on every mountain and
hill and in the cracks of the rocks. [17]I see everything they do. They cannot hide from me the
things they do; their sin is not hidden from my
eyes. [18]I will pay back the people of Judah twice
for every one of their sins, because they have
made my land unclean.[d] They have filled my
country with their hateful idols."

19LORD, you are my strength and my
protection,
my safe place in times of trouble.
The nations will come to you from all over
the world
and say, "Our ancestors had only false
gods,
useless idols that didn't help them.
20Can people make gods for themselves?
They will not really be gods!"

21The LORD says, "So I will teach those who
make idols.
This time I will teach them
about my power and my strength.
Then they will know
that my name is the LORD.

Judah's Guilty Heart

17 "The sin of the people of Judah is
written with an iron tool.
Their sins were cut with a hard point into
the stone that is their hearts.
Their sins were cut into the corners of their
altars.
2Even their children remember
their altars to idols and their Asherah[d] idols
beside the green trees
and on the high hills.
3My mountain in the open country
and your wealth and treasures
I will give away to other people.
I will give away the places of worship in
your country,
because you sinned by worshiping there.
4You will lose the land I gave you,
and it is your own fault.
I will let your enemies take you as their
slaves
to a land you have never known.
This is because you have made my anger
burn like a hot fire,
and it will burn forever."

Trusting in Humans or God

5This is what the LORD says:
"A curse is placed on those who trust other
people,
who depend on humans for strength,
who have stopped trusting the LORD.
6They are like a bush in a desert
that grows in a land where no one lives,
a hot and dry land with bad soil.
They don't know about the good things God
can give.

DECISION MAKING

What Do You Believe?

The book Walden Two tells about scientists who pulled a trick on some sheep. First, they fenced them in with an electrified wire. The sheep figured out pretty quickly that they should stay away from the wire.

Then the scientists replaced the wire with a piece of string. Not knowing the difference, the sheep stayed away from the string too. They even taught their young to stay away from the string. The young sheep believed that the string was dangerous, because that's what the older sheep taught them.

Humans may not believe in electrified string, but we surely listen to a lot of things other people tell us. God warns us to put our trust in him, not in other people. He used Jeremiah to warn the people of Israel to trust in him and not be led astray by other people. Read about it in **Jeremiah 17:5–8**.

- How are the sheep in the experiment like the people described in this passage?
- According to this passage, how should you evaluate others' advice so that you don't end up hurting yourself and others?

CONSIDER . . .

- listening to your favorite radio station and writing down the messages you hear in several songs. Do you trust those messages?
- keeping a list this week of the messages you hear about yourself from your friends (for example, "you're pretty," "you're a clown," "you're strange") and deciding if you agree with those messages.

FOR MORE, SEE . . .

- Exodus 32:1–35 (p. 89)
- Psalm 146:3–6 (p. 563)
- 2 Corinthians 11:12–15 (p. 1202)

7“But the person who trusts in the LORD will
be blessed.
The LORD will show him that he can be
trusted.
8He will be strong, like a tree planted near
water
that sends its roots by a stream.
It is not afraid when the days are hot;
its leaves are always green.
It does not worry in a year when no rain
comes;
it always produces fruit.

9“More than anything else, a person's mind is
evil
and cannot be healed.
No one truly understands it.
10But I, the LORD, look into a person's heart
and test the mind.
So I can decide what each one deserves;
I can give each one the right payment for
what he does.”

11Like a bird hatching an egg it did not lay,
so are the people who get rich by cheating.
When their lives are half finished, they will
lose their riches.
At the end of their lives, it will be clear
they were fools.

12From the beginning, our Temple[d] has been
honored
as a glorious throne for God.
13LORD, hope of Israel,
those who leave you will be shamed.
People who quit following the LORD will be
like a name written in the dust,
because they have left the LORD, the spring
of living water.

Jeremiah's Third Complaint

14LORD, heal me, and I will truly be healed.
Save me, and I will truly be saved.
You are the one I praise.
15The people of Judah keep asking me,
“Where is the word from the LORD?
Let's see that message come true!”
16LORD, I didn't run away from being the
shepherd you wanted.
I didn't want the terrible day to come.
You know everything I have said;
you see all that is happening.
17Don't be a terror to me.
I run to you for safety in times of trouble.
18Make those who are hurting me be ashamed,
but don't bring shame to me.
Let them be terrified,
but keep me from terror.
Bring the day of disaster on my enemies.
Destroy them, and destroy them again.

Keeping the Sabbath Holy

19This is what the LORD said to me: “Go and
stand at the People's Gate of Jerusalem, where
the kings of Judah go in and out. And then go to
all the other gates of Jerusalem. 20Say to them
there: ‘Hear the word of the LORD, kings of Judah,
all you people of Judah, and all who live in Jerusalem, who come through these gates into the city.
21This is what the LORD says: Be careful not to
carry a load on the Sabbath[d] day or bring it
through the gates of Jerusalem. 22Don't take a
load out of your houses on the Sabbath or do any
work on that day. But keep the Sabbath as a holy
day, as I commanded your ancestors. 23But your
ancestors did not listen or pay attention to me.
They were very stubborn and did not listen. I punished them, but it didn't do any good. 24But you
must be careful to obey me, says the LORD. You
must not bring a load through the gates of Jerusalem on the Sabbath, but you must keep the Sabbath as a holy day and not do any work on that
day.
25“ ‘If you obey this command, kings who sit on
David's throne will come through the gates of Jerusalem with their officers. They will come riding
in chariots and on horses, along with the people
of Judah and Jerusalem. And the city of Jerusalem
will have people living in it forever. 26People will
come to Jerusalem from the villages around it,
from the towns of Judah, from the land of Benjamin, from the western hills, from the mountains,
and from southern Judah. They will all bring to
the Temple[d] of the LORD burnt offerings, sacrifices, grain offerings, incense,[d] and offerings to
show thanks to God. 27But you must obey me and
keep the Sabbath day as a holy day. You must not
carry any loads into Jerusalem on the Sabbath. If
you don't obey me, I will start a fire at the gates
of Jerusalem, and it will burn until it burns even
the strong towers. And it will not be put out.’ ”

The Potter and the Clay

18 This is the word the LORD spoke to Jeremiah: 2“Go down to the potter's house,
and I will give you my message there.” 3So I went
down to the potter's house and saw him working
at the potter's wheel. 4He was using his hands to
make a pot from clay, but something went wrong
with it. So he used that clay to make another pot
the way he wanted it to be.
5Then the LORD spoke his word to me: 6“Family of Israel, can't I do the same thing with you?”
says the LORD. “You are in my hands like the clay
in the potter's hands. 7There may come a time
when I will speak about a nation or a kingdom
that I will pull up by its roots or that I will pull
down to destroy it. 8But if the people of that nation stop doing the evil they have done, I will

change my mind and not carry out my plans to
bring disaster to them. 9There may come another
time when I will speak about a nation that I will
build up and plant. 10But if I see it doing evil by
not obeying me, I will change my mind and not
carry out my plans to do good for them.

> **SIDELIGHT:** The potter (Jeremiah 18:1–4) had an important job in the ancient world. Pottery was preferred over leather or baskets, because it lasted longer, held liquids better, and protected things from animals and insects. Even broken pottery was useful. People etched notes on it because leather and papyrus—the paper of the day—were too expensive.

11"So, say this to the people of Judah and those
who live in Jerusalem: 'This is what the LORD
says: I am preparing disaster for you and making
plans against you. So stop doing evil. Change your
ways and do what is right.' 12But the people of
Judah will answer, 'It won't do any good to try!
We will continue to do what we want. Each of us
will do what his stubborn, evil heart wants!' "

13So this is what the LORD says:
"Ask the people in other nations this
 question:
'Have you ever heard anything like this?'
The people of Israel have done a horrible
 thing.
14The snow on the mountains of Lebanon
 never melts from the rocks.
Its cool, flowing streams
 do not dry up.
15But my people have forgotten me.
 They burn incense to worthless idols
and have stumbled in what they do
 and in the old ways of their ancestors.
They walk along back roads
 and on poor highways.
16So Judah's country will become an empty
 desert.
People will not stop making fun of it.
They will shake their heads as they pass by;
 they will be shocked at how the country
 was destroyed.
17Like a strong east wind,
 I will scatter them before their enemies.
At that awful time they will not see me
 coming to help them;
 they will see me leaving."

Jeremiah's Fourth Complaint

18Then the people said, "Come, let's make
plans against Jeremiah. Surely the teaching of the
law by the priest will not be lost. We will still have
the advice from the wise men and the words of
the prophets.[d] So let's ruin him by telling lies
about him. We won't pay attention to anything he
says."

19LORD, listen to me.
 Listen to what my accusers are saying!
20Good should not be paid back with evil,
 but they have dug a pit in order to kill me.
Remember that I stood before you
 and asked you to do good things for these
 people
 and to turn your anger away from them.
21So now, let their children starve,
 and let their enemies kill them with
 swords.
Let their wives lose their children and
 husbands.
 Let the men from Judah be put to death
 and the young men be killed with swords
 in battle.
22Let them cry out in their houses
 when you bring an enemy against them
 suddenly.
Let all this happen, because my enemies have
 dug a pit to capture me
 and have hidden traps for my feet.
23LORD, you know
 about all their plans to kill me.
Don't forgive their crimes
 or erase their sins from your mind.
Make them fall from their places;
 punish them while you are angry.

Judah Is like a Broken Jar

19 This is what the LORD said to me: "Go
and buy a clay jar from a potter. 2Take
some of the older leaders of the people and the
priests, and go out to the Valley of Ben Hinnom,
near the front of the Potsherd Gate. There speak
the words I tell you. 3Say, 'Kings of Judah and
people of Jerusalem, listen to this message from
the LORD. This is what the LORD All-Powerful, the
God of Israel, says: I will soon bring a disaster on
this place that will amaze and frighten everyone
who hears about it. 4The people of Judah have
quit following me. They have made this a place
for foreign gods. They have burned sacrifices to
other gods that neither they, nor their ancestors,
nor the kings of Judah had ever known before.
They filled this place with the blood of innocent
people. 5They have built places on hilltops to worship Baal,[d] where they burn their children in the
fire to Baal. That is something I did not command
or speak about; it never even entered my mind.
6Now people call this place the Valley of Ben Hinnom or Topheth, but the days are coming, says

the LORD, when people will call it the Valley of
Killing.
7“ ‘At this place I will ruin the plans of the people of Judah and Jerusalem. The enemy will chase
them, and I will have them killed with swords. I
will make their dead bodies food for the birds and
wild animals. 8I will completely destroy this city.
People will make fun of it and shake their heads
when they pass by. They will be shocked when
they see how the city was destroyed. 9An enemy
army will surround the city and will not let anyone go out to get food. I will make the people so
hungry that they will eat the bodies of their own
sons and daughters, and then they will begin to
eat each other.’
10“While the people with you are watching,
break that jar. 11Then say this: ‘The LORD All-
Powerful says: I will break this nation and this
city just as someone breaks a clay jar that cannot
be put back together again. The dead people will
be buried here in Topheth, because there is no
other place for them. 12This is what I will do to
these people and to this place, says the LORD. I
will make this city like Topheth. 13The houses in
Jerusalem and the king’s palaces will become as
unclean[d] as this place, Topheth, because the people worshiped gods on the roofs[n] of their houses.
They worshiped the stars and burned incense[d] to
honor them and gave drink offerings to gods.’ ”
14When Jeremiah left Topheth where the LORD
had sent him to prophesy,[d] he went to the LORD’s
Temple,[d] stood in the courtyard, and said to all
the people: 15“This is what the LORD All-
Powerful, the God of Israel, says: ‘I will soon
bring disaster to Jerusalem and the villages around
it, as I said I would. This will happen because the
people are very stubborn and do not listen at all
to what I say.’ ”

Pashhur Will Be Captured

20 Pashhur son of Immer was a priest and
the highest officer in the Temple[d] of the
LORD. When he heard Jeremiah prophesying[d] in
the Temple courtyard, 2he had Jeremiah the
prophet beaten. And he locked Jeremiah’s hands
and feet between large blocks of wood at the Upper Gate of Benjamin of the LORD’s Temple. 3The
next day when Pashhur took Jeremiah out of the
blocks of wood, Jeremiah said to him, “The
LORD’s name for you is not Pashhur. Now his
name for you is Terror on Every Side. 4This is
what the LORD says: ‘I will soon make you a terror
to yourself and to all your friends. You will watch
enemies killing your friends with swords. And I
will give all the people of Judah to the king of
Babylon, who will take them away as captives to
Babylon and then will kill them with swords. 5I
will give all the wealth of this city to its enemies—its goods, its valuables, and the treasures
of the kings of Judah. The enemies will carry all
those valuables off to Babylon. 6And Pashhur, you
and everyone in your house will be taken captive.
You will be forced to go to Babylon, where you
will die and be buried, you and your friends to
whom you have prophesied lies.’ ”

Jeremiah’s Fifth Complaint

7LORD, you tricked me, and I was fooled.
You are stronger than I am, so you won.
I have become a joke;
everyone makes fun of me all day long.
8Every time I speak, I shout.
I am always shouting about violence and destruction.
I tell the people about the message I received from the LORD,
but this only brings me insults.
The people make fun of me all day long.
9Sometimes I say to myself,
“I will forget about the LORD.
I will not speak anymore in his name.”
But then his message becomes like a burning fire inside me,
deep within my bones.
I get tired of trying to hold it inside of me,
and finally, I cannot hold it in.
10I hear many people whispering about me:
“Terror on every side!
Tell on him! Let’s tell the rulers about him.”
My friends are all just waiting for me to make some mistake.
They are saying,
“Maybe we can trick him
so we can defeat him
and pay him back.”
11But the LORD is with me like a strong warrior,
so those who are chasing me will trip and fall;
they will not defeat me.
They will be ashamed because they have failed,
and their shame will never be forgotten.
12LORD All-Powerful, you test good people;
you look deeply into the heart and mind of a person.
I have told you my arguments against these people,
so let me see you give them the punishment they deserve.

roofs In Bible times houses were built with flat roofs. The roof was used for drying things such as flax and fruit; and it was used as an extra room, as a place for worship, and as a place to sleep in the summer.

13 Sing to the LORD!
Praise the LORD!
He saves the life of the poor
from the power of the wicked.

Jeremiah's Sixth Complaint

14 Let there be a curse on the day I was born;
let there be no blessing on the day when
my mother gave birth to me.
15 Let there be a curse on the man
who brought my father the news:
"You have a son!"
This made my father very glad.
16 Let that man be like the towns
the LORD destroyed without pity.
Let him hear loud crying in the morning
and battle cries at noon,
17 because he did not kill me before I was born.
Then my mother would have been my
grave;
she would have stayed pregnant forever.
18 Why did I have to come out of my mother's
body?
All I have known is trouble and sorrow,
and my life will end in shame.

God Rejects King Zedekiah's Request

21 This is the word that the LORD spoke to
Jeremiah. It came when Zedekiah king
of Judah sent Pashhur son of Malkijah and the
priest Zephaniah son of Maaseiah to Jeremiah.
2 They said, "Ask the LORD for us what will happen, because Nebuchadnezzar king of Babylon is
attacking us. Maybe the LORD will do miracles[d]
for us as he did in the past so Nebuchadnezzar
will stop attacking us and leave."
3 But Jeremiah answered them, "Tell King Zedekiah this: 4 'Here is what the LORD, the God of
Israel, says: You have weapons of war in your
hands to defend yourselves against the king of
Babylon and the Babylonians, who are all around
the city wall. But I will make those weapons useless. Soon I will bring them into the center of this
city. 5 In my anger, my very great anger, I myself
will fight against you with my great power and
strength. 6 I will kill everything living in Jerusalem—both people and animals. They will die
from terrible diseases. 7 Then, says the LORD, I'll
hand over Zedekiah king of Judah, his officers,
and the people in Jerusalem who do not die from
the terrible diseases or battle or hunger, to Nebuchadnezzar king of Babylon. I will let those win
who want to kill the people of Judah, so the people of Judah and Jerusalem will be killed in war.
Nebuchadnezzar will not show any mercy or pity
or feel sorry for them!'
8 "Also tell this to the people of Jerusalem: 'This
is what the LORD says: I will let you choose to live
or die. 9 Anyone who stays in Jerusalem will die in
war or from hunger or from a terrible disease. But
anyone who goes out of Jerusalem and surrenders
to the Babylonians who are attacking you will
live. Anyone who leaves the city will save his life
as if it were a prize won in war. 10 I have decided
to make trouble for this city and not to help it,
says the LORD. I will give it to the king of Babylon,
and he will burn it with fire.'
11 "Say to Judah's royal family: 'Hear the word
of the LORD. 12 Family of David, this is what the
LORD says:
You must judge people fairly every morning.
Save the person who has been robbed
from the power of his attacker.
If you don't, I will become very angry.
My anger will be like a fire that no one can
put out,
because you have done evil things.

13 " 'Jerusalem, I am against you,
you who live on top of the mountain
over this valley, says the LORD.
You say, "No one can attack us
or come into our strong city."
14 But I will give you the punishment you
deserve, says the LORD.
I will start a fire in your forests
that will burn up everything around you!' "

Judgment Against Evil Kings

22 This is what the LORD says: "Go down to
the palace of the king of Judah and
prophesy[d] this message there: 2 'Hear the word of
the LORD, king of Judah, who rules from David's
throne. You and your officers, and your people
who come through these gates, listen! 3 This is
what the LORD says: Do what is fair and right.
Save the one who has been robbed from the
power of his attacker. Don't mistreat or hurt the
foreigners, orphans, or widows. Don't kill innocent people here. 4 If you carefully obey these
commands, kings who sit on David's throne will
come through the gates of this palace with their
officers and people, riding in chariots and on
horses. 5 But if you don't obey these commands,
says the LORD, I swear by my own name that this
king's palace will become a ruin.' "
6 This is what the LORD says about the palace
where the king of Judah lives:
"You are tall like the forests of Gilead,
like the mountaintops of Lebanon.
But I will truly make you into a desert,
into towns where no one lives.
7 I will send men to destroy the palace,
each with his weapons.
They will cut up your strong, beautiful cedar
beams
and throw them into the fire.
8 "People from many nations will pass by this

city and ask each other, 'Why has the LORD done such a terrible thing to Jerusalem, this great city?'
9And the answer will be: 'Because the people of Judah quit following the agreement with the LORD their God. They worshiped and served other gods.' "

Judgment Against Jehoahaz

10Don't cry for the dead king or be sad about
 him.
But cry painfully for the king who is being
 taken away,
because he will never return
 or see his homeland again.

11This is what the LORD says about Jehoahaz son of Josiah who became king of Judah after his father died and who has left this place: "He will never return. 12He will die where he has been taken captive, and he will not see this land again."

Judgment Against Jehoiakim

13"How terrible it will be for one who builds
 his palace by doing evil,
who cheats people so he can build its upper
 rooms.
He makes his own people work for nothing
 and does not pay them.
14He says, 'I will build a great palace for myself
 with large upper rooms.'
So he builds it with large windows
 and uses cedar wood for the walls,
 which he paints red.

15"Does having a lot of cedar in your house
 make you a great king?
Your father was satisfied to have food and
 drink.
He did what was right and fair,
 so everything went well for him.
16He helped those who were poor and needy,
 so everything went well for him.
That is what it means to know God,"
 says the LORD.
17"But you only look for and think about
 what you can get dishonestly.
You are even willing to kill innocent people
 to get it.
You feel free to hurt people and to steal
 from them."
18So this is what the LORD says to Jehoiakim son of Josiah king of Judah:
"The people of Judah will not cry when
 Jehoiakim dies,
saying: 'Oh, my brother,' or 'Oh, my
 sister.'
They will not cry for him, saying:
 'Oh, master,' or 'Oh, my king.'
19They will bury him like a donkey,
 dragging his body away
 and throwing it outside the gates of
 Jerusalem.

20"Judah, go up to Lebanon and cry out.
 Let your voice be heard in Bashan.
Cry out from Abarim,
 because all your friends are destroyed!
21Judah, when you were successful, I warned
 you,
 but you said, 'I won't listen.'
You have acted like this since you were
 young;
 you have not obeyed me.
22Like a storm, my punishment will blow all
 your shepherds away
 and send your friends into captivity.
Then you will really be ashamed and
 disgraced
 because of all the wicked things you did.
23King, you live in your palace,
 cozy in your rooms of cedar.
But when your punishment comes, how you
 will groan
 like a woman giving birth to a baby!

Judgment upon Jehoiachin

24"As surely as I live," says the LORD, "Jehoiachin son of Jehoiakim king of Judah, even if you
were a signet[d] ring on my right hand, I would still
pull you off. 25I will hand you over to Nebuchadnezzar king of Babylon and to the Babylonians—
those people you fear because they want to kill
you. 26I will throw you and your mother into another country. Neither of you was born there, but
both of you will die there. 27They will want to
come back, but they will never be able to return."

28Jehoiachin is like a broken pot someone
 threw away;
 he is like something no one wants.
Why will Jehoiachin and his children be
 thrown out
 and sent into a foreign land?
29Land, land, land of Judah,
 hear the word of the LORD!
30This is what the LORD says:
"Write this down in the record about
 Jehoiachin:
 He is a man without children,
 a man who will not be successful in his
 lifetime.
And none of his descendants will be
 successful;
 none will sit on the throne of David
 or rule in Judah."

The Evil Leaders of Judah

23 "How terrible it will be for the leaders of Judah, who are scattering and destroying my people," says the LORD.

2They are responsible for the people, so the
LORD, the God of Israel, says to them: "You have
scattered my people and forced them away and
not taken care of them. So I will punish you for
the evil things you have done," says the LORD. 3"I
sent my people to other countries, but I will
gather those who are left alive and bring them
back to their own country. Then they will have
many children and grow in number. 4I will place
new leaders over my people, who will take care
of them. And my people will not be afraid or terrified again, and none of them will be lost," says the
LORD.

The Good Branch Will Come

5"The days are coming," says the LORD,
"when I will raise up a good branch in
David's family.
He will be a king who will rule in a wise
way;
he will do what is fair and right in the
land.
6In his time Judah will be saved,
and Israel will live in safety.
This will be his name:
The LORD Does What Is Right.
7"So the days are coming," says the LORD, "when
people will not say again: 'As surely as the LORD
lives, who brought Israel out of Egypt . . .' 8But
people will say something new: 'As surely as the
LORD lives, who brought the descendants of Israel
from the land of the north and from all the countries where he had sent them away. . .' Then the
people of Israel will live in their own land."

False Prophets Will Be Punished

9A message to the prophets:[d]
My heart is broken.
All my bones shake.
I'm like someone who is drunk,
like someone who has been overcome with
wine.
This is because of the LORD
and his holy words.
10The land of Judah is full of people who are
guilty of adultery.[d]
Because of this, the LORD cursed the land.
It has become a very sad place,
and the pastures have dried up.
The people are evil

LEADERSHIP

Who'll Pay for It?

Stephanie Fishkin had nothing to do with the senior class prank that caused damages of about fourteen hundred dollars to a small park on school grounds. She didn't destroy the park's cherry tree, break the branches off the hackberry tree, or saw through the split-rail fence. But it was her picture that appeared on the front page of the "Denver Post" with the news account of the vandalism.

Why? Because as senior class president, Stephanie was responsible for answering to the press. She and the other class officers also had the responsibility to pay for the damage out of the class treasury. They had planned to donate those funds to Denver Children's Hospital or to a scholarship fund.

Ironically, the park had been built as a memorial to a student who died in 1974. The student's parents spent at least ten thousand dollars of their own money to build the park. This family, at the very least, deserved an apology. Whose responsibility was that?

Most class presidents consider that position to be an honor. But being a leader, Stephanie found out, also carries responsibility. In Judah, God held the leaders responsible for misguiding his people. See what God has to say to them in **Jeremiah 23:1–6**.

- Why do you think Stephanie and the leaders of Judah were held accountable for the things happening around them?
- What are some ways you can serve as a leader for God's people?

CONSIDER. . .

- helping your family by taking responsibility for a household chore without being asked.
- offering your leadership in your school or church for a project that needs to be done, and then responsibly completing it.

FOR MORE, SEE. . .

- Micah 3:9–12 (p. 864)
- Matthew 23:13–36 (p. 949)
- 2 Peter 2:1–3 (p. 1311)

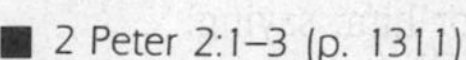

and use their power in the wrong way.

11"Both the prophets and the priests live as if
there were no God.
I have found them doing evil things even in
my own Temple,"[d] says the LORD.
12"So they will be in danger.
They will be forced into darkness
where they will be defeated.
I will bring disaster on them
in the year I punish them," says the LORD.

13"I saw the prophets of Samaria
do something wrong.
Those prophets prophesied by Baal[d]
and led my people Israel away.
14And I have seen the prophets of Jerusalem
do terrible things.
They are guilty of adultery
and live by lies.
They encourage evil people to keep on doing
evil,
so the people don't stop sinning.
All of those people are like the city of Sodom.
The people of Jerusalem are like the city of
Gomorrah to me!"

15So this is what the LORD All-Powerful says
about the prophets:
"I will make those prophets eat bitter food
and drink poisoned water,
because the prophets of Jerusalem spread
wickedness
through the whole country."

16This is what the LORD All-Powerful says:
"Don't pay attention to what those prophets
are saying to you.
They are trying to fool you.
They talk about visions their own minds
made up,
not about visions from me.
17They say to those who hate me:
'The LORD says: You will have peace.'
They say to all those who are stubborn and
do as they please:
'Nothing bad will happen to you.'
18But none of these prophets has stood in the
meeting of angels
to see or hear the message of the LORD.
None of them has paid close attention to
his message.
19Look, the punishment from the LORD
will come like a storm.
His anger will be like a hurricane.
It will come swirling down on the heads of
those wicked people.
20The LORD's anger will not stop
until he finishes what he plans to do.
When that day is over,
you will understand this clearly.

21I did not send those prophets,
but they ran to tell their message.
I did not speak to them,
but they prophesied anyway.
22But if they had stood in the meeting of
angels,
they would have told my message to my
people.
They would have turned the people from
their evil ways
and from doing evil.

23"I am a God who is near," says the LORD.
"I am also a God who is far away."
24"No one can hide
where I cannot see him," says the LORD.
"I fill all of heaven and earth," says the
LORD.

25"I have heard the prophets who prophesy lies
in my name. They say, 'I have had a dream! I have
had a dream!' 26How long will this continue in the
minds of these lying prophets? They prophesy
from their own wishful thinking. 27They are trying to make the people of Judah forget me by telling each other these dreams. In the same way,
their ancestors forgot me and worshiped Baal. 28Is
straw the same thing as wheat?" says the LORD.
"If a prophet wants to tell about his dreams, let
him! But let the person who hears my message
speak it truthfully! 29Isn't my message like a
fire?" says the LORD. "Isn't it like a hammer that
smashes a rock?

30"So I am against the false prophets," says the
LORD. "They keep stealing words from each other
and say they are from me. 31I am against the false
prophets," says the LORD. "They use their own
words and pretend it is a message from me. 32I am
against the prophets who prophesy false dreams,"
says the LORD. "They mislead my people with
their lies and false teachings! I did not send them
or command them to do anything for me. They
can't help the people of Judah at all," says the
LORD.

The Sad Message from the Lord

33"Suppose the people of Judah, a prophet,[d] or
a priest asks you: 'Jeremiah, what is the message
from the LORD?' You will answer them and say,
'You are a heavy load to the LORD, and I will
throw you down, says the LORD.' 34A prophet or
a priest or one of the people might say, 'This is a
message from the LORD.' That person has lied, so
I will punish him and his whole family. 35This is
what you will say to each other: 'What did the
LORD answer?' or 'What did the LORD say?' 36But
you will never again say, 'The message of the
LORD,' because the only message you speak is
your own words. You have changed the words of
our God, the living God, the LORD All-Powerful.

37This is how you should speak to the prophets: 'What answer did the LORD give you?' or 'What did the LORD say?' 38But don't say, 'The message from the LORD.' If you use these words, this is what the LORD says: Because you called it a 'message from the LORD,' though I told you not to use those words, 39I will pick you up and throw you away from me, along with Jerusalem, which I gave to your ancestors and to you. 40And I will make a disgrace of you forever; your shame will never be forgotten."

The Good and Bad Figs

24 Nebuchadnezzar king of Babylon captured Jehoiachin son of Jehoiakim and king of Judah, his officers, and all the craftsmen and metalworkers of Judah. He took them away from Jerusalem and brought them to Babylon. It was then that the LORD showed me two baskets of figs arranged in front of the Temple[d] of the LORD. 2One of the baskets had very good figs in it, like figs that ripen early in the season. But the other basket had figs too rotten to eat.

3The LORD said to me, "What do you see, Jeremiah?"

I answered, "I see figs. The good figs are very good, but the rotten figs are too rotten to eat."

4Then the LORD spoke his word to me: 5"This is what the LORD, the God of Israel, says: 'I sent the people of Judah out of their country to live in the country of Babylon. I think of those people as good, like these good figs. 6I will look after them and bring them back to the land of Judah. I will not tear them down, but I will build them up. I will not pull them up, but I will plant them so they can grow. 7I will make them want to know me, that I am the LORD. They will be my people, and I will be their God, because they will return to me with their whole hearts.

8" 'But the bad figs are too rotten to eat.' So this is what the LORD says: 'Zedekiah king of Judah, his officers, and all the people from Jerusalem who are left alive, even those who live in Egypt, will be like those rotten figs. 9I will make those people hated as an evil people by all the kingdoms of the earth. People will make fun of them and tell

HONESTY

Slow to Heal

After placing second at the regional karate tournament, Dan McCarty got an invitation to nationals. But one week before the trip, he tore the ligaments in his ankle and ended up in a cast.

Still, nothing would stop Dan. He convinced his parents to let him make the trip anyway, promising just to watch the tournament. Once on his way, he told his karate instructor that the doctor had put him in a cast only as a precaution. He said he had both his doctor's and parents' permission to participate. Since it was a removable cast, he took it off when he got to the tournament and competed. He even won a few matches.

Although the cast was back on when he got home, his parents figured out what he had done by the way he talked about the competition. They felt angry and betrayed!

Dan paid for his scheme: His ankle healed much more slowly than it would have. Luckily, the ankle wasn't permanently damaged.

Dan falsely used the authority of his doctor and parents to back up his lies to his instructor. In a similar way, false prophets appealed to God's authority to back up their lies in **Jeremiah 23:23–30**.

- Why were Dan's karate instructor and the people in the passage quick to accept lies?
- When people say, "Honest to God!" do you believe their story more than you would have otherwise? Why or why not?

CONSIDER . . .

- tracking down the source of a rumor you've heard at school and finding out how much is true.
- Mark Twain's humorous thought on lying: "If you tell the truth you don't have to remember anything." Think of a time you've lied. Then make a list of all the other lies you had to tell to support it.

FOR MORE, SEE . . .

- Psalm 139:1–18 (p. 561)
- Matthew 5:33–37 (p. 915)
- 1 John 4:1–6 (p. 1319)

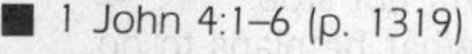

jokes about them and point fingers at them and curse them everywhere I scatter them. 10I will send war, hunger, and disease against them. I will attack them until they have all been killed. Then they will no longer be in the land I gave to them and their ancestors.' "

SIDELIGHT: If you have trouble figuring out all the oracles, history, and stories in the book of Jeremiah, read a summary of his ministry in Jeremiah 25. This may be the first "Reader's Digest Condensed Book."

A Summary of Jeremiah's Preaching

25 This is the message that came to Jeremiah concerning all the people of Judah. It came in the fourth year that Jehoiakim son of Josiah was king of Judah and the first year Nebuchadnezzar was king of Babylon. 2This is the message Jeremiah the prophet[d] spoke to all the people of Judah and Jerusalem:

3The LORD has spoken his word to me again and again for these past twenty-three years. I have been a prophet since the thirteenth year of Josiah son of Amon king of Judah. I have spoken messages from the LORD to you from that time until today, but you have not listened.

4The LORD has sent all his servants the prophets to you over and over again, but you have not listened or paid any attention to them. 5Those prophets have said, "Stop your evil ways. Stop doing what is wrong so you can stay in the land that the LORD gave to you and your ancestors to live in forever. 6Don't follow other gods to serve them or to worship them. Don't make me, the LORD, angry by worshiping idols that are the work of your own hands, or I will punish you."

7"But you people of Judah did not listen to me," says the LORD. "You made me angry by worshiping idols that were the work of your own hands, so I punished you."

8So this is what the LORD All-Powerful says: "Since you have not listened to my messages, 9I will send for all the peoples of the north," says the LORD, "along with my servant Nebuchadnezzar king of Babylon. I will bring them all against Judah, those who live there, and all the nations around you, too. I will completely destroy all those countries and leave them in ruins forever. People will be shocked when they see how badly I have destroyed those countries. 10I will bring an end to the sounds of joy and happiness, the sounds of brides and bridegrooms, and the sound of people grinding meal. And I will take away the light of the lamp. 11That whole area will be an empty desert, and these nations will be slaves of the king of Babylon for seventy years.

12"But when the seventy years have passed, I will punish the king of Babylon and his entire nation for their evil," says the LORD. "I will make that land a desert forever. 13I will make happen all the terrible things I said about Babylonia — everything Jeremiah prophesied about all those foreign nations, the warnings written in this book. 14Even the Babylonians will have to serve many nations and many great kings. I will give them the punishment they deserve for all their own hands have done."

Judgment on the Nations

15The LORD, the God of Israel, said this to me: "My anger is like the wine in a cup. Take it from my hand and make all the nations, to whom I am sending you, drink all of my anger from this cup. 16They will drink my anger and stumble about and act like madmen because of the war I am going to send among them."

17So I took the cup from the LORD's hand and went to those nations and made them drink from it. 18I served this wine to the people of Jerusalem and the towns of Judah, and the kings and officers of Judah, so they would become a ruin. Then people would be shocked and would insult them and speak evil of them. And so it has been to this day. 19I also made these people drink of the LORD's anger: the king of Egypt, his servants, his officers, all his people, 20and all the foreigners there; all the kings of the land of Uz; all the kings of the Philistines (the kings of the cities of Ashkelon, Gaza, Ekron, and the people left at Ashdod); 21the people of Edom, Moab, and Ammon; 22all the kings of Tyre and Sidon; all the kings of the coastal countries to the west; 23the people of Dedan and Tema and Buz; all who cut their hair short; 24all the kings of Arabia; and the kings of the people who live in the desert; 25all the kings of Zimri, Elam, and Media; 26and all the kings of the north, near and far, one after the other. I made all the kingdoms on earth drink from the cup of the LORD's anger, but the king of Babylon will drink from this cup after all the others.

27"Then say to them, 'This is what the LORD All-Powerful, the God of Israel, says: Drink this cup of my anger. Get drunk from it and vomit. Fall down and don't get up because of the war I am sending among you!'

28"If they refuse to take the cup from your hand and drink, say to them, 'The LORD All-Powerful says this: You must drink from this cup. 29Look! I am already bringing disaster on Jerusalem, the city that is called by my name. Do you think you will not be punished? You will be punished! I am sending war on all the people of the earth, says the LORD All-Powerful.'

30“You, Jeremiah, will prophesy[d] against them
with all these words. Say to them:

‘The LORD will roar from heaven
and will shout from his Holy Temple.[d]
He will roar loudly against his land.
He will shout like people who walk on grapes
to make wine;
he will shout against all who live on the
earth.
31The noise will spread all over the earth,
because the LORD will accuse all the
nations.
He will judge and tell what is wrong with all
people,
and he will kill the evil people with a
sword,’ ” says the LORD.

32This is what the LORD All-Powerful says:
“Disasters will soon spread
from nation to nation.
They will come like a powerful storm
from the faraway places on earth.”

33At that time those killed by the LORD will reach
from one end of the earth to the other. No one
will cry for them or gather up their bodies and
bury them. They will be left lying on the ground
like dung.

34Cry, you leaders! Cry out loud!
Roll around in the dust, leaders of the
people!
It is now time for you to be killed.
You will fall and be scattered,
like pieces of a broken jar.
35There will be no place for the leaders to
hide;
they will not escape.
36I hear the sound of the leaders shouting.
I hear the leaders of the people crying
loudly,
because the LORD is destroying their land.
37Those peaceful pastures will be like an empty
desert,
because the LORD is very angry.
38Like a lion, he has left his den.
Their land has been destroyed
because of the terrible war he brought,
because of his fierce anger.

Jeremiah's Lesson at the Temple

26 This message came from the LORD soon
after Jehoiakim son of Josiah became
king of Judah. 2This is what the LORD said: “Jeremiah, stand in the courtyard of the Temple[d] of the
LORD. Give this message to all the people of the
towns of Judah who are coming to worship at the
Temple of the LORD. Tell them everything I tell
you to say; don't leave out a word. 3Maybe they
will listen and stop their evil ways. If they will, I
will change my mind about bringing on them the
disaster that I am planning because of the evil
they have done. 4Say to them: ‘This is what the
LORD says: You must obey me and follow my
teachings that I gave you. 5You must listen to
what my servants the prophets[d] say to you. I have
sent them to you again and again, but you did not
listen. 6If you don't obey me, I will destroy my
Temple in Jerusalem as I destroyed my Holy Tent[d]
at Shiloh. When I do, people all over the world
will curse Jerusalem.’ ”

7The priests, the prophets, and all the people
heard Jeremiah speaking these words in the Temple of the LORD. 8When Jeremiah finished speaking everything the LORD had commanded him to
say, the priests, prophets, and all the people
grabbed Jeremiah. They said, “You must die!
9How dare you prophesy in the name of the LORD
that this Temple will be destroyed like the one at
Shiloh! How dare you say that Jerusalem will become a desert without anyone to live in it!” And
all the people crowded around Jeremiah in the
Temple of the LORD.

10Now when the officers of Judah heard about
what was happening, they came out of the king's
palace and went up to the Temple of the LORD
and took their places at the entrance of the New
Gate. 11Then the priests and prophets said to the
officers and all the other people, “Jeremiah should
be killed. He prophesied against Jerusalem, and
you heard him yourselves.”

12Then Jeremiah spoke these words to all the
officers of Judah and all the other people: “The
LORD sent me to say everything you have heard
about this Temple and this city. 13Now change
your lives and start doing good and obey the LORD
your God. Then he will change his mind and not
bring on you the disaster he has told you about.
14As for me, I am in your power. Do to me what
you think is good and right. 15But be sure of one
thing. If you kill me, you will be guilty of killing
an innocent person. You will make this city and
everyone who lives in it guilty, too! The LORD
truly sent me to you to give you this message.”

16Then the officers and all the people said to the
priests and the prophets, “Jeremiah must not be
killed. What he told us comes from the LORD our
God.”

17Then some of the older leaders of Judah stood
up and said to all the people, 18“Micah, from the
city of Moresheth, was a prophet during the time
Hezekiah was king of Judah. Micah said to all the
people of Judah, ‘This is what the LORD All-
Powerful says:

Jerusalem will be plowed like a field.
It will become a pile of rocks,
and the hill where the Temple stands will
be covered with bushes.’

19“Hezekiah king of Judah and the people of

Judah did not kill Micah. You know that Hezekiah feared the LORD and tried to please the LORD.
So the LORD changed his mind and did not bring
on Judah the disaster he had promised. If we hurt
Jeremiah, we will bring a terrible disaster on ourselves!"
20(Now there was another man who prophesied in the name of the LORD. His name was Uriah
son of Shemaiah from the city of Kiriath Jearim.
He preached the same things against Jerusalem
and the land of Judah that Jeremiah did. 21When
King Jehoiakim, all his army officers, and all the
leaders of Judah heard Uriah preach, King Jehoiakim wanted to kill Uriah. But Uriah heard about
it and was afraid. So he escaped to Egypt. 22Then
King Jehoiakim sent Elnathan son of Acbor and
some other men to Egypt, 23and they brought
Uriah back from Egypt. Then they took him to
King Jehoiakim, who had Uriah killed with a
sword. His body was thrown into the burial place
where poor people are buried.)
24Ahikam son of Shaphan supported Jeremiah.
So Ahikam did not hand Jeremiah over to be
killed by the people.

Nebuchadnezzar Is Made Ruler

27 The LORD spoke his word to Jeremiah
soon after Zedekiah son of Josiah was
made king of Judah. 2This is what the LORD said
to me: "Make a yoke[d] out of straps and poles, and
put it on the back of your neck. 3Then send messages to the kings of Edom, Moab, Ammon, Tyre,
and Sidon by their messengers who have come
to Jerusalem to see Zedekiah king of Judah. 4Tell
them to give this message to their masters: 'The
LORD All-Powerful, the God of Israel, says: "Tell
your masters: 5I made the earth, its people, and
all its animals with my great power and strength.
I can give the earth to anyone I want. 6Now I have
given all these lands to Nebuchadnezzar king of
Babylon, my servant. I will make even the wild
animals obey him. 7All nations will serve Nebuchadnezzar and his son and grandson. Then the
time will come for Babylon to be defeated, and

PEER PRESSURE

Quick Comeback

Kevin Carter's alcohol and drug abuse started as a simple desire to be "one of the guys." Kevin wanted to fit in with his older brother and his brother's friends. Drinking and getting high were ways to do that.

Before long, Kevin went from feeling peer pressure to delivering it. "I became the bad influence," he remembers. He would encourage friends to get drunk at parties, and he persuaded people who had never used drugs to get high.

One day, when Kevin couldn't obtain any drugs or alcohol, he lost his temper and was beaten up in a fight. Then he saw himself in the mirror—and realized how desperate he was. Kevin entered treatment for alcoholism and drug abuse. Thankfully, he's been able to stay clean and sober for ten months. And peer pressure hasn't deterred him.

Kevin still sees some of his old friends who drink. But they don't try to get Kevin to drink. And if they did, Kevin would know how to respond. "You've made your choice to use or drink," he'd say. "Please respect my choice not to."

Jeremiah's peers wanted him to stop preaching God's word to them. They used the ultimate peer pressure threat: Stop preaching, or we'll kill you. See how he responded in **Jeremiah 26:8–15**.

- What are the differences between Kevin's friends and the people of Jeremiah's time?
- How is peer pressure today different from the peer pressure in this passage?

CONSIDER. . .

- talking with a parent about the negative peer pressure he or she experiences—and how he or she deals with it.
- asking a close friend to form a partnership for positive peer pressure and perhaps writing a "contract" of specific ways you'll help each other.

FOR MORE, SEE. . .

- Daniel 3 (p. 809)
- Matthew 5:10–12 (p. 912)
- Acts 4:1–22 (p. 1103)

many nations and great kings will make Babylon
their servant.
8" ' "But if some nations or kingdoms refuse to
serve Nebuchadnezzar king of Babylon and refuse
to be under his control, I will punish them with
war, hunger, and terrible diseases, says the LORD.
I will use Nebuchadnezzar to destroy them. 9So
don't listen to your false prophets,[d] those who use
magic to tell the future, those who explain
dreams, the mediums,[d] or magicians. They all tell
you, 'You will not be slaves to the king of Babylon.' 10They are telling you lies that will cause
you to be taken far from your homeland. I will
force you to leave your homes, and you will die
in another land. 11But the nations who put themselves under the control of the king of Babylon
and serve him I will let stay in their own country,
says the LORD. The people from those nations will
live in their own land and farm it." ' "
12I gave the same message to Zedekiah king of
Judah. I said, "Put yourself under the control of
the king of Babylon and serve him, and you will
live. 13Why should you and your people die from
war, hunger, or disease, as the LORD said would
happen to those who do not serve the king of Babylon? 14But the false prophets are saying, 'You will
never be slaves to the king of Babylon.' Don't listen to them because they are prophesying lies to
you! 15'I did not send them,' says the LORD. 'They
are prophesying lies and saying the message is
from me. So I will send you away, Judah. And you
and those prophets who prophesy to you will
die.' "
16Then I, Jeremiah, said to the priests and all
the people, "This is what the LORD says: Those
false prophets are saying, 'The Babylonians will
soon return what they took from the Temple[d] of
the LORD.' Don't listen to them! They are prophesying lies to you. 17Don't listen to those prophets.
But serve the king of Babylon, and you will live.
There is no reason for you to cause Jerusalem to
become a ruin. 18If they are prophets and have the
message from the LORD, let them pray to the LORD
All-Powerful. Let them ask that the items which
are still in the Temple of the LORD and in the
king's palace and in Jerusalem not be taken away
to Babylon.
19"This is what the LORD All-Powerful says
about those items left in Jerusalem: the pillars, the
large bronze bowl, which is called the Sea, the
stands that can be moved, and other things.
20Nebuchadnezzar king of Babylon did not take
these away when he took as captives Jehoiachin
son of Jehoiakim king of Judah and all the other
important people from Judah and Jerusalem to
Babylon. 21This is what the LORD All-Powerful,
the God of Israel, says about the items left in the
Temple of the LORD and in the king's palace and
in Jerusalem: 22'All of them will also be taken to
Babylon. And they will stay there until the day I
go to get them,' says the LORD. 'Then I will bring
them back and return them to this place.' "

The False Prophet Hananiah

28 It was in that same year, in the fifth
month of Zedekiah's fourth year as king
of Judah, soon after he began to rule. The
prophet[d] Hananiah son of Azzur, from the town
of Gibeon, spoke to me in the Temple[d] of the
LORD in front of the priests and all the people. He
said: 2"The LORD All-Powerful, the God of Israel,
says: 'I have broken the yoke[d] the king of Babylon
has put on Judah. 3Before two years are over, I
will bring back everything that Nebuchadnezzar
king of Babylon took to Babylon from the LORD's
Temple. 4I will also bring back Jehoiachin son of
Jehoiakim king of Judah and all the other captives
from Judah who went to Babylon,' says the LORD.
'So I will break the yoke the king of Babylon put
on Judah.' "
5Then the prophet Jeremiah spoke to the
prophet Hananiah in front of the priests and all
the people who were standing in the Temple[d] of
the LORD. 6He said, "Amen! Let the LORD really
do that! May the LORD make the message you
prophesy come true. May he bring back here everything from the LORD's Temple and all the people who were taken as captives to Babylon.
7"But listen to what I am going to say to you
and all the people. 8There were prophets long before we became prophets, Hananiah. They prophesied that war, hunger, and terrible diseases
would come to many countries and great kingdoms. 9But if a prophet prophesies that we will
have peace and that message comes true, he can
be recognized as one truly sent by the LORD."
10Then the prophet Hananiah took the yoke off
Jeremiah's neck and broke it. 11Hananiah said in
front of all the people, "This is what the LORD
says: 'In the same way I will break the yoke of
Nebuchadnezzar king of Babylon. He put that
yoke on all the nations of the world, but I will
break it before two years are over.' " After Hananiah had said that, Jeremiah left the Temple.
12The LORD spoke his word to Jeremiah after
the prophet Hananiah had broken the yoke off of
the prophet Jeremiah's neck. 13The LORD said,
"Go and tell Hananiah, 'This is what the LORD
says: You have broken a wooden yoke, but I will
make a yoke of iron in its place! 14The LORD All-
Powerful, the God of Israel, says: I will put a yoke
of iron on the necks of all these nations to make
them serve Nebuchadnezzar king of Babylon, and
they will be slaves to him. I will even give Nebuchadnezzar control over the wild animals.' "
15Then the prophet Jeremiah said to the
prophet Hananiah, "Listen, Hananiah! The LORD
did not send you, and you have made the people

of Judah trust in lies. 16So this is what the LORD says: 'Soon I will remove you from the earth. You will die this year, because you taught the people to turn against the LORD.' "

17Hananiah died in the seventh month of that same year.

A Letter to the Captives in Babylon

29 This is the letter that Jeremiah the prophet[d] sent from Jerusalem to the older leaders who were among the captives, the priests, and the prophets. He sent it to all the other people Nebuchadnezzar had taken as captives from Jerusalem to Babylon. 2(This letter was sent after all these people were taken away: Jehoiachin the king and the queen mother; the officers and leaders of Judah and Jerusalem; and the craftsmen and metalworkers from Jerusalem.) 3Zedekiah king of Judah sent Elasah son of Shaphan and Gemariah son of Hilkiah to Babylon to Nebuchadnezzar king of Babylon. So Jeremiah gave them this letter to carry to Babylon:

4This is what the LORD All-Powerful, the God of Israel, says to all those people I sent away from Jerusalem as captives to Babylon: 5"Build houses and settle in the land. Plant gardens and eat the food they grow. 6Get married and have sons and daughters. Find wives for your sons, and let your daughters be married so they also may have sons and daughters. Have many children in Babylon; don't become fewer in number. 7Also do good things for the city where I sent you as captives. Pray to the LORD for the city where you are living, because if good things happen in the city, good things will happen to you also." 8The LORD All-Powerful, the God of Israel, says: "Don't let the prophets among you and the people who do magic fool you. Don't listen to their dreams. 9They are prophesying lies to you, saying that their message is from me. But I did not send them," says the LORD.

10This is what the LORD says: "Babylon will be powerful for seventy years. After that time I will come to you, and I will keep my promise to bring you back to Jerusalem. 11I say this because I know what I am planning for you," says the LORD. "I have good plans for you, not plans to hurt you. I will give you hope and a good future. 12Then you will call my name. You will come to me and pray to me, and I will listen to you. 13You will search for me. And when you search for me with all your heart, you will find me! 14I will let you find me," says the LORD. "And I will bring you back from your captivity. I forced you to leave this place, but I will gather you from all the nations, from the places I have sent you as captives," says the LORD. "And I will bring you back to this place."

15You might say, "The LORD has given us prophets here in Babylon."

16But the LORD says this about the king who is sitting on David's throne now and all the other people still in Jerusalem, your relatives who did not go as captives to Babylon with you. 17The LORD All-Powerful says: "I will soon send war, hunger, and terrible diseases against those still in Jerusalem. I will make them like bad figs that are too rotten to eat. 18I will chase them with war, hunger, and terrible diseases. I will make them hated by all the kingdoms of the earth. People will curse them and be shocked and will use them as a shameful example wherever I make them go. 19This is because they have not listened to my message," says the LORD. "I sent my message to them again and again through my servants, the prophets, but they did not listen," says the LORD.

20You captives, whom I forced to leave Jerusalem and go to Babylon, listen to the message from the LORD. 21The LORD All-Powerful, the God of Israel, says this about Ahab son of Kolaiah and Zedekiah son of Maaseiah: "These two men have been prophesying lies to you, saying that their message is from me. But soon I will hand over those two prophets to Nebuchadnezzar king of Babylon, and he will kill them in front of you. 22Because of them, all the captives from Judah in Babylon will use this curse: 'May the LORD treat you like Zedekiah and Ahab, whom the king of Babylon burned in the fire.' 23They have done evil things among the people of Israel. They are guilty of adultery[d] with their neighbors' wives. They have also spoken lies and said those lies were a message from me. I did not tell them to do that. I know what they have done; I am a witness to it," says the LORD.

24Also give a message to Shemaiah from the Nehelamite family. 25The LORD All-Powerful, the God of Israel, says: "Shemaiah, you sent letters in your name to all the people in Jerusalem, to the priest Zephaniah son of Maaseiah, and to all the priests. 26You said to Zephaniah, 'The LORD has made you priest in place of Jehoiada. You are to be in charge of the Temple[d] of the LORD. You should arrest any madman who acts like a prophet. Lock his hands and feet between wooden blocks, and put iron rings around his neck. 27Now Jeremiah from Anathoth is acting like a prophet. So why haven't you arrested him? 28Jeremiah has sent this message to us in Babylon:

You will be there for a long time, so build houses and settle down. Plant gardens and eat what they grow.' "

[29]Zephaniah the priest read the letter to Jeremiah the prophet. [30]Then the LORD spoke his word to Jeremiah: [31]"Send this message to all the captives in Babylon: 'This is what the LORD says about Shemaiah the Nehelamite: Shemaiah has prophesied to you, but I did not send him. He has made you believe a lie. [32]So the LORD says, I will soon punish Shemaiah the Nehelamite and his family. He will not see the good things I will do for my people, says the LORD. None of his family will be left alive among the people, because he has taught the people to turn against me.' "

> **SIDELIGHT:** Though most of Jeremiah is bad news, chapters 30 to 33 are good news. These chapters have been called the "Book of Consolation" or the "Little Book of Comfort" because of their message of hope.

Promises of Hope

30 These are the words that the LORD spoke to Jeremiah. [2]The LORD, the God of Israel, said: "Jeremiah, write in a book all the words I have spoken to you. [3]The days will come when I will bring Israel and Judah back from captivity," says the LORD. "I will return them to the land I gave their ancestors, and they will own it!" says the LORD.

[4]The LORD spoke this message about the people of Israel and Judah: [5]This is what the LORD said:

"We hear people crying from fear.
They are afraid; there is no peace.
[6]Ask this question, and consider it:
A man cannot have a baby.
So why do I see every strong man
holding his stomach in pain like a woman having a baby?
Why is everyone's face turning white like a dead man's face?
[7]This will be a terrible day!
There will never be another time like this.
This is a time of great trouble for the people of Jacob,
but they will be saved from it."

[8]The LORD All-Powerful says, "At that time
I will break the yoke[a] from their necks
and tear off the ropes that hold them.
Foreign people will never again make my people slaves.
[9]They will serve the LORD their God
and David their king,
whom I will send to them.

[10]"So people of Jacob, my servants, don't be afraid.
Israel, don't be frightened," says the LORD.
"I will soon save you from that faraway place where you are captives.
I will save your family from that land.
The people of Jacob will be safe and have peace again;
there will be no enemy to frighten them.
[11]I am with you and will save you,"
says the LORD.
"I will completely destroy all those nations
where I scattered you,
but I will not completely destroy you.
I will punish you fairly,
but I will still punish you."

[12]This is what the LORD said:
"You people have a wound that cannot be cured;
your injury will not heal.
[13]There is no one to argue your case
and no cure for your sores.
So you will not be healed.
[14]All those nations who were your friends have forgotten you.
They don't care about you.
I have hurt you as an enemy would.
I punished you very hard,
because your guilt was so great
and your sins were so many.
[15]Why are you crying out about your injury?
There is no cure for your pain.
I did these things to you because of your great guilt,
because of your many sins.
[16]But all those nations that destroyed you will now be destroyed.
All your enemies will become captives in other lands.
Those who stole from you will have their own things stolen.
Those who took things from you in war
will have their own things taken.
[17]I will bring back your health
and heal your injuries," says the LORD,
"because other people forced you away.
They said about you, 'No one cares about Jerusalem!' "

[18]This is what the LORD said:
"I will soon make the tents of Jacob's people
as they used to be,
and I will have pity on Israel's houses.
The city will be rebuilt on its hill of ruins,
and the king's palace will stand in its proper place.

[19]People in those places will sing songs of
praise.
There will be the sound of laughter.
I will give them many children
so their number will not be small.
I will bring honor to them
so no one will look down on them.
[20]Their descendants[d] will be as they were in
the old days.
I will set them up as a strong people before
me,
and I will punish the nations who have hurt
them.
[21]One of their own people will lead them;
their ruler will come from among them.
He will come near to me when I invite him.
Who would dare to come to me
uninvited?" says the LORD.
[22]"So you will be my people,
and I will be your God."
[23]Look! It is a storm from the LORD!
He is angry and has gone out to punish the
people.
Punishment will come like a storm
crashing down on the evil people.
[24]The LORD will stay angry
until he finishes punishing the people.
He will stay angry
until he finishes the punishment he
planned.
When that day comes,
you will understand this.

The New Israel

31 The LORD says, "At that time I will be
God of all Israel's family groups, and
they will be my people."

[2]This is what the LORD says:
"The people who were not killed by the
enemy's sword
found help in the desert.
I came to give rest to Israel."

CELEBRATING

Remembering Matt

Matt Floyd, seventeen, finished writing his talk for the upcoming retreat and attended a planning meeting on Sunday, but he never gave his talk. Three days later, while hiking in the mountains, Matt lost his footing and fell to his death.

Matt's death shocked the other retreat team members. But over the next few weeks, they pulled together and learned how to celebrate even in the face of tragedy. They attended Matt's funeral and celebrated the seventeen years of life God had granted him. They celebrated the gift of Matt's fun-loving friendship that each of them had experienced.

Then they went on with the retreat, introducing other teenagers to the God whom Matt knew. Matt's talk was read at the time he was scheduled to give it. Kids cried as they listened to his words and remembered his voice. Some of the team members wore woven-yarn rings to remind them of Matt's friendship. At the end of the weekend, they offered those rings to God.

"When Matt died we thought about canceling the retreat," said one of the planning team members. "But I'm glad we didn't. God brought us closer together and helped us celebrate the blessings Matt had brought us."

Matt's friends learned that even in the midst of tragedies, we can celebrate God's goodness. Read how God encourages celebration—in hard times as well as good ones—in **Jeremiah 31:1–17**.

- What role does God play in the celebrations for Matt and the ones described in the passage?
- How do these celebrations compare to your ideas about celebrating?

CONSIDER...

- celebrating something God has done for you the next time you are going through a tough situation.
- writing your thoughts and memories of a relative or friend who has died, celebrating what that person meant to you.

FOR MORE, SEE...

- Nehemiah 8:9–12 (p. 434)
- Psalm 150 (p. 565)
- Luke 1:68–79 (p. 1002)

[3]And from far away the LORD appeared to his
people and said,
"I love you people
with a love that will last forever.
That is why I have continued
showing you kindness.
[4]People of Israel, I will build you up again,
and you will be rebuilt.
You will pick up your tambourines[d] again
and dance with those who are joyful.
[5]You will plant vineyards again
on the hills around Samaria.
The farmers will plant them
and enjoy their fruit.
[6]There will be a time when watchmen in the
mountains of Ephraim shout this
message:
'Come, let's go up to Jerusalem to worship
the LORD our God!' "

[7]This is what the LORD says:
"Be happy and sing for the people of Jacob.
Shout for Israel, the greatest of the nations.
Sing your praises and shout this:
'LORD, save your people,
those who are left alive from the nation of
Israel!'
[8]Look, I will soon bring Israel from the
country in the north,
and I will gather them from the faraway
places on earth.
Some of the people are blind and crippled.
Some of the women are pregnant, and
some are ready to give birth.
A great many people will come back.
[9]They will be crying as they come,
but they will pray as I bring them back.
I will lead those people by streams of water
on an even road where they will not
stumble.
I am Israel's father,
and Israel is my firstborn[d] son.

[10]"Nations, listen to the message from the
LORD.
Tell this message in the faraway lands by
the sea:
'The one who scattered the people of Israel
will bring them back,
and he will watch over his people like a
shepherd.'
[11]The LORD will pay for the people of Jacob
and will buy them back from people
stronger than they were.
[12]The people of Israel will come to the high
points of Jerusalem
and shout for joy.
Their faces will shine with happiness about
all the good things from the LORD:
the grain, new wine, oil, young sheep, and
young cows.
They will be like a garden that has plenty of
water,
and they will not be troubled anymore.
[13]Then young women of Israel will be happy
and dance,
the young men and old men also.
I will change their sadness into happiness;
I will give them comfort and joy instead of
sadness.
[14]The priests will have more than enough
sacrifices,
and my people will be filled with the good
things I give them!" says the LORD.

[15]This is what the LORD says:
"A voice was heard in Ramah
of painful crying and deep sadness:
Rachel crying for her children.
She refused to be comforted,
because her children are dead!"

[16]But this is what the LORD says:
"Stop crying;
don't let your eyes fill with tears.
You will be rewarded for your work!" says
the LORD.
"The people will return from their enemy's
land.
[17]So there is hope for you in the future," says
the LORD.
"Your children will return to their own
land.

[18]"I have heard Israel moaning:
'LORD, you punished me, and I have
learned my lesson.
I was like a calf that had never been
trained.
Take me back so that I may come back.
You truly are the LORD my God.
[19]LORD, after I wandered away from you,
I changed my heart and life.
After I understood,
I beat my breast with sorrow.
I was ashamed and disgraced,
because I suffered for the foolish things I
did when I was young.'

[20]"You know that Israel is my dear son,
The child I love.
Yes, I often speak against Israel,
but I still remember him.
I love him very much,
and I want to comfort him," says the LORD.

[21]"People of Israel, fix the road signs.
Put up signs to show you the way home.
Watch the road.

Pay attention to the road on which you
travel.
People of Israel, come home,
come back to your towns.
22You are an unfaithful daughter.
How long will you wander before you
come home?
The LORD has made something new happen
in the land:
A woman will go seeking a man."

23The LORD All-Powerful, the God of Israel,
says: "I will again do good things for the people
of Judah. At that time the people in the land of
Judah and its towns will again use these words:
'May the LORD bless you, home of what is good,
holy mountain.' 24People in all the towns of Judah
will live together in peace. Farmers and those
who move around with their flocks will live together in peace. 25I will give rest and strength to
those who are weak and tired."
26After hearing that, I, Jeremiah, woke up and
looked around. My sleep had been very pleasant.

27The LORD says, "The time is coming when I
will help the families of Israel and Judah and their
children and animals to grow. 28In the past I
watched over Israel and Judah, to pull them up
and tear them down, to destroy them and bring
them disaster. But now I will watch over them to
build them up and make them strong," says the
LORD.

29"At that time people will no longer say:
'The parents have eaten sour grapes,
and that caused the children to grind their
teeth from the sour taste.'
30Instead, each person will die for his own sin; the
person who eats sour grapes will grind his own
teeth.

The New Agreement

31"Look, the time is coming," says the LORD,
"when I will make a new agreement
with the people of Israel
and the people of Judah.
32It will not be like the agreement
I made with their ancestors

PROMISES

Changing Lives

Aristides Alvarado, twenty, is a junior at Renssalaer Polytechnic Institute in upstate New York. But when he was a sixth grader, most people who knew him gave him less than a 50 percent chance of graduating from high school.

Fortunately, "most people" didn't include Eugene M. Lang.

Lang is a wealthy businessman, in fact, a millionaire. A few years ago, he returned to his elementary school—Public School 121 in East Harlem, New York—now one of the poorest schools in the United States. He promised the sixty-one sixth-graders, including Aristides, that if they graduated from high school he would pay for their college education.

Lang is keeping that promise. He helped those students through their junior and senior high school years, paying for workshops, cultural trips, even tutors to help them stay in school. About one-half of the original sixty-one are in college, and their education is being paid for through Lang's "I Have a Dream" Foundation.

The students, who call themselves "Dreamers," are deeply grateful that Lang is keeping his promise. "Mr. Lang was one of the first people who took a personal interest in me and made me look at my life in a different way," says Aristides. "I know I'm going to make it. And someday I'll be big—real big—and pay the tuition for my class of dreamers."

Lang and his friends aren't the only ones keeping promises these days. Read about God's promises in **Jeremiah 31:27–37**.

- What effects might Lang's or God's promises have on the people involved?
- What choices must you make to receive the benefits of God's promises?

CONSIDER...

- reading Jesus' teaching in the Beatitudes (Matthew 5:1–12, p. 0000). Imagine Jesus using your name in his promises for believers.
- keeping a promise you've neglected.

FOR MORE, SEE...

- Lamentations 3:22–25 (p. 757)
- Matthew 7:7–11 (p. 919)
- John 2:18–22 (p. 1060)

when I took them by the hand
to bring them out of Egypt.
I was a husband to them,
but they broke that agreement," says the
LORD.
33"This is the agreement I will make
with the people of Israel at that time," says
the LORD:
"I will put my teachings in their minds
and write them on their hearts.
I will be their God,
and they will be my people.
34People will no longer have to teach their
neighbors and relatives
to know the LORD,
because all people will know me,
from the least to the most important," says
the LORD.
"I will forgive them for the wicked things
they did,
and I will not remember their sins
anymore."

The Lord Will Never Leave Israel

35The LORD makes the sun shine in the day
and the moon and stars to shine at night.
He stirs up the sea so that its waves crash on
the shore.
The LORD All-Powerful is his name.
This is what the LORD says:
36"Only if these laws should ever fail,"
says the LORD,
"will Israel's descendants[d] ever stop
being a nation before me."

37This is what the LORD says:
"Only if people can measure the sky above
and learn the secrets of the earth below,
will I reject all the descendants of Israel
because of what they have done," says the
LORD.

The New Jerusalem

38The LORD says, "The time is coming when
Jerusalem will be rebuilt for me—everything
from the Tower of Hananel to the Corner Gate.
39The measuring line will stretch from the Corner
Gate straight to the hill of Gareb. Then it will turn
to the place named Goah. 40The whole valley
where dead bodies and ashes are thrown, and all
the terraces out to the Kidron Valley on the east
as far as the corner of the Horse Gate—all that
area will be holy to the LORD. The city of Jerusalem will never again be torn down or destroyed."

Jeremiah Buys a Field

32 This is the word the LORD spoke to Jeremiah in the tenth year Zedekiah was
king of Judah, which was the eighteenth year of
Nebuchadnezzar. 2At that time the army of the
king of Babylon was surrounding Jerusalem. Jeremiah the prophet was under arrest in the courtyard of the guard, which was at the palace of the
king of Judah.
3Zedekiah king of Judah had put Jeremiah in
prison there. Zedekiah had asked, "Why have you
prophesied[d] the things you have?" (Jeremiah had
said, "This is what the LORD says: 'I will soon
hand the city of Jerusalem over to the king of Babylon, and he will capture it. 4Zedekiah king of Judah will not escape from the Babylonian army,
but he will surely be handed over to the king of
Babylon. And he will speak to the king of Babylon
face to face and see him with his own eyes. 5The
king will take Zedekiah to Babylon, where he will
stay until I have punished him,' says the LORD. 'If
you fight against the Babylonians, you will not
succeed.' ")
6While Jeremiah was in prison, he said, "The
LORD spoke this word to me: 7Your cousin Hanamel, son of your uncle Shallum, will come to you
soon. Hanamel will say to you, 'Jeremiah, you are
my nearest relative, so buy my field near the town
of Anathoth. It is your right and your duty to buy
that field.'
8"Then it happened just as the LORD had said.
My cousin Hanamel came to me in the courtyard
of the guard and said to me, 'Buy for yourself my
field near Anathoth in the land of Benjamin. It is
your right and duty to buy it and own it.' So I
knew this was a message from the LORD.
9"I bought the field at Anathoth from my
cousin Hanamel, weighing out seven ounces of
silver for him. 10I signed the record and sealed it
and had some people witness it. I also weighed
out the silver on the scales. 11Then I took both
copies of the record of ownership—the one that
was sealed that had the demands and limits of
ownership, and the one that was not sealed.
12And I gave them to Baruch son of Neriah, the
son of Mahseiah. My cousin Hanamel, the other
witnesses who signed the record of ownership, and many Jews sitting in the courtyard of
the guard saw me give the record of ownership
to Baruch.
13"With all the people watching, I told Baruch,
14'This is what the LORD All-Powerful, the God of
Israel, says: Take both copies of the record of
ownership—the sealed copy and the copy that
was not sealed—and put them in a clay jar so
they will last a long time. 15This is what the LORD
All-Powerful, the God of Israel, says: In the future
my people will once again buy houses and fields
for grain and vineyards in the land of Israel.'
16"After I gave the record of ownership to Baruch son of Neriah, I prayed to the LORD, 17Oh,
Lord GOD, you made the skies and the earth with
your very great power. There is nothing too hard

for you to do. 18You show love and kindness to thousands of people, but you also bring punishment to children for their parents' sins. Great and powerful God, your name is the LORD All-Powerful. 19You plan and do great things. You see everything that people do, and you reward people for the way they live and for what they do. 20You did miracles[d] and wonderful things in the land of Egypt. You have continued doing them in Israel and among the other nations even until today. So you have become well known. 21You brought your people, the Israelites, out of Egypt using signs and miracles and your great power and strength. You brought great terror on everyone. 22You gave them this land that you promised to their ancestors long ago, a fertile land. 23They came into this land and took it for their own, but they did not obey you or follow your teachings. They did not do everything you commanded. So you made all these terrible things happen to them.

24"Look! The enemy has surrounded the city and has built roads to the top of the walls to capture it. Because of war, hunger, and terrible diseases, the city will be handed over to the Babylonians who are attacking it. You said this would happen, and now you see it is happening. 25But now, Lord GOD, you tell me, 'Buy the field with silver and call in witnesses.' You tell me this while the Babylonian army is ready to capture the city."

26Then the LORD spoke this word to Jeremiah: 27"I am the LORD, the God of every person on the earth. Nothing is impossible for me. 28So this is what the LORD says: I will soon hand over the city of Jerusalem to the Babylonian army and to Nebuchadnezzar king of Babylon, who will capture it. 29The Babylonian army is already attacking the city of Jerusalem. They will soon enter it and start a fire to burn down the city and its houses. The people of Jerusalem offered sacrifices to Baal[d] on the roofs[n] of those same houses and poured out drink offerings to other idols to make me angry. 30From their youth, the people of Israel and Judah have done only the things I said were wrong. They have made me angry by worshiping idols made with their own hands," says the LORD. 31"From the day Jerusalem was built until now, this city has made me angry, so angry that I must remove it from my sight. 32I will destroy it, because of all the evil the people of Israel and Judah have done. The people, their kings and officers, their priests and prophets, all the people of Judah, and the people of Jerusalem have made me angry. 33They turned their backs to me, not their faces. I tried to teach them again and again, but they wouldn't listen or learn. 34They put their hateful idols in the place where I have chosen to be worshiped, so they made it unclean.[d] 35In the Valley of Ben Hinnom they built places to worship Baal so they could burn their sons and daughters as sacrifices to Molech.[d] But I never commanded them to do such a hateful thing. It never entered my mind that they would do such a thing and cause Judah to sin.

36"You are saying, 'Because of war, hunger, and terrible diseases, the city will be handed over to the king of Babylon.' But the LORD, the God of Israel, says about Jerusalem: 37I forced the people of Israel and Judah to leave their land, because I was furious and very angry with them. But soon I will gather them from all the lands where I forced them to go, and I will bring them back to this place, where they may live in safety. 38The people of Israel and Judah will be my people, and I will be their God. 39I will make them truly want to be one people with one goal. They will truly want to worship me all their lives, for their own good and for the good of their children after them.

40"I will make an agreement with them that will last forever. I will never turn away from them; I will always do good to them. I will make them want to respect me so they will never turn away from me. 41I will enjoy doing good to them. And with my whole being I will surely plant them in this land and make them grow."

42This is what the LORD says: "I have brought this great disaster to the people of Israel and Judah. In the same way I will bring the good things that I promise to do for them. 43You are saying, 'This land is an empty desert, without people or animals. It has been handed over to the Babylonians.' But in the future, people will again buy fields in this land. 44They will use their money to buy fields. They will sign and seal their agreements and call in witnesses. They will again buy fields in the land of Benjamin, in the area around Jerusalem, in the towns of Judah and in the mountains, in the western hills, and in southern Judah. I will make everything as good for them as it once was," says the LORD.

The Promise of the Lord

33 While Jeremiah was still locked up in the courtyard of the guards, the LORD spoke his word to him a second time: 2"These are the words of the LORD, who made the earth, shaped it, and gave it order, whose name is the LORD: 3'Judah, pray to me, and I will answer you. I will tell you important secrets you have never heard before.' 4This is what the LORD, the God of Israel, says about the houses in Jerusalem and the royal

roofs In Bible times houses were built with flat roofs. The roof was used for drying things such as flax and fruit. And it was used as an extra room, as a place for worship, and as a place to sleep in the summer.

palaces of Judah that have been torn down to be
used in defense of the attack by the Babylonian
army: 5'Some people will come to fight against
the Babylonians. They will fill these houses with
the bodies of people I killed in my hot anger. I
have turned away from this city because of all the
evil its people have done.
6" 'But then I will bring health and healing to
the people there. I will heal them and let them
enjoy great peace and safety. 7I will bring Judah
and Israel back from captivity and make them
strong countries as in the past. 8They sinned
against me, but I will wash away that sin. They
did evil and turned away from me, but I will forgive them. 9Then 'Jerusalem' will be to me a
name that brings joy! And people from all nations
of the earth will praise it when they hear about
the good things I am doing there. They will be
surprised and shocked at all the good things and
the peace I will bring to Jerusalem.'
10"You are saying, 'Our country is an empty
desert, without people or animals.' But this is
what the LORD says: It is now quiet in the streets
of Jerusalem and in the towns of Judah, without
people or animals, but it will be noisy there soon!
11There will be sounds of joy and gladness and the
happy sounds of brides and bridegrooms. There
will be the sounds of people bringing to the Temple[d] of the LORD their offerings of thanks to the LORD. They will say,

'Praise the LORD All-Powerful,
because the LORD is good!
His love continues forever!'

They will say this because I will again do good things for Judah, as I did in the beginning," says the LORD.
12This is what the LORD All-Powerful says:
"This place is empty now, without people or animals. But there will be shepherds in all the towns of Judah and pastures where they let their flocks
rest. 13Shepherds will again count their sheep as
the sheep walk in front of them. They will count them in the mountains and in the western hills, in southern Judah and the land of Benjamin, and around Jerusalem and the other towns of Judah!" says the LORD.

The Good Branch

14The LORD says, "The time is coming when I will do the good thing I promised to the people of Israel and Judah.
15In those days and at that time,
I will make a good branch sprout from
David's family.
He will do what is fair and right in the
land.

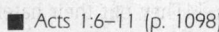

FUTURE

Will Peace Ever Come?

"The atomic bomb is another weapon in the arsenal of righteousness." —Harry S Truman, U.S. president

"The atomic age is here to stay—but are we?" —Bennett Cerf, publisher

"The way to win an atomic war is to make certain it never starts." —Omar Bradley, U.S. Army general

"There is no evil in the atom—only in men's souls." —Adlai Stevenson, statesman

The future can seem uncertain and dangerous, and the spread of nuclear weapons adds to that uncertainty. But, even in difficult times, God keeps his promises. Read one of God's promises for the future in **Jeremiah 33:14–16**.

- God promises a Savior in the passage. Do you think that promise includes being saved from nuclear weapons and war? Why or why not?
- How does your future look? How does faith in Christ affect the way you look at your future?

CONSIDER . . .

- each day asking God to guide some part of your future. For example, Monday: Who will I marry? Tuesday: What career should I choose?
- writing one paragraph on how you would like to be remembered after your death. Choose one thing to do this week to help you toward your goals.

FOR MORE, SEE . . .

- Genesis 9:8–17 (p. 11)
- Matthew 6:25–34 (p. 918)
- Acts 1:6–11 (p. 1098)

16At that time Judah will be saved,
and the people of Jerusalem will live in safety.
The branch will be named:
The LORD Does What Is Right."

17This is what the LORD says: "Someone from David's family will always sit on the throne of the family of Israel. 18And there will always be priests from the family of Levi. They will always stand before me to offer burnt offerings and grain offerings and sacrifices to me."

19The LORD spoke his word to Jeremiah, saying: 20"This is what the LORD says: I have an agreement with day and night that they will always come at the right times. If you could change that agreement, 21only then could you change my agreement with David and Levi. Only then would my servant David not have a descendant[d] ruling as king on David's throne. And only then would the family of Levi not be priests serving me in the Temple.[d] 22But I will give many descendants to my servant David and to the family group of Levi who serve me in the Temple. They will be as many as the stars in the sky that no one can count. They will be as many as the grains of sand on the seashore that no one can measure."

23The LORD spoke his word to Jeremiah, saying: 24"Jeremiah, have you heard what the people are saying? They say: 'The LORD turned away from the two families of Israel and Judah that he chose.' Now they don't think of my people as a nation anymore!"

25This is what the LORD says: "If I had not made my agreement with day and night, and if I had not made the laws for the sky and earth, 26only then would I turn away from Jacob's descendants. And only then would I not let the descendants of David my servant rule over the descendants of Abraham, Isaac, and Jacob. But I will be kind to them and cause good things to happen to them again."

A Warning to Zedekiah

34 The LORD spoke his word to Jeremiah when Nebuchadnezzar king of Babylon was fighting against Jerusalem and all the towns around it. Nebuchadnezzar had with him all his army and the armies of all the kingdoms and peoples he ruled. 2This is what the LORD, the God of Israel, said: "Jeremiah, go to Zedekiah king of Judah and tell him: 'This is what the LORD says: I will soon hand the city of Jerusalem over to the king of Babylon, and he will burn it down! 3You will not escape from the king of Babylon; you will surely be captured and handed over to him. You will see the king of Babylon with your own eyes, and he will talk to you face to face. And you will go to Babylon. 4But, Zedekiah king of Judah, listen to the promise of the LORD. This is what the LORD says about you: You will not be killed with a sword. 5You will die in a peaceful way. As people made funeral fires to honor your ancestors, the kings who ruled before you, so people will make a funeral fire to honor you. They will cry for you and sadly say, "Ah, master!" I myself make this promise to you, says the LORD.' "

6So Jeremiah the prophet[d] gave this message to Zedekiah in Jerusalem. 7This was while the army of the king of Babylon was fighting against Jerusalem and the cities of Judah that had not yet been taken—Lachish and Azekah. These were the only strong, walled cities left in the land of Judah.

Slaves Are Mistreated

8The LORD spoke his word to Jeremiah. This was after King Zedekiah had made an agreement with all the people in Jerusalem to free all the Hebrew slaves. 9Everyone was supposed to free his Hebrew slaves, both male and female. No one was to keep a fellow Jew as a slave. 10All the officers and all the people accepted this agreement; they agreed to free their male and female slaves and no longer keep them as slaves. So all the slaves were set free. 11But after that, the people who had slaves changed their minds. So they took back the people they had set free and made them slaves again.

12Then the LORD spoke his word to Jeremiah: 13"This is what the LORD, the God of Israel, says: I brought your ancestors out of Egypt where they were slaves and made an agreement with them. 14I said to your ancestors: 'At the end of every seven years, each one of you must set his Hebrew slaves free. If a fellow Hebrew has sold himself to you, you must let him go free after he has served you for six years.' But your ancestors did not listen or pay attention to me. 15A short time ago you changed your hearts and did what I say is right. Each of you gave freedom to his fellow Hebrews who were slaves. And you even made an agreement before me in the place where I have chosen to be worshiped. 16But now you have changed your minds. You have shown you do not honor me. Each of you has taken back the male and female slaves you had set free, and you have forced them to become your slaves again.

17"So this is what the LORD says: You have not obeyed me. You have not given freedom to your fellow Hebrews, neither relatives nor friends. But now I will give freedom, says the LORD, to war, to terrible diseases, and to hunger. I will make you hated by all the kingdoms of the earth. 18I will hand over the men who broke my agreement, who have not kept the promises they made before me. They cut a calf into two pieces before me and walked between the pieces.[n] 19These people made the agreement before me by walking between the pieces of the calf: the leaders of Judah and Jerusalem, the officers of the court, the priests, and all the people of the land. 20So I will hand them over to their enemies and to everyone who wants to kill them. Their bodies will become food for the birds of the air and for the wild animals of the earth. 21I will hand Zedekiah king of Judah and his officers over to their enemies, and to everyone who wants to kill them, and to the army of the king of Babylon, even though they have left Jerusalem. 22I will give the order, says the LORD, to bring the Babylonian army back to Jerusalem. It will fight against Jerusalem, capture it, set it on fire, and burn it down. I will destroy the towns in Judah so that they become ruins where no one lives!"

The Recabite Family Obeys God

35 When Jehoiakim son of Josiah was king of Judah, the LORD spoke his word to Jeremiah, saying: 2"Go to the family of Recab. Invite them to come to one of the side rooms of the Temple[d] of the LORD, and offer them wine to drink."

3So I went to get Jaazaniah son of Jeremiah,[n] the son of Habazziniah. And I gathered all of Jaazaniah's brothers and sons and the whole family of the Recabites together. 4Then I brought them into the Temple of the LORD. We went into the room of the sons of Hanan son of Igdaliah, who was a man of God. The room was next to the one where the officers stay and above the room of Maaseiah son of Shallum, the doorkeeper in the Temple. 5Then I put some bowls full of wine and some cups before the men of the Recabite family. And I said to them, "Drink some wine."

6But the Recabite men answered, "We never drink wine. Our ancestor Jonadab son of Recab gave us this command: 'You and your descendants[d] must never drink wine. 7Also you must never build houses, plant seeds, or plant vineyards, or do any of those things. You must live only in tents. Then you will live a long time in the land where you are wanderers.' 8So we Recabites have obeyed everything Jonadab our ancestor commanded us. Neither we nor our wives, sons, or daughters ever drink wine. 9We never build houses in which to live, or own fields or vineyards, or plant crops. 10We have lived in tents and have obeyed everything our ancestor Jonadab commanded us. 11But when Nebuchadnezzar king of Babylon attacked Judah, we said to each other, 'Come, we must enter Jerusalem so we can escape the Babylonian army and the Aramean army.' So we have stayed in Jerusalem."

12Then the LORD spoke his word to Jeremiah: 13"This is what the LORD All-Powerful, the God of Israel, says: Jeremiah, go and tell the men of Judah and the people of Jerusalem: 'You should learn a lesson and obey my message,' says the LORD. 14'Jonadab son of Recab ordered his descendants not to drink wine, and that command has been obeyed. Until today they have obeyed their ancestor's command; they do not drink wine. But I, the LORD, have given you messages again and again, but you did not obey me. 15I sent all my servants the prophets to you again and again, saying, "Each of you must stop doing evil. You must change and be good. Do not follow other gods to serve them. If you obey me, you will live in the land I have given to you and your ancestors." But you have not listened to me or paid attention to my message. 16The descendants of Jonadab son of Recab obeyed the commands their ancestor gave them, but the people of Judah have not obeyed me.'

17"So the LORD God All-Powerful, the God of Israel, says: 'I will soon bring every disaster I said would come to Judah and to everyone living in Jerusalem. I spoke to those people, but they refused to listen. I called out to them, but they did not answer me.' "

18Then Jeremiah said to the Recabites, "This is what the LORD All-Powerful, the God of Israel, says: 'You have obeyed the commands of your ancestor Jonadab and have followed all of his teachings; you have done everything he commanded.' 19So this is what the LORD All-Powerful, the God of Israel, says: 'There will always be a descendant of Jonadab son of Recab to serve me.' "

Jehoiakim Burns Jeremiah's Scroll

36 The LORD spoke this word to Jeremiah during the fourth year that Jehoiakim son of Josiah was king of Judah: 2"Get a scroll. Write on it all the words I have spoken to you about Israel and Judah and all the nations. Write everything from when I first spoke to you, when Josiah was king, until now. 3Maybe the family of Judah will hear what disasters I am planning to bring on them and will stop doing wicked things. Then I would forgive them for the sins and the evil things they have done."

4So Jeremiah called for Baruch son of Neriah. Jeremiah spoke the messages the LORD had given him, and Baruch wrote those messages on the scroll. 5Then Jeremiah commanded Baruch, "I cannot go to the Temple[d] of the LORD. I must stay

They . . . pieces. This showed that the men were willing to be killed, like this animal, if they did not keep their agreement.
Jeremiah Not the prophet Jeremiah, but a different man with the same name.

here. [6]So I want you to go to the Temple of the LORD on a day when the people are giving up eating. Read from the scroll to all the people of Judah who come into Jerusalem from their towns. Read the messages from the LORD, which are the words you wrote on the scroll as I spoke them to you.

SIDELIGHT: Baruch was Jeremiah's secretary and friend who recorded the prophet's thoughts on scrolls made from treated animal skins (Jeremiah 36:4). Baruch was an important citizen of Jerusalem and probably served as a royal clerk. That made working with Jeremiah an occupational hazard, since Jeremiah was rarely on the king's good side.

[7]Perhaps they will ask the LORD to help them. Perhaps each one will stop doing wicked things, because the LORD has announced that he is very angry with them." [8]So Baruch son of Neriah did everything Jeremiah the prophet[d] told him to do. In the LORD's Temple he read aloud the scroll that had the LORD's messages written on it.

[9]In the ninth month of the fifth year that Jehoiakim son of Josiah was king, a special time to give up eating was announced. All the people of Jerusalem and everyone who had come into Jerusalem from the towns of Judah were supposed to give up eating to honor the LORD. [10]At that time Baruch read to all the people there the scroll containing Jeremiah's words. He read the scroll in the Temple of the LORD in the room of Gemariah son of Shaphan, a royal secretary. That room was in the upper courtyard at the entrance of the New Gate of the Temple.

[11]Micaiah son of Gemariah, the son of Shaphan, heard all the messages from the LORD that were on the scroll. [12]Micaiah went down to the royal secretary's room in the king's palace where all of the officers were sitting: Elishama the royal secretary; Delaiah son of Shemaiah; Elnathan son of Acbor; Gemariah son of Shaphan; Zedekiah son of Hananiah; and all the other officers. [13]Micaiah told those officers everything he had heard Baruch read to the people from the scroll.

[14]Then the officers sent a man named Jehudi son of Nethaniah to Baruch. (Nethaniah was the son of Shelemiah, who was the son of Cushi.) Jehudi said to Baruch, "Bring the scroll that you read to the people and come with me."

So Baruch son of Neriah took the scroll and went with Jehudi to the officers. [15]Then the officers said to Baruch, "Please sit down and read the scroll to us."

So Baruch read the scroll to them. [16]When the officers heard all the words, they became afraid and looked at each other. They said to Baruch, "We must certainly tell the king about these words." [17]Then the officers asked Baruch, "Tell us, please, where did you get all these words you wrote on the scroll? Did you write down what Jeremiah said to you?"

[18]"Yes," Baruch answered. "Jeremiah spoke them all to me, and I wrote them down with ink on this scroll."

[19]Then the officers said to Baruch, "You and Jeremiah must go and hide, and don't tell anyone where you are."

[20]The officers put the scroll in the room of Elishama the royal secretary. Then they went to the king in the courtyard and told him all about the scroll. [21]So King Jehoiakim sent Jehudi to get the scroll. Jehudi brought the scroll from the room of Elishama the royal secretary and read it to the king and to all the officers who stood around the king. [22]It was the ninth month of the year, so King Jehoiakim was sitting in the winter apartment. There was a fire burning in a small firepot in front of him. [23]After Jehudi had read three or four columns, the king cut those columns off of the scroll with a penknife and threw them into the firepot. Finally, the whole scroll was burned in the fire. [24]King Jehoiakim and his servants heard everything that was said, but they were not frightened! They did not tear their clothes to show their sorrow. [25]Elnathan, Delaiah, and Gemariah even tried to talk King Jehoiakim out of burning the scroll, but he would not listen to them. [26]Instead, the king ordered Jerahmeel son of the king, Seraiah son of Azriel, and Shelemiah son of Abdeel to arrest Baruch the secretary and Jeremiah the prophet. But the LORD had hidden them.

SIDELIGHT: If you've ever written a long, difficult report in school, you know how scary it can be to have the teacher grade it. Imagine how Jeremiah felt when the king, after hearing what Jeremiah had written, cut up and burned his scroll (Jeremiah 36:20–26). Jeremiah didn't give up, though. He wrote an even longer book to replace the burned one (Jeremiah 36:27–32).

[27]So King Jehoiakim burned the scroll where Baruch had written all the words Jeremiah had spoken to him. Then the LORD spoke his word to Jeremiah: [28]"Get another scroll. Write all the words on it that were on the first scroll that Jehoiakim king of Judah burned up. [29]Also say this to Jehoiakim king of Judah: 'This is what the LORD

says: You burned up that scroll and said, "Why, Jeremiah, did you write on it 'the king of Babylon will surely come and destroy this land and the people and animals in it'?" 30So this is what the LORD says about Jehoiakim king of Judah: Jehoiakim's descendants[d] will not sit on David's throne. When Jehoiakim dies, his body will be thrown out on the ground. It will be left out in the heat of the day and in the cold frost of the night. 31I will punish Jehoiakim and his children and his servants, because they have done evil things. I will bring disasters upon them and upon all the people in Jerusalem and Judah — everything I promised but which they refused to hear.' "

32So Jeremiah took another scroll and gave it to Baruch son of Neriah, his secretary. As Jeremiah spoke, Baruch wrote on the scroll the same words that were on the scroll Jehoiakim king of Judah had burned in the fire. And many similar words were added to the second scroll.

Jeremiah in Prison

37 Nebuchadnezzar king of Babylon had appointed Zedekiah son of Josiah to be king of Judah. Zedekiah took the place of Jehoiachin son of Jehoiakim. 2But Zedekiah, his servants, and the people of Judah did not listen to the words the LORD had spoken through Jeremiah the prophet.[d]

3Now King Zedekiah sent Jehucal son of Shelemiah and the priest Zephaniah son of Maaseiah with a message to Jeremiah the prophet. This was the message: "Jeremiah, please pray to the LORD our God for us."

4At that time Jeremiah had not yet been put into prison. So he was free to go anywhere he wanted. 5The army of the king of Egypt had marched from Egypt toward Judah. Now the Babylonian army had surrounded the city of Jerusalem. When they heard about the Egyptian army marching toward them, the Babylonian army left Jerusalem.

6The LORD spoke his word to Jeremiah the prophet: 7"This is what the LORD, the God of Israel, says: Jehucal and Zephaniah, I know Zedekiah king of Judah sent you to seek my help. Tell this to King Zedekiah: 'The army of the king of Egypt came here to help you, but they will go back to Egypt. 8After that, the Babylonian army will return and attack Jerusalem and capture it and burn it down.'

9"This is what the LORD says: People of Jerusalem, do not fool yourselves. Don't say, 'The Babylonian army will surely leave us alone.' They will not! 10Even if you defeated all of the Babylonian army that is attacking you and there were only a few injured men left in their tents, they would come from their tents and burn down Jerusalem!"

11So the Babylonian army left Jerusalem to fight the army of the king of Egypt. 12Now Jeremiah tried to travel from Jerusalem to the land of Benjamin to get his share of the property that belonged to his family. 13When Jeremiah got to the Benjamin Gate of Jerusalem, the captain in charge of the guards arrested him. The captain's name was Irijah son of Shelemiah son of Hananiah. Irijah said, "You are leaving us to join the Babylonians!"

14But Jeremiah said to Irijah, "That's not true! I am not leaving to join the Babylonians." Irijah refused to listen to Jeremiah, so he arrested Jeremiah and took him to the officers of Jerusalem. 15Those rulers were very angry with Jeremiah and beat him. Then they put him in jail in the house of Jonathan the royal secretary, which had been made into a prison. 16So those people put Jeremiah into a cell in a dungeon, and Jeremiah was there for a long time.

17Then King Zedekiah sent for Jeremiah and had him brought to the palace. Zedekiah asked him in private, "Is there any message from the LORD?"

Jeremiah answered, "Yes, there is. Zedekiah, you will be handed over to the king of Babylon." 18Then Jeremiah said to King Zedekiah, "What crime have I done against you or your officers or the people of Jerusalem? Why have you thrown me into prison? 19Where are your prophets that prophesied this message to you: 'The king of Babylon will not attack you or this land of Judah?' 20But now, my master, king of Judah, please listen to me, and please do what I ask of you. Do not send me back to the house of Jonathan the royal secretary, or I will die there!"

21So King Zedekiah gave orders for Jeremiah to be put under guard in the courtyard of the guard and to be given bread each day from the street of the bakers until there was no more bread in the city. So he stayed under guard in the courtyard of the guard.

Jeremiah Is Thrown into a Well

38 Shephatiah son of Mattan, Gedaliah son of Pashhur, Jehucal son of Shelemiah, and Pashhur son of Malkijah heard what Jeremiah was telling all the people. He said: 2"This is what the LORD says: 'Everyone who stays in Jerusalem will die from war, or hunger, or terrible diseases. But everyone who surrenders to the Babylonian army will live; they will escape with their lives and live.' 3And this is what the LORD says: 'This city of Jerusalem will surely be handed over to the army of the king of Babylon. He will capture this city!' "

4Then the officers said to the king, "Jeremiah must be put to death! He is discouraging the soldiers who are still in the city, and all the people, by what he is saying to them. He does not want good to happen to us; he wants to ruin us."

5King Zedekiah said to them, "Jeremiah is in
your control. I cannot do anything to stop you."
6So the officers took Jeremiah and put him into
the well of Malkijah, the king's son, which was in
the courtyard of the guards. The officers used
ropes to lower Jeremiah into the well, which did
not have any water in it, only mud. And Jeremiah
sank down into the mud.

SIDELIGHT: Talk about being "the pits"! Jeremiah's "well of a jail" (Jeremiah 38:6) was a muddy cistern, a plastered hole in the ground that could have been twenty feet deep. It was originally used as a water supply.

7But Ebed-Melech, a Cushite and a servant in
the palace, heard that the officers had put Jeremiah into the well. As King Zedekiah was sitting
at the Benjamin Gate, 8Ebed-Melech left the palace and went to the king. Ebed-Melech said to
him, 9"My master and king, these rulers have
acted in an evil way. They have treated Jeremiah
the prophet badly. They have thrown him into a
well and left him there to die! When there is no
more bread in the city, he will starve to death."
10Then King Zedekiah commanded Ebed-
Melech the Cushite, "Take thirty men from the
palace and lift Jeremiah the prophet out of the
well before he dies."
11So Ebed-Melech took the men with him and
went to a room under the storeroom in the palace. He took some old rags and worn-out clothes
from that room. Then he let those rags down with
some ropes to Jeremiah in the well. 12Ebed-
Melech the Cushite said to Jeremiah, "Put these
old rags and worn-out clothes under your arms to
be pads for the ropes." So Jeremiah did as Ebed-
Melech said. 13The men pulled Jeremiah up with
the ropes and lifted him out of the well. And Jeremiah stayed under guard in the courtyard of the
guard.

Zedekiah Questions Jeremiah

14Then King Zedekiah sent someone to get Jeremiah the prophet[d] and bring him to the third entrance to the Temple[d] of the LORD. The king said
to Jeremiah, "I am going to ask you something.
Do not hide anything from me, but tell me everything honestly."
15Jeremiah said to Zedekiah, "If I give you an
answer, you will surely kill me. And even if I give
you advice, you will not listen to me."
16But King Zedekiah made a secret promise to
Jeremiah, "As surely as the LORD lives who has
given us breath and life, I will not kill you. And
I promise not to hand you over to the officers who
want to kill you."
17Then Jeremiah said to Zedekiah, "This is
what the LORD God All-Powerful, the God of Israel, says: 'If you surrender to the officers of the
king of Babylon, your life will be saved. Jerusalem
will not be burned down, and you and your family
will live. 18But if you refuse to surrender to the
officers of the king of Babylon, Jerusalem will be
handed over to the Babylonian army, and they
will burn it down. And you yourself will not escape from them.' "
19Then King Zedekiah said to Jeremiah, "I'm
afraid of some Jews who have already gone over
to the side of the Babylonian army. If the Babylonians hand me over to them, they will treat me
badly."
20But Jeremiah answered, "The Babylonians
will not hand you over to the Jews. Obey the
LORD by doing what I tell you. Then things will
go well for you, and your life will be saved. 21But
if you refuse to surrender to the Babylonians, the
LORD has shown me what will happen. 22All the
women left in the palace of the king of Judah will
be brought out and taken to the important officers
of the king of Babylon. Your women will make
fun of you with this song:

'Your good friends misled you
and were stronger than you.
While your feet were stuck in the mud,
they left you.'

23"All your wives and children will be brought
out and given to the Babylonian army. You yourself will not even escape from them. You will be
taken prisoner by the king of Babylon, and Jerusalem will be burned down."
24Then Zedekiah said to Jeremiah, "Do not tell
anyone that I have been talking to you, or you will
die. 25If the officers find out I talked to you, they
will come to you and say, 'Tell us what you said
to King Zedekiah and what he said to you. Don't
keep any secrets from us. If you don't tell us everything, we will kill you.' 26If they ask you, tell
them, 'I was begging the king not to send me back
to Jonathan's house to die.' "
27All the officers did come to question Jeremiah. So he told them everything the king had
ordered him to say. Then the officers said no more
to Jeremiah, because no one had heard what Jeremiah and the king had discussed.
28So Jeremiah stayed under guard in the courtyard of the guard until the day Jerusalem was captured.

The Fall of Jerusalem

39 This is how Jerusalem was captured:
Nebuchadnezzar king of Babylon
marched against Jerusalem with his whole army
and surrounded the city to attack it. This was dur-

ing the tenth month of the ninth year Zedekiah was king of Judah. 2This lasted until the ninth day of the fourth month in Zedekiah's eleventh year. Then the city wall was broken through. 3And all these officers of the king of Babylon came into Jerusalem and sat down at the Middle Gate: Nergal-Sharezer of the district of Samgar; Nebo-Sarsekim, a chief officer; Nergal-Sharezer, an important leader; and all the other important officers.

4When Zedekiah king of Judah and all his soldiers saw them, they ran away. They left Jerusalem at night and went out from the king's garden. They went through the gate that was between the two walls and then headed toward the Jordan Valley. 5But the Babylonian army chased them and caught up with Zedekiah in the plains of Jericho. They captured him and took him to Nebuchadnezzar king of Babylon, who was at the town of Riblah in the land of Hamath. There Nebuchadnezzar passed his sentence on Zedekiah. 6At Riblah the king of Babylon killed Zedekiah's sons and all the important officers of Judah as Zedekiah watched. 7Then he put out Zedekiah's eyes. He put bronze chains on Zedekiah and took him to Babylon.

8The Babylonians set fire to the palace and to the houses of the people, and they broke down the walls around Jerusalem. 9Nebuzaradan, commander of the king's special guards, took the people left in Jerusalem, those captives who had surrendered to him earlier, and the rest of the people of Jerusalem, and he took them all away to Babylon. 10But Nebuzaradan, commander of the guard, left some of the poorest people of Judah behind. They owned nothing, but that day he gave them vineyards and fields.

SIDELIGHT: The eighteen-month siege of Jerusalem by the Babylonians was a grueling experience for Jeremiah (Jeremiah 39:1–10). Lamentations 4 (p. 758) describes the horrible conditions, including starvation and cannibalism.

11Nebuchadnezzar king of Babylon had given these orders about Jeremiah through Nebuzaradan, commander of the guard: 12"Find Jeremiah and take care of him. Do not hurt him, but do for him whatever he asks you." 13So Nebuchadnezzar sent these men for Jeremiah: Nebuzaradan, commander of the guards; Nebushazban, a chief officer; Nergal-Sharezer, an important leader; and all the other officers of the king of Babylon. 14They had Jeremiah taken out of the courtyard of the guard. Then they turned him over to Gedaliah son of Ahikam son of Shaphan, who had orders to take Jeremiah back home. So they took him home, and he stayed among the people left in Judah.

15While Jeremiah was guarded in the courtyard, the LORD spoke his word to him: 16"Jeremiah, go and tell Ebed-Melech the Cushite this message: 'This is what the LORD All-Powerful, the God of Israel, says: Very soon I will make my words about Jerusalem come true through disaster, not through good times. You will see everything come true with your own eyes. 17But I will save you on that day, Ebed-Melech, says the LORD. You will not be handed over to the people you fear. 18I will surely save you, Ebed-Melech. You will not die from a sword, but you will escape and live. This will happen because you have trusted in me, says the LORD.' "

Jeremiah Is Set Free

40 The LORD spoke his word to Jeremiah after Nebuzaradan, commander of the guards, had set Jeremiah free at the city of Ramah. He had found Jeremiah in Ramah bound in chains with all the captives from Jerusalem and Judah who were being taken away to Babylon. 2When commander Nebuzaradan found Jeremiah, Nebuzaradan said to him, "The LORD your God announced this disaster would come to this place. 3And now the LORD has done everything he said he would do. This disaster happened because the people of Judah sinned against the LORD and did not obey him. 4But today I am freeing you from the chains on your wrists. If you want to, come with me to Babylon, and I will take good care of you. But if you don't want to come, then don't. Look, the whole country is open to you. Go wherever you wish." 5Before Jeremiah turned to leave, Nebuzaradan said, "Or go back to Gedaliah son of Ahikam, the son of Shaphan. The king of Babylon has chosen him to be governor over the towns of Judah. Go and live with Gedaliah among the people, or go anywhere you want."

Then Nebuzaradan gave Jeremiah some food and a present and let him go. 6So Jeremiah went to Gedaliah son of Ahikam at Mizpah and stayed with him there. He lived among the people who were left behind in Judah.

The Short Rule of Gedaliah

7Some officers and their men from the army of Judah were still out in the open country. They heard that the king of Babylon had put Gedaliah son of Ahikam in charge of the people who were left in the land: the men, women, and children who were the poorest. They were the ones who were not taken to Babylon as captives. 8So these soldiers came to Gedaliah at Mizpah: Ishmael son of Nethaniah, Johanan and Jonathan sons of Kareah, Seraiah son of Tanhumeth, the sons of Ephai the Netophathite, Jaazaniah son of the Maacathite, and their men.

9Gedaliah son of Ahikam, the son of Shaphan, made a promise to them, saying, "Do not be afraid to serve the Babylonians. Stay in the land and serve the king of Babylon. Then everything will go well for you. 10I myself will live in Mizpah and will speak for you before the Babylonians who come to us here. Harvest the wine, the summer fruit, and the oil, and put what you harvest in your storage jars. Live in the towns you control."

11The Jews in Moab, Ammon, Edom, and other countries also heard that the king of Babylon had left a few Jews alive in the land. And they heard the king of Babylon had chosen Gedaliah as governor over them. (Gedaliah was the son of Ahikam, the son of Shaphan.) 12When the people of Judah heard this news, they came back to Judah from all the countries where they had been scattered. They came to Gedaliah at Mizpah and gathered a large harvest of wine and summer fruit.

13Johanan son of Kareah and all the army officers of Judah still in the open country came to Gedaliah at Mizpah. 14They said to him, "Don't you know that Baalis king of the Ammonite people wants you dead? He has sent Ishmael son of Nethaniah to kill you." But Gedaliah son of Ahikam did not believe them.

15Then Johanan son of Kareah spoke to Gedaliah in private at Mizpah. He said, "Let me go and kill Ishmael son of Nethaniah. No one will know anything about it. We should not let Ishmael kill you. Then all the Jews gathered around you would be scattered to different countries again, and the few people of Judah who are left alive would be lost."

16But Gedaliah son of Ahikam said to Johanan son of Kareah, "Do not kill Ishmael! The things you are saying about Ishmael are not true."

41 In the seventh month Ishmael son of Nethaniah and ten of his men came to Gedaliah son of Ahikam at Mizpah. (Nethaniah was the son of Elishama.) Now Ishmael was a member of the king's family and had been one of the officers of the king of Judah. While they were eating a meal with Gedaliah at Mizpah, 2Ishmael and his ten men got up and killed Gedaliah son of Ahikam, the son of Shaphan, with a sword. (Gedaliah was the man the king of Babylon had chosen as governor over Judah.) 3Ishmael also killed all the Jews and the Babylonian soldiers who were there with Gedaliah at Mizpah.

4The day after Gedaliah was murdered, before anyone knew about it, 5eighty men came to Mizpah bringing grain offerings and incense[d] to the Temple[d] of the LORD. Those men from Shechem, Shiloh, and Samaria had shaved off their beards, torn their clothes, and cut themselves.[n] 6Ishmael son of Nethaniah went out from Mizpah to meet them, crying as he walked. When he met them, he said, "Come with me to meet Gedaliah son of Ahikam." 7So they went into Mizpah. Then Ishmael son of Nethaniah and his men killed seventy of them and threw the bodies into a deep well. 8But the ten men who were left alive said to Ishmael, "Don't kill us! We have wheat and barley and oil and honey that we have hidden in a field." So Ishmael let them live and did not kill them with the others. 9Now the well where he had thrown all the bodies had been made by King Asa as a part of his defenses against Baasha king of Israel. But Ishmael son of Nethaniah put dead bodies in it until it was full.

10Ishmael captured all the other people in Mizpah: the king's daughters and all the other people who were left there. They were the ones whom Nebuzaradan commander of the guard had chosen Gedaliah son of Ahikam to take care of. So Ishmael son of Nethaniah captured those people, and he started to cross over to the country of the Ammonites.

11Johanan son of Kareah and all his army officers with him heard about all the evil things Ishmael son of Nethaniah had done. 12So they took their men and went to fight Ishmael son of Nethaniah and caught him near the big pool of water at Gibeon. 13When the captives Ishmael had taken saw Johanan and the army officers, they were glad. 14So all the people Ishmael had taken captive from Mizpah turned around and ran to Johanan son of Kareah. 15But Ishmael son of Nethaniah and eight of his men escaped from Johanan and ran away to the Ammonites.

16So Johanan son of Kareah and all his army officers saved the captives that Ishmael son of Nethaniah had taken from Mizpah after he murdered Gedaliah son of Ahikam. Among those left alive were soldiers, women, children, and palace officers. And Johanan brought them back from the town of Gibeon.

The Escape to Egypt

17-18Johanan and the other army officers were afraid of the Babylonians. Since the king of Babylon had chosen Gedaliah son of Ahikam to be governor of Judah but Ishmael son of Nethaniah had murdered him, Johanan was afraid that the Babylonians would be angry. So they decided to run away to Egypt. On the way they stayed at Geruth Kimham, near the town of Bethlehem.

42 While there, Johanan son of Kareah and Jezaniah son of Hoshaiah went to Jeremiah the prophet.[d] All the army officers and all

shaved . . . themselves The men did this to show they were sad about the Temple in Jerusalem being destroyed.

the people, from the least important to the greatest, went along, too. 2They said to him, "Jeremiah, please listen to what we ask. Pray to the LORD your God for all the people left alive from the family of Judah. At one time there were many of us, but you can see that there are few of us now. 3So pray that the LORD your God will tell us where we should go and what we should do."

4Then Jeremiah the prophet answered, "I understand what you want me to do. I will pray to the LORD your God as you have asked. I will tell you everything he says and not hide anything from you."

5Then the people said to Jeremiah, "May the LORD be a true and loyal witness against us if we don't do everything the LORD your God sends you to tell us. 6It does not matter if we like the message or not. We will obey the LORD our God, to whom we are sending you. We will obey what he says so good things will happen to us."

7Ten days later the LORD spoke his word to Jeremiah. 8Then Jeremiah called for Johanan son of Kareah, the army officers with him, and all the other people, from the least important to the greatest. 9Jeremiah said to them, "You sent me to ask the LORD for what you wanted. This is what the God of Israel says: 10'If you will stay in Judah, I will build you up and not tear you down. I will plant you and not pull you up, because I am sad about the disaster I brought on you. 11Now you fear the king of Babylon, but don't be afraid of him. Don't be afraid of him,' says the LORD, 'because I am with you. I will save you and rescue you from his power. 12I will be kind to you, and he will also treat you with mercy and let you stay in your land.'

13"But if you say, 'We will not stay in Judah,' you will disobey the LORD your God. 14Or you might say, 'No, we will go and live in Egypt. There we will not see war, or hear the trumpets of war, or be hungry.' 15If you say that, listen to the message of the LORD, you who are left alive from Judah. This is what the LORD All-Powerful, the God of Israel, says: 'If you make up your mind to go and live in Egypt, these things will happen: 16You are afraid of war, but it will find you in the land of Egypt. And you are worried about hunger, but it will follow you into Egypt, and you will die there. 17Everyone who goes to live in Egypt will die in war or from hunger or terrible disease. No one who goes to Egypt will live; no one will escape the terrible things I will bring to them.'

18"This is what the LORD All-Powerful, the God of Israel, says: 'I showed my anger against the people of Jerusalem. In the same way I will show my anger against you when you go to Egypt. Other nations will speak evil of you. People will be shocked by what will happen to you. You will become a curse word, and people will insult you. And you will never see Judah again.'

19"You who are left alive in Judah, the LORD has told you, 'Don't go to Egypt.' Be sure you understand this; I warn you today 20that you are making a mistake that will cause your deaths. You sent me to the LORD your God, saying, 'Pray to the LORD our God for us. Tell us everything the LORD our God says, and we will do it.' 21So today I have told you, but you have not obeyed the LORD your God in all that he sent me to tell you. 22So now be sure you understand this: You want to go to live in Egypt, but you will die there by war, hunger, or terrible diseases."

43

So Jeremiah finished telling the people the message from the LORD their God; he told them everything the LORD their God had sent him to tell them.

2Azariah son of Hoshaiah, Johanan son of Kareah, and some other men were too proud. They said to Jeremiah, "You are lying! The LORD our God did not send you to say, 'You must not go to Egypt to live there.' 3Baruch son of Neriah is causing you to be against us. He wants you to hand us over to the Babylonians so they can kill us or capture us and take us to Babylon."

4So Johanan, the army officers, and all the people disobeyed the LORD's command to stay in Judah. 5But Johanan son of Kareah and the army officers led away those who were left alive from Judah. They were the people who had run away from the Babylonians to other countries but then had come back to live in Judah. 6They led away the men, women, and children, and the king's daughters. Nebuzaradan commander of the guard had put Gedaliah son of Ahikam son of Shaphan in charge of those people. Johanan also took Jeremiah the prophet[d] and Baruch son of Neriah. 7These people did not listen to the LORD. So they all went to Egypt to the city of Tahpanhes.

SIDELIGHT: Tahpanhes (Jeremiah 43:7) was an Egyptian border fortress in the delta area of the Nile River. It would be the first city that refugees from Israel would reach when they entered Egypt.

8In Tahpanhes the LORD spoke his word to Jeremiah: 9"Take some large stones. Bury them in the clay in the brick pavement in front of the king of Egypt's palace in Tahpanhes. Do this while the Jews are watching you. 10Then say to them, 'This is what the LORD All-Powerful, the God of Israel, says: I will soon send for my servant, Nebuchad-

nezzar king of Babylon. I will set his throne over
these stones I have buried, and he will spread his
covering for shade above them. 11He will come
here and attack Egypt. He will bring death to
those who are supposed to die. He will make prisoners of those who are to be taken captive, and
he will bring war to those who are to be killed
with a sword. 12Nebuchadnezzar will set fire to
the temples of the gods of Egypt and burn them.
And he will take the idols away as captives. As a
shepherd wraps himself in his clothes, so Nebuchadnezzar will wrap Egypt around him. Then he
will safely leave Egypt. 13He will destroy the stone
pillars in the temple of the sun god in Egypt, and
he will burn down the temples of the gods of
Egypt.' "

Disaster in Egypt

44 Jeremiah received a message from the
LORD for all the Jews living in Egypt—in
the cities of Migdol, Tahpanhes, Memphis, and in
southern Egypt. This was the message: 2"The
LORD All-Powerful, the God of Israel, says: You
saw all the terrible things I brought on Jerusalem
and the towns of Judah, which are ruins today
with no one living in them. 3It is because the people who lived there did evil. They made me angry
by burning incense[d] and worshiping other gods
that neither they nor you nor your ancestors ever
knew. 4I sent all my servants, the prophets,[d] to
you again and again. By them I said to you, 'Don't
do this terrible thing that I hate.' 5But they did not
listen or pay attention. They did not stop doing
evil things and burning incense to other gods. 6So
I showed my great anger against them. I poured
out my anger in the towns of Judah and the
streets of Jerusalem so they are only ruins and
piles of stones today.
7"Now the LORD All-Powerful, the God of Israel, says: Why are you doing such great harm to
yourselves? You are cutting off the men and
women, children and babies from the family of
Judah, leaving yourselves without anyone from
the family of Judah. 8Why do you want to make
me angry by making idols? Why do you burn incense to the gods of Egypt, where you have come
to live? You will destroy yourselves. Other nations
will speak evil of you and make fun of you. 9Have
you forgotten about the evil things your ancestors
did? And have you forgotten the evil the kings
and queens of Judah did? Have you forgotten
about the evil you and your wives did? These
things were done in the country of Judah and in
the streets of Jerusalem. 10Even to this day the
people of Judah are still too proud. They have not
learned to respect me or to follow my teachings.
They have not obeyed the laws I gave you and
your ancestors.
11"So this is what the LORD All-Powerful, the
God of Israel, says: I am determined to bring disasters on you. I will destroy the whole family of
Judah. 12The few who were left alive from Judah
were determined to go to Egypt and settle there,
but they will all die in Egypt. They will be killed
in war or die from hunger. From the least important to the greatest, they will be killed in war or
die from hunger. Other nations will speak evil
about them. People will be shocked by what has
happened to them. They will become a curse
word, and people will insult them. 13I will punish
those people who have gone to live in Egypt, just
as I punished Jerusalem, using swords, hunger,
and terrible diseases. 14Of the people of Judah
who were left alive and have gone to live in
Egypt, none will escape my punishment. They
want to return to Judah and live there, but none
of them will live to return to Judah, except a few
people who will escape."
15A large group of the people of Judah who
lived in southern Egypt were meeting together.
Among them were many women of Judah who
were burning incense to other gods, and their
husbands knew it. All these people said to Jeremiah, 16"We will not listen to the message from
the LORD that you spoke to us. 17We promised to
make sacrifices to the Queen Goddess,[d] and we
will certainly do everything we promised. We will
burn incense and pour out drink offerings to worship her, just as we, our ancestors, kings, and officers did in the past. All of us did these things in
the towns of Judah and in the streets of Jerusalem.
At that time we had plenty of food and were successful, and nothing bad happened to us. 18But
since we stopped making sacrifices to the Queen
Goddess and stopped pouring out drink offerings
to her, we have had great problems. Our people
have also been killed in war and by hunger."
19The women said, "Our husbands knew what
we were doing. We had their permission to burn
incense to the Queen Goddess and to pour out
drink offerings to her. Our husbands knew we
were making cakes that looked like her and were
pouring out drink offerings to her."
20Then Jeremiah spoke to all the people—men
and women—who answered him. 21He said to
them, "The LORD remembered that you and your
ancestors, kings and officers, and the people of the
land burned incense in the towns of Judah and in
the streets of Jerusalem. He remembered and
thought about it. 22Then he could not be patient
with you any longer. He hated the terrible things
you did. So he made your country an empty
desert, where no one lives. Other people curse
that country. And so it is today. 23All this happened because you burned incense to other gods.
You sinned against the LORD. You did not obey
him or follow his teachings or the laws he gave
you. You did not keep your part of the agreement

with him. So this disaster has happened to you. It
is there for you to see."
24Then Jeremiah said to all those men and
women, "People of Judah who are now in Egypt,
hear the word of the LORD: 25The LORD All-
Powerful, the God of Israel, says: You and your
wives did what you said you would do. You said,
'We will certainly keep the promises we made.
We promised to make sacrifices to the Queen
Goddess and to pour out drink offerings to her.'
So, go ahead. Do the things you promised, and
keep your promises. 26But hear the word of
the LORD. Listen, all you Jews living in Egypt. The
LORD says, 'I have sworn by my great name: The
people of Judah now living in Egypt will never
again use my name to make promises. They will
never again say in Egypt, "As surely as the Lord
GOD lives. . ." 27I am watching over them, not to
take care of them, but to hurt them. The Jews
who live in Egypt will die from swords or hunger
until they are all destroyed. 28A few will escape
being killed by the sword and will come back
to Judah from Egypt. Then, of the people of Judah
who came to live in Egypt, those who are left alive
will know if my word or their word came true. 29I
will give you a sign that I will punish you here in
Egypt,' says the LORD. 'When you see it happen,
you will know that my promises to hurt you will
really happen.' 30This is what the LORD says:
'Hophra king of Egypt has enemies who want to
kill him. Soon I will hand him over to his enemies
just as I handed Zedekiah king of Judah over to
Nebuchadnezzar king of Babylon, who wanted to
kill him.' "

A Message to Baruch

45 It was the fourth year that Jehoiakim son
of Josiah was king of Judah. Jeremiah the
prophet[d] told these things to Baruch son of Neriah, and Baruch wrote them on a scroll: 2"This
is what the LORD, the God of Israel, says to you,
Baruch: 3You have said, 'How terrible it is for me!
The LORD has given me sorrow along with my
pain. I am tired because of my suffering and cannot rest.' "
4The LORD said, "Say this to Baruch: 'This is
what the LORD says: I will soon tear down what
I have built, and I will pull up what I have planted
everywhere in Judah. 5Baruch, you are looking for
great things for yourself. Don't look for them, because I will bring disaster on all the people, says
the LORD. You will have to go many places, but
I will let you escape alive wherever you go.' "

Messages to the Nations

46 The LORD spoke this word to Jeremiah
the prophet[d] about the nations:
2This message is to Egypt. It is about the army
of Neco king of Egypt, which was defeated at the
city of Carchemish on the Euphrates River by
Nebuchadnezzar king of Babylon. This was in
the fourth year that Jehoiakim son of Josiah was
king of Judah. This is the LORD's message to
Egypt:

3"Prepare your shields, large and small,
and march out for battle!
4Harness the horses
and get on them!
Go to your places for battle
and put on your helmets!
Polish your spears.
Put on your armor!
5What do I see?
That army is terrified,
and the soldiers are running away.
Their warriors are defeated.
They run away quickly
without looking back.
There is terror on every side!" says the
LORD.
6"The fast runners cannot run away;
the strong soldiers cannot escape.
They stumble and fall
in the north, by the Euphrates River.
7Who is this, rising up like the Nile River,
like strong, fast rivers?
8Egypt rises up like the Nile River,
like strong, fast rivers.
Egypt says, 'I will rise up and cover the
earth.
I will destroy cities and the people in
them!'
9Horsemen, charge into battle!
Chariot drivers, drive hard!
March on, brave soldiers—
soldiers from the countries of Cush and Put
who carry shields,
soldiers from Lydia who use bows.
10"But that day belongs to the Lord GOD
All-Powerful.
At that time he will give those people the
punishment they deserve.
The sword will kill until it is finished,
until it satisfies its thirst for their blood.
The Lord GOD All-Powerful will offer a
sacrifice
in the land of the north, by the Euphrates
River.
11"Go up to Gilead and get some balm,[d]
people of Egypt!
You have prepared many medicines,
but they will not work;
you will not be healed.
12The nations have heard of your shame,
and your cries fill all the earth.
One warrior has run into another;
both of them have fallen down together!"

13This is the message the LORD spoke to Jeremiah the prophet[d] about Nebuchadnezzar king of
Babylon's coming to attack Egypt:

14"Announce this message in Egypt, and preach
it in Migdol.
Preach it also in the cities of Memphis and
Tahpanhes:
'Get ready for war,
because the battle is all around you.'
15Egypt, why were your warriors killed?
They could not stand because the LORD
pushed them down.
16They stumbled again and again
and fell over each other.
They said, 'Get up. Let's go back
to our own people and our homeland.
We must get away from our enemy's
sword!'
17In their homelands those soldiers called out,
'The king of Egypt is only a lot of noise.
He missed his chance for glory!' "

18The King's name is the LORD All-Powerful.
He says, "As surely as I live,
a powerful leader will come.
He will be like Mount Tabor among the
mountains,
like Mount Carmel by the sea.
19People of Egypt, pack your things
to be taken away as captives,
because Memphis will be destroyed.
It will be a ruin, and no one will live there.

20"Egypt is like a beautiful young cow,
but a horsefly is coming
from the north to attack her.
21The hired soldiers in Egypt's army
are like fat calves,
because even they all turn and run away
together;
they do not stand strong against the attack.
Their time of destruction is coming;
they will soon be punished.
22Egypt is like a hissing snake that is trying to
escape.
The enemy comes closer and closer.
They come against Egypt with axes
like men who cut down trees.
23They will chop down Egypt's army
as if it were a great forest," says the LORD.
"There are more enemy soldiers than
locusts;[d]
there are too many to count.
24The people of Egypt will be ashamed.
They will be handed over to the enemy
from the north."

25The LORD All-Powerful, the God of Israel,
says: "Very soon I will punish Amon, the god of
the city of Thebes. And I will punish Egypt, her
kings, her gods, and the people who depend on
the king. 26I will hand those people over to their
enemies, who want to kill them. I will give them
to Nebuchadnezzar king of Babylon and his officers. But in the future, Egypt will live in peace as
it once did," says the LORD.

A Message to Israel

27"People of Jacob, my servants, don't be
afraid;
don't be frightened, Israel.
I will surely save you from those faraway
places
and your children from the lands where
they are captives.
The people of Jacob will have peace and
safety again,
and no one will make them afraid.
28People of Jacob, my servants, do not be
afraid,
because I am with you," says the LORD.
"I will completely destroy the many different
nations
where I scattered you.
But I will not completely destroy you.
I will punish you fairly,
but I will not let you escape your
punishment."

A Message to the Philistines

47 Before the king of Egypt attacked the city
of Gaza, the LORD spoke his word to Jeremiah the prophet.[d] This message is to the Philistine people.

2This is what the LORD says:
"See, the enemy is gathering in the north like
rising waters.
They will become like an overflowing
stream
and will cover the whole country like a flood,
even the towns and the people living in
them.
Everyone living in that country
will cry for help;
the people will cry painfully.
3They will hear the sound of the running
horses
and the noisy chariots
and the rumbling chariot wheels.
Parents will not help their children to safety,
because they will be too weak to help.
4The time has come
to destroy all the Philistines.
It is time to destroy all who are left alive
who could help the cities of Tyre and
Sidon.
The LORD will soon destroy the Philistines,
those left alive from the island of Crete.

5The people from the city of Gaza will be sad
and shave their heads.
The people from the city of Ashkelon will
be made silent.
Those left alive from the valley,
how long will you cut yourselves?[n]

6"You cry, 'Sword of the LORD,
how long will you keep fighting?
Return to your holder.
Stop and be still.'
7But how can his sword rest
when the LORD has given it a command?
He has ordered it
to attack Ashkelon and the seacoast."

A Message to Moab

48 This message is to the country of Moab. This is what the LORD All-Powerful, the God of Israel, says:

"How terrible it will be for the city of Nebo,
because it will be ruined.
The town of Kiriathaim will be disgraced and
captured;
the strong city will be disgraced and
shattered.
2Moab will not be praised again.
Men in the town of Heshbon plan Moab's
defeat.
They say, 'Come, let us put an end to that
nation!'
Town of Madmen,[n] you will also be
silenced.
The sword will chase you.
3Listen to the cries from the town of
Horonaim,
cries of much confusion and destruction.
4Moab will be broken up.
Her little children will cry for help.
5Moab's people go up the path to the town of
Luhith,
crying loudly as they go.
On the road down to Horonaim,
cries of pain and suffering can be heard.
6Run! Run for your lives!
Go like a bush being blown through the
desert.
7You trust in the things you do and in your
wealth,
so you also will be captured.
The god Chemosh[d] will go into captivity
and his priests and officers with him.
8The destroyer will come against every town;
not one town will escape.
The valley will be ruined,
and the high plain will be destroyed,
as the LORD has said.
9Give wings to Moab,
because she will surely leave her land.
Moab's towns will become empty,
with no one to live in them.
10A curse will be on anyone who doesn't do
what the LORD says,
and a curse will be on anyone who holds
back his sword from killing.

11"The people of Moab have never known
trouble.
They are like wine left to settle;
they have never been poured from one jar to
another.
They have not been taken into captivity.
So they taste as they did before,
and their smell has not changed.
12A time is coming," says the LORD,
"When I will send people to pour you from
your jars.
They will empty Moab's jars
and smash her jugs.
13The people of Israel trusted that god in the
town of Bethel,
and they were ashamed when there was no
help.
In the same way Moab will be ashamed of
their god Chemosh.

14"You cannot say, 'We are warriors!
We are brave men in battle!'
15The destroyer of Moab and her towns has
arrived.
Her best young men will be killed!" says
the King,
whose name is the LORD All-Powerful.
16"The end of Moab is near,
and she will soon be destroyed.
17All you who live around Moab,
all you who know her, cry for her.
Say, 'The ruler's power is broken;
Moab's power and glory are gone.'

18"You people living in the town of Dibon,
come down from your place of honor
and sit on the dry ground,
because the destroyer of Moab has come
against you.
And he has destroyed your strong, walled
cities.
19You people living in the town of Aroer,
stand next to the road and watch.
See the man running away and the woman
escaping.
Ask them, 'What happened?'

sad and . . . yourselves The people did these things to show their sadness.
Madmen This name sounds like the Hebrew word for "be silenced."

20Moab is filled with shame, because she is
ruined.
Cry, Moab, cry out!
Announce at the Arnon River
that Moab is destroyed.
21People on the high plain have been punished.
Judgment has come to these towns:
Holon, Jahzah, and Mephaath;
22 Dibon, Nebo, and Beth Diblathaim;
23 Kiriathaim, Beth Gamul, and Beth Meon;
24 Kerioth and Bozrah.
Judgment has come to all the towns of
Moab, far and near.
25Moab's strength has been cut off,
and its arm broken!" says the LORD.

26"The people of Moab thought they were
greater than the LORD,
so punish them until they act as if they are
drunk.
Moab will fall and roll around in its own
vomit,
and people will even make fun of it.
27Moab, you made fun of Israel.
Israel was caught in the middle of a gang of
thieves.
When you spoke about Israel,
you shook your head and acted as if you
were better than it.
28People in Moab, leave your towns empty
and go live among the rocks.
Be like a dove that makes its nest
at the entrance of a cave.

29"We have heard that the people of Moab are
proud,
very proud.
They are proud, very proud,
and in their hearts they think they are
important."
30The LORD says,
"I know Moab's great pride, but it is
useless.
Moab's bragging accomplishes nothing.
31So I cry sadly for Moab,
for everyone in Moab.
I moan for the people from the town of Kir
Hareseth.
32I cry with the people of the town of Jazer
for you, the grapevines of the town of
Sibmah.
In the past your vines spread all the way to
the sea,
as far as the sea of Jazer.
But the destroyer has taken over
your fruit and grapes.
33Joy and happiness are gone
from the large, rich fields of Moab.
I have stopped the flow of wine from the
winepresses.[d]
No one walks on the grapes with shouts of
joy.
There are shouts,
but not shouts of joy.

34"Their crying can be heard from Moabite
towns,
from Heshbon to Elealeh and Jahaz.
It can be heard from Zoar as far away as
Horonaim and Eglath Shelishiyah.
Even the waters of Nimrim are dried up.
35I will stop Moab
from making burnt offerings at the places of
worship
and from burning incense[d] to their gods,"
says the LORD.

36"My heart cries sadly for Moab like a flute
playing a funeral song.
It cries like a flute for the people from Kir
Hareseth.
The money they made has all been taken
away.
37Every head has been shaved
and every beard cut off.
Everyone's hands are cut,
and everyone wears rough cloth around his
waist.[n]

SIDELIGHT: If you meet someone with a scraggly beard or long hair, don't assume he's just a scruffy guy. Maybe he read Jeremiah 48:37, which says that clipped beards and shaved heads were signs of disgrace and defeat. Don't tell that to any hair stylists!

38People are crying on every roof[n] in Moab
and in every public square.
There is nothing but sadness,
because I have broken Moab
like a jar no one wants," says the LORD.
39"Moab is shattered! The people are crying!
Moab turns away in shame!
People all around her make fun of her.
The things that happened fill them with
great fear."

40This is what the LORD says:

Every head . . . waist. The people did these things to show their sadness for those who had died.
roof In Bible times houses were built with flat roofs. The roof was used for drying things such as flax and fruit. And it was used as an extra room, as a place for worship, and as a place to sleep in the summer.

"Look! Someone is coming, like an eagle
diving down from the sky
and spreading its wings over Moab.
41The towns of Moab will be captured,
and the strong, walled cities will be
defeated.
At that time Moab's warriors will be
frightened,
like a woman who is having a baby.
42The nation of Moab will be destroyed,
because they thought they were greater
than the LORD.
43Fear, deep pits, and traps wait for you,
people of Moab," says the LORD.
44"People will run from fear,
but they will fall into the pits.
Anyone who climbs out of the pits
will be caught in the traps.
I will bring the year of punishment to Moab,"
says the LORD.

45"People have run from the powerful enemy
and have gone to Heshbon for safety.
But fire started in Heshbon;
a blaze has spread from the hometown of
Sihon king of Moab.
It burned up the leaders of Moab
and destroyed those proud people.
46How terrible it is for you, Moab!
The people who worship Chemosh have
been destroyed.
Your sons have been taken captive,
and your daughters have been taken away.

47"But in days to come,
I will make good things happen again to
Moab," says the LORD.

This ends the judgment on Moab.

A Message to Ammon

49 This message is to the Ammonite people.
This is what the LORD says:
"Do you think that Israel has no children?
Do you think there is no one to take the
land when the parents die?
If that were true, why did Molech[d] take
Gad's land
and why did Molech's people settle in
Gad's towns?"
2The LORD says,
"The time will come when I will make
Rabbah,
the capital city of the Ammonites, hear the
battle cry.
It will become a hill covered with ruins,
and the towns around it will be burned.
Those people forced Israel out of that land,
but now Israel will force them out!" says
the LORD.

3"People in the town of Heshbon, cry sadly
because the town of Ai is destroyed!
Those who live in Rabbah, cry out!
Put on your rough cloth to show your
sadness, and cry loudly.
Run here and there for safety inside the
walls,
because Molech will be taken captive
and his priests and officers with him.
4You brag about your valleys
and about the fruit in your valleys.
You are like an unfaithful child
who believes his treasures will save him.
You think, 'Who would attack me?'
5I will soon bring terror on you
from everyone around you,"
says the Lord GOD All-Powerful.
"You will all be forced to run away,
and no one will be able to gather you.

6"But the time will come
when I will make good things happen to
the Ammonites again,"
says the LORD.

A Message to Edom

7This message is to Edom. This is what the
LORD All-Powerful says:
"Is there no more wisdom in the town of
Teman?
Can the wise men of Edom no longer give
good advice?
Have they lost their wisdom?
8You people living in the town of Dedan,
run away and hide in deep caves,
because I will bring disaster on the people of
Esau.
It is time for me to punish them.
9If workers came and picked the grapes from
your vines,
they would leave a few grapes behind.
If robbers came at night,
they would steal only enough for
themselves.
10But I will strip Edom bare.
I will find all their hiding places,
so they will not be able to hide from me.
The children, relatives, and neighbors will
die,
and Edom will be no more.
11Leave the orphans, and I will take care of
them.
Your widows also can trust in me."

12This is what the LORD says: "Some people did
not deserve to be punished, but they had to drink
from the cup of suffering anyway. People of
Edom, you deserve to be punished, so you will
not escape punishment. You must certainly drink
from the cup of suffering." 13The LORD says, "I

swear by my own name that the city of Bozrah will become a pile of ruins! People will be shocked by what happened there. They will insult that city and speak evil of it. And all the towns around it will become ruins forever."

14I have heard a message from the LORD.
A messenger has been sent among the nations, saying,
"Gather your armies to attack it!
Get ready for battle!"

15"Soon I will make you the smallest of nations,
and you will be greatly hated by everyone.
16Edom, you frightened other nations,
but your pride has fooled you.
You live in the hollow places of the cliff
and control the high places of the hills.
Even if you build your home as high as an eagle's nest,
I will bring you down from there," says the LORD.

17"Edom will be destroyed.
People who pass by will be shocked to see the destroyed cities,
and they will be amazed at all her injuries.
18Edom will be destroyed like the cities of Sodom and Gomorrah
and the towns around them," says the LORD.
"No one will live there!
No one will stay in Edom."

19"Like a lion coming up from the thick bushes near the Jordan River
to attack a strong pen for sheep,
I will suddenly chase Edom from its land.
Who is the one I have chosen to do this?
There is no one like me,
no one who can take me to court.
None of their leaders can stand up against me."

20So listen to what the LORD has planned to do against Edom.
Listen to what he has decided to do to the people in the town of Teman.
He will surely drag away the young ones of Edom.
Their hometowns will surely be shocked at what happens to them.
21At the sound of Edom's fall, the earth will shake.
Their cry will be heard all the way to the Red Sea.
22The LORD is like an eagle swooping down
and spreading its wings over the city of Bozrah.
At that time Edom's soldiers will become very frightened,
like a woman having a baby.

A Message to Damascus

23This message is to the city of Damascus:
"The towns of Hamath and Arpad are put to shame,
because they have heard bad news.
They are discouraged.
They are troubled like the tossing sea.
24The city of Damascus has become weak.
The people want to run away;
they are ready to panic.
The people feel pain and suffering,
like a woman giving birth to a baby.
25Damascus was a city of my joy.
Why have the people not left that famous city yet?
26Surely the young men will die in the city squares,
and all her soldiers will be killed at that time," says the LORD All-Powerful.
27"I will set fire to the walls of Damascus,
and it will completely burn the strong cities of King Ben-Hadad."

A Message to Kedar and Hazor

28This message is to the tribe[d] of Kedar and the kingdoms of Hazor, which Nebuchadnezzar king of Babylon defeated. This is what the LORD says:
"Go and attack the people of Kedar,
and destroy the people of the East.
29Their tents and flocks will be taken away.
Their belongings will be carried off—
their tents, all their goods, and their camels.
Men will shout to them,
'Terror on every side!'

30"Run away quickly!
People in Hazor, find a good place to hide!" says the LORD.
"Nebuchadnezzar king of Babylon has made plans against you
and wants to defeat you.

31"Get up! Attack the nation that is comfortable,
that is sure no one will defeat it," says the LORD.
"It does not have gates or fences to protect it.
Its people live alone.
32The enemy will steal their camels
and their large herds of cattle as war prizes.
I will scatter the people who cut their hair short to every part of the earth,
and I will bring disaster on them from everywhere," says the LORD.

[33]"The city of Hazor will become a home for
wild dogs;
it will be an empty desert forever.
No one will live there,
and no one will stay in it."

A Message to Elam

[34]Soon after Zedekiah became king of Judah,
the LORD spoke this word to Jeremiah the
prophet.[d] This message is to the nation of Elam.
[35]This is what the LORD All-Powerful says:
"I will soon break Elam's bow,
its greatest strength.
[36]I will bring the four winds against Elam
from the four corners of the skies.
I will scatter its people everywhere the four
winds blow;
its captives will go to every nation.
[37]I will terrify Elam in front of their enemies,
who want to destroy them.
I will bring disaster to Elam
and show them how angry I am!" says the
LORD.
"I will send a sword to chase Elam
until I have killed them all.
[38]I will set up my throne in Elam to show that
I am king,
and I will destroy its king and its officers!"
says the LORD.
[39]"But I will make good things happen to Elam
again
in the future," says the LORD.

A Message to Babylon

50 This is the message the LORD spoke to
Babylon and the Babylonian people
through Jeremiah the prophet.[d]
[2]"Announce this to the nations.
Lift up a banner and tell them.
Speak the whole message and say:
'Babylon will be captured.
The god Bel[d] will be put to shame,
and the god Marduk[d] will be afraid.
Babylon's gods will be put to shame,
and her idols will be afraid!'
[3]A nation from the north will attack Babylon
and make it like an empty desert.
No one will live there;
both people and animals will run away."

[4]The LORD says, "At that time
the people of Israel and Judah will come
together.
They will cry and look for the LORD their
God.
[5]Those people will ask how to go to Jerusalem
and will start in that direction.
They will come and join themselves to the
LORD.
They will make an agreement with him
that will last forever,
an agreement that will never be forgotten.

[6]"My people have been like lost sheep.
Their leaders have led them in the wrong
way
and made them wander around in the
mountains and hills.
They forgot where their resting place was.
[7]Whoever saw my people hurt them.
And those enemies said, 'We did nothing
wrong.
Those people sinned against the LORD, their
true resting place,
the God their fathers trusted.'

[8]"Run away from Babylon,
and leave the land of the Babylonians.
Be like the goats that lead the flock.
[9]I will soon bring against Babylon
many great nations from the north.
They will take their places for war against it,
and it will be captured by people from the
north.
Their arrows are like trained soldiers
who do not return from war with empty
hands.
[10]The enemy will take all the wealth from the
Babylonians.
Those enemy soldiers will get all they
want," says the LORD.

[11]"Babylon, you are excited and happy,
because you took my land.
You dance around like a young cow in the
grain.
Your laughter is like the neighing of male
horses.
[12]Your mother will be very ashamed;
the woman who gave birth to you will be
disgraced.
Soon Babylonia will be the least important of
all the nations.
She will be an empty, dry desert.
[13]Because of the LORD's anger,
no one will live there.
She will be completely empty.
Everyone who passes by Babylon will be
shocked.
They will shake their heads when they see
all her injuries.

[14]"Take your positions for war against Babylon,
all you soldiers with bows.
Shoot your arrows at Babylon! Do not save
any of them,
because Babylon has sinned against the
LORD.
[15]Soldiers around Babylon, shout the war cry!

Babylon has surrendered, her towers have fallen,
and her walls have been torn down.
The LORD is giving her people the punishment they deserve.
You nations should give her what she deserves;
do to her what she has done to others.
16Don't let the people from Babylon plant their crops
or gather the harvest.
The soldiers treated their captives cruelly.
Now, let everyone go back home.
Let everyone run to his own country.

17"The people of Israel are like a flock of sheep that are scattered
from being chased by lions.
The first lion to eat them up
was the king of Assyria.
The last lion to crush their bones
was Nebuchadnezzar king of Babylon."

18So this is what the LORD All-Powerful, the
God of Israel, says:
"I will punish the king of Babylon and his country
as I punished the king of Assyria.
19But I will bring the people of Israel back to their own pasture.
They will eat on Mount Carmel and in Bashan.
They will eat and be full
on the hills of Ephraim and Gilead."
20The LORD says,
"At that time people will try to find Israel's guilt,
but there will be no guilt.
People will try to find Judah's sins,
but no sins will be found,
because I will leave a few people alive from Israel and Judah,
and I will forgive their sins.

21"Attack the land of Merathaim.
Attack the people who live in Pekod.
Chase them, kill them, and completely destroy them.
Do everything I commanded you!" says the LORD.

22"The noise of battle can be heard all over the country;
it is the noise of much destruction.
23Babylon was the hammer of the whole earth,
but how broken and shattered that hammer is now.
It is truly the most ruined
of all the nations.
24Babylon, I set a trap for you,
and you were caught before you knew it.
You fought against the LORD,
so you were found and taken prisoner.
25The LORD has opened up his storeroom
and brought out the weapons of his anger,
because the Lord GOD All-Powerful has work to do
in the land of the Babylonians.
26Come against Babylon from far away.
Break open her storehouses of grain.
Pile up her dead bodies like heaps of grain.
Completely destroy Babylon
and do not leave anyone alive.
27Kill all the young men in Babylon;
let them be killed like animals.
How terrible it will be for them, because the time has come for their defeat;
it is time for them to be punished.
28Listen to the people running to escape the country of Babylon!
They are telling Jerusalem
how the LORD our God is punishing Babylon as it deserves
for destroying his Temple.[d]

29"Call for the archers
to come against Babylon.
Tell them to surround the city,
and let no one escape.
Pay her back for what she has done;
do to her what she has done to other nations.
Babylon acted with pride against the LORD,
the Holy One of Israel.
30So her young men will be killed in her streets.
All her soldiers will die on that day," says the LORD.
31"Babylon, you are too proud, and I am against you,"
says the Lord GOD All-Powerful.
"The time has come
for you to be punished.
32Proud Babylon will stumble and fall,
and no one will help her get up.
I will start a fire in her towns,
and it will burn up everything around her."

33This is what the LORD All-Powerful says:
"The people of Israel
and Judah are slaves.
The enemy took them as prisoners
and won't let them go.
34But God is strong and will buy them back.
His name is the LORD All-Powerful.
He will surely defend them with power
so he can give rest to their land.
But he will not give rest to those living in Babylon."
35The LORD says,

"Let a sword kill the people living in Babylon
and her officers and wise men!
36Let a sword kill her false prophets,[d]
and they will become fools.
Let a sword kill her warriors,
and they will be full of terror.
37Let a sword kill her horses and chariots
and all the soldiers hired from other countries!
Then they will be like frightened women.
Let a sword attack her treasures,
so they will be taken away.
38Let a sword attack her waters
so they will be dried up.
She is a land of idols,
and the people go crazy with fear over them.

39"Desert animals and hyenas will live there,
and owls will live there,
but no people will ever live there again.
She will never be filled with people again.
40God completely destroyed the cities of Sodom and Gomorrah
and the towns around them," says the LORD.
"In the same way no people will live in Babylon,
and no human being will stay there.

41"Look! An army is coming from the north.
A powerful nation and many kings
are coming together from all around the world.
42Their armies have bows and spears.
The soldiers are cruel and have no mercy.
As the soldiers come riding on their horses,
the sound is loud like the roaring sea.
They stand in their places, ready for battle.
They are ready to attack you, city of Babylon.
43The king of Babylon heard about those armies,
and he became helpless with fear.
Distress has gripped him.
His pain is like that of a woman giving birth to a baby.

44"Like a lion coming up from the thick bushes near the Jordan River
to attack a strong pen for sheep,
I will suddenly chase the people of Babylon from their land.
Who is the one I have chosen to do this?
There is no one like me,
no one who can take me to court.
None of their leaders can stand up against me."

45So listen to what the LORD has planned to do against Babylon.
Listen to what he has decided to do to the people in the city of Babylon.
He will surely drag away the young ones of Babylon.
Their hometowns will surely be shocked at what happens to them.
46At the sound of Babylon's capture, the earth will shake.
People in all nations will hear Babylon's cry of distress.

51

This is what the LORD says:
"I will soon cause a destroying wind to blow
against Babylon and the Babylonian people.
2I will send foreign people to destroy Babylon
like a wind that blows chaff[d] away.
They will destroy the land.
Armies will surround the city
when the day of disaster comes upon her.
3Don't let the Babylonian soldiers prepare their bows to shoot.
Don't even let them put on their armor.
Don't feel sorry for the young men of Babylon,
but completely destroy her army.
4They will be killed in the land of the Babylonians
and will die in her streets.
5The Lord GOD All-Powerful
did not leave Israel and Judah,
even though they were completely guilty
in the presence of the Holy One of Israel.
6"Run away from Babylon
and save your lives!
Don't stay and be killed because of Babylon's sins.
It is time for the LORD to punish Babylon;
he will give Babylon the punishment she deserves.
7Babylon was like a gold cup in the LORD's hand
that made the whole earth drunk.
The nations drank Babylon's wine,
so they went crazy.
8Babylon has suddenly fallen and been broken.
Cry for her!
Get balm[d] for her pain,
and maybe she can be healed.

9"Foreigners in Babylon say, 'We tried to heal Babylon,
but she cannot be healed.
So let us leave her and each go to his own country.
Babylon's punishment is as high as the sky;
it reaches to the clouds.'

10"The people of Judah say, 'The LORD has shown us to be right.
Come, let us tell in Jerusalem

what the LORD our God has done.'

11"Sharpen the arrows!
Pick up your shields!
The LORD has stirred up the kings of the Medes,
because he wants to destroy Babylon.
The LORD will punish them as they deserve
for destroying his Temple.[d]
12Lift up a banner against the walls of Babylon!
Bring more guards.
Put the watchmen in their places,
and get ready for a secret attack!
The LORD will certainly do what he has planned
and what he said he would do against the people of Babylon.
13People of Babylon, you live near much water
and are rich with many treasures,
but your end as a nation has come.
It is time to stop you from robbing other nations.
14The LORD All-Powerful has promised in his own name:
'Babylon, I will surely fill you with so many enemy soldiers they will be like a swarm of locusts.[d]
They will stand over you and shout their victory.'

15"The LORD made the earth by his power.
He used his wisdom to build the world
and his understanding to stretch out the skies.
16When he thunders, the waters in the skies roar.
He makes clouds rise in the sky all over the earth.
He sends lightning with the rain
and brings out the wind from his storehouses.

17"People are so stupid and know so little.
Goldsmiths are made ashamed by their idols,
because those statues are only false gods.
They have no breath in them.
18They are worth nothing; people make fun of them.
When they are judged, they will be destroyed.
19But God, who is Jacob's Portion,[d] is not like the idols.
He made everything,
and he chose Israel to be his special people.
The LORD All-Powerful is his name.

20"You are my war club,
my battle weapon.
I use you to smash nations.
I use you to destroy kingdoms.
21I use you to smash horses and riders.
I use you to smash chariots and drivers.
22I use you to smash men and women.
I use you to smash old people and young people.
I use you to smash young men and young women.
23I use you to smash shepherds and flocks.
I use you to smash farmers and oxen.
I use you to smash governors and officers.

24"But I will pay back Babylon and all the Babylonians for all the evil things they did to Jerusalem in your sight," says the LORD.

25The LORD says,
"Babylon, you are a destroying mountain,
and I am against you.
You have destroyed the whole land.
I will put my hand out against you.
I will roll you off the cliffs,
and I will make you a burned-out mountain.
26People will not find any rocks in Babylon big enough for cornerstones.[d]
People will not take any rocks from Babylon to use for the foundation of a building,
because your city will be just a pile of ruins forever," says the LORD.

27"Lift up a banner in the land!
Blow the trumpet among the nations!
Get the nations ready for battle against Babylon.
Call these kingdoms of Ararat, Minni, and Ashkenaz to fight against her.
Choose a commander to lead the army against Babylon.
Send so many horses that they are like a swarm of locusts.
28Get the nations ready for battle against Babylon—
the kings of the Medes,
their governors and all their officers,
and all the countries they rule.
29The land shakes and moves in pain,
because the LORD will do what he has planned to Babylon.
He will make Babylon an empty desert,
where no one will live.
30Babylon's warriors have stopped fighting.
They stay in their protected cities.
Their strength is gone,
and they have become like frightened women.
Babylon's houses are burning.
The bars of her gates are broken.
31One messenger follows another;
messenger follows messenger.

They announce to the king of Babylon
that his whole city has been captured.
32The river crossings have been captured,
and the swamplands are burning.
All of Babylon's soldiers are terribly afraid."

33This is what the LORD All-Powerful, the God of Israel, says:
"The city of Babylon is like a threshing[d] floor,
where people crush the grain at harvest time.
The time to harvest Babylon is coming soon."
34"Nebuchadnezzar king of Babylon has defeated and destroyed us.
In the past he took our people away,
and we became like an empty jar.
He was like a giant snake that swallowed us.
He filled his stomach with our best things.
Then he spit us out.
35Babylon did terrible things to hurt us.
Now let those things happen to Babylon,"
say the people of Jerusalem.
"The people of Babylon killed our people.
Now let them be punished for what they did," says Jerusalem.

36So this is what the LORD says:
"I will soon defend you, Judah,
and make sure that Babylon is punished.
I will dry up Babylon's sea
and make her springs become dry.
37Babylon will become a pile of ruins,
a home for wild dogs.
People will be shocked by what happened there.
No one will live there anymore.
38Babylon's people roar like young lions;
they growl like baby lions.
39While they are stirred up,
I will give a feast for them
and make them drunk.
They will shout and laugh.
And they will sleep forever and never wake up!" says the LORD.
40"I will take the people of Babylon to be killed.
They will be like lambs,
like sheep and goats waiting to be killed.

41"How Babylon has been defeated!
The pride of the whole earth has been taken captive.
People from other nations are shocked at what happened to Babylon,
and the things they see make them afraid.
42The sea has risen over Babylon;
its roaring waves cover her.
43Babylon's towns are ruined and empty.
It has become a dry, desert land,
a land where no one lives.
People do not even travel through Babylon.
44I will punish the god Bel[d] in Babylon.
I will make him spit out what he has swallowed.
Nations will no longer come to Babylon;
even the wall around the city will fall.

45"Come out of Babylon, my people!
Run for your lives!
Run from the LORD's great anger.
46Don't lose courage;
rumors will spread through the land, but don't be afraid.
One rumor comes this year, and another comes the next year.
There will be rumors of terrible fighting in the country,
of rulers fighting against rulers.
47The time will surely come
when I will punish the idols of Babylon,
and the whole land will be disgraced.
There will be many dead people lying all around.
48Then heaven and earth and all that is in them
will shout for joy about Babylon.
They will shout because the army comes from the north
to destroy Babylon," says the LORD.

49"Babylon must fall, because she killed people from Israel.
She killed people from everywhere on earth.
50You who have escaped being killed with swords,
leave Babylon! Don't wait!
Remember the LORD in the faraway land
and think about Jerusalem."

51"We people of Judah are disgraced,
because we have been insulted.
We have been shamed,
because strangers have gone into
the holy places of the LORD's Temple!"[d]

52So the LORD says, "The time is coming soon
when I will punish the idols of Babylon.
Wounded people will cry with pain
all over that land.
53Even if Babylon grows until she touches the sky,
and even if she makes her highest cities strong,
I will send people to destroy her," says the LORD.

54"Sounds of people crying are heard in Babylon.
Sounds of people destroying things

are heard in the land of the Babylonians.
55 The LORD is destroying Babylon
and making the loud sounds of the city
become silent.
Enemies come roaring in like ocean waves.
The roar of their voices is heard all around.
56 The army has come to destroy Babylon.
Her soldiers have been captured,
and their bows are broken,
because the LORD is a God who punishes
people for the evil they do.
He gives them the full punishment they
deserve.
57 I will make Babylon's rulers and wise men
drunk,
and her governors, officers, and soldiers,
too.
Then they will sleep forever and never wake
up," says the King,
whose name is the LORD All-Powerful.

58 This is what the LORD All-Powerful says:
"Babylon's thick wall will be completely
pulled down
and her high gates burned.
The people will work hard, but it won't help;
their work will only become fuel for the
flames!"

A Message to Babylon

59 This is the message that Jeremiah the
prophet[d] gave to the officer Seraiah son of Neriah,
who was the son of Mahseiah. Seraiah went to
Babylon with Zedekiah king of Judah in the fourth
year Zedekiah was king of Judah. His duty was to
arrange the king's food and housing on the trip.
60 Jeremiah had written on a scroll all the terrible
things that would happen to Babylon, all these
words about Babylon. 61 Jeremiah said to Seraiah,
"As soon as you come to Babylon, be sure to read
this message so all the people can hear you.
62 Then say, 'LORD, you have said that you will
destroy this place so that no people or animals will
live in it. It will be an empty ruin forever.' 63 After
you finish reading this scroll, tie a stone to it and
throw it into the Euphrates River. 64 Then say, 'In
the same way Babylon will sink and will not rise
again because of the terrible things I will make
happen here. Her people will fall.' "

The words of Jeremiah end here.

The Fall of Jerusalem

52 Zedekiah was twenty-one years old
when he became king, and he was king
in Jerusalem for eleven years. His mother's name
was Hamutal daughter of Jeremiah,[n] and she was
from Libnah. 2 Zedekiah did what the LORD said
was wrong, just as Jehoiakim had done. 3 All this
happened in Jerusalem and Judah because the
LORD was angry with them. Finally, he threw
them out of his presence.

Zedekiah turned against the king of Babylon.
4 Then Nebuchadnezzar king of Babylon marched
against Jerusalem with his whole army. They
made a camp around the city and built devices all
around the city walls to attack it. This happened
on Zedekiah's ninth year, tenth month, and tenth
day as king. 5 And the city was under attack until
Zedekiah's eleventh year as king.

6 By the ninth day of the fourth month, the hunger was terrible in the city; there was no food for
the people to eat. 7 Then the city wall was broken
through, and the whole army of Judah ran away
at night. They left the city through the gate between the two walls by the king's garden. Even
though the Babylonians were surrounding the
city, Zedekiah and his men headed toward the
Jordan Valley.

8 But the Babylonian army chased King Zedekiah and caught him in the plains of Jericho. All
of his army was scattered from him. 9 So the Babylonians captured Zedekiah and took him to the
king of Babylon at the town of Riblah in the land
of Hamath. There he passed sentence on Zedekiah. 10 At Riblah the king of Babylon killed Zedekiah's sons as he watched. The king also killed
all the officers of Judah. 11 Then he put out Zedekiah's eyes, and put bronze chains on him, and
took him to Babylon. And the king kept Zedekiah
in prison there until the day he died.

12 Nebuzaradan, commander of the king's special guards and servant of the king of Babylon,
came to Jerusalem on the tenth day of the fifth
month. This was in Nebuchadnezzar's nineteenth
year as king of Babylon. 13 Nebuzaradan set fire to
the Temple[d] of the LORD, the palace, and all the
houses of Jerusalem; every important building
was burned. 14 The whole Babylonian army, led by
the commander of the king's special guards, broke
down all the walls around Jerusalem. 15 Nebuzaradan, the commander of the king's special guards,
took captive some of the poorest people, those
who were left in Jerusalem, those who had surrendered to the king of Babylon, and the skilled
craftsmen who were left in Jerusalem. 16 But Nebuzaradan left behind some of the poorest people
of the land to take care of the vineyards and fields.

17 The Babylonians broke into pieces the bronze
pillars, the bronze stands, and the large bronze
bowl, called the Sea, which were in the Temple
of the LORD. Then they carried all the bronze
pieces to Babylon. 18 They also took the pots, shovels, wick trimmers, bowls, dishes, and all the
bronze objects used to serve in the Temple. 19 The

Jeremiah This is not the prophet Jeremiah but a different man with the same name.

commander of the king's special guards took away bowls, pans for carrying hot coals, large bowls, pots, lampstands, pans, and bowls used for drink offerings. He took everything that was made of pure gold or silver.

20There was so much bronze that it could not be weighed: two pillars, the large bronze bowl called the Sea with the twelve bronze bulls under it, and the movable stands, which King Solomon had made for the Temple of the LORD.

21Each of the pillars was about twenty-seven feet high, eighteen feet around, and hollow inside. The wall of each pillar was three inches thick. 22The bronze capital[d] on top of the one pillar was about seven and one-half feet high. It was decorated with a net design and bronze pomegranates[d] all around it. The other pillar also had pomegranates and was like the first pillar. 23There were ninety-six pomegranates on the sides of the pillars. There was a total of a hundred pomegranates above the net design.

> **SIDELIGHT:** If you think allowances are just for kids, read Jeremiah 52:34, which tells about an allowance for King Jehoiachin. Archaeologists have uncovered actual records that show the allowances the king and his family received.

24The commander of the king's special guards took as prisoners Seraiah the chief priest, Zephaniah the priest next in rank, and the three doorkeepers. 25He also took from the city the officer in charge of the soldiers, seven people who advised the king, the royal secretary who selected people for the army, and sixty other men from Judah who were in the city when it fell. 26Nebuzaradan, the commander, took these people and brought them to the king of Babylon at the town of Riblah. 27There at Riblah, in the land of Hamath, the king had them killed.

So the people of Judah were led away from their country as captives. 28This is the number of the people Nebuchadnezzar took away as captives: in the seventh year, 3,023 Jews; 29in Nebuchadnezzar's eighteenth year, 832 people from Jerusalem; 30in Nebuchadnezzar's twenty-third year, Nebuzaradan, commander of the king's special guards, took 745 Jews as captives.

In all 4,600 people were taken captive.

Jehoiachin Is Set Free

31Jehoiachin king of Judah was in prison in Babylon for thirty-seven years. The year Evil-Merodach became king of Babylon he let Jehoiachin king of Judah out of prison. He set Jehoiachin free on the twenty-fifth day of the twelfth month. 32Evil-Merodach spoke kindly to Jehoiachin and gave him a seat of honor above the seats of the other kings who were with him in Babylon. 33So Jehoiachin put away his prison clothes, and for the rest of his life, he ate at the king's table. 34Every day the king of Babylon gave Jehoiachin an allowance. This lasted as long as he lived, until the day Jehoiachin died.

LAMENTATIONS

Why Read This Book:

- Find ways to express grief to God (Lamentations 1—2).
- Learn about taking responsibility for choices and consequences (Lamentations 3—4).
- Be encouraged to turn to God in times of trouble (Lamentations 5).

Behind the Scenes:

All of Jerusalem was in ruins.
Babylonians had surrounded the city and then burned it to the ground.
Children, women and men had been killed.
Desolation was everywhere.
Everything the Jews had known and loved was gone.
Full of sorrow, the five poems in Lamentations were written.
Grief is evident in each of the poems.
Hope shines through only toward the end of the book.
In future years, people read the book in times of sorrow.
Jews read it each year in August to remember the Temple's destruction and to repent of their sins.

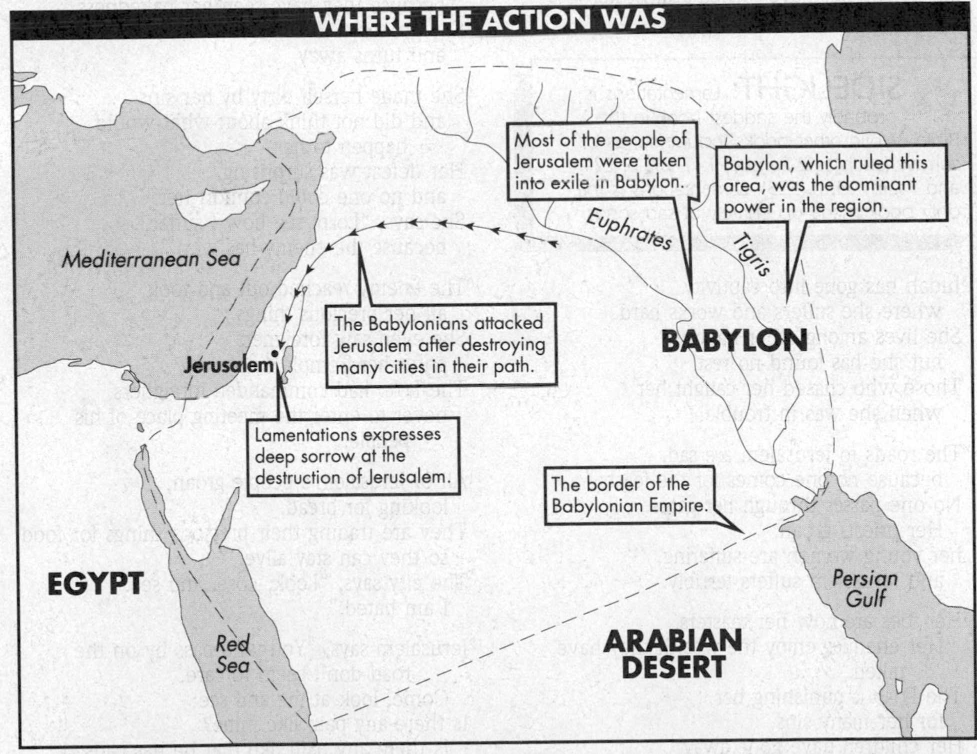
WHERE THE ACTION WAS
Most of the people of Jerusalem were taken into exile in Babylon.
Babylon, which ruled this area, was the dominant power in the region.
Euphrates
Tigris
Mediterranean Sea
The Babylonians attacked Jerusalem after destroying many cities in their path.
BABYLON
Jerusalem
Lamentations expresses deep sorrow at the destruction of Jerusalem.
The border of the Babylonian Empire.
EGYPT
Persian Gulf
ARABIAN DESERT
Red Sea

WHEN THE ACTION WAS

- 1000BC
- The kingdom was split between Israel and Judah
- 750BC
- The Northern Kingdom (Israel) fell to Assyria
- Jerusalem was destroyed by the Babylonians
- The poems in Lamentations were written
- The Jews began returning from exile
- 500BC
- 250BC
- BC/AD
- Jesus was born

Behind the Scenes (cont.): Knowing God's love can help through times of crisis like this.

Like the lines above, each stanza in the five poems in Lamentations begins with a different consecutive letter of the Hebrew alphabet—twenty-two letters in all. Of course, we can't see the structure in English, because the translated words are different. But the ancient Hebrews understood that the poems expressed their sorrow from beginning to end, "from A to Z."

Jerusalem Cries over Her Loss

1 Jerusalem once was full of people,
but now the city is empty.
Jerusalem once was a great city among the nations,
but now she[n] is like a widow.
She was like a queen of all the other cities,
but now she is a slave.

2She cries loudly at night,
and tears are on her cheeks.
There is no one to comfort her;
all who loved her are gone.
All her friends have turned against her
and are now her enemies.

> **SIDELIGHT:** Lamentations is probably the saddest book in the Bible. While other books include songs of sorrow (such as 2 Samuel 1:17–27, p. 274, and Psalm 74, p. 525), Lamentations is the only book made up entirely of sad songs.

3Judah has gone into captivity
where she suffers and works hard.
She lives among other nations,
but she has found no rest.
Those who chased her caught her
when she was in trouble.

4The roads to Jerusalem are sad,
because no one comes for the feasts.
No one passes through her gates.
Her priests groan,
her young women are suffering,
and Jerusalem suffers terribly.

5Her foes are now her masters.
Her enemies enjoy the wealth they have taken.
The LORD is punishing her
for her many sins.
Her children have gone away
as captives of the enemy.

6The beauty of Jerusalem
has gone away.
Her rulers are like deer
that cannot find food.
They are weak
and run from the hunters.

7Jerusalem is suffering and homeless.
She remembers all the good things
from the past.
But her people were defeated by the enemy,
and there was no one to help her.
When her enemies saw her,
they laughed to see her ruined.

8Jerusalem sinned terribly,
so she has become unclean.[d]
Those who honored her now hate her,
because they have seen her nakedness.
She groans
and turns away.

9She made herself dirty by her sins
and did not think about what would happen to her.
Her defeat was surprising,
and no one could comfort her.
She says, "LORD, see how I suffer,
because the enemy has won."

10The enemy reached out and took
all her precious things.
She even saw foreigners
enter her Temple.[d]
The LORD had commanded foreigners
never to enter the meeting place of his people.

11All of Jerusalem's people groan,
looking for bread.
They are trading their precious things for food
so they can stay alive.
The city says, "Look, LORD, and see.
I am hated."

12Jerusalem says, "You who pass by on the road don't seem to care.
Come, look at me and see:
Is there any pain like mine?
Is there any pain like that he has caused me?
The LORD has punished me
on the day of his great anger.

13"He sent fire from above
that went down into my bones.

she In this poem the city of Jerusalem is described as a woman.

He stretched out a net for my feet
and turned me back.
He made me so sad and lonely
that I am weak all day.

14"He has noticed my sins;
they are tied together by his hands;
they hang around my neck.
He has turned my strength into weakness.
The Lord has handed me over
to those who are stronger than I.

15"The Lord has rejected
all my mighty men inside my walls.
He brought an army against me
to destroy my young men.
As if in a winepress,[d] the Lord has crushed
the capital city of Judah.

16"I cry about these things;
my eyes overflow with tears.
There is no one near to comfort me,
no one who can give me strength again.
My children are left sad and lonely,
because the enemy has won."

17Jerusalem reaches out her hands,
but there is no one to comfort her.
The LORD commanded the people of Jacob
to be surrounded by their enemies.
Jerusalem is now unclean
like those around her.

18Jerusalem says, "The LORD is right,
but I refused to obey him.
Listen, all you people,
and look at my pain.
My young women and men
have gone into captivity.

19"I called out to my friends,
but they turned against me.
My priests and my older leaders
have died in the city
while looking for food
to stay alive.

20"Look at me, LORD. I am upset
and greatly troubled.
My heart is troubled,
because I have been so stubborn.
Out in the streets, the sword kills;
inside the houses, death destroys.

21"People have heard my groaning,
and there is no one to comfort me.
All my enemies have heard of my trouble,
and they are happy you have done this to me.
Now bring that day you have announced
so that my enemies will be like me.

22"Look at all their evil.
Do to them what you have done to me
because of all my sins.
I groan over and over again,
and I am afraid."

The Lord Destroyed Jerusalem

2 Look how the Lord in his anger
has brought Jerusalem to shame.
He has thrown down the greatness of Israel
from the sky to the earth;
he did not remember the Temple,[d] his footstool,
on the day of his anger.

2The Lord swallowed up without mercy
all the houses of the people of Jacob;
in his anger he pulled down
the strong places of Judah.
He threw her kingdom and its rulers
down to the ground in dishonor.

3In his anger he has removed
all the strength of Israel;
he took away his power from Israel
when the enemy came.
He burned against the people of Jacob like a flaming fire
that burns up everything around it.

4Like an enemy, he prepared to shoot his bow,
and his hand was against us.
Like an enemy, he killed
all the good-looking people;
he poured out his anger like fire
on the tents of Jerusalem.

5The Lord was like an enemy;
he swallowed up Israel.
He swallowed up all her palaces
and destroyed all her strongholds.[d]
He has caused more moaning and groaning for Judah.

6He cut down his Temple like a garden;
he destroyed the meeting place.
The LORD has made Jerusalem forget
the set feasts and Sabbath[d] days.
He has rejected the king and the priest
in his great anger.

7The Lord has rejected his altar
and abandoned his Temple.
He has handed over to the enemy
the walls of Jerusalem's palaces.
Their uproar in the LORD's Temple
was like that of a feast day.

8The LORD planned to destroy
the wall around Jerusalem.
He measured the wall

and did not stop himself from destroying it.
He made the walls and defenses sad;
together they have fallen.

9Jerusalem's gates have fallen to the ground;
he destroyed and smashed the bars of the gates.
Her king and her princes are among the nations.
The teaching of the LORD has stopped,
and the prophets[d] do not have
visions from the LORD.

10The older leaders of Jerusalem
sit on the ground in silence.
They throw dust on their heads
and put on rough cloth to show their sadness.
The young women of Jerusalem
bow their heads to the ground in sorrow.

11My eyes have no more tears,
and I am sick to my stomach.
I feel empty inside,
because my people have been destroyed.
Children and babies are fainting
in the streets of the city.

12They ask their mothers,
"Where is the grain and wine?"
They faint like wounded soldiers
in the streets of the city
and die in their mothers' arms.

13What can I say about you, Jerusalem?
What can I compare you to?
What can I say you are like?
How can I comfort you, Jerusalem?
Your ruin is as deep as the sea.
No one can heal you.

14Your prophets saw visions,
but they were false and worth nothing.
They did not point out your sins
to keep you from being captured.
They preached what was false
and led you wrongly.

15All who pass by on the road
clap their hands at you;
they make fun of Jerusalem
and shake their heads.
They ask, "Is this the city that people called
the most beautiful city,
the happiest place on earth?"

16All your enemies open their mouths
to speak against you.
They make fun and grind their teeth in anger.
They say, "We have swallowed you up.
This is the day we were waiting for!
We have finally seen it happen."

17The LORD has done what he planned;
he has kept his word
that he commanded long ago.
He has destroyed without mercy,
and he has let your enemies laugh at you.
He has strengthened your enemies.

18The people cry out to the Lord.
Wall of Jerusalem,
let your tears flow
like a river day and night.
Do not stop
or let your eyes rest.

19Get up, cry out in the night,
even as the night begins.
Pour out your heart like water
in prayer to the Lord.
Lift up your hands in prayer to him
for the life of your children
who are fainting with hunger
on every street corner.

20Jerusalem says: "Look, LORD, and see
to whom you have done this.
Women eat their own babies,
the children they have cared for.
Priests and prophets are killed
in the Temple of the Lord.

21"People young and old
lie outside on the ground.
My young women and young men
have been killed by the sword.
You killed them on the day of your anger;
you killed them without mercy.

22"You invited terrors to come against me on every side,
as if you were inviting them to a feast.
No one escaped or remained alive
on the day of the LORD's anger.
My enemy has killed
those I cared for and brought up."

The Meaning of Suffering

3 I am a man who has seen the suffering
that comes from the rod of the LORD's anger.
2He led me
into darkness, not light.
3He turned his hand against me
again and again, all day long.

4He wore out my flesh and skin
and broke my bones.
5He surrounded me with sadness
and attacked me with grief.
6He made me sit in the dark,
like those who have been dead a long time.

7He shut me in so I could not get out;

he put heavy chains on me.
8I cry out and beg for help,
but he ignores my prayer.
9He blocked my way with a stone wall
and led me in the wrong direction.

10He is like a bear ready to attack me,
like a lion in hiding.
11He led me the wrong way and let me stray
and left me without help.
12He prepared to shoot his bow
and made me the target for his arrows.

13He shot me in the kidneys
with the arrows from his bag.
14I was a joke to all my people,
who make fun of me with songs all day
long.
15The LORD filled me with misery;
he made me drunk with suffering.

16He broke my teeth with gravel
and trampled me into the dirt.
17I have no more peace.
I have forgotten what happiness is.
18I said, "My strength is gone,
and I have no hope in the LORD."

19LORD, remember my suffering and my misery,
my sorrow and trouble.
20Please remember me
and think about me.
21But I have hope
when I think of this:

22The LORD's love never ends;
his mercies never stop.
23They are new every morning;
LORD, your loyalty is great.
24I say to myself, "The LORD is mine,
so I hope in him."

25The LORD is good to those who hope in him,
to those who seek him.
26It is good to wait quietly
for the LORD to save.
27It is good for someone to work hard
while he is young.

28He should sit alone and be quiet;
the LORD has given him hard work to do.
29He should bow down to the ground;
maybe there is still hope.
30He should let anyone slap his cheek;
he should be filled with shame.

31The Lord will not reject
his people forever.

SUFFERING

Lord, Remember Me

After dating for seven months, Brad, seventeen, and Angie, sixteen, broke up. "It was a really hard breakup," Brad remembers. "Part of me didn't want to do it, and part did."

For about three months afterward, Brad was severely depressed. "Angie was a source of energy for me," he explains. "After the breakup, I'd think about her and sigh and wonder why it had to happen."

Brad felt pretty bad sometimes, but he didn't blame God for what happened. In fact, he believes God got him through the loss, even if God's guidance wasn't clear. And he believes God's love came through his parents and friends, who listened as he shared his feelings. "What kept me going," he remembers, "was knowing that whatever happens, happens for the best."

Even though Brad was going through a tough time, he sensed God was with him. Read how the writer of **Lamentations 3:1–24** expresses a much greater disappointment and pain.

- If Brad wrote a poem about his breakup, what would be the similarities and differences between Brad's poem and this passage?
- What does God's love have to do with times of suffering, both in biblical times and today?

CONSIDER . . .

- watching an old comedy routine, such as one from Laurel and Hardy. Sometimes laughter gives perspective to difficult times.
- volunteering to serve on phone hot lines, in a shelter, or with another group that helps people through crises.

FOR MORE, SEE . . .

- 2 Kings 24:18—25:21 (p. 357)
- Psalm 22 (p. 493)
- 2 Corinthians 12:7–10 (p. 1203)

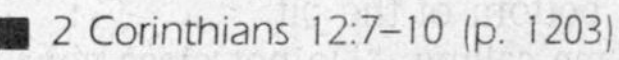

[32]Although he brings sorrow,
he also has mercy and great love.
[33]He does not like to punish people
or make them sad.

[34]He sees if any prisoner of the earth
is crushed under his feet;
[35]he sees if someone is treated unfairly
before the Most High God;
[36]the Lord sees
if someone is cheated in his case in court.

[37]Nobody can speak and have it happen
unless the Lord commands it.
[38]Both bad and good things
come by the command of the Most High God.
[39]No one should complain
when he is punished for his sins.

[40]Let us examine and see what we have done
and then return to the LORD.
[41]Let us lift up our hands and pray from our hearts
to God in heaven:
[42]"We have sinned and turned against you,
and you have not forgiven us.

[43]"You wrapped yourself in anger and chased us;
you killed us without mercy.
[44]You wrapped yourself in a cloud,
and no prayer could get through.
[45]You made us like scum and trash
among the other nations.

[46]"All of our enemies
open their mouths and speak against us.
[47]We have been frightened and fearful,
ruined and destroyed."
[48]Streams of tears flow from my eyes,
because my people are destroyed.

[49]My tears flow continually,
without stopping,
[50]until the LORD looks down
and sees from heaven.
[51]I am sad when I see
what has happened to all the women of my city.

[52]Those who are my enemies for no reason
hunted me like a bird.
[53]They tried to kill me in a pit;
they threw stones at me.
[54]Water came up over my head,
and I said, "I am going to die."
[55]I called out to you, LORD,
from the bottom of the pit.
[56]You heard me calling, "Do not close your ears
and ignore my gasps and shouts."
[57]You came near when I called to you;
you said, "Don't be afraid."

[58]Lord, you have taken my case
and given me back my life.
[59]LORD, you have seen how I have been wronged.
Now judge my case for me.
[60]You have seen how my enemies took revenge on me
and made evil plans against me.

[61]LORD, you have heard their insults
and all their evil plans against me.
[62]The words and thoughts of my enemies
are against me all the time.
[63]Look! In everything they do
they make fun of me with songs.

[64]Pay them back, LORD,
for what they have done.
[65]Make them stubborn,
and put your curse on them.
[66]Chase them in anger, LORD,
and destroy them from under your heavens.

SIDELIGHT: Because only priests were allowed to enter the Most Holy Place in the Temple, the Babylonian trampling of the Temple (Lamentations 4:1) was difficult to cope with. In fact, the Temple's destruction was even more tragic to the devout Jew than the devastation in the rest of Jerusalem.

The Attack on Jerusalem

4 See how the gold has lost its shine,
how the pure gold has dulled!
The stones of the Temple[d] are scattered
at every street corner.

[2]The precious people of Jerusalem
were more valuable than gold,
but now they are thought of as clay jars
made by the hands of a potter.

[3]Even wild dogs give their milk
to feed their young,
but my people are cruel
like ostriches in the desert.

[4]The babies are so thirsty
their tongues stick to the roofs of their mouths.
Children beg for bread,
but no one gives them any.

[5]Those who once ate fine foods
are now starving in the streets.
People who grew up wearing nice clothes

now pick through trash piles.

6My people have been punished
more than Sodom was.
Sodom was destroyed suddenly,
and no hands reached out to help her.

7Our princes were purer than snow,
and whiter than milk.
Their bodies were redder than rubies;
they looked like sapphires.

8But now they are blacker than coal,
and no one recognizes them in the streets.
Their skin hangs on their bones;
it is as dry as wood.

9Those who were killed in the war were better off
than those killed by hunger.
They starve in pain and die,
because there is no food from the field.

10With their own hands kind women
cook their own children.
They became food
when my people were destroyed.

11The LORD turned loose all of his anger;
he poured out his strong anger.
He set fire to Jerusalem,
burning it down to the foundations.

12Kings of the earth and people of the world
could not believe
that enemies and foes
could enter the gates of Jerusalem.

13It happened because her prophets[d] sinned
and her priests did evil.
They killed in the city
those who did what was right.

14They wandered in the streets
as if they were blind.
They were dirty with blood,
so no one would touch their clothes.

15"Go away! You are unclean,"[d] people shouted at them.
"Get away! Get away! Don't touch us!"
So they ran away and wandered.
Even the other nations said, "Don't stay here."

16The LORD himself scattered them
and did not look after them anymore.
No one respects the priests
or honors the older leaders.

17Also, our eyes grew tired,
looking for help that never came.
We kept watch from our towers
for a nation to save us.

18Our enemies hunted us,
so we could not even walk in the streets.
Our end is near. Our time is up.
Our end has come.

19Those who chased us
were faster than eagles in the sky.
They ran us into the mountains
and ambushed us in the desert.

20The LORD's appointed king, who was our very breath,
was caught in their traps.
We had said about him, "We will be protected by him
among the nations."

21Be happy and glad, people of Edom,
you who live in the land of Uz.
The cup of God's anger will come to you;
then you will get drunk and go naked.

22Your punishment is complete, Jerusalem.
He will not send you into captivity again.
But the LORD will punish the sins of Edom;
he will uncover your evil.

A Prayer to the Lord

5 Remember, LORD, what happened to us.
Look and see our disgrace.
2Our land has been turned over to strangers;
our houses have been given to foreigners.
3We are like orphans with no father;
our mothers are like widows.
4We have to buy the water we drink;
we must pay for the firewood.
5Those who chase after us want to catch us by the neck.
We are tired and find no rest.
6We made an agreement with Egypt
and with Assyria to get enough food.
7Our ancestors sinned against you, but they are gone;
now we suffer because of their sins.
8Slaves have become our rulers,
and no one can save us from them.
9We risk our lives to get our food;
we face death in the desert.
10Our skin is hot like an oven;
we burn with starvation.
11The enemy abused the women of Jerusalem
and the girls in the cities of Judah.
12Princes were hung by the hands;
they did not respect our older leaders.
13The young men ground grain at the mill,
and boys stumbled under loads of wood.
14The older leaders no longer sit at the city gates;
the young men no longer sing.
15We have no more joy in our hearts;
our dancing has turned to sadness.

16The crown has fallen from our head.
How terrible it is because we sinned.
17Because of this we are afraid,
and now our eyes are dim.
18Mount Zion[d] is empty,
and wild dogs wander around it.

19But you rule forever, LORD.
You will be King from now on.
20Why have you forgotten us for so long?
Have you left us forever?
21Bring us back to you, LORD, and we will return.
Make our days as they were before,
22or have you completely rejected us?
Are you so angry with us?

EZEKIEL

Why Read This Book:

- Be encouraged by God's extraordinary efforts to call his people back to himself (Ezekiel 1—24).
- Take comfort in the promises God made through the prophet Ezekiel (Ezekiel 33—48).

Behind the Scenes:

"PROPHET SEES UFO!" the headline would have screamed if tabloid newspapers had been around in Ezekiel's time.

The story would reveal how Ezekiel, the prophet, saw the sky opening up, glowing lights in the sky, fire, and something like glowing metal in the middle of a cloud. Then, the story would continue, the prophet saw creatures—creatures who, the writer suggests, were probably aliens.

Finally—and this was the best part—a voice above the creatures boomed out. When Ezekiel looked up, he saw an amazing throne. It was all so powerful he was knocked off his feet.

But the prophet didn't see a UFO. The prophet saw a vision of God, as described in the first chapter of Ezekiel.

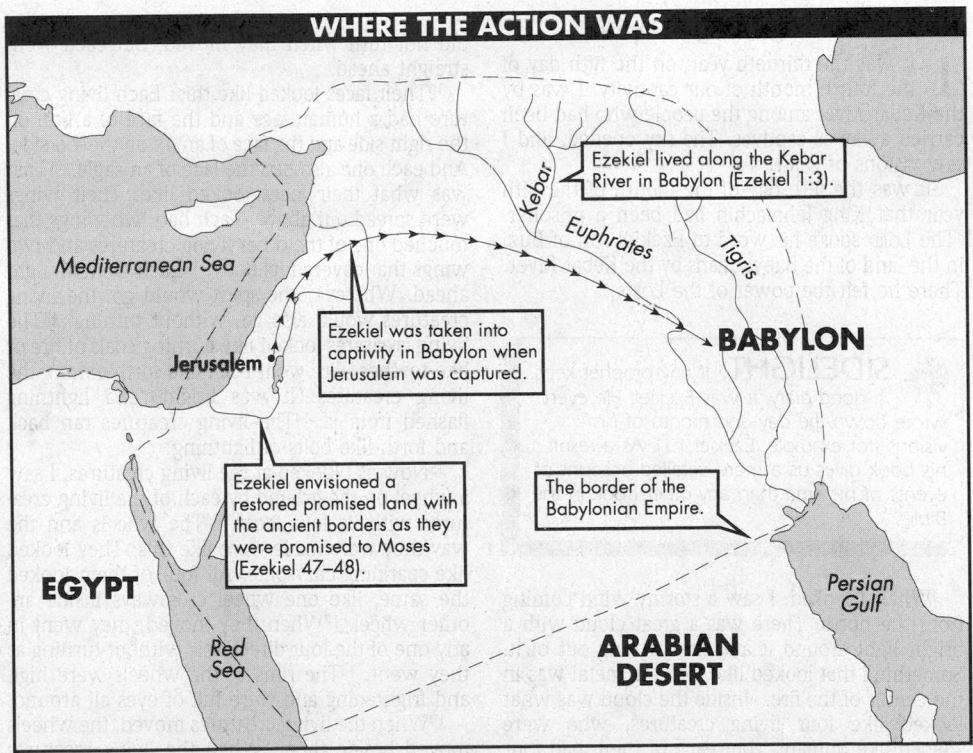

WHERE THE ACTION WAS

Mediterranean Sea
Jerusalem
EGYPT
Red Sea
Kebar
Euphrates
Tigris
BABYLON
ARABIAN DESERT
Persian Gulf
Ezekiel lived along the Kebar River in Babylon (Ezekiel 1:3).
Ezekiel was taken into captivity in Babylon when Jerusalem was captured.
Ezekiel envisioned a restored promised land with the ancient borders as they were promised to Moses (Ezekiel 47–48).
The border of the Babylonian Empire.

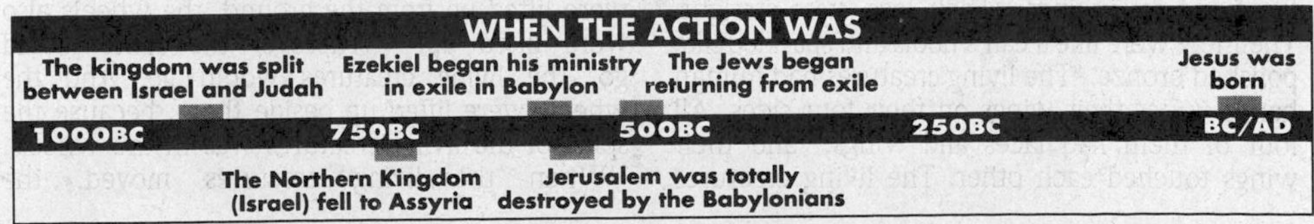

Ezekiel began his ministry in exile in Babylon

Behind the Scenes (cont.):

This unusual book is filled with such stories. Ezekiel lived during the most difficult time in the Old Testament. Jerusalem had been destroyed, and the people—including Ezekiel—had been taken into exile, mostly in Babylon. The people couldn't understand what had happened to their beloved, holy city. Had God abandoned them?

Through visions, strange actions, and symbolic language, the prophet interpreted what had happened to the city and his people. First, he told how the people of Judah got themselves into trouble by refusing to listen to earlier prophets or to follow God. So God had used the invading Babylonians to punish the people.

Yet God had not abandoned his chosen people, Ezekiel insisted. Because of God's love and trustworthiness, he would restore the city to them and renew his relationship with them. They would respond to his gift by returning to him. At that point, God would again comfort his people.

As Ezekiel describes his dreams and visions, it's sometimes hard to understand the prophet's underlying message. In fact, from the beginning scholars have been stumped by the specific meanings of passages.

But beneath all the unusual language, poetry, and imagery is a consistent message that still has meaning for us today: Through everything, God wants people to "know that I am the Lord God"—a phrase that's repeated more than sixty times through the book.

Ezekiel's Vision of Living Creatures

1 It was the thirtieth year, on the fifth day of
the fourth month of our captivity. I was by
the Kebar River among the people who had been
carried away as captives. The sky opened, and I
saw visions of God.
2It was the fifth day of the month of the fifth
year that King Jehoiachin had been a prisoner.
3The LORD spoke his word to Ezekiel son of Buzi
in the land of the Babylonians by the Kebar River.
There he felt the power of the LORD.

> **SIDELIGHT:** If any prophet kept a good diary, it was Ezekiel. He even wrote down the day and month of his visions (for example, Ezekiel 1:1). As a result, his book gives us a more detailed account of events of his time than any other book in the Bible.

4When I looked, I saw a stormy wind coming
from the north. There was a great cloud with a
bright light around it and fire flashing out of it.
Something that looked like glowing metal was in
the center of the fire. 5Inside the cloud was what
looked like four living creatures, who were
shaped like humans, 6but each of them had four
faces and four wings. 7Their legs were straight.
Their feet were like a calf's hoofs and sparkled like
polished bronze. 8The living creatures had human
hands under their wings on their four sides. All
four of them had faces and wings, 9and their
wings touched each other. The living creatures
did not turn when they moved, but each went
straight ahead.
10Their faces looked like this: Each living creature had a human face and the face of a lion on
the right side and the face of an ox on the left side.
And each one also had the face of an eagle. 11That
was what their faces looked like. Their wings
were spread out above. Each had two wings that
touched one of the other living creatures and two
wings that covered its body. 12Each went straight
ahead. Wherever the spirit would go, the living
creatures would also go, without turning. 13The
living creatures looked like burning coals of fire or
like torches. Fire went back and forth among the
living creatures. It was bright, and lightning
flashed from it. 14The living creatures ran back
and forth like bolts of lightning.
15Now as I looked at the living creatures, I saw
a wheel on the ground by each of the living creatures with its four faces. 16The wheels and the
way they were made were like this: They looked
like sparkling chrysolite. All four of them looked
the same, like one wheel crossways inside another wheel. 17When they moved, they went in
any one of the four directions, without turning as
they went. 18The rims of the wheels were high
and frightening and were full of eyes all around.
19When the living creatures moved, the wheels
moved beside them. When the living creatures
were lifted up from the ground, the wheels also
were lifted up. 20Wherever the spirit would
go, the living creatures would go. And the
wheels were lifted up beside them, because the
spirit of the living creatures was in the wheels.
21When the living creatures moved, the

wheels moved. When the living creatures stopped, the wheels stopped. And when the living creatures were lifted from the ground, the wheels were lifted beside them, because the spirit of the living creatures was in the wheels.

22Now, over the heads of the living creatures was something like a dome that sparkled like ice and was frightening. 23And under the dome the wings of the living creatures were stretched out straight toward one another. Each living creature also had two wings covering its body. 24I heard the sound of their wings, like the roaring sound of the sea, as they moved. It was like the voice of God Almighty, a roaring sound like a noisy army. When the living creatures stopped, they lowered their wings.

25A voice came from above the dome over the heads of the living creatures. When the living creatures stopped, they lowered their wings. 26Now above the dome there was something that looked like a throne. It looked like a sapphire gem. And on the throne was a shape like a human. 27Then I noticed that from the waist up the shape looked like glowing metal with fire inside. From the waist down it looked like fire, and a bright light was all around. 28The surrounding glow looked like the rainbow in the clouds on a rainy day. It seemed to look like the glory of the LORD. So when I saw it, I bowed facedown on the ground and heard a voice speaking.

The Lord Speaks to Ezekiel

2 He said to me, "Human, stand up on your feet so I may speak with you." 2While he spoke to me, the Spirit[d] entered me and put me on my feet. Then I heard the LORD speaking to me.

3He said, "Human, I am sending you to the people of Israel. That nation has turned against me and broken away from me. They and their ancestors have sinned against me until this very day. 4I am sending you to people who are stubborn and who do not obey. You will say to them, 'This is what the Lord GOD says.' 5They may listen, or they may not, since they are a people who have turned against me. But they will know that a prophet[d] has been among them. 6You, human, don't be afraid of the people or their words. Even though they may be like thorny branches and stickers all around you, and though you may feel like you live with poisonous insects, don't be afraid. Don't be afraid of their words or their looks, because they are a people who turn against me. 7But speak my words to them. They may listen, or they may not, because they turn against me. 8But you, human, listen to what I say to you. Don't turn against me as those people do. Open your mouth and eat what I am giving you."

9Then I looked and saw a hand stretched out to me, and a scroll was in it. 10He opened the scroll in front of me. Funeral songs, sad writings, and words about troubles were written on the front and back.

3 Then the LORD said to me, "Human, eat what you find; eat this scroll. Then go and speak to the people of Israel." 2So I opened my mouth, and he gave me the scroll to eat.

3He said to me, "Human, eat this scroll which I am giving you, and fill your stomach with it." Then I ate it, and it was as sweet as honey in my mouth.

> **SIDELIGHT:** You've eaten gummy bears, right? How about "Gummy Scrolls"? Ezekiel tried them and said they tasted like honey—even though they were full of gloomy messages (Ezekiel 3:1–3). For Ezekiel, eating God's message symbolized accepting God's mission to tell the news to the Jews.

4Then he said to me, "Human, go to the people of Israel, and speak my words to them. 5You are not being sent to people whose speech you can't understand, whose language is difficult. You are being sent to Israel. 6You are not being sent to many nations whose speech you can't understand, whose language is difficult, whose words you cannot understand. If I had sent you to them, they would have listened to you. 7But the people of Israel will not be willing to listen to you, because they are not willing to listen to me. Yes, all the people of Israel are stubborn and will not obey. 8See, I now make you as stubborn and as hard as they are. 9I am making you as hard as a diamond, harder than stone. Don't be afraid of them or be frightened by them, though they are a people who turn against me."

10Also, he said to me, "Human, believe all the words I will speak to you, and listen carefully to them. 11Then go to the captives, your own people, and say to them, 'The Lord GOD says this.' Tell them this whether they listen or not."

12Then the Spirit lifted me up, and I heard a loud rumbling sound behind me, saying, "Praise the glory of the LORD in heaven." 13I heard the wings of the living creatures touching each other and the sound of the wheels by them. It was a loud rumbling sound. 14So the Spirit lifted me up and took me away. I was unhappy and angry, and I felt the great power of the LORD. 15I came to the captives from Judah, who lived by the Kebar River at Tel Abib. I sat there seven days where these people lived, feeling shocked.

Israel's Warning

16After seven days the LORD spoke his word to me again. He said, 17"Human, I now make you a watchman for Israel. Any time you hear a word from my mouth, warn them for me. 18When I say to the wicked, 'You will surely die,' you must warn them so they may live. If you don't speak out to warn the wicked to stop their evil ways, they will die in their sin. But I will hold you responsible for their death. 19If you warn the wicked and they do not turn from their wickedness or their evil ways, they will die because of their sin. But you will have saved your life.

20"Again, those who do right may turn away from doing good and do evil. If I make something bad happen to them, they will die. Because you have not warned them, they will die because of their sin, and the good they did will not be remembered. But I will hold you responsible for their deaths. 21But if you have warned those good people not to sin, and they do not sin, they will surely live, because they believed the warning. And you will have saved your life."

22Then I felt the power of the LORD there. He said to me, "Get up and go out to the plain. There I will speak to you." 23So I got up and went out to the plain. I saw the glory of the LORD standing there, like the glory I saw by the Kebar River, and I bowed facedown on the ground.

24Then the Spirit[d] entered me and made me stand on my feet. He spoke to me and said, "Go, shut yourself up in your house. 25As for you, human, the people will tie you up with ropes so that you will not be able to go out among them. 26Also, I will make your tongue stick to the roof of your mouth so you will be silent. You will not be able to argue with the people, even though they turn against me. 27But when I speak to you, I will open your mouth, and you will say to them, 'The Lord GOD says this.' Those who will listen, let them listen. Those who refuse, let them refuse, because they are a people who turn against me.

The Map of Jerusalem

4 "Now, human, get yourself a brick, put it in front of you, and draw a map of Jerusalem on it. 2Then surround it with an army. Build battle works against the city and a dirt road to the top of the city walls. Set up camps around it, and put heavy logs in place to break down the walls. 3Then get yourself an iron plate and set it up like an iron wall between you and the city. Turn your face toward the city as if to attack it and then attack. This is a sign to Israel.

4"Then lie down on your left side, and take the guilt of Israel on yourself. Their guilt will be on you for the number of days you lie on your left side. 5I have given you the same number of days

HONESTY

The Whole Truth

Jessica knew she was in trouble when the car skidded and slid on the wet road, hitting the curb hard enough to ruin a front wheel. Even though no one was hurt, the disabled car would not move.

When she got home, Jessica told her parents what had happened. She admitted having seven people in her compact car, and driving faster than the speed limit. Then she described the damage.

"What I didn't tell them was that a friend was driving my car," she says.

Jessica's paying for the damage now with money from her part-time job. She's afraid that if she tells her parents the whole truth, she will slide into even more trouble. Jessica's parents might appreciate her honesty and not punish her more severely. God, too, appreciates honesty. He expects it even when it may cause more trouble than keeping silent. He demanded that Ezekiel tell the people the whole truth in **Ezekiel 3:16–21**.

- Why might it be difficult for Jessica or Ezekiel to be completely honest?
- How can you be honest with a friend who is doing something wrong and still preserve the friendship?

C O N S I D E R . . .

- warning a friend about something he or she is doing that's wrong.
- discussing with your friends when, if ever, it's okay to tell white lies.

F O R M O R E , S E E . . .

- Genesis 3:1–9 (p. 4)
- 2 Samuel 12:1–14 (p. 284)
- Acts 5:1–11 (p. 1104)

as the years of the people's sin. So you will have
the guilt of Israel's sin on you for three hundred
ninety days.

> **SIDELIGHT:** To get God's message across, Ezekiel resorted to dramatic measures. Once he lay on his left side for three hundred ninety days to symbolize the siege of Jerusalem (Ezekiel 4:4–8). Another time he burned his hair (Ezekiel 5:1–3) to symbolize military defeat for Jerusalem. You won't see those object lessons in Sunday school!

6"After you have finished these three hundred
ninety days, lie down a second time, on your right
side. You will then have the guilt of Judah on you.
I will give it to you for forty days, a day for each
year of their sin. 7Then you will look toward Jerusalem, which is being attacked. With your arm
bare, you will prophesy[d] against Jerusalem. 8I will
put ropes on you so you cannot turn from one side
to the other until you have finished the days of
your attack on Jerusalem.
9"Take wheat, barley, beans, small peas, and
millet seeds, and put them in one bowl, and make
them into bread for yourself. You will eat it the
three hundred ninety days you lie on your side.
10You will eat eight ounces of food every day at
set times. 11You will drink about two-thirds of a
quart of water every day at set times. 12Eat your
food as you would eat a barley cake, baking it over
human dung where the people can see." 13Then
the LORD said, "In the same way Israel will eat
unclean[d] food among the nations where I force
them to go."
14But I said, "No, Lord GOD! I have never been
made unclean. From the time I was young until
now I've never eaten anything that died by itself
or was torn by animals. Unclean meat has never
entered my mouth."

> **SIDELIGHT:** When God told Ezekiel to cook his food over human excrement (Ezekiel 4:9–14), the prophet refused because human excrement was considered unclean (see Deuteronomy 23:12–14, p. 181). But dried cow dung was—and still is—a common fuel in the Near East.

15"Very well," he said. "Then I will give you
cow's dung instead of human dung to use for your
fire to bake your bread."
16He also said to me, "Human, I am going to
cut off the supply of bread to Jerusalem. They will
eat the bread that is measured out to them, and
they will worry as they eat. They will drink water
that is measured out to them, and they will be in
shock as they drink it. 17This is because bread and
water will be hard to find. The people will be
shocked at the sight of each other, and they will
become weak because of their sin.

Ezekiel Cuts His Hair

5 "Now, human, take a sharp sword, and use
it like a barber's razor to shave your head
and beard. Then take scales and weigh and divide
the hair. 2Burn one-third with fire in the middle
of the city when the days of the attack on Jerusalem are over. Then take one-third and cut it up
with the knife all around the city. And scatter
one-third to the wind. This is how I will chase
them with a sword. 3Also take a few of these hairs
and tie them in the folds of your clothes. 4Take a
few more and throw them into the fire and burn
them up. From there a fire will spread to all the
people of Israel.
5"This is what the Lord GOD says: This is Jerusalem. I have put her at the center of the nations
with countries all around her. 6But she has refused to obey my laws and has been more evil
than the nations. She has refused to obey my
rules, even more than nations around her. The
people of Jerusalem have rejected my laws and
have not lived by my rules.
7"So this is what the Lord GOD says: You have
caused more trouble than the nations around you.
You have not followed my rules or obeyed my
laws. You have not even obeyed the laws of the
nations around you.
8"So this is what the Lord GOD says: I myself
am against you, and I will punish you as the nations watch. 9I will do things among you that I
have not done before and that I will never do anything like again, because you do the things I hate.
10So parents among you will eat their children,
and children will eat their parents. I will punish
you and will scatter to the winds all who are left
alive. 11So the Lord GOD says: You have made my
Temple[d] unclean[d] with all your evil idols and the
hateful things you do. Because of this, as surely as
I live, I will cut you off. I will have no pity, and
I will show no mercy. 12A third of you will die by
disease or be destroyed by hunger inside your
walls. A third will fall dead by the sword outside
your walls. And a third I will scatter in every direction as I chase them with a sword. 13Then my
anger will come to an end. I will use it up against
them, and then I will be satisfied. Then they will
know that I, the LORD, have spoken. After I have
carried out my anger against them, they will
know how strongly I felt.
14"I will make you a ruin and a shame among

the nations around you, to be seen by all who pass by. 15Then the nations around you will shame you and make fun of you. You will be a warning and a terror to them. This will happen when I punish you in my great anger. I, the LORD, have spoken. 16I will send a time of hunger to destroy you, and then I will make your hunger get even worse, and I will cut off your supply of food. 17I will send a time of hunger and wild animals against you, and they will kill your children. Disease and death will sweep through your people, and I will bring the sword against you to kill you. I, the LORD, have spoken."

Prophecies Against the Mountains

6 Again the LORD spoke his word to me, saying: 2"Human, look toward the mountains of Israel, and prophesy[d] against them. 3Say, 'Mountains of Israel, listen to the word of the Lord GOD. The Lord GOD says this to the mountains, the hills, the ravines, and the valleys: I will bring a sword against you, and I will destroy your places of idol worship. 4Your altars will be destroyed and your incense[d] altars broken down. Your people will be killed in front of your idols. 5I will lay the dead bodies of the Israelites in front of their idols, and I will scatter your bones around your altars. 6In all the places you live, cities will become empty. The places of idol worship will be ruined; your altars will become lonely ruins. Your idols will be broken and brought to an end. Your incense altars will be cut down, and the things you made will be wiped out. 7Your people will be killed and fall among you. Then you will know that I am the LORD.

8" 'But I will leave some people alive; some will not be killed by the nations when you are scattered among the foreign lands. 9Then those who have escaped will remember me, as they live among the nations where they have been taken as captives. They will remember how I was hurt because they were unfaithful to me and turned away from me and desired to worship their idols. They will hate themselves because of the evil things they did that I hate. 10Then they will know that I am the LORD. I did not bring this terrible thing on them for no reason.

11" 'This is what the Lord GOD says: Clap your hands, stamp your feet, and groan because of all the hateful, evil things the people of Israel have done. They will die by war, hunger, and disease. 12The person who is far away will die by disease. The one who is nearby will die in war. The person who is still alive and has escaped these will die from hunger. So I will carry out my anger on them. 13Their people will lie dead among their idols around the altars, on every high hill, on all the mountain tops, and under every green tree and leafy oak—all the places where they offered sweet-smelling incense to their idols. Then you will know that I am the LORD. 14I will use my power against them to make the land empty and wasted from the desert to Diblah, wherever they live. Then they will know that I am the LORD.' "

Ezekiel Tells of the End

7 Again the LORD spoke his word to me, saying: 2"Human, the Lord GOD says this to the land of Israel: An end! The end has come on the four corners of the land. 3Now the end has come for you, and I will send my anger against you. I will judge you for the way you have lived, and I will make you pay for all your actions that I hate. 4I will have no pity on you; I will not hold back punishment from you. Instead, I will make you pay for the way you have lived and for your actions that I hate. Then you will know that I am the LORD.

SIDELIGHT: Why does God repeatedly address Ezekiel as "human"? (See Ezekiel 7:2, for example.) It was simply to remind the prophet of the huge difference between God and people.

5"This is what the Lord GOD says: Disaster on top of disaster is coming. 6The end has come! The end has come! It has stirred itself up against you! Look! It has come! 7Disaster has come for you who live in the land! The time has come; the day of confusion is near. There will be no happy shouting on the mountains. 8Soon I will pour out my anger against you; I will carry out my anger against you. I will judge you for the way you have lived and will make you pay for everything you have done that I hate. 9I will show no pity, and I will not hold back punishment. I will pay you back for the way you have lived and the things you have done that I hate. Then you will know that I am the LORD who punishes.

10"Look, the day is here. It has come. Disaster has come, violence has grown, and there is more pride than ever. 11Violence has grown into a weapon for punishing wickedness. None of the people will be left—none of that crowd, none of their wealth, and nothing of value. 12The time has come; the day has arrived. Don't let the buyer be happy or the seller be sad, because my burning anger is against the whole crowd. 13Sellers will not return to the land they have sold as long as they live, because the vision against all that crowd will not be changed. Because of their sins, they will not save their lives. 14They have blown the trumpet, and everything is ready.

But no one is going to the battle, because my anger is against all that crowd.

15"The sword is outside, and disease and hunger are inside. Whoever is in the field will die by the sword. Hunger and disease will destroy those in the city. 16Those who are left alive and who escape will be on the mountains, moaning like doves of the valleys about their own sin. 17All hands will hang weakly with fear, and all knees will become weak as water. 18They will put on rough cloth to show how sad they are. They will tremble all over with fear. Their faces will show their shame, and all their heads will be shaved. 19The people will throw their silver into the streets, and their gold will be like trash. Their silver and gold will not save them from the LORD's anger. It will not satisfy their hunger or fill their stomachs, because it caused them to fall into sin. 20They were proud of their beautiful jewelry and used it to make their idols and their evil statues, which I hate. So I will turn their wealth into trash. 21I will give it to foreigners as loot from war and to the most evil people in the world as treasure, and they will dishonor it. 22I will also turn away from the people of Israel, and they will dishonor my treasured place. Then robbers will enter and dishonor it.

23"Make chains for captives, because the land is full of bloody crimes and the city is full of violence. 24So I will bring the worst of the nations to take over the people's houses. I will also end the pride of the strong, and their holy places will be dishonored. 25When the people are suffering greatly, they will look for peace, but there will be none. 26Disaster will come on top of disaster, and rumor will be added to rumor. Then they will try to get a vision from a prophet;[d] the teachings of God from the priest and the advice from the older leaders will be lost. 27The king will cry greatly, the prince will give up hope, and the hands of the people who own land will shake with fear. I will punish them for the way they have lived. The way they have judged others is the way I will judge them. Then they will know that I am the LORD."

Ezekiel's Vision of Jerusalem

8 It was the sixth year, on the fifth day of the sixth month of our captivity. I was sitting in my house with the older leaders of Judah in front of me. There I felt the power of the Lord GOD. 2I looked and saw something that looked like a human. From the waist down it looked like fire, and from the waist up it looked like bright glowing metal. 3It stretched out the shape of a hand and caught me by the hair on my head. The Spirit[d] lifted me up between the earth and the sky. He took me in visions of God to Jerusalem, to the entrance to the north gate of the inner courtyard of the Temple.[d] In the courtyard was the idol that caused God to be jealous. 4I saw the glory of the God of Israel there, as I had seen on the plain.

5Then he said to me, "Human, now look toward the north." So I looked up toward the north, and in the entrance north of the gate of the altar was the idol that caused God to be jealous.

6He said to me, "Human, do you see what they are doing? Do you see how many hateful things the people of Israel are doing here that drive me far away from my Temple? But you will see things more hateful than these."

7Then he brought me to the entry of the courtyard. When I looked, I saw a hole in the wall. 8He said to me, "Human, dig through the wall." So I dug through the wall and saw an entrance.

9Then he said to me, "Go in and see the hateful, evil things they are doing here." 10So I entered and looked, and I saw every kind of crawling thing and hateful beast and all the idols of the people of Israel, carved on the wall all around. 11Standing in front of these carvings and idols were seventy of the older leaders of Israel and Jaazaniah son of Shaphan. Each man had his pan for burning incense[d] in his hand, and a sweet-smelling cloud of incense was rising.

12Then he said to me, "Human, have you seen what the older leaders of Israel are doing in the dark? Have you seen each man in the room of his own idol? They say, 'The LORD doesn't see us. The LORD has left the land.' " 13He also said to me, "You will see even more hateful things that they are doing."

14Then he brought me to the entrance of the north gate of the Temple of the LORD, where I saw women sitting and crying for Tammuz.[n] 15He said to me, "Do you see, human? You will see things even more hateful than these."

16Then he brought me into the inner courtyard of the Temple. There I saw about twenty-five men at the entrance to the Temple of the LORD, between the porch and the altar. With their backs turned to the Temple of the LORD, they faced east and were worshiping the sun in the east.

17He said to me, "Do you see, human? Is it unimportant that the people of Judah are doing the hateful things they have done here? They have filled the land with violence and made me continually angry. Look, they are insulting me every way they can. 18So I will act in anger. I will have no pity, nor will I show mercy. Even if they shout in my ears, I won't listen to them."

Tammuz Tammuz was a god in Babylon. Every year people thought this god died when the plants died. After they cried for him, they believed he came back to life and the plants lived again.

Vision of the Angels

9 Then he shouted with a loud voice in my ears, "You who are chosen to punish this city, come near with your weapon in your hand." 2Then six men came from the direction of the upper gate, which faces north, each with his powerful weapon in his hand. Among them was a man dressed in linen with a writing case at his side. The men went in and stood by the bronze altar.

3Then the glory of the God of Israel went up from above the creatures with wings, where it had been, to the place in the Temple[d] where the door opened. He called to the man dressed in linen who had the writing case at his side. 4He said to the man, "Go through Jerusalem and put a mark on the foreheads of the people who groan and cry about all the hateful things being done among them."

SIDELIGHT: The mark of Ezekiel 9:4 was the taw, the last letter of the Hebrew alphabet. This is one I.D. you wouldn't want to be without; those in the vision without the mark were killed.

5As I listened, he said to the other men, "Go through the city behind the man dressed in linen and kill. Don't pity anyone, and don't show mercy. 6Kill and destroy old men, young men and women, little children, and older women, but don't touch any who have the mark on them. Start at my Temple." So they started with the older leaders who were in front of the Temple.

7Then he said to the men, "Make the Temple unclean,[d] and fill the courtyards with those who have been killed. Go out!" So the men went out and killed the people in the city. 8While the men were killing the people, I was left alone. I bowed facedown on the ground and I cried out, "Oh, Lord GOD! Will you destroy everyone left alive in Israel when you turn loose your anger on Jerusalem?"

9Then he said to me, "The sin of the people of Israel and Judah is very great. The land is filled with people who murder, and the city is full of people who are not fair. The people say, 'The LORD has left the land, and the LORD does not see.' 10But I will have no pity, nor will I show mercy. I will bring their evil back on their heads."

11Then the man dressed in linen with the writing case at his side reported, "I have done just as you commanded me."

The Coals of Fire

10 Then I looked and saw in the dome above the heads of the living creatures something like a sapphire gem which looked like a throne. 2The LORD said to the man dressed in linen, "Go in between the wheels under the living creatures, fill your hands with coals of fire from between the living creatures, and scatter the coals over the city."

As I watched, the man with linen clothes went in. 3Now the living creatures were standing on the south side of the Temple[d] when the man went in. And a cloud filled the inner courtyard. 4Then the glory of the LORD went up from the living creatures and stood over the door of the Temple. The Temple was filled with the cloud, and the courtyard was full of the brightness from the glory of the LORD. 5The sound of the wings of the living creatures was heard all the way to the outer courtyard. It was like the voice of God Almighty when he speaks.

6When the LORD commanded the man dressed in linen, "Take fire from between the wheels, from between the living creatures," the man went in and stood by a wheel. 7One living creature put out his hand to the fire that was among them, took some of the fire, and put it in the hands of the man dressed in linen. Then the man took the fire and went out.

The Wheels and the Creatures

8Something that looked like a human hand could be seen under the wings of the living creatures. 9I saw the four wheels by the living creatures, one wheel by each living creature. The wheels looked like shining chrysolite. 10All four wheels looked alike: Each looked like a wheel crossways inside another wheel. 11When the wheels moved, they went in any of the directions that the four living creatures faced. The wheels did not turn about, and the living creatures did not turn their bodies as they went. 12All their bodies, their backs, their hands, their wings, and the wheels were full of eyes all over. Each of the four living creatures had a wheel. 13I heard the wheels being called "whirling wheels." 14Each living creature had four faces. The first face was the face of a creature with wings. The second face was a human face, the third was the face of a lion, and the fourth was the face of an eagle.

15Then the living creatures flew up. They were the same living creatures I had seen by the Kebar River. 16When the living creatures moved, the wheels moved beside them. When the living creatures lifted their wings to fly up from the ground, the wheels did not leave their place beside them. 17When the living creatures stopped, the wheels stopped. When the creatures went up, the wheels went up also, because the spirit of the living creatures was in the wheels.

18Then the glory of the LORD left the door of the Temple[d] and stood over the living creatures. 19As

I watched, the living creatures spread their wings and flew up from the ground, with the wheels beside them. They stood where the east gate of the Temple of the LORD opened, and the glory of the God of Israel was over them.

20These were the living creatures I had seen under the God of Israel by the Kebar River. I knew they were called cherubim.[d] 21Each one had four faces and four wings, and under their wings were things that looked like human hands. 22Their faces looked the same as the ones I had seen by the Kebar River. They each went straight ahead.

Prophecies Against Evil Leaders

11 The Spirit[d] lifted me up and brought me to the front gate of the Temple[d] of the LORD, which faces east. I saw twenty-five men where the gate opens, among them Jaazaniah son of Azzur and Pelatiah son of Benaiah, who were leaders of the people. 2Then the LORD said to me, "Human, these are the men who plan evil and give wicked advice in this city of Jerusalem. 3They say, 'It is almost time for us to build houses. This city is like a cooking pot, and we are like the best meat.' 4So prophesy[d] against them, prophesy, human."

5Then the Spirit of the LORD entered me and told me to say: "This is what the LORD says: You have said these things, people of Israel, and I know what you are thinking. 6You have killed many people in this city, filling its streets with their bodies.

7"So this is what the Lord GOD says: Those people you have killed and left in the middle of the city are like the best meat, and this city is like the cooking pot. But I will force you out of the city. 8You have feared the sword, but I will bring a sword against you, says the Lord GOD. 9I will force you out of the city and hand you over to strangers and punish you. 10You will die by the sword. I will punish you at the border of Israel so you will know that I am the LORD. 11This city will not be your cooking pot, and you will not be the best meat in the middle of it. I will punish you at the border of Israel. 12Then you will know that I am the LORD. You did not live by my rules or obey my laws. Instead, you did the same things as the nations around you."

13As I prophesied, Pelatiah son of Benaiah died. Then I bowed facedown on the ground and shouted with a loud voice, "Oh no, Lord GOD! Will you completely destroy the Israelites who are left alive?"

Promise to Those Remaining

14The LORD spoke his word to me, saying, 15"Human, the people still in Jerusalem have spoken about your own relatives and all the people of Israel who are captives with you, saying, 'They are far from the LORD. This land has been given to us as our property.'

16"So say, 'This is what the Lord GOD says: I sent the people far away among the nations and scattered them among the countries. But for a little while I have become a Temple[d] to them in the countries where they have gone.'

17"So say: 'This is what the Lord GOD says: I will gather you from the nations and bring you together from the countries where you have been scattered. Then I will give you back the land of Israel.'

18"When they come to this land, they will remove all the evil idols and all the hateful images. 19I will give them a desire to respect me completely, and I will put inside them a new way of thinking. I will take out the stubborn heart of stone from their bodies, and I will give them an obedient heart of flesh. 20Then they will live by my rules and obey my laws and keep them. They will be my people, and I will be their God. 21But those who want to serve their evil statues and hateful idols, I will pay back for their evil ways, says the Lord GOD."

Ezekiel's Vision Ends

22Then the living creatures lifted their wings with the wheels beside them, and the glory of the God of Israel was above them. 23The glory of the LORD went up from inside Jerusalem and stopped on the mountain on the east side of the city. 24The Spirit[d] lifted me up and brought me to the captives who had been taken from Judah to Babylonia. This happened in a vision given by the Spirit of God, and then the vision I had seen ended. 25And I told the captives from Judah all the things the LORD had shown me.

Ezekiel Moves Out

12 Again the LORD spoke his word to me, saying: 2"Human, you are living among a people who refuse to obey. They have eyes to see, but they do not see, and they have ears to hear, but they do not hear, because they are a people who refuse to obey.

3"So, human, pack your things as if you will be taken away captive, and walk away like a captive in the daytime with the people watching. Move from your place to another with the people watching. Maybe they will understand, even though they are a people who refuse to obey. 4During the day when the people are watching, bring out the things you would pack as captive. At evening, with the people watching, leave your place like those who are taken away as captives from their country. 5Dig a hole through the wall while they watch, and bring your things out through it. 6Lift them onto your shoulders with

the people watching, and carry them out in the
dark. Cover your face so you cannot see the
ground, because I have made you a sign to
the people of Israel."
7I did these things as I was commanded. In the
daytime I brought what I had packed as if I were
being taken away captive. Then in the evening I
dug through the wall with my hands. I brought
my things out in the dark and carried them on my
shoulders as the people watched.
8Then in the morning the LORD spoke his word
to me, saying: 9"Human, didn't Israel, who refuses to obey, ask you, 'What are you doing?'
10"Say to them, 'This is what the Lord GOD
says: This message is about the king in Jerusalem
and all the people of Israel who live there.' 11Say,
'I am a sign to you.'
"The same things I have done will be done to
the people in Jerusalem. They will be taken away
from their country as captives. 12The king among
them will put his things on his shoulder in the
dark and will leave. The people will dig a hole
through the wall to bring him out. He will cover
his face so he cannot see the ground. 13But I will
spread my net over him, and he will be caught in
my trap. Then I will bring him to Babylon in the
land of the Babylonians. He will not see that land,
but he will die there. 14All who are around the
king—his helpers and all his army—I will scatter
in every direction, and I will chase them with a
sword.
15"They will know that I am the LORD when I
scatter them among the nations and spread them
among the countries. 16But I will save a few of
them from the sword and from hunger and disease. Then they can tell about their hateful actions among the nations where they go. Then
they will know that I am the LORD."

The Lesson of Ezekiel's Shaking

17The LORD spoke his word to me, saying:
18"Human, tremble as you eat your food, and
shake with fear as you drink your water. 19Then
say to the people of the land: 'This is what the
Lord GOD says about the people who live in Jerusalem in the land of Israel: They will eat their food
with fear and drink their water in shock, because
their land will be stripped bare because of the violence of the people who live in it. 20The cities
where people live will become ruins, and the land
will become empty. Then you will know that I am
the LORD.' "

The Visions Will Come True

21The LORD spoke his word to me, saying:
22"Human, what is this saying you have in the
land of Israel: 'The days go by and every vision
comes to nothing'? 23So say to them, 'This is what
the Lord GOD says: I will make them stop saying
this, and nobody in Israel will use this saying anymore.' But tell them, 'The time is near when every vision will come true. 24There will be no more
false visions or pleasing prophecies[d] inside the nation of Israel, 25but I, the LORD, will speak. What
I say will be done, and it will not be delayed. You
refuse to obey, but in your time I will say the
word and do it, says the Lord GOD.' "
26The LORD spoke his word to me, saying:
27"Human, the people of Israel are saying, 'The
vision that Ezekiel sees is for a time many years
from now. He is prophesying about times far
away.'
28"So say to them: 'The Lord GOD says this:
None of my words will be delayed anymore.
What I have said will be done, says the Lord
GOD.' "

Ezekiel Speaks Against False Prophets

13 The LORD spoke his word to me, saying:
2"Human, prophesy[d] against the prophets of Israel. Say to those who make up their own
prophecies: 'Listen to the word of the LORD. 3This
is what the Lord GOD says: How terrible it will be
for the foolish prophets who follow their own
ideas and have not seen a vision from me! 4People
of Israel, your prophets have been like wild dogs
hunting to kill and eat among ruins. 5Israel is like
a house in ruins, but you have not gone up into
the broken places or repaired the wall. So how
can Israel hold back the enemy in the battle on
the LORD's day of judging? 6Your prophets see
false visions and prophesy lies. They say, "This is
the message of the LORD," when the LORD has not
sent them. But they still hope their words will
come true. 7You said, "This is the message of the
LORD," but that is a false vision. Your prophecies
are lies, because I have not spoken.
8" 'So this is what the Lord GOD says: Because
you prophets spoke things that are false and saw
visions that do not come true, I am against you,
says the Lord GOD. 9I will punish the prophets
who see false visions and prophesy lies. They will
have no place among my people. Their names will
not be written on the list of the people of Israel,
and they will not enter the land of Israel. Then
you will know that I am the Lord GOD.
10" 'It is because they lead my people the
wrong way by saying, "Peace!" when there is no
peace. When the people build a weak wall, the
prophets cover it with whitewash to make it look
strong. 11So tell those who cover a weak wall with
whitewash that it will fall down. Rain will pour
down, hailstones will fall, and a stormy wind will
break the wall down. 12When the wall has fallen,
people will ask you, "Where is the whitewash you
used on the wall?"
13" 'So this is what the Lord GOD says: I will
break the wall with a stormy wind. In my anger

rain will pour down, and hailstones will destroy the wall. 14I will tear down the wall on which you put whitewash. I will level it to the ground so that people will see the wall's foundation. And when the wall falls, you will be destroyed under it. Then you will know that I am the LORD. 15So I will carry out my anger on the wall and against those who covered it with whitewash. Then I will tell you, "The wall is gone, and those who covered it with whitewash are gone. 16The prophets of Israel who prophesy to Jerusalem and who see visions of peace for the city, when there is no peace, will be gone, says the Lord GOD." '

False Women Prophets

17"Now, human, look toward the women among your people who make up their own prophecies.[d] Prophesy against them. 18Say, 'This is what the Lord GOD says: How terrible it will be for women who sew magic charms on their wrists and make veils of every length to trap people! You ruin the lives of my people but try to save your own lives. 19For handfuls of barley and pieces of bread, you have dishonored me among my people. By lying to my people, who listen to lies, you have killed people who should not die, and you have kept alive those who should not live.

20" 'So this is what the Lord GOD says: I am against your magic charms, by which you trap people as if they were birds. I will tear those charms off your arms, and I will free those people you have trapped like birds. 21I will also tear off your veils and save my people from your hands. They will no longer be trapped by your power. Then you will know that I am the LORD. 22By your lies you have caused those who did right to be sad, when I did not make them sad. And you have encouraged the wicked not to stop being wicked, which would have saved their lives. 23So you will not see false visions or prophesy anymore, and I will save my people from your power so you will know that I am the LORD.' "

Stop Worshiping Idols

14 Some of the older leaders of Israel came to me and sat down in front of me. 2Then the LORD spoke his word to me, saying: 3"Human, these men want to worship idols. They put up evil things that cause people to sin. Should I allow them to ask me for help? 4So speak to them and tell them, 'This is what the Lord GOD says: When any of the people of Israel want to worship idols and put up evil things that cause people to sin and then come to the prophet,[d] I, the LORD, will answer them myself for worshiping idols. 5Then I will win back my people Israel, who have left me because of all their idols.'

6"So say to the people of Israel, 'This is what the Lord GOD says: Change your hearts and lives, and stop worshiping idols. Stop doing all the things I hate. 7Any of the Israelites or foreigners in Israel can separate themselves from me by wanting to worship idols or by putting up the things that cause people to sin. Then if they come to the prophet to ask me questions, I, the LORD, will answer them myself. 8I will reject them. I will make them a sign and an example, and I will separate them from my people. Then you will know that I am the LORD.

9" 'But if the prophet is tricked into giving a prophecy, it is because I, the LORD, have tricked that prophet to speak. Then I will use my power against him and destroy him from among my people Israel. 10The prophet will be as guilty as the one who asks him for help; both will be responsible for their guilt. 11Then the nation of Israel will not leave me anymore or make themselves unclean[d] anymore with all their sins. They will be my people, and I will be their God, says the Lord GOD.' "

> **SIDELIGHT:** If Ezekiel's mother were living, she might have washed his mouth out with soap when he talked about pagan idols (Ezekiel 14:1–11). His term for these idols literally means "dung balls" or "animal dung." Ezekiel uses the term thirty-nine times, but it only appears nine times in the rest of the Old Testament.

Jerusalem Will Not Be Spared

12The LORD spoke his word to me, saying: 13"Human, if the people of a country sin against me by not being loyal, I will use my power against them. I will cut off their supply of food and send a time of hunger, destroying both people and animals. 14Even if three great men like Noah, Daniel, and Job were in that country, their goodness could save only themselves, says the Lord GOD.

15"Or I might send wild animals into that land, leaving the land empty and without children. Then no one would pass through it because of the animals. 16As surely as I live, says the Lord GOD, even if Noah, Daniel, and Job were in the land, they could not save their own sons or daughters. They could save only themselves, but that country would become empty.

17"Or I might bring a war against that country. I might say, 'Let a war be fought in that land,' in this way destroying its people and its animals. 18As surely as I live, says the Lord GOD, even if those three men were in the land, they could not save their sons or daughters. They could save only themselves.

19"Or I might cause a disease to spread in that

country. I might pour out my anger against it, destroying and killing people and animals. 20As surely as I live, says the Lord GOD, even if Noah, Daniel, and Job were in the land, they could not save their son or daughter. They could save only themselves because they did what was right.

21"This is what the Lord GOD says: My plans for Jerusalem are much worse! I will send my four terrible punishments against it—war, hunger, wild animals, and disease—to destroy its people and animals. 22But some people will escape; some sons and daughters will be led out. They will come out to you, and you will see what happens to people who live as they did. Then you will be comforted after the disasters I have brought against Jerusalem, after all the things I have brought against it. 23You will be comforted when you see what happens to them for living as they did, because you will know there was a good reason for what I did to Jerusalem, says the Lord GOD."

Story of the Vine

15 The LORD spoke his word to me, saying: 2"Human, is the wood of the vine better than the wood of any tree in the forest? 3Can wood be taken from the vine to make anything? Can you use it to make a peg on which to hang something? 4If the vine is thrown into the fire for fuel, and the fire burns up both ends and starts to burn the middle, is it useful for anything? 5When the vine was whole, it couldn't be made into anything. When the fire has burned it completely, it certainly cannot be made into anything."

6So this is what the Lord GOD says: "Out of all the trees in the forest, I have given the wood of the vine as fuel for fire. In the same way I have given up the people who live in Jerusalem 7and will turn against them. Although they came through one fire, fire will still destroy them. When I turn against them, you will know that I am the LORD. 8So I will make the land empty, because the people have not been loyal, says the Lord GOD."

The Lord's Kindness to Jerusalem

16 The LORD spoke his word to me, saying: 2"Human, tell Jerusalem about her hateful actions. 3Say, 'This is what the Lord GOD says to Jerusalem: Your beginnings and your ancestors were in the land of the Canaanites. Your father was an Amorite, and your mother was a Hittite. 4On the day you were born, your cord[n] was not cut. You were not washed with water to clean you. You were not rubbed with salt or wrapped in cloths. 5No one felt sorry enough for you to do any of these things for you. No, you were thrown out into the open field, because you were hated on the day you were born.

SIDELIGHT: Who needs baby lotion when you have salt? In ancient times, people would rub salt on newborn babies (Ezekiel 16:4). They might have thought it had medical value, or they might have done it because of superstition.

6" 'When I passed by and saw you kicking about in your blood, I said to you, "Live!" 7I made you grow like a plant in the field. You grew up and became tall and became like a beautiful jewel. Your breasts formed, and your hair grew, but you were naked and without clothes.

8" 'Later when I passed by you and looked at you, I saw that you were old enough for love. So I spread my robe over you and covered your nakedness. I also made a promise to you and entered into an agreement with you so that you became mine, says the Lord GOD.

9" 'Then I bathed you with water, washed all the blood off of you, and put oil on you. 10I put beautiful clothes made with needlework on you and put sandals of fine leather on your feet. I wrapped you in fine linen and covered you with silk. 11I put jewelry on you: bracelets on your arms, a necklace around your neck, 12a ring in your nose, earrings in your ears, and a beautiful crown on your head. 13So you wore gold and silver. Your clothes were made of fine linen, silk, and beautiful needlework. You ate fine flour, honey, and olive oil. You were very beautiful and became a queen. 14Then you became famous among the nations, because you were so beautiful. Your beauty was perfect, because of the glory I gave you, says the Lord GOD.

Jerusalem Becomes a Prostitute

15" 'But you trusted in your beauty. You became a prostitute,[d] because you were so famous. You had sexual relations with anyone who passed by. 16You took some of your clothes and made your places of worship colorful. There you carried on your prostitution. These things should not happen; they should never occur. 17You also took your beautiful jewelry, made from my gold and silver I had given you, and you made for yourselves male idols so you could be a prostitute with them. 18Then you took your clothes with beautiful needlework and covered the idols. You gave my oil and incense[d] as an offering to them. 19Also, you took the bread I gave you, the fine flour, oil,

cord The umbilical cord that gives the unborn baby food and air from its mother.

and honey I gave you to eat, and you offered them
before the gods as a pleasing smell. This is what
happened, says the Lord God.
20" 'But your sexual sins were not enough for
you. You also took your sons and daughters who
were my children, and you sacrificed them to the
idols as food. 21You killed my children and offered
them up in fire to the idols. 22While you did all
your hateful acts and sexual sins, you did not remember when you were young, when you were
naked and had no clothes and were left in your
blood.
23" 'How terrible! How terrible it will be for
you, says the Lord God. After you did all these
evil things, 24you built yourself a place to worship
gods. You made for yourself a place of worship in
every city square. 25You built a place of worship
at the beginning of every street. You made your
beauty hateful, offering your body for sex to anyone who passed by, so your sexual sins became
worse and worse. 26You also had sexual relations
with the Egyptians, who were your neighbors and
partners in sexual sin. Your sexual sins became
even worse, and they caused me to be angry. 27So
then, I used my power against you and took away
some of your land. I let you be defeated by those
who hate you, the Philistine women, who were
ashamed of your evil ways. 28Also, you had sexual
relations with the Assyrians, because you could
not be satisfied. Even though you had sexual relations with them, you still were not satisfied. 29You
did many more sexual sins in Babylonia, the land
of traders, but even this did not satisfy you.
30" 'Truly your will is weak, says the Lord God.
You do all the things a stubborn prostitute does.
31You built your place to worship gods at the beginning of every street, and you made places of
worship in every city square. But you were not
like a prostitute when you refused to accept payment.
32" 'You are a wife who is guilty of adultery.[d]
You desire strangers instead of your husband.
33Men pay prostitutes, but you pay all your lovers
to come to you. And they come from all around
for sexual relations. 34So you are different from
other prostitutes. No man asks you to be a prostitute, and you pay money instead of having money
paid to you. Yes, you are different.

The Prostitute Is Judged

35" 'So, prostitute,[d] hear the word of the Lord.
36This is what the Lord God says: You showed
your nakedness to other countries. You uncovered your body in your sexual sins with them as
your lovers and with all your hateful idols. You
killed your children and offered their blood to
your idols. 37So I will gather all your lovers with
whom you found pleasure. Yes, I will gather all
those you loved and those you hated. I will gather
them against you from all around, and I will strip
you naked in front of them so they can see your
nakedness. 38I will punish you as women guilty of
adultery[d] or as murderers are punished. I will put
you to death because I am angry and jealous. 39I
will also hand you over to your lovers. They will
tear down your places of worship and destroy
other places where you worship gods. They will
tear off your clothes and take away your jewelry,
leaving you naked and bare. 40They will bring a
crowd against you to throw stones at you and to
cut you into pieces with their swords. 41They will
burn down your houses and will punish you in
front of many women. I will put an end to your
sexual sins, and you will no longer pay your lovers. 42Then I will rest from my anger against you,
and I will stop being jealous. I will be quiet and
not angry anymore.
43" 'Because you didn't remember when you
were young, but have made me angry in all these
ways, I will repay you for what you have done,
says the Lord God. Didn't you add sexual sins to
all your other acts which I hate?
44" 'Everyone who uses wise sayings will say
this about you: "The daughter is like her mother."
45You are like your mother, who hated her husband and children. You are also like your sisters,
who hated their husbands and children. Your
mother was a Hittite, and your father was an Amorite. 46Your older sister is Samaria, who lived
north of you with her daughters; your younger
sister is Sodom, who lived south of you with her
daughters. 47You not only followed their ways and
did the hateful things they did, but you were soon
worse than they were in all your ways. 48As surely
as I live, says the Lord God, this is true. Your
sister Sodom and her daughters never did what
you and your daughters have done.
49" 'This was the sin of your sister Sodom: She
and her daughters were proud and had plenty of
food and lived in great comfort, but she did not
help the poor and needy. 50So Sodom and her
daughters were proud and did things I hate in
front of me. So I got rid of them when I saw what
they did. 51Also, Samaria did not do half the sins
you do; you have done more hateful things than
they did. So you make your sisters look good because of all the hateful things you have done.
52You will suffer disgrace, because you have provided an excuse for your sisters. They are better
than you are. Your sins were even more terrible
than theirs. Feel ashamed and suffer disgrace, because you made your sisters look good.
53" 'But I will give back to Sodom and her
daughters the good things they once had. I will
give back to Samaria and her daughters the good
things they once had. And with them I will also
give back the good things you once had 54so you
may suffer disgrace and feel ashamed for all the

things you have done. You even gave comfort to your sisters in their sins. 55Your sisters, Sodom with her daughters and Samaria with her daughters, will return to what they were before. You and your daughters will also return to what you were before. 56You humiliated your sister Sodom when you were proud, 57before your evil was uncovered. And now the Edomite women and their neighbors humiliate you. Even the Philistine women humiliate you. Those around you hate you. 58This is your punishment for your terrible sins and for actions that I hate, says the LORD.

God Keeps His Promises

59" 'This is what the Lord GOD says: I will do to you what you have done. You hated and broke the agreement you promised to keep. 60But I will remember my agreement I made with you when you were young, and I will make an agreement that will continue forever with you. 61Then you will remember what you have done and feel ashamed when you receive your sisters—both your older and your younger sisters. I will give them to you like daughters, but not because they share in my agreement with you. 62I will set up my agreement with you, and you will know that I am the LORD. 63You will remember what you did and feel ashamed. You will not open your mouth again because of your shame, when I forgive you for all the things you have done, says the Lord GOD.' "

The Eagle and the Vine

17 The LORD spoke his word to me, saying: 2"Human, give a riddle and tell a story to the people of Israel. 3Say, 'This is what the Lord GOD says: A giant eagle with big wings and long feathers of many different colors came to Lebanon and took hold of the top of a cedar tree. 4He pulled off the top branch and brought it to a land of traders, where he planted it in a city of traders.

5" 'The eagle took some seed from the land and planted it in a good field near plenty of water. He planted it to grow like a willow tree. 6It sprouted and became a low vine that spread over the ground. The branches turned toward the eagle, but the roots were under the eagle. So the seed became a vine, and its branches grew, sending out leaves.

7" 'But there was another giant eagle with big wings and many feathers. The vine then bent its roots toward this eagle. It sent out its branches from the area where it was planted toward the eagle so he could water it. 8It had been planted in a good field by plenty of water so it could grow branches and give fruit. It could have become a fine vine.'

9"Say to them, 'This is what the Lord GOD says: The vine will not continue to grow. The first eagle will pull up the vine's roots and strip off its fruit. Then the vine and all its new leaves will dry up and die. It will not take a strong arm or many people to pull the vine up by its roots. 10Even if it is planted again, it will not continue to grow. It will completely dry up and die when the east wind hits it in the area where it grew.' "

Zedekiah Against Nebuchadnezzar

11Then the LORD spoke his word to me, saying: 12"Say now to the people who refuse to obey: 'Do you know what these things mean?' Say: 'The king of Babylon came to Jerusalem and took the king and important men of Jerusalem and brought them to Babylon. 13Then he took a member of the family of the king of Judah and made an agreement with him, forcing him to take an oath. The king also took away the leaders of Judah 14to make the kingdom weak so it would not be strong again. Then the kingdom of Judah could continue only by keeping its agreement with the king of Babylon. 15But the king of Judah turned against the king of Babylon by sending his messengers to Egypt and asking them for horses and many soldiers. Will the king of Judah succeed? Will the one who does such things escape? He cannot break the agreement and escape.

16" 'As surely as I live, says the Lord GOD, he will die in Babylon, in the land of the king who made him king of Judah. The king of Judah hated his promise to the king of Babylon and broke his agreement with him. 17The king of Egypt with his mighty army and many people will not help the king of Judah in the war. The Babylonians will build devices to attack the cities and to kill many people. 18The king of Judah showed that he hated the promise by breaking the agreement. He promised to support Babylon, but he did all these things. So he will not escape.

19" 'So this is what the Lord GOD says: As surely as I live, this is true: I will pay back the king of Judah for hating my promise and breaking my agreement. 20I will spread my net over him, and he will be caught in my trap. Then I will bring him to Babylon, where I will punish him for the unfaithful acts he did against me. 21All the best of his soldiers who escape will die by the sword, and those who live will be scattered to every wind. Then you will know that I, the LORD, have spoken.

22" 'This is what the Lord GOD says: I myself will also take a young branch from the top of a cedar tree, and I will plant it. I will cut off a small twig from the top of the tree's young branches, and I will plant it on a very high mountain. 23I will plant it on the high mountain of Israel. Then it will grow branches and give fruit and become a great cedar tree. Birds of every kind will build nests in it and live in the shelter of the tree's branches. 24Then all the trees in the countryside will know that I am the LORD. I bring down the high tree and make the low tree tall. I dry up the green tree and make the dry tree grow. I am the LORD. I have spoken, and I will do it.' "

God Is Fair

18 The LORD spoke his word to me, saying: 2"What do you mean by using this saying about the land of Israel:

'The parents have eaten sour grapes,
 and that caused the children to grind their
  teeth from the sour taste'?

3"As surely as I live, says the Lord GOD, this is true: You will not use this saying in Israel anymore. 4Every living thing belongs to me. The life of the parent is mine, and the life of the child is mine. The person who sins is the one who will die.

5"Suppose a person is good and does what is fair and right. 6He does not eat at the mountain places of worship. He does not look to the idols of Israel for help. He does not have sexual relations with his neighbor's wife or with a woman during her time of monthly bleeding. 7He does not mistreat anyone but returns what was given as a promise for a loan. He does not rob other people. He gives bread to the hungry and clothes to those who have none. 8He does not lend money to get too much interest or profit. He keeps his hand from doing wrong. He judges fairly between one person and another. 9He lives by my rules and obeys my laws faithfully. Whoever does these things is good and will surely live, says the Lord GOD.

10"But suppose this person has a wild son who murders people and who does any of these other things. 11(But the father himself has not done any of these things.) This son eats at the mountain places of worship. He has sexual relations with his neighbor's wife. 12He mistreats the poor and needy. He steals and refuses to return what was promised for a loan. He looks to idols for help. He does things which I hate. 13He lends money for too much interest and profit. Will this son live? No, he will not live! He has done all these hateful things, so he will surely be put to death. He will be responsible for his own death.

14"Now suppose this son has a son who has seen all his father's sins, but after seeing them does not do those things. 15He does not eat at the mountain places of worship. He does not look to the idols of Israel for help. He does not have sexual relations with his neighbor's wife. 16He does not mistreat anyone or keep something promised for a loan or steal. He gives bread to the hungry and clothes to those who have none. 17He keeps his hand from doing wrong. He does not take too much interest or profit when he lends money. He obeys my laws and lives by my rules. He will not die for his father's sin; he will surely live. 18But his father took other people's money unfairly and robbed his brother and did what was wrong among his people. So he will die for his own sin.

19"But you ask, 'Why is the son not punished for the father's sin?' The son has done what is fair and right. He obeys all my rules, so he will surely live. 20The person who sins is the one who will die. A child will not be punished for a parent's sin, and a parent will not be punished for a child's sin. Those who do right will enjoy the results of their own goodness; evil people will suffer the results of their own evil.

21"But suppose the wicked stop doing all the sins they have done and obey all my rules and do what is fair and right. Then they will surely live; they will not die. 22Their sins will be forgotten. Because they have done what is right, they will live. 23I do not really want the wicked to die, says the Lord GOD. I want them to stop their bad ways and live.

24"But suppose good people stop doing good and do wrong and do the same hateful things the wicked do. Will they live? All their good acts will be forgotten, because they became unfaithful. They have sinned, so they will die because of their sins.

25"But you say, 'What the Lord does isn't fair.' Listen, people of Israel. I am fair. It is what you do that is not fair! 26When good people stop doing good and do wrong, they will die because of it. They will die, because they did wrong. 27When the wicked stop being wicked and do what is fair and right, they will save their lives. 28Because they thought about it and stopped doing all the sins they had done, they will surely live; they will not die. 29But the people of Israel still say, 'What the Lord does isn't fair.' People of Israel, I am fair. It is what you do that is not fair.

30"So I will judge you, people of Israel; I will judge each of you by what you do, says the Lord GOD. Change your hearts and stop all your sinning so sin will not bring your ruin. 31Get rid of all the sins you have done, and get for yourselves a new heart and a new way of thinking. Why do you want to die, people of Israel? 32I do not want anyone to die, says the Lord GOD, so change your hearts and lives so you may live.

A Sad Song for Israel

19 "Sing a funeral song for the leaders of Israel. 2Say:

'Your mother was like a female lion.
She lay down among the young lions.
 She had many cubs.
3When she brought up one of her cubs,
 he became a strong lion.
He learned to tear the animals he hunted,

and he ate people.
4The nations heard about him.
He was trapped in their pit,
and they brought him with hooks
to the land of Egypt.

5" 'The mother lion waited and saw
that there was no hope for her cub.
So she took another one of her cubs
and made him a strong lion.
6This cub roamed among the lions.
He was now a strong lion.
He learned to tear the animals he hunted,
and he ate people.
7He tore down their strong places
and destroyed their cities.
The land and everything in it
were terrified by the sound of his roar.
8Then the nations came against him
from areas all around,
and they spread their net over him.
He was trapped in their pit.
9Then they put him into a cage with chains
and brought him to the king of Babylon.
They put him into prison
so his roar could not be heard again
on the mountains of Israel.

10" 'Your mother was like a vine in your vineyard,
planted beside the water.
The vine had many branches and gave much fruit,
because there was plenty of water.
11The vine had strong branches,
good enough for a king's scepter.[d]
The vine became tall
among the thick branches.
And it was seen, because it was tall
with many branches.
12But it was pulled up by its roots in anger
and thrown down to the ground.
The east wind dried it up.
Its fruit was torn off.
Its strong branches were broken off
and burned up.
13Now the vine is planted in the desert,
in a dry and thirsty land.
14Fire spread from the vine's main branch,
destroying its fruit.
There is not a strong branch left on it
that could become a scepter for a king.'

This is a funeral song; it is to be used as a funeral song."

Israel Has Refused God

20 It was the seventh year of our captivity, in the fifth month, on the tenth day of the month. Some of the older leaders of Israel
came to ask about the LORD and sat down in front
of me.
2The LORD spoke his word to me, saying: 3"Human, speak to the older leaders of Israel and say
to them: 'This is what the Lord GOD says: Did
you come to ask me questions? As surely as I live,
I will not let you ask me questions.'
4"Will you judge them? Will you judge them,
human? Let them know the hateful things their
ancestors did. 5Say to them: 'This is what the
Lord GOD says: When I chose Israel, I made a
promise to the descendants[d] of Jacob. I made myself known to them in Egypt, and I promised
them, "I am the LORD your God." 6At that time
I promised them I would bring them out of Egypt
into a land I had found for them, a fertile land, the
best land in the world. 7I said to them, "Each one
of you must throw away the hateful idols you
have seen and liked. Don't make yourselves unclean[d] with the idols of Egypt. I am the LORD your
God."
8" 'But they turned against me and refused to
listen to me. They did not throw away the hateful
idols which they saw and liked; they did not give
up the idols of Egypt. Then I decided to pour out
my anger against them while they were still in
Egypt. 9But I acted for the sake of my name so it
would not be dishonored in full view of the nations where the Israelites lived. I made myself
known to the Israelites with a promise to bring
them out of Egypt while the nations were watching. 10So I took them out of Egypt and brought
them into the desert. 11I gave them my rules and
told them about my laws, by which people will
live if they obey them. 12I also gave them my Sabbaths[d] to be a sign between us so they would
know that I am the LORD who made them holy.
13" 'But in the desert Israel turned against me.
They did not follow my rules, and they rejected
my laws, by which people will live if they obey
them. They dishonored my Sabbaths. Then I decided to pour out my anger against them and destroy them in the desert. 14But I acted for the sake
of my name so it would not be dishonored in full
view of the nations who watched as I had brought
the Israelites out of Egypt. 15And in the desert I
swore to the Israelites that I would not bring them
into the land I had given them. It is a fertile land,
the best land in the world. 16This was because
they rejected my laws and did not follow my
rules. They dishonored my Sabbaths and wanted
to worship their idols. 17But I had pity on them.
I did not destroy them or put an end to them in
the desert. 18I said to their children in the desert,
"Don't live by the rules of your parents, or obey
their laws. Don't make yourselves unclean with
their idols. 19I am the LORD your God. Live by my
rules, obey my laws, and follow them. 20Keep my
Sabbaths holy, and they will be a sign between me

and you. Then you will know that I am the LORD
your God."
21" 'But the children turned against me. They
did not live by my rules, nor were they careful to
obey my laws, by which people will live if they
obey them. They dishonored my Sabbaths. So I
decided to pour out my anger against them in the
desert. 22But I held back my anger. I acted for the
sake of my name so it would not be dishonored
in full view of the nations who watched as I
brought the Israelites out. 23And in the desert I
swore to the Israelites that I would scatter them
among the nations and spread them among the
countries, 24because they had not obeyed my
laws. They had rejected my rules and dishonored
my Sabbaths and worshiped the idols of their parents. 25I also allowed them to follow rules that
were not good and laws by which they could not
live. 26I let the Israelites make themselves unclean
by the gifts they brought to their gods when they
sacrificed their first children in the fire. I wanted
to terrify them so they would know that I am the
LORD.'
27"So, human, speak to the people of Israel. Say
to them, 'This is what the Lord GOD says: Your
ancestors spoke against me by being unfaithful to
me in another way. 28When I had brought them
into the land I promised to give them, they saw
every high hill and every leafy tree. There they
offered their sacrifices to gods. They brought offerings that made me angry and burned their incense[d] and poured out their drink offerings.
29Then I said to them: What is this high place
where you go to worship?' " (It is still called High
Place today.)
30"So say to the people of Israel: 'This is what
the Lord GOD says: Are you going to make yourselves unclean as your ancestors did? Are you going to be unfaithful and desire their hateful idols?
31When you offer your children as gifts and sacrifice them in the fire, you are making yourselves
unclean with all your idols even today. So, people
of Israel, should I let you ask me questions? As
surely as I live, says the Lord GOD, I will not accept questions from you.
32" 'What you want will not come true. You
say, "We want to be like the other nations, like
the people in other lands. We want to worship
idols made of wood and stone." 33As surely as I
live, says the Lord GOD, I will use my great power
and strength and anger to rule over you. 34I will
bring you out from the foreign nations. With my
great power and strength and anger I will gather
you from the lands where you are scattered. 35I
will bring you among the nations as I brought
your ancestors into the desert with Moses. There
I will judge you face to face. 36I will judge you the
same way I judged your ancestors in the desert of
the land of Egypt, says the Lord GOD. 37I will
count you like sheep and will bring you into line
with my agreement. 38I will get rid of those who
refuse to obey me and who turn against me. I will
bring them out of the land where they are now
living, but they will never enter the land of Israel.
Then you will know that I am the LORD.
39" 'This is what the Lord GOD says: People of
Israel, go serve your idols for now. But later you
will listen to me; you will not continue to dishonor my holy name with your gifts and gods.
40On my holy mountain, the high mountain of Israel, all Israel will serve me in the land, says the
Lord GOD. There I will accept you. There I will
expect your offerings, the first harvest of your offerings, and all your holy gifts. 41I will accept you
like the pleasing smell of sacrifices when I bring
you out from the foreign nations and gather you
from the lands where you are scattered. Then
through you I will show how holy I am so the
nations will see. 42When I bring you into the land
of Israel, the land I promised your ancestors, you
will know that I am the LORD. 43There you will
remember everything you did that made you un
clean, and then you will hate yourselves for all the
evil things you have done. 44I will deal with you
for the sake of my name, not because of your evil
ways or unclean actions. Then you will know I
am the LORD, people of Israel, says the Lord
GOD.' "

Babylon, the Lord's Sword

45Now the LORD spoke his word to me, saying:
46"Human, look toward the south. Prophesy[d]
against the south and against the forest of the
southern area. 47Say to that forest: 'Hear the word
of the LORD. This is what the Lord GOD says: I am
ready to start a fire in you that will destroy all your
green trees and all your dry trees. The flames that
burn will not be put out. Every face from south
to north will feel their heat. 48Then all the people
will see that I, the LORD, have started the fire. It
will not be put out.' "
49Then I said, "Ah, Lord GOD! The people are
saying about me, 'He is only telling stories.' "

21 Then the LORD spoke his word to me,
saying: 2"Human, look toward Jerusa-
lem and speak against the holy place. Prophesy[d]
against the land of Israel. 3Say to Israel: 'This is
what the LORD says: I am against you. I will pull
my sword out of its holder, and I will cut off from
you both the wicked and those who do right. 4Be-
cause I am going to cut off the wicked and those
who do right, my sword will come out from its
holder and attack all people from south to north.
5Then all people will know that I, the LORD, have
pulled my sword out from its holder. My sword
will not go back in again.'
6"So, human, groan with breaking heart and
great sadness. Groan in front of the people.

7When they ask you, 'Why are you groaning?' you
will say, 'Because of what I have heard is going
to happen. When it happens, every heart will melt
with fear, and all hands will become weak. Everyone will be afraid; all knees will become weak as
water. Look, it is coming, and it will happen, says
the Lord GOD.' "

8The LORD spoke his word to me, saying: 9"Human, prophesy and say, 'This is what the Lord
says:

A sword, a sword,
made sharp and polished.
10It is made sharp for the killing.
It is polished to flash like lightning.

" 'You are not happy about this horrible punishment by the sword. But my son Judah, you did
not change when you were only beaten with a
rod.

11The sword should be polished.
It is meant to be held in the hand.
It is made sharp and polished,
ready for the hand of a killer.
12Shout and yell, human,
because the sword is meant for my people,
for all the rulers of Israel.
They will be killed by the sword,
along with my people.
So beat your chest in sadness.

13" 'The test will come. And Judah, who is
hated by the armies of Babylon, will not last, says
the Lord GOD.'

14"So, human, prophesy
and clap your hands.
Let the sword strike
two or three times.
It is a sword meant for killing,
a sword meant for much killing.
This sword surrounds the people to be
killed.
15Their hearts will melt with fear,
and many people will die.
I have placed the killing sword
at all their city gates.
Oh! The sword is made to flash like
lightning.
It is held, ready for killing.
16Sword, cut on the right side;
then cut on the left side.
Cut anywhere your blade is turned.
17I will also clap my hands
and use up my anger.
I, the LORD, have spoken."

Jerusalem to Be Destroyed

18The LORD spoke his word to me, saying:
19"Human, mark two roads that the king of Babylon and his sword can follow. Both of these roads
will start from the same country. And make signs
where the road divides and one way goes toward
the city. 20Mark one sign to show the road he can
take with his sword to Rabbah in the land of the
Ammonites. Mark the other sign to show the road
to Judah and Jerusalem, which is protected with
strong walls. 21The king of Babylon has come to
where the road divides, and he is using magic. He
throws lots[d] with arrows and asks questions of his
family idols. He looks at the liver of a sacrificed
animal to learn where he should go. 22The lot in
his right hand tells him to go to Jerusalem. It tells
him to use logs to break down the city gates, to
shout the battle cry and give the order to kill, and
to build a dirt road to the top of the walls and
devices to attack the walls. 23The people of Jerusalem have made agreements with other nations to
help them fight Babylon. So they will think this
prediction is wrong, but it is really proof of their
sin, and they will be captured.

SIDELIGHT: Using arrows to predict the future (Ezekiel 21:21) was a favorite Babylonian divination (magic trick) to help make decisions—as some people use tarot cards, tea leaves, and horoscopes today. The person would shake the arrows and then throw them on the ground. Their formation would tell what to do.

24"So this is what the Lord GOD says: 'You have
shown how sinful you are by turning against the
LORD. Your sins are seen in all the things you do.
Because of this proof against you, you will be
taken captive by the enemy.

25" 'You unclean[d] and evil leader of Israel, you
will be killed! The time of your final punishment
has come. 26This is what the Lord GOD says: Take
off the royal turban, and remove the crown.
Things will change. Those who are important
now will be made unimportant, and those who
are unimportant now will be made important. 27A
ruin! A ruin! I will make it a ruin! This place will
not be rebuilt until the one comes who has a right
to be king. Then I will give him that right.'

The Punishment of Ammon

28"And you, human, prophesy[d] and say: 'This
is what the Lord GOD says about the people of
Ammon and their insults:

A sword, a sword
is pulled out of its holder.
It is polished to kill and destroy,
to flash like lightning!
29Prophets[d] see false visions about you
and prophesy lies about you.
The sword will be put on the necks

of these unclean[d] and evil people.
Their day of judging has come;
the time of final punishment has come.
30Put the sword back in its holder.
I will judge you
in the place where you were created,
in the land where you were born.
31I will pour out my anger against you
and blast you with the fire of my anger.
I will hand you over to cruel men,
experts in destruction.
32You will be like fuel for the fire;
you will die in the land.
You will not be remembered,
because I, the LORD, have spoken.' "

The Sins of Jerusalem

22 The LORD spoke his word to me, saying:
2"And you, human, will you judge? Will
you judge the city of murderers? Then tell her
about all her hateful acts. 3You are to say: 'This
is what the Lord GOD says: You are a city that kills
those who come to live there. You make yourself
unclean[d] by making idols. 4You have become
guilty of murder and have become unclean by
your idols which you have made. So you have
brought your time of punishment near; you
have come to the end of your years. That is why
I have made you a shame to the nations and
why all lands laugh at you. 5Those near and
those far away laugh at you with your bad
name, you city full of confusion.
6" 'Jerusalem, see how each ruler of Israel in
you has been trying to kill people. 7The people in
you hate their fathers and mothers. They mistreat
the foreigners in you and wrong the orphans and
widows in you. 8You hate my holy things and dishonor my Sabbaths.[d] 9The men in you tell lies to
cause the death of others. The people in you eat
food offered to idols at the mountain places of
worship, and they take part in sexual sins. 10The
men in you have sexual relations with their fathers' wives and with women who are unclean,
during their time of monthly bleeding. 11One man
in you does a hateful act with his neighbor's wife,
while another has shamefully made his daughter-
in-law unclean sexually. And another forces his
half sister to have sexual relations with him. 12The
people in you take money to kill others. You take
unfair interest and profits and make profits by mistreating your neighbor. And you have forgotten
me, says the Lord GOD.
13" 'So, Jerusalem, I will shake my fist at you for
stealing money and for murdering people. 14Will
you still be brave and strong when I punish you?
I, the LORD, have spoken, and I will act. 15I will
scatter you among the nations and spread you
through the countries. That is how I will get rid
of your uncleanness. 16But you, yourself, will be
dishonored in the sight of the nations. Then you
will know that I am the LORD.' "

Israel Is Worthless

17The LORD spoke his word to me, saying:
18"Human, the people of Israel have become useless like scum to me. They are like the copper, tin,
iron, and lead left in the furnace when silver is
purified. 19So this is what the Lord GOD says: 'Because you have become useless like scum, I am
going to put you together inside Jerusalem. 20Peo-
ple put silver, copper, iron, lead, and tin together
inside a furnace to melt them down in a blazing
fire. In the same way I will gather you in my hot
anger and put you together in Jerusalem and melt
you down. 21I will put you together and make you
feel the heat of my anger. You will be melted
down inside Jerusalem. 22As silver is melted in a
furnace, you will be melted inside the city. Then
you will know that I, the LORD, have poured out
my anger on you.' "

Sins of the People

23The LORD spoke his word to me, saying:
24"Human, say to the land, 'You are a land that
has not had rain or showers when God is angry.'
25Like a roaring lion that tears the animal it has
caught, Israel's rulers make evil plans. They have
destroyed lives and have taken treasure and valuable things. They have caused many women to
become widows. 26Israel's priests do cruel things
to my teachings and do not honor my holy things.
They make no difference between holy and unholy things, and they teach there is no difference
between clean[d] and unclean things. They do not
remember my Sabbaths,[d] so I am dishonored by
them. 27Like wolves tearing a dead animal, Jerusalem's leaders have killed people for profit. 28And
the prophets[d] try to cover this up by false visions
and by lying messages. They say, 'This is what the
Lord GOD says' when the LORD has not spoken.
29The people cheat others and steal. They hurt
people who are poor and needy. They cheat foreigners and do not treat them fairly.
30"I looked for someone to build up the walls
and to stand before me where the walls are broken to defend these people so I would not have
to destroy them. But I could not find anyone. 31So
I let them see my anger. I destroyed them with an
anger that was like fire because of all the things
they have done, says the Lord GOD."

Samaria and Jerusalem

23 The LORD spoke his word to me, saying:
2"Human, a woman had two daughters.
3While they were young, they went to Egypt and
became prostitutes.[d] They let men touch and hold
their breasts. 4The older girl was named Oholah,
and her sister was named Oholibah. They became

my wives and had sons and daughters. Oholah is Samaria, and Oholibah is Jerusalem.[n]

5"While still my wife, Samaria had sexual relations with other men. She had great sexual desire for her lovers, men from Assyria. The Assyrians were warriors and 6wore blue uniforms. They were all handsome young captains and lieutenants riding on horseback. 7Samaria became a prostitute for all the important men in Assyria and made herself unclean[d] with all the idols of everyone she desired. 8She continued the prostitution she began in Egypt. When she was young, she had slept with men, and they touched her breasts and had sexual relations with her.

9"So I handed her over to her lovers, the Assyrians, that she wanted so badly. 10They stripped her naked and took away her sons and daughters. Then they killed her with a sword. Women everywhere began talking about how she had been punished.

11"Her sister Jerusalem saw what happened, but she became worse than her sister in her sexual desire and prostitution. 12She also desired the Assyrians, who were all soldiers in beautiful uniforms—handsome young captains and lieutenants riding horses. 13I saw that both girls were alike; both were prostitutes.

14"But Jerusalem went even further. She saw carvings of Babylonian men on a wall. They wore red 15and had belts around their waists and turbans on their heads. They all looked like chariot officers born in Babylonia. 16When she saw them, she wanted to have sexual relations with them and sent messengers to them in Babylonia. 17So these Babylonian men came and had sexual relations with her and made her unclean. After that, she became sick of them. 18But she continued her prostitution so openly that everyone knew about it. And I finally became sick of her, as I had her sister. 19But she remembered how she was a young prostitute in Egypt, so she took part in even more prostitution. 20She wanted men who behaved like animals in their sexual desire. 21In the same way you desired to do the sinful things you had done in Egypt. There men touched and held your young breasts.

God's Judgment on Jerusalem

22"So, Jerusalem, this is what the Lord GOD says: You are tired of your lovers. So now I will make them angry with you and have them attack you from all sides. 23Men from Babylon and all Babylonia and men from Pekod, Shoa, and Koa will attack you. All the Assyrians will attack you: handsome young captains and lieutenants, all of them important men and all riding horses. 24Those men will attack with great armies and with their weapons, chariots, and wagons. They will surround you with large and small shields and with helmets. And I will give them the right to punish you, and they will give you their own kind of punishment. 25Then you will see how strong my anger can be when they punish you in their anger. They will cut off your noses and ears. They will take away your sons and daughters, and those who are left will be burned. 26They will take off your clothes and steal your jewelry. 27I will put a stop to the sinful life you began when you were in Egypt so that you will not desire it or remember Egypt anymore.

28"This is what the Lord GOD says: You became tired of your lovers, but I am going to hand you over to those men you now hate. 29They will treat you with hate and take away everything you worked for, leaving you empty and naked. Everyone will know about the sinful things you did. Your sexual sins 30have brought this on you. You have had sexual relations with the nations and made yourselves unclean[d] by worshiping their idols. 31You did the same things your sister did, so you will get the same punishment, like a bitter cup to drink.

32"This is what the Lord GOD says:

You will drink the same cup your sister did,
  and that cup is deep and wide.
Everyone will make fun of you,
  because the cup is full.
33It will make you miserable and drunk.
  It is the cup of fear and ruin.
  It is the cup of your sister Samaria.
34You will drink everything in it,
  and then you will smash it
  and tear at your breasts.
I have spoken, says the Lord GOD.

35"So this is what the Lord GOD says: You have forgotten me and turned your back on me. So you will be punished for your sexual sins."

Judgment on Samaria and Jerusalem

36The LORD said to me: "Human, will you judge Samaria and Jerusalem, showing them their hateful acts? 37They are guilty of adultery[d] and murder. They have taken part in adultery with their idols. They even offered our children as sacrifices in the fire to be food for these idols. 38They have also done this to me: They made my Temple[d] unclean[d] at the same time they dishonored my Sabbaths.[d] 39They sacrificed their children to their idols. Then they entered my Temple at that very time to dishonor it. That is what they did inside my Temple!

40"They even sent for men from far away, who

Oholah . . . Jerusalem Throughout this chapter Samaria is used in place of Oholah, and Jerusalem is used in place of Oholibah.

came after a messenger was sent to them. The
two sisters bathed themselves for them, painted
their eyes, and put on jewelry. 41They sat on a fine
bed with a table set before it, on which they put
my incense[d] and my oil.
42"There was the noise of a reckless crowd in
the city. Common people gathered, and drunkards were brought from the desert. They put
bracelets on the wrists of the two sisters and beautiful crowns on their heads. 43Then I said about
the one who was worn out by her acts of adultery,
'Let them continue their sexual sins with her. She
is nothing but a prostitute.'[d] 44They kept going to
her as they would go to a prostitute. So they continued to go to Samaria and Jerusalem, these
shameful women. 45But men who do right will
punish them as they punish women who take part
in adultery and who murder people, because they
are guilty of adultery and murder.
46"This is what the Lord GOD says: Bring together a mob against Samaria and Jerusalem, and
hand them over to be frightened and robbed.
47Let the mob kill them by throwing stones at
them, and let them cut them down with their
swords. Let them kill their sons and daughters
and burn their houses down.
48"So I will put an end to sexual sins in the
land. Then all women will be warned, and they
will not do the sexual sins you have done. 49You
will be punished for your sexual sins and the sin
of worshiping idols. Then you will know that I am
the Lord GOD."

The Pot and the Meat

24 The LORD spoke his word to me in the
ninth year of our captivity, in the tenth
month, on the tenth day of the month. He said:
2"Human, write down today's date, this very
date. The king of Babylon has surrounded Jerusalem this very day. 3And tell a story to the people
who refuse to obey me. Say to them: 'This is what
the Lord GOD says:

Put on the pot; put it on
and pour water in it.
4Put in the pieces of meat,
the best pieces—the legs and the shoulders.
Fill it with the best bones.
5 Take the best of the flock,
and pile wood under the pot.
Boil the pieces of meat
until even the bones are cooked.

6" 'This is what the Lord GOD says:
How terrible it will be for the city of
murderers!
How terrible it will be for the rusty pot
whose rust will not come off!
Take the meat out of it, piece by piece.
Don't choose any special piece.
7" 'The blood from her killings is still in the
city.
She poured the blood on the bare rock.
She did not pour it on the ground
where dust would cover it.
8To stir up my anger and revenge,
I put the blood she spilled on the bare rock
so it will not be covered.

9" 'So this is what the Lord GOD says:
How terrible it will be for the city of
murderers!
I myself will pile the wood high for
burning.
10Pile up the wood
and light the fire.
Finish cooking the meat.
Mix in the spices,
and let the bones burn.
11Then set the empty pot on the coals
so it may become hot and its copper sides
glow.
The dirty scum stuck inside it may then melt
and its rust burn away.
12But efforts to clean the pot have failed.
Its heavy rust cannot be removed,
even in the fire.

13" 'By your sinful action you have become unclean.[d] I wanted to cleanse you, but you are still
unclean. You will never be cleansed from your sin
until my anger against you is carried out.
14" 'I, the LORD, have spoken. The time has
come for me to act. I will not hold back punishment or feel pity or change my mind. I will judge
you by your ways and actions, says the Lord
GOD.' "

The Death of Ezekiel's Wife

15Then the LORD spoke his word to me, saying:
16"Human, I am going to take your wife from you,
the woman you look at with love. She will die
suddenly, but you must not be sad or cry loudly
for her or shed any tears. 17Groan silently; do not
cry loudly for the dead. Tie on your turban, and
put your sandals on your feet. Do not cover your
face, and do not eat the food people eat when
they are sad about a death."
18So I spoke to the people in the morning, and
my wife died in the evening. The next morning
I did as I had been commanded.
19Then the people asked me, "Tell us, what do
the things you are doing mean for us?"
20Then I said to them, "The LORD spoke his
word to me. He said, 21'Say to the people of Israel,
This is what the Lord GOD says: I am going to
dishonor my Temple.[d] You think it gives you
strength. You are proud of it, and you look at it
with love and tenderness. But your sons and
daughters that you left behind in Jerusalem will

fall dead by the sword. 22When that happens, you are to act as I have: you are not to cover your face, and you are not to eat the food people eat when they are sad about a death. 23Your turbans must stay on your heads, and your sandals on your feet. You must not cry loudly, but you must rot away in your sins and groan to each other. 24So Ezekiel is to be an example for you. You must do all the same things he did. When all this happens, you will know that I am the Lord GOD.'

> **SIDELIGHT:** If God had allowed Ezekiel to grieve for his wife, there would have been no flowers or nice funeral clothes. Under normal circumstances, the prophet would have gone barefoot, worn sackcloth, and sprinkled ashes on his head. To learn why he did none of them read Ezekiel 24:15–24.

25"And as for you, human, this is how it will be. I will take away the Temple that gives them strength and joy, that makes them proud. They look at it with love, and it makes them happy. And I will take away their sons and daughters also. 26At that time a person who escapes will come to you with information for you to hear. 27At that very time your mouth will be opened. You will speak and be silent no more. So you will be a sign for them, and they will know that I am the LORD."

Prophecy Against Ammon

25 The LORD spoke his word to me, saying: 2"Human, look toward the people of Ammon and prophesy[d] against them. 3Say to them, 'Hear the word of the Lord GOD. This is what the Lord GOD says: You were glad when my Temple[d] was dishonored, when the land of Israel was ruined, and when the people of Judah were taken away as captives. 4So I am going to give you to the people of the East to be theirs. They will set up their camps among you and make their homes among you. They will eat your fruit and drink your milk. 5I will make the city of Rabbah a pasture for camels and the land of Ammon a resting place for sheep. Then you will know that I am the LORD. 6This is what the Lord GOD says: You have clapped your hands and stamped your feet; you have laughed about all the insults you made against the land of Israel. 7So I will use my power against you. I will give you to the nations as if you were treasures taken in war. I will wipe you out of the lands so you will no longer be a nation, and I will destroy you. Then you will know that I am the LORD.'

Prophecy Against Moab and Edom

8"This is what the Lord GOD says: 'Moab and Edom say, "The people of Judah are like all the other nations." 9So I am going to take away the cities that protect Moab's borders, the best cities in that land: Beth Jeshimoth, Baal Meon, and Kiriathaim. 10Then I will give Moab, along with the Ammonites, to the people of the East as their possession. Then, along with the Ammonites, Moab will not be a nation anymore. 11So I will punish the people of Moab, and they will know that I am the LORD.'

Prophecy Against Edom

12"This is what the Lord GOD says: 'Edom took revenge on the people of Judah, and the Edomites became guilty because of it. 13So this is what the Lord GOD says: I will use my power against Edom, killing every human and animal in it. And I will destroy Edom all the way from Teman to Dedan as they die in battle. 14I will use my people Israel to take revenge on Edom. So the Israelites will do to Edom what my hot anger demands. Then the Edomites will know what my revenge feels like, says the Lord GOD.'

Prophecy Against Philistia

15"This is what the Lord GOD says: 'The Philistines have taken revenge with hateful hearts. Because of their strong hatred, they have tried to destroy Judah. 16So this is what the Lord GOD says: I will use my power against the Philistines. I will kill the Kerethites, and I will destroy those people still alive on the coast of the Mediterranean Sea. 17I will punish them in my anger and do great acts of revenge to them. They will know that I am the LORD when I take revenge on them.'"

Prophecy Against Tyre

26 It was the eleventh year of our captivity, on the first day of the month. The LORD spoke his word to me, saying: 2"Human, the city of Tyre has spoken against Jerusalem: 'The city that traded with the nations is destroyed. Now we can be the trading center. Since the city of Jerusalem is ruined, we can make money.' 3So this is what the Lord GOD says: I am against you, Tyre. I will bring many nations against you, like the sea beating its waves on your island shores. 4They will destroy the walls of Tyre and pull down her towers. I will also scrape away her ruins and make her a bare rock. 5Tyre will be an island where fishermen dry their nets. I have spoken, says the Lord GOD. The nations will steal treasures from Tyre. 6Also, her villages on the shore across from the island will be destroyed by war. Then they will know that I am the LORD.

Nebuchadnezzar to Attack Tyre

7"This is what the Lord GOD says: I will bring a king from the north against Tyre. He is Nebuchadnezzar king of Babylon, the greatest king, with his horses, chariots, horsemen, and a great army.
8He will fight a battle and destroy your villages on the shore across from the island. He will set up devices to attack you. He will build a road of earth to the top of the walls. He will raise his shields against you.
9He will bring logs to pound through your city walls, and he will break down your towers with his iron bars.
10His horses will be so many that they will cover you with their dust. Your walls will shake at the noise of horsemen, wagons, and chariots. The king of Babylon will enter your city gates as men enter a city where the walls are broken through.
11The hoofs of his horses will run over your streets. He will kill your army with the sword, and your strong pillars will fall down to the ground.
12Also, his men will take away your riches and will steal the things you sell. They will break down your walls and destroy your nice houses. They will throw your stones, wood, and trash into the sea.
13So I will stop your songs; the music of your harps will not be heard anymore.
14I will make you a bare rock, and you will be a place for drying fishing nets. You will not be built again, because I, the LORD, have spoken, says the Lord GOD.

15"This is what the Lord GOD says to Tyre: The people who live along the seacoast will shake with fear when they hear about your defeat. Those of you who are injured and dying will groan.
16Then all the leaders of the seacoast will get down from their thrones, take off their beautiful needlework clothes, and show how afraid they are. They will sit on the ground and tremble all the time. When they see you, they will be shocked.
17They will begin singing a funeral song about you and will say to you:

'Tyre, you famous city, you have been
destroyed!
You have lost your sea power!
You and your people
had great power on the seas.
You made everyone around you
afraid of you.
18Now the people who live by the coast
tremble,
now that you have fallen.
The islands of the sea
are afraid because you have been defeated.'

19"This is what the Lord GOD says: I will make you an empty city, like cities that have no people living in them. I will bring the deep ocean waters over you, and the Mediterranean Sea will cover you.
20At that time I will send you down to the place of the dead to join those who died long ago. I will make you live with the dead below the earth in places that are like old ruins. You will not come back from there or have any place in the world of the living again.
21Other people will be afraid of what happened to you, and it will be the end of you. People will look for you, but they will never find you again, says the Lord GOD."

SIDELIGHT: The island city of Tyre (Ezekiel 27) was perhaps the major shipping city in the Middle East in Old Testament times. After the Babylonians destroyed Jerusalem, they besieged Tyre for thirteen years, but didn't conquer it. Instead, the city and the empire reached a peaceful settlement.

A Funeral Song for Tyre

27 The LORD spoke his word to me, saying:
2"Human, sing a funeral song for the city of Tyre.
3Speak to Tyre, which has ports for the Mediterranean Sea and is a place for trade for the people of many lands along the seacoast. 'This is what the Lord GOD says:

Tyre, you have said,
"I am like a beautiful ship."
4You were at home on the high seas.
Your builders made your beauty perfect.
5They made all your boards
of fir trees from Mount Hermon.
They took a cedar tree from Lebanon
to make a ship's mast for you.
6They made your oars
from oak trees from Bashan.
They made your deck
from cypress trees from the coast of Cyprus
and set ivory into it.
7Your sail of linen with designs sewed on it
came from Egypt
and became like a flag for you.
Your cloth shades over the deck were blue
and purple
and came from the island of Cyprus.
8Men from Sidon and Arvad used oars to row
you.
Tyre, your skilled men were the sailors on
your deck.
9Workers of Byblos were with you,
putting caulk[n] in your ship's seams.
All the ships of the sea and their sailors
came alongside to trade with you.

10" 'Men of Persia, Lydia, and Put

caulk Something like tar put between the boards of a ship to make it waterproof.

were warriors in your navy
and hung their shields and helmets on your sides.
They made you look beautiful.
11Men of Arvad and Cilicia
guarded your city walls all around.
Men of Gammad
were in your watchtowers
and hung their shields around your walls.
They made your beauty perfect.

12" 'People of Tarshish became traders for you because of your great wealth. They traded your goods for silver, iron, tin, and lead.

13" 'People of Greece, Tubal, and Meshech became merchants for you. They traded your goods for slaves and items of bronze.

14" 'People of Beth Togarmah traded your goods for work horses, war horses, and mules.

15" 'People of Rhodes became merchants for you, selling your goods on many coastlands. They brought back ivory tusks and valuable black wood as your payment.

16" 'People of Aram became traders for you, because you had so many good things to sell. They traded your goods for turquoise, purple cloth, cloth with designs sewed on, fine linen, coral, and rubies.

17" 'People of Judah and Israel became merchants for you. They traded your goods for wheat from Minnith, and for honey, olive oil, and balm.[d]

18-19" 'People of Damascus became traders for you because you have many good things and great wealth. They traded your goods for wine from Helbon, wool from Zahar, and barrels of wine from Izal. They received wrought iron, cassia,[d] and sugar cane in payment for your good things.

20" 'People of Dedan became merchants for you, trading saddle blankets for riding.

21" 'People of Arabia and all the rulers of Kedar became traders for you. They received lambs, male sheep, and goats in payment for you.

22" 'The merchants of Sheba and Raamah became merchants for you. They traded your goods for all the best spices, valuable gems, and gold.

23" 'People of Haran, Canneh, Eden, and the traders of Sheba, Asshur, and Kilmad became merchants for you.
24They were paid with the best clothes, blue cloth, cloth with designs sewed on, carpets of many colors, and tightly wound ropes.

25" 'Trading ships
carried the things you sold.
You were like a ship full of heavy cargo
in the middle of the sea.
26The men who rowed you
brought you out into the high seas,
but the east wind broke you to pieces
in the middle of the sea.
27Your wealth, your trade, your goods,
your seamen, your sailors, your workers,
your traders, your warriors,
and everyone else on board
sank into the sea
on the day your ship was wrecked.
28The people on the shore shake with fear
when your sailors cry out.
29All the men who row
leave their ships;
the seamen and the sailors of other ships
stand on the shore.
30They cry loudly about you;
they cry very much.
They throw dust on their heads
and roll in ashes to show they are sad.
31They shave their heads for you,
and they put on rough cloth to show they are upset.
They cry and sob for you;
they cry loudly.
32And in their loud crying
they sing a funeral song for you:
"No one was ever destroyed like Tyre,
surrounded by the sea."
33When the goods you traded went out over the seas,
you met the needs of many nations.
With your great wealth and goods,
you made kings of the earth rich.
34But now you are broken by the sea
and have sunk to the bottom.
Your goods and all the people on board
have gone down with you.
35All those who live along the shore
are shocked by what happened to you.
Their kings are terribly afraid,
and their faces show their fear.
36The traders among the nations hiss at you.
You have come to a terrible end,
and you are gone forever.' "

Prophecy Against the King of Tyre

28 The LORD spoke his word to me, saying:
2"Human, say to the ruler of Tyre: 'This is what the Lord GOD says:
Because you are proud,
you say, "I am a god.
I sit on the throne of a god
in the middle of the seas."
You think you are as wise as a god,
but you are a human, not a god.
3You think you are wiser than Daniel.
You think you can find out all secrets.
4Through your wisdom and understanding
you have made yourself rich.
You have gained gold and silver
and have saved it in your storerooms.

[5]Through your great skill in trading,
you have made your riches grow.
You are too proud
because of your riches.

[6]" 'So this is what the Lord GOD says:
You think you are wise
like a god,
[7]but I will bring foreign people against you,
the cruelest nation.
They will pull out their swords
and destroy all that your wisdom has built,
and they will dishonor your greatness.
[8]They will kill you;
you will die a terrible death
like those who are killed at sea.
[9]While they are killing you,
you will not be able to say anymore, "I am
a god."
You will be only a human, not a god,
when your murderers kill you.
[10]You will die like an unclean[d] person;
foreigners will kill you.

I have spoken, says the Lord GOD.' "

[11]The LORD spoke his word to me, saying:
[12]"Human, sing a funeral song for the king of
Tyre. Say to him: 'This is what the Lord GOD
says:
You were an example of what was perfect,
full of wisdom and perfect in beauty.
[13]You had a wonderful life,
as if you were in Eden, the garden of God.
Every valuable gem was on you:
ruby, topaz, and emerald,
yellow quartz, onyx, and jasper,
sapphire, turquoise, and chrysolite.
Your jewelry was made of gold.
It was prepared on the day you were
created.
[14]I appointed a living creature to guard you.
I put you on the holy mountain of God.
You walked among the gems that shined
like fire.
[15]Your life was right and good
from the day you were created,
until evil was found in you.
[16]Because you traded with countries far away,
you learned to be cruel, and you sinned.
So I threw you down in disgrace from the
mountain of God.
And the living creature who guarded you
forced you out from among the gems that
shined like fire.
[17]You became too proud
because of your beauty.
You ruined your wisdom
because of your greatness.
I threw you down to the ground.
Your example taught a lesson to other
kings.
[18]You dishonored your places of worship
through your many sins and dishonest
trade.
So I set on fire the place where you lived,
and the fire burned you up.
I turned you into ashes on the ground
for all those watching to see.
[19]All the nations who knew you
are shocked about you.
Your punishment was so terrible,
and you are gone forever.' "

Prophecy Against Sidon

[20]The LORD spoke his word to me, saying:
[21]"Human, look toward the city of Sidon and
prophesy[d] against her. [22]Say: 'This is what the
Lord GOD says:
I am against you, Sidon,
and I will show my glory among you.
People will know that I am the LORD
when I have punished Sidon;
I will show my holiness by defeating her.
[23]I will send diseases to Sidon,
and blood will flow in her streets.
Those who are wounded in Sidon will fall
dead,
attacked from all sides.
Then they will know that I am the LORD.

God Will Help Israel

[24]" 'No more will neighboring nations be like
thorny branches or sharp stickers to hurt Israel.
Then they will know that I am the Lord GOD.
[25]" 'This is what the Lord GOD says: I will
gather the people of Israel from the nations where
they are scattered. I will show my holiness when
the nations see what I do for my people. Then
they will live in their own land—the land I gave
to my servant Jacob. [26]They will live safely in the
land and will build houses and plant vineyards.
They will live in safety after I have punished all
the nations around who hate them. Then they
will know that I am the LORD their God.' "

Prophecy Against Egypt

29 It was the tenth year of our captivity, in
the tenth month, on the twelfth day of
the month. The LORD spoke his word to me, saying: [2]"Human, look toward the king of Egypt, and
prophesy[d] against him and all Egypt. [3]Say: 'This
is what the Lord GOD says:
I am against you, king of Egypt.
You are like a great crocodile that lies in
the Nile River.
You say, "The Nile is mine;
I made it for myself."
[4]But I will put hooks in your jaws,

and I will make the fish of the Nile stick to
your sides.
I will pull you up out of your rivers,
with all the fish sticking to your sides.
5I will leave you in the desert,
you and all the fish from your rivers.
You will fall onto the ground;
you will not be picked up or buried.
I have given you to the wild animals
and to the birds of the sky for food.
6Then all the people who live in Egypt will know
that I am the LORD.

" 'Israel tried to lean on you for help, but you
were like a crutch made out of a weak stalk of
grass. 7When their hands grabbed you, you splint-
ered and tore open their shoulders. When they
leaned on you, you broke and made all their backs
twist.

8" 'So this is what the Lord GOD says: I will
cause an enemy to attack you and kill your people
and animals. 9Egypt will become an empty desert.
Then they will know that I am the LORD.

" 'Because you said, "The Nile River is mine,
and I have made it," 10I am against you and your
rivers. I will destroy the land of Egypt and make
it an empty desert from Migdol in the north to
Aswan in the south, all the way to the border of
Cush. 11No person or animal will walk through it,
and no one will live in Egypt for forty years. 12I
will make the land of Egypt the most deserted
country of all. Her cities will be the most deserted of all ruined cities for forty years. I will scatter the Egyptians among the nations, spreading
them among the countries.

13" 'This is what the Lord GOD says: After forty
years I will gather Egypt from the nations where
they have been scattered. 14I will bring back the
Egyptian captives and make them return to southern Egypt, to the land they came from. They will
become a weak kingdom there. 15It will be the
weakest kingdom, and it will never again rule
other nations. I will make it so weak it will never
again rule over the nations. 16The Israelites will
never again depend on Egypt. Instead, Egypt's
punishment will remind the Israelites of their sin
in turning to Egypt for help. Then they will know
that I am the Lord GOD.' "

Egypt Is Given to Babylon

17It was the twenty-seventh year of our captivity, in the first month, on the first day of the
month. The LORD spoke his word to me, saying:
18"Human, Nebuchadnezzar king of Babylon
made his army fight hard against Tyre. Every soldier's head was rubbed bare, and every shoulder
was rubbed raw. But Nebuchadnezzar and his
army gained nothing from fighting Tyre. 19So this
is what the Lord GOD says: I will give the land of
Egypt to Nebuchadnezzar king of Babylon. He
will take away Egypt's people and its wealth and
its treasures as pay for his army. 20I am giving
Nebuchadnezzar the land of Egypt as a reward for
working hard for me, says the Lord GOD.

21"At that time I will make Israel grow strong
again, and I will let you, Ezekiel, speak to them.
Then they will know that I am the LORD."

Egypt Will Be Punished

30 The LORD spoke his word to me, saying:
2"Human, prophesy[d] and say, 'This is
what the Lord GOD says:
Cry and say,
"The terrible day is coming."
3The day is near;
the LORD's day of judging is near.
It is a cloudy day
and a time when the nations will be
judged.
4An enemy will attack Egypt,
and Cush will tremble with fear.
When the killing begins in Egypt,
her wealth will be taken away,
and her foundations will be torn down.

5Cush, Put, Lydia, Arabia, Libya, and some of my
people who had made an agreement with Egypt
will fall dead in war.

6" 'This is what the LORD says:
Those who fight on Egypt's side will fall.
The power she is proud of will be lost.
The people in Egypt will fall dead in war
from Migdol in the north to Aswan in the
south,
says the Lord GOD.
7They will be the most deserted lands.
Egypt's cities will be the worst of cities that
lie in ruins.
8Then they will know that I am the LORD
when I set fire to Egypt
and when all those nations on her side are
crushed.

9" 'At that time I will send messengers in ships
to frighten Cush, which now feels safe. The people of Cush will tremble with fear when Egypt is
punished. And that time is sure to come.

10" 'This is what the Lord GOD says:
I will destroy great numbers of people in
Egypt
through the power of Nebuchadnezzar king
of Babylon.
11Nebuchadnezzar and his army,
the cruelest army of any nation,
will be brought in to destroy the land.
They will pull out their swords against Egypt
and will fill the land with those they kill.
12I will make the streams of the Nile River
become dry land,
and then I will sell the land to evil people.

I will destroy the land and everything in it
through the power of foreigners.

I, the LORD, have spoken.

Egypt's Idols Are Destroyed

13" 'This is what the Lord GOD says:
I will destroy the idols
and take away the statues of gods from the city of Memphis.
There will no longer be a leader in Egypt,
and I will spread fear through the land of Egypt.
14I will make southern Egypt empty
and start a fire in Zoan
and punish Thebes.
15And I will pour out my anger against Pelusium,
the strong place of Egypt.
I will destroy great numbers of people in Thebes.
16I will set fire to Egypt.
Pelusium will be in great pain.
The walls of Thebes will be broken open,
and Memphis will have troubles every day.
17The young men of Heliopolis and Bubastis
will fall dead in war,
and the people will be taken away as captives.
18In Tahpanhes the day will be dark
when I break Egypt's power.
Then she will no longer be proud of her power.
A cloud will cover Egypt,
and her villages will be captured and taken away.
19So I will punish Egypt,
and they will know I am the LORD.' "

Egypt Becomes Weak

20It was in the eleventh year of our captivity, in
the first month, on the seventh day of the month.
The LORD spoke his word to me, saying: 21"Human, I have broken the powerful arm of the king
of Egypt. It has not been tied up, so it will not get
well. It has not been wrapped with a bandage, so
it will not be strong enough to hold a sword in
war. 22So this is what the Lord GOD says: I am
against the king of Egypt. I will break his arms,
both the strong arm and the broken arm, and I
will make the sword fall from his hand. 23I will
scatter the Egyptians among the nations, spreading them among the countries. 24I will make the
arms of the king of Babylon strong and put my
sword in his hand. But I will break the arms of the
king of Egypt. Then when he faces the king of
Babylon, he will cry out in pain like a dying person. 25So I will make the arms of the king of Babylon strong, but the arms of the king of Egypt will
fall. Then people will know that I am the LORD
when I put my sword into the hand of the king
of Babylon and he uses it in war against Egypt.
26Then I will scatter the Egyptians among the nations, spreading them among the countries. Then
they will know that I am the LORD."

A Cedar Tree

31 It was in the eleventh year of our captivity, in the third month, on the first day
of the month. The LORD spoke his word to me,
saying: 2"Human, say to the king of Egypt and his
people:

'No one is like you in your greatness.
3Assyria was once like a cedar tree in Lebanon
with beautiful branches that shaded the forest.
It was very tall;
its top was among the clouds.
4Much water made the tree grow;
the deep springs made it tall.
Rivers flowed
around the bottom of the tree
and sent their streams
to all other trees in the countryside.
5So the tree was taller
than all the other trees in the countryside.
Its limbs became long and big
because of so much water.
6All the birds of the sky
made their nests in the tree's limbs.
And all the wild animals
gave birth under its branches.
All great nations
lived in the tree's shade.
7So the tree was great and beautiful,
with its long branches,
because its roots reached down to much water.
8The cedar trees in the garden of God
were not as great as it was.
The pine trees
did not have such great limbs.
The plane trees
did not have such branches.
No tree in the garden of God
was as beautiful as this tree.
9I made it beautiful
with many branches,
and all the trees of Eden in the garden of God
wanted to be like it.

10" 'So this is what the Lord GOD says: The tree
grew tall. Its top reached the clouds, and it became proud of its height. 11So I handed it over to
a mighty ruler of the nations for him to punish it.
Because it was evil, I got rid of it. 12The cruelest
foreign nation cut it down and left it. The tree's

branches fell on the mountains and in all the valleys, and its broken limbs were in all the ravines
of the land. All the nations of the earth left the
shade of that tree. 13The birds of the sky live on
the fallen tree. The wild animals live among the
tree's fallen branches. 14So the trees that grow by
the water will not be proud to be tall; they will
not put their tops among the clouds. None of the
trees that are watered well will grow that tall,
because they all are meant to die and go under the
ground. They will be with people who have died
and have gone down to the place of the dead.

15" 'This is what the Lord GOD says: On the day
when the tree went down to the place of the
dead, I made the deep springs cry loudly. I covered them and held back their rivers, and the
great waters stopped flowing. I dressed Lebanon
in black to show her sadness about the great tree,
and all the trees in the countryside were sad about
it. 16I made the nations shake with fear at the
sound of the tree falling when I brought it down
to the place of the dead. It went to join those who
have gone down to the grave. Then all the trees
of Eden and the best trees of Lebanon, all the
well-watered trees, were comforted in the place
of the dead below the earth. 17These trees had
also gone down with the great tree to the place
of the dead. They joined those who were killed in
war and those among the nations who had lived
under the great tree's shade.

18" 'So no tree in Eden is equal to you, Egypt,
in greatness and honor, but you will go down to
join the trees of Eden in the place below the earth.
You will lie among unclean[d] people, with those
who were killed in war.

" 'This is about the king of Egypt and all his
people, says the Lord GOD.' "

A Funeral Song

32 It was in the twelfth year of our captivity, in the twelfth month, on the first day
of the month. The LORD spoke his word to me,
saying: 2"Human, sing a funeral song about the
king of Egypt. Say to him:

'You are like a young lion among the nations.
You are like a crocodile in the seas.
You splash around in your streams
and stir up the water with your feet,
making the rivers muddy.

3" 'This is what the Lord GOD says:
I will spread my net over you,
and I will use a large group of people
to pull you up in my net.
4Then I will throw you on the land
dropping you onto the ground.
I will let the birds of the sky rest on you
and all the animals of the earth eat you
until they are full.
5I will scatter your flesh on the mountains
and fill the valleys with what is left of you.
6I will drench the land with your flowing
blood
as far as the mountains,
and the ravines will be full of your flesh.
7When I make you disappear,
I will cover the sky and make the stars
dark.
I will cover the sun with a cloud,
and the moon will not shine.
8I will make all the shining lights in the sky
become dark over you;
I will bring darkness over your land,
says the Lord GOD.
9I will cause many people to be afraid
when I bring you as a captive into other
nations,
to lands you have not known.
10I will cause many people to be shocked about
you.
Their kings will tremble with fear because
of you
when I swing my sword in front of them.
They will shake every moment
on the day you fall;
each king will be afraid for his own life.

11" 'So this is what the Lord GOD says:
The sword of the king of Babylon
will attack you.
12I will cause your people to fall
by the swords of mighty soldiers,
the most terrible in the world.
They will destroy the pride of Egypt
and all its people.
13I will also destroy all Egypt's cattle
which live alongside much water.
The foot of a human will not stir the water,
and the hoofs of cattle will not muddy it
anymore.
14So I will let the Egyptians' water become
clear.
I will cause their rivers to run as smoothly
as olive oil,
says the Lord GOD.
15When I make the land of Egypt empty
and take everything that is in the land,
when I destroy all those who live in Egypt,
then they will know that I am the LORD.'

16"This is the funeral song people will sing for
Egypt. The women of the nations will sing it; they
will sing a funeral song for Egypt and all its people, says the Lord GOD."

Egypt to Be Destroyed

17It was in the twelfth year of our captivity, on
the fifteenth day of the month. The LORD spoke
his word to me, saying: 18"Human, cry for the

people of Egypt. Bring down Egypt, together with
the women of the powerful nations; bring them
down to the place of the dead below the earth to
join those who go to the place of the dead. 19Say
to them: 'Are you more beautiful than others? Go
lie down in death with those who are unclean.'[d]
20The Egyptians will fall among those killed in
war. The sword is ready; the enemy will drag
Egypt and all her people away. 21From the place
of the dead the leaders of the mighty ones will
speak about the king of Egypt and the nations
which help him: 'The unclean, those killed in
war, have come down here and lie dead.'

22"Assyria and all its army lie dead there. The
graves of their soldiers are all around. All were
killed in war, 23and their graves were put in the
deepest parts of the place of the dead. Assyria's
army lies around its grave. When they lived on
earth, they frightened people, but now all of them
have been killed in war.

24"The nation of Elam is there with all its army
around its grave. All of them were killed in war.
They had frightened people on earth and were
unclean, so they went down to the lowest parts
of the place of the dead. They must carry their
shame with those who have gone down to the
place of the dead. 25A bed has been made for Elam
with all those killed in war. The graves of her soldiers are all around her. All Elam's people are unclean, killed in war. They frightened people when
they lived on earth, but now they must carry their
shame with those who have gone down to the
place of the dead. Their graves are with the rest
who were killed.

26"Meshech and Tubal are there with the
graves of all their soldiers around them. All of
them are unclean and have been killed in war.
They also frightened people when they lived on
earth. 27But they are not buried with the other
soldiers who were killed in battle long ago, those
who went with their weapons of war to the place
of the dead. These soldiers had their swords laid
under their heads and their shields on their bodies. These mighty soldiers used to frighten people
when they lived on earth.

28"You, king of Egypt, will be broken and lie
among those who are unclean, who were killed
in war.

29"Edom is there also, with its kings and all its
leaders. They were mighty, but now they lie in
death with those killed in war, with those who
are unclean, with those who have gone down to
the place of the dead.

30"All the rulers of the north and all the Sidonians are there. Their strength frightened people,
but they have gone down in shame with those
who were killed. They are unclean, lying with
those killed in war. They carry their shame with
those who have gone down to the place of the
dead.

31"The king of Egypt and his army will see
these who have been killed in war. Then he will
be comforted for all his soldiers killed in war, says
the Lord GOD. 32I made people afraid of the king
of Egypt while he lived on earth. But he and all
his people will lie among those who are unclean,
who were killed in war, says the Lord GOD."

Ezekiel Is Watchman for Israel

33 The LORD spoke his word to me, saying:
2"Human, speak to your people and say
to them: 'Suppose I bring a war against a land.
The people of the land may choose one of their
men and make him their watchman. 3When he
sees the enemy coming to attack the land, he will
blow the trumpet and warn the people. 4If they
hear the sound of the trumpet but do nothing, the
enemy will come and kill them. They will be responsible for their own deaths. 5They heard the
sound of the trumpet but didn't do anything. So
they are to blame for their own deaths. If they had
done something, they would have saved their
own lives. 6But if the watchman sees the enemy
coming to attack and does not blow the trumpet,
the people will not be warned. Then if the enemy
comes and kills any of them, they have died because of their own sin. But I will punish the
watchman for their deaths.'

7"You, human, are the one I have made a
watchman for Israel. If you hear a word from my
mouth, you must warn them for me. 8Suppose I
say to the wicked: 'Wicked people, you will
surely die,' but you don't speak to warn the
wicked to stop doing evil. Then they will die because they were sinners, but I will punish you for
their deaths. 9But if you warn the wicked to stop
doing evil and they do not stop, they will die because they were sinners. But you have saved your
life.

10"So you, human, say to Israel: 'You have said:
Surely our law-breaking and sins are hurting us.
They will kill us. What can we do so we will live?'
11Say to them: 'The Lord GOD says: As surely as
I live, I do not want any who are wicked to die.
I want them to stop doing evil and live. Stop! Stop
your wicked ways! You don't want to die, do you,
people of Israel?'

12"Human, say to your people: 'The goodness
of those who do right will not save them when
they sin. The evil of wicked people will not cause
them to be punished if they stop doing it. If good
people sin, they will not be able to live by the
good they did earlier.' 13If I tell good people, "You
will surely live," they might think they have done
enough good and then do evil. Then none of the
good things they did will be remembered. They
will die because of the evil they have done. 14Or,

if I say to the wicked people, "You will surely die," they may stop sinning and do what is right and honest. 15For example, they may return what somebody gave them as a promise to repay a loan, or pay back what they stole. If they live by the rules that give life and do not sin, then they will surely live, and they will not die. 16They will not be punished for any of their sins. They now do what is right and fair, so they will surely live.

17"Your people say: 'The way of the Lord is not fair.' But it is their own ways that are not fair. 18When the good people stop doing good and do evil, they will die for their evil. 19But when the wicked stop doing evil and do what is right and fair, they will live. 20You still say: 'The way of the Lord is not fair.' Israel, I will judge all of you by your own ways."

The Fall of Jerusalem Explained

21It was in the twelfth year of our captivity, on the fifth day of the tenth month. A person who had escaped from Jerusalem came to me and said, "Jerusalem has been captured." 22Now I had felt the power of the LORD on me the evening before. He had made me able to talk again before this person came to me. I could speak; I was not without speech anymore.

23Then the LORD spoke his word to me, saying: 24"Human, people who live in the ruins in the land of Israel are saying: 'Abraham was only one person, yet he was given the land as his own. Surely the land has been given to us, who are many, as our very own.' 25So say to them: 'This is what the Lord GOD says: You eat meat with the blood still in it, you ask your idols for help, and you murder people. Should you then have the land as your very own? 26You depend on your sword and do terrible things which I hate. Each of you has sexual relations with his neighbor's wife. So should you have the land?'

27"Say to them: 'This is what the Lord GOD says: As surely as I live, those who are among the city ruins in Israel will be killed in war. I will cause those who live in the country to be eaten by wild animals. People hiding in the strongholds[d] and caves will die of disease. 28I will make the land an empty desert. The people's pride in the land's power will end. The mountains of Israel will become empty so that no one will pass through them. 29They will know that I am the LORD when I make the land an empty desert because of the things they have done that I hate.'

30"But as for you, human, your people are talking about you by the walls and in the doorways of houses. They say to each other: 'Come now, and hear the message from the LORD.' 31So they come to you in crowds as if they were really ready to listen. They sit in front of you as if they were my people and hear your words, but they will not obey them. With their mouths they tell me they love me, but their hearts desire their selfish profits. 32To your people you are nothing more than a singer who sings love songs and has a beautiful voice and plays a musical instrument well. They hear your words, but they will not obey them.

SIDELIGHT: If Ezekiel were a preacher today, he would probably have a big following. Ezekiel 33:32 tells how people were so attracted to his style and his beautiful voice that they didn't hear his challenging message.

33"When this comes true, and it surely will happen, then the people will know that a prophet[d] has been among them."

The Leaders Are like Shepherds

34 The LORD spoke his word to me, saying: 2"Human, prophesy[d] against the leaders of Israel, who are like shepherds. Prophesy and say to them: 'This is what the Lord GOD says: How terrible it will be for the shepherds of Israel who feed only themselves! Why don't the shepherds feed the flock? 3You eat the milk curds, and you clothe yourselves with the wool. You kill the fat sheep, but you do not feed the flock. 4You have not made the weak strong. You have not healed the sick or put bandages on those that were hurt. You have not brought back those who strayed away or searched for the lost. But you have ruled the sheep with cruel force. 5The sheep were scattered, because there was no shepherd, and they became food for every wild animal. 6My flock wandered over all the mountains and on every high hill. They were scattered all over the face of the earth, and no one searched or looked for them.

7" 'So, you shepherds, hear the word of the LORD. This is what the Lord GOD says: 8As surely as I live, my flock has been caught and eaten by all the wild animals, because the flock has no shepherd. The shepherds did not search for my flock. No, they fed themselves instead of my flock. 9So, you shepherds, hear the word of the LORD. 10This is what the Lord GOD says: I am against the shepherds. I will blame them for what has happened to my sheep and will not let them tend the flock anymore. Then the shepherds will stop feeding themselves, and I will take my flock from their mouths so they will no longer be their food.

11" 'This is what the Lord GOD says: I, myself,

will search for my sheep and take care of them.
12As a shepherd takes care of his scattered flock
when it is found, I will take care of my sheep. I
will save them from all the places where they
were scattered on a cloudy and dark day. 13I will
bring them out from the nations and gather them
from the countries. I will bring them to their own
land and pasture them on the mountains of Israel,
in the ravines, and in all the places where people
live in the land. 14I will feed them in a good pasture, and they will eat grass on the high mountains of Israel. They will lie down on good ground
where they eat grass, and they will eat in rich
grassland on the mountains of Israel. 15I will feed
my flock and lead them to rest, says the Lord
GOD. 16I will search for the lost, bring back those
that strayed away, put bandages on those that
were hurt, and make the weak strong. But I will
destroy those sheep that are fat and strong. I
will tend the sheep with fairness.

17" 'This is what the Lord GOD says: As for you,
my flock, I will judge between one sheep and another, between the male sheep and the male
goats. 18Is it not enough for you to eat grass in the
good land? Must you crush the rest of the grass
with your feet? Is it not enough for you to drink
clear water? Must you make the rest of the water
muddy with your feet? 19Must my flock eat what
you crush, and must they drink what you make
muddy with your feet?

20" 'So this is what the Lord GOD says to them:
I, myself, will judge between the fat sheep and the
thin sheep. 21You push with your side and with
your shoulder, and you knock down all the weak
sheep with your horns until you have forced them
away. 22So I will save my flock; they will not
be hurt anymore. I will judge between one sheep
and another. 23Then I will put over them one
shepherd, my servant David. He will feed them
and tend them and be their shepherd. 24Then I,

SELFISHNESS

Abused Privileges

Jenny Carlsen felt honored to be selected for the Vocal Ensemble, a special choir at her school. The group was invited to compete at the state music conference, held at a hotel. After the performance, the judges raved and gave the group top honors. Jenny felt proud to be a member of the group.

The choir director gave the singers some free time before returning home. Many of them felt pretty rowdy. How could they have fun?

First, they tried monopolizing the elevators and escalators. Jenny joined in.

They began shouting and screaming, disrupting others who had come for the conference. Jenny did too.

Some invaded the hotel pharmacy, where one member was kicked out after fooling around with a pair of crutches. Others dumped ash trays on the floor.

Finally, the hotel manager demanded to see the director. When the director learned what was going on, she discontinued the Vocal Ensemble on the spot. "I gave you free time as a reward for performing well," she said angrily, "but you selfishly violated my trust and other people's rights."

Now Jenny is not so proud to have been a part of the Ensemble. "It's a memory that you wish wasn't a memory," she says.

Like the members of the Vocal Ensemble, God's people receive special honors and privileges. When God promised special gifts for his people in **Ezekiel 34:11–24**, he also warned them not to selfishly abuse them.

- What do this passage and Jenny's story have to say about selfishness?
- What gifts has God given you that you must be careful not to selfishly abuse?

CONSIDER . . .

- drawing four circles on a sheet of paper, one each for family, time, money, and friends. In each circle, list one way you can be less selfish this coming week, and then do all four ideas.
- asking forgiveness from someone whose trust you've broken or with whom you've acted selfishly.

FOR MORE, SEE . . .

- Exodus 16:11–21 (p. 74)
- Mark 12:1–12 (p. 987)
- 1 Corinthians 11:20–22 (p. 1181)

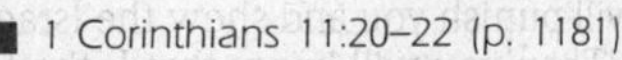

the LORD, will be their God, and my servant David will be a ruler among them. I, the LORD, have spoken.

25“ ‘I will make an agreement of peace with my sheep and will remove harmful animals from the land. Then the sheep will live safely in the desert and sleep in the woods. 26I will bless them and let them live around my hill. I will cause the rains to come when it is time; there will be showers to bless them. 27Also the trees in the countryside will give their fruit, and the land will give its harvest. And the sheep will be safe on their land. Then they will know that I am the LORD when I break the bars of their captivity and save them from the power of those who made them slaves. 28They will not be led captive by the nations again. The wild animals will not eat them, but they will live safely, and no one will make them afraid. 29I will give them a place famous for its good crops, so they will no longer suffer from hunger in the land. They will not suffer the insults of other nations anymore. 30Then they will know that I, the LORD their God, am with them. The nation of Israel will know that they are my people, says the Lord GOD. 31You, my human sheep, are the sheep I care for, and I am your God, says the Lord GOD.’ ”

Prophecy Against Edom

35 The LORD spoke his word to me, saying: 2“Human, look toward Edom and prophesy[d] against it. 3Say to it: ‘This is what the Lord GOD says: I am against you, Edom. I will stretch out my hand against you and make you an empty desert. 4I will destroy your cities, and you will become empty. Then you will know that I am the LORD.

5“ ‘You have always been an enemy of Israel. You let them be defeated in war when they were in trouble at the time of their final punishment. 6So the Lord GOD says, as surely as I live, I will let you be murdered. Murder will chase you. Since you did not hate murdering people, murder will chase you. 7I will make Edom an empty ruin and destroy everyone who goes in or comes out of it. 8I will fill its mountains with those who are killed. Those killed in war will fall on your hills, in your valleys, and in all your ravines. 9I will make you a ruin forever; no one will live in your cities. Then you will know that I am the LORD.

10“ ‘You said, “These two nations, Israel and Judah, and these two lands will be ours. We will take them for our own.” But the LORD was there. 11So this is what the Lord GOD says: As surely as I live, I will treat you just as you treated them. You were angry and jealous because you hated them. So I will punish you and show the Israelites who I am. 12Then you will know that I, the LORD, have heard all your insults against the mountains of Israel. You said, “They have been ruined. They have been given to us to eat.” 13You have not stopped your proud talk against me. I have heard you. 14This is what the Lord GOD says: All the earth will be happy when I make you an empty ruin. 15You were happy when the land of Israel was ruined, but I will do the same thing to you. Mount Seir and all Edom, you will become an empty ruin. Then you will know that I am the LORD.’ ”

Israel to Come Home

36 “Human, prophesy[d] to the mountains of Israel and say: ‘Mountains of Israel, hear the word of the LORD. 2This is what the Lord GOD says: The enemy has said about you, “Now the old places to worship gods have become ours.” ’ 3So prophesy and say: ‘This is what the Lord GOD says: They have made you an empty ruin and have crushed you from all around. So you became a possession of the other nations. People have talked and whispered against you. 4So, mountains of Israel, hear the word of the Lord GOD. The Lord GOD speaks to the mountains, hills, ravines, and valleys, to the empty ruins and abandoned cities that have been robbed and laughed at by the other nations. 5This is what the Lord GOD says: I speak in hot anger against the other nations. I speak against the people of Edom, who took my land for themselves with joy and with hate in their hearts. They forced out the people and took their pastureland.’ 6So prophesy about the land of Israel and say to the mountains, hills, ravines, and valleys: ‘This is what the Lord GOD says: I speak in my jealous anger, because you have suffered the insults of the nations. 7So this is what the Lord GOD says: I promise that the nations around you will also have to suffer insults.

8“ ‘But you, mountains of Israel, will grow branches and fruit for my people, who will soon come home. 9I am concerned about you; I am on your side. You will be plowed, and seed will be planted in you. 10I will increase the number of people who live on you, all the people of Israel. The cities will have people living in them, and the ruins will be rebuilt. 11I will increase the number of people and animals living on you. They will grow and have many young. You will have people living on you as you did before, and I will make you better off than at the beginning. Then you will know that I am the LORD. 12I will cause my people Israel to walk on you and own you, and you will belong to them. You will never again take their children away from them.

13“ ‘This is what the Lord GOD says: People say about you, “You eat people and take children from your nation.” 14But you will not eat people anymore or take away the children, says the Lord GOD. 15I will not make you listen to insults from the nations anymore; you will not suffer shame

from them anymore. You will not cause your nation to fall anymore, says the Lord God.' "

The Lord Acts for Himself

16The Lord spoke his word to me again, saying: 17"Human, when the nation of Israel was living in their own land, they made it unclean[d] by
their ways and the things they did. Their ways
were like a woman's uncleanness in her time of
monthly bleeding. 18So I poured out my anger
against them, because they murdered in the land
and because they made the land unclean with
their idols. 19I scattered them among the nations,
and they were spread through the countries. I
punished them for how they lived and what they
did. 20They dishonored my holy name in the nations where they went. The nations said about
them: 'These are the people of the Lord, but they
had to leave the land which he gave them.' 21But
I had concern for my holy name, which the nation
of Israel had dishonored among the nations where
they went.

22"So say to the people of Israel, 'This is what
the Lord God says: Israel, I am going to act, but
not for your sake. I will do something to help my
holy name, which you have dishonored among
the nations where you went. 23I will prove the
holiness of my great name, which has been dishonored among the nations. You have dishonored
it among these nations, but the nations will know
that I am the Lord when I prove myself holy before their eyes, says the Lord God.

24" 'I will take you from the nations and gather
you out of all the lands and bring you back into
your own land. 25Then I will sprinkle clean water
on you, and you will be clean. I will cleanse you
from all your uncleanness and your idols. 26Also,
I will teach you to respect me completely, and I
will put a new way of thinking inside you. I will
take out the stubborn hearts of stone from your
bodies, and I will give you obedient hearts of
flesh. 27I will put my Spirit[d] inside you and help
you live by my rules and carefully obey my laws.
28You will live in the land I gave to your ancestors,
and you will be my people, and I will be your
God. 29So I will save you from all your uncleanness. I will command the grain to come and grow;
I will not allow a time of hunger to hurt you. 30I
will increase the harvest of the field so you will
never again suffer shame among the nations because of hunger. 31Then you will remember your
evil ways and actions that were not good, and you
will hate yourselves because of your sins and your
terrible acts that I hate. 32I want you to know that
I am not going to do this for your sake, says the
Lord God. Be ashamed and embarrassed about
your ways, Israel.

33" 'This is what the Lord God says: This is
what will happen on the day I cleanse you from
all your sins: I will cause the cities to have people
living in them again, and the destroyed places will
be rebuilt. 34The empty land will be plowed so it
will no longer be a ruin for everyone who passes
by to see. 35They will say, "This land was ruined,
but now it has become like the garden of Eden.
The cities were destroyed, empty, and ruined, but
now they are protected and have people living in
them." 36Then those nations still around you will
know that I, the Lord, have rebuilt what was destroyed and have planted what was empty. I, the
Lord, have spoken, and I will do it.'

37"This is what the Lord God says: I will let
myself be asked by the people of Israel to do this
for them again: I will make their people grow in
number like a flock. 38They will be as many as the
flocks brought to Jerusalem during her holy feasts.
Her ruined cities will be filled with flocks of people. Then they will know that I am the Lord."

The Vision of Dry Bones

37 I felt the power of the Lord on me, and
he brought me out by the Spirit[d] of the
Lord and put me down in the middle of a valley.
It was full of bones. 2He led me around among the
bones, and I saw that there were many bones in
the valley and that they were very dry. 3Then he
asked me, "Human, can these bones live?"

I answered, "Lord God, only you know."

4He said to me, "Prophesy[d] to these bones and
say to them, 'Dry bones, hear the word of the
Lord. 5This is what the Lord God says to the
bones: I will cause breath to enter you so you will
come to life. 6I will put muscles on you and flesh
on you and cover you with skin. Then I will put
breath in you so you will come to life. Then you
will know that I am the Lord.' "

7So I prophesied as I was commanded. While
I prophesied, there was a noise and a rattling. The
bones came together, bone to bone. 8I looked and
saw muscles come on the bones, and flesh grew,
and skin covered the bones. But there was no
breath in them.

9Then he said to me, "Prophesy to the wind.[n]
Prophesy, human, and say to the wind, 'This is
what the Lord God says: Wind, come from the
four winds, and breathe on these people who
were killed so they can come back to life.' " 10So
I prophesied as the Lord commanded me. And
the breath came into them, and they came to life
and stood on their feet, a very large army.

11Then he said to me, "Human, these bones are
like all the people of Israel. They say, 'Our bones
are dried up, and our hope has gone. We are destroyed.' 12So, prophesy and say to them, 'This is

wind This Hebrew word could also mean "breath" or "spirit."

what the Lord GOD says: My people, I will open
your graves and cause you to come up out of your
graves. Then I will bring you into the land of Israel. 13My people, you will know that I am the
LORD when I open your graves and cause you to
come up from them. 14And I will put my Spirit
inside you, and you will come to life. Then I will
put you in your own land. And you will know that
I, the LORD, have spoken and done it, says the
LORD.' "

Judah and Israel Back Together

15The LORD spoke his word to me, saying,
16"Human, take a stick and write on it, 'For Judah
and all the Israelites with him.' Then take another
stick and write on it, 'The stick of Ephraim, for
Joseph and all the Israelites with him.' 17Then join
them together into one stick so they will be one
in your hand.
18"When your people say to you, 'Explain to us
what you mean by this,' 19say to them, 'This is
what the Lord GOD says: I will take the stick for
Joseph and the tribes[d] of Israel with him, which
is in the hand of Ephraim, and I will put it with
the stick of Judah. I will make them into one stick,
and they will be one in my hand.' 20Hold the
sticks on which you wrote these names in your
hand so the people can see them. 21Say to the
people, 'This is what the Lord GOD says: I am
going to take the people of Israel from among the
nations where they have gone. I will gather them
from all around and bring them into their own
land. 22I will make them one nation in the land,
on the mountains of Israel. One king will rule all
of them. They will never again be two nations;
they will not be divided into two kingdoms anymore. 23They will not continue to make themselves unclean[d] by their idols, their statues of gods

DISCOURAGEMENT

God Is Here

Todd Petracek thought his relationship with Erin Chatham was over. First, he had acted like a jerk by often teasing her past the point of it being funny. Then he wouldn't apologize. Worse, he wouldn't even admit he had done anything wrong. Each time they talked, things seemed to get worse.

Finally, confused and hurt, Erin told Todd she hated him. She said she didn't think she could ever respect or trust him again.

By the time Todd got home that night, he wondered if they would ever speak again. He did the only thing he could think to do in such a discouraging situation: He prayed. Todd asked God to help him with what was left of his friendship with Erin.

Todd believes God answered his prayer. He believes God helped Erin call him the next night, to ask if they could get together and talk. And God helped Erin and Todd both see the situation more clearly.

They realized that Todd was afraid of getting too close to Erin, since they would soon be leaving for colleges three thousand miles apart. So he had acted as he did as a way of pulling away from her.

God helped Todd to be sorry for his actions, and he helped Erin to forgive Todd. Now, they are good friends, at peace with each other.

When a situation seems discouraging, there's still hope in God. In time, and with prayer, God will use your discouragements to help you grow and to help you know him better. That's the lesson God taught Todd and Erin. It's also the lesson in **Ezekiel 37:1–14**.

- What are the similarities between God's actions with Todd and Erin and God's actions in this passage?
- In what ways might God respond to your prayers in times that seem hopeless?

CONSIDER . . .

- calling someone who is discouraged and inviting him or her out for a Coke.
- writing "I can do all things through Christ, because he gives me strength" (Philippians 4:13, p. 1235) on credit-card size pieces of paper. Then have them laminated. Keep one for yourself, and give others to discouraged people.

FOR MORE, SEE . . .

- Psalm 121 (p. 554)
- John 11:1–44 (p. 1076)
- Ephesians 2:1–10 (p. 1219)

which I hate, or by their sins. I will save them
from all the ways they sin and turn against me,
and I will make them clean. Then they will be my
people, and I will be their God.
24“ ‘My servant David will be their king, and
they will all have one shepherd. They will live
by my rules and obey my laws. 25They will
live on the land I gave to my servant Jacob, the
land in which your ancestors lived. They will all
live on the land forever: they, their children,
and their grandchildren. David my servant will
be their king forever. 26I will make an agreement of peace with them, an agreement that continues forever. I will put them in their land and
make them grow in number. Then I will put my
Temple[d] among them forever. 27The place where
I live will be with them. I will be their God,
and they will be my people. 28When my Temple
is among them forever, the nations will know
that I, the LORD, make Israel holy.’ ”

Prophecy Against Gog

38 The LORD spoke his word to me, saying,
2“Human, look toward Gog of the land
of Magog, the chief ruler of the nations of Meshech and Tubal. Prophesy[d] against him 3and say,
‘The Lord GOD says this: I am against you, Gog,

> **SIDELIGHT:** Gog and Magog sound like they might be creatures from a strange horror movie (Ezekiel 38:2). Actually, they are the names of an unknown king and nation hostile to Israel. Wonder if their soldiers looked like giant lizards?

chief ruler of Meshech and Tubal. 4I will turn you
around and put hooks in your jaws. And I will
bring you out with all your army, horses, and
horsemen, all of whom will be dressed in beautiful uniforms. They will be a large army with large
and small shields and all having swords. 5Persia,
Cush, and Put will be with them, all of them having shields and helmets. 6There will also be Gomer with all its troops and the nation of Togarmah
from the far north with all its troops—many nations with you.
7“ ‘Be prepared. Be prepared, you and all the
armies that have come together to make you their
commander. 8After a long time you will be called
for service. After those years you will come into
a land that has been rebuilt from war. The people
in the land will have been gathered from many
nations to the mountains of Israel, which were
empty for a long time. These people were brought
out from the nations, and they will all be living in
safety. 9You will come like a storm. You, all your
troops, and the many nations with you will be like
a cloud covering the land.
10“ ‘This is what the Lord GOD says: At that
time ideas will come into your mind, and you will
think up an evil plan. 11You will say, “I will march
against a land of towns without walls. I will attack
those who are at rest and live in safety. All of
them live without city walls or gate bars or gates.
12I will capture treasures and take loot. I will turn
my power against the rebuilt ruins that now have
people living in them. I will attack these people
who have been gathered from the nations, who
have become rich with farm animals and property, who live at the center of the world.”
13Sheba, Dedan, and the traders of Tarshish, with
all its villages, will say to you, “Did you come to
capture treasure? Did you bring your troops together to take loot? Did you bring them to carry
away silver and gold and to take away farm animals and property?” ’
14“So prophesy, human, and say to Gog, ‘This
is what the Lord GOD says: Now that my people
Israel are living in safety, you will know about it.
15You will come with many people from your
place in the far north. You will have a large group
with you, a mighty army, all riding on horses.
16You will attack my people Israel like a cloud that
covers the land. This will happen in the days to
come when I bring you against my land. Gog,
then the nations will know me when they see me
prove how holy I am in what I do through you.
17“ ‘This is what the Lord GOD says: You are
the one about whom I spoke in past days. I spoke
through my servants, the prophets of Israel, who
prophesied for many years that I would bring you
against them. 18This is what will happen: On the
day Gog attacks the land of Israel, I will become
very angry, says the Lord GOD. 19With jealousy
and great anger I tell you that at that time there
will surely be a great earthquake in Israel. 20The
fish of the sea, the birds of the sky, the wild animals, everything that crawls on the ground, and
all the people on the earth will shake with fear
before me. Also the mountains will be thrown
down, the cliffs will fall, and every wall will fall
to the ground. 21Then I will call for a war against
Gog on all my mountains, says the Lord GOD. Everyone's sword will attack the soldier next to him.
22I will punish Gog with disease and death. I will
send a heavy rain with hailstones and burning sulfur on Gog, his army, and the many nations with
him. 23Then I will show how great I am. I will
show my holiness, and I will make myself known
to the many nations that watch. Then they will
know that I am the LORD.’

The Death of Gog and His Army

39 “Human, prophesy[d] against Gog and say,
‘This is what the Lord GOD says: I am

against you, Gog, chief ruler of Meshech and Tubal. 2I will turn you around and lead you. I will bring you from the far north and send you to attack the mountains of Israel. 3I will knock your bow out of your left hand and throw down your arrows from your right hand. 4You, all your troops, and the nations with you will fall dead on the mountains of Israel. I will let you be food for every bird that eats meat and for every wild animal. 5You will lie fallen on the ground, because I have spoken, says the Lord GOD. 6I will send fire on Magog and those who live in safety on the coastlands. Then they will know that I am the LORD.

7" 'I will make myself known among my people Israel, and I will not let myself be dishonored anymore. Then the nations will know that I am the LORD, the Holy One in Israel. 8It is coming! It will happen, says the Lord GOD. The time I talked about is coming.

9" 'Then those who live in the cities of Israel will come out and make fires with the enemy's weapons. They will burn them, both large and small shields, bows and arrows, war clubs, and spears. They will use the weapons to burn in their fires for seven years. 10They will not need to take wood from the field or chop firewood from the forests, because they will make fires with the weapons. In this way they will take the treasures of those who took their treasures; they will take the loot of those who took their loot, says the Lord GOD.

11" 'At that time I will give Gog a burial place in Israel, in the Valley of the Travelers, east of the Dead Sea.[d] It will block the road for travelers. Gog and all his army will be buried there, so people will call it The Valley of Gog's Army.

12" 'The people of Israel will be burying them for seven months to make the land clean[d] again. 13All the people in the land will bury them, and they will be honored on the day of my victory, says the Lord GOD.

14" 'The people of Israel will choose men to work through the land to make it clean. Along with others, they will bury Gog's soldiers still lying dead on the ground. After the seven months are finished, they will still search. 15As they go through the land, anyone who sees a human bone is to put a marker by it. The sign will stay there until the gravediggers bury the bone in The Valley of Gog's Army. 16A city will be there named Hamonah. So they will make the land clean again.'

17"Human, this is what the Lord GOD says: Speak to every kind of bird and wild animal: 'Come together, come! Come together from all around to my sacrifice, a great sacrifice which I will prepare for you on the mountains of Israel. Eat flesh and drink blood! 18You are to eat the flesh of the mighty and drink the blood of the rulers of the earth as if they were fat animals from Bashan: male sheep, lambs, goats, and bulls. 19You are to eat and drink from my sacrifice which I have prepared for you, eating fat until you are full and drinking blood until you are drunk. 20At my table you are to eat until you are full of horses and riders, mighty men and all kinds of soldiers,' says the Lord GOD.

21"I will show my glory among the nations. All the nations will see my power when I punish them. 22From that time onward the people of Israel will know that I am the LORD their God. 23The nations will know Israel was taken away captive because they turned against me. So I turned away from them and handed them over to their enemies until all of them died in war. 24Because of their uncleanness[d] and their sins, I punished them and turned away from them.

25"So this is what the Lord GOD says: Now I will bring the people of Jacob back from captivity, and I will have mercy on the whole nation of Israel. I will not let them dishonor me. 26The people will forget their shame and how they rejected me when they live again in safety on their own land with no one to make them afraid. 27I will bring the people back from other lands and gather them from the lands of their enemies. So I will use my people to show many nations that I am holy. 28Then my people will know that I am the LORD their God, because I sent them into captivity among the nations, but then I brought them back to their own land, leaving no one behind. 29I will not turn away from them anymore, because I will put my Spirit[d] into the people of Israel, says the Lord GOD."

SIDELIGHT: Ezekiel's final vision is packed with measurements for a restored temple in Jerusalem (chapters 40—48). Its total floor space was about eight hundred sixty-one square feet, which is about the size of three large bedrooms today.

The New Temple

40 It was the twenty-fifth year of our captivity, at the beginning of the year, on the tenth day of the month. It was in the fourteenth year after Jerusalem was captured. On that same day I felt the power of the LORD, and he brought me to Jerusalem. 2In the visions of God he brought me to the land of Israel and put me down on a very high mountain. On the south of the mountain there were some buildings that looked like a city. 3He took me closer to the buildings, and I saw a man who looked as if he were made of bronze, standing in the gateway. He had a cord

made of linen and a stick in his hand, both for
measuring. 4The man said to me, "Human, look
with your eyes and hear with your ears. Pay attention to all that I will show you, because that's why
you have been brought here. Tell the people of
Israel all that you see."

The East Gateway

5I saw a wall that surrounded the Temple[a]
area. The measuring stick in the man's hand was
ten and one-half feet long. So the man measured
the wall, which was ten and one-half feet thick
and ten and one-half feet high.
6Then the man went to the east gateway. He
went up its steps and measured the opening of the
gateway. It was ten and one-half feet deep. 7The
rooms for the guards were ten and one-half feet
long and ten and one-half feet wide. The walls
that came out between the guards' rooms were
about nine feet thick. The opening of the gateway
next to the porch that faced the Temple was ten
and one-half feet deep.
8Then the man measured the porch of the gateway. 9It was about fourteen feet deep, and its side
walls were three and one-half feet thick. The
porch of the gateway faced the Temple.
10On each side of the east gateway were three
rooms, which measured the same on each side.
The walls between each room were the same
thickness. 11The man measured the width of the
entrance to the gateway, which was seventeen
and one-half feet wide. The width of the gate was
about twenty-three feet. 12And there was a low
wall about twenty-one inches high in front of each
room. The rooms were ten and one-half feet on
each side. 13The man measured the gateway from
the roof of one room to the roof of the opposite
room. It was about forty-four feet from one door
to the opposite door. 14The man also measured
the porch, which was about thirty-five feet wide.
The courtyard was around the porch. 15From the
front of the outer side of the gateway to the front
of the porch of the inner side of the gateway was
eighty-seven and one-half feet. 16The rooms and
porch had small windows on both sides. The windows were narrower on the side facing the gateway. Carvings of palm trees were on each side
wall of the rooms.

The Outer Courtyard

17Then the man brought me into the outer
courtyard where I saw rooms and a pavement of
stones all around the court. Thirty rooms were
along the edge of the paved walkway. 18The pavement ran alongside the gates and was as deep as
the gates were wide. This was the lower pavement. 19Then the man measured from the outer
wall to the inner wall. The outer court between
these two walls was one hundred seventy-five
feet on the east and on the north.

The North Gateway

20The man measured the length and width of
the north gateway leading to the outer courtyard.
21Its three rooms on each side, its inner walls, and
its porch measured the same as the first gateway.
It was eighty-seven and one-half feet long and
forty-four feet wide. 22Its windows, porch, and
carvings of palm trees measured the same as the
east gateway. Seven steps went up to the gateway, and the gateway's porch was at the inner
end. 23The inner courtyard had a gateway across
from the northern gateway like the one on the
east. The man measured it and found it was one
hundred seventy-five feet from inner gateway to
outer gateway.

The South Gateway

24Then the man led me south where I saw a
gateway facing south. He measured its inner walls
and its porch, and they measured the same as the
other gateways. 25The gateway and its porch had
windows all around like the other gateways. It
was eighty-seven and one-half feet long and forty-
four feet wide. 26Seven steps went up to this gateway. Its porch was at the inner end, and it had
carvings of palm trees on its inner walls. 27The
inner courtyard had a gateway on its south side.
The man measured from gate to gate on the south
side, which was one hundred seventy-five feet.

The Inner Courtyard

28Then the man brought me through the south
gateway into the inner courtyard. The inner south
gateway measured the same as the gateways in
the outer wall. 29The inner south gateway's
rooms, inner walls, and porch measured the same
as the gateways in the outer wall. There were
windows all around the gateway and its porch.
The gateway was eighty-seven and one-half feet
long and forty-four feet wide. 30Each porch of
each inner gateway was about forty-four feet long
and about nine feet wide. 31The inner south gateway's porch faced the outer courtyard. Carvings
of palm trees were on its side walls, and its stairway had eight steps.
32The man brought me into the inner courtyard
on the east side. He measured the inner east gateway, and it was the same as the other gateways.
33The inner east gateway's rooms, inside walls,
and porch measured the same as the other gateways. Windows were all around the gateway and
its porch. The inner east gateway was eighty-
seven and one-half feet long and forty-four feet
wide. 34Its porch faced the outer courtyard. Carvings of palm trees were on its inner walls on each
side, and its stairway had eight steps.

35Then the man brought me to the inner north gateway. He measured it, and it was the same as the other gateways. 36Its rooms, inner walls, and porch measured the same as the other gateways. There were windows all around the gateway, which was eighty-seven and one-half feet long and forty-four feet wide. 37Its porch faced the outer courtyard. Carvings of palm trees were on its inner walls on each side, and its stairway had eight steps.

Rooms for Preparing Sacrifices

38There was a room with a door that opened onto the porch of the inner north gateway. In this room the priests washed animals for the burnt offerings. 39There were two tables on each side of the porch, on which animals for burnt offerings, sin offerings, and penalty offerings were killed. 40Outside, by each side wall of the porch, at the entrance to the north gateway, were two more tables. 41So there were four tables inside the gateway, and four tables outside. In all there were eight tables on which the priests killed animals for sacrifices. 42There were four tables made of cut stone for the burnt offering. These tables were about three feet long, three feet wide, and about two feet high. On these tables the priests put their tools which they used to kill animals for burnt offerings and the other sacrifices. 43Double shelves three inches wide were put up on all the walls. The flesh for the offering was put on the tables.

The Priests' Rooms

44There were two rooms in the inner courtyard. One was beside the north gateway and faced south. The other room was beside the south gateway and faced north. 45The man said to me, "The room which faces south is for the priests who serve in the Temple[d] area, 46while the room that faces north is for the priests who serve at the altar. This second group of priests are descendants[d] of Zadok, the only descendants of Levi who can come near the LORD to serve him."

47The man measured the inner courtyard. It was a square—one hundred seventy-five feet long and one hundred seventy-five feet wide. The altar was in front of the Temple.

The Temple Porch

48The man brought me to the porch of the Temple[d] and measured each side wall of the porch. Each was about nine feet thick. The doorway was twenty-four and one-half feet wide. The side walls of the doorway were each about five feet wide. 49The porch was thirty-five feet long and twenty-one feet wide, with ten steps leading up to it. Pillars were by the side walls, one on each side of the entrance.

The Holy Place of the Temple

41 The man brought me to the Holy Place and measured its side walls, which were each ten and one-half feet thick. 2The entrance was seventeen and one-half feet wide. The walls alongside the entrance were each about nine feet wide. The man measured the Holy Place, which was seventy feet long and thirty-five feet wide.

3Then the man went inside and measured the side walls of the next doorway. Each was three and one-half feet thick. The doorway was ten and one-half feet wide, and the walls next to it were each more than twelve feet thick. 4Then the man measured the room at the end of the Holy Place. It was thirty-five feet long and thirty-five feet wide. The man said to me, "This is the Most Holy Place."

5Then the man measured the wall of the Temple,[d] which was ten and one-half feet thick. There were side rooms seven feet wide all around the Temple. 6The side rooms were on three different stories, each above the other, with thirty rooms on each story. All around the Temple walls there were ledges for the side rooms. The upper rooms rested on the ledges but were not attached to the Temple walls. 7The side rooms around the Temple were wider on each higher story, so rooms were wider on the top story. A stairway went up from the lowest story to the highest through the middle story.

8I also saw that the Temple had a raised base all around. Its edge was the foundation for the side rooms, and it was ten and one-half feet thick. 9The outer wall of the side rooms was about nine feet thick. There was an open area between the side rooms of the Temple 10and some other rooms. It was thirty-five feet wide and went all around the Temple. 11The side rooms had doors which led to the open area around the outside of the Temple. One door faced north, and the other faced south. The open area was about nine feet wide all around.

12The building facing the private area at the west side was one hundred twenty-two and one-half feet wide. The wall around the building was about nine feet thick and one hundred fifty-seven and one-half feet long.

13Then the man measured the Temple. It was one hundred seventy-five feet long. The private area, including the building and its walls, was in all one hundred seventy-five feet long. 14Also the front of the Temple and the private area on its east side were one hundred seventy-five feet wide.

15The man measured the length of the building facing the private area on the west side, and it was one hundred seventy-five feet from one wall to the other.

The Holy Place, the Most Holy Place, and the

outer porch [16]had wood panels on the walls. By the doorway, the Temple had wood panels on the walls. The wood covered all the walls from the floor up to the windows, [17]up to the part of the wall above the entrance.

All the walls inside the Most Holy Place and the Holy Place, and on the outside, in the porch, [18]had carvings of creatures with wings and palm trees. A palm tree was between each carved creature, and every creature had two faces. [19]One was a human face looking toward the palm tree on one side. The other was a lion's face looking toward the palm tree on the other side. They were carved all around the Temple walls. [20]From the floor to above the entrance, palm trees and creatures with wings were carved. The walls of the Holy Place [21]had square doorposts. In front of the Most Holy Place was something that looked like [22]an altar of wood. It was more than five feet high and three feet wide. Its corners, base, and sides were wood. The man said to me, "This is the table that is in the presence of the LORD." [23]Both the Holy Place and the Most Holy Place had double doors. [24]Each of the doors had two pieces that would swing open. [25]Carved on the doors of the Holy Place were palm trees and creatures with wings, like those carved on the walls. And there was a wood roof over the front Temple porch. [26]There were windows and palm trees on both side walls of the porch. The side rooms of the Temple were also covered by a roof over the stairway.

The Priests' Rooms

42 Then the man led me north out into the outer courtyard and to the rooms across from the private area and the building. [2]These rooms on the north side were one hundred seventy-five feet long and eighty-seven and one-half feet wide. [3]There was thirty-five feet of the inner courtyard between them and the Temple. On the other side, they faced the stone pavement of the outer courtyard. The rooms were built in three stories like steps and had balconies. [4]There was a path on the north side of the rooms, which was seventeen and one-half feet wide and one hundred seventy-five feet long. Doors led into the rooms from this path. [5]The top rooms were narrower, because the balconies took more space from them. The rooms on the first and second stories of the building were wider. [6]The rooms were on three stories. They did not have pillars like the pillars of the courtyards. So the top rooms were farther back than those on the first and second stories. [7]There was a wall outside parallel to the rooms and to the outer courtyard. It ran in front of the rooms for eighty-seven and one-half feet. [8]The row of rooms along the outer courtyard was eighty-seven and one-half feet long, and the rooms that faced the Temple were about one hundred seventy-five feet long. [9]The lower rooms had an entrance on the east side so a person could enter them from the outer courtyard, [10]at the start of the wall beside the courtyard.

There were rooms on the south side, which were across from the private area and the building. [11]These rooms had a path in front of them. They were like the rooms on the north with the same length and width and the same doors. [12]The doors of the south rooms were like the doors of the north rooms. There was an entrance at the open end of a path beside the wall, so a person could enter at the east end.

[13]The man said to me, "The north and south rooms across from the private area are holy rooms. There the priests who go near the LORD will eat the most holy offerings. There they will put the most holy offerings: the grain offerings, sin offerings, and the penalty offerings, because the place is holy. [14]The priests who enter the Holy Place must leave their serving clothes there before they go into the outer courtyard, because these clothes are holy. After they put on other clothes, they may go to the part of the Temple area which is for the people."

Outside the Temple Area

[15]When the man finished measuring inside the Temple[d] area, he brought me out through the east gateway. He measured the area all around. [16]The man measured the east side with the measuring stick; it was eight hundred seventy-five feet by the measuring stick. [17]He measured the north side; it was eight hundred seventy-five feet by the measuring stick. [18]He measured the south side; it was eight hundred seventy-five feet by the measuring stick.[19]He went around to the west side; it measured eight hundred seventy-five feet by the measuring stick. [20]So he measured the Temple area on all four sides. The Temple area had a wall all around it that was eight hundred seventy-five feet long and eight hundred seventy-five feet wide. It separated what was holy from that which was not holy.

The Lord Among His People

43 Then the man led me to the outer east gateway, [2]and I saw the glory of the God of Israel coming from the east. It sounded like the roar of rushing water, and its brightness made the earth shine. [3]The vision I saw was like the vision I had seen when the LORD came to destroy the city and also like the vision I had seen by the Kebar River. I bowed facedown on the ground. [4]The glory of the LORD came into the Temple[d] area through the east gateway.

[5]Then the Spirit[d] picked me up and brought me into the inner courtyard. There I saw the LORD's

glory filling the Temple. 6As the man stood at my
side, I heard someone speaking to me from inside
the Temple. 7The voice from the Temple said to
me, "Human, this is my throne and the place
where my feet rest. I will live here among the
Israelites forever. The people of Israel will not
make my holy name unclean[d] again. Neither the
people nor their kings will make it unclean with
their sexual sins or with the dead bodies of their
kings. 8The kings made my name unclean by putting their doorway next to my doorway, and their
doorpost next to my doorpost so only a wall separated me from them. When they did their acts
that I hate, they made my holy name unclean, and
so I destroyed them in my anger. 9Now let them
stop their sexual sins and take the dead bodies of
their kings far away from me. Then I will live
among them forever.

10"Human, tell the people of Israel about the
Temple so they will be ashamed of their sins. Let
them think about the plan of the Temple. 11If they
are ashamed of all they have done, let them know
the design of the Temple and how it is built. Show
them its exits and entrances, all its designs, and
also all its rules and teachings. Write the rules as
they watch so they will obey all the teachings and
rules about the Temple. 12This is the teaching
about the Temple: All the area around the top of
the mountain is most holy. This is the teaching
about the Temple.

The Altar

13"These are the measurements of the altar, using the measuring stick. The altar's gutter is
twenty-one inches high and twenty-one inches
wide, and its rim is about nine inches around its
edge. And the altar is this tall: 14From the ground
up to the lower ledge, it measures three and one-
half feet. It is twenty-one inches wide. It measures
seven feet from the smaller ledge to the larger
ledge and is twenty-one inches wide. 15The place
where the sacrifice is burned on the altar is seven
feet high, with its four corners shaped like horns
and reaching up above it. 16It is square, twenty-
one feet long and twenty-one feet wide. 17The upper ledge is also square, twenty-four and one-half
feet long and twenty-four and one-half feet wide.
The rim around the altar is ten and one-half
inches wide, and its gutter is twenty-one inches
wide all around. Its steps are on the east side."

18Then the man said to me, "Human, this is
what the Lord GOD says: These are the rules for
the altar. When it is built, use these rules to offer
burnt offerings and to sprinkle blood on it. 19You
must give a young bull as a sin offering to the
priests, the Levites who are from the family of
Zadok and who come near me to serve me, says
the Lord GOD. 20Take some of the bull's blood and
put it on the four corners of the altar, on the four
corners of the ledge, and all around the rim. This
is how you will make the altar pure and ready for
God's service. 21Then take the bull for the sin offering and burn it in the proper place in the Temple[d] area, outside the Temple building.

22"On the second day offer a male goat that has
nothing wrong with it for a sin offering. The
priests will make the altar pure and ready for
God's service as they did with the young bull.
23When you finish making the altar pure and
ready, offer a young bull and a male sheep from
the flock, which have nothing wrong with them.
24You must offer them in the presence of the
LORD, and the priests are to throw salt on them
and offer them as a burnt offering to the LORD.

25"You must prepare a goat every day for seven
days as a sin offering. Also, the priests must prepare a young bull and male sheep from the flock,
which have nothing wrong with them. 26For
seven days the priests are to make the altar pure
and ready for God's service. Then they will give
the altar to God. 27After these seven days, on the
eighth day, the priests must offer your burnt offerings and your fellowship offerings on the altar.
Then I will accept you, says the Lord GOD."

The Outer East Gate

44 Then the man brought me back to the
outer east gateway of the Temple[d] area,
but the gate was shut. 2The LORD said to me,
"This gate will stay shut; it will not be opened. No
one may enter through it, because the LORD God
of Israel has entered through it. So it must stay
shut. 3Only the ruler himself may sit in the gateway to eat a meal in the presence of the LORD. He
must enter through the porch of the gateway and
go out the same way."

4Then the man brought me through the outer
north gate to the front of the Temple. As I looked,
I saw the glory of the LORD filling the Temple of
the LORD, and I bowed facedown on the ground.

5The LORD said to me, "Human, pay attention.
Use your eyes to see, and your ears to hear. See
and hear everything I tell you about all the rules
and teachings of the Temple of the LORD. Pay attention to the entrance to the Temple and to all
the exits from the Temple area. 6Then speak to
those who refuse to obey. Say to the people of
Israel, 'This is what the Lord GOD says: Stop doing all your acts that I hate, Israel! 7You brought
foreigners into my Holy Place who were not circumcised[d] in the flesh and had not given themselves to serving me. You dishonored my Temple
when you offered me food, fat, and blood. You
broke my agreement by all the things you did that
I hate. 8You did not take care of my holy things
yourselves but put foreigners in charge of my
Temple. 9This is what the Lord GOD says: Foreigners who are not circumcised in flesh and who

do not give themselves to serving me may not
enter my Temple. Not even a foreigner living
among the people of Israel may enter.
10“ ‘But the Levites who stopped obeying me
when Israel left me and who followed their idols
must be punished for their sin. 11These Levites are
to be servants in my Holy Place. They may guard
the gates of the Temple and serve in the Temple
area. They may kill the animals for the burnt offering and the sacrifices for the people. They may
stand before the people to serve them. 12But these
Levites helped the people worship their idols and
caused the people of Israel to fall, so I make this
promise: They will be punished for their sin, says
the Lord God. 13They will not come near me to
serve as priests, nor will they come near any of my
holy things or the most holy offerings. But they
will be made ashamed of the things they did that
I hate. 14I will put them in charge of taking care
of the Temple area, all the work that must be
done in it.
15“ ‘But the priests who are Levites and descendants[d] of Zadok took care of my Holy Place when
Israel left me, so they may come near to serve me.
They may stand in my presence to offer me the fat
and blood of the animals they sacrifice, says the
Lord God. 16They are the only ones who may enter my Holy Place. Only they may come near my
table to serve me and take care of the things I gave
them to do.
17“ ‘When they enter the gates of the inner
courtyard, they must wear linen robes. They must
not wear wool to serve at the gates of the inner
courtyard or in the Temple. 18They will wear
linen turbans on their heads and linen underclothes. They will not wear anything that makes
them perspire. 19When they go out into the outer
courtyard to the people, they must take off their
serving clothes before they go. They must leave
these clothes in the holy rooms and put on other
clothes. Then they will not let their holy clothes
hurt the people.
20“ ‘They must not shave their heads or let
their hair grow long but must keep the hair of
their heads trimmed. 21None of the priests may
drink wine when they enter the inner courtyard.
22The priests must not marry widows or divorced
women. They may marry only virgins[d] from the
people of Israel or widows of priests. 23They must
teach my people the difference between what is
holy and what is not holy. They must help my
people know what is unclean[d] and what is clean.
24“ ‘In court they will act as judges. When they
judge, they will follow my teachings. They must
obey my laws and my rules at all my special feasts
and keep my Sabbaths[d] holy.
25“ ‘They must not go near a dead person, making themselves unclean.[d] But they are allowed to
make themselves unclean if the dead person is
their father, mother, son, daughter, brother, or a
sister who has not married. 26After a priest has
been made clean again, he must wait seven days.
27Then he may go into the inner courtyard to
serve in the Temple, but he must offer a sin offering for himself, says the Lord God.
28“ ‘These are the rules about the priests and
their property: They will have me instead of property. You will not give them any land to own in
Israel; I am what they will own. 29They will eat
the grain offerings, sin offerings, and penalty offerings. Everything Israel gives to me will be theirs.
30The best fruits of all the first harvests and all the
special gifts offered to me will belong to the
priests. You will also give to the priests the first
part of your grain that you grind and so bring a
blessing on your family. 31The priests must not eat
any bird or animal that died a natural death or one
that has been torn by wild animals.’

The Land Is Divided

45 “ ‘When you divide the land for the Israelite tribes[d] by throwing lots,[d] you must
give a part of the land to belong to the Lord. It
will be about seven miles long and about six miles
wide; all of this land will be holy. 2From this land,
an area eight hundred seventy-five feet square
will be for the Temple.[d] There will be an open
space around the Temple that is eighty-seven and
one-half feet wide. 3In the holy area you will measure a part about seven miles long and three miles
wide, and in it will be the Most Holy Place. 4This
holy part of the land will be for the priests who
serve in the Temple, who come near to the Lord
to serve him. It will be a place for the priests’
houses and for the Temple. 5Another area about
seven miles long and more than three miles wide
will be for the Levites, who serve in the Temple
area. It will belong to them so they will have cities
in which to live.
6“ ‘You must give the city an area that is about
one and one-half miles wide and about seven
miles long, along the side of the holy area. It will
belong to all the people of Israel.
7“ ‘The ruler will have land on both sides of the
holy area and the city. On the west of the holy
area, his land will reach to the Mediterranean
Sea. On the east of the holy area, his land will
reach to the eastern border. It will be as long as
the land given to each tribe. 8Only this land will
be the ruler’s property in Israel. So my rulers will
not be cruel to my people anymore, but they will
let each tribe in the nation of Israel have its share
of the land.
9“ ‘This is what the Lord God says: You have
gone far enough, you rulers of Israel! Stop being
cruel and hurting people, and do what is right and
fair. Stop forcing my people out of their homes,
says the Lord God. 10You must have honest

scales, an honest dry measurement and an honest
liquid measurement. 11The dry measure and the
liquid measure will be the same: The liquid measure will always be a tenth of a homer,[n] and the
ephah will always be a tenth of a homer. The measurement they follow will be the homer. 12The
shekel[n] will be worth twenty gerahs, and a mina
will be worth sixty shekels.

Offerings and Holy Days

13“ ‘This is the gift you should offer: a sixth of
an ephah from every homer of wheat, and a sixth
of an ephah from every homer of barley. 14The
amount of oil you are to offer is a tenth of a bath
from each cor. (Ten baths make a homer and also
make a cor.) 15You should give one sheep from
each flock of two hundred from the watering
places of Israel. All these are to be offered for the
grain offerings, burnt offerings, and fellowship offerings to remove sins so you will belong to God,
says the Lord GOD. 16All people in the land will
give this special offering to the ruler of Israel. 17It
will be the ruler's responsibility to supply the
burnt offerings, grain offerings, and drink offerings. These offerings will be given at the feasts, at
the New Moons,[d] on the Sabbaths,[d] and at all the
other feasts of Israel. The ruler will supply the sin
offerings, grain offerings, and fellowship offerings
to pay for the sins of Israel.

18“ ‘This is what the Lord GOD says: On the
first day of the first month take a young bull that
has nothing wrong with it. Use it to make the
Temple[d] pure and ready for God's service. 19The
priest will take some of the blood from this sin
offering and put it on the doorposts of the Temple,
on the four corners of the ledge of the altar, and
on the posts of the gate to the inner courtyard.
20You will do the same thing on the seventh day
of the month for anyone who has sinned by accident or without knowing it. This is how you make
the Temple pure and ready for God's service.

Passover Feast Offerings

21“ ‘On the fourteenth day of the first month
you will celebrate the Feast[d] of Passover. It will be
a feast of seven days when you eat bread made
without yeast. 22On that day the ruler must offer
a bull for himself and for all the people of the land
as a sin offering. 23During the seven days of the
feast he must offer seven bulls and seven male
sheep that have nothing wrong with them. They
will be burnt offerings to the LORD, which the
ruler will offer every day of the seven days of the
feast. He must also offer a male goat every day as
a sin offering. 24The ruler must give as a grain
offering one-half bushel for each bull and one-half
bushel for each sheep. He must give a gallon of
olive oil for each half bushel.

25“ ‘Beginning on the fifteenth day of the seventh month, when you celebrate the Feast[d] of
Shelters, the ruler will supply the same things for
seven days: the sin offerings, burnt offerings,
grain offerings, and the olive oil.

Rules for Worship

46 “ ‘This is what the Lord GOD says: The
east gate of the inner courtyard will stay
shut on the six working days, but it will be
opened on the Sabbath[d] day and on the day of the
New Moon.[d] 2The ruler will enter from outside
through the porch of the gateway and stand by
the gatepost, while the priests offer the ruler's
burnt offering and fellowship offering. The ruler
will worship at the entrance of the gateway, and
then he will go out. But the gate will not be shut
until evening. 3The people of the land will worship at the entrance of that gateway in the presence of the LORD on the Sabbaths and New
Moons. 4This is the burnt offering the ruler will
offer to the LORD on the Sabbath day: six male
lambs that have nothing wrong with them and a
male sheep that has nothing wrong with it. 5He
must give a half-bushel grain offering with the
male sheep, but he may give as much grain offering with the lambs as he pleases. He must also
give a gallon of olive oil for each half bushel of
grain. 6On the day of the New Moon he must
offer a young bull that has nothing wrong with it.
He must also offer six lambs and a male sheep that
have nothing wrong with them. 7The ruler must
give a half-bushel grain offering with the bull and
one-half bushel with the male sheep. With the
lambs, he may give as much grain as he pleases.
But he must give a gallon of olive oil for each half
bushel of grain. 8When the ruler enters, he must
go in through the porch of the gateway, and he
must go out the same way.

9“ ‘When the people of the land come into the
LORD's presence at the special feasts, those who
enter through the north gate to worship must go
out through the south gate. Those who enter
through the south gate must go out through the
north gate. They must not return the same way
they entered; everyone must go out the opposite
way. 10The ruler will go in with the people when
they go in and go out with them when they go
out.

11“ ‘At the feasts and regular times of worship
one-half bushel of grain must be offered with a
young bull, and one-half bushel of grain must be

homer The Hebrew word means “donkey-load.” It measured about five dry bushels or one hundred seventy-five liquid quarts. So an ephah was about one-half bushel, and a bath was about eighteen quarts.
shekel In Ezekiel's time a shekel weighed about two-fifths of an ounce.

offered with a male sheep. But with an offering of
lambs, the ruler may give as much grain as he
pleases. He should give a gallon of olive oil for
each half bushel of grain. 12The ruler may give an
offering as a special gift to the LORD; it may be a
burnt offering or fellowship offering. When he
gives it to the LORD, the inner east gate is to be
opened for him. He must offer his burnt offering
or his fellowship offering as he does on the Sabbath[d] day. Then he will go out, and the gate will
be shut after he has left.

13" 'Every day you will give a year-old lamb that
has nothing wrong with it for a burnt offering to
the LORD. Do it every morning. 14Also, you must
offer a grain offering with the lamb every morning. For this you will give three and one-third
quarts of grain and one and one-third quarts of
olive oil, to make the fine flour moist, as a grain
offering to the LORD. This is a rule that must be
kept from now on. 15So you must always give the
lamb, together with the grain offering and the olive oil, every morning as a burnt offering.

Rules for the Ruler

16" 'This is what the Lord GOD says: If the ruler
gives a gift from his land to any of his sons, that
land will belong to the son and then to the son's
children. It is their property passed down from
their family. 17But if the ruler gives a gift from his
land to any of his servants, that land will belong
to the servant only until the year of freedom.
Then the land will go back to the ruler. Only the
ruler's sons may keep a gift of land from the ruler.
18The ruler must not take any of the people's land,
forcing them out of their land. He must give his
sons some of his own land so my people will not
be scattered out of their own land.' "

The Special Kitchens

19The man led me through the entrance at the
side of the gateway to the priests' holy rooms that
face north. There I saw a place at the west end.
20The man said to me, "This is where the priests
will boil the meat of the penalty offering and sin
offering and bake the grain offering. Then they
will not need to bring these holy offerings into the
outer courtyard, because that would hurt the people."

21Then the man brought me out into the outer
courtyard and led me to its four corners. In each
corner of the courtyard was a smaller courtyard.
22Small courtyards were in the four corners of the
courtyard. Each small courtyard was the same
size, seventy feet long and fifty-two and one-half
feet wide. 23A stone wall was around each of the
four small courtyards, and places for cooking
were built in each of the stone walls. 24The man
said to me, "These are the kitchens where those
who work in the Temple[d] will boil the sacrifices
offered by the people."

The River from the Temple

47 The man led me back to the door of the
Temple,[d] and I saw water coming out
from under the doorway and flowing east. (The
Temple faced east.) The water flowed down from
the south side wall of the Temple and then south
of the altar. 2The man brought me out through
the outer north gate and led me around outside
to the outer east gate. I found the water coming
out on the south side of the gate.

3The man went toward the east with a line in
his hand and measured about one-third of a mile.
Then he led me through water that came up to
my ankles. 4The man measured about one-third of
a mile again and led me through water that came
up to my knees. Then he measured about one-
third of a mile again and led me through water up
to my waist. 5The man measured about one-third
of a mile again, but it was now a river that I could
not cross. The water had risen too high; it was
deep enough for swimming; it was a river that no
one could cross. 6The man asked me, "Human, do
you see this?"

Then the man led me back to the bank of the
river. 7As I went back, I saw many trees on both
sides of the river. 8The man said to me, "This water will flow toward the eastern areas and go
down into the Jordan Valley. When it enters the
Dead Sea,[d] it will become fresh. 9Everywhere the
river goes, there will be many fish. Wherever this
water goes the Dead Sea will become fresh, and
so where the river goes there will be many living
things. 10Fishermen will stand by the Dead Sea.
From En Gedi all the way to En Eglaim there will
be places to spread fishing nets. There will be
many kinds of fish in the Dead Sea, as many as in
the Mediterranean Sea. 11But its swamps and
marshes will not become fresh; they will be left
for salt. 12All kinds of fruit trees will grow on both
banks of the river, and their leaves will not dry
and die. The trees will have fruit every month,

SIDELIGHT: In its current state, the Dead Sea is hardly a healthy habitat for the "many kinds of fish" that Ezekiel sees in his vision (Ezekiel 47:8–10). The surface of this body of water is 1,294 feet below sea level, and 25 percent of the sea is minerals—making it the saltiest and most uninhabitable sea in the world. It would take a true miracle for water to become fresh when it left the Dead Sea.

because the water for them comes from the Temple. The fruit from the trees will be used for food,
and their leaves for medicine."

Borders of the Land

13This is what the Lord God says: "These are
the borders of the land to be divided among the
twelve tribes[d] of Israel. Joseph will have two parts
of land. 14You will divide the land equally. I promised to give it to your ancestors, so this land will
belong to you as family property.
15"This will be the border line of the land: "On
the north side it will start at the Mediterranean
Sea. It will go through Hethlon, toward Lebo Hamath and on to the towns of Zedad, 16Berothah,
and Sibraim on the border between Damascus
and Hamath. Then it will go on to the town of
Hazer Hatticon on the border of the country of
Hauran. 17So the border line will go from the
Mediterranean Sea east to the town of Hazar
Enan, where the land belonging to Damascus and
Hamath lies on the north side. This will be the
north side of the land.
18"On the east side the border runs south from
a point between Hauran and Damascus. It will go
along the Jordan between Gilead and the land of
Israel and will continue to the town of Tamar on
the Dead Sea.[d] This will be the east side of the
land.
19"On the south side the border line will go east
from Tamar all the way to the waters of Meribah
Kadesh. Then it will run along the brook of Egypt
to the Mediterranean Sea. This will be the south
side of the land.
20"On the west side the Mediterranean Sea will
be the border line up to a place across from Lebo
Hamath. This will be the west side of your land.
21"You will divide this land among the tribes of
Israel. 22You will divide it as family property for
yourselves and for the foreigners who live and
have children among you. You are to treat these
foreigners the same as people born in Israel; they
are to share the land with the tribes of Israel. 23In
whatever tribe the foreigner lives, you will give
him some land," says the Lord God.

Dividing the Land

48 "These are the areas of the tribes[d]
named here: Dan will have one share at
the northern border. It will go from the sea
through Hethlon to Lebo Hamath, all the way to
Hazar Enan, where Damascus lies to the north. It
will stop there next to Hamath. This will be Dan's
northern border from the east side to the Mediterranean Sea on the west side.
2"South of Dan's border, Asher will have one
share. It will go from the east side to the west
side.
3"South of Asher's border, Naphtali will have
one share. It will go from the east side to the west
side.
4"South of Naphtali's border, Manasseh will
have one share. It will go from the east side to the
west side.
5"South of Manasseh's border, Ephraim will
have one share. It will go from the east side to the
west side.
6"South of Ephraim's border, Reuben will have
one share. It will go from the east side to the west
side.
7"South of Reuben's border, Judah will have
one share. It will go from the east side to the west
side.
8"South of Judah's border will be the holy area
which you are to give. It will be about seven miles
wide and as long and wide as one of the tribes'
shares. It will run from the east side to the west
side. The Temple[d] will be in the middle of this
area.
9"The share which you will give the Lord will
be about seven miles long and three miles wide.
10The holy area will be divided among these people. The priests will have land about seven miles
long on the north and south sides, and three miles
wide on the west and east sides. The Temple of
the Lord will be in the middle of it. 11This land
is for the priests who are given the holy duty of
serving the Lord. They are the descendants[d] of
Zadok who did my work and did not leave me
when Israel and the Levites left me. 12They will
have as their share a very holy part of the holy
portion of the land. It will be next to the land of
the Levites.
13"Alongside the land for the priests, the Levites will have a share about seven miles long and
three miles wide; its full length will be about
seven miles and its full width about three miles.
14The Levites are not to sell or trade any of this
land. They are not to let anyone else own any of
this best part of the land, because it belongs to the
Lord.

City Property

15"The rest of the area will be about one and
one-half miles wide and seven miles long. It will
not be holy but will belong to the city and be used
for homes and pastures. The city will be in the
middle of it. 16These are the city's measurements: the north side will be about one mile,
the south side about one mile, the east side
about one mile, and the west side about one
mile. 17The city's land for pastures will be about
four hundred thirty-seven feet on the north, four
hundred thirty-seven feet on the south, four hundred thirty-seven feet on the east, and four
hundred thirty-seven feet on the west. 18Along the
long side of the holy area there will be left three
miles on the east and three miles on the west. It

will be used to grow food for the city workers.
19 The city workers from all the tribes[d] of Israel
will farm this land. 20 This whole area will be
square, seven miles by seven miles. You shall give
to the LORD the holy share along with the city
property.

21 "Land that is left over on both sides of the
holy area and city property will belong to the
ruler. That land will extend east of the holy area
to the eastern border and west of it to the Mediterranean Sea. Both of these areas run the length
of the lands of the tribes, and they belong to the
ruler. The holy area with the Holy Place of the
Temple[d] will be in the middle. 22 The Levites' land
and the city property will be in the middle of
the lands belonging to the ruler. Those lands
will be between Judah's border and Benjamin's
border.

The Other Tribes' Land

23 "Here is what the rest of the tribes will receive: Benjamin will have one share. It will go
from the east side to the Mediterranean Sea on
the west side.

24 "South of Benjamin's land, Simeon will have
one share. It will go from the east side to the west
side.

25 "South of Simeon's land, Issachar will have
one share. It will go from the east side to the west
side.

26 "South of Issachar's land, Zebulun will have
one share. It will go from the east side to the west
side.

27 "South of Zebulun's land, Gad will have one
share. It will go from the east side to the west
side.

28 "The southern border of Gad's land will go
east from Tamar on the Dead Sea[d] to the waters
of Meribah Kadesh. Then it will run along the
brook of Egypt to the Mediterranean Sea.

29 "This is the land you will divide among the
tribes of Israel to be their shares," says the Lord
GOD.

The Gates of the City

30 "These will be the outside borders of the city:
The north side will measure more than one mile.
31 There will be three gates facing north: Reuben's
Gate, Judah's Gate, and Levi's Gate, named for
the tribes[d] of Israel.

32 "The east side will measure more than one
mile. There will be three gates facing east: Joseph's Gate, Benjamin's Gate, and Dan's Gate.

33 "The south side will measure more than one
mile. There will be three gates facing south: Simeon's Gate, Issachar's Gate, and Zebulun's Gate.

34 "The west side will measure more than one
mile. There will be three gates facing west: Gad's
Gate, Asher's Gate, and Naphtali's Gate.

35 "The city will measure about six miles
around. From then on the name of the city will
be The LORD Is There."

DANIEL

Why Read This Book:

- Find courage to stand against pressure to compromise your beliefs (Daniel 1—6).
- Be assured that God works through history to fulfill his purposes (Daniel 7—12).

Behind the Scenes:

After moving to a new town, he quickly became popular. People respected him. Then he started getting pressured to compromise—to do things he knew were wrong. Saying no would have been easier if the people pressuring him weren't so important. He had to please them, didn't he?

It sounds like something that could happen today, right? But it's a story set twenty-five hundred years ago. Daniel had been dragged off to Babylon (modern-day Iraq) when the empire conquered Judah. Because of Daniel's ability to interpret dreams, the king chose him to be an important adviser.

But Daniel's career took a downward turn when he resisted the pressure to set aside his faith and worship the king. Because he wouldn't give in, he was sent to die in a den of lions, but God's power protected him. Through everything, Daniel remained faithful to God.

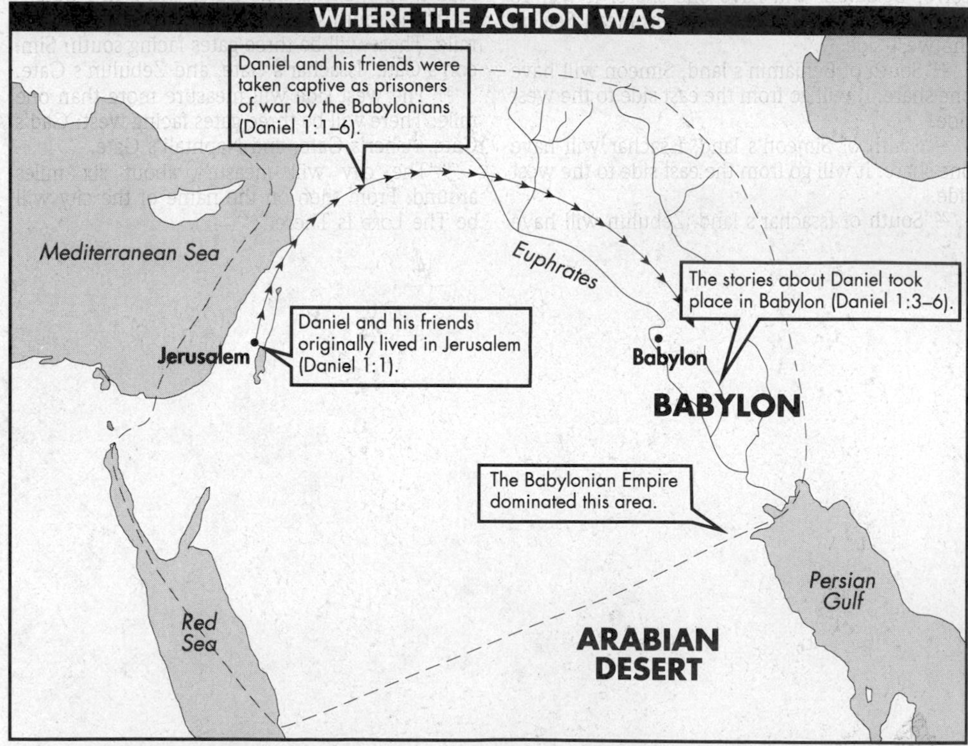

WHERE THE ACTION WAS
Daniel and his friends were taken captive as prisoners of war by the Babylonians (Daniel 1:1–6).
Mediterranean Sea
Euphrates
The stories about Daniel took place in Babylon (Daniel 1:3–6).
Daniel and his friends originally lived in Jerusalem (Daniel 1:1).
Jerusalem
Babylon
BABYLON
The Babylonian Empire dominated this area.
Persian Gulf
Red Sea
ARABIAN DESERT

WHEN THE ACTION WAS

- 1000BC — David was Israel's king
- 750BC — The Northern Kingdom (Israel) fell to Assyria
- The Southern Kingdom (Judah) fell, and Daniel was taken to Babylon
- 500BC — People began returning to Jerusalem from Babylon
- 250BC
- BC/AD — Jesus was born

Behind the Scenes (cont.): The book of Daniel has two parts. In the first part (chapters 1—6), we read the heroic story of Daniel and his friends. Then chapters 7—12 consist of Daniel's unusual visions that include strange symbols and heavenly messengers that proclaim God's Word.

Though parts of Daniel are difficult to understand, the book's underlying message is consistent: God is in control of history. Even when things get rough and we are under pressure, we can know that God is working to protect his people and advance his purposes in the world. We, like Daniel, should rely on God and remain faithful to God, no matter what happens.

Daniel Taken to Babylon

1 During the third year that Jehoiakim was king of Judah, Nebuchadnezzar king of Babylon came to Jerusalem and surrounded it with his army. 2The Lord allowed Nebuchadnezzar to capture Jehoiakim king of Judah. Nebuchadnezzar also took some of the things from the Temple[d] of God, which he carried to Babylonia and put in the temple of his gods.

3Then King Nebuchadnezzar ordered Ashpenaz, his chief officer, to bring some of the Israelite men into his palace. He wanted them to be from important families, including the family of the king of Judah. 4King Nebuchadnezzar wanted only young Israelite men who had nothing wrong with them. They were to be handsome and well educated, capable of learning and understanding, and able to serve in his palace. Ashpenaz was to teach them the language and writings of the Babylonians. 5The king gave the young men a certain amount of food and wine every day, just like the food he ate. The young men were to be trained for three years, and then they would become servants of the king of Babylon. 6Among those young men were Daniel, Hananiah, Mishael, and Azariah from the people of Judah.

> **SIDELIGHT:** In Old Testament times, names had important meanings. All four of the Israelites' names in Daniel 1:6 included syllables meaning God (El) or the Lord God (Yah). So these faithful men probably weren't excited when they were given Babylonian names, some of which included the names of false gods.

7Ashpenaz, the chief officer, gave them Babylonian names. Daniel's new name was Belteshazzar, Hananiah's was Shadrach, Mishael's was Meshach, and Azariah's was Abednego.

8Daniel decided not to eat the king's food or drink his wine because that would make him unclean.[d] So he asked Ashpenaz for permission not to make himself unclean in this way.

9God made Ashpenaz, the chief officer, want to be kind and merciful to Daniel, 10but Ashpenaz said to Daniel, "I am afraid of my master, the king. He ordered me to give you this food and drink. If you begin to look worse than other young men your age, the king will see this. Then he will cut off my head because of you."

11Ashpenaz had ordered a guard to watch Daniel, Hananiah, Mishael, and Azariah. 12Daniel said to the guard, "Please give us this test for ten days: Don't give us anything but vegetables to eat and water to drink. 13After ten days compare how we look with how the other young men look who eat the king's food. See for yourself and then decide how you want to treat us, your servants."

14So the guard agreed to test them for ten days. 15After ten days they looked healthier and better fed than all the young men who ate the king's food. 16So the guard took away the king's special food and wine, feeding them vegetables instead.

17God gave these four young men wisdom and the ability to learn many things that people had written and studied. Daniel could also understand visions and dreams.

18At the end of the time set for them by the king, Ashpenaz brought all the young men to King Nebuchadnezzar. 19The king talked to them and found that none of the young men were as good as Daniel, Hananiah, Mishael, and Azariah. So those four young men became the king's servants. 20Every time the king asked them about something important, they showed much wisdom and understanding. They were ten times better than all the fortune-tellers and magicians in his kingdom! 21So Daniel continued to be the king's servant until the first year Cyrus was king.

Nebuchadnezzar's Dream

2 During Nebuchadnezzar's second year as king, he had dreams that bothered him and kept him awake at night. 2So the king called for his fortune-tellers, magicians, wizards, and wise men, because he wanted them to tell him what he had dreamed. They came in and stood in front of the king.

3Then the king said to them, "I had a dream that bothers me, and I want to know what it means."

4The wise men answered the king in the Aramaic language, "O king, live forever! Please tell us, your servants, your dream. Then we will tell you what it means."

5King Nebuchadnezzar said to them, "I meant what I said. You must tell me the dream and what it means. If you don't, I will have you torn apart, and I will turn your houses into piles of stones. 6But if you tell me my dream and its meaning, I will reward you with gifts and great honor. So tell me the dream and what it means."

7Again the wise men said to the king, "Tell us, your servants, the dream, and we will tell you what it means."

8King Nebuchadnezzar answered, "I know you are trying to get more time, because you know that I meant what I said. 9If you don't tell me my dream, you will be punished. You have all agreed to tell me lies and wicked things, hoping things will change. Now, tell me the dream so that I will know you can tell me what it really means!"

10The wise men answered the king, saying, "No one on earth can do what the king asks! No great and powerful king has ever asked the fortune-tellers, magicians, or wise men to do this; 11the king is asking something that is too hard. Only the gods could tell the king this, but the gods do not live among people."

12When the king heard their answer, he became very angry. He ordered that all the wise men of Babylon be killed. 13So King Nebuchadnezzar's order to kill the wise men was announced, and men were sent to look for Daniel and his friends to kill them.

14Arioch, the commander of the king's guards, was going to kill the wise men of Babylon. But Daniel spoke to him with wisdom and skill, 15saying, "Why did the king order such a terrible punishment?" Then Arioch explained everything to Daniel. 16So Daniel went to King Nebuchadnezzar and asked for an appointment so that he could tell the king what his dream meant.

17Then Daniel went to his house and explained the whole story to his friends Hananiah, Mishael, and Azariah. 18Daniel asked his friends to pray that the God of heaven would show them mercy and help them understand this secret so he and his friends would not be killed with the other wise men of Babylon.

19During the night God explained the secret to Daniel in a vision. Then Daniel praised the God of heaven. 20Daniel said:

"Praise God forever and ever,
because he has wisdom and power.
21He changes the times and seasons of the year.
He takes away the power of kings
and gives their power to new kings.
He gives wisdom to those who are wise
and knowledge to those who understand.
22He makes known secrets that are deep and hidden;
he knows what is hidden in darkness,
and light is all around him.
23I thank you and praise you, God of my ancestors,
because you have given me wisdom and power.
You told me what we asked of you;
you told us about the king's dream."

The Meaning of the Dream

24Then Daniel went to Arioch, the man King Nebuchadnezzar had chosen to kill the wise men of Babylon. Daniel said to him, "Don't put the wise men of Babylon to death. Take me to the king, and I will tell him what his dream means."

25Very quickly Arioch took Daniel to the king and said, "I have found a man among the captives from Judah who can tell the king what his dream means."

26The king asked Daniel, who was also called Belteshazzar, "Are you able to tell me what I dreamed and what it means?"

27Daniel answered, "No wise man, magician, or fortune-teller can explain to the king the secret he has asked about. 28But there is a God in heaven who explains secret things, and he has shown King Nebuchadnezzar what will happen at a later time. This is your dream, the vision you saw while lying on your bed: 29O king, as you were lying there, you thought about things to come. God, who can tell people about secret things, showed you what is going to happen. 30God also told this secret to me, not because I have greater wisdom than any other living person, but so that you may know what it means. In that way you will understand what went through your mind.

31"O king, in your dream you saw a huge, shiny, and frightening statue in front of you. 32The head of the statue was made of pure gold. Its chest and arms were made of silver. Its stomach and the upper part of its legs were made of bronze. 33The lower part of the legs were made of iron, while its feet were made partly of iron and partly of baked clay. 34While you were looking at the statue, you saw a rock cut free, but no human being touched the rock. It hit the statue on its feet of iron and clay and smashed them. 35Then the iron, clay, bronze, silver, and gold broke to pieces at the same time. They became like chaff[d] on a threshing[d] floor in the summertime; the wind blew them away, and there was nothing left. Then the rock that hit the statue became a very large mountain that filled the whole earth.

36"That was your dream. Now we will tell the king what it means. 37O king, you are the greatest king. God of heaven has given you a kingdom, power, strength, and glory. 38Wherever people,

wild animals, and birds live, God made you ruler
over them. King Nebuchadnezzar, you are the
head of gold on that statue.

39"Another kingdom will come after you, but it
will not be as great as yours. Next a third kingdom, the bronze part, will rule over the earth.
40Then there will be a fourth kingdom, strong as
iron. In the same way that iron crushes and
smashes things to pieces, the fourth kingdom will
smash and crush all the other kingdoms.

41"You saw that the statue's feet and toes were
partly baked clay and partly iron. That means the
fourth kingdom will be a divided kingdom. It will
have some of the strength of iron in it, just as you
saw iron was mixed with clay. 42The toes of the
statue were partly iron and partly clay. So the
fourth kingdom will be partly strong like iron and
partly breakable like clay. 43You saw the iron
mixed with clay, but iron and clay do not hold
together. In the same way the people of the fourth
kingdom will be a mixture, but they will not be
united as one people.

44"During the time of those kings, the God of
heaven will set up another kingdom that will
never be destroyed or given to another group of
people. This kingdom will crush all the other
kingdoms and bring them to an end, but it will
continue forever.

45"King Nebuchadnezzar, you saw a rock cut
from a mountain, but no human being touched it.
The rock broke the iron, bronze, clay, silver, and
gold to pieces. In this way the great God showed
you what will happen. The dream is true, and you
can trust this explanation."

46Then King Nebuchadnezzar fell facedown on
the ground in front of Daniel. The king honored
him and commanded that an offering and incense[d] be presented to him. 47Then the king said
to Daniel, "Truly I know your God is the greatest
of all gods, the Lord of all the kings. He tells people about things they cannot know. I know this is
true, because you were able to tell these secret
things to me."

48Then the king gave Daniel many gifts plus an
important position in his kingdom. Nebuchadnezzar made him ruler over the whole area of Babylon and put him in charge of all the wise men of
Babylon. 49Daniel asked the king to make Shadrach, Meshach, and Abednego leaders over the
area of Babylon, so the king did as Daniel asked.
Daniel himself became one of the people who
stayed at the royal court.

The Gold Idol and Blazing Furnace

3 King Nebuchadnezzar made a gold statue
ninety feet high and nine feet wide and set
it up on the plain of Dura in the area of Babylon.
2Then he called for the leaders: the governors,
assistant governors, captains of the soldiers, people who advised the king, keepers of the treasury,
judges, rulers, and all other officers in his kingdom. He wanted them to come to the special service for the statue he had set up. 3So they all came
for the special service and stood in front of the
statue that King Nebuchadnezzar had set up.
4Then the man who made announcements for the
king said in a loud voice, "People, nations, and
those of every language, this is what you are commanded to do: 5When you hear the sound of the
horns, flutes, lyres,[d] zithers,[n] harps, pipes, and all
the other musical instruments, you must bow
down and worship the gold statue that King Nebuchadnezzar has set up. 6Anyone who doesn't
bow down and worship will immediately be
thrown into a blazing furnace."

7Now people, nations, and those who spoke every language were there. When they heard the
sound of the horns, flutes, lyres, zithers, pipes,
and all the other musical instruments, they
bowed down and worshiped the gold statue King
Nebuchadnezzar had set up.

8Then some Babylonians came up to the king
and began speaking against the men of Judah.
9They said to King Nebuchadnezzar, "O king, live
forever! 10O king, you gave a command that everyone who heard the horns, lyres, zithers, harps,
pipes, and all the other musical instruments
would have to bow down and worship the gold
statue. 11Anyone who wouldn't do this was to be
thrown into a blazing furnace. 12O king, there are
some men of Judah whom you made officers in
the area of Babylon that did not pay attention to
your order. Their names are Shadrach, Meshach,
and Abednego. They do not serve your gods and
do not worship the gold statue you have set up."

13Nebuchadnezzar became very angry and
called for Shadrach, Meshach, and Abednego.
When they were brought to the king, 14Nebu-
chadnezzar said, "Shadrach, Meshach, and Abednego, is it true that you do not serve my gods nor
worship the gold statue I have set up? 15In a moment you will again hear the sound of the horns,
flutes, lyres, zithers, harps, pipes, and all the other
musical instruments. If you bow down and worship the statue I made, that will be good. But if
you do not worship it, you will immediately be
thrown into the blazing furnace. What god will be
able to save you from my power then?"

16Shadrach, Meshach, and Abednego answered
the king, saying, "Nebuchadnezzar, we do not
need to defend ourselves to you. 17If you throw us
into the blazing furnace, the God we serve is able
to save us from the furnace. He will save us from
your power, O king. 18But even if God does not

zithers Musical instruments with thirty to forty strings.

save us, we want you, O king, to know this: We will not serve your gods or worship the gold statue you have set up."

19Then Nebuchadnezzar was furious with Shadrach, Meshach, and Abednego, and he changed his mind. He ordered the furnace to be heated seven times hotter than usual. 20Then he commanded some of the strongest soldiers in his army to tie up Shadrach, Meshach, and Abednego and throw them into the blazing furnace.

21So Shadrach, Meshach, and Abednego were tied up and thrown into the blazing furnace while still wearing their robes, trousers, turbans, and other clothes. 22The king's command was very strict, and the furnace was made so hot that the flames killed the strong soldiers who threw Shadrach, Meshach, and Abednego into the furnace. 23Firmly tied, Shadrach, Meshach, and Abednego fell into the blazing furnace.

24Then King Nebuchadnezzar was so surprised that he jumped to his feet. He asked the men who advised him, "Didn't we tie up only three men and throw them into the fire?"

They answered, "Yes, O king."

25The king said, "Look! I see four men walking around in the fire. They are not tied up, and they are not burned. The fourth man looks like a son of the gods."

26Then Nebuchadnezzar went to the opening of the blazing furnace and shouted, "Shadrach, Meshach, and Abednego, come out! Servants of the Most High God, come here!"

So Shadrach, Meshach, and Abednego came out of the fire. 27When they came out, the governors, assistant governors, captains of the soldiers, and royal advisers crowded around them and saw that the fire had not harmed their bodies. Their hair was not burned, their robes were not burned, and they didn't even smell like smoke!

SIDELIGHT: *We can hope that Shadrach, Meshach, and Abednego weren't wearing any jewelry when they were thrown into the blazing furnace (Daniel 3:16–27). The furnace would have been one used to smelt metals. Archaeologists have uncovered this kind of furnace, which is about nine feet in diameter.*

28Then Nebuchadnezzar said, "Praise the God of Shadrach, Meshach, and Abednego. Their God has sent his angel and saved his servants from the fire! These three men trusted their God and refused to obey my command. They were willing to die rather than serve or worship any god other than their own. 29So I now give this command: Anyone from any nation or language who says anything against the God of Shadrach, Meshach, and Abednego will be torn apart and have his house turned into a pile of stones. No other god can save his people like this." 30Then the king promoted Shadrach, Meshach, and Abednego in the area of Babylon.

Nebuchadnezzar's Dream of a Tree

4 King Nebuchadnezzar sent this letter to the people, nations, and those who speak every language in all the world:

I wish you peace and great wealth!

2The Most High God has done miracles[d] and wonderful things for me that I am happy to tell you about.

3His wonderful acts are great,
and his miracles are mighty.
His kingdom goes on forever,
and his rule continues from now on.

4I, Nebuchadnezzar, was happy and successful at my palace, 5but I had a dream that made me afraid. As I was lying on my bed, I saw pictures and visions in my mind that alarmed me. 6So I ordered all the wise men of Babylon to come to me and tell me what my dream meant. 7The fortune-tellers, magicians, and wise men came, and I told them about the dream. But they could not tell me what it meant.

8Finally, Daniel came to me. (I called him Belteshazzar to honor my god, because the spirit of the holy gods is in him.) I told my dream to him. 9I said, "Belteshazzar, you are the most important of all the fortune-tellers. I know that the spirit of the holy gods is in you, so there is no secret that is too hard for you to understand. This was what I dreamed; tell me what it means. 10These are the visions I saw while I was lying in my bed: I looked, and there in front of me was a tree standing in the middle of the earth. And it was very tall. 11The tree grew large and strong. The top of the tree touched the sky and could be seen from anywhere on earth. 12The leaves of the tree were beautiful. It had plenty of good fruit on it, enough food for everyone. The wild animals found shelter under the tree, and the birds lived in its branches. Every animal ate from it.

13"As I was looking at those things in the vision while lying on my bed, I saw an observer, a holy angel coming down from heaven. 14He spoke very loudly and said, 'Cut down the tree and cut off its branches. Strip off its leaves and scatter its fruit. Let the animals under the tree run away, and let the birds in its branches fly away. [15]But leave the stump and its roots in the ground with a band of iron and bronze around it; let it stay in the field with the grass around it.

" 'Let the man become wet with dew, and let him live among the animals and plants of the earth. [16]Let him not think like a human any longer, but let him have the mind of an animal for seven years.

[17]" 'The observers gave this command; the holy ones declared the sentence. This is so all people may know that the Most High God rules over every kingdom on earth. God gives those kingdoms to anyone he wants, and he chooses people to rule them who are not proud.'

[18]"That is what I, King Nebuchadnezzar, dreamed. Now Belteshazzar,[n] tell me what the dream means. None of the wise men in my kingdom can explain it to me, but you can, because the spirit of the holy gods is in you."

Daniel Explains the Dream

[19]Then Daniel, who was called Belteshazzar, was very quiet for a while, because his understanding of the dream frightened him. So the king said, "Belteshazzar, do not let the dream or its meaning make you afraid."

Then Belteshazzar answered, "My master, I wish the dream were about your enemies, and I wish its meaning were for those who are against you! [20]You saw a tree in your dream that grew large and strong. Its top touched the sky, and it could be seen from all over the earth. [21]Its leaves were beautiful, and it had plenty of fruit for everyone to eat. It was a home for the wild animals, and its branches were nesting places for the birds. [22]O king, you are that tree! You have become great and powerful, like the tall tree that touched the sky. Your power reaches to the far parts of the earth.

[23]"O king, you saw an observer, a holy angel, coming down from heaven who said, 'Cut down the tree and destroy it. But leave the stump and its roots in the ground with a band of iron and bronze around it; leave it in the field with the grass. Let him become wet with dew and live like a wild animal for seven years.'

[24]"This is the meaning of the dream, O king. The Most High God has commanded these things to happen to my master the king: [25]You will be forced away from people to live among the wild animals. People will feed you grass like an ox, and dew from the sky will make you wet. Seven years will pass, and then you will learn this lesson: The Most High God is ruler over every kingdom on earth, and he gives those kingdoms to anyone he chooses.

[26]"Since the stump of the tree and its roots were left in the ground, your kingdom will be given back to you when you learn that one in heaven rules your kingdom. [27]So, O king, please accept my advice. Stop sinning and do what is right. Stop doing wicked things and be kind to the poor. Then you might continue to be successful."

The King's Dream Comes True

[28]All these things happened to King Nebuchadnezzar. [29]Twelve months later as he was walking on the roof[n] of his palace in Babylon, [30]he said, "I have built this great Babylon as my royal home. I built it by my power to show my glory and my majesty."

[31]The words were still in his mouth when a voice from heaven said, "King Nebuchadnezzar, these things will happen to you: Your royal power has been taken away from you. [32]You will be forced away from people. You will live with the wild animals and will be fed grass like an ox. Seven years will pass before you learn this lesson: The Most High God rules over every kingdom on earth and gives those kingdoms to anyone he chooses."

[33]Immediately the words came true. Nebuchadnezzar was forced to go away from people, and he began eating grass like an ox. He became wet from dew. His hair grew long like the feathers of an eagle, and his nails grew like the claws of a bird.

SIDELIGHT: The power-hungry, grass-chomping King Nebuchadnezzar may have suffered from pica, an unnatural craving for unusual objects (Daniel 4:33). It's the same word used for pregnant women who crave clay or paint!

[34]At the end of that time, I, Nebuchadnezzar, looked up toward heaven, and I could think normally again! Then I gave praise to the Most High God; I gave honor and glory to him who lives forever.

Belteshazzar Another name for Daniel.
roof In Bible times houses were built with flat roofs. The roof was used for drying things such as flax and fruit. And it was used as an extra room, as a place for worship, and as a place to sleep in the summer.

God's rule is forever,
and his kingdom continues for all time.
35People on earth
are not truly important.
God does what he wants
with the powers of heaven
and the people on earth.
No one can stop his powerful hand
or question what he does.

36At that time I could think normally again, and God gave back my great honor and power and returned the glory to my kingdom. The people who advised me and the royal family came to me for help again. I became king again and was even greater and more powerful than before. 37Now I, Nebuchadnezzar, give praise and honor and glory to the King of heaven. Everything he does is right and fair, and he is able to make proud people humble.

The Writing on the Wall

5 King Belshazzar gave a big banquet for a thousand royal guests and drank wine with them. 2As Belshazzar was drinking his wine, he gave orders to bring the gold and silver cups that his ancestor Nebuchadnezzar had taken from the Temple[d] in Jerusalem. This was so the king, his royal guests, his wives, and his slave women[d] could drink from those cups. 3So they brought the gold cups that had been taken from the Temple of God in Jerusalem. And the king and his royal guests, his wives, and his slave women drank from them. 4As they were drinking, they praised their gods, which were made from gold, silver, bronze, iron, wood, and stone.

5Suddenly the fingers of a person's hand appeared and began writing on the plaster of the wall, near the lampstand in the royal palace. The king watched the hand as it wrote.

6King Belshazzar was very frightened. His face turned white, his knees knocked together, and he could not stand up because his legs were too weak. 7The king called for the magicians, wise men, and wizards of Babylon and said to them, "Anyone who can read this writing and explain it will receive purple clothes fit for a king and a gold chain around his neck. And I will make that person the third highest ruler in the kingdom."

8Then all the king's wise men came in, but they could not read the writing or tell the king what it meant. 9King Belshazzar became even more afraid, and his face became even whiter. His royal guests were confused.

10Then the king's mother, who had heard the voices of the king and his royal guests, came into the banquet room. She said, "O king, live forever! Don't be afraid or let your face be white with fear! 11There is a man in your kingdom who has the spirit of the holy gods. In the days of your father, this man showed understanding, knowledge, and wisdom like the gods. Your father, King Nebuchadnezzar, put this man in charge of all the wise men, fortune-tellers, magicians, and wizards. 12The man I am talking about is named Daniel, whom the king named Belteshazzar. He was very smart and had knowledge and understanding. He could explain dreams and secrets and could answer very hard problems. Call for Daniel. He will tell you what the writing on the wall means."

13So they brought Daniel to the king, and the king asked, "Is your name Daniel? Are you one of the captives my father the king brought from Judah? 14I have heard that the spirit of the gods is in you, and that you are very smart and have knowledge and extraordinary understanding. 15The wise men and magicians were brought to me to read this writing and to explain what it means, but they could not explain it. 16I have heard that you are able to explain what things mean and can find the answers to hard problems. Read this writing on the wall and explain it to me. If you can, I will give you purple clothes fit for a king and a gold chain to wear around your neck. And you will become the third highest ruler in the kingdom."

17Then Daniel answered the king, "You may keep your gifts for yourself, or you may give those rewards to someone else. But I will read the writing on the wall for you and will explain to you what it means.

18"O king, the Most High God made your father Nebuchadnezzar a great, important, and powerful king. 19Because God made him important, all the people, nations, and those who spoke every language were very frightened of Nebuchadnezzar. If he wanted someone to die, he killed that person. If he wanted someone to live, he let that person live. Those he wanted to promote, he promoted. Those he wanted to be less important, he made less important.

20"But Nebuchadnezzar became too proud and stubborn, so he was taken off his royal throne. His glory was taken away. 21He was forced away from people, and his mind became like the mind of an animal. He lived with the wild donkeys and was fed grass like an ox and became wet with dew. These things happened to him until he learned his lesson: The Most High God rules over every kingdom on earth, and he sets anyone he chooses over those kingdoms.

22"Belshazzar, you already knew these things, because you are a descendant[d] of Nebuchadnezzar. Still you have not been sorry for what you have done. 23Instead, you have set yourself against the Lord of heaven. You ordered the drinking cups from the Temple of the Lord to be brought to you. Then you and your royal guests, your wives, and your slave women drank wine from them. You praised the gods of silver, gold, bronze, iron, wood, and stone that are not really gods; they cannot see or hear or understand anything. You did not honor God, who has power over your life and everything you do. 24So God sent the hand that wrote on the wall.

25"These are the words that were written on the wall: 'Mene, mene, tekel, and parsin.'

26"This is what the words mean: Mene: God has counted the days until your kingdom will end. 27Tekel: You have been weighed on the scales and found not good enough. 28Parsin: Your kingdom is being divided and will be given to the Medes and the Persians."

29Then Belshazzar gave an order for Daniel to be dressed in purple clothes and to have a gold chain put around his neck. And it was announced that Daniel was the third highest ruler in the king dom. 30That very same night Belshazzar, king of the Babylonian people, was killed. 31So Darius the Mede became the new king when he was sixty-two years old.

Daniel and the Lions

6 Darius thought it would be a good idea to choose one hundred twenty governors who would rule his kingdom. 2He chose three men as supervisors over those governors, and Daniel was one of the supervisors. The supervisors were to ensure that the governors did not try to cheat the king. 3Daniel showed that he could do the work better than the other supervisors and governors, so the king planned to put Daniel in charge of the whole kingdom. 4Because of this, the other supervisors and governors tried to find reasons to accuse Daniel about his work in the government. But they could not find anything wrong with him or any reason to accuse him, because he was trustworthy and not lazy or dishonest. 5Finally these men said, "We will never find any reason to accuse Daniel unless it is about the law of his God."

6So the supervisors and governors went as a group to the king and said: "King Darius, live forever! 7The supervisors, assistant governors, governors, the people who advise you, and the captains of the soldiers have all agreed that you should make a new law for everyone to obey: For the next thirty days no one should pray to any god or human except to you, O king. Anyone who doesn't obey will be thrown into the lions' den. 8Now, O king, make the law and sign your name to it so that it cannot be changed, because then it will be a law of the Medes and Persians and cannot be canceled." 9So King Darius signed the law.

10Even though Daniel knew that the new law had been written, he went to pray in an upstairs room in his house, which had windows that opened toward Jerusalem. Three times each day Daniel would kneel down to pray and thank God, just as he always had done.

SIDELIGHT: Daniel really wanted God's attention when he dropped to his knees in prayer (Daniel 6:10). His fellow Jews normally stood when they addressed God.

11Then those men went as a group and found Daniel praying and asking God for help. 12So they went to the king and talked to him about the law he had made. They said, "Didn't you sign a law that says no one may pray to any god or human except you, O king? Doesn't it say that anyone who disobeys during the next thirty days will be thrown into the lions' den?"

The king answered, "Yes, that is the law, and the laws of the Medes and Persians cannot be canceled."

13Then they said to the king, "Daniel, one of the captives from Judah, is not paying attention to you, O king, or to the law you signed. Daniel still prays to his God three times every day." 14The king became very upset when he heard this. He wanted to save Daniel, and he worked hard until sunset trying to think of a way to save him.

15Then those men went as a group to the king. They said, "Remember, O king, the law of the Medes and Persians says that no law or command given by the king can be changed."

16So King Darius gave the order, and Daniel was brought in and thrown into the lions' den. The king said to Daniel, "May the God you serve all the time save you!" 17A big stone was brought and placed over the opening of the lions' den. Then the king used his signet[d] ring and the rings of his royal officers to put special seals[d] on the rock. This ensured that no one would move the rock and bring Daniel out. 18Then King Darius went back to his palace. He did not eat that night, he did not have any entertainment brought to him, and he could not sleep.

19The next morning King Darius got up at dawn and hurried to the lions' den. 20As he came near the den, he was worried. He called out to Daniel, "Daniel, servant of the living God! Has your God that you always worship been able to save you from the lions?"

21Daniel answered, "O king, live forever! 22My God sent his angel to close the lions' mouths. They have not hurt me, because my God knows

I am innocent. I never did anything wrong to you,
O king."
23King Darius was very happy and told his servants to lift Daniel out of the lions' den. So they
lifted him out and did not find any injury on him,
because Daniel had trusted in his God.
24Then the king commanded that the men who
had accused Daniel be brought to the lions' den.
They, their wives, and their children were thrown
into the den. The lions grabbed them before they
hit the floor of the den and crushed their bones.
25Then King Darius wrote a letter to all people
and all nations, to those who spoke every language in the world:

I wish you great peace and wealth.

26I am making a new law for people in
every part of my kingdom. All of you must
fear and respect the God of Daniel.

Daniel's God is the living God;
he lives forever.
His kingdom will never be destroyed,
and his rule will never end.
27God rescues and saves people
and does mighty miracles[d]
in heaven and on earth.
He is the one who saved Daniel
from the power of the lions.

28So Daniel was successful during the time Darius was king and when Cyrus the Persian was
king.

Daniel's Dream about Four Animals

7 In Belshazzar's first year as king of Babylon,
Daniel had a dream. He saw visions as he
was lying on his bed, and he wrote down what he
had dreamed.
2Daniel said: "I saw my vision at night. In the
vision the wind was blowing from all four directions, which made the sea very rough. 3I saw four
huge animals come up from the sea, and each animal was different from the others.
4"The first animal looked like a lion, but had
wings like an eagle. I watched this animal until its
wings were torn off. It was lifted from the ground
so that it stood up on two feet like a human, and
it was given the mind of a human.
5Then I saw a second animal before me that
looked like a bear. It was raised up on one of its
sides and had three ribs in its mouth between its
teeth. It was told, 'Get up and eat all the meat you
want!'
6"After that, I looked, and there before me was
another animal. This animal looked like a leopard
with four wings on its back that looked like a
bird's wings. This animal had four heads and was
given power to rule.
7"After that, in my vision at night I saw in front
of me a fourth animal that was cruel, terrible, and
very strong. It had large iron teeth. It crushed and
ate what it killed, and then it walked on whatever
was left. This fourth animal was different from
any animal I had seen before, and it had ten
horns.
8"While I was thinking about the horns, another horn grew up among them. It was a little
horn with eyes like a human's eyes. It also had a
mouth, and the mouth was bragging. The little
horn pulled out three of the other horns.
9"As I looked,
thrones were put in their places,
and God, who has been alive forever, sat
on his throne.
His clothes were white like snow,
and the hair on his head was white like
wool.
His throne was made from fire,
and the wheels of his throne were blazing
with fire.
10A river of fire was flowing
from in front of him.
Many thousands of angels were serving him,
and millions of angels stood before him.
Court was ready to begin,
and the books were opened.
11"I kept on looking because the little horn was
bragging. I kept watching until finally the fourth
animal was killed. Its body was destroyed, and it
was thrown into the burning fire. 12(The power
and rule of the other animals had been taken from
them, but they were permitted to live for a certain
period of time.)
13"In my vision at night I saw in front of me
someone who looked like a human being coming
on the clouds in the sky. He came near God, who
has been alive forever, and he was led to God.
14He was given authority, glory, and the strength
of a king. People of every tribe,[d] nation, and language will serve him. His rule will last forever,
and his kingdom will never be destroyed.

The Meaning of the Dream

15"I, Daniel, was worried. The visions that
went through my mind frightened me. 16I came
near one of those standing there and asked what
all this meant.
"So he told me and explained to me what these
things meant: 17'The four great animals are four
kingdoms that will come from the earth. 18But the
holy people who belong to the Most High God
will receive the power to rule and will have the
power to rule forever, from now on.'
19"Then I wanted to know what the fourth animal meant, because it was different from all the
others. It was very terrible and had iron teeth and
bronze claws. It was the animal that crushed and
ate what it killed and then walked on whatever

was left. 20I also wanted to know about the ten
horns on its head and about the little horn that
grew there. It had pulled out three of the other
ten horns and looked greater than the others. It
had eyes and a mouth that kept bragging. 21As I
watched, the little horn began making war against
God's holy people and was defeating them 22until
God, who has been alive forever, came. He
judged in favor of the holy people who belong to
the Most High God; then the time came for them
to receive the power to rule.
23"And he explained this to me: 'The fourth
animal is a fourth kingdom that will come on the
earth. It will be different from all the other kingdoms and will destroy people all over the world.
It will walk on and crush the whole earth. 24The
ten horns are ten kings who will come from this
fourth kingdom. After those ten kings are gone,
another king will come. He will be different from
the kings who ruled before him, and he will defeat three of the other kings. 25This king will speak
against the Most High God, and he will hurt and
kill God's holy people. He will try to change times
and laws that have already been set. The holy people that belong to God will be in that king's power
for three and one-half years.
26" 'But the court will decide what should happen. The power of the king will be taken away,
and his kingdom will be completely destroyed.
27Then the holy people who belong to the Most
High God will have the power to rule. They will
rule over all the kingdoms under heaven with
power and greatness, and their power to rule will
last forever. People from all the other kingdoms
will respect and serve them.'
28"That was the end of the dream. I, Daniel,
was very afraid. My face became white from fear,
but I kept everything to myself."

Daniel's Vision

8 During the third year of King Belshazzar's
rule, I, Daniel, saw another vision, which
was like the first one. 2In this vision I saw myself
in the capital city of Susa, in the area of Elam. I
was standing by the Ulai Canal 3when I looked up
and saw a male sheep standing beside the canal.
It had two long horns, but one horn was longer

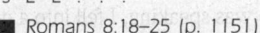

PERSISTENCE

What Do You See?

El Salvador suffered a devastating earthquake in 1986. Thousands of people were hurt and killed, and many buildings were destroyed. Carlos, Raphael and Cecilia, like most other people, were initially overwhelmed by the suffering and destruction. Soon, however, they organized their church's youth group to help. They began by sweeping and mopping floors at their church, which sheltered three hundred refugees. Then they expanded into day care, tutoring, and health-care programs. Seeing the amazing results of their work kept the young people going, even when they felt tired or overwhelmed.

They saw their work as the Christian challenge. Although the earthquake disaster eventually passed, they continued to help the victims of their country's civil war. Their belief in Jesus gave them strength to keep going.

"People must be involved together if progress is to be made," Cecilia explains. "We must be informed of needs in today's world and learn to see through the eyes of Jesus." That's where hope begins.

Daniel faced a similar situation that seemed overwhelming. Read about how he found hope in his vision in **Daniel 7:9–14**.

- How did visions of hope motivate the Salvadoran youth group and help Daniel in his troubles?
- Why might Christian hope give you more strength to persist in difficult times?

CONSIDER . . .

- drawing a symbol for one of the obstacles you face and then drawing a large cross through it. Tape it to your mirror to give you strength to persist in spite of those obstacles.
- reading the newspaper and, for one week, asking God to give hope to those who are hurt or discouraged.

FOR MORE, SEE . . .

- Psalm 71 (p. 523)
- Matthew 26:62–66 (p. 958)
- Romans 8:18–25 (p. 1151)

and newer than the other. 4I watched the sheep
charge to the west, the north, and the south. No
animal could stand before him, and none could
save another animal from his power. He did whatever he wanted and became very powerful.
5While I was watching this, I saw a male goat
come from the west. This goat had one large horn
between his eyes that was easy to see. He crossed
over the whole earth so fast that his feet hardly
touched the ground.
6In his anger the goat charged the sheep with
the two horns that I had seen standing by the
canal. 7I watched the angry goat attack the sheep
and break the sheep's two horns. The sheep was
not strong enough to stop it. The goat knocked
the sheep to the ground and then walked all over
him. No one was able to save the sheep from the
goat, 8so the male goat became very great. But
when he was strong, his big horn broke off and
four horns grew in place of the one big horn.
Those four horns pointed in four different directions and were easy to see.
9Then a little horn grew from one of those four
horns, and it became very big. It grew to the
south, the east, and toward the beautiful land of
Judah. 10That little horn grew until it reached to
the sky. It even threw some of the army of heaven
to the ground and walked on them! 11That little
horn set itself up as equal to God, the Commander of heaven's armies. It stopped the daily
sacrifices that were offered to him, and the Temple,[d] the place where people worshiped him, was
pulled down. 12Because there was a turning away
from God, the people stopped the daily sacrifices.
Truth was thrown down to the ground, and the
horn was successful in everything it did.
13Then I heard a holy angel speaking. Another
holy angel asked the first one, "How long will the
things in this vision last — the daily sacrifices, the
turning away from God that brings destruction,
the Temple[d] being pulled down, and the army of
heaven being walked on?"
14The angel said to me, "This will happen for
twenty-three hundred evenings and mornings.
Then the holy place will be repaired."
15I, Daniel, saw this vision and tried to understand what it meant. In it I saw someone who
looked like a man standing near me. 16And I heard
a man's voice calling from the Ulai Canal: "Gabriel, explain the vision to this man."
17Gabriel came to where I was standing. When
he came close to me, I was very afraid and bowed
facedown on the ground. But Gabriel said to me,
"Human being, understand that this vision is
about the time of the end."
18While Gabriel was speaking, I fell into a deep
sleep with my face on the ground. Then he
touched me and lifted me to my feet. 19He said,
"Now, I will explain to you what will happen in
the time of God's anger. Your vision was about
the set time of the end.
20"You saw a male sheep with two horns,
which are the kings of Media and Persia. 21The
male goat is the king of Greece, and the big horn
between its eyes is the first king. 22The four horns
that grew in the place of the broken horn are four
kingdoms. Those four kingdoms will come from
the nation of the first king, but they will not be
as strong as the first king.
23"When the end comes near for those kingdoms, a bold and cruel king who tells lies will
come. This will happen when many people have
turned against God. 24This king will be very powerful, but his power will not come from himself.
He will cause terrible destruction and will be successful in everything he does. He will destroy
powerful people and even God's holy people.
25This king will succeed by using lies and force.
He will think that he is very important. He will
destroy many people without warning; he will try
to fight even the Prince of princes! But that cruel
king will be destroyed, and not by human power.
26"The vision that has been shown to you about
these evenings and mornings is true. But seal up
the vision, because those things won't happen for
a long time."

SIDELIGHT: When Daniel was told to seal the vision (Daniel 8:26), it probably involved writing it on a scroll, then rolling up the scroll, tying it shut, and fastening the ties with clay. The clay was then imprinted with a ring or stamp with a special seal or emblem on it. Then all the documents were placed in clay jars for safe-keeping.

27I, Daniel, became very weak and was sick for
several days after that vision. Then I got up and
went back to work for the king, but I was very
upset about the vision. I didn't understand what
it meant.

Daniel's Prayer

9 These things happened during the first year
Darius son of Xerxes was king over Babylon.
He was a descendant[d] of the Medes. 2During Darius' first year as king, I, Daniel, was reading the
Scriptures.[d] I saw that the LORD told Jeremiah
that Jerusalem would be empty ruins for seventy
years.
3Then I turned to the Lord God and prayed and
asked him for help. I did not eat any food. To
show my sadness, I put on rough cloth and sat in
ashes. 4I prayed to the LORD my God and told him

about all of our sins. I said, "Lord, you are a great God who causes fear and wonder. You keep your agreement of love with all who love you and obey your commands.

5"But we have sinned and done wrong. We have been wicked and turned against you, your commands, and your laws. 6We did not listen to your servants, the prophets, who spoke for you to our kings, our leaders, our ancestors, and all the people of the land.

7"Lord, you are good and right, but we are full of shame today—the people of Judah and Jerusalem, all the people of Israel, those near and far whom you scattered among many nations because they were not loyal to you. 8LORD, we are all ashamed. Our kings and leaders and our fathers are ashamed, because we have sinned against you.

9"But, Lord our God, you show us mercy and forgive us even though we have turned against you. 10We have not obeyed the LORD our God or the teachings he gave us through his servants, the prophets. 11All the people of Israel have disobeyed your teachings and have turned away, refusing to obey you. So you brought on us the curses and promises of punishment written in the Teachings of Moses, the servant of God, because we sinned against you.

12"You said these things would happen to us and our leaders, and you made them happen; you brought on us a great disaster. Nothing has ever been done on earth like what was done to Jerusalem. 13All this disaster came to us just as it is written in the Teachings of Moses. But we have not pleaded with the LORD our God. We have not stopped sinning. We have not paid attention to your truth. 14The LORD was ready to bring the disaster on us, and he did it because the LORD our God is right in everything he does. But we still did not obey him.

15"Lord our God, you used your power and brought us out of Egypt. Because of that, your name is known even today. But we have sinned and have done wrong. 16Lord, you do what is right, but please do not be angry with Jerusalem, your city on your holy hill. Because of our sins and the evil things done by our ancestors, people all around insult and make fun of Jerusalem and your people.

17"Now, our God, hear the prayers of your servant. Listen to my prayer for help, and for your sake do good things for your holy place that is in ruins. 18My God, pay attention and hear me. Open your eyes and see all the terrible things that have happened to us. See how our lives have been ruined and what has happened to the city that is called by your name. We do not ask these things because we are good; instead, we ask because of your mercy. 19Lord, listen! Lord, forgive! Lord, hear us and do something! For your sake, don't wait, because your city and your people are called by your name."

Gabriel's Explanation

20While I was saying these things in my prayer to the LORD, my God, confessing my sins and the sins of the people of Israel and praying for God's holy hill, 21Gabriel came to me. (I had seen him in my last vision.) He came flying quickly to me about the time of the evening sacrifice, while I was still praying. 22He taught me and said to me, "Daniel, I have come to give you wisdom and to help you understand. 23When you first started praying, an answer was given, and I came to tell you, because God loves you very much. So think about the message and understand the vision.

24"God has ordered four hundred ninety years for your people and your holy city for these reasons: to stop people from turning against God; to put an end to sin; to take away evil; to bring in goodness that continues forever; to bring about the vision and prophecy;[d] and to appoint a most holy place.

25"Learn and understand these things. A command will come to rebuild Jerusalem. The time from this command until the appointed leader comes will be forty-nine years and four hundred thirty-four years. Jerusalem will be rebuilt with streets and a trench filled with water around it, but it will be built in times of trouble. 26After the four hundred thirty-four years the appointed leader will be killed; he will have nothing. The people of the leader who is to come will destroy the city and the holy place. The end of the city will come like a flood, and war will continue until the end. God has ordered that place to be completely destroyed. 27That leader will make firm an agreement with many people for seven years. He will stop the offerings and sacrifices after three and one-half years. A destroyer will do terrible things until the ordered end comes to the destroyed city."

Daniel's Vision of a Man

10 During Cyrus' third year as king of Persia, Daniel, whose name was Belteshazzar, received a vision about a great war. It was a true message that Daniel understood.

2At that time I, Daniel, had been very sad for three weeks. 3I did not eat any fancy food or meat, or drink any wine, or use any perfumed oil for three weeks.

4On the twenty-fourth day of the first month, I was standing beside the great Tigris River. 5While standing there, I looked up and saw a man dressed in linen clothes with a belt of fine gold wrapped around his waist. 6His body was like shiny yellow quartz. His face was bright like lightning, and his eyes were like fire. His arms and legs were shiny like polished bronze, and his voice sounded like the roar of a crowd.

7I, Daniel, was the only person who saw the vision. The men with me did not see it, because they were so frightened that they ran away and hid. 8So I was left alone, watching this great vision. I lost my strength, my face turned white like a dead person, and I was helpless. 9Then I heard the man in the vision speaking. As I listened, I fell into a deep sleep with my face on the ground.

10Then a hand touched me and set me on my hands and knees. I was so afraid that I was shaking. 11The man in the vision said to me, "Daniel, God loves you very much. Think carefully about the words I will speak to you, and stand up, because I have been sent to you." When he said this, I stood up, but I was still shaking.

12Then the man said to me, "Daniel, do not be afraid. Some time ago you decided to get understanding and to humble yourself before your God. Since that time God has listened to you, and I have come because of your prayers. 13But the prince of Persia has been fighting against me for twenty-one days. Then Michael, one of the most important angels, came to help me, because I had been left there with the king of Persia. 14Now I have come to explain to you what will happen to your people, because the vision is about a time in the future."

15While he was speaking to me, I bowed facedown and could not speak. 16Then one who looked like a man touched my lips, so I opened my mouth and started to speak. I said to the one standing in front of me, "Master, I am upset and afraid because of what I saw in the vision. I feel helpless. 17Master, how can I, your servant, talk with you? My strength is gone, and it is hard for me to breathe."

18The one who looked like a man touched me again and gave me strength. 19He said, "Daniel, don't be afraid. God loves you very much. Peace be with you. Be strong now; be courageous."

When he spoke to me, I became stronger and said, "Master, speak, since you have given me strength."

20Then he said, "Daniel, do you know why I have come to you? Soon I must go back to fight against the prince of Persia. When I go, the prince of Greece will come, 21but I must first tell you what is written in the Book of Truth. No one stands with me against these enemies except Michael, the angel ruling over your people.

11 In the first year that Darius the Mede was king, I stood up to support Michael in his fight against the prince of Persia.

Kingdoms of the South and North

2"Now then, Daniel, I tell you the truth: Three more kings will rule in Persia, and then a fourth king will come. He will be much richer than all the kings of Persia before him and will use his riches to get power. He will stir up everyone against the kingdom of Greece. 3Then a mighty king will come, who will rule with great power and will do anything he wants. 4After that king has come, his kingdom will be broken up and divided out toward the four parts of the world. His kingdom will not go to his descendants,[d] and it will not have the power that he had, because his kingdom will be pulled up and given to other people.

5"The king of the South will become strong, but one of his commanders will become even stronger. He will begin to rule his own kingdom with great power. 6Then after a few years, a new friendship will develop. The daughter of the king of the South will marry the king of the North in order to bring peace. But she will not keep her power, and his family will not last. She, her husband, her child, and those who brought her to that country will be killed.

7"But a person from her family will become king of the South and will attack the armies of the king of the North. He will go into that king's strong, walled city and will fight and win. 8He will take their gods, their metal idols, and their valuable things made of silver and gold back to Egypt. Then he will not bother the king of the North for a few years. 9Next, the king of the North will attack the king of the South, but he will be beaten back to his own country.

10"The sons of the king of the North will prepare for war. They will get a large army together that will move through the land very quickly, like a powerful flood. Later, that army will come back and fight all the way to the strong, walled city of the king of the South. 11Then the king of the South will become very angry and will march out to fight against the king of the North. The king of the North will have a large army, but he will lose the battle, 12and the soldiers will be carried away. The king of the South will then be very proud and will kill thousands of soldiers from the northern army, but he will not continue to be successful. 13The king of the North will gather another army, larger than the first one. After several years he will attack with a large army and many weapons.

14"In those times many people will be against the king of the South. Some of your own people who love to fight will turn against the king of the South, thinking it is time for God's promises to come true. But they will fail. 15Then the king of the North will come. He will build ramps to the tops of the city walls and will capture a strong, walled city. The southern army will not have the power to fight back; even their best soldiers will not be strong enough to stop the northern army.

16So the king of the North will do whatever he
wants; no one will be able to stand against him.
He will gain power and control in the beautiful
land of Israel and will have the power to destroy
it. 17The king of the North will decide to use all
his power to fight against the king of the South,
but he will make a peace agreement with the king
of the South. The king of the North will give one
of his daughters as a wife to the king of the South
so that he can defeat him. But those plans will not
succeed or help him. 18Then the king of the North
will turn his attention to cities along the coast of
the Mediterranean Sea and will capture them. But
a commander will put an end to the pride of the
king of the North, turning his pride back on him.
19After that happens the king of the North will go
back to the strong, walled cities of his own country, but he will lose his power. That will be the
end of him.

20"The next king of the North will send out a
tax collector so he will have plenty of money. In
a few years that ruler will be killed, although he
will not die in anger or in a battle.

21"That ruler will be followed by a very cruel
and hated man, who will not have the honor of
being from a king's family. He will attack the kingdom when the people feel safe, and he will take
power by lying to the people. 22He will sweep
away in defeat large and powerful armies and
even a prince who made an agreement. 23Many
nations will make agreements with that cruel and
hated ruler, but he will lie to them. He will gain
much power, but only a few people will support
him. 24The richest areas will feel safe, but that
cruel and hated ruler will attack them. He will
succeed where his ancestors did not. He will rob
the countries he defeats and will give those things
to his followers. He will plan to defeat and destroy
strong cities, but he will be successful for only a
short time.

25"That very cruel and hated ruler will have a
large army that he will use to stir up his strength
and courage. He will attack the king of the South.
The king of the South will gather a large and very
powerful army and prepare for war. But the people who are against him will make secret plans,
and the king of the South will be defeated. 26Peo-
ple who were supposed to be his good friends will
try to destroy him. His army will be swept away
in defeat; many of his soldiers will be killed in
battle. 27Those two kings will want to hurt each
other. They will sit at the same table and lie to
each other, but it will not do either one any good,
because God has set a time for their end to come.
28The king of the North will go back to his own
country with much wealth. Then he will decide
to go against the holy agreement. He will take
action and then return to his own country.

29"At the right time the king of the North will
attack the king of the South again, but this time
he will not be successful as he was before. 30Ships
from the west will come and fight against the king
of the North, so he will be afraid. Then he will
return and show his anger against the holy agreement. He will be good to those who have stopped
obeying the holy agreement.

31"The king of the North will send his army to
make the Temple[d] in Jerusalem unclean.[d] They
will stop the people from offering the daily sacrifice, and then they will set up the destroying terror. 32The king of the North will tell lies and cause
those who have not obeyed God to be ruined. But
those who know God and obey him will be strong
and fight back.

33"Those who are wise will help the others understand what is happening. But they will be
killed with swords, or burned, or taken captive, or
robbed of their homes and possessions. These
things will continue for many days. 34When the
wise ones are suffering, they will get a little help,
but many who join the wise ones will not help
them in their time of need. 35Some of the wise
ones will be killed. But the hard times must come
so they can be made stronger and purer and without faults until the time of the end comes. Then,
at the right time, the end will come.

The King Who Praises Himself

36"The king of the North will do whatever he
wants. He will brag about himself and praise himself and think he is even better than a god. He will
say things against the God of gods that no one has
ever heard. And he will be successful until all the
bad things have happened. Then what God has
planned to happen will happen. 37The king of the
North will not care about the gods his ancestors
worshiped or the god that women worship. He
won't care about any god. Instead, he will make
himself more important than any god. 38The king
of the North will worship power and strength,
which his ancestors did not worship. He will
honor the god of power with gold and silver, expensive jewels and gifts. 39That king will attack
strong, walled cities with the help of a foreign
god. He will give much honor to the people who
join him, making them rulers in charge of many
other people. And he will make them pay him for
the land they rule.

40"At the time of the end, the king of the South
will fight a battle against the king of the North.
The king of the North will attack with chariots,
soldiers on horses, and many large ships. He will
invade many countries and sweep through their
lands like a flood. 41The king of the North will
attack the beautiful land of Judah. He will defeat
many countries, but Edom, Moab, and the leaders
of Ammon will be saved from him. 42The king of
the North will show his power in many countries;

Egypt will not escape. 43The king will get treasures of gold and silver and all the riches of Egypt.
The Libyan and Nubian people will obey him.
44But the king of the North will hear news from
the east and the north that will make him afraid
and angry. He will go to destroy completely many
nations. 45He will set up his royal tents between
the sea and the beautiful mountain where the
holy Temple[d] is built. But, finally, his end will
come, and no one will help him.

The Time of the End

12 "At that time Michael, the great prince
who protects your people, will stand up.
There will be a time of much trouble, the worst
time since nations have been on earth, but your
people will be saved. Everyone whose name is
written in God's book will be saved. 2Many people who have already died will live again. Some
of them will wake up to have life forever, but
some will wake up to find shame and disgrace

SIDELIGHT: Rise and shine!
Daniel 12:2 is the clearest reference in the Old Testament to the resurrection of the dead. Another possible reference is found in Isaiah 26:19 (p. 642).

forever. 3The wise people will shine like the
brightness of the sky. Those who teach others
to live right will shine like stars forever and
ever.
4"But you, Daniel, close up the book and seal
it. These things will happen at the time of the end.
Many people will go here and there to find true
knowledge."

ETERNAL LIFE

Going the Distance

At the age of nineteen, Canadian Terry Fox lost his right leg to cancer. After the amputation, he became a discouraged and bitter young man. He assumed he was stuck in a wheelchair forever and felt cheated out of the "normal" things in life.

Trying to provide some motivation, Terry's former basketball coach showed him an article about a one-legged man who competed in the New York Marathon. The article ignited a sense of challenge in Terry. "If he can do it, so can I," Terry thought.

Gradually, Terry began to set goals for himself and decided to take more control of his life. He began to build his body and find ways to run with an artificial limb. He perfected the stride that came to be called the "Fox Trot." He was soon running frequently and feeling good about his life.

On April 12, 1980, Terry started his "marathon of hope," a solo run across Canada to raise money for cancer research. Four and one-half months later, after covering 3,317 miles and raising twenty-four million dollars, he had to stop. The cancer had spread to his lungs. Terry was hospitalized, and pneumonia set in. He died at the age of twenty-two.

Terry remains a dramatic symbol of hope and courage to Canada and to the world. "I wanted to show people that just because they are disabled, it's not the end," he said.

His memory will live for many, many years.

All of us need more of that kind of hope and courage. Read about the rewards in **Daniel 12:1–3** for those who trust in God for strength to go the distance.

- What hope and encouragement would Terry have found in this passage as he struggled to complete his transcontinental trek?
- If you were to be remembered forever, how would you like to be remembered?

CONSIDER . . .

- completing this sentence as many ways as possible: "When I think of eternal life, I imagine . . ."
- drawing a star and writing the name of a person you respect on it (see verse 3) and then thanking God for that person each day this week.

FOR MORE, SEE . . .

- Ezekiel 37:1–14 (p. 793)
- Mark 13:1–12 (p. 989)
- 1 Corinthians 15:12–28 (p. 1187)

5Then I, Daniel, looked, and saw two other
men. One was standing on my side of the river,
and the other was standing on the far side. 6The
man who was dressed in linen was standing over
the water in the river. One of the two men spoke
to him and asked, "How long will it be before
these amazing things come true?"

7The man dressed in linen, who stood over the
water, raised his hands toward heaven. And I
heard him swear by the name of God who lives
forever, "It will be for three and one-half years.
The power of the holy people will finally be
broken, and then all these things will come
true."

8I heard the answer, but I did not really understand, so I asked, "Master, what will happen after
all these things come true?"

9He answered, "Go your way, Daniel. The message is closed up and sealed until the time of the
end. 10Many people will be made clean,[d] pure,
and spotless, but the wicked will continue to be
wicked. Those wicked people will not understand
these things, but the wise will understand them.

11"The daily sacrifice will be stopped. Then, after 1,290 days from that time, the destroying terror will be set up. 12Those who wait for the end
of the 1,335 days will be happy.

13"As for you, Daniel, go your way until the
end. You will get your rest, and at the end you
will rise to receive your reward."

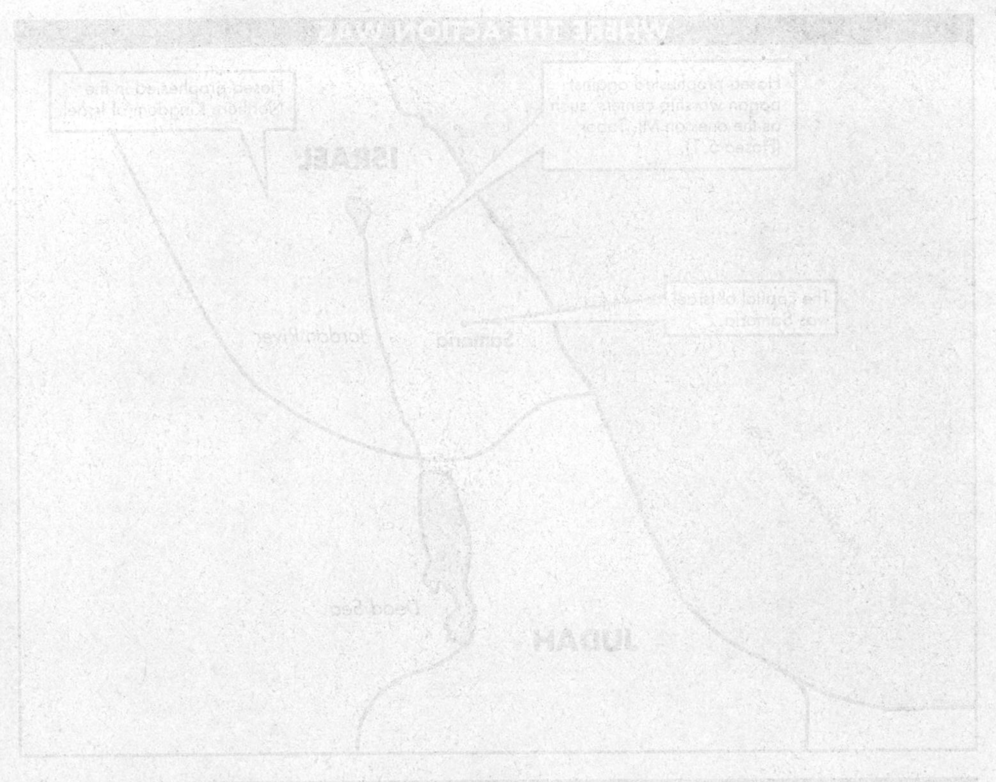

HOSEA

Why Read This Book:

- Discover how strong God's love is (Hosea 1—3).
- Learn what can happen when people turn from God (Hosea 6—10).
- Find assurance in God's love and forgiveness (Hosea 11—14).

Behind the Scenes:

Imagine God telling someone to marry a prostitute. Then imagine that man remaining faithful to his bride even after she returned to her old job.

As improbable as that situation may sound, it is what happened in the book of Hosea. The prophet Hosea married Gomer, a prostitute. She was unfaithful to him, yet he continued to love her and forgive her. Even though her unfaithfulness hurt him, Hosea never stopped loving his unfaithful wife.

Hosea's life symbolized God's relationship to Israel. God had tried to build a relationship with the Israelites. But time after time, the Israelites had turned to other "lovers"—other gods. Yet God's love wouldn't let Israel go.

Hosea preached in the Northern Kingdom (Israel) in the eighth century B.C. It was a time of prosperity, so the people didn't listen to him. But years of immorality

WHERE THE ACTION WAS

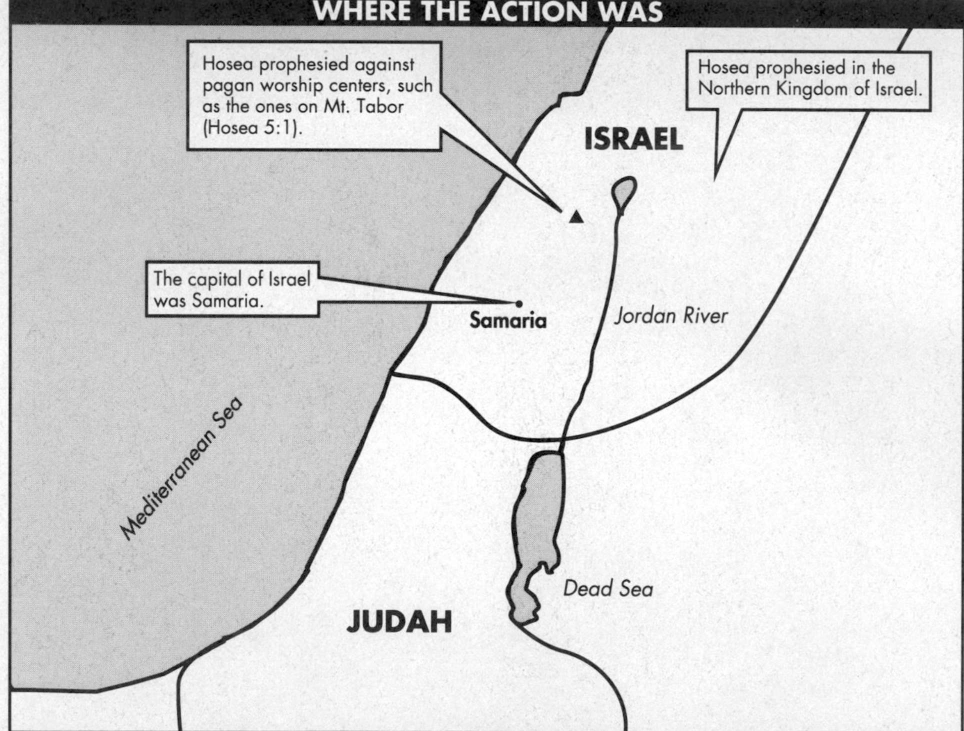
Hosea prophesied against pagan worship centers, such as the ones on Mt. Tabor (Hosea 5:1).
Hosea prophesied in the Northern Kingdom of Israel.
ISRAEL
The capital of Israel was Samaria.
Samaria
Jordan River
Mediterranean Sea
Dead Sea
JUDAH

WHEN THE ACTION WAS

The kingdom was split between Israel and Judah — **Hosea ministered in Israel** — **The Jews began returning from exile** — **Jesus was born**

1000BC — **750BC** — **500BC** — **250BC** — **BC/AD**

Saul was Israel's king — **The Northern Kingdom (Israel) fell to Assyria** — **The Southern Kingdom (Judah) fell to Babylon**

Behind the Scenes (cont.): and unfaithfulness followed, leading to Israel's destruction in 722 B.C. by the Assyrians.

The book of Hosea tells the story of a prophet's pleading with the people to stop turning away from God and to recognize God's everlasting and tender love. Through the prophet, God says, "I want faithful love. . . . I want people to know me. . . ." (Hosea 6:6). This central message in Hosea is a message for all time!

---

1 The LORD spoke his word to Hosea son of
Beeri during the time that Uzziah, Jotham,
Ahaz, and Hezekiah were kings of Judah and Jero-
boam son of Jehoash was king of Israel.

Hosea's Wife and Children

2When the LORD began speaking through Hosea, the LORD said to him, "Go, and marry an unfaithful woman and have unfaithful children,
because the people in this country have
been completely unfaithful to the LORD." 3So
Hosea married Gomer daughter of Diblaim, and
she became pregnant and gave birth to Hosea's
son.

4The LORD said to Hosea, "Name him Jezreel,
because soon I will punish the family of Jehu for
the people they killed at Jezreel. In the future I
will put an end to the kingdom of Israel 5and
break the power of Israel's army in the Valley of
Jezreel."

6Gomer became pregnant again and gave birth
to a daughter. The LORD said to Hosea, "Name
her Lo-Ruhamah,[n] because I will not pity Israel
anymore, nor will I forgive them. 7But I will show
pity to the people of Judah. I will save them, but
not by using bows or swords, horses or horsemen,
or weapons of war. I, the LORD their God, will
save them."

8After Gomer had stopped nursing Lo-
Ruhamah, she became pregnant again and gave
birth to another son. 9The LORD said, "Name him
Lo-Ammi,[n] because you are not my people, and
I am not your God.

God's Promise to Israel

10"But the number of the Israelites will become
like the grains of sand of the sea, which no one
can measure or count. They were called, 'You are
not my people,' but later they will be called 'children of the living God.' 11The people of Judah and
Israel will join together again and will choose one
leader for themselves. They will come up from
the land, because the day of Jezreel[n] will be truly
great.

2 "You are to call your brothers, 'my people,'
and your sisters, 'you have been shown pity.'

God Speaks About Israel

2"Plead with your mother.[n]
Accuse her, because she is no longer my wife,
and I am no longer her husband.
Tell her to stop acting like a prostitute,[d]
to stop behaving like an unfaithful wife.
3If she refuses, I will strip her naked
and leave her bare like the day she was born.
I will make her dry like a desert,
like a land without water,
and I will kill her with thirst.
4I will not take pity on her children,
because they are the children of a prostitute.
5Their mother has acted like a prostitute;
the one who became pregnant with them
has acted disgracefully.
She said, 'I will chase after my lovers,[n]
who give me my food and water,
wool and flax, wine and olive oil.'
6So I will block her road with thornbushes;
I will build a wall around her
so she cannot find her way.
7She will run after her lovers,
but she won't catch them.
She will look for them,
but she won't find them.

> **SIDELIGHT:** If you've been teased because your parents gave you an unusual name, imagine how Jezreel, Lo-Ruhamah, and Lo-Ammi felt (Hosea 1:4–9). Their names meant, respectively, "God plants," "not pitied," and "not my people."

Lo-Ruhamah This name in Hebrew means "not pitied."
Lo-Ammi This name in Hebrew means "not my people."
Jezreel This name in Hebrew means "God plants."
mother Refers to the nation of Israel here.
lovers Refers to the nations surrounding Israel, who led Israel to worship false gods.

Then she will say, 'I will go back to my first
husband,[n]
because life was better then for me than it
is now.'
8But she does not know that I was the one
who gave her grain, new wine, and oil.
I gave her much silver and gold,
but she used it for Baal.[d]

9"So I will come back and take away my grain
at harvest time
and my new wine when it is ready.
I will take back my wool and linen
that covered her nakedness.
10So I will show her nakedness to her
lovers,
and no one will save her from me.
11I will put an end to all her celebrations:
her yearly festivals, her New Moon[d]
festivals, and her Sabbaths.[d]
I will stop all of her special feasts.
12I will destroy her vines and fig trees,
which she said were her pay from her
lovers.
I will turn them into a forest,
and wild animals will eat them.
13I will punish her for all the times
she burned incense[d] to the Baals.
She put on her rings and jewelry
and went chasing after her lovers,
but she forgot me!"
says the LORD.

14"So I am going to attract her;
I will lead her into the desert
and speak tenderly to her.
15There I will give her back her vineyards,
and I will make the Valley of Trouble a
door of hope.
There she will respond as when she was
young,
as when she came out of Egypt."

husband Refers to God here.

FOLLOWING GOD

Going to the Desert

Sometimes it was so difficult to think clearly back home. Danny Washington had grown up in the noise, clamor, and confusion of inner-city Philadelphia. Similar confusion filled his own life. Arrested for a series of minor crimes, Danny was assigned to a juvenile delinquent treatment program.

Now here he was on a mountain ridge in West Virginia, participating in a wilderness challenge course—nineteen days of mountain living. The course had been frustrating so far. His feelings of frustration and anger from the inner city followed him. He had snapped at the advisers because of the cold and the rain, the long days of hiking with backpacks, and getting lost. Why couldn't he ever just relax and handle the situation? Why did he always feel so angry and out of control?

Sitting under the quiet, star-filled sky, Danny tried to sort out his feelings of failure by talking with Bob, his group adviser. They talked about thoughts and fears for a long time. Then Bob said, "If there were just one gift I could give you, it'd be the gift of peace—the peace that begins with accepting yourself as loved by God."

Tears welled in Danny's eyes. In the silence of the wilderness, Danny felt the quiet peace and acceptance of God for the first time.

Sometimes following God requires us to leave our usual surroundings and go to a quiet place to hear his message. In **Hosea 2:14–20** read how God would become more real in the wilderness.

- How is God's message to Israel similar to the one that Danny heard?
- How does the passage's theme compare with your own ideas of what it means to follow God?

CONSIDER . . .

- taking a long walk by yourself and listening for ways God wants you to serve him.
- serving God through a quiet act of kindness, such as listening to someone without interrupting, or donating your time and money to a ministry you support.

FOR MORE, SEE . . .

- Exodus 3:1–6 (p. 60)
- Matthew 4:1–11 (p. 910)
- Luke 9:28–36 (p. 1019)

16The LORD says, "In the future she will call
me 'my husband';
no longer will she call me 'my baal.'[n]
17I will never let her say the names of Baal
again;
people won't use their names anymore.
18At that time I will make an agreement for
them
with the wild animals, the birds, and the
crawling things.
I will smash from the land
the bow and the sword and the weapons of
war,
so my people will live in safety.
19And I will make you my promised bride
forever.
I will be good and fair;
I will show you my love and mercy.
20I will be true to you as my promised bride,
and you will know the LORD.

21"At that time I will speak to you," says the
LORD.
"I will speak to the skies,
and they will give rain to the earth.
22The earth will produce grain, new wine, and
oil;
much will grow because my people are
called Jezreel.[n]
23I will plant my people in the land,
and I will show pity to the one I had called
'not shown pity.'
I will say, 'You are my people'
to those I had called 'not my people.'
And they will say to me, 'You are our
God.' "

SIDELIGHT: Hosea's wife, Gomer, probably wasn't an ordinary prostitute (Hosea 3:1). Most likely she was a cult prostitute—or cult priestess—in the temples of the false god Baal. The Baal religion included a variety of fertility rites thought to bring rain and a bountiful harvest.

Hosea Buys a Wife

3 The LORD said to me again, "Go, show your
love to a woman loved by someone else,
who has been unfaithful to you. In the same way
the LORD loves the people of Israel, even though
they worship other gods and love to eat the raisin
cakes."[n]
2So I bought her for six ounces of silver and ten
bushels of barley. 3Then I told her, "You must
wait for me for many days. You must not be a
prostitute,[d] and you must not have sexual relations with any other man. I will act the same way
toward you."
4In the same way Israel will live many days
without a king or leader, without sacrifices or
holy stone pillars, and without the holy vest[d] or
an idol. 5After this, the people of Israel will return
to the LORD their God and follow him and the
king from David's family. In the last days they
will turn in fear to the LORD, and he will bless
them.

The Lord's Word Against Israel

4 People of Israel, listen to the LORD's
message.
The LORD has this
against you who live in the land:
"The people are not true, not loyal to God,
nor do those who live in the land even
know him.
2Cursing, lying, killing, stealing and adultery[d]
are everywhere.
One murder follows another.
3Because of this the land dries up,
and all its people are dying.
Even the wild animals and the birds of the
air
and the fish of the sea are dying.

God's Case Against the Priests

4"No one should accuse
or blame another person.
Don't blame the people, you priests,
when they quarrel with you.
5You will be ruined in the day,
and your prophets[d] will be ruined with you
in the night.
I will also destroy your mother.[n]
6My people will be destroyed,
because they have no knowledge.
You have refused to learn,
so I will refuse to let you be priests to me.
You have forgotten the teachings of your
God,
so I will forget your children.
7The more priests there are,
the more they sin against me.
I will take away their honor
and give them shame.
8Since the priests live off the sin offerings of
the people,

baal Another Hebrew word for husband, but it was the same word as the god Baal.
Jezreel This name in Hebrew means "God plants."
raisin cakes This food was eaten in the feasts that honored false gods.
mother Here "mother" refers to the nation of Israel.

they want the people to sin more and
more.
9The priests are as wrong as the people,
and I will punish them both for what they
have done.
I will repay them for the wrong they have
done.

10"They will eat
but not have enough;
they will have sexual relations with the
prostitutes,[d]
but they will not have children,
because they have left the LORD
to give themselves to 11prostitution,
to old and new wine,
which take away their ability to understand.

God's Case Against the People

12"My people ask wooden idols for advice;
they ask those sticks of wood to advise
them!
Like prostitutes, they have chased after other
gods
and have left their own God.
13They make sacrifices on the tops of the
mountains.
They burn offerings on the hills,
under oaks, poplars, and other trees,
because their shade is nice.
So your daughters become prostitutes,
and your daughters-in-law are guilty of
adultery.[d]

14"But I will not punish your daughters
for becoming prostitutes,
nor your daughters-in-law
for their sins of adultery.
I will not punish them,
because the men have sexual relations with
prostitutes
and offer sacrifices with the temple
prostitutes.
A foolish people will be ruined.

15"Israel, you act like a prostitute,
but do not be guilty toward the LORD.
Don't go to Gilgal
or go up to Beth Aven.[n]
Don't make promises,
saying, 'As surely as the LORD lives . . .'
16The people of Israel are stubborn
like a stubborn young cow.
Now the LORD will feed them
like lambs in the open country.
17The Israelites have chosen to worship idols,
so leave them alone.
18When they finish their drinking,
they completely give themselves to being
prostitutes;
they love these disgraceful ways.
19They will be swept away as if by a
whirlwind,
and their sacrifices will bring them only
shame.

God's Word Against the Leaders

5 "Listen, you priests.
Pay attention, people of Israel.
Listen, royal family,
because you will all be judged.
You have been like a trap at Mizpah
and like a net spread out at Mount Tabor.
2You have done many evil things,
so I will punish you all.
3I know all about the people of Israel;
what they have done is not hidden from
me.
Now that Israel acts like a prostitute,[d]
it has made itself unclean.[d]

4"They will not give up their deeds
and return to their God.
They are determined to be unfaithful to me;
they do not know the LORD.
5Israel's pride testifies against them.
The people of Israel will stumble because of
their sin,
and the people of Judah will stumble with
them.
6They will come to worship the LORD,
bringing their flocks and herds,
but they will not be able to find him,
because he has left them.
7They have not been true to the LORD;
they are children who do not belong to
him.
So their false worship
will destroy them and their land.

8"Blow the horn in Gibeah
and the trumpet in Ramah.
Give the warning at Beth Aven,
and be first into battle, people of Benjamin.
9Israel will be ruined
on the day of punishment.
To the tribes[d] of Israel
I tell the truth.
10The leaders of Judah are like those
who steal other people's land.
I will pour my punishment over them
like a flood of water.
11Israel is crushed by the punishment,
because it decided to follow idols.
12I am like a moth to Israel,
like a rot to the people of Judah.

Gilgal . . . Beth Aven Cities in Israel where people worshiped false gods.

[13]"When Israel saw its illness
and Judah saw its wounds,
Israel went to Assyria for help
and sent to the great king of Assyria.
But he cannot heal you
or cure your wounds.
[14]I will be like a lion to Israel,
like a young lion to Judah.
I will attack them
and tear them to pieces.
I will drag them off,
and no one will be able to save them.
[15]Then I will go back to my place
until they suffer for their guilt and turn
back to me.
In their trouble they will look for me."

The People Are Not Faithful

6 "Come, let's go back to the LORD.
He has hurt us, but he will heal us.
He has wounded us, but he will bandage
our wounds.
[2]In two days he will put new life in us;
on the third day he will raise us up
so that we may live in his presence [3]and
know him.

FOLLOWING GOD

Shape Up or Ship Out

Even as a child, Nadja Salerno-Sonnenberg was a "natural" on the violin. Nadja could play the most difficult violin music as easily as most people breathe or sleep. She made her official concert debut with the Philadelphia Orchestra at the age of ten.

"When I was young I was very talented. I still am, but I rode on that talent for such a long time," Nadja says.

"At age fourteen, I'd walk on stage and whip off the Carmen Fantasy as if I were Heifetz, because I had the ability in my fingers. At sixteen, I was still kind of whipping it off. At seventeen or eighteen, I walked on stage and stumbled all over it. I finally realized how difficult it was to play the violin." So, incredibly, Nadja abandoned her instrument while already a student at Juilliard School of Music.

Her teacher at Juilliard, Dorothy DeLay, had previously taught some of the world's best violinists. She grew angry with Nadja's "going through the motions" and her mediocre effort. When Nadja began showing up for lessons without her violin, Dorothy told her to shape up or ship out. "She was threatening to throw me out of class," says Nadja. "I was petrified."

Jolted out of her complacency, Nadja followed her teacher's demand: intense, dedicated practice. She entered the prestigious Naumburg Competition. "I was like a horse with blinders on. My goal was to make the finals so that everybody would know I was still out there," she says.

Everybody watched in awe as, at age twenty, she played her way to becoming the youngest first-prize winner in the competition's history. She's gone on to perform for astonished audiences at sold-out concerts around the world.

Just as Nadja once "went through the motions" of violin lessons, the people in Hosea's time were "going through the motions" of faith. Instead of following God, they paid him token attention with ritualistic animal sacrifices. God, through Hosea, shares his anger about this dull, ho-hum faith. Read what God does want in **Hosea 6:1–6**.

■ Why did Nadja's teacher and God become angry with empty efforts?
■ How would your life change if you more intensely followed God's desire that you love him faithfully? How might your church be different? your world?

CONSIDER . . .

■ making two columns on a sheet of paper, one headed by "Dull, dead faith" and the other by "God-following faith." List as many activities as you can think of that fit each category. Pick one from the God-following column and do it.
■ spending more time each day in prayer and reading the Bible to get to know God.

FOR MORE, SEE . . .

■ Micah 6:8 (p. 866)
■ Matthew 22:34–40 (p. 948)
■ Colossians 3:12–17 (p. 1241)

Let's try to learn about the LORD;
He will come to us as surely as the dawn comes.
He will come to us like rain,
like the spring rain that waters the ground."

4The LORD says, "Israel, what should I do with you?
Judah, what should I do with you?
Your faithfulness is like a morning mist,
like the dew that goes away early in the day.
5I have warned you by my prophets[d]
that I will kill you and destroy you.
My justice comes out like bright light.
6I want faithful love
more than I want animal sacrifices.
I want people to know me
more than I want burnt offerings.
7But they have broken the agreement as Adam did;
they have been unfaithful to me.
8Gilead is a city of people who do evil;
their footprints are bloody.
9The priests are like robbers waiting to attack people;
they murder people on the road to Shechem[n]
and do wicked things.
10I have seen horrible things in Israel.
Look at Israel's prostitution;[d]
Israel has become unclean.[d]

11"Judah, I have set a harvest time for you
when I will make the lives of my people good again.

7 When I heal Israel,
Israel's sin will go away,
and so will Samaria's evil.

"They cheat a lot!
Thieves break into houses,
and robbers are in the streets.
2It never enters their minds
that I remember all their evil deeds.
The bad things they do are all around them;
they are right in front of me.

Israel's Evil Kings

3"They make the king happy with their wickedness;
their rulers are glad with their lies.
4But all of them are traitors.
They are like an oven heated by a baker.
While he mixes the dough,
he does not need to stir up the fire.
5The kings get so drunk they get sick every day.
The rulers become crazy with wine;
they make agreements with those who do not know the true God.
6They burn like an oven;
their hearts burn inside them.
All night long their anger is low,
but when morning comes, it becomes a roaring fire.
7All these people are as hot as an oven;
they burn up their rulers.
All their kings fall,
and no one calls on me.

> SIDELIGHT: During Hosea's career, Israelite politics were about as stable as the fault-line under Los Angeles. In only twenty-five years, the prophet saw the reign of six kings—four of whom were assassinated. That's probably what Hosea 7:7 refers to.

Israel and the Other Nations

8"Israel mixes with other nations;
he is like a pancake cooked only on one side.
9Foreign nations have eaten up his strength,
but he doesn't know it.
Israel is weak and feeble, like an old man,
but he doesn't know it.
10Israel's pride will cause their defeat;
they will not turn back to the LORD their God
or look to him for help in all this.
11Israel has become like a pigeon—
easy to fool and stupid.
First they call to Egypt for help.
Then they run to Assyria.
12When they go, I will catch them in a net,
I will bring them down like birds from the sky;
I will punish them countless times for their evil.
13How terrible for them because they left me!
They will be destroyed, because they turned against me.
I want to save them,
but they have spoken lies against me.
14They do not call to me from their hearts.
They just lie on their beds and cry.
They come together to ask for grain and new wine,
but they really turn away from me.

Shechem A city of safety where people could go for protection.

[15]Though I trained them and gave them strength,
they have made evil plans against me.
[16]They did not turn to the Most High God.
They are like a loose bow that can't shoot.
Because their leaders brag about their strength,
they will be killed with swords,
and the people in Egypt
will laugh at them.

Israel Has Trusted Wrong Things

8 "Put the trumpet to your lips and give the warning!
The enemy swoops down on the LORD's people like an eagle.
The Israelites have broken my agreement
and have turned against my teachings.
[2]They cry out to me,
'Our God, we in Israel know you!'
[3]But Israel has rejected what is good,
so the enemy will chase them.
[4]They chose their own kings
without asking my permission.
They chose their own leaders,
people I did not know.
They made their silver and gold into idols,
and for all this they will be destroyed.
[5]I hate the calf-shaped idol of Israel!
I am very angry with the people.
How long will they remain unclean?[d]
[6]The idol is something a craftsman made;
it is not God.
Israel's calf-shaped idol
will surely be smashed to pieces.

[7]"Israel's foolish plans are like planting the wind,
but they will harvest a storm.
Like a stalk with no head of grain,
it produces nothing.
Even if it produced something,
other nations would eat it.
[8]Israel is eaten up;
the people are mixed among the other nations
and have become useless to me.
[9]Israel is like a wild donkey all by itself.
They have run to Assyria;
They have hired other nations to protect them.
[10]Although Israel is mixed among the nations,
I will gather them together.
They will become weaker and weaker
as they suffer under the great king of Assyria.

[11]"Although Israel built more altars to remove sin,
they have become altars for sinning.
[12]I have written many teachings for them,
but they think the teachings are strange and foreign.
[13]The Israelites offer sacrifices to me as gifts
and eat the meat,
but the LORD is not pleased with them.
He remembers the evil they have done,
and he will punish them for their sins.
They will be slaves again as they were in Egypt.
[14]Israel has forgotten their Maker and has built palaces;
Judah has built many strong, walled cities.
But I will send fire on their cities
and destroy their strong buildings."

Israel's Punishment

9 Israel, do not rejoice;
don't shout for joy as the other nations do.
You have been like a prostitute[d] against your God.
You love the pay of prostitutes on every threshing[d] floor.
[2]But the threshing floor and the winepress will not feed the people,
and there won't be enough new wine.
[3]The people will not stay in the LORD's land.
Israel will return to being captives as they were in Egypt,
and in Assyria they will eat food that they are not allowed to eat.
[4]The Israelites will not give offerings of wine to the LORD;
they will not give him sacrifices.
Their sacrifices will be like food that is eaten at a funeral;
it is unclean,[d] and everyone who eats it becomes unclean.
Their food will only satisfy their hunger;
they cannot sacrifice it in the Temple.[d]
[5]What will you do then on the day of feasts
and on the day of the LORD's festival?
[6]Even if the people are not destroyed,
Egypt will capture them;
Memphis[n] will bury them.
Weeds will grow over their silver treasures,
and thorns will drive them out of their tents.
[7]The time of punishment has come,
the time to pay for sins.
Let Israel know this:
You think the prophet[d] is a fool,
and you say the spiritual person is crazy.

Memphis A city in Egypt famous for its tombs.

You have sinned very much,
and your hatred is great.
8Is Israel a watchman?
Are God's people prophets?
Everywhere Israel goes, traps are set for him.
He is an enemy in God's house.
9The people of Israel have gone deep into sin
as the people of Gibeah[n] did.
The Lord will remember the evil things they have done,
and he will punish their sins.

10"When I found Israel,
it was like finding grapes in the desert.
Your ancestors were like
finding the first figs on the fig tree.
But when they came to Baal Peor,
they began worshiping an idol,
and they became as hateful as the thing they worshiped.
11Israel's glory will fly away like a bird;
there will be no more pregnancy, no more births, no more getting pregnant.
12But even if the Israelites bring up children,
I will take them all away.
How terrible it will be for them
when I go away from them!
13I have seen Israel, like Tyre,
given a pleasant place.
But the people of Israel will soon bring out
their children to be killed."
14LORD, give them what they should have.
What will you give them?
Make their women unable to have children;
give them dried-up breasts that cannot feed their babies.

15"The Israelites were very wicked in Gilgal,
so I have hated them there.
Because of the sinful things they have done,
I will force them to leave my land.
I will no longer love them;
their leaders have turned against me.
16Israel is beaten down;
its root is dying, and it has no fruit.
If they have more children,
I will kill the children they love."

17God will reject them,
because they have not obeyed him;
they will wander among the nations.

Israel Will Pay for Sin

10 Israel is like a large vine
that produced plenty of fruit.
As the people became richer,
they built more altars for idols.
As their land became better,
they put up better stone pillars to honor gods.
2Their heart was false,
and now they must pay for their guilt.
The LORD will break down their altars;
he will destroy their holy stone pillars.

3Then they will say, "We have no king,
because we didn't honor the LORD.
As for the king,
he couldn't do anything for us."
4They make many false promises
and agreements which they don't keep.
So people sue each other in court;
they are like poisonous weeds growing in a plowed field.
5The people from Israel are worried about
the calf-shaped idol at Beth Aven.
The people will cry about it,
and the priests will cry about it.
They used to shout for joy about its glory,
6but it will be carried off to Assyria
as a gift to the great king.
Israel will be disgraced,
and the people will be ashamed for not obeying.
7Israel will be destroyed;
its king will be like a chip of wood floating on the water.
8The places of false worship will be destroyed,
the places where Israel sins.
Thorns and weeds will grow up
and cover their altars.
Then they will say to the mountains, "Cover us!"
and to the hills, "Fall on us!"

9"Israel, you have sinned since the time of Gibeah,[n]
and the people there have continued sinning.
But war will surely overwhelm them in Gibeah,
because of the evil they have done there.
10When I am ready,
I will come to punish them.
Nations will come together against them,
and they will be punished for their double sins.
11Israel is like a well-trained young cow
that likes to thresh[d] grain.
I will put a yoke[d] on her neck
and make her work hard in the field.
Israel will plow,
and Judah will break up the ground.

Gibeah The sins of the people of Gibeah caused a civil war. See Judges 19-21.

12I said, 'Plant goodness,
harvest the fruit of loyalty,
plow the new ground of knowledge.
Look for the LORD until he comes
and pours goodness on you like water.'
13But you have plowed evil
and harvested trouble;
you have eaten the fruit of your lies.
Because you have trusted in your own power
and your many soldiers,
14your people will hear the noise of battle,
and all your strong, walled cities will be destroyed.
It will be like the time King Shalman
destroyed Beth Arbel in battle,
when mothers and their children were bashed to death.
15The same will happen to you, people of Bethel,
because you did so much evil.
When the sun comes up,
the king of Israel will die.

God's Love for Israel

11 "When Israel was a child, I loved him,
and I called my son out of Egypt.
2But when I called the people of Israel,
they went away from me.
They offered sacrifices to the Baals[d]
and burned incense[d] to the idols.
3It was I who taught Israel to walk,
and I took them by the arms,
but they did not understand
that I had healed them.
4I led them with cords of human kindness,
with ropes of love.
I lifted the yoke[d] from their neck
and bent down and fed them.

5"The Israelites will become captives again, as they were in Egypt,
and Assyria will become their king,
because they refuse to turn back to God.
6War will sweep through their cities
and will destroy them
and kill them because of their wicked plans.
7My people have made up their minds
to turn away from me.
The prophets[d] call them to turn to me,
but none of them honors me at all.

8"Israel, how can I give you up?
How can I give you away, Israel?
I don't want to make you like Admah
or treat you like Zeboiim.[n]
My heart beats for you,
and my love for you stirs up my pity.
9I won't punish you in my anger,
and I won't destroy Israel again.
I am God and not a human;
I am the Holy One, and I am among you.
I will not come against you in anger.
10They will go after the LORD,
and he will roar like a lion.
When he roars,
his children will hurry to him from the west.
11They will come swiftly
like birds from Egypt
and like doves from Assyria.
I will settle them again in their homes,"
says the LORD.

The Lord Is Against Israel

12Israel has surrounded me with lies;
the people have made evil plans.
And Judah turns against God,
the faithful Holy One.

12 What Israel does is as useless as chasing the wind;
he chases the east wind all day.
They tell more and more lies
and do more and more violence.
They make agreements with Assyria,
and they send a gift of olive oil to Egypt.
2The LORD also has some things against Judah.
He will punish Israel for what they have done;
he will give them what they deserve.
3Their ancestor Jacob held on to his brother's heel
while the two of them were being born.
When he grew to be a man,
he wrestled with God.
4When Jacob wrestled with the angel and won,
he cried and asked for his blessing.
Later, God met with him at Bethel
and spoke with him there.
5It was the LORD God All-Powerful;
the LORD is his great name.
6You must return to your God;
love him, do what is just,
and always trust in him as your God.

7The merchants use dishonest scales;
they like to cheat people.
8Israel said, "I am rich! I am someone with power!"
All their money will do them no good
because of the sins they have done.

9"But I am the LORD your God,
who brought you out of Egypt.
I will make you live in tents again

Admah . . . Zeboiim Two other cities destroyed when God destroyed Sodom and Gomorrah.

as you used to do on worship days.
10I spoke to the prophets[d]
and gave them many visions;
through them, I taught my lessons to you."

11The people of Gilead are evil,
worth nothing.
Though people sacrifice bulls at Gilgal,
their altars will become like piles of stone
in a plowed field.
12Your ancestor Jacob fled to Northwest
Mesopotamia
where he worked to get a wife;
he tended sheep to pay for her.
13Later the LORD used a prophet
to bring Jacob's descendants[d] out of Egypt;
he used a prophet
to take care of the Israelites.
14But the Israelites made the Lord angry when
they killed other people,
and they deserve to die for their crimes.
The Lord will make them pay
for the disgraceful things they have done.

The Final Word Against Israel

13 People used to fear the tribe[d] of
Ephraim;
they were important people in Israel.
But they sinned by worshiping Baal,[d]
so they must die.
2But they still keep on sinning more and
more.
They make idols of their silver,
idols that are cleverly made,
the work of a craftsman.
Yet the people of Israel say to each other,
"Kiss those calf idols and sacrifice to them."
3So those people will be like the morning
mist;
they will disappear like the morning dew.
They will be like chaff[d] blown from the
threshing[d] floor,
like smoke going out a window.

4"I, the LORD, have been your God
since you were in the land of Egypt.
You should have known no other God except
me.
I am the only one who saves.
5I cared for them in the desert
where it was hot and dry.
6I gave them food, and they became full and
satisfied.
But then they became too proud and forgot
me.
7That is why I will be like a lion to them,
like a leopard waiting by the road.
8I will attack like a bear robbed of her cubs,
ripping their bodies open.
I will devour them like a lion
and tear them apart like a wild animal.

9"Israel, I will destroy you.
Who will be your helper then?
10What good is your king?
Can he save you in any of your towns?
What good are your leaders?
You said, 'Give us a king and leaders.'
11So I gave you a king, but only in anger,
and I took him away in my great anger.
12The sins of Israel are on record,
stored away, waiting for punishment.
13The pain of birth will come for him,
but he is like a foolish baby
who won't come out of its mother's womb.

SIDELIGHT: Childbirth was much more dangerous in Old Testament times than it is today in most places (Hosea 13:13). Many a woman died during childbirth because she couldn't deliver her child.

14Will I save them from the place of the dead?
Will I rescue them from death?
Where is your sickness, death?
Where is your pain, place of death?
I will show them no mercy.
15Israel is doing well among the nations,
but the LORD will send a wind from the
east,
coming from the desert,
that will dry up his springs and wells of
water.
He will destroy from their treasure houses
everything of value.
16The nation of Israel will be ruined,
because it fought against God.
The people of Israel will die in war;
their children will be torn to pieces,
and their pregnant women will be ripped
open."

Israel Returns to God

14 Israel, return to the LORD your God,
because your sins have made you fall.
2Come back to the LORD
and say these words to him:
"Take away all our sin
and kindly receive us,
and we will keep the promises we made to
you.
3Assyria cannot save us,
nor will we trust in our horses.
We will not say again, 'Our gods,'
to the things our hands have made.
You show mercy to orphans."

4The LORD says,
"I will forgive them for leaving me
and will love them freely,
because I am not angry with them
anymore.
5I will be like the dew to Israel,
and they will blossom like a lily.
Like the cedar trees in Lebanon,
their roots will be firm.
6They will be like spreading branches,
like the beautiful olive trees
and the sweet-smelling cedars in Lebanon.
7The people of Israel will again live under my
protection.
They will grow like the grain,
they will bloom like a vine,
and they will be as famous as the wine of
Lebanon.
8Israel, have nothing to do with idols.
I, the LORD, am the one who answers your
prayers and watches over you.
I am like a green pine tree;
your blessings come from me."
9A wise person will know these things,
and an understanding person will take them
to heart.
The LORD's ways are right.
Good people live by following them,
but those who turn against God die
because of them.

JOEL

Why Read This Book:

- See how forgiveness begins with a change of heart (Joel 2).
- Hear Joel announce a new life for the faithful (Joel 3).

Behind the Scenes:

In the 1930s, the United States was devastated by the Great Depression. Crops died in the "dust bowls." People lost their jobs. The whole nation was in trouble. People who lived through those years will never forget them.

Judah faced a similar catastrophe, except its land was attacked by locusts. These insects destroyed all vegetation, attacking fields, trees, and vineyards. The swarms turned farmland into desert. The people had never seen anything like it.

The prophet Joel interpreted what was happening to the land as a sign of God's judgment on the people. He called them to repent for turning away from God. In the end, Joel predicted, God's judgment would be much worse than a plague of locusts if the people didn't turn back to God. Restoration and blessing would come only if the people turned back to God.

We don't know much about the prophet Joel, but his central message is a message for all time: God will judge those who oppose him and will bless those who follow him.

WHEN THE ACTION WAS

Saul was Israel's king — 1000BC

The kingdom was split between Israel and Judah

Possible time of Joel's life

The Northern Kingdom (Israel) fell to Assyria — 750BC

The Southern Kingdom (Judah) fell to Babylon

Jews began returning from exile — 500BC

250BC

Jesus was born — BC/AD

Locusts Destroy the Crops

1 The LORD spoke his word to Joel son of Pethuel:

2Older leaders, listen to this message.
Listen to me, all you who live in the land.
Nothing like this has ever happened during your lifetime
or during your ancestors' lifetimes.

> **SIDELIGHT:** The name Joel is common in the Old Testament (Joel 1:1). Twelve other people share this name (for examples, see 1 Samuel 8:2, p. 251, and Nehemiah 11:9, p. 437). The name means "The Lord is God" or "The Lord is my God."

3Tell your children about these things,
let your children tell their children,
and let your grandchildren tell their children.
4What the cutting locusts have left,
the swarming locusts have eaten;
what the swarming locusts have left,
the hopping locusts have eaten,
and what the hopping locusts have left,
the destroying locusts[n] have eaten.
5Drunks, wake up and cry!
All you people who drink wine, cry!
Cry because your wine
has been taken away from your mouths.
6A powerful nation has come into my land
with too many soldiers to count.
It has teeth like a lion,
jaws like a female lion.
7It has made my grapevine a waste
and made my fig tree a stump.
It has stripped all the bark off my trees
and left the branches white.
8Cry as a young woman cries
when the man she was going to marry has died.

> **SIDELIGHT:** The locust invasion described in Joel 1 wasn't a unique event. As recently as 1915 and 1930, the Middle East has been ravaged by plagues of these insects.

9There will be no more grain or drink offerings
to offer in the Temple[d] of the LORD.
Because of this, the priests,
the servants of the LORD, are sad.
10The fields are ruined;
the ground is dried up.
The grain is destroyed,
the new wine is dried up,
and the olive oil runs out.
11Be sad, farmers.
Cry loudly, you who grow grapes.
Cry for the wheat and the barley.
Cry because the harvest of the field is lost.
12The vines have become dry,
and the fig trees are dried up.
The pomegranate[d] trees, the date palm trees,
the apple trees—
all the trees in the field have died.
And the happiness of the people has died, too.
13Priests, put on your rough cloth and cry to show your sadness.
Servants of the altar, cry out loud.
Servants of my God,
keep your rough cloth on all night to show your sadness.
Cry because there will be no more grain or drink offerings
to offer in the Temple of your God.
14Call for a day when no one eats food!
Tell everyone to stop work!
Bring the older leaders
and everyone who lives in the land
to the Temple of the LORD your God,
and cry out to the LORD.
15What a terrible day it will be!
The LORD's day of judging is near,
when punishment will come
like a destroying attack from the Almighty.
16Our food is taken away
while we watch.
Joy and happiness are gone
from the Temple of our God.
17Though we planted fig seeds,
they lie dry and dead in the dirt.
The barns are empty and falling down.
The storerooms for grain have been broken down,
because the grain has dried up.
18The animals are groaning!
The herds of cattle wander around confused,
because they have no grass to eat;
even the flocks of sheep suffer.

cutting . . . locusts These are different names for an insect like a large grasshopper. The locust can quickly destroy trees, plants, and crops, and in this destruction Joel sees a warning. God will cause this type of destruction when he punishes his people.

[19]LORD, I am calling to you for help,
because fire has burned up the open pastures,
and flames have burned all the trees in the field.
[20]Wild animals also need your help.
The streams of water have dried up,
and fire has burned up the open pastures.

The Coming Day of Judgment

2 Blow the trumpet in Jerusalem;
shout a warning on my holy mountain.
Let all the people who live in the land shake with fear,
because the LORD's day of judging is coming;
it is near.
[2]It will be a dark, gloomy day,
cloudy and black.
Like the light at sunrise,
a great and powerful army will spread over the mountains.
There has never been anything like it before,
and there will never be anything like it again.
[3]In front of them a fire destroys;
in back of them a flame burns.
The land in front of them is like the garden of Eden;
the land behind them is like an empty desert.
Nothing will escape from them.
[4]They look like horses,
and they run like war horses.
[5]It is like the noise of chariots
rumbling over the tops of the mountains,
like the noise of a roaring fire
burning dry stalks.
They are like a powerful army lined up for battle.

GOD'S POWER

The Big Blast

For one hundred twenty-three years Mount St. Helens slept quietly. Whenever geologists looked down the throat of the Washington volcano, all they found were ash and ice. Then, on March 20, 1980, earthquakes shook the area. Within a week the volcano began spewing steam and ash into the air.

At first, people were frightened. But as weeks went by and nothing happened, they grew accustomed to living next to an active volcano. They got tired of hearing warnings of possible disaster. In fact, a carnival-like attitude prevailed, and the volcano's small eruptions became a source of entertainment.

On May 18, Mount St. Helens was rattled by another series of earthquakes. This time a huge section of the northern slope came crashing down the mountain. Two minutes later, the mountain exploded. The explosion, heard two hundred miles away, was louder and more powerful than an atomic bomb. A billowing cloud of ash shot more than twelve miles into the air. More than one hundred eighty-five square miles of forest land were leveled. Hundreds of thousands of trees vaporized, clouds of gray ash filled the air, and the land was left barren.

The predicted eruption had come.

Like many of the people who scoffed at the predictions of Mount St. Helens's eruption, most of the people in Joel's time paid little attention to the prophet's warnings that the Lord's judgment was soon to come. Read how the prophet describes God's warnings in **Joel 2:1–2**.

- Why do you think many of the people living near Mount St. Helens and those who heard Joel's prophecy of God's power didn't believe the warnings?
- What warning signs should you be paying attention to?

CONSIDER . . .

- riding a bicycle and viewing God's power in nature as you ride.
- reading Revelation (p. 1331) and comparing John's visions of God's power to the ones in Joel.

FOR MORE, SEE . . .

- Psalm 98 (p. 538)
- Matthew 12:33–37 (p. 929)
- 2 Peter 3:1–13 (p. 1313)

6When they see them, nations shake with fear,
and everyone's face becomes pale.

7They charge like soldiers;
they climb over the wall like warriors.
They all march straight ahead
and do not move off their path.
8They do not run into each other,
because each walks in line.
They break through all efforts to stop them
and keep coming.
9They run into the city.
They run at the wall
and climb into the houses,
entering through windows like thieves.

SIDELIGHT: The Israelites couldn't keep the locusts out of their houses (Joel 2:9), because they didn't have screens or glass windows. Instead, their windows had wooden latticework in them. I would check in the sheets before climbing into bed, wouldn't you?

10Before them, earth and sky shake.
The sun and the moon become dark,
and the stars stop shining.
11The LORD shouts out orders
to his army.
His army is very large!
Those who obey him are very strong!
The LORD's day of judging
is an overwhelming and terrible day.
No one can stand up against it!

Change Your Hearts

12The LORD says, "Even now, come back to me
with all your heart.
Go without food, and cry and be sad."

13Tearing your clothes is not enough to show
you are sad;
let your heart be broken.
Come back to the LORD your God,
because he is kind and shows mercy.
He doesn't become angry quickly,
and he has great love.
He can change his mind about doing harm.
14Who knows? Maybe he will turn back to you
and leave behind a blessing for you.
Grain and drink offerings belong to the LORD
your God.

15Blow the trumpet in Jerusalem;
call for a day when no one eats food.
Tell everyone to stop work.
16Bring the people together
and make the meeting holy for the LORD.
Bring together the older leaders,
as well as the children,
and even babies that still feed at their
mothers' breasts.
The bridegroom should come from his room,
the bride from her bedroom.
17The priests, the LORD's servants, should cry
between the altar and the entrance to the
Temple.[d]
They should say, "LORD, have mercy on your
people.
Don't let them be put to shame;
don't let other nations make fun of them.
Don't let people in other nations ask,
'Where is their God?' "

The Lord Restores the Land

18Then the LORD became concerned about his
land
and felt sorry for his people.
19He said to them:
"I will send you grain, new wine, and olive
oil,
so that you will have plenty.
No more will I shame you
among the nations.
20I will force the army from the north to leave
your land
and go into a dry, empty land.
Their soldiers in front will be forced into the
Dead Sea,[d]
and those in the rear into the
Mediterranean Sea.
Their bodies will rot and stink.
The LORD has surely done a wonderful
thing!"

21Land, don't be afraid;
be happy and full of joy,
because the LORD has done a wonderful
thing.
22Wild animals, don't be afraid,
because the open pastures have grown
grass.
The trees have given fruit;
the fig trees and the grapevines have grown
much fruit.
23So be happy, people of Jerusalem;
be joyful in the LORD your God.
Because he does what is right,
he has brought you rain;
he has sent the fall rain
and the spring rain for you, as before.
24And the threshing[d] floors will be full of grain;
the barrels will overflow with new wine
and olive oil.

The Lord Speaks

25"Though I sent my great army against you—

those swarming locusts and hopping locusts,
the destroying locusts and the cutting
locusts[n] that ate your crops—
I will pay you back
for those years of trouble.
26Then you will have plenty to eat
and be full.
You will praise the name of the LORD your
God,
who has done miracles[d] for you.
My people will never again be shamed.
27Then you will know that I am among the
people of Israel,
that I am the LORD your God,
and there is no other God.
My people will never be shamed again.

28"After this,
I will pour out my Spirit[d] on all kinds of
people.
Your sons and daughters will prophesy,[d]
your old men will dream dreams,
and your young men will see visions.
29At that time I will pour out my Spirit
also on male slaves and female
slaves.
30I will show miracles
in the sky and on the earth:
blood, fire, and thick smoke.
31The sun will become dark,
the moon red as blood,
before the overwhelming and terrible day of
the LORD comes.
32Then anyone who calls on the LORD
will be saved,
because on Mount Zion[d] and in Jerusalem
there will be people who will be saved,
just as the LORD has said.
Those left alive after the day of punishment
are the people whom the LORD called.

swarming . . . locusts These are different names for an insect like a large grasshopper. The locust can quickly destroy trees, plants, and crops, and in this destruction, Joel sees a warning. God will cause this type of destruction when he punishes his people.

FORGIVENESS

Change of Heart

When their only son was killed by a drunk driver, Frank and Elizabeth Morris had just one wish: revenge. "We wanted him dead," Mrs. Morris admits, talking about the killer.

Tommy Pigage pleaded guilty to the charge and was sent to jail. The Morrises were angry at the court for not punishing him more severely. In time, however, they realized their bitterness stopped them from getting on with their lives. They decided to visit Tommy in jail.

Tommy expressed deep remorse for killing their son and admitted that he deserved his punishment. The Morrises were moved by his sensitivity and honesty. "I didn't want my son's death to be totally in vain," Mrs. Morris says. "And in my heart I know that if he could, my son would tell us to forgive Tommy."

The Morrises' decision to forgive not only freed them from their bitterness, but also started a change in Tommy's life. He quit drinking and turned to God. The Morrises continue to visit Tommy regularly and support him in his struggle with alcoholism. "The accident already wiped out one very special life. I don't want to see it waste Tommy's life, too," Mrs. Morris says.

The giving and receiving of forgiveness is necessary for living in Christ. To change their lives, the Morrises needed to forgive—and Tommy needed their forgiveness. Read **Joel 2:12–19** for God's plea for people to change their hearts.

- How is the Morrises' (and Tommy's) change of heart similar to what God required of the people in Joel's time?
- Is forgiveness the same thing as fairness? Why or why not?

CONSIDER . . .

- making a paper heart and listing on it people you need to forgive. Ask God to help you forgive them.
- taking the risk of asking forgiveness from someone you've hurt.

FOR MORE, SEE . . .

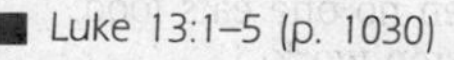

- Psalm 51 (p. 511)
- Matthew 5:21–26 (p. 913)
- Luke 13:1–5 (p. 1030)

Punishment for Judah's Enemies

3 "In those days and at that time,
when I will make things better for Judah
and Jerusalem,
2 I will gather all the nations together
and bring them down into the Valley
Where the LORD Judges.
There I will judge them,
because those nations scattered my own
people Israel
and forced them to live in other nations.
They divided up my land
3 and threw lots[d] for my people.
They traded boys for prostitutes,[d]
and they sold girls to buy wine to drink.

4 "Tyre and Sidon and all of you regions of Philistia! What did you have against me? Were you
punishing me for something I did, or were you
doing something to hurt me? I will very quickly
do to you what you have done to me. 5 You took
my silver and gold, and you put my precious treasures in your temples. 6 You sold the people of Judah and Jerusalem to the Greeks so that you could
send them far from their land.
7 "You sent my people to that faraway place, but
I will get them and bring them back, and I will do
to you what you have done to them. 8 I will sell
your sons and daughters to the people of Judah,
and they will sell them to the Sabean people far
away." The LORD said this.

God Judges the Nations

9 Announce this among the nations:
Prepare for war!
Wake up the soldiers!
Let all the men of war come near and
attack.
10 Make swords from your plows,
and make spears from your hooks for
trimming trees.
Let even the weak person say,
"I am a soldier."
11 All of you nations, hurry,

CREATION

Trashed Out

Marion Stoddart and her family watched their nice neighborhood on the Nashua River in Groton, Massachusetts, become a dumping ground for industrial waste and trash. Once beautiful, the river bank was scattered with litter, discarded appliances, and abandoned cars. The river smelled like a sewer.

Finally, Marion realized she could either move away or rescue the Nashua River, which was so polluted that people said it was "too thick to pour and too thin to plow." She organized other concerned residents in the community to reclaim the river.

They showed labor unions, business leaders, and politicians how everyone would benefit from making the river "fishable and swimmable." They even got the governor's attention by giving him a bottle of filthy river water to keep on his desk until the Nashua was clean again. Slowly, the various users of the river did their part to stop polluting and to clean up the mess, due in large part to Mrs. Stoddart's group. Mrs. Stoddart says it is possible for ordinary people to reclaim their world for good.

"You don't have to be real smart to make a difference," she says. "You just have to persuade the people with power, the people who care, and be really committed, persistent, and honest."

It is not God's will that we trash his creation. In **Joel 2:21–27** read of God's desire for the land's health and vitality.

- How does Mrs. Stoddart's crusade for the Nashua River compare to God's will for the land in Joel?
- From your reading of the passage, what do you think is God's will for the way we are to use the earth?

CONSIDER . . .

- choosing one way today to show God's love for creation by reducing the amount of trash you create.
- leading a group from your school or church in cleaning up a riverbank, a public park, or a lake shore where you live.

FOR MORE, SEE . . .

- Genesis 1 (p. 2)
- Psalm 104 (p. 541)

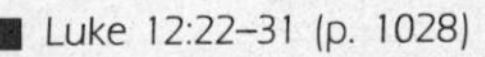

- Luke 12:22–31 (p. 1028)

and come together in that place.
LORD, send your soldiers
to gather the nations.

12"Wake up, nations,
and come to attack in the Valley Where the LORD Judges.
There I will sit to judge
all the nations on every side.
13Swing the cutting tool,
because the harvest is ripe.
Come, walk on them as you would walk on grapes to get their juice,
because the winepress[d] is full
and the barrels are spilling over,
because these people are so evil!"

14There are huge numbers of people
in the Valley of Decision,[n]
because the LORD's day of judging is near
in the Valley of Decision.
15The sun and the moon will become dark,
and the stars will stop shining.
16The LORD will roar like a lion from Jerusalem;
his loud voice will thunder from that city,
and the sky and the earth will shake.
But the LORD will be a safe place for his people,
a strong place of safety for the people of Israel.

17"Then you will know that I, the LORD your God,
live on my holy Mount Zion.[d]
Jerusalem will be a holy place,
and strangers will never even go through it again.

A New Life Promised for Judah

18"On that day wine will drip from the mountains,
milk will flow from the hills,
and water will run through all the ravines of Judah.
A fountain will flow from the Temple[d] of the LORD
and give water to the valley of acacia trees.
19But Egypt will become empty,
and Edom an empty desert,
because they were cruel to the people of Judah.
They killed innocent people in that land.
20But there will always be people living in Judah,
and people will live in Jerusalem from now on.
21Egypt and Edom killed my people,
so I will definitely punish them."

The LORD lives in Jerusalem!

Valley of Decision This is like the name Valley Where the LORD Judges in 3:2 and 3:12.

AMOS

Why Read This Book:

- Read of the Lord's punishment for injustice (Amos 1—2).
- Be warned about vanity and self-centeredness (Amos 6).
- See the Lord's reaction to those who oppress the poor (Amos 8).

Behind the Scenes:

Amos was one angry farmer! All around him were smug, satisfied people. The nation was prosperous and secure. Surely God was on Israel's side. So why was Amos angry?

Because underneath the veneer of prosperity was religious and moral corruption. People had acquired their wealth by stepping on the poor. They relied on military might instead of God. Their worship was superficial. In short, they had forgotten what it meant to follow God.

Though he lived in the southern kingdom of Judah, Amos preached to the people of Israel in the north. He took his strong, uncompromising message straight to the religious authorities of his day. Instead of listening to him, they threw him out. Sometimes the truth is hard to hear.

In the same way Amos challenged the Israelites to reconsider their priorities, he

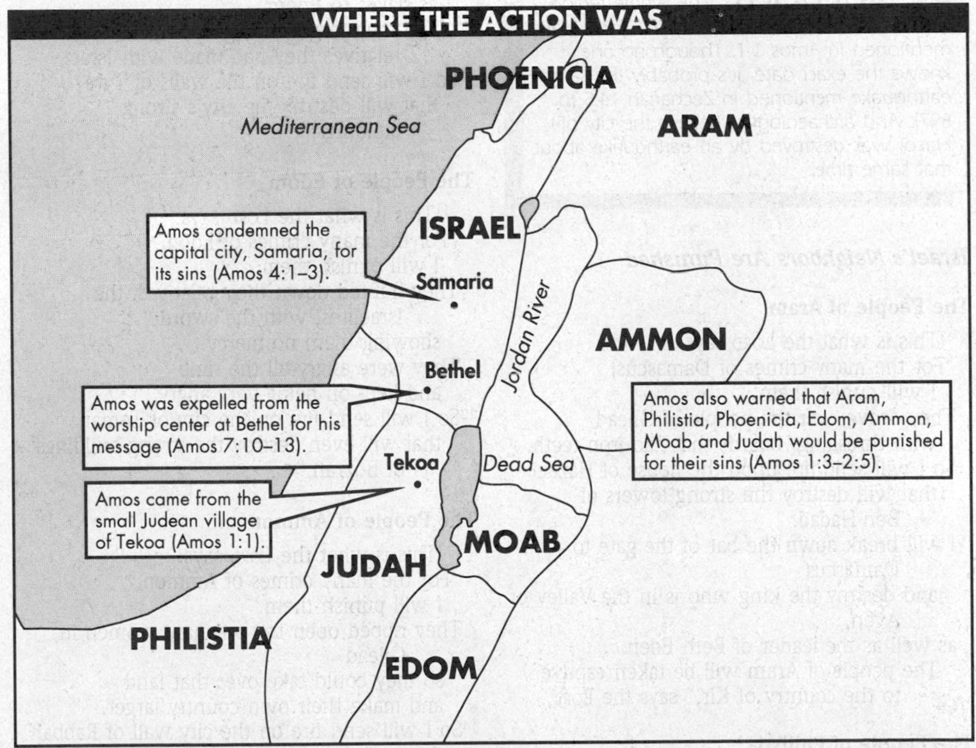

WHERE THE ACTION WAS
PHOENICIA
Mediterranean Sea
ARAM
ISRAEL
Amos condemned the capital city, Samaria, for its sins (Amos 4:1–3).
Samaria
Jordan River
AMMON
Bethel
Amos was expelled from the worship center at Bethel for his message (Amos 7:10–13).
Amos also warned that Aram, Philistia, Phoenicia, Edom, Ammon, Moab and Judah would be punished for their sins (Amos 1:3–2:5).
Tekoa
Dead Sea
Amos came from the small Judean village of Tekoa (Amos 1:1).
MOAB
JUDAH
PHILISTIA
EDOM

WHEN THE ACTION WAS

1000BC	750BC	500BC	250BC	BC/AD
The kingdom was split between Israel and Judah	Amos prophesied to Israel	The Jews began returning from exile		Jesus was born
Saul was Israel's king	The Northern Kingdom (Israel) fell to Assyria	The Southern Kingdom (Judah) fell to Babylon		

Behind the Scenes (cont.): challenges us. In the climax to his book, he reminds us what God wants from us: "Let justice flow like a river, and let goodness flow like a stream that never stops" (Amos 5:24).

---

1 These are the words of Amos, one of the
shepherds from the town of Tekoa. He saw
this vision about Israel two years before the earthquake. It was at the time Uzziah was king of
Judah and Jeroboam son of Jehoash was king
of Israel.
2Amos said,
"The LORD will roar from Jerusalem;
he will send his voice from Jerusalem.
The pastures of the shepherds will become dry,
and even the top of Mount Carmel will dry up."

> **SIDELIGHT:** The whole region of Israel was shaken by the earthquake mentioned in Amos 1:1. Though no one knows the exact date, it's probably the same earthquake mentioned in Zechariah 14:5 (p. 897). And archaeologists believe the city of Hazor was destroyed by an earthquake about that same time.

Israel's Neighbors Are Punished

The People of Aram

3This is what the LORD says:
"For the many crimes of Damascus,
I will punish them.
They drove over the people of Gilead
with threshing[d] boards that had iron teeth.
4So I will send fire upon the house of Hazael
that will destroy the strong towers of Ben-Hadad.
5I will break down the bar of the gate to Damascus
and destroy the king who is in the Valley of Aven,
as well as the leader of Beth Eden.
The people of Aram will be taken captive
to the country of Kir," says the LORD.

The People of Philistia

6This is what the LORD says:
"For the many crimes of Gaza,
I will punish them.
They sold all the people of one area
as slaves to Edom.
7So I will send a fire on the walls of Gaza
that will destroy the city's strong buildings.
8I will destroy the king of the city of Ashdod,
as well as the leader of Ashkelon.
Then I will turn against the people of the city of Ekron,
and the last of the Philistines will die," says the Lord GOD.

The People of Phoenicia

9This is what the LORD says:
"For the many crimes of Tyre,
I will punish them.
They sold all the people of one area
as slaves to Edom,
and they forgot the agreement among
relatives they had made with Israel.
10So I will send fire on the walls of Tyre
that will destroy the city's strong buildings."

The People of Edom

11This is what the LORD says:
"For the many crimes of Edom,
I will punish them.
They hunted down their relatives, the Israelites, with the sword,
showing them no mercy.
They were angry all the time
and kept on being very angry.
12So I will send fire on the city of Teman
that will even destroy the strong buildings of Bozrah." [n]

The People of Ammon

13This is what the LORD says:
"For the many crimes of Ammon,
I will punish them.
They ripped open the pregnant women in Gilead
so they could take over that land
and make their own country larger.
14So I will send fire on the city wall of Rabbah
that will destroy its strong buildings.
It will come during a day of battle,
during a stormy day with strong winds.
15Then their king and leaders will be taken captive;

Teman . . . Bozrah Since Teman was in northern Edom and Bozrah was in southern Edom, this means the whole country will be destroyed.

they will all be taken away together," says
the LORD.

The People of Moab

2 This is what the LORD says:
"For the many crimes of Moab,
I will punish them.
They burned the bones of the king of Edom
into lime.
2So I will send fire on Moab
that will destroy the strong buildings of the
city of Kerioth.
The people of Moab will die in a great noise,
in the middle of the sounds of war and
trumpets.
3So I will bring an end to the king of Moab,
and I will kill all its leaders with him," says
the LORD.

The People of Judah

4This is what the LORD says:
"For the many crimes of Judah,
I will punish them.
They rejected the teachings of the LORD
and did not keep his commands;
they followed the same gods
as their ancestors had followed.
5So I will send fire on Judah,
and it will destroy the strong buildings of
Jerusalem."

Israel Is Punished

6This is what the LORD says:
"For the many crimes of Israel,
I will punish them.
For silver, they sell people who have done
nothing wrong;
they sell the poor to buy a pair of sandals.
7They walk on poor people as if they were
dirt,
and they refuse to be fair to those who are
suffering.
Fathers and sons have sexual relations with
the same woman,
and so they ruin my holy name.
8As they worship at their altars,
they lie down on clothes taken from the
poor.
They fine people,
and with that money they buy wine to
drink in the house of their god.
9"But it was I who destroyed the Amorites
before them,
who were tall like cedar trees and as strong
as oaks—
I destroyed them completely.
10It was I who brought you from the land of
Egypt
and led you for forty years through the
desert
so I could give you the land of the
Amorites.
11I made some of your children to be prophets[d]
and some of your young people to be
Nazirites.[d]
People of Israel, isn't this true?" says the
LORD.
12"But you made the Nazirites drink wine
and told the prophets not to prophesy.
13Now I will make you get stuck,
as a wagon loaded with grain gets stuck.
14No one will escape, not even the fastest
runner.
Strong people will not be strong enough;
warriors will not be able to save
themselves.
15Soldiers with bows and arrows will not stand
and fight,
and even fast runners will not get away;
soldiers on horses will not escape alive.
16At that time even the bravest warriors
will run away without their armor," says
the LORD.

Warning to Israel

3 Listen to this word that the LORD has spoken
against you, people of Israel, against the
whole family he brought out of Egypt.
2"I have chosen only you
out of all the families of the earth,
so I will punish you
for all your sins."
3Two people will not walk together
unless they have agreed to do so.
4A lion in the forest does not roar
unless it has caught an animal;
it does not growl in its den
when it has caught nothing.
5A bird will not fall into a trap
where there is no bait;
the trap will not spring shut
if there is nothing to catch.
6When a trumpet blows a warning in a city,
the people tremble.
When trouble comes to a city,
the LORD has caused it.
7Before the Lord GOD does anything,
he tells his plans to his servants the
prophets.[d]
8The lion has roared!
Who wouldn't be afraid?
The Lord GOD has spoken.
Who will not prophesy?
9Announce this to the strong buildings of
Ashdod
and to the strong buildings of Egypt:

"Come to the mountains of Samaria,
where you will see great confusion
and people hurting others."

10"The people don't know how to do what is right," says the LORD.
"Their strong buildings are filled with treasures they took by force from others."

11So this is what the Lord GOD says:
"An enemy will take over the land
and pull down your strongholds;[d]
he will take the treasures out of your strong buildings."

12This is what the LORD says:
"A shepherd might save from a lion's mouth
only two leg bones or a scrap of an ear of his sheep.
In the same way only a few Israelites in Samaria will be saved—
people who now sit on their beds
and on their couches."

13"Listen and be witnesses against the family of
Jacob," says the Lord GOD, the God All-Powerful.

14"When I punish Israel for their sins,
I will also destroy the altars at Bethel.
The corners of the altar will be cut off,
and they will fall to the ground.
15I will tear down the winter house,
together with the summer house.
The houses decorated with ivory will be destroyed,
and the great houses will come to an end,"
says the LORD.

SIDELIGHT: If rich people today built like the rich people in Amos's day, elephants would certainly be extinct. A great sign of wealth was to have ivory inlays in furniture and paneling in your house (Amos 3:15). Amos wasn't impressed.

Israel Will Not Return

4 Listen to this message, you cows of
Bashan[n] on the Mountain of Samaria.
You take things from the poor
and crush people who are in need.
Then you command your husbands,
"Bring us something to drink!"
2The Lord GOD has promised this:
"Just as surely as I am a holy God,
the time will come
when you will be taken away by hooks,
and what is left of you with fishhooks.
3You will go straight out of the city
through holes in the walls,
and you will be thrown on the garbage dump," says the LORD.

4"Come to the city of Bethel and sin;
come to Gilgal and sin even more.
Offer your sacrifices every morning,
and bring one-tenth of your crops every three days.
5Offer bread made with yeast as a sacrifice to show your thanks,
and brag about the special offerings you bring,
because this is what you love to do,
Israelites," says the Lord GOD.

6"I did not give you any food in your cities,
and there was not enough to eat in any of your towns,
but you did not come back to me," says the LORD.
7"I held back the rain from you
three months before harvest time.
Then I let it rain on one city
but not on another.
Rain fell on one field,
but another field got none and dried up.
8People weak from thirst went from town to town for water,
but they could not get enough to drink.
Still you did not come back to me," says the LORD.
9"I made your crops die from disease and mildew.[d]
When your gardens and your vineyards got larger,
locusts[d] ate your fig and olive trees.
But still you did not come back to me,"
says the LORD.
10"I sent disasters against you,
as I did to Egypt.
I killed your young men with swords,
and your horses were taken from you.
I made you smell the stink from all the dead bodies,
but still you did not come back to me,"
says the LORD.
11"I destroyed some of you
as I destroyed Sodom and Gomorrah.
You were like a burning stick pulled from a fire,
but still you did not come back to me,"
says the LORD.

Bashan Amos compares the rich, lazy women of Samaria to well-fed cows from Bashan, a place known for its rich animal pastures.

12"So this is what I will do to you, Israel;
because I will do this to you,
get ready to meet your God, Israel."

13He is the one who makes the mountains
and creates the wind
and makes his thoughts known to people.
He changes the dawn into darkness
and walks over the mountains of the earth.
His name is the LORD God All-Powerful.

Israel Needs to Repent

5 Listen to this funeral song that I sing about
you, people of Israel.
2"The young girl Israel has fallen,
and she will not rise up again.
She was left alone in her own land,
and there is no one to help her up."

3This is what the Lord GOD says:
"If a thousand soldiers leave a city,
only a hundred will return;
if a hundred soldiers leave a city,
only ten will return."

4This is what the LORD says to the nation of
Israel:
"Come to me and live.
5 But do not look in Bethel
or go to Gilgal,
and do not go down to Beersheba.
The people of Gilgal will be taken away as
captives,
and Bethel will become nothing."
6Come to the LORD and live,
or he will move like fire against the
descendants[d] of Joseph.
The fire will burn Bethel,
and there will be no one to put it out.
7You turn justice upside down,
and you throw on the ground what is right.

8God is the one who made the star groups
Pleiades and Orion;
he changes darkness into the morning light,
and the day into dark night.
He calls for the waters of the sea
to pour out on the earth.
The LORD is his name.
9He destroys the protected city;
he ruins the strong, walled city.

10You hate those who speak in court against
evil,
and you can't stand those who tell the
truth.
11You walk on poor people,
forcing them to give you grain.
You have built fancy houses of cut stone,
but you will not live in them.
You have planted beautiful vineyards,
but you will not drink the wine from them.
12I know your many crimes,
your terrible sins.
You hurt people who do right,
you take money to do wrong,
and you keep the poor from getting justice
in court.
13In such times the wise person will keep
quiet,
because it is a bad time.

14Try to do good, not evil,
so that you will live,
and the LORD God All-Powerful will be with
you
just as you say he is.
15Hate evil and love good;
be fair in the courts.
Maybe the LORD God All-Powerful will be
kind
to the people of Joseph who are left alive.

16This is what the Lord, the LORD God All-
Powerful, says:
"People will be crying in all the streets;
they will be saying, 'Oh, no!' in the public
places.
They will call the farmers to come and weep
and will pay people to cry out loud for
them.
17People will be crying in all the vineyards,
because I will pass among you to punish
you," says the LORD.

SIDELIGHT: The people in Amos's time expected "the day of the LORD" to be a sunny picnic, but Amos countered with a dark vision of inescapable terror (Amos 5:18–19). You can run, but you can't hide!

The Lord's Day of Judging

18How terrible it will be for you who want
the LORD's day of judging to come.
Why do you want that day to come?
It will bring darkness for you, not light.
19It will be like someone who runs from a lion
and meets a bear,
or like someone who goes into his house
and puts his hand on the wall,
and then is bitten by a snake.
20So the LORD's day of judging will bring
darkness, not light;
it will be very dark, not light at all.

21The LORD says, "I completely hate your
feasts;

I cannot stand your religious meetings.
22If you offer me burnt offerings and grain offerings,
I won't accept them.
You bring your best fellowship offerings of fattened cattle,
but I will ignore them.
23Take the noise of your songs away from me!
I won't listen to the music of your harps.
24But let justice flow like a river,
and let goodness flow like a stream that never stops.

25"People of Israel, you did not bring me sacrifices and offerings
while you traveled in the desert for forty years.
26You have carried with you
your king, the god Sakkuth,
and Kaiwan your idol,
and the star gods you have made.
27So I will send you away as captives beyond Damascus,"
says the LORD, whose name is the God All-Powerful.

Israel Will Be Destroyed

6 How terrible it will be for those who have an easy life in Jerusalem,
for those who feel safe living on Mount Samaria.
You think you are the important people of the best nation in the world;
the Israelites come to you for help.
2Go look at the city of Calneh,
and from there go to the great city Hamath;
then go down to Gath of the Philistines.
You are no better than these kingdoms.
Your land is no larger than theirs.

HYPOCRISY

Empty Words

In her high school, Shannon Smith usually hung around with a close group of five or six girls. One of the fringe members of the group, Joanna, was a common topic of conversation when she wasn't around. Even though Joanna could be fun, the group didn't really like her.

When Joanna was with the other girls, they always acted friendly. But after she left, they would go back to talking about her. "We all did it," Shannon says. "We were nice to her when she was around but destroyed her behind her back. It was kind of a habit to talk bad about her."

After a while, Shannon realized the group was being hypocritical. "You really couldn't tell whether or not we liked Joanna," she says. "I began to feel funny about the way we were treating her."

Shannon soon realized she couldn't believe much of what the group said. Their words were often empty. So Shannon left the group. What do they say about me now that I'm not around? she wonders.

Just as Shannon's group was hypocritical in saying one thing but doing another, the people in Amos's time participated in Temple worship, but behaved in ways opposite to God's desires. In **Amos 5:18–24**, the people of Israel are rebuked because their sinful actions didn't match their pious words.

- What was hypocritical about the way the group treated Joanna and the way the people worshiped God in the passage?
- How do you think God's desire for justice, as expressed in the passage, applies to your own worship?

CONSIDER . . .

- keeping a list of times you have been hypocritical—when your actions were different from your beliefs. Pray for integrity and offer the list to God.
- calling your friends' attention to their mistreatment of someone else, but doing so in a Christian manner.

FOR MORE, SEE . . .

- Psalm 62 (p. 517)
- Matthew 6:2–6 (p. 917)
- Luke 13:10–17 (p. 1031)

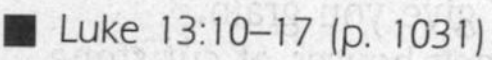

3 You put off the day of punishment,
but you bring near the day when you can
do evil to others.
4 You lie on beds decorated with ivory
and stretch out on your couches.
You eat tender lambs
and fattened calves.
5 You make up songs on your harps,
and, like David, you compose songs on
musical instruments.
6 You drink wine by the bowlful
and use the best perfumed lotions.
But you are not sad over the ruin of Israel,
7 so you will be some of the first ones taken as
slaves.
Your feasting and lying around will come to
an end.

8 The Lord GOD made this promise; the LORD
God All-Powerful says:
"I hate the pride of the Israelites,
and I hate their strong buildings,
so I will let the enemy take the city
and everything in it."

9 At that time there might be only ten people
left alive in just one house, but they will also die.
10 When the relatives come to get the bodies to
take them outside, one of them will call to the
other and ask, "Are there any other dead bodies
with you?"
That person will answer, "No."
Then the one who asked will say, "Hush! We
must not say the name of the LORD."

11 The LORD has given the command;
the large house will be broken into
pieces,
and the small house into bits.
12 Horses do not run on rocks,
and people do not plow rocks with
oxen.
But you have changed fairness into
poison;
you have changed what is right into
a bitter taste.
13 You are happy that the town of Lo Debar
was captured,

SELF-ESTEEM

It's What's Inside

Brandon Edwards had been selling balloons all afternoon. A little boy suddenly appeared across the street and watched him intently for at least thirty minutes. Finally the boy spoke, "Hey, Mister, do you think the green balloons can fly as high as the other balloons?"

"Of course," said Brandon, not paying him much attention.

After several minutes, the young boy asked, "Hey, Mister, do you think the red balloons can fly as high as the other balloons?"

"Of course," Brandon replied.

A few minutes passed and the boy asked, "Hey, Mister, how about the black balloons? Do you think the black balloons can fly as high as the other balloons?"

Brandon walked across the street to the boy, gave him a balloon, and said, "It's not the color of the balloon that makes it fly. It's what's inside the balloon that makes it fly."

It's "what's inside" that makes us "fly" in our relationship with God. Read **Amos 6:1–7** to see why God rebukes Israel for ignoring the source of real worth and value.

- How was the distorted self-esteem of the people in the passage like the boy's belief that colors affect balloon aerodynamics?
- How much do the images of materialism in the passage reflect your own values and self-esteem or your feelings of security?

CONSIDER

- listing the values—not the material things—that would improve your self-esteem and then doing one thing today to grow in the one value you believe is most important.
- joining a peer ministry or peer counseling group to help others (and yourself) grow in good self-esteem.

FOR MORE, SEE . . .

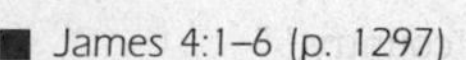

- Proverbs 22:1–4 (p. 586)
- Philippians 2:1–4 (p. 1230)
- James 4:1–6 (p. 1297)

and you say, "We have taken Karnaim[n] by
our own strength."

14The LORD God All-Powerful says,
"Israel, I will bring a nation against you
that will make your people suffer from Lebo
Hamath in the north
to the valley south of the Dead Sea."[d]

The Vision of Locusts

7 This is what the Lord GOD showed me: He
was forming a swarm of locusts,[d] after the
king had taken his share of the first crop and the
second crop had just begun growing. 2When
the locusts ate all the crops in the country, I
said, "Lord GOD, forgive us. How could Israel
live through this? It is too small already!"
3So the LORD changed his mind about this. "It
will not happen," said the LORD.

The Vision of Fire

4This is what the Lord GOD showed me: The
Lord GOD was calling for fire to come down like
rain. It burned up the deep water and was going
to burn up the land. 5Then I cried out, "Lord
GOD, stop! How could Israel live through this? It
is too small already."
6So the LORD changed his mind about this too.
"It will not happen," said the Lord GOD.

The Vision of the Plumb Line

7This is what he showed me: The Lord stood
by a straight wall, with a plumb line[d] in his hand.
8The LORD said to me, "Amos, what do you see?"
I said, "A plumb line."
Then the Lord said, "See, I will put a plumb
line among my people Israel to show how
crooked they are. I will not look the other way
any longer.

9"The places where Isaac's descendants[d]
worship will be destroyed,
Israel's holy places will be turned into
ruins,
and I will attack King Jeroboam's family
with the sword."

Amaziah Speaks Against Amos

10Amaziah, a priest at Bethel, sent this message
to Jeroboam king of Israel: "Amos is making evil
plans against you with the people of Israel. He has
been speaking so much that this land can't hold
all his words. 11This is what Amos has said:
'Jeroboam will die by the sword,
and the people of Israel will be taken as
captives
out of their own country.' "

12Then Amaziah said to Amos, "Seer,[d] go back
right now to Judah. Do your prophesying[d] and
earn your living there, 13but don't prophesy anymore here at Bethel. This is the king's holy place,
and it is the nation's temple."
14Then Amos answered Amaziah, "I do not
make my living as a prophet, nor am I a member
of a group of prophets. I make my living as a shepherd, and I take care of sycamore trees. 15But the

SIDELIGHT: When Amos said he took care of sycamore trees (Amos 7:14)—which bore figs—he did more than pick their fruit once a year. To ensure good fruit from these trees, the farmer had to slit the top of each fig as it grew.

LORD took me away from tending the flock and
said to me, 'Go, prophesy to my people Israel.'
16So listen to the LORD's word. You tell me,
'Don't prophesy against Israel,
and stop prophesying against the
descendants of Isaac.'

17"Because you have said this, the LORD says:
'Your wife will become a prostitute[d] in the
city,
and your sons and daughters will be killed
with swords.
Other people will measure your land and
divide it among themselves,
and you will die in a foreign country.
The people of Israel will definitely be taken
from their own land as captives.' "

The Vision of Ripe Fruit

8 This is what the Lord GOD showed me: a
basket of summer fruit. 2He said to me,
"Amos, what do you see?"
I said, "A basket of summer fruit."
Then the LORD said to me, "An end[n] has come
for my people Israel, because I will not overlook
their sins anymore.
3"On that day the palace songs will become funeral songs," says the Lord GOD. "There will be
dead bodies thrown everywhere! Silence!"

4Listen to me, you who walk on helpless
people,
you who are trying to destroy the poor
people of this country, saying,
5"When will the New Moon[d] festival be over
so we can sell grain?
When will the Sabbath[d] be over
so we can bring out wheat to sell?

Lo Debar . . . Karnaim These were cities in Israel that the Israelites had captured in war.
end The Hebrew word for "end" sounds like the Hebrew word for "summer fruit."

We can charge them more
and give them less,
and we can change the scales to cheat the people.
6We will buy poor people for silver,
and needy people for the price of a pair of sandals.
We will even sell the wheat that was swept up from the floor."

7The LORD has sworn by his name, the Pride of
Jacob, "I will never forget everything that these
people did.
8The whole land will shake because of it,
and everyone who lives in the land will cry for those who died.
The whole land will rise like the Nile;
it will be shaken, and then it will fall
like the Nile River in Egypt."

9The Lord GOD says:
"At that time I will cause the sun to go down at noon
and make the earth dark on a bright day.
10I will change your festivals into days of crying for the dead,
and all your songs will become songs of sadness.
I will make all of you wear rough cloth to show your sadness;
I will make you shave your heads as well.

JUSTICE

Making a Difference

By most measures, Robert Hayes was set for life. Graduating near the top of his law school class at New York University, he landed a six-figure salary with an elite Wall Street law firm. He was on the way to becoming a partner which would have paid him three hundred thousand dollars to nine hundred thousand dollars a year for the rest of his life.

The only problem with his fast-track career was the morning walk to the subway. He began noticing "the assorted bums sleeping in doorways and begging for handouts." Gradually, he says, he started talking with the people, asking them how they ended up on the streets. He "got curious and then got angry," as he describes it, when he learned how tens of thousands of New Yorkers barely survived day-to-day, bounced from one filthy shelter to another.

He visited all sorts of shelters, flophouses and organizations struggling to help the homeless. His law firm allowed him time to sue the state to do more for the homeless. In time he founded the New York Coalition for the Homeless and then the National Coalition for the Homeless.

Hayes came to realize that his life's work wasn't in Wall Street; it was with the people of the streets. "I realized what I wanted to do in life," he says. "So I did it." He resigned from his firm, leaving behind wealth and prestige, to become a lawyer for the homeless in a tiny office with flickering fluorescent lights.

"You achieve a balance in life," he says to people now. "You don't have to become Mother Teresa, but you can decide to make less and have the freedom to help people, and to make a difference."

Robert Hayes's reaction to the mistreatment of the homeless is a lot like Amos's reaction to how the Israelites treated the poor, as described in **Amos 8:4–8**.

- How are Robert Hayes's actions different from the unjust ones God condemns in the passage?
- What oppression of the poor as described by Amos do you see in your town or city?

CONSIDER . . .

- learning about the homeless people near you, and then volunteering your time to organizations that help them.
- donating to an organization that helps homeless people, such as the National Coalition for the Homeless (1621 Connecticut Ave. NW, Suite 400, Washington, DC 20009).

FOR MORE, SEE . . .

- Psalm 146 (p. 563)
- Isaiah 32:1–5 (p. 647)
- Luke 16:19–31 (p. 1038)

I will make it like a time of crying for the
death of an only son,
and its end like the end of an awful day."

11The Lord GOD says: "The days are coming
when I will cause a time of hunger in the
land.
The people will not be hungry for bread or
thirsty for water,
but they will be hungry for words from the
LORD.
12They will wander from the Mediterranean
Sea to the Dead Sea,[d]
from the north to the east.
They will search for the word of the LORD,
but they won't find it.
13At that time the beautiful young women and
the young men
will become weak from thirst.
14They make promises by the idol in Samaria
and say, 'As surely as the god of Dan
lives . . . '
and, 'As surely as the god of Beersheba[n]
lives, we promise . . . '
So they will fall
and never get up again."

Israel Will Be Destroyed

9 I saw the Lord standing by the altar, and he
said:
"Smash the top of the pillars
so that even the bottom of the doors will
shake.
Make the pillars fall on the people's heads;
anyone left alive I will kill with a sword.
Not one person will get away;
no one will escape.
2If they dig down as deep as the place of the
dead,
I will pull them up from there.
If they climb up into heaven,
I will bring them down from there.
3If they hide at the top of Mount Carmel,
I will find them and take them away.
If they try to hide from me at the bottom of
the sea,
I will command a snake to bite them.

SIDELIGHT: If you were looking for a good place to hide, Mt. Carmel would be an excellent choice (Amos 9:3). It's a wooded mountain filled with honeycomb-like caves, and it juts out over the Mediterranean Sea. Yet it's still not a good enough hiding place to escape from God.

4If they are captured and taken away by their
enemies,
I will command the sword to kill them.
I will keep watch over them,
but I will keep watch to give them trouble,
not to do them good."

5The Lord GOD All-Powerful touches the land,
and the land shakes.
Then everyone who lives in the land cries
for the dead.
The whole land rises like the Nile River
and falls like the river of Egypt.
6The LORD builds his upper rooms above the
skies;
he sets their foundations on the earth.
He calls for the waters of the sea
and pours them out on the land.
The LORD is his name.

7The LORD says,
"Israel, you are no different to me than the
people of Cush.
I brought Israel out of the land of Egypt,
and the Philistines from Crete,
and the Arameans from Kir.
8I, the Lord GOD, am watching the sinful
kingdom Israel.
I will destroy it
from off the earth,
but I will not completely destroy
Jacob's descendants,"[d] says the LORD.
9"I am giving the command
to scatter the nation of Israel among all
nations.
It will be like someone shaking grain through
a strainer,
but not even a tiny stone falls through.
10All the sinners among my people
will die by the sword—
those who say,
'Nothing bad will happen to us.'

The Lord Promises to Restore Israel

11"The kingdom of David is like a fallen tent,
but in that day I will set it up again
and mend its broken places.
I will rebuild its ruins
as it was before.
12Then Israel will take over what is left of
Edom
and the other nations that belong to me,"
says the LORD,
who will make it happen.

13The LORD says, "The time is coming when
there will be all kinds of food.

Dan . . . Beersheba Dan was the city farthest north in Israel, and Beersheba was the city farthest south.

People will still be harvesting crops
when it's time to plow again.
People will still be taking the juice from grapes
when it's time to plant again.
Wine will drip from the mountains
and pour from the hills.
14I will bring my people Israel back from captivity;
they will build the ruined cities again,
and they will live in them.
They will plant vineyards and drink the wine from them;
they will plant gardens and eat their fruit.
15I will plant my people on their land,
and they will not be pulled out again
from the land which I have given them,"
says the LORD your God.

OBADIAH

Why Read This Book:

- Learn what can happen to a nation that's filled with false pride (Obadiah 2–8).
- See how the righteous will be victorious (Obadiah 17–21).

Behind the Scenes:

If you think you've seen real rivalries on the basketball court or football field, you haven't seen real rivalries. Israel vs. Edom—now that's a real rivalry!

Even though they were close neighbors, these two countries had been rivals for hundreds of years. They fought over control of trade routes. Then when Israel was sacked by major empires, Edom not only didn't help but actually shared in the war booty! All this from a nation of people who were actually related to Israel. Esau, the father of the Edomites, was the brother of Jacob (who was also called Israel). (See Genesis 25:30, p. 30.)

Into the middle of this rivalry steps the prophet Obadiah. He describes God's anger at Edom for not helping oppressed people and for rejoicing over the Israelites' misfortune. And he predicts that Edom will be destroyed for its sinfulness, and the nation of Israel will have the final victory.

Obadiah's message was more than a motivational talk at a pep rally for the

WHERE THE ACTION WAS

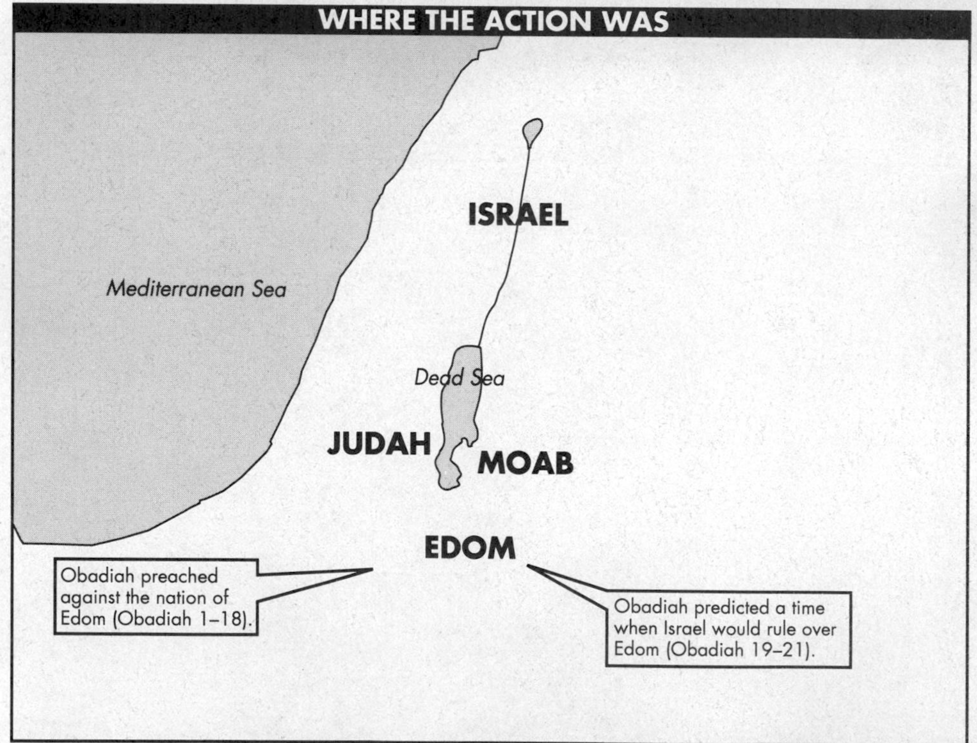
ISRAEL
Mediterranean Sea
Dead Sea
JUDAH
MOAB
EDOM
Obadiah preached against the nation of Edom (Obadiah 1–18).
Obadiah predicted a time when Israel would rule over Edom (Obadiah 19–21).

WHEN THE ACTION WAS

Obadiah may have lived

Obadiah may have lived

The Jews began returning from exile

Jesus was born

1000BC — 750BC — 500BC — 250BC — BC/AD

Saul was Israel's king

The Northern Kingdom (Israel) fell to Assyria

The Southern Kingdom (Judah) fell to Babylon

Behind the Scenes (cont.): Israelites. At times, it was harsh and full of revenge. God will correct the injustice by bringing down the Edomites, Obadiah said. His message reminds us to care for the weak around us and to keep hopeful even when we feel overwhelmed and beaten down. God will be victorious in the end!

The shortest book in the Old Testament, Obadiah only has one chapter. So its verses are numbered without chapter markings.

The Lord Will Punish the Edomites

1 This is the vision of Obadiah.

This is what the Lord God says about Edom: [n]
We have heard a message from the Lord.
A messenger has been sent among the
nations, saying,
"Attack! Let's go attack Edom!"

The Lord Speaks to the Edomites

2 "Soon I will make you the smallest of
nations.
You will be greatly hated by everyone.
3 Your pride has fooled you,

Edom The Edomites were the people who came from Esau, Jacob's twin brother. They were enemies of the Israelites.

SIN

Laughing at Others' Troubles

"What am I doing here?" Dan Gallager kept asking himself. About the last place he expected to be during his summer vacation was knee-deep in water and mud far from home. But that's exactly where he was, digging a trench for a water line.

Dan was in Appalachia with his youth group, repairing homes for the poor. "I knew in my mind that I was doing the right thing. But I was tired and wet, and I had just ruined my best pair of basketball shoes," Dan says.

The house was run-down, but it was home to a family of seven. In addition to the water line, the house needed siding, paint, and a new porch. While the other young people worked on the building, Dan dug the trench for the water pipe.

"What's wrong with this lazy family, anyway?" Dan thought to himself. "I began to wonder why they didn't just fix all of this themselves. How could they live without running water?" He started making sarcastic jokes to the other workers about the people who lived there.

As the group finished for the day and prepared to go back to their host church for dinner, the mother of the family, Mrs. Hoffman, came out of the house to talk to Dan. She was carrying a new pair of basketball shoes. "I saw how your sneakers got ruined today," she said to Dan. "These look to be about your size. I'd appreciate it if you would take them. Thanks for all you're doing for us."

Dan just stood there, feeling guilty about the cruel words he had spoken and thought. As he got in the van to leave, he wondered who was really helping whom.

Our actions and words don't go unnoticed. Read in **Obadiah 12–14** how the Lord reacts to those who laugh at people's troubles.

- How is Dan's attitude toward the Appalachian family similar to the sin of laughing at others' troubles described in the passage?
- How do you usually feel about yourself after laughing at someone's troubles or problems?

CONSIDER . . .

- saying a word of encouragement to a family member who has had a hard day.
- befriending a student at your school who is often laughed at or picked on.

FOR MORE, SEE . . .

- Proverbs 19:17 (p. 584)
- John 8:1–11 (p. 1070)
- Galatians 6:1–6 (p. 1213)

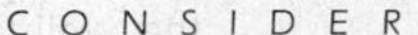

you who live in the hollow places of the
cliff.
Your home is up high,
you who say to yourself,
'No one can bring me down to the
ground.'
4Even if you fly high like the eagle
and make your nest among the stars,
I will bring you down from there," says the
LORD.
5"You will really be ruined!
If thieves came to you,
if robbers came by night,
they would steal only enough for
themselves.
If workers came and picked the grapes from
your vines,
they would leave a few behind.
6But you, Edom, will really lose everything!
People will find all your hidden treasures!

SIDELIGHT: Some people hide their money under mattresses, but the Edomites reportedly squirreled their wealth in the red cliffs south of the Dead Sea where they lived (Obadiah 6). Obadiah mentions "treasures" on an average of every seventh verse.

7All the people who are your friends
will force you out of the land.
The people who are at peace with you
will trick you and defeat you.
Those who eat your bread with you now
are planning a trap for you,
and you will not notice it."
8The LORD says, "On that day
I will surely destroy the wise people from
Edom,
and those with understanding from the
mountains of Edom.
9Then, city of Teman, your best warriors will
be afraid,
and everyone from the mountains of Edom
will be killed.
10You did violence to your relatives, the
Israelites,
so you will be covered with shame
and destroyed forever.
11You stood aside without helping
while strangers carried Israel's treasures
away.
When foreigners entered Israel's city gate
and threw lots[d] to decide what part of
Jerusalem they would take,
you were like one of them.

Commands That Edom Broke

12"Edom, do not laugh at your brother Israel in
his time of trouble
or be happy about the people of Judah when
they are destroyed.
Do not brag when cruel things are done to
them.
13Do not enter the city gate of my people
in their time of trouble
or laugh at their problems
in their time of trouble.
Do not take their treasures
in their time of trouble.
14Do not stand at the crossroads
to destroy those who are trying to escape.
Do not capture those who escape alive and
turn them over to their enemy
in their time of trouble.

The Nations Will Be Judged

15"The LORD's day of judging is coming soon
to all the nations.
The same evil things you did to other people
will happen to you;
they will come back upon your own head.
16Because you drank in my Temple,[d]
all the nations will drink on and on.
They will drink and drink
until they disappear.
17But on Mount Zion[d] some will escape the
judgment,
and it will be a holy place.
The people of Jacob will take back their land
from those who took it from them.
18The people of Jacob will be like a fire
and the people of Joseph[n] like a flame.
But the people of Esau[n] will be like dry
stalks.
The people of Jacob will set them on fire
and burn them up.
There will be no one left of the people of
Esau."
This will happen because the LORD has said
it.
19Then God's people will regain southern Judah
from Edom;
they will take back the mountains of Edom.
They will take back the western hills
from the Philistines.
They will regain the lands of Ephraim and
Samaria,

people of Jacob . . . Joseph The people who came from Jacob and Joseph, or the Israelites.
people of Esau The people who came from Esau, or the Edomites.

and Benjamin will take over Gilead.
20People from Israel who once were forced to leave their homes
will take the land of the Canaanites,
all the way to Zarephath.
People from Judah who once were forced to leave Jerusalem and live in Sepharad
will take back the cities of southern Judah.
21Powerful warriors will go up on Mount Zion,
where they will rule the people living on Edom's mountains.
And the kingdom will belong to the LORD.

JONAH

Why Read This Book:

- Discover truth in a story of a prophet who was reluctant to do what God wanted him to do (Jonah 1—2).
- See that God's love and mercy are for all the world (Jonah 3—4).

Behind the Scenes:

Being chosen to be a leader or to fill an office is always a great honor. But you probably wouldn't last long in the position if you simply basked in the glow of being chosen. You would have to fulfill the tasks and responsibilities—some that you might not like—that come with the honor.

The Jews had been chosen by God to be his special people. Through history, God had guided and protected them. But what responsibilities for the rest of the world did that honor include? Should God's people shut off the world, focusing on their gifts from God? Or should they take the story of God's love to the rest of the world?

The story of Jonah addressed this dilemma. God called the prophet Jonah to go preach at Nineveh, the heathen capital of Assyria. Not wanting to preach to non-Jewish people—especially pagans whose cruelty and barbaric actions were widely known—Jonah went the opposite direction. Like many Israelites, he enjoyed God's mercy on Israel but wanted all enemies to be destroyed.

God wouldn't let Jonah off from his mission, though. Through a storm and a big fish, God got Jonah's attention and turned him around. Reluctantly, Jonah went to Nineveh and preached, and the whole city turned to God. But Jonah wasn't happy. He went to sulk and complain about God sparing the Ninevites from destruction.

God responded with a message that's at the heart of the book: "Shouldn't I show concern for the great city Nineveh, which has people who do not know right from wrong . . . ?" (Jonah 4:11).

Jonah's story reminds all God's followers that no one has a "corner" on God.

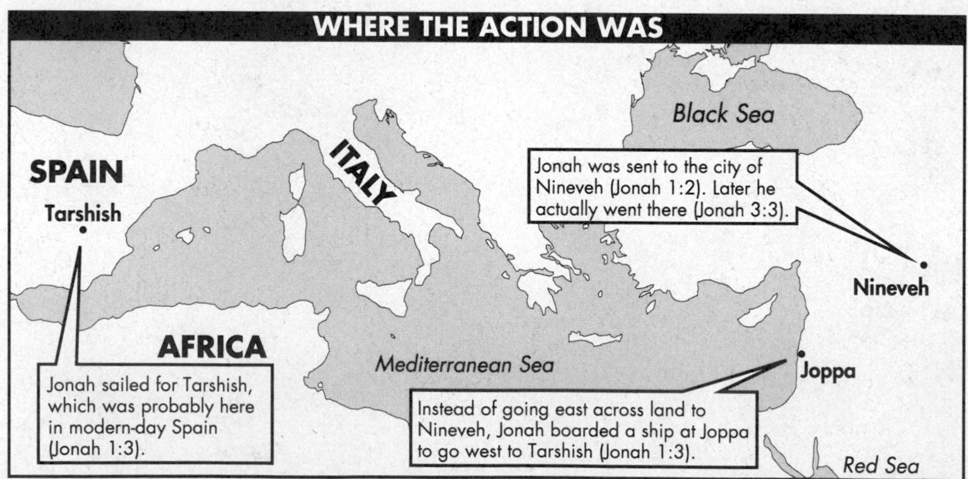
WHERE THE ACTION WAS
Black Sea
SPAIN
Tarshish
ITALY
Jonah was sent to the city of Nineveh (Jonah 1:2). Later he actually went there (Jonah 3:3).
Nineveh
AFRICA
Mediterranean Sea
Joppa
Jonah sailed for Tarshish, which was probably here in modern-day Spain (Jonah 1:3).
Instead of going east across land to Nineveh, Jonah boarded a ship at Joppa to go west to Tarshish (Jonah 1:3).
Red Sea

WHEN THE ACTION WAS

- 1000BC
- Saul was Israel's king
- The kingdom was split between Israel and Judah
- 750BC
- The prophet Jonah lived
- The Northern Kingdom (Israel) fell to Assyria
- The Southern Kingdom (Judah) fell to Babylon
- 500BC
- The Jews began returning from exile
- 250BC
- BC/AD
- Jesus was born

Behind the Scenes (cont.): God wants his people to tell others about his love. As Jesus said in Luke 5:32 (p. 1012), "I have not come to invite good people but sinners to change their hearts and lives."

God Calls and Jonah Runs

1 The LORD spoke his word to Jonah son of
Amittai: 2"Get up, go to the great city of Nineveh, and preach against it, because I see the evil
things they do."
3But Jonah got up to run away from the LORD
by going to Tarshish. He went to the city of Joppa,
where he found a ship that was going to the city
of Tarshish. Jonah paid for the trip and went
aboard, planning to go to Tarshish to run away
from the LORD.

SIDELIGHT: The name Jonah (Jonah 1:1) means "dove," which may have been a traditional symbol for the nation of Israel (see Psalm 74:19–21, p. 526).

4But the LORD sent a great wind on the sea,
which made the sea so stormy that the ship was
in danger of breaking apart. 5The sailors were
afraid, and each man cried to his own god. They
began throwing the cargo from the ship into the
sea to make the ship lighter.
But Jonah had gone down far inside the ship to
lie down, and he fell fast asleep. 6The captain of
the ship came and said, "Why are you sleeping?
Get up and pray to your god! Maybe your god will
pay attention to us, and we won't die!"
7Then the men said to each other, "Let's throw
lots[d] to see who caused these troubles to happen
to us."
When they threw lots, the lot showed that the
trouble had happened because of Jonah. 8Then
they said to him, "Tell us, who caused our trouble? What is your job? Where do you come from?
What is your country? Who are your people?"
9Then Jonah said to them, "I am a Hebrew. I
fear the LORD, the God of heaven, who made the
sea and the land."
10The men were very afraid, and they asked
Jonah, "What terrible thing did you do?" (They
knew he was running away from the LORD because he had told them.)
11Since the wind and the waves of the sea were
becoming much stronger, they said to him, "What
should we do to you to make the sea calm down
for us?"
12Jonah said to them, "Pick me up, and throw
me into the sea, and then it will calm down. I
know it is my fault that this great storm has come
on you."
13Instead, the men tried to row the ship back
to the land, but they could not, because the sea
was becoming more stormy.

Jonah's Punishment

14So the men cried to the LORD, "LORD, please
don't let us die because of this man's life; please
don't think we are guilty of killing an innocent
person. LORD, you have caused all this to happen;
you wanted it this way." 15So they picked up Jonah and threw him into the sea, and the sea
became calm. 16Then they began to fear the
LORD very much; they offered a sacrifice to
the LORD and made promises to him.
17The LORD caused a big fish to swallow Jonah,
and Jonah was inside the fish three days and three
nights.

SIDELIGHT: Being swallowed by a big fish may have been a bit of divine comedy (Jonah 1:17). In an ancient kind of writing known as cuneiform the name Nineveh may have been represented by a box with a fish inside.

2 While Jonah was inside the fish, he prayed
to the LORD his God and said,
2"When I was in danger,
I called to the LORD,
and he answered me.
I was about to die,
so I cried to you,
and you heard my voice.
3You threw me into the sea,
down, down into the deep sea.
The water was all around me,
and your powerful waves flowed over me.
4I said, 'I was driven out of your presence,
but I hope to see your Holy Temple[d] again.'
5The waters of the sea closed around my
throat.
The deep sea was all around me;
seaweed was wrapped around my head.
6When I went down to where the mountains
of the sea start to rise,
I thought I was locked in this prison
forever,
but you saved me from the pit of death,
LORD my God.

[7]"When my life had almost gone,
I remembered the LORD.
I prayed to you,
and you heard my prayers in your Holy Temple.

[8]"People who worship useless idols
give up their loyalty to you.
[9]But I will praise and thank you
while I give sacrifices to you,
and I will keep my promises to you.
Salvation comes from the LORD!"

[10]Then the LORD spoke to the fish, and the fish threw up Jonah onto the dry land.

God Calls and Jonah Obeys

3 The LORD spoke his word to Jonah again and said, [2]"Get up, go to the great city Nineveh, and preach to it what I tell you to say."

[3]So Jonah obeyed the LORD and got up and went to Nineveh. It was a very large city; just to walk across it took a person three days. [4]After Jonah had entered the city and walked for one day, he preached to the people, saying, "After forty days, Nineveh will be destroyed!"

[5]The people of Nineveh believed God. They announced that they would stop eating for a while, and they put on rough cloth to show their sadness. All the people in the city did this, from the most important to the least important.

[6]When the king of Nineveh heard this news, he got up from his throne, took off his robe, and covered himself with rough cloth and sat in ashes to show how upset he was.

SIDELIGHT: The rough cloth the king put on when he heard about Nineveh's sins would make polyester feel like fine silk (Jonah 3:6). It was probably made of scratchy goat hair. Wearing it next to the skin virtually guaranteed discomfort. It was the common clothing to wear during times of repentance or mourning.

[7]He sent this announcement through Nineveh:

By command of the king and his important men: No person or animal, herd or flock, will be allowed to taste anything. Do not let them eat food or drink water. [8]But every person and animal should be covered with rough cloth, and people should cry loudly to

THANKFULNESS

A Simple Thank You

When she was three years old, Lisa Greene was pulled from the flames engulfing her home in Brooklyn, New York. She spent three months in a hospital, where she recovered from severe burns.

Fourteen years later, as her high school graduation approached, she decided to track down the firefighter who saved her life. With the fire department's help she located Lt. Marvin Bunch, who had retired to Las Vegas. Lisa invited him to her graduation so she could thank him.

"I always wanted to thank him personally, and I wanted to show him that it really was worthwhile saving my life," Lisa explains. "I have a future—I'm going to college—and it's all because of him." Moved by her gratitude, Lt. Bunch returned to New York to share Lisa's happiness.

Jonah, too, experienced being saved from a life-threatening situation. Read of Jonah's thankfulness to God in **Jonah 2:2–9**.

- How was Lisa's experience similar to Jonah's?
- When was the last time you thanked God for saving you?

CONSIDER . . .

- drawing a "wheel of thankfulness" (a circle with pie-shaped wedges), writing the things you're thankful to God for in the spaces. Offer a prayer thanking God for them.
- giving a small present as "thanks" to someone who has helped you through a difficult time.

FOR MORE, SEE . . .

- Psalm 65 (p. 518)
- Luke 17:11–19 (p. 1040)
- 1 Thessalonians 5:12–18 (p. 1249)

God. Everyone must turn away from evil living and stop doing harm all the time. 9Who
knows? Maybe God will change his mind.
Maybe he will stop being angry, and then we
will not die.

10When God saw what the people did, that
they stopped doing evil, he changed his mind and
did not do what he had warned. He did not punish them.

God's Mercy Makes Jonah Angry

4 But this made Jonah very unhappy, and he
became angry. 2He prayed to the LORD,
"When I was still in my own country this is what
I said would happen, and that is why I quickly ran
away to Tarshish. I knew that you are a God who
is kind and shows mercy. You don't become angry quickly, and you have great love. I knew you
would choose not to cause harm. 3So now I ask
you, LORD, please kill me. It is better for me to die
than to live."

4Then the LORD said, "Do you think it is right
for you to be angry?"

5Jonah went out and sat down east of the city.
There he made a shelter for himself and sat in the
shade, waiting to see what would happen to the

FORGIVENESS

Personal Peace

By 1938, when eighteen-year-old Joseph Mavsar left home to study for the ministry, he had heard many sermons about forgiveness. In a few years, however, he would know how hard it would become to live out those sermons.

In 1941, Italy invaded Yugoslavia and occupied Joseph's village. The family's troubles increased when his father, a respected leader, refused to join the local Communist resistance.

The family gathered for Christmas, 1942. Two days later, the Communists attacked the house and killed Joseph's parents, four of his brothers and his only sister. Joseph and his twelve-year-old brother, Bill, jumped from a second-floor window and fled to the woods. The Communists burned the others' bodies and stole the family's property.

Just two brothers of the large family survived the war.

Joseph came to the United States in 1948 as a minister. He amazed some and shocked others as he preached forgiveness for the war crimes. Although he wanted the truth of the crimes against his family to be known, he still preached forgiveness.

As the twenty-fifth anniversary of his ordination approached, however, Joseph still struggled to personally forgive the people who had killed his family and taken all its possessions. Then a cousin in Yugoslavia wrote to Joseph, telling him that some of the killers were haunted by what they had done. "Come back and make peace with them," the cousin wrote.

Joseph returned to his village and found one of the Communists living in his father's house. "As I shook this man's hand and told him I forgave him," Joseph remembers, "he thanked me over and over, and said it was the best day of his life."

In his old age, Joseph continued to preach forgiveness. "In life we cannot be happy unless we're able to forgive," he said. "We must forgive, no matter how painful the hurt."

He knows what he's talking about.

Sometimes offenses seem too great to ever be forgiven. Read in **Jonah 3:1–10** how the Lord forgives the people of Nineveh for their many sins.

- Jonah did not want to forgive Nineveh (Jonah 4:1). How do Joseph and Jonah differ in their willingness to forgive?
- Have you ever found it difficult to forgive someone, even though it was necessary for your own peace of mind?

CONSIDER . . .

- forgiving someone who has hurt you, even though it's difficult to do.
- making the first move to restore a damaged relationship within your family or peers.

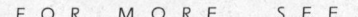

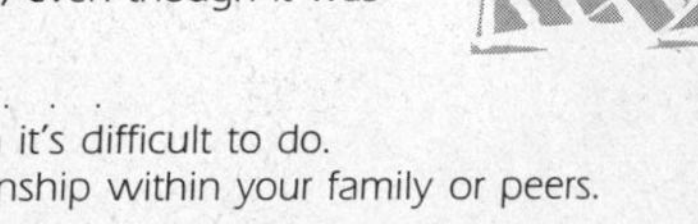

FOR MORE, SEE . . .

- Joel 2:12–19 (p. 837)
- Luke 23:26–34 (p. 1053)
- Acts 10:43 (p. 1115)

city. [6]The LORD made a plant grow quickly up
over Jonah, which gave him shade and helped
him to be more comfortable. Jonah was very
pleased to have the plant. [7]But the next day when
the sun rose, God sent a worm to attack the plant
so that it died.

[8]As the sun rose higher in the sky, God sent a
very hot east wind to blow, and the sun became
so hot on Jonah's head that he became very weak
and wished he were dead. He said, "It is better for
me to die than to live."

[9]But God said to Jonah, "Do you think it is right
for you to be angry about the plant?"

Jonah answered, "It is right for me to be angry! I am so angry I could die!"

[10]And the LORD said, "You are so concerned for
that plant even though you did nothing to make
it grow. It appeared one day, and the next day it
died. [11]Then shouldn't I show concern for the
great city Nineveh, which has more than one
hundred twenty thousand people who do not
know right from wrong, and many animals, too?"

MICAH

Why Read This Book:

- See God's judgment on a nation that didn't follow him (Micah 1–2).
- Find out what happens when leaders' actions are unjust (Micah 3).
- Be encouraged by God's promise for the future (Micah 7).

Behind the Scenes: Everything was falling apart, but no one seemed to notice. And when people were confronted with their problems, they just rolled their eyes, unwilling to listen to a message that seemed so farfetched.

That was the prophet Micah's situation. When he started preaching in Judah, its northern neighbor, Israel, was about to be conquered by the Assyrians. And, he believed, the same fate awaited Judah because of its injustice to the poor and its immoral leadership.

The book of Micah is a collection of Micah's sermons about God's punishment of Judah. Yet Micah also saw hope and redemption in the future. Because of God's mercy, Micah said, God would reclaim the Israelites and establish a kingdom of eternal peace.

The heart of Micah's message summarized what most of the prophets called

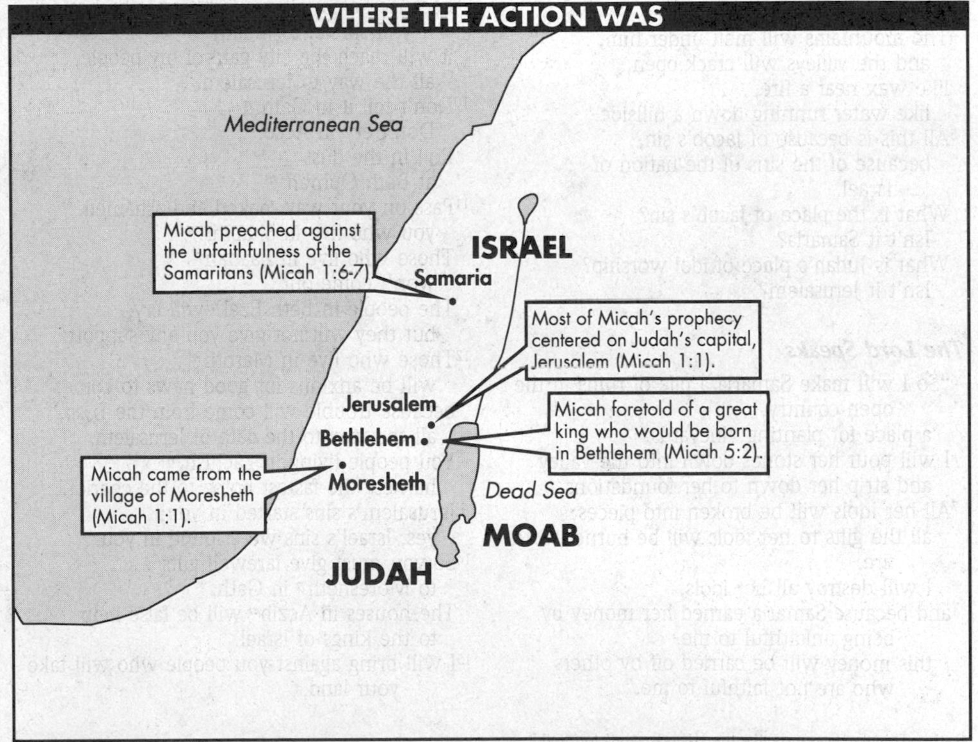
WHERE THE ACTION WAS
Mediterranean Sea
Micah preached against the unfaithfulness of the Samaritans (Micah 1:6-7).
ISRAEL
Samaria
Most of Micah's prophecy centered on Judah's capital, Jerusalem (Micah 1:1).
Jerusalem
Bethlehem
Micah foretold of a great king who would be born in Bethlehem (Micah 5:2).
Micah came from the village of Moresheth (Micah 1:1).
Moresheth
Dead Sea
MOAB
JUDAH

WHEN THE ACTION WAS

- The kingdom was split between Israel and Judah
- Micah prophesied in Jerusalem
- The Jews began returning from exile
- Jesus was born

1000BC — 750BC — 500BC — 250BC — BC/AD

- Saul was Israel's king
- The Northern Kingdom (Israel) fell to Assyria
- The Southern Kingdom (Judah) fell to Babylon

Behind the Scenes (cont.): people to do: "The Lord has told you, human, what is good; he has told you what he wants from you: to do what is right to other people, love being kind to others, and live humbly, obeying your God" (Micah 6:8). It's a message that's just as relevant today as it was more than twenty-five hundred years ago.

Samaria and Israel to Be Punished

1 During the time that Jotham, Ahaz, and Hezekiah were kings of Judah, the word of the LORD came to Micah, who was from Moresheth. He saw these visions about Samaria and Jerusalem.

2Hear this, all you nations;
listen, earth and all you who live on it.
The Lord GOD will be a witness against you,
the Lord from his Holy Temple.[d]
3See, the LORD is coming out of his place;
he is coming down to walk on the tops of the mountains.
4The mountains will melt under him,
and the valleys will crack open,
like wax near a fire,
like water running down a hillside.
5All this is because of Jacob's sin,
because of the sins of the nation of Israel.
What is the place of Jacob's sin?
Isn't it Samaria?
What is Judah's place of idol worship?
Isn't it Jerusalem?

The Lord Speaks

6"So I will make Samaria a pile of ruins in the open country,
a place for planting vineyards.
I will pour her stones down into the valley
and strip her down to her foundations.
7All her idols will be broken into pieces;
all the gifts to her idols will be burned with fire.
I will destroy all her idols,
and because Samaria earned her money by being unfaithful to me,
this money will be carried off by others
who are not faithful to me."

SIDELIGHT: Micah has sometimes been called the "wailing prophet," based on Micah 1:8. He's not the only one who went "barefoot and naked" to make a point. Isaiah attracted attention the same way, in Isaiah 20:2–4 (p. 637).

Micah's Great Sadness

8I will moan and cry because of this evil,
going around barefoot and naked.
I will cry loudly like the wild dogs
and make sad sounds like the owls do,
9because Samaria's wound cannot be healed.
It will spread to Judah;
it will reach the city gate of my people,
all the way to Jerusalem.
10Don't tell it in Gath.[n]
Don't cry in Acco.[n]
Roll in the dust
at Beth Ophrah.[n]
11Pass on your way, naked and ashamed,
you who live in Shaphir.[n]
Those who live in Zaanan[n]
won't come out.
The people in Beth Ezel[n] will cry,
but they will not give you any support.
12Those who live in Maroth[n]
will be anxious for good news to come,
because trouble will come from the LORD,
all the way to the gate of Jerusalem.
13You people living in Lachish,[n]
harness the fastest horse to the chariot.
Jerusalem's sins started in you;
yes, Israel's sins were found in you.
14So you must give farewell gifts
to Moresheth[n] in Gath.
The houses in Aczib[n] will be false help
to the kings of Israel.
15I will bring against you people who will take your land,

Gath This name sounds like the Hebrew word for "tell."
Acco This name sounds like the Hebrew word for "cry."
Beth Ophrah This name means "house of dust."
Shaphir This name means "beautiful."
Zanaan This name sounds like the Hebrew word for "come out."
Beth Ezel This name means "house by the side of another," suggesting help or support.
Maroth This name sounds like the Hebrew word for "sad" or "miserable."
Lachish This name sounds like the Hebrew word for "horses."
Moresheth This may be a play on the word "engaged," referring to a farewell gift to a bride.
Aczib This name means "lie" or "trick."

you who live in Mareshah.[n]
The glory of Israel
will go in to Adullam.
16Cut off your hair to show you are sad
for the children you love.
Make yourself bald like the eagle,
because your children will be taken away
to a foreign land.

The Evil Plans of People

2 How terrible it will be for people who
plan wickedness,
who lie on their beds and make evil plans.
When the morning light comes, they do what
they planned,
because they have the power to do so.
2They want fields, so they take them;
they want houses, so they take them away.
They cheat people to get their houses;
they rob them even of their property.

3That is why the LORD says:
"Look, I am planning trouble against such
people,
and you won't be able to save yourselves.
You will no longer walk proudly,
because it will be a terrible time.
4At that time people will make fun of you
and sing this sad song about you:
'We are completely ruined;
the LORD has taken away my people's land.
Yes, he has taken it away from me
and divided our fields among our
enemies!' "
5So you will have no one from the LORD's
people
to throw lots[d] to divide the land.

Micah Is Asked Not to Prophesy

6The prophets say, "Don't prophesy[d] to us!
Don't prophesy about these things!
Nothing to make us feel bad will happen!"
7But I must say this, people of Jacob:
The LORD is becoming angry about what
you have done.
My words are welcome
to the person who does what is right.
8But you are fighting against my people like an
enemy.
You take the coats from people who pass
by;
you rob them of their safety;
you plan war.
9You've forced the women of my people
from their nice houses;
you've taken my glory
from their children forever.
10Get up and leave.
This is not your place of rest anymore.
You have made this place unclean,[d]
and it is doomed to destruction.
11But you people want a false prophet
who will tell you nothing but lies.
You want one who promises to prophesy
good things for you
if you give him wine and beer.
He's just the prophet for you.

The Lord Promises to Rescue His People

12"Yes, people of Jacob, I will bring all of you
together;
I will bring together all those left alive in
Israel.
I will put them together like sheep in a pen,
like a flock in its pasture;
the place will be filled with many people.
13Someone will open the way and lead the
people out.
The people will break through the gate and
leave the city where they were held
captive.
Their king will go out in front of them,
and the LORD will lead them."

The Leaders of Israel Are Guilty of Evil

3 Then I said,
"Listen, leaders of the people of Jacob;
listen, you rulers of the nation of Israel.
You should know how to decide cases fairly,
2 but you hate good and love evil.
You skin my people alive
and tear the flesh off their bones.
3You eat my people's flesh
and skin them and break their bones;
you chop them up like meat for the pot,
like meat in a cooking pan.
4They will cry to the LORD,
but he won't answer them.
At that time he will hide his face from them,
because what they have done is evil."

5The LORD says this about the prophets[d] who
teach his people the wrong way of living:
"If these prophets are given food to eat,
they shout, 'Peace!'
But if someone doesn't give them what they
ask for,
they call for a holy war against that person.
6So it will become like night for them,
without visions.
It will become dark for them, without any
way to tell the future.
The sun is about to set for the prophets;
their day will become dark.

Mareshah This name sounds like the Hebrew word for a person who captures other cities and lands.

7The seers[d] will be ashamed;
the people who see the future will be embarrassed.
Yes, all of them will cover their mouths,
because there will be no answer from God."

Micah Is an Honest Prophet of God

8But I am filled with power,
with the Spirit[d] of the LORD,
and with justice and strength,
to tell the people of Jacob how they have turned against God,
and the people of Israel how they have sinned.
9Leaders of Jacob and rulers of Israel,
listen to me,
you who hate fairness
and twist what is right.
10You build Jerusalem by murdering people;
you build it with evil.
11Its judges take money
to decide who wins in court.
Its priests only teach for pay,
and its prophets[d] only look into the future when they get paid.
But they lean on the LORD and say,
"The LORD is here with us,
so nothing bad will happen to us."
12Because of you,
Jerusalem will be plowed like a field.
The city will become a pile of rocks,
and the hill on which the Temple[d] stands
will be covered with bushes.

The Mountain of the Lord

4 In the last days
the mountain on which the LORD's Temple[d] stands
will become the most important of all mountains.
It will be raised above the hills,
and people from other nations will come streaming to it.
2Many nations will come and say,
"Come, let us go up to the mountain of the LORD,
to the Temple of the God of Jacob,
so that he can teach us his ways,
and we can obey his teachings."
His teachings will go out from Jerusalem,
the word of the LORD from that city.
3The Lord will judge many nations;
he will make decisions about strong nations that are far away.
They will hammer their swords into plow blades
and their spears into hooks for trimming trees.
Nations will no longer raise swords against other nations;
they will not train for war anymore.
4Everyone will sit under his own vine and fig tree,
and no one will make them afraid,
because the LORD All-Powerful has said it.
5All other nations may follow their own gods,
but we will follow the LORD our God
forever and ever.

6The LORD says, "At that time,
I will gather the crippled;
I will bring together those who were sent away,
those whom I caused to have trouble.
7I will keep alive those who were crippled,
and I will make a strong nation of those who were sent away.
The LORD will be their king in Mount Zion[d]
from now on and forever.
8And you, watchtower of the flocks,[n] hill of Jerusalem,
to you will come the kingdom as in the past.
Jerusalem, the right to rule will come again to you."

Why the Israelites Must Go to Babylon

9Now, why do you cry so loudly?
Is your king gone?
Have you lost your helper,
so that you are in pain, like a woman trying to give birth?
10People of Jerusalem, strain and be in pain.
Be like a woman trying to give birth,
because now you must leave the city
and live in the field.
You will go to Babylon,
but you will be saved from that place.
The LORD will go there
and buy you back from your enemies.

11But now many nations
have come to fight against you,
saying, "Let's destroy Jerusalem.
We will look at her and be glad we have defeated her."
12But they don't know
what the LORD is thinking;
they don't understand his plan.
He has gathered them like bundles of grain
to the threshing[d] floor.

watchtower . . . flocks This probably means a part of Jerusalem. The leaders would be like shepherds in a tower watching their sheep.

13“Get up and beat them, people of Jerusalem.
I will make you strong as if you had horns of iron
and hoofs of bronze.
You will beat many nations into small pieces
and give their wealth to the LORD,
their treasure to the Lord of all the earth.”

5 So, strong city, gather your soldiers together,
because we are surrounded and attacked.
They will hit the leader of Israel
in the face with a club.

SIDELIGHT: The book of Micah has been important to Christians, partly because of Micah 5:2. Matthew 2:6 (p. 907) says this prophecy was fulfilled when Jesus was born in Bethlehem.

The Ruler to Be Born in Bethlehem

2“But you, Bethlehem Ephrathah,
though you are too small to be among the army groups from Judah,
from you will come one who will rule Israel for me.
He comes from very old times,
from days long ago.”

3The LORD will give up his people
until the one who is having a baby gives birth;
then the rest of his relatives will return
to the people of Israel.
4At that time the ruler of Israel will stand
and take care of his people
with the LORD’s strength
and with the power of the name of the LORD his God.
The Israelites will live in safety,
because his greatness will reach all over the earth.
5 He will bring peace.

LEADERSHIP

A Leader Who Overcame

He grew up in the country, an area so rural that he had to study on his own because it was too far to travel to the nearest school. In fact, by the time he was an adult, his total official schooling amounted to no more than one year. His parents were uneducated; his mother was unable to read or write.

His family wasn’t rich, so he had to stay around the homestead with his brothers and sisters to help keep up the farm. Because of his limited traveling, he knew very little of the world outside of Illinois until he was eighteen years old.

Small town, no schooling, unfamiliar with the world. With a background like that, you might not expect this person to become one of the greatest leaders in U.S. history: Abraham Lincoln.

There’s more to being a leader than where you were brought up, whether you’re rich, or whom you know. Lincoln was a good leader because of his wisdom, honesty, and trustworthiness. People felt confident under his leadership. Read **Micah 5:2–4** to find out about another world leader born in the “backwoods” town of Bethlehem in Judah.

- What similarities are there between Abraham Lincoln and Jesus? What differences are there?
- Which obstacles might keep a person from becoming a leader? Which obstacles are possible for a leader to overcome?

CONSIDER . . .

- choosing two leadership qualities you admire and developing those qualities in yourself.
- getting involved with underprivileged children and encouraging them to overcome obstacles.

FOR MORE, SEE . . .

- Exodus 4:10–17 (p. 62)
- Matthew 2:1–6 (p. 907)
- 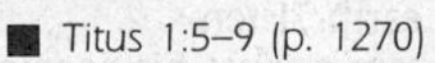Titus 1:5–9 (p. 1270)

Rescue and Punishment

Assyria will surely come into our country
and walk over our large buildings.
We will set up seven shepherds,
eight leaders of the people.
6They will destroy the Assyrians with their
swords;
they will conquer the land of Assyria with
their swords drawn.
They will rescue us from the Assyrians when
they come into our land,
when they walk over our borders.

7Then the people of Jacob who are left alive
will be to other people
like dew from the LORD
or rain on the grass—
it does not wait for human beings;
it does not pause for any person.
8Those of Jacob's people who are left alive
will be scattered among many nations and
peoples.
They will be like a lion among the animals of
the forest,
like a young lion in a flock of sheep:
As it goes, it jumps on them
and tears them to pieces,
and no one can save them.
9So you will raise your fist in victory over
your enemies,
and all your enemies will be destroyed.

10The LORD says, "At that time,
I will take your horses from you
and destroy your chariots.
11I will destroy the cities in your country
and tear down all your defenses.
12I will take away the magic charms you use
so you will have no more fortune-tellers.
13I will destroy your statues of gods
and the stone pillars you worship
so that you will no longer worship
what your hands have made.
14I will tear down Asherah[d] idols from you
and destroy your cities.
15In my anger and rage,
I will pay back the nations that have not
listened."

The Lord's Case

6 Now hear what the LORD says:
"Get up; plead your case in front of the
mountains;
let the hills hear your story.
2Mountains, listen to the LORD's legal case.
Foundations of the earth, listen.
The LORD has a legal case against his people,
and he will accuse Israel."
3He says, "My people, what did I do to you?
How did I make you tired of me?
Tell me.
4I brought you from the land of Egypt
and freed you from slavery;
I sent Moses, Aaron, and Miriam to you.
5My people, remember
the evil plans of Balak king of Moab
and what Balaam son of Beor told Balak.
Remember what happened from Acacia to
Gilgal
so that you will know the LORD does what
is right!"

6You say, "What can I bring with me
when I come before the LORD,
when I bow before God on high?
Should I come before him with burnt
offerings,
with year-old calves?
7Will the LORD be pleased with a thousand
male sheep?
Will he be pleased with ten thousand rivers
of oil?
Should I give my first child for the evil I have
done?
Should I give my very own child for my
sin?"
8The LORD has told you, human, what is
good;
he has told you what he wants from you:
to do what is right to other people,
love being kind to others,
and live humbly, obeying your God.

9The voice of the LORD calls to the city,
and the wise person honors him.
So pay attention to the rod of punishment;
pay attention to the One who threatens to
punish.
10Are there still in the wicked house
wicked treasures
and the cursed false measure?
11Can I forgive people who cheat others
with wrong weights and scales?
12The rich people of the city
do cruel things.
Its people tell lies;
they do not tell the truth.
13As for me, I will make you sick.
I will attack you, ruining you because of
your sins.
14You will eat, but you won't become full;
you will still be hungry and empty.
You will store up, but save nothing,
and what you store up, the sword will
destroy.
15You will plant,
but you won't harvest.

You will step on your olives,
but you won't get any oil from them.
You will crush the grapes,
but you will not drink the new wine.
16This is because you obey the laws of King
Omri
and do all the things that Ahab's family
does;
you follow their advice.
So I will let you be destroyed.
The people in your city will be laughed at,
and other nations will make fun of you.

The Evil That People Do

7 Poor me! I am like a hungry man,
and all the summer fruit has been
picked—
there are no grapes left to eat,
none of the early figs I love.
2All of the faithful people are gone;
there is not one good person left in this
country.
Everyone is waiting to kill someone;
everyone is trying to trap someone
else.
3With both hands they are doing evil.
Rulers ask for money,
and judges' decisions are bought for a
price.
Rich people tell what they want,
and they get it.
4Even the best of them is like a thornbush;
the most honest of them is worse than a
prickly plant.

SERVICE

Not Just Lip Service

Monika Tirrell's life was pretty protected and carefree. She went to a private school in a Chicago suburb. Although she had gone on several ministry projects, she had never gotten involved in ministry on a consistent basis.

Until her private college's "Day of Prayer." As her work project for the day, she chose a one-day, clean-up crew at the Chicago Gospel League, a shelter for battered and homeless women. When Monika first entered the shelter, she felt as though the women would not accept her and would say to themselves, "Who do you think you are, anyway?"

But after that first visit, Monika and a few friends decided to help out at Gospel League regularly. They promised to return to the shelter every Saturday morning to do whatever was needed.

Monika knew that a few hours a week probably would not make a huge difference in the women's daily hardships. But Monika and her friends wanted to try.

Monika began leading a Bible study and focused on something the women had little of: security. "They couldn't be secure in anything—spouse, home, family, job," Monika said. "Even Gospel League was just a temporary shelter."

Through the Bible studies, Monika encouraged the women to share their experiences and prayer concerns. The women opened up and showed Monika more of what their lives were like. After the studies, Monika and the other volunteers stayed to talk individually with the residents.

Monika readily admits that while the Bible studies did the Gospel League women some good, the entire experience had a more definite long-term effect on her. Monika now wants to commit her life to living with and helping the poor and needy.

Through volunteering at the shelter, Monika learned what it means to serve God. Read **Micah 6:1–8** to see what God said to the Israelites about what it means to serve and follow him.

■ How did Monika fulfill what God says he wants from people in verse 8?
■ How can you fulfill verse 8 in your own life?

CONSIDER . . .

■ being kind to others by saying one kind thing to someone each day.
■ learning about helping professions such as social worker, minister, doctor or counselor. Pray about whether God would have you invest your life in helping others.

FOR MORE, SEE . . .

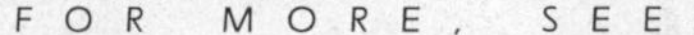

■ Ecclesiastes 12:13–14 (p. 607)
■ Ephesians 2:4–10 (p. 1219)
■ Mark 9:33–37 (p. 980)

The day that your watchmen[n] warned you
about has come.
Now they will be confused.
5Don't believe your neighbor
or trust a friend.
Don't say anything,
even to your wife.
6A son will not honor his father,
a daughter will turn against her mother,
and a daughter-in-law will be against her
mother-in-law;
a person's enemies will be members of his
own family.

The Lord's Kindness

7Israel says, "I will look to the LORD for help.
I will wait for God to save me;
my God will hear me.
8Enemy, don't laugh at me.
I have fallen, but I will get up again.
I sit in the shadow of trouble now,
but the LORD will be a light for me.
9I sinned against the LORD,
so he was angry with me,
but he will defend my case in court.
He will bring about what is right for me.
Then he will bring me out into the light,
and I will see him set things right.
10Then my enemies will see this,
and they will be ashamed,
those who said to me,
'Where is the LORD your God?'
I will look down on them.
They will get walked on, like mud in the
street."

Israel Will Return

11The time will come when your walls will be
built again,
when your country will grow.
12At that time your people will come back to
you
from Assyria and the cities of Egypt,
and from Egypt to the Euphrates River,
and from sea to sea and mountain to
mountain.
13The earth will be ruined for the people who
live in it
because of their deeds.

A Prayer to God

14So shepherd your people with your stick;
tend the flock of people who belong to
you.
That flock now lives alone in the forest
in the middle of a garden land.
Let them feed in Bashan and Gilead
as in days long ago.

15"As in the days when I brought you out of
Egypt,
I will show them miracles."[d]

16When the nations see those miracles,
they will no longer brag about their power.
They will put their hands over their mouths,
refusing to listen.
17They will crawl in the dust like a snake,
like insects crawling on the ground.
They will come trembling from their holes to
the LORD our God
and will turn in fear before you.
18There is no God like you.
You forgive those who are guilty of sin;
you don't look at the sins of your people
who are left alive.
You will not stay angry forever,
because you enjoy being kind.
19You will have mercy on us again;
you will conquer our sins.
You will throw away all our sins
into the deepest part of the sea.

SIDELIGHT: Micah's name means, "Who is like God?" He answers the question in Micah 7:18–19. No one is. In fact, the Lord is so great he tosses our darkest sins into the ocean. Since the Middle Ages, Orthodox Jews have visited a river or other body of water on the Jewish New Year and repeated verse 19 three times while tossing bread crumbs on the water.

20You will be true to the people of Jacob,
and you will be kind to the people of
Abraham
as you promised to our ancestors long
ago.

watchmen Another name for prophets. The prophets were like guards who stood on a city's wall and watched for trouble coming from far away.

NAHUM

Why Read This Book:

- Discover how God can become angry when people don't follow him (Nahum 1).
- See how God's justice is victorious in the end (Nahum 2—3).

Behind the Scenes:

Think of the most powerful force in all the universe. Now imagine that force being angry. Scary, isn't it?

Nineveh—the capital of Assyria—heated God's anger to a boiling point. The Assyrians had captured and destroyed Israel. For about two hundred and fifty years, the brutal Assyrians had attacked and persecuted Israel and Judah. As a result, the city of Nineveh had come to symbolize everything evil.

The prophet Nahum announced the downfall of Nineveh, using a series of poems to convey his message. In these poems, we see God's anger at unrighteousness, and we see the wickedness of this city. Compare the book of Nahum to the book of Jonah (p. 856), which also focuses on Nineveh. The comparison gives you a better sense of the many dimensions of God's personality. And in both books, we're reminded that God's strength extends to the whole world.

WHERE THE ACTION WAS

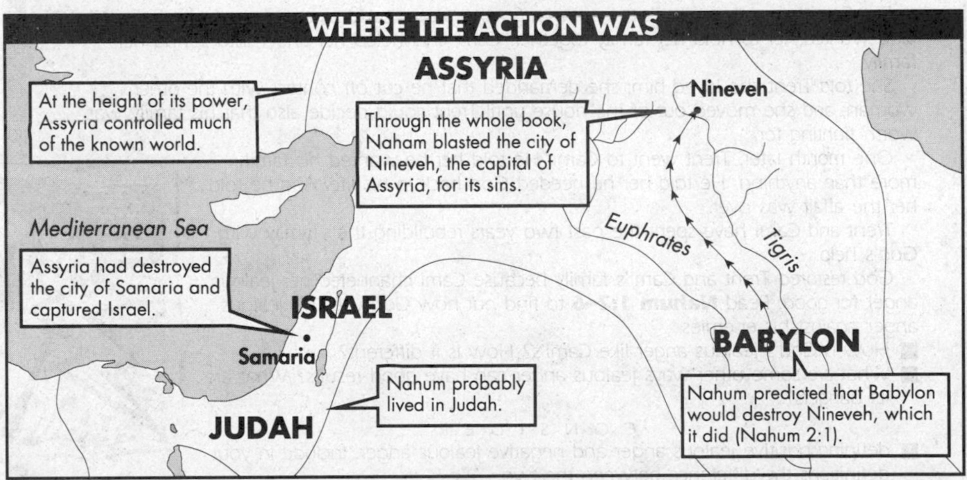

WHEN THE ACTION WAS

1000BC	Saul was Israel's king
750BC	The Northern Kingdom (Israel) fell to Assyria
	Nahum preached against Nineveh, the Assyrian capital
	The Babylonians destroyed the city of Nineveh
500BC	The Jews began returning from exile
250BC	
BC/AD	Jesus was born

1 This is the message for the city of Nineveh.[n] This is the book of the vision of Nahum, who was from the town of Elkosh.

The Lord Is Angry with Nineveh

[2]The LORD is a jealous God who punishes;
the LORD punishes and is filled with anger.
The LORD punishes those who are against him,
and he stays angry with his enemies.
[3]The LORD does not become angry quickly,
and his power is great.
The LORD will not let the guilty go unpunished.
Where the LORD goes, there are whirlwinds and storms,
and the clouds are the dust beneath his feet.
[4]He speaks to the sea and makes it dry;
he dries up all the rivers.
The areas of Bashan and Carmel dry up,
and the flowers of Lebanon dry up.
[5]The mountains shake in front of him,
and the hills melt.
The earth trembles when he comes;
the world and all who live in it shake with fear.
[6]No one can stay alive when he is angry;
no one can survive his strong anger.

Nineveh The capital city of the country of Assyria. Nahum uses Nineveh to stand for all of Assyria.

ANGER

Jealous Anger

After ten years of marriage and three kids, Trent Davis's commitment to his family began to wane. He started spending more time at the plant, and he was distant whenever he was home. Finally, he told his wife, Cami, that he had been having an affair for more than a year. He was confused, he said, and guilt-ridden. He didn't expect Cami to forgive him, and even if she did, he wasn't sure he wanted the marriage to continue.

Cami was crushed. Their marriage had seemed so stable. Although they had fought more lately, Trent had always seemed to be a good father and husband.

Emotions flooded Cami. Sadness. Fear. Confusion. But, most of all, anger. She wanted to hurt the woman who had intruded into her family. "I hate her," Cami cried. "If I see her, I'll probably kill her—and maybe Trent too."

But Cami knew that wasn't the answer. So she prayed, and as she prayed, she believed God wanted her to hold her family together. Cami channeled her anger into saving her family.

She told Trent she loved him; she demanded that he cut off contact with the other woman; and she moved out of the house until Trent could decide also that his family was worth fighting for.

One month later, Trent went to Cami. He told her he wanted his family more than anything. He told her he needed God back in his life. And he told her the affair was over.

Trent and Cami have spent the past two years rebuilding their family with God's help.

God restored Trent and Cami's family because Cami channeled her jealous anger for good. Read **Nahum 1:2–6** to find out how God uses his jealous anger against his enemies.

- How is God's jealous anger like Cami's? How is it different?
- What are some other ways jealous anger can have good results? What are its dangers?

CONSIDER . . .

- defining positive jealous anger and negative jealous anger. Include in your definitions the difference between the two.
- asking your parents or other married adults how they have seen jealous anger in their relationship have positive or negative results.

FOR MORE SEE

- Hosea 11:1–11 (p. 831)
- Jonah 4:1–11 (p. 859)
- John 2:12–16 (p. 1060)

His anger is poured out like fire;
the rocks are smashed by him.

7The LORD is good,
giving protection in times of trouble.
He knows who trusts in him.
8But like a rushing flood,
he will completely destroy Nineveh;
he will chase his enemies until he kills them.

SIDELIGHT: New York City is called "the Big Apple" because it is a place where so much power, action, glamor, and tradition are centered. Nineveh was the "Big Apple" of Nahum's day—a fast-lane city surrounded by a seven-and-a-half-mile-long wall with fifteen gates. It also was surrounded by a 150-foot-wide moat. The party's over, though. A few mounds are all that remain of the city.

9The LORD will completely destroy
anyone making plans against him.
Trouble will not come a second time.
10Those people will be like tangled thorns
or like people drunk from their wine;
they will be burned up quickly like dry weeds.
11Someone has come from Nineveh
who makes evil plans against the LORD
and gives wicked advice.

12This is what the LORD says:
"Although Assyria is strong and has many people,
it will be defeated and brought to an end.
Although I have made you suffer, Judah,
I will make you suffer no more.
13Now I will free you from their control
and tear away your chains."
14The LORD has given you this command, Nineveh:
"You will not have descendants[d] to carry on your name.
I will destroy the idols and metal images
that are in the temple of your gods.
I will make a grave for you,
because you are wicked."

15Look, there on the hills,
someone is bringing good news!
He is announcing peace!
Celebrate your feasts, people of Judah,
and give your promised sacrifices to God.
The wicked will not come to attack you again;
they have been completely destroyed.

Nineveh Will Be Defeated

2 The destroyer[n] is coming to attack you, Nineveh.
Guard the defenses.
Watch the road.
Get ready.
Gather all your strength!
2Destroyers have destroyed God's people
and ruined their vines,
but the LORD will bring back Jacob's greatness
like Israel's greatness.

3The shields of his soldiers are red;
the army is dressed in red.
The metal on the chariots flashes like fire
when they are ready to attack;
their horses are excited.
4The chariots race through the streets
and rush back and forth through the city squares.
They look like torches;
they run like lightning.

5He[n] calls his officers,
but they stumble on the way.
They hurry to the city wall,
and the shield is put into place.
6The river gates are thrown open,
and the palace is destroyed.
7It has been announced that the people of Nineveh
will be captured and carried away.
The slave girls moan like doves
and beat their breasts, because they are sad.
8Nineveh is like a pool,
and now its water is draining away.
"Stop! Stop!" the people yell,
but no one turns back.
9Take the silver!
Take the gold!
There is no end to the treasure—
piles of wealth of every kind.
10Nineveh is robbed, ruined, and destroyed.
The people lose their courage, and their knees knock.
Stomachs ache, and everyone's face grows pale.

11Where is the lions'[n] den
and the place where they feed their young?

destroyer The Babylonians, the Scythians, and the Medes destroyed Nineveh.
He This probably means the king of Assyria.
lions' The symbol of Assyria was the lion.

Where did the lion, lioness, and cubs go
without being afraid?
12The lion killed enough for his cubs,
enough for his mate.
He filled his cave with the animals he
caught;
he filled his den with meat he had killed.

13"I am against you, Nineveh,"
says the LORD All-Powerful.
"I will burn up your chariots in smoke,
and the sword will kill your young lions.
I will stop you from hunting down others
on the earth,
and your messengers' voices
will no longer be heard."

It Will Be Terrible for Nineveh

3 How terrible it will be for the city that
has killed so many.
It is full of lies
and goods stolen from other countries.
It is always killing somebody.
2Hear the sound of whips
and the noise of the wheels.
Hear horses galloping
and chariots bouncing along!
3Horses are charging,
swords are shining,
spears are gleaming!
Many are dead;
their bodies are piled up—
too many to count.
People stumble over the dead bodies.

SIDELIGHT: The wartime cruelty of the Assyrians (Nahum 3:3) would have been similar to the terrible things that happened to the Jewish people in World War II. One Assyrian king bragged of building pyramids of chopped-off heads outside the enemy's city. Other kings stacked corpses like firewood near the conquered city's gates.

4The city was like a prostitute;[d]
she was charming and a lover of magic.
She made nations slaves with her
prostitution[d]
and her witchcraft.[d]
5"I am against you, Nineveh," says the LORD
All-Powerful.
"I will pull your dress up over your face
and show the nations your nakedness
and the kingdoms your shame.
6I will throw filthy garbage on you
and make a fool of you.
I will make people stare at you.
7Everyone who sees you will run away and
say,
'Nineveh is in ruins. Who will cry for her?'
Nineveh, where will I find anyone to
comfort you?"

8You are no better than Thebes,[n]
who sits by the Nile River
with water all around her.
The river was her defense;
the waters were like a wall around her.
9Cush and Egypt gave her endless strength;
Put and Libya supported her.
10But Thebes was captured
and went into captivity.
Her small children were beaten to death
at every street corner.
Lots[d] were thrown for her important men,
and all of her leaders were put in chains.

11Nineveh, you will be drunk, too.
You will hide;
you will look for a place safe from the
enemy.
12All your defenses are like fig trees with ripe
fruit.
When the tree is shaken, the figs fall into
the mouth of the eater.
13Look at your soldiers.
They are all women!
The gates of your land
are wide open for your enemies;
fire has burned the bars of your gates.

14Get enough water before the long war
begins.
Make your defenses strong!
Get mud,
mix clay,
make bricks!
15There the fire will burn you up.
The sword will kill you;
like grasshoppers eating crops, the battle
will completely destroy you.
Grow in number like hopping locusts;[d]
grow in number like swarming locusts!
16Your traders are more than the stars in the
sky,
but like locusts, they strip the land and
then fly away.
17Your guards are like locusts.
Your officers are like swarms of locusts
that hang on the walls on a cold day.
When the sun comes up, they fly away,
and no one knows where they have gone.

Thebes A great city in Egypt.

18King of Assyria, your rulers are asleep;
your important men lie down to rest.
Your people have been scattered on the mountains,
and there is no one to bring them back.

19Nothing can heal your wound;
your injury will not heal.
Everyone who hears about you applauds,
because everyone has felt your endless cruelty.

HABAKKUK

Why Read This Book:

- Listen to what God says about why wicked people prosper (Habakkuk 1–2).
- Learn the importance of waiting patiently for God (Habakkuk 3).

Behind the Scenes:

Sometimes it's hard to understand what God is doing in the world. Bad people seem to do great while good people suffer. Is God absent? Isn't he in control? Doesn't he have the power to control things? Or is God not a righteous God?

The prophet Habakkuk had those tough questions, and he wasn't afraid to ask them directly to God. His book takes the form of a question-and-answer session with God. Habakkuk asks the questions, and then God, through visions, gives answers:

Habakkuk: God, why don't you deliver your people from injustice?
God: Be patient. I've got it under control. The evil people will be punished.
Habakkuk: Why do you wait silently while wicked people destroy other people?
God: Justice will come. Live faithfully, and you will be rewarded.

WHERE THE ACTION WAS

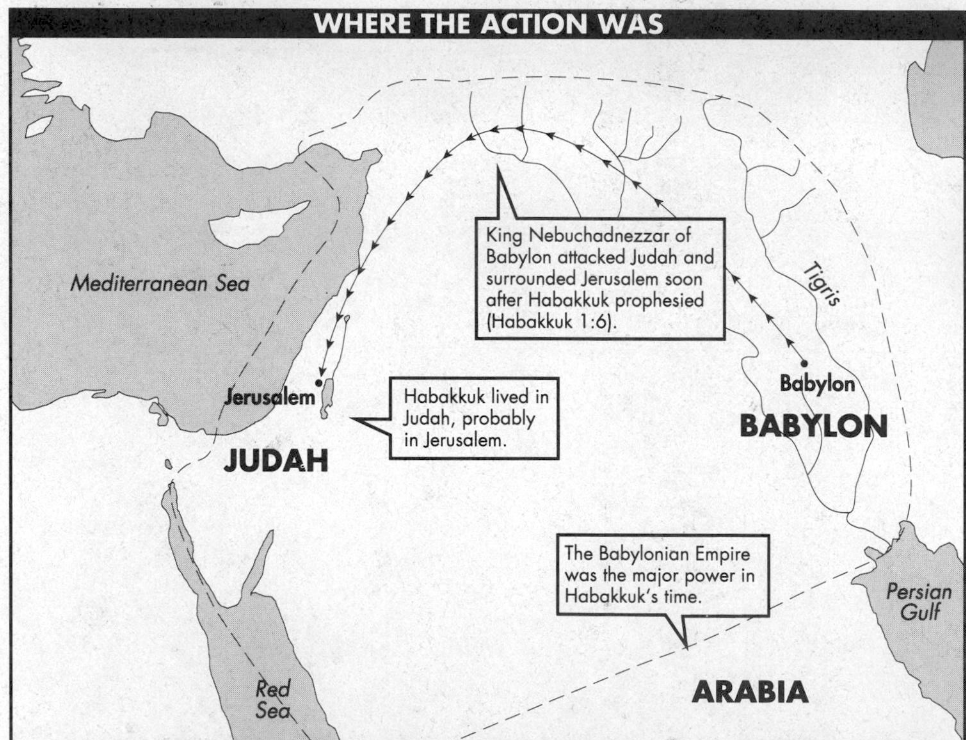
Mediterranean Sea
King Nebuchadnezzar of Babylon attacked Judah and surrounded Jerusalem soon after Habakkuk prophesied (Habakkuk 1:6).
Tigris
Jerusalem
Habakkuk lived in Judah, probably in Jerusalem.
Babylon
BABYLON
JUDAH
The Babylonian Empire was the major power in Habakkuk's time.
Persian Gulf
Red Sea
ARABIA

WHEN THE ACTION WAS

The kingdom was split between Israel and Judah
Habakkuk lived
The Jews began returning from exile
Jesus was born
1000BC
750BC
500BC
250BC
BC/AD
Saul was Israel's king
Habakkuk's prophecy was fulfilled when Babylon attacked Jerusalem

Behind the Scenes (cont.): This short book is filled with comfort for people who suffer unjustly and for those who have trouble finding meaning in life. Not only does the prophet take honest questions to God, but the answers convince him that God is faithful and powerful.

"I will still be glad in the LORD," Habakkuk concludes. "I will rejoice in God my Savior. The Lord GOD is my strength" (Habakkuk 3:18–19a). It's a reassuring message of faith and hope for all people who see life as meaningless or who suffer unjustly.

---

1 This is the message Habakkuk the prophet received.[d]

Habakkuk Complains

2LORD, how long must I ask for help
and you ignore me?
I cry out to you about violence,
but you do not save us!
3Why do you make me see wrong things
and make me look at trouble?
People are destroying things and hurting
others in front of me;
they are arguing and fighting.
4So the teachings are weak,
and justice never comes.
Evil people gain while good people
lose;
the judges no longer make fair decisions.

DISCOURAGEMENT

Is There Hope?

Bill Evans had volunteered to stay all night at the homeless shelter, hoping he would be able to make a difference, hoping conditions might somehow change, hoping to feel needed and useful.

The only thing Bill felt as he left the old building, though, was discouragement. As he left the shelter, he was glad to be free from the smell of old clothes, the sight of loneliness, and the sounds of sadness.

He knew one thing: This type of service wasn't for him. He felt he wasn't helpful and could do no good. Why do anything?

As Bill opened his car door, he prayed, "God, why don't you do something?"

Bill thought of how the men in the shelter would accept anything—stale food, old clothing, a heartless handshake—and accept it with thanks and gratitude.

"They settle for so little, but they need so much," Bill said to himself.

Then it hit Bill almost as an answer to his questioning prayer. The poor were so open for gifts; they would be the most happy and pleased to receive God's gift of grace and eternal life.

"It's no wonder, God," Bill thought, "that you came to the poor and needy. They are the most accepting and grateful of all."

Like Bill, Habakkuk felt discouraged. And like Bill, Habakkuk turned to God with his discouragement. Read about Habakkuk's discouragement in **Habakkuk 1:1–3**.

- How was Habakkuk's response to discouragement similar to Bill's? How was it different?
- If Habakkuk were alive today, what things might he complain to God about? How might God answer those complaints?

CONSIDER . . .

- listing the complaints you make to God when you're discouraged. Keep the list with you for a week and then review it to see how God may have answered the questions.
- volunteering your time to spend a day with a young child and encouraging the child with positive words.

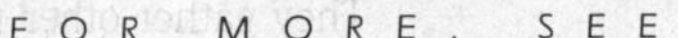

FOR MORE, SEE . . .

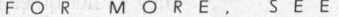

- Zephaniah 3:14–18 (p. 884)
- Luke 6:20–26 (p. 1012)
- Romans 8:31–39 (p. 1152)

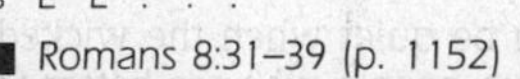

The Lord Answers

5"Look at the nations!
Watch them and be amazed and shocked.
I will do something in your lifetime
that you won't believe even when you are told about it.

SIDELIGHT: We know hardly anything about the prophet Habakkuk, but his name may give us a clue (Habakkuk 1:1). It means "embracer" or "a garden plant." Makes you wonder if he was a couch potato!

6I will use the Babylonians,
those cruel and wild people
who march across the earth
and take lands that don't belong to them.
7They scare and frighten people.
They do what they want to do
and are good only to themselves.
8Their horses are faster than leopards
and quicker than wolves at sunset.
Their horse soldiers attack quickly;
they come from places far away.
They attack quickly, like an eagle swooping down for food.
9 They all come to fight.
Nothing can stop them.
Their prisoners are as many as the grains of sand.
10They laugh at kings
and make fun of rulers.
They laugh at all the strong, walled cities
and build dirt piles to the top of the walls to capture them.
11Then they leave like the wind and move on.
They are guilty of worshiping their own strength."

Habakkuk Complains Again

12LORD, you live forever,
my God, my holy God.
We will not die.
LORD, you have chosen the Babylonians to punish people;
our Rock,[d] you picked them to punish.
13Your eyes are too good to look at evil;
you cannot stand to see those who do wrong.
So how can you put up with those evil people?
How can you be quiet when the wicked swallow up people who are better than they are?
14You treat people like fish in the sea,
like sea animals without a leader.
15The enemy brings them in with hooks.
He catches them in his net
and drags them in his fishnet.
So he rejoices and sings for joy.

SIDELIGHT: Wearing nose jewelry may be fashionable at different times, but people probably wouldn't be attracted to the "hooks" mentioned in Habakkuk 1:15. The verse may refer to the Assyrian practice of leading prisoners of war by a rope that was attached to a hook pierced through the nose or lower lip.

16The enemy offers sacrifices to his net
and burns incense[d] to worship it,
because it lets him live like the rich
and enjoy the best food.
17Will he keep on taking riches with his net?
Will he go on destroying people without showing mercy?

2 I will stand like a guard to watch
and place myself at the tower.
I will wait to see what he will say to me;
I will wait to learn how God will answer my complaint.

The Lord Answers

2The LORD answered me:
"Write down the vision;
write it clearly on clay tablets
so whoever reads it can run to tell others.
3It is not yet time for the message to come true,
but that time is coming soon;
the message will come true.
It may seem like a long time,
but be patient and wait for it,
because it will surely come;
it will not be delayed.
4The evil nation is very proud of itself;
it is not living as it should.
But those who are right with God will live by trusting in him.

5"Just as wine can trick a person,
those who are too proud will not last,
because their desire is like a grave's desire for death,
and like death they always want more.
They gather other nations for themselves
and collect for themselves all the countries.
6But all the nations the Babylonians have hurt will laugh at them.
They will make fun of the Babylonians

and say, 'How terrible it will be for the one
that steals many things.
How long will that nation get rich by
forcing others to pay them?'

7"One day the people from whom you have
taken money will turn against you.
They will realize what is happening and
make you shake with fear.
Then they will take everything you
have.
8Because you have stolen from many nations,
those who are left will take much from
you.
This is because you have killed many people,
destroying countries and cities and everyone
in them.

9"How terrible it will be for the nation that
becomes rich by doing wrong,
thinking they will live in a safe place
and escape harm.
10Because you have made plans to destroy
many people,
you have made your own houses ashamed
of you.
Because of it, you will lose your lives.
11The stones of the walls will cry out against
you,
and the boards that support the roof will
agree that you are wrong.

12"How terrible it will be for the nation that
kills people to build a city,
that wrongs others to start a town.
13The LORD All-Powerful will send fire
to destroy what those people have built;
all the nations' work will be for nothing.
14Then, just as water covers the sea,
people everywhere will know the LORD's
glory.

15"How terrible for the nation that makes its
neighbors drink,
pouring from the jug of wine until they are
drunk
so that it can look at their naked bodies.
16You Babylonians will be filled with disgrace,
not respect.
It's your turn to drink and fall to the
ground like a drunk person.
The cup of anger from the LORD's right hand
is coming around to you.
You will receive disgrace, not respect.

PATIENCE

Pumping Iron

Push. Squeeze. Pump. Pain.

These are just a few of the things Matt Davis goes through each day as he works out with weights at the gym. All that pumping and breathing and clanging and lifting get tiring after a while. Matt has not only had to struggle with moving weights around, but he's had difficulty moving his schedule around to make room for the daily two-hour workout.

You would think that as tired as Matt gets each day he would be bulging with muscles. Not yet. Oh, he's seen improvement. That's what keeps him going. But Matt looks around the gym at other guys and realizes he has a long way to go to get his body to its full potential.

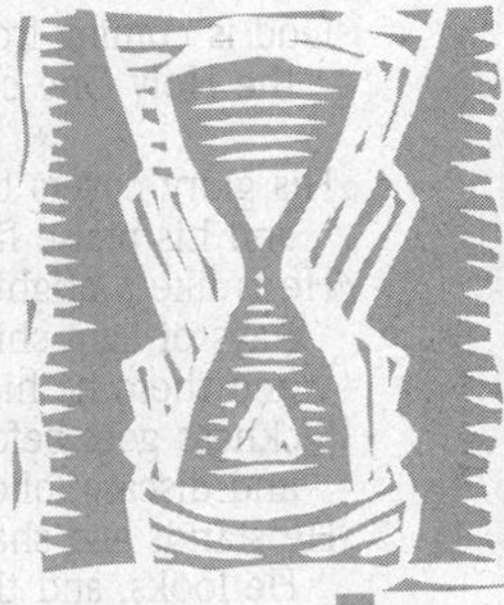

Every now and then Matt considers taking a shortcut in his training. He's struggling with the temptation of turning to steroids—drugs that could boost his muscle growth—or quitting his training totally. Every now and then Matt finds his patience wearing thin. He wants results fast.

Habakkuk felt a similar struggle with patience as he waited for God to take action against God's enemies. Read about God's answer in **Habakkuk 2:1–4**.

- How is Matt's struggle with patience similar to Habakkuk's?
- When have you been impatient like Habakkuk and Matt?

CONSIDER . . .

- writing things that you are impatient about and committing yourself to be patient as you wait for God to work them out.
- carrying a small, tablet-shaped stone in your pocket or purse to remind you to be patient and trust God.

FOR MORE, SEE . . .

- Job 38:1–15 (p. 475)
- Hebrews 6:10–12 (p. 1281)
- James 5:7–8 (p. 1299)

17You hurt many people in Lebanon,
but now you will be hurt.
You killed many animals there,
and now you must be afraid
because of what you did
to that land, those cities, and the people
who lived in them.

The Message About Idols

18"An idol does no good, because a human
made it;
it is only a statue that teaches lies.
The one who made it expects his own work
to help him,
but he makes idols that can't even speak!
19How terrible it will be for the one who says
to a wooden statue, 'Come to life!'
How terrible it will be for the one who
says to a silent stone, 'Get up!'
It cannot tell you what to do.
It is only a statue covered with gold and
silver;
there is no life in it.
20The LORD is in his Holy Temple;[d]
all the earth should be silent in his
presence."

Habakkuk's Prayer

3 This is the prayer of Habakkuk the prophet,[d]
on shigionoth.[d]

2LORD, I have heard the news about you;
I am amazed at what you have done.
LORD, do great things once again in our time;
make those things happen again in our own
days.
Even when you are angry,
remember to be kind.

3God is coming from Teman;
the Holy One comes from Mount Paran.[n]
Selah[d]
His glory covers the skies,
and his praise fills the earth.
4He is like a bright light.
Rays of light shine from his hand,
and there he hides his power.
5Sickness goes before him,
and disease follows behind him.
6He stands and shakes the earth.
He looks, and the nations shake with fear.
The mountains, which stood for ages, break
into pieces;
the old hills fall down.
God has always done this.
7I saw that the tents of Cushan were in
trouble
and that the tents of Midian trembled.
8LORD, were you angry at the rivers,
or were you angry at the streams?
Were you angry with the sea
when you rode your horses and chariots of
victory?[n]
9You uncovered your bow
and commanded many arrows to be
brought to you. *Selah*
You split the earth with rivers.
10 The mountains saw you and shook with
fear.
The rushing water flowed.
The sea made a loud noise,
and its waves rose high.
11The sun and moon stood still in the sky;
they stopped when they saw the flash of
your flying arrows
and the gleam of your shining spear.
12In anger you marched on the earth;
in anger you punished the nations.
13You came out to save your people,
to save your chosen one.
You crushed the leader of the wicked ones
and took everything he had, from head to
toe. *Selah*
14With the enemy's own spear you stabbed the
leader of his army.
His soldiers rushed out like a storm to
scatter us.
They were happy
as they were robbing the poor people in
secret.
15But you marched through the sea with your
horses,
stirring the great waters.

16I hear these things, and my body trembles;
my lips tremble when I hear the sound.
My bones feel weak,
and my legs shake.

But I will wait patiently for the day of
disaster
that will come to the people who attack us.
17Fig trees may not grow figs,
and there may be no grapes on the vines.
There may be no olives growing
and no food growing in the fields.

Teman . . . Paran God is seen as again coming from the direction of Mount Sinai. He came from Sinai when he rescued his people from Egypt.
sea . . . victory This is probably talking about the Israelites crossing the Red Sea.

There may be no sheep in the
pens
and no cattle in the barns.
18But I will still be glad in the LORD;
I will rejoice in God my Savior.
19The Lord GOD is my strength.
He makes me like a deer that does not
stumble
so I can walk on the steep mountains.

For the director of music. On my stringed instruments.

ZEPHANIAH

Why Read This Book:

- Discover what moral corruption can do to people (Zephaniah 1—2).
- Hear the promise of God's comfort for the faithful (Zephaniah 3).

Behind the Scenes:

Have you ever had a really lousy day—so lousy that you were glad to go to bed to get it over with? When you woke up the next morning, you were determined to start out fresh, and you did everything you could to make sure the next day would be better.

In a sense, the people of Judah had just had a lousy hundred years. Their land had been controlled by the Assyrians. But now they had gained independence. They were ready to start a new day—to rebuild their nation and start over. King Josiah would lead them to new political strength.

But the people needed religious renewal as well. Domination by foreign powers had brought with it foreign customs and pagan gods. The Canaanite religion, Baalism, flourished in the country.

The prophet Zephaniah saw the corruption in the land and warned the people

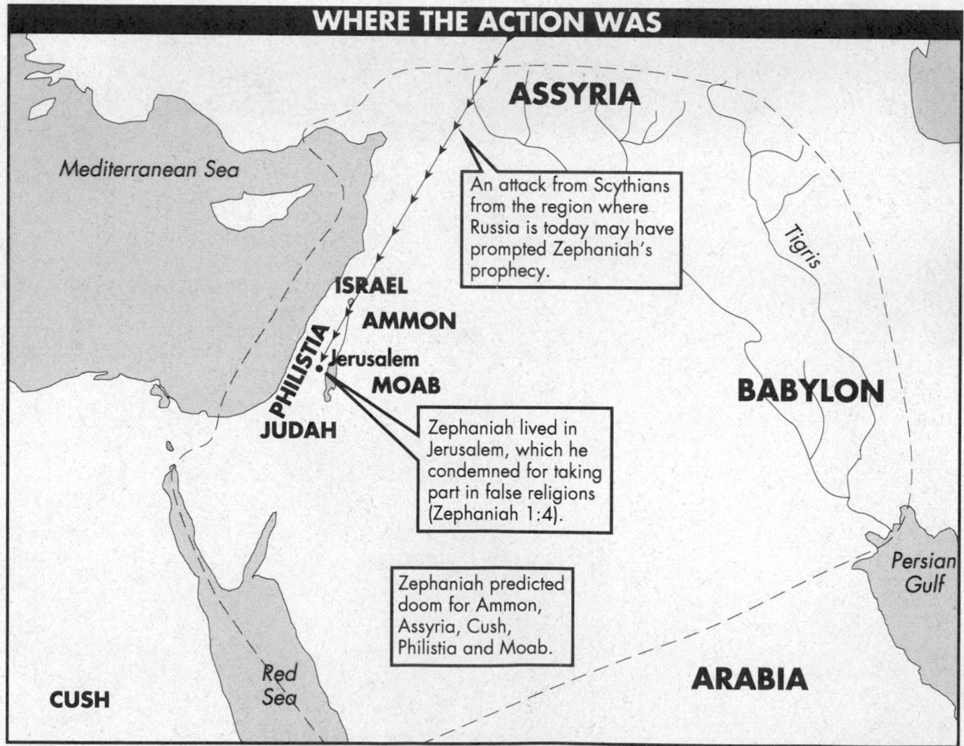

WHERE THE ACTION WAS
ASSYRIA
Mediterranean Sea
An attack from Scythians from the region where Russia is today may have prompted Zephaniah's prophecy.
Tigris
ISRAEL
AMMON
PHILISTIA
Jerusalem
MOAB
JUDAH
BABYLON
Zephaniah lived in Jerusalem, which he condemned for taking part in false religions (Zephaniah 1:4).
Persian Gulf
Zephaniah predicted doom for Ammon, Assyria, Cush, Philistia and Moab.
Red Sea
CUSH
ARABIA

WHEN THE ACTION WAS

1000BC	750BC	500BC	250BC	BC/AD

- The kingdom was split between Israel and Judah
- Saul was Israel's king
- The Northern Kingdom (Israel) fell to Assyria
- Zephaniah prophesied in Judah
- The Southern Kingdom (Judah) fell to Babylon
- The Jews began returning from exile
- Jesus was born

Behind the Scenes (cont.): to change. As a prophet in Jerusalem, his ministry was probably influential in getting King Josiah to institute widespread religious reform based on the book of Deuteronomy (p. 160).

Zephaniah's message to the people was that God would judge Judah for turning away from him. The book is filled with terrifying images of doom and punishment on "the LORD's day of judging" (Zephaniah 1:14). But the book ends on a positive note, describing a time when people would return to God and the nation would be restored.

The book of Zephaniah has a message that's similar to that of many prophets: Disaster will ultimately come for those who turn away from God. But God will build a new, lasting relationship with those who repent and serve him faithfully.

---

1 This is the word of the LORD that came through Zephaniah while Josiah son of Amon was king of Judah. Zephaniah was the son of Cushi, who was the son of Gedaliah. Gedaliah was the son of Amariah, who was the son of Hezekiah.

The Lord's Judgment

2"I will sweep away everything
from the earth," says the LORD.
3"I will sweep away the people and animals;
I will destroy the birds in the air
and the fish of the sea.
I will ruin the evil people,
and I will remove human beings from the earth," says the LORD.

The Future of Judah

4"I will punish Judah
and all the people living in Jerusalem.
I will remove from this place
all signs of Baal,[d] the false priests, and the other priests.
5I will destroy those who worship
the stars from the roofs,[n]
and those who worship and make promises
by both the LORD and the god Molech,[d]

> **SIDELIGHT:** The false religion of Baalism included numerous terrible practices, including human sacrifices, temple prostitution, and astrology. Making matters worse, the Israelites often tried to mix these false religions with true religion—and practice them both at the same time (Zephaniah 1:4–5)!

6and those who turned away from the LORD,
and those who quit following the LORD and praying to him for direction.
7Be silent before the Lord GOD,
because the LORD's day for judging people is coming soon.
The LORD has prepared a sacrifice;
he has made holy his invited guests.
8On the day of the LORD's sacrifice,
I, the LORD, will punish the princes and the king's sons
and all those who wear foreign clothes.
9On that day I will punish those who worship Dagon,[d]
those who hurt others and tell lies in the temples of their gods.

10"On that day," says the LORD,
"a cry will be heard at the Fish Gate.
A wail will come from the new area of the city,
and a loud crash will echo from the hills.
11Cry, you people living in the market area,
because all the merchants will be dead;
all the silver traders will be gone.
12At that time I, the LORD, will search Jerusalem with lamps.
I will punish those who are satisfied with themselves,
who think, 'The LORD won't help us or punish us.'
13Their wealth will be stolen
and their houses destroyed.
They may build houses,
but they will not live in them.
They may plant vineyards,
but they will not drink any wine from them.

The Lord's Day of Judging

14"The LORD's day of judging is coming soon;
it is near and coming fast.
The cry will be very sad on the day of the LORD;
even soldiers will cry.
15That day will be a day of anger,
a day of terror and trouble,

roofs In Bible times houses were built with flat roofs. The roof was used for drying things such as flax and fruit. And it was used as an extra room, as a place for worship, and as a place to sleep in the summer.

a day of destruction and ruin,
a day of darkness and gloom,
a day of clouds and blackness,
16a day of alarms and battle cries.
'Attack the strong, walled cities!
Attack the corner towers!'
17I will make life hard on the people;
they will walk around like the blind,
because they have sinned against the LORD.
Their blood will be poured out like dust,
and their insides will be dumped like trash.
18On the day that God will show his anger,
neither their silver nor gold will save them.
The LORD's anger will be like a fire
that will burn up the whole world;
suddenly he will bring an end, yes, an end
to everyone on earth."

The Lord Asks People to Change

2 Gather together, gather,
you unwanted people.
2Do it before it's too late,
before you are blown away like chaff,[d]
before the LORD's terrible anger reaches you,
before the day of the LORD's anger comes to you.
3Come to the LORD, all you who are not proud,
who obey his laws.
Do what is right. Learn to be humble.
Maybe you will escape
on the day the LORD shows his anger.

Philistia Will Be Punished

4No one will be left in the city of Gaza,
and the city of Ashkelon will be destroyed.
Ashdod will be empty by noon,

MONEY

Look Where It Got Them

Who, in 1923, was:

- president of the United States' largest steel company?
- president of the largest gas company?
- president of the New York Stock Exchange?
- the greatest wheat speculator in America?
- the "Great Bear" of Wall Street?

In their day, these people made lots of money. They would have been considered the most successful men in the world. But look at what became of these "successful" moneybags:

- The president of the largest steel company, Charles Schwab, died penniless.
- The president of the largest gas company, Howard Hopson, went insane.
- The president of the New York Stock Exchange, Richard Whitney, was released from prison to die at home.
- Arthur Cutten, the greatest wheat speculator, died overseas— penniless and homeless.
- Mr. C. Rivermore, the "Great Bear" of Wall Street, committed suicide.

Although these men had wealth and worldly success, their "kingdom" fell. They had based their lives and priorities on money, and money couldn't meet all their needs.

God wanted the people in Zephaniah's day to base their lives and priorities on much more than money. Read **Zephaniah 1:7–18** to learn more about God's directions and the limitations of money.

- How are the men's lives in this story like the lives of the people in this passage?
- According to the Bible passage, what will happen to those who trust in money and riches?

CONSIDER . . .

- giving some of your money and prized possessions to someone less fortunate.
- keeping track of the money you spend this week and evaluating whether your spending is pleasing to God.

FOR MORE, SEE . . .

- Ecclesiastes 7:11–12 (p. 604)
- Matthew 6:19–34 (p. 918)
- Mark 10:17–31 (p. 982)

and the people of Ekron will be chased
away.
5How terrible it will be for you who live by
the Mediterranean Sea,
you Philistines!
The word of the LORD is against you,
Canaan, land of the Philistines.

"I will destroy you
so that no one will be left."
6The land by the Mediterranean Sea, in which
you live,
will become pastures, fields for shepherds,
and pens for sheep.
7It will belong to the descendants[d] of Judah
who are left alive.
There they will let their sheep eat grass.
At night they will sleep
in the houses of Ashkelon.
The LORD their God will pay attention to
them
and will make their life good again.

Moab and Ammon Will Be Punished

8"I have heard the insults of the country of
Moab
and the threats of the people of Ammon.
They have insulted my people
and have taken their land."
9So the LORD All Powerful, the God of Israel,
says,
"As surely as I live,
Moab will be destroyed like Sodom,
and Ammon will be destroyed like
Gomorrah[n]—
a heap of weeds, a pit of salt,
and a ruin forever.
Those of my people who are left alive will
take whatever they want from them;
those who are left from my nation will take
their land."
10This is what Moab and Ammon get for being
proud,
because they insulted and made fun of the
people of the LORD All-Powerful.
11The LORD will frighten them,
because he will destroy all the gods of the
earth.
Then everyone in faraway places
will worship him wherever they are.

Cush and Assyria Will Be Destroyed

12"You Cushites also
will be killed by my sword."
13Then the LORD will turn against the north
and destroy Assyria.
He will make Nineveh
a ruin as dry as a desert.
14Flocks and herds will lie down there,
and all wild animals.
The owls and crows will sit
on the stone pillars.
The owl will hoot through the windows,
trash will be in the doorways,
and the wooden boards of the buildings
will be gone.

SIDELIGHT: The nation of Cush (Zephaniah 2:12–14) is modern-day Ethiopia. By pairing Assyria and Cush in this passage, the prophet shows the broadness of God's judgment, since the two nations were in the extreme north and south of the known world at that time.

15This is the happy and safe city
that thinks there is no one else as strong as
it is.
But what a ruin it will be,
a place where wild animals live.
All those who pass by will make fun
and shake their fists.

Jerusalem Will Be Punished

3 How terrible for the wicked, stubborn city
of Jerusalem,
which hurts its own people.
2It obeys no voice;
it can't be taught to do right.
It doesn't trust the LORD;
it doesn't worship its God.
3Its officers are like roaring lions.
Its rulers are like hungry wolves that attack
in the evening,
and in the morning nothing is left of those
they attacked.
4Its prophets[d] are proud;
they are people who cannot be trusted.
Its priests don't respect holy things;
they break God's teachings.
5But the LORD is good, and he is there in that
city.
He does no wrong.
Every morning he governs the people fairly;
every day he can be trusted.
But evil people are not ashamed of what
they do.

6"I have destroyed nations;
their towers were ruined.
I made their streets empty
so no one goes there anymore.

Sodom . . . Gomorrah Two cities God destroyed because the people were so evil.

Their cities are ruined;
no one lives there at all.
7I said, 'Surely now Jerusalem will respect me
and will accept my teaching.'
Then the place where they lived would not
be destroyed,
and I would not have to punish them.
But they were still eager
to do evil in everything they did.
8Just wait," says the LORD.
"Some day I will stand up as a witness.
I have decided that I will gather nations
and assemble kingdoms.
I will pour out my anger on them,
all my strong anger.
My anger will be like fire
that will burn up the whole world.

A New Day for God's People

9"Then I will give the people of all nations
pure speech
so that all of them will speak the name of
the LORD
and worship me together.
10People will come from where the Nile River
begins;
my scattered people will come with gifts for
me.
11Then Jerusalem will not be ashamed
of the wrongs done against me,
because I will remove from this city
those who like to brag;
there will never be any more proud people
on my holy mountain in Jerusalem.
12But I will leave in the city
the humble and those who are not proud,
and they will trust in the LORD.
13Those who are left alive in Israel won't do
wrong
or tell lies;
they won't trick people with their words.
They will eat and lie down
with no one to make them afraid."

A Happy Song

14Sing, Jerusalem.
Israel, shout for joy!
Jerusalem, be happy
and rejoice with all your heart.
15The LORD has stopped punishing you;
he has sent your enemies away.
The King of Israel, the LORD, is with you;

HAPPINESS

Glad You're Here . . . Finally

Jim felt terribly out of place. Everyone at the party knew everybody. Except Jim. He knew no one. And no one knew him. Jim was sure everyone was staring, wondering why he even came. He looked at the front door constantly, hoping someone he knew would walk in.

Finally Jim could take no more. He reached for his coat and started walking to the front door. As he stepped outside, he heard a familiar voice call from the street.

"Jim! Sorry I'm late. I stopped by to get Janet and the others. How's the party?"

Jim's eyes brightened as he recognized Terry and five other friends.

"Fine! The party's great . . . now that you're here."

Jim learned that good friends can add to happiness. Find out how a trustworthy friend brought happiness to Israel in **Zephaniah 3:14–18**.

- What made Jim and the people in this passage happy?
- How is having God with us the same as having a close friend with us? How is it different?

CONSIDER . . .

- rereading the scripture passage with your own name in place of "Jerusalem," "Israel," and "you."
- writing a poem about a close friend or family member who makes you happy and then sending the poem to that person.

FOR MORE, SEE

- Psalm 146 (p. 563)
- Proverbs 16:20 (p. 581)
- John 16:16–24 (p. 1087)

you will never again be afraid of being
harmed.
16On that day Jerusalem will be told,
"Don't be afraid, city of Jerusalem.
Don't give up.
17The LORD your God is with you;
the mighty One will save you.
He will rejoice over you.
You will rest in his love;
he will sing and be joyful about you."

18"I will take away the sadness planned for
you,
which would have made you very ashamed.
19At that time I will punish
all those who harmed you.
I will save my people who cannot walk
and gather my people who have been
thrown out.
I will give them praise and honor
in every place where they were shamed.
20At that time I will gather you;
at that time I will bring you back home.
I will give you honor and praise
from people everywhere
when I make things go well again for you,
as you will see with your own eyes," says
the LORD.

HAGGAI

Why Read This Book:

- Understand the importance of focusing on God's priorities instead of our own desires (Haggai 1).
- See the excitement of working together for God's glory (Haggai 2).

Behind the Scenes:

If you've ever moved, you know what it's like to get settled. You have to find your way around the neighborhood. You have to make new friends. You have to settle into a job or a school. In short, you stay busy getting your new life together.

The Jewish people were in that kind of situation. They had just returned to Judah after being captives in Babylon. They were caught up in planting crops, repairing homes, and earning a living.

But something was missing. While the Jews were enjoying their new freedom in their nice homes, God's Temple lay in ruins. So the people were permitted to return from Persia to rebuild the Temple. God sent the prophet Haggai to show the Jews that their priorities were wrong, that they were being selfish and materialistic.

Building the Temple was important for the Jews, not so they would have a place to worship, but as a symbol of God's leadership and lordship in the nation. It was the "place" of God's personal contact with his people. Haggai believed the completed Temple would bring hope to a people who were depressed and struggling.

Haggai's ministry involved motivating people to complete God's Temple, which had been started almost twenty years earlier. He was successful, too; within three weeks, the people had started work on the Temple again. And four years later, the Temple was complete.

Though we don't face the challenge of building a Temple in Jerusalem, the book of Haggai still has important reminders for us. It reminds us to keep our

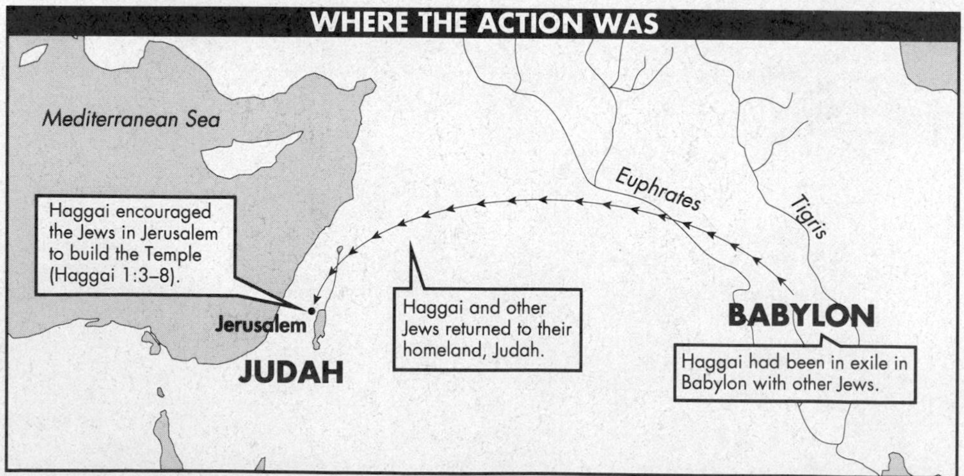
WHERE THE ACTION WAS
Mediterranean Sea
Euphrates
Tigris
Haggai encouraged the Jews in Jerusalem to build the Temple (Haggai 1:3–8).
Jerusalem
JUDAH
Haggai and other Jews returned to their homeland, Judah.
BABYLON
Haggai had been in exile in Babylon with other Jews.
WHEN THE ACTION WAS
The kingdom was split between Israel and Judah
The Jews began returning from exile
The rebuilt Temple was completed
Jesus was born
1000BC
750BC
500BC
250BC
BC/AD
Saul was Israel's king
The Southern Kingdom (Judah) fell to Babylon
Haggai began to preach

Behind the Scenes (cont.): priorities straight. And it reminds us to make God the center of our lives—just as the Temple was the center of life for the Jewish people.

It Is Time to Build the Temple

1 The prophet[d] Haggai spoke the word of the
LORD to Zerubbabel son of Shealtiel, the governor of Judah, and to Joshua son of Jehozadak,
the high priest. This message came in the second
year that Darius was king, on the first day of the
sixth month:
2"This is what the LORD All-Powerful says: 'The
people say the right time has not come to rebuild
the Temple[d] of the LORD.'"
3Then Haggai the prophet spoke the word of
the LORD: 4"Is it right for you to be living in fancy
houses while the Temple is still in ruins?"
5This is what the LORD All-Powerful says:
"Think about what you have done. 6You have
planted much, but you harvest little. You eat, but
you do not become full. You drink, but you are
still thirsty. You put on clothes, but you are not
warm enough. You earn money, but then you
lose it all as if you had put it into a purse full of
holes."
7This is what the LORD All-Powerful says:
"Think about what you have done. 8Go up to the
mountains, bring back wood, and build the Temple. Then I will be pleased with it and be honored," says the LORD. 9"You look for much, but
you find little. When you bring it home, I destroy
it. Why?" asks the LORD All-Powerful. "Because
you all work hard for your own houses while my
house is still in ruins! 10Because of what you have
done, the sky holds back its rain and the ground
holds back its crops. 11I have called for a time
without rain on the land, and on the mountains,
and on the grain, the new wine, the olive oil, the
plants which the earth produces, the people, the
farm animals, and all the work of your hands."

SIDELIGHT: The warning of a dry time that would ruin the harvest was scary, since the Jews depended on the crops to survive (Haggai 1:11). The olive tree, for example, was used for food, fuel, medicine, and anointing oil. Plus it was used in sacrifices and for building furniture. Olive trees covered the countryside, even growing on rocky hillsides.

PRIORITIES

The Way to Bee

It has no single home of its own. It makes nothing for itself. Yet the bee constantly works from one flower to another, gathering nectar on its legs and carrying it back to the hive.

The other bees—all with their own tasks—work the nectar into food, building the hive and feeding the queen.

Because the bee's main concern is the hive and its community, all other needs are taken care of—food, shelter, family, and job. Through working together, bees create a strong community with their main priority in place: the survival of the hive.

Through the prophet Haggai, God also spoke about priorities. Read **Haggai 1:5–11** to find out what God says about priorities.

- How is God asking the people of Israel to be like bees?
- What might God be telling you to make your top priority?

C O N S I D E R . . .

- pledging to give one-tenth of all the money you make this year to your church.
- asking your pastor for ways to help around the church building and gathering a group of friends to help do those things.

F O R M O R E , S E E . . .

- Genesis 25:27–34 (p. 30)
- Matthew 13:44–46 (p. 932)
- Matthew 19:16–26 (p. 942)

12Zerubbabel son of Shealtiel and Joshua son of
Jehozadak, the high priest, and all the rest of the
people who were left alive obeyed the LORD their
God and the message from Haggai the prophet,
because the LORD their God had sent him. And
the people feared the LORD.

13Haggai, the LORD's messenger, gave the
LORD's message to the people, saying, "The LORD
says, 'I am with you.' " 14The LORD stirred up Zerubbabel son of Shealtiel, the governor of Judah,
and Joshua son of Jehozadak, the high priest, and
all the rest of the people who were left alive. So
they came and worked on the Temple of their
God, the LORD All-Powerful. 15They began on the
twenty-fourth day of the sixth month in the second year Darius was king.

The Beauty of the Temple

2 On the twenty-first day of the seventh
month, the LORD spoke his word through
Haggai the prophet,[d] saying, 2"Speak to Zerubbabel son of Shealtiel, governor of Judah, and to
Joshua son of Jehozadak, the high priest, and to
the rest of the people who are left alive. Say, 3'Do
any of you remember how great the Temple[d] was
before it was destroyed? What does it look like
now? Doesn't it seem like nothing to you?' 4But
the LORD says, 'Zerubbabel, be brave. Also,
Joshua son of Jehozadak, the high priest, be brave.
And all you people who live in the land, be brave,'
says the LORD. 'Work, because I am with you,'
says the LORD All-Powerful. 5'I made a promise to
you when you came out of Egypt, and my Spirit[d]
is still with you. So don't be afraid.'

6"This is what the LORD All-Powerful says: 'In
a short time I will once again shake the heavens
and the earth, the sea and the dry land. 7I will
shake all the nations, and they will bring their
wealth. Then I will fill this Temple with glory,'
says the LORD All-Powerful. 8'The silver is mine,
and the gold is mine,' says the LORD All-Powerful.
9'The new Temple will be greater than the one
before,' says the LORD All-Powerful. 'And in this
place I will give peace,' says the LORD All-
Powerful."

10On the twenty-fourth day of the ninth month
in the second year Darius was king, the LORD
spoke his word to Haggai the prophet, saying,
11"This is what the LORD All-Powerful says: 'Ask
the priests for a teaching. 12Suppose a person carries in the fold of his clothes some meat made
holy for the LORD. If that fold touches bread,
cooked food, wine, olive oil, or some other food,
will that be made holy?' "

The priests answered, "No."

13Then Haggai said, "A person who touches a
dead body will become unclean.[d] If he touches
any of these foods, will it become unclean, too?"

The priests answered, "Yes, it would become
unclean."

14Then Haggai answered, "The LORD says,
'This is also true for the people of this nation.
They are unclean, and everything they do with
their hands is unclean to me. Whatever they offer
at the altar is also unclean.

15" 'Think about this from now on! Think
about how it was before you started laying stones
on top of stones to build the Temple of the LORD.
16A person used to come to a pile of grain expecting to find twenty basketfuls, but there were only
ten. And a person used to come to the wine vat
to take out fifty jarfuls, but only twenty were
there. 17I destroyed your work with diseases, mildew,[d] and hail, but you still did not come back to
me,' says the LORD. 18'It is the twenty-fourth day
of the ninth month, the day in which the people
finished working on the foundation of the Temple
of the LORD. From now on, think about these
things: 19Do you have seeds for crops still in the
barn? Your vines, fig trees, pomegranates,[d] and
olive trees have not given fruit yet. But from now
on I will bless you!' "

The Lord Makes a Promise to Zerubbabel

20Then the LORD spoke his word a second time
to Haggai on the twenty-fourth day of the month.
He said, 21"Tell Zerubbabel, the governor of Judah, 'I am going to shake the heavens and the
earth. 22I will destroy the foreign kingdoms and
take away the power of the kingdoms of the nations. I will destroy the chariots and their riders.
The horses will fall with their riders, as people kill
each other with swords.' 23The LORD All-Powerful
says, 'On that day I will take you, Zerubbabel son
of Shealtiel, my servant,' says the LORD, 'and I
will make you important like my signet[d] ring, because I have chosen you!' says the LORD All-
Powerful."

ZECHARIAH

Why Read This Book:

- Be challenged to follow God and do his will (Zechariah 1—8).
- Find encouragement in knowing a glorious, peaceful future awaits God's people (Zechariah 9—14).

Behind the Scenes:

When you work on something, you like to see results. You want to know that your hard work will be worth the time and energy you've invested.

The people of Israel also wanted to see results when they started rebuilding their Temple. They wanted to know they would be blessed for what they were doing.

The prophet Zechariah was there to assure them and encourage them. Like his colleague Haggai (p. 886), who ministered during the same time, Zechariah believed completing the Temple would be the first step for bringing God's kingdom to earth.

Zechariah's encouragement came in a series of visions about the Temple (Zechariah 1.7—6.8). Each vision in the first part of the book shows activity between heaven and earth. They each show a world that's changing, and they have a universal theme—that God is bigger than the Temple or Judah. Through each vision, Zechariah encourages the people to rebuild the Temple and to focus on following God so they will be ready for the coming of God's kingdom.

The second part of Zechariah (chapters 9—14) has a different focus. It concentrates on the coming kingdom of God instead of the Temple. In the coming age, the wicked will be destroyed and the righteous will be saved. This new kingdom will focus on justice, kindness, and mercy rather than rituals of religion.

The book of Zechariah has been treasured by Christians because many of its images of the Messiah (such as the Prince of Peace, Zechariah 9:9–10), foreshadow Jesus Christ's life and ministry. Just as Zechariah offered encouragement, hope, and joy to the people of his day, the book offers encouragement, hope, and joy to us today.

WHEN THE ACTION WAS

Saul was Israel's king

The Northern Kingdom (Israel) fell to Assyria

Jews began returning from exile

Jesus was born

1000BC — **750BC** — **500BC** — **250BC** — **BC/AD**

The kingdom was split between Israel and Judah

The Southern Kingdom (Judah) fell to Babylon

Zechariah had his visions

The Lord Calls His People Back

1 In the eighth month of the second year Darius was king, the LORD spoke his word to the prophet[d] Zechariah son of Berekiah, who was the son of Iddo. The LORD said, 2"The LORD was very angry with your ancestors. 3So tell the people: This is what the LORD All-Powerful says: 'Return to me, and I will return to you,' says the LORD All-Powerful. 4Don't be like your ancestors. In the past the prophets said to them: This is what the LORD All-Powerful says: 'Stop your evil ways and evil actions.' But they wouldn't listen or pay attention to me, says the LORD. 5Your ancestors are dead, and those prophets didn't live forever. 6I commanded my words and laws to my servants the prophets, and they preached to your ancestors, who returned to me. They said, 'The LORD All-Powerful did as he said he would. He punished us for the way we lived and for what we did.' "

SIDELIGHT: The "Z" section of the phone book would have been a lot thicker in biblical times than it is today. The name Zechariah (Zechariah 1:1) was used for more than thirty people in the Bible, including a gatekeeper (1 Chronicles 26:2, p. 381), a harpist (1 Chronicles 15:20, p. 373), a trumpet-blowing priest (1 Chronicles 15:24, p. 373), and the father of John the Baptist (Luke 1:5, p. 1000). The Zechariah in this book was a prophet and probably a priest.

The Vision of the Horses

7It was on the twenty-fourth day of the eleventh month, which is the month of Shebat, in Darius's second year as king. The LORD spoke his word to the prophet[d] Zechariah son of Berekiah, who was the son of Iddo.

8During the night I had a vision. I saw a man riding a red horse. He was standing among some myrtle trees in a ravine, with red, brown, and white horses behind him.

9I asked, "What are these, sir?"

The angel who was talking with me answered, "I'll show you what they are."

10Then the man standing among the myrtle trees explained, "They are the ones the LORD sent through all the earth."

11Then they spoke to the LORD's angel, who was standing among the myrtle trees. They said, "We have gone through all the earth, and everything is calm and quiet."

12Then the LORD's angel asked, "LORD All-Powerful, how long will it be before you show mercy to Jerusalem and the cities of Judah? You have been angry with them for seventy years now." 13So the LORD answered the angel who was talking with me, and his words were comforting and good.

14Then the angel who was talking to me said to me, "Announce this: This is what the LORD All-Powerful says: 'I have a strong love for Jerusalem. 15And I am very angry with the nations that feel so safe. I was only a little angry at them, but they made things worse.'

16"So this is what the LORD says: 'I will return to Jerusalem with mercy. My Temple[d] will be rebuilt,' says the LORD All-Powerful, 'and the measuring line will be used to rebuild Jerusalem.'

17"Also announce: This is what the LORD All-Powerful says: 'My towns will be rich again. The LORD will comfort Jerusalem again, and I will again choose Jerusalem.' "

The Vision of the Horns

18Then I looked up and saw four animal horns. 19I asked the angel who was talking with me, "What are these?"

He said, "These are the horns that scattered the people of Judah, Israel, and Jerusalem."

20Then the LORD showed me four craftsmen. 21I asked, "What are they coming to do?"

He answered, "They have come to scare and throw down the horns. These horns scattered the people of Judah so that no one could even lift up his head. These horns stand for the nations that attacked the people of Judah and scattered them."

The Vision of the Measuring Line

2 Then I looked up and saw a man holding a line for measuring things. 2I asked him, "Where are you going?"

He said to me, "I am going to measure Jerusalem, to see how wide and how long it is."

3Then the angel who was talking with me left, and another angel came out to meet him. 4The second angel said to him, "Run and tell that young man, 'Jerusalem will become a city without walls, because there will be so many people and cattle in it. 5I will be a wall of fire around it,' says the LORD. 'And I will be the glory within it.'

6"Oh no! Oh no! Run away from Babylon, because I have scattered you like the four winds of heaven," says the LORD.

7"Oh no, Jerusalem! Escape, you who live right in Babylon." 8This is what the LORD All-Powerful says: "After he has honored me and sent me against the nations who took your possessions— because whoever touches you hurts what is precious to me— 9I will shake my hand against them so that their slaves will rob them."

Then you will know that the LORD All-Powerful sent me.

10“Shout and be glad, Jerusalem. I am coming, and I will live among you,” says the LORD. 11“At that time people from many nations will join with the LORD and will become my people. Then I will live among you, and you will know that the LORD All-Powerful has sent me to you. 12The LORD will take Judah as his own part of the holy land, and Jerusalem will be his chosen city again. 13Be silent, everyone, in the presence of the LORD. He is coming out of the holy place where he lives.”

The Vision of the High Priest

3 Then he showed me Joshua, the high priest, standing in front of the LORD's angel. And Satan was standing by Joshua's right side to accuse him. 2The LORD said to Satan, “The LORD says no to you, Satan! The LORD who has chosen Jerusalem says no to you! This man was like a burning stick pulled from the fire.”

3Joshua was wearing dirty clothes and was standing in front of the angel. 4The angel said to those standing in front of him, “Take off those dirty clothes.”

Then the angel said to Joshua, “Look, I have taken away your sin from you, and I am giving you beautiful, fine clothes.”

5Then I said, “Put a clean turban on his head.” So they put a clean turban on his head and dressed him while the LORD's angel stood there.

6Then the LORD's angel said to Joshua, 7“This is what the LORD All-Powerful says: ‘If you do as I tell you and serve me, you will be in charge of my Temple[d] and my courtyards. And I will let you be with these angels who are standing here.

8“ ‘Listen, Joshua, the high priest, and your friends who are sitting in front of you. They are symbols of what will happen. I am going to bring my servant called the Branch. 9Look, I put this stone in front of Joshua, a stone with seven sides. I will carve a message on it,’ says the LORD All-Powerful. ‘And in one day I will take away the sin of this land.’

10“The LORD All-Powerful says, ‘In that day, each of you will invite your neighbor to sit under your own grapevine and under your own fig tree.’ ”

The Vision of the Lampstand

4 Then the angel who was talking with me returned and woke me up as if I had been asleep. 2He asked me, “What do you see?”

I said, “I see a solid gold lampstand with a bowl at the top. And there are seven lamps and also seven places for wicks. 3There are two olive trees by it, one on the right of the bowl and the other on the left.”

4I asked the angel who talked with me, “Sir, what are these?”

5The angel said, “Don't you know what they are?”

“No, sir,” I said.

6Then he told me, “This is the word of the LORD to Zerubbabel: ‘You will not succeed by your own strength or power, but by my Spirit,’[d] says the LORD All-Powerful.

7“Who are you, big mountain? In front of Zerubbabel you will become flat land, and he will bring out the topmost stone, shouting, ‘It's beautiful! It's beautiful!’ ”

8Then the LORD spoke his word to me again, saying, 9“Zerubbabel has laid the foundation of this Temple,[d] and he will complete it. Then you will know that the LORD All-Powerful has sent me to you.

10“The people should not think that small beginnings are unimportant. They will be happy when they see Zerubbabel with tools, building the Temple.

“(These are the seven eyes of the LORD, which look back and forth across the earth.)”

11Then I asked the angel, “What are the two olive trees on the right and left of the lampstand?”

12I also asked him, “What are the two olive branches beside the two gold pipes, from which the olive oil flows to the lamps?”

13He answered, “Don't you know what they are?”

“No, sir,” I said.

14So he said, “They are symbols of the two who have been appointed to serve the LORD of all the earth.”

> **SIDELIGHT:** Though the flying scroll of Zechariah 5 had impressive dimensions, it doesn't hold the record. Archaeologists have discovered scrolls that would stretch almost half the length of a football field. Try fitting one of those textbooks into your locker!

The Vision of the Flying Scroll

5 I looked up again and saw a flying scroll. 2The angel asked me, “What do you see?”

I answered, “I see a flying scroll, thirty feet long and fifteen feet wide.”

3And he said to me, “This is the curse that will go all over the land. One side says every thief will be taken away. The other side says everyone who makes false promises will be taken away. 4The LORD All-Powerful says, ‘I will send it to the houses of thieves and to those who use my name to make false promises. The scroll will stay in that person's house and destroy it with its wood and stones.’ ”

The Vision of the Woman

5Then the angel who was talking with me came
forward and said to me, "Look up and see what
is going out."
6"What is it?" I asked.
He answered, "It is a measuring basket going
out." He also said, "It is a symbol of the people's
sins in all the land."
7Then the lid made of lead was raised, and
there was a woman sitting inside the basket. 8The
angel said, "The woman stands for wickedness."
Then he pushed her back into the basket and put
the lid back down.
9Then I looked up and saw two women going
out with the wind in their wings. Their wings
were like those of a stork, and they lifted up the
basket between earth and the sky.
10I asked the angel who was talking with me,
"Where are they taking the basket?"
11"They are going to Babylonia to build a temple for it," he answered. "When the temple is
ready, they will set the basket there in its place."

The Vision of the Four Chariots

6 I looked up again and saw four chariots going out between two mountains, mountains
of bronze. 2Red horses pulled the first chariot.
Black horses pulled the second chariot. 3White
horses pulled the third chariot, and strong, spotted horses pulled the fourth chariot. 4I asked the
angel who was talking with me, "What are these,
sir?"
5He said, "These are the four spirits of heaven.
They have just come from the presence of the
Lord of the whole world. 6The chariot pulled by
the black horses will go to the land of the north.
The white horses will go to the land of the west,
and the spotted horses will go to the land of the
south."
7When the powerful horses went out, they
were eager to go through all the earth. So he said,
"Go through all the earth," and they did.
8Then he called to me, "Look, the horses that
went north have caused my spirit to rest in the
land of the north."

A Crown for Joshua

9The LORD spoke his word to me, saying,
10"Take silver and gold from Heldai, Tobijah, and
Jedaiah, who were captives in Babylon. Go that
same day to the house of Josiah son of Zephaniah,
who came from Babylon. 11Make the silver and
gold into a crown, and put it on the head of
Joshua son of Jehozadak, the high priest. 12Tell
him this is what the LORD All-Powerful says: 'A
man whose name is the Branch will branch out
from where he is, and he will build the Temple[d] of the LORD. 13One man[n] will build the
Temple of the LORD, and the other[n] will receive
honor. One man will sit on his throne and rule,
and the other will be a priest on his throne. And
these two men will work together in peace.'
14The crown will be kept in the Temple of the
LORD to remind Heldai, Tobijah, Jedaiah, and Josiah son of Zephaniah. 15People living far away
will come and build the Temple of the LORD.
Then you will know the LORD All-Powerful has
sent me to you. This will happen if you completely obey the LORD your God."

SIDELIGHT: Going without food for religious reasons is called "fasting" (Zechariah 7). Like Zechariah, Jesus considered faithfulness to God more important than fasting (Matthew 6:16–18, p. 918). Anybody hungry?

The People Should Show Mercy

7 In the fourth year Darius was king, on the
fourth day of the ninth month, which is
called Kislev, the LORD spoke his word to Zechariah. 2The city of Bethel sent Sharezer, Regem-
Melech, and their men to ask the LORD a question. 3They went to the prophets[d] and priests who
were at the Temple[d] of the LORD All-Powerful.
The men said, "For years in the fifth month of
each year we have shown our sadness and gone
without food. Should we continue to do this?"
4The LORD All-Powerful spoke his word to me,
saying, 5"Tell the priests and the people in the
land: 'For seventy years you went without food
and cried in the fifth and seventh months, but that
was not really for me. 6And when you ate and
drank, it was really for yourselves. 7The LORD
used the earlier prophets to say the same thing,
when Jerusalem and the surrounding towns were
at peace and wealthy, and people lived in the
southern area and the western hills.' "
8And the LORD spoke his word to Zechariah
again, saying, 9"This is what the LORD All-
Powerful says: 'Do what is right and true. Be kind
and merciful to each other. 10Don't hurt widows
and orphans, foreigners or the poor; don't even
think of doing evil to somebody else.'
11"But they refused to pay attention; they were
stubborn and did not want to listen anymore.
12They made their hearts as hard as rock and
would not listen to the teachings of the LORD All-
Powerful. And they would not hear the words he

One man This probably refers to Zerubbabel.
other This probably refers to Joshua.

sent by his Spirit through the earlier prophets. So
the LORD All-Powerful became very angry.
13" 'When I called to them, they would not listen. So when they called to me, I would not
listen,' says the LORD All-Powerful. 14'I scattered them like a hurricane to other countries
they did not know. This good land was left so
ruined behind them that no one could live
there. They had made the desired land a ruin.' "

The Lord Will Bless Jerusalem

8 The LORD All-Powerful spoke his word, saying, 2This is what the LORD All-Powerful
says: "I have a very strong love for Jerusalem. My
strong love for her is like a fire burning in me."
3This is what the LORD says: "I will return to
Jerusalem and live in it. Then it will be called the
City of Truth, and the mountain of the LORD All-
Powerful will be called the Holy Mountain."
4This is what the LORD All-Powerful says: "Old
men and old women will again sit along Jerusalem's streets, each carrying a cane because of age.
5And the streets will be filled with boys and girls
playing."
6This is what the LORD All-Powerful says:
"Those who are left alive then may think it is too
difficult to happen, but it is not too difficult for
me," says the LORD All-Powerful. 7This is what
the LORD All-Powerful says: "I will save my people from countries in the east and west. 8I will
bring them back, and they will live in Jerusalem.
They will be my people, and I will be their good
and loyal God."
9This is what the LORD All-Powerful says:
"Work hard, you who are hearing these words
today. The prophets spoke these words when the
foundation was laid for the house of the LORD All-
Powerful, for the building of the Temple.[d] 10Be-
fore that time there was no money to hire people
or animals. People could not safely come and go
because of the enemies; I had turned everyone
against his neighbor. 11But I will not do to these
people who are left what I did in the past," says
the LORD All-Powerful.
12"They will plant their seeds in peace, their
grapevines will have fruit, the ground will give
good crops, and the sky will send rain. I will give
all this to the people who are left alive. 13Judah
and Israel, your names have been used as curses
in other nations. But I will save you, and you will
become a blessing. So don't be afraid; work
hard."
14This is what the LORD All-Powerful says:
"When your ancestors made me angry, I planned
to punish you. I did not change my mind," says
the LORD All-Powerful. 15"But now I will do
something different. I am planning to do good to
Jerusalem and Judah. So don't be afraid. 16These
are the things you should do: Tell each other the
truth. In the courts judge with truth and complete
fairness. 17Do not make plans to hurt your neighbors, and don't love false promises. I hate all these
things," says the LORD.
18The LORD All-Powerful spoke his word to me
again. 19This is what the LORD All-Powerful says:
"The special days when you give up eating in the
fourth, fifth, seventh, and tenth months will become good, joyful, happy feasts in Judah. But you
must love truth and peace."
20This is what the LORD All-Powerful says:
"Many people from many cities will still come to
Jerusalem. 21People from one city will go and say
to those from another city, 'We are going to pray
to the LORD and to ask the LORD All-Powerful for
help. Come and go with us.' 22Many people and
powerful nations will come to worship the
LORD All-Powerful in Jerusalem and to pray to
the LORD for help."
23This is what the LORD All-Powerful says: "At
that time, ten men from different countries will
come and take hold of a Judean by his coat. They
will say to him, 'Let us go with you, because we
have heard that God is with you.' "

Punishment on Israel's Enemies

9 This message is the word of the LORD.
The message is against the land of
Hadrach
and the city of Damascus.
The tribes[d] of Israel and all people
belong to the LORD.
2The message is also against the city of
Hamath, on the border,
and against Tyre and Sidon, with their skill.
3Tyre has built a strong wall for herself.
She has piled up silver like dust
and gold like the mud in the streets.
4But the Lord will take away all she has
and destroy her power on the sea.
That city will be destroyed by fire.
5The city of Ashkelon will see it and be afraid.
The people of Gaza will shake with fear,
and the people of Ekron will lose hope.
No king will be left in Gaza,
and no one will live in Ashkelon anymore.
6Foreigners will live in Ashdod,
and I will destroy the pride of the
Philistines.
7I will stop them from drinking blood
and from eating forbidden food.
Those left alive will belong to God.
They will be leaders in Judah,
and Ekron will become like the Jebusites.
8I will protect my Temple[d]
from armies who would come or go.
No one will hurt my people again,
because now I am watching them.

The King Is Coming

9Rejoice greatly, people of Jerusalem!
Shout for joy, people of Jerusalem!
Your king is coming to you.
He does what is right, and he saves.
He is gentle and riding on a donkey,
on the colt of a donkey.

SIDELIGHT: The limousine of the ancient world was a white warhorse. But Zechariah pictures the future king of Jerusalem on a donkey—the biblical equivalent of an economy car (Zechariah 9:9; see also Matthew 21:5, p. 944).

10I will take away the chariots from Ephraim
and the horses from Jerusalem.
The bows used in war will be broken.
The king will talk to the nations about peace.
His kingdom will go from sea to sea,
and from the Euphrates River to the ends of the earth.

11As for you, because of the blood of the agreement with you
I will set your prisoners free from the waterless pit.
12You prisoners who have hope,
return to your place of safety.
Today I am telling you
that I will give you back twice as much as before.
13I will use Judah like a bow
and Ephraim like the arrows.
Jerusalem, I will use your men
to fight the men of Greece.
I will use you like a warrior's sword.
14Then the LORD will appear above them,
and his arrows will shoot like lightning.
The Lord GOD will blow the trumpet,
and he will march in the storms of the south.
15The LORD All-Powerful will protect them;
they will destroy the enemy with slingshots.
They will drink and shout like drunk men.
They will be filled like a bowl
used for sprinkling blood at the corners of the altar.
16On that day the LORD their God will save them
as if his people were sheep.
They will shine in his land
like jewels in a crown.
17They will be so pretty and beautiful.
The young men will grow strong on the grain
and the young women on new wine.

The Lord's Promises

10 Ask the LORD for rain during the springtime rains.
The LORD is the one who makes the clouds.
He sends the showers
and gives everyone green fields.
2Idols tell lies;
fortune-tellers see false visions
and tell about false dreams.
The comfort they give is worth nothing.
So the people are like lost sheep.
They are abused, because there is no shepherd.

3The LORD says, "I am angry at my shepherds,
and I will punish the leaders.
I, the LORD All-Powerful, care
for my flock, the people of Judah.
I will make them like my proud war horses.
4From Judah will come the cornerstone,[d]
and the tent peg,
the battle bow,
and every ruler.
5Together they will be like soldiers
marching to battle through muddy streets.
The LORD is with them,
so they will fight and defeat the horsemen.
6"I will strengthen the people of Judah
and save the people of Joseph.
I will bring them back,
because I care about them.
It will be as though
I had never left them,
because I am the LORD their God,
and I will answer them.
7The people of Ephraim will be strong like soldiers;
they will be glad as when they have drunk wine.
Their children will see it and rejoice;
they will be happy in the LORD.
8I will call my people
and gather them together.
I will save them,
and they will grow in number as they grew in number before.
9I have scattered them among the nations,
but in those faraway places, they will remember me.
They and their children will live and return.
10I will bring them back from the land of Egypt
and gather them from Assyria.
I will bring them to Gilead and Lebanon
until there isn't enough room for them all.

11They will come through the sea of trouble.
The waves of the sea will be calm,
and the Nile River will dry up.
I will defeat Assyria's pride
and destroy Egypt's power over other
countries.
12I will make my people strong,
and they will live as I say," says the LORD.

11 Lebanon, open your gates
so fire may burn your cedar trees.[n]
2Cry, pine trees, because the cedar has fallen,
because the tall trees are ruined.
Cry, oaks in Bashan,
because the mighty forest has been cut
down.
3Listen to the shepherds crying
because their rich pastures are destroyed.
Listen to the lions roaring
because the lovely land of the Jordan River
is ruined.

The Two Shepherds

4This is what the LORD my God says: "Feed the flock that are about to be killed. 5Their buyers kill them and are not punished. Those who sell them say, 'Praise the LORD, I am rich.' Even the shepherds don't feel sorry for their sheep. 6I don't feel sorry anymore for the people of this country," says the LORD. "I will let everyone be under the power of his neighbor and king. They will bring trouble to the country, and I will not save anyone from them."

7So I fed the flock about to be killed, particularly the weakest ones. Then I took two sticks; I called one Pleasant and the other Union, and I fed the flock. 8In one month I got rid of three shepherds. The flock did not pay attention to me, and I got impatient with them. 9I said, "I will no longer take care of you like a shepherd. Let those that are dying die, and let those that are to be destroyed be destroyed. Let those that are left eat each other."

10Then I broke the stick named Pleasant to break the agreement God made with all the nations. 11That day it was broken. The weak ones in the flock who were watching me knew this message was from the LORD.

12Then I said, "If you want to pay me, pay me. If not, then don't." So they paid me thirty pieces of silver.

13The LORD said to me, "Throw the money to the potter." That is how little they thought I was worth.[n] So I took the thirty pieces of silver and threw them to the potter in the Temple[d] of the LORD.

14Then I broke the second stick, named Union, to break the brotherhood between Judah and Israel.

15Then the LORD said to me, "Get the things used by a foolish shepherd again, 16because I am going to get a new shepherd for the country. He will not care for the dying sheep, or look for the young ones, or heal the injured ones, or feed the healthy. But he will eat the best sheep and tear off their hoofs.

17"How terrible it will be for the useless
shepherd
who abandoned the flock.
A sword will strike his arm and his right eye.
His arm will lose all its strength,
and his right eye will go blind."

Jerusalem Will Be Saved

12 This message is the word of the LORD to Israel. This is what the LORD says, who stretched out the skies, and laid the foundations of the earth, and put the human spirit within: 2"I will make Jerusalem like a cup of poison to the nations around her. They will come and attack Jerusalem and Judah. 3One day all the nations on earth will come together to attack Jerusalem, but I will make it like a heavy rock; anyone who tries to move it will get hurt. 4At that time I will confuse every horse and cause its rider to go crazy," says the LORD. "I will watch over Judah, but I will blind all the horses of the enemies. 5Then the leaders of Judah will say to themselves, 'The people of Jerusalem are strong, because the LORD All-Powerful is their God.'

6"At that time I will make the leaders of Judah like a fire burning a stack of wood or like a fire burning straw. They will destroy all the people around them left and right. But the people of Jerusalem will remain safe.

7"The LORD will save the homes of Judah first so that the honor given to David's family and to the people of Jerusalem won't be greater than the honor given to Judah. 8At that time the LORD will protect the people in Jerusalem. Then even the weakest of them will be strong like David. And the family of David will be like God, like an angel of the LORD in front of them. 9At that time I will go to destroy all the nations that attack Jerusalem.

Crying for the One They Stabbed

10"I will pour out on David's family and the people in Jerusalem a spirit of kindness and mercy. They will look at me, the one they have stabbed, and they will cry like someone crying over the death of an only child. They will be as

trees In this poem, trees, bushes, and animals stand for leaders of countries around Judah.
worth This was a small amount. It was about the price paid for a slave.

sad as someone who has lost a firstborn[d] son. 11At
that time there will be much crying in Jerusalem,
like the crying for Hadad Rimmon in the plain of
Megiddo. 12The land will cry, each family by itself: the family of David by itself and their wives
by themselves, the family of Nathan by itself and
their wives by themselves, 13the family of Levi by
itself and their wives by themselves, the family of
Shimei by itself and their wives by themselves,
14and all the rest of the families by themselves and
their wives by themselves.

13 "At that time a fountain will be open for
David's descendants[d] and for the people
of Jerusalem to cleanse them of their sin and uncleanness."
2The LORD All-Powerful says, "At that time I
will get rid of the names of the idols from the
land; no one will remember them anymore. I will
also remove the prophets[d] and unclean[d] spirits
from the land. 3If a person continues to prophesy,
his own father and mother, the ones who gave
birth to him, will tell him, 'You have told lies using the LORD's name, so you must die.' When he
prophesies, his own father and mother who gave
birth to him will stab him.
4"At that time the prophets will be ashamed of
their visions and prophecies. They won't wear the
prophet's clothes made of hair to trick people.
5Each of them will say, 'I am not a prophet. I am
a farmer and have been a farmer since I was
young.' 6But someone will ask, 'What are the
deep cuts on your body?' And each will answer,
'I was hurt at my friend's house.'

SIDELIGHT: If false prophets tried to get new jobs, they would have had trouble hiding their previous occupation. The deep cuts on their bodies (Zechariah 13:6) were probably self-inflicted while they were prophesying.

The Shepherd Is Killed

7"Sword, hit the shepherd.
Attack the man who is my friend,"
says the LORD All-Powerful.
"Kill the shepherd,
and the sheep will scatter,
and I will punish the little ones."

SADNESS

Stabbed in the Back

Youth leader Denise McNeil felt cheated and abused by her youth group. After returning from a recent retreat, she discovered that one of the older teenagers had bought and supplied liquor for the kids on the trip. All the kids knew about the alcohol, but no one had told Denise.

When the group returned home, the word got out. Parents called Denise the next day, asking how such a thing could happen.

Denise had no idea how it had happened. That was what made it so embarrassing. She thought she knew the group. Now she wasn't so sure. She had trusted the kids. Now she could make no promises.

Denise spent the next month talking to all the kids who were on the retreat. She shared her anger, pain, and sadness. She also showed the group she still loved them. Then she worked—against heavy opposition—to plan another youth retreat, one that could be done right.

When the kids saw how much Denise cared for them and how they had abused her trust in them, they felt sad and sorry. The sadness they felt was much like the sadness described in **Zechariah 12:7–10**.

- How did Denise's youth group act like the people described in verse 10?
- According to this passage, how does God feel when we disobey?

CONSIDER

- listening carefully to a friend the next time he or she is sad.
- rewriting Zechariah 12:7–9, substituting your own name for "the people of Judah," "the people in Jerusalem," and "the family of David." Read the passage to yourself when you're down.

FOR MORE, SEE

- Job 2:11–13 (p. 453)
- Mark 15:33–34 (p. 995)
- Luke 19:41–44 (p. 1045)

8 The LORD says, "Two-thirds of the people
through all the land will die. They will be
gone,
and one-third will be left.
9 The third that is left I will test with fire,
purifying them like silver,
testing them like gold.
Then they will call on me,
and I will answer them.
I will say, 'You are my people,'
and they will say, 'The LORD is our God.' "

The Day of Punishment

14 The LORD's day of judging is coming
when the wealth you have taken will be
divided among you.
2 I will bring all the nations together to fight Jerusalem. They will capture the city and rob the
houses and attack the women. Half the people
will be taken away as captives, but the rest of the
people won't be taken from the city.
3 Then the LORD will go to war against those
nations; he will fight as in a day of battle. 4 On that
day he will stand on the Mount of Olives,[d] east of
Jerusalem. The Mount of Olives will split in two,
forming a deep valley that runs east and west.
Half the mountain will move toward the north,
and half will move toward the south. 5 You will
run through this mountain valley to the other
side, just as you ran from the earthquake when
Uzziah was king of Judah. Then the LORD my God
will come and all the holy ones with him.
6 On that day there will be no light, cold, or
frost. 7 There will be no other day like it, and the
LORD knows when it will come. There will be no
day or night; even at evening it will still be light.
8 At that time fresh water will flow from Jerusalem. Half of it will flow east to the Dead Sea,[d] and
half will flow west to the Mediterranean Sea. It
will flow summer and winter.
9 Then the LORD will be king over the whole
world. At that time there will be only one LORD,
and his name will be the only name.
10 All the land south of Jerusalem from Geba to
Rimmon will be turned into a plain. Jerusalem
will be raised up, but it will stay in the same place.
The city will reach from the Benjamin Gate and
to the First Gate to the Corner Gate, and from the
Tower of Hananel to the king's winepresses.[d]
11 People will live there, and it will never be destroyed again. Jerusalem will be safe.
12 But the LORD will bring a terrible disease on
the nations that fought against Jerusalem. Their
flesh will rot away while they are still standing up.
Their eyes will rot in their sockets, and their
tongues will rot in their mouths. 13 At that time
the LORD will cause panic. Everybody will grab his
neighbor, and they will attack each other. 14 The
people of Judah will fight in Jerusalem. And the
wealth of the nations around them will be collected — much gold, silver, and clothes. 15 A similar disease will strike the horses, mules, camels,
donkeys, and all the animals in the camps.
16 All of those left alive of the people who came
to fight Jerusalem will come back to Jerusalem
year after year to worship the King, the LORD All-
Powerful, and to celebrate the Feast[d] of Shelters.
17 Anyone from the nations who does not go to
Jerusalem to worship the King, the LORD All-
Powerful, will not have rain fall on his land. 18 If
the Egyptians do not go to Jerusalem, they will
not have rain. Then the LORD will send them the
same terrible disease he sent the other nations
that did not celebrate the Feast of Shelters. 19 This
will be the punishment for Egypt and any nation
which does not go to celebrate the Feast of Shelters.
20 At that time the horses' bells will have written on them: HOLY TO THE LORD. The cooking pots
in the Temple[d] of the LORD will be like the holy
altar bowls. 21 Every pot in Jerusalem and Judah
will be holy to the LORD All-Powerful, and everyone who offers sacrifices will be able to take food
from them and cook in them. At that time there
will not be any buyers or sellers in the Temple of
the LORD All-Powerful.

MALACHI

Why Read This Book:

- Learn how to be loyal when things are tough (Malachi 1—2).
- Claim God's promise in the midst of discouragement (Malachi 3).

Behind the Scenes:

Everything was supposed to be better now. The Jewish people returned to Jerusalem from exile, excited by the promises of Haggai (p. 886) and Zechariah (p. 889) about the coming of God's kingdom. But many years had passed, and life seemed about like it had been—if not worse.

The community was still poor. Droughts and locusts continually ruined crops. Families were falling apart by divorce and adultery. The poor were being abused. And, worst of all, people had forgotten their faith. They just went through the motions of worshiping God.

In short, times were hard and God seemed far away. Why even try? the people seemed to say. They were upset and impatient. It seemed that God had not carried through with his part of the agreement.

Enter Malachi, whose name means "my messenger." He pointed out how the country's priests were abusing or neglecting their God-given responsibilities. Their failure, the prophet said, was the main reason things hadn't gotten any better. The prophet then challenged people to return to their faith. Then, at the time of judgment, the faithful would receive God's blessing.

When things don't go as we expect or hope, it's easy to think God has let us down. And it's easy to relax our faith. But the book of Malachi urges us to stay strong. God loves us and is faithful, even when we can't see him working. We can have courage and hope in knowing that, in the end, God has a great future for all who follow him.

WHEN THE ACTION WAS

1000BC	Saul was Israel's king
	The kingdom was split between Israel and Judah
750BC	The Northern Kingdom (Israel) fell to Assyria
	The Southern Kingdom (Judah) fell to Babylon
500BC	Jews began returning from exile
	Malachi ministered in Jerusalem
250BC	
BC/AD	Jesus was born

1 This message is the word of the LORD given to Israel through Malachi.

God Loves Israel

2The LORD said, "I have loved you."

But you ask, "How have you loved us?"

The LORD said, "Esau and Jacob were brothers. I loved Jacob, 3but I hated Esau. I destroyed his mountain country and left his land to the wild dogs of the desert."

4The people of Edom might say, "We were destroyed, but we will go back and rebuild the ruins."

But the LORD All-Powerful says, "If they rebuild them, I will destroy them. People will say, 'Edom is a wicked country. The LORD is always angry with the Edomites.' 5You will see these things with your own eyes. And you will say, 'The LORD is great, even outside the borders of Israel!' "

The Priests Don't Respect God

6The LORD All-Powerful says, "A child honors his father, and a servant honors his master. I am a father, so why don't you honor me? I am a master, so why don't you respect me? You priests do not respect me.

"But you ask, 'How have we shown you disrespect?'

7"You have shown it by bringing unclean[d] food to my altar.

"But you ask, 'What makes it unclean?'

"It is unclean because you don't respect the altar of the LORD. 8When you bring blind animals as sacrifices, that is wrong. When you bring crippled and sick animals, that is wrong. Try giving them to your governor. Would he be pleased with you? He wouldn't accept you," says the LORD All-Powerful.

9"Now ask God to be kind to you, but he won't accept you with such offerings," says the LORD All-Powerful.

10"I wish one of you would close the Temple[d] doors so that you would not light useless fires on my altar! I am not pleased with you and will not accept your gifts," says the LORD All-Powerful. 11"From the east to the west I will be honored among the nations. Everywhere they will bring incense[d] and clean offerings to me, because I will be honored among the nations," says the LORD All-Powerful.

12"But you don't honor me. You say about the Lord's altar, 'It is unclean, and the food has no worth.' 13You say, 'We are tired of doing this,' and you sniff at it in disgust," says the LORD All-Powerful.

"And you bring hurt, crippled, and sick animals as gifts. You bring them as gifts, but I won't accept them from you," says the LORD. 14"The person who cheats will be cursed. He has a male animal in his flock and promises to offer it, but then he offers to the Lord an animal that has something wrong with it. I am a great king," says the LORD All-Powerful, "and I am feared by all the nations.

Rules for Priests

2 "Priests, this command is for you. 2Listen to me. Pay attention to what I say. Honor my name," says the LORD All-Powerful. "If you don't, I will send a curse on you and on your blessings. I have already cursed them, because you don't pay attention to what I say.

3"I will punish your descendants.[d] I will smear your faces with the animal insides left from your feasts, and you will be thrown away with it. 4Then you will know that I am giving you this command so my agreement with Levi will continue," says the LORD All-Powerful. 5"My agreement for priests was with the tribe[d] of Levi. I promised them life and peace so they would honor me. And they did honor me and fear me. 6They taught the true teachings and spoke no lies. With peace and honesty they did what I said they should do, and they kept many people from sinning.

7"A priest should teach what he knows, and people should learn the teachings from him, because he is the messenger of the LORD All-Powerful. 8But you priests have stopped obeying me. With your teachings you have caused many people to do wrong. You have broken the agreement with the tribe[d] of Levi!" says the LORD All-Powerful. 9"You have not been careful to do what I say, but instead you take sides in court cases. So I have caused you to be hated and disgraced in front of everybody."

Judah Was Not Loyal to God

10We all have the same father; the same God made us. So why do people break their promises to each other and show no respect for the agreement our ancestors made with God? 11The people of Judah have broken their promises. They have done something God hates in Israel and Jerusalem: The people of Judah did not respect the Temple[d] that the LORD loves, and the men of Judah married women who worship foreign gods. 12Whoever does this might bring offerings to the LORD All-Powerful, but the LORD will still cut that person off from the community of Israel.

13This is another thing you do. You cover the LORD's altar with your tears. You cry and moan, because he does not accept your offerings and is not pleased with what you bring. 14You ask, "Why?" It is because the LORD sees how you treated the wife you married when you were young. You broke your promise to her, even though she was your partner and you had an

agreement with her. [15]God made husbands and
wives to become one body and one spirit for his
purpose—so they would have children who are
true to God.

So be careful, and do not break your promise
to the wife you married when you were young.

[16]The LORD God of Israel says, "I hate divorce.
And I hate people who do cruel things as easily as
they put on clothes," says the LORD All-Powerful.

So be careful. And do not break your trust.

The Special Day of Judging

[17]You have tired the LORD with your words.
You ask, "How have we tired him?"

You did it by saying, "The LORD thinks anyone
who does evil is good, and he is pleased with
them." Or you asked, "Where is the God who is
fair?"

3 The LORD All-Powerful says, "I will send my
messenger, who will prepare the way for
me. Suddenly, the Lord you are looking for will
come to his Temple;[d] the messenger of the agreement, whom you want, will come." [2]No one can
live through that time; no one can survive when
he comes. He will be like a purifying fire and like
laundry soap. [3]Like someone who heats and puri-
fies silver, he will purify the Levites and make
them pure like gold and silver. Then they will
bring offerings to the LORD in the right way. [4]And
the LORD will accept the offerings from Judah and
Jerusalem, as it was in the past. [5]The LORD All-
Powerful says, "Then I will come to you and
judge you. I will be quick to testify against those
who take part in evil magic, adultery,[d] and lying
under oath, those who cheat workers of their pay
and who cheat widows and orphans, those who
are unfair to foreigners, and those who do not
respect me.

Stealing from God

[6]"I the LORD do not change. So you descendants[d] of Jacob have not been destroyed. [7]Since
the time of your ancestors, you have disobeyed
my rules and have not kept them. Return to me,

GOD'S POWER

The Power of Right

Laura Frey, the senior class president, had a remarkable power over the students at her school. The whole gymnasium could be full, and all Laura needed to do to quiet things down was to stand up, look out over the crowd, and wait. Within a minute the whole gym would be quiet.

Where did Laura get her power?

Ask her fellow students:

"I trust her. If she says she's going to do something, she always does her best to do it."

Ask her teachers:

"She's truthful and honest. She owns up to her mistakes and will always try to do better. She even helps others through their mistakes."

Ask her friends' parents:

"I like her sincerity. Laura will listen to my daughter if she has a problem. She's a good friend who's there for others."

People had no reason to doubt Laura and countless reasons to admire her.

As you get to know God, you'll discover a God who has the ultimate powerful qualities of trust, honesty, and sincerity. Read **Malachi 3:1–4** about the promised "messenger" of God whose power is like a purifying fire. This "messenger" is the promised Messiah, the Son of God.

- How much greater is God's power in Malachi than that of leaders like Laura?
- What area of your life needs the purifying power of God?

CONSIDER . . .

- choosing one of the symbols of God's power from the passage (matches, laundry soap, silver, or gold) and keeping it in your room as a reminder of God's power.
- wearing something gold or silver every day this week to remind you to pray for God's purifying power in your life.

FOR MORE, SEE . . .

- Psalm 51:10–13 (p. 511)
- Isaiah 25:1–5 (p. 640)
- Revelation 21:1–8 (p. 1347)

and I will return to you," says the LORD All-
Powerful.

"But you ask, 'How can we return?'

8"Should a person rob God? But you are robbing me.

"You ask, 'How have we robbed you?'

"You have robbed me in your offerings and the
tenth of your crops. 9So a curse is on you, because
the whole nation has robbed me. 10Bring to the
storehouse a full tenth of what you earn so there
will be food in my house. Test me in this," says
the LORD All-Powerful. "I will open the windows
of heaven for you and pour out all the blessings
you need. 11I will stop the insects so they won't
eat your crops. The grapes won't fall from your
vines before they are ready to pick," says the
LORD All-Powerful. 12"All the nations will call you
blessed, because you will have a pleasant country," says the LORD All-Powerful.

SIDELIGHT: Your church ushers might not appreciate broccoli in the Sunday plate, but the storehouse of Malachi 3:10 welcomed such agricultural gifts. Every third year, these barns opened their doors to the poor and priests (see Deuteronomy 14:28–29, p. 174).

The Lord's Promise of Mercy

13The LORD says, "You have said terrible things
about me.

"But you ask, 'What have we said about you?'

14"You have said, 'It is useless to serve God. It
did no good to obey his laws and to show the
LORD All-Powerful that we were sorry for what
we did. 15So we say that proud people are happy.
Evil people succeed. They challenge God and get
away with it.' "

16Then those who honored the LORD spoke
with each other, and the LORD listened and heard
them. The names of those who honored the LORD
and respected him were written in his presence in
a book to be remembered.

17The LORD All-Powerful says, "They belong to
me; on that day they will be my very own. As a
parent shows mercy to his child who serves him,
I will show mercy to my people. 18You will again
see the difference between good and evil people,
between those who serve God and those who
don't.

SIN

Unfair Acquisitions

It didn't seem fair to Alicia Hall. She needed a new dress just as much as Donna Sims. She wanted the cassette tapes just as much as Donna. She liked chocolate just as much as Donna. She even wanted a new car stereo just as much as Donna.

But unlike Donna, she wasn't willing to steal and cheat to get them.

It wasn't fair.

Alicia sometimes hoped that Donna would get caught shoving a tape into her purse or wearing a new dress out of a store or lying to her insurance company about the "theft" of her old car stereo.

But Alicia didn't stay honest just because she was afraid of being caught. She was honest because she knew it was the right thing to do. She knew that others were hurt by Donna's stealing and lies. Alicia also knew that God would not approve of Donna's dishonesty.

Dishonesty will separate you from God. Read **Malachi 4:1–2** to find out how God will deal with those who do evil things and those who honor God.

- According to the scripture, what punishment awaits dishonest and greedy people like Donna?
- How can you honor God and receive the goodness and healing he promises in this passage?

CONSIDER . . .

- confronting any friends who shoplift.
- returning to their rightful owners any items you've stolen.

FOR MORE, SEE . . .

- Genesis 3 (p. 4)
- 1 Corinthians 3:12–15 (p. 1171)
- 1 John 4:1–6 (p. 1319)

The Day of the Lord's Judging

4 "There is a day coming that will burn like a
hot furnace, and all the proud and evil people will be like straw. On that day they will be
completely burned up so that not a root or branch
will be left," says the LORD All-Powerful. 2"But for
you who honor me, goodness will shine on you
like the sun, with healing in its rays. You will
jump around, like well-fed calves. 3Then you
will crush the wicked like ashes under your
feet on the day I will do this," says the LORD
All-Powerful.

4"Remember the teaching of Moses my servant, those laws and rules I gave to him on Mount
Sinai for all the Israelites.

5"But I will send you Elijah the prophet[d] before
that great and terrifying day of the LORD's judging.
6Elijah will help parents love their children and
children love their parents. Otherwise, I will
come and put a curse on the land."

NEW TESTAMENT

MATTHEW

Why Read This Book:

- Learn how Jesus filled the role of the Messiah—the Savior whose coming was anticipated in the Old Testament (Matthew 1—3).
- Find guidelines for living (Matthew 5—7).
- Understand Jesus' power as shown through many miracles and stories (Matthew 8—20).
- See what happened to Jesus that led to his death and resurrection (Matthew 21—28).

Behind the Scenes:

When candidates announce they are running for political office, the press begins a flurry of investigation. Reporters check the candidate's background and experience. Where is he from? What's her family like? Is he trustworthy? Has she done what she says she's done?

The book of Matthew is something like stories about new candidates. This Gospel digs into Jesus' background. It tells his relationship to the Jewish faith—how he fulfills Old Testament prophecies about a Messiah or Savior. That's why the book quotes Old Testament passages more than any other book in the New

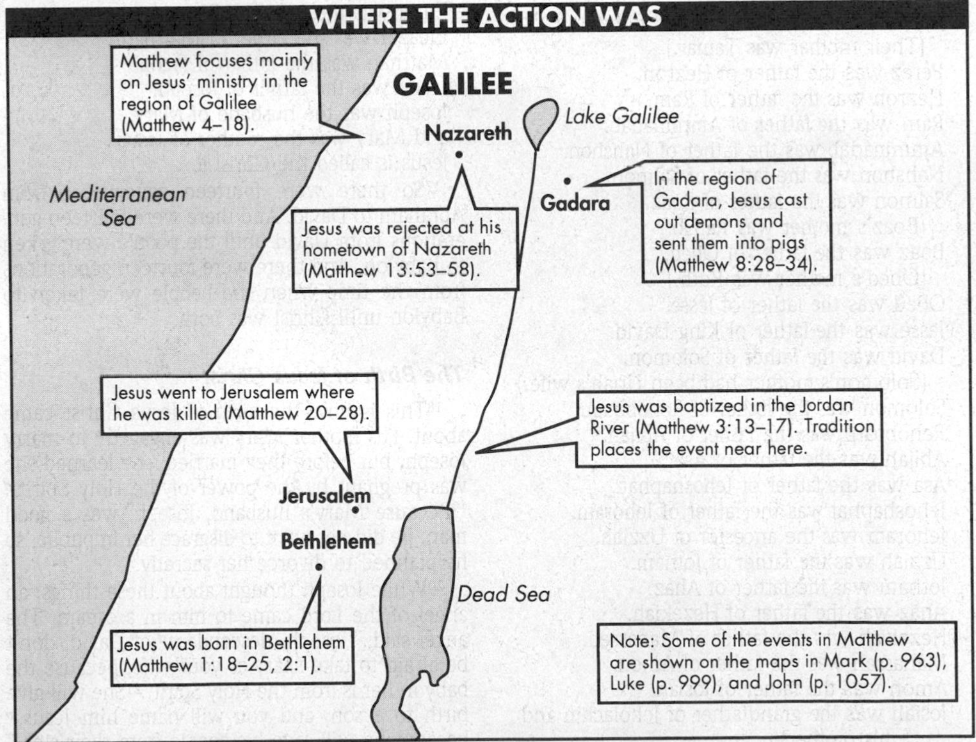
WHERE THE ACTION WAS
Matthew focuses mainly on Jesus' ministry in the region of Galilee (Matthew 4–18).
GALILEE
Lake Galilee
Nazareth
Mediterranean Sea
Gadara
In the region of Gadara, Jesus cast out demons and sent them into pigs (Matthew 8:28–34).
Jesus was rejected at his hometown of Nazareth (Matthew 13:53–58).
Jesus went to Jerusalem where he was killed (Matthew 20–28).
Jesus was baptized in the Jordan River (Matthew 3:13–17). Tradition places the event near here.
Jerusalem
Bethlehem
Dead Sea
Jesus was born in Bethlehem (Matthew 1:18–25, 2:1).
Note: Some of the events in Matthew are shown on the maps in Mark (p. 963), Luke (p. 999), and John (p. 1057).

WHEN THE ACTION WAS

BC/AD	25AD	50AD	75AD	100AD

- Jesus was born (BC/AD)
- Jesus began his ministry
- Jesus was crucified, rose from the dead, and went to heaven
- Paul began his missionary work
- Fire destroyed Rome
- Romans destroyed the Temple in Jerusalem

Behind the Scenes (cont.): Testament. And because the Jews expected a political messiah to establish a kingdom on earth, this book emphasizes Jesus' teachings about what his kingdom would be like.

The book of Matthew uses a straightforward, biographical approach to tell stories of Jesus' life and teachings. It begins by telling about his birth (chapters 1—2), then focuses on his ministry, primarily around Lake Galilee, where he grew up (chapters 3—18). Then the book moves to tell about events in Jerusalem that ultimately led to Jesus' death (chapters 19—27). The book concludes with Jesus' resurrection and last instructions to his disciples (chapter 28).

Matthew is a good source for examining what Jesus did and said while he was on earth. By reading it, we learn what Jesus expects of us if we intend to follow him.

The Family History of Jesus

1 This is the family history of Jesus Christ. He came from the family of David, and David came from the family of Abraham.
2Abraham was the father[n] of Isaac.
Isaac was the father of Jacob.
Jacob was the father of Judah and his brothers.
3Judah was the father of Perez and Zerah.
(Their mother was Tamar.)
Perez was the father of Hezron.
Hezron was the father of Ram.
4Ram was the father of Amminadab.
Amminadab was the father of Nahshon.
Nahshon was the father of Salmon.
5Salmon was the father of Boaz.
(Boaz's mother was Rahab.)
Boaz was the father of Obed.
(Obed's mother was Ruth.)
Obed was the father of Jesse.
6Jesse was the father of King David.
David was the father of Solomon.
(Solomon's mother had been Uriah's wife.)
7Solomon was the father of Rehoboam.
Rehoboam was the father of Abijah.
Abijah was the father of Asa.
8Asa was the father of Jehoshaphat.
Jehoshaphat was the father of Jehoram.
Jehoram was the ancestor of Uzziah.
9Uzziah was the father of Jotham.
Jotham was the father of Ahaz.
Ahaz was the father of Hezekiah.
10Hezekiah was the father of Manasseh.
Manasseh was the father of Amon.
Amon was the father of Josiah.
11Josiah was the grandfather of Jehoiachin and his brothers.
(This was at the time that the people were taken to Babylon.)
12After they were taken to Babylon:
Jehoiachin was the father of Shealtiel.
Shealtiel was the grandfather of Zerubbabel.
13Zerubbabel was the father of Abiud.
Abiud was the father of Eliakim.
Eliakim was the father of Azor.
14Azor was the father of Zadok.
Zadok was the father of Akim.
Akim was the father of Eliud.
15Eliud was the father of Eleazar.
Eleazar was the father of Matthan.
Matthan was the father of Jacob.
16Jacob was the father of Joseph.
Joseph was the husband of Mary,
and Mary was the mother of Jesus.
Jesus is called the Christ.[d]

17So there were fourteen generations from
Abraham to David. And there were fourteen generations from David until the people were taken
to Babylon. And there were fourteen generations
from the time when the people were taken to
Babylon until Christ was born.

The Birth of Jesus Christ

18This is how the birth of Jesus Christ came
about. His mother Mary was engaged[n] to marry
Joseph, but before they married, she learned she
was pregnant by the power of the Holy Spirit.[d]
19Because Mary's husband, Joseph, was a good
man, he did not want to disgrace her in public, so
he planned to divorce her secretly.
20While Joseph thought about these things, an
angel of the Lord came to him in a dream. The
angel said, "Joseph, descendant[d] of David, don't
be afraid to take Mary as your wife, because the
baby in her is from the Holy Spirit. 21She will give
birth to a son, and you will name him Jesus,[n]
because he will save his people from their sins."
22All this happened to bring about what the
Lord had said through the prophet:[d] 23"The virgin[d] will be pregnant. She will have a son, and

father "Father" in Jewish lists of ancestors can sometimes mean grandfather or more distant relative.
engaged For the Jewish people an engagement was a lasting agreement, which could only be broken by a divorce. If a bride was unfaithful, it was considered adultery, and she could be put to death.
Jesus The name Jesus means "salvation."

they will name him Immanuel,"[n] which means
"God is with us."
24When Joseph woke up, he did what the
Lord's angel had told him to do. Joseph took Mary
as his wife, 25but he did not have sexual relations
with her until she gave birth to the son. And Joseph named him Jesus.

Wise Men Come to Visit Jesus

2 Jesus was born in the town of Bethlehem in
Judea during the time when Herod was king.
When Jesus was born, some wise men from the
east came to Jerusalem. 2They asked, "Where is
the baby who was born to be the king of the Jews?
We saw his star in the east and have come to
worship him."
3When King Herod heard this, he was troubled,
as well as all the people in Jerusalem. 4Herod
called a meeting of all the leading priests and
teachers of the law and asked them where the
Christ[d] would be born. 5They answered, "In the
town of Bethlehem in Judea. The prophet[d] wrote
about this in the Scriptures:[d]
6'But you, Bethlehem, in the land of Judah,
are important among the tribes[d] of Judah.
A ruler will come from you

"The virgin . . . Immanuel" Quotation from Isaiah 7:14.

FOLLOWING GOD

Taking a Stand

As a young man in Germany, Martin Luther feared he wasn't good enough for God. He even became a monk, hoping to avoid God's anger. Luther tested the patience of other monks as he beat himself with whips and slept without a blanket in the frigid German winter. He confessed every tiny thought or deed, just in case it might be evil.

Regardless of his quirks, Luther grew as a highly skilled Bible professor. But he still felt spiritually distressed by his fear of an angry, judging God. While preparing lectures on the Psalms and later on Paul's letter to the Romans, he discovered something that would change his life: He couldn't earn God's approval. God loved him as he was! He knew now that God really loved him, no matter how unlovable he was. He was happy for the first time in his life. He began teaching and preaching his newfound faith, and criticizing many church policies of the day.

Predictably, the religious authorities disapproved. A long-standing rewards system required people to earn their salvation. The authorities gave Luther a clear choice: Take back everything he had written and said, or be kicked out of the church, lose his job and perhaps lose his life.

Luther had to choose between following God and going along with the system. At a dramatic trial before several authorities, he looked at his accusers and said, "Here I stand. I can do no other."

He was thrown out of the church, and he had to hide in a remote castle from would-be assassins. Yet, his view of a loving God instead of a punishing one ignited the flame that grew into a bonfire of church reform in the sixteenth century.

In **Matthew 1:18–25**, Joseph, like Luther, had to choose between following God and taking the easy way out.

- What factors might have made both Luther's and Joseph's decisions difficult?
- Do you ever find yourself facing a situation in which following God looks like the most difficult way? What direction or comfort does this Bible story give you?

CONSIDER . . .

- writing out a tough decision you're now facing. Based on what you have read in the passage, list your options for following God, and choose.
- encouraging friends who are facing hard choices to follow God's direction, although it may seem difficult.

FOR MORE, SEE . . .

- Exodus 3:1–15 (p. 60)
- Luke 2:1–7 (p. 1003)
- 1 Timothy 4:6–10 (p. 1258)

who will be like a shepherd for my people
Israel.' " *Micah 5:2*
7Then Herod had a secret meeting with the
wise men and learned from them the exact time
they first saw the star. 8He sent the wise men to
Bethlehem, saying, "Look carefully for the child.
When you find him, come tell me so I can worship him too."
9After the wise men heard the king, they left.
The star that they had seen in the east went before them until it stopped above the place where
the child was. 10When the wise men saw the star,
they were filled with joy. 11They came to the
house where the child was and saw him with his
mother, Mary, and they bowed down and worshiped him. They opened their gifts and gave him
treasures of gold, frankincense,[d] and myrrh.[d]
12But God warned the wise men in a dream not
to go back to Herod, so they returned to their own
country by a different way.

Jesus' Parents Take Him to Egypt

13After they left, an angel of the Lord came to
Joseph in a dream and said, "Get up! Take the
child and his mother and escape to Egypt, because
Herod is starting to look for the child so he can
kill him. Stay in Egypt until I tell you to return."
14So Joseph got up and left for Egypt during the
night with the child and his mother. 15And Joseph
stayed in Egypt until Herod died. This happened

WORSHIP

Enjoying God's Gifts

Sean Sutcliffe hated Sunday mornings. "Sunday meant church, and that meant boring," he said. He felt boredom start with the first note of the organ, and steadily suffered as worship went on. The best part to him was driving out of the church parking lot on the way to lunch.

"Much of what happened there just didn't seem important," he said. "We sang a few old songs, read a few scriptures, listened to somebody talk for thirty minutes—how did any of that really worship God?"

The only thing that kept Sean's interest in church was the youth group. One Sunday evening, the group gathered at a nearby lake. They started a campfire, and somebody played soft guitar while everyone watched a spectacular sunset. Sean sat in silence, enjoying the sunset's reflection on the still lake, until the last pink streak faded in the sky. "That's the most beautiful thing I've ever seen," he said.

Caroline McGee overheard him. She had been sitting so quietly he hadn't noticed her. She asked him, "Do you think God hears us when we say things like that? Do you think God likes it when we enjoy a sunset?"

"Yeah," Sean replied. Then suddenly something "clicked" for Sean about worship. "Maybe part of worship is enjoying something God made," he said. "To watch a sunset, or a butterfly, or the rain, and to be thankful that God had such good taste. Am I right?"

The next time he worshiped at church, he looked around at the people. Many of their faces wore the same expression of awe Sean had felt at the lake. Maybe this feeling of "wow!" is worship, he thought. It isn't the motions you go through. It's when you see or hear or remember things so good that you have to catch your breath, and then thank and praise God for them.

In **Matthew 2:1–12**, read about the "wow!" the wise men must have felt when they saw and worshiped the infant Jesus.

- In what ways might the wise men have felt as Sean did while he watched the sunset?
- When have you experienced a sense of "wow!" in worship, either in or out of church?

CONSIDER . . .

- noticing the ways your church worships God and finding out the meaning of each part of the service.
- visiting a few other churches with your family or friends, and seeing what each church does differently.

FOR MORE, SEE . . .

- Psalm 19:1–6 (p. 492)
- Luke 9:28–36 (p. 1019)
- Revelation 4:1–11 (p. 1335)

to bring about what the Lord had said through the prophet:[d] "I called my son out of Egypt."[n]

Herod Kills the Baby Boys

16When Herod saw that the wise men had tricked him, he was furious. So he gave an order to kill all the baby boys in Bethlehem and in the surrounding area who were two years old or younger. This was in keeping with the time he learned from the wise men. 17So what God had said through the prophet[d] Jeremiah came true:

18"A voice was heard in Ramah
of painful crying and deep sadness:
Rachel crying for her children.
She refused to be comforted,
because her children are dead." *Jeremiah 31:15*

Joseph and Mary Return

19After Herod died, an angel of the Lord spoke
to Joseph in a dream while he was in Egypt. 20The
angel said, "Get up! Take the child and his
mother and go to the land of Israel, because the

"I called . . . Egypt." Quotation from Hosea 11:1.

FREEDOM

Going to a Safe Place

White journalist Donald Woods openly opposed the South African government's cruel policies toward its black people. In the early 1970s, Woods began to publish a newspaper that chronicled the government's repressive actions.

Woods befriended several leaders in the black liberation movement, including Steve Biko; and he grew even more committed to freedom for blacks. In spite of government and police warnings, Woods refused to turn his back on his friends.

The political situation soon worsened in South Africa. The police stepped up arrests of black leaders, who were later found tortured and often dead. In 1977, Steve Biko was arrested. Woods worked furiously for his friend's release, but faced unbending opposition from officials.

When Woods personally discovered the dead body of his tortured friend, he blasted the official explanation that Biko's death was accidental. While questioning the doctor who had determined the cause of Biko's death, Woods heard the doctor tearfully admit to falsifying the autopsy report. Woods, in his raging grief, openly accused the government of murdering Biko. South Africa's response was to arrest Woods.

After Woods was held under house arrest for three months, his friends in the liberation movement devised a plan for him to escape from the country. After escaping the guards, he crossed the country disguised as a priest. Along the way, sympathizers risked their lives to see him safely along. But he finally made it to the bordering country of Lesotho.

Woods's family also escaped and joined him in Lesotho. They moved to England, where Woods wrote the story of South Africa's cruelty. If he had not been able to escape, his story and Steve Biko's would not have been told. Because of changes in South Africa, Woods has been able to return. His story—and others like it—directly influenced these changes.

Joseph, Mary, and Jesus also had to flee from their country so Jesus could grow up and fulfill God's purpose for him. Read their story in **Matthew 2:13–23**.

- Why did Joseph and Mary and Donald Woods temporarily leave their homes instead of facing their persecutors?
- Have you ever had to leave a "comfort zone" in your life to follow God? What happened?

CONSIDER. . .

- watching the movie Cry Freedom (about Donald Woods) and talking about whether God's freedom is similar or different, and why.
- looking up the word freedom in the dictionary, and then defining "Christian freedom" in your own words.

FOR MORE, SEE. . .

- Exodus 12:31–50 (p. 69)
- John 8:31–36 (p. 1072)
- Galatians 5:13–15 (p. 1212)

people who were trying to kill the child are now
dead."

> **SIDELIGHT:** The "three kings" traditionally associated with Matthew 2:1–12 were probably neither "three" nor "kings." Some sources suggest as many as a hundred of these philosophers, doctors, and astrologers visited Jesus. Now that would make a Christmas play! The traditional idea of "three" comes from the three gifts they brought—gold, frankincense, and myrrh.

21So Joseph took the child and his mother and
went to Israel. 22But he heard that Archelaus was
now king in Judea since his father Herod had
died. So Joseph was afraid to go there. After being
warned in a dream, he went to the area of Galilee,
23to a town called Nazareth, and lived there. And
so what God had said through the prophets[d] came
true: "He will be called a Nazarene."[n]

The Work of John the Baptist

3 About that time John the Baptist[d] began
preaching in the desert area of Judea. 2John
said, "Change your hearts and lives because the
kingdom of heaven is near." 3John the Baptist is
the one Isaiah the prophet[d] was talking about
when he said:

"This is a voice of one
 who calls out in the desert:
'Prepare the way for the Lord.
 Make the road straight for him.' " *Isaiah 40:3*

4John's clothes were made from camel's hair,
and he wore a leather belt around his waist. For
food, he ate locusts[d] and wild honey. 5Many people came from Jerusalem and Judea and all the
area around the Jordan River to hear John. 6They
confessed their sins, and he baptized them in the
Jordan River.

7Many of the Pharisees[d] and Sadducees[d] came
to the place where John was baptizing people.
When John saw them, he said, "You are all
snakes! Who warned you to run away from God's
coming punishment? 8Do the things that show
you really have changed your hearts and lives.
9And don't think you can say to yourselves, 'Abraham is our father.' I tell you that God could make
children for Abraham from these rocks. 10The ax
is now ready to cut down the trees, and every tree
that does not produce good fruit will be cut down
and thrown into the fire.[n]

11"I baptize you with water to show that your
hearts and lives have changed. But there is one
coming after me who is greater than I am, whose
sandals I am not good enough to carry. He will
baptize you with the Holy Spirit[d] and fire. 12He
will come ready to clean the grain, separating the
good grain from the chaff.[d] He will put the good
part of the grain into his barn, but he will burn the
chaff with a fire that cannot be put out."[n]

Jesus Is Baptized by John

13At that time Jesus came from Galilee to the
Jordan River and wanted John to baptize him.
14But John tried to stop him, saying, "Why do you
come to me to be baptized? I need to be baptized
by you!"

15Jesus answered, "Let it be this way for now.
We should do all things that are God's will." So
John agreed to baptize Jesus.

16As soon as Jesus was baptized, he came up
out of the water. Then heaven opened, and he
saw God's Spirit[d] coming down on him like a
dove. 17And a voice from heaven said, "This is my
Son, whom I love, and I am very pleased with
him."

> **SIDELIGHT:** John the Baptist's diet wouldn't go over well at an all-church potluck dinner. He dined on locusts and wild honey (Matthew 3:4). Some people speculate that he might have been part of the desert Qumran community, people who lived in caves in cliffs above the Dead Sea. In the Qumran caves, some of the earliest manuscripts of the Bible and other writings—known as the Dead Sea Scrolls—were discovered in 1947.

The Temptation of Jesus

4 Then the Spirit[d] led Jesus into the desert to
be tempted by the devil. 2Jesus ate nothing
for forty days and nights. After this, he was very
hungry. 3The devil came to Jesus to tempt him,
saying, "If you are the Son of God, tell these rocks
to become bread."

4Jesus answered, "It is written in the Scriptures,[d] 'A person does not live by eating only
bread, but by everything God says.' "[n]

Nazarene A person from the city of Nazareth, a name probably meaning "branch" (see Isaiah 11:1).
The ax . . . fire. This means that God is ready to punish his people who do not obey him.
He will . . . out. This means that Jesus will come to separate good people from bad people, saving the good and punishing the bad.
'A person . . . says.' Quotation from Deuteronomy 8:3.

5Then the devil led Jesus to the holy city of
Jerusalem and put him on a high place of the Temple.[d] 6The devil said, "If you are the Son of God,
jump down, because it is written in the Scriptures:

'He has put his angels in charge of you.
They will catch you in their hands
so that you will not hit your foot on a
rock.' " *Psalm 91:11-12*

7Jesus answered him, "It also says in the Scriptures, 'Do not test the Lord your God.' "[n]

8Then the devil led Jesus to the top of a very
high mountain and showed him all the kingdoms
of the world and all their splendor. 9The devil
said, "If you will bow down and worship me, I
will give you all these things."

10Jesus said to the devil, "Go away from me,
Satan! It is written in the Scriptures, 'You must
worship the Lord your God and serve only
him.' "[n]

11So the devil left Jesus, and angels came and
took care of him.

'Do . . . God.' Quotation from Deuteronomy 6:16.
'You . . . him.' Quotation from Deuteronomy 6:13.

GOD'S WILL

God's Surprises

It was February, and time to begin rehearsals for Wheeler High School's senior play. Trina Cook eagerly auditioned for a part, convinced she would make the cast. But when the list was posted, Trina couldn't find her name on it.

She tried to hide her disappointment as she walked toward her last class of the day. Mr. Hendon, the director, caught up with her. "Trina," he said, "I meant to talk to you before the names were posted. We know you would have worked hard and done a good job for us. But you've had a lot of honors already, so we decided to let some of the others have a chance. I hope you're not too disappointed."

"Thanks, Mr. Hendon," she answered. "Thanks for explaining it to me." She still felt sad, but she didn't want him to know. In a way, she understood what he was saying.

A week later, Trina cringed as sharp pains shot through her stomach. Soon she was in the hospital, recovering from an emergency appendectomy. Mr. Hendon came to visit her. "It's a good thing you didn't put me in the senior play," she said. "You'd be looking for a replacement now."

A few weeks later, the missions committee at Trina's church decided to produce a drama about a woman who had spent her life in missions efforts. By this time Trina had regained her strength. She was chosen to play the leading role.

At every rehearsal, the cast prayed that God would use their efforts through the play to touch someone's heart.

Trina had no idea that she would be the one whose heart would be touched: On the evening of the performance, she committed her life to God's service and went on to be a missionary.

Disappointments, closed doors, and unexpected events often lead to surprises of God's will for our lives. Just as Trina was surprised by her road to a missionary career, John the Baptist was surprised to learn that God's will was for him to baptize the Messiah, instead of vice versa. You'll find the story of Jesus' baptism in **Matthew 3:13–17**.

- Why were both John the Baptist and Trina surprised by God's will?
- How has God used ironic or unusual circumstances in your life to do his will? How did you respond in those situations?

C O N S I D E R . . .

- writing a list of prayer concerns. As you pray, follow each with, "We know that in everything God works for the good of those who love him" (Romans 8:28, p. 1151).
- thinking of unexpected events that have happened to you in the last month, and how God might be leading you. Then act on one of those leads.

F O R M O R E , S E E . . .

- Isaiah 55:8–11 (p. 674)
- Luke 3:1–20 (p. 1005)
- 1 Corinthians 1:18–25 (p. 1168)

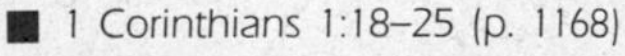

Jesus Begins Work in Galilee

12When Jesus heard that John had been put in prison, he went back to Galilee. 13He left Nazareth and went to live in Capernaum, a town near Lake Galilee, in the area near Zebulun and Naphtali. 14Jesus did this to bring about what the prophet[d] Isaiah had said:

15"Land of Zebulun and land of Naphtali
along the sea,
beyond the Jordan River.
This is Galilee where the non-Jewish people
live.
16These people who live in darkness
will see a great light.
They live in a place covered with the
shadows of death,
but a light will shine on them." *Isaiah 9:1-2*

Jesus Chooses Some Followers

17From that time Jesus began to preach, saying, "Change your hearts and lives, because the kingdom of heaven is near."

18As Jesus was walking by Lake Galilee, he saw two brothers, Simon (called Peter) and his brother Andrew. They were throwing a net into the lake because they were fishermen. 19Jesus said, "Come follow me, and I will make you fish for people." 20So Simon and Andrew immediately left their nets and followed him.

21As Jesus continued walking by Lake Galilee, he saw two other brothers, James and John, the sons of Zebedee. They were in a boat with their father Zebedee, mending their nets. Jesus told them to come with him. 22Immediately they left the boat and their father, and they followed Jesus.

Jesus Teaches and Heals People

23Jesus went everywhere in Galilee, teaching in the synagogues,[d] preaching the Good News[d] about the kingdom of heaven, and healing all the people's diseases and sicknesses. 24The news about Jesus spread all over Syria, and people brought all the sick to him. They were suffering from different kinds of diseases. Some were in great pain, some had demons,[d] some were epileptics,[n] and some were paralyzed. Jesus healed all of them. 25Many people from Galilee, the Ten Towns,[n] Jerusalem, Judea, and the land across the Jordan River followed him.

Jesus Teaches the People

5 When Jesus saw the crowds, he went up on a hill and sat down. His followers came to him, 2and he began to teach them, saying:

3"Those people who know they have great
spiritual needs are happy,
because the kingdom of heaven belongs to
them.
4Those who are sad now are happy,
because God will comfort them.
5Those who are humble are happy,
because the earth will belong to them.
6Those who want to do right more than
anything else are happy,
because God will fully satisfy them.
7Those who show mercy to others are happy,
because God will show mercy to them.
8Those who are pure in their thinking are
happy,
because they will be with God.
9Those who work to bring peace are happy,
because God will call them his children.
10Those who are treated badly for doing good
are happy,
because the kingdom of heaven belongs to
them.

11"People will insult you and hurt you. They will lie and say all kinds of evil things about you because you follow me. But when they do, you will be happy. 12Rejoice and be glad, because you have a great reward waiting for you in heaven. People did the same evil things to the prophets[d] who lived before you.

You Are like Salt and Light

13"You are the salt of the earth. But if the salt loses its salty taste, it cannot be made salty again. It is good for nothing, except to be thrown out and walked on.

14"You are the light that gives light to the world. A city that is built on a hill cannot be hidden. 15And people don't hide a light under a bowl. They put it on a lampstand so the light shines for all the people in the house. 16In the same way, you should be a light for other people. Live so that they will see the good things you do and will praise your Father in heaven.

The Importance of the Law

17"Don't think that I have come to destroy the law of Moses or the teaching of the prophets.[d] I have not come to destroy them but to bring about what they said. 18I tell you the truth, nothing will disappear from the law until heaven and earth are gone. Not even the smallest letter or the smallest part of a letter will be lost until everything has happened. 19Whoever refuses to obey any command and teaches other people not to obey that

epileptics People with a disease that causes them sometimes to lose control of their bodies and maybe faint, shake strongly, or not be able to move.

Ten Towns In Greek, called "Decapolis." It was an area east of Lake Galilee that once had ten main towns.

command will be the least important in the kingdom of heaven. But whoever obeys the commands and teaches other people to obey them will
be great in the kingdom of heaven. 20I tell you
that if you are no more obedient than the teachers
of the law and the Pharisees,[d] you will never enter the kingdom of heaven.

Jesus Teaches About Anger

21"You have heard that it was said to our people long ago, 'You must not murder anyone.[n]
Anyone who murders another will be judged.'
22But I tell you, if you are angry with a brother or
sister,[n] you will be judged. If you say bad things
to a brother or sister, you will be judged by the
council. And if you call someone a fool, you will
be in danger of the fire of hell.

23"So when you offer your gift to God at the
altar, and you remember that your brother or sister has something against you, 24leave your gift
there at the altar. Go and make peace with that
person, and then come and offer your gift.

You . . . anyone. Quotation from Exodus 20:13; Deuteronomy 5:17.
brother . . . sister Although the Greek text reads "brother" here and throughout this book, Jesus' words were meant for the entire church, including men and women.

HAPPINESS

The Secret of Real Happiness

Young Francesco had it all: money, friends, power. His father was one of the wealthiest businessmen in the city-state of Assisi, in twelfth-century Italy. Francesco partied away his teenage years, often carousing in the streets until dawn.

But something was missing. When the parties ended, he felt depressed.

To try to find happiness and purpose, Francesco trained to be a knight. At twenty-one, he gallantly rode off to war against the neighboring city-state of Perugia. After a disastrous battlefield decision, he and his soldiers were taken prisoners. In a dungeon Francesco caught a fever that almost killed him. The enemy released him, and he somehow stumbled back to Assisi. He had left as a proud knight; he returned as a sad, sick failure.

These experiences made Francesco reexamine his life. He spent days in prayer, poring over Jesus' Sermon on the Mount in Matthew 5—7. He saw a chance for genuine happiness by following Jesus' teachings about storing treasures in heaven instead of on earth, not worrying about tomorrow, and trusting God. He began to run through meadows, singing like the birds and flinging his arms open to embrace the wind and sun. He gave away all his possessions and lived in caves because he didn't want to be burdened with "things." He traded his expensive clothing for a shepherd's robe.

His relationships with other people changed too. For the first time, he was happy. He spent his days helping the poor, homeless, and disabled. He went to the local leper colony and embraced people who had once nauseated him. He attracted several friends who shared his poverty and worked beside him, ministering to the poor of their community.

Francesco was named St. Francis shortly after his death, and remains one of the most beloved of all Christians. Eight hundred years later, people still seek the secret to the happiness St. Francis of Assisi found.

One of the passages that changed Francesco's life was **Matthew 5:1–12**. Read how Jesus' secret to happiness transformed St. Francis's life.

- What do you find in Jesus' words that could so powerfully change Francesco's depression to happiness?
- How does Jesus' secret for happiness compare to what you've been taught about happiness?

CONSIDER . . .

- looking at the "things" in your bedroom that make you happy and asking yourself which of them would make Jesus happy.
- writing each verse of this passage on a separate card, and then putting a different one on your mirror for eight days.

FOR MORE, SEE . . .

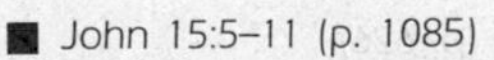

- Psalm 4 (p. 483)
- Luke 6:17–49 (p. 1012)
- John 15:5–11 (p. 1085)

25 "If your enemy is taking you to court, become
friends quickly, before you go to court. Otherwise, your enemy might turn you over to the
judge, and the judge might give you to a guard to
put you in jail. 26 I tell you the truth, you will not
leave there until you have paid everything you
owe.

Jesus Teaches About Sexual Sin

27 "You have heard that it was said, 'You must
not be guilty of adultery.'[n] 28 But I tell you that if
anyone looks at a woman and wants to sin sexually with her, in his mind he has already done that
sin with the woman. 29 If your right eye causes you
to sin, take it out and throw it away. It is better
to lose one part of your body than to have your
whole body thrown into hell. 30 If your right hand
causes you to sin, cut it off and throw it away. It
is better to lose one part of your body than for
your whole body to go into hell.

Jesus Teaches About Divorce

31 "It was also said, 'Anyone who divorces his
wife must give her a written divorce paper.'[n]
32 But I tell you that anyone who divorces his wife
forces her to be guilty of adultery.[d] The only reason for a man to divorce his wife is if she has
sexual relations with another man. And anyone

'You . . . adultery.' Quotation from Exodus 20:14; Deuteronomy 5:18.
'Anyone . . . divorce paper.' Quotation from Deuteronomy 24:1.

SHARING FAITH

Salt and Light

Brett Clanton's image of a homeless person had always been of a bag lady rummaging through dumpsters. He was afraid of poor people. And he was a little scared as he and his youth group traveled to San Antonio, Texas, to help in a homeless shelter for a week.

Brett and the other young people spent their days with homeless families—serving food, helping them find clothing, reading the Bible with them, playing with their children. By the end of the week the image of the faceless bag lady was gone from Brett's mind. These people were now his friends.

The group went to the city's famous river walk on their last evening of the trip, and they saw street people along the way. "I saw a man asleep on a bench, and I started to make a wide path to avoid him, and I suddenly realized that I knew him!" Brett later told the church. "I knew his name, where he was from—and I wasn't afraid. Then I realized that all homeless people have names and home towns, and that becoming homeless could happen to any of us."

One Wednesday evening the young people shared their experiences with the whole church. The next day, several of the adults from Brett's church attended a meeting of more than thirty-five area ministers. These adults had been so moved by the young people's stories that they shared them with leaders from the other churches.

The truth that Brett and the others had learned in San Antonio had spread from a few teenagers to an entire church, and then to a gathering of area ministers. The group now sponsors a task force on local poverty and hunger. The young people energized the task force members to respond to poverty in their community.

Brett discovered the contagious power of being the salt of the earth and light of the world as Jesus describes in **Matthew 5:13–16**. Jesus promises that when faith is shared, things change.

- How did Brett's youth group act as salt and light in San Antonio and in their home town?
- How can you be "salt and light" in your world, as Jesus describes in the passage?

CONSIDER . . .

- telling someone you know about your faith this week.
- choosing two people you know who seem most like "salt and light" and asking them what they've learned as they have shared their faith.

FOR MORE, SEE . . .

- Isaiah 9:2–7 (p. 626)
- 2 Corinthians 4:1–6 (p. 1194)
- 1 John 1:5–6 (p. 1316)

who marries that divorced woman is guilty of
adultery.

Make Promises Carefully

33"You have heard that it was said to our people long ago, 'Don't break your promises, but
keep the promises you make to the Lord.'[n] 34But
I tell you, never swear an oath. Don't swear an
oath using the name of heaven, because heaven
is God's throne. 35Don't swear an oath using the
name of the earth, because the earth belongs to
God. Don't swear an oath using the name of Jerusalem, because that is the city of the great King.
36Don't even swear by your own head, because
you cannot make one hair on your head become
white or black. 37Say only yes if you mean yes,
and no if you mean no. If you say more than yes
or no, it is from the Evil One.

Don't Fight Back

38"You have heard that it was said, 'An eye for
an eye, and a tooth for a tooth.'[n] 39But I tell you,
don't stand up against an evil person. If someone
slaps you on the right cheek, turn to him the other

'Don't . . . Lord.' This refers to Leviticus 19:12; Numbers 30:2; Deuteronomy 23:21.
'An eye . . . tooth.' Quotation from Exodus 21:24; Leviticus 24:20; Deuteronomy 19:21.

ANGER

Beating the Bully

Life wasn't going well for twelve-year-old Keith Jenkins. His parents had recently divorced, and he and his mom had moved from their farm to a nearby city. Keith felt alone in his new school, which seemed huge. But now there was another problem. Another student, Brian, had threatened to beat up Keith after school. And he meant it.

After the last bell on Thursday, Keith tried to slip out of school without being seen. He wanted to get home quickly. As he turned a corner, Brian was waiting for him.

Keith's heart pounded with fear. Brian attacked and landed blow after blow. Keith tried to fight back, but Brian was several years older and much stronger. After a few minutes of a one-sided fight, Brian left his victim lying on the sidewalk. Keith got up slowly and walked the rest of the way home. At the front door, his mother saw his torn clothes, his bloody face and hands. Keith told what happened and asked, "Mom, why are people like that? Why does Brian like to hurt other people?"

"I don't know, honey," she answered. "It doesn't make sense. There must be something wrong with him." Keith knew that she was upset, though she was trying to hide her anger toward Brian.

Later that evening, Keith looked at his reflection in the hall mirror. His face was already puffy and purple. He looked at his mom and said, "I look pretty weird, don't I?"

She laughed, and then he began to laugh. "You've certainly looked better," she said, with a sad smile. "How do you feel?"

"Sore," he said. "And a little scared. But you know what? I'm not really mad at Brian. What you said about there being something wrong—I think there is. I thought I'd hate him. But I don't. I feel kind of sorry for him. I don't think anybody likes him. Maybe that's why he does those things."

Jesus offers several ways to respond when we're angered and hurt by others. In **Matthew 5:17–26**, read how Jesus might have reacted in Keith's situation.

- Did Keith react in the way Jesus commands? Why or why not?
- If Brian had beaten you up, how would you have handled your anger and hurt? What are some ways to handle the situation according to the passage?

CONSIDER . . .

- watching how some TV characters handle their anger. What would happen in the real world if people handled their anger in those ways?
- making peace with someone with whom you have a conflict before the next time you attend worship.

FOR MORE, SEE . . .

- Proverbs 15:1 (p. 580)
- Matthew 5:38–48 (p. 915)
- Ephesians 4:17–32 (p. 1223)

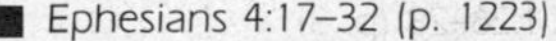

cheek also. 40If someone wants to sue you in court
and take your shirt, let him have your coat also.
41If someone forces you to go with him one mile,
go with him two miles. 42If a person asks you for
something, give it to him. Don't refuse to give to
someone who wants to borrow from you.

SIDELIGHT: The coat (or robe) in Matthew 5:40 was a prized possession in Jesus' day. It was often the only protection poor people had from cold nights. That's why the Old Testament protected it (Exodus 22:26–27, p. 81). And rich people showed their wealth by the number and quality of coats or robes they had (see James 5:1–2, p. 1299).

Love All People

43"You have heard that it was said, 'Love your
neighbor[n] and hate your enemies.' 44But I say to
you, love your enemies. Pray for those who hurt
you. 45If you do this, you will be true children of
your Father in heaven. He causes the sun to rise
on good people and on evil people, and he sends
rain to those who do right and to those who do
wrong. 46If you love only the people who love

Love your neighbor Quotation from Leviticus 19:18.

SEXUALITY

A Special Gift

Anna Bradley, thirteen, felt her life turning upside down. Her body was changing so fast she couldn't figure out what was happening. Along with the physical changes, she had new feelings she didn't understand.

A couple of years earlier, she didn't even like being around boys. Now she was fascinated by them. Especially Larry. He was so cute! She hung around outside the science lab just to see him when he came out. When he said "hi" to her in the hall, she felt like she was melting inside. "What's going on here?" she asked herself. "What's happening to me?"

She finally got the courage to ask her youth leader, Deanna.

"You're beginning to change from a young girl into a young woman," Deanna said.

"You mean my feelings—these desires—aren't bad?"

"How could they be bad if God put them there? But God also expects you to use this gift wisely."

"But what will the kids at school say if I tell them I want to stay a virgin until I marry? What will boys say if I go on a date with them?"

"You can tell them this is your decision, and that's all there is to it. If they're your friends, they'll respect your decision."

"What about the waiting part? Will it be hard to control myself all that time?"

"You can do it. People can control themselves—although some may not think they can, and many simply don't want to. But it's possible, and it'll be worth it. You'll discover how God's gift of sexuality is so wonderful in a committed marriage relationship."

Jesus considered sexuality a special gift from God. As such he spoke of the serious consequence of sex being used outside of marriage. **Matthew 5:27–37** has some rather harsh things to say about specific sexual behaviors. Read the passage and think about what Anna might think as she reads it.

- How does Deanna's advice relate to Jesus' teaching in the passage?
- Why do you think Jesus took sexual relations so seriously?

CONSIDER . . .

- talking about sexuality with a parent or an adult whom you trust. Write your questions first if that's helpful. Be honest about your feelings.
- organizing a discussion group at your church—perhaps a panel with adults and youth—on issues involving sexuality and teenagers.

FOR MORE, SEE . . .

- Genesis 1:26–28 (p. 3)
- Song of Solomon 2:1–17 (p. 609)
- 1 Corinthians 7:1–15 (p. 1174)

you, you will get no reward. Even the tax collectors do that. [47]And if you are nice only to your friends, you are no better than other people. Even those who don't know God are nice to their friends. [48]So you must be perfect, just as your Father in heaven is perfect.

Jesus Teaches About Giving

6 "Be careful! When you do good things, don't do them in front of people to be seen by them. If you do that, you will have no reward from your Father in heaven.

[2]"When you give to the poor, don't be like the hypocrites.[d] They blow trumpets in the synagogues[d] and on the streets so that people will see them and honor them. I tell you the truth, those hypocrites already have their full reward. [3]So when you give to the poor, don't let anyone know what you are doing. [4]Your giving should be done in secret. Your Father can see what is done in secret, and he will reward you.

Jesus Teaches About Prayer

[5]"When you pray, don't be like the hypocrites.[d]

PEACE

The Second Mile

Tracy Collins pulled her car into the driveway and groaned when she saw that the front door was ajar. "Not again!" she fumed. She knew her apartment had been robbed for the third time.

When the police arrived, they helped her take inventory of what was missing. "Not that there was much left to take," she said. "He really cleaned me out the first time."

The police were virtually positive who the thief was. After the previous burglary, one of the officers had let the name slip: Tim O'Conner. They recognized his "style." A warrant for his arrest had been issued months earlier.

Tracy worked in an inner-city mission distributing food and clothing to needy people. Among the volunteers were adults placed on probation for nonviolent crimes. Instead of going to jail, they were required to provide community service.

Several weeks after the third burglary, Tracy interviewed a new probationer, filling out a form that would record the hours worked. "What's your name?" she asked, her pen ready on the correct line.

"Tim O'Conner," he said.

Tracy choked, and looked into the young man's eyes. He sat calmly, waiting for the next question. He was well-dressed, well-groomed, and had good manners. She shook her head as if to clear it, and turned the document back to the first page, searching for the line that would tell her why he had been convicted. "Burglary of a habitation," it read.

"Is something wrong?" he asked in a polite voice.

"He has no idea I'm one of his victims," she thought angrily. Then her anger turned into compassion as she wondered what made him break into other people's homes. "No," she answered. "Let's finish this form."

After they finished the interview, Tim was given an assignment. "Thanks," he said. "I'm glad the judge sent me here."

"So am I," Tracy said.

Tracy was surprised when she didn't feel like striking back at Tim. Then she realized Jesus' words in **Matthew 5:38–48** must have helped her handle her anger in a peaceful manner.

- In light of the passage, do you think Tracy did the right thing?
- Does "turning the other cheek" mean that Jesus wants people to walk all over your rights? Why or why not?

CONSIDER

- listing the "normal" ways for handling conflicts, and then listing the "cheek-turning," peaceful ways next to them. Promise yourself to "turn the other cheek" the next time a conflict arises.
- walking away from a fight or keeping your cool in an argument in the future.

FOR MORE, SEE . . .

- Psalm 37 (p. 503)
- Luke 6:27–36 (p. 1013)
- Colossians 3:12–13 (p. 1241)

They love to stand in the synagogues[d] and on the
street corners and pray so people will see them.
I tell you the truth, they already have their full
reward. 6When you pray, you should go into your
room and close the door and pray to your Father
who cannot be seen. Your Father can see what is
done in secret, and he will reward you.

> **SIDELIGHT:** Jews in Jesus' day had plenty of opportunities to give to people in need, which could lead to the problems Jesus talked about in Matthew 6:1–4. Jerusalem had a "chamber of secrets" where people quietly left gifts. Then the needy could slip in unnoticed and claim goods without embarrassment.

7"And when you pray, don't be like those people who don't know God. They continue saying
things that mean nothing, thinking that God will
hear them because of their many words. 8Don't
be like them, because your Father knows the
things you need before you ask him. 9So when
you pray, you should pray like this:
'Our Father in heaven,
may your name always be kept holy.
10May your kingdom come
and what you want be done,
here on earth as it is in heaven.
11Give us the food we need for each day.
12Forgive us for our sins,
just as we have forgiven those who sinned
against us.
13And do not cause us to be tempted,
but save us from the Evil One.'
14Yes, if you forgive others for their sins, your Father in heaven will also forgive you for your sins.
15But if you don't forgive others, your Father in
heaven will not forgive your sins.

Jesus Teaches About Worship

16"When you give up eating,[n] don't put on a
sad face like the hypocrites.[d] They make their
faces look sad to show people they are giving up
eating. I tell you the truth, those hypocrites already have their full reward. 17So when you give
up eating, comb your hair and wash your face.
18Then people will not know that you are giving
up eating, but your Father, whom you cannot see,
will see you. Your Father sees what is done in
secret, and he will reward you.

God Is More Important than Money

19"Don't store treasures for yourselves here on
earth where moths and rust will destroy them and
thieves can break in and steal them. 20But store
your treasures in heaven where they cannot be
destroyed by moths or rust and where thieves
cannot break in and steal them. 21Your heart will
be where your treasure is.
22"The eye is a light for the body. If your eyes
are good, your whole body will be full of light.
23But if your eyes are evil, your whole body will
be full of darkness. And if the only light you have
is really darkness, then you have the worst darkness.
24"No one can serve two masters. The person will hate one master and love the other,
or will follow one master and refuse to follow
the other. You cannot serve both God and
worldly riches.

Don't Worry

25"So I tell you, don't worry about the food or
drink you need to live, or about the clothes you
need for your body. Life is more than food, and
the body is more than clothes. 26Look at the birds
in the air. They don't plant or harvest or store
food in barns, but your heavenly Father feeds
them. And you know that you are worth much
more than the birds. 27You cannot add any time
to your life by worrying about it.
28"And why do you worry about clothes? Look
at how the lilies in the field grow. They don't
work or make clothes for themselves. 29But I tell
you that even Solomon with his riches was not
dressed as beautifully as one of these flowers.
30God clothes the grass in the field, which is alive
today but tomorrow is thrown into the fire. So
you can be even more sure that God will clothe
you. Don't have so little faith! 31Don't worry and
say, 'What will we eat?' or 'What will we drink?'
or 'What will we wear?' 32The people who don't
know God keep trying to get these things, and
your Father in heaven knows you need them.
33The thing you should want most is God's kingdom and doing what God wants. Then all these
other things you need will be given to you. 34So
don't worry about tomorrow, because tomorrow
will have its own worries. Each day has enough
trouble of its own.

Be Careful About Judging Others

7 "Don't judge other people, or you will be
judged. 2You will be judged in the same way
that you judge others, and the amount you give
to others will be given to you.
3"Why do you notice the little piece of dust in
your friend's eye, but you don't notice the big
piece of wood in your own eye? 4How can you say

give up eating This is called "fasting." The people would give up eating for a special time of prayer and worship to God. It was also done to show sadness and disappointment.

to your friend, 'Let me take that little piece of dust out of your eye'? Look at yourself! You still have that big piece of wood in your own eye. 5You hypocrite![d] First, take the wood out of your own eye. Then you will see clearly to take the dust out of your friend's eye.

6"Don't give holy things to dogs, and don't throw your pearls before pigs. Pigs will only trample on them, and dogs will turn to attack you.

Ask God for What You Need

7"Ask, and God will give to you. Search, and you will find. Knock, and the door will open for you. 8Yes, everyone who asks will receive. Everyone who searches will find. And everyone who knocks will have the door opened.

9"If your children ask for bread, which of you would give them a stone? 10Or if your children ask for a fish, would you give them a snake? 11Even though you are bad, you know how to give good gifts to your children. How much more your heavenly Father will give good things to those who ask him!

The Most Important Rule

12"Do to others what you want them to do to you. This is the meaning of the law of Moses and the teaching of the prophets.[d]

The Way to Heaven Is Hard

13"Enter through the narrow gate. The gate is wide and the road is wide that leads to hell, and many people enter through that gate. 14But the gate is small and the road is narrow that leads to true life. Only a few people find that road.

WORRYING

Sweating It Out

Jason Taylor stood at the coach's door, staring a long time at the recently posted roster. There it was: His name was on the list. He had made the junior varsity basketball team. Jason let out a deep sigh of relief and offered a silent thanks to God.

Anxiety was Jason's trademark. He worried about everything. In the two-day waiting period between tryouts and team roster, Jason couldn't sleep, concentrate on school, or eat much of anything. These worries were added to his stress of being a new kid in school. His family had moved from Georgia to Seattle over the summer.

His new friend Marc, seeing Jason staring at the roster, came over and shared Jason's happy time. "I knew you'd make it," Marc said, slapping him on the back. "Congratulations!"

Jason shook his head. "Since seventh grade," he said, "I had been looking forward to going to Stone Mountain High. Coach Wilson said I had a good chance of making junior varsity there this year. But then Dad told us we'd have to move here to Seattle because of his transfer to the new branch office. I didn't think I'd have a chance to make the team here. I've been sweating it out all summer. It even made me get off to a bad start on my grades."

"I told you there wasn't anything to worry about," Marc said.

"Easy for you to say," Jason thought. Suddenly a new worry hit Jason: "What if I'm not good enough to start?"

People today worry about many things, as did the people in Jesus' earthly ministry. He reminded them often not to worry. Read Jesus' practical teachings about worrying in **Matthew 6:25–34**.

- How could the analogy of the birds and flowers apply to Jason's life? How are the two kinds of worry different?
- If God doesn't want you to use time for worrying, how does he want you to use it?

CONSIDER . . .

- taking ten to fifteen minutes to watch a bird. Why do you think Jesus saw birds as examples of how you could live?
- listing some things you're worried about. Analyze each item on the list and decide if it's something you can change or something you should leave in God's hands.

FOR MORE, SEE . . .

- Psalm 46 (p. 508)
- Luke 10:41–42 (p. 1024)
- Philippians 4:5–7 (p. 1234)

People Know You by Your Actions

15"Be careful of false prophets.[d] They come to
you looking gentle like sheep, but they are really
dangerous like wolves. 16You will know these
people by what they do. Grapes don't come from
thornbushes, and figs don't come from thorny
weeds. 17In the same way, every good tree produces good fruit, but a bad tree produces bad
fruit. 18A good tree cannot produce bad fruit, and
a bad tree cannot produce good fruit. 19Every tree
that does not produce good fruit is cut down and
thrown into the fire. 20In the same way, you will
know these false prophets by what they do.

21"Not all those who say that I am their Lord
will enter the kingdom of heaven. The only people who will enter the kingdom of heaven are
those who do what my Father in heaven wants.
22On the last day many people will say to me,
'Lord, Lord, we spoke for you, and through you
we forced out demons[d] and did many miracles.'[d]
23Then I will tell them clearly, 'Get away from
me, you who do evil. I never knew you.'

Two Kinds of People

24"Everyone who hears my words and obeys
them is like a wise man who built his house on
rock. 25It rained hard, the floods came, and the
winds blew and hit that house. But it did not fall,
because it was built on rock. 26Everyone who
hears my words and does not obey them is like
a foolish man who built his house on sand.
27It rained hard, the floods came, and the winds
blew and hit that house, and it fell with a big
crash."

28When Jesus finished saying these things, the
people were amazed at his teaching, 29because he
did not teach like their teachers of the law. He
taught like a person who had authority.

Jesus Heals a Sick Man

8 When Jesus came down from the hill, great
crowds followed him. 2Then a man with a
skin disease came to Jesus. The man bowed down
before him and said, "Lord, you can heal me if
you will."

3Jesus reached out his hand and touched the
man and said, "I will. Be healed!" And immediately the man was healed from his disease. 4Then
Jesus said to him, "Don't tell anyone about this.
But go and show yourself to the priest[n] and offer

show . . . priest The law of Moses said a priest must say when a Jewish person with a skin disease was well.

CULTS

Deadly Deception

Malaya is home for a species of praying mantis that's made a career of looking like a flower. But this "flower" kills unsuspecting bugs.

Pink, petal-like structures flank its spindly legs. Part of its green thorax simulates the stem of an orchid. A few brown markings here and there make it look slightly wilted. When a soft breeze blows, the mantis even simulates the flower's gentle, swaying motion.

But this unusual insect is as deadly as it is beautiful. If a butterfly mistakes the mantis for an orchid, the mantis strikes with frightful speed and captures the butterfly in pink, vice-like forelegs.

Like butterflies, Christians need to be aware that not everything is as it appears. Many cults may look appealing, just as the praying mantis looks like an orchid to an unsuspecting butterfly. Learn how you can watch out for this kind of deception in **Matthew 7:15–29**.

- How is a butterfly captured by a praying mantis like those who build their houses on the sand?
- Who are some modern-day "false prophets" or groups you have heard of or been contacted by? How might Jesus react to them?

C O N S I D E R . . .

- praying for ways to resist the temptations of cults, and then investing time to grow in your faith in Christ.
- praying for those caught in cults, and sharing your faith with non-Christians.

F O R M O R E , S E E . . .

- 1 Kings 18:1–40 (p. 323)
- Mark 13:14–23 (p. 990)
- 2 Peter 2:1–22 (p. 1311)

the gift Moses commanded[n] for people who are
made well. This will show the people what I have
done."

Jesus Heals a Soldier's Servant

5When Jesus entered the city of Capernaum, an
army officer came to him, begging for help. 6The
officer said, "Lord, my servant is at home in bed.
He can't move his body and is in much pain."
7Jesus said to the officer, "I will go and heal
him."
8The officer answered, "Lord, I am not worthy
for you to come into my house. You only need to
command it, and my servant will be healed. 9I,
too, am a man under the authority of others, and
I have soldiers under my command. I tell one soldier, 'Go,' and he goes. I tell another soldier,
'Come,' and he comes. I say to my servant, 'Do
this,' and my servant does it.
10When Jesus heard this, he was amazed. He
said to those who were following him, "I tell you
the truth, this is the greatest faith I have found,
even in Israel. 11Many people will come from the
east and from the west and will sit and eat with
Abraham, Isaac, and Jacob in the kingdom of
heaven. 12But those people who should be in the
kingdom will be thrown outside into the darkness, where people will cry and grind their teeth
with pain."
13Then Jesus said to the officer, "Go home.
Your servant will be healed just as you believed
he would." And his servant was healed that same
hour.

Jesus Heals Many People

14When Jesus went to Peter's house, he saw
that Peter's mother-in-law was sick in bed with a
fever. 15Jesus touched her hand, and the fever left
her. Then she stood up and began to serve Jesus.
16That evening people brought to Jesus many
who had demons.[d] Jesus spoke and the demons
left them, and he healed all the sick. 17He did
these things to bring about what Isaiah the
prophet[d] had said:

"He took our suffering on him
and carried our diseases." *Isaiah 53:4*

People Want to Follow Jesus

18When Jesus saw the crowd around him, he
told his followers to go to the other side of the
lake. 19Then a teacher of the law came to Jesus
and said, "Teacher, I will follow you any place
you go."
20Jesus said to him, "The foxes have holes to
live in, and the birds have nests, but the Son of
Man[d] has no place to rest his head."
21Another man, one of Jesus' followers, said to
him, "Lord, first let me go and bury my father."
22But Jesus told him, "Follow me, and let the
people who are dead bury their own dead."

Jesus Calms a Storm

23Jesus got into a boat, and his followers went
with him. 24A great storm arose on the lake so
that waves covered the boat, but Jesus was sleeping. 25His followers went to him and woke him,
saying, "Lord, save us! We will drown!"
26Jesus answered, "Why are you afraid? You
don't have enough faith." Then Jesus got up and
gave a command to the wind and the waves, and
it became completely calm.
27The men were amazed and said, "What kind
of man is this? Even the wind and the waves obey
him!"

Jesus Heals Two Men with Demons

28When Jesus arrived at the other side of the
lake in the area of the Gadarene[n] people, two
men who had demons[d] in them met him. These
men lived in the burial caves and were so dangerous that people could not use the road by
those caves. 29They shouted, "What do you want
with us, Son of God? Did you come here to torture us before the right time?"
30Near that place there was a large herd of pigs
feeding. 31The demons begged Jesus, "If you
make us leave these men, please send us into that
herd of pigs."
32Jesus said to them, "Go!" So the demons left
the men and went into the pigs. Then the whole
herd rushed down the hill into the lake and were
drowned. 33The herdsmen ran away and went
into town, where they told about all of this and
what had happened to the men who had demons.
34Then the whole town went out to see Jesus.
When they saw him, they begged him to leave
their area.

Jesus Heals a Paralyzed Man

9 Jesus got into a boat and went back across
the lake to his own town. 2Some people
brought to Jesus a man who was paralyzed and
lying on a mat. When Jesus saw the faith of these
people, he said to the paralyzed man, "Be encouraged, young man. Your sins are forgiven."
3Some of the teachers of the law said to themselves, "This man speaks as if he were God. That
is blasphemy!"[n]
4Knowing their thoughts, Jesus said, "Why are

Moses commanded Read about this in Leviticus 14:1-32.
Gadarene From Gadara, an area southeast of Lake Galilee.
blasphemy Saying things against God or not showing respect for God.

you thinking evil thoughts? 5Which is easier: to
say, 'Your sins are forgiven,' or to tell him, 'Stand
up and walk'? 6But I will prove to you that the
Son of Man[d] has authority on earth to forgive
sins." Then Jesus said to the paralyzed man,
"Stand up, take your mat, and go home." 7And
the man stood up and went home. 8When the
people saw this, they were amazed and praised
God for giving power like this to human beings.

Jesus Chooses Matthew

9When Jesus was leaving, he saw a man named
Matthew sitting in the tax collector's booth. Jesus
said to him, "Follow me," and he stood up and
followed Jesus.
10As Jesus was having dinner at Matthew's
house, many tax collectors and "sinners" came
and ate with Jesus and his followers. 11When the
Pharisees[d] saw this, they asked Jesus' followers,
"Why does your teacher eat with tax collectors
and sinners?"
12When Jesus heard them, he said, "It is not the
healthy people who need a doctor, but the sick.

SIDELIGHT: As a tax collector, Matthew was hardly Mr. Popularity (Matthew 9:9–13). He could tax you for crossing a bridge—and also tax your cart, its axle, and the engine (or donkey). And you thought toll roads were bad!

13Go and learn what this means: 'I want kindness
more than I want animal sacrifices.'[n] I did
not come to invite good people but to invite sinners."

'I want . . . sacrifices.' Quotation from Hosea 6:6.

NON-CHRISTIANS

How to Win Friends

Carlos Trujillo thought he had found a simple solution to negative peer influence: just avoid non-Christians. But then he got a job at a fast-food restaurant.

Because he was a team worker, Carlos often helped others finish their work. One day he helped Todd, another worker, wipe off the last table before their shift ended.

"Thanks for your help, Carlos," Todd said. "I've really got to hustle tonight because I have to study for a huge chemistry exam tomorrow. Mrs. Stafford's tests are really tough."

"You take chemistry from Mrs. Stafford, too?" Carlos asked. "Why don't we study together?"

Todd and Carlos spent two hours at the library reviewing for the test. Although he later learned that Todd had never been inside a church, Carlos discovered they had a lot in common. "Maybe," Carlos thought, "God has a good reason for Todd and me to be friends."

Over time, Carlos began to reach out in friendship to other non-Christians. His initial fear of how non-Christians would be a bad influence on him quickly disappeared. In fact, he discovered that many of his non-Christian friends were hungry for the truth of Christ.

In **Matthew 9:9–13**, Jesus chose to eat with Matthew, a tax collector, and other "sinners." This action raised pious eyebrows among the religious leaders. Read Jesus' response to their criticism.

- Why might the Pharisees have agreed with Carlos's initial plan to avoid non-Christians?
- What do these verses say to you about reaching non-Christians in your world?

CONSIDER

- inviting someone at school or at work to attend church with you, or bringing that person to your next youth group outing.
- taking time this week to establish a relationship with a non-Christian or unchurched friend.

FOR MORE, SEE . . .

- Isaiah 56:1–8 (p. 675)
- Luke 12:8–9 (p. 1027)
- James 2:14–26 (p. 1295)

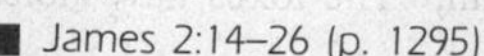

Jesus' Followers Are Criticized

14Then the followers of John[n] came to Jesus and said, "Why do we and the Pharisees[d] often give up eating for a certain time,[n] but your followers don't?"

15Jesus answered, "The friends of the bridegroom are not sad while he is with them. But the time will come when the bridegroom will be taken from them, and then they will give up eating.

16"No one sews a patch of unshrunk cloth over a hole in an old coat. If he does, the patch will shrink and pull away from the coat, making the hole worse. 17Also, people never pour new wine into old leather bags. Otherwise, the bags will break, the wine will spill, and the wine bags will be ruined. But people always pour new wine into new wine bags. Then both will continue to be good."

Jesus Gives Life to a Dead Girl and Heals a Sick Woman

18While Jesus was saying these things, a leader of the synagogue[d] came to him. He bowed down before Jesus and said, "My daughter has just died. But if you come and lay your hand on her, she will live again." 19So Jesus and his followers stood up and went with the leader.

20Then a woman who had been bleeding for twelve years came behind Jesus and touched the edge of his coat. 21She was thinking, "If I can just touch his clothes, I will be healed."

22Jesus turned and saw the woman and said, "Be encouraged, dear woman. You are made well because you believed." And the woman was healed from that moment on.

23Jesus continued along with the leader and went into his house. There he saw the funeral musicians and many people crying. 24Jesus said, "Go away. The girl is not dead, only asleep." But the people laughed at him. 25After the crowd had been thrown out of the house, Jesus went into the girl's room and took hold of her hand, and she stood up. 26The news about this spread all around the area.

Jesus Heals More People

27When Jesus was leaving there, two blind men followed him. They cried out, "Have mercy on us, Son of David!"[d]

28After Jesus went inside, the blind men went with him. He asked the men, "Do you believe that I can make you see again?"

They answered, "Yes, Lord."

29Then Jesus touched their eyes and said, "Because you believe I can make you see again, it will happen." 30Then the men were able to see. But Jesus warned them strongly, saying, "Don't tell anyone about this." 31But the blind men left and spread the news about Jesus all around that area.

32When the two men were leaving, some people brought another man to Jesus. This man could not talk because he had a demon[d] in him. 33After Jesus forced the demon to leave the man, he was able to speak. The crowd was amazed and said, "We have never seen anything like this in Israel."

34But the Pharisees[d] said, "The prince of demons is the one that gives him power to force demons out."

35Jesus traveled through all the towns and villages, teaching in their synagogues,[d] preaching the Good News[d] about the kingdom, and healing all kinds of diseases and sicknesses. 36When he saw the crowds, he felt sorry for them because they were hurting and helpless, like sheep without a shepherd. 37Jesus said to his followers, "There are many people to harvest but only a few workers to help harvest them. 38Pray to the Lord, who owns the harvest, that he will send more workers to gather his harvest."[n]

Jesus Sends Out His Apostles

10 Jesus called his twelve followers together and gave them authority to drive out evil spirits and to heal every kind of disease and sickness. 2These are the names of the twelve apostles:[d] Simon (also called Peter) and his brother Andrew; James son of Zebedee, and his brother John; 3Philip and Bartholomew; Thomas and Matthew, the tax collector; James son of Alphaeus, and Thaddaeus; 4Simon the Zealot[d] and Judas Iscariot, who turned against Jesus.

5Jesus sent out these twelve men with the following order: "Don't go to the non-Jewish people or to any town where the Samaritans[d] live. 6But go to the people of Israel, who are like lost sheep. 7When you go, preach this: 'The kingdom of heaven is near.' 8Heal the sick, raise the dead to life again, heal those who have skin diseases, and force demons[d] out of people. I give you these powers freely, so help other people freely. 9Don't carry any money with you — gold or silver or copper. 10Don't carry a bag or extra clothes or sandals or a walking stick. Workers should be given what they need.

11"When you enter a city or town, find some

John John the Baptist, who preached to people about Christ's coming (Matthew 3, Luke 3).
give up . . . time This is called "fasting." The people would give up eating for a special time of prayer and worship to God. It was also done to show sadness and disappointment.
"There are . . . harvest." As a farmer sends workers to harvest the grain, Jesus sends his followers to bring people to God.

worthy person there and stay in that home until
you leave. 12When you enter that home, say,
'Peace be with you.' 13If the people there welcome you, let your peace stay there. But if they
don't welcome you, take back the peace you
wished for them. 14And if a home or town refuses
to welcome you or listen to you, leave that place
and shake its dust off your feet.[n] 15I tell you the
truth, on the Judgment Day it will be better for
the towns of Sodom and Gomorrah[n] than for the
people of that town.

Jesus Warns His Apostles

16"Listen, I am sending you out like sheep
among wolves. So be as smart as snakes and as
innocent as doves. 17Be careful of people, because
they will arrest you and take you to court and
whip you in their synagogues.[d] 18Because of me
you will be taken to stand before governors and
kings, and you will tell them and the non-Jewish
people about me. 19When you are arrested, don't
worry about what to say or how to say it. At that
time you will be given the things to say. 20It will
not really be you speaking but the Spirit of your
Father speaking through you.

21"Brothers will give their own brothers to be
killed, and fathers will give their own children to
be killed. Children will fight against their own

shake . . . feet. A warning. It showed that they had rejected these people.
Sodom and Gomorrah Two cities that God destroyed because the people were so evil.

SICKNESS

Giving the World Friends

Rebecca Smathers, a high school junior, dances, walks, and runs. No big deal for most of us—but for Rebecca those abilities prove God's power. For not long ago, she was almost completely paralyzed.

In her freshman year, Rebecca felt her muscles slowly becoming numb. She started avoiding golf and softball practices. Play rehearsals caused excruciating pain. Her mother finally took her to a doctor, and Rebecca was admitted to the hospital that same day.

A spinal tap confirmed she had Guillain Barr Syndrome, a rare condition in which a virus attacks the nervous system, causing paralysis in all of the motor functions. Although she began various drug and physical treatments, Rebecca's condition worsened. "The syndrome spread, and I could no longer sit upright in bed by myself," she recalls.

Doctors gave her little chance for recovery. However, Rebecca believes the care and prayers of others made the difference. "My spirits have been strengthened because of the love from family and friends," Rebecca says. "Daily I received phone calls, cards, and flowers. My room was crowded with friends every day. It was a time for fellowship and support, not only for me, but also for my family and friends."

The doctors continued treatment, and Rebecca slowly recovered.

"Some people say the Lord doesn't give us answers we can see or touch, yet we all see and touch our family and friends," Rebecca says. "The Lord answered my prayers with a family who stroked my hair and sat next to me day and night while I lay motionless.

"The Lord brought me friends who told me, 'You will get better, because I'm praying for you.' I thank God for the answers he's given me."

Rebecca's doctors were amazed at the healing power of faith. Yet **Matthew 9:35—10:8** tells how Jesus commissioned the disciples to heal the sick.

- How well did the people who prayed and stayed with Rebecca follow Jesus' commission to the apostles?
- Why does God care not only about your physical health, but also your spiritual health?

CONSIDER. . .

- doing one activity this week to better your health and well-being.
- visiting someone in a hospital or nursing home and praying with him or her.

FOR MORE, SEE. . .

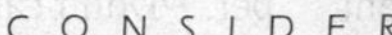

- 2 Kings 20:1–11 (p. 327)
- Psalm 30:2–3 (p. 498)
- Luke 18:35–43 (p. 1043)

parents and have them put to death. 22All people
will hate you because you follow me, but those
people who keep their faith until the end will be
saved. 23When you are treated badly in one city,
run to another city. I tell you the truth, you will
not finish going through all the cities of Israel before the Son of Man[d] comes.
24"A student is not better than his teacher, and
a servant is not better than his master. 25A student
should be satisfied to become like his teacher; a
servant should be satisfied to become like his master. If the head of the family is called Beelzebul,[d]
then the other members of the family will be
called worse names!

Fear God, Not People

26"So don't be afraid of those people, because
everything that is hidden will be shown. Everything that is secret will be made known. 27I tell
you these things in the dark, but I want you to tell
them in the light. What you hear whispered in
your ear you should shout from the housetops.
28Don't be afraid of people, who can kill the body
but cannot kill the soul. The only one you should
fear is the one who can destroy the soul and the
body in hell. 29Two sparrows cost only a penny,
but not even one of them can die without your
Father's knowing it. 30God even knows how
many hairs are on your head. 31So don't be
afraid. You are worth much more than many sparrows.

Tell People About Your Faith

32"All those who stand before others and say
they believe in me, I will say before my Father in
heaven that they belong to me. 33But all who
stand before others and say they do not believe in
me, I will say before my Father in heaven that
they do not belong to me.
34"Don't think that I came to bring peace to the
earth. I did not come to bring peace, but a sword.

SELF-ESTEEM

Playing Your Part

The second-period algebra test had been a disaster for Charlene Markham. Then she had slipped and fallen in the hallway in front of two dozen other students. As she sat in sixth-period band practice, her mind was everywhere except on the sheets of music.

"Sometimes I wonder if my being here at Springbrook High makes any difference at all," she thought as the band music filled the room. "It's like the flutists' part in this medley. All you can hear are the trumpets and trombones, anyway."

As an experiment, Charlene raised the flute to her lips but only pretended to play. "See," she thought after the piece, "no one even noticed."

Just before the bell rang, Mr. Westmore, the band director, instructed the students to put away their instruments. Then he asked Charlene to stay after the bell.

"Why didn't you play in the Sousa medley?" he asked.

Charlene was stunned that he knew what she had done. She didn't answer him.

"Charlene," he said kindly, yet firmly, "we need every part in a piece of music to make it complete. The director looks for everyone to be playing his or her part."

Somehow Charlene felt better knowing she had been missed. "Maybe I have a part to play after all," she thought. Learn what Jesus says about your importance in **Matthew 10:24–33**.

- How does the Bible passage speak to Charlene's feelings of worthlessness?
- How does knowing that God loves you affect your feelings about yourself?

CONSIDER . . .

- investing thirty minutes today in an activity for your own growth, health and well-being.
- listing all of the "sections" in God's "band" (the church) you can think of, such as pastors, leaders, choirs and so forth. Pick the one section that you're most interested in, and volunteer to "play" in it.

FOR MORE, SEE . . .

- Psalm 8:3–9 (p. 486)
- Romans 5:1–11 (p. 1145)
- 1 Corinthians 12:12–31 (p. 1182)

35I have come so that
'a son will be against his father,
a daughter will be against her mother,
a daughter-in-law will be against her
mother-in-law.
36 A person's enemies will be members of his
own family.' *Micah 7:6*
37"Those who love their father or mother more
than they love me are not worthy to be my followers. Those who love their son or daughter more
than they love me are not worthy to be my followers. 38Whoever is not willing to carry the cross
and follow me is not worthy of me. 39Those who
try to hold on to their lives will give up true life.
Those who give up their lives for me will hold on
to true life. 40Whoever accepts you also accepts
me, and whoever accepts me also accepts the One
who sent me. 41Whoever meets a prophet[d] and
accepts him will receive the reward of a prophet.
And whoever accepts a good person because that
person is good will receive the reward of a good
person. 42Those who give one of these little ones
a cup of cold water because they are my followers
will truly get their reward."

Jesus and John the Baptist

11 After Jesus finished telling these things
to his twelve followers, he left there
and went to the towns in Galilee to teach and
preach.
2John the Baptist[d] was in prison, but he heard
about what Christ was doing. So John sent some
of his followers to Jesus. 3They asked him, "Are
you the One who is to come, or should we wait
for someone else?"
4Jesus answered them, "Go tell John what you
hear and see: 5The blind can see, the crippled can
walk, and people with skin diseases are healed.
The deaf can hear, the dead are raised to life, and
the Good News[d] is preached to the poor. 6Those
who do not stumble in their faith because of me
are blessed."
7As John's followers were leaving, Jesus began
talking to the people about John. Jesus said,
"What did you go out into the desert to see? A
reed[n] blown by the wind? 8What did you go out
to see? A man dressed in fine clothes? No, those
who wear fine clothes live in kings' palaces. 9So

reed It means that John was not ordinary or weak like grass blown by the wind.

PRIORITIES

Doing the Right Thing

Dad appeared in Marcia Sloan's bedroom doorway. "What's all this I hear about you going to a Christian college next year?" he asked.

This was the moment she had been dreading. "It's true, Dad. That's what I've decided."

"Ever since you started going to that church, you've been getting weird ideas," he said. "If you want to go to medical school, you'll need the quality of education that you can get at a state school."

Then he dropped the ultimatum: "If you go to that Christian college, don't look to us for financial support."

Marcia's father kept his promise. But Marcia firmly believed that the Christian college was God's will for her.

Marcia's freshman year in college was difficult. Because she had to pay her own tuition, she worked several hours part-time in the evenings. But she kept going, knowing she had made a smart choice.

Jesus cautioned that following him would not always be easy. Read in **Matthew 10:34–42** about the difficult choices Christians may face.

- How was Marcia's predicament like that described in the passage?
- What does this passage say about your priorities in your family and in other areas of life?

CONSIDER . . .

- giving encouragement to a Christian friend whose parents are not believers.
- taking your mom or dad out for dessert after dinner one night this week, and talking with them about your goals and priorities.

FOR MORE, SEE . . .

- Genesis 22:1–18 (p. 25)
- Exodus 20:12 (p. 78)
- 1 John 3:1–3 (p. 1318)

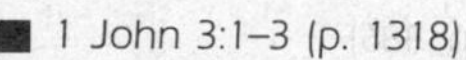

why did you go out? To see a prophet?[d] Yes, and
I tell you, John is more than a prophet. 10This was
written about him:

'I will send my messenger ahead of you,
who will prepare the way for you.' *Malachi 3:1*

11I tell you the truth, John the Baptist is greater
than any other person ever born, but even the
least important person in the kingdom of heaven
is greater than John. 12Since the time John the
Baptist came until now, the kingdom of heaven
has been going forward in strength, and people
have been trying to take it by force. 13All the
prophets and the law of Moses told about what
would happen until the time John came. 14And if
you will believe what they said, you will believe
that John is Elijah, whom they said would come.
15You people who can hear me, listen!

16"What can I say about the people of this time?
What are they like? They are like children sitting
in the marketplace, who call out to each other,

17'We played music for you, but you did not
dance;
we sang a sad song, but you did not cry.'

18John came and did not eat or drink like other
people. So people say, 'He has a demon.'[d] 19The
Son of Man[d] came, eating and drinking, and people say, 'Look at him! He eats too much and
drinks too much wine, and he is a friend of tax
collectors and sinners.' But wisdom is proved to
be right by what it does."

Jesus Warns Unbelievers

20Then Jesus criticized the cities where he did
most of his miracles,[d] because the people did not
change their lives and stop sinning. 21He said,
"How terrible for you, Korazin! How terrible for
you, Bethsaida! If the same miracles I did in you
had happened in Tyre and Sidon,[n] those people
would have changed their lives a long time ago.
They would have worn rough cloth and put ashes

Tyre and Sidon Towns where wicked people lived.

FAITH

The Faith Difference

Next time friends ask you, "Does your faith make a difference?" remember these statistics about teenagers in the United States*:

1. Teenagers who have never used illegal drugs—61 percent of regular churchgoers, versus 39 percent of nonchurchgoers.
2. Teenagers who have never had sexual intercourse—61 percent of regular churchgoers, versus 35 percent of nonchurchgoers.
3. Teenagers who believe in a personal God—87 percent of regular churchgoers, versus 64 percent of nonchurchgoers.
4. Teenagers who read the Bible weekly—58 percent of regular churchgoers, versus 17 percent of nonchurchgoers.
5. Teenagers who plan to go to college—57 percent of regular churchgoers, versus 33 percent of nonchurchgoers.

Faith isn't a "heady" thing. It's something that affects everything we do. As the statistics above illustrate, a committed faith makes a visible, real difference in the way we live. In **Matthew 11:2–11** the followers of John the Baptist asked Jesus whether he was the Christ. Read how he responded.

- Why is faith a powerful force in the miracles of Jesus as well as the behavior of regular churchgoers?
- What difference does faith make in your own life? Have you seen the signs of God's work that are listed in the passage?

CONSIDER . . .

- surveying your own behavior in comparison to the statistics. How well did you fit the categories?
- drawing up your own survey and interviewing both churchgoers and nonchurchgoers. Share your results with others at church and school.

FOR MORE, SEE . . .

- Judges 6:11–24 (p. 222)
- Luke 13:1–9 (p. 1030)
- James 5:13–18 (p. 1299)

*Eugene C. Roehlkepartain ed., The Youth Ministry Resource Book; (Loveland, CO: Group Books, 1988).

on themselves to show they had changed. 22But
I tell you, on the Judgment Day it will be better
for Tyre and Sidon than for you. 23And you, Capernaum,[n] will you be lifted up to heaven? No,
you will be thrown down to the depths. If the
miracles I did in you had happened in Sodom,[n]
its people would have stopped sinning, and it
would still be a city today. 24But I tell you, on the
Judgment Day it will be better for Sodom than for
you."

Jesus Offers Rest to People

25At that time Jesus said, "I praise you, Father,
Lord of heaven and earth, because you have hidden these things from the people who are wise
and smart. But you have shown them to those
who are like little children. 26Yes, Father, this is
what you really wanted.
27"My Father has given me all things. No one
knows the Son, except the Father. And no one
knows the Father, except the Son and those
whom the Son chooses to tell.
28"Come to me, all of you who are tired and
have heavy loads, and I will give you rest. 29Ac-
cept my teachings and learn from me, because I
am gentle and humble in spirit, and you will find
rest for your lives. 30The teaching that I ask you
to accept is easy; the load I give you to carry is
light."

Jesus Is Lord of the Sabbath

12 At that time Jesus was walking through
some fields of grain on a Sabbath[d] day.
His followers were hungry, so they began to pick
the grain and eat it. 2When the Pharisees[d] saw
this, they said to Jesus, "Look! Your followers
are doing what is unlawful to do on the Sabbath
day."
3Jesus answered, "Have you not read what David did when he and the people with him were
hungry? 4He went into God's house, and he and
those with him ate the holy bread, which was
lawful only for priests to eat. 5And have you not
read in the law of Moses that on every Sabbath
day the priests in the Temple[d] break this law
about the Sabbath day? But the priests are not
wrong for doing that. 6I tell you that there is
something here that is greater than the Temple.

Korazin . . . Bethsaida . . . Capernaum Towns by Lake Galilee where Jesus preached to the people.
Sodom A city that God destroyed because the people were so evil.

WORRYING

Making It Through Your Day

Why did everyone else seem to have such a carefree life? Stacy Campbell wondered.

For more than a year her mother had been threatening to leave her father. Her school counselor told her she would have to raise her grades in physics and math if she ever wanted to take engineering in college. While other students received allowances, Stacy worked long hours at a "lousy" part-time job. And Grandma Campbell had just gone into a nursing home because she couldn't care for herself anymore.

Stacy usually fell into bed after midnight. But she often had trouble going to sleep. Even in her sleep she couldn't find rest; the day's problems crept into her dreams.

But then one evening she stumbled across a way to unwind at day's end. She began to spend a little time reading her Bible and praying just before going to bed. In time, this habit helped to settle her down, set her mind at peace and place her day's troubles in God's care.

Jesus offered ways to cope with the stresses of life. Read about his promise in **Matthew 11:25–30**.

- What truth in this passage did Stacy stumble upon?
- What kinds of stresses do you have that you can take to Jesus?

CONSIDER . . .

- writing a thank-you note to Jesus for helping you cope with problems.
- setting aside ten minutes a day for one week for Bible reading and prayer. Perhaps begin by reading a psalm (p. 482) and a chapter of Proverbs (p. 568) each day. Many of the psalms are prayers you can use.

FOR MORE, SEE . . .

- Psalm 4 (p. 483)
- Luke 11:5–13 (p. 1024)
- Jude 24–25 (p. 1330)

7The Scripture[d] says, 'I want kindness more than
I want animal sacrifices.'[n] You don't really know
what those words mean. If you understood them,
you would not judge those who have done nothing wrong.
8"So the Son of Man[d] is Lord of the Sabbath
day."

SIDELIGHT: It was hard not to break Sabbath laws in Jesus' day (Matthew 12:1–8). The Pharisees believed thirty-nine different actions violated Sabbath laws. You couldn't take a trip, light a fire, get a drink, or pick up anything that weighed more than two figs. How much does a TV remote control weigh?

Jesus Heals a Man's Hand

9Jesus left there and went into their synagogue,[d] 10where there was a man with a crippled
hand. They were looking for a reason to accuse
Jesus, so they asked him, "Is it right to heal on the
Sabbath[d] day?"[n]
11Jesus answered, "If any of you has a sheep,
and it falls into a ditch on the Sabbath day, you
will help it out of the ditch. 12Surely a human
being is more important than a sheep. So it is lawful to do good things on the Sabbath day."
13Then Jesus said to the man with the crippled
hand, "Hold out your hand." The man held out
his hand, and it became well again, like the other
hand. 14But the Pharisees[d] left and made plans to
kill Jesus.

Jesus Is God's Chosen Servant

15Jesus knew what the Pharisees[d] were doing,
so he left that place. Many people followed him,
and he healed all who were sick. 16But Jesus
warned the people not to tell who he was. 17He
did these things to bring about what Isaiah the
prophet[d] had said:

18"Here is my servant whom I have chosen.
 I love him, and I am pleased with him.
I will put my Spirit[d] upon him,
 and he will tell of my justice to all people.
19He will not argue or cry out;
 no one will hear his voice in the streets.
20He will not break a crushed blade of grass
 or put out even a weak flame
until he makes justice win the victory.
21 In him will the non-Jewish people find
 hope." *Isaiah 42:1-4*

Jesus' Power Is from God

22Then some people brought to Jesus a man
who was blind and could not talk, because he had
a demon.[d] Jesus healed the man so that he could
talk and see. 23All the people were amazed and
said, "Perhaps this man is the Son of David!"[d]
24When the Pharisees[d] heard this, they said,
"Jesus uses the power of Beelzebul,[d] the ruler of
demons, to force demons out of people."
25Jesus knew what the Pharisees were thinking, so he said to them, "Every kingdom that is
divided against itself will be destroyed. And any
city or family that is divided against itself will not
continue. 26And if Satan forces out himself, then
Satan is divided against himself, and his kingdom
will not continue. 27You say that I use the power
of Beelzebul to force out demons. If that is true,
then what power do your people use to force out
demons? So they will be your judges. 28But if I use
the power of God's Spirit[d] to force out demons,
then the kingdom of God has come to you.
29"If anyone wants to enter a strong person's
house and steal his things, he must first tie up the
strong person. Then he can steal the things from
the house.
30"Whoever is not with me is against me. Whoever does not work with me is working against
me. 31So I tell you, people can be forgiven for every sin and everything they say against God. But
whoever speaks against the Holy Spirit will not be
forgiven. 32Anyone who speaks against the Son of
Man[d] can be forgiven, but anyone who speaks
against the Holy Spirit will not be forgiven, now
or in the future.

People Know You by Your Words

33"If you want good fruit, you must make the
tree good. If your tree is not good, it will have bad
fruit. A tree is known by the kind of fruit it produces. 34You snakes! You are evil people, so how
can you say anything good? The mouth speaks the
things that are in the heart. 35Good people have
good things in their hearts, and so they say good
things. But evil people have evil in their hearts, so
they say evil things. 36And I tell you that on the
Judgment Day people will be responsible for every
careless thing they have said. 37The words
you have said will be used to judge you. Some
of your words will prove you right, but some of
your words will prove you guilty."

The People Ask for a Miracle

38Then some of the Pharisees[d] and teachers of
the law answered Jesus, saying, "Teacher, we
want to see you work a miracle[d] as a sign."
39Jesus answered, "Evil and sinful people are

'I . . . sacrifices.' Quotation from Hosea 6:6.
"Is it right . . . day?" It was against Jewish law to work on the Sabbath day.

the ones who want to see a miracle for a sign. But no sign will be given to them, except the sign of the prophet[d] Jonah. 40Jonah was in the stomach of the big fish for three days and three nights. In the same way, the Son of Man[d] will be in the grave three days and three nights. 41On the Judgment Day the people from Nineveh[n] will stand up with you people who live now, and they will show that you are guilty. When Jonah preached to them, they were sorry and changed their lives. And I tell you that someone greater than Jonah is here. 42On the Judgment Day, the Queen of the South[n] will stand up with you people who live today. She will show that you are guilty, because she came from far away to listen to Solomon's wise teaching. And I tell you that someone greater than Solomon is here.

People Today Are Full of Evil

43"When an evil spirit comes out of a person, it travels through dry places, looking for a place to rest, but it doesn't find it. 44So the spirit says, 'I will go back to the house I left.' When the spirit comes back, it finds the house still empty, swept clean, and made neat. 45Then the evil spirit goes out and brings seven other spirits even more evil than it is, and they go in and live there. So the person has even more trouble than before. It is the same way with the evil people who live today."

Jesus' True Family

46While Jesus was talking to the people, his mother and brothers stood outside, trying to find a way to talk to him. 47Someone told Jesus, "Your mother and brothers are standing outside, and they want to talk to you."

48He answered, "Who is my mother? Who are my brothers?" 49Then he pointed to his followers and said, "Here are my mother and my brothers. 50My true brother and sister and mother are those who do what my Father in heaven wants."

A Story About Planting Seed

13 That same day Jesus went out of the house and sat by the lake. 2Large crowds gathered around him, so he got into a boat and sat down, while the people stood on the shore. 3Then Jesus used stories to teach them many things. He said: "A farmer went out to plant his seed. 4While he was planting, some seed fell by the road, and the birds came and ate it all up. 5Some seed fell on rocky ground, where there wasn't much dirt. That seed grew very fast, because the ground was not deep. 6But when the sun rose, the plants dried up, because they did not have deep roots. 7Some other seed fell among thorny weeds, which grew and choked the good plants. 8Some other seed fell on good ground where it grew and produced a crop. Some plants made a hundred times more, some made sixty times more, and some made thirty times more. 9You people who can hear me, listen."

Why Jesus Used Stories to Teach

10The followers came to Jesus and asked, "Why do you use stories to teach the people?"

11Jesus answered, "You have been chosen to know the secrets about the kingdom of heaven, but others cannot know these secrets. 12Those who have understanding will be given more, and they will have all they need. But those who do not have understanding, even what they have will be taken away from them. 13This is why I use stories to teach the people: They see, but they don't really see. They hear, but they don't really hear or understand. 14So they show that the things Isaiah said about them are true:

'You will listen and listen, but you will not
understand.
You will look and look, but you will not
learn.
15For the minds of these people have become
stubborn.
They do not hear with their ears,
and they have closed their eyes.
Otherwise they might really understand
what they see with their eyes
and hear with their ears.
They might really understand in their minds
and come back to me and be healed.'

Isaiah 6:9-10

16But you are blessed, because you see with your eyes and hear with your ears. 17I tell you the truth, many prophets[d] and good people wanted to see the things that you now see, but they did not see them. And they wanted to hear the things that you now hear, but they did not hear them.

Jesus Explains the Seed Story

18"So listen to the meaning of that story about the farmer. 19What is the seed that fell by the road? That seed is like the person who hears the message about the kingdom but does not understand it. The Evil One comes and takes away what was planted in that person's heart. 20And what is the seed that fell on rocky ground? That seed is like the person who hears the teaching and quickly accepts it with joy. 21But he does not let the teaching go deep into his life, so he keeps it

Nineveh The city where Jonah preached to warn the people. Read Jonah 3.
Queen of the South The Queen of Sheba. She traveled a thousand miles to learn God's wisdom from Solomon. Read 1 Kings 10:1-13.

only a short time. When trouble or persecution comes because of the teaching he accepted, he quickly gives up.
22And what is the seed that fell among the thorny weeds? That seed is like the person who hears the teaching but lets worries about this life and the temptation of wealth stop that teaching from growing. So the teaching does not produce fruit[n] in that person's life.
23But what is the seed that fell on the good ground? That seed is like the person who hears the teaching and understands it. That person grows and produces fruit, sometimes a hundred times more, sometimes sixty times more, and sometimes thirty times more."

A Story About Wheat and Weeds

24Then Jesus told them another story: "The kingdom of heaven is like a man who planted good seed in his field.
25That night, when everyone was asleep, his enemy came and planted weeds among the wheat and then left.
26Later, the wheat sprouted and the heads of grain grew, but the weeds also grew.
27Then the man's servants came to him and said, 'You planted good seed in your field. Where did the weeds come from?'
28The man answered, 'An enemy planted weeds.' The servants asked, 'Do you want us to pull up the weeds?'
29The man answered, 'No, because when you pull up the weeds, you might also pull up the wheat.
30Let the weeds and the wheat grow together until the harvest time. At harvest time I will tell the workers, "First gather the weeds and tie them together to be burned. Then gather the wheat and bring it to my barn." ' "

Stories of Mustard Seed and Yeast

31Then Jesus told another story: "The kingdom of heaven is like a mustard seed that a man planted in his field.
32That seed is the smallest of all seeds, but when it grows, it is one of the largest garden plants. It becomes big enough for the wild birds to come and build nests in its branches."
33Then Jesus told another story: "The kingdom of heaven is like yeast that a woman took and hid in a large tub of flour until it made all the dough rise."
34Jesus used stories to tell all these things to the

produce fruit To produce fruit means to have in your life the good things God wants.

FOLLOWING GOD

Tuned In

One beautiful spring morning, an experienced hiker was walking with a friend down Fifth Avenue in Manhattan. The streets rumbled with the sounds of weekday rush-hour traffic. Suddenly the hiker stopped. "Listen," he said. "I hear a cricket."

"That's nonsense!" his friend scoffed. "Why do you think you hear a lowly cricket in all this downtown uproar?"

"I'm sure I do," the hiker said. "Watch this." He pulled a dime from his pocket and dropped it on the pavement. Almost all of the people nearby stopped at the sound of the coin hitting the concrete.

"All of us are tuned to certain things," the hiker said to his friend. "Our ears hear what they are tuned to. Mine happen to be tuned to crickets."

In a similar way we need to be open to God's word. Jesus said we need "eyes to see" and "ears to hear" before we can tune in to the gospel. Read how to gain a new view of your faith in **Matthew 13:1–23**.

- How was the hiker's hearing the cricket like the ability to hear Jesus' message?
- Why do you think Jesus compares following God to being the "good ground" for the seed of faith?

CONSIDER...

- looking around your room or yard as if you've never seen it before. What do you see, hear or feel that's gone unnoticed? Then do the same process at your church. How can you follow God in ways you may not have noticed?
- listing three specific things you can do in the next week to better see and hear ways to follow God.

FOR MORE, SEE...

- 1 Samuel 3:1–21 (p. 247)
- Isaiah 42:18–20 (p. 659)
- 1 Corinthians 13:8–13 (p. 1184)

people; he always used stories to teach them.
35This is as the prophet[d] said:

"I will speak using stories;
I will tell things that have been secret since
the world was made." *Psalm 78:2*

Jesus Explains About the Weeds

36Then Jesus left the crowd and went into the
house. His followers came to him and said, "Explain to us the meaning of the story about the
weeds in the field."

37Jesus answered, "The man who planted the
good seed in the field is the Son of Man.[d] 38The
field is the world, and the good seed are all of
God's children who belong to the kingdom. The
weeds are those people who belong to the Evil
One. 39And the enemy who planted the bad seed
is the devil. The harvest time is the end of the
world, and the workers who gather are God's angels.
40"Just as the weeds are pulled up and burned
in the fire, so it will be at the end of the world.
41The Son of Man will send out his angels, and
they will gather out of his kingdom all who cause
sin and all who do evil. 42The angels will throw
them into the blazing furnace, where the people
will cry and grind their teeth with pain. 43Then
the good people will shine like the sun in the kingdom of their Father. You people who can hear
me, listen.

Stories of a Treasure and a Pearl

44"The kingdom of heaven is like a treasure hidden in a field. One day a man found the treasure,
and then he hid it in the field again. He was so
happy that he went and sold everything he owned
to buy that field.
45"Also, the kingdom of heaven is like a man
looking for fine pearls. 46When he found a very
valuable pearl, he went and sold everything he
had and bought it.

A Story of a Fishing Net

47"Also, the kingdom of heaven is like a net
that was put into the lake and caught many different kinds of fish. 48When it was full, the fishermen
pulled the net to the shore. They sat down and
put all the good fish in baskets and threw away
the bad fish. 49It will be this way at the end of the
world. The angels will come and separate the evil
people from the good people. 50The angels will
throw the evil people into the blazing furnace,
where people will cry and grind their teeth with
pain."

SIN

A Crafty Enemy

Life in the Arctic would be pretty safe for a ringed seal if it weren't for its enemy the polar bear.

This crafty predator probably uses more strategies than any other animal in capturing and killing its prey. It may spend thirty minutes in the water approaching a resting seal on an ice floe, surfacing silently to see where the prey is and then submerging again. It may drift like a small harmless iceberg to within striking distance, and then explode from the water so suddenly and ferociously that the seal has no time to react.

When it's stalking on the ice, the polar bear slithers along on its chest and forelegs. It will build mounds of snow to hide behind while it waits at the edge of a breathing hole. It can surface in the seal's den and catch it sleeping there. Or it can dive so quickly into the den from above that the seal cannot escape.

We, too, must be wary of a crafty enemy. You can read about the enemy in Jesus' parable of the wheat and weeds in **Matthew 13:24–30**.

- How are the polar bear's tactics similar to the enemy's in the passage?
- How can you be prepared for the traps of the enemy in your life?

CONSIDER . . .

- separating the forms of entertainment that you enjoy into categories of "wheat" and "weeds." Consider giving up one (or more) of the "weeds."
- looking up references to "Satan" and "devil" in the "Dictionary with Topical Concordance" at the back of this Bible (p. 1350). Share what you learn with friends.

FOR MORE, SEE . . .

- Genesis 3:1–9 (p. 4)
- Hebrews 3:12–14 (p. 1279)
- 1 Peter 5:8–9 (p. 1308)

51Jesus asked his followers, "Do you understand all these things?"

They answered, "Yes, we understand."

52Then Jesus said to them, "So every teacher of the law who has been taught about the kingdom of heaven is like the owner of a house. He brings out both new things and old things he has saved."

Jesus Goes to His Hometown

53When Jesus finished teaching with these stories, he left there.
54He went to his hometown and taught the people in the synagogue,[d] and they were amazed. They said, "Where did this man get this wisdom and this power to do miracles?[d]
55He is just the son of a carpenter. His mother is Mary, and his brothers are James, Joseph, Simon, and Judas.
56And all his sisters are here with us. Where then does this man get all these things?"
57So the people were upset with Jesus.

But Jesus said to them, "A prophet[d] is honored everywhere except in his hometown and in his own home."

58So he did not do many miracles there because they had no faith.

How John the Baptist Was Killed

14 At that time Herod, the ruler of Galilee, heard the reports about Jesus.
2So he said to his servants, "Jesus is John the Baptist,[d] who has risen from the dead. That is why he can work these miracles."[d]

3Sometime before this, Herod had arrested John, tied him up, and put him into prison. Herod did this because of Herodias, who had been the wife of Philip, Herod's brother.
4John had been telling Herod, "It is not lawful for you to be married to Herodias."
5Herod wanted to kill John, but he was afraid of the people, because they believed John was a prophet.[d]

6On Herod's birthday, the daughter of Herodias danced for Herod and his guests, and she pleased him.
7So he promised with an oath to give her anything she wanted.
8Herodias told her daughter what to ask for, so she said to Herod, "Give me the head of John the Baptist here on a platter."
9Although King Herod was very sad, he had made a promise, and his dinner guests had heard him. So Herod ordered that what she asked for be

HAPPINESS

Real Treasure

When seventeen-year-old Derek Green bought his first car—a "previously owned" model—he expected to hit the road and leave his problems in the dust.

The car, Derek expected, would give him more time to do as he pleased. It would get him out of the house and away from his parents' fighting all the time. It would surely improve his standing with girls.

But only a week later, with three friends in the car, a fan belt broke on the way to a football game.

One month later, he had to buy two new tires.

Now he discovered, twenty miles from home, that the radiator was leaking. As the traffic swished past on the freeway, Derek and his friend Phil sat in the front seat of the car, watching the steam rise from under the hood.

"I always looked forward to owning my own car," Derek said. "But sometimes I feel as if the car owns me."

Derek learned an ageless truth that the more things we acquire, the more they use our time and energy. Possessions rarely bring the happiness expected, and often bring just the opposite. The Bible talks often about the spiritual kingdom and the only true happiness. Read three of Jesus' parables on the kingdom in **Matthew 13:44–52**.

- What are the differences between Derek's car and the "treasure hidden in a field" mentioned in the passage?
- What is the true value of the things you treasure?

CONSIDER . . .

- praying that God will help you value the things in life that truly last.
- interviewing an elderly Christian about the things that have meant the most in his or her lifetime.

FOR MORE, SEE . . .

- Ecclesiastes 3:1–8 (p. 600)
- Philippians 4:4–9 (p. 1234)
- Revelation 3:14–22 (p. 1335)

done. 10He sent soldiers to the prison to cut off
John's head. 11And they brought it on a platter
and gave it to the girl, and she took it to her
mother. 12John's followers came and got his body
and buried it. Then they went and told Jesus.

More than Five Thousand Fed

13When Jesus heard what had happened to
John, he left in a boat and went to a lonely place
by himself. But the crowds heard about it and followed him on foot from the towns. 14When he
arrived, he saw a great crowd waiting. He felt
sorry for them and healed those who were sick.
15When it was evening, his followers came to
him and said, "No one lives in this place, and it
is already late. Send the people away so they can
go to the towns and buy food for themselves."
16But Jesus answered, "They don't need to go
away. You give them something to eat."
17They said to him, "But we have only five
loaves of bread and two fish."
18Jesus said, "Bring the bread and the fish to
me." 19Then he told the people to sit down on the
grass. He took the five loaves and the two fish
and, looking to heaven, he thanked God for the
food. Jesus divided the bread and gave it to his
followers, who gave it to the people. 20All the people ate and were satisfied. Then the followers
filled twelve baskets with the leftover pieces of
food. 21There were about five thousand men there
who ate, not counting women and children.

> **SIDELIGHT:** The fish mentioned in Matthew 14:17–21 may have referred to the small, sardine-like fish that were plentiful in Lake Galilee. The poor usually ate this fish with barley bread.

Jesus Walks on the Water

22Immediately Jesus told his followers to get
into the boat and go ahead of him across the lake.
He stayed there to send the people home. 23After
he had sent them away, he went by himself up
into the hills to pray. It was late, and Jesus was
there alone. 24By this time, the boat was already
far away from land. It was being hit by waves,
because the wind was blowing against it.
25Between three and six o'clock in the morning, Jesus came to them, walking on the water.
26When his followers saw him walking on the water, they were afraid. They said, "It's a ghost!"
and cried out in fear.
27But Jesus quickly spoke to them, "Have courage! It is I. Do not be afraid."
28Peter said, "Lord, if it is really you, then command me to come to you on the water."
29Jesus said, "Come."
And Peter left the boat and walked on the water to Jesus. 30But when Peter saw the wind and
the waves, he became afraid and began to sink.
He shouted, "Lord, save me!"
31Immediately Jesus reached out his hand and
caught Peter. Jesus said, "Your faith is small. Why
did you doubt?"
32After they got into the boat, the wind became
calm. 33Then those who were in the boat worshiped Jesus and said, "Truly you are the Son of
God!"
34When they had crossed the lake, they came
to shore at Gennesaret. 35When the people there
recognized Jesus, they told people all around
there that Jesus had come, and they brought all
their sick to him. 36They begged Jesus to let them
touch just the edge of his coat, and all who
touched it were healed.

Obey God's Law

15 Then some Pharisees[d] and teachers of
the law came to Jesus from Jerusalem.
They asked him, 2"Why don't your followers obey
the unwritten laws which have been handed
down to us? They don't wash their hands before
they eat."
3Jesus answered, "And why do you refuse to
obey God's command so that you can follow your
own teachings? 4God said, 'Honor your father and
your mother,'[n] and 'Anyone who says cruel
things to his father or mother must be put to
death.'[n] 5But you say a person can tell his father
or mother, 'I have something I could use to help
you, but I have given it to God already.' 6You
teach that person not to honor his father or his
mother. You rejected what God said for the sake
of your own rules. 7You are hypocrites![d] Isaiah
was right when he said about you:
8'These people show honor to me with words,
but their hearts are far from me.
9Their worship of me is worthless.
The things they teach are nothing but
human rules.' " *Isaiah 29:13*
10After Jesus called the crowd to him, he said,
"Listen and understand what I am saying. 11It is
not what people put into their mouths that makes
them unclean.[d] It is what comes out of their
mouths that makes them unclean."
12Then his followers came to him and asked,
"Do you know that the Pharisees are angry because of what you said?"

'Honor . . . mother.' Quotation from Exodus 20:12; Deuteronomy 5:16.
'Anyone . . . death.' Quotation from Exodus 21:17.

13Jesus answered, "Every plant that my Father
in heaven has not planted himself will be pulled
up by the roots. 14Stay away from the Pharisees;
they are blind leaders. And if a blind person leads
a blind person, both will fall into a ditch."
15Peter said, "Explain the example to us."
16Jesus said, "Do you still not understand?
17Surely you know that all the food that enters the
mouth goes into the stomach and then goes out
of the body. 18But what people say with their
mouths comes from the way they think; these are
the things that make people unclean. 19Out of the
mind come evil thoughts, murder, adultery,[d] sexual sins, stealing, lying, and speaking evil of others. 20These things make people unclean; eating
with unwashed hands does not make them unclean."

Jesus Helps a Non-Jewish Woman

21Jesus left that place and went to the area of
Tyre and Sidon. 22A Canaanite woman from that
area came to Jesus and cried out, "Lord, Son of
David,[d] have mercy on me! My daughter has a
demon,[d] and she is suffering very much."
23But Jesus did not answer the woman. So his
followers came to Jesus and begged him, "Tell the
woman to go away. She is following us and shouting."
24Jesus answered, "God sent me only to the lost
sheep, the people of Israel."
25Then the woman came to Jesus again and
bowed before him and said, "Lord, help me!"
26Jesus answered, "It is not right to take the
children's bread and give it to the dogs."

FEAR

The Handicap

Curt Ryan was "cool." Nothing seemed to unnerve him. That's why the youth group was surprised when he strongly objected to the idea of a weekend service retreat at a home for mentally and physically disabled people.

"Why don't you like the idea?" someone asked.

"It's stupid, that's all!" Curt said.

"Are you scared, or what?" someone else asked.

"Yeah, right," Curt responded sarcastically.

The group decided to go ahead, and planned the retreat. Curt grudgingly went along, and kept up his "cool" veneer. But inside, Curt was afraid of the people at the home. He coped with his fear by avoiding any contact with residents.

But he couldn't avoid the dance. Curt walked in late and leaned against a wall in a dark corner. Sally, one of the residents, saw him and rushed up in her wheelchair. She tugged at his arm. "Dance with me," she pleaded.

He pretended he had not heard her.

"Please dance with me," she persisted. "Please?"

Reluctantly, Curt agreed. Although he felt awkward at first, Curt's fears soon faded. He discovered Sally was fun. She had a sharp wit. Sally actually made Curt feel comfortable.

"I was scared," he admitted later. "I didn't know what to expect. Then I saw the love and care these people give. They are just like me. I am the one who was handicapped."

Like Curt's fear of the residents, Peter, one of Jesus' disciples, often suffered from fear. Read how he was afraid to walk on water in **Matthew 14:22–33**.

- How are Curt's and Peter's reactions to fear similar?
- Would you have stayed in the boat or gotten out to walk on the water? Why?

C O N S I D E R . . .

- dividing a piece of paper equally. On the left side list fears. On the right side list ways to overcome fears. Share it with a friend. Pray for one another.
- taking a step this week in overcoming one of your fears. For example, if you're shy, go up to someone at school or church and introduce yourself.

F O R M O R E , S E E . . .

- Psalm 27 (p. 497)
- Mark 4:35–41 (p. 972)
- 1 Corinthians 2:1–5 (p. 1168)

27The woman said, "Yes, Lord, but even the
dogs eat the crumbs that fall from their masters'
table."
28Then Jesus answered, "Woman, you have
great faith! I will do what you asked." And at that
moment the woman's daughter was healed.

Jesus Heals Many People

29After leaving there, Jesus went along the
shore of Lake Galilee. He went up on a hill and
sat there.
30Great crowds came to Jesus, bringing with
them the lame, the blind, the crippled, those who
could not speak, and many others. They put them
at Jesus' feet, and he healed them. 31The crowd
was amazed when they saw that people who
could not speak before were now able to speak.
The crippled were made strong. The lame could
walk, and the blind could see. And they praised
the God of Israel for this.

More than Four Thousand Fed

32Jesus called his followers to him and said, "I
feel sorry for these people, because they have already been with me three days, and they have
nothing to eat. I don't want to send them away
hungry. They might faint while going home."
33His followers asked him, "How can we get
enough bread to feed all these people? We are far
away from any town."
34Jesus asked, "How many loaves of bread do
you have?"
They answered, "Seven, and a few small fish."
35Jesus told the people to sit on the ground.
36He took the seven loaves of bread and the fish
and gave thanks to God. Then he divided the food
and gave it to his followers, and they gave it to the
people. 37All the people ate and were satisfied.
Then his followers filled seven baskets with the
leftover pieces of food. 38There were about four
thousand men there who ate, besides women and
children. 39After sending the people home, Jesus
got into the boat and went to the area of Maga-
dan.

The Leaders Ask for a Miracle

16 The Pharisees[d] and Sadducees[d] came to
Jesus, wanting to trick him. So they
asked him to show them a miracle[d] from God.
2Jesus answered, "At sunset you say we will

PERSISTENCE

Go for the Gold

In 1972 Mark Spitz was an Olympic hero. He competed in seven swimming events, won seven gold medals, and set seven world records. Spitz remains a legend.

Almost twenty years later, Spitz is attempting a comeback. He wants to compete again in the Olympics, hoping to beat his time in the 100-meter butterfly. That time would have placed him eighth in the 1988 Olympics.

It takes persistence to prepare for competition. Spitz admits the closest he's been to water since his 1972 accomplishments is in the shower or his son's wading pool.

Why do it? "I just want to see if I can," Spitz says. "God gifted me with a certain talent and ability. You've got to get hungry if you want to prove something. I'm hungry to prove myself."

His coach believes in Spitz. "If anyone can do it, Mark can," he says. "He's a winner, a master competitor."

In a way similar to Spitz's dedication to his swimming dream, a woman pursued Jesus to heal her daughter. Read **Matthew 15:21–28** to see how she showed great persistence and faith.

- How is Spitz's persistence similar to the mother's in the passage?
- When have you been persistent like the mother? What happened?

CONSIDER . . .

- looking for examples of persistent people in newspapers or on television. What qualities do they possess? Write five of those qualities on a card. Tape it to your mirror as a reminder.
- setting a realistic goal for a project or task you've been putting off. Share it with a friend and ask him or her to help you reach your goal.

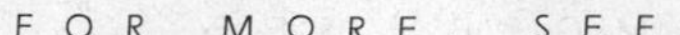

FOR MORE, SEE . . .

- Ruth 1:1–18 (p. 239)
- Mark 5:25–34 (p. 972)
- Ephesians 6:10–20 (p. 1226)

have good weather, because the sky is red. 3And in the morning you say that it will be a rainy day, because the sky is dark and red. You see these signs in the sky and know what they mean. In the same way, you see the things that I am doing now, but you don't know their meaning. 4Evil and sinful people ask for a miracle as a sign, but they will not be given any sign, except the sign of Jonah."[n] Then Jesus left them and went away.

Guard Against Wrong Teachings

5Jesus' followers went across the lake, but they had forgotten to bring bread. 6Jesus said to them, "Be careful! Beware of the yeast of the Pharisees[d] and the Sadducees."[d]

7His followers discussed the meaning of this, saying, "He said this because we forgot to bring bread."

8Knowing what they were talking about, Jesus asked them, "Why are you talking about not having bread? Your faith is small. 9Do you still not understand? Remember the five loaves of bread that fed the five thousand? And remember that you filled many baskets with the leftovers? 10Or the seven loaves of bread that fed the four thousand and the many baskets you filled then also? 11I was not talking to you about bread. Why don't you understand that? I am telling you to beware of the yeast of the Pharisees and the Sadducees." 12Then the followers understood that Jesus was not telling them to beware of the yeast used in bread but to beware of the teaching of the Pharisees and the Sadducees.

> **SIDELIGHT:** The city of Caesarea Philippi (Matthew 16:13) where Peter declared Jesus was God's Son, was north of Lake Galilee in an area that wasn't Jewish. In fact, it had a pagan shrine to Pan, a Greek and Roman nature god.

Peter Says Jesus Is the Christ

13When Jesus came to the area of Caesarea Philippi, he asked his followers, "Who do people say the Son of Man[d] is?"

14They answered, "Some say you are John the Baptist.[d] Others say you are Elijah, and still others say you are Jeremiah or one of the prophets."[d]

15Then Jesus asked them, "And who do you say I am?"

16Simon Peter answered, "You are the Christ,[d] the Son of the living God."

17Jesus answered, "You are blessed, Simon son of Jonah, because no person taught you that. My Father in heaven showed you who I am. 18So I tell you, you are Peter.[n] On this rock I will build my church, and the power of death will not be able to defeat it. 19I will give you the keys of the kingdom of heaven; the things you don't allow on earth will be the things that God does not allow, and the things you allow on earth will be the things that God allows." 20Then Jesus warned his followers not to tell anyone he was the Christ.

Jesus Says that He Must Die

21From that time on Jesus began telling his followers that he must go to Jerusalem, where the older Jewish leaders, the leading priests, and the teachers of the law would make him suffer many things. He told them he must be killed and then be raised from the dead on the third day.

22Peter took Jesus aside and told him not to talk like that. He said, "God save you from those things, Lord! Those things will never happen to you!"

23Then Jesus said to Peter, "Go away from me, Satan![n] You are not helping me! You don't care about the things of God, but only about the things people think are important."

24Then Jesus said to his followers, "If people want to follow me, they must give up the things they want. They must be willing even to give up their lives to follow me. 25Those who want to save their lives will give up true life, and those who give up their lives for me will have true life. 26It is worth nothing for them to have the whole world if they lose their souls. They could never pay enough to buy back their souls. 27The Son of Man[d] will come again with his Father's glory and with his angels. At that time, he will reward them for what they have done. 28I tell you the truth, some people standing here will see the Son of Man coming with his kingdom before they die."

Jesus Talks with Moses and Elijah

17 Six days later, Jesus took Peter, James, and John, the brother of James, up on a high mountain by themselves. 2While they watched, Jesus' appearance was changed; his face became bright like the sun, and his clothes became white as light. 3Then Moses and Elijah[n] appeared to them, talking with Jesus.

4Peter said to Jesus, "Lord, it is good that we

sign of Jonah Jonah's three days in the fish are like Jesus' three days in the tomb. The story about Jonah is in the book of Jonah.

Peter The Greek name "Peter," like the Aramaic name "Cephas," means "rock."

Satan Name for the devil, meaning "the enemy." Jesus means that Peter was talking like Satan.

Moses and Elijah Two of the most important Jewish leaders in the past. Moses had given them the law, and Elijah was an important prophet.

are here. If you want, I will put up three tents
here—one for you, one for Moses, and one for
Elijah."

SIDELIGHT: When Peter suggested camping out in Matthew 17:4, he may have been thinking about the annual Feast of Shelters. During this harvest festival, Jews from everywhere came to Jerusalem and built shelters or booths in the streets and town square—anywhere with a little space. It made for bad traffic jams, but was cheaper than staying in a hotel.

5While Peter was talking, a bright cloud covered them. A voice came from the cloud and said,
"This is my Son, whom I love, and I am very
pleased with him. Listen to him!"
6When his followers heard the voice, they were
so frightened they fell to the ground. 7But Jesus
went to them and touched them and said, "Stand
up. Don't be afraid." 8When they looked up, they
saw Jesus was now alone.
9As they were coming down the mountain,
Jesus commanded them not to tell anyone about
what they had seen until the Son of Man[d] had
risen from the dead.
10Then his followers asked him, "Why do the
teachers of the law say that Elijah must come
first?"
11Jesus answered, "They are right to say that
Elijah is coming and that he will make everything
the way it should be. 12But I tell you that Elijah
has already come, and they did not recognize
him. They did to him whatever they wanted to
do. It will be the same with the Son of Man; those
same people will make the Son of Man suffer."
13Then the followers understood that Jesus was
talking about John the Baptist.[d]

Jesus Heals a Sick Boy

14When Jesus and his followers came back to
the crowd, a man came to Jesus and bowed before

FAITH

T-e-a-c-h-e-r

A fever left Helen Keller blind and deaf at birth. She was imprisoned in a dark, silent world.

In 1887, when Helen was seven, Anne Sullivan, herself partially blind, became Helen's teacher. Anne had great vision and hope. She believed Helen held untapped and unseen abilities.

Months passed with very little progress, but Anne still believed.

Then, finally, Anne witnessed the results of faith. Helen was playing at the water pump. Anne finger-spelled "w-a-t-e-r" into her free hand. Anne wrote in her journal, "The word coming so close upon the sensation of cold water rushing over her hand seemed to startle her. A new light came into her face. She understood! Then turning around she asked my name. I spelled "T-e-a-c-h-e-r."

Thanks to Anne's faith, Helen's dark, lonely life opened wide to the light of communication and learning. Helen graduated with honors from Radcliffe College, and went on to a distinguished career as an educator, speaker and author. Helen and "Teacher" were lifelong companions.

"Teacher's" faith brought Helen out of darkness and into light. In **Matthew 16:13–20**, read how Jesus had faith in Peter, even when Peter wasn't sure of his own faith.

- How was Anne's and Helen's friendship similar to Jesus' and Peter's?
- Anne's faith enabled her to teach Helen. Peter's faith helped him become a church leader. What does your faith help you do?

C O N S I D E R . . .

- helping young children grow in their faith by volunteering to help one Sunday in the church nursery, Sunday school or vacation church school.
- writing a Haiku poem that expresses faith. A Haiku poem has three lines. The first and third lines each have seven syllables. The middle line has five.

F O R M O R E , S E E . . .

- Nehemiah 9:6–8 (p. 435)
- Mark 8:27–38 (p. 979)
- Hebrews 11 (p. 1287)

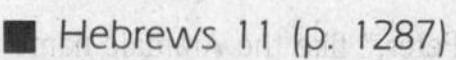

him. 15The man said, "Lord, have mercy on my son. He has epilepsy[n] and is suffering very much, because he often falls into the fire or into the water. 16I brought him to your followers, but they could not cure him."

17Jesus answered, "You people have no faith, and your lives are all wrong. How long must I put up with you? How long must I continue to be patient with you? Bring the boy here." 18Jesus commanded the demon[d] inside the boy. Then the demon came out, and the boy was healed from that time on.

19The followers came to Jesus when he was alone and asked, "Why couldn't we force the demon out?"

20Jesus answered, "Because your faith is too small. I tell you the truth, if your faith is as big as a mustard seed, you can say to this mountain, 'Move from here to there,' and it will move. All things will be possible for you." 21 [n]

Jesus Talks About His Death

22While Jesus' followers were gathering in Galilee, he said to them, "The Son of Man[d] will be handed over to people, 23and they will kill him. But on the third day he will be raised from the dead." And the followers were filled with sadness.

Jesus Talks About Paying Taxes

24When Jesus and his followers came to Capernaum, the men who collected the Temple[d] tax came to Peter. They asked, "Does your teacher pay the Temple tax?"

25Peter answered, "Yes, Jesus pays the tax."

Peter went into the house, but before he could speak, Jesus said to him, "What do you think? The kings of the earth collect different kinds of taxes. But who pays the taxes—the king's children or others?"

26Peter answered, "Other people pay the taxes."

Jesus said to Peter, "Then the children of the king don't have to pay taxes. 27But we don't want to upset these tax collectors. So go to the lake and fish. After you catch the first fish, open its mouth and you will find a coin. Take that coin and give it to the tax collectors for you and me."

Who Is the Greatest?

18 At that time the followers came to Jesus and asked, "Who is greatest in the kingdom of heaven?"

2Jesus called a little child to him and stood the child before his followers. 3Then he said, "I tell you the truth, you must change and become like little children. Otherwise, you will never enter the kingdom of heaven. 4The greatest person in the kingdom of heaven is the one who makes himself humble like this child.

5"Whoever accepts a child in my name accepts me. 6If one of these little children believes in me, and someone causes that child to sin, it would be better for that person to have a large stone tied around the neck and be drowned in the sea. 7How terrible for the people of the world because of the things that cause them to sin. Such things will happen, but how terrible for the one who causes them to happen! 8If your hand or your foot causes you to sin, cut it off and throw it away. It is better for you to lose part of your body and live forever than to have two hands and two feet and be thrown into the fire that burns forever. 9If your eye causes you to sin, take it out and throw it away. It is better for you to have only one eye and live forever than to have two eyes and be thrown into the fire of hell.

A Lost Sheep

10"Be careful. Don't think these little children are worth nothing. I tell you that they have angels in heaven who are always with my Father in heaven. 11 [n]

12"If a man has a hundred sheep but one of the sheep gets lost, he will leave the other ninety-nine on the hill and go to look for the lost sheep. 13I tell you the truth, he is happier about that one sheep than about the ninety-nine that were never lost. 14In the same way, your Father in heaven does not want any of these little children to be lost.

When a Person Sins Against You

15"If your fellow believer sins against you, go and tell him in private what he did wrong. If he listens to you, you have helped that person to be your brother or sister again. 16But if he refuses to listen, go to him again and take one or two other people with you. 'Every case may be proved by two or three witnesses.'[n] 17If he refuses to listen to them, tell the church. If he refuses to listen to the church, then treat him like a person who does not believe in God or like a tax collector.

18"I tell you the truth, the things you don't allow on earth will be the things God does not allow. And the things you allow on earth will be the things that God allows.

19"Also, I tell you that if two of you on earth

epilepsy A disease that causes a person sometimes to lose control of his body and maybe faint, shake strongly, or not be able to move.
Verse 21 Some Greek copies add verse 21: "That kind of spirit comes out only if you use prayer and give up eating."
Verse 11 Some Greek copies add verse 11: "The Son of Man came to save lost people."
'Every . . . witnesses.' Quotation from Deuteronomy 19:15.

agree about something and pray for it, it will be
done for you by my Father in heaven. 20This is
true because if two or three people come together
in my name, I am there with them."

An Unforgiving Servant

21Then Peter came to Jesus and asked, "Lord,
when my fellow believer sins against me, how
many times must I forgive him? Should I forgive
him as many as seven times?"
22Jesus answered, "I tell you, you must forgive
him more than seven times. You must forgive him
even if he does wrong to you seventy-seven times.
23"The kingdom of heaven is like a king who
decided to collect the money his servants owed
him. 24When the king began to collect his money,
a servant who owed him several million dollars
was brought to him. 25But the servant did not
have enough money to pay his master, the king.
So the master ordered that everything the servant
owned should be sold, even the servant's wife
and children. Then the money would be used to
pay the king what the servant owed.
26"But the servant fell on his knees and begged,
'Be patient with me, and I will pay you everything
I owe.' 27The master felt sorry for his servant and
told him he did not have to pay it back. Then he
let the servant go free.
28"Later, that same servant found another servant who owed him a few dollars. The servant
grabbed him around the neck and said, 'Pay me
the money you owe me!'
29"The other servant fell on his knees and
begged him, 'Be patient with me, and I will pay
you everything I owe.'
30"But the first servant refused to be patient. He

FRIENDS

I Hate You!

"What's going on?" Dad asked Suzanne, his fourteen-year-old daughter. "I was outside the house and heard your screaming."

"I hate her!" Suzanne yelled. "How could Vicki do this to me?" Suzanne Hinton and Vicki Linder had grown up together. As kids they had played with Barbie dolls and built tree forts. They had walked to school together and shared lunches. In middle school they were still friends.

Then Jean Lawlor moved to town. Jean caused trouble. To Suzanne it seemed Jean enjoyed setting Suzanne and Vicki against each other.

Dad listened as Suzanne alternated between crying and telling him what was going on. Jean had told Vicki that Suzanne was interested in Todd, Vicki's boyfriend. Jean later told Vicki that Suzanne had asked Todd out on a date, which wasn't true. Suzanne and Vicki had just argued on the phone, screaming at each other before Vicki slammed down the receiver.

"Can you believe it?" Suzanne wailed. "Vicki believed Jean—not me! I hate Jean! And Vicki! They betrayed me!"

"Sounds like you have a major conflict," Dad said.

"It's their fault!" Suzanne cried.

"The issue is: What are you going to do?" Dad said.

Sooner or later, conflict will erupt in most friendships. Jesus taught his followers several guidelines for dealing with conflict. Read **Matthew 18:15–20** and see how Suzanne, Vicki, and Jean might find ways to settle their differences.

- If Suzanne follows Jesus' teachings, what can she do to resolve her conflict with Vicki and Jean?
- How might Jesus' prescription for dealing with conflict help you in your friendships?

CONSIDER . . .

- making a list of friends with whom you have conflicts. Pray daily for strength to help you deal with these conflicts.
- writing about a friendship that's bothering you. Using Jesus' plan as a model, write your own plan for improving the friendship. What will you do and say?

FOR MORE, SEE . . .

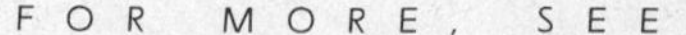

- Genesis 4:1–15 (p. 7)
- Luke 6:27–36 (p. 1013)
- Galatians 2:11–14 (p. 1207)

threw the other servant into prison until he could
pay everything he owed. 31When the other servants saw what had happened, they were very
sorry. So they went and told their master all that
had happened.
32"Then the master called his servant in and
said, 'You evil servant! Because you begged me to
forget what you owed, I told you that you did not
have to pay anything. 33You should have showed
mercy to that other servant, just as I showed
mercy to you.' 34The master was very angry and
put the servant in prison to be punished until he
could pay everything he owed.
35"This king did what my heavenly Father will
do to you if you do not forgive your brother or
sister from your heart."

Jesus Teaches About Divorce

19 After Jesus said all these things, he left
Galilee and went into the area of Judea
on the other side of the Jordan River. 2Large
crowds followed him, and he healed them there.
3Some Pharisees[d] came to Jesus and tried to
trick him. They asked, "Is it right for a man to
divorce his wife for any reason he chooses?"
4Jesus answered, "Surely you have read in the
Scriptures:[d] When God made the world, 'he
made them male and female.'[n] 5And God said,
'So a man will leave his father and mother and be
united with his wife, and the two will become
one body.'[n] 6So there are not two, but one. God
has joined the two together, so no one should separate them."
7The Pharisees asked, "Why then did Moses
give a command for a man to divorce his wife by
giving her divorce papers?"
8Jesus answered, "Moses allowed you to divorce your wives because you refused to accept
God's teaching, but divorce was not allowed in
the beginning. 9I tell you that anyone who di-

'he made . . . female.' Quotation from Genesis 1:27 or 5:2.
'So . . . body.' Quotation from Genesis 2:24.

FORGIVENESS

So Sorry

Kerrie Trent was in trouble, and she knew it. She hadn't even cracked the textbook, and the history exam would determine her grade in the class.

She sat behind Matt Kimmerly, who was a smart student. He would help, she thought. "Psst, Matt," she whispered, poking him with her pencil. "Question five. Gimme a clue."

Matt shrugged.

Kerrie poked him again with the pencil. Matt turned. "Cut it out," he hissed.

"Matt, come up here, and bring your exam," interrupted Ms. Miller, the history teacher. As Matt walked to Ms. Miller's desk, Kerrie pretended to work on her exam.

"I won't tolerate cheating," Ms. Miller said quietly to Matt. She tossed the exam into the wastebasket. Matt tried to explain what had happened, but she didn't believe him. "Take your seat, and be quiet for the rest of the period," she snapped.

Kerrie saw Matt's face as he walked back toward his seat. His eyes showed his deep anger and hurt. "Why?" he whispered. Kerrie looked away.

As school let out, Kerrie saw Matt in the hall and tried to tell him how sorry she was. But Matt ignored her. At midnight, she still couldn't get Matt's hurt out of her mind. She knew what to do. "Tomorrow," she thought, "I'll tell Ms. Miller what really happened, but will Matt ever forgive me?"

Both Kerrie and Matt could learn from the story Jesus told in **Matthew 18:21–35**.

- How is Kerrie's and Matt's struggle similar to the one in Jesus' story?
- Which character in Jesus' parable do you identify with most often? Why?

C O N S I D E R . . .

- listing things you find difficult to forgive. Put them in order, from least to most difficult to forgive. What factors make forgiveness difficult?
- thinking of two people: one who has hurt you most, and one you have hurt the most. Pray for strength, and then do one thing to help bring forgiveness to both people.

F O R M O R E , S E E . . .

- Jonah 3 (p. 858)
- Micah 7:18–20 (p. 868)
- Luke 17:1–4 (p. 1039)

vorces his wife and marries another woman is guilty of adultery.[d] The only reason for a man to divorce his wife is if his wife has sexual relations with another man."

10The followers said to him, "If that is the only reason a man can divorce his wife, it is better not to marry."

11Jesus answered, "Not everyone can accept this teaching, but God has made some able to accept it. 12There are different reasons why some men cannot marry. Some men were born without the ability to become fathers. Others were made that way later in life by other people. And some men have given up marriage because of the kingdom of heaven. But the person who can marry should accept this teaching about marriage."[n]

> **SIDELIGHT:** Divorce has always been a controversial subject—even in Jesus' day. While some religious leaders said someone could only get a divorce because of unfaithfulness, others argued that a husband could divorce a wife for burning supper, wearing the wrong thing in public, or even talking to another man. Jesus entered the debate in Matthew 19:1–12.

Jesus Welcomes Children

13Then the people brought their little children to Jesus so he could put his hands on them[n] and pray for them. His followers told them to stop, 14but Jesus said, "Let the little children come to me. Don't stop them, because the kingdom of heaven belongs to people who are like these children." 15After Jesus put his hands on the children, he left there.

A Rich Young Man's Question

16A man came to Jesus and asked, "Teacher, what good thing must I do to have life forever?"

17Jesus answered, "Why do you ask me about what is good? Only God is good. But if you want to have life forever, obey the commands."

18The man asked, "Which commands?"

Jesus answered, " 'You must not murder anyone; you must not be guilty of adultery;[d] you must not steal; you must not tell lies about your neighbor; 19honor your father and mother;[n] and love your neighbor as you love yourself.' "[n]

20The young man said, "I have obeyed all these things. What else do I need to do?"

21Jesus answered, "If you want to be perfect, then go and sell your possessions and give the money to the poor. If you do this, you will have treasure in heaven. Then come and follow me."

22But when the young man heard this, he left sorrowfully, because he was rich.

23Then Jesus said to his followers, "I tell you the truth, it will be hard for a rich person to enter the kingdom of heaven. 24Yes, I tell you that it is easier for a camel to go through the eye of a needle than for a rich person to enter the kingdom of God."

25When Jesus' followers heard this, they were very surprised and asked, "Then who can be saved?"

26Jesus looked at them and said, "This is something people cannot do, but God can do all things."

27Peter said to Jesus, "Look, we have left everything and followed you. So what will we have?"

28Jesus said to them, "I tell you the truth, when the age to come has arrived, the Son of Man[d] will sit on his great throne. All of you who followed me will also sit on twelve thrones, judging the twelve tribes[d] of Israel. 29And all those who have left houses, brothers, sisters, father, mother, children, or farms to follow me will get much more than they left, and they will have life forever. 30Many who have the highest place now will have the lowest place in the future. And many who have the lowest place now will have the highest place in the future.

A Story About Workers

20 "The kingdom of heaven is like a person who owned some land. One morning, he went out very early to hire some people to work in his vineyard. 2The man agreed to pay the workers one coin[n] for working that day. Then he sent them into the vineyard to work. 3About nine o'clock the man went to the marketplace and saw some other people standing there, doing nothing. 4So he said to them, 'If you go and work in my vineyard, I will pay you what your work is worth.' 5So they went to work in the vineyard. The man went out again about twelve o'clock and three o'clock and did the same thing. 6About five o'clock the man went to the marketplace again and saw others standing there. He asked them, 'Why did you stand here all day doing nothing?' 7They answered, 'No one gave us a job.' The man said to them, 'Then you can go and work in my vineyard.'

8"At the end of the day, the owner of the vine-

But . . . marriage. This may also mean, "The person who can accept this teaching about not marrying should accept it."
put his hands on them Showing that Jesus gave special blessings to these children.
'You . . . mother.' Quotation from Exodus 20:12-16; Deuteronomy 5:16-20.
'love . . . yourself.' Quotation from Leviticus 19:18.
coin A Roman denarius. One coin was the average pay for one day's work.

yard said to the boss of all the workers, 'Call the
workers and pay them. Start with the last people
I hired and end with those I hired first.'
9"When the workers who were hired at five
o'clock came to get their pay, each received one
coin. 10When the workers who were hired first
came to get their pay, they thought they would be
paid more than the others. But each one of them
also received one coin. 11When they got their
coin, they complained to the man who owned the
land. 12They said, 'Those people were hired last
and worked only one hour. But you paid them the
same as you paid us who worked hard all day in
the hot sun.' 13But the man who owned the vineyard said to one of those workers, 'Friend, I am
being fair to you. You agreed to work for one coin.
14So take your pay and go. I want to give the man
who was hired last the same pay that I gave you.
15I can do what I want with my own money. Are
you jealous because I am good to those people?'
16"So those who have the last place now will
have the first place in the future, and those who
have the first place now will have the last place
in the future."

Jesus Talks About His Own Death

17While Jesus was going to Jerusalem, he took
his twelve followers aside privately and said to

JUSTICE

It's Not Fair!

For months, Laura Steiner, seventeen, prepared her chemistry project for the area science fair competition. In previous years Laura had won several ribbons, but she had never won a chance to go to state. As a senior, this was her last chance.

Laura's fourteen-year-old brother, Kenneth, a freshman, also entered the science fair. Scientific concepts came to him easier than they did to Laura. Kenneth put together his project on the solar system in just a few days.

On the opening day of the fair, Laura, Kenneth, and their parents arrived in the family car. Laura rushed to see her project that simulated a nuclear reaction, while her brother and parents went to see Kenneth's entry. Laura couldn't wait to see the prize she expected from the judges.

But there was no ribbon. "Have the judges been here?" she cried. Yes, they have, she was told. "Then there's been some mistake!"

Kenneth ran up to Laura. "I won first prize!" yelled Kenneth. "I'm going to state!"

"That's unfair!" wailed Laura, who started sobbing. "Your project isn't even unique."

When she had settled down a bit, her parents tried to comfort her, but weren't very successful. "It just isn't fair," Laura muttered time and again. "I worked so hard, but Kenneth just threw his together at the last minute."

Then Mom reminded her of a time when Laura and Kenneth were younger. "Remember when you beat Kenneth in the skiing competition, after he had taught you to ski?" Mom asked. "He didn't think that was fair, but you didn't mind winning."

Laura was still disappointed, but started feeling happy for her brother. "Congratulations, and good luck at state," she finally told him.

No doubt you have been told, "Life isn't fair." Laura obviously found this out. God's view of justice and fairness puzzled many of the people in Jesus' time. Many assumed God would be better to them than to others. Read Jesus' response to their assumption in **Matthew 20:1–16**.

- How are Laura's complaints similar to those of the vineyard workers in Jesus' parable?
- If you were one of the first workers hired, how would you have felt? What would your reaction have been if you were among the last hired?

C O N S I D E R . . .

- looking for examples of "fairness" and "justice" in the news. Talk with your friends about whether these examples fit their views.
- asking a lawyer or judge to define justice. Ask your pastor to define justice. Then come up with your own definition.

F O R M O R E , S E E . . .

- Job 8:3–6 (p. 457)
- Luke 14:12–24 (p. 1032)
- 2 Thessalonians 1:3–12 (p. 1252)

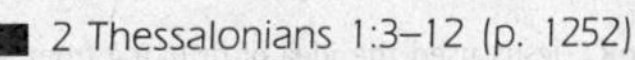

them, 18“Look, we are going to Jerusalem. The Son of Man[d] will be turned over to the leading priests and the teachers of the law, and they will say that he must die. 19They will give the Son of Man to the non-Jewish people to laugh at him and beat him with whips and crucify him. But on the third day, he will be raised to life again.”

A Mother Asks Jesus a Favor

20Then the wife of Zebedee came to Jesus with her sons. She bowed before him and asked him to do something for her.

21Jesus asked, “What do you want?”

She said, “Promise that one of my sons will sit at your right side and the other will sit at your left side in your kingdom.”

22But Jesus said, “You don’t understand what you are asking. Can you drink the cup that I am about to drink?”[n]

The sons answered, “Yes, we can.”

23Jesus said to them, “You will drink from my cup. But I cannot choose who will sit at my right or my left; those places belong to those for whom my Father has prepared them.”

24When the other ten followers heard this, they were angry with the two brothers.

> **SIDELIGHT:** James and John, the sons of Zebedee, were nicknamed “the sons of thunder” (Matthew 20:20–24; see Mark 3:17, p. 969). The nicknames may have come from their booming voices or their short tempers. Either way, the name would look great on a wrestling team roster.

25Jesus called all the followers together and said, “You know that the rulers of the non-Jewish people love to show their power over the people. And their important leaders love to use all their authority. 26But it should not be that way among you. Whoever wants to become great among you must serve the rest of you like a servant. 27Whoever wants to become first among you must serve the rest of you like a slave. 28In the same way, the Son of Man[d] did not come to be served. He came to serve others and to give his life as a ransom for many people.”

Jesus Heals Two Blind Men

29When Jesus and his followers were leaving Jericho, a great many people followed him. 30Two blind men sitting by the road heard that Jesus was going by, so they shouted, “Lord, Son of David,[d] have mercy on us!”

31The people warned the blind men to be quiet, but they shouted even more, “Lord, Son of David, have mercy on us!”

32Jesus stopped and said to the blind men, “What do you want me to do for you?”

33They answered, “Lord, we want to see.”

34Jesus felt sorry for the blind men and touched their eyes, and at once they could see. Then they followed Jesus.

Jesus Enters Jerusalem as a King

21 As Jesus and his followers were coming closer to Jerusalem, they stopped at Bethphage at the hill called the Mount of Olives.[d] From there Jesus sent two of his followers 2and said to them, “Go to the town you can see there. When you enter it, you will quickly find a donkey tied there with its colt. Untie them and bring them to me. 3If anyone asks you why you are taking the donkeys, say that the Master needs them, and he will send them at once.”

4This was to bring about what the prophet[d] had said:

5“Tell the people of Jerusalem,
‘Your king is coming to you.
He is gentle and riding on a donkey,
on the colt of a donkey.’ ”

Isaiah 62:11; Zechariah 9:9

6The followers went and did what Jesus told them to do. 7They brought the donkey and the colt to Jesus and laid their coats on them, and Jesus sat on them. 8Many people spread their coats on the road. Others cut branches from the trees and spread them on the road. 9The people were walking ahead of Jesus and behind him, shouting,

“Praise[n] to the Son of David![d]
God bless the One who comes in the name
of the Lord! *Psalm 118:26*
Praise to God in heaven!”

10When Jesus entered Jerusalem, all the city was filled with excitement. The people asked, “Who is this man?”

11The crowd said, “This man is Jesus, the prophet from the town of Nazareth in Galilee.”

Jesus Goes to the Temple

12Jesus went into the Temple[d] and threw out all the people who were buying and selling there. He turned over the tables of those who were exchanging different kinds of money, and he upset the benches of those who were selling doves.

drink . . . drink Jesus used the idea of drinking from a cup to ask if they could accept the same terrible things that would happen to him.

Praise Literally, “Hosanna,” a Hebrew word used at first in praying to God for help. At this time it was probably a shout of joy used in praising God or his Messiah.

13Jesus said to all the people there, "It is written in the Scriptures,[d] 'My Temple will be called a house for prayer.'[n] But you are changing it into a 'hideout for robbers.' "[n]

14The blind and crippled people came to Jesus in the Temple, and he healed them. 15The leading priests and the teachers of the law saw that Jesus was doing wonderful things and that the children were praising him in the Temple, saying, "Praise[n] to the Son of David."[d] All these things made the priests and the teachers of the law very angry.

16They asked Jesus, "Do you hear the things these children are saying?"

Jesus answered, "Yes. Haven't you read in the Scriptures, 'You have taught children and babies to sing praises'?"[n]

17Then Jesus left and went out of the city to Bethany, where he spent the night.

The Power of Faith

18Early the next morning, as Jesus was going back to the city, he became hungry. 19Seeing a fig tree beside the road, Jesus went to it, but there were no figs on the tree, only leaves. So Jesus said to the tree, "You will never again have fruit." The tree immediately dried up.

20When his followers saw this, they were amazed. They asked, "How did the fig tree dry up so quickly?"

21Jesus answered, "I tell you the truth, if you have faith and do not doubt, you will be able to do what I did to this tree and even more. You will be able to say to this mountain, 'Go, fall into the sea.' And if you have faith, it will happen. 22If you believe, you will get anything you ask for in prayer."

Leaders Doubt Jesus' Authority

23Jesus went to the Temple,[d] and while he was teaching there, the leading priests and the older leaders of the people came to him. They said, "What authority do you have to do these things? Who gave you this authority?"

24Jesus answered, "I also will ask you a question. If you answer me, then I will tell you what authority I have to do these things. 25Tell me: When John baptized people, did that come from God or just from other people?"

They argued about Jesus' question, saying, "If we answer, 'John's baptism was from God,' Jesus will say, 'Then why didn't you believe him?' 26But if we say, 'It was from people,' we are afraid of what the crowd will do because they all believe that John was a prophet."[d]

27So they answered Jesus, "We don't know."

Jesus said to them, "Then I won't tell you what authority I have to do these things.

A Story About Two Sons

28"Tell me what you think about this: A man had two sons. He went to the first son and said, 'Son, go and work today in my vineyard.' 29The son answered, 'I will not go.' But later the son changed his mind and went. 30Then the father went to the other son and said, 'Son, go and work today in my vineyard.' The son answered, 'Yes, sir, I will go and work,' but he did not go. 31Which of the two sons obeyed his father?"

The priests and leaders answered, "The first son."

Jesus said to them, "I tell you the truth, the tax collectors and the prostitutes[d] will enter the kingdom of God before you do. 32John came to show you the right way to live. You did not believe him, but the tax collectors and prostitutes believed him. Even after seeing this, you still refused to change your ways and believe him.

A Story About God's Son

33"Listen to this story: There was a man who owned a vineyard. He put a wall around it and dug a hole for a winepress[d] and built a tower. Then he leased the land to some farmers and left for a trip. 34When it was time for the grapes to be picked, he sent his servants to the farmers to get his share of the grapes. 35But the farmers grabbed the servants, beat one, killed another, and then killed a third servant with stones. 36So the man sent some other servants to the farmers, even more than he sent the first time. But the farmers did the same thing to the servants that they had done before. 37So the man decided to send his son to the farmers. He said, 'They will respect my son.' 38But when the farmers saw the son, they said to each other, 'This son will inherit the vineyard. If we kill him, it will be ours!' 39Then the farmers grabbed the son, threw him out of the vineyard, and killed him. 40So what will the owner of the vineyard do to these farmers when he comes?"

41The priests and leaders said, "He will surely kill those evil men. Then he will lease the vineyard to some other farmers who will give him his share of the crop at harvest time."

'My Temple . . . prayer.' Quotation from Isaiah 56:7.
'hideout for robbers.' Quotation from Jeremiah 7:11.
Praise Literally, "Hosanna," a Hebrew word used at first in praying to God for help. At this time it was probably a shout of joy used in praising God or his Messiah.
'You . . . praises' Quotation from the Septuagint (Greek) version of Psalm 8:2.

[42]Jesus said to them, "Surely you have read this
in the Scriptures:[d]

'The stone that the builders rejected
became the cornerstone.[d]
The Lord did this,
and it is wonderful to us.' *Psalm 118:22-23*

[43]"So I tell you that the kingdom of God will be
taken away from you and given to people who do
the things God wants in his kingdom. [44]The person who falls on this stone will be broken, and on
whomever that stone falls, that person will be
crushed."[n]

[45]When the leading priests and the Pharisees[d]
heard these stories, they knew Jesus was talking
about them. [46]They wanted to arrest him, but
they were afraid of the people, because the people
believed that Jesus was a prophet.[d]

Verse 44 Some copies do not have verse 44.

A Story About a Wedding Feast

22 Jesus again used stories to teach the people. He said, [2]"The kingdom of heaven is
like a king who prepared a wedding feast for his
son. [3]The king invited some people to the feast.
When the feast was ready, the king sent his servants to tell the people, but they refused to come.

[4]"Then the king sent other servants, saying,
'Tell those who have been invited that my feast
is ready. I have killed my best bulls and calves for
the dinner, and everything is ready. Come to the
wedding feast.'

[5]"But the people refused to listen to the servants and left to do other things. One went to
work in his field, and another went to his business. [6]Some of the other people grabbed the servants, beat them, and killed them. [7]The king was

HYPOCRISY

Sunday Christians

It was Saturday night and Jay Nelson was ready to party. On Saturday nights all streets led to the warehouse. After a tough week at school, it was party time!

The warehouse was in a secluded spot at the edge of town. The party was in full swing when Jay arrived. Beer flowed freely. People danced wildly to the full-volume music.

"Hey, Jay," a familiar voice cried.

Jay turned to see Chris Freedman, a new kid at school.

"I didn't know you'd be here," Chris said.

"Oh, yeah," Jay said easily as he hoisted a can of beer. "This is the place for all the cool people."

The next morning Jay's head was pounding. He dragged himself off to Sunday school. The teacher met him at the door. "Jay," she said. "There's someone new I'd like you to meet, Chris Freedman."

Chris's eyes widened. "This is great!" he said. "My folks made me come. But you're here, so this must be the cool place to be, huh?"

"Class," the teacher said. "Today's lesson will focus on telling others about God's love. Jay, would you please lead us in prayer?"

As he prayed, Jay had to come face-to-face with his own hypocrisy. Jesus told stories about living with integrity. Read one in **Matthew 21:28–32**.

- Which son in Jesus' story is most like Jay? Why?
- How are you like the son who said he wouldn't work but went anyway?
- How are you like the son who said he would work but didn't?

C O N S I D E R . . .

- looking up "hypocrite" in a dictionary. Jot down the definitions. Read what Jesus says about hypocrisy in Matthew 7:1–5, p. 918, and Matthew 23:1–12, p. 948. Write Jesus' advice under the definitions. Keep the paper as a reminder to guard against hypocrisy in your life.
- noticing the sets on TV shows you watch this week—how the sets make the show seem "real" when it isn't at all. Then think of one "set" in your life and do one thing today to be more authentic.

F O R M O R E , S E E . . .

- Psalm 51 (p. 511)
- Matthew 7:1–5 (p. 918)
- Luke 11:37–44 (p. 1026)

furious and sent his army to kill the murderers
and burn their city.
8"After that, the king said to his servants, 'The
wedding feast is ready. I invited those people, but
they were not worthy to come. 9So go to the
street corners and invite everyone you find to
come to my feast.' 10So the servants went into the
streets and gathered all the people they could
find, both good and bad. And the wedding hall
was filled with guests.
11"When the king came in to see the guests, he
saw a man who was not dressed for a wedding.
12The king said, 'Friend, how were you allowed
to come in here? You are not dressed for a wedding.'
But the man said nothing. 13So the king told
some servants, 'Tie this man's hands and feet.
Throw him out into the darkness, where people
will cry and grind their teeth with pain.'
14"Yes, many people are invited, but only a few
are chosen."

Is It Right to Pay Taxes or Not?

15Then the Pharisees[d] left that place and made
plans to trap Jesus in saying something wrong.

PRIORITIES

What Are You Worth?

"I'm worth $353.21 today," Craig Madison remarked as he modeled the clothes he had purchased during his shopping binge. "These," he said as he removed new sunglasses, "$40."

"This leather jacket—$100. Check out these running shoes—$80." Craig continued to tick off his value in new goods, including sales tax.

A few months later, Craig joined his church's drama group, which traveled all summer across the country. When the group arrived in a town, members would set up a huge circus tent and perform several times. It was hard work, but lots of fun.

The least favorite part for Craig was the afternoon matinee, a play especially for young children. Craig didn't like little kids. They "bugged" him, he said. Until the group performed at an orphanage.

Almost immediately, six-year-old Billy liked Craig. Wherever Craig sat, Billy climbed in his lap. During the performance, Billy watched the play with awe. At one point, Billy yelled, "Hi, Craig!"

After the performance, Billy was back in Craig's lap. "Do you believe in this Jesus guy?" Billy asked.

"Yeah, I think so," Craig said.

"You think he'd love me?" Billy pressed.

"He loves everyone," Craig said.

"No one ever loved me before," Billy said.

Craig didn't know what to say. Suddenly all his possessions didn't seem so important. He handed his sunglasses to Billy. "Are these worth a lot?" Billy asked.

"Just $40," said Craig. "But Billy, you're worth much, much more. That's what Jesus is about."

Sometimes it's easy to forget what's really important. To help keep us on track, Jesus told a parable in **Matthew 22:1–14** about life's priorities. He wanted the people to know that his top priority is to live for God and do his will.

- How is Craig's initial love of stuff like the attitude of the wedding guests? Why did his priorities change?
- How are your priorities sometimes like those of the wedding guests?

CONSIDER . . .

- reviewing your activities of the past week. Which of them reflect your desires for the best use of time? Which ones don't?
- inviting your parent to list his or her priorities for you while you list your own. Compare the lists and discuss differences and similarities.

FOR MORE, SEE . . .

- Ecclesiastes 2:1–11 (p. 599)
- Luke 12:13–21 (p. 1027)
- 1 Timothy 6:17–19 (p. 1261)

16They sent some of their own followers and some people from the group called Herodians.[n] They said, "Teacher, we know that you are an honest man and that you teach the truth about God's way. You are not afraid of what other people think about you, because you pay no attention to who they are. 17So tell us what you think. Is it right to pay taxes to Caesar[d] or not?"

18But knowing that these leaders were trying to trick him, Jesus said, "You hypocrites![d] Why are you trying to trap me? 19Show me a coin used for paying the tax." So the men showed him a coin.[n] 20Then Jesus asked, "Whose image and name are on the coin?"

21The men answered, "Caesar's."

Then Jesus said to them, "Give to Caesar the things that are Caesar's, and give to God the things that are God's."

22When the men heard what Jesus said, they were amazed and left him and went away.

Some Sadducees Try to Trick Jesus

23That same day some Sadducees[d] came to Jesus and asked him a question. (Sadducees believed that people would not rise from the dead.) 24They said, "Teacher, Moses said if a married man dies without having children, his brother must marry the widow and have children for him. 25Once there were seven brothers among us. The first one married and died. Since he had no children, his brother married the widow. 26Then the second brother also died. The same thing happened to the third brother and all the other brothers. 27Finally, the woman died. 28Since all seven men had married her, when people rise from the dead, whose wife will she be?"

29Jesus answered, "You don't understand, because you don't know what the Scriptures[d] say, and you don't know about the power of God. 30When people rise from the dead, they will not marry, nor will they be given to someone to marry. They will be like the angels in heaven. 31Surely you have read what God said to you about rising from the dead. 32God said, 'I am the God of Abraham, the God of Isaac, and the God of Jacob.'[n] God is the God of the living, not the dead."

33When the people heard this, they were amazed at Jesus' teaching.

The Most Important Command

34When the Pharisees[d] learned that the Sadducees[d] could not argue with Jesus' answers to them, the Pharisees met together. 35One Pharisee, who was an expert on the law of Moses, asked Jesus this question to test him: 36"Teacher, which command in the law is the most important?"

37Jesus answered, " 'Love the Lord your God with all your heart, all your soul, and all your mind.'[n] 38This is the first and most important command. 39And the second command is like the first: 'Love your neighbor as you love yourself.'[n] 40All the law and the writings of the prophets[d] depend on these two commands."

Jesus Questions the Pharisees

41While the Pharisees[d] were together, Jesus asked them, 42"What do you think about the Christ?[d] Whose son is he?"

They answered, "The Christ is the Son of David."[d]

43Then Jesus said to them, "Then why did David call him 'Lord'? David, speaking by the power of the Holy Spirit,[d] said,

44'The Lord said to my Lord:
Sit by me at my right side,
until I put your enemies under your
control.'
Psalm 110:1

45David calls the Christ 'Lord,' so how can the Christ be his son?"

46None of the Pharisees could answer Jesus' question, and after that day no one was brave enough to ask him any more questions.

Jesus Accuses Some Leaders

23 Then Jesus said to the crowds and to his followers, 2"The teachers of the law and the Pharisees[d] have the authority to tell you what the law of Moses says. 3So you should obey and follow whatever they tell you, but their lives are not good examples for you to follow. They tell you to do things, but they themselves don't do them. 4They make strict rules and try to force people to obey them, but they are unwilling to help those who struggle under the weight of their rules.

5"They do good things so that other people will see them. They make the boxes[n] of Scriptures[d] that they wear bigger, and they make their special prayer clothes very long. 6Those Pharisees and teachers of the law love to have the most important seats at feasts and in the synagogues.[d] 7They love people to greet them with respect in the marketplaces, and they love to have people call them 'Teacher.'

Herodians A political group that followed Herod and his family.
coin A Roman denarius. One coin was the average pay for one day's work.
'I am . . . Jacob.' Quotation from Exodus 3:6.
'Love . . . mind.' Quotation from Deuteronomy 6:5.
'Love . . . yourself.' Quotation from Leviticus 19:18.
boxes Small leather boxes containing four important Scriptures. Some Jews tied these to the forehead and left arm, probably to show they were very religious.

8"But you must not be called 'Teacher,' because you have only one Teacher, and you are all
brothers and sisters together. 9And don't call any
person on earth 'Father,' because you have one
Father, who is in heaven. 10And you should not
be called 'Master,' because you have only one
Master, the Christ.[d] 11Whoever is your servant is
the greatest among you. 12Whoever makes himself great will be made humble. Whoever makes
himself humble will be made great.
13"How terrible for you, teachers of the law and
Pharisees! You are hypocrites![d] You close the door
for people to enter the kingdom of heaven. You
yourselves don't enter, and you stop others who
are trying to enter. 14 [n]
15"How terrible for you, teachers of the law and
Pharisees! You are hypocrites! You travel across
land and sea to find one person who will change
to your ways. When you find that person, you
make him more fit for hell than you are.
16"How terrible for you! You guide the people,
but you are blind. You say, 'If people swear by the
Temple[d] when they make a promise, that means
nothing. But if they swear by the gold that is in
the Temple, they must keep that promise.' 17You
are blind fools! Which is greater: the gold or the
Temple that makes that gold holy? 18And you say,
'If people swear by the altar when they make a
promise, that means nothing. But if they swear by
the gift on the altar, they must keep that promise.'
19You are blind! Which is greater: the gift or
the altar that makes the gift holy? 20The person
who swears by the altar is really using the altar
and also everything on the altar. 21And the person who swears by the Temple is really using
the Temple and also everything in the Temple.
22The person who swears by heaven is also using God's throne and the One who sits on that
throne.
23"How terrible for you, teachers of the law and
Pharisees! You are hypocrites! You give to God
one-tenth of everything you earn—even your

Verse 14 Some Greek copies add verse 14: "How terrible for you, teachers of the law and Pharisees. You are hypocrites. You take away widows' houses, and you say long prayers so that people will notice you. So you will have a worse punishment."

HYPOCRISY

Being an Example

Stuart Jacobs attended the same high school as David Springer. Stuart was a "brain." He got A's in all his courses except gym. He wore thick glasses, stuttered, and looked like an unmade bed. He had few friends. Stuart didn't fit in.

David heard about a game some guys had started to play at lunch at one of the school's doorways. A long, sloping ramp led to the door. David arrived and found Stuart chasing quarters down the ramp. The guys took turns rolling quarters. Stuart, who longed for acceptance from the guys, always chased the quarters. If he caught them before a certain crack in the ramp, he got to keep them. He didn't realize he was being laughed at.

"C'mon, David!" his friends called, "It's your turn to roll a quarter for Stuart."

David didn't know what to do. He didn't want to disappoint the guys, but he didn't want to hurt Stuart's feelings, either.

His pastor's words during a recent sermon came back to him, "You may be the only one through whom others see Christ."

"What am I going to do?" David wondered.

Jesus told his followers that their words needed to reflect their actions. Read how Jesus taught about the differences between real faith and fake faith in **Matthew 23:1–12**.

- If David followed his pastor's advice and Jesus' teachings, what did he do?
- Have you ever sensed your faith was just an act? How can you change?

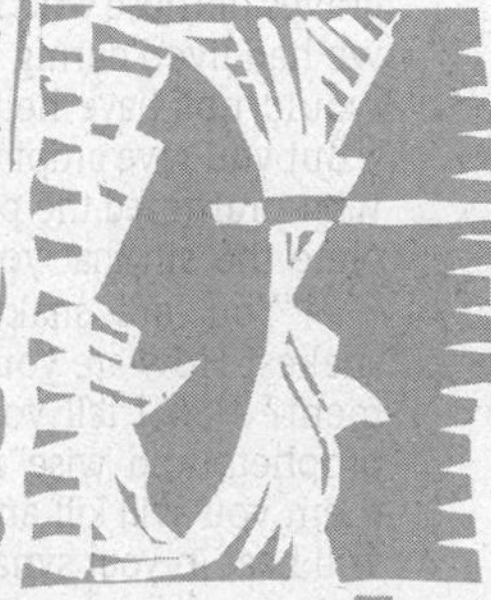

CONSIDER . . .

- writing a variety of conclusions to David's story based on Jesus' teachings in the passage.
- identifying one way you can "make yourself humble" this week, and do it.

FOR MORE, SEE . . .

- Leviticus 19:15–18 (p. 116)
- Mark 12:28–44 (p. 988)
- Luke 6:37–42 (p. 1013)

mint, dill, and cumin.[n] But you don't obey the really important teachings of the law—justice, mercy, and being loyal. These are the things you should do, as well as those other things. 24You guide the people, but you are blind! You are like a person who picks a fly out of a drink and then swallows a camel![n]

> **SIDELIGHT:** When Jesus criticized the Pharisees for picking flies out of their drinks (Matthew 23:24), he mentioned one of the five smallest items in the Bible. Others are fleas (1 Samuel 24:14, p. 267), ants (Proverbs 6:6, p. 572), tiny pen marks (Matthew 5:18, p. 912), and mustard seeds (Mark 4:31, p. 972).

25"How terrible for you, teachers of the law and Pharisees! You are hypocrites! You wash the outside of your cups and dishes, but inside they are full of things you got by cheating others and by pleasing only yourselves. 26Pharisees, you are blind! First make the inside of the cup clean, and then the outside of the cup can be truly clean.

27"How terrible for you, teachers of the law and Pharisees! You are hypocrites! You are like tombs that are painted white. Outside, those tombs look fine, but inside, they are full of the bones of dead people and all kinds of unclean things. 28It is the same with you. People look at you and think you are good, but on the inside you are full of hypocrisy and evil.

29"How terrible for you, teachers of the law and Pharisees! You are hypocrites! You build tombs for the prophets,[d] and you show honor to the graves of those who lived good lives. 30You say, 'If we had lived during the time of our ancestors, we would not have helped them kill the prophets.' 31But you give proof that you are children of those who murdered the prophets. 32And you will complete the sin that your ancestors started.

33"You are snakes! A family of poisonous snakes! How are you going to escape God's judgment? 34So I tell you this: I am sending to you prophets and wise men and teachers. Some of them you will kill and crucify. Some of them you will beat in your synagogues and chase from town to town. 35So you will be guilty for the death of all the good people who have been killed on earth—from the murder of that good man Abel to the murder of Zechariah[n] son of Berakiah, whom you murdered between the Temple and the altar. 36I tell you the truth, all of these things will happen to you people who are living now.

Jesus Feels Sorry for Jerusalem

37"Jerusalem, Jerusalem! You kill the prophets[d] and stone to death those who are sent to you. Many times I wanted to gather your people as a hen gathers her chicks under her wings, but you did not let me. 38Now your house will be left completely empty. 39I tell you, you will not see me again until that time when you will say, 'God bless the One who comes in the name of the Lord.' "[n]

The Temple Will Be Destroyed

24

As Jesus left the Temple[d] and was walking away, his followers came up to show him the Temple's buildings. 2Jesus asked, "Do you see all these buildings? I tell you the truth, not one stone will be left on another. Every stone will be thrown down to the ground."

3Later, as Jesus was sitting on the Mount of Olives,[d] his followers came to be alone with him. They said, "Tell us, when will these things happen? And what will be the sign that it is time for you to come again and for this age to end?"

4Jesus answered, "Be careful that no one fools you. 5Many will come in my name, saying, 'I am the Christ,'[d] and they will fool many people. 6You will hear about wars and stories of wars that are coming, but don't be afraid. These things must happen before the end comes. 7Nations will fight against other nations; kingdoms will fight against other kingdoms. There will be times when there is no food for people to eat, and there will be earthquakes in different places. 8These things are like the first pains when something new is about to be born.

9"Then people will arrest you, hand you over to be hurt, and kill you. They will hate you because you believe in me. 10At that time, many will lose their faith, and they will turn against each other and hate each other. 11Many false prophets[d] will come and cause many people to believe lies. 12There will be more and more evil in the world, so most people will stop showing their love for each other. 13But those people who keep their faith until the end will be saved. 14The Good News[d] about God's kingdom will be preached in all the world, to every nation. Then the end will come.

mint, dill, and cumin Small plants grown in gardens and used for spices. Only very religious people would be careful enough to give a tenth of these plants.
You . . . camel! Meaning, "You worry about the smallest mistakes but commit the biggest sin."
Abel . . . Zechariah In the order of the books of the Hebrew Old Testament, the first and last men to be murdered.
'God . . . Lord.' Quotation from Psalm 118:26.

15"Daniel the prophet spoke about 'the destroying terror.'[n] You will see this standing in the holy
place." (You who read this should understand
what it means.) 16"At that time, the people in Judea should run away to the mountains. 17If people
are on the roofs[n] of their houses, they must not
go down to get anything out of their houses. 18If
people are in the fields, they must not go back to
get their coats. 19At that time, how terrible it will
be for women who are pregnant or have nursing
babies! 20Pray that it will not be winter or a Sabbath[d] day when these things happen and you
have to run away, 21because at that time there
will be much trouble. There will be more trouble
than there has ever been since the beginning of
the world until now, and nothing as bad will ever
happen again. 22God has decided to make that terrible time short. Otherwise, no one would go on
living. But God will make that time short to help
the people he has chosen. 23At that time, someone might say to you, 'Look, there is the Christ!'
Or another person might say, 'There he is!'
But don't believe them. 24False Christs and false
prophets will come and perform great wonders
and miracles.[d] They will try to fool even the
people God has chosen, if that is possible.
25Now I have warned you about this before
it happens.

26"If people tell you, 'The Christ is in the
desert,' don't go there. If they say, 'The Christ is
in the inner room,' don't believe it. 27When the

'the destroying terror' Mentioned in Daniel 9:27; 12:11 (see also Daniel 11:31).

roof In Bible times houses were built with flat roofs. The roof was used for drying things such as flax and fruit. And it was used as an extra room, as a place for worship, and as a place to sleep in the summer.

LEADERSHIP

Leading a Just Cause

On November 1, 1872, Susan B. Anthony walked into a polling place, demanding to be registered to vote. She voted in the national election. Two weeks later a U.S. marshal arrested her for "voting without lawful right." The judge wouldn't allow a jury trial. Her sentence was to pay a $100 fine and the cost of the trial. "Your Honor," declared Anthony. "I shall never pay one dollar of your unjust penalty."

She never did.

Anthony was long-familiar with the controversy and conflict of reform movements. Years earlier, she had worked for the American Anti-Slavery Society. She regarded slavery as evil and un-Christian. She published the first women's newspaper and organized the first women's union. Now Anthony was at the front of the National Women's Suffrage Movement, working tirelessly for women's voting rights.

The work was often discouraging. The press mocked her. She was denied entry into meetings. She was attacked by angry mobs. But these persecutions didn't stop her. She lectured, lobbied Congress and organized petitions.

In 1920, Anthony's efforts helped to pass the Nineteenth Amendment to the U.S. Constitution, assuring everyone the right to vote regardless of gender. But Anthony never got the chance to vote under the new amendment. She had died fourteen years earlier.

Those who lead movements for justice usually suffer ridicule, persecution, and sometimes death. Read in **Matthew 23:34–39**, what Jesus thinks about those who persecute the prophets of God.

- Why do you think people fear and persecute leaders such as Susan B. Anthony and the ones Jesus describes?
- When has your unpopular stance caused you persecution?

CONSIDER...

- reading through one of the prophets of the Old Testament such as Amos (p. 842), trying to understand why his messages were ridiculed and rejected.
- listening to leaders who have differing opinions, keeping your mind open for truth—even if it's uncomfortable.

FOR MORE, SEE...

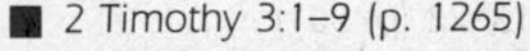

- Jeremiah 3:11–13 (p. 694)
- Ezekiel 20:13–20 (p. 776)
- 2 Timothy 3:1–9 (p. 1265)

Son of Man[d] comes, he will be seen by everyone,
like lightning flashing from the east to the west.
28Wherever the dead body is, there the vultures
will gather.

29"Soon after the trouble of those days,
'the sun will grow dark,
and the moon will not give its light.
The stars will fall from the sky.
And the powers of the heavens will be
shaken.' *Isaiah 13:10; 34:4*

30"At that time, the sign of the Son of Man will
appear in the sky. Then all the peoples of the
world will cry. They will see the Son of Man coming on clouds in the sky with great power and
glory. 31He will use a loud trumpet to send
his angels all around the earth, and they will
gather his chosen people from every part of the
world.

32"Learn a lesson from the fig tree: When its
branches become green and soft and new leaves
appear, you know summer is near. 33In the same
way, when you see all these things happening,
you will know that the time is near, ready to
come. 34I tell you the truth, all these things will
happen while the people of this time are still living. 35Earth and sky will be destroyed, but the
words I have said will never be destroyed.

When Will Jesus Come Again?

36"No one knows when that day or time will
be, not the angels in heaven, not even the Son.
Only the Father knows. 37When the Son of Man[d]
comes, it will be like what happened during
Noah's time. 38In those days before the flood, people were eating and drinking, marrying and giving
their children to be married, until the day Noah
entered the boat. 39They knew nothing about
what was happening until the flood came and destroyed them. It will be the same when the Son
of Man comes. 40Two men will be in the field.
One will be taken, and the other will be left.
41Two women will be grinding grain with a

FUTURE

The Rock

In San Francisco Bay an abandoned penitentiary sits on Alcatraz Island. For years it served as a prison for hardened criminals. Its prisoners called it "The Rock."

Whitey Thompson was a "solid con." He grew up in an abusive home. He ran away. Whitey seemed to have no future.

After a failed bank robbery, Whitey was sent to jail, where he fought with guards and other prisoners. Being sent to "The Rock" seemed logical. It was end of the line for those considered hopeless criminals.

Ironically, Whitey's life turned around at Alcatraz. Whitey began to think about his future, which led him to find hope in Jesus.

Instead of killing time, he learned new skills, including painting. He painted beautiful landscapes. Guards, prisoners, and visitors admired his art.

Whitey was released directly from Alcatraz to the streets. It wasn't easy to keep looking toward the future and to build a new life. But Whitey finds strength in Jesus.

Now Whitey returns to Alcatraz as a guest of the National Park Service, which runs the former prison as a tourist attraction. His eyes twinkle when tourists ask how he survived. "Here I was on The Rock," he says. "Now I've found the true Rock."

The future lies in Jesus. In **Matthew 24:36–44**, read Jesus' promises to return. This promise not only gives hope for the future, but also a reason for living today, as Whitey discovered.

- What did Whitey discover in Jesus to help him find hope for his future?
- How does knowing Christ will return affect your view of your future?

CONSIDER . . .

- making a list of the things you want to achieve. Keep the scripture in mind. If Jesus came tomorrow would you be ready?
- telling a cynical friend about the hope for the future you have in Jesus.

FOR MORE, SEE . . .

- Psalm 33:13–22 (p. 501)
- Luke 12:35–40 (p. 1028)
- 1 Thessalonians 5:1–11 (p. 1248)

mill.[n] One will be taken, and the other will be
left.

42"So always be ready, because you don't know
the day your Lord will come. 43Remember this: If
the owner of the house knew what time of night
a thief was coming, the owner would watch and
not let the thief break in. 44So you also must be
ready, because the Son of Man will come at a time
you don't expect him.

45"Who is the wise and loyal servant that the
master trusts to give the other servants their food
at the right time? 46When the master comes and
finds the servant doing his work, the servant will
be blessed. 47I tell you the truth, the master will
choose that servant to take care of everything he
owns. 48But suppose that evil servant thinks to
himself, 'My master will not come back soon,'
49and he begins to beat the other servants and eat
and get drunk with others like him? 50The master
will come when that servant is not ready and is
not expecting him. 51Then the master will cut
him in pieces and send him away to be with the
hypocrites,[d] where people will cry and grind their
teeth with pain.

A Story About Ten Bridesmaids

25 "At that time the kingdom of heaven will
be like ten bridesmaids who took their
lamps and went to wait for the bridegroom. 2Five
of them were foolish and five were wise. 3The five
foolish bridesmaids took their lamps, but they did
not take more oil for the lamps to burn. 4The wise

mill Two large, round, flat rocks used for grinding grain to make flour.

DECISION MAKING

Always Be Ready

Kent Andrews was discouraged as he drove to work. He could hear Mom's words from a few months ago echo in his mind. "Kent, you must get your act together," she'd said. "It's your senior year and time is running out. You need to decide about college. Don't you want to go?"

What a worry wart, he had thought at the time. Of course he wanted to go to college. His grades were okay. He just needed to decide where to go. Weren't they all the same? Kent was sick of school anyway, and wanted to have fun with his friends in his senior year.

Kent hadn't counted on the state standardized test. The state allowed students to graduate only if they passed the basic skills test. Fairly easy stuff—if you were ready. But it had seemed a better idea to Kent to party than to study.

Kent had failed the test. He had missed the admissions deadlines for most colleges anyway, and most of the financial aid had already been doled out.

So, instead of receiving his diploma with his friends, Kent had watched graduation from the bleachers in the school gym. Instead of packing for college in the fall like his friends, he was sacking groceries at a local supermarket.

As Kent tied his apron for work, he thought about his friends in college. He realized it was his own fault he wasn't there with them. Next year, Kent vowed, I'll be ready.

Jesus told a story about poor preparation and poor decisions. Read it in **Matthew 25:1–13**.

- How are the stories of Kent and the ten girls similar? How did poor decision making play a role in both stories?
- When have you had to live with the consequences of a poor decision similar to that of the ten girls in Jesus' story? How would better decisions have helped you?

CONSIDER. . .

- dividing a piece of paper in half. On the left side list things about which you have made poor decisions in the past. On the right side write one thing you could do in each instance to make a better choice next time.
- asking a parent to tell about a tough decision he or she has made and what happened as a result of the choice.

FOR MORE, SEE. . .

- Proverbs 8:10 (p. 573)
- Luke 12:35–48 (p. 1028)
- John 7:16–18 (p. 1069)

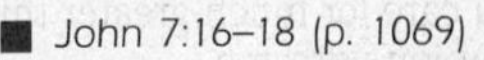

bridesmaids took their lamps and more oil in jars.
5Because the bridegroom was late, they became
sleepy and went to sleep.
6"At midnight someone cried out, 'The bridegroom is coming! Come and meet him!' 7Then all
the bridesmaids woke up and got their lamps
ready. 8But the foolish ones said to the wise, 'Give
us some of your oil, because our lamps are going
out.' 9The wise bridesmaids answered, 'No, the
oil we have might not be enough for all of us. Go
to the people who sell oil and buy some for yourselves.'
10"So while the five foolish bridesmaids went to
buy oil, the bridegroom came. The bridesmaids
who were ready went in with the bridegroom to
the wedding feast. Then the door was closed and
locked.
11"Later the others came back and said, 'Sir, sir,
open the door to let us in.' 12But the bridegroom
answered, 'I tell you the truth, I don't want to
know you.'
13"So always be ready, because you don't know
the day or the hour the Son of Man[d] will come.

A Story About Three Servants

14"The kingdom of heaven is like a man who
was going to another place for a visit. Before he
left, he called for his servants and told them to
take care of his things while he was gone. 15He
gave one servant five bags of gold, another servant
two bags of gold, and a third servant one bag of
gold, to each one as much as he could handle.
Then he left. 16The servant who got five bags
went quickly to invest the money and earned five
more bags. 17In the same way, the servant who
had two bags invested them and earned two
more. 18But the servant who got one bag went out
and dug a hole in the ground and hid the master's
money.
19"After a long time the master came home and
asked the servants what they did with his money.
20The servant who was given five bags of gold
brought five more bags to the master and said,
'Master, you trusted me to care for five bags of
gold, so I used your five bags to earn five more.'
21The master answered, 'You did well. You are a
good and loyal servant. Because you were loyal
with small things, I will let you care for much
greater things. Come and share my joy with me.'
22"Then the servant who had been given two
bags of gold came to the master and said, 'Master,
you gave me two bags of gold to care for, so I used
your two bags to earn two more.' 23The master
answered, 'You did well. You are a good and loyal
servant. Because you were loyal with small
things, I will let you care for much greater things.
Come and share my joy with me.'
24"Then the servant who had been given one
bag of gold came to the master and said, 'Master,
I knew that you were a hard man. You harvest
things you did not plant. You gather crops where
you did not sow any seed. 25So I was afraid and
went and hid your money in the ground. Here is
your bag of gold.' 26The master answered, 'You
are a wicked and lazy servant! You say you knew
that I harvest things I did not plant and that I
gather crops where I did not sow any seed. 27So
you should have put my gold in the bank. Then,
when I came home, I would have received my
gold back with interest.'
28"So the master told his other servants, 'Take
the bag of gold from that servant and give it to the
servant who has ten bags of gold. 29Those who
have much will get more, and they will have
much more than they need. But those who do not
have much will have everything taken away from
them.' 30Then the master said, 'Throw that useless servant outside, into the darkness where people will cry and grind their teeth with pain.'

The King Will Judge All People

31"The Son of Man[d] will come again in his great
glory, with all his angels. He will be King and sit
on his great throne. 32All the nations of the world
will be gathered before him, and he will separate
them into two groups as a shepherd separates the
sheep from the goats. 33The Son of Man will put
the sheep on his right and the goats on his left.
34"Then the King will say to the people on his
right, 'Come, my Father has given you his blessing. Receive the kingdom God has prepared for
you since the world was made. 35I was hungry,
and you gave me food. I was thirsty, and you gave
me something to drink. I was alone and away
from home, and you invited me into your house.
36I was without clothes, and you gave me something to wear. I was sick, and you cared for me.
I was in prison, and you visited me.'
37"Then the good people will answer, 'Lord,
when did we see you hungry and give you food,
or thirsty and give you something to drink?
38When did we see you alone and away from
home and invite you into our house? When did
we see you without clothes and give you something to wear? 39When did we see you sick or in
prison and care for you?'
40"Then the King will answer, 'I tell you the
truth, anything you did for even the least of my
people here, you also did for me.'
41"Then the King will say to those on his left,
'Go away from me. You will be punished. Go into
the fire that burns forever that was prepared
for the devil and his angels. 42I was hungry, and
you gave me nothing to eat. I was thirsty,
and you gave me nothing to drink. 43I was alone
and away from home, and you did not invite
me into your house. I was without clothes, and

you gave me nothing to wear. I was sick and in prison, and you did not care for me.'
44"Then those people will answer, 'Lord, when
did we see you hungry or thirsty or alone and
away from home or without clothes or sick or in
prison? When did we see these things and not
help you?'
45"Then the King will answer, 'I tell you the
truth, anything you refused to do for even the
least of my people here, you refused to do for me.'
46"These people will go off to be punished forever, but the good people will go to live forever."

The Plan to Kill Jesus

26 After Jesus finished saying all these
things, he told his followers, 2"You
know that the day after tomorrow is the day of the
Passover[d] Feast. On that day the Son of Man[d] will
be given to his enemies to be crucified."
3Then the leading priests and the older Jewish
leaders had a meeting at the palace of the high
priest, named Caiaphas. 4At the meeting, they
planned to set a trap to arrest Jesus and kill him.
5But they said, "We must not do it during the
feast, because the people might cause a riot."

Perfume for Jesus' Burial

6Jesus was in Bethany at the house of Simon,
who had a skin disease. 7While Jesus was there,
a woman approached him with an alabaster[d] jar
filled with expensive perfume. She poured this
perfume on Jesus' head while he was eating.

SERVICE

Are You Jesus?

Eric Schwartz dressed in army surplus fatigues and roared through the city on his motorcycle. He wore his hair long and his beard full, which made him look older than his eighteen years. Eric was proud of his tough image—it was his "style."

Because of his tough image, it was no surprise when he was arrested for shoplifting. Since Eric was a first-time offender, the judge sentenced him to several hours of community service instead of jail.

Eric chose to "do his time" at The Shepherd's Table, a soup kitchen for the homeless. He peeled potatoes, served food, and mopped floors. The sights, sounds, and smells depressed him. It was a place for the poor, broken, lonely, and afraid—people who reminded him a lot of himself.

Eric began to talk with the people. He had expected to find just a bunch of drunken bums, but, instead, he met a surprising variety of people caught in the poverty trap.

There was a Vietnam War veteran who worked, but never had money at month's end. An older woman had lost her home after her husband had died. A young mother with three small children lived in one room. A family who had lost a farm struggled to find work in the city. The stories broke his heart.

He didn't feel so "tough" after a while. In fact, he began to enjoy how he felt when he served others. One evening after supper, he was wiping tables when he felt a tug at his camouflage pants. A young girl looked up to him.

"Mister," whispered the child. "Are you Jesus?"

The question startled him. "Huh?" he asked, confused.

"You must be Jesus," she insisted. "Momma told me Jesus loves poor people like us."

When Eric shared the story with the soup kitchen manager, she showed him **Matthew 25:31–46**. "That's why we're here," she said.

- What did serving teach Eric about being Jesus' follower?
- When have you seen someone as Jesus describes: hungry, thirsty, sick, without warm clothes, alone, or imprisoned? What was your reaction?

CONSIDER . . .

- listing all the people with whom you come in contact in a typical day. Decide something you can do to serve those people.
- thinking of Jesus each time you see someone in need. How do your thoughts affect your attitude toward that person?

FOR MORE, SEE . . .

- Lamentations 3:26–27 (p. 757)
- Luke 10:25–37 (p. 1022)
- John 13:1–17 (p. 1080)

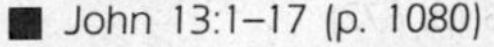

[8]His followers were upset when they saw
the woman do this. They asked, "Why waste
that perfume? [9]It could have been sold for a
great deal of money and the money given to
the poor."

[10]Knowing what had happened, Jesus said,
"Why are you troubling this woman? She did an
excellent thing for me. [11]You will always have
the poor with you, but you will not always
have me. [12]This woman poured perfume on
my body to prepare me for burial. [13]I tell you
the truth, wherever the Good News[d] is
preached in all the world, what this woman has
done will be told, and people will remember
her."

Judas Becomes an Enemy of Jesus

[14]Then one of the twelve apostles, Judas Iscar-
iot, went to talk to the leading priests. [15]He said,
"What will you pay me for giving Jesus to you?"
And they gave him thirty silver coins. [16]After that,
Judas watched for the best time to turn Jesus in.

Jesus Eats the Passover Meal

[17]On the first day of the Feast[d] of Unleavened
Bread, the followers came to Jesus. They said,
"Where do you want us to prepare for you to eat
the Passover[d] meal?"

[18]Jesus answered, "Go into the city to a certain
man and tell him, 'The Teacher says: The chosen

FRIENDS

Diary of a Backstabber

November 1: I knew something was wrong when I came out from work and saw Drew. He should have been at basketball practice. "I need to talk to you," he said, and my stomach tightened. "Lisa, I hate to do this, but there's no good way to break up. . ."

He droned on, but I didn't hear anything past the "break up" part. "And I want to still be friends," he said. FRIENDS! He dumps me and still wants to be friends!

November 30: I can't stand seeing Drew at school. And now he's hanging around the mall with his skateboarding friends.

December 6: Tonight I saw some workers dismantling a Winter Wonderland display at the mall lobby. When I got to the store, I asked my manager what happened.

"It was skateboarders," she said. "A bunch of 'em sneaked in after hours and trashed the whole thing. They rode their skateboards all over, using the fake snowdrifts as ramps."

December 11: During prayer requests at youth group, I spoke up. "I think we should pray for Drew, since the incident at the mall with the skateboarders and all."

December 13: The rumors about Drew spread to school. Then in fifth hour, he was called out of class. After school let out, I ran into him. He didn't look good.

"Are you okay?" I asked, surprised that I felt so concerned.

"Yeah, I guess so," Drew answered. "Have you heard what everyone's saying about me, Lisa?"

"Uh, yeah," I stammered, not looking him in the eye.

"It wasn't us!" he says. "Sure, we hang around the mall some, but we'd never do something like that. I can't imagine who'd think we had. You don't know who turned in our names, do you?"

"No, Drew I don't," I said. Because she felt hurt, Lisa betrayed Drew and got him into a lot of trouble. We don't know Judas's motives for betraying Jesus, but we do know what happened. Read about it in **Matthew 26:14–25**.

- What feelings might Lisa and Judas have experienced as each betrayed a friend?
- If you had been in the room with Jesus and the disciples, what would you have said or done?

CONSIDER

- making a commitment not to betray your friends by spreading rumors or gossip about them.
- forgiving a friend who has betrayed you. Try to settle your differences.

FOR MORE, SEE . . .

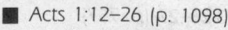

- Isaiah 53:4–6 (p. 672)
- Mark 14:10–21 (p. 991)
- Acts 1:12–26 (p. 1098)

time is near. I will have the Passover with my followers at your house.' " 19The followers did what Jesus told them to do, and they prepared the Passover meal.

20In the evening Jesus was sitting at the table with his twelve followers. 21As they were eating, Jesus said, "I tell you the truth, one of you will turn against me."

22This made the followers very sad. Each one began to say to Jesus, "Surely, Lord, I am not the one who will turn against you, am I?"

23Jesus answered, "The man who has dipped his hand with me into the bowl is the one who will turn against me. 24The Son of Man[d] will die, just as the Scriptures[d] say. But how terrible it will be for the person who hands the Son of Man over to be killed. It would be better for him if he had never been born."

25Then Judas, who would give Jesus to his enemies, said to Jesus, "Teacher, surely I am not the one, am I?"

Jesus answered, "Yes, it is you."

The Lord's Supper

26While they were eating, Jesus took some bread and thanked God for it and broke it. Then he gave it to his followers and said, "Take this bread and eat it; this is my body."

27Then Jesus took a cup and thanked God for it and gave it to the followers. He said, "Every one of you drink this. 28This is my blood which is the new agreement that God makes with his people. This blood is poured out for many to forgive their sins. 29I tell you this: I will not drink of this fruit of the vine[n] again until that day when I drink it new with you in my Father's kingdom."

30After singing a hymn, they went out to the Mount of Olives.[d]

Jesus' Followers Will Leave Him

31Jesus told his followers, "Tonight you will all stumble in your faith on account of me, because it is written in the Scriptures:[d]

'I will kill the shepherd,
and the sheep will scatter.' *Zechariah 13:7*

32But after I rise from the dead, I will go ahead of you into Galilee."

33Peter said, "Everyone else may stumble in their faith because of you, but I will not."

34Jesus said, "I tell you the truth, tonight before the rooster crows you will say three times that you don't know me."

35But Peter said, "I will never say that I don't know you! I will even die with you!" And all the other followers said the same thing.

Jesus Prays Alone

36Then Jesus went with his followers to a place called Gethsemane. He said to them, "Sit here while I go over there and pray." 37He took Peter and the two sons of Zebedee with him, and he began to be very sad and troubled. 38He said to them, "My heart is full of sorrow, to the point of death. Stay here and watch with me."

39After walking a little farther away from them, Jesus fell to the ground and prayed, "My Father, if it is possible, do not give me this cup[n] of suffering. But do what you want, not what I want." 40Then Jesus went back to his followers and found them asleep. He said to Peter, "You men could not stay awake with me for one hour? 41Stay awake and pray for strength against temptation. The spirit wants to do what is right, but the body is weak."

42Then Jesus went away a second time and prayed, "My Father, if it is not possible for this painful thing to be taken from me, and if I must do it, I pray that what you want will be done."

43Then he went back to his followers, and again he found them asleep, because their eyes were heavy. 44So Jesus left them and went away and prayed a third time, saying the same thing.

45Then Jesus went back to his followers and said, "Are you still sleeping and resting? The time has come for the Son of Man[d] to be handed over to sinful people. 46Get up, we must go. Look, here comes the man who has turned against me."

Jesus Is Arrested

47While Jesus was still speaking, Judas, one of the twelve apostles,[d] came up. With him were many people carrying swords and clubs who had been sent from the leading priests and the older Jewish leaders of the people. 48Judas had planned to give them a signal, saying, "The man I kiss is Jesus. Arrest him." 49At once Judas went to Jesus and said, "Greetings, Teacher!" and kissed him.

50Jesus answered, "Friend, do what you came to do."

Then the people came and grabbed Jesus and arrested him. 51When that happened, one of Jesus' followers reached for his sword and pulled it out. He struck the servant of the high priest and cut off his ear.

52Jesus said to the man, "Put your sword back in its place. All who use swords will be killed with swords. 53Surely you know I could ask my Father, and he would give me more than twelve armies of angels. 54But it must happen this way to bring about what the Scriptures[d] say."

fruit of the vine Product of the grapevine; this may also be translated "wine."
cup Jesus is talking about the terrible things that will happen to him. Accepting these things will be very hard, like drinking a cup of something bitter.

55Then Jesus said to the crowd, "You came to get me with swords and clubs as if I were a criminal. Every day I sat in the Temple[d] teaching, and you did not arrest me there. 56But all these things have happened so that it will come about as the prophets[d] wrote." Then all of Jesus' followers left him and ran away.

Jesus Before the Leaders

57Those people who arrested Jesus led him to the house of Caiaphas, the high priest, where the teachers of the law and the older Jewish leaders were gathered. 58Peter followed far behind to the courtyard of the high priest's house, and he sat down with the guards to see what would happen to Jesus.

59The leading priests and the whole Jewish council tried to find something false against Jesus so they could kill him. 60Many people came and told lies about him, but the council could find no real reason to kill him. Then two people came and said, 61"This man said, 'I can destroy the Temple[d] of God and build it again in three days.' "

62Then the high priest stood up and said to Jesus, "Aren't you going to answer? Don't you have something to say about their charges against you?" 63But Jesus said nothing.

SIDELIGHT: Practically every legal rule was broken to convict Jesus (Matthew 26:57–67). Jewish law prohibited trials at night, during Passover, and without legitimate witnesses—all of which happened in Jesus' trial. Any good judge would declare a mistrial today.

Again the high priest said to Jesus, "I command you by the power of the living God: Tell us if you are the Christ,[d] the Son of God."

64Jesus answered, "Those are your words. But I tell you, in the future you will see the Son of Man[d] sitting at the right hand of God, the Powerful One, and coming on clouds in the sky."

65When the high priest heard this, he tore his clothes and said, "This man has said things that are against God! We don't need any more witnesses; you all heard him say these things against God. 66What do you think?"

The people answered, "He should die."

67Then the people there spat in Jesus' face and beat him with their fists. Others slapped him. 68They said, "Prove to us that you are a prophet,[d] you Christ! Tell us who hit you!"

Peter Says He Doesn't Know Jesus

69At that time, as Peter was sitting in the courtyard, a servant girl came to him and said, "You also were with Jesus of Galilee."

70But Peter said to all the people there that he was never with Jesus. He said, "I don't know what you are talking about."

71When he left the courtyard and was at the gate, another girl saw him. She said to the people there, "This man was with Jesus of Nazareth."

72Again, Peter said he was never with him, saying, "I swear I don't know this man Jesus!"

73A short time later, some people standing there went to Peter and said, "Surely you are one of those who followed Jesus. The way you talk shows it."

74Then Peter began to place a curse on himself and swear, "I don't know the man." At once, a rooster crowed. 75And Peter remembered what Jesus had told him: "Before the rooster crows, you will say three times that you don't know me." Then Peter went outside and cried painfully.

Jesus Is Taken to Pilate

27 Early the next morning, all the leading priests and older leaders of the people decided that Jesus should die. 2They tied him, led him away, and turned him over to Pilate, the governor.

Judas Kills Himself

3Judas, the one who had given Jesus to his enemies, saw that they had decided to kill Jesus. Then he was very sorry for what he had done. So he took the thirty silver coins back to the priests and the leaders, 4saying, "I sinned; I handed over to you an innocent man."

The leaders answered, "What is that to us? That's your problem, not ours."

5So Judas threw the money into the Temple.[d] Then he went off and hanged himself.

6The leading priests picked up the silver coins in the Temple and said, "Our law does not allow us to keep this money with the Temple money, because it has paid for a man's death." 7So they decided to use the coins to buy Potter's Field as a place to bury strangers who died in Jerusalem. 8That is why that field is still called the Field of Blood. 9So what Jeremiah the prophet[d] had said came true: "They took thirty silver coins. That is how little the Israelites thought he was worth. 10They used those thirty silver coins to buy the potter's field, as the Lord commanded me."[n]

Pilate Questions Jesus

11Jesus stood before Pilate the governor, and

"They . . . commanded me." See Zechariah 11:12-13 and Jeremiah 32:6-9.

Pilate asked him, "Are you the king of the Jews?"

Jesus answered, "Those are your words."

12When the leading priests and the older leaders accused Jesus, he said nothing.

13So Pilate said to Jesus, "Don't you hear them accusing you of all these things?"

14But Jesus said nothing in answer to Pilate, and Pilate was very surprised at this.

Pilate Tries to Free Jesus

15Every year at the time of Passover[d] the governor would free one prisoner whom the people chose. 16At that time there was a man in prison, named Barabbas, who was known to be very bad. 17When the people gathered at Pilate's house, Pilate said, "Whom do you want me to set free: Barabbas or Jesus who is called the Christ?"[d] 18Pilate knew that the people turned Jesus in to him because they were jealous.

19While Pilate was sitting there on the judge's seat, his wife sent this message to him: "Don't do anything to that man, because he is innocent. Today I had a dream about him, and it troubled me very much."

20But the leading priests and older leaders convinced the crowd to ask for Barabbas to be freed and for Jesus to be killed.

21Pilate said, "I have Barabbas and Jesus. Which do you want me to set free for you?"

The people answered, "Barabbas."

22Pilate asked, "So what should I do with Jesus, the one called the Christ?"

They all answered, "Crucify him!"

23Pilate asked, "Why? What wrong has he done?"

But they shouted louder, "Crucify him!"

24When Pilate saw that he could do nothing about this and that a riot was starting, he took some water and washed his hands[n] in front of the crowd. Then he said, "I am not guilty of this man's death. You are the ones who are causing it!"

25All the people answered, "We and our children will be responsible for his death."

26Then he set Barabbas free. But Jesus was beaten with whips and handed over to the soldiers to be crucified.

27The governor's soldiers took Jesus into the governor's palace, and they all gathered around him. 28They took off his clothes and put a red robe on him. 29Using thorny branches, they made a crown, put it on his head, and put a stick in his right hand. Then the soldiers bowed before Jesus and made fun of him, saying, "Hail, King of the Jews!" 30They spat on Jesus. Then they took his stick and began to beat him on the head. 31After they finished, the soldiers took off the robe and put his own clothes on him again. Then they led him away to be crucified.

Jesus Is Crucified

32As the soldiers were going out of the city with Jesus, they forced a man from Cyrene, named Simon, to carry the cross for Jesus. 33They all came to the place called Golgotha, which means the Place of the Skull. 34The soldiers gave Jesus wine mixed with gall[n] to drink. He tasted the wine but refused to drink it. 35When the soldiers had crucified him, they threw lots[d] to decide who would get his clothes. 36The soldiers sat there and continued watching him. 37They put a sign above Jesus' head with a charge against him. It said: THIS IS JESUS, THE KING OF THE JEWS. 38Two robbers were crucified beside Jesus, one on the right and the other on the left. 39People walked by and insulted Jesus and shook their heads, 40saying, "You said you could destroy the Temple[d] and build it again in three days. So save yourself! Come down from that cross if you are really the Son of God!"

41The leading priests, the teachers of the law, and the older Jewish leaders were also making fun of Jesus. 42They said, "He saved others, but he can't save himself! He says he is the king of Israel! If he is the king, let him come down now from the cross. Then we will believe in him. 43He trusts in God, so let God save him now, if God really wants him. He himself said, 'I am the Son of God.' " 44And in the same way, the robbers who were being crucified beside Jesus also insulted him.

Jesus Dies

45At noon the whole country became dark, and the darkness lasted for three hours. 46About three o'clock Jesus cried out in a loud voice, "Eli, Eli, lama sabachthani?" This means, "My God, my God, why have you rejected me?"

47Some of the people standing there who heard this said, "He is calling Elijah."

48Quickly one of them ran and got a sponge and filled it with vinegar and tied it to a stick and gave it to Jesus to drink. 49But the others said, "Don't bother him. We want to see if Elijah will come to save him."

50But Jesus cried out again in a loud voice and died.

51Then the curtain in the Temple[n] was torn into two pieces, from the top to the bottom. Also, the earth shook and rocks broke apart. 52The

washed his hands He did this as a sign to show that he wanted no part in what the people did.
gall Probably a drink of wine mixed with drugs to help a person feel less pain.
curtain in the Temple A curtain divided the Most Holy Place from the other part of the Temple. That was the special building in Jerusalem where God commanded the Jewish people to worship him.

graves opened, and many of God's people who
had died were raised from the dead. 53They came
out of the graves after Jesus was raised from the
dead and went into the holy city, where they appeared to many people.

54When the army officer and the soldiers guarding Jesus saw this earthquake and everything else
that happened, they were very frightened and
said, "He really was the Son of God!"

55Many women who had followed Jesus from
Galilee to help him were standing at a distance
from the cross, watching. 56Mary Magdalene, and
Mary the mother of James and Joseph, and the
mother of James and John were there.

Jesus Is Buried

57That evening a rich man named Joseph, a follower of Jesus from the town of Arimathea, came
to Jerusalem. 58Joseph went to Pilate and asked to
have Jesus' body. So Pilate gave orders for the soldiers to give it to Joseph. 59Then Joseph took the
body and wrapped it in a clean linen cloth. 60He
put Jesus' body in a new tomb that he had cut out
of a wall of rock, and he rolled a very large stone
to block the entrance of the tomb. Then Joseph
went away. 61Mary Magdalene and the other
woman named Mary were sitting near the tomb.

The Tomb of Jesus Is Guarded

62The next day, the day after Preparation[d] Day,
the leading priests and the Pharisees[d] went to Pilate. 63They said, "Sir, we remember that while
that liar was still alive he said, 'After three days
I will rise from the dead.' 64So give the order for
the tomb to be guarded closely till the third day.
Otherwise, his followers might come and steal the
body and tell people that he has risen from the
dead. That lie would be even worse than the first
one."

65Pilate said, "Take some soldiers and go guard
the tomb the best way you know." 66So they all
went to the tomb and made it safe from thieves

SADNESS

Does Anybody Care?

"Louise!" Mom yelled. "Joyce is on the phone!" Joyce Berg was Louise Stone's best friend. They were inseparable.

Joyce's voice was soft when Louise picked up the phone. It didn't sound like her.

"Louise, my dad died," Joyce said.

Silence.

Louise's mind raced. She knew he had been sick. But Joyce and Louise were only sixteen. Parents don't die now!

"What can I do?" Louise asked.

"Can you come over?" Joyce replied.

Louise went. The sadness was overwhelming. Joyce was quiet. Her mom cried a lot. Her brother stayed in his room. Louise babysat, answered phones, collected casseroles from visitors. She went to the funeral and hugged Joyce a lot.

Back home Mom and Louise talked. "I couldn't do anything," Louise said as she wept. "It was awful. I couldn't take away her sadness. I didn't know how to tell her I cared."

For several weeks both Joyce and Louise remained sad. Although they knew this was temporary, they didn't realize that the death of Joyce's dad would leave them vulnerable to sad feelings for months, even years. There was no way to avoid their grief; it was just something to go through.

Sadness and grief are normal feelings when someone close to you dies. After Jesus was crucified, his friends were terribly sad. Read what they did in **Matthew 27:57–61**.

- What feelings seem common to Jesus' friends and Louise?
- What ways might this the passage suggest for helping hurting friends?

CONSIDER . . .

- making a list of your hurting friends. Carry it with you. It will remind you to reach out to those friends, especially after the immediate crisis has passed.
- memorizing Romans 8:38–39, p. 1153. Use it to strengthen you in sad times.

FOR MORE, SEE . . .

- Ecclesiastes 7:2–4 (p. 603)
- Luke 23:44–56 (p. 1053)
- John 11:28–44 (p. 1077)

by sealing the stone in the entrance and putting soldiers there to guard it.

Jesus Rises from the Dead

28 The day after the Sabbath[d] day was the
first day of the week. At dawn on the
first day, Mary Magdalene and another woman
named Mary went to look at the tomb.
2At that time there was a strong earthquake. An
angel of the Lord came down from heaven, went
to the tomb, and rolled the stone away from the
entrance. Then he sat on the stone. 3He was shining as bright as lightning, and his clothes were
white as snow. 4The soldiers guarding the tomb
shook with fear because of the angel, and they
became like dead men.
5The angel said to the women, "Don't be
afraid. I know that you are looking for Jesus, who
has been crucified. 6He is not here. He has risen
from the dead as he said he would. Come and see
the place where his body was. 7And go quickly
and tell his followers, 'Jesus has risen from the
dead. He is going into Galilee ahead of you, and
you will see him there.'" Then the angel said,
"Now I have told you."

> **SIDELIGHT:** The stones in front of tombs in Jesus' day were large, disk-shaped boulders (Matthew 28:2). They were placed in grooves so that they would roll down and block the entrance to the cave-like tombs, making them difficult to move.

8The women left the tomb quickly. They were
afraid, but they were also very happy. They ran to
tell Jesus' followers what had happened. 9Sud-
denly, Jesus met them and said, "Greetings." The

FOLLOWING GOD

Not Me, Lord!

"How do I know what God wants me to do?" Beth Berger asked her pastor. Beth was a college junior struggling with her future. She was home on Christmas break, looking for a summer job.

"Obviously, you want to follow God," Pastor Jones said. "Try listening. You'll be surprised at what you hear."

"I don't want to be a pastor!" Beth shot back. "I'm not sure I feel called to do that."

"You don't have to be in full-time ministry to follow God," he said quietly. "Following God takes different paths. Why not explore other possibilities?"

Beth stayed open to God's calling. She was offered a position for the summer at a church camp. She accepted. She worked with children, led Bible studies, planned and led worship and music, cared for animals and camped outdoors. She listened for God and learned what it meant to be a follower.

She returned to college energized for her senior year. "I discovered I'm good at things like teaching. I even like Bible studies," she wrote to Pastor Jones. "I still don't know what I'll do. But I'll keep finding ways to follow God."

Beth learned that following God may at first seem scary. But after the initial "Yes, send me," serving God brings adventure, growth and true joy. Read **Matthew 28:16–20** to find Jesus' commission and promise for those who agree to follow him.

- What did Beth learn about following God? How is this similar to Jesus' command?
- How do you follow God? How do you seek to make others followers of God?

CONSIDER . . .

- writing a scenario in which you befriend people who have never heard about Jesus. How will you teach them about faith?
- listing the ways the careers you're interested in could minister and spread God's kingdom.

FOR MORE, SEE . . .

- Exodus 3 (p. 60)
- John 21 (p. 1094)
- Acts 1:7–11 (p. 1098)

women came up to him, took hold of his feet, and
worshiped him. [10]Then Jesus said to them, "Don't
be afraid. Go and tell my followers to go on to
Galilee, and they will see me there."

The Soldiers Report to the Leaders

[11]While the women went to tell Jesus' followers, some of the soldiers who had been guarding
the tomb went into the city to tell the leading
priests everything that had happened. [12]Then the
priests met with the older Jewish leaders and
made a plan. They paid the soldiers a large
amount of money [13]and said to them, "Tell the
people that Jesus' followers came during the night
and stole the body while you were asleep. [14]If the
governor hears about this, we will satisfy him and
save you from trouble." [15]So the soldiers kept the
money and did as they were told. And that story
is still spread among the Jewish people even today.

Jesus Talks to His Followers

[16]The eleven followers went to Galilee to the
mountain where Jesus had told them to go. [17]On
the mountain they saw Jesus and worshiped him,
but some of them did not believe it was really
Jesus. [18]Then Jesus came to them and said, "All
power in heaven and on earth is given to me. [19]So
go and make followers of all people in the world.
Baptize them in the name of the Father and the
Son and the Holy Spirit.[d] [20]Teach them to obey
everything that I have taught you, and I will
be with you always, even until the end of this
age."

MARK

Why Read This Book:

- Learn about the healings and miracles Jesus performed (Mark 2—8).
- Listen to Jesus' teachings about following him (Mark 9—12).
- See how Jesus was victorious even though people killed him (Mark 14—16).

Behind the Scenes:

The Gospel of Mark is a lot like an evening newscast. It's filled with short, quick "news bites" about Jesus' life. It moves quickly from scene to scene, and is filled with action and drama.

Unlike a newsmagazine, it doesn't linger on any scene. Instead, it cuts quickly from one scene to the next. So Mark is packed with simple, vivid stories. The Greek word translated "immediately" or "then" appears more than forty times in just sixteen chapters!

The book begins with a short segment on John the Baptist, who announced Jesus' coming. Then it tells about Jesus' miracles and activities in the region of Lake Galilee. Finally, the action moves to Jerusalem, where Jesus was arrested and killed. Then he rose from the grave.

Unlike the other three Gospels, this book appears to be addressed to people

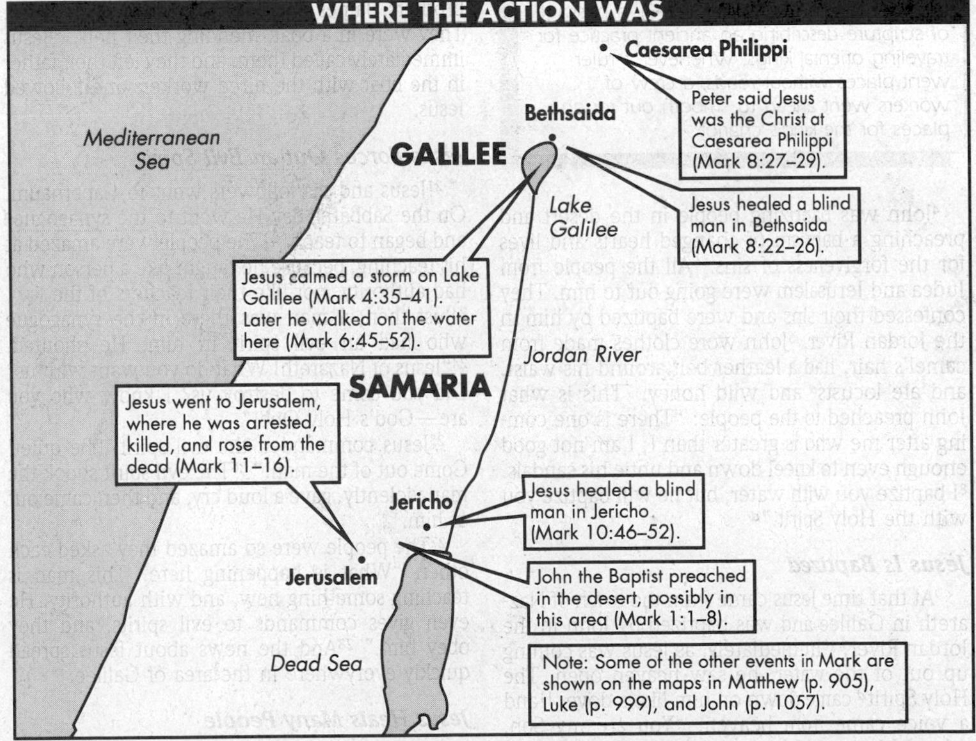

WHERE THE ACTION WAS
Caesarea Philippi
Peter said Jesus was the Christ at Caesarea Philippi (Mark 8:27–29).
Bethsaida
Mediterranean Sea
GALILEE
Jesus healed a blind man in Bethsaida (Mark 8:22–26).
Lake Galilee
Jesus calmed a storm on Lake Galilee (Mark 4:35–41). Later he walked on the water here (Mark 6:45–52).
Jordan River
SAMARIA
Jesus went to Jerusalem, where he was arrested, killed, and rose from the dead (Mark 11–16).
Jesus healed a blind man in Jericho (Mark 10:46–52).
Jericho
John the Baptist preached in the desert, possibly in this area (Mark 1:1–8).
Jerusalem
Dead Sea
Note: Some of the other events in Mark are shown on the maps in Matthew (p. 905), Luke (p. 999), and John (p. 1057).

WHEN THE ACTION WAS

BC/AD	25AD	50AD	75AD	100AD
Jesus was born	Jesus was crucified, rose from the dead, and went to heaven	Paul began his missionary work	Fire destroyed Rome	
	Jesus began his ministry		Romans destroyed the Temple in Jerusalem	

Behind the Scenes (cont.): who weren't from the area where Jesus lived. Since this audience wasn't as familiar with stories about Jesus, this book is a simple introduction to who Jesus was, what he did and why he came into the world.

So it's a great place to begin learning the basics!

John Prepares for Jesus

1 This is the beginning of the Good News[d] about Jesus Christ, the Son of God,[n] [2]as the prophet[d] Isaiah wrote:

"I will send my messenger ahead of you,
who will prepare your way." *Malachi 3:1*

[3]"This is a voice of one
who calls out in the desert:
'Prepare the way for the Lord.
Make the road straight for him.' " *Isaiah 40:3*

> **SIDELIGHT:** John the Baptist quoted from Isaiah about preparing the way for the Lord (Mark 1:2–3), a passage of scripture describing an ancient practice for traveling oriental kings. Whenever a ruler went places without roads, a crew of workers went ahead to smooth out rough places for the king's chariot.

[4]John was baptizing people in the desert and preaching a baptism of changed hearts and lives for the forgiveness of sins. [5]All the people from Judea and Jerusalem were going out to him. They confessed their sins and were baptized by him in the Jordan River. [6]John wore clothes made from camel's hair, had a leather belt around his waist, and ate locusts[d] and wild honey. [7]This is what John preached to the people: "There is one coming after me who is greater than I; I am not good enough even to kneel down and untie his sandals. [8]I baptize you with water, but he will baptize you with the Holy Spirit."[d]

Jesus Is Baptized

[9]At that time Jesus came from the town of Nazareth in Galilee and was baptized by John in the Jordan River. [10]Immediately, as Jesus was coming up out of the water, he saw heaven open. The Holy Spirit[d] came down on him like a dove, [11]and a voice came from heaven: "You are my Son, whom I love, and I am very pleased with you."

[12]Then the Spirit sent Jesus into the desert. [13]He was in the desert forty days and was tempted by Satan. He was with the wild animals, and the angels came and took care of him.

Jesus Chooses Some Followers

[14]After John was put in prison, Jesus went into Galilee, preaching the Good News[d] from God. [15]He said, "The right time has come. The kingdom of God is near. Change your hearts and lives and believe the Good News!"

[16]When Jesus was walking by Lake Galilee, he saw Simon[n] and his brother Andrew throwing a net into the lake because they were fishermen. [17]Jesus said to them, "Come follow me, and I will make you fish for people." [18]So Simon and Andrew immediately left their nets and followed him.

[19]Going a little farther, Jesus saw two more brothers, James and John, the sons of Zebedee. They were in a boat, mending their nets. [20]Jesus immediately called them, and they left their father in the boat with the hired workers and followed Jesus.

Jesus Forces Out an Evil Spirit

[21]Jesus and his followers went to Capernaum. On the Sabbath[d] day He went to the synagogue[d] and began to teach. [22]The people were amazed at his teaching, because he taught like a person who had authority, not like their teachers of the law. [23]Just then, a man was there in the synagogue who had an evil spirit in him. He shouted, [24]"Jesus of Nazareth! What do you want with us? Did you come to destroy us? I know who you are — God's Holy One!"

[25]Jesus commanded the evil spirit, "Be quiet! Come out of the man!" [26]The evil spirit shook the man violently, gave a loud cry, and then came out of him.

[27]The people were so amazed they asked each other, "What is happening here? This man is teaching something new, and with authority. He even gives commands to evil spirits, and they obey him." [28]And the news about Jesus spread quickly everywhere in the area of Galilee.

Jesus Heals Many People

[29]As soon as Jesus and his followers left the synagogue,[d] they went with James and John to the home of Simon[n] and Andrew. [30]Simon's mother-in-law was sick in bed with a fever, and the people told Jesus about her. [31]So Jesus went to her

the Son of God Some Greek copies omit these words.
Simon Simon's other name was Peter.

bed, took her hand, and helped her up. The fever
left her, and she began serving them.
32That evening, after the sun went down, the
people brought to Jesus all who were sick and had
demons[d] in them. 33The whole town gathered at
the door. 34Jesus healed many who had different
kinds of sicknesses, and he forced many demons
to leave people. But he would not allow the demons to speak, because they knew who he was.
35Early the next morning, while it was still
dark, Jesus woke and left the house. He went to
a lonely place, where he prayed. 36Simon and his
friends went to look for Jesus. 37When they found
him, they said, "Everyone is looking for you!"
38Jesus answered, "We should go to other
towns around here so I can preach there too. That
is the reason I came." 39So he went everywhere
in Galilee, preaching in the synagogues and forcing out demons.

Jesus Heals a Sick Man

40A man with a skin disease came to Jesus. He
fell to his knees and begged Jesus, "You can heal
me if you will."
41Jesus felt sorry for the man, so he reached out
his hand and touched him and said, "I will. Be
healed!" 42Immediately the disease left the man,
and he was healed.
43Jesus told the man to go away at once, but he
warned him strongly, 44"Don't tell anyone about
this. But go and show yourself to the priest. And
offer the gift Moses commanded for people who
are made well.[n] This will show the people what
I have done." 45The man left there, but he began
to tell everyone that Jesus had healed him, and so
he spread the news about Jesus. As a result, Jesus
could not enter a town if people saw him. He
stayed in places where nobody lived, but people
came to him from everywhere.

Moses . . . well Read about this in Leviticus 14:1-32.

FOLLOWING GOD

Leaving Everything

Li Tang grew up in the Chinese capital of Beijing. All her life, Li's family and friends had taught her that God was not real. Li believed what others told her, but she hoped that someday she would find that there really is a God.

When Li was seventeen years old, she found a Bible in an old library. She opened it and began reading about God loving people and sending his Son to the world.

Li was amazed. Why had she never heard about this before? She wanted to know more about this God and follow him. How could she? She decided she would leave everything—her family, her friends and even her country—to follow Jesus.

Her parents weren't thrilled with Li's decision to study Christianity, but they wanted her to be happy. Many of her friends couldn't understand why she wanted to leave. Wasn't ancestor worship good enough for her?

Li moved to England to study and learn more about Jesus so she could someday return to tell others about him. While there, she met Christians who helped her learn and grow.

"You really experience the change in your life," Li reflected after she decided to follow Jesus. "It's really a difference."

Jesus asked people to follow him. Often, following meant leaving many things behind. Yet following also meant gaining a friend like Jesus. Read about Jesus' first followers in **Mark 1:14–20.**

- How did what Li had to give up compare with what the disciples had to give up to follow Jesus?
- What have you had to give up to follow Jesus? What do you need to give up now to follow Jesus more fully?

CONSIDER. . .

- making a small, wooden cross to carry in your pocket or purse as a reminder of what it means to follow Jesus.
- interviewing two Christian friends about what it means to them to follow Jesus.

FOR MORE, SEE. . .

- Ruth 1:11–18 (p. 240)
- Matthew 4:12–22 (p. 912)
- John 1:35–42 (p. 1059)

Jesus Heals a Paralyzed Man

2 A few days later, when Jesus came back to
Capernaum, the news spread that he was at
home. 2Many people gathered together so that
there was no room in the house, not even outside
the door. And Jesus was teaching them God's
message. 3Four people came, carrying a paralyzed
man. 4Since they could not get to Jesus because
of the crowd, they dug a hole in the roof right
above where he was speaking. When they got
through, they lowered the mat with the paralyzed
man on it. 5When Jesus saw the faith of these
people, he said to the paralyzed man, "Young
man, your sins are forgiven."
6Some of the teachers of the law were sitting
there, thinking to themselves, 7"Why does this
man say things like that? He is speaking as if he
were God. Only God can forgive sins."
8Jesus knew immediately what these teachers
of the law were thinking. So he said to them,
"Why are you thinking these things? 9Which is
easier: to tell this paralyzed man, 'Your sins are
forgiven,' or to tell him, 'Stand up. Take your mat
and walk'? 10But I will prove to you that the Son
of Man[d] has authority on earth to forgive sins." So
Jesus said to the paralyzed man, 11"I tell you,
stand up, take your mat, and go home." 12Imme-
diately the paralyzed man stood up, took his mat,
and walked out while everyone was watching
him.
The people were amazed and praised God.
They said, "We have never seen anything like
this!"
13Jesus went to the lake again. The whole
crowd followed him there, and he taught them.
14While he was walking along, he saw a man
named Levi son of Alphaeus, sitting in the tax collector's booth. Jesus said to him, "Follow me,"
and he stood up and followed Jesus.
15Later, as Jesus was having dinner at Levi's

FORGIVENESS

The Christmas Gift

"I can't stand him! He's the one who left us. Why should I have to ruin my Christmas by spending it with him?" Juanita shouted at her mother through sobs.

"Honey, that was three years ago," Ellen Gonzales said. She put her hand on her daughter's shoulder. "A lot has happened since then. We're different people now—and happier too."

"That doesn't make it right. He still left us," Juanita countered.

Ellen sat down beside Juanita. "Your father needed work, and there was nothing here for him. He had to go someplace where he could feel useful and needed. I never believed he really wanted to leave us."

"But he did leave us," Juanita said. "And he never came back."

"You're right. But that doesn't mean he doesn't love you. Now he wants you to understand, to forgive him, and to get to know him again. Could you please forgive your father and go to his house for a few days for Christmas?" Ellen asked sympathetically.

"I guess I never really understood why he left, Mom." Juanita thought for a moment, then said, "I don't really want to, but I guess I could spend part of my Christmas vacation with Dad."

As Juanita reached for the phone, Ellen smiled and said quietly, "Maybe forgiveness can be your Christmas gift to your dad."

Forgiveness can bring healing to people and relationships. Read **Mark 2:1–12** to see how Jesus' miracle resulted in forgiveness and healing.

- How did Jesus' and Juanita's forgiveness bring about healing?
- Who needs a healing word of forgiveness from you?

CONSIDER . . .

- calling someone you've not talked with for a long time because of a misunderstanding.
- listing people you need to forgive, forgiving each person and then performing an act of service for each one to bring about healing.

FOR MORE, SEE . . .

- Psalm 130 (p. 557)
- Luke 5:17–26 (p. 1011)
- Hebrews 12:14–15 (p. 1290)

house, many tax collectors and "sinners" were
eating there with Jesus and his followers. Many

> **SIDELIGHT:** Most of Jesus' ministry took place around Lake Galilee (for example, see Mark 2:13–14). This lake is the world's lowest fresh-water lake, with a surface 680 feet below sea level. Despite the lake's prominence in Jesus' ministry, it's only mentioned three times in the Old Testament (Numbers 34:11, p. 157; Joshua 12:3, p. 205; and Joshua 13:27, p. 206).

people like this followed Jesus. [16]When the teachers of the law who were Pharisees[d] saw Jesus eating with the tax collectors and "sinners," they
asked his followers, "Why does he eat with tax
collectors and sinners?"
[17]Jesus heard this and said to them, "It is not
the healthy people who need a doctor, but the
sick. I did not come to invite good people but to
invite sinners."

Jesus' Followers Are Criticized

[18]Now the followers of John[n] and the Phari-
sees[d] often gave up eating for a certain time.[n]
Some people came to Jesus and said, "Why do
John's followers and the followers of the Phari-

John John the Baptist, who preached to the Jewish people about Christ's coming (Mark 1:4-8).
gave . . . time This is called "fasting." The people would give up eating for a special time of prayer and worship to God. It was also done to show sadness and disappointment.

CELEBRATING

Party Blues

Allison Vollaro's graduation party really drew a crowd. She had invited all her friends, which came to around thirty. Beyond that, her parents had invited several relatives and friends.

People filled every nook and corner in the house. A group of guys talked and joked on the sun deck. Several of the girls gathered in the kitchen and laughed at each other's stories. And a large assortment of other people crammed into the living room, talking about the graduation ceremony and chuckling at the antics of some of the kids.

Everyone was having a great time. Everyone, that is, except Allison. She stood quietly in a corner of the kitchen, only half-listening to the girls' conversation.

"What's wrong, Al?" asked Kriss Mitchell, walking quietly over to Allison. "You seem lost in your thoughts."

"Yeah, I guess I am," Allison said with a weak smile. "It's just that now that I'm out of school, I don't know what's going to happen to my friendships. I love you all so much; it makes me sad to think of you not being in my life anymore."

Kriss touched Allison on the arm. "Hey, listen, none of us knows what's going to happen from one day to the next. We may all get to stay together forever, or we may not. We just can't know for sure. But," Kriss added with a smile, "we're here today. So let's go join the others and have some fun, okay? After all, it is your party."

"Okay, okay," Allison said jokingly. Then she reached out and grabbed Kriss's hand. "Thanks, Kriss. I needed to hear that."

Kriss helped Allison realize the importance of celebrating good things that come along, even though they may not last. Jesus helped his disciples understand the same truth. Read the story Jesus used in **Mark 2:18–22**.

- How was Allison like the Pharisees' disciples in this passage?
- How can you celebrate Jesus' presence in your life, as this passage directs?

CONSIDER . . .

- writing all the ways Jesus reveals his presence in your life, then thanking God for being so real to you.
- throwing a party to celebrate friendship and God's love.

FOR MORE, SEE . . .

- Isaiah 62:1–9 (p. 682)
- Matthew 9:14–17 (p. 923)
- John 3:25–30 (p. 1062)

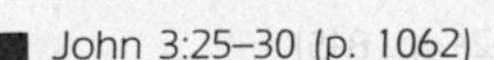

sees often give up eating, but your followers
don't?"
19Jesus answered, "The friends of the bridegroom do not give up eating while the bridegroom is still with them. As long as the
bridegroom is with them, they cannot give up
eating. 20But the time will come when the bridegroom will be taken from them, and then they
will give up eating.
21"No one sews a patch of unshrunk cloth
over a hole in an old coat. Otherwise, the patch
will shrink and pull away—the new patch
will pull away from the old coat. Then the
hole will be worse. 22Also, no one ever pours
new wine into old leather bags. Otherwise,
the new wine will break the bags, and the
wine will be ruined along with the bags. But
new wine should be put into new leather bags."

Jesus Is Lord of the Sabbath

23One Sabbath[d] day, as Jesus was walking
through some fields of grain, his followers began
to pick some grain to eat. 24The Pharisees[d] said to
Jesus, "Why are your followers doing what is not
lawful on the Sabbath day?"
25Jesus answered, "Have you never read what
David did when he and those with him were hungry and needed food? 26During the time of Abiathar the high priest, David went into God's house
and ate the holy bread, which is lawful only for
priests to eat. And David also gave some of the
bread to those who were with him."
27Then Jesus said to the Pharisees, "The Sabbath day was made to help people; they were not
made to be ruled by the Sabbath day. 28So then,
the Son of Man[d] is Lord even of the Sabbath day."

FREEDOM

Free to Choose

Angela Ferrara stared out the window of her second-story bedroom. Her father had just told the family he was taking a job in California. They would move at the end of February.

Angela cried as she thought about the friends she would have to leave and the basketball team she would have to quit. It wasn't fair. She wanted to be angry at her dad for moving during her last year in junior high school. If only they could wait until June.

She had pleaded with her parents not to move, but they wouldn't change their minds. Angela had no choice. The family would have to stay together, and she knew her parents expected her to cooperate.

"Can I come in?"

Surprised, Angela turned and saw her dad standing in the doorway of her room. Angela hesitated. "Yeah, I guess," she said finally..

"Your mother and I have been thinking. And we think you're old enough to make good decisions about your life, Angela," her dad began. "You may stay with your Aunt Sarah until school is out if you'd like to."

Angela's expression changed from disgust to a smile. "You mean I have a choice?" Angela asked incredulously. "I can decide for myself?"

"We don't want the family to be separated," her dad said. "But, on the other hand, we don't want to force you to make a move in the middle of the school year. It's up to you."

Angela's parents trusted her to make a responsible decision. In a similar way, God gives us guidelines for our lives, but trusts us to use those guidelines responsibly. Read **Mark 2:23—3:6** to see how Jesus encouraged people to follow those guidelines.

- What similarities are there between Jesus' use of guidelines and Angela's parents' decision to let Angela decide for herself?
- What kind of judging attitudes have you had toward people that are similar to the Pharisees' attitudes?

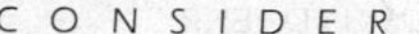

CONSIDER. . .

- talking to your parents about the purpose of family rules you don't understand.
- asking kids from other Christian churches about their beliefs. Celebrate the freedom you each have to be different!

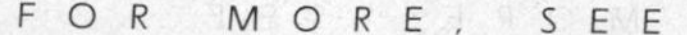

FOR MORE, SEE. . .

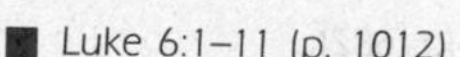

- Amos 5:21–24 (p. 845)
- Matthew 12:1–14 (p. 928)
- Luke 6:1–11 (p. 1012)

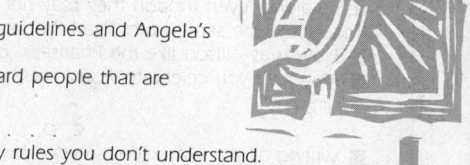

Jesus Heals a Man's Hand

3 Another time when Jesus went into a synagogue,[d] a man with a crippled hand was there. 2Some people watched Jesus closely to see if he would heal the man on the Sabbath[d] day so they could accuse him.

3Jesus said to the man with the crippled hand, "Stand up here in the middle of everyone."

4Then Jesus asked the people, "Which is lawful on the Sabbath day: to do good or to do evil, to save a life or to kill?" But they said nothing to answer him.

5Jesus was angry as he looked at the people, and he felt very sad because they were stubborn. Then he said to the man, "Hold out your hand." The man held out his hand and it was healed. 6Then the Pharisees[d] left and began making plans with the Herodians[n] about a way to kill Jesus.

Many People Follow Jesus

7Jesus left with his followers for the lake, and a large crowd from Galilee followed him. 8Also many people came from Judea, from Jerusalem, from Idumea, from the lands across the Jordan River, and from the area of Tyre and Sidon. When they heard what Jesus was doing, many people came to him. 9When Jesus saw the crowds, he told his followers to get a boat ready for him to keep people from crowding against him. 10He had healed many people, so all the sick were pushing toward him to touch him. 11When evil spirits saw Jesus, they fell down before him and shouted, "You are the Son of God!" 12But Jesus strongly warned them not to tell who he was.

Jesus Chooses His Twelve Apostles

13Then Jesus went up on a mountain and called to him the men he wanted, and they came to him. 14Jesus chose twelve men and called them apostles.[d] He wanted them to be with him, and he wanted to send them out to preach 15and to have the authority to force demons[d] out of people. 16These are the twelve men he chose: Simon (Jesus named him Peter), 17James and John, the sons of Zebedee (Jesus named them Boanerges, which means "Sons of Thunder"), 18Andrew, Philip, Bartholomew, Matthew, Thomas, James the son of Alphaeus, Thaddaeus, Simon the Zealot,[d] 19and Judas Iscariot, who later turned against Jesus.

Some People Say Jesus Has a Devil

20Then Jesus went home, but again a crowd gathered. There were so many people that Jesus and his followers could not eat. 21When his family heard this, they went to get him because they thought he was out of his mind. 22But the teachers of the law from Jerusalem were saying, "Beelzebul[d] is living inside him! He uses power from the ruler of demons[d] to force demons out of people."

23So Jesus called the people together and taught them with stories. He said, "Satan will not force himself out of people. 24A kingdom that is divided cannot continue, 25and a family that is divided cannot continue. 26And if Satan is against himself and fights against his own people, he cannot continue; that is the end of Satan. 27No one can enter a strong person's house and steal his things unless he first ties up the strong person. Then he can steal things from the house. 28I tell you the truth, all sins that people do and all the things people say against God can be forgiven. 29But anyone who speaks against the Holy Spirit[d] will never be forgiven; he is guilty of a sin that continues forever."

30Jesus said this because the teachers of the law said that he had an evil spirit inside him.

Jesus' True Family

31Then Jesus' mother and brothers arrived. Standing outside, they sent someone in to tell him to come out. 32Many people were sitting around Jesus, and they said to him, "Your mother and brothers are waiting for you outside."

33Jesus asked, "Who are my mother and my brothers?" 34Then he looked at those sitting around him and said, "Here are my mother and my brothers! 35My true brother and sister and mother are those who do what God wants."

A Story About Planting Seed

4 Again Jesus began teaching by the lake. A great crowd gathered around him, so he sat down in a boat near the shore. All the people stayed on the shore close to the water. 2Jesus taught them many things, using stories. He said, 3"Listen! A farmer went out to plant his seed. 4While he was planting, some seed fell by the road, and the birds came and ate it up. 5Some seed fell on rocky ground where there wasn't much dirt. That seed grew very fast, because the ground was not deep. 6But when the sun rose, the plants dried up because they did not have deep roots. 7Some other seed fell among thorny weeds, which grew and choked the good plants. So those plants did not produce a crop. 8Some other seed fell on good ground and began to grow. It got taller and produced a crop. Some plants made thirty times more, some made sixty times more, and some made a hundred times more."

9Then Jesus said, "You people who can hear me, listen!"

Herodians A political group that followed Herod and his family.

Jesus Tells Why He Used Stories

10Later, when Jesus was alone, the twelve apostles[d] and others around him asked him about the stories.

> **SIDELIGHT:** Jesus' story about planting seeds (Mark 4:1–9) not only has spiritual truth, but tells a lot about farming in those days. After plowing a field, farmers would walk through the field scattering seeds around the field. Then they would go back over the field dragging branches across to cover the seeds and protect them from birds and strong winds.

11Jesus said, "You can know the secret about the kingdom of God. But to other people I tell everything by using stories 12so that:

'They will look and look, but they will not
learn.
They will listen and listen, but they will not
understand.
If they did learn and understand,
they would come back to me and be
forgiven.' "
Isaiah 6:9-10

Jesus Explains the Seed Story

13Then Jesus said to his followers, "Don't you understand this story? If you don't, how will you understand any story? 14The farmer is like a person who plants God's message in people.
15Sometimes the teaching falls on the road. This is like the people who hear the teaching of God, but Satan quickly comes and takes away the teaching that was planted in them. 16Others
are like the seed planted on rocky ground. They hear the teaching and quickly accept it with joy. 17But since they don't allow the teaching to go deep into their lives, they keep it only a short time. When trouble or persecution comes because of the teaching they accepted, they quickly give up. 18Others are like the seed
planted among the thorny weeds. They hear

EVIL

Fearful Escape

Susan Platt was small, tired, and afraid. Her troubled eyes continually darted around the crowded bus stop. Everyone looked suspicious to Susan and made her want to run somewhere—anywhere—to get away from those who might find her and take her back.

Susan had a good reason to be afraid. Although she looked like any other teenager in Los Angeles, Susan was different from most. For the past six years, Susan had been involved in a coven that pledged itself to worship Satan. It had seemed fun when she started. Now, at eighteen, she wanted out.

Susan pulled at the sleeves of her sweater. Her arms must not be seen. They would expose her. Carved into her flesh were Satanic symbols to identify her as a devout Satanist. These marks were only an outward sign of the evil she had witnessed.

Susan had met some Christians a few years earlier. They had tried to tell her the truth about God's love and had offered to help her escape to a new way of life. She had refused then, but now she was going to find them.

Susan scanned the bus stop one last time. Seeing that no one was following her, she breathed a sigh of relief. As she climbed up the bus steps, Susan thought about how each step she took brought her closer to the freedom Jesus offered.

Since the beginning of time, Satan has lied to people, telling them his way is right and God's way is evil. **Mark 3:20–35** shows one instance when Satan convinced people that Jesus himself had an evil spirit.

- Why did Susan and the people in Jesus' day fear Satan?
- What promise do you see in this passage that helps you in the face of evil?

CONSIDER . . .

- praying for your church and family to be united so they can stand against evil.
- identifying an evil influence in your life and working to get rid of it.

FOR MORE, SEE . . .

- Genesis 3 (p. 4)
- Matthew 9:32–34 (p. 923)
- John 10:19–21 (p. 1075)

the teaching, [19]but the worries of this life, the
temptation of wealth, and many other evil
desires keep the teaching from growing and
producing fruit[n] in their lives. [20]Others are
like the seed planted in the good ground. They
hear the teaching and accept it. Then they
grow and produce fruit—sometimes thirty
times more, sometimes sixty times more, and
sometimes a hundred times more."

Use What You Have

[21]Then Jesus said to them, "Do you hide a lamp
under a bowl or under a bed? No! You put the
lamp on a lampstand. [22]Everything that is hidden
will be made clear and every secret thing will be
made known. [23]You people who can hear me, listen!

[24]"Think carefully about what you hear. The
way you give to others is the way God will give
to you, but God will give you even more. [25]Those
who have understanding will be given more.
But those who do not have understanding,
even what they have will be taken away from
them."

Jesus Uses a Story About Seed

[26]Then Jesus said, "The kingdom of God is like
someone who plants seed in the ground. [27]Night
and day, whether the person is asleep or awake,
the seed still grows, but the person does not know
how it grows. [28]By itself the earth produces grain.
First the plant grows, then the head, and then all
the grain in the head. [29]When the grain is ready,
the farmer cuts it, because this is the harvest
time."

A Story About Mustard Seed

[30]Then Jesus said, "How can I show you what
the kingdom of God is like? What story can I use
to explain it? [31]The kingdom of God is like a mustard seed, the smallest seed you plant in the
ground. [32]But when planted, this seed grows and
becomes the largest of all garden plants. It produces large branches, and the wild birds can
make nests in its shade."

[33]Jesus used many stories like these to teach
the crowd God's message—as much as they
could understand. [34]He always used stories to

producing fruit To produce fruit means to have in your life the good things God wants.

FAITH

It's Alive!

Witness, if you will, one of the most efficient, self-contained structures in nature. It possesses—on its own—almost everything it needs to survive and grow. It has its own coat, its own embryo and its own food supply.

It can even impregnate itself. That's right; each one has the male and female components it needs to create a fertilized egg.

The reproductive system is incredible, but it does need extra help to grow. After fertilization, it remains dormant until warm, moist conditions promote germination.

Then its coat softens and the metabolism rate in the cells increases. It drinks water and even starts "breathing," while a simple digestion begins. The digested food travels to new areas of growth that emerge when cell division begins.

And congratulations, Mr. and Mrs. Seed, it's a plant!

The incredible seed is a lot like the kingdom of God. Read **Mark 4:26–34** to see how.

- How is a seed's reproductive system like faith's growth process in you?
- According to this passage, what benefits can come from faith's growth in you? What benefits can come from many people growing in faith?

CONSIDER

- working in a garden and drawing other parallels between the plant world and faith. Write your own parable to illustrate those parallels.
- choosing one quality from 2 Peter 1:5–9 (p. 1311) to add to your faith. Create one project to help develop that quality.

FOR MORE, SEE

- Ecclesiastes 11:1–6 (p. 606)
- Matthew 13:24–32 (p. 931)
- Luke 13:18–20 (p. 1031)

teach them. But when he and his followers were alone, Jesus explained everything to them.

Jesus Calms a Storm

35That evening, Jesus said to his followers, "Let's go across the lake." 36Leaving the crowd behind, they took him in the boat just as he was. There were also other boats with them. 37A very strong wind came up on the lake. The waves came over the sides and into the boat so that it was already full of water. 38Jesus was at the back of the boat, sleeping with his head on a cushion. His followers woke him and said, "Teacher, don't you care that we are drowning!"

39Jesus stood up and commanded the wind and said to the waves, "Quiet! Be still!" Then the wind stopped, and it became completely calm.

40Jesus said to his followers, "Why are you afraid? Do you still have no faith?"

41The followers were very afraid and asked each other, "Who is this? Even the wind and the waves obey him!"

A Man with Demons Inside Him

5 Jesus and his followers went to the other side of the lake to the area of the Gerasene people. 2When Jesus got out of the boat, instantly a man with an evil spirit came to him from the burial caves. 3This man lived in the caves, and no one could tie him up, not even with a chain. 4Many times people had used chains to tie the man's hands and feet, but he always broke them off. No one was strong enough to control him. 5Day and night he would wander around the burial caves and on the hills, screaming and cutting himself with stones. 6While Jesus was still far away, the man saw him, ran to him, and fell down before him.

7The man shouted in a loud voice, "What do you want with me, Jesus, Son of the Most High God? I command you in God's name not to torture me!" 8He said this because Jesus was saying to him, "You evil spirit, come out of the man."

9Then Jesus asked him, "What is your name?"

He answered, "My name is Legion,[n] because we are many spirits." 10He begged Jesus again and again not to send them out of that area.

11A large herd of pigs was feeding on a hill near there. 12The demons[d] begged Jesus, "Send us into the pigs; let us go into them." 13So Jesus allowed them to do this. The evil spirits left the man and went into the pigs. Then the herd of pigs — about two thousand of them — rushed down the hill into the lake and were drowned.

14The herdsmen ran away and went to the town and to the countryside, telling everyone about this. So people went out to see what had happened. 15They came to Jesus and saw the man who used to have the many evil spirits, sitting, clothed, and in his right mind. And they were frightened. 16The people who saw this told the others what had happened to the man who had the demons living in him, and they told about the pigs. 17Then the people began to beg Jesus to leave their area.

18As Jesus was getting back into the boat, the man who was freed from the demons begged to go with him.

19But Jesus would not let him. He said, "Go home to your family and tell them how much the Lord has done for you and how he has had mercy on you." 20So the man left and began to tell the people in the Ten Towns[n] about what Jesus had done for him. And everyone was amazed.

Jesus Gives Life to a Dead Girl and Heals a Sick Woman

21When Jesus went in the boat back to the other side of the lake, a large crowd gathered around him there. 22A leader of the synagogue,[d] named Jairus, came there, saw Jesus, and fell at his feet. 23He begged Jesus, saying again and again, "My daughter is dying. Please come and put your hands on her so she will be healed and will live." 24So Jesus went with him.

A large crowd followed Jesus and pushed very close around him. 25Among them was a woman who had been bleeding for twelve years. 26She had suffered very much from many doctors and had spent all the money she had, but instead of improving, she was getting worse. 27When the woman heard about Jesus, she came up behind him in the crowd and touched his coat. 28She thought, "If I can just touch his clothes, I will be healed." 29Instantly her bleeding stopped, and she felt in her body that she was healed from her disease.

30At once Jesus felt power go out from him. So he turned around in the crowd and asked, "Who touched my clothes?"

31His followers said, "Look at how many people are pushing against you! And you ask, 'Who touched me?' "

32But Jesus continued looking around to see who had touched him. 33The woman, knowing that she was healed, came and fell at Jesus' feet. Shaking with fear, she told him the whole truth. 34Jesus said to her, "Dear woman, you are made well because you believed. Go in peace; be healed of your disease."

Legion Means very many. A legion was about five thousand men in the Roman army.
Ten Towns In Greek, called "Decapolis." It was an area east of Lake Galilee that once had ten main towns.

35While Jesus was still speaking, some people
came from the house of the synagogue leader.
They said, "Your daughter is dead. There is no
need to bother the teacher anymore."
36But Jesus paid no attention to what they said.
He told the synagogue leader, "Don't be afraid;
just believe."
37Jesus let only Peter, James, and John the
brother of James go with him. 38When they came
to the house of the synagogue leader, Jesus found
many people there making lots of noise and crying
loudly. 39Jesus entered the house and said to
them, "Why are you crying and making so much
noise? The child is not dead, only asleep." 40But
they laughed at him. So, after throwing them out
of the house, Jesus took the child's father and
mother and his three followers into the room
where the child was. 41Taking hold of the girl's
hand, he said to her, "Talitha, koum!" (This
means, "Young girl, I tell you to stand up!") 42At
once the girl stood right up and began walking.
(She was twelve years old.) Everyone was completely amazed. 43Jesus gave them strict orders
not to tell people about this. Then he told them
to give the girl something to eat.

Jesus Goes to His Hometown

6 Jesus left there and went to his hometown,
and his followers went with him. 2On the
Sabbath[d] day he taught in the synagogue.[d] Many
people heard him and were amazed, saying,
"Where did this man get these teachings? What
is this wisdom that has been given to him? And
where did he get the power to do miracles?[d] 3He
is just the carpenter, the son of Mary and the
brother of James, Joseph, Judas, and Simon. And
his sisters are here with us." So the people were
upset with Jesus.
4Jesus said to them, "A prophet[d] is honored everywhere except in his hometown and with his
own people and in his own home." 5So Jesus was
not able to work any miracles there except to heal
a few sick people by putting his hands on them.
6He was amazed at how many people had no
faith.
Then Jesus went to other villages in that area
and taught. 7He called his twelve followers together and got ready to send them out two by two
and gave them authority over evil spirits. 8This is
what Jesus commanded them: "Take nothing for
your trip except a walking stick. Take no bread,

SICKNESS

Miracles Happen

Doris Flynn's face was streaked with tears. "They say there's no hope," she sobbed, reaching for another tissue. "My granddaughter has a tumor the size of a baseball. It has completely surrounded her kidneys."

She continued haltingly: "The doctors aren't sure if other organs are involved. They don't think she'll live long."

Betty Hall placed her hand on Doris's shoulder. "Miracles do happen, Doris. We need to pray for a miracle."

"I've given up on God. Even he can't heal Wendy now. And besides, I don't think he's listening anymore."

Doris was wrong. Even the doctors were wrong. A new medicine was added to Wendy's treatment, and she was healed.

God heals. He can use doctors, nurses, and medicine to accomplish his purposes. Sometimes he even heals without their help. Read **Mark 5:21–43** to see how Jesus healed two people.

- How were the three healings—Wendy, the woman (verses 25–34) and the little girl—different from each other?
- Does God still heal the way Jesus did in this passage?

C O N S I D E R . . .

- writing a letter as though you were going to send it to someone who asked for healing and didn't receive it. Encourage that imaginary person to accept God's will.
- walking down the hallway of a local hospital and silently praying for God's healing for each patient.

F O R M O R E , S E E

- Psalm 103:1–5 (p. 540)
- Matthew 9:1–26 (p. 921)
- James 5:13–18 (p. 1299)

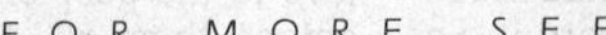

no bag, and no money in your pockets. 9Wear sandals, but take only the clothes you are wearing. 10When you enter a house, stay there until you leave that town. 11If the people in a certain place refuse to welcome you or listen to you, leave that place. Shake its dust off your feet[n] as a warning to them."

12So the followers went out and preached that people should change their hearts and lives. 13They forced many demons[d] out and put olive oil on many sick people and healed them.

How John the Baptist Was Killed

14King Herod heard about Jesus, because he was now well known. Some people said, "He is John the Baptist,[d] who has risen from the dead. That is why he can work these miracles."[d]

15Others said, "He is Elijah."[n]

Other people said, "Jesus is a prophet,[d] like the prophets who lived long ago."

16When Herod heard this, he said, "I killed John by cutting off his head. Now he has risen from the dead!"

17Herod himself had ordered his soldiers to arrest John and put him in prison in order to please his wife, Herodias. She had been the wife of Philip, Herod's brother, but then Herod had married her. 18John had been telling Herod, "It is not lawful for you to be married to your brother's wife." 19So Herodias hated John and wanted to kill him. But she couldn't, 20because Herod was afraid of John and protected him. He knew John was a good and holy man. Also, though John's preaching always bothered him, he enjoyed listening to John.

21Then the perfect time came for Herodias to cause John's death. On Herod's birthday, he gave a dinner party for the most important government leaders, the commanders of his army, and the most important people in Galilee. 22When the daughter of Herodias came in and danced, she pleased Herod and the people eating with him.

So King Herod said to the girl, "Ask me for anything you want, and I will give it to you." 23He promised her, "Anything you ask for I will give to you — up to half of my kingdom."

24The girl went to her mother and asked, "What should I ask for?"

Her mother answered, "Ask for the head of John the Baptist."[d]

25At once the girl went back to the king and said to him, "I want the head of John the Baptist right now on a platter."

26Although the king was very sad, he had made a promise, and his dinner guests had heard it. So he did not want to refuse what she asked. 27Immediately the king sent a soldier to bring John's head. The soldier went and cut off John's head in the prison 28and brought it back on a platter. He gave it to the girl, and the girl gave it to her mother. 29When John's followers heard this, they came and got John's body and put it in a tomb.

SIDELIGHT: Herod the Great wasn't the great guy his name might imply. Besides beheading John the Baptist (Mark 6:14–29), he murdered his own kids, prompting the saying, "It's safer to be Herod's pig than Herod's son."

More than Five Thousand Fed

30The apostles[d] gathered around Jesus and told him about all the things they had done and taught. 31Crowds of people were coming and going so that Jesus and his followers did not even have time to eat. He said to them, "Come away by yourselves, and we will go to a lonely place to get some rest."

32So they went in a boat by themselves to a lonely place. 33But many people saw them leave and recognized them. So from all the towns they ran to the place where Jesus was going, and they got there before him. 34When he arrived, he saw a great crowd waiting. He felt sorry for them, because they were like sheep without a shepherd. So he began to teach them many things.

35When it was late in the day, his followers came to him and said, "No one lives in this place, and it is already very late. 36Send the people away so they can go to the countryside and towns around here to buy themselves something to eat."

37But Jesus answered, "You give them something to eat."

They said to him, "We would all have to work a month to earn enough money to buy that much bread!"

38Jesus asked them, "How many loaves of bread do you have? Go and see."

When they found out, they said, "Five loaves and two fish."

39Then Jesus told his followers to have the people sit in groups on the green grass. 40So they sat in groups of fifty or a hundred. 41Jesus took the five loaves and two fish and, looking up to heaven, he thanked God for the food. He divided the bread and gave it to his followers for them to give to the people. Then he divided the two fish among them all. 42All the people ate and were satisfied. 43The followers filled twelve baskets

Shake . . . feet A warning. It showed that they were rejecting these people.
Elijah A man who spoke for God and who lived hundreds of years before Christ. See 1 Kings 17.

with the leftover pieces of bread and fish. [44]There
were five thousand men who ate.

Jesus Walks on the Water

[45]Immediately Jesus told his followers to get
into the boat and go ahead of him to Bethsaida
across the lake. He stayed there to send the people home. [46]After sending them away, he went
into the hills to pray.

[47]That night, the boat was in the middle of the
lake, and Jesus was alone on the land. [48]He saw
his followers struggling hard to row the boat, because the wind was blowing against them. Between three and six o'clock in the morning, Jesus
came to them, walking on the water, and he
wanted to walk past the boat. [49]But when they
saw him walking on the water, they thought he
was a ghost and cried out. [50]They all saw him and
were afraid. But quickly Jesus spoke to them and
said, "Have courage! It is I. Do not be afraid."
[51]Then he got into the boat with them, and the
wind became calm. The followers were greatly
amazed. [52]They did not understand about the miracle of the five loaves, because their minds were
closed.

[53]When they had crossed the lake, they came
to shore at Gennesaret and tied the boat there.
[54]When they got out of the boat, people immedi-

HUNGER AND POVERTY

The Multiplication Principle

"We have only three thousand cans. I wanted to collect ten thousand," Kristen Green complained to Mr. Rossetti, the principal of St. Francis De Sales High School in Columbus, Ohio. Mr. Rossetti was the one who had asked Kristen to chair her school's canned food drive for the soup kitchen.

Mr. Rossetti listened but didn't say much. Later that day during the school pep rally, he surprised Kristen by asking her to speak to the students about the food drive.

Kristen spoke about a man she had met at the local soup kitchen who each night asked for an extra plate of food for his dying wife. Kristen also told about a hungry woman who shared her orange with the person sitting beside her. She continued, "We think of starving people being in Ethiopia, but these people live three blocks from this school." Kristen challenged the students to meet the goal of ten thousand cans of food in the next week.

After the pep rally, students asked Kristen how they could help. Suddenly everyone was mobilized: The football team went door to door in the Columbus neighborhoods, asking for donations of canned goods. The Fellowship of Christian Athletes collected $1,500 worth of food in one night. Kristen and a friend asked area grocers for food donations.

By Wednesday, the goal of ten thousand cans was met—a goal people had thought was unrealistic. (Only four thousand cans had been collected the year before.) Kristen decided not to tell anyone the goal was reached before the deadline. On Friday, people cheered when she announced the total: 17,299 cans!

Kristen and others filled three school buses with the food. As they delivered the food to the soup kitchen, people standing in line thanked them and patted them on the back.

"We knew we were making a difference," Kristen says. "People were going to be able to eat."

Jesus and his disciples were also confronted with the challenge of feeding hungry people. Read **Mark 6:30–44** to see how Jesus fed a hungry mob.

- How is the multiplication of canned food at De Sales High similar to Jesus multiplying food for the multitude? How is it different?
- How have you seen Jesus increase your gifts or resources to help others?

CONSIDER. . .

- giving up eating a meal and spending time in prayer for those who have less to eat than you do. Donate the money you would have spent on the meal to World Vision, Special Programs, Pasadena, CA 91131, or to another relief agency.
- organizing a canned food drive at your church or school.

FOR MORE, SEE. . .

- 2 Kings 4:42–44 (p. 337)
- Matthew 14:13–21 (p. 934)
- John 6:1–15 (p. 1066)

ately recognized Jesus. 55They ran everywhere in
that area and began to bring sick people on mats
wherever they heard he was. 56And everywhere
he went — into towns, cities, or countryside — the
people brought the sick to the marketplaces. They
begged him to let them touch just the edge of his
coat, and all who touched it were healed.

Obey God's Law

7 When some Pharisees[d] and some teachers of
the law came from Jerusalem, they gathered
around Jesus. 2They saw that some of Jesus' followers ate food with hands that were not clean,[d]
that is, they hadn't washed them. 3(The Pharisees
and all the Jews never eat before washing their
hands in a special way according to their unwritten laws. 4And when they buy something in the
market, they never eat it until they wash themselves in a special way. They also follow many
other unwritten laws, such as the washing of
cups, pitchers, and pots.)
5The Pharisees and the teachers of the law said
to Jesus, "Why don't your followers obey the unwritten laws which have been handed down to
us? Why do your followers eat their food with
hands that are not clean?"
6Jesus answered, "Isaiah was right when he
spoke about you hypocrites.[d] He wrote,

'These people show honor to me with words,
but their hearts are far from me.
7Their worship of me is worthless.
The things they teach are nothing but
human rules.' *Isaiah 29:13*

8You have stopped following the commands of
God, and you follow only human teachings."
9Then Jesus said to them, "You cleverly ignore
the commands of God so you can follow your
own teachings. 10Moses said, 'Honor your father
and your mother,'[n] and 'Anyone who says cruel
things to his father or mother must be put to
death.'[n] 11But you say a person can tell his father
or mother, 'I have something I could use to help
you, but it is Corban — a gift to God.' 12You no
longer let that person use that money for his fa-

'Honor . . . mother' Quotation from Exodus 20:12; Deuteronomy 5:16.
'Anyone . . . death.' Quotation from Exodus 21:17.

HYPOCRISY

An Open Letter to God

Craig Mackey was tired of seeing what he called "the Dr. Jekyll and Mr. Hyde" sides of his father. In his frustration, he wrote this letter to God.

Dear God,

There are a few things I just don't understand about people and the way they act. Let me tell you what I mean.

Take my dad, for example. Don't get me wrong. He's a nice guy; he goes to church with us and everything. But when it comes to his business, he really changes. Dad's always talking about how he really "got the best of that guy" in a business deal or how he "beat her out of a contract." It just doesn't seem very Christian.

Oh, and another place is on the highway. My dad gets really angry at other drivers and sometimes even yells at them.

And, oh well, I guess I just don't understand. It just doesn't seem very Christian.

Can you help me understand, God?

Craig

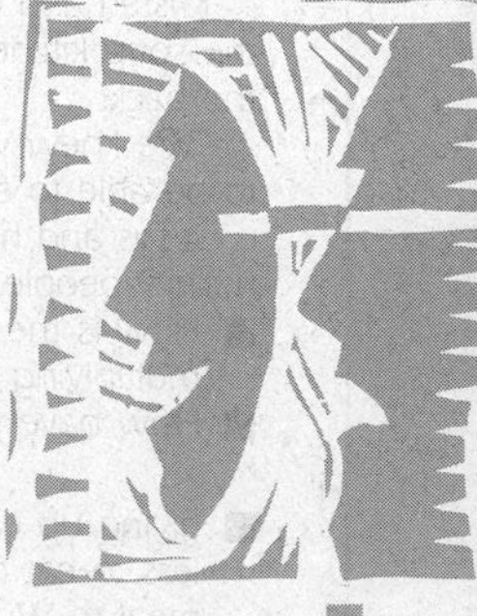

Hypocrisy is common. Even in Jesus' day, Jesus' followers were troubled by hypocrites. Read **Mark 7:1–23** to learn more about the situation.

- What was hypocritical about Craig's dad's actions and the Pharisees' actions?
- According to this passage, what's the cure for hypocrisy?

C O N S I D E R . . .

- evaluating your own life for any hypocrisies and applying the "cure" to get rid of them.
- writing a letter to Craig that responds to his frustrations.

F O R   M O R E ,   S E E . . .

- Isaiah 29:13–14 (p. 645)
- Matthew 15:1–20 (p. 934)
- Romans 14:13–18 (p. 1160)

ther or his mother. 13By your own rules, which
you teach people, you are rejecting what God
said. And you do many things like that."
14After Jesus called the crowd to him again, he
said, "Every person should listen to me and understand what I am saying. 15There is nothing
people put into their bodies that makes them unclean. People are made unclean by the things that
come out of them." 16 [n]
17When Jesus left the people and went into the
house, his followers asked him about this story.
18Jesus said, "Do you still not understand? Surely
you know that nothing that enters someone from
the outside can make that person unclean. 19It
does not go into the mind, but into the stomach.
Then it goes out of the body." (When Jesus said
this, he meant that no longer was any food unclean for people to eat.)
20And Jesus said, "The things that come out of
people are the things that make them unclean.
21All these evil things begin inside people, in the
mind: evil thoughts, sexual sins, stealing, murder,
adultery,[d] 22greed, evil actions, lying, doing sinful
things, jealousy, speaking evil of others, pride,
and foolish living. 23All these evil things come
from inside and make people unclean."

Jesus Helps a Non-Jewish Woman

24Jesus left that place and went to the area
around Tyre. When he went into a house, he did
not want anyone to know he was there, but he
could not stay hidden. 25A woman whose daughter had an evil spirit in her heard that he was
there. So she quickly came to Jesus and fell at his
feet. 26She was Greek, born in Phoenicia, in Syria.
She begged Jesus to force the demon[d] out of her
daughter.
27Jesus told the woman, "It is not right to take
the children's bread and give it to the dogs. First
let the children eat all they want."
28But she answered, "Yes, Lord, but even the
dogs under the table can eat the children's
crumbs."
29Then Jesus said, "Because of your answer,
you may go. The demon has left your daughter."
30The woman went home and found her
daughter lying in bed; the demon was gone.

Jesus Heals a Deaf Man

31Then Jesus left the area around Tyre and
went through Sidon to Lake Galilee, to the area
of the Ten Towns.[n] 32While he was there, some
people brought a man to him who was deaf and
could not talk plainly. The people begged Jesus to
put his hand on the man to heal him.
33Jesus led the man away from the crowd, by
himself. He put his fingers in the man's ears and
then spit and touched the man's tongue. 34Look-
ing up to heaven, he sighed and said to the man,
"Ephphatha!" (This means, "Be opened.") 35In-
stantly the man was able to hear and to use his
tongue so that he spoke clearly.
36Jesus commanded the people not to tell anyone about what happened. But the more he commanded them, the more they told about it. 37They
were completely amazed and said, "Jesus does everything well. He makes the deaf hear! And those
who can't talk he makes able to speak."

More than Four Thousand People Fed

8 Another time there was a great crowd with
Jesus that had nothing to eat. So Jesus called
his followers and said, 2"I feel sorry for these people, because they have already been with me for
three days, and they have nothing to eat. 3If I send
them home hungry, they will faint on the way.
Some of them live a long way from here."
4Jesus' followers answered, "How can we get
enough bread to feed all these people? We are far
away from any town."
5Jesus asked, "How many loaves of bread do
you have?"
They answered, "Seven."
6Jesus told the people to sit on the ground.
Then he took the seven loaves, gave thanks to
God, and divided the bread. He gave the pieces to
his followers to give to the people, and they did
so. 7The followers also had a few small fish. After
Jesus gave thanks for the fish, he told his followers
to give them to the people also. 8All the people ate
and were satisfied. Then his followers filled seven
baskets with the leftover pieces of food. 9There
were about four thousand people who ate. After
they had eaten, Jesus sent them home. 10Then
right away he got into a boat with his followers
and went to the area of Dalmanutha.

SIDELIGHT: Jesus had conflicts with the Pharisees (Mark 8:11) throughout his ministry. These leaders were respected for their accurate interpretations of Jewish law. The historian Josephus estimates that six thousand Pharisees lived in Palestine during Jesus' years.

The Leaders Ask for a Miracle

11The Pharisees[d] came to Jesus and began to
ask him questions. Hoping to trap him, they asked
Jesus for a miracle[d] from God. 12Jesus sighed

Verse 16 Some Greek copies add verse 16: "You people who can hear me, listen!"
Ten Towns In Greek, called "Decapolis." It was an area east of Lake Galilee that once had ten main towns.

deeply and said, "Why do you people ask for a
miracle as a sign? I tell you the truth, no sign will
be given to you." 13Then Jesus left the Pharisees
and went in the boat to the other side of the lake.

Guard Against Wrong Teachings

14His followers had only one loaf of bread with
them in the boat; they had forgotten to bring
more. 15Jesus warned them, "Be careful! Beware
of the yeast of the Pharisees[d] and the yeast of
Herod."

16His followers discussed the meaning of this,
saying, "He said this because we have no bread."
17Knowing what they were talking about, Jesus
asked them, "Why are you talking about not having bread? Do you still not see or understand? Are
your minds closed? 18You have eyes, but you
don't really see. You have ears, but you don't
really listen. Remember when 19I divided five
loaves of bread for the five thousand? How many
baskets did you fill with leftover pieces of food?"
They answered, "Twelve."
20"And when I divided seven loaves of bread
for the four thousand, how many baskets did you
fill with leftover pieces of food?"
They answered, "Seven."
21Then Jesus said to them, "Don't you understand yet?"

Jesus Heals a Blind Man

22Jesus and his followers came to Bethsaida.
There some people brought a blind man to Jesus
and begged him to touch the man. 23So Jesus took
the blind man's hand and led him out of the village. Then he spit on the man's eyes and put his
hands on the man and asked, "Can you see
now?"
24The man looked up and said, "Yes, I see people, but they look like trees walking around."
25Again Jesus put his hands on the man's eyes.

SICKNESS

She Made a Difference

In the 1940s, more than 500,000 people in the city of Calcutta (5 percent of the city's population) literally lived and died in the streets. With summer temperatures normally above 115 degrees and winter temperatures hovering in the high 90s, the city could seem like hell on earth. It was there that the "poorest of the poor" lived, plagued by leprosy, tuberculosis, pneumonia and, most of all, poverty.

What hope was there in such a place? Surely no one could make a difference there. But Agnes thought differently. She believed that God was calling her to bring hope to these poor and downtrodden people.

In her journal, Agnes, now known as Mother Teresa, described her first day in the slums as a day of meeting Christ. She met Christ face to face there—the hungry Christ, the naked Christ, the sick Christ, the homeless Christ. She said the touch of him in this distressing disguise gave her great joy, peace, and strength.

So, clad in a white sari edged with blue, Mother Teresa began her work. She and a group of nuns taught the children of the poor. They provided care for lepers who could get help nowhere else. They built shelters and hospitals so the poor would have a place out of the streets. They fed the hungry and loved the unlovable. They literally changed the face of Calcutta.

Jesus' love flowed through Mother Teresa to touch people. Jesus' love always makes a difference. When Jesus touches sick people, their lives are never the same. Read **Mark 7:31–37** and imagine how the sick people who met Jesus must have felt.

- How is Mother Teresa's hands-on approach to ministry like Jesus' approach?
- Which of Jesus' actions in this passage are most important to people who are sick?

CONSIDER

- doing a task that you don't like to do (such as cleaning a bathroom) for a homebound member of your church.
- talking to your pastor about how your church can minister to people with AIDS.

FOR MORE, SEE.

- Leviticus 13 (p. 108)
- Matthew 8:1–4 (p. 920)
- Luke 17:11–19 (p. 1040)

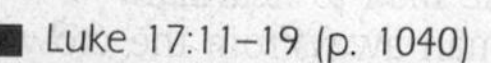

Then the man opened his eyes wide and they were healed, and he was able to see everything clearly. 26Jesus told him to go home, saying, "Don't go into the town."

Peter Says Jesus Is the Christ

27Jesus and his followers went to the towns around Caesarea Philippi. While they were traveling, Jesus asked them, "Who do people say I am?"

28They answered, "Some say you are John the Baptist.[d] Others say you are Elijah,[n] and others say you are one of the prophets."[d]

29Then Jesus asked, "But who do you say I am?"

Peter answered, "You are the Christ."[d]

30Jesus warned his followers not to tell anyone who he was.

31Then Jesus began to teach them that the Son of Man[d] must suffer many things and that he would be rejected by the older Jewish leaders, the leading priests, and the teachers of the law. He told them that the Son of Man must be killed and then rise from the dead after three days. 32Jesus told them plainly what would happen. Then Peter took Jesus aside and began to tell him not to talk like that. 33But Jesus turned and looked at his followers. Then he told Peter not to talk that way. He said, "Go away from me, Satan![n] You don't care about the things of God, but only about things people think are important."

34Then Jesus called the crowd to him, along with his followers. He said, "If people want to follow me, they must give up the things they want. They must be willing even to give up their lives to follow me. 35Those who want to save their lives will give up true life. But those who give up their lives for me and for the Good News[d] will have true life. 36It is worth nothing for them to have the whole world if they lose their souls. 37They could never pay enough to buy back their souls. 38The people who live now are living in a sinful and evil time. If people are ashamed of me and my teaching, the Son of Man[d] will be ashamed of them when he comes with his Father's glory and with the holy angels."

9 Then Jesus said to the people, "I tell you the truth, some people standing here will see the kingdom of God come with power before they die."

Jesus Talks with Moses and Elijah

2Six days later, Jesus took Peter, James, and John up on a high mountain by themselves. While they watched, Jesus' appearance was changed. 3His clothes became shining white, whiter than any person could make them. 4Then Elijah and Moses[n] appeared to them, talking with Jesus.

5Peter said to Jesus, "Teacher, it is good that we are here. Let us make three tents—one for you, one for Moses, and one for Elijah." 6Peter did not know what to say, because he and the others were so frightened.

7Then a cloud came and covered them, and a voice came from the cloud, saying, "This is my Son, whom I love. Listen to him!"

8Suddenly Peter, James, and John looked around, but they saw only Jesus there alone with them.

9As they were coming down the mountain, Jesus commanded them not to tell anyone about what they had seen until the Son of Man[d] had risen from the dead.

10So the followers obeyed Jesus, but they discussed what he meant about rising from the dead.

11Then they asked Jesus, "Why do the teachers of the law say that Elijah must come first?"

12Jesus answered, "They are right to say that Elijah must come first and make everything the way it should be. But why does the Scripture[d] say that the Son of Man will suffer much and that people will treat him as if he were nothing? 13I tell you that Elijah has already come. And people did to him whatever they wanted to do, just as the Scriptures said it would happen."

Jesus Heals a Sick Boy

14When Jesus, Peter, James, and John came back to the other followers, they saw a great crowd around them and the teachers of the law arguing with them. 15But as soon as the crowd saw Jesus, the people were surprised and ran to welcome him.

16Jesus asked, "What are you arguing about?"

17A man answered, "Teacher, I brought my son to you. He has an evil spirit in him that stops him from talking. 18When the spirit attacks him, it throws him on the ground. Then my son foams at the mouth, grinds his teeth, and becomes very stiff. I asked your followers to force the evil spirit out, but they couldn't."

19Jesus answered, "You people have no faith. How long must I stay with you? How long must I put up with you? Bring the boy to me."

20So the followers brought him to Jesus. As soon as the evil spirit saw Jesus, it made the boy lose control of himself, and he fell down and rolled on the ground, foaming at the mouth.

Elijah A man who spoke for God and who lived hundreds of years before Christ. See 1 Kings 17.
Satan Name for the devil meaning "the enemy." Jesus means that Peter was talking like Satan.
Elijah and Moses Two of the most important Jewish leaders in the past. Moses had given them the law, and Elijah was an important prophet.

21Jesus asked the boy's father, "How long has
this been happening?"
The father answered, "Since he was very
young. 22The spirit often throws him into a fire
or into water to kill him. If you can do anything for him, please have pity on us and help
us."
23Jesus said to the father, "You said, 'If you
can!' All things are possible for the one who believes."
24Immediately the father cried out, "I do believe! Help me to believe more!"
25When Jesus saw that a crowd was quickly
gathering, he ordered the evil spirit, saying, "You
spirit that makes people unable to hear or speak,
I command you to come out of this boy and never
enter him again!"
26The evil spirit screamed and caused the boy
to fall on the ground again. Then the spirit came
out. The boy looked as if he were dead, and many
people said, "He is dead!" 27But Jesus took
hold of the boy's hand and helped him to stand
up.
28When Jesus went into the house, his followers began asking him privately, "Why couldn't we
force that evil spirit out?"
29Jesus answered, "That kind of spirit can only
be forced out by prayer."

Jesus Talks About His Death

30Then Jesus and his followers left that place
and went through Galilee. He didn't want anyone
to know where he was, 31because he was teaching his followers. He said to them, "The Son of
Man[d] will be handed over to people, and they will
kill him. After three days, he will rise from the
dead." 32But the followers did not understand
what Jesus meant, and they were afraid to ask
him.

Who Is the Greatest?

33Jesus and his followers went to Capernaum.
When they went into a house there, he asked
them, "What were you arguing about on the
road?" 34But the followers did not answer, because their argument on the road was about
which one of them was the greatest.
35Jesus sat down and called the twelve apostles[d] to him. He said, "Whoever wants to be the
most important must be last of all and servant of
all."

FAITH

Over a Cliff

Ethan Magness peered anxiously over his shoulder down the steep cliff. The bottom of the deep ravine appeared to be miles away. Standing on the edge of the rocks, he heard the rappelling instructor yell, "Just lean straight back into the air; the ropes will hold you."

"I can't lean back," Ethan thought. "How do I know the ropes will hold me?"

"Come on, Ethan, are you afraid?" Ellie asked.

Sweat poured down his face as he thought about the cliff. He was afraid, but he didn't want anyone to know it—especially not Ellie.

"Come on, Ethan," the instructor encouraged. "It's all right; just have faith in the ropes. They'll hold you."

Ethan held his breath and leaned back. He was swinging in the air, but the ropes did hold! Cautiously, he let out the tension on the rope and slid down. Finally he reached the bottom. Whew!

Just as it took faith for Ethan to rappel, it also took faith for the disciples to believe in Jesus. Read **Mark 9:1–9** to see an experience the disciples had with Jesus.

- How is Ethan's faith in his ropes similar to the faith the disciples needed to believe in Jesus?
- How can you overcome hard-to-believe things that stand in the way of your faith in Jesus?

CONSIDER . . .

- listing obstacles to your faith on separate sheets of paper and tearing up each sheet.
- doing one risky thing to demonstrate your faith. For example, tell a non-Christian friend about Jesus or take a stand for or against a social issue.

FOR MORE, SEE . . .

- Psalm 130 (p. 557)
- Matthew 17:1–9 (p. 937)
- Luke 9:28–36 (p. 1019)

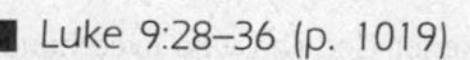

36Then Jesus took a small child and had him
stand among them. Taking the child in his arms,
he said, 37"Whoever accepts a child like this in my
name accepts me. And whoever accepts me accepts the One who sent me."

Anyone Not Against Us Is for Us

38Then John said, "Teacher, we saw someone
using your name to force demons[d] out of a person. We told him to stop, because he does not
belong to our group."
39But Jesus said, "Don't stop him, because anyone who uses my name to do powerful things will
not easily say evil things about me. 40Whoever is
not against us is with us. 41I tell you the truth,
whoever gives you a drink of water because you
belong to the Christ[d] will truly get his reward.
42"If one of these little children believes in me,
and someone causes that child to sin, it would be
better for that person to have a large stone tied
around his neck and be drowned in the sea. 43If
your hand causes you to sin, cut it off. It is better
for you to lose part of your body and live forever
than to have two hands and go to hell, where the
fire never goes out. 44 [n] 45If your foot causes you
to sin, cut it off. It is better for you to lose part of
your body and to live forever than to have two
feet and be thrown into hell. 46 [n] 47If your eye
causes you to sin, take it out. It is better for you
to enter the kingdom of God with only one eye
than to have two eyes and be thrown into hell.
48In hell the worm does not die; the fire is never
put out. 49Every person will be salted with fire.
50"Salt is good, but if the salt loses its salty taste,
you cannot make it salty again. So, be full of salt,
and have peace with each other."

Verse 44 Some Greek copies of Mark add verse 44, which is the same as verse 48.
Verse 46 Some Greek copies of Mark add verse 46, which is the same as verse 48.

POPULARITY

Everyone Is Going

Sam Collins slammed his locker shut. It was Friday afternoon; the final bell had rung. He needed to catch Roy and Justin before they got on their bus to be sure all of them were meeting at the football game that night.

As Sam turned from his locker, his foot caught on a wheel. It was Alex O'Brien's wheelchair. Alex had broken his neck the previous spring in a diving accident and was paralyzed from the shoulders down.

"Hey, Sam, what are you guys doin' tonight?" Alex asked.

"Well, uh. . . ." Sam hesitated as his eyes searched the hall for the other guys, but Alex didn't wait for an answer.

"Would you like to come over to my place? My mom said she'd pick up some videos. Could you open my locker and put away the books in my backpack, please?"

Sam impatiently unloaded the backpack, opened the locker, and deposited the books. As Sam closed the locker, Alex asked again, "Well? What about tonight?"

Sam glanced down the empty hallway. The buses were pulling away. It was too late to make plans with Justin and Roy. Alex needed a friend. But everyone would be going to the game.

Sam thought for a moment and then smiled at Alex. "What time do you want me to come over?"

The disciples also had to make a decision about what it meant to be popular. They were arguing about who was the greatest or most popular. **Read Mark 9:30–37** to see how Jesus turned the tables on them.

■ How would Sam's actions make him important in the kingdom of God?
■ When have you had to decide between doing what's popular and what's right? How was that experience like the incident in this passage?

CONSIDER . . .

■ having lunch with an unpopular classmate.
■ doing a household chore that everyone in your family dislikes doing.

FOR MORE, SEE . . .

■ Proverbs 11:24–26 (p. 577)
■ Matthew 18:1–5 (p. 939)

■ Philippians 2:5–7 (p. 1230)

Jesus Teaches About Divorce

10 Then Jesus left that place and went into
the area of Judea and across the Jordan

> **SIDELIGHT:** In the original
> Greek language of the New
> Testament, the word for "hell" (Mark 9:45–49)
> is Gehenna, which is based on the Hebrew
> name of the Hinnom Valley southwest of
> Jerusalem. The description is appropriate. In
> ancient times, this valley was used for infant
> sacrifices (see Jeremiah 32:35, p. 729). It later
> became Jerusalem's smelly garbage dump—
> not a place you would want to spend
> eternity!

River. Again, crowds came to him, and he taught
them as he usually did.
2Some Pharisees[d] came to Jesus and tried to
trick him. They asked, "Is it right for a man to
divorce his wife?"
3Jesus answered, "What did Moses command
you to do?"
4They said, "Moses allowed a man to write out
divorce papers and send her away." [n]
5Jesus said, "Moses wrote that command for
you because you were stubborn. 6But when God
made the world, 'he made them male and female.' [n] 7'So a man will leave his father and
mother and be united with his wife, 8and the two
will become one body.' [n] So there are not two,
but one. 9God has joined the two together, so no
one should separate them."
10Later, in the house, his followers asked Jesus
again about the question of divorce. 11He answered, "Anyone who divorces his wife and marries another woman is guilty of adultery[d] against
her. 12And the woman who divorces her husband
and marries another man is also guilty of adultery."

Jesus Accepts Children

13Some people brought their little children to
Jesus so he could touch them, but his followers
told them to stop. 14When Jesus saw this, he was
upset and said to them, "Let the little children
come to me. Don't stop them, because the kingdom of God belongs to people who are like these
children. 15I tell you the truth, you must accept
the kingdom of God as if you were a little child,
or you will never enter it." 16Then Jesus took the
children in his arms, put his hands on them, and
blessed them.

A Rich Young Man's Question

17As Jesus started to leave, a man ran to him
and fell on his knees before Jesus. The man asked,
"Good teacher, what must I do to have life forever?"
18Jesus answered, "Why do you call me good?
Only God is good. 19You know the commands:
'You must not murder anyone. You must not be
guilty of adultery.[d] You must not steal. You must
not tell lies about your neighbor. You must not
cheat. Honor your father and mother.' " [n]
20The man said, "Teacher, I have obeyed all
these things since I was a boy."
21Jesus, looking at the man, loved him and said,
"There is one more thing you need to do. Go and
sell everything you have, and give the money to
the poor, and you will have treasure in heaven.
Then come and follow me."
22He was very sad to hear Jesus say this, and he
left sorrowfully, because he was rich.
23Then Jesus looked at his followers and said,
"How hard it will be for the rich to enter the kingdom of God!"
24The followers were amazed at what Jesus
said. But he said again, "My children, it is very
hard to enter the kingdom of God! 25It is easier
for a camel to go through the eye of a needle
than for a rich person to enter the kingdom of
God."
26The followers were even more surprised and
said to each other, "Then who can be saved?"
27Jesus looked at them and said, "This is something people cannot do, but God can. God can do
all things."
28Peter said to Jesus, "Look, we have left everything and followed you."
29Jesus said, "I tell you the truth, all those who
have left houses, brothers, sisters, mother, father,
children, or farms for me and for the Good News[d]
30will get more than they left. Here in this world
they will have a hundred times more homes,
brothers, sisters, mothers, children, and fields.
And with those things, they will also suffer for
their belief. But in the age that is coming they will
have life forever. 31Many who have the highest
place now will have the lowest place in the future. And many who have the lowest place now
will have the highest place in the future."

Jesus Talks About His Death

32As Jesus and the people with him were on the

"Moses . . . away." Quotation from Deuteronomy 24:1.
'he made . . . female.' Quotation from Genesis 1:27.
'So . . . body.' Quotation from Genesis 2:24.
'You . . . mother.' Quotation from Exodus 20:12-16; Deuteronomy 5:16-20.

road to Jerusalem, he was leading the way. His
followers were amazed, but others in the crowd
who followed were afraid. Again Jesus took the
twelve apostles[d] aside and began to tell them
what was about to happen in Jerusalem. 33He
said, "Look, we are going to Jerusalem. The Son
of Man[d] will be turned over to the leading priests
and the teachers of the law. They will say that he
must die, and they will turn him over to the non-
Jewish people, 34who will laugh at him and spit
on him. They will beat him with whips and crucify him. But on the third day, he will rise to life
again."

Two Followers Ask Jesus a Favor

35Then James and John, sons of Zebedee, came
to Jesus and said, "Teacher, we want to ask you
to do something for us."
36Jesus asked, "What do you want me to do for
you?"
37They answered, "Let one of us sit at your
right side and one of us sit at your left side in your
glory in your kingdom."
38Jesus said, "You don't understand what you
are asking. Can you drink the cup that I must
drink? And can you be baptized with the
same kind of baptism that I must go through?"[n]
39They answered, "Yes, we can."
Jesus said to them, "You will drink the same
cup that I will drink, and you will be baptized with the same baptism that I must go
through. 40But I cannot choose who will sit at
my right or my left; those places belong to
those for whom they have been prepared."
41When the other ten followers heard this, they
began to be angry with James and John.
42Jesus called them together and said, "The
non-Jewish people have rulers. You know that
those rulers love to show their power over the
people, and their important leaders love to use all
their authority. 43But it should not be that way
among you. Whoever wants to become great
among you must serve the rest of you like a servant. 44Whoever wants to become the first among
you must serve all of you like a slave. 45In the
same way, the Son of Man[d] did not come to be
served. He came to serve others and to give his
life as a ransom for many people."

Can you . . . through? Jesus was asking if they could suffer the same terrible things that would happen to him.

FAITH

Christmas In June, July . . .

Corky Adams is unique. He's a real trendsetter. For example, he always wears one red sock and one green sock to remind himself that every day is Christmas. His socks are a perfect reflection of the way he lives his Christian faith with others.

Corky often plays with children and talks with elderly folks in his neighborhood. Once he drove a thousand miles to comfort someone whose friend had died suddenly. He is also a gifted photographer who captures the best of each person he photographs.

Corky is a joy to be around. His beaming smile lights up his cheeks as though he were Santa Claus himself. When friends see him, their natural reaction is to smile and give him a hug. His faith is alive with wonder and joy—much like the excitement of a child who has just discovered that dirt and water make mud.

What's most amazing about Corky, though, is that he's thirty-five years old!

Jesus, himself, challenges us, no matter how old or young we are, to live the childlike faith and joy that Corky lives each day. Read **Mark 10:13–16** to see how Jesus requires childlike faith.

- How does Corky reflect the kingdom of God in a childlike way?
- In what ways do you feel challenged to be more childlike in your own faith?

CONSIDER . . .

- listing the questions you had about God as a child, then writing the answers you have discovered as you've grown.
- playing with a little child. Build with blocks; paint with your fingers. Read stories. Notice the childlike qualities, such as curiosity, innocence, and trust. Then work at applying those qualities to your faith.

FOR MORE, SEE . . .

- Isaiah 11:1–6 (p. 629)
- Mark 9:33–37 (p. 980)
- Romans 8:14–17 (p. 1150)

Jesus Heals a Blind Man

46Then they came to the town of Jericho. As
Jesus was leaving there with his followers and a
great many people, a blind beggar named Bartimaeus son of Timaeus was sitting by the road.
47When he heard that Jesus from Nazareth was
walking by, he began to shout, "Jesus, Son of David,[d] have mercy on me!"
48Many people warned the blind man to be
quiet, but he shouted even more, "Son of David,
have mercy on me!"
49Jesus stopped and said, "Tell the man to come
here."
So they called the blind man, saying, "Cheer
up! Get to your feet. Jesus is calling you." 50The
blind man jumped up, left his coat there, and
went to Jesus.
51Jesus asked him, "What do you want me to
do for you?"
The blind man answered, "Teacher, I want to
see."
52Jesus said, "Go, you are healed because you
believed." At once the man could see, and he followed Jesus on the road.

Jesus Enters Jerusalem as a King

11 As Jesus and his followers were coming
closer to Jerusalem, they came to the
towns of Bethphage and Bethany near the Mount
of Olives.[d] From there Jesus sent two of his followers 2and said to them, "Go to the town you
can see there. When you enter it, you will quickly
find a colt tied, which no one has ever ridden.
Untie it and bring it here to me. 3If anyone asks
you why you are doing this, tell him its Master
needs the colt, and he will send it at once."
4The followers went into the town, found a colt
tied in the street near the door of a house, and
untied it. 5Some people were standing there and
asked, "What are you doing? Why are you untying that colt?" 6The followers answered the way
Jesus told them to answer, and the people let
them take the colt.
7They brought the colt to Jesus and put their
coats on it, and Jesus sat on it. 8Many people
spread their coats on the road. Others cut
branches in the fields and spread them on the
road. 9The people were walking ahead of Jesus
and behind him, shouting,

MONEY

What's Important?

"I have made many millions, but they have brought me no happiness. I would barter them all for the days I sat on an office stool in Cleveland and counted myself rich on $3 a week." —John Rockefeller, a multi-millionaire

"The care of $200 million is too great a load for any brain or back to bear. It is enough to kill anyone. There is no pleasure in it." —W.H. Vanderbilt, who inherited a fortune

"I am the most miserable man on earth." —John Jacob Astor, who died leaving $5 million

"Millionaires seldom smile." —Andrew Carnegie, a millionaire

Each of these people, who had lots of money, knew other things were more important than money. Jesus tried to teach the same lesson to the young man in **Mark 10:17–30**. Read how he responded.

- How is what Jesus said similar to the quotes from these millionaires?
- How does your "wealth" help or hinder your faith?

CONSIDER . . .

- drawing a treasure chest and "filling" it with all the things that are most valuable to you. Evaluate what Jesus would think of your treasure.
- giving someone $10 with no strings attached and for no particular reason—just for the fun of it. How does it make you feel?

FOR MORE, SEE . . .

- Deuteronomy 14:22–29 (p. 174)
- Luke 21:1–4 (p. 1047)
- Acts 3:1–10 (p. 1100)

"Praise[n] God!
God bless the One who comes in the name
of the Lord! *Psalm 118:26*
10God bless the kingdom of our father David!
That kingdom is coming!
Praise to God in heaven!"
11Jesus entered Jerusalem and went into the
Temple.[d] After he had looked at everything, since
it was already late, he went out to Bethany with
the twelve apostles.[d]
12The next day as Jesus was leaving Bethany,
he became hungry. 13Seeing a fig tree in leaf
from far away, he went to see if it had any figs
on it. But he found no figs, only leaves, because
it was not the right season for figs. 14So Jesus
said to the tree, "May no one ever eat fruit from
you again." And Jesus' followers heard him say
this.

Jesus Goes to the Temple

15When Jesus returned to Jerusalem, he went
into the Temple[d] and began to throw out those
who were buying and selling there. He turned
over the tables of those who were exchanging different kinds of money, and he upset the benches
of those who were selling doves. 16Jesus refused
to allow anyone to carry goods through the Temple courts. 17Then he taught the people, saying,
"It is written in the Scriptures,[d] 'My Temple will
be called a house for prayer for people from all
nations.'[n] But you are changing God's house into
a 'hideout for robbers.' "[n]
18The leading priests and the teachers of the
law heard all this and began trying to find a way
to kill Jesus. They were afraid of him, because all
the people were amazed at his teaching. 19That
evening, Jesus and his followers left the city.

Praise Literally, "Hosanna," a Hebrew word used at first in praying to God for help, but at this time it was probably a shout of joy used in praising God or his Messiah.
'My Temple . . . nations.' Quotation from Isaiah 56:7.
'hideout for robbers.' Quotation from Jeremiah 7:11.

SERVICE

Volunteer of the Year

Wanted: Class clown. Poor study habits a must.

If you asked her teachers, this job advertisement fit Denise Delgado perfectly. She never did her homework, and she was constantly cutting up in class. Denise had a definite gift of getting people to notice her.

Yet, Denise also had a gift her teachers failed to recognize. During her senior year, Denise volunteered at a special school for autistic children. Autistic children are difficult to work with because they seldom respond to those around them. However, Denise loved working with the kids. She soaked in any affirmation they would give her—a nod of the head, the glance of an eye, or a rare smile. Teachers and parents alike marveled at Denise's success in helping their children.

When she graduated, the special school awarded Denise a scholarship to study special education. The "class clown" even became a celebrity when the local United Way recognized her as the Youth Volunteer of the Year.

Like Denise early in high school, Jesus' followers sometimes searched for recognition among their peers. They didn't understand that Jesus required them to be servants first of all. John and James were two such people. Read about their encounter with Jesus in **Mark 10:35–45**.

- How was Denise's response similar to the challenge Jesus gave his followers?
- Which servant characteristics that Jesus talks about in this passage do you have?

CONSIDER. . .

- encouraging someone you usually compete with, and being excited when he or she does something better than you.
- going to a sports event and writing down the encouraging things people say to their favorite team. Use those things to encourage the people around you.

FOR MORE, SEE. . .

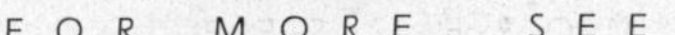

- 1 Samuel 3:1–10 (p. 247)
- Luke 22:24–27 (p. 1049)
- John 13:1–17 (p. 1080)

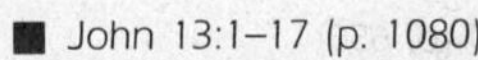

The Power of Faith

20The next morning as Jesus was passing by
with his followers, they saw the fig tree dry and
dead, even to the roots. 21Peter remembered the
tree and said to Jesus, "Teacher, look! The fig tree
you cursed is dry and dead!"

> **SIDELIGHT:** The people whom Jesus threw out of the Temple were merchants who took advantage of those in Jerusalem on religious pilgrimages (Mark 11:15–17). They exchanged foreign currency for money to use in the Temple—with an extra charge, of course. Others sold doves to be used in Temple sacrifices.

22Jesus answered, "Have faith in God. 23I tell
you the truth, you can say to this mountain, 'Go,
fall into the sea.' And if you have no doubts in
your mind and believe that what you say will happen, God will do it for you. 24So I tell you to believe that you have received the things you ask for
in prayer, and God will give them to you. 25When
you are praying, if you are angry with someone,
forgive him so that your Father in heaven will also
forgive your sins." 26 [n]

Leaders Doubt Jesus' Authority

27Jesus and his followers went again to Jerusalem. As Jesus was walking in the Temple,[d] the
leading priests, the teachers of the law, and the
older leaders came to him. 28They said to him,
"What authority do you have to do these things?
Who gave you this authority?"
29Jesus answered, "I will ask you one question.
If you answer me, I will tell you what authority
I have to do these things. 30Tell me: When John
baptized people, was that authority from God or
just from other people?"
31They argued about Jesus' question, saying, "If
we answer, 'John's baptism was from God,' Jesus
will say, 'Then why didn't you believe him?' 32But

Verse 26 Some early Greek copies add verse 26: "But if you don't forgive other people, then your Father in heaven will not forgive your sins."

PERSISTENCE

The Long Run

"We don't know if your baby will live through the night," the doctors told two-pound Patti Maslowski's new parents. She was born in 1966, when few babies born three months premature survived.

But Patti was a fighter from the start.

By the time she reached high school, she was an excellent student and an all-district volleyball star. She was also the regional track champion in the 3,200-meter run. When she finished eighth in her first state track meet, everyone was confident she had a great running future.

But then a back injury before her junior year changed her plans. No longer could she run like she used to. So she found a new way to give of herself—by becoming the track team manager.

Patti explains why she perseveres: "My persistence comes from making the most of each opportunity I'm given. I wasn't expected to live in the first place, so now I just want to use the gifts I've been blessed with to the best of my ability."

At one point in Jesus' ministry, he met a blind man who also exhibited Patti's perseverance. Read about the blind man in **Mark 10:46–52**.

- Why did Patti and the blind man persevere?
- How does your faith in Jesus help you persevere in pursuing your goals?

CONSIDER. . .

- making a plan of action to improve performance in one area of your life. Then spend the time needed to make progress. Evaluate your progress every month.
- setting short- and long-term goals. Write them in a pocket calendar, and keep the calendar in your purse or wallet.

FOR MORE, SEE. . .

- Isaiah 35:1–10 (p. 650)
- Luke 5:17–25 (p. 1011)
- Hebrews 10:32–39 (p. 1287)

if we say, 'It was from other people,' the crowd
will be against us." (These leaders were afraid of
the people, because all the people believed that
John was a prophet.[d])
33 So they answered Jesus, "We don't know."
Jesus said to them, "Then I won't tell you what
authority I have to do these things."

A Story About God's Son

12 Jesus began to use stories to teach the
people. He said, "A man planted a vineyard. He put a wall around it and dug a hole for
a winepress[d] and built a tower. Then he leased
the land to some farmers and left for a trip.
2 When
it was time for the grapes to be picked, he sent a
servant to the farmers to get his share of the
grapes.
3 But the farmers grabbed the servant and
beat him and sent him away empty-handed.
4 Then the man sent another servant. They hit him
on the head and showed no respect for him.
5 So
the man sent another servant, whom they killed.
The man sent many other servants; the farmers
beat some of them and killed others.
6 "The man had one person left to send, his son
whom he loved. He sent him last of all, saying,
'They will respect my son.'
7 "But the farmers said to each other, 'This son
will inherit the vineyard. If we kill him, it will be
ours.'
8 So they took the son, killed him, and
threw him out of the vineyard.
9 "So what will the owner of the vineyard do?
He will come and kill those farmers and will give
the vineyard to other farmers.
10 Surely you have
read this Scripture:[d]

'The stone that the builders rejected
became the cornerstone.[d]
11 The Lord did this,
and it is wonderful to us.' " *Psalm 118:22-23*

12 The Jewish leaders knew that the story was
about them. So they wanted to find a way to arrest Jesus, but they were afraid of the people. So
the leaders left him and went away.

Is It Right to Pay Taxes or Not?

13 Later, the Jewish leaders sent some Phari-

WORSHIP

1964

On August 18, 1964, the Beatles boarded a plane in London and flew to San Francisco to begin their first coast-to-coast concert tour of North America. The "Fab Four" expected to perform before more people in their thirty-one-day tour than any other act in music history. What they didn't expect was "Beatlemania."

When the musicians arrived, they were greeted at the airport by five thousand screaming fans. At the hotel where they stayed, they were greeted by four thousand more. And that was just the beginning.

In the months that followed, the Beatles found themselves confronted by mobs raging with excitement. The foursome often had to travel in secret to avoid crowds. At their concerts, the music was often drowned out by excited, screaming fans.

Some might think the Beatles loved the attention. But they didn't.

"It wasn't as much fun for us as it was for all of you," commented George Harrison, the band's guitarist, when asked about Beatlemania. People worshiped the Beatles—even though they were just human beings and didn't really deserve that kind of adoration.

Everyone longs to worship something, to have a hero to look up to. That was true even in Jesus' time. **Mark 11:1–11** describes a worship scene that resembled Beatlemania—except the one worshiped was worthy of people's praise. Check it out.

- How is the story in the passage like Beatlemania?
- If you had been in Jerusalem at the time of the passage, how would you have worshiped Jesus? How do you worship him today?

CONSIDER . . .

- going to a Christian concert to discover a new way to worship.
- writing a song or poem of worship to Jesus, thanking him for what he's done for you.

FOR MORE, SEE . . .

- Psalm 66 (p. 519)
- Matthew 21:1–11 (p. 944)
- Luke 19:28–40 (p. 1045)

sees[d] and Herodians[n] to Jesus to trap him in saying something wrong. 14They came to him and
said, "Teacher, we know that you are an honest
man. You are not afraid of what other people
think about you, because you pay no attention to
who they are. And you teach the truth about
God's way. Tell us: Is it right to pay taxes to Caesar[d] or not? 15Should we pay them, or not?"

But knowing what these men were really trying to do, Jesus said to them, "Why are you trying
to trap me? Bring me a coin to look at." 16They
gave Jesus a coin, and he asked, "Whose image
and name are on the coin?"

They answered, "Caesar's."

17Then Jesus said to them, "Give to Caesar the
things that are Caesar's, and give to God the
things that are God's." The men were amazed at
what Jesus said.

Some Sadducees Try to Trick Jesus

18Then some Sadducees[d] came to Jesus and
asked him a question. (Sadducees believed that
people would not rise from the dead.) 19They said,
"Teacher, Moses wrote that if a man's brother
dies, leaving a wife but no children, then that man
must marry the widow and have children for his
brother. 20Once there were seven brothers. The
first brother married and died, leaving no children. 21So the second brother married the widow,
but he also died and had no children. The same
thing happened with the third brother. 22All seven
brothers married her and died, and none of the
brothers had any children. Finally the woman
died too. 23Since all seven brothers had married
her, when people rise from the dead, whose wife
will she be?"

24Jesus answered, "Why don't you understand?
Don't you know what the Scriptures[d] say, and
don't you know about the power of God? 25When
people rise from the dead, they will not marry,
nor will they be given to someone to marry. They
will be like the angels in heaven. 26Surely you
have read what God said about people rising from
the dead. In the book in which Moses wrote
about the burning bush,[n] it says that God told
Moses, 'I am the God of Abraham, the God of
Isaac, and the God of Jacob.'[n] 27God is the God
of the living, not the dead. You Sadducees are
wrong!"

The Most Important Command

28One of the teachers of the law came and
heard Jesus arguing with the Sadducees.[d] Seeing
that Jesus gave good answers to their questions,
he asked Jesus, "Which of the commands is most
important?"

29Jesus answered, "The most important command is this: 'Listen, people of Israel! The Lord
our God is the only Lord. 30Love the Lord your
God with all your heart, all your soul, all your
mind, and all your strength.'[n] 31The second
command is this: 'Love your neighbor as
you love yourself.'[n] There are no commands
more important than these."

32The man answered, "That was a good answer, Teacher. You were right when you said
God is the only Lord and there is no other God
besides him. 33One must love God with all his
heart, all his mind, and all his strength. And one
must love his neighbor as he loves himself. These
commands are more important than all the animals and sacrifices we offer to God."

34When Jesus saw that the man answered him
wisely, Jesus said to him, "You are close to the
kingdom of God." And after that, no one was
brave enough to ask Jesus any more questions.

35As Jesus was teaching in the Temple,[d] he
asked, "Why do the teachers of the law say that
the Christ[d] is the son of David? 36David himself,
speaking by the Holy Spirit,[d] said:

'The Lord said to my Lord:
Sit by me at my right side,
until I put your enemies under your
control.' *Psalm 110:1*

37David himself calls the Christ 'Lord,' so how can
the Christ be his son?" The large crowd listened
to Jesus with pleasure.

38Jesus continued teaching and said, "Beware
of the teachers of the law. They like to walk
around wearing fancy clothes, and they love for
people to greet them with respect in the marketplaces. 39They love to have the most important
seats in the synagogues[d] and at feasts. 40But they
cheat widows and steal their houses and then try
to make themselves look good by saying long
prayers. They will receive a greater punishment."

True Giving

41Jesus sat near the Temple[d] money box and
watched the people put in their money. Many
rich people gave large sums of money. 42Then a
poor widow came and put in two small copper
coins, which were only worth a few cents.

43Calling his followers to him, Jesus said, "I tell
you the truth, this poor widow gave more than all
those rich people. 44They gave only what they did
not need. This woman is very poor, but she gave
all she had; she gave all she had to live on."

Herodians A political group that followed Herod and his family.
burning bush Read Exodus 3:1-12 in the Old Testament.
'I am . . . Jacob.' Quotation from Exodus 3:6.
'Listen . . . strength.' Quotation from Deuteronomy 6:4-5.
'Love . . . yourself.' Quotation from Leviticus 19:18.

The Temple Will Be Destroyed

13 As Jesus was leaving the Temple,[d] one of
his followers said to him, "Look,
Teacher! How beautiful the buildings are! How
big the stones are!"
2Jesus said, "Do you see all these great buildings? Not one stone will be left on another. Every
stone will be thrown down to the ground."

> **SIDELIGHT:** Jesus' prediction that the Temple would be destroyed (Mark 13:1–2) came true within about forty years. In A.D. 70, the Romans surrounded and sacked Jerusalem, burning the Temple to the ground. Today, the Muslim shrine called the "Dome of the Rock" stands on the Temple site.

3Later, as Jesus was sitting on the Mount of Olives,[d] opposite the Temple, he was alone with Peter, James, John, and Andrew. They asked Jesus,
4"Tell us, when will these things happen? And
what will be the sign that they are going to happen?"
5Jesus began to answer them, "Be careful that
no one fools you. 6Many people will come in my
name, saying, 'I am the One,' and they will fool
many people. 7When you hear about wars and
stories of wars that are coming, don't be afraid.
These things must happen before the end comes.
8Nations will fight against other nations, and kingdoms against other kingdoms. There will be earthquakes in different places, and there will be times
when there is no food for people to eat. These
things are like the first pains when something
new is about to be born.
9"You must be careful. People will arrest you
and take you to court and beat you in their synagogues.[d] You will be forced to stand before kings
and governors, to tell them about me. This will
happen to you because you follow me. 10But before these things happen, the Good News[d] must
be told to all people. 11When you are arrested and
judged, don't worry ahead of time about what
you should say. Say whatever is given you to say

GIVING

Under Construction

Stephen Chang was shy and short. He was one of those teenagers who seemed to slip into the background at big events. He was so quiet that most of the time no one noticed he was even there.

One thing, however, that did stand out about Stephen was how hard he worked. When the youth group picked up leaves for a fund-raiser, Stephen had the most bags of leaves. And when litter filled the youth group room during a meeting, Stephen stayed after to clean up.

It was Stephen's hard work that Joe Heaton recalled when he asked him to design a planter box for a youth group prayer service. Stephen responded enthusiastically, immediately drawing up blueprints for the planter. He created a large cross-shaped planter box. It was beautiful.

The youth group members then planted mustard seeds in the box. As the seeds grew, tended by Stephen's loving care, they reminded the class members of their own growth as Christians.

Aside from Joe, few people knew it was Stephen who had created the planter. No one even knew Stephen had cared for the plants.

In some ways, Stephen is like the widow Jesus talked about in **Mark 12:38–44**. Read this passage to discover Jesus' message.

- How were Stephen's gifts like the kind of giving Jesus described?
- According to this passage, what are things we should not do to be "religious"?

C O N S I D E R . . .

- doing something anonymously to help someone. For example, you could send money to someone, or you could rake someone's leaves without his knowing about it.
- committing to contribute a percentage of your income to your church.

F O R M O R E , S E E . . .

- Malachi 3:8–12 (p. 901)
- Matthew 6:19–24 (p. 918)
- 1 Timothy 6:6–10 (p. 1260)

at that time, because it will not really be you
speaking; it will be the Holy Spirit.[d]
12"Brothers will give their own brothers to be
killed, and fathers will give their own children to
be killed. Children will fight against their own
parents and cause them to be put to death. 13All
people will hate you because you follow me, but
those people who keep their faith until the end
will be saved.
14"You will see 'the destroying terror'[n] standing where it should not be." (You who read this
should understand what it means.) "At that time,
the people in Judea should run away to the mountains. 15If people are on the roofs[n] of their
houses, they must not go down or go inside to get
anything out of their houses. 16If people are in the
fields, they must not go back to get their coats.
17At that time, how terrible it will be for women
who are pregnant or have nursing babies! 18Pray
that these things will not happen in winter, 19be-
cause those days will be full of trouble. There will
be more trouble than there has ever been since
the beginning, when God made the world, until
now, and nothing as bad will ever happen again.
20God has decided to make that terrible time
short. Otherwise, no one would go on living.
But God will make that time short to help the
people he has chosen. 21At that time, someone
might say to you, 'Look, there is the Christ!'[d]
Or another person might say, 'There he is!'
But don't believe them. 22False Christs and false
prophets[d] will come and perform great wonders and miracles.[d] They will try to fool even
the people God has chosen, if that is possible.
23So be careful. I have warned you about all
this before it happens.
24"During the days after this trouble comes,
'the sun will grow dark,
and the moon will not give its light.
25The stars will fall from the sky.

'the destroying terror' Mentioned in Daniel 9:27; 12:11 (cf. Daniel 11:31).
roofs In Bible times houses were built with flat roofs. The roof was used for drying things such as flax and fruit. And it was used as an extra room, as a place for worship, and as a place to sleep in the summer.

FUTURE

Be Prepared

NEW MADRID, MO.—In November 1990, grocery store shelves were cleared and ice chests packed with emergency items such as food, water, first-aid kits, flashlights and radios. People were frightened. Some people wouldn't even sleep in their own homes; they slept in their cars and pick-up trucks instead. Many residents even left the area.

"I'm terrified of this," resident Anna Harper said. "I feel like it's some terminal illness. I don't want to believe it, but there is so much talk about it."

Residents of this small town were preparing for the earthquake that Iben Browning, a business consultant from New Mexico, had predicted. He said tidal forces were unusually high and could trigger an earthquake of 6.5 to 7.5 on the Richter scale forty-eight hours before or after December 3, along the New Madrid Fault.

While many residents of the small town scurried about to prepare for the catastrophe, others were calm about it. After all, these residents said, it's not as though they didn't already know they were living on a fault line.

December 3 came and went, and there was no earthquake.

In **Mark 13:24–33**, Jesus warns his followers of a certain day they need to be prepared for in the future.

- According to this passage, no one knows when Jesus will return. To prepare for that day, which people should we be like—the people who prepared at the last minute or those who were ready at all times?
- If Jesus were to return today, would you be ready?

CONSIDER . . .

- deciding what things you would put in an "emergency kit" to prepare for the end of the world; for example, faith or courage. Think about what you need to do to have those things ready.
- asking your pastor or youth leader to teach a course on the "end times."

FOR MORE, SEE . . .

- Genesis 9:1–17 (p. 10)
- Luke 21:25–36 (p. 1048)
- 1 Thessalonians 4:13—5:11 (p. 1248)

And the powers of the heavens will be
shaken.' *Isaiah 13:10; 34:4*

26"Then people will see the Son of Man[d] coming in clouds with great power and glory. 27Then he will send his angels all around the earth to gather his chosen people from every part of the earth and from every part of heaven.

28"Learn a lesson from the fig tree: When its branches become green and soft and new leaves appear, you know summer is near. 29In the same way, when you see these things happening, you will know that the time is near, ready to come. 30I tell you the truth, all these things will happen while the people of this time are still living. 31Earth and sky will be destroyed, but the words I have said will never be destroyed.

32"No one knows when that day or time will be, not the angels in heaven, not even the Son. Only the Father knows. 33Be careful! Always be ready, because you don't know when that time will be. 34It is like a man who goes on a trip. He leaves his house and lets his servants take care of it, giving each one a special job to do. The man tells the servant guarding the door always to be watchful. 35So always be ready, because you don't know when the owner of the house will come back. It might be in the evening, or at midnight, or in the morning while it is still dark, or when the sun rises. 36Always be ready. Otherwise he might come back suddenly and find you sleeping. 37I tell you this, and I say this to everyone: 'Be ready!' "

The Plan to Kill Jesus

14 It was now only two days before the Passover[d] and the Feast[d] of Unleavened Bread. The leading priests and teachers of the law were trying to find a trick to arrest Jesus and kill him. 2But they said, "We must not do it during the feast, because the people might cause a riot."

A Woman with Perfume for Jesus

3Jesus was in Bethany at the house of Simon, who had a skin disease. While Jesus was eating there, a woman approached him with an alabaster[d] jar filled with very expensive perfume, made of pure nard.[d] She opened the jar and poured the perfume on Jesus' head.

4Some who were there became upset and said to each other, "Why waste that perfume? 5It was worth a full year's work. It could have been sold and the money given to the poor." And they got very angry with the woman.

6Jesus said, "Leave her alone. Why are you troubling her? She did an excellent thing for me. 7You will always have the poor with you, and you can help them anytime you want. But you will not always have me. 8This woman did the only thing she could do for me; she poured perfume on my body to prepare me for burial. 9I tell you the truth, wherever the Good News[d] is preached in all the world, what this woman has done will be told, and people will remember her."

> **SIDELIGHT:** The perfume the woman poured on Jesus' feet at Bethany (Mark 14:3–9) might have made many modern perfumes seem cheap. Called spikenard, it was taken from pink-blossomed plants in the Himalayan Mountains of northern India.

Judas Becomes an Enemy of Jesus

10One of the twelve apostles, Judas Iscariot, went to talk to the leading priests to offer to hand Jesus over to them. 11These priests were pleased about this and promised to pay Judas money. So he watched for the best time to turn Jesus in.

Jesus Eats the Passover Meal

12It was now the first day of the Feast[d] of Unleavened Bread when the Passover[d] lamb was sacrificed. Jesus' followers said to him, "Where do you want us to go and prepare for you to eat the Passover meal?"

13Jesus sent two of his followers and said to them, "Go into the city and a man carrying a jar of water will meet you. Follow him. 14When he goes into a house, tell the owner of the house, 'The Teacher says: Where is my guest room in which I can eat the Passover meal with my followers?' 15The owner will show you a large room upstairs that is furnished and ready. Prepare the food for us there."

16So the followers left and went into the city. Everything happened as Jesus had said, so they prepared the Passover meal.

17In the evening, Jesus went to that house with the twelve. 18While they were all eating, Jesus said, "I tell you the truth, one of you will turn against me—one of you eating with me now."

19The followers were very sad to hear this. Each one began to say to Jesus, "I am not the one, am I?"

20Jesus answered, "It is one of the twelve—the one who dips his bread into the bowl with me. 21The Son of Man[d] will die, just as the Scriptures[d] say. But how terrible it will be for the person who hands the Son of Man over to be killed. It would be better for him if he had never been born."

The Lord's Supper

22While they were eating, Jesus took some bread and thanked God for it and broke it. Then he gave it to his followers and said, "Take it; this is my body."

23Then Jesus took a cup and thanked God for
it and gave it to the followers, and they all drank
from the cup.
24Then Jesus said, "This is my blood which is
the new agreement that God makes with his people. This blood is poured out for many. 25I tell you
the truth, I will not drink of this fruit of the vine[n]
again until that day when I drink it new in the
kingdom of God."
26After singing a hymn, they went out to the
Mount of Olives.[d]

Jesus' Followers Will Leave Him

27Then Jesus told the followers, "You will all
stumble in your faith, because it is written in the
Scriptures:[d]

'I will kill the shepherd,
and the sheep will scatter.' *Zechariah 13:7*

28But after I rise from the dead, I will go ahead of
you into Galilee."
29Peter said, "Everyone else may stumble in
their faith, but I will not."
30Jesus answered, "I tell you the truth, tonight
before the rooster crows twice you will say three
times you don't know me."
31But Peter insisted, "I will never say that I
don't know you! I will even die with you!" And
all the other followers said the same thing.

Jesus Prays Alone

32Jesus and his followers went to a place called
Gethsemane. He said to them, "Sit here while I
pray." 33Jesus took Peter, James, and John with
him, and he began to be very sad and troubled.
34He said to them, "My heart is full of sorrow, to
the point of death. Stay here and watch."
35After walking a little farther away from them,
Jesus fell to the ground and prayed that, if possible, he would not have this time of suffering. 36He
prayed, "Abba,[n] Father! You can do all things.
Take away this cup[n] of suffering. But do what
you want, not what I want."
37Then Jesus went back to his followers and
found them asleep. He said to Peter, "Simon, are

fruit of the vine Product of the grapevine; this may also be translated "wine."
Abba Name that a child called his father.
cup Jesus is talking about the terrible things that will happen to him. Accepting these things will be very hard, like drinking a cup of something bitter.

DEATH

Loving Memories

"Peace I leave with you." That's the message Rudy Beranek lived and died.

Peace and hope. Those were Rudy's constant themes in life. And as he prepared for his death, he continued to share those gifts.

He invited two funeral homes to work together on his funeral services, because the funeral director of each was his close friend. He then asked two flower shops to design floral arrangements, again, because he valued each shop owner's friendship.

For Rudy, the most important thing in life was people working together for the good of all, sharing their gifts and appreciating others' gifts. It was as if by inviting businesses to collaborate in preparing with him for his death that he was inviting them to recognize what was most important in life.

Rudy also asked people at each church he had served to donate college scholarships for children to have a Christian education. And he invited each church's choir to share its gift of song at his funeral.

He wanted no one to be left out. In short, Rudy said "I love you" to the people whom his life had touched.

Jesus, like Rudy, shared his life as he gathered his friends together for his last meal. Read about this special gathering in **Mark 14:12–26**.

- How did Jesus, like Rudy, prepare people for his death?
- How can you remember Jesus' death for you every day?

CONSIDER . . .

- visiting the grave or a favorite spot of a friend or relative who has died. Recall the ways that person taught you through his or her life.
- creating a symbol of Jesus' death and carrying it in your pocket or purse every day.

FOR MORE, SEE . . .

- Exodus 12:1–17 (p. 67)
- Luke 22:7–20 (p. 1049)
- John 13:21–30 (p. 1081)

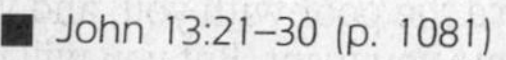

you sleeping? Couldn't you stay awake with me for one hour? 38Stay awake and pray for strength against temptation. The spirit wants to do what is right, but the body is weak."

39Again Jesus went away and prayed the same thing. 40Then he went back to his followers, and again he found them asleep, because their eyes were very heavy. And they did not know what to say to him.

41After Jesus prayed a third time, he went back to his followers and said to them, "Are you still sleeping and resting? That's enough. The time has come for the Son of Man[d] to be handed over to sinful people. 42Get up, we must go. Look, here comes the man who has turned against me."

Jesus Is Arrested

43At once, while Jesus was still speaking, Judas, one of the twelve apostles,[d] came up. With him were many people carrying swords and clubs who had been sent from the leading priests, the teachers of the law, and the older Jewish leaders.

44Judas had planned a signal for them, saying, "The man I kiss is Jesus. Arrest him and guard him while you lead him away." 45So Judas went straight to Jesus and said, "Teacher!" and kissed him. 46Then the people grabbed Jesus and arrested him. 47One of his followers standing nearby pulled out his sword and struck the servant of the high priest and cut off his ear.

48Then Jesus said, "You came to get me with swords and clubs as if I were a criminal. 49Every day I was with you teaching in the Temple,[d] and you did not arrest me there. But all these things have happened to make the Scriptures[d] come true." 50Then all of Jesus' followers left him and ran away.

51A young man, wearing only a linen cloth, was following Jesus, and the people also grabbed him. 52But the cloth he was wearing came off, and he ran away naked.

Jesus Before the Leaders

53The people who arrested Jesus led him to the house of the high priest, where all the leading priests, the older Jewish leaders, and the teachers of the law were gathered. 54Peter followed far behind and entered the courtyard of the high priest's house. There he sat with the guards, warming himself by the fire.

55The leading priests and the whole Jewish council tried to find something that Jesus had done wrong so they could kill him. But the council could find no proof of anything. 56Many people came and told false things about him, but all said different things—none of them agreed.

57Then some people stood up and lied about Jesus, saying, 58"We heard this man say, 'I will destroy this Temple[d] that people made. And three days later, I will build another Temple not made by people.' " 59But even the things these people said did not agree.

60Then the high priest stood before them and asked Jesus, "Aren't you going to answer? Don't you have something to say about their charges against you?" 61But Jesus said nothing; he did not answer.

The high priest asked Jesus another question: "Are you the Christ,[d] the Son of the blessed God?"

62Jesus answered, "I am. And in the future you will see the Son of Man[d] sitting at the right hand of God, the Powerful One, and coming on clouds in the sky."

63When the high priest heard this, he tore his clothes and said, "We don't need any more witnesses! 64You all heard him say these things against God. What do you think?"

They all said that Jesus was guilty and should die. 65Some of the people there began to spit at Jesus. They blindfolded him and beat him with their fists and said, "Prove you are a prophet!"[d] Then the guards led Jesus away and beat him.

Peter Says He Doesn't Know Jesus

66While Peter was in the courtyard, a servant girl of the high priest came there. 67She saw Peter warming himself at the fire and looked closely at him.

Then she said, "You also were with Jesus, that man from Nazareth."

68But Peter said that he was never with Jesus. He said, "I don't know or understand what you are talking about." Then Peter left and went toward the entrance of the courtyard. And the rooster crowed.[n]

69The servant girl saw Peter there, and again she said to the people who were standing nearby, "This man is one of those who followed Jesus." 70Again Peter said that it was not true.

A short time later, some people were standing near Peter saying, "Surely you are one of those who followed Jesus, because you are from Galilee, too."

71Then Peter began to place a curse on himself and swear, "I don't know this man you're talking about!"

72At once, the rooster crowed the second time. Then Peter remembered what Jesus had told him: "Before the rooster crows twice, you will say three times that you don't know me." Then Peter lost control of himself and began to cry.

And . . . crowed. A few, early Greek copies leave out this phrase.

Pilate Questions Jesus

15 Very early in the morning, the leading
priests, the older leaders, the teachers of the law, and all the Jewish council decided what to do with Jesus. They tied him, led him away, and turned him over to Pilate, the governor.
2Pilate asked Jesus, "Are you the king of the Jews?"

Jesus answered, "Those are your words."
3The leading priests accused Jesus of many
things. 4So Pilate asked Jesus another question, "You can see that they are accusing you of many things. Aren't you going to answer?"
5But Jesus still said nothing, so Pilate was very surprised.

Pilate Tries to Free Jesus

6Every year at the time of the Passover[d] the governor would free one prisoner whom the people chose.
7At that time, there was a man named Barabbas in prison who was a rebel and had committed murder during a riot.
8The crowd came to

PEER PRESSURE

Curfew Capers

"It's our last night at camp. Can't we please stay up late to talk?" Missy Goette and Michael Davenport begged.

The two spokespeople had been designated by their peers to negotiate an extended curfew with Wayne Broderick, the camp director. Wayne listened patiently. Then he reminded them that "we all agreed on Sunday evening that the camp curfew would be midnight. We still have one day's activities to rest up for, so we will not change the curfew."

Missy and Michael reluctantly agreed and relayed the news to their friends. Most accepted the verdict.

Nonetheless, Mary McCain and Justin Weimer convinced Missy to secretly rendezvous at 4 A.M. to celebrate their last night together.

Just after leaving their dorms, the three friends came face-to-face with Wayne.

"What are you doing out here?" he growled.

Missy tried to explain: "We were just talking. We wanted to have more time together before we have to leave."

"What about curfew?" asked Wayne.

"We agreed to a midnight curfew," Justin admitted.

Wayne continued by asking, "What are the consequences for breaking a guideline?"

Mary spoke quietly as tears filled her eyes. "We have to call our parents to pick us up from camp early."

After daybreak, Wayne had the three call their parents. Soon they were heading homeward with their families.

Peer pressure, like that Mary, Justin, and Missy experienced, can be destructive. Read **Mark 15:1–20** to see how a type of peer pressure led to Jesus' death.

- Why did Pilate, the crowd who shouted for Barabbas to be released, and the kids who came together at 4 A.M. give in to pressure?
- If you had been in the shouting crowd, how would you have withstood the pressure to kill Jesus? How can you use those same actions to withstand peer pressure today?

CONSIDER . . .

- listing situations in which you experience strong peer pressure to do wrong. Beside each situation, write what you can do or say to withstand the pressure.
- forming a "Pressure Valve Team" with friends. Whenever a teammate is pressured to do something wrong, relieve that negative pressure by providing positive pressure to do what's right.

FOR MORE, SEE . . .

- Proverbs 1:10–19 (p. 568)
- Luke 23:1–25 (p. 1052)
- John 18:28—19:16 (p. 1091)

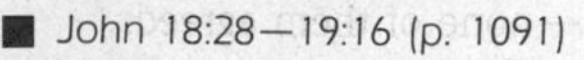

Pilate and began to ask him to free a prisoner as he always did.

9So Pilate asked them, "Do you want me to free the king of the Jews?" 10Pilate knew that the leading priests had turned Jesus in to him because they were jealous. 11But the leading priests had persuaded the people to ask Pilate to free Barabbas, not Jesus.

12Then Pilate asked the crowd again, "So what should I do with this man you call the king of the Jews?"

13They shouted, "Crucify him!"

14Pilate asked, "Why? What wrong has he done?"

But they shouted even louder, "Crucify him!"

15Pilate wanted to please the crowd, so he freed Barabbas for them. After having Jesus beaten with whips, he handed Jesus over to the soldiers to be crucified.

SIDELIGHT: The kind of beating Jesus experienced (Mark 15:15) was a gruesome practice among the Romans. The whip was made of leather, lead, and bone, and could tear out eyes, sever veins, and rip open stomachs. It was a customary part of the death sentence.

16The soldiers took Jesus into the governor's palace (called the Praetorium) and called all the other soldiers together. 17They put a purple robe on Jesus and used thorny branches to make a crown for his head. 18They began to call out to him, "Hail, King of the Jews!" 19The soldiers beat Jesus on the head many times with a stick. They spit on him and made fun of him by bowing on their knees and worshiping him. 20After they finished, the soldiers took off the purple robe and put his own clothes on him again. Then they led him out of the palace to be crucified.

Jesus Is Crucified

21A man named Simon from Cyrene, the father of Alexander and Rufus, was coming from the fields to the city. The soldiers forced Simon to carry the cross for Jesus. 22They led Jesus to the place called Golgotha, which means the Place of the Skull. 23The soldiers tried to give Jesus wine mixed with myrrh[d] to drink, but he refused. 24The soldiers crucified Jesus and divided his clothes among themselves, throwing lots[d] to decide what each soldier would get.

25It was nine o'clock in the morning when they crucified Jesus. 26There was a sign with this charge against Jesus written on it: THE KING OF THE JEWS. 27They also put two robbers on crosses beside Jesus, one on the right, and the other on the left. 28 [n] 29People walked by and insulted Jesus and shook their heads, saying, "You said you could destroy the Temple[d] and build it again in three days. 30So save yourself! Come down from that cross!"

31The leading priests and the teachers of the law were also making fun of Jesus. They said to each other, "He saved other people, but he can't save himself. 32If he is really the Christ,[d] the king of Israel, let him come down now from the cross. When we see this, we will believe in him." The robbers who were being crucified beside Jesus also insulted him.

Jesus Dies

33At noon the whole country became dark, and the darkness lasted for three hours. 34At three o'clock Jesus cried in a loud voice, "Eloi, Eloi, lama sabachthani." This means, "My God, my God, why have you rejected me?"

35When some of the people standing there heard this, they said, "Listen! He is calling Elijah."

36Someone there ran and got a sponge, filled it with vinegar, tied it to a stick, and gave it to Jesus to drink. He said, "We want to see if Elijah will come to take him down from the cross."

37Then Jesus cried in a loud voice and died.

38The curtain in the Temple[n] was torn into two pieces, from the top to the bottom. 39When the army officer who was standing in front of the cross saw what happened when Jesus died, he said, "This man really was the Son of God!"

40Some women were standing at a distance from the cross, watching; among them were Mary Magdalene, Salome, and Mary the mother of James and Joseph. (James was her youngest son.) 41These women had followed Jesus in Galilee and helped him. Many other women were also there who had come with Jesus to Jerusalem.

Jesus Is Buried

42This was Preparation[d] Day. (That means the day before the Sabbath[d] day.) That evening, 43Joseph from Arimathea was brave enough to go to Pilate and ask for Jesus' body. Joseph, an important member of the Jewish council, was one of the people who was waiting for the kingdom of God to come. 44Pilate was amazed that Jesus would have already died, so he called the army officer who had guarded Jesus and asked him if Jesus had already died. 45The officer told Pilate that he was

Verse 28 Some Greek copies add verse 28: "And the Scripture came true that says, 'They put him with criminals.' "
curtain in the Temple A curtain divided the Most Holy Place from the other part of the Temple. That was the special building in Jerusalem where God commanded the Jewish people to worship him.

dead, so Pilate told Joseph he could have the body. [46]Joseph bought some linen cloth, took the body down from the cross, and wrapped it in the linen. He put the body in a tomb that was cut out of a wall of rock. Then he rolled a very large stone to block the entrance of the tomb. [47]And Mary Magdalene and Mary the mother of Joseph saw the place where Jesus was laid.

> **SIDELIGHT:** Most people who were crucified in Jesus' day were left on the cross or were simply discarded in a mass grave. By requesting Jesus' body for burial, Joseph saved Jesus from that final indignity (Mark 15:42–47).

Jesus Rises from the Dead

16 The day after the Sabbath[d] day, Mary Magdalene, Mary the mother of James, and Salome bought some sweet-smelling spices to put on Jesus' body. [2]Very early on that day, the first day of the week, soon after sunrise, the women were on their way to the tomb. [3]They said to each other, "Who will roll away for us the stone that covers the entrance of the tomb?"

[4]Then the women looked and saw that the stone had already been rolled away, even though it was very large. [5]The women entered the tomb and saw a young man wearing a white robe and sitting on the right side, and they were afraid.

[6]But the man said, "Don't be afraid. You are looking for Jesus from Nazareth, who has been crucified. He has risen from the dead; he is not here. Look, here is the place they laid him. [7]Now go and tell his followers and Peter, 'Jesus is going into Galilee ahead of you, and you will see him there as he told you before.' "

[8]The women were confused and shaking with fear, so they left the tomb and ran away. They did not tell anyone about what happened, because they were afraid.

Verses 9-20 are not included in two of the best and oldest Greek manuscripts of Mark.

Some Followers See Jesus

[[9]After Jesus rose from the dead early on the first day of the week, he showed himself first to Mary Magdalene. One time in the past, he had forced seven demons[d] out of her. [10]After Mary saw Jesus, she went and told his followers, who were very sad and were crying. [11]But Mary told

JESUS CHRIST

Unexpected Savior

Jesus painted no pictures. Yet some of the greatest artists were inspired by him to paint their greatest works.

Jesus wrote no poetry. Yet hundreds of the world's greatest poems pay tribute to him.

Jesus composed no music. Yet Haydn, Handel, Beethoven, Bach, and other great musicians wrote some of their greatest music to praise him.

Jesus preached and taught for only three years. The philosopher Socrates taught for forty years, Plato for fifty years, and Aristotle for forty years. Yet more people follow what Jesus taught than follow the three philosophers combined.

Jesus died on a cross as a criminal. Yet even a guard who helped put him to death recognized that he was God's Son. Read **Mark 15:33–39** to see how Jesus showed he was God's Son even in his death.

- What unexpected things do you see in Jesus' life as described by the passage and by the comparisons above?
- How does this passage strengthen your faith in Jesus as God's Son?

CONSIDER . . .

- listing everything you would expect a king to do. Then compare it to what you read in the Bible about Jesus. Identify similarities and differences.
- rereading the passage, putting yourself in the place of the officer. How would you have responded to this situation? What would you have said?

FOR MORE, SEE . . .

- Isaiah 53 (p. 672)
- Matthew 16:21–28 (p. 937)
- John 19:28–37 (p. 1092)

them that Jesus was alive. She said that she had
seen him, but the followers did not believe her.
12Later, Jesus showed himself to two of his followers while they were walking in the country,
but he did not look the same as before. 13These
followers went back to the others and told them
what had happened, but again, the followers did
not believe them.

Jesus Talks to the Apostles

14Later Jesus showed himself to the eleven
apostles while they were eating, and he criticized
them because they had no faith. They were stubborn and refused to believe those who had seen
him after he had risen from the dead.
15Jesus said to his followers, "Go everywhere in
the world, and tell the Good News[d] to everyone.
16Anyone who believes and is baptized will be
saved, but anyone who does not believe will be
punished. 17And those who believe will be able to
do these things as proof: They will use my name
to force out demons.[d] They will speak in new languages.[n] 18They will pick up snakes and drink
poison without being hurt. They will touch the
sick, and the sick will be healed."
19After the Lord Jesus said these things to his
followers, he was carried up into heaven, and he
sat at the right side of God. 20The followers went
everywhere in the world and told the Good News
to people, and the Lord helped them. The Lord
proved that the Good News they told was true by
giving them power to work miracles.[d]]

languages This can also be translated "tongues."

LIFE

A Light in the Darkness

Devon Sparks was heavily into drugs by the time he was fourteen. After being arrested for helping his friends steal a radio, he was placed in an alternative school. But he kept slipping further and further downhill.

He became more distant from his family and friends. And he started using drugs daily to try to escape the pain he felt inside.

One day Devon couldn't stand the pain any longer. He hated himself, and he didn't want to go on living. He felt trapped. The darkness was overwhelming, and he just couldn't see a way out.

Finally, he cried out to God. "Please," he pleaded, "please help me."

Almost immediately he sensed a peace and calm inside, as if the darkness was replaced with a new hope. In the next weeks, he began attending Narcotics Anonymous support meetings and joined a Christian fellowship. Devon had a new beginning.

"Turning my life over to God's direction is the toughest decision I've ever made," Devon later explained. "But my faith is beginning to pay off. I'm making new friends. I found a job. I'm taking art classes. I feel alive. It's a day-to-day struggle to stay free of drugs, but I'm headed in the right direction for once in my life."

Devon was beginning to experience the life and power of Jesus' resurrection. Read about the resurrection in **Mark 16:1–8**.

- How was Devon's new life similar to Jesus' resurrection? How was it different?
- How is your response to Jesus' resurrection like or unlike the women's reactions in this passage?

CONSIDER . . .

- asking God to "roll away" an obstacle in your life with his resurrection power.
- listing the ways you can "stop the pain" you may be experiencing like Devon stopped his pain. Ask others for help if you need to.

FOR MORE, SEE . . .

- Exodus 14 (p. 70)
- Matthew 28:1–10 (p. 961)
- John 20:1–18 (p. 1093)

SHARING FAITH

Pass It On!

Geri Rainbolt was frightened when she stepped up to the microphone. She wasn't sure God could use her story to help other people. But she began speaking anyway.

"Two years ago I went out drinking with several friends. I drank so much I passed out. My friends panicked. Was I dying? Would I be okay? They didn't know what to do.

"So they drove me to Kristi Coll's house. Her parents would know what to do. They were always around when we needed them.

"Kristi's parents called my dad. He came and picked me up, drove me home and carried me to my room. I don't remember anything—just waking up the next morning.

"My dad came in to talk with me. Tears filled his eyes. He was so afraid of losing me.

"Right then, I realized I never knew how much I could hurt my father. I really love him, but I had hurt him.

"And that's the message I want to share with you today. The things that keep me—that keep us—from loving our parents or friends are the same things that can keep us from growing in our relationship with God."

The room was silent as the teenagers soaked in the truth of Geri's message. Geri could sense God's power as she stepped away from the microphone. She had indeed passed on a truth about faith they all needed to hear.

In **Mark 16:19–20**, Jesus' first followers experienced the same power in telling others about Jesus.

■ How is Geri's talk similar to the disciples telling the Good News? How is it different?

■ How can you tell others the Good News?

C O N S I D E R . . .

■ telling a non-Christian friend about Jesus.

■ asking your pastor or youth leader to lead a training course on telling others about Christ.

F O R M O R E , S E E . . .

■ 1 Kings 18 (p. 323)

■ Luke 24:44–53 (p. 1056)

■ Acts 1:1–14 (p. 1098)

LUKE

Why Read This Book:

- Discover the Bible's only stories about Jesus' childhood (Luke 2).
- See how Jesus ministered to all people, especially the poor and the outcast (Luke 4—8).
- Enjoy some of Jesus' most famous stories (Luke 10, 15—16).
- Learn how Jesus gave his life for our sins (Luke 22—24).

Behind the Scenes:

Imagine never hearing that Jesus was laid in a manger when he was born (Luke 2:7–11). Imagine not knowing the parable of the Good Samaritan (Luke 10:25–37). Or the parable of the son who left home, which is also known as the Prodigal Son (Luke 15:11–32). Imagine not knowing about Jesus' encounter with Zacchaeus (Luke 19:1–10).

We wouldn't have any of these stories without the Gospel of Luke. Though the books of Matthew, Mark, and John tell many stories about Jesus, they don't include about one-third of the material in Luke. Luke is the most complete account of Jesus' life. Written by a doctor, it's a detailed, organized picture of Jesus' life and ministry.

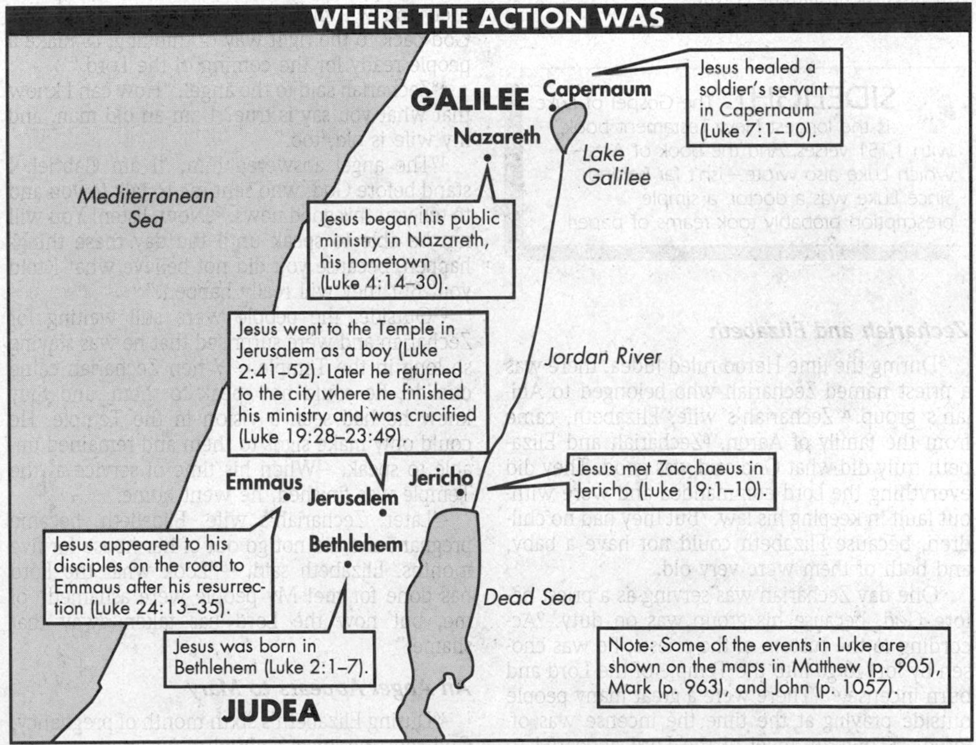
WHERE THE ACTION WAS
GALILEE
Capernaum
Jesus healed a soldier's servant in Capernaum (Luke 7:1–10).
Nazareth
Lake Galilee
Mediterranean Sea
Jesus began his public ministry in Nazareth, his hometown (Luke 4:14–30).
Jesus went to the Temple in Jerusalem as a boy (Luke 2:41–52). Later he returned to the city where he finished his ministry and was crucified (Luke 19:28–23:49).
Jordan River
Emmaus
Jerusalem
Jericho
Jesus met Zacchaeus in Jericho (Luke 19:1–10).
Bethlehem
Jesus appeared to his disciples on the road to Emmaus after his resurrection (Luke 24:13–35).
Dead Sea
Jesus was born in Bethlehem (Luke 2:1–7).
Note: Some of the events in Luke are shown on the maps in Matthew (p. 905), Mark (p. 963), and John (p. 1057).
JUDEA
WHEN THE ACTION WAS
Jesus was born
Jesus was crucified, rose from the dead, and went to heaven
Paul began his missionary work
Fire destroyed Rome
BC/AD
25AD
50AD
75AD
100AD
Jesus began his ministry
Romans destroyed the Temple in Jerusalem

Behind the Scenes (cont.): As you read the Gospel of Luke, you'll discover some important emphases. First, this book emphasizes that Jesus came for all people, not just the Jews. You'll also see Jesus' particular concern for women, the poor and the outcasts of the world. Then the book shows Jesus as God's Spirit-led Son who came to offer eternal life to all people who follow him.

Luke 19:10 says that "the Son of Man came to find lost people and save them." This book tells, in detail, the story of his coming. If you like the Gospel of Luke, check out the sequel: the book of Acts (p. 1097). It's written by the same author, and continues the story where Luke leaves off.

Luke Writes About Jesus' Life

1 Many have tried to report on the things that
happened among us. 2They have written the
same things that we learned from others—the
people who saw those things from the beginning
and served God by telling people his message.
3Since I myself have studied everything carefully
from the beginning, most excellent[n] Theophilus,
it seemed good for me to write it out for you. I
arranged it in order 4to help you know that what
you have been taught is true.

> **SIDELIGHT:** The Gospel of Luke is the longest New Testament book, with 1,151 verses. And the book of Acts—which Luke also wrote—isn't far behind. Since Luke was a doctor, a simple prescription probably took reams of paper!

Zechariah and Elizabeth

5During the time Herod ruled Judea, there was
a priest named Zechariah who belonged to Abijah's group.[n] Zechariah's wife, Elizabeth, came
from the family of Aaron. 6Zechariah and Elizabeth truly did what God said was good. They did
everything the Lord commanded and were without fault in keeping his law. 7But they had no children, because Elizabeth could not have a baby,
and both of them were very old.

8One day Zechariah was serving as a priest before God, because his group was on duty. 9Ac-
cording to the custom of the priests, he was chosen by lot[d] to go into the Temple of the Lord and
burn incense.[d] 10There were a great many people
outside praying at the time the incense was offered. 11Then an angel of the Lord appeared to
Zechariah, standing on the right side of the incense table. 12When he saw the angel, Zechariah
was startled and frightened. 13But the angel said
to him, "Zechariah, don't be afraid. God has
heard your prayer. Your wife, Elizabeth, will give
birth to a son, and you will name him John. 14He
will bring you joy and gladness, and many people
will be happy because of his birth. 15John will be
a great man for the Lord. He will never drink
wine or beer, and even from birth, he will be filled
with the Holy Spirit.[d] 16He will help many people
of Israel return to the Lord their God. 17He will go
before the Lord in spirit and power like Elijah. He
will make peace between parents and their children and will bring those who are not obeying
God back to the right way of thinking, to make a
people ready for the coming of the Lord."

18Zechariah said to the angel, "How can I know
that what you say is true? I am an old man, and
my wife is old, too."

19The angel answered him, "I am Gabriel. I
stand before God, who sent me to talk to you and
to tell you this good news. 20Now, listen! You will
not be able to speak until the day these things
happen, because you did not believe what I told
you. But they will really happen."

21Outside, the people were still waiting for
Zechariah and were surprised that he was staying
so long in the Temple. 22When Zechariah came
outside, he could not speak to them, and they
knew he had seen a vision in the Temple. He
could only make signs to them and remained unable to speak. 23When his time of service at the
Temple was finished, he went home.

24Later, Zechariah's wife, Elizabeth, became
pregnant and did not go out of her house for five
months. Elizabeth said, 25"Look what the Lord
has done for me! My people were ashamed[n] of
me, but now the Lord has taken away that
shame."

An Angel Appears to Mary

26During Elizabeth's sixth month of pregnancy,
God sent the angel Gabriel to Nazareth, a town
in Galilee, 27to a virgin.[d] She was engaged to
marry a man named Joseph from the family of
David. Her name was Mary. 28The angel came to

excellent This word was used to show respect to an important person like a king or ruler.
Abijah's group The Jewish priests were divided into twenty-four groups. See 1 Chronicles 24.
ashamed The Jewish people thought it was a disgrace for women not to have children.

her and said, "Greetings! The Lord has blessed
you and is with you."
29But Mary was very startled by what the angel
said and wondered what this greeting might
mean.
30The angel said to her, "Don't be afraid, Mary;
God has shown you his grace. 31Listen! You will
become pregnant and give birth to a son, and you
will name him Jesus. 32He will be great and
will be called the Son of the Most High. The
Lord God will give him the throne of King David,
his ancestor. 33He will rule over the people
of Jacob forever, and his kingdom will never
end."
34Mary said to the angel, "How will this happen since I am a virgin?"
35The angel said to Mary, "The Holy Spirit[d] will
come upon you, and the power of the Most High
will cover you. For this reason the baby will be
holy and will be called the Son of God. 36Now
Elizabeth, your relative, is also pregnant with a
son though she is very old. Everyone thought she
could not have a baby, but she has been pregnant
for six months. 37God can do anything!"
38Mary said, "I am the servant of the Lord. Let
this happen to me as you say!" Then the angel
went away.

Mary Visits Elizabeth

39Mary got up and went quickly to a town in
the hills of Judea. 40She came to Zechariah's
house and greeted Elizabeth. 41When Elizabeth
heard Mary's greeting, the unborn baby inside her
jumped, and Elizabeth was filled with the Holy
Spirit.[d] 42She cried out in a loud voice, "God has
blessed you more than any other woman, and he
has blessed the baby to which you will give birth.
43Why has this good thing happened to me, that
the mother of my Lord comes to me? 44When I
heard your voice, the baby inside me jumped with
joy. 45You are blessed because you believed that
what the Lord said to you would really happen."

Mary Praises God

46Then Mary said,
"My soul praises the Lord;
47 my heart rejoices in God my Savior,
48because he has shown his concern for his
humble servant girl.

GOD'S POWER

Power in Letting Go

Joni Eareckson loved to swim when she was young. She was an excellent diver too, and had even thought about trying out for the Olympics.

When she was seventeen, Joni and her friends went swimming in Chesapeake Bay. Joni dove into the unfamiliar waters, expecting to feel that cool, free-floating feeling she had come to love. Instead, she felt nothing. As her head struck the bottom, her spinal cord snapped—leaving her paralyzed from the neck down for the rest of her life.

Joni felt depressed and angry at the prospect of spending the rest of her life in a wheelchair. Most of her anger was aimed at God. "Oh God, how can you do this to me?" she prayed. "What have you done to me?"

Though God has never healed her physically, he did heal Joni's soul. And over the years she has grown into a beautiful free spirit. She sums it up this way: "When I had no choice but acceptance, trust, and surrender . . . it was as if I had finally gained emotional independence—through complete dependence on God."

Read **Luke 1:26–38** to see how God brought forth life in another teenage girl because she was ready to accept, trust, and surrender.

- How was Mary's response to God's actions different from or similar to Joni's?
- In what specific ways would you like to see God's power change your life?

CONSIDER. . .

- underlining the verses in this passage that speak most to you, and memorizing them.
- asking God to help you understand his unlimited power and the ways he chooses to use (or not to use) it.

FOR MORE, SEE. . .

- Psalm 31:14–24 (p. 500)
- 2 Corinthians 12:7–10 (p. 1203)

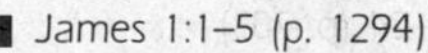

- James 1:1–5 (p. 1294)

From now on, all people will say that I am
blessed,
49 because the Powerful One has done great
things for me.
His name is holy.
50God will show his mercy forever and ever
to those who worship and serve him.
51He has done mighty deeds by his power.
He has scattered the people who are
proud
and think great things about themselves.
52He has brought down rulers from their
thrones
and raised up the humble.
53He has filled the hungry with good things
and sent the rich away with nothing.
54He has helped his servant, the people of
Israel,
remembering to show them mercy
55as he promised to our ancestors,
to Abraham and to his children forever."
56Mary stayed with Elizabeth for about three
months and then returned home.

The Birth of John

57When it was time for Elizabeth to give birth,
she had a boy. 58Her neighbors and relatives heard
how good the Lord was to her, and they rejoiced
with her.
59When the baby was eight days old, they came
to circumcise[d] him. They wanted to name him
Zechariah because this was his father's name,
60but his mother said, "No! He will be named
John."
61The people said to Elizabeth, "But no one in
your family has this name." 62Then they made
signs to his father to find out what he would like
to name him.
63Zechariah asked for a writing tablet and
wrote, "His name is John," and everyone was surprised. 64Immediately Zechariah could talk again,
and he began praising God. 65All their neighbors
became alarmed, and in all the mountains of Judea people continued talking about all these
things. 66The people who heard about them wondered, saying, "What will this child be?" because
the Lord was with him.

Zechariah Praises God

67Then Zechariah, John's father, was filled with
the Holy Spirit and prophesied:[d]
68"Let us praise the Lord, the God of Israel,
because he has come to help his people and
has given them freedom.

BRAGGING

A Tale of Two Teenagers

Ted and Ed were graduating seniors. One was voted most popular; the other most respected. Both graduated with many awards.

Ed never talked about himself. He never seemed to mind not being in the spotlight.

But Ted had to be the center of attention. If he thought others missed the significance of his accomplishments, he quickly filled them in.

They were two of the state's best cross-country runners. Ted almost always finished first, and Ed almost always came in right behind him. They were both comfortable with that, and always managed to congratulate and praise each other after a race. In their final state meet, however, Ed finished first. Ted couldn't congratulate or praise him, or even accept congratulations for himself. He was only comfortable with being Number One.

Ted bragged a lot to get attention, but Ed didn't. Read **Luke 1:39–56** to see how God blessed a young girl, who didn't brag or take credit for herself.

- If Mary were in high school today, what do you think she would be like?
- Are you more like Ed or Ted? How does Mary's prayer in this passage apply to you?

C O N S I D E R . . .

- drawing a line with two endpoints labeled ED and TED. Place a pencil point where you think you fit on the line, and another where you would like to be on the line. Ask God to help you reach your goal.
- thinking of someone you know who is like Ed, and spending more time with that person.

F O R M O R E , S E E . . .

- Jeremiah 9:23–24 (p. 703)
- Romans 12:3–5 (p. 1157)
- Philippians 2:5–11 (p. 1230)

69He has given us a powerful Savior
from the family of God's servant David.
70He said that he would do this
through his holy prophets[d] who lived long ago:
71He promised he would save us from our enemies
and from the power of all those who hate us.
72He said he would give mercy to our fathers
and that he would remember his holy promise.
73God promised Abraham, our father,
74 that he would save us from the power of our enemies
so we could serve him without fear,
75being holy and good before God as long as we live.
76"Now you, child, will be called a prophet of the Most High God.
You will go before the Lord to prepare his way.
77You will make his people know that they will be saved
by having their sins forgiven.
78With the loving mercy of our God,
a new day from heaven will dawn upon us.
79It will shine on those who live in darkness,
in the shadow of death.
It will guide us into the path of peace."

80And so the child grew up and became strong
in spirit. John lived in the desert until the time
when he came out to preach to Israel.

The Birth of Jesus

2 At that time, Augustus Caesar[d] sent an order
that all people in the countries under Roman
rule must list their names in a register. 2This was
the first registration;[n] it was taken while Quirinius was governor of Syria. 3And all went to their
own towns to be registered.

4So Joseph left Nazareth, a town in Galilee, and
went to the town of Bethlehem in Judea, known
as the town of David. Joseph went there because
he was from the family of David. 5Joseph registered with Mary, to whom he was engaged[n] and
who was now pregnant. 6While they were in
Bethlehem, the time came for Mary to have the
baby, 7and she gave birth to her first son. Because
there were no rooms left in the inn, she wrapped
the baby with pieces of cloth and laid him in a box
where animals are fed.

Shepherds Hear About Jesus

8That night, some shepherds were in the fields
nearby watching their sheep. 9Then an angel of

> **SIDELIGHT:** When Mary wrapped Jesus with cloths (Luke 2:7), he probably couldn't move his arms because he was wrapped so tightly. In biblical times, people believed a good six-month "wrapping" prevented arms and legs from becoming crooked.

the Lord stood before them. The glory of the Lord
was shining around them, and they became very
frightened. 10The angel said to them, "Do not be
afraid. I am bringing you good news that will be
a great joy to all the people. 11Today your Savior
was born in the town of David. He is Christ,[d] the
Lord. 12This is how you will know him: You will
find a baby wrapped in pieces of cloth and lying
in a feeding box."

13Then a very large group of angels from
heaven joined the first angel, praising God and
saying:

14"Give glory to God in heaven,
and on earth let there be peace among the people who please God."

15When the angels left them and went back to
heaven, the shepherds said to each other, "Let's
go to Bethlehem. Let's see this thing that has happened which the Lord has told us about."

16So the shepherds went quickly and found
Mary and Joseph and the baby, who was lying in
a feeding box. 17When they had seen him, they
told what the angels had said about this child.
18Everyone was amazed at what the shepherds
said to them. 19But Mary treasured these things
and continued to think about them. 20Then the
shepherds went back to their sheep, praising God
and thanking him for everything they had seen
and heard. It had been just as the angel had told
them.

21When the baby was eight days old, he was
circumcised[d] and was named Jesus, the name
given by the angel before the baby began to grow
inside Mary.

Jesus Is Presented in the Temple

22When the time came for Mary and Joseph to
do what the law of Moses taught about being
made pure,[n] they took Jesus to Jerusalem to
present him to the Lord. 23(It is written in the law

registration Census. A counting of all the people and the things they own.
engaged For the Jewish people, an engagement was a lasting agreement. It could only be broken by divorce.
pure The law of Moses said that forty days after a Jewish woman gave birth to a son, she must be cleansed by a ceremony at the Temple. Read Leviticus 12:2-8.

of the Lord: "Every firstborn[d] male shall be given to the Lord.")[n] 24Mary and Joseph also went to offer a sacrifice, as the law of the Lord says: "You must sacrifice two doves or two young pigeons."[n]

Simeon Sees Jesus

25In Jerusalem lived a man named Simeon who was a good man and godly. He was waiting for the time when God would take away Israel's sorrow, and the Holy Spirit[d] was in him. 26Simeon had been told by the Holy Spirit that he would not die before he saw the Christ[d] promised by the Lord.
27The Spirit led Simeon to the Temple.[d] When Mary and Joseph brought the baby Jesus to the Temple to do what the law said they must do,
28Simeon took the baby in his arms and thanked God:

29"Now, Lord, you can let me, your servant,
die in peace as you said.
30With my own eyes I have seen your
salvation,
31 which you prepared before all people.
32It is a light for the non-Jewish people to see
and an honor for your people, the
Israelites."

33Jesus' father and mother were amazed at what Simeon had said about him. 34Then Simeon blessed them and said to Mary, "God has chosen this child to cause the fall and rise of many in Israel. He will be a sign from God that many people will not accept 35so that the thoughts of many will be made known. And the things that will happen will make your heart sad, too."

Anna Sees Jesus

36There was a prophetess,[d] Anna, from the family of Phanuel in the tribe[d] of Asher. Anna was very old. She had once been married for seven years. 37Then her husband died, and she was a widow for eighty-four years. Anna never left the Temple but worshiped God, going without food and praying day and night. 38Standing there at that time, she thanked God and spoke about Jesus to all who were waiting for God to free Jerusalem.

Joseph and Mary Return Home

39When Joseph and Mary had done everything the law of the Lord commanded, they went home to Nazareth, their own town in Galilee. 40The little child grew and became strong. He was filled with wisdom, and God's goodness was upon him.

"Every . . . Lord." Quotation from Exodus 13:2.
"You . . . pigeons." Quotation from Leviticus 12:8.

WORSHIP

Awesome Stuff

When you look up at the sky on a clear night, did you know:

- the nearest star to earth is four light-years away?
- the light your eyeball sees from a star may have begun its journey toward you—at 186,000 miles per second—before the birth of Christ?
- some of the stars you see in a night sky may not be stars but whole galaxies? They may be millions of stars that are so incredibly far away they appear to be just one pinpoint of light.
- our little corner of the universe is one of only a few places with light and activity? Most of space is vast emptiness with no stars or planets.
- the earth's place in the universe may be comparable to the place occupied by a grain of sand in our world? Awe-inspiring, isn't it? In **Luke 2:8–21** the shepherds also learned how worship can grow out of seeing beyond ourselves into God's awesome realm.
- How do the facts of Jesus' birth and the vastness of our universe compare or contrast?
- What does it tell you to know that the same God who made and watches over us became a human just so we could know him?

C O N S I D E R . . .

- listing five ways you can worship God more, then doing them.
- sitting under a starry sky and pondering God's vast power.

F O R M O R E , S E E . . .

- Psalm 8:3–9 (p. 486)
- Habbakuk 3:17–19 (p. 878)
- Acts 4:24–31 (p. 1104)

Jesus As a Boy

41Every year Jesus' parents went to Jerusalem
for the Passover[d] Feast. 42When he was twelve
years old, they went to the feast as they always
did. 43After the feast days were over, they started
home. The boy Jesus stayed behind in Jerusalem,
but his parents did not know it. 44Thinking that
Jesus was with them in the group, they traveled
for a whole day. Then they began to look for him
among their family and friends. 45When they did
not find him, they went back to Jerusalem to look
for him there. 46After three days they found Jesus
sitting in the Temple[d] with the teachers, listening
to them and asking them questions. 47All who
heard him were amazed at his understanding and
answers. 48When Jesus' parents saw him, they
were astonished. His mother said to him, "Son,
why did you do this to us? Your father and I were
very worried about you and have been looking for
you."
49Jesus said to them, "Why were you looking
for me? Didn't you know that I must be in my
Father's house?" 50But they did not understand
the meaning of what he said.
51Jesus went with them to Nazareth and was
obedient to them. But his mother kept in her
mind all that had happened. 52Jesus became wiser
and grew physically. People liked him, and he
pleased God.

The Preaching of John

3 It was the fifteenth year of the rule of Tiberius Caesar.[d] These men were under Caesar:
Pontius Pilate, the ruler of Judea; Herod, the ruler
of Galilee; Philip, Herod's brother, the ruler of
Iturea and Trachonitis; and Lysanias, the ruler of
Abilene. 2Annas and Caiaphas were the high
priests. At this time, the word of God came to
John son of Zechariah in the desert. 3He went all
over the area around the Jordan River preaching
a baptism of changed hearts and lives for the forgiveness of sins. 4As it is written in the book of
Isaiah the prophet:[d]

"This is a voice of one
who calls out in the desert:

FAMILY

Laboratory of Faith

"Jen, I don't want to leave." Jen Peters knew Kay Stone was serious. "Christianity is so much easier here. Everyone follows God, gets along, and it feels so good to get away from the pressure."

Kay's youth group had spent a weekend together in a mountain cabin. They had had a lot of fun and spent time learning about God. But now it was time to go home.

"Maybe I should take time off from school and stay here—or maybe even go to school in another town," Kay wondered aloud.

A few caring questions from Jen helped Kay talk about the real issue in her life. She was under stress at home, and the weekend away had provided a sense of escape. She didn't want to go back to the way it was.

"Kay, God has taught you much this weekend. And for every lesson he teaches, he provides a laboratory to test your new understanding and put it to work. Your family just might be your laboratory."

Kay thought for a moment, then nodded in agreement.

"Yeah," Kay sighed. "I guess there's no better place for God to help me grow."

Good or bad, families can challenge you to grow as a person and a Christian. **Luke 2:22–40** speaks of how God used Jesus' family to help him.

- Why does Kay need her family, even though things are hard? Why did Jesus need his family?
- Who are the "Simeons" and "Annas" in your life who help you see God's work in your life and your family? Why are these people important to you?

CONSIDER . . .

- telling your parent one good lesson you have learned because of your family.
- talking to a trusted adult if your family struggles feel overwhelming.

FOR MORE, SEE . . .

- Proverbs 22:6 (p. 586)
- Matthew 12:46–50 (p. 930)
- Ephesians 6:1–3 (p. 1225)

'Prepare the way for the Lord.
Make the road straight for him.
5 Every valley should be filled in,
and every mountain and hill should be
made flat.
Roads with turns should be made straight,
and rough roads should be made smooth.
6 And all people will know about the salvation
of God!' " *Isaiah 40:3-5*

7 To the crowds of people who came to be baptized by John, he said, "You are all snakes! Who
warned you to run away from God's coming punishment? 8 Do the things that show you really
have changed your hearts and lives. Don't begin
to say to yourselves, 'Abraham is our father.' I tell
you that God could make children for Abraham
from these rocks. 9 The ax is now ready to cut
down the trees, and every tree that does not produce good fruit will be cut down and thrown into
the fire."[n]

10 The people asked John, "Then what should
we do?"

11 John answered, "If you have two shirts, share
with the person who does not have one. If you
have food, share that also."

12 Even tax collectors came to John to be baptized. They said to him, "Teacher, what should
we do?"

13 John said to them, "Don't take more taxes
from people than you have been ordered to take."

14 The soldiers asked John, "What about us?
What should we do?"

John said to them, "Don't force people to give
you money, and don't lie about them. Be satisfied
with the pay you get."

15 Since the people were hoping for the Christ[d]
to come, they wondered if John might be the
one.

16 John answered everyone, "I baptize you with
water, but there is one coming who is greater

The ax . . . fire. This means that God is ready to punish his people who do not obey him.

SPIRITUAL GROWTH

Who Am I?

When Brian Ziegler was a boy, he used to love to make mud pies by the outdoor faucet on the side of his house. His mom would give him old pie pans, and he'd fill them with just the right mix of dirt and water.

"You had to be careful to mix it right," Brian recalls. "Too much dirt, and your pie would crumble. Too much water, and it would ooze."

As Brian got older, he didn't make mud pies as often. But he still enjoyed working with his hands to create. In junior high, Brian got into an art class and learned the basics of sculpture design.

"I was hooked from then on," Brian says with a smile. "I loved the idea of taking an image in my hands, and making it a reality in the clay. It's been fun ever since!"

Brian now works as a sculptor part-time after school. He has won several awards for his work through the school system, and plans to attend an art school in New York after he graduates.

"I want to design sculptures like you see around big corporate skyscrapers," says Brian, "and still have my own business."

Brian grins. "Wow, I never realized you could turn making mud pies into a career."

Brian's interest and skill in sculpting grew as he got older. In the same way, our ability to understand and appreciate God grows as we get older and expose ourselves to more of God's ways. Jesus also experienced this spiritual growth process. Read about it in **Luke 2:41–52**, especially verse 52.

- What do Jesus and Brian have in common based on the passage?
- How have you "continued to learn more and more" in the past year?

CONSIDER . . .

- thinking about all the ways you have changed in the past year, and thanking God for helping you grow spiritually.
- keeping a prayer journal to help log spiritual growth in your life.

FOR MORE, SEE . . .

- 1 Samuel 2:26 (p. 247)
- Ephesians 4:4–16 (p. 1222)
- 1 Corinthians 13:11–13 (p. 1184)

than I am. I am not good enough to untie his sandals. He will baptize you with the Holy Spirit[d] and fire. 17He will come ready to clean the grain, separating the good grain from the chaff.[d] He will put the good part of the grain into his barn, but he will burn the chaff with a fire that cannot be put out."[n] 18And John continued to preach the Good News,[d] saying many other things to encourage the people.

19But John spoke against Herod, the governor, because of his sin with Herodias, the wife of Herod's brother, and because of the many other evil things Herod did. 20So Herod did something even worse: He put John in prison.

Jesus Is Baptized by John

21When all the people were being baptized by John, Jesus also was baptized. While Jesus was praying, heaven opened 22and the Holy Spirit[d] came down on him in the form of a dove. Then a voice came from heaven, saying, "You are my Son, whom I love, and I am very pleased with you."

The Family History of Jesus

23When Jesus began his ministry, he was about thirty years old. People thought that Jesus was Joseph's son.

Joseph was the son[n] of Heli.
24Heli was the son of Matthat.
Matthat was the son of Levi.
Levi was the son of Melki.
Melki was the son of Jannai.
Jannai was the son of Joseph.
25Joseph was the son of Mattathias.
Mattathias was the son of Amos.
Amos was the son of Nahum.
Nahum was the son of Esli.
Esli was the son of Naggai.
26Naggai was the son of Maath.
Maath was the son of Mattathias.
Mattathias was the son of Semein.
Semein was the son of Josech.
Josech was the son of Joda.
27Joda was the son of Joanan.
Joanan was the son of Rhesa.
Rhesa was the son of Zerubbabel.

He will . . . out. This means that Jesus will come to separate good people from bad people, saving the good and punishing the bad.

son "Son" in Jewish lists of ancestors can sometimes mean grandson or more distant relative.

JUSTICE

Quiet Disasters

If forty thousand people were to die from an earthquake or hurricane, would it make the news? Of course.

But forty thousand people die every day—from hunger. And when was the last time you saw that on the news?

If you saw a rich person feasting while a poor child starved at the doorstep, would you be angry? Of course.

But did you know that the United States has less than 6 percent of the world's population, yet consumes more than 33 percent of the world's resources?

It may be hard to see yourself as superwealthy, especially when you compare your income with those of kids around you. But when compared to the average world citizen, you have great wealth. And you have a lot to offer a hurting world.

Luke 3:1–18 records John's advice to the people of his day who practiced "religion," but weren't supporting "justice." Read the passage to hear the warning he gives them—and us.

- What group of people might John relay his message to today?
- According to this passage, how should we define justice?

CONSIDER . . .

- writing a short speech that John the Baptist might deliver to your church.
- doing something to promote justice in the world. For example, spearhead a canned food drive, or volunteer at a local relief agency.

FOR MORE, SEE . . .

- Jeremiah 2:34–35 (p. 694)
- Matthew 3:1–12 (p. 910)
- John 1:19–34 (p. 1059)

Zerubbabel was the grandson of Shealtiel.
Shealtiel was the son of Neri.
28 Neri was the son of Melchi.
Melchi was the son of Addi.
Addi was the son of Cosam.
Cosam was the son of Elmadam.
Elmadam was the son of Er.
29 Er was the son of Joshua.
Joshua was the son of Eliezer.
Eliezer was the son of Jorim.
Jorim was the son of Matthat.
Matthat was the son of Levi.
30 Levi was the son of Simeon.
Simeon was the son of Judah.
Judah was the son of Joseph.
Joseph was the son of Jonam.
Jonam was the son of Eliakim.
31 Eliakim was the son of Melea.
Melea was the son of Menna.
Menna was the son of Mattatha.
Mattatha was the son of Nathan.
Nathan was the son of David.
32 David was the son of Jesse.
Jesse was the son of Obed.
Obed was the son of Boaz.
Boaz was the son of Salmon.
Salmon was the son of Nahshon.
33 Nahshon was the son of Amminadab.
Amminadab was the son of Admin.
Admin was the son of Arni.
Arni was the son of Hezron.
Hezron was the son of Perez.
Perez was the son of Judah.
34 Judah was the son of Jacob.
Jacob was the son of Isaac.
Isaac was the son of Abraham.
Abraham was the son of Terah.
Terah was the son of Nahor.
35 Nahor was the son of Serug.
Serug was the son of Reu.
Reu was the son of Peleg.
Peleg was the son of Eber.
Eber was the son of Shelah.
36 Shelah was the son of Cainan.
Cainan was the son of Arphaxad.
Arphaxad was the son of Shem.
Shem was the son of Noah.
Noah was the son of Lamech.
37 Lamech was the son of Methuselah.
Methuselah was the son of Enoch.
Enoch was the son of Jared.
Jared was the son of Mahalalel.
Mahalalel was the son of Kenan.
38 Kenan was the son of Enosh.
Enosh was the son of Seth.
Seth was the son of Adam.
Adam was the son of God.

Jesus Is Tempted by the Devil

4 Jesus, filled with the Holy Spirit,[d] returned
from the Jordan River. The Spirit led Jesus
into the desert 2 where the devil tempted Jesus for
forty days. Jesus ate nothing during that time, and
when those days were ended, he was very hungry.

3 The devil said to Jesus, "If you are the Son of
God, tell this rock to become bread."

4 Jesus answered, "It is written in the Scriptures:[d] 'A person does not live by eating only bread.' "[n]

5 Then the devil took Jesus and showed him all
the kingdoms of the world in an instant. 6 The
devil said to Jesus, "I will give you all these kingdoms and all their power and glory. It has all been
given to me, and I can give it to anyone I wish.
7 If you worship me, then it will all be yours."
8 Jesus answered, "It is written in the Scriptures: 'You must worship the Lord your God and
serve only him.' "[n]

9 Then the devil led Jesus to Jerusalem and put
him on a high place of the Temple.[d] He said to
Jesus, "If you are the Son of God, jump down. 10 It
is written in the Scriptures:

'He has put his angels in charge of you
to watch over you.' *Psalm 91:11*

11 It is also written:

'They will catch you in their hands
so that you will not hit your foot on a
rock.' " *Psalm 91:12*

12 Jesus answered, "But it also says in the Scriptures: 'Do not test the Lord your God.' "[n]

13 After the devil had tempted Jesus in every
way, he left him to wait until a better time.

Jesus Teaches the People

14 Jesus returned to Galilee in the power of the
Holy Spirit,[d] and stories about him spread all
through the area. 15 He began to teach in their synagogues,[d] and everyone praised him.

SIDELIGHT: *If you don't like being noticed when you visit different churches, you wouldn't have visited many synagogues in Jesus' day. It was customary for the synagogue leader to invite visitors to address the congregation. Jesus took advantage of the opportunity to preach in Luke 4:14–19.*

'A person . . . bread.' Quotation from Deuteronomy 8:3.
'You . . . him.' Quotation from Deuteronomy 6:13.
'Do . . . God.' Quotation from Deuteronomy 6:16.

16Jesus traveled to Nazareth, where he had
grown up. On the Sabbath[d] day he went to the
synagogue, as he always did, and stood up to read.
17The book of Isaiah the prophet[d] was given to
him. He opened the book and found the place
where this is written:

18"The Lord has put his Spirit in me,
because he appointed me to tell the Good
News[d] to the poor.
He has sent me to tell the captives they are
free
and to tell the blind that they can see
again. *Isaiah 61:1*
God sent me to free those who have been
treated unfairly *Isaiah 58:6*
19 and to announce the time when the Lord
will show his kindness." *Isaiah 61:2*

20Jesus closed the book, gave it back to the assistant, and sat down. Everyone in the synagogue
was watching Jesus closely. 21He began to say to
them, "While you heard these words just now,
they were coming true!"

22All the people spoke well of Jesus and were
amazed at the words of grace he spoke. They
asked, "Isn't this Joseph's son?"

23Jesus said to them, "I know that you will tell
me the old saying: 'Doctor, heal yourself.' You
want to say, 'We heard about the things you did
in Capernaum. Do those things here in your own

SIN

Proving Self

In his small high school in upstate New York, Josh Hartley was a star. He played everything from baseball to football, and enjoyed knowing he had helped win most of the trophies in the school display case. Some people thought he was stuck-up, but that didn't bother him much. The important thing was that everyone knew who Josh Hartley was.

Then things changed. Josh's mother got a new job in another part of the state. So Josh had to move from his small-town school to a supersize suburban school near New York City.

No problem, thought Josh. I may not be able to play every sport here, but I can still make my mark somewhere.

But time after time, Josh met with disappointment. He would try out, but when teams were posted, his name never appeared. And even if he had made the teams, the trophy case filled an entire hallway of the school. No chance of recognition there.

For the first time in his life Josh began to get in trouble. It was little things at first—skipping school and picking fights between classes. But then the problems began to get worse. Josh seemed out of control. He didn't care about school anymore, or much of anything else.

One year later, Josh was put in the county correctional center for arson. He had torched the high school field house.

Josh was released from prison on the condition that he receive counseling. After much therapy and prayer, Josh's attitude and outlook on life improved.

After Josh got out of prison, he told his parents, "I just didn't know who I was anymore. I wasn't an athlete. I didn't belong anywhere. So I found other ways to prove myself and get noticed."

Josh tried to prove himself in unhealthy ways. In **Luke 4:1–13** Satan also tempted Jesus to prove his identity by sinning against God. Read the passage to see how Jesus defeated the temptation to sin.

- What temptations did both Josh and Jesus face?
- Based on Jesus' example, what can you do to keep from sinning the next time you're tempted?

CONSIDER . . .

- identifying ways you want to "prove yourself and get noticed." Talk about one of the ways with a parent or trusted friend.
- telling a trusted friend about a sin you struggle with and asking him or her to pray for you.

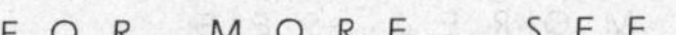

FOR MORE, SEE . . .

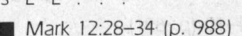

- Genesis 3:1–6 (p. 4)
- Matthew 4:1–11 (p. 910)
- Mark 12:28–34 (p. 988)

town!' " 24Then Jesus said, "I tell you the truth,
a prophet is not accepted in his hometown. 25But
I tell you the truth, there were many widows in
Israel during the time of Elijah. It did not rain in
Israel for three and one-half years, and there was
no food anywhere in the whole country. 26But Elijah was sent to none of those widows, only to a
widow in Zarephath, a town in Sidon. 27And there
were many with skin diseases living in Israel during the time of the prophet Elisha. But none of
them were healed, only Naaman, who was from
the country of Syria."

28When all the people in the synagogue heard
these things, they became very angry. 29They got
up, forced Jesus out of town, and took him to the
edge of the cliff on which the town was built.
They planned to throw him off the edge, 30but
Jesus walked through the crowd and went on his
way.

Jesus Forces Out an Evil Spirit

31Jesus went to Capernaum, a city in Galilee,
and on the Sabbath[d] day, he taught the people.
32They were amazed at his teaching, because he
spoke with authority. 33In the synagogue[d] a man
who had within him an evil spirit shouted in a
loud voice, 34"Jesus of Nazareth! What do you
want with us? Did you come to destroy us? I
know who you are—God's Holy One!"

35Jesus commanded the evil spirit, "Be quiet!
Come out of the man!" The evil spirit threw the
man down to the ground before all the people and
then left the man without hurting him.

36The people were amazed and said to each
other, "What does this mean? With authority and
power he commands evil spirits, and they come
out." 37And so the news about Jesus spread to every place in the whole area.

Jesus Heals Many People

38Jesus left the synagogue[d] and went to the
home of Simon.[n] Simon's mother-in-law was sick
with a high fever, and they asked Jesus to help
her. 39He came to her side and commanded the

Simon Simon's other name was Peter.

GOD'S WILL

Against the Grain

In the spring of 1981, a worker at a nuclear weapons plant near Amarillo, Texas, made an appointment to see Bishop Leroy Matthiesen of the diocese of Amarillo.

"I'm pushing sixty," said Bill Hobbles. "I've worked for Pantex for seventeen years, and I'm worried that, as a Christian, what I'm doing with my life may be morally wrong."

Bishop Matthiesen listened to Bill's dilemma, and decided to take action. Knowing that the plant was a cornerstone of the local economy, the bishop issued a public statement calling for workers in the nuclear-weapons industry to search their consciences and consider quitting and finding other jobs.

He was accused of treason in the papers and was publicly invited to accept a one-way ticket to the totalitarian country of his choice. Moreover, a local agency cut off all funds for one of his social-service programs.

An important part of living out our faith means following God's will as we understand it—even when our view is unpopular. And as Jesus found in **Luke 4:16–30**, sometimes it's hardest to follow God's will when we are with those who know us best.

- How is the bishop's experience like Jesus' experience in the passage? How are their experiences different?
- Drawing from the passage, how should you respond when you feel you must take a stand that others—even Christians—disagree with?

CONSIDER . . .

- choosing one way you will stand up for your beliefs at school, even though it may be unpopular with some people. For example, stick up for someone who is being picked on or take a stand on a controversial issue.
- writing out all the questions you have about God's will for your life and then talking to your youth pastor about them.

FOR MORE, SEE . . .

- Jeremiah 1:4–10 (p. 691)
- Mark 6:1–6 (p. 973)
- Romans 12:1–2 (p. 1157)

fever to leave. It left her, and immediately she got
up and began serving them.
40When the sun went down, the people
brought those who were sick to Jesus. Putting his
hands on each sick person, he healed every one
of them. 41Demons[d] came out of many people,
shouting, "You are the Son of God." But Jesus
commanded the demons and would not allow
them to speak, because they knew Jesus was the
Christ.[d]
42At daybreak, Jesus went to a lonely place, but
the people looked for him. When they found him,
they tried to keep him from leaving. 43But Jesus
said to them, "I must preach about God's kingdom to other towns, too. This is why I was sent."
44Then he kept on preaching in the synagogues[d] of Judea.

Jesus' First Followers

5 One day while Jesus was standing beside
Lake Galilee, many people were pressing all
around him to hear the word of God. 2Jesus saw
two boats at the shore of the lake. The fishermen
had left them and were washing their nets. 3Jesus
got into one of the boats, the one that belonged
to Simon,[n] and asked him to push off a little from
the land. Then Jesus sat down and continued to
teach the people from the boat.
4When Jesus had finished speaking, he said to
Simon, "Take the boat into deep water, and put
your nets in the water to catch some fish."
5Simon answered, "Master, we worked hard all
night trying to catch fish, and we caught nothing.
But you say to put the nets in the water, so I will."
6When the fishermen did as Jesus told them, they
caught so many fish that the nets began to break.
7They called to their partners in the other boat to
come and help them. They came and filled both
boats so full that they were almost sinking.
8When Simon Peter saw what had happened,
he bowed down before Jesus and said, "Go away
from me, Lord. I am a sinful man!" 9He and the
other fishermen were amazed at the many fish
they caught, as were 10James and John, the sons
of Zebedee, Simon's partners.
Jesus said to Simon, "Don't be afraid. From
now on you will fish for people." 11When the men
brought their boats to the shore, they left everything and followed Jesus.

Jesus Heals a Sick Man

12When Jesus was in one of the towns, there
was a man covered with a skin disease. When he
saw Jesus, he bowed down before him and begged him,
"Lord, you can heal me if you will."
13Jesus reached out his hand and touched the
man and said, "I will. Be healed!" Immediately
the disease disappeared. 14Then Jesus said, "Don't
tell anyone about this, but go and show yourself
to the priest[n] and offer a gift for your healing, as
Moses commanded.[n] This will show the people
what I have done."
15But the news about Jesus spread even more.
Many people came to hear Jesus and to be healed
of their sicknesses, 16but Jesus often slipped away
to be alone so he could pray.

Jesus Heals a Paralyzed Man

17One day as Jesus was teaching the people, the
Pharisees[d] and teachers of the law from every
town in Galilee and Judea and from Jerusalem
were there. The Lord was giving Jesus the power
to heal people. 18Just then, some men were carrying on a mat a man who was paralyzed. They
tried to bring him in and put him down before
Jesus. 19But because there were so many people
there, they could not find a way in. So they went
up on the roof and lowered the man on his mat
through the ceiling into the middle of the crowd
right before Jesus. 20Seeing their faith, Jesus said,
"Friend, your sins are forgiven."

> **SIDELIGHT:** If you think access to buildings is a new problem for disabled people, read Luke 5:18–20. The friends probably had to dig through layers of clay, reeds, grass, and branches to make a hole in the roof, since that's how most roofs were made in Jesus' time. The roofs were supported by wooden beams, which stretched from wall to wall.

21The Jewish teachers of the law and the Pharisees thought to themselves, "Who is this man
who is speaking as if he were God? Only God can
forgive sins."
22But Jesus knew what they were thinking and
said, "Why are you thinking these things?
23Which is easier: to say, 'Your sins are forgiven,'
or to say, 'Stand up and walk'? 24But I will prove
to you that the Son of Man[d] has authority on earth
to forgive sins." So Jesus said to the paralyzed
man, "I tell you, stand up, take your mat, and go
home."
25At once the man stood up before them,
picked up his mat, and went home, praising God.
26All the people were fully amazed and began
to praise God. They were filled with much re-

Simon Simon's other name was Peter.
show . . . priest The law of Moses said a priest must say when a Jewish person with a skin disease was well.
Moses commanded Read about this in Leviticus 14:1-32.

spect and said, "Today we have seen amazing
things!"

Levi Follows Jesus

27After this, Jesus went out and saw a tax collector named Levi sitting in the tax collector's
booth. Jesus said to him, "Follow me!" 28So Levi
got up, left everything, and followed him.
29Then Levi gave a big dinner for Jesus at his
house. Many tax collectors and other people were
eating there, too. 30But the Pharisees[d] and the
men who taught the law for the Pharisees began
to complain to Jesus' followers, "Why do you eat
and drink with tax collectors and sinners?"
31Jesus answered them, "It is not the healthy
people who need a doctor, but the sick. 32I have
not come to invite good people but sinners to
change their hearts and lives."

Jesus Answers a Question

33They said to Jesus, "John's followers often
give up eating[n] for a certain time and pray, just
as the Pharisees[d] do. But your followers eat and
drink all the time."
34Jesus said to them, "You cannot make the
friends of the bridegroom give up eating while he
is still with them. 35But the time will come when
the bridegroom will be taken away from them,
and then they will give up eating."
36Jesus told them this story: "No one takes
cloth off a new coat to cover a hole in an old coat.
Otherwise, he ruins the new coat, and the cloth
from the new coat will not be the same as the old
cloth. 37Also, no one ever pours new wine into
old leather bags. Otherwise, the new wine will
break the bags, the wine will spill out, and the
leather bags will be ruined. 38New wine must be
put into new leather bags. 39No one after drinking
old wine wants new wine, because he says, 'The
old wine is better.' "

Jesus Is Lord over the Sabbath

6 One Sabbath[d] day Jesus was walking
through some fields of grain. His followers
picked the heads of grain, rubbed them in their
hands, and ate them. 2Some Pharisees[d] said,
"Why do you do what is not lawful on the Sabbath day?"
3Jesus answered, "Have you not read what David did when he and those with him were hungry? 4He went into God's house and took and ate
the holy bread, which is lawful only for priests to
eat. And he gave some to the people who were
with him." 5Then Jesus said to the Pharisees,
"The Son of Man[d] is Lord of the Sabbath day."

Jesus Heals a Man's Hand

6On another Sabbath[d] day Jesus went into the
synagogue[d] and was teaching, and a man with a
crippled right hand was there. 7The teachers of
the law and the Pharisees[d] were watching closely
to see if Jesus would heal on the Sabbath day so
they could accuse him. 8But he knew what they
were thinking, and he said to the man with the
crippled hand, "Stand up here in the middle of
everyone." The man got up and stood there.
9Then Jesus said to them, "I ask you, which is
lawful on the Sabbath day: to do good or to do
evil, to save a life or to destroy it?" 10Jesus looked
around at all of them and said to the man, "Hold
out your hand." The man held out his hand, and
it was healed.
11But the Pharisees and the teachers of the law
were very angry and discussed with each other
what they could do to Jesus.

Jesus Chooses His Apostles

12At that time Jesus went off to a mountain to
pray, and he spent the night praying to God. 13The
next morning, Jesus called his followers to him
and chose twelve of them, whom he named apostles:[d] 14Simon (Jesus named him Peter), his
brother Andrew, James, John, Philip, Bartholomew, 15Matthew, Thomas, James son of Alphaeus, Simon (called the Zealot[d]), 16Judas son of
James, and Judas Iscariot, who later turned Jesus
over to his enemies.

Jesus Teaches and Heals

17Jesus and the apostles[d] came down from the
mountain, and he stood on level ground. A large
group of his followers was there, as well as many
people from all around Judea, Jerusalem, and the
seacoast cities of Tyre and Sidon. 18They all came
to hear Jesus teach and to be healed of their sicknesses, and he healed those who were troubled
by evil spirits. 19All the people were trying to
touch Jesus, because power was coming from him
and healing them all.
20Jesus looked at his followers and said,
"You people who are poor are happy,
because the kingdom of God belongs to
you.
21You people who are now hungry are happy,
because you will be satisfied.
You people who are now crying are happy,
because you will laugh with joy.
22"People will hate you, shut you out, insult
you, and say you are evil because you follow the
Son of Man.[d] But when they do, you will be
happy. 23Be full of joy at that time, because you
have a great reward waiting for you in heaven.

give up eating This is called "fasting." The people would give up eating for a special time of prayer and worship to God. It was also done to show sadness and disappointment.

Their ancestors did the same things to the prophets.[d]

24“But how terrible it will be for you who are
rich,
because you have had your easy life.
25How terrible it will be for you who are full
now,
because you will be hungry.
How terrible it will be for you who are
laughing now,
because you will be sad and cry.

26“How terrible when everyone says only good
things about you, because their ancestors said the
same things about the false prophets.

Love Your Enemies

27“But I say to you who are listening, love your
enemies. Do good to those who hate you, 28bless
those who curse you, pray for those who are cruel
to you. 29If anyone slaps you on one cheek, offer
him the other cheek, too. If someone takes your
coat, do not stop him from taking your shirt.
30Give to everyone who asks you, and when
someone takes something that is yours, don’t ask
for it back. 31Do to others what you would want
them to do to you. 32If you love only the people
who love you, what praise should you get? Even
sinners love the people who love them. 33If you
do good only to those who do good to you, what
praise should you get? Even sinners do that! 34If
you lend things to people, always hoping to get
something back, what praise should you get?
Even sinners lend to other sinners so that they can
get back the same amount! 35But love your enemies, do good to them, and lend to them without
hoping to get anything back. Then you will have
a great reward, and you will be children of the
Most High God, because he is kind even to people
who are ungrateful and full of sin. 36Show mercy,
just as your Father shows mercy.

Look at Yourselves

37“Don’t judge other people, and you will not
be judged. Don’t accuse others of being guilty,
and you will not be accused of being guilty. Forgive, and you will be forgiven. 38Give, and you
will receive. You will be given much. Pressed
down, shaken together, and running over, it will
spill into your lap. The way you give to others is
the way God will give to you.”

39Jesus told them this story: “Can a blind person lead another blind person? No! Both of them
will fall into a ditch. 40A student is not better than
the teacher, but the student who has been fully
trained will be like the teacher.

41“Why do you notice the little piece of dust in
your friend’s eye, but you don’t notice the big
piece of wood in your own eye? 42How can you
say to your friend, ‘Friend, let me take that little
piece of dust out of your eye’ when you cannot
see that big piece of wood in your own eye! You
hypocrite![d] First, take the wood out of your own
eye. Then you will see clearly to take the dust out
of your friend’s eye.

Two Kinds of Fruit

43“A good tree does not produce bad fruit, nor
does a bad tree produce good fruit. 44Each tree is
known by its own fruit. People don’t gather figs
from thornbushes, and they don’t get grapes from
bushes. 45Good people bring good things out of
the good they stored in their hearts. But evil people bring evil things out of the evil they stored in
their hearts. People speak the things that are in
their hearts.

Two Kinds of People

46“Why do you call me, ‘Lord, Lord,’ but do not
do what I say? 47I will show you what everyone
is like who comes to me and hears my words and
obeys. 48That person is like a man building a
house who dug deep and laid the foundation on
rock. When the floods came, the water tried to
wash the house away, but it could not shake it,
because the house was built well. 49But the one
who hears my words and does not obey is like a
man who built his house on the ground without
a foundation. When the floods came, the house
quickly fell and was completely destroyed.”

Jesus Heals a Soldier’s Servant

7 When Jesus finished saying all these things
to the people, he went to Capernaum.
2There was an army officer who had a servant
who was very important to him. The servant was
so sick he was nearly dead. 3When the officer
heard about Jesus, he sent some older Jewish
leaders to him to ask Jesus to come and heal his
servant. 4The men went to Jesus and begged him,
saying, “This officer is worthy of your help. 5He
loves our people, and he built us a synagogue.”[d]

6So Jesus went with the men. He was getting
near the officer’s house when the officer sent
friends to say, “Lord, don’t trouble yourself, because I am not worthy to have you come into my
house. 7That is why I did not come to you myself.
But you only need to command it, and my servant
will be healed. 8I, too, am a man under the authority of others, and I have soldiers under my
command. I tell one soldier, ‘Go,’ and he goes.
I tell another soldier, ‘Come,’ and he comes.
I say to my servant, ‘Do this,’ and my servant
does it.”

9When Jesus heard this, he was amazed. Turning to the crowd that was following him, he said,
“I tell you, this is the greatest faith I have found
anywhere, even in Israel.”

[10]Those who had been sent to Jesus went back
to the house where they found the servant in
good health.

Jesus Brings a Man Back to Life

[11]Soon afterwards Jesus went to a town called
Nain, and his followers and a large crowd traveled
with him. [12]When he came near the town gate,
he saw a funeral. A mother, who was a widow,
had lost her only son. A large crowd from the
town was with the mother while her son was being carried out. [13]When the Lord saw her, he felt
very sorry for her and said, "Don't cry." [14]He
went up and touched the coffin, and the people
who were carrying it stopped. Jesus said, "Young
man, I tell you, get up!" [15]And the son sat up and
began to talk. Then Jesus gave him back to his
mother.

[16]All the people were amazed and began praising God, saying, "A great prophet[d] has come to
us! God has come to help his people."

[17]This news about Jesus spread through all Judea and into all the places around there.

John Asks a Question

[18]John's followers told him about all these
things. He called for two of his followers [19]and
sent them to the Lord to ask, "Are you the One
who is to come, or should we wait for someone
else?"

SIDELIGHT: The coffin where the boy lay when Jesus brought him back to life (Luke 7:11–15) wasn't like coffins today. In fact, it was probably just a board on which they laid the body. Just like today, wealthier people sometimes had more elaborate "funeral biers," as they were called.

[20]When the men came to Jesus, they said,
"John the Baptist[d] sent us to you with this question: 'Are you the One who is to come, or should
we wait for someone else?' "

[21]At that time, Jesus healed many people of

LEADERSHIP

Fish Out of Water

"Whales Commit Mass Suicide"

The 1986 newspaper headline alerted the community in Cape Cod about the baffling incident that had happened the night before. A herd, or "pod," of ninety-four whales beached themselves on the shores of Cape Cod. They just swam up onto the sand and died.

That wasn't the first or last time whales have committed this strange act around the world. Newspapers periodically report stories of whales beaching themselves.

Several theories try to explain why whales do this. One of them is that the whales are following a basic herd instinct. Every pod has a leader. And if the leader becomes ill or disoriented, it might react by beaching itself. But since it's the leader, the other whales simply follow, even though it means death.

Sound crazy? Maybe, but it's not so unlike the way many people act. It's easy to follow leaders who say they have got the right answers, or know the truth.

People who pretend to have life's answers but live destructively are called hypocrites. In **Luke 6:39–49**, Jesus was saddened and angered to find hypocrisy in the religious leaders around him.

- How is the lead whale like the blind leaders Jesus talks about in this passage?
- What leaders do kids follow, even though the leaders' lifestyles seem destructive?

CONSIDER . . .

- listing "good fruits" and "bad fruits" you see in your own life, then asking God to take away the bad fruit.
- telling people whom you look to as leaders about the "good fruits" you see in their lives.

FOR MORE, SEE . . .

- Isaiah 29:13 (p. 645)
- Amos 8:4–8 (p. 848)
- James 1:19–27 (p. 1294)

their sicknesses, diseases, and evil spirits, and he
gave sight to many blind people. 22Then Jesus answered John's followers, "Go tell John what you
saw and heard here. The blind can see, the crippled can walk, and people with skin diseases are
healed. The deaf can hear, the dead are raised to
life, and the Good News[d] is preached to the poor.
23Those who do not stumble in their faith because
of me are blessed!"

24When John's followers left, Jesus began talking to the people about John: "What did you go
out into the desert to see? A reed[n] blown by the
wind? 25What did you go out to see? A man
dressed in fine clothes? No, people who have fine
clothes and much wealth live in kings' palaces.
26But what did you go out to see? A prophet?[d]
Yes, and I tell you, John is more than a prophet.
27This was written about him:

'I will send my messenger ahead of you,
who will prepare the way for you.' *Malachi 3:1*

28I tell you, John is greater than any other person
ever born, but even the least important person in
the kingdom of God is greater than John."

29(When the people, including the tax collectors, heard this, they all agreed that God's teaching was good, because they had been baptized by
John. 30But the Pharisees[d] and experts on the law
refused to accept God's plan for themselves; they
did not let John baptize them.)

31Then Jesus said, "What shall I say about the
people of this time? What are they like? 32They
are like children sitting in the marketplace, calling
to one another and saying,

'We played music for you, but you did not
dance;
we sang a sad song, but you did not cry.'

33John the Baptist came and did not eat bread or
drink wine, and you say, 'He has a demon[d] in
him.' 34The Son of Man[d] came eating and drinking, and you say, 'Look at him! He eats too much
and drinks too much wine, and he is a friend of
tax collectors and sinners!' 35But wisdom is
proved to be right by what it does."

A Woman Washes Jesus' Feet

36One of the Pharisees[d] asked Jesus to eat with

reed It means that John was not ordinary or weak like grass blown by the wind.

FAITH

Surrender

In Officer's Training School, Roger Curtis learned to speak to an officer in a specific way. First you say, "Sir." Then you say your name, "Candidate Curtis." Then you answer the question or respond to the officer. Then finish with, "Sir." Officers try their hardest to confuse you. For example:

Officer: "Candidate Curtis!"
Candidate: "Sir, Candidate Curtis, yes, Sir!"
Officer: "You've got a thread on your uniform, Curtis!"
Candidate: "Sir, Candidate Curtis, yes, Sir!"
Officer: "Tell you what I'm gonna do; I'm gonna pull it, and I want you to make a noise like a cannon."
Candidate: "Sir, Candidate Curtis, yes, Sir!"
Officer: "I pulled it!"
Candidate: "Sir, Candidate Curtis, boom, Sir!"

Maybe this approach sounds foolish to you. But in battle, the most important thing soldiers can do is to place themselves completely under the authority of their superior—even if they don't understand the reasoning behind the orders. That's real faith. **Luke 7:1–10** describes another soldier who understood that kind of faith, and reaped the benefits of it.

- How is the soldier in this passage like Candidate Curtis?
- Is your faith as strong as the officer's in this passage? Why or why not?

CONSIDER. . .

- trusting God with a part of your life you have never had the faith to let go of before.
- memorizing Hebrews 11:1 (p. 1287), to learn God's definition of faith.

FOR MORE, SEE. . .

- Genesis 22:1–18 (p. 25)
- Matthew 14:22–35 (p. 934)
- Hebrews 11 (p. 1287)

him, so Jesus went into the Pharisee's house and
sat at the table. 37A sinful woman in the town
learned that Jesus was eating at the Pharisee's
house. So she brought an alabaster[d] jar of perfume
38and stood behind Jesus at his feet, crying. She
began to wash his feet with her tears, and she
dried them with her hair, kissing them many
times and rubbing them with the perfume.
39When the Pharisee who asked Jesus to come to
his house saw this, he thought to himself, "If Jesus
were a prophet,[d] he would know that the woman
touching him is a sinner!"

40Jesus said to the Pharisee, "Simon, I have
something to say to you."

Simon said, "Teacher, tell me."

41Jesus said, "Two people owed money to the
same banker. One owed five hundred coins[n] and
the other owed fifty. 42They had no money to pay
what they owed, but the banker told both of them
they did not have to pay him. Which person will
love the banker more?"

43Simon, the Pharisee, answered, "I think it
would be the one who owed him the most
money."

Jesus said to Simon, "You are right." 44Then
Jesus turned toward the woman and said to Simon, "Do you see this woman? When I came into
your house, you gave me no water for my feet,
but she washed my feet with her tears and dried
them with her hair. 45You gave me no kiss of
greeting, but she has been kissing my feet since I
came in. 46You did not put oil on my head, but she

coins Roman denarii. One coin was the average pay for one day's work.

NON-CHRISTIANS

Beyond the Great Divide

Janice Jenson was a riot. There was just no denying that. Tasha Smith hated her world history course, but Janice, who sat next to her, had a way of summing up every lecture that made it all seem like a funny movie. Her silly faces and off-the-wall comments sent Tasha rolling every time.

Tasha had to admit she liked Janice. But that made Tasha uneasy. She wasn't sure she was supposed to like Janice.

Janice had a reputation for wildness around school. She was a heavy drinker and usually had a whole string of boyfriends begging for her attention—which she freely gave. She was bad news, and everybody knew it.

"Tasha, why are hanging around with that girl?" her church friends would sometimes ask. "She could hurt your Christian witness."

Before long, Tasha began to get angry about her friends' attitude—and the internal struggle over Janice she still fought.

"How will people who don't know you ever get the chance if I'm unwilling to get to know them first?" Tasha asked God one day.

"They won't," a voice seemed to respond. Tasha smiled. She knew what she had to do now. She gladly spends time with her non-Christian friends—and shares Christ's love with them.

Tasha struggled with accepting non-Christians when others thought it was wrong. Jesus had to deal with the same problem within the religious community of his time. Read about his encounter with a "sinful woman" in **Luke 7:36–50**.

- What feelings do Tasha's church friends and the Pharisee in the passage share?
- If Jesus were a student in your school, whom might he spend the most time with?

CONSIDER . . .

- scanning your yearbook and asking God to lead you to people he wants you to spend time with.
- talking with your youth pastor about doing a youth group study on friendship evangelism.

FOR MORE, SEE . . .

- Isaiah 61:1–2 (p. 680)
- John 4:1–41 (p. 1063)
- 2 Corinthians 6:14–18 (p. 1199)

poured perfume on my feet. [47]I tell you that her many sins are forgiven, so she showed great love. But the person who is forgiven only a little will love only a little."

[48]Then Jesus said to her, "Your sins are forgiven."

[49]The people sitting at the table began to say among themselves, "Who is this who even forgives sins?"

[50]Jesus said to the woman, "Because you believed, you are saved from your sins. Go in peace."

The Group with Jesus

8 After this, while Jesus was traveling through some cities and small towns, he preached and told the Good News[d] about God's kingdom. The twelve apostles[d] were with him, [2]and also some women who had been healed of sicknesses and evil spirits: Mary, called Magdalene, from whom seven demons[d] had gone out; [3]Joanna, the wife of Chuza (the manager of Herod's house); Susanna; and many others. These women used their own money to help Jesus and his apostles.

A Story About Planting Seed

[4]When a great crowd was gathered, and people were coming to Jesus from every town, he told them this story:

[5]"A farmer went out to plant his seed. While he was planting, some seed fell by the road. People walked on the seed, and the birds ate it up. [6]Some seed fell on rock, and when it began to grow, it died because it had no water. [7]Some seed fell among thorny weeds, but the weeds grew up with it and choked the good plants. [8]And some seed fell on good ground and grew and made a hundred times more."

As Jesus finished the story, he called out, "You people who can hear me, listen!"

[9]Jesus' followers asked him what this story meant.

[10]Jesus said, "You have been chosen to know the secrets about the kingdom of God. But I use stories to speak to other people so that:

'They will look, but they may not see.
They will listen, but they may not
understand.' *Isaiah 6:9*

[11]"This is what the story means: The seed is God's message. [12]The seed that fell beside the road is like the people who hear God's teaching, but the devil comes and takes it away from them so they cannot believe it and be saved. [13]The seed that fell on rock is like those who hear God's teaching and accept it gladly, but they don't allow the teaching to go deep into their lives. They believe for a while, but when trouble comes, they give up. [14]The seed that fell among the thorny weeds is like those who hear God's teaching, but they let the worries, riches, and pleasures of this life keep them from growing and producing good fruit. [15]And the seed that fell on the good ground is like those who hear God's teaching with good, honest hearts and obey it and patiently produce good fruit.

Use What You Have

[16]"No one after lighting a lamp covers it with a bowl or hides it under a bed. Instead, the person puts it on a lampstand so those who come in will see the light. [17]Everything that is hidden will become clear, and every secret thing will be made known. [18]So be careful how you listen. Those who have understanding will be given more. But those who do not have understanding, even what they think they have will be taken away from them."

Jesus' True Family

[19]Jesus' mother and brothers came to see him, but there was such a crowd they could not get to him. [20]Someone said to Jesus, "Your mother and your brothers are standing outside, wanting to see you."

[21]Jesus answered them, "My mother and my brothers are those who listen to God's teaching and obey it!"

Jesus Calms a Storm

[22]One day Jesus and his followers got into a boat, and he said to them, "Let's go across the lake." And so they started across. [23]While they were sailing, Jesus fell asleep. A very strong wind blew up on the lake, causing the boat to fill with water, and they were in danger.

[24]The followers went to Jesus and woke him, saying, "Master! Master! We will drown!"

Jesus got up and gave a command to the wind and the waves. They stopped, and it became calm. [25]Jesus said to his followers, "Where is your faith?"

The followers were afraid and amazed and said to each other, "Who is this that commands even the wind and the water, and they obey him?"

A Man with Demons Inside Him

[26]Jesus and his followers sailed across the lake from Galilee to the area of the Gerasene people. [27]When Jesus got out on the land, a man from the town who had demons[d] inside him came to Jesus. For a long time he had worn no clothes and had lived in the burial caves, not in a house. [28]When he saw Jesus, he cried out and fell down before him. He said with a loud voice, "What do you want with me, Jesus, Son of the Most High God? I beg you, don't torture me!" [29]He said this because Jesus was commanding the evil spirit to come out of the man. Many times it had taken

hold of him. Though he had been kept under guard and chained hand and foot, he had broken his chains and had been forced by the demon out into a lonely place.

30Jesus asked him, "What is your name?"

He answered, "Legion,"[n] because many demons were in him. 31The demons begged Jesus not to send them into eternal darkness.[n] 32A large herd of pigs was feeding on a hill, and the demons begged Jesus to allow them to go into the pigs. So Jesus allowed them to do this. 33When the demons came out of the man, they went into the pigs, and the herd ran down the hill into the lake and was drowned.

34When the herdsmen saw what had happened, they ran away and told about this in the town and the countryside. 35And people went to see what had happened. When they came to Jesus, they found the man sitting at Jesus' feet, clothed and in his right mind, because the demons were gone. But the people were frightened. 36The people who saw this happen told the others how Jesus had made the man well. 37All the people of the Gerasene country asked Jesus to leave, because they were all very afraid. So Jesus got into the boat and went back to Galilee.

38The man whom Jesus had healed begged to go with him, but Jesus sent him away, saying, 39"Go back home and tell people how much God has done for you." So the man went all over town telling how much Jesus had done for him.

Jesus Gives Life to a Dead Girl and Heals a Sick Woman

40When Jesus got back to Galilee, a crowd welcomed him, because everyone was waiting for him. 41A man named Jairus, a leader of the synagogue,[d] came to Jesus and fell at his feet, begging him to come to his house. 42Jairus' only daughter, about twelve years old, was dying.

While Jesus was on his way to Jairus' house, the people were crowding all around him. 43A woman was in the crowd who had been bleeding for twelve years, but no one was able to heal her. 44She came up behind Jesus and touched the edge of his coat, and instantly her bleeding stopped. 45Then Jesus said, "Who touched me?"

When all the people said they had not touched him, Peter said, "Master, the people are all around you and are pushing against you."

46But Jesus said, "Someone did touch me, because I felt power go out from me." 47When the woman saw she could not hide, she came forward, shaking, and fell down before Jesus. While all the people listened, she told why she had touched him and how she had been instantly healed. 48Jesus said to her, "Dear woman, you are made well because you believed. Go in peace."

49While Jesus was still speaking, someone came from the house of the synagogue leader and said to him, "Your daughter is dead. Don't bother the teacher anymore."

50When Jesus heard this, he said to Jairus, "Don't be afraid. Just believe, and your daughter will be well."

51When Jesus went to the house, he let only Peter, John, James, and the girl's father and mother go inside with him. 52All the people were crying and feeling sad because the girl was dead, but Jesus said, "Stop crying. She is not dead, only asleep."

53The people laughed at Jesus because they knew the girl was dead. 54But Jesus took hold of her hand and called to her, "My child, stand up!" 55Her spirit came back into her, and she stood up at once. Then Jesus ordered that she be given something to eat. 56The girl's parents were amazed, but Jesus told them not to tell anyone what had happened.

Jesus Sends Out the Apostles

9 Jesus called the twelve apostles[d] together and gave them power and authority over all demons[d] and the ability to heal sicknesses. 2He sent the apostles out to tell about God's kingdom and to heal the sick. 3He said to them, "Take nothing for your trip, neither a walking stick, bag, bread, money, or extra clothes. 4When you enter a house, stay there until it is time to leave. 5If people do not welcome you, shake the dust off of your feet[n] as you leave the town, as a warning to them."

6So the apostles went out and traveled through all the towns, preaching the Good News[d] and healing people everywhere.

Herod Is Confused About Jesus

7Herod, the governor, heard about all the things that were happening and was confused, because some people said, "John the Baptist[d] has risen from the dead." 8Others said, "Elijah has come to us." And still others said, "One of the prophets[d] who lived long ago has risen from the dead." 9Herod said, "I cut off John's head, so who is this man I hear such things about?" And Herod kept trying to see Jesus.

More than Five Thousand Fed

10When the apostles[d] returned, they told Jesus

"Legion" Means very many. A legion was about five thousand men in the Roman army.
eternal darkness Literally, "the abyss," something like a pit or a hole that has no end.
shake . . . feet A warning. It showed that they had rejected these people.

everything they had done. Then Jesus took them with him to a town called Bethsaida where they could be alone together. [11]But the people learned where Jesus went and followed him. He welcomed them and talked with them about God's kingdom and healed those who needed to be healed.

[12]Late in the afternoon, the twelve apostles came to Jesus and said, "Send the people away. They need to go to the towns and countryside around here and find places to sleep and something to eat, because no one lives in this place."

[13]But Jesus said to them, "You give them something to eat."

They said, "We have only five loaves of bread and two fish, unless we go buy food for all these people." [14](There were about five thousand men there.)

Jesus said to his followers, "Tell the people to sit in groups of about fifty people."

[15]So the followers did this, and all the people sat down. [16]Then Jesus took the five loaves of bread and two fish, and looking up to heaven, he thanked God for the food. Then he divided the food and gave it to the followers to give to the people. [17]They all ate and were satisfied, and what was left over was gathered up, filling twelve baskets.

Jesus Is the Christ

[18]One time when Jesus was praying alone, his followers were with him, and he asked them, "Who do the people say I am?"

[19]They answered, "Some say you are John the Baptist.[d] Others say you are Elijah.[n] And others say you are one of the prophets[d] from long ago who has come back to life."

[20]Then Jesus asked, "But who do you say I am?"

Peter answered, "You are the Christ[d] from God."

[21]Jesus warned them not to tell anyone, saying, [22]"The Son of Man[d] must suffer many things. He will be rejected by the older Jewish leaders, the leading priests, and the teachers of the law. He will be killed and after three days will be raised from the dead."

[23]Jesus said to all of them, "If people want to follow me, they must give up the things they want. They must be willing to give up their lives daily to follow me. [24]Those who want to save their lives will give up true life. But those who give up their lives for me will have true life. [25]It is worth nothing for them to have the whole world if they themselves are destroyed or lost. [26]If people are ashamed of me and my teaching, then the Son of Man[d] will be ashamed of them when he comes in his glory and with the glory of the Father and the holy angels. [27]I tell you the truth, some people standing here will see the kingdom of God before they die."

Jesus Talks with Moses and Elijah

[28]About eight days after Jesus said these things, he took Peter, John, and James and went up on a mountain to pray. [29]While Jesus was praying, the appearance of his face changed, and his clothes became shining white. [30]Then two men, Moses and Elijah,[n] were talking with Jesus. [31]They appeared in heavenly glory, talking about his departure which he would soon bring about in Jerusalem. [32]Peter and the others were very sleepy, but when they awoke fully, they saw the glory of Jesus and the two men standing with him. [33]When Moses and Elijah were about to leave, Peter said to Jesus, "Master, it is good that we are here. Let us make three tents — one for you, one for Moses, and one for Elijah." (Peter did not know what he was talking about.)

[34]While he was saying these things, a cloud came and covered them, and they became afraid as the cloud covered them. [35]A voice came from the cloud, saying, "This is my Son, whom I have chosen. Listen to him!"

[36]When the voice finished speaking, only Jesus was there. Peter, John, and James said nothing and told no one at that time what they had seen.

Jesus Heals a Sick Boy

[37]The next day, when they came down from the mountain, a large crowd met Jesus. [38]A man in the crowd shouted to him, "Teacher, please come and look at my son, because he is my only child. [39]An evil spirit seizes my son, and suddenly he screams. It causes him to lose control of himself and foam at the mouth. The evil spirit keeps on hurting him and almost never leaves him. [40]I begged your followers to force the evil spirit out, but they could not do it."

[41]Jesus answered, "You people have no faith, and your lives are all wrong. How long must I stay with you and put up with you? Bring your son here."

[42]While the boy was coming, the demon[d] threw him on the ground and made him lose control of himself. But Jesus gave a strong command to the evil spirit and healed the boy and gave him

Elijah A man who spoke for God and who lived hundreds of years before Christ. See 1 Kings 17.
Moses and Elijah Two of the most important Jewish leaders in the past. Moses had given them the law, and Elijah was an important prophet.

back to his father. 43All the people were amazed at the great power of God.

Jesus Talks About His Death

While everyone was wondering about all that Jesus did, he said to his followers, 44"Don't forget what I tell you now: The Son of Man[d] will be handed over to people." 45But the followers did not understand what this meant; the meaning was hidden from them so they could not understand. But they were afraid to ask Jesus about it.

Who Is the Greatest?

46Jesus' followers began to have an argument about which one of them was the greatest. 47Jesus knew what they were thinking, so he took a little child and stood the child beside him. 48Then Jesus said, "Whoever accepts this little child in my name accepts me. And whoever accepts me accepts the One who sent me, because whoever is least among you all is really the greatest."

Anyone Not Against Us Is for Us

49John answered, "Master, we saw someone using your name to force demons[d] out of people. We told him to stop, because he does not belong to our group."

50But Jesus said to him, "Don't stop him, because whoever is not against you is for you."

A Town Rejects Jesus

51When the time was coming near for Jesus to depart, he was determined to go to Jerusalem. 52He sent some men ahead of him, who went into a town in Samaria to make everything ready for him. 53But the people there would not welcome him, because he was set on going to Jerusalem. 54When James and John, followers of Jesus, saw this, they said, "Lord, do you want us to call fire down from heaven and destroy those people?"[n]

Verse 54 Here, some Greek copies add: ". . . as Elijah did."

DECISION MAKING

A Soldier Decides

On June 5, 1944, Dwight Eisenhower sat at a table surrounded by all his advisers. The decision, however, was his alone.

It appeared there just might be a brief break in the horrible weather they were having. The question was whether to send the largest amphibious invasion force ever assembled across the stormy English Channel to attack Hitler's "Fortress Europe." Their efforts had been fruitless before, but the success of this mission was essential if the war was to be won.

Conditions of tide and moon wouldn't be right again for weeks, and by then the element of surprise could be lost. On the other hand, the predicted gale force winds in the channel could swamp the landing crafts and drown the entire army before it reached shore. All the eyes looked to General Eisenhower. He knew if he made the wrong choice, the results could be disastrous. After long minutes of silence, he spoke.

"We go!" he said.

The D-Day invasion was on, and the outcome of the war was decided—in favor of Britain and the Allies.

Making big decisions is hard, especially since we usually don't know all the consequences of our choices. In **Luke 9:51–62**, Jesus pointed out that important decisions can involve letting go of the past and taking a stand.

- How was General Eisenhower unlike the would-be followers in this passage?
- Are you willing to say to Jesus, "I'll follow you any place you go"? If not, what's holding you back?

CONSIDER . . .

- writing out all the important decisions you need to make soon and asking advice from several people you trust.
- asking your parent or youth leader to give his or her insight on how you can make better decisions.

FOR MORE, SEE . . .

- Joshua 24:14–15 (p. 214)
- Proverbs 8 (p. 573)
- Acts 5:1–11 (p. 1104)

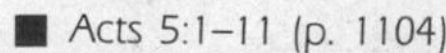

55But Jesus turned and scolded them. 56Then[n]
they went to another town.

SIDELIGHT: The disciples' reaction to Jesus' not being welcomed in a Samaritan town (Luke 9:51–56) would have been common in Jesus' day, given the hatred between Jews and Samaritans at that time. A hundred years earlier, Jews had destroyed a Samaritan temple. Then, during the night, Samaritans had strewn human bones on the steps of the Jewish Temple in Jerusalem. To see Jesus' attitude toward the Samaritans, read John 4:5–10 (p. 1063).

Following Jesus

57As they were going along the road, someone
said to Jesus, "I will follow you any place you go."
58Jesus said to them, "The foxes have holes to
live in, and the birds have nests, but the Son of
Man[d] has no place to rest his head."
59Jesus said to another man, "Follow me!"
But he said, "Lord, first let me go and bury my
father."
60But Jesus said to him, "Let the people who
are dead bury their own dead. You must go and
tell about the kingdom of God."
61Another man said, "I will follow you, Lord,
but first let me go and say good-bye to my family."
62Jesus said, "Anyone who begins to plow a
field but keeps looking back is of no use in the
kingdom of God."

Jesus Sends Out the Seventy-Two

10 After this, the Lord chose seventy-two[n]
others and sent them out in pairs ahead
of him into every town and place where he
planned to go. 2He said to them, "There are a
great many people to harvest, but there are only
a few workers. So pray to God, who owns the
harvest, that he will send more workers to help
gather his harvest. 3Go now, but listen! I am sending you out like sheep among wolves. 4Don't
carry a purse, a bag, or sandals and don't waste
time talking with people on the road. 5Before you
go into a house, say, 'Peace be with this house.'
6If peaceful people live there, your blessing of
peace will stay with them, but if not, then your
blessing will come back to you. 7Stay in the peaceful house, eating and drinking what the people
there give you. A worker should be given his pay.
Don't move from house to house. 8If you go into
a town and the people welcome you, eat what
they give you. 9Heal the sick who live there, and
tell them, 'The kingdom of God is near you.' 10But
if you go into a town, and the people don't welcome you, then go into the streets and say,
11'Even the dirt from your town that sticks to our
feet we wipe off against you.[n] But remember that
the kingdom of God is near.' 12I tell you, on the
Judgment Day it will be better for the people of
Sodom[n] than for the people of that town.

Jesus Warns Unbelievers

13"How terrible for you, Korazin! How terrible
for you, Bethsaida! If the miracles[d] I did in you
had happened in Tyre and Sidon,[n] those people
would have changed their lives long ago. They
would have worn rough cloth and put ashes on
themselves to show they had changed. 14But on
the Judgment Day it will be better for Tyre and
Sidon than for you. 15And you, Capernaum,[n] will
you be lifted up to heaven? No! You will be
thrown down to the depths!
16"Whoever listens to you listens to me, and
whoever refuses to accept you refuses to accept
me. And whoever refuses to accept me refuses to
accept the One who sent me."

Satan Falls

17When the seventy-two[n] came back, they
were very happy and said, "Lord, even the demons[d] obeyed us when we used your name!"
18Jesus said, "I saw Satan fall like lightning from
heaven. 19Listen, I have given you power to walk
on snakes and scorpions, power that is greater
than the enemy has. So nothing will hurt you.
20But you should not be happy because the spirits
obey you but because your names are written in
heaven."

Jesus Prays to the Father

21Then Jesus rejoiced in the Holy Spirit[d] and
said, "I praise you, Father, Lord of heaven and
earth, because you have hidden these things from
the people who are wise and smart. But you have
shown them to those who are like little children.
Yes, Father, this is what you really wanted.
22"My Father has given me all things. No one
knows who the Son is, except the Father. And no

Verse 55-56 Some copies read: "But Jesus turned and scolded them. And Jesus said, 'You don't know what kind of spirit you belong to. 56The Son of Man did not come to destroy the souls of people but to save them.' Then"
seventy-two Many Greek copies read seventy.
dirt . . . you A warning. It showed that they had rejected these people.
Sodom City that God destroyed because the people were so evil.
Tyre and Sidon Towns where wicked people lived.
Korazin, Bethsaida, Capernaum Towns by Lake Galilee where Jesus preached to the people.

one knows who the Father is, except the Son and
those whom the Son chooses to tell."
23 Then Jesus turned to his followers and said
privately, "You are blessed to see what you now
see. 24 I tell you, many prophets[d] and kings
wanted to see what you now see, but they did
not, and they wanted to hear what you now hear,
but they did not."

The Good Samaritan

25 Then an expert on the law stood up to test
Jesus, saying, "Teacher, what must I do to get life
forever?"
26 Jesus said, "What is written in the law? What
do you read there?"
27 The man answered, "Love the Lord your God
with all your heart, all your soul, all your strength,
and all your mind."[n] Also, "Love your neighbor
as you love yourself."[n]
28 Jesus said to him, "Your answer is right. Do
this and you will live."
29 But the man, wanting to show the importance of his question, said to Jesus, "And who is
my neighbor?"
30 Jesus answered, "As a man was going down
from Jerusalem to Jericho, some robbers attacked
him. They tore off his clothes, beat him, and left
him lying there, almost dead. 31 It happened that
a Jewish priest was going down that road. When
he saw the man, he walked by on the other side.
32 Next, a Levite[n] came there, and after he went
over and looked at the man, he walked by on the

"Love . . . mind." Quotation from Deuteronomy 6:5.
"Love . . . yourself." Quotation from Leviticus 19:18.
Levite Levites were members of the tribe of Levi who helped the Jewish priests with their work in the Temple. Read 1 Chronicles 23:24-32.

SHARING FAITH

Unknown Soldiers

Spitballs and paper airplanes were flying everywhere. One student was demonstrating his amazing mastery of crude sounds. Poor Edward Kimball. He was only nineteen, but he was responsible for this Sunday school class of half-crazed junior high boys. He did his best, but they were more concerned about spitballs, practical jokes, and nasty sounds than about God.

Ed was warm, gentle, and shy. But to the boys, he came across as dull. Many adults had serious doubts about Ed's future as a Sunday school teacher.

But Ed was persistent. He really cared about those boys. Realizing his weaknesses as a teacher, he decided he might be more successful meeting the boys one-to-one. One sunny day in April he paced up and down a Boston street, trying to get up nerve to walk into a shoe store where Dwight, one of his students, worked. Finally he did. In frightened, faltering words he told Dwight how God had made a difference in his life. When he looked up the boy was crying.

Not many people today remember what Ed did. Thousands of lives, however, were touched by Dwight L. Moody, the famous evangelist, who on that day in 1855 was led to faith in Christ by Edward Kimball.

It wasn't easy for Ed to share his faith. In **Luke 10:1–12**, Jesus explains that the way won't be easy, but his heart will guide and strengthen us as we obey him.

■ Do you think some of the seventy-two people in this passage felt as "ungifted" as Ed did? Why did Jesus choose them? (See especially verse 2.)

■ According to this passage, which quality was most important to Jesus: talent or obedience? Why is that?

CONSIDER . . .

■ asking God to show you how you can be more obedient to him in sharing your faith.

■ reading a book about Dwight L. Moody's life and ministry.

FOR MORE, SEE

■ Isaiah 6:1–8 (p. 622)
■ Matthew 28:16–20 (p. 962)
■ Mark 6:7–13 (p. 973)

other side of the road. 33 Then a Samaritan[n] traveling down the road came to where the hurt man
was. When he saw the man, he felt very sorry for
him. 34 The Samaritan went to him, poured olive
oil and wine[n] on his wounds, and bandaged
them. Then he put the hurt man on his own donkey and took him to an inn where he cared for
him. 35 The next day, the Samaritan brought out
two coins,[n] gave them to the innkeeper, and
said, 'Take care of this man. If you spend more
money on him, I will pay it back to you when I
come again.' "
36 Then Jesus said, "Which one of these three
men do you think was a neighbor to the man who
was attacked by the robbers?"
37 The expert on the law answered, "The one
who showed him mercy."

SIDELIGHT: The Jerusalem-to-Jericho road where the man was robbed in Jesus' story (Luke 10:30) was notoriously dangerous. With a 3,600 foot drop in only seventeen miles, this narrow, steep, twisting path—nicknamed "The Bloody Way"—was the notorious hangout of robbers.

Samaritan Samaritans were people from Samaria. These people were part Jewish, but the Jews did not accept them as true Jews. Samaritans and Jews disliked each other.
olive oil and wine Oil and wine were used like medicine to soften and clean wounds.
coins Roman denarii. One coin was the average pay for one day's work.

SERVICE

Sweating on a Shingle

Minnie Burgeon wasn't looking forward to the rainy season.

"Oh, it's worse now than it was before they worked on it," says Minnie, who last year paid $2,000 to replace the roof on her home.

The roofing company Minnie used had done several jobs in her area—mostly for the elderly—and then had disappeared.

Minnie had no money to get the roof replaced again, so she contacted the Samaritan Connection, a service organization that matches people in need with volunteer labor.

The timing was bad. It was June, and hot. Everyone wanted to be swimming and boating, not baking on a rooftop. One youth group volunteered its time and energy for Minnie, but once the group members had spent a few hours tearing shingles off the sweltering roof, their resolve to help others waned.

"Hey, I'm sorry, but I don't think I can stay very long. I've got stuff around the house I'm supposed to do."

"Yeah, I've got a date tonight, and I've gotta do my hair."

"I told a friend I'd meet her at the mall in a little while, so I can't stay long."

The leader knew he had to do something or lose the whole work crew. He brought them downstairs to meet Minnie. She pointed to the water stains above her bed and talked about how she would lie in bed and worry as water dripped on her. Then she said, "Jesus has been good to me to send me you Samaritans."

Nobody left. Nobody complained again. They all finished the job and felt great. Minnie was no longer just a "service project." She was a neighbor.

Read **Luke 10:25–37** to find out who God says your neighbor is.

- How is your youth group like the one in the story? How is it like the men who encountered the hurt man in the passage?
- What can you do to become more like the Samaritan in the passage?

CONSIDER . . .

- helping a friend or neighbor with a job around the house.
- listing four ways you could serve others better and then doing one each week for the next four weeks.

FOR MORE, SEE . . .

- Matthew 22:34–46 (p. 948)
- Mark 12:28–34 (p. 988)
- Philippians 2:1–4 (p. 1230)

Jesus said to him, "Then go and do what he
did."

Mary and Martha

38While Jesus and his followers were traveling,
Jesus went into a town. A woman named Martha
let Jesus stay at her house. 39Martha had a sister
named Mary, who was sitting at Jesus' feet and
listening to him teach. 40But Martha was busy
with all the work to be done. She went in and
said, "Lord, don't you care that my sister has left
me alone to do all the work? Tell her to help me."
41But the Lord answered her, "Martha, Martha, you are worried and upset about many
things. 42Only one thing is important. Mary has
chosen the better thing, and it will never be taken
away from her."

Jesus Teaches About Prayer

11 One time Jesus was praying in a certain
place. When he finished, one of his followers said to him, "Lord, teach us to pray as John
taught his followers."
2Jesus said to them, "When you pray, say:
'Father, may your name always be kept holy.
May your kingdom come.
3Give us the food we need for each day.
4Forgive us for our sins,
because we forgive everyone who has done
wrong to us.
And do not cause us to be tempted.' "

Continue to Ask

5Then Jesus said to them, "Suppose one of you
went to your friend's house at midnight and said
to him, 'Friend, loan me three loaves of bread. 6A
friend of mine has come into town to visit me, but
I have nothing for him to eat.' 7Your friend inside
the house answers, 'Don't bother me! The door
is already locked, and my children and I are in
bed. I cannot get up and give you anything.' 8I tell
you, if friendship is not enough to make him get
up to give you the bread, your boldness will make

WORRYING

First Letter Home

Dear Mom and Dad,

I hate college! I wish I were back home in Toledo in high school. I worry about tests. I worry about dates. I worry if anyone likes me. My studying never feels like it does me any good. I don't feel comfortable with friends like I did in high school. I even wake up and worry about the weather.

I never used to worry! What's happening to me?

Love, Moira

Dear Moira,

Sorry to hear you're so worried. We could tell you "don't worry," but even we know better.

One suggestion: Don't rely on others, or your accomplishments, or your busyness for your self-concept. If you do, there'll be lots of worry in your future. Take some time and sit still with God. He has less worrisome ways of helping us know who we are—apart from those other things. Rely on him to show you what he thinks of you.

Love, Mom & Dad

P.S. Don't worry!

Moira Jackson needed to see that she was loved and accepted just as she was, without doing anything. Read how Jesus helped another busy, fretful, worrying woman see that truth in **Luke 10:38–42**.

- Can you think of a time you acted like Martha in this passage?
- How would your "worry level" change if you had a better sense of God's love for you?

C O N S I D E R . . .

- sitting for five minutes in God's presence and just listening.
- writing out all your concerns and then talking to God about each one.

F O R   M O R E ,   S E E . . .

- Psalm 131 (p. 558)
- Matthew 6:25–34 (p. 918)
- 1 Peter 5:6–7 (p. 1308)

him get up and give you whatever you need. 9So
I tell you, ask, and God will give to you. Search,
and you will find. Knock, and the door will open
for you. 10Yes, everyone who asks will receive.
The one who searches will find. And everyone
who knocks will have the door opened. 11If your
children ask for a fish, which of you would give
them a snake instead? 12Or, if your children ask
for an egg, would you give them a scorpion?
13Even though you are bad, you know how to give
good things to your children. How much more
your heavenly Father will give the Holy Spirit[d] to
those who ask him!"

Jesus' Power Is from God

14One time Jesus was sending out a demon[d]
that could not talk. When the demon came out,
the man who had been unable to speak, then
spoke. The people were amazed. 15But some of
them said, "Jesus uses the power of Beelzebul,[d]
the ruler of demons, to force demons out of people."
16Other people, wanting to test Jesus, asked
him to give them a sign from heaven. 17But knowing their thoughts, he said to them, "Every kingdom that is divided against itself will be destroyed. And a family that is divided against itself
will not continue. 18So if Satan is divided against
himself, his kingdom will not continue. You say
that I use the power of Beelzebul to force out demons. 19But if I use the power of Beelzebul to
force out demons, what power do your people use
to force demons out? So they will be your judges.
20But if I use the power of God to force out
demons, then the kingdom of God has come to
you.
21"When a strong person with many weapons
guards his own house, his possessions are safe.
22But when someone stronger comes and defeats
him, the stronger one will take away the weapons
the first man trusted and will give away the possessions.
23"Anyone who is not with me is against me,
and anyone who does not work with me is working against me.

The Empty Person

24"When an evil spirit comes out of a person,
it travels through dry places, looking for a place to
rest. But when it finds no place, it says, 'I will go
back to the house I left.' 25And when it comes

PRAYER

Countdown to Victory

"Oh, I'll never get it right. There's just no cure. It's hopeless."

Maybe that's what a lot of scientists were thinking in the first part of the twentieth century, when a disease called polio crippled and killed millions. Hundreds of researchers looked frantically for a cure. But it seemed like an impossible task. Then in 1954, Dr. Jonas Salk announced that after two hundred attempts he had developed a vaccine. This terrible disease disappeared virtually overnight.

Later, a reporter asked Dr. Salk how it felt to have had two hundred failures and only one success. Salk replied that he had never experienced two hundred failures. He had learned two hundred lessons. And those lessons had enabled him to create a usable vaccine. Rather than viewing each unsuccessful attempt as a tragedy, Dr. Salk chose to see it as an opportunity to learn.

Dr. Salk saw a need and didn't stop until the need was met. Similarly, persistent prayer is what Jesus recommends as one of the best ways to find answers in life. Read the story Jesus told in **Luke 11:1–13**.

- How is Dr. Salk like the man who needed bread in Jesus' story?
- Based on the passage, how should you pray about problems you really care about?

CONSIDER. . .

- writing about seven concerns that are important to you, and praying about a different concern each day this week.
- making a pact with a friend to become your "prayer partner" for the next month. Meet at least once a week to share requests and pray for each other.

FOR MORE, SEE. . .

- Psalm 130 (p. 557)
- Matthew 6:1–15 (p. 917)
- Luke 18:1–8 (p. 1041)

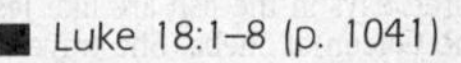

back, it finds that house swept clean and made neat. 26 Then the evil spirit goes out and brings seven other spirits more evil than it is, and they go in and live there. So the person has even more trouble than before."

People Who Are Truly Happy

27 As Jesus was saying these things, a woman in the crowd called out to Jesus, "Happy is the mother who gave birth to you and nursed you."

28 But Jesus said, "No, happy are those who hear the teaching of God and obey it."

The People Want a Miracle

29 As the crowd grew larger, Jesus said, "The people who live today are evil. They want to see a miracle[d] for a sign, but no sign will be given them, except the sign of Jonah.[n] 30 As Jonah was a sign for those people who lived in Nineveh, the Son of Man[d] will be a sign for the people of this time. 31 On the Judgment Day the Queen of the South[n] will stand up with the people who live now. She will show they are guilty, because she came from far away to listen to Solomon's wise teaching. And I tell you that someone greater than Solomon is here. 32 On the Judgment Day the people of Nineveh will stand up with the people who live now, and they will show that you are guilty. When Jonah preached to them, they were sorry and changed their lives. And I tell you that someone greater than Jonah is here.

Be a Light for the World

33 "No one lights a lamp and puts it in a secret place or under a bowl, but on a lampstand so the people who come in can see. 34 Your eye is a light for the body. When your eyes are good, your whole body will be full of light. But when your eyes are evil, your whole body will be full of darkness. 35 So be careful not to let the light in you become darkness. 36 If your whole body is full of light, and none of it is dark, then you will shine bright, as when a lamp shines on you."

Jesus Accuses the Pharisees

37 After Jesus had finished speaking, a Pharisee[d] asked Jesus to eat with him. So Jesus went in and sat at the table. 38 But the Pharisee was surprised when he saw that Jesus did not wash his hands[n] before the meal. 39 The Lord said to him, "You Pharisees clean the outside of the cup and the dish, but inside you are full of greed and evil. 40 You foolish people! The same one who made what is outside also made what is inside. 41 So give what is in your dishes to the poor, and then you will be fully clean. 42 How terrible for you Pharisees! You give God one-tenth of even your mint, your rue, and every other plant in your garden. But you fail to be fair to others and to love God. These are the things you should do while continuing to do those other things. 43 How terrible for you Pharisees, because you love to have the most important seats in the synagogues,[d] and you love to be greeted with respect in the marketplaces. 44 How terrible for you, because you are like hidden graves, which people walk on without knowing."

Jesus Talks to Experts on the Law

45 One of the experts on the law said to Jesus, "Teacher, when you say these things, you are insulting us, too."

46 Jesus answered, "How terrible for you, you experts on the law! You make strict rules that are very hard for people to obey, but you yourselves don't even try to follow those rules. 47 How terrible for you, because you build tombs for the prophets[d] whom your ancestors killed! 48 And now you show that you approve of what your ancestors did. They killed the prophets, and you build tombs for them! 49 This is why in his wisdom God said, 'I will send prophets and apostles[d] to them. They will kill some, and they will treat others cruelly.' 50 So you who live now will be punished for the deaths of all the prophets who were killed since the beginning of the world— 51 from the killing of Abel to the killing of Zechariah,[n] who died between the altar and the Temple.[d] Yes, I tell you that you who are alive now will be punished for them all.

52 "How terrible for you, you experts on the law. You have taken away the key to learning about God. You yourselves would not learn, and you stopped others from learning, too."

53 When Jesus left, the teachers of the law and the Pharisees[d] began to give him trouble, asking him questions about many things, 54 trying to catch him saying something wrong.

Don't Be Like the Pharisees

12 So many thousands of people had gathered that they were stepping on each other. Jesus spoke first to his followers, saying, "Beware of the yeast of the Pharisees,[d] because they are hypocrites.[d] 2 Everything that is hidden will be shown, and everything that is secret will be made known. 3 What you have said in the dark will be heard in the light, and what you have

sign of Jonah Jonah's three days in the fish are like Jesus' three days in the tomb. See Matthew 12:40.
Queen of the South The Queen of Sheba. She traveled a thousand miles to learn God's wisdom from Solomon. Read 1 Kings 10:1-3.
wash his hands This was a Jewish religious custom that the Pharisees thought was very important.
Abel . . . Zechariah In the Hebrew Old Testament, the first and last men to be murdered.

whispered in an inner room will be shouted from
the housetops.
4"I tell you, my friends, don't be afraid of people who can kill the body but after that can do
nothing more to hurt you. 5I will show you the
one to fear. Fear the one who has the power to
kill you and also to throw you into hell. Yes, this
is the one you should fear.
6"Five sparrows are sold for only two pennies,
and God does not forget any of them. 7But God
even knows how many hairs you have on your
head. Don't be afraid. You are worth much more
than many sparrows.

Don't Be Ashamed of Jesus

8"I tell you, all those who stand before others
and say they believe in me, I, the Son of Man,[d]
will say before the angels of God that they belong to me. 9But all who stand before others
and say they do not believe in me, I will say before the angels of God that they do not belong
to me.
10"Anyone who speaks against the Son of Man[d]
can be forgiven, but anyone who speaks against
the Holy Spirit[d] will not be forgiven.
11"When you are brought into the synagogues[d]
before the leaders and other powerful people,
don't worry about how to defend yourself or what
to say. 12At that time the Holy Spirit will teach
you what you must say."

Jesus Warns Against Selfishness

13Someone in the crowd said to Jesus,
"Teacher, tell my brother to divide with me the
property our father left us."
14But Jesus said to him, "Who said I should

BRAGGING

Cliffhangers

Pugslie Selman was by far the biggest kid around, and he didn't mind letting everyone know it. In a neighborhood full of tough guys, this loner was the undisputed champion. His real name was John, but nobody used it. The few guys he hung around with called him "Pugs," and most everyone else simply tried to stay out of his way.

Today was different, though. Instead of pushing people around, Pugs was on a ledge forty feet high, crying like a baby. He had come rock climbing with his buddies, and now he was stuck. He was afraid to try to go back down the way he had come up, but he couldn't trust the rope around his waist (or the boy who was holding it) enough to lean out and grab the rock above his head. So he clung to the cliff and cried.

Predictably, everyone on the ground laughed at Pugslie. They were yelling and joking about the "giant wimp." But then things changed. Paul Woods, a little guy that Pugslie liked to push around, climbed up the cliff face. "Everything will be all right, Pugs, " said Paul. "You'll be fine. Just follow me."

Then Paul climbed ahead of Pugslie, showing him each place to put his feet and hands. Before long, the guys on the ground were cheering Pugslie as he climbed over the top of the cliff and raised his fist into the air.

Pugslie is still big, and he's still tough. But because of Paul, Pugslie doesn't brag about his size so much. Paul showed Pugs that everyone has special gifts.

Jesus told a story about another man who thought he was big and tough. Like Pugslie, he had an "I'm the best" attitude. Read about his "fall" in **Luke 12:13–21**.

- What similarities can you see between Pugslie and the rich man in the passage?
- In what ways do you "store things up" for yourself? What does this passage say to you about that?

CONSIDER . . .

- listing the positive qualities of three of your friends and thanking God for giving them those gifts.
- looking up the word humility in the dictionary, and asking God to help you be humble.

FOR MORE, SEE . . .

- Daniel 4:19–37 (p. 811)
- 1 Corinthians 1:26–31 (p. 1168)
- Ephesians 2:8–9 (p. 1219)

judge or decide between you?" 15Then Jesus said
to them, "Be careful and guard against all kinds
of greed. Life is not measured by how much one
owns."

16Then Jesus told this story: "There was a rich
man who had some land, which grew a good
crop. 17He thought to himself, 'What will I do? I
have no place to keep all my crops.' 18Then he
said, 'This is what I will do: I will tear down my
barns and build bigger ones, and there I will store
all my grain and other goods. 19Then I can say
to myself, "I have enough good things stored to
last for many years. Rest, eat, drink, and enjoy
life!"'

20"But God said to him, 'Foolish man! Tonight your life will be taken from you. So who
will get those things you have prepared for yourself?'

21"This is how it will be for those who store up
things for themselves and are not rich toward
God."

SIDELIGHT: The rich man in Jesus' story (Luke 12:16–21) would probably have been a millionaire today. Most farmers stored their food supply in clay jars of various sizes. To have a barn or grain silo would indicate extreme wealth. Archaeologists have discovered some underground grain silos that are twenty-five feet wide and more than twenty feet deep.

Don't Worry

22Jesus said to his followers, "So I tell you,
don't worry about the food you need to live, or
about the clothes you need for your body. 23Life
is more than food, and the body is more than
clothes. 24Look at the birds. They don't plant or
harvest, they don't have storerooms or barns, but
God feeds them. And you are worth much more
than birds. 25You cannot add any time to your life
by worrying about it. 26If you cannot do even the
little things, then why worry about the big things?
27Consider how the lilies grow; they don't work
or make clothes for themselves. But I tell you that
even Solomon with his riches was not dressed as
beautifully as one of these flowers. 28God clothes
the grass in the field, which is alive today but tomorrow is thrown into the fire. So how much
more will God clothe you? Don't have so little
faith! 29Don't always think about what you will
eat or what you will drink, and don't keep worrying. 30All the people in the world are trying to get
these things, and your Father knows you need
them. 31But seek God's kingdom, and all the
other things you need will be given to you.

Don't Trust in Money

32"Don't fear, little flock, because your Father
wants to give you the kingdom. 33Sell your possessions and give to the poor. Get for yourselves
purses that will not wear out, the treasure in
heaven that never runs out, where thieves can't
steal and moths can't destroy. 34Your heart will be
where your treasure is.

Always Be Ready

35"Be dressed, ready for service, and have your
lamps shining. 36Be like servants who are waiting
for their master to come home from a wedding
party. When he comes and knocks, the servants
immediately open the door for him. 37They will be
blessed when their master comes home, because
he sees that they were watching for him. I tell you
the truth, the master will dress himself to serve
and tell the servants to sit at the table, and he will
serve them. 38Those servants will be happy when
he comes in and finds them still waiting, even if
it is midnight or later.

39"Remember this: If the owner of the house
knew what time a thief was coming, he would
not allow the thief to enter his house. 40So you
also must be ready, because the Son of Man[d] will
come at a time when you don't expect him!"

Who Is the Trusted Servant?

41Peter said, "Lord, did you tell this story to us
or to all people?"

42The Lord said, "Who is the wise and trusted
servant that the master trusts to give the other
servants their food at the right time? 43When the
master comes and finds the servant doing his
work, the servant will be blessed. 44I tell you the
truth, the master will choose that servant to take
care of everything he owns. 45But suppose the servant thinks to himself, 'My master will not come
back soon,' and he begins to beat the other servants, men and women, and to eat and drink and
get drunk. 46The master will come when that servant is not ready and is not expecting him. Then
the master will cut him in pieces and send him
away to be with the others who don't obey.

47"The servant who knows what his master
wants but is not ready, or who does not do what
the master wants, will be beaten with many
blows! 48But the servant who does not know
what his master wants and does things that
should be punished will be beaten with few
blows. From everyone who has been given much,
much will be demanded. And from the one
trusted with much, much more will be expected.

Jesus Causes Division

49"I came to set fire to the world, and I
wish it were already burning! 50I have a bap-

tism[n] to suffer through, and I feel very
troubled until it is over. 51Do you think I came
to give peace to the earth? No, I tell you, I came
to divide it. 52From now on, a family with five
people will be divided, three against two, and
two against three. 53They will be divided: father
against son and son against father, mother against
daughter and daughter against mother, mother-
in-law against daughter-in-law and daughter-
in-law against mother-in-law."

Understanding the Times

54Then Jesus said to the people, "When you see
clouds coming up in the west, you say, 'It's going
to rain,' and it happens. 55When you feel the wind
begin to blow from the south, you say, 'It will be
a hot day,' and it happens. 56Hypocrites![d] You
know how to understand the appearance of the
earth and sky. Why don't you understand what is
happening now?

I . . . baptism Jesus was talking about the suffering he would soon go through.

MONEY

It's Only Money!

By the time he was thirty, Millard Fuller had achieved the American Dream. He was worth more than $1 million and lived a lifestyle that showed it. He drove a fancy car, lived in a huge house, owned lots of land, and generally enjoyed the things his money could buy. He and his wife, Linda, had just about anything that a young couple could want, except. . . .

Except what? Well, they weren't sure. All Millard and Linda did know was that they weren't happy.

"We just thought there must be something more to life," Millard explains.

On the advice of a friend, Millard and Linda turned to God. They spent time reading the Bible and praying with other Christians at Koinonia Farms. What could they do? What should they do?

"By seeing other Christians' lifestyles," explains Linda, "we quickly saw there was much more to life than the success money can bring. We realized God had a purpose for us. And we were determined to find out what it was."

Finally, they received the answer to their prayers. They believed God wanted them to start something new. Something big. They believed God wanted them to start over.

So they did. They sold off their businesses and their big house, and gave the money away. They sold their land, their boats, their horses, their cattle. In fact, they got rid of just about everything.

After this, they didn't go on tour to brag about how kind they were, or how many points they had earned with God. Instead, they continued to pray about what God was calling them toward. For more than five years, they worked at various mission stations, continuing to pray. Finally, at God's prompting, they formed Habitat for Humanity, a world-wide group that seeks to eliminate all substandard housing. Because the Fullers were able to give everything away and listen to God, thousands of families go to bed each night in safe, secure homes.

One of the passages that helped the Fullers make their decision was **Luke 12:32–40**. Read it and see if you can understand their actions.

- How did these verses influence the Fullers?
- What can you do to apply Jesus' words in this passage?

CONSIDER. . .

- deciding to give a specific portion of your money to your church or other charity.
- keeping a list of all the money you spend in a week. Sit down with your list and see who really determines how you spend it. Then pray for the freedom to give everything to God.

FOR MORE, SEE. . .

- Isaiah 58:6–11 (p. 677)
- Matthew 6:19–21 (p. 918)
- 2 Corinthians 9:6–9 (p. 1201)

Settle Your Problems

57“Why can’t you decide for yourselves what is
right? 58If your enemy is taking you to court, try
hard to settle it on the way. If you don’t, your
enemy might take you to the judge, and the judge
might turn you over to the officer, and the officer
might throw you into jail. 59I tell you, you will not
get out of there until you have paid everything
you owe.”

Change Your Hearts

13 At that time some people were there
who told Jesus that Pilate[n] had killed
some people from Galilee while they were worshiping. He mixed their blood with the blood of
the animals they were sacrificing to God. 2Jesus
answered, “Do you think this happened to them
because they were more sinful than all others
from Galilee? 3No, I tell you. But unless you
change your hearts and lives, you will be destroyed as they were! 4What about those eighteen
people who died when the tower of Siloam fell on
them? Do you think they were more sinful than
all the others who live in Jerusalem? 5No, I tell
you. But unless you change your hearts and lives,
you will all be destroyed too!”

The Useless Tree

6Jesus told this story: “A man had a fig tree
planted in his vineyard. He came looking for some
fruit on the tree, but he found none. 7So the man
said to his gardener, ‘I have been looking for fruit
on this tree for three years, but I never find any.
Cut it down. Why should it waste the ground?’
8But the servant answered, ‘Master, let the tree
have one more year to produce fruit. Let me dig

Pilate Pontius Pilate was the Roman governor of Judea from A.D. 26 to A.D. 36.

SPIRITUAL GROWTH

Every Day Counts

Tim Richard was a friend of mine, in an unusual way. We met by accident and had very little in common. We liked different foods, different sports, different girls, and we each had our own definition of a “good time.” We did share two things, though: we had the same birthday and we loved the same God. Sometimes this was all we could agree on, but we usually enjoyed our time together.

When we were eighteen, Tim died suddenly of a heart attack. He said he wasn’t feeling well, and he passed out by the time the paramedics got to him. He was dead hours later. Through my tears, I realized that I didn’t have anyone to share my birthday with. And I wasn’t so sure about the God that I loved. Why did this happen? Everybody knows that teenagers aren’t supposed to die, right?

A few days later, Tim’s family and friends got together to mourn his death. As we sat around talking, somebody told a story about Tim that brought a smile to our faces. Before long, all of Tim’s old jokes were flying, along with stories of how his short life had touched each of us. In that conversation, we saw that Tim had tried to live each day as though it were an important chance to serve God and others.

I think of my friend Tim often, because his life and death challenged me. I realized I don’t know what will happen. So I must work to make each day count.

When people asked Jesus about their friends who had died, he gave them a challenge to use their days well. Read about it in **Luke 13:1–9**.

- How is Tim’s story like the stories in the passage?
- What can you do to prepare yourself to “bear fruit” and so avoid being like the useless tree in the passage?

CONSIDER . . .

- imagining that you have only two weeks to live. Decide what your priorities would be, then do them.
- buying two small potted plants and taking one to a person who is sick, elderly or shut-in. Keep the other in your room as a reminder to pray for your special friend—and as a reminder to always try to bear fruit for God’s kingdom.

FOR MORE, SEE . . .

- Psalm 90 (p. 535)
- Matthew 7:15–23 (p. 920)
- Galatians 6:7–10 (p. 1214)

up the dirt around it and put on some fertilizer. 9If the tree produces fruit next year, good. But if not, you can cut it down.' "

Jesus Heals on the Sabbath

10Jesus was teaching in one of the synagogues[d] on the Sabbath[d] day. 11A woman was there who, for eighteen years, had an evil spirit in her that made her crippled. Her back was always bent; she could not stand up straight. 12When Jesus saw her, he called her over and said, "Woman, you are free from your sickness." 13Jesus put his hands on her, and immediately she was able to stand up straight and began praising God.

14The synagogue leader was angry because Jesus healed on the Sabbath day. He said to the people, "There are six days when one has to work. So come to be healed on one of those days, and not on the Sabbath day."

15The Lord answered, "You hypocrites![d] Doesn't each of you untie your work animals and lead them to drink water every day—even on the Sabbath day? 16This woman that I healed, a daughter of Abraham, has been held by Satan for eighteen years. Surely it is not wrong for her to be freed from her sickness on a Sabbath day!" 17When Jesus said this, all of those who were criticizing him were ashamed, but the entire crowd rejoiced at all the wonderful things Jesus was doing.

Stories of Mustard Seed and Yeast

18Then Jesus said, "What is God's kingdom like? What can I compare it with? 19It is like a mustard seed that a man plants in his garden. The seed grows and becomes a tree, and the wild birds build nests in its branches."

20Jesus said again, "What can I compare God's kingdom with? 21It is like yeast that a woman took and hid in a large tub of flour until it made all the dough rise."

The Narrow Door

22Jesus was teaching in every town and village as he traveled toward Jerusalem. 23Someone said to Jesus, "Lord, will only a few people be saved?"

Jesus said, 24"Try hard to enter through the narrow door, because many people will try to enter there, but they will not be able. 25When the owner of the house gets up and closes the door, you can stand outside and knock on the door and say, 'Sir, open the door for us.' But he will answer, 'I don't know you or where you come from.' 26Then you will say, 'We ate and drank with you, and you taught in the streets of our town.' 27But he will say to you, 'I don't know you or where you come from. Go away from me, all you who do evil!' 28You will cry and grind your teeth with pain when you see Abraham, Isaac, Jacob, and all the prophets[d] in God's kingdom, but you yourselves thrown outside. 29People will come from the east, west, north, and south and will sit down at the table in the kingdom of God. 30There are those who have the lowest place in life now who will have the highest place in the future. And there are those who have the highest place now who will have the lowest place in the future."

Jesus Will Die in Jerusalem

31At that time some Pharisees[d] came to Jesus and said, "Go away from here! Herod wants to kill you!"

32Jesus said to them, "Go tell that fox Herod, 'Today and tomorrow I am forcing demons[d] out and healing people. Then, on the third day, I will reach my goal.' 33Yet I must be on my way today and tomorrow and the next day. Surely it cannot be right for a prophet[d] to be killed anywhere except in Jerusalem.

34"Jerusalem, Jerusalem! You kill the prophets and stone to death those who are sent to you. Many times I wanted to gather your people as a hen gathers her chicks under her wings, but you would not let me. 35Now your house is left completely empty. I tell you, you will not see me until that time when you will say, 'God bless the One who comes in the name of the Lord.' "[n]

Healing on the Sabbath

14 On a Sabbath[d] day, when Jesus went to eat at the home of a leading Pharisee,[d] the people were watching Jesus very closely. 2And in front of him was a man with dropsy.[n] 3Jesus said to the Pharisees and experts on the law, "Is it right or wrong to heal on the Sabbath day?" 4But they would not answer his question. So Jesus took the man, healed him, and sent him away. 5Jesus said to the Pharisees and teachers of the law, "If your child or ox falls into a well on the Sabbath day, will you not pull him out quickly?" 6And they could not answer him.

Don't Make Yourself Important

7When Jesus noticed that some of the guests were choosing the best places to sit, he told this story: 8"When someone invites you to a wedding feast, don't take the most important seat, because someone more important than you may have been invited. 9The host, who invited both of you, will come to you and say, 'Give this person your seat.' Then you will be embarrassed and will have

'God . . . Lord.' Quotation from Psalm 118:26.
dropsy A sickness that causes the body to swell larger and larger.

to move to the last place. 10So when you are invited, go sit in a seat that is not important. When
the host comes to you, he may say, 'Friend, move
up here to a more important place.' Then all the
other guests will respect you. 11All who make
themselves great will be made humble, but those
who make themselves humble will be made
great."

You Will Be Rewarded

12Then Jesus said to the man who had invited
him, "When you give a lunch or a dinner, don't
invite only your friends, your family, your other
relatives, and your rich neighbors. At another
time they will invite you to eat with them, and
you will be repaid. 13Instead, when you give a
feast, invite the poor, the crippled, the lame, and
the blind. 14Then you will be blessed, because
they have nothing and cannot pay you back. But
you will be repaid when the good people rise from
the dead."

A Story About a Big Banquet

15One of those at the table with Jesus heard
these things and said to him, "Happy are the people who will share in the meal in God's kingdom."
16Jesus said to him, "A man gave a big banquet

ETERNAL LIFE

Good Enough

Terry Wilson's favorite saying seemed to be "good enough."

"Hey, Terry!" his friend, Josh Simms, yelled. "How'd baseball tryouts go?"

"Good enough," he said.

"Did you clean your room?" Terry's mom would ask.

"Good enough," was the inevitable response.

"What about that song you were working on for Sunday, Terry?" his youth minister asked. "Will it be ready for Sunday service?"

The amazing thing about Terry is that whatever he did, it almost always was good enough. He usually did make the team or pass the test or win the award. If he wanted to, Terry could make anything he tried come out "good enough." It was even more surprising that he usually accomplished these feats without trying too hard. If a particular task was too demanding or required too much commitment, Terry simply shifted his energy into something else that promised an easier victory.

One summer Terry asked his friend Josh to be his prayer partner. They arranged to meet each week, and it started out well.

But then Terry started coming late, or not at all. Josh was always there, but Terry eventually quit. The commitment was too much, it seemed. That fall, after leaving home for the first time, Terry called Josh, in tears. He was so lonely and felt so "dead" inside. Josh sympathized with his friend and prayed for him, but there was little else he could do. If Terry's faith wasn't "good enough," it was his own fault.

Terry discovered that living the Christian life wasn't as easy as other things he had tried. And he had trouble paying the price to follow God. When Jesus talked about living with God forever, he said that it starts with giving your all to live for God here on earth. Listen to his words in **Luke 13:22–30**.

- What did Jesus say to the people who, like Terry, thought their lives were "good enough" to be worthy of eternal life?
- What are obstacles that keep you from the "narrow road" that leads to living with God forever?

CONSIDER . . .

- writing a short story or poem that describes what you think life in heaven will be like.
- selecting five goals that will help you walk the "narrow road" of eternal life with God. Put a copy of them in an envelope and give it to a trusted friend. Ask him or her to mail it to you in six months. Do your best to achieve the goals!

FOR MORE, SEE . . .

- Hosea 6:1–6 (p. 827)
- Matthew 7:13–23 (p. 919)
- Hebrews 6:7–12 (p. 1281)

and invited many people. [17]When it was time to
eat, the man sent his servant to tell the guests,
'Come. Everything is ready.'
[18]"But all the guests made excuses. The first
one said, 'I have just bought a field, and I must go
look at it. Please excuse me.' [19]Another said, 'I
have just bought five pairs of oxen; I must go and
try them. Please excuse me.' [20]A third person
said, 'I just got married; I can't come.' [21]So the
servant returned and told his master what had
happened. Then the master became angry and
said, 'Go at once into the streets and alleys of
the town, and bring in the poor, the crippled,
the blind, and the lame.' [22]Later the servant
said to him, 'Master, I did what you commanded,
but we still have room.' [23]The master said to the
servant, 'Go out to the roads and country lanes,
and urge the people there to come so my house
will be full. [24]I tell you, none of those whom I invited first will eat with me.' "

SIDELIGHT: A party invitation in Jesus' day (Luke 14:15–24) included the day but never the hour. When the party was ready, slaves would go get the guests. To reject an invitation you had earlier accepted was the ultimate insult—as this story illustrates!

FRIENDS

A New Kind of Friend

Seventeen-year-old Amanda Hughes doesn't worry much about friends. Her attractive smile, engaging personality and sincere personal warmth make people simply want to be with her.

When she went on the service project, Amanda wasn't concerned about being in a new group. Questions like "will they like me?" never entered her mind. She was just excited about this new experience.

Amanda was surprised the first day she worked. She had expected to work on new home construction, interacting only with her crew. But her crew was renovating an existing home—a home full of people, one of whom, Charles, was close to her own age. For perhaps the first time in her life, she was nervous about making a friend. Her skin was a different color, and her life experience was vastly different. She and Charles seemed to have little in common.

Amanda cried as she told her prayer group of her desire to befriend Charles and his family. How could she do it? They were just so different.

One day, instead of taking her break with the work crew, she challenged Charles to a game of basketball. It was no contest, but they had a great time. The next day, he offered to help her paint, and again they had a lot of fun.

On their last work day, Amanda asked Charles if she could have his address and write to him.

"That'd be great," he exclaimed.

After exchanging addresses and phone numbers, they exchanged hugs. Amanda laughed inside as she thought about her confusion, and thanked God for helping bring two of his children just a little bit closer.

Sometimes we're friends only with those who are just like us. See how Jesus felt about that subject by reading **Luke 14:7–14**.

- How did Amanda demonstrate her understanding of Jesus' words in this passage?
- What do these verses say about you and your circle of friends?

CONSIDER . . .

- sending an anonymous letter to one of your friends. Fill it with encouragement from scripture, as well as other affirmations.
- arranging for your youth group to visit another church, preferably one of a different tradition and location (for instance, if you're in the suburbs, visit a city church). See what you can learn from each other.

FOR MORE, SEE . . .

- Ruth 1 (p. 239)
- Philemon 4–7 (p. 1274)
- 1 John 4:13–21 (p. 1319)

The Cost of Being Jesus' Follower

[25]Large crowds were traveling with Jesus, and
he turned and said to them, [26]"If anyone comes
to me but loves his father, mother, wife, children,
brothers, or sisters — or even life — more than me,
he cannot be my follower. [27]Whoever is not willing to carry the cross and follow me cannot be my
follower. [28]If you want to build a tower, you first
sit down and decide how much it will cost, to see
if you have enough money to finish the job. [29]If
you don't, you might lay the foundation, but you
would not be able to finish. Then all who would
see it would make fun of you, [30]saying, 'This person began to build but was not able to finish.'
[31]"If a king is going to fight another king, first
he will sit down and plan. He will decide if he and
his ten thousand soldiers can defeat the other king
who has twenty thousand soldiers. [32]If he can't,
then while the other king is still far away, he will
send some people to speak to him and ask for
peace. [33]In the same way, you must give up everything you have to be my follower.

Don't Lose Your Influence

[34]"Salt is good, but if it loses its salty taste, you
cannot make it salty again. [35]It is no good for the
soil or for manure; it is thrown away.

"You people who can hear me, listen."

A Lost Sheep, a Lost Coin

15 The tax collectors and sinners all came
to listen to Jesus. [2]But the Pharisees[d] and
the teachers of the law began to complain: "Look,
this man welcomes sinners and even eats with
them."

[3]Then Jesus told them this story: [4]"Suppose
one of you has a hundred sheep but loses one of
them. Then he will leave the other ninety-nine
sheep in the open field and go out and look for the

FOLLOWING GOD

The Choice to Follow

André Bolte is a likable guy. He's athletic, funny, good-looking, and charming. In fact, when André joined the youth group at First Church, attendance went up. He was eager to learn more about following God and making friends.

André was also eager to please others. So it wasn't long before he agreed to participate in Bible study, Sunday school and other activities. After a few years, you couldn't go to any youth group event without seeing André or hearing how wonderful he was. And he was a great follower of God.

As time passed, André stayed active in the group. But new things came up, too. He started playing sports at school. He joined a couple of academic clubs. He got a new girlfriend. He got a job and a car.

André didn't want his friends to think he had forgotten them, so he kept volunteering for jobs in the group. He got so busy, though, that he began to do them poorly, or just forgot about them.

He still comes around the youth group occasionally. Not long ago, he came to encourage the younger kids to keep active—"Just like I am," he said. They didn't say much, though. Afterward, Michelle Jones commented: "André is a lot of talk and no action. He never does what he says he will. It seems pretty useless to me."

André wanted to follow God, but his overloaded lifestyle got in the way. When people asked Jesus what it takes to truly follow God, he had them make some hard choices. Read Jesus' requirements in **Luke 14:25–33**.

- How is André's situation like that of the king mentioned in the passage?
- What does this passage say about your priorities and following God?

CONSIDER . . .

- listing your top five priorities in life and taping the list to your mirror. Each day, pray for the chance to follow God in those areas of your life.
- keeping a daily log for the coming week, writing down everything you do and how long it takes. At the end of the week, compare your daily log to your priorities. What does it say about your schedule?

FOR MORE, SEE . . .

- Psalm 119:105–115 (p. 553)
- Luke 9:23–26 (p. 1019)
- Philippians 3:8–11 (p. 1232)

lost sheep until he finds it. 5And when he finds it,
he happily puts it on his shoulders 6and goes
home. He calls to his friends and neighbors and
says, 'Be happy with me because I found my lost
sheep.' 7In the same way, I tell you there is more
joy in heaven over one sinner who changes his
heart and life, than over ninety-nine good people
who don't need to change.

8"Suppose a woman has ten silver coins,[n] but
loses one. She will light a lamp, sweep the house,
and look carefully for the coin until she finds it.
9And when she finds it, she will call her friends
and neighbors and say, 'Be happy with me because I have found the coin that I lost.' 10In the
same way, there is joy in the presence of the angels of God when one sinner changes his heart
and life."

The Son Who Left Home

11Then Jesus said, "A man had two sons. 12The
younger son said to his father, 'Give me my share
of the property.' So the father divided the property between his two sons. 13Then the younger
son gathered up all that was his and traveled far
away to another country. There he wasted his
money in foolish living. 14After he had spent everything, a time came when there was no food
anywhere in the country, and the son was poor

silver coins Roman denarii. One coin was the average pay for one day's work.

GOD'S LOVE

Stubborn Love

Stan Geary sat dumbfounded at the dining room table in Arlo Lane's house. For years Arlo had told stories about how he hated his mom because she didn't really care about him. Arlo had accused her of trying to control him, choose his friends for him, even determine the music he listened to.

He didn't really believe his mother loved him.

Arlo's mom had wanted him to stop smoking marijuana. She told him how hurtful the drug is, how addictive it can be. But Arlo claimed it was all a front—his mom just wanted to control him. She got her pleasure out of ruling his life, he thought.

But now, Stan didn't know what to believe. He knew at least some of Arlo's stories must have been true, but a quick glance around the table told him that they weren't true anymore. As Arlo and his mom laughed and joked, it was obvious that something—no, everything—had changed.

Stan didn't understand it, but he liked it. Later, when the guys were outside working on Arlo's ten-speed bike, Stan asked what had changed.

"It was awesome," Arlo said. "After one of our battles, Mom and I were both really upset. She started crying, you know? I yelled something like, 'What do you have to cry about?' She said she was crying because she loved me, and the drugs were hurting me."

"At that moment I looked at her and realized she was telling the truth. I don't know how—something just clicked inside. I realized she really does love me. So we decided to start all over again. It hasn't been easy, but I've quit smoking marijuana. Things have gotten a lot better!"

Arlo discovered how God's love can change things for the better. Jesus told stories that show how God's love can change people's lives. Check them out in **Luke 15:1–10**.

- How do you think the love Jesus talked about in this passage helped Arlo's relationship with his mom to change?
- What can you do to help you feel God's love for you?

CONSIDER . . .

- writing what you think God's love is like, then comparing your ideas with 1 Corinthians 13:4–7.
- reading the words to "Amazing Grace" from a hymnal. Rewrite them to fit your own life. Then sing your own song of thanks to God for his love!

FOR MORE, SEE . . .

- Zephaniah 3:14–17 (p. 884)
- John 3:16 (p. 1062)

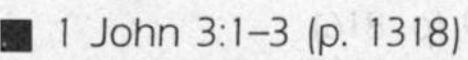

- 1 John 3:1–3 (p. 1318)

and hungry. 15So he got a job with one of the
citizens there who sent the son into the fields to
feed pigs. 16The son was so hungry that he
wanted to eat the pods the pigs were eating, but
no one gave him anything. 17When he realized
what he was doing, he thought, 'All of my father's
servants have plenty of food. But I am here, almost dying with hunger. 18I will leave and return
to my father and say to him, "Father, I have
sinned against God and have done wrong to you.
19I am no longer worthy to be called your son, but
let me be like one of your servants." ' 20So the son
left and went to his father.

"While the son was still a long way off, his father saw him and felt sorry for his son. So the
father ran to him and hugged and kissed him.
21The son said, 'Father, I have sinned against God
and have done wrong to you. I am no longer worthy to be called your son.' 22But the father said to
his servants, 'Hurry! Bring the best clothes and
put them on him. Also, put a ring on his finger
and sandals on his feet. 23And get our fat calf and
kill it so we can have a feast and celebrate. 24My
son was dead, but now he is alive again! He was
lost, but now he is found!' So they began to celebrate.

25"The older son was in the field, and as he
came closer to the house, he heard the sound of
music and dancing. 26So he called to one of the
servants and asked what all this meant. 27The servant said, 'Your brother has come back, and your
father killed the fat calf, because your brother
came home safely.' 28The older son was angry and
would not go in to the feast. So his father went
out and begged him to come in. 29But the older
son said to his father, 'I have served you like a
slave for many years and have always obeyed your
commands. But you never gave me even a young
goat to have at a feast with my friends. 30But your
other son, who wasted all your money on prostitutes,[d] comes home, and you kill the fat calf for
him!' 31The father said to him, 'Son, you are al-

REBELLION

I'm Outta Here

"Have you seen Liz?" the nervous voice asked. "It's past midnight and she's not home yet. We had another argument. . . . Her mother and I are . . . worried."

How could this be happening? Liz Cole was great—very popular and liked by everyone in her group. Her parents were model church members. They seemed like the "perfect" family. But this night revealed that they weren't so "perfect" after all.

Three hours later, Liz came up the front steps. She looked angry. "I'm outta here. I just came home for some clothes."

"Your dad and I were worried, " her mother said.

She sneered. "I've got nothing to say to you."

But then she sat down, crying. She cried for a long time. In fact, all three of them did. And it turned out that they had plenty to say to each other. Before long, they were talking about how this "perfect" family had been spending a lot of energy concentrating on the rules and regulations involved with being so perfect, and not enough time telling how much they loved each other. The word love was used a lot more that night than it had been in a long time.

The Coles now know they don't have the perfect family. But they do love each other and have created a family where rebellion has been replaced by gentleness, respect, and forgiveness.

Liz's family was almost torn apart by rebellion. Jesus told a story about another family that dealt with rebellion. Read about it in **Luke 15:11–32**.

- What similarities and differences do you see between Liz's story and the one Jesus told?
- What things make you feel like rebelling? What might this passage say to you?

CONSIDER . . .

- walking around your block three times. Each time, pray about a different problem in your family life that makes you feel like rebelling.
- rewriting the story in Luke 15:11–32 to fit your family situation.

FOR MORE, SEE . . .

- Daniel 9:3–19 (p. 816)
- John 3:16–21 (p. 1062)
- Hebrews 3:12—4:13 (p. 1279)

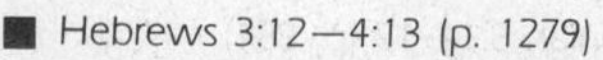

ways with me, and all that I have is yours. 32We
had to celebrate and be happy because your
brother was dead, but now he is alive. He was
lost, but now he is found.' "

True Wealth

16 Jesus also said to his followers, "Once
there was a rich man who had a manager to take care of his business. This manager
was accused of cheating him. 2So he called the
manager in and said to him, 'What is this I hear
about you? Give me a report of what you have
done with my money, because you can't be my
manager any longer.' 3The manager thought
to himself, 'What will I do since my master
is taking my job away from me? I am not
strong enough to dig ditches, and I am
ashamed to beg. 4I know what I'll do so that
when I lose my job people will welcome me
into their homes.'
5"So the manager called in everyone who owed
the master any money. He asked the first one,
'How much do you owe?' 6He answered, 'Eight
hundred gallons of olive oil.' The manager said to
him, 'Take your bill, sit down quickly, and write
four hundred gallons.' 7Then the manager asked
another one, 'How much do you owe?' He answered, 'One thousand bushels of wheat.' Then
the manager said to him, 'Take your bill and write
eight hundred bushels.' 8So, the master praised
the dishonest manager for being smart. Yes,
worldly people are smarter with their own kind
than spiritual people are.
9"I tell you, make friends for yourselves using
worldly riches so that when those riches are gone,
you will be welcomed in those homes that continue forever. 10Whoever can be trusted with a
little can also be trusted with a lot, and whoever
is dishonest with a little is dishonest with a lot. 11If
you cannot be trusted with worldly riches, then
who will trust you with true riches? 12And if you
cannot be trusted with things that belong to
someone else, who will give you things of your
own?
13"No servant can serve two masters. The servant will hate one master and love the other, or

MONEY

Tool or Master?

Money was tight for John Wesley. When he began his ministry in the 1700s, he had to budget to survive. After making careful calculations, he determined that he would need about sixty-five dollars a year to live on. Remember, this was a long time ago! Because there was little inflation during that time, John stayed on that yearly budget for the rest of his life. When he first made that decision, his annual income was about seventy dollars. John was able to give away five dollars that first year.

Later in his life, after he had written several books and become a famous minister, his income often exceeded three thousand dollars per year. But John still held to his budget and lived on sixty-five dollars. He gave the rest of the money to people who needed it or to charities that would help tell others about God's love for them.

How could John do this? Was it hard? We don't know the answers to those questions. All we do know is that at an early age John Wesley decided to make sure that money would be his servant, not his master.

John Wesley, who started the Christian movement we know as Methodism, understood the truth Jesus talks about in **Luke 16:1–13**. Read the passage to learn Jesus' view on money.

- How did John Wesley apply Jesus' teaching in this passage to his own life?
- How would heeding these verses change your spending habits?

CONSIDER . . .

- looking through the advertisements of two or three current magazines to see what they reveal about our society's view of money and material goods. How does society's view of money compare with Jesus'?
- making a commitment to give money to a worthwhile organization, such as your denomination's hunger-relief program, or an interdenominational hunger-relief organization.

FOR MORE, SEE . . .

- Proverbs 30:7–9 (p. 594)
- Luke 16:19–31 (p. 1038)
- James 1:9–11 (p. 1294)

will follow one master and refuse to follow the
other. You cannot serve both God and worldly
riches."

God's Law Cannot Be Changed

14The Pharisees,[d] who loved money, were listening to all these things and made fun of Jesus.
15He said to them, "You make yourselves look
good in front of people, but God knows what is
really in your hearts. What is important to people
is hateful in God's sight.
16"The law of Moses and the writings of the
prophets[d] were preached until John[n] came. Since
then the Good News[d] about the kingdom of God
is being told, and everyone tries to enter it by
force. 17It would be easier for heaven and earth to
pass away than for the smallest part of a letter in
the law to be changed.

Divorce and Remarriage

18"If a man divorces his wife and marries another woman, he is guilty of adultery,[d] and the
man who marries a divorced woman is also guilty
of adultery."

The Rich Man and Lazarus

19Jesus said, "There was a rich man who always
dressed in the finest clothes and lived in luxury
every day. 20And a very poor man named Lazarus,
whose body was covered with sores, was laid at
the rich man's gate. 21He wanted to eat only the
small pieces of food that fell from the rich man's
table. And the dogs would come and lick his
sores. 22Later, Lazarus died, and the angels carried him to the arms of Abraham.[d] The rich man
died, too, and was buried. 23In the place of the
dead, he was in much pain. The rich man saw

John John the Baptist, who preached to people about Christ's coming (Matthew 3, Luke 3).

DECISION MAKING

But I Didn't Think . . .

Sixteen-year-old Alan McPherson was in a daze as he walked out of Mr. Lloyd's English class. His friends and classmates swirled by him in a rush to get to sixth period for their final exam of the day.

"How was I supposed to know all that stuff?" he asked out loud.

"Oh, come on, Alan," said his friend, Casey Adams. "You've known for weeks that our whole exam would come from Moby Dick. Don't act surprised now."

"Yeah, but it all seemed so complicated. There were so many details!"

"Tell the truth, Alan. Did you even read the book?" he asked.

He moaned. "Of course not! You know I watched the movie. It's a stupid book anyway. What do I care about Ahab and the Pequod or whatever? I didn't have time. I thought all I'd need was the basic plot, not every little detail."

"You know whose fault that is," Casey sighed as he left Alan by the lockers. "See ya later."

Alan did know whose fault it was. If only he could turn back the clock, he thought. If only he had made the right decision. Then he could have passed the test.

Alan made the wrong decision, and suffered for it. Fortunately, Alan's test was not a life-or-death matter. **Luke 16:19–31** records a story about another man's exam. But this man's test had eternal consequences.

■ What similarities do you think exist between Alan and the rich man in the passage?

■ How was the decision the rich man faced like decisions you face in life?

CONSIDER . . .

■ using a concordance to find times Jesus talked about the importance of making wise choices. Look up "wisdom," "choice," "decide," or "decision."

■ listing all the decisions you face right now, and asking your youth leader for advice on what choices would be best.

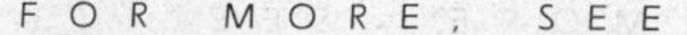

FOR MORE, SEE . . .

■ Proverbs 8:10–11 (p. 573)

■ Isaiah 58:3–9 (p. 676)

■ Romans 7:15–25 (p. 1148)

Abraham far away with Lazarus at his side. 24He
called, 'Father Abraham, have mercy on me! Send
Lazarus to dip his finger in water and cool my
tongue, because I am suffering in this fire!' 25But
Abraham said, 'Child, remember when you were
alive you had the good things in life, but bad
things happened to Lazarus. Now he is comforted
here, and you are suffering. 26Besides, there is a
big pit between you and us, so no one can cross
over to you, and no one can leave there and come
here.' 27The rich man said, 'Father, then please
send Lazarus to my father's house. 28I have five
brothers, and Lazarus could warn them so that
they will not come to this place of pain.' 29But
Abraham said, 'They have the law of Moses and
the writings of the prophets;[d] let them learn from
them.' 30The rich man said, 'No, father Abraham! If someone goes to them from the dead,
they would believe and change their hearts and
lives.' 31But Abraham said to him, 'If they will
not listen to Moses and the prophets, they
will not listen to someone who comes back
from the dead.' "

SIDELIGHT: To say that the rich man in Luke 16:19–31 wore "the finest clothes" would indicate the man spent a lot of money on his wardrobe. The outer clothes were purple, a sign of true wealth and royalty. Some of his clothes might have been made out of an Egyptian yellowed flax that was so luxurious it was called "woven air."

Sin and Forgiveness

17 Jesus said to his followers, "Things that
cause people to sin will happen, but how
terrible for the person who causes them to happen! 2It would be better for you to be thrown into
the sea with a large stone around your neck than
to cause one of these little ones to sin. 3So be
careful!

"If another follower sins, warn him, and if he
is sorry and stops sinning, forgive him. 4If he sins
against you seven times in one day and says that
he is sorry each time, forgive him."

FRIENDS

Helping Each Other

Everyone wants friends, and those friends have a great influence on our lives. That influence can be harmful, as it is when people push us to vandalize property, get sexually involved, or use drugs. But—as students in an Atlanta, Georgia, high school discovered—friends can also be positive influences.

Older teenagers decided they could use their influence on younger teenagers to make a positive difference. So they started a program to convince junior high kids that they could avoid sex before marriage and still be popular.

Did it make a difference?

- By the end of the eighth grade, students who didn't participate in the program were five times more likely to be sexually active than those who participated.
- A year later, the rate of sexual activity among those who had gone through this "peer-to-peer" program was 33 percent less than the rate of those not in the program.

Jesus talked about how friends can affect each other's behavior. He told people to use "positive peer pressure," rather than give in to others' sin. Read all about it in **Luke 17:1–10**.

- How does the Atlanta high school story relate to this passage?
- How does this passage help you evaluate your friendships? How does it challenge you to help your friends?

CONSIDER...

- listing activities you could do with your friends that would be both fun and positive.
- spending more time with the strong Christians in your youth group.

FOR MORE, SEE...

- Exodus 32:1–29 (p. 89)
- Romans 1:11–12 (p. 1141)
- James 5:19–20 (p. 1300)

How Big Is Your Faith?

5The apostles[d] said to the Lord, "Give us more
faith!"

6The Lord said, "If your faith were the size of
a mustard seed, you could say to this mulberry
tree, 'Dig yourself up and plant yourself in the
sea,' and it would obey you.

Be Good Servants

7"Suppose one of you has a servant who has
been plowing the ground or caring for the sheep.
When the servant comes in from working in the
field, would you say, 'Come in and sit down to
eat'? 8No, you would say to him, 'Prepare something for me to eat. Then get yourself ready and
serve me. After I finish eating and drinking, you
can eat.' 9The servant does not get any special
thanks for doing what his master commanded.
10It is the same with you. When you have done
everything you are told to do, you should say, 'We
are unworthy servants; we have only done the
work we should do.' "

Be Thankful

11While Jesus was on his way to Jerusalem, he
was going through the area between Samaria and
Galilee. 12As he came into a small town, ten men
who had a skin disease met him there. They did
not come close to Jesus 13but called to him,
"Jesus! Master! Have mercy on us!"

14When Jesus saw the men, he said, "Go and
show yourselves to the priests."[n]

As the ten men were going, they were healed.
15When one of them saw that he was healed, he
went back to Jesus, praising God in a loud voice.
16Then he bowed down at Jesus' feet and thanked

show . . . priests The law of Moses said a priest must say when a Jewish person with a skin disease became well.

THANKFULNESS

Attitude of Gratitude

Bruce Hallman's father shook his head doubtfully. "I don't see how we can do it, son," he said.

Bruce knew his father was right, but it still hurt to think about missing the big trip. All of the guys in the jazz band were looking forward to that summer trip, but Bruce's dad had been unemployed for a while. So money was tight—too tight to allow an eleventh grader to go to Europe for a month.

As Bruce left the room, he asked God to somehow show him a way. He continued to pray about it, and not long afterward a family in his church asked him to do some yardwork. Not much, but it was something. Soon more jobs came in, mostly from families who knew that Bruce was saving his money for the trip.

All spring, Bruce was busier than he had ever been. And that summer, he went to Europe with the band. The families he had worked for had provided the means to get there.

That was a long time ago, but Bruce hasn't forgotten those families. He's a youth minister now, committed to helping kids find their way out of rough spots. "I know I can't go back and thank all those families who helped me," Bruce says. "I don't even remember some of their names. But I figure I can express my thanks to God for all the good things in my life by helping others."

Sometimes we only think of thankfulness when something really special happens to us. People like Bruce, though, understand what Jesus said about always being thankful. Read Jesus' words in **Luke 17:11–19**.

- How is Bruce like the leper who returned to Jesus?
- What things in your life make you feel like running after Jesus just to say "thanks!"?

CONSIDER . . .

- writing a letter to God, thanking him for all the good things in your life.
- keeping stamps and blank postcards handy all the time. When people do something nice for you, send them a note of thanks.

FOR MORE, SEE . . .

- Psalm 100 (p. 539)
- Acts 3:1–10 (p. 1100)

- 1 Thessalonians 5:15–18 (p. 1249)

him. (And this man was a Samaritan.[d]) 17 Jesus said, "Weren't ten men healed? Where are the other nine? 18 Is this Samaritan the only one who came back to thank God?" 19 Then Jesus said to him, "Stand up and go on your way. You were healed because you believed."

SIDELIGHT: The "skin disease" described in Luke 17:11–19 is often called leprosy. It was a dreaded disease, and people who had it were isolated from other people because they were unclean (see Leviticus 13:42–46, p. 109). Most scholars agree leprosy in the Bible isn't the same disease we call leprosy today, but it's not clear exactly what the disease was.

God's Kingdom Is Within You

20 Some of the Pharisees[d] asked Jesus, "When will the kingdom of God come?"

Jesus answered, "God's kingdom is coming, but not in a way that you will be able to see with your eyes. 21 People will not say, 'Look, here it is!' or, 'There it is!' because God's kingdom is within[n] you."

22 Then Jesus said to his followers, "The time will come when you will want very much to see one of the days of the Son of Man.[d] But you will not see it. 23 People will say to you, 'Look, there he is!' or, 'Look, here he is!' Stay where you are; don't go away and search.

When Jesus Comes Again

24 "When the Son of Man[d] comes again, he will shine like lightning, which flashes across the sky and lights it up from one side to the other. 25 But first he must suffer many things and be rejected by the people of this time. 26 When the Son of Man comes again, it will be as it was when Noah lived. 27 People were eating, drinking, marrying, and giving their children to be married until the day Noah entered the boat. Then the flood came and killed them all. 28 It will be the same as during the time of Lot. People were eating, drinking, buying, selling, planting, and building. 29 But the day Lot left Sodom,[n] fire and sulfur rained down from the sky and killed them all. 30 This is how it will be when the Son of Man comes again.

31 "On that day, a person who is on the roof and whose belongings are in the house should not go inside to get them. A person who is in the field should not go back home. 32 Remember Lot's wife.[n] 33 Those who try to keep their lives will lose them. But those who give up their lives will save them. 34 I tell you, on that night two people will be sleeping in one bed; one will be taken and the other will be left. 35 There will be two women grinding grain together; one will be taken, and the other will be left." 36 [n]

37 The followers asked Jesus, "Where will this be, Lord?"

Jesus answered, "Where there is a dead body, there the vultures will gather."

God Will Answer His People

18 Then Jesus used this story to teach his followers that they should always pray and never lose hope. 2 "In a certain town there was a judge who did not respect God or care about people. 3 In that same town there was a widow who kept coming to this judge, saying, 'Give me my rights against my enemy.' 4 For a while the judge refused to help her. But afterwards, he thought to himself, 'Even though I don't respect God or care about people, 5 I will see that she gets her rights. Otherwise she will continue to bother me until I am worn out.' "

6 The Lord said, "Listen to what the unfair judge said. 7 God will always give what is right to his people who cry to him night and day, and he will not be slow to answer them. 8 I tell you, God will help his people quickly. But when the Son of Man[d] comes again, will he find those on earth who believe in him?"

Being Right with God

9 Jesus told this story to some people who thought they were very good and looked down on everyone else: 10 "A Pharisee[d] and a tax collector both went to the Temple[d] to pray. 11 The Pharisee stood alone and prayed, 'God, I thank you that I am not like other people who steal, cheat, or take part in adultery,[d] or even like this tax collector. 12 I give up eating[n] twice a week, and I give one-tenth of everything I get!'

13 "The tax collector, standing at a distance, would not even look up to heaven. But he beat on his chest because he was so sad. He said, 'God, have mercy on me, a sinner.' 14 I tell you, when this man went home, he was right with God, but the Pharisee was not. All who make themselves great will be made humble, but all who make themselves humble will be made great."

within Or "among."
Sodom City that God destroyed because the people were so evil.
Lot's wife A story about what happened to Lot's wife is found in Genesis 19:15-17, 26.
Verse 36 A few Greek copies add verse 36: "Two people will be in the field. One will be taken, and the other will be left."
give up eating This is called "fasting." The people would give up eating for a special time of prayer and worship to God. It was also done to show sadness and disappointment.

Who Will Enter God's Kingdom?

15Some people brought even their babies to
Jesus so he could touch them. When the followers
saw this, they told them to stop. 16But Jesus called
for the children, saying, "Let the little children
come to me. Don't stop them, because the kingdom of God belongs to people who are like these
children. 17I tell you the truth, you must accept
the kingdom of God as if you were a child, or you
will never enter it."

A Rich Man's Question

18A certain leader asked Jesus, "Good Teacher,
what must I do to have life forever?"
19Jesus said to him, "Why do you call me good?
Only God is good. 20You know the commands:
'You must not be guilty of adultery.[d] You must not
murder anyone. You must not steal. You must
not tell lies about your neighbor. Honor your
father and mother.' "[n]
21But the leader said, "I have obeyed all these
commands since I was a boy."
22When Jesus heard this, he said to him, "There
is still one more thing you need to do. Sell
everything you have and give it to the poor,
and you will have treasure in heaven. Then
come and follow me." 23But when the man
heard this, he became very sad, because he
was very rich.
24Jesus looked at him and said, "It is very hard
for rich people to enter the kingdom of God. 25It
is easier for a camel to go through the eye of a
needle than for a rich person to enter the kingdom
of God."

Who Can Be Saved?

26When the people heard this, they asked,
"Then who can be saved?"
27Jesus answered, "God can do things that are
not possible for people to do."

'You . . . mother.' Quotation from Exodus 20:12-16; Deuteronomy 5:16-20.

BRAGGING

Maximum Ruler

In October 1989, pictures of General Manuel Noriega shaking his fist at the world made headlines everywhere. As dictator of the country of Panama, he'd just thwarted an attempt to remove him from power. Some reports indicated he tortured and murdered as many as seventy-five rebel soldiers after the attempted coup.

Noriega controlled the Panamanian government pridefully, as if he owned it. He held mock elections where his people frightened away voters. He reportedly financed his lifestyle through illegal drug trade and commonly mocked and belittled his enemies, including the United States.

In December, his arrogance reached its peak. He boasted that he was Panama's "maximum leader," daring anyone to disagree.

Someone did.

That month the United States invaded Panama and removed Noriega from power. Within days, he was on his way to face drug charges in a Florida courtroom.

On New Year's Day, the world again saw Manuel Noriega's picture in the headlines. This time, though, the pictures showed a handcuffed man dressed in prison clothes being taken away to jail.

Jesus talked about how God views bragging and prideful people. Read what he said in **Luke 18:9–14**.

- What attitude did both General Noriega and the Pharisee in this passage display?
- How can pride interfere in your relationship with Christ?

CONSIDER . . .

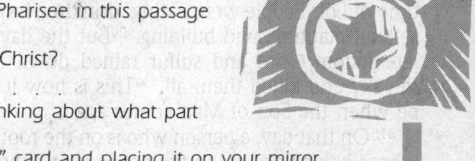

- looking up the word pride in a dictionary and thinking about what part pride plays in bragging.
- writing the second half of Luke 18:14 on a 4" X 6" card and placing it on your mirror as an encouragement to avoid arrogance.

FOR MORE, SEE . . .

- Jeremiah 9:23–24 (p. 703)
- 1 Corinthians 4:6–7 (p. 1172)
- James 4:13–17 (p. 1298)

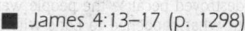

[28]Peter said, "Look, we have left everything
and followed you."
[29]Jesus said, "I tell you the truth, all those who
have left houses, wives, brothers, parents, or children for the kingdom of God [30]will get much
more in this life. And in the age that is coming,
they will have life forever."

Jesus Will Rise from the Dead

[31]Then Jesus took the twelve apostles[d] aside
and said to them, "We are going to Jerusalem.
Everything the prophets[d] wrote about the Son of
Man[d] will happen. [32]He will be turned over to
those who are not Jews. They will laugh at him,
insult him, spit on him, [33]beat him with whips,
and kill him. But on the third day, he will rise to
life again." [34]The apostles did not understand this;
the meaning was hidden from them, and they did
not realize what was said.

Jesus Heals a Blind Man

[35]As Jesus came near the city of Jericho, a blind
man was sitting beside the road, begging. [36]When
he heard the people coming down the road, he
asked, "What is happening?"
[37]They told him, "Jesus, from Nazareth, is going by."
[38]The blind man cried out, "Jesus, Son of David,[d] have mercy on me!"
[39]The people leading the group warned the
blind man to be quiet. But the blind man shouted
even more, "Son of David, have mercy on me!"
[40]Jesus stopped and ordered the blind man to
be brought to him. When he came near, Jesus
asked him, [41]"What do you want me to do for
you?"
He said, "Lord, I want to see."
[42]Jesus said to him, "Then see. You are healed
because you believed."
[43]At once the man was able to see, and he followed Jesus, thanking God. All the people who
saw this praised God.

Zacchaeus Meets Jesus

19 Jesus was going through the city of
Jericho. [2]A man was there named

SELF-ESTEEM

Geek in Glasses

The workers in the Los Angeles Lakers' front office first noticed Kurt Rambis during training camp. "Who invited the geek in the glasses to camp?" they asked.

On the court Kurt adjusted his black horn-rimmed glasses and continued his workout. With 20/400 vision, thick, scraggly hair and an awkward style, no one expected him to make one of the best teams in basketball.

Despite the way others looked at him, Kurt still believed he had much to contribute to the Lakers. It didn't matter if he didn't look or play like the other guys, as long as what he did made this a better—and winning—team.

And Kurt Rambis was right.

He not only made the team but became a starter. He earned a reputation as a tough defensive player and rebounder. Through the 1980s his talents helped the Lakers win four NBA championships. During his time there, the Lakers became known as the "team of the '80s."

Not bad for a "geek in glasses."

Kurt believed his deficiency shouldn't stop him from striving to reach his potential. The Bible tells about someone else who got recognition even though others looked down on him. Read Zacchaeus's story in **Luke 19:1–10**.

- How are Kurt Rambis and Zacchaeus similar? different?
- How does seeing the way Jesus treated Zacchaeus help you believe in your own potential?

CONSIDER . . .

- listing things you like about yourself and thanking God for making you special.
- giving one sincere compliment to your friends, family, or others each day for the next week.

FOR MORE, SEE . . .

- Judges 6:11–16; 7:19–22 (p. 222)
- 1 Samuel 16:1–13 (p. 258)
- 1 Timothy 4:12 (p. 1259)

Zacchaeus, who was a very important tax collector, and he was wealthy. 3He wanted to see
who Jesus was, but he was not able because he
was too short to see above the crowd. 4He ran
ahead to a place where Jesus would come,
and he climbed a sycamore tree so he could
see him. 5When Jesus came to that place, he
looked up and said to him, "Zacchaeus, hurry
and come down! I must stay at your house
today."
6Zacchaeus came down quickly and welcomed
him gladly. 7All the people saw this and began to complain, "Jesus is staying with a sinner!"
8But Zacchaeus stood and said to the Lord, "I
will give half of my possessions to the poor. And
if I have cheated anyone, I will pay back four
times more."
9Jesus said to him, "Salvation has come to this
house today, because this man also belongs to the
family of Abraham. 10The Son of Man[d] came to
find lost people and save them."

SIDELIGHT: Asking to stay at Zacchaeus's house, as Jesus did in Luke 19:1–10, would have been seen as scandalous. As a tax collector, Zacchaeus was thought of as a thief or a swindler. Many tax collectors would charge more than the fair amount and keep the "profits" for themselves—a practice approved by the Roman government.

A Story About Three Servants

11As the people were listening to this, Jesus told
them a story because he was near Jerusalem and
they thought God's kingdom would appear immediately. 12He said: "A very important man went to
a country far away to be made a king and then to
return home. 13So he called ten of his servants
and gave a coin[n] to each servant. He said, 'Do
business with this money until I get back.' 14But
the people in the kingdom hated the man. So they

coin A Greek "mina." One mina was enough money to pay a person for working three months.

MONEY

Earning Potential

Norm Wakefield has a lot to be proud of.

His son Joel earns a good salary during the school year as a physical education teacher. During summers Joel works as a trainer for baseball's Oakland Athletics. Through his work in Oakland, he has earned a World Series championship ring, valued at seven thousand dollars.

Norm's daughter Annette may never make as much money as Joel. Hampered by a learning disability, she'll take a little longer than usual to finish high school. During the summer she earns the minimum wage working with kids at the community center. She also gets income from babysitting. When she took part in the Special Olympics, she did well enough to win a second-place ribbon.

When Norm was asked to speak at a junior high graduation, he took with him to show both Joel's championship ring and Annette's track ribbon. Their abilities brought them different rewards monetarily. But in their father's eyes, they are both champions.

Annette and Joel both did their best. Jesus talks about God's view of making the most of what you have. Read his words in **Luke 19:11–27**.

- Which character in the passage is most like Joel? like Annette? like you?
- According to this passage, what does God expect you to do with the gifts he has given you?

C O N S I D E R . . .

- evaluating how thoughtfully you spend your money.
- looking for ways you can invest what God has given you—whether it's money or talents—to make the most of what God has given to you.

F O R   M O R E ,   S E E . . .

- Ecclesiastes 5:10–17 (p. 603)
- Matthew 6:31–33 (p. 918)
- Matthew 25:14–30 (p. 954)

sent a group to follow him and say, 'We don't
want this man to be our king.'
15"But the man became king. When he returned home, he said, 'Call those servants who
have my money so I can know how much they
earned with it.'
16"The first servant came and said, 'Sir, I
earned ten coins with the one you gave me.'
17The king said to the servant, 'Excellent! You are
a good servant. Since I can trust you with small
things, I will let you rule over ten of my cities.'
18"The second servant said, 'Sir, I earned five
coins with your one.' 19The king said to this servant, 'You can rule over five cities.'
20"Then another servant came in and said to
the king, 'Sir, here is your coin which I wrapped
in a piece of cloth and hid. 21I was afraid of you,
because you are a hard man. You even take
money that you didn't earn and gather food that
you didn't plant.' 22Then the king said to the servant, 'I will condemn you by your own words,
you evil servant. You knew that I am a hard man,
taking money that I didn't earn and gathering
food that I didn't plant. 23Why then didn't you put
my money in the bank? Then when I came back,
my money would have earned some interest.'
24"The king said to the men who were standing
by, 'Take the coin away from this servant and give
it to the servant who earned ten coins.' 25They
said, 'But sir, that servant already has ten coins.'
26The king said, 'Those who have will be given
more, but those who do not have anything will
have everything taken away from them. 27Now
where are my enemies who didn't want me to be
king? Bring them here and kill them before me.' "

Jesus Enters Jerusalem as a King

28After Jesus said this, he went on toward Jerusalem. 29As Jesus came near Bethphage and Bethany, towns near the hill called the Mount of Olives,[d] he sent out two of his followers. 30He said,
"Go to the town you can see there. When you
enter it, you will find a colt tied there, which no
one has ever ridden. Untie it and bring it here to
me. 31If anyone asks you why you are untying it,
say that the Master needs it."
32The two followers went into town and found
the colt just as Jesus had told them. 33As they
were untying it, its owners came out and asked
the followers, "Why are you untying our colt?"
34The followers answered, "The Master needs
it." 35So they brought it to Jesus, threw their coats
on the colt's back, and put Jesus on it. 36As Jesus
rode toward Jerusalem, others spread their coats
on the road before him.
37As he was coming close to Jerusalem, on the
way down the Mount of Olives, the whole crowd
of followers began joyfully shouting praise to God
for all the miracles[d] they had seen. 38They said,

"God bless the king who comes in the name
of the Lord! *Psalm 118:26*
There is peace in heaven and glory to God!"

39Some of the Pharisees[d] in the crowd said to
Jesus, "Teacher, tell your followers not to say
these things."
40But Jesus answered, "I tell you, if my followers didn't say these things, then the stones would
cry out."

Jesus Cries for Jerusalem

41As Jesus came near Jerusalem, he saw the city
and cried for it, 42saying, "I wish you knew today
what would bring you peace. But now it is hidden
from you. 43The time is coming when your enemies will build a wall around you and will hold
you in on all sides. 44They will destroy you and all
your people, and not one stone will be left on
another. All this will happen because you did not
recognize the time when God came to save you."

Jesus Goes to the Temple

45Jesus went into the Temple[d] and began to
throw out the people who were selling things
there. 46He said, "It is written in the Scriptures,[d]
'My Temple will be a house for prayer.'[n] But you
have changed it into a 'hideout for robbers'!"[n]
47Jesus taught in the Temple every day. The
leading priests, the experts on the law, and some
of the leaders of the people wanted to kill Jesus.
48But they did not know how they could do it,
because all the people were listening closely to
him.

Jewish Leaders Question Jesus

20 One day Jesus was in the Temple,[d]
teaching the people and telling them the
Good News.[d] The leading priests, teachers of the
law, and older Jewish leaders came up to talk
with him, 2saying, "Tell us what authority you
have to do these things? Who gave you this authority?"
3Jesus answered, "I will also ask you a question. Tell me: 4When John baptized people, was
that authority from God or just from other people?"
5They argued about this, saying, "If we answer,
'John's baptism was from God,' Jesus will say,
'Then why did you not believe him?' 6But if we
say, 'It was from other people,' all the people will
stone us to death, because they believe John was
a prophet."[d] 7So they answered that they didn't
know where it came from.

'My Temple . . . prayer.' Quotation from Isaiah 56:7.
'hideout for robbers' Quotation from Jeremiah 7:11.

[8]Jesus said to them, "Then I won't tell you
what authority I have to do these things."

A Story About God's Son

[9]Then Jesus told the people this story: "A man
planted a vineyard and leased it to some farmers.
Then he went away for a long time. [10]When it
was time for the grapes to be picked, he sent a
servant to the farmers to get some of the grapes.
But they beat the servant and sent him away
empty-handed. [11]Then he sent another servant.
They beat this servant also, and showed no respect for him, and sent him away empty-handed.
[12]So the man sent a third servant. The farmers
wounded him and threw him out. [13]The owner of
the vineyard said, 'What will I do now? I will send
my son whom I love. Maybe they will respect
him.' [14]But when the farmers saw the son, they
said to each other, 'This son will inherit the vineyard. If we kill him, it will be ours.' [15]So the farmers threw the son out of the vineyard and killed
him.

"What will the owner of this vineyard do to
them? [16]He will come and kill those farmers and
will give the vineyard to other farmers."

When the people heard this story, they said,
"Let this never happen!"

[17]But Jesus looked at them and said, "Then
what does this verse mean:

'The stone that the builders rejected
became the cornerstone'?[d] *Psalm 118:22*

[18]Everyone who falls on that stone will be broken,
and the person on whom it falls, that person will
be crushed!"

[19]The teachers of the law and the leading
priests wanted to arrest Jesus at once, because
they knew the story was about them. But they
were afraid of what the people would do.

Is It Right to Pay Taxes or Not?

[20]So they watched Jesus and sent some spies
who acted as if they were sincere. They wanted
to trap Jesus in saying something wrong so they
could hand him over to the authority and power
of the governor. [21]So the spies asked Jesus,
"Teacher, we know that what you say and teach

EVIL

Grim Snapshots

In April, fifteen-year-old Jason Thomas was thrilled to receive a new pair of expensive sneakers. In May he was dead. Someone had strangled him, stolen his shoes, and left his body.

Due to an accident as an infant, Carol Miller suffers from severe physical handicaps. Many in the youth group have reached out to her in spite of the differences. Yet, one day a young girl insensitively told Carol she thought Carol was disgusting and hated being around her. The girl walked away leaving Carol to cry alone.

When the Detroit Pistons won their second straight NBA championship, the city wanted to "celebrate." Looting and rioting caused untold damage. Hundreds were injured. Seven people were killed.

Bad news, huh? We would like to say those things never happened, or just sweep them under a rug somewhere. But they did happen. And other bad things continue to happen all around us, all the time.

While we are sometimes tempted to close our eyes to evil in the world, Jesus never avoided the reality of evil. However, he was also quick to point out that God can and will triumph over it. Read a parable he told about evil in **Luke 20:9–19**.

- What motivates people to mistreat each other the way they did in the parable and the snapshots above?
- How do you see God's power conquering evil in the world as this passage describes?

CONSIDER . . .

- praying for God to use you to overcome evil with good.
- writing letters of encouragement through a pen pal program to a prison inmate.

FOR MORE, SEE . . .

- Proverbs 24:19–20 (p. 588)
- Matthew 21:33–43 (p. 945)
- Romans 12:17–21 (p. 1158)

is true. You pay no attention to who people are, and you always teach the truth about God's way. 22Tell us, is it right for us to pay taxes to Caesar[d] or not?"

23But Jesus, knowing they were trying to trick him, said, 24"Show me a coin. Whose image and name are on it?"

They said, "Caesar's."

25Jesus said to them, "Then give to Caesar the things that are Caesar's, and give to God the things that are God's."

26So they were not able to trap Jesus in anything he said in the presence of the people. And being amazed at his answer, they became silent.

> **SIDELIGHT:** The Sadducees—who didn't believe in the resurrection of the dead (Luke 20:27)—were major rivals of the Pharisees in Jesus' time. In later years, the Sadducees were often considered heretics by other Jews.

Some Sadducees Try to Trick Jesus

27Some Sadducees,[d] who believed people would not rise from the dead, came to Jesus. 28They asked, "Teacher, Moses wrote that if a man's brother dies and leaves a wife but no children, then that man must marry the widow and have children for his brother. 29Once there were seven brothers. The first brother married and died, but had no children. 30Then the second brother married the widow, and he died. 31And the third brother married the widow, and he died. The same thing happened with all seven brothers; they died and had no children. 32Finally, the woman died also. 33Since all seven brothers had married her, whose wife will she be when people rise from the dead?"

34Jesus said to them, "On earth, people marry and are given to someone to marry. 35But those who will be worthy to be raised from the dead and live again will not marry, nor will they be given to someone to marry. 36In that life they are like angels and cannot die. They are children of God, because they have been raised from the dead. 37Even Moses clearly showed that the dead are raised to life. When he wrote about the burning bush,[n] he said that the Lord is 'the God of Abraham, the God of Isaac, and the God of Jacob.'[n] 38God is the God of the living, not the dead, because all people are alive to him."

39Some of the teachers of the law said, "Teacher, your answer was good." 40No one was brave enough to ask him another question.

Is the Christ the Son of David?

41Then Jesus said, "Why do people say that the Christ[d] is the Son of David?[d] 42In the book of Psalms, David himself says:

'The Lord said to my Lord:
Sit by me at my right side,
43 until I put your enemies under your
control.'[n] *Psalm 110:1*

44David calls the Christ 'Lord,' so how can the Christ be his son?"

Jesus Accuses Some Leaders

45While all the people were listening, Jesus said to his followers, 46"Beware of the teachers of the law. They like to walk around wearing fancy clothes, and they love for people to greet them with respect in the marketplaces. They love to have the most important seats in the synagogues[d] and at feasts. 47But they cheat widows and steal their houses and then try to make themselves look good by saying long prayers. They will receive a greater punishment."

True Giving

21 As Jesus looked up, he saw some rich people putting their gifts into the Temple[d] money box.[n] 2Then he saw a poor widow putting two small copper coins into the box. 3He said, "I tell you the truth, this poor widow gave more than all those rich people. 4They gave only what they did not need. This woman is very poor, but she gave all she had to live on."

The Temple Will Be Destroyed

5Some people were talking about the Temple[d] and how it was decorated with beautiful stones and gifts offered to God.

But Jesus said, 6"As for these things you are looking at, the time will come when not one stone will be left on another. Every stone will be thrown down."

7They asked Jesus, "Teacher, when will these things happen? What will be the sign that they are about to take place?"

8Jesus said, "Be careful so you are not fooled. Many people will come in my name, saying, 'I am the One' and, 'The time has come!' But don't follow them. 9When you hear about wars and riots, don't be afraid, because these things must happen first, but the end will come later."

10Then he said to them, "Nations will fight

burning bush Read Exodus 3:1-12 in the Old Testament.
'the God of . . . Jacob' These words are taken from Exodus 3:6.
until . . . control Literally, "until I make your enemies a footstool for your feet."
money box A special box in the Jewish place of worship where people put their gifts to God.

against other nations, and kingdoms against other
kingdoms. 11In various places there will be great
earthquakes, sicknesses, and a lack of food. Fearful events and great signs will come from heaven.
12"But before all these things happen, people
will arrest you and treat you cruelly. They will
judge you in their synagogues[d] and put you in jail
and force you to stand before kings and governors, because you follow me. 13But this will give
you an opportunity to tell about me. 14Make up
your minds not to worry ahead of time about
what you will say. 15I will give you the wisdom
to say things that none of your enemies will be
able to stand against or prove wrong. 16Even your
parents, brothers, relatives, and friends will turn
against you, and they will kill some of you. 17All
people will hate you because you follow me. 18But
none of these things can really harm you. 19By
continuing to have faith you will save your lives.

Jerusalem Will Be Destroyed

20"When you see armies all around Jerusalem,
you will know it will soon be destroyed. 21At that
time, the people in Judea should run away to the mountains. The people in Jerusalem must get out, and those who are near the city should not go in.
22These are the days of punishment to bring about
all that is written in the Scriptures.[d] 23How terrible it will be for women who are pregnant or have nursing babies! Great trouble will come upon this land, and God will be angry with these people.
24They will be killed by the sword and taken
as prisoners to all nations. Jerusalem will be crushed by non-Jewish people until their time is over.

Don't Fear

25"There will be signs in the sun, moon, and
stars. On earth, nations will be afraid and confused because of the roar and fury of the sea.
26People will be so afraid they will faint, wondering what is happening to the world, because the powers of the heavens will be shaken. 27Then
people will see the Son of Man[d] coming in a cloud with power and great glory. 28When these things
begin to happen, look up and hold your heads

PEER PRESSURE

Friends in Deed

Lance O'Pry was a student at Lamar High School in Rosenberg, Texas, when he learned he had cancer. He was told he would have to undergo painful chemotherapy if he hoped to live.

For Lance the pain was even harder to take knowing the treatment would make his hair fall out. Would he fit in at school? What would his friends say? Would they avoid him because they were embarrassed by his baldness? Would he be laughed at and mocked? He knew his classmates' reactions could make having the awful disease even more unbearable.

What he didn't know—but soon discovered—was that his friends really cared. To make sure Lance would fit in, Jason, Korl, Mac, Tim, Johnny, Donnie, Jeff, and Doug all shaved their heads.

A stranger to Rosenberg might wonder why nine students at Lamar High study, laugh, joke and go on dates wearing shiny, bald heads. But one of those bald heads knows the power of positive peer pressure. That makes all the difference.

Peer pressure can be good or bad. The Bible talks about a negative kind of peer pressure that many Christians will face. Read **Luke 21:5–19**, especially verse 16, to find out more about it.

- Lance faced rejection at school. How will Christians face rejection by the world, according to this passage?
- What encouragement does this passage give you to stand up to pressure from people who try to get you to compromise what you believe?

CONSIDER . . .

- making a list of pressures that challenge your relationships with God and your friends, then asking your youth leader for advice on how to overcome those pressures.
- making a pact with your friends to always encourage each other to follow God.

FOR MORE, SEE . . .

- 1 Samuel 20:28–42 (p. 264)
- Matthew 10:16–23 (p. 924)
- 1 Corinthians 15:33 (p. 1188)

high, because the time when God will free you is near!"

Jesus' Words Will Live Forever

29Then Jesus told this story: "Look at the fig tree and all the other trees. 30When their leaves appear, you know that summer is near. 31In the same way, when you see these things happening, you will know that God's kingdom is near.

32"I tell you the truth, all these things will happen while the people of this time are still living. 33Earth and sky will be destroyed, but the words I have spoken will never be destroyed.

Be Ready All the Time

34"Be careful not to spend your time feasting, drinking, or worrying about worldly things. If you do, that day might come on you suddenly, 35like a trap on all people on earth. 36So be ready all the time. Pray that you will be strong enough to escape all these things that will happen and that you will be able to stand before the Son of Man."[d]

37During the day, Jesus taught the people in the Temple,[d] and at night he went out of the city and stayed on the Mount of Olives.[d] 38Every morning all the people got up early to go to the Temple to listen to him.

Judas Becomes an Enemy of Jesus

22 It was almost time for the Feast[d] of Unleavened Bread, called the Passover[d] Feast. 2The leading priests and teachers of the law were trying to find a way to kill Jesus, because they were afraid of the people.

3Satan entered Judas Iscariot, one of Jesus' twelve apostles.[d] 4Judas went to the leading priests and some of the soldiers who guarded the Temple[d] and talked to them about a way to hand Jesus over to them. 5They were pleased and agreed to give Judas money. 6He agreed and watched for the best time to hand Jesus over to them when he was away from the crowd.

Jesus Eats the Passover Meal

7The Day of Unleavened[d] Bread came when the Passover[d] lambs had to be sacrificed. 8Jesus said to Peter and John, "Go and prepare the Passover meal for us to eat."

9They asked, "Where do you want us to prepare it?" 10Jesus said to them, "After you go into the city, a man carrying a jar of water will meet you. Follow him into the house that he enters, 11and tell the owner of the house, 'The Teacher says: Where is the guest room in which I may eat the Passover meal with my followers?' 12Then he will show you a large, furnished room upstairs. Prepare the Passover meal there."

13So Peter and John left and found everything as Jesus had said. And they prepared the Passover meal.

The Lord's Supper

14When the time came, Jesus and the apostles[d] were sitting at the table. 15He said to them, "I wanted very much to eat this Passover[d] meal with you before I suffer. 16I will not eat another Passover meal until it is given its true meaning in the kingdom of God."

17Then Jesus took a cup, gave thanks, and said, "Take this cup and share it among yourselves. 18I will not drink again from the fruit of the vine[n] until God's kingdom comes."

19Then Jesus took some bread, gave thanks, broke it, and gave it to the apostles, saying, "This is my body, which I am giving for you. Do this to remember me." 20In the same way, after supper, Jesus took the cup and said, "This cup is the new agreement that God makes with his people. This new agreement begins with my blood which is poured out for you.

Who Will Turn Against Jesus?

21"But one of you will turn against me, and his hand is with mine on the table. 22What God has planned for the Son of Man[d] will happen, but how terrible it will be for that one who turns against the Son of Man."

23Then the apostles[d] asked each other which one of them would do that.

Be Like a Servant

24The apostles[d] also began to argue about which one of them was the most important. 25But Jesus said to them, "The kings of the non-Jewish people rule over them, and those who have authority over others like to be called 'friends of the people.' 26But you must not be like that. Instead, the greatest among you should be like the youngest, and the leader should be like the servant. 27Who is more important: the one sitting at the table or the one serving? You think the one at the table is more important, but I am like a servant among you.

28"You have stayed with me through my struggles. 29Just as my Father has given me a kingdom, I also give you a kingdom 30so you may eat and drink at my table in my kingdom. And you will sit on thrones, judging the twelve tribes[d] of Israel.

Don't Lose Your Faith!

31"Simon, Simon, Satan has asked to test all of you as a farmer sifts his wheat. 32I have prayed that you will not lose your faith! Help your brothers be stronger when you come back to me."

fruit of the vine Product of the grapevine; this may also be translated "wine."

33But Peter said to Jesus, "Lord, I am ready to go with you to prison and even to die with you!"

34But Jesus said, "Peter, before the rooster crows this day, you will say three times that you don't know me."

Be Ready for Trouble

35Then Jesus said to the apostles,[d] "When I sent you out without a purse, a bag, or sandals, did you need anything?"

They said, "No."

36He said to them, "But now if you have a purse or a bag, carry that with you. If you don't have a sword, sell your coat and buy one. 37The Scripture[d] says, 'He was treated like a criminal,'[n] and I tell you this scripture must have its full meaning. It was written about me, and it is happening now."

38His followers said, "Look, Lord, here are two swords."

He said to them, "That is enough."

Jesus Prays Alone

39Jesus left the city and went to the Mount of Olives,[d] as he often did, and his followers went with him. 40When he reached the place, he said to them, "Pray for strength against temptation."

41Then Jesus went about a stone's throw away from them. He kneeled down and prayed, 42"Father, if you are willing, take away this cup[n] of suffering. But do what you want, not what I want." 43Then an angel from heaven appeared to him to strengthen him. 44Being full of pain, Jesus prayed even harder. His sweat was like drops of blood falling to the ground. 45When he finished praying, he went to his followers and found them asleep because of their sadness. 46Jesus said to them, "Why are you sleeping? Get up and pray for strength against temptation."

Jesus Is Arrested

47While Jesus was speaking, a crowd came up, and Judas, one of the twelve apostles,[d] was leading them. He came close to Jesus so he could kiss him.

48But Jesus said to him, "Judas, are you using the kiss to give the Son of Man[d] to his enemies?"

49When those who were standing around him

'He . . . criminal' Quotation from Isaiah 53:12.
cup Jesus is talking about the painful things that will happen to him. Accepting these things will be hard, like drinking a cup of something bitter.

JEALOUSY

When Others Succeed

"Few men have the strength to honor a friend's success without envy." —Aeschylus

"Lots of people know a good thing the minute the other fellow sees it first." —Job E. Hedges

"The man who keeps busy helping the man below him won't have time to envy the man above him—and there may not be anybody above him anyway." —Henrietta C. Mears

"The greatest among you should be like the youngest, and the leader should be like the servant." —Jesus Christ

For more about what Jesus said to his jealous disciples—who were arguing about prestige—read **Luke 22:24–30**.

- What similarities and differences are there between what Jesus said and what these famous people said about jealousy?
- How are you like and unlike the disciples in the passage? What would Jesus say to you?

CONSIDER . . .

- stopping yourself next time you feel jealous toward someone. Instead, do an act of service for that person.
- setting three goals for the coming week that will help you overcome jealous feelings you have toward someone you know.

FOR MORE, SEE . . .

- Genesis 37:2–28 (p. 42)
- 1 Samuel 18:6–11 (p. 262)

- 1 Peter 2:1 (p. 1303)

saw what was happening, they said, "Lord,
should we strike them with our swords?" 50And
one of them struck the servant of the high priest
and cut off his right ear.
51Jesus said, "Stop! No more of this." Then he
touched the servant's ear and healed him.
52Those who came to arrest Jesus were the
leading priests, the soldiers who guarded the
Temple,[d] and the older Jewish leaders. Jesus said
to them, "You came out here with swords and
clubs as though I were a criminal. 53I was with
you every day in the Temple, and you didn't arrest me there. But this is your time—the time
when darkness rules."

Peter Says He Doesn't Know Jesus

54They arrested Jesus, and led him away, and
brought him into the house of the high priest. Peter followed far behind them. 55After the soldiers
started a fire in the middle of the courtyard and
sat together, Peter sat with them. 56A servant girl
saw Peter sitting there in the firelight, and looking
closely at him, she said, "This man was also with
him."
57But Peter said this was not true; he said,
"Woman, I don't know him."
58A short time later, another person saw Peter
and said, "You are also one of them."
But Peter said, "Man, I am not!"
59About an hour later, another man insisted,
"Certainly this man was with him, because he is
from Galilee, too."
60But Peter said, "Man, I don't know what you
are talking about!"
At once, while Peter was still speaking, a
rooster crowed. 61Then the Lord turned and
looked straight at Peter. And Peter remembered
what the Lord had said: "Before the rooster crows
this day, you will say three times that you don't
know me." 62Then Peter went outside and cried
painfully.

The People Make Fun of Jesus

63The men who were guarding Jesus began
making fun of him and beating him.
64They blindfolded him and said, "Prove that
you are a prophet,[d] and tell us who hit you."
65They said many cruel things to Jesus.

GOD'S WILL

Daring to Follow

Bruce Olson believed strongly that God wanted him to live with the savage Motilone Indians in the jungles of South America. So, this skinny, shy, Minnesota boy set out to find them.

The Motilones were an isolated and fierce group. They hated white people and had killed or wounded all who tried to contact them. Bruce's first encounter with them came when they shot an arrow through his thigh. Then they captured him and forced him to walk hours to their village.

The months that followed were filled with pain, hunger and loneliness. But Bruce wouldn't give up. God had sent him. Eventually Bruce learned the Motilones' language and began communicating with his captors. They called him "Bruchko."

The Motilones have now come to love and respect Bruchko. Through him many people have met Jesus and have benefited from Bruchko's medical and agricultural expertise.

All because he dared to follow God.

Bruce knew what God wanted him to do, and he wouldn't stop until he had accomplished it. Jesus also refused to give up on God's will. Read about his experience in **Luke 22:39–46**, when he prayed the night before he was to suffer beatings and a cruel death.

- Knowing it would be hard, why do you think both Jesus and Bruchko insisted on following God's leadership?
- Jesus followed God's will all his life. What makes following God's will possible even when it's tough for you?

C O N S I D E R . . .

- placing an object in your room that will remind you to seek God's desires.
- reading Bruce Olson's autobiography, titled Bruchko, published by Creation House.

F O R M O R E , S E E . . .

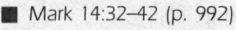

- Psalm 143:8–11 (p. 562)
- Matthew 26:36–46 (p. 957)
- Mark 14:32–42 (p. 992)

Jesus Before the Leaders

66When day came, the council of the older
leaders of the people, both the leading priests and
the teachers of the law, came together and led
Jesus to their highest court. 67They said, "If you
are the Christ,[d] tell us."
Jesus said to them, "If I tell you, you will not
believe me. 68And if I ask you, you will not answer. 69But from now on, the Son of Man[d] will sit
at the right hand of the powerful God."
70They all said, "Then are you the Son of God?"
Jesus said to them, "You say that I am."
71They said, "Why do we need witnesses now?
We ourselves heard him say this."

Pilate Questions Jesus

23 Then the whole group stood up and led
Jesus to Pilate.[n] 2They began to accuse
Jesus, saying, "We caught this man telling things
that mislead our people. He says that we should
not pay taxes to Caesar,[d] and he calls himself the
Christ,[d] a king."
3Pilate asked Jesus, "Are you the king of the
Jews?"
Jesus answered, "Those are your words."
4Pilate said to the leading priests and the people, "I find nothing against this man."
5They were insisting, saying, "But Jesus makes
trouble with the people, teaching all around Judea. He began in Galilee, and now he is here."

Pilate Sends Jesus to Herod

6Pilate heard this and asked if Jesus was from
Galilee. 7Since Jesus was under Herod's authority,
Pilate sent Jesus to Herod, who was in Jerusalem
at that time. 8When Herod saw Jesus, he was very
glad, because he had heard about Jesus and had
wanted to meet him for a long time. He was hoping to see Jesus work a miracle.[d] 9Herod asked
Jesus many questions, but Jesus said nothing.

Pilate Pontius Pilate was the Roman governor of Judea from A.D. 26 to A.D. 36.

SUFFERING

The Price of Goals

In West Perrine, Florida, Lee Lawrence had a dream.

"Can you imagine," he said, "all the churches in the neighborhood . . . marching up Homestead Avenue to let the drug pushers know we won't take it anymore?"

The drug dealers didn't like Lee or his vision. Twice he was shot at while getting out of his car. The grocery store he owned was vandalized; then someone tried to burn it down. Refusing to give up, Lee got several pushers arrested. His store became a drug-free haven for the neighborhood kids.

The dealers vowed to strike back.

In March 1989, Lee walked outside his store and was met by a man shooting a semiautomatic rifle. The first shot knocked Lee to the ground. A second man shot Lee again as he lay on the pavement. Minutes later he was dead. But his vision was not.

On Lee Lawrence's funeral day, more than three thousand people from area churches linked arms and marched up Homestead Avenue singing, "We shall overcome: drugs and crime must go!"

It was a dream come true. And the start of a turnaround in West Perrine.

Lee was willing to face hardship—even death—to see his goal become a reality. Jesus also endured hardship because of his mission to reclaim humanity from sin. Read about it in **Luke 22:63–71**.

- What price were both Lee and Jesus willing to pay to see their goals become reality?
- How was Jesus' response in this passage like the way you respond when others attack your faith? How is your response different from Jesus'?

CONSIDER . . .

- writing down three goals you would be willing to suffer for.
- looking through a newspaper to find three people who are suffering for doing right, and praying for them each day this week.

FOR MORE, SEE . . .

- Exodus 3:6–10 (p. 60)
- Mark 14:62–65 (p. 993)
- 1 Peter 2:18–25 (p. 1305)

10The leading priests and teachers of the law were standing there, strongly accusing Jesus. 11After Herod and his soldiers had made fun of Jesus, they dressed him in a kingly robe and sent him back to Pilate. 12In the past, Pilate and Herod had always been enemies, but on that day they became friends.

Jesus Must Die

13Pilate called the people together with the leading priests and the Jewish leaders. 14He said to them, "You brought this man to me, saying he makes trouble among the people. But I have questioned him before you all, and I have not found him guilty of what you say. 15Also, Herod found nothing wrong with him; he sent him back to us. Look, he has done nothing for which he should die. 16So, after I punish him, I will let him go free." 17 [n]

18But the people shouted together, "Take this man away! Let Barabbas go free!" 19(Barabbas was a man who was in prison for his part in a riot in the city and for murder.)

20Pilate wanted to let Jesus go free and told this to the crowd. 21But they shouted again, "Crucify him! Crucify him!"

22A third time Pilate said to them, "Why? What wrong has he done? I can find no reason to kill him. So I will have him punished and set him free."

23But they continued to shout, demanding that Jesus be crucified. Their yelling became so loud that 24Pilate decided to give them what they wanted. 25He set free the man who was in jail for rioting and murder, and he handed Jesus over to them to do with him as they wished.

Jesus Is Crucified

26As they led Jesus away, Simon, a man from Cyrene, was coming in from the fields. They forced him to carry Jesus' cross and to walk behind him.

27A large crowd of people was following Jesus, including some women who were sad and crying for him. 28But Jesus turned and said to them, "Women of Jerusalem, don't cry for me. Cry for yourselves and for your children. 29The time is coming when people will say, 'Happy are the women who cannot have children and who have no babies to nurse.' 30Then people will say to the mountains, 'Fall on us!' And they will say to the hills, 'Cover us!' 31If they act like this now when life is good, what will happen when bad times come?" [n]

32There were also two criminals led out with Jesus to be put to death. 33When they came to a place called the Skull, the soldiers crucified Jesus and the criminals — one on his right and the other on his left. 34Jesus said, "Father, forgive them, because they don't know what they are doing." [n]

> **SIDELIGHT:** If Jesus had been crucified like most Roman prisoners were executed, he was probably nailed to a capital T-shaped (Roman) cross rather than the Italian cross that most churches now display (Luke 23:32–33).

The soldiers threw lots[d] to decide who would get his clothes. 35The people stood there watching. And the leaders made fun of Jesus, saying, "He saved others. Let him save himself if he is God's Chosen One, the Christ."[d]

36The soldiers also made fun of him, coming to Jesus and offering him some vinegar. 37They said, "If you are the king of the Jews, save yourself!" 38At the top of the cross these words were written: THIS IS THE KING OF THE JEWS.

39One of the criminals on a cross began to shout insults at Jesus: "Aren't you the Christ? Then save yourself and us."

40But the other criminal stopped him and said, "You should fear God! You are getting the same punishment he is. 41We are punished justly, getting what we deserve for what we did. But this man has done nothing wrong." 42Then he said, "Jesus, remember me when you come into your kingdom."

43Jesus said to him, "I tell you the truth, today you will be with me in paradise." [n]

Jesus Dies

44It was about noon, and the whole land became dark until three o'clock in the afternoon, 45because the sun did not shine. The curtain in the Temple[n] was torn in two. 46Jesus cried out in a loud voice, "Father, I give you my life." After Jesus said this, he died.

47When the army officer there saw what happened, he praised God, saying, "Surely this was a good man!"

48When all the people who had gathered there

Verse 17 A few Greek copies add verse 17: "Every year at the Passover Feast, Pilate had to release one prisoner to the people."
If . . . come? Literally, "If they do these things in the green tree, what will happen in the dry?"
Verse 34 Some early Greek copies do not have this part of the verse.
paradise A place where people who are obedient to God go when they die.
curtain in the Temple A curtain divided the Most Holy Place from the other part of the Temple, the special building in Jerusalem where God commanded the Jewish people to worship him.

to watch saw what happened, they returned
home, beating their chests because they were so
sad. 49But those who were close friends of Jesus,
including the women who had followed him from
Galilee, stood at a distance and watched.

Joseph Takes Jesus' Body

50There was a good and religious man named
Joseph who was a member of the Jewish council.
51But he had not agreed to the other leaders' plans
and actions against Jesus. He was from the Jewish
town of Arimathea and was waiting for the kingdom of God to come. 52Joseph went to Pilate to
ask for the body of Jesus. 53He took the body
down from the cross, wrapped it in cloth, and put
it in a tomb that was cut out of a wall of rock. This
tomb had never been used before. 54This was late
on Preparation[d] Day, and when the sun went
down, the Sabbath[d] day would begin.
55The women who had come from Galilee with
Jesus followed Joseph and saw the tomb and how
Jesus' body was laid. 56Then the women left to
prepare spices and perfumes.
On the Sabbath day they rested, as the law of
Moses commanded.

Jesus Rises from the Dead

24 Very early on the first day of the week,
at dawn, the women came to the tomb,
bringing the spices they had prepared. 2They
found the stone rolled away from the entrance of
the tomb, 3but when they went in, they did not
find the body of the Lord Jesus. 4While they were
wondering about this, two men in shining clothes
suddenly stood beside them. 5The women were
very afraid and bowed their heads to the ground.
The men said to them, "Why are you looking for
a living person in this place for the dead? 6He is
not here; he has risen from the dead. Do you remember what he told you in Galilee? 7He said the
Son of Man[d] must be handed over to sinful people, be crucified, and rise from the dead on the

FORGIVENESS

Lasting Impact

Dr. Boris Kornfeld was a prisoner in Siberia. Because of his medical skills, he regularly performed surgery for both prisoners and staff.

One day while repairing a guard's artery, which had been cut by a knife wound, he seriously considered stitching the wound in a way that would cause the guard to bleed to death. Shocked by his own hatred and bitterness, he quietly said the words from the Lord's Prayer:

"Forgive us for our sins, just as we have forgiven those who sinned against us."

Weeks later, Dr. Kornfeld was examining a patient who had just had surgery for cancer. Sensing a spiritual depth in the man, Kornfeld retold the story of the earlier incident. He shared his secret faith with the patient.

That night, someone who was angry at the doctor sneaked into his sleeping quarters and smashed his head. Kornfeld died a few hours later.

But his confession did not die. The patient who heard it became a Christian. When he left the prison camp, he went on to tell the world of his experiences there.

The patient was the Christian writer Aleksandr Solzhenitsyn.

Dr. Kornfeld's forgiveness of guards in the terrible prison camps had a great impact on Solzhenitsyn's life—and, as a result, on the world. The Bible tells of an even greater sacrifice and act of forgiveness—Jesus dying on the cross for all people's sins. Read about the forgiveness in **Luke 23:26–43**.

- How was Dr. Kornfeld's forgiveness of the guard like and unlike Jesus' forgiveness of the thief in the passage?
- If you were watching Jesus on the cross, and knew he was God's son, what would you ask forgiveness for?

C O N S I D E R . . .

- writing a short song to thank God for forgiving you.
- creating a symbol of forgiveness and putting it in your locker or on your notebooks at school to remind you that God's forgiveness is always available.

F O R M O R E , S E E . . .

- Isaiah 53:1–12 (p. 672)
- Mark 15:21–21 (p. 995)
- John 19:17–27 (p. 1092)

third day." [8]Then the women remembered what
Jesus had said.

[9]The women left the tomb and told all these
things to the eleven apostles[d] and the other followers. [10]It was Mary Magdalene, Joanna, Mary
the mother of James, and some other women who
told the apostles everything that had happened at
the tomb. [11]But they did not believe the women,
because it sounded like nonsense. [12]But Peter got
up and ran to the tomb. Bending down and looking in, he saw only the cloth that Jesus' body had
been wrapped in. Peter went away to his home,
wondering about what had happened.

Jesus on the Road to Emmaus

[13]That same day two of Jesus' followers were
going to a town named Emmaus, about seven
miles from Jerusalem. [14]They were talking about
everything that had happened. [15]While they were
talking and discussing, Jesus himself came near
and began walking with them, [16]but they were
kept from recognizing him. [17]Then he said,
"What are these things you are talking about
while you walk?"

The two followers stopped, looking very sad.
[18]The one named Cleopas answered, "Are you
the only visitor in Jerusalem who does not know
what just happened there?"

[19]Jesus said to them, "What are you talking
about?"

They said, "About Jesus of Nazareth. He was a
prophet[d] who said and did many powerful things
before God and all the people. [20]Our leaders and
the leading priests handed him over to be sentenced to death, and they crucified him. [21]But we
were hoping that he would free Israel. Besides
this, it is now the third day since this happened.
[22]And today some women among us amazed us.
Early this morning they went to the tomb, [23]but
they did not find his body there. They came and
told us that they had seen a vision of angels who
said that Jesus was alive! [24]So some of our group
went to the tomb, too. They found it just as the
women said, but they did not see Jesus."

[25]Then Jesus said to them, "You are foolish and
slow to believe everything the prophets said.
[26]They said that the Christ[d] must suffer these
things before he enters his glory." [27]Then starting
with what Moses and all the prophets had said
about him, Jesus began to explain everything that
had been written about himself in the Scriptures.[d]

[28]They came near the town of Emmaus, and
Jesus acted as if he were going farther. [29]But they
begged him, "Stay with us, because it is late; it is
almost night." So he went in to stay with them.

[30]When Jesus was at the table with them, he
took some bread, gave thanks, divided it, and

LIFE

Good News

Bob Delker's family members mourned the day he died, but they also knew others would live now because of him. Bob had decided to give his body to medicine. That meant that people who desperately needed organ donations would receive them. For these people, Bob's death brought new life.

A few received badly needed bone transplants. Some critically injured burn victims received skin grafts. Corneas from Bob's eyes allowed two blind people to see.

In all, Bob's final gift helped thirty-four people. Countless others have been inspired to become organ donors because of Bob's example.

Bob's death brought new life to many people. Similarly, the sad news of Jesus' death meant the possibility of new life for all people everywhere, for Jesus rose from the dead. But unlike Bob Delker, Jesus didn't stay dead. Read **Luke 24:1–11** to discover what happened.

- How is an organ transplant a little like Jesus' coming back from the dead?
- How does Jesus' rising from the dead make a difference in your life?

CONSIDER . . .

- listing the ways that Christ's death has given you life.
- growing a plant in your room as a reminder of the spiritual life Jesus gives you.

FOR MORE, SEE . . .

- Psalm 36:7–9 (p. 502)
- Mark 16:1–8 (p. 996)
- John 20:1–18 (p. 1093)

gave it to them. 31And then, they were allowed to
recognize Jesus. But when they saw who he was,
he disappeared. 32They said to each other, "It felt
like a fire burning in us when Jesus talked to us
on the road and explained the Scriptures to us."

33So the two followers got up at once and went
back to Jerusalem. There they found the eleven
apostles[d] and others gathered. 34They were saying, "The Lord really has risen from the dead! He
showed himself to Simon."

35Then the two followers told what had happened on the road and how they recognized Jesus
when he divided the bread.

Jesus Appears to His Followers

36While the two followers were telling this,
Jesus himself stood right in the middle of them
and said, "Peace be with you."

37They were fearful and terrified and thought
they were seeing a ghost. 38But Jesus said, "Why
are you troubled? Why do you doubt what you
see? 39Look at my hands and my feet. It is I myself! Touch me and see, because a ghost does not
have a living body as you see I have."

40After Jesus said this, he showed them his
hands and feet. 41While they still could not believe it because they were amazed and happy,
Jesus said to them, "Do you have any food here?"
42They gave him a piece of broiled fish. 43While
the followers watched, Jesus took the fish and ate
it.

44He said to them, "Remember when I was
with you before? I said that everything written
about me must happen — everything in the law of
Moses, the books of the prophets,[d] and the
Psalms."

45Then Jesus opened their minds so they could
understand the Scriptures.[d] 46He said to them, "It
is written that the Christ[d] would suffer and rise
from the dead on the third day 47and that a
change of hearts and lives and forgiveness of sins
would be preached in his name to all nations,
starting at Jerusalem. 48You are witnesses of these
things. 49I will send you what my Father has
promised, but you must stay in Jerusalem until
you have received that power from heaven."

Jesus Goes Back to Heaven

50Jesus led his followers as far as Bethany, and
he raised his hands and blessed them. 51While he
was blessing them, he was separated from them
and carried into heaven. 52They worshiped him
and returned to Jerusalem very happy. 53They
stayed in the Temple[d] all the time, praising God.

JOHN

Why Read This Book:

- Be reminded that Jesus Christ is fully human and fully divine (John 1).
- Find stories that reveal Jesus' glory as giver of eternal life (John 2—11).
- Learn the importance of Jesus' death and resurrection (John 13—21).

Behind the Scenes:

Imagine meeting someone for the first time. The conversation begins with "Hi, I'm Barb. I go to Central High. I live in Rogers Park." If the conversation continues, you might talk about hobbies, interests, background, and other information.

But you still wouldn't really know that person. If you saw each other regularly, you would begin to understand each other's personality, values, and uniquenesses.

In some ways, the first three Gospels (Matthew, p. 906; Mark, p. 964; and Luke, p. 1000) are like the first part of a relationship with Jesus Christ. Through these books, we get to know stories about Jesus and what he did. But the Gospel of John digs deeper into who Jesus was, why he lived and the meaning of his life.

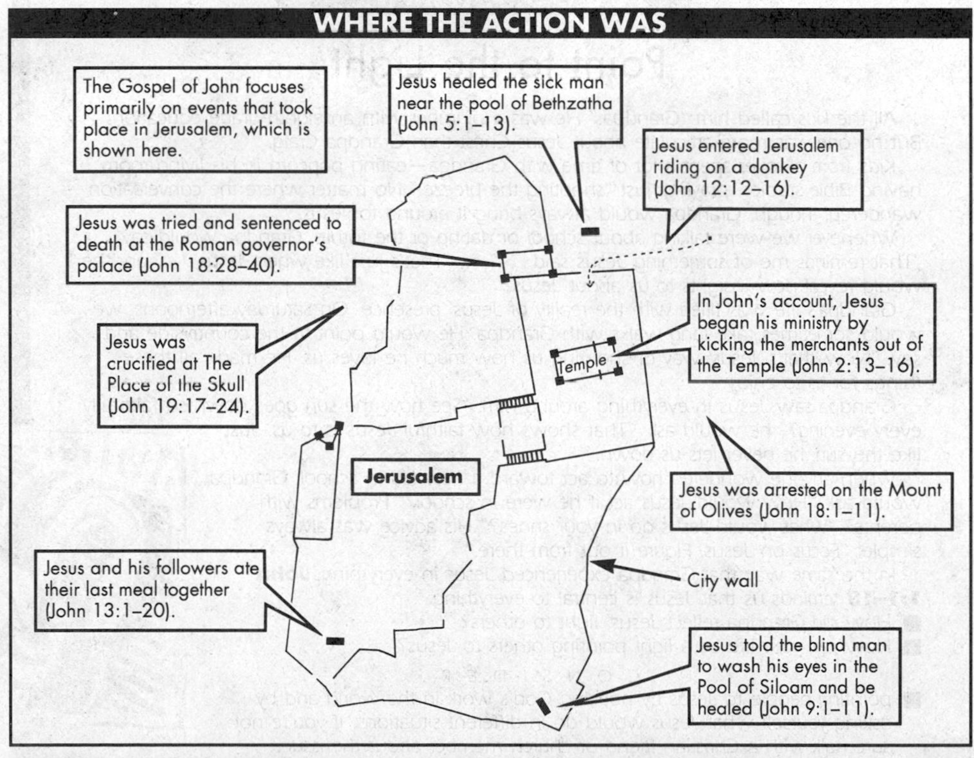
WHERE THE ACTION WAS
The Gospel of John focuses primarily on events that took place in Jerusalem, which is shown here.
Jesus healed the sick man near the pool of Bethzatha (John 5:1–13).
Jesus entered Jerusalem riding on a donkey (John 12:12–16).
Jesus was tried and sentenced to death at the Roman governor's palace (John 18:28–40).
In John's account, Jesus began his ministry by kicking the merchants out of the Temple (John 2:13–16).
Temple
Jesus was crucified at The Place of the Skull (John 19:17–24).
Jerusalem
Jesus was arrested on the Mount of Olives (John 18:1–11).
Jesus and his followers ate their last meal together (John 13:1–20).
City wall
Jesus told the blind man to wash his eyes in the Pool of Siloam and be healed (John 9:1–11).

WHEN THE ACTION WAS

- **Jesus was born** — BC/AD
- **Jesus began his ministry** — c. 25AD
- **Jesus was crucified, rose from the dead, and went to heaven** — c. 30AD
- 50AD
- **Fire destroyed Rome** — c. 64AD
- **Romans destroyed the Temple in Jerusalem** — c. 70AD
- 75AD
- 100AD

Behind the Scenes (cont.):

This fourth Gospel is quite different from the other three. Like the others, it tells about what Jesus said and did. But it goes a step further by interpreting Jesus' significance as God's Son.

Many new believers turn first to this Gospel to discover what it means to be a Christian. That's not surprising, given the book's purpose as stated in John 20:31: "These [things] are written so that you may believe that Jesus is the Christ, the Son of God. Then, by believing, you may have life through his name."

Christ Comes to the World

1 In the beginning there was the Word.[n] The
Word was with God, and the Word was
God. 2He was with God in the beginning. 3All
things were made by him, and nothing was made
without him. 4In him there was life, and that life
was the light of all people. 5The Light shines in the
darkness, and the darkness has not overpowered
it.

6There was a man named John[n] who was sent
by God. 7He came to tell people the truth about
the Light so that through him all people could

Word The Greek word is "logos," meaning any kind of communication; it could be translated "message." Here, it means Christ, because Christ was the way God told people about himself.

John John the Baptist, who preached to people about Christ's coming (Matthew 3, Luke 3).

JESUS CHRIST

Point to the Light

All the kids called him "Grandpa." He was a plumber with an eighth-grade education. But no one was more articulate about Jesus Christ than Grandpa Craig.

Kids from all over spent a lot of time with Grandpa—eating popcorn in his living room, having Bible studies, praying, just "shooting the breeze." No matter where the conversation wandered, though, Grandpa would always bring it around to Jesus.

Whenever we were talking about school or dating or the future, Grandpa would say, "That reminds me of something Jesus said . . ." or, "That's just like when Jesus . . ." and he would reveal new insights to us about Jesus.

Grandpa's life was filled with the reality of Jesus' presence. On Saturday afternoons, we would sometimes take long walks with Grandpa. He would point to the countryside and say, "Now, that's Jesus' way of showing us how much he loves us. He made all these things for us to enjoy."

Grandpa saw Jesus in everything around him. "See how the sun goes down so faithfully every evening?" he would ask. "That shows how faithful Jesus is to us. Just like the sun, he never lets us down."

When anyone wondered how to act toward a new kid in school, Grandpa would ask, "How would Jesus act if he were in school?" Problems with parents? "What would Jesus do in your shoes?" His advice was always simple: "Focus on Jesus. Figure it out from there."

In the same way that Grandpa experienced Jesus in everything, **John 1:1–18** reminds us that Jesus is central to everything.

- How did Grandpa reflect Jesus' light to others?
- How can your life be a light pointing others to Jesus?

C O N S I D E R . . .

- pointing people to Jesus by noticing God's work in the world and by asking yourself what Jesus would do in different situations. If you're not sure, talk with a Christian friend or church member about the issue.
- taking a nature walk and sitting down to list all the ways Jesus is revealed through creation and then sharing your list with a friend.

F O R M O R E , S E E . . .

- Isaiah 53:1—12 (p. 672)
- Philippians 2:5—11 (p. 1230)
- Colossians 1:15—20 (p. 1239)

hear about the Light and believe. 8John was not
the Light, but he came to tell people the truth
about the Light. 9The true Light that gives light to
all was coming into the world!
10The Word was in the world, and the world
was made by him, but the world did not know
him. 11He came to the world that was his own,
but his own people did not accept him. 12But to
all who did accept him and believe in him he gave
the right to become children of God. 13They did
not become his children in any human way—by
any human parents or human desire. They were
born of God.
14The Word became a human and lived among
us. We saw his glory—the glory that belongs to
the only Son of the Father—and he was full of

> **SIDELIGHT:** Did you know Jesus was a great camper? When John 1:14 says "The Word became a human and lived among us," the literal Greek words say he "pitched his tent" among us. No fancy houses here!

grace and truth. 15John tells the truth about him
and cries out, saying, "This is the One I told you
about: 'The One who comes after me is greater
than I am, because he was living before me.' "
16Because he was full of grace and truth, from
him we all received one gift after another. 17The
law was given through Moses, but grace and truth
came through Jesus Christ. 18No one has ever
seen God. But God the only Son is very close to
the Father,[n] and he has shown us what God is
like.

John Tells People About Jesus

19Here is the truth John[n] told when the Jews
in Jerusalem sent priests and Levites to ask him,
"Who are you?"
20John spoke freely and did not refuse to answer. He said, "I am not the Christ."[d]
21So they asked him, "Then who are you? Are
you Elijah?"[n]
He answered, "No, I am not."
"Are you the Prophet?"[n] they asked.
He answered, "No."
22Then they said, "Who are you? Give us an
answer to tell those who sent us. What do you say
about yourself?"
23John told them in the words of the prophet
Isaiah:

"I am the voice of one
calling out in the desert:
'Make the road straight for the Lord.' "
Isaiah 40:3

24Some Pharisees[d] who had been sent asked
John: 25"If you are not the Christ or Elijah or the
Prophet, why do you baptize people?"
26John answered, "I baptize with water, but
there is one here with you that you don't know
about. 27He is the One who comes after me. I am
not good enough to untie the strings of his sandals."
28This all happened at Bethany on the other
side of the Jordan River, where John was baptizing people.
29The next day John saw Jesus coming toward
him. John said, "Look, the Lamb of God,[n] who
takes away the sin of the world! 30This is the One
I was talking about when I said, 'A man will come
after me, but he is greater than I am, because he
was living before me.' 31Even I did not know who
he was, although I came baptizing with water so
that the people of Israel would know who he is."
32-33Then John said, "I saw the Spirit come
down from heaven in the form of a dove and rest
on him. Until then I did not know who the Christ
was. But the God who sent me to baptize with
water told me, 'You will see the Spirit[d] come
down and rest on a man; he is the One who will
baptize with the Holy Spirit.' 34I have seen this
happen, and I tell you the truth: This man is the
Son of God."

The First Followers of Jesus

35The next day John[n] was there again with
two of his followers. 36When he saw Jesus walking by, he said, "Look, the Lamb of God!"[n]
37The two followers heard John say this, so
they followed Jesus. 38When Jesus turned and saw
them following him, he asked, "What are you
looking for?"
They said, "Rabbi, where are you staying?"
("Rabbi" means "Teacher.")
39He answered, "Come and see." So the two
men went with Jesus and saw where he was staying and stayed there with him that day. It was
about four o'clock in the afternoon.
40One of the two men who followed Jesus after
they heard John speak about him was Andrew,
Simon Peter's brother. 41The first thing Andrew

But . . . Father This could be translated, "But the only God is very close to the Father." Also, some Greek copies say, "But the only Son is very close to the Father."
John John the Baptist, who preached to people about Christ's coming (Matthew 3, Luke 3).
Elijah A man who spoke for God. He lived hundreds of years before Christ and was expected to return before Christ (Malachi 4:5-6).
Prophet They probably meant the prophet that God told Moses he would send (Deuteronomy 18:15-19).
Lamb of God Name for Jesus. Jesus is like the lambs that were offered for a sacrifice to God.

did was to find his brother Simon and say to him,
"We have found the Messiah." ("Messiah" means
"Christ."[d])
42Then Andrew took Simon to Jesus. Jesus
looked at him and said, "You are Simon son of
John. You will be called Cephas." ("Cephas"
means "Peter."[n])
43The next day Jesus decided to go to Galilee.
He found Philip and said to him, "Follow me."
44Philip was from the town of Bethsaida, where
Andrew and Peter lived. 45Philip found Nathanael
and told him, "We have found the man that Moses wrote about in the law, and the prophets[d] also
wrote about him. He is Jesus, the son of Joseph,
from Nazareth."
46But Nathanael said to Philip, "Can anything
good come from Nazareth?"
Philip answered, "Come and see."
47As Jesus saw Nathanael coming toward him,
he said, "Here is truly an Israelite. There is nothing false in him."
48Nathanael asked, "How do you know me?"
Jesus answered, "I saw you when you were under the fig tree, before Philip told you about me."
49Then Nathanael said to Jesus, "Teacher, you
are the Son of God; you are the King of Israel."
50Jesus said to Nathanael, "Do you believe simply because I told you I saw you under the fig
tree? You will see greater things than that." 51And
Jesus said to them, "I tell you the truth, you will
all see heaven open and 'angels of God going up
and coming down'[n] on the Son of Man."[d]

The Wedding at Cana

2 Two days later there was a wedding in the
town of Cana in Galilee. Jesus' mother was
there, 2and Jesus and his followers were also invited to the wedding. 3When all the wine was
gone, Jesus' mother said to him, "They have no
more wine."
4Jesus answered, "Dear woman, why come to
me? My time has not yet come."
5His mother said to the servants, "Do whatever
he tells you to do."
6In that place there were six stone water jars
that the Jews used in their washing ceremony.[n]
Each jar held about twenty or thirty gallons.
7Jesus said to the servants, "Fill the jars with
water." So they filled the jars to the top.
8Then he said to them, "Now take some out
and give it to the master of the feast."
So they took the water to the master. 9When
he tasted it, the water had become wine. He did
not know where the wine came from, but the
servants who had brought the water knew. The
master of the wedding called the bridegroom
10and said to him, "People always serve the best
wine first. Later, after the guests have been drinking awhile, they serve the cheaper wine. But you
have saved the best wine till now."
11So in Cana of Galilee Jesus did his first miracle.[d] There he showed his glory, and his followers
believed in him.

SIDELIGHT: The wedding at Cana (John 2:1–11) wouldn't have involved a short ceremony followed by a cake-and-punch reception. In Jesus' day, weddings usually lasted about a week. On the first day, the couple exchanged vows under a canopy. Then, for the next six days or more, the couple and all the guests celebrated with dancing, games, music, food, and wine.

Jesus in the Temple

12After this, Jesus went to the town of Capernaum with his mother, brothers, and followers.
They stayed there for just a few days. 13When it
was almost time for the Jewish Passover[d] Feast,
Jesus went to Jerusalem. 14In the Temple[d] he
found people selling cattle, sheep, and doves. He
saw others sitting at tables, exchanging different
kinds of money. 15Jesus made a whip out of cords
and forced all of them, both the sheep and cattle,
to leave the Temple. He turned over the tables
and scattered the money of those who were exchanging it. 16Then he said to those who were
selling pigeons, "Take these things out of here!
Don't make my Father's house a place for buying
and selling!"
17When this happened, the followers remembered what was written in the Scriptures:[d] "My
strong love for your Temple completely controls
me."[n]
18The Jews said to Jesus, "Show us a miracle[d]
to prove you have the right to do these things."
19Jesus answered them, "Destroy this temple,
and I will build it again in three days."
20The Jews answered, "It took forty-six years to
build this Temple! Do you really believe you can
build it again in three days?"
21(But the temple Jesus meant was his own
body. 22After Jesus was raised from the dead, his
followers remembered that Jesus had said this.

Peter The Greek name "Peter," like the Aramaic name "Cephas," means "rock."
'angels . . . down' These words are from Genesis 28:12.
washing ceremony The Jewish people washed themselves in special ways before eating, before worshiping in the Temple, and at other special times.
"My . . . me." Quotation from Psalm 69:9.

Then they believed the Scripture[d] and the words
Jesus had said.)
23When Jesus was in Jerusalem for the Passover
Feast, many people believed in him because they
saw the miracles he did. 24But Jesus did not trust
himself to them because he knew them all. 25He
did not need anyone to tell him about people, because he knew what was in people's minds.

Nicodemus Comes to Jesus

3 There was a man named Nicodemus who
was one of the Pharisees[d] and an important
Jewish leader. 2One night Nicodemus came to
Jesus and said, "Teacher, we know you are a
teacher sent from God, because no one can do the
miracles[d] you do unless God is with him."
3Jesus answered, "I tell you the truth, unless
one is born again, he cannot be in God's kingdom."
4Nicodemus said, "But if a person is already
old, how can he be born again? He cannot enter
his mother's body again. So how can a person be
born a second time?"
5But Jesus answered, "I tell you the truth, unless one is born from water and the Spirit,[d] he
cannot enter God's kingdom. 6Human life comes
from human parents, but spiritual life comes from
the Spirit. 7Don't be surprised when I tell you,
'You must all be born again.' 8The wind blows
where it wants to and you hear the sound of it,
but you don't know where the wind comes from
or where it is going. It is the same with every
person who is born from the Spirit."
9Nicodemus asked, "How can this happen?"
10Jesus said, "You are an important teacher in
Israel, and you don't understand these things? 11I
tell you the truth, we talk about what we know,
and we tell about what we have seen, but you
don't accept what we tell you. 12I have told you
about things here on earth, and you do not be-

ANGER

Constructive Anger

They wander the streets late at night in the toughest parts of town. Jackets with their emblem let anyone who can see know exactly who they are.

They are not the Crips or Bloods. They are not even a gang. They are "Mad Dads"—men who have dedicated themselves to fight the influences of gangs and substance abuse in Omaha, Nebraska.

Neighborhoods feel the difference when the Mad Dads come around. These men educate adults about the needs of young people. They clean up gang graffiti, work with local businesses to find jobs for kids who need them, and encourage kids to stay in school and out of trouble.

Often, volunteer patrols of Mad Dads watch for gang or drug-related activities, and then report them to the police.

Mad Dads formed out of the founders' shared anger against gang violence and drug pushing in their neighborhoods. They finally got angry enough to take positive action.

Eddie Staton, one of the founders, said, "For too long, we, as black men, were silent. And people took our silence to mean we didn't care about drugs, alcohol, or gangs. So we took action. As parents, as black fathers in particular . . . we are actively involved in preventative measures against the influences of gangs, drugs, and alcohol."

Jesus became angry at bad influences too. Read **John 2:12–22** to see what Jesus did with his anger.

- How are the Mad Dads' actions like Jesus' actions in this passage? How are they different?
- When have you been so angry at wrongdoing that you took action against it like Jesus or the Mad Dads did?

C O N S I D E R . . .

- stopping the next time you get angry, and praying that your anger will produce something positive.
- memorizing Ephesians 4:26, p. 1224. What does the verse mean to you? Meditate on it so it can help you the next time you are angry.

F O R M O R E , S E E . . .

- Psalm 103:7–13 (p. 540)
- Ephesians 4:26–27 (p. 1224)
- James 1:19–20 (p. 1294)

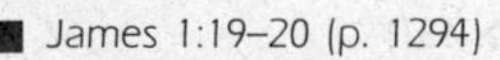

lieve me. So you will not believe me if I tell you
about things of heaven. 13The only one who has
ever gone up to heaven is the One who came
down from heaven—the Son of Man.[d]
14"Just as Moses lifted up the snake in the
desert,[n] the Son of Man must also be lifted up.
15So that everyone who believes can have eternal
life in him.
16"God loved the world so much that he gave
his one and only Son so that whoever believes in
him may not be lost, but have eternal life. 17God
did not send his Son into the world to judge the
world guilty, but to save the world through him.
18People who believe in God's Son are not judged
guilty. Those who do not believe have already
been judged guilty, because they have not believed in God's one and only Son. 19They are
judged by this fact: The Light has come into the
world, but they did not want light. They wanted
darkness, because they were doing evil things.
20All who do evil hate the light and will not come
to the light, because it will show all the evil things
they do. 21But those who follow the true way
come to the light, and it shows that the things
they do were done through God."

Jesus and John the Baptist

22After this, Jesus and his followers went into
the area of Judea, where he stayed with his followers and baptized people. 23John was also baptizing in Aenon, near Salim, because there was
plenty of water there. People were going there to
be baptized. 24(This was before John was put into
prison.)
25Some of John's followers had an argument
with a Jew about religious washing.[n] 26So they
came to John and said, "Teacher, remember the
man who was with you on the other side of the
Jordan River, the one you spoke about so much?
He is baptizing, and everyone is going to him."
27John answered, "A man can get only what
God gives him. 28You yourselves heard me say, 'I

Moses . . . desert When the Israelites were dying from snake bites, God told Moses to put a brass snake on a pole. The people who looked at the snake were healed (Numbers 21:4-9).
religious washing The Jewish people washed themselves in special ways before eating, before worshiping in the Temple, and at other special times.

ETERNAL LIFE

The Ultimate Price

Brian Watkins had been in New York City before. Brian loved the annual trip his family made from Provo, Utah, to watch the U.S. Open together in New York.

One Sunday during the 1990 tournament, Brian was waiting with his parents in a Manhattan subway station when a gang approached them. Surrounding the Watkinses, they robbed Brian's father, then began beating Brian's mother.

Brian fought back to defend his mother. The attackers turned from Brian's mother to Brian. In the struggle, one of the robbers pulled a knife and stabbed Brian to death.

Brian Watkins paid the ultimate price because he couldn't stand watching the ones he loved be hurt. Jesus, God's Son, willingly paid the ultimate price for us because he doesn't want us to be hurt forever.

In **John 3:1–21**, Jesus talks about the gift of eternal life that his death would provide.

- How were Brian's feelings for his parents like God's desires for us? How were they different?
- According to this passage (especially verses 16–18), what must we do to receive all God desires for us?

CONSIDER . . .

- writing John 3:16 on paper, placing it in a box, and gift wrapping the box. Give the box to a friend to keep in his or her room as a reminder of God's gift of eternal life.
- asking your pastor or youth leader what eternal life is, then comparing the answer to what Jesus said in this passage.

FOR MORE, SEE . . .

- Isaiah 12 (p. 631)
- 1 Timothy 1:12–17 (p. 1256)
- 1 John 5:1–12 (p. 1319)

am not the Christ,[d] but I am the one sent to prepare the way for him.' 29The bride belongs only to the bridegroom. But the friend who helps the bridegroom stands by and listens to him. He is thrilled that he gets to hear the bridegroom's voice. In the same way, I am really happy. 30He must become greater, and I must become less important.

The One Who Comes from Heaven

31"The One who comes from above is greater than all. The one who is from the earth belongs to the earth and talks about things on the earth. But the One who comes from heaven is greater than all. 32He tells what he has seen and heard, but no one accepts what he says. 33Whoever accepts what he says has proven that God is true. 34The One whom God sent speaks the words of God, because God gives him the Spirit[d] fully. 35The Father loves the Son and has given him power over everything. 36Those who believe in the Son have eternal life, but those who do not obey the Son will never have life. God's anger stays on them."

Jesus and a Samaritan Woman

4 The Pharisees[d] heard that Jesus was making and baptizing more followers than John, 2although Jesus himself did not baptize people, but his followers did. 3Jesus knew that the Pharisees had heard about him, so he left Judea and went back to Galilee. 4But on the way he had to go through the country of Samaria.

5In Samaria Jesus came to the town called Sychar, which is near the field Jacob gave to his son Joseph. 6Jacob's well was there. Jesus was tired from his long trip, so he sat down beside the well. It was about twelve o'clock noon. 7When a Samaritan[d] woman came to the well to get some water, Jesus said to her, "Please give me a drink." 8(This happened while Jesus' followers were in town buying some food.)

9The woman said, "I am surprised that you ask me for a drink, since you are a Jewish man and I am a Samaritan woman." (Jewish people are not friends with Samaritans.[n])

10Jesus said, "If you only knew the free gift of God and who it is that is asking you for water, you would have asked him, and he would have given you living water."

11The woman said, "Sir, where will you get this living water? The well is very deep, and you have nothing to get water with. 12Are you greater than Jacob, our father, who gave us this well and drank from it himself along with his sons and flocks?"

13Jesus answered, "Everyone who drinks this water will be thirsty again, 14but whoever drinks the water I give will never be thirsty. The water I give will become a spring of water gushing up inside that person, giving eternal life."

15The woman said to him, "Sir, give me this water so I will never be thirsty again and will not have to come back here to get more water."

16Jesus told her, "Go get your husband and come back here."

17The woman answered, "I have no husband."

Jesus said to her, "You are right to say you have no husband. 18Really you have had five husbands, and the man you live with now is not your husband. You told the truth."

19The woman said, "Sir, I can see that you are a prophet.[d] 20Our ancestors worshiped on this mountain, but you Jews say that Jerusalem is the place where people must worship."

21Jesus said, "Believe me, woman. The time is coming when neither in Jerusalem nor on this mountain will you actually worship the Father. 22You Samaritans worship something you don't understand. We understand what we worship, because salvation comes from the Jews. 23The time is coming when the true worshipers will worship the Father in spirit and truth, and that time is here already. You see, the Father too is actively seeking such people to worship him. 24God is spirit, and those who worship him must worship in spirit and truth."

25The woman said, "I know that the Messiah is coming." (Messiah is the One called Christ.[d]) "When the Messiah comes, he will explain everything to us."

26Then Jesus said, "I am he—I, the one talking to you."

27Just then his followers came back from town and were surprised to see him talking with a woman. But none of them asked, "What do you want?" or "Why are you talking with her?"

28Then the woman left her water jar and went back to town. She said to the people, 29"Come and see a man who told me everything I ever did. Do you think he might be the Christ?" 30So the people left the town and went to see Jesus.

SIDELIGHT: Jesus risked getting into lots of trouble when he talked with the Samaritan woman (see John 4:1–30). Jewish law forbade teachers to speak to women, Jews to talk to Samaritans, and the "righteous" to mingle with "sinners." Kinda made it hard to have any friends, don't you think?

Jewish people . . . Samaritans. This can also be translated "Jewish people don't use things that Samaritans have used."

[31]Meanwhile, his followers were begging him,
"Teacher, eat something."
[32]But Jesus answered, "I have food to eat that
you know nothing about."
[33]So the followers asked themselves, "Did
somebody already bring him food?"
[34]Jesus said, "My food is to do what the One
who sent me wants me to do and to finish his
work. [35]You have a saying, 'Four more months till
harvest.' But I tell you, open your eyes and look
at the fields ready for harvest now. [36]Already, the
one who harvests is being paid and is gathering
crops for eternal life. So the one who plants and
the one who harvests celebrate at the same time.
[37]Here the saying is true, 'One person plants, and
another harvests.' [38]I sent you to harvest a crop
that you did not work on. Others did the work,
and you get to finish up their work."[n]
[39]Many of the Samaritans in that town believed
in Jesus because of what the woman said: "He
told me everything I ever did." [40]When the Samaritans came to Jesus, they begged him to stay
with them, so he stayed there two more days.
[41]And many more believed because of the things
he said.
[42]They said to the woman, "First we believed
in Jesus because of your speech, but now we believe because we heard him ourselves. We know

But I . . . their work. As a farmer sends workers to harvest grain, Jesus sends his followers out to bring people to God.

JUDGING OTHERS

Prejudice

The bell rang. Creative writing was over for another day. Burt Moore stared at his short story.

His classmates walked by, some commenting as they passed. "What an imagination you have in there!" Burt wasn't sure if it was a compliment or not. "I'd love to hear you try reading it yourself, freak." He was sure that wasn't a compliment.

Burt waited for the classroom traffic to clear, then made his way to his next class: trigonometry.

Mr. Springer, his teacher, greeted him at the doorway. "Hi, Burt!" he yelled. "How are you today?"

Burt just nodded and wondered, once again, why people treated him like he was deaf.

When Burt began attending public school in junior high, one of the toughest adjustments was learning how to interact with others. Some people were great. They shared Burt's interest in chess and science fiction, and made special efforts to make him their friend. Others, though, openly insulted him for being different.

Burt learned a lot about prejudice in junior high and high school. Because of his severe cerebral palsy, some people expected Burt to be stupid. He always took special pleasure in blowing away stereotypes by writing a creative short story or taking the toughest math class offered.

Burt was different from others in some ways. His speech was often difficult to understand. He communicated by typing with touchsticks strapped to his hands. And he traveled by moving a joystick attached to his wheelchair.

But Burt had a lot more in common with those around him than many people thought. A lot of them refused to see beyond his wheelchair or his inability to speak as they did. And their prejudice was tough on Burt.

Jesus also had to overcome people's prejudice. Read **John 4:5–42** about how Jesus dealt with prejudice toward himself and others.

- How did Burt break down prejudice in the same way Jesus did?
- What prejudices do you have? How would Jesus respond to those prejudices?

CONSIDER . . .

- writing a letter to the editor of your school or local newspaper concerning a prejudice you see. Describe ways to combat that prejudice.
- regularly eating lunch at school with someone who has been hurt by prejudice.

FOR MORE, SEE . . .

- Psalm 9:7–10 (p. 487)
- Acts 10:1–33 (p. 1114)
- Galatians 3:26–29 (p. 1210)

that this man really is the Savior of the world."

Jesus Heals an Officer's Son

43 Two days later, Jesus left and went to Galilee. 44 (Jesus had said before that a prophet[d] is not respected in his own country.) 45 When Jesus arrived in Galilee, the people there welcomed him. They had seen all the things he did at the Passover[d] Feast in Jerusalem, because they had been there, too.

46 Jesus went again to visit Cana in Galilee where he had changed the water into wine. One of the king's important officers lived in the city of Capernaum, and his son was sick. 47 When he heard that Jesus had come from Judea to Galilee, he went to Jesus and begged him to come to Capernaum and heal his son, because his son was almost dead. 48 Jesus said to him, "You people must see signs and miracles[d] before you will believe in me."

49 The officer said, "Sir, come before my child dies."

50 Jesus answered, "Go. Your son will live."

The man believed what Jesus told him and went home. 51 On the way the man's servants came and met him and told him, "Your son is alive."

52 The man asked, "What time did my son begin to get well?"

They answered, "Yesterday at one o'clock the fever left him."

53 The father knew that one o'clock was the exact time that Jesus had said, "Your son will live." So the man and all the people who lived in his house believed in Jesus.

54 That was the second miracle Jesus did after coming from Judea to Galilee.

Jesus Heals a Man at a Pool

5 Later Jesus went to Jerusalem for a special Jewish feast. 2 In Jerusalem there is a pool with five covered porches, which is called Bethzatha[n] in the Jewish language.[n] This pool is near the Sheep Gate. 3 Many sick people were lying on the porches beside the pool. Some were blind, some were crippled, and some were paralyzed.[n] 5 A man was lying there who had been sick for thirty-eight years. 6 When Jesus saw the man and knew that he had been sick for such a long time, Jesus asked him, "Do you want to be well?"

7 The sick man answered, "Sir, there is no one to help me get into the pool when the water starts moving. While I am coming to the water, someone else always gets in before me."

8 Then Jesus said, "Stand up. Pick up your mat and walk." 9 And immediately the man was well; he picked up his mat and began to walk.

The day this happened was a Sabbath[d] day. 10 So the Jews said to the man who had been healed, "Today is the Sabbath. It is against our law for you to carry your mat on the Sabbath day."

11 But he answered, "The man who made me well told me, 'Pick up your mat and walk.' "

12 Then they asked him, "Who is the man who told you to pick up your mat and walk?"

13 But the man who had been healed did not know who it was, because there were many people in that place, and Jesus had left.

14 Later, Jesus found the man at the Temple[d] and said to him, "See, you are well now. Stop sinning so that something worse does not happen to you."

15 Then the man left and told the Jews that Jesus was the one who had made him well.

16 Because Jesus was doing this on the Sabbath day, the Jews began to persecute him. 17 But Jesus said to them, "My Father never stops working, and so I keep working, too."

18 This made the Jews try still harder to kill him. They said, "First Jesus was breaking the law about the Sabbath day. Now he says that God is his own Father, making himself equal with God!"

Jesus Has God's Authority

19 But Jesus said, "I tell you the truth, the Son can do nothing alone. The Son does only what he sees the Father doing, because the Son does whatever the Father does. 20 The Father loves the Son and shows the Son all the things he himself does. But the Father will show the Son even greater things than this so that you can all be amazed. 21 Just as the Father raises the dead and gives them life, so also the Son gives life to those he wants to. 22 In fact, the Father judges no one, but he has given the Son power to do all the judging 23 so that all people will honor the Son as much as they honor the Father. Anyone who does not honor the Son does not honor the Father who sent him.

24 "I tell you the truth, whoever hears what I say and believes in the One who sent me has eternal life. That person will not be judged guilty but has already left death and entered life. 25 I tell you the truth, the time is coming and is already here when the dead will hear the voice of the Son of God, and those who hear will have life. 26 Life comes from the Father himself, and he has allowed the Son to have life in himself as well.

Bethzatha Also called Bethsaida or Bethesda, a pool of water north of the Temple in Jerusalem.
Jewish language Hebrew or Aramaic, the languages of the Jewish people in the first century.
Verse 3 Some Greek copies add "and they waited for the water to move." A few later copies add verse 4: "Sometimes an angel of the Lord came down to the pool and stirred up the water. After the angel did this, the first person to go into the pool was healed from any sickness he had."

27And the Father has given the Son the power to judge, because he is the Son of Man.[d] 28Don't be surprised at this: A time is coming when all who are dead and in their graves will hear his voice. 29Then they will come out of their graves. Those who did good will rise and have life forever, but those who did evil will rise to be judged guilty.

Jesus Is God's Son

30"I can do nothing alone. I judge only the way I am told, so my judgment is fair. I don't try to please myself, but I try to please the One who sent me.

31"If only I tell people about myself, what I say is not true. 32But there is another who tells about me, and I know that the things he says about me are true.

33"You have sent people to John, and he has told you the truth. 34It is not that I accept such human telling; I tell you this so you can be saved. 35John was like a burning and shining lamp, and you were happy to enjoy his light for a while.

36"But I have a proof about myself that is greater than that of John. The things I do, which are the things my Father gave me to do, prove that the Father sent me. 37And the Father himself who sent me has given proof about me. You have never heard his voice or seen what he looks like. 38His teaching does not live in you, because you don't believe in the One the Father sent. 39You carefully study the Scriptures[d] because you think they give you eternal life. They do in fact tell about me, 40but you refuse to come to me to have that life.

41"I don't need praise from people. 42But I know you—I know that you don't have God's love in you. 43I have come from my Father and speak for him, but you don't accept me. But when another person comes, speaking only for himself, you will accept him. 44You try to get praise from each other, but you do not try to get the praise that comes from the only God. So how can you believe? 45Don't think that I will stand before the Father and say you are wrong. The one who says you are wrong is Moses, the one you hoped would save you. 46If you really believed Moses, you would believe me, because Moses wrote about me. 47But if you don't believe what Moses wrote, how can you believe what I say?"

More than Five Thousand Fed

6 After this, Jesus went across Lake Galilee (or, Lake Tiberias). 2Many people followed him because they saw the miracles[d] he did to heal the sick. 3Jesus went up on a hill and sat down there with his followers. 4It was almost the time for the Jewish Passover[d] Feast.

5When Jesus looked up and saw a large crowd coming toward him, he said to Philip, "Where can we buy enough bread for all these people to eat?" 6(Jesus asked Philip this question to test him, because Jesus already knew what he planned to do.)

7Philip answered, "We would all have to work a month to buy enough bread for each person to have only a little piece."

8Another one of his followers, Andrew, Simon Peter's brother, said, 9"Here is a boy with five loaves of barley bread and two little fish, but that is not enough for so many people."

> **SIDELIGHT:** There were three types of bread in Jesus' day: small loaves (that would look like our biscuits), round loaves (about the size of basketballs), and flat loaves (large, bread-like pancakes). The boy who gave loaves to Jesus gave the first type (John 6:9). His were made from barley, indicating he was probably poor.

10Jesus said, "Tell the people to sit down." This was a very grassy place, and about five thousand men sat down there. 11Then Jesus took the loaves of bread, thanked God for them, and gave them to the people who were sitting there. He did the same with the fish, giving as much as the people wanted.

12When they had all had enough to eat, Jesus said to his followers, "Gather the leftover pieces of fish and bread so that nothing is wasted." 13So they gathered up the pieces and filled twelve baskets with the pieces left from the five barley loaves.

14When the people saw this miracle[d] that Jesus did, they said, "He must truly be the Prophet[n] who is coming into the world."

15Jesus knew that the people planned to come and take him by force and make him their king, so he left and went into the hills alone.

Jesus Walks on the Water

16That evening Jesus' followers went down to Lake Galilee. 17It was dark now, and Jesus had not yet come to them. The followers got into a boat and started across the lake to Capernaum. 18By now a strong wind was blowing, and the waves on the lake were getting bigger. 19When they had rowed the boat about three or four miles, they saw Jesus walking on the water, coming toward the boat. The followers were afraid, 20but Jesus said to them, "It is I. Do not be afraid." 21Then they were glad to take him into the boat. At once

Prophet They probably meant the prophet that God told Moses he would send (Deuteronomy 18:15-19).

the boat came to land at the place where they
wanted to go.

The People Seek Jesus

22The next day the people who had stayed on
the other side of the lake knew that Jesus had not
gone in the boat with his followers but that they
had left without him. And they knew that only
one boat had been there. 23But then some boats
came from Tiberias and landed near the place
where the people had eaten the bread after the
Lord had given thanks. 24When the people saw
that Jesus and his followers were not there now,
they got into boats and went to Capernaum to
find Jesus.

Jesus, the Bread of Life

25When the people found Jesus on the other
side of the lake, they asked him, "Teacher, when
did you come here?"
26Jesus answered, "I tell you the truth, you
aren't looking for me because you saw me do
miracles.[d] You are looking for me because you
ate the bread and were satisfied. 27Don't work
for the food that spoils. Work for the food
that stays good always and gives eternal life.
The Son of Man[d] will give you this food, because on him God the Father has put his power."
28The people asked Jesus, "What are the things
God wants us to do?"
29Jesus answered, "The work God wants you to
do is this: Believe the One he sent."
30So the people asked, "What miracle will you
do? If we see a miracle, we will believe you. What
will you do? 31Our fathers ate the manna[d] in the

PRIORITIES

Proms and Personalities

"So who are you going to the prom with this year?" Heather Keith asked.

"I'm waiting for Brett to ask me. He's got the greatest car, and his parents have loads of money. So I know we'd have a blast," Laurie Hull answered.

"I didn't know you liked Brett Howard. How long has this been going on?"

Laurie tossed her hair back. "Oh, I don't like him."

Heather didn't have to say anything. Her shocked look said it all.

"I don't have to like him to go to the prom with him," Laurie explained. "I just think we'd look good together. And he can afford the kind of evening I want."

Over the next few weeks, Laurie asked her friends to drop hints to Brett. She even teased him at lunch one day, asking if he had anyone with whom to share his Trans Am for the prom.

A week before the prom, though, Brett hadn't asked Laurie to the prom. Three other guys had asked the bubbly cheerleader, but Laurie thought they were too weird. They didn't have very much money, and she wasn't about to be seen with any of them.

Prom night came, and Laurie stayed home watching television. While her friends had a great time, Laurie ate popcorn and wondered why Brett had never asked her.

Laurie had focused on what she could get from people, rather than on the people themselves. But when she did, she came up empty-handed.

Jesus frequently challenged people to make people rather than things a priority. Read **John 6:24–51** to see how people tended to give Jesus' miracles higher priority than they gave Jesus himself.

- What was most important to Laurie and the people in this passage?
- How can you make people a priority in your life?

CONSIDER . . .

- looking at your class members' photographs in a recent yearbook. Ask God to help you focus on your classmates as people and not on what you can get from them.
- telling five friends or family members the things you appreciate about them. Focus only on inner qualities and not on what you can get from them.

FOR MORE, SEE . . .

- 1 Samuel 16:6–13 (p. 258)
- Matthew 6:25–34 (p. 918)

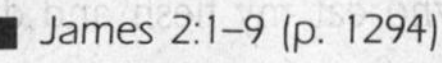

- James 2:1–9 (p. 1294)

desert. This is written in the Scriptures:[d] 'He gave them bread from heaven to eat.' "[n]

32Jesus said, "I tell you the truth, it was not Moses who gave you bread from heaven; it is my Father who is giving you the true bread from heaven. 33God's bread is the One who comes down from heaven and gives life to the world."

34The people said, "Sir, give us this bread always."

35Then Jesus said, "I am the bread that gives life. Whoever comes to me will never be hungry, and whoever believes in me will never be thirsty. 36But as I told you before, you have seen me and still don't believe. 37The Father gives me my people. Every one of them will come to me, and I will always accept them. 38I came down from heaven to do what God wants me to do, not what I want to do. 39Here is what the One who sent me wants me to do: I must not lose even one whom God gave me, but I must raise them all on the last day. 40Those who see the Son and believe in him have eternal life, and I will raise them on the last day. This is what my Father wants."

41The Jews began to complain about Jesus because he said, "I am the bread that comes down from heaven." 42They said, "This is Jesus, the son of Joseph. We know his father and mother. How can he say, 'I came down from heaven'?"

43But Jesus answered, "Stop complaining to each other. 44The Father is the One who sent me. No one can come to me unless the Father draws him to me, and I will raise that person up on the last day. 45It is written in the prophets,[d] 'They will all be taught by God.'[n] Everyone who listens to the Father and learns from him comes to me. 46No one has seen the Father except the One who is from God; only he has seen the Father. 47I tell you the truth, whoever believes has eternal life. 48I am the bread that gives life. 49Your ancestors ate the manna in the desert, but still they died. 50Here is the bread that comes down from heaven. Anyone who eats this bread will never die. 51I am the living bread that came down from heaven. Anyone who eats this bread will live forever. This bread is my flesh, which I will give up so that the world may have life."

52Then the Jews began to argue among themselves, saying, "How can this man give us his flesh to eat?"

53Jesus said, "I tell you the truth, you must eat the flesh of the Son of Man and drink his blood. Otherwise, you won't have real life in you. 54Those who eat my flesh and drink my blood have eternal life, and I will raise them up on the last day. 55My flesh is true food, and my blood is true drink. 56Those who eat my flesh and drink my blood live in me, and I live in them. 57The living Father sent me, and I live because of the Father. So whoever eats me will live because of me. 58I am not like the bread your ancestors ate. They ate that bread and still died. I am the bread that came down from heaven, and whoever eats this bread will live forever." 59Jesus said all these things while he was teaching in the synagogue[d] in Capernaum.

The Words of Eternal Life

60When the followers of Jesus heard this, many of them said, "This teaching is hard. Who can accept it?"

61Knowing that his followers were complaining about this, Jesus said, "Does this teaching bother you? 62Then will it also bother you to see the Son of Man[d] going back to the place where he came from? 63It is the Spirit that gives life. The flesh doesn't give life. The words I told you are spirit, and they give life. 64But some of you don't believe." (Jesus knew from the beginning who did not believe and who would turn against him.) 65Jesus said, "That is the reason I said, 'If the Father does not bring a person to me, that one cannot come.' "

66After Jesus said this, many of his followers left him and stopped following him.

67Jesus asked the twelve followers, "Do you want to leave, too?"

68Simon Peter answered him, "Lord, where would we go? You have the words that give eternal life. 69We believe and know that you are the Holy One from God."

70Then Jesus answered, "I chose all twelve of you, but one of you is a devil."

71Jesus was talking about Judas, the son of Simon Iscariot. Judas was one of the twelve, but later he was going to turn against Jesus.

Jesus' Brothers Don't Believe

7 After this, Jesus traveled around Galilee. He did not want to travel in Judea, because the Jews there wanted to kill him. 2It was time for the Jewish Feast[d] of Shelters. 3So Jesus' brothers said to him, "You should leave here and go to Judea so your followers there can see the miracles[d] you do. 4Anyone who wants to be well known does not hide what he does. If you are doing these things, show yourself to the world." 5(Even Jesus' brothers did not believe in him.)

6Jesus said to his brothers, "The right time for me has not yet come, but any time is right for you. 7The world cannot hate you, but it hates me, because I tell it the evil things it does. 8So you go to the feast. I will not go yet to this feast, because the

'He gave . . . eat.' Quotation from Psalm 78:24.
'They . . . God.' Quotation from Isaiah 54:13.

right time for me has not yet come." 9After saying
this, Jesus stayed in Galilee.
10But after Jesus' brothers had gone to the feast,
Jesus went also. But he did not let people see him.
11At the feast the Jews were looking for him and
saying, "Where is that man?"
12Within the large crowd there, many people
were whispering to each other about Jesus. Some
said, "He is a good man."
Others said, "No, he fools the people." 13But no
one was brave enough to talk about Jesus openly,
because they were afraid of the Jews.

Jesus Teaches at the Feast

14When the feast was about half over, Jesus
went to the Temple[d] and began to teach. 15The
Jews were amazed and said, "This man has never
studied in school. How did he learn so much?"
16Jesus answered, "The things I teach are not
my own, but they come from him who sent me.
17If people choose to do what God wants, they
will know that my teaching comes from God and
not from me. 18Those who teach their own ideas
are trying to get honor for themselves. But those
who try to bring honor to the one who sent him
speak the truth, and there is nothing false in
them. 19Moses gave you the law,[n] but none of
you obeys that law. Why are you trying to kill
me?"
20The people answered, "A demon[d] has come
into you. We are not trying to kill you."
21Jesus said to them, "I did one miracle,[d] and
you are all amazed. 22Moses gave you the law
about circumcision.[d] (But really Moses did not
give you circumcision; it came from our ancestors.) And yet you circumcise a baby on a Sabbath[d] day. 23If a baby can be circumcised on a
Sabbath day to obey the law of Moses, why are
you angry at me for healing a person's whole body
on the Sabbath day? 24Stop judging by the way
things look, but judge by what is really right."

Is Jesus the Christ?

25Then some of the people who lived in Jerusa-

law Moses gave God's people the law that God gave him on Mount Sinai (Exodus 34:29-32).

LIFE

Along for the Ride

Angie Baldwin had kept quiet about her heart problem so long that even the memories of surgeries and long hospital stays didn't seem real to her. She lived the life of an amazingly active, fun-loving eighth grader.

So when her school band took a trip to an amusement park, Angie reluctantly delivered her mother's note to the band director. The note said Angie shouldn't ride the "thrill rides."

Angie refused at first to join her boyfriend on one of the park's featured thrill rides. She kept quiet about her heart while he teased her about being chicken.

Angie finally gave in. The initial ride kind of took her breath, but she wasn't feeling too bad at the end of it.

Just as her second venture was beginning, Angie passed out. The ride operator stopped the ride, got Angie out, and called an ambulance.

Three hours later, Angie was having another heart surgery. In the middle of the operation, her heart stopped for twenty seconds. Angie might have died had she not been plugged into life-support equipment.

Angie has fully recovered, but her brush with death has made her more aware of how fragile life can be. And she's more open about her heart condition and her restrictions.

Life is a wonderful gift. Read **John 6:59–69** to see how Jesus said he was the only one who could give life.

- What words of assurance would Angie find in the passage?
- What do you appreciate most about the life Jesus has given you?

CONSIDER . . .

- buying or picking a flower to display in your room as a reminder of the gift of life.
- spending an afternoon taking pictures of the things you most enjoy about life, then creating a photo arrangement once they are developed.

FOR MORE, SEE . . .

- Leviticus 17:10–14 (p. 114)
- Psalm 104:33–35 (p. 542)
- Hebrews 9:11–15 (p. 1284)

lem said, "This is the man they are trying to kill. 26But he is teaching where everyone can see and hear him, and no one is trying to stop him. Maybe the leaders have decided he really is the Christ.[d] 27But we know where this man is from. And when the real Christ comes, no one will know where he comes from."

28Jesus, teaching in the Temple,[d] cried out, "Yes, you know me, and you know where I am from. But I have not come by my own authority. I was sent by the One who is true, whom you don't know. 29But I know him, because I am from him, and he sent me."

30When Jesus said this, the people tried to take him. But no one was able to touch him, because it was not yet the right time. 31But many of the people believed in Jesus. They said, "When the Christ comes, will he do more miracles[d] than this man has done?"

The Leaders Try to Arrest Jesus

32The Pharisees[d] heard the crowd whispering these things about Jesus. So the leading priests and the Pharisees sent some Temple[d] guards to arrest him. 33Jesus said, "I will be with you a little while longer. Then I will go back to the One who sent me. 34You will look for me, but you will not find me. And you cannot come where I am."

35The Jews said to each other, "Where will this man go so we cannot find him? Will he go to the Greek cities where our people live and teach the Greek people there? 36What did he mean when he said, 'You will look for me, but you will not find me,' and 'You cannot come where I am'?"

Jesus Talks About the Spirit

37On the last and most important day of the feast Jesus stood up and said in a loud voice, "Let anyone who is thirsty come to me and drink. 38If anyone believes in me, rivers of living water will flow out from that person's heart, as the Scripture[d] says." 39Jesus was talking about the Holy Spirit.[d] The Spirit had not yet been given, because Jesus had not yet been raised to glory. But later, those who believed in Jesus would receive the Spirit.

The People Argue About Jesus

40When the people heard Jesus' words, some of them said, "This man really is the Prophet."[n]

41Others said, "He is the Christ."[d]

Still others said, "The Christ will not come from Galilee. 42The Scripture[d] says that the Christ will come from David's family and from Bethlehem, the town where David lived." 43So the people did not agree with each other about Jesus. 44Some of them wanted to arrest him, but no one was able to touch him.

Some Leaders Won't Believe

45The Temple[d] guards went back to the leading priests and the Pharisees,[d] who asked, "Why didn't you bring Jesus?"

46The guards answered, "The words he says are greater than the words of any other person who has ever spoken!"

47The Pharisees answered, "So Jesus has fooled you also! 48Have any of the leaders or the Pharisees believed in him? No! 49But these people, who know nothing about the law, are under God's curse."

50Nicodemus, who had gone to see Jesus before, was in that group.[n] He said, 51"Our law does not judge a man without hearing him and knowing what he has done."

52They answered, "Are you from Galilee, too? Study the Scriptures,[d] and you will learn that no prophet[d] comes from Galilee."

Some early Greek manuscripts do not contain 7:53–8:11.

[53And everyone left and went home.

The Woman Caught in Adultery

8 Jesus went to the Mount of Olives.[d] 2But early in the morning he went back to the Temple,[d] and all the people came to him, and he sat and taught them. 3The teachers of the law and the Pharisees[d] brought a woman who had been caught in adultery.[d] They forced her to stand before the people. 4They said to Jesus, "Teacher, this woman was caught having sexual relations with a man who is not her husband. 5The law of Moses commands that we stone to death every woman who does this. What do you say we should do?" 6They were asking this to trick Jesus so that they could have some charge against him.

But Jesus bent over and started writing on the ground with his finger. 7When they continued to ask Jesus their question, he raised up and said, "Anyone here who has never sinned can throw the first stone at her." 8Then Jesus bent over again and wrote on the ground.

9Those who heard Jesus began to leave one by one, first the older men and then the others. Jesus was left there alone with the woman standing before him. 10Jesus raised up again and asked her,

Prophet They probably meant the prophet God told Moses he would send (Deuteronomy 18:15-19).
Nicodemus . . . group. The story about Nicodemus going and talking to Jesus is in John 3:1-21.

"Woman, where are they? Has no one judged you guilty?"

11She answered, "No one, sir."

Then Jesus said, "I also don't judge you guilty. You may go now, but don't sin anymore."]

Jesus Is the Light of the World

12Later, Jesus talked to the people again, saying, "I am the light of the world. The person who follows me will never live in darkness but will have the light that gives life."

13The Pharisees[d] said to Jesus, "When you talk about yourself, you are the only one to say these things are true. We cannot accept what you say."

14Jesus answered, "Yes, I am saying these things about myself, but they are true. I know where I came from and where I am going. But you don't know where I came from or where I am going. 15You judge by human standards. I am not judging anyone. 16But when I do judge, my judging is true, because I am not alone. The Father who sent me is with me. 17Your own law says that when two witnesses say the same thing, you must accept what they say. 18I am one of the witnesses who speaks about myself, and the Father who sent me is the other witness."

SIDELIGHT: When the teachers of the law and the Pharisees brought the woman caught in adultery to Jesus, they were more interested in tricking Jesus than in doing what was right (John 8:1–11). Though the woman was "caught in adultery," they didn't accuse the man involved—even though the law demanded that both be executed if guilty (Leviticus 20:10, p. 117).

SEXUALITY

Once Forgiven, What Then?

Stephanie Broussard silently wept as Ross Walker sat next to her in the front seat of his dad's Buick, buttoning his shirt. The silence seemed to swallow them.

"Ross, we said we'd never do this again," she finally said through her tears.

"Well, we didn't mean to. . . . It just happened," Ross responded.

"That's what you always say." The two sat silently for a long time, and then Stephanie finally spoke, "I don't think we should see each other anymore."

Ross didn't say anything. He just stared out the window. But Stephanie knew by his sniffling that he was crying.

Stephanie reached across and touched his arm. "I'm sorry, Ross, but I just can't keep doing this to us—or to God. We just keep doing it over and over, and then asking God to forgive us."

Ross jerked his head around and looked at Stephanie. "But God does forgive us, Steph," Ross argued. "We won't do it again."

Stephanie started crying even harder. "No, Ross, we say that every time. I'm serious this time. We can't keep sinning and expect God to forgive us. I love you, but this hurts too much. Please take me home."

In **John 8:1–11**, Jesus faced a woman caught in sexual sin. Read what he said to her.

- How are Ross and Stephanie similar to the woman caught in adultery? How are they different?
- What does this passage tell us about Jesus' perspective on sexual sin and the person who commits it? What is there in your life that needs to hear his "don't sin anymore"?

CONSIDER. . .

- evaluating the movies you watch or music you listen to and deciding what view of sexuality they promote.
- acting on one area of your life where Jesus is telling you to "go and not sin anymore." Tell a friend or parent about the area, and ask that person to support you in your decision.

FOR MORE, SEE. . .

- Psalm 51:1–19 (p. 511)
- I Corinthians 6:12–20 (p. 1174)
- Ephesians 6:10–18 (p. 1226)

19They asked, "Where is your father?"
Jesus answered, "You don't know me or my
Father. If you knew me, you would know my Father, too." 20Jesus said these things while he was
teaching in the Temple,[d] near where the money
is kept. But no one arrested him, because the right
time for him had not yet come.

The People Misunderstand Jesus

21Again, Jesus said to the people, "I will leave
you, and you will look for me, but you will die in
your sins. You cannot come where I am going."
22So the Jews asked, "Will Jesus kill himself? Is
that why he said, 'You cannot come where I am
going'?"
23Jesus said, "You people are from here below,
but I am from above. You belong to this world,
but I don't belong to this world. 24So I told you
that you would die in your sins. Yes, you will die
in your sins if you don't believe that I am he."
25They asked, "Then who are you?"
Jesus answered, "I am what I have told you
from the beginning. 26I have many things to say
and decide about you. But I tell people only the
things I have heard from the One who sent me,
and he speaks the truth."
27The people did not understand that he was
talking to them about the Father. 28So Jesus said
to them, "When you lift up the Son of Man,[d] you
will know that I am he. You will know that these
things I do are not by my own authority but that
I say only what the Father has taught me. 29The
One who sent me is with me. I always do what
is pleasing to him, so he has not left me alone."
30While Jesus was saying these things, many people believed in him.

Freedom from Sin

31So Jesus said to the Jews who believed in
him, "If you continue to obey my teaching, you
are truly my followers. 32Then you will know the
truth, and the truth will make you free."
33They answered, "We are Abraham's children,
and we have never been anyone's slaves. So why
do you say we will be free?"
34Jesus answered, "I tell you the truth, everyone who lives in sin is a slave to sin. 35A slave does
not stay with a family forever, but a son belongs
to the family forever. 36So if the Son makes you
free, you will be truly free. 37I know you are Abraham's children, but you want to kill me because
you don't accept my teaching. 38I am telling you
what my Father has shown me, but you do what
your father has told you."
39They answered, "Our father is Abraham."
Jesus said, "If you were really Abraham's children, you would do the things Abraham did. 40I
am a man who has told you the truth which I
heard from God, but you are trying to kill me.
Abraham did nothing like that. 41So you are doing
the things your own father did."
But they said, "We are not like children who
never knew who their father was. God is our Father; he is the only Father we have."
42Jesus said to them, "If God were really your
Father, you would love me, because I came from
God and now I am here. I did not come by my
own authority; God sent me. 43You don't understand what I say, because you cannot accept my
teaching. 44You belong to your father the devil,
and you want to do what he wants. He was a
murderer from the beginning and was against the
truth, because there is no truth in him. When he
tells a lie, he shows what he is really like, because
he is a liar and the father of lies. 45But because I
speak the truth, you don't believe me. 46Can any
of you prove that I am guilty of sin? If I am telling
the truth, why don't you believe me? 47The person who belongs to God accepts what God says.
But you don't accept what God says, because you
don't belong to God."

Jesus Is Greater than Abraham

48The Jews answered, "We say you are a Samaritan[d] and have a demon[d] in you. Are we not
right?"
49Jesus answered, "I have no demon in me. I
give honor to my Father, but you dishonor me. 50I
am not trying to get honor for myself. There is
One who wants this honor for me, and he is the
judge. 51I tell you the truth, whoever obeys my
teaching will never die."
52The Jews said to Jesus, "Now we know that
you have a demon in you! Even Abraham and the
prophets[d] died. But you say, 'Whoever obeys my
teaching will never die.' 53Do you think you are
greater than our father Abraham, who died? And
the prophets died, too. Who do you think you
are?"
54Jesus answered, "If I give honor to myself,
that honor is worth nothing. The One who gives
me honor is my Father, and you say he is your
God. 55You don't really know him, but I know
him. If I said I did not know him, I would be a
liar like you. But I do know him, and I obey what
he says. 56Your father Abraham was very happy
that he would see my day. He saw that day and
was glad."
57The Jews said to him, "You have never seen
Abraham! You are not even fifty years old."
58Jesus answered, "I tell you the truth, before
Abraham was even born, I am!" 59When Jesus
said this, the people picked up stones to throw at
him. But Jesus hid himself, and then he left the
Temple.[d]

Jesus Heals a Man Born Blind

9 As Jesus was walking along, he saw a man
who had been born blind. 2His followers
asked him, "Teacher, whose sin caused this man
to be born blind—his own sin or his parents'
sin?"
3Jesus answered, "It is not this man's sin or his
parents' sin that made him be blind. This man
was born blind so that God's power could be
shown in him. 4While it is daytime, we must continue doing the work of the One who sent me.
Night is coming, when no one can work. 5While
I am in the world, I am the light of the world."
6After Jesus said this, he spit on the ground and
made some mud with it and put the mud on the
man's eyes. 7Then he told the man, "Go and wash
in the Pool of Siloam." (Siloam means Sent.) So
the man went, washed, and came back seeing.
8The neighbors and some people who had earlier seen this man begging said, "Isn't this the
same man who used to sit and beg?"
9Some said, "He is the one," but others said,
"No, he only looks like him."
The man himself said, "I am the man."
10They asked, "How did you get your sight?"
11He answered, "The man named Jesus made
some mud and put it on my eyes. Then he told me
to go to Siloam and wash. So I went and washed,
and then I could see."
12They asked him, "Where is this man?"
"I don't know," he answered.

SIDELIGHT: Sending the blind man to wash in the Pool of Siloam would clearly have been symbolic for the people in Jesus' day (John 9:7). This pool was the source for water used for religious ceremonies. It was also Jerusalem's primary water source.

Pharisees Question the Healing

13Then the people took to the Pharisees[d] the

SIN

Blind Side

"I actually thought no one could tell I was drinking." Josh Perez studied his hands for a moment before he looked up at the group. "I got caught the first time I got drunk. I thought about quitting then. But my friends were into it, so I kept drinking with them."

Josh paused and took a deep breath. Then he continued, "Before long, I didn't need them as an excuse to drink. I enjoyed it so much I drank every chance I could." A few other teenagers in the group nodded knowingly. Josh relaxed a bit.

"I figured I was maintaining pretty well. I kept my position on the baseball team and my grades hadn't slipped too far. I tried to be careful with curfews and covering the alcohol on my breath.

"One day, my dad made some comment to me about how I was gonna end up just like him. That shocked me! Dad's an alcoholic. And it scared me.

"So I talked to my youth leader, and he suggested I get into this support group," Josh said as his eyes swept over the teenagers seated in a circle. "I really thought I had everyone fooled. I guess the only one blind to my drinking problem was me."

Jesus encountered blind people of all kinds. Read **John 9:1–41** to see the key to true sight.

- What are the similarities and differences between Josh's blindness and the Pharisees' blindness? Between Josh's blindness and that of the man blind from birth?
- What does this Bible passage tell us about being blind to sin?

CONSIDER . . .

- asking God to open your eyes to areas where you are blind to sin.
- asking a good friend to tell you about a blind spot in your life, then working to change it.

FOR MORE, SEE . . .

- Isaiah 6:9–10 (p. 623)
- Matthew 15:1–20 (p. 934)

- Ephesians 5:6–15 (p. 1224)

man who had been blind. 14The day Jesus had made mud and healed his eyes was a Sabbath[d] day. 15So now the Pharisees asked the man, "How did you get your sight?"

He answered, "He put mud on my eyes, I washed, and now I see."

16So some of the Pharisees were saying, "This man does not keep the Sabbath day, so he is not from God."

But others said, "A man who is a sinner can't do miracles[d] like these." So they could not agree with each other.

17They asked the man again, "What do you say about him since it was your eyes he opened?"

The man answered, "He is a prophet."[d]

18The Jews did not believe that he had been blind and could now see again. So they sent for the man's parents 19and asked them, "Is this your son who you say was born blind? Then how does he now see?"

20His parents answered, "We know that this is our son and that he was born blind. 21But we don't know how he can now see. We don't know who opened his eyes. Ask him. He is old enough to speak for himself." 22His parents said this because they were afraid of the Jews, who had already decided that anyone who said Jesus was the Christ[d] would be put out of the synagogue.[d] 23That is why his parents said, "He is old enough. Ask him."

24So for the second time, they called the man who had been blind. They said, "You should give God the glory by telling the truth. We know that this man is a sinner."

25He answered, "I don't know if he is a sinner. One thing I do know: I was blind, and now I see."

26They asked, "What did he do to you? How did he make you see again?"

27He answered, "I already told you, and you didn't listen. Why do you want to hear it again? Do you want to become his followers, too?"

28Then they insulted him and said, "You are his follower, but we are followers of Moses. 29We know that God spoke to Moses, but we don't even know where this man comes from."

30The man answered, "This is a very strange thing. You don't know where he comes from, and yet he opened my eyes. 31We all know that God does not listen to sinners, but he listens to anyone who worships and obeys him. 32Nobody has ever heard of anyone giving sight to a man born blind. 33If this man were not from God, he could do nothing."

34They answered, "You were born full of sin! Are you trying to teach us?" And they threw him out.

Spiritual Blindness

35When Jesus heard that they had thrown him out, Jesus found him and said, "Do you believe in the Son of Man?"[d]

36He asked, "Who is the Son of Man, sir, so that I can believe in him?"

37Jesus said to him, "You have seen him. The Son of Man is the one talking with you."

38He said, "Lord, I believe!" Then the man worshiped Jesus.

39Jesus said, "I came into this world so that the world could be judged. I came so that the blind[n] would see and so that those who see will become blind."

40Some of the Pharisees[d] who were nearby heard Jesus say this and asked, "Are you saying we are blind, too?"

41Jesus said, "If you were blind, you would not be guilty of sin. But since you keep saying you see, your guilt remains."

The Shepherd and His Sheep

10 Jesus said, "I tell you the truth, the person who does not enter the sheepfold by the door, but climbs in some other way, is a thief and a robber. 2The one who enters by the door is the shepherd of the sheep. 3The one who guards the door opens it for him. And the sheep listen to the voice of the shepherd. He calls his own sheep by name and leads them out. 4When he brings all his sheep out, he goes ahead of them, and they follow him because they know his voice. 5But they will never follow a stranger. They will run away from him because they don't know his voice." 6Jesus told the people this story, but they did not understand what it meant.

SIDELIGHT: When Jesus described a sheepfold in John 10:1–6, his listeners would have understood immediately, since sheep were the most common animal of that region. Sheepfolds consisted of low buildings to protect the flock during bad weather, and an outdoor pen that had a wall around it. The wall was covered with sharp thorny brush to keep out thieves and predators.

Jesus Is the Good Shepherd

7So Jesus said again, "I tell you the truth, I am the door for the sheep. 8All the people who came before me were thieves and robbers. The sheep did not listen to them. 9I am the door, and the person who enters through me will be saved and

blind Jesus is talking about people who are spiritually blind, not physically blind.

will be able to come in and go out and find pasture. [10]A thief comes to steal and kill and destroy, but I came to give life—life in all its fullness.

[11]"I am the good shepherd. The good shepherd gives his life for the sheep. [12]The worker who is paid to keep the sheep is different from the shepherd who owns them. When the worker sees a wolf coming, he runs away and leaves the sheep alone. Then the wolf attacks the sheep and scatters them. [13]The man runs away because he is only a paid worker and does not really care about the sheep.

[14-15]"I am the good shepherd. I know my sheep, as the Father knows me. And my sheep know me, as I know the Father. I give my life for the sheep. [16]I have other sheep that are not in this flock, and I must bring them also. They will listen to my voice, and there will be one flock and one shepherd. [17]The Father loves me because I give my life so that I can take it back again. [18]No one takes it away from me; I give my own life freely. I have the right to give my life, and I have the right to take it back. This is what my Father commanded me to do."

[19]Again the Jews did not agree with each other because of these words of Jesus. [20]Many of them said, "A demon[d] has come into him and made him crazy. Why listen to him?"

[21]But others said, "A man who is crazy with a demon does not say things like this. Can a demon open the eyes of the blind?"

Jesus Is Rejected

[22]The time came for the Feast[d] of Dedication at Jerusalem. It was winter, [23]and Jesus was walking in the Temple[d] in Solomon's Porch.[d] [24]The Jews gathered around him and said, "How long will you make us wonder about you? If you are the Christ,[d] tell us plainly."

[25]Jesus answered, "I told you already, but you did not believe. The miracles[d] I do in my Father's name show who I am. [26]But you don't believe, because you are not my sheep. [27]My sheep listen to my voice; I know them, and they follow me. [28]I give them eternal life, and they will never die, and no one can steal them out of my hand. [29]My Father gave my sheep to me. He is greater than all, and no person can steal my sheep out of my Father's hand. [30]The Father and I are one."

GOD'S LOVE

Shepherds and Sheep

Sheep can be incredibly smart. For instance, most sheep can distinguish their shepherd's voice from any other voice. A few exceptional sheep can even be taught how to come when called and how to sit like a dog (well, almost) on command.

On the other hand, sheep can seem completely brainless. It's not unusual to see sheep trying to walk through a barbed wire fence or casually strolling straight off the edge of a cliff. To make matters worse, where one goes, others tend to follow.

The hardest thing about being a shepherd is keeping the sheep where they should be. Certain sheep seem determined to go where they could be harmed. Modern shepherds use a device called a "hobbler" on sheep's hind legs to keep them from moving freely. Before hobblers were invented, shepherds often broke a sheep's leg to keep it from the great danger of wandering away from the flock. It was all part of caring for the sheep.

Jesus seemed to understand sheep well. Read **John 10:1–30** to discover how Jesus saw his followers as sheep and himself as their shepherd.

- How is Jesus' care of his people similar to the care of a shepherd for sheep?
- How are people today—including yourself—like sheep?

CONSIDER . . .

- underlining the things in this passage that the shepherd does and circling the things sheep do. Then turn to Psalm 23, p. 495, and do the same thing.
- reading A Shepherd Looks at Psalm 23 by W. Phillip Keller (Zondervan) to learn more about sheep and their shepherd.

FOR MORE, SEE . . .

- Psalm 23 (p. 495)
- Ezekiel 34:11–31 (p. 790)
- Luke 15:1–7 (p. 1034)

[31]Again the Jews picked up stones to kill Jesus.
[32]But he said to them, "I have done many good
works from the Father. Which of these good
works are you killing me for?"

[33]The Jews answered, "We are not killing you
because of any good work you did, but because
you speak against God. You are only a human, but
you say you are the same as God!"

[34]Jesus answered, "It is written in your law that
God said, 'I said, you are gods.'[n] [35]This Scripture[d] called those people gods who received
God's message, and Scripture is always true. [36]So
why do you say that I speak against God because
I said, 'I am God's Son'? I am the one God chose
and sent into the world. [37]If I don't do what my
Father does, then don't believe me. [38]But if I do
what my Father does, even though you don't believe in me, believe what I do. Then you will
know and understand that the Father is in me and
I am in the Father."

[39]They tried to take Jesus again, but he escaped
from them.

[40]Then he went back across the Jordan River to
the place where John had first baptized. Jesus
stayed there, [41]and many people came to him and
said, "John never did a miracle, but everything
John said about this man is true." [42]And in that
place many believed in Jesus.

The Death of Lazarus

11 A man named Lazarus was sick. He lived
in the town of Bethany, where Mary and
her sister Martha lived. [2]Mary was the woman
who later put perfume on the Lord and wiped his
feet with her hair. Mary's brother was Lazarus,
the man who was now sick. [3]So Mary and Martha
sent someone to tell Jesus, "Lord, the one you
love is sick."

[4]When Jesus heard this, he said, "This sickness
will not end in death. It is for the glory of God,
to bring glory to the Son of God." [5]Jesus loved
Martha and her sister and Lazarus. [6]But when he
heard that Lazarus was sick, he stayed where he
was for two more days. [7]Then Jesus said to his
followers, "Let's go back to Judea."

[8]The followers said, "But Teacher, the Jews

'I . . . gods.' Quotation from Psalm 82:6.

DEATH

Sharing Sadness

They went through the church doors, signed the guest registry and made their way to a back pew. Neither of them knew Polly's father, but they had decided to go to his funeral because Polly Brinkman was their classmate.

It wasn't a comfortable situation for Steve Parks or Don Shackelford, but they couldn't begin to imagine how tough it must have been for Polly. As they filed past the open coffin after the service, Polly looked up at them and kind of smiled and cried at the same time.

The next Thursday Polly came back to school and made it a point to talk with Don and Steve before class. "I really want to thank you guys for being at my dad's funeral Saturday. It means a lot to me," Polly said.

"We didn't know what else we could do to help," Don offered.

"That was enough," Polly said. "Just knowing I had friends there made a difference. I didn't feel so alone. Your being around made the service easier to take. It was like you shared some of the hurt."

Jesus understood what it was like to grieve with friends. Read **John 11:1–45** to see how Jesus shared his friends' grief and how Jesus' presence at a funeral made a difference.

- How did Steve's and Don's actions compare with Jesus' actions?
- What does Jesus' reactions to Lazarus's death teach us about dealing with sadness?

CONSIDER . . .

- telling a trusted friend about the death of someone who was important to you. Openly express your emotions.
- asking your pastor or youth leader to help you and a group of friends devise things you can do when a friend's family member dies.

FOR MORE, SEE . . .

- Isaiah 61:1–3 (p. 680)
- Romans 12:9–15 (p. 1157)
- Revelation 21:1–4 (p. 1347)

there tried to stone you to death only a short time ago. Now you want to go back there?"

9Jesus answered, "Are there not twelve hours in the day? If anyone walks in the daylight, he will not stumble, because he can see by this world's light. 10But if anyone walks at night, he stumbles because there is no light to help him see."

11After Jesus said this, he added, "Our friend Lazarus has fallen asleep, but I am going there to wake him."

12The followers said, "But Lord, if he is only asleep, he will be all right."

13Jesus meant that Lazarus was dead, but his followers thought he meant Lazarus was really sleeping. 14So then Jesus said plainly, "Lazarus is dead. 15And I am glad for your sakes I was not there so that you may believe. But let's go to him now."

16Then Thomas (the one called Didymus) said to the other followers, "Let us also go so that we can die with him."

Jesus in Bethany

17When Jesus arrived, he learned that Lazarus had already been dead and in the tomb for four days. 18Bethany was about two miles from Jerusalem. 19Many of the Jews had come there to comfort Martha and Mary about their brother.

20When Martha heard that Jesus was coming, she went out to meet him, but Mary stayed home. 21Martha said to Jesus, "Lord, if you had been here, my brother would not have died. 22But I know that even now God will give you anything you ask."

23Jesus said, "Your brother will rise and live again."

24Martha answered, "I know that he will rise and live again in the resurrection[n] on the last day."

25Jesus said to her, "I am the resurrection and the life. Those who believe in me will have life even if they die. 26And everyone who lives and believes in me will never die. Martha, do you believe this?"

27Martha answered, "Yes, Lord. I believe that you are the Christ,[d] the Son of God, the One coming to the world."

Jesus Cries

28After Martha said this, she went back and talked to her sister Mary alone. Martha said, "The Teacher is here and he is asking for you." 29When Mary heard this, she got up quickly and went to Jesus. 30Jesus had not yet come into the town but was still at the place where Martha had met him. 31The Jews were with Mary in the house, comforting her. When they saw her stand and leave quickly, they followed her, thinking she was going to the tomb to cry there.

32But Mary went to the place where Jesus was. When she saw him, she fell at his feet and said, "Lord, if you had been here, my brother would not have died."

33When Jesus saw Mary crying and the Jews who came with her also crying, he was upset and was deeply troubled. 34He asked, "Where did you bury him?"

"Come and see, Lord," they said.

35Jesus cried.

36So the Jews said, "See how much he loved him."

37But some of them said, "If Jesus opened the eyes of the blind man, why couldn't he keep Lazarus from dying?"

Jesus Raises Lazarus

38Again feeling very upset, Jesus came to the tomb. It was a cave with a large stone covering the entrance. 39Jesus said, "Move the stone away."

Martha, the sister of the dead man, said, "But, Lord, it has been four days since he died. There will be a bad smell."

SIDELIGHT: Lazarus had been dead four days before Jesus arrived (John 11:39). That would have made bringing him back to life particularly miraculous to people in Jesus' day. They believed that a soul stayed with a body for three days and then left.

40Then Jesus said to her, "Didn't I tell you that if you believed you would see the glory of God?"

41So they moved the stone away from the entrance. Then Jesus looked up and said, "Father, I thank you that you heard me. 42I know that you always hear me, but I said these things because of the people here around me. I want them to believe that you sent me." 43After Jesus said this, he cried out in a loud voice, "Lazarus, come out!" 44The dead man came out, his hands and feet wrapped with pieces of cloth, and a cloth around his face.

Jesus said to them, "Take the cloth off of him and let him go."

The Plan to Kill Jesus

45Many of the Jews, who had come to visit Mary and saw what Jesus did, believed in him. 46But some of them went to the Pharisees[d] and told them what Jesus had done. 47Then the lead-

resurrection Being raised from the dead to live again.

ing priests and Pharisees called a meeting of the
Jewish council. They asked, "What should we do?
This man is doing many miracles.[d] 48If we let him
continue doing these things, everyone will believe
in him. Then the Romans will come and take
away our Temple[d] and our nation."
49One of the men there was Caiaphas, the high
priest that year. He said, "You people know nothing! 50You don't realize that it is better for one
man to die for the people than for the whole nation to be destroyed."
51Caiaphas did not think of this himself. As high
priest that year, he was really prophesying[d] that
Jesus would die for the Jewish nation 52and for
God's scattered children to bring them all together and make them one.
53That day they started planning to kill Jesus.
54So Jesus no longer traveled openly among the
Jews. He left there and went to a place near the
desert, to a town called Ephraim and stayed there
with his followers.
55It was almost time for the Jewish Passover[d]
Feast. Many from the country went up to Jerusalem before the Passover to do the special things
to make themselves pure. 56The people looked for
Jesus and stood in the Temple asking each other,
"Is he coming to the Feast? What do you think?"
57But the leading priests and the Pharisees had
given orders that if anyone knew where Jesus
was, he must tell them. Then they could arrest
him.

Jesus with Friends in Bethany

12 Six days before the Passover[d] Feast,
Jesus went to Bethany, where Lazarus
lived. (Lazarus is the man Jesus raised from the
dead.) 2There they had a dinner for Jesus. Martha
served the food, and Lazarus was one of the people eating with Jesus. 3Mary brought in a pint of
very expensive perfume made from pure nard.[d]
She poured the perfume on Jesus' feet, and then
she wiped his feet with her hair. And the sweet
smell from the perfume filled the whole house.
4Judas Iscariot, one of Jesus' followers who
would later turn against him, was there. Judas
said, 5"This perfume was worth three hundred
coins.[n] Why wasn't it sold and the money given
to the poor?" 6But Judas did not really care about
the poor; he said this because he was a thief. He
was the one who kept the money box, and he
often stole from it.
7Jesus answered, "Leave her alone. It was right

coins One coin, a denarius, was the average pay for one day's work.

SERVICE

Life on the Altar

Chuckie Johnston could be making a lot of money selling drugs. Or he could have a steady job as a bodyguard in his old neighborhood. Instead, he lives and works with former addicts at Boston Outreach, a Christian rehabilitation program.

Chuckie could have been part of a network that destroyed thousands of lives. Instead, he is helping hundreds of people break the bondage of drug abuse.

Gertrude Falk could have been a school administrator in a good school in the United States. She could have lived in a beautiful home and retired with a great pension. Rather, she has spent all of her adult life living in a modest home on a little island in Haiti. Thousands of kids over the years have received an education, medical care, adequate nutrition, and a chance to hear about Jesus Christ because of Gertrude's gifts.

Chuckie and Gertrude have given their lives to serve others. They have no regrets, because they know the secret of service—gratitude. In **John 12:1–11**, we read that Mary also knew the secret of service.

- In what ways is Mary's service similar to or different from Chuckie's and Gertrude's service to the Lord?
- If Jesus were in your house today, how might you serve him?

CONSIDER. . .

- listing all the things God has done for you and thanking him for those things.
- becoming involved in an ongoing act of service to others by joining a volunteer service organization.

FOR MORE, SEE. . .

- Isaiah 1:11–17 (p. 617)
- Romans 12:1–2 (p. 1157)
- James 1:26–27 (p. 1294)

for her to save this perfume for today, the day for
me to be prepared for burial. 8You will always
have the poor with you, but you will not always
have me."

The Plot Against Lazarus

9A large crowd of Jews heard that Jesus was in
Bethany. So they went there to see not only Jesus
but Lazarus, whom Jesus raised from the dead.
10So the leading priests made plans to kill Lazarus,
too. 11Because of Lazarus many of the Jews were
leaving them and believing in Jesus.

Jesus Enters Jerusalem

12The next day a great crowd who had come to
Jerusalem for the Passover[d] Feast heard that Jesus
was coming there. 13So they took branches of
palm trees and went out to meet Jesus, shouting,

"Praise[n] God!
God bless the One who comes in the name
of the Lord!
God bless the King of Israel!" *Psalm 118:25-26*

14Jesus found a colt and sat on it. This was as
the Scripture[d] says,

15"Don't be afraid, people of Jerusalem!
Your king is coming,
sitting on the colt of a donkey." *Zechariah 9:9*

16The followers of Jesus did not understand this
at first. But after Jesus was raised to glory, they
remembered that this had been written about him
and that they had done these things to him.

People Tell About Jesus

17There had been many people with Jesus
when he raised Lazarus from the dead and told
him to come out of the tomb. Now they were
telling others about what Jesus did. 18Many people went out to meet Jesus, because they had
heard about this miracle.[d] 19So the Pharisees[d] said
to each other, "You can see that nothing is going
right for us. Look! The whole world is following
him."

Jesus Talks About His Death

20There were some Greek people, too, who
came to Jerusalem to worship at the Passover[d]
Feast. 21They went to Philip, who was from Bethsaida in Galilee, and said, "Sir, we would like to
see Jesus." 22Philip told Andrew, and then Andrew and Philip told Jesus.

23Jesus said to them, "The time has come for
the Son of Man[d] to receive his glory. 24I tell you
the truth, a grain of wheat must fall to the ground
and die to make many seeds. But if it never dies,
it remains only a single seed. 25Those who love
their lives will lose them, but those who hate their
lives in this world will keep true life forever.
26Whoever serves me must follow me. Then my
servant will be with me everywhere I am. My
Father will honor anyone who serves me.

27"Now I am very troubled. Should I say, 'Father, save me from this time'? No, I came to this
time so I could suffer. 28Father, bring glory to your
name!"

Then a voice came from heaven, "I have
brought glory to it, and I will do it again."
29The crowd standing there, who heard the
voice, said it was thunder.

But others said, "An angel has spoken to him."

30Jesus said, "That voice was for your sake, not
mine. 31Now is the time for the world to be
judged; now the ruler of this world will be
thrown down. 32If I am lifted up from the earth,
I will draw all people toward me." 33Jesus said this
to show how he would die.

34The crowd said, "We have heard from the
law that the Christ[d] will live forever. So why do
you say, 'The Son of Man must be lifted up'? Who
is this 'Son of Man'?"

35Then Jesus said, "The light will be with you
for a little longer, so walk while you have the
light. Then the darkness will not catch you. If you
walk in the darkness, you will not know where
you are going. 36Believe in the light while you still
have it so that you will become children of light."
When Jesus had said this, he left and hid himself
from them.

Some People Won't Believe in Jesus

37Though Jesus had done many miracles[d] in
front of the people, they still did not believe in
him. 38This was to bring about what Isaiah the
prophet[d] had said:

"Lord, who believed what we told them?
Who saw the Lord's power in this?"
Isaiah 53:1

39This is why the people could not believe: Isaiah
also had said,

40"He has blinded their eyes,
and he has closed their minds.
Otherwise they would see with their eyes
and understand in their minds
and come back to me and be healed."
Isaiah 6:10

41Isaiah said this because he saw Jesus' glory and
spoke about him.

42But many believed in Jesus, even many of the
leaders. But because of the Pharisees,[d] they did
not say they believed in him for fear they would
be put out of the synagogue.[d] 43They loved praise
from people more than praise from God.

44Then Jesus cried out, "Whoever believes in

Praise Literally, "Hosanna," a Hebrew word used at first in praying to God for help, but at this time it was probably a shout of joy used in praising God or his Messiah.

me is really believing in the One who sent me.
45Whoever sees me sees the One who sent me. 46I
have come as light into the world so that whoever
believes in me would not stay in darkness.
47"Anyone who hears my words and does not
obey them, I do not judge, because I did not come
to judge the world, but to save the world. 48There
is a judge for those who refuse to believe in me
and do not accept my words. The word I have
taught will be their judge on the last day. 49The
things I taught were not from myself. The Father
who sent me told me what to say and what to
teach. 50And I know that eternal life comes from
what the Father commands. So whatever I say is
what the Father told me to say."

Jesus Washes His Followers' Feet

13 It was almost time for the Jewish Passover[d] Feast. Jesus knew that it was time
for him to leave this world and go back to the
Father. He had always loved those who were his
own in the world, and he loved them all the way
to the end.
2Jesus and his followers were at the evening
meal. The devil had already persuaded Judas Iscariot, the son of Simon, to turn against Jesus.
3Jesus knew that the Father had given him power
over everything and that he had come from God
and was going back to God. 4So during the meal
Jesus stood up and took off his outer clothing.
Taking a towel, he wrapped it around his waist.
5Then he poured water into a bowl and began to
wash the followers' feet, drying them with the
towel that was wrapped around him.
6Jesus came to Simon Peter, who said to him,
"Lord, are you going to wash my feet?"
7Jesus answered, "You don't understand now
what I am doing, but you will understand later."
8Peter said, "No, you will never wash my feet."
Jesus answered, "If I don't wash your feet, you
are not one of my people."
9Simon Peter answered, "Lord, then wash not
only my feet, but wash my hands and my head,
too!"
10Jesus said, "After a person has had a bath, his
whole body is clean. He needs only to wash his
feet. And you men are clean,[d] but not all of you."
11Jesus knew who would turn against him, and
that is why he said, "Not all of you are clean."
12When he had finished washing their feet, he

DEATH

Life From the Ashes

Forest fires swept through nearly half of Yellowstone National Park's 2.2 million acres in the summer of 1988. At first, it seemed life in the park could never be the same. The fire seemed like a total disaster.

But it wasn't. Foresters pointed out that lodgepole pine trees had cones on them that would only open under intense heat—almost as though they were designed to respond to a forest fire. Yellowstone's dry climate kept dead wood from decaying quickly, so the ashes from the fire provided nutrients to the ground that could actually mean better growth for years to come. Bluebirds and woodpeckers would benefit from open areas the fire had created. Other animals would flourish with the nearly tenfold increase in plant species that the newly fortified and uncovered earth could offer.

No one at Yellowstone looks forward to forest fires. But it is known that fires, however devastating they seem, don't mean the end of things.

The devastation of death can be sudden and tragic—like the devastation of a forest fire. But new life can result. Read **John 12:20–36** to discover what Jesus said about death and new growth.

- How might an ecologist's attitude toward forest fires be like Jesus' attitude toward death?
- What does the Bible passage say to you about death?

CONSIDER . . .

- writing on a sheet of paper about an area of your life in which you need to give something up and then burying the paper in your backyard. A week later, dig it up and evaluate your progress in letting go.
- walking through a park or forest to notice examples in nature of how death gives way to new growth.

FOR MORE, SEE . . .

- Ecclesiastes 3:1–8 (p. 600)
- 2 Corinthians 4:16—5:10 (p. 1196)
- 1 John 1:5–7 (p. 1316)

put on his clothes and sat down again. He asked,
"Do you understand what I have just done for
you? 13You call me 'Teacher' and 'Lord,' and you
are right, because that is what I am. 14If I, your
Lord and Teacher, have washed your feet, you
also should wash each other's feet. 15I did this as
an example so that you should do as I have done
for you. 16I tell you the truth, a servant is not
greater than his master. A messenger is not
greater than the one who sent him. 17If you know
these things, you will be happy if you do them.
18"I am not talking about all of you. I know
those I have chosen. But this is to bring about
what the Scripture[d] said: 'The man who ate at my
table has turned against me.'[n] 19I am telling you
this now before it happens so that when it happens, you will believe that I am he. 20I tell you the
truth, whoever accepts anyone I send also accepts
me. And whoever accepts me also accepts the
One who sent me."

Jesus Talks About His Death

21After Jesus said this, he was very troubled. He
said openly, "I tell you the truth, one of you will
turn against me."
22The followers all looked at each other, because they did not know whom Jesus was talking
about. 23One of the followers sitting[n] next to

'The man . . . me.' Quotation from Psalm 41:9.
sitting Literally, "lying." The people of that time ate lying down and leaning on one arm.

SERVICE

The Lowly Star

Jerry Richardson was an all-state running back and linebacker for a high school football team that was considered one of the best in the nation. He was fast. He was remarkably strong. And opposing players hated to see him walk onto the field.

Jerry's teammate, Scott Cunningham, on the other hand, was nothing special on the football field. He played Jerry's same position on offense—running back. He made the team only because the head coach found a place for every player who lasted through the rigorous two-a-day practices. Scott boasted few athletic skills, but he did have the courage to pick himself up after each ferocious hit and do it all again.

Since he rarely played in games, Scott never knew the thrill of the crowd chanting his name after a big play. What he heard, most often, was "Jer-ry! Jer-ry! Jer-ry!"

That's why what happened at the yearbook-signing party after Scott and Jerry's senior year was so remarkable. Scott saw Jerry walking toward him with a smile on his face.

Softly Jerry said, "I'd like to sign your yearbook, Scott. Would you sign mine?"

Scott nervously handed over his yearbook. A couple of minutes later, Jerry handed it back, smiled and squeezed Scott's shoulder. Scott never saw Jerry again. But he will always remember what Jerry wrote in his yearbook: "You have to be the greatest influence on me because of the size of your heart. You are the best player I know, from the standpoint of desire and heart. Glad to have you on my side. Luck always, Jerry."

Just as Jerry humbled himself in front of his classmates, Jesus humbled himself and washed his disciples' feet—a task normally reserved for servants, not kings. Read about it in **John 13:1–17**.

- How was Jerry's note to Scott similar to Jesus' washing the disciple's feet?
- At first, some of Jesus' disciples were uncomfortable with Jesus washing their feet. How would you feel if someone like Jerry washed your feet or did something equal to that?

CONSIDER . . .

- thinking about someone in your life who could use some encouragement. Write a note to that person, listing the qualities you appreciate about him or her. Sign the note and then secretly slip it into his or her locker or notebook.
- planning a get-together for your friends and inviting someone who is normally not invited to parties or events.

FOR MORE, SEE . . .

- Nehemiah 5:1–13 (p. 431)
- Matthew 20:20–28 (p. 944)
- Galatians 5:13–15 (p. 1212)

Jesus was the follower Jesus loved. 24Simon Peter
motioned to him to ask Jesus whom he was talking about.
25That follower leaned closer to Jesus and
asked, "Lord, who is it?"
26Jesus answered, "I will dip this bread into the
dish. The man I give it to is the man who will turn
against me." So Jesus took a piece of bread,
dipped it, and gave it to Judas Iscariot, the son of
Simon. 27As soon as Judas took the bread, Satan
entered him. Jesus said to him, "The thing that
you will do—do it quickly." 28No one at the table
understood why Jesus said this to Judas. 29Since
he was the one who kept the money box, some
of the followers thought Jesus was telling him to
buy what was needed for the feast or to give
something to the poor.
30Judas took the bread Jesus gave him and immediately went out. It was night.
31When Judas was gone, Jesus said, "Now the
Son of Man[d] receives his glory, and God receives
glory through him. 32If God receives glory
through him, then God will give glory to the Son

SIDELIGHT: Parents may tell kids to wash their hands before dinner, but they probably don't insist on clean feet. In Jesus' day, washing feet was important, since people wore sandals and their feet got sore from walking everywhere. But, more importantly, washing a guest's feet was a sign of hospitality (John 13:1–20). Try it next time you have a party!

FRIENDS

The Tough Choice

Melissa Spencer had a secret problem. Two months earlier, she and her boyfriend Matt had had sexual intercourse. It was her first time. Now she was pregnant. And Matt, immature and desperate, was pressuring her to "get rid" of the baby. When Melissa refused, he beat her. Life seemed dark and hopeless to her. She was afraid to tell anyone about her problems, especially her single mom.

But Melissa's best friend, Jessica Bullard, knew, and that secret tormented Jessica. Melissa had made Jessica promise to keep quiet about her secret.

"If you tell anyone," warned Melissa, "I'll hate you forever." But Jessica could barely contain her rage when she saw how Matt was abusing Melissa.

Though she knew she was risking a strong friendship, Jessica decided to get help for Melissa before it was too late. She asked to meet with Melissa's aunt and uncle and, sobbing, told them Melissa's story.

They thanked Jessica for her honesty and courage, then they found Melissa and gently confronted her with the truth. After Melissa's initial shock, she broke down crying, asking them for help.

Melissa was angry with Jessica for violating her trust. But in less than a week, she forgave Jessica and told her how relieved she was that Jessica had told.

Melissa got the help she needed. And she gave birth to a healthy little girl who was adopted by a couple who could never have children.

Just as Jessica risked something important to her for the good of her friend, Jesus encourages those who follow him to love each other with a self-sacrificing love. Read about this kind of love in **John 13:31–35**.

- How is Jessica's decision to tell Melissa's secret similar to Jesus' decision to go to the cross?
- What's one way you can love your best friend the way Jesus loved his disciples?

CONSIDER . . .

- talking to a friend who has been doing something that concerns you.
- making a pact with a friend, promising each other to be open to criticism and direction regarding the choices you each make in life.

FOR MORE, SEE . . .

- 1 Samuel 20 (p. 263)
- Proverbs 17:17 (p. 582)
- 1 John 4:7–8 (p. 1319)

through himself. And God will give him glory quickly."

33Jesus said, "My children, I will be with you only a little longer. You will look for me, and what I told the Jews, I tell you now: Where I am going you cannot come.

34"I give you a new command: Love each other. You must love each other as I have loved you. 35All people will know that you are my followers if you love each other."

Peter Will Say He Doesn't Know Jesus

36Simon Peter asked Jesus, "Lord, where are you going?"

Jesus answered, "Where I am going you cannot follow now, but you will follow later."

37Peter asked, "Lord, why can't I follow you now? I am ready to die for you!"

38Jesus answered, "Are you ready to die for me? I tell you the truth, before the rooster crows, you will say three times that you don't know me."

Jesus Comforts His Followers

14 Jesus said, "Don't let your hearts be troubled. Trust in God, and trust in me. 2There are many rooms in my Father's house; I would not tell you this if it were not true. I am going there to prepare a place for you. 3After I go and prepare a place for you, I will come back and take you to be with me so that you may be where I am. 4You know the way to the place where I am going."

5Thomas said to Jesus, "Lord, we don't know where you are going. So how can we know the way?"

6Jesus answered, "I am the way, and the truth, and the life. The only way to the Father is through me. 7If you really knew me, you would know my Father, too. But now you do know him, and you have seen him."

8Philip said to him, "Lord, show us the Father. That is all we need."

DOUBT

Riding Out the Storm

Robin Graham is the youngest person in history to sail around the world alone. But success didn't come easily for him. He left on his three-year odyssey as a sixteen-year-old boy thrill-seeker. Adventure was like a drug to him.

His trip changed something deep inside him. A violent storm almost capsized his little sloop, the Dove. In the midst of the torrent, the Dove's mast snapped in two, and Robin barely survived a waterspout—a water-filled tornado.

But that wasn't the worst of it. When his boat entered the doldrums, a windless, currentless part of the ocean near the equator, Robin almost went crazy with despair and doubt. At one point, he completely gave up hope that he would ever make it out of the doldrums, so he splashed kerosene all over his boat and set it on fire. Fortunately, Robin snapped to his senses and doused the fire before it did serious damage.

Three years after his departure, Robin sailed into the Los Angeles harbor to cheering crowds, honking cars, and blasting steam whistles. He had made it. And, more importantly, he had wrestled two great enemies—doubt and despair—and found himself stronger as a result.

Robin Graham is a courageous hero. But he had crippling doubts about himself, just like the "heroes of the faith" who first followed Jesus. Read about them in **John 14:1–14**.

- How were Robin's doubts like the doubts the disciples experienced after Jesus told them he was leaving them?
- What doubts have you had about your life that seem impossible for God to solve?

CONSIDER . . .

- writing on paper, "The one thing I doubt the most is. . ." and finishing the sentence. Then ask a friend to pray with you about your doubt.
- writing out one nagging doubt you have about God. Then tape your "doubt" to a specific date on a calendar at least a week from today. Ask God to give you insight into your doubt by that date.

FOR MORE, SEE . . .

- Jonah (p. 857)
- Matthew 14:22–33 (p. 934)
- James 1:2–8 (p. 1294)

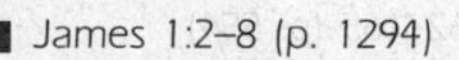

9Jesus answered, "I have been with you a long
time now. Do you still not know me, Philip?
Whoever has seen me has seen the Father. So
why do you say, 'Show us the Father'? 10Don't
you believe that I am in the Father and the Father
is in me? The words I say to you don't come from
me, but the Father lives in me and does his own
work. 11Believe me when I say that I am in the
Father and the Father is in me. Or believe because
of the miracles[d] I have done. 12I tell you the truth,
whoever believes in me will do the same things
that I do. Those who believe will do even greater
things than these, because I am going to the Father. 13And if you ask for anything in my name,
I will do it for you so that the Father's glory will
be shown through the Son. 14If you ask me for
anything in my name, I will do it.

The Promise of the Holy Spirit

15"If you love me, you will obey my commands. 16I will ask the Father, and he will give
you another Helper[n] to be with you forever—
17the Spirit[d] of truth. The world cannot accept
him, because it does not see him or know him.
But you know him, because he lives with you and
he will be in you.

18"I will not leave you all alone like orphans; I
will come back to you. 19In a little while the world
will not see me anymore, but you will see me.
Because I live, you will live, too. 20On that day

Helper "Counselor" or "Comforter." Jesus is talking about the Holy Spirit.

PEACE

The True Champion

Four decades after his death, an obscure Scottish sprinter named Eric Liddell became a household name after the Oscar-winning movie Chariots of Fire profiled his heroics in the 1924 Olympic Games. The movie told of Liddell's strong Christian convictions, his competitive spirit that was harnessed by his love for God, and his decision to drop out of the Olympic 100-meter dash because the race was scheduled for Sunday, a day he believed was to be a day of rest for Christians.

Later, Liddell shocked the sports world by competing in and winning the Olympic 400-meter race—an event he had not intended to enter. The actor who played Liddell in the film, Ian Charleson, said, "What I admired about him was his serenity. My whole personality changed during the time I was doing the part. I became very slow and laconic."

After his Olympic victory, Liddell returned to China where he continued his work as a Christian missionary. When war broke out, he and other Westerners were rounded up by Japanese troops and held as "civil internees." During Liddell's two years in the camp, he was cut off from his wife and children. Liddell worked long hours—with little complaint—to organize a sports and recreation program for teenagers. He also helped people in any way he could and tutored students at night.

Toward the end of the war, Liddell died fighting the onslaught of a brain tumor. He died the same way he always ran—fighting for every inch on the outside, but at peace inside.

Annie Buchan, a close friend, was with him when he died. Before slipping into a coma from which he would never recover, Eric told his friend, "Annie, it's complete surrender."

Eric Liddell knew by experience the kind of peace Jesus promises those who follow him. Read about that peace in **John 14:15–29**.

- Have you experienced the kind of peace Eric Liddell knew and Jesus talked about?
- What does the passage tell you about how to know God's peace? What's one thing in your life you feel you need peace about?

C O N S I D E R . . .

- watching for times you don't feel at peace, then stopping to pray for fifteen seconds.
- planning to take a few hours or even a day or two for a "personal retreat" with God. Spend the time reading the Bible, praying and worshiping.

F O R M O R E , S E E . . .

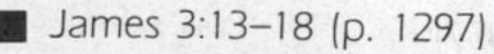

- Psalm 119:162–165 (p. 554)
- Philippians 4:6–9 (p. 1234)
- James 3:13–18 (p. 1297)

you will know that I am in my Father, and that
you are in me and I am in you. 21Those who know
my commands and obey them are the ones who
love me, and my Father will love those who love
me. I will love them and will show myself to
them."
22Then Judas (not Judas Iscariot) said, "But,
Lord, why do you plan to show yourself to us and
not to the rest of the world?"
23Jesus answered, "If people love me, they will
obey my teaching. My Father will love them, and
we will come to them and make our home with
them. 24Those who do not love me do not obey
my teaching. This teaching that you hear is not
really mine; it is from my Father, who sent me.
25"I have told you all these things while I am
with you. 26But the Helper will teach you everything and will cause you to remember all that I
told you. This Helper is the Holy Spirit whom the
Father will send in my name.
27"I leave you peace; my peace I give you. I do
not give it to you as the world does. So don't let
your hearts be troubled or afraid. 28You heard me
say to you, 'I am going, but I am coming back to
you.' If you loved me, you should be happy that
I am going back to the Father, because he is
greater than I am. 29I have told you this now, before it happens, so that when it happens, you will
believe. 30I will not talk with you much longer,
because the ruler of this world is coming. He has
no power over me, 31but the world must know
that I love the Father, so I do exactly what the
Father told me to do.
"Come now, let us go.

Jesus Is Like a Vine

15 "I am the true vine; my Father is the gardener. 2He cuts off every branch of mine
that does not produce fruit. And he trims and
cleans every branch that produces fruit so that it
will produce even more fruit. 3You are already
clean[d] because of the words I have spoken to you.
4Remain in me, and I will remain in you. A branch
cannot produce fruit alone but must remain in the
vine. In the same way, you cannot produce fruit
alone but must remain in me.
5"I am the vine, and you are the branches. If
any remain in me and I remain in them, they produce much fruit. But without me they can do
nothing. 6If any do not remain in me, they are like
a branch that is thrown away and then dies. People pick up dead branches, throw them into the
fire, and burn them. 7If you remain in me and
follow my teachings, you can ask anything you
want, and it will be given to you. 8You should
produce much fruit and show that you are my
followers, which brings glory to my Father. 9I
loved you as the Father loved me. Now remain in
my love. 10I have obeyed my Father's commands,
and I remain in his love. In the same way, if you
obey my commands, you will remain in my love.
11I have told you these things so that you can have
the same joy I have and so that your joy will be
the fullest possible joy.

SIDELIGHT: Jesus' listeners would have quickly understood Jesus' comparison of himself to the vine in John 15:1–11, since vineyards were common in Israel. Growing a good harvest of grapes required intensive, long-term work. Each year, the vines had to be pruned heavily, hoed, thinned, and sometimes irrigated. Without such care, the harvest would be poor and the grapes bitter.

12"This is my command: Love each other as I
have loved you. 13The greatest love a person can
show is to die for his friends. 14You are my friends
if you do what I command you. 15I no longer call
you servants, because a servant does not know
what his master is doing. But I call you friends,
because I have made known to you everything I
heard from my Father. 16You did not choose me;
I chose you. And I gave you this work: to go and
produce fruit, fruit that will last. Then the Father
will give you anything you ask for in my name.
17This is my command: Love each other.

Jesus Warns His Followers

18"If the world hates you, remember that it
hated me first. 19If you belonged to the world, it
would love you as it loves its own. But I have
chosen you out of the world, so you don't belong
to it. That is why the world hates you. 20Remem-
ber what I told you: A servant is not greater than
his master. If people did wrong to me, they will
do wrong to you, too. And if they obeyed my
teaching, they will obey yours, too. 21They will do
all this to you on account of me, because they do
not know the One who sent me. 22If I had not
come and spoken to them, they would not be
guilty of sin, but now they have no excuse for
their sin. 23Whoever hates me also hates my Father. 24I did works among them that no one else
has ever done. If I had not done these works, they
would not be guilty of sin. But now they have
seen what I have done, and yet they have hated
both me and my Father. 25But this happened so
that what is written in their law would be true:
'They hated me for no reason.'[n]

'They . . . reason.' These words could be from Psalm 35:19 or Psalm 69:4.

26"I will send you the Helper[n] from the Father; he is the Spirit of truth who comes from the
Father. When he comes, he will tell about me,
27and you also must tell people about me, because
you have been with me from the beginning.

16 "I have told you these things to keep you
from giving up. 2People will put you out
of their synagogues.[d] Yes, the time is coming
when those who kill you will think they are offering service to God. 3They will do this because
they have not known the Father and they have
not known me. 4I have told you these things now
so that when the time comes you will remember
that I warned you.

The Work of the Holy Spirit

"I did not tell you these things at the beginning,
because I was with you then. 5Now I am going
back to the One who sent me. But none of you
asks me, 'Where are you going?' 6Your hearts are
filled with sadness because I have told you these
things. 7But I tell you the truth, it is better for you
that I go away. When I go away, I will send the
Helper[n] to you. If I do not go away, the Helper

Helper "Counselor" or "Comforter." Jesus is talking about the Holy Spirit.

SPIRITUAL GROWTH

Cheri's Gift

Michele remembers exactly why she tried to meet Cheri Bruce the first time. They sang together in the Girls Performance Choir their senior year, and Cheri's talent dazzled Michele. Cheri wrote her own songs and could play piano with the kind of intensity and skill Michele envied.

But there was something about Cheri that defied description. She had an honesty about her—a fearless security that made Michele feel safe and challenged at the same time.

One day Michele decided to stay after choir and talk to Cheri. That became the first of many long, intense conversations. The inner strength Michele had always sensed in Cheri was rooted, she found, in a deep faith in Christ.

She seemed to know more about God than anyone Michele had ever met. Michele herself had grown up going to church, and had opinions about God. But Cheri told Michele about a God she had come to know personally.

One day as they rode together in her car, Cheri said, "The Bible says God hates sin, and that's why it's so important for us to recognize our sin and ask God's forgiveness."

"So what?" Michele said. "I don't drink, swear, smoke, or do drugs. I don't have anything to confess."

But Cheri didn't miss a beat. "Michele, all of us sin. I know you've lied to your parents about going out with that older actor guy you met. Don't you realize that lying to your parents is sin in God's eyes?"

Cheri was getting a little too bold, and suddenly Michele felt very uncomfortable. "If I'm a Christian and you're a Christian, why are we so different?" Michele asked.

"The big question is, 'How much do you need God in your life?'," Cheri responded. "Everyone needs God, but not everyone knows they need him."

That conversation in the car has been locked in Michele's memory since that day, because that day she really put her faith in Christ and began spending time in prayer, Bible reading, and church so as to grow closer to Jesus—as Jesus told all Christians to do in **John 15:1–17**.

- Did Cheri love Michele the way Jesus commanded his followers to love? Why or why not?
- What kind of "spiritual fruit" do you see ripening in your life?

CONSIDER. . .

- inviting someone you respect spiritually to have lunch with you.
- asking someone who gardens to explain how a plant produces fruit. Then ask God to make you produce more "spiritual fruit" in your life.

FOR MORE, SEE

- Psalm 1 (p. 482)
- Matthew 7:24–27 (p. 920)
- Matthew 13:3–23 (p. 930)

will not come. 8When the Helper comes, he will
prove to the people of the world the truth about
sin, about being right with God, and about judgment. 9He will prove to them that sin is not believing in me. 10He will prove to them that being
right with God comes from my going to the Father and not being seen anymore. 11And the
Helper will prove to them that judgment happened when the ruler of this world was judged.
12"I have many more things to say to you, but
they are too much for you now. 13But when the
Spirit[a] of truth comes, he will lead you into all
truth. He will not speak his own words, but he
will speak only what he hears, and he will tell you
what is to come. 14The Spirit of truth will bring
glory to me, because he will take what I have to
say and tell it to you. 15All that the Father has is
mine. That is why I said that the Spirit will take
what I have to say and tell it to you.

Sadness Will Become Happiness

16"After a little while you will not see me, and
then after a little while you will see me again."
17Some of the followers said to each other,
"What does Jesus mean when he says, 'After a
little while you will not see me, and then
after a little while you will see me again'? And
what does he mean when he says, 'Because I am
going to the Father'?" 18They also asked, "What
does he mean by 'a little while'? We don't understand what he is saying."
19Jesus saw that the followers wanted to ask

HOLY SPIRIT

The Improbable Disciple

Nicky Cruz was a murderous, uncontrollable gang leader who had killed before and would likely kill again. Without overstating the truth, Cruz was the most unlikely prospect for Christian conversion. He was also one of the first gang members whom David Wilkerson, a rural minister, met on the rough streets of New York City.

Wilkerson left his comfortable surroundings and started a missionary outreach to gang members in New York during the late 1960s. He was idealistic, and sometimes his efforts to gain a foothold for Christ among the vicious gang culture failed miserably.

Time after time, Nicky rejected David's pleas to seek God's forgiveness—once threatening the thin, quaking minister with a knife to his throat. But David replied, "You can cut me to pieces, Nicky, but every piece will still cry out, 'I love you.' "

David invited Nicky to attend a city-wide revival meeting he was organizing for gang members. Impressed by the man's courage, Nicky told David he and his gang would be there.

Nicky did show up at the revival, and David invited him to collect the offering. Nicky and his gang did and then headed for the backstage exit, snickering at the gullible preacher.

But on the way out, Nicky felt a heavy, almost overpowering weight on his shoulders. He stopped. He couldn't escape the fearful truth: The Jesus about whom David had spoken required something of him. Nicky and his gang returned to meet David on stage. At the end of the meeting, Nicky told David, "I've given my heart to God."

Today Nicky works with tough, inner-city teenagers, helping them turn from drugs and violence and follow Christ. Jesus said one of the Holy Spirit's main responsibilities is to prove the truth to people who are like Nicky Cruz used to be. Read about the Holy Spirit in **John 16:4–15**.

- According to verse 8, how did the Holy Spirit influence Nicky Cruz's change of heart?
- When have you felt the Holy Spirit working with you? Explain.

C O N S I D E R . . .

- listing ten words that could replace the word "Holy" and ten words that could replace the word "Spirit." Mix and match the words to come up with combinations such as "Perfect Presence" or "Pure Companion."
- spending five minutes at the end of each day, thinking of ways the Holy Spirit was with you throughout the day.

F O R M O R E , S E E . . .

- Psalm 51:10–13 (p. 511)
- Luke 11:5–13 (p. 1024)

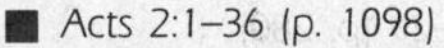

- Acts 2:1–36 (p. 1098)

him about this, so he said to them, "Are you asking each other what I meant when I said, 'After
a little while you will not see me, and then
after a little while you will see me again'? 20I tell
you the truth, you will cry and be sad, but the
world will be happy. You will be sad, but your
sadness will become joy. 21When a woman gives
birth to a baby, she has pain, because her time
has come. But when her baby is born, she forgets the pain, because she is so happy that a child
has been born into the world. 22It is the same
with you. Now you are sad, but I will see you
again and you will be happy, and no one will take
away your joy. 23In that day you will not ask me
for anything. I tell you the truth, my Father will
give you anything you ask for in my name. 24Un-
til now you have not asked for anything in my
name. Ask and you will receive, so that your joy
will be the fullest possible joy.

Victory over the World

25"I have told you these things, using stories
that hide the meaning. But the time will come
when I will not use stories like that to tell you
things; I will speak to you in plain words about
the Father. 26In that day you will ask the Father
for things in my name. I mean, I will not need to
ask the Father for you. 27The Father himself loves
you. He loves you because you loved me and believed that I came from God. 28I came from the
Father into the world. Now I am leaving the
world and going back to the Father."

29Then the followers of Jesus said, "You are
speaking clearly to us now and are not using stories that are hard to understand. 30We can see
now that you know all things. You can answer a
person's question even before it is asked. This
makes us believe you came from God."

31Jesus answered, "So now you believe? 32Lis-
ten to me; a time is coming when you will be
scattered, each to his own home. That time is
now here. You will leave me alone, but I am
never really alone, because the Father is with me.
33"I told you these things so that you can have
peace in me. In this world you will have trouble,
but be brave! I have defeated the world."

SIDELIGHT: Jesus' prayer in John 17 is the longest prayer in the New Testament. But Nehemiah holds the record for the longest Bible prayer with his prayer of praise, confession, and covenant in Nehemiah 9:5–37 (p. 434).

Jesus Prays for His Followers

17 After Jesus said these things, he looked
toward heaven and prayed, "Father, the
time has come. Give glory to your Son so that the

PRAYER

Do You Have a Prayer?

Does prayer have a place in your life? Read about other teenagers' prayer attitudes and practices as discovered in a Search Institute survey:

- Eighty-three percent say they often pray for God's help when they have problems.
- Eighty-three percent say they often pray that God will help other people.
- Sixty-five percent say they pray at least once a week outside church and other than before meals.
- Yet only 15 percent say personal prayer is an important influence in their life.
- No wonder 90 percent of teenagers are interested in learning how to pray.

Read **John 17:1–26** to see how Jesus prayed.

- What might the teenagers in the survey ask Jesus if they talked to him about his prayer?
- What does Jesus' prayer in this passage reveal about what is most important to him? How are your own priorities reflected in your prayers?

CONSIDER . . .

- making a prayer list of the people and things you consider most important to pray for. Use it daily, and keep track of answers.
- forming a prayer group to study prayer and pray together each week.

FOR MORE, SEE . . .

- 2 Samuel 7:18–29 (p. 280)
- Ephesians 6:18–19 (p. 1226)
- Hebrews 4:14–16 (p. 1279)

Son can give glory to you. 2You gave the Son
power over all people so that the Son could give
eternal life to all those you gave him. 3And this is
eternal life: that people know you, the only true
God, and that they know Jesus Christ, the One
you sent. 4Having finished the work you gave
me to do, I brought you glory on earth. 5And
now, Father, give me glory with you; give me
the glory I had with you before the world was
made.

6"I showed what you are like to those you gave
me from the world. They belonged to you, and
you gave them to me, and they have obeyed your
teaching. 7Now they know that everything you
gave me comes from you. 8I gave them the teachings you gave me, and they accepted them. They
knew that I truly came from you, and they believed that you sent me. 9I am praying for them.
I am not praying for people in the world but for
those you gave me, because they are yours. 10All
I have is yours, and all you have is mine. And my
glory is shown through them. 11I am coming to
you; I will not stay in the world any longer. But
they are still in the world. Holy Father, keep them
safe by the power of your name, the name you
gave me, so that they will be one, just as you and
I are one. 12While I was with them, I kept them
safe by the power of your name, the name you
gave me. I protected them, and only one of them,
the one worthy of destruction, was lost so that the
Scripture[d] would come true.

13"I am coming to you now. But I pray these
things while I am still in the world so that these
followers can have all of my joy in them. 14I have
given them your teaching. And the world has
hated them, because they don't belong to the
world, just as I don't belong to the world. 15I am
not asking you to take them out of the world but
to keep them safe from the Evil One. 16They don't
belong to the world, just as I don't belong to the
world. 17Make them ready for your service
through your truth; your teaching is truth. 18I
have sent them into the world, just as you sent me
into the world. 19For their sake, I am making myself ready to serve so that they can be ready for
their service of the truth.

20"I pray for these followers, but I am also praying for all those who will believe in me because
of their teaching. 21Father, I pray that they can be
one. As you are in me and I am in you, I pray that
they can also be one in us. Then the world will
believe that you sent me. 22I have given these people the glory that you gave me so that they can be
one, just as you and I are one. 23I will be in them
and you will be in me so that they will be completely one. Then the world will know that you
sent me and that you loved them just as much as
you loved me.

24"Father, I want these people that you gave
me to be with me where I am. I want them to see
my glory, which you gave me because you loved
me before the world was made. 25Father, you are
the One who is good. The world does not know
you, but I know you, and these people know you
sent me. 26I showed them what you are like, and
I will show them again. Then they will have the
same love that you have for me, and I will live in
them."

Jesus Is Arrested

18 When Jesus finished praying, he went
with his followers across the Kidron Valley. On the other side there was a garden, and
Jesus and his followers went into it.

2Judas knew where this place was, because
Jesus met there often with his followers. Judas
was the one who turned against Jesus. 3So Judas
came there with a group of soldiers and some
guards from the leading priests and the Pharisees.[d] They were carrying torches, lanterns, and
weapons.

4Knowing everything that would happen to
him, Jesus went out and asked, "Who is it you are
looking for?"

5They answered, "Jesus from Nazareth."

"I am he," Jesus said. (Judas, the one who
turned against Jesus, was standing there with
them.) 6When Jesus said, "I am he," they moved
back and fell to the ground.

7Jesus asked them again, "Who is it you are
looking for?"

They said, "Jesus of Nazareth."

8"I told you that I am he," Jesus said. "So if you
are looking for me, let the others go." 9This happened so that the words Jesus said before would
come true: "I have not lost any of the ones you
gave me."

10Simon Peter, who had a sword, pulled it out
and struck the servant of the high priest, cutting
off his right ear. (The servant's name was Mal-
chus.) 11Jesus said to Peter, "Put your sword back.
Shouldn't I drink the cup[n] the Father gave me?"

Jesus Is Brought Before Annas

12Then the soldiers with their commander and
the Jewish guards arrested Jesus. They tied him
13and led him first to Annas, the father-in-law of
Caiaphas, the high priest that year. 14Caiaphas
was the one who told the Jews that it would be
better if one man died for all the people.

cup Jesus is talking about the painful things that will happen to him. Accepting these things will be very hard, like drinking a cup of something bitter.

Peter Says He Doesn't Know Jesus

15 Simon Peter and another one of Jesus' followers went along after Jesus. This follower knew the
high priest, so he went with Jesus into the high
priest's courtyard. 16 But Peter waited outside near
the door. The follower who knew the high
priest came back outside, spoke to the girl at
the door, and brought Peter inside. 17 The girl
at the door said to Peter, "Aren't you also one
of that man's followers?"
Peter answered, "No, I am not!"
18 It was cold, so the servants and guards had
built a fire and were standing around it, warming
themselves. Peter also was standing with them,
warming himself.

The High Priest Questions Jesus

19 The high priest asked Jesus questions about
his followers and his teaching. 20 Jesus answered,
"I have spoken openly to everyone. I have always

FEAR

Letting Go

Brad Parks, Dean Brown, and Eric Unrau grew up together. In the summer they played football, rode trail bikes, and shot BB guns. In the fall they signed up for the same classes and held all-night Monopoly tournaments. In the winter they skied; in the spring they went camping. The years they had spent together made them feel like brothers.

But during their senior year in high school, something changed. Dean and Eric started drinking. They insisted on seeing the raunchiest movies in town. They each talked about how far they had gotten with their girlfriends.

All the while, Brad went along with them. But he felt worse and worse about himself. The changes he saw in Dean and Eric disgusted him. But Brad didn't have many friends in school. He couldn't risk alienating the ones he did have. He was afraid they would reject him. For months, this fear overpowered the sick feeling he had whenever he was with his friends.

One night, Dean called Brad and told him to be ready to leave for the movies in a half-hour.

"What are we going to see?" asked Brad.

"Eric found out how to sneak into a steamy show downtown. It starts in an hour."

Something broke in Brad. He was angry about his wasted weekends, about the terrible things he had said and done with his friends, and about letting God down.

"I'm sorry. I just can't go with you guys tonight," Brad said. "I can't stand the kind of movies we've seen lately. I'm not going to do that kind of stuff with you anymore."

Shocked, Dean tried to convince Brad to come anyway. But Brad wouldn't budge. Furious, Dean hung up the phone.

Dean and Eric abruptly broke off all contact with Brad. They spread terrible rumors about him at school and threatened to beat him up. A five-minute conversation had cost Brad his two closest friends. But it won him something far more valuable: the ability to face his fears and overcome them.

Just as Brad struggled to stand up to his friends, the apostle Peter was too afraid to admit he followed Jesus when he thought his life might be threatened. Read about Peter's struggle in **John 18:1–27**.

- How were Brad's fears similar to the apostle Peter's fears? How were they different?
- If you had been in Peter's shoes, what would you have said to the people who asked if you knew Jesus?

CONSIDER . . .

- writing one thing you have been afraid to tell a friend this last month, then thinking of a creative way to face your fear.
- listing the activities and topics of conversation you have participated in with your friends this last week. Circle things Jesus would never do or say, and mark a star beside things he would do or say.

FOR MORE, SEE . . .

- Psalm 118:5–9 (p. 549)
- Matthew 10:26–32 (p. 925)
- Acts 2:14–42 (p. 1099)

taught in synagogues[d] and in the Temple,[d] where all the Jews come together. I never said anything in secret. [21]So why do you question me? Ask the people who heard my teaching. They know what I said."

[22]When Jesus said this, one of the guards standing there hit him. The guard said, "Is that the way you answer the high priest?"

> **SIDELIGHT:** The sword Simon Peter used in John 18:10–11 was probably similar to a modern machete. Roman soldiers of this time used lightweight, well-balanced swords that were about two feet long for close-range combat. The sword is the most common weapon mentioned in the Bible, appearing more than four hundred times from Genesis to Revelation.

[23]Jesus answered him, "If I said something wrong, then show what it was. But if what I said is true, why do you hit me?"

[24]Then Annas sent Jesus, who was still tied, to Caiaphas the high priest.

Peter Says Again He Doesn't Know Jesus

[25]As Simon Peter was standing and warming himself, they said to him, "Aren't you one of that man's followers?"

Peter said it was not true; he said, "No, I am not."

[26]One of the servants of the high priest was there. This servant was a relative of the man whose ear Peter had cut off. The servant said, "Didn't I see you with him in the garden?"

[27]Again Peter said it wasn't true. At once a rooster crowed.

Jesus Is Brought Before Pilate

[28]Early in the morning they led Jesus from Caiaphas's house to the Roman governor's palace. They would not go inside the palace, because they did not want to make themselves unclean;[n] they wanted to eat the Passover[d] meal. [29]So Pilate went outside to them and asked, "What charges do you bring against this man?"

[30]They answered, "If he were not a criminal, we wouldn't have brought him to you."

[31]Pilate said to them, "Take him yourselves and judge him by your own law."

"But we are not allowed to put anyone to death," the Jews answered. [32](This happened so that what Jesus said about how he would die would come true.)

[33]Then Pilate went back inside the palace and called Jesus to him and asked, "Are you the king of the Jews?"

[34]Jesus said, "Is that your own question, or did others tell you about me?"

[35]Pilate answered, "I am not Jewish. It was your own people and their leading priests who handed you over to me. What have you done wrong?"

[36]Jesus answered, "My kingdom does not belong to this world. If it belonged to this world, my servants would fight so that I would not be given over to the Jews. But my kingdom is from another place."

[37]Pilate said, "So you are a king!"

Jesus answered, "You are the one saying I am a king. This is why I was born and came into the world: to tell people the truth. And everyone who belongs to the truth listens to me."

[38]Pilate said, "What is truth?" After he said this, he went out to the Jews again and said to them, "I find nothing against this man. [39]But it is your custom that I free one prisoner to you at Passover time. Do you want me to free the 'king of the Jews'?"

[40]They shouted back, "No, not him! Let Barabbas go free!" (Barabbas was a robber.)

19

Then Pilate ordered that Jesus be taken away and whipped. [2]The soldiers made a crown from some thorny branches and put it on Jesus' head and put a purple robe around him. [3]Then they came to him many times and said, "Hail, King of the Jews!" and hit him in the face.

[4]Again Pilate came out and said to them, "Look, I am bringing Jesus out to you. I want you to know that I find nothing against him." [5]So Jesus came out, wearing the crown of thorns and the purple robe. Pilate said to them, "Here is the man!"

[6]When the leading priests and the guards saw Jesus, they shouted, "Crucify him! Crucify him!"

But Pilate answered, "Crucify him yourselves, because I find nothing against him."

[7]The Jews answered, "We have a law that says he should die, because he said he is the Son of God."

[8]When Pilate heard this, he was even more afraid. [9]He went back inside the palace and asked Jesus, "Where do you come from?" But Jesus did not answer him. [10]Pilate said, "You refuse to speak to me? Don't you know I have power to set you free and power to have you crucified?"

[11]Jesus answered, "The only power you have over me is the power given to you by God. The

unclean Going into a non-Jewish place would make them unfit to eat the Passover Feast, according to Jewish law.

man who turned me in to you is guilty of a greater
sin."
12After this, Pilate tried to let Jesus go. But the
Jews cried out, "Anyone who makes himself king
is against Caesar. If you let this man go, you are
no friend of Caesar."
13When Pilate heard what they were saying, he
brought Jesus out and sat down on the judge's
seat at the place called The Stone Pavement. (In
the Jewish language[n] the name is Gabbatha.)
14It was about noon on Preparation[d] Day of Passover[d] week. Pilate said to the Jews, "Here is your
king!"
15They shouted, "Take him away! Take him
away! Crucify him!"

Pilate asked them, "Do you want me to crucify your king?"

The leading priests answered, "The only king we have is Caesar."
16So Pilate handed Jesus over to them to be crucified.

Jesus Is Crucified

The soldiers took charge of Jesus. 17Carrying
his own cross, Jesus went out to a place called
The Place of the Skull, which in the Jewish language[n] is called Golgotha. 18There they crucified
Jesus. They also crucified two other men, one on
each side, with Jesus in the middle. 19Pilate wrote
a sign and put it on the cross. It read: JESUS OF
NAZARETH, THE KING OF THE JEWS. 20The sign was
written in the Jewish language, in Latin, and in
Greek. Many of the Jews read the sign, because
the place where Jesus was crucified was near
the city. 21The leading Jewish priests said to Pilate, "Don't write, 'The King of the Jews.' But
write, 'This man said, "I am the King of the
Jews." ' "
22Pilate answered, "What I have written, I have
written."
23After the soldiers crucified Jesus, they took
his clothes and divided them into four parts, with
each soldier getting one part. They also took his
long shirt, which was all one piece of cloth, woven from top to bottom. 24So the soldiers said to
each other, "We should not tear this into parts.
Let's throw lots[d] to see who will get it." This
happened so that this Scripture would come
true:[d]

"They divided my clothes among them,
and they threw lots[d] for my clothing."

Psalm 22:18

So the soldiers did this.

SIDELIGHT: *The "long shirt" the soldiers gambled for (John 19:23–24) was, in reality, like Jesus' undergarment. Crucifixions were often done with the criminals naked to make the execution even more humiliating.*

25Standing near his cross were Jesus' mother,
his mother's sister, Mary the wife of Clopas, and
Mary Magdalene. 26When Jesus saw his mother
and the follower he loved standing nearby, he said
to his mother, "Dear woman, here is your son."
27Then he said to the follower, "Here is your
mother." From that time on, the follower took her
to live in his home.

Jesus Dies

28After this, Jesus knew that everything had
been done. So that the Scripture[d] would come
true, he said, "I am thirsty."[n] 29There was a jar
full of vinegar there, so the soldiers soaked a
sponge in it, put the sponge on a branch of a hyssop plant, and lifted it to Jesus' mouth. 30When
Jesus tasted the vinegar, he said, "It is finished."
Then he bowed his head and died.
31This day was Preparation[d] Day, and the next
day was a special Sabbath[d] day. Since the Jews did
not want the bodies to stay on the cross on the
Sabbath day, they asked Pilate to order that the
legs of the men be broken[n] and the bodies be
taken away. 32So the soldiers came and broke the
legs of the first man on the cross beside Jesus.
Then they broke the legs of the man on the other
cross beside Jesus. 33But when the soldiers came
to Jesus and saw that he was already dead, they
did not break his legs. 34But one of the soldiers
stuck his spear into Jesus' side, and at once blood
and water came out. 35(The one who saw this
happen is the one who told us this, and whatever
he says is true. And he knows that he tells the
truth, and he tells it so that you might believe.)
36These things happened to make the Scripture
come true: "Not one of his bones will be broken."[n] 37And another Scripture says, "They will
look at the one they stabbed."[n]

Jesus Is Buried

38Later, Joseph from Arimathea asked Pilate if
he could take the body of Jesus. (Joseph was a
secret follower of Jesus, because he was afraid of
the Jews.) Pilate gave his permission, so Joseph

Jewish language Hebrew or Aramaic, the languages of the Jewish people in the first century.
"I am thirsty." Read Psalms 22:15; 69:21.
broken The breaking of their bones would make them die sooner.
"Not one . . . broken." Quotation from Psalm 34:20. The idea is from Exodus 12:46; Numbers 9:12.
"They . . . stabbed." Quotation from Zechariah 12:10.

came and took Jesus' body away. 39Nicodemus,
who earlier had come to Jesus at night, went with
Joseph. He brought about seventy-five pounds of
myrrh[d] and aloes.[d] 40These two men took Jesus'
body and wrapped it with the spices in pieces of
linen cloth, which is how the Jewish people bury
the dead. 41In the place where Jesus was crucified, there was a garden. In the garden was a new
tomb that had never been used before. 42The men
laid Jesus in that tomb because it was nearby, and
the Jews were preparing to start their Sabbath[d]
day.

Jesus' Tomb Is Empty

20 Early on the first day of the week, Mary
Magdalene went to the tomb while it
was still dark. When she saw that the large stone
had been moved away from the tomb, 2she ran to
Simon Peter and the follower whom Jesus loved.
Mary said, "They have taken the Lord out of the
tomb, and we don't know where they have put
him."
3So Peter and the other follower started for the
tomb. 4They were both running, but the other follower ran faster than Peter and reached the tomb
first. 5He bent down and looked in and saw the
strips of linen cloth lying there, but he did not go
in. 6Then following him, Simon Peter arrived and
went into the tomb and saw the strips of linen
lying there. 7He also saw the cloth that had been
around Jesus' head, which was folded up and laid
in a different place from the strips of linen. 8Then
the other follower, who had reached the tomb
first, also went in. He saw and believed. 9(They
did not yet understand from the Scriptures[d] that
Jesus must rise from the dead.)

DEATH

Good-bye to a Pigtail-Puller

Danny Finnegan was Irish through and through. His red hair clashed with his light blue eyes—eyes that always seemed to laugh with mischief. Danny and his wife were Christine's parents' best friends. And he was the only adult she can remember who made a special effort to make her feel important.

In church on Sundays he would always sit behind Christine, where he could tug on her pigtails without ever taking his eyes off the minister. He would ride with Christine's family in the station wagon after church because he had never learned how to drive. And always, he would lean back and shout over the dull roar created by her brothers and sisters, "Christine, please sing 'Danny Boy' for me. You have such a beautiful voice. Please, Christine, sing for me."

Beaming with pride, she would always oblige. And when she had sung the last note, she always heard Danny's hearty laugh amid her brothers' and sisters' groans.

Danny loved Christine. He was one of those people you're sure will live forever just because a world without Danny wouldn't seem a whole world at all.

But one day Danny's doctor told him he was dying of cancer. Though years had passed since Danny had pulled on Christine's pigtails in church, she was stunned. She wrote Danny a long, loving letter when she heard he wouldn't last much longer.

A month later, Danny died. But before he slipped away, he made one last phone call to Christine's parents to tell them about "the most beautiful letter."

It was hard to see someone die who had been so full of life. Joseph and Nicodemus knew what it was like to lose somebody who made life worth living. Read about what they did for Jesus in **John 19:38–42**.

■ How was the letter to Danny Finnegan like Joseph's and Nicodemus's burying Jesus?

■ If you had been there, what would have been your first reaction to Jesus' death? What would you have done for Jesus?

CONSIDER . . .

■ writing a letter to a friend or relative, telling him or her how your life has been enriched by his or her presence in it.

■ asking someone who has lost a loved one to talk about that loved one.

FOR MORE, SEE

■ Psalm 116 (p. 548)

■ Luke 24:1–8 (p. 1054)

■ Hebrews 9:23–28 (p. 1285)

Jesus Appears to Mary Magdalene

10Then the followers went back home. 11But
Mary stood outside the tomb, crying. As she was
crying, she bent down and looked inside the
tomb. 12She saw two angels dressed in white, sitting where Jesus' body had been, one at the head
and one at the feet.
13They asked her, "Woman, why are you crying?"
She answered, "They have taken away my
Lord, and I don't know where they have put
him." 14When Mary said this, she turned around
and saw Jesus standing there, but she did not
know it was Jesus.
15Jesus asked her, "Woman, why are you crying? Whom are you looking for?"
Thinking he was the gardener, she said to him,
"Did you take him away, sir? Tell me where you
put him, and I will get him."
16Jesus said to her, "Mary."
Mary turned toward Jesus and said in the Jewish language,[n] "Rabboni." (This means Teacher.)
17Jesus said to her, "Don't hold on to me, because I have not yet gone up to the Father. But
go to my brothers and tell them, 'I am going back
to my Father and your Father, to my God and
your God.'"
18Mary Magdalene went and said to the followers, "I saw the Lord!" And she told them what
Jesus had said to her.

Jesus Appears to His Followers

19When it was evening on the first day of the
week, the followers were together. The doors
were locked, because they were afraid of the
Jews. Then Jesus came and stood right in the middle of them and said, "Peace be with you." 20After
he said this, he showed them his hands and his
side. The followers were thrilled when they saw
the Lord.
21Then Jesus said again, "Peace be with you. As
the Father sent me, I now send you." 22After he
said this, he breathed on them and said, "Receive
the Holy Spirit.[d] 23If you forgive anyone his sins,
they are forgiven. If you don't forgive them, they
are not forgiven."

Jesus Appears to Thomas

24Thomas (called Didymus), who was one of
the twelve, was not with them when Jesus came.
25The other followers kept telling Thomas, "We
saw the Lord."
But Thomas said, "I will not believe it until I
see the nail marks in his hands and put my finger
where the nails were and put my hand into his
side."
26A week later the followers were in the house
again, and Thomas was with them. The doors
were locked, but Jesus came in and stood right in
the middle of them. He said, "Peace be with you."
27Then he said to Thomas, "Put your finger here,
and look at my hands. Put your hand here in my
side. Stop being an unbeliever and believe."
28Thomas said to him, "My Lord and my God!"
29Then Jesus told him, "You believe because
you see me. Those who believe without seeing
me will be truly happy."

Why John Wrote This Book

30Jesus did many other miracles[d] in the presence of his followers that are not written in this
book. 31But these are written so that you may believe that Jesus is the Christ,[d] the Son of God.
Then, by believing, you may have life through his
name.

Jesus Appears to Seven Followers

21 Later, Jesus showed himself to his followers again—this time at Lake Galilee.[n] This is how he showed himself: 2Some of
the followers were together: Simon Peter,
Thomas (called Didymus), Nathanael from Cana
in Galilee, the two sons of Zebedee, and two
other followers. 3Simon Peter said, "I am going
out to fish."
The others said, "We will go with you." So they
went out and got into the boat. They fished that
night but caught nothing.
4Early the next morning Jesus stood on the
shore, but the followers did not know it was
Jesus. 5Then he said to them, "Friends, did you
catch any fish?"
They answered, "No."
6He said, "Throw your net on the right side of
the boat, and you will find some." So they did,
and they caught so many fish they could not pull
the net back into the boat.
7The follower whom Jesus loved said to Peter,
"It is the Lord!" When Peter heard him say this,
he wrapped his coat around himself. (Peter had
taken his clothes off.) Then he jumped into the
water. 8The other followers went to shore in the
boat, dragging the net full of fish. They were not
very far from shore, only about a hundred yards.
9When the followers stepped out of the boat and
onto the shore, they saw a fire of hot coals. There
were fish on the fire, and there was bread.
10Then Jesus said, "Bring some of the fish you
just caught."
11Simon Peter went into the boat and pulled
the net to the shore. It was full of big fish, one

Jewish language Hebrew or Aramaic, the languages of the Jewish people in the first century.
Lake Galilee Literally, "Sea of Tiberias."

hundred fifty-three in all, but even though there were so many, the net did not tear.
12Jesus said to them, "Come and eat." None of the followers dared ask him, "Who are you?" because they knew it was the Lord.
13Jesus came and took the bread and gave it to them, along with the fish.
14This was now the third time Jesus showed himself to his followers after he was raised from the dead.

> **SIDELIGHT:** Barbecued fish for breakfast, anyone? That's what Jesus served when he appeared to his disciples (see John 21:4–13). Cooking fish on an open, charcoal fire was common in Jesus' day. He may have served them musht fish (now known as St. Peter's fish), which is one of the most common fish in Lake Galilee.

Jesus Talks to Peter

15When they finished eating, Jesus said to Simon Peter, "Simon son of John do you love me more than these?"

He answered, "Yes, Lord, you know that I love you."

Jesus said, "Feed my lambs."

16Again Jesus said, "Simon son of John do you love me?"

He answered, "Yes, Lord, you know that I love you."

Jesus said, "Take care of my sheep."

17A third time he said, "Simon son of John do you love me?"

DOUBT

The Death of Doubt

Tim Simpson and his brothers had fought with their dad through the years. He was a salesman, a community leader, a church leader and a strong disciplinarian. He expected a lot from his four sons; his standards were high and generally inflexible. Going to church wasn't an option; it was expected.

Tim loved his dad, but it had always been a fearful, distant love. He had never really known, deep inside, whether his dad loved him. He saw God the same way—as a fearful, distant ruler he was forced to obey. So he wasn't sure if God loved him either. Until one cold November day.

Tim's dad had asked Tim to go out to breakfast with him—just the two of them. Tim didn't know what to think. *What have I done?* he wondered.

So Tim and his dad climbed into the family's beat-up station wagon and went to breakfast together. They didn't say much in the car, and Tim could see that his dad had something important to tell him.

After a tense, awkward breakfast, his dad laid down his fork, looked at Tim and said: "I know we haven't always seen eye to eye. And I know I've made life tough on you. But I don't ever want you to forget what I'm about to say to you. I love you as much as a father can love his son. And nothing will ever change that."

The words came with a power and a peace that enveloped Tim. Something changed between him and his dad in that moment. And something changed between Tim and God in that moment.

Tim felt, for the first time, the assurance of God's love for him.

Like Tim, the disciples sometimes had a hard time believing God. They doubted many of the promises Jesus had told them. And the chief doubter among them was Thomas. Read about Thomas's doubt in **John 20:19–31**.

- How did Tim's doubts about his father's love for him compare to Thomas's doubts about Jesus rising from the dead?
- When have you doubted the love of someone close to you?

CONSIDER . . .

- taking a twenty-minute walk and asking God to demonstrate his love for you in something you see.
- reaffirming your love to a friend or family member who may be doubting your love.

FOR MORE, SEE . . .

- Job 40—41 (p. 477)
- Luke 24:13–53 (p. 1055)
- Romans 14:14–23 (p. 1160)

Peter was hurt because Jesus asked him the third time, "Do you love me?" Peter said, "Lord, you know everything; you know that I love you!"

He said to him, "Feed my sheep.
18I tell you the truth, when you were younger, you tied your own belt and went where you wanted. But when you are old, you will put out your hands and someone else will tie you and take you where you don't want to go."
19(Jesus said this to show how Peter would die to give glory to God.) Then Jesus said to Peter, "Follow me!"

20Peter turned and saw that the follower Jesus loved was walking behind them. (This was the follower who had leaned against Jesus at the supper and had said, "Lord, who will turn against you?")
21When Peter saw him behind them, he asked Jesus, "Lord, what about him?"

22Jesus answered, "If I want him to live until I come back, that is not your business. You follow me."

23So a story spread among the followers that this one would not die. But Jesus did not say he would not die. He only said, "If I want him to live until I come back, that is not your business."

24That follower is the one who is telling these things and who has now written them down. We know that what he says is true.

25There are many other things Jesus did. If every one of them were written down, I suppose the whole world would not be big enough for all the books that would be written.

CELEBRATING

A Dark Victory

All year long, Tracy Howell's volleyball coach assured the team they were the best in the state. For most of the year, the state rankings agreed with her. Hilltop High's varsity volleyball team ranked Number One going into the district playoffs. Winning the district championship was the first step on the way to the state championship.

But Hilltop lost its first three playoff matches. One more, and they were out. With each loss, the girls became more depressed. Before their fourth match, the coach couldn't even get them "up" for it. The fans stayed away when they began losing.

Privately, Tracy told her best friend, "I know we're good, but I don't think we can win."

Hilltop's ranking slipped to sixth in state, and the experts labeled them the "dark horse" in the state playoffs. Seeded next to last in the tournament, Hilltop was paired against the best teams in state. They won their first match and surprised even themselves. In the second match, they lost their first game, but won the last two. They went into the state finals with renewed fan support.

In the third match, the games were tight. Hilltop won the first game, 18–16, but lost the second, 17–15. When the last point was scored in the final game, Hilltop had won 19–17.

The fans rushed onto the court and mobbed the Hilltop players. In the middle of the screaming crowd, Tracy felt out of place. She expected to feel all the ecstatic emotions she had dreamed of. But she felt more relief than anything.

That same joyful relief is what Jesus' disciples must have felt when Jesus rose from the dead and showed himself to them. Read about the disciples' experience in **John 21:1–14**.

- How do Tracy's up-and-down emotions compare with the disciples' emotions after Jesus was crucified and then appeared to them?
- When have you felt the kind of joy the disciples experienced on the shores of Lake Galilee? Explain.

CONSIDER . . .

- sending a "Celebrate Life" box to a faraway friend. Include confetti, party hats, party favors, snacks, and notes of encouragement to celebrate life.
- celebrating Christmas—the birth of Jesus—one day during the next two weeks. Plan a party, invite your friends, decorate in Christmas colors and ornaments, watch Christmas movies on video, and close by thanking God for his goodness in sending Christ.

FOR MORE, SEE . . .

- Psalm 126 (p. 555)
- Luke 15:1–7 (p. 1034)
- James 1:2–4 (p. 1294)

ACTS

Why Read This Book:

- Discover how the Christian church was born (Acts 1—9).
- Recognize that God wants all people to have faith in him (Acts 10—12).
- Be encouraged to tell others about your faith, as the early Christians did (Acts 13—28).

Behind the Scenes:

It looked like everything was over. Jesus was dead—executed by the Romans. After three years with Jesus, the disciples weren't sure what to do next. Maybe go back to fishing and tax-collecting and the other things they did before Jesus came along.

But three days later, Jesus rose from the dead, and the world has never been the same. The book of Acts tells how that event began changing the world.

Written by Luke, Acts picks up where the Gospel of Luke (p. 1000) leaves off. It tells how Jesus went up into heaven, then sent his Holy Spirit fifty days later (Acts 2). The rest of the book tells how the Good News of Jesus Christ spread rapidly throughout the world. Most of the book focuses on two people: Peter and Paul. Peter had been Jesus' disciple, and he quickly became a prominent leader in the early church. Through the book of Acts, we see him struggling to learn—and teach others—what it means to follow Jesus. Peter became a courageous leader who risked his life many times to share his faith.

Unlike Peter, Paul began as an enemy of Christians. But through a miraculous conversion (Acts 9), he became a devout Christian and great church leader. Acts tells about his travels to spread the Good News. And Acts provides the context for many of the topics Paul writes about in his letters (such as 1 Corinthians, p. 1167 and Philippians, p. 1229).

Acts tells about a time Christians were endangered by religious and political authorities. Many churches had to meet in hiding, and Christian leaders were

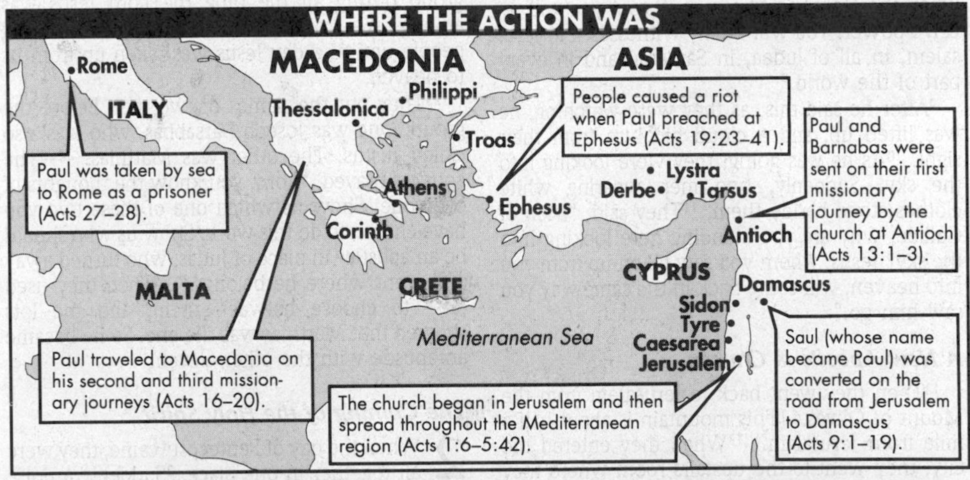
WHERE THE ACTION WAS
MACEDONIA
ASIA
Rome
ITALY
Philippi
Thessalonica
Troas
People caused a riot when Paul preached at Ephesus (Acts 19:23–41).
Paul and Barnabas were sent on their first missionary journey by the church at Antioch (Acts 13:1–3).
Paul was taken by sea to Rome as a prisoner (Acts 27–28).
Lystra
Derbe
Tarsus
Athens
Ephesus
Corinth
Antioch
CYPRUS
MALTA
CRETE
Damascus
Sidon
Tyre
Caesarea
Jerusalem
Mediterranean Sea
Saul (whose name became Paul) was converted on the road from Jerusalem to Damascus (Acts 9:1–19).
Paul traveled to Macedonia on his second and third missionary journeys (Acts 16–20).
The church began in Jerusalem and then spread throughout the Mediterranean region (Acts 1:6–5:42).

WHEN THE ACTION WAS

Jesus was born — The church began soon after Jesus went to heaven — Paul began his missionary work — Fire destroyed Rome

BC/AD — 25AD — 50AD — 75AD — 100AD

Jesus began his ministry — Paul became a Christian — Romans destroyed the Temple in Jerusalem

Behind the Scenes (cont.): regularly thrown in jail—or killed—for what they believed and taught. Yet the early Christians didn't back down. Their determination can encourage us to live our faith and tell others about it—even when we are tempted to hide it.

Luke Writes Another Book

1 To Theophilus.
The first book I wrote was about everything
Jesus began to do and teach 2until the day he was
taken up into heaven. Before this, with the help
of the Holy Spirit,[d] Jesus told the apostles he had
chosen what they should do. 3After his death, he
showed himself to them and proved in many
ways that he was alive. The apostles saw Jesus
during the forty days after he was raised from the
dead, and he spoke to them about the kingdom of
God. 4Once when he was eating with them, he
told them not to leave Jerusalem. He said, "Wait
here to receive the promise from the Father
which I told you about. 5John baptized people
with water, but in a few days you will be baptized
with the Holy Spirit."

Jesus Is Taken Up Into Heaven

6When the apostles[d] were all together, they
asked Jesus, "Lord, are you now going to give the
kingdom back to Israel?"
7Jesus said to them, "The Father is the only
One who has the authority to decide dates and
times. These things are not for you to know. 8But
when the Holy Spirit[d] comes to you, you will receive power. You will be my witnesses—in Jerusalem, in all of Judea, in Samaria, and in every
part of the world."
9After he said this, as they were watching, he
was lifted up, and a cloud hid him from their
sight. 10As he was going, they were looking into
the sky. Suddenly, two men wearing white
clothes stood beside them. 11They said, "Men of
Galilee, why are you standing here looking into
the sky? Jesus, whom you saw taken up from you
into heaven, will come back in the same way you
saw him go."

A New Apostle Is Chosen

12Then they went back to Jerusalem from the
Mount of Olives.[d] (This mountain is about half a
mile from Jerusalem.) 13When they entered the
city, they went to the upstairs room where they
were staying. Peter, John, James, Andrew, Philip,
Thomas, Bartholomew, Matthew, James son of
Alphaeus, Simon (known as the Zealot[d]), and Judas son of James were there. 14They all continued
praying together with some women, including
Mary the mother of Jesus, and Jesus' brothers.
15During this time there was a meeting of the
believers (about one hundred twenty of them).
Peter stood up and said, 16-17"Brothers and sisters,[n] in the Scriptures[d] the Holy Spirit[d] said
through David something that must happen involving Judas. He was one of our own group and
served together with us. He led those who arrested Jesus." 18(Judas bought a field with the
money he got for his evil act. But he fell to his
death, his body burst open, and all his intestines
poured out. 19Everyone in Jerusalem learned
about this so they named this place Akeldama. In
their language Akeldama means "Field of Blood.")
20"In the Book of Psalms," Peter said, "this is written:

'May his place be empty;
leave no one to live in it.' *Psalm 69:25*

And it is also written:

'Let another man replace him as leader.' *Psalm 109:8*

21-22"So now a man must become a witness
with us of Jesus' being raised from the dead. He
must be one of the men who were part of our
group during all the time the Lord Jesus was
among us—from the time John was baptizing
people until the day Jesus was taken up from us
to heaven."
23They put the names of two men before the
group. One was Joseph Barsabbas, who was also
called Justus. The other was Matthias. 24-25The
apostles prayed, "Lord, you know the thoughts of
everyone. Show us which one of these two you
have chosen to do this work. Show us who should
be an apostle[d] in place of Judas, who turned away
and went where he belongs." 26Then they used
lots[d] to choose between them, and the lots
showed that Matthias was the one. So he became
an apostle with the other eleven.

The Coming of the Holy Spirit

2 When the day of Pentecost[d] came, they were
all together in one place. 2Suddenly a noise
like a strong, blowing wind came from heaven
and filled the whole house where they were sitting. 3They saw something like flames of fire that
were separated and stood over each person there.

Brothers and sisters Although the Greek text says "Brothers" here and throughout this book, the words of the speakers were meant for the entire church, including men and women.

4They were all filled with the Holy Spirit,[d] and
they began to speak different languages[n] by the
power the Holy Spirit was giving them.

SIDELIGHT: Before the birth of the church, Pentecost (Acts 2:1–4) was a major time of celebration among Jews. This festival celebrated the wheat harvest with religious ceremonies, eating, drinking, and music. The festivities surrounding the event may be why skeptics thought the disciples were drunk (Acts 2:13).

5There were some religious Jews staying in Jerusalem who were from every country in the
world. 6When they heard this noise, a crowd
came together. They were all surprised, because
each one heard them speaking in his own language. 7They were completely amazed at this.
They said, "Look! Aren't all these people that we
hear speaking from Galilee? 8Then how is it possible that we each hear them in our own languages? We are from different places: 9Parthia,
Media, Elam, Mesopotamia, Judea, Cappadocia,
Pontus, Asia, 10Phrygia, Pamphylia, Egypt, the areas of Libya near Cyrene, Rome 11(both Jews and
those who had become Jews), Crete, and Arabia.
But we hear them telling in our own languages
about the great things God has done!" 12They
were all amazed and confused, asking each other,
"What does this mean?"
13But others were making fun of them, saying,
"They have had too much wine."

Peter Speaks to the People

14But Peter stood up with the eleven apostles,[d]
and in a loud voice he spoke to the crowd: "My
fellow Jews, and all of you who are in Jerusalem,
listen to me. Pay attention to what I have to say.
15These people are not drunk, as you think; it is
only nine o'clock in the morning! 16But Joel the
prophet[d] wrote about what is happening here today:
17'God says: In the last days
I will pour out my Spirit[d] on all kinds of
people.
Your sons and daughters will prophesy.[d]
Your young men will see visions,
and your old men will dream dreams.

languages This can also be translated "tongues."

HOLY SPIRIT

The Third Rail

The largest subway in the world is in New York City. It is an electric-powered, underground railway system. Every day, the system's 6,200 cars carry 3.5 million people to their destinations. Each year, more than a billion people use the subway.

The subway trains get their power through a "third rail," which runs alongside the 723 miles of subway tracks and supplies 600 volts of electricity to each train.

Without the third rail's power, the whole system would fail, and millions of people would be stranded. At all times, the successful operation of the subway system depends on the power of the third rail. Like the third rail is the subway's source of power, the Holy Spirit is the source of power for Christians. As we connect with the Spirit, we have the power we need to live the Christian life. Read **Acts 2:1–21** to discover how the Holy Spirit first empowered Christians.

- As the third rail empowers the subway, how does the Holy Spirit empower Christians?
- According to this passage, what are some evidences of the Holy Spirit's power?

C O N S I D E R . . .

- telling people from another culture about Jesus. Depend on the Holy Spirit to help you communicate clearly.
- finding out about the beginning of your congregation. What similarities do you see between that beginning and the beginning of the church in Acts 2?

F O R M O R E , S E E . . .

- Joel 2:28–29 (p. 838)
- John 14:15–26 (p. 1084)
- 1 Corinthians 12:1–11 (p. 1181)

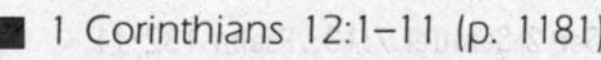

18At that time I will pour out my Spirit
also on my male slaves and female slaves,
and they will prophesy.
19I will show miracles[d]
in the sky and on the earth:
blood, fire, and thick smoke.
20The sun will become dark,
the moon red as blood,
before the overwhelming and glorious day
of the Lord will come.
21Then anyone who calls on the Lord
will be saved.' *Joel 2:28-32*

22"People of Israel, listen to these words: Jesus
from Nazareth was a very special man. God
clearly showed this to you by the miracles,[d] wonders, and signs he did through Jesus. You all know
this, because it happened right here among you.
23Jesus was given to you, and with the help of
those who don't know the law, you put him to
death by nailing him to a cross. But this was God's
plan which he had made long ago; he knew all
this would happen. 24God raised Jesus from the
dead and set him free from the pain of death, because death could not hold him. 25For David said
this about him:

'I keep the Lord before me always.
Because he is close by my side,
I will not be hurt.
26So I am glad, and I rejoice.
Even my body has hope,
27because you will not leave me in the grave.
You will not let your Holy One rot.
28You will teach me how to live a holy life.
Being with you will fill me with joy.'
Psalm 16:8-11

29"Brothers and sisters, I can tell you truly that
David, our ancestor, died and was buried. His
grave is still here with us today. 30He was a
prophet[d] and knew God had promised him that
he would make a person from David's family a
king just as he was.[n] 31Knowing this before it
happened, David talked about the Christ[d] rising
from the dead. He said:

'He was not left in the grave.
His body did not rot.'

32So Jesus is the One whom God raised from the
dead. And we are all witnesses to this. 33Jesus was
lifted up to heaven and is now at God's right side.
The Father has given the Holy Spirit[d] to Jesus as
he promised. So Jesus has poured out that Spirit,
and this is what you now see and hear. 34David
was not the one who was lifted up to heaven, but
he said:

'The Lord said to my Lord,
"Sit by me at my right side,
35 until I put your enemies under your
control." '[n]
Psalm 110:1

36"So, all the people of Israel should know this
truly: God has made Jesus — the man you nailed
to the cross — both Lord and Christ."
37When the people heard this, they felt guilty
and asked Peter and the other apostles, "What
shall we do?"
38Peter said to them, "Change your hearts and
lives and be baptized, each one of you, in the
name of Jesus Christ for the forgiveness of your
sins. And you will receive the gift of the Holy
Spirit. 39This promise is for you, for your children,
and for all who are far away. It is for everyone the
Lord our God calls to himself."
40Peter warned them with many other words.
He begged them, "Save yourselves from the evil
of today's people!" 41Then those people who accepted what Peter said were baptized. About
three thousand people were added to the number
of believers that day. 42They spent their time
learning the apostles' teaching, sharing, breaking
bread,[n] and praying together.

The Believers Share

43The apostles[d] were doing many miracles[d] and
signs, and everyone felt great respect for God.
44All the believers were together and shared everything. 45They would sell their land and the
things they owned and then divide the money
and give it to anyone who needed it. 46The believers met together in the Temple[d] every day. They
ate together in their homes, happy to share their
food with joyful hearts. 47They praised God and
were liked by all the people. Every day the Lord
added those who were being saved to the group
of believers.

Peter Heals a Crippled Man

3 One day Peter and John went to the Temple[d]
at three o'clock, the time set each day for the
afternoon prayer service. 2There, at the Temple
gate called Beautiful Gate, was a man who had
been crippled all his life. Every day he was carried
to this gate to beg for money from the people going into the Temple. 3The man saw Peter and
John going into the Temple and asked them for
money. 4Peter and John looked straight at him
and said, "Look at us!" 5The man looked at them,
thinking they were going to give him some

God . . . was See 2 Samuel 7:13; Psalm 132:11.
until . . . control Literally, "until I make your enemies a footstool for your feet."
breaking bread This may mean a meal as in verse 46, or the Lord's Supper, the special meal Jesus told his followers to eat to remember him (Luke 22:14-20).

money. 6 But Peter said, "I don't have any silver
or gold, but I do have something else I can give
you. By the power of Jesus Christ from Nazareth,
stand up and walk!" 7 Then Peter took the man's
right hand and lifted him up. Immediately the
man's feet and ankles became strong. 8 He jumped
up, stood on his feet, and began to walk. He went
into the Temple with them, walking and jumping
and praising God. 9-10 All the people recognized
him as the crippled man who always sat by the
Beautiful Gate begging for money. Now they saw
this same man walking and praising God, and
they were amazed. They wondered how this
could happen.

Peter Speaks to the People

11 While the man was holding on to Peter and
John, all the people were amazed and ran to them
at Solomon's Porch.[d] 12 When Peter saw this, he
said to them, "People of Israel, why are you surprised? You are looking at us as if it were our own
power or goodness that made this man walk.
13 The God of Abraham, Isaac, and Jacob, the God
of our ancestors, gave glory to Jesus, his servant.
But you handed him over to be killed. Pilate decided to let him go free, but you told Pilate you
did not want Jesus. 14 You did not want the One
who is holy and good but asked Pilate to give you

CHURCH

The Place to Belong

Rebecca Fisher yearned to fit in. She wanted people to like her and be her friend. That's why she joined every organization she could at school. She still didn't feel like she fit in, but at least she was busy.

During French club meeting one day, Lee Brungardt invited Rebecca to church. She grimaced at the thought, remembering the church she had attended with her mother years before. Each service had been one long, boring sermon with her mom telling her to be quiet. That was not Rebecca's idea of fun. She "had a commitment already," she lied to Lee.

But Lee persisted. Finally Rebecca agreed to endure one service—just to get him to leave her alone.

She didn't say much to him. When Lee and Rebecca arrived for Sunday school the next Sunday morning, the kids were standing around talking and laughing. Several of them recognized Rebecca and welcomed her. During the Bible study, the teacher called Rebecca by name and asked her opinion. Several kids invited Rebecca and Lee to sit with them during the worship service. And during the sermon, the pastor told interesting stories. Rebecca never felt bored.

After the worship service, all the kids went to Jason Hawley's house for lunch and to complete plans for their mission project. Rebecca helped make posters.

All the way home, Rebecca couldn't stop talking about how much she had liked Lee's church. "It just seems like I fit there, you know?" she commented.

"Yeah, I know." Lee smiled. "So, I guess you'll need a ride next week?"

Rebecca laughed and asked, "What do you think?"

People are attracted to places where people really care and teach God's Word. Read **Acts 2:36–47** to see how the first church attracted people by the way its people lived and worshiped together.

- How does the church in Acts compare with Lee's church?
- Which qualities does the Acts church have in common with your church? Which qualities of this church are different from your church's?

CONSIDER . . .

- befriending visitors who come to your church. Ask them to sit with you or invite them to other church activities.
- doing a specific job in your church, such as greeting visitors or writing for the newsletter. Become one of the people who makes church more of what God wants it to be.

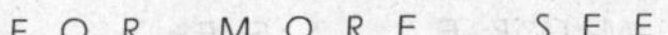

FOR MORE, SEE . . .

- Isaiah 2:2–5 (p. 618)
- Acts 4:32–35 (p. 1104)
- Romans 12 (p. 1157)

a murderer[n] instead. 15And so you killed the One
who gives life, but God raised him from the dead.
We are witnesses to this. 16It was faith in Jesus
that made this crippled man well. You can see this
man, and you know him. He was made completely well because of trust in Jesus, and you all
saw it happen!
17"Brothers and sisters, I know you did those
things to Jesus because neither you nor your leaders understood what you were doing. 18God said
through the prophets[d] that his Christ[d] would suffer and die. And now God has made these things
come true in this way. 19So you must change your
hearts and lives! Come back to God, and he will
forgive your sins. Then the Lord will send the
time of rest. 20And he will send Jesus, the One he
chose to be the Christ. 21But Jesus must stay in
heaven until the time comes when all things will
be made right again. God told about this time long
ago when he spoke through his holy prophets.
22Moses said, 'The Lord your God will give you a
prophet like me, who is one of your own people.
You must listen to everything he tells you. 23Any-
one who does not listen to that prophet will die,
cut off from God's people.'[n] 24Samuel, and all the
other prophets who spoke for God after Samuel,
told about this time now. 25You are descendants[d]
of the prophets. You have received the agreement
God made with your ancestors. He said to your
father Abraham, 'Through your descendants[d] all
the nations on the earth will be blessed.'[n] 26God
has raised up his servant Jesus and sent him to

murderer Barabbas, the man the crowd asked Pilate to set free instead of Jesus (Luke 23:18).
'The Lord . . . people.' Quotation from Deuteronomy 18:15, 19.
'Through . . . blessed.' Quotation from Genesis 22:18; 26:4.

GOD'S LOVE

Power to Heal

"Hey, freak! Why don't you join the circus?"

"Aaagh! It's Frankenstein's brother."

Rocky Dennis had heard cruel jeers like this all his life. Rocky had been born with a disease known as lionitis. This disease multiplied calcium deposits at an abnormal rate throughout Rocky's skull and progressively disfigured Rocky's face.

But Rocky displayed remarkable friendship, joy, and confidence—even with the people who were most cruel. He wouldn't accept rejection. When people made fun of his face, he responded with better jokes. Rocky loved people in a way that made them forget what he looked like. His comfort with himself put other people at ease.

Mask, the movie about Rocky's life, portrays how Rocky loved a blind and beautiful teenage girl. Because the girl couldn't see his physical deformity, his inner beauty captured her heart. Rocky opened up the world to her. He showed her color by placing things in her hands: Blue was an ice cube; red was a hot rock; the hot rock cooled to pink; white was a mass of cotton balls.

But not everyone could see Rocky's beauty. After meeting Rocky, the blind girl's parents blocked further contact with him. The only girl who had ever really seen Rocky was taken away from him.

Rocky had reason to be frustrated, angry and sad. But he overcame bad with good. He continued to care for people and was patient with those who were blinded by his deformity.

Jesus also knew the pain of rejection, but he kept loving people anyway, as we see in **Acts 3:11–19**.

- How were Rocky's attitude and actions similar to Jesus' attitude and actions?
- According to this passage, what is the Christlike way to respond to rejection?

CONSIDER . . .

- listing things you could say to people who reject you.
- developing a friendship with someone other people reject.

FOR MORE, SEE . . .

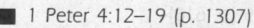

- Isaiah 53:1–6 (p. 672)
- Matthew 5:43–48 (p. 916)
- 1 Peter 4:12–19 (p. 1307)

you first to bless you by turning each of you away
from doing evil."

Peter and John at the Council

4 While Peter and John were speaking to the
people, Jewish priests, the captain of the soldiers that guarded the Temple,[d] and Sadducees[d]
came up to them. 2They were upset because the
two apostles[d] were teaching the people and were
preaching that people will rise from the dead
through the power of Jesus. 3The Jewish leaders
grabbed Peter and John and put them in jail. Since
it was already night, they kept them in jail until
the next day. 4But many of those who had heard
Peter and John preach believed the things they
said. There were now about five thousand in the
group of believers.
5The next day the Jewish rulers, the older Jewish leaders, and the teachers of the law met in
Jerusalem. 6Annas the high priest, Caiaphas, John,
and Alexander were there, as well as everyone
from the high priest's family. 7They made Peter
and John stand before them and then asked them,
"By what power or authority did you do this?"
8Then Peter, filled with the Holy Spirit,[d] said to
them, "Rulers of the people and you older leaders,
9are you questioning us about a good thing that
was done to a crippled man? Are you asking us
who made him well? 10We want all of you and all
the Jewish people to know that this man was
made well by the power of Jesus Christ from Nazareth. You crucified him, but God raised him from
the dead. This man was crippled, but he is now
well and able to stand here before you because of
the power of Jesus. 11Jesus is

'the stone[n] that you builders rejected,
which has become the cornerstone.'[d]

Psalm 118:22

12Jesus is the only One who can save people. His
name is the only power in the world that has been
given to save people. We must be saved through
him."
13The Jewish leaders saw that Peter and John
were not afraid to speak, and they understood
that these men had no special training or education. So they were amazed. Then they realized

stone A symbol meaning Jesus.

SHARING FAITH

Responding to Opportunities

"C'mon, Manuel. Don't let me down! Mrs. Reece trusts you," Rick Jantzen pleaded. "She would let you into the classroom to use the lab at night, and you could copy the test key while you're there. She'd never know."

"I just can't. I can't use Mrs. Reece's trust that way," Manuel Salazar said. "And besides, it's wrong to cheat."

"Why can't you do it just this once? No one will know!" Rick persisted.

"I will know and so will Jesus," Manuel answered.

"But Jesus wants you to make good grades, doesn't he?" Rick challenged.

"Yeah, he does. This just isn't the way to make those good grades."

Rick finally quit pressuring Manuel to compromise his faith. In fact, over time Rick even started asking Manuel questions about "this Jesus who runs your life."

Caught in a tough situation, Manuel shared his faith by showing how it influenced his actions. Read how Peter and John took advantage of an opportunity to talk about Jesus in **Acts 4:1–13**.

- What obstacles did Manuel and Peter have to overcome to talk about their faith?
- What basic facts about Jesus did Peter consider essential in discussing his faith?

CONSIDER . . .

- writing down ways you could share your faith with a non-Christian. Use one of these ways with someone this week.
- enlisting a friend to role-play faith-sharing situations. Role-play talking to people who are skeptical, open, rebellious or interested.

FOR MORE, SEE . . .

- Daniel 1:3–16 (p. 807)
- Matthew 10:16–20 (p. 924)
- Colossians 4:5–6 (p. 1243)

that Peter and John had been with Jesus. 14Be-
cause they saw the healed man standing there beside the two apostles, they could say nothing
against them. 15After the Jewish leaders ordered
them to leave the meeting, they began to talk to
each other. 16They said, "What shall we do with
these men? Everyone in Jerusalem knows they
have done a great miracle,[d] and we cannot say it
is not true. 17But to keep it from spreading among
the people, we must warn them not to talk to
people anymore using that name."

18So they called Peter and John in again and
told them not to speak or to teach at all in the
name of Jesus. 19But Peter and John answered
them, "You decide what God would want.
Should we obey you or God? 20We cannot keep
quiet. We must speak about what we have seen
and heard." 21The Jewish leaders warned the
apostles again and let them go free. They could
not find a way to punish them, because all the
people were praising God for what had been
done. 22The man who received the miracle of
healing was more than forty years old.

> **SIDELIGHT:** The council before which Peter appeared in Acts 4:1–22 was the Sanhedrin, the Jewish equivalent of the Supreme Court. It was likely composed of Jerusalem's religious and political leaders. Its main job was to protect Jewish life, custom, and law.

The Believers Pray

23After Peter and John left the meeting of Jewish leaders, they went to their own group and told
them everything the leading priests and the older
Jewish leaders had said to them. 24When the believers heard this, they prayed to God together,
"Lord, you are the One who made the sky, the
earth, the sea, and everything in them. 25By the
Holy Spirit,[d] through our father David your servant, you said:

'Why are the nations so angry?
Why are the people making useless plans?
26The kings of the earth prepare to fight,
and their leaders make plans together
against the Lord
and his Christ.'[d] *Psalm 2:1-2*

27These things really happened when Herod, Pontius Pilate, those who are not Jews, and the Jewish people all came together against Jesus here in
Jerusalem. Jesus is your holy servant, the One you
made to be the Christ. 28These people made your
plan happen because of your power and your will.
29And now, Lord, listen to their threats. Lord,
help us, your servants, to speak your word without fear. 30Help us to be brave by showing us your
power to heal. Give proofs and make miracles[d]
happen by the power of Jesus, your holy servant."

31After they had prayed, the place where they
were meeting was shaken. They were all filled
with the Holy Spirit,[d] and they spoke God's word
without fear.

The Believers Share

32The group of believers were united in their
hearts and spirit. All those in the group acted as
though their private property belonged to everyone in the group. In fact, they shared everything.
33With great power the apostles[d] were telling people that the Lord Jesus was truly raised from the
dead. And God blessed all the believers very
much. 34No one in the group needed anything.
From time to time those who owned fields or
houses sold them, brought the money, 35and gave
it to the apostles. Then the money was given to
anyone who needed it.

36One of the believers was named Joseph, a Levite born in Cyprus. The apostles called him Barnabas (which means "one who encourages").
37Joseph owned a field, sold it, brought the
money, and gave it to the apostles.

Ananias and Sapphira Die

5 But a man named Ananias and his wife Sapphira sold some land. 2He kept back part of
the money for himself; his wife knew about this
and agreed to it. But he brought the rest of the
money and gave it to the apostles.[d] 3Peter said,
"Ananias, why did you let Satan rule your
thoughts to lie to the Holy Spirit[d] and to keep for
yourself part of the money you received for the
land? 4Before you sold the land, it belonged to
you. And even after you sold it, you could have
used the money any way you wanted. Why did
you think of doing this? You lied to God, not to
us!" 5-6When Ananias heard this, he fell down and
died. Some young men came in, wrapped up his
body, carried it out, and buried it. And everyone
who heard about this was filled with fear.

7About three hours later his wife came in, but
she did not know what had happened. 8Peter said
to her, "Tell me, was the money you got for your
field this much?"

Sapphira answered, "Yes, that was the price."

9Peter said to her, "Why did you and your husband agree to test the Spirit of the Lord? Look!
The men who buried your husband are at the
door, and they will carry you out." 10At that moment Sapphira fell down by his feet and died.
When the young men came in and saw that she
was dead, they carried her out and buried her beside her husband. 11The whole church and all the
others who heard about these things were filled
with fear.

The Apostles Heal Many

12The apostles[d] did many signs and miracles[d]
among the people. And they would all meet together on Solomon's Porch.[d] 13None of the others
dared to join them, but all the people respected
them. 14More and more men and women believed in the Lord and were added to the group
of believers. 15The people placed their sick on
beds and mats in the streets, hoping that when
Peter passed by at least his shadow might fall on
them. 16Crowds came from all the towns around
Jerusalem, bringing their sick and those who were
bothered by evil spirits, and all of them were
healed.

Leaders Try to Stop the Apostles

17The high priest and all his friends (a group
called the Sadducees[d]) became very jealous.
18They took the apostles[d] and put them in jail.
19But during the night, an angel of the Lord
opened the doors of the jail and led the apostles
outside. The angel said, 20"Go stand in the Tem-

PRIORITIES

Who's the Boss?

Richard Wurmbrand fidgeted in his chair as he listened to Gheorghe Gheorghiu-Dej, the Communist Party boss, deliver his speech. Gheorghe promised the post-World War II clergy of Romania that his government would pay the clergy from tax revenues if communism and Christianity would work together.

Most of the audience cheered, and a leader promised that the clergy would cooperate with the state.

But Richard didn't cheer. He had already been imprisoned and beaten several times for his faith. He knew speaking out could again cost him his freedom.

Richard's wife, Sabrina, sat beside him. "Go and wash this shame from the face of Christ!" she demanded.

Richard pleaded that he would probably be taken away if he spoke out against the communists.

"I don't need a coward," Sabrina replied.

Gathering his courage, Richard asked permission to speak and was welcomed forward by the organizers, who apparently anticipated a unity speech. Instead, Richard began by saying it was the duty of pastors to glorify God, not earthly powers. He encouraged the clergy to support the eternal kingdom of God, not the fleeting powers of Romania.

As he continued, someone suddenly began to clap. And another person also clapped. Soon, the clapping erupted into waves of applause.

"Stop! Your right to speak has been withdrawn," ordered the Minister of Cults ("cults" included religious bodies of all kinds in Romania).

"My right to speak comes from God," Richard declared. He kept speaking until his microphone was disconnected.

Soon after, Richard was imprisoned. The Romanian communists instituted their state religion and the Ministry of Cults ran the church.

Like Richard, the apostles recognized the priority of obeying God and speaking out for him. Read **Acts 5:17–32** to see how they spoke out for Jesus even when threatened by imprisonment.

- Based on the story and the Bible passage, what were the top priorities for Richard Wurmbrand and the apostles?
- When have you faced opposition for your faith? How was that experience like and unlike the scripture passage?

CONSIDER . . .

- making a poster of Acts 5:29 and writing around the border five priorities you believe God wants you to follow. Then make a weekly schedule that reflects those priorities.
- talking with a friend about times you have had to do something unpopular to make your faith your top priority.

FOR MORE, SEE . . .

- Psalm 119:17–24 (p. 550)
- Matthew 10:32–36 (p. 925)
- 2 Corinthians 11:23–29 (p. 1202)

ple[d] and tell the people everything about this new life." 21When the apostles heard this, they obeyed and went into the Temple early in the morning and continued teaching.

When the high priest and his friends arrived, they called a meeting of the Jewish leaders and all the important older Jewish men. They sent some men to the jail to bring the apostles to them. 22But, upon arriving, the officers could not find the apostles. So they went back and reported to the Jewish leaders. 23They said, "The jail was closed and locked, and the guards were standing at the doors. But when we opened the doors, the jail was empty!" 24Hearing this, the captain of the Temple guards and the leading priests were confused and wondered what was happening.

25Then someone came and told them, "Listen! The men you put in jail are standing in the Temple teaching the people." 26Then the captain and his men went out and brought the apostles back. But the soldiers did not use force, because they were afraid the people would stone them to death.

27The soldiers brought the apostles to the meeting and made them stand before the Jewish leaders. The high priest questioned them, 28saying, "We gave you strict orders not to continue teaching in that name. But look, you have filled Jerusalem with your teaching and are trying to make us responsible for this man's death."

29Peter and the other apostles answered, "We must obey God, not human authority! 30You killed Jesus by hanging him on a cross. But God, the God of our ancestors, raised Jesus up from the dead! 31Jesus is the One whom God raised to be on his right side, as Leader and Savior. Through him, all Jewish people could change their hearts and lives and have their sins forgiven. 32We saw all these things happen. The Holy Spirit,[d] whom God has given to all who obey him, also proves these things are true."

33When the Jewish leaders heard this, they became angry and wanted to kill them. 34But a Pharisee[d] named Gamaliel stood up in the meeting. He was a teacher of the law, and all the people respected him. He ordered the apostles to leave the meeting for a little while. 35Then he said, "People of Israel, be careful what you are planning to do to these men. 36Remember when Theudas appeared? He said he was a great man, and about four hundred men joined him. But he was killed, and all his followers were scattered; they were able to do nothing. 37Later, a man named Judas came from Galilee at the time of the registration.[n] He also led a group of followers and was killed, and all his followers were scattered. 38And so now I tell you: Stay away from these men, and leave them alone. If their plan comes from human authority, it will fail. 39But if it is from God, you will not be able to stop them. You might even be fighting against God himself!"

The Jewish leaders agreed with what Gamaliel said. 40They called the apostles in, beat them, and told them not to speak in the name of Jesus again. Then they let them go free. 41The apostles left the meeting full of joy because they were given the honor of suffering disgrace for Jesus. 42Every day in the Temple and in people's homes they continued teaching the people and telling the Good News — that Jesus is the Christ.[d]

SIDELIGHT: Relationships between Jews and non-Jewish people were strained in Bible times. This prejudice shows up in Acts 6:1 where Greek (non-Jewish) Christians complained that their widows weren't receiving a fair share of the church's distributions. The book of Acts is filled with other stories that highlight the tensions between Jewish and non-Jewish Christians.

Seven Leaders Are Chosen

6 The number of followers was growing. But during this same time, the Greek-speaking followers had an argument with the other Jewish followers. The Greek-speaking widows were not getting their share of the food that was given out every day. 2The twelve apostles[d] called the whole group of followers together and said, "It is not right for us to stop our work of teaching God's word in order to serve tables. 3So, brothers and sisters, choose seven of your own men who are good, full of the Spirit[d] and full of wisdom. We will put them in charge of this work. 4Then we can continue to pray and to teach the word of God."

5The whole group liked the idea, so they chose these seven men: Stephen (a man with great faith and full of the Holy Spirit), Philip,[n] Procorus, Nicanor, Timon, Parmenas, and Nicolas (a man from Antioch who had become a Jew). 6Then they put these men before the apostles, who prayed and laid their hands[n] on them.

7The word of God was continuing to spread. The group of followers in Jerusalem increased, and a great number of the Jewish priests believed and obeyed.

registration Census. A counting of all the people and the things they own.
Philip Not the apostle named Philip.
laid their hands The laying on of hands had many purposes, including the giving of a blessing, power, or authority.

Stephen Is Accused

8Stephen was richly blessed by God who gave
him the power to do great miracles[d] and signs
among the people. 9But some Jewish people were
against him. They belonged to the synagogue[d] of
Free Men[n] (as it was called), which included
Jewish people from Cyrene, Alexandria, Cilicia,
and Asia. They all came and argued with Stephen.
10But the Spirit[d] was helping him to speak with
wisdom, and his words were so strong that they
could not argue with him. 11So they secretly
urged some men to say, "We heard Stephen speak
against Moses and against God."
12This upset the people, the older Jewish leaders, and the teachers of the law. They came and
grabbed Stephen and brought him to a meeting of
the Jewish leaders. 13They brought in some people to tell lies about Stephen, saying, "This man
is always speaking against this holy place and the
law of Moses. 14We heard him say that Jesus from
Nazareth will destroy this place and that Jesus
will change the customs Moses gave us." 15All the
people in the meeting were watching Stephen
closely and saw that his face looked like the face
of an angel.

Stephen's Speech

7 The high priest said to Stephen, "Are these
things true?"
2Stephen answered, "Brothers and fathers, lis-

Free Men Jewish people who had been slaves or whose fathers had been slaves, but were now free.

HONESTY

Rumors

"Shhhhh! There she is."

The girls in the back of the room stopped giggling and whispering when Zoe Ketner arrived at her first-period world history class on Monday morning.

"What's going on?" Zoe asked uncomfortably as she sat next to her best friend, Marlene Riddle.

Marlene shot a dirty look at the girls in the back of the room: "Someone is saying you're 'easy,' " she said. "There's a note in the guys' bathroom that says 'Zoe's fine, so get in line.' "

Zoe couldn't believe it. She felt like someone had just kicked her in the chest.

Just then, Mark Warren leaned across the aisle and asked, "Hey, Zoe, can I be next in line?"

Zoe burst into tears and ran from the room. Her mind raced as she stumbled through the empty hallway. Where could such a false rumor have come from? Who could say such ugly things?

Then she remembered what Ben Pullman, her ex-boyfriend, had said. After begging her not to break up, he warned that she would be sorry if she did.

"This must be what he meant," Zoe thought as she leaned against a locker and slid down to sit on the floor.

Zoe knew it would take a long time to clear her reputation. But she was determined that, no matter what, it would be cleared.

"Lord," she prayed, "help me be strong." Zoe maintained her high standards in dating, and in time the rumors died down.

Stephen was also a victim of lies and rumors, but he remained faithful to God, as we read in **Acts 6:8–15**.

- How could Zoe and Stephen be strong in the face of lies and rumors?
- When has someone told lies about you the way these people did about Stephen? How did you respond?

CONSIDER. . .

- thinking of a tactful way to respond to people who spread rumors. Always talk to the person who is being talked about rather than spread rumors.
- deciding what you will do to clear your reputation if someone spreads dishonest rumors about you.

FOR MORE, SEE

- Leviticus 19:16–17 (p. 116)
- Matthew 26:57–68 (p. 958)
- James 3:1–12 (p. 1296)

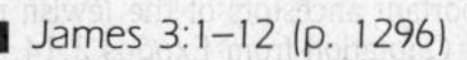

ten to me. Our glorious God appeared to Abraham, our ancestor, in Mesopotamia before he lived in Haran. 3God said to Abraham, 'Leave your country and your relatives, and go to the land I will show you.'[n] 4So Abraham left the country of Chaldea and went to live in Haran. After Abraham's father died, God sent him to this place where you now live. 5God did not give Abraham any of this land, not even a foot of it. But God promised that he would give this land to him and his descendants,[d] even before Abraham had a child. 6This is what God said to him: 'Your descendants will be strangers in a land they don't own. The people there will make them slaves and will mistreat them for four hundred years. 7But I will punish the nation where they are slaves. Then your descendants will leave that land and will worship me in this place.'[n] 8God made an agreement with Abraham, the sign of which was circumcision.[d] And so when Abraham had his son Isaac, Abraham circumcised him when he was eight days old. Isaac also circumcised his son Jacob, and Jacob did the same for his sons, the twelve ancestors[n] of our people.

9"Jacob's sons became jealous of Joseph and sold him to be a slave in Egypt. But God was with him 10and saved him from all his troubles. The king of Egypt liked Joseph and respected him because of the wisdom God gave him. The king made him governor of Egypt and put him in charge of all the people in his palace.

11"Then all the land of Egypt and Canaan became so dry that nothing would grow, and the people suffered very much. Jacob's sons, our ancestors, could not find anything to eat. 12But when Jacob heard there was grain in Egypt, he sent his sons there. This was their first trip to Egypt. 13When they went there a second time, Joseph told his brothers who he was, and the king learned about Joseph's family. 14Then Joseph sent messengers to invite Jacob, his father, to come to Egypt along with all his relatives (seventy-five persons altogether). 15So Jacob went down to Egypt, where he and his sons died. 16Later their bodies were moved to Shechem and put in a grave there. (It was the same grave Abraham had bought for a sum of money from the sons of Hamor in Shechem.)

17"The promise God made to Abraham was soon to come true, and the number of people in Egypt grew large. 18Then a new king, who did not know who Joseph was, began to rule Egypt. 19This king tricked our people and was cruel to our ancestors, forcing them to leave their babies outside to die. 20At this time Moses was born, and he was very beautiful. For three months Moses was cared for in his father's house. 21When they put Moses outside, the king's daughter adopted him and raised him as if he were her own son. 22The Egyptians taught Moses everything they knew, and he was a powerful man in what he said and did.

23"When Moses was about forty years old, he thought it would be good to visit his own people, the people of Israel. 24Moses saw an Egyptian mistreating an Israelite, so he defended the Israelite and punished the Egyptian by killing him. 25Moses thought his own people would understand that God was using him to save them, but they did not. 26The next day when Moses saw two men of Israel fighting, he tried to make peace between them. He said, 'Men, you are brothers. Why are you hurting each other?' 27The man who was hurting the other pushed Moses away and said, 'Who made you our ruler and judge? 28Are you going to kill me as you killed the Egyptian yesterday?'[n] 29When Moses heard him say this, he left Egypt and went to live in the land of Midian where he was a stranger. While Moses lived in Midian, he had two sons.

30"Forty years later an angel appeared to Moses in the flames of a burning bush as he was in the desert near Mount Sinai. 31When Moses saw this, he was amazed and went near to look closer. Moses heard the Lord's voice say, 32'I am the God of your ancestors, the God of Abraham, Isaac, and Jacob.'[n] Moses began to shake with fear and was afraid to look. 33The Lord said to him, 'Take off your sandals, because you are standing on holy ground. 34I have seen the troubles my people have suffered in Egypt. I have heard their cries and have come down to save them. And now, Moses, I am sending you back to Egypt.'[n]

35"This Moses was the same man the two men of Israel rejected, saying, 'Who made you a ruler and judge?'[n] Moses is the same man God sent to be a ruler and savior, with the help of the angel that Moses saw in the burning bush. 36So Moses led the people out of Egypt. He worked miracles[d] and signs in Egypt, at the Red Sea,[d] and then in the desert for forty years. 37This is the same Moses that said to the people of Israel, 'God will give you a prophet[d] like me, who is one of your own

'Leave . . . you.' Quotation from Genesis 12:1.
'Your descendants . . . place.' Quotation from Genesis 15:13-14 and Exodus 3:12.
twelve ancestors Important ancestors of the Jewish people; the leaders of the twelve Jewish tribes.
'Who . . . yesterday?' Quotation from Exodus 2:14.
'I am . . . Jacob.' Quotation from Exodus 3:6.
'Take . . . Egypt.' Quotation from Exodus 3:5-10.
'Who . . . judge?' Quotation from Exodus 2:14.

people.'[n] 38This is the Moses who was with the
gathering of the Israelites in the desert. He was
with the angel that spoke to him at Mount Sinai,
and he was with our ancestors. He received
commands from God that give life, and he gave
those commands to us.
39"But our ancestors did not want to obey Moses. They rejected him and wanted to go back to
Egypt. 40They said to Aaron, 'Make us gods who
will lead us. Moses led us out of Egypt, but we
don't know what has happened to him.'[n] 41So the
people made an idol that looked like a calf. Then
they brought sacrifices to it and were proud of
what they had made with their own hands. 42But
God turned against them and did not try to stop
them from worshiping the sun, moon, and stars.
This is what is written in the book of the prophets: God says,

'People of Israel, you did not bring me
sacrifices and offerings
while you traveled in the desert for forty
years.
43You have carried with you
the tent to worship Molech[d]
and the idols of the star god Rephan that
you made to worship.
So I will send you away beyond Babylon.'

Amos 5:25-27

44"The Holy Tent[d] where God spoke to our ancestors was with them in the desert. God told Moses how to make this Tent, and he made it like the
plan God showed him. 45Later, Joshua led our ancestors to capture the lands of the other nations.
Our people went in, and God forced the other
people out. When our people went into this new
land, they took with them this same Tent they
had received from their ancestors. They kept it
until the time of David, 46who pleased God and
asked God to let him build a house for him, the
God of Jacob. 47But Solomon was the one who
built the Temple.[d]
48"But the Most High does not live in houses
that people build with their hands. As the prophet
says:

49'Heaven is my throne,
and the earth is my footstool.
So do you think you can build a house for
me? says the Lord.
Do I need a place to rest?
50Remember, my hand made all these things!' "

Isaiah 66:1-2

51Stephen continued speaking: "You stubborn
people! You have not given your hearts to God,
nor will you listen to him! You are always against
what the Holy Spirit[d] is trying to tell you, just as
your ancestors were. 52Your ancestors tried to
hurt every prophet who ever lived. Those prophets said long ago that the One who is good would
come, but your ancestors killed them. And now
you have turned against and killed the One who
is good. 53You received the law of Moses, which
God gave you through his angels, but you haven't
obeyed it."

Stephen Is Killed

54When the leaders heard this, they became furious. They were so mad they were grinding their
teeth at Stephen. 55But Stephen was full of the
Holy Spirit.[d] He looked up to heaven and saw the
glory of God and Jesus standing at God's right
side. 56He said, "Look! I see heaven open and the
Son of Man[d] standing at God's right side."
57Then they shouted loudly and covered their
ears and all ran at Stephen. 58They took him out
of the city and began to throw stones at him to kill
him. And those who told lies against Stephen left
their coats with a young man named Saul.
59While they were throwing stones, Stephen
prayed, "Lord Jesus, receive my spirit." 60He fell
on his knees and cried in a loud voice, "Lord, do
not hold this sin against them." After Stephen said
this, he died.

8 Saul agreed that the killing of Stephen was
good.

Troubles for the Believers

On that day the church of Jerusalem began to
be persecuted,[d] and all the believers, except the
apostles,[d] were scattered throughout Judea and
Samaria.
2And some religious people buried Stephen and
cried loudly for him. 3Saul was also trying to destroy the church, going from house to house,
dragging out men and women and putting them
in jail. 4And wherever they were scattered, they
told people the Good News.[d]

Philip Preaches in Samaria

5Philip[n] went to the city of Samaria and
preached about the Christ.[d] 6When the people
there heard Philip and saw the miracles[d] he was
doing, they all listened carefully to what he said.
7Many of these people had evil spirits in them, but
Philip made the evil spirits leave. The spirits made
a loud noise when they came out. Philip also
healed many weak and crippled people there. 8So
the people in that city were very happy.
9But there was a man named Simon in that
city. Before Philip came there, Simon had practiced magic and amazed all the people of Samaria.

'God . . . people.' Quotation from Deuteronomy 18:15.
'Make . . . him.' Quotation from Exodus 32:1.
Philip Not the apostle named Philip.

He bragged and called himself a great man. 10All
the people — the least important and the most important — paid attention to Simon, saying, "This
man has the power of God, called 'the Great
Power'!" 11Simon had amazed them with his
magic so long that the people became his followers. 12But when Philip told them the Good News[d]
about the kingdom of God and the power of Jesus
Christ, men and women believed Philip and were
baptized. 13Simon himself believed, and after he
was baptized, he stayed very close to Philip.
When he saw the miracles and the powerful
things Philip did, Simon was amazed.
14When the apostles[d] who were still in Jerusalem heard that the people of Samaria had accepted the word of God, they sent Peter and John
to them. 15When Peter and John arrived, they
prayed that the Samaritan believers might receive
the Holy Spirit.[d] 16These people had been baptized in the name of the Lord Jesus, but the
Holy Spirit had not yet come upon any of them.
17Then, when the two apostles began laying
their hands on the people, they received the
Holy Spirit.

18Simon saw that the Spirit was given to
people when the apostles laid their hands on
them. So he offered the apostles money, 19saying,
"Give me also this power so that anyone on
whom I lay my hands will receive the Holy
Spirit."
20Peter said to him, "You and your money
should both be destroyed, because you thought
you could buy God's gift with money. 21You cannot share with us in this work since your heart is
not right before God. 22Change your heart! Turn
away from this evil thing you have done, and pray
to the Lord. Maybe he will forgive you for thinking this. 23I see that you are full of bitter jealousy
and ruled by sin."
24Simon answered, "Both of you pray for me to
the Lord so the things you have said will not happen to me."
25After Peter and John told the people what
they had seen Jesus do and after they had spoken
the message of the Lord, they went back to Jerusalem. On the way, they went through many Samaritan towns and preached the Good News to
the people.

ANGER

Rage

Ann, thirteen, appeared to be a model student and a devoted daughter. But one night, Ann brought two guys into her bedroom and called her father to come upstairs. Using a knife and a length of pipe, the three teenagers slashed and bludgeoned him to death. Ann had been psychologically abused by her father.

Alan, fourteen, was the school scapegoat. Gangly and clumsy, with few friends, he was the target of daily harassment and beatings. One morning in late January, Alan headed to school carrying one of his father's high-power rifles and ammunition. When he got there, he opened fire in the hallway, killing the school's principal and wounding two teachers and one student. He thought his actions might win his harsh father's approval.

A group of Jewish leaders, religious and proper, faithfully practiced the regulations of their faith. When Stephen, a Christian disciple, started preaching about Jesus, the Jewish leaders went berserk. They carried Stephen out of the city and hurled stones at him until he was dead.

Read **Acts 7:51–60** to get the full story of how these Jewish leaders let their anger lead to destruction.

- What caused Ann's, Alan's, and the Jewish leaders' rage?
- Why was Stephen able to respond to his killers the way he did?

CONSIDER . . .

- counting to ten before expressing your anger so you won't do something you'll later regret.
- seeking professional help if your anger turns to rage. Protect yourself and others by learning how to handle anger.

FOR MORE, SEE . . .

- Deuteronomy 13:6–11 (p. 173)
- Ephesians 4:26–32 (p. 1224)
- James 1:19–20 (p. 1294)

Philip Teaches an Ethiopian

[26]An angel of the Lord said to Philip,[n] "Get
ready and go south to the road that leads down
to Gaza from Jerusalem—the desert road." [27]So
Philip got ready and went. On the road he saw a
man from Ethiopia, a eunuch.[d] He was an important officer in the service of Candace, the queen
of the Ethiopians; he was responsible for taking care of all her money. He had gone to Jerusalem to worship. [28]Now, as he was on his way
home, he was sitting in his chariot reading from
the Book of Isaiah, the prophet.[d] [29]The Spirit[d]
said to Philip, "Go to that chariot and stay near
it."

[30]So when Philip ran toward the chariot, he
heard the man reading from Isaiah the prophet.
Philip asked, "Do you understand what you are
reading?"

[31]He answered, "How can I understand unless
someone explains it to me?" Then he invited
Philip to climb in and sit with him. [32]The portion
of Scripture[d] he was reading was this:

"He was like a sheep being led to be killed.
He was quiet, as a lamb is quiet while its
wool is being cut;
he never opened his mouth.
33 He was shamed and was treated unfairly.
He died without children to continue his
family.
His life on earth has ended." *Isaiah 53:7-8*

[34]The officer said to Philip, "Please tell me,
who is the prophet talking about—himself or
someone else?" [35]Philip began to speak, and starting with this same Scripture, he told the man the
Good News[d] about Jesus.

[36]While they were traveling down the road,
they came to some water. The officer said, "Look,
here is water. What is stopping me from being

Philip Not the apostle named Philip.

BIBLE STUDY

Creative Questions

"Lately I've been wondering if there really is a God," Kevin Morgan said and looked down at his shoes. "I mean, how do I know Christianity isn't just wishful thinking?"

Kevin looked around the room for someone to answer his questions. Everyone was silent.

Finally, Jeremy Coffey spoke up. "I like to hit it from the opposite point of view. I try to prove there isn't a God."

Then everyone started talking at once.

"That leads to even harder questions," said someone in the corner. "How can you explain everything in this world if there isn't a Creator?"

"And why do people get mad at things like murder and child abuse if there isn't a God who shows the difference between right and wrong?"

"Yeah! And what about people's need for religion? Why would they want to worship God if there is no God?"

The questions went on and on. Finally, the kids were silent. Jeremy looked around and smiled. "Believing there is no God takes more faith than realizing there is one," he said. "Thanks for stretching my faith."

There's nothing wrong with sincere questions because they lead to real answers. An Ethiopian asked questions that led to faith in Jesus in **Acts 8:26–40**.

- How do you think his questions led Kevin to deeper faith? How did the Ethiopian's questions lead him to God's salvation?
- What questions would you ask about the passage the Ethiopian had read?

C O N S I D E R . . .

- listing the questions you have about God and searching for answers to those questions.
- writing down questions as you read the Bible. Ask these questions during Sunday school or youth group.

F O R M O R E , S E E . . .

- Isaiah 53:7–8 (p. 672)
- John 20:24–29 (p. 1094)
- Hebrews 6:1–3 (p. 1280)

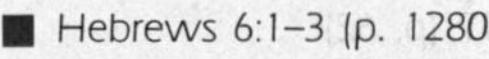

baptized?" [37] [n] [38]Then the officer commanded
the chariot to stop. Both Philip and the officer
went down into the water, and Philip baptized
him. [39]When they came up out of the water, the
Spirit of the Lord took Philip away; the officer
never saw him again. And the officer continued
on his way home, full of joy. [40]But Philip appeared
in a city called Azotus and preached the Good
News in all the towns on the way from Azotus to
Caesarea.

SIDELIGHT: Acts 8:26–40 tells of what is likely the conversion of the first African. He came from an area south of Egypt called Nubia. Philip had traveled about fifty miles from Jerusalem to witness to this man.

Saul Is Converted

9 In Jerusalem Saul was still threatening the
followers of the Lord by saying he would kill
them. So he went to the high priest [2]and asked
him to write letters to the synagogues[d] in the city
of Damascus. Then if Saul found any followers of
Christ's Way, men or women, he would arrest
them and bring them back to Jerusalem.

[3]So Saul headed toward Damascus. As he came
near the city, a bright light from heaven suddenly
flashed around him. [4]Saul fell to the ground and
heard a voice saying to him, "Saul, Saul! Why are
you persecuting me?"

[5]Saul said, "Who are you, Lord?"

The voice answered, "I am Jesus, whom you
are persecuting. [6]Get up now and go into the city.
Someone there will tell you what you must do."

[7]The people traveling with Saul stood there but
said nothing. They heard the voice, but they saw

Verse 37 Some late copies of Acts add verse 37: "Philip answered, 'If you believe with all your heart, you can.' The officer said, 'I believe that Jesus Christ is the Son of God.' "

FOLLOWING GOD

Show and Tell

Charles Blondin stretched an eleven-hundred-foot tightrope across Niagara Falls on June 30, 1859. About twenty-five thousand spectators gathered to watch the incredible stunt. Charles stood in front of the crowd and asked, "How many believe I can walk across Niagara Falls?"

"We believe!" the crowd roared. And so Charles walked safely across Niagara Falls, one hundred sixty feet in the air.

Five days later, he asked, "How many believe I can walk across Niagara Falls blindfolded and pushing a wheelbarrow?"

The crowd cheered. And Charles did it again.

Two weeks later, the crowd gathered again. "How many believe I can walk across with a person on my back?" he asked.

The crowd screamed: "Of course! We believe!"

Charles looked straight at a person in the front. "You, sir. Climb on!" The man refused.

There's a big difference between talking about faith and acting on that faith. In **Acts 9:1–20**, Saul and Ananias both learned what it meant to act on their faith.

- Which was most difficult to act on: Charles's challenge or Jesus' instructions to Saul and Ananias? Why?
- What did Ananias's actions communicate to Saul?

C O N S I D E R . . .

- becoming an "Ananias" to a friend who is struggling with his or her faith. Provide encouragement and support as that person searches for what it means to follow God.
- writing the story of a time when you have experienced God's love. Then tell a friend your story.

F O R M O R E , S E E . . .

- Exodus 4:1–17 (p. 62)
- Acts 22:1–16 (p. 1132)
- James 2:14–18 (p. 1295)

no one. [8]Saul got up from the ground and opened his eyes, but he could not see. So those with Saul took his hand and led him into Damascus. [9]For three days Saul could not see and did not eat or drink.

[10]There was a follower of Jesus in Damascus named Ananias. The Lord spoke to Ananias in a vision, "Ananias!"

Ananias answered, "Here I am, Lord."

[11]The Lord said to him, "Get up and go to Straight Street. Find the house of Judas,[n] and ask for a man named Saul from the city of Tarsus. He is there now, praying. [12]Saul has seen a vision in which a man named Ananias comes to him and lays his hands on him. Then he is able to see again."

[13]But Ananias answered, "Lord, many people have told me about this man and the terrible things he did to your holy people in Jerusalem. [14]Now he has come here to Damascus, and the leading priests have given him the power to arrest everyone who worships you."

[15]But the Lord said to Ananias, "Go! I have chosen Saul for an important work. He must tell about me to those who are not Jews, to kings, and to the people of Israel. [16]I will show him how much he must suffer for my name."

[17]So Ananias went to the house of Judas. He laid his hands on Saul and said, "Brother Saul, the Lord Jesus sent me. He is the one you saw on the road on your way here. He sent me so that you can see again and be filled with the Holy Spirit."[d] [18]Immediately, something that looked like fish scales fell from Saul's eyes, and he was able to see again! Then Saul got up and was baptized. [19]After he ate some food, his strength returned.

Saul Preaches in Damascus

Saul stayed with the followers of Jesus in Damascus for a few days. [20]Soon he began to preach about Jesus in the synagogues,[d] saying, "Jesus is the Son of God."

[21]All the people who heard him were amazed. They said, "This is the man who was in Jerusalem trying to destroy those who trust in this name! He came here to arrest the followers of Jesus and take them back to the leading priests."

[22]But Saul grew more powerful. His proofs that Jesus is the Christ[d] were so strong that the Jewish people in Damascus could not argue with him.

[23]After many days, some Jewish people made plans to kill Saul. [24]They were watching the city gates day and night, but Saul learned about their plan. [25]One night some followers of Saul helped him leave the city by lowering him in a basket through an opening in the city wall.

Saul Preaches in Jerusalem

[26]When Saul went to Jerusalem, he tried to join the group of followers, but they were all afraid of him. They did not believe he was really a follower. [27]But Barnabas accepted Saul and took him to the apostles.[d] Barnabas explained to them that Saul had seen the Lord on the road and the Lord had spoken to Saul. Then he told them how boldly Saul had preached in the name of Jesus in Damascus.

[28]And so Saul stayed with the followers, going everywhere in Jerusalem, preaching boldly in the name of the Lord. [29]He would often talk and argue with the Jewish people who spoke Greek, but they were trying to kill him. [30]When the followers learned about this, they took Saul to Caesarea and from there sent him to Tarsus.

[31]The church everywhere in Judea, Galilee, and Samaria had a time of peace and became stronger. Respecting the Lord by the way they lived, and being encouraged by the Holy Spirit,[d] the group of believers continued to grow.

Peter Heals Aeneas

[32]As Peter was traveling through all the area, he visited God's people who lived in Lydda. [33]There he met a man named Aeneas, who was paralyzed and had not been able to leave his bed for the past eight years. [34]Peter said to him, "Aeneas, Jesus Christ heals you. Stand up and make your bed." Aeneas stood up immediately. [35]All the people living in Lydda and on the Plain of Sharon saw him and turned to the Lord.

Peter Heals Tabitha

[36]In the city of Joppa there was a follower named Tabitha (whose Greek name was Dorcas). She was always doing good deeds and kind acts. [37]While Peter was in Lydda, Tabitha became sick and died. Her body was washed and put in a room upstairs. [38]Since Lydda is near Joppa and the followers in Joppa heard that Peter was in Lydda, they sent two messengers to Peter. They begged him, "Hurry, please come to us!" [39]So Peter got ready and went with them. When he arrived, they took him to the upstairs room where all the widows stood around Peter, crying. They showed him the shirts and coats Tabitha had made when she was still alive. [40]Peter sent everyone out of the room and kneeled and prayed. Then he turned to the body and said, "Tabitha, stand up." She opened her eyes, and when she saw Peter, she sat up. [41]He gave her his hand and helped her up. Then he called the saints[d] and the widows into the room and showed them that Tabitha was alive. [42]People everywhere in Joppa learned about

Judas This is not either of the apostles named Judas.

this, and many believed in the Lord. 43Peter stayed in Joppa for many days with a man named Simon who was a tanner.

Peter Teaches Cornelius

10 At Caesarea there was a man named Cornelius, an officer in the Italian group of the Roman army. 2Cornelius was a religious man. He and all the other people who lived in his house worshiped the true God. He gave much of his money to the poor and prayed to God often. 3One afternoon about three o'clock, Cornelius clearly saw a vision. An angel of God came to him and said, "Cornelius!"

4Cornelius stared at the angel. He became afraid and said, "What do you want, Lord?"

The angel said, "God has heard your prayers. He has seen that you give to the poor, and he remembers you. 5Send some men now to Joppa to bring back a man named Simon who is also called Peter. 6He is staying with a man, also named Simon, who is a tanner and has a house beside the sea." 7When the angel who spoke to Cornelius left, Cornelius called two of his servants and a soldier, a religious man who worked for him. 8Cornelius explained everything to them and sent them to Joppa.

9About noon the next day as they came near Joppa, Peter was going up to the roof[n] to pray. 10He was hungry and wanted to eat, but while the food was being prepared, he had a vision. 11He saw heaven opened and something coming down that looked like a big sheet being lowered to earth by its four corners. 12In it were all kinds of animals, reptiles, and birds. 13Then a voice said to Peter, "Get up, Peter; kill and eat."

14But Peter said, "No, Lord! I have never eaten food that is unholy or unclean."[d]

15But the voice said to him again, "God has made these things clean so don't call them 'unholy'!" 16This happened three times, and at once the sheet was taken back to heaven.

17While Peter was wondering what this vision meant, the men Cornelius sent had found Simon's house and were standing at the gate. 18They asked, "Is Simon Peter staying here?"

19While Peter was still thinking about the vision, the Spirit[d] said to him, "Listen, three men are looking for you. 20Get up and go downstairs. Go with them without doubting, because I have sent them to you."

21So Peter went down to the men and said, "I am the one you are looking for. Why did you come here?"

22They said, "A holy angel spoke to Cornelius, an army officer and a good man; he worships God. All the Jewish people respect him. The angel told Cornelius to ask you to come to his house so that he can hear what you have to say." 23So Peter asked the men to come in and spend the night.

The next day Peter got ready and went with them, and some of the followers from Joppa joined him. 24On the following day they came to Caesarea. Cornelius was waiting for them and had called together his relatives and close friends. 25When Peter entered, Cornelius met him, fell at his feet, and worshiped him. 26But Peter helped him up, saying, "Stand up. I too am only a human." 27As he talked with Cornelius, Peter went inside where he saw many people gathered. 28He said, "You people understand that it is against our Jewish law for Jewish people to associate with or visit anyone who is not Jewish. But God has shown me that I should not call any person 'unholy' or 'unclean.' 29That is why I did not argue when I was asked to come here. Now, please tell me why you sent for me."

30Cornelius said, "Four days ago, I was praying in my house at this same time — three o'clock in the afternoon. Suddenly, there was a man standing before me wearing shining clothes. 31He said, 'Cornelius, God has heard your prayer and has seen that you give to the poor and remembers you. 32So send some men to Joppa and ask Simon Peter to come. Peter is staying in the house of a man, also named Simon, who is a tanner and has a house beside the sea.' 33So I sent for you immediately, and it was very good of you to come. Now we are all here before God to hear everything the Lord has commanded you to tell us."

34Peter began to speak: "I really understand now that to God every person is the same. 35In every country God accepts anyone who worships him and does what is right. 36You know the message that God has sent to the people of Israel is the Good News[d] that peace has come through Jesus Christ. Jesus is the Lord of all people! 37You know what has happened all over Judea, beginning in Galilee after John[n] preached to the people about baptism. 38You know about Jesus from Nazareth, that God gave him the Holy Spirit[d] and power. You know how Jesus went everywhere doing good and healing those who were ruled by the devil, because God was with him. 39We saw what Jesus did in Judea and in Jerusalem, but the Jews in Jerusalem killed him by hanging him on a cross. 40Yet, on the third day, God raised Jesus to life and caused him to be seen, 41not by all the people, but only by the witnesses God had already cho-

roof In Bible times houses were built with flat roofs. The roof was used for drying things such as flax and fruit. And it was used as an extra room, as a place for worship, and as a place to sleep in the summer.

John John the Baptist, who preached to people about Christ's coming (Luke 3).

sen. And we are those witnesses who ate and
drank with him after he was raised from the dead.
42He told us to preach to the people and to tell
them that he is the one whom God chose to be
the judge of the living and the dead. 43All the
prophets say it is true that all who believe in Jesus
will be forgiven of their sins through Jesus'
name."

44While Peter was still saying this, the Holy
Spirit[d] came down on all those who were listening. 45The Jewish believers who came with Peter
were amazed that the gift of the Holy Spirit had
been given even to those who were not Jews.
46These Jewish believers heard them speaking in
different languages[n] and praising God. Then Peter said, 47"Can anyone keep these people from
being baptized with water? They have received
the Holy Spirit just as we did!" 48So Peter ordered
that they be baptized in the name of Jesus Christ.
Then they asked Peter to stay with them for a few
days.

Peter Returns to Jerusalem

11 The apostles[d] and the believers in Judea
heard that some who were not Jewish
had accepted God's teaching too. 2But when Peter came to Jerusalem, some Jewish believers argued with him. 3They said, "You went into the
homes of people who are not circumcised[d] and
ate with them!"

4So Peter explained the whole story to them.
5He said, "I was in the city of Joppa, and while I
was praying, I had a vision. I saw something that
looked like a big sheet being lowered from heaven
by its four corners. It came very close to me. 6I
looked inside it and saw animals, wild beasts, reptiles, and birds. 7I heard a voice say to me, 'Get
up, Peter. Kill and eat.' 8But I said, 'No, Lord! I
have never eaten anything that is unholy or unclean.'[d] 9But the voice from heaven spoke again,
'God has made these things clean, so don't call
them unholy.' 10This happened three times. Then
the whole thing was taken back to heaven.

languages This can also be translated "tongues."

JUDGING OTHERS

The Color of Hatred

"It's not that blacks are bad," John Metzger says. "There are quite a few, well, not quite a few, but a sizable number of nonwhites who are intelligent."

John is a racist. He believes whites are the "chosen people"—that all nonwhite races should live in their own territories, away from whites. He is also the leader of the Aryan Youth Movement, otherwise known as "skinheads."

John doesn't look like a skinhead. His blond hair is cut conservatively. He has a respectable job and dresses like most guys his age.

But John's racist beliefs are deeply ingrained. His father leads a group of adult racists called the White Aryan Resistance. When other kids were growing up with stories about Goldilocks and the three bears, John listened to stories of hatred and prejudice at his father's knee.

Skinheads in John's Aryan Youth Movement have been linked to such brutalities as beating people to death, terrorizing people of nonwhite origin, and even nailing a former skinhead to a cross. And they have done these things all in the name of preserving their race.

Prejudice has blinded John and other racists to the fact that God loves all people the same. In **Acts 10:34–48**, Peter challenges the people of his day to see others from God's perspective and lay aside their prejudices.

- How was prejudice in Peter's day different from John Metzger's prejudice? How are they similar?
- According to this passage, what is the cure for prejudice?

CONSIDER . . .

- observing people in a mall. Evaluate which people you do or don't have prejudices toward. Then ask God to remove any prejudices you may have.
- getting to know someone you have prejudged. Think about the ways the person is different from what you had expected.

FOR MORE, SEE . . .

- Genesis 3:20 (p. 6)
- John 4:1–27 (p. 1063)
- Acts 11:1–18 (p. 1115)

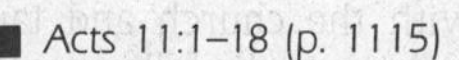

11 Right then three men who were sent to me from
Caesarea came to the house where I was staying.
12 The Spirit[d] told me to go with them without
doubting. These six believers here also went with
me, and we entered the house of Cornelius. 13 He
told us about the angel he saw standing in his
house. The angel said to him, 'Send some men to
Joppa and invite Simon Peter to come. 14 By the
words he will say to you, you and all your family
will be saved.' 15 When I began my speech, the
Holy Spirit came on them just as he came on us
at the beginning. 16 Then I remembered the words
of the Lord. He said, 'John baptized with water,
but you will be baptized with the Holy Spirit.'
17 Since God gave them the same gift he gave us
who believed in the Lord Jesus Christ, how could
I stop the work of God?"

18 When the Jewish believers heard this, they
stopped arguing. They praised God and said, "So
God is allowing even those who are not Jewish to
turn to him and live."

The Good News Comes to Antioch

19 Many of the believers were scattered when
they were persecuted after Stephen was killed.
Some of them went as far as Phoenicia, Cyprus,
and Antioch telling the message to others, but
only to Jews. 20 Some of these believers were people from Cyprus and Cyrene. When they came to
Antioch, they spoke also to Greeks, telling them
the Good News[d] about the Lord Jesus. 21 The Lord
was helping the believers, and a large group of
people believed and turned to the Lord.

22 The church in Jerusalem heard about all
of this, so they sent Barnabas to Antioch.
23-24 Barnabas was a good man, full of the Holy
Spirit[d] and full of faith. When he reached Antioch
and saw how God had blessed the people, he was
glad. He encouraged all the believers in Antioch
always to obey the Lord with all their hearts, and
many people became followers of the Lord.

25 Then Barnabas went to the city of Tarsus to
look for Saul, 26 and when he found Saul, he
brought him to Antioch. For a whole year Saul
and Barnabas met with the church and taught
many people there. In Antioch the followers were
called Christians for the first time.

> **SIDELIGHT:** The name "Christian" (Acts 11:26) may have originally been an insult. It meant "devotees of the Anointed One" or "followers of Christ." The term was widely used by the end of the first century.

27 About that time some prophets[d] came from
Jerusalem to Antioch. 28 One of them, named Agabus, stood up and spoke with the help of the Holy
Spirit. He said, "A very hard time is coming to the
whole world. There will be no food to eat." (This
happened when Claudius ruled.) 29 The believers
all decided to help the followers who lived in Judea, as much as each one could. 30 They gathered
the money and gave it to Barnabas and Saul, who
brought it to the elders[d] in Judea.

Herod Agrippa Hurts the Church

12 During that same time King Herod began to mistreat some who belonged to
the church. 2 He ordered James, the brother of
John, to be killed by the sword. 3 Herod saw that
the Jewish people liked this, so he decided to arrest Peter, too. (This happened during the time of
the Feast[d] of Unleavened Bread.)

4 After Herod arrested Peter, he put him in jail
and handed him over to be guarded by sixteen
soldiers. Herod planned to bring Peter before the
people for trial after the Passover[d] Feast. 5 So Peter
was kept in jail, but the church prayed earnestly
to God for him.

Peter Leaves the Jail

6 The night before Herod was to bring him to
trial, Peter was sleeping between two soldiers,
bound with two chains. Other soldiers were
guarding the door of the jail. 7 Suddenly, an angel
of the Lord stood there, and a light shined in the
cell. The angel struck Peter on the side and woke
him up. "Hurry! Get up!" the angel said. And the
chains fell off Peter's hands. 8 Then the angel told
him, "Get dressed and put on your sandals." And
Peter did. Then the angel said, "Put on your coat
and follow me." 9 So Peter followed him out, but
he did not know if what the angel was doing was
real; he thought he might be seeing a vision.
10 They went past the first and second guards and
came to the iron gate that separated them from
the city. The gate opened by itself for them, and
they went through it. When they had walked
down one street, the angel suddenly left him.

11 Then Peter realized what had happened. He
thought, "Now I know that the Lord really sent
his angel to me. He rescued me from Herod and
from all the things the Jewish people thought
would happen."

12 When he considered this, he went to the
home of Mary, the mother of John Mark. Many
people were gathered there, praying. 13 Peter
knocked on the outside door, and a servant girl
named Rhoda came to answer it. 14 When she recognized Peter's voice, she was so happy she forgot
to open the door. Instead, she ran inside and told
the group, "Peter is at the door!"

15 They said to her, "You are crazy!" But she

kept on saying it was true, so they said, "It must be Peter's angel."

16Peter continued to knock, and when they opened the door, they saw him and were amazed. 17Peter made a sign with his hand to tell them to be quiet. He explained how the Lord led him out of the jail, and he said, "Tell James and the other believers what happened." Then he left to go to another place.

18The next day the soldiers were very upset and wondered what had happened to Peter. 19Herod looked everywhere for him but could not find him. So he questioned the guards and ordered that they be killed.

The Death of Herod Agrippa

Later Herod moved from Judea and went to the city of Caesarea, where he stayed. 20Herod was very angry with the people of Tyre and Sidon, but the people of those cities all came in a group to him. After convincing Blastus, the king's personal servant, to be on their side, they asked Herod for peace, because their country got its food from his country.

21On a chosen day Herod put on his royal robes, sat on his throne, and made a speech to the people. 22They shouted, "This is the voice of a god, not a human!" 23Because Herod did not give the glory to God, an angel of the Lord immediately caused him to become sick, and he was eaten by worms and died.

24God's message continued to spread and reach people.

25After Barnabas and Saul finished their task in Jerusalem, they returned to Antioch, taking John Mark with them.

Barnabas and Saul Are Chosen

13 In the church at Antioch there were these prophets[d] and teachers: Barnabas, Simeon (also called Niger), Lucius (from the city of Cyrene), Manaen (who had grown up with Herod, the ruler), and Saul. 2They were all worshiping the Lord and giving up eating for a certain time.[n] During this time the Holy Spirit[d] said to them, "Set apart for me Barnabas and Saul to do a special work for which I have chosen them."

3So after they gave up eating and prayed, they laid their hands on[n] Barnabas and Saul and sent them out.

Barnabas and Saul in Cyprus

4Barnabas and Saul, sent out by the Holy Spirit,[d] went to the city of Seleucia. From there they sailed to the island of Cyprus. 5When they came to Salamis, they preached the Good News[d] of God in the Jewish synagogues.[d] John Mark was with them to help.

6They went across the whole island to Paphos where they met a Jewish magician named Bar-Jesus. He was a false prophet[d] 7who always stayed close to Sergius Paulus, the governor and a smart man. He asked Barnabas and Saul to come to him, because he wanted to hear the message of God. 8But Elymas, the magician, was against them. (Elymas is the name for Bar-Jesus in the Greek language.) He tried to stop the governor from believing in Jesus. 9But Saul, who was also called Paul, was filled with the Holy Spirit. He looked straight at Elymas 10and said, "You son of the devil! You are an enemy of everything that is right! You are full of evil tricks and lies, always trying to change the Lord's truths into lies. 11Now the Lord will touch you, and you will be blind. For a time you will not be able to see anything—not even the light from the sun."

Then everything became dark for Elymas, and he walked around, trying to find someone to lead him by the hand. 12When the governor saw this, he believed because he was amazed at the teaching about the Lord.

Paul and Barnabas Leave Cyprus

13Paul and those with him sailed from Paphos and came to Perga, in Pamphylia. There John Mark left them to return to Jerusalem. 14They continued their trip from Perga and went to Antioch, a city in Pisidia. On the Sabbath[d] day they went into the synagogue[d] and sat down. 15After the law of Moses and the writings of the prophets[d] were read, the leaders of the synagogue sent a message to Paul and Barnabas: "Brothers, if you have any message that will encourage the people, please speak."

16Paul stood up, raised his hand, and said, "You Israelites and you who worship God, please listen! 17The God of the Israelites chose our ancestors. He made the people great during the time they lived in Egypt, and he brought them out of that country with great power. 18And he was patient with them for forty years in the desert. 19God destroyed seven nations in the land of Canaan and gave the land to his people. 20All this happened in about four hundred fifty years.

"After this, God gave them judges until the time of Samuel the prophet. 21Then the people asked for a king, so God gave them Saul son of Kish. Saul was from the tribe[d] of Benjamin and was king for forty years. 22After God took him away, God made David their king. God said about

giving up . . . time This is called "fasting." The people would give up eating for a special time of prayer and worship to God. It was also done to show sadness and disappointment.

laid their hands on The laying on of hands had many purposes, including the giving of a blessing, power, or authority.

him: 'I have found in David son of Jesse the kind
of man I want. He will do all I want him to do.'
23So God has brought Jesus, one of David's
descendants,[d] to Israel to be its Savior,[d] as he
promised. 24Before Jesus came, John[n] preached
to all the people of Israel about a baptism of
changed hearts and lives. 25When he was finishing his work, he said, 'Who do you think I am?
I am not the Christ.[d] He is coming later, and I am
not worthy to untie his sandals.'
26"Brothers, sons of the family of Abraham, and
those of you who are not Jews who worship God,
listen! The news about this salvation has been
sent to us. 27Those who live in Jerusalem and
their leaders did not realize that Jesus was the
Savior. They did not understand the words that
the prophets wrote, which are read every Sabbath[d] day. But they made them come true when
they said Jesus was guilty. 28They could not find
any real reason for Jesus to be put to death, but
they asked Pilate to have him killed. 29When they
had done to him all that the Scriptures[d] had said,
they took him down from the cross and laid him
in a tomb. 30But God raised him up from the dead!
31After this, for many days, those who had gone
with Jesus from Galilee to Jerusalem saw him.
They are now his witnesses to the people. 32We
tell you the Good News[d] about the promise God
made to our ancestors. 33God has made this promise come true for us, his children, by raising
Jesus from the dead. We read about this also in
Psalm 2:

> 'You are my Son.
> Today I have become your Father.' *Psalm 2:7*

34God raised Jesus from the dead, and he will
never go back to the grave and become dust. So
God said:

> 'I will give you the holy and sure blessings
> that I promised to David.' *Isaiah 55:3*

35But in another place God says:

> 'You will not let your Holy One rot.' *Psalm 16:10*

36David did God's will during his lifetime. Then
he died and was buried beside his ancestors, and
his body did rot in the grave. 37But the One God
raised from the dead did not rot in the grave.
38-39Brothers, understand what we are telling you:
You can have forgiveness of your sins through
Jesus. The law of Moses could not free you from
your sins. But through Jesus everyone who believes is free from all sins. 40Be careful! Don't let
what the prophets said happen to you:

John John the Baptist, who preached to people about Christ's coming (Luke 3).

BIBLE STUDY

Putting the Pieces Together

Jigsaw puzzles can drive you crazy. When first you dump hundreds of jigsaw puzzle pieces from the box, you fear you will never get the puzzle together. But because you know the pieces have to fit together eventually, you separate border pieces from inside pieces. The border goes together reasonably well, so you move on to notice pieces that are related and may form a figure in the puzzle.

Each time you fit a piece, you feel more hopeful. Completing certain sections may bring cries of victory and, "Come see what we finished!" Sometimes along the way, it gets discouraging, but you keep at it. Bit by bit, the picture begins to take shape. The pieces are no longer meaningless but related and relevant. When only a few pieces remain, you can see exactly where they belong. The triumph of the final assembly makes the hours of work worth it.

Sometimes Bible study can be like a jigsaw puzzle. Understanding the Bible and the God described in it also happens piece by piece. In **Acts 13:22–33**, Paul put together some pieces about Jesus for his listeners.

- How is this passage like the picture on the front of a puzzle box?
- What are the three most important pieces to you in this passage?

CONSIDER . . .

- listing at least ten things you already understand about Jesus.
- keeping a journal of discoveries you make during group and individual Bible studies. Reread this journal to remind yourself of the pieces of truth you've learned.

FOR MORE, SEE . . .

- Deuteronomy 6:4–9 (p. 167)
- Romans 15:4 (p. 1161)
- 2 Timothy 3:14–17 (p. 1266)

[41]'Listen, you people who doubt!
You can wonder, and then die.
I will do something in your lifetime
that you won't believe even when you are
told about it!' " *Habakkuk 1:5*

[42]While Paul and Barnabas were leaving the
synagogue, the people asked them to tell them
more about these things on the next Sabbath.
[43]When the meeting was over, many Jews and
those who had changed to the Jewish religion and
who worshiped God followed Paul and Barnabas
from that place. Paul and Barnabas were persuading them to continue trusting in God's grace.
[44]On the next Sabbath day, almost everyone in
the city came to hear the word of the Lord. [45]See-
ing the crowd, the Jewish people became very
jealous and said insulting things and argued
against what Paul said. [46]But Paul and Barnabas
spoke very boldly, saying, "We must speak the
message of God to you first. But you refuse to
listen. You are judging yourselves not worthy of
having eternal life! So we will now go to the people of other nations. [47]This is what the Lord told
us to do, saying:

'I have made you a light for the nations;
you will show people all over the world the
way to be saved.' " *Isaiah 49:6*

[48]When those who were not Jewish heard Paul
say this, they were happy and gave honor to the
message of the Lord. And the people who were
chosen to have life forever believed the message.
[49]So the message of the Lord was spreading
through the whole country. [50]But the Jewish people stirred up some of the important religious
women and the leaders of the city. They started
trouble against Paul and Barnabas and forced
them out of their area. [51]So Paul and Barnabas
shook the dust off their feet[n] and went to Ico-

shook . . . feet A warning. It showed that they had rejected these people.

JEALOUSY

A Door to Greater Evil

Report card day. Dale Castle dreaded walking into his house. He figured his parents had already seen Denise's report card, and he knew his would never compare to hers.

"They'll probably give her a new car or something for every A," Dale thought to himself.

As Dale opened the front door, he heard his parents talking in the living room.

"Denise, this is an outstanding report card—as usual," his dad gushed.

"We're so proud of you, honey. You've worked so hard," his mother added.

Dale tried to sneak by his parents, but just as he rounded the corner his mother called out: "Dale, come here. Let's see how you did this semester."

"Oh great," Dale thought, "here comes World War III." Dale walked into the living room and handed his mother his crumpled report card from his back pocket.

She unfolded it and said, "Well, these are fine grades, son." Then she handed it to his dad.

"Hmmm," his dad mused. "Looks like you brought up that grade in biology. Good work."

"Yeah, right," Dale fumed. "I know it's not as good as Denise's. Nothing I do is ever as good as her."

He stormed out of the room, leaving his family in shock.

Dale let his jealousy of Denise affect his response to his parents. In **Acts 13:44–52**, some Jewish leaders allowed their jealousy to affect the way they treated Paul and Barnabas.

- Why were Dale and the Jewish leaders jealous? What were the consequences of Dale's and the Jewish leaders' jealousy?
- When have you been jealous of someone? What were the consequences of your jealousy?

CONSIDER. . .

- making a list of your talents and things you are good at, then reading the list when you are tempted to be jealous of someone else.
- thanking God for someone you are jealous of. Be excited when that person does well.

FOR MORE, SEE. . .

- Genesis 37 (p. 42)
- Psalm 37:1–8 (p. 503)
- Acts 17:5–9 (p. 1124)

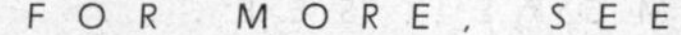

nium. [52]But the followers were filled with joy and
the Holy Spirit.[d]

Paul and Barnabas in Iconium

14 In Iconium, Paul and Barnabas went as
usual to the Jewish synagogue.[d] They
spoke so well that a great many Jews and Greeks
believed. [2]But some of the Jews who did not believe excited the non-Jewish people and turned
them against the believers. [3]Paul and Barnabas
stayed in Iconium a long time and spoke bravely
for the Lord. He showed that their message about
his grace was true by giving them the power to
work miracles[d] and signs. [4]But the city was divided. Some of the people agreed with the Jews,
and others believed the apostles.[d]

[5]Some who were not Jews, some Jews, and
some of their rulers wanted to mistreat Paul and
Barnabas and to stone them to death. [6]When Paul
and Barnabas learned about this, they ran away to
Lystra and Derbe, cities in Lycaonia, and to the
areas around those cities. [7]They announced the
Good News[d] there, too.

Paul in Lystra and Derbe

[8]In Lystra there sat a man who had been born
crippled; he had never walked. [9]As this man was
listening to Paul speak, Paul looked straight at
him and saw that he believed God could heal
him. [10]So he cried out, "Stand up on your feet!"
The man jumped up and began walking around.
[11]When the crowds saw what Paul did, they
shouted in the Lycaonian language, "The gods
have become like humans and have come down
to us!" [12]Then the people began to call Barnabas
"Zeus"[n] and Paul "Hermes,"[n] because he was

"Zeus" The Greeks believed in many gods, of whom Zeus was most important.
"Hermes" The Greeks believed he was a messenger for the other gods.

HEROES

Admire, Don't Worship

Mandy Rios admired everything about her pastor. When he first came to her church, she was immediately drawn to his dynamic personality, warm smile and genuine concern for people.

The pastor always had time to listen. He always talked about how great the young people of the church were, praising their character and service. Mandy believed that God must be just like her pastor.

Whenever the youth group had a controversial discussion, Mandy would go to her pastor later and ask what he thought. Mandy would explain what he said in the next youth group meeting. To Mandy, he knew everything.

Eleven months after coming to Mandy's church, her pastor left suddenly to go to another church. He answered none of Mandy's letters, nor did he return her phone calls. He never even said good-bye.

Mandy was crushed and heartbroken. How could he treat her church like this? How could he treat her like this when she had respected him so much? Mandy felt betrayed. Could she ever trust a pastor again?

Worshiping a person always leads to disappointment. Her pastor turned out to be human—with human faults and inconsistencies. In **Acts 14:8–18**, God used Paul and Barnabas to work miracles, but even they weren't worthy of worship.

- What led Mandy to worship her pastor, and the people to worship Paul and Barnabas?
- Based on Paul's and Barnabas's words, what are appropriate ways to treat spiritual leaders?

CONSIDER . . .

- thanking God for the good qualities of people you admire. Ask God to help you keep your admiration in proper perspective.
- getting to know someone you admire and learning about his or her human and less-admirable qualities as well.

FOR MORE, SEE . . .

- Exodus 20:2–6 (p. 78)
- Daniel 3 (p. 809)
- 1 Corinthians 4:1–7 (p. 1172)

the main speaker. 13The priest in the temple of
Zeus, which was near the city, brought some bulls
and flowers to the city gates. He and the people
wanted to offer a sacrifice to Paul and Barnabas.
14But when the apostles,[d] Barnabas and Paul,
heard about it, they tore their clothes. They ran
in among the people, shouting, 15"Friends, why
are you doing these things? We are only human
beings like you. We are bringing you the Good
News[d] and are telling you to turn away from
these worthless things and turn to the living God.
He is the One who made the sky, the earth, the
sea, and everything in them. 16In the past, God let
all the nations do what they wanted. 17Yet he
proved he is real by showing kindness, by giving
you rain from heaven and crops at the right times,
by giving you food and filling your hearts with
joy." 18Even with these words, they were barely
able to keep the crowd from offering sacrifices to
them.

SIDELIGHT: Paul and Barnabas faced a real case of mistaken identity when they visited Lystra, a town in the center of modern-day Turkey (Acts 14:8–18). The people in the region believed a myth that the Greek gods Zeus and Hermes had previously visited the area. When Paul and Barnabas healed a cripple, the people thought the gods had returned, putting the Christian missionaries in an awkward situation.

19Then some Jewish people came from Antioch
and Iconium and persuaded the people to turn
against Paul. So they threw stones at him and
dragged him out of town, thinking they had killed
him. 20But the followers gathered around him,
and he got up and went back into the town. The
next day he and Barnabas left and went to the city
of Derbe.

The Return to Antioch in Syria

21Paul and Barnabas told the Good News[d] in
Derbe, and many became followers. Paul and Barnabas returned to Lystra, Iconium, and Antioch,
22making the followers of Jesus stronger and helping them stay in the faith. They said, "We must
suffer many things to enter God's kingdom."
23They chose elders[d] for each church, by praying
and giving up eating for a certain time.[n] These
elders had trusted the Lord, so Paul and Barnabas
put them in the Lord's care.
24Then they went through Pisidia and came to
Pamphylia. 25When they had preached the message in Perga, they went down to Attalia. 26And
from there they sailed away to Antioch where the
believers had put them into God's care and had
sent them out to do this work. Now they had finished.
27When they arrived in Antioch, Paul and Barnabas gathered the church together. They told the
church all about what God had done with them
and how God had made it possible for those who
were not Jewish to believe. 28And they stayed
there a long time with the followers.

The Meeting at Jerusalem

15 Then some people came to Antioch from
Judea and began teaching the non-
Jewish believers: "You cannot be saved if you are
not circumcised[d] as Moses taught us." 2Paul and
Barnabas were against this teaching and argued
with them about it. So the church decided to send
Paul, Barnabas, and some others to Jerusalem
where they could talk more about this with the
apostles[d] and elders.[d]
3The church helped them leave on the trip, and
they went through the countries of Phoenicia and
Samaria, telling all about how those who were
not Jewish had turned to God. This made all the
believers very happy. 4When they arrived in Jerusalem, they were welcomed by the apostles, the
elders, and the church. Paul, Barnabas, and the
others told about everything God had done with
them. 5But some of the believers who belonged to
the Pharisee[d] group came forward and said, "The
non-Jewish believers must be circumcised. They
must be told to obey the law of Moses."
6The apostles and the elders gathered to consider this problem. 7After a long debate, Peter
stood up and said to them, "Brothers, you know
that in the early days God chose me from among
you to preach the Good News[d] to those who are
not Jewish. They heard the Good News from
me, and they believed. 8God, who knows the
thoughts of everyone, accepted them. He showed
this to us by giving them the Holy Spirit,[d] just as
he did to us. 9To God, those people are not different from us. When they believed, he made their
hearts pure. 10So now why are you testing God by
putting a heavy load around the necks of the non-
Jewish believers? It is a load that neither we nor
our ancestors were able to carry. 11But we believe
that we and they too will be saved by the grace
of the Lord Jesus."
12Then the whole group became quiet. They
listened to Paul and Barnabas tell about all the
miracles[d] and signs that God did through them
among the non-Jewish people. 13After they finished speaking, James said, "Brothers, listen to

giving . . . time This is called "fasting." The people would give up eating for a special time of prayer and worship to God. It was also done to show sadness and disappointment.

me. 14Simon has told us how God showed his love
for the non-Jewish people. For the first time he is
accepting from among them a people to be his
own. 15The words of the prophets[d] agree with this
too:

16'After these things I will return.
 The kingdom of David is like a fallen tent.
But I will rebuild its ruins,
 and I will set it up.
17Then those people who are left alive may ask
  the Lord for help,
 and the other nations that belong to me,
says the Lord,
 who will make it happen.
18 And these things have been known for a
  long time.' *Amos 9:11-12*

19"So I think we should not bother the non-
Jewish people who are turning to God. 20Instead,
we should write a letter to them telling them
these things: Stay away from food that has been
offered to idols (which makes it unclean[d]), any
kind of sexual sin, eating animals that have been
strangled, and blood. 21They should do these
things, because for a long time in every city the
law of Moses has been taught. And it is still read
in the synagogue[d] every Sabbath[d] day."

Letter to Non-Jewish Believers

22The apostles,[d] the elders,[d] and the whole
church decided to send some of their men with
Paul and Barnabas to Antioch. They chose Judas
Barsabbas and Silas, who were respected by the
believers. 23They sent the following letter with
them:

From the apostles and elders, your brothers.

To all the non-Jewish believers in Antioch,
Syria, and Cilicia:

Greetings!

24We have heard that some of our group
have come to you and said things that trouble and upset you. But we did not tell them
to do this. 25We have all agreed to choose
some messengers and send them to you with
our dear friends Barnabas and Paul— 26peo-
ple who have given their lives to serve our
Lord Jesus Christ. 27So we are sending Judas
and Silas, who will tell you the same things.
28It has pleased the Holy Spirit[d] that you
should not have a heavy load to carry, and
we agree. You need to do only these things:
29Stay away from any food that has been offered to idols, eating any animals that have
been strangled, and blood, and any kind of
sexual sin. If you stay away from these
things, you will do well.

Good-bye.

30So they left Jerusalem and went to Antioch
where they gathered the church and gave them
the letter. 31When they read it, they were very
happy because of the encouraging message. 32Ju-
das and Silas, who were also prophets,[d] said many
things to encourage the believers and make them
stronger. 33After some time Judas and Silas were
sent off in peace by the believers, and they went
back to those who had sent them. 34 [n]

35But Paul and Barnabas stayed in Antioch and,
along with many others, preached the Good
News[d] and taught the people the message of the
Lord.

Paul and Barnabas Separate

36After some time, Paul said to Barnabas, "We
should go back to all those towns where we
preached the message of the Lord. Let's visit the
believers and see how they are doing."

37Barnabas wanted to take John Mark with
them, 38but he had left them at Pamphylia; he did
not continue with them in the work. So Paul did
not think it was a good idea to take him. 39Paul
and Barnabas had such a serious argument about
this that they separated and went different ways.
Barnabas took Mark and sailed to Cyprus, 40but
Paul chose Silas and left. The believers in Antioch
put Paul into the Lord's care, 41and he went
through Syria and Cilicia, giving strength to the
churches.

Timothy Goes with Paul

16 Paul came to Derbe and Lystra, where a
follower named Timothy lived. Timo-
thy's mother was Jewish and a believer, but his
father was a Greek.

2The believers in Lystra and Iconium respected
Timothy and said good things about him. 3Paul
wanted Timothy to travel with him, but all the
Jews living in that area knew that Timothy's father was Greek. So Paul circumcised[d] Timothy to
please the Jews. 4Paul and those with him traveled from town to town and gave the decisions
made by the apostles[d] and elders[d] in Jerusalem
for the people to obey. 5So the churches became stronger in the faith and grew larger every
day.

Paul Is Called Out of Asia

6Paul and those with him went through the areas of Phrygia and Galatia since the Holy Spirit[d]
did not let them preach the Good News[d] in the
country of Asia. 7When they came near the country of Mysia, they tried to go into Bithynia, but the
Spirit of Jesus did not let them. 8So they passed by
Mysia and went to Troas. 9That night Paul saw in

Verse 34 Some Greek copies add verse 34: ". . . but Silas decided to remain there."

a vision a man from Macedonia. The man stood and begged, "Come over to Macedonia and help us." 10After Paul had seen the vision, we immediately prepared to leave for Macedonia, understanding that God had called us to tell the Good News to those people.

Lydia Becomes a Christian

11We left Troas and sailed straight to the island of Samothrace. The next day we sailed to Neapolis.[n] 12Then we went by land to Philippi, a Roman colony[n] and the leading city in that part of Macedonia. We stayed there for several days.

13On the Sabbath[d] day we went outside the city gate to the river where we thought we would find a special place for prayer. Some women had gathered there, so we sat down and talked with them. 14One of the listeners was a woman named Lydia from the city of Thyatira whose job was selling purple cloth. She worshiped God, and he opened her mind to pay attention to what Paul was saying. 15She and all the people in her house were baptized. Then she invited us to her home, saying, "If you think I am truly a believer in the Lord, then come stay in my house." And she persuaded us to stay with her.

Neapolis City in Macedonia. It was the first city Paul visited on the continent of Europe.
Roman colony A town begun by Romans with Roman laws, customs, and privileges.

GOD'S WILL

Close to Your Heart

Sandra Graham was one semester away from high school graduation, and she had no idea what she would do with her life. She had been praying for God to show her his will, but still there were no answers.

One Sunday after church, Ted Holt, a Sunday school teacher, asked Sandra to come home with his family of eight for dinner.

All through the meal, they talked about Sandra's plans after graduation. "What do you think God wants you to do, Sandra?" Ted asked as they finished dessert.

"I don't know. I've been praying about it, but God just doesn't seem to answer," Sandra lamented.

Ted's voice softened. "What do you want to do?" he asked.

"God's will," she answered.

Again, Ted asked, "But what do you want to do?"

Sandra was confused. "That's it. I want to do God's will."

Ted smiled. "Sandra, I have six kids, and I want nothing more than for each of my kids to be happy. I'll do almost anything to make that happen."

Sandra nodded, not sure what this had to do with her decision.

Ted laughed heartily when he saw her confusion. "Sandra, God is your father, and he wants you to be happy. He's probably been showing you all the time what his will is."

"He has?" Sandra asked incredulously.

"Yes, he has. Look into your heart. I'll bet your desires will point you toward God's will."

Sandra did find God's will. After she graduated from college, she used her love for drama to teach others how to communicate their faith. In **Acts 16:6–10**, Paul also found God's will.

- What was Ted trying to help Sandra learn about finding God's will? In the passage, how did God show his will to Paul and the others?
- Do you think God still reveals his will to people as he did in the passage? In what other ways do people learn God's will?

CONSIDER

- keeping track of what happens to you in the coming week. See if any patterns emerge that show God leading you in a particular direction.
- interviewing an older person in your church about what he or she has learned about discovering and doing God's will.

FOR MORE, SEE...

- Psalm 32:6–11 (p. 500)
- Matthew 6:9–13 (p. 918)
- Luke 22:41–43 (p. 1050)

Paul and Silas in Jail

16 Once, while we were going to the place for prayer, a servant girl met us. She had a special spirit[n] in her, and she earned a lot of money for her owners by telling fortunes. 17 This girl followed Paul and us, shouting, "These men are servants of the Most High God. They are telling you how you can be saved."

18 She kept this up for many days. This bothered Paul, so he turned and said to the spirit, "By the power of Jesus Christ, I command you to come out of her!" Immediately, the spirit came out.

19 When the owners of the servant girl saw this, they knew that now they could not use her to make money. So they grabbed Paul and Silas and dragged them before the city rulers in the marketplace. 20 They brought Paul and Silas to the Roman rulers and said, "These men are Jews and are making trouble in our city. 21 They are teaching things that are not right for us as Romans to do."

22 The crowd joined the attack against them. The Roman officers tore the clothes of Paul and Silas and had them beaten with rods. 23 Then Paul and Silas were thrown into jail, and the jailer was ordered to guard them carefully. 24 When he heard this order, he put them far inside the jail and pinned their feet down between large blocks of wood.

25 About midnight Paul and Silas were praying and singing songs to God as the other prisoners listened. 26 Suddenly, there was a strong earthquake that shook the foundation of the jail. Then all the doors of the jail broke open, and all the prisoners were freed from their chains. 27 The jailer woke up and saw that the jail doors were open. Thinking that the prisoners had already escaped, he got his sword and was about to kill himself.[n] 28 But Paul shouted, "Don't hurt yourself! We are all here."

29 The jailer told someone to bring a light. Then he ran inside and, shaking with fear, fell down before Paul and Silas. 30 He brought them outside and said, "Men, what must I do to be saved?"

31 They said to him, "Believe in the Lord Jesus and you will be saved — you and all the people in your house." 32 So Paul and Silas told the message of the Lord to the jailer and all the people in his house. 33 At that hour of the night the jailer took Paul and Silas and washed their wounds. Then he and all his people were baptized immediately. 34 After this the jailer took Paul and Silas home and gave them food. He and his family were very happy because they now believed in God.

35 The next morning, the Roman officers sent the police to tell the jailer, "Let these men go free."

36 The jailer said to Paul, "The officers have sent an order to let you go free. You can leave now. Go in peace."

37 But Paul said to the police, "They beat us in public without a trial, even though we are Roman citizens.[n] And they threw us in jail. Now they want to make us go away quietly. No! Let them come themselves and bring us out."

38 The police told the Roman officers what Paul said. When the officers heard that Paul and Silas were Roman citizens, they were afraid. 39 So they came and told Paul and Silas they were sorry and took them out of jail and asked them to leave the city. 40 So when they came out of the jail, they went to Lydia's house where they saw some of the believers and encouraged them. Then they left.

Paul and Silas in Thessalonica

17 Paul and Silas traveled through Amphipolis and Apollonia and came to Thessalonica where there was a Jewish synagogue.[d] 2 Paul went into the synagogue as he always did, and on each Sabbath[d] day for three weeks, he talked with the Jews about the Scriptures.[d] 3 He explained and proved that the Christ[d] must die and then rise from the dead. He said, "This Jesus I am telling you about is the Christ." 4 Some of the Jews were convinced and joined Paul and Silas, along with many of the Greeks who worshiped God and many of the important women.

5 But the Jews became jealous. So they got some evil men from the marketplace, formed a mob, and started a riot. They ran to Jason's house, looking for Paul and Silas, wanting to bring them out to the people. 6 But when they did not find them, they dragged Jason and some other believers to the leaders of the city. The people were yelling, "These people have made trouble everywhere in the world, and now they have come here too! 7 Jason is keeping them in his house. All of them do things against the laws of Caesar,[d] saying there is another king, called Jesus."

8 When the people and the leaders of the city heard these things, they became very upset. 9 They made Jason and the others put up a sum of money. Then they let the believers go free.

Paul and Silas Go to Berea

10 That same night the believers sent Paul and Silas to Berea where they went to the Jewish syna-

spirit This was a spirit from the devil, which caused her to say she had special knowledge.
kill himself He thought the leaders would kill him for letting the prisoners escape.
Roman citizens Roman law said that Roman citizens must not be beaten before they had a trial.

gogue.[d] 11These Jews were more willing to listen
than the Jews in Thessalonica. The Bereans were
eager to hear what Paul and Silas said and studied
the Scriptures[d] every day to find out if these
things were true. 12So, many of them believed, as
well as many important Greek women and men.
13But the Jews in Thessalonica learned that Paul
was preaching the word of God in Berea, too. So
they came there, upsetting the people and making
trouble. 14The believers quickly sent Paul away to
the coast, but Silas and Timothy stayed in Berea.
15The people leading Paul went with him to Athens. Then they carried a message from Paul back
to Silas and Timothy for them to come to him as
soon as they could.

Paul Preaches in Athens

16While Paul was waiting for Silas and Timothy
in Athens, he was troubled because he saw that
the city was full of idols. 17In the synagogue,[d] he
talked with the Jews and the Greeks who worshiped God. He also talked every day with people
in the marketplace.
18Some of the Epicurean and Stoic philosophers[n] argued with him, saying, "This man

Epicurean and Stoic philosophers Philosophers were those who searched for truth. Epicureans believed that pleasures, especially pleasures of the mind, were the goal of life. Stoics believed that life should be without feelings of joy or grief.

FRIENDS

A Way Out

Keivan McClure was delighted to land a job at the steak house. He needed every penny he could earn for college. Few of his co-workers were Christians, but Keivan didn't let that bother him. He tried to make friends with them, and he talked about faith and church when he had a chance.

One night after closing, the entire crew decided to go to a drive-in movie and out for pizza. The chosen movie was one with lots of violence and nudity, so Keivan decided not to go.

"I'll meet you after the movie for pizza," Keivan said.

"What's the matter? Our movie choice not good enough for Mr. Holier-Than-Thou?" one of the crew chided.

Keivan knew he didn't deserve that, so he just repeated his request: "That's not what I said or meant. I'll see you for pizza."

"Yeah, right, church-boy," another crew member taunted. "You can't handle the scary stuff, so you're running away."

Most of the other crew members laughed. Keivan didn't know what to say.

Finally, Conrad Langley, the crew leader, spoke up. "Hey, get off his back," he said. "Keivan's a Christian and doesn't watch that junk. I'm a Christian too, and I'm not going either."

The crew was silent. Keivan was surprised. He knew Conrad was a nice guy, but Conrad had never said anything about being a Christian before.

After that night, things got better at work. Keivan and Conrad became close friends, and the crew members showed more respect for their beliefs.

Committed Christian friends. They're a great help when the going gets rough. In **Acts 17:1–15**, Paul and Silas were rescued from discouraging circumstances by friends who cared.

- How was the way Conrad helped Keivan similar to the way the believers helped Paul?
- When has someone helped you in the same way the believers helped Paul? When have you supported another Christian?

CONSIDER . . .

- keeping a journal where you write about times you are discouraged. Later, re-read entries and reflect on how God pulled you through.
- encouraging a Christian friend who is in a difficult situation to be strong and hang in there.

FOR MORE, SEE . . .

- Ecclesiastes 4:9–12 (p. 602)
- Matthew 10:21–23 (p. 924)
- 1 Timothy 1:1–3 (p. 1256)

doesn't know what he is talking about. What is
he trying to say?" Others said, "He seems to be
telling us about some other gods," because Paul
was telling them about Jesus and his rising from
the dead. 19They got Paul and took him to a
meeting of the Areopagus,[n] where they said,
"Please explain to us this new idea you have
been teaching. 20The things you are saying are
new to us, and we want to know what this teaching means." 21(All the people of Athens and
those from other countries who lived there always used their time to talk about the newest
ideas.)

22Then Paul stood before the meeting of the
Areopagus and said, "People of Athens, I can see
you are very religious in all things. 23As I was going through your city, I saw the objects you worship. I found an altar that had these words written
on it: TO A GOD WHO IS NOT KNOWN. You worship
a god that you don't know, and this is the God I
am telling you about! 24The God who made the
whole world and everything in it is the Lord of the
land and the sky. He does not live in temples built
by human hands. 25This God is the One who gives
life, breath, and everything else to people. He
does not need any help from them; he has everything he needs. 26God began by making one person, and from him came all the different people
who live everywhere in the world. God decided
exactly when and where they must live. 27God
wanted them to look for him and perhaps search
all around for him and find him, though he is not
far from any of us: 28'We live in him. We walk in
him. We are in him.' Some of your own poets
have said: 'For we are his children.' 29Since we
are God's children, you must not think that God
is like something that people imagine or make
from gold, silver, or rock. 30In the past, people did
not understand God, and he ignored this. But
now, God tells all people in the world to change
their hearts and lives. 31God has set a day that
he will judge all the world with fairness, by the
man he chose long ago. And God has proved
this to everyone by raising that man from the
dead!"

32When the people heard about Jesus being
raised from the dead, some of them laughed. But
others said, "We will hear more about this from
you later." 33So Paul went away from them. 34But
some of the people believed Paul and joined him.
Among those who believed was Dionysius, a
member of the Areopagus, a woman named Dam-
aris, and some others.

Areopagus A council or group of important leaders in Athens. They were like judges.

NON-CHRISTIANS

A Starting Place

Jay Dugan is a talented musician. His friend explained God as a director who "conducts" every element of life to move in harmony.

Amanda Roady has moved nine times in eleven years. Her friend explained God as the friend who goes with us no matter where we move or what new situation we face.

Jason Gaddy is a soccer star. His friend explained God as a coach who insists on practice, works to tone our life muscles, teaches strategy for difficult experiences, and cheers every play from the sidelines.

Some Greek leaders thought there must be a god they did not know. In **Acts 17:22–31**, Paul focused on their understanding of that god to guide them to a full knowledge of the true God.

- Why is it effective to explain God by using things people already understand?
- What images did Paul use to describe God in this passage?

CONSIDER . . .

- underlining phrases about God in Acts 17:22–31 that someone who has never been in church could understand. Use these phrases to explain God to your non-Christian friends.
- thinking of a way to explain Jesus to a non-Christian friend. Begin with an image your friend will relate to.

FOR MORE, SEE . . .

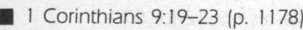

- Exodus 3:12–15 (p. 60)
- John 4:5–25 (p. 1063)
- 1 Corinthians 9:19–23 (p. 1178)

Paul in Corinth

18 Later Paul left Athens and went to Corinth. 2Here he met a Jew named Aquila who had been born in the country of Pontus. But Aquila and his wife, Priscilla, had recently moved to Corinth from Italy, because Claudius[n] commanded that all Jews must leave Rome. Paul went to visit Aquila and Priscilla. 3Because they were tentmakers, just as he was, he stayed with them and worked with them. 4Every Sabbath[d] day he talked with the Jews and Greeks in the synagogue,[d] trying to persuade them to believe in Jesus.

> **SIDELIGHT:** Claudius (Acts 18:2) ruled Rome thirteen years and was partially paralyzed. He kicked Christians out of Rome for allegedly starting riots that threatened the Roman peace—a common charge against early Christians.

5Silas and Timothy came from Macedonia and joined Paul in Corinth. After this, Paul spent all his time telling people the Good News,[d] showing the Jews that Jesus is the Christ.[d] 6But they would not accept Paul's teaching and said some evil things. So he shook off the dust from his clothes[n] and said to them, "If you are not saved, it will be your own fault! I have done all I can do! After this, I will go only to those who are not Jewish." 7Paul left the synagogue and moved into the home of Titius Justus, next to the synagogue. This man worshiped God. 8Crispus was the leader of that synagogue, and he and all the people living in his house believed in the Lord. Many others in Corinth also listened to Paul and believed and were baptized.

9During the night, the Lord told Paul in a vision: "Don't be afraid. Continue talking to people and don't be quiet. 10I am with you, and no one will hurt you because many of my people are in this city." 11Paul stayed there for a year and a half, teaching God's word to the people.

Paul Is Brought Before Gallio

12When Gallio was the governor of the country of Southern Greece, some of the Jews came together against Paul and took him to the court. 13They said, "This man is teaching people to worship God in a way that is against our law."

14Paul was about to say something, but Gallio spoke to the Jews, saying, "I would listen to you Jews if you were complaining about a crime or some wrong. 15But the things you are saying are only questions about words and names—arguments about your own law. So you must solve this problem yourselves. I don't want to be a judge of these things." 16And Gallio made them leave the court.

17Then they all grabbed Sosthenes, the leader of the synagogue,[d] and beat him there before the court. But this did not bother Gallio.

Paul Returns to Antioch

18Paul stayed with the believers for many more days. Then he left and sailed for Syria, with Priscilla and Aquila. At Cenchrea Paul cut off his hair,[n] because he had made a promise to God. 19Then they went to Ephesus, where Paul left Priscilla and Aquila. While Paul was there, he went into the synagogue[d] and talked with the Jews. 20When they asked him to stay with them longer, he refused. 21But as he left, he said, "I will come back to you again if God wants me to." And so he sailed away from Ephesus.

22When Paul landed at Caesarea, he went and gave greetings to the church in Jerusalem. After that, Paul went to Antioch. 23He stayed there for a while and then left and went through the regions of Galatia and Phrygia. He traveled from town to town in these regions, giving strength to all the followers.

Apollos in Ephesus and Corinth

24A Jew named Apollos came to Ephesus. He was born in the city of Alexandria and was a good speaker who knew the Scriptures[d] well. 25He had been taught about the way of the Lord and was always very excited when he spoke and taught the truth about Jesus. But the only baptism Apollos knew about was the baptism that John[n] taught. 26Apollos began to speak very boldly in the synagogue,[d] and when Priscilla and Aquila heard him, they took him to their home and helped him better understand the way of God. 27Now Apollos wanted to go to the country of Southern Greece. So the believers helped him and wrote a letter to the followers there, asking them to accept him. These followers had believed in Jesus because of God's grace, and when Apollos arrived, he helped them very much. 28He argued very strongly with the Jews before all the people, clearly proving with the Scriptures that Jesus is the Christ.[d]

Claudius The emperor (ruler) of Rome, A.D. 41-54.
shook . . . clothes This was a warning to show that Paul was finished talking to the Jews in that city.
cut . . . hair Jews did this to show that the time of a special promise to God was finished.
John John the Baptist, who preached to people about Christ's coming (Luke 3).

Paul in Ephesus

19 While Apollos was in Corinth, Paul was
visiting some places on the way to Ephesus. There he found some followers [2]and asked
them, "Did you receive the Holy Spirit[d] when you
believed?"
They said, "We have never even heard of a
Holy Spirit."
[3]So he asked, "What kind of baptism did you
have?"
They said, "It was the baptism that John[n]
taught."
[4]Paul said, "John's baptism was a baptism of
changed hearts and lives. He told people to believe in the one who would come after him, and
that one is Jesus."
[5]When they heard this, they were baptized in
the name of the Lord Jesus. [6]Then Paul laid his
hands on them,[n] and the Holy Spirit came upon
them. They began speaking different languages[n]
and prophesying.[d] [7]There were about twelve people in this group.
[8]Paul went into the synagogue[d] and spoke out
boldly for three months. He talked with the Jews
and persuaded them to accept the things he said
about the kingdom of God. [9]But some of the Jews
became stubborn. They refused to believe and
said evil things about the Way of Jesus before all
the people. So Paul left them, and taking the followers with him, he went to the school of a man
named Tyrannus. There Paul talked with people
every day [10]for two years. Because of his work,
every Jew and Greek in the country of Asia heard
the word of the Lord.

John John the Baptist, who preached to people about Christ's coming (Luke 3).
laid his hands on them The laying on of hands had many purposes, including the giving of a blessing, power, or authority.
languages This can also be translated "tongues."

FAITH

Growing Up

Checkmark the items that are true of your relationship with God. I understand God better now than when I first started learning about him. I genuinely enjoy being involved in activities related to my faith. God helps me love and care for people. My relationships are better as a result of my faith in God. I understand scripture better than I used to. I ask God to help me solve problems. My friends and family know I'm a Christian. I take time each day to pray. I know God loves me. I ask God to forgive me when I do something wrong. I am honest with God about my feelings. I tell people about Jesus. My relationship with God deeply influences my actions.

Now rate yourself:

- 6 to 13 checkmarks—Your faith is definitely growing. You are experiencing the type of growth described in Acts 19:1–7.
- 3 to 5 checkmarks—Be careful that your faith is not stagnating. Read the items you didn't checkmark, and begin building those things into your life. Be encouraged by Acts 19:1–7.
- 0 to 2 checkmarks—Your faith is wilting. Water it with the Word of God and get involved with other Christians soon—before your faith withers. Be challenged by Acts 19:1–7.

In **Acts 19:1–7**, Paul explained truth that the followers did not know. When they heard all that God had done for them, they were changed—and their faith could grow.

- How did Paul help people's faith grow? What items in the checklist would be true for the people in the passage?
- How did the people in this passage express their faith?

CONSIDER . . .

- pretending it's yearbook signing time. Write an entry to Jesus telling ways your relationship has grown, what you appreciate about him and how you hope your relationship will grow in the next year.
- choosing one item from the checklist to begin building into your life.

FOR MORE, SEE . . .

- Psalm 15 (p. 488)
- 1 Corinthians 3:1–9 (p. 1169)
- Colossians 1:9–14 (p. 1238)

The Sons of Sceva

11God used Paul to do some very special miracles.[d] 12Some people took handkerchiefs and
clothes that Paul had used and put them on the
sick. When they did this, the sick were healed and
evil spirits left them.

13But some Jews also were traveling around
and making evil spirits go out of people. They
tried to use the name of the Lord Jesus to force
the evil spirits out. They would say, "By the same
Jesus that Paul talks about, I order you to come
out!" 14Seven sons of Sceva, a leading Jewish
priest, were doing this.

15But one time an evil spirit said to them, "I
know Jesus, and I know about Paul, but who are
you?"

16Then the man who had the evil spirit jumped
on them. Because he was so much stronger than
all of them, they ran away from the house naked
and hurt. 17All the people in Ephesus — Jews and
Greeks — learned about this and were filled with
fear and gave great honor to the Lord Jesus.
18Many of the believers began to confess openly
and tell all the evil things they had done. 19Some
of them who had used magic brought their magic
books and burned them before everyone. Those
books were worth about fifty thousand silver
coins.[n]

20So in a powerful way the word of the Lord
kept spreading and growing.

21After these things, Paul decided to go to Jerusalem, planning to go through the countries of
Macedonia and Southern Greece and then on to
Jerusalem. He said, "After I have been to Jerusalem, I must also visit Rome." 22Paul sent Timothy
and Erastus, two of his helpers, ahead to Macedonia, but he himself stayed in Asia for a while.

Trouble in Ephesus

23And during that time, there was some serious
trouble in Ephesus about the Way of Jesus. 24A
man named Demetrius, who worked with silver,
made little silver models that looked like the temple of the goddess Artemis.[n] Those who did this
work made much money. 25Demetrius had a
meeting with them and some others who did the
same kind of work. He told them, "Men, you
know that we make a lot of money from our business. 26But look at what this man Paul is doing.
He has convinced and turned away many people
in Ephesus and in almost all of Asia! He says the
gods made by human hands are not real. 27There
is a danger that our business will lose its good
name, but there is also another danger: People
will begin to think that the temple of the great
goddess Artemis is not important. Her greatness
will be destroyed, and Artemis is the goddess that
everyone in Asia and the whole world worships."

28When the others heard this, they became
very angry and shouted, "Artemis, the goddess of
Ephesus, is great!" 29The whole city became confused. The people grabbed Gaius and Aristarchus,
who were from Macedonia and were traveling
with Paul, and ran to the theater. 30Paul wanted
to go in and talk to the crowd, but the followers
did not let him. 31Also, some leaders of Asia who
were friends of Paul sent him a message, begging
him not to go into the theater. 32Some people
were shouting one thing, and some were shouting
another. The meeting was completely confused;
most of them did not know why they had come
together. 33The Jews put a man named Alexander
in front of the people, and some of them told him
what to do. Alexander waved his hand so he
could explain things to the people. 34But when
they saw that Alexander was a Jew, they all
shouted the same thing for two hours: "Great is
Artemis of Ephesus!"

35Then the city clerk made the crowd be quiet.
He said, "People of Ephesus, everyone knows that
Ephesus is the city that keeps the temple of the
great goddess Artemis and her holy stone[n] that
fell from heaven. 36Since no one can say this is not
true, you should be quiet. Stop and think before
you do anything. 37You brought these men here,
but they have not said anything evil against our
goddess or stolen anything from her temple. 38If
Demetrius and those who work with him have a
charge against anyone they should go to the
courts and judges where they can argue with each
other. 39If there is something else you want to talk
about, it can be decided at the regular town meeting of the people. 40I say this because some people
might see this trouble today and say that we are
rioting. We could not explain this, because there
is no real reason for this meeting." 41After the city
clerk said these things, he told the people to go
home.

Paul In Macedonia and Greece

20 When the trouble stopped, Paul sent for
the followers to come to him. After he
encouraged them and then told them good-bye,
he left and went to the country of Macedonia. 2He
said many things to strengthen the followers in
the different places on his way through Macedonia. Then he went to Greece, 3where he stayed
for three months. He was ready to sail for Syria,
but some Jews were planning something against
him. So Paul decided to go back through Macedo-

fifty thousand silver coins Probably drachmas. One coin was enough to pay a worker for one day's labor.
Artemis A Greek goddess that the people of Asia Minor worshiped.
holy stone Probably a meteorite or stone that the people thought looked like Artemis.

nia to Syria. 4The men who went with him were Sopater son of Pyrrhus, from the city of Berea; Aristarchus and Secundus, from the city of Thessalonica; Gaius, from Derbe; Timothy; and Tychicus and Trophimus, two men from the country of Asia. 5These men went on ahead and waited for us at Troas. 6We sailed from Philippi after the Feast[d] of Unleavened Bread. Five days later we met them in Troas, where we stayed for seven days.

Paul's Last Visit to Troas

7On the first day of the week,[n] we all met together to break bread,[n] and Paul spoke to the group. Because he was planning to leave the next day, he kept on talking until midnight. 8We were all together in a room upstairs, and there were many lamps in the room. 9A young man named Eutychus was sitting in the window. As Paul continued talking, Eutychus was falling into a deep sleep. Finally, he went sound asleep and fell to the ground from the third floor. When they picked him up, he was dead. 10Paul went down to Eutychus, knelt down, and put his arms around him. He said, "Don't worry. He is alive now." 11Then Paul went upstairs again, broke bread, and ate. He spoke to them a long time, until it was early morning, and then he left. 12They took the young man home alive and were greatly comforted.

The Trip from Troas to Miletus

13We went on ahead of Paul and sailed for the city of Assos, where he wanted to join us on the ship. Paul planned it this way because he wanted to go to Assos by land. 14When he met us there, we took him aboard and went to Mitylene. 15We sailed from Mitylene and the next day came to a place near Chios. The following day we sailed to Samos, and the next day we reached Miletus. 16Paul had already decided not to stop at Ephesus, because he did not want to stay too long in the country of Asia. He was hurrying to be in Jerusalem on the day of Pentecost,[d] if that were possible.

The Elders from Ephesus

17Now from Miletus Paul sent to Ephesus and called for the elders[d] of the church. 18When they came to him, he said, "You know about my life from the first day I came to Asia. You know the way I lived all the time I was with you. 19The Jews made plans against me, which troubled me very much. But you know I always served the Lord unselfishly, and I often cried. 20You know I preached to you and did not hold back anything that would help you. You know that I taught you in public and in your homes. 21I warned both Jews and Greeks to change their lives and turn to God and believe in our Lord Jesus. 22But now I must obey the Holy Spirit[d] and go to Jerusalem. I don't know what will happen to me there. 23I know only that in every city the Holy Spirit tells me that troubles and even jail wait for me. 24I don't care about my own life. The most important thing is that I complete my mission, the work that the Lord Jesus gave me—to tell people the Good News[d] about God's grace.

25"And now, I know that none of you among whom I was preaching the kingdom of God will ever see me again. 26So today I tell you that if any of you should be lost, I am not responsible, 27because I have told you everything God wants you to know. 28Be careful for yourselves and for all the people the Holy Spirit has given to you to care for. You must be like shepherds to the church of God,[n] which he bought with the death of his own son. 29I know that after I leave, some people will come like wild wolves and try to destroy the flock. 30Also, some from your own group will rise up and twist the truth and will lead away followers after them. 31So be careful! Always remember that for three years, day and night, I never stopped warning each of you, and I often cried over you.

32"Now I am putting you in the care of God and the message about his grace. It is able to give you strength, and it will give you the blessings God has for all his holy people. 33When I was with you, I never wanted anyone's money or fine clothes. 34You know I always worked to take care of my own needs and the needs of those who were with me. 35I showed you in all things that you should work as I did and help the weak. I taught you to remember the words Jesus said: 'It is more blessed to give than to receive.' "

36When Paul had said this, he knelt down with all of them and prayed. 37-38And they all cried because Paul had said they would never see him again. They put their arms around him and kissed him. Then they went with him to the ship.

Paul Goes to Jerusalem

21 After we all said good-bye to them, we sailed straight to the island of Cos. The next day we reached Rhodes, and from there we went to Patara. 2There we found a ship going to Phoenicia, so we went aboard and sailed away. 3We sailed near the island of Cyprus, seeing it to

first day of the week Sunday, which for the Jews began at sunset on our Saturday. But if in this part of Asia a different system of time was used, then the meeting was on our Sunday night.

break bread Probably the Lord's Supper, the special meal that Jesus told his followers to eat to remember him (Luke 22:14-20).

of God Some Greek copies say, "of the Lord."

the north, but we sailed on to Syria. We stopped at Tyre because the ship needed to unload its cargo there. 4We found some followers in Tyre and stayed with them for seven days. Through the Holy Spirit[d] they warned Paul not to go to Jerusalem. 5When we finished our visit, we left and continued our trip. All the followers, even the women and children, came outside the city with us. After we all knelt on the beach and prayed, 6we said good-bye and got on the ship, and the followers went back home.

7We continued our trip from Tyre and arrived at Ptolemais, where we greeted the believers and stayed with them for a day. 8The next day we left Ptolemais and went to the city of Caesarea. There we went into the home of Philip the preacher,[d] one of the seven helpers,[n] and stayed with him. 9He had four unmarried daughters who had the gift of prophesying.[d] 10After we had been there for some time, a prophet named Agabus arrived from Judea. 11He came to us and borrowed Paul's belt and used it to tie his own hands and feet. He said, "The Holy Spirit says, 'This is how the Jews in Jerusalem will tie up the man who wears this belt. Then they will give him to those who are not Jews.' "

12When we all heard this, we and the people there begged Paul not to go to Jerusalem. 13But he said, "Why are you crying and making me so sad? I am not only ready to be tied up in Jerusalem, I am ready to die for the Lord Jesus!"

14We could not persuade him to stay away from Jerusalem. So we stopped begging him and said, "We pray that what the Lord wants will be done."

15After this, we got ready and started on our way to Jerusalem. 16Some of the followers from Caesarea went with us and took us to the home of Mnason, where we would stay. He was from Cyprus and was one of the first followers.

Paul Visits James

17In Jerusalem the believers were glad to see us. 18The next day Paul went with us to visit James, and all the elders[d] were there. 19Paul greeted them and told them everything God had done among the non-Jewish people through him. 20When they heard this, they praised God. Then they said to Paul, "Brother, you can see that many thousands of Jews have become believers. And they think it is very important to obey the law of Moses. 21They have heard about your teaching, that you tell the Jews who live among those who are not Jews to leave the law of Moses. They have heard that you tell them not to circumcise[d] their children and not to obey Jewish customs. 22What should we do? They will learn that you have come. 23So we will tell you what to do: Four of our men have made a promise to God. 24Take these men with you and share in their cleansing ceremony.[n] Pay their expenses so they can shave their heads.[n] Then it will prove to everyone that what they have heard about you is not true and that you follow the law of Moses in your own life. 25We have already sent a letter to the non-Jewish believers. The letter said: 'Do not eat food that has been offered to idols, or blood, or animals that have been strangled. Do not take part in sexual sin.' "

26The next day Paul took the four men and shared in the cleansing ceremony with them. Then he went to the Temple[d] and announced the time when the days of the cleansing ceremony would be finished. On the last day an offering would be given for each of the men.

27When the seven days were almost over, some Jews from Asia saw Paul at the Temple. They caused all the people to be upset and grabbed Paul. 28They shouted, "People of Israel, help us! This is the man who goes everywhere teaching against the law of Moses, against our people, and against this Temple. Now he has brought some Greeks into the Temple and has made this holy place unclean!"[d] 29(The Jews said this because they had seen Trophimus, a man from Ephesus, with Paul in Jerusalem. The Jews thought that Paul had brought him into the Temple.)

SIDELIGHT: When Paul was accused of making the Temple unclean, he was being accused of a crime punishable by death (Acts 21:28). Archaeologists have found a temple inscription that says: "No foreigner is to enter. . . . Whoever is caught will render himself liable to the consequent penalty of death."

30All the people in Jerusalem became upset. Together they ran, took Paul, and dragged him out of the Temple. The Temple doors were closed immediately. 31While they were trying to kill Paul, the commander of the Roman army in Jerusalem learned that there was trouble in the whole city. 32Immediately he took some officers and soldiers and ran to the place where the crowd was gathered. When the people saw them, they stopped beating Paul. 33The commander went to Paul and arrested him. He told his soldiers to tie Paul with

helpers The seven men chosen for a special work described in Acts 6:1-6.
cleansing ceremony The special things Jews did to end the Nazirite promise.
shave their heads The Jews did this to show that their promise was finished.

two chains. Then he asked who he was and what
he had done wrong. 34Some in the crowd were
yelling one thing, and some were yelling another.
Because of all this confusion and shouting, the
commander could not learn what had happened.
So he ordered the soldiers to take Paul to the army
building. 35When Paul came to the steps, the soldiers had to carry him because the people were
ready to hurt him. 36The whole mob was following them, shouting, "Kill him!"

37As the soldiers were about to take Paul into
the army building, he spoke to the commander,
"May I say something to you?"

The commander said, "Do you speak Greek?
38I thought you were the Egyptian who started
some trouble against the government not long
ago and led four thousand killers out to the
desert."

39Paul said, "No, I am a Jew from Tarsus in the
country of Cilicia. I am a citizen of that important
city. Please, let me speak to the people."

40The commander gave permission, so Paul
stood on the steps and waved his hand to quiet
the people. When there was silence, he spoke to
them in the Jewish language.[n]

Paul Speaks to the People

22 Paul said, "Friends, fellow Jews, listen to
my defense to you." 2When the Jews
heard him speaking the Jewish language,[n] they
became very quiet. Paul said, 3"I am a Jew, born
in Tarsus in the country of Cilicia, but I grew up
in this city. I was a student of Gamaliel,[n] who
carefully taught me everything about the law of
our ancestors. I was very serious about serving
God, just as are all of you here today. 4I persecuted the people who followed the Way of Jesus,
and some of them were even killed. I arrested
men and women and put them in jail. 5The high
priest and the whole council of older Jewish leaders can tell you this is true. They gave me letters
to the Jewish brothers in Damascus. So I was going there to arrest these people and bring them
back to Jerusalem to be punished.

6"About noon when I came near Damascus, a
bright light from heaven suddenly flashed all
around me. 7I fell to the ground and heard a voice
saying, 'Saul, Saul, why are you persecuting me?'
8I asked, 'Who are you, Lord?' The voice said, 'I
am Jesus from Nazareth whom you are persecuting.' 9Those who were with me did not hear the
voice, but they saw the light. 10I said, 'What shall
I do, Lord?' The Lord answered, 'Get up and go
to Damascus. There you will be told about all the
things I have planned for you to do.' 11I could not
see, because the bright light had made me blind.
So my companions led me into Damascus.

12"There a man named Ananias came to me.
He was a religious man; he obeyed the law of
Moses, and all the Jews who lived there respected
him. 13He stood by me and said, 'Brother Saul, see
again!' Immediately I was able to see him. 14He
said, 'The God of our ancestors chose you long
ago to know his plan, to see the Righteous One,
and to hear words from him. 15You will be his
witness to all people, telling them about what you
have seen and heard. 16Now, why wait any
longer? Get up, be baptized, and wash your sins
away, trusting in him to save you.'

17"Later, when I returned to Jerusalem, I was
praying in the Temple,[d] and I saw a vision. 18I saw
the Lord saying to me, 'Hurry! Leave Jerusalem
now! The people here will not accept the truth
about me.' 19But I said, 'Lord, they know that in
every synagogue[d] I put the believers in jail and
beat them. 20They also know I was there when
Stephen, your witness, was killed. I stood there
agreeing and holding the coats of those who were
killing him!' 21But the Lord said to me, 'Leave
now. I will send you far away to the non-Jewish
people.' "

22The crowd listened to Paul until he said this.
Then they began shouting, "Kill him! Get him out
of the world! He should not be allowed to live!"
23They shouted, threw off their coats,[n] and
threw dust into the air.[n]
24Then the commander ordered the soldiers to
take Paul into the army building and beat him. He
wanted to make Paul tell why the people were
shouting against him like this. 25But as the soldiers
were tying him up, preparing to beat him, Paul
said to an officer nearby, "Do you have the right
to beat a Roman citizen[n] who has not been
proven guilty?"

26When the officer heard this, he went to the
commander and reported it. The officer said, "Do
you know what you are doing? This man is a Roman citizen."

27The commander came to Paul and said, "Tell
me, are you really a Roman citizen?"

He answered, "Yes."

28The commander said, "I paid a lot of money
to become a Roman citizen."

But Paul said, "I was born a citizen."

29The men who were preparing to question
Paul moved away from him immediately. The
commander was frightened because he had already tied Paul, and Paul was a Roman citizen.

Jewish language Hebrew or Aramaic, the languages of the Jews in the first century.
Gamaliel A very important teacher of the Pharisees, a Jewish religious group (Acts 5:34).
threw off their coats This showed that the Jews were very angry with Paul.
threw dust into the air This showed even greater anger.
Roman citizen Roman law said that Roman citizens must not be beaten before they had a trial.

Paul Speaks to Jewish Leaders

30The next day the commander decided to learn why the Jews were accusing Paul. So he ordered the leading priests and the Jewish council to meet. The commander took Paul's chains off. Then he brought Paul out and stood him before their meeting.

23 Paul looked at the Jewish council and said, "Brothers, I have lived my life without guilt feelings before God up to this day." 2Ananias,[n] the high priest, heard this and told the men who were standing near Paul to hit him on the mouth. 3Paul said to Ananias, "God will hit you, too! You are like a wall that has been painted white. You sit there and judge me, using the law of Moses, but you are telling them to hit me, and that is against the law."

4The men standing near Paul said to him, "You cannot insult God's high priest like that!"

5Paul said, "Brothers, I did not know this man was the high priest. It is written in the Scriptures,[d] 'You must not curse a leader of your people.' "[n]

6Some of the men in the meeting were Sadducees,[d] and others were Pharisees.[d] Knowing this, Paul shouted to them, "My brothers, I am a Pharisee, and my father was a Pharisee. I am on trial here because I believe that people will rise from the dead."

7When Paul said this, there was an argument between the Pharisees and the Sadducees, and the group was divided. 8(The Sadducees do not believe in angels or spirits or that people will rise from the dead. But the Pharisees believe in them all.) 9So there was a great uproar. Some of the teachers of the law, who were Pharisees, stood up and argued, "We find nothing wrong with this man. Maybe an angel or a spirit did speak to him."

10The argument was beginning to turn into such a fight that the commander was afraid the Jews would tear Paul to pieces. So he told the soldiers to go down and take Paul away and put him in the army building.

11The next night the Lord came and stood by Paul. He said, "Be brave! You have told people in Jerusalem about me. You must do the same in Rome."

12In the morning some of the Jews made a plan to kill Paul, and they took an oath not to eat or drink anything until they had killed him. 13There were more than forty Jews who made this plan. 14They went to the leading priests and the older Jewish leaders and said, "We have taken an oath not to eat or drink until we have killed Paul. 15So this is what we want you to do: Send a message to the commander to bring Paul out to you as though you want to ask him more questions. We will be waiting to kill him while he is on the way here."

16But Paul's nephew heard about this plan and went to the army building and told Paul. 17Then Paul called one of the officers and said, "Take this young man to the commander. He has a message for him."

18So the officer brought Paul's nephew to the commander and said, "The prisoner, Paul, asked me to bring this young man to you. He wants to tell you something."

19The commander took the young man's hand and led him to a place where they could be alone. He asked, "What do you want to tell me?"

20The young man said, "The Jews have decided to ask you to bring Paul down to their council meeting tomorrow. They want you to think they are going to ask him more questions. 21But don't believe them! More than forty men are hiding and waiting to kill Paul. They have all taken an oath not to eat or drink until they have killed him. Now they are waiting for you to agree."

22The commander sent the young man away, ordering him, "Don't tell anyone that you have told me about their plan."

Paul Is Sent to Caesarea

23Then the commander called two officers and said, "I need some men to go to Caesarea. Get two hundred soldiers, seventy horsemen, and two hundred men with spears ready to leave at nine o'clock tonight. 24Get some horses for Paul to ride so he can be taken to Governor Felix safely." 25And he wrote a letter that said:

> 26From Claudius Lysias.
> To the Most Excellent Governor Felix:
> Greetings.
>
> 27The Jews had taken this man and planned to kill him. But I learned that he is a Roman citizen, so I went with my soldiers and saved him. 28I wanted to know why they were accusing him, so I brought him before their council meeting. 29I learned that the Jews said Paul did some things that were wrong by their own laws, but no charge was worthy of jail or death. 30When I was told that some of the Jews were planning to kill Paul, I sent him to you at once. I also told those Jews to tell you what they have against him.

31So the soldiers did what they were told and took Paul and brought him to the city of Antipatris that night. 32The next day the horsemen went with Paul to Caesarea, but the other soldiers went back to the army building in Jerusalem. 33When

Ananias This is not the same man named Ananias in Acts 22:12.
'You . . . people.' Quotation from Exodus 22:28.

the horsemen came to Caesarea and gave the letter to the governor, they turned Paul over to him. 34The governor read the letter and asked Paul, "What area are you from?" When he learned that Paul was from Cilicia, 35he said, "I will hear your case when those who are against you come here, too." Then the governor gave orders for Paul to be kept under guard in Herod's palace.

Paul Is Accused

24 Five days later Ananias, the high priest, went to the city of Caesarea with some of the older Jewish leaders and a lawyer named Tertullus. They had come to make charges against Paul before the governor. 2Paul was called into the meeting, and Tertullus began to accuse him, saying, "Most Excellent Felix! Our people enjoy much peace because of you, and many wrong things in our country are being made right through your wise help. 3We accept these things always and in every place, and we are thankful for them. 4But not wanting to take any more of your time, I beg you to be kind and listen to our few words. 5We have found this man to be a troublemaker, stirring up the Jews everywhere in the world. He is a leader of the Nazarene[d] group. 6Also, he was trying to make the Temple[d] unclean,[d] but we stopped him.[n] 8By asking him questions yourself, you can decide if all these things are true." 9The other Jews agreed and said that all of this was true.

10When the governor made a sign for Paul to speak, Paul said, "Governor Felix, I know you have been a judge over this nation for a long time. So I am happy to defend myself before you. 11You can learn for yourself that I went to worship in Jerusalem only twelve days ago. 12Those who are accusing me did not find me arguing with anyone in the Temple or stirring up the people in the synagogues[d] or in the city. 13They cannot prove the things they are saying against me now. 14But I will tell you this: I worship the God of our ancestors as a follower of the Way of Jesus. The Jews say that the Way of Jesus is not the right way. But I believe everything that is taught in the law of Moses and that is written in the books of the Prophets.[d] 15I have the same hope in God that they have—the hope that all people, good and bad, will surely be raised from the dead. 16This is why I always try to do what I believe is right before God and people.

17"After being away from Jerusalem for several years, I went back to bring money to my people and to offer sacrifices. 18I was doing this when they found me in the Temple. I had finished the cleansing ceremony and had not made any trouble; no people were gathering around me. 19But there were some Jews from the country of Asia who should be here, standing before you. If I have really done anything wrong, they are the ones who should accuse me. 20Or ask these Jews here if they found any wrong in me when I stood before the Jewish council in Jerusalem. 21But I did shout one thing when I stood before them: 'You are judging me today because I believe that people will rise from the dead!' "

22Felix already understood much about the Way of Jesus. He stopped the trial and said, "When commander Lysias comes here, I will decide your case." 23Felix told the officer to keep Paul guarded but to give him some freedom and to let his friends bring what he needed.

Paul Speaks to Felix and His Wife

24After some days Felix came with his wife, Drusilla, who was Jewish, and asked for Paul to be brought to him. He listened to Paul talk about believing in Christ Jesus. 25But Felix became afraid when Paul spoke about living right, self-control, and the time when God will judge the world. He said, "Go away now. When I have more time, I will call for you." 26At the same time Felix hoped that Paul would give him some money, so he often sent for Paul and talked with him.

> **SIDELIGHT:** *The Judean governor Felix was greedy, brutal, and incompetent. He once killed four hundred men suspected of terrorist activities—without a trial. When Paul wouldn't pay him a bribe, Felix left the apostle in jail for two years, until Felix was succeeded in office (Acts 24:1–27).*

27But after two years, Felix was replaced by Porcius Festus as governor. But Felix had left Paul in prison to please the Jews.

Paul Asks to See Caesar

25 Three days after Festus became governor, he went from Caesarea to Jerusalem. 2There the leading priests and the important Jewish leaders made charges against Paul before Festus. 3They asked Festus to do them a favor. They wanted him to send Paul back to Jerusalem, because they had a plan to kill him on the way. 4But Festus answered that Paul would be kept in Caesarea and that he himself was returning there soon. 5He said, "Some of your leaders should go

Verse 6 Some Greek copies add 6b-8a: "And we wanted to judge him by our own law. 7But the officer Lysias came and used much force to take him from us. 8And Lysias commanded those who wanted to accuse Paul to come to you."

with me. They can accuse the man there in Caesarea, if he has really done something wrong."
6Festus stayed in Jerusalem another eight or ten
days and then went back to Caesarea. The next
day he told the soldiers to bring Paul before him.
Festus was seated on the judge's seat 7when Paul
came into the room. The Jewish people who had
come from Jerusalem stood around him, making
serious charges against him, which they could not
prove. 8This is what Paul said to defend himself:
"I have done nothing wrong against the Jewish
law, against the Temple,[d] or against Caesar."[d]
9But Festus wanted to please the Jews. So he
asked Paul, "Do you want to go to Jerusalem for
me to judge you there on these charges?"
10Paul said, "I am standing at Caesar's judgment seat now, where I should be judged. I have
done nothing wrong to the Jews; you know this
is true. 11If I have done something wrong and the
law says I must die, I do not ask to be saved from
death. But if these charges are not true, then no
one can give me to them. I want Caesar to hear
my case!"
12Festus talked about this with his advisors.
Then he said, "You have asked to see Caesar, so
you will go to Caesar!"

Paul Before King Agrippa

13A few days later King Agrippa and Bernice
came to Caesarea to visit Festus. 14They stayed
there for some time, and Festus told the king
about Paul's case. Festus said, "There is a man
that Felix left in prison. 15When I went to Jerusalem, the leading priests and the older Jewish leaders there made charges against him, asking me to
sentence him to death. 16But I answered, 'When
a man is accused of a crime, Romans do not hand
him over until he has been allowed to face his
accusers and defend himself against their
charges.' 17So when these Jews came here to
Caesarea for the trial, I did not waste time. The
next day I sat on the judge's seat and commanded
that the man be brought in. 18The Jews stood up
and accused him, but not of any serious crime as
I thought they would. 19The things they said were
about their own religion and about a man named
Jesus who died. But Paul said that he is still alive.
20Not knowing how to find out about these questions, I asked Paul, 'Do you want to go to Jerusalem and be judged there?' 21But he asked to be
kept in Caesarea. He wants a decision from the
emperor.[n] So I ordered that he be held until I
could send him to Caesar.[d]"
22Agrippa said to Festus, "I would also like to
hear this man myself."
Festus said, "Tomorrow you will hear him."
23The next day Agrippa and Bernice appeared
with great show, acting like very important people. They went into the judgment room with the
army leaders and the important men of Caesarea.
Then Festus ordered the soldiers to bring Paul in.
24Festus said, "King Agrippa and all who are gathered here with us, you see this man. All the Jewish people, here and in Jerusalem, have complained to me about him, shouting that he should
not live any longer. 25When I judged him, I found
no reason to order his death. But since he asked
to be judged by Caesar, I decided to send him.
26But I have nothing definite to write the emperor
about him. So I have brought him before all of
you—especially you, King Agrippa. I hope you
can question him and give me something to write.
27I think it is foolish to send a prisoner to Caesar
without telling what charges are against him."

Paul Defends Himself

26 Agrippa said to Paul, "You may now
speak to defend yourself."
Then Paul raised his hand and began to speak.
2He said, "King Agrippa, I am very happy to stand
before you and will answer all the charges the
Jewish people make against me. 3You know so
much about all the Jewish customs and the things
the Jews argue about, so please listen to me patiently.
4"All the Jewish people know about my whole
life, how I lived from the beginning in my own
country and later in Jerusalem. 5They have
known me for a long time. If they want to, they
can tell you that I was a good Pharisee.[d] And the
Pharisees obey the laws of the Jewish religion
more carefully than any other group. 6Now I am
on trial because I hope for the promise that God
made to our ancestors. 7This is the promise that
the twelve tribes[d] of our people hope to receive
as they serve God day and night. My king, the
Jews have accused me because I hope for this
same promise! 8Why do any of you people think
it is impossible for God to raise people from the
dead?
9"I, too, thought I ought to do many things
against Jesus from Nazareth. 10And that is what I
did in Jerusalem. The leading priests gave me the
power to put many of God's people in jail, and
when they were being killed, I agreed it was a
good thing. 11In every synagogue,[d] I often punished them and tried to make them speak against
Jesus. I was so angry against them I even went to
other cities to find them and punish them.
12"One time the leading priests gave me permission and the power to go to Damascus. 13On
the way there, at noon, I saw a light from heaven.
It was brighter than the sun and flashed all around
me and those who were traveling with me. 14We

emperor The ruler of the Roman Empire, which was almost all the known world.

all fell to the ground. Then I heard a voice speaking to me in the Jewish language,[n] saying, 'Saul,
Saul, why are you persecuting me? You are only
hurting yourself by fighting me.' 15I said, 'Who are
you, Lord?' The Lord said, 'I am Jesus, the one
you are persecuting. 16Stand up! I have chosen
you to be my servant and my witness—you will
tell people the things that you have seen and the
things that I will show you. This is why I have
come to you today. 17I will keep you safe from
your own people and also from those who are not
Jewish. I am sending you to them 18to open their
eyes so that they may turn away from darkness to
the light, away from the power of Satan and to
God. Then their sins can be forgiven, and they
can have a place with those people who have
been made holy by believing in me.'

19"King Agrippa, after I had this vision from
heaven, I obeyed it. 20I began telling people that
they should change their hearts and lives and turn
to God and do things to show they really had
changed. I told this first to those in Damascus,
then in Jerusalem, and in every part of Judea, and
also to those who are not Jewish. 21This is why
the Jews took me and were trying to kill me in the
Temple.[d] 22But God has helped me, and so I stand
here today, telling all people, small and great,
what I have seen. But I am saying only what Moses and the prophets[d] said would happen— 23that
the Christ[d] would die, and as the first to rise from
the dead, he would bring light to the Jewish and
non-Jewish people."

Paul Tries to Persuade Agrippa

24While Paul was saying these things to defend
himself, Festus said loudly, "Paul, you are out of
your mind! Too much study has driven you
crazy!"

25Paul said, "Most excellent Festus, I am not
crazy. My words are true and sensible. 26King
Agrippa knows about these things, and I can
speak freely to him. I know he has heard about all
of these things, because they did not happen off
in a corner. 27King Agrippa, do you believe what
the prophets[d] wrote? I know you believe."

28King Agrippa said to Paul, "Do you think you
can persuade me to become a Christian in such a
short time?"

29Paul said, "Whether it is a short or a long
time, I pray to God that not only you but every
person listening to me today would be saved and
be like me—except for these chains I have."

30Then King Agrippa, Governor Festus, Bernice, and all the people sitting with them stood up
31and left the room. Talking to each other, they
said, "There is no reason why this man should die
or be put in jail." 32And Agrippa said to Festus,
"We could let this man go free, but he has asked
Caesar[d] to hear his case."

Paul Sails for Rome

27 It was decided that we would sail for Italy. An officer named Julius, who served
in the emperor's[n] army, guarded Paul and some
other prisoners. 2We got on a ship that was from
the city of Adramyttium and was about to sail to
different ports in the country of Asia. Aristarchus,
a man from the city of Thessalonica in Macedonia, went with us. 3The next day we came to Sidon. Julius was very good to Paul and gave him
freedom to go visit his friends, who took care of
his needs. 4We left Sidon and sailed close to the
island of Cyprus, because the wind was blowing
against us. 5We went across the sea by Cilicia and
Pamphylia and landed at the city of Myra, in
Lycia. 6There the officer found a ship from Alexandria that was going to Italy, so he put us on it.

7We sailed slowly for many days. We had a
hard time reaching Cnidus because the wind was
blowing against us, and we could not go any farther. So we sailed by the south side of the island
of Crete near Salmone. 8Sailing past it was hard.
Then we came to a place called Fair Havens, near
the city of Lasea.

9We had lost much time, and it was now dangerous to sail, because it was already after the Day
of Cleansing.[n] So Paul warned them, 10"Men, I
can see there will be a lot of trouble on this trip.
The ship, the cargo, and even our lives may be
lost." 11But the captain and the owner of the ship
did not agree with Paul, and the officer believed
what the captain and owner of the ship said.
12Since that harbor was not a good place for the
ship to stay for the winter, most of the men decided that the ship should leave. They hoped we
could go to Phoenix and stay there for the winter.
Phoenix, a city on the island of Crete, had a harbor which faced southwest and northwest.

The Storm

13When a good wind began to blow from the
south, the men on the ship thought, "This is the
wind we wanted, and now we have it." So they
pulled up the anchor, and we sailed very close to
the island of Crete. 14But then a very strong wind
named the "northeaster" came from the island.
15The ship was caught in it and could not sail
against it. So we stopped trying and let the wind

Jewish language Hebrew or Aramaic, the languages of the Jews in the first century.
emperor The ruler of the Roman Empire, which was almost all the known world.
Day of Cleansing An important Jewish holy day in the fall of the year. This was the time of year that bad storms arose on the sea.

carry us. 16When we went below a small island
named Cauda, we were barely able to bring in the
lifeboat. 17After the men took the lifeboat in, they
tied ropes around the ship to hold it together. The
men were afraid that the ship would hit the sand-
banks of Syrtis,[n] so they lowered the sail and let
the wind carry the ship. 18The next day the storm
was blowing us so hard that the men threw out
some of the cargo. 19A day later with their own
hands they threw out the ship's equipment.
20When we could not see the sun or the stars for
many days, and the storm was very bad, we lost
all hope of being saved.

21After the men had gone without food for a
long time, Paul stood up before them and said,
"Men, you should have listened to me. You
should not have sailed from Crete. Then you
would not have all this trouble and loss. 22But
now I tell you to cheer up because none of you
will die. Only the ship will be lost. 23Last night an
angel came to me from the God I belong to and
worship. 24The angel said, 'Paul, do not be afraid.
You must stand before Caesar.[d] And God has
promised you that he will save the lives of everyone sailing with you.' 25So men, have courage. I
trust in God that everything will happen as his
angel told me. 26But we will crash on an island."

27On the fourteenth night we were still being
carried around in the Adriatic Sea.[n] About midnight the sailors thought we were close to land,
28so they lowered a rope with a weight on the end
of it into the water. They found that the water
was one hundred twenty feet deep. They went a
little farther and lowered the rope again. It was
ninety feet deep. 29The sailors were afraid that we
would hit the rocks, so they threw four anchors
into the water and prayed for daylight to come.
30Some of the sailors wanted to leave the ship,
and they lowered the lifeboat, pretending they
were throwing more anchors from the front of the
ship. 31But Paul told the officer and the other soldiers, "If these men do not stay in the ship, your
lives cannot be saved." 32So the soldiers cut the
ropes and let the lifeboat fall into the water.

33Just before dawn Paul began persuading all
the people to eat something. He said, "For the
past fourteen days you have been waiting and
watching and not eating. 34Now I beg you to eat
something. You need it to stay alive. None of you
will lose even one hair off your heads." 35After he
said this, Paul took some bread and thanked God
for it before all of them. He broke off a piece and
began eating. 36They all felt better and started eating, too. 37There were two hundred seventy-six
people on the ship. 38When they had eaten all
they wanted, they began making the ship lighter
by throwing the grain into the sea.

The Ship Is Destroyed

39When daylight came, the sailors saw land.
They did not know what land it was, but they saw
a bay with a beach and wanted to sail the ship to
the beach if they could. 40So they cut the ropes to
the anchors and left the anchors in the sea. At the
same time, they untied the ropes that were holding the rudders. Then they raised the front sail
into the wind and sailed toward the beach. 41But
the ship hit a sandbank. The front of the ship
stuck there and could not move, but the back of
the ship began to break up from the big waves.

42The soldiers decided to kill the prisoners so
none of them could swim away and escape. 43But
Julius, the officer, wanted to let Paul live and did
not allow the soldiers to kill the prisoners. Instead
he ordered everyone who could swim to jump
into the water first and swim to land. 44The rest
were to follow using wooden boards or pieces of
the ship. And this is how all the people made it
safely to land.

SIDELIGHT: Paul often experienced rough waters while sailing (Acts 27:13–44). Storms, a common occurrence in the Mediterranean Sea, made travel hazardous for wooden trading ships. Today, one Greek island, only nine miles long, has four hundred churches that were built by sailors who were fulfilling vows they made to God in the midst of perilous storms.

Paul on the Island of Malta

28 When we were safe on land, we learned
that the island was called Malta. 2The
people who lived there were very good to us. Because it was raining and very cold, they made a
fire and welcomed all of us. 3Paul gathered a pile
of sticks and was putting them on the fire when
a poisonous snake came out because of the heat
and bit him on the hand. 4The people living on
the island saw the snake hanging from Paul's
hand and said to each other, "This man must be
a murderer! He did not die in the sea, but Justice[n] does not want him to live." 5But Paul shook
the snake off into the fire and was not hurt. 6The
people thought that Paul would swell up or fall
down dead. They waited and watched him for a
long time, but nothing bad happened to him. So
they changed their minds and said, "He is a god!"

Syrtis Shallow area in the sea near the Libyan coast.
Adriatic Sea The sea between Greece and Italy, including the central Mediterranean.
Justice The people thought there was a god named Justice who would punish bad people.

7There were some fields around there owned
by Publius, an important man on the island. He
welcomed us into his home and was very good to
us for three days. 8Publius' father was sick with a
fever and dysentery.[n] Paul went to him, prayed,
and put his hands on the man and healed him.
9After this, all the other sick people on the island
came to Paul, and he healed them, too. 10-11The
people on the island gave us many honors. When
we were ready to leave, three months later, they
gave us the things we needed.

Paul Goes to Rome

We got on a ship from Alexandria that had
stayed on the island during the winter. On the
front of the ship was the sign of the twin gods.[n]
12We stopped at Syracuse for three days. 13From
there we sailed to Rhegium. The next day a wind
began to blow from the south, and a day later we
came to Puteoli. 14We found some believers there
who asked us to stay with them for a week. Finally, we came to Rome. 15The believers in Rome
heard that we were there and came out as far as
the Market of Appius[n] and the Three Inns[n] to
meet us. When Paul saw them, he was encouraged and thanked God.

Paul in Rome

16When we arrived at Rome, Paul was allowed
to live alone, with the soldier who guarded him.
17Three days later Paul sent for the Jewish leaders there. When they came together, he said,
"Brothers, I have done nothing against our people
or the customs of our ancestors. But I was arrested in Jerusalem and given to the Romans. 18Af-
ter they asked me many questions, they could find
no reason why I should be killed. They wanted to
let me go free, 19but the Jewish people there argued against that. So I had to ask to come to Rome
to have my trial before Caesar.[d] But I have no
charge to bring against my own people. 20That is
why I wanted to see you and talk with you. I am
bound with this chain because I believe in the
hope of Israel."
21They answered Paul, "We have received no
letters from Judea about you. None of our Jewish
brothers who have come from there brought
news or told us anything bad about you. 22But we
want to hear your ideas, because we know that
people everywhere are speaking against this religious group."
23Paul and the Jewish people chose a day for a
meeting and on that day many more of the Jews
met with Paul at the place he was staying. He
spoke to them all day long. Using the law of Moses and the prophets'[d] writings, he explained the
kingdom of God, and he tried to persuade them
to believe these things about Jesus. 24Some believed what Paul said, but others did not. 25So
they argued and began leaving after Paul said one
more thing to them: "The Holy Spirit[d] spoke the
truth to your ancestors through Isaiah the
prophet, saying,
26'Go to this people and say:
You will listen and listen, but you will not
understand.
You will look and look, but you will not
learn,
27because these people have become stubborn.
They don't hear with their ears,
and they have closed their eyes.
Otherwise, they might really understand
what they see with their eyes
and hear with their ears.
They might really understand in their minds
and come back to me and be healed.'

Isaiah 6:9-10

28"I want you to know that God has also sent
his salvation to those who are not Jewish, and
they will listen!" 29 [n]
30Paul stayed two full years in his own rented
house and welcomed all people who came to visit
him. 31He boldly preached about the kingdom of
God and taught about the Lord Jesus Christ, and
no one tried to stop him.

dysentery A sickness like diarrhea.
twin gods Statues of Castor and Pollux, gods in old Greek tales.
Market of Appius A town about twenty-seven miles from Rome.
Three Inns A town about thirty miles from Rome.
Verse 29 Some late Greek copies add verse 29: "After Paul said this, the Jews left. They were arguing very much with each other."

ROMANS

Why Read This Book:

- Understand that all people have sinned (Romans 1—3).
- Learn how Jesus Christ pays for our sins (Romans 4—8).
- Be challenged to live the Christian life (Romans 12—15).

Behind the Scenes:

Suppose a school friend sat down with you in the cafeteria and asked, out of the blue, "What do you believe?" What would you say?

The Book of Romans is the apostle Paul's answer to that question: What do you believe? For more than twenty years, he had been a missionary, spreading the good news about Jesus Christ. He wanted to visit the Roman church, but before he went, he wanted the Roman Christians to understand what he believed.

So he wrote them this letter, which many people believe is the best, most powerful summary of Christian beliefs in the Bible. The letter explains how all people have sinned and how God sent Jesus to pay for those sins and make people right with God (Romans 3:22–28). Then it explains what it means to live as Christians.

The Book of Romans is packed with powerful statements about God and faith. From this book we can learn how God's love for us overcomes the power of sin in our lives and how we can live lives that please God.

WHERE THE ACTION WAS

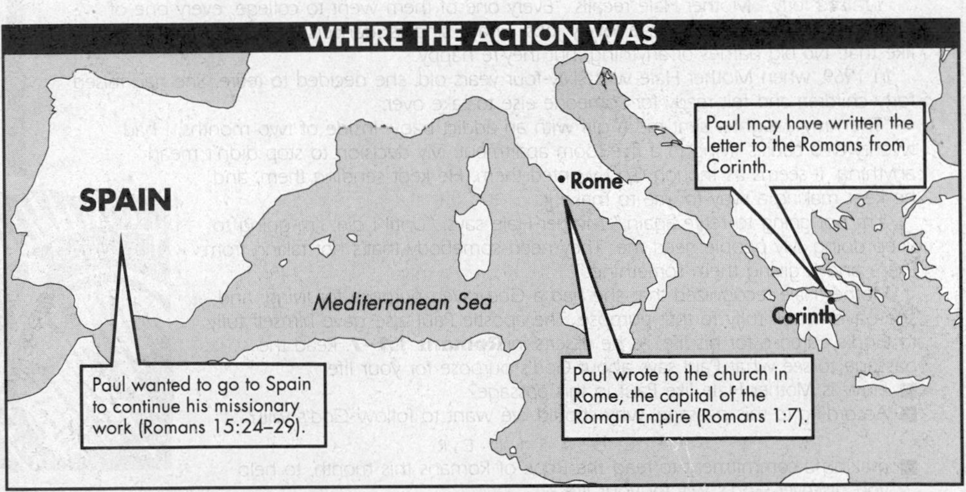

Paul may have written the letter to the Romans from Corinth.
Rome
SPAIN
Mediterranean Sea
Corinth
Paul wanted to go to Spain to continue his missionary work (Romans 15:24–29).
Paul wrote to the church in Rome, the capital of the Roman Empire (Romans 1:7).

WHEN THE ACTION WAS

Above the timeline: Jesus was born — The church began soon after Jesus went to heaven — Paul began his missionary work — Fire destroyed Rome

BC/AD — 25AD — 50AD — 75AD — 100AD

Below the timeline: Jesus began his ministry — Paul became a Christian — Paul wrote Romans — Romans destroyed the Temple in Jerusalem

1 From Paul, a servant of Christ Jesus. God
called me to be an apostle[d] and chose me to
tell the Good News.[d]
2 God promised this Good News long ago
through his prophets,[d] as it is written in the Holy
Scriptures.[d] 3-4 The Good News is about God's
Son, Jesus Christ our Lord. As a man, he was born
from the family of David. But through the Spirit[d]
of holiness he was appointed to be God's Son with
great power by rising from the dead. 5 Through
Christ, God gave me the special work of an apostle, which was to lead people of all nations to believe and obey. I do this work for him. 6 And you
who are in Rome are also called to belong to Jesus
Christ.
7 To all of you in Rome whom God loves and
has called to be his holy people:

Grace and peace to you from God our Father and the Lord Jesus Christ.

A Prayer of Thanks

8 First I want to say that I thank my God
through Jesus Christ for all of you, because people
everywhere in the world are talking about your
faith. 9 God, whom I serve with my whole heart
by telling the Good News[d] about his Son, knows

GOD'S WILL

Mother Hale

"My husband and I had dreams of what we were going to do with our children," recalls Clara McBride Hale of her life in the early part of the 1900s. "We dreamed that they'd grow up and be what they want to be and have a good life."

But Clara's husband died when their children, Lorraine and Nathan, were five and six. And during that time, untrained women could only work domestic jobs, such as housecleaning. Clara had to support her children, but she didn't want to leave them alone all day while she went to work.

"So I decided to take in other people's children," Clara continues. "They were coming for five days and going home Saturday and Sunday. But they got so they didn't want to go home. They wanted to stay with me altogether. So the parents would give me an extra dollar, and that meant I kept them all the time."

What started as a "survival" business bloomed into a lifetime ministry for Clara, who came to be known by the children and their parents as "Mother Hale."

"I raised forty," Mother Hale recalls. "Every one of them went to college, every one of them graduated, and they have lovely jobs. I have singers, dancers, preachers, and things like that. No big names or anything, but they're happy."

In 1969, when Mother Hale was sixty-four years old, she decided to retire. She had raised forty children and felt ready for someone else to take over.

"Then my daughter sent me a girl with an addict baby. Inside of two months, I had twenty-two babies living in a five-room apartment. My decision to stop didn't mean anything. It seems as though God wanted them. He kept sending them, and he kept making a way for me to make it.

"I'm not going to retire again," Mother Hale says. "Until I die, I'm going to keep doing. My people need me. They need somebody that's not taking from them and is giving them something."

Mother Hale recognized that she had a God-given purpose for living, and she gave herself fully to that purpose. The apostle Paul also gave himself fully to God's purpose for his life, as he asserts in **Romans 1:1–7**. Read the passage to see what Paul says about God's purpose for your life.

- How is Mother Hale like Paul in this passage?
- According to this passage, why should we want to follow God's will?

CONSIDER . . .

- making a commitment to read the Book of Romans this month, to help you discover God's will for your life.
- writing out God's purpose for your life according to the passage. Then pray for God to make his purpose become reality in your life.

FOR MORE, SEE . . .

- Jeremiah 1:4–8 (p. 691)
- Matthew 12:46–50 (p. 930)
- 1 Thessalonians 4:3–8 (p. 1247)

that I always mention you 10every time I pray. I
pray that I will be allowed to come to you, and

SIDELIGHT: The recipients of the letter to the Romans lived in the capital of the giant, powerful Roman Empire (Romans 1:7). The Romans built a 250,000-mile long highway system that would have circled the equator ten times if it had been one long road.

this will happen if God wants it. 11I want very
much to see you, to give you some spiritual gift
to make you strong. 12I mean that I want us to
help each other with the faith we have. Your faith
will help me, and my faith will help you. 13Broth-
ers and sisters,[n] I want you to know that I
planned many times to come to you, but this has
not been possible. I wanted to come so that I
could help you grow spiritually as I have helped
the other non-Jewish people.

14I have a duty to all people — Greeks and those
who are not Greeks, the wise and the foolish.
15That is why I want so much to preach the Good
News to you in Rome.

16I am proud of the Good News, because it is
the power God uses to save everyone who believes — to save the Jews first, and also to save
those who are not Jews. 17The Good News shows
how God makes people right with himself — that
it begins and ends with faith. As the Scripture[d]
says, "But those who are right with God will live
by trusting in him."[n]

All People Have Done Wrong

18God's anger is shown from heaven against all
the evil and wrong things people do. By their own
evil lives they hide the truth. 19God shows his anger because some knowledge of him has been
made clear to them. Yes, God has shown himself
to them. 20There are things about him that people
cannot see — his eternal power and all the things
that make him God. But since the beginning of
the world those things have been easy to understand by what God has made. So people have no
excuse for the bad things they do. 21They knew
God, but they did not give glory to God or thank
him. Their thinking became useless. Their foolish
minds were filled with darkness. 22They said they
were wise, but they became fools. 23They traded
the glory of God who lives forever for the worship
of idols made to look like earthly people, birds,
animals, and snakes.

24Because they did these things, God left them
and let them go their sinful way, wanting only to
do evil. As a result, they became full of sexual sin,
using their bodies wrongly with each other.
25They traded the truth of God for a lie. They worshiped and served what had been created instead
of the God who created those things, who should
be praised forever. Amen.

26Because people did those things, God left
them and let them do the shameful things they
wanted to do. Women stopped having natural sex
and started having sex with other women. 27In
the same way, men stopped having natural sex
and began wanting each other. Men did shameful
things with other men, and in their bodies they
received the punishment for those wrongs.

28People did not think it was important to have
a true knowledge of God. So God left them and
allowed them to have their own worthless thinking and to do things they should not do. 29They
are filled with every kind of sin, evil, selfishness,
and hatred. They are full of jealousy, murder,
fighting, lying, and thinking the worst about each
other. They gossip 30and say evil things about
each other. They hate God. They are rude and
conceited and brag about themselves. They in-
vent ways of doing evil. They do not obey their
parents. 31They are foolish, they do not keep their
promises, and they show no kindness or mercy to
others. 32They know God's law says that those
who live like this should die. But they themselves
not only continue to do these evil things, they
applaud others who do them.

You People Also Are Sinful

2 If you think you can judge others, you are
wrong. When you judge them, you are really
judging yourself guilty, because you do the same
things they do. 2God judges those who do wrong
things, and we know that his judging is right.
3You judge those who do wrong, but you do
wrong yourselves. Do you think you will be able
to escape the judgment of God? 4He has been very
kind and patient, waiting for you to change, but
you think nothing of his kindness. Perhaps you do
not understand that God is kind to you so you will
change your hearts and lives. 5But you are stubborn and refuse to change, so you are making
your own punishment even greater on the day he
shows his anger. On that day everyone will see
God's right judgments. 6God will reward or punish every person for what that person has done.
7Some people, by always continuing to do good,
live for God's glory, for honor, and for life that has
no end. God will give them life forever. 8But other

Brothers and sisters Although the Greek text says "Brothers" here and throughout this book, Paul's words were meant for the entire church, including men and women.
"But those . . . him." Quotation from Habakkuk 2:4.

people are selfish. They refuse to follow truth and,
instead, follow evil. God will give them his punishment and anger. 9He will give trouble and suffering to everyone who does evil—to the Jews
first and also to those who are not Jews. 10But he
will give glory, honor, and peace to everyone who
does good—to the Jews first and also to those
who are not Jews. 11For God judges all people in
the same way.

12People who do not have the law and who are
sinners will be lost, although they do not have the
law. And, in the same way, those who have the
law and are sinners will be judged by the law.
13Hearing the law does not make people right
with God. It is those who obey the law who will
be right with him. 14(Those who are not Jews do
not have the law, but when they freely do what
the law commands, they are the law for themselves. This is true even though they do not have
the law. 15They show that in their hearts they
know what is right and wrong, just as the law
commands. And they show this by their consciences. Sometimes their thoughts tell them they
did wrong, and sometimes their thoughts tell
them they did right.) 16All these things will happen on the day when God, through Christ Jesus,
will judge people's secret thoughts. The Good
News[d] that I preach says this.

The Jews and the Law

17What about you? You call yourself a Jew. You
trust in the law of Moses and brag that you are
close to God. 18You know what he wants you to
do and what is important, because you have
learned the law. 19You think you are a guide for
the blind and a light for those who are in darkness. 20You think you can show foolish people
what is right and teach those who know nothing.
You have the law; so you think you know everything and have all truth. 21You teach others, so
why don't you teach yourself? You tell others not
to steal, but you steal. 22You say that others must
not take part in adultery,[d] but you are guilty of
that sin. You hate idols, but you steal from temples. 23You brag about having God's law, but you
bring shame to God by breaking his law, 24just as
the Scriptures[d] say: "Those who are not Jews
speak against God's name because of you."[n]

25If you follow the law, your circumcision[d] has
meaning. But if you break the law, it is as if you
were never circumcised. 26People who are not
Jews are not circumcised, but if they do what the
law says, it is as if they were circumcised. 27You
Jews have the written law and circumcision, but
you break the law. So those who are not circumcised in their bodies, but still obey the law, will
show that you are guilty. 28They can do this because a person is not a true Jew if he is only a Jew
in his physical body; true circumcision is not only
on the outside of the body. 29A person is a Jew
only if he is a Jew inside; true circumcision is
done in the heart by the Spirit,[d] not by the written
law. Such a person gets praise from God rather
than from people.

3 So, do Jews have anything that other people
do not have? Is there anything special about
being circumcised? 2Yes, of course, there is in every way. The most important thing is this: God
trusted the Jews with his teachings. 3If some Jews
were not faithful to him, will that stop God from
doing what he promised? 4No! God will continue
to be true even when every person is false. As the
Scriptures[d] say:

"So you will be shown to be right when you
speak,
and you will win your case." *Psalm 51:4*

5When we do wrong, that shows more clearly
that God is right. So can we say that God is wrong
to punish us? (I am talking as people might talk.)
6No! If God could not punish us, he could not
judge the world.

7A person might say, "When I lie, it really gives
him glory, because my lie shows God's truth. So
why am I judged a sinner?" 8It would be the same
to say, "We should do evil so that good will
come." Some people find fault with us and say we
teach this, but they are wrong and deserve the
punishment they will receive.

All People Are Guilty

9So are we Jews better than others? No! We
have already said that Jews and those who are not
Jews are all guilty of sin. 10As the Scriptures[d] say:

"There is no one who always does what is
right,
not even one.
11 There is no one who understands.
There is no one who looks to God for help.
12All have turned away.
Together, everyone has become useless.
There is no one who does anything good;
there is not even one." *Psalm 14:1-3*
13"Their throats are like open graves;
they use their tongues for telling lies."
Psalm 5:9
"Their words are like snake poison." *Psalm 140:3*
14 "Their mouths are full of cursing and hate."
Psalm 10:7
15"They are always ready to kill people.
16 Everywhere they go they cause ruin and
misery.
17They don't know how to live in peace."
Isaiah 59:7-8
18 "They have no fear of God." *Psalm 36:1*

"Those . . . you." Quotation from Isaiah 52:5; Ezekiel 36:20.

19We know that the law's commands are for
those who have the law. This stops all excuses
and brings the whole world under God's judgment, 20because no one can be made right with
God by following the law. The law only shows us
our sin.

How God Makes People Right

21But God has a way to make people right with
him without the law, and he has now shown us
that way which the law and the prophets[d] told us
about. 22God makes people right with himself
through their faith in Jesus Christ. This is true for
all who believe in Christ, because all people are
the same: 23All have sinned and are not good
enough for God's glory, 24and all need to be made
right with God by his grace, which is a free gift.
They need to be made free from sin through Jesus
Christ. 25God gave him as a way to forgive sin
through faith in the blood of Jesus' death. This
showed that God always does what is right and
fair, as in the past when he was patient and did
not punish people for their sins. 26And God gave
Jesus to show today that he does what is right.
God did this so he could judge rightly and so he
could make right any person who has faith in
Jesus.

27So do we have a reason to brag about ourselves? No! And why not? It is the way of faith
that stops all bragging, not the way of trying to
obey the law. 28A person is made right with God
through faith, not through obeying the law. 29Is
God only the God of the Jews? Is he not also the
God of those who are not Jews? 30Of course he is,
because there is only one God. He will make Jews
right with him by their faith, and he will also
make those who are not Jews right with him
through their faith. 31So do we destroy the law by
following the way of faith? No! Faith causes us to
be what the law truly wants.

The Example of Abraham

4 So what can we say that Abraham,[n] the father of our people, learned about faith? 2If

Abraham Most respected ancestor of the Jews. Every Jew hoped to see Abraham.

FORGIVENESS

Only a Car

Uncle Carl let Derek borrow his new, red convertible for the prom. It was less than two weeks old.

The magical night ended much too early for Derek, about 3 A.M., when he dropped off his date at her house and started the long drive across town to home. The next thing he knew, he was waking up, skidding madly across the deserted suburban road, scraping the side of the car against a guardrail before he could come to a stop.

He drove home, parked the car against the curb, and sat on the front porch, waiting for morning to come. His stomach was in a knot. He didn't even try to sleep.

At 8 A.M., Derek stood next to his uncle as he silently examined the foot-wide scar that now marred the fender and door of his new car. Uncle Carl's breathing was slow and measured. The silence seemed to go on forever.

How could Derek ever make this up to him? How could he pay for the damage or heal the hurt he saw in his face?

Finally, the older man placed his hand on Derek's shoulder and gave it a reassuring squeeze. He shrugged, smiled a lopsided smile, and said, "It's only a car."

At that moment, Derek knew something of the kind of forgiveness Paul was talking about when he wrote **Romans 3:21–28**.

- How is Uncle Carl's act of forgiveness like the forgiveness Paul talks about in this passage?
- According to the passage, how do we receive God's forgiveness?

CONSIDER . . .

- writing about a way someone has hurt you recently and then tearing up the paper and forgiving the hurt.
- talking to a friend you've hurt and asking for forgiveness.

FOR MORE, SEE . . .

- Psalm 103:10–13 (p. 540)
- Luke 6:27–36 (p. 1013)
- Hebrews 8:10–13 (p. 1283)

Abraham was made right by the things he did, he
had a reason to brag. But this is not God's view,
3 because the Scripture[d] says, "Abraham believed
God, and God accepted Abraham's faith, and that
faith made him right with God." [n]

4 When people work, their pay is not given as
a gift, but as something earned. 5 But people cannot do any work that will make them right with
God. So they must trust in him, who makes even
evil people right in his sight. Then God accepts
their faith, and that makes them right with him.
6 David said the same thing. He said that people
are truly blessed when God, without paying attention to good deeds, makes people right with himself.

7 "Happy are they
whose sins are forgiven,
whose wrongs are pardoned.
8 Happy is the person
whom the Lord does not consider guilty."

Psalm 32:1-2

9 Is this blessing only for those who are circum-

"Abraham . . . God." Quotation from Genesis 15:6.

FAITH

Free Approval

Ed Marx really liked Julie Hempstead. In fact, he was totally crazy about her. Julie was funny, smart, beautiful—everything Ed wanted in a girl. For weeks, Ed watched Julie as she went from class to class. He watched her while she ate lunch. He watched her as she walked home from school.

Finally, after weeks of planning, he got up the nerve to ask her out.

"Hi, Ed. What's up?" Julie asked with that smile Ed loved so much.

"Um, I was wondering . . ." he said, clearing his throat. "I was wondering if you'd like to go do something Friday night." Ed couldn't believe his heart could pound so hard.

"Sure, I'd love to," Julie responded without missing a beat.

That was the first of many evenings together for the new couple. Julie really liked Ed. He was funny and sensitive. And, of course, Ed liked Julie, but he couldn't believe she could be interested in him.

As they continued to date, Ed kept doing things for Julie to keep her interested. He bought her gifts. He offered to run errands for her. One day, he even offered her his car so she wouldn't have to walk to school.

"Ed, I don't want your car," Julie said.

"It's okay, really," Ed assured her. "I want you to have it."

"No, Ed, you don't understand." Julie took a deep breath. "You don't need to try so hard. I already like you. You really don't need to do anything to win my love. So just relax, okay? You're starting to drive me crazy."

Ed felt embarrassed. "It's hard to believe, that's all," he said.

"Well, believe it," Julie said, grinning, and she kissed him.

Ed had a hard time believing Julie could love him unless he did things to earn her affection. **Romans 4:1–12** tells a similar story about Abraham, who discovered that God's favor is also based on believing. Read the passage to see why we can't earn God's approval through our actions.

- How does Ed's response to Julie differ from Abraham's response to God in the passage?
- According to the passage, what does God require for you to have a relationship with him?

C O N S I D E R . . .

- thinking of ways you might try to earn God's love and then asking God to help you accept his love by faith.
- writing out how you think God sees you, and having your youth leader do the same.
- Compare the two descriptions, and ask God to increase your faith to believe the truth about how he sees you.

F O R M O R E , S E E . . .

- Genesis 15:1–6 (p. 16)
- Galatians 3:6–27 (p. 1209)
- Ephesians 2:8–9 (p. 1219)

cised[d] or also for those who are not circumcised?
We have already said that God accepted Abraham's faith and that faith made him right with
God. 10So how did this happen? Did God accept
Abraham before or after he was circumcised? It
was before his circumcision. 11Abraham was circumcised to show that he was right with God
through faith before he was circumcised. So Abraham is the father of all those who believe but are
not circumcised; he is the father of all believers
who are accepted as being right with God. 12And
Abraham is also the father of those who have
been circumcised and who live following the faith
that our father Abraham had before he was circumcised.

God Keeps His Promise

13Abraham[n] and his descendants[d] received the
promise that they would get the whole world. He
did not receive that promise through the law, but
through being right with God by his faith. 14If people could receive what God promised by following the law, then faith is worthless. And God's
promise to Abraham is worthless, 15because the
law can only bring God's anger. But if there is no
law, there is nothing to disobey.

16So people receive God's promise by having
faith. This happens so the promise can be a free
gift. Then all of Abraham's children can have that
promise. It is not only for those who live under
the law of Moses but for anyone who lives with
faith like that of Abraham, who is the father of us
all. 17As it is written in the Scriptures:[d] "I am making you a father of many nations."[n] This is true
before God, the God Abraham believed, the God
who gives life to the dead and who creates something out of nothing.

18There was no hope that Abraham would have
children. But Abraham believed God and continued hoping, and so he became the father of many
nations. As God told him, "Your descendants also
will be too many to count."[n] 19Abraham was almost a hundred years old, much past the age for
having children, and Sarah could not have children. Abraham thought about all this, but his faith
in God did not become weak. 20He never doubted
that God would keep his promise, and he never
stopped believing. He grew stronger in his faith
and gave praise to God. 21Abraham felt sure that
God was able to do what he had promised. 22So,
"God accepted Abraham's faith, and that faith
made him right with God."[n] 23Those words
("God accepted Abraham's faith") were written
not only for Abraham 24but also for us. God will
accept us also because we believe in the One who
raised Jesus our Lord from the dead. 25Jesus was
given to die for our sins, and he was raised from
the dead to make us right with God.

Right with God

5 Since we have been made right with God by
our faith, we have peace with God. This happened through our Lord Jesus Christ, 2who has
brought us into that blessing of God's grace that
we now enjoy. And we are happy because of the
hope we have of sharing God's glory. 3We also
have joy with our troubles, because we know that
these troubles produce patience. 4And patience
produces character, and character produces hope.
5And this hope will never disappoint us, because
God has poured out his love to fill our hearts. He
gave us his love through the Holy Spirit,[d] whom
God has given to us.

6When we were unable to help ourselves, at
the moment of our need, Christ died for us, although we were living against God. 7Very few
people will die to save the life of someone else.
Although perhaps for a good person someone
might possibly die. 8But God shows his great love
for us in this way: Christ died for us while we
were still sinners.

9So through Christ we will surely be saved
from God's anger, because we have been made
right with God by the blood of Christ's death.
10While we were God's enemies, he made friends
with us through the death of his Son. Surely, now
that we are his friends, he will save us through his
Son's life. 11And not only that, but now we are
also very happy in God through our Lord Jesus
Christ. Through him we are now God's friends
again.

Adam and Christ Compared

12Sin came into the world because of what one
man did, and with sin came death. This is why
everyone must die—because everyone sinned.
13Sin was in the world before the law of Moses,
but sin is not counted against us as breaking a
command when there is no law. 14But from the
time of Adam to the time of Moses, everyone had
to die, even those who had not sinned by breaking a command, as Adam had.

Adam was like the One who was coming in the
future. 15But God's free gift is not like Adam's sin.
Many people died because of the sin of that one
man. But the grace from God was much greater;

Abraham Most respected ancestor of the Jews. Every Jew hoped to see Abraham.
"I . . . nations." Quotation from Genesis 17:5.
"Your . . . count." Quotation from Genesis 15:5.
"God . . . God." Quotation from Genesis 15:6.

many people received God's gift of life by the
grace of the one man, Jesus Christ. 16After Adam
sinned once, he was judged guilty. But the gift of
God is different. God's free gift came after many
sins, and it makes people right with God. 17One
man sinned, and so death ruled all people because
of that one man. But now those people who accept God's full grace and the great gift of being
made right with him will surely have true life and
rule through the one man, Jesus Christ.

18So as one sin of Adam brought the punishment of death to all people, one good act that
Christ did makes all people right with God. And
that brings true life for all. 19One man disobeyed
God, and many became sinners. In the same way,
one man obeyed God, and many will be made
right. 20The law came to make sin worse. But
when sin grew worse, God's grace increased.
21Sin once used death to rule us, but God gave
people more of his grace so that grace could rule
by making people right with him. And this brings
life forever through Jesus Christ our Lord.

Dead to Sin but Alive in Christ

6 So do you think we should continue sinning
so that God will give us even more grace?

> **SIDELIGHT:** Adam—the man in the Garden of Eden (Genesis 1–4, p. 2)—seems to get blamed for more than his share of sin in Romans 5:12–21. But don't feel too sorry for him. Paul uses Adam to represent all people. That's not surprising when you know that "adam" means "human."

2No! We died to our old sinful lives, so how can
we continue living with sin? 3Did you forget that
all of us became part of Christ when we were
baptized? We shared his death in our baptism.
4When we were baptized, we were buried with
Christ and shared his death. So, just as Christ was

FRIENDS

What Are Friends For?

Sometimes Lisa Kretch got frustrated with her friends. It seemed like she was constantly bailing them out of something.

Take Coreen Mills for instance. She was flunking algebra. And Nancy Olton had just broken up with her boyfriend and was depressed all the time. Luann Winger was gaining weight like crazy, and all she did was complain about it and eat.

And as if that weren't enough, last week all three of these friends had gone to a party and had drunk several beers. Lisa had to drive them home so they wouldn't have a wreck.

Sometimes it seemed like Lisa's friends were trying to cause her problems. It was all getting to be too much. Too much concern, too much pain.

Maybe she should just find new friends, she thought. It would sure make her life easier. But . . .

"Hi, Lisa!" Coreen said, setting her tray down beside Lisa's at the cafeteria table. "Boy, this algebra is a bear. Can you help me with a couple of things?"

This was it. The true test. Was Lisa strong enough? She gathered her courage, took a deep breath, paused, and said, "Sure, Coreen. What are friends for?" And she meant it.

Lisa learned that friendship means commitment, even when friends disappoint you. **Romans 5:1–19** calls God our friend. Read the passage to discover how committed he is to us.

- How is Lisa's friendship with her friends like God's friendship with us in Jesus Christ?
- How can you model your friendship with God in human friendships?

CONSIDER . . .

- writing down the names of three friends and praying for them each day this week.
- writing a card, buying a flower, or doing a favor for a friend, just to say I'm committed to you.

FOR MORE, SEE . . .

- Job 2:11–13 (p. 453)
- Proverbs 17:17 (p. 582)
- John 15:13–16 (p. 1085)

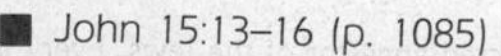

raised from the dead by the wonderful power of
the Father, we also can live a new life.
[5]Christ died, and we have been joined with him
by dying too. So we will also be joined with
him by rising from the dead as he did. [6]We know
that our old life died with Christ on the cross
so that our sinful selves would have no power
over us and we would not be slaves to sin. [7]Any-
one who has died is made free from sin's control.
[8]If we died with Christ, we know we will also
live with him. [9]Christ was raised from the dead,
and we know that he cannot die again. Death has
no power over him now. [10]Yes, when Christ died,
he died to defeat the power of sin one time—
enough for all time. He now has a new life, and
his new life is with God. [11]In the same way, you
should see yourselves as being dead to the power
of sin and alive with God through Christ Jesus.
[12]So, do not let sin control your life here on
earth so that you do what your sinful self wants
to do. [13]Do not offer the parts of your body to
serve sin, as things to be used in doing evil. Instead, offer yourselves to God as people who have
died and now live. Offer the parts of your body to
God to be used in doing good. [14]Sin will not be
your master, because you are not under law but
under God's grace.

Be Slaves of Righteousness

[15]So what should we do? Should we sin because we are under grace and not under law? No!
[16]Surely you know that when you give yourselves

FREEDOM

A Slave to Freedom

Tom Stipe wouldn't have been late for Biology 101 if he hadn't fallen. And he wouldn't have fallen if he hadn't been running. And he wouldn't have been running if he had gotten out of bed on time.

But he didn't get out of bed on time. He had forgotten to set his alarm. And his roommate—a guy he could hardly stand—hadn't bothered to wake him up, even though they were in the same class.

College wasn't everything Tom had hoped it would be.

It wasn't the classes. They were hard, sure, but Tom was no stranger to the books. And it wasn't the basketball practice. Practice was always rough, but you expected that and planned for it. It wasn't even Jack, the bothersome roommate. Tom had roomed with his brother at home, and they had rarely gotten along for more than a few minutes at a time.

It was the freedom, Tom realized with a start. Or, more to the point, it was the responsibility that came with the freedom. That was the part Tom disliked.

In high school, Tom had resented the way everyone controlled his time. His mother woke him in the morning. His teachers prodded him to work during the day and sent work home with him at night. Tom longed to be free.

But now that he was in college, Tom discovered that the freedom he had longed for came with one looming catch: responsibility. He was free to do what he wanted, but he also had to live with the consequences of his actions.

Tom learned that freedom and responsibility always come together. **Romans 6:1–12** talks about freedom too, and the responsibility that comes with it.

- How is Tom's struggle with freedom similar to the struggle for freedom Paul writes about in the passage?
- What does the passage say we need to do to gain freedom?

CONSIDER . . .

- drawing a line down the center of a page. On the left side, list all the freedoms you want to gain. On the right, list all the responsibilities that will come with those freedoms. With a parent, design a plan for helping you gain those freedoms responsibly.
- evaluating how you use your free time to see if you use it responsibly. If not, start using some of your time to do something on a regular basis to serve others.

FOR MORE, SEE . . .

- Psalm 119:41–48 (p. 551)
- John 8:31–32, 34–36 (p. 1072)
- 1 Peter 2:16 (p. 1304)

like slaves to obey someone, then you are really
slaves of that person. The person you obey is your
master. You can follow sin, which brings spiritual
death, or you can obey God, which makes you
right with him. 17In the past you were slaves to
sin—sin controlled you. But thank God, you fully
obeyed the things that you were taught. 18You
were made free from sin, and now you are slaves
to goodness. 19I use this example because this is
hard for you to understand. In the past you offered the parts of your body to be slaves to sin and
evil; you lived only for evil. In the same way now
you must give yourselves to be slaves of goodness.
Then you will live only for God.

20In the past you were slaves to sin, and goodness did not control you. 21You did evil things,
and now you are ashamed of them. Those things
only bring death. 22But now you are free from sin
and have become slaves of God. This brings you
a life that is only for God, and this gives you life
forever. 23When people sin, they earn what sin
pays—death. But God gives us a free gift—life
forever in Christ Jesus our Lord.

An Example from Marriage

7 Brothers and sisters, all of you understand
the law of Moses. So surely you know that
the law rules over people only while they are
alive. 2For example, a woman must stay married
to her husband as long as he is alive. But if her
husband dies, she is free from the law of marriage.
3But if she marries another man while her husband is still alive, the law says she is guilty of adultery.[d] But if her husband dies, she is free from the
law of marriage. Then if she marries another man,
she is not guilty of adultery.

4In the same way, my brothers and sisters, your
old selves died, and you became free from the law
through the body of Christ. This happened so that
you might belong to someone else—the One who
was raised from the dead—and so that we might
be used in service to God. 5In the past, we were
ruled by our sinful selves. The law made us want
to do sinful things that controlled our bodies, so
the things we did were bringing us death. 6In the
past, the law held us like prisoners, but our old
selves died, and we were made free from the law.
So now we serve God in a new way with the
Spirit,[d] and not in the old way with written rules.

Our Fight Against Sin

7You might think I am saying that sin and the
law are the same thing. That is not true. But the
law was the only way I could learn what sin
meant. I would never have known what it means
to want to take something belonging to someone
else if the law had not said, "You must not want
to take your neighbor's things."[n] 8And sin found
a way to use that command and cause me to want
all kinds of things I should not want. But without
the law, sin has no power. 9I was alive before I
knew the law. But when the law's command
came to me, then sin began to live, 10and I died.
The command was meant to bring life, but for me
it brought death. 11Sin found a way to fool me by
using the command to make me die.

12So the law is holy, and the command is holy
and right and good. 13Does this mean that something that is good brought death to me? No! Sin
used something that is good to bring death to me.
This happened so that I could see what sin is
really like; the command was used to show that
sin is very evil.

The War Within Us

14We know that the law is spiritual, but I am
not spiritual since sin rules me as if I were its
slave. 15I do not understand the things I do. I do
not do what I want to do, and I do the things I
hate. 16And if I do not want to do the hated things
I do, that means I agree that the law is good. 17But
I am not really the one who is doing these hated
things; it is sin living in me that does them. 18Yes,
I know that nothing good lives in me—I mean
nothing good lives in the part of me that is earthly
and sinful. I want to do the things that are good,
but I do not do them. 19I do not do the good
things I want to do, but I do the bad things I do
not want to do. 20So if I do things I do not want
to do, then I am not the one doing them. It is sin
living in me that does those things.

21So I have learned this rule: When I want to
do good, evil is there with me. 22In my mind, I am
happy with God's law. 23But I see another law
working in my body, which makes war against
the law that my mind accepts. That other law
working in my body is the law of sin, and it makes
me its prisoner. 24What a miserable man I am!
Who will save me from this body that brings me
death? 25I thank God for saving me through Jesus
Christ our Lord!

So in my mind I am a slave to God's law, but
in my sinful self I am a slave to the law of sin.

Be Ruled by the Spirit

8 So now, those who are in Christ Jesus are
not judged guilty. 2Through Christ Jesus the
law of the Spirit[d] that brings life made me free
from the law that brings sin and death. 3The law
was without power, because the law was made
weak by our sinful selves. But God did what the
law could not do. He sent his own Son to earth
with the same human life that others use for sin.
By sending his Son to be an offering to pay for sin,

"You . . . things." Quotation from Exodus 20:17.

God used a human life to destroy sin. [4]He did this
so that we could be the kind of people the law
correctly wants us to be. Now we do not live following our sinful selves, but we live following the
Spirit.
[5]Those who live following their sinful selves
think only about things that their sinful selves want.
But those who live following the Spirit are
thinking about the things the Spirit wants them to
do. [6]If people's thinking is controlled by the sinful
self, there is death. But if their thinking is controlled by the Spirit, there is life and peace. [7]When
people's thinking is controlled by the sinful self,
they are against God, because they refuse to obey
God's law and really are not even able to
obey God's law. [8]Those people who are ruled by
their sinful selves cannot please God.
[9]But you are not ruled by your sinful selves.
You are ruled by the Spirit, if that Spirit of God
really lives in you. But the person who does not
have the Spirit of Christ does not belong to Christ.
[10]Your body will always be dead because of sin.

DRUGS AND ALCOHOL

Not Alone . . .

Seven years, five months, three days. That's how long Shelly Everett had been sober. Counting today. And she didn't mind talking about it to her fellow Alcoholics Anonymous (AA) members. It helped her stick with recovery.

"I started drinking in high school," she explained. "But I didn't start abusing it until I was in college. By the time I was out of school and in a career position, I was an alcoholic."

Shelly went on to tell how a marriage and the addition of two children didn't change her drinking habits much. "I managed to keep up with my responsibilities, both at home and at work," she said. "As long as I did that, I convinced myself that I had it under control."

But then things changed. A messy divorce. Trouble at work. And a daughter who almost died from rheumatic fever.

"I began to drink more often—for comfort, and sometimes, to forget. Eventually, events in my life began to blur together. I was never sober.

"And the worse I felt about myself the more I drank. Finally, I just wanted to die. So I tried to drink myself to death. Five days later I woke up in a hospital room attached to a bunch of machines. The doctors say I didn't even know who I was. I lay there and cried. I couldn't eat. I couldn't sleep. I was a failure. I couldn't even kill myself right." Shelly pulled a tissue from the box beside her. The AA leader motioned her to continue.

"Then," she went on, "the hospital chaplain walked in, and there's this little dumpy woman with him. They both just sit down by my bed. And this little dumpy woman asked, 'You wanna quit drinking?' "

Now Shelly's tears came in full flood. "I just bawled like a baby. I wanted to quit, but I didn't know how! Then she says, 'You don't have to do it alone. You've got me and Reverend Benjamin here and a whole flock of folks willing to help. And you've got God, too, honey. Don't forget about God.' "

Shelly blew her nose on the tissue and looked around at the faces of her friends. "For the first time I realized I wasn't alone. And I haven't had a drink since that day—all because you, and God, are keeping me sober."

Shelly learned she wasn't alone in her struggle. And God made a difference in her life. The apostle Paul made a similar discovery. Read about it in **Romans 7:14–25**.

- How is Shelly's addiction like the "battle" Paul describes in this passage?
- What are ways God shows that he is with you when you're pressured to use alcohol or drugs?

C O N S I D E R . . .

- encouraging a friend who is dealing with issues like Shelly's to seek professional help.
- finding an appropriate support group in your community if you struggle with a drinking or drug problem. Your pastor or a counselor can help you.

F O R M O R E , S E E . . .

- Proverbs 23:29–32 (p. 588)
- Isaiah 5:11–12 (p. 621)
- Luke 21:34–36 (p. 1049)

But if Christ is in you, then the Spirit gives you
life, because Christ made you right with God.
11God raised Jesus from the dead, and if God's
Spirit is living in you, he will also give life to your
bodies that die. God is the One who raised Christ
from the dead, and he will give life through his
Spirit that lives in you.
12So, my brothers and sisters, we must not be
ruled by our sinful selves or live the way our sinful
selves want. 13If you use your lives to do the
wrong things your sinful selves want, you will die
spiritually. But if you use the Spirit's help to stop
doing the wrong things you do with your body,
you will have true life.
14The true children of God are those who let
God's Spirit lead them. 15The Spirit we received
does not make us slaves again to fear; it makes us
children of God. With that Spirit we cry out, "Father."[n] 16And the Spirit himself joins with our
spirits to say we are God's children. 17If we are
God's children, we will receive blessings from
God together with Christ. But we must suffer as
Christ suffered so that we will have glory as Christ
has glory.

"Father" Literally, "Abba, Father." Jewish children called their fathers "Abba."

SPIRITUAL GROWTH

Living for God

To buy or not to buy. That was the question.

Carrie Munson was the only one in her class who didn't have a school jacket. Well, nearly the only one. Most of the kids had them—navy blue and white, with a hood that rolled up into the zippered collar when you didn't want it over your head.

And Cline's Sporting Goods had a special offer this weekend. They would put the school name on the back of the coat and your initials on the front—no charge. But only if you bought it this weekend.

"Let's see," Carrie thought aloud. "That's a savings of . . . $8 for the school name and $3 for my initials . . . that's $11 savings!"

True, it wasn't a fortune, but with Carrie's meager allowance, every penny counted.

There was just one problem. Carrie had pledged to give $13 each month to the church to help fund the new homeless shelter. And if she bought the jacket, she would have only $11 left.

That's $2 short, Carrie thought. And the pledge is due this Sunday.

"Ugh!" Carrie grunted in frustration. Why had she made such a big pledge? Thirteen dollars! That was almost a fourth of her income! And besides, the jacket was on sale now. If Carrie didn't buy it this weekend, it would cost her $11 dollars more next week, and she wouldn't have enough money then—especially if she paid her pledge.

"What should I do?" Carrie asked, looking at the ceiling of the sporting goods store. Slowly, her eyebrows unfurled, her tense shoulders relaxed, and she walked out of the store—away from the jacket she wanted.

When Carrie got home, she went to her bedroom, pulled $13 out of her purse, and put it in the Bible next to her bed.

"If you want me to have the jacket, you'll provide a way," she prayed. "But I don't want to break my promise to you just to get what I want."

Carrie discovered it's not always easy to do what's right, especially when our own desires get in the way. **Romans 8:6–17** talks about why spiritual growth is sometimes hard.

- How is the conflict described in this passage like what happened to Carrie?
- According to this passage, what should you do the next time your own desires conflict with God's?

CONSIDER . . .

- asking God's forgiveness for times you have chosen your desires over his.
- listing all the ways your desires might conflict with God's and asking God to help you grow through following his desires for your life.

FOR MORE, SEE . . .

- Psalm 1:1–3 (p. 482)
- Colossians 3:1–10 (p. 1241)
- Hebrews 12:1–13 (p. 1289)

Our Future Glory

[18]The sufferings we have now are nothing compared to the great glory that will be shown to us.
[19]Everything God made is waiting with excitement for God to show his children's glory completely. [20]Everything God made was changed to
become useless, not by its own wish but because
God wanted it and because all along there was
this hope: [21]that everything God made would be
set free from ruin to have the freedom and glory
that belong to God's children.

[22]We know that everything God made has
been waiting until now in pain, like a woman
ready to give birth. [23]Not only the world, but we
also have been waiting with pain inside us. We
have the Spirit[d] as the first part of God's promise.
So we are waiting for God to finish making us his
own children, which means our bodies will be
made free. [24]We were saved, and we have this
hope. If we see what we are waiting for, that is
not really hope. People do not hope for something
they already have. [25]But we are hoping for something we do not have yet, and we are waiting for
it patiently.

[26]Also, the Spirit helps us with our weakness.
We do not know how to pray as we should. But
the Spirit himself speaks to God for us, even begs
God for us with deep feelings that words cannot
explain. [27]God can see what is in people's hearts.
And he knows what is in the mind of the Spirit,
because the Spirit speaks to God for his people in
the way God wants.

[28]We know that in everything God works for
the good of those who love him. They are the

PATIENCE

Looking Back

Pierce Richman had been a Christian about six months before the problems started.

What problems? "Well, I lost my job," Pierce recalls. "Then the transmission on my car went out, and I had no money to repair it. But that wasn't the real problem. My girlfriend broke up with me. I really wanted to marry this girl, but she said I wasn't what she wanted in a husband. That really hurt."

About that time Pierce's old desires began to well up. Before he had become a Christian at age eighteen, he had lived a loose lifestyle, filled with drinking and taking drugs and sleeping with girlfriends.

"I came to Christ to get away from all that," he recalls. "But when all these problems started, I began to feel really insecure. It was all I could do not to go out and get drunk or call up one of my old girlfriends. I felt gross inside. I began to wonder whether I was really a Christian."

But Pierce didn't go back to his old lifestyle. Even though he didn't understand why all these things were happening to him, he knew God was in control. So he waited.

"Things didn't get better right away," Pierce says, "but I knew I had made the right decision. And that helped me believe even more that, if I was patient, God would come through for me. And he did!"

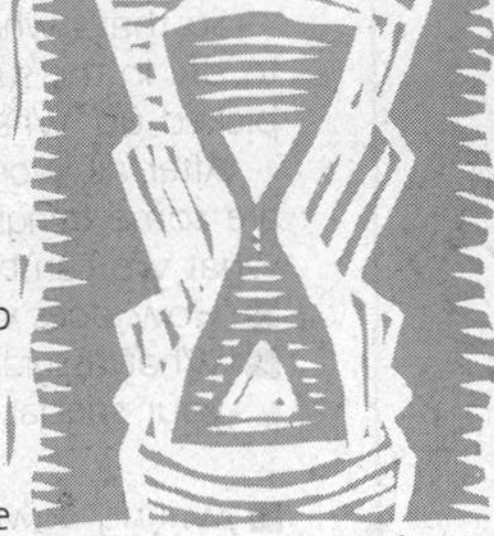

Pierce and his girlfriend got back together, and he got a new job—better than the other one. Now Pierce knows the value of obeying God even when you don't know what God is doing.

Pierce learned that becoming like Christ takes patience. Paul talked about how all creation is waiting patiently for us to become like Christ. Read why in **Romans 8:22–30.**

- How does Pierce demonstrate the patience the passage describes?
- According to the passage, what is God's ultimate purpose for you? Why do we need patience to wait for his purpose to be fulfilled?

CONSIDER . . .

- dreaming about the kind of person you want to be ten years from now. Then ask God to give you patience to let him make you into the person he wants you to be.
- working on a project that takes a long time to finish, such as a quilt or a model ship. Use the experience to learn more about patience.

FOR MORE, SEE . . .

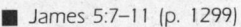

- Lamentations 3:25–26 (p. 757)
- Hebrews 11:8–16 (p. 1288)
- James 5:7–11 (p. 1299)

people he called, because that was his plan. 29God
knew them before he made the world, and he
decided that they would be like his Son so that
Jesus would be the firstborn[n] of many brothers.
30God planned for them to be like his Son; and
those he planned to be like his Son, he also called;
and those he called, he also made right with
him; and those he made right, he also glorified.

God's Love in Christ Jesus

31So what should we say about this? If God is
with us, no one can defeat us. 32He did not spare
his own Son but gave him for us all. So with Jesus,
God will surely give us all things. 33Who can accuse the people God has chosen? No one, because
God is the One who makes them right. 34Who can
say God's people are guilty? No one, because
Christ Jesus died, but he was also raised from the
dead, and now he is on God's right side, begging God for us. 35Can anything separate us from
the love Christ has for us? Can troubles or problems or sufferings or hunger or nakedness or
danger or violent death? 36As it is written in the
Scriptures:[d]

"For you we are in danger of death all the
time.

firstborn Here this probably means that Christ was the first in God's family to share God's glory.

WORRYING

Let It Rain!

When Ray Jordon was a teenager, his friend Scott Wright and he would help bale hay each summer for seventy-year-old Bailey Tag, a rancher who lived near their town. Mr. Tag baled the hay onto the ground. Then he would drive the tractor, and Ray would walk behind it, picking up bales and throwing them up to Scott on the wagon, where he would stack them.

It was hot, miserable, sticky, dirty work. But the pay was good.

One day as the three ate their lunches under a big oak tree, the sky began to darken in the west and the sound of thunder rolled toward them.

Mr. Tag sat, eating his apple and looking at the clouds. "Beautiful, aren't they?" he remarked. "Rain'll cool things off a might, I 'spect."

"What about the hay?" Scott asked.

Mr. Tag looked at his apple. "Let me finish this, and we'll get the hay to the barn. We've got time."

Scott looked at Ray, and they both looked out over the field where the other bales waited to be picked up.

"Mr. Tag," said Ray, "those clouds look like they're moving this way."

He looked at them, paused, then nodded. "Maybe."

Ray swept the field with his arm. "But, what about the other bales? I mean, what if the rain is moving this way? What'll we do?"

Mr. Tag looked at Ray, smiled around a bite of his apple and winked. "Why, we'll let it rain," he said. "What else can we do?"

So that's what they did. They let it rain. The bales got wet, and they had to dry in the sun for a few days before they could be picked up. But they got picked up. What else could have been done?

After all, worrying wouldn't stop the rain. **Romans 8:31–39** says there are some things we never have to worry about. Read the passage to find out what we can be sure of.

- How does worrying about the hay differ from worrying about God's love?
- What assurance do these verses offer you when you worry about losing your special relationship with God?

C O N S I D E R . . .

- writing down all the things you worry about, then crossing out the ones you can't do anything about. Create a plan for doing something about the others.
- reading a fun novel, going camping, or doing something similar—to help you let go of your worries and trust God.

F O R   M O R E ,   S E E . . .

- Psalm 91 (p. 535)
- Psalm 131 (p. 558)
- Matthew 6:25–34 (p. 918)

People think we are worth no more than
sheep to be killed." *Psalm 44:22*

37But in all these things we have full victory
through God who showed his love for us. 38Yes,
I am sure that neither death, nor life, nor angels,
nor ruling spirits, nothing now, nothing in the future, no powers, 39nothing above us, nothing below us, nor anything else in the whole world will
ever be able to separate us from the love of God
that is in Christ Jesus our Lord.

God and the Jewish People

9 I am in Christ, and I am telling you the truth;
I do not lie. My conscience is ruled by the
Holy Spirit,[d] and it tells me I am not lying. 2I have
great sorrow and always feel much sadness. 3I
wish I could help my Jewish brothers and sisters,
my people. I would even wish that I were cursed
and cut off from Christ if that would help them.
4They are the people of Israel, God's chosen children. They have seen the glory of God, and they
have the agreements that God made between
himself and his people. God gave them the law of
Moses and the right way of worship and his promises. 5They are the descendants[d] of our great ancestors, and they are the earthly family into which
Christ was born, who is God over all. Praise him
forever![n] Amen.

6It is not that God failed to keep his promise to
them. But only some of the people of Israel are
truly God's people,[n] 7and only some of Abraham's[n] descendants are true children of Abraham. But God said to Abraham: "The descendants I promised you will be from Isaac."[n] 8This
means that not all of Abraham's descendants are
God's true children. Abraham's true children are
those who become God's children because of the
promise God made to Abraham. 9God's promise
to Abraham was this: "At the right time I will
return, and Sarah will have a son."[n] 10And that
is not all. Rebekah's sons had the same father, our
father Isaac. 11-12But before the two boys were
born, God told Rebekah, "The older will serve the
younger."[n] This was before the boys had done
anything good or bad. God said this so that the
one chosen would be chosen because of God's
own plan. He was chosen because he was the one
God wanted to call, not because of anything he
did. 13As the Scripture[d] says, "I loved Jacob, but
I hated Esau."[n]

14So what should we say about this? Is God
unfair? In no way. 15God said to Moses, "I will
show kindness to anyone to whom I want to
show kindness, and I will show mercy to anyone
to whom I want to show mercy."[n] 16So God will
choose the one to whom he decides to show
mercy; his choice does not depend on what people want or try to do. 17The Scripture says to the
king of Egypt: "I made you king for this reason:
to show my power in you so that my name will
be talked about in all the earth."[n] 18So God
shows mercy where he wants to show mercy, and
he makes stubborn the people he wants to make
stubborn.

19So one of you will ask me: "Then why does
God blame us for our sins? Who can fight his
will?" 20You are only human, and human beings
have no right to question God. An object should
not ask the person who made it, "Why did you
make me like this?" 21The potter can make anything he wants to make. He can use the same clay
to make one thing for special use and another
thing for daily use.

22It is the same way with God. He wanted to
show his anger and to let people see his power.
But he patiently stayed with those people he was
angry with—people who were made ready to be
destroyed. 23He waited with patience so that he
could make known his rich glory to the people
who receive his mercy. He has prepared these
people to have his glory, 24and we are those people whom God called. He called us not from the
Jews only but also from those who are not Jews.
25As the Scripture says in Hosea:

"I will say, 'You are my people'
to those I had called 'not my people.'
And I will show my love
to those people I did not love." *Hosea 2:1, 23*

26"They were called,
'You are not my people,'
but later they will be called
'children of the living God.'" *Hosea 1:10*

27And Isaiah cries out about Israel:

"The people of Israel are many,
like the grains of sand by the sea.
But only a few of them will be saved,
28 because the Lord will quickly and
completely punish the people on the
earth." *Isaiah 10:22-23*

29It is as Isaiah said:

born . . . forever! This can also mean, "born. May God, who rules over all things, be praised forever!"
God's people Literally, "Israel," the people God chose to bring his blessings to the world.
Abraham Most respected ancestor of the Jews. Every Jew hoped to see Abraham.
"The descendants . . . Isaac." Quotation from Genesis 21:12.
"At . . . son." Quotation from Genesis 18:10, 14.
"The older . . . younger." Quotation from Genesis 25:23.
"I . . . Esau." Quotation from Malachi 1:2-3.
"I . . . mercy." Quotation from Exodus 33:19.
"I . . . earth." Quotation from Exodus 9:16.

"The Lord All-Powerful
allowed a few of our descendants to live.
Otherwise we would have been completely
destroyed
like the cities of Sodom and Gomorrah."[n]

Isaiah 1:9

30So what does all this mean? Those who are
not Jews were not trying to make themselves
right with God, but they were made right with
God because of their faith. 31The people of Israel
tried to follow a law to make themselves right
with God. But they did not succeed, 32because
they tried to make themselves right by the things
they did instead of trusting in God to make them
right. They stumbled over the stone that causes
people to stumble. 33As it is written in the Scripture:

"I will put in Jerusalem a stone that causes
people to stumble,
a rock that makes them fall.
Anyone who trusts in him will never be
disappointed."

Isaiah 8:14; 28:16

SIDELIGHT: Early Christians often argued about what was required to be a Christian (Romans 9:1–33). Some Jewish Christians wanted the non-Jewish ones to obey all the Jewish laws. If their beliefs had won the day, we would all have to eat kosher pickles!

10

Brothers and sisters, the thing I want
most is for all the Jews to be saved. That
is my prayer to God. 2I can say this about them:
They really try to follow God, but they do not
know the right way. 3Because they did not know
the way that God makes people right with him,
they tried to make themselves right in their own
way. So they did not accept God's way of making
people right. 4Christ ended the law so that everyone who believes in him may be right with God.
5Moses writes about being made right by following the law. He says, "A person who obeys
these things will live because of them."[n] 6But
this is what the Scripture says about being made
right through faith: "Don't say to yourself, 'Who
will go up into heaven?' " (That means, "Who
will go up to heaven and bring Christ down to
earth?") 7"And do not say, 'Who will go down
into the world below?' " (That means, "Who will
go down and bring Christ up from the dead?")
8This is what the Scripture says: "The word is
near you; it is in your mouth and in your heart."[n]
That is the teaching of faith that we are telling. 9If
you use your mouth to say, "Jesus is Lord," and
if you believe in your heart that God raised Jesus
from the dead, you will be saved. 10We believe
with our hearts, and so we are made right with
God. And we use our mouths to say that we believe, and so we are saved. 11As the Scripture says,
"Anyone who trusts in him will never be disappointed."[n] 12That Scripture says "anyone" because there is no difference between those who
are Jews and those who are not. The same Lord
is the Lord of all and gives many blessings to all
who trust in him, 13as the Scripture says, "Anyone
who calls on the Lord will be saved."[n]
14But before people can ask the Lord for help,
they must believe in him; and before they can
believe in him, they must hear about him; and for
them to hear about the Lord, someone must tell
them; 15and before someone can go and tell them,
that person must be sent. It is written, "How
beautiful is the person who comes to bring good
news."[n]
16But not all the Jews accepted the good news.
Isaiah said, "Lord, who believed what we told
them?"[n] 17So faith comes from hearing the Good
News,[d] and people hear the Good News when
someone tells them about Christ.
18But I ask: Didn't people hear the Good
News? Yes, they heard—as the Scripture says:

"Their message went out through all the
world;
their words go everywhere on earth."

Psalm 19:4

19Again I ask: Didn't the people of Israel understand? Yes, they did understand. First, Moses
says:

"I will use those who are not a nation to
make you jealous.
I will use a nation that does not understand
to make you angry."

Deuteronomy 32:21

20Then Isaiah is bold enough to say:

"I was found by those who were not asking
me for help.
I made myself known to people who were
not looking for me."

Isaiah 65:1

21But about Israel God says,

"All day long I stood ready to accept
people who disobey and are stubborn."

Isaiah 65:2

Sodom and Gomorrah Two cities that God destroyed because the people were so evil.
"A person . . . them." Quotation from Leviticus 18:5.
Verses 6-8 Quotations from Deuteronomy 9:4; 30:12-14; Psalm 107:26.
"Anyone . . . disappointed." Quotation from Isaiah 28:16.
"Anyone . . . saved." Quotation from Joel 2:32.
"How . . . news." Quotation from Isaiah 52:7.
"Lord, . . . them?" Quotation from Isaiah 53:1.

God Shows Mercy to All People

11 So I ask: Did God throw out his people?
No! I myself am an Israelite from the
family of Abraham, from the tribe[d] of Benjamin.
2God chose the Israelites to be his people before
they were born, and he has not thrown his people
out. Surely you know what the Scripture[d] says
about Elijah, how he prayed to God against the
people of Israel. 3"Lord," he said, "they have
killed your prophets,[d] and they have destroyed
your altars. I am the only prophet left, and now
they are trying to kill me, too."[n] 4But what answer did God give Elijah? He said, "But I have left
seven thousand people in Israel who have never
bowed down before Baal."[n] 5It is the same now.
There are a few people that God has chosen by his
grace. 6And if he chose them by grace, it is not for
the things they have done. If they could be made
God's people by what they did, God's gift of grace
would not really be a gift.

"They . . . too." Quotation from 1 Kings 19:10, 14.
"But . . . Baal." Quotation from 1 Kings 19:18.

SHARING FAITH

Why Didn't You Say Something?

Mark Shipp went to church on Sundays. He didn't make a big thing of it, but he sang in the choir and went to Bible study. He was even on the youth council. Mark was trying to do what was right without being . . . pushy.

Just about every Friday, his school buddy, Jack, would invite him to play touch football: "So, what'cha got planned this weekend, Mark?"

Mark would shrug, "Oh, you know . . ."

"Tell me about it! Clean this, straighten that, mow the grass, wash the car! I work harder on Saturdays than I do on school days."

Mark would smile knowingly and shrug, "That's the truth."

"That's why I take Sunday off. Me, Tim, Larry, and some other guys get together in the morning to play football. Do ya wanna come?"

Mark would evade the question, "Oh, I'd like to, Jack. I really would, but I can't. I've already made plans."

"Sure. Well, if you ever change your mind, the invitation stands," Jack would say and then off he would go with a smile.

Then one Friday late in the year, the ritual took a different turn.

Mark had just evaded the question, explaining that he really wanted to play touch football but couldn't, and Jack just nodded as usual. But this time, Jack didn't walk away. He just stood there, looking at Mark.

Finally, he spoke. "Mark, for the past year I've invited you to play touch football, but you can't because you go to church."

Mark was caught off guard. "Oh, well, yeah, I go to church, but that . . ."

"For a year I've been inviting you to play football, and never once have you invited me to church," Jack continued, scratching his head. "Why?"

Mark needed to read Paul's admonition in **Romans 10:8–18** to learn how important it is to tell others about your faith in Christ and not just assume they don't want to know.

- What does this passage say about Mark's attitude toward telling others about his faith in Christ?
- According to the passage, why is it important that you tell others about your faith in Christ?

C O N S I D E R . . .

- putting your faith story into words. How, in a hundred words, has your faith affected your life?
- inviting a non-Christian friend to go to church with you this Sunday.

F O R M O R E , S E E . . .

- Jeremiah 1:4–8 (p. 691)
- Matthew 10:32–33 (p. 925)
- Acts 2 (p. 1098)

7So this is what has happened: Although the
Israelites tried to be right with God, they did not
succeed, but the ones God chose did become
right with him. The others were made stubborn
and refused to listen to God. 8As it is written in
the Scriptures:[d]

"God gave the people a dull mind so they
could not understand." *Isaiah 29:10*
"He closed their eyes so they could not see
and their ears so they could not hear.
This continues until today." *Deuteronomy 29:4*

9And David says:

"Let their own feasts trap them and cause
their ruin;
let their feasts cause them to stumble and
be paid back.
10Let their eyes be closed so they cannot see
and their backs be forever weak from
troubles." *Psalm 69:22-23*

11So I ask: When the Jews fell, did that fall destroy them? No! But their mistake brought salvation to those who are not Jews, in order to make
the Jews jealous. 12The Jews' mistake brought
rich blessings for the world, and the Jews' loss
brought rich blessings for the non-Jewish people.
So surely the world will receive much richer
blessings when enough Jews become the kind of
people God wants.

13Now I am speaking to you who are not Jews.
I am an apostle[d] to those who are not Jews, and
since I have that work, I will make the most of it.
14I hope I can make my own people jealous and,
in that way, help some of them to be saved.
15When God turned away from the Jews, he became friends with other people in the world. So
when God accepts the Jews, surely that will bring
them life after death.

16If the first piece of bread is offered to God,
then the whole loaf is made holy. If the roots of
a tree are holy, then the tree's branches are holy
too.

17It is as if some of the branches from an olive
tree have been broken off. You non-Jewish people
are like the branch of a wild olive tree that has
been joined to that first tree. You now share the
strength and life of the first tree, the Jews. 18So do
not brag about those branches that were broken
off. If you brag, remember that you do not support
the root, but the root supports you. 19You will say,
"Branches were broken off so that I could be
joined to their tree." 20That is true. But those
branches were broken off because they did not
believe, and you continue to be part of the tree
only because you believe. Do not be proud, but be
afraid. 21If God did not let the natural branches of
that tree stay, then he will not let you stay if you
don't believe.

22So you see that God is kind and also very
strict. He punishes those who stop following him.
But God is kind to you, if you continue following
in his kindness. If you do not, you will be cut off
from the tree. 23And if the Jews will believe in
God again, he will accept them back. God is able
to put them back where they were. 24It is not natural for a wild branch to be part of a good tree.
And you who are not Jews are like a branch cut
from a wild olive tree and joined to a good olive
tree. But since those Jews are like a branch that
grew from the good tree, surely they can be joined
to their own tree again.

25I want you to understand this secret, brothers
and sisters, so you will understand that you do not
know everything: Part of Israel has been made
stubborn, but that will change when many who
are not Jews have come to God. 26And that is how
all Israel will be saved. It is written in the Scriptures:

"The Savior will come from Jerusalem;
he will take away all evil from the family of
Jacob.[n]
27And I will make this agreement with those
people
when I take away their sins."
Isaiah 59:20-21; 27:9

28The Jews refuse to accept the Good News,[d]
so they are God's enemies. This has happened to
help you who are not Jews. But the Jews are still
God's chosen people, and he loves them very
much because of the promises he made to their
ancestors. 29God never changes his mind about
the people he calls and the things he gives them.
30At one time you refused to obey God. But now
you have received mercy, because those people
refused to obey. 31And now the Jews refuse to
obey, because God showed mercy to you. But
this happened so that they also can receive
mercy from him. 32God has given all people over
to their stubborn ways so that he can show
mercy to all.

Praise to God

33Yes, God's riches are very great, and his wisdom and knowledge have no end! No one can
explain the things God decides or understand his
ways. 34As the Scripture[d] says,

"Who has known the mind of the Lord,
or who has been able to give him advice?"
Isaiah 40:13
35"No one has ever given God anything
that he must pay back." *Job 41:11*

36Yes, God made all things, and everything continues through him and for him. To him be the
glory forever! Amen.

Jacob Father of the twelve family groups of Israel, the people God chose to be his people.

Give Your Lives to God

12 So brothers and sisters, since God has
shown us great mercy, I beg you to offer
your lives as a living sacrifice to him. Your offering
must be only for God and pleasing to him, which
is the spiritual way for you to worship. 2Do not
change yourselves to be like the people of this
world, but be changed within by a new way of
thinking. Then you will be able to decide what
God wants for you; you will know what is good
and pleasing to him and what is perfect. 3Because
God has given me a special gift, I have something
to say to everyone among you. Do not think you
are better than you are. You must decide what
you really are by the amount of faith God has
given you. 4Each one of us has a body with many
parts, and these parts all have different uses. 5In
the same way, we are many, but in Christ we are
all one body. Each one is a part of that body, and
each part belongs to all the other parts. 6We all
have different gifts, each of which came because
of the grace God gave us. The person who has the
gift of prophecy[d] should use that gift in agreement
with the faith. 7Anyone who has the gift of serving
should serve. Anyone who has the gift of teaching should teach. 8Whoever has the gift of
encouraging others should encourage. Whoever
has the gift of giving to others should give freely.
Anyone who has the gift of being a leader should
try hard when he leads. Whoever has the gift of
showing mercy to others should do so with joy.

9Your love must be real. Hate what is evil, and
hold on to what is good. 10Love each other like
brothers and sisters. Give each other more honor
than you want for yourselves. 11Do not be lazy but
work hard, serving the Lord with all your heart.
12Be joyful because you have hope. Be patient
when trouble comes, and pray at all times.

GOD'S LOVE

Free Gifts

Aaron Spell volunteered in an inner-city free store, where he sorted used clothing and helped people pick out things they needed.

One Friday, while Aaron was walking to the bus stop near the store, he passed a house that was having a yard sale. He recognized one of the kids as the child of a woman who often came to the free store. After a few moments of talking to the child, he began to recognize more than just the little boy.

There, piled on the old card tables, were stacks of blue jeans, sweatshirts, socks, shoes, and mittens that Aaron had seen earlier that week at the free store. He was outraged! These people didn't take the clothing from the store because they needed it. They took it so they could sell it! What a rip-off!

"It just doesn't seem right," Aaron complained to Jim Knudson, the store manager, later that week. "We gave them those clothes so they'd have something to wear, not so they could sell them."

"Well, it seems they needed the clothes either way," responded Jim. "They needed the clothes to sell for cash so they could buy other things. Besides, we help these people because we care about them, not because they always respond the way we want them to."

"It sounds risky," Aaron said.

"Love always is," answered Jim.

Jim helped Aaron see that their love wasn't something people should have to earn. God's love is like that too. Read **Romans 11:29–36** to find a description of God's merciful gift of love for us.

- How is the free store like God's love for us?
- What would happen to your relationship with God if his love depended on your doing what he wanted?

CONSIDER . . .

- writing out five reasons God's love can never be taken away from you. Read Romans 8:31–39 for a few hints.
- giving a dollar to someone you meet who is in need—without knowing how that person will use the money.

FOR MORE, SEE . . .

- Psalm 103:6–14 (p. 540)
- Ephesians 2:4–7 (p. 1219)
- 1 John 4:7–12 (p. 1319)

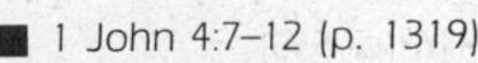

13Share with God's people who need help. Bring
strangers in need into your homes.
14Wish good for those who harm you; wish
them well and do not curse them. 15Be happy
with those who are happy, and be sad with those
who are sad. 16Live in peace with each other. Do
not be proud, but make friends with those who
seem unimportant. Do not think how smart you
are.
17If someone does wrong to you, do not pay
him back by doing wrong to him. Try to do what
everyone thinks is right. 18Do your best to live in
peace with everyone. 19My friends, do not try to
punish others when they wrong you, but wait
for God to punish them with his anger. It is written: "I will punish those who do wrong; I will
repay them,"[n] says the Lord. 20But you should
do this:

"If your enemy is hungry, feed him;
if he is thirsty, give him a drink.
Doing this will be like pouring burning coals
on his head."

Proverbs 25:21-22

"I . . . them" Quotation from Deuteronomy 32:35.

FOLLOWING GOD

Bouncing Betties

The Bouncing Betty was the worst kind of land mine in the Vietnam War. It was loaded with a spring so when you stepped on it, it flew into the air, about waist high, then exploded. It was designed to blow people apart and to strike terror in the hearts of young soldiers.

The plan worked on Craig Morrison.

He was on patrol one day with five other guys and this little Vietnamese guy who was supposed to be their guide. They had been out about three hours, walking quietly through the bush, just looking and listening and trying not to get shot.

Then they came to a clearing, maybe a hundred feet across. The situation had "Bouncing Betty" written all over it. And Craig just knew snipers were hiding in the jungle on the other side, waiting for him and his buddies to step into that clearing. But the bush was too thick to go around the clearing, so they had no choice but to go through.

The Vietnamese guide signaled for quiet and pointed to his feet then spread his fingers on both hands. "Stay quiet," he whispered. "Follow me. Place your feet where I place mine. Stay ten yards behind the guy in front of you."

Craig had never been so scared in his life. The guide went ten yards out into the clearing and then motioned for Craig to follow.

Slowly now. Despite his fears, he managed to keep putting his feet in the impressions left by the guide. He kept his head down, waiting for a sniper's bullet to send him to the ground.

And then it was over. He took a deep breath and realized he had made it across. Shaking violently, he looked up and saw the little Vietnamese guy smiling at him. It was nice to have someone in whose steps you could walk.

Craig learned that to get through rough times he had to deny his own desires and follow someone he could trust, someone who knew the way. **Romans 12:1–16** talks about God as the one who knows the way for our lives. Read the passage to see how we can walk in his steps.

- How is the way Craig followed the guide similar to the way you follow God?
- According to the passage, why should you follow God? (See verses 1–2.)

C O N S I D E R . . .

- asking your youth leader to read Romans 12:6–8. Have the leader tell you which gifts he thinks you have. Then ask God to give you more opportunities to use your gift.
- writing how your life would change if you walked each day in Christ's steps by following his instructions in this passage.

F O R   M O R E ,   S E E . . .

- Psalm 119:9–16 (p. 550)
- Luke 9:23–26 (p. 1019)
- Luke 14:25–33 (p. 1034)

21 Do not let evil defeat you, but defeat evil by
doing good.

Christians Should Obey the Law

13 All of you must yield to the government
rulers. No one rules unless God has
given him the power to rule, and no one rules
now without that power from God. 2 So those
who are against the government are really against
what God has commanded. And they will bring
punishment on themselves. 3 Those who do right
do not have to fear the rulers; only those who do
wrong fear them. Do you want to be unafraid of
the rulers? Then do what is right, and they will
praise you. 4 The ruler is God's servant to help
you. But if you do wrong, then be afraid. He has
the power to punish; he is God's servant to punish those who do wrong. 5 So you must yield to the
government, not only because you might be punished, but because you know it is right.
6 This is also why you pay taxes. Rulers are
working for God and give their time to their

GOVERNMENT

An Inch Is as Good as a Mile

Darren Smithers wrote a column for his high school newspaper. It wasn't a big column, but it was fun. He wrote humorously about cafeteria food, class workload, or the latest bungle of the notoriously bad basketball team. He had gotten the job because his best friend, Mitch Salinas, was the editor. And much to their surprise, the column had become one of the paper's most popular features, even among kids who attended other schools.

One Monday on the way to class, Darren saw a student in a wheelchair and an older woman trying—unsuccessfully—to push the wheelchair over the curb.

When Darren stopped to help, he noticed a wheelchair ramp cut into the curb just a few yards away. But the yellow paint that marked it off had faded, and someone had parked in front of it.

"Unbelievable," Darren said, shaking his head.

"Believe it," said the student in the wheelchair, whose name was Bruce McCoy. "It happens all the time. That's why my mom has to come with me. More than half the ramps haven't been painted in five years. People just ignore them."

Darren smelled a story. He agreed to meet Bruce and his mom the next day. They would bring their extra wheelchair, and Darren would spend the day trying to get around school in it.

That's how Darren discovered that the main elevator stopped two inches below the floor level (as good as two miles when you're in a wheelchair). He had trouble negotiating the super-narrow doors in the band room. And he discovered high water fountains everywhere and over a hundred obstacles all over the campus. And that was in just six hours!

The next day, Darren wrote about his experiences, but somehow that just didn't seem like enough. He also attended student council meetings and talked to the principal about the problem.

A few months later, Darren talked to Bruce again. But this time his mom wasn't with him. "She doesn't need to come with me anymore," he said. "For some reason, the principal just seemed to wake up."

"Maybe somebody tapped him on the shoulder," Darren said.

Romans 13:1–10 encourages us to do what's right in serving our government. In Paul's day, that meant carefully following the laws laid out by Rome. But in today's democracy, it can mean helping to shape policy—just as Darren did. Read the passage to see what else Paul said about your relationship with the government.

- Would Paul have approved of Darren's actions? Why or why not?
- What's one thing you can do to apply this passage to your situation?

CONSIDER

- running for a place in your school's student council.
- writing a letter to your congressional representative, relating your concerns about the disabled, education, or some other issue you care about.

FOR MORE, SEE...

- 1 Samuel 8:1–22 (p. 251)
- Matthew 22:17–21 (p. 948)
- 1 Peter 2:13–17 (p. 1304)

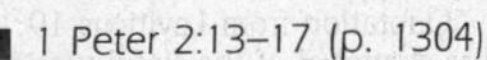

work. [7]Pay everyone, then, what you owe. If you owe any kind of tax, pay it. Show respect and honor to them all.

> **SIDELIGHT:** Relations with the government were important to Roman Christians, since they lived in the capital city. When Paul wrote Romans 13:1–7, about obeying the government, Christians were tolerated—sometimes even protected—by the state. Within a few years, though, Christians would face the constant threat of torture and execution.

Loving Others

[8]Do not owe people anything, except always owe love to each other, because the person who loves others has obeyed all the law. [9]The law says, "You must not be guilty of adultery.[d] You must not murder anyone. You must not steal. You must not want to take your neighbor's things."[n] All these commands and all others are really only one rule: "Love your neighbor as you love yourself."[n] [10]Love never hurts a neighbor, so loving is obeying all the law.

[11]Do this because we live in an important time. It is now time for you to wake up from your sleep, because our salvation is nearer now than when we first believed. [12]The "night"[n] is almost finished, and the "day"[n] is almost here. So we should stop doing things that belong to darkness and take up the weapons used for fighting in the light. [13]Let us live in a right way, like people who belong to the day. We should not have wild parties or get drunk. There should be no sexual sins of any kind, no fighting or jealousy. [14]But clothe yourselves with the Lord Jesus Christ and forget about satisfying your sinful self.

Do Not Criticize Other People

14 Accept into your group someone who is weak in faith, and do not argue about opinions. [2]One person believes it is right to eat all kinds of food.[n] But another, who is weak, believes it is right to eat only vegetables. [3]The one who knows that it is right to eat any kind of food must not reject the one who eats only vegetables. And the person who eats only vegetables must not think that the one who eats all foods is wrong, because God has accepted that person. [4]You cannot judge another person's servant. The master decides if the servant is doing well or not. And the Lord's servant will do well because the Lord helps him do well.

[5]Some think that one day is more important than another, and others think that every day is the same. Let all be sure in their own mind. [6]Those who think one day is more important than other days are doing that for the Lord. And those who eat all kinds of food are doing that for the Lord, and they give thanks to God. Others who refuse to eat some foods do that for the Lord, and they give thanks to God. [7]We do not live or die for ourselves. [8]If we live, we are living for the Lord, and if we die, we are dying for the Lord. So living or dying, we belong to the Lord.

[9]The reason Christ died and rose from the dead to live again was so he would be Lord over both the dead and the living. [10]So why do you judge your brothers or sisters in Christ? And why do you think you are better than they are? We will all stand before God to be judged, [11]because it is written in the Scriptures:[d]

" 'As surely as I live,' says the Lord,
'Everyone will bow before me;
everyone will say that I am God.' "

Isaiah 45:23

[12]So each of us will have to answer to God.

Do Not Cause Others to Sin

[13]For that reason we should stop judging each other. We must make up our minds not to do anything that will make another Christian sin. [14]I am in the Lord Jesus, and I know that there is no food that is wrong to eat. But if a person believes something is wrong, that thing is wrong for him. [15]If you hurt your brother's or sister's faith because of something you eat, you are not really following the way of love. Do not destroy someone's faith by eating food he thinks is wrong, because Christ died for him. [16]Do not allow what you think is good to become what others say is evil. [17]In the kingdom of God, eating and drinking are not important. The important things are living right with God, peace, and joy in the Holy Spirit.[d] [18]Anyone who serves Christ by living this way is pleasing God and will be accepted by other people.

[19]So let us try to do what makes peace and helps one another. [20]Do not let the eating of food destroy the work of God. All foods are all right to

"You . . . things." Quotation from Exodus 20:13-15, 17.
"Love . . . yourself." Quotation from Leviticus 19:18.
"night" This is used as a symbol of the sinful world we live in. This world will soon end.
"day" This is used as a symbol of the good time that is coming, when we will be with God.
all . . . food The Jewish law said there were some foods Jews should not eat. When Jews became Christians, some of them did not understand they could now eat all foods.

eat, but it is wrong to eat food that causes someone else to sin. 21It is better not to eat meat or
drink wine or do anything that will cause your
brother or sister to sin.
22Your beliefs about these things should be kept
secret between you and God. People are happy if
they can do what they think is right without feeling guilty. 23But those who eat something without
being sure it is right are wrong because they did
not believe it was right. Anything that is done
without believing it is right is a sin.

15 We who are strong in faith should help
the weak with their weaknesses, and not
please only ourselves. 2Let each of us please our
neighbors for their good, to help them be stronger
in faith. 3Even Christ did not live to please himself. It was as the Scriptures[d] said: "When people
insult you, it hurts me."[n] 4Everything that was
written in the past was written to teach us. The
Scriptures give us patience and encouragement so
that we can have hope. 5Patience and encouragement come from God. And I pray that God will
help you all agree with each other the way Christ
Jesus wants. 6Then you will all be joined together,
and you will give glory to God the Father of our
Lord Jesus Christ. 7Christ accepted you, so you
should accept each other, which will bring glory
to God. 8I tell you that Christ became a servant
of the Jews to show that God's promises to the
Jewish ancestors are true. 9And he also did this so

"When . . . me." Quotation from Psalm 69:9.

DRUGS AND ALCOHOL

The Lost Weekend

"It was just beer. It wasn't like they were alcoholics or drug addicts or anything, right?"

The teenagers in the small Sunday school class nodded their heads, but they didn't speak. What was there to say? So JoAnn Pearson kept talking.

"Well, so we'd do it every weekend. We'd usually go to a ball game or a dance or a party or something on Friday night. Then we'd go get some beer and chips and stuff and go back to Lonnie Brock's house. Her parents were never home.

"Then we'd just drink beer all weekend. Just, you know, get a buzz on Friday and keep it until Sunday night. Then, after a while it was more than a buzz. We started getting really drunk. And we'd just stay drunk all weekend.

"To tell you the truth, it was getting kinda scary, but I didn't know what to do. Then, one day I woke up with a terrible hangover. I was so wasted. And it was Sunday and I didn't know where I was. I mean, I couldn't remember anything that had happened since Friday night. That really scared me.

"I remember kneeling next to the commode in the bathroom and thinking, whoa, this has gone too far. I lost a whole weekend.

"And that's why I'm here," JoAnn concluded. "I decided to go to church more and see if God could help me straighten out my life. He can, can't he?"

"Yes, he can," said Chip Shoenig. "And we'll be there to help too. Right, guys?"

And everyone nodded.

JoAnn learned the hard way that to be free she had to turn away from alcohol. **Romans 13:11–14** also talks about the need to turn away from drunkenness to follow God. Read the passage to see what it says about drinking and drugs.

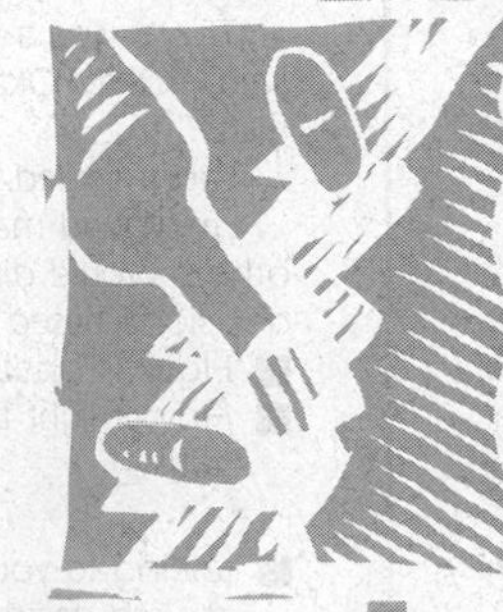

- According to this passage, how did JoAnn's decision move her from darkness to light?
- What reasons does the passage give for avoiding drunkenness?

CONSIDER . . .

- examining your own drug or alcohol use in light of this passage. What would God want you to do (or stop doing)?
- helping a drug-abusing friend find help through a local substance abuse program or your church.

FOR MORE, SEE . . .

- Proverbs 23:19–21 (p. 587)
- Luke 21:34–36 (p. 1049)
- Galatians 5:16–25 (p. 1212)

that those who are not Jews could give glory to
God for the mercy he gives to them. It is written
in the Scriptures:

"So I will praise you among the non-Jewish
people.
I will sing praises to your name." *Psalm 18:49*

10The Scripture also says,
"Be happy, you who are not Jews, together
with his people." *Deuteronomy 32:43*

11Again the Scripture says,
"All you who are not Jews, praise the Lord.
All you people, sing praises to him."
Psalm 117:1

12And Isaiah says,
"A new king will come from the family of
Jesse.[n]
He will come to rule over the non-Jewish
people,
and they will have hope because of him."
Isaiah 11:10

13I pray that the God who gives hope will fill
you with much joy and peace while you trust in
him. Then your hope will overflow by the power
of the Holy Spirit.[d]

Paul Talks About His Work

14My brothers and sisters, I am sure that
you are full of goodness. I know that you have
all the knowledge you need and that you are
able to teach each other. 15But I have written
to you very openly about some things I wanted

Jesse Jesse was the father of David, king of Israel. Jesus was from their family.

DECISION MAKING

Different Strokes for Different Folks

"I'd be mortified!" Rachael Whalen said.

"Everyone would laugh at us!" Dora Parolini shouted.

"We can't let her do it. We'll just have to talk to her, that's all," Janeen Holt reasoned.

Laura Booker shook her head and tried to calm them. "It won't do any good. Her church says you can't wear skirts or dresses above the knee."

"But that's stupid," said Dora. "How can you be a cheerleader and not wear a short skirt? Everyone does it!"

"Yeah," Janeen added. "And besides, Linda knew when she tried out that we wore short skirts."

"Why can't we just let her wear her skirt longer than ours?" Laura asked. "Is it really such a big deal? I mean, I don't think there's anything wrong with our outfits. But if she does, why can't we let her do it her way?"

Rachael sighed loudly. "They're called uniforms! We're supposed to look the same."

"I still don't think it's that big a deal," Laura said. "We're talking about two inches of fabric. No one's asking us to lengthen our skirts. She just wants to be allowed to wear hers longer."

There was a long pause as Laura looked at the other girls. Finally Rachael said, "Okay! Okay, I guess it's all right. Different strokes for different folks, huh?"

Laura smiled. It was nice to know that sometimes everyone could "win."

Linda had made a decision based on her beliefs, even though she knew others would disagree. **Romans 14:5–12** challenges us all to make decisions based on our faith.

- How is Linda like the people mentioned in the passage?
- How might this passage affect the way you make decisions about your faith?

CONSIDER...

- talking to your youth leader about your church's beliefs. Ask how your church decided to believe the things it does.
- making decisions about your lifestyle based on what the Bible teaches. Work toward changing activities that go against your beliefs.

FOR MORE, SEE...

- 1 Kings 12:1–20 (p. 316)
- Matthew 7:13–14 (p. 919)
- Acts 5:12–32 (p. 1105)

you to remember. I did this because God gave
me this special gift: 16to be a minister of Christ
Jesus to those who are not Jews. I served God
by teaching his Good News,[d] so that the non-
Jewish people could be an offering that God
would accept—an offering made holy by the
Holy Spirit.[d]
17So I am proud of what I have done for God
in Christ Jesus. 18I will not talk about anything
except what Christ has done through me in leading those who are not Jews to obey God. They
have obeyed God because of what I have said and
done, 19because of the power of miracles[d] and the
great things they saw, and because of the power
of the Holy Spirit. I preached the Good News
from Jerusalem all the way around to Illyricum,
and so I have finished that part of my work. 20I
always want to preach the Good News in places
where people have never heard of Christ, because
I do not want to build on the work someone else
has already started. 21But it is written in the Scriptures:[d]

"Those who were not told about him will
see,

FRIENDS

Accepted

Karen Flock carried her tray into the cafeteria, looking for her friends. As usual, they were sitting by the windows, in the traditional "senior corner." Karen carried her tray to the table and sat down, but she had trouble staying with their conversation. Her mind was on something else.

A girl named Amy.

Amy Powell was a freshman whom Karen had seen at church. Amy was new to the school and, Karen could see, desperately lonely. Amy ate her lunch alone every day. Not because she wanted to—you could see that in her eyes. She ate alone because sophomores, juniors, and seniors didn't eat with underclassmen, and other freshmen were afraid to eat with her.

They weren't afraid of Amy. It was Kara Holland they were afraid of. Kara was queen of the freshman class. She and her "court" of five pretty girls ruled freshman society. They decided who was "in" and who was "out," and, for undisclosed reasons, Amy was definitely "out."

The more Karen thought about Amy's situation, the more angry she became. It's time to stop this dumb game, she thought. So Karen picked up her tray and walked across the cafeteria to where Amy was sitting. Amy wouldn't look up at her, so she said, "Hi, Amy."

"Hi."

"Is this seat saved?" she asked, pulling out a chair and sitting down.

"No." She looked up briefly, then back to her plate.

"So, how do you like the school?"

Amy shrugged.

"Hi, Amy!" two voices said as they walked by. Girls. Freshmen. Then they giggled.

Now Amy looked up at Karen. She smiled, shyly.

It would be okay, now, she knew. No freshman ever questioned the acceptance of a senior.

Karen accepted Amy even though others had rejected her. Paul talks about the foolishness of rejecting others, since we have all been accepted equally by Christ. Read what else Paul said about accepting others in **Romans 15:4–13**.

■ Based on this passage, what might Paul have said to Karen and her friends?
■ How does knowing that Christ has accepted other people help you accept them too?

C O N S I D E R . . .

■ sitting by people you don't know this week and getting to know them.
■ thinking of people at school or church whom you don't like and asking God to help you accept them as he does.

F O R M O R E , S E E . . .

■ Job 2:11–13 (p. 453)
■ 1 Samuel 18:1–4 (p. 262)
■ John 13:20 (p. 1081)

and those who have not heard about him
will understand." *Isaiah 52:15*

Paul's Plan to Visit Rome

22This is the reason I was stopped many times from coming to you. 23Now I have finished my work here. Since for many years I have wanted to come to you, 24I hope to visit you on my way to Spain. After I enjoy being with you for a while, I hope you can help me on my trip. 25Now I am going to Jerusalem to help God's people. 26The believers in Macedonia and Southern Greece were happy to give their money to help the poor among God's people at Jerusalem. 27They were happy to do this, and really they owe it to them. These who are not Jews have shared in the Jews' spiritual blessings, so they should use their material possessions to help the Jews. 28After I am sure the poor in Jerusalem get the money that has been given for them, I will leave for Spain and stop and visit you. 29I know that when I come to you I will bring Christ's full blessing.

30Brothers and sisters, I beg you to help me in my work by praying to God for me. Do this because of our Lord Jesus and the love that the Holy Spirit[d] gives us. 31Pray that I will be saved from the non-believers in Judea and that this help I bring to Jerusalem will please God's people there. 32Then, if God wants me to, I will come to you with joy, and together you and I will have a time of rest. 33The God who gives peace be with you all. Amen.

Greetings to the Christians

16 I recommend to you our sister Phoebe, who is a helper[n] in the church in Cenchrea. 2I ask you to accept her in the Lord in the way God's people should. Help her with anything she needs, because she has helped me and many other people also.

3Give my greetings to Priscilla and Aquila, who work together with me in Christ Jesus 4and who risked their own lives to save my life. I am thankful to them, and all the non-Jewish churches are thankful as well. 5Also, greet for me the church that meets at their house.

Greetings to my dear friend Epenetus, who was the first person in the country of Asia to follow Christ. 6Greetings to Mary, who worked very hard for you. 7Greetings to Andronicus and Junia, my relatives, who were in prison with me. They are very important apostles. They were believers in Christ before I was. 8Greetings to Ampliatus, my dear friend in the Lord. 9Greetings to Urbanus, a worker together with me for Christ. And greetings to my dear friend Stachys. 10Greetings to Apelles, who was tested and proved that he truly loves Christ. Greetings to all those who are in the family of Aristobulus. 11Greetings to Herodion, my fellow citizen. Greetings to all those in the family of Narcissus who belong to the Lord. 12Greetings to Tryphena and Tryphosa, women who work very hard for the Lord. Greetings to my dear friend Persis, who also has worked very hard for the Lord. 13Greetings to Rufus, who is a special person in the Lord, and to his mother, who has been like a mother to me also. 14Greetings to Asyncritus, Phlegon, Hermes, Patrobas, Hermas, and all the brothers who are with them. 15Greetings to Philologus and Julia, Nereus and his sister, and Olympas, and to all God's people with them. 16Greet each other with a holy kiss. All of Christ's churches send greetings to you.

17Brothers and sisters, I ask you to look out for those who cause people to be against each other and who upset other people's faith. They are against the true teaching you learned, so stay away from them. 18Such people are not serving our Lord Christ but are only doing what pleases themselves. They use fancy talk and fine words to fool the minds of those who do not know about evil. 19All the believers have heard that you obey, so I am very happy because of you. But I want you to be wise in what is good and innocent in what is evil.

20The God who brings peace will soon defeat Satan and give you power over him.

The grace of our Lord Jesus be with you.

21Timothy, a worker together with me, sends greetings, as well as Lucius, Jason, and Sosipater, my relatives.

22I am Tertius, and I am writing this letter from Paul. I send greetings to you in the Lord.

23Gaius is letting me and the whole church here use his home. He also sends greetings to you, as do Erastus, the city treasurer, and our brother Quartus. 24 [n]

25Glory to God who can make you strong in

SIDELIGHT: Since the early Christians didn't have churches to go to, they usually met in homes (Romans 16:3–5). Priscilla and Aquila might have been wealthy and had a large house where Christians could gather for worship. You would probably have to clean your room more often if this were still standard practice.

helper Literally, "deaconess." This might mean the same as one of the special women helpers in 1 Timothy 3:11.
Verse 24 Some Greek copies add verse 24: "The grace of our Lord Jesus Christ be with all of you. Amen."

faith by the Good News[d] that I tell people and by
the message about Jesus Christ. The message
about Christ is the secret that was hidden for long
ages past but is now made known. 26It has been
made clear through the writings of the prophets.[d]
And by the command of the eternal God it is
made known to all nations that they might believe
and obey.

27To the only wise God be glory forever
through Jesus Christ! Amen.

BIBLE STUDY

Recipe

Ray Marx had baked bread before. Hundreds of times.

Well, two times anyway.

"It's a simple loaf of white bread. How hard could that be?" Ray wondered aloud. "A little yeast, a little oil, a little flour—nothing to it."

Ray put all the ingredients into the big bowl his mother always used, added more flour until the mixture was a big ball, and dumped it onto the counter.

As Ray kneaded the dough he imagined how surprised and happy his parents would be when he presented his homemade bread for breakfast the next morning. It was their twenty-fifth anniversary.

Ray covered the big ball of dough with a light coating of butter, flipped it into the bowl, covered it with plastic wrap, and set it aside in a warm corner of the room to rise.

"See, nothing to it," he said smugly. "Didn't even have to look at the recipe."

Now all he had to do was wait for it to rise. Thirty minutes. Nothing. An hour. Nothing.

"It just sat there in the bowl like a . . . like a big lump of dough. Why wasn't it rising?" Ray asked himself.

He checked the expiration date on the yeast package. No problem; it wouldn't expire for another three months. So what could it be?

Reluctantly, he went to the cookbook.

"Let's see," he mused. "Flour, oil, yeast, sugar . . ."

"Sugar! Of course!"

Without sugar, the yeast couldn't do its job. No wonder the bread wasn't rising! He had left out a small but vital ingredient.

Ray's bread couldn't rise without sugar. In the same way, Paul says that a Christian can't reach a mature faith without having the right ingredients in his or her life. Read **Romans 16:22–27** to see what those ingredients are.

- What, according to Paul, is the effect of God's message on people's lives?
- According to this passage, what ingredients might you be lacking to bring you to Christian maturity?

CONSIDER . . .

- asking your parent or Sunday school teacher to give you a recipe for Bible study. Ask what steps you should follow in studying the Bible.
- regularly attending your youth group's weekly Bible study. If you don't have one, ask your youth leader to start one.

FOR MORE, SEE . . .

- Joshua 1:8 (p. 195)
- Psalm 19:7–11 (p. 492)
- Revelation 1:1–3 (p. 1332)

1 CORINTHIANS

Why Read This Book:

- Hear down-to-earth advice about dealing with church problems (1 Corinthians 1—10).
- Learn the importance of working together as Christians (1 Corinthians 11—13).
- Discover the promise of Christ's victory over death (1 Corinthians 14—16).

Behind the Scenes:

If you have ever gone on a road trip with a band, youth group, or sports team, you know what it's like. At first, everything goes well. Everyone has fun being together. But as the miles and days pass, things get tense. Roommates have fights. Bossy people get on other people's nerves. Clowns become irritating. By the time you're home, you're glad you only see those people a few hours a day!

The Christians at Corinth may have had similar feelings. Located in one of the largest and most important cities in Greece, church members came from all over the world. Their backgrounds were different. Their incomes were different. Their beliefs were different. And those differences were dividing the church. To complicate things, many were immature Christians.

In this letter to the Corinthians, the apostle Paul addresses the issues that were dividing the church. These included competition, pride, differences in theology, sexual immorality, lawsuits, marriage and singleness, food offered to idols, and worship. He expresses his beliefs on the issues, challenging the church to follow Christ in all things.

At the heart of the letter, Paul focuses on what it means to be Christians together (1 Corinthians 12—13), respecting each other's uniqueness and gifts, and, above all, loving each other with God's love.

This letter is a problem-solving letter. As you read, you can almost picture Paul referring to a list of questions he has heard from the people, then answering each one. His advice is specific and practical.

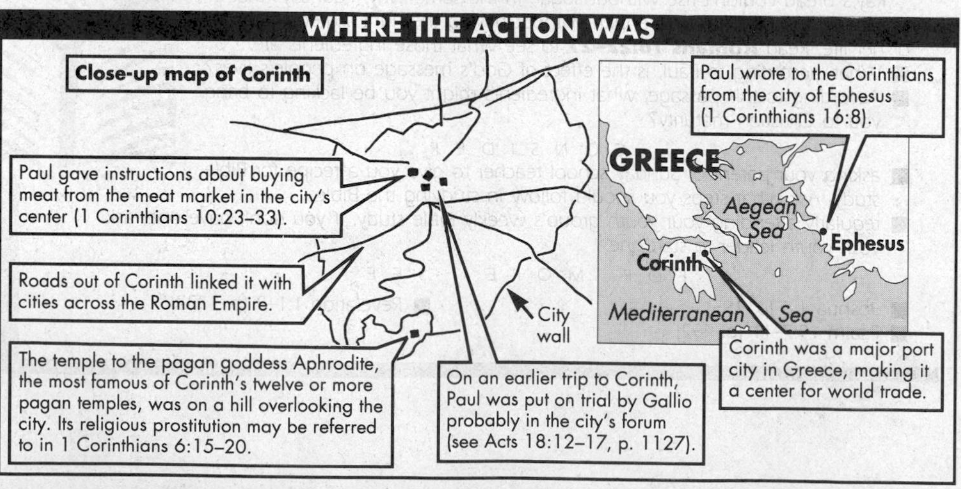

WHERE THE ACTION WAS
Close-up map of Corinth
Paul gave instructions about buying meat from the meat market in the city's center (1 Corinthians 10:23–33).
Roads out of Corinth linked it with cities across the Roman Empire.
The temple to the pagan goddess Aphrodite, the most famous of Corinth's twelve or more pagan temples, was on a hill overlooking the city. Its religious prostitution may be referred to in 1 Corinthians 6:15–20.
On an earlier trip to Corinth, Paul was put on trial by Gallio probably in the city's forum (see Acts 18:12–17, p. 1127).
City wall
Paul wrote to the Corinthians from the city of Ephesus (1 Corinthians 16:8).
GREECE
Aegean Sea
Ephesus
Corinth
Mediterranean Sea
Corinth was a major port city in Greece, making it a center for world trade.

WHEN THE ACTION WAS

BC/AD — 25AD — 50AD — 75AD — 100AD

- Jesus was born
- The church began soon after Jesus went to heaven
- Paul began his missionary work
- Fire destroyed Rome
- Jesus began his ministry
- Paul founded the church in Corinth
- Paul wrote 1 Corinthians
- Romans destroyed the Temple in Jerusalem

Behind the Scenes (cont.): In many ways, the Corinthian Christians lived in a culture a lot like ours. They faced many of the same temptations and problems we face today. This book gives a unique glimpse into their world. And it gives us practical insights into how to live in our complex world today.

---

1 From Paul. God called me to be an apostle[d]
of Christ Jesus because that is what God
wanted. Also from Sosthenes, our brother in
Christ.
2To the church of God in Corinth, to you
who have been made holy in Christ Jesus.
You were called to be God's holy people with
all people everywhere who pray in the name
of the Lord Jesus Christ—their Lord and ours:
3Grace and peace to you from God our Father
and the Lord Jesus Christ.

Paul Gives Thanks to God

4I always thank my God for you because of the
grace God has given you in Christ Jesus. 5I thank
God because in Christ you have been made rich

HEROES

How Hard They Fall

Phil Edwards's youth group was selected to sing at a Christian music conference. The young people were so excited; they would be singing on the same stage as many contemporary Christian artists.

Phil hoped to meet some of the musicians—especially those in one particular band. Phil had their albums, and he had gone to a few of their concerts. He had T-shirts with their group logo on them, and his room was plastered with their posters. Phil was even a trivia expert on the group. He could tell you the band members' birthdays, birthplaces, favorite foods and even their pet peeves. Phil practically worshiped this band!

On the day of the performance, when Phil and his youth group went backstage to prepare for the performance, Phil was distracted. He searched the area to get a glimpse of the band.

He didn't have to look far. He heard arguing from a back corner and looked to see the lead guitarist yelling at a stagehand. Two other band members were smoking under a No Smoking sign by the door, and the lead singer was walking right toward Phil.

As the singer walked past, Phil touched the singer's shoulder to get his attention.

"Hey, punk! What do you think this is? Public property?" the singer growled and jerked away.

Phil couldn't even speak. He just melted back into his group in shock.

When Phil went home that night, he tore down all his posters and shoved them into his trash can. He couldn't believe he had been so stupid. Phil had thought these guys were perfect just because they could sing. Phil vowed he would never again forget that even famous people are just human, and can disappoint others.

Knowing whom to trust and admire isn't a new problem. People back in Bible times also had a hard time figuring out just who should be their hero. Read about one such struggle in **1 Corinthians 1:1–17**.

- In what ways is Phil's "hero worship" similar to that of the Corinthians in this passage? In what ways is it different?
- According to this passage (especially verses 10–13), what happens if we worship human heroes?

CONSIDER. . .

- evaluating whether people whom you admire deserve your respect. Then look for heroes that point you toward Christ.
- going out with your best friend for "hero" sandwiches at your local sub shop. With every bite, give one reason that only Jesus can be a real hero.

FOR MORE, SEE. . .

- Proverbs 4:20–27 (p. 571)
- Romans 15:1–6 (p. 1161)
- 1 Timothy 4:12–16 (p. 1259)

in every way, in all your speaking and in all your knowledge. [6]Just as our witness about Christ has been guaranteed to you, [7]so you have every gift from God while you wait for our Lord Jesus Christ to come again. [8]Jesus will keep you strong until the end so that there will be no wrong in you on the day our Lord Jesus Christ comes again. [9]God, who has called you to share everything with his Son, Jesus Christ our Lord, is faithful.

SIDELIGHT: You have heard of the Suez Canal in Egypt and the Panama Canal in Panama. But have you heard of the Corinth Track? Because Corinth was located on a small strip of land (see map, p. 1166), the city built a five-mile rock track across the land to roll cargo and small ships. By using this track, sailors not only had a shorter trip, but they avoided a dangerous sea journey.

Problems in the Church

[10]I beg you, brothers and sisters,[n] by the name of our Lord Jesus Christ that all of you agree with each other and not be split into groups. I beg that you be completely joined together by having the same kind of thinking and the same purpose. [11]My brothers and sisters, some people from Chloe's family have told me quite plainly that there are quarrels among you. [12]This is what I mean: One of you says, "I follow Paul"; another says, "I follow Apollos"; another says, "I follow Peter"; and another says, "I follow Christ." [13]Christ has been divided up into different groups! Did Paul die on the cross for you? No! Were you baptized in the name of Paul? No! [14]I thank God I did not baptize any of you except Crispus and Gaius [15]so that now no one can say you were baptized in my name. [16](I also baptized the family of Stephanas, but I do not remember that I baptized anyone else.) [17]Christ did not send me to baptize people but to preach the Good News.[d] And he sent me to preach the Good News without using words of human wisdom so that the cross[n] of Christ would not lose its power.

Christ Is God's Power and Wisdom

[18]The teaching about the cross is foolishness to those who are being lost, but to us who are being saved it is the power of God. [19]It is written in the Scriptures:[d]

"I will cause the wise men to lose their
  wisdom;
I will make the wise men unable to
  understand."
Isaiah 29:14

[20]Where is the wise person? Where is the educated person? Where is the skilled talker of this world? God has made the wisdom of the world foolish. [21]In the wisdom of God the world did not know God through its own wisdom. So God chose to use the message that sounds foolish to save those who believe. [22]The Jews ask for miracles,[d] and the Greeks want wisdom. [23]But we preach a crucified Christ. This is a big problem to the Jews, and it is foolishness to those who are not Jews. [24]But Christ is the power of God and the wisdom of God to those people God has called—Jews and Greeks. [25]Even the foolishness of God is wiser than human wisdom, and the weakness of God is stronger than human strength.

[26]Brothers and sisters, look at what you were when God called you. Not many of you were wise in the way the world judges wisdom. Not many of you had great influence. Not many of you came from important families. [27]But God chose the foolish things of the world to shame the wise, and he chose the weak things of the world to shame the strong. [28]He chose what the world thinks is unimportant and what the world looks down on and thinks is nothing in order to destroy what the world thinks is important. [29]God did this so that no one can brag in his presence. [30]Because of God you are in Christ Jesus, who has become for us wisdom from God. In Christ we are put right with God, and have been made holy, and have been set free from sin. [31]So, as the Scripture[d] says, "If someone wants to brag, he should brag only about the Lord."[n]

The Message of Christ's Death

2 Dear brothers and sisters, when I came to you, I did not come preaching God's secret with fancy words or a show of human wisdom. [2]I decided that while I was with you I would forget about everything except Jesus Christ and his death on the cross. [3]So when I came to you, I was weak and fearful and trembling. [4]My teaching and preaching were not with words of human wisdom that persuade people but with proof of the power that the Spirit[d] gives. [5]This was so that your faith would be in God's power and not in human wisdom.

brothers and sisters Although the Greek text says "brothers" here and throughout this book, Paul's words were meant for the entire church, including men and women.
cross Paul uses the cross as a picture of the gospel, the story of Christ's death and rising from the dead to pay for people's sins. The cross, or Christ's death, was God's way to save people.
"If . . . Lord." Quotation from Jeremiah 9:24.

God's Wisdom

6However, I speak a wisdom to those who are
mature. But this wisdom is not from this world or
from the rulers of this world, who are losing their
power. 7I speak God's secret wisdom, which he
has kept hidden. Before the world began, God
planned this wisdom for our glory. 8None of the
rulers of this world understood it. If they had,
they would not have crucified the Lord of glory.
9But as it is written in the Scriptures:[d]

"No one has ever seen this,
 and no one has ever heard about it.
No one has ever imagined
 what God has prepared for those
 who love him." *Isaiah 64:4*

10But God has shown us these things through
the Spirit.[d]
The Spirit searches out all things, even the deep
secrets of God. 11Who knows the thoughts that
another person has? Only a person's spirit that
lives within him knows his thoughts. It is the
same with God. No one knows the thoughts of
God except the Spirit of God. 12Now we did not
receive the spirit of the world, but we received
the Spirit that is from God so that we can know
all that God has given us. 13And we speak about
these things, not with words taught us by human
wisdom but with words taught us by the Spirit.
And so we explain spiritual truths to spiritual people. 14A person who does not have the Spirit does
not accept the truths that come from the Spirit of
God. That person thinks they are foolish and cannot understand them, because they can only be
judged to be true by the Spirit. 15The spiritual
person is able to judge all things, but no one
can judge him. The Scripture says:

16"Who has known the mind of the Lord?
 Who has been able to teach him?" *Isaiah 40:13*

But we have the mind of Christ.

Following People Is Wrong

3 Brothers and sisters, in the past I could not
talk to you as I talk to spiritual people. I had
to talk to you as I would to people without the
Spirit—babies in Christ. 2The teaching I gave you
was like milk, not solid food, because you were

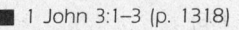

PRIORITIES

Is This All There Is?

When Howard Hughes was forty-five, he was one of the most glamorous men in America. He owned an airline and hotels around the world. He dated actresses, flew exotic test aircraft, and worked on top-secret CIA contracts.

Twenty years later, Howard Hughes was the world's richest man—with $2.3 billion. But he was also one of the world's most pathetic. He lived in small, dark rooms in his hotels. He preferred to keep his life without sun and without joy. He had a scraggly beard down to his waist, long hair, and two-inch-long fingernails. His body had wasted away to a mere one hundred pounds.

He spent most of his time watching movies over and over—sometimes watching the same movie 150 times. He lay naked in bed, deathly afraid of germs. Life had lost its meaning for him.

Finally, emaciated and hooked on drugs, Howard Hughes died at age sixty-seven, because he didn't have a medical device his company had helped to develop.

Howard Hughes had it all—worldly wisdom, wealth, power, fame. He had all the things the world considers important. But they weren't enough. Read **1 Corinthians 1:18–31** to see what Paul says is really important in life.

- How was Howard Hughes's life an illustration of this passage?
- According to this passage, what does God say is most important for Christians?

CONSIDER . . .

- doing something "foolish"—such as helping someone who doesn't deserve it—as a sign of your faith.
- tearing out words and pictures from a magazine that show what the world says is important and what God says is important. Make a separate pile for each category.

FOR MORE, SEE . . .

- Psalm 139:1–18 (p. 561)
- 2 Corinthians 11:16–31 (p. 1202)
- 1 John 3:1–3 (p. 1318)

not able to take solid food. And even now you are
not ready. [3]You are still not spiritual, because
there is jealousy and quarreling among you, and
this shows that you are not spiritual. You are acting like people of the world. [4]One of you says, "I
belong to Paul," and another says, "I belong to
Apollos." When you say things like this, you are
acting like people of the world.
[5]Is Apollos important? No! Is Paul important?
No! We are only servants of God who helped you
believe. Each one of us did the work God gave us
to do. [6]I planted the seed, and Apollos watered it.
But God is the One who made it grow. [7]So the
one who plants is not important, and the one who
waters is not important. Only God, who makes
things grow, is important. [8]The one who plants
and the one who waters have the same purpose,
and each will be rewarded for his own work. [9]We
are God's workers, working together; you are like
God's farm, God's house.

SIDELIGHT: Even though Apollos isn't mentioned much in the Bible, he appears to have been an influential church leader. For a while he was a leader in Corinth, and may have been a better preacher than Paul (1 Corinthians 3:1–9).

[10]Using the gift God gave me, I laid the foundation of that house like an expert builder. Others
are building on that foundation, but all people
should be careful how they build on it. [11]The
foundation that has already been laid is Jesus
Christ, and no one can lay down any other foun-

SCHOOL

The Powerful Way

It was disgusting! While Scott Douglas was at the evening play practice, someone had smeared animal guts all over his car. Scott just stood in the parking lot, looking shocked.

Things had not been the same since he had seriously committed his life to Christ. Many of his friends didn't understand. They thought Scott was snubbing them when he wouldn't party with them. The verbal abuse came first. Then a few flattened tires. Then vicious rumors.

But this? This was sick!

Scott's best friend, Jeff Stevens, walked up behind him. When he noticed the car, Jeff blew up. "Man! . . . I can't believe . . . the nerve of those. . . ." Jeff was so angry he couldn't even finish his sentences. "We know who's behind this," he fumed. "Enough is enough! Let's go bash some heads!"

Scott shook his head and began to smile. "No way. Two bucks and some elbow grease, and we'll never know it happened. Besides, aren't we supposed to act more like Jesus? Do you think Jesus would bash heads now?"

Jeff looked at his friend and began to smile. "You're something, buddy. You're also right. Okay. To the car wash we go!"

Scott Douglas had plenty of reasons to take revenge. But, instead, Scott prayed for those people and treated them as he would anyone else. People noticed. During his final months at high school, people who knew what Scott had been through asked what his secret was.

It was tough for Scott to live the Christian life at school. But because he didn't fight back, Scott's actions demonstrated God's power. To find out more about demonstrating God's power at school, read **1 Corinthians 2:1–11**.

- How do Scott's actions show the difference between God's wisdom and the world's wisdom?
- According to this passage, what should be our attitude as we talk about and demonstrate our faith?

C O N S I D E R . . .

- imagining you were with Paul when he was experiencing some of the feelings he talks about in this passage. Write what you would say to encourage him.
- demonstrating God's power at school by not getting angry if people ridicule your faith.

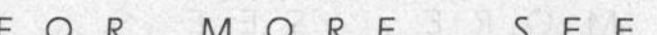

F O R M O R E , S E E . . .

- Joshua 6 (p. 198)
- Ephesians 3:14–21 (p. 1222)
- 2 Timothy 1:6–8 (p. 1263)

dation. [12]But if people build on that foundation,
using gold, silver, jewels, wood, grass, or straw,
[13]their work will be clearly seen, because the Day
of Judgment[n] will make it visible. That Day will
appear with fire, and the fire will test everyone's
work to show what sort of work it was. [14]If the
building that has been put on the foundation still
stands, the builder will get a reward. [15]But if the
building is burned up, the builder will suffer loss.
The builder will be saved, but it will be as one
who escaped from a fire.

[16]Don't you know that you are God's temple
and that God's Spirit[d] lives in you? [17]If anyone
destroys God's temple, God will destroy that person, because God's temple is holy and you are
that temple.

[18]Do not fool yourselves. If you think you are
wise in this world, you should become a fool so
that you can become truly wise, [19]because the
wisdom of this world is foolishness with God. It
is written in the Scriptures,[d] "He catches those
who are wise in their own clever traps."[n] [20]It is
also written in the Scriptures, "The Lord knows
what wise people think. He knows their thoughts
are just a puff of wind."[n] [21]So you should not
brag about human leaders. All things belong to
you: [22]Paul, Apollos, and Peter; the world, life,
death, the present, and the future—all these be-

Day of Judgment The day Christ will come to judge all people and take his people home to live with him.
"He . . . traps." Quotation from Job 5:13.
"The Lord . . . wind." Quotation from Psalm 94:11.

POPULARITY

It's Not Who You Know . . .

Even in grade school, Steven Curtis Chapman faced a dilemma: to be popular by the "in" crowd's terms or to be popular on his own terms. Steven's faith was important to him, and he didn't want to compromise it.

At the same time, he just wanted to be everyone's friend. "I wanted to get along with everybody," Steven, the 1990 Gospel Music Association's Artist of the Year, explains now. So he decided to live what he believed and hope people would like him anyway.

It wasn't easy. He used to get together to play guitars with one guy. "Then [this guy] went the direction of the jock crowd," Steven recalls. "I went into music. He was the cool sports guy that everybody wanted to be friends with, and I saw this split happening and it really bothered me."

It didn't seem right that they couldn't be friends, just because they had different interests.

So Steven challenged the system. He continued to be himself and pursue interests even if they were "unpopular." He tried to be the best Christian he could be, and he treated people the same—no matter what clique they were in.

By the end of his high school years, people recognized what Steven had done. Steven's classmates voted to give him the highest honors possible at Heath High School, naming him "Mr. Heath" and "Mr. Senior."

Steven thinks he got the awards, "not so much for myself, but as a representative of a group of people who said, 'We are going to stand for what's good and right.'"

Steven had proven that it's not whom you know but who you are that matters most of all. Read **1 Corinthians 3:1–23** to see how Paul helped the Corinthian church understand this principle.

- Why do people such as Steven's classmates and the Corinthians value having the right connections? How does this attitude divide people?
- What does this passage tell us we should focus on, instead of focusing on popularity?

CONSIDER . . .

- evaluating whether your efforts to be popular please God.
- working with friends to create a "Popularity/Clique Survey" to distribute at school. Determine how cliques affect relationships.

FOR MORE, SEE . . .

- Daniel 1:1–21 (p. 807)
- Mark 10:42–45 (p. 983)
- 3 John 2–8 (p. 1326)

long to you. [23]And you belong to Christ, and
Christ belongs to God.

Apostles Are Servants of Christ

4 People should think of us as servants of
Christ, the ones God has trusted with his secrets. [2]Now in this way those who are trusted
with something valuable must show they are worthy of that trust. [3]As for myself, I do not care if I
am judged by you or by any human court. I do not
even judge myself. [4]I know of no wrong I have
done, but this does not make me right before the
Lord. The Lord is the One who judges me. [5]So do
not judge before the right time; wait until the
Lord comes. He will bring to light things that are
now hidden in darkness, and will make known
the secret purposes of people's hearts. Then God
will praise each one of them.
[6]Brothers and sisters, I have used Apollos and
myself as examples so you could learn through us
the meaning of the saying, "Follow only what is
written in the Scriptures."[d] Then you will not be
more proud of one person than another. [7]Who
says you are better than others? What do you
have that was not given to you? And if it was
given to you, why do you brag as if you did not
receive it as a gift?
[8]You think you already have everything you
need. You think you are rich. You think you have
become kings without us. I wish you really were
kings so we could be kings together with you.
[9]But it seems to me that God has put us apostles[d]
in last place, like those sentenced to die. We are

SERVICE

Worthy of the Trust

"Son, please don't go."

Bill Dukes's eyes met his father's. "Dad, I believe God wants me in Brazil this year. We've been waiting on the missionary board for a long time. Now the appointment is here. I've got to go."

Bill nearly broke down as he watched his dad's eyes fill with tears. The doctors didn't think Bill's dad had long to live. If Bill left for Brazil, his father might die before Bill could come home.

"Look, Dad, I know you want me to stay. I want to be around you too. But I have to ask what God wants. And as far as I can tell now, he wants me in Brazil."

As Bill drove away from his parents' house, his mind replayed doubts others had expressed about his decision:

"A wife, one boy, and a baby on the way. You're crazy!"

"Do you really think God would call you away from your father now?"

"We need pastors in this country. Why don't you stay?"

Bill weighed his options. Jesus had given him so much that Bill felt he had a responsibility to fulfill.

For eight years, Bill and his family worked in South America. And, against all predictions by doctors and the expectations of Bill's family, Bill's father was alive to welcome him home.

"I'm convinced that God is faithful," Bill says, "especially in those times when someone has to make a hard choice to be faithful in serving God."

The Corinthian Christians needed to be reminded of the same thing, and so do we. Read how Paul makes the point clear in **1 Corinthians 4:1–5**.

- How would Bill's feelings about his life compare with Paul's feelings in this passage?
- How do you feel about God's knowing and judging the secrets of your heart?

CONSIDER . . .

- thanking God for a servant whose faithfulness has helped you in some way. Ask God to help you do the same for someone else.
- evaluating any commitments to serve you have made and haven't kept. Begin fulfilling those commitments this week.

FOR MORE, SEE . . .

- Joshua 24:14–15 (p. 214)
- Luke 16:10–12 (p. 1037)
- Ephesians 4:11–16 (p. 1223)

like a show for the whole world to see—angels
and people. 10We are fools for Christ's sake, but
you are very wise in Christ. We are weak, but you
are strong. You receive honor, but we are
shamed. 11Even to this very hour we do not have
enough to eat or drink or to wear. We are often
beaten, and we have no homes in which to live.
12We work hard with our own hands for our food.
When people curse us, we bless them. When they
hurt us, we put up with it. 13When they tell evil
lies about us, we speak nice words about them.
Even today, we are treated as though we were the
garbage of the world—the filth of the earth.

14I am not trying to make you feel ashamed. I
am writing this to give you a warning as my own
dear children. 15For though you may have ten
thousand teachers in Christ, you do not have
many fathers. Through the Good News[d] I became
your father in Christ Jesus, 16so I beg you, please
follow my example. 17That is why I am sending to
you Timothy, my son in the Lord. I love Timothy,
and he is faithful. He will help you remember my
way of life in Christ Jesus, just as I teach it in all
the churches everywhere.

18Some of you have become proud, thinking
that I will not come to you again. 19But I will
come to you very soon if the Lord wishes. Then
I will know what the proud ones do, not what
they say, 20because the kingdom of God is present
not in talk but in power. 21Which do you want:
that I come to you with punishment or with love
and gentleness?

Wickedness in the Church

5 It is actually being said that there is sexual
sin among you. And it is a kind that does not
happen even among people who do not know
God. A man there has his father's wife. 2And you
are proud! You should have been filled with sadness so that the man who did this should be put
out of your group. 3I am not there with you in
person, but I am with you in spirit. And I have
already judged the man who did that sin as if I
were really there. 4When you meet together in
the name of our Lord Jesus, and I meet with you
in spirit with the power of our Lord Jesus, 5then
hand this man over to Satan. So his sinful self[n]
will be destroyed, and his spirit will be saved on
the day of the Lord.

6Your bragging is not good. You know the saying, "Just a little yeast makes the whole batch of
dough rise." 7Take out all the old yeast so that you
will be a new batch of dough without yeast,
which you really are. For Christ, our Passover[d]
lamb, has been sacrificed. 8So let us celebrate this
feast, but not with the bread that has the old
yeast—the yeast of sin and wickedness. Let us
celebrate this feast with the bread that has no
yeast—the bread of goodness and truth.

9I wrote you in my earlier letter not to associate
with those who sin sexually. 10But I did not mean
you should not associate with those of this world
who sin sexually, or with the greedy, or robbers,
or those who worship idols. To get away from
them you would have to leave this world. 11I am
writing to tell you that you must not associate
with those who call themselves believers in Christ
but who sin sexually, or are greedy, or worship
idols, or abuse others with words, or get drunk,
or cheat people. Do not even eat with people like
that.

12-13It is not my business to judge those who are
not part of the church. God will judge them. But
you must judge the people who are part of the
church. The Scripture[d] says, "You must get rid of
the evil person among you."[n]

> **SIDELIGHT:** Corinth was known for lawsuits (1 Corinthians 6:1). Trials were social events, and sitting on the jury was a privilege. One record tells of a jury with six thousand people on it.

Judging Problems Among Christians

6 When you have something against another
Christian, how can you bring yourself to go
before judges who are not right with God? Why
do you not let God's people decide who is right?
2Surely you know that God's people will judge the
world. So if you are to judge the world, are you
not able to judge small cases as well? 3You know
that in the future we will judge angels, so surely
we can judge the ordinary things of this life. 4If
you have ordinary cases that must be judged, are
you going to appoint people as judges who mean
nothing to the church? 5I say this to shame you.
Surely there is someone among you wise enough
to judge a complaint between believers. 6But now
one believer goes to court against another believer—and you do this in front of unbelievers!

7The fact that you have lawsuits against each
other shows that you are already defeated. Why
not let yourselves be wronged? Why not let yourselves be cheated? 8But you yourselves do wrong
and cheat, and you do this to other believers!

9-10Surely you know that the people who do
wrong will not inherit God's kingdom. Do not be
fooled. Those who sin sexually, worship idols,
take part in adultery,[d] those who are male prosti-

sinful self Literally, "flesh." This could also mean his body.
"You . . . you." Quotation from Deuteronomy 17:7; 19:19; 22:21, 24; 24:7.

tutes,[d] or men who have sexual relations with
other men, those who steal, are greedy, get
drunk, lie about others, or rob — these people will
not inherit God's kingdom. 11In the past, some of
you were like that, but you were washed clean.
You were made holy, and you were made right
with God in the name of the Lord Jesus Christ and
in the Spirit of our God.

Use Your Bodies for God's Glory

12"I am allowed to do all things," but all things
are not good for me to do. "I am allowed to do
all things," but I will not let anything make me its
slave. 13"Food is for the stomach, and the stomach
for food," but God will destroy them both. The
body is not for sexual sin but for the Lord, and the
Lord is for the body. 14By his power God has
raised the Lord from the dead and will also raise
us from the dead. 15Surely you know that your
bodies are parts of Christ himself. So I must never
take the parts of Christ and join them to a prostitute![d] 16It is written in the Scriptures,[d] "The two
will become one body."[n] So you should know
that anyone who joins with a prostitute becomes
one body with the prostitute. 17But the one who
joins with the Lord is one spirit with the Lord.
18So run away from sexual sin. Every other sin
people do is outside their bodies, but those who
sin sexually sin against their own bodies. 19You
should know that your body is a temple for the
Holy Spirit[d] who is in you. You have received
the Holy Spirit from God. So you do not belong
to yourselves, 20because you were bought by God
for a price. So honor God with your bodies.

About Marriage

7 Now I will discuss the things you wrote me
about. It is good for a man not to have sexual
relations with a woman. 2But because sexual sin
is a danger, each man should have his own wife,
and each woman should have her own husband.
3The husband should give his wife all that he
owes her as his wife. And the wife should give her
husband all that she owes him as her husband.

"The two . . . body." Quotation from Genesis 2:24.

BRAGGING

Honest to God!

Nothing ordinary ever seemed to happen to Ray Fulton. His stories of extravagant family vacations, chance meetings of famous people, and doing unbelievable feats were too amazing to be true. When Henry McCormick questioned the facts of his stories, Ray would get defensive. He would insist he was being truthful by pledging, "Honest to God!"

Finally, Henry caught Ray in a blatant lie. One Saturday morning he called to tell Henry he had gotten a ticket to a rock concert that had been sold out for more than two months. He wouldn't show Henry the ticket for fear of losing it, he said, nor would he explain how he got it. Yet he tried to make Henry believe he had an "inside" source. He promised to tell all about the concert the next day.

But that night, during the very hour of the concert, Henry spotted Ray with his family at a mall more than fifty miles from the concert site! Henry confronted Ray the next day, and he still insisted he had been at the concert. When Henry told him he had seen him at the mall, he finally admitted he had exaggerated a little—but he had bought the group's latest album, he said.

Henry's friendship with Ray crumbled after that. He was tired of sorting truth from fiction whenever Ray bragged. Bragging ruined Henry's friendship with Ray. Read **1 Corinthians 5:6–8** to see what Paul thought about bragging.

- How was Ray's bragging like the yeast Paul writes about in this passage?
- What effects has bragging had in your relationships?

CONSIDER

- listing specific ways people can keep from bragging.
- asking God to show you if you have been guilty of bragging. If so, tell the modest truth to the people you bragged to.

FOR MORE, SEE

- Isaiah 10:8–15 (p. 628)
- Jeremiah 9:23–24 (p. 703)
- James 4:13–17 (p. 1298)

4The wife does not have full rights over her own body; her husband shares them. And the husband does not have full rights over his own body; his wife shares them. 5Do not refuse to give your bodies to each other, unless you both agree to stay away from sexual relations for a time so you can give your time to prayer. Then come together again so Satan cannot tempt you because of a lack of self-control. 6I say this to give you permission to stay away from sexual relations for a time. It is not a command to do so. 7I wish that everyone were like me, but each person has his own gift from God. One has one gift, another has another gift.

8Now for those who are not married and for the widows I say this: It is good for them to stay unmarried as I am. 9But if they cannot control themselves, they should marry. It is better to marry than to burn with sexual desire.

10Now I give this command for the married people. (The command is not from me; it is from the Lord.) A wife should not leave her husband. 11But if she does leave, she must not marry again, or she should make up with her husband. Also the husband should not divorce his wife.

12For all the others I say this (I am saying this, not the Lord): If a Christian man has a wife who is not a believer, and she is happy to live with him, he must not divorce her. 13And if a Christian woman has a husband who is not a believer, and he is happy to live with her, she must not divorce him. 14The husband who is not a believer is made holy through his believing wife. And the wife who is not a believer is made holy through her believing husband. If this were not true, your children would not be clean,[d] but now your children are holy.

15But if those who are not believers decide to leave, let them leave. When this happens, the Christian man or woman is free. But God called us to live in peace. 16Wife, you don't know; maybe you will save your husband. And husband, you don't know; maybe you will save your wife.

Live as God Called You

17But in any case each one of you should continue to live the way God has given you to live—the way you were when God called you. This is a rule I make in all the churches. 18If a man was already circumcised[d] when he was called, he should not undo his circumcision. If a man was without circumcision when he was called, he should not be circumcised. 19It is not important if a man is circumcised or not. The important thing is obeying God's commands. 20Each one of you should stay the way you were when God called

DRUGS AND ALCOHOL

Serving Something

"I never believed I'd lose control." For the first time in two years, Mikal Hun's eyes, mind and heart were clear. And it was the first time she had ever discussed her alcohol addiction with Carl Nelson, her youth leader.

"I didn't become alcoholic overnight. It was a gradual thing for me. First, it was an occasional sneak drink at a friend's house when her parents were gone. Then it was a few beers at parties. It wasn't long before I needed drinks. Before and after school as well as during lunch break, and even between classes—any time was the right time because I needed them just to feel human."

Choking back tears, Mikal continued: "I couldn't see it then because of my addiction. But I now know I sold myself into slavery—one drink at a time. My body, my heart, my mind became a slave to beer and wine coolers."

As Mikal covered her face and sobbed, a warm tear slowly rolled from Carl's eye and down his cheek. He felt with her the tragedy of her experience and recalled the warning in **1 Corinthians 6:12–20**.

- How did the slavery Paul warned of become a reality in Mikal's life?
- How can food or sex, like alcohol, enslave people?

CONSIDER . . .

- looking at magazine ads for alcoholic beverages. Determine what the advertisers are communicating about using alcohol.
- talking with an adult if you have a problem with drugs and alcohol.

FOR MORE, SEE . . .

- Proverbs 20:1 (p. 584)
- Matthew 4:8–11 (p. 911)
- Romans 1:18–25 (p. 1141)

you. 21If you were a slave when God called you, do not let that bother you. But if you can be free, then make good use of your freedom. 22Those who were slaves when the Lord called them are free persons who belong to the Lord. In the same way, those who were free when they were called are now Christ's slaves. 23You all were bought at a great price, so do not become slaves of people. 24Brothers and sisters, each of you should stay as you were when you were called, and stay there with God.

Questions About Getting Married

25Now I write about people who are not married. I have no command from the Lord about this; I give my opinion. But I can be trusted, because the Lord has shown me mercy. 26The present time is a time of trouble, so I think it is good for you to stay the way you are. 27If you have a wife, do not try to become free from her. If you are not married, do not try to find a wife. 28But if you decide to marry, you have not sinned. And if a girl who has never married decides to marry, she has not sinned. But those who marry will have trouble in this life, and I want you to be free from trouble.

29Brothers and sisters, this is what I mean: We do not have much time left. So starting now, those who have wives should live as if they had no wives. 30Those who are crying should live as if they were not crying. Those who are happy should live as if they were not happy. Those who buy things should live as if they own nothing. 31Those who use the things of the world should live as if they were not using them, because this world in its present form will soon be gone.

32I want you to be free from worry. A man who is not married is busy with the Lord's work, trying to please the Lord. 33But a man who is married is busy with things of the world, trying to please his wife. 34He must think about two things — pleasing his wife and pleasing the Lord. A woman who is not married or a girl who has never married is busy with the Lord's work. She wants to be holy in body and spirit. But a married woman is busy with things of the world, as to how she can please her husband. 35I am saying this to help you, not to limit you. But I want you to live in the right way, to give yourselves fully to the Lord without concern for other things.

36If a man thinks he is not doing the right thing with the girl he is engaged to, if she is almost past the best age to marry and he feels he should marry her, he should do what he wants. They should get married. It is no sin. 37But if a man is sure in his mind that there is no need for marriage, and has

LOVE

Keeping in Focus

- The best way to draw a straight line is to focus on its ending point.
- The best way to take a test is to shut out all distractions and focus only on the questions.
- The best way to drive a car safely is to focus on the road and the traffic around you.
- The best way to become an accomplished musician or athlete is to focus your time and talent on training and practice.
- The best way to build lifelong friendships is to focus on being friendly and communicating honestly.
- The best way to accomplish things is to focus on goals.
- The best way to love God is to focus on knowing Christ and doing his will.

For more about the importance of keeping love's focus, read **1 Corinthians 7:29–35**.

- How does focusing on loving God affect the way you use your time?
- What things listed in this passage distract you from focusing your love on God?

C O N S I D E R . . .

- asking God to reveal any distractions in your life that keep you from focusing your love on him.
- transforming the relationships in your life to help you focus on loving God. For example, you and a friend could have a Bible study together, or you and your mom or dad could pray together once a week.

F O R M O R E , S E E . . .

- Genesis 5:21–24 (p. 8)
- Matthew 10:34–38 (p. 925)
- Philippians 3:12–14 (p. 1232)

his own desires under control, and has decided
not to marry the one to whom he is engaged, he
is doing the right thing. 38So the man who marries
his girl does right, but the man who does not
marry will do better.
39A woman must stay with her husband as long
as he lives. But if her husband dies, she is free to
marry any man she wants, but she must marry in
the Lord. 40The woman is happier if she does not
marry again. This is my opinion, but I believe I
also have God's Spirit.

About Food Offered to Idols

8 Now I will write about meat that is sacrificed
to idols. We know that "we all have knowledge." Knowledge puffs you up with pride, but
love builds up. 2If you think you know something,
you do not yet know anything as you should. 3But
if any person loves God, that person is known by
God.
4So this is what I say about eating meat sacrificed to idols: We know that an idol is really nothing in the world, and we know there is only one
God. 5Even though there are things called gods,
in heaven or on earth (and there are many "gods"
and "lords"), 6for us there is only one God—our
Father. All things came from him, and we live for
him. And there is only one Lord—Jesus Christ.
All things were made through him, and we also
were made through him.
7But not all people know this. Some people are
still so used to idols that when they eat meat, they
still think of it as being sacrificed to an idol. Because their conscience is weak, when they eat it,
they feel guilty. 8But food will not bring us closer
to God. Refusing to eat does not make us less
pleasing to God, and eating does not make us better in God's sight.
9But be careful that your freedom does not
cause those who are weak in faith to fall into sin.
10You have "knowledge," so you eat in an idol's
temple.[n] But someone who is weak in faith
might see you eating there and be encouraged to
eat meat sacrificed to idols while thinking it is

idol's temple Building where a god is worshiped.

FREEDOM

Free to Do Good

Holly Boyd was overweight. All the kids made fun of her when she tried to play games with them. And when refreshments were served, they would say things such as "Hurry! Hide the food. Here comes Holly."

One night after youth group, youth leader Max Barrett found Holly crying in an empty room.

She told Max about how much it hurt when kids made fun of her and how she wanted to lose weight but couldn't. Max couldn't relate to Holly's weight problem; he was a runner and never seemed to gain weight. But he could empathize with the pain she felt.

"I'll tell you what, Holly," he offered, "you give up sweets and so will I. And why don't you start running with me?"

Holly agreed. The two ran together three times a week. And at youth group meetings while the kids were eating junk food, Max and Holly munched on veggies.

In four months, Holly had lost thirty pounds. She felt better about herself. Holly told Max she couldn't have done it without him.

Max could have eaten whatever he wanted, but he gave up his freedom to help Holly. Read **1 Corinthians 8:1–13** to see how Paul encourages Christians to use their freedom to help others.

- How do Max's actions demonstrate the principles of this passage?
- How would your friends describe your use of the freedom you have in Jesus Christ?

CONSIDER. . .

- changing an area of your life if your freedom is hurting others.
- talking to a new Christian and asking what he or she thinks about how Christians use their freedom.

FOR MORE, SEE. . .

- Deuteronomy 30:11–20 (p. 187)
- 1 Corinthians 10:23–24 (p. 1180)

- 1 Timothy 4:10–12 (p. 1259)

wrong to do so. 11This weak believer for whom Christ died is ruined because of your "knowledge." 12When you sin against your brothers and sisters in Christ like this and cause them to do what they feel is wrong, you are also sinning against Christ. 13So if the food I eat causes them to fall into sin, I will never eat meat again so that I will not cause any of them to sin.

Paul Is like the Other Apostles

9 I am a free man. I am an apostle.[d] I have seen Jesus our Lord. You people are all an example of my work in the Lord. 2If others do not accept me as an apostle, surely you do, because you are proof that I am an apostle in the Lord.

3This is the answer I give people who want to judge me: 4Do we not have the right to eat and drink? 5Do we not have the right to bring a believing wife with us when we travel as do the other apostles and the Lord's brothers and Peter? 6Are Barnabas and I the only ones who must work to earn our living? 7No soldier ever serves in the army and pays his own salary. No one ever plants a vineyard without eating some of the grapes. No person takes care of a flock without drinking some of the milk.

8I do not say this by human authority; God's law also says the same thing. 9It is written in the law of Moses: "When an ox is working in the grain, do not cover its mouth to keep it from eating."[n] When God said this, was he thinking only about oxen? No. 10He was really talking about us. Yes, that Scripture[d] was written for us, because it goes on to say: "The one who plows and the one who works in the grain should hope to get some of the grain for their work." 11Since we planted spiritual seed among you, is it too much if we should harvest from you some things for this life? 12If others have the right to get something from you, surely we have this right, too. But we do not use it. No, we put up with everything ourselves so that we will not keep anyone from believing the Good News[d] of Christ. 13Surely you know that those who work at the Temple[d] get their food from the Temple, and those who serve at the altar get part of what is offered at the altar. 14In the same way, the Lord has commanded that those who tell the Good News should get their living from this work.

15But I have not used any of these rights. And I am not writing this now to get anything from you. I would rather die than to have my reason for bragging taken away. 16Telling the Good News does not give me any reason for bragging. Telling the Good News is my duty—something I must do. And how terrible it will be for me if I do not tell the Good News. 17If I preach because it is my own choice, I have a reward. But if I preach and it is not my choice to do so, I am only doing the duty that was given to me. 18So what reward do I get? This is my reward: that when I tell the Good News I can offer it freely. I do not use my full rights in my work of preaching the Good News.

19I am free and belong to no one. But I make myself a slave to all people to win as many as I can. 20To the Jews I became like a Jew to win the Jews. I myself am not ruled by the law. But to those who are ruled by the law I became like a person who is ruled by the law. I did this to win those who are ruled by the law. 21To those who are without the law I became like a person who is without the law. I did this to win those people who are without the law. (But really, I am not without God's law—I am ruled by Christ's law.) 22To those who are weak, I became weak so I could win the weak. I have become all things to all people so I could save some of them in any way possible. 23I do all this because of the Good News and so I can share in its blessings.

24You know that in a race all the runners run, but only one gets the prize. So run to win! 25All those who compete in the games use self-control so they can win a crown. That crown is an earthly thing that lasts only a short time, but our crown will never be destroyed. 26So I do not run without a goal. I fight like a boxer who is hitting something—not just the air. 27I treat my body hard and make it my slave so that I myself will not be disqualified after I have preached to others.

SIDELIGHT: Paul's reference to "running the race" in 1 Corinthians 9:24–27 would have reminded the Corinthians of the Isthmian Games, held every two years in Corinth's coliseum. These games were the most famous athletic competition of their time except for the ancient Olympics. The games might have included wrestling, boxing, chariot races, and foot races.

Warnings from Israel's Past

10 Brothers and sisters, I want you to know what happened to our ancestors who followed Moses. They were all under the cloud and all went through the sea. 2They were all baptized as followers of Moses in the cloud and in the sea. 3They all ate the same spiritual food, 4and all drank the same spiritual drink. They drank from that spiritual rock that followed them, and that

"When an ox . . . eating." Quotation from Deuteronomy 25:4.

rock was Christ. 5But God was not pleased with
most of them, so they died in the desert.
6And these things happened as examples for us,
to stop us from wanting evil things as those people
did. 7Do not worship idols, as some of them did.
Just as it is written in the Scriptures:[d] "They sat
down to eat and drink, and then they got up and
sinned sexually."[n] 8We must not take part in sexual sins, as some of them did. In one day twenty-
three thousand of them died because of their sins.
9We must not test Christ as some of them did;
they were killed by snakes. 10Do not complain as
some of them did; they were killed by the angel
that destroys.
11The things that happened to those people are
examples. They were written down to teach us,
because we live in a time when all these things of
the past have reached their goal. 12If you think
you are strong, you should be careful not to fall.
13The only temptation that has come to you is that
which everyone has. But you can trust God, who
will not permit you to be tempted more than you
can stand. But when you are tempted, he will also
give you a way to escape so that you will be able
to stand it.
14So, my dear friends, run away from the worship of idols. 15I am speaking to you as to intelligent people; judge for yourselves what I say. 16We
give thanks for the cup of blessing,[n] which is a
sharing in the blood of Christ. And the bread that
we break is a sharing in the body of Christ. 17Be-
cause there is one loaf of bread, we who are many
are one body, because we all share that one loaf.
18Think about the Israelites: Do not those who
eat the sacrifices share in the altar? 19I do not
mean that the food sacrificed to an idol is important. I do not mean that an idol is anything at all.
20But I say that what is sacrificed to idols is offered
to demons,[d] not to God. And I do not want you
to share anything with demons. 21You cannot
drink the cup of the Lord and the cup of demons
also. You cannot share in the Lord's table and the

"They . . . sexually." Quotation from Exodus 32:6.
cup of blessing The cup of the fruit of the vine that Christians thank God for and drink at the Lord's Supper.

SHARING FAITH

Giving It All

In 1873, Lottie Moon went to China as a missionary. She reached out to the Chinese people in the face of tremendous persecution, and she challenged Christians back in the United States to give more money to help people hear the gospel.

In 1911, war and famine hit China. Lottie was evacuated to Japan, but she regularly gave a large part of her small salary to her starving Chinese friends.

She wrote to her mission board asking for help time and again. But the board was heavily in debt and could hardly pay its missionary salaries. Nothing was budgeted for famine relief.

The famine worsened. Lottie drew out the last of her savings from a bank to send to relief workers. "I pray that no missionary will ever be as lonely as I have been," she wrote in her bank book.

Lottie vowed not to eat as long as her Chinese friends were starving. On Christmas Eve night, 1912, she lapsed into unconsciousness. The nurse who was with her watched her clasping and unclasping her hands in the Chinese fashion of greeting. The nurse bent over her and heard her saying the name of a Chinese friend. Even in her last minutes, Lottie's heart and mind were focused on the people she loved.

Lottie Moon died, having given everything she had to the Chinese people. Paul writes about this kind of love in **1 Corinthians 9:16–27**.

- How did Lottie Moon demonstrate this passage with her life?
- How can the methods in this passage help you effectively reach a non-Christian friend?

CONSIDER. . .

- getting to know a non-Christian friend so you can share your faith.
- giving to a missionary organization to help spread the gospel.

FOR MORE, SEE. . .

- Isaiah 61 (p. 680)
- Matthew 10:1–15 (p. 923)
- Matthew 28:16–20 (p. 962)

table of demons. 22Are we trying to make the Lord
jealous? We are not stronger than he is, are we?

How to Use Christian Freedom

23"We are allowed to do all things," but all
things are not good for us to do. "We are allowed
to do all things," but not all things help others
grow stronger. 24Do not look out only for yourselves. Look out for the good of others also.
25Eat any meat that is sold in the meat market.
Do not ask questions to see if it is meat you think
is wrong to eat. 26You may eat it, "because the
earth belongs to the Lord, and everything in it."[n]
27Those who are not believers may invite you
to eat with them. If you want to go, eat anything
that is put before you. Do not ask questions to see
if you think it might be wrong to eat. 28But if anyone says to you, "That food was offered to idols,"
do not eat it. Do not eat it because of that person
who told you and because eating it might be
thought to be wrong. 29I don't mean you think it
is wrong, but the other person might. But why,
you ask, should my freedom be judged by someone else's conscience? 30If I eat the meal with
thankfulness, why am I criticized because of
something for which I thank God?
31The answer is, if you eat or drink, or if you
do anything, do it all for the glory of God. 32Never
do anything that might hurt others—Jews,
Greeks, or God's church— 33just as I, also, try to
please everybody in every way. I am not trying to
do what is good for me but what is good for most
people so they can be saved.

11 Follow my example, as I follow the example of Christ.

Being Under Authority

2I praise you because you remember me in everything, and you follow closely the teachings just
as I gave them to you. 3But I want you to understand this: The head of every man is Christ, the
head of a woman is the man,[n] and the head of

"because . . . it" Quotation from Psalms 24:1; 50:12; 89:11.
the man This could also mean "her husband."

SEXUALITY

It Could Happen to Me

As Christians, Todd Pierce and Larry Gatchell shared the same sexual values. Both believed it was important to wait until marriage to have sexual intercourse. But Todd and Larry differed in their attitude toward the temptation.

"No problem!" Todd would often say. "That's not going to happen to me. I can wait."

But Larry would say: "Hey, it's a problem for me. I know it could happen to me."

Because of their different perspectives, Todd and Larry lived different lifestyles. Convinced of his ability to remain chaste, Todd flirted with girls, and with the danger of becoming sexually involved. Barely a teenager, Todd began to solo date with his "steady" girlfriends.

Realizing his own vulnerability to become sexually active, Larry didn't take the same risks as Todd. Larry would usually group date and never got too serious with any girl.

Todd and Larry met together once a week before school to pray and read the Bible. One day, as Todd read the scripture aloud, Larry heard Todd's voice crack, then go silent. Looking up, he saw Todd wiping tears from his eyes.

After a while, Todd spoke: "I've really blown it, Larry. I said I'd never do it before marriage, but I did. I guess I only fooled myself by thinking I was too strong to be so weak."

Read **1 Corinthians 10:1–13**, to see Paul's warnings about temptation.

- Which of these verses do you believe would have spoken the strongest to Todd?
- What ways has God provided to help us deal with sexual temptation?

CONSIDER . . .

- designing an "escape plan" for whenever you are tempted with sexual sin.
- listing situations when you might be tempted sexually. Then decide how you will avoid those situations.

FOR MORE, SEE . . .

- Genesis 39:6–12 (p. 45)
- 2 Samuel 11 (p. 283)
- Ephesians 5:1–5 (p. 1224)

Christ is God. 4Every man who prays or prophesies[d] with his head covered brings shame to his head. 5But every woman who prays or prophesies with her head uncovered brings shame to her head. She is the same as a woman who has her head shaved. 6If a woman does not cover her head, she should have her hair cut off. But since it is shameful for a woman to cut off her hair or to shave her head, she should cover her head. 7But a man should not cover his head, because he is the likeness and glory of God. But woman is man's glory. 8Man did not come from woman, but woman came from man. 9And man was not made for woman, but woman was made for man. 10So that is why a woman should have a symbol of authority on her head, because of the angels.

11But in the Lord women are not independent of men, and men are not independent of women. 12This is true because woman came from man, but also man is born from woman. But everything comes from God. 13Decide this for yourselves: Is it right for a woman to pray to God with her head uncovered? 14Even nature itself teaches you that wearing long hair is shameful for a man. 15But long hair is a woman's glory. Long hair is given to her as a covering. 16Some people may still want to argue about this, but I would add that neither we nor the churches of God have any other practice.

The Lord's Supper

17In the things I tell you now I do not praise you, because when you come together you do more harm than good. 18First, I hear that when you meet together as a church you are divided, and I believe some of this. 19(It is necessary to have differences among you so that it may be clear which of you really have God's approval.) 20When you come together, you are not really eating the Lord's Supper.[n] 21This is because when you eat, each person eats without waiting for the others. Some people do not get enough to eat, while others have too much to drink. 22You can eat and drink in your own homes! You seem to think God's church is not important, and you embarrass those who are poor. What should I tell you? Should I praise you? I do not praise you for doing this.

23The teaching I gave you is the same teaching I received from the Lord: On the night when the Lord Jesus was handed over to be killed, he took bread 24and gave thanks for it. Then he broke the bread and said, "This is my body; it is for you. Do this to remember me." 25In the same way, after they ate, Jesus took the cup. He said, "This cup is the new agreement that is sealed with the blood of my death. When you drink this, do it to remember me." 26Every time you eat this bread and drink this cup you are telling others about the Lord's death until he comes.

27So a person who eats the bread or drinks the cup of the Lord in a way that is not worthy of it will be guilty of sinning against the body and the blood of the Lord. 28Look into your own hearts before you eat the bread and drink the cup, 29because all who eat the bread and drink the cup without recognizing the body eat and drink judgment against themselves. 30That is why many in your group are sick and weak, and many have died. 31But if we judged ourselves in the right way, God would not judge us. 32But when the Lord judges us, he punishes us so that we will not be destroyed along with the world.

33So my brothers and sisters, when you come together to eat, wait for each other. 34Anyone who is too hungry should eat at home so that in meeting together you will not bring God's judgment on yourselves. I will tell you what to do about the other things when I come.

Gifts from the Holy Spirit

12 Now, brothers and sisters, I want you to understand about spiritual gifts. 2You know the way you lived before you were believers. You let yourselves be influenced and led away to worship idols — things that could not speak. 3So I want you to understand that no one who is speaking with the help of God's Spirit says, "Jesus be cursed." And no one can say, "Jesus is Lord," without the help of the Holy Spirit.[d]

4There are different kinds of gifts, but they are all from the same Spirit. 5There are different ways to serve but the same Lord to serve. 6And there are different ways that God works through people but the same God. God works in all of us in everything we do. 7Something from the Spirit can be seen in each person, for the common good. 8The Spirit gives one person the ability to speak with wisdom, and the same Spirit gives another the ability to speak with knowledge. 9The same Spirit gives faith to one person. And, to another, that one Spirit gives gifts of healing. 10The Spirit gives to another person the power to do miracles,[d] to another the ability to prophesy.[d] And he gives to another the ability to know the difference between good and evil spirits. The Spirit gives one person the ability to speak in different kinds of languages[n] and to another the ability to interpret those languages. 11One Spirit, the same Spirit, does all these things, and the Spirit decides what to give each person.

Lord's Supper The meal Jesus told his followers to eat to remember him (Luke 22:14-20).
languages This can also be translated "tongues."

The Body of Christ Works Together

12A person's body is only one thing, but it has
many parts. Though there are many parts to a
body, all those parts make only one body. Christ
is like that also. 13Some of us are Jews, and some
are Greeks. Some of us are slaves, and some are
free. But we were all baptized into one body
through one Spirit.[d] And we were all made to
share in the one Spirit.
14The human body has many parts. 15The foot
might say, "Because I am not a hand, I am not
part of the body." But saying this would not stop
the foot from being a part of the body. 16The ear
might say, "Because I am not an eye, I am not part
of the body." But saying this would not stop the
ear from being a part of the body. 17If the whole
body were an eye, it would not be able to hear.
If the whole body were an ear, it would not be
able to smell. 18-19If each part of the body were the
same part, there would be no body. But truly God
put all the parts, each one of them, in the body
as he wanted them. 20So then there are many
parts, but only one body.
21The eye cannot say to the hand, "I don't need
you!" And the head cannot say to the foot, "I
don't need you!" 22No! Those parts of the body
that seem to be the weaker are really necessary.
23And the parts of the body we think are less deserving are the parts to which we give the most
honor. We give special respect to the parts we
want to hide. 24The more respectable parts of our
body need no special care. But God put the body
together and gave more honor to the parts that
need it 25so our body would not be divided. God
wanted the different parts to care the same for
each other. 26If one part of the body suffers, all the
other parts suffer with it. Or if one part of our
body is honored, all the other parts share its honor.
27Together you are the body of Christ, and each
one of you is a part of that body. 28In the church
God has given a place first to apostles,[d] second to
prophets,[d] and third to teachers. Then God has

WORSHIP

Remember Me?

The second Sunday in March is a special day for Sharon Ebell's family. Each year on this date, her family gathers for a meal. When the table is cleared, the family photo albums are brought out and passed around.

Everyone smiles and giggles to see how each family member has changed from picture to picture over the years. The giggles sometimes erupt into laughter when the pictures prompt funny stories about family members. Sharon's favorite is the one about her dad being chased by a skunk when he was a teenager.

And there are always tears when the family sees the photos of its absent members. No eye is dry when photos of Jonathan, Sharon's younger brother, are passed around. He died of cystic fibrosis when he was five.

Some of Sharon's friends think her family's habit is a little weird. A few have even wondered if it isn't like worshiping the dead.

But Sharon shrugs off their comments. "It's just how we remember the people who've been important to our family. I never met my grandparents, but I feel like I know them. I've seen their pictures and heard stories about them at least once a year for as long as I can remember," she explains. "I don't think we worship our dead relatives; we just celebrate their lives."

As Christians, we don't worship the dead. But we do worship one who died and rose from the dead. Read **1 Corinthians 11:23–26** to see how Paul explains one way in which Christians can celebrate Jesus' life and work.

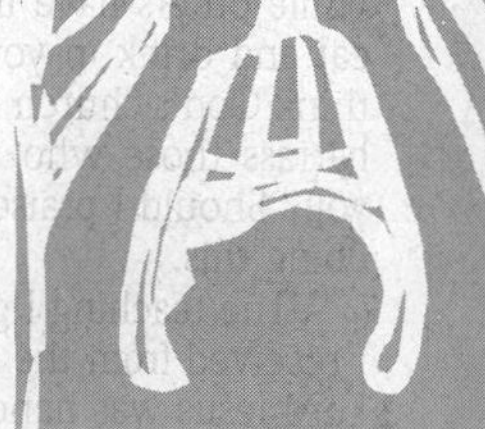

- How is the celebration Paul describes similar to the celebration in Sharon's family? How is it different?
- What do you do in your church and life to remember Jesus?

CONSIDER

- creating other celebrations to remember Jesus. For example, a candlelight dinner could remind you that Jesus is the light of the world.
- talking with your pastor about the ways your church follows this scripture.

FOR MORE, SEE

- Exodus 12:14–20 (p. 68)
- Exodus 16:31–36 (p. 74)
- Luke 22:14–20 (p. 1049)

given a place to those who do miracles,[d] those who have gifts of healing, those who can help others, those who are able to govern, and those who can speak in different languages.[n] 29Not all are apostles. Not all are prophets. Not all are teachers. Not all do miracles. 30Not all have gifts of healing. Not all speak in different languages. Not all interpret those languages. 31But you should truly want to have the greater gifts.

Love Is the Greatest Gift

And now I will show you the best way of all.

13 I may speak in different languages[n] of
people or even angels. But if I do not
have love, I am only a noisy bell or a crashing
cymbal. 2I may have the gift of prophecy.[d] I may
understand all the secret things of God and have

languages This can also be translated "tongues."

SIDELIGHT: The Bible's famous "love chapter" (1 Corinthians 13) stands in sharp contrast to the kind of "love" for which Corinth was infamous. Above Corinth on the hill of Acropolis was the temple of Aphrodite, who was the Greek goddess of love. Prostitute-priestesses worked in that temple, supposedly "cleansing" men of sin through perverse sexual acts.

SELF-ESTEEM

Be Yourself

Susan Klopp wanted to be like Melody Malen. Melody was smart. She was in the National Honor Society. And teachers said Melody was the best student in their classes.

Susan wanted that recognition too. So she started doing what Melody did. When Melody got a wedge haircut, Susan did the same. When Melody joined the yearbook staff, so did Susan.

But as Susan got involved with the yearbook staff, she began to doubt herself. She felt out of place. Susan hated matching all the mug shots with the names of the students. She liked talking, not working by herself writing about the rifle team's accomplishments.

Susan's best friend, Gina Andrews, confronted Susan one day.

"What are you trying to do? You looked better in long hair," Gina said.

"What's wrong with my hair?" Susan asked.

"It's just not you," Gina replied. "Just like you should be on the debate team, not the yearbook staff. You're a better debater than a writer. In fact, if you didn't have that nose, I'd swear you were just another Melody."

"That's not true!" Susan sputtered.

"Oh, no?" Gina asked. "Just look in the mirror sometime. And ask yourself who you are."

At first Susan dismissed Gina's comments. But the more she worked on the yearbook, the emptier she felt. Susan missed her friend Gina. She missed being on the debate team. She missed her old self.

So Susan quit the yearbook staff, realizing that she had to choose her own life—not copy Melody's. Susan started hanging around with Gina and joined the debate team again. It felt good to be back.

Susan finally recognized the importance of being herself and using her own talents. Read **1 Corinthians 12:1–11** to see what Paul says about gifts.

- What does this passage say about whether it was wise for Susan to copy Melody?
- How does this passage make you feel about your own gifts, or about the gifts of others?

CONSIDER. . .

- meeting with your Christian friends to identify each other's gifts.
- rereading this passage with your family, substituting your name and other family members' names who best fit the gifts described.

FOR MORE, SEE. . .

- Genesis 49:2–28 (p. 54)
- Romans 12:4–8 (p. 1157)
- Ephesians 4:11–12 (p. 1223)

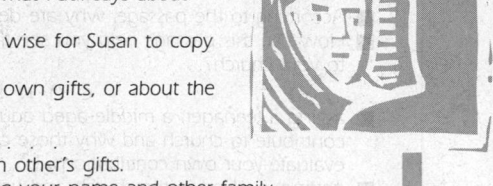

all knowledge, and I may have faith so great I can
move mountains. But even with all these things,
if I do not have love, then I am nothing. [3]I may
give away everything I have, and I may even give
my body as an offering to be burned.[n] But I gain
nothing if I do not have love.

[4]Love is patient and kind. Love is not jealous,
it does not brag, and it is not proud. [5]Love is not
rude, is not selfish, and does not get upset with
others. Love does not count up wrongs that have
been done. [6]Love is not happy with evil but is
happy with the truth. [7]Love patiently accepts all
things. It always trusts, always hopes, and always
remains strong.

[8]Love never ends. There are gifts of prophecy,[d]
but they will be ended. There are gifts of speaking
in different languages, but those gifts will stop.
There is the gift of knowledge, but it will come to
an end. [9]The reason is that our knowledge and
our ability to prophesy are not perfect. [10]But
when perfection comes, the things that are not
perfect will end. [11]When I was a child, I talked
like a child, I thought like a child, I reasoned like
a child. When I became a man, I stopped those
childish ways. [12]It is the same with us. Now we
see a dim reflection, as if we were looking into a
mirror, but then we shall see clearly. Now I know
only a part, but then I will know fully, as God has
known me. [13]So these three things continue forever: faith, hope, and love. And the greatest of
these is love.

Desire Spiritual Gifts

14 You should seek after love, and you
should truly want to have the spiritual
gifts, especially the gift of prophecy.[d] [2]I will explain why. Those who have the gift of speaking in
different languages[n] are not speaking to people;
they are speaking to God. No one understands

Verse 3 Other Greek copies read: "hand over my body in order that I may brag."
languages This can also be translated "tongues."

CHURCH

Watching Every Detail

Michelangelo spent four years painting the 132-foot-long by 44-foot-wide ceiling of the Sistine Chapel. Every day for hours, Michelangelo would lie on his back on the scaffolding, perfecting the details of the continuous, unbroken compositions that contained hundreds of figures from the book of Genesis.

The color. The curves of the lines. The facial expressions. The shadows. The hair. The noses. The fingers. Every detail was important.

But the ceiling was sixty feet from the floor. Those admiring Michelangelo's work could see the mastery of his work, but they couldn't see the details from so far away.

One day one of Michelangelo's friends asked Michelangelo why he spent so many hours painstakingly perfecting each detail—details no one would ever be able to see. "After all, who will know whether it is perfect or not?" Michelangelo's friend asked.

"I will," Michelangelo replied.

Michelangelo saw the many possibilities of details for the ceiling of the Sistine Chapel. And he knew when all those details came together, they would make a masterpiece.

That's what **1 Corinthians 12:12–27** is all about. Read what Paul says about the importance of many parts making one body—the church.

- According to the passage, why are details so important?
- How can this passage help you see the important gifts each person brings to your church?

CONSIDER . . .

- asking a teenager, a middle-aged adult, and a senior citizen ways they contribute to church and why those contributions are important. Then evaluate your own contributions.
- getting involved in the church and using your talents. If you sing, join the choir. If you're good at art, make posters to publicize events.

FOR MORE, SEE . . .

- 1 Kings 5:5–18 (p. 308)
- Colossians 3:11–17 (p. 1241)
- 1 Peter 4:7–11 (p. 1306)

them; they are speaking secret things through the
Spirit.[d] 3But those who prophesy are speaking to
people to give them strength, encouragement,
and comfort. 4The ones who speak in different
languages are helping only themselves, but those
who prophesy are helping the whole church. 5I
wish all of you had the gift of speaking in different
kinds of languages, but more, I wish you would
prophesy. Those who prophesy are greater than
those who can only speak in different languages—unless someone is there who can explain what is said so that the whole church can
be helped.
6Brothers and sisters, will it help you if I come
to you speaking in different languages? No! It will
help you only if I bring you a new truth or some
new knowledge, or prophecy, or teaching. 7It is
the same as with lifeless things that make
sounds—like a flute or a harp. If they do not
make clear musical notes, you will not know
what is being played. 8And in a war, if the trumpet does not give a clear sound, who will prepare
for battle? 9It is the same with you. Unless you
speak clearly with your tongue, no one can understand what you are saying. You will be talking
into the air! 10It may be true that there are all
kinds of sounds in the world, and none is without
meaning. 11But unless I understand the meaning
of what someone says to me, I will be a foreigner
to him, and he will be a foreigner to me. 12It is the

LOVE

Love Never Ends

Everyone knew Lisa Wilson and Gregg Hillburn as Lisa and Gregg—almost as though their names were one word. They had been dating for four years. They cheered for the football team together. They ate lunch together. They did everything together. Nothing could separate them.

Until Gregg started to party.

At first he and Lisa went to parties to be with their friends. Sure there was alcohol, but Lisa and Gregg didn't drink.

After a while, though, Gregg began accepting a glass of beer. Then he started getting drunk. Lisa hated it.

Sometimes Lisa tried talking to Gregg about the problem. But he always got mad. One time he even broke up with her on the spot and called her nasty names. Lisa wanted to scream back at him, but instead she went to his parents.

Tears streaked Lisa's face as she told Gregg's mom and dad what was happening. After she finished, Gregg's dad told Lisa about his own former drinking problem. He knew Gregg needed professional help.

Over the next few months, Lisa wanted to give up on Gregg. Although he was seeing a professional counselor, he was furious at Lisa for "turning him in." He accused her of ruining his life. And he said he never wanted to see her again.

But Lisa patiently waited for Gregg to recover. Although Gregg's words hurt her, Lisa hung on to her memories of the Gregg she first knew. When Gregg eventually admitted his problem, he thanked Lisa for loving him during the times when he was so unlovable.

Lisa loved Gregg with the kind of love described in **1 Corinthians 13:1–13**. Through the tough times, Lisa stuck with Gregg, and a few years later they were married. Gregg has remained sober to this day.

- How do Lisa's actions reflect the message of this scripture?
- How can this passage help you know what true love is all about?

CONSIDER . . .

- copying this scripture passage onto the inside cover of a notebook. The next time someone stretches your patience, read this scripture for advice on how to respond.
- hanging in there with a friend or relative you are about to give up on. Keep loving this person through a difficult time.

FOR MORE, SEE . . .

- Song of Solomon 8:6–7 (p. 614)
- Matthew 5:43–48 (p. 916)
- Romans 13:9–10 (p. 1160)

same with you. Since you want spiritual gifts very
much, seek most of all to have the gifts that help
the church grow stronger.
13The one who has the gift of speaking in a different language should pray for the gift to interpret what is spoken. 14If I pray in a different language, my spirit is praying, but my mind does
nothing. 15So what should I do? I will pray with
my spirit, but I will also pray with my mind. I will
sing with my spirit, but I will also sing with my
mind. 16If you praise God with your spirit, those
persons there without understanding cannot say
amen[n] to your prayer of thanks, because they do
not know what you are saying. 17You may be
thanking God in a good way, but the other person
is not helped.
18I thank God that I speak in different kinds of
languages more than all of you. 19But in the
church meetings I would rather speak five words
I understand in order to teach others than thousands of words in a different language.
20Brothers and sisters, do not think like children. In evil things be like babies, but in your
thinking you should be like adults. 21It is written
in the Scriptures:[d]

"With people who use strange words and
foreign languages
I will speak to these people.
But even then they will not listen to me,"
Isaiah 28:11-12

says the Lord.
22So the gift of speaking in different kinds of
languages is a proof for those who do not believe,
not for those who do believe. And prophecy is for
people who believe, not for those who do not believe. 23Suppose the whole church meets together
and everyone speaks in different languages. If
some people come in who do not understand or

amen To say amen means to agree with the things that were said.

FRIENDS

Inside Lingo

What do the following acronyms mean?

- MS-DOS
- SIMM
- SCSI
- MB
- ROM
- RAM
- DPI
- RGB
- PC
- CD-ROM
- CPU

If you know computers, you probably know what most of these acronyms stand for. And when you talk with other computer people, you might rattle off these abbreviations and have a great conversation.

But if you don't work with computers, few of these abbreviations make any sense. And you may feel left out when others use them around you.

Cliques work in a similar way. People on the "inside" may talk the same way, act the same way, and like the same kinds of things. They easily exclude others and make them feel unwanted.

In **1 Corinthians 14:13–20**, Paul talks about including other people in worship, and his advice has a lot to say about cliques.

- According to this passage, why is it better to speak five understandable words than thousands of words that no one understands? What does this say about cliques?
- How did you feel not knowing what the words at the beginning of this devotion were all about? What does the Scripture say to you about "insiders" and "outsiders"?

C O N S I D E R . . .

- getting together with your friends and discussing ways you exclude others. Choose one way to improve.
- thumbing through your yearbook, looking for someone who used to be—but is no longer—in your group of friends. Call that person and ask how he or she is doing.

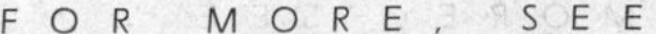
F O R M O R E , S E E . . .

- Ruth 2 (p. 240)
- Jonah 4 (p. 859)
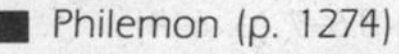
- Philemon (p. 1274)

do not believe, they will say you are crazy. 24But suppose everyone is prophesying and some people come in who do not believe or do not understand. If everyone is prophesying, their sin will be shown to them, and they will be judged by all that they hear. 25The secret things in their hearts will be made known. So they will bow down and worship God saying, "Truly, God is with you."

Meetings Should Help the Church

26So, brothers and sisters, what should you do? When you meet together, one person has a song, and another has a teaching. Another has a new truth from God. Another speaks in a different language,[n] and another person interprets that language. The purpose of all these things should be to help the church grow strong. 27When you meet together, if anyone speaks in a different language, it should be only two, or not more than three, who speak. They should speak one after the other, and someone else should interpret. 28But if there is no interpreter, then those who speak in a different language should be quiet in the church meeting. They should speak only to themselves and to God.

29Only two or three prophets[d] should speak, and the others should judge what they say. 30If a message from God comes to another person who is sitting, the first speaker should stop. 31You can all prophesy one after the other. In this way all the people can be taught and encouraged. 32The spirits of prophets are under the control of the prophets themselves. 33God is not a God of confusion but a God of peace.

As is true in all the churches of God's people, 34women should keep quiet in the church meetings. They are not allowed to speak, but they must yield to this rule as the law says. 35If they want to learn something, they should ask their own husbands at home. It is shameful for a woman to speak in the church meeting. 36Did God's teaching come from you? Or are you the only ones to whom it has come?

37Those who think they are prophets or spiritual persons should understand that what I am writing to you is the Lord's command. 38Those who ignore this will be ignored by God.

39So my brothers and sisters, you should truly want to prophesy. But do not stop people from using the gift of speaking in different kinds of languages. 40But let everything be done in a right and orderly way.

The Good News About Christ

15 Now, brothers and sisters, I want you to remember the Good News[d] I brought to you. You received this Good News and continue strong in it. 2And you are being saved by it if you continue believing what I told you. If you do not, then you believed for nothing.

3I passed on to you what I received, of which this was most important: that Christ died for our sins, as the Scriptures[d] say; 4that he was buried and was raised to life on the third day as the Scriptures say; 5and that he was seen by Peter and then by the twelve apostles.[d] 6After that, Jesus was seen by more than five hundred of the believers at the same time. Most of them are still living today, but some have died. 7Then he was seen by James and later by all the apostles. 8Last of all he was seen by me—as by a person not born at the normal time. 9All the other apostles are greater than I am. I am not even good enough to be called an apostle, because I persecuted the church of God. 10But God's grace has made me what I am, and his grace to me was not wasted. I worked harder than all the other apostles. (But it was not I really; it was God's grace that was with me.) 11So if I preached to you or the other apostles preached to you, we all preach the same thing, and this is what you believed.

We Will Be Raised from the Dead

12Now since we preached that Christ was raised from the dead, why do some of you say that people will not be raised from the dead? 13If no one is ever raised from the dead, then Christ has not been raised. 14And if Christ has not been raised, then our preaching is worth nothing, and your faith is worth nothing. 15And also, we are guilty of lying about God, because we testified of him that he raised Christ from the dead. But if people are not raised from the dead, then God never raised Christ. 16If the dead are not raised, Christ has not been raised either. 17And if Christ has not been raised, then your faith has nothing to it; you are still guilty of your sins. 18And those in Christ who have already died are lost. 19If our hope in Christ is for this life only, we should be pitied more than anyone else in the world.

20But Christ has truly been raised from the dead—the first one and proof that those who sleep in death will also be raised. 21Death has come because of what one man did, but the rising from death also comes because of one man. 22In Adam all of us die. In the same way, in Christ all of us will be made alive again. 23But everyone will be raised to life in the right order. Christ was first to be raised. When Christ comes again, those who belong to him will be raised to life, 24and then the end will come. At that time Christ will destroy all rulers, authorities, and powers, and he will hand over the kingdom to God the Father. 25Christ must rule until he puts all enemies under his con-

language This can also be translated "tongue."

trol. 26The last enemy to be destroyed will be
death. 27The Scripture[d] says that God put all
things under his control.[n] When it says "all
things" are under him, it is clear this does not
include God himself. God is the One who put everything under his control. 28After everything has
been put under the Son, then he will put himself
under God, who had put all things under him.
Then God will be the complete ruler over everything.

29If the dead are never raised, what will people
do who are being baptized for the dead? If the
dead are not raised at all, why are people being
baptized for them?

30And what about us? Why do we put ourselves in danger every hour? 31I die every day.
That is true, brothers and sisters, just as it is true
that I brag about you in Christ Jesus our Lord. 32If
I fought wild animals in Ephesus only with human hopes, I have gained nothing. If the dead are
not raised, "Let us eat and drink, because tomorrow we will die."[n]

33Do not be fooled: "Bad friends will ruin good
habits." 34Come back to your right way of thinking and stop sinning. Some of you do not know
God—I say this to shame you.

SIDELIGHT: Though Paul probably didn't fight wild animals himself (1 Corinthians 15:32), it's likely he is referring to the Roman "sport" of putting prisoners in an arena, then releasing wild animals to maul the prisoners while huge crowds watched. Animals used in this activity included lions, bears, leopards, rhinoceroses, crocodiles, tigers, and elephants. A decade after Paul wrote this letter, Christians faced this kind of persecution.

What Kind of Body Will We Have?

35But someone may ask, "How are the dead
raised? What kind of body will they have?" 36Fool-
ish person! When you sow a seed, it must die in

God put . . . control. From Psalm 8:6.
"Let us . . . die." Quotation from Isaiah 22:13; 56:12.

FAITH

Stick With It

It's not easy to become an emperor butterfly. To emerge into the world, the butterfly must force its way through the neck of a flask-shaped cocoon. Getting through this opening takes hours of intense struggle. The insect must squirm and wiggle to push its way through the confining threads.

If you watched an emperor butterfly's struggle, you might feel sorry for the struggling insect and snip the confining threads to make an easier exit. But if you did, the butterfly would never develop its wings. Instead, it would spend most of its life crawling, never able to spread its wings and fly.

Entomologists who study this butterfly believe the pressure on the insect's body forces the essential juices into the wings, thus preparing the wings for flight. Without the pressure, the wings would never become strong.

Sometimes having faith is difficult. Like the emperor butterfly, we struggle. We feel overwhelmed—tested. And we wish someone could step in and take away the struggle.

But our faith grows through those struggles, as Paul reminds us in **1 Corinthians 15:1–11**.

- According to this passage, what are we to continue to believe in?
- How can the example of the people's faith in this passage encourage you when you struggle with your faith?

C O N S I D E R . . .

- calling one of your grandparents or an older person in your congregation. Ask that person about his or her faith journey—including the ups and downs.
- talking to a friend about the ways you have grown after a difficult time.

F O R M O R E , S E E . . .

- Genesis 22 (p. 25)
- Daniel 3 (p. 809)
- Hebrews 11 (p. 1287)

the ground before it can live and grow. 37And
when you sow it, it does not have the same
"body" it will have later. What you sow is only a
bare seed, maybe wheat or something else. 38But
God gives it a body that he has planned for it,
and God gives each kind of seed its own body.
39All things made of flesh are not the same: People
have one kind of flesh, animals have another,
birds have another, and fish have another. 40Also
there are heavenly bodies and earthly bodies. But
the beauty of the heavenly bodies is one kind,
and the beauty of the earthly bodies is another.
41The sun has one kind of beauty, the moon has
another beauty, and the stars have another. And
each star is different in its beauty.

42It is the same with the dead who are raised
to life. The body that is "planted" will ruin and
decay, but it is raised to a life that cannot be destroyed. 43When the body is "planted," it is without honor, but it is raised in glory. When the body
is "planted," it is weak, but when it is raised, it
is powerful. 44The body that is "planted" is a
physical body. When it is raised, it is a spiritual
body.

There is a physical body, and there is also a
spiritual body. 45It is written in the Scriptures:[d]
"The first man, Adam, became a living person."[n]
But the last Adam became a spirit that gives life.
46The spiritual did not come first, but the physical
and then the spiritual. 47The first man came from
the dust of the earth. The second man came
from heaven. 48People who belong to the earth
are like the first man of earth. But those people
who belong to heaven are like the man of heav-
en. 49Just as we were made like the man of earth,
so we will also be made like the man of heaven.

50I tell you this, brothers and sisters: Flesh and
blood cannot have a part in the kingdom of God.
Something that will ruin cannot have a part in
something that never ruins. 51But look! I tell you
this secret: We will not all sleep in death, but we
will all be changed. 52It will take only a second—
as quickly as an eye blinks—when the last trumpet sounds. The trumpet will sound, and those
who have died will be raised to live forever, and
we will all be changed. 53This body that can be
destroyed must clothe itself with something that
can never be destroyed. And this body that dies
must clothe itself with something that can never
die. 54So this body that can be destroyed will
clothe itself with that which can never be destroyed, and this body that dies will clothe itself
with that which can never die. When this happens, this Scripture will be made true:

"Death is destroyed forever in victory." *Isaiah 25:8*

55"Death, where is your victory?
Death, where is your pain?" *Hosea 13:14*

"The first . . . person." Quotation from Genesis 2:7.

DEATH

Life After Death?

What do teenagers think about death? According to a Gallup Youth Poll, two-thirds of teenagers believe in life after death. But while most teenagers believe in life after death, most teenagers also fear death. According to a Youth Monitor Poll:

- Three out of four teenagers worry that one of their parents will die.
- Half worry about themselves dying.
- Two other major worries—being in a car accident or a plane crash—also hint at this fear of death.

Fearing death is natural for most people. But Paul says death isn't final for Christians. Read about the other side of death in **1 Corinthians 15:12–28**.

- Why does Paul talk about Christ when explaining being raised from the dead?
- How does this passage help you deal with your fears about death?

C O N S I D E R . . .

- going to a church cemetery and reading the epitaphs on gravestones. Decide how you can develop the faith and hope indicated by the sayings.
- drinking a soft drink with your youth leader and talking about your fears concerning death.

F O R M O R E , S E E . . .

- Isaiah 57:1–2 (p. 675)
- John 5:24–29 (p. 1065)
- Hebrews 2:14–15 (p. 1278)

56Death's power to hurt is sin, and the power of
sin is the law. 57But we thank God! He gives us
the victory through our Lord Jesus Christ.
58So my dear brothers and sisters, stand strong.
Do not let anything change you. Always give
yourselves fully to the work of the Lord, because
you know that your work in the Lord is never
wasted.

The Gift for Other Believers

16 Now I will write about the collection of
money for God's people. Do the same
thing I told the Galatian churches to do: 2On the
first day of every week, each one of you should
put aside money as you have been blessed. Save
it up so you will not have to collect money after
I come. 3When I arrive, I will send whomever you
approve to take your gift to Jerusalem. I will send
them with letters of introduction, 4and if it seems
good for me to go also, they will go along with
me.

Paul's Plans

5I plan to go through Macedonia, so I will come
to you after I go through there. 6Perhaps I will stay
with you for a time or even all winter. Then you
can help me on my trip, wherever I go. 7I do not
want to see you now just in passing. I hope to stay
a longer time with you if the Lord allows it. 8But
I will stay at Ephesus until Pentecost,[d] 9because a
good opportunity for a great and growing work
has been given to me now. And there are many
people working against me.
10If Timothy comes to you, see to it that he has
nothing to fear with you, because he is working
for the Lord just as I am. 11So none of you should
treat Timothy as unimportant, but help him on his
trip in peace so that he can come back to me.
I am expecting him to come with the brothers.
12Now about our brother Apollos: I strongly encouraged him to visit you with the other brothers.
He did not at all want to come now; he will come
when he has the opportunity.

Paul Ends His Letter

13Be alert. Continue strong in the faith. Have
courage, and be strong. 14Do everything in love.
15You know that the family of Stephanas were
the first believers in Southern Greece and that
they have given themselves to the service of
God's people. I ask you, brothers and sisters, 16to
follow the leading of people like these and anyone
else who works and serves with them.

ETERNAL LIFE

We Will All Be Changed

Coal, buried deep within the earth, sometimes encounters intense pressure and heat. When it does, over time, a diamond results.

Under the right conditions, the mineral beryl transforms into an emerald, another precious stone. But if beryl contains impurities and undergoes the same conditions, the result is aquamarine—which is only a semiprecious stone.

When rocks with specks of gold are melted, the weighty gold deposits sink to the bottom, and the impurities are scraped from the top. After the process is repeated several times, only pure gold remains.

As minerals change under the right conditions, our bodies will change at death. In **1 Corinthians 15:35–58**, Paul talks about the transformation and refining that will occur in our bodies.

- How will the change in our bodies be similar to what happens to coal, beryl, and gold-specked rocks? How will it be different?
- How does the value of eternal life compare to the value of precious stones?

C O N S I D E R . . .

- drawing a picture of what you think heaven will be like.
- hanging a "We Will All Be Changed" sign in your closet to remind you how our earthly bodies will change.

F O R M O R E , S E E . . .

- Psalm 73:23–28 (p. 525)
- Job 19:25–27 (p. 463)
- Revelation 22:1–5 (p. 1348)

17I am happy that Stephanas, Fortunatus, and
Achaicus have come. You are not here, but they
have filled your place. 18They have refreshed my
spirit and yours. You should recognize the value
of people like these.

19The churches in the country of Asia send
greetings to you. Aquila and Priscilla greet you in
the Lord, as does the church that meets in their
house. 20All the brothers and sisters here send
greetings. Give each other a holy kiss when you
meet.

21I, Paul, am writing this greeting with my own
hand.

22If anyone does not love the Lord, let him be
separated from God—lost forever!

Come, O Lord!

23The grace of the Lord Jesus be with you.

24My love be with all of you in Christ Jesus.

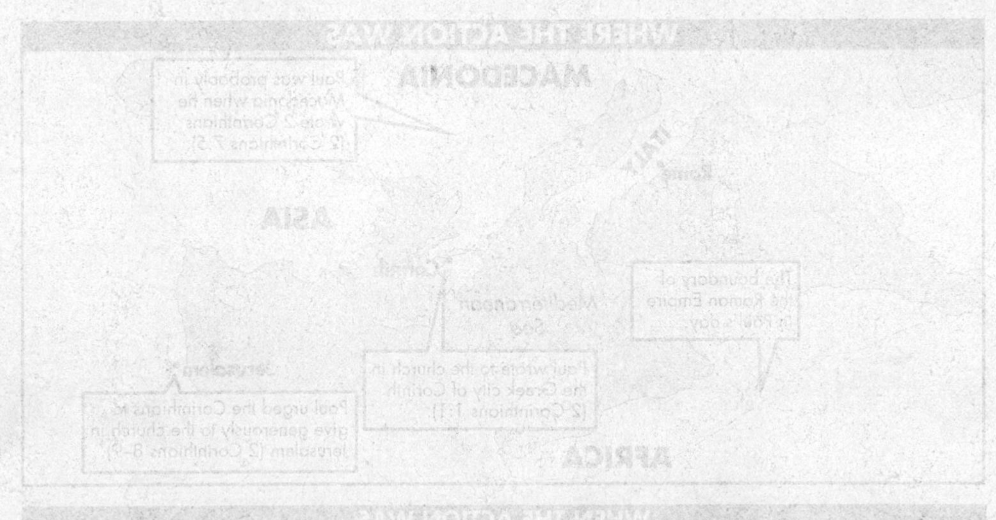

2 CORINTHIANS

Why Read This Book:

- Explore what it means to be a minister for Christ (2 Corinthians 1—7).
- Be challenged to give generously to God's work (2 Corinthians 8—9).
- See what Christians have to brag about (2 Corinthians 10—13).

Behind the Scenes:

"One of the striking differences between a cat and a lie is that the cat has only nine lives." —Mark Twain, American humorist

The apostle Paul wouldn't have laughed at that quote while he was writing 2 Corinthians. Any mention of lying would not have been a laughing matter.

Just three or four years earlier, Paul had started the church in Corinth, a major city in modern-day Greece. He had carefully guided and helped the people grow in their faith, as can be seen in 1 Corinthians (p. 1166). The church was special to him.

But then someone started spreading lies and rumors about Paul, trying to discredit him. He was inconsistent, they said. He was deceptive, arrogant, and boastful. He didn't have the right credentials. He was emotionally unstable. And the list continued. Even worse, the people believed the lies, and were turning to other, false leaders for guidance.

The slanderous lies angered and upset Paul personally. But he worried most that the church was being led away from Jesus Christ. Though he didn't like doing it, Paul's enemies had forced him to defend his ministry. He sent a harsh, stinging letter, which we don't have (see 2 Corinthians 2:3–4). He demanded that the church turn away from the false teachers and discipline the person who insulted him. Much to the apostle's relief, the church followed his advice and reaffirmed its loyalty to him (see 2 Corinthians 7:6–16). The crisis was over.

In 2 Corinthians, a thankful Paul rebuilds the relationship that had been strained by the sharp words. He also clears up any remaining misunderstanding that might

WHERE THE ACTION WAS

MACEDONIA
Paul was probably in Macedonia when he wrote 2 Corinthians (2 Corinthians 7:5).
ITALY
Rome
ASIA
Corinth
The boundary of the Roman Empire in Paul's day.
Mediterranean Sea
Paul wrote to the church in the Greek city of Corinth (2 Corinthians 1:1).
Jerusalem
Paul urged the Corinthians to give generously to the church in Jerusalem (2 Corinthians 8–9).
AFRICA

WHEN THE ACTION WAS

BC/AD — 25AD — 50AD — 75AD — 100AD

- Jesus was born
- Jesus began his ministry
- The church began soon after Jesus went to heaven
- Paul began his missionary work
- Paul founded the church in Corinth
- Paul wrote 2 Corinthians
- Fire destroyed Rome
- Romans destroyed the Temple in Jerusalem

Behind the Scenes (cont.): be present in the church. Finally, he urges the Corinthians to give generously to the offering he was collecting for the struggling church in Jerusalem.

Because of the conflict that prompted the letter, 2 Corinthians gives us an intimate picture of the struggles and dangers Paul faced because of his ministry. In the process, the book gives us a detailed picture of what it means to follow Christ and to be a minister of the Good News.

Though the book focuses on being a minister, its insights and guidance apply to all Christians. It gives courage to overcome discouragement. It encourages us to share freely with others. And it reminds us to find our strength in Christ. That's good advice for all people!

---

1 From Paul, an apostle[d] of Christ Jesus. I am
an apostle because that is what God wanted.
Also from Timothy our brother in Christ.
To the church of God in Corinth, and to all of
God's people everywhere in Southern Greece:
2Grace and peace to you from God our Father
and the Lord Jesus Christ.

SIDELIGHT: The Corinthian church was made up of a diverse group of people who came to this major city from around the world. Paul hints at this when he addresses them in 2 Corinthians 1:2 with "grace," a Greek greeting, and "peace," a Hebrew greeting.

Paul Gives Thanks to God

3Praise be to the God and Father of our Lord
Jesus Christ. God is the Father who is full of
mercy and all comfort. 4He comforts us every
time we have trouble, so when others have trouble, we can comfort them with the same comfort
God gives us. 5We share in the many sufferings of
Christ. In the same way, much comfort comes to
us through Christ. 6If we have troubles, it is for
your comfort and salvation, and if we have comfort, you also have comfort. This helps you to accept patiently the same sufferings we have. 7Our
hope for you is strong, knowing that you share in
our sufferings and also in the comfort we receive.
8Brothers and sisters,[n] we want you to know
about the trouble we suffered in Asia. We had
great burdens there that were beyond our own
strength. We even gave up hope of living. 9Truly,
in our own hearts we believed we would die. But
this happened so we would not trust in ourselves
but in God, who raises people from the dead.
10God saved us from these great dangers of death,
and he will continue to save us. We have put our
hope in him, and he will save us again. 11And you
can help us with your prayers. Then many people
will give thanks for us—that God blessed us because of their many prayers.

The Change in Paul's Plans

12This is what we are proud of, and I can say
it with a clear conscience: In everything we have
done in the world, and especially with you, we
have had an honest and sincere heart from God.
We did this by God's grace, not by the kind of
wisdom the world has. 13-14We write to you only
what you can read and understand. And I hope
that as you have understood some things about
us, you may come to know everything about us.
Then you can be proud of us, as we will be proud
of you on the day our Lord Jesus Christ comes
again.
15I was so sure of all this that I made plans to
visit you first so you could be blessed twice. 16I
planned to visit you on my way to Macedonia and
again on my way back. I wanted to get help from
you for my trip to Judea. 17Do you think that I
made these plans without really meaning it? Or
maybe you think I make plans as the world does,
so that I say yes, yes and at the same time no, no.
18But if you can believe God, you can believe
that what we tell you is never both yes and no.
19The Son of God, Jesus Christ, that Silas and Timothy and I preached to you, was not yes and no.
In Christ it has always been yes. 20The yes to all
of God's promises is in Christ, and through Christ
we say yes to the glory of God. 21Remember, God
is the One who makes you and us strong in
Christ. God made us his chosen people. 22He put
his mark on us to show that we are his, and he
put his Spirit[d] in our hearts to be a guarantee for
all he has promised.
23I tell you this, and I ask God to be my witness
that this is true: The reason I did not come back
to Corinth was to keep you from being punished
or hurt. 24We are not trying to control your faith.
You are strong in faith. But we are workers with
you for your own joy.

2 So I decided that my next visit to you would
not be another one to make you sad. 2If I

Brothers and sisters Although the Greek text says "Brothers" here and throughout this book, Paul's words were meant for the entire church, including men and women.

make you sad, who will make me glad? Only you can make me glad—particularly the person whom I made sad. 3I wrote you a letter for this reason: that when I came to you I would not be made sad by the people who should make me happy. I felt sure of all of you, that you would share my joy. 4When I wrote to you before, I was very troubled and unhappy in my heart, and I wrote with many tears. I did not write to make you sad, but to let you know how much I love you.

Forgive the Sinner

5Someone there among you has caused sadness, not to me, but to all of you. I mean he caused sadness to all in some way. (I do not want to make it sound worse than it really is.) 6The punishment that most of you gave him is enough for him. 7But now you should forgive him and comfort him to keep him from having too much sadness and giving up completely. 8So I beg you to show that you love him. 9I wrote you to test you and to see if you obey in everything. 10If you forgive someone, I also forgive him. And what I have forgiven—if I had anything to forgive—I forgave it for you, as if Christ were with me. 11I did this so that Satan would not win anything from us, because we know very well what Satan's plans are.

Paul's Concern in Troas

12When I came to Troas to preach the Good News[d] of Christ, the Lord gave me a good opportunity there. 13But I had no peace, because I did not find my brother Titus. So I said good-bye to them at Troas and went to Macedonia.

Victory Through Christ

14But thanks be to God, who always leads us in victory through Christ. God uses us to spread his knowledge everywhere like a sweet-smelling perfume. 15Our offering to God is this: We are the sweet smell of Christ among those who are being saved and among those who are being lost. 16To those who are lost, we are the smell of death that brings death, but to those who are being saved, we are the smell of life that brings life. So who is able to do this work? 17We do not sell the word of God for a profit as many other people do. But in Christ we speak the truth before God, as messengers of God.

Servants of the New Agreement

3 Are we starting to brag about ourselves again? Do we need letters of introduction to you or from you, like some other people? 2You yourselves are our letter, written on our hearts, known and read by everyone. 3You show that you are a letter from Christ sent through us. This letter is not written with ink but with the Spirit[d] of the living God. It is not written on stone tablets[n] but on human hearts.

4We can say this, because through Christ we feel certain before God. 5We are not saying that we can do this work ourselves. It is God who makes us able to do all that we do. 6He made us able to be servants of a new agreement from himself to his people. This new agreement is not a written law, but it is of the Spirit. The written law brings death, but the Spirit gives life.

7The law that brought death was written in words on stone. It came with God's glory, which made Moses' face so bright that the Israelites could not continue to look at it. But that glory later disappeared. 8So surely the new way that brings the Spirit has even more glory. 9If the law that judged people guilty of sin had glory, surely the new way that makes people right with God has much greater glory. 10That old law had glory, but it really loses its glory when it is compared to the much greater glory of this new way. 11If that law which disappeared came with glory, then this new way which continues forever has much greater glory.

12We have this hope, so we are very bold. 13We are not like Moses, who put a covering over his face so the Israelites would not see it. The glory was disappearing, and Moses did not want them to see it end. 14But their minds were closed, and even today that same covering hides the meaning when they read the old agreement. That covering is taken away only through Christ. 15Even today, when they read the law of Moses, there is a covering over their minds. 16But when a person changes and follows the Lord, that covering is taken away. 17The Lord is the Spirit, and where the Spirit of the Lord is, there is freedom. 18Our faces, then, are not covered. We all show the Lord's glory, and we are being changed to be like him. This change in us brings ever greater glory, which comes from the Lord, who is the Spirit.

Preaching the Good News

4 God, with his mercy, gave us this work to do, so we don't give up. 2But we have turned away from secret and shameful ways. We use no trickery, and we do not change the teaching of God. We teach the truth plainly, showing everyone who we are. Then they can know in their hearts what kind of people we are in God's sight. 3If the Good News[d] that we preach is hidden, it is hidden only to those who are lost. 4The devil who rules this world has blinded the minds of those who do not believe. They cannot see the

stone tablets Meaning the law of Moses that was written on stone tablets (Exodus 24:12; 25:16).

light of the Good News—the Good News about
the glory of Christ, who is exactly like God. 5We
do not preach about ourselves, but we preach that
Jesus Christ is Lord and that we are your servants
for Jesus. 6God once said, "Let the light shine out
of the darkness!" This is the same God who made
his light shine in our hearts by letting us know the
glory of God that is in the face of Christ.

Spiritual Treasure in Clay Jars

7We have this treasure from God, but we are
like clay jars that hold the treasure. This shows
that the great power is from God, not from us.
8We have troubles all around us, but we are not
defeated. We do not know what to do, but we do
not give up the hope of living. 9We are persecuted, but God does not leave us. We are hurt

SIDELIGHT: Hiding treasures in clay jars was a common practice in biblical times, since people wouldn't suspect anything valuable was in the cheap jar (2 Corinthians 4:7). It's sort of like hiding your money in a sock.

NON-CHRISTIANS

Trying Too Hard

Dave Hildebrant tried to live a perfect Christian life. He went to church and was active in his youth group. He faithfully read the Bible and shared his faith with others.

Dave's problem was that he got carried away.

At school Dave constantly talked about his beliefs. In history class he challenged everything his teacher said. In science class he blasted theories and ideas as un-Christian. During lunch he commented on others' food, telling them that God wanted them to treat their bodies like a temple. Between classes he witnessed in the halls.

At first, teachers and students listened to him. But soon, people around him grew irritated. Teachers began to cut him off, and students just laughed. The more they laughed or ignored him the harder he tried. Finally, even other Christians began to sneer. They started calling him "the preacher" and "super Christian."

Holly Myers was also a Christian. Although she, too, was tired of Dave's style, she felt sorry when others put him down. One day Dave complained to Holly that no one ever listened.

"Maybe you're trying too hard," Holly suggested. "After all, we don't have to be preaching all the time. We just need to let God's love shine through."

Over the next few weeks, whenever Holly saw Dave she just smiled. For a long time Dave didn't seem to have heard her. He just kept on preaching and witnessing, and students kept on making fun of him.

Slowly, Dave began following Holly's advice. He still lived out his faith, but instead of being obnoxious, he expressed it with a smile, a kind word or an offer of help. And, for the first time, people began responding positively to Dave's efforts.

Sometimes we get so tied up in trying to convert others that we don't let God's love show through us to non-Christians. Read **2 Corinthians 4:3–12** to discover more about the treasure of God's love and how to share your faith with the world.

- How does Dave's discovery relate to Paul's belief that we are clay jars holding the treasure of God's love?
- How have you shared God's treasure with a non-Christian?

CONSIDER . . .

- asking God to teach you how to respect others while you share your beliefs with them.
- inviting a friend who doesn't go to church to come with you to worship. Introduce him or her to your Christian friends.

FOR MORE, SEE . . .

- Genesis 18:16–33 (p. 20)
- Matthew 28:16–20 (p. 962)
- Colossians 3:12–17 (p. 1241)

sometimes, but we are not destroyed. 10We carry
the death of Jesus in our own bodies so that the
life of Jesus can also be seen in our bodies. 11We
are alive, but for Jesus we are always in danger of
death so that the life of Jesus can be seen in our
bodies that die. 12So death is working in us, but
life is working in you.
13It is written in the Scriptures,[d] "I believed, so
I spoke."[n] Our faith is like this, too. We believe,
and so we speak. 14God raised the Lord Jesus from
the dead, and we know that God will also raise
us with Jesus. God will bring us together with
you, and we will stand before him. 15All these
things are for you. And so the grace of God that
is being given to more and more people will bring
increasing thanks to God for his glory.

Living by Faith

16So we do not give up. Our physical body is
becoming older and weaker, but our spirit inside
us is made new every day. 17We have small troubles for a while now, but they are helping us gain
an eternal glory that is much greater than the
troubles. 18We set our eyes not on what we see
but on what we cannot see. What we see will last
only a short time, but what we cannot see will
last forever.

5 We know that our body—the tent we live in
here on earth—will be destroyed. But when
that happens, God will have a house for us. It will
not be a house made by human hands; instead, it
will be a home in heaven that will last forever.
2But now we groan in this tent. We want God to

"I . . . spoke." Quotation from Psalm 116:10.

FAITH

Unseen Water

Frank Zeigler's ranch in Wyoming had been in his family for years, but had never been used. It was full of cactus and rocks. Surely the land could be used for something, Frank thought. He thought of raising sheep, but sheep couldn't live there without water. He thought of mining the minerals that had been discovered long ago, but there was no water to process the ore.

Frank felt he was missing something—something he couldn't see. He just needed water, but there was none for miles around.

"I know there is more," he told his wife. "I just know there is. God is always giving us gifts, but half the time we don't see them."

One day as he rode across the barren range, he suddenly stopped. He piled up five or six rocks and called a drilling company. Frank told them to drill a deep water well where he had piled the rocks.

At first the owners laughed. "There's no water on that land. You know that," they teased.

But he insisted. "I just have a feeling it's there," he said. Finally they agreed to drill. Months later, they hit water almost one mile underground.

Astonished, the drilling crew asked how he knew water was down there. Frank shrugged. "I just knew," he said. "I guess I had the faith that there was more there than my eyes could see."

As Frank did, it's important for us to have faith not just in things seen but in things unseen as well. To learn more, read **2 Corinthians 4:13–18**.

- How does Frank's search for water parallel the faith described in the passage? How does it differ?
- Which part of this passage gives you the greatest sense of hope in your faith?

CONSIDER . . .

- thinking about things you know exist even though you can't see them, such as air and electricity. List ways you know God exists even though you can't see him.
- stepping out in faith in an area where you may not have all the "facts" but still believe what you're doing is God's will.

FOR MORE, SEE . . .

- Psalm 116 (p. 548)
- Romans 8:18–28 (p. 1151)
- Colossians 3:1–4 (p. 1241)

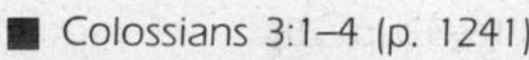

give us our heavenly home, 3because it will clothe
us so we will not be naked. 4While we live in this
body, we have burdens, and we groan. We do not
want to be naked, but we want to be clothed with
our heavenly home. Then this body that dies will
be fully covered with life. 5This is what God made
us for, and he has given us the Spirit[d] to be a
guarantee for this new life.

6So we always have courage. We know that
while we live in this body, we are away from the
Lord. 7We live by what we believe, not by what
we can see. 8So I say that we have courage. We
really want to be away from this body and be at
home with the Lord. 9Our only goal is to please
God whether we live here or there, 10because we
must all stand before Christ to be judged. Each of
us will receive what we should get—good or
bad—for the things we did in the earthly body.

Becoming Friends with God

11Since we know what it means to fear the
Lord, we try to help people accept the truth about
us. God knows what we really are, and I hope
that in your hearts you know, too. 12We are not
trying to prove ourselves to you again, but we are
telling you about ourselves so you will be proud
of us. Then you will have an answer for those
who are proud about things that can be seen
rather than what is in the heart. 13If we are out
of our minds, it is for God. If we have our right
minds, it is for you. 14The love of Christ controls
us, because we know that One died for all, so all
have died. 15Christ died for all so that those who
live would not continue to live for themselves. He
died for them and was raised from the dead so
that they would live for him.

16From this time on we do not think of anyone
as the world does. In the past we thought of
Christ as the world thinks, but we no longer think
of him in that way. 17If anyone belongs to Christ,
there is a new creation. The old things have gone;
everything is made new! 18All this is from God.
Through Christ, God made peace between us and
himself, and God gave us the work of telling ev-

FOLLOWING GOD

Daring to Believe

Christopher Wren, a young English architect in the early 1700s, had the chance of a lifetime. He had won the job of building a new cathedral in London. He prayed and worked to design a cathedral with a magnificently arched ceiling stretching toward heaven.

But when the church was almost finished, other architects in London claimed the building was flawed. They said six additional pillars were needed or else the roof would fall.

Wren genuinely believed God was guiding him in building the cathedral. Still, the other architects were older and more experienced. So, instead of reacting angrily, he listened and prayed. After much discussion he agreed to add the pillars.

At least that's what everyone thought.

After the cathedral was finished, Wren left London. Fifty years later, after his death, workers were repainting the ceiling when they discovered something strange. Each of the six additional pillars was a few inches short of the vaulted ceiling.

Wren had been right. And he had proven it.

Like Christopher Wren we are called to follow God as best we know how, which often requires courage and creativity. To learn more about following God read **2 Corinthians 5:6–17**.

- How does Christopher Wren's decision to follow God's call in his heart relate to Paul's advice to live by believing in Christ?
- How have you made choices that reflect the challenge of verse 9? What happened?

CONSIDER. . .

- choosing a creative way to follow God this week, such as writing, drawing, painting, or singing.
- interviewing your pastor, a teacher, or a friend about times he or she struggled with decisions to follow God, and what happened.

FOR MORE, SEE. . .

- Isaiah 65:17–25 (p. 686)
- John 14:1–7 (p. 1083)
- Philippians 1:19–20 (p. 1230)

eryone about the peace we can have with him.
[19]God was in Christ, making peace between the
world and himself. In Christ, God did not hold the
world guilty of its sins. And he gave us this message of peace. [20]So we have been sent to speak for
Christ. It is as if God is calling to you through us.
We speak for Christ when we beg you to be at
peace with God. [21]Christ had no sin, but God
made him become sin so that in Christ we could
become right with God.

6 We are workers together with God, so we
beg you: Do not let the grace that you received from God be for nothing. [2]God says,

"At the right time I heard your prayers.
On the day of salvation I helped you."

Isaiah 49:8

I tell you that the "right time" is now, and the
"day of salvation" is now.

[3]We do not want anyone to find fault with our
work, so nothing we do will be a problem for anyone. [4]But in every way we show we are servants
of God: in accepting many hard things, in troubles, in difficulties, and in great problems. [5]We are
beaten and thrown into prison. We meet those
who become upset with us and start riots. We
work hard, and sometimes we get no sleep or
food. [6]We show we are servants of God by our
pure lives, our understanding, patience, and kind-

SERVICE

Doing What We Can

Joanni Glade wasn't like the other kids in the youth group. Born with the neuromuscular disease Charcot-marie-toothe, she couldn't walk without crutches.

This was her first year in the youth group, and though she had been very active, the other kids assumed she wouldn't go on the two-week summer service project. But Joanni shocked them when she made it clear she was going.

A few youth group members went to Joanni. "We know you want to go, but don't you think it would be better for everyone if you stayed at home?" they asked. "Aren't you afraid you'll get hurt?" Joanni firmly replied she was going.

When the group arrived at the service project, their assignment was to repair a home in the middle of a dry, treeless yard. Everyone had an assignment. Some kids repaired the roof, some replaced siding, and some painted.

Joanni began painting, but quickly discovered she didn't have the strength to lift the brush over and over. By the end of the first day she felt like a failure. "I guess everyone was right. I really am useless here," she thought.

The same people who had talked to her earlier approached her again. "Maybe it would be better if you went home," they urged. "It's not that we don't care; it's just that we're here to help these other people." After a while Joanni disappeared, and no one could find her. Later she reappeared with a tired but happy smile on her face.

The next day Joanni didn't go with the group to the work site. An hour later, a supply truck arrived at the work site with lumber, nails, shingles and water. Joanni sat in the cab with a list of supplies. For two weeks Joanni kept track of supplies and saw to it that work groups had what they needed. By the end of the project, the project directors talked about hiring her the next year as their supply coordinator.

Joanni took the message of **2 Corinthians 5:20–6:10** seriously. In spite of the doubts of others she served God in her own unique way.

- How were Joanni's actions similar to the kind of service the passage talks about?
- When have you served God and others in ways that are reflected in this passage? What was the result?

C O N S I D E R . . .

- taking an inventory of your skills, gifts and abilities, and deciding how you can use them in God's service.
- including people with disabilities as full and equal servants in your youth group and church.

F O R M O R E , S E E . . .

- Jeremiah 1:4–10 (p. 691)
- Matthew 4:16–19 (p. 912)
- James 2:14–26 (p. 1295)

ness, by the Holy Spirit,[d] by true love, 7by speaking the truth, and by God's power. We use our
right living to defend ourselves against everything. 8Some people honor us, but others blame

> **SIDELIGHT:** Paul was no stranger to the local bars—prison bars, that is (2 Corinthians 6:5). According to Clement of Rome, Paul was imprisoned at least seven times. Among the places he was locked up were Philippi, Jerusalem, and Rome. Paul's life ended in prison when he was executed by the Roman government.

us. Some people say evil things about us, but others say good things. Some people say we are liars,
but we speak the truth. 9We are not known, but
we are well known. We seem to be dying, but we
continue to live. We are punished, but we are not
killed. 10We have much sadness, but we are always rejoicing. We are poor, but we are making
many people rich in faith. We have nothing, but
really we have everything.
11We have spoken freely to you in Corinth and
have opened our hearts to you. 12Our feelings of
love for you have not stopped, but you have
stopped your feelings of love for us. 13I speak to
you as if you were my children. Do to us as we
have done—open your hearts to us.

Warning About Non-Christians

14You are not the same as those who do not
believe. So do not join yourselves to them. Good
and bad do not belong together. Light and darkness cannot share together. 15How can Christ and
Belial, the devil, have any agreement? What can
a believer have together with a nonbeliever?
16The temple of God cannot have any agreement
with idols, and we are the temple of the living
God. As God said: "I will live with them and walk
with them. And I will be their God, and they will
be my people."[n]

17"Leave those people,
and be separate, says the Lord.
Touch nothing that is unclean,[d]
and I will accept you."

Isaiah 52:11; Ezekiel 20:34, 41

18"I will be your father,
and you will be my sons and daughters,
says the Lord Almighty." *2 Samuel 7:14; 7:8*

7 Dear friends, we have these promises from
God, so we should make ourselves pure—
free from anything that makes body or soul unclean. We should try to become holy in the way
we live, because we respect God.

Paul's Joy

2Open your hearts to us. We have not done
wrong to anyone, we have not ruined the faith of
anyone, and we have not cheated anyone. 3I do
not say this to blame you. I told you before that
we love you so much we would live or die with
you. 4I feel very sure of you and am very proud
of you. You give me much comfort, and in all of
our troubles I have great joy.
5When we came into Macedonia, we had no
rest. We found trouble all around us. We had
fighting on the outside and fear on the inside. 6But
God, who comforts those who are troubled, comforted us when Titus came. 7We were comforted,
not only by his coming but also by the comfort
you gave him. Titus told us about your wish to see
me and that you are very sorry for what you did.
He also told me about your great care for me, and
when I heard this, I was much happier.
8Even if my letter made you sad, I am not sorry
I wrote it. At first I was sorry, because it made you
sad, but you were sad only for a short time. 9Now
I am happy, not because you were made sad, but
because your sorrow made you change your lives.
You became sad in the way God wanted you to,
so you were not hurt by us in any way. 10The kind
of sorrow God wants makes people change their
hearts and lives. This leads to salvation, and you
cannot be sorry for that. But the kind of sorrow
the world has brings death. 11See what this sorrow—the sorrow God wanted you to have—has
done to you: It has made you very serious. It
made you want to prove you were not wrong. It
made you angry and afraid. It made you want to
see me. It made you care. It made you want the
right thing to be done. You proved you were innocent in the problem. 12I wrote that letter, not because of the one who did the wrong or because
of the person who was hurt. I wrote the letter
so you could see, before God, the great care
you have for us. 13That is why we were comforted.
Not only were we very comforted, we were
even happier to see that Titus was so happy. All
of you made him feel much better. 14I bragged to
Titus about you, and you showed that I was right.
Everything we said to you was true, and you have
proved that what we bragged about to Titus is
true. 15And his love for you is stronger when he
remembers that you were all ready to obey. You
welcomed him with respect and fear. 16I am very
happy that I can trust you fully.

"I . . . people." Quotation from Leviticus 26:11-12; Jeremiah 32:38; Ezekiel 37:27.

Christian Giving

8 And now, brothers and sisters, we want you
to know about the grace God gave the
churches in Macedonia. 2They have been tested
by great troubles, and they are very poor. But they
gave much because of their great joy. 3I can tell
you that they gave as much as they were able and
even more than they could afford. No one told
them to do it. 4But they begged and pleaded with
us to let them share in this service for God's people. 5And they gave in a way we did not expect:
They first gave themselves to the Lord and to us.
This is what God wants. 6So we asked Titus to
help you finish this special work of grace since he
is the one who started it. 7You are rich in everything—in faith, in speaking, in knowledge, in
truly wanting to help, and in the love you learned
from us. In the same way, be strong also in the
grace of giving.
8I am not commanding you to give. But I want
to see if your love is true by comparing you with
others that really want to help. 9You know the
grace of our Lord Jesus Christ. You know that
Christ was rich, but for you he became poor so
that by his becoming poor you might become
rich.
10This is what I think you should do: Last year
you were the first to want to give, and you were
the first who gave. 11So now finish the work you
started. Then your "doing" will be equal to your
"wanting to do." Give from what you have. 12If
you want to give, your gift will be accepted. It will
be judged by what you have, not by what you do
not have. 13We do not want you to have troubles
while other people are at ease, but we want ev-

GIVING

The Little Things

Linda Dale was Judy Grantham's friend, and she had come on the ski trip to be with Judy. The Bible studies and prayertimes were okay, but she had really come to ski. After a day of skiing, Linda was on the bus, feeling exhausted and cold. Her socks were soaked and the bus was freezing. Shivering and surrounded by people she barely knew, she hoped Judy would come soon.

Jennifer Davis was cold, too. She was a regular group member, and noticed Linda sitting alone, cold and miserable. Going over to Linda, she asked, "Are you okay? You look like a Popsicle."

"I'm just so cold," Linda said. "My feet are freezing. Maybe Judy will have an extra pair of dry socks she can loan me."

"I have an extra pair of socks I'd be glad to give you," Jennifer said.

Linda hesitated, but then she said, "Would you? That would be wonderful."

Jennifer found the socks and gave them to Linda, along with some dry gloves and a scarf. By the time Judy boarded the bus, Linda and Jennifer were laughing about their day of skiing.

Later that night Linda asked Judy, "Why did Jennifer give me all those clothes when she was just as cold as I was?"

"Because giving is a part of being a Christian," Judy said. Then they talked for hours about why Judy was a Christian, and what it meant to give.

After the ski trip, Linda began coming to youth group regularly. While she still enjoyed the fun stuff, she also began asking more questions during Bible studies and offered prayers during worship. It took a while, but slowly she developed a solid faith.

In a world that assumes life's purpose is to take and keep, Jennifer's giving showed Linda that Christianity is different. Jennifer took **2 Corinthians 8:5–15** to heart.

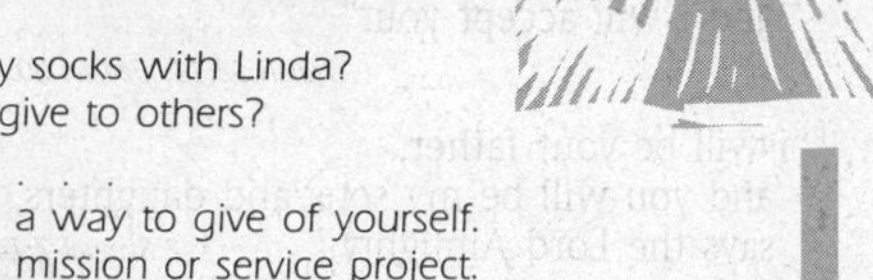

- Looking at the passage, why did Jennifer share dry socks with Linda?
- In what ways does the passage challenge you to give to others?

CONSIDER . . .

- doing one unexpected chore around the house as a way to give of yourself.
- organizing a benefit fund-raiser to help a Christian mission or service project.

FOR MORE, SEE . . .

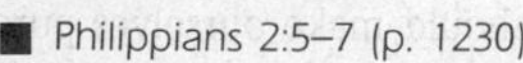

- Exodus 22:25–27 (p. 81)
- Acts 20:32–35 (p. 1130)
- Philippians 2:5–7 (p. 1230)

erything to be equal. 14At this time you have
plenty. What you have can help others who are
in need. Then later, when they have plenty, they
can help you when you are in need, and all will
be equal. 15As it is written in the Scriptures,[d] "The
person who gathered more did not have too
much, nor did the person who gathered less have
too little."[n]

Titus and His Companions Help

16I thank God because he gave Titus the same
love for you that I have. 17Titus accepted what we
asked him to do. He wanted very much to go to
you, and this was his own idea. 18We are sending
with him the brother who is praised by all the
churches because of his service in preaching the
Good News.[d] 19Also, this brother was chosen by
the churches to go with us when we deliver this
gift of money. We are doing this service to bring
glory to the Lord and to show that we really want
to help.

20We are being careful so that no one will criticize us for the way we are handling this large gift.
21We are trying hard to do what the Lord accepts
as right and also what people think is right.

22Also, we are sending with them our brother,
who is always ready to help. He has proved this
to us in many ways, and he wants to help even
more now, because he has much faith in you.

23Now about Titus—he is my partner who is
working with me to help you. And about the
other brothers—they are sent from the churches,
and they bring glory to Christ. 24So show these
men the proof of your love and the reason we are
proud of you. Then all the churches can see it.

Help for Fellow Christians

9 I really do not need to write you about this
help for God's people. 2I know you want to
help. I have been bragging about this to the people in Macedonia, telling them that you in Southern Greece have been ready to give since last
year. And your desire to give has made most of
them ready to give also. 3But I am sending the
brothers to you so that our bragging about you in
this will not be empty words. I want you to be
ready, as I said you would be. 4If any of the people
from Macedonia come with me and find that you
are not ready, we will be ashamed that we were
so sure of you. (And you will be ashamed, too!)
5So I thought I should ask these brothers to go to
you before we do. They will finish getting in order
the generous gift you promised so it will be ready
when we come. And it will be a generous gift—
not one that you did not want to give.

6Remember this: The person who plants a little
will have a small harvest, but the person who
plants a lot will have a big harvest. 7Each one
should give as you have decided in your heart to
give. You should not be sad when you give, and
you should not give because you feel forced to
give. God loves the person who gives happily.
8And God can give you more blessings than you
need. Then you will always have plenty of everything—enough to give to every good work. 9It is
written in the Scriptures:[d]

"He gives freely to the poor.
The things he does are right and will
continue forever." *Psalm 112:9*

10God is the One who gives seed to the farmer
and bread for food. He will give you all the seed
you need and make it grow so there will be a great
harvest from your goodness. 11He will make you
rich in every way so that you can always give
freely. And your giving through us will cause
many to give thanks to God. 12This service you do
not only helps the needs of God's people, it also
brings many more thanks to God. 13It is a proof
of your faith. Many people will praise God because you obey the Good News[d] of Christ—the
gospel you say you believe—and because you
freely share with them and with all others. 14And
when they pray, they will wish they could be with
you because of the great grace that God has given
you. 15Thanks be to God for his gift that is too
wonderful for words.

Paul Defends His Ministry

10 I, Paul, am begging you with the gentleness and the kindness of Christ. Some
people say that I am easy on you when I am with
you and bold when I am away. 2They think we
live in a worldly way, and I plan to be very bold
with them when I come. I beg you that when I
come I will not need to use that same boldness
with you. 3We do live in the world, but we do not
fight in the same way the world fights. 4We fight
with weapons that are different from those the
world uses. Our weapons have power from God
that can destroy the enemy's strong places. We
destroy people's arguments 5and every proud
thing that raises itself against the knowledge of
God. We capture every thought and make it give
up and obey Christ. 6We are ready to punish anyone there who does not obey, but first we want
you to obey fully.

7You must look at the facts before you. If you
feel sure that you belong to Christ, you must remember that we belong to Christ just as you do.
8It is true that we brag freely about the authority
the Lord gave us. But this authority is to build you
up, not to tear you down. So I will not be
ashamed. 9I do not want you to think I am trying
to scare you with my letters. 10Some people say,

"The person . . . little." Quotation from Exodus 16:18.

"Paul's letters are powerful and sound important, but when he is with us, he is weak. And his speaking is nothing." [11]They should know this: We are not there with you now, so we say these things in letters. But when we are there with you, we will show the same authority that we show in our letters.

SIDELIGHT: Paul may have been a great missionary, but he would have never made it on the front of a fashion magazine. A nonbiblical book called Acts of Paul and Thecla described him as "a man small of stature, with bald head and crooked legs . . . with eyebrows meeting and nose somewhat hooked." His critics said: "He is weak. And his speaking is nothing" (2 Corinthians 10:10).

[12]We do not dare to compare ourselves with those who think they are very important. They use themselves to measure themselves, and they judge themselves by what they themselves are. This shows that they know nothing. [13]But we will not brag about things outside the work that was given us to do. We will limit our bragging to the work that God gave us, and this includes our work with you. [14]We are not bragging too much, as we would be if we had not already come to you. But we have come to you with the Good News[d] of Christ. [15]We limit our bragging to the work that is ours, not what others have done. We hope that as your faith continues to grow, you will help our work to grow much larger. [16]We want to tell the Good News in the areas beyond your city. We do not want to brag about work that has already been done in another person's area. [17]But, "If someone wants to brag, he should brag only about the Lord."[n] [18]It is not those who say they are good who are accepted but those who the Lord thinks are good.

Paul and the False Apostles

11 I wish you would be patient with me even when I am a little foolish, but you are already doing that. [2]I am jealous over you with a jealousy that comes from God. I promised to give you to Christ, as your only husband. I want to give you as his pure bride. [3]But I am afraid that your minds will be led away from your true and pure following of Christ just as Eve was tricked by the snake with his evil ways. [4]You are very patient with anyone who comes to you and preaches a different Jesus from the one we preached. You are very willing to accept a spirit or gospel that is different from the Spirit[d] and Good News[d] you received from us.

[5]I do not think that those "great apostles" are any better than I am. [6]I may not be a trained speaker, but I do have knowledge. We have shown this to you clearly in every way.

[7]I preached God's Good News to you without pay. I made myself unimportant to make you important. Do you think that was wrong? [8]I accepted pay from other churches, taking their money so I could serve you. [9]If I needed something when I was with you, I did not trouble any of you. The brothers who came from Macedonia gave me all that I needed. I did not allow myself to depend on you in any way, and I will never depend on you. [10]No one in Southern Greece will stop me from bragging about that. I say this with the truth of Christ in me. [11]And why do I not depend on you? Do you think it is because I do not love you? God knows that I love you.

[12]And I will continue doing what I am doing now, because I want to stop those people from having a reason to brag. They would like to say that the work they brag about is the same as ours. [13]Such men are not true apostles[d] but are workers who lie. They change themselves to look like apostles of Christ. [14]This does not surprise us. Even Satan changes himself to look like an angel of light.[n] [15]So it does not surprise us if Satan's servants also make themselves look like servants who work for what is right. But in the end they will be punished for what they do.

Paul Tells About His Sufferings

[16]I tell you again: No one should think I am a fool. But if you think so, accept me as you would accept a fool. Then I can brag a little, too. [17]When I brag because I feel sure of myself, I am not talking as the Lord would talk but as a fool. [18]Many people are bragging about their lives in the world. So I will brag too. [19]You are wise, so you will gladly be patient with fools! [20]You are even patient with those who order you around, or use you, or trick you, or think they are better than you, or hit you in the face. [21]It is shameful to me to say this, but we were too "weak" to do those things to you!

But if anyone else is brave enough to brag, then I also will be brave and brag. (I am talking as a fool.) [22]Are they Hebrews?[n] So am I. Are they Israelites? So am I. Are they from Abraham's family? So am I. [23]Are they serving Christ? I am serving him more. (I am crazy to talk like this.) I have

"If . . . Lord." Quotation from Jeremiah 9:24.
angel of light Messenger from God. The devil fools people so that they think he is from God.
Hebrews A name for the Jews that some Jews were very proud of.

worked much harder than they. I have been in prison more often. I have been hurt more in beatings. I have been near death many times. 24Five times the Jews have given me their punishment of thirty-nine lashes with a whip. 25Three different times I was beaten with rods. One time I was almost stoned to death. Three times I was in ships that wrecked, and one of those times I spent a night and a day in the sea. 26I have gone on many travels and have been in danger from rivers, thieves, my own people, the Jews, and those who are not Jews. I have been in danger in cities, in places where no one lives, and on the sea. And I have been in danger with false Christians. 27I have done hard and tiring work, and many times I did not sleep. I have been hungry and thirsty, and many times I have been without food. I have been cold and without clothes. 28Besides all this, there is on me every day the load of my concern for all the churches. 29I feel weak every time someone is weak, and I feel upset every time someone is led into sin.

30If I must brag, I will brag about the things that show I am weak. 31God knows I am not lying. He is the God and Father of the Lord Jesus Christ, and he is to be praised forever. 32When I was in Damascus, the governor under King Aretas wanted to arrest me, so he put guards around the city. 33But my friends lowered me in a basket through a hole in the city wall. So I escaped from the governor.

A Special Blessing in Paul's Life

12 I must continue to brag. It will do no good, but I will talk now about visions and revelations[n] from the Lord. 2I know a man in Christ who was taken up to the third heaven fourteen years ago. I do not know whether the man was in his body or out of his body, but God knows. 3-4And I know that this man was taken up to paradise.[n] I don't know if he was in his body or away from his body, but God knows. He heard things he is not able to explain, things that no human is allowed to tell. 5I will brag about a man like that, but I will not brag about myself, except about my weaknesses. 6But if I wanted to brag about myself, I would not be a fool, because I would be telling the truth. But I will not brag about myself. I do not want people to think more of me than what they see me do or hear me say.

7So that I would not become too proud of the wonderful things that were shown to me, a painful physical problem[n] was given to me. This problem was a messenger from Satan, sent to beat me and keep me from being too proud. 8I begged the Lord three times to take this problem away from me. 9But he said to me, "My grace is enough for you. When you are weak, my power is made perfect in you." So I am very happy to brag about my weaknesses. Then Christ's power can live in me. 10For this reason I am happy when I have weaknesses, insults, hard times, sufferings, and all kinds of troubles for Christ. Because when I am weak, then I am truly strong.

Paul's Love for the Christians

11I have been talking like a fool, but you made me do it. You are the ones who should say good things about me. I am worth nothing, but those "great apostles" are not worth any more than I am! 12When I was with you, I patiently did the things that prove I am an apostle[d]—signs, wonders, and miracles.[d] 13So you received everything that the other churches have received. Only one thing was different: I was not a burden to you. Forgive me for this!

14I am now ready to visit you the third time, and I will not be a burden to you. I want nothing from you, except you. Children should not have to save up to give to their parents. Parents should save to give to their children. 15So I am happy to give everything I have for you, even myself. If I love you more, will you love me less?

16It is clear I was not a burden to you, but you think I was tricky and lied to catch you. 17Did I cheat you by using any of the messengers I sent to you? No, you know I did not. 18I asked Titus to go to you, and I sent our brother with him. Titus did not cheat you, did he? No, you know that Titus and I did the same thing and with the same spirit.

19Do you think we have been defending ourselves to you all this time? We have been speaking in Christ and before God. You are our dear friends, and everything we do is to make you stronger. 20I am afraid that when I come, you will not be what I want you to be, and I will not be what you want me to be. I am afraid that among you there may be arguing, jealousy, anger, selfish fighting, evil talk, gossip, pride, and confusion. 21I am afraid that when I come to you again, my God will make me ashamed before you. I may be saddened by many of those who have sinned because they have not changed their hearts or turned from their sexual sins and the shameful things they have done.

Final Warnings and Greetings

13 I will come to you for the third time. "Every case must be proved by two or

revelations Revelation is making known a truth that was hidden.
paradise A place where good people go when they die.
painful physical problem Literally, "thorn in the flesh."

three witnesses."[n] 2When I was with you the
second time, I gave a warning to those who had
sinned. Now I am away from you, and I give a
warning to all the others. When I come to you
again, I will not be easy with them. 3You want
proof that Christ is speaking through me. My
proof is that he is not weak among you, but he is
powerful. 4It is true that he was weak when he
was killed on the cross, but he lives now by God's
power. It is true that we are weak in Christ, but
for you we will be alive in Christ by God's power.

5Look closely at yourselves. Test yourselves to
see if you are living in the faith. You know that
Jesus Christ is in you—unless you fail the test.
6But I hope you will see that we ourselves have
not failed the test. 7We pray to God that you will
not do anything wrong. It is not important to see
that we have passed the test, but it is important
that you do what is right, even if it seems we have
failed. 8We cannot do anything against the truth,
but only for the truth. 9We are happy to be weak,
if you are strong, and we pray that you will become complete. 10I am writing this while I am
away from you so that when I come I will not
have to be harsh in my use of authority. The Lord
gave me this authority to build you up, not to tear
you down.

11Now, brothers and sisters, I say good-bye.
Try to be complete. Do what I have asked you
to do. Agree with each other, and live in peace.
Then the God of love and peace will be with
you.

SIDELIGHT: *Want to start rumors in your youth group? Then put 2 Corinthians 13:12 into practice. This custom of kissing other Christians arose spontaneously in the early church, and later became a regular part of worship. It's still a custom in some Near Eastern cultures.*

12Greet each other with a holy kiss. 13All of
God's holy people send greetings to you.

14The grace of the Lord Jesus Christ, the love
of God, and the fellowship of the Holy Spirit[d] be
with you all.

"Every . . . witnesses." Quotation from Deuteronomy 19:15.

GALATIANS

Why Read This Book:

- See the dangers of listening to false teachers (Galatians 1—2).
- Discover the freedom we have through faith in Christ (Galatians 3).
- Find out how Christians should use their freedom (Galatians 5—6).

Behind the Scenes:

What do you have to do to be a Christian? Do you have to practice certain rituals? Do you have to follow certain rules?

Those were controversial questions in the early church, as we discover in Paul's letter to the Galatians. Not long before, Paul had started the churches in Galatia. But soon after he left, people began questioning his beliefs and authority. They said non-Jewish people who became Christians also had to follow Jewish laws and rituals to be true Christians—a perspective that was splitting the early church (see Acts 15, p. 1121).

When Paul heard what was happening, he wrote this letter to confront the problem. "You have already accepted the Good News. If anyone is preaching something different to you, he should be judged guilty!" he blasts in Galatians 1:9. Then Paul gets to the heart of the Christian faith. He explains that people can't do anything to earn God's promises. Those promises are free gifts for all people, to be received by faith in Christ. Instead of being the law's prisoners, Christians live in freedom.

Someone always seems to be telling us that serving God means following a long list of dos and don'ts. Paul's letter to the Galatians reminds us that being a Christian isn't a matter of what we do or don't do; it's a matter of accepting what Jesus Christ did for us. Now that's Good News!

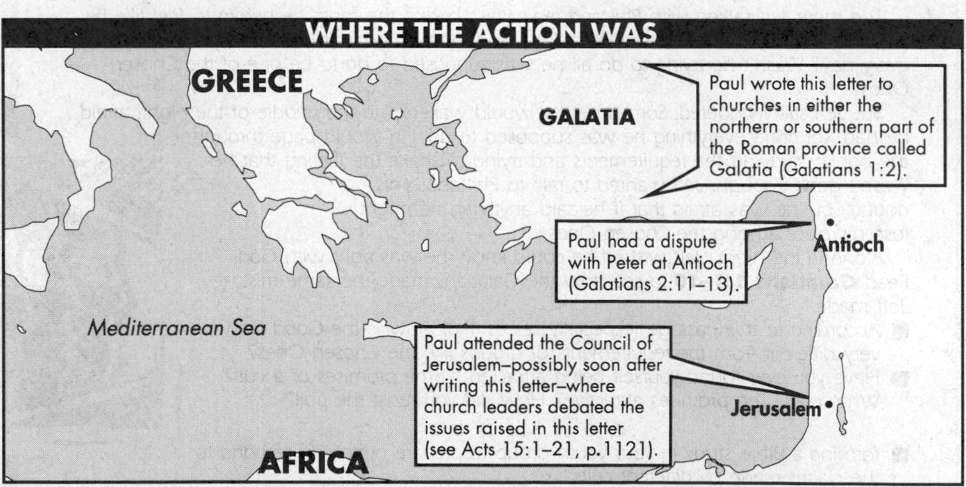
WHERE THE ACTION WAS
GREECE
GALATIA
Paul wrote this letter to churches in either the northern or southern part of the Roman province called Galatia (Galatians 1:2).
Paul had a dispute with Peter at Antioch (Galatians 2:11–13).
Antioch
Mediterranean Sea
Paul attended the Council of Jerusalem–possibly soon after writing this letter–where church leaders debated the issues raised in this letter (see Acts 15:1–21, p.1121).
Jerusalem
AFRICA

WHEN THE ACTION WAS

- BC/AD: Jesus was born
- 20AD: Jesus began his ministry
- 30AD: The church began soon after Jesus went to heaven; Paul became a Christian
- 40AD
- 50AD: Paul started churches in Galatia; Paul wrote Galatians
- 60AD: Fire destroyed Rome
- 70AD: Romans destroyed the Temple in Jerusalem

1 From Paul, an apostle.[d] I was not chosen to
be an apostle by human beings, nor was I
sent from human beings. I was made an apostle
through Jesus Christ and God the Father who
raised Jesus from the dead. 2This letter is also from
all those of God's family[n] who are with me.
To the churches in Galatia:[n]
3Grace and peace to you from God our Father
and the Lord Jesus Christ. 4Jesus gave himself for
our sins to free us from this evil world we live in,
as God the Father planned. 5The glory belongs to
God forever and ever. Amen.

The Only Good News

6God, by his grace through Christ, called you to
become his people. So I am amazed that you are
turning away so quickly and believing something
different than the Good News.[d] 7Really, there is
no other Good News. But some people are confusing you; they want to change the Good News

those . . . family The Greek text says "brothers."
Galatia Probably the same country where Paul preached and began churches on his first missionary trip. Read the book of Acts, chapters 13 and 14.

CULTS

Good News, Bad News

Jeff Davis had gone to church off and on since he was little, but he had never felt he really needed God. That is, until last summer. Nearly everything Jeff did seemed to go wrong. He got fired from his summer job, then he totaled his car. Now his dad had moved out and wanted a divorce. Jeff began to wonder if maybe he could use help with his life.

He immediately thought of Phil Rogers. Nothing seemed to faze him. He seemed to have an inside track on the supernatural. He constantly read spiritual books and encouraged other kids to read them.

So Jeff started talking with Phil during lunch. Phil had an answer for every question Jeff asked. He made everything seem so simple and clear-cut. Phil talked about what it took to be one of the "Chosen Ones"—a new religious group Phil was involved with. "Wow," Jeff thought. "This guy really knows his stuff!"

Of course, Phil explained the Bible differently than Jeff had ever heard, but Phil seemed to know what he was talking about. It all seemed so simple. All you had to do is follow a list of rules and requirements, and you would be fine.

The more Jeff talked with Phil and read Phil's books, the more he began to feel like he, too, might finally be on the inside track to God. After all, wasn't he learning new things every day? Wasn't he trying to do all he was supposed to do to be one of the Chosen Ones?

But Jeff still wondered. Sometimes he would wake up in the middle of the night, afraid he had not done everything he was supposed to do. He would page through the books, studying the requirements and trying to shake the feeling that he wasn't good enough. Jeff wanted to talk to Phil about his doubts, but he was afraid that if he said anything, he might lose his place among the Chosen Ones.

Alone in the night, Jeff wished he could know he was right with God. Read **Galatians 1:1–10** to see how the Galatians made the same mistake Jeff made.

- According to this passage (especially verses 4–6), how is the Good News very different from the requirements of groups like the Chosen Ones?
- Have you ever found yourself being attracted by the promises of a cult? What made the promises attractive? How did you resist the pull?

CONSIDER . . .

- forming a Bible study in your youth group to prepare people to respond to the claims made by different cults.
- sharing the Good News with someone in a cult. Take an older Christian with you who knows about the specific cult.

FOR MORE, SEE

- Deuteronomy 13:1–4 (p. 173)
- Matthew 7:13–20 (p. 919)
- 1 John 4:1–6 (p. 1319)

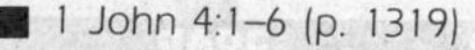

of Christ. 8We preached to you the Good News. So if we ourselves, or even an angel from heaven, should preach to you something different, we should be judged guilty! 9I said this before, and now I say it again: You have already accepted the Good News. If anyone is preaching something different to you, he should be judged guilty!

> **SIDELIGHT:** If Paul wrote Galatians early in his missionary career—as some scholars believe—it may have been the first New Testament book written, dated less than twenty years after Jesus lived. Other scholars think either 1 Thessalonians (p. 1244) or James (p. 1293) was the first book written.

10Do you think I am trying to make people accept me? No, God is the One I am trying to please. Am I trying to please people? If I still wanted to please people, I would not be a servant of Christ.

Paul's Authority Is from God

11Brothers and sisters,[n] I want you to know that the Good News[d] I preached to you was not made up by human beings. 12I did not get it from humans, nor did anyone teach it to me, but Jesus Christ showed it to me.

13You have heard about my past life in the Jewish religion. I attacked the church of God and tried to destroy it. 14I was becoming a leader in the Jewish religion, doing better than most other Jews of my age. I tried harder than anyone else to follow the teachings handed down by our ancestors.

15But God had special plans for me and set me apart for his work even before I was born. He called me through his grace 16and showed his son to me so that I might tell the Good News about him to those who are not Jewish. When God called me, I did not get advice or help from any person. 17I did not go to Jerusalem to see those who were apostles[d] before I was. But, without waiting, I went away to Arabia and later went back to Damascus.

18After three years I went to Jerusalem to meet Peter and stayed with him for fifteen days. 19I met no other apostles, except James, the brother of the Lord. 20God knows that these things I write are not lies. 21Later, I went to the areas of Syria and Cilicia.

22In Judea the churches in Christ had never met me. 23They had only heard it said, "This man who was attacking us is now preaching the same faith that he once tried to destroy." 24And these believers praised God because of me.

Other Apostles Accepted Paul

2 After fourteen years I went to Jerusalem again, this time with Barnabas. I also took Titus with me. 2I went because God showed me I should go. I met with the believers there, and in private I told their leaders the Good News[d] that I preach to the non-Jewish people. I did not want my past work and the work I am now doing to be wasted. 3Titus was with me, but he was not forced to be circumcised,[d] even though he was a Greek. 4We talked about this problem because some false believers had come into our group secretly. They came in like spies to overturn the freedom we have in Christ Jesus. They wanted to make us slaves. 5But we did not give in to those false believers for a minute. We wanted the truth of the Good News to continue for you.

6Those leaders who seemed to be important did not change the Good News that I preach. (It doesn't matter to me if they were "important" or not. To God everyone is the same.) 7But these leaders saw that I had been given the work of telling the Good News to those who are not Jewish, just as Peter had the work of telling the Jews. 8God gave Peter the power to work as an apostle[d] for the Jewish people. But he also gave me the power to work as an apostle for those who are not Jews. 9James, Peter, and John, who seemed to be the leaders, understood that God had given me this special grace, so they accepted Barnabas and me. They agreed that they would go to the Jewish people and that we should go to those who are not Jewish. 10The only thing they asked us was to remember to help the poor—something I really wanted to do.

Paul Shows that Peter Was Wrong

11When Peter came to Antioch, I challenged him to his face, because he was wrong. 12Peter ate with the non-Jewish people until some Jewish people sent from James came to Antioch. When they arrived, Peter stopped eating with those who weren't Jewish, and he separated himself from them. He was afraid of the Jews. 13So Peter was a hypocrite,[d] as were the other Jewish believers who joined with him. Even Barnabas was influenced by what these Jewish believers did. 14When I saw they were not following the truth of the Good News,[d] I spoke to Peter in front of them all.

Brothers and sisters Although the Greek text says "Brothers" here and throughout this book, Paul's words were meant for the entire church, including men and women.

I said, "Peter, you are a Jew, but you are not living
like a Jew. You are living like those who are not
Jewish. So why do you now try to force those who
are not Jewish to live like Jews?"
15 We were not born as non-Jewish "sinners,"
but as Jews. 16 Yet we know that a person is made
right with God not by following the law, but by
trusting in Jesus Christ. So we, too, have put our
faith in Christ Jesus, that we might be made right
with God because we trusted in Christ. It is not
because we followed the law, because no one
can be made right with God by following the
law.
17 We Jews came to Christ, trying to be made
right with God, and it became clear that we are
sinners, too. Does this mean that Christ encourages sin? No! 18 But I would really be wrong to
begin teaching again those things that I gave up.
19 It was the law that put me to death, and I died
to the law so that I can now live for God. 20 I was
put to death on the cross with Christ, and I do not
live anymore—it is Christ who lives in me. I still
live in my body, but I live by faith in the Son of
God who loved me and gave himself to save me.
21 By saying these things I am not going against
God's grace. Just the opposite, if the law could
make us right with God, then Christ's death
would be useless.

FAITH

You'd Better Believe It!

Pastor Crosby offered to take everyone out for pizza after Bible study. The kids cheered. Then the pastor disappeared upstairs to make a phone call.

"Did you hear that?" David asked James. "He's gonna buy us pizza!"

"There's no such thing as a free lunch, Dave. Look over there." James pointed toward a pile of brand new brooms, mops, buckets and sponges stacked against the wall. "When Crosby gets back, he's gonna tell us we've gotta clean the basement to pay for our lunch."

David had to admit James's theory made sense.

"Well, I'm starving," James continued. "If we gotta clean up, we might as well get going." He walked over and picked up one of the brooms.

"What are you guys doing?" Laura Moore asked.

"Well, what are you doing?" David asked sarcastically.

Laura was confused. "I'm waiting to go to lunch."

The boys laughed. "The sooner we get this basement cleaned, the sooner we can eat," David said, raising a storm of dust with his broom.

Laura started coughing. "You guys are making a big mess."

A few minutes later, Pastor Crosby walked into the dust storm. "What's going on down here? I thought I told you guys we were going out to lunch."

David stepped forward with a sheepish grin. "We figured you'd have us clean the basement before lunch, so we decided to get a head start."

"I just ordered pizzas at that new restaurant across town," Pastor Crosby said. "Let's go!"

James and David didn't believe their pastor's promise. Read **Galatians 2:11–21** to see how the apostle Peter didn't have faith in God's promises to him.

- How is the boys' lack of faith in their pastor's promise similar to Peter's lack of faith in God's promises?
- How have you acted like Peter in this passage and not believed God loves you and accepts you?

CONSIDER. . .

- making a list of good deeds you have done to make God love and accept you. Then tear up the list to symbolize that faith—not good deeds—earns eternal life.
- looking for "free" offers of things that really aren't free. Compare these things to God's free gift of eternal life through faith. Think about why it's hard for people to believe God's gift is really free.

FOR MORE, SEE. . .

- Genesis 15:1–6 (p. 16)
- Romans 3:21–31 (p. 1143)
- Ephesians 2:4–10 (p. 1219)

Blessing Comes Through Faith

3 You people in Galatia were told very clearly
about the death of Jesus Christ on the cross.
But you were foolish; you let someone trick you.
2Tell me this one thing: How did you receive the
Holy Spirit?[d] Did you receive the Spirit by following the law? No, you received the Spirit because
you heard the Good News[d] and believed it. 3You
began your life in Christ by the Spirit. Now are
you trying to make it complete by your own
power? That is foolish. 4Were all your experiences
wasted? I hope not! 5Does God give you the Spirit
and work miracles[d] among you because you follow the law? No, he does these things because
you heard the Good News and believed it.

6The Scriptures[d] say the same thing about Abraham: "Abraham believed God, and God accepted
Abraham's faith, and that faith made him right
with God."[n] 7So you should know that the true
children of Abraham are those who have faith.
8The Scriptures, telling what would happen in the
future, said that God would make the non-Jewish
people right through their faith. This Good News
was told to Abraham beforehand, as the Scripture
says: "All nations will be blessed through you."[n]
9So all who believe as Abraham believed are
blessed just as Abraham was. 10But those who depend on following the law to make them right are
under a curse, because the Scriptures say, "Any
one will be cursed who does not always obey
what is written in the Book of the Law."[n] 11Now
it is clear that no one can be made right with God
by the law, because the Scriptures say, "Those
who are right with God will live by trusting in
him."[n] 12The law is not based on faith. It says, "A
person who obeys these things will live because
of them."[n] 13Christ took away the curse the law
put on us. He changed places with us and put
himself under that curse. It is written in the Scriptures, "Anyone whose body is displayed on a
tree[n] is cursed." 14Christ did this so that God's
blessing promised to Abraham might come
through Jesus Christ to those who are not Jews.
Jesus died so that by our believing we could receive the Spirit that God promised.

The Law and the Promise

15Brothers and sisters, let us think in human
terms: Even an agreement made between two
persons is firm. After that agreement is accepted
by both people, no one can stop it or add anything
to it. 16God made promises both to Abraham and
to his descendant.[d] God did not say, "and to your
descendants." That would mean many people.
But God said, "and to your descendant." That
means only one person; that person is Christ.
17This is what I mean: God had an agreement
with Abraham and promised to keep it. The law,
which came four hundred thirty years later, cannot change that agreement and so destroy God's
promise to Abraham. 18If the law could give us
Abraham's blessing, then the promise would not
be necessary. But that is not possible, because
God freely gave his blessings to Abraham through
the promise he had made.

19So what was the law for? It was given to
show that the wrong things people do are against
God's will. And it continued until the special
descendant, who had been promised, came. The
law was given through angels who used Moses for
a mediator[n] to give the law to people. 20But a
mediator is not needed when there is only one
side, and God is only one.

The Purpose of the Law of Moses

21Does this mean that the law is against God's
promises? Never! That would be true only if the
law could make us right. But God did not give a
law that can bring life. 22Instead, the Scriptures[d]
showed that the whole world is bound by sin.
This was so the promise would be given through
faith to people who believe in Jesus Christ.

> **SIDELIGHT:** The Greek word translated "guardian" in Galatians 3:24 could almost be translated "babysitter." It refers to the person—usually a slave—who was responsible for taking care of young children (see also Galatians 4:1–7, p. 1210). Possibly half of the population of the Roman Empire were slaves during New Testament times.

23Before this faith came, we were all held prisoners by the law. We had no freedom until God
showed us the way of faith that was coming. 24In
other words, the law was our guardian leading us
to Christ so that we could be made right with God
through faith. 25Now the way of faith has come,
and we no longer live under a guardian.

"Abraham . . . God." Quotation from Genesis 15:6.
"All . . . you." Quotation from Genesis 12:3 and 18:18.
"Anyone . . . Law." Quotation from Deuteronomy 27:26.
"Those . . . him." Quotation from Habakkuk 2:4.
"A person . . . them." Quotation from Leviticus 18:5.
displayed on a tree Deuteronomy 21:22-23 says that when a person was killed for doing wrong, the body was hung on a tree to show shame. Paul means that the cross of Jesus was like that.
mediator A person who helps one person talk to or give something to another person.

[26-27]You were all baptized into Christ, and so
you were all clothed with Christ. This means that
you are all children of God through faith in Christ
Jesus. [28]In Christ, there is no difference between
Jew and Greek, slave and free person, male and
female. You are all the same in Christ Jesus. [29]You
belong to Christ, so you are Abraham's descendants.[d] You will inherit all of God's blessings because of the promise God made to Abraham.

4 I want to tell you this: While those who will
inherit their fathers' property are still children, they are no different from slaves. It does not
matter that the children own everything. [2]While
they are children, they must obey those who are
chosen to care for them. But when the children
reach the age set by their fathers, they are free. [3]It
is the same for us. We were once like children,
slaves to the useless rules of this world. [4]But
when the right time came, God sent his Son who
was born of a woman and lived under the law.
[5]God did this so he could buy freedom for those
who were under the law and so we could become
his children.

[6]Since you are God's children, God sent the
Spirit of his Son into your hearts, and the Spirit[d]
cries out, "Father."[n] [7]So now you are not a slave;
you are God's child, and God will give you the
blessing he promised, because you are his child.

"Father" Literally, "Abba, Father." Jewish children called their fathers "Abba."

JUDGING OTHERS

Inside Out

In this corner: Harold Milburn, Sunday school superintendent, board member, businessman. Gray suit and tie, starched shirt, thick glasses.

In that corner: Josh Kincaid, would-be radical, always off on some wild project to save the world, usually involving loud music. Orange-dyed mohawk, ripped jeans, T-shirt, earring.

Mohawk sizes up Starched Shirt. "He'll turn me down before I even ask. Old people are like that. Narrow-minded, afraid of anything new."

Starched Shirt sizes up Mohawk: "Oh, boy. Here we go. Another crazy idea. And if I say no, he'll call me old-fashioned."

"Hi, Josh. What's up?"

"We want to fix up the old fellowship hall for a place to have a weekly Bible study."

Starched Shirt frowns.

So does Mohawk. "I knew it," he thinks. "You think anybody who doesn't look like you can't be trusted."

"Hmmm," Starched Shirt muses. "These kids sure dress funny, but their hearts are in the right place."

"Sounds like a great idea to me," Starched Shirt finally says. "What's your first topic?"

Mohawk is down for the count. "Uh, the importance of prayer," he manages to get out.

"Now there's a subject I could always use some help with," Starched Shirt says.

"Well, Mr. Milburn," Mohawk grins, "why don't you join us sometime?"

Though people may be different on the outside, they are the same in Jesus Christ. Read this truth in **Galatians 3:23–29**.

- How are Starched Shirt and Mohawk—or as it says in this passage, a Jew and a Greek—no different in Christ?
- What criteria besides what is in this passage have you used to judge another Christian?

CONSIDER . . .

- tearing out pictures of five people from a magazine. On each picture, write five preconceptions you have about people like that person. Check your perceptions by getting to know people in each category.
- visiting a church with a different culture. For example, if you are from a Spanish-speaking church, visit a Vietnamese church.

FOR MORE, SEE . . .

- 1 Samuel 16:1–13 (p. 258)
- Romans 2:28–29 (p. 1142)
- 2 Corinthians 5:11–12 (p. 1197)

Paul's Love for the Christians

[8]In the past you did not know God. You were
slaves to gods that were not real. [9]But now you
know the true God. Really, it is God who knows
you. So why do you turn back to those weak and
useless rules you followed before? Do you want to
be slaves to those things again? [10]You still follow
teachings about special days, months, seasons,
and years. [11]I am afraid for you, that my work for
you has been wasted.
[12]Brothers and sisters, I became like you, so I
beg you to become like me. You were very good
to me before. [13]You remember that it was because
of an illness that I came to you the first time,
preaching the Good News.[d] [14]Though my sickness was a trouble for you, you did not hate me
or make me leave. But you welcomed me as an
angel from God, as if I were Jesus Christ himself!
[15]You were very happy then, but where is that joy
now? I am ready to testify that you would have
taken out your eyes and given them to me if that
were possible. [16]Now am I your enemy because
I tell you the truth?
[17]Those people[n] are working hard to persuade

Those people They are the false teachers who were bothering the believers in Galatia (Galatians 1:7).

GOD'S LOVE

Too Good to Be True?

"Yours Free! Just Call and Claim Your Prize! No Obligation!" It was a once-in-a-lifetime offer that Jackie Sondheim couldn't refuse when it arrived in the mail.

Sure, Jackie had heard that some of these offers were scams. But this looked like a sure bet. It guaranteed she would get "a luxurious fur coat" or a "limited edition Mercedes sports car with all the extras."

"Everyone's a winner" the card boasted. "Call now to learn what you won!"

"What could it hurt," Jackie thought to herself, picking up the phone.

Sure enough, she had won! The fur coat was being packed for her. And, the contest's agent asked if she would also consider another special offer. For only $395 (charge it, if you like), she could receive beauty tips from "the nation's foremost beauty experts" in an exclusive newsletter for teenage girls called "Lookin' Good."

Plus, she would have access to a toll-free "Looks Line." She could call the number any time, day or night, and receive personal consultations on anything from shoes to eye shadow—for the rest of her life. It was just a one-time fee, Jackie told herself. And it was good for a lifetime. So she placed her order with her mom's credit card.

Jackie's excitement turned to displeasure when she received the genuine dyed rabbit fur coat. She knew she had been taken when the one-page "Lookin' Good" newsletter arrived, complete with revolutionary beauty tips such as "thoroughly wash your face each night before going to bed."

Something that had seemed like a dream just a few days earlier now seemed like a nightmare. It had sounded too good to be true. And it was.

All around us are too-good-to-be-true offers. Most are hoaxes. **Galatians 4:4–7** tells about an offer of God's love that seems too good to be true, but really is true!

- What differences do you see between the once-in-a-lifetime offer Jackie fell for and the once-for-all-times offer of God's love that's described in the passage?
- What parts of God's offer of love are most appealing to you? How have you responded to that offer?

CONSIDER . . .

- using the form and style of a junk-mail offer to write a postcard about God's offer of love. Send it to a friend who needs some encouragement.
- talking to a friend who was adopted about what it feels like to be specially chosen by parents. Discuss similarities and differences between that experience and the experience of being a child of God.

FOR MORE, SEE . . .

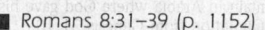

- Isaiah 64:8–9 (p. 685)
- Matthew 7:7–11 (p. 919)
- Romans 8:31–39 (p. 1152)

you, but this is not good for you. They want
to persuade you to turn against us and follow
only them. 18It is good for people to show
interest in you, but only if their purpose is
good. This is always true, not just when I am
with you. 19My little children, again I feel the
pain of childbirth for you until you truly become like Christ. 20I wish I could be with you
now and could change the way I am talking
to you, because I do not know what to think
about you.

The Example of Hagar and Sarah

21Some of you still want to be under the law.
Tell me, do you know what the law says? 22The
Scriptures[d] say that Abraham had two sons. The
mother of one son was a slave woman, and the
mother of the other son was a free woman.
23Abraham's son from the slave woman was born
in the normal human way. But the son from the
free woman was born because of the promise God
made to Abraham.

24This story teaches something else: The two
women are like the two agreements between God
and his people. One agreement is the law that
God made on Mount Sinai,[n] and the people
who are under this agreement are like slaves. The
mother named Hagar is like that agreement. 25She
is like Mount Sinai in Arabia and is a picture of the
earthly Jewish city of Jerusalem. This city and its
people, the Jews, are slaves to the law. 26But the
heavenly Jerusalem, which is above, is like the
free woman. She is our mother. 27It is written in
the Scriptures:

"Be happy, Jerusalem.
You are like a woman who never gave
birth to children.
Start singing and shout for joy.
You never felt the pain of giving birth,
but you will have more children
than the woman who has a husband."

Isaiah 54:1

28My brothers and sisters, you are God's children because of his promise, as Isaac was then.
29The son who was born in the normal way
treated the other son badly. It is the same today.
30But what does the Scripture say? "Throw out
the slave woman and her son. The son of the slave
woman should not inherit anything. The son of
the free woman should receive it all."[n] 31So, my
brothers and sisters, we are not children of the
slave woman, but of the free woman.

Keep Your Freedom

5 We have freedom now, because Christ made
us free. So stand strong. Do not change and
go back into the slavery of the law. 2Listen, I Paul
tell you that if you go back to the law by being
circumcised,[d] Christ does you no good. 3Again, I
warn every man: If you allow yourselves to be
circumcised, you must follow all the law. 4If you
try to be made right with God through the law,
your life with Christ is over—you have left God's
grace. 5But we have the true hope that comes
from being made right with God, and by the Spirit
we wait eagerly for this hope. 6When we are in
Christ Jesus, it is not important if we are circumcised or not. The important thing is faith—the
kind of faith that works through love.

SIDELIGHT: Circumcision (Galatians 5:2–6) was an important ritual for Jews, symbolizing bringing a baby boy into God's family. A festive occasion marked each circumcision, which was usually performed by the boy's father.

7You were running a good race. Who stopped
you from following the true way? 8This change
did not come from the One who chose you. 9Be
careful! "Just a little yeast makes the whole batch
of dough rise." 10But I trust in the Lord that you
will not believe those different ideas. Whoever is
confusing you with such ideas will be punished.

11My brothers and sisters, I do not teach that a
man must be circumcised. If I teach circumcision,
why am I still being attacked? If I still taught circumcision, my preaching about the cross would
not be a problem. 12I wish the people who are
bothering you would castrate[n] themselves!

13My brothers and sisters, God called you to be
free, but do not use your freedom as an excuse to
do what pleases your sinful self. Serve each other
with love. 14The whole law is made complete in
this one command: "Love your neighbor as you
love yourself."[n] 15If you go on hurting each other
and tearing each other apart, be careful, or you
will completely destroy each other.

The Spirit and Human Nature

16So I tell you: Live by following the Spirit.[d]
Then you will not do what your sinful selves
want. 17Our sinful selves want what is against the

Mount Sinai Mountain in Arabia where God gave his laws to Moses (Exodus 19 and 20).
"Throw . . . all." Quotation from Genesis 21:10.
castrate To cut off part of the male sex organ. Paul uses this word because it is similar to "circumcision." Paul wanted to show that he is very upset with the false teachers.
"Love . . . yourself." Quotation from Leviticus 19:18.

Spirit, and the Spirit wants what is against our
sinful selves. The two are against each other, so
you cannot do just what you please. [18]But if
the Spirit is leading you, you are not under the
law.
[19]The wrong things the sinful self does are
clear: being sexually unfaithful, not being pure,
taking part in sexual sins, [20]worshiping gods, doing witchcraft,[d] hating, making trouble, being
jealous, being angry, being selfish, making people
angry with each other, causing divisions among
people, [21]feeling envy, being drunk, having wild
and wasteful parties, and doing other things like
these. I warn you now as I warned you before:
Those who do these things will not inherit God's
kingdom. [22]But the Spirit produces the fruit of
love, joy, peace, patience, kindness, goodness,
faithfulness, [23]gentleness, self-control. There is no
law that says these things are wrong. [24]Those who
belong to Christ Jesus have crucified their own
sinful selves. They have given up their old selfish
feelings and the evil things they wanted to do.
[25]We get our new life from the Spirit, so we
should follow the Spirit. [26]We must not be proud
or make trouble with each other or be jealous of
each other.

Help Each Other

6 Brothers and sisters, if someone in your
group does something wrong, you who are
spiritual should go to that person and gently help
make him right again. But be careful, because you
might be tempted to sin, too. [2]By helping each
other with your troubles, you truly obey the law
of Christ. [3]If anyone thinks he is important when
he really is not, he is only fooling himself. [4]Each
person should judge his own actions and not compare himself with others. Then he can be proud
for what he himself has done. [5]Each person must
be responsible for himself.

SERVICE

Free to Serve

The 1970s. "Feathered" hair, disco, the Bee Gees.

And Watergate.

The scandal of Watergate led to the first resignation by an American president since the nation was founded. It was a turbulent time, full of suspicion, intrigue, distrust, and power-hungry leaders. In the middle of it was Charles W. Colson.

Chuck Colson was a presidential aide for Richard Nixon. He was one of several White House personnel who were sentenced to prison for their involvement in the Watergate scandal. Colson served seven months.

Before he was sent to prison, Colson became a Christian. And while in prison, he saw firsthand the tremendous obstacles facing prisoners, ex-prisoners, and their families. "Rather than rehabilitating, prisons have become breeding grounds for crime," he says.

After his release from prison, Colson could have done like many people. He could have forgotten about his prison experience and gone on with his life. But he chose not to forget. He founded Prison Fellowship, a Christian outreach to inmates. Today, Colson regularly visits prisons and works for prison reform in the United States and in countries around the world.

Because of Colson's organization, nearly forty thousand volunteers work in more than six hundred prisons in the United States alone. His dedicated concern has resulted in the changed lives of thousands of inmates and families.

Chuck Colson turned his freedom into an opportunity to help those in prison. **Galatians 5:13–26** talks about the relationship between freedom and service. Read the passage to discover why God sets people free.

- How does Colson's choice to serve prisoners reflect this passage?
- How have you used your freedom in Christ as an avenue to serve others?

C O N S I D E R . . .

- using some of your "free time" to serve other people.
- becoming a pen pal with a prison inmate, or contacting Prison Fellowship, Box 17500, Washington, DC 20041, to see how you can serve in your area.

F O R M O R E , S E E . . .

- Leviticus 19:17–18 (p. 116)
- 1 Corinthians 10:23–24 (p. 1180)
- Philippians 2:4–7 (p. 1230)

[6]Anyone who is learning the teaching of God should share all the good things he has with his teacher.

Life Is like Planting a Field

[7]Do not be fooled: You cannot cheat God. People harvest only what they plant. [8]If they plant to satisfy their sinful selves, their sinful selves will bring them ruin. But if they plant to please the Spirit,[d] they will receive eternal life from the Spirit. [9]We must not become tired of doing good. We will receive our harvest of eternal life at the right time if we do not give up. [10]When we have the opportunity to help anyone, we should do it. But we should give special attention to those who are in the family of believers.

Paul Ends His Letter

[11]See what large letters I use to write this myself. [12]Some people are trying to force you to be circumcised[d] so the Jews will accept them. They are afraid they will be attacked if they follow only

SIDELIGHT: Paul may have had a lot to say, but he probably didn't have good handwriting (Galatians 6:11). From Galatians 4:13–15 (p. 1211), some scholars think he might have had poor eyesight, because he thanks them for their generosity in being willing to take out their eyes and give them to him.

FRIENDS

When Friends Fail

Scott Perkins couldn't believe his eyes. There was Jason Haas, smoking a cigarette and laughing with the rest of the lunchtime crowd in the student parking lot.

"Didn't I tell you he was a phony?" Denise Rambo whispered. "I wish he'd stop coming to church altogether and hang out with his real friends."

"Hmmm," Scott thought. "I wonder what's going on here."

The next morning, he bumped into Jason between classes. "Wanna grab a burger for lunch?" Scott asked.

Jason looked down. "I don't think so."

Scott put his hand on Jason's shoulder. "Hey, you haven't been yourself lately. I wish we could talk about it."

Jason brushed him off. "I know what you want to talk about—you and Denise and everyone else. You're gonna be all nice and buy me a burger and then jump all over my case for being a big, bad sinner. Well, I don't want to hear it."

He turned to leave, but Scott grabbed his arm. "Wait a second. Number one, you're no bigger or worse a sinner than I am. Number two, I know if I suddenly had a total personality change I'd want my friends to investigate. And number three, you're buying your own burger."

Jason smiled. "Okay. You win. There are a couple of things I wouldn't mind talking about. And you're probably the only guy I know who'd care enough to listen."

Scott understood what it meant to be a real friend. Read **Galatians 6:1–10** to learn about the responsibilities of Christian friendship.

- Who most closely lived out this scripture: Scott or Denise?
- When have you acted out this scripture to help a fellow Christian who's done something wrong? When has another Christian gently corrected you? What were the results of either time?

CONSIDER...

- developing a friendship with an older Christian. Discuss your own areas of weakness with your new friend and ask him or her to help you avoid stumbling into sin.
- starting a prayer group with your friends. Discuss ways to draw closer and watch out for one another.

FOR MORE, SEE...

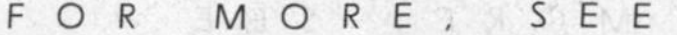

- Proverbs 27:6, 9–10 (p. 591)
- Luke 22:31–32 (p. 1049)
- Hebrews 10:24–25 (p. 1286)

the cross of Christ.[n] 13Those who are circumcised do not obey the law themselves, but they
want you to be circumcised so they can brag
about what they forced you to do. 14I hope I
will never brag about things like that. The cross
of our Lord Jesus Christ is my only reason for
bragging. Through the cross of Jesus my world
was crucified, and I died to the world. 15It is
not important if a man is circumcised or uncircumcised. The important thing is being the
new people God has made. 16Peace and mercy to
those who follow this rule—and to all of God's
people.

17So do not give me any more trouble. I have
scars on my body that show[n] I belong to Christ
Jesus.

18My brothers and sisters, the grace of our Lord
Jesus Christ be with your spirit. Amen.

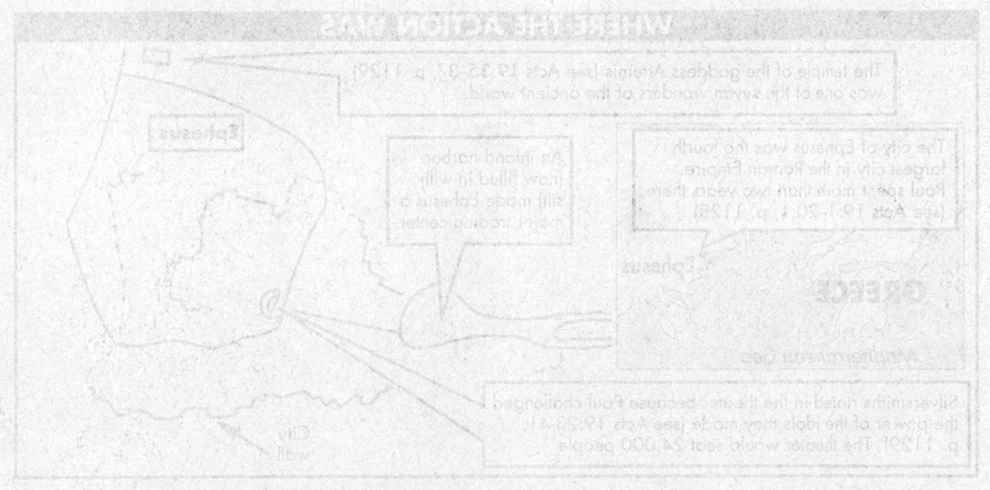

cross of Christ Paul uses the cross as a picture of the gospel, the story of Christ's death and rising from the dead to pay for our sins. The cross, or Christ's death, was God's way to save us.

that show Many times Paul was beaten and whipped by people who were against him because he was teaching about Christ. The scars were from these beatings.

EPHESIANS

Why Read This Book:

- Discover the blessings we have because we belong to Christ (Ephesians 1—3).
- Learn how to be united in our relationships with others (Ephesians 4—6:4).
- Gather the armor you need to follow God (Ephesians 6:10–20).

Behind the Scenes:

Has anything ever happened to you that was so great that you couldn't help but burst into song? When you read the book of Ephesians, you get the feeling the author felt that way about being a Christian.

The book is like a grand musical celebration of the Christian faith. It sings about God, Christ, human redemption, the church, God's power, and unity in Christ. Many people describe it as the climax of the New Testament.

Probably intended for several churches in Asia, including Ephesus, the book focuses on God's eternal purpose in establishing the universal church on earth. No matter what their background or nationality, all people are called to become part of Christ's body, which is both a privilege and a responsibility.

The first part of the book (Ephesians 1—3) uses prayers and praise to describe God's plan to unite all things in Christ. The second part (Ephesians 4—6) describes Christians' role in fulfilling God's plan.

As Christians, we come from various backgrounds, and attend different churches. Yet we share in the same blessings from God, and are called to live our lives according to Christ's example.

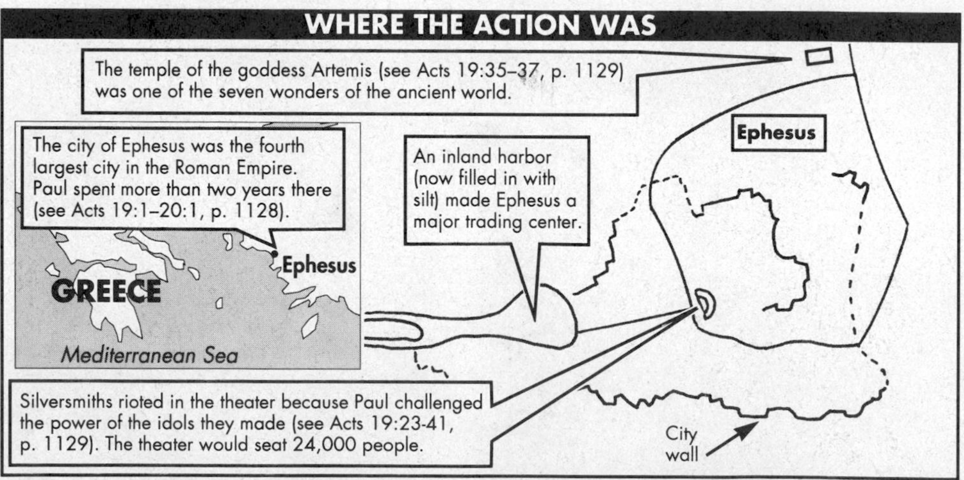

WHERE THE ACTION WAS
The temple of the goddess Artemis (see Acts 19:35–37, p. 1129) was one of the seven wonders of the ancient world.
The city of Ephesus was the fourth largest city in the Roman Empire. Paul spent more than two years there (see Acts 19:1–20:1, p. 1128).
An inland harbor (now filled in with silt) made Ephesus a major trading center.
Ephesus
Ephesus
GREECE
Mediterranean Sea
Silversmiths rioted in the theater because Paul challenged the power of the idols they made (see Acts 19:23-41, p. 1129). The theater would seat 24,000 people.
City wall

WHEN THE ACTION WAS

Jesus was born	The church began soon after Jesus went to heaven	Paul began his missionary work	Paul may have written Ephesians in prison	Fire destroyed Rome

BC/AD — 20AD — 30AD — 40AD — 50AD — 60AD — 70AD

Jesus began his ministry	Paul became a Christian	Paul worked in Ephesus for more than two years	Romans destroyed the Temple in Jerusalem

1 From Paul, an apostle[d] of Christ Jesus. I am
an apostle because that is what God wanted.
To God's holy people living in Ephesus, believers in Christ Jesus:
2Grace and peace to you from God our Father
and the Lord Jesus Christ.

Spiritual Blessings in Christ

3Praise be to the God and Father of our Lord
Jesus Christ. In Christ, God has given us every
spiritual blessing in the heavenly world. 4That is,
in Christ, he chose us before the world was made
so that we would be his holy people—people
without blame before him. 5Because of his love,
God had already decided to make us his own children through Jesus Christ. That was what he
wanted and what pleased him, 6and it brings
praise to God because of his wonderful grace. God
gave that grace to us freely, in Christ, the One he
loves. 7In Christ we are set free by the blood of
his death, and so we have forgiveness of sins.
How rich is God's grace, 8which he has given to
us so fully and freely. God, with full wisdom and
understanding, 9let us know his secret purpose.
This was what God wanted, and he planned to do
it through Christ. 10His goal was to carry out his
plan, when the right time came, that all things in

FORGIVENESS

Putting Up Bail

"Now I've done it," Bob Logan thought as he slammed his fist into the dashboard. The nose of his car was buried in someone's hedge, and red and blue lights were flashing in his rear-view mirror.

To make matters worse, Bob had been drinking. He hoped the police officer would be kind. More than that, he hoped his dad would be. This was the third time this year Bob had wrecked his car, and he figured his dad would explode when he found out.

Bob was arrested and allowed one phone call home. His mother cried as he told her what had happened. No one bailed Bob out; he spent the night in jail. He thought he would never be able to face his parents again.

In the morning, an officer yelled at Bob to get up and follow him. Bob left the stench of the cell and stepped into the white light of the police station. The first person Bob saw was his dad, standing with his hat in his hands, looking at the floor.

"Thanks . . ." Bob started and then stopped, unsure of how his dad would react. His dad looked up, and Bob saw the compassion in his eyes.

"Come on, Son," he said, "let's get out of here."

As they walked out of the station, Bob tried to explain. "Dad, I'm so sorry. It'll never happen again. I promise."

"Bob, you've made some big mistakes—mistakes that could've killed you," his dad responded.

Bob tried to speak, but his dad stopped him. "Son, I love you, and we're going to get through this together."

Although Bob's father forgave him, Bob still suffered some heavy consequences: He lost his license for ninety days, and it took him six months to repay the bail money. But Bob's relationship with his dad remained strong.

Being forgiven by his dad set Bob free. **Ephesians 1:1–10** describes how our Heavenly Father has set us free.

- How is Bob's experience of forgiveness like the forgiveness described in this passage? How is it different?
- According to this passage, what are the benefits of God's forgiveness to those who are in Christ?

C O N S I D E R . . .

- forgiving someone and setting that person free.
- making a card that says "Christians Aren't Perfect, Just Forgiven." Put it by your bed and think about its meaning each time you see it this week.

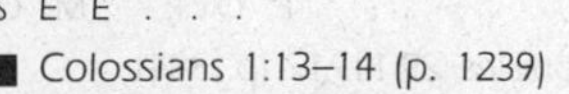

F O R M O R E , S E E . . .

- Psalm 103 (p. 540)
- Romans 3:21–26 (p. 1143)
- Colossians 1:13–14 (p. 1239)

heaven and on earth would be joined together in
Christ as the head.

> **SIDELIGHT:** Many scholars believe this letter was originally circulated among many churches, since the earliest manuscripts do not include the words "in Ephesus" in Ephesians 1:1. In the second century A.D., one source called this letter the "letter to the Laodiceans"—another city in Asia Minor.

11 In Christ we were chosen to be God's people,
because from the very beginning God had decided
this in keeping with his plan. And he is the One
who makes everything agree with what he decides and wants. 12 We are the first people who
hoped in Christ, and we were chosen so that we
would bring praise to God's glory. 13 So it is with
you. When you heard the true teaching—the
Good News[d] about your salvation—you believed
in Christ. And in Christ, God put his special mark
of ownership on you by giving you the Holy
Spirit[d] that he had promised. 14 That Holy Spirit is
the guarantee that we will receive what God
promised for his people until God gives full freedom to those who are his—to bring praise to
God's glory.

Paul's Prayer

15 That is why since I heard about your faith in
the Lord Jesus and your love for all God's people,
16 I have not stopped giving thanks to God for you.
I always remember you in my prayers, 17 asking
the God of our Lord Jesus Christ, the glorious Father, to give you a spirit of wisdom and revelation[d] so that you will know him better. 18 I pray
also that you will have greater understanding in
your heart so you will know the hope to which he
has called us and that you will know how rich and
glorious are the blessings God has promised his
holy people. 19 And you will know that God's

GOD'S POWER

Batteries Included

Tony DeFazio might never have turned around except for the ministry of Richard Parks. A street kid, Tony ran away from his home in Newport, Oregon, when he was only eleven years old. He lived on handouts for a while but soon found that selling drugs earned him a better living. He was in and out of various homes and schools for seven years.

Then when he was eighteen, he met Richard on a street corner in Portland. Richard, a reformed street kid himself, was dedicated to getting kids off the streets through his work in an inner-city church. Richard found Tony a place to live and helped him get a job in a nearby gas station. He helped turn Tony around.

Tony was just one of many kids whom Richard reached with his love. When the local police heard about Richard's ministry, they asked how they could get involved. They figured their additional resources would expand the program, add energy and make it more effective.

After learning about the program, one officer remarked: "That's great. We'd be glad to help. But can we leave out the stuff about Jesus?"

Overhearing the question, Tony replied: "Hey man, you might as well take out the batteries. Jesus is what makes it work!"

Tony knew God's power was what had changed his life. This same power is available to all Christians, as we read in **Ephesians 1:15–23**.

- According to this passage, how is God's power different from earthly powers?
- How does this passage say to tap into God's power supply?

CONSIDER . . .

- writing a radio commercial announcing the benefits of God's power. Read the commercial to a friend or family member.
- applying God's power to your life in an area in which you have felt weak. Pray and work together with God to change that weakness.

FOR MORE, SEE . . .

- 1 Chronicles 29:11–12 (p. 384)
- Acts 1:7–8 (p. 1098)
- Ephesians 3:20–21 (p. 1222)

power is very great for us who believe. That
power is the same as the great strength 20God
used to raise Christ from the dead and put him at
his right side in the heavenly world. 21God has put
Christ over all rulers, authorities, powers, and
kings, not only in this world but also in the next.
22God put everything under his power and made
him the head over everything for the church,
23which is Christ's body. The church is filled with
Christ, and Christ fills everything in every way.

We Now Have Life

2 In the past you were spiritually dead because
of your sins and the things you did against
God. 2Yes, in the past you lived the way the world
lives, following the ruler of the evil powers that
are above the earth. That same spirit is now working in those who refuse to obey God. 3In the past
all of us lived like them, trying to please our sinful
selves and doing all the things our bodies and
minds wanted. We should have suffered God's
anger because of the way we were. We were the
same as all other people.

4But God's mercy is great, and he loved us very
much. 5Though we were spiritually dead because
of the things we did against God, he gave us new
life with Christ. You have been saved by God's
grace. 6And he raised us up with Christ and gave
us a seat with him in the heavens. He did this for
those in Christ Jesus 7so that for all future time he
could show the very great riches of his grace by
being kind to us in Christ Jesus. 8I mean that you
have been saved by grace through believing. You
did not save yourselves; it was a gift from God. 9It
was not the result of your own efforts, so you can-

PEACE

Enemy in My House

Ellie Gamble and her father were best friends. She had always run to him when she was hurt. But when Ellie was in junior high, everything changed. Her father began spending more time away from home. And when he was home, he and Ellie's mother fought all the time.

One day after school, Ellie found her mother lying across her bed, crying. The closet doors hung open, and her father's clothes were gone. Ellie's father had been having an affair and had moved out. Ellie couldn't believe it. She felt betrayed. How could her dad walk out on her like this?

Within three months, Ellie's parents were together, trying to restore their marriage. But Ellie couldn't see herself loving her father again. She avoided him. She even put a "No Men Allowed" sign on her bedroom door.

When Ellie went away to college, she was relieved to get away from the tense relationship with her dad. But during her freshman year, she heard the gospel and decided to follow Christ.

Her life began to change. She realized God wanted to rebuild her relationship with her dad. While home one weekend, Ellie cried as she told her dad she forgave him and asked him to forgive her.

From that point on, there was peace in Ellie's home—the kind of peace that made her homesick for time with her father.

God's love brought peace between Ellie and her dad. Read **Ephesians 2:4–22** to see how Christ also broke down the walls and established peace between the Jews and those who were not Jews.

- How was Ellie's broken relationship with her dad like the broken relationship between Jewish and non-Jewish people? How was it different?
- How can Christ break down walls of hatred between you and other people you know?

CONSIDER. . .

- asking God to reveal any walls in your relationships that need to be broken down.
- making peace with someone from whom you feel separated by giving that person a brick or rock and explaining that you want to break down the "wall" between you.

FOR MORE, SEE. . .

- Psalm 120:6–7 (p. 554)
- Romans 9 (p. 1153)
- Hebrews 12:14–15 (p. 1290)

not brag about it. [10]God has made us what we are. In Christ Jesus, God made us to do good works, which God planned in advance for us to live our lives doing.

One in Christ

[11]You were not born Jewish. You are the people the Jews call "uncircumcised."[n] Those who call you "uncircumcised" call themselves "circumcised."[d] (Their circumcision is only something they themselves do on their bodies.) [12]Remember that in the past you were without Christ. You were not citizens of Israel, and you had no part in the agreements[n] with the promise that God made to his people. You had no hope, and you did not know God. [13]But now in Christ Jesus, you who were far away from God are brought near through the blood of Christ's death. [14]Christ himself is our peace. He made both Jewish people and those who are not Jews one people. They were separated as if there were a wall between them, but Christ broke down that wall of hate by giving his own body. [15]The Jewish law had many commands and rules, but Christ ended that law. His purpose was to make the two groups of people become one new people in him and in this way make peace. [16]It was also Christ's purpose to end the hatred between the two groups, to make them into one body, and to bring them back to God. Christ did all this with his death on the cross. [17]Christ came and preached peace to you who were far away from God, and to those who were near to God. [18]Yes, it is through Christ we all have the right to come to the Father in one Spirit.[d]

[19]Now you who are not Jewish are not foreigners or strangers any longer, but are citizens together with God's holy people. You belong to God's family. [20]You are like a building that was built on the foundation of the apostles[d] and prophets.[d] Christ Jesus himself is the most important stone[n] in that building, [21]and that whole building is joined together in Christ. He makes it grow and become a holy temple in the Lord. [22]And in Christ you, too, are being built together with the Jews into a place where God lives through the Spirit.

uncircumcised People not having the mark of circumcision as the Jews had.
agreements The agreements that God gave to his people in the Old Testament.
most important stone Literally, "cornerstone." The first and most important stone in a building.

GOD'S LOVE

Unbelievable!

Imagine that the thickness of the page you are reading is the distance from Earth to the sun (93 million miles). With this scale, consider the following:

- The distance to the nearest star in our galaxy would be a 71-foot-high stack of paper.
- The diameter of our own galaxy (100,000 light years) would be a 310-mile stack.
- The edge of our known universe would be a 31 million-mile pile of paper.

And that's just the beginning! Astronomers tell us our galaxy is a family of more than 100 billion stars and that there are as many as 100 billion other galaxies in the universe. Each of these galaxies may have hundreds of millions of planets like our Earth.

Unfathomable? Incomprehensible? Beyond understanding?

Yes. But something even more vast than the universe is God's love for us. Read Paul's prayer in **Ephesians 3:14–21** to see how great God's love is.

- How accurate a comparison is God's love to the universe?
- How does knowing that God's love for you has no limits affect you?

CONSIDER . . .

- making a sign about God's love for you. Hang it where you will see it each morning, and remember that God's love for you has no limits.
- gazing at the stars on a clear night. For each star you see, thank God for a way he has shown his love for you.

FOR MORE, SEE . . .

- Psalm 36:5–10 (p. 502)
- John 13:34–35 ((p. 1083)
- Romans 8:35–39 (p. 1152)

Paul's Work in Telling the Good News

3 So I, Paul, am a prisoner of Christ Jesus for
you who are not Jews. 2Surely you have
heard that God gave me this work through his
grace to help you. 3He let me know his secret by
showing it to me. I have already written a little
about this. 4If you read what I wrote then, you
can see that I truly understand the secret about
the Christ.[d] 5People who lived in other times
were not told that secret. But now, through the
Spirit,[d] God has shown that secret to his holy
apostles[d] and prophets.[d] 6This is that secret: that
through the Good News[d] those who are not Jews
will share with the Jews in God's blessing.
They belong to the same body, and they share
together in the promise that God made in Christ
Jesus.

7By God's special gift of grace given to me
through his power, I became a servant to tell that
Good News. 8I am the least important of all God's
people, but God gave me this gift—to tell those
who are not Jews the Good News about the riches
of Christ, which are too great to understand fully.
9And God gave me the work of telling all people
about the plan for his secret, which has been hidden in him since the beginning of time. He is the
One who created everything. 10His purpose was
that through the church all the rulers and powers
in the heavenly world will now know God's wisdom, which has so many forms. 11This agrees
with the purpose God had since the beginning of
time, and he carried out his plan through Christ
Jesus our Lord. 12In Christ we can come before
God with freedom and without fear. We can do
this through faith in Christ. 13So I ask you not to
become discouraged because of the sufferings I
am having for you. My sufferings are for your
glory.

> **SIDELIGHT:** To describe Jesus as the "most important stone" or cornerstone (Ephesians 2:20) makes him essential for the "building." When construction workers started building, they would first place one stone—the cornerstone—and then line up all the walls based on this stone.

CHURCH

Friends or Foes?

After several months of fighting among Westside Church members, the get-rid-of-the-pastor side won. Pastor Howard fought back tears as he announced his resignation on Sunday morning. He packed up his office and home, and moved away within a month.

Many church members on the keep-the-pastor side were angry and disillusioned; most of them left the Westside Church within six months. Some went to other churches. But some stayed away from the church for years.

Those who stayed at Westside Church hired a new pastor—one they were sure they would like much better than Pastor Howard. But in less than two years, the church members were fighting again. They ordered the new pastor to leave, and the cycle began again.

After watching the church destroy itself for the second time, one of the young people commented, "I don't think you can even call this place a church—anyway, I don't think it's what God meant for the church to be."

This teenager's perception fits the description of the church in **Ephesians 4:1–6**. Read this scripture to see what God wants the church to be like.

- If Westside Church members had applied these verses to their situation, how would the outcome have been different?
- How can you use this passage to promote unity within your church?

CONSIDER. . .

- encouraging your youth group to pray weekly for your church to be united.
- talking to your pastor about creating an annual "Unity Award" for church members who consistently promote unity in your church.

FOR MORE, SEE. . .

- Psalm 133 (p. 558)
- Titus 3:9–11 (p. 1271)
- 1 Peter 3:8–12 (p. 1306)

The Love of Christ

14So I bow in prayer before the Father 15from
whom every family in heaven and on earth gets
its true name. 16I ask the Father in his great glory
to give you the power to be strong inwardly
through his Spirit.[d] 17I pray that Christ will live in
your hearts by faith and that your life will be
strong in love and be built on love. 18And I pray
that you and all God's holy people will have the
power to understand the greatness of Christ's
love — how wide and how long and how high and
how deep that love is. 19Christ's love is greater
than anyone can ever know, but I pray that you
will be able to know that love. Then you can be
filled with the fullness of God.

20With God's power working in us, God can do
much, much more than anything we can ask or
imagine. 21To him be glory in the church and in
Christ Jesus for all time, forever and ever. Amen.

The Unity of the Body

4 I am in prison because I belong to the Lord.
God chose you to be his people, so I urge you
now to live the life to which God called you. 2Al-
ways be humble, gentle, and patient, accepting
each other in love. 3You are joined together with
peace through the Spirit,[d] so make every effort to
continue together in this way. 4There is one body
and one Spirit, and God called you to have one
hope. 5There is one Lord, one faith, and one baptism. 6There is one God and Father of everything.
He rules everything and is everywhere and is in
everything.

SIDELIGHT: Christian unity is central to the book of Ephesians. The word "one" appears seven times in Ephesians 4:4–6 alone!

7Christ gave each one of us the special gift of
grace, showing how generous he is. 8That is why
it says in the Scriptures,[d]

"When he went up to the heights,
he led a parade of captives,
and he gave gifts to people." *Psalm 68:18*

CULTS

Hazardous to Your Health

Jim Jones was an ordained minister who thought he was the messiah. Jones demanded total allegiance from his followers, telling them he was going to create the perfect society—free from hate, crime, and lack of anything.

People believed him. They sold everything they had and gave it to Jones. Nearly a thousand people followed Jones to Guyana in South America, where he established a settlement called Jonestown.

In 1978, Leo Ryan, a United States representative from California traveled to Jonestown to investigate rumors that Jones was holding some people against their will. In fear of being caught, Jones had Ryan and three journalists who accompanied Ryan killed. Then to destroy all evidence of his lies and deceit, Jones ordered his followers to take poison in a religious ceremony. More than nine hundred people—including Jones himself—died in what is now called the "Jonestown Massacre."

The people in Jonestown didn't recognize Jim Jones's lies. **Ephesians 4:11–16** warns us to be mature so we can recognize false teachings.

- How were the people in Jim Jones's church like the babies described in this passage?
- Has anyone ever tried to lead you down the wrong path like this passage talks about? How did the truth help you stay on God's path?

C O N S I D E R . . .

- talking to your pastor or other church leader about the elements of truth that your own church emphasizes.
- asking your pastor or youth leader to lead a study on a new "religious movement" to discover whether or not it is founded on the truth.

F O R M O R E , S E E . . .

- Proverbs 4 (p. 570)
- Romans 1:18–32 (p. 1141)
- Philippians 4:8–9 (p. 1234)

9When it says, "He went up," what does it
mean? It means that he first came down to the
earth. 10So Jesus came down, and he is the same
One who went up above all the sky. Christ did
that to fill everything with his presence. 11And
Christ gave gifts to people—he made some to be
apostles,[d] some to be prophets,[d] some to go and
tell the Good News,[d] and some to have the work
of caring for and teaching God's people. 12Christ
gave those gifts to prepare God's holy people for
the work of serving, to make the body of Christ
stronger. 13This work must continue until we
are all joined together in the same faith and
in the same knowledge of the Son of God. We
must become like a mature person, growing un-
until we become like Christ and have his perfection.
14Then we will no longer be babies. We will
not be tossed about like a ship that the waves
carry one way and then another. We will not be
influenced by every new teaching we hear from
people who are trying to fool us. They make plans
and try any kind of trick to fool people into following the wrong path. 15No! Speaking the truth with
love, we will grow up in every way into Christ,
who is the head. 16The whole body depends on
Christ, and all the parts of the body are joined and
held together. Each part does its own work to
make the whole body grow and be strong with
love.

The Way You Should Live

17In the Lord's name, I tell you this. Do not
continue living like those who do not believe.
Their thoughts are worth nothing. 18They do not
understand, and they know nothing, because they
refuse to listen. So they cannot have the life that
God gives. 19They have lost all feeling of shame,
and they use their lives for doing evil. They continually want to do all kinds of evil. 20But what
you learned in Christ was not like this. 21I know
that you heard about him, and you are in him, so
you were taught the truth that is in Jesus. 22You
were taught to leave your old self—to stop living
the evil way you lived before. That old self becomes worse, because people are fooled by the
evil things they want to do. 23But you were taught
to be made new in your hearts, 24to become a
new person. That new person is made to be like
God—made to be truly good and holy.
25So you must stop telling lies. Tell each other
the truth, because we all belong to each other in

ANGER

Handle With Care

Clarisse Olson wasn't having a good day. Her boyfriend broke up with her before her first class. She got her math test back and knew her parents would not be pleased with the score. She missed lunch. And then she mouthed off at her P.E. teacher.

She shook her head as she recalled the incident.

"Come on, Clarisse," Mr. Eaton had yelled. "You can't do push-ups with your fanny in the air. Try fifty more, and do them right this time!"

Clarisse felt the anger well up inside her as she started over again. "One . . . two . . . three . . ." she counted.

"I'd like to see you do fifty push-ups, you fat slob," Clarisse mumbled—a little louder than she intended.

Now she was sitting in the detention room while everyone else in school was in a pep assembly for the homecoming game.

"If only I'd kept my mouth shut," Clarisse moaned.

Sometimes our anger can get us into trouble. Read the warning about anger in **Ephesians 4:25—5:2**.

- According to this passage, did Clarisse's anger lead to sin or not?
- How can you be angry, and yet not sin?

CONSIDER . . .

- listing three things that make you angry. Beside each one, write a brief description of how you can handle the situation without sinning.
- resolving to deal quickly with things that make you angry.

FOR MORE, SEE . . .

- Psalm 4 (p. 483)
- Proverbs 22:24–25 (p. 587)

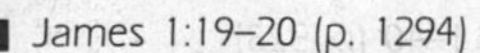

- James 1:19–20 (p. 1294)

the same body.[n] 26When you are angry, do not sin, and be sure to stop being angry before the end of the day. 27Do not give the devil a way to defeat you. 28Those who are stealing must stop stealing and start working. They should earn an honest living for themselves. Then they will have something to share with those who are poor.

29When you talk, do not say harmful things, but say what people need—words that will help others become stronger. Then what you say will do good to those who listen to you. 30And do not make the Holy Spirit[d] sad. The Spirit is God's proof that you belong to him. God gave you the Spirit to show that God will make you free when the final day comes. 31Do not be bitter or angry or mad. Never shout angrily or say things to hurt others. Never do anything evil. 32Be kind and loving to each other, and forgive each other just as God forgave you in Christ.

Living in the Light

5 You are God's children whom he loves, so try to be like him. 2Live a life of love just as Christ loved us and gave himself for us as a sweet-smelling offering and sacrifice to God.

3But there must be no sexual sin among you, or any kind of evil or greed. Those things are not right for God's holy people. 4Also, there must be no evil talk among you, and you must not speak foolishly or tell evil jokes. These things are not right for you. Instead, you should be giving thanks to God. 5You can be sure of this: No one will have a place in the kingdom of Christ and of God who sins sexually, or does evil things, or is greedy. Anyone who is greedy is serving a false god.

6Do not let anyone fool you by telling you things that are not true, because these things will bring God's anger on those who do not obey him. 7So have nothing to do with them. 8In the past you were full of darkness, but now you are full of light in the Lord. So live like children who belong to the light. 9Light brings every kind of goodness, right living, and truth. 10Try to learn what pleases the Lord. 11Have nothing to do with the things done in darkness, which are not worth anything. But show that they are wrong. 12It is shameful even to talk about what those people do in secret. 13But the light makes all things easy to see, 14and everything that is made easy to see can become light. This is why it is said:

"Wake up, sleeper!
Rise from death,
and Christ will shine on you."

15So be very careful how you live. Do not live

Tell . . . body. Quotation from Zechariah 8:16.

DECISION MAKING

Who's Gonna Know?

Rob was having the time of his life on tour in Germany with his community orchestra—and no parents! There were chaperones, of course, but Rob was making his own decisions and loving every minute of it.

On Saturday night, Rob's friends went out to get their first taste of German beer. Most band members were excited to take advantage of Germany's lax alcohol laws.

Rob wasn't sure. He didn't feel quite right about going. It seemed to be an okay thing to do in Germany, but it wasn't something he would do at home.

But then he thought, "Who's gonna know?"

"I'd know," Rob finally told himself, after remembering the advice in **Ephesians 5:6–20**. See how this passage can help you make tough decisions.

- What principles do you find in this passage that Rob may have used in making his decision?
- How can you use the passage's advice in a decision you face now?

C O N S I D E R . . .

- praying and writing about what God wants you to do with your life.
- writing a letter to a friend who's facing a tough decision. Include the passage's advice on decision making.

F O R M O R E , S E E . . .

- 1 Kings 18:1–40 (p. 323)
- Romans 12:1–2 (p. 1157)
- James 1:5–8 (p. 1294)

like those who are not wise, but live wisely. [16]Use every chance you have for doing good, because these are evil times. [17]So do not be foolish but learn what the Lord wants you to do. [18]Do not be drunk with wine, which will ruin you, but be filled with the Spirit.[d] [19]Speak to each other with psalms, hymns, and spiritual songs, singing and making music in your hearts to the Lord. [20]Always give thanks to God the Father for everything, in the name of our Lord Jesus Christ.

Wives and Husbands

[21]Yield to obey each other because you respect Christ.

[22]Wives, yield to your husbands, as you do to the Lord, [23]because the husband is the head of the wife, as Christ is the head of the church. And he is the Savior of the body, which is the church. [24]As the church yields to Christ, so you wives should yield to your husbands in everything.

[25]Husbands, love your wives as Christ loved the church and gave himself for it [26]to make it belong to God. Christ used the word to make the church clean by washing it with water. [27]He died so that he could give the church to himself like a bride in all her beauty. He died so that the church could be pure and without fault, with no evil or sin or any other wrong thing in it. [28]In the same way, husbands should love their wives as they love their own bodies. The man who loves his wife loves himself. [29]No one ever hates his own body, but feeds and takes care of it. And that is what Christ does for the church, [30]because we are parts of his body. [31]The Scripture says, "So a man will leave his father and mother and be united with his wife, and the two will become one body."[n] [32]That secret is very important—I am talking about Christ and the church. [33]But each one of you must love his wife as he loves himself, and a wife must respect her husband.

Children and Parents

6 Children, obey your parents as the Lord wants, because this is the right thing to do. [2]The command says, "Honor your father and

"So . . . body." Quotation from Genesis 2:24.

FAMILY

Wolf Packs

When people think of wolves, they sometimes visualize a lonely silhouette on a hill, howling at the moon. Some picture the predator, sneaking up on an unsuspecting flock of sheep.

Much the opposite is true of wolves. While wolves do hunt, they most often prey on the sick or old animals in a herd, leaving the healthy animals to reproduce and protect the others. And wolves are seldom lonely. They live together with other wolves in families called packs.

Within the pack, adult wolves work together to hunt and to feed the younger members of the family. After a time of training, the young wolves take their place alongside the adults to hunt and to care for the next generation. Wolves rarely fight among themselves. But they will stand together, defending their home from attack by outsiders.

Experts believe wolves stay together as families because they have a kind of love for each other. Human family members also have certain responsibilities that help maintain order. Read about these responsibilities in **Ephesians 6:1–4**.

- How is a wolf pack like the family described in this passage? How is it different?
- From this passage, what is your role in your family?

C O N S I D E R . . .

- writing out one thing you could do to improve your role in your family. Then do it.
- obeying your parents this week, even when they ask you to do something you don't want to.

F O R M O R E , S E E . . .

- Proverbs 23:22–25 (p. 588)
- Matthew 15:3–9 (p. 934)
- Colossians 3:18–21 (p. 1242)

mother."[n] This is the first command that has a
promise with it— 3"Then everything will be well
with you, and you will have a long life on the
earth."[n]
4Fathers, do not make your children angry, but
raise them with the training and teaching of the
Lord.

Slaves and Masters

5Slaves, obey your masters here on earth with
fear and respect and from a sincere heart, just as
you obey Christ. 6You must do this not only while
they are watching you, to please them. With all
your heart you must do what God wants as people
who are obeying Christ. 7Do your work with enthusiasm. Work as if you were serving the Lord,
not as if you were serving only men and women.
8Remember that the Lord will give a reward to
everyone, slave or free, for doing good.
9Masters, in the same way, be good to your
slaves. Do not threaten them. Remember that the
One who is your Master and their Master is in
heaven, and he treats everyone alike.

Wear the Full Armor of God

10Finally, be strong in the Lord and in his great
power. 11Put on the full armor of God so that you
can fight against the devil's evil tricks. 12Our fight
is not against people on earth but against the rulers and authorities and the powers of this world's
darkness, against the spiritual powers of evil in
the heavenly world. 13That is why you need to put
on God's full armor. Then on the day of evil you
will be able to stand strong. And when you have
finished the whole fight, you will still be standing.
14So stand strong, with the belt of truth tied
around your waist and the protection of right living on your chest. 15On your feet wear the Good
News[d] of peace to help you stand strong. 16And
also use the shield of faith with which you can
stop all the burning arrows of the Evil One. 17Ac-
cept God's salvation as your helmet, and take the
sword of the Spirit,[d] which is the word of God.
18Pray in the Spirit at all times with all kinds of
prayers, asking for everything you need. To do
this you must always be ready and never give up.
Always pray for all God's people.

"Honor . . . mother." Quotation from Exodus 20:12; Deuteronomy 5:16.
"Then . . . earth." Quotation from Exodus 20:12; Deuteronomy 5:16.

FOLLOWING GOD

Spiritual Armor-All

Kremmling, Colorado, was a small mountain town of fifteen hundred where nothing out of the ordinary ever happened. Then police found a graffiti-emblazoned shack where someone had set up an altar with a satanic bible and plotted to vandalize churches and sacrifice animals.

"Major things like this never happen in Kremmling," Jody Cordova said. "It's kind of scary. I wrack my brain trying to figure out the people in town who would do this."

The townspeople were frightened. Some were even hysterical, threatening to carry handguns while taking children trick-or-treating on Halloween.

People were puzzled and concerned. They couldn't believe the dark side of the spiritual world could invade their little town the way it had.

Ephesians 6:10–20 warns not to be caught off guard in spiritual battles. Read the passage to see how Christians can protect themselves.

- How might this passage help the people of Kremmling respond to their situation? Which piece of armor would help them most?
- Which pieces of your armor are weakest? Which are strongest?

C O N S I D E R . . .

- writing on a bookmark the words to represent each of the pieces of armor in the passage. Keep the bookmark in one of your school books to remind you to stay prepared.
- choosing the pieces of your armor that are weakest. Begin to strengthen those pieces this week.

F O R M O R E S E E . . .

- 1 Samuel 17 (p. 260)
- Matthew 8:28–34 (p. 921)
- James 4:7–10 (p. 1298)

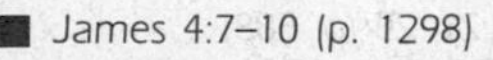

19Also pray for me that when I speak, God will
give me words so that I can tell the secret of the
Good News without fear. 20I have been sent to
preach this Good News, and I am doing that now,
here in prison. Pray that when I preach the Good
News I will speak without fear, as I should.

> **SIDELIGHT:** The "shield of faith" in Ephesians 6:16 is a comparison to the large Roman shield used by heavily armed soldiers. This shield was designed to protect against burning darts, one of the most dangerous weapons of the time. When the dart hit the shield, it sunk into wood, and the flame was extinquished.

Final Greetings

21I am sending to you Tychicus, our brother
whom we love and a faithful servant of the Lord's
work. He will tell you everything that is happening with me. Then you will know how I am and
what I am doing. 22I am sending him to you for
this reason — so that you will know how we are,
and he can encourage you.
23Peace and love with faith to you from God
the Father and the Lord Jesus Christ. 24Grace to
all of you who love our Lord Jesus Christ with
love that never ends.

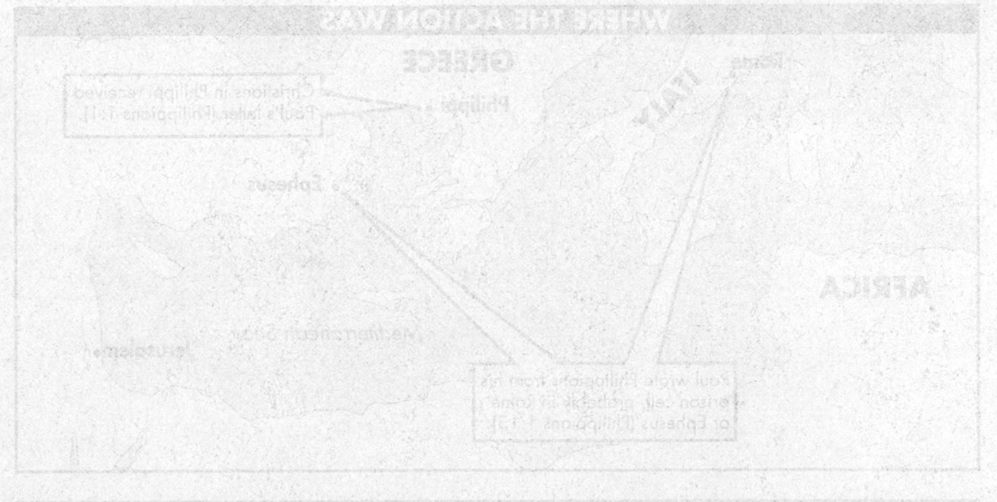

PHILIPPIANS

Why Read This Book?

- Discover how serving other people serves Christ (Philippians 1—2).
- Learn why growing in faith is so important (Philippians 3).
- Learn Paul's secret of having joy amidst suffering (Philippians 4).

Behind the Scenes:

Paul spent his life telling the Good News of Jesus Christ and starting new churches. But what did he get for it? He was put on trial, run out of town, stoned, beaten with rods, and thrown in prison several times. In addition, other Christians misunderstood and opposed him.

In short, Paul had plenty of reason to be gloomy and depressed. But, as we learn in Philippians, Paul felt just the opposite. In fact, this short letter from Paul is probably the most upbeat, cheerful book in the Bible.

Part of the reason he was happy was that the Christians in Philippi had heard about his imprisonment and had taken up a collection for him. Their love and concern made Paul deeply grateful, and Paul thanks them in this letter.

But the most important reason for Paul's happiness is clear in the letter. "To me the only important thing about living is Christ," he writes, "and dying would be profit for me" (Philippians 1:21).

The Romans could chain Paul's body, but they couldn't chain Paul's heart. And in this letter to his friends at Philippi, the apostle shares his secret for facing difficult circumstances with a song on his lips and joy in his heart.

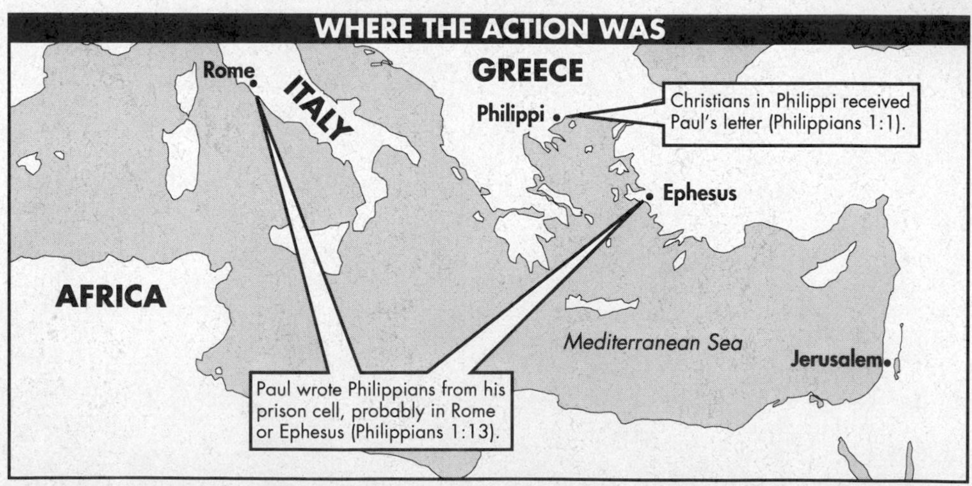
WHERE THE ACTION WAS
Rome
ITALY
GREECE
Philippi
Christians in Philippi received Paul's letter (Philippians 1:1).
Ephesus
AFRICA
Mediterranean Sea
Jerusalem
Paul wrote Philippians from his prison cell, probably in Rome or Ephesus (Philippians 1:13).

WHEN THE ACTION WAS

Jesus was born — BC/AD
The church began soon after Jesus went to heaven
Jesus began his ministry — 25AD
Paul started the church in Philippi
Paul began his missionary work — 50AD
Paul wrote Philippians
Fire destroyed Rome
Romans destroyed the Temple in Jerusalem — 75AD
100AD

1 From Paul and Timothy, servants of Christ
Jesus.
To all of God's holy people in Christ Jesus who
live in Philippi, including your elders[d] and deacons:[d]
2Grace and peace to you from God our Father
and the Lord Jesus Christ.

Paul's Prayer

3I thank my God every time I remember you,
4always praying with joy for all of you. 5I thank
God for the help you gave me while I preached
the Good News[d]—help you gave from the first
day you believed until now. 6God began doing a
good work in you, and I am sure he will continue
it until it is finished when Jesus Christ comes
again.
7And I know that I am right to think like this
about all of you, because I have you in my heart.
All of you share in God's grace with me while I
am in prison and while I am defending and proving the truth of the Good News. 8God knows that
I want to see you very much, because I love all
of you with the love of Christ Jesus.
9This is my prayer for you: that your love will
grow more and more; that you will have knowl-

SIDELIGHT: A woman, Lydia, was the first person baptized in Europe. She was probably a leader in the early Philippian church (see Acts 16:11–15, p. 1123), but she may not have stayed there long, since she made a living as a traveling merchant who sold purple-dyed cloth.

FRIENDS

First-String Help

Wyatt Jordan was a sure bet to make second-string quarterback, right behind his best friend Todd Andrews. That is, until Todd suddenly quit the team.

Steve Lowry congratulated Wyatt the morning after Todd quit. Steve was especially excited; now he would be second-string quarterback, right behind Wyatt.

"Yeah, thanks," Wyatt said with a lot less enthusiasm. He knew there was only one reason his friend would quit the team: Things must be getting worse at home. It had been a rough summer at the Andrews's family farm, with financial problems and Todd's dad being sick.

Of course, Todd's mom had insisted that her son play football. "Your brothers can bring in the harvest without you or your father," she had said. But at the first practice, Todd warned Wyatt that he might have to give up football to work on the farm.

During Wyatt's first practice as the starting quarterback, Coach Larson put the ball in Wyatt's hands.

"You're my man now," the coach said and blew his whistle.

"This is ridiculous," Wyatt thought. "The only reason I picked up a football in the first place was because of Todd. How can I do this when I know he's having a tough time right now?"

Wyatt walked off the field toward the coach, stopping first to give Steve the football. "Where are you going?" an astonished Steve asked.

"Farming," Wyatt answered.

Wyatt is the kind of friend we all want when we are having problems. Read **Philippians 1:3–11** to discover how Paul felt about friends who helped him when life was difficult.

- How do Wyatt's actions reflect the kind of friendship Paul is thankful for in this passage?
- How does the kind of friendship displayed in this passage make a difference in relationships?

CONSIDER

- praying Philippians 1:9–11 for each of your friends.
- making a scrapbook for a friend, with mementos of what his or her friendship has meant to you. Then present the scrapbook to your friend.

FOR MORE, SEE...

- Exodus 17:8–13 (p. 75)
- Mark 14:32–42 (p. 992)
- Philemon 10–14 (p. 1274)

edge and understanding with your love; 10that you will see the difference between good and bad and will choose the good; that you will be pure and without wrong for the coming of Christ; 11that you will do many good things with the help of Christ to bring glory and praise to God.

Paul's Troubles Help the Work

12I want you brothers and sisters[n] to know that what has happened to me has helped to spread the Good News.[d] 13All the palace guards and everyone else knows that I am in prison because I am a believer in Christ. 14Because I am in prison, most of the believers have become more bold in Christ and are not afraid to speak the word of God.

15It is true that some preach about Christ because they are jealous and ambitious, but others preach about Christ because they want to help. 16They preach because they have love, and they know that God gave me the work of defending the Good News. 17But the others preach about Christ for selfish and wrong reasons, wanting to make trouble for me in prison.

18But it doesn't matter. The important thing is that in every way, whether for right or wrong reasons, they are preaching about Christ. So I am happy, and I will continue to be happy. 19Because you are praying for me and the Spirit of Jesus Christ is helping me, I know this trouble will bring my freedom. 20I expect and hope that I will not fail Christ in anything but that I will have the courage now, as always, to show the greatness of Christ in my life here on earth, whether I live or die. 21To me the only important thing about living is Christ, and dying would be profit for me. 22If I continue living in my body, I will be able to work for the Lord. I do not know what to choose—living or dying. 23It is hard to choose between the two. I want to leave this life and be with Christ, which is much better, 24but you need me here in my body. 25Since I am sure of this, I know I will stay with you to help you grow and have joy in your faith. 26You will be very happy in Christ Jesus when I am with you again.

27Only one thing concerns me: Be sure that you live in a way that brings honor to the Good News of Christ. Then whether I come and visit you or am away from you, I will hear that you are standing strong with one purpose, that you work together as one for the faith of the Good News, 28and that you are not afraid of those who are against you. All of this is proof that your enemies will be destroyed but that you will be saved by God. 29God gave you the honor not only of believing in Christ but also of suffering for him, both of which bring glory to Christ. 30When I was with you, you saw the struggles I had, and you hear about the struggles I am having now. You yourselves are having the same kind of struggles.

2 Does your life in Christ give you strength? Does his love comfort you? Do we share together in the spirit? Do you have mercy and kindness? 2If so, make me very happy by having the same thoughts, sharing the same love, and having one mind and purpose. 3When you do things, do not let selfishness or pride be your guide. Instead, be humble and give more honor to others than to yourselves. 4Do not be interested only in your own life, but be interested in the lives of others.

Be Unselfish like Christ

5In your lives you must think and act like Christ Jesus.

6Christ himself was like God in everything.
But he did not think that being equal with
God was something to be used for his
own benefit.
7But he gave up his place with God and made
himself nothing.
He was born to be a man
and became like a servant.
8And when he was living as a man,
he humbled himself and was fully obedient
to God,
even when that caused his death—death
on a cross.
9So God raised him to the highest place.
God made his name greater than every
other name
10so that every knee will bow to the name of
Jesus—
everyone in heaven, on earth, and under
the earth.
11And everyone will confess that Jesus Christ is
Lord
and bring glory to God the Father.

Be the People God Wants You to Be

12My dear friends, you have always obeyed God when I was with you. It is even more important that you obey now while I am away from you. Keep on working to complete your salvation with fear and trembling, 13because God is working in you to help you want to do and be able to do what pleases him.

14Do everything without complaining or arguing. 15Then you will be innocent and without any wrong. You will be God's children without fault. But you are living with crooked and mean people all around you, among whom you shine like stars in the dark world. 16You offer the teaching that

brothers and sisters Although the Greek text says "brothers" here and throughout this book, Paul's words were meant for the entire church, including men and women.

gives life. So when Christ comes again, I can be
happy because my work was not wasted. I ran the
race and won.
17Your faith makes you offer your lives as a sacrifice in serving God. If I have to offer my own
blood with your sacrifice, I will be happy and full
of joy with all of you. 18You also should be happy
and full of joy with me.

Timothy and Epaphroditus

19I hope in the Lord Jesus to send Timothy to
you soon. I will be happy to learn how you are.
20I have no one else like Timothy, who truly cares
for you. 21Other people are interested only in their
own lives, not in the work of Jesus Christ. 22You
know the kind of person Timothy is. You know he
has served with me in telling the Good News,[d] as
a son serves his father. 23I plan to send him to you
quickly when I know what will happen to me. 24I
am sure that the Lord will help me to come to you
soon.
25Epaphroditus, my brother in Christ, works
and serves with me in the army of Christ. When
I needed help, you sent him to me. I think now
that I must send him back to you, 26because he
wants very much to see all of you. He is worried
because you heard that he was sick. 27Yes, he was
sick, and nearly died, but God had mercy on him
and me too so that I would not have more sadness. 28I want very much to send him to you so
that when you see him you can be happy, and I
can stop worrying about you. 29Welcome him in
the Lord with much joy. Give honor to people like
him, 30because he almost died for the work of

DEATH

After AIDS

For Dale Pullen, a childhood filled with rejection became a life of rejection. His parents' failed marriage contributed to his own broken marriages. A need to escape problems led to drug and alcohol addictions. A desire for some kind of acceptance led to homosexuality. And homosexuality led to AIDS.

Abandoned by family and friends, Dale faced death alone. He was ready to end his life when Jeanne Cottrell, a Christian friend, invited Dale into her home. Through Jeanne's caring, Dale eventually decided to follow Christ.

What changes occurred in the heart of this beaten, lonely man! He experienced the release of forgiveness from his past. For the first time in his life, he felt genuine acceptance and unconditional love. And he had a place to belong with people who cared for him.

As his body weakened, Dale's spirit grew stronger and stronger. He was revitalized by his newfound hope in Christ. Dale directed his energy to reaching out with the love of Jesus to those who needed it most.

He visited AIDS patients at a local hospital and shared his story with many dying people who had also been rejected. He spoke at churches and support groups, and he explained how God's love reaches even those whom some find unlovable. He spent his time eagerly giving and receiving love.

"I don't know how long I'm going to live, but I want to live the rest of my days for the Lord," Dale told his friends.

After several months, Dale died. Those who were touched by Dale's life felt a tremendous loss. But at the same time, they rejoiced because they knew Dale was at peace and happy to be with Jesus.

Paul faced death peacefully under different circumstances. Read **Philippians 1:21–27** to see Paul's attitude toward living and dying.

- How were Dale's and Paul's attitudes about life affected by what they thought about death?
- According to this passage, what is the purpose of life and death?

CONSIDER . . .

- thinking of the number one reason you have to live, then putting more energy into that activity.
- discussing your feelings about death with a Christian friend. Think about how your priorities look from a heavenly perspective.

FOR MORE, SEE . . .

- Psalm 42 (p. 507)
- Romans 14:7–8 (p. 1160)
- Galatians 2:20–21 (p. 1208)

Christ. He risked his life to give me the help you could not give in your service to me.

SIDELIGHT: If Epaphroditus's sickness had been a fever (see Philippians 2:26–27), he might have been treated by hanging a bag around his neck, a bag that included seven hairs from seven old dogs—a common treatment in New Testament times.

The Importance of Christ

3 My brothers and sisters, be full of joy in the
Lord. It is no trouble for me to write the
same things to you again, and it will help you to
be more ready. [2]Watch out for those who do evil,
who are like dogs, who demand to cut[n] the body.
[3]We are the ones who are truly circumcised.[d] We
worship God through his Spirit,[d] and our pride is
in Christ Jesus. We do not put trust in ourselves
or anything we can do, [4]although I might be able
to put trust in myself. If anyone thinks he has a
reason to trust in himself, he should know that I
have greater reason for trusting in myself. [5]I was
circumcised eight days after my birth. I am from
the people of Israel and the tribe[d] of Benjamin.
I am a Hebrew, and my parents were Hebrews. I
had a strict view of the law, which is why I became a Pharisee.[d] [6]I was so enthusiastic I tried to
hurt the church. No one could find fault with the
way I obeyed the law of Moses. [7]Those things
were important to me, but now I think they are
worth nothing because of Christ. [8]Not only those
things, but I think that all things are worth nothing compared with the greatness of knowing
Christ Jesus my Lord. Because of him, I have lost
all those things, and now I know they are worthless trash. This allows me to have Christ [9]and to
belong to him. Now I am right with God, not because I followed the law, but because I believed
in Christ. God uses my faith to make me right
with him. [10]I want to know Christ and the power
that raised him from the dead. I want to share in
his sufferings and become like him in his death.
[11]Then I have hope that I myself will be raised
from the dead.

Continuing Toward Our Goal

[12]I do not mean that I am already as God wants
me to be. I have not yet reached that goal, but I
continue trying to reach it and to make it mine.

cut The word in Greek is like the word "circumcise," but it means "to cut completely off."

CHURCH

Sticking Together

When a flock of geese fly south for the winter, they fly in a V-shaped formation. If they didn't, they would never reach their destination.

Researchers have found that the V-shaped formation helps geese fly at least 71 percent farther than they could fly alone, because each bird creates an updraft for the one behind it, making flying easier.

If one goose falls out of formation, the wind resistance slows down the bird. If it doesn't act quickly, it will not be able to keep up with its flock. So, it quickly gets back into formation.

Like geese, Christians need to work together in the church. Read **Philippians 2:1–11** to learn how.

- How is the geese's V-shaped formation like the passage's description of Christians working together?
- How does being with other Christians encourage you in your faith?

C O N S I D E R . . .

- writing your name and the names of other people in a V-shaped pattern to symbolize how you support each other. Thank God for people in the church who lead and support you.
- talking to your youth leader or a Sunday school teacher about how you can create an "updraft" to support and encourage others in your church.

F O R M O R E , S E E . . .

- Psalm 133:1–3 (p. 558)
- Mark 9:33–37 (p. 980)
- Acts 2:44–47 (p. 1100)

Christ wants me to do that, which is the reason
he made me his. 13Brothers and sisters, I know
that I have not yet reached that goal, but there is
one thing I always do. Forgetting the past and
straining toward what is ahead, 14I keep trying to
reach the goal and get the prize for which God
called me through Christ to the life above.

15All of us who are spiritually mature should
think this way, too. And if there are things you do
not agree with, God will make them clear to you.
16But we should continue following the truth we
already have.

17Brothers and sisters, all of you should try to
follow my example and to copy those who live
the way we showed you. 18Many people live like
enemies of the cross of Christ. I have often told
you about them, and it makes me cry to tell you
about them now. 19In the end, they will be destroyed. They do whatever their bodies want,
they are proud of their shameful acts, and they
think only about earthly things. 20But our homeland is in heaven, and we are waiting for our Savior, the Lord Jesus Christ, to come from heaven.
21By his power to rule all things, he will change
our simple bodies and make them like his own
glorious body.

POPULARITY

Impressive!

Mark Lester was assigned to work with class president Barry Clark on a biology class project. Who could have foreseen that working together a few nights a week for a month might actually lead to a friendship?

Barry and Mark had little in common. Barry was popular, owned a fancy car, and partied with the "in" crowd. Mark had a few friends from church, rode a bike, and spent his weekends with the youth group.

But one Friday night at the basketball game, Barry asked Mark to sit with him in the bleacher section informally reserved for football players, cheerleaders—anybody but Mark Lester. Not even in his wildest dreams could Mark have pictured himself sitting in the bleachers right in front of Tracy Watkins and spending more time talking to her than watching the game!

Mark was so enamored with his sudden change of fortune that he had to ask Tracy to repeat herself. The next time, she said it so loudly everyone heard her—including Barry. "If you can find a way to get us some beer, I'll go out with you after the game," she shouted above the crowd's roar.

Barry's expression said he was very impressed. Mark pretended to watch the basketball game for a second. It was the final quarter, and time was running out. But another clock was ticking in the bleachers. Mark knew the more important contest was taking place right where he sat.

"Well," he began, then hesitated.

Tracy frowned and glanced at Barry, who grinned, leaned forward, and teased, "If you won't take her out, Mark, I guess I'll have to."

Mark gripped the bleacher with both hands and, with all the enthusiasm he could muster, grinned back at Barry through gritted teeth. "Go for it, Barry," he stuttered. The clock ran out. The buzzer sounded. The game had been close, but Mark knew he had won.

Mark had chosen to be popular with God rather than people. Read **Philippians 3:8–11** to see how Paul had a similar attitude.

- How does Mark's decision reflect Paul's philosophy in this passage?
- How can "knowing Christ" be greater than what the world offers?

CONSIDER . . .

- giving up something that might make you popular if it stands in the way of your knowing Christ.
- asking a parent to recall the popular people in his or her high school, then finding out what has happened to them.

FOR MORE, SEE . . .

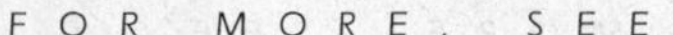

- Joshua 24:14–27 (p. 214)
- John 5:41–44 (p. 1066)
- Galatians 1:9–10 (p. 1207)

What the Christians Are to Do

4 My dear brothers and sisters, I love you and
want to see you. You bring me joy and make
me proud of you, so stand strong in the Lord as
I have told you.
2I ask Euodia and Syntyche to agree in the
Lord. 3And I ask you, my faithful friend, to help
these women. They served with me in telling the
Good News,[d] together with Clement and others
who worked with me, whose names are written
in the book of life.[n]
4Be full of joy in the Lord always. I will say
again, be full of joy.
5Let everyone see that you are gentle and kind.
The Lord is coming soon. 6Do not worry about
anything, but pray and ask God for everything you
need, always giving thanks. 7And God's peace,
which is so great we cannot understand it, will
keep your hearts and minds in Christ Jesus.
8Brothers and sisters, think about the things

SIDELIGHT: When Paul said our "homeland is in heaven" (Philippians 3:20), he literally said Christians live in a colony of heaven. The Philippian Christians would have seen this as a great privilege, since Philippi was a colony of the Roman Empire (see Acts 16:12, p. 1123). Being a colony meant Philippi had special privileges, including self-government, exemption from control by regional governments, and exemption from many taxes.

book of life God's book that has the names of all God's chosen people (Revelation 3:5; 21:27).

PERSISTENCE

Sticking With It

Wilma Rudolph dreamed of competing in the Olympics. But she had everything stacked against her.

She was born prematurely in a Tennessee shack, weighing only four and one-half pounds. Scarlet fever and polio struck, partially paralyzing her left leg, and forcing her to wear a steel brace.

Wilma remembers: "My father was the one who sort of babied me and was sympathetic. . . . My mother was the one who made me work, made me believe that one day it would be possible for me to walk without braces." Wilma's mother told her that, with persistence, she could follow her dreams in life.

So at age nine, Wilma did away with the braces. Four years later she developed a rhythmic stride and entered her first race. She came in last.

But she didn't give up.

"I worked very hard for the next four years," Wilma recalls. "I was self-motivated and motivated by my family. It took sheer determination to be able to run a hundred yards and remember all of the mechanics that go along with it. It takes steady nerves and being a fighter to stay out there."

In the 1960 Olympics, Wilma Rudolph set the world record in the 100-meter dash. She also won the 200-meter sprints and ran the anchor leg for the United States 400-meter relay team. She was the first American woman to win three gold medals in track and field at a single Olympiad.

Wilma Rudolph learned the lesson of **Philippians 3:12–21**. Read the passage to discover the key to persistence.

- In light of the passage, why was Wilma persistent?
- What was Paul's spiritual goal, according to this passage? How can this passage help you persist in reaching such a goal?

CONSIDER . . .

- watching part of a sports event on television. Look for evidences of persistence, then apply what you learn to a challenge you face.
- setting a specific goal to help you grow in your faith and persisting to meet that goal this week.

FOR MORE, SEE . . .

- Psalm 37:23–24 (p. 504)
- Luke 9:57–62 (p. 1021)
- 1 Timothy 6:11–16 (p. 1260)

that are good and worthy of praise. Think about
the things that are true and honorable and right
and pure and beautiful and respected. 9Do what
you learned and received from me, what I told
you, and what you saw me do. And the God who
gives peace will be with you.

> **SIDELIGHT:** The words joy and rejoice occur in some form sixteen times in Philippians (for example, Philippians 4:4). Even in prison, Paul's thoughts were focused on joy!

Paul Thanks the Christians

10I am very happy in the Lord that you have
shown your care for me again. You continued to
care about me, but there was no way for you to
show it. 11I am not telling you this because I need
anything. I have learned to be satisfied with the
things I have and with everything that happens.
12I know how to live when I am poor, and I know
how to live when I have plenty. I have learned the
secret of being happy at any time in everything
that happens, when I have enough to eat and
when I go hungry, when I have more than I need
and when I do not have enough. 13I can do all
things through Christ, because he gives me
strength.
14But it was good that you helped me when I
needed it. 15You Philippians remember when I
first preached the Good News[d] there. When I left
Macedonia, you were the only church that gave
me help. 16Several times you sent me things I
needed when I was in Thessalonica. 17Really, it is

PEACE

Beyond Understanding

The ringing telephone pierced the night. "Hello, Mrs. Gibson. This is Officer Rogers with the highway patrol."

Norma's throat tightened, but she managed to gulp: "Yes, what is it?"

"It's your daughter, Cassandra. There's been an accident." Shocked, Norma sobbed uncontrollably and dropped the phone. Her husband, Neil, grabbed it and learned that Cassandra was still alive, but that she had extensive head injuries and was unconscious. The Flight for Life helicopter was flying her to an Oklahoma City hospital.

When Neil and Norma arrived at the hospital, Cassandra was in a coma. Her head was bruised and swollen. Her back was broken, and her body lay lifeless. Her heart had stopped once in the helicopter, but the paramedics had restarted it. Surgeons were inserting a catheter into Cassandra's skull to relieve the pressure on her brain.

During the surgery, Norma prayed in the hospital chapel. As she read her Bible, an overwhelming peace filled her. She couldn't explain what she felt, especially with her daughter so close to death. All she knew was that God seemed near and that he would take care of Cassandra.

For days, Neil and Norma rarely left Cassandra's side. Norma's prayers surprised even her, because they were filled with thanksgiving rather than questioning or pleading. Her heart was filled with God's peace.

It took a long time for Cassandra to recover, and much of what happened in the weeks after the accident is now a blur to her. But every hour is vivid to Neil and Norma. They were joyful that their daughter was alive.

In **Philippians 4:1–9**, Paul describes the secret to having a joy that is greater than life's difficulties. Read it to understand Norma's experience.

- Which actions or attitudes from this passage did Norma have that resulted in peace?
- Which ones can most help you experience God's peace?

C O N S I D E R . . .

- listing the nine steps to peace—one step from each verse in this passage. Choose one step you can take to experience God's peace.
- planning with a friend to pray together during difficult times.

F O R M O R E , S E E . . .

- Psalm 25 (p. 496)
- Luke 6:17–23 (p. 1012)

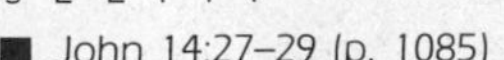

- John 14:27–29 (p. 1085)

not that I want to receive gifts from you, but I
want you to have the good that comes from giving. 18 And now I have everything, and more. I
have all I need, because Epaphroditus brought
your gift to me. It is like a sweet-smelling sacrifice
offered to God, who accepts that sacrifice and is
pleased with it. 19 My God will use his wonderful
riches in Christ Jesus to give you everything you
need. 20 Glory to our God and Father forever and
ever! Amen.

21 Greet each of God's people in Christ. Those
who are with me send greetings to you. 22 All of
God's people greet you, particularly those from
the palace of Caesar.[d]

23 The grace of the Lord Jesus Christ be with
you all.

COLOSSIANS

Why Read This Book?

- Learn the importance of following only Jesus Christ (Colossians 1).
- Discover how to respond to false teachers (Colossians 2).
- Find guidelines for living a Christian life (Colossians 3—4).

Behind the Scenes:

ESP. Astrology. Witchcraft. Ghosts. UFOs. Tarot cards. Ouija boards. The Loch Ness monster. Mysterious things can intrigue and attract us.

We are not the only people who can be fascinated with these kinds of things. Early Christians in Colosse were attracted to the same kinds of mysterious or supernatural things. Someone apparently came into the church and began teaching people to worship angels and cosmic powers. Jesus is fine, they argued, but these other mysterious powers controlled human destiny and gave secret knowledge (Colossians 2:16–23).

This letter to the Colossians challenges these false teachers. But instead of picking apart their arguments, the letter goes on the offensive, telling the Colossians the truth about Jesus Christ. "He ranks higher than everything that has been made," the letter states. "Christ is all that is important" (Colossians 1:15, 3:11).

The letter's advice to the Colossians is good advice for all people in all times. When we feel tempted to look for power in other, mysterious things, this book reminds us of the source of true power. And when someone suggests we need to do something else for salvation, Colossians assures us that Jesus is all we need.

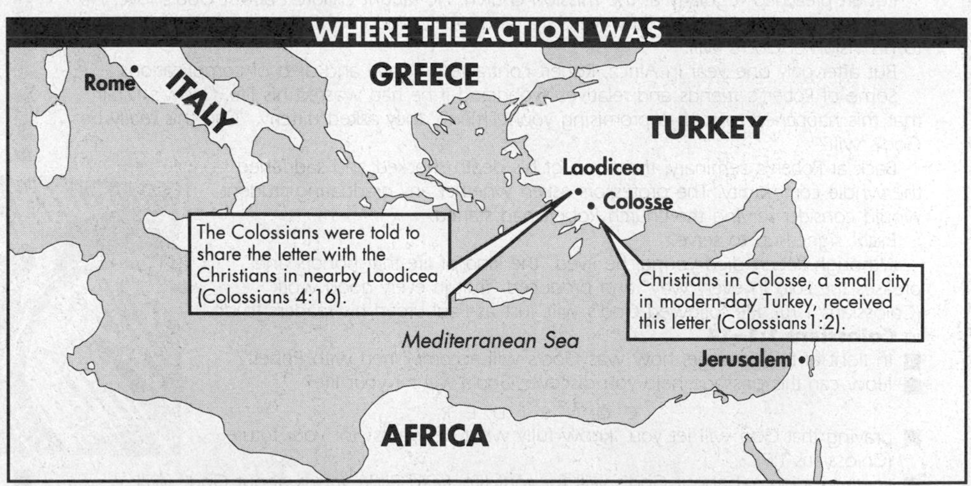
WHERE THE ACTION WAS
Rome
ITALY
GREECE
TURKEY
Laodicea
Colosse
The Colossians were told to share the letter with the Christians in nearby Laodicea (Colossians 4:16).
Christians in Colosse, a small city in modern-day Turkey, received this letter (Colossians1:2).
Mediterranean Sea
Jerusalem
AFRICA

WHEN THE ACTION WAS

BC/AD	25AD	50AD	75AD	100AD

- Jesus was born
- The church began soon after Jesus went to heaven
- Paul began his missionary work
- Fire destroyed Rome
- Jesus began his ministry
- Paul became a Christian
- Paul wrote this letter to the Colossians
- Romans destroyed the Temple in Jerusalem

1 From Paul, an apostle[d] of Christ Jesus. I am
an apostle because that is what God wanted.
Also from Timothy, our brother.
2To the holy and faithful brothers and sisters[n]
in Christ that live in Colosse:
Grace and peace to you from God our Father.
3In our prayers for you we always thank God,
the Father of our Lord Jesus Christ, 4because we
have heard about the faith you have in Christ
Jesus and the love you have for all of God's people. 5You have this faith and love because of your
hope, and what you hope for is kept safe for you
in heaven. You learned about this hope when you
heard the message about the truth, the Good
News[d] 6that was told to you. Everywhere in the
world that Good News is bringing blessings and
is growing. This has happened with you, too,
since you heard the Good News and understood
the truth about the grace of God. 7You learned
about God's grace from Epaphras, whom we love.
He works together with us and is a faithful servant
of Christ for us. 8He also told us about the love
you have from the Holy Spirit.[d]
9Because of this, since the day we heard about
you, we have continued praying for you, asking
God that you will know fully what he wants. We
pray that you will also have great wisdom and
understanding in spiritual things 10so that you will
live the kind of life that honors and pleases the
Lord in every way. You will produce fruit in every
good work and grow in the knowledge of God.
11God will strengthen you with his own great

brothers and sisters Although the Greek text says "brothers" here and throughout this book, Paul's words were meant for the entire church, including men and women.

GOD'S WILL

A Life Pleasing God

From childhood, Robert Beck knew he wanted to be a missionary to Africa. Every day he kept his goal foremost in his mind. He read magazine articles and books and watched TV news reports and documentaries on Africa. In school he wrote stories and reports about the African people.

After graduating from high school, Robert earned a bachelor's degree, then completed seminary. After almost twenty years of education, Robert finally was ready to start on his goal. He began a church in Africa.

Robert preached regularly at the mission church. He taught children about God's love. He befriended the people when they were sick and lonely, and cheerfully devoted all his time to his vision of God's will.

But after only one year in Africa, Robert contracted malaria and died of complications.

Some of Robert's friends and relatives wondered if he had wasted his life. "How's it fair that this happened to such a promising young man?" they asked bitterly. "Can this really be God's will?"

Back at Robert's seminary, the news of his death shocked and saddened the whole community. The professors asked whether any graduating student would consider serving the church Robert had started.

Eight signed up to serve.

Although Robert died young, he lived "the kind of life that honors and pleases the Lord in every way" and produced "fruit in every good work" (Colossians 1:10). He followed God's will, just as Paul urged his readers to do in **Colossians 1:1–14**.

- In light of this passage, how was God's will accomplished with Robert?
- How can this passage help you discover God's will for your life?

CONSIDER . . .

- praying that God will let you "know fully what he wants" for your future (Colossians 1:9).
- keeping a journal about God's will for your life. Read Bible verses about God's will (see below) and write your thoughts as you apply those verses to decisions you are facing.

FOR MORE, SEE . . .

- Psalm 40:8–10 (p. 505)
- Matthew 6:9–13 (p. 918)
- Mark 3:31–35 (p. 969)

power so that you will not give up when troubles come, but you will be patient. 12And you will joyfully give thanks to the Father who has made you able to have a share in all that he has prepared for his people in the kingdom of light. 13God has freed us from the power of darkness, and he brought us into the kingdom of his dear Son. 14The Son paid for our sins, and in him we have forgiveness.

The Importance of Christ

15No one can see God, but Jesus Christ is exactly like him. He ranks higher than everything that has been made. 16Through his power all things were made—things in heaven and on earth, things seen and unseen, all powers, authorities, lords, and rulers. All things were made through Christ and for Christ. 17He was there before anything was made, and all things continue because of him. 18He is the head of the body, which is the church. Everything comes from him. He is the first one who was raised from the dead. So in all things Jesus has first place. 19God was pleased for all of himself to live in Christ. 20And through Christ, God has brought all things back to himself again—things on earth and things in heaven. God made peace through the blood of Christ's death on the cross.

SIDELIGHT: The city of Colosse (Colossians 1:2) was once a major mill town, known for its wool-working and cloth-dying industries. In fact, a widely used dark red wool cloth was known as colossinum. However, the city had declined by the time this letter was written, and may have been devastated by a major earthquake in A.D. 60 or 61.

21At one time you were separated from God. You were his enemies in your minds, and the evil things you did were against God. 22But now God has made you his friends again. He did this through Christ's death in the body so that he might bring you into God's presence as people who are holy, with no wrong, and with nothing of which God can judge you guilty. 23This will

FORGIVENESS

The Face of Hatred

Just before Leonardo da Vinci began painting the Last Supper, he argued bitterly with a fellow painter. Da Vinci was so enraged that he decided to paint the face of his enemy as the face of Judas Iscariot. That way the hated painter's face would be preserved for ages in the face of the disciple who betrayed Jesus.

Da Vinci painted the face of Judas quickly. At first he took delight as everyone who came by recognized the face of the other painter in Judas.

Work on the other disciples' portraits continued. Da Vinci tried several times to start Jesus' face, but couldn't make any progress. Something seemed to baffle him, frustrating his best efforts.

In time, da Vinci saw his hatred of the other painter as the problem holding him back from finishing his work. Only after repainting the face of Judas was he able to paint Jesus' face and complete his masterpiece.

In his work on the Last Supper, da Vinci learned something important about forgiveness. **Colossians 1:15–29** has a similar lesson as it explains how Christ came to forgive—to end the separation between God and people.

- How was Leonardo da Vinci's separation from his fellow painter like humanity's separation from God as described in the passage?
- How do you feel when you are forgiven? How do you feel when you forgive someone else?

CONSIDER. . .

- confessing your sin to God, and, if you can, to an adult you trust. It may help you feel God's forgiveness.
- closing your eyes and thinking about the face of someone you need to forgive. Then imagine the face of Jesus next to that person's, and ask God to help you forgive that person.

FOR MORE, SEE. . .

- Psalm 79:8–9 (p. 529)
- Luke 6:37–38 (p. 1013)
- Romans 5:1–11 (p. 1145)

happen if you continue strong and sure in your
faith. You must not be moved away from the hope
brought to you by the Good News that you heard.
That same Good News has been told to everyone
in the world, and I, Paul, help in preaching that
Good News.

Paul's Work for the Church

24I am happy in my sufferings for you. There are
things that Christ must still suffer through his
body, the church. I am accepting, in my body, my
part of these things that must be suffered. 25I became a servant of the church because God gave
me a special work to do that helps you, and that
work is to tell fully the message of God. 26This
message is the secret that was hidden from everyone since the beginning of time, but now it is
made known to God's holy people. 27God decided
to let his people know this rich and glorious secret
which he has for all people. This secret is Christ
himself, who is in you. He is our only hope for
glory. 28So we continue to preach Christ to each
person, using all wisdom to warn and to teach
everyone, in order to bring each one into God's
presence as a mature person in Christ. 29To do
this, I work and struggle, using Christ's great
strength that works so powerfully in me.

2 I want you to know how hard I work for
you, those in Laodicea, and others who have
never seen me. 2I want them to be strengthened
and joined together with love so that they may be
rich in their understanding. This leads to their
knowing fully God's secret, that is, Christ himself.
3In him all the treasures of wisdom and knowledge are safely kept.

4I say this so that no one can fool you by arguments that seem good, but are false. 5Though I am
absent from you in my body, my heart is with you,

CULTS

Fatal Attraction

DeAnne Shackly was an average high school senior. Her grades were average: Bs and Cs in most subjects. Her interest in school was average: She thought school was okay, but she would much rather play tennis or watch television. Her social life was average: an occasional date or evening out with some friends.

DeAnne couldn't wait to graduate from high school and get on with life. She didn't know what she wanted, but she knew it had to be more interesting than what she was doing.

One day after school, DeAnne went to the beach. There, some members of a religious group approached her. DeAnne had never heard of the group. But because they offered her a chance to belong, to take part in something greater than herself, she joined them.

After two years DeAnne decided the cult had manipulated her for its own ends. The group had offered "answers" to tough questions, but then told her to stop asking questions—to "just believe." It used her to raise money by selling flowers, candy, and other things, but when she asked where all the money was going, she was told it wasn't her concern.

Finally, she dropped out. She felt sick about the two years she had wasted. "Why was I attracted to that group?" she later asked herself. "I was a typical kid with a comfortable lifestyle. Why did I change my life so drastically? I wasn't that unhappy."

The Colossian Christians experienced a similar attraction to false beliefs. **Colossians 2:1–15** warns the early Christians not to be fooled by empty teachings.

- How might DeAnne's response to the cult have been different if she had listened to the warnings in this passage?
- How can you recognize false teachers today, according to the passage?

CONSIDER . . .

- making a list of Paul's warnings about false teachers. Refer to it when someone offers you quick, appealing answers to tough questions.
- asking your pastor or youth leader to get literature from cult groups and asking his help evaluating the groups' claims in light of scripture.

FOR MORE, SEE . . .

- Deuteronomy 13:1–5 (p. 173)
- Matthew 24:23–25 (p. 951)
- 2 Peter 2:17–22 (p. 1312)

and I am happy to see your good lives and your strong faith in Christ.

> **SIDELIGHT:** Unlike most of Paul's letters, the letter to the Colossians was written to a church Paul apparently never visited (Colossians 2:1). Scholars suggest that the church may have been started by Epaphras, a native of the city who was in prison with Paul (Colossians 4:12, p. 1243).

Continue to Live in Christ

6As you received Christ Jesus the Lord, so continue to live in him. 7Keep your roots deep in him and have your lives built on him. Be strong in the faith, just as you were taught, and always be thankful.

8Be sure that no one leads you away with false and empty teaching that is only human, which comes from the ruling spirits of this world, and not from Christ. 9All of God lives in Christ fully (even when Christ was on earth), 10and you have a full and true life in Christ, who is ruler over all rulers and powers.

11Also in Christ you had a different kind of circumcision,[d] a circumcision not done by hands. It was through Christ's circumcision, that is, his death, that you were made free from the power of your sinful self. 12When you were baptized, you were buried with Christ, and you were raised up with him through your faith in God's power that was shown when he raised Christ from the dead. 13When you were spiritually dead because of your sins and because you were not free from the power of your sinful self, God made you alive with Christ, and he forgave all our sins. 14He canceled the debt, which listed all the rules we failed to follow. He took away that record with its rules and nailed it to the cross. 15God stripped the spiritual rulers and powers of their authority. With the cross, he won the victory and showed the world that they were powerless.

Don't Follow People's Rules

16So do not let anyone make rules for you about eating and drinking or about a religious feast, a New Moon[d] Festival, or a Sabbath[d] day. 17These things were like a shadow of what was to come. But what is true and real has come and is found in Christ. 18Do not let anyone disqualify you by making you humiliate yourself and worship angels. Such people enter into visions, which fill them with foolish pride because of their human way of thinking. 19They do not hold tightly to Christ, the head. It is from him that all the parts of the body are cared for and held together. So it grows in the way God wants it to grow.

20Since you died with Christ and were made free from the ruling spirits of the world, why do you act as if you still belong to this world by following rules like these: 21"Don't eat this," "Don't taste that," "Don't even touch that thing"? 22These rules refer to earthly things that are gone as soon as they are used. They are only man-made commands and teachings. 23They seem to be wise, but they are only part of a man-made religion. They make people pretend not to be proud and make them punish their bodies, but they do not really control the evil desires of the sinful self.

Your New Life in Christ

3 Since you were raised from the dead with Christ, aim at what is in heaven, where Christ is sitting at the right hand of God. 2Think only about the things in heaven, not the things on earth. 3Your old sinful self has died, and your new life is kept with Christ in God. 4Christ is our life, and when he comes again, you will share in his glory.

5So put all evil things out of your life: sexual sinning, doing evil, letting evil thoughts control you, wanting things that are evil, and greed. This is really serving a false god. 6These things make God angry.[n] 7In your past, evil life you also did these things.

8But now also put these things out of your life: anger, bad temper, doing or saying things to hurt others, and using evil words when you talk. 9Do not lie to each other. You have left your old sinful life and the things you did before. 10You have begun to live the new life, in which you are being made new and are becoming like the One who made you. This new life brings you the true knowledge of God. 11In the new life there is no difference between Greeks and Jews, those who are circumcised[d] and those who are not circumcised, or people who are foreigners, or Scythians.[n] There is no difference between slaves and free people. But Christ is in all believers, and Christ is all that is important.

12God has chosen you and made you his holy people. He loves you. So always do these things: Show mercy to others, be kind, humble, gentle, and patient. 13Get along with each other, and forgive each other. If someone does wrong to you, forgive that person because the Lord forgave you. 14Do all these things; but most important, love each other. Love is what holds you all together in

These . . . angry Some Greek copies add: "against the people who do not obey God."
Scythians The Scythians were known as very wild and cruel people.

perfect unity. [15]Let the peace that Christ gives
control your thinking, because you were all called
together in one body[n] to have peace. Always be
thankful. [16]Let the teaching of Christ live in you
richly. Use all wisdom to teach and instruct each
other by singing psalms, hymns, and spiritual
songs with thankfulness in your hearts to God.
[17]Everything you do or say should be done to obey
Jesus your Lord. And in all you do, give thanks to
God the Father through Jesus.

Your New Life with Other People

[18]Wives, yield to the authority of your husbands, because this is the right thing to do in the Lord.

[19]Husbands, love your wives and be gentle with them.

[20]Children, obey your parents in all things, because this pleases the Lord.

[21]Fathers, do not nag your children. If you are
too hard to please, they may want to stop trying.

> **SIDELIGHT:** If you feel like you have read some of Colossians somewhere else, you might be right. The book is filled with passages that closely parallel Ephesians (for example, compare Colossians 3:16–17 with Ephesians 5:19–20, p. 1225). In fact, about half of Ephesians' 155 verses also have similarities to verses in Colossians.

[22]Slaves, obey your masters in all things. Do not
obey just when they are watching you, to gain
their favor, but serve them honestly, because you
respect the Lord. [23]In all the work you are doing,

body The spiritual body of Christ, meaning the church or his people.

FOLLOWING GOD

Wake Up!

In high school, George shyly kept to himself. His few friends thought he was a nice guy, but nobody, including himself, thought he had much talent or potential. In fact, they seemed rarely to think anything of him. That was okay with George, since he rarely thought about anything anyway. He was content just to exist without any goals, dreams, or ideas.

About the only thing George enjoyed was driving around town in his car. It seemed a way to pass empty hours. But one day another car slammed into George's, sending his car off the road toward a tree. George was thrown from the car just before it smashed into the tree.

When George regained consciousness, he kept hearing the police say how lucky he was. George suffered minor injuries, but the car was totaled.

George's near tragedy awakened him to the reality of his empty life. Deciding he wanted to live for more than driving his car, he poured himself into many new interests, including filmmaking. A few years after his accident, George Lucas entertained millions with American Graffiti, the Star Wars trilogy, and the Indiana Jones movies.

George Lucas was lucky: He lost his car, but gained a new purpose in life. **Colossians 3:1–10** tells Christians to "wake up" to a whole, new life that is far more important than any new career.

- How does George Lucas's awakening to life illustrate Paul's challenge to live a different way in Christ? How is it different?
- In light of this passage, how is your "old life" different from your "new life in Christ"?

CONSIDER

- writing on one side of a sheet of paper things that are different because of your "new life in Christ." On the back, write out temptations you can avoid because of this new life. Thank God for giving you strength.
- trying a new skill or interest that might help you follow God's will. Focus your attention on gifts you believe God has given you.

FOR MORE, SEE...

- Habakkuk 3:2 (p. 878)
- Luke 9:24 (p. 1019)
- Revelation 21:1–5 (p. 1347)

work the best you can. Work as if you were doing
it for the Lord, not for people. 24Remember that
you will receive your reward from the Lord,
which he promised to his people. You are serving
the Lord Christ. 25But remember that anyone who
does wrong will be punished for that wrong, and
the Lord treats everyone the same.

4 Masters, give what is good and fair to your
slaves. Remember that you have a Master in
heaven.

What the Christians Are to Do

2Continue praying, keeping alert, and always
thanking God. 3Also pray for us that God will give
us an opportunity to tell people his message. Pray
that we can preach the secret that God has made
known about Christ. This is why I am in prison.
4Pray that I can speak in a way that will make it
clear, as I should.

5Be wise in the way you act with people who
are not believers, making the most of every opportunity.
6When you talk, you should always be
kind and pleasant so you will be able to answer
everyone in the way you should.

News About the People with Paul

7Tychicus is my dear brother in Christ and a
faithful minister and servant with me in the Lord.
He will tell you all the things that are happening
to me. 8This is why I am sending him: so you may
know how we are and he may encourage you. 9I
send him with Onesimus, a faithful and dear
brother in Christ, and one of your group. They
will tell you all that has happened here.

10Aristarchus, a prisoner with me, and Mark,
the cousin of Barnabas, greet you. (I have already
told you what to do about Mark. If he comes,
welcome him.) 11Jesus, who is called Justus, also
greets you. These are the only Jewish believers
who work with me for the kingdom of God, and
they have been a comfort to me.

12Epaphras, a servant of Jesus Christ, from your
group, also greets you. He always prays for you
that you will grow to be spiritually mature and
have everything God wants for you. 13I know he
has worked hard for you and the people in Laodicea
and in Hierapolis. 14Demas and our dear
friend Luke, the doctor, greet you.

15Greet the brothers in Laodicea. And greet
Nympha and the church that meets in her house.
16After this letter is read to you, be sure it is also
read to the church in Laodicea. And you read the
letter that I wrote to Laodicea. 17Tell Archippus,
"Be sure to finish the work the Lord gave you."

18I, Paul, greet you and write this with my own
hand. Remember me in prison. Grace be with
you.

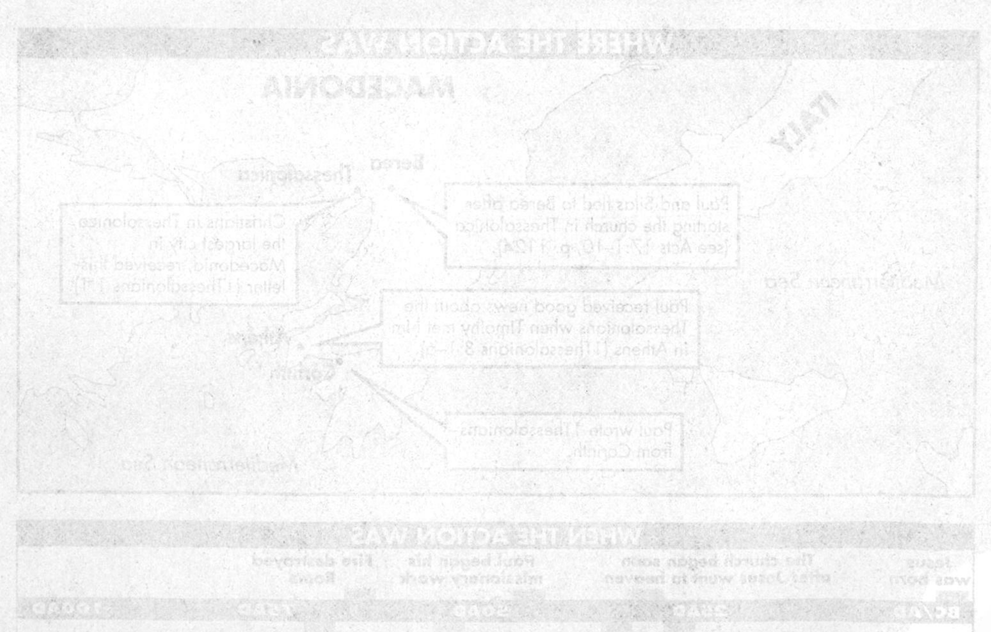

1 THESSALONIANS

Why Read This Book:

- Be encouraged to stand up for your faith even when those around you make fun of you (1 Thessalonians 2—3).
- See the importance of growing strong in faith (1 Thessalonians 4—5).

Behind the Scenes:

Summer camp was sensational. You had fun. You made friends. You grew in your faith. Around the campfire the final night, you were sure your life would never be the same because of your renewed faith. Then you went home. Your enthusiasm wore off as you faced the realities of everyday life. Would your new commitment last?

The Thessalonians might have felt the same way. Paul had come to their city, and they had become Christians. Then, suddenly, Paul was run out of town, and the new Christians were left in a hostile city without their leader. Could they stick to their faith? Would their faith keep growing?

Paul wrote this letter to encourage the new Christians and to explain why he left so quickly. He says how happy he is that they are "hanging in there" through all the troubles they face. He challenges them to keep growing in their faith. And he encourages them to look beyond persecution to the day when the Lord will come again.

Just as the letter encouraged the Thessalonians, it encourages new (and longtime) Christians today. It challenges us to hold firmly to our faith and to press on toward becoming mature Christians—even when we don't feel the spiritual "highs" we might have experienced at first.

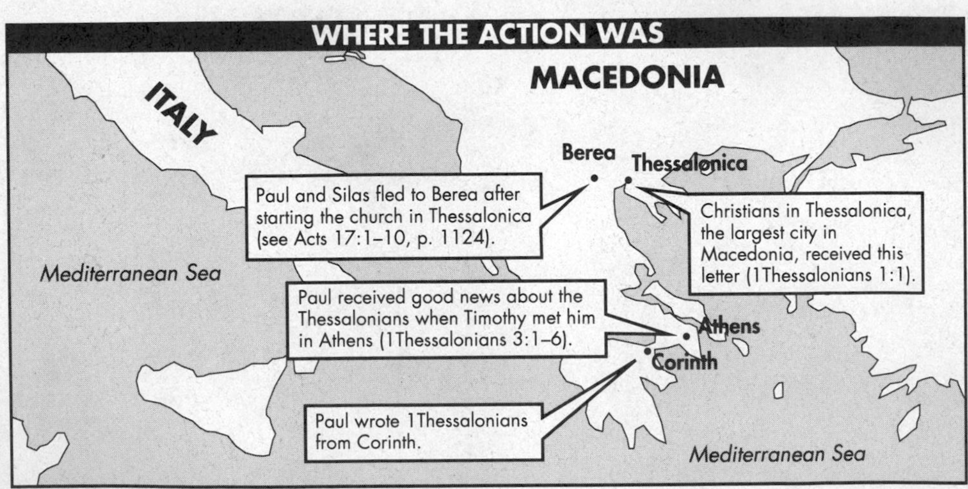

WHERE THE ACTION WAS
MACEDONIA
ITALY
Berea
Thessalonica
Paul and Silas fled to Berea after starting the church in Thessalonica (see Acts 17:1–10, p. 1124).
Christians in Thessalonica, the largest city in Macedonia, received this letter (1Thessalonians 1:1).
Mediterranean Sea
Paul received good news about the Thessalonians when Timothy met him in Athens (1Thessalonians 3:1–6).
Athens
Corinth
Paul wrote 1Thessalonians from Corinth.
Mediterranean Sea

WHEN THE ACTION WAS

Jesus born | The church began soon after Jesus went to heaven | Paul began his missionary work | Fire destroyed Rome

AD | 25AD | 50AD | 75AD | 100AD

Jesus began his ministry | Paul became a Christian | Paul wrote 1 Thessalonians | Romans destroyed the Temple in Jerusalem

1 From Paul, Silas, and Timothy.
To the church in Thessalonica, the church in
God the Father and the Lord Jesus Christ:
Grace and peace to you.

The Faith of the Thessalonians

2We always thank God for all of you and mention you when we pray. 3We continually recall
before God our Father the things you have done
because of your faith and the work you have done
because of your love. And we thank him that you
continue to be strong because of your hope in our
Lord Jesus Christ.
4Brothers and sisters,[n] God loves you, and we
know he has chosen you, 5because the Good
News[d] we brought to you came not only with
words, but with power, with the Holy Spirit,[d] and
with sure knowledge that it is true. Also you

> **SIDELIGHT:** If all the New Testament books appeared in the Bible in the order they were actually written, 1 Thessalonians might come first (with the possible exception of Galatians, p. 1206 or James, p. 1294). It is believed to have been written only twenty years after Jesus was crucified and rose from the dead.

know how we lived when we were with you in
order to help you. 6And you became like us and
like the Lord. You suffered much, but still you
accepted the teaching with the joy that comes

Brothers and sisters Although the Greek text says "Brothers" here and throughout this book, Paul's words were meant for the entire church, including men and women.

SPIRITUAL GROWTH

Spreading Love Around

Maria Mayo sat quietly in her pew through the whole organ postlude. She couldn't get the pastor's sermon on using God-given talents out of her head. She knew she had talents such as playing the guitar, but she had never thought of how she might use them for God.

Then Maria began remembering all her church friends. One friend played the piano, another played drums, and two could sing. Maybe they should form a Christian band.

Maria approached her friends, and they agreed. After practicing for several months, the band began volunteering to perform at retreats, youth gatherings, children's camps, and church services. Maria thoroughly enjoyed the band and hoped the music was helping people grow in faith.

But she really couldn't tell.

Several years later, Maria was asked to lead music for a denominational youth gathering. After an opening service, one teenager grabbed her and asked, "Did you lead music at Circle R seven summers ago?"

Maria vaguely remembered that the old band had played there. The young person continued, "That summer was the first time I heard about Jesus. I'm starting college now and want to go into the ministry. Thanks for the seed you planted."

Even though Maria didn't know how God was using her at the time, Maria spread the Good News—just as Paul spread the Good News. In **1 Thessalonians 1:1–10** we read about how the Thessalonians heard the Good News, grew in faith, and "became an example to all the believers."

- How might Paul say Maria's faith is like the Thessalonians' faith?
- The passage describes how the Thessalonians grew through several stages in their faith. What stage is your faith in?

CONSIDER . . .

- deciding how God might use you to be an example of faith to those around you. Look in the passage for specific ideas.
- taking a potted plant to someone who needs cheering up—as a symbol of your spiritual growth.

FOR MORE, SEE . . .

- Jeremiah 17:7–8 (p. 711)
- 1 Corinthians 12:1–11 (p. 1181)
- Hebrews 5:12–14 (p. 1280)

from the Holy Spirit. 7So you became an example
to all the believers in Macedonia and Southern
Greece. 8And the Lord's teaching spread from you
not only into Macedonia and Southern Greece,
but now your faith in God has become known
everywhere. So we do not need to say anything
about it. 9People everywhere are telling about the
way you accepted us when we were there with
you. They tell how you stopped worshiping idols
and began serving the living and true God. 10And
you wait for God's Son, whom God raised from
the dead, to come from heaven. He is Jesus, who
saves us from God's angry judgment that is sure
to come.

Paul's Work in Thessalonica

2 Brothers and sisters, you know our visit to
you was not a failure. 2Before we came to
you, we suffered in Philippi. People there insulted
us, as you know, and many people were against
us. But our God helped us to be brave and to tell
you his Good News.[d] 3Our appeal does not come
from lies or wrong reasons, nor were we trying to
trick you. 4But we speak the Good News because
God tested us and trusted us to do it. When we
speak, we are not trying to please people, but
God, who tests our hearts. 5You know that we
never tried to influence you by saying nice things
about you. We were not trying to get your
money; we had no selfishness to hide from you.

SIDELIGHT: Most pastors and missionaries are not in it for the money. Paul certainly wasn't (1 Thessalonians 2:5, 9). In addition to his missionary work, Paul also worked as a tentmaker (see Acts 18:3, p. 1127) so he wouldn't have to take money from the churches he started.

God knows that this is true. 6We were not looking
for human praise, from you or anyone else, 7even
though as apostles[d] of Christ we could have used
our authority over you.
But we were very gentle with you, like a
mother caring for her little children. 8Because we
loved you, we were happy to share not only God's
Good News with you, but even our own lives.
You had become so dear to us! 9Brothers and sisters, I know you remember our hard work and
difficulties. We worked night and day so we

LEADERSHIP

Gentle Leadership

She didn't look like a dynamic leader. She didn't look like a dynamic anything. In fact, you probably wouldn't notice her in a crowd—smoky gray hair, out-of-fashion glasses, thin figure, pencil behind her ear. Yet in the twenty years she taught high school English, Elsie Cannery powerfully influenced her students' lives. She gently prodded and encouraged them to use their creativity and sharpen their thinking skills.

Elsie was available to her students night and day. She told them to call her at home any time they needed to talk to someone about school or any part of their lives.

Ninety percent of her students went on to graduate from college.

As Elsie Cannery made a difference in her students' lives, the apostles made a difference in the new Christians' lives. See the similarities in **1 Thessalonians 2:1–13**.

- How are Elsie Cannery's leadership qualities like those of the apostles?
- How is your leadership style similar to the one Paul describes in the passage? How is it different?

CONSIDER . . .

- listing all the words you can to describe Christian leadership. Read the passage to give you ideas. Check the "leadership" words that also describe you. How strong is your leadership ability?
- thinking about one leader you admire a lot (a family member, friend, pastor, teacher). Talk to that person. Ask how he or she chose a profession. Ask about the qualities to strive for as a leader.

FOR MORE, SEE . . .

- Proverbs 12:14 (p. 577)
- Ephesians 2:9–10 (p. 1219)
- James 2:14–17 (p. 1295)

would not burden any of you while we preached
God's Good News to you.
10When we were with you, we lived in a holy
and honest way, without fault. You know this is
true, and so does God. 11You know that we
treated each of you as a father treats his own children. 12We encouraged you, we urged you, and
we insisted that you live good lives for God, who
calls you to his glorious kingdom.

13Also, we always thank God because when
you heard his message from us, you accepted it as
the word of God, not the words of humans. And
it really is God's message which works in you
who believe. 14Brothers and sisters, your experiences have been like those of God's churches in
Christ that are in Judea.[n] You suffered from the
people of your own country, as they suffered from
the Jews, 15who killed both the Lord Jesus and the
prophets[d] and forced us to leave that country.
They do not please God and are against all people.
16They try to stop us from teaching those who are
not Jews so they may be saved. By doing this, they
are increasing their sins to the limit. The anger of
God has come to them at last.

Paul Wants to Visit Them Again

17Brothers and sisters, though we were separated from you for a short time, our thoughts
were still with you. We wanted very much to see
you and tried hard to do so. 18We wanted to come
to you. I, Paul, tried to come more than once, but
Satan stopped us. 19You are our hope, our joy, and
the crown we will take pride in when our Lord
Jesus Christ comes. 20Truly you are our glory and
our joy.

3 When we could not wait any longer, we decided it was best to stay in Athens alone 2and
send Timothy to you. Timothy, our brother,
works with us for God and helps us tell people the
Good News[d] about Christ. We sent him to
strengthen and encourage you in your faith 3so
none of you would be upset by these troubles.
You yourselves know that we must face these
troubles. 4Even when we were with you, we told
you we all would have to suffer, and you know
it has happened. 5Because of this, when I could
wait no longer, I sent Timothy to you so I could
learn about your faith. I was afraid the devil had
tempted you, and then our hard work would have
been wasted.

6But Timothy now has come back to us from
you and has brought us good news about your
faith and love. He told us that you always remember us in a good way and that you want to see us
just as much as we want to see you. 7So, brothers
and sisters, while we have much trouble and suffering, we are encouraged about you because of
your faith. 8Our life is really full if you stand strong
in the Lord. 9We have so much joy before our God
because of you. We cannot thank him enough for
all the joy we feel. 10Night and day we continue
praying with all our heart that we can see you
again and give you all the things you need to
make your faith strong.

11Now may our God and Father himself and
our Lord Jesus prepare the way for us to come to
you. 12May the Lord make your love grow more
and multiply for each other and for all people so
that you will love others as we love you. 13May
your hearts be made strong so that you will be
holy and without fault before our God and Father
when our Lord Jesus comes with all his holy ones.

A Life that Pleases God

4 Brothers and sisters, we taught you how to
live in a way that will please God, and you
are living that way. Now we ask and encourage
you in the Lord Jesus to live that way even more.
2You know what we told you to do by the authority of the Lord Jesus. 3God wants you to be holy
and to stay away from sexual sins. 4He wants each
of you to learn to control your own body[n] in a
way that is holy and honorable. 5Don't use your
body for sexual sin like the people who do not
know God. 6Also, do not wrong or cheat another
Christian in this way. The Lord will punish people
who do those things as we have already told you
and warned you. 7God called us to be holy and
does not want us to live in sin. 8So the person
who refuses to obey this teaching is disobeying
God, not simply a human teaching. And God is
the One who gives us his Holy Spirit.[d]

SIDELIGHT: The church in Thessalonica would have been in an excellent position to love all the "Christians in all of Macedonia" (1 Thessalonians 4:10). The city was the capital of its province, so its residents had contact with people from all over the province.

9We do not need to write you about having
love for your Christian family, because God has
already taught you to love each other. 10And truly
you do love the Christians in all of Macedonia.
Brothers and sisters, now we encourage you to
love them even more.
11Do all you can to live a peaceful life. Take

Judea The Jewish land where Jesus lived and taught and where the church first began.
learn . . . body This might also mean "learn to live with your own wife."

care of your own business, and do your own work
as we have already told you. 12If you do, then
people who are not believers will respect you, and
you will not have to depend on others for what
you need.

The Lord's Coming

13Brothers and sisters, we want you to know
about those Christians who have died so you will
not be sad, as others who have no hope. 14We
believe that Jesus died and that he rose again. So,
because of him, God will raise with Jesus those
who have died. 15What we tell you now is the
Lord's own message. We who are living when the
Lord comes again will not go before those who
have already died. 16The Lord himself will come
down from heaven with a loud command, with
the voice of the archangel,[n] and with the trumpet call of God. And those who have died believing in Christ will rise first. 17After that, we who
are still alive will be gathered up with them in the
clouds to meet the Lord in the air. And we will
be with the Lord forever. 18So encourage each
other with these words.

Be Ready for the Lord's Coming

5 Now, brothers and sisters, we do not need to
write you about times and dates. 2You know

archangel The leader among God's angels or messengers.

HAPPINESS

Creating Happiness

Jorge and Juanita Hernandez were having a horrible spring as they watched their parents' unhappy marriage disintegrate. Dinners were filled with tension, evenings filled with fighting, mornings filled with angry silence.

In time, their parents decided to divorce.

On one hand, Jorge and Juanita were relieved because the constant tension would end. But they were sad because their family, as they knew it, would also end. They would have to live with one parent and visit the other.

Jorge spent the next several weeks stewing about the divorce, watching television, being alone, and skipping church and school activities. "I don't care what my parents do, and I don't care what I do," Jorge told Juanita.

Juanita thought just the opposite. "I'm hurting, but I know others are hurting worse than I am," she replied. "I want to help some of those people."

So Juanita signed up for a youth group trip to Mexico. On the trip, Juanita and other group members sang songs in prisons, presented puppet plays, read stories, and played with the village kids. Although she was sad about her parents, she dealt with that sadness by reaching out to others.

Her Mexico experience gave Juanita a new perspective on happiness. "I saw how others with a lot less than I have are happy," she said. "In some ways we need to make our own happiness."

In the midst of her sadness, Juanita created happiness for herself by reaching out to others. Read about similar feelings of happiness and joy in **1 Thessalonians 3:9–13**.

■ What encouragement would Juanita find by reading this passage? What parts of this passage show the meaning of true happiness, even when things aren't going well?

C O N S I D E R . . .

■ writing on your calendar what makes you happiest each day of the upcoming week. See if there's a pattern. Are you happiest when you are reaching out to others?

■ choosing one thing that makes you happy and doing that for someone else. For example, if you're happy when a friend calls you on the phone and says, "I was just thinking about you," think of another person, and call him or her.

F O R M O R E , S E E . . .

■ Psalm 43:4–5 (p. 507)

■ Proverbs 8:3–36 (p. 573)

■ James 5:7–11 (p. 1299)

very well that the day the Lord comes again will
be a surprise, like a thief that comes in the night.
3While people are saying, "We have peace and we
are safe," they will be destroyed quickly. It is like
pains that come quickly to a woman having a
baby. Those people will not escape. 4But you,
brothers and sisters, are not living in darkness,
and so that day will not surprise you like a thief.
5You are all people who belong to the light and to
the day. We do not belong to the night or to darkness. 6So we should not be like other people who
are sleeping, but we should be alert and have self-
control. 7Those who sleep, sleep at night. Those
who get drunk, get drunk at night. 8But we belong to the day, so we should control ourselves.
We should wear faith and love to protect us, and
the hope of salvation should be our helmet. 9God
did not choose us to suffer his anger but to have
salvation through our Lord Jesus Christ. 10Jesus
died for us so that we can live together with him,
whether we are alive or dead when he comes.
11So encourage each other and give each other
strength, just as you are doing now.

Final Instructions and Greetings

12Now, brothers and sisters, we ask you to appreciate those who work hard among you, who
lead you in the Lord and teach you. 13Respect
them with a very special love because of the work
they do.

Live in peace with each other. 14We ask you,
brothers and sisters, to warn those who do not
work. Encourage the people who are afraid. Help
those who are weak. Be patient with everyone.
15Be sure that no one pays back wrong for wrong,
but always try to do what is good for each other
and for all people.

16Always be joyful. 17Pray continually, 18and
give thanks whatever happens. That is what God
wants for you in Christ Jesus.

19Do not hold back the work of the Holy
Spirit.[d] 20Do not treat prophecy[d] as if it were
unimportant. 21But test everything. Keep what
is good, 22and stay away from everything that is
evil.

23Now may God himself, the God of peace,
make you pure, belonging only to him. May your

DEATH

We Have Hope

Dennis Harwell was in high school when his parents had a baby girl. The birth was a major celebration, because Dennis's parents had wanted another child since he was four years old. Years of trying, years of crying, years of suffering through three miscarriages finally produced Dennis's baby sister, whom they named Sarah.

Dennis and his parents were overjoyed with the new addition to their family. They fixed up a nursery and designed a playroom. They planned a special outing each weekend. They thoroughly enjoyed their new family member.

Their joy lasted six short months. One morning they woke up to discover Sarah had died in her sleep. Dennis and his parents were numb with grief. The doctors determined the cause of death was Sudden Infant Death Syndrome (SIDS). They told the family not to blame themselves, that it is virtually impossible to prevent a SIDS death.

Although Dennis and his parents felt a bit comforted by the doctors, they were still devastated by Sarah's death. As Dennis tried to work through his grief, he read **1 Thessalonians 4:13–14**. Dennis shared the passage with his parents, and they were all comforted by its words of hope.

- How were Dennis and his family comforted by this passage?
- How does it feel to know that someday you will see Christian loved ones who have died?

CONSIDER . . .

- writing a memorial letter to someone you loved who has died. Keep the letter as a reminder of this special person.
- thinking of someone who has recently lost a loved one. Call, write, visit, or take that person out to eat. Offer a little comfort.

FOR MORE, SEE . . .

- Isaiah 25:7–8 (p. 640)
- Romans 8:37–39 (p. 1153)
- 2 Timothy 1:9–10 (p. 1263)

whole self—spirit, soul, and body—be kept safe
and without fault when our Lord Jesus Christ
comes. 24You can trust the One who calls you to
do that for you.
25Brothers and sisters, pray for us.
26Give each other a holy kiss when you meet.
27I tell you by the authority of the Lord to read this
letter to all the believers.
28The grace of our Lord Jesus Christ be with
you.

FOLLOWING GOD

Get Ready!

A beginning-of-the-year notice was issued to all seniors at Franklin High: "A surprise senior fitness test will be given near the end of the school year," the notice read. "You won't know the exact day or time. You will be tested on strength, flexibility, and endurance. The highest scorer will receive a $1,000 scholarship to the college of his or her choice. This is your only notice. Be prepared!"

Steven Killain read the notice and decided to prepare right away for the test. He wanted to win the scholarship money, so it meant getting in shape, staying in shape, and staying alert for the test.

He regularly jogged, stretched, and lifted weights. He ate nutritious foods. Some of his friends thought he was crazy. "Why don't you relax a while?" they asked. "You'll have plenty of time to get ready later."

But Steve wanted to be ready whenever or wherever the test was announced. He wanted to win.

When the test was announced, all seniors competed. Most were not physically fit. Most could not even finish the long-distance run, jumping jacks, or push-ups. Not only did Steve complete all test areas, he took first place in all of them. Steve won the $1,000.

In **1 Thessalonians 5:1–11** we read about being alert and ready for the Lord's coming. Like Steve, we don't want to be caught unprepared.

■ What "be prepared" qualities did Steve possess that you also see recommended for believers in this passage?

■ How can you grow more awake and alert in following God so that you are not caught unprepared when the Lord comes?

CONSIDER. . .

■ consciously going through one day's activities as if it were the day Jesus were coming. How did you act differently? the same?

■ hanging a "Be Prepared" sign in your closet to remind you to live each day to the fullest and be ready for Christ's return.

FOR MORE, SEE. . .

■ Daniel 12:1–13 (p. 820)
■ Matthew 22:1–14 (p. 946)
■ 2 Peter 3:8–13 (p. 1313)

2 THESSALONIANS

Why Read This Book:

- Learn how God is with us now and in the future (2 Thessalonians 1).
- Find hope and comfort in God's love in the midst of life's tough times (2 Thessalonians 2—3).

Behind the Scenes:

You are about to graduate. You have passed all your classes, but you still have one English test left to go. You don't think the test will make any difference on your grade or transcript. How hard will you study?

The Thessalonian Christians were in a similar situation. They had been told that "the day of the Lord" (Christ's Second Coming) had already come, and some believed it. As a result, they didn't think they had anything to worry about, since they would all go to heaven soon. So they quit work, sat around lazily, meddled in other people's business, and depended on the church for charity. Worst of all, people decided they didn't really have to worry about growing spiritually.

Second Thessalonians challenged these actions, saying the day of the Lord had not come and would not come for some time. Instead of sitting lazily, waiting for the end, Christians should be working hard and seeking to grow in their faith.

Sometimes it can be tempting to be so excited about God's gift of eternal life that we stop working. Second Thessalonians reminds us that God has a purpose for us on earth, and we are called to do God's work in this world. We are called to keep growing in our faith even in the face of persecution.

WHEN THE ACTION WAS

Jesus was born — BC/AD

Jesus began his ministry — 25AD

The church began soon after Jesus went to heaven

Paul began his missionary work

2 Thessalonians may have been written — 50AD

Fire destroyed Rome

Romans destroyed the Temple in Jerusalem — 75AD

100AD

1 From Paul, Silas, and Timothy.
To the church in Thessalonica in God our
Father and the Lord Jesus Christ:
2Grace and peace to you from God the Father
and the Lord Jesus Christ.

Paul Talks About God's Judgment

3We must always thank God for you, brothers
and sisters.[n] This is only right, because your faith
is growing more and more, and the love that every one of you has for each other is increasing.
4So we brag about you to the other churches of
God. We tell them about the way you continue
to be strong and have faith even though you are
being treated badly and are suffering many troubles.
5This is proof that God is right in his judgment.
He wants you to be counted worthy of his kingdom for which you are suffering. 6God will do
what is right. He will give trouble to those who
trouble you. 7And he will give rest to you who are
troubled and to us also when the Lord Jesus appears with burning fire from heaven with his powerful angels. 8Then he will punish those who do
not know God and who do not obey the Good
News[d] about our Lord Jesus Christ. 9Those people
will be punished with a destruction that continues forever. They will be kept away from the Lord

brothers and sisters Although the Greek text says "brothers" here and throughout this book, Paul's words were meant for the entire church, including men and women.

SUFFERING

When a Dream Dies

It was unbelievable! Doug Hutchcraft would be able to play junior varsity football. And he was just a sophomore. His summer of intense training and his "killer instinct" were paying off. Maybe he would reach his lifelong dream of playing professional football.

During preseason workouts, Doug was ruthless. Once he noticed another guy's blood on his jersey after a workout, and he wouldn't let his mom wash the jersey.

Then one day during the cool-down drills after a scrimmage, Doug caught a cleat in the turf, spun around, and fell—with another guy on top of him. He heard a snap. "I tried to stand," Doug said. "It was impossible. My right knee felt like water."

Doug spent his whole sophomore year waiting for the badly torn ligament in his knee to heal. But at the beginning of the next season, Doug's coaches said he would need a doctor's release to play. So he went to see the team doctor of the New York Giants. "I can't sign a release allowing you to play," the doctor told him. "If you play football with this injury, you won't get through the season without ruining your knee for the rest of your life."

Doug's dream of playing football died. "I felt bitter," he later said. "I didn't think I deserved it. I had led a clean life, unlike most of the other players I knew. So why did God seem to be coming down so hard on me?"

The answer to Doug's question came later when he realized how football had replaced God in his life. "It hit me: I hadn't been living for the only thing that endures," he said. "Even if I'd been successful in the sport, the glory might have lasted six or eight years more, only if I got to the pros. But what was that compared to eternity?"

When the Thessalonians received this letter, they also were wondering why they had to suffer for their faith. **Second Thessalonians 1:1–12** encourages them to hang on because God will be victorious in the end.

- What perspective on their suffering might Doug and the Thessalonians have gotten from this letter?
- How might knowing you will experience peace with God in the future help you through troubles right now?

CONSIDER . . .

- praying for God's comfort and strength to help you through troubles you are facing at home, school, church, or work.
- writing all of the troubles you're now experiencing. Pray that God will strengthen you and help you grow in your faith through these troubles.

FOR MORE, SEE . . .

- Isaiah 9:2–7 (p. 626)
- Matthew 7:7–11 (p. 919)
- 1 Peter 3:8–22 (p. 1306)

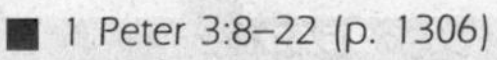

and from his great power. 10This will happen on the day when the Lord Jesus comes to receive glory because of his holy people. And all the people who have believed will be amazed at Jesus. You will be in that group, because you believed what we told you.

> **SIDELIGHT:** In the first century, being a Christian could be hazardous to your health (2 Thessalonians 1:4). The Roman historian Tacitus describes how Emperor Nero tortured Christians in Rome by dipping them in tar and setting them on fire to illuminate his race track at night.

11That is why we always pray for you, asking our God to help you live the kind of life he called you to live. We pray that with his power God will help you do the good things you want and perform the works that come from your faith. 12We pray all this so that the name of our Lord Jesus Christ will have glory in you, and you will have glory in him. That glory comes from the grace of our God and the Lord Jesus Christ.

Evil Things Will Happen

2 Brothers and sisters, we have something to say about the coming of our Lord Jesus Christ and the time when we will meet together with him. 2Do not become easily upset in your thinking or afraid if you hear that the day of the Lord has already come. Someone may say this in a prophecy[d] or in a message or in a letter as if it came from us. 3Do not let anyone fool you in any way. That day of the Lord will not come until the turning away[n] from God happens and the Man of Evil, who is on his way to hell, appears. 4He will be against and put himself above anything called God or anything that people worship. And that Man of Evil will even go into God's Temple[d] and sit there and say that he is God.

5I told you when I was with you that all this would happen. Do you not remember? 6And now you know what is stopping that Man of Evil so he will appear at the right time. 7The secret power of evil is already working in the world, but there is one who is stopping that power. And he will continue to stop it until he is taken out of the way. 8Then that Man of Evil will appear, and the Lord Jesus will kill him with the breath that comes from his mouth and will destroy him with the glory of his coming. 9The Man of Evil will come by the power of Satan. He will have great power, and he will do many different false miracles,[d] signs, and wonders. 10He will use every kind of evil to trick those who are lost. They will die, because they refused to love the truth. (If they loved the truth, they would be saved.) 11For this reason God sends them something powerful that leads them away from the truth so they will believe a lie. 12So all those will be judged guilty who did not believe the truth, but enjoyed doing evil.

You Are Chosen for Salvation

13Brothers and sisters, whom the Lord loves, God chose you from the beginning to be saved. So we must always thank God for you. You are saved by the Spirit[d] that makes you holy and by your faith in the truth. 14God used the Good News[d] that we preached to call you to be saved so you can share in the glory of our Lord Jesus Christ. 15So, brothers and sisters, stand strong and continue to believe the teachings we gave you in our speaking and in our letter.

16-17May our Lord Jesus Christ himself and God our Father encourage you and strengthen you in every good thing you do and say. God loved us, and through his grace he gave us a good hope and encouragement that continues forever.

Pray for Us

3 And now, brothers and sisters, pray for us that the Lord's teaching will continue to spread quickly and that people will give honor to that teaching, just as happened with you. 2And pray that we will be protected from stubborn and evil people, because not all people believe.

3But the Lord is faithful and will give you strength and will protect you from the Evil One. 4The Lord makes us feel sure that you are doing and will continue to do the things we told you. 5May the Lord lead your hearts into God's love and Christ's patience.

The Duty to Work

6Brothers and sisters, by the authority of our Lord Jesus Christ we command you to stay away from any believer who refuses to work and does not follow the teaching we gave you. 7You yourselves know that you should live as we live. We were not lazy when we were with you. 8And when we ate another person's food, we always paid for it. We worked very hard night and day so we would not be an expense to any of you. 9We had the right to ask you to help us, but we worked to take care of ourselves so we would be an example for you to follow. 10When we were with you, we gave you this rule: "Anyone who refuses to work should not eat."

11We hear that some people in your group refuse to work. They do nothing but busy them-

turning away Or "the rebellion."

selves in other people's lives. [12]We command those people and beg them in the Lord Jesus Christ to work quietly and earn their own food. [13]But you, brothers and sisters, never become tired of doing good.

SIDELIGHT: Slouches, beware! If you don't work, you don't eat. That's what 2 Thessalonians 3:11–13 says to people who sat around waiting for Christ's Second Coming. The original Greek language is a pun. It could be translated, "No loaf for loafers!"

[14]If some people do not obey what we tell you in this letter, then take note of them. Have nothing to do with them so they will feel ashamed. [15]But do not treat them as enemies. Warn them as fellow believers.

Final Words

[16]Now may the Lord of peace give you peace at all times and in every way. The Lord be with all of you.

[17]I, Paul, end this letter now in my own handwriting. All my letters have this to show they are from me. This is the way I write.

[18]The grace of our Lord Jesus Christ be with you all.

GOD'S LOVE

Tough Times

The Jefferson family experienced the pits of despair. Mr. Jefferson, a fantastic, energetic, loving husband and father, was killed in a car accident. He left a wife, an eighteen-year-old daughter, and a sixteen-year-old son. How would the family survive this horribly lonely and tough time?

Their church rallied around them. People volunteered to mow their yard and repair their house. Church members cooked and served meals every day right after the death and once a week throughout the following year. The church collected a special offering for their immediate expenses and found a job for Mrs. Jefferson. Church friends supported the family throughout that tough first year with phone calls, visits, cards, and gifts.

The Jeffersons wrote this thank-you to their congregation: "Through your prayers, dear friends, we have been comforted. Through your kind acts we have been soothed. We experienced God's love through you and your love. You made an unbearable experience bearable."

As the church comforted the Jeffersons, **2 Thessalonians 2:13–3:5** promises that God's love will comfort Christians who suffer.

- How is the love shown to the Jeffersons by their congregation like the love that comforted the early Christians?
- How does God's love comfort you through tough times?

CONSIDER . . .

- circling the word love each time you read your Bible over the next several days. Count the number of "loves." Notice how God's love for you is stressed throughout the Bible. Consider starting your reading with the passages listed below.
- letting God's love shine through you. Think of someone who is sad or lonely (for example, a new person at school or an elderly church member who has lost a spouse). Surprise that person with a present or a card.

FOR MORE, SEE . . .

- Psalm 89:1–2 (p. 534)
- Matthew 11:28–30 (p. 928)
- Romans 5:6–8 (p. 1145)

1 TIMOTHY

Why Read This Book:

- Learn how to guard against false teaching (1 Timothy 1).
- Find out what to look for in a good church leader (1 Timothy 2—5).
- See what is really important in life (1 Timothy 6).

Behind the Scenes:

When you begin using a computer, you could just turn it on and start punching keys, hoping you will hit the right ones to make something happen. But, more likely, you will begin by reading the machine's operations manual. There you will find step-by-step things to do to use the machine correctly.

The first Christians didn't have experience running a church. Many times they tried different things, hoping they were right. But they also needed an "operations manual."

First Timothy was just what they needed. It gives church leaders specific guidance on running a church: choosing leaders, dealing with false teachings, and order in worship, for example. It's called a "pastoral letter" because it focuses on the work of pastors. The two other pastoral letters in the Bible are 2 Timothy (p. 1263) and Titus (p. 1270).

Just because 1 Timothy was originally written about church leaders doesn't mean pastors are the only ones who can benefit from reading it. The book helps all Christians learn the differences between true and false teachings. And it gives practical guidance on how to live as Christians.

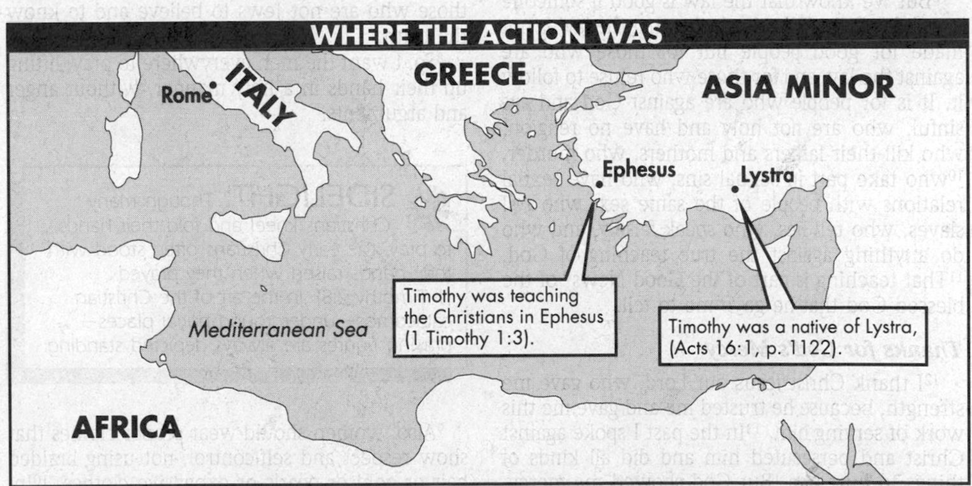

WHERE THE ACTION WAS
GREECE
ASIA MINOR
Rome
ITALY
Ephesus
Lystra
Mediterranean Sea
AFRICA
Timothy was teaching the Christians in Ephesus (1 Timothy 1:3).
Timothy was a native of Lystra, (Acts 16:1, p. 1122).

WHEN THE ACTION WAS

- **Jesus was born** — BC/AD
- **Jesus began his ministry**
- **The church began soon after Jesus went to heaven**
- 25AD
- **Paul became a Christian**
- **Timothy traveled with Paul on numerous trips**
- 50AD
- **I Timothy may have been written**
- **Fire destroyed Rome**
- **Romans destroyed the Temple in Jerusalem**
- 75AD
- 100AD

1 From Paul, an apostle[d] of Christ Jesus, by the command of God our Savior and Christ Jesus our hope.

2To Timothy, a true child to me because you believe:

Grace, mercy, and peace from God the Father and Christ Jesus our Lord.

SIDELIGHT: Genealogies were hot fads in Bible times (1 Timothy 1:4). Alexander the Great even made up his own family tree, linking him with such Greek gods as Hercules and Achilles.

Warning Against False Teaching

3I asked you to stay longer in Ephesus when I went into Macedonia so you could command some people there to stop teaching false things. 4Tell them not to spend their time on stories that are not true and on long lists of names in family histories. These things only bring arguments; they do not help God's work, which is done in faith. 5The purpose of this command is for people to have love, a love that comes from a pure heart and a good conscience and a true faith. 6Some people have missed these things and turned to useless talk. 7They want to be teachers of the law, but they do not understand either what they are talking about or what they are sure about.

8But we know that the law is good if someone uses it lawfully. 9We also know that the law is not made for good people but for those who are against the law and for those who refuse to follow it. It is for people who are against God and are sinful, who are not holy and have no religion, who kill their fathers and mothers, who murder, 10who take part in sexual sins, who have sexual relations with people of the same sex, who sell slaves, who tell lies, who speak falsely, and who do anything against the true teaching of God. 11That teaching is part of the Good News[d] of the blessed God that he gave me to tell.

Thanks for God's Mercy

12I thank Christ Jesus our Lord, who gave me strength, because he trusted me and gave me this work of serving him. 13In the past I spoke against Christ and persecuted him and did all kinds of things to hurt him. But God showed me mercy, because I did not know what I was doing. I did not believe. 14But the grace of our Lord was fully given to me, and with that grace came the faith and love that are in Christ Jesus.

15What I say is true, and you should fully accept it: Christ Jesus came into the world to save sinners, of whom I am the worst. 16But I was given mercy so that in me, the worst of all sinners, Christ Jesus could show that he has patience without limit. His patience with me made me an example for those who would believe in him and have life forever. 17To the King that rules forever, who will never die, who cannot be seen, the only God, be honor and glory forever and ever. Amen.

18Timothy, my child, I am giving you a command that agrees with the prophecies[d] that were given about you in the past. I tell you this so you can follow them and fight the good fight. 19Continue to have faith and do what you know is right. Some people have rejected this, and their faith has been shipwrecked. 20Hymenaeus and Alexander have done that, and I have given them to Satan so they will learn not to speak against God.

Some Rules for Men and Women

2 First, I tell you to pray for all people, asking God for what they need and being thankful to him. 2Pray for rulers and for all who have authority so that we can have quiet and peaceful lives full of worship and respect for God. 3This is good, and it pleases God our Savior, 4who wants all people to be saved and to know the truth. 5There is one God and one way human beings can reach God. That way is through Christ Jesus, who is himself human. 6He gave himself as a payment to free all people. He is proof that came at the right time. 7That is why I was chosen to tell the Good News[d] and to be an apostle.[d] (I am telling the truth; I am not lying.) I was chosen to teach those who are not Jews to believe and to know the truth.

8So, I want the men everywhere to pray, lifting up their hands in a holy manner, without anger and arguments.

SIDELIGHT: Though many Christians kneel and fold their hands to pray, the early Christians often stood with their hands raised when they prayed (1 Timothy 2:8). In the art of the Christian catacombs—underground burial places—praying figures are always depicted standing.

9Also, women should wear proper clothes that show respect and self-control, not using braided hair or gold or pearls or expensive clothes. 10Instead, they should do good deeds, which is right for women who say they worship God.

11Let a woman learn by listening quietly and being ready to cooperate in everything. 12But I do not allow a woman to teach or to have authority over a man, but to listen quietly, 13because Adam was formed first and then Eve. 14And Adam was

not tricked, but the woman was tricked and became a sinner. 15But she will be saved through
having children if they continue in faith, love, and
holiness, with self-control.

Elders in the Church

3 What I say is true: Anyone wanting to become an elder[d] desires a good work. 2An elder must not give people a reason to criticize him,
and he must have only one wife. He must be self-
controlled, wise, respected by others, ready to
welcome guests, and able to teach. 3He must not
drink too much wine or like to fight, but rather
be gentle and peaceable, not loving money. 4He
must be a good family leader, having children
who cooperate with full respect. 5(If someone
does not know how to lead the family, how can
that person take care of God's church?) 6But an
elder must not be a new believer, or he might be
too proud of himself and be judged guilty just as
the devil was. 7An elder must also have the respect of people who are not in the church so he
will not be criticized by others and caught in the
devil's trap.

Deacons in the Church

8In the same way, deacons[d] must be respected
by others, not saying things they do not mean.
They must not drink too much wine or try to get
rich by cheating others. 9With a clear conscience

FORGIVENESS

Accidents Happen

Tyler Hanson and Troy Carr crouched low when they heard a twig snap. Peering through the brush, they saw the buck.

"I'll circle to his left. You circle to his right," Troy whispered.

Tyler nodded and started crawling to the right.

As the buck wandered closer, Tyler slowly rose and pointed his rifle.

But Troy's shot pierced the silence first, and Tyler fell to the ground before he could shoot.

When Tyler awoke eight hours later at the hospital, he couldn't see. He had been shot in the eye, his doctors explained. A glass eye would replace his destroyed eye.

Tyler seethed. "How could his best friend do this to him?" he asked himself.

When Troy visited Tyler for the first time, Tyler refused to speak to him. He folded his arms and wouldn't face Troy. When Troy hung around too long, Tyler exploded. "Get out of here! Leave me alone!"

After Tyler settled down, he and Troy talked. The buck had jumped right before Troy pulled the trigger. "It was an accident. I jerked the gun to hit him," Troy explained. "But instead, I hit you. Please, don't hate me."

It took weeks for Tyler to talk to Troy—let alone forgive him. But finally Tyler realized forgiveness was the only way to heal the bitterness inside him. And when he forgave Troy, the two became close again.

"Yes, I lost my eye," Tyler told Troy two months after the accident, "but I didn't need to lose a friend, too."

Tyler and Troy understood the importance of mercy and forgiveness, which is what **1 Timothy 1:12–17** is all about. Read what the writer says about mercy.

- How is Troy like the writer in this passage? How are they different? Why were Troy and the writer of 1 Timothy thankful for the forgiveness they received?
- How might God's forgiveness help you deal with the sins you've committed?

C O N S I D E R . . .

- praying about the wrongs you have done and asking God for forgiveness. Write "You are forgiven" on a note, and post it on your mirror.
- inviting someone you need to forgive to an ice cream shop. Buy the person a treat, talk about the problem, and forgive the person. Ask your forgiven friend to forgive you.

F O R M O R E , S E E . . .

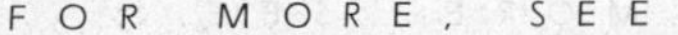
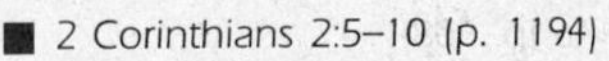

- Genesis 50:15–21 (p. 56)
- Matthew 6:14–15 (p. 918)
- 2 Corinthians 2:5–10 (p. 1194)

they must follow the secret of the faith that God made known to us. 10Test them first. Then let them serve as deacons if you find nothing wrong in them. 11In the same way, women[n] must be respected by others. They must not speak evil of others. They must be self-controlled and trustworthy in everything. 12Deacons must have only one wife and be good leaders of their children and their own families. 13Those who serve well as deacons are making an honorable place for themselves, and they will be very bold in their faith in Christ Jesus.

The Secret of Our Life

14Although I hope I can come to you soon, I am writing these things to you now. 15Then, even if I am delayed, you will know how to live in the family of God. That family is the church of the living God, the support and foundation of the truth. 16Without doubt, the secret of our life of worship is great:

He was shown to us in a human body,
  proved right in spirit,[d]
and seen by angels.
  He was preached to those who are not
    Jews,
believed in by the world,
  and taken up in glory.

A Warning About False Teachers

4 Now the Holy Spirit[d] clearly says that in the later times some people will stop believing the faith. They will follow spirits that lie and teachings of demons.[d] 2Such teachings come from the false words of liars whose consciences are destroyed as if by a hot iron. 3They forbid people to marry and tell them not to eat certain foods which God created to be eaten with thanks by people who believe and know the truth. 4Everything God made is good, and nothing should be refused if it is accepted with thanks, 5because it is made holy by what God has said and by prayer.

Be a Good Servant of Christ

6By telling these things to the brothers and sis-

women This might mean the wives of the deacons, or it might mean women who serve in the same way as deacons.

PRAYER

Pray for All People

"I'm shipping out tonight to Saudi Arabia. I'll see you when I get back."

Darlene Wachs hung up the phone. Saudi Arabia? Her boyfriend Greg Richter was going to Saudi Arabia with the U.S. armed forces. She didn't even know where Saudi Arabia was!

She said a quick prayer, asking God to keep Greg safe.

Darlene swallowed the lump in her throat and searched for a world atlas. She was terrified something could happen to Greg, but she wanted at least to know where he was going.

During the worship service on Sunday, her pastor said, "Let's pray for all people," and then listed different parts of the world, including Saudi Arabia. Darlene's mind usually wandered during those prayers, since the places seemed so far away and irrelevant to her life. But this time she paid attention.

What happened in Saudi Arabia really did affect her life.

When Darlene's boyfriend suddenly went overseas, she understood the importance of praying for all people. **1 Timothy 2:1–4** expands our prayer concerns beyond ourselves and reminds us God cares for the whole world.

- How does praying for a country such as Saudi Arabia fit the message of this scripture?
- Which countries and rulers should you pray for today?

C O N S I D E R . . .

- reading the international section of your newspaper. Ask members of your church to pray for the people mentioned there.
- looking at a world atlas, and praying for people in different parts of the world. Pray for them each evening.

F O R   M O R E ,   S E E . . .

- Psalm 46 (p. 508)
- Ephesians 6:18–20 (p. 1226)
- James 5:13–18 (p. 1299)

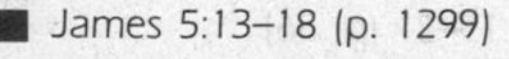

ters,[n] you will be a good servant of Christ Jesus. You will be made strong by the words of the faith and the good teaching which you have been following. 7But do not follow foolish stories that disagree with God's truth, but train yourself to serve God. 8Training your body helps you in some ways, but serving God helps you in every way by bringing you blessings in this life and in the future life, too. 9What I say is true, and you should fully accept it. 10This is why we work and struggle: We hope in the living God who is the Savior of all people, especially of those who believe.

SIDELIGHT: When 1 Timothy 4:8 talks about training your body, the original Greek word for training is the same as gymnastics in English. And the word gymnastics comes from the word for nude, since athletes worked out in the nude. Today we just have to put up with gang showers!

11Command and teach these things. 12Do not let anyone treat you as if you are unimportant because you are young. Instead, be an example to the believers with your words, your actions, your love, your faith, and your pure life. 13Until I come, continue to read the Scriptures[d] to the people, strengthen them, and teach them. 14Use the gift you have, which was given to you through prophecy[d] when the group of elders[d] laid their hands on[n] you. 15Continue to do those things; give your life to doing them so your progress may be seen by everyone. 16Be careful in your life and in your teaching. If you continue to live and teach rightly, you will save both yourself and those who listen to you.

Rules for Living with Others

5 Do not speak angrily to an older man, but plead with him as if he were your father. Treat younger men like brothers, 2older women like mothers, and younger women like sisters. Always treat them in a pure way.

3Take care of widows who are truly widows. 4But if a widow has children or grandchildren, let them first learn to do their duty to their own family and to repay their parents or grandparents. That pleases God. 5The true widow, who is all alone, puts her hope in God and continues to pray night and day for God's help. 6But the widow who uses her life to please herself is really dead while she is alive. 7Tell the believers to do these things so that no one can criticize them. 8Whoever does not care for his own relatives, especially his own family members, has turned against the faith and is worse than someone who does not believe in God.

9To be on the list of widows, a woman must be at least sixty years old. She must have been faithful to her husband. 10She must be known for her good works—works such as raising her children, welcoming strangers, washing the feet of God's people, helping those in trouble, and giving her life to do all kinds of good deeds.

11But do not put younger widows on that list. After they give themselves to Christ, they are pulled away from him by their physical needs, and then they want to marry again. 12They will be judged for not doing what they first promised to do. 13Besides that, they learn to waste their time, going from house to house. And they not only waste their time but also begin to gossip and busy themselves with other people's lives, saying things they should not say. 14So I want the younger widows to marry, have children, and manage their homes. Then no enemy will have any reason to criticize them. 15But some have already turned away to follow Satan.

16If any woman who is a believer has widows in her family, she should care for them herself. The church should not have to care for them. Then it will be able to take care of those who are truly widows.

17The elders[d] who lead the church well should receive double honor, especially those who work hard by speaking and teaching, 18because the Scripture[d] says: "When an ox is working in the grain, do not cover its mouth to keep it from eating,"[n] and "A worker should be given his pay."[n]

19Do not listen to someone who accuses an elder, without two or three witnesses. 20Tell those who continue sinning that they are wrong. Do this in front of the whole church so that the others will have a warning.

21Before God and Christ Jesus and the chosen angels, I command you to do these things without showing favor of any kind to anyone.

22Think carefully before you lay your hands on[n] anyone, and don't share in the sins of others. Keep yourself pure.

23Stop drinking only water, but drink a little wine to help your stomach and your frequent sicknesses.

brothers and sisters Although the Greek text says "brothers" here and throughout this book, Paul's words refer to the entire church, including men and women.
laid their hands on The laying on of hands had many purposes, including the giving of a blessing, power, or authority.
"When . . . eating," Quotation from Deuteronomy 25:4.
"A worker . . . pay." Quotation from Luke 10:7.
lay your hands on The laying on of hands had many purposes, including the giving of a blessing, power, or authority.

24 The sins of some people are easy to see even
before they are judged, but the sins of others are
seen only later. 25 So also good deeds are easy to
see, but even those that are not easily seen cannot
stay hidden.

6 All who are slaves under a yoke[d] should
show full respect to their masters so no one
will speak against God's name and our teaching.
2 The slaves whose masters are believers should
not show their masters any less respect because
they are believers. They should serve their masters even better, because they are helping believers they love.

You must teach and preach these things.

False Teaching and True Riches

3 Anyone who has a different teaching does not
agree with the true teaching of our Lord Jesus
Christ and the teaching that shows the true way
to serve God. 4 This person is full of pride and understands nothing, but is sick with a love for arguing and fighting about words. This brings jealousy,
fighting, speaking against others, evil mistrust,
5 and constant quarrels from those who have evil
minds and have lost the truth. They think that
serving God is a way to get rich.

6 Serving God does make us very rich, if we are
satisfied with what we have. 7 We brought nothing into the world, so we can take nothing out.
8 But, if we have food and clothes, we will be satisfied with that. 9 Those who want to become rich
bring temptation to themselves and are caught in
a trap. They want many foolish and harmful
things that ruin and destroy people. 10 The love of
money causes all kinds of evil. Some people have
left the faith, because they wanted to get more
money, but they have caused themselves much
sorrow.

Some Things to Remember

11 But you, man of God, run away from all those
things. Instead, live in the right way, serve God,
have faith, love, patience, and gentleness. 12 Fight
the good fight of faith, grabbing hold of the life
that continues forever. You were called to have
that life when you confessed the good confession
before many witnesses. 13 In the sight of God, who
gives life to everything, and of Christ Jesus, I give

MONEY

More and More

Disappointed by her mom's refusal to buy the expensive dress she wanted for her junior prom, Janice Nielsen vowed her senior prom would be different.

So, at the start of her senior year, Janice landed a job as a cashier in a video store. All year she worked hard. From each paycheck, she diligently put away money for the prom dress and other prom expenses.

During March and April, Janice tried on dress after dress. She wanted to buy just the right one—the one that would make her happy.

The morning after the prom, Janice sat in her room and cried. The night had been wonderful. Her dress was beautiful. The limousine ride was fun. But now it was all over. The hundreds of dollars she had spent had not brought the happiness she expected.

She felt betrayed, especially when she compared her senior prom to her junior prom. After all, she had had just as much fun at the junior prom, even though her dress had cost much less.

Janice thought money would buy her happiness. As you read **1 Timothy 6:6–16**, consider what truly makes Christians rich.

- What advice in this passage could help Janice understand the ultimate result of the love of money?
- When do you get caught up in wanting more? How could the advice in the passage help you avoid that trap?

C O N S I D E R . . .

- analyzing your use of money in three categories: spending, saving and giving. Based on what you read in the passage, what do you need to do with your money?
- beginning a tithe (giving 10 percent of your income) to your church.

F O R M O R E , S E E . . .

- Joshua 7:19–26 (p. 200)
- Proverbs 15:27 (p. 581)
- Hebrews 13:5–6 (p. 1291)

you a command. Christ Jesus made the good confession when he stood before Pontius Pilate. 14 Do
what you were commanded to do without wrong
or blame until our Lord Jesus Christ comes again.
15 God will make that happen at the right time. He
is the blessed and only Ruler, the King of all kings
and the Lord of all lords. 16 He is the only One who
never dies. He lives in light so bright no one can
go near it. No one has ever seen God, or can see
him. May honor and power belong to God forever. Amen.

17 Command those who are rich with things of
this world not to be proud. Tell them to hope in
God, not in their uncertain riches. God richly
gives us everything to enjoy. 18 Tell the rich people
to do good, to be rich in doing good deeds, to be
generous and ready to share. 19 By doing that, they
will be saving a treasure for themselves as a strong
foundation for the future. Then they will be able
to have the life that is true life.

20 Timothy, guard what God has trusted to you.
Stay away from foolish, useless talk and from the
arguments of what is falsely called "knowledge."
21 By saying they have that "knowledge," some
have missed the true faith.

Grace be with you.

> **SIDELIGHT:** Saying that Jesus Christ is "King of all kings and the Lord of all lords" (1 Timothy 6:15) was a bold statement in the midst of the persecution the early Christians faced. Near the end of the first century, the Roman emperor Domitian demanded that his subjects address him as "Lord and God." Christians who refused were threatened, exiled, and put to death.

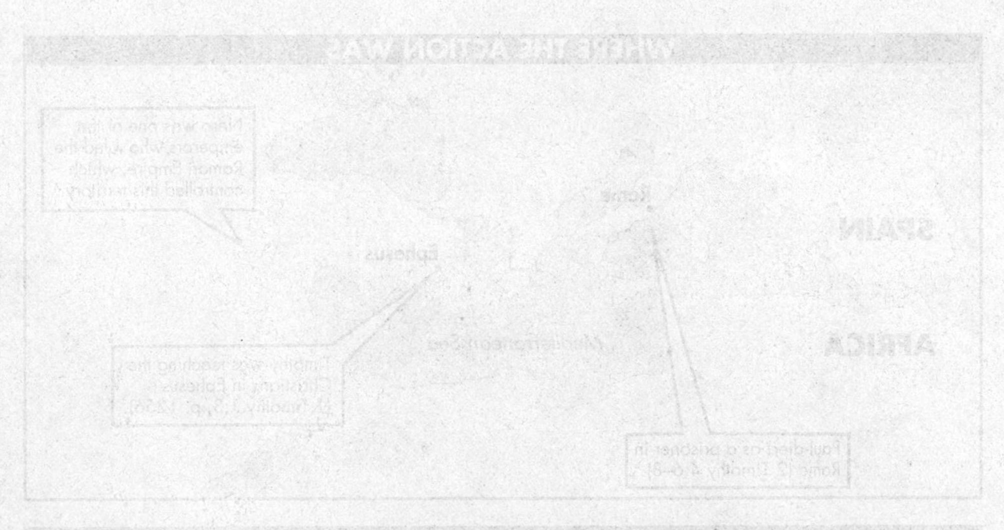

2 TIMOTHY

Why Read This Book:

- Be encouraged to keep following God, even when you face danger for doing it (2 Timothy 1—2).
- Find out how to make it through tough times (2 Timothy 3—4).

Behind the Scenes:

People who know they are soon to die often divide up their belongings and ask those around them to finish the projects they have started. Paul knew he was facing death (2 Timothy 4:6–8), so he wrote this letter to hand off the baton of ministry for Timothy to carry on.

Second Timothy captures what a retiring leader would say to a new leader. It gives lots of encouragement. It gives advice on how to become a leader. And it says that the road will be rocky and rough at times, but we should remain strong anyway.

While 1 Timothy gives instructions on how to run a church, 2 Timothy is a personal letter—like one you would write to a close friend. It encourages Christians facing tough times, since the Roman leader was persecuting Christians. And it can encourage us to stick to our faith today, even when people try to pull us away.

WHERE THE ACTION WAS

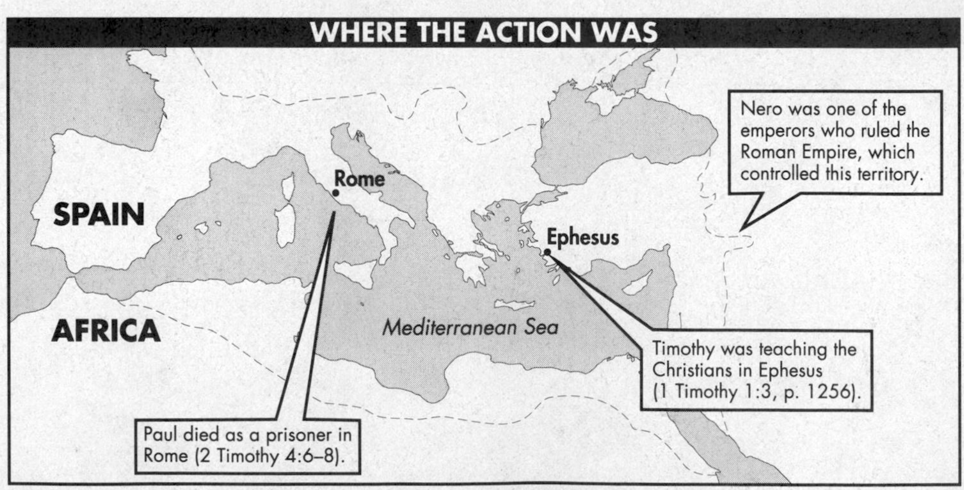

Nero was one of the emperors who ruled the Roman Empire, which controlled this territory.
Rome
SPAIN
Ephesus
AFRICA
Mediterranean Sea
Timothy was teaching the Christians in Ephesus (1 Timothy 1:3, p. 1256).
Paul died as a prisoner in Rome (2 Timothy 4:6–8).

WHEN THE ACTION WAS

Jesus was born — The church began soon after Jesus went to heaven — Timothy traveled with Paul on numerous trips — Fire destroyed Rome

BC/AD — 25AD — 50AD — 75AD — 100AD

Jesus began his ministry — Paul became a Christian — 2 Timothy may have been written — Romans destroyed the Temple in Jerusalem

1 From Paul, an apostle[d] of Christ Jesus by the
will of God. God sent me to tell about the
promise of life that is in Christ Jesus.
2To Timothy, a dear child to me:
Grace, mercy, and peace to you from God the
Father and Christ Jesus our Lord.

Encouragement for Timothy

3I thank God as I always mention you in my
prayers, day and night. I serve him, doing what I
know is right as my ancestors did. 4Remembering
that you cried for me, I want very much to see
you so I can be filled with joy. 5I remember your
true faith. That faith first lived in your grandmother Lois and in your mother Eunice, and I
know you now have that same faith. 6This is why
I remind you to keep using the gift God gave you
when I laid my hands on[n] you. Now let it grow,
as a small flame grows into a fire. 7God did not
give us a spirit that makes us afraid but a spirit of
power and love and self-control.
8So do not be ashamed to tell people about our
Lord Jesus, and do not be ashamed of me, in
prison for the Lord. But suffer with me for the
Good News.[d] God, who gives us the strength to
do that, 9saved us and made us his holy people.
That was not because of anything we did ourselves but because of God's purpose and grace.
That grace was given to us through Christ Jesus
before time began, 10but it is now shown to us by
the coming of our Savior Christ Jesus. He de-

laid my hands on The laying on of hands had many purposes, including the giving of a blessing, power, or authority.

SHARING FAITH

What to Say?

Megan Taylor abruptly dropped out of church. She had been going regularly for several months, so the group noticed her absence immediately. Her friend Jeanne Murray went over to Megan's house to ask what was wrong.

"I'm just not good enough to be a Christian," Megan replied. "I sometimes swear when I get mad. I think bad things sometimes. And I just don't feel like I set a good example for other people."

"But you don't need to be perfect or know all the answers," Jeanne said.

Megan just shook her head, and Jeanne struggled to find the right words to help her friend. "You're always so giving, and Christians are giving," Jeanne said.

"I'm not more giving than anybody else," Megan replied.

Jeanne didn't know how to respond. The more she thought, the more frustrated she became. She finally blurted out, "You are a Christian, Megan. But if I were really a good friend, I'd know how to help you."

Megan paused. "You're right. You're absolutely right."

"Huh?" a puzzled Jeanne asked.

"You just told me why I can still be a Christian," Megan said. "We've been friends a long time, right? But sometimes we don't feel like we're good friends. It's the same with being a Christian. At times, I may feel like a failure. But as long as I'm trying, I'm doing okay. You really helped me, Jeanne. Thanks."

As Jeanne walked home, she still wondered how she had helped Megan. So, she simply thanked God for giving her the words to say. Jeanne's willingness to witness was a lot like **2 Timothy 1:3–14**.

- How did Jeanne share her faith with Megan? How was her experience like and unlike the passage?
- What does this passage say about sharing your faith with others?

C O N S I D E R . . .

- telling your family why you are a Christian. Ask how family members see you sharing your faith.
- dropping a postcard to someone struggling with his or her faith, encouraging that person like 2 Timothy offers encouragement.

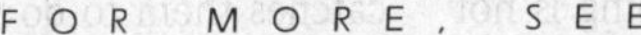
F O R M O R E , S E E . . .

- Exodus 4:1–12 (p. 62)
- Luke 9:1–6 (p. 1018)
- 1 Corinthians 1:18–31 (p. 1168)

stroyed death, and through the Good News he showed us the way to have life that cannot be destroyed. 11I was chosen to tell that Good News and to be an apostle[d] and a teacher. 12I am suffering now because I tell the Good News, but I am not ashamed, because I know Jesus, the One in whom I have believed. And I am sure he is able to protect what he has trusted me with until that day.[n] 13Follow the pattern of true teachings that you heard from me in faith and love, which are in Christ Jesus. 14Protect the truth that you were given; protect it with the help of the Holy Spirit[d] who lives in us.

SIDELIGHT: Like his mentor Paul (2 Timothy 1:8), Timothy also experienced persecution for his faith, according to Hebrews 13:23 (p. 1292). He was imprisoned but released. Paul was apparently executed while a prisoner in Rome.

15You know that everyone in the country of Asia has left me, even Phygelus and Hermogenes. 16May the Lord show mercy to the family of Onesiphorus, who has often helped me and was not ashamed that I was in prison. 17When he came to Rome, he looked eagerly for me until he found me. 18May the Lord allow him to find mercy from the Lord on that day. You know how many ways he helped me in Ephesus.

A Loyal Soldier of Christ Jesus

2 You then, Timothy, my child, be strong in the grace we have in Christ Jesus. 2You should teach people whom you can trust the things you and many others have heard me say. Then they will be able to teach others. 3Share in the troubles we have like a good soldier of Christ Jesus. 4A soldier wants to please the enlisting officer, so no one serving in the army wastes time with everyday matters. 5Also an athlete who takes part in a contest must obey all the rules in order to win. 6The farmer who works hard should be the first person to get some of the food that was grown. 7Think about what I am saying, because the Lord will give you the ability to understand everything.

8Remember Jesus Christ, who was raised from the dead, who is from the family of David. This is the Good News[d] I preach, 9and I am suffering because of it to the point of being bound with chains like a criminal. But God's teaching is not in chains. 10So I patiently accept all these troubles so that those whom God has chosen can have the salvation that is in Christ Jesus. With that salvation comes glory that never ends.

11This teaching is true:

If we died with him, we will also live with
him.
12 If we accept suffering, we will also rule
with him.
If we refuse to accept him, he will refuse to
accept us.
13 If we are not faithful, he will still be
faithful,
because he cannot be false to himself.

A Worker Pleasing to God

14Continue teaching these things, warning people in God's presence not to argue about words. It does not help anyone, and it ruins those who listen. 15Make every effort to give yourself to God as the kind of person he will accept. Be a worker who is not ashamed and who uses the true teaching in the right way. 16Stay away from foolish, useless talk, because that will lead people further away from God. 17Their evil teaching will spread like a sickness inside the body. Hymenaeus and Philetus are like that. 18They have left the true teaching, saying that the rising from the dead has already taken place, and so they are destroying the faith of some people. 19But God's strong foundation continues to stand. These words are written on the seal: "The Lord knows those who belong to him,"[n] and "Everyone who wants to belong to the Lord must stop doing wrong."

20In a large house there are not only things made of gold and silver, but also things made of wood and clay. Some things are used for special purposes, and others are made for ordinary jobs. 21All who make themselves clean[d] from evil will be used for special purposes. They will be made holy, useful to the Master, ready to do any good work.

22But run away from the evil young people like to do. Try hard to live right and to have faith, love, and peace, together with those who trust in the Lord from pure hearts. 23Stay away from foolish and stupid arguments, because you know they grow into quarrels. 24And a servant of the Lord must not quarrel but must be kind to everyone, a good teacher, and patient. 25The Lord's servant must gently teach those who disagree. Then maybe God will let them change their minds so they can accept the truth. 26And they may wake up and escape from the trap of the devil, who catches them to do what he wants.

day The day Christ will come to judge all people and take his people to live with him.
"The Lord . . . him" Quotation from Numbers 16:5.

The Last Days

3 Remember this! In the last days there will be
many troubles, 2because people will love
themselves, love money, brag, and be proud.
They will say evil things against others and will
not obey their parents or be thankful or be the
kind of people God wants. 3They will not love
others, will refuse to forgive, will gossip, and will
not control themselves. They will be cruel, will
hate what is good, 4will turn against their friends,
and will do foolish things without thinking. They
will be conceited, will love pleasure instead of
God, 5and will act as if they serve God but will not
have his power. Stay away from those people.
6Some of them go into homes and get control of
silly women who are full of sin and are led by
many evil desires. 7These women are always
learning new teachings, but they are never able to
understand the truth fully. 8Just as Jannes and
Jambres were against Moses, these people are
against the truth. Their thinking has been ruined,
and they have failed in trying to follow the faith.
9But they will not be successful in what they do,

SIDELIGHT: When 2 Timothy 3:2 cautions Timothy about people who love only themselves and money, it pegs the culture of Ephesus, where Timothy ministered. Nicknamed the treasure house of the ancient world, the major seaport city of Ephesus was famous for selfish, materialistic living.

PATIENCE

Worth the Wait

For thirty years, Rosa Parks bristled at the inequalities all around her. Because she was black, she had to ride in the back of the bus. Her skin color made everything more difficult for her in the segregated South.

On her way home from work in 1955, in Montgomery, Alabama, Rosa boarded a bus and filled a vacant seat. She was exhausted. Her neck, shoulders and back ached from sewing alterations all day. A few white people boarded the bus after Rosa, and they all found seats, except for one white man.

The bus driver asked someone to give up a seat, meaning that a black person was to give up a seat for the white person. Since Rosa sat in a seat closest to the front and closest to the aisle, everyone looked at her. But Rosa would not budge. Finally two police officers arrested her.

Rosa's arrest stirred an uproar in the black community. People were furious at the unfairness of forcing a black woman to give up her seat on a bus to a white man just because of her skin color.

People gathered at Dexter Avenue Baptist Church to organize a bus boycott that made history and brought Martin Luther King, Jr., to national attention. The 381-day boycott required intense patience and endurance as the organizers set up car pools to transport workers who relied on bus transportation. The boycott succeeded when Montgomery buses were ordered desegregated in 1956. No longer would blacks be forced to give up their seats for whites.

Because of Rosa Parks's patience and the patience of the boycott leaders, the civil rights movement of the 1950s and 1960s was born. By refusing to budge and by being patient to see segregation crumble, Rosa showed the patience reflected in **2 Timothy 2:8–13**.

- How are the patience and suffering mentioned in this passage like the patience and suffering of blacks in the boycott?
- How could this passage help you to be more patient during tough times?

C O N S I D E R . . .

- asking God for patience to deal with a problem you are facing, and then being patient.
- talking with your family about creating a rule for silently counting to fifteen when someone tries a family member's patience.

F O R M O R E , S E E . . .

- Numbers 11:4–20 (p. 136)
- Romans 8:16–18 (p. 1150)
- 1 Peter 4:12–19 (p. 1307)

because as with Jannes and Jambres, everyone
will see that they are foolish.

Obey the Teachings

10But you have followed what I teach, the way
I live, my goal, faith, patience, and love. You
know I never give up. 11You know how I have
been hurt and have suffered, as in Antioch, Iconium, and Lystra. I have suffered, but the Lord
saved me from all those troubles. 12Everyone who
wants to live as God desires, in Christ Jesus, will
be hurt. 13But people who are evil and cheat others will go from bad to worse. They will fool others, but they will also be fooling themselves.

14But you should continue following the teachings you learned. You know they are true, because you trust those who taught you. 15Since you
were a child you have known the Holy Scriptures[d] which are able to make you wise. And that
wisdom leads to salvation through faith in Christ
Jesus. 16All Scripture is given by God and is useful
for teaching, for showing people what is wrong in
their lives, for correcting faults, and for teaching
how to live right. 17Using the Scriptures, the
person who serves God will be capable, having
all that is needed to do every good work.

4 I give you a command in the presence of
God and Christ Jesus, the One who will
judge the living and the dead, and by his coming
and his kingdom: 2Preach the Good News.[d] Be
ready at all times, and tell people what they need
to do. Tell them when they are wrong. Encourage
them with great patience and careful teaching,
3because the time will come when people will
not listen to the true teaching but will find many
more teachers who please them by saying the
things they want to hear. 4They will stop listening
to the truth and will begin to follow false stories.
5But you should control yourself at all times, accept troubles, do the work of telling the Good
News, and complete all the duties of a servant of
God.

BIBLE STUDY

Take Time to Learn

Reading the Bible is important, right? But do you do it? Many Christian teenagers don't, indicates Teenage Magazine:

- Thirteen percent of Christian teenagers say they never read their Bible.
- Only eight percent say they read the Bible every day.
- Forty-four percent say they read the Bible only when they feel like it.
- And the rest, thirty-five percent, read the Bible a few times a week, or less.

Why don't Christian teenagers read the Bible? Teenagers say the top five reasons are:

1. They get busy.
2. They would rather do something else.
3. They think the Bible is boring.
4. They don't know how to study the Bible.
5. They forget to read it.

The Bible has been called the most printed and the least read of all books. Adults and teenagers alike cannot grow as Christians without the life-changing guidance of the Bible. Teenagers might get a lot from the Bible if they read it knowing the value of scripture as described in **2 Timothy 3:14–4:5**.

- According to this passage, of what value is Bible study to the Christian's life?
- What can you do to make Bible study an important part of your everyday life?

C O N S I D E R . . .

- asking your youth minister or pastor for tips on how to make Bible study easier and more effective.
- spending one week reading through one of the Gospels (Matthew, Mark, Luke, or John) with a friend, meeting every day at lunch to discuss what you have learned in your reading.

F O R M O R E , S E E . . .

- Psalm 119:97–104 (p. 552)
- John 5:39 (p. 1066)
- 2 Timothy 1:13–14 (p. 1264)

6My life is being given as an offering to God,
and the time has come for me to leave this life.
7I have fought the good fight, I have finished the
race, I have kept the faith. 8Now, a crown is being
held for me—a crown for being right with God.
The Lord, the judge who judges rightly, will give
the crown to me on that day[n]—not only to me
but to all those who have waited with love for
him to come again.

Personal Words

9Do your best to come to me as soon as you
can, 10because Demas, who loved this world, left
me and went to Thessalonica. Crescens went to
Galatia, and Titus went to Dalmatia. 11Luke is the
only one still with me. Get Mark and bring him
with you when you come, because he can help
me in my work here. 12I sent Tychicus to Ephesus. 13When I was in Troas, I left my coat there
with Carpus. So when you come, bring it to me,
along with my books, particularly the ones written on parchment.[n]

> **SIDELIGHT:** Have trouble misplacing things? Take heart. So did the apostle Paul. He left his coat in Troas (2 Timothy 4:13), which was more than a hundred miles from Ephesus, and close to a thousand miles from Rome—the two places he might have been when he asked the people to send the coat to him. This coat was probably a heavy cloak that would have kept Paul warmer in a damp prison cell.

14Alexander the metalworker did many harmful things against me. The Lord will punish him
for what he did. 15You also should be careful that

day The day Christ will come to judge all people and take his people to live with him.
parchment A writing paper made from the skins of sheep.

PERSISTENCE

Dream Big

He always dreamed of playing football, but many obstacles blocked his dream.

His church discouraged playing the game. His parents weren't keen on the idea, but eventually they let him try out for the sport. In seventh grade, he went out for the team—even though he was too small to fit in a uniform.

Once on the field playing defense, the odds of his making the team seemed even worse. "The coach put me up against the biggest fullback on the team," he recalls. "I didn't know what to do. I yelled and grabbed him around the legs. He carried me for a few yards, and I finally tackled him."

After that first courageous tackle, the coach let the boy play. Although he lacked size, the coach saw a "won't-give-up" persistence in the kid. And he showed an intensity the coach rarely saw.

Many years later, after high school and college football, this persistent player was drafted by the Chicago Bears. And in 1985 and 1988 Mike Singletary, the 6-foot, 230-pound linebacker, was named the NFL Defensive Player of the Year.

His seventh-grade persistence paid off for Mike Singletary. He lives the message of persistence in **2 Timothy 4:6–18**.

- How is Mike Singletary like the writer of 2 Timothy, especially in verse 16 of this passage?
- What hobby, sport, or talent have you considered giving up on? How should you decide whether to stick with it or not?

CONSIDER . . .

- identifying someone who has stuck with something after almost quitting. Write or call that person, encouraging him or her to hang in there.
- looking at the people around you—friends, family, teachers. Choose one person you can talk to when you feel like quitting.

FOR MORE, SEE . . .

- 1 Samuel 17:1–54 (p. 260)
- Acts 20:24 (p. 1130)
- 1 Corinthians 9:24–27 (p. 1178)

he does not hurt you, because he fought strongly
against our teaching.
16The first time I defended myself, no one
helped me; everyone left me. May they be forgiven. 17But the Lord stayed with me and gave me
strength so I could fully tell the Good News[d] to
all those who are not Jews. So I was saved from
the lion's mouth. 18The Lord will save me when
anyone tries to hurt me, and he will bring me
safely to his heavenly kingdom. Glory forever and
ever be the Lord's. Amen.

Final Greetings

19Greet Priscilla and Aquila and the family of
Onesiphorus. 20Erastus stayed in Corinth, and I
left Trophimus sick in Miletus. 21Try as hard as
you can to come to me before winter.
Eubulus sends greetings to you. Also Pudens,
Linus, Claudia, and all the brothers and sisters in
Christ greet you.
22The Lord be with your spirit. Grace be with
you.

TITUS

Why Read This Book:

- Find out what it takes to be a Christian leader (Titus 1).
- Discover how to live as a Christian (Titus 2—3).

Behind the Scenes:

Suppose you knew a group of people who lied, bickered, and were greedy? Most likely you would write them off as evil people and wouldn't hang around with them. And what if these people said they were Christians? You would probably call them hypocrites—then switch churches.

Yet that is the kind of people Titus encountered when he went to Crete, an island infamous for its tough people. Years earlier, a poet from the island had written: "Cretans are always liars, evil animals, and lazy people who do nothing but eat" (Titus 1:12).

But instead of writing off these people, Titus had gone to work with them, helping them grow in their faith. It was a tough missionary assignment. The letter to Titus encourages the leader and gives the people practical advice on how to overcome their past, sinful practices and to begin living a new life in Christ.

This short letter is full of help for effective Christian living. It summarizes the basics of the Christian faith, and encourages all people to live lives that are pleasing to God.

WHERE THE ACTION WAS

Black Sea
MACEDONIA
ITALY
DALMATIA
Before going to Crete, Titus had traveled with Paul in Macedonia (2 Corinthians 7:5–16, p. 1199).
Later in life, Titus ministered in Dalmatia, which is in modern-day Yugoslavia (2 Timothy 4:10, p. 1267).
CRETE
Titus was working on the island of Crete (Titus 1:5).
AFRICA
Mediterranean Sea

WHEN THE ACTION WAS

- BC/AD — Jesus was born
- Jesus began his ministry
- 25AD — The church began soon after Jesus went to heaven
- Paul became a Christian
- Paul began his missionary work
- 50AD — Titus may have been written
- Fire destroyed Rome
- 75AD — Romans destroyed the Temple in Jerusalem
- 100AD

1 From Paul, a servant of God and an apostle[d] of Jesus Christ. I was sent to help the faith of God's chosen people and to help them know the truth that shows people how to serve God. 2That faith and that knowledge come from the hope for life forever, which God promised to us before time began. And God cannot lie. 3At the right time God let the world know about that life through preaching. He trusted me with that work, and I preached by the command of God our Savior.

4To Titus, my true child in the faith we share:

Grace and peace from God the Father and Christ Jesus our Savior.

Titus' Work in Crete

5I left you in Crete so you could finish doing the things that still needed to be done and so you could appoint elders[d] in every town, as I directed you. 6An elder must not be guilty of doing wrong, must have only one wife, and must have believing children. They must not be known as children who are wild and do not cooperate. 7As God's manager, an elder must not be guilty of doing wrong, being selfish, or becoming angry quickly. He must not drink too much wine, like to fight, or try to get rich by cheating others. 8An elder must be ready to welcome guests, love what is good, be wise, live right, and be holy and self-controlled. 9By holding on to the trustworthy word just as we teach it, an elder can help people by using true teaching, and he can show those who are against the true teaching that they are wrong.

> **SIDELIGHT:** When Titus 1:8 says elders must accept others into their homes, it means more than just giving them a glass of iced tea. If a stranger stopped at the door, a hospitable person was expected to feed, lodge, protect, and clothe the stranger, if necessary. The Greek word for hospitality literally meant "lover of strangers."

10There are many people who refuse to cooperate, who talk about worthless things and lead others into the wrong way—mainly those who say all who are not Jews must be circumcised.[d] 11These people must be stopped, because they are upsetting whole families by teaching things they should not teach, which they do to get rich by cheating people. 12Even one of their own prophets said, "Cretans are always liars, evil animals, and lazy people who do nothing but eat." 13The words that prophet said are true. So firmly tell those people they are wrong so they may become strong in the faith, 14not accepting Jewish false stories and the commands of people who reject the truth. 15To those who are pure, all things are pure, but to those who are full of sin and do not believe, nothing is pure. Both their minds and their consciences have been ruined. 16They say they know God, but their actions show they do not accept him. They are hateful people, they refuse to obey, and they are useless for doing anything good.

Following the True Teaching

2 But you must tell everyone what to do to follow the true teaching. 2Teach older men to be self-controlled, serious, wise, strong in faith, in love, and in patience.

3In the same way, teach older women to be holy in their behavior, not speaking against others or enslaved to too much wine, but teaching what is good. 4Then they can teach the young women to love their husbands, to love their children, 5to be wise and pure, to be good workers at home, to be kind, and to yield to their husbands. Then no one will be able to criticize the teaching God gave us.

6In the same way, encourage young men to be wise. 7In every way be an example of doing good deeds. When you teach, do it with honesty and seriousness. 8Speak the truth so that you cannot be criticized. Then those who are against you will be ashamed because there is nothing bad to say about us.

9Slaves should yield to their own masters at all times, trying to please them and not arguing with them. 10They should not steal from them but should show their masters they can be fully trusted so that in everything they do they will make the teaching of God our Savior attractive.

11That is the way we should live, because God's grace that can save everyone has come. 12It teaches us not to live against God nor to do the evil things the world wants to do. Instead, that grace teaches us to live now in a wise and right way and in a way that shows we serve God. 13We should live like that while we wait for our great hope and the coming of the glory of our great God and Savior Jesus Christ. 14He gave himself for us so he might pay the price to free us from all evil and to make us pure people who belong only to him—people who are always wanting to do good deeds.

15Say these things and encourage the people and tell them what is wrong in their lives, with all authority. Do not let anyone treat you as if you were unimportant.

The Right Way to Live

3 Remind the believers to yield to the authority of rulers and government leaders, to obey

them, to be ready to do good, 2to speak no evil
about anyone, to live in peace, and to be gentle
and polite to all people.
3In the past we also were foolish. We did not
obey, we were wrong, and we were slaves to
many things our bodies wanted and enjoyed. We
spent our lives doing evil and being jealous. People hated us, and we hated each other. 4But when
the kindness and love of God our Savior was
shown, 5he saved us because of his mercy. It was
not because of good deeds we did to be right with
him. He saved us through the washing that made
us new people through the Holy Spirit.[d] 6God
poured out richly upon us that Holy Spirit through
Jesus Christ our Savior. 7Being made right with
God by his grace, we could have the hope of receiving the life that never ends.
8This teaching is true, and I want you to be sure
the people understand these things. Then those
who believe in God will be careful to use their
lives for doing good. These things are good and
will help everyone.
9But stay away from those who have foolish
arguments and talk about useless family histories
and argue and quarrel about the law. Those things
are worth nothing and will not help anyone. 10Af-
ter a first and second warning, avoid someone
who causes arguments. 11You can know that such
people are evil and sinful; their own sins prove
them wrong.

Some Things to Remember

12When I send Artemas or Tychicus to you,
make every effort to come to me at Nicopolis, because I have decided to stay there this winter.
13Do all you can to help Zenas the lawyer and

FOLLOWING GOD

The Fun Factor

Tom Harrington didn't think Christianity was much fun. There were so many rules and commandments. No getting drunk. No swearing. No messing around with girls. No making fun of other people. To be a Christian, he thought, meant wearing a stern face, singing slow hymns and eating tuna casseroles at potluck dinners.

His view of Christianity brightened when he saw in his youth minister's office a painting of a laughing Jesus.

Tom never imagined Jesus laughing before. He had always thought of Jesus as quiet and somber—someone who never smiled and spoke only in wise-sounding tones. Could Jesus really be fun?

This image of Jesus laughing made Tom look again at the stories of Jesus in the Gospels. He saw hints of Jesus' humor and began to see in the stories the Jesus of the painting. He started going to youth group, where he met Christians who had fun. They had joy, too, even when life wasn't great.

As Tom grew in faith, his own view of fun changed. Instead of calling friends to go get drunk, he called a Christian friend. Sometimes they just talked and laughed. Other times they watched comedies. Whatever they did, they enjoyed it, without hurting themselves.

Like Tom, the early Christians also had trouble knowing how Christians should live. **Titus 2:11–3:7** describes the joy of living a Christian life that is freeing and hopeful, not dull and rigid.

- How does the picture of a laughing Jesus match the good news of God's gift that is described in this passage?
- How could you implement these guidelines in your life and enjoy following them at the same time? What in the passage gives reason to celebrate following God?

CONSIDER . . .

- looking around your church for positive, fun, or joyful images of faith in paintings, pictures, banners, and books. Think about how these images of joy compare to the world's view of fun.
- meeting with your Christian friends and thinking of ideas for joyful ways to follow Christ.

FOR MORE, SEE . . .

- Isaiah 6:1–8 (p. 622)
- Ephesians 4:31–32 (p. 1224)
- Philippians 4:4–9 (p. 1234)

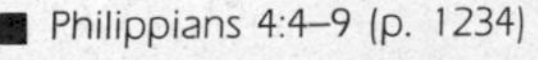

Apollos on their journey so that they have everything they need. 14Our people must learn to use their lives for doing good deeds to provide what is necessary so that their lives will not be useless.

15All who are with me greet you. Greet those who love us in the faith.

Grace be with you all.

SIDELIGHT: The reason Paul says he plans to spend the winter in Nicopolis (Titus 3:12) was that ships stopped sailing during the stormy winter months. The practice would have made it hard to get to Grandma's for Christmas!

PHILEMON

Why Read This Book:

- Learn how to treat fellow Christians (Philemon 4–7).
- Discover how to see others as friends in Christ (Philemon 8–21).

Behind the Scenes:

Onesimus, a slave, deserved to die. He had stolen from his master, then run away. Under Roman law, a runaway slave had no rights. Disobedience meant possible beatings, tortuous brandings on the face and even crucifixion.

But something had happened since Onesimus had left his master. He had become a Christian through Paul's influence. And making the matter even more complicated, his master Philemon was also a Christian. Onesimus knew he should return to his master, but he also knew he could die if he went back.

So Paul wrote this letter to persuade Philemon to forgive Onesimus and welcome him back as a Christian friend. Instead of telling Philemon to punish Onesimus, Paul asked that the wrongdoing be charged to Paul.

Though we no longer live with slavery, we, like Philemon, may be tempted to look down on people because of the color of their skin, the amount of money they have, or what they wear. And we may treat them as second-class citizens and think we are first class. Philemon challenges all of us to rethink those prejudices.

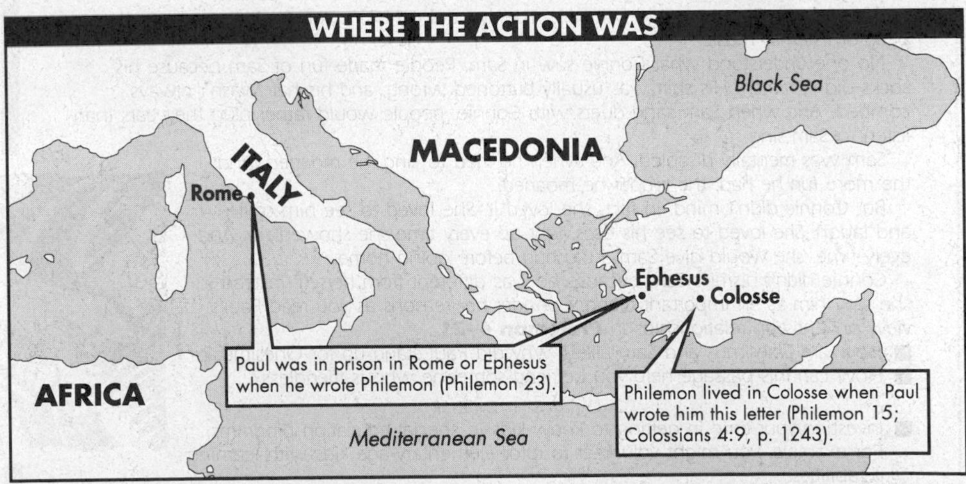
WHERE THE ACTION WAS
Black Sea
MACEDONIA
ITALY
Rome
Ephesus
Colosse
AFRICA
Mediterranean Sea
Paul was in prison in Rome or Ephesus when he wrote Philemon (Philemon 23).
Philemon lived in Colosse when Paul wrote him this letter (Philemon 15; Colossians 4:9, p. 1243).

WHEN THE ACTION WAS

BC/AD	Jesus was born
	Jesus began his ministry
	The church began soon after Jesus went to heaven
25AD	
	Paul became a Christian
	Paul began his missionary work
50AD	Paul wrote Philemon
	Fire destroyed Rome
	Romans destroyed the Temple in Jerusalem
75AD	
100AD	

1From Paul, a prisoner of Christ Jesus, and from
Timothy, our brother.
To Philemon, our dear friend and worker with
us; 2to Apphia, our sister; to Archippus, a worker
with us; and to the church that meets in your
home:
3Grace and peace to you from God our Father
and the Lord Jesus Christ.

Philemon's Love and Faith

4I always thank my God when I mention you
in my prayers, 5because I hear about the love
you have for all God's holy people and the
faith you have in the Lord Jesus. 6I pray that
the faith you share may make you understand every blessing we have in Christ. 7I have great joy
and comfort, my brother, because the love you
have shown to God's people has refreshed them.

Accept Onesimus as a Brother

8So, in Christ, I could be bold and order you to
do what is right. 9But because I love you, I am
pleading with you instead. I, Paul, an old man
now and also a prisoner for Christ Jesus, 10am
pleading with you for my child Onesimus, who
became my child while I was in prison. 11In the
past he was useless to you, but now he has become useful for both you and me.
12I am sending him back to you, and with him
I am sending my own heart. 13I wanted to keep
him with me so that in your place he might help
me while I am in prison for the Good News.[d]
14But I did not want to do anything without asking you first so that any good you do for me will
be because you want to do it, not because I forced
you. 15Maybe Onesimus was separated from you
for a short time so you could have him back forever— 16no longer as a slave, but better than a
slave, as a loved brother. I love him very much,
but you will love him even more, both as a person
and as a believer in the Lord.
17So if you consider me your partner, welcome

SIDELIGHT: Slavery was common in the Roman Empire in Paul's day. According to some estimates, there were about sixty million slaves in the Empire—up to half the total population.

FRIENDS

A Friend in Everyone

Everyone liked Connie Klein. But nobody liked Sam Bush—except Connie.

After school, Connie would visit Sam. They would go biking, go for long walks in the park, or listen to music.

No one understood what Connie saw in Sam. People made fun of Sam because his socks didn't match. His shirt was usually buttoned wrong, and his hair wasn't always combed. And when Sam sang duets with Connie, people would rather plug their ears than listen to Sam sing.

Sam was mentally disabled. And when he tried to sing, he moaned. And the more fun he had, the louder he moaned.

But Connie didn't mind. In fact, she loved it. She loved to see him smile and laugh. She loved to see his eyes light up every time she showed up. And every time, she would give Sam a big hug before going home.

Connie didn't dismiss Sam because he was different from herself. Instead she saw him as an important friend. Consider her reasons as you read Paul's view on Christian relationships in **Philemon 4–21**.

- How are Onesimus and Sam alike? Why did Paul stand up for Onesimus?
- How can this passage help you befriend someone who is friendless?

C O N S I D E R . . .

- investing your time in getting to know kids in special education programs. For example, you might volunteer to tutor elementary-age kids with learning disabilities.
- asking someone you don't like very well to join you for popcorn. Get to know the person by asking a lot of questions.

F O R M O R E , S E E

- 1 Samuel 20:1–42 (p. 263)
- Matthew 25:34–46 (p. 954)
- 1 Timothy 6:11–16 (p. 1260)

Onesimus as you would welcome me. [18]If he has
done anything wrong to you or if he owes you
anything, charge that to me. [19]I, Paul, am writing
this with my own hand. I will pay it back, and I
will say nothing about what you owe me for your
own life. [20]So, my brother, I ask that you do this
for me in the Lord: Refresh my heart in Christ. [21]I
write this letter, knowing that you will do what
I ask you and even more.
[22]One more thing—prepare a room for me in
which to stay, because I hope God will answer
your prayers and I will be able to come to you.

Final Greetings

[23]Epaphras, a prisoner with me for Christ Jesus,
sends greetings to you. [24]And also Mark, Aristarchus, Demas, and Luke, workers together with
me, send greetings.
[25]The grace of our Lord Jesus Christ be with
your spirit.

HEBREWS

Why Read This Book:

- Discover how Jesus Christ fulfilled God's promises (Hebrews 1—7).
- Learn about the sacrifice Jesus made for us (Hebrews 8—10).
- Be challenged to stay strong in your faith (Hebrews 11—13).

Behind the Scenes:

Imagine a courtroom scene. The jury has heard persuasive testimony from many different people. Now the jury is about to go behind closed doors to come to a verdict about whether Christianity does hold the truth. But first the lawyers will present their closing arguments.

The book of Hebrews is like a closing argument in defense of Christianity. Using careful logic and referring often to testimony, the writer shows that Jesus Christ is the Son of God and worthy of our faith. The book compares and contrasts Jesus with all of Old Testament history and argues that Jesus is the climax of everything in the past.

So, the author concludes, "Let us look only to Jesus, the One who began our faith and who makes it perfect. . . . Think about Jesus' example. . . . So do not get tired and stop trying" (Hebrews 12:2–3).

We don't know how the original readers responded to the eloquent argument in Hebrews. But we do know that the book has become a treasured source of encouragement and hope for Christians through the centuries. Just as this letter encouraged its first readers to hold strong to their faith, it can do the same for us today.

WHEN THE ACTION WAS

Jesus was born	BC/AD	
The church began soon after Jesus went to heaven	25AD	Jesus began his ministry
Paul began his missionary work		Paul became a Christian
Fire destroyed Rome	50AD	Hebrews was written
	75AD	Romans destroyed the Temple in Jerusalem
	100AD	

God Spoke Through His Son

1 In the past God spoke to our ancestors through the prophets[d] many times and in many different ways. 2But now in these last days God has spoken to us through his Son. God has chosen his Son to own all things, and through him he made the world. 3The Son reflects the glory of God and shows exactly what God is like. He holds everything together with his powerful word. When the Son made people clean from their sins, he sat down at the right side of God, the Great One in heaven. 4The Son became much greater than the angels, and God gave him a name that is much greater than theirs.

SIDELIGHT: No one really knows who wrote Hebrews. Suggestions have included Paul, Apollos, Luke, Barnabas, Clement of Rome, Silas, Philip, and Priscilla. In the third century, Origen probably had the right idea when he wrote, "Who wrote the epistle God alone knows certainly."

5This is because God never said to any of the angels,

"You are my Son.
Today I have become your Father." *Psalm 2:7*

Nor did God say of any angel,

"I will be his Father,
and he will be my Son." *2 Samuel 7:14*

6And when God brings his firstborn Son into the world, he says,

"Let all God's angels worship him."[n] *Psalm 97:7*

7This is what God said about the angels:

"God makes his angels become like winds.
He makes his servants become like flames of fire." *Psalm 104:4*

8But God said this about his Son:

"God, your throne will last forever and ever.
You will rule your kingdom with fairness.
9You love right and hate evil,
so God has chosen you from among your friends;
he has set you apart with much joy." *Psalm 45:6-7*

10God also says,

"Lord, in the beginning you made the earth,
and your hands made the skies.
11They will be destroyed, but you will remain.
They will all wear out like clothes.
12You will fold them like a coat.
And, like clothes, you will change them.
But you never change,
and your life will never end." *Psalm 102:25-27*

13And God never said this to an angel:

"Sit by me at my right side
until I put your enemies under your control."[n] *Psalm 110:1*

14All the angels are spirits who serve God and are sent to help those who will receive salvation.

Our Salvation Is Great

2 So we must be more careful to follow what we were taught. Then we will not stray
away from the truth. 2The teaching God spoke
through angels was shown to be true, and anyone
who did not follow it or obey it received the punishment that was earned. 3So surely we also will
be punished if we ignore this great salvation. The
Lord himself first told about this salvation, and it
was proven true to us by those who heard him.
4God also proved it by using wonders, great signs,
many kinds of miracles,[d] and by giving people
gifts through the Holy Spirit,[d] just as he wanted.

Christ Became like Humans

5God did not choose angels to be the rulers of
the new world that was coming, which is what
we have been talking about. 6It is written in the
Scriptures,[d]

"Why are people important to you?
Why do you take care of human beings?
7You made them a little lower than the angels
and crowned them with glory and honor.
8 You put all things under their control." *Psalm 8:4-6*

When God put everything under their control,
there was nothing left that they did not rule. Still,
we do not yet see them ruling over everything.
9But we see Jesus, who for a short time was made
lower than the angels. And now he is wearing a
crown of glory and honor because he suffered and
died. And by God's grace, he died for everyone.

10God is the One who made all things, and all
things are for his glory. He wanted to have many
children share his glory, so he made the One who
leads people to salvation perfect through suffering.

11Jesus, who makes people holy, and those who
are made holy are from the same family. So he is
not ashamed to call them his brothers and sisters.[n] 12He says,

"Then, I will tell my fellow Israelites about you;

"Let . . . him." These words are found in Deuteronomy 32:43 in the Septuagint, the Greek version of the Old Testament, and in a Hebrew copy among the Dead Sea Scrolls.
until . . . control Literally, "until I make your enemies a footstool for your feet."
brothers and sisters Although the Greek text says "brothers" here and throughout this book, the writer's words were meant for the entire church, including men and women.

I will praise you in the public meeting." *Psalm 22:22*

13He also says,
"I will trust in God." *Isaiah 8:17*
And he also says,
"I am here, and with me are the children
God has given me." *Isaiah 8:18*

14Since these children are people with physical
bodies, Jesus himself became like them. He did
this so that, by dying, he could destroy the one
who has the power of death — the devil — 15and
free those who were like slaves all their lives because of their fear of death. 16Clearly, it is not
angels that Jesus helps, but the people who are
from Abraham.[n] 17For this reason Jesus had
to be made like his brothers in every way so he
could be their merciful and faithful high priest in
service to God. Then Jesus could bring forgiveness for their sins. 18And now he can help those
who are tempted, because he himself suffered
and was tempted.

Jesus Is Greater than Moses

3 So all of you holy brothers and sisters, who
were called by God, think about Jesus, who
was sent to us and is the high priest of our faith.
2Jesus was faithful to God as Moses was in God's
family. 3Jesus has more honor than Moses, just as
the builder of a house has more honor than the
house itself. 4Every house is built by someone, but
the builder of everything is God himself. 5Moses
was faithful in God's family as a servant, and he
told what God would say in the future. 6But
Christ is faithful as a Son over God's house. And
we are God's house if we keep on being very sure
about our great hope.

We Must Continue to Follow God

7So it is as the Holy Spirit[d] says:
"Today listen to what he says.
8Do not be stubborn as in the past
when you turned against God,
when you tested God in the desert.
9There your ancestors tried me and tested me
and saw the things I did for forty years.
10I was angry with them.
I said, 'They are not loyal to me
and have not understood my ways.'
11I was angry and made a promise,

Abraham Most respected ancestor of the Jews. Every Jew hoped to see Abraham.

SHARING FAITH

Can You Tell the Difference?

When she graduated from college, Bev Johnson became a short-term missionary at a school in Japan. Each day she led a Bible study and taught English to the Japanese.

Each day an elderly woman came to the Bible study. She sat quietly in the back of the room and rushed out when it ended. And each day Bev grew more curious about the silent woman.

One day after the Bible study, Bev walked quickly to the woman and began a conversation. The woman spoke excellent English. She told Bev she had heard of Jesus since she was a young girl. The woman owned a Bible and knew much of it by heart.

"Are you a Christian?" Bev asked.

"No, no I'm not," the woman said, "but I've seen Christians, and I'm watching to see if Jesus makes any difference in their lives."

From that incident, Bev learned how people need to see Jesus in Christians. Read how Jesus can shine through us in **Hebrews 2:9–18**.

- How does the older woman's statement to Bev relate to this passage?
- Why do you think God, in Jesus, became a person for us to know?

CONSIDER . . .

- listing all the ways Jesus showed what God is like, such as loving all people, and so on. Choose one of those ways to show how you follow Christ.
- letting at least one other person know this week how Christ has made a difference in your life.

FOR MORE, SEE . . .

- Isaiah 57:14–21 (p. 676)
- Matthew 20:29–34 (p. 944)
- John 11:28–43 (p. 1077)

'They will never enter my rest.' "[n]
Psalm 95:7-11

12So brothers and sisters, be careful that none
of you has an evil, unbelieving heart that will turn
you away from the living God. 13But encourage
each other every day while it is "today."[n] Help
each other so none of you will become hardened
because sin has tricked you. 14We all share in
Christ if we keep till the end the sure faith we had
in the beginning. 15This is what the Scripture[d]
says:

"Today listen to what he says.
Do not be stubborn as in the past
when you turned against God." Psalm 95:7-8

16Who heard God's voice and was against him? It
was all those people Moses led out of Egypt.
17And with whom was God angry for forty years?
He was angry with those who sinned, who died
in the desert. 18And to whom was God talking
when he promised that they would never enter
his rest? He was talking to those who did not obey
him. 19So we see they were not allowed to enter
and have God's rest, because they did not believe.

> **SIDELIGHT:** If Hebrews had been submitted as a term paper, it probably would have gotten a good grade for research and documentation. The book quotes from the Old Testament more than eighty times, including Psalm 95:7–11 (p. 537) in Hebrews 3:7–11.

4 Now, since God has left us the promise that
we may enter his rest, let us be very careful
so none of you will fail to enter. 2The Good News[d]
was preached to us just as it was to them. But the
teaching they heard did not help them, because
they heard it but did not accept it with faith. 3We
who have believed are able to enter and have
God's rest. As God has said,

"I was angry and made a promise,
'They will never enter my rest.' " Psalm 95:11

But God's work was finished from the time he
made the world. 4In the Scriptures[d] he talked
about the seventh day of the week: "And on the
seventh day God rested from all his works."[n]
5And again in the Scripture God said, "They will
never enter my rest."

6It is still true that some people will enter God's
rest, but those who first heard the way to be saved
did not enter, because they did not obey. 7So God
planned another day, called "today." He spoke
about that day through David a long time later in
the same Scripture used before:

"Today listen to what he says.
Do not be stubborn." Psalm 95:7-8

8We know that Joshua[n] did not lead the people
into that rest, because God spoke later about another day. 9This shows that the rest[n] for God's
people is still coming. 10Anyone who enters God's
rest will rest from his work as God did. 11Let us
try as hard as we can to enter God's rest so that
no one will fail by following the example of those
who refused to obey.

12God's word is alive and working and is
sharper than a double-edged sword. It cuts all the
way into us, where the soul and the spirit are
joined, to the center of our joints and bones. And
it judges the thoughts and feelings in our hearts.
13Nothing in all the world can be hidden from
God. Everything is clear and lies open before him,
and to him we must explain the way we have
lived.

Jesus Is Our High Priest

14Since we have a great high priest, Jesus the
Son of God, who has gone into heaven, let us hold
on to the faith we have. 15For our high priest is
able to understand our weaknesses. When he
lived on earth, he was tempted in every way that
we are, but he did not sin. 16Let us, then, feel very
sure that we can come before God's throne where
there is grace. There we can receive mercy and
grace to help us when we need it.

5 Every high priest is chosen from among
other people. He is given the work of going
before God for them to offer gifts and sacrifices for
sins. 2Since he himself is weak, he is able to be
gentle with those who do not understand and
who are doing wrong things. 3Because he is weak,
the high priest must offer sacrifices for his own
sins and also for the sins of the people.

4To be a high priest is an honor, but no one
chooses himself for this work. He must be called
by God as Aaron[n] was. 5So also Christ did not
choose himself to have the honor of being a high
priest, but God chose him. God said to him,

"You are my Son.
Today I have become your Father." Psalm 2:7

6And in another Scripture[d] God says,

"You are a priest forever,

rest A place of rest God promised to give his people.
"today" This word is taken from verse 7. It means that it is important to do these things now.
"And . . . works." Quotation from Genesis 2:2.
Joshua After Moses died, Joshua became leader of the Jewish people and led them into the land that God promised to give them.
rest Literally, "sabbath rest," meaning a sharing in the rest that God began after he created the world.
Aaron Aaron was Moses' brother and the first Jewish high priest.

a priest like Melchizedek."[n] *Psalm 110:4*
7 While Jesus lived on earth, he prayed to God
and asked God for help. He prayed with loud cries
and tears to the One who could save him from
death, and his prayer was heard because he
trusted God. 8 Even though Jesus was the Son of
God, he learned obedience by what he suffered.
9 And because his obedience was perfect, he was
able to give eternal salvation to all who obey him.
10 In this way God made Jesus a high priest, a
priest like Melchizedek.

Warning Against Falling Away

11 We have much to say about this, but it is hard
to explain because you are so slow to understand.
12 By now you should be teachers, but you need
someone to teach you again the first lessons of
God's message. You still need the teaching that is
like milk. You are not ready for solid food. 13 Anyone who lives on milk is still a baby and knows
nothing about right teaching. 14 But solid food is
for those who are grown up. They have practiced
in order to know the difference between good and
evil.

6 So let us go on to grown-up teaching. Let us
not go back over the beginning lessons we
learned about Christ. We should not again start
teaching about faith in God and about turning
away from those acts that lead to death. 2 We
should not return to the teaching about bap-

Melchizedek A priest and king who lived in the time of Abraham. (Read Genesis 14:17-24.)

FOLLOWING GOD

When the Going Gets Tough . . .

Isabella Baumfree was an African-American slave born to a Dutch owner in Ulster County, New York, about 1797. She was separated from her family and sold twice before she was twelve. Slave life was never easy. Even after she was set free in 1827, she barely survived as a domestic helper in New York City.

After the Civil War began, Isabella left New York to "travel up an' down the land showin' the people their sins an' bein' a sign unto them." She even changed her name to Sojourner Truth.

Sojourner Truth became famous for her unique style of preaching. Although she couldn't read or write, she preached a message of freedom for slaves, women, and the poor. She spoke in a heavy Dutch accent, knew the Bible well, and drew stares by wrapping a turban around her head.

Because blacks—especially black women—were routinely oppressed, Sojourner Truth found the going difficult. But she kept at it, hardened by her life of slavery and struggle. Her fame spread; she even met with President Lincoln in 1864.

Fame doesn't always equal popularity, as Sojourner Truth found out. She often preached and lectured before hostile audiences. Many times she was told her mission was hopeless. "I don't care any more for your talk than I do for the bite of a flea," someone told her.

"Perhaps not," she replied, "but the Lord willing, I'll keep you scratchin'."

Sojourner Truth knew following God requires commitment and endurance. So did the writer of Hebrews. And, in **Hebrews 4:1–13**, the writer promises that endurance and commitment will not go unrewarded.

- How was Sojourner Truth's persistence in her mission like the challenge of the passage to stay obedient to God? How did she embody the theme of verses 12–13?
- What does the passage say about those who truly follow God versus those who just say they do?

C O N S I D E R . . .

- taking an unpopular stand on an issue because you believe it's what God wants you to do.
- listing things you would honestly die for. Decide how to follow those priorities better this week.

F O R M O R E , S E E . . .

- Deuteronomy 33:26–29 (p. 193)
- Luke 10:25–37 (p. 1022)
- Acts 7:51–60 (p. 1109)

tisms,[n] about laying on of hands,[n] about the raising of the dead and eternal judgment. 3And we will go on to grown-up teaching if God allows.
4Some people cannot be brought back again to a changed life. They were once in God's light, and enjoyed heaven's gift, and shared in the Holy Spirit.[d] 5They found out how good God's word is, and they received the powers of his new world.
6But they fell away from Christ. It is impossible to bring them back to a changed life again, because they are nailing the Son of God to a cross again and are shaming him in front of others.

7Some people are like land that gets plenty of rain. The land produces a good crop for those who work it, and it receives God's blessings. 8Other people are like land that grows thorns and weeds and is worthless. It is in danger of being cursed by God and will be destroyed by fire.
9Dear friends, we are saying this to you, but we really expect better things from you that will lead to your salvation. 10God is fair; he will not forget the work you did and the love you showed for him by helping his people. And he will remember that you are still helping them. 11We want each

baptisms The word here may refer to Christian baptism, or it may refer to the Jewish ceremonial washings.
laying on of hands The laying on of hands had many purposes, including the giving of a blessing, power, or authority.

GOD'S LOVE

Storm Trackers

When people on the Atlantic coast hear hurricane warnings, most board up their windows and evacuate the coastline. They know hurricanes can whip across the ocean with winds of more than 150 miles per hour and raise the ocean level by twenty feet.

But while most people are getting away from a hurricane, storm trackers aboard their WC-130 aircraft are headed straight into the storm. It takes ten to forty-five seconds to fly through the swirling clouds around the eye of the storm. Once in the storm's eye, the crew flies from one end of the eye to the other, tracking the hurricane's path and measuring its conditions.

These missions are extremely dangerous. The plane can be struck by lightning, or its jet engines sometimes stall because of the sheets of water kicked up by the storm. At times the winds are so strong that one pilot cannot steer the plane alone.

"Everything is whipping around," says storm tracker Scott Maddox, describing a typical mission. "You have one pilot with both hands on the throttle and the other one on the automatic pilot, using it to bring the plane straight and level in air that is battering it in all directions."

Why do they go on these dangerous missions? Because without their efforts, more people would lose their lives in hurricanes. While satellite pictures warn when a hurricane is approaching land, they cannot measure wind speeds, barometric pressure, temperatures, or sea swells in the middle of the storm. That information is vital for forecasting when, where, and with how much force a hurricane will hit land.

Because they risk their lives on dangerous missions, storm trackers gain information that saves people's lives. Because of his love, God sent his Son Jesus on an even more deadly mission: to come to earth to save us and pay for our sins. Read about this unbelievable love in **Hebrews 4:14–5:10**.

- How do the storm trackers illustrate the kind of self-sacrificing love that is described in this passage? What makes God's love even more amazing?
- How does knowing about God's love and Christ's sacrifice for you affect the way you live?

CONSIDER...

- looking in the newspaper this week for stories of people who take great risks to save the lives of others. Thank God for these human examples of the kind of love God has for people.
- writing "Thanks for Your Love, God" at the top of a sheet of paper. Then fill the paper with words that show how you have experienced God's love. Keep the sheet in your Bible as a reminder, and add to it when you think of something new.

FOR MORE, SEE...

- Daniel 9:1–9 (p. 816)
- Matthew 7:7–11 (p. 919)
- Romans 3:21–26 (p. 1143)

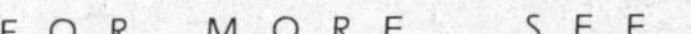
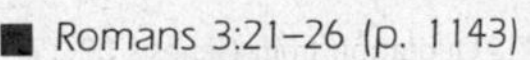

of you to go on with the same hard work all your
lives so you will surely get what you hope for.
12We do not want you to become lazy. Be like
those who through faith and patience will receive
what God has promised.

> **SIDELIGHT:** Many scholars believe Hebrews may have originally been a sermon, partly because the author mentions speaking in several places (for example, Hebrews 6:9). If it was originally a sermon, it would have taken about fifty minutes to read aloud—not too long for an early Christian worship service. Their services often included "breaking bread" (communion), teaching, preaching, singing, praying, prophesying, and reading letters. Hope they had padded pews!

13God made a promise to Abraham. And as
there is no one greater than God, he used himself
when he swore to Abraham, 14saying, "I will
surely bless you and give you many descendants."[n] 15Abraham waited patiently for this to
happen, and he received what God promised.
16People always use the name of someone
greater than themselves when they swear. The
oath proves that what they say is true, and this
ends all arguing. 17God wanted to prove that his
promise was true to those who would get what he
promised. And he wanted them to understand
clearly that his purposes never change, so he
made an oath. 18These two things cannot change:
God cannot lie when he makes a promise, and he
cannot lie when he makes an oath. These things
encourage us who came to God for safety. They
give us strength to hold on to the hope we have
been given. 19We have this hope as an anchor for
the soul, sure and strong. It enters behind the curtain in the Most Holy Place in heaven, 20where
Jesus has gone ahead of us and for us. He has
become the high priest forever, a priest like Melchizedek.[n]

The Priest Melchizedek

7 Melchizedek[n] was the king of Salem and a
priest for God Most High. He met Abraham
when Abraham was coming back after defeating
the kings. When they met, Melchizedek blessed
Abraham, 2and Abraham gave him a tenth of everything he had brought back from the battle.
First, Melchizedek's name means "king of goodness," and he is king of Salem, which means "king
of peace." 3No one knows who Melchizedek's father or mother was,[n] where he came from, when
he was born, or when he died. Melchizedek is
like the Son of God; he continues being a priest
forever.
4You can see how great Melchizedek was.
Abraham, the great father, gave him a tenth of
everything that he won in battle. 5Now the law
says that those in the tribe[d] of Levi who become
priests must collect a tenth from the people—
their own people—even though the priests and
the people are from the family of Abraham. 6Mel-
chizedek was not from the tribe of Levi, but he
collected a tenth from Abraham. And he blessed
Abraham, the man who had God's promises.
7Now everyone knows that the more important
person blesses the less important person. 8Priests
receive a tenth, even though they are only men
who live and then die. But Melchizedek, who received a tenth from Abraham, continues living, as
the Scripture[d] says. 9We might even say that Levi,
who receives a tenth, also paid it when Abraham
paid Melchizedek a tenth. 10Levi was not yet
born, but he was in the body of his ancestor when
Melchizedek met Abraham.

> **SIDELIGHT:** If you think Melchizedek (Hebrews 7:1) is a hard name to say, try the Bible's longest name: Maher-Shalal-Hash-Baz, the name of Isaiah's son (Isaiah 8:1, p. 625).

11The people were given the law[n] based on a
system of priests from the tribe of Levi, but they
could not be made perfect through that system.
So there was a need for another priest to come,
a priest like Melchizedek, not Aaron. 12And when
a different kind of priest comes, the law must be
changed, too. 13We are saying these things about
Christ, who belonged to a different tribe. No one
from that tribe ever served as a priest at the altar.
14It is clear that our Lord came from the tribe of
Judah, and Moses said nothing about priests belonging to that tribe.

Jesus Is like Melchizedek

15And this becomes even more clear when we
see that another priest comes who is like Melchizedek.[n] 16He was not made a priest by human
rules and laws but through the power of his life,
which continues forever. 17It is said about him,

"I . . . descendants." Quotation from Genesis 22:17.
Melchizedek A priest and king who lived in the time of Abraham. (Read Genesis 14:17-24.)
No . . . was Literally, "Melchizedek was without father, without mother, without genealogy."
The . . . law This refers to the people of Israel who were given the law of Moses.

"You are a priest forever,
  a priest like Melchizedek." *Psalm 110:4*

18The old rule is now set aside, because it was weak and useless. 19The law of Moses could not make anything perfect. But now a better hope has been given to us, and with this hope we can come near to God. 20It is important that God did this with an oath. Others became priests without an oath, 21but Christ became a priest with God's oath. God said:

"The Lord has made a promise
  and will not change his mind.
'You are a priest forever.'" *Psalm 110:4*

22This means that Jesus is the guarantee of a better agreement[n] from God to his people.

23When one of the other priests died, he could not continue being a priest. So there were many priests. 24But because Jesus lives forever, he will never stop serving as priest. 25So he is able always to save those who come to God through him because he always lives, asking God to help them.

26Jesus is the kind of high priest we need. He is holy, sinless, pure, not influenced by sinners, and he is raised above the heavens. 27He is not like the other priests who had to offer sacrifices every day, first for their own sins, and then for the sins of the people. Christ offered his sacrifice only once and for all time when he offered himself. 28The law chooses high priests who are people with weaknesses, but the word of God's oath came later than the law. It made God's Son to be the high priest, and that Son has been made perfect forever.

Jesus Is Our High Priest

8 Here is the point of what we are saying: We have a high priest who sits on the right side of God's throne in heaven. 2Our high priest serves in the Most Holy Place, the true place of worship that was made by God, not by humans.

3Every high priest has the work of offering gifts and sacrifices to God. So our high priest must also offer something to God. 4If our high priest were now living on earth, he would not be a priest, because there are already priests here who follow the law by offering gifts to God. 5The work they do as priests is only a copy and a shadow of what is in heaven. This is why God warned Moses when he was ready to build the Holy Tent:[d] "Be very careful to make everything by the plan I showed you on the mountain."[n] 6But the priestly work that has been given to Jesus is much greater than the work that was given to the other priests. In the same way, the new agreement that Jesus brought from God to his people is much greater than the old one. And the new agreement is based on promises of better things.

7If there had been nothing wrong with the first agreement,[n] there would have been no need for a second agreement. 8But God found something wrong with his people. He says:

"Look, the time is coming, says the Lord,
  when I will make a new agreement
with the people of Israel
  and the people of Judah.
9It will not be like the agreement
  I made with their ancestors
when I took them by the hand
  to bring them out of Egypt.
But they broke that agreement,
  and I turned away from them, says the
    Lord.
10This is the agreement I will make
  with the people of Israel at that time, says
    the Lord.
I will put my teachings in their minds
  and write them on their hearts.
I will be their God,
  and they will be my people.
11People will no longer have to teach their
    neighbors and relatives
  to know the Lord,
because all people will know me,
  from the least to the most important.
12I will forgive them for the wicked things they
    did,
  and I will not remember their sins
    anymore." *Jeremiah 31:31-34*

13God called this a new agreement, so he has made the first agreement old. And anything that is old and worn out is ready to disappear.

The Old Agreement

9 The first agreement[n] had rules for worship and a man-made place for worship. 2The Holy Tent[d] was set up for this. The first area in the Tent was called the Holy Place. In it were the lamp and the table with the bread that was made holy for God. 3Behind the second curtain was a room called the Most Holy Place. 4In it was a golden altar for burning incense[d] and the Ark[d] covered with gold that held the old agreement. Inside this Ark was a golden jar of manna,[d] Aaron's rod that once grew leaves, and the stone tablets of the old agreement. 5Above the Ark were the creatures that showed God's glory, whose wings reached over the lid. But we cannot tell everything about these things now.

agreement God gives a contract or agreement to his people. For the Jews, this agreement was the law of Moses. But now God has given a better agreement to his people through Christ.
"Be . . . mountain." Quotation from Exodus 25:40.
first agreement The contract God gave the Jewish people when he gave them the law of Moses.

6When everything in the Tent was made ready
in this way, the priests went into the first room
every day to worship. 7But only the high priest
could go into the second room, and he did that
only once a year. He could never enter the inner
room without taking blood with him, which he
offered to God for himself and for sins the people
did without knowing they did them. 8The Holy
Spirit[d] uses this to show that the way into the
Most Holy Place was not open while the system
of the old Holy Tent was still being used. 9This is
an example for the present time. It shows that the
gifts and sacrifices offered cannot make the conscience of the worshiper perfect. 10These gifts and
sacrifices were only about food and drink and special washings. They were rules for the body, to be
followed until the time of God's new way.

The New Agreement

11But when Christ came as the high priest of
the good things we now have, he entered the
greater and more perfect tent. It is not made by
humans and does not belong to this world.
12Christ entered the Most Holy Place only once—
and for all time. He did not take with him the
blood of goats and calves. His sacrifice was his
own blood, and by it he set us free from sin forever. 13The blood of goats and bulls and the ashes
of a cow are sprinkled on the people who are unclean,[d] and this makes their bodies clean again.
14How much more is done by the blood of Christ.
He offered himself through the eternal Spirit[n] as
a perfect sacrifice to God. His blood will make our
consciences pure from useless acts so we may
serve the living God.
15For this reason Christ brings a new agreement from God to his people. Those who are
called by God can now receive the blessings he
has promised, blessings that will last forever. They
can have those things because Christ died so that

Spirit This refers to the Holy Spirit, to Christ's own spirit, or to the spiritual and eternal nature of his sacrifice.

SIN

Unexpected Forgiveness

Dawn Hammond and Craig Meadows had been dating for about a year. Both were sixteen. When Dawn stopped coming to youth group meetings, Donna Richards, her youth leader, dropped by after school to see if she was okay.

She obviously wasn't.

Dawn confessed her relationship with Craig had gotten very physical. "I think I'm pregnant," she said.

She and Craig had had sex on a date four weeks earlier. "It just happened. We didn't plan it," she kept saying.

"Have you told your parents?" Donna asked.

"No!" she screamed. "They would absolutely die if they knew!"

"That's not the main issue," Donna said. "They need to know, and you need their help."

Donna promised to stay with Dawn until her parents came home from work. When Dawn told them the news, they were upset at first, but they assured Dawn they loved her. What she had done was wrong, but it didn't change the way they felt about her. She was their daughter.

Dawn learned a hard lesson about sex before marriage. She also learned a lot about the kind of forgiveness and acceptance written about in **Hebrews 9:11–28**.

- How was forgiveness by Dawn's parents like and unlike the forgiveness described in this passage? How did the price Dawn's parents paid in the story differ from the price Christ paid in the passage?
- How are our sins forgiven, according to the passage?

CONSIDER . . .

- talking with a trusted adult about a sin you're struggling with.
- defining the word "sin," using this passage and the ones listed in "For More, See . . ." for guidance. Find out whether your friends agree with your definition. Check it out with your youth leader too.

FOR MORE, SEE . . .

- Genesis 4:1–12 (p. 7)
- Romans 3:21–26 (p. 1143)
- Romans 6:12–14 (p. 1147)

the people who lived under the first agreement
could be set free from sin.
16When there is a will,[n] it must be proven that
the one who wrote that will is dead. 17A will
means nothing while the person is alive; it can be
used only after the person dies. 18This is why even
the first agreement could not begin without blood
to show death. 19First, Moses told all the people
every command in the law. Next he took the
blood of calves and mixed it with water. Then he
used red wool and a branch of the hyssop plant
to sprinkle it on the book of the law and on all the
people. 20He said, "This is the blood that begins
the Agreement that God commanded you to
obey."[n] 21In the same way, Moses sprinkled the
blood on the Holy Tent[d] and over all the things
used in worship. 22The law says that almost everything must be made clean by blood, and sins cannot be forgiven without blood to show death.

Christ's Death Takes Away Sins

23So the copies of the real things in heaven had
to be made clean[d] by animal sacrifices. But the
real things in heaven need much better sacrifices.
24Christ did not go into the Most Holy Place made
by humans, which is only a copy of the real one.
He went into heaven itself and is there now before God to help us. 25The high priest enters the
Most Holy Place once every year with blood that
is not his own. But Christ did not offer himself
many times. 26Then he would have had to suffer
many times since the world was made. But Christ
came only once and for all time at just the right
time to take away all sin by sacrificing himself.
27Just as everyone must die once and be judged,
28so Christ was offered as a sacrifice one time to
take away the sins of many people. And he will
come a second time, not to offer himself for sin,
but to bring salvation to those who are waiting for
him.

10 The law is only an unclear picture of the
good things coming in the future; it is
not the real thing. The people under the law offer
the same sacrifices every year, but these sacrifices
can never make perfect those who come near to
worship God. 2If the law could make them perfect, the sacrifices would have already stopped.
The worshipers would be made clean, and they
would no longer have a sense of sin. 3But these
sacrifices remind them of their sins every year,
4because it is impossible for the blood of bulls and
goats to take away sins.
5So when Christ came into the world, he said:
"You do not want sacrifices and offerings,
but you have prepared a body for me.
6You do not ask for burnt offerings
and offerings to take away sins.
7Then I said, 'Look, I have come.
It is written about me in the book.
God, I have come to do what you want.' "
Psalm 40:6-8

8In this Scripture[d] he first said, "You do not want
sacrifices and offerings. You do not ask for burnt
offerings and offerings to take away sins." (These
are all sacrifices that the law commands.) 9Then
he said, "Look, I have come to do what you
want." God ends the first system of sacrifices
so he can set up the new system. 10And because
of this, we are made holy through the sacrifice
Christ made in his body once and for all time.
11Every day the priests stand and do their religious service, often offering the same sacrifices.
Those sacrifices can never take away sins. 12But
after Christ offered one sacrifice for sins, forever,
he sat down at the right side of God. 13And now
Christ waits there for his enemies to be put under
his power. 14With one sacrifice he made perfect
forever those who are being made holy.

> **SIDELIGHT:** When Hebrews 10:1 talks about making "the same sacrifices every year," it refers to the annual Jewish holiday of Yom Kippur. On this day, the high priest would symbolically transfer the sins of Israel to a goat (known as a scapegoat). Then the goat would be carried away to the desert where it—along with the sins—would be lost and forgotten (see Leviticus 16:7–10, 20–22, p. 113).

15The Holy Spirit[d] also tells us about this. First
he says:
16"This is the agreement[n] I will make
with them at that time, says the Lord.
I will put my teachings in their hearts
and write them on their minds." *Jeremiah 31:33*
17Then he says:
"Their sins and the evil things they do—
I will not remember anymore." *Jeremiah 31:34*
18Now when these have been forgiven, there is no
more need for a sacrifice for sins.

Continue to Trust God

19So, brothers and sisters, we are completely
free to enter the Most Holy Place without fear

will A legal document that shows how a person's money and property are to be distributed at the time of death. This is the same word in Greek as "agreement" in verse 15.
"This . . . obey." Quotation from Exodus 24:8.
agreement God gives a contract or agreement to his people. For the Jews, this agreement was the law of Moses. But now God has given a better agreement to his people through Christ.

because of the blood of Jesus' death. 20We can
enter through a new and living way that Jesus
opened for us. It leads through the curtain—
Christ's body. 21And since we have a great priest
over God's house, 22let us come near to God with
a sincere heart and a sure faith, because we have
been made free from a guilty conscience, and our
bodies have been washed with pure water. 23Let
us hold firmly to the hope that we have confessed,
because we can trust God to do what he promised.

24Let us think about each other and help each
other to show love and do good deeds. 25You
should not stay away from the church meetings,
as some are doing, but you should meet together
and encourage each other. Do this even more as
you see the day[n] coming.

26If we decide to go on sinning after we have
learned the truth, there is no longer any sacrifice
for sins. 27There is nothing but fear in waiting for
the judgment and the terrible fire that will destroy
all those who live against God. 28Anyone who refused to obey the law of Moses was found guilty
from the proof given by two or three witnesses.
He was put to death without mercy. 29So what do
you think should be done to those who do not

day The day Christ will come to judge all people and take his people to live with him.

CHURCH

Family of Friends

Jeremy Carr had had a rough life. His parents were divorced, and he had bounced between one parent and the other. When he signed up for summer youth camp, everyone was surprised, since he had shown little interest in church before.

After they arrived at the camp, the campers were split into groups of ten, each including an adult counselor. The group would stay together for a week.

Jeremy started acting up immediately. His counselor and the other kids tried to include him, but he ignored their kind gestures. He acted rude, obnoxious and selfish.

Finally the camp director, Cheryl Bolte, met with him after supper. When she asked Jeremy what he didn't like about his group, he said, "All they do is sit around and talk about their problems. I'm bored."

Cheryl explained to Jeremy that they were trying to build relationships, and that he was choosing not to be a part. "You don't have to participate, but you must respect other people's feelings," she said.

Jeremy spent the next day listening. He watched the group care for each other. Before he knew it, he told the group about his family and how much he hated moving back and forth between parents.

The group listened. Then one of the guys spoke. "We will be family for you, if you'll let us," he offered Jeremy, and the others agreed.

Jeremy couldn't believe it at first. But through the week, the campers' concern and their openness to him convinced him.

On the last day of camp, Jeremy thanked the group. "I've never known what it meant to have a real family, until this week," he said. "I know things still won't be easy at home, but I know at least ten people who care."

Fortunately for Jeremy, he experienced the love of a group of committed Christians who wouldn't give up on him. In **Hebrews 10:19–39**, the writer talks about this kind of commitment to the family of God.

- While at camp, how well did Jeremy's group live up to this passage's message?
- According to this passage, why do we need the church?

CONSIDER . . .

- praying for someone at church whom you think is incredibly rude or obnoxious. Then pray for help in understanding that person.
- accepting the care and concern of others if they invite you to church youth group meetings or outings. You may find new friends there.

FOR MORE, SEE . . .

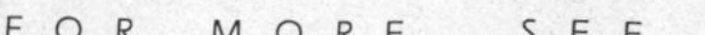

- Isaiah 65:1–2 (p. 685)
- Matthew 16:13–20 (p. 937)
- Acts 2:43–47 (p. 1100)

respect the Son of God, who look at the blood of
the agreement that made them holy as no different from others' blood, who insult the Spirit[d] of
God's grace? Surely they should have a much
worse punishment. 30We know that God said, "I
will punish those who do wrong; I will repay
them."[n] And he also said, "The Lord will judge
his people."[n] 31It is a terrible thing to fall into the
hands of the living God.

32Remember those days in the past when you
first learned the truth. You had a hard struggle
with many sufferings, but you continued strong.
33Sometimes you were hurt and attacked before
crowds of people, and sometimes you shared with
those who were being treated that way. 34You
helped the prisoners. You even had joy when all
that you owned was taken from you, because you
knew you had something better and more lasting.
35So do not lose the courage you had in the
past, which has a great reward. 36You must hold
on, so you can do what God wants and receive
what he has promised. 37For in a very short time,

"The One who is coming will come
and will not be delayed.
38The person who is right with me
will live by trusting in me.
But if he turns back with fear,
I will not be pleased with him." *Habakkuk 2:3-4*

39But we are not those who turn back and are
lost. We are people who have faith and are saved.

What Is Faith?

11 Faith means being sure of the things we
hope for and knowing that something is
real even if we do not see it. 2Faith is the reason
we remember great people who lived in the past.
3It is by faith we understand that the whole
world was made by God's command so what we

"I . . . them." Quotation from Deuteronomy 32:35.
"The Lord . . . people." Quotation from Deuteronomy 32:36; Psalm 135:14.

FAITH

A Voice in the Dark

A youth group was enjoying a week of climbing and cave exploration at Flat Rock, near Fredericksburg, Texas. David Yankton, an experienced wilderness guide, led the group. He'd brought along his six-year-old daughter, Kelly Jo, to hike with them.

On the second day, David led the group as it explored a nearby cave. He allowed just one flashlight. At the entrance there was plenty of light and the group moved along rapidly. As they sank deeper into the cave, however, the darkness thickened. Finally, the cave was so dark the hikers couldn't walk a step without clear directions from the person in front of them.

At one point in the darkness, Kelly Jo panicked and screamed out what the rest of the group felt: "Daddy, don't leave me!"

From the darkness came David's calming voice. "Kelly Jo, I'm right in front of you, leading the way." That was all she needed to hear. In fact, the whole group felt better after hearing David's voice.

The writer of Hebrews wanted Christians to understand how faith sometimes requires believing in things that can't be seen or heard. The writer gives examples in **Hebrews 11:1–16** of others who acted in faith even though they didn't know exactly where or how God was leading them.

- How were Kelly Jo and the group like some of the examples the writer mentions in this passage?
- When have you trusted in God even though you didn't know what was going to happen? How does that experience help you trust God now?

CONSIDER. . .

- trying something new in your faith, such as singing in the choir, or helping with mission or service projects.
- listing the ways you trust others, such as letting someone drive you somewhere or relying on others for food. Compare the list with the ways you trust God will take care of you.

FOR MORE, SEE. . .

- Genesis 12:1–5 (p. 14)
- Mark 4:35–41 (p. 972)
- Romans 4:13–25 (p. 1145)

see was made by something that cannot be seen.
4It was by faith that Abel offered God a better
sacrifice than Cain did. God said he was pleased
with the gifts Abel offered and called Abel a good
man because of his faith. Abel died, but through
his faith he is still speaking.
5It was by faith that Enoch was taken to heaven
so he would not die. He could not be found, because God had taken him away. Before he was
taken, the Scripture[d] says that he was a man who
truly pleased God. 6Without faith no one can
please God. Anyone who comes to God must believe that he is real and that he rewards those who
truly want to find him.
7It was by faith that Noah heard God's warnings about things he could not yet see. He obeyed
God and built a large boat to save his family. By
his faith, Noah showed that the world was wrong,
and he became one of those who are made right
with God through faith.
8It was by faith Abraham obeyed God's call to
go to another place God promised to give him. He
left his own country, not knowing where he was
to go. 9It was by faith that he lived like a foreigner
in the country God promised to give him. He lived
in tents with Isaac and Jacob, who had received
that same promise from God. 10Abraham was
waiting for the city[n] that has real foundations—
the city planned and built by God.
11He was too old to have children, and Sarah
could not have children. It was by faith that Abraham was made able to become a father, because
he trusted God to do what he had promised.
12This man was so old he was almost dead, but
from him came as many descendants as there are
stars in the sky. Like the sand on the seashore,
they could not be counted.
13All these great people died in faith. They did
not get the things that God promised his people,
but they saw them coming far in the future and
were glad. They said they were like visitors and
strangers on earth. 14When people say such
things, they show they are looking for a country
that will be their own. 15If they had been thinking
about the country they had left, they could have
gone back. 16But they were waiting for a better
country—a heavenly country. So God is not
ashamed to be called their God, because he has
prepared a city for them.
17It was by faith that Abraham, when God
tested him, offered his son Isaac as a sacrifice.
God made the promises to Abraham, but Abraham was ready to offer his own son as a sacrifice.
18God had said, "The descendants I promised you
will be from Isaac."[n] 19Abraham believed that
God could raise the dead, and really, it was as if
Abraham got Isaac back from death.
20It was by faith that Isaac blessed the future of
Jacob and Esau. 21It was by faith that Jacob, as he
was dying, blessed each one of Joseph's sons.
Then he worshiped as he leaned on the top of his
walking stick.
22It was by faith that Joseph, while he was dying, spoke about the Israelites leaving Egypt and
gave instructions about what to do with his body.
23It was by faith that Moses' parents hid him for
three months after he was born. They saw that
Moses was a beautiful baby, and they were not
afraid to disobey the king's order.
24It was by faith that Moses, when he grew up,
refused to be called the son of the king of Egypt's
daughter. 25He chose to suffer with God's people
instead of enjoying sin for a short time. 26He
thought it was better to suffer for the Christ[d] than
to have all the treasures of Egypt, because he was
looking for God's reward. 27It was by faith that
Moses left Egypt and was not afraid of the king's
anger. Moses continued strong as if he could see
the God that no one can see. 28It was by faith that
Moses prepared the Passover[d] and spread the
blood on the doors so the one who brings death
would not kill the firstborn[d] sons of Israel.
29It was by faith that the people crossed the Red
Sea as if it were dry land. But when the Egyptians
tried it, they were drowned.
30It was by faith that the walls of Jericho fell
after the people had marched around them for
seven days.
31It was by faith that Rahab, the prostitute,[d]
welcomed the spies and was not killed with those
who refused to obey God.

> **SIDELIGHT:** If you think you have had a hard life, read Hebrews 11:32–38. When verse 37 talks about being "cut in half," it may refer to the prophet Isaiah (p. 617), who, according to tradition, met this fate.

32Do I need to give more examples? I do not
have time to tell you about Gideon, Barak, Samson, Jephthah, David, Samuel, and the prophets.[d]
33Through their faith they defeated kingdoms.
They did what was right, received God's promises, and shut the mouths of lions. 34They stopped
great fires and were saved from being killed with
swords. They were weak, and yet were made

city The spiritual "city" where God's people live with him. Also called "the heavenly Jerusalem." (See Hebrews 12:22.)
"The descendants . . . Isaac." Quotation from Genesis 21:12.

strong. They were powerful in battle and defeated
other armies. 35Women received their dead relatives raised back to life. Others were tortured and
refused to accept their freedom so they could be
raised from the dead to a better life. 36Some were
laughed at and beaten. Others were put in chains
and thrown into prison. 37They were stoned to
death, they were cut in half, and they were killed
with swords. Some wore the skins of sheep and
goats. They were poor, abused, and treated badly.
38The world was not good enough for them! They
wandered in deserts and mountains, living in
caves and holes in the earth.
39All these people are known for their faith, but
none of them received what God had promised.
40God planned to give us something better so that
they would be made perfect, but only together
with us.

Follow Jesus' Example

12 We have around us many people whose lives tell us what faith means. So let us run the race that is before us and never give up. We should remove from our lives anything that would get in the way and the sin that so easily holds us back.
2Let us look only to Jesus, the One
who began our faith and who makes it perfect. He
suffered death on the cross. But he accepted the
shame as if it were nothing because of the joy that

PERSISTENCE

Learning to Win

It seemed to Sylvia Snyder that Coach Riker had no trust in the girls' basketball team. "The woman's impossible to please," Sylvia complained to her parents.

Sylvia remembered the end of the previous season when Coach Riker said they had the talent to be one of the state's best teams. "The question is, do you want to be the best?" she had asked.

"Yes!" they had all shouted. So, Sylvia and her teammates dedicated themselves to that goal.

When practice began again, Coach Riker worked the girls hard. Each daily practice turned into three grueling hours of pain and sweat. The coach never let up on them. She made them run extra laps, enforced a curfew, and monitored their grades. Sylvia was so frustrated she was ready to quit.

"I don't think I can take it anymore," Sylvia told her youth minister. "Coach Riker won't let up on us. She thinks practice is the most important thing in the world."

Sylvia's youth minister heard her frustration. "I know it's tough for you," he said. "But you and the rest of the team made a commitment at the end of last season. You knew it wouldn't be easy, so hang in there at least until the end of this season."

The season did end. The girls played hard and won the district. They went on to win third place at the state tournament. At the end of their final game, they carried out Coach Riker on their shoulders.

The next Sunday, the youth minister asked Sylvia whether she was glad she didn't quit. "I just didn't realize at the time that Coach Riker knew what she was doing," Sylvia said. "All of it—the practices, drills, monitoring our homework—helped us achieve our goal."

The writer of Hebrews knew life is often difficult. Things don't always go the way we plan. **Hebrews 12:1–13** explains the importance of being persistent in our lives as Christians.

- How could Sylvia's attitude have been different if she had read this passage?
- How does this passage apply to being persistent in your own life?

CONSIDER . . .

- taking on the next step of the hardest task, school project, or job you are facing.
- making a goal for your spiritual life for the next week (such as reading from your Bible three times). Tell your goal to two friends so they can pray for you and encourage you to stick with your goal. Talk about what you are learning from your reading.

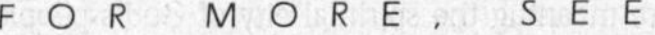

FOR MORE, SEE . . .

- Isaiah 42:1–4 (p. 657)
- Luke 18:1–5 (p. 1041)
- Ephesians 6:10–18 (p. 1226)

God put before him. And now he is sitting at the
right side of God's throne. 3Think about Jesus' example. He held on while wicked people were doing evil things to him. So do not get tired and stop
trying.

God Is like a Father

4You are struggling against sin, but your struggles have not yet caused you to be killed. 5You
have forgotten the encouraging words that call
you his children:

"My child, don't think the Lord's discipline is
worth nothing,
and don't stop trying when he corrects you.
6The Lord disciplines those he loves,
and he punishes everyone he accepts as his
child." *Proverbs 3:11-12*

7So hold on through your sufferings, because
they are like a father's discipline. God is treating
you as children. All children are disciplined by
their fathers. 8If you are never disciplined (and
every child must be disciplined), you are not true
children. 9We have all had fathers here on earth
who disciplined us, and we respected them. So it
is even more important that we accept discipline
from the Father of our spirits so we will have life.
10Our fathers on earth disciplined us for a short
time in the way they thought was best. But God
disciplines us to help us, so we can become holy
as he is. 11We do not enjoy being disciplined. It is
painful, but later, after we have learned from it,
we have peace, because we start living in the right
way.

Be Careful How You Live

12You have become weak, so make yourselves
strong again. 13Live in the right way so that you
will be saved and your weakness will not cause
you to be lost.

14Try to live in peace with all people, and try
to live free from sin. Anyone whose life is not holy
will never see the Lord. 15Be careful that no one
fails to receive God's grace and begins to cause
trouble among you. A person like that can ruin
many of you. 16Be careful that no one takes part
in sexual sin or is like Esau and never thinks about
God. As the oldest son, Esau would have received
everything from his father, but he sold all that for
a single meal. 17You remember that after Esau did
this, he wanted to get his father's blessing, but his
father refused. Esau could find no way to change
what he had done, even though he wanted the
blessing so much that he cried.

18You have not come to a mountain that can be
touched and that is burning with fire. You have
not come to darkness, sadness, and storms. 19You
have not come to the noise of a trumpet or to the
sound of a voice like the one the people of Israel
heard and begged not to hear another word.
20They did not want to hear the command: "If
anything, even an animal, touches the mountain,
it must be put to death with stones."[n] 21What
they saw was so terrible that Moses said, "I am
shaking with fear."[n]

22But you have come to Mount Zion,[n] to the
city of the living God, the heavenly Jerusalem.
You have come to thousands of angels gathered
together with joy. 23You have come to the meeting of God's firstborn[n] children whose names are
written in heaven. You have come to God, the
judge of all people, and to the spirits of good people who have been made perfect. 24You have
come to Jesus, the One who brought the new
agreement from God to his people, and you have
come to the sprinkled blood[n] that has a better
message than the blood of Abel.[n]

25So be careful and do not refuse to listen when
God speaks. Others refused to listen to him when
he warned them on earth, and they did not escape. So it will be worse for us if we refuse to
listen to God who warns us from heaven. 26When
he spoke before, his voice shook the earth, but
now he has promised, "Once again I will shake
not only the earth but also the heavens."[n] 27The
words "once again" clearly show us that everything that was made — things that can be
shaken — will be destroyed. Only the things that
cannot be shaken will remain.

28So let us be thankful, because we have a kingdom that cannot be shaken. We should worship
God in a way that pleases him with respect and
fear, 29because our God is like a fire that burns
things up.

13 Keep on loving each other as brothers
and sisters. 2Remember to welcome
strangers, because some who have done this have
welcomed angels without knowing it. 3Remem-
ber those who are in prison as if you were in
prison with them. Remember those who are suffering as if you were suffering with them.

4Marriage should be honored by everyone, and
husband and wife should keep their marriage

"If . . . stones." Quotation from Exodus 19:12-13.
"I . . . fear." Quotation from Deuteronomy 9:19.
Mount Zion Another name for Jerusalem, here meaning the spiritual city of God's people.
firstborn The first son born in a Jewish family was given the most important place in the family and received special blessings. All of God's children are like that.
sprinkled blood The blood of Jesus' death.
Abel The son of Adam and Eve, who was killed by his brother Cain (Genesis 4:8).
"Once . . . heavens." Quotation from Haggai 2:6, 21.

pure. God will judge as guilty those who take part
in sexual sins. 5Keep your lives free from the love
of money, and be satisfied with what you have.
God has said,

"I will never leave you;
I will never forget you." *Deuteronomy 31:6*

6So we can be sure when we say,

"I will not be afraid, because the Lord is my
helper.
People can't do anything to me." *Psalm 118:6*

7Remember your leaders who taught God's
message to you. Remember how they lived and
died, and copy their faith. 8Jesus Christ is the
same yesterday, today, and forever.

9Do not let all kinds of strange teachings lead
you into the wrong way. Your hearts should be
strengthened by God's grace, not by obeying rules
about foods, which do not help those who obey
them.

10We have a sacrifice, but the priests who serve
in the Holy Tent[d] cannot eat from it. 11The high
priest carries the blood of animals into the Most
Holy Place where he offers this blood for sins. But
the bodies of the animals are burned outside the
camp. 12So Jesus also suffered outside the city to
make his people holy with his own blood. 13So let
us go to Jesus outside the camp, holding on as he
did when we are abused.

14Here on earth we do not have a city that lasts
forever, but we are looking for the city that we
will have in the future. 15So through Jesus let us
always offer to God our sacrifice of praise, coming
from lips that speak his name. 16Do not forget to
do good to others, and share with them, because
such sacrifices please God.

17Obey your leaders and act under their authority. They are watching over you, because they are
responsible for your souls. Obey them so that they
will do this work with joy, not sadness. It will not
help you to make their work hard.

18Pray for us. We are sure that we have a clear
conscience, because we always want to do the
right thing. 19I especially beg you to pray so that
God will send me back to you soon.

20-21I pray that the God of peace will give you
every good thing you need so you can do what he

WORSHIP

Why Doesn't God Talk?

On the Thursday before Easter at the children's home, the children enjoyed a candlelight service in the chapel. The kids entered in their usual loud way. But, as soon as they saw the candles they became very quiet. Their eyes showed anticipation, as if something were about to happen.

After a moving service, Jason, Jenny, and Tina—three older children who lived at the home—came to talk to the chaplain. They wanted to know why God doesn't always seem as close as he was that evening.

"If God would talk to me, you know, out loud, it would be a lot easier to be a Christian," Jenny said.

The others agreed. "Why doesn't God just speak to us in church?" Jason asked.

Seven-year-old Kimberly, who had been listening, suddenly spoke up. "God does talk to you," she said to the other three. "Maybe you just don't always listen."

The writer of Hebrews describes how God speaks to us in worship. The writer of Hebrews knew that his readers, like the kids at the children's home, needed guidance for hearing God's message in worship. In **Hebrews 12:18–25** you will find more on hearing God in worship.

- Would the writer of Hebrews agree or disagree with Kimberly? Why or why not?
- How might you be more open to God's talking with you, according to the passage?

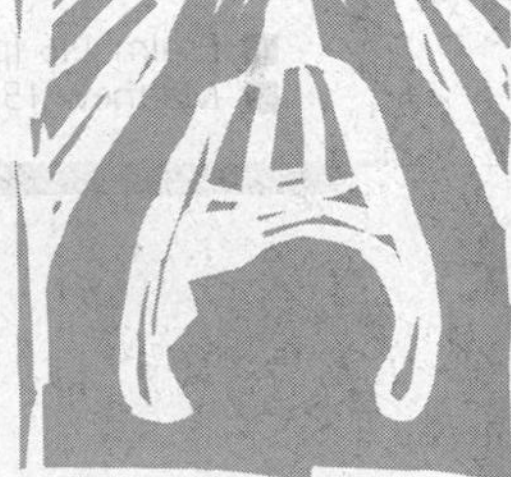

C O N S I D E R . . .

- spending a few minutes in prayer just before you go to a worship service this week, asking God to help you hear him better.
- volunteering to take a more active role one week in your church's worship service. See your pastor or minister of worship to see how you can participate.

F O R M O R E , S E E . . .

- Exodus 3:1–6 (p. 60)
- Psalm 95 (p. 537)
- Matthew 21:12–16 (p. 944)

wants. God raised from the dead our Lord Jesus, the Great Shepherd of the sheep, because of the blood of his death. His blood began the eternal agreement that God made with his people. I pray that God will do in us what pleases him, through Jesus Christ, and to him be glory forever and ever. Amen.

22My brothers and sisters, I beg you to listen patiently to this message I have written to encourage you, because it is not very long. 23I want you to know that our brother Timothy has been let out of prison. If he arrives soon, we will both come to see you.

24Greet all your leaders and all of God's people. Those from Italy send greetings to you.

25Grace be with you all.

SERVICE

When You See It

The Seventh Street Church youth group regularly went on outings. One night when the kids were returning in a church van from a pizza party, they saw an elderly woman waving for help in a bad section of town. Her car was broken down and she was alone. The kids immediately wanted to stop and help.

The car's battery was dead, and no one had jumper cables. The woman was afraid to leave her car there, and the kids didn't want to leave her there. So they decided to push her car to the nearest service station.

Eleven kids and one youth minister began pushing the woman's old Ford LTD through two miles of the worst section of town. More than once, people offered to take the car off their hands. The group pushed for what seemed forever. When a service station came into view, everyone cheered.

The woman was so grateful that she cried. "Not even my neighbors are so kind to me," she said. She took each member of the group by the hand and gave each one a hug and a smile.

As the group boarded the van for home, the woman thanked them again. "It takes special people to see a need and meet it where it is," she said.

The writer of Hebrews reminds Christians that serving each other is important. **Hebrews 13:1–8** offers several examples of how to love and care for others.

- How does the youth group's willingness to help compare with the message of the passage?
- What specific teachings from the passage apply to your life today?

CONSIDER. . .

- calling someone who has done something for you recently and letting that person know you appreciate the caring.
- doing something for someone in need. Look for needs you can meet, such as cutting grass or running an errand.

FOR MORE, SEE. . .

- Psalm 146 (p. 563)
- Matthew 15:21–28 (p. 935)
- Luke 7:1–10 (p. 1013)

JAMES

Why Read This Book:

- Learn how to handle temptation, testing and trouble (James 1).
- Understand the connection between what you believe and what you do (James 2—3).
- See what can happen when you let God be in charge of your life (James 4—5).

Behind the Scenes:

If someone says, "Would you mind taking out the garbage?" it's easy to forget or find some excuse for not doing it. But suppose someone says, "Take out the garbage!" It's hard to ignore the demand or find an excuse not to do it.

The book of James is like the second example. Its guidance is so clear that it is hard to ignore. "Do not become angry easily" (James 1:19). "Never think some people are more important than others" (James 2:1). "Do not tell evil lies about each other" (James 4:11). In fact, James has more than fifty direct commands in just five chapters!

While much of the New Testament focuses on what Christians believe, James focuses on how Christians behave. Some early Christians apparently thought they could do whatever they wanted because God would forgive them anyway. But James warns them that "if people say they have faith, but do nothing, their faith is worth nothing" (James 2:14).

This short book is loaded with advice on putting our faith into action. It covers many areas of life we continue to struggle with: handling money, relations between the rich and poor, bragging, judging others, being patient. The book is as practical today as when it was written almost two thousand years ago.

WHERE THE ACTION WAS

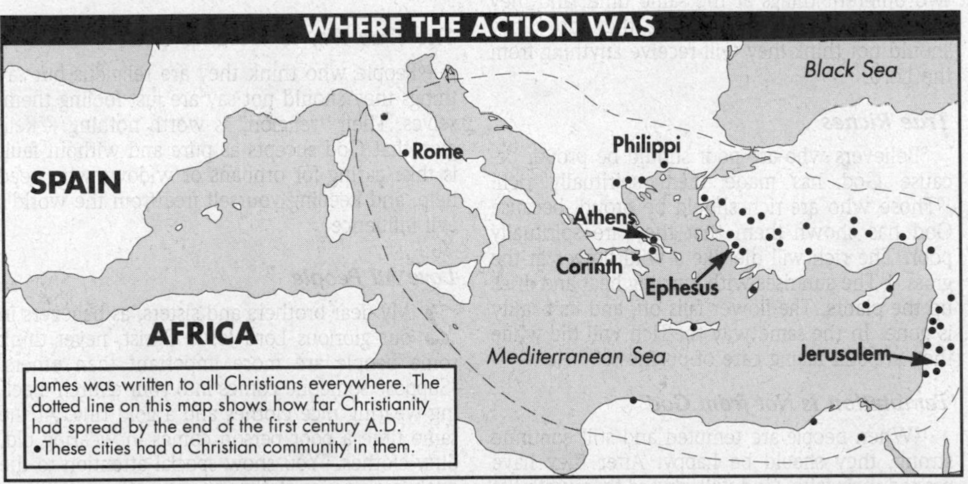

James was written to all Christians everywhere. The dotted line on this map shows how far Christianity had spread by the end of the first century A.D.
•These cities had a Christian community in them.

WHEN THE ACTION WAS

BC/AD — 20AD — 30AD — 40AD — 50AD — 60AD — 70AD

- Jesus was born
- Jesus began his ministry
- The church began soon after Jesus went to heaven
- Paul became a Christian
- Paul began his missionary work
- James may have been written
- Fire destroyed Rome
- Romans destroyed the Temple in Jerusalem

1 From James, a servant of God and of the
Lord Jesus Christ.
To all of God's people who are scattered every-
where in the world:

Greetings.

Faith and Wisdom

2My brothers and sisters,[n] when you have
many kinds of troubles, you should be full of joy,
3because you know that these troubles test your

> **SIDELIGHT:** James was a common name in the first century, so we are not positive who wrote this letter. One theory is that the author was a brother of Jesus. This James became the leader of the Jerusalem church and later was put to death because of his faith.

faith, and this will give you patience. 4Let your
patience show itself perfectly in what you do.
Then you will be perfect and complete and will
have everything you need. 5But if any of you
needs wisdom, you should ask God for it. He is
generous and enjoys giving to all people, so he
will give you wisdom. 6But when you ask God,
you must believe and not doubt. Anyone who
doubts is like a wave in the sea, blown up and
down by the wind. 7-8Such doubters are thinking
two different things at the same time, and they
cannot decide about anything they do. They
should not think they will receive anything from
the Lord.

True Riches

9Believers who are poor should be proud, because God has made them spiritually rich.
10Those who are rich should be proud, because
God has shown them that they are spiritually
poor. The rich will die like a wild flower in the
grass. 11The sun rises with burning heat and dries
up the plants. The flower falls off, and its beauty
is gone. In the same way the rich will die while
they are still taking care of business.

Temptation Is Not from God

12When people are tempted and still continue
strong, they should be happy. After they have
proved their faith, God will reward them with life
forever. God promised this to all those who love
him. 13When people are tempted, they should not
say, "God is tempting me." Evil cannot tempt
God, and God himself does not tempt anyone.
14But people are tempted when their own evil desire leads them away and traps them. 15This desire
leads to sin, and then the sin grows and brings
death.
16My dear brothers and sisters, do not be fooled
about this. 17Every good action and every perfect
gift is from God. These good gifts come down
from the Creator of the sun, moon, and stars, who
does not change like their shifting shadows.
18God decided to give us life through the word of
truth so we might be the most important of all the
things he made.

Listening and Obeying

19My dear brothers and sisters, always be willing to listen and slow to speak. Do not become
angry easily, 20because anger will not help you
live the right kind of life God wants. 21So put out
of your life every evil thing and every kind of
wrong. Then in gentleness accept God's teaching
that is planted in your hearts, which can save you.
22Do what God's teaching says; when you only
listen and do nothing, you are fooling yourselves.
23Those who hear God's teaching and do nothing
are like people who look at themselves in a mirror. 24They see their faces and then go away and
quickly forget what they looked like. 25But the
truly happy people are those who carefully study
God's perfect law that makes people free, and
they continue to study it. They do not forget what
they heard, but they obey what God's teaching
says. Those who do this will be made happy.

The True Way to Worship God

26People who think they are religious but say
things they should not say are just fooling themselves. Their "religion" is worth nothing. 27Reli-
gion that God accepts as pure and without fault
is this: caring for orphans or widows who need
help, and keeping yourself free from the world's
evil influence.

Love All People

2 My dear brothers and sisters, as believers in
our glorious Lord Jesus Christ, never think
some people are more important than others.
2Suppose someone comes into your church meeting wearing nice clothes and a gold ring. At the
same time a poor person comes in wearing old,
dirty clothes. 3You show special attention to the
one wearing nice clothes and say, "Please, sit here
in this good seat." But you say to the poor person,
"Stand over there," or, "Sit on the floor by my
feet." 4What are you doing? You are making some
people more important than others, and with evil

brothers and sisters Although the Greek text says "brothers" here and throughout this book, James' words were meant for the entire church, including men and women.

thoughts you are deciding that one person is better.

SIDELIGHT: Wearing a gold ring (James 2:2) was a sign of great wealth in New Testament times. People who wanted to show off their wealth would cover their fingers with rings, often several on each finger. They would even rent rings when they particularly wanted to impress people. Imagine the limousine they would hire to go to the senior prom!

5Listen, my dear brothers and sisters! God
chose the poor in the world to be rich with faith
and to receive the kingdom God promised to
those who love him. 6But you show no respect to
the poor. The rich are always trying to control
your lives. They are the ones who take you to
court. 7And they are the ones who speak against
Jesus, who owns you.
8This royal law is found in the Scriptures:[d]
"Love your neighbor as you love yourself."[n] If
you obey this law, you are doing right. 9But if you
treat one person as being more important than
another, you are sinning. You are guilty of breaking God's law. 10A person who follows all of God's
law but fails to obey even one command is guilty
of breaking all the commands in that law. 11The
same God who said, "You must not be guilty of
adultery,"[d,n] also said, "You must not murder
anyone."[n] So if you do not take part in adultery
but you murder someone, you are guilty of breaking all of God's law. 12In everything you say and
do, remember that you will be judged by the law
that makes people free. 13So you must show
mercy to others, or God will not show mercy to
you when he judges you. But the person who
shows mercy can stand without fear at the judgment.

Faith and Good Works

14My brothers and sisters, if people say they
have faith, but do nothing, their faith is worth
nothing. Can faith like that save them? 15A
brother or sister in Christ might need clothes or
food. 16If you say to that person, "God be with
you! I hope you stay warm and get plenty to eat,"
but you do not give what that person needs, your

"Love . . . yourself." Quotation from Leviticus 19:18.
"You . . . adultery." Quotation from Exodus 20:14 and Deuteronomy 5:18.
"You . . . anyone." Quotation from Exodus 20:13 and Deuteronomy 5:17.

BIBLE STUDY

A Word From Your Sponsor

If you're a typical teenager, by the time you graduate from high school, you'll have watched eighteen to twenty thousand hours of television. An hour of television may carry fifteen to twenty-five advertisements. Thus, a typical eighteen year old has seen about three to four hundred thousand advertisements.

How many of those ads do you think eighteen year olds can remember?

Probably no one could recall more than a few hundred. Even lower would be the number of ads to which the typical teenager responded by purchasing the product.

We simply tune out much of what we hear.

But **James 1:17–27** says we can't afford to "tune out" when we hear God's teaching. Tune in the passage.

- What does James say about those "who hear God's teaching and do nothing"—the way most of us treat commercials?
- According to James, who is "the truly happy person?" How might your life change if you were to remember and act on more of God's teaching?

CONSIDER . . .

- telling a Christian friend what you read in the Bible today. Doing so can help you remember it and apply it to your own life.
- taking notes the next time you hear a sermon in church.

FOR MORE, SEE . . .

- Joshua 1:6–9 (p. 195)
- Psalm 119:1–16 (p. 550)
- Luke 11:27–28 (p. 1026)

words are worth nothing. 17In the same way, faith
that is alone — that does nothing — is dead.
18Someone might say, "You have faith, but I
have deeds." Show me your faith without doing
anything, and I will show you my faith by what
I do. 19You believe there is one God. Good! But
the demons[d] believe that, too, and they tremble
with fear.
20You foolish person! Must you be shown that
faith that does nothing is worth nothing? 21Abra-
ham, our ancestor, was made right with God by
what he did when he offered his son Isaac on the
altar. 22So you see that Abraham's faith and the
things he did worked together. His faith was
made perfect by what he did. 23This shows the full
meaning of the Scripture[d] that says: "Abraham believed God, and God accepted Abraham's faith,
and that faith made him right with God."[n] And
Abraham was called God's friend.[n] 24So you see
that people are made right with God by what they
do, not by faith only.
25Another example is Rahab, a prostitute,[d] who
was made right with God by something she did.
She welcomed the spies into her home and
helped them escape by a different road.
26Just as a person's body that does not have a
spirit is dead, so faith that does nothing is dead!

Controlling the Things We Say

3 My brothers and sisters, not many of you
should become teachers, because you know
that we who teach will be judged more strictly.
2We all make many mistakes. If people never said
anything wrong, they would be perfect and able
to control their entire selves, too. 3When we put
bits into the mouths of horses to make them obey

"Abraham . . . God." Quotation from Genesis 15:6.
God's friend These words about Abraham are found in 2 Chronicles 20:7 and Isaiah 41:8.

JUDGING OTHERS

A Perfect Ten?

Peggy Reynolds and her friends moved down the food line in the music camp dining hall. Two guys serving food watched Peggy and the other girls, and grinned. When she got near them, they reached under the counter, pulled out two cardboard signs with numbers, and put them on a high ledge behind them. "Nine" and "five," Peggy thought, reading the cards. "I wonder what they mean?"

When Peggy's friend Marie got to the same place in line, the guys changed the numbers to an "eight" and a "six." By now everybody had stopped eating to watch. When the next girl in line received a "nine" and a "seven," people cheered. "They're rating us," Peggy suddenly realized. Her face turned red.

Peggy and her friends laughed uncomfortably as the two guys continued to rate girls as they passed in line. Then Terri Smith got in line. She wasn't "perfect" looking and was a bit overweight. Peggy dreaded how the guys might rate Terri. But as she passed through the line, the guys just ignored her. They didn't rate her at all. Then, when other "better looking" girls came up in the line, the guys resumed their rating game.

But the game wasn't funny to Peggy. She felt judged, and imagined how hurt Terri probably felt.

Sometimes it may seem like fun to judge other people, but being judged is rarely funny. Read in **James 2:1–17** what James wrote about treating people as though they are more important than others.

- What does James say is wrong with judging people like the guys were rating the girls at the camp?
- When have you unfairly judged someone because of clothes or grades or skill at sports? What makes us fall into doing things like that?

C O N S I D E R . . .

- thinking about one person you have judged. The next time you see this person, say, "Hi."
- watching this week how often you put people down. Whenever you realize you have put someone down, quickly say something that builds the person up too.

F O R   M O R E ,   S E E . . .

- 1 Samuel 16:7 (p. 258)
- Matthew 7:1–5 (p. 918)
- Romans 12:14–16 (p. 1158)

us, we can control their whole bodies. [4]Also a
ship is very big, and it is pushed by strong winds.
But a very small rudder controls that big ship,
making it go wherever the pilot wants. [5]It is the
same with the tongue. It is a small part of the
body, but it brags about great things.

A big forest fire can be started with only a little
flame. [6]And the tongue is like a fire. It is a whole
world of evil among the parts of our bodies. The
tongue spreads its evil through the whole body.
The tongue is set on fire by hell, and it starts a fire
that influences all of life. [7]People can tame every
kind of wild animal, bird, reptile, and fish, and
they have tamed them, [8]but no one can tame the
tongue. It is wild and evil and full of deadly poison. [9]We use our tongues to praise our Lord and
Father, but then we curse people, whom God
made like himself. [10]Praises and curses come from
the same mouth! My brothers and sisters, this
should not happen. [11]Do good and bad water flow
from the same spring? [12]My brothers and sisters,
can a fig tree make olives, or can a grapevine
make figs? No! And a well full of salty water cannot give good water.

True Wisdom

[13]Are there those among you who are truly
wise and understanding? Then they should show
it by living right and doing good things with a
gentleness that comes from wisdom. [14]But if you
are selfish and have bitter jealousy in your hearts,
do not brag. Your bragging is a lie that hides the
truth. [15]That kind of "wisdom" does not come
from God but from the world. It is not spiritual;
it is from the devil. [16]Where jealousy and selfishness are, there will be confusion and every kind
of evil. [17]But the wisdom that comes from God is
first of all pure, then peaceful, gentle, and easy to
please. This wisdom is always ready to help those
who are troubled and to do good for others. It is
always fair and honest. [18]People who work for
peace in a peaceful way plant a good crop of right-
living.

Give Yourselves to God

4 Do you know where your fights and argu
ments come from? They come from the selfish desires that war within you. [2]You want things,
but you do not have them. So you are ready to kill
and are jealous of other people, but you still cannot get what you want. So you argue and fight.
You do not get what you want, because you do
not ask God. [3]Or when you ask, you do not
receive because the reason you ask is wrong.

BRAGGING

Spain's Greatest Matador . . . Almost

Though only twenty-one years old, Jose Cubero had leaped to fame as one of Spain's most spectacular matadors. In bullfight after bullfight, he had daringly whirled and dodged his way to triumph.

It was no surprise, then, when he made especially quick work of a bull during a routine bullfight. Thrusting his sword one last time, Jose watched the bull collapse onto the dirt of the arena. Jose had performed well, and he knew it. He turned arrogantly to bask in the crowd's applause.

Enjoying the roaring cheers, Jose was unaware that the bull behind him was not dead. The bull suddenly rose and lunged, one of its horns piercing the matador from the back. Jose Cubero, a rising young star, was dead.

When we have done well, we like to get people's attention. We like to listen to the cheers. But James reminds us in **James 3:13–18** to do "good things with a gentleness that comes from wisdom." Boasting of our actions is a dangerous practice.

- What else might James have told Jose Cubero about bragging?
- What do you think makes people eager to brag? Why might Christians have less need to brag?

C O N S I D E R . . .

- noticing, as you watch television today, which characters brag. How do you feel about these characters?
- writing on a card this saying: "There's no limit to the amount of good you can do if you don't care who gets the credit." Place it where you will see it.

F O R M O R E , S E E . . .

- Daniel 4:28–37 (p. 811)
- Luke 14:7–11 (p. 1031)

- Philippians 2:3–11 (p. 1230)

You want things so you can use them for your
own pleasures.
4So, you are not loyal to God! You should know
that loving the world is the same as hating God.
Anyone who wants to be a friend of the world
becomes God's enemy. 5Do you think the Scripture[d] means nothing that says, "The Spirit[d] that
God made to live in us wants us for himself
alone."[n] 6But God gives us even more grace, as
the Scripture says,

"God is against the proud,
but he gives grace to the humble."

Proverbs 3:34

7So give yourselves completely to God. Stand
against the devil, and the devil will run from you.
8Come near to God, and God will come near to
you. You sinners, clean sin out of your lives. You
who are trying to follow God and the world at the
same time, make your thinking pure. 9Be sad, cry,
and weep! Change your laughter into crying and
your joy into sadness. 10Don't be too proud in the
Lord's presence, and he will make you great.

You Are Not the Judge

11Brothers and sisters, do not tell evil lies about
each other. If you speak against your fellow believers or judge them, you are judging and speaking against the law they follow. And when you are
judging the law, you are no longer a follower of
the law. You have become a judge. 12God is the
only Lawmaker and Judge. He is the only One
who can save and destroy. So it is not right for you
to judge your neighbor.

Let God Plan Your Life

13Some of you say, "Today or tomorrow we
will go to some city. We will stay there a year, do
business, and make money." 14But you do not
know what will happen tomorrow! Your life is
like a mist. You can see it for a short time, but
then it goes away. 15So you should say, "If the
Lord wants, we will live and do this or that."
16But now you are proud and you brag. All of this
bragging is wrong. 17Anyone who knows the right
thing to do, but does not do it, is sinning.

"The Spirit . . . alone." These words may be from Exodus 20:5.

GOD'S WILL

Lump on an All-Star's Arm

"Cancer came into my life as a small thing," remembers all-star baseball pitcher Dave Dravecky, talking about the small lump that had appeared on his throwing arm.

"The San Francisco Giants had clinched the division," Dave says. "We were making ready for what every baseball player works for, and most never experience: postseason play. So I had things on my mind other than a little, painless lump."

But the lump on his arm didn't go away. It grew. The next year the tumor had to be removed, along with 50 percent of Dave's deltoid muscle. "Short of a miracle," the cancer specialist said, "Dave will never pitch again."

Through therapy and exercise, Dave did come back. But in his second game the next season, he broke his arm, and his career came to an abrupt and painful halt.

"There's a bittersweet quality to my retirement from baseball," he says. "I've learned to put my life in God's hands. I had to learn to do what was within my grasp, one day at a time, and leave control of the rest to God."

James 4:13–17 reminds us that the future is in God's hands.

- What would both Dave Dravecky and James say we should expect from the future?
- What are you hoping and planning to do in the next several months? When you think about these plans, does God come into your mind?

CONSIDER . . .

- evaluating your dreams for the future in light of this passage on God's will.
- writing on an envelope, "It's in God's hands." Whenever you are worried about something in the future you cannot control, write out your worry on a slip of paper and place it in the envelope.

FOR MORE, SEE . . .

- Psalm 139 (p. 561)
- Proverbs 16:1, 9 (p. 581)
- Luke 12:22–31 (p. 1028)

A Warning to the Rich

5 You rich people, listen! Cry and be very sad
because of the troubles that are coming to
you. [2]Your riches have rotted, and your clothes
have been eaten by moths. [3]Your gold and silver
have rusted, and that rust will be a proof that you
were wrong. It will eat your bodies like fire. You
saved your treasure for the last days. [4]The pay you
did not give the workers who mowed your fields
cries out against you, and the cries of the workers
have been heard by the Lord All-Powerful. [5]Your
life on earth was full of rich living and pleasing
yourselves with everything you wanted. You
made yourselves fat, like an animal ready to be
killed. [6]You have judged guilty and then murdered innocent people, who were not against you.

Be Patient

[7]Brothers and sisters, be patient until the Lord
comes again. A farmer patiently waits for his valuable crop to grow from the earth and for it to receive the autumn and spring rains. [8]You, too,
must be patient. Do not give up hope, because the
Lord is coming soon. [9]Brothers and sisters, do not
complain against each other or you will be judged
guilty. And the Judge is ready to come! [10]Brothers
and sisters, follow the example of the prophets[d]
who spoke for the Lord. They suffered many hard
things, but they were patient. [11]We say they are
happy because they did not give up. You have
heard about Job's patience, and you know the
Lord's purpose for him in the end. You know
the Lord is full of mercy and is kind.

Be Careful What You Say

[12]My brothers and sisters, above all, do not use
an oath when you make a promise. Don't use the
name of heaven, earth, or anything else to prove
what you say. When you mean yes, say only yes,
and when you mean no, say only no so you will
not be judged guilty.

The Power of Prayer

[13]Anyone who is having troubles should pray.

PATIENCE

Endless Paddling

"Come on, guys! Hurry up!" Sherri Rohrer's youth leader called from a silver canoe a hundred yards ahead. Sherri felt she would never catch up, let alone finish the ten-day trip.

They had broken camp at 9:00 A.M. It was now 3:00 P.M., and they still had miles to paddle. The wind blew against them, and the hard paddling took its toll on many out-of-shape bodies. "I can't wait to get there," Sherri complained to her canoeing partner. "Where's a motor for this thing? My arms feel dead."

As Sherri lifted her paddle out of the water, she watched the drops fall back into the dark Maine river. She thought about how she had waited all year for this trip. She and the other group members had worked hard—spaghetti dinners, car washes, bake sales. Her excitement had grown as the trip date approached. It had been hard to wait.

Now that the trip was here, she sometimes wondered whether it had been worth all the excitement. She grew tired of still waiting—for rest, for dinner, and for free time to relax.

As Sherri had trouble being patient on the canoe trip, Christians sometimes tire of waiting for things to get better. **James 5:7–11** encourages believers to keep a patient faith, because things will get better.

- How might James's advice help Sherri?
- What does James say we can look forward to if we are patient? How can knowing that Jesus is coming help you be patient today?

C O N S I D E R . . .

- listing things you are waiting for. Ask God to give you hope while you wait.
- getting a calendar and marking the date of an upcoming "big event" in your life. Sprinkle short notes on dates along the way to encourage you while you wait.

F O R   M O R E ,   S E E . . .

- Job 2:11–13 (p. 453) and 42:10–17 (p. 479)
- Isaiah 40:27–31 (p. 656)
- Matthew 7:7–11 (p. 919)

Anyone who is happy should sing praises. [14]Any-
one who is sick should call the church's elders.[d]
They should pray for and pour oil on the person[n]
in the name of the Lord. [15]And the prayer that is
said with faith will make the sick person well; the
Lord will heal that person. And if the person has
sinned, the sins will be forgiven. [16]Confess your
sins to each other and pray for each other so God
can heal you. When a believing person prays,
great things happen. [17]Elijah was a human being
just like us. He prayed that it would not rain, and
it did not rain on the land for three and a half
years! [18]Then Elijah prayed again, and the rain
came down from the sky, and the land produced
crops again.

SIDELIGHT: Using oil as medicine was a common practice in Bible times (James 5:14). The good Samaritan in Jesus' parable poured oil on the victim's wounds (Luke 10:34, p. 1023). People who had headaches probably had the greasiest heads in town!

Saving a Soul

[19]My brothers and sisters, if one of you wanders away from the truth, and someone helps that
person come back, [20]remember this: Anyone who
brings a sinner back from the wrong way will save
that sinner's soul from death and will cause many
sins to be forgiven.

pour oil on the person Oil was used in the name of the Lord as a sign that the person was now set apart for God's special attention and care.

1 PETER

Why Read This Book:

- See the benefits of the salvation God offers you (1 Peter 1:3—2:10).
- Discover how Christians should live (1 Peter 2:11—4:11).
- Learn how to grow even when suffering (1 Peter 4:12—5:11).

Behind the Scenes:

You may have experienced the old prank: Someone writes "KICK ME" on a sheet of paper, then puts it on your back without your knowing it. Suddenly everyone starts laughing at you. Some kick you. You feel angry and embarrassed.

The Christians who received 1 Peter had similar feelings, though the reasons were much different and much more serious. They had become Christians in a pagan culture. And the Christian label brought ridicule, persecution, and suffering.

Some of these Christians might have felt embarrassed about their faith. They may have been tempted to get rid of the Christian "label." Maybe being a Christian wasn't worth all this pain.

This letter encourages the early Christians to stick with their faith, even in the midst of their suffering. It gives them practical advice on how to live with the pain. It reminds them that their circumstances don't have to control their joy and hope in life. God is in control, and he cares about their suffering.

Sometimes it is hard being a Christian. People may make fun of our choices. They may call us names. But this letter encourages us to stay strong in our faith, for in the end God will give victory to his faithful.

WHERE THE ACTION WAS

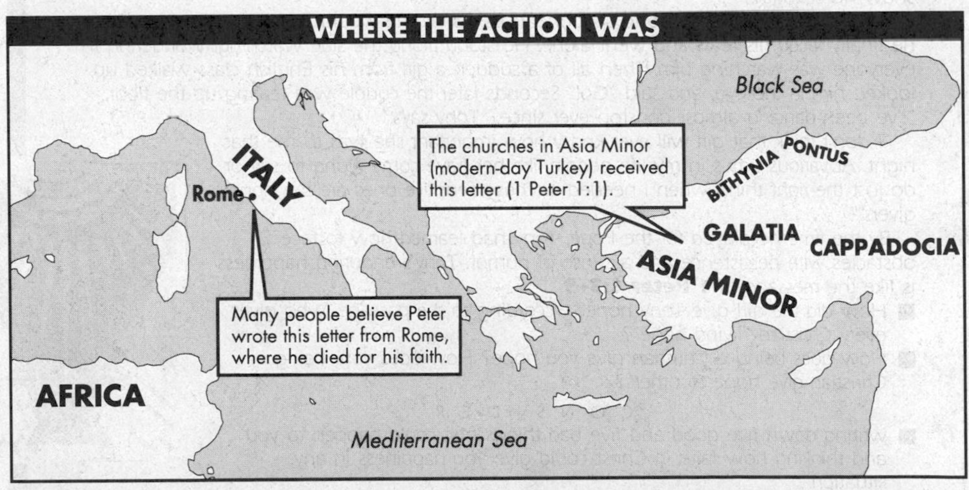

Black Sea
The churches in Asia Minor (modern-day Turkey) received this letter (1 Peter 1:1).
PONTUS
BITHYNIA
ITALY
Rome
GALATIA
CAPPADOCIA
ASIA MINOR
Many people believe Peter wrote this letter from Rome, where he died for his faith.
AFRICA
Mediterranean Sea

WHEN THE ACTION WAS

- BC/AD — Jesus was born
- Jesus began his ministry
- The church began soon after Jesus went to heaven
- 25AD
- Paul began his missionary work
- 50AD
- Fire destroyed Rome, and Roman persecution of Christians began
- 1 Peter may have been written
- 75AD
- The Roman emperor increased persecution of Christians
- 100AD

1 From Peter, an apostle[d] of Jesus Christ.
To God's chosen people who are away from
their homes and are scattered all around the countries of Pontus, Galatia, Cappadocia, Asia, and Bithynia. 2God planned long ago to choose you by
making you his holy people, which is the Spirit's[d]
work. God wanted you to obey him and to be
made clean by the blood of the death of Jesus
Christ.
Grace and peace be yours more and more.

We Have a Living Hope

3Praise be to the God and Father of our Lord
Jesus Christ. In God's great mercy he has caused
us to be born again into a living hope, because
Jesus Christ rose from the dead. 4Now we hope
for the blessings God has for his children. These
blessings, which cannot be destroyed or be
spoiled or lose their beauty, are kept in heaven for
you. 5God's power protects you through your
faith until salvation is shown to you at the end of

HAPPINESS

The Hope Giver

Tony Melendez amazed 100 million TV viewers in 1987 as he played the guitar with his feet and sang for Pope John Paul II. "Tony," the Pope said, after embracing the performer, "you are giving hope to all of us. My wish to you is to continue giving this hope to all the people."

Born without arms, Tony is normal in every other way. But he had struggled for years to be accepted.

Without persistence, Tony might never have graduated from high school. When he transferred from special education into a "normal" English class, all eyes watched him when he walked into the classroom. He shrugged off his backpack, pulled out a notebook with his toes and put it on the floor. Then he grabbed a pencil between his two biggest toes and began taking notes. Even the teacher had stopped the discussion of Moby Dick to watch. Everyone stared in silence.

"Somebody had to break the silence," Tony recalled. "Hope the floor is clean," he said with a grin. "If it isn't, I'll have to turn in a dirty paper." The students and teacher roared with laughter, then class continued. It was one of the many awkward times he had to show his strength.

Still, Tony was afraid to go to school dances—afraid he would be rejected by girls. But he finally faced his fears and went alone. He stood along the side watching, wondering if everyone was watching him. Then all of a sudden a girl from his English class walked up, looked him in the eye, and said "Go!" Seconds later the couple was tearing up the floor. "I've been dancing almost nonstop ever since," Tony says.

"I don't think that girl will ever know how important she was to me that night. At various times in my life people like her have come along to say or do just the right thing when I needed it. These sensitive ones are the hope givers."

By the time he played for the Pope, Tony had learned how to face obstacles with persistence and a sense of humor. Tony's enduring happiness is like the message of **1 Peter 1:3–9**.

- How did the girl give Tony hope? According to the passage, who gives every Christian "living hope"?
- How does being a Christian give you hope? How does your being a Christian give hope to others?

CONSIDER . . .

- writing down five good and five bad things that could happen to you and thinking how faith in Christ could give you happiness in any situation.
- interviewing someone who has suffered great tragedy, but whose life still is characterized by joy.

FOR MORE, SEE . . .

- Job 5:17 (p. 454)
- John 15:11 (p. 1085)
- James 1:2–4 (p. 1294)

time. 6This makes you very happy, even though now for a short time different kinds of troubles may make you sad. 7These troubles come to prove that your faith is pure. This purity of faith is worth more than gold, which can be proved to be pure by fire but will ruin. But the purity of your faith will bring you praise and glory and honor when Jesus Christ is shown to you. 8You have not seen Christ, but still you love him. You cannot see him now, but you believe in him. So you are filled with a joy that cannot be explained, a joy full of glory. 9And you are receiving the goal of your faith — the salvation of your souls.

10The prophets[d] searched carefully and tried to learn about this salvation. They prophesied about the grace that was coming to you. 11The Spirit[d] of Christ was in the prophets, telling in advance about the sufferings of Christ and about the glory that would follow those sufferings. The prophets tried to learn about what the Spirit was showing them, when those things would happen, and what the world would be like at that time. 12It was shown them that their service was not for themselves but for you, when they told about the truths you have now heard. Those who preached the Good News[d] to you told you those things with the help of the Holy Spirit who was sent from heaven — things into which angels desire to look.

A Call to Holy Living

13So prepare your minds for service and have self-control. All your hope should be for the gift of grace that will be yours when Jesus Christ is shown to you. 14Now that you are obedient children of God do not live as you did in the past. You did not understand, so you did the evil things you wanted. 15But be holy in all you do, just as God, the One who called you, is holy. 16It is written in the Scriptures:[d] "You must be holy, because I am holy."[n]

17You pray to God and call him Father, and he judges each person's work equally. So while you are here on earth, you should live with respect for God. 18You know that in the past you were living in a worthless way, a way passed down from the people who lived before you. But you were saved from that useless life. You were bought, not with something that ruins like gold or silver, 19but with the precious blood of Christ, who was like a pure and perfect lamb. 20Christ was chosen before the world was made, but he was shown to the world in these last times for your sake. 21Through Christ you believe in God, who raised Christ from the dead and gave him glory. So your faith and your hope are in God.

22Now that you have made your souls pure by obeying the truth, you can have true love for your Christian brothers and sisters.[n] So love each other deeply with all your heart. 23You have been born again, and this new life did not come from something that dies, but from something that cannot die. You were born again through God's living message that continues forever. 24The Scripture says,

"All people are like the grass,
  and all their glory is like the flowers of the
    field.
The grass dies and the flowers fall,
25 but the word of the Lord will live forever."
Isaiah 40:6-8

And this is the word that was preached to you.

Jesus Is the Living Stone

2 So then, rid yourselves of all evil, all lying, hypocrisy,[d] jealousy, and evil speech. 2As newborn babies want milk, you should want the pure and simple teaching. By it you can grow up and be saved, 3because you have already examined and seen how good the Lord is.

4Come to the Lord Jesus, the "stone"[n] that lives. The people of the world did not want this stone, but he was the stone God chose, and he was precious. 5You also are like living stones, so let yourselves be used to build a spiritual temple — to be holy priests who offer spiritual sacrifices to God. He will accept those sacrifices through Jesus Christ. 6The Scripture[d] says:

"I will put a stone in the ground in
    Jerusalem.
  Everything will be built on this important
    and precious rock.
Anyone who trusts in him
  will never be disappointed." *Isaiah 28:16*

7This stone is worth much to you who believe. But to the people who do not believe,

"the stone that the builders rejected
  has become the cornerstone."[d] *Psalm 118:22*

8Also, he is

"a stone that causes people to stumble,
  a rock that makes them fall." *Isaiah 8:14*

They stumble because they do not obey what God says, which is what God planned to happen to them.

9But you are a chosen people, royal priests, a holy nation, a people for God's own possession. You were chosen to tell about the wonderful acts of God, who called you out of darkness into his wonderful light. 10At one time you were not a people, but now you are God's people. In the past

"You must be . . . holy." Quotation from Leviticus 11:45; 19:2; 20:7.
brothers and sisters Although the Greek text says "brothers" here and throughout this book, Peter's words were meant for the entire church, including men and women.
"stone" The most important stone in God's spiritual temple or house (his people).

you had never received mercy, but now you have received God's mercy.

Live for God

11 Dear friends, you are like foreigners and strangers in this world. I beg you to avoid the evil things your bodies want to do that fight against your soul. 12 People who do not believe are living all around you and might say that you are doing wrong. Live such good lives that they will see the good things you do and will give glory to God on the day when Christ comes again.

Yield to Every Human Authority

13 For the Lord's sake, yield to the people who have authority in this world: the king, who is the highest authority, 14 and the leaders who are sent by him to punish those who do wrong and to praise those who do right. 15 It is God's desire that by doing good you should stop foolish people from saying stupid things about you. 16 Live as free people, but do not use your freedom as an excuse to do evil. Live as servants of God. 17 Show respect for all people: Love the brothers and sisters of God's family, respect God, honor the king.

LOVE

Given, Not Earned

The argument was brutal. Rochelle Mattison's parents didn't want her to go to the party. They didn't know the guy throwing it, didn't know his parents, didn't know who was going to be there, and didn't know what the teenagers would be doing.

"You're eighteen years old, Rochelle," her father said. "We won't forbid you to go. But if you ignore our wishes on this, don't expect us to honor your wishes on other things . . . including the use of the car."

They thought withholding the car would stop her.

But it didn't. "I'm tired of you using the car to force me to do what you want," she shot back. "Just keep the car! I don't need it! I've got friends who'll take me to parties!"

With that, she stormed out, called her friends from a pay phone, and headed for the party. Rochelle savored her apparent victory.

But then she arrived at the party. It was wild. Heavy drinking. Too many people. No adults around. She wanted to leave. But her "friends" had left without her, and everyone else at the party had been drinking. She was left to walk seven miles home. She stood alone outside, wondering what to do.

"Hey, Beautiful! Want a lift?" a voice said from a car pulling up behind her. Rochelle felt a surge of fear, and looked for somewhere to run. But when she glanced over her shoulder at the car, she saw her dad's smiling face.

She got in. Dad spoke first. "Dina called," he explained. "She said they tried to find you before they left but it was too crowded. They wanted to get out of there before their car got blocked in."

"I didn't think you'd be willing to come and get me," Rochelle said. "Not after the things I said and did."

Dad pulled the car over and turned to look at her. "Hey," he said. "You're my daughter. I love you. Nothing you say or do can ever change that."

Rochelle learned something about true love that night. **First Peter 1:17–23** talks about the kind of love Rochelle felt from her dad.

- According to the passage, how is Rochelle's dad's love for her like God's love for us?
- How might your life change if you trusted and accepted God's love as described in 1 Peter?

CONSIDER . . .

- comparing your parents' love with God's love. Share your observations with your mom or dad.
- talking with a grandparent, aunt, or uncle about times when someone had to discipline your mom or dad. How was that person's love like God's love for you?

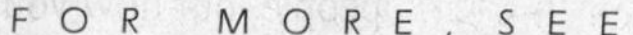

FOR MORE, SEE . . .

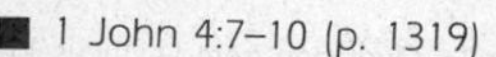

- Deuteronomy 7:7–9 (p. 168)
- Romans 4:1–8 (p. 1143)
- 1 John 4:7–10 (p. 1319)

Follow Christ's Example

[18]Slaves, yield to the authority of your masters
with all respect, not only those who are good and
kind, but also those who are dishonest. [19]A person
might have to suffer even when it is unfair, but if
he thinks of God and stands the pain, God is
pleased. [20]If you are beaten for doing wrong, there
is no reason to praise you for being patient in your
punishment. But if you suffer for doing good, and
you are patient, then God is pleased. [21]This is
what you were called to do, because Christ suffered for you and gave you an example to follow.
So you should do as he did.
[22]"He had never sinned,
and he had never lied." *Isaiah 53:9*
[23]People insulted Christ, but he did not insult
them in return. Christ suffered, but he did not
threaten. He let God, the One who judges rightly,
take care of him. [24]Christ carried our sins in his
body on the cross so we would stop living for sin
and start living for what is right. And you are
healed because of his wounds. [25]You were like
sheep that wandered away, but now you have
come back to the Shepherd and Protector of your
souls.

SIDELIGHT: Because the early Christians were viewed suspiciously, 1 Peter 2:12 urges them to "live good lives" so people would not accuse them of wrongdoing. Among other things, early Christians were falsely accused of eating children because they followed Jesus' command to eat his body and drink his blood in the Communion (also called the Lord's Supper) (see 1 Corinthians 11:23–26, p. 1181).

SELF-ESTEEM

Paying the Price

More than anything, Frank Simms wanted to join the Lords. What a great feeling it would be, he thought, to wear the gang jacket, to be accepted by the guys, to be tough.

But membership in the Lords came with a price. One of the initiation rites was to beat up another guy, steal his expensive shoes, then wear those shoes the next day.

Jimmy Pantelli was chosen as Frank's target. Frank worked out a plan for the attack and left home late one afternoon with a baseball bat. He cornered Jimmy and told him to hand over his shoes.

But Jimmy refused, and a fight broke out. By the time it was over, Frank had been arrested, and Jimmy had been taken to the hospital.

Three months later, Frank still sat in jail, awaiting trial for attempted murder. Jimmy still lay in a coma. Frank wondered why it had all backfired. Why hadn't Jimmy just given him the shoes?

"I wanted to be somebody, that's all," Frank explained. "I just wanted to belong." But nothing could help him feel less guilty for wrecking Jimmy's life, nor reduce the serious consequences of his crime.

Frank was paying the price for his violent attempts to be accepted. **First Peter 2:2–10** shows how Jesus offers a different foundation for building self-esteem.

- If Frank were to read and follow this passage, what would it tell him about feeling chosen, accepted, and important?
- Whenever you feel shaky in your self-esteem, how might this passage help you improve your view?

CONSIDER . . .

- listing the groups you would like to belong to, along with the need they could fill for you. What price would you pay to belong, and how would your self-esteem benefit from belonging?
- choosing one person whom you think would truly help you change for the better, and befriend that person.

FOR MORE, SEE . . .

- Isaiah 8:12–14 (p. 626)
- Hosea 2:23 (p. 825)
- 2 Corinthians 6:3–10 (p. 1198)

Wives and Husbands

3 In the same way, you wives should yield to your husbands. Then, if some husbands do not obey God's teaching, they will be persuaded to believe without anyone's saying a word to them. They will be persuaded by the way their wives live. 2Your husbands will see the pure lives you live with your respect for God. 3It is not fancy hair, gold jewelry, or fine clothes that should make you beautiful. 4No, your beauty should come from within you—the beauty of a gentle and quiet spirit that will never be destroyed and is very precious to God. 5In this same way the holy women who lived long ago and followed God made themselves beautiful, yielding to their own husbands. 6Sarah obeyed Abraham, her husband, and called him her master. And you women are true children of Sarah if you always do what is right and are not afraid.

> **SIDELIGHT:** When 1 Peter 3:3–4 says true beauty comes from the inside, it would not have made the jewelry merchants happy. In those times, women would decorate their hair with elaborate combs and hairpins, some of which were made of gold.

7In the same way, you husbands should live with your wives in an understanding way, since they are weaker than you. But show them respect, because God gives them the same blessing he gives you—the grace that gives true life. Do this so that nothing will stop your prayers.

Suffering for Doing Right

8Finally, all of you should be in agreement, understanding each other, loving each other as family, being kind and humble. 9Do not do wrong to repay a wrong, and do not insult to repay an insult. But repay with a blessing, because you yourselves were called to do this so that you might receive a blessing. 10The Scripture[d] says,

"A person must do these things
  to enjoy life and have many happy days.
He must not say evil things,
  and he must not tell lies.
11He must stop doing evil and do good.
  He must look for peace and work for it.
12The Lord sees the good people
  and listens to their prayers.
But the Lord is against
  those who do evil." *Psalm 34:12-16*

13If you are trying hard to do good, no one can really hurt you. 14But even if you suffer for doing right, you are blessed.

"Don't be afraid of what they fear;
  do not dread those things." *Isaiah 8:12-13*

15But respect Christ as the holy Lord in your hearts. Always be ready to answer everyone who asks you to explain about the hope you have, 16but answer in a gentle way and with respect. Keep a clear conscience so that those who speak evil of your good life in Christ will be made ashamed. 17It is better to suffer for doing good than for doing wrong if that is what God wants. 18Christ himself suffered for sins once. He was not guilty, but he suffered for those who are guilty to bring you to God. His body was killed, but he was made alive in the spirit. 19And in the spirit he went and preached to the spirits in prison 20who refused to obey God long ago in the time of Noah. God was waiting patiently for them while Noah was building the boat. Only a few people—eight in all—were saved by water. 21And that water is like baptism that now saves you—not the washing of dirt from the body, but the promise made to God from a good conscience. And this is because Jesus Christ was raised from the dead. 22Now Jesus has gone into heaven and is at God's right side ruling over angels, authorities, and powers.

Change Your Lives

4 Since Christ suffered while he was in his body, strengthen yourselves with the same way of thinking Christ had. The person who has suffered in the body is finished with sin. 2Strengthen yourselves so that you will live here on earth doing what God wants, not the evil things people want. 3In the past you wasted too much time doing what nonbelievers enjoy. You were guilty of sexual sins, evil desires, drunkenness, wild and drunken parties, and hateful idol worship. 4Nonbelievers think it is strange that you do not do the many wild and wasteful things they do, so they insult you. 5But they will have to explain this to God, who is ready to judge the living and the dead. 6For this reason the Good News[d] was preached to those who are now dead. Even though they were judged like all people, the Good News was preached to them so they could live in the spirit as God lives.

Use God's Gifts Wisely

7The time is near when all things will end. So think clearly and control yourselves so you will be able to pray. 8Most importantly, love each other deeply, because love will cause many sins to be forgiven. 9Open your homes to each other, without complaining. 10Each of you has received a gift to use to serve others. Be good servants of God's various gifts of grace. 11Anyone who speaks should speak words from God. Anyone who

serves should serve with the strength God gives
so that in everything God will be praised through
Jesus Christ. Power and glory belong to him forever and ever. Amen.

Suffering as a Christian

12My friends, do not be surprised at the terrible
trouble which now comes to test you. Do not
think that something strange is happening to you.
13But be happy that you are sharing in Christ's
sufferings so that you will be happy and full of joy
when Christ comes again in glory. 14When people
insult you because you follow Christ, you are
blessed, because the glorious Spirit,[d] the Spirit of
God, is with you. 15Do not suffer for murder,
theft, or any other crime, nor because you trouble
other people. 16But if you suffer because you are
a Christian, do not be ashamed. Praise God because you wear that name. 17It is time for judg
ment to begin with God's family. And if that judging begins with us, what will happen to those
people who do not obey the Good News[d] of God?
18"If it is very hard for a good person to be
saved,
the wicked person and the sinner will
surely be lost!"[n]
19So those who suffer as God wants should
trust their souls to the faithful Creator as they continue to do what is right.

The Flock of God

5 Now I have something to say to the elders[d]
in your group. I also am an elder. I have seen
Christ's sufferings, and I will share in the glory
that will be shown to us. I beg you to 2shepherd
God's flock, for whom you are responsible. Watch
over them because you want to, not because you
are forced. That is how God wants it. Do it because you are happy to serve, not because you
want money. 3Do not be like a ruler over people
you are responsible for, but be good examples to
them. 4Then when Christ, the Chief Shepherd,

"If . . . lost!" Quotation from Proverbs 11:31 in the Septuagint, the Greek version of the Old Testament.

SUFFERING

The Cost of Faith

"Hey, man," said Bill Miller to his friend Jose Castano. "I don't want to hear about your Jesus! Leave me alone!"

The words broke Jose's heart. Bill had been his best friend since eighth grade. But now, three years later, their friendship was in jeopardy because Jose had become a Christian and had let his friends know.

Bill had confronted Jose at a friend's party, accusing him of "thinking you're better than everyone else" because Jose had chosen not to drink anymore.

"Let me know when you get over this religion stuff," Bill had said. "Maybe then we can be friends again." At that, Bill left Jose standing alone. Jose feared he had just lost his best friend.

"No one ever told me that being a Christian could hurt this bad or cost so much," Jose muttered to himself as he went home after the party. "Maybe it's just not worth it. I thought being a Christian meant life got better, not more painful."

As we grow in faith, we change. Sometimes friends change with us. Sometimes they don't. This change may cause some pain. **First Peter 4:12–19** reminds us that being a Christian does not insulate us from pain and suffering. In fact, Peter lets us know that we can expect it as we grow in Christ. He also reminds us that some things are worth suffering for.

- What comfort or understanding might this passage give to Jose in the loss of his friendship with Bill?
- When have you paid a cost for your faith? How did you grow from that experience?

CONSIDER . . .

- praying for a friend whom you know is suffering right now.
- reading about the life of a Christian martyr. Your pastor can help you find such a story.

FOR MORE, SEE . . .

- Psalm 56:1–4 (p. 514)
- John 15:18–21 (p. 1085)
- 1 Peter 2:19–25 (p. 1305)

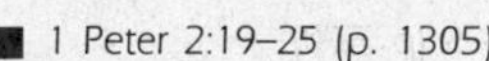

comes, you will get a glorious crown that will never lose its beauty.

SIDELIGHT: If you were a star athlete in Peter's day, you might receive a palm branch (suitable for hanging) and a wreath of olive leaves, parsley, celery leaves, or ivy. These wreaths were a source of great pride, but, like a bouquet of roses, they didn't last long. Maybe that is one reason 1 Peter 5:4 urges chasing crowns that would not need watering!

5In the same way, younger people should be willing to be under older people. And all of you should be very humble with each other.

"God is against the proud,
but he gives grace to the humble."

Proverbs 3:34

6Be humble under God's powerful hand so
he will lift you up when the right time comes.
7Give all your worries to him, because he cares
about you.
8Control yourselves and be careful! The devil,
your enemy, goes around like a roaring lion looking for someone to eat. 9Refuse to give in to him,
by standing strong in your faith. You know that your Christian family all over the world is having the same kinds of suffering.
10And after you suffer for a short time, God, who gives all grace, will make everything right. He will make you strong and support you and keep you from falling. He called you to share in his glory in Christ, a glory that will continue forever. 11All power is his forever and ever. Amen.

SIDELIGHT: When 1 Peter 5:13 mentions Babylon, it probably refers to Rome, the capital of the Roman Empire. (The comparison comes from the common practice of using Babylon as a "code name" for Rome.) By the time 1 Peter was written, the historic city of Babylon was just a small, insignificant village.

Final Greetings

12I wrote this short letter with the help of Silas, who I know is a faithful brother in Christ. I

WORRYING

Weighty Worries

Dwight Evans has played baseball with the Boston Red Sox for almost two decades. He has hit more than 350 home runs, batted in 1,200 runs and had 2,000 hits. His salary matches his accomplishments. He shouldn't have much to worry about, right?

But he does. His two teenage sons suffer from neurofibromatosis, a genetic disorder that causes tumors on the skin. Both sons have had numerous surgeries and radiation treatments. Since the disease is incurable, their future remains uncertain.

"It's very easy to feel sorry for ourselves," Evans says. What keeps Evans and his wife from being overwhelmed with worries? Their faith. "I can't tell you the number of times we've just gotten down on our knees and prayed," he explains. "We have faith in God to carry us through."

Like the Evans family, the early Christians needed assurance that God would deliver them from worries. Bible texts such as **1 Peter 5:6–11** helped them put life in perspective.

- How might this passage give hope and comfort to the Evans family?
- How does the passage, especially verse 7, speak to whatever worries you right now?

C O N S I D E R . . .

- memorizing verse 7 to encourage you when worries get you down.
- keeping a list of troubles and prayers. Over time, review the list, remembering how God helped you endure various problems.

F O R M O R E , S E E . . .

- Proverbs 3:3–5 (p. 570)
- Matthew 11:28–30 (p. 928)
- Revelation 2:8–11 (p. 1333)

wrote to encourage you and to tell you that
this is the true grace of God. Stand strong in
that grace.
13The church in Babylon, who was chosen like
you, sends you greetings. Mark, my son in Christ,
also greets you. 14Give each other a kiss of Christian love when you meet.

Peace to all of you who are in Christ.

2 PETER

Why Read This Book:

- Be assured that the Christian faith is true (2 Peter 1).
- Learn how to respond to false teaching (2 Peter 2).
- Anticipate Christ's return (2 Peter 3).

Behind the Scenes:

Walking on rocks is fairly easy if you have a good pair of shoes. But what happens when even a small pebble inches its way inside your shoe? The pain and annoyance are almost unbearable. Something has to be done!

Think of 2 Peter as dealing with a pebble in the church's shoe. The early church expected false teachings outside the church, and these Christians had learned to protect themselves from those false teachings. But then, like an annoying pebble, false teachings entered the church. Some people were accepting the teachings as truth. But 2 Peter challenged them to get rid of the "pebble" before it caused more problems.

This hard-hitting letter urges believers to counteract false "knowledge" with true knowledge. It exposes the false beliefs of those who said Jesus would not come again. And it attacks those who lived sinful lives by abusing their freedom in Christ. Christ is coming again, the letter proclaims. And Christians should live moral lives as they wait for that return.

This short letter challenges us today, just as it challenged its original readers. Watch out for false teachers. Live lives that follow God's commands. And wait with anticipation for Christ to come again.

WHEN THE ACTION WAS

Jesus was born — **The church began soon after Jesus went to heaven** — **Paul began his missionary work** — **Fire destroyed Rome**

BC/AD — **25AD** — **50AD** — **75AD** — **100AD**

Jesus began his ministry — **2 Peter may have been written** — **The Roman emperor increased persecution of Christians**

1 From Simon Peter, a servant and apostle[d] of Jesus Christ.

To you who have received a faith as valuable as ours, because our God and Savior Jesus Christ does what is right.

2 Grace and peace be given to you more and more, because you truly know God and Jesus our Lord.

> **SIDELIGHT:** If you want to read a short version of 2 Peter, check out Jude (p. 1329). About nineteen of the twenty-five verses in Jude are similar to verses in 2 Peter.

God Has Given Us Blessings

3 Jesus has the power of God, by which he has given us everything we need to live and to serve God. We have these things because we know him. Jesus called us by his glory and goodness. 4 Through these he gave us the very great and precious promises. With these gifts you can share in being like God, and the world will not ruin you with its evil desires.

5 Because you have these blessings, do your best to add these things to your lives: to your faith, add goodness; and to your goodness, add knowledge; 6 and to your knowledge, add self-control; and to your self-control, add patience; and to your patience, add service for God; 7 and to your service for God, add kindness for your brothers and sisters in Christ; and to this kindness, add love. 8 If all these things are in you and are growing, they will help you to be useful and productive in your knowledge of our Lord Jesus Christ. 9 But anyone who does not have these things cannot see clearly. He is blind and has forgotten that he was made clean from his past sins.

10 My brothers and sisters,[n] try hard to be certain that you really are called and chosen by God. If you do all these things, you will never fall. 11 And you will be given a very great welcome into the eternal kingdom of our Lord and Savior Jesus Christ.

12 You know these things, and you are very strong in the truth, but I will always help you remember them. 13 I think it is right for me to help you remember as long as I am in this body. 14 I know I must soon leave this body, as our Lord Jesus Christ has shown me. 15 I will try my best so that you may be able to remember these things even after I am gone.

We Saw Christ's Glory

16 When we told you about the powerful coming of our Lord Jesus Christ, we were not telling just smart stories that someone invented. But we saw the greatness of Jesus with our own eyes. 17 Jesus heard the voice of God, the Greatest Glory, when he received honor and glory from God the Father. The voice said, "This is my Son, whom I love, and I am very pleased with him." 18 We heard that voice from heaven while we were with Jesus on the holy mountain.

19 This makes us more sure about the message the prophets[d] gave. It is good for you to follow closely what they said as you would follow a light shining in a dark place, until the day begins and the morning star rises in your hearts. 20 Most of all, you must understand this: No prophecy in the Scriptures[d] ever comes from the prophet's own interpretation. 21 No prophecy ever came from what a person wanted to say, but people led by the Holy Spirit[d] spoke words from God.

False Teachers

2 There used to be false prophets[d] among God's people, just as you will have some false teachers in your group. They will secretly teach things that are wrong—teachings that will cause people to be lost. They will even refuse to accept the Master, Jesus, who bought their freedom. So they will bring quick ruin on themselves. 2 Many will follow their evil ways and say evil things about the way of truth. 3 Those false teachers only want your money, so they will use you by telling you lies. Their judgment spoken against them long ago is still coming, and their ruin is certain.

4 When angels sinned, God did not let them go free without punishment. He sent them to hell and put them in caves of darkness where they are being held for judgment. 5 And God punished the world long ago when he brought a flood to the world that was full of people who were against him. But God saved Noah, who preached about being right with God, and seven other people with him. 6 And God also destroyed the evil cities of Sodom and Gomorrah[n] by burning them until they were ashes. He made those cities an example of what will happen to those who are against God. 7 But he saved Lot from those cities. Lot, a good man, was troubled because of the filthy lives of evil people. 8 (Lot was a good man, but because he lived with evil people every day, his good heart was hurt by the evil things he saw and heard.) 9 So the Lord knows how to save those who serve him when troubles come. He will hold evil people and

brothers and sisters Although the Greek text reads "brothers" here and throughout this book, Peter's words were meant for the entire church, including men and women.

Sodom and Gomorrah Two cities God destroyed because the people were so evil.

punish them, while waiting for the Judgment Day. 10That punishment is especially for those who live by doing the evil things their sinful selves want and who hate authority.

These false teachers are bold and do anything they want. They are not afraid to speak against the angels. 11But even the angels, who are much stronger and more powerful than false teachers, do not accuse them with insults before the Lord. 12But these people speak against things they do not understand. They are like animals that act without thinking, animals born to be caught and killed. And, like animals, these false teachers will be destroyed. 13They have caused many people to suffer, so they themselves will suffer. That is their pay for what they have done. They take pleasure in openly doing evil, so they are like dirty spots and stains among you. They delight in trickery while eating meals with you. 14Every time they look at a woman they want her, and their desire for sin is never satisfied. They lead weak people into the trap of sin, and they have taught their hearts to be greedy. God will punish them! 15These false teachers left the right road and lost their way, following the way Balaam went. Balaam was the son of Beor, who loved being paid for doing wrong. 16But a donkey, which cannot talk, told Balaam he was sinning. It spoke with a man's voice and stopped the prophet's crazy thinking.

17Those false teachers are like springs without water and clouds blown by a storm. A place in the blackest darkness has been kept for them. 18They brag with words that mean nothing. By their evil desires they lead people into the trap of sin — people who are just beginning to escape from others who live in error. 19They promise them freedom, but they themselves are not free. They are slaves of things that will be destroyed. For people are slaves of anything that controls them. 20They were made free from the evil in the world by knowing our Lord and Savior Jesus Christ. But if they return to evil things and those things control them, then it is worse for them than it was before. 21Yes, it would be better for them to have never known the right way than to know it and to turn away from the holy teaching that was given to them. 22What they did is like this true saying: "A

BIBLE STUDY

God's Love Letter

Have you ever received love letters? No doubt you read them differently than you would read junk mail or a form letter inviting you to join Latin club. Indeed, author Mortimer Adler says that when we read a love letter, we:

- read every word three ways,
- read between the lines,
- weigh each sentence,
- perceive the color of each word, and,
- look for deep meaning, even in the punctuation.

When you are in love, you read a love letter over and over, carefully, and in depth.

If the Bible were a letter, what kind of letter would it be for you? Would it be "junk mail"? Would it be boring "required reading" such as a literature assignment? Or, would it be a "love letter" from God to you?

The writer of **2 Peter 1:16–21** guarantees that the life and message of Jesus Christ is not "junk mail." It's a love letter from God.

- Why might someone who loves God learn more from the Bible than someone who doesn't love God?
- How might reading more of God's "love letters" in the Bible help you face life's problems and decisions?

CONSIDER

- listing reasons why people study the Bible, and then choosing which one is your top reason.
- reading the Gospel of Matthew over the next month (one chapter per day) as if it were addressed particularly to you.

FOR MORE, SEE . . .

- Jeremiah 23:25–29 (p. 717)
- Acts 17:11 (p. 1125)
- Hebrews 4:12–16 (p. 1279)

dog goes back to what it has thrown up,"[n] and,
"After a pig is washed, it goes back and rolls in the
mud."

Jesus Will Come Again

3 My friends, this is the second letter I have
written you to help your honest minds remember. 2I want you to think about the words
the holy prophets[d] spoke in the past, and remember the command our Lord and Savior gave us
through your apostles.[d] 3It is most important for
you to understand what will happen in the last
days. People will laugh at you. They will live doing the evil things they want to do. 4They will say,
"Jesus promised to come again. Where is he? Our
fathers have died, but the world continues the
way it has been since it was made." 5But they do
not want to remember what happened long ago.
By the word of God heaven was made, and the
earth was made from water and with water.
6Then the world was flooded and destroyed with
water. 7And that same word of God is keeping
heaven and earth that we now have in order to
be destroyed by fire. They are being kept for the
Judgment Day and the destruction of all who are
against God.
8But do not forget this one thing, dear friends:
To the Lord one day is as a thousand years, and
a thousand years is as one day. 9The Lord is not
slow in doing what he promised—the way some
people understand slowness. But God is being patient with you. He does not want anyone to be
lost, but he wants all people to change their hearts
and lives.
10But the day of the Lord will come like a thief.
The skies will disappear with a loud noise. Everything in them will be destroyed by fire, and the
earth and everything in it will be burned up.[n]

"A dog . . . up" Quotation from Proverbs 26:11.
will be burned up Many Greek copies say, "will be found." One copy says, "will disappear."

FUTURE

Party Now?

"Why shouldn't I party?" protested sixteen-year-old Joe Williams at a youth group meeting. "The world might not even be around when I'm twenty."

Joe didn't see much hope for the future. He read newspapers and newsmagazines to keep up with world events. The more Joe read, the more he became a sarcastic pessimist.

"We're either gonna die in a nuclear war or from poisoning our environment," he would say. His cynical attitude began to affect his views on life issues. He still received good grades, but he no longer enjoyed learning

At one time in junior high, Joe had held to high values about issues such as sex, alcohol use, and the environment. In his dark gloom about the future, however, those values seemed irrelevant to him.

"I just hang out, watch some TV, and look out for a good time," he said. "I want to live it up now while I still can."

Joe said his dark view of the future might have something to do with his uncertainty about God. "I don't even know if God can get us out of this mess, or even if he cares," he said. "I'm living for now and for me. I wish there were hope somewhere, but I don't see any right now."

Joe's views of the future negatively affected how he lived every day. In contrast, **2 Peter 3:8–13** offers a hopeful message that can positively affect how we live now.

- If Joe were to read this passage, what hope or encouragement about the future might he find?
- How does knowing that the future rests in God's hands influence the way you live your life?

CONSIDER . . .

- living like God is in complete control of your day.
- setting three important goals to reach in the next five years, based on your reading of the passage.

FOR MORE, SEE . . .

- Isaiah 65:17–25 (p. 686)
- Mark 13:32–37 (p. 991)
- Revelation 21:1–5 (p. 1347)

[11]In that way everything will be destroyed. So
what kind of people should you be? You should
live holy lives and serve God, [12]as you wait for
and look forward to the coming of the day of God.
When that day comes, the skies will be destroyed
with fire, and everything in them will melt with
heat. [13]But God made a promise to us, and we are
waiting for a new heaven and a new earth where
goodness lives.

SIDELIGHT: According to 2 Peter 3:15–16, you are in good company if you sometimes have trouble understanding Romans (p. 1140) or other books that Paul wrote. Peter did too. This passage is a rare example of a New Testament author giving another New Testament book the authority of scripture.

[14]Dear friends, since you are waiting for this to
happen, do your best to be without sin and without fault. Try to be at peace with God. [15]Remem-
ber that we are saved because our Lord is patient.
Our dear brother Paul told you the same thing
when he wrote to you with the wisdom that God
gave him. [16]He writes about this in all his letters.
Some things in Paul's letters are hard to understand, and people who are ignorant and weak in
faith explain these things falsely. They also falsely
explain the other Scriptures,[d] but they are destroying themselves by doing this.

[17]Dear friends, since you already know about
this, be careful. Do not let those evil people lead
you away by the wrong they do. Be careful so you
will not fall from your strong faith. [18]But grow in
the grace and knowledge of our Lord and Savior
Jesus Christ. Glory be to him now and forever!
Amen.

1 JOHN

Why Read This Book:

- Find out how to grow closer to God (1 John 1—2).
- See what it's like to be part of God's family (1 John 3—4).
- Be assured of life with God after death (1 John 5).

Behind the Scenes:

When you read the book of 1 John, you almost have the feeling that a grandfather has gathered his grandchildren around a fire to talk. You can see his love for them sparkling in his eyes, and you know from the way they look at him that they respect him a great deal.

As he talks to his "children," as he calls them, you can feel the warmth. He reassures them of God's love for them. He gently coaxes them to believe in and follow God.

But he also has another purpose. He is worried that the younger Christians are hearing mixed messages about Jesus Christ. People—known as gnostics—are saying that Jesus wasn't really human; he was only divine. Furthermore, they were arguing that they could do whatever they wanted to do with their bodies, because the physical body was separate from the spiritual nature.

The grandfather knows these ideas are wrong. Jesus was both fully human and fully divine. And what the body does certainly affects the spirit—for better or worse. So the grandfather challenges the false teaching and urges his children to stick to the truth.

Of course, 1 John isn't really a fireside chat between a grandfather and his grandchildren. It's a letter or sermon written to Christians to help them grow in their faith and to counteract the false teaching that was gaining influence among the early Christians.

Yet the true spirit of the letter comes through when we imagine the love and warmth that comes when we sit around a fireplace, listening to the advice of a wise grandfather. Not only did the words encourage and challenge the original hearers to keep following God, but they challenge and encourage us today.

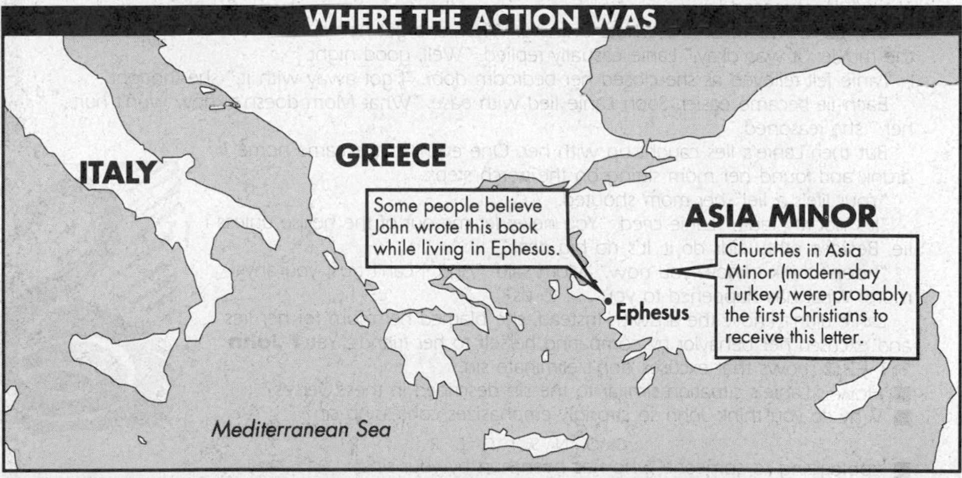
WHERE THE ACTION WAS
ITALY
GREECE
ASIA MINOR
Some people believe John wrote this book while living in Ephesus.
Churches in Asia Minor (modern-day Turkey) were probably the first Christians to receive this letter.
Ephesus
Mediterranean Sea

WHEN THE ACTION WAS

BC/AD		25AD		50AD		75AD		100AD

- Jesus was born (BC/AD)
- The church began soon after Jesus went to heaven
- Jesus began his ministry
- Paul became a Christian
- Paul began his missionary work
- Fire destroyed Rome
- Romans destroyed the Temple in Jerusalem
- I John was written

1 We write you now about what has always
existed, which we have heard, we have seen
with our own eyes, we have looked at, and we
have touched with our hands. We write to you
about the Word[n] that gives life. 2He who gives
life was shown to us. We saw him and can give
proof about it. And now we announce to you that
he has life that continues forever. He was with
God the Father and was shown to us. 3We announce to you what we have seen and heard, because we want you also to have fellowship with
us. Our fellowship is with God the Father and
with his Son, Jesus Christ. 4We write this to you
so you can be full of joy with us.

God Forgives Our Sins

5Here is the message we have heard from
Christ and now announce to you: God is light,[n]
and in him there is no darkness at all. 6So if we
say we have fellowship with God, but we continue living in darkness, we are liars and do not
follow the truth. 7But if we live in the light, as
God is in the light, we can share fellowship with
each other. Then the blood of Jesus, God's Son,
cleanses us from every sin.
8If we say we have no sin, we are fooling ourselves, and the truth is not in us. 9But if we confess our sins, he will forgive our sins, because we
can trust God to do what is right. He will cleanse
us from all the wrongs we have done. 10If we say
we have not sinned, we make God a liar, and we
do not accept God's teaching.

Jesus Is Our Helper

2 My dear children, I write this letter to you
so you will not sin. But if anyone does sin,
we have a helper in the presence of the Father—
Jesus Christ, the One who does what is right. 2He

Word The Greek word is "logos," meaning any kind of communication. Here, it means Christ, who was the way God told people about himself.
light Here, this word is used as a symbol of God's goodness or truth.

SIN

No Excuses

Lanie Pritchard remembers the first time she lied to her mom about where she was going. "Janet, Kate, and I are going to a movie," she lied without looking straight into her mom's eyes.

Could her mom tell she was lying? Lanie couldn't tell, so she quickly left the house.

The party blared away when the three girls arrived. "See, it wasn't so hard to fool your mom," Janet teased Lanie.

Still, Lanie was tense the whole evening. When she got home, her mom asked about the movie. "It was okay," Lanie casually replied. "Well, good night."

Lanie felt relieved as she closed her bedroom door. "I got away with it," she thought.

Each lie became easier. Soon Lanie lied with ease. "What Mom doesn't know won't hurt her," she reasoned.

But then Lanie's lies caught up with her. One evening she came home drunk and found her mom sitting on the porch steps.

"Your life's a lie!" her mom shouted.

"It's not my fault," Lanie cried. "You never let me out of the house unless I lie. Besides, other kids do it. It's no big deal."

"I don't think I know you now," Mom said. "And, I can't trust you anymore. What has happened to you . . . to us?"

Lanie didn't know the answer. Instead, she blamed her mom for her lies and excused her behavior by comparing herself to her friends. Yet **1 John 1:1—2:2** shows that excuses don't eliminate sin.

- How is Lanie's situation similar to the sin described in these verses?
- Why do you think John so strongly emphasizes confessing sin?

CONSIDER . . .

- apologizing to someone who has been hurt by your sins.
- selecting a verse from the passage that conveys the "no excuses" idea. Write the verse on a small card and memorize it.

FOR MORE, SEE . . .

- Genesis 3:1–13 (p. 4)
- Psalm 51:1–13 (p. 511)
- Luke 15:11–24 (p. 1035)

is the way our sins are taken away, and not only our sins but the sins of all people.

SIDELIGHT: Perhaps the biggest heresy (wrong doctrine) that the early church faced involved the gnostic understanding of evil. Gnostics—whose name came from the word for "knowledge"—believed evil was simply an error that grew out of ignorance; the person who did wrong was not really responsible. First John responded that people are responsible for their sins and must be forgiven to be right with God (1 John 1:9; 2:2).

3We can be sure that we know God if we obey his commands. 4Anyone who says, "I know God," but does not obey God's commands is a liar, and the truth is not in that person. 5But if someone obeys God's teaching, then in that person God's love has truly reached its goal. This is how we can be sure we are living in God: 6Whoever says that he lives in God must live as Jesus lived.

The Command to Love Others

7My dear friends, I am not writing a new command to you but an old command you have had from the beginning. It is the teaching you have already heard. 8But also I am writing a new command to you, and you can see its truth in Jesus and in you, because the darkness is passing away, and the true light is already shining.

9Anyone who says, "I am in the light,"[n] but hates a brother or sister,[n] is still in the darkness. 10Whoever loves a brother or sister lives in the light and will not cause anyone to stumble in his faith. 11But whoever hates a brother or sister is in darkness, lives in darkness, and does not know where to go, because the darkness has made that person blind.

12I write to you, dear children,
because your sins are forgiven through
Christ.
13I write to you, parents,
because you know the One who existed
from the beginning.
I write to you, young people,
because you have defeated the Evil One.
14I write to you, children,
because you know the Father.
I write to you, parents,
because you know the One who existed
from the beginning.
I write to you, young people,
because you are strong;
the teaching of God lives in you,
and you have defeated the Evil One.

15Do not love the world or the things in the world. If you love the world, the love of the Father is not in you. 16These are the ways of the world: wanting to please our sinful selves, wanting the sinful things we see, and being too proud of what we have. None of these come from the Father, but all of them come from the world. 17The world and everything that people want in it are passing away, but the person who does what God wants lives forever.

Reject the Enemies of Christ

18My dear children, these are the last days. You have heard that the enemy of Christ[d] is coming, and now many enemies of Christ are already here. This is how we know that these are the last days. 19These enemies of Christ were in our fellowship, but they left us. They never really belonged to us; if they had been a part of us, they would have stayed with us. But they left, and this shows that none of them really belonged to us.

20You have the gift[n] that the Holy One gave you, so you all know the truth. 21I do not write to you because you do not know the truth but because you do know the truth. And you know that no lie comes from the truth.

22Who is the liar? It is the person who does not accept Jesus as the Christ. This is the enemy of Christ: the person who does not accept the Father and his Son. 23Whoever does not accept the Son does not have the Father. But whoever confesses the Son has the Father, too.

24Be sure you continue to follow the teaching you heard from the beginning. If you continue to follow what you heard from the beginning, you will stay in the Son and in the Father. 25And this is what the Son promised to us—life forever.

26I am writing this letter about those people who are trying to lead you the wrong way. 27Christ gave you a special gift that is still in you, so you do not need any other teacher. His gift teaches you about everything, and it is true, not false. So continue to live in Christ, as his gift taught you.

28Yes, my dear children, live in him so that when Christ comes back, we can be without fear and not be ashamed in his presence. 29If you

light Here, this word is used as a symbol of God's goodness or truth.
brother or sister Although the Greek text says "brother" here and throughout this book, the writer's words were meant for the entire church, including men and women.
gift This might mean the Holy Spirit, or it might mean teaching or truth as in verse 24.

know that Christ is all that is right, you know that
all who do right are God's children.

We Are God's Children

3 The Father has loved us so much that we are
called children of God. And we really are his
children. The reason the people in the world do
not know us is that they have not known him.
[2]Dear friends, now we are children of God, and
we have not yet been shown what we will be in
the future. But we know that when Christ comes
again, we will be like him, because we will see
him as he really is. [3]Christ is pure, and all who
have this hope in Christ keep themselves pure like
Christ.
[4]The person who sins breaks God's law. Yes,
sin is living against God's law. [5]You know that
Christ came to take away sins and that there is no
sin in Christ. [6]So anyone who lives in Christ does
not go on sinning. Anyone who goes on sinning
has never really understood Christ and has never
known him.
[7]Dear children, do not let anyone lead you the
wrong way. Christ is all that is right. So to be like
Christ a person must do what is right. [8]The devil
has been sinning since the beginning, so anyone
who continues to sin belongs to the devil. The
Son of God came for this purpose: to destroy the
devil's work.
[9]Those who are God's children do not continue
sinning, because the new life from God remains
in them. They are not able to go on sinning, because they have become children of God. [10]So we
can see who God's children are and who the
devil's children are: Those who do not do what
is right are not God's children, and those who do
not love their brothers and sisters are not God's
children.

We Must Love Each Other

[11]This is the teaching you have heard from the
beginning: We must love each other. [12]Do not be
like Cain who belonged to the Evil One and killed
his brother. And why did he kill him? Because the
things Cain did were evil, and the things his
brother did were good.

FOLLOWING GOD

Life at the Top

Lynn Hill has always been at the top of everything. When she was a kid, she was at the top of trees, telephone poles, even street lights. Now she is on top of cliffs and mountains as one of the world's leading rock climbers. She is one of the few people who has defied gravity and scaled cliffs that are "steeper" than vertical.

Lynn has gotten to be so good because she dedicates her life to her climbing. A picture taken the day after her wedding shows how important climbing is to her. It shows her and her new husband—also a climber, of course—in full wedding attire hanging from a rope off cliffs near their home.

Lynn knows how important it is to not become lax in her climbing techniques. Once she fell seventy-five feet down a cliff because she forgot to tie a simple knot on her safety rope. A tree branch slowed her fall and saved her life, though she was injured.

"The rock is a tool for learning and understanding," she says. "When you get to the top, you've conquered something inside as well."

Lynn's dedication to climbing illustrates the kind of dedication Christians should have in following God. **First John 3:1–24** encourages Christians not to be distracted from following God.

- What parallels do you see between Lynn's dedication to rock climbing and the passage's guidance about being a Christian?
- How have other Christians encouraged you and kept you dedicated to following God?

CONSIDER . . .

- thinking about everything you did in the past twenty-four hours. Decide which things helped you follow God and which ones did not.
- asking a Christian friend to help you overcome a sin that keeps you from following God, with the kind of dedication Lynn has for rock climbing.

FOR MORE, SEE . . .

- Psalm 95:1–11 (p. 537)
- Romans 7:14–25 (p. 1148)
- Ephesians 5:1–11 (p. 1224)

13Brothers and sisters, do not be surprised when the people of the world hate you. 14We know we have left death and have come into life because we love each other. Whoever does not love is still dead. 15Everyone who hates a brother or sister is a murderer,[n] and you know that no murderers have eternal life in them. 16This is how we know what real love is: Jesus gave his life for us. So we should give our lives for our brothers and sisters. 17Suppose someone has enough to live and sees a brother or sister in need, but does not help. Then God's love is not living in that person. 18My children, we should love people not only with words and talk, but by our actions and true caring.

SIDELIGHT: When 1 John 3:13 told believers not to be surprised that the world hates them, it was speaking to an everyday reality for Christians at that time in Asia Minor. Even the Roman historian Tacitus, who lived during that time, wrote that Romans hated the Christians.

19-20This is the way we know that we belong to the way of truth. When our hearts make us feel guilty, we can still have peace before God. God is greater than our hearts, and he knows everything. 21My dear friends, if our hearts do not make us feel guilty, we can come without fear into God's presence. 22And God gives us what we ask for because we obey God's commands and do what pleases him. 23This is what God commands: that we believe in his Son, Jesus Christ, and that we love each other, just as he commanded. 24The people who obey God's commands live in God, and God lives in them. We know that God lives in us because of the Spirit[d] God gave us.

Warning Against False Teachers

4 My dear friends, many false prophets[d] have gone out into the world. So do not believe every spirit, but test the spirits to see if they are from God. 2This is how you can know God's Spirit:[d] Every spirit who confesses that Jesus Christ came to earth as a human is from God. 3And every spirit who refuses to say this about Jesus is not from God. It is the spirit of the enemy of Christ,[d] which you have heard is coming, and now he is already in the world.

4My dear children, you belong to God and have defeated them; because God's Spirit, who is in you, is greater than the devil, who is in the world. 5And they belong to the world, so what they say is from the world, and the world listens to them. 6But we belong to God, and those who know God listen to us. But those who are not from God do not listen to us. That is how we know the Spirit that is true and the spirit that is false.

Love Comes from God

7Dear friends, we should love each other, because love comes from God. Everyone who loves has become God's child and knows God. 8Whoever does not love does not know God, because God is love. 9This is how God showed his love to us: He sent his one and only Son into the world so that we could have life through him. 10This is what real love is: It is not our love for God; it is God's love for us in sending his Son to be the way to take away our sins.

11Dear friends, if God loved us that much we also should love each other. 12No one has ever seen God, but if we love each other, God lives in us, and his love is made perfect in us.

13We know that we live in God and he lives in us, because he gave us his Spirit.[d] 14We have seen and can testify that the Father sent his Son to be the Savior of the world. 15Whoever confesses that Jesus is the Son of God has God living inside, and that person lives in God. 16And so we know the love that God has for us, and we trust that love.

God is love. Those who live in love live in God, and God lives in them. 17This is how love is made perfect in us: that we can be without fear on the day God judges us, because in this world we are like him. 18Where God's love is, there is no fear, because God's perfect love drives out fear. It is punishment that makes a person fear, so love is not made perfect in the person who fears.

19We love because God first loved us. 20If people say, "I love God," but hate their brothers or sisters, they are liars. Those who do not love their brothers and sisters, whom they have seen, cannot love God, whom they have never seen. 21And God gave us this command: Those who love God must also love their brothers and sisters.

Faith in the Son of God

5 Everyone who believes that Jesus is the Christ[d] is God's child, and whoever loves the Father also loves the Father's children. 2This is how we know we love God's children: when we love God and obey his commands. 3Loving God means obeying his commands. And God's commands are not too hard for us, 4because everyone who is a child of God conquers the world. And this is the victory that conquers the world—our faith. 5So the one who wins against the world is

Everyone . . . murderer If one person hates a brother or sister, then in the heart that person has killed that brother or sister. Jesus taught about this sin to his followers (Matthew 5:21-26).

the person who believes that Jesus is the Son of
God.
6Jesus Christ is the One who came by water[n]
and blood.[n] He did not come by water only, but
by water and blood. And the Spirit[d] says that this
is true, because the Spirit is the truth. 7So there
are three witnesses that tell us about Jesus: 8the
Spirit, the water, and the blood; and these three
witnesses agree. 9We believe people when they
say something is true. But what God says is more
important, and he has told us the truth about his
own Son. 10Anyone who believes in the Son of
God has the truth that God told us. Anyone who
does not believe makes God a liar, because that
person does not believe what God told us about
his Son. 11This is what God told us: God has given
us eternal life, and this life is in his Son. 12Who-
ever has the Son has life, but whoever does not
have the Son of God does not have life.

We Have Eternal Life Now

13I write this letter to you who believe in the
Son of God so you will know you have eternal life.
14And this is the boldness we have in God's presence: that if we ask God for anything that agrees
with what he wants, he hears us. 15If we know he
hears us every time we ask him, we know we
have what we ask from him.
16If anyone sees a brother or sister sinning (sin
that does not lead to eternal death), that person
should pray, and God will give the sinner life. I
am talking about people whose sin does not lead
to eternal death. There is sin that leads to death.
I do not mean that a person should pray about

water This probably means the water of Jesus' baptism.
blood This probably means the blood of Jesus' death.

LOVE

The First Step

"But I don't even like her," Michelle Benson complained to Angie Stone after the camp Bible study. "So how am I going to love her?"

No one could remember what started the feud between Cindy and Michelle. They had known each other since childhood, and seemed always in conflict. They accused each other of telling lies; they fought over boyfriends; they over-competed in classes.

Angie suggested that Christian love goes beyond liking what others do. "It's a conscious decision to care," Angie explained.

Michelle frowned. "No matter what she does, I have to love her?"

"Loving people who love us is easy," said Angie. "Loving difficult people makes Christian love unique."

Michelle walked away, frustrated by Angie's words. During the week at camp, however, Michelle watched others build new relationships and mend damaged ones. People who had not gotten along at first seemed to make peace with each other.

At the last campfire, the camp director urged the kids to settle differences with those whom they had hurt during the year. Michelle wanted to go to Cindy, but held back, fearing rejection.

Suddenly she saw Cindy coming straight toward her with tears in her eyes. "I'm sorry," Michelle heard Cindy say. The girls hugged and cried. Healing began.

Loving others even when you don't like them is tough, but it is possible. In **1 John 4:7–12**, look for unique qualities of Christian love in action.

- How did Michelle's initial attitude toward Cindy influence her relationship with God, according to this passage?
- Why is loving others easier when you understand how God loves you?

CONSIDER

- making the first move to mend a damaged relationship with a family member or friend.
- asking several friends to go out for hamburgers, including someone who is difficult for you to love. Try to get to know that person better.

FOR MORE, SEE . . .

- Deuteronomy 6:5 (p. 167)
- Matthew 5:43–48 (p. 916)
- 1 Peter 4:8–9 (p. 1306)

that sin. 17Doing wrong is always sin, but there is
sin that does not lead to eternal death.
18We know that those who are God's children
do not continue to sin. The Son of God keeps
them safe, and the Evil One cannot touch them.
19We know that we belong to God, but the Evil
One controls the whole world. 20We also know
that the Son of God has come and has given us
understanding so that we can know the True
One. And our lives are in the True One and in his
Son, Jesus Christ. He is the true God and the eternal life.
21So, dear children, keep yourselves away from
gods.

DISCOURAGEMENT

Hope Breakers and Makers

Did you ever experience a day when everything went wrong? Sometimes the day seems like one disappointing event after another. These disappointments can be called "hope breakers." Hope breakers can lead to outright discouragement if they persist. Which of these hope breakers seem familiar to you?

■ threats of war in the world
■ fights with your parents
■ an accident in the family car
■ breaking up with a girlfriend/boyfriend
■ making a poor grade on a test
■ doubting your Christian beliefs
■ too much homework
■ criticism from others
■ feeling alone

Hope can overcome discouragement. Hope reminds you of a brighter future. Which of the events below are hope makers for you?

■ feeling good about your life
■ scoring high on a hard test
■ giving and receiving Christian love from others
■ making the team
■ enjoying a beautiful day
■ knowing God loves you
■ getting a fantastic job
■ having a great time with friends
■ renewing a broken friendship

John offered reassurance and hope to Christians who had experienced too many hope breakers. Read John's hope-making ideas in **1 John 5:1–15**.

■ How do the hope breakers and hope makers described above compare to the ones in this passage?
■ What phrases in this passage offer you the most hope?

CONSIDER . . .

■ writing out the promises and assurances in this passage. Post the list on your locker door.
■ acting as a hope maker to a discouraged friend by offering encouragement, time or help.

FOR MORE, SEE . . .

■ Psalm 42 (p. 507)
■ John 15:18–27 (p. 1085)
■ Romans 8:35–39 (p. 1152)

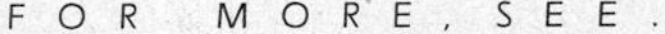

2 JOHN

Why Read This Book:

- Learn ways to show Christian love (2 John 1–6).
- Examine the danger of listening to false teachers (2 John 7–11).

Behind the Scenes:

The musical-movie The Music Man tells about a swindling, traveling salesman who goes into gullible towns offering to start bands for the kids. Then when people get excited and give him money for uniforms and instruments, he slips out of town, laughing about the trick.

The early Christians faced a similar situation. Because they were always open and loving to strangers, false teachers would take advantage of their openness. These teachers would get into the church and begin spreading false teachings. (For a description of the teachings, see the introduction to 1 John, p. 1315.)

Second John was written to warn churches not to welcome people who bring false teaching into the church. The short letter encourages them to keep loving each other. But, at the same time, it urges them to stay far away from false teachers.

As Christians, we too need to be open and loving to each other. But we also need to be on guard against people who present teachings that contradict the Bible. Second John challenges us to carefully evaluate others' statements before accepting them as true.

While 2 John warns against welcoming false teachers, 3 John (p. 1325) gives the other side of the issue. It focuses on the importance of being hospitable toward fellow believers. Read the two letters together for a balanced picture.

WHEN THE ACTION WAS

Jesus was born

The church began soon after Jesus went to heaven

Paul began his missionary work

Fire destroyed Rome

2 John was written

BC/AD — 25AD — 50AD — 75AD — 100AD

Jesus began his ministry

Paul became a Christian

Romans destroyed the Temple in Jerusalem

[1]From the Elder.[n]
To the chosen lady[n] and her children:
I love all of you in the truth,[n] and all those who know the truth love you. [2]We love you because of the truth that lives in us and will be with us forever.
[3]Grace, mercy, and peace from God the Father and his Son, Jesus Christ, will be with us in truth and love.
[4]I was very happy to learn that some of your children are following the way of truth, as the Father commanded us. [5]And now, dear lady, this is not a new command but is the same command we have had from the beginning. I ask you that we all love each other. [6]And love means living the way God commanded us to live. As you have heard from the beginning, his command is this: Live a life of love.
[7]Many false teachers are in the world now who do not confess that Jesus Christ came to earth as a human. Anyone who does not confess this is a false teacher and an enemy of Christ.[d] [8]Be careful yourselves that you do not lose everything you have worked for, but that you receive your full reward.

SIDELIGHT: If other books in the New Testament are letters (such as 1 Corinthians, p. 1167), then 2 John is more like a postcard. With only thirteen verses, it is the shortest book in the Bible. One reason it may have been short is so it could fit on a single sheet of papyrus, the paper of the day (2 John 12).

Elder "Elder" means an older person. It can also mean a special leader in the church (as in Titus 1:5).
lady This might mean a woman, or in this letter it might mean a church. If it is a church, then "her children" would be the people of the church.
truth The truth or "Good News" about Jesus Christ that joins all believers together.

CULTS

Christian Frauds

Amy Vanderhoof had just turned sixteen when she was approached by a friendly guy at the mall who engaged her in a conversation about God. The guy's enthusiasm about his beliefs impressed Amy. He invited her to a Bible study the next Tuesday evening. Already active in her church, Amy thought it sounded fun, so she went.

The Bible study began with upbeat songs. Then the teacher began his talk. He started calmly, but grew more energized as he taught. He held the Bible while he spoke, and he even referred to a Bible story Amy recognized. It all sounded real, acceptable, and safe.

Amy grew more involved. After attending several more Bible studies, she agreed to go with the group on a weekend retreat.

She never returned home.

Frantically, her parents tried to contact her, but the leaders kept them away. Soon her parents learned that she had "voluntarily" moved to a cult center in another state. Despite constant effort, Amy's parents never heard from her again.

Although the cult leaders used scripture, prayer, and other Christian-sounding ideas, Jesus Christ wasn't their focus. Since the beginning, false teachers have plagued the church. False teachers greatly concerned the writer of 2 John. Check out John's criteria for a false teacher in **2 John 7–11**.

- How could John's warning have helped Amy?
- What current false teachers or groups do you recognize from John's description?

CONSIDER . . .

- becoming aware of cults operating in your area. What do they believe? How do they recruit?
- seeking to understand more of Christ's teachings so that you will know when a false teacher "goes beyond" them (verse 9).

FOR MORE, SEE . . .

- Daniel 6:7–23 (p. 813)
- John 14:5–7 (p. 1083)
- 2 Timothy 4:3–5 (p. 1266)

9Anyone who goes beyond Christ's teaching
and does not continue to follow only his teaching does not have God. But whoever continues
to follow the teaching of Christ has both the
Father and the Son. 10If someone comes to you
and does not bring this teaching, do not welcome
or accept that person into your house. 11If you
welcome such a person, you share in the evil
work.

12I have many things to write to you, but I do
not want to use paper and ink. Instead, I hope to
come to you and talk face to face so we can be full
of joy. 13The children of your chosen sister[n] greet
you.

sister Sister of the "lady" in verse 1. This might be another woman or another church.

3 JOHN

Why Read This Book:

- Consider how Christians can support one another (3 John 1–8).
- See how much damage one negative leader can do (3 John 9–11).

Behind the Scenes:

Suppose a visitor walked in to your Sunday school class. Would you welcome him or her? Would you invite the visitor home for dinner? And suppose the visitor expressed different views from yours during the discussion. Would you be open to those views? Or would you cut the person off?

The two central characters in 3 John would answer those questions quite differently. Gaius (3 John 1) would probably welcome the visitor and listen closely to his or her views. Diotrephes (3 John 9) would probably shun the visitor and squelch his or her opinions.

The situation in 3 John was different from a Sunday school class, of course. Gaius was welcoming missionaries sent by "the Elder" (3 John 1), and the writer thanks him for it. Diotrephes refused to welcome these missionaries. In fact, he tried to kick out of the church anyone who did welcome them.

Like 2 John (p. 1323), 3 John focuses on welcoming and showing love to fellow Christians. Taken together, these two letters tell a lot about the church. On the one hand, Christians are called to love, accept and serve one another in Christ. At the same time, Christians are to be on guard against false teachers. These two themes are as relevant to Christians today as they were back then.

WHEN THE ACTION WAS

BC/AD	25AD	50AD	75AD	100AD

- Jesus was born (BC/AD)
- Jesus began his ministry
- The church began soon after Jesus went to heaven
- Paul became a Christian
- Paul began his missionary work
- Fire destroyed Rome
- Romans destroyed the Temple in Jerusalem
- 3 John was written

[1]From the Elder.[n]
To my dear friend Gaius, whom I love in the
truth:[n]
[2]My dear friend, I know your soul is doing fine,
and I pray that you are doing well in every way
and that your health is good. [3]I was very happy
when some brothers and sisters[n] came and told
me about the truth in your life and how you are
following the way of truth. [4]Nothing gives me
greater joy than to hear that my children are following the way of truth.
[5]My dear friend, it is good that you help the
brothers and sisters, even those you do not know.
[6]They told the church about your love. Please
help them to continue their trip in a way worthy
of God. [7]They started out in service to Christ, and
they have been accepting nothing from nonbelievers. [8]So we should help such people; when we
do, we share in their work for the truth.

SIDELIGHT: Since motels in ancient times were notoriously dirty, flea-infested, and expensive, travelers often stayed in people's homes—without any advance notice (3 John 5–8). "Oh, Mom! Guess who's coming to dinner."

[9]I wrote something to the church, but Diotrephes, who loves to be their leader, will not listen
to us. [10]So if I come, I will talk about what Diotrephes is doing, about how he lies and says evil
things about us. But more than that, he refuses to

Elder "Elder" means an older person. It can also mean a special leader in the church (as Titus 1:5).
truth The truth or "Good News" about Jesus Christ that joins all believers together.
brothers and sisters Although the Greek text says "brothers" here and throughout this book, the writer's words were meant for the entire church, including men and women.

SERVICE

Thanks for Coming

"Dear Mack,

"Thank you for coming so far away to teach me 'bout Jesus. I have fun. I miss you, but I'll read the Bible you gave me. I love you!— Wesley."

Mack Kemper smiled when he read the scrawled words on notebook paper. The unexpected thanks made Mack's week.

For five busy days, five hundred miles from home, twenty-two teenagers had used songs, crafts, and recreation to show Jesus' love to children in a small church. Eight-year-old Wesley Wilke was among the children who heard the exciting news about Jesus.

The summer trip had been Mack's first mission project. He didn't know what to expect, or whether the kids would like him. But Wesley had taken a special liking to Mack. Toward week's end, Wesley had asked Mack how he could make Jesus his friend. Mack had handed his own Bible to Wesley and had prayed with him. On the last day, Wesley had given Mack the short letter.

At the teenagers' final meeting before returning home, Mack read Wesley's letter. "I think I understand a little more about the song 'Jesus Loves Me, This I Know,' " Mack explained. "Now, I've seen it in action." From the back of the room the simple song began and grew as others joined in.

Mack found out how Christian service often helps the giver as much as the receiver. Read how John stressed the value of Christian service in **3 John 5–8**.

- How did Wesley benefit from Mack's serving? How did Mack benefit from the serving?
- How can John's idea of Christian service help both those receiving and those giving the service?

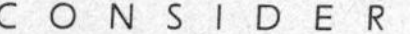

CONSIDER . . .

- serving someone who needs help this week.
- asking to serve on your youth group's or church's missions or outreach committee.

FOR MORE SEE . . .

- Proverbs 11:24–25 (p. 577)
- John 13:4–17 (p. 1080)
- 1 Peter 5:2–7 (p. 1307)

accept the other brothers and sisters; he even stops those who do want to accept them and puts them out of the church.

11My dear friend, do not follow what is bad; follow what is good. The one who does good belongs to God. But the one who does evil has never known God.

12Everyone says good things about Demetrius, and the truth agrees with what they say. We also speak well of him, and you know what we say is true.

13I have many things I want to write you, but
I do not want to use pen and ink. 14I hope to see
you soon and talk face to face. 15Peace to you. The friends here greet you. Please greet each friend there by name.

JUDE

Why Read This Book:

- Test others' beliefs against the truth of Jesus Christ (Jude 1–4).
- Focus on the dangers of listening to false teachers (Jude 5–16).
- Be challenged to stay strong in your faith (Jude 17–24).

Behind the Scenes:

Termites can destroy a building before you even know they are there. The wood might look fine from the outside, but inside the termites have hollowed the beams. If you don't discover the damage soon enough and get rid of the insects, the building can become so weak that it can't be salvaged.

The early church had to deal with false teachers who were like termites in the church. They had sneaked into the church with lies about Jesus and salvation. Unless the church got rid of the false teachers, they could weaken or even destroy the church.

Jude urges the church to get rid of the termites!—"to fight hard for the faith that was given the holy people of God" (Jude 3). These false teachers evidently believed that their freedom encouraged them to follow the modern philosophy: "If it feels good, do it." These people will be punished by God in the end, the author says, but in the meantime their loose morals, hypocrisy, rejection of authority, and divisiveness were infecting the church.

How should the Christians deal with the false teachers? By being strong in their own faith, Jude says. By praying. By focusing on God's love. By waiting patiently for Jesus Christ. And even though Christians hate and avoid what these sinful people do, Christians should reach out to them with God's love (Jude 20–23).

As Christians, we regularly encounter people who believe and act differently from us. How do we respond to them? The book of Jude offers positive guidance.

WHEN THE ACTION WAS

Jesus was born
The church began soon after Jesus went to heaven
Paul began his missionary work
Fire destroyed Rome

BC/AD — 25AD — 50AD — 75AD — 100AD

Jesus began his ministry
Paul became a Christian
Jude may have been written
Romans destroyed the Temple in Jerusalem

[1]From Jude, a servant of Jesus Christ and a
brother of James.
To all who have been called by God. God the
Father loves you, and you have been kept safe in
Jesus Christ:
[2]Mercy, peace, and love be yours richly.

God Will Punish Sinners

[3]Dear friends, I wanted very much to write you
about the salvation we all share. But I felt the
need to write you about something else: I want
to encourage you to fight hard for the faith that
was given the holy people of God once and for all
time. [4]Some people have secretly entered your
group. Long ago the prophets[d] wrote about these
people who will be judged guilty. They are against
God and have changed the grace of our God into
a reason for sexual sin. They also refuse to accept
Jesus Christ, our only Master and Lord.
[5]I want to remind you of some things you already know: Remember that the Lord saved his
people by bringing them out of the land of Egypt.
But later he destroyed all those who did not believe. [6]And remember the angels who did not
keep their place of power but left their proper
home. The Lord has kept these angels in darkness, bound with everlasting chains, to be judged
on the great day. [7]Also remember the cities of

FOLLOWING GOD

Standing Alone

At a large youth convention, thirty-two teams competed for a $500 prize in a Bible quiz game called the "Holy Word Squares." Most teams had five members. But one team had only one person, a shy thirteen-year-old named Chris Bailey.

Chris was short, skinny and wore heavy glasses. He had been so excited about the Bible quiz that he had tried to find four other youth-group kids to team up with him. But they were not interested; they had other things to do besides practice for a Bible game.

Their rejection didn't stop Chris. He entered the competition alone—a one-person "team." For weeks before the contest, Chris studied the Bible and "scrimmaged" with his youth minister. He got better and better.

When Chris's youth group got to the convention, the other kids went swimming while Chris began to compete. No one took him seriously, until he won a preliminary round. Then he won the next round. Then the semifinals. By the final game, everyone was curious about this one-person team.

More than seven hundred people eagerly awaited the final round with Chris against a five-member team. First, the other team won. Then Chris won. The tournament all came down to one, tie-breaking game.

Each side answered question after question. When the round was almost over, Chris took the lead. Then he correctly answered the final question. He had won!

As Chris raised his arms in victory, his youth group swarmed around him in celebration. The crowd gave him a screaming, standing ovation.

His group cheered again when he announced that he was giving the prize money to the group. Pizza was on him!

Despite the way he was treated at first, Chris stuck with what he believed. His story illustrates the kind of determination and faith **Jude 17–25** urges all Christians to have as they seek to follow God.

- How was Chris's solitary stand like the ways Jude tells believers to keep following God?
- What situations do you encounter in which this passage can encourage you to keep following God?

CONSIDER . . .

- rating from one to ten your willingness to act on your faith, with ten as the highest. Why did you rate yourself as you did?
- practicing sharing your faith with a Christian friend. Then share it with a non-Christian friend.

FOR MORE, SEE . . .

- Psalm 113 (p. 547)
- 1 Thessalonians 5:12–22 (p. 1249)
- 1 Peter 2:4–10 (p. 1303)

Sodom and Gomorrah[n] and the other towns
around them. In the same way they were full of
sexual sin and people who desired sexual relations that God does not allow. They suffer the
punishment of eternal fire, as an example for all
to see.
8It is the same with these people who have entered your group. They are guided by dreams and
make themselves filthy with sin. They reject
God's authority and speak against the angels.
9Not even the archangel[n] Michael, when he argued with the devil about who would have the
body of Moses, dared to judge the devil guilty.
Instead, he said, "The Lord punish you." 10But
these people speak against things they do not understand. And what they do know, by feeling, as
dumb animals know things, are the very things
that destroy them. 11It will be terrible for them.
They have followed the way of Cain, and for
money they have given themselves to doing the
wrong that Balaam did. They have fought against
God as Korah did, and like Korah, they surely will
be destroyed. 12They are like dirty spots in your
special Christian meals you share. They eat with
you and have no fear, caring only for themselves.
They are clouds without rain, which the wind
blows around. They are autumn trees without
fruit that are pulled out of the ground. So they are
twice dead. 13They are like wild waves of the sea,
tossing up their own shameful actions like foam.
They are like stars that wander in the sky. A place
in the blackest darkness has been kept for them
forever.
14Enoch, the seventh descendant[d] from Adam,
said about these people: "Look, the Lord is coming with many thousands of his holy angels to
15judge every person. He is coming to punish all
who are against God for all the evil they have
done against him. And he will punish the sinners
who are against God for all the evil they have said
against him."
16These people complain and blame others, doing the evil things they want to do. They brag
about themselves, and they flatter others to get
what they want.

SIDELIGHT: Don't look for the quotation by Enoch in the Old Testament (Jude 14–15). This is a direct quote from a book known as 1 Enoch, which is part of the sixty-five documents known as the Pseudepigrapha. Christians don't consider these books part of scripture, but the books were widely read and quoted in New Testament times.

A Warning and Things to Do

17Dear friends, remember what the apostles[d] of
our Lord Jesus Christ said before. 18They said to
you, "In the last times there will be people who
laugh about God, following their own evil desires
which are against God." 19These are the people
who divide you, people whose thoughts are only
of this world, who do not have the Spirit.[d]
20But dear friends, use your most holy faith to
build yourselves up, praying in the Holy Spirit.
21Keep yourselves in God's love as you wait for
the Lord Jesus Christ with his mercy to give you
life forever.
22Show mercy to some people who have
doubts. 23Take others out of the fire, and save
them. Show mercy mixed with fear to others,
hating even their clothes which are dirty from
sin.

Praise God

24God is strong and can help you not to fall. He
can bring you before his glory without any wrong
in you and can give you great joy. 25He is the only
God, the One who saves us. To him be glory,
greatness, power, and authority through Jesus
Christ our Lord for all time past, now, and
forever. Amen.

Sodom and Gomorrah Two cities God destroyed because they were so evil.
archangel The leader among God's angels or messengers.

REVELATION

Why Read This Book:

- Hear warnings about problems in churches (Revelation 1—3).
- See God's power against the forces of evil (Revelation 4—11).
- Be comforted by God's promise of hope for all his people (Revelation 12—22).

Behind the Scenes:

A blood-red moon. A lamb with seven horns and seven eyes. Locusts with golden crowns. White, red, black, and pale horses. A giant, red dragon. A sea of glass mixed with fire.

These images sound like they are straight out of a science-fiction movie. But they are not; they are from the book of Revelation, the last book of the Bible. They make the book exciting and mysterious . . . and confusing.

This book can be so difficult to understand because it is "apocalyptic" literature. This literature uses mysterious visions and symbolic language to describe God's victory over the troubles of this world. Most often, this kind of literature was written during tough times, when the church was being persecuted. One reason for using the images and symbols was to use symbols that Christians would understand, but others would not.

That's certainly true of the book of Revelation. At the time, Christians were under attack by the Roman authorities. The Romans demanded that all people worship the emperor. Many Christians refused, and many were executed.

The book of Revelation was written to give hope and courage to these persecuted Christians. Scholars view the symbols, events and visions in Revelation in different ways. Some of the major perspectives include:

- The book describes the first-century situation, and all the events described in it have taken place.
- The book contains predictions for a long chain of events that will conclude with Christ's Second Coming.

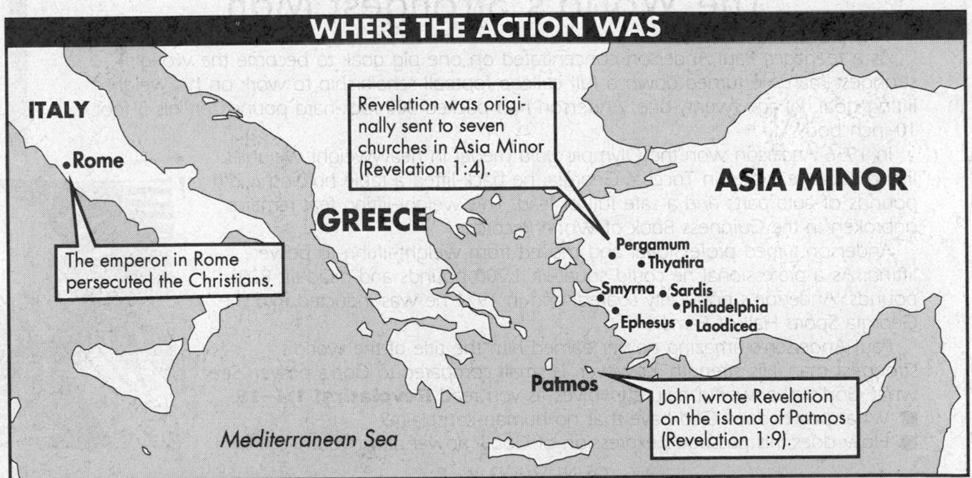

WHEN THE ACTION WAS

Jesus was born	BC/AD
The church began soon after Jesus went to heaven	
Paul began his missionary work	
Fire destroyed Rome	
The book of Revelation was written	

Timeline: BC/AD — 25AD — 50AD — 75AD — 100AD

Below timeline: Jesus began his ministry; Paul became a Christian; Romans destroyed the Temple in Jerusalem

Behind the Scenes (cont.):

- The visions describe the final days before the end of the world, and do not relate directly to biblical times.
- The book does not predict the future; rather, it uses symbolic language to teach religious truth about God's victory over evil.

Regardless of the specific perspective, central themes are clear. God is powerful. Jesus Christ reigns forever. Those who suffer for Christ will ultimately share his victory. Revelation gives a message of hope and encouragement for all people in all times.

John Tells About This Book

1 This is the revelation[n] of Jesus Christ,
which God gave to him, to show his servants
what must soon happen. And Jesus sent his angel
to show it to his servant John, 2who has told everything he has seen. It is the word of God; it is
the message from Jesus Christ. 3Happy is the one
who reads the words of God's message, and
happy are the people who hear this message and
do what is written in it. The time is near when all
of this will happen.

Jesus' Message to the Churches

4From John.
To the seven churches in the country of Asia:
Grace and peace to you from the One who is
and was and is coming, and from the seven spirits
before his throne, 5and from Jesus Christ. Jesus is
the faithful witness, the first among those raised
from the dead. He is the ruler of the kings of the
earth.
He is the One who loves us, who made us free
from our sins with the blood of his death. 6He
made us to be a kingdom of priests who serve God
his Father. To Jesus Christ be glory and power
forever and ever! Amen.
7Look, Jesus is coming with the clouds, and everyone will see him, even those who stabbed him.
And all peoples of the earth will cry loudly because of him. Yes, this will happen! Amen.
8The Lord God says, "I am the Alpha and the

revelation A making known of truth that has been hidden.

GOD'S POWER

The World's Strongest Man

As a teenager, Paul Anderson concentrated on one big goal: to become the world's strongest man. He turned down a full college football scholarship to work on his weight-lifting goal. By age twenty-one, Anderson had packed 300 rock-hard pounds on his 5-foot, 10-inch body.

In 1956 Anderson won the Olympic gold medal in heavyweight weight-lifting. One year later in Toccoa, Georgia, he back-lifted a table holding 6,270 pounds of auto parts and a safe full of lead. This weight-lifting feat remains unbroken in the Guinness Book of World Records.

Anderson turned professional and moved from weight-lifting to power-lifting. As a professional he could squat-lift 1,200 pounds and dead-lift 820 pounds. Anderson's popularity soared, and in 1974 he was inducted into the Georgia Sports Hall of Fame.

Paul Anderson's amazing power earned him the title of the world's strongest man. His strength, however, is small compared to God's power. See what God's all-powerful nature involves as you read **Revelation 1:4–18**.

- What power does God have that no human can claim?
- How does this passage's expression of God's power affect your life?

CONSIDER . . .

- watching for evidence of God's power around you while you go through this day.
- designing a symbol or logo representing God's power described in these verses.

FOR MORE, SEE . . .

- Psalm 46 (p. 508)
- Isaiah 40:12–31 (p. 655)
- Luke 18: 27–39 (p. 1042)

Omega.[n] I am the One who is and was and is coming. I am the Almighty."

9I, John, am your brother. All of us share with Christ in suffering, in the kingdom, and in patience to continue. I was on the island of Patmos,[n] because I had preached the word of God

> **SIDELIGHT:** The island of Patmos, where John wrote Revelation (Revelation 1:9), was the Alcatraz of the Roman Empire. Religious and political prisoners were banished to this island prison, which is only about ten miles long.

and the message about Jesus. 10On the Lord's day I was in the Spirit,[d] and I heard a loud voice behind me that sounded like a trumpet. 11The voice said, "Write what you see in a book and send it to the seven churches: to Ephesus, Smyrna, Pergamum, Thyatira, Sardis, Philadelphia, and Laodicea."

12I turned to see who was talking to me. When I turned, I saw seven golden lampstands 13and someone among the lampstands who was "like a Son of Man."[n] He was dressed in a long robe and had a gold band around his chest. 14His head and hair were white like wool, as white as snow, and his eyes were like flames of fire. 15His feet were like bronze that glows hot in a furnace, and his voice was like the noise of flooding water. 16He held seven stars in his right hand, and a sharp double-edged sword came out of his mouth. He looked like the sun shining at its brightest time.

17When I saw him, I fell down at his feet like a dead man. He put his right hand on me and said, "Do not be afraid. I am the First and the Last. 18I am the One who lives; I was dead, but look, I am alive forever and ever! And I hold the keys to death and to the place of the dead. 19So write the things you see, what is now and what will happen later. 20Here is the secret of the seven stars that you saw in my right hand and the seven golden lampstands: The seven lampstands are the seven churches, and the seven stars are the angels of the seven churches.

To the Church in Ephesus

2 "Write this to the angel of the church in Ephesus:

"The One who holds the seven stars in his right hand and walks among the seven golden lampstands says this: 2I know what you do, how you work hard and never give up. I know you do not put up with the false teachings of evil people. You have tested those who say they are apostles[d] but really are not, and you found they are liars. 3You have patience and have suffered troubles for my name and have not given up.

4"But I have this against you: You have left the love you had in the beginning. 5So remember where you were before you fell. Change your hearts and do what you did at first. If you do not change, I will come to you and will take away your lampstand from its place. 6But there is something you do that is right: You hate what the Nicolaitans[n] do, as much as I.

7"Every person who has ears should listen to what the Spirit[d] says to the churches. To those who win the victory I will give the right to eat the fruit from the tree of life, which is in the garden of God.

To the Church in Smyrna

8"Write this to the angel of the church in Smyrna:

"The One who is the First and the Last, who died and came to life again, says this: 9I know your troubles and that you are poor, but really you are rich! I know the bad things some people say about you. They say they are Jews, but they are not true Jews. They are a synagogue[d] that belongs to Satan. 10Do not be afraid of what you are about to suffer. I tell you, the devil will put some of you in prison to test you, and you will suffer for ten days. But be faithful, even if you have to die, and I will give you the crown of life.

11"Everyone who has ears should listen to what the Spirit[d] says to the churches. Those who win the victory will not be hurt by the second death.

To the Church in Pergamum

12"Write this to the angel of the church in Pergamum:

"The One who has the sharp, double-edged sword says this: 13I know where you live. It is where Satan has his throne. But you are true to me. You did not refuse to tell about your faith in me even during the time of Antipas, my faithful witness who was killed in your city, where Satan lives.

14"But I have a few things against you: You have some there who follow the teaching of Balaam. He taught Balak how to cause the people of Israel to sin by eating food offered to idols and by taking part in sexual sins. 15You also have some who follow the teaching of the Nicolaitans.[n] 16So

Alpha and the Omega The first and last letters of the Greek alphabet. This means "the beginning and the end."
Patmos A small island in the Aegean Sea, near the coast of Asia Minor (modern Turkey).
"like . . . Man" "Son of Man" is a name Jesus called himself. See dictionary.
Nicolaitans This is the name of a religious group that followed false beliefs and ideas.

change your hearts and lives. If you do not, I will come to you quickly and fight against them with the sword that comes out of my mouth.

17“Everyone who has ears should listen to what the Spirit[d] says to the churches.

“I will give some of the hidden manna[d] to everyone who wins the victory. I will also give to each one who wins the victory a white stone with a new name written on it. No one knows this new name except the one who receives it.

To the Church in Thyatira

18“Write this to the angel of the church in Thyatira:

“The Son of God, who has eyes that blaze like fire and feet like shining bronze, says this: 19I know what you do. I know about your love, your faith, your service, and your patience. I know that you are doing more now than you did at first. 20“But I have this against you: You let that woman Jezebel spread false teachings. She says she is a prophetess,[d] but by her teaching she leads my people to take part in sexual sins and to eat food that is offered to idols. 21I have given her time to change her heart and turn away from her sin, but she does not want to change. 22So I will throw her on a bed of suffering. And all those who take part in adultery[d] with her will suffer greatly if they do not turn away from the wrongs she does. 23I will also kill her followers. Then all the churches will know I am the One who searches hearts and minds, and I will repay each of you for what you have done.

24“But others of you in Thyatira have not followed her teaching and have not learned what some call Satan’s deep secrets. I say to you that I will not put any other load on you. 25Only continue in your loyalty until I come.

26“I will give power over the nations to everyone who wins the victory and continues to be obedient to me until the end.

27‘You will rule over them with an iron rod,
as when pottery is broken into pieces.’

Psalm 2:9

28This is the same power I received from my Father. I will also give him the morning star. 29Everyone who has ears should listen to what the Spirit[d] says to the churches.

To the Church in Sardis

3 “Write this to the angel of the church in Sardis:

“The One who has the seven spirits and the seven stars says this: I know what you do. People say that you are alive, but really you are dead. 2Wake up! Make yourselves stronger before what you have left dies completely. I have found that what you are doing is less than what my God wants. 3So do not forget what you have received and heard. Obey it, and change your hearts and lives. So you must wake up, or I will come like a thief, and you will not know when I will come to you. 4But you have a few there in Sardis who have kept their clothes unstained, so they will walk with me and will wear white clothes, because they are worthy. 5Those who win the victory will be dressed in white clothes like them. And I will not erase their names from the book of life, but I will say they belong to me before my Father and before his angels. 6Everyone who has ears should listen to what the Spirit[d] says to the churches.

> **SIDELIGHT:** Mathematicians, arise! Numbers have an important role in Revelation, with many having symbolic significance. For example, seven (Revelation 3:1) symbolizes completeness; four signifies the created universe (Revelation 7:1, p. 1337); and twelve symbolizes the church or Israel (Revelation 21:12–14, p. 1348).

To the Church in Philadelphia

7“Write this to the angel of the church in Philadelphia:

“This is what the One who is holy and true, who holds the key of David, says. When he opens a door, no one can close it. And when he closes it, no one can open it. 8I know what you do. I have put an open door before you, which no one can close. I know you have a little strength, but you have obeyed my teaching and were not afraid to speak my name. 9Those in the synagogue[d] that belongs to Satan say they are Jews, but they are not true Jews; they are liars. I will make them come before you and bow at your feet, and they will know that I have loved you. 10You have obeyed my teaching about not giving up your faith. So I will keep you from the time of trouble that will come to the whole world to test those who live on earth.

11“I am coming soon. Continue strong in your faith so no one will take away your crown. 12I will make those who win the victory pillars in the temple of my God, and they will never have to leave it. I will write on them the name of my God and the name of the city of my God, the new Jerusalem,[n] that comes down out of heaven from my God. I will also write on them my new name. 13Everyone who has ears should listen to what the Spirit[d] says to the churches.

Jerusalem This name is used to mean the spiritual city God built for his people. See Revelation 21-22.

To the Church in Laodicea

14"Write this to the angel of the church in Laodicea:

"The Amen,[n] the faithful and true witness, the beginning of all God has made, says this: 15I know what you do, that you are not hot or cold. I wish that you were hot or cold! 16But because you are lukewarm—neither hot, nor cold—I am ready to spit you out of my mouth. 17You say, 'I am rich, and I have become wealthy and do not need anything.' But you do not know that you are really miserable, pitiful, poor, blind, and naked. 18I advise you to buy from me gold made pure in fire so you can be truly rich. Buy from me white clothes so you can be clothed and so you can cover your shameful nakedness. Buy from me medicine to put on your eyes so you can truly see.

19"I correct and punish those whom I love. So be eager to do right, and change your hearts and lives. 20Here I am! I stand at the door and knock. If you hear my voice and open the door, I will come in and eat with you, and you will eat with me.

21"Those who win the victory will sit with me on my throne in the same way that I won the victory and sat down with my Father on his throne. 22Everyone who has ears should listen to what the Spirit[d] says to the churches."

John Sees Heaven

4 After the vision of these things I looked, and there before me was an open door in heaven. And the same voice that spoke to me before, that sounded like a trumpet, said, "Come up here, and I will show you what must happen after this." 2Immediately I was in the Spirit,[d] and before me was a throne in heaven, and someone was sitting on it. 3The One who sat on the throne looked like precious stones, like jasper and carnelian. All around the throne was a rainbow the color of an emerald. 4Around the throne there were twenty-four other thrones with twenty-four elders sitting on them. They were dressed in white and had golden crowns on their heads. 5Lightning flashes and noises and thundering came from the throne. Before the throne seven lamps were burning, which are the seven spirits of God. 6Also before the throne there was something that looked like a sea of glass, clear like crystal.

In the center and around the throne were four living creatures with eyes all over them, in front and in back. 7The first living creature was like a lion. The second was like a calf. The third had a face like a man. The fourth was like a flying eagle. 8Each of these four living creatures had six wings and was covered all over with eyes, inside and out. Day and night they never stop saying:

"Holy, holy, holy is the Lord God Almighty.
He was, he is, and he is coming."

9These living creatures give glory, honor, and thanks to the One who sits on the throne, who lives forever and ever. 10Then the twenty-four elders bow down before the One who sits on the throne, and they worship him who lives forever and ever. They put their crowns down before the throne and say:

11"You are worthy, our Lord and God,
to receive glory and honor and power,
because you made all things.
Everything existed and was made,
because you wanted it."

5 Then I saw a scroll in the right hand of the One sitting on the throne. The scroll had writing on both sides and was kept closed with seven seals. 2And I saw a powerful angel calling in a loud voice, "Who is worthy to break the seals and open the scroll?" 3But there was no one in heaven or on earth or under the earth who could open the scroll or look inside it. 4I cried hard because there was no one who was worthy to open the scroll or look inside. 5But one of the elders said to me, "Do not cry! The Lion[n] from the tribe[d] of Judah, David's descendant,[d] has won the victory so that he is able to open the scroll and its seven seals."

6Then I saw a Lamb standing in the center of the throne and in the middle of the four living creatures and the elders. The Lamb looked as if he had been killed. He had seven horns and seven eyes, which are the seven spirits of God that were sent into all the world. 7The Lamb came and took the scroll from the right hand of the One sitting on the throne. 8When he took the scroll, the four living creatures and the twenty-four elders bowed down before the Lamb. Each one of them had a harp and golden bowls full of incense,[d] which are the prayers of God's holy people. 9And they all sang a new song to the Lamb:

SIDELIGHT: Ancient scrolls (Revelation 5:1) were created by beating papyrus (a reed found in the Nile River) into sheets (often about 8″ × 10″) and sewing them together. A scroll of Revelation—written on both sides to save money—would have been about fifteen feet long.

Amen Used here as a name for Jesus; it means to agree fully that something is true.
Lion Here refers to Christ.

"You are worthy to take the scroll
and to open its seals,
because you were killed,
and with the blood of your death you
bought people for God
from every tribe, language, people, and
nation.
10You made them to be a kingdom of priests
for our God,
and they will rule on the earth."
11Then I looked, and I heard the voices of many
angels around the throne, and the four living creatures, and the elders. There were thousands and
thousands of angels, 12saying in a loud voice:
"The Lamb who was killed is worthy
to receive power, wealth, wisdom, and
strength,
honor, glory, and praise!"
13Then I heard all creatures in heaven and on
earth and under the earth and in the sea saying:
"To the One who sits on the throne
and to the Lamb
be praise and honor and glory and power
forever and ever."
14The four living creatures said, "Amen," and
the elders bowed down and worshiped.

6 Then I watched while the Lamb opened the
first of the seven seals. I heard one of the
four living creatures say with a voice like thunder,
"Come!" 2I looked, and there before me was a
white horse. The rider on the horse held a bow,
and he was given a crown, and he rode out, determined to win the victory.
3When the Lamb opened the second seal, I
heard the second living creature say, "Come!"
4Then another horse came out, a red one. Its rider
was given power to take away peace from the
earth and to make people kill each other, and he
was given a big sword.
5When the Lamb opened the third seal, I heard
the third living creature say, "Come!" I looked,
and there before me was a black horse, and its
rider held a pair of scales in his hand. 6Then I
heard something that sounded like a voice coming from the middle of the four living creatures.
The voice said, "A quart of wheat for a day's pay,
and three quarts of barley for a day's pay, and do
not damage the olive oil and wine!"

WORSHIP

Worship's Many Faces

Christians are free to worship in varied and unique ways. There is no one right way to worship, as evidenced by the thousands of denominations and churches through the ages. Many churches today worship in ways shaped by traditions hundreds of years old. For example:

- Some Christians lift their voices in song, but use no musical instruments in their worship services.
- Many Christians sing hymns accompanied by pipe organs. They may use familiar prayers and liturgies through the service.
- Other Christians have informal worship styles that include contemporary music and spontaneous applause.
- Some Christians raise their hands above their heads when they pray and worship.
- And some Christians hold meetings without a formal program or a minister. Instead of a set order of worship, they gather in silence. They speak when they feel moved to pray, read a Bible passage or share a thought.

As these examples show, Christians worship God in many different ways. But they all have the central purpose of worship in mind that is found in **Revelation 5:11–14**.

- How do different expressions of worship capture the worship described in this vision?
- What feelings about worship does the passage bring out in you?

CONSIDER . . .

- finding ways your church has incorporated this passage in its worship services.
- planning a worship service with other young people. Ask your pastor to let you share in leading worship for the whole church.

FOR MORE, SEE

- Psalm 100 (p. 539)
- Isaiah 6:1–8 (p. 622)
- John 4:19–24 (p. 1063)

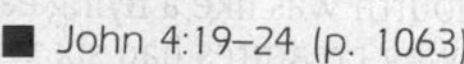

7When the Lamb opened the fourth seal, I heard the voice of the fourth living creature say, "Come!" 8I looked, and there before me was a pale horse. Its rider was named death, and Hades[n] was following close behind him. They were given power over a fourth of the earth to kill people by war, by starvation, by disease, and by the wild animals of the earth.

9When the Lamb opened the fifth seal, I saw under the altar the souls of those who had been killed because they were faithful to the word of God and to the message they had received. 10These souls shouted in a loud voice, "Holy and true Lord, how long until you judge the people of the earth and punish them for killing us?" 11Then each one of them was given a white robe and was told to wait a short time longer. There were still some of their fellow servants and brothers and sisters[n] in the service of Christ who must be killed as they were. They had to wait until all of this was finished.

12Then I watched while the Lamb opened the sixth seal, and there was a great earthquake. The sun became black like rough black cloth, and the whole moon became red like blood. 13And the stars in the sky fell to the earth like figs falling from a fig tree when the wind blows. 14The sky disappeared as a scroll when it is rolled up, and every mountain and island was moved from its place.

15Then the kings of the earth, the rulers, the generals, the rich people, the powerful people, the slaves, and the free people hid themselves in caves and in the rocks on the mountains. 16They called to the mountains and the rocks, "Fall on us. Hide us from the face of the One who sits on the throne and from the anger of the Lamb! 17The great day for their anger has come, and who can stand against it?"

The 144,000 People of Israel

7 After the vision of these things I saw four angels standing at the four corners of the earth. The angels were holding the four winds of the earth to keep them from blowing on the land or on the sea or on any tree. 2Then I saw another angel coming up from the east who had the seal of the living God. And he called out in a loud voice to the four angels to whom God had given power to harm the earth and the sea. 3He said to them, "Do not harm the land or the sea or the trees until we mark with a sign the foreheads of the people who serve our God." 4Then I heard how many people were marked with the sign. There were one hundred forty-four thousand from every tribe[d] of the people of Israel.

5From the tribe of Judah twelve thousand
were marked with the sign,
from the tribe of Reuben twelve thousand,
from the tribe of Gad twelve thousand,
6from the tribe of Asher twelve thousand,
from the tribe of Naphtali twelve thousand,
from the tribe of Manasseh twelve thousand,
7from the tribe of Simeon twelve thousand,
from the tribe of Levi twelve thousand,
from the tribe of Issachar twelve thousand,
8from the tribe of Zebulun twelve thousand,
from the tribe of Joseph twelve thousand,
and from the tribe of Benjamin twelve thousand were marked with the sign.

The Great Crowd Worships God

9After the vision of these things I looked, and there was a great number of people, so many that no one could count them. They were from every nation, tribe,[d] people, and language of the earth. They were all standing before the throne and before the Lamb, wearing white robes and holding palm branches in their hands. 10They were shouting in a loud voice, "Salvation belongs to our God, who sits on the throne, and to the Lamb." 11All the angels were standing around the throne and the elders and the four living creatures. They all bowed down on their faces before the throne and worshiped God, 12saying, "Amen! Praise, glory, wisdom, thanks, honor, power, and strength belong to our God forever and ever. Amen!"

13Then one of the elders asked me, "Who are these people dressed in white robes? Where did they come from?"

14I answered, "You know, sir."

And the elder said to me, "These are the people who have come out of the great distress. They have washed their robes[n] and made them white in the blood of the Lamb. 15Because of this, they are before the throne of God. They worship him day and night in his temple. And the One who sits on the throne will be present with them. 16Those people will never be hungry again, and they will never be thirsty again. The sun will not hurt them, and no heat will burn them, 17because the Lamb at the center of the throne will be their shepherd. He will lead them to springs of water that give life. And God will wipe away every tear from their eyes."

Hades The unseen world of the dead.
brothers and sisters Although the Greek text says "brothers" here and throughout this book, both men and women would have been included.
washed their robes This means they believed in Jesus so that their sins could be forgiven by Christ's blood.

The Seventh Seal

8 When the Lamb opened the seventh seal,
there was silence in heaven for about half an
hour. [2]And I saw the seven angels who stand before God and to whom were given seven trumpets.

[3]Another angel came and stood at the altar,
holding a golden pan for incense.[d] He was given
much incense to offer with the prayers of all
God's holy people. The angel put this offering on
the golden altar before the throne. [4]The smoke
from the incense went up from the angel's hand
to God with the prayers of God's people. [5]Then
the angel filled the incense pan with fire from the
altar and threw it on the earth, and there were

SIDELIGHT: Since no one had invented lick-and-seal envelopes in Bible times, people would fold or roll up documents, tie string around them, and press a lump of clay over the knot (Revelation 8:1). Then the sender would stamp the hardening clay with a special ring or seal, which was intended to be broken only by the appropriate person.

SADNESS

The Worst Year of Her Life

Lexie Byers had looked forward to her junior year. She did not know it would be her life's worst.

Early in the fall her mother was diagnosed with leukemia. Her dad quit his job to help care for her mom. Money, time, and energy were scarce. And, Lexie carried a difficult class load.

"I had to take care of the house, feed everyone, and plow through my schoolwork," she recalls. "It was tough, but I got along somehow."

One day, however, her mother entered the hospital for one final, risky operation to fight the leukemia. "When the surgeons came out of the operating room, I could tell by the way they looked at me that she was gone," she says.

After the funeral, Lexie's life changed dramatically. Her father, in deep grief, wandered about the house. One day Lexie found a For Sale sign in their front yard. "It's too painful for me to live here," her father said.

Lexie watched her dad fall apart. Unable to find work and desperately lonely, her father returned to his hometown. Lexie faced the difficult choice: either live with her older sister and finish at her present school, or go with her father. Even though she missed her dad, Lexie stayed with her sister.

What sustained her through this sad time? "Christian friends and a caring church got me through the experience," she says. "I couldn't pray, because I was mad at God. All I'd do was cry. These friends just kept loving me, even when I was unlovely."

Lexie went on to college, where she's majoring in engineering. Her father, in time, overcame his grief and went on with his life. "My world fell apart in eleventh grade," Lexie reflects. "Our family suffered a lot. But with God's help, we made it through, and that's what matters."

Everyone experiences pain, disappointment, and uncontrollable events. When those sad times seem overwhelming, Christians can turn to passages such as **Revelation 7:9–17** for a message of hope.

- What hope could Lexie gain from these verses?
- How could these verses help you deal with sadness in your life?

CONSIDER . . .

- doing something positive to help you get out of the blues. Try visiting a friend, watching a comedy film, or exercising.
- visiting someone who is having a sad time. Take fresh flowers, cookies, or a small gift to show you care.

FOR MORE, SEE . . .

- Psalm 40:1–3 (p. 505)
- Ecclesiastes 3:1–8 (p. 600)
- Hebrews 10:23–25 (p. 1286)

flashes of lightning, thunder and loud noises, and an earthquake.

The Seven Angels and Trumpets

6Then the seven angels who had the seven trumpets prepared to blow them.

7The first angel blew his trumpet, and hail and fire mixed with blood were poured down on the earth. And a third of the earth, and all the green grass, and a third of the trees were burned up.

8Then the second angel blew his trumpet, and something that looked like a big mountain, burning with fire, was thrown into the sea. And a third of the sea became blood, 9a third of the living things in the sea died, and a third of the ships were destroyed.

10Then the third angel blew his trumpet, and a large star, burning like a torch, fell from the sky. It fell on a third of the rivers and on the springs of water. 11The name of the star is Wormwood.[n] And a third of all the water became bitter, and many people died from drinking the water that was bitter.

12Then the fourth angel blew his trumpet, and a third of the sun, and a third of the moon, and a third of the stars were struck. So a third of them became dark, and a third of the day was without light, and also the night.

13While I watched, I heard an eagle that was flying high in the air cry out in a loud voice, "Trouble! Trouble! Trouble for those who live on the earth because of the remaining sounds of the trumpets that the other three angels are about to blow!"

9 Then the fifth angel blew his trumpet, and I saw a star fall from the sky to the earth. The star was given the key to the deep hole that leads to the bottomless pit. 2Then it opened up the hole that leads to the bottomless pit, and smoke came up from the hole like smoke from a big furnace. Then the sun and sky became dark because of the smoke from the hole. 3Then locusts[d] came down to the earth out of the smoke, and they were given the power to sting like scorpions.[n] 4They were told not to harm the grass on the earth or any plant or tree. They could harm only the people who did not have the sign of God on their foreheads. 5These locusts were not given the power to kill anyone, but to cause pain to the people for five months. And the pain they felt was like the pain a scorpion gives when it stings someone. 6During those days people will look for a way to die, but they will not find it. They will want to die, but death will run away from them.

7The locusts looked like horses prepared for battle. On their heads they wore what looked like crowns of gold, and their faces looked like human faces. 8Their hair was like women's hair, and their teeth were like lions' teeth. 9Their chests looked like iron breastplates, and the sound of their wings was like the noise of many horses and chariots hurrying into battle. 10The locusts had tails with stingers like scorpions, and in their tails was their power to hurt people for five months. 11The locusts had a king who was the angel of the bottomless pit. His name in the Hebrew language is Abaddon and in the Greek language is Apollyon.[n]

12The first trouble is past; there are still two other troubles that will come.

13Then the sixth angel blew his trumpet, and I heard a voice coming from the horns on the golden altar that is before God. 14The voice said to the sixth angel who had the trumpet, "Free the four angels who are tied at the great river Euphrates." 15And they let loose the four angels who had been kept ready for this hour and day and month and year so they could kill a third of all people on the earth. 16I heard how many troops on horses were in their army — two hundred million.

17The horses and their riders I saw in the vision looked like this: They had breastplates that were fiery red, dark blue, and yellow like sulfur. The heads of the horses looked like heads of lions, with fire, smoke, and sulfur coming out of their mouths. 18A third of all the people on earth were killed by these three terrible disasters coming out of the horses' mouths: the fire, the smoke, and the sulfur. 19The horses' power was in their mouths and in their tails; their tails were like snakes with heads, and with them they hurt people.

20The other people who were not killed by these terrible disasters still did not change their hearts and turn away from what they had made with their own hands. They did not stop worshiping demons[d] and idols made of gold, silver, bronze, stone, and wood — things that cannot see or hear or walk. 21These people did not change their hearts and turn away from murder or evil magic, from their sexual sins or stealing.

The Angel and the Small Scroll

10 Then I saw another powerful angel coming down from heaven dressed in a cloud with a rainbow over his head. His face was like the sun, and his legs were like pillars of fire. 2The angel was holding a small scroll open in his

Wormwood Name of a very bitter plant; used here to give the idea of bitter sorrow.
scorpions A scorpion is an insect that stings with a bad poison.
Abaddon, Apollyon Both names mean "Destroyer."

hand. He put his right foot on the sea and his left foot on the land. 3Then he shouted loudly like the roaring of a lion. And when he shouted, the voices of seven thunders spoke. 4When the seven thunders spoke, I started to write. But I heard a voice from heaven say, "Keep hidden what the seven thunders said, and do not write them down."

5Then the angel I saw standing on the sea and on the land raised his right hand to heaven, 6and he made a promise by the power of the One who lives forever and ever. He is the One who made the skies and all that is in them, the earth and all that is in it, and the sea and all that is in it. The angel promised, "There will be no more waiting! 7In the days when the seventh angel is ready to blow his trumpet, God's secret will be finished. This secret is the Good News[d] God told to his servants, the prophets."[d]

8Then I heard the same voice from heaven again, saying to me: "Go and take the open scroll that is in the hand of the angel that is standing on the sea and on the land."

9So I went to the angel and told him to give me the small scroll. And he said to me, "Take the scroll and eat it. It will be sour in your stomach, but in your mouth it will be sweet as honey." 10So I took the small scroll from the angel's hand and ate it. In my mouth it tasted sweet as honey, but after I ate it, it was sour in my stomach. 11Then I was told, "You must prophesy[d] again about many peoples, nations, languages, and kings."

The Two Witnesses

11 I was given a measuring stick like a rod, and I was told, "Go and measure the temple[d] of God and the altar, and count the people worshiping there. 2But do not measure the yard outside the temple. Leave it alone, because it has been given to those who are not God's people. And they will trample on the holy city for forty-two months. 3And I will give power to my two witnesses to prophesy[d] for one thousand two hundred sixty days, and they will be dressed in rough cloth to show their sadness."

4These two witnesses are the two olive trees and the two lampstands that stand before the Lord of the earth. 5And if anyone tries to hurt them, fire comes from their mouths and kills their enemies. And if anyone tries to hurt them in whatever way, in that same way that person will die. 6These witnesses have the power to stop the sky from raining during the time they are prophesying. And they have power to make the waters become blood, and they have power to send every kind of trouble to the earth as many times as they want.

7When the two witnesses have finished telling their message, the beast that comes up from the bottomless pit will fight a war against them. He will defeat them and kill them. 8The bodies of the two witnesses will lie in the street of the great city where the Lord was killed. This city is named Sodom[n] and Egypt, which has a spiritual meaning. 9Those from every race of people, tribe,[d] language, and nation will look at the bodies of the two witnesses for three and one-half days, and they will refuse to bury them. 10People who live on the earth will rejoice and be happy because these two are dead. They will send each other gifts, because these two prophets brought much suffering to those who live on the earth.

11But after three and one-half days, God put the breath of life into the two prophets again. They stood on their feet, and everyone who saw them became very afraid. 12Then the two prophets heard a loud voice from heaven saying, "Come up here!" And they went up into heaven in a cloud as their enemies watched.

13In the same hour there was a great earthquake, and a tenth of the city was destroyed. Seven thousand people were killed in the earthquake, and those who did not die were very afraid and gave glory to the God of heaven.

14The second trouble is finished. Pay attention: The third trouble is coming soon.

The Seventh Trumpet

15Then the seventh angel blew his trumpet. And there were loud voices in heaven, saying:

"The power to rule the world
now belongs to our Lord and his Christ,[d]
and he will rule forever and ever."

16Then the twenty-four elders, who sit on their thrones before God, bowed down on their faces and worshiped God. 17They said:

"We give thanks to you, Lord God Almighty,
who is and who was,
because you have used your great power
and have begun to rule!
18The people of the world were angry,
but your anger has come.
The time has come to judge the dead
and to reward your servants the prophets[d]
and your holy people,
all who respect you, great and small.
The time has come to destroy those who
destroy the earth!"

19Then God's temple[d] in heaven was opened. The Ark[d] that holds the agreement God gave to his people could be seen in his temple. Then there were flashes of lightning, noises, thunder, an earthquake, and a great hailstorm.

Sodom City that God destroyed because the people were so evil.

The Woman and the Dragon

12 And then a great wonder appeared in heaven: A woman was clothed with the sun, and the moon was under her feet, and a crown of twelve stars was on her head. 2She was pregnant and cried out with pain, because she was about to give birth. 3Then another wonder appeared in heaven: There was a giant red dragon with seven heads and seven crowns on each head. He also had ten horns. 4His tail swept a third of the stars out of the sky and threw them down to the earth. He stood in front of the woman who was ready to give birth so he could eat her baby as soon as it was born. 5Then the woman gave birth to a son who will rule all the nations with an iron rod. And her child was taken up to God and to his throne. 6The woman ran away into the desert to a place God prepared for her where she would be taken care of for one thousand two hundred sixty days.

7Then there was a war in heaven. Michael[n] and his angels fought against the dragon, and the dragon and his angels fought back. 8But the dragon was not strong enough, and he and his angels lost their place in heaven. 9The giant dragon was thrown down out of heaven. (He is that old snake called the devil or Satan, who tricks the whole world.) The dragon with his angels was thrown down to the earth.

10Then I heard a loud voice in heaven saying:

"The salvation and the power and the
 kingdom of our God
and the authority of his Christ[d] have now
 come.
The accuser of our brothers and sisters,
 who accused them day and night before
 our God,
 has been thrown down.
11And our brothers and sisters defeated him
 by the blood of the Lamb's death
 and by the message they preached.
They did not love their lives so much
 that they were afraid of death.
12So rejoice, you heavens
 and all who live there!
But it will be terrible for the earth and the
 sea,
 because the devil has come down to you!
He is filled with anger,
 because he knows he does not have much
 time."

13When the dragon saw he had been thrown down to the earth, he hunted for the woman who had given birth to the son. 14But the woman was given the two wings of a great eagle so she could fly to the place prepared for her in the desert. There she would be taken care of for three and one-half years, away from the snake. 15Then the snake poured water out of its mouth like a river toward the woman so the flood would carry her away. 16But the earth helped the woman by opening its mouth and swallowing the river that came from the mouth of the dragon. 17Then the dragon was very angry at the woman, and he went off to make war against all her other children—those who obey God's commands and who have the message Jesus taught.

18And the dragon stood on the seashore.

SIDELIGHT: The reign of the Roman Emperor Nero (often paralleled with the first beast in Revelation 13) was marked by terrible crimes, destruction, and persecution of Christians. When he sent someone to murder his own mother, she bared her body and cried, "Strike my womb because it bore a Nero!"

The Two Beasts

13 Then I saw a beast coming up out of the sea. It had ten horns and seven heads, and there was a crown on each horn. A name against God was written on each head. 2This beast looked like a leopard, with feet like a bear's feet and a mouth like a lion's mouth. And the dragon gave the beast all of his power and his throne and great authority. 3One of the heads of the beast looked as if it had been killed by a wound, but this death wound was healed. Then the whole world was amazed and followed the beast. 4People worshiped the dragon because he had given his power to the beast. And they also worshiped the beast, asking, "Who is like the beast? Who can make war against it?"

5The beast was allowed to say proud words and words against God, and it was allowed to use its power for forty-two months. 6It used its mouth to speak against God, against God's name, against the place where God lives, and against all those who live in heaven. 7It was given power to make war against God's holy people and to defeat them. It was given power over every tribe,[d] people, language, and nation. 8And all who live on earth will worship the beast—all the people since the beginning of the world whose names are not written in the Lamb's book of life. The Lamb is the One who was killed.

9Anyone who has ears should listen:

10If you are to be a prisoner,
 then you will be a prisoner.

Michael The archangel—leader among God's angels or messengers (Jude 9).

If you are to be killed with the sword,
then you will be killed with the sword.
This means that God's holy people must have patience and faith.

11Then I saw another beast coming up out of the earth. It had two horns like a lamb, but it spoke like a dragon. 12This beast stands before the first beast and uses the same power the first beast has. By this power it makes everyone living on earth worship the first beast, who had the death wound that was healed. 13And the second beast does great miracles[d] so that it even makes fire come down from heaven to earth while people are watching. 14It fools those who live on earth by the miracles it has been given the power to do. It does these miracles to serve the first beast. The second beast orders people to make an idol to honor the first beast, the one that was wounded by the deadly sword but sprang to life again. 15The second beast was given power to give life to the idol of the first one so that the idol could speak. And the second beast was given power to command all who will not worship the image of the beast to be killed. 16The second beast also forced all people, small and great, rich and poor, free and slave, to have a mark on their right hand or on their forehead. 17No one could buy or sell without this mark, which is the name of the beast or the number of its name. 18This takes wisdom. Let the one who has understanding find the meaning of the number, which is the number of a person. Its number is six hundred sixty-six.

The Song of the Saved

14 Then I looked, and there before me was the Lamb standing on Mount Zion.[n] With him were one hundred forty-four thousand people who had his name and his Father's name written on their foreheads. 2And I heard a sound from heaven like the noise of flooding water and like the sound of loud thunder. The sound I heard was like people playing harps. 3And they sang a new song before the throne and before the four living creatures and the elders. No one could learn the new song except the one hundred forty-four thousand who had been bought from the earth. 4These are the ones who did not do sinful things with women, because they kept themselves pure. They follow the Lamb every place he goes. These one hundred forty-four thousand were bought from among the people of the earth as people to be offered to God and the Lamb. 5They were not guilty of telling lies; they are without fault.

The Three Angels

6Then I saw another angel flying high in the air. He had the eternal Good News[d] to preach to those who live on earth—to every nation, tribe,[d] language, and people. 7He preached in a loud voice, "Fear God and give him praise, because the time has come for God to judge all people. So worship God who made the heavens, and the earth, and the sea, and the springs of water."

8Then the second angel followed the first angel and said, "Ruined, ruined is the great city of Babylon! She made all the nations drink the wine of the anger of her adultery."[d]

9Then a third angel followed the first two angels, saying in a loud voice: "If anyone worships the beast and his idol and gets the beast's mark on the forehead or on the hand, 10that one also will drink the wine of God's anger, which is prepared with all its strength in the cup of his anger. And that person will be put in pain with burning sulfur before the holy angels and the Lamb. 11And the smoke from their burning pain will rise forever and ever. There will be no rest, day or night, for those who worship the beast and his idol or who get the mark of his name." 12This means God's holy people must be patient. They must obey God's commands and keep their faith in Jesus.

13Then I heard a voice from heaven saying, "Write this: Happy are the dead who die from now on in the Lord."

The Spirit[d] says, "Yes, they will rest from their hard work, and the reward of all they have done stays with them."

The Earth Is Harvested

14Then I looked, and there before me was a white cloud, and sitting on the white cloud was One who looked like a Son of Man.[n] He had a gold crown on his head and a sharp sickle[n] in his hand. 15Then another angel came out of the temple and called out in a loud voice to the One who was sitting on the cloud, "Take your sickle and harvest from the earth, because the time to harvest has come, and the fruit of the earth is ripe." 16So the One who was sitting on the cloud swung his sickle over the earth, and the earth was harvested.

17Then another angel came out of the temple in heaven, and he also had a sharp sickle. 18And then another angel, who has power over the fire, came from the altar. This angel called to the angel with the sharp sickle, saying, "Take your sharp sickle and gather the bunches of grapes from the earth's vine, because its grapes are ripe." 19Then the an-

Mount Zion Another name for Jerusalem; here meaning the spiritual city of God's people.
Son of Man "Son of Man" is a name Jesus called himself. See dictionary.
sickle A farming tool with a curved blade. It was used to harvest grain.

gel swung his sickle over the earth. He gathered
the earth's grapes and threw them into the great
winepress[d] of God's anger. 20They were trampled
in the winepress outside the city, and blood
flowed out of the winepress as high as horses' bri-
dles for a distance of about one hundred eighty
miles.

The Last Troubles

15 Then I saw another wonder in heaven
that was great and amazing. There were
seven angels bringing seven disasters. These are
the last disasters, because after them, God's anger
is finished.
2I saw what looked like a sea of glass mixed
with fire. All of those who had won the victory
over the beast and his idol and over the number
of his name were standing by the sea of glass.
They had harps that God had given them. 3They
sang the song of Moses, the servant of God, and
the song of the Lamb:

"You do great and wonderful things, *Psalm 111:2*
  Lord God Almighty. *Amos 3:13*
Everything the Lord does is right and true, *Psalm 145:17*
  King of the nations.
4Everyone will respect you, Lord, *Jeremiah 10:7*
  and will honor you.
Only you are holy.
All the nations will come
  and worship you, *Psalm 86:9-10*
because the right things you have done
  are now made known." *Deuteronomy 32:4*

5After this I saw that the temple (the Tent[d] of
the Agreement) in heaven was opened. 6And the
seven angels bringing the seven disasters came
out of the temple. They were dressed in clean,
shining linen and wore golden bands tied around
their chests. 7Then one of the four living creatures
gave to the seven angels seven golden bowls filled
with the anger of God, who lives forever and
ever. 8The temple was filled with smoke from the
glory and the power of God, and no one could
enter the temple until the seven disasters of the
seven angels were finished.

The Bowls of God's Anger

16 Then I heard a loud voice from the temple saying to the seven angels, "Go and
pour out the seven bowls of God's anger on the
earth."
2The first angel left and poured out his bowl on
the land. Then ugly and painful sores came upon
all those who had the mark of the beast and who
worshiped his idol.
3The second angel poured out his bowl on the
sea, and it became blood like that of a dead man,
and every living thing in the sea died.
4The third angel poured out his bowl on the
rivers and the springs of water, and they became
blood. 5Then I heard the angel of the waters saying:

"Holy One, you are the One who is and who
  was.
You are right to decide to punish these evil
  people.
6They have poured out the blood of your holy
  people and your prophets.[d]
So now you have given them blood to
  drink as they deserve."

7And I heard a voice coming from the altar saying:

"Yes, Lord God Almighty,
  the way you punish evil people is right and
  fair."

8The fourth angel poured out his bowl on the
sun, and he was given power to burn the people
with fire. 9They were burned by the great heat,
and they cursed the name of God, who had control over these disasters. But the people refused to
change their hearts and lives and give glory to
God.
10The fifth angel poured out his bowl on the
throne of the beast, and darkness covered its kingdom. People gnawed their tongues because of the
pain. 11They also cursed the God of heaven because of their pain and the sores they had, but
they refused to change their hearts and turn away
from the evil things they did.
12The sixth angel poured out his bowl on the
great river Euphrates so that the water in the river
was dried up to prepare the way for the kings
from the east to come. 13Then I saw three evil
spirits that looked like frogs coming out of the
mouth of the dragon, out of the mouth of the
beast, and out of the mouth of the false prophet.[d]
14These evil spirits are the spirits of demons,[d]
which have power to do miracles.[d] They go out
to the kings of the whole world to gather them
together for the battle on the great day of God
Almighty.
15"Listen! I will come as a thief comes! Happy
are those who stay awake and keep their clothes
on so that they will not walk around naked and
have people see their shame."
16Then the evil spirits gathered the kings to-

SIDELIGHT: Revelation 16:15 isn't a warning to wear pajamas in bed. According to Jewish laws of the time, the captain of the Temple would check up on the Temple police at night. If someone was asleep on duty, his clothes were taken off and burned, and he was sent away naked and disgraced. Anyone want an extra cup of coffee?

gether to the place that is called Armageddon in the Hebrew language.

[17]The seventh angel poured out his bowl into the air. Then a loud voice came out of the temple from the throne, saying, "It is finished!" [18]Then there were flashes of lightning, noises, thunder, and a big earthquake — the worst earthquake that has ever happened since people have been on earth. [19]The great city split into three parts, and the cities of the nations were destroyed. And God remembered the sins of Babylon the Great, so he gave that city the cup filled with the wine of his terrible anger. [20]Then every island ran away, and mountains disappeared. [21]Giant hailstones, each weighing about a hundred pounds, fell from the sky upon people. People cursed God for the disaster of the hail, because this disaster was so terrible.

The Woman on the Animal

17 Then one of the seven angels who had the seven bowls came and spoke to me. He said, "Come, and I will show you the punishment that will be given to the great prostitute,[d] the one sitting over many waters. [2]The kings of the earth sinned sexually with her, and the people of the earth became drunk from the wine of her sexual sin."

[3]Then the angel carried me away by the Spirit[d] to the desert. There I saw a woman sitting on a red beast. It was covered with names against God written on it, and it had seven heads and ten horns. [4]The woman was dressed in purple and red and was shining with the gold, precious jewels, and pearls she was wearing. She had a golden cup in her hand, a cup filled with evil things and the uncleanness of her sexual sin. [5]On her forehead a title was written that was secret. This is what was written:

THE GREAT BABYLON
MOTHER OF PROSTITUTES
AND OF THE EVIL THINGS OF THE EARTH

[6]Then I saw that the woman was drunk with the blood of God's holy people and with the blood of those who were killed because of their faith in Jesus.

When I saw the woman, I was very amazed. [7]Then the angel said to me, "Why are you amazed? I will tell you the secret of this woman and the beast she rides — the one with seven heads and ten horns. [8]The beast you saw was once alive but is not alive now. But soon it will come up out of the bottomless pit and go away to be destroyed. There are people who live on earth whose names have not been written in the book of life since the beginning of the world. They will be amazed when they see the beast, because he was once alive, is not alive now, but will come again.

[9]"You need a wise mind to understand this. The seven heads on the beast are seven mountains where the woman sits. [10]And they are seven kings. Five of the kings have already been destroyed, one of the kings lives now, and another has not yet come. When he comes, he must stay a short time. [11]The beast that was once alive, but is not alive now, is also an eighth king. He belongs to the first seven kings, and he will go away to be destroyed.

[12]"The ten horns you saw are ten kings who have not yet begun to rule, but they will receive power to rule with the beast for one hour. [13]All ten of these kings have the same purpose, and they will give their power and authority to the beast. [14]They will make war against the Lamb, but the Lamb will defeat them, because he is Lord of lords and King of kings. He will defeat them with his called, chosen, and faithful followers."

[15]Then the angel said to me, "The waters that you saw, where the prostitute sits, are peoples, races, nations, and languages. [16]The ten horns and the beast you saw will hate the prostitute. They will take everything she has and leave her naked. They will eat her body and burn her with fire. [17]God made the ten horns want to carry out his purpose by agreeing to give the beast their power to rule, until what God has said comes about. [18]The woman you saw is the great city that rules over the kings of the earth."

Babylon Is Destroyed

18 After the vision of these things, I saw another angel coming down from heaven. This angel had great power, and his glory made the earth bright. [2]He shouted in a powerful voice:

"Ruined, ruined is the great city of Babylon!
She has become a home for demons[d]
and a prison for every evil spirit,
and a prison for every unclean[d] bird and unclean beast.
[3]She has been ruined, because all the peoples of the earth
have drunk the wine of the desire of her sexual sin.
She has been ruined also because the kings of the earth
have sinned sexually with her,
and the merchants of the earth
have grown rich from the great wealth of her luxury."

[4]Then I heard another voice from heaven saying:

"Come out of that city, my people,
so that you will not share in her sins,
so that you will not receive the disasters that will come to her.
[5]Her sins have piled up as high as the sky,

and God has not forgotten the wrongs she
has done.
6Give that city the same as she gave to others.
Pay her back twice as much as she did.
Prepare wine for her that is twice as strong
as the wine she prepared for others.
7She gave herself much glory and rich living.
Give her that much suffering and sadness.
She says to herself, 'I am a queen sitting on
my throne.
I am not a widow; I will never be sad.'
8So these disasters will come to her in one
day:
death, and crying, and great hunger,
and she will be destroyed by fire,
because the Lord God who judges her is
powerful."

9The kings of the earth who sinned sexually
with her and shared her wealth will see the
smoke from her burning. Then they will cry and
be sad because of her death. 10They will be afraid
of her suffering and stand far away and say:

"Terrible! How terrible for you, great city,
powerful city of Babylon,
because your punishment has come in one
hour!"

11And the merchants of the earth will cry and
be sad about her, because now there is no one to
buy their cargoes— 12cargoes of gold, silver, jewels, pearls, fine linen, purple cloth, silk, red cloth;
all kinds of citron wood and all kinds of things
made from ivory, expensive wood, bronze, iron,
and marble; 13cinnamon, spice, incense,[d] myrrh,[d]
frankincense,[d] wine, olive oil, fine flour, wheat,
cattle, sheep, horses, carriages, slaves, and human
lives.

14The merchants will say,
"Babylon, the good things you wanted are
gone from you.
All your rich and fancy things have
disappeared.
You will never have them again."

15The merchants who became rich from selling to
her will be afraid of her suffering and will stand
far away. They will cry and be sad 16and say:

"Terrible! How terrible for the great city!
She was dressed in fine linen, purple and
red cloth,
and she was shining with gold, precious
jewels, and pearls!
17All these riches have been destroyed in one
hour!"

Every sea captain, every passenger, the sailors,
and all those who earn their living from the sea
stood far away from Babylon. 18As they saw the
smoke from her burning, they cried out loudly,
"There was never a city like this great city!" 19And
they threw dust on their heads and cried out,
weeping and being sad. They said:

"Terrible! How terrible for the great city!
All the people who had ships on the sea
became rich because of her wealth!
But she has been destroyed in one hour!
20Be happy because of this, heaven!
Be happy, God's holy people and apostles[d]
and prophets![d]
God has punished her because of what she
did to you."

21Then a powerful angel picked up a large
stone, like one used for grinding grain, and threw
it into the sea. He said:

"In the same way, the great city of Babylon
will be thrown down,
and it will never be found again.
22The music of people playing harps and other
instruments, flutes, and trumpets,
will never be heard in you again.
No workman doing any job
will ever be found in you again.
The sound of grinding grain
will never be heard in you again.
23The light of a lamp
will never shine in you again,
and the voices of a bridegroom and bride
will never be heard in you again.
Your merchants were the world's great
people,
and all the nations were tricked by your
magic.
24You are guilty of the death of the prophets
and God's holy people
and all who have been killed on earth."

People in Heaven Praise God

19 After this vision and announcement I
heard what sounded like a great many
people in heaven saying:

"Hallelujah![n]
Salvation, glory, and power belong to our
God,
2 because his judgments are true and right.
He has punished the prostitute[d]
who made the earth evil with her sexual
sin.
He has paid her back for the death of his
servants."

3Again they said:
"Hallelujah!
She is burning, and her smoke will rise
forever and ever."

4Then the twenty-four elders and the four living creatures bowed down and worshiped God,
who sits on the throne. They said:
"Amen, Hallelujah!"

Hallelujah This means "praise God!"

5Then a voice came from the throne, saying:
"Praise our God, all you who serve him
and all you who honor him, both small and
great!"

> **SIDELIGHT:** Bowing (Revelation 19:4) was a common greeting in Bible times. However, there was more variety than we have with handshakes. Depending on whom you were greeting, you could lightly nod your head or give a complete, bend-at-the-waist, face-down bow.

6Then I heard what sounded like a great many
people, like the noise of flooding water, and like
the noise of loud thunder. The people were saying:
"Hallelujah!
Our Lord God, the Almighty, rules.
7Let us rejoice and be happy
and give God glory,
because the wedding of the Lamb has come,
and the Lamb's bride has made herself
ready.
8Fine linen, bright and clean, was given to her
to wear."
(The fine linen means the good things done by
God's holy people.)
9And the angel said to me, "Write this: Happy
are those who have been invited to the wedding
meal of the Lamb!" And the angel said, "These
are the true words of God."
10Then I bowed down at the angel's feet to
worship him, but he said to me, "Do not worship
me! I am a servant like you and your brothers and
sisters who have the message of Jesus. Worship
God, because the message about Jesus is the spirit
that gives all prophecy."[d]

The Rider on the White Horse

11Then I saw heaven opened, and there before
me was a white horse. The rider on the horse is
called Faithful and True, and he is right when he
judges and makes war. 12His eyes are like burning
fire, and on his head are many crowns. He has a
name written on him, which no one but himself
knows. 13He is dressed in a robe dipped in blood,
and his name is the Word of God. 14The armies
of heaven, dressed in fine linen, white and clean,
were following him on white horses. 15Out of the
rider's mouth comes a sharp sword that he will
use to defeat the nations, and he will rule them
with a rod of iron. He will crush out the wine in
the winepress[d] of the terrible anger of God the
Almighty. 16On his robe and on his upper leg was
written this name: KING OF KINGS AND LORD OF
LORDS.
17Then I saw an angel standing in the sun, and
he called with a loud voice to all the birds flying
in the sky: "Come and gather together for the
great feast of God 18so that you can eat the bodies
of kings, generals, mighty people, horses and their
riders, and the bodies of all people — free, slave,
small, and great."
19Then I saw the beast and the kings of the
earth. Their armies were gathered together to
make war against the rider on the horse and his
army. 20But the beast was captured and with him
the false prophet[d] who did the miracles[d] for the
beast. The false prophet had used these miracles
to trick those who had the mark of the beast and
worshiped his idol. The false prophet and the
beast were thrown alive into the lake of fire that
burns with sulfur. 21And their armies were killed
with the sword that came out of the mouth of the
rider on the horse, and all the birds ate the bodies
until they were full.

The Thousand Years

20 I saw an angel coming down from
heaven. He had the key to the bottomless pit and a large chain in his hand. 2The angel
grabbed the dragon, that old snake who is the
devil and Satan, and tied him up for a thousand
years. 3Then he threw him into the bottomless
pit, closed it, and locked it over him. The angel
did this so he could not trick the people of the
earth anymore until the thousand years were
ended. After a thousand years he must be set free
for a short time.
4Then I saw some thrones and people sitting on
them who had been given the power to judge.
And I saw the souls of those who had been killed
because they were faithful to the message of Jesus
and the message from God. They had not worshiped the beast or his idol, and they had not received the mark of the beast on their foreheads or
on their hands. They came back to life and ruled
with Christ for a thousand years. 5(The others that
were dead did not live again until the thousand
years were ended.) This is the first raising of the
dead. 6Happy and holy are those who share in this
first raising of the dead. The second death has no
power over them. They will be priests for God
and for Christ and will rule with him for a thousand years.
7When the thousand years are over, Satan will
be set free from his prison. 8Then he will go out
to trick the nations in all the earth — Gog and Magog — to gather them for battle. There are so
many people they will be like sand on the seashore. 9And Satan's army marched across the
earth and gathered around the camp of God's people and the city God loves. But fire came down

from heaven and burned them up. 10And Satan,
who tricked them, was thrown into the lake of
burning sulfur with the beast and the false
prophet.[d] There they will be punished day and
night forever and ever.

People of the World Are Judged

11Then I saw a great white throne and the One
who was sitting on it. Earth and sky ran away
from him and disappeared. 12And I saw the dead,
great and small, standing before the throne. Then
books were opened, and the book of life was
opened. The dead were judged by what they had
done, which was written in the books. 13The sea
gave up the dead who were in it, and Death and
Hades[n] gave up the dead who were in them.
Each person was judged by what he had done.
14And Death and Hades were thrown into the
lake of fire. The lake of fire is the second death.
15And anyone whose name was not found written
in the book of life was thrown into the lake of fire.

The New Jerusalem

21 Then I saw a new heaven and a new
earth. The first heaven and the first earth
had disappeared, and there was no sea anymore.
2And I saw the holy city, the new Jerusalem,[n]
coming down out of heaven from God. It was prepared like a bride dressed for her husband. 3And
I heard a loud voice from the throne, saying,
"Now God's presence is with people, and he will
live with them, and they will be his people. God
himself will be with them and will be their God.
4He will wipe away every tear from their eyes,
and there will be no more death, sadness, crying,
or pain, because all the old ways are gone."

SIDELIGHT: To dress the bride (Revelation 21:2) in Bible times was about as expensive as it can be today. The bride's face was made up to look glossy and shiny. Her hair was braided with gold and pearls. She was dressed in inherited family treasures. People borrowed what they couldn't buy.

5The One who was sitting on the throne said,
"Look! I am making everything new!" Then he
said, "Write this, because these words are true
and can be trusted."

Hades The place of the dead.
new Jerusalem The spiritual city where God's people live with him.

DEATH

Fear of Dying

"Thank you for flying with us," crackled the flight attendant's voice over the intercom after the jet landed. "And we encourage you to be extra careful on the most dangerous part of your journey: driving to your final destination in a car."

Many people fear flying, yet the odds of dying in a commercial airplane crash are only about 1 in 800,000. You're more likely to die by choking on food than in a plane crash.

In fact, all of the following are more dangerous than flying, based on the number of fatalities for each: car accidents, falls, fires and burns, drownings, shootings, poisonings.

Many people fear the way they will die more than they fear death itself. The Bible, however, promises Christians that God has overcome death. **Revelation 21:1–6** offers a hopeful description of life with God beyond death.

- What does this picture of heaven say to people's many fears about dying?
- How does the passage speak to your own fears about death?

CONSIDER...

- selecting a story about death from the newspaper and using it to discuss your feelings about death with a friend or trusted adult.
- imagining what someone who has died might be experiencing in heaven. Thank God for his gift of eternal life that overcomes death.

FOR MORE, SEE...

- Psalm 23 (p. 495)
- Luke 23:32–43 (p. 1053)
- 1 Corinthians 15:12–23 (p. 1187)

6The One on the throne said to me, "It is finished. I am the Alpha and the Omega,[n] the Beginning and the End. I will give free water from
the spring of the water of life to anyone who is
thirsty. 7Those who win the victory will receive
this, and I will be their God, and they will be my
children. 8But cowards, those who refuse to believe, who do evil things, who kill, who sin sexually, who do evil magic, who worship idols, and
who tell lies—all these will have a place in the
lake of burning sulfur. This is the second death."
9Then one of the seven angels who had the
seven bowls full of the seven last troubles came
to me, saying, "Come with me, and I will show
you the bride, the wife of the Lamb." 10And the
angel carried me away by the Spirit[d] to a very
large and high mountain. He showed me the holy
city, Jerusalem, coming down out of heaven from
God. 11It was shining with the glory of God and
was bright like a very expensive jewel, like a jasper, clear as crystal. 12The city had a great high
wall with twelve gates with twelve angels at the
gates, and on each gate was written the name of
one of the twelve tribes[d] of Israel. 13There were
three gates on the east, three on the north, three
on the south, and three on the west. 14The walls
of the city were built on twelve foundation
stones, and on the stones were written the names
of the twelve apostles[d] of the Lamb.
15The angel who talked with me had a measuring rod made of gold to measure the city, its gates,
and its wall. 16The city was built in a square, and
its length was equal to its width. The angel measured the city with the rod. The city was twelve
thousand stadia[n] long, twelve thousand stadia
wide, and twelve thousand stadia high. 17The angel also measured the wall. It was one hundred
forty-four cubits[n] high, by human measurements, which the angel was using. 18The wall was
made of jasper, and the city was made of pure
gold, as pure as glass. 19The foundation stones of
the city walls were decorated with every kind of
jewel. The first foundation was jasper, the second
was sapphire, the third was chalcedony, the
fourth was emerald, 20the fifth was onyx, the
sixth was carnelian, the seventh was chrysolite,
the eighth was beryl, the ninth was topaz, the
tenth was chrysoprase, the eleventh was jacinth,
and the twelfth was amethyst. 21The twelve gates
were twelve pearls, each gate having been made
from a single pearl. And the street of the city was
made of pure gold as clear as glass.
22I did not see a temple in the city, because the
Lord God Almighty and the Lamb are the city's
temple. 23The city does not need the sun or the
moon to shine on it, because the glory of God is
its light, and the Lamb is the city's lamp. 24By its
light the people of the world will walk, and the
kings of the earth will bring their glory into it.
25The city's gates will never be shut on any day,
because there is no night there. 26The glory and
the honor of the nations will be brought into it.
27Nothing unclean[d] and no one who does shameful things or tells lies will ever go into it. Only
those whose names are written in the Lamb's
book of life will enter the city.

22

Then the angel showed me the river of
the water of life. It was shining like crystal and was flowing from the throne of God and
of the Lamb 2down the middle of the street of the
city. The tree of life was on each side of the river.
It produces fruit twelve times a year, once each
month. The leaves of the tree are for the healing
of all the nations. 3Nothing that God judges guilty
will be in that city. The throne of God and of the
Lamb will be there, and God's servants will worship him. 4They will see his face, and his name
will be written on their foreheads. 5There will
never be night again. They will not need the light
of a lamp or the light of the sun, because the Lord
God will give them light. And they will rule as
kings forever and ever.
6The angel said to me, "These words can be
trusted and are true." The Lord, the God of the
spirits of the prophets,[d] sent his angel to show his
servants the things that must happen soon.
7"Listen! I am coming soon! Happy is the one
who obeys the words of prophecy in this book."
8I, John, am the one who heard and saw these
things. When I heard and saw them, I bowed
down to worship at the feet of the angel who
showed these things to me. 9But the angel said to
me, "Do not worship me! I am a servant like you,
your brothers the prophets, and all those who
obey the words in this book. Worship God!"
10Then the angel told me, "Do not keep secret
the words of prophecy in this book, because the
time is near for all this to happen. 11Let whoever
is doing evil continue to do evil. Let whoever is
unclean continue to be unclean. Let whoever
is doing right continue to do right. Let whoever is holy continue to be holy."
12"Listen! I am coming soon! I will bring my
reward with me, and I will repay each one of you
for what you have done. 13I am the Alpha and the
Omega,[n] the First and the Last, the Beginning
and the End.
14"Happy are those who wash their robes[n] so

Alpha and the Omega The first and last letters of the Greek alphabet. This means "the beginning and the end."
stadia One stadion was a distance of about two hundred yards; about one-eighth of a Roman mile.
cubits A cubit is about half a yard, the length from the elbow to the tip of the little finger.
wash their robes This means they believed in Jesus so that their sins could be forgiven by Christ's blood.

that they will receive the right to eat the fruit from
the tree of life and may go through the gates into
the city. 15Outside the city are the evil people,
those who do evil magic, who sin sexually, who
murder, who worship idols, and who love lies and
tell lies.
16"I, Jesus, have sent my angel to tell you these
things for the churches. I am the descendant[d]
from the family of David, and I am the bright
morning star."
17The Spirit[d] and the bride say, "Come!" Let
the one who hears this say, "Come!" Let whoever
is thirsty come; whoever wishes may have the
water of life as a free gift.
18I warn everyone who hears the words of the
prophecy of this book: If anyone adds anything to
these words, God will add to that person the disasters written about in this book. 19And if anyone
takes away from the words of this book of prophecy, God will take away that one's share of the
tree of life and of the holy city, which are written
about in this book.
20Jesus, the One who says these things are true,
says, "Yes, I am coming soon."

Amen. Come, Lord Jesus!

21The grace of the Lord Jesus be with all.
Amen.

ETERNAL LIFE

A Bit of Heaven

Three hundred teenage tourists gathered in the Swiss Alps, 7,100 feet above sea level. Rising even higher on one side were craggy, snow-capped peaks. A huge glacier stretched out on the other side, seemingly unaffected by the warm July day.

The group gathered for outdoor worship, which began with a trio of alpine horns echoing hymns across the valley. The minister shared the Good News of Christ. Then voices joined together to close the service with familiar choruses of praise to God.

The day passed quickly, filled with hugs, songs, shouts of pleasure, helping hands, huge smiles, and incredible sights. As the teenagers waited to return to Grindelwald on Europe's longest chair lift, several girls talked about the experience.

"I hope heaven's like this," said one of the girls.

"Heaven's going to be even better!" said another.

God's promise of eternal life in heaven is even better! Read the promise in **Revelation 22:12–21**.

- What do you think made the girls think of heaven during their outing in Switzerland? How do you think the mountain experience compares to heaven itself?
- What difference does God's promise of eternal life make in your everyday living?

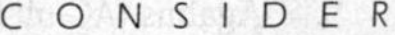

- remembering a time when you felt overwhelmed by nature's majesty as a reminder of God's greatness.
- asking yourself what you need to do to respond to the invitation in verse 17: "Let whoever is thirsty come; whoever wishes may have the water of life as a free gift."

FOR MORE, SEE . . .

- Psalm 16:9–11 (p. 489)
- Matthew 19:16–30 (p. 942)
- John 4:5–42 (p. 1063)

Dictionary

A

Aaron (AIR-ohn) *older brother of Moses.*
- before the king of Egypt, Exodus 4:14-16; 5:1-5; 7:1-2
- death of, Numbers 20:22-29

Abba (AB-uh) *word for "father" in Aramaic.*
- Jesus called God "Abba," Mark 14:36
- we can call God "Abba," Romans 8:15; Galatians 4:6

Abednego (a-BED-nee-go) *one of the three friends of Daniel whom God protected from the fiery furnace.*
- refused the king of Babylon's food, Daniel 1:3-17
- thrown into the fiery furnace, Daniel 3

Abel (AY-bul) *the second son of Adam and Eve.*
- born to Adam and Eve, Genesis 4:2
- approved by God, Genesis 4:3-4; Hebrews 11:4
- murdered by Cain, Genesis 4:8; 1 John 3:12

Abib (ah-BEEB) *first month of the Jewish calendar, about the time of year as our March or April; also called "Nisan"; means "young ears of grain."*
- the time the Israelites left Egypt, Exodus 13:3-4
- the time for the Feast of Unleavened Bread, Exodus 23:15; 34:18

Abigail, sister of David (AB-eh-gale) 1 Chronicles 2:13-17

Abigail, wife of Nabal
- brought food to David, 1 Samuel 25:14-35
- became David's wife, 1 Samuel 25:36-42

Abijah, king of Judah (a-BY-jah) 1 Kings 15:1-8; 2 Chronicles 13:1–14:1

Abijah, son of Jeroboam
- death of, 1 Kings 14:1-18

Abijah, son of Samuel, 1 Samuel 8:1-3

ability
- given by God, 2 Corinthians 3:5-6
- through Christ, Philippians 4:13
- differing abilities, 1 Corinthians 12:7-11

Abimelech, king of Gerar (a-BIM-eh-lek)
- tried to take Sarah as his wife, Genesis 20

Abimelech, king of the Philistines
- tried to take Rebekah as his wife, Genesis 26:6-11

Abimelech, son of Gideon
- birth of, Judges 8:29-31
- murdered his brothers, Judges 9:1-6
- defeated the people of Shechem, Judges 9:22-45
- burned the Tower of Shechem, Judges 9:46-49
- death of, Judges 9:50-55

Abishai (a-BISH-eye) *nephew of King David.*
- served in David's army, 2 Samuel 23:18-19; 1 Chronicles 18:12-13
- saved David's life, 2 Samuel 21:15-17

Abner (AB-nur) *commander of Saul's army.*
- at Goliath's defeat, 1 Samuel 17:55-57
- made Ish-Bosheth king of Israel, 2 Samuel 2:8-10
- later loyal to David, 2 Samuel 3:6-21
- killed by Joab, 2 Samuel 3:22-27

Abraham (AY-bra-ham) *father of the Jewish nation.*
- called from Ur by God, Genesis 12:1-4
- lied about Sarai, Genesis 12:10-20
- separated from Lot, Genesis 13
- God's agreement with, Genesis 15; 17
- name changed, Genesis 17:3-6
- father of Isaac, Genesis 21:1-7
- offered Isaac as a sacrifice, Genesis 22:1-19
- father of the faithful, Romans 4
- God's friend, James 2:23

Absalom (AB-sah-lum) *one of David's sons.*
- turned against David, 2 Samuel 15–18:8
- killed by Joab, 2 Samuel 18:9-15

abstain (ab-STAIN) *to keep from doing something.*
- from food offered to idols, Acts 15:20
- from evil, 1 Thessalonians 5:22
- from lust, 1 Peter 2:11

abyss (uh-BISS) See "bottomless pit."

accept
- a prophet not accepted, Luke 4:24
- accepted by God, Acts 10:35; 15:7-8; Romans 14:3
- each other, Romans 14:1; 15:7
- Jesus, John 12:48

accuse
- Jesus accused by the Jews, Matthew 27:12-13; Mark 15:3; Luke 6:7
- Paul accused by the Jews, Acts 23:27-29; 26:7
- the Devil, as the accuser, Revelation 12:10

Achaia (a-KA-yuh) See "Greece."

Achan (AY-can) *an Israelite who disobeyed God during the battle of Jericho, Joshua 7*

Achish (AY-kish) *king of the Philistine city of Gath.*
- David pretends to be insane, 1 Samuel 21:10-15
- David in his army, 1 Samuel 27; 29

actions
- judged by, Proverbs 20:11; Matthew 11:19; Galatians 6:4
- of love, 1 John 3:18
- of goodness, Matthew 5:16

Adam (AD-um) *the first man.*
- created by God, Genesis 1:26–2:25
- disobeyed God, Genesis 3
- compared to Christ, 1 Corinthians 15:21-22,45-49

adder, *a poisonous snake.* See "snake."

Adonijah (ad-oh-NY-jah) *David's fourth son.*
- son of Haggith, 2 Samuel 3:4
- tried to become king, 1 Kings 1
- killed by Solomon, 1 Kings 2:12-25

Adoni-Zedek (a-DOH-ny-ZEE-dek) *an Amorite king of Jerusalem.*
- defeated by Joshua, Joshua 10:1-28

Adullam (a-DOO-lum) *a city about thirteen miles from Bethlehem.*
- David hid in a cave there, 2 Samuel 23:13

adultery (ah-DUL-ter-ee) *breaking a marriage promise by having sexual relations with someone other than your husband or wife.*
- "You must not be guilty of adultery," Exodus 20:14
- Christ teaches about, Matthew 5:27-32; Luke 16:18
- woman caught in adultery, John 8:1-11

advice
- given by Ahithophel, 2 Samuel 15:30–17:23
- given to Rehoboam, 1 Kings 12:1-15
- teachings about, Proverbs 11:14; 12:5,15; 19:20

Agabus (AG-uh-bus) *a Christian prophet.*
- warned the people, Acts 11:27-30
- warned Paul about going to Jerusalem, Acts 21:10-11

Agag (AY-gag) *king of the Amalekites.*
- captured by Saul, 1 Samuel 15

agreement *a contract, promise, or covenant.*
- with Noah, Genesis 9:1-17
- with Abraham, Genesis 15; 17:1-14
- Ark of the Agreement, Exodus 25:10-22; 1 Samuel 4–5; 2 Samuel 6:1-15
- with the Israelites, Exodus 19:3-8,24; Deuteronomy 29
- new agreement, 2 Corinthians 2:12–3:18
- difference between the old and new agreements, Hebrews 8–10

Agrippa (uh-GRIP-pah) See "Herod Agrippa."

Ahab (AY-hab) *evil king of Israel who was married to Jezebel.*
- worshiped Baal, 1 Kings 16:29-33
- had Naboth killed, 1 Kings 21
- death of, 1 Kings 22:1-40

Ahasuerus (ah-HAZ-oo-EE-rus) *Hebrew word for the Greek name Xerxes.* See "Xerxes."

Ahaz, *twelfth king of Judah,* 2 Kings 16; 2 Chronicles 28

Ahaziah, king of Judah (ay-ha-ZY-uh) 2 Chronicles 22:1-9

Ahaziah, son of Ahab
- king of Israel, 1 Kings 22:40-53

Ahijah, great-grandson of Eli (a-HY-jah) 1 Samuel 14:1-23

Ahijah, the prophet
- told Jeroboam the kingdom would be divided, 1 Kings 11:29-39
- told that Jeroboam's son would die, 1 Kings 14:1-18

Ahimelech, the high priest (a-HIM-eh-lek)
- helped David, 1 Samuel 21:1-9

Ahimelech, the Hittite warrior, 1 Samuel 26:6

Ahithophel (a-HITH-oh-fel) *gave advice to King David.*
- helped Absalom rebel against David, 1 Samuel 15:31; 16:15–17:23

Ai (AY-eye) *a city completely destroyed by the Israelites,* Joshua 7–8:28

Akeldama (a-KEL-dah-mah) *field bought with the money Judas received for betraying Jesus,* Matthew 27:3-10; Acts 1:18-19

alabaster (AL-a-bass-ter) *light-colored stone with streaks or stripes through it,* Matthew 26:7; Mark 14:3; Luke 7:37

alamoth (AL-a-moth) *a musical word, which may mean "like a flute" or "high-pitched,"* Psalm 46

All-Powerful, *a name for God,* 1 Chronicles 11:9; Psalm 24:10; Isaiah 6:3-5; Malachi 3:1-17

Almighty, *a name for God.*
- "I am God Almighty," Genesis 17:1
- "I appeared to Abraham . . . by the name, God Almighty," Exodus 6:3
- "Holy, holy, holy is the Lord God Almighty," Revelation 4:8

almond
- design of the lampstands in Holy Tent, Exodus 25:31-36
- Aaron's stick produced, Numbers 17:8

aloes (AL-ohs) *oils from sweet-smelling sap of certain trees; used to make perfume and medicine and to prepare bodies for burial,* Psalm 45:8; Proverbs 7:17
- used to prepare Jesus' body for burial, John 19:39

Alpha and Omega (AL-fah and oh-MAY-guh) *the first and last letters of the Greek alphabet, like our A and Z.*
- used to describe Jesus, Revelation 1:8; 21:6; 22:13

altar (ALL-ter) *a place where sacrifices, gifts, or prayers were offered to a god.*
- built by Noah, Genesis 8:20
- built by Abraham, Genesis 22:9
- for burnt offerings, Exodus 27:1-8
- for incense, Exodus 30:1-10
- corners of, Exodus 27:2; 30:10; 1 Kings 1:50
- for the Temple, 2 Chronicles 4:1

Amalekites (AM-a-lah-kites) *fierce, fighting people who descended from Esau; they were enemies of Israel and were finally wiped out during the time of Hezekiah.*
- enemies of Israel, Exodus 17:8-16; 1 Samuel 15
- destroyed by King Hezekiah, 1 Chronicles 4:43

Amasa (AM-a-sa) *leader of Absalom's army when he rebelled against David,* 2 Samuel 17:25
- made leader of David's army, 2 Samuel 19:13
- killed by Joab, 2 Samuel 20:1-10

Amaziah (am-ah-ZY-uh) *the ninth king of Judah,* 2 Kings 14; 2 Chronicles 25

amen (AY-MEN or AH-MEN) *Hebrew word for "that is right,"* 1 Chronicles 16:36; Psalm 106:48; 1 Corinthians 14:16
- "Amen. Come, Lord Jesus!" Revelation 22:20

Ammonites (AM-on-ites) *descendants of Lot's son, Ben-Ammi,* Genesis 19:36-38
- enemies of Israel, Judges 10:6–11:33; 1 Samuel 11; 2 Samuel 10:1-14
- worshiped Molech, 1 Kings 11:5

Amon (AM-on) *the fifteenth king of Judah,* 2 Kings 21:18-26; 2 Chronicles 33:20-25
- an ancestor of Jesus, Matthew 1:10

Amorites (AM-or-ites) *a group of wicked people who worshiped false gods and lived in Canaan when the Israelites arrived.*
- defeated by Israel, Numbers 21:21-32; Joshua 10:1–11:14

Amos (AY-mos) *a prophet who warned Israel of God's punishment for disobedience.*
- a shepherd from Tekoa, Amos 1:1
- his visions, Amos 7–9:10

Anak/Anakites (A-nak/AN-uh-kites) *a group of large, fighting people who lived in Canaan when the Israelites arrived.*
- feared by the twelve spies, Numbers 13:22,28,33; Deuteronomy 1:26-28
- defeated by Joshua, Joshua 11:21-23

Ananias, husband of Sapphira (an-uh-NY-us)
- killed for lying to the Holy Spirit, Acts 5:1-6

Ananias, a Christian in Damascus
- helped Saul of Tarsus, Acts 9:10-19; 22:12-16

Ananias, the high priest
- at Paul's trial, Acts 23:1-5

Andrew, *a fisherman and brother of the apostle Peter.*
- chosen by Jesus to be an apostle, Mark 1:16-18; 3:13-19
- brought Peter to Jesus, John 1:40-42
- waited with the apostles in Jerusalem, Acts 1:13

angel (AIN-jel) *a heavenly being.*
- rescued Lot from Sodom, Genesis 19:1-22
- led Israel to Canaan, Exodus 23:20-23; 32:34
- announced Jesus' birth, Matthew 1:20-21; Luke 1:26-37; 2:8-15
- helped Jesus, Matthew 4:11; Luke 22:43
- helped the apostles, Acts 5:19-20; 12:6-10
- will bring judgment, Matthew 13:24-50; 24:31
- archangel, 1 Thessalonians 4:16; Jude 9
- less than Christ, Hebrews 1:4-14; 1 Peter 3:22
- rebellious angels, 2 Peter 2:4; Jude 6
- serving in heaven, Revelation 7–10

anger, *wrath.*
- of God toward people, John 3:36; Romans 1:18; 2:5-6; Colossians 3:5-6
- saved from God's anger by Christ, Romans 5:9; 1 Thessalonians 1:10; 5:9
- warnings against, Matthew 5:21-22; Ephesians 4:26,31; James 1:19-20

animal
- created by God, Genesis 1:20-25
- to be ruled by people, Genesis 1:26
- named by Adam, Genesis 2:19-20
- saved by Noah, Genesis 6:19-20
- clean, Leviticus 11:1-3,9; Deuteronomy 14:3-6
- unclean, Leviticus 11:4-8,10-12,26-44; Deuteronomy 14:7-8

Annas (AN-us) *a high priest of the Jews during Jesus' lifetime,* Luke 3:2; John 18:13
- questioned Peter and John, Acts 4:5-22

anoint (uh-NOINT) *to pour oil on.*
- to appoint a priest, Exodus 28:41; 40:13
- to appoint a king, 1 Samuel 10:1; 16:12-13; 2 Kings 9:6
- the Holy Tent, Numbers 7:1
- to heal sickness, Mark 6:13; James 5:14

Anti-Christ (AN-tee KRYST) See "enemy of Christ."

Antioch in Pisidia (AN-tee-ahk) *a small city in the country of Pisidia.*
- Paul preached there, Acts 13:14-15

Antioch in Syria, *third largest city in the Roman Empire.*
- Saul and Barnabus preached there, Acts 11:19-26
- followers first called "Christians" there, Acts 11:26
- Peter in Antioch, Galatians 2:11-12

• Paul preached there, Acts 13:14-15

Apollos (uh-POL-us) *an educated Jew from Alexandria.*
• taught by Aquila and Priscilla, Acts 18:24-28
• preached to the Corinthians, 1 Corinthians 1:12; 3:4-6
• friend of Paul, Titus 3:13

apostle (uh-POS-'l) *someone who is sent off. Jesus chose these twelve special followers and sent them to tell the Good News about him to the whole world.*
• twelve chosen by Jesus, Mark 3:14-19
• Matthias chosen, Acts 1:12-26
• Paul chosen, 1 Corinthians 15:3-11; 2 Corinthians 12:11-12
• duties and powers of, Luke 9:1-6; Acts 5:12-16; 8:18
• leaders of the church, Acts 15; 16:4; 1 Corinthians 12:28
• false apostles, 2 Corinthians 11:13; Revelation 2:2

appearance
• not to judge by, 1 Samuel 16:7; John 7:24
• deceiving, Matthew 23:27-28
• of Jesus, Isaiah 53:2; Philippians 2:7

Aquila (AK-wi-lah) *a Jewish Christian from Rome.*
• friend of Paul, Acts 18:2-3; Romans 16:3-5
• taught Apollos, Acts 18:24-28

Arabah (AIR-uh-bah) *the Hebrew word for the Jordan Valley.* See "Jordan Valley."

Arabah, Sea of, See "Dead Sea."

Aram (AIR-um) *a country northeast of Israel,* 1 Kings 11:25; 15:18; 2 Kings 5:1; Isaiah 7:1
• known as "Syria" in the New Testament, Matthew 4:24; Acts 15:23

Aramaic (AIR-uh-MAY-ik) *the language of the people in the nation of Aram.*
• common language of the Jews, 2 Kings 18:26; John 19:13,17,20; Acts 21:40

Ararat (AIR-uh-rat) *a group of mountains located in what is now Turkey and the Soviet Union.*
• Noah's boat landed there, Genesis 8:14

Araunah (a-RAW-nah) *a Jebusite who was also called Ornan.*
• sold his threshing floor to King David, 2 Samuel 24:15-25; 1 Chronicles 21:18-28

archangel (ark-AIN-jel) *the leader of God's angels,* 1 Thessalonians 4:16; Jude 9

Areopagus (AI R-ee-OP-uh-gus) *a council or group of important leaders in Athens.*
• Paul spoke there, Acts 17:16-34

argue
• the apostles argued, Mark 9:33-37; Luke 9:46-48
• avoid arguments, Philippians 2:14; 2 Timothy 2:23-26; Titus 3:9
• Michael argued with the devil, Jude 9

Aristarchus (air-i-STAR-kus) *a man from Thessalonica who often traveled with Paul,* Acts 27:2; Colossians 4:10; Philemon 24

ark, Noah's, *the huge boat that Noah built to save his family from the flood God sent to cover the earth.* See "boat."

Ark of the Agreement, *a special box made of acacia wood and gold. Inside were the stone tablets on which the Ten Commandments were written. Later, a pot of manna and Aaron's walking stick were also put into the Ark. It was to remind the people of Israel of God's promise to be with them.*
• building of, Exodus 25:10-22; 37:1-9
• crossing the Jordan River, Joshua 3:1-17
• captured by the Philistines, 1 Samuel 4–7:1
• touched by Uzzah, 2 Samuel 6:1-8; 1 Chronicles 13
• placed in the Temple, 2 Chronicles 5:2-10
• contents of, Hebrews 9:4-5

Ark of the Covenant, See "Ark of the Agreement."

armor
• of Saul, 1 Samuel 17:38-39; 31:9-10
• of God, Ephesians 6:10-17

arrest
• John the Baptist arrested, Matthew 14:3; Mark 6:17
• Jesus arrested, Matthew 26:50-57; Mark 14:44-50; John 18:1-14
• Peter arrested, Acts 12:1-4
• Paul arrested, Acts 28:17-20

Artaxerxes (ar-tah-ZERK-sees) *the title or name of Persian kings,* Ezra 4:7; Nehemiah 2:1
• his letter to Ezra, Ezra 7:11-26

Artemis (AR-tuh-mis) *a goddess that many Greeks worshiped,* Acts 19:23-41

Asa (AY-sah) *the third king of Judah,* 1 Kings 15:9-24; 2 Chronicles 14–16

Asaph (AY-saf) *a leader of singers when David was king,* 1 Chronicles 16:5,7; 25:1-2; 2 Chronicles 5:12
• songs of, Psalms 73–83

ascension (uh-SIN-shun) *lifted up; used to describe Jesus' return to heaven,* Acts 1:2-11; 2:32-33

ashamed
• of Jesus, Mark 8:38; Luke 9:26; 2 Timothy 1:8
• for suffering as a Christian, 1 Peter 4:16

Ashdod (ASH-dahd) *one of the five strong, walled cities of the Philistines; called Azotus in the New Testament.*
• Ark of the Agreement there, 1 Samuel 5:1-8
• later called "Azotus," Acts 8:40

Asherah (ah-SHIR-ah) *a Canaanite goddess thought to be the wife of the god Baal.*
• worshiped by Israelites, 1 Kings 14:14-15,22-23; 15:13
• worship forbidden, Exodus 34:13-14; Deuteronomy 16:21-22

Ashkelon (ASH-keh-lon) *one of the five important cities of the Philistines,* Judges 1:18; Zephaniah 2:4,7
• thirty of its men killed by Samson, Judges 14:19

Ashtoreth (ASH-toh-reth) *a goddess of the people of Assyria and Canaan. At times the Israelites forgot God and built idols to worship her.* Judges 2:13; 1 Samuel 7:3-4; 12:10
• worshiped by Solomon, 1 Kings 11:5,33

Asia (AY-zhuh) *the western part of the country now called "Turkey."*
• Paul preached there, Acts 19:10,26
• seven churches of, Revelation 1:4

assembly (a-SEM-blee) *a meeting; a group of people gathered for a purpose.*
• of the church, Hebrews 10:24-25
• conduct in, James 2:1-4

assurance (uh-SHURE-ans) *with confidence; without doubts.*
• about the gospel, 1 Thessalonians 1:5
• before God, Hebrews 10:22-23; 1 John 5:14-15
• faith as, Hebrews 11:1

Assyria (uh-SEER-ee-uh) *a powerful nation north and east of Israel.*
• enemy of Israel, 2 Kings 15:19-20; 17:3-6
• enemy of Judah, 2 Kings 18:13–19:36; Isaiah 36–37:37

Astarte (ah-STAR-tay) *another name for the goddess Ashtoreth.* See "Ashtoreth."

Athaliah (ath-uh-LY-uh) *the only woman who ruled over Judah,* 2 Kings 11; 2 Chronicles 22:10–23:21

Athens (ATH-enz) *the leading city of the country of Greece.*
• Paul preached there, Acts 17:16-34

atonement (uh-TONE-ment) *to remove or forgive sins.*
• through animal sacrifices, Exodus 30:10; Leviticus 17:11; Numbers 25:13
• through faith in the blood of Jesus' death, Romans 3:25; Hebrews 2:17; 9:22; 10:11-12

Atonement, Day of, See "Cleansing, Day of."

Augustus Caesar (aw-GUS-tus SEE-zer) *or Caesar Augustus, the first Roman emperor,* Luke 2:1

authority (uh-THAR-uh-tee) *power or right to control.*

- proper use of, Matthew 20:25-26; Luke 22:24-30; Titus 2:15
- respect for, Luke 20:20-26; Romans 13:1-7; 1 Timothy 2:2; 1 Peter 2:13-17; Hebrews 13:17
- Jesus' authority, Matthew 7:29; 9:6; Mark 11:27-33; Luke 5:24; John 5:19-29

B

Baal (BAY-el) *a god of the Canaanites; "Baal" was the common word for "master, lord." He was known as the son of Dagon, or the son of El, who was known as the father of the false gods.*
- worshiped by Israelites, Judges 2:10-11; Jeremiah 11:13
- Elijah defeated prophets of Baal, 1 Kings 18:1-40
- Baal worship destroyed by Jehu, 2 Kings 10:18-28

Baal-Zebub, See "Beelzebul."

Baasha (BAY-ah-shah) *the third king of Israel,* 1 Kings 15:27–16:7; 2 Chronicles 16:1-6; Jeremiah 41:9

Babel (BAY-bel) *a tower built to reach the sky,* Genesis 11:1-9

baby
- Moses as, Exodus 2:1-10
- Solomon determined mother of, 1 Kings 3:16-28
- Elizabeth's, Luke 1:39-44
- Jesus as, Luke 2:6-21
- as a symbol of new Christians, 1 Peter 2:2

Babylon (BAB-uh-lun) *city on the Euphrates River; capital of Babylonia.*
- captives in Babylon, Psalm 137:1; Jeremiah 29:10
- destruction predicted, Jeremiah 51:36-37
- as a symbol of evil, Revelation 14:8; 17:5

Babylonians (bab-e-LONE-e-unz) *people of the country Babylonia.* Also called "Chaldeans."
- capture warned by Jeremiah, Jeremiah 21; 25
- captured the people of Judah, 2 Kings 20:12-18; 24–25; Jeremiah 39:1-10
- Daniel in Babylon, Daniel 1–4
- released Israelite captives, Ezra 2

Balaam (BAY-lum) *a prophet from Midian.*
- asked by Balak to prophesy, Numbers 22–24; 2 Peter 2:15-16; Revelation 2:14
- death of, Numbers 31:8

balm, *oil from a plant used as medicine,* Genesis 37:25; Jeremiah 8:22; 51:8; Ezekiel 27:17

Baptist, John the (BAP-tist) *someone who baptizes. John, a relative of Jesus, was called this because he baptized many people.* Matthew 3:1-6
- condemned Pharisees and Sadducees, Matthew 3:7-10
- preached about Jesus, Matthew 3:11-12
- baptized Jesus, Matthew 3:13-17
- in prison, Matthew 11:1-6; Luke 7:18-23
- described by Jesus, Matthew 11:7-12; 17:10-13; Luke 7:24-28
- death of, Matthew 14:1-12; Mark 6:14-29
- baptism of, Matthew 21:25-26; Acts 10:37; 18:25; 19:3-4
- Jesus mistaken for, Matthew 16:13-14; Mark 8:27-28; Luke 9:18-19

baptism (BAP-tiz-em) *dipping or immersing.*
- by John, Matthew 3:6; Mark 1:4; Luke 3; Acts 19:3
- of Jesus, Matthew 3:13-17
- examples of, Acts 2:38-41; 8:36-38; 16:15,33
- with fire, Matthew 3:11; Luke 3:16
- with the Holy Spirit, Mark 1:8; Acts 1:5; 11:16

Barabbas (bah-RAB-us) *a robber who had murdered someone in Jerusalem.* He was freed instead of Jesus. Matthew 27:15-26; Mark 15:6-11

Barak (BAY-rak) *a leader of Israel's army when Deborah was judge,* Judges 4–5

Bar-Jesus, See "Elymas."

barley (BAR-lee) *a type of grain.*
- harvest of, Ruth 1:22; 2:17,23; 2 Samuel 21:9
- loaves of, John 6:9-13

barn
- storing in, Matthew 6:26
- rich man's, Luke 12:16-20

Barnabas (BAR-nah-bus) *an encourager who helped the apostles,* Acts 4:36; 11:23
- worked with Paul, Acts 11:26; 13–15
- influenced by hypocrites, Galatians 2:13

Bartholomew (bar-THOL-oh-mew) *one of the twelve apostles of Jesus,* Matthew 10:3; Mark 3:18; Luke 6:14; Acts 1:13

Bartimaeus (bar-teh-MAY-us) *a blind man who was healed by Jesus,* Mark 10:46-52

Baruch (BAH-rook) *a friend of the prophet Jeremiah,* Jeremiah 36

Bathsheba (bath-SHE-buh) *the mother of Solomon and wife of David,* 2 Samuel 11–12:25; 1 Kings 1–2; 22

beatitude (bee-A-ti-tyood) *blessed or happy; often used for Jesus' teaching in Matthew 5:3-12; Luke 6:20-22.*

Beelzebul (bee-EL-ze-bull) *false god of the Philistines; in the New Testament it often refers to the devil.*
- name for Satan, Matthew 12:24; Mark 3:22; Luke 11:15

Beersheba (beer-SHE-buh) *the town farthest south in the land of Judah,* 2 Samuel 3:10; 2 Chronicles 30:5
- Abraham made an agreement there, Genesis 21:14-34

beg
- Jesus begged by demons, Matthew 8:28-34; Mark 5:1-13; Luke 8:26-33
- Jesus begged by people, Matthew 14:36; Mark 7:24-26,32; 8:22

beggar
- Bartimaeus, Mark 10:46-52
- Lazarus, Luke 16:19-31
- at Beautiful Gate, Acts 3:1-10
- man born blind, John 9:1-12

Bel, a false god of the Babylonians, Jeremiah 50:2; 51:44

believe
- in God, Acts 16:34; Romans 4:24
- in Jesus, Matthew 18:6; John 12:44; 14:11-12; 1 John 5:10
- in the Good News, Mark 1:15; 11:24; Acts 15:7
- rewards of believing, Matthew 21:22; John 20:31; 1 Thessalonians 2:13
- a lie, 2 Thessalonians 2:11

believers (be-LEE-vers) *the followers of Jesus,* John 3:16; Acts 4:32; 5:14; Galatians 6:10

Belshazzar (bell-SHAZ-er) *a ruler of Babylon,* Daniel 5

Belteshazzar (BELL-teh-SHAZ-er) *the Babylonian name that Nebuchadnezzar gave to Daniel,* Daniel 4:8; 5:12

Benaiah (bee-NAY-uh) *the captain of David's bodyguard,* 2 Samuel 23:20-23
- commander of Solomon's army, 1 Kings 2:34-35

Ben-Hadad (ben-HAY-dad) *two or three Syrian kings who often fought against Israel,* 1 Kings 20:1-34; 2 Kings 6:24–8:15

Benjamin (BEN-jah-min) *the youngest son of Jacob and Rachel.*
- birth of, Genesis 35:16-20
- reunited with Joseph, Genesis 42–45

Bernice (bur-NY-see) *the oldest daughter of Herod Agrippa I,* Acts 25:13–26:32

Bethany (BETH-uh-nee) *a small town about two miles from Jerusalem.*
- home of Mary, Martha, and Lazarus, John 11:1; 12:1
- home of Simon, Mark 14:3

Bethel (BETH-el) *a town about twelve miles north of Jerusalem.*
- named by Jacob, Genesis 28:10-19
- Jeroboam built idols there, 1 Kings 12:26-33

Bethesda (be-THES-da) See "Bethzatha, pool of."
Bethlehem (BETH-le-hem) *a small town five miles from Jerusalem.*
- hometown of King David, 1 Samuel 16:1,13
- birthplace of Jesus, Matthew 2:1; Luke 2:15-17

Bethsaida (beth-SAY-ih-duh) *a city in Galilee and home of Peter, Andrew, and Philip,* John 1:44; 12:21
- rejected Jesus, Matthew 11:20-21; Luke 10:13

Bethzatha, pool of (beth-ZAY-tha) *a pool in Jerusalem near the Sheep Gate.*
- Jesus healed a man there, John 5:1-18

betray (be-TRAY) *to turn against.*
- families against each other, Mark 13:12-13
- Jesus betrayed, Matthew 26:20-25; Mark 14:18-46; John 13:2-30

birds
- created by God, Genesis 1:20-21
- saved by Noah, Genesis 6:19-20; 7:1-3
- unclean, Leviticus 11:13-19
- cared for by God, Matthew 6:25-27; Luke 12:24

birth
- spiritual birth, John 1:13; 3:3-8; 1 Peter 1:23

bishop, See "elder."
bitter
- water, Exodus 15:22-25; Numbers 5:18-27; Revelation 8:11
- herbs, Exodus 12:8

bitterness (BIT-er-nes) *sorrow or pain; anger or hatred.*
- warning against, Acts 8:23; Ephesians 4:31; James 3:14

blasphemy (BLAS-feh-mee) *saying things against God or not showing respect for God.*
- examples of, 1 Timothy 1:13; Revelation 13:6
- warnings against, Matthew 12:31-32; Mark 3:28-29
- Jesus accused of, Matthew 9:3; 26:65; Mark 2:6-7; John 10:36

blessing (BLES-ing) *a gift from God; asking God's favor on.*
- promised to Abraham, Genesis 12:1-3
- Isaac blessed Jacob, Genesis 27:1-41
- from God, Acts 3:25; Romans 10:12; 15:27; Hebrews 6:7
- by Jesus, Mark 10:16; Luke 24:50; John 1:16
- by each other, Luke 6:28; 1 Corinthians 4:12; 1 Peter 3:9

blind
- the blind healed, Matthew 9:27-31; 15:30; Mark 8:22-26; John 9
- Saul struck blind, Acts 9:8-9
- spiritually blind, Matthew 23:16-26; John 9:35-41; 2 Peter 1:5-9

blood, *sometimes used to mean "death."*
- water turned into, Exodus 7:14-24
- used in the Passover, Exodus 12:13-23
- not to be eaten, Leviticus 3:17; Deuteronomy 12:16; 1 Samuel 14:31-34
- of animal sacrifices, Leviticus 1; 3; 4; Hebrews 9:12-13; 10:4
- of Christ, Matthew 26:28; Romans 5:9; Hebrews 9:14; 1 John 1:7

boasting, See "bragging."
boat, *ark.*
- built by Noah, Genesis 6:11-21
- of the apostles, Matthew 4:21-22; John 21:3-11
- used by Jesus, Matthew 8:23; 13:2; 14:13-34

body
- made of dust, Genesis 2:7; 3:19
- health of, Proverbs 3:7-8; 4:20-22; 14:30
- attitudes toward, Matthew 6:25; Romans 6:13; Ephesians 5:29
- warnings against misuse, Romans 8:13; 1 Corinthians 6:18-20; 1 Thessalonians 4:5

body of Christ, *sometimes means Jesus' human body; also a way of describing Christians.*
- Christ's physical body, John 2:19-21; 19:38; Acts 2:31; 1 Corinthians 11:24; 1 Timothy 3:16; 1 Peter 3:18
- the Church as Christ's spiritual body, Romans 12:5; 1 Corinthians 12:12-31; Ephesians 1:23; 4:4; 5:23

bone
- "whose bones came from my bones," Genesis 2:23
- Ezekiel's vision of, Ezekiel 37:1-14
- none of Jesus' bones to be broken, John 19:36

book, *parchments, scroll.*
- Book of the Teachings, Deuteronomy 30:10; Joshua 1:8; 2 Chronicles 34:14-32; Ezra 8
- book of life, Philippians 4:3; Revelation 3:5; 13:8; 20:12; 21:27
- "Jesus did many other miracles. . .not written in this book." John 20:30
- "the whole world would not be big enough for all the books," John 21:25

bottomless pit, *the place where the devil and his demons live,* Luke 8:31; Revelation 9:1-11; 11:7; 17:8; 20:1-3
box of Scriptures, *small leather boxes that some Jews tied to their foreheads and left arms; also called "phylacteries" or "frontlets."*
- held the Law of Moses, Deuteronomy 6:6-8
- Jesus criticized misuse of, Matthew 23:5

bragging, *boasting.*
- warnings against, Proverbs 27:1; 2 Corinthians 10:12-18; James 4:16; Jude 16
- about the Lord, 1 Corinthians 1:31; 2 Corinthians 10:17; Galatians 6:14

bread, *the most important food in New Testament times; usually made of barley or wheat.*
- to feed 5,000 people, Matthew 14:13-21; Mark 6:30-44; Luke 9:10-17; John 6:1-13
- to feed 4,000 people, Matthew 15:32-39; Mark 8:1-10
- Jesus, the bread of life, John 6:25-59
- "A person does not live by eating only bread." Matthew 4:4; Luke 4:4
- "Give us the food we need for each day." Luke 11:3
- in the Lord's Supper, Luke 22:19; Acts 20:7; 1 Corinthians 10:16; 11:17-34

bread that shows we are in God's presence, *twelve loaves of bread that were kept on the table in the Holy Tent and later in the Temple; also called "Bread of the Presence" or "showbread,"* Leviticus 24:5-9
- eaten by David, Matthew 12:3-4; Mark 2:25-26; Luke 6:4

bride, Song of Solomon 4:8-12
- belongs to the bridegroom, John 3:29
- of Christ, Revelation 21:2,9

bridegroom
- sun compared to, Psalm 19:5
- Jesus compared to, Matthew 9:15; Mark 2:19-20; Luke 5:34
- Jesus' story of, Matthew 25:1-13
- at Jesus' first miracle, John 2:9

brother, *a family member; people from the same country; or Christians.*
- physical brothers, Proverbs 18:24; Matthew 19:29; Mark 12:18-23
- Jesus' brothers, Matthew 13:55; Mark 3:31; John 2:12; 7:3; Acts 1:14; 1 Corinthians 9:5
- spiritual brothers, Romans 8:29; 12:10; 1 Timothy 6:2; Hebrews 2:11; 1 Peter 2:17

burn
- sacrifices, Exodus 29:10-42; Leviticus 1–4
- incense, Exodus 30:7-8; Numbers 16:40; Jeremiah 48:35; Luke 1:9
- Jericho burned by Israelites, Joshua 6:24
- idols burned by Josiah, 2 Kings 23:4-20
- jealousy like a fire, Psalm 79:5

- chaff, Matthew 3:12; Luke 3:17
- lake of burning sulfur, Revelation 21:8

burnt offerings, *a whole animal sacrificed as a gift to God.*
- rules about, Leviticus 1; 6:8-13; Numbers 28–29
- less important than obedience, 1 Samuel 15:22; Psalm 51:16-19
- less important than love, Hosea 6:6; Mark 12:32-33

bury, Matthew 8:21-22; Luke 9:59-60
- Abraham buried Sarah, Genesis 23
- Jacob not to be buried in Egypt, Genesis 47:29-30; 50:1-14
- strangers, Matthew 27:7
- in baptism, Romans 6:4

C

Caesar (SEE-zer) *a famous Roman family; used as the title of the Roman emperors.*
- Augustus, Luke 2:1
- Tiberius, Luke 3:1; 20:22; John 19:12
- Claudius, Acts 11:28; 17:7; 18:2
- Nero, Acts 25:8; 27:24; Philippians 4:22

Caesarea (SES-uh-REE-uh) *a city on the Mediterranean Sea,* Acts 10:1; 21:8; 23:32

Caesarea Philippi (SES-uh-REE-uh fih-LIP-eye) *a city at the base of Mount Hermon,* Matthew 16:13; Mark 8:27

Caiaphas (KAY-uh-fus) *the Jewish high priest from A.D. 18 to 36.*
- plotted to kill Jesus, Matthew 26:3-5; John 11:45-54
- father-in-law to Annas, John 18:13
- at Jesus' trial, Matthew 26:57-67
- questioned Peter and John, Acts 4:5-22

Cain, *the first son of Adam and Eve.*
- killed his brother Abel, Genesis 4:1-24; 1 John 3:12

Caleb (KAY-leb) *one of the twelve men Moses sent to spy out Canaan.*
- explored Canaan, Numbers 13–14
- given the city of Hebron, Joshua 14:6-15

calf
- gold idol, Exodus 32:1-20; 1 Kings 12:26-30; 2 Kings 10:28-29
- fatted, Luke 15:23,27,30

camel, Genesis 37:25; 1 Samuel 30:17; 1 Kings 10:2
- Rebekah watered Abraham's camels, Genesis 24:10-20
- "easier for a camel to go through the eye of a needle," Matthew 19:24; Mark 10:25; Luke 18:25
- "swallows a camel," Matthew 23:24

Cana (KAY-nah) *a small town near the city of Nazareth in Galilee.*
- place of Jesus' first miracle, John 2:1-11

Canaan (KAY-nun) *land God promised to the Israelites,* Leviticus 25:38; Numbers 13:2; 33:51; Psalm 105:11

Capernaum (kay-PUR-nay-um) *a city on the western shore of Lake Galilee.*
- Jesus lived there, Matthew 4:12-13
- Jesus healed there, Matthew 8:5-13; Luke 4:31-41
- rejected Jesus, Matthew 11:23-24

capital, *the top of a pillar, usually decorated with beautiful carvings.*
- in the Temple, 1 Kings 7:16-20; 2 Kings 25:17

captive
- Israelites as captives, Deuteronomy 28:41; 2 Kings 25:21; Jeremiah 30:3

cassia (CASH-ah) *a pleasant-smelling powder. Its odor is like the bark of the cinnamon plant.* Exodus 30:23-24; Psalm 45:8

census (SIN-sus) *a count of the number of people who live in an area.*
- the Israelites counted, Numbers 1:2; 26:2
- ordered by David, 1 Chronicles 21:1-2
- ordered by Augustus Caesar, Luke 2:1-3

centurion (sin-TUR-ree-un) *a Roman army officer who commanded a hundred soldiers.*
- centurion's servant healed by Jesus, Matthew 8:5-13; Luke 7:1-10
- at Jesus' death, Matthew 27:54; Mark 15:39; Luke 23:47
- Cornelius, Acts 10

Cephas (SEE-fuss) *the Aramaic word for "rock"; in Greek, "Peter." Jesus gave this name to the apostle Simon.* John 1:42

chaff (CHAF) *the husk of a head of grain. Farmers would toss the grain and chaff into the air. Since the chaff is lighter, the wind would blow it away, and the good grain would fall back to the threshing floor.*
- sinners to be destroyed like chaff, Psalms 1:4; 35:5; Matthew 3:12; Luke 3:17

Chaldeans, See "Babylonians."

change of heart and life, *repentance.*
- commanded, Matthew 3:2; Mark 1:15; Luke 13:3; Acts 3:19; 17:30
- causes of, Romans 2:4; 2 Corinthians 7:9-10
- examples of, Matthew 12:41; Luke 11:32

chariot
- Egyptians' chariots destroyed, Exodus 14:5-28
- of fire, 2 Kings 2:11; 6:17
- Ethiopian taught in a chariot, Acts 8:27-31

Chemosh (KEE-mosh) *a god of the Moabites,* Jeremiah 48:13
- worshiped by Solomon, 1 Kings 11:7

cherubim (CHAIR-uh-bim) *heavenly beings with wings and the faces of men and animals.*
- guarded the garden of Eden, Genesis 3:24
- on the Ark of the Agreement, Exodus 25:18-22; 1 Kings 6:23-28
- seen by Ezekiel, Ezekiel 10:1-20

children
- of God, John 1:12; Romans 8:14; 1 Peter 1:14; 1 John 3:1-10
- training of, Ephesians 6:4; Colossians 3:21
- obedience of, Ephesians 6:1; Colossians 3:20; 1 Timothy 3:4
- become like, Matthew 18:3-4
- "Let the little children come to me," Matthew 19:14; Mark 10:14; Luke 18:16

chosen
- Israelites chosen by God, Deuteronomy 7:7-8; 9:4-5; Isaiah 44:1
- people chosen by God, Romans 8:33; Ephesians 1:4-5; 2 Timothy 2:10; 1 Peter 1:2; 2:9
- Jesus chosen by God, Hebrews 1:2; 1 Peter 2:4

Christ (KRYST) *anointed (or chosen) one. Jesus is the Christ, chosen by God to save people from their sins.*
- active in creation, John 1:1-3; Colossians 1:15-17; Hebrews 1:2,10
- equal with God, John 5:23; 10:30; Philippians 2:6; Colossians 2:9; Hebrews 1:3
- purpose of his death, Romans 5:6; 14:9; Hebrews 9:28; 1 Peter 3:18
- gives life, John 5:21; 6:35; 10:28; 11:25; 14:6
- as Savior, Matthew 1:21; John 12:47
- as judge, Matthew 10:32-33; 25:31-46; John 5:22; Acts 17:31
- living in Christians, John 17:23; Romans 8:10; 2 Corinthians 1:21; Ephesians 3:17
- his return, Acts 1:11; 1 Thessalonians 5:1-11; Hebrews 9:28; 2 Peter 3:10
- enemy of, 1 John 2:18,22; 4:3; 2 John 7

Christians (KRIS-chuns) *Christ's followers,* Acts 11:26; 26:28; 1 Peter 4:16

church
- established by Christ, Matthew 16:18
- Christ as its head, Ephesians 1:22; 5:23; Colossians 1:18

- Christ died for, Ephesians 5:25
- activities of, Acts 12:5; 1 Corinthians 14:26-40; 1 Timothy 5:16; Hebrews 10:24-25

circumcision (SIR-kum-SIH-zhun) *the cutting off of the foreskin of the male sex organ; each Jewish boy was circumcised on the eighth day after he was born; this was done as a sign of the agreement God had made with his people, the Jews.*
- commanded by God, Genesis 17; Leviticus 12:1-3
- spiritual circumcision, Philippians 3:3; Colossians 2:11

city of refuge, See "safety, city of."

Claudius (CLAW-dee-us) *the fourth Roman emperor. He ruled from A.D. 41 to 54.* Acts 11:28; 17:7; 18:2

clean, *the state of a person, animal, or action that is pleasing to God. Under the Teachings of Moses, unclean animals could not be eaten. People who were considered clean could live and serve God normally.*
- clean and unclean animals, Deuteronomy 14:1-21; Mark 7:19; Acts 10
- clean and unclean people, Leviticus 13
- spiritually clean, Ephesians 5:26; Hebrews 9:14; 2 Peter 1:9

Cleansing, Day of, *the Day of Atonement; the most special day of the year for the Israelites when the high priest could go into the Most Holy Place. Animals were sacrificed for the sins of the people as a sign that people were cleansed of their sins for a year.*
- rules about, Leviticus 23:26-32; 25:9

cloud
- Israel led by pillar of cloud, Exodus 13:21
- cloud as small as a fist, 1 Kings 18:44
- Jesus leaves and will return in clouds, Luke 21:27; Acts 1:9; 1 Thessalonians 4:17; Revelation 1:7

Colossae (koh-LAH-see) *a city in the country of Turkey,* Colossians 1:1-2

comfort, *to help ease someone's pain, grief, or trouble.*
- bad comforters, Job 16:2
- by shepherd's rod, Psalm 23:4
- from God, Isaiah 49:13; Matthew 5:4; 2 Corinthians 1:3-4
- from the Holy Spirit, John 14:16-18

commands
- to be taught, Deuteronomy 6:1-7; Matthew 5:19
- to be obeyed, Deuteronomy 8:6; Proverbs 19:16; John 15:10
- a new command, John 13:34
- to love, Galatians 5:14; 1 Timothy 1:5; 2 John 6

communion (KUH-myu-nyun) See "Lord's Supper."

complain
- Pharisees complained, Luke 5:30
- disciples complained, John 6:61
- warnings against, Philippians 2:14

concubine (KON-kyu-bine) See "slave woman."

condemn (kun-DIM) *to judge someone guilty of doing wrong,* John 3:16-18; Romans 2:1; 8:1

coney, See "rock badger."

confess
- admitting sin, Psalm 32:5; Proverbs 28:13; James 5:16; 1 John 1:9
- admitting Christ is Lord, Romans 10:9-10; Philippians 2:11; 1 Timothy 6:12; 1 John 4:2-3

confidence (KON-fuh-dens) *a feeling of assurance; trust.*
- from the Lord, 2 Thessalonians 3:4; 2 Timothy 1:7
- in Christ, Philippians 4:13
- before God, 1 John 3:21

conscience (KON-shunts) *a person's belief about what is right and wrong.*
- Paul's good conscience, Acts 23:1
- commanded to have a good conscience, 1 Timothy 3:9; Hebrews 9:14
- a troubled conscience, Hebrews 10:22; 1 John 3:20
- a corrupt conscience, 1 Timothy 4:2; Titus 1:15

contentment, *satisfaction.*
- Paul learned, Philippians 4:11
- with possessions, Luke 3:14; 1 Timothy 6:6; Hebrews 13:5

conversion (kon-VER-zhun) *a person's turning toward God and becoming a Christian.*
- examples of, Acts 9:1-22; 11:19-21; 1 Thessalonians 1:9

coral (KOR-al) *a type of limestone that forms in the ocean,* Job 28:18; Ezekiel 27:16

Corinth (KOR-inth) *a large seaport in the country of Greece.*
- Paul preached there, Acts 18:1-11
- Paul's letters to the church there, 1 and 2 Corinthians

Cornelius (kor-NEEL-yus) *a Roman army officer in charge of a hundred soldiers,* Acts 10

cornerstone, *the most important stone at the corner of the base of a building; Jesus is called the cornerstone of the new law.*
- Christ as the cornerstone, Ephesians 2:20; 1 Peter 2:4-8

council (KOWN-s'l) *or meeting; the highest Jewish court in the days of Jesus.*
- Jesus before the council, Matthew 26:57-68; Mark 14:53-65
- apostles before the council, Acts 4:1-22; 22:30–23:10
- Stephen before the council, Acts 6:18–7

courage
- need for, Joshua 1:6-9; Psalm 27:14; 1 Corinthians 16:13; Philippians 1:20
- examples of, Acts 4:13; 5:17-32; 20:22-24

court, courtyard, *part of a building that has walls, but no roof. The Temple had four courts:*
- the Court of the Non-Jews (Gentiles), a large open area just inside the walls of Herod's Temple, Mark 11:15-17; John 10:23; Acts 3:11
- the Court of Women, the next area, where both men and women were allowed, Mark 12:41-44
- the Court of Israel, the inner area of the Temple, where only Jewish men were allowed
- the Court of the Priests, the innermost court in the Temple, where only priests were allowed, Matthew 23:35

covenant (KUV-eh-nant) See "agreement."

covet (KUV-et) *to want strongly something that belongs to someone else.*
- forbidden by God, Exodus 20:17; Romans 13:9; Hebrews 13:5

creation
- of the world, Genesis 1–2; Job 38–41; Psalm 8; Isaiah 40:21-26; John 1:1-3; Hebrews 11:3

creator, *one who makes something out of nothing.*
- God as our Maker, Deuteronomy 32:6
- "Remember your Creator," Ecclesiastes 12:1

Crete (KREET) *an island in the Mediterranean Sea.*
- Paul visited there, Acts 27:7; Titus 1:5

cross, *two rough beams of wood nailed together; criminals were killed on crosses.*
- Jesus died on a cross, Matthew 27:31-50; Mark 15:20-37; Luke 23:26-46; John 19:16-30
- importance of, 1 Corinthians 1:18; 2:2; Galatians 6:14; Ephesians 2:16; Colossians 2:13-14
- as a symbol of death to oneself, Matthew 10:38; Luke 9:23; Romans 6:6; Galatians 5:24

crown, *a special band worn around the head.*
- a king's crown, Psalm 21:2-3; Song of Solomon 3:11; Revelation 12:3
- of thorns, Matthew 27:29; Mark 15:17; John 19:2
- of victory, 1 Corinthians 9:25; 2 Timothy 4:8; 1 Peter 5:4

crucifixion (kroo-suh-FIK-shun) *to be killed on a cross. See "cross."*

cubit (KU-bit) *a measurement in Bible times; about eighteen inches,* Revelation 21:17
cud, *an animal's food that is chewed slightly, swallowed, brought up, then chewed more completely a second time,* Leviticus 11; Deuteronomy 14
cup
• of the king of Egypt, Genesis 40:11
• of Joseph, Genesis 44:1-17
• of Lord's Supper, Matthew 26:27-29; Mark 14:22-25; Luke 22:17-20; 1 Corinthians 11:25-29
• of anger, Isaiah 51:17-23
• of water, Matthew 10:42; Mark 9:41
cupbearer, *the officer who tasted and served the king his wine.*
• to the king of Egypt, Genesis 40
• Nehemiah, cupbearer to Artaxerxes, Nehemiah 1:11
curse
• from God, Deuteronomy 11:26-29; John 7:49; Galatians 3:10-13
• forbidden to people, Matthew 15:4; Romans 12:14; James 3:9-10
• response to, Luke 6:28; 1 Corinthians 4:12
curtain
• of the Holy Tent, Exodus 26:1-2; 36:9
• of the Temple, Matthew 27:51; Mark 15:38; Luke 23:45
Cush, *a country in Africa,* Genesis 2:13; Psalm 68:31; Isaiah 18; 20
Cush, grandson of Noah, Genesis 10
Cyprus (SY-prus) *an island in the Mediterranean Sea,* Acts 11:19-20; 13:4; 15:39
Cyrene (sy-REE-nee) *a city in North Africa,* Acts 2:10; 6:9
• Simon of, Matthew 27:32; Mark 15:21; Luke 23:26
Cyrus (SY-rus) *a king of Persia,* Daniel 1:21
• sent captives home, Ezra 1; 6
• chosen by God, Isaiah 44:28–45:13

D

Dagon (DAY-gon) *a false god of the Philistines,* Judges 16:23; 1 Samuel 5:2-7; 1 Chronicles 10:10
Damascus (duh-MAS-kus) *a city forty miles east of Lake Galilee.*
• a chief city of Syria, 1 Kings 15:18; 2 Chronicles 24:23
• condemned by Amos, Amos 1:3,5
• Paul converted there, Acts 9:1-22
Dan, a city
• Israel's most northern city, Judges 20:1; 2 Samuel 16:11
Dan, son of Jacob, Genesis 30:6; 49:16-17; Joshua 19:40-48
Daniel (DAN-yel) *a Hebrew captive taken to Babylon as a young man.*
• taken to Babylon, Daniel 1:1-6
• became king's servant, Daniel 1:7-21
• explained Nebuchadnezzar's dreams, Daniel 2; 4
• read the writing on the wall, Daniel 5
• thrown into lions' den, Daniel 6
• his visions, Daniel 7; 8; 10
• a prophet, Matthew 24:15
Darius Hystaspes (dah-RYE-us his-TAHS-peez) *a ruler of Persia who allowed the Jews to finish rebuilding the Temple,* Ezra 5–6
Darius the Mede, *the king of Persia who made Daniel an important ruler under him,* Daniel 5:31–6:28; Haggai 1:1; Zechariah 1:1
darkness, *having no light; a symbol of evil.*
• before creation, Genesis 1:2
• as a plague, Exodus 10:21-23
• at Jesus' death, Matthew 27:45; Mark 15:33; Luke 23:44-45
• spiritual, John 1:5; Romans 13:12; Colossians 1:13
• as punishment, Matthew 8:12; 2 Peter 2:17; Jude 6; 13
David (DAY-vid) *Israel's greatest king.*
• son of Jesse, 1 Samuel 16:13-23
• played harp for Saul, 1 Samuel 16:14-23
• killed Goliath, 1 Samuel 17
• friend of Jonathan, 1 Samuel 18:1-4; 19:1-7; 20
• chased by Saul, 1 Samuel 18–19; 23:7-29
• protected Saul, 1 Samuel 24; 26
• became king, 2 Samuel 2:1-7; 5:1-14
• married Bathsheba, 2 Samuel 11–12:25
• reign of, 2 Samuel 5–1 Kings 1
• not allowed to build the Temple, 2 Samuel 7:1-17
• death of, 1 Kings 2:1-11
• Jesus as son of David, Matthew 22:42-45; Luke 1:27; 20:41-44
deacon (DEE-kun) *a person chosen to serve the church in special ways,* Philippians 1:1; 1 Timothy 3:8-13
Dead Sea, *large lake at the south end of the Jordan River. Several small streams flow into it, but it has no outlet. It is so salty that nothing lives in it. It is also called the "Sea of Arabah," the "Salt Sea," and the "Eastern Sea."* Genesis 14:3; Numbers 34:3,12; Joshua 3:16
deaf, *unable or unwilling to hear.*
• healed, Matthew 11:5; Luke 7:22
• and dumb spirit, Mark 9:25
death
• a result of sin, Genesis 2:16-17; Romans 5:12; 6:23; 1 Corinthians 15:21
• Christ's victory over, 1 Corinthians 15:24-26,54-57; 2 Timothy 1:10; Hebrews 2:14; Revelation 1:18
• spiritual death, Ephesians 2:1; Colossians 2:13
Deborah (DEB-oh-rah) *the only woman judge over Israel,* Judges 4–5
Decapolis (dee-KAP-oh-lis) *ten towns in an area southeast of Lake Galilee,* Matthew 4:25; Mark 5:20; 7:31
Delilah (dee-LYE-luh) *an evil Philistine woman whom Samson loved,* Judges 16:4-20
Demas (DEE-mus) *a Christian who helped the apostle Paul when Paul was in prison.*
• worked with Paul, Colossians 4:14; Philemon 24
• left Paul, 2 Timothy 4:10
Demetrius (deh-MEE-tree-us) *a silver worker in Ephesus,* Acts 19:23-27,38
demon, *an evil spirit from the devil. Sometimes demons lived in people, but Jesus could force them out.*
• people possessed by, Matthew 8:28-32; 9:32-33; Mark 7:24-30; 9:17-29
• Jesus accused of demon possession, Mark 3:22; John 7:20; 8:48; 10:20-21
• demons recognized Jesus, Mark 1:23-26; 3:11-12; 5:7-8; Acts 19:15; James 2:19
deny (di-NY) *refusing to believe the truth.*
• denying Christ, Matthew 10:32-33; 2 Timothy 2:12; 1 John 2:22-23
• Peter denied Christ, Matthew 26:34-35,69-75
descendants (de-SIN-dants) *family members who are born to a person or his children; grandchildren, great-grandchildren, great-great-grandchildren and so on,* Genesis 13:14-16; 15:12-16
devil (DEV-'l) *Satan; a spirit and the enemy of God and humans.*
• Jesus tempted by, Matthew 4:1-11; Luke 4:1-13
• children of, John 8:41-44; Acts 13:10; 1 John 3:7-10
• people to oppose, Ephesians 4:27; 6:11; James 4:7
Didymus (DID-ee-mus) *another name for Thomas, one of Jesus' apostles,* John 11:16; 20:24; 21:2
disciple (dih-SYE-p'l) See "follower."
disease
• a result of sin, Exodus 15:26; Deuteronomy 7:15; 28:60-61
• healed by Jesus, Matthew 4:23-24; 15:30-31; 21:14; Luke 7:21
• healed by apostles, Acts 5:12-16; 9:32-35; 14:8-10; 19:11-12; 28:8-9

disobedience
- brought sin, Romans 5:19
- to be punished, 2 Corinthians 10:6; Hebrews 4:11

divide
- heavens and earth, Genesis 1:6-8
- Red Sea, Exodus 14:16,21
- family against itself, Matthew 12:25; Mark 3:25; Luke 11:17

divorce
- teachings about, Deuteronomy 22:13-19,28-29; 24:1-4; Matthew 5:31-32; 19:1-12; 1 Corinthians 7:10-16

dog
- drinking water like a dog, Judges 7:5-6
- returns to its vomit, Proverbs 26:11; 2 Peter 2:22
- licked Ahab's blood, 1 Kings 22:38
- licked Lazarus's sores, Luke 16:20-21

door
- Jesus as the door, John 10:1
- "Knock, and the door will open," Luke 11:9-10
- "I stand at the door and knock." Revelation 3:20

donkey
- Balaam's, Numbers 22:21-30
- jawbone of, Judges 15:15-17
- ridden by Jesus, Matthew 21:1-7

Dorcas (DOR-kus) *Tabitha; a Christian woman known for helping the poor.*
- raised from the dead, Acts 9:36-43

dove, *a small bird similar to a pigeon; often a symbol for love, peace, and the Holy Spirit.*
- sent out by Noah, Genesis 8:8-12
- form taken by the Spirit of God, Matthew 3:16; Mark 1:10
- sellers of, John 2:14-16

dreams
- Joseph's, Genesis 37:1-11
- the king of Egypt's, Genesis 41:1-36
- Nebuchadnezzar's, Daniel 2; 4
- angel appeared to Joseph, Matthew 1:20-21; 2:13,19
- "your old men will dream dreams," Acts 2:17

drunkenness
- Noah became drunk, Genesis 9:20-23
- warnings against, Romans 13:13; 1 Corinthians 6:10; Ephesians 5:18; 1 Peter 4:3

E

eagle
- "to rise up as an eagle," Isaiah 40:31

earth
- creation of, Genesis 1:9-10; Jeremiah 51:15
- belongs to God, Exodus 19:5; Psalm 24:1

earthquake
- experienced by Elijah, 1 Kings 19:11-12
- at the death of Jesus, Matthew 27:51-54
- at Jesus' resurrection, Matthew 28:2
- experienced by Paul and Silas, Acts 16:25-26

Ebal (EE-buhl) *a mountain in Samaria next to Mount Gerizim.*
- place to announce curses, Deuteronomy 11:29; 27:12-13; Joshua 8:30-35

Eden, garden of (EE-den) *the home God created for Adam and Eve,* Genesis 2:8–3:24; Ezekiel 36:35; Joel 2:3

Edom (EE-dum) *Esau; the land where Esau's descendants lived.*
- the land of Esau, Genesis 36:8-9
- refused to let Israelites pass through, Numbers 20:14-21; Judges 11:17-18
- broke away from Judah, 2 Kings 8:20-22
- to be punished, Jeremiah 49:7-22; Ezekiel 25:12-14; Obadiah

education
- of Moses, Acts 7:22
- of children, Deuteronomy 6:1-7
- brings wisdom, Proverbs 8:33; 22:6

Eglon (EGG-lon) *a king of Moab,* Judges 3:12-25

Egypt (EE-jipt) *a country in the northeast part of Africa.*
- Joseph there, Genesis 39–50
- Israelites there, Genesis 46:5-34; Exodus 1; Acts 7:9-38
- Israelites left, Exodus 12:31-51
- Jesus there, Matthew 2:13-15

Ehud (EE-hud) *the second judge of Israel,* Judges 3:12-30

elder (EL-der) *older men who led God's people; appointed leaders in the church.*
- leaders of the Jews, Numbers 11:16-25; Deuteronomy 19:11-12; Matthew 21:23; Acts 4:5-7
- leaders of the church, Acts 11:30; 14:23; 15:2; 16:4
- duties and qualities, Acts 20:28; 1 Timothy 3:1-7; Titus 1:6-9; 1 Peter 5:1-3

Eleazar (el-ee-A-zar) *son of Aaron.*
- birth of, Exodus 6:23-25
- Moses became angry with, Leviticus 10:16-20
- a high priest, Numbers 3:32
- divided the promised land, Numbers 34:17

election, *process of selecting.* See "chosen."

Eli (EE-lye) *a priest and the next-to-last judge of Israel.*
- trained Samuel, 1 Samuel 1:9-28; 2:11; 3
- didn't discipline his sons, 1 Samuel 2:12-36
- death of, 1 Samuel 4:1-18

Elihu (ee-LYE-hew) *the fourth of Job's friends to try to explain Job's troubles,* Job 32–37

Elijah (ee-LIE-juh) *a prophet who spoke for God.*
- fed by ravens, 1 Kings 17:1-6
- brought boy to life, 1 Kings 17:7-24
- against prophets of Baal, 1 Kings 18:1-40
- condemned Ahab, 1 Kings 21:17-29
- taken to heaven, 2 Kings 2:1-12
- appeared with Jesus, Matthew 17:1-13; Mark 9:2-13; Luke 9:28-36

Elisha (ee-LYE-shuh) *the prophet who took Elijah's place as God's messenger.*
- received Elijah's spirit, 2 Kings 2:9-14
- helped a Shunammite woman, 2 Kings 4:1-36
- miracles of, 2 Kings 2:19-22; 4:38-44; 6:1-7
- healed Naaman, 2 Kings 5
- death of, 2 Kings 13:14-20

Elizabeth (ee-LIZ-uh-beth) *the wife of Zechariah, a priest.*
- mother of John the Baptist, Luke 1:5-25,57-66
- visited by Mary, Luke 1:39-45

Elkanah (el-KAY-nuh) *the father of Samuel,* 1 Samuel 1–2:11

Elymas (EL-ih-mus) *Bar-Jesus; a magician in the city of Paphos in Cyprus,* Acts 13:4-12

Emmaus (ee-MAY-us) *a town seven miles from Jerusalem.*
- Jesus appeared to disciples near there, Luke 24:13-39

encourage
- encouragement from God, Romans 15:4-5
- Christians to encourage each other, 1 Thessalonians 5:14; 2 Timothy 4:2; Hebrews 3:13; 10:24-25
- examples of encouragement, Acts 11:23; 13:15; 15:31-32

endurance, See "patience."

enemy
- attitude toward, Exodus 23:4-5; Matthew 5:43-48; Luke 6:27-36; Romans 12:20
- God's enemies, Romans 5:10; Philippians 3:18-19; James 4:4

enemy of Christ, *the anti-Christ,* 1 John 2:18,22; 4:3; 2 John 7

Enoch (E-nuk) *a man who walked with God,* Genesis 5:21-24; Hebrews 11:5

enrollment, See "census."

envy, See "jealousy."

Epaphras (EP-ah-fruhs) *a Christian who started the church at Colossae,* Colossians 1:7-8; 4:12-13; Philemon 23

Epaphroditus (ee-PAF-ro-DYE-tus) *a Christian in the church at Philippi,* Philippians 2:25-30; 4:18

ephah (EE-fah) *a common measurement for dry materials, about twenty quarts,* Exodus 16:36
Ephesus (EF-eh-sus) *the capital city in the Roman state of Asia.*
• Paul's work there, Acts 18:18-20; 1 Corinthians 16:8-9
• church there, Ephesians 1:1; Revelation 2:1-7
ephod (EF-ahd) See "vest, holy."
Ephraim (EE-frah-im) *Joseph's younger son,* Genesis 41:50-52; 48:8-20
• descendants of, Numbers 26:35; Joshua 16:5-10
equality (ee-KWAHL-eh-tee) *being identical in value.*
• in death, Ecclesiastes 3:19-20
• of Jewish and non-Jewish people, Romans 10:12
• in Christ, Galatians 3:26-28
Esau (EE-saw) See "Edom."
Esther (ES-ter) *a Jewish girl who became the wife of Ahasuerus, King of Persia,* Esther 1–10
• became queen, Esther 1–2:18
• learned of the plan to kill the Jews, Esther 3–4
• saved the Jews, Esther 5–8
eternal, See "forever."
eternal life, *the new kind of life promised to those who follow Jesus.*
• conditions for, Mark 10:17-31; John 3:14-15; 12:25; 17:3; Galatians 6:7-8
• source of, John 6:27-29; 10:28; Titus 1:2, 1 John 5:11-12
Ethiopia, *earlier called "Cush."* See "Cush."
eunuch (YOU-nuk) *a man who cannot have sexual relations. In Bible times, eunuchs were often high officers in royal palaces or armies.* 2 Kings 9:32; Esther 2:3; Isaiah 56:3-5; Acts 8:26-40
Euphrates (you-FRAY-teez) *a long, important river in Bible lands.*
• in the garden of Eden, Genesis 2:10-14
• a boundary, Genesis 15:18; 1 Kings 4:21; 2 Kings 24:7
Eutychus (YOU-ti-cus) *a young man in the city of Troas who was brought back to life,* Acts 20:7-12
evangelist (ee-VAN-juh-list) *someone who tells the Good News.*
• Philip, the evangelist, Acts 21:8
• as a gift from Christ, Ephesians 4:11
Eve (EEV) *the first woman.*
• created by God, Genesis 2:18-25
• tricked by Satan, Genesis 3; 2 Corinthians 11:3; 1 Timothy 2:13-14
everlasting, *living forever; eternal.*
• God, Genesis 21:33; Nehemiah 9:5; Isaiah 40:28
• Christ, Isaiah 9:6
• kingdom, Daniel 4:3; 2 Peter 1:11
• fire, Matthew 18:8,25,41
• gospel, Revelation 14:6
evil
• warnings against, Amos 5:15; Romans 12:9; 1 Thessalonians 5:22
• to be punished, Proverbs 24:20; Isaiah 13:11
evil spirit, See "demon."
eye
• "eye for eye," Exodus 21:23-24; Matthew 5:38
• wood in, Matthew 7:3-5; Luke 6:41-42
eyewitness, *one who sees an occurrence and reports on it.*
• of Jesus' life, Luke 1:2; 2 Peter 1:16; 1 John 1:1
Ezekiel (ee-ZEEK-yel) *a prophet during the time the Jews were captured by the Babylonians,* Ezekiel 1:3
• his vision of dry bones, Ezekiel 37:1-14
Ezra (EZ-ra) *the leader of a group of Israelites who were allowed to return to Jerusalem from Babylon,* Ezra 7–10; Nehemiah 8

F

faith (FAYTH) *belief and trust.*
• definition of, Hebrews 11:1
• sources of, Romans 1:20; 10:17
• examples of, Matthew 8:5-10; 15:21-28; Hebrews 11
• power of, Matthew 17:20-21; Ephesians 6:16
• made right with God by, Romans 4:3; 5:1; Philippians 3:9
• salvation by, Mark 16:15-16; John 5:24; 20:31; Romans 10:9; Galatians 2:16
• blessings by, Galatians 3:1-14; Ephesians 3:12; 1 Peter 1:5
• continue in, 2 Corinthians 13:5; Colossians 1:23; 1 Timothy 1:19; 2 Timothy 2:22
• lack of, Matthew 8:26; 14:31; 16:8
faithful (FAYTH-ful) honest, loyal, *true.*
• God is faithful, Deuteronomy 32:3-4; Isaiah 49:7; 2 Timothy 2:13; Hebrews 3:6; Revelation 19:11
• God's people must be faithful, Matthew 25:21; Revelation 2:10; 14:12; 17:14
fall, *sometimes used to describe the first sin.*
• Adam and Eve sinned, Genesis 3
false
• gods, Exodus 20:3; Deuteronomy 4:28; 1 Chronicles 16:26
• prophets, Deuteronomy 13:1-11; 18:22; Jeremiah 14:13-16; Matthew 7:15
• Christs, Matthew 24:24; Mark 13:22
• apostles, 2 Corinthians 11:13
• brothers, Galatians 2:4
• teachers, 2 Peter 2:1
family
• of believers, Galatians 6:10; Hebrews 2:11; 1 Peter 4:17
famine (FAM-un) *a time of hunger when there is very little food.*
• in Egypt, Genesis 41:30-31,53-57
• in Moab, Ruth 1:1
• in Israel, 1 Kings 17:1
• in Jerusalem during Claudius's rule, Acts 11:27-28
fasting (FAST-ing) *giving up food for a while.*
• to show sorrow, 1 Samuel 1:11-12; 2 Samuel 12:15-22
• of Jesus, Matthew 4:1-2
• how to fast, Matthew 6:16-18
• combined with prayer, Ezra 8:23; Luke 5:33; Acts 13:1-3
father
• to be honored, Exodus 20:12; Ephesians 6:2
• commands to, Colossians 3:21
• God as Father, Matthew 6:9; 23:9; 2 Corinthians 6:18; Galatians 4:6; Hebrews 12:4-11
fear, *a feeling of being afraid, or one of deep respect.*
• of God, Matthew 10:26-31; Luke 23:40
• overcoming, 2 Timothy 1:7; Hebrews 13:6; 1 John 4:18
• "your salvation. . .with fear and trembling," Philippians 2:12
feast (FEEST) *a special meal and celebration for a certain purpose.*
• Feast of Dedication, an eight-day celebration for the Jews that showed they were thankful that the Temple had been cleansed again, John 10:22
• Feast of Harvest, see "Feast of Weeks."
• Feast of Purim (PURE-rim) reminded the Israelites of how they were saved from death during the time of Queen Esther, Esther 9:18-32
• Feast of Shelters, "Feast of Booths" or "Feast of Tents"; reminded the Israelites of how God had taken care of them when they left Egypt and lived in tents in the wilderness, Exodus 23:16; Deuteronomy 16:13-17
• Feast of Unleavened Bread, or "Passover"; reminded the Israelites how God brought them out of Egyptian slavery, Exodus 12:1-30; Numbers 28:16-25; Deuteronomy 16:1-8
• Feast of Weeks, or "Pentecost," the "Feast of Harvest," or the "Day of Firstfruits"; a feast of thanksgiving for the summer harvest, Exodus 34:22; Leviticus 23:15-22; Numbers 28:26-31

Felix (FEE-lix) *the Roman governor of Judea from A.D. 52 to 54.*
- put Paul on trial, Acts 23:23-24; 24

fellowship (FEL-o-ship) *sharing friendship and love with others.*
- with Christ, Matthew 18:20; 1 Corinthians 1:9; 1 John 1:3
- with the Holy Spirit, 2 Corinthians 13:14; Philippians 2:1
- with believers, Acts 2:42; 1 John 1:7

Festus (FES-tus) *governor of Judea after Felix.*
- put Paul on trial, Acts 25–26

fighting
- against evil, 2 Corinthians 10:3-6; Ephesians 6:12
- "fight the good fight," 1 Timothy 1:18
- "I have fought the good fight." 2 Timothy 4:7

fire, *used by God as a sign of his presence and power.*
- the burning bush, Exodus 3:1-6
- pillar of, Exodus 13:21-22
- chariot of, 2 Kings 2:11
- wrong kind of, Numbers 26:61
- fiery furnace, Daniel 3:25
- baptism of, Matthew 3:11
- of punishment, Matthew 5:22; 13:41-42; Mark 9:43; 2 Thessalonians 1:8; Hebrews 10:27
- everything destroyed by fire, 2 Peter 3:10
- evidence of the Holy Spirit, Acts 2:3

firstborn (FIRST-born) *the oldest child in a family; the firstborn son in a Jewish family received a double share of his father's wealth and became the leader of the family when his father died.*
- Esau sold his rights, Genesis 25:27-34
- Israelites as God's firstborn, Exodus 4:22; Jeremiah 31:9
- death of, Exodus 11:1-8
- given to God, Exodus 13:1-16

firstfruits (FIRST-fruits) *the first and best crops and animals the Israelites raised and gave to God at harvest time,* Exodus 34:26; Numbers 28:26; Deuteronomy 18:3-4

fish
- clean and unclean, Deuteronomy 14:9-10
- used in miracles, Matthew 14:17; Luke 5:1-7; John 21:1-13

flax (FLAKS) *a plant used to make clothing and ropes,* Exodus 9:31; Isaiah 19:9
- used by Rahab, Joshua 2:6

flood, Genesis 6:9–8; Matthew 24:37-39; 2 Peter 3:5-6

follower (FAHL-o-wer) *a person who is learning from someone else; a "disciple."*
- of John, Matthew 9:14; 11:2; Mark 2:18
- of Christ, Matthew 11:1; 28:18-20; John 19:38; Acts 6:1-7; 11:26

fool, *someone who is not wise,* Proverbs 10:8-23; 17:7-28; 26:1-12
- examples of, Matthew 7:24-27; 25:1-13
- rejects God, Psalms 14:1; 53:1; Romans 1:20-23

footwashing, *done as an act of hospitality in Bible times because people wore sandals.*
- examples of, 1 Samuel 25:41; Luke 7:44; John 13:1-17

forever
- God's love continues forever, 1 Chronicles 16:34; Psalm 136
- praise God forever, Psalm 44:8; Romans 9:5
- be with God forever, 1 Thessalonians 4:17; 1 John 2:17
- Jesus lives forever, Hebrews 7:24
- "word of the Lord will live forever," 1 Peter 1:25

forgiveness
- of others, Matthew 6:14-15; 18:21-35; Mark 11:25; Luke 17:3-4
- by God, Luke 24:47-48; Acts 10:43; Ephesians 1:7; 1 John 1:9
- not given, Matthew 12:31-32; Mark 3:28-29; Luke 12:10; John 20:19-23
- "Father, forgive them," Luke 23:34

fornication (for-ni-KAY-shun) *having sexual relations with someone to whom you are not married.* See "adultery."

fountain, Proverbs 10:11; 13:14; 14:27; 16:22

frankincense (FRANK-in-senz) *a very expensive, sweet smelling perfume,* Exodus 30:34; Revelation 18:13
- given to Jesus, Matthew 2:11

freedom, *having liberty; not being a slave.*
- given to Jesus, Matthew 2:11
- in Christ, 2 Corinthians 3:17; Galatians 5:1; Hebrews 2:15
- from sin, Romans 6; 8:2; Hebrews 9:15
- to be used wisely, 1 Corinthians 8:9; Galatians 5:13; 1 Peter 2:16
- "truth will make you free," John 8:32

friend
- characteristics of, Proverbs 17:17; 18:24
- of Jesus, John 15:13-15
- Abraham, as a friend of God, James 2:23

frontlet, See "box of Scriptures."

fruit, *often used to mean "result."*
- spiritual, Matthew 7:15-20; John 15:1-17; Colossians 1:10
- of the Spirit, Galatians 5:22

fulfill (full-FILL) *to give the full meaning or to cause something to come true.*
- prophecy fulfilled, Matthew 2:14-15,17-18; Luke 4:16-21; 24:44-46; John 19:24

furnace
- Shadrach, Meshach, and Abednego thrown into, Daniel 3
- hell compared to, Matthew 13:42

G

Gabriel (GAY-bree-el) *an angel of God.*
- seen in a vision, Daniel 8:16; 9:21-27
- announced Jesus' birth, Luke 1:8-20,26-38

Gad, *a prophet*
- David's seer, 1 Samuel 22:5; 2 Samuel 24:11-19

Gad, son of Jacob
- birth of, Genesis 30:9-11
- land of, Deuteronomy 33:20-21; Joshua 22:1-4
- tribe of, Numbers 26:15

Gadarenes (gad-uh-REENZ) *people who lived in Gadara, southeast of Lake Galilee,* Matthew 8:28-34

Galatia (guh-LAY-shuh) *a district of Asia,* Acts 16:6; 18:23; Galatians 1:2; 1 Corinthians 16:1

Galilee (GAL-i-lee) *the country between the Jordan River and the Mediterranean Sea,* 2 Kings 15:29; Matthew 4:23; 21:11; John 7:1

Galilee, Lake (GAL-i-lee) *or "Sea of Galilee," "Sea of Kinnereth," "Lake of Gennesaret," "Sea of Tiberias"; a lake thirteen miles long and eight miles wide.*
- Jesus preached there, Matthew 4:12-22; 8:23-27; John 6:1-2,16-21

Gallio (GAL-ee-oh) *a Roman governor in the country of Achaia.*
- refused to punish Paul, Acts 18:12-17

Gamaliel (guh-MAY-lee-el) *a Pharisee and Jewish teacher of the Law of Moses.*
- prevented deaths of Peter and John, Acts 5:17-40
- Paul's teacher, Acts 22:1-3

gate
- Samson removed, Judges 16:3
- narrow, Matthew 7:13-14
- of heaven, Revelation 21:21

Gath, *one of the Philistines' five strong cities,* Joshua 13:3; 1 Samuel 21:10-12
- captured Ark taken there, 1 Samuel 5:1-10
- home of Goliath, 1 Samuel 17:4

Gaza (GAY-zuh) *one of the Philistines' five strong cities,*

Joshua 13:3; Judges 1:18; 1 Samuel 6:17; Amos 1:6; Acts 8:26
• Samson in prison there, Judges 16
gazelle (gah-ZEL) *an animal of the antelope family; known for its beauty and speed,* Deuteronomy 12:15; 1 Chronicles 12:8
Gedaliah (ged-uh-LYE-uh) *made governor of Judah by Nebuchadnezzar after capturing Jerusalem,* 2 Kings 25:22-26; Jeremiah 39:14–41:18
Gehazi (geh-HAY-zye) *a servant of the prophet Elisha.*
• and the Shunammite woman, 2 Kings 4:8-37
• and Naaman, 2 Kings 5:1-27
Gehenna, See "Hinnom."
genealogy (jee-nee-AHL-o-jee) *a list of the descendants in a family.*
• of Jesus, Matthew 1:1-17; Luke 3:23-38
generosity (jen-uh-RAHS-et-ee) *unselfishness.*
• shown to Ruth, Ruth 2:14-16
• to the needy, Nehemiah 8:10
• rewarded, Proverbs 11:25; Matthew 7:11
Gennesaret, Lake of, See "Galilee, Lake."
Gentiles (JEN-tiles) *anyone not Jewish.*
• received the Good News, Acts 10:44-45; 11:18; Romans 11:11-15; Ephesians 3:6-8
• conflict with the Jews, Acts 15:5-11; Galatians 2:11-14
Gerasenes (GER-un-seenz) *or "Gadarenes."* See "Gadarenes."
Gerizim (GER-i-zim) *a mountain next to Mount Ebal about thirty miles north of Jerusalem.*
• blessings announced from there, Deuteronomy 11:29; 27:12; Joshua 8:33
Gethsemane (geth-SEM-uh-nee) *a garden of olive trees just outside Jerusalem.*
• Jesus arrested there, Matthew 26:36-56; Mark 14:32-50
Gibeah (GIB-ee-uh) *a city about three miles north of Jerusalem,* Judges 19:12–20:43; 1 Samuel 10:26
Gibeon (GIB-ee-uhn) *a town about six miles northwest of Jerusalem.*
• Joshua defeated Amorites there, Joshua 9–10
Gideon (GID-ee-uhn) *the judge who led Israel to defeat the Midianites,* Judges 6:1–8:35
• angel appeared to, Judges 6:11-24
• destroyed Baal idol, Judges 6:25-32
• defeated Midianites, Judges 6:33–8:21
• the sign of the fleece, Judges 6:36-40
• built an idol, Judges 8:22-27
• death of, Judges 8:28-32
• hero of faith, Hebrews 11:32-34
gifts, *talents or abilities.*
• spiritual, Romans 12:6-8; 1 Corinthians 7:7; 12; 14:1-25; Ephesians 4:7
Gihon (GYE-hohn) *a spring outside the walls of Jerusalem,* 1 Kings 1:38-39; 2 Chronicles 32:30; 33:14
Gilead (GIL-ee-ad) *the area that Israel owned east of the Jordan River,* Numbers 32; Deuteronomy 3:10-16
Gilgal (GIL-gal) *the first place the Israelites camped after entering the promised land,* Joshua 4:19–5:12
gittith (GIT-tith) *probably a musical word and a musical instrument,* Psalms 8; 81; 84
giving
• examples of generous giving, Mark 12:43; Acts 10:2; 11:29-30; 2 Corinthians 8:3-5
• proper attitude toward, Matthew 6:3-4; Romans 12:8; 1 Corinthians 13:3; 2 Corinthians 9:7
gleaning (GLEEN-ing) *to gather grain left in the field after harvest,* Ruth 2
glory, *visible sign of God's greatness.*
• appeared in a cloud, Exodus 16:10; 24:16-17
• seen by Moses, Exodus 33:18-23
• "The heavens tell the glory of God," Psalm 19:1
• seen by Ezekiel, Ezekiel 1:26-28; 3:23; 8:4
• at Jesus' birth, Luke 2:8-14
• of Jesus, Luke 9:28-32
• seen by Stephen, Acts 7:55
• in the temple in heaven, Revelation 15:8
gluttony (GLUH-tun-ee) *eating too much.*
• warnings against, Deuteronomy 21:20; Proverbs 23:20-21
• Jesus accused of, Matthew 11:19; Luke 7:34
goat
• for a sin offering, Leviticus 9:3
• divided from sheep, Matthew 25:32-33
• blood of, Hebrews 9:12-13; 10:4
God, *the One who made the world and everything in it.* See also "glory."
• the creator, Genesis 1; Acts 17:24; Romans 1:25
• nearness of, Acts 17:27-28; James 4:8
• goodness of, Matthew 19:17; Acts 14:17; Romans 2:4; 1 John 4:7-11
• eternal nature of, Psalm 102:24-28; 1 Timothy 1:17; 6:16
• names of, Exodus 3:13-14; 1 Timothy 6:15; Hebrews 12:9; James 1:17; 5:4
• power of, Job 9:4-19; Isaiah 40:12-31; Matthew 19:26
• mercy of, Exodus 20:6; Numbers 14:18; Ephesians 2:4
• justice of, Psalm 67:4; Acts 17:31; Romans 2:2
golden calf, *an idol made to worship false gods.*
• made by Aaron, Exodus 32:1-24
• made by Jeroboam, 1 Kings 12:26-33
golden rule, *a name often used for Jesus' command. "Do to others what you want them to do to you,"* Matthew 7:12; Luke 6:31
Golgotha (GOL-guh-thuh) *Calvary; the hill where Jesus was crucified,* Matthew 27:33; Mark 15:22; John 19:17
Goliath (go-LYE-eth) *the giant from Gath whom David killed,* 1 Samuel 17
Gomorrah (goh-MOR-ruh) *an evil city near Sodom.*
• destroyed by God, Genesis 18:17–19:29; Matthew 10:11-15; 2 Peter 2:6
Good News, *also called the "gospel." Jesus died on the cross, was buried, and came back to life so people can be saved.* Mark 1:1; Acts 5:42; 13:26-39
• power of, Romans 1:16-17; Colossians 1:5-6; 1 Corinthians 15:2
• preached by the apostles, Luke 9:6; Acts 8:25; Philippians 1:5,12-14
Goshen (GO-shen) *an area in the Nile delta of Egypt.*
• home for Joseph's family, Genesis 45:9-10; 47:1-6,27
gospel (GOS-p'l) *"good news." The first four books of the New Testament are called the gospels because they tell the good news of what Jesus has done for us. See "Good News."*
gossip
• to be avoided, Romans 1:28-32; 2 Corinthians 12:20; 1 Timothy 5:13
government (GUV-er-ment) *group of people in charge of managing and making laws for people in a country, state, or city.*
• to be obeyed, Matthew 22:15-21; Romans 13:1-7; Titus 3:1; 1 Peter 2:13-17
governor
• Joseph, governor of Egypt, Genesis 42:6
• Nehemiah, governor of Judah, Nehemiah 5:14
• Pilate, governor of Judea, Matthew 27:2
• Felix, governor of Judea, Acts 23:26
grace, *God's kindness and love shown to us, even though we do not deserve them.*
• source of, Ephesians 3:7; Hebrews 4:14-16
• saved by, Acts 15:11; Romans 3:24; Ephesians 2:5-8; 2 Timothy 1:9
• misuse of, Romans 6; Galatians 5:4; Jude 4
grandchildren
• a blessing, Ruth 4:15; Proverbs 17:6
• inherit grandparents' wealth, Proverbs 13:22
grave, See "tomb."
Great Sea, See "Mediterranean Sea."

Greece, *once the most powerful nation in southeast Europe. Northern Greece was called "Macedonia." Southern Greece was called "Achaia."*
- Paul preached there, Acts 16:11-12; 20:1-6

greed, *selfish desire for more than one's share of something.*
- never satisfied, Proverbs 27:20
- beware of, Luke 12:15
- love of money, 1 Timothy 6:10

Greek
- the language of Greece, John 19:20; Acts 21:37; Revelation 9:11
- the people from Greece, Acts 14:1; 16:1; Colossians 3:11

grief
- of David for Absalom, 2 Samuel 18:33
- of the disciples, Matthew 17:23; John 16:6

guidance (GYD-ns) *direction.*
- by God, Exodus 13:21
- of the humble, Psalm 25:9
- of the Holy Spirit, John 16:15

guilt, *fact of having done wrong; regret, shame.*
- for improper worship, 1 Corinthians 11:27
- for breaking the Law, James 2:10
- cleansed of, Job 33:9; Isaiah 6:7; Hebrews 10:22

H

Habakkuk (ha-BAK-uk) *a prophet who wrote about the same time as Jeremiah,* Habakkuk 1–3

Hades (HAY-deez) *the world of the dead,* Revelation 6:8; 20:13-14

Hagar (HAY-gar) *Sarah's slave girl.*
- gave birth to Ishmael, Genesis 16
- sent away by Sarah, Genesis 21:8-21

Haggai (HAG-ay-eye) *a prophet in Jerusalem when the Israelites came back from Babylon,* Ezra 5:1; 6:14; Haggai 1–2

half-tribe, *one of the two parts of the tribe of Manasseh. One half-tribe settled east of the Jordan and the other settled west of the Jordan.* Joshua 1:12-15; 13:8-9; 22

Ham, *the son of Noah,* Genesis 6:10; 9:18-19; 10:6

Haman (HAY-man) *the chief officer under Ahasuerus, King of Persia.*
- planned to kill the Jews, Esther 3–6
- hanged, Esther 7

hands, laying on, *a ceremony where a person places his hands upon another.*
- for healing, Mark 5:23; 6:5; Luke 4:40
- to receive the Holy Spirit, Acts 8:17-19; 19:6
- for blessing, Mark 10:16; Acts 13:3

Hannah (HAN-uh) *the mother of Samuel,* 1 Samuel 1–2:21

happiness
- of the people of God, Psalms 144:15; 146:5; Proverbs 16:20; Matthew 5:3-12
- comes from wisdom, Proverbs 3:13

Haran (HAY-ran)
- Abraham's brother, Genesis 11:26-31
- home of Abraham, Genesis 11:31–12:5

harlot, See "prostitute."

harp, *the favorite musical instrument of the Jews.*
- first played, Genesis 4:21
- played by David, 1 Samuel 16:23; 18:10-11
- to praise God, Psalms 33:2; 71:22; 150:3

harvest
- of the poor, Ruth 2
- as a symbol, Matthew 9:37-38; 13:24-30,39; Revelation 14:14-16

hate
- seven things God hates, Proverbs 6:16-19
- a time to, Ecclesiastes 3:8
- of the world toward Jesus, John 15:18
- equal to murder, 1 John 3:15
- commands against, Galatians 5:19-21; 1 John 4:19-21

head
- a part of the body, Genesis 3:15; Psalm 23:5; Matthew 8:20; 1 Corinthians 12:21; Revelation 14:14
- a leader, Ephesians 1:22; 5:23; Colossians 1:18

heal
- a time to, Ecclesiastes 3:3
- by faith, Matthew 9:21-22; James 5:15
- "Doctor, heal yourself." Luke 4:23

heart, *the mind or feelings; not the physical heart that pumps blood,* Deuteronomy 6:5; Matthew 22:37

heaven
- *the home of God,* Matthew 5:34; Mark 16:19; John 3:13; Revelation 4
- angel spoke from, Genesis 21:17; 22:11
- opened, Matthew 3:16; Acts 7:56; 10:11
- fire from, 2 Kings 1:10-14; 1 Chronicles 21:26
- third heaven, 2 Corinthians 12:2
- the new heaven, Revelation 21:1-4
- kingdom of, Matthew 3:2; 5:3,19-20

Hebrews (HEE-brooz) *another name for the Jewish people,* Exodus 7:16; 2 Corinthians 11:22; Philippians 3:5

Hebron (HEE-bron) *a city about twenty miles southwest of Jerusalem,* Genesis 13:18; Numbers 13:22; 2 Samuel 2:1-11

heir (AIR) *the person who inherits what belongs to a relative. Because through Christ we can be adopted children of God, Christians are heirs to God's riches.*
- Abraham's heir, Genesis 15:3-4
- heir of God, Romans 8:17; Galatians 4:7

hell
- home of the devil and his angels, 2 Peter 2:4
- future home of sinners, Matthew 10:28; 23:33; Revelation 21:8
- descriptions of, Matthew 13:42; Mark 9:47-48; James 3:6; Revelation 14:11

helmet
- worn in battle, 1 Samuel 17:5; Ezekiel 23:24
- a symbol of salvation, Isaiah 59:17; Ephesians 6:17; 1 Thessalonians 5:8

help
- the stone of help, 1 Samuel 7:12
- the Holy Spirit as helper, Romans 8:26; Philippians 1:19
- from God, Psalms 46:1; 121:1-2; Isaiah 41:10
- commanded, 1 Thessalonians 5:14; Hebrews 6:10

Herod I (HEH-rud) *"Herod the Great"; king of Palestine from 40 to 4 B.C.,* Matthew 2:1; Luke 1:5

Herod Agrippa I (uh-GRIP-a) *King of Palestine from A.D. 41 to 44,* Acts 12:1

Herod Agrippa II, *King of Palestine from A.D. 52 to 70,* Acts 25:13–26:32

Herod Antipas (AN-ti-pus) *King of Palestine from 4 B.C. to about A.D. 39,* Matthew 14:1; Mark 6:14; Luke 23:7

Herodias (heh-ROW-dee-us) *the granddaughter of Herod I.*
- asked for John's head, Matthew 14:3-12; Mark 6:17-28; Luke 3:19

Hezekiah (hez-eh-KY-uh) *one of the good kings of Judah.*
- destroyed idols, 2 Kings 18:1-8; 2 Chronicles 29–31
- attacked by Assyria, 2 Kings 18:9–19:37; 2 Chronicles 32:1-23; Isaiah 36–37
- life extended by God, 2 Kings 20:1-11; Isaiah 38
- death of, 2 Kings 20:12-21; 2 Chronicles 32:24-33

higgaion (hig-GI-on) *probably a time to think quietly during a song,* Psalm 9:16

high place, *a place to worship gods,* 1 Kings 14:23; 2 Chronicles 31:1; 33:3

high priest, *the most important religious leader of the Jewish people.*
- rules for, Leviticus 21:10-15
- of the Jews, Exodus 29:30; Numbers 35:25; Matthew 26:3; Acts 23:2

- Jesus as, Hebrews 2:17; 3:1; 4:14–5:10; 8:1-6

Hilkiah (hil-KY-ah) *high priest when Josiah was King,* 2 Kings 22–23; 2 Chronicles 34

Hinnom, Valley of (HIN-num) *an area where trash was burned just outside of Jerusalem; also called "Gehenna,"* Joshua 15:8; 18:16; Nehemiah 11:30

Hiram (HY-rum) *King of Tyre when David and Solomon were kings over Israel.*
- supplied trees for Solomon's Temple, 2 Samuel 5:11; 1 Kings 5:1-18; 9:11-27; 10:22

Hittites (HIT-tites) *people who lived in what is now Turkey,* Genesis 23:1-16; Exodus 3:8; Joshua 1:4; 1 Samuel 11:3

holy (HO-lee) *pure, belonging to and willing to serve God.*
- holiness of God, Leviticus 11:45; Isaiah 6:3; Hebrews 12:10; Revelation 4:8
- holy kiss, Romans 16:16
- people to be holy, Ephesians 1:4; Colossians 1:22-23; 3:2; 1 Peter 1:15-16

Holy of Holies, See "Most Holy Place."

Holy Place, *a room in the Holy Tent and the Temple,* Exodus 26:31-35; 28:29; Leviticus 6:30; 1 Kings 8:10-11

Holy Spirit (HO-lee SPIH-rit) *one of the three persons of God. The Holy Spirit helped the apostles do miracles and led men to write God's word; he lives in Christians today.*
- in creation, Genesis 1:2
- living in Christians, John 14:15-17; 1 Corinthians 6:19; Galatians 4:6
- as a helper, John 14:25-26; 16:7-15; Romans 8:1-27; Galatians 5:22-25
- filled with, Luke 1:15; Acts 2:4; 7:55; 11:23-24
- sin against, Matthew 12:31; Acts 5:3; 1 Thessalonians 5:19; Hebrews 10:29

Holy Tent, See "Meeting Tent."

honest
- heart, Luke 8:15
- people, 2 Kings 12:15
- answer, Proverbs 24:26
- commanded, Mark 10:19; Philippians 4:8

honor
- for the old, Leviticus 19:32
- from God, 1 Samuel 2:30
- comes from humility, Proverbs 15:33
- to the deserving, Romans 13:7
- shown to parents, Exodus 20:12; Matthew 15:4
- shown to God, Proverbs 3:9; John 5:23; Revelation 4:9
- not shown to a prophet in his own town, Matthew 13:57

hope, *looking forward to something you really expect to happen.*
- reason for, Romans 5:3-5; 15:4; 2 Thessalonians 2:16; 1 Peter 1:13
- nature of, Romans 8:24-25
- results of, Colossians 1:5; Hebrews 6:18

Hophni (HOF-nee) *an evil son of Eli the priest,* 1 Samuel 2:12-34; 3:11–4:18

Horeb, Mount, See "Sinai."

horses, Exodus 14:9; 1 Kings 10:26-29; Psalm 33:16-17; James 3:3

Hosanna (ho-ZAN-ah) *a shout of joy in praising God,* Matthew 21:9,15; Mark 11:9; John 12:13

Hosea (ho-SEE-uh) *a prophet who lived about seven hundred years before Christ.*
- his unfaithful wife, Hosea 1
- his warnings to Israel, Hosea 2; 4–14

hospitality
- of Abraham, Genesis 18:1-16
- teachings about, Romans 12:13; 1 Timothy 3:2; 5:9-10; 1 Peter 4:9

hosts, *armies; God is called the "Lord of hosts."* See "Lord of hosts."

Huldah (HUL-duh) *a woman prophet,* 2 Kings 22:14-20; 2 Chronicles 34:22-28

humble (HUM-bul) *not bragging or calling attention to yourself.*
- Moses as example of, Numbers 12:3
- humility commanded, Luke 14:7-11; 22:24-27; Ephesians 4:2; Philippians 2:3
- Jesus' humility, Philippians 2:5-8

hunger
- feeding the hungry, Matthew 25:34-35; Romans 12:20
- spiritual, John 6:35; 1 Peter 2:2

husband
- responsibilities of, 1 Corinthians 7:3-5; Ephesians 5:25-33; Colossians 3:19; 1 Peter 3:7

hymn (HIM) *a song that teaches us about God or praises him,* Matthew 26:30; Ephesians 5:19; Colossians 3:16
- Jesus and apostles sang, Matthew 26:30; Mark 14:26
- teachings about, Ephesians 5:19; Colossians 3:16

hypocrisy (hi-POK-ri-see) *acting as if one is good when that is not true,* Matthew 23:28; 1 Peter 2:1

hypocrite (HIP-oh-krit) *a person who acts as if he is good but isn't.*
- warnings about, Matthew 6:2,5,16; 7:3-5; Luke 13:15-17
- Pharisees as hypocrites, Matthew 15:1-9; 23:13-32

hyssop (HIS-op) *a small bushy plant; marjoram,* Exodus 12:22; Leviticus 14:4,6; John 19:29

I

Iconium (eye-KOH-nee-um) *a city in Galatia where Paul preached,* Acts 14:1-7,19-23

idol (EYE-d'l) *a statue of a false god.* See also "Baal," "Chemosh," "Molech."
- worship of, 2 Kings 17:12-17; Acts 17:16-23; 19:24; Romans 1:25
- warnings against worship of, Leviticus 19:4; Deuteronomy 6:14-15; 1 Corinthians 5:10-11; 6:9-10
- Baal, 1 Kings 18:17-40
- Chemosh, Numbers 21:29
- Molech, Jeremiah 32:35

ignorance (IG-nur-rance) *a lack of knowledge.*
- not an excuse, Leviticus 5:17

image, *likeness.*
- God's, Genesis 1:26-27
- Caesar's, Luke 20:24
- the Lord's, 2 Corinthians 3:18
- Jesus in God's image, Hebrews 1:3

immorality (IM-mor-RAL-i-tee) *evil; sinfulness.* See also "sin."
- warnings against, 1 Corinthians 5:9-11; 6:9-10; Galatians 5:19-21; Ephesians 5:5

immortality (IM-mor-TAL-i-tee) *life after death,* Job 14:1-14; Daniel 12:1-2; 1 Corinthians 15:12-58; 2 Timothy 1:10. See also "eternal life."

impossible
- people cannot do, Matthew 19:26
- for God to lie, Hebrews 6:18
- without faith to please God, Hebrews 11:6

incense (IN-sents) *a spice burned to make a sweet smell.*
- altar of, Exodus 30:1-10,34-38; Revelation 8:3-5
- used in worship, Psalm 141:2
- as a gift, Matthew 2:11

inheritance (in-HEH-ri-tence) *something valuable that is handed down within a family.*
- of land, Numbers 36:8; Deuteronomy 3:28; Psalm 25:13

iniquity, See "sin."

inn, *a place for travelers to spend the night,* Luke 2:7; 10:34

innocence (IN-uh-sens) *not guilty of sin.*
- of Adam and Eve, Genesis 2:25
- declared by Job, Job 34:5

• declared by Pilate, Matthew 27:24

inspiration (IN-spi-RAY-shun) *"God-breathed." It is used to mean that the Bible writers wrote what God wanted them to write.* 2 Timothy 3:16; 2 Peter 1:20-21

Isaac (EYE-zak) *the son of Abraham and Sarah.*
• birth of, Genesis 21:1-4
• offered as a sacrifice, Genesis 22:1-19
• married Rebekah, Genesis 24
• tricked by Jacob, Genesis 27
• hero of faith, Hebrews 11:20

Isaiah (eye-ZAY-uh) *prophet who lived about seven hundred years before Christ.*
• became a prophet, Isaiah 6:1-8
• prophesied to Hezekiah, 2 Kings 19–20
• prophecies fulfilled, Matthew 3:3; 4:14; 13:14-15

Ish-Bosheth (ish-BOW-sheth) *son of Saul,* 2 Samuel 2:8–4

Ishmael (ISH-may-el) *son of Abraham and Hagar.*
• birth of, Genesis 16:2-16
• sent away from Abraham's camp, Genesis 21:8-21

Israel, kingdom of (IZ-rah-el) *the northern kingdom which had ten tribes.*
• beginning of, 1 Kings 11:27–12
• fall of, 2 Kings 17:1-18
• rulers of, 1 Kings 15:25–16; 22:51-53; 2 Kings 13; 14:23–17:6

Israel, son of Isaac, *Hebrew for "he who wrestles with God." Jacob's name was changed to Israel when he struggled with an angel at Bethel.* Genesis 32:22-28; 35:9-10. See also "Jacob."
• name given to Jacob's descendants, Genesis 49:28; Exodus 4:22; Psalm 22:23; Romans 9:3-5

Issachar (IS-uh-car) *a son of Jacob and Leah,* Genesis 30:18
• his descendants, Numbers 1:28-29; 26:23

ivory (EYE-voh-ree) *a creamy white bone that comes from elephant tusks,* 1 Kings 10:18; 22:39; Psalm 45:8

J

Jabbok River (JAB-ok) *a stream about fifty miles long that runs into the Jordan River,* Numbers 21:24; Joshua 12:2; Judges 11:13

Jabesh Gilead (JAY-besh GIL-ee-ad) *a small town on the east side of the Jordan River,* Judges 21:6-14; 2 Samuel 2:4-7

Jabin, king of Hazor (JAY-bin) *led a group of kings against the Israelites,* Joshua 11:1-11

Jabin, king of Canaan, *defeated by Israel when Deborah was judge,* Judges 4

Jacob (JAY-cub) *one of the sons of Isaac.*
• cheated Esau, Genesis 25:29-34
• tricked Isaac, Genesis 27:1-29
• his dream of a ladder to heaven, Genesis 28:10-22
• tricked by his sons, Genesis 37:10-22
• moved to Egypt, Genesis 45:25–47:12
• hero of faith, Hebrews 11:20-21

Jacob's Portion (JAY-cubs POR-shun) *a name for God, meaning he cares for Jacob's people,* Jeremiah 10:16; 51:19

jailer, *a keeper of a jail.*
• of Paul and Silas, Acts 16:23

Jairus (jay-EYE-rus) *a ruler of the synagogue.*
• Jesus brought his daughter back to life, Matthew 9:18-26; Mark 5:21-43; Luke 8:40-56

James, brother of Jesus, Matthew 13:55; Acts 12:17; 21:18
• later an apostle, Galatians 1:19

James, son of Alphaeus, *an apostle,* Matthew 10:3; Mark 3:18; Luke 6:15; Acts 1:13

James, son of Zebedee, *an apostle of Jesus and a brother of the apostle John,* Matthew 10:2; Mark 10:35; Acts 12:2

Japheth (JAY-fith) *one of Noah's three sons,* Genesis 5:32; 7:13; 9:18-27; 10:1-5

Jashar, Book of, *a book mentioned in the Bible, but not part of it,* Joshua 10:12-13; 2 Samuel 1:17-27

Jason (JAY-son) *a Christian in Thessalonica,* Acts 17:5-9

jealousy
• to describe God, Exodus 20:5; 34:14; Deuteronomy 5:9
• examples of, Genesis 37:11; 1 Samuel 18:19; Matthew 27:18; Acts 5:17
• warnings against, Romans 13:13; 1 Corinthians 13:4; 1 Timothy 6:4; 1 Peter 2:1

Jebusites (JEB-you-sites) *people who lived around Jerusalem before the time of David,* Joshua 15:63; Judges 19:10-11; 2 Samuel 4:6-8

Jehoahaz, son of Jehu (jeh-HO-uh-haz) *King of Israel who lived about eight hundred years before Christ,* 2 Kings 13:1-9

Jehoahaz, son of Josiah, *King of Judah for only three months,* 2 Kings 23:31-34; 2 Chronicles 36:1-4

Jehoash (jeh-HO-ash) *a king of Israel,* 2 Kings 13:10–14:16

Jehoiachin (jeh-HO-uh-kin) *the next-to-last king of Judah.*
• surrendered to Babylon, 2 Kings 24:8-17
• in Babylon, 2 Kings 25:27-30

Jehoiada (jeh-HO-yah-duh) *the chief priest in Jerusalem during Joash's rule,* 2 Kings 11– 12; 2 Chronicles 22:11–24

Jehoiakim (jeh-HO-uh-kim) *king of Judah about 600 B.C.,* 2 Kings 23:34–24:6
• tried to kill Jeremiah, Jeremiah 26:1-23
• burned Jeremiah's scroll, Jeremiah 36:1-23

Jehoram (jeh-HOR-am) *or "Joram"; the fifth king of Judah,* 2 Kings 8:16-29; 2 Chronicles 21:4-20

Jehoshaphat (jeh-HOSH-uh-fat) *one of the good kings of Judah.*
• faithful to God, 2 Chronicles 17:1-9
• appointed judges, 2 Chronicles 19:4-11
• defeated Moab and Ammon, 2 Chronicles 20

Jehovah (jeh-HOVE-uh) *a name for God; also translated "LORD,"* Exodus 3:15; 6:3; Deuteronomy 28:58; Psalm 83:18

Jehu (JEE-hew) *an army captain who became king of Israel.*
• appointed as king, 2 Kings 9:1-13
• killed Joram and Ahaziah, 2 Kings 9:14-29
• stopped Baal worship, 2 Kings 10:18-35

Jephthah (JEF-thuh) *one of the judges of Israel.*
• fought the Ammonites, Judges 11:1-29,32-33
• his vow, Judges 11:30-31,34-39
• fought the people of Ephraim, Judges 12:2-7

Jeremiah (jer-eh-MY-ah) *a prophet who warned the people of Judah,* Jeremiah 1–52
• became a prophet, Jeremiah 1:1-10
• songs of, 2 Chronicles 35:25
• his prophecies fulfilled, 2 Chronicles 36:21-22; Matthew 2:17; 27:9
• wrote a scroll, Jeremiah 36

Jericho (JEHR-ih-ko) *probably the oldest city in the world,* Mark 10:46; Luke 10:30; 19:1
• fall of, Joshua 2–6
• rebuilt, 1 Kings 16:34

Jeroboam, son of Jehoash (jeh-ro-BO-am) *a king of Israel,* 2 Kings 14:23-29; Amos 7:7-17

Jeroboam, son of Nebat, *first ruler of the northern kingdom of Israel.*
• given ten tribes by God, 1 Kings 11:26-40
• built idols, 1 Kings 12:26-33
• warned by God, 1 Kings 13:1-34
• death of his son, 1 Kings 14:1-20

Jerusalem (jeh-ROO-suh-lem) *"Zion" or "City of David"; the greatest city of Palestine.*
• the City of David, 2 Samuel 5:6-7
• captured by Babylonians, 2 Chronicles 36:15-23

- Jews returned to, Ezra 1–2
- the new Jerusalem, Galatians 4:26; Hebrews 12:22; Revelation 3:12; 21–22

Jesse (JEH-see) *father of King David,* 1 Samuel 16–17; 1 Chronicles 2:13-15; Luke 3:32; Romans 15:12

Jesus (JEE-zus) *"Savior"; the son of God.* See also "Christ," "Son of David," "Son of Man."
- birth and childhood of, Matthew 1–2; Luke 1–2
- temptation of, Matthew 4:1-11; Mark 1:12-13; Luke 4:1-13
- miracles of, Matthew 8–9; Mark 6:30-56; Luke 17:11; 22:50-51; John 2:1; 11
- appeared with Moses and Elijah, Matthew 17:1-13; Mark 9:2-13; Luke 9:28-36
- forced men from the Temple, Matthew 21:12-13; John 2:13-17
- the Last Supper, Matthew 26:17-30; Luke 22:1-20; John 13
- trial and death of, Matthew 26:57–27:66; Mark 15; Luke 22:66–23:56; John 18–19
- appearances after resurrection, Matthew 28; Mark 16; Luke 24; John 20–21; 1 Corinthians 15:5-8
- Son of God, Matthew 3:16-17; 26:63-64; John 1:14

Jethro (JETH-row) *father of Moses' wife,* Exodus 2:16-21
- advised Moses, Exodus 18

Jews (JOOZ) *first, the tribe of Judah; later, any of the twelve tribes,* Ezra 4:12; Esther 3–10; Acts 2:5
- against Jesus, John 5:16-18; 7:1,32-36; 10:25-42
- Jesus, king of, Matthew 2:2; 27:11-14,29; John 19:17-22
- and non-Jewish people, 1 Corinthians 12:13; Galatians 3:28; Colossians 3:11

Jezebel (JEZ-eh-bell) *the evil wife of King Ahab.*
- married Ahab, 1 Kings 16:31
- killed the Lord's prophets, 1 Kings 18:4-14
- killed Naboth, 1 Kings 21:1-23
- death of, 2 Kings 9:30-37

Jezreel (JEZ-reel) *the name of a town and a valley near the Jordan River,* Judges 6:33; 1 Kings 21:1; 2 Kings 8:29

Joab (JO-ab) *the commander of King David's army,* 2 Samuel 2:12–3; 10–11; 14; 18– 20; 24; 1 Kings 1–2

Joanna (jo-ANN-uh) *a woman Jesus healed,* Luke 8:2-3; 23:55–24:11

Joash, Gideon's father (JO-ash)
- protected Gideon, Judges 6:28-32

Joash, son of Ahaziah, *became king of Judah when he was seven,* 2 Kings 11–12; 2 Chronicles 22:10–24

Job (JOBE) *a wealthy man who honored God.*
- ruined by Satan, Job 1–2:10
- wealth restored, Job 42:7
- example of patience, James 5:11

Joel (JO-el) *a prophet who wrote the book of Joel,* Joel 1–3; Acts 2:16

Johanan (jo-HAY-nan) *a Jewish army captain,* Jeremiah 40:8–43

John, the apostle, *one of the sons of Zebedee.*
- called by Jesus, Mark 1:19-20
- at Jesus' transfiguration, Mark 9:2
- with Jesus in Gethsemane, Mark 14:33-42
- in the early church, Acts 3–4
- writer of Revelation, Revelation 1:1-4,9

John the Baptist, *Jesus' relative and the son of Elizabeth and Zechariah the priest.*
- birth of, Luke 1:5-25,57-80
- preached at the Jordan River, Matthew 3:1-12
- baptized Jesus, Matthew 3:13-17
- killed by Herod, Matthew 14:1-12

John Mark, See "Mark."

Jonah (JO-nah) *a prophet whom God told to preach to the city of Nineveh.*
- ran from God, Jonah 1:1-3
- swallowed by a fish, Jonah 1:4–2:10
- went to Nineveh, Jonah 3
- complained to God, Jonah 4
- the sign of, Matthew 12:38-41; 16:4; Luke 11:29-32

Jonathan (JAH-nah-thun) *the oldest son of King Saul.*
- David's friend, 1 Samuel 18:1-4
- saved David's life, 1 Samuel 19:1-7; 20
- death of, 1 Samuel 31:2

Joppa (JOP-uh) *a city on the coast of Palestine,* Jonah 1:3
- Peter preached there, Acts 9:36-42; 10:9-36

Joram (JO-ram) *son of Ahab; also a king of Israel,* 2 Kings 3:1-3; 8:29; 9:14-29

Jordan (JOR-d'n) *the only large river in Palestine.*
- Israelites crossed, Joshua 3
- Jesus baptized in, Matthew 3:13-17; Mark 1:9-11

Jordan Valley, *the valley along the Jordan River,* Deuteronomy 1:1; 3:17; Joshua 11:2

Joseph of Arimathea (JOZ-uf) *took the body of Jesus down from the cross and buried it in a tomb Joseph had dug for himself,* Matthew 27:57-60; Mark 15:42-46; Luke 23:50-54

Joseph of Nazareth, *husband of Mary, Jesus' mother.*
- angel appeared to, Matthew 1:18-24
- went to register in Bethlehem, Luke 2:4-7
- took Jesus to the Temple, Luke 2:21-52

Joseph, son of Jacob, *one of the twelve sons of Israel.*
- sold into slavery, Genesis 37
- put into prison, Genesis 39
- interpreted dreams, Genesis 40–41
- reunited with family, Genesis 42–50

Joshua (JAH-shoo-ah) *leader of the Israelites into the promised land.*
- spied out Canaan, Numbers 13
- chosen to replace Moses, Numbers 27:12-23; Deuteronomy 34:9-10
- conquered Canaan, Joshua 1; 3–12
- death of, Joshua 23–24

Josiah (jo-SY-uh) *king of Judah about 640 to 609 B.C.*
- became king, 2 Kings 22:1-2
- found the lost laws of God, 2 Kings 22:3-20
- gave the law to the people, 2 Kings 23:1-30

Jotham, youngest son of Gideon (JO-tham) Judges 9:1-21,57

Jotham, son of Uzziah, *a king of Judah,* 2 Kings 15:32-38; 2 Chronicles 27

joy, Psalm 43:4; John 15:11; 17:13; 1 Thessalonians 1:6
- a fruit of the Holy Spirit, Galatians 5:22
- God as the source, Psalms 43:4; 45:7; Romans 15:13
- joy from the Holy Spirit, Luke 10:21; Romans 14:17; Galatians 5:22; 1 Thessalonians 1:6

Jubilee (JOO-bih-lee) *a Jewish celebration that took place once every fifty years. Israelites were to let the soil rest, to free their slaves, and to return land and houses to their first owners or their descendants.* Leviticus 25; 27:17-24; Numbers 36:4

Judah, son of Jacob (JOO-duh) Genesis 29:35
- saved Joseph, Genesis 37:26-27
- deceived by Tamar, Genesis 38
- reunited with Joseph, Genesis 43–44
- tribe of, Numbers 1:26-27; 26:20-22; Joshua 15
- Jesus, a descendant of, Matthew 1:2-3; Luke 3:33-34; Revelation 5:5

Judah, kingdom of, *the southern kingdom when Israel split in two.*
- beginning of, 1 Kings 11:27–12:20
- rulers of, 1 Kings 14:21–15:24; 22:41-50; 2 Kings 8:16-29; 11–12; 14–16; 18–24
- fall of, 2 Kings 24:18–25:22

Judas Iscariot (JOO-dus is-CARE-ee-ut) *apostle who handed Jesus over to be killed.*
- chosen by Jesus, Matthew 10:4; Mark 3:19
- apostles' treasurer, John 12:4-6; 13:27-29
- betrayed Jesus, Matthew 26:14-16,47-50; Luke 22:1-6; John 6:70-71; 13:2,21-30

• death of, Matthew 27:3-5
Judas, brother of Jesus, Matthew 13:55; Mark 6:3
Judas, son of James
• an apostle, Luke 6:16; Acts 1:13
Jude (JOOD) *brother of James,* Jude 1
Judea (joo-DEE-uh) *the land of the Jews,* Matthew 2:1; 3:1; Luke 1:5; 3:1; Acts 1:8
judges (JUHG-es) *leaders of Israel prior to the kings,* Judges 2:16-19; 3:7–4; 10–12; 1 Samuel 8:1-5
judging
• warnings against, Matthew 7:1-5; 1 Corinthians 4:5; James 4:11-12
• good kinds of judging, 1 Corinthians 5:12; 6:2; 10:15
• God's judging of people, Matthew 11:22; Acts 17:31; 2 Peter 2:9; 3:7
Judgment Day (JUJ-ment) *the day Christ will judge all people,* Matthew 11:20-24; 12:33-37; 2 Peter 2:9-10; 3:7-13
Julius (JOOL-yus) *a Roman soldier in charge of Paul while Paul was taken to Rome,* Acts 27:1-3
justify (JUS-teh-fy) *to make someone right with God,* Romans 3:24; 5:1; Galatians 2:16; Titus 3:7

K

Kadesh/Kadesh Barnea (KAY-desh BAR-nee-uh) *a town in the Desert of Zin,* Numbers 20:1-21; Joshua 10:41
Kenites (KEE-nites) *a tribe of early metal workers,* Genesis 15:19; Judges 1:16; 4:11; 1 Samuel 27:10
Kerethites (KAIR-uh-thites) *King David's bodyguards,* 2 Samuel 8:18; 1 Kings 1:38
Keturah (keh-TOO-ruh) *Abraham's second wife,* Genesis 25:1-4; 1 Chronicles 1:32-33
key, *something that solves or explains.*
• to God's kingdom, Matthew 16:19
• to death, Revelation 1:18
Kidron Valley (KEH-dron) *a valley between Jerusalem and the Mount of Olives,* 2 Samuel 15:23; John 18:1
• idols burned there, 1 Kings 15:13; 2 Kings 23:4
kill
• Cain killed, Genesis 4:10-11
• laws against, Exodus 20:13
• of baby boys, Exodus 1:16; Matthew 2:16
• Jesus killed, Matthew 27:31-50; Mark 15:20-37; Luke 23:25-46; John 19:16-30
kindness
• of God, Exodus 34:6-7; Jeremiah 9:24; Romans 2:4; Ephesians 2:4-7
• commanded, 2 Corinthians 6:6; Ephesians 4:32; Colossians 3:12; 2 Peter 1:5-7
king
• King of kings, 1 Timothy 6:15; Revelation 17:14
kingdom (KING-d'm) *the kingdom of heaven is God ruling in the lives of his people.*
• the nature of, Matthew 5:19-20; 19:14; Luke 17:20-21; Romans 14:17
• parables of, Matthew 13:24-52; 18:23-35; 20:1-16; 25:1-30; Mark 4:30-33; Luke 13:18-21
• belongs to, Matthew 5:3,10; 19:14
Kiriath Jearim (KEER-yath JEE-ah-rim) *a town in the hills about twelve miles west of Jerusalem,* 1 Samuel 6:20–7:20; 1 Chronicles 13:5-6; 2 Chronicles 1:4
Kish, *father of Saul,* 1 Samuel 9:1-2
Kishon (KY-shon) *the name of a valley and a stream,* Judges 4:13; 5:21; 1 Kings 18:40
kiss, *a greeting of friendship, love, or respect.*
• of Judas, Matthew 26:48-49; Mark 14:44-45; Luke 22:47-48
• holy kiss, Romans 16:16; 1 Corinthians 16:20; 1 Peter 5:14
Kittim (KEH-tim) *the island of Cyprus,* Genesis 10:4; Numbers 24:24; 1 Chronicles 1:7; Isaiah 23:1,12
kneel
• Solomon kneeled before God, 1 Kings 8:54
• Daniel kneeled before God, Daniel 6:10
• everyone to kneel before Jesus, Philippians 2:10
knock
• "knock, and the door will open," Matthew 7:7
• at the door, Luke 13:25
• Peter knocked, Acts 12:13,16
• Jesus knocks, Revelation 3:20
knowledge
• tree of, Genesis 2:9,17
• value of, Proverbs 1:7; 8:10; 18:15; 24:5; 2 Peter 1:5-6
• lack of, Hosea 4:6; Romans 1:28
• limitations of, 1 Corinthians 8:1-2; 13:2,8-10
Kohath (KO-hath) *a son of Levi,* Exodus 6:16-20; Numbers 3:17-19
Kohathites (KO-hath-ites) *descendants of Kohath.*
• worked in the Holy Tent and Temple, Numbers 3:27-31; 4:1-20; 1 Chronicles 9:17-32
Korah (KO-ruh) *the musician,* Psalms 42; 44–49; 84
Korah, son of Izhar, *rebelled against Moses,* Numbers 16:1-40

L

Laban (LAY-ban) *father of Leah and Rachel.*
• Jacob worked for, Genesis 29:13-30
• divided his flocks with Jacob, Genesis 30:29-43
• chased Jacob, Genesis 31:19-55
Lachish (LAY-kish) *a city about thirty miles southwest of Jerusalem.*
• Joshua defeated, Joshua 10
lake
• of Galilee, Luke 5:1-2; 8:22-23,33
• of fire, Revelation 19:20
• of sulfur, Revelation 20:10; 21:8
lamb (LAM) *an animal that the Jews often offered as a gift to God.*
• as sacrifice, Genesis 4:4; Exodus 12:3-10; Leviticus 3:6-11; 4:32-35; 5:6; 14:24-25
• Jesus, the lamb of God, John 1:29,36; 1 Corinthians 5:7; 1 Peter 1:19; Revelation 5–7
Lamech, a descendant of Cain (LAY-mek) Genesis 4:18-24
Lamech, son of Methuselah, *the father of Noah,* Genesis 5:28-31
lamp, *a small bowl that held a wick and burned olive oil, thus giving light,* Matthew 25:1-13; Luke 8:16-18
• "Your word is like a lamp for my feet," Psalm 119:105
lampstand, *a holder for a lamp.*
• in the Holy Tent, Exodus 25:31-40; Numbers 8:1-4
• in the Temple, 1 Kings 7:49
• symbol of the church, Revelation 1:12-13,20
language
• world spoke only one, Genesis 11:1,6
• confused at Babel, Genesis 11:7,9
• Aramaic, 2 Kings 18:26; Ezra 4:7; John 19:20
• Latin, John 19:20
• Greek, John 19:20; Acts 21:37
Laodicea (lay-ah-deh-SEE-uh) *a town in what is now Turkey,* Colossians 4:13-16; Revelation 3:14-22
Last Supper, *the meal Jesus ate with his followers the night before his death,* Matthew 26:17-30; Mark 14:12-26; Luke 22:7-20; 1 Corinthians 11:23-26
Latin (LAT-in) *the language spoken by the Romans during New Testament times,* John 19:20
laughter
• Sarah laughed, Genesis 18:12
• mouths filled with, Psalm 126:2
• sorrow better than, Ecclesiastes 7:3
• changed into crying, James 4:9
law
• as rules, Romans 4:15; 6:14-15; Galatians 5:18

• as God's rules or teachings, Psalm 119; Romans 7:22; 8:7; James 1:25; 1 John 3:4
Law of Moses, See "Teachings of Moses."
laying on of hands, See "hands, laying on."
Lazarus of Bethany (LAZ-uh-rus) *a brother to Mary and Martha and a friend of Jesus,* John 11:1-45; 12:1-11
Lazarus, the beggar, Luke 16:19-31
laziness
• brings poverty, Proverbs 10:4
• not to be fed, 2 Thessalonians 3:10
leadership
• blind, Matthew 15:14
• of own family, 1 Timothy 3:5
• elders worthy of honor, 1 Timothy 5:17
Leah (LEE-uh) *a wife of Jacob,* Genesis 29:15-35; 30:9-21; 49:31
leather, Leviticus 13:47-59; Matthew 3:4
leaven, See "yeast."
Lebanon (LEH-beh-nun) *a country north of Israel.*
• cedars of, 1 Kings 5:1-11; Ezra 3:7
• prophecy of Lebanon's fall, Isaiah 10:34
Legion (LEE-jun) *a man who had many evil spirits in him,* Mark 5:9; Luke 8:30
lend
• money, Exodus 22:25
• borrower, a servant to lender, Proverbs 22:7
• sinners to sinners, Luke 6:34
• to enemies, Luke 6:35
leprosy (LEH-prah-see) *bad skin disease. A person with leprosy was called a leper and had to live outside the city.* Leviticus 13:45-46
• disease of Naaman, 2 Kings 5:1-27
• healed by Jesus, Matthew 8:2-3; Luke 7:11-19
Leviathan (lee-VI-ah-than) *a sea monster; possibly a crocodile,* Job 3:8; 41:1; Psalm 74:14; Isaiah 27:1
Levites (LEE-vites) *descendants of Levi, one of Jacob's sons.*
• served as priests, Numbers 1:47-53; 8:5-26; Deuteronomy 10:8-9; 18:1-8
• towns assigned to, Joshua 21
liar
• better to be poor, Proverbs 19:22
• Satan as a, John 8:44
• Cretans as, Titus 1:12
• to be punished, Revelation 21:8
lid on the Ark of the Agreement, *the mercy seat; the gold lid on the Ark of the Agreement,* Exodus 25:17-22; Hebrews 9:5
life
• breath of, Genesis 2:7
• book of, Philippians 4:3; Revelation 3:5; 21:27
• in the blood, Leviticus 17:14
• length of, Psalm 90:10
• true life, John 12:25
• "I am the. . .life." John 14:6
• eternal, John 5:24-29; 6:35-51
light
• creation of, Genesis 1:3-4
• of the world, Matthew 5:14
• God is, 1 Timothy 6:16; 1 John 1:5
• Jesus is, John 1:4-9; 3:19-20; 8:12; 12:46
• God's word is light, Psalm 119:105
• symbol of God's presence, 2 Corinthians 4:6; Ephesians 5:8-9; 1 Peter 2:9
linen (LEH-nin) *a type of cloth made from the flax plant.*
• used for priests' clothes, Exodus 28:39-42; Leviticus 6:10
• used for royal clothes, Esther 8:15
• Jesus' body wrapped in, Matthew 27:59
lion
• killed by Samson, Judges 14:5-18
• killed by David, 1 Samuel 17:34-37
• devil like a lion, 1 Peter 5:8
lips
• touched by hot coal, Isaiah 6:5-7
loaves
• used to feed five thousand, Matthew 14:17-19
• used to feed four thousand, Matthew 15:34-38
locust (LO-cust) *an insect that looks like a grasshopper. They travel in large groups and can destroy crops.*
• as a plague, Exodus 10:3-19; Deuteronomy 28:38-42; Joel 1:1-4; Nahum 3:15-17
• food for John the Baptist, Matthew 3:4; Mark 1:6
Lord, *master or one who is in control; ruler of all the world and universe.*
• God as Lord, Exodus 3:15; 7:16; Psalms 31:5; 106:48
• Jesus as Lord, Acts 2:36; 1 Corinthians 8:6; Philippians 2:11; 1 Peter 3:15
• Holy Spirit as Lord, 2 Corinthians 3:18
Lord of hosts, *one of the names used for God; also called "Lord All-Powerful" and "Lord Sabaoth,"* 1 Chronicles 11:9; Psalm 24:10; Isaiah 6:3-5; Malachi 3:1-17
Lord's day
• the first day of the week, Acts 20:7; Revelation 1:10
• as the Judgment Day, 1 Corinthians 5:5; 2 Corinthians 1:14; 1 Thessalonians 5:2; 2 Peter 3:10
Lord's Prayer, *the name often given to the model prayer Jesus taught his followers,* Matthew 6:9-13; Luke 11:1-4
Lord's Supper, *the meal Jesus' followers eat to remember how he died for them; also called "communion."*
• beginning of, Matthew 26:26-29; Mark 14:22-25; Luke 22:14-20
• examples of, Acts 20:7; 1 Corinthians 10:16; 11:17-34
Lot, *Abraham's nephew,* Genesis 11:27-30
• divided land with Abram, Genesis 13
• captured, Genesis 14:1-16
• escaped destruction of Sodom, Genesis 19:1-29
• death of wife, Genesis 19:15-26
lots, *sticks, stones, or pieces of bone thrown like dice to decide something. Often God controlled the result of the lots to let people know what he wanted them to do.*
• Canaan divided by, Numbers 26:55-56
• Jonah found guilty by, Jonah 1:7
• Jesus' clothes divided by, Luke 23:34
• Matthias chosen by, Acts 1:26
love, *a strong feeling of affection, loyalty and concern for someone.*
• love of God commanded, Deuteronomy 6:5; 11:1; Matthew 22:36-38
• of God for people, Psalm 36; John 3:16; Romans 5:8; 8:39; Ephesians 1:4; 1 John 4:10-11
• of people for God, 1 Corinthians 8:3; 1 John 5:3
• of Christ for people, John 13:1; 15:9; Romans 8:35; Galatians 2:20; 1 John 3:16
• of people for Christ, Matthew 10:37; 1 Corinthians 16:22; 1 Peter 1:8
• of people for each other, Leviticus 19:18; Luke 6:27-35; John 13:34-35; 1 Corinthians 13; 1 John 4:7
Luke, *a non-Jewish doctor who often traveled with the apostle Paul,* Colossians 4:14; 2 Timothy 4:11
lust, *wanting something evil.*
• to be avoided, Proverbs 6:25; Matthew 5:28; Colossians 3:5; 1 Thessalonians 4:5
• typical of the ungodly, Romans 1:26; 1 Peter 4:3
Lydia (LID-ee-uh) *a woman from the city of Thyatira who sold purple cloth,* Acts 16:13-15,40
lying
• warnings against, Ephesians 4:25; Colossians 3:9; Revelation 21:8
• devil as a liar, John 8:44
• to the Holy Spirit, Acts 5:1-6

lyre (LIRE) *a musical instrument with strings, similar to a harp,* 1 Chronicles 15:16; Psalms 33:2; 81:2

Lystra (LIS-tra) *a city of Lycaonia.*

- Paul preached there, Acts 14:6-20; 16:1; 2 Timothy 3:11

M

Macedonia (mas-eh-DOH-nee-uh) *the northern part of Greece.*

- Paul preached there, Acts 16:6-10; 20:1-6; 1 Corinthians 16:5-9; Philippians 4:15

Machpelah (mack-PEE-luh) *the land Abraham bought from Ephron, the Hittite.*

- Sarah buried there, Genesis 23:7-19
- Abraham buried there, Genesis 25:7-10
- Jacob buried there, Genesis 49:29-33; 50:12-13

magic (MAJ-ik) *trying to use the power of evil spirits to make unnatural things happen.*

- magicians of Egypt, Genesis 41:8; Exodus 7:11-12
- condemned, Leviticus 19:26; 20:27; Deuteronomy 18:10-12
- Simon the magician, Acts 8:9-24
- Elymas the magician, Acts 13:6-11
- Ephesian magicians burn their books, Acts 19:17-19

mahalath (mah-HAY-lath) *probably a musical word; may be the name of a tune or may mean to dance and shout,* Psalms 53; 88

Malachi (MAL-uh-ky) *a prophet who lived about the time of Nehemiah. He wrote the last book of the Old Testament.* Malachi 1:1

man, *humankind; a male.*

- created by God, Genesis 1:26-27; 2:7-23
- born of woman, Job 14:1
- important to God, Psalm 8:4-8
- woman created for, 1 Corinthians 11:9

Manasseh, son of Hezekiah (mah-NASS-uh) *a king of Judah for fifty-five years,* 2 Kings 21:1-17; 2 Chronicles 33:1-20

Manasseh, son of Joseph, *older brother of Ephraim. His descendants were the tribe of Manasseh.* Genesis 41:51; 46:20; 48:1-20

- descendants of, Numbers 1:34; 26:29-34; Joshua 13:8-13; 17
- eastern half-tribe, Joshua 1:12-17; 22
- western half-tribe, Joshua 21:5,25; 22:7

manger (MAIN-jur) *a box where animals are fed,* Luke 2:6-17

manna (MAN-ah) *the white, sweet-tasting food God gave the people of Israel in the wilderness. It appeared on the ground during the night so they could gather it in the morning.*

- God sent to Israel, Exodus 16:11-36; Joshua 5:10-12
- kept in the Ark, Exodus 16:31-34; Hebrews 9:1-4

Manoah (mah-NO-uh) *the father of Samson,* Judges 13

Marduk (MAR-dook) *a god of the Babylonians. The Babylonians believed that people were evil because Marduk had created them from the blood of an evil god.* Jeremiah 50:2

Mark, *John Mark; a cousin to Barnabas; traveled with Paul and Barnabas and wrote the Gospel of Mark,* Acts 12:12,25; 13:5; Colossians 4:10; 2 Timothy 4:11

- left Paul, Acts 13:13
- traveled with Barnabas, Acts 15:36-41

marketplace, *usually a large open area inside a city where people came to buy and sell goods,* Matthew 20:3; Mark 7:4; 12:38; Luke 7:32; Acts 16:19

marriage

- teachings about, Mark 10:6-9; 1 Corinthians 7:1-16; Hebrews 13:4; 1 Timothy 5:14
- authority in, Ephesians 5:21; Colossians 3:18

Mars Hill, See "Areopagus."

Martha (MAR-thuh) *the sister of Mary and Lazarus who lived in Bethany.*

- criticized Mary, Luke 10:38-42
- at death of Lazarus, John 11:17-44

martyr (MAR-ter) *"witness"; one who knows about something. Later, martyr came to mean a person who was killed for being a witness.*

- Stephen, first Christian martyr, Acts 7:54-60
- James killed, Acts 12:2
- heroes of faith killed, Hebrews 11:32-37

Mary Magdalene (MAG-duh-lun) *a follower of Jesus from the town of Magdala; the first person to see Jesus after he came back to life.*

- at Jesus' death, Matthew 27:55-56,61
- saw Jesus after his resurrection, Matthew 28:1-10; Mark 16:1-11; John 20:10-18

Mary, mother of Jesus

- engaged to marry Joseph, Matthew 1:18-25; Luke 2:4-5
- angel appeared to, Luke 1:26-45
- birth of Jesus, Luke 2:6-21
- with Jesus in Jerusalem, Luke 2:41-52
- at wedding in Cana, John 2:1-10
- at Jesus' death, John 19:25-27
- with the apostles, Acts 1:14

Mary of Bethany, *sister of Martha and Lazarus, and a friend of Jesus.*

- sat at Jesus' feet, Luke 10:38-42
- at death of Lazarus, John 11:1-45
- poured oil on Jesus' feet, John 12:1-8

maskil (MAS-kil) *probably a description of the kind of song that some of the Psalms were,* Psalms 32, 42, 44, 45

master, *lord; ruler.*

- "No one can serve two masters." Matthew 6:24
- not to be called, Matthew 23:10
- to be obeyed, Ephesians 6:5
- how to treat slaves, Ephesians 6:9
- in heaven, Ephesians 6:9; Colossians 4:1
- Jesus as, Luke 5:5; 8:24; 17:13

Matthew (MATH-you) *also called Levi; a tax collector; wrote the Gospel of Matthew,* Matthew 9:9-10; 10:3; Acts 1:13

Matthias (muh-THY-us) *chosen to be an apostle after Judas Iscariot killed himself,* Acts 1:15-26

meat

- given by God in the wilderness, Exodus 16:1-15; Numbers 11:4-34; Psalm 78:27
- eating meat sacrificed to idols, Acts 15:20; 1 Corinthians 8; 10:25-32

Medes (MEEDS) *the people who lived in Media, which is called "Iran" today,* 2 Kings 17:6; Ezra 6:2; Esther 1:3-19; Daniel 5:28; 6:8-15

mediator (MEE-dee-a-ter) *a go-between.*

- Jesus as, 1 Timothy 2:5

medicine

- happy heart as, Proverbs 17:22

Mediterranean Sea (med-ih-teh-RANE-ih-an) *a large sea west of Canaan; also called the "Great Sea" or the "Western Sea,"* Numbers 34:6-7; Joshua 1:4

medium (MEED-ee-um) *a person who tries to help living people talk to the spirits of the dead.*

- condemned, Leviticus 19:31; Deuteronomy 18:11-13; Isaiah 8:19-20
- of Endor, 1 Samuel 28
- Josiah destroyed mediums, 2 Kings 23:24

Meeting Tent, *"Tabernacle" or "Holy Tent"; a special tent where the Israelites worshiped God. It was used from the time they left Egypt until Solomon built the Temple in Jerusalem.*

- description of, Exodus 25–27
- set up, Exodus 39:32–40:36

Megiddo (meh-GID-oh) *important town in northern Israel where many battles were fought. The book of Revelation tells about a great battle between good and evil at "Armageddon," which means "the hill of*

Megiddo." Joshua 12:8-21; 2 Kings 23:29-30; Revelation 16:16

Melchizedek (mel-KIZ-ih-dek) *priest and king who worshiped God in the time of Abraham,* Genesis 14:17-24
- Christ compared to, Hebrews 5:4-10; 7

Mene, mene, tekel, parsin (MEE-nee, TEE-kul, PAR-sun) *the words written on the wall by a mysterious hand at Belshazzar's feast,* Daniel 5

Mephibosheth (me-FIB-o-sheth) *crippled son of Jonathan,* 2 Samuel 4:4
- David's agreement with, 2 Samuel 9
- tricked by Ziba, 2 Samuel 16:1-4; 19:24-30

Merab (MEE-rab) *daughter of King Saul,* 1 Samuel 14:49; 18:17-19

Merarites (mee-RAY-rites) *descendants of Merari, a son of Levi; they were responsible for caring for the frame of the Holy Tent,* Numbers 3:17,33-37; 4:29-33

mercy (MUR-see) *kindness and forgiveness.*
- God's mercy to people, Exodus 34:6; Deuteronomy 4:31; Luke 1:50; Ephesians 2:4
- people's mercy to each other, Matthew 5:7; James 2:13

mercy seat, See "lid on the Ark of the Agreement."

Mesha (MEE-shuh) *an evil king of Moab,* 2 Kings 3:4-27

Meshach (MEE-shack) *friend of Daniel who was put in the fiery furnace,* Daniel 1–3

messenger, 1 Samuel 23:27; 1 Kings 19:2
- John the Baptist as, Matthew 11:10; Mark 1:2; Luke 7:27
- of Satan, 2 Corinthians 12:7

Messiah (muh-SYE-uh) *"anointed one"; the Greek word for Messiah is "Christ." Christians believe that Jesus is the Messiah or the Christ.* John 1:40-41; 4:25-26

Methuselah (meh-THOO-zeh-lah) *lived 969 years, longer than anyone else in the Bible; the son of Enoch and the grandfather of Noah,* Genesis 5:21-27

Micah (MY-cuh) *a prophet who told the people of Israel and Judah about their sins,* Micah 1–7

Micaiah (mi-KAY-uh) *a prophet of God,* 1 Kings 22:8-28; 2 Chronicles 18

Michael (MY-kul) *the archangel of God,* Jude 9; Revelation 12:7

Michal (MY-kul) *a daughter of Saul and wife of David,* 1 Samuel 18:20-29; 19:11-17; 2 Samuel 3:13-16
- criticized David, 2 Samuel 6:16-23

Michmash (MIK-mash) *a hilly area about seven miles northeast of Jerusalem,* 1 Samuel 13:23–14:23; Isaiah 10:28

Midian (MID-ee-un) *a son of Abraham; his descendants were called "Midianites,"* Genesis 25:1-6
- Joseph sold to, Genesis 37:18-36
- Jethro, a descendant of, Exodus 2:15-21
- enemy of Israel, Judges 6–7

midnight
- when the firstborn of Egypt died, Exodus 12:29
- Paul and Silas freed from jail, Acts 16:25-26
- Paul preached until, Acts 20:7

miktam (MIK-tam) *a kind of song that may describe some of the Psalms. It may mean that it is a sad song or a song about danger.* Psalms 16; 56–60

mildew (MIL-doo) *a growth that appears on things that have been damp for a long time,* Leviticus 13:47-59; 14:33-54

milk, 1 Peter 2:2

millstones, *huge stones used for grinding grain into flour or meal,* Deuteronomy 24:6; Matthew 18:6; Luke 17:1-2
- used to kill Abimelech, Judges 9:53; 2 Samuel 11:21

minister (MIN-i-ster) *servant; one who lives serving God and others,* Romans 15:15-16; Colossians 4:7

miracle (MEER-ih-k'l) *"wonderful thing"; a great event which can be done only by God's help. Miracles are special signs to show God's power.*
- purpose of, Exodus 10:1-2; Mark 2:8-12; John 2:11; Acts 3:1-10
- over nature, Exodus 14:21-22; Joshua 10:12-13; Matthew 8:23-27; 14:22-32; 21:18-22
- of healing, Matthew 8:14-17; 9:27-31; Mark 7:31-37; Acts 14:3
- of bringing people back to life, Mark 5:21-43; John 11:1-44; Acts 9:36-43

Miriam (MEER-ee-um) *the sister of Moses and Aaron.*
- watched over Moses, Exodus 2:1-8
- song of, Exodus 15:19-21
- punished, Numbers 12:1-15
- death of, Numbers 20:1

mistress (MISS-tres) *a female head of the household,* Proverbs 30:21-23
- Hagar as, Genesis 16:4-9

Mizpah (MIZ-pah) *the place where Jacob and Laban made a pile of stones to remind them of their agreement not to be angry with each other,* Genesis 31:44-49

Mizpah, *the city, a few miles north of Jerusalem,* Judges 11:29-34; 1 Samuel 7:5-16; 2 Kings 25:23

Moab (MO-ab) *the country on the east side of the Dead Sea.*
- fought with Israel, Numbers 22:1–25:9; Judges 3:12-30
- home of Ruth, Ruth 1:2,4
- rebelled against Israel, 2 Kings 3:4-27

mob
- against Paul, Acts 17:5; 21:30-36

Molech (MO-lek) *a god of the Canaanite people. Those who worshiped Molech often sacrificed their own children to him by burning them on altars.* Leviticus 18:21; 20:1-5; 2 Kings 23:10; Jeremiah 32:35

money, *Many kinds of money were used in Bible days–gold, silver, and copper.*
- proper attitudes toward, Luke 16:13; Hebrews 13:5; 1 Timothy 3:3; 6:10

moneychangers, *people who traded money from other countries for Jewish money.*
- of the Temple, Matthew 21:12-13; Mark 11:15-17; Luke 19:45-46; John 2:13-16

Mordecai (MOR-deh-kye) *a man who helped Esther to save the Jews from death.*
- discovered a plot, Esther 2:19-23
- asked Esther to help, Esther 4
- honored by the king, Esther 6

Moriah (moh-RYE-uh) *the land where Abraham went to sacrifice Isaac,* Genesis 22:2
- site of the Temple, 2 Chronicles 3:1

mortar (MORE-tar) *a stone bowl where grain is ground into flour by pounding; also, the sticky material that holds bricks together,* Genesis 11:3; Exodus 1:14

Moses (MO-zez) *the man who led God's people out of the land of Egypt; the author of the first five books of the Old Testament.*
- birth of, Exodus 2:1-10
- in Midian, Exodus 2:11–4:17
- led Israel out of Egypt, Exodus 4:18–12:51; 13:17-31
- received the law, Exodus 20–31
- struck the rock, Numbers 20:1-13
- death of, Deuteronomy 31:14–34:12

Most Holy Place, *the inner and most special room in the Holy Tent and the Temple.*
- rules about, Leviticus 16:2-20
- in the Temple, 1 Kings 6:16-35
- entered by Christ, Hebrews 9:3-25

mother-in-law
- law about, Deuteronomy 27:23
- of Ruth, Ruth 1:3-4
- Peter's, Matthew 8:14-15; Luke 4:38-39
- family against, Matthew 10:35; Luke 12:53

mothers
- treatment of, Exodus 20:12; 21:15,17; Leviticus 19:3;

Proverbs 1:8; 13:1; 23:22, 25; Matthew 15:4; 1 Timothy 5:2,4

Mount of Olives, *a hill covered with olive trees near Jerusalem; site of the garden of Gethsemane,* Matthew 21:1; 24:3; John 8:1
- David cried there, 2 Samuel 15:30
- Jesus prayed there, Luke 22:39-53
- Jesus ascended from there, Acts 1:6-12

Mount Sinai (SYE-nye) *a mountain in the Sinai Peninsula.*
- Lord spoke with Moses there, Exodus 24:16; Acts 7:30,38
- law given on, Exodus 31:18

Mount Zion (ZI-on) *one of the hills on which Jerusalem was built; later, it became another name for the whole city of Jerusalem; also a name for heaven.*
- hill of Jerusalem, 2 Kings 19:31; Psalm 48:2,11; Isaiah 24:23
- as heaven, Hebrews 12:22; Revelation 14:1

mourning (MORN-ing) *showing sadness, especially when someone has died.*
- examples of, Genesis 50:3; Deuteronomy 34:8; 1 Samuel 31:11-13

murder
- laws against, Exodus 20:13; Deuteronomy 5:17; Matthew 5:21
- committed by Barabbas, Mark 15:7
- devil as a murderer, John 8:44
- full of, Romans 1:29

music
- to the Lord, Judges 5:3; Ephesians 5:19
- in the Temple, 1 Chronicles 25:6-7

myrrh (MUR) *sweet-smelling liquid taken from certain trees and shrubs; used as a perfume and a painkiller,* Genesis 37:25; 43:11; Proverbs 7:17
- given to Jesus, Matthew 2:11; Mark 15:23
- used in Jesus' burial, John 19:39-40

mystery (MIH-ster-ee) *a secret.*
- revealed by God, Daniel 2:28
- of the message of Christ, Romans 16:25-26; Colossians 2:2; 4:3
- of Gentiles also being saved, Ephesians 3:1-6; Colossians 1:25-27
- of life after death, 1 Corinthians 15:51

N

Naaman (NAY-uh-mun) *a commander of the Aramean army; healed by Elisha of a skin disease,* 2 Kings 5; Luke 4:27

Nabal (NAY-bal) *husband of Abigail.*
- refused to help David, 1 Samuel 25:2-13
- saved by Abigail, 1 Samuel 25:14-35
- death of, 1 Samuel 25:36-38

Naboth (NAY-both) *killed by Jezebel so she could steal his vineyard,* 1 Kings 21

Nadab (NAY-dab) *son of Aaron.*
- saw God, Exodus 24:1-11
- death of, Leviticus 10:1; Numbers 3:4; 26:61

Nahum (NAY-hum) *a prophet of God; wrote the book of Nahum,* Nahum 1–3

naked
- Adam and Eve, Genesis 2:25
- realization of nakedness, Genesis 3:7-10
- born, Job 1:21

Naomi (nay-OH-me) *mother-in-law of Ruth,* Ruth 1:1-5
- returned to Bethlehem, Ruth 1:6-22
- encouraged Ruth, Ruth 2:19–3:4
- became a grandmother, Ruth 4:13-17

Naphtali (NAF-tuh-lye) *the sixth son of Jacob; his descendants were the tribe of Naphtali,* Genesis 30:7-8; Numbers 26:48-50; Joshua 19:32-39

nard, *an expensive perfume which was imported from India,* Song of Solomon 4:13; Mark 14:3; John 12:3

Nathan (NAY-thun) *a prophet during the time of David and Solomon,* 1 Kings 1
- told David not to build the Temple, 2 Samuel 7:1-17
- told David the parable of the lamb, 2 Samuel 12:1-25

Nathanael (nuh-THAN-yul) *one of Jesus' twelve apostles; probably called "Bartholomew."* John 1:43-51

nation
- formed and spread, Genesis 10:32
- against nation, Mark 13:8
- Good News preached to every one, Revelation 14:6

Nazarene (NAZ-uh-reen) *a person from the town of Nazareth. Jesus was called a Nazarene, so his followers sometimes were also called Nazarenes.* Matthew 2:21-23; Acts 24:5

Nazareth (NAZ-uh-reth) *the city in Galilee where Jesus grew up,* Matthew 2:21-23; Luke 4:16-30; John 1:45-46

Nazirite (NAZ-e-rite) *a special promise made to God, which had rules about eating certain foods and cutting the hair.*
- rules for, Numbers 6:1-21
- made by Samson, Judges 13:2-7; 16:17

Nebo, god of the Babylonians (NEE-boh) Isaiah 46:1

Nebo, the mountain
- Moses died there, Deuteronomy 34:1-5

Nebuchadnezzar (neb-you-kud-NEZ-zur) *a Babylonian king.*
- conquered Jerusalem, 2 Kings 24–25; 2 Chronicles 36
- his dreams, Daniel 2; 4
- and fiery furnace, Daniel 3

Nebuzaradan (NEB-you-ZAR-ah-dan) *the commander of Nebuchadnezzar's army.*
- captured Jerusalem, 2 Kings 25:8-12; Jeremiah 39:8-14; 40:1-6

Neco (NECK-o) *king of Egypt from 609 to 594 B.C.*
- killed King Josiah, 2 Kings 23:29-37; 2 Chronicles 35:20-27
- captured Jehoahaz, 2 Chronicles 36:1-4
- defeated by Nebuchadnezzar, Jeremiah 46:2

Nehemiah (NEE-uh-MY-uh) *led the first group of Israelites back to Jerusalem from Babylon.*
- sent to Jerusalem, Nehemiah 2
- rebuilt walls of Jerusalem, Nehemiah 3–4; 6
- as governor, Nehemiah 8:9; 10:1

neighbor
- teachings about, Exodus 20:16-17; Leviticus 19:13-18; Proverbs 3:27-29; Matthew 19:19; Luke 10:25-37

Nephilim (NEF-eh-lim) *people who were famous for being large and strong. The ten spies who were afraid to enter Canaan had seen the Nephilim who lived there.* Genesis 6:4; Numbers 13:30-33

Ner (NUR) *father of Kish,* 1 Chronicles 8:33; 9:36,39

net
- fishing with, Matthew 4:18; Luke 5:5,6; John 21:6-11
- kingdom of heaven like, Matthew 13:47

new
- a new song, Psalms 40:3; 98:1
- a new name, Isaiah 62:2; Revelation 2:17
- new mercies every morning, Lamentations 3:22-23
- a new heart, Ezekiel 18:31; 36:26
- a new life, Romans 6:4; Ephesians 4:23-24; Colossians 3:10; 1 Peter 1:3
- a new agreement, Jeremiah 31:31; 1 Corinthians 11:25; Hebrews 8:8; 9:15; 12:24
- a new heaven and earth, 2 Peter 3:13; Revelation 21:1

New Moon, *a Jewish feast held on the first day of the month. It was celebrated with animal sacrifices and the blowing of trumpets. It was to dedicate the month to the Lord.* Numbers 10:10; 2 Chronicles 2:4; 8:13; Psalm 81:3; Isaiah 1:11-17

Nicodemus (nick-uh-DEE-mus) *an important Jewish ruler*

and teacher. Jesus taught him about spiritual life. John 3:1-21; 7:45-53; 19:38-42

night, *can refer to ordinary darkness or be a symbol of distress, judgment, or evil.*
- created by God, Genesis 1:5; Psalm 19:1-2
- time of distress, Psalms 30:5; 42:8; 77:6
- time of judgment, John 9:4
- symbol of evil, 1 Thessalonians 5:5
- no night in heaven, Revelation 21:25

Nile River, *a river in Africa more than twenty-five hundred miles long.*
- baby Moses placed there, Exodus 2:1-10
- turned to blood, Exodus 7:14-25
- produced plague of frogs, Exodus 8:1-15

Nineveh (NIN-eh-vuh) *one of the oldest and most important cities in the world. For many years it was the capital of Assyria.* Genesis 10:8-11
- Jonah preached there, Jonah 1:1-2; 3–4; Matthew 12:41
- Nahum prophesied against, Nahum 1–3

Noah (NO-uh) *saved his family and the animals from the flood.*
- built the boat, Genesis 6:8-22
- saved from the flood, Genesis 7–8
- agreement with God, Genesis 9:1-17

Nob, *a town where priests lived during the days of King Saul,* 1 Samuel 21:1

noise
- joyful, Psalm 66:1
- of many people, Isaiah 17:12
- skies will disappear with, 2 Peter 3:10

noon
- sun to go down at, Amos 8:9
- bright light at, Acts 22:6

O

oath, *a promise or vow.*
- rules about, Matthew 5:33-37; 23:16-22; James 5:12
- God's oath, Hebrews 6:16-18
- examples of, 1 Samuel 14:24-28; 1 Kings 1:29-30; Psalm 132:1-12

Obadiah (oh-buh-DYE-uh) *a prophet of God who warned the Edomites they would be punished,* Obadiah 1-21

obedience
- to God, Leviticus 25:18; Deuteronomy 27:10; Acts 5:29
- to parents, Ephesians 6:1; Colossians 3:20
- to government, Romans 13:1-7; Titus 3:1-2; Matthew 22:17-21
- punishment for disobedience, Ephesians 5:6; 2 Thessalonians 1:8; 1 Timothy 1:9

offering (AW-fer-ing) *a gift or sacrifice.* See "sacrifice."
- brought by Cain, Genesis 4:3-5
- of non-Jewish people, Romans 15:16
- of Christ, Hebrews 10:5-18

Og (AHG) *the king of Bashan who was defeated by the Israelites,* Numbers 21:33-35; Deuteronomy 3:1-11

oil, *in Bible times usually means olive oil; used for cooking, medicine, burning in lamps, and anointing.* See "anoint."
- for lamps, Exodus 25:5-6; Matthew 25:1-10
- as medicine, Luke 10:34
- in offerings, Leviticus 2; 14:12-31
- in cooking, 1 Kings 17:10-16

ointment, See "perfume."

olive (OL-iv) *a small fruit; its oil was used in anointing ceremonies and as medicine.* See "oil."
- leaf, Genesis 8:11
- trees, Deuteronomy 6:11; 1 Samuel 8:14; Habakkuk 3:17; John 18:1

Omega, See "Alpha and Omega."

Omri (AHM-rih) *an evil king of Israel,* 1 Kings 16:15-28

Onesimus (oh-NES-ih-mus) *the slave of a Christian named Philemon,* Colossians 4:9; Philemon

Onesiphorus (OH-nih-SIF-uh-russ) *a Christian friend of Paul who lived in Ephesus,* 2 Timothy 1:16-18; 4:19

onyx (AHN-ix) *a precious stone with layers of black and white running through it,* Genesis 2:12; Job 28:16
- used in the holy vest, Exodus 25:7; 28:9-14; 39:6-7,13

Orpah (OR-pah) *the sister-in-law of Ruth,* Ruth 1:3-14

Ophir (OH-fur) *a land known for its gold and beautiful trees. Its location is uncertain.* Psalm 45:9; Isaiah 13:12
- Solomon traded with Ophir, 1 Kings 9:28; 10:11; 1 Chronicles 29:4

oven, *fire was built in the bottom of a clay barrel to bake bread,* Exodus 8:3; Leviticus 2:4; Hosea 7:4

oxen
- not to be coveted, Exodus 20:17
- as offering, Numbers 7:12-83
- not to be denied food, Deuteronomy 25:4; 1 Corinthians 9:9
- Elisha plowed with, 1 Kings 19:19-21
- pulled the cart containing the Ark, 1 Chronicles 13:9

P

pain
- of a woman in childbirth, Genesis 3:16; Isaiah 13:8; Romans 8:22; Galatians 4:19,27
- not found in the new Jerusalem, Revelation 21:4

palace
- of David, 2 Samuel 5:11-12
- of Solomon, 1 Kings 7:1-12

palm tree, *a tall tree with long, fan-shaped branches growing out of the top; gives dates for food and wood for building,* Exodus 15:27; Nehemiah 8:15
- Jericho, city of, Deuteronomy 34:3; Judges 1:16; 3:13
- branches spread before Jesus, John 12:12-13

papyrus (puh-PY-rus) *a tall reed that grows in swampy places; used to make paper,* Job 8:11; 9:26

parable (PARE-uh-b'l) *a story that teaches a lesson by comparing two things.*
- of the kingdom of God, Matthew 13; 20:1-16
- of the lost sheep, coin, and son, Luke 15:1-31
- of the Judgment Day, Matthew 25

Paradise (PARE-uh-dice) *"garden"; a place where God's people go when they die,* Luke 23:43; 2 Corinthians 12:3-4

Paran (PAY-ran) *a desert area between Egypt and Canaan,* Genesis 21:20; Numbers 10:12; 12:16; 13:1-26

parchment (PARCH-ment) *a writing material made from the skin of sheep or goats,* 2 Timothy 4:13

parents
- responsibilities of, Ephesians 6:4; Colossians 3:21

Passover Feast (PASS-o-ver FEEST) *an important holy day for the Jews in the spring of each year. They ate a special meal on this day to remind them that God had freed them from being slaves in Egypt.*
- first Passover, Exodus 12:1-30
- commanded, Numbers 9:1-14
- celebrated by Jesus, Matthew 26:2,17-19

patience (PAY-shentz) *to handle pain or difficult times calmly and without complaining.*
- of God, Romans 2:4; 2 Peter 3:9
- teachings about, 1 Corinthians 13:4,7; Hebrews 6:12
- comes from the Holy Spirit, Galatians 5:22
- commanded, Romans 12:12; Ephesians 4:2; 1 Thessalonians 5:14; James 5:7-8

Patmos (PAT-mus) *a small, rocky island in the Aegean Sea between Greece and Turkey,* Revelation 1:9

Paul, *the Roman name for "Saul." Saul was a Jew, born in the city of Tarsus. He became an apostle and a great servant of God.*
- conversion of, Acts 9:1-22

- name changed from "Saul," Acts 13:9
- healings by, Acts 14:8-10; 19:11-12; 20:7-12; 28:1-11
- imprisoned, Acts 23:35–28:31
- death of, 2 Timothy 4:6-8

peace
- from God, Psalm 29:11; John 14:27; Romans 5:1
- commanded, Romans 12:18; 14:17-19; Colossians 3:15
- Prince of Peace, Isaiah 9:6
- from the Holy Spirit, Galatians 5:22

pearl (PURL), Matthew 7:6; 1 Timothy 2:9; Revelation 21:21
- parable of, Matthew 13:45-46

Pekah (PEE-kuh) *an evil king of Israel,* 2 Kings 15:25–16:9; Isaiah 7:1-10

Pekahiah (peck-uh-HI-uh) *an evil king of Israel,* 2 Kings 15:22-26

Pelethites (PELL-eh-thites) *King David's bodyguards,* 2 Samuel 15:18; 20:6-7,23

Peninnah (pe-NIN-uh) *a wife of Elkanah,* 1 Samuel 1:2-6

Pentecost (PEN-tee-cost) *a Jewish feast day celebrating the summer harvest. The apostles began telling the Good News on Pentecost after Jesus died.* Acts 2:1-41; 20:16; 1 Corinthians 16:8

perfect
- describing Jesus, Hebrews 2:10; 5:9; 7:28
- describing God, Psalm 18:30; Matthew 5:48
- God's perfect law, James 1:25
- will of God, Romans 12:2
- love, 1 John 4:18
- people made perfect, 2 Corinthians 13:11; Hebrews 10:1-14; 11:40; 12:23

perfume
- used in idol worship, Isaiah 57:9
- poured on Jesus' feet, Mark 14:3-9; Luke 7:36-39; John 12:3

Pergamum (PER-guh-mum) *a town in the Roman province of Asia in what is now Turkey,* Revelation 2:12-17

persecution (PUR-seh-CUE-shun) *trying to hurt people. Christians in the New Testament times were often persecuted by being put in jail or killed.*
- blessings with, Matthew 5:11-12; 1 Peter 3:8-17
- examples of, Acts 8:1-4; 1 Peter 3:13-15
- response to, Matthew 5:44; Romans 12:14; 1 Corinthians 4:12; 2 Corinthians 12:2
- of Christians, Matthew 13:21; 2 Timothy 3:12

Persia (PUR-zhuh) *a powerful country during the last years of the Old Testament; now called "Iran."*
- defeated Babylon, 2 Chronicles 36:20-23
- let captives return to Jerusalem, Ezra 1:1-11

Peter, *a fisherman; he and his brother, Andrew, were the first two apostles Jesus chose. First called " Simon" or "Peter," Jesus changed his name to "Cephas," which means "rock."*
- called to follow Jesus, Matthew 4:18-20
- walked on water, Matthew 14:22-33
- at the Last Supper, John 13:1-11
- defended Jesus, John 18:10-11
- denied Jesus, Mark 14:66-72; Luke 22:54-62
- preached the Good News, Acts 2:14-40
- an elder in the church, 1 Peter 5:1

pharaoh (FAY-row) *the title given to the kings of Egypt.*
- made Joseph ruler of Egypt, Genesis 40–47
- made Israelites slaves, Exodus 1–14

Pharisees (FARE-ih-seez) *"the separate people"; they followed the Jewish religious laws and customs very strictly. Jesus often spoke against them for their religious teachings and traditions.*
- practices of, Matthew 9:14; 15:1-9; Mark 7:1-13; Luke 7:30
- against Jesus, Matthew 12:14; 22:15; John 8:1-6
- criticized by Jesus, Matthew 5:20; Matthew 23

Philadelphia (fill-uh-DEL-fee-uh) *a city in the country now called "Turkey,"* Revelation 3:7-13

Philemon (fih-LEE-mun) *a Christian in the city of Colossae,* Philemon 1-25

Philip, the apostle (FIL-ip) *friend of Peter and Andrew.*
- called by Jesus, John 1:43
- brought Nathanael to Jesus, John 1:44-50
- brought Greeks to Jesus, John 12:21-22

Philip, the evangelist, *a Greek-speaking Jew chosen to serve in the church in Jerusalem.*
- preached in Samaria, Acts 8:5-13
- preached to the Ethiopian, Acts 8:26-39
- his daughters prophesied, Acts 21:8-9

Philip, the tetrarch, *son of Herod I and Cleopatra.*
- ruler of Iturea and Trachonitis, Luke 3:1

Philippi (fih-LIP-eye) *a city in northeastern Greece,* Philippians 1:1; 4:15
- Paul in jail there, Acts 16:11-40

Philistines (FIL-ih-steens) *people who were Israel's enemy for many years; worshiped false gods.*
- Samson defeated, Judges 15–16
- captured the Ark of the Agreement, 1 Samuel 4–6
- David defeated, 1 Samuel 17–18; 2 Samuel 5:17-25; 21:15-22

Phinehas, son of Eleazar (FIN-ee-us) *a priest and grandson of Aaron,* Numbers 25:1-13

Phinehas, son of Eli, *an evil priest,* 1 Samuel 1:3; 2:34; 4:4-11

Phoebe (FEE-beh) *a woman in the church in Cenchrea,* Romans 16:1

Phoenicia (foh-NEE-shuh) *an early name for the land on the east coast of the Mediterranean Sea; called "Lebanon" today,* Mark 7:26; Acts 11:19; 15:3

phylactery (fil-LAK-tur-ee) See "box of Scriptures."

pigs
- considered unclean, Leviticus 11:7
- snout of, Proverbs 11:22
- "don't throw your pearls before pigs." Matthew 7:6
- demons sent into, Matthew 8:30-33; Mark 5:11-13; Luke 8:32-33
- fed by prodigal son, Luke 15:15-16

Pilate, Pontius (PIE-lut, PON-shus) *the Roman governor of Judea from A.D. 26 to 36,* Luke 3:1; 13:1
- handed Jesus over to be killed, Matthew 27; Mark 15; Luke 23; John 18:28–19:38

pillar (PILL-ur) *a large stone that is set upright; also a tall column of stone that supports the roof of a building.*
- of Jacob, Genesis 28:18-22
- to worship false gods, 2 Kings 17:9-12
- in the Temple, 1 Kings 7:6,15-22
- of cloud and fire, Exodus 13:21-22; 14:19-24; 33:8-10

Pisgah, Mount (PIS-guh) *one of the high spots on Mount Nebo where Moses stood to see into the promised land,* Numbers 23:14; Deuteronomy 3:27; 34:1

plague (PLAYG) *a disaster. God sent ten plagues on the land of Egypt so the Egyptians would set the Israelites free.*
- on the Egyptians, Exodus 7–11
- on the Israelites, Exodus 32:35; Numbers 11:31-33; 16:41-50; 25:1-9

plumb line (PLUM LINE) *a string with a rock or other weight on one end. People used it to see if a wall was straight.*
- symbol for God's judging, 2 Kings 21:10-13; Amos 7:7-8

pomegranate (PAHM-gran-it) *a reddish fruit about the size of an apple,* Numbers 13:23; Joel 1:12
- design on priests' clothing, Exodus 28:33-34
- design of Temple decorations, 1 Kings 7:18-20

poor
- God's care for, Psalm 140:12; Proverbs 22:22-23; Matthew 11:5; James 2:5

- treatment of, Leviticus 19:9-10; Matthew 25:34-36; Luke 14:12-14

possessions
- promised land given to Israelites, Genesis 17:8; Numbers 32:22; Joshua 1:11
- proper attitudes toward, Ecclesiastes 5:10– 6:6; Luke 12:13-21; Acts 2:45; 1 John 3:17
- danger of, Matthew 19:22
- sold by Christians, Acts 2:45

Potiphar (POT-ih-fur) *an officer for the king of Egypt. He put Joseph in charge of his household.* Genesis 39

pottage (POT-edge) *a thick vegetable soup or stew,* Genesis 25:29-34; 2 Kings 4:38-41

potter (POT-ur) *a person who makes pots and dishes out of clay.*
- as a symbol of God, Jeremiah 18:1-6

power
- of Jesus, Matthew 24:30; 28:18; Luke 6:19
- of the Spirit, Luke 4:14; Acts 1:8; Romans 15:19
- of Satan, Acts 26:18
- of the apostles, Luke 9:1; Acts 4:33

praetorium (pray-TORE-ee-um) *the governor's palace in New Testament times,* Matthew 27:27; Acts 23:35

praise (PRAYZ) *to say good things about someone or something. God's people can praise him by singing, praying, and by living the way he tells us to live.* 1 Chronicles 16:4-7; Psalms 103; 104; 145–150

prayer
- teachings about, Matthew 5:44-45; 21:18-22; Philippians 4:6; James 5:15-16
- Jesus' model prayer, Matthew 6:5-15

preach, *to give a talk on a religious subject; to tell the Good News.*
- Jonah preached to Nineveh, Jonah 3:2-4
- John preached, Matthew 3:1; Mark 1:4; Luke 3:3
- Jesus preached, Matthew 4:17; Mark 2:2; Luke 4:43-44
- Good News preached, Acts 8:25,40; Galatians 2:7; 1 Thessalonians 2:9
- preaching commanded, 2 Timothy 4:2

Preparation Day (prep-a-RAY-shun DAY) *the day before the Sabbath day. On that day the Jews prepared for the Sabbath.* Luke 23:54; John 19:14,31

pride
- warnings against, Romans 12:3; 1 Corinthians 13:4; Philippians 2:3; James 4:6

priest (PREEST) *in the Old Testament, a servant of God who worked in the Holy Tent or Temple. See also "high priest."*
- clothes for, Exodus 28
- appointing of, Exodus 29:1-37
- rules for, Leviticus 21–22:16

Priscilla (prih-SIL-uh) *a friend of Paul,* Acts 18:1-4,18-19; Romans 16:3-4
- taught Apollos, Acts 18:24-26

prison
- Joseph in prison, Genesis 39:20–41:40
- Peter in prison, Acts 5:17-20
- Paul in prison, Acts 16:23-34

prodigal (PRAH-dih-gul) *careless and wasteful.*
- the prodigal son, Luke 15:11-32

promise
- from God, Joshua 1:3; 1 Kings 8:20; Galatians 3:14; Ephesians 3:6
- first commandment with, Ephesians 6:2
- Lord is not slow in keeping, 2 Peter 2:9

prophecy (PRAH-feh-see) *a message; God speaking through chosen people called "prophets,"* Ezekiel 14:9; 1 Thessalonians 5:20; 2 Peter 1:20-21

prophesy (PRAH-fes-sy) *to speak a prophecy,* Acts 2:17-18. See "prophecy."
- a spiritual gift, 1 Corinthians 14:1-5

prophet (PRAH-fet) *a messenger; one who is able, with God's help, to tell God's message correctly. Sometimes prophets told what would happen in the future.* Matthew 11:13-14
- how to judge, Deuteronomy 13:1-5; 18:21-22
- examples of, Ezra 5:1; Jeremiah 1:1-9; Matthew 3:3
- false prophets, Deuteronomy 13:1-5

prophetess (PRAH-feh-tess) *a female prophet,* Exodus 15:20; Judges 4:4; 2 Kings 22:14; Luke 2:36. See "prophet."

prostitute (PRAH-sti-toot) *a person who sells his or her body for sex.*
- warnings against, 1 Corinthians 6:15
- examples of, Genesis 38:15-16; Jeremiah 3:1-3; Hosea 3:2-3; Matthew 21:32

proverbs (PRAH-verbs) *wise sayings. The book of Proverbs contains many wise sayings that tell how to live a good and happy life.* 1 Kings 4:32; Proverbs

psalm (SAHM) *a song. The book of Psalms is like a songbook.* Ephesians 5:19; Colossians 3:16

publican (PUB-leh-kun) See "tax collector."

Publius (POOB-lih-us) *an important man of the island of Malta,* Acts 28:7-8

Pul, See "Tiglath-Pileser."

punishment
- of Cain, Genesis 4:13
- everlasting, Matthew 25:46; 2 Thessalonians 1:8-9
- for rejecting Jesus, Hebrews 10:29
- by government, Romans 13:4; 1 Peter 2:14

pure
- gold, Exodus 25:11-39; 37; 1 Kings 6:20-21
- heart, Psalm 51:10; Matthew 5:8
- describing Jesus, Hebrews 7:26
- describing people, Job 4:17; 15:14; Philippians 1:10; Titus 1:15
- water, Hebrews 10:22

Purim, See "Feast of Purim."

purple, *a color that, in Bible times, was worn by kings, queens, and other rich people. Purple cloth was expensive because the purple dye came from special shellfish.* Exodus 25:1-4; Judges 8:26; Mark 15:17; Acts 16:14

Q

quail (KWALE) *a brownish-white bird.*
- given by God to Israel, Exodus 16:11-13; Numbers 11:31-34; Psalm 105:40

quarrel
- Israelites quarreled with Moses, Exodus 17:1-7

Queen Goddess, *Ishtar; a goddess of the Babylonians,* Jeremiah 7:18; 44:15-29

Queen of Heaven, See "Queen Goddess."

queen of Sheba, See "Sheba, queen of."

question
- Solomon questioned by queen of Sheba, 1 Kings 10:1-3
- Jesus questioned, Mark 8:11; Luke 23:9; John 8:6
- asked by Jesus, Matthew 21:24
- apostles questioned by Jews, Acts 4:7; 5:27

quiet
- words, Ecclesiastes 9:17
- riot quieted, Acts 19:35-36
- life, 1 Thessalonians 4:11; 1 Timothy 2:2

Quirinius (kwy-RIN-ee-us) *the Roman governor of Syria when Jesus was born,* Luke 2:1-3

quiver (KWIH-vur) *a bag to hold arrows,* Psalm 127:5; Isaiah 49:2

R

Rabbah (RAB-uh) *the capital city of the Ammonites,* 2 Samuel 11:1; 12:26-29; Ezekiel 25:5

rabbi/rabboni (RAB-eye/rah-BONE-eye) *teacher. Jesus' followers often called him "rabbi" as a sign of respect.* John 1:38; 20:16

Rachel (RAY-chel) *a wife of Jacob and the mother of Benjamin and Joseph.*
- married Jacob, Genesis 29:1-30
- gave birth to Joseph, Genesis 30:22-24
- stole Laban's idols, Genesis 31:19-35
- death of, Genesis 35:16-20

Rahab, the dragon (RAY-hab) *In a well-known story, Rahab was defeated. Egypt was sometimes called Rahab to show that it would be defeated.* Job 9:13; Isaiah 30:7

Rahab, the prostitute, *a woman in Jericho. She hid the Israelite spies and helped them escape.*
- hid the spies, Joshua 2:1-21
- rescued from Jericho, Joshua 6:16-25
- an example of faith, Hebrews 11:31; James 2:25

rainbow
- a sign of God's agreement with people, Genesis 9:8-17

raisin, 1 Samuel 25:18; 30:12; 1 Chronicles 12:40

ram, *a male sheep.*
- offered instead of Isaac, Genesis 22:13
- used for burnt offerings, Exodus 29; Leviticus 8:18-29; Numbers 28:11–29:37
- with two horns, Daniel 8:3-22

Ramah (RAY-muh) *a town about five miles north of Jerusalem,* Jeremiah 31:15; Matthew 2:18

Rameses (RAM-eh-seez) *one of the cities built by the Israelites when they were slaves in Egypt,* Exodus 1:11; 12:37; Numbers 33:3

Ramoth Gilead (RAY-moth GIL-ee-ad) *one of the cities of safety on the east side of the Jordan River,* Joshua 20:8; 1 Kings 4:13; 2 Kings 8:28–9:14

ransom, *a payment that frees a captive.*
- Jesus as a ransom for sins, Matthew 20:28; 1 Timothy 2:6; Hebrews 9:15

Rapha (RAY-fa) *a leader of a group of people in Canaan who may have been giants. The descendants of Rapha are called "Rephaites."* 2 Samuel 21:15-22; Joshua 13:12

raven, *a large black bird similar to a crow which eats dead things.*
- sent out by Noah, Genesis 8:7
- fed Elijah, 1 Kings 17:4-6

read
- the Book of the Teachings, Joshua 8:34-35; Nehemiah 8:2-9
- reading the teachings commanded, Deuteronomy 17:18-19; 31:9-13
- brings happiness, Revelation 1:3

Rebekah (ree-BEK-uh) *the wife of Isaac and the mother of Jacob and Esau.*
- married Isaac, Genesis 24
- gave birth to Jacob and Esau, Genesis 25:19-26
- helped deceive Isaac, Genesis 27
- buried at Machpelah, Genesis 49:31

redeem (ree-DEEM) *to buy something back or to buy a slave's freedom.*
- property, Leviticus 25:23-34; Ruth 4:3-6
- slave, Leviticus 25:47-49
- redeemed by God, 1 Corinthians 6:20; Galatians 4:5; Titus 2:14

Red Sea, *Sea of Reeds; a large body of water between Africa and Arabia.*
- Israelites crossed, Exodus 13:17–14:31

refuge, *a place of safety or protection.*
- God as our refuge, Deuteronomy 33:27; 2 Samuel 22:3; Psalms 18:2; 31:2; 71:3; 91:2
- city of, Numbers 35:6-34; Joshua 20

Rehoboam (ree-ho-BO-um) *son of Solomon who took his place as king.*
- became king, 1 Kings 11:41-43
- Israel rebelled against, 1 Kings 12:1-24
- strengthened Judah, 2 Chronicles 11:5-17
- disobeyed God, 2 Chronicles 12

rejoice
- commanded to, Matthew 5:11-12; Romans 12:15; Philippians 4:4; 1 Peter 4:13
- examples of, 1 Samuel 6:13; Nehemiah 12:43

remission (rih-MISH-un) See "forgiveness."

remnant (REM-nant) *a small part that is left; a name used for the Jews who were left alive after their captivity in Babylon.*
- of Israelites who returned to Jerusalem, Ezra 9:15; Nehemiah 1:2; Isaiah 10:20-22

repent (ree-PENT) *being sorry for doing something wrong and not continuing to do that wrong. See "change of heart and life."*

Rephaites, See "Rapha."

respect
- to parents, Leviticus 19:3; 1 Timothy 3:4
- between husbands and wives, Ephesians 5:33; 1 Peter 3:7
- to all people, 1 Peter 2:17; 3:16

rest
- on the seventh day, Genesis 2:2; Exodus 31:15; Hebrews 4:4
- given by the Lord, Psalm 95:11; Jeremiah 6:16; Matthew 11:28
- heaven as a place of rest, Revelation 14:13

resurrection (REZ-uh-REK-shun) *a dead person's coming back to life.*
- of Jesus, Matthew 28:1-10; Mark 16; Luke 24; John 20–21; Acts 2:24-32; Romans 1:4
- of God's people, John 6:39; Acts 24:15; 1 Corinthians 15; Philippians 3:10-11; Hebrews 11:35

Reuben (ROO-ben) *oldest of Jacob's twelve sons.*
- birth of, Genesis 29:32
- tried to save Joseph, Genesis 37:18-29
- descendants of, Exodus 6:14; Numbers 1:20; Joshua 13:15-23

revelation (rev-uh-LAY-shun) *showing plainly something that has been hidden,* 2 Corinthians 12:1; Revelation 1:1-3

revenge
- warnings against, Leviticus 19:18; Romans 12:19; 1 Thessalonians 5:15; 1 Peter 3:9

reward
- in heaven, Matthew 5:12
- for obedience, Psalm 19:11
- for what a person does, Matthew 6:1-18; 10:42; 16:27; Colossians 3:24
- children as a reward, Psalm 127:3

Rhoda (ROAD-uh) *a servant girl in the home of John Mark's mother,* Acts 12:6-17

righteousness (RY-chuss-ness) *being right with God and doing what is right.*
- explained, Romans 3:19-26; 2 Corinthians 5:21; 6:4-7; Philippians 3:8-9
- Abraham as an example of, Romans 4:3
- right living, 2 Corinthians 6:7; Ephesians 5:9; 1 Timothy 6:11; 1 Peter 2:24

robber
- Temple as a hideout for, Jeremiah 7:11; Matthew 21:13
- attacked man on road to Jericho, Luke 10:30
- killed with Jesus, Matthew 27:38-44; John 18:40

roof
- spies hid there, Joshua 2:6
- David saw Bathsheba from there, 2 Samuel 11:2
- built room for Elisha there, 2 Kings 4:8-10
- man lowered through, Mark 2:3-4
- Peter prayed there, Acts 10:9

Rock, *often used as a name for God. As a large rock is strong and provides a hiding place, so God is strong and protects us from our enemies.* Genesis 49:24; 2 Samuel 22:32-49; Psalm 19:14

rock badger (ROK BAD-jur) *a coney; a small, tailless animal like a rabbit that hides among the mountain gorges and rocky areas of Arabia,* Psalm 104:18; Proverbs 30:26

Rome, *the capital city of the Roman Empire at the time of Christ,* Acts 2:10; 18:2; Romans 1:7
- Paul sent there, Acts 23:11; 28:14-15

Ruth (ROOTH) *a widow from Moab.*
- moved to Judah, Ruth 1
- worked in Boaz's field, Ruth 2
- married Boaz, Ruth 3–4
- birth of Obed, Ruth 4:13-22

S

Sabbath (SAB-uth) *means "rest"; the seventh day of the Jewish week; the Jews' day to worship God. They were not allowed to work on this day.*
- commands about, Exodus 20:8-11; 31:12-17
- Jesus is Lord of, Matthew 12:1-13; Mark 2:23-28; Luke 6:1-11

sackcloth (SAK-cloth) *a type of clothing made from rough cloth; worn by people to show their sadness,* Genesis 37:33-35; Esther 4:1; Matthew 11:21

sacrifice (SAK-rih-fice) *to give something valuable to God.*
- burnt sacrifices, Leviticus 6:8-13
- drink sacrifices, Leviticus 23:13; Numbers 15:5; 28:7
- penalty sacrifices, Leviticus 7:1-10
- fellowship sacrifices, Leviticus 3; 7:11-27
- sin sacrifices, Leviticus 4
- limits of, Hebrews 9; 10
- living sacrifice, Romans 12:1

Sadducees (SAD-you-seez) *a Jewish religious group that didn't believe in angels or resurrection; they believed only the first five books of the Old Testament were true.*
- challenged Jesus, Matthew 22:23-33
- arrested Peter and John, Acts 4:1-3
- arrested the apostles, Acts 5:17-42
- Paul spoke to the council, Acts 23:1-9

safety, city of, *city of refuge. In Bible times, someone who had accidentally killed another person could go to a city of safety for protection. As long as he was there, the dead person's relative could not punish him.*
- rules about, Numbers 35:6-34; Joshua 20

saffron (SAF-ron) *a purple flower; parts of it are used as a spice,* Song of Solomon 4:14

saint, *holy person; another word for "Christian,"* Acts 9:41; Romans 1:7; 1 Corinthians 14:33

Salem (SAY-lem) *means "peace"; an old name for Jerusalem.*
- home of Melchizedek, Genesis 14:18; Hebrews 7:1-2

Salome, daughter of Herodias (sah-LO-mee)
- had John the Baptist killed, Matthew 14:3-12; Mark 6:17-29

Salome, wife of Zebedee, *the mother of the apostles James and John,* Mark 15:40; 16:1

salt
- used to preserve foods, Job 6:6; Mark 9:50
- Lot's wife turned into salt, Genesis 19:15-26
- "You are the salt of the earth," Matthew 5:13

Salt Sea, See "Dead Sea."

salvation (sal-VAY-shun) *being rescued from danger; being saved from sin and its punishment.*
- as God's gift, John 3:16; Ephesians 2:8; Titus 2:11
- through Christ, Acts 4:12; 1 Thessalonians 5:9; 1 Timothy 1:15; Hebrews 5:7-9
- as a helmet, Ephesians 6:17; 1 Thessalonians 5:8
- urgency of, 2 Corinthians 6:2; Hebrews 2:3
- rejoice in, Psalms 9:14; 13:5; 51:12; Isaiah 25:9

Samaritan (sah-MEHR-ih-ton) *a person from the area of Samaria in Palestine. These people were only partly Jewish, so the Jews hated them.* John 4:9
- Jesus taught a Samaritan woman, John 4:1-42
- story of the good Samaritan, Luke 10:25-37

Samson (SAM-son) *one of Israel's judges; he was famous for his great strength.*
- birth of, Judges 13
- married a Philistine, Judges 14–15
- tricked by Delilah, Judges 16:4-22
- death of, Judges 16:23-31
- hero of faith, Hebrews 11:32

Samuel (SAM-u-el) *the last judge in Israel.*
- birth of, 1 Samuel 1:1-20
- worked in the Temple, 1 Samuel 1:21–2:26
- became a prophet, 1 Samuel 3
- appointed Saul as king, 1 Samuel 10
- appointed David as king, 1 Samuel 16:1-13
- death of, 1 Samuel 25:1

Sanballat (san-BAL-lat) *governor of Samaria who tried to stop Nehemiah from rebuilding the walls of Jerusalem,* Nehemiah 4–6

sanctify (SANK-teh-fy) *to make holy or ready for service to God,* John 17:17-19; 1 Corinthians 6:11; 1 Peter 1:2

sanctuary (SANK-choo-air-ee) See "Holy Place."

sand
- Abraham's descendants as numerous as, Genesis 22:17; 32:12
- Job's days as numerous as, Job 29:18
- house built on, Matthew 7:26-27

Sanhedrin (san-HEE-drin) See "council."

Sapphira (sah-FY-ruh) *wife of Ananias.*
- lied to the Holy Spirit, Acts 5:1-11

Sarah (SAIR-uh) *wife of Abraham,* Genesis 11:29-30
- gave Hagar to Abraham, Genesis 16:1-6
- name changed from "Sarai," Genesis 17:15-16
- gave birth to Isaac, Genesis 21:1-7
- death of, Genesis 23

Satan (SAY-ton) *means "enemy"; the devil; the enemy of God and man.*
- encouraged David to sin, 1 Chronicles 21:1
- tested Job, Job 1:6-12; 2:1-7
- tempted Jesus, Luke 4:1-13
- a fallen angel, Luke 10:18-19
- to be thrown into lake of fire, Revelation 20:10

Saul, king of Israel
- appointed king, 1 Samuel 9–10
- disobeyed God, 1 Samuel 15
- tried to kill David, 1 Samuel 19; 23:7-29
- death of, 1 Samuel 31

Saul of Tarsus, Acts 13:9. See "Paul."

savior
- God as Savior, Psalm 25:5; Isaiah 45:21; Luke 1:47; 1 Timothy 1:1
- Christ as Savior, Luke 2:11; John 4:42; Ephesians 5:23; Titus 2:13

scarlet (SCAR-let) *a bright red color,* Exodus 26:1; Joshua 2:18; Isaiah 1:18; Matthew 27:28

scepter (SEP-tur) *a wand or a rod that the king holds; a sign of his power,* Esther 4:11; Psalm 60:7

scourge (SKURJ) *to beat someone with a whip or stick,* 1 Kings 12:11
- Jesus scourged, Matthew 27:26; Mark 15:15
- Paul scourged, Acts 21:32; 2 Corinthians 11:24

scribe, *to write, to count, and to put in order. In New Testament times scribes were men who wrote copies of the Scriptures.*
- Ezra as scribe, Nehemiah 8:1
- against Jesus, Matthew 15:1-9
- condemned by Jesus, Matthew 23:13-36

Scriptures (SCRIP-churs) *special writings of God's word for people. When the word Scriptures is used in the New Testament, it usually means the Old Testament. Later, it came to mean the whole Bible.*

• fulfilled, Matthew 26:52-54; John 19:24,28,36
• given by God, 2 Timothy 3:16
scroll, *a long roll of paper used for writing,* Deuteronomy 17:18; Jeremiah 36; Revelation 5:1-5
Scythians (SITH-ee-unz) *a group of wandering people who lived near the Black Sea,* Colossians 3:11
Sea of Galilee, See "Galilee, Lake."
Sea of Reeds, See "Red Sea."
seal, *a tool with a design or picture carved on it. Kings pressed this seal into wax and used it like a signature. Sometimes these seals were worn as rings.*
• examples of, 1 Kings 21:8; Esther 8:8
seed
• created by God, Genesis 1:11,12,29
• parables of, Matthew 13:1-43
seer, *another name for prophet.* See "prophet."
Selah (SEE-lah) *probably a musical direction; used in the Psalms. It may mean to pause. The word was not intended to be spoken when reading the psalm.* Psalms 3:2,4,8; 89:4,37,45,48
Sennacherib (sen-AK-ur-ib) *king of Assyria from 705 to 681 B.C.*
• attacked Jerusalem, 2 Kings 18:13–19; 2 Chronicles 32:1-23; Isaiah 36–37
Sermon on the Mount, *a sermon Jesus preached as he was sitting on the side of a mountain near Lake Galilee,* Matthew 5–7
serpent, See "snake."
servant
• of the Lord, Deuteronomy 34:5; Joshua 2:8; 1 Kings 11:32; Luke 1:38
• Jesus as a, Philippians 2:7
• parable of, Matthew 25:14-30
• Jesus' followers to be, Matthew 20:25-27
Seth, *the third son of Adam and Eve,* Genesis 4:25-26; 5:6-8; Luke 3:38
Shadrach (SHAYD-rak) *a friend of Daniel.*
• taken into captivity, Daniel 1
• became a leader, Daniel 2:49
• saved from the furnace, Daniel 3
Shallum, king of Israel (SHAL-um) *ruled for only one month in 752 B.C.,* 2 Kings 15:10-15
Shalmaneser (shal-mah-NEE-zer) *a king of Assyria,* 2 Kings 17:1-6; 18:9
Shaphan (SHAY-fan) *an assistant to King Josiah,* 2 Kings 22:3-14; 2 Chronicles 34:8-21
sharing
• commanded, Luke 3:11; Romans 12:13; 1 Timothy 6:18
• examples of, Acts 2:42-47; 4:32; 2 Corinthians 8:1-4
Sharon (SHAIR-un) *the plain in Palestine along the coast of the Mediterranean Sea,* 1 Chronicles 5:16; 27:29; Song of Solomon 2:1; Isaiah 33:9
sheaf (SHEEF) *a bundle of grain stalks that have been cut and tied together,* Genesis 37:7; Leviticus 23:10; Job 24:10
Sheba, queen of (SHE-buh) *a queen who came to visit Solomon and see his wealth,* 1 Kings 10:1-13
Shebna (SHEB-nuh) *the manager of the palace for King Hezekiah,* 2 Kings 18:17–19:4; Isaiah 36:1–37:4
sheep
• God's people compared to, Ezekiel 34; John 10:1-18; 1 Peter 2:25
• parable of, Luke 15:1-7
Shem, *Noah's oldest son,* Genesis 6:10; 7:13; 10:21-31
sheminith (SHEM-ih-nith) *a musical term in the Psalms that means an octave (eight notes); may mean to use an instrument with eight strings,* Psalms 6; 12
shepherd
• David as, 1 Samuel 17:15,34-36
• Lord as, Psalm 23
• Jesus, the good shepherd, John 10:1-18
• elders as, 1 Peter 5:1-4
Sheshbazzar (shesh-BAZ-ur) *governor of the Jews in 538 B.C.,* Ezra 1:7-11; 5:13-16
shiggaion (shi-GY-on) *probably a musical term; used in the Psalms; may mean that the psalm is a sad song,* Psalm 7
shigionoth (shi-GY-o-noth) *probably a musical term,* Habakkuk 3:1
Shiloh (SHY-lo) *a town north of Jerusalem.*
• location of the Holy Tent, Joshua 18:1,8; Judges 18:31; Jeremiah 7:12
Shimei (SHIM-ee-i) *a relative of King Saul.*
• cursed David, 2 Samuel 16:5-14
• asked forgiveness, 2 Samuel 19:16-23
• death of, 1 Kings 2:36-46
ship, 1 Kings 9:26-28; 22:48; Acts 27
Shishak (SHY-shak) *king of Egypt during the time of Solomon and Rehoboam.*
• attacked Jerusalem, 1 Kings 14:25-28; 2 Chronicles 12:1-9
showbread, See "bread that shows we are in God's presence."
Shunammite (SHOO-nah-mite) *a person from Shunem, a town in northern Israel.*
• Shunammite woman took care of Elisha, 2 Kings 4:8-17
• her son raised from the dead, 2 Kings 4:18-37
• given back her land, 2 Kings 8:1-6
sickle (SICK-ul) *a tool for cutting grain,* Revelation 14:14-19
Sidon (SY-don) *a Phoenician city on the coast of the Mediterranean Sea,* Genesis 10:19; Matthew 11:21-22; Mark 7:31; Acts 27:3-4
siege mound (SEEJ) *dirt piled against a city wall to make it easier for attackers to climb up and attack the city,* 2 Samuel 20:15; Isaiah 37:33; Jeremiah 6:6
signet ring (SIG-net RING) *a ring worn by a king or other important person. It had his seal on it.* Genesis 41:42; Esther 3:10; 8:2-10; Daniel 6:17. See "seal."
Sihon (SY-hon) *a king of the Amorites when the Israelites came out of Egypt.*
• refused to let Israelites pass, Numbers 21:21-31; Deuteronomy 2:24-37
Silas (SY-lus) *also "Silvanus"; a teacher in the church in Jerusalem who often traveled with Paul.*
• sent to the Gentiles, Acts 15:22-23; 17:16
• joined Paul in Corinth, Acts 18:5
• helped with Peter's letter, 1 Peter 5:12
Siloam, pool of (sy-LO-um) *a pool of water in Jerusalem,* John 9:1-12
Silvanus (sil-VAY-nus) See "Silas."
Simeon of Jerusalem (SIM-ee-un) *a godly man who saw baby Jesus in the Temple,* Luke 2:25-35
Simeon, son of Israel, *one of the twelve sons of Israel,* Genesis 29:33; 42:23-36
• descendants of, Numbers 1:22-23; 26:12-14
Simon, brother of Jesus (SY-mun) Matthew 13:55
Simon of Cyrene (sy-REE-ni) *carried the cross of Jesus,* Matthew 27:32; Mark 15:21; Luke 23:26
Simon Peter, See "Peter."
Simon, the magician, *tried to buy the power of the Holy Spirit,* Acts 8:9-24
Simon, the Zealot, *an apostle of Jesus,* Matthew 10:4; Mark 3:18; Luke 6:15; Acts 1:13
sin, *a word, thought, or act against the law of God.*
• offering for, Leviticus 4; 6:24-30; Hebrews 7:27; 10:4-12
• committed by everyone, Romans 3:23; 1 John 1:8-10
• Christ died for, Romans 4:25; 1 Corinthians 15:3; 1 Peter 2:24; 1 John 2:2; 3:5
• results of, Isaiah 59:2; Romans 6:23; Ephesians 2:1; Hebrews 12:1

Sinai (SY-ny) *a mountain in the desert between Egypt and Canaan.*
- Moses received the Ten Commandments there, Exodus 19–20

singing, *a way of praising God and teaching each other,* Judges 5:3; Psalm 30:4; Ephesians 5:19; Colossians 3:16

Sisera (SIS-er-uh) *captain of a Canaanite army,* Judges 4

slave
- rules about, Exodus 21:1-11,16,26-32; Ephesians 6:5-9; 1 Timothy 6:1-2

slave woman, *concubine; she bore children for her master but was not considered equal to a wife.*
- Hagar as, Genesis 16:1-3
- of Solomon, 1 Kings 11:2-3

sleep
- God never sleeps, Psalm 121:4
- danger of, Proverbs 6:10-11
- Eutychus fell asleep, Acts 20:9
- to awake from, Romans 13:11
- a gift from the Lord, Psalm 127:2

sling, *a weapon for throwing rocks,* Judges 20:16; 1 Samuel 17:39-50; 2 Kings 3:24-25

slothful (SLAWTH-ful) *lazy and undependable,* Proverbs 6:6-11; 13:4; Matthew 25:26; Hebrews 6:12

sluggard, See "slothful."

snake
- sticks became snakes, Exodus 7:8-13
- bronze snake made by Moses, Numbers 21:4-9; John 3:14
- Paul bitten by, Acts 28:1-6

Sodom (SOD-um) *a town known for its evil people.*
- destroyed, Genesis 18:17–19:29
- symbol of evil, Matthew 10:11-15; 11:20-24; Revelation 11:8

soldier
- arrested Jesus, John 18:12-13
- made fun of Jesus, Matthew 27:27-31; Luke 23:11
- at Jesus' death, Matthew 27:32-37; Luke 23:26-38,47; John 19:1-3,16-24,28-35
- lied about Jesus' resurrection, Matthew 28:11-15
- Cornelius, Acts 10:1
- guarded Peter, Acts 12:6
- Christian compared to, 2 Timothy 2:3-4

Solomon (SOL-o-mon) *a son of David; famous for his wisdom.*
- became king, 1 Kings 1:28-53
- wisdom of, 1 Kings 3:1-15; 4:29-34
- made a wise decision, 1 Kings 3:16-28
- built the Temple, 1 Kings 6; 7:13-51
- visited by the queen of Sheba, 1 Kings 10:1-13; Matthew 12:42
- married many women, 1 Kings 11:1-8
- death of, 1 Kings 11:40-41

Solomon's Porch (SOL-o-mon's PORCH) *a covered courtyard on the east side of the Temple,* 1 Kings 7:6; John 10:23; Acts 3:11; 5:12

Son of David, *a name the Jews used for the Christ because the Savior was to come from the family of King David,* Matthew 1:1; 9:27; 15:22; 21:9

Son of Man, *a name Jesus called himself. It showed that he was God's Son, but he was also a human being.* Matthew 24:30; Mark 13:26; Luke 21:27; 22:69-70

sorcery (SOR-sir-ee) *trying to put magical spells on people or harming them by magic,* Acts 8:9-25; 19:18-19
- warnings against, Leviticus 19:26; Deuteronomy 18:14-15; 2 Kings 17:17

soul (SOLE) *what makes a person alive. Sometimes the Bible writers used words like "heart" and "soul" to mean a person's whole being or the person himself.*
- "destroy the soul and the body," Matthew 10:28
- losing, Matthew 16:26
- "all your heart and all your soul," Matthew 22:37
- joined with the spirit, Hebrews 4:12

sower, *someone who plants seeds to grow into crops,* Matthew 13:1-43; 2 Corinthians 9:6

Spirit (SPIH-rit) See "Holy Spirit."

spirit, *the part of humans that was made to be like God because God is spirit. The New Testament also talks about evil spirits.* Isaiah 26:9; 1 Thessalonians 5:23; James 2:26
- evil spirit, Matthew 12:43; Mark 1:23; 5:2; Luke 4:33

spiritual gifts, *special talents or abilities that God gives his people,* Romans 12:6-8; 1 Corinthians 12:1-11; 14; Ephesians 4:7-13

spring, *a natural fountain,* Genesis 7:11; Exodus 15:27

staff, *a shepherd's walking stick,* Exodus 4:1-5; 7:8-12; Numbers 20:6-11; Psalm 23:4

steal, See also "robber."
- commands against, Exodus 20:15; Matthew 19:18; Romans 13:9; Ephesians 4:28

Stephen (STEE-ven) *one of the seven men chosen to serve the church in Jerusalem; the first martyr for Christ.*
- chosen to serve the church, Acts 6:5-6
- killed by the Jews, Acts 6:8–7:60

stoning, *a way of killing someone by throwing rocks at him.*
- commanded, Deuteronomy 17:2-7
- Naboth stoned, 1 Kings 21:13
- Stephen stoned, Acts 7:54-60
- Paul stoned, Acts 14:19

strength
- love God with all your strength, Deuteronomy 6:5; Mark 12:30
- God as the source, Psalms 18:1; 73:26; Philippians 4:13; 1 Peter 4:11

stronghold, *a fortress, a well protected place,* 1 Samuel 22:4; 2 Samuel 5:17

suffering
- proper attitude toward, 2 Corinthians 1:3-7; James 5:10
- value of, Romans 8:17-18; 1 Peter 3:8-17
- of Jesus, Isaiah 53:3-10; Luke 24:26,46; Philippians 3:10; Hebrews 2:18

swaddling clothes, *pieces of cloth that were wrapped around a newborn baby in Jesus' time,* Luke 2:7 12

sword
- of fire, Genesis 3:24
- a weapon, Joshua 5:13; 1 Samuel 17:45; Matthew 26:51-52
- the word of God, Ephesians 6:17; Hebrews 4:12

Sychar (SY-kar) *a small town in Samaria near Jacob's well,* John 4:5-6

synagogue (SIN-uh-gog) *"a meeting." By the first century, the Jews met in synagogues to read and study the Scriptures. The building was also used as the Jewish court and as a school.*
- Jesus taught in, Matthew 4:23; Mark 1:21; Luke 4:16-17
- Paul spoke there, Acts 17:1,10

Syria (SEER-ee-uh) *an area north of Galilee and east of the Mediterranean Sea; called "Aram" in Old Testament times.* See "Aram."
- enemy of Israel, 1 Kings 11:25; 20:1-34; 2 Kings 13:22-25
- learned about Jesus, Matthew 4:24

T

tabernacle (TAB-er-NAK-'l) See "Meeting Tent."

tablets of the agreement, *two flat stones on which God wrote the Ten Commandments.*
- given to Moses, Exodus 19–20; 24:12-18
- broken by Moses, Exodus 32:15-19
- the second tablets, Exodus 34:1-4

- in the Most Holy Place, Hebrews 9:4

Tabitha (TAB-eh-thuh) See "Dorcas."

Tabor, Mount (TAY-bur) *in the Valley of Jezreel about twelve miles from Lake Galilee,* Judges 4:6-16; Psalm 89:12

tambourine (tam-bah-REEN) *a musical instrument that is beaten to keep rhythm,* Exodus 15:20; 1 Samuel 18:6; Psalm 81:2

Tarshish (TAR-shish) *a city somewhere on the western side of the Mediterranean Sea,* Jonah 1:3; 4:2

Tarsus (TAR-sus) *the most important city in Cilicia, which is now the country of Turkey,* Acts 9:30; 11:25-26
- home of Paul, Acts 9:11; 21:39; 22:3

tax collector, *a Jew hired by the Romans to collect taxes,* Matthew 9:10-11
- Matthew, Matthew 10:3; Luke 5:27
- Zacchaeus, Luke 19:1-10

teacher
- Jesus called a, Matthew 8:19; Mark 10:17; John 1:38; 3:2
- in the church, Romans 12:7; Ephesians 4:11; 1 Timothy 4:13
- false, 1 Timothy 4:1-5; 2 Peter 2:1
- to be judged more strictly, James 3:1

teaching
- commanded, Deuteronomy 6:1-7; Matthew 28:20; 2 Timothy 2:2,14-15; Titus 2

Teachings of Moses, *or the "Law of Moses,"* Deuteronomy 31:24-26; Joshua 23:6; Nehemiah 8
- purpose of, Romans 3:20; 5:20; Galatians 3:21-25
- limitations of, Romans 8:3; Galatians 2:19; Hebrews 10:1

temple (TEM-p'l) *a building where people worship. God told the Jewish people to worship him at the Temple in Jerusalem.*
- Solomon's Temple, 1 Kings 6–8; 2 Chronicles 2–7
- the Temple rebuilt, Ezra 3
- the body as a temple, John 2:19-22; 1 Corinthians 3:16-17; 6:19-20; 2 Corinthians 6:16

temptation (temp-TAY-shun) *the devil's attempt to get us to do something wrong.*
- Jesus tempted, Matthew 4:1-11; Luke 4:1-13; Hebrews 4:15-16
- a way of escape from, 1 Corinthians 10:13
- source of, James 1:13-15

Ten Commandments, *the rules God gave Moses on Mount Sinai,* Exodus 20:1-20; 31:18; 34:1-28; Deuteronomy 5:1-22

tent
- Abram's tents, Genesis 13:18
- peg, Judges 4:21-22
- makers of, Acts 18:3

Tent, See "Meeting Tent."

Thaddaeus (THAD-ee-us) *one of the twelve apostles,* Matthew 10:3; Mark 3:18

thankfulness, Psalm 107:1; 1 Thessalonians 5:8; Hebrews 12:28

Theophilus (thee-AHF-ih-lus) *the person to whom the books of Luke and Acts were written,* Luke 1:1-4; Acts 1:1

Thessalonica (THES-ah-lah-NY-kah) *the capital of the country of Macedonia, which is now northern Greece,* 1 Thessalonians 1:1; 2 Thessalonians 1:1
- Paul preached there, Acts 17:1-9

Thomas (TOM-us) *Didymus; one of the twelve apostles,* Matthew 10:2-3
- questioned Jesus, John 14:5-7
- saw Jesus after resurrection, John 20:24-29; 21:2

thorn, *sharp points on a branch or stem of a plant.*
- as a curse on Adam, Genesis 3:17-18
- crown of, Matthew 27:29; Mark 15:17; John 19:2-5

threshing floor, *a place where farmers separated grain from chaff. This was done by beating the stalks on the hard ground, throwing them in the air, and letting the wind blow the chaff away.*
- angel visited Gideon there, Judges 6:11
- David bought, 2 Samuel 24:16-25

throne
- king's throne, 1 Kings 10:18-19
- God's throne, Matthew 5:34; Hebrews 4:16; Revelation 3:21; 4

Thummim (THUM-im) *the Urim and Thummim may have been gems. They were attached to the holy vest of the high priest and were used to learn God's will.* Exodus 28:29-30; Leviticus 8:8; Deuteronomy 33:8

Thyatira (THY-ah-TY-rah) *an important city in Asia famous for its purple cloth,* Acts 16:13-14; Revelation 1:11; 2:18-29

Tiberius Caesar (tie-BEER-ee-us SEE-zur) *Roman emperor during the last half of Jesus' life,* Luke 3:1

Tiglath-Pileser (TIG-lath-peh-LEE-zur) *king of Assyria who helped Ahaz;* also called "Pul."
- attacked Israel, 2 Kings 15:19-20
- rescued Ahaz, 2 Kings 16:7-10

Tigris (TY-gris) *a great river in the eastern part of the Bible lands,* Genesis 2:14; Daniel 10:4

Timothy (TIM-oh-thee) *close friend and helper of the apostle Paul.*
- helped Paul, Acts 16:1-3; 17:13-16; 1 Corinthians 4:17; 2 Corinthians 1:19
- instructed by Paul, 1 and 2 Timothy

tithe (TIETH) *"tenth." The Jews were told to give one-tenth of what they earned to God.* Leviticus 27:30-32; Deuteronomy 12:1-6; Luke 11:42; 18:12

Titus (TIE-tus) *trusted friend and helper of the apostle Paul.*
- helped Corinthians, 2 Corinthians 7:6-7,13-15; 8:6,16,23
- appointed elders, Titus 1:4-5
- Paul's instructions to, Titus 1–3

Tobiah (toe-BY-uh) *tried to keep Nehemiah from rebuilding the walls of Jerusalem,* Nehemiah 2:10-20; 6:10-19; 13:4-9

tomb
- of Lazarus, John 11:38-44
- of Jesus, Matthew 27:57–28:15; Mark 15:42–16:30; Luke 23:50–24:12; John 19:38–20:9

tongue
- lying tongue hated by God, Proverbs 6:16-17
- cannot be tamed, James 3:2-12

tower of Babel, See "Babel."

transfiguration (tranz-fig-you-RAY-shun) *"to change." Jesus was transfigured in front of Peter, James, and John when his face and clothes began to shine brightly.* Matthew 17:1-9; Mark 9:2-9; Luke 9:28-36

tree
- of knowledge of good and evil, Genesis 2:9; 3:3
- of life, Genesis 2:9; Revelation 2:7; 22:2,14
- people compared to, Psalms 1:3; 92:12; Jeremiah 17:8; Matthew 3:10; 12:33
- cross described as a tree, Galatians 3:13

trespass, See "sin."

tribe, *all descendants of a certain person. The twelve tribes of Israel were descendants of the twelve sons of Jacob, who was later named "Israel."* Numbers 1–2
- Canaan divided among, Joshua 13:7-33; 15–19

triumphal entry (tri-UMF-ul) *the time Jesus entered Jerusalem just before his death,* Matthew 21:1-11; Mark 11:1-19; Luke 19:28-44; John 12:12-15

Troas (TRO-az) *one of the most important cities in northwest Asia,* Acts 16:8-10; 20:5-12; 2 Corinthians 2:12

Trophimus *(TROF-eh-mus) non-Jewish Christian who*

traveled with Paul, Acts 20:3-4; 21:27-29; 2 Timothy 4:20

trumpet (TRUM-pet) *in Bible times it was made from animal horns; used to call an army together or announce something important,* Numbers 10:2-10; Joshua 6:4-20; 1 Corinthians 15:52

trust
- a duty, Luke 16:11; 1 Corinthians 4:2; Titus 2:10
- in God, Psalm 20:7; Proverbs 3:5; 16:20; Romans 4:5; 10:11; 1 Peter 2:6
- in lesser things, Psalms 49:13-14; 118:9; Proverbs 11:28; Isaiah 2:22

truth
- speaking honestly, Psalm 15:2; Proverbs 16:13
- God's message, John 17:17; Romans 1:25; Ephesians 1:13; 1 John 1:6

tunic (TOO-nik) *a kind of coat,* Exodus 28:39-40; John 19:23

Tychicus (TIK-ih-kus) *Christian from Asia who did important jobs for Paul,* Acts 20:4; Ephesians 6:21-22; Colossians 4:7-9

Tyre (TIRE) *large, important city in Phoenicia, which is now part of the country of Lebanon,* Mark 7:24-31; Acts 12:20
- Hiram, king of, 2 Samuel 5:11; 1 Kings 9:10-14; 2 Chronicles 2
- a wicked city, Matthew 11:21-22; Luke 10:13-14

U

uncircumcised, See "circumcision."

unclean, *the state of a person, animal or action that was not pleasing to God. In the Old Testament God said certain animals were unclean and were not to be eaten. If a person disobeyed the rules about being clean, he was called unclean and could not serve God until he was made clean again.* See "clean."
- unclean animals, Leviticus 11; Acts 10:9-15
- unclean people, Leviticus 12–15
- God declared everyone to be clean, Acts 10

unleavened bread (un-LEV-'nd BREAD) *bread made without yeast.*
- used in the Passover Feast, Exodus 12:20; Deuteronomy 16:1-4

Unleavened Bread, Day of, *the first day of the Feast of Unleavened Bread or Passover,* Matthew 26:17; Luke 22:7

upper room, *upstairs room in a house.*
- Jesus and his followers met there, Mark 14:14-15; Luke 22:9-12

Ur, *a great city thousands of years ago; today in the country of Iraq.*
- home of Abram, Genesis 11:28-31

Uriah (you-RY-uh) *a soldier in King David's army.*
- killed by David, 2 Samuel 11

Urim (YOUR-im) See "Thummim."

Uzzah (UZ-uh) *touched the Ark of the Agreement and died,* 2 Samuel 6:1-8; 1 Chronicles 13:1-14

Uzziah (uh-ZY-uh) *a king of Judah,* 2 Kings 15:13-15; 2 Chronicles 26; Isaiah 6:1

V

Vashti (VASH-ty) *the wife of Ahasuerus, king of Persia,* Esther 1:1-20

veil (VALE) *a head covering usually worn by women; also, a curtain in the Temple.*
- worn by women, Genesis 24:65; Song of Solomon 4:1; Isaiah 3:19
- the Temple veil, Matthew 27:51; Mark 15:38; Luke 23:45

vest, holy, *"ephod"; a special type of clothing for the priests in the Old Testament. The holy vest for the high priest had gold and gems on it.*
- description of, Exodus 25:7; 28:6-14; 39:2-7
- one made by Micah, Judges 17:1-5; 18:14-20
- worn by David, 2 Samuel 6:14

vine
- fruit of the, Matthew 26:29; Mark 14:25; Luke 22:18
- Jesus as the, John 15:1-11

vineyard
- Naboth's, 1 Kings 21
- parables of, Matthew 20:1-16; 21:28-46; Mark 12:1-12; Luke 20:9-19

virgin (VUR-jin) *person who has not had sexual relations,* Deuteronomy 22:13-29; Isaiah 7:14; Matthew 1:23; Luke 1:34

vision (VIZ-zhun) *like a dream. God often spoke to his people in visions.*
- of Abram, Genesis 15:1
- of Daniel, Daniel 2:19
- of Peter and Cornelius, Acts 10:1-16
- of Paul, Acts 16:9

vow, *a special and serious promise often made to God.*
- rules about, Numbers 30; Deuteronomy 23:21-23
- the Nazirite, Numbers 6:1-21
- of Jephthah, Judges 11:29-40
- of Paul, Acts 18:18

W

war
- rumors of, Matthew 24:6-7; Mark 13:7-8; Luke 21:9-10
- spiritual, 2 Corinthians 10:3-4
- will end, Micah 4:1-3

watchman
- examples of, 2 Samuel 18:24-27; Psalm 130:6
- prophets as watchmen, Ezekiel 3:17; Micah 7:4

water
- in creation, Genesis 1:1-2,6-10
- bitter, Exodus 15:22-27
- from a rock, Exodus 17:1-7
- for David, 2 Samuel 23:15-17
- drink of, Matthew 10:42; Mark 9:41
- Jesus walked on, Matthew 14:22-36
- turned to wine, John 2:1-11
- living water, John 4:1-15

"Way, the," *one of the earliest names given to Christians. Jesus said he was "the way" to reach God.* Acts 9:1-2; 19:9,23; 22:4; 24:14,22

wedding, Matthew 22:1-14; Luke 14:8; John 2:1-11

Western Sea, See "Mediterranean Sea."

widow
- examples of, Ruth 4:10; 1 Kings 17:8-24; Luke 21:2-4
- care for, Deuteronomy 24:17-22; 1 Timothy 5:3-16; James 1:27

wife
- man united with, Genesis 2:24
- the good wife, Proverbs 31:10-31
- teachings about, 1 Corinthians 7:1-16
- responsibility of, Ephesians 5:21-24,33; Colossians 3:18; 1 Peter 3:1

wine
- danger of, Proverbs 20:1; Ephesians 5:18
- at wedding in Cana, John 2:1-11
- for the stomach, 1 Timothy 5:23

winepress, *a pit where grapes were mashed to get the juice out. The winepress is sometimes used to describe how enemy armies will defeat people as if they were grapes crushed in a winepress.*
- examples of, Judges 6:11; Matthew 21:33
- as a symbol of punishment, Lamentations 1:15; Revelation 14:19-20; 19:15

wisdom (WIZ-d'm) *understanding what is really important in life. This wisdom comes from God.* Proverbs 1:1-2,7; 2; 4
- Solomon asked for, 1 Kings 4:29-34

- source of, James 1:5
- a parable about, Matthew 25:1-13

wise men, "magi"; *men who studied the stars,* Genesis 41:8; Exodus 7:11; Matthew 2:1-12

witchcraft, *using the power of the devil to do magic.*
- warnings against, Deuteronomy 18:10-12; Galatians 5:19-21
- examples of, 2 Kings 9:22; 2 Chronicles 33:6

witness, Acts 1:8,22; 2:32; 22:14-15

woman
- created by God, Genesis 2:22-23
- how to treat a, 1 Timothy 5:2,14

word, *in the Bible often means God's message to us in the Scriptures. Jesus is called the "Word" because he shows us what God is like.*
- like a lamp, Psalm 119:105
- like a sword, Hebrews 4:12
- living in God's people, John 15:7; Colossians 3:16; 1 John 2:14
- lasts forever, Matthew 24:35; 1 Peter 1:25
- people's words, Proverbs 12:25; 25:11; Matthew 12:36-37
- as a message, 1 Peter 1:24-25; 1 John 2:14
- Jesus as the "Word," John 1:1-5,14; 1 John 1:1-2

world, *the planet Earth; also the people on this earth who follow Satan.*
- as the Earth, 2 Samuel 22:16; Psalm 18:15
- as a symbol of wickedness, Romans 12:2; Ephesians 2:2

worship, *to praise and serve God.*
- commanded, Exodus 34:14; Luke 4:8; John 4:20-24

X-Y

Xerxes (ZERK-sees) *a king of Persia; also called "Ahasuerus,"* Esther 1–10

yeast (YEEST) *an ingredient used to make breads and cakes rise; used in the New Testament to stand for a person's influence over others.* See also "unleavened bread."
- as a symbol for influence, Mark 8:15; Luke 13:21

yoke, *a wooden frame that fits on the necks of animals to hold them together while working.*
- examples of, Deuteronomy 21:3; 1 Kings 19:19-21

youth
- "Remember your Creator," Ecclesiastes 12:1
- teachings about, 1 Timothy 4:12

Z

Zacchaeus (za-KEE-us) *Jewish tax collector in the city of Jericho,* Luke 19:1-8

Zadok (ZAY-dok) *priest who helped King David,* 2 Samuel 15:24-36; 17:15-21; 1 Kings 1:18-45

Zarephath (ZAIR-eh-fath) *a Canaanite town where the prophet Elijah helped a widow,* 1 Kings 17:8-24; Luke 4:25-26

Zealots (ZEL-ots) *a group of Jewish men also called "Enthusiasts." They hated the Romans for controlling their home country, and they planned to force the Romans out.*
- Simon, the Zealot, Matthew 10:4; Mark 3:18; Luke 6:15; Acts 1:13

Zebedee (ZEB-uh-dee) *a fisherman on Lake Galilee,* Matthew 4:21-22; 20:20; Mark 1:19-20; Luke 5:10; John 21:2

Zechariah, father of John the Baptist, (ZEK-uh-RY-uh) *a Jewish priest,* Luke 1:5-25,57-80

Zechariah, king of Israel, *ruled for only six months; killed by Shallum,* 2 Kings 14:29; 15:8-11

Zechariah, son of Berekiah, *a prophet who wrote the next-to-the-last book in the Old Testament,* Ezra 5:1; Zechariah 1–14

Zechariah, son of Jehoiada, *a priest who taught the people to serve God,* 2 Chronicles 24:20-25

Zedekiah, son of Josiah, (zed-ee-KY-uh) *the last king of Judah,* 2 Kings 24:16–25:7

Zedekiah, son of Kenaanah, *a false prophet during the time of King Ahab,* 1 Kings 22:1-24

Zedekiah, son of Maaseiah, *a false prophet in Babylon during the time of Jeremiah,* Jeremiah 29:21-23

Zephaniah (zef-uh-NY-uh) *a prophet who lived when Josiah was king of Judah; wrote the short book of Zephaniah,* Zephaniah 1:1

Zerubbabel (zeh-RUB-uh-bull) *governor of Jerusalem after the Jews had been in captivity in Babylon for seventy years.*
- returned from exile, Ezra 2:2
- built the altar of God, Ezra 3:1-6
- rebuilt the Temple, Ezra 3:7-10; 5:2

Ziba (ZY-buh) *a servant of Saul,* 2 Samuel 9:1-11; 16:1-4; 19:24-30

Zimri (ZIM-rye) *a king of Israel,* 1 Kings 16:11-20

Zion (ZY-on) *a hill inside the city of Jerusalem.* See "Mount Zion."

Ziph (ZIF) *a city about twenty-five miles south of Jerusalem,* 1 Samuel 23:14-28; 26:1-25

Zipporah (zih-PO-ruh) *the wife of Moses,* Exodus 2:15-22; 4:24-26; 18:1-3

zither (ZITH-ur) *a type of musical instrument that had about forty strings on it,* Ezekiel 3:5,7,10,15